THE NORTON ANTHOLOGY OF DRAMA

SHORTER EDITION

THE NORTON ANTHOLOGY OF DRAMA

J. ELLEN GAINOR
CORNELL UNIVERSITY

STANTON B. GARNER JR.
UNIVERSITY OF TENNESSEE

MARTIN PUCHNER
COLUMBIA UNIVERSITY

SHORTER EDITION

W. W. NORTON & COMPANY
NEW YORK · LONDON

W. W. Norton & Company has been independent since its founding in 1923, when William Warder Norton and Mary D. Herter Norton first published lectures delivered at the People's Institute, the adult education division of New York City's Cooper Union. The firm soon expanded its program beyond the Institute, publishing books by celebrated academics from America and abroad. By mid-century, the two major pillars of Norton's publishing program—trade books and college texts—were firmly established. In the 1950s, the Norton family transferred control of the company to its employees, and today—with a staff of four hundred and a comparable number of trade, college, and professional titles published each year—W. W. Norton & Company stands as the largest and oldest publishing house owned wholly by its employees.

Printed in the United States of America
First Edition

Editor: Peter Simon
Manuscript Editor: Alice Falk
Reference Editor: Michael Fleming
Assistant Editor: Conor Sullivan
Marketing Associate: Katie Hannah
Electronic Media Editor: Eileen Connell
Project Editors: Kari Gulbrandsen, Pamela Lawson, Barbara Necol, Paula Noonan
Photo Research: Trish Marx, Julie Tesser
Permissions Management: Nancy J. Rodwan
Book Design: Jo Anne Metsch
Production Manager: Benjamin Reynolds
Managing Editor, College: Marian Johnson

Composition by the Westchester Book Group
Manufacturing by R. R. Donnelley & Sons—Crawfordsville, IN

Library of Congress Cataloging-in-Publication Data

The Norton anthology of drama, shorter edition / [edited by] J. Ellen Gainor, Stanton B. Garner, Jr., Martin Puchner.—1st ed.
p. cm.
Includes bibliographical references and index.
ISBN 978-0-393-93412-0 (pbk.)
1. Drama—Collections. I. Gainor, J. Ellen. II. Garner, Stanton B., 1955–
III. Puchner, H. Martin.
PN6112.N68 2009
808.2—dc22

2009028409

W. W. Norton & Company, Inc., 500 Fifth Avenue, New York, N.Y. 10110
wwnorton.com
W. W. Norton & Company Ltd., Castle House, 75/76 Wells Street, London W1T 3QT

2 3 4 5 6 7 8 9 0

Contents

Preface

DRAMA, one of the oldest of the arts, is also the most multifaceted. Grounded in the different mediums of writing and physical enactment, it offers pleasures both to the spectators of its theatrical realizations and to the solitary reader. In preparing *The Norton Anthology of Drama,* the editors have been mindful of this dual allegiance, and we have taken as our guiding principle that drama is at once a literary document, speaking to us across a vast expanse of time and space, and a live event, taking place in the here and now. Most of the plays collected here can be experienced in theaters today, or at least be seen in performance on film, videotape, or DVD. But even those that are rarely performed in the contemporary era are presented in *The Norton Anthology of Drama* with considerable attention to their life on the stage.

The presentation of plays in *The Norton Anthology of Drama* reflects a commitment to the richness and internationality of the dramatic tradition and to the dialogues that mark dramatic performance across languages, borders, and periods. Most anthologies organize their plays into historical and geographical units with such headings as "Greek Drama," "Renaissance Drama," and "Contemporary Drama." One of the chief results of this kind of demarcation is the separation of Western traditions from non-Western ones, as if these existed in isolation from one another. We, on the other hand, rely on chronology to organize our plays (using actual or estimated dates of first performance, and substituting publication or composition dates for those plays not originally written for performance or plays whose performance was significantly delayed). This decision reflects our belief that theater is historically and geographically more fluid than unit "boxes" imply. We believe, too, that what we call "Western" and "non-Western" texts are marked by concurrent developments across cultures and by similarities of form, subject, and even performance conditions that traditional theatrical and dramatic histories neglect. Chronological presentation allows surprising juxtapositions: Zeami's noh masterpiece *Atsumori* with *Everyman,* Behn's *The Rover* with Sor Juana's *Loa* for *The Divine Narcissus,* and Arthur Miller's *Death of a Salesman* with Tawfiq al-Hakim's *Song of Death.* It also enhances flexibility of course development and organization—*The Norton Anthology of Drama* makes possible many different courses while mandating no specific approach. At the same time, those who desire a presentation of theatrical history that emphasizes historical periods and national traditions will find this structure in the anthology's General Introduction.

In determining the table of contents for this anthology, the editors were guided by the desire to select the most thematically rich, performatively engaging, and pedagogically compelling plays available—plays that respond to the historical, cultural, literary, and theatrical contexts in which they were written in new, often groundbreaking, ways. Among the plays assembled here are two masterpieces of the twentieth-century stage for which *The Norton Anthology of Drama* has secured exclusive anthology publication rights. One of these—Tennessee Williams's *A Streetcar Named Desire*—is numbered in the greatest plays from the modern American theater, while the other—Samuel Beckett's *Waiting for Godot*—is widely considered the century's most important and influential dramatic work. The inclusion of *Waiting for Godot* is particularly significant. Since its publication in 1952, Beckett's greatest play has been available in English only in editions from its American and British publishers. It has never before appeared in a general drama anthology, complete with annotation and critical introduction. Our presentation of twentieth-century drama is immeasurably enriched by its presence.

To ensure that reading classic plays written in languages other than English is a lively experience for students, we have selected vibrant translations that speak in a modern idiom while respecting the spirit and sense of the original. When no existing version satisfied us, we commissioned a new one. Whether commissioned specifically for *The Norton Anthology of Drama* or published previously, the translations in this anthology are all not only engaging and accessible on the page but also eminently *performable*. Indeed, several of our translators are themselves playwrights. For example, our translation of Molière's *Tartuffe*, by the playwright Constance Congdon, premiered at the Two Rivers Theater in 2006 and is now coming alive on other stages throughout North America.

In balancing the literary with the theatrical, we have designed an anthology that will work in both English and theater classrooms. For the instructor of dramatic literature courses at the introductory and advanced levels, the plays in *The Norton Anthology of Drama* reward textual attention of a literary kind while also encouraging analysis of the play's performance possibilities. For the theater instructor, the anthology provides theatrically vibrant texts in actable editions and translations. Students encountering drama for the first time will discover how powerfully the language of these plays comes alive on the tongue, and experienced and inexperienced students alike will find the versions here to be ideal for in-class performance as well as for line and scene reading. The teaching of drama can be conducted through a range of classroom activities, and *The Norton Anthology of Drama* has been designed to facilitate as many as possible.

Like the Norton anthologies of British, American, and world literatures; *The Norton Anthology of Theory and Criticism*; and the other anthologies with which Norton has shaped classroom teaching over the years, *The Norton Anthology of Drama* provides students and instructors with a wealth of introductory and editorial support. The substantial General Introduction opens by exploring the relationship between dramatic literature and theatrical performance, and it concludes with a discussion of the challenges and opportunities of reading plays as scripts for performance. This final section—"Reading Drama / Imagining Theater"—is designed to give students approaching drama for the first time the tools they need to understand a uniquely hybrid form. The "Short History of Theater and Drama," which makes up the central part of the introduction, provides a detailed yet brisk overview of the political, social, and theatrical contexts within which drama has been embedded through the ages and across the globe.

We illustrate this history—and the headnotes that accompany each play—with vivid images of theaters, playwrights, actors, and audiences; pictures from acting manuals; and other figures related to theatrical performance. Given the importance of manuscript and print culture to the development and dissemination of drama, we have also included examples of the textual appearance of drama: manuscript pages, woodcuts, early printings. Together with images from the other arts (painting and sculpture, for instance), this anthology's generous illustrations convey a rich experience of the visual, performative, and textual cultures from which drama has emerged. Although we have decided to omit pictures from contemporary performances of classic plays, the website that accompanies *The Norton Anthology of Drama* does offer such images of its plays, thereby giving students a glimpse of the creative work performed by actors and directors as they reframe and reimagine plays onstage.

Supplemented by the substantial yet concise historical survey that opens the anthology, the headnotes that accompany each selection offer detailed, accessible introductions to the plays. These headnotes include summaries of the author's life and career, the specific historical and cultural contexts of the play in question, production information (where pertinent), and consideration of the play's importance in terms of its historical period and the broader history of drama and theater. The headnotes also include a discussion of the plays themselves, though we have taken care not to "explain" the plays to students, instead raising issues that will enable them to interpret the works on their own. For those interested in delving more deeply into the subject matter, we provide a carefully chosen and annotated bibliography of books and articles on each play and author. Throughout the headnote and bibliography, the editors have emphasized usefulness, readability, and student interest.

Similar care has been taken with the dramatic texts and their annotations. We have done everything possible to ensure that the texts in *The Norton Anthology of Drama* are the most authoritative ones available; if competing versions of these texts exist, we have selected the ones that are endorsed by contemporary scholarly consensus. In cases in which there is more than one version of a play—Marlowe's *Doctor Faustus,* and Shaw's *Pygmalion,* for instance—we have selected the text that reflects the playwright's earliest theatrical vision. Our edition of *Hamlet*—a play with one of the most complicated and contested textual histories in world drama—is accompanied by a brief summary of that textual history, an overview of recent attempts to establish or resist an "authoritative" text, and a rationale for the version of the text included here. At the levels of selection and copyediting, we have devoted an exceptional amount of attention to ensuring that the text as it appears here is the most correct published version available.

Whereas other drama anthologies occasionally present historically and linguistically challenging plays without any annotations at all, *The Norton Anthology of Drama* provides footnotes and marginal glosses whenever an unfamiliar word, phrase, or historical/cultural reference risks interfering with a student's understanding of the text. We have tried to avoid cluttering plays with such material—we assume that students have access to a dictionary—but we have worked to annotate those words and references whose significance is obscured or hidden by historical remoteness. A number of our plays—including *Godot*—are annotated here for the first time, and we hope that even those plays that have been annotated before have been given a fresh presentation through our footnotes and marginal glosses.

Anthologies of drama, students and instructors have long agreed, are unwieldy affairs, encompassing as they do twenty-five centuries of drama in phone-book-size volumes. *The Norton Anthology of Drama,* by contrast, has been published in a format that fits comfortably in the hand and on a lap, with the play-texts appearing on easy-to-read, single-column pages.

Finally, the many resources in *The Norton Anthology of Drama*—the General Introduction, individual headnotes, bibliographies, and textual annotations—are complemented by resources outside the anthology itself. An Instructor's Manual by Zander Brietzke, written in consultation with the editors, provides valuable material for teaching both large survey courses and smaller lectures and seminars. This guide presents the most important topics that might be covered in a lecture on a given play; it also suggests creative classroom exercises for students who want to explore the complexities of a scene by performing it in class. Topics and exercises focus on particular passages and scenes, yet also cover larger themes, as do the handy paper topics provided for each play. Teachers will also find a list of prominent productions in the Instructor's Manual, along with a list of the best film adaptations that might be used in class or for further study. Of additional help is an extensive companion website, wwnorton.com/drama. Among other things, it offers students extensive review materials, a comprehensive glossary of terms, a guide to writing about drama, excerpts from well-known statements of drama theory, and "Plays in Performance" features, which present an illustrated overview of significant performances and their critical reception.

Coming from theater and literature departments, the editors of *The Norton Anthology of Drama* bring the perspectives of these overlapping disciplines to the project of compiling a compact anthology of dramatic literature. We have been aided in our efforts by a number of contributing editors, who have taken responsibilities for plays and playwrights that require special expertise. Numerous other scholars have lent knowledge and experience to this project—reading drafts of the headnotes and General Introduction; clarifying points of fact and interpretation; providing nuance, when needed, to prevent historical overgeneralization; and helping us track down and identify historical images for the anthology. Their names are mentioned in the Acknowledgments section that follows. *The Norton Anthology of Drama,* in short, has been a deeply collaborative process, in which scholars from a number of areas have pooled their expertise to produce the most complete, informative, and engaging anthology of its kind.

Acknowledgments

A project of this magnitude cannot reach its final form without the help and encouragement of many people beyond those whose names appear on the book's cover. Given our appreciation of and love for the collaborative art of theater, we editors of *The Norton Anthology of Drama* are especially sensitive to the countless ways in which we have been helped and inspired by others.

CONTRIBUTING EDITORS

First, we would like to acknowledge the following scholars, who lent us their expertise by editing and introducing specific plays:

Dina Ahmed Amin (Villanova University), *Song of Death*

Art Borreca (University of Iowa), *Angels in America: Millennium Approaches*

Karen Brazell (Cornell University), *Atsumori*

Thomas Cartelli (Muhlenberg College), *The Tragical History of the Life and Death of Doctor Faustus*

Ivo Kamps (University of Mississippi), *Hamlet; Twelfth Night*

Evan Darwin Winet (University of Pittsburgh), *Snow in Midsummer*

Each of these scholars has played a critical role in making the anthology what it is, and we are grateful to have had the opportunity to collaborate with them. In addition, we would like to thank Virginia Scott and Constance Congdon, whose translation of *Tartuffe* was undertaken specifically for *The Norton Anthology of Drama*.

We would also like to acknowledge the following people and institutions who provided us with advice, encouragement, administrative support, research assistance, and constructive critiques: Misty G. Anderson, Stephen Bottoms, Zander Brietzke, Meghan Brodie, Bruce E. Bursten, Debra Castillo, Amanda Claybaugh, Leonard Conolly, Jonah Corne, James E. Diamond, Kat Empson, John Ernest, David St. John and Loie Faulkner, Helene Foley, Mary and Charles Gainor, Alison Maerker Garner, Helen Elizabeth Garner, Stanton and Lydia Garner, Monika Gay, Helen Gilbert, Sandra Gilbert, Amy Gillingham, Esther Liu Godfrey, S. E. Gontarski, David Goslee, Cindy Grey, Laura L. Howes, Alexander C. Y. Huang, Shari Huhndorf, Veronica Kelly, William Kennedy, Daphne Lei, Mechele Leon, Diana Looser, Calvin MacLean, Charles Maland, Jonathan Marks, Meagan Michelson, Judith Milhous, Fred Muratori and the Reference and Interlibrary Loan Staff of Cornell University Libraries, Natalia Pevukhin, Alison G. Power, Gregary Racz,

Samuel C. Ramer, Jeffrey Rusten, Sabine Sörgel, Miriam Thaggert, Judith Thompson, Shawkat Toorawa, Dennis Walder, Judith Welch, Pamela Whaley, Katharina Wilson, Katherine Young, John Zomchick, the Yale Repertory Theatre, and the staff of the University of Tennessee Library Interlibrary Loan and Library Express departments.

We also acknowledge Bert Cardullo, who first proposed the anthology to Norton and who brought the original editorial team together.

The publisher and editors are grateful to all of the educators who responded to Norton surveys, questionnaires, and review requests during the early stages of this project. The anthology's shape has changed considerably over the years, in large part because of the good suggestions offered by the following people, whom we thank one and all: Michael Abbott, Gordon S. Armstrong, Yashdip S. Bains, Beulah Baker, Claudia Barnett, Susan Bennett, Linda Ben-Zvi, Robin Bernstein, Dallas Boggs, Scott Boltwood, Kazimierz Braun, Sybil Brinberg, Sarah Bryant-Bertail, Jackson R. Bryer, Ruth Cantrell, Anne Cattaneo, Dorothy Chansky, Kenneth Cox, Margaret Croskery, Marsha Cummins, Richard Cunningham, Koos Daley, Lynda Del Valle, William Demastes, Carlos Dews, Betty Diamond, Maria-Elena Doyle, Robert Duxbury, Michael Erickson, Chris Fisher, Terezinha Fonseca, Valerie L. Gager, Fanni Green, Elissa Guralnick, Janet Haedicke, Jerry Harris, Kevin J. Harty, David Hay, Woody Hood, David Hopes, Elisabeth Schulz Hostetter, Helen M. Housley, Keith N. Hull, William Hutchings, Bill Jenkins, Walter H. Johnson, P. Pennington Jones, Helen Killoran, Matthew Kinservik, Robert Knopf, Michael Kohler, David Kranes, Damon Kupper, James H. Lake, Penne J. Laubenthal, Bruce Leland, Paul M. Levitt, John L'Heureux, Stanley V. Longman, Wayne Luckman, Thomas Luddy, William Luhr, Kevin M. Lynch, Sue Mach, William MacLennan, Philip Manwell, Deborah Martinson, Cary Mazer, Joseph McCadden, Adrienne McCormick, Kirk Melnikoff, Lorraine Mercer, Naomi Miller, Lamata Mitchell, Kathleen Monahan, Deborah J. Montuori, Jonathan Morse, Joan Navarre, I. Nunnari, Pat Onion, Terry Otten, Howard Pearce, June Pulliam, Marjean D. Purinton, Rebecca Rumbo, William Streitberger, Wilbur Thomas, Randolph Umberger, Mardi Valgemae, Martine Van Elk, Ronald Wainscott, Albert Wertheim, David Wheeler, Lisa Whitney, Kayla Wiggins, Don B. Wilmeth, Janet S. Wolf, Leigh Woods, Joyce Wszalek, Kate Wulle, Trisha Yarbrough, Yvonne Yaw, Rick Yeatman, John T. Young, and Kelly Younger.

THE NORTON ANTHOLOGY OF DRAMA

SHORTER EDITION

Introduction

DRAMA AND THEATER

Audiences gather in a hillside amphitheater under the eastern Mediterranean sun to watch the impersonated figures of Greek myth play out their heroic, terrifying stories. In Kyoto, Japan, the sweep of robes on a railed wooden bridge announces the entry of a masked noh actor, who moves and gestures in front of his aristocratic audience with stylized precision. In London, a group of traveling players are given advice on acting by a Danish prince while the spectators who crowd the theater—aldermen, midwives, apprentices—enjoy the irony of actors meditating on their craft. In Paris, two tramps sitting by a tree on a country road share conversation and stage routines that barely conceal their anguish; an audience, seated in the dark, bears witness to their starkly contemporary situation.

The history of theater and dramatic performance is, in many ways, the history of moments such as these. The collaborative product of actors, playwrights, designers, directors, and spectators, theater achieves its magic in the live moment, rich with its sounds, sights, and feelings. The immediacy of the audience-stage encounter renders the act of theater-making magical and unique. Like other art forms—such as novels, paintings, and movies—theater constructs imaginative worlds that we can marvel at, be moved by, and learn from. Unlike these other forms, however, theater puts its worlds into live motion, in real time. In a kind of alchemy, theater takes the realm of fiction and brings it to life with living beings whose interactions take place before our eyes. At the same time, it takes the experiences of everyday life and transforms them through the magic of performance into something more powerful, deeply felt, and artful than the daily exchanges we witness and participate in. The actor stands in for us, embodies our hopes and fears, boldly enacts what is forbidden or only dreamed of. And like the theater itself, the actor introduces us to the pleasures inherent in recognition, imitation, and the intensity of a life passionately observed and lived.

Theater is the art of the moment, and its ability to captivate us with its illusion is linked to its magical but always precarious sleight of hand. Theater is the most ephemeral of vehicles—a performance, once finished, is lost to time—and the unrepeatability of its accomplishments is a major source of its power. Unlike film, which fixes action in celluloid or other media, theater takes place in the actual, in the here and now that it shares with its spectators, and its illusions are inseparable from its precariousness. Not surprisingly, the most memorable playgoing experiences are often those when something goes wrong—a stage chair collapses, a piece of stage machinery fails, an understudy is rushed on during the middle of a performance when the main actor falls ill—and the carefully constructed dramatic illusion hangs in the balance.

Central to the act of theater-making is the dramatic text, play-text, or script, which serves as the fictional and narrative foundation of the theatrical event. Whether these texts are loosely sketched, as in the improvisational performances of the Renaissance commedia dell'arte, or highly detailed in plot, setting, characterization, and dialogue, the use of scripted narratives is one of the principal features distinguishing theater from other performance types. With the invention of writing, these texts became artworks in and of themselves, and drama assumed its place as the first "literary" form, no longer exclusively dependent on performance for its realization. Plays were available in manuscript form to the educated elite of ancient Greece and Rome; classical India, China, and Japan; and medieval Europe; and after the invention of the printing press in the fifteenth century, they became available to an expanding popular readership. The plays of WILLIAM SHAKESPEARE and TENNESSEE WILLIAMS share space on twenty-first-century bookstore shelves with the novels of Jane Austen and Cormac McCarthy. But the literary dimension of dramatic works remains inseparable from performance—actual, possible, historical, imagined—with the result that drama has different aims and reference points than do more exclusively literary forms. To read a novel is to project characters, actions, and locations within an imaginative realm that is guided and limited by the words on the page; it is to undertake a mental and emotional activity that resembles dreaming more than it does the actions we engage in daily. To read a play, in contrast, is to encounter a text whose primary purpose, with rare exceptions, is to make something happen in real space and time with actors whose bodies and voices are the drama's principal instruments. In this sense, a play resembles a symphonic score, whose printed notations are directions for the production of musical sound. Even those plays that we refer to as "closet dramas," which were usually not performed when written—whether because of political, technical, or cultural barriers or because their authors preferred them to be read or recited rather than subjected to the stage's inherent limitations—often seem to have been created with some ideal performance in mind.

As the final section of this introduction ("Reading Drama, Imagining Theater") will discuss in more detail, drama invites the reader to put her- or himself in the position of a theater artist, alive to the possibilities and choices that bring a play to life, imagining the different ways that a scene, line, or gesture might look, sound, and feel when performed. Being attentive to the conditions of performance allows one to appreciate the features that characterize drama as a literary and theatrical form: the necessary economy of its action, setting, and characterization, which are denied the leisure of novelistic description; the centrality of spoken language, which provides access to offstage and subjective worlds; and the preoccupation with questions of role-playing, impersonation, and the many ways in which we perform for the benefit of others and ourselves. In the absence of an omniscient narrator or other guiding authorial consciousness, drama emerges through the interplay of its characters, who enact their stories in the theater and on the imagined stage of one's reading. The power of these stories resides in the immediacy of the actors and their interactions with the theater environment, which of course includes the audience.

Humans have always told each other stories. From the earliest times for which we have physical or documentary evidence, we have acted our stories for each other. We donned costumes and masks, wielded props, and later created designated places—theaters—where we use the immediacy of live performance to communicate the powerful experiences that have shaped us. Like other forms of organized social performance—games, festivities,

Spectators watch a performance of Anton Chekhov's *Three Sisters* at the Guthrie Theater in Minneapolis, 1963.

storytelling, athletic displays, civic ceremonies, political events, and rituals—these encounters are deeply embedded in specific historical, social, and cultural con texts. To study the history of theater and drama is to confront a range of historical junctures, social and institutional practices, and cultural forms. It is also to encounter one of the most enduring of human activities: make-believe, the act of making oneself other than oneself for purposes of entertainment, commemoration, communication, or devotion.

Through performance and its rituals, we confirm our shared humanity—we acknowledge the importance of each other's existence and suggest that our lives are of value. Collectively, we generate forms of community while articulating the meanings that lend shape to our lives. The sense of communion and reciprocal awareness engendered by live performance, and the dramatic texts written for it, transcends cultures and history; it is foundational to who we are as living beings. As prehistoric cave paintings indicate, imitation and ritual were part of the earliest human societies. We are performers by nature. Although theater and drama are relative latecomers to human history (having been around for a mere 2,500 years), the activities they draw on are as old as humanity itself.

A SHORT HISTORY OF THEATER

The origins of theater—and hence of drama—have long been a subject of scholarly debate. We possess little material evidence concerning the development of theatrical activity in most cultures, and what generalizations we might draw from it are complicated by the fact that the earliest forms of theater were the product of a variety of social, political, and religious forces. However, those studying different dramatic traditions have found theater to be closely connected to hunting, fertility, and other rituals in those early societies where it emerged. The nature of this connection has been debated by scholars, but the consensus view is that theatrical activity represented an extension of ritual's symbolic forms of representation into nonritual contexts. The rituals of early societies involved the enactment of religious and mythic narratives by privileged participants—shaman, priest, ruler, sacrificial victim—and these performances could become quite elaborate. In Egypt, rituals commemorating the death and resurrection of Osiris, a god associated with fertility, took place at the sacred site of Abydos as early as 2500 B.C.E. Evidence suggests that the dramatic events of Osiris's life may have been performed by priests and that these performances were accompanied by lavish spectacle.

Ritual differs from theater, of course, in that its prescribed actions, passed down from generation to generation, are designed to effect change in the natural or spiritual worlds. The ritual performances of Egypt remained tied to their religious and dynastic functions and never developed in the direction of theater. In those cultures in which theater did emerge, symbolic performance asserted itself as an object of interest in its own right, thereby paving the way for institutions, practitioners, and audiences who conceived of theater as a communal artistic activity. The earliest of these transitions—and one of the most important for the subsequent history of theater and drama—occurred in Greece in the fifth century B.C.E.

Greek Theater

ORIGINS OF GREEK THEATER

The theater of classical Greece looms large in the history of Western theater. Not only did the emergence of theater as an institution in Athens during the fifth century B.C.E. establish the world's first theatrical culture, but the characters who confronted their fate on the Greek stage—Orestes, Oedipus, Antigone, Medea—remain among the most imposing characters in the dramatic repertoire. Yet despite the importance of Greek theater to the history of Western drama, little is known about its origins. Scholars have depended, for the most part, on the scattered remarks of later classical writers who were themselves speculating about events hundred of years in the past. Archaeological findings, the history of words associated with the theater, and vase paintings have since provided additional hints as to how the first Greek theaters came into existence. Most scholars subscribe to the notion that the origins of Greek theater lie in religious rituals. Ancient Greek religious life included many different types of ceremonies and public performances: funeral services, festivals celebrating the seasons or individual gods, processions and competitions. But which of these performances provided the decisive impulse is much harder to pinpoint. The Greek word for tragedy, *tragōidia,* originally meant "goat song" and therefore seems to associate tragedy with ritual practices involving the killing of a goat. Other theories hold that theater emerged from rituals performed at the tombs of heroes.

Though we know little about either the goat song or the ritual performances at tombs, other cultural practices that aided the development of theater are much better documented. Among them are the public performances of storytellers, or *rhapsōidoi,* who recited stories of gods and mythical humans to large audiences. The first theorist of theater, the philosopher Plato (ca. 427–ca. 347 B.C.E.), emphasized the similarities between public recitations of epic poetry and simple dramatic performances. What is still the most convincing theory about the origin of Greek theater was developed by Aristotle (384–322 B.C.E.), who wrote a generation after his teacher Plato. Aristotle claimed that theater emerged from a specific ceremony honoring Dionysus, a god associated with fertility, agriculture, wine, and (by extension) physical and spiritual intoxication. During the Attic ceremony honoring him, a chorus and a chorus leader (*koryphaios*) sang and danced a hymn composed in a particular form known as the *dithyrambos.* According to Aristotle, these ritual performances formed the basis for later dramatic performance. The Greek language reinforces Aristotle's claim, for the choral

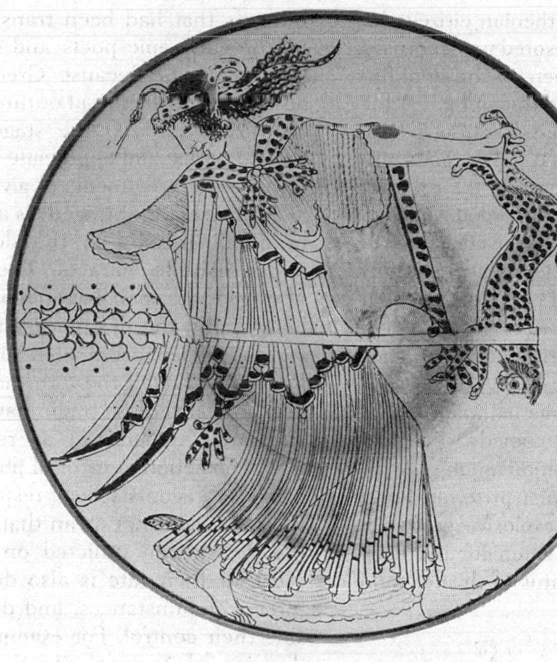

This image, a detail from a *kylix* (a wine cup) painted by the so-called Brygos Painter in the early fifth century B.C.E., depicts a devotee (a *bacchante* or *maenad*) of the god Dionysus performing a ritualized dance. In her right hand is a *thrysus*, an ivy-covered staff that was an important part of sacred rituals.

performers of dithyrambs were called *tragōidoi*, pointing once again to the later word for tragedy.

The association of theater with the dithyrambs performed in the honor of Dionysus makes sense for many reasons. The first Greek playwright, Thespis (sixth century B.C.E.), whose plays have all been lost, is credited with adding an individual performer to the dithyrambic chorus and chorus leader, and thus enabling dramatic interaction to emerge. Because Thespis himself is said to have performed this newly individual role, he is considered by many to be the world's first actor, and his name has given us the word *thespian*. From this point on the chorus (or chorus leader) was not limited to reciting a hymn but could impersonate an imaginary figure by engaging in a dialogue with the newly introduced actor. The Greek word for actor, *hypokritēs*, by the way, still exists in the English word *hypocrite*, whose now largely negative meaning underscores that acting involves imitation and pretense. Subsequent playwrights added more actors to increase the possibilities for dialogue between individuals, although the chorus remained an important component of Greek, and subsequently of Roman, theater.

Another reason for associating theater with the Dionysian dithyrambs is that the first known Greek plays were performed at the City Dionysia, one of four Athenian festivals (another was the Rural Dionysia) held during the winter in honor of the god. Over the course of the fifth century, when Greek theater was at its height, other festivals incorporated dramatic performances, but the City Dionysia remained the most important event for theater. The City Dionysia, which attracted many visitors from other city-states and from outside Greece, was a multiday affair, whose focus was various competitions. The first was a competition of dithyrambs, first organized around 600 B.C.E., among the four (later ten) "tribes" (*phylai*)—the administrative and military divisions to which all Athenian citizens belonged. Each tribe sponsored two choruses, one consisting of fifty men, the other of fifty boys. Although these dithyrambic performances centered on the worship of Dionysus, they soon included other gods and myths as well. As early as 534 B.C.E., when Thespis became the first recorded winner of the prize for tragedy, plays were added to the program. By the beginning of the fifth century, a system was in place: each dramatist had to compose three tragedies, which were followed by the performance of a short satirical work (called a *satyr play*). Somewhat later, around 486 B.C.E., another type of drama was added: comedy. The City Dionysia held a competition among the different playwrights for first prize, an honor that helped spark the explosive growth in the number of plays written for the occasion and raising the status of theater more generally.

GREEK TRAGEDY

One development necessary for drama to emerge from these various rituals and performances was the invention of writing and the spread of literacy. Greek rituals did not include written scripts but were instead based on formulaic and orally transmitted incantations, hymns, and performances. Likewise, dithyrambic and epic poems were originally memorized and improvised by the performers, but not composed as literature. The first epics to be preserved in writing were those attributed to Homer (ca. 750–700 B.C.E.), the *Iliad* and the *Odyssey;* and in the late seventh century, Arion (active 628–625 B.C.E.) was apparently the first to write down his own dithyrambs (none of which have survived). Consequently, Homer and Arion are considered by some to be the first tragedians, though they did not actually write plays.

The earliest extant tragedies all date from the fifth century and were written by three playwrights: Aeschylus (ca. 525–456 B.C.E.), SOPHOCLES (ca. 496–406 B.C.E.), and EURIPIDES (ca. 480–ca. 406 B.C.E.). These plays are set in a mythical past (with one exception—Aeschylus's *Persians,* which takes place during the Persian Wars), using the stories of gods and heroic humans that had been transmitted orally by the early epic poets and subsequently written down. Because Greek audiences already knew the broad outlines of the stories dramatized on the stage, they were able to notice and appreciate subtle differences in the treatments of given myths.

At the center of tragedy is a conflict that eventually results in the downfall of a larger-than-life character. The protagonists of tragedy are socially and morally elevated beings, and the destruction they undergo results, in part, from what Aristotle called *hamartia;* though the term has sometimes been translated as "tragic flaw," it is more accurately understood as referring to a mistaken action or error of judgment. That tragic protagonists bear responsibility for their fate does not mean that they deserve the destruction inflicted on them, however, for their fate is also determined by forces, circumstances, and dilemmas outside their control. For example, while the decision of Antigone (in Sophocles' play of the same name) to bury her brother Polyneices follows the religious imperative, obeying that imperative brings her into conflict with her uncle Creon, the king of Thebes, who has declared him a traitor and therefore has forbidden his burial. Faced with this set of forces not of her making—one, a social and religious mandate; the other, a legal prohibition—Antigone has no alternative but to choose her tragic fate. Similarly, the protagonist of Sophocles' *OEDIPUS THE KING* (ca. 428 B.C.E.), who unknowingly killed his father and married his mother, must accept punishment for deeds performed not with malicious intent but with an overweening pride and belief in his own invulnerability. Ironically, the man of action and the solver of the Sphinx's riddle proves rash in his actions and blind to fate's riddle in his own life. Virtues and flaws, the notion of *hamartia* may also suggest, are intimately tied up in each other: we can trust our talents and strengths too much and learn, in the outcome of our actions, that they are both the reason for our good fortune and the cause of our demise.

As these tragic conflicts unfold, the protagonists find themselves in another contentious relation, namely with the chorus. Not surprisingly, given its origins in choral dithyrambs, tragedy retained the chorus as an important element. Reflecting the perspective of the community, this body observes and comments on the actions and entanglements of the protagonists, trying to rein in their excesses and restore order to the civic realm. The chorus also reminds the audience of the background story of a given myth and often engages the protagonists in a dialogue that draws out the motives of their actions. In keeping with the evolving nature of Greek tragedy during the fifth century, the role of the chorus underwent changes. As dramatic characters grew in number, complexity, and importance, the role of the chorus lessened.

This detail from the so-called Pronomos Vase, painted in the late fifth century B.C.E., depicts actors preparing for a satyr play.

The complexity of the relations between individual actors and the chorus shaped the typical structure of Greek tragedy. Greek tragedies begin either with a prologue that sets the scene or with the entrance—*parodos*—of the chorus. The main body of the tragedy is then composed of a sequence of episodes—*epeisodia,* scenes in which the main actors talk to one another or to the chorus—and choral songs without dialogue, *stasima.* At the end of the play, the characters and the chorus leave the stage in what is called the *exodos.* Greek tragedy, in other words, was a highly structured and formalized art form in which dialogue between two individual actors, today the main component of drama, was relatively unimportant. Instead, choral lyrics and the dialogue between chorus and protagonist took up most of the play. Playwrights used different styles of language and meter to distinguish between the different sections of tragedy. Choral lyrics were a form of poetry highly elevated in diction and intricately composed, while the exchanges between the chorus and individual characters, though still quite stylized, were more conversational. The dialogues in iambic meter between the individual characters, though they too were artfully wrought, were closer still to everyday speech. Such differentiation can clearly be seen in the works of Euripides, who, writing slightly later than Aeschylus and Sophocles, attempted to bring the language of tragedy nearer to the language actually spoken by the audience.

As noted above, in its mature form the City Dionysia included a competition in which each dramatist presented three tragedies followed by a satyr play. Unfortunately, because only one complete satyr play has survived—Euripides' *Cyclops*—it is difficult to generalize about the genre. They plays seem to have dealt with the same mythical and heroic figures and stories as tragedies but irreverently, as burlesque. Accordingly, their language was apparently more colloquial than that of tragedy. The satyr play remained closely connected to Dionysus, for in Greek mythology satyrs were half-human and half-bestial creatures who formed part of his retinue, and the leader of the chorus in satyr plays was Silenus, a satyr who was a constant companion of the god. The satyr play provided the audience with comic relief at the end of a daylong performance of tragedies.

GREEK COMEDY

The satyr play, despite its comic elements, belonged to a genre distinct from comedy. Although comedies had not originally been part of festival competitions, they were incorporated into the City Dionysia festival around 486 B.C.E. The origins of comedy also lie in ritual, most likely in rites that featured groups of men wearing representations of large *phalloi* (male sexual organs) and animal masks. A second source for Greek comedy was a form of mime—short, improvised sketches treating everyday situations humorously. These foundations are visible in what is called Old Comedy, which developed in the fifth century; its only remaining examples are the plays of ARISTOPHANES (ca. 450–ca. 385 B.C.E.), although the names of other comic playwrights are known to us, including Magnes (active 472 B.C.E.) and Aristophanes' main rival, Eupolis (ca. 445–ca. 411 B.C.E.). The choruses of comedy may well represent animals or inanimate objects—Aristophanes' plays have such titles as *The Frogs, The Wasps,* and *The Clouds*—and they often treat explicitly sexual themes. In contrast to both tragedy and the satyr play, comedies take as their subject matter not the gods and heroes of Greek mythology but rather the everyday life of contemporary Athenians, and the topics they engage range from the long Peloponnesian War with Sparta (which provides the background to *LYSISTRATA* [411 B.C.E.], Aristophanes' best-known play) to public personalities such as the philosopher Socrates. Like tragedy, Old Comedy begins with a prologue, which is followed by the entry of the chorus; it contains passages of dialogue; and it concludes with the exit of all the characters. It also features an added element: a section called the *parabasis* (literally, "digression") in which the chorus addresses the audience directly, discussing political and social problems and sometimes praising the playwright. In the *parabasis* and throughout each play, classical comedy engages with political and social issues much more directly than tragedy, although it does so comically, drawing on fantasy, humor that frequently is ribald, and farce.

THE GREEK STAGE

The main performance venue for Athenian theater was the Dionysus theater, located in the hill just below the Acropolis, an elevated area on which stood the Parthenon and which served as the city's religious and political center. Given the elaborate nature of later Greek and Roman theaters, the Dionysus theater in the fifth century was surprisingly simple. A large *amphitheatron,* holding between 14,000 to 17,000 audience members, was built into the hillside, with seating provided by temporary wooden benches. At the center of the amphitheater was the *orchēstra* (or "dancing place"), a semicircle in whose middle stood the *thymelē,* a raised stone used as an altar or a table. Behind the *orchēstra* stood a wooden structure, the *skēnē,* which served as a place where actors could change masks and costumes and, through one or more doors, appear and disappear from the stage. The area in front of the *skēnē* would later be known as the *paraskēnion,* a term from which the modern word *proscenium* derives. On either side of the *skēnē* were passageways.

This physical arrangement was used by the Greek dramatists in increasingly complex ways. The passageways aided the elaborate entrances and exits of the chorus, while the *orchēstra* was the place where the dances performed by the chorus and the interaction between chorus and individual actors took place. The altar or table could be used by individual actors to hide and suddenly appear. The *skēnē* at the back of the performance area provided even more theatrical possibilities. For example, playwrights placed messengers and other figures on its roof, where they could be on the lookout and describe battles and other scenes they pretended to see on its other side (a stage device called *teichoskopeia,* or "watching from a wall"). The doors in the *skēnē* were used not only to aid entrances and exits but also to suddenly reveal characters. To heighten the effect of the doors, a rolling platform, or *ekkyklēma,* was employed to roll the body of a killed character in front of the audience or to make other dramatic disclosures. Such a device was especially important since almost all physical violence—the blinding of Oedipus, for example, or Medea's murder of her children—occurred offstage, often (the audience was led to believe) within the scene building. A second mechanism became increasingly popular: a crane called a *mēchanē*, which could move characters through the air into the space in front of the scene building. Euripides, in particular, used such cranes to introduce gods, who would resolve the plot and mete out punishment at the end of his tragedies; this device became well-known by its Latin name, *deus ex machina* (god from a machine). Various forms of painted panels were probably employed on the stage as well, though little is known about their appearance and function.

Because theater was an integral part of civic and religious festivals, an elaborate system of rules and practices governed the production of plays. A leading figure of the Athenian government, an *archōn eponymos*, selected from among the wealthy citizens a *chorēgos*, or producer, who would provide the funds for the chorus, while the city government provided the funds for the playwright and the leading actors. The playwrights were responsible for rehearsals and sometimes even performed in their own plays. The number of performers was strictly limited. The chorus probably contained twelve to fifteen members, although as many as fifty may have appeared in some early plays of Aeschylus. The number of individual actors was even more crucial, because it directly affected how many characters were available to the playwright. Aeschylus's early plays used two actors, who could take on different roles over the course of a play—but obviously, no more than two speaking parts could be present simultaneously. Either Aeschylus or, more likely, his younger rival Sophocles took the decisive step of introducing a third actor, thereby expanding the playwright's options considerably.

One reason why actors could change so easily from one role to the next was the relative simplicity of their costumes. A thick, richly colored garment covered their bodies; large, high boots made them appear larger than life; and a mask made from either fabric or wood covered their entire face. Given the size of the theater and the bulkiness of their costumes, the actors had to rely on large gestures rather than on small, intimate reactions, and in masks they lacked any recourse to facial expressions.

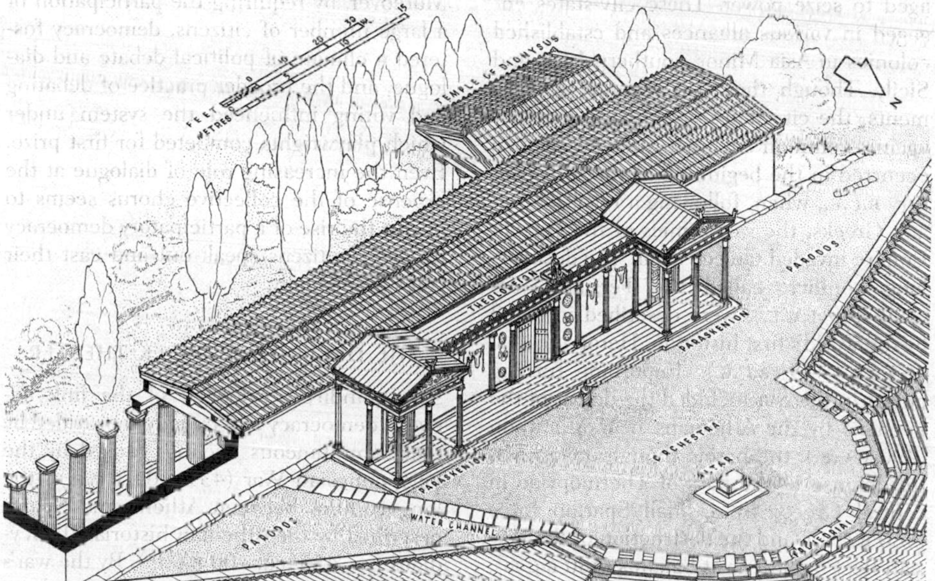

A reconstruction of the Dionysus theater by the theater and architectural scholar Richard Leacroft. An actor stands in the *orchēstra*, while another stands on the roof of the *skēnē*.

Scenes of dialogue alternated with the elaborate dances of the chorus. The performance of Greek plays was accompanied by music, provided mainly by the flute—it was a flute player who led the entrance of the chorus at the beginning of the play—but various other wind and percussion instruments were employed as well. Today's audiences and readers can easily overlook the significance of music, which is generally little used in contemporary revivals of Greek plays, but the scholars and artists who attempted to revive Greek tragedy during the European Renaissance were very conscious of its importance. Indeed, this awareness led to the creation of opera, a form of theater that relies primarily on music and song and only secondarily on spoken dialogue.

THEATER AND ATHENIAN DEMOCRACY

The emergence and rise of Greek theater is intimately tied to the political history of Greece. Greece was not a unified nation but rather a network of city-states—Athens, Sparta, Corinth, and Thebes, among others—ruled by kings or, from the seventh century onward, by nobles who had managed to seize power. These city-states engaged in various alliances and established colonies in Asia Minor, southern Italy, and Sicily. Though they had separate governments, the city-states could band together against common enemies. Such an alliance occurred in the beginning of the fifth century B.C.E., when, following a revolt of Asiatic Greeks, the vast armies of the Persian Empire invaded Greece itself. The decades-long conflict, called the Persian Wars (499–449 B.C.E.), were described in detail by the world's first historian, Herodotus (ca. 484–ca. 425 B.C.E.). Important turning points in the war included the defeat of the Persians by the Athenians near Marathon (490 B.C.E.), the heroic though unsuccessful defense of the pass of Thermopylae in central Greece by a small Spartan force (480 B.C.E.), and the destruction of the Persian fleet by Athens at Salamis (480 B.C.E.), a battle that was critical to Persia's subsequent defeat.

The crucial role of Athens in winning this victory led to its increasing dominance over the rest of Greece, and it built a largely seaborne empire consisting of allies, dependent states, and colonies. It was during this time of military dominance that Athens became a cosmopolitan center for the arts—the birthplace of Greek theater and the center of many other intellectual and cultural pursuits, such as philosophy (although many philosophers living in Athens were foreign-born). Equally important was the development in Athens of an early form of democracy that involved all adult male citizens in the governance of the Athenian empire, serving in the courts, military offices, and other administrative posts. Women, slaves, and foreigners, it is important to note, were not considered citizens. Moreover, though it was a predecessor of modern democracies, Athenian democracy included many features that might strike today's citizens as odd, such as the choosing of important positions by lot (to avoid favoritism). Many scholars consider the rise of Athenian theater and of democracy to be related developments. It is likely that most of the city's inhabitants, including Athenian women and slaves of both sexes, were allowed to attend theater performances, though only adult male citizens could perform in the chorus and as individual actors. Moreover, by requiring the participation of a large number of citizens, democracy fostered a climate of political debate and dialogue, and the broader practice of debating and voting influenced the system under which playwrights competed for first prize. Even the increasing role of dialogue at the expense of the collective chorus seems to mirror the rise of a participatory democracy in which citizens speak out and cast their votes individually.

THE DECLINE OF GREEK THEATER

Strong indirect evidence of the link between democracy and tragedy is provided by their simultaneous decline, caused by the Peloponnesian War (431–404 B.C.E.)—the long conflict between Athens and Sparta described by the Athenian historian Thucydides (ca. 455–ca. 400 B.C.E.). By the war's end, Athens had lost its empire and, at least temporarily, its democracy. Though Greek theater continued to develop—chiefly through the emergence, in the following

The ruins of the theater at Epidaurus, Greece. The theater was built in the middle of the fourth century B.C.E.

century, of New Comedy, whose main practitioner was the playwright Menander (ca. 342–ca. 292 B.C.E.) and whose plays depended much less on fantastic plots and conceits than had their Old Comedy predecessors—by the end of the fifth century the most important era of Greek theater had come to an end.

GREEK THEORIES OF DRAMA

The fourth century's contribution to theater history was the work of two authors who together provided the first written theories of drama: Plato and Aristotle. Though Plato did not take up the subject separately, his philosophy as a whole is deeply engaged with the theater as medium and institution. All of his works were written as dialogues, and although there is no evidence of their performance before large audiences, they may have been recited by students in his Academy, the school that he founded (which took its name from its site, a park sacred to the legendary hero Academus). In these dialogues, Plato—or, more precisely, his main character, Socrates—is often critical of tragedy and comedy as well as of actors, arguing that drama and other works of art offer mere representations of the world and therefore stand in the way of the pursuit of truth, which consists of knowledge of the things themselves. Drawn to the exchange of ideas but suspicious of the seductions of theatrical performance, Plato offered his own philosophical dialogues as an alternative form of drama.

Plato's student Aristotle, by contrast, devoted an entire treatise to the subject of tragedy, describing its classifications, elements, and structure and examining its effect on spectators. In his widely influential *Poetics*, probably composed around 330 B.C.E., Aristotle discusses the origin of tragedy in dithyrambic hymns, the nature of the heroic protagonist, the function of the chorus, and what he considers to be the six crucial elements of theater: plot, character, thought, diction, music, and spectacle (the last is accorded a marginal position in his descriptive hierarchy). He also emphasizes certain plot elements, such as sudden reversals (*peripeteiai*) and the moment of recognition (*anagnōrisis*), and insists that unlike epic poetry, with its meandering plots, tragedy should present a single, unified action. This focus mandates that the action of tragedy be confined to short periods of time, typically one day, and to a single place. Renaissance commentators on the *Poetics* turned these recommendations into the three unities—of time, place, and action—that, according to the strictures of what became known as neoclassical theory, must be maintained by playwrights.

In response to Plato's attack on theatrical representation, Aristotle defended actors by arguing that the drive to imitate, *mimēsis,* was a common human trait and served as a source of pleasure. Perhaps the most influential term introduced in this treatise was *katharsis,* the purging or cleansing of emotions that was the desired effect of tragedy on the audience. Whereas Plato had argued that the extreme emotions depicted in tragedy could have adverse effects on the audience and therefore recommended that playwrights, like other artists, be banished from his ideal republic, Aristotle held that tragedy provided a release, a *katharsis,* of those stirred-up emotions—particularly fear and pity—and that dramatic art thus served a socially therapeutic function. The disagreement between Plato and Aristotle about the value of theater, the reaction of the audience, and the status of actors has persisted to the present—in our debates, for instance, about depictions of violence onstage and on the screen. Much as the playwrights of the fifth century B.C.E. have continued to influence theater history, so the philosophers of the fourth century still shape our thinking about theater.

Roman Theater

The decline of Athens, which at its height had dependent colonies in Italy (where Greeks from several city-states had settled as early as the eighth century B.C.E.), coincided with the rise and expanding influence of Rome. By the middle of the third century B.C.E., the city-state of Rome had managed to unify most of Italy under its leadership, and its victory over its North African rival, Carthage, in the First Punic War (264–241 B.C.E.) enabled Rome to extend its hegemony over Sicily as well as parts of Greece itself. One hundred years later, Rome had absorbed the entire Greek world, on its way to becoming one of the largest empires ever created.

Even though Rome was a rising military power, its art, literature, philosophy, and theater remained heavily influenced by those of Greece. Like Greek theater, Roman theater was performed in the context of civic festivals, here called *ludi,* which by 240 B.C.E. included both tragedies and comedies. The most important of these festivals were the *Ludi Romani,* which honored not Dionysus (or his Roman counterpart, Bacchus) but Jupiter, chief of the gods. This and other festivities differed from their Greek counterparts in significant ways. Influenced by the earlier performance practices of the Etruscans, who belonged to an earlier civilization (centered in present-day Tuscany and part of Umbria) that reached its height in the sixth century B.C.E., the festivities of early Rome included a variety of nondramatic entertainments—chariot races, prize-

Roman masks—one tragic, one comic—as depicted in a wall mosaic from the first century B.C.E.

fighting, dance, farce—that vied with dramatic performance for the spectators' attention. Relatively few early Roman tragedies and comedies survive, although it is clear that most were adaptations of existing Greek plays, which were introduced to Rome in 240 B.C.E. The first known dramatists in Rome, Livius Andronicus (ca. 284–ca. 204 B.C.E.) and Gnaeus Naevius (ca. 270–201 B.C.E.), adapted both Greek tragedies and comedies into Latin, while later playwrights, including the tragedians Quintus Ennius (239–169 B.C.E.) and Lucius Accius (170–ca. 86 B.C.E.), specialized in one or the other genre. Even though Roman tragedies were mostly versions of Greek ones, Roman playwrights introduced considerable alterations, changes, and innovations; far from being a sign of unoriginality, adaptation thus became a special art form. Whereas the Greek playwrights had used known stories and characters in composing their plays, Roman playwrights perfected a more elaborate technique of imitation by working from established dramatic models.

ROMAN COMEDY

Though both tragedies and comedies were performed in Roman theaters, comedy was the genre in which Roman playwrights excelled. Roman comedians could look back at a long tradition of farce, and they drew especially on Atellan farce, a burlesque form based on improvisation and a small set of stock characters that took its name from Atella, a town near Naples in southern Italy. These improvised sketches and stock characters remained popular throughout the history of Rome and beyond, influencing such later theater traditions as Italy's commedia dell'arte. At the same time, a more literary form of comedy, based on Greek Old and New Comedy, was developing. The two most famous Roman playwrights—Titus Maccius Plautus (ca. 254–ca. 184 B.C.E.) and Terence (Publius Terentius Afer, ca. 190–159 B.C.E.)—were authors of such comedies. The most important changes Plautus and Terence made to their Greek models were eliminating the chorus and significantly expanding the use of music, thereby turning their comedies into a kind of musical theater.

EMPIRE AND SPECTACLE

The height of Roman drama, as represented by Plautus and Terence, occurred under the Roman Republic, a political system that allowed a limited number of citizens to participate in government and prevented any single individual from gaining supreme power. It was under the Republic that Rome established its dominance through the Second Punic War with Carthage (218–201 B.C.E.) and finally defeated and destroyed Carthage in 146 at the end of the Third Punic War (149–146 B.C.E.). Rome now dominated not only Italy and Greece

This detail from a Roman mosaic depicts a *venation*—a battle between a leopard and a gladiator.

but also large parts of northern Africa. The resulting flow of wealth and power to Rome increasingly undermined republican institutions, and the Republic gave way to an empire with an absolute ruler. Under the emperors—beginning with Augustus (63 B.C.E.–14 C.E.)—Rome expanded its empire as far as England, Germany, France, Spain, and the Balkans and controlled the entire Mediterranean basin.

The increasing scale of the Roman Empire, and the unheard-of concentration of wealth and power in Rome itself, fueled a tendency toward expensive and lavish spectacles, comparable perhaps to blockbuster Hollywood action films today. These nondramatic varieties of performance, most of them significantly more spectacular than anything seen on the dramatic stage, came to overshadow tragedy and comedy. Among these new public entertainments were chariot races held in sizable arenas, the largest of which, the Circus Maximus in Rome, accommodated more than 60,000 spectators. Other spectacles included elaborately orchestrated, and often lethal, sea battles, which sometimes involved thousands of participants; contests called *venationes,* in which wild animals fought against one another or against humans; and of course the most emblematic and notorious of Roman spectacles—gladiatorial contests, which featured hand-to-hand combat to the death. Although their appetite for staged (but real) violence was voracious, Romans weren't entirely bloodthirsty in their entertainment preferences; pantomime and short comic sketches of mime performances were also very popular.

CLOSET TRAGEDY

The overwhelming popularity of nondramatic entertainments led to a decline of traditional dramatic forms, especially tragedy and comedy. Writers with literary ambitions therefore began to create "closet dramas," plays designed to be recited at small, private gatherings or to be read in private. In fact, the most famous Roman tragic dramatist, Lucius Annaeus Seneca (4 B.C.E.–65 C.E.), wrote only closet dramas, and his plays were never performed on the great Roman stages of the time. Modeled on Greek tragedy, Seneca's tragedies are composed in an intricate, literary Latin that became a model for many subsequent writers. That these dramas were not written to be performed did not make them less violent. Indeed, unlike Greek tragedy, which had hidden most of its violence offstage, Seneca required that the audience or readers envision it as happening in their "sight." Though few in his own time would have known of his plays, they proved enormously influential on later playwrights, including the Elizabethan playwrights Thomas Kyd and WILLIAM SHAKESPEARE.

THE ROMAN STAGE

Although plays had been written in Latin since the third century B.C.E., the first permanent theater—erected at Pompeii—was not built until 55 B.C.E. Before that time, temporary stages (often quite stable and elaborate) were used for dramatic and other performances. Modeled on their Greek predecessors, Roman theaters included large amphitheaters for the audience; these could be built into hills, like Greek theaters, or erected on level ground. The amphitheater formed a semicircle similar to the Greek *orchēstra,* which was closed on one side by a building, the *scaena,* which was the counterpart of the Greek *skēnē*. In their adaptation from one society to another, however, the function and proportions of these elements changed significantly. For example, the *orchēstra* was used by the chorus, but its Roman equivalent was occupied—as it is in today's theaters—by the most privileged of the audience members. The action of the play took place on a raised stage, or *pulpitum,* located in front of the scene building, which was significantly larger and more elaborate than its Greek predecessor. Supported by several sets of columns and often ornately decorated, the scene building could be many stories high—a change that had profound implications. Unlike the audience of Greek theater, whose view of the stage was framed by landscape and sky, the Roman audience looked entirely at the artificial world created on a stage.

Even as playwrights such as Seneca withdrew from the stage, the Roman taste for spectacle—races, parades, festivals, and staged battles—led to the development of

A digital reconstruction of the interior of the theater of Pompey in Rome. This image—based on a collaborative research project by Richard Beacham, James E. Packer, and John Burge—was generated by the King's Visualization Lab and is copyright © King's College London.

elaborate stage machinery. Roman theater producers not only instituted the stage curtain but also invented sliding panels, cranes, and a type of elevator with which actors or animals could be lifted onto the stage from below. They also introduced more complex, three-dimensional stage decorations, extensive stage props, and even live animals. The actors, called *histriones* in Latin, were not, as had originally been the case in Greece, talented citizen amateurs; instead, they were theater professionals, some of whom were slaves. Their acting style ranged from burlesque and conversational for comedy to more formal and declamatory for tragedy. Costumes and masks were mostly fashioned on Greek models.

THE DECLINE AND INFLUENCE OF ROMAN THEATER

Roman theater declined significantly with the rise of Christianity, which won official toleration in 313 C.E. when the emperor Constantine I issued the Edict of Milan; it soon became the dominant religion in the Roman Empire. Christian clergy were highly critical of theater and in particular its actors, declaring the attendance of theater cause for excommunication and denying actors the holy sacraments (a practice that remained in place in some parts of Europe well into the modern era). Yet despite the theater's waning under Christianity, the influence of classical theater would reverberate through the centuries. The architecture of Roman theater buildings helped shape Renaissance stage design, for example, and Roman comedy and tragedy were important models for English Renaissance playwrights, who often knew of Greek works only through their Roman adaptations and translations. Equally vital for Renaissance theater was Rome's most significant critic, the poet Quintus Horatius Flaccus, known as Horace (65–8 B.C.E.), whose *Ars Poetica* (*The Art of Poetry* [ca. 10 B.C.E.]) discusses the origins, forms, and ends of drama. Recommending such formal practices as the division of plays into five acts, Horace also offered a powerfully moral conception of drama's function. Not only should playwrights cater to their audiences, he asserted, they should also serve as moral instructors: their works, in other words, should prove useful (*utile*) as well as pleasing (*dulce*). In keeping with this conception of theater's social role, he argued against the more fantastic, spectacular, and violent aspects of Roman theater. Like those of Aristotle, his views on drama were taken up by later theorists of drama and theater.

Although Roman theater was in many ways derivative, the influence of its drama, architecture, and practice on subsequent theater history was even greater than that of its Greek predecessor and model. The plays of Plautus, Terence, and Seneca inspired the work of later playwrights, and Roman theater technology—much of it described in *De Architectura* (*On Architecture*), written in the first century B.C.E. by the architect and engineer Vitruvius—made important contributions to theater design during the European Renaissance. One of the most lasting legacies of Roman theater may be the division it opened up between drama as a literary genre and stage as a site of spectacle. In later centuries, in the great ages of world theater, drama and theater have often worked hand in hand; but at times they have become estranged, leading to forms of literary drama disconnected from a theater system mainly interested in extravagant spectacle. To the extent that this division still informs our theater today—when, for example, lavish Broadway spectacles divert attention from serious plays—we are still in the process of working through the inheritance of Roman theater.

Classical Indian Theater

During the millennium after Greece and Rome established the outlines of European theatrical culture, the foundations were being laid for separate traditions in Asia. The earliest, and arguably the most influential, form of Asian theater emerged in India, home to one of the world's oldest civilizations. By 2500 B.C.E. the Indus Valley civilization had introduced city-states and a technologically advanced agricultural society in northwestern and western India. Its decline was caused in part by internal weakness and in part by the incursions of the Aryans, a nomadic people from northern Iran or central Asia. By 1500 B.C.E., the Indian subcontinent had been settled by the Aryans, who developed the Vedic civilization that would subsequently shape Indian history and culture. Central to this culture were the Vedas, or scriptures, that constituted the founding texts of Hinduism (the earliest of these, the *Rig-Veda*, was composed between 1500 and 1000 B.C.E.). Written in Sanskrit, these texts inspired a number of further writings; among them were two epic poems, the *Mahabharata* and the *Ramayana* (both written between 500 and 200 B.C.E.), which exerted a vast influence on later literature and theater in India and Southeast Asia. The Aryans also introduced the system of caste, or social stratification, that divided Indian society into four groups: priests, warriors and rulers, traders and merchants, and workers and peasants. The caste system, which provided the social framework of classical Indian drama and the audience that attended it, remains influential in today's India despite laws mandating equality of treatment for all members of society.

ORIGINS OF INDIAN THEATER

The scarcity of available historical evidence prevents us from knowing much about the origins of Indian, or Sanskrit, theater. In some Vedic rituals priests performed symbolic gestures, and these actions occasionally involved impersonating a represented figure, but it is impossible to tell whether these rites were the seeds of a more purely theatrical tradition. The *Mahabharata* makes references to performers (*nata*), though it is not known if actors were among them. Unlike Greece, India has no surviving theater structures from this period. The earliest plays extant, which date from the first century C.E., display a sophistication that suggests a long period of prior development, but there is no way of determining when a literary theater was first established. What evidence we do have concerning the Sanskrit theater comes from the plays that have survived from later centuries and from the *Natyasastra* (*The Art of Theater*), a compendious treatise on the nature and purpose of dramatic performance ascribed to Bharata Muni and written sometime between 300 B.C.E. and 200 C.E. Longer and more detailed than Aristotle's *Poetics*, the *Natyasastra* includes information concerning acting, theater and stage structures, theater organization, music, dance, playwriting, and aesthetics.

AUDIENCE, PLAYHOUSE, AND ACTORS

Theatrical performances during the classical age of Sanskrit theater (100–900 C.E.) apparently were offered on occasions ranging from sacred festivals to the coronation of kings, marriages, births, or the return of travelers. Although Bharata writes that the ideal spectator for such performances was learned and of high birth, members of all four castes (seated separately) seem to have attended. The *Natyasastra* describes three types of playhouses (square, triangular, and rectangular) and three sizes that these buildings could assume (small, medium-sized, and large), but focuses mainly on a rectangular building measuring 96 by 48 feet. Such a playhouse should resemble a cave, so that the actors' voices would resonate. Its interior was divided into two equal areas, with one half (called the *prekshagriha*) devoted to seating an audience that would have probably included no more than 500 spectators. The other half

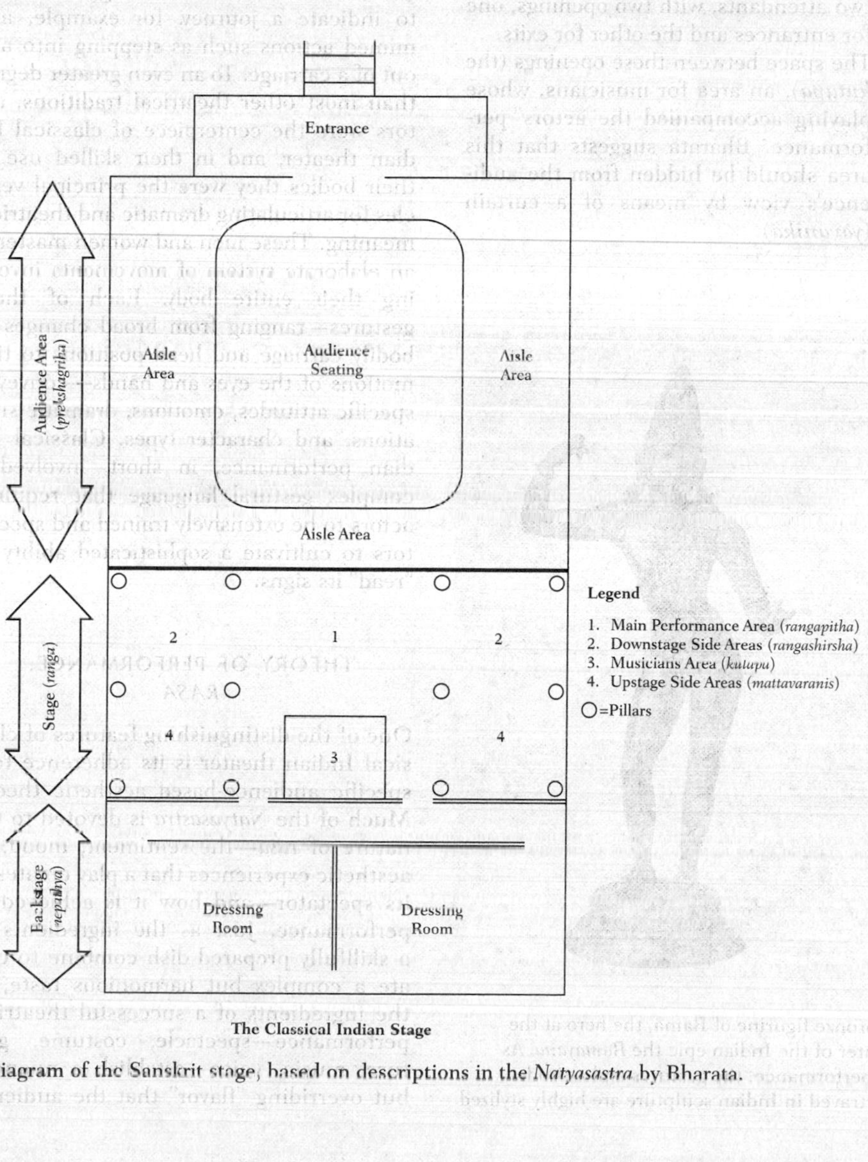

The Classical Indian Stage

A diagram of the Sanskrit stage, based on descriptions in the *Natyasastra* by Bharata.

was itself divided in two: its back half (the *nepathya*) served as a backstage and dressing room, and its front half (the *ranga*) represented the performance area. The performance area, in turn, contained a number of distinct zones:

1. The main performance space (*rangapitha*) at the center of the stage.
2. The upstage area (*rangashirsha*), which stretched across the width of the performance space, between the back wall and the front performance area. Demarcating the back of this area was an ornamented curtain, possibly held by two attendants, with two openings, one for entrances and the other for exits.
3. The space between these openings (the *kutapa*), an area for musicians, whose playing accompanied the actors' performance. Bharata suggests that this area should be hidden from the audience's view by means of a curtain (*yavanika*).

A bronze figurine of Rama, the hero at the center of the Indian epic the *Ramayana*. As in performance, the gestures and attitudes portrayed in Indian sculpture are highly stylized.

4. Two downstage side areas (*mattavaranis*) flanking the main performance space.

These separate but contiguous acting areas made possible the fluid narrative structure of Sanskrit drama, in which dramatic action shifts between different locations and events and encounters can be staged simultaneously.

Apart from general decorations, which could serve a symbolic function, there were few props and no scenery on the classical Indian stage. Location and specific actions were indicated through a fixed repertoire of highly stylized movements. Actors walked around the stage in a circle to indicate a journey, for example, and mimed actions such as stepping into and out of a carriage. To an even greater degree than most other theatrical traditions, actors were the centerpiece of classical Indian theater, and in their skilled use of their bodies they were the principal vehicles for articulating dramatic and theatrical meaning. These men and women mastered an elaborate system of movements involving their entire body. Each of these gestures—ranging from broad changes in bodily carriage and head positions to tiny motions of the eyes and hands—conveyed specific attitudes, emotions, dramatic situations, and character types. Classical Indian performance, in short, involved a complex gestural language that required actors to be extensively trained and spectators to cultivate a sophisticated ability to "read" its signs.

THEORY OF PERFORMANCE: *RASA*

One of the distinguishing features of classical Indian theater is its adherence to a specific audience-based aesthetic theory. Much of the *Natyasastra* is devoted to the nature of *rasa*—the sentiment, mood, or aesthetic experiences that a play creates in its spectator—and how it is achieved in performance. Just as the ingredients of a skillfully prepared dish combine to create a complex but harmonious taste, so the ingredients of a successful theatrical performance—spectacle, costume, gesture, music, voice—establish a nuanced but overriding "flavor" that the audience can savor. The *Natyasastra* catalogues eight basic *rasas* (a ninth was added by later commentators) and associates these with eight permanent (and thirty-three transitory) human emotions, or *bhavas*. As actors portray these emotions, the spectator experiences the corresponding *rasa*. The effect, akin to that of any good meal, is a sense of aesthetic fullness and satisfaction.

CLASSICAL INDIAN DRAMA

About two dozen Sanskrit plays have survived to the present day, and they demonstrate the formal richness of classical Indian drama. Though Bharata describes ten major categories of play, two types were dominant on the classical Indian stage: *nataka* plays, whose stories are drawn from mythology or history, deal with exploits of kings and heroes; and *prakarana* plays are characterized by invented stories and less exalted characters. All plays combine a central story with numerous subsidiary plots, interweaving the serious and the comic. Indian dramatists employed both verse and prose in their plays and a mixture of Sanskrit and the popular dialects collectively known as Prakrit. The former is reserved for characters of high social standing, whereas the latter is spoken by characters of lesser station.

Most of the finest Sanskrit plays were written during the Gupta dynasty (ca. 320–ca. 550 C.E.), a period that witnessed a golden age of science, mathematics, literature, and philosophy in India. Major playwrights during this period include Bhasa, the author of thirteen surviving plays; Kalidasa, whose epic romance *Shakuntala* is considered by many to be the finest Sanskrit play; and Shudraka, whose lengthy masterpiece *The Little Clay Cart* (ca. 100–300 C.E.) is excerpted in this anthology. Important Sanskrit drama continued to be written through the seventh century. Subsequent Indian history was marked by political instability as the court culture that helped sustain Sanskrit drama was threatened by a series of invasions by Muslim armies from the north from the tenth century onward. Sanskrit theater had largely disappeared as a cultural form by 1000 C.E.

Classical Chinese Theater

ORIGINS OF CHINESE THEATER

China, another of the world's oldest civilizations, has one of its richest performance and theater histories. Ancient Chinese scholars described performances synthesizing dance, music, and poetry as early as the reign of the legendary sage-ruler Yi Shun (2300–2205 B.C.E.), and shamanistic and court rituals involving dance and music were attributed to the Shang dynasty (1600–1045 B.C.E.). There are records dating to the first millennium B.C.E. of court entertainments—performed by jesters and others—that included music, dance, and mime. The integration of various activities in these earliest Chinese performances anticipates the capacious scope of later Chinese theater. The Chinese word that would later be used for "play" (*xi*) also meant "game," and it could be used to describe acrobatics, sports, and other kinds of entertainment. This highly theatrical synthesis of performance forms has flourished in Chinese theater to the present day, as the popularity of Beijing opera—a style of theater combining dance, music, storytelling, acrobatics, and martial arts—demonstrates.

THEATER DURING THE TANG AND SONG DYNASTIES

Theater and other forms of entertainment thrived during the Tang and Song dynasties, whose rulers held power in China between the seventh and thirteenth centuries C.E. During the Tang dynasty (618–907 C.E.), dance stories, skits, shadow and puppet plays, and a popular genre of play satirizing corrupt officials thrived at court and in the marketplace, as did circuslike performances and other forms of staged spectacle. Storytelling flourished as well, in forms that included the oral presentation of religious and secular stories by preachers attempting to disseminate Buddhism to nonliterate audiences. It was during the Tang period that Emperor Minghuang—considered the patron of Chinese theater—established the Pear Orchard Conservatory, the first academy in China devoted to the training of actors and other performers.

During the Song dynasty (960–1279), a period that saw a rise in commerce and the growth and social diversification of Chinese urban centers, amusement centers called "tile districts" (*wazi*) were organized in major cities. These centers, which provided a wide variety of entertainment, included theaters—as many as fifty in the tile districts of the northern capital Bianliang (modern-day Kaifeng)—that could seat up to several thousand spectators. The most accomplished players also performed at the emperor's palace, while itinerant players performed in villages and elsewhere on temporary stages. In addition to viewing such activities as tightrope walking, storytelling, and puppetry, audiences in the tile districts of northern China (a region that was taken over from the Song emperor by invaders from Manchuria in 1127 and ruled thereafter by the Jin dynasty) were entertained by the performance of *zaju:* variety shows that featured dramatic sketches accompanied by musical performance, comic routines, dancing, and acrobatics. In the southern provinces (which remained under Song rule), a separate form of theater known as *nanxi* developed during this period. Longer than their counterparts presented in the north and more intricate in story lines, *nanxi* made use of folk music and a array of familiar character types that influenced subsequent Chinese drama.

YUAN DRAMA: *ZAJU*

Though *nanxi* and the *zaju* have clear dramatic elements, it was not until the Yuan dynasty (1234–1368), when first part and later all of China was under Mongol occupation, that drama flourished as a literary genre. As the Venetian explorer Marco Polo (1254–1324) reported during his travels to the court of Kublai Khan (1215–1294), greatest of the Mongol emperors, China during the Yuan dynasty was a land of prosperity and cultural achievement, enjoying the fruits of increased trade and cultural exchange with western Asia and Europe. Contemporary records mention the titles of some 700 plays written during this period—of which 163 have been preserved, many of them in collections compiled during the late Ming dynasty (1368–1644)—and the names of roughly 550 dramatists, including GUAN HANQING (ca. 1245–ca. 1322), the most prolific and best known of the Yuan playwrights. In its quantity and sophistication, Yuan drama has often been compared to that of Elizabethan and Jacobean England. One of the reasons for its flourishing is that Chinese scholars, who had traditionally served in government posts, found themselves excluded from civil service under Mongol rule; they therefore turned their attention to other careers, such as writing. To appeal to a popular audience, these scholars abandoned the classical Chinese of Confucius (Kong Fuzi, ca. 551–479 B.C.E.)—whose ethical teachings constituted a pillar of traditional Chinese society—and helped develop the vernacular as a dramatic language. The result was a richly poetic drama, literary in conception yet deeply grounded in the performance traditions of Chinese theater.

Most of this drama is referred to as "Yuan *zaju*," to distinguish it from the earlier form of northern theater. These plays treated subjects ranging from the historical, legendary, and supernatural to the contemporary. They told stories of love, war, political intrigue, adventure, religious conversion, domestic drama, crime, and judicial punishment. Their characters—covering a broad spectrum, from gods, emperors, and generals to hermits, outlaws, concubines, and ordinary people—derive from an array of popular types. Yuan *zaju* plays are typically four acts long, though shorter wedge acts (*xiezi*) may be added when additional plot material is required, and they include from ten to twenty songs, all performed by the main character. These songs, often of great poetic beauty, are the lyrical center of *zaju* plays. The remainder of the dramatic action is conveyed through speech and dialogue. In keeping with the Confucian emphasis on right and wrong and on the importance of correct conduct, *zaju* plays end with justice served, even when (as in Guan Hanqing's *SNOW IN MIDSUMMER*) a play's hero or heroine dies.

ACTORS AND STAGE

Yuan acting troupes included men and women performers, and both men and women played male and female roles. From the scattered evidence we possess—

Yuan troupe onstage, from a 1324 temple wall painting in the northern Chinese province of Shanxi.

including a fourteenth-century colored mural from a temple in the northern province of Shanxi that depicts a Yuan acting troupe onstage—we know that actors wore ornate, colorful costumes and highly stylized makeup. Though the physical structure of the stage most likely varied with the venue and performance occasion, the stage depicted in the Shanxi mural—consisting of a bare tile floor with entrances on either side of a decorative wall painting in the rear—was probably typical. There was no formal scenery on the Yuan stage and props were minimal. Musicians performed onstage, and their instruments included the flute, gong, clapper, drum, and a lute-like instrument known as a *pipa*. The audience of these Yuan performers seems to have represented a wide range of Chinese society, from the Mongol emperors and their courts down to merchants, peasants, and poor laborers. Yuan *zaju* was a drama that appealed to educated and uneducated spectators alike.

THE RISE OF *NANXI*

Zaju continued to be popular into the Ming dynasty, which assumed power in 1368 after a rebellion drove the Yuan from power, but in the fourteenth century it was rivaled and eventually eclipsed by the reemergence of *nanxi* drama in the southern provinces and its development into a form markedly different from the theater found in the north. *Nanxi* plays are longer than *zaju* plays, and they contain a variable number of acts (as many as fifty or more, each with its own title). Singing is not restricted to a single character; instead, songs are performed by two or more singers, and sometimes by choruses. Acted to the accompaniment of a bamboo flute, *nanxi* plays drew on folk music, and their overall atmosphere in performance was elegiac. Although *zaju* is considered China's premier classical drama, the development of a "southern style" of drama proved to be more influential. A number of the distinctive character types of *nanxi* drama, in fact, remain popular on today's Chinese stage.

Classical Japanese Theater

When Westerners think of Asian theater, it is the theater of Japan that most often comes to mind. In part, this can be explained by the cultural distinctiveness of Japan's theatrical and dramatic traditions: the meditative dance theater of noh, the stylized acrobatics of kabuki, the sophisticated gestures of bunraku puppet theater. But it also has to do with the preservation of such theatrical traditions through centuries of political and social change. In a country devoted to ritual, ceremony, and other forms of tradition, theatrical practices have been handed down with the formal exactitude of the tea ceremony. As a result, we can come to understand the development of Japanese theater not only by reading histories of theater but by attending live performances.

ORIGINS OF JAPANESE THEATER

Although archaeologists have uncovered clay representations of singers, dancers, and musical instruments from as early as the third century B.C.E., the earliest manifestations of what we would consider theater in Japan were dance-based ritual celebrations collectively known as *kagura*. These performances were connected with Shintoism, a prehistoric religion devoted to the worship of gods and spirits who represented aspects of the natural world. Versions of *kagura* were performed at Shinto shrines by shamanistic priestesses, at the imperial court, and in villages during harvest and other annual festivals. Other theatrical forms emerged in the centuries after Buddhism was introduced to Japan between 538 and 552 C.E., a period during which continental Asian culture was embraced by the imperial court. In the seventh and eighth centuries, two forms of dance theater came from China via Korea: *gigaku*, a Buddhist dance play in which masked figures moved in procession, and *bugaku*, a stately court entertainment that eventually included dances from India, Tibet, and Vietnam in addition to those from China and Korea.

Other popular forms of entertainment also flourished during this time, involving music, dance, masked pantomime, and in some instances acrobatics, juggling, and tightrope walking. Several of these traditions had dramatic components, including *sarugaku* (monkey entertainment), a form of variety theater containing comic dialogues and short skits that came to be performed at Buddhist temples. By the thirteenth century, the dramatic and performance elements of these entertainments had become increasingly sophisticated, and the form was given the name *sarugaku noh*. The term *noh*, which means "skill" or "craft," eventually stood alone as a theatrical category.

THE EMERGENCE OF NOH THEATER: KANAMI AND ZEAMI

The emergence of noh theater reflected the political and social changes that Japan had undergone during the previous two centuries. In 1192 the Japanese emperor relinquished rule of the country to samurai generals, whose rising military and economic power had made them the country's dominant social class. These generals, who gave themselves the title *shogun*, presided over wealthy courts in Kamakura and later Kyoto and established a feudal society with rigidly demarcated social strata. Although many cultural forms that had found favor in the imperial court fell out of fashion, the shoguns patronized the arts, including the theater of *sarugaku noh*. In 1374, Kanami Kiyotsugu (1333–1384), head of one of the country's *sarugaku noh* troupes, performed before the young shogun Ashikaga

Yoshimitsu (1358–1408). So impressed was the shogun that he became Kanami's patron and took the performer's son, ZEAMI MOTOKIYO (1363–1443), who was also an accomplished actor, as his companion and lover.

It was through the efforts of Kanami and Zeami that noh became an autonomous form. An innovator by temperament, Kanami combined elements of existing performance traditions into a dramatic form adapted to the tastes of the shogunate and lower warrior classes. Kanami amalgamated popular songs, dance, music, and poetry within an aesthetic of meditative deliberateness and restraint drawn from Zen Buddhism. Limiting his plays to a single protagonist, he advocated a style of acting based on authenticity of physical and vocal characterization. After Kanami's death, Zeami, who would become one of the most important figures in the history of Japanese theater, extended and refined his father's theatrical innovations. In a number of theoretical writings, including the seven-volume *Kadensho* (1400–02), Zeami discussed the intricacies of noh acting, the relationship of noh theater to its audience, and the aesthetic concepts underlying noh performance, such as *yugen,* which denotes suggestive beauty, gracefulness, and an awareness of life's impermanence. In addition to being noh's chief theoretician and one of its greatest actors, Zeami was also its most accomplished playwright, authoring nearly half of the 240 surviving plays that constitute the noh repertoire.

NOH DRAMA

The stories of noh plays are drawn from mythology, legend, and history, particularly (as in Zeami's *ATSUMORI* [ca. 1400]) the twelfth-century civil war between rival samurai clans. The main character (or *shite*) is often a ghost, demon, or tormented person who cannot find rest because of his or her past deeds. In the typical two-act structure, the central character appears disguised in the first act and is revealed in the second. He or she speaks an elevated, highly literary verse, and frequently quotes classical Chinese and Japanese poetry. Other established roles include the main character's companion (*tsure*); a third party (*waki*), frequently a priest, who encounters the main character in the first

The *shite*, or primary actor, in a contemporary performance of the noh drama *The Lady Aoi*. Note the mask, costume, folding fan, and stylized gesture of the performer. In the background sit the *hayashikata*, or musicians.

act; and a servant or commoner (*kyogen*), whose language is colloquial and who often provides a narrative summary in the interlude between acts. An onstage chorus sings many of the characters' lines and narrates events within the dramatic action, while three or four onstage musicians accompany the play with drums and flute. The climax of a noh play takes the form of a ritualized dance.

Noh dramas fall into five categories: plays about gods; warrior plays; plays about women, or "wig plays"; miscellaneous plays, including plays about madness and plays about the present time; and demon plays, in which the main character is a good or evil supernatural being. In a traditional noh program, plays from each of these categories were performed, in the order given. Between the plays, farcical sketches known as *kyogen* (wild words) were performed by the same actors who took the colloquial roles in the noh drama. A *nohgaku* program (the term refers to the combination of *noh* and *kyogen* in performance) took seven or eight hours to complete.

ACTORS

The actors of noh drama, who were male—a tradition maintained in all but a few noh companies today—were dressed in elaborate, highly formal silk costumes. These costumes, which included kimonos for male characters, involved variously layered inner and outer garments. Actors were usually wigged. Among the most celebrated features of noh theater are the masks that the main character and his or her companion wore. Treasured for their craftsmanship and elegant yet simple design, these masks offered stylized representations of the established noh character types: male and female, old and young, human and supernatural. Actors in other roles wore masklike makeup. In contrast to the richness of visual presentation that characterized the actors thus attired, the physical setting and props in noh performance were minimal. Movable structures were used to represent a hut, boat, mountain, and other features, while handheld props served to represent emotional states and a range of other objects. A folding fan, for instance, one of the main props in noh theater, could be used to stand for a sword, a flute, or other item. The handling of physical objects formed part of the broader choreography of noh performance, which involved slow, deliberate movement and symbolic, meditative gestures. The acts of walking and dancing, for example, called for painstaking control of body position and motion, and years of training were required for the actor to master such simple gestures as lifting an arm or raising a hand to the eyes, the symbol of weeping.

THE NOH STAGE

Drawn to its formal precision and ceremonial nature, later dramatists and theater artists have sought to appropriate elements of the noh for the modern theater (*Four Plays for Dancers,* published in 1921 by the Irish playwright and poet William Butler Yeats, represents one such attempt). To an extent unrivaled in world theater, however, traditional noh performance is inseparable from the stage for which it was written. The configuration, dimensions, and materials of this stage were standardized during the seventeenth century and have remained unchanged in noh theaters to the present day. The main stage, roughly 18 feet square and raised about 2½ feet above the ground, consists of a polished surface of Japanese cypress with four pillars, roughly 15 feet high, that support a temple-like roof. The audience sits in front of and to the left of this stage. A visible backstage area, at the front of which the musicians sit, features a wooden wall with painted pine trees, while an area to the audience's right of the main acting area is occupied by the chorus, who sit in two rows facing the stage.

One of the most characteristic features of the noh stage is the *hashigakiri,* a railed passageway or bridge that extends from the side of the backstage area on the audience's left to a dressing (or "mirror") room, from which actors make their entrances and to which they exit. A secondary exit to the right of the backstage area is used by the chorus and stage attendants. Reverberating jars are placed under the main stage, backstage, and bridge to provide additional resonance and to amplify the sound of characters walking and stomping their feet. Specific areas of the stage are associated

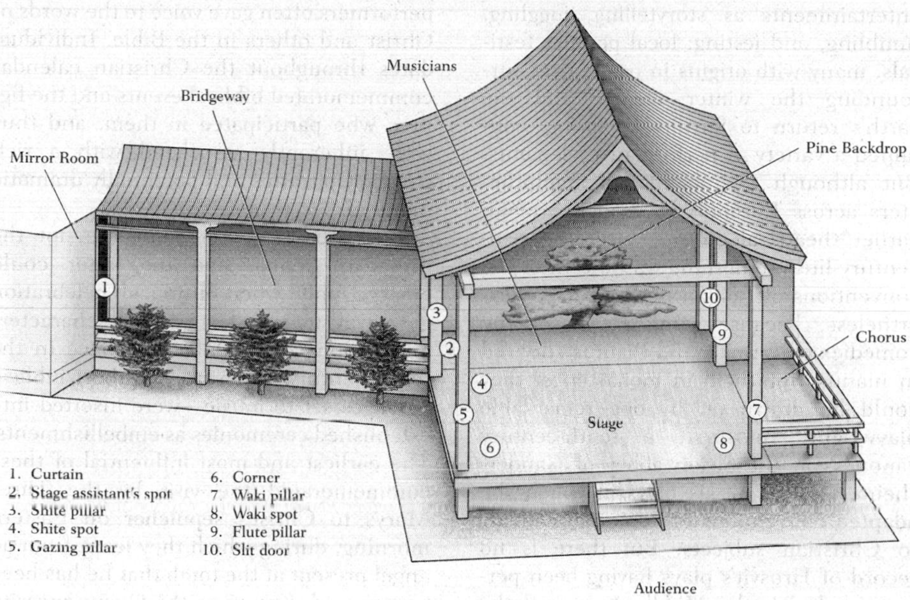

with individual characters and with conventionally assigned functions. The pillar that stands where the bridge meets the stage, for instance, known as the *shite*-pillar, is where the main character stops to announce his name upon entering the stage area.

LATER NOH THEATER

The conventions of modern-day noh theater were standardized during the Tokugawa shogunate (1603–1867), a period when the center of government was moved to Edo (modern-day Tokyo) and the hierarchies of Japanese society were institutionalized to a greater extent. Noh theater companies assumed their modern form as hereditary heads (*iemoto*) were made responsible for preserving the traditions of the major schools of noh. Rooted in the practices and accomplishments of its early masters, noh became an art for connoisseurs; although amateur noh companies found support among the commoners, its principal audience was courtly and upper class.

KABUKI AND BUNRAKU

By the early seventeenth century, other theatrical forms had emerged to satisfy the tastes of a rising urban middle class. Kabuki—a form of dramatic theater involving music, dance, and acrobatics; ornate costumes and makeup; extensive scenery; and spectacular tricks of stage technology—developed in the early decades of the 1600s from the lively, often erotic, dances that temple maidens performed at religious shrines. The performance of kabuki, which was restricted to adult males in 1653, became a highly conventional and stylized art, and its practitioners—including the popular *onnagata,* or actor of female roles—require decades of training. Bunraku, an elaborate form of puppet (or doll) theater that developed out of earlier puppet and storytelling traditions, also became popular during this period. Like noh, which can be seen in specially built theaters throughout Japan, these centuries-old theater forms remain popular on today's stage.

Medieval European Theater

EUROPE AFTER THE ROMAN EMPIRE

The disintegration of the Roman Empire between the fifth and sixth centuries C.E. marked the end of organized theatrical activity in western and central Europe as it had been practiced in classical Rome. Itinerant groups of performers traveled through southern Europe offering such entertainments as storytelling, juggling, tumbling, and jesting; local popular festivals, many with origins in pagan rites surrounding the winter solstice and the earth's return to fertility in spring, contained a variety of performative elements. But although the abandoned amphitheaters across Europe gave evidence of an earlier theatrical culture, after the sixth century little to nothing was known of the conventions of Roman performance. Nevertheless, because some copies of the comedies of Terence and Plautus survived in manuscripts held in monasteries, they could be drawn on by one remarkable playwright: HROTSVIT, a tenth-century canoness at the Saxon abbey of Gandersheim, who wrote six plays in which she adapted conventions of Terentian comedy to Christian subjects. But there is no record of Hrosvit's plays having been performed during the Middle Ages, and the impact of the Roman playwrights before the Renaissance was limited to scholars and to literary circles; they had no affect on theatrical practice.

EARLY CHURCH DRAMA

A major reason for the absence of organized theater during this era was the opposition of the Christian Church to all such activities. Throughout the Middle Ages (and much of the early modern period), church authorities and moralists denounced theater and other forms of spectacle and impersonation as idolatrous, obscene, and dangerous in their effects on the audience members' passions. Ironically, this same church served as the major site for the reemergence of theater in medieval Europe—but perhaps not surprisingly, since the Catholic liturgy is itself a performed spectacle. During the medieval mass, priests wearing ornate robes officiated before spectators gathered in designated locations within enclosed structures. Processions and other forms of ceremony marked holy days throughout the year, while each day's canonical "offices" or "hours" (such as matins and vespers) were marked by services of their own. Chanting during the liturgy was often antiphonal—with passages sung alternately by two choirs, much like dialogue—and singer-performers often gave voice to the words of Christ and others in the Bible. Individual dates throughout the Christian calendar commemorated biblical events and the figures who participated in them, and thus were inherently associated with a rich trove of narrative and potentially dramatic material.

But ritual and ceremony are not the same as drama, and the latter could emerge only when liturgical celebration gave way to a wider range of characters and actions. This shift took place in the tenth century, when *tropes*—short biblical passages set to music—were inserted into established ceremonies as embellishments. The earliest and most influential of these commemorated the visit by the Three Marys to Christ's sepulcher on Eastern morning, during which they learn from an angel present at the tomb that he has been resurrected. Known as the *Quem quaeritis* trope after its opening line ("Whom are you seeking?"), this chanted dialogue rapidly gained popularity and by the late tenth century had inspired similar tropes

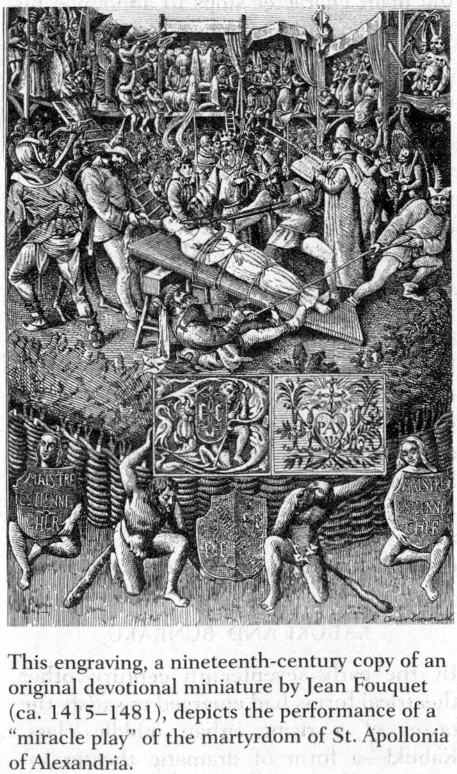

This engraving, a nineteenth-century copy of an original devotional miniature by Jean Fouquet (ca. 1415–1481), depicts the performance of a "miracle play" of the martyrdom of St. Apollonia of Alexandria.

connected with the Christmas liturgy. The connections eventually encompassed other events from the Christmas season, and the *Quem quaeritis* tropes developed into full-length Easter dramas. In their earliest forms liturgical tropes were performed in Benedictine monasteries for fellow monastics; but as cathedrals and other large church buildings were constructed in the eleventh and twelfth centuries, the lay congregations became audiences for these religious performances.

By the twelfth century, church drama had so expanded in scope and complexity that some works—the Christmas and Passion plays from the Benediktbeuern Abbey in Bavarian Germany, for example—were performed outside the context of the liturgy. Eventually, as part of this natural progression, the plays came to be performed outside the context of the church. The range of suitable dramatic subjects grew to include figures and events from the Old and the New Testament: the raising of Lazarus, Daniel in the lion's den, and the conversion of St. Paul, to name a few. Plays commemorating the lives of saints—often called "miracle plays" because they recounted the miracles or martyrdoms that led to the protagonist's conversion—mixed narratives of conflict and romantic adventure with moral exempla. Versions of these saints' plays were written and performed into the late Middle Ages.

CORPUS CHRISTI CYCLES

In a parallel development, religious plays began to be written in the national languages of central and western Europe (rather than the Latin of the church), and during the fourteenth and fifteenth centuries these vernacular forms developed into elaborate dramatic cycles of short plays, or pageants. The most notable of these cycle plays were performed in conjunction with the Feast of Corpus Christi (literally, "The Body of Christ"), a holy day—proposed by Pope Urban IV in 1264 and instituted by the church in 1311—celebrating the redemptive presence of the Holy Eucharist. This feast day, which occurred in late spring or early summer, included an outdoor procession in which the host was displayed; eventually, taking advantage of the generally favorable weather and the longer period of daylight, performers took an entire day and sometimes more to mount plays dramatizing events from biblical history. Though more limited versions of these cycles were performed on the Continent, the best-known achievements in this extended dramatic form were England's Corpus Christi plays, which dramatized the history of the world from the fall of the angels and the creation to the Last Judgment. Local records and the manuscripts of individual plays note performances in London, Coventry, Norwich, Newcastle-on-Tyne, and elsewhere in England, but the great majority of the surviving cycle plays come from just four towns, apparently all in the north: York, Wakefield, Chester, and N Town (where N stands for *nomen*—Latin for "name"—suggesting that this cycle was performed by touring players who would insert whatever name was appropriate as they traveled across the countryside). These cycles are quite extensive, containing between twenty-five pageants (the Chester cycle) to forty-eight (the York cycle). Although English cycle drama was performed as early as 1376, most Corpus Christi plays date from the fifteenth century. This distinctive form of drama continued to be performed—scholars have speculated that as a youth, WILLIAM SHAKESPEARE may have seen a performance of the Coventry cycle; by the late sixteenth century, however, it was effectively suppressed by the newly established Church of England.

The development of theatrical activity on such a scale was made possible by the growth of medieval towns and the formation of guilds: that is, associations governing the practice of individual crafts and trades, which participated in town government and played a major role in both the religious and nonreligious aspects of civic life. In northern England, guilds assumed primary responsibility for the production of the Corpus Christi plays, which therefore are also called "mystery cycles" (the word *mystery*, derived from the Latin *mysterium*, referred to a craft, trade, or profession known only to a few). This arrangement indicates that the cycle plays performed a civic as well as religious function. Given responsibility for individual pageants, guilds provided actors, scenery, costumes, props, and other theatrical elements and materials. In some cases guilds were assigned plays for which they seemed particularly suited: the shipwrights would be given the Noah plays, for instance, while the goldsmiths produced plays about the Three Kings.

STAGING

The manner in which individual Corpus Christi cycles were staged remains a matter of debate. Although practice varied from town to town, there is evidence of two forms of staging: processional and fixed. In certain cities, such as York and Coventry, plays were mounted on pageant wagons that performed, in procession, before spectators gathered at designated viewing sites throughout the town. Scholars disagree on the structure and appearance of these wagons: some speculate that they had two levels (the lower serving as a dressing room), while others argue for a single-platform structure. In addition to the acting area, performers occasionally acted in the street surrounding the pageant wagon; in the Nativity pageant, one of two surviving plays from Coventry, the actor playing Herod "rages in the pagond [pageant wagon] and in the street also." In the alternative staging method, all plays were performed at stationary locations. It is also possible that some combination of processional and fixed staging was practiced: for instance, pageant wagons may have paraded through the town with the actors arranged in tableaux, then gathered in a circle at an open place where they could serve as stages for an audience that stood within the circle's periphery and moved from play to play.

Whether presented on pageant wagons or at fixed locations, the Corpus Christi cycles drew on a staging convention that had characterized medieval drama since its liturgical beginnings. The acting area had two components: one or more structures

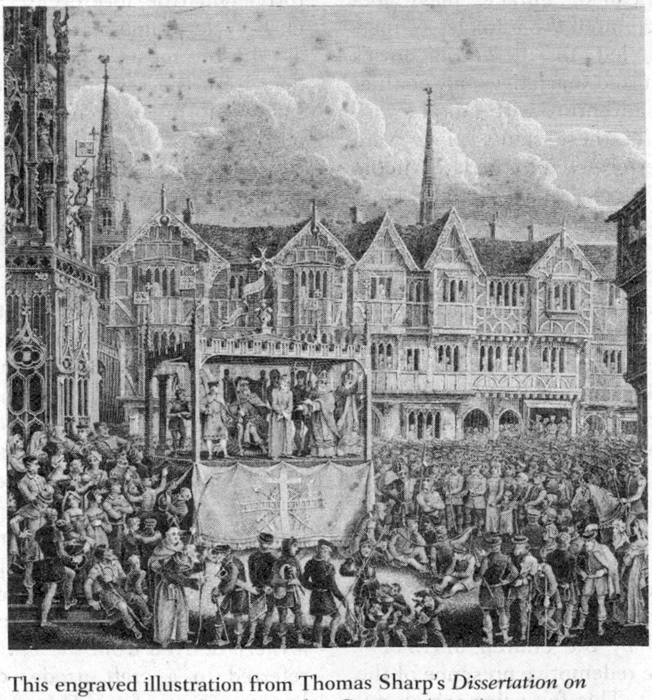

This engraved illustration from Thomas Sharp's *Dissertation on the Pageants Anciently Performed at Coventry* (1825) presents an imaginative reconstruction of the performance of a pageant play in Coventry, England.

called *sedes* (mansions) and a nonlocalized playing space adjacent to these that was known as the *platea* (courtyard, or place). The former, usually represented by decorative booths, oriented the dramatic action to specific locations (Heaven, Hell, palace, house, manger), while the latter allowed for extensions of the action into more indeterminate spaces beyond the *sedes*. Financed by prosperous guilds and engineered by skilled craftsmen, Corpus Christi performances could be awe-inspiring affairs, with special effects and elaborate technical devices. Cranes enabled characters to ascend, descend, and fly between locations, while the Hell's Mouth through which sinners were dragged relied on an elaborate contraption of pulleys and smoke-ejecting bellows. Costumes included everyday medieval garments, ecclesiastical vestments, and—in the case of heavenly beings, who wore gilded masks, and devils, who were given the features of grotesque animals—nonnaturalistic adornments.

DRAMATIC TEXTS

Individual plays, or pageants, within specific cycles vary in length, structure, and style. Some are very formal and rely heavily on long-standing conventions, while others combine biblical narratives with scenes and characters from medieval life. Because the authors of these plays often embellished the biblical accounts with more realistic incidents and characterizations, the Corpus Christi cycles established links between sacred history and the world of their audiences. Indeed, the plays reveal as much about the medieval world as they do about the biblical episodes they take as their subjects. Among the greatest of these works blending the sacred and everyday is by an author whom later scholars call the Wakefield Master. This unidentified playwright, whose plays display a command of vernacular dialects, complex characterization, and realistic situations, wrote *The Second Shepherds' Play* (ca. 1475), which parallels and contrasts the scene of the Nativity with a rustic sheep-stealing episode. By counterpointing the mystery of Christ's Incarnation with the earthiness of fallen humanity, this widely known play demonstrates the use of comedy in Corpus Christi drama. Its folk elements remind us of popular forms of entertainment and celebration—folk festivals, songs and stories, mummers' plays (i.e., seasonal folk plays)—and of the drama that emerged from them in the later Middle Ages. In this tradition are the farces of the German poet and dramatist Hans Sachs (1494–1576), written for the festivities of Shrovetide, the three days preceding Lent.

MORALITY PLAYS

At the same time that the mystery cycles were being organized in the late fourteenth century, a different form of religious drama was emerging in England and France: the morality play. Like the Corpus Christi pageants, this drama was concerned with human salvation—but rather than exploring sin and redemption across the vast landscape of human and divine history, as did the cycles, morality plays focused on the moral life of the individual Christian. Written in the mode of allegory, in which abstract ideas and categories of individuals are given concrete form, morality drama featured a representative figure of humanity—Mankind, Everyman, Well-Advised, Ill-Advised—whose identity is universal rather than historical, biblical, or individual. This character interacts with figures personifying virtues and vices, who typically seek to win his soul in a battle between temptation and spiritual obedience. Whereas Corpus Christi plays occasionally employed allegorical characters, morality drama derived neither from these plays nor from the liturgical drama that preceded them. In addition to reflecting the general fondness for allegory in the Middle Ages—Prudentius's poem *Psychomachia* (fourth century C.E.), which introduced the competition of virtues and vices, was widely influential throughout the medieval period—morality drama likely drew on Pater Noster (or Lord's Prayer) plays; these were dramatizations of the seven deadly sins, performed in England during the fourteenth and fifteenth centuries. Since no Pater Noster plays have survived, specific relationships between the two dramatic forms cannot be established.

The oldest extant English morality play is a dramatic fragment titled *The Pride of*

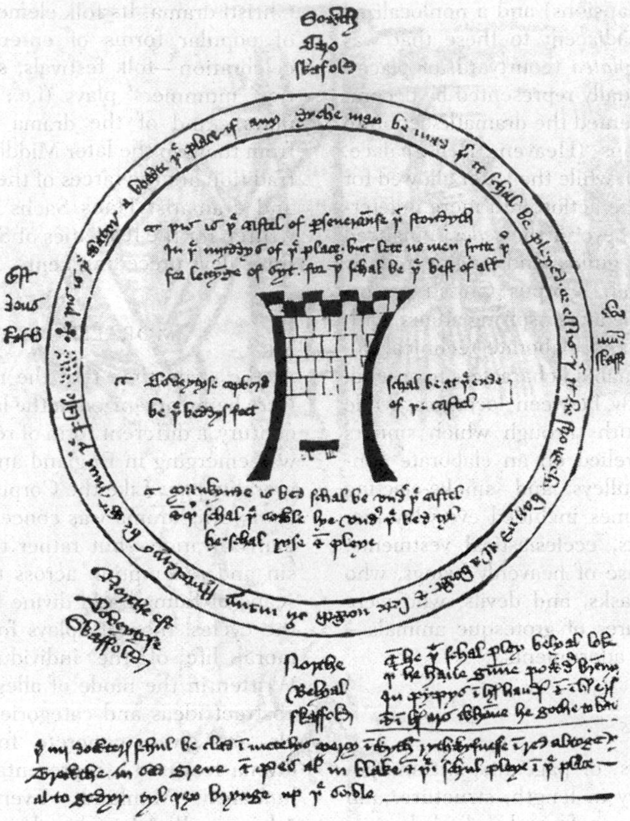

Diagram for staging *The Castle of Perseverance*, from a fifteenth-century manuscript.

Life (ca. 1350). Only a few plays from the following 160 years have survived, but they indicate the drama's variety of forms and staging practices. The longest and most complex of the English moralities, *The Castle of Perseverance* (ca. 1405–25), presents the life of its protagonist Mankind from birth to death, the struggle over his soul by virtues and vices, a debate between Body and Soul, the parliament of heaven, and the final judgment on Mankind's soul. The manuscript for this play, which includes a diagram, offers particular insight into its staging. Located outdoors, the performance area of *The Castle of Perseverance* consisted of a circular playing space with a structure indicating Mankind's castle in the center and five mansions on the periphery. The later *Mankind* (ca. 1465–70), by contrast, was performed before rural audiences by an itinerant group of professional or semiprofessional actors. The staging requirements were necessarily simple—a few props, a small booth for entrances and exits—and the play could be staged both in an open courtyard and indoors. The play itself combines the story of the farmer Mankind's temptation, fall, and repentance with wide-ranging comic business, most having to do with the devil and his attendant mischief-figures. Finally, the best known of the moralities, EVERYMAN (ca. 1510, translated from a 1495 Dutch original), eschews the drama of temptation for the more somber story of Everyman's journey to death and final judgment. Although textual evidence suggests that the play was written for a playing area with fixed structures, there are no records of its actual performance.

During the sixteenth century, morality drama became broadly popular with audiences across the social spectrum. A growing number of morality plays were performed in public and private venues throughout England by troupes of professional actors—the direct precursors of the acting companies of Shakespeare's time. As the intellectual and religious climate of England changed in response to Renaissance humanism (a revival in the study of classical literature, science, and philosophy) and to the Reformation (a movement to reform the Catholic Church that led to the founding of Protestant religious denominations), morality drama evolved in its subject matter as well as its ideological function. In the hands of such Tudor humanist writers as Henry Medwall (1462–1501?) and John Skelton (ca. 1460–1529), morality plays engaged with increasingly secular subjects, addressing issues of philosophy, social relations, and politics in addition to moral and religious questions. In this form they frequently resembled Tudor interludes (indoor dramatic entertainments that were usually performed in noble households, guild halls, and schools). During the religious controversies of the English Reformation, morality drama was employed by Catholics and Protestants to dramatize their doctrinal and political divisions. Even more profoundly than the Corpus Christi cycles, which were cumbersome in structure and rooted in a medieval religious consensus that no longer applied in sixteenth-century England, morality plays helped shape subsequent English drama. Because their allegorical conventions were adaptable to a range of issues and ideologies, these plays provided a dramatic structure for such Elizabethan and Jacobean plays as CHRISTOPHER MARLOWE'S *DOCTOR FAUSTUS* (ca. 1588). Certainly, the legacy of the Vice characters, with their conniving but theatrically appealing horseplay, can be seen clearly in such later dramatic masterpieces as Ben Jonson's *Volpone* (1606).

Theater in Early Modern Europe, 1500–1700

As European theater developed between 1500 and 1700, it was affected by a range of political, economic, social, artistic, and religious changes that were transforming the region and its relationship to the rest of the world. The term *early modern*, which is often used to designate the period in European history between the end of the Middle Ages and the beginning of the Industrial Revolution, focuses attention on those developments that inaugurated the world we know today: the rise of science and accelerating technological innovation, the growth of cities and the emergence of mercantile economies, New World exploration and colonization, and the transformations of church and state through reformation, absolutism, and revolution. But as the competing term *Renaissance*—applied to the fifteenth and sixteenth centuries—suggests, this period is also characterized by a powerful look backward to the classical era of Greece and Rome and to the social, artistic, and intellectual values that scholars, newly given access to many of its rediscovered texts, found there. As they combined the new and the old in fruitful, and also volatile, ways, the years 1500–1700 were a period of unprecedented discovery and rediscovery in the visual, plastic, architectural, and musical arts. But arguably it was theater—where audiences in England, Spain, France, and elsewhere in Europe saw their world represented in action—that witnessed the greatest accomplishments during this extraordinary period.

THE EUROPEAN RENAISSANCE: HUMANISM AND THE CLASSICAL PAST

The European Renaissance played a crucial role in the transformations that Europe underwent in the fifteenth and sixteenth centuries. The term *Renaissance*, which means "rebirth," was first used in 1550 by the artist and critic Giorgio Vasari (1511–1574) to refer to the rediscovery of classical values—which, he claimed, had been eclipsed during the Middle Ages by Christianity and the "barbarian" cultures of northern Europe—in the paintings of Giotto (ca. 1267–1337) and later Florentine artists. This view of medieval civilization as a dark age compared to the civilizations of Greece and Rome is, of course, inaccurate, as is any absolute demarcation between the later Middle Ages and the Renaissance. Europe in the 1500s remained in many ways medieval. But the turn to the classical world represented a driving force behind humanism, the dominant intellectual movement in Renaissance Europe, and it effected a profound shift of cultural direction. Convinced that the civilizations of Greece and Rome represented the highest point of human achievement and that modern Europe should cultivate their ideals and emulate their accomplishments, scholars devoted themselves to the rediscovery, translation, and textual study of classical works, many of which had been preserved in European monasteries and in the libraries of the Byzantine Empire and Islamic Spain. The invention of the printing press in 1450 by Johann Gutenberg (ca. 1400–1468) accelerated the process by which these texts and Renaissance commentaries on them were disseminated.

The deepening understanding of Greek and Roman writers, and of classical civilization as a whole, revolutionized the fields of literature and the arts. The Italian writers Petrarch (Francesco Petrarca, 1304–1374) and Giovanni Boccaccio (1313–1375) urged their peers to study Greek and Roman writers, and the influence of authors, literary forms, historical subjects, and mythological characters from the classical period was widespread in the literature of the next three centuries. Though it is a mistake to see this expanding interest as a departure from the religious concerns of medieval literature—most Renaissance writers explored classical materials in the context of Christian belief—an intensifying concern with human experience and the things of the world makes itself felt throughout the literature of this period, including its finest: the essays of Michel de Montaigne (1533–1592), for example, and the picaresque fiction of Miguel de Cervantes (1547–1616). A similar interest in the world as it is lived and observed is apparent in the work of Leonardo da Vinci (1452–1519), Michelangelo (1475–1564), and other Renaissance artists, who abandoned the flat, often ornamental surfaces of medieval art for more lifelike representations of the human figure and the visible world.

PATRONAGE

The Renaissance as a cultural phenomenon was closely linked to the increasing urbanization and the changing economic and political landscapes of European society. The movement began in the city-states of Italy, where rulers competed with each other to be patrons of scholarship, literature, and the other arts. Here, as elsewhere in Europe, wealth and power were increasingly concentrated in the hands of princes and other monarchs, civic authorities, and an expanding merchant class, and these groups sought to enhance their prestige by funding art, architecture, literature, music, and lavish spectacles. The most prominent of the Italian cultural centers was Florence, which served—under the rule of Lorenzo de' Medici (1449–1492), "the Magnificent"—as a home for humanists, artists, poets, and philosophers. Later centers of patronage included the courts of England's Elizabeth I and James I, Spain's Philip II, and France's Louis XIV. Acting companies, whose members had previously operated on the margins of society, also benefited from the patronage system during the sixteenth and seventeenth centuries. Even as it earned money from the London playgoing public, for instance, the company to which WILLIAM SHAKESPEARE belonged—the Lord Chamberlain's Men, later renamed the King's Men—enjoyed the support, protection, and legitimation conferred by courtly patronage.

SCIENCE AND THE "NEW PHILOSOPHY"

As Renaissance humanism reevaluated medieval learning in light of earlier classical traditions, it profoundly altered established fields of knowledge and inquiry. In the field of political philosophy, for instance, the Italian theorist Niccolò Machiavelli (1469–1527) proposed a view of politics and government in which the maintenance and exercise of power, not moral authority, were the ultimate justification for political action. So controversial were these ideas that his very name became synonymous with cunning and ruthless self-interest. The argument between older and newer conceptions of the world

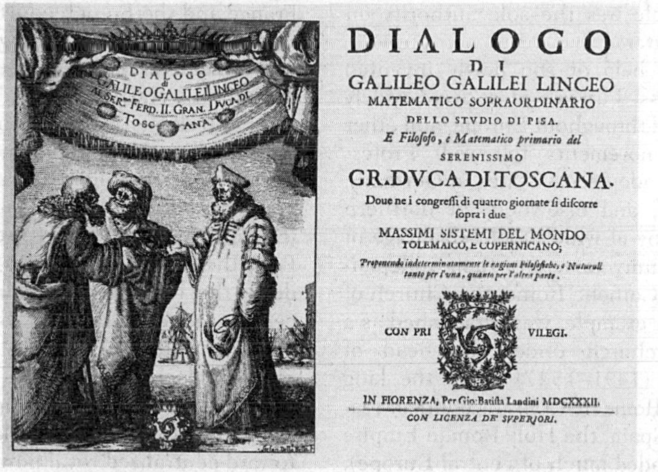

The title page and engraved frontispiece of Galileo's *Dialogue Concerning the Two Chief World Systems*, published in Florence in 1632. In the book, Galileo argued in favor of Copernicus's model of the solar system, in which the planets revolve around the sun, and against the older Ptolemaic system, which placed the earth at the center of the known universe. The engraving shows Aristotle (left), Ptolemy (center), and Copernicus (right).

was a defining feature of the scientific revolution that took place during the sixteenth and seventeenth centuries. In 1543 Nicolaus Copernicus (1473–1543) published his treatise demonstrating that the earth orbited the sun, thereby refuting the geocentric model that had dominated classical and medieval understanding of the heavens.

Further astronomical discoveries were made by Galileo Galilei (1564–1642), who relied on an improved version of the recently invented telescope to make direct celestial observations. The use of empirical observation, experimentation, and inductive reasoning (i.e., drawing general conclusions from data) represented a shift from the more abstract procedures applied by medieval scholars of the natural world. While Aristotle and classical authorities continued to influence Renaissance science and its social practice—the theories of human physiology set forth by the Greek physician Galen (129–ca. 199 C.E.) remained popular during the period, for example—and while most early modern scientists reconciled their scientific methods and discoveries with a literal belief in the Bible, the scientific method worked to undermine traditional notions of authority. As the poet John Donne wrote of recent scientific discoveries in 1611, "[T]he new Philosophy calls all in doubt."

REFORMATION AND COUNTER-REFORMATION

By 1600, the spirits of inquiry and individualism had challenged the authority of the Catholic Church and, in the process, redrawn the political and religious map of Europe. The Protestant Reformation began as a call for reform within the church in 1517, when Martin Luther (1483–1546) wrote a series of theses protesting the sale of indulgences (the remission of temporal punishment for sins) on behalf of the pope. Luther's opposition to the abuses of the Catholic Church quickly expanded to include a broader challenge to its authority. Believing that the church had lost contact with the fundamental truths of Christianity, Luther rejected the doctrine that salvation required the intercession of a religious clergy, arguing instead that salvation was a function of faith alone and that the Bible was the sole authority on spiritual matters.

With the help of the newly invented printing press, Luther's ideas were widely disseminated throughout Europe, and other Protestant movements followed. Protestantism was adopted by states in Germany, Scandinavia, and elsewhere in northern Europe, many of which took advantage of this opportunity to assert their independence from Catholic Rome; the Church of England, for example, was established as a Protestant church under the head of Henry VIII (1491–1547) when the king broke from Rome in 1534 for political reasons. Italy, Spain, the Holy Roman Empire (which included much of central Europe), and eventually France remained within a reviving Catholicism that consolidated its doctrine at the Council of Trent (1545–63) and extended its authority through the Counter-Reformation that followed. Wars, rebellions, and the persecution of religious minorities within states swept across Europe as Catholics, state-sponsored Protestant majorities, and more radical Protestant sects confronted each other over matters of faith, doctrine, and religious and social hierarchy. The conflict between nations that resulted from the Reformation would not begin to be resolved until the Peace of Westphalia, which ended Europe's devastating Thirty Years War (1618–48).

MONARCHY AND GOVERNMENT

Religious controversy and the political turmoil it precipitated contributed to the changing shapes of monarchy and government during the early modern period. In the late sixteenth and early seventeenth centuries, power was increasingly centralized in the hands of monarchs, who justified this movement toward absolutism by invoking the doctrine of the divine right of kings—the right to rule by virtue of birth, a right bestowed by God alone. France offers the most striking example of this development. Following the religious wars that divided the country in the 1500s and the continuation of civil disturbances and political intrigues in the first half of the 1600s, Louis XIV (1638–1715), the "Sun King," assumed the throne in 1643 and began a seventy-two-year reign that saw France and the French court achieve a position of dominance throughout Europe. The statement that is famously attributed to him—"L'état, c'est moi" ("I am the state")—reflects his power over the country's nobility, laws, military, and growing bureaucracy. His model was followed by other European monarchs such as Frederick William I (1688–1740) of Prussia and Peter the Great (1672–1725) of Russia; indeed, the latter built a palace in the recently founded city of St. Petersburg explicitly intended to rival Louis' monumental palace at Versailles.

Absolutism did not triumph everywhere in Europe, however. In England the moves toward centralized royal power undertaken by the Tudor monarchs Henry VII, Henry VIII, and Elizabeth I were checked by Parliament in the 1600s: the Stuart king Charles I (1600–1649) was beheaded in 1649 during the English Civil War, and for the following eleven years—a period divided into the Commonwealth and the Protectorate—England was subject to parliamentary and military rule. The Stuart monarchy was restored in 1660 with the crowning of Charles II (1630–1685), but the next forty years, known as the Restoration, witnessed the overthrow of his brother and successor, the Catholic James II (1633–1701), as a result of conflicts with his Protestant Parliament. Similar clashes awaited European monarchs in the eighteenth century.

NEW WORLD ENCOUNTERS

No overview of early modern Europe would be complete that failed to acknowledge the profound shift in European consciousness brought about by the encounter with the Western Hemisphere. In the Middle Ages Europeans had traveled through Asia by land as far east as Kublai Khan's China, and by 1500 the Portuguese had explored the west coast of Africa. But the "discovery" of an inhabited land across the ocean by the Italian-born Spanish explorer Christopher Columbus (1451–1506), who landed in the Caribbean in 1492 while seeking a western sea route to Asia, had consequences that reached much further. The success of this and subsequent expeditions prompted a race for conquest and settlement of the Americas by Spain and other European powers competing for resources, territorial possessions, and prestige. Over the next hundred years, the Spanish colonized an area stretching from eastern and southern South America to what is today Mexico and much of the United States, while Portugal, the Netherlands, France, and England also established colonies in the New World. The first permanent English settlement was Jamestown (located in the colony of Virginia) in 1607, and by the end of the seventeenth century England's colonial holdings encompassed a good deal of eastern North America.

The history of European colonialism in the Americas is, without doubt, a dark one. The indigenous peoples of South, Central, and North America suffered violence, exploitation, death by disease, and forced conversions, and the relationships between colonizer and colonized were shaped by military power, economic interests, and the religious fervor of missionaries. Europe's colonization of the New World inaugurated a transatlantic system of trade that would eventually bring African slaves to the Americas as part of a highly organized exchange of labor, resources, and commodities. At the same time, even as New World settlers may have sought to Europeanize the indigenous peoples and societies they encountered, their own world was transformed by the contact. Materially, Europe benefited from the introduction of new commodities, such as tobacco, corn, and previously unknown medications. But as Renaissance travel literature reveals, the encounter with the New World also fundamentally changed Europeans' awareness of their recently expanded world. When four delegates (or "kings," as they were called) from the Iroquois Confederacy visited London and Queen Anne's court in 1710, they inspired a fascination whose intensity reveals how deeply their newly discovered hemisphere had penetrated the early modern imagination.

PROFESSIONAL THEATER, 1500–1700

Theater played an important part in the emergence of early modern Europe. As a medium of impersonation and display, theater spoke to a deeply theatricalized society where power was asserted through spectacles, performances, and rituals of display. The spirits of individualism and inquiry found a natural home in an art form in which characters grappled with their destinies on a public stage, and spectators who flocked to attend these performances saw the concerns of their world illuminated and explored. As defenders and critics debated its moral authority, European

55An engraving from the mid-1600s showing actors onstage at the Hôtel de Bourgogne.

theater during this period exerted unprecedented social influence.

The years 1500–1700 saw wide-ranging developments in the institution and practices of theater. In addition to those performances that took place in court, private, and university settings, the first professional theaters, public and private, opened in Europe during the second half of the sixteenth century. Paris had the Hôtel de Bourgogne, built in 1548; London the short-lived Red Lion, in 1567; and Madrid the Corral de la Cruz, in 1579; and by 1600 these major cities—and several in Italy—had become thriving theatrical centers. Many of these early theater buildings employed staging arrangements used in courtyard and other outdoor performance venues—the major public theaters of London, such as the Globe, were open-air theaters and contained stages that extended into the audience. But the development of theater architecture and scenic practices during this period was also influenced by the rediscovery of the treatise on architecture by the Roman engineer and architect Vitruvius. Italian architects and theorists drew on it in determining the theater's shape, the relationship between stage and auditorium, and the design of tragic, comic, and pastoral scenes. During the seventeenth and eighteenth centuries, Italian stage design became influential throughout Europe, as such innovations were introduced as the use of perspective, a form of visual representation that creates the impression of three-dimensionality and distance. As it gained popularity, the simultaneous staging that characterized the medieval period and continued into early modern production was replaced by a spatially unified visual field. Italian designers also pioneered the use of the proscenium, an archway or a frame that would become characteristic of European stage design from the late sixteenth to nineteenth centuries.

As the sophistication of theater technology grew, stage design and scenic effects became increasingly elaborate. The spectacular staging for which the theaters of seventeenth-century Italy, France, and Spain became particularly well-known—multiple scenery changes, flying chariots, hidden grottoes, lavish pictorial effects—were manifestations of the baroque style that dominated European arts during this period. The baroque, which stresses exuberance, monumentality, and ornateness, achieved its highest realization in court performances, when royalty spent large sums for the work of Italy's leading designers and those who studied their innovations. This movement toward greater spectacle was accelerated by the development of opera during the 1600s.

COMMEDIA DELL'ARTE

The establishment of theater as a public, private, and courtly institution was paralleled by the professionalization of actors and others involved in theatrical productions. Acting companies operated in England and on the Continent throughout the sixteenth century, and these troupes often performed in other countries in addition to their own. The most widely known were the *commedia dell'arte* (literally, "comedy of art") players who emerged in Italy in the mid-1500s, performed throughout Europe, and occupied an important place in European theatrical history into the eighteenth century. These troupes—which consisted of ten to twelve actors, both male and female—presented comic scenarios centering on love and intrigue. While the narrative outlines of these scenarios were established in advance, their performance depended on improvisation and the use of comic routines or improvisational asides known as *lazzi*. Popular with audiences, *lazzi* were often ingenious bits of comic business that players used to enliven their performances, such as using a wooden arm to slip away from a beating, or engaging in acrobatic contortions in order to catch a flea. Commedia dell'arte actors portrayed a range of stock characters—some masked and some unmasked—that included lovers, masters, and servants (known as *zanni*). Among the best known of the masked characters are Pantalone, a rich miser, and Arlecchino (or Harlequin), an acrobatic servant with a distinctive motley-colored costume.

Commedia dell'arte companies were organized on the sharing plan, an arrangement that enabled performers to share in the risks and profits of their companies. It was just one of the forms of economic

A sixteenth-century engraving of two commedia actors dancing.

organization that acting companies throughout Europe used as actors, managers, playwrights, and others participated in the expanding business of theater. Performing at Europe's courts (often under the patronage of royalty and nobility) while also operating within a newly established network of public and private playhouses, theater companies in the late 1500s and 1600s began to enjoy some measure of economic security. At the same time, the life of theater professionals remained a hard one, with actors and playwrights often living on the edge of poverty and under the threat of debtors' prison. Theater and the profession of acting were regarded with the social ambivalence and antitheatrical prejudice that early modern Europe inherited from the medieval period. In Catholic and Protestant countries alike, the theater was regularly associated with immorality, and such charges came from secular as well as religious sources. Relationships with state and civic authorities were often equally fraught. Dramatic censorship was instituted in Spain and England, and the theater was subject to a range of restrictive laws throughout Europe. Although the licensing of theaters that took place during the 1600s conferred greater legitimacy on the companies that gained state approval, the implementation of such policies had the effect of bringing theatrical activity even more firmly under government control.

THE DRAMA OF EARLY MODERN EUROPE

The profound changes in Europe between 1500 and 1700 and the accompanying theatrical developments helped ensure that the era would become one of the most prominent in the creation of dramatic literature. The rediscovery, translation, and publication of Greek and Roman plays spurred widespread interest in classical drama, and the translation into Italian of Aristotle's *Poetics* in 1549 helped ignite a debate over Aristotelian dramatic theory that lasted into the eighteenth century. Through the efforts of sixteenth-century Italian and French commentators, Aristotle's treatise was interpreted and codified into neoclassical precepts concerning decorum, verisimilitude, dramatic probability, concentrated action, and uniformity of subject and tone. The dramatic unities of time, place, and action, for example, dictated that the playwright not strain a spectator's credulity by having events take place over more than one day and in more than one location and that the play be restricted to a single, focused plotline. Noble characters were appropriate to tragedy, while those of lower social station belonged to the domain of comedy. Neoclassical theory had its greatest impact on the drama of Italy and France; but even in England and Spain, where dramatists generally eschewed its precepts for more episodic, stylistically varied dramatic styles, debates over classical authority took place.

Early in the sixteenth century, comedy, tragedy, tragicomedy, pastoral, and dramatic satire were strongly influenced by classical models. But as the academic performance of plays in Latin gave way to plays written in the vernacular, the drama of early modern Europe began drawing more strongly on native performance traditions inherited from the Middle Ages. The result was a rich tapestry of dramatic styles, ranging from the multiple, episodic plots of Elizabethan and Jacobean English drama to the classical simplicity of the plays of JEAN RACINE (1639–1699). As part of a larger theatrical field that included religious performances, royal pageants, civic commemorations, and such popular forms as mumming, drama during the period 1500–1700 entertained a variety of spectators in numerous venues. Concentrated in Europe's major cities, this drama reflected a lively urban culture and the early stirrings of national self-awareness. And although many of its most enduring technological, performative, and theoretical innovations arose in Italy, the theater of early modern Europe found its highest dramatic achievement in England, Spain, and France.

English Theater, 1576–1642

In 1576, when the actor, manager, and theatrical entrepreneur James Burbage (1531–1597) built the Theatre in Shoreditch (an area to the northeast of the City of London), the commercial theater was in its infancy in England. The performance of plays and other theatrical activity had, of course, enjoyed popularity earlier in the sixteenth century. Dramatists influenced by Renaissance humanism wrote comedies, tragedies, and moral interludes that made use of classical and medieval models alike; they were performed in a variety of places, including at court and in noble households, schools, universities, and London's legal societies, the Inns of Court. Among the best known of these earlier plays are *Ralph Roister Doister* (ca. 1553) and *Gammer Gurton's Needle* (1552–53), two early English comedies, and Thomas Norton and Thomas Sackville's *Gorboduc* (1561), generally considered the first English tragedy. Traveling actors brought mummings, farces, and other forms of popular dramatic entertainment to local communities, and Corpus Christi plays continued to be staged throughout England until the 1570s, when their performance was effectively halted by royal edict. But the expansion of dramatic activity that would make London one of the most vibrant theatrical centers in Europe did not occur until the commercial theater was established during the century's final quarter.

PUBLIC AND PRIVATE THEATERS

In England, as elsewhere in Europe, the construction of theater buildings was essential to the institutionalization of theater. Theater buildings in London were of two kinds: public and private. Burbage's Theatre established the model for subsequent public theaters. Polygonal in shape, it contained three tiers of audience galleries surrounding a roughly circular, unroofed yard. We have sufficient information about this and other public theaters built between 1577 and 1623—notably the Swan, the Rose, the Fortune, and the Globe, which was built in Southwark (on the southern side of the Thames) with timber from the dismantled Theatre in 1599—to know that the stage for these theaters extended into the yard at a height of approximately 5 feet. Partly roofed, this stage featured a structure at the rear known as the *tiring house,* which included two doors for entrances and exits and one or two balcony levels that could be used for audience seating, music, and scenes requiring actors to perform above stage level (the so-called balcony scene in SHAKESPEARE's *Romeo and Juliet* [1595], for example). A trapdoor on the stage floor allowed ghosts and other characters to ascend from a darkened cellar (sometimes referred to as

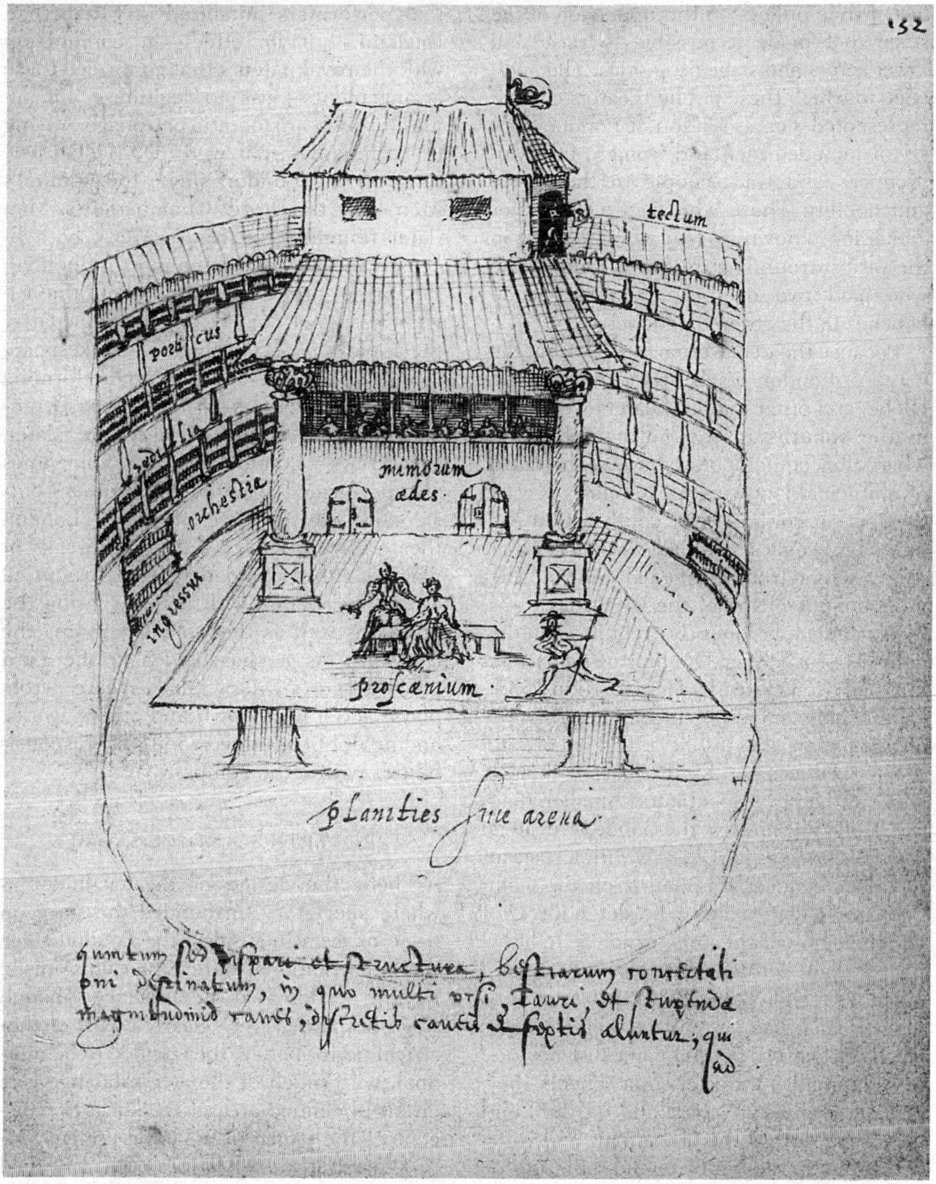

This sketch of the Swan Theater—a copy of an original by a late-sixteenth-century Dutch visitor to London named Johannes de Witt—is the only surviving contemporary likeness of the inside of an Elizabethan theater. Latin words or phrases identify the major parts of the theater: the *proscaenium* (the flat, open stage); the *mimorum aedes* (a dressing room for the actors); the *planities sive arena* (the "yard," in which spectators could stand in front of the stage); the *tectum* (the roof); the *porticus* (covered gallery); the *sedilia* (seats); the *orchestra* (seats for important spectators); and the *ingressus* (the entry into the various galleries).

hell), while pulleys on the underside of the stage roof made it possible to raise and lower actors and stage properties. The audience to which these public theaters catered represented a cross section of London society; it included men and women, from apprentices and tradespeople to the gentry and nobility. Those who paid a penny for admission, known as *groundlings,* stood in the yard surrounding the stage, while those who paid two or three pennies sat on benches in the covered galleries.

Because theaters were banned within the City of London itself, the Theatre, the Globe, and other public theaters were built in the suburbs to the north and south, where they could operate beyond the reach of municipal law. Most of London's private theaters, in contrast, were built within city limits on properties known as *liberties* that were exempt from municipal control. The most famous of these, the Blackfriars, was built and subsequently rebuilt on the grounds of a former Dominican monastery that had been closed by Henry VIII in 1538. With substantially higher admission charges than the public theaters, private theaters entertained a more socially homogeneous body of spectators. Smaller than the public playhouses, these indoor theaters were designed as long rooms with a stage at one end, benches for seating on the main floor, and galleries along the side walls. Unlike the open-air theaters, which were lit by natural light, private theaters were illuminated by candlelight. Until 1609, performances at London's private theaters were given exclusively by companies of boy actors; originally formed at choir schools, they became popular at court and on the London stage during the late 1500s and early 1600s but subsequently fell out of favor.

ACTING COMPANIES

An essential contribution to the rise of professional theater in late sixteenth-century England was a legal shift in the status of actors. In 1572 the government of Elizabeth I passed a law decreeing that itinerant actors and entertainers be arrested and punished as vagabonds if they could not demonstrate that they belonged to the household of a nobleman. The law underscored the socially marginal world that performers inhabited in Elizabethan England, but its effect—in conjunction with the royal patents that confirmed these arrangements—was to legitimize companies through aristocratic patronage. Among the companies that were licensed to perform on the London stage, the Admiral's Men and the Lord Chamberlain's Men (later renamed the King's Men), both licensed in 1594, were the most influential; the former produced the plays of CHRISTOPHER MARLOWE (1564–1593) and the latter the plays of William Shakespeare (1564–1616). In addition to performing in specific theaters—Shakespeare's company played at the Globe and, later, Blackfriars—London theatrical companies also performed at court and on tours outside the city (a necessity when London theaters were closed during outbreaks of plague). Adult companies were structured as sharing plans, with actors sharing the profits as well as the work of running the company. As a shareholder in the Lord Chamberlain's Men, Shakespeare wrote plays, acted in his own and others' works, and no doubt assumed additional responsibilities within the company.

PROPERTIES AND COSTUMES

As befit the design of theater buildings where spectators surrounded the stage on three or even four sides, the London stage was presentational rather than illusionistic in how it addressed the audience. Though stage properties were clearly a part of theatrical performance, they tended to be minimal, with much of the action taking place on an undefined area of the stage reminiscent of the *platea* of medieval drama. Setting, when it was specified, was established more through verbal description than through stage properties. Costumes, on the other hand, were often quite elaborate, with visually luxurious pieces provided by the nobility or purchased by the companies themselves. Whereas actresses were allowed to perform on the Continent, only male actors performed on the London stage before the closing of the theaters in 1642. Women's roles were usually played by boy actors within the companies, a practice that Shakespeare's Cleopatra (played by a boy) alludes to when she imagines her story being performed on a Roman stage: "I shall see / Some squeaking Cleopatra boy my greatness / I'th' posture of a whore." But what may seem like limitations to the modern eye were opportunities for exceptional displays of acting skill by the period's many renowned performers, including the most celebrated actor of his day, Richard Burbage (James Burbage's son, 1568–1619).

PLAYWRIGHTS AND PLAYS

The proliferation of theaters and the rising demand for theatrical entertainment created intense competition for new plays, and a professional class of playwrights emerged to meet this demand. Shakespeare earned enough money from his playwriting and other theatrical efforts to purchase a large house and property in Stratford-upon-Avon, but not all playwrights had equal success, and they often turned their hands to pamphleteering and other activities in London's booming print market. Forced to work under the eye of the Master of the Revels, who in 1581 was granted the power to license plays (and thereby to act as government censor), playwrights were subject to arrest, imprisonment, and even torture if they addressed controversial subjects in their plays. Because plays belonged to the companies that purchased them, playwrights had no rights over their production or publication. Nor were plays accorded the literary standing of poetry and other more strictly literary forms. Company-authorized and pirated versions of plays occasionally appeared in inexpensive quarto editions (on small-sized paper), but it wasn't until 1616, when Ben Jonson (1572–1637) published his plays under the title *The Works of Benjamin Jonson,* that a dramatist presumed to accord his works the status of literary art. Like most of his contemporary dramatists, Shakespeare showed little interest in the publication of his plays, and it was only in 1623, seven years after his death, that two of his colleagues published his plays in a large-format edition, subsequently known as the First Folio.

The drama of Renaissance England was rich and varied, combining the eloquence of dramatic poetry with the vibrant particularity of contemporary life. During the 1580s and 1590s, the London stage offered a wealth of plays in the genres of comedy, tragedy, dramatic pastoral, and history play. With *The Spanish Tragedy* (1587), Thomas Kyd (1558–1594) inaugurated the genre of revenge tragedy that was to prove popular during the reigns of Elizabeth and James, and before his premature death (in 1593) Marlowe wrote a half-dozen or so tragedies and history plays that remain among the finest of their age. Elizabethan comedy ranged from the pastoral and romantic plays of Robert Greene (1558–1592) to Jonson's early satiric comedies. The exuberance that characterizes much of this drama reflected the optimism of an England that was asserting itself as a European power (the English defeat of the Spanish Armada occurred in 1588). This attitude changed in the years preceding Elizabeth's death in 1603, and the drama of the early seventeenth century was marked by a darkening of tone and subject matter. Shakespeare's greatest tragedies were written during this period, as were the plays of John Webster (1579–1630s?) and other tragic dramatists. In the area of comedy, the closing years of the sixteenth century and the first quarter of the seventeenth saw the sharpening of dramatic satire; a proliferation of city comedies (plays whose characters are drawn from London's urban classes) in the drama of Thomas Middleton (1580–1627), Thomas Dekker (ca. 1572–1632), and others; and the popularity of a hybrid genre—tragicomedy—in the plays of Francis Beaumont (ca. 1584–1616) and John Fletcher (1579–1625). The years of Charles I's reign (1625–49) saw the tragedies of John Ford (1586–1639?) and the genteel comedies of James Shirley (1596–1666).

COURT THEATER: MASQUES

The early seventeenth century also witnessed a flowering of theatrical activity in the courts of James I and Charles I. The Stuart court masque was an elaborate form of entertainment that featured lavish spectacle, music, singing, dance, and allegorical or mythological plots celebrating monarchical authority. Jonson was the leading writer of masques during this period, and he worked in collaboration with the architect and stage designer Inigo Jones (1573–

Costume design by Inigo Jones for Ben Jonson's *The Masque of Queens* (1609).

1652), who introduced important aspects of Italian stage design to the English theater. Like the court ballets that were performed in France during the reign of Louis XIV later in the century, the Stuart masques reflect the profound relationship between theatricality and the performance of power in the early modern state.

CIVIL WAR, COMMONWEALTH, AND THE CLOSING OF THE THEATERS

This relationship came to an end during the English Civil War (1642–49), which was followed by the Commonwealth and the Protectorate (1649–60); those eighteen years witnessed the overthrow of the English monarchy by a Puritan-dominated Parliament and the closing of the theaters by parliamentary decree in 1642. The Globe was torn down in 1644 to make room for tenements, and other theaters were subsequently dismantled or allowed to fall into disrepair. Theatrical activity was not entirely eliminated during these years—dramatic performances were given at private houses and other nontheatrical venues, and in the 1650s the musical dramas of William Davenant (1606–1668) marked the beginning of English opera—but the great age of Tudor and Stuart theater had come to a decisive end.

Spanish Theater, 1580–1700

During the sixteenth and seventeenth centuries, a period known as the "Golden Age" of Spanish literature and art, dramatic theater in Spain achieved a level of excellence that rivaled that of SHAKESPEARE's England. The rise of theater and the distinctive shapes it assumed reflected the history of Spain's emergence as a European and global power. During the medieval period much of Spain was under Moslem rule, and the slow reconquest of the Iberian peninsula by Christian armies was not completed until the Battle of Granada in 1492. The kingdoms of Aragon and Castile were joined by the marriage of Ferdinand II (1452–1516) and Isabella I (1451–1504) in 1469, and the resultant unified Spain extended its power through further dynastic alliances and an overseas empire that included vast areas of North, Central, and South America.

While other areas of Europe were feeling the initial shocks of the Protestant Reformation, the Catholic Church consolidated its authority in Spain and, through the office of the Spanish Inquisition, kept religious division beyond its borders. Spain's unique history strongly affected its theatrical development. The centuries of Moslem occupation gave Spanish drama and Spanish literature as a whole their most distinctive theme—that of honor; at the same time, the pervasive Catholicism of Spanish life during the later period ensured that the religious and secular theaters, which were diverging elsewhere in Europe, remained unusually close.

RELIGIOUS DRAMA: THE *AUTO SACRAMENTALE*

The most widely produced form of religious drama in sixteenth- and seventeenth-century Spain was the *auto sacramentale*. Performed, like the earlier mystery cycles throughout Europe, on the Feast of Corpus Christi, *autos sacramentales* celebrated the mystery of the Eucharist in stories mixing the human, the supernatural, and the allegorical. To put on the *autos,* the players used two-story *carros,* or wagons, which were first paraded through Madrid and other cities and towns as part of the Corpus Christi procession and then positioned behind a portable or fixed outdoor stage. Two *carros* were used for each performance until the mid-1600s, when the number was expanded to four (and later to eight). Early *autos* were produced by trade guilds, but by the mid-sixteenth century the responsibility had passed to municipal authorities, who often spent considerable amounts to stage them. Enormously popular events that brought together civic and church authority, *autos sacramentales* were performed by professional acting troupes hired specifically for these occasions, and they commanded the talents of Spain's leading dramatists.

PUBLIC THEATER: THE *CORRALES*

Although there was dramatic and theatrical activity—including the performance of secular plays for academic, aristocratic, and popular audiences—in the early and mid-sixteenth century, it was not until the 1570s that a professional public theater was fully established in Spain's major cities. Not surprisingly, the country's theatrical center was Madrid, which in 1561 became the capital under Philip II (1527–1598). The Corral de la Cruz, Madrid's first permanent theater, was built in 1579; it was followed by the Corral del Príncipe in 1583. Like the open-air theaters of Elizabethan England, the design of the *corrales,* or Spanish public theaters, derived from courtyard performances. The *corrales* were constructed within square or rectangular courtyards enclosed on three sides by buildings. A raised stage with permanent backdrop and upper levels was placed on one end of the courtyard, and an open space, or *patio,* for standing spectators was located directly in front of it. In the seventeenth century several rows of benches or stools (called *taburetes*) were installed immediately in front of the stage on a raised platform. On either side of the patio, a section of seats in ascending rows known as the *gradas* extended to the second story. Above the *alojería* (refreshment booth) at the end of the courtyard facing the stage, galleries accommodated additional spectators. The first of these, the *cazuela,* provided seating for women, while higher galleries accommodated officials from the city of Madrid and the Council of Castile and (above them) clergymen and intellectuals. The windows of buildings above the *gradas* served as box seats (*aposentos*), and additional levels of boxed seats or open galleries were available at the third- and fourth-floor levels. The lively, sometimes unruly, audiences who attended performances in the *corrales* represented a cross section of Madrid society.

The Corral de Comedias de Almagro, built in 1628 and restored in the 1950s, is the only surviving *corral.* Seats for the audience are positioned in an enclosed courtyard, while the rows of seats known as *gradas* ascend on either side.

From its inception the public theater in Madrid was embedded in the city's institutional structures. The *corrales* were originally licensed to confraternities, or charitable organizations, which used theatrical performance as a means of raising money to support hospitals and aid the poor. This arrangement lasted until 1615, when the city of Madrid assumed control of the theaters and the distribution of their revenues for charitable purposes. The theatrical companies it hired—consisting of actor-managers (*autores*), actors, apprentices, and others involved in the productions—were subject to government regulation. After 1603 only licensed companies could operate in Spain, and the number of licenses was limited. Actors who were not hired by these companies joined *compañías de la legua* (companies of the road), which performed throughout the countryside. No company was allowed to perform in any one place for more than two months of the year, and only one could perform there at any one time (more were permitted in Madrid and Seville). As a result, even licensed companies regularly traveled between cities. Women actors were licensed to perform in 1587, but this practice sparked such controversy that a royal decree was issued in 1599 stipulating that only those women married to members of the company perform and that male and female actors not dress in the clothing of the opposite sex. Compromises in response to this final restriction were frequent, however, and actresses who played women disguised as men regularly wore male clothing down to the waist with a skirt below.

THEATER AT COURT

Court performances, which had been infrequent in Spain during the sixteenth century, began to be mounted in the seventeenth century with a splendor that rivaled that displayed in Italy and France. During the reign of Philip III (r. 1598–1621), professional productions and masque-like entertainments involving elaborate settings, costumes, and special effects were given in one of the halls in the Alcázar (the royal palace). When a new palace, the Buen Retiro, was completed on the outskirts of Madrid in 1633, it became the center for court entertainments, which reached their high point during the reign of Philip IV (r. 1621–65). Under the supervision of Italian set designers who were brought to the Spanish court to oversee and engineer these performances, spectacular entertainments were staged both within the palace—a permanent theater, the Coliseo, was constructed there in 1640—and outdoors on the palace grounds. For a 1635 production of *Love Is the Greatest Enchantment* by Pedro Calderón de la Barca (1600–1681), the Tuscan hydraulics engineer, scenographer, and landscape designer Cosimo (Cosme) Lotti (d. 1643) built a special stage above the waters of a lake, managed to have a silver chariot drawn across the water's surface by two large fish, and transformed a mountain into a palace.

SPANISH GOLDEN AGE DRAMA

The drama of Spain's Golden Age represents one of the period's greatest achievements. Those plays that were performed by early professional troupes in Spain were written by actor-managers for the companies they ran—hence, these versatile men of the theater were given the full title *autores de comedias*. By the 1590s, a class of professional dramatists had emerged to satisfy the increasing demand for original dramatic scripts. The *comedia nueva* (new drama)—or *comedia*, as it became known less formally—proved to be the most popular and enduring dramatic form written during the Spanish Golden Age. Consisting of three-act plays in varying verse forms, *comedia nueva* mixed high and low, tragedy and comedy, in plots that were drawn from history, mythology, legend, Italian *novelle* and other literary sources, the Bible, popular ballads, and the everyday life of country and town. Among its specialized subgenres were the *comedias de capa y espada* (cape and sword plays), which featured stories of romance and intrigue, and *comedias de costumbres* (comedies of manners). Popular character types in the *comedia* included the *cabellero* (gentleman), *galán* (cavalier or gallant), *dama* (lady), and *gracioso* (comic character, or fool, whose actions often parallel the actions of those of superior rank).

Of the many playwrights who contributed to the *comedia nueva*, none played a greater role in its development and success than Lope de Vega (1562–1635), a towering figure in Spanish Golden Age drama and one of the most prolific dramatists ever to write for the stage. He wrote as many as 1,500 plays (of which 470 have survived), and his output included *comedias, autos sacramentales,* and *loas* (prologues) and *entremeses* (interludes), which were performed before and between the acts of plays, respectively. In *The New Art of Writing Plays* (1609), his treatise on dramatic theory, Lope defended his disregard for the classical rules of playwriting in favor of variety and "the likeness of truth." Other dramatists followed in his footsteps—including Tirso de Molina (Gabriel Téllez, ca. 1584–1648), whose play *The Trickster of Seville* is the earliest known version of the Don Juan story—but none achieved a more prominent position in seventeenth-century Spanish theater than Pedro Calderón de la Barca. Calderón—whose plays are marked by meticulous craftsmanship, linguistic complexity, and richness of metaphor—became a leading figure in the *corrales* and in the court of Philip IV, where much of his dramatic activity was concentrated. He also became the leading author of *autos sacramentales;* so exceptional was his mastery of this form that between 1647 and 1681 he wrote all of the *autos* produced in Madrid.

THE LEGACY OF GOLDEN AGE DRAMA

Calderón's death is generally considered to mark the end of Spanish Golden Age drama. Those dramatists who followed in his footsteps conformed to established models rather than pursuing innovation. While spectacular productions continued to be undertaken at court through the end of the century, the heyday of both the court theater and public *corrales* had passed. In their decline they mirrored the condition of Spain itself, which had been weakened and demoralized by a century of wars, declining wealth, and waning influence. Yet during its Golden Age, Spain had achieved one of Europe's most vibrant theatrical cultures, and its dramatic legacy was felt throughout the Continent (particularly in France) and in the world beyond its shores. Colonizing armies and Spanish missionaries brought drama and theatrical performance to the Philippines and the Americas, and the colonial drama that appeared there retained its Spanish heritage (the Philippine vernacular drama known as *komedya,* for instance, derived from European romances brought to the islands by Spanish soldiers). The more developed colonial societies produced dramatists who worked within the forms and conventions of Golden Age drama. The Mexican scholar, poet, and nun SOR JUANA INÉS DE LA CRUZ (1648?–1695), one of the finest writers of the Spanish Golden Age, composed nearly thirty *autos sacramentales,* comedies, and *loas.* The theater of sixteenth- and seventeenth-century Spain, in other words, provided the world with its first truly global drama.

French Theater, 1630–1700

THEATER IN PARIS

During the second half of the seventeenth century, France established one of the most admired and emulated dramatic traditions in Europe. Yet the theatrical institutions needed to underpin this achievement developed significantly later there than they did in Italy, England, and Spain. The delay was largely attributable to external factors, most importantly the Wars of Religion between Catholics and French Protestants (known as Huguenots) that paralyzed the country from 1562 to 1598. The early history of the public theater in Paris certainly did not bode well for establishing an urban theatrical culture. The Hôtel de Bourgogne, Paris's first public theater, was built in 1548 by the Confrérie de la Passion, an association of Paris merchants and tradesmen that had been organized in 1402 to produce religious plays and thereafter held a monopoly on theatrical productions of all kinds in Paris. By the end of the century the Confrérie had ceased to perform plays and was leasing its theater for short periods to theater companies from outside Paris. But traveling companies often avoided Paris, because the cost of renting the Hôtel de Bourgogne was substantial, and because the Confrérie enforced its monopoly by charging a fee to companies who chose to perform elsewhere in the city. The capital lacked a resident theater company until 1629, when a permanent company was allowed to occupy the Hôtel de Bourgogne. In 1634 a second theater—the Théâtre de Marais—opened in a converted tennis court (the sport, popular among the nobility, was played on enclosed courts with a gallery for spectators; these structures often served as theaters in the seventeenth century). It housed a second permanent company, and after a fire in 1644 the theater was rebuilt with many technical improvements. Though Paris had not been without theatrical entertainment during the early decades of the 1600s—commedia dell'arte troupes performed in the city, farce was widely popular, and the foundations of a French dramatic tradition were laid by Alexandre Hardy (ca. 1572–1632), who composed hundreds of tragedies, tragicomedies, and pastoral plays—it was not until the 1630s that the theater became a regular pastime for Paris's middle and upper classes.

STATE PATRONAGE

The growing status of French theater during this time owed much to the support of those in positions of power. Cardinal Richelieu (1585–1642), chief minister to Louis XIII (1601–1643) and one of the figures most responsible for the centralization of power in the French monarchy, was a strong supporter of the arts, and under his patronage the theater acquired a legitimacy it had previously lacked. Richelieu awarded a subsidy to the theater company that occupied the Marais, inaugurating the practice whereby all major French companies received government subsidies. In addition, he had a theater built in his private palace, the Palais Cardinal (renamed the Palais Royal when the palace came under the control of the crown); it was the first in France to include the proscenium arch and side wings characteristic of Italian stage design. The strong link between theater and the French state that Richelieu helped establish was a defining feature of the reigns of Louis XIII and Louis XIV—and this link achieved its clearest institutional expression in 1680, when the latter merged Paris's two leading theater companies to form Europe's first national theater, the Comédie Française.

THEATERS AND AUDIENCE

Like the indoor tennis courts that preceded them and continued to be used as venues for theatrical productions, the public theaters of Paris were rectangular structures, typically long and narrow, with an auditorium for the public and a stage that

An engraving from 1641 showing the stage, complete with proscenium arch and perspectival stage scenery in the background, of the Palais Cardinal.

included room, as the century progressed, for increasingly sophisticated technical machinery. The main floor of the auditorium consisted of a pit (*parterre*) for standing spectators with benches along the wall. The side and rear walls contained three rows of galleries, the first two of which were divided into boxes (*loges*). At the rear of the *parterre* and below the boxes rose the *amphithéâtre,* a section whose rows were raked to provide a better angle for viewing the stage. Both stage and auditorium were illuminated by candlelight. For much of the first half of the seventeenth century, scenic practice followed the conventions of medieval drama, with dramatic locales represented by the separate scenic structures called *mansions.* But as Italian scene design was adopted in the public theaters, the Parisian stage incorporated the spatially unifying principles of perspective staging. Any increase in dramatic illusion that might have resulted from perspective staging, though, was offset by the lively presence of the spectators, whose appearance and behavior in the Paris theater often constituted a performance in their own right. Perhaps more distracting to the actors than the unruly occupants of the *parterre* were those spectators who were allowed to sit onstage during performances. A cross section of Paris society, including the nobility and, on occasion, the king himself, made up the audience.

NEOCLASSICISM AND FRENCH DRAMA

The triumph of Italian scene design, with its concentration on single locations, was aided by the growing influence of neoclassicism on seventeenth-century French drama. During the 1630s and 1640s a number of French authors and intellectuals championed the "rules" that earlier Renaissance commentators had drawn from Aristotle's *Poetics,* and the principles advocated by neoclassical theory (including the dramatic unities) were given official sanction by the newly formed Académie Française. The authority and validity of neoclassicism were fiercely debated, particularly as its strictures might apply to the genre of tragedy. The most passionately argued of these debates concerned *Le Cid* (1636–37), a tragedy written by

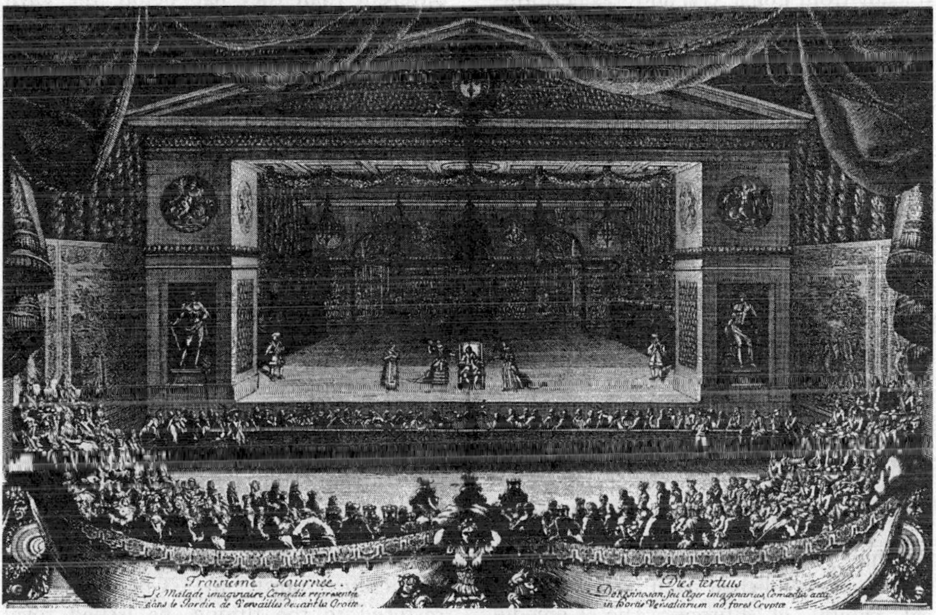
Troisième Journée.
Le Malade imaginaire, Comédie représentée dans le Jardin de Versailles devant la Grotte.
Dies tertius

An engraving showing the performance of Molière's *The Imaginary Invalid,* in 1664, before Louis XIV and his court.

France's leading playwright at the time, Pierre Corneille (1606–1684). Those who attacked Corneille's play for not observing the principles of verisimilitude, decorum, and purity of genre were supported by the Académie, which entered the debate at the request of Richelieu. Although some writers continued to resist, the principles of neoclassical theory became widely adopted by French playwrights. That these principles could be artistically enabling as well as prescriptive is demonstrated by the formally elegant, psychologically complex plays of Jean Racine (1639–1699), France's greatest tragic dramatist.

French comedy also attained a pinnacle of excellence in the later seventeenth century, chiefly through the plays of JEAN-BAPTISTE POQUELIN (1621?–1673), better known by his stage name, MOLIÈRE. Like SHAKESPEARE, Molière was a man of the theater as well as a writer, and his career as a dramatist is intertwined with the professions of actor and company manager. After years touring the French provinces, the theatrical troupe that Molière had helped found in 1643 settled in the French capital. By the 1660s the company had established itself in the Palais Royal, had been awarded an annual subsidy from Louis XIV, and was performing to great acclaim at court and before the Parisian public. Much of this acclaim resulted from Molière's dramatic contributions: farces influenced by the commedia dell'arte, court spectacles, ballets, and, most of all, the comedies of manners in which Molière offered lively and satirical portraits of French society. These plays were not without their controversies—*TARTUFFE* (1664–69), Molière's comic investigation of religious hypocrisy, was attacked on religious grounds and banned from performance for five years—but they quickly became standards of the classical French repertoire.

THE DECLINE OF COURT INFLUENCE

By the end of the seventeenth century, Paris had established itself as the theatrical capital of Europe. The Comédie Française was the leading theatrical company of its time, and under the influence of Jean-Baptiste Lully (1632–1687) French opera had become equally renowned. The brilliance of the theatrical arts in seventeenth-century France owed much to the splendor of the French court, which displayed its power through the culture of spectacle. After Louis XIV moved his court and France's nobility outside Paris to the newly built Palace of Versailles in 1682, however, the role in French theater of the court and its literary tastes declined. As in England at the turn of the eighteenth century, in France public theater was left to thrive on its own terms. That Paris continued to exert a strong influence on European theater in the centuries that followed is powerful testimony to the theater that Corneille, Racine, and Molière helped build.

English Theater, 1660–1700

RESTORATION AND THEATER

When Charles II, eldest son of the executed Charles I, made his triumphant return in 1660 after eighteen years of parliamentary rule, both the monarchy and the public theater were reestablished in England. But the intervening years ensured that both institutions looked very different than they had before the Civil War. Restoration theater (1660–1700) was the product of a largely aristocratic culture, and it catered to a much narrower audience than had the theater of Elizabeth I and James I. Rejecting the Puritanism of the Commonwealth and Protectorate, upper-class Restoration London was an intensely social world, and the licentiousness, materialism, social competition, and love of wit for which the elite society of this period is notorious found ample representation onstage.

The emergence of this theater owes much to broader European theatrical developments. During their exile in France, Charles II and members of his court grew familiar with the theatrical culture that flourished under Louis XIV, and the theater that they helped establish upon their return reflected their taste for Continental stagecraft. Shortly after Charles II was restored to the throne, he issued royal patents to William Davenant (1606–1668) and Thomas Killigrew (1612–1683) to

An early-nineteenth-century engraving of the interior of the Duke's Theatre in Lincoln's Inn Fields during the reign of Charles II.

form theatrical companies and purchase or build theaters. Because the few theaters that survived the Civil War were unable to meet the technical requirements of Italian scenic innovations—sliding upstage shutters and side wings that made possible rapid scene changes, trapdoors, and flying machinery, for instance—new theaters were built to accommodate the new technology. The King's Company (managed by Killigrew and sponsored by Charles II himself) first used an indoor tennis court but soon was performing at the newly built Theatre Royal on Bridges Street; when this burned down in 1672 they performed at a new structure on the same site, the Drury Lane Theatre. The Duke's Company (managed by Davenant and sponsored by the duke of York, the future king James II) used the Lincoln's Inn Fields Theatre (a converted tennis court) and, after 1671, the Dorset Garden Theatre. Given that the patented companies held a monopoly over theatrical production in London—merging in 1682 (after the King's Company fell into dire financial straits) to form the United Company, an arrangement that lasted until 1695—these buildings were the center of London's theatrical life.

PLAYHOUSES, AUDIENCE, AND ACTORS

Restoration playhouses were small structures when compared with the open-air theaters that were built in London in the late sixteenth century. The stage featured a proscenium arch with a curved apron (or open floor) extending into the audience and to the side. The main floor of the auditorium (or pit) contained benches, and these were surrounded on the side and rear by boxed seats and galleries. The play-watching experience in this setting was intimate. Restoration theaters accommodated no more than 600 spectators, and all were seated within 35 feet or so of the stage. Boxes allowed spectators to sit above the sides of the stage (and hence be prominently displayed to the rest of the audience), and by the end of the century spectators were routinely seated onstage. Auditorium and stage were both lit by candelabra, with the result that actors and their spectators were equally illuminated. Restoration actors often played on the forestage (near the audience), and they delivered their lines as much to the spectators as to the play's other characters. It was not uncommon for spectators, who could be quite unruly in the Restoration theater, to interrupt a play by addressing the actors themselves.

As these practices and behaviors begin to suggest, the relationship between Restoration spectators and the performances they attended was marked by mutual interaction and display. Attending the theater was a popular activity for the upper classes of London society and for the king, and the theater became a microcosm of this aristocratic world, its relationships (overt and covert), and its social distinctions. Men and women came to the theater arrayed in the latest fashions, and the theater became an arena for displaying symbols of social distinction. Women—some of them prostitutes—often wore masks (or *vizards*) to disguise their identities, and the rendezvous that were arranged through this and other stratagems mirrored the sexual intrigue being performed onstage. The introduction of women actors for the first time on the English stage contributed to the sexually charged atmosphere of Restoration theaters. Charles II, who had seen actresses perform on the Continent, justified their inclusion in the name of moral reformation, since their presence would eliminate transvestism—boys dressing as women. But the theatrical display of female bodies onstage became an erotic attraction in its own right, particularly when women actors dressed as men, donning tight-fitting, knee-length pants in what were called *breeches roles.* Contemporary moralists viewed actresses as a symbol of the theater's licentiousness; and while their general accusation was unfair, it was certainly true that some actresses did have affairs with theatergoers. Charles II, a well-known libertine, numbered the actress Nell Gwynn (1650–1687) among his many mistresses.

RESTORATION DRAMA

The drama of Restoration England assumed a number of characteristic forms. Even the revivals of English plays written before the Civil War—chiefly, the works of Beaumont and Fletcher, Shakespeare, and JONSON—were often adapted to reflect contemporary tastes and conventions. During this period heroic tragedy flourished; it featured larger-than-life characters, exotic locales, and elevated—occasionally ranting—dramatic verse. Other tragedies written during this time observed the principles of French neoclassicism, such as the concentration of dramatic action according to the dramatic "unities." Adherence to these principles was not as strict in England as it was in France, however, and Restoration tragedy continued to be influenced by Shakespeare and by earlier English dramatic conventions. In his 1668 *An Essay of Dramatic Poesy,* the period's most significant work of dramatic theory, John Dryden (1611–1700)—a leading writer of tragic and other drama—defended "the honour of our *English* writers" against those who overvalued French dramatic models.

But it was in comedy that the Restoration's achievements were most dazzling. Set in contemporary London, the Restoration comedy of manners featured gallants (or rakes), ladies, jealous husbands, cast-off mistresses, unsophisticated country visitors, fops, and clever servants engaged in often predatory games of intrigue and seduction. The wit and wordplay that characterize these plays reflect the importance of language, innuendo, and verbal disguise to Restoration stage interactions. Many of the plays contain a secondary plot involving conventional lovers, but the theatrical energies of the finest Restoration comedies—*The Country Wife* (1675), by William Wycherley (1641–1716); *The Man of Mode* (1676), by George Etherege (1636–1692); *THE ROVER* (written in two parts, 1677, 1681), by APHRA BEHN (1640–1689), England's first professional woman playwright; and *The Way of the World* (1700), by William Congreve (1670–1729)—are located in the central, equally matched "wit" couple. The lens provided by these interactions enabled playwrights to investigate fashion, marriage as a social contract, authenticity, masculinity, and social difference. By the end of the century, however, Restoration comedy faced opposition from a growing middle-class audience that rejected its libertinism, amorality, and elitism. When Jeremy Collier (1650–1726), an English clergyman, published *A Short View of the Immorality and Profaneness of the English Stage* in 1698, his attack hastened the end of a comic form that had outlived the courtly world of Charles II.

Eighteenth-Century Theater

The eighteenth century in Europe was characterized by stability and change; it was a period when the new rubbed uncomfortably against the old, and the outlines of the modern world began to emerge with unprecedented clarity. Throughout the century many of the artistic forms that had traditionally been preferred by the social elite continued to thrive. However, the social and economic transformations that would lead, by century's end, to the beginning of the Industrial Revolution hastened the growth of a middle class with its own interests, moral expectations, and tastes. Neoclassicism retained considerable authority on the Continent throughout the century, and the influence of classical ideals was evident in movements in literature, art, architecture, and music late in the century, but these were countered by the growing middle-class demand for nonelite literary and cultural forms such as the novel, which—with the help of an expanding popular press—by 1800 had become a literary form in its own right.

THE ENLIGHTENMENT

The eighteenth century was also the period of the Enlightenment, a philosophical movement centered in France that stressed the authority of reason and universally valid principles in human affairs. While some of the age's thinkers approved of the authoritarian rule of such "enlightened despots" as Frederick the Great (1712–1786) of Prussia and Catherine the Great (1729–1796) of Russia, the Enlightenment's main proponents challenged arbitrary authority and advocated limits to state power. The writings of such theorists as Jean-Jacques Rousseau (1712–1778), who argued that a social contract between individuals constitutes the only legitimate form of political order, established the foundations of modern democracy and were an important influence on the American Revolution (1775–83), the French Revolution (1789–99), and the Latin American revolutions of the early nineteenth century.

THEATERS AND ACTORS

The public theaters of eighteenth-century Europe offered a variety of entertainments—pantomime, comic opera, burlesque, and other popular performance forms in addition to serious and comic drama—to an audience whose numbers grew throughout the century. To accommodate this increase in spectators and keep up with the latest trends in stage design and technology, the major theaters of the period were expanded, renovated, and sometimes replaced by newer, larger buildings. Established theaters and theatrical companies continued to dominate theatrical life in Europe's capitals, usually as a result of government licensing,

A painting by William Hogarth of a scene from John Gay's popular ballad opera *The Beggar's Opera*. Note the audience members onstage in boxes.

though theatrical activity beyond these theaters enjoyed periods of popularity. In London (the capital of what was now known as Great Britain, following the union of England and Scotland in 1707), a number of unlicensed theaters operating in the 1720s and 1730s contributed to a lively theatrical scene that produced the long-running ballad opera *The Beggar's Opera* (1728), by John Gay (1685–1732), and satirical burlesques directed at the government of Sir Robert Walpole (1676–1745), who was in effect Britain's prime minister (a title not yet in official usage). In part as a reaction to this satirical activity, the Theatrical Licensing Act, which confirmed the Drury Lane and Covent Garden as London's only licensed theaters and empowered the Lord Chamberlain to approve plays for performance, was passed in 1737. In Paris, the monopoly of the Comédie Française and the Opéra was challenged by nonlicensed troupes that performed as part of the city's seasonal fairs. These troupes, which presented comic operas, pantomimes, and (by the end of the century) comic and noncomic drama, eventually established themselves as year-round companies housed on the fashionable Boulevard du Temple.

Although theater as an institution changed less in the eighteenth century than in earlier centuries, scenic practice underwent a number of modifications designed to intensify the stage's visual realism. The symmetries of classical perspective were relinquished in favor of angled perspectives, which allowed the scene to be viewed from varying points of view, and mid- and late-century designers introduced picturesque landscapes, historical and exotic locales, and increasingly sophisticated atmospheric settings made possible, in part, by advances in lighting and sound effects. Another development that reinforced the increasing illusionism of the eighteenth-century stage in London and Paris was the removal from it of spectators, a change that was complete by the middle of the century.

Although by modern standards eighteenth-century acting remained stylized in gesture and vocal delivery, in this area, too, practitioners shifted toward realism—and away from rhetorical modes of delivery. David Garrick (1717–1779), the century's greatest English actor, was praised for his natural style of acting, and similar advances in realistic performance took place on the Continent. To be sure, these efforts to bring the stage closer to life were limited in their aspirations and accomplishments. But though realism would not become a fully formed theatrical aesthetic until the nineteenth century, the first steps toward it were taken in the eighteenth.

EIGHTEENTH-CENTURY DRAMA

In the eighteenth century, the genres of tragedy and comedy underwent a number of important modifications that reflected the tastes of a growing middle-class audience and its largely conservative moral outlook. Tragedy, which had traditionally been concerned with actions of the ruling classes, set in historical and mythological locales, was expanded to include the events and scenes of ordinary life. The pioneering play in the subgenre of domestic tragedy was *The London Merchant* (1731), by the English playwright George Lillo (1693–1739), which centered on the downfall and moral reclamation of a London apprentice. Comedy was similarly modified as the values of wit, ingenuity, and sexual titillation gave way to noble feeling, moral elevation, and what Sir Richard Steele (1672–1729), one of the new subgenre's earliest champions, called "a joy too exquisite for laughter." Sentimental comedy (known in France as *comédie larmoyante*, or "tearful comedy") became popular throughout Europe during the eighteenth century.

Traditional tragedy and comedy had their supporters and practitioners, as well. For example, the French philosopher and writer Voltaire (François-Marie Arouet, 1694–1778) wrote intricate tragedies in the elevated style, and the Irish-born London playwrights Oliver Goldsmith (ca. 1730–1774) and Richard Brinsley Sheridan (1751–1816) championed "laughing comedy" against the drama of sentimentality. In Italy Carlo Goldoni (1707–1793) reformed Italian comedy by transforming the improvisational drama of the commedia dell'arte into a literary genre. While eliminating the bawdiness and nonrealistic devices of the commedia, he nonetheless succeeded in preserving the tradition's comic spirit. Overall, though, sentimental drama and the century's other dramatic innovations crossed and, because of their popularity, undermined the boundaries between the traditional genres. In the 1750s Denis Diderot (1713–1784), one of the leading figures of the French Enlightenment, advocated a genre midway between tragedy and comedy: the *drame bourgeois*, which would take the social and familial problems of the middle class as its subject. Though it produced few plays of note during the late eighteenth century, the *drame bourgeois* was an important precursor to the social problem plays of HENRIK IBSEN (1828–1906) and later modern dramatists.

GERMAN THEATER AND DRAMA

One of the most important theatrical developments in the eighteenth century was the rise of established theater beyond its traditional centers in Italy, Spain, England, and France. This expansion was most striking in the German states of northern and central Europe. Although Vienna was one of the leading centers of opera in the late seventeenth century and troupes of professional actors performed at courts and in public settings throughout German-speaking Europe, an organized German theater did not develop until the eighteenth century. The Thirty Years War, which was fought largely on German soil, had devastated the region in the seventeenth century, and the territories that in the late nineteenth century would become modern Germany consisted of numerous small states within a declining Holy Roman Empire. With the region's resources scattered over a large area rather than concentrated in a capital or in other urban centers, it fell to the individual states to establish and support public theaters. The Hamburg National Theater, established in 1767, was a short-lived venture that paved the way for state-subsidized theaters elsewhere in German-speaking Europe. The Gotha Court Theater was founded in 1775, the Imperial and National Theater of Vienna in 1776, and the Court and National Theater of Mannheim in 1779. Of the numerous state theaters that followed these, the most significant were the Royal National Theater, established in Berlin in 1786, and the Weimar Court Theater (1791), which produced plays by two of the century's greatest dramatists, Johann Wolfgang von Goethe (1749–1832) and Friedrich von Schiller (1759–1805). Though these theaters operated independently of each other, their founding reflected a broad cultural concern with the expression of German national identity.

Despite being a relative newcomer to the European dramatic tradition, German drama of the mid- and late eighteenth century was significant in its experimentation and the range of its literary achievement. Gotthold Ephraim Lessing (1729–1781), an early advocate of sentimental drama, wrote plays that dealt with national, social, and philosophical themes and was instrumental in freeing German drama from the influence of French neoclassicism. His *Hamburg Dramaturgy*, a series of essays published in 1767 and 1768, was one of the century's most important works of dramatic theory. A more radical break with neoclassicism was achieved by the playwrights of the *Sturm und Drang* (storm and stress) movement, a revolt against Enlightenment rationalism that flourished between the late 1760s and early 1780s. The drama written as part of this movement—including early plays by Goethe and Schiller—explored intense emotion, nature, rebellion against society, and violent action in irregular, often episodic plots.

Goethe and Schiller eventually rejected *Sturm und Drang* for the "Weimar classicism" of their work created between the former's visit to Italy in 1786–88 and the latter's death in 1805. Ranging over modern European history, classical mythology, and philosophy, the plays of this period pursued the values of harmony, wholeness, and aesthetic distance. This desire to provide Germany with a classical tradition reflected a revived interest in the classical world in late eighteenth-century Europe—the ruins of Herculaneum and Pompeii, which offered Europeans a mesmerizing portrait of Roman life preserved in the ashes of Mount Vesuvius's eruption of 79 C.E., were discovered in Italy in 1709 and 1748. The resultant drama embodied the aesthetic values of beauty, harmony, and form rather than the prescriptive neoclassicism of

An illustration of a scene from one of Schiller's *Sturm und Drang* dramas, *Kabale und Liebe* (1784).

earlier centuries. At the same time, this drama drew its subjects from a Europe facing a period of political and aesthetic changes. Indeed, Goethe's masterpiece, the poetic drama *Faust* (written in two parts, 1808, 1831), owes as much to the Romanticism that flourished in the next century as it does to the classical past.

Romanticism and Melodrama, 1800–1880

THE AGE OF REVOLUTION

At the end of the eighteenth century, two events fundamentally changed the political and cultural landscape of the Western world: the American Revolution and the French Revolution. The American Revolution severed England from its most prosperous colony and launched a radical experiment in democracy in the New World. A few years later, the French Revolution showed that even in Europe the old order was not impervious to change. Begun as a relatively modest revolt against the excesses of a king seeking absolute power, the French Revolution became radical when the lower orders and their revolutionary leaders turned against the aristocracy with increasing violence. The twin revolutions had far-reaching consequences, as neighboring countries watched them and their aftermaths with astonishment, enthusiasm, and fear. Soon, they would be directly affected as well, when Napoleon Bonaparte (1769–1821) rose from the French revolutionary forces to conquer much of Europe, propelled by a powerful army and the promise of freedom from local tyranny. Even after Napoleon had been defeated and the political map of Europe reordered in 1815 at the Congress of Vienna, what historians now term the Age of Revolution would continue well into the second half of the nineteenth century.

ROMANTICISM AND THE THEATER

The two revolutions changed more than the political order of two countries: they also altered how Western societies thought about themselves, with marked effects on cultural institutions and the arts. The French and the American revolutions had been inspired by Enlightenment philosophers such as Voltaire (François-Marie Arouet, 1694–1778), Immanuel Kant (1724–1804), and Thomas Jefferson (1743–1826), who had advocated new social organizations based not on religious beliefs but on rational planning and thought. But as the social upheavals of these revolutions grew more and more violent and unsettling, the Enlightenment insistence on pure reason lost some of its currency. Reflecting these changing historical and intellectual currents, the generation of writers, artists, and thinkers following the revolutions articulated the movement known as Romanticism. The Romantics did not reject the Enlightenment and its social experiments entirely, but they considered its more extreme claims with skepticism. They consequently placed greater emphasis on subjective experience and even on irrational desires and beliefs, which had been rejected by the Enlightenment. By the same token, they turned against the restrained, rational movement in the arts known as classicism.

Whereas artists adhering to classicism respected the boundaries between styles and poetic forms, the Romantics created unusual mixtures and sometimes left their works deliberately in fragments. Ruins of medieval architecture were prized over classical buildings, and folk arts such as fairy tales or rustic idylls over Greek and Roman models.

These developments changed the face of drama and theater as well. Indeed, the battles between the advocates of classicist theater and those of the new Romantic theater were often fierce. The French writer Victor Hugo (1802–1885), whose preface to the play *Cromwell* (1827) served as a manifesto of Romanticism, aroused the ire of traditionalists by rejecting the unities of time and place, advocating the use of historically accurate stage settings, and calling for a theatrical art that included the sublime and the grotesque. So intense were the passions of classicists and romanticists over the future of French theater that the performances of Hugo's play *Hernani* (1830) at the Comédie Française were interrupted by sustained outbursts by supporters and detractors.

An illustration, by Jean Albert Grand-Carteret, of the audience disturbances that followed the final scene of Victor Hugo's *Hernani* at its premiere in 1830.

Like many of their contemporaries, Romantic playwrights developed an ambivalent attitude toward the French Revolution. In the early nineteenth century Georg Büchner (1813–1837) wanted to bring the legacy of the French Revolution to Germany, where the political system was especially hierarchical and repressive. He even wrote a tragedy about one of the leaders of the French Revolution—*Danton's*

This late-eighteenth-century engraving of King Lear in the storm indicates the passionate intensity with which Shakespeare was often performed on the Romantic stage.

Death (1835), a sympathetic portrait of Georges-Jacques Danton (1759–1794). Other Romantics, such as William Wordsworth (1770–1850) and Samuel Taylor Coleridge (1772–1834), became much more disenchanted with the French Revolution, foregrounding not its social gains but its violence. But though they were divided in their attitudes toward the political and social upheavals of their time, the Romantics could agree on many other things. One was the eminence of WILLIAM SHAKESPEARE, which lead to a revival of the playwright across Europe; French and German Romantics treated the Elizabethan playwright as their most important predecessor. What the Romantics admired in Shakespeare was precisely what classicism had rejected: namely, the mixing of high and low characters and of comedy and tragedy, as well as the fantastic events depicted in Shakespeare's romances.

CLOSET DRAMA

Despite the fascination with theater in general and Shakespeare in particular, Romantic drama was characterized by an increasing distance from the theater audience. Although plays such as Hugo's *Hernani* enjoyed controversy and success on the popular stage, many dramas written by the great Romantic writers either were not performed during their lifetimes or received limited, private performances or readings. Such plays written for reading only, or *closet dramas,* form the most significant genre of dramatic literature during the Romantic era. Among them are *The Borderers* (1796), by Wordsworth; *The Death of Empedocles* (1798; unfinished), by Friedrich Hölderlin (1770–1843); *Remorse* (1813), by Coleridge; *Manfred* (1817), by Lord Byron (1788–1824); *The Cenci* (1819), by Percy Bysshe Shelley (1792–1822); and the plays of Alfred de Musset (1810–1857).

THEATERS AND ACTORS

The increasing division between dramatic literature and theatrical performance had to do both with the preferences of writers and with the state of the theater industry. Poets distrusted theater managers and actors, choosing instead to write for the reading public only. At the same time, theaters—which, throughout Europe, continued to expand in size during the nineteenth century—catered to the tastes of the general public by putting on lavish spectacles. (When a similar estrangement between dramatic authors and theater managers had occurred in imperial Rome, Seneca likewise wrote only for readers or small recitations and left the theater to the popular entertainments then dominating the stage.) The demand for such spectacles drove innovation, and thus nineteenth-century theater history is dominated by a series of technical developments—including the use of gaslights (first introduced around 1825) and limelights, an early form of spotlight that greatly enhanced designers' ability to create theatrical illusions and effects. The public also desired equestrian as well as nautical plays, as new traps, elevators, moving panoramas, and, later on, revolving stages expanded the range of theatrical possibilities. Other developments were more in tune with cultural tastes and ideas dominant in the Romantic era. As general interest in the distant past grew, audiences began to pay more attention to historically accurate costumes and sets. At the same time, celebrated actors such as England's Edmund Kean (1787–1833)—famous for his interpretation of Shakespeare—and France's Frédérick Lemaître (1800–1876) developed a Romantic acting style, based on the expression of strong emotions. Such performances may have seemed spontaneous and authentic, but in fact many Romantic actors, who were given little time for rehearsal, followed manuals of gesture and expression.

MELODRAMA

Though most poets refused to write plays for the stage, a second group of writers were only too willing to supply the theaters of Europe with the popular drama they needed. The most popular type of play during this period was melodrama, which suited the public's taste for spectacle, music, and easily digestible characters and plots. The term *melodrama* is taken from the French *melodrame*, which joins the Greek word for music (*melos*) to drama; it was first applied in the late eighteenth century to plays with musical interludes that employ an easily recognizable dramatic formula and unambiguous moral contrasts. Drawing on a set of stock characters—the villain, the hapless maiden in distress, and the hero—melodramatic plots involve extraordinary coincidences and hinge on sudden revelations and encounters. France was the birthplace of melodrama, and its king was René-Charles Guilbert de Pixérécourt (1773–1844). Another prominent author of melodrama was the Irish writer Dion Boucicault (1820?–1890). Boucicault not only wrote popular plays set in Ireland, such as *The Colleen Bawn* (1860), but after spending several years in the United States he set several notable plays there as well, including *The Octoroon; or, Life in Louisiana* (1859).

Both in England and in France, many melodramas were produced by adapting novels to the stage. It was a time when the novel experienced an unprecedented rise in status and appeal, and many of the era's most accomplished writers turned their hands to fiction. Prime candidates for adaptation were the immensely popular novels of Charles Dickens (1812–1870). In France, novels by Alexandre Dumas père (1802–1870) and his son, Alexandre Dumas fils (1824–1895), were adapted by the two authors themselves, among them the former's *The Three Musketeers* (1844) and *The Count of Monte Christo* (1845) and the latter's *La Dame aux camélias* (in English known as *Camille;* 1848), which also became the libretto for Giuseppe Verdi's opera *La Traviata* (1853). Because of Paris's dominant cultural position, nineteenth-century French melodramas were imported into many European countries and more distant lands.

Sarah Bernhardt in the title role of Victorien Sardou's *Theodora* (1884).

THE WELL-MADE PLAY

Alongside melodrama, French playwrights perfected another, related form of drama, the so-called *well-made play* (a name borrowed from the French *pièce bien-fait*). The well-made play was based not on spectacle and music but on complicated, intricately constructed plots. Playwrights relied on well-known techniques such as overheard conversations, mistaken identities, sudden appearances and disappearances, and other forms of confusion that culminated in the main scene of the play—the confrontation of the main antagonists—followed by the final resolution. Because everything in a well-made play led up to such a scene, it was called *scène à faire,* the obligatory scene that "had to be done." Masters of the well-made play included Augustin-Eugène Scribe (1791–1861), who wrote more than 300 plays, and the even more popular Victorien Sardou (1831–1908), who composed several plays specifically for the greatest star of the French nineteenth-century stage, Sarah Bernhardt (1844–1923). Sardou so dominated the second half of the nineteenth century that GEORGE BERNARD SHAW (1856–1950), a radical reformer of the well-made play, referred to his drama as "sardoodledom." Like melodrama, the well-made play was an extremely popular export, imitated everywhere.

EUROPE AT MIDCENTURY

The ever-more sophisticated spectacles, melodramas, and well-made plays were created in the context of Europe's larger economic and political developments. The Age of Revolution had come to a second climax with the Europe-wide revolution of 1848, during which the countries of Continental Europe suffered through protests, strikes, and overturned governments. The revolution of 1848 gave expression to the social consequences of rapid, though uneven, industrialization in various regions of Europe, including the large-scale movements of people to urban centers, the emergence of an industrial proletariat, and the triumph of a bourgeois class. What followed was a period of political reaction and a new focus on economic gains. It was a time when England and France in particular secured and expanded their empires, and from those holdings outside Europe they drew enormous resources. The financial speculation that attended such enterprises as the building of the railroads led a fortunate few to amass unheard-of fortunes, especially in the 1870s and 1880s. This new accumulation of wealth contributed to the development of extravagant and lavish spectacles, the expansion of theaters, and an emphasis on technical developments.

NATIONALISM AND THE THEATER

The nineteenth century was also the century of nationalism, as growing numbers of countries attempted to establish and affirm their own native traditions and values. Nationalists called for national theaters to showcase the new (or old) national self-consciousness, on the model of the Comédie Française, the foremost theater of France. Theatrically the most remarkable of those efforts was undertaken by Richard Wagner (1813–1883) in Germany. Wagner sought to integrate dramatic literature, music, and acting, as well as all the other components of theater such as set design and lighting, into a new and complete synthesis—what he labeled the *Gesamtkunstwerk* (total work of art). Single-handedly, he wrote the libretti, composed the music, and influenced the staging of his operas, which he called music-dramas, at the opera house in Bayreuth newly built under his supervision, the Festspielhaus (Festival Theater). Because Wagner wanted to immerse his spectators in the power of theatrical illusion, he inaugurated what are today common theatrical methods such as dimming the light in the auditorium and hiding the orchestra to encourage the audience to focus exclusively on the stage. Though Wagner himself relied on Romantic plots and folktales, many later theater practitioners, such as the Swiss designer Adolphe Appia (1862–1928), took their inspiration from him as they attempted to create a new and modern theater.

THEATER IN THE UNITED STATES, 1800–1900

The quest for national identity was no less urgent in the United States, but it took a very different form. Theatrical activity in colonial America was recorded in the 1600s, and the first theater was built in Williamsburg, Virginia, in 1716. Even after the American Revolution was over and independence from England had been won, many economic and cultural ties between the newly formed United States of America and its former mother country remained in place. One particularly strong connection was their theaters. In the United States in the late eighteenth century, theatrical activity was largely restricted to the cities of Philadelphia, New York, Boston, and Charleston, South Carolina, and the small but growing number of resident professional companies was dominated by English-born actors and actors who had been trained in England. While the United States produced its own playwrights—including Mercy Otis Warren (1728–1814) and Royall Tyler (1757–1826)—English plays constituted most of the dramatic repertoire well into the nineteenth century.

During the nineteenth century, a new and genuinely American theater culture appeared, owing in no small part to the country's first native-born acting star. Edwin Forrest (1806–1872) established an American school of acting based on a heroic style that relied on grand, physical gestures

The Astor Place Riot, New York City, 1849.

and speech that appealed to popular audiences. While Forrest stayed in America, Charlotte Cushman (1816–1876), the first famous American actress, moved to England once she had become well known, proving that England still had greater cachet and rewards for an ambitious actor. In 1849 the relation between the United States and England, and more specifically the difference between the English and the more physical American acting schools, led to violence. In New York City, both Forrest and the visiting English actor William Charles Macready (1793–1873) were playing Macbeth. The two men were longtime rivals, and when thousands of followers of Forrest invaded the Astor Place Opera House to stop Macready's performance, with thousands more outside, the mayor called out the National Guard. Guardsmen fired into the crowd, and at least twenty-two died in what has become known as the Astor Place Riot.

STAGING RACE

While Americans were fighting for cultural independence, there emerged in the United States another type of theater not found in England or any other part of Europe: the minstrel show. Initially its players were white performers in blackface, their skins darkened with burnt cork or shoe polish, but African American minstrel troupes soon appeared as well. Musicians and singers would form a semicircle, and they would alternate between songs, dances, and short bits of dialogue, mostly between two characters—Tambo (a player of the tambourine) and Bones (a player of the bones, a clacking folk instrument made of bones or wood)—seated at either end of the semicircle, or between them and an interlocutor who sat in the middle. The minstrel show relied on racial stereotypes, for whether whites represented African Americans, as was most often the case, or African Americans made up the troupe, they had to conform to the stereotyped routines that were initially established by white performers and demanded by the predominantly white audiences. In this way, the minstrel show, America's most popular form of theatrical entertainment in the nineteenth century, was part of the fabric of American racism even as it established an American, and especially an African American, performance tradition.

America's most popular play of the nineteenth century also dealt with race relations. Harriet Beecher Stowe's (1811–1896) immensely influential novel *Uncle Tom's Cabin* (1851–52), which some have credited with having helped to start the U.S. Civil War (1861–65) through its moving depiction of the plight of slaves, inspired numerous dramatic adaptations; the most famous was an 1852 version by George L. Aiken (1830–1876), which had the longest run—more than 300 performances—of any single production in nineteenth-century America. Aiken's dramatization was largely faithful to Stowe's antislavery stance, but many other adaptations simply reverted to racial stereotypes. These adaptations, known as Tom shows, helped establish "Uncle Tom" as a derogatory label for African Americans who appeared to make their peace with slavery and suppression rather than rebelling against them. While minstrel shows and the dramatizations of *Uncle Tom's Cabin* played a central role in nineteenth-century American theater, other representations of black life or slavery rarely appeared onstage. As so often in the history of drama, dramatists at odds with popular taste had to write for a smaller reading public instead, as the African American writer and former slave William Wells Brown (1814–1884) did with his play *The Escape; or, A Leap for Freedom* (1858).

Modern Theater, 1880–1945

THEATER AND THE MODERN WORLD

In the era of Romanticism, theatrical performance and dramatic literature had increasingly drifted apart. During the last two decades of the nineteenth century, however, serious writers were finally drawn to the theater once more. This did not mean that they sought to please the tastes of popular audiences. Indeed, modern drama was often characterized by a tension, even antagonism, between dramatists and audiences, an antagonism sometimes provoked by the playwrights themselves. Riling up audiences had been part of theater history for some time, as demonstrated by various nineteenth-century clashes in theaters, but now an adversarial relationship between producers and consumers became expected. The history of modern drama frequently involved confrontations between supporters of innovation and hostile audiences unprepared for new subjects, dramatic structures, and theatrical techniques. Whether by design or not, being controversial became the very condition for being modern.

Many modern dramatists earned their notoriety by engaging and often confronting audiences with challenging subjects and unusual forms. They wanted to restore theater's serious, moral function and to challenge, rather than please, their audience. To that end, they depicted the most vexing moral problems and dilemmas of their time. During the late nineteenth and early twentieth centuries, Europe and North America underwent a number of profound changes: new technologies, scientific advancement, urbanism, the proliferation of nationalist movements, changing class relationships, an accelerating economic transition from agriculture to industry, and new theories of human nature (including Marxism, Darwinism, and Freudianism).

Challenging the conventions and complacency of late nineteenth and early twentieth century society, modern playwrights addressed the impact of these and other changes. The Norwegian dramatist HENRIK IBSEN (1828–1906) depicted public hypocrisy, restrictive social conventions, and such taboo subjects as hereditary syphilis. His play *A Doll House* (1879), which exposes the hypocrisies and inequalities of Victorian marriage, was denounced in newspapers, sermons, and books. GEORGE BERNARD SHAW (1856–1950), who championed his Norwegian contemporary in *The Quintessence of Ibsenism* (1891), wrote about prostitution and woman's emancipation in *Mrs. Warren's Profession* (1893) and expressed his idiosyncratic form of socialism in such plays as *Man and Superman* (1903). The German writer Gerhart Hauptmann (1862–1946) used his play *The Weavers* (1892) to call attention to the degrading conditions of weavers, while the Swedish playwright AUGUST STRINDBERG (1849–1912) depicted the ruthless battle between the sexes in *MISS JULIE* (1888). Even OSCAR WILDE (1854–1900), who delighted audiences with *THE IMPORTANCE OF BEING EARNEST*

Eleonora Duse as Rebecca in the 1906 production of Ibsen's *Rosmersholm* at the National Theater of Christiana. Rebecca rejects not only the Christian religion but also the entire structure of Christian ethics.

(1895) and other social comedies, violated conventional expectations with *Salomé* (1894), a play based on a sexually charged episode in the New Testament that describes the decapitation of St. John the Baptist. What united these playwrights was that all struggled with official censors; many of their plays could be presented only to small, private audiences because they were banned.

Though provocative themes and characters drew the most immediate hostile reaction, dramatists also deviated radically from the established rules governing dramatic forms. Many modernists criticized and ridiculed the most popular nineteenth century dramas, such as melodramas and well-made plays. Ibsen and Shaw borrowed the conventions of the well-made play but interrupted its smooth, technically structured plots with lengthy dialogues, set speeches, and other devices that shifted dramatic attention from incidents to social and psychological issues. In such later plays as *The Dream Play* (1902) and *The Ghost Sonata* (1907), Strindberg abandoned dramatic rules for the logic of dreams. Seeking to capture the nuances of everyday life, ANTON CHEKHOV (1860–1904) rejected the stock characters and heightened dramatic incidents of the contemporary Russian theater for a drama of understatement, indirection, and psychological nuance. Traditional forms, when they were used, were adapted to new purposes, and new forms were developed to respond to a changing modern world.

THE INDEPENDENT THEATER MOVEMENT: NATURALISM

These modern playwrights could present their work to the public because of the opening of small, independent theaters intended to provide an alternative to the larger commercial theaters. Particularly important in this respect was André Antoine's (1858–1943) Théâtre Libre in Paris, which introduced the plays of Ibsen, among others. In London the Independent Theatre, founded by J. T. Grein (1862–1935), was devoted to the same task, and later Shaw and Harley Granville-Barker (1877–1946) would find a home at the Court Theatre. In Berlin it was the Freie Bühne of Otto Brahm (1856–1912) and in Moscow the Moscow Art Theater of Konstanin Stanislavsky (1863–1938) that made available performance venues for modern drama. All the theaters named above were associated with naturalism, a movement that originated in France in the 1860s and advocated that literature and art must faithfully present reality, with the writer and artist assuming the position of an objective scientist.

In its concern with the accurate portrayal of human beings and the external world, naturalism represented an extension of the realist movement that came to dominate European and North American art and literature during the middle of the nineteenth century and remains a powerful aesthetic current in today's theater. A reaction against the idealizing tendencies of Romanticism, realism seeks to depict contemporary life and society directly, unmediated by art's distorting conventions. The plays of Ibsen and Chekhov and the early plays of Shaw, which address social realities in recognizably contemporary settings, fall under this rubric. Naturalism differs from realism in that it relies on a more scientifically grounded understanding of the relation between individuals and their environment. Inspired by Charles Darwin (1809–1882) and his theory of natural selection, naturalists believed that humans are not free agents choosing their own destiny but rather are creatures determined by their environment, their physiology, and the social conditions under which they live. In the arts, the chief proponent of naturalism was Émile Zola (1840–1902), who influenced Antoine, Grein, Brahm, and other directors associated with naturalism in the theater. Dramatists who were strongly affected by naturalism include Strindberg and Hauptmann.

MODERN ACTING

Naturalism changed not only the nature of plays but also the modes of staging them. The movement led to an increased emphasis on realistic stage props and décor and a rejection of the histrionic acting practiced in the nineteenth-century commercial theater. The Russian actor and director Konstantin Stanislavsky, for example, pioneered a new acting system based on the actor's psychology and emotions. For performances of Ibsen, he even imported Norwegian furniture to help the actors merge with their roles. What Stanislavsky did for individual roles, George II, the duke of Saxe-Meiningen (1826–1914), did for groups, introducing new systems of ensemble acting and bringing vivid crowds to the stage. Modern plays, with their new and daring female roles, also made it possible for a new generation of female stars to emerge and contribute to a truly modern acting style. Among them were Eleonora Duse (1958–1924) in Italy, Elizabeth Robins (1862–1952) in England, and Eva Le Gallienne (1899–1991) in the United States. In developing their signature roles, many of these actresses chose characters from Ibsen's plays.

AESTHETICISM AND SYMBOLISM

Naturalism was not the only movement that sought to break with the conventions of nineteenth-century theater. Indeed, the rapidity with which such movements followed one another, and their strenuous and public efforts to present a distinctive rationale for artistic innovation, became a distinctive feature of modernism. Aestheticism, which advocated the primacy of beauty over values such as social or political utility, was particularly associated with Oscar Wilde (although Wilde himself was well aware of the importance of societal forces; he expressed a commitment to socialism and suffered prosecution as a homosexual). Symbolism focused on rarified meanings, subjectivity, and suggestion rather than common idioms or everyday speech. Symbolist playwrights included Maurice Maeterlinck (Belgium, 1862–1949), Madame Rachilde (France, 1860–

A set-design sketch by Adolphe Appia, ca. 1910. Note the abstract pattern of lines and angles.

1953), William Butler Yeats (Ireland, 1865–1939), and Aleksandr Blok (Russia, 1880–1921). Symbolism also entailed a return to exalted and poetic speeches and a preference for simple, symbolic designs over the cluttered stage sets of naturalism. Symbolist design was championed especially in Paris, in Aurélien Lugné-Poe's (1869–1940) Théâtre de l'Œuvre. In England, the abstract sets of Edward Gordon Craig (1872–1966) had many affinities with symbolism, as did the monumental and abstract designs of Adolphe Appia (1862–1928).

THEATER AND THE AVANT-GARDE

The battles between different movements became more pronounced and complicated in the first decades of the twentieth century. A host of "isms," often announced through manifestos and declarations, emerged virtually overnight, and many disappeared as quickly. Among those that made a mark was futurism, mostly based in Italy and Russia, which was initiated by F. T. Marinetti (1876–1944). Inspired by an enthusiasm for technology and machines—the products of a belated but rapid industrialization in northern Italy—Marinetti sought to banish the human actor from the theater, relying instead on puppets, machines, and other inanimate objects. He also rejected well-structured plays in favor of short episodes of discontinuous actions and effects. Futurism was followed by Dadaism, which pushed the anarchic provocations of the futurists to an extreme. In the Cabaret Voltaire, which flourished in Zurich during World War I (1914–18), Tristan Tzara (1896–1963) and other Dadaists presented nonsense poems, manifestos, musical pieces, and masked performances of various kinds, often simultaneously. Like futurism, Dadaism quickly became an international movement with followers in the major European cities and beyond. When Dadaism declined in Paris in the early twenties, many of its adherents joined the movement of surrealism, which was led by André Breton (1896–1966). Influenced by the psychoanalytic theory of Sigmund Freud (1865–1939), surrealism focused on

A photograph of the original 1935 production of Antonin Artaud's *Les Cenci*. Based on an Italian story of incest, torture, and patricide, the play embodies the Theater of Cruelty that Artaud espoused in *The Theater and Its Double*. Artaud, in the role of Count Cenci, stands in front.

spontaneous associations, drifting thoughts, and dream images. The surrealists were also interested in earlier writers who shared their concerns, including the provocateur Alfred Jarry (1873–1907), who had written crude and funny plays violating almost all strictures of decency and proper form. His scatological, grotesque, and irreverent play *Ubu the King* (1896) became an icon of the surrealist movement. The most influential theater maker associated with surrealism (even though he left the movement after a quarrel with Breton) was Antonin Artaud (1896–1948), who, under the name Theater of Cruelty, advocated a primal, physical theater inspired not just by ancient rituals but also by the slapstick comedy of the Marx Brothers. Artaud's writings on theater, which were published on 1938 under the title *The Theater and Its Double,* drew on images such as the plague, primitive myths, and the "animated hieroglyphics" of Balinese theater to establish theater as an antidote to the decadence of modern life.

The increasingly strident movements of the early twentieth century are often grouped together under the classification *avant-garde*. Originally a military term used to designate the advance corps of an army, in the early nineteenth century *avant-garde* became a political label applied to radical and advanced groups seeking social change. It was only in the second half of the nineteenth century that the notion of the avant-garde infiltrated the arts, allowing artists of various movements to present themselves as ahead of everyone else. Yet because the avant-garde groups maintained ties to their political roots, their formation must be understood in the context of the political history of the early twentieth century, and they often strongly promoted socialism, anarchism, or, as in the case of the Italian futurists, fascism. Indeed, the Futurists were extreme Italian nationalists, advocating war as an end in itself as well as a form of self-aggrandizement. The Dadaists, by contrast, formed in opposition to World War I and came to embrace an international socialism as a way to destroy the old class-based societies. They shared that aim with surrealists, many of whom joined various communist parties. Even more closely linked to socialism were the Russian futurists, who participated in the Russian October Revolution of 1917 and strove through artistic means to help it succeed.

POLITICAL THEATER: BRECHT

Socialism had an immense effect on many artists and thinkers of the first half of the twentieth century and later, including those not associated with the more extreme avant-garde movements. The most influential political playwright was BERTOLT BRECHT (1898–1956), who developed a new form of drama and performance called Epic Theater, which relied on a number of techniques meant to interrupt the flow of plot and acting. Brecht believed that such interruptions would ensure that audiences actively ponder, rather than passively consume, the theatrical spectacle. He had also learned from the director Erwin Piscator (1893–1966) the value of bringing many art forms, including film (still relatively new at the time), into the theater, and he collaborated with composers such as Kurt Weill (1900–1950) on new, presentational forms of opera and other forms of musical theater. Brecht, Piscator, and Weill, together with many other European writers and theater makers, fled to the United States during the Nazi era and exerted considerable influence on theater and music there. Besides these émigrés, the best-known political writer in the United States was Clifford Odets (1906–1963), whose plays depicted the plight of working-class families and often included rousing calls for a socialist society.

CULTURAL RENEWAL: IRELAND AND THE UNITED STATES

Not all theaters in the early twentieth century were dominated by avant-garde and socialist plays. The Abbey Theatre (1904) in Dublin, for example, was devoted to gaining the cultural independence of Ireland, which for centuries had been under England's control; it thus followed the nineteenth-century movement for national theaters in European countries other than those—England, France, Spain, and Italy—that had traditionally dominated theater. One of its founding members, Lady Augusta Gregory (1852–1932), advocated a return to the Irish language, which had long been marginalized by English colonizers and settlers. The playwrights associated with the theater took varied approaches to drama. While Ireland's leading poet William Butler Years composed dense, difficult plays filled with highly

A scene from the original 1928 production of *The Threepenny Opera*, a collaboration between the composer Kurt Weill and Bertolt Brecht.

A photograph of the Provincetown Players original production of Eugene O'Neill's *All God's Chill'un Got Wings* (1924). Paul Robeson, seated, played the lead role.

poetic language and mostly set in a mythical past, John Millington Synge (1871–1909) wrote in a more colloquial, highly lyrical idiom. His plays, which undercut romanticized views of the Irish peasantry, proved controversial with the theatergoing Dublin public; so jarring was his presentation of rural Ireland in *The Playboy of the Western World* (1907) that it sparked theatrical riots and a long dispute that threatened the existence of the Abbey Theatre and the Irish Theatre Movement of which it was part.

Cultural independence was also the purpose of the Provincetown Players in the United States, a small theater troupe devoted to presenting new and challenging plays by American playwrights such as SUSAN GLASPELL (1876–1948) and Eugene O'Neill (1888–1953). Founded in Cape Cod and then moved to New York City, the company was part of the so-called Little Theatre Movement of the 1910s and 1920s in the United States. This movement, which was inspired by Europe's alternative theater movement of the late nineteenth century, provided the space for staging new and experimental plays without the financial constraints of the commercial theater, which by the late nineteenth century was dominated by New York's Broadway theaters and by touring productions of successful shows that took star performers to theaters in an extensive network across the United States. Some modern playwrights, such as O'Neill, both participated in the Little Theatre Movement and managed to have their plays performed on Broadway, where the largest and most elegant commercial theaters were located. Broadway still retains its unique status, as demonstrated by the distinction drawn today between Broadway, off-Broadway, and even off-off-Broadway theaters.

TRAGEDY, METATRAGEDY, METATHEATER

While the era of modern drama saw an unprecedented explosion of new forms of drama and theater, a number of playwrights also sought to return to one of the oldest dramatic forms: tragedy. In the eyes of Ibsen, the bourgeois family and its struggle against the overwhelming power of the past created the conditions for modern tragedy to take place. A similar view led Eugene O'Neill to adapt Greek tragedies to contemporary America, as in *Mourning Becomes Electra* (1931), and to write new tragedies based on his own family, as in *Long Day's Journey into Night* (written 1941; produced 1956). Other playwrights in the United States followed his lead: such dramatists as TENNESSEE WILLIAMS (1911–1983), ARTHUR MILLER (1915–2005), Sam Shepard (b. 1943), David Mamet (b. 1947), and Edward Albee (b. 1928) have all explored the intersection of the tragic and the everyday in American life, as characters grapple with the economic, social, and personal challenges of their modern world. Another set of playwrights turned to remote, rural settings in search for appropriate material for modern tragedies. The Spaniard Federico García Lorca (1898–1936), for example, set such tragedies as *The House of Bernarda Alba* (1936) in Andalusia, and Synge turned to the remote western coast of Ireland for *Riders to the Sea* (1904), a play that was later adapted by the Caribbean writer

Derek Walcott (b. 1930) in *The Sea at Dauphin* (1957).

A second group of modern playwrights were also drawn to tragedy but did not believe that it was suitable for the modern world. Instead, they wrote plays *about* tragedy—what they called metatragedy or *metatheater*—that focused on the nature of role-playing and the relationship between reality and theatrical illusion. The best-known writer of metatragedies was the Italian LUIGI PIRANDELLO (1867–1936), whose plays—such as the influential *SIX CHARACTERS IN SEARCH OF AN AUTHOR* (1921)—are mirrored cabinets in which characters adopt roles, pretend to be mad, or philosophize, in self-referential ways, about the nature of theater itself. Another prominent writer of metatragedies was the French Jean Genet (1910–1986). Originally a novelist, Genet turned to the theater because of his fascination with costumes and role-playing, and his plays create intricate layers of pretense that are never entirely peeled back. The turn to metatheater proved influential throughout modern and contemporary drama—nontragic as well as tragic—and a self-conscious awareness of theatrical reality is an important part of the twentieth- and early twenty-first-century stage.

WAR, REVOLUTION, AND DEPRESSION: 1900–1945

The explosion of forms, the emergence of politically driven avant-gardes, the return to tragedy, and the rise of metatheater were all responses to the unprecedented turmoil of the first half of the twentieth century in Europe and elsewhere. Nineteenth-century industrialization had effected profound changes in how people lived and worked, leading scores of men and women who formerly had labored in agriculture or trades to join the urban proletariat. The revolutions and wars of the first half of the twentieth century were fueled by these changes. Social unrest was everywhere, even in the relatively stable United States, and the Russian Revolution of 1917 was only one of its most striking manifestations. The unforeseen horrors of World War I, in which the European nations brought on themselves incalculable loss of life, showed once and for all the destructive potential of advances in technology and industrialization. European self-confidence, as well as the belief in progress and the upward course of civilization more generally, was dashed. Peace brought only short-lived relief, as the worldwide stock market crash of 1929 and

Figures silhouetted by the U.S. Constitution in a production of *Triple-A Plowed Under* sponsored by the Federal Theater Project during the 1930s. This play, one of the earliest and best-known of the "living newspapers," addressed the plight of American farmers during the Depression.

the depression that followed it threw the global economy into a crisis—one that, unlike the war, affected the United States as much as it did Europe. Faced with the Great Depression, President Franklin Delano Roosevelt (1882–1945) undertook, as part of his New Deal, an ambitious public works program, which included unprecedented sponsorship of the theater. During its brief existence (1935–39), the Federal Theatre Project rejuvenated theatrical activity across the country and pioneered such innovative forms as the "living newspaper," which addressed social and political issues in innovative, multimedia productions. Other changes affected the theater arts as well. Economic turmoil and racism in the South encouraged the great migration of African Americans to northern cities, which helped make New York's Harlem a cultural center for the arts in the 1910s and 1920s. African American musicians and jazz flourished, and so did such writers, intellectuals, and playwrights of the Harlem Renaissance as Zora Neale Hurston (1891–1960) and LANGSTON HUGHES (1902–1967).

In Europe of the twenties and thirties, fascism and Nazism were on the rise, and soon England and the Continent, the United States, and the world as a whole would be plunged into another and even bloodier war. The cataclysm of World War II (1939–45) brought to a close the era of modern drama that began with Ibsen and other groundbreaking figures of the later nineteenth century, and it cleared the way for new movements and playwrights who would explore the emerging outlines of the contemporary world. The period 1880–1945—which opened with Thomas Edison's first public demonstration of the incandescent lightbulb on December 31, 1879, and ended with the atomic bombing of Hiroshima and Nagasaki in August 1945—was a time of profound and unsettling changes that inevitably affected playwrights. They participated in the political, ideological, and social movements and changes around them, contributing with their plays and performances to urgent debates, problems, and opportunities. They responded to these unsettling times in their stark and jagged plays, in which all the old forms, structures, and certainties seemed to have fallen apart. In the process, they gave rise to the most innovative and influential era of theater-making since the Renaissance. The varied forms of dramatic art that they introduced would influence the shape of theater for generations.

Postwar Theater, 1945–1970

THE POSTWAR WORLD

In political, social, and cultural terms, the latter half of the twentieth century was shaped by the second of two global wars and by the geopolitical changes that followed in its wake. World War II, which was fought between the Axis powers (Germany, Italy, Japan) and the Allies (Britain, France, the Soviet Union, the United States, and China), claimed 60 million military and civilian lives, including 11 million who died in German-controlled concentration camps (6 million of them Jews killed in the Holocaust) and as many as 200,000 who died as a result of the atomic bombs that the United States dropped on the Japanese cities of Hiroshima and Nagasaki. With much of Europe and parts of Asia devastated by warfare, the United States emerged from World War II as the world's dominant military, industrial, and economic power, though its unilateral supremacy proved to be short-lived. The Soviet Union, which successfully tested its own atomic bomb in 1949, established its influence over the countries of Eastern Europe, while the revolution led by Mao Zedong (1893–1976) ended with a communist government ruling mainland China. By 1950 the international landscape had been redrawn between two competing economic and ideological blocs—a capitalist "West" and a communist "East"—and the cold war that would dominate the world for the next forty years was well under way. Although the United States and the Soviet Union avoided direct military confrontation during this period, their struggle for ideological supremacy played itself out in a series of regional wars—notably in Korea, Vietnam, and Afghanistan—and in the internal politics of countries throughout Asia, Africa, and Latin America. They competed as well in the fields of science, technology, culture, and sports. No symbol was more resonant of this bipolar world than the city of Berlin, which was divided into western and eastern sectors by the Berlin Wall, a literal version of the "Iron Curtain" that divided not just Germany but Europe as a whole.

The 1950s inaugurated a period of prosperity for North America, Western Europe, and Japan, and the middle class established itself more firmly as the arbiter of social values. After years of wartime austerity, many in the West began to enjoy the benefits of a thriving consumer-oriented economy that catered to domestic households and an emergent youth subculture. On the surface, the 1950s was a decade of materialism and conformity, a period during which social stability was reinforced—particularly in the United States, where a new "Red Scare," like the one that had followed the Russian Revolution, inflamed anticommunist sentiment in the late 1940s and early 1950s—by the fears of enemy infiltration and nuclear war. Yet many of the social problems that would erupt in the following decade were already visible. The civil rights movement on behalf of African Americans took definitive shape in the United States in the mid-1950s, and London was the site of clashes between white youths and West Indian immigrants in the Notting Hill race riots of 1958. In 1954 France became involved in a war in Algeria that ended eight years later with the independence of its oldest major colony. Decolonization was under way around the globe, as the former holdings of European empires became newly independent countries in what was soon being called the Third World. Even in those nations under Soviet control—the Warsaw Pact countries of Eastern Europe—there were disturbances, as citizens in client states sought more autonomy. In 1956 the Soviet Union brutally suppressed the Hungarian Revolution, as it would Czechoslovakia's "Prague Spring" in 1968.

Driven by these and other impulses for change, an increasing number of challenges arose in the 1960s to the social consensus that had largely prevailed in the United States and Western Europe since the end of World War II. A growing number of intellectuals and activists condemned the inequalities of Western capitalism from the points of view of Marxism/socialism and anarchism, and to their social critique were added the voices of radical trade unionists, an emerging youth subculture, Black Power advocates in the United States, and members of such issue-specific movements as the Campaign for Nuclear Disarmament in Britain and the international protests against the United States' war in Vietnam (1961–73). These movements came to a head in Paris in May 1968, when an escalating series of strikes by students and workers brought France to a standstill and nearly toppled the government of Charles de Gaulle (1890–1970). Similar uprisings took place elsewhere, and it seemed—for the moment, at least—as if capitalism itself was under siege.

POSTWAR THEATER: EXPANSION, CONTINUITY, AND INNOVATION

During the years 1945–70 theater and drama underwent their own changes, many of which intensified trends that had emerged earlier in the century—while others signaled important new directions for the late twentieth-century stage. Even as London, Paris, Berlin, Moscow, New York, Toronto, and other major cities continued to serve and grow as important theatrical centers, more theaters were built and more residential theater companies formed outside these cities. Regional and provincial theaters were established, a number of annual theatrical festivals—such as those in Avignon, France; Edinburgh, Scotland; and Stratford, Ontario—were founded and expanded, and smaller theaters were opened in cities to provide opportunities for productions that the larger commercial theaters were unwilling or unable to undertake. The period also saw the founding of a number of state-sponsored theaters and theater companies, such as London's National Theatre, which was established in 1963. Like other new theaters and companies, these venues opened the way for new kinds of techniques, performance aesthetics outside the mainstream, and unconventional dramatic texts.

Though new theatrical theorists emerged, much of the innovation of these years reflected the influence of two earlier writers: BERTOLT BRECHT and Antonin Artaud.

Brecht's Epic Theater—specifically, its presentational devices and acting style, as well as its view of theater as a medium for social analysis and intervention—maintained a powerful hold on European political theater, while Artaud's conception of a total theater that would surround its audience and address it on a visceral level had a profound impact on the environmental theater movements of the 1960s and the pioneering work of the Polish director Jerzy Grotowski (1933–1999). Both of these traditions helped the theater of the mid-twentieth century to meet one of its greatest challenges: rediscovering its performative uniqueness during an age when competition from film, radio, and television was increasing.

POSTWAR FRENCH THEATER: ABSURDISM

The psychological and social impact of World War II on midcentury drama was felt most immediately in France, where the absurdists established themselves as one of the most important groups of postwar dramatists. The term *absurdism* was not coined until 1961, when the critic and scholar Martin Esslin (1918–2002) published his influential study *The Theater of the Absurd*, and the dramatists who were included under this label are as notable for their differences as for their similarities. But the word does underscore a shared rejection of conventional dramatic structures and a skepticism toward rationality, language, and the coherent subject of traditional philosophy and drama. As they confronted a universe apparently bereft of meaning, divine or otherwise, they echoed the assumptions of Jean-Paul Sartre (1905–1980), Albert Camus (1913–1960), and other proponents of philosophical existentialism, while the dramatic features that defined their plays—nonlinearity, antirealism, lack of traditional coherence, nonsensical language, metadramatic awareness, and the mixture of tragedy, comedy, and farce in a modern form of tragicomedy—owed much to the experiments of Dada, surrealism, and other avant-garde movements earlier in the century. Eugène Ionesco (1909–1994) and JEAN GENET (1910–1986) are among the most prominent of the playwrights whose works show the influence of absurdism, though no figure in this tradition had a greater impact on the drama that followed than the Irish-born playwright SAMUEL BECKETT (1906–1989),

In Eugène Ionesco's *The Bald Soprano*, a classic example of Theater of the Absurd, characters engage in nonsensical banter that calls into question the nature of communication in modern society. Pictured here is the 1950 production at the Théâtre Noctambules in Paris, directed by Nicolas Bataille.

whose play *WAITING FOR GODOT* (1952)—first performed in Paris in 1953—changed the landscape of postwar theater. Although it originated in France, absurdism exerted a pronounced influence on international drama during the 1950s and 1960s. Its challenge to arbitrary forms of order lent itself to social and political critique in the hands of Eastern European dissidents such as the Czech playwright Václav Havel (b. 1936) and dramatists living under repressive regimes throughout the Third World.

POSTWAR GERMAN THEATER: THE BRECHTIAN LEGACY

Postwar drama followed a different trajectory in Germany and the other German-speaking countries of central Europe. Most of Germany's theaters had been destroyed during the war, and the governments of both West Germany and East Germany embarked on major efforts to rebuild their countries' cultural infrastructure. The drama that was written for these theaters in the 1950s dealt mainly with social and political issues, and the subjects of guilt and responsibility loomed particularly large for a people confronting their collective role in World War II. Aiding the development of political theater were Bertolt Brecht's return to East Germany after his self-imposed exile during the Nazi period and the founding of the Berliner Ensemble in 1949 by Brecht and his wife, the actress Helene Weigel (1900–1971). The Berliner Ensemble put Brecht's theories of rehearsal and production into practice and in performing to audiences at home and abroad established Brecht's plays and the "Brechtian style" as major forces in the contemporary theater. In the German-speaking theater Brecht's influence was manifest in the drama of a new generation of playwrights, many of whom adopted the Brechtian focus on social and political issues and employed Brechtian techniques, though usually without the doctrinaire and, at times, utopian Marxism that often shaped Brecht's plays. The Swiss playwright Friedrich Dürrenmatt (1921–1990) made Brechtian and absurdist techniques part of his pessimistic dramatic vision of humanity in the postwar world, while the German playwright Peter Weiss (1916–1982) brought elements of Artaud's Theater of Cruelty to a Brechtian concern with history. Weiss's dramas of the mid- and late 1960s—such as *The Investigation* (1965), which examines the Holocaust through the theatrical re-creation of war crimes testimony—were written in the style of documentary theater, a genre that other dramatists embraced during the decade.

POSTWAR BRITISH THEATER: THE WELFARE STATE AND ITS DISCONTENTS

In the ten years immediately following the war, the theater in Britain gave little evidence of the important role it would play in the history of contemporary drama. The country itself was undergoing historic changes: in 1945 Clement Attlee's (1883–1967) Labour Party achieved a landslide victory over the incumbent prime minister and wartime hero Winston Churchill (1874–1965), and the following six years saw the establishment of the British welfare state. One sign of the increasing role of government in society was the creation of the Arts Council of Great Britain, an independent, government-funded body that—for the first time in Britain—provided state subsidies for the arts. But these changes in society left little mark on the London theater, which for the most part was sustaining itself on an uninspiring diet of West End productions. Two events caused a seismic shift. In 1955 Beckett's *Waiting for Godot* was given its London premiere, and in the following year *Look Back in Anger*, by the playwright John Osborne (1929–1994), electrified the theater world; it was produced by the London Stage Company, a noncommercial company specifically formed to support new playwrights. Osborne's play expressed the restlessness and anger of a generation at odds with the materialism and oppressive class structure of Britain in the mid-1950s, and it reflected the disillusionment permeating an imperial power in the twilight of its ascendancy. Along with the work of the Theatre Workshop—a company in a working-class area in East London that, under the leadership of Joan Littlewood (1914–2002), produced plays

Jimmy Porter (played by Kenneth Haigh) plays his trumpet to distract himself from his cramped quarters and the complacency of postwar Britain in the original 1956 Royal Court production of John Osborne's *Look Back in Anger*.

by such working-class playwrights as Shelagh Delaney (b. 1939)—*Look Back in Anger* opened the door for a new generation of dramatists grappling with social class and other issues central to British national identity.

The subsequent development of social and political theater in Britain was influenced by Brecht's theories and practices; indeed, over the next two decades Brechtian dramaturgy and stagecraft found their widest application outside Germany in British theater. The Berliner Ensemble visited London in 1956 (the year of Brecht's death) and 1965, and its epic style influenced a number of left-wing directors, designers, and playwrights. John Arden (b. 1930) and Edward Bond (b. 1934) belong to the first generation of British dramatists who employed the strategies and techniques of Brechtian theater to strikingly original ends. The Brechtian turn in British drama received greater impetus in the aftermath of 1968, when a new generation of socialist playwrights—inspired by the revolutionary events in Paris and elsewhere and aided by the abolition of government censorship, which had been in effect since the Theatrical Licensing Act of 1737—made Brechtian devices a cornerstone of their more radical political drama. John McGrath (1935–2002), Howard Brenton (b. 1942), and David Hare (b. 1947) are only a few of the many dramatists who drew on Brecht in the 1970s and early 1980s. Among the women playwrights who sought to adapt Brecht within the politics of an emerging feminist movement, CARYL CHURCHILL (b. 1938)—whose plays range with deliberate abandon through space and time in treating their historical and contemporary subjects—is the most accomplished and widely known. This intensification of political playwriting after the events of 1968 was matched by a proliferation of radical (or "fringe") theater groups throughout Britain and Northern Ireland.

PINTER, STOPPARD, ORTON

Other playwrights and dramatic currents helped define postwar British theater. The influence of Samuel Beckett was apparent in the drama of Harold Pinter (b. 1930) and Tom Stoppard (b. 1937), two of the country's leading contemporary playwrights. Pinter combined the indeterminacy and linguistic evasions of Beckettian drama with the often gritty realism of interactions within the lower, middle, and upper strata of Britain's class-based society. Stoppard, who was born in Czechoslovakia, drew on Beckett in a technically virtuoso, philosophically sophisticated drama that also has more than a passing kinship to GEORGE BERNARD SHAW's "drama of ideas." Joining Stoppard in reworking the English comic tradition was Joe Orton (1933–1967), whose plays of the mid-1960s exploited the farcical, the macabre, and the surface gentility of English drawing-room comedy within an anarchic drama of sexual desire pursued across boundaries of gender, sexual identity, and class.

POSTWAR AMERICAN THEATER: EXPRESSIVE REALISM, METHOD ACTING

Theater in the United States achieved one of its greatest flowerings in the years immediately following World War II. While Europe found it necessary to revive—and in many cases, rebuild—its theatrical institutions, the Broadway theaters that represented the center of theatrical life in the United States had been left relatively untouched by the war. But with few exceptions—the plays of Thornton Wilder (1897–1975), for instance—this theater had produced little of substance since the mid-1930s. The rebirth of American theater that followed the end of the war resulted from the collaboration between a group of visionary theatrical practitioners and two emerging dramatists—TENNESSEE WILLIAMS (1911–1983) and ARTHUR MILLER (1915–2005)—whose innovative dramaturgy was put to work in plays that captured the aspirations and anxieties of postwar America. The designer Jo Mielziner (1901–1976) pioneered an expressive or "subjective" stage realism that presented the theatrical categories of present and past, here and there, exterior and interior with poetic fluidity. Using the stage designs of Mielziner and under the direction of Elia Kazan (1909–2003), such plays as Williams's *A STREETCAR NAMED DESIRE* (1947) and Miller's *DEATH OF A SALESMAN* (1949) explored the shifting landscapes of memory and desire on a stage where the external world was at once materially real and evanescent. Such plays created a need for performers to convey greater psychological complexity, and it was met by contemporary developments in American acting. Continuing the interest in Konstantin Stanislavsky's psychological approach to acting that had marked the work of the Group Theater in the 1930s, the Actors Studio (founded in 1947 by members of the earlier company) promoted method acting, a performance style that emphasized psychological motivation, intention, and the importance of subtext in the presentation of dramatic characters. This approach, perhaps most famously realized in the theatrical and film performances of Marlon Brando (1924–2004), dominated American acting through the 1950s.

Director Elia Kazan and playwright Arthur Miller sitting on Jo Mielziner's set for the 1949 Broadway production of *Death of a Salesman.*

OFF-BROADWAY AND OFF-OFF-BROADWAY THEATER

Even as Broadway played a central role in presenting a revitalized American drama, its historically dominant role in American theater was challenged during the postwar years. In an attempt to diversify and expand theatrical activity outside the city of New York, a number of regional theaters were formed with resident companies presenting an annual season of plays. Among the most prominent of these are the Alley Theatre (Houston, 1947), the Arena Stage (Washington, 1950), and the Guthrie Theater (Minneapolis, 1963). Within New York, the increasing conservatism of Broadway theaters in the face of rising production costs led to the opening of off-Broadway theaters. Like the Little Theater Movement of the 1910s, off-Broadway theater involved smaller buildings that often were some distance from the main commercial theater district, and because these spaces served smaller audiences—between 100 and 499 spectators—they could be used to produce plays that the larger Broadway houses found too risky. European writers such as Beckett and Ionesco saw the first New York productions of their plays in off-Broadway theaters, as did a number of new American playwrights, including Edward Albee (b. 1928). Off-Broadway also played a significant role in the careers of more established American playwrights. The 1956 production of *The Iceman Cometh* by Circle in the Square, one of the decade's most important off-Broadway theaters, revived interest in the plays of EUGENE O'NEILL (1888–1953) and thus helped lead to the Broadway premiere of ***LONG DAY'S JOURNEY INTO NIGHT*** that same year.

But by the end of the 1950s, off-Broadway theaters were themselves dealing with rising costs; they therefore became more reluctant to gamble on experimental plays or on unproven writers and increasingly reliant on productions whose commercial success seemed guaranteed. In response, off-off-Broadway theaters were founded throughout New York. These low-budget theaters—which were located in coffeehouses, church buildings, various basements, and wherever else space was available—provided opportunities for a generation of younger dramatists with strong antiestablishment leanings and experimental creative interests. During the 1960s—in Caffe Cino (1958), La MaMa Experimental Theatre Club (1961), Judson Poets' Theater (1961), and elsewhere—they launched the careers of such prominent contemporary playwrights as Maria Irene Fornes (b. 1930) and Sam Shepard (b. 1943). The often radical plays produced in these venues took part in the experimentation more broadly under way in 1960s American theater. For example, under the leadership of Joseph Chaikin (1935–2003), the Open Theater rejected the psychological realism of method acting for a form of acting rooted in improvisation, role-playing, and transformation. Communal theater groups, such as the Living Theater (which had been

Playwright Luis Valdez, right, founder of El Teatro Campesino, with the United Farm Workers president, Cesar Chavez, in front of New York's Winter Garden Theater in 1979. *Zoot Suit*, by Valdez, was the first Chicano play to be performed on Broadway.

founded as an off-Broadway company in 1947), explored a radically participatory theater in which the division between performer and audience became almost imperceptible. Other theater groups—the Free Southern Theater, the Bread and Puppet Theater, and El Teatro Campesino, to name a few—used agitprop techniques, puppetry, and populist theater traditions to engage with social issues such as civil rights, the conditions of migrant farmworkers, and the Vietnam War.

AFRICAN AMERICAN THEATER

The years 1945–70 also saw the rise of contemporary African American drama. Drama and theater, of course, had played a central role in the Harlem Renaissance during the 1920s and 1930s, most notably in the plays of LANGSTON HUGHES (1902–1967), and the government-funded Federal Theatre Project of the 1930s had provided work for African American theater professionals through the "Negro units" that were established in New York and other cities. But it was not until Lorraine Hansberry's (1930–1965) play *A Raisin in the Sun,* which had an acclaimed run on Broadway in 1959, that serious African American drama claimed the attention of mainstream audiences. A product of the 1950s civil rights movement, the play also anticipated the more radical political and cultural movements of the decade that followed. African American theater of the 1960s reflected a deepening militancy; the plays of Amiri Baraka (b. 1934), for instance, reveal the author's growing separatism and revolutionary convictions, while the Black Arts Repertory Theatre (1965) that Baraka helped establish in Harlem was at the forefront of the militant Black Arts Movement. These and other dramatists of the 1950s and 1960s laid the groundwork for such later African American playwrights as Ntozake Shange (b. 1948), AUGUST WILSON (1945–2005), and SUZAN-LORI PARKS (b. 1964).

Contemporary Theater

THE CONTEMPORARY WORLD

The term *contemporary,* always imprecise, is particularly elusive when applied to today's historical moment. In a world of accelerated change where international events, technological developments, and cultural trends follow each other with dizzying speed—the past of even a few years ago can seem like another age. Much has transpired during the period from the end of the 1960s through the first decade of the twenty-first century, and these years could be subdivided into smaller segments, each with its defining issues and preoccupations. Over the time since 1970, a world has emerged markedly different than that of the postwar years, and the overall trends and transformations of those decades have led to a present whose outlines we are still coming to understand.

In the past forty years a number of pivotal events have remapped the international geopolitical landscape, and two have been particularly important in their immediate and long-range consequences. As the result of intensifying pressure from the outside and the weaknesses of their own economic and social systems, which were unable to adapt to a changing global economy, the Soviet Union and its satellite states rejected communism in favor of Western-style capitalist economies in the years 1989–91, thereby bringing an end to the cold war that had defined international relations since the end of World War II. The fall of the Berlin Wall in November 1989 was the most visual symbol of this rapid change that took the form of peaceful and violent revolutions throughout the former Eastern Bloc, the unification of Germany, the dissolution of the Soviet Union in 1991, and the wars among the newly independent states of the former Yugoslavia. The second major shift was the rise of Islamist militancy as a social and political force. Islamic fundamentalists in Iran overthrew the monarchy of the shahs in 1979, replacing it with a revolutionary Islamic republic; in the 1980s, foreign volunteers joined an Afghan national resistance movement in what they viewed as a fight for Islam and drove the Soviet Union out of Afghanistan (1979–89). Such successes helped foster the growth of organized terrorist organizations, leading to the attacks on the World Trade Center and the Pentagon on September 11, 2001, and the subsequent wars in Afghanistan and Iraq.

THEATER AND GLOBALIZATION

Even more important in shaping the contemporary world than these geopolitical and ideological changes have been developments in the transnational spheres of capital and finance, corporate organization, information, communications, and culture. The world's economy has become literally global: the flow of goods, services, money, and information is increasingly unfettered, as traders move currencies and corporations reconfigure labor forces, production networks, management operations, and marketing strategies without respect to national borders. This process of globalization has been supported by innovations in information and communications technology—most notably, personal and network computing, cellular and electronic communications, and the rapid expansion of the Internet, which has made possible unprecedented access to information. Culture and the arts also show the effects of the global economy, as the products of high, popular, and mass (or commercial) culture reflect an ever-richer dialogue between the local and global. American teenagers read graphic novels that borrow from the latest in Japanese anime, while fans in Asia, Europe, and South America follow the steadily internationalizing game of American basketball. Music and other cultural products circulate between societies, and these encounters generate hybrid forms that draw on and transform both national and more localized styles and traditions.

Not surprisingly, the field of theater has adapted itself to—and been shaped by—this globalizing, technological world. Though one can still speak of national theaters, the activities of theater and drama have become increasingly internationalized over the twentieth and early twenty-first centuries. The 1913 Nobel Prize in Literature was won by the Indian poet and playwright Rabindranath Tagore (1861–1941), whose play *The Post Office* had been performed by Dublin's Abbey Theatre earlier that year; the 2000 prize was awarded to the Chinese playwright and novelist Gao Xingjian (b. 1940). Playwrights, theatrical companies, and productions cross borders with ease, and the encounter of cultural traditions has become both a subject and a collaborative aesthetic of theatrical production. The 1985 theatrical adaptation of the Hindu epic the *Mahabharata* by the British director Peter Brook (b. 1925) was produced at the Avignon Festival in France with actors from sixteen countries; over the next four years it toured internationally. More recently, the French Canadian director, writer, and performer Robert Lepage (b. 1957) has produced a number of

The 1987 production at the Theatre des Bouffes du Nord of *Mahabharata*, directed by Peter Brook.

theatrical pieces that combine international performance styles in narratives about history, migration, and cultural identity that span the globe. These, too, have been performed around the world. Other prominent contemporary directors—such as Ariane Mnouchkine (b. 1939) and Robert Wilson (b. 1941)—similarly are international theater figures.

THEATER AND MEDIA

One reason for the internationalism of contemporary theater is the shifting relationship of the performing arts to the expanding field of media technologies. For much of the twentieth century, theater was forced to compete with a series of emerging media: film, radio, tape recording, and television. In a number of cases, it responded by incorporating these technologies into its repertoire of staging practices: onstage projections in Brechtian theater, for example, and the disembodied voices of BECKETT's late plays. In the century's final decades, the line separating theater from film and other media continued to blur. The American playwright Sam Shepard's (b. 1943) reputation owes as much to his work as a film actor as it does to his theater work, while David Mamet (b. 1947) writes as frequently for cinema as he does for the stage. Plays are regularly adapted for film and television—vastly more people saw TONY KUSHNER's (b. 1956) *ANGELS IN AMERICA* (1991–92) on HBO in 2003 (and subsequently on videotape) than saw it in the theater—and noteworthy productions of such plays as CHEKHOV's *Uncle Vanya* are available for video libraries. As it becomes less reliant on specific performance sites, in other words, theater is more transportable than it has ever been.

The shifting boundary between theater and other media—and the resultant blurring of the distinction between elite and mass culture— is also reflected in the influence of postmodernism on contemporary theater and drama. *Postmodernism,* a term most frequently applied to developments in architecture, the visual arts, and literature in the second half of the twentieth century, denotes a style (or set of styles) that challenges the Enlightenment and modernist belief in metanarratives (i.e., overarching frameworks of meaning) and abandons historical analysis in favor of juxtaposing historical and contemporary elements in the mode of quotation or pastiche.

The theater has also responded to competing media technologies by asserting its uniqueness in the actuality of the theatrical moment and the proximity of live actor to spectator. This impulse, which marked the activities of theater groups influenced by Artaud and the performances of the Living Theater and other communal theater groups of the 1960s, manifested itself in the work of performance artists who began presenting their work in the United States during the 1970s. These artists, often working solo, appeared at a range of locations inside and outside the theater; their performances, which could be scripted or unscripted, often involved the performer's body in situations or encounters that addressed various issues pertaining to social representation, politics, and other matters. By the 1980s, though, even these artists were engaging with contemporary media culture in their performances.

INTERNATIONAL THEATER

In keeping with the overall trend of globalization, in the twentieth and early twenty-first centuries the importance of theater outside Europe and the United States has increased. The rise of national theaters outside Italy, Britain, France, Spain, and Germany is connected to the political and cultural nationalisms that gathered force in Europe and other areas of the world in the late nineteenth and twentieth centuries. From Mexico to Ireland to Egypt, plays were produced that embraced newly emerging cultural identities, often within theaters that were built and designated as national sites. The dramatists who helped drive these movements frequently were influenced by traditional and modern European dramatic forms, and in this sense their dramatic writing represented an attempt to bring Western modernity to local theatrical cultures. This pattern can be observed in Japan, China, and India, where Western-influenced plays entered ancient theatrical traditions. Many of the most influential figures in international theater during the past century brought Western traditions into dialogue with indigenous theatrical, dramatic, and narrative forms. The Egyptian playwright TAWFIQ AL-HAKIM (1898–1987), for instance—who lived in Paris for several years during the 1920s—helped establish an Arabic literary dramatic tradition by applying Western dramatic forms and techniques to traditional Arabic story material (such as *The Thousand and One Nights*). Al-Hakim's plays after 1950, like those of playwrights who followed in his footsteps, addressed the political and social issues of the contemporary Arab world.

POSTCOLONIAL THEATER

The internationalization of drama after the end of World War II received a strong impetus from the decolonization movements that led to the dismantling of Europe's global empires. India achieved its independence from Great Britain in 1947, and by 1970 all but a few of the British, French, and other European colonies in Africa, Asia, and the Caribbean had followed suit. In most cases independence followed intense campaigns by nationalist groups, such as the Viet Minh (the full form of its name means "League for the Independence of Vietnam") of Ho Chi Minh (1890–1969) in French Indochina and the Mouvement National Congolais of Patrice Lumumba (1925–1961) in the Belgian Congo. The newly independent countries faced their own formidable challenges: poverty and underdevelopment; corrupt, often repressive governments; outside political interference; economic exploitation; and tribal, ethnic, and sectarian divisions, in addition to the pervasive political, social, and economic legacies of colonial rule. The unbalanced power relations between indigenous peoples and long-established populations of white settlers caused wide economic disparities, which had political consequences. For example, in South Africa, which became independent of Great Britain in 1910, a system known as *apartheid* (an Afrikaans word that means "separate") restricted political power to citizens of British and Dutch ancestry and legally classified all persons within the country into one of four racial groups. Until it was abolished in 1994, black citizens were forced to live and work in so-called homelands (only those with a work permit could live in a city), were forced into a separate education system, and were compelled to carry government-issued passes for identification. Other former colonies, as well as those nation-states that achieved independence when the Soviet Union dissolved in 1991, have had to deal with their own legacies of colonial suppression.

The term *postcolonial* is frequently used in discussions of national identity in a world still coming to terms with the effects of colonialism—or, according to some, now living under a neocolonial system of new economic and cultural dependencies. The term is often applied to literature and other cultural forms—such as theater—within those nations previously subjected to colonial rule. *Postcolonial*, in this sense, refers less to the historical period after colonialism than it does to the inheritance of a system whose tensions and contradictions—social, psychological, and cultural—remain very much alive. Postcolonial writers and other artists address the metropolitan centers that historically dominated their nations and societies (most prominently, London and Paris), but they do so as subjects who have been partly formed by those centers and their language, educational system, social structures, and culture. Literature, theater, and other postcolonial art forms establish relationships between native and colonial traditions; explore the influence of imperial ideologies, power structures, and discourses on contemporary perceptions and relations; and look for ways in which those who live in postcolonial societies can achieve new forms of identity and cultural resistance.

Postcolonial dramatists, whose work represents one of the most vibrant and important currents in contemporary theater, have been at the forefront of those seeking to rewrite the received traditions of Western culture from a postcolonial point of view. The Nigerian playwright Wole Soyinka (b. 1934), who studied in England and worked with the Royal Court Theatre in London before returning to his native country in the late 1950s, draws on the rituals and festivals of Nigeria's Yoruba culture as well as on European dramatic models in plays that address the impact of colonialism and the tyranny of oppressive

Actor-playwrights Percy Mtwa and Mbongeni Ngema in *Woza Albert!*, a play about apartheid performed in 1983 at the Market Theater in Johannesburg.

regimes that followed in its wake. The West Indian playwright Derek Walcott (b. 1930) has also sought fusions of Western and indigenous performance forms, drawing on Caribbean folklore, dance, storytelling, and linguistic patois while celebrating the hybridization of the region's multiple cultures. Because language was central to the dynamics of colonial subjugation—local languages were usually subordinated to an "official" tongue and, in some countries, were even outlawed—the politics of language is an important subject of postcolonial drama. Many of these plays include non-European languages—Gaelic, Zulu, Bengali—within a broadened field of linguistic interaction.

The term *postcolonial* is also used to refer to playwrights who live in the former "settlement colonies," predominantly English-speaking countries where white settlers adopted their own version of British culture and whose relations with London, for most of the colonial period, were largely autonomous. In Canada, which became a dominion in 1867 and achieved legislative independence in 1931, drama challenging the dominant Anglo-Canadian culture has been produced by the country's French-speaking minority—including the leading Quebecois playwright, Michel Tremblay (b. 1942)—and such Native American playwrights as Tomson Highway (Cree, b. 1951). In Australia, which was settled as a British penal colony in the late eighteenth century, a national history that includes the displacement of the indigenous population has been explored by such writers as the Aboriginal playwright Jack Davis (1917–2000) and the white Australian Louis Nowra (b. 1950). And no postcolonial drama is more socially urgent than that which was produced within apartheid South Africa by writers such as Athol Fugard (b. 1932), Zakes Mda (b. 1948), and Maishe Maponya (b. 1951), many of them associated with the pioneering multiracial Market Theatre in Johannesburg (established 1976).

THEATER AND DIVERSITY

The social, cultural, and psychological changes associated with postcolonialism, it is important to note, extend beyond the nations that had been imperial holdings. Many former colonial subjects were among the immigrants who streamed into Europe to work in the decades after World War II, and this growing population of naturalized citizens—South Asians, West Indians, and Africans in Britain; North Africans in France; Turks in West Germany—has redrawn the racial profile of societies that once were homogeneous. Throughout western Europe, cities have become more cosmopolitan—a cosmopolitanism deepened at the end of the twentieth century and the beginning of the twenty-first by the economic integration of nations within the European Union and the liberalization of economies in eastern Europe. The effects on the contemporary theater of Britain, Ireland, and the Continent have been profound. Second- and third-generation writers from immigrant populations—Hanif Kureishi (b. 1954) and Ayub Khan-Din (b. 1961) in Britain, for instance—who find themselves between two cultures and belonging completely to neither, have created plays that explore their often conflicted position, while playwrights from culturally dominant racial groups have produced a drama increasingly concerned with the changing face of nationhood.

A different version of this cultural evolution is evident in the United States, where immigration has been central to national self-definition since the metaphor of the "melting pot" was first used in 1782. Though it has traditionally been assumed that immigrants and their descendents would surrender their particular racial and ethnic differences for a dominant, shared "Americanness," this stance has been replaced in recent decades by an embrace of cultural uniqueness and ethnic/racial identity. Following the development of a contemporary African American drama in the 1950s and 1960s, the American theater has seen the emergence of Asian American drama in the work of DAVID HENRY HWANG (b. 1957) and others, Chicano/a drama, and—since the 1990s—Arab American drama. The growing political and cultural assertiveness of the continent's original inhabitants has also produced an impressive body of Native American drama. This drama is sometimes the product of theater groups, such as the U.S.-based Spiderwoman Theater, that draw on Native American storytelling and performance traditions.

More broadly, the theater has begun to include a wider range of voices and experiences that traditionally have been marginalized within, or excluded from, the stage. The roots of this expansion lie in the "identity" or "liberation" movements that have gathered strength in recent decades in Europe, North America, and other areas of the world. The contemporary women's movement, for example, which burgeoned in the 1970s, has produced a rich body of drama concerned with women's experience, the meaning of "woman" in traditional representations, and the changing manifestations of gender in the late twentieth and early twenty-first centuries. This drama has often formed part of an explicit feminist project to challenge male-directed theatrical practices, institutions, and notions of authorship, and it has sometimes been produced by companies employing newer, more collaborative forms of theatrical practice.

Gay and lesbian drama has also gained a prominent voice in the contemporary theater. Though homosexual rights groups existed in Europe and the United States earlier in the century, agitation for the rights and recognition of gay, lesbian, bisexual, and transgendered individuals did not come to the attention of the general public until the late 1960s. The Sexual Offenses Act of 1967 decriminalized most sexual acts between adults in Britain, and the 1969 Stonewall riots in New York galvanized the gay liberation movement in the United States. Perhaps because of its interest in role-playing and its tolerance for unconventional identities, the modern theater has attracted an impressive number of homosexual and bisexual playwrights, including OSCAR WILDE (1854–1900), Gertrude Stein (1874–1946), Federico García Lorca (1898–1936), TENNESSEE WILLIAMS (1911–1983), Jean Genet (1910–1986), Lorraine Hansberry (1930–1965), Edward Albee (b. 1928), and Joe Orton (1933–1967). Yet only in the 1970s did an openly gay and lesbian drama emerge in its own right. Among the leading writers of this drama is the American playwright TONY KUSHNER, whose two-part dramatic fantasia *ANGELS IN AMERICA* was one of a number of plays during the 1980s and 1990s that addressed the AIDS epidemic. Important authors of lesbian drama include the contemporary American playwright and performance artist Holly Hughes (b. 1955).

THEATER IN THE TWENTY-FIRST CENTURY

As the works of these and other contemporary playwrights indicate, theater remains deeply responsive to social movements, cultural developments, and historical shifts and transformations. As the twenty-first century unfolds, theater—a medium at once traditional and new—offers a unique perspective on the issues and preoccupations of a changing world. One of the oldest of the arts, theater brings nearly 2,500 years of performance forms and dramatic texts to the current historical moment. At the same time, theater is one of the most immediate of the representational arts, grounded in the physical presence of the actor's body and the irreproducible occasion of live performance. Old plays are performed in new contexts, and the resulting dialogue frames both present and past in mutually illuminating ways. *HAMLET* (1600–01) has been performed thousands of times, but every time the Danish prince picks up Yorick's skull—a stage prop—he does it for different audiences in a performance interaction that changes from moment to moment. Its sensitivity to audience and occasion makes theater exceptionally responsive to the complex web of issues, relationships, and interactions that make up the present moment. For this reason, many of the contemporary theater's most important activities have taken place not in traditional theater buildings but in the squares, community centers, and other sites where people gather and work. Health and theater workers have used theater as a vehicle for vaccination campaigns in South America, AIDS education in Africa, and trauma therapy for those victimized by violence around the world. In these and other forms, theater remains deeply important in regions that may not have access to other media, in cultures that rely for education less on print than on oral modes of transmitting information, and with marginalized social groups in other societies.

Theater is more international than it has ever been, and in its emerging and time-honored forms it constitutes an important part of the global cultural landscape. As the expansion and proliferation of media continue in this digitalizing age of multiple entertainment sources, theater and drama carry on traditions that have been handed down for centuries, reworking these conventions in often striking ways and making them responsive to a new century's changing realities.

READING DRAMA, IMAGINING THEATER

For those of us who are used to reading novels and short stories, opening the text of a play can come as something of a surprise. Characters are identified before the story ever begins, in a listing (often labeled *dramatis personae*) that seems more like the entries in an address book than the stuff of literature. Instead of the designations "he said" or "she said" that embed what these characters say within a novel's or short story's unfolding narrative, dialogue is presented directly, with the speakers' names indicated on the left-hand margin. Stage directions indicate when characters enter or exit the dramatic scene, how they move around in relation to each other, and how they handle the objects of their material world. The very world they inhabit feels constrained—even claustrophobic—next to the expansive, shifting settings of *Don Quixote* or *War and Peace*.

Features such as these point to the essential difference between drama and more strictly literary forms such as fiction and poetry. While the term *playwright* means "maker of plays," the written text that we pick up to read provides only a part of the larger phenomenon we call *performance*. Its meanings, in other words, are not limited to the private worlds created by readers as they encounter words on a page. Rather, the printed play is a blueprint for something that happens in real time and space before an audience. The dramatic text in performance thus depends not on a single literary author but on the collective artistry of actors, designers, directors, and others involved in theatrical production. Even those plays—known as "closet dramas"—that were written with the expectation that they would never (or could never) be performed in an actual theater generate imaginative scenarios that have more in common with an audience's experience of watching a play than with a solitary reader's enjoyment. The fact that plays are written with some form of theater in mind—that they exist as dramatic scripts as well as literary works—ensures that the pleasures associated with dramatic art are rich and complex.

As a consequence, to read drama well requires a theatrical imagination attuned to the possible realizations of the dramatic script onstage. The first time we encounter an unfamiliar play, we seek and respond to its narrative—the story it is telling us. But we cannot fully appreciate the impact of such a play unless we consider *how* that story is told and what kind of performance it suggests. Reading plays is an active process—a creative collaboration with the dramatist that takes place in the mind of the reader. As a way of conceiving the dramatic world of a play, it may be helpful to start by envisioning its physical environment, or setting. Where and when is the play set? What and where are the key markers in that location (a door, for example, or a throne)? Some playwrights—particularly those who write under the influence of theatrical realism—include a great deal of information about the play's physical environment, making the stage materialize by supplying a wealth of particular detail. Other dramatic texts provide minimal, or no, setting specifications; for example, SAMUEL BECKETT'S *WAITING FOR GODOT* (1952) includes the famously minimalist direction "A country road. A tree. Evening." Plays written before the nineteenth century often lack place descriptions and depend on the dramatic action and dialogue to establish what is onstage. The plays of SHAKESPEARE and his contemporaries, for example, establish location through economical, highly evocative verbal description. Knowing something about the production conventions in use during specific periods can help you re-create how a play might have looked to its original audience, but it should not limit your imagination. As the history of theatrical performance indicates, plays are adaptable to other kinds of theaters, stage resources, and production practices.

When visualizing this physical environment, you may wish to make a rough sketch of the scenic environment (or environments) indicated within the dramatic text, so that you can visualize how the characters and locale interact in each scene. Some theatrical terminology is useful here. In many theatrical traditions, locations and movement on stage are designated by a gridlike pattern. The section farthest away from the audience is considered *upstage,* while the area closest to them is *downstage.* Unless otherwise indicated, the sides of the stage are noted from the actor's perspective; hence, *stage right* will be to the actor's right, and *stage left* will be to the actor's left. The midpoint of the stage is called its *center.* Thus, for example, an actor might be told to enter through a door up right and to move (or "cross") to sit on a chair down left. When imagining the layout of a particular scene, it is important to be aware of who is onstage and where, at all times, even when these characters participate only silently in what is going on. Though the presence of such characters may be easy to forget, they may prove pivotal to the action of individual scenes.

Try to envision each character's appearance, as well as how much flexibility there may be in matching the bodily reality of a given actor to the physical description of the character. At some times and in some places, the correspondence between bodily appearance and role has been fairly conventionalized, with recognizable "types" recurring in similar dramatic performances. But even such roles can be taken by actors who vary in appearance, bearing, age, and manner, or even play against type. Throughout theater history, for example, what we now call cross-gender casting and cross-racial casting have been important elements of performance. As part of your effort to visualize the play in performance, you might cast known actors in your imaginary staging to make it more vivid, then substitute others to see how different personalities and styles of acting might shape a role differently. Here, too, the text can be your guide. Is the performance required by the text naturalistic or stylized, comic or serious? In some cases—the stylized theater of Japanese noh, for example—the answer is clear, and by imposing antithetical acting styles you may violate the play's aesthetic underpinnings. In most cases, however, access to a range of acting styles can liberate possibilities within the dramatic text, offering new perspectives and opening it up to new theatrical energies.

In addition, it is useful to pay close attention to what characters say and how they say it. Language is the playwright's principal means for revealing characters and their dramatic world, and the play relies mainly on the spoken word to communicate with its audience. Dramatic speech often reveals important information about the characters, including their class position, geographic origin (especially through dialect), and personality. In the absence of a narrator who might make known to us a character's inner thoughts and feelings, speech is the conduit through which the play's figures disclose their hopes, fears, and intentions. Such characterization rests not simply on what a specific character says but also on what is said about him or her. Indeed, the richness of a dramatic portrait is often the product of multiple—and differing—accounts, observations, and perspectives offered by a play's characters.

Language, of course, is more than information, and nowhere is this truer than in the theater, where language exists not to be read but to be spoken. The words on the page of a dramatic text are designed for the mouth, and as chosen by the best dramatists their sounds fill and guide the mouth, position the body in specific attitudes, and occupy the stage with their acoustic power. When the playwright John Millington Synge wrote that "in a good play every speech should be as fully flavored as a nut or apple," he was referring not just to his own use of Irish dialect but to the linguistic and syntactical richness that makes all great dialogue a kind of vocal music. When bringing a play to theatrical life in your mind, read its lines aloud, feel the emotions they stir in your body, and enjoy the music that they create within your room. By yourself or with a friend, read some of the dialogue, noticing the contrapuntal rhythms that characters establish when they speak together. Even when reading translations—such as the ones included in this anthology, which were selected with vocal and other forms of performability in mind—you can feel such cadences and musicality. Along with the other sounds that a play may require—the ritualized foot stamping of the noh actor, the swish of regal costumes, Feste's lute in Shakespeare's TWELFTH NIGHT (1600–01)—the spoken word makes up the soundscape of dramatic performance. Reading with an awareness of this aural power can enhance your understanding and appreciation of drama.

While noting that the spoken language is a primary determinant of dramatic and theatrical meaning, we must not ignore the other elements that reinforce or complicate the acts of expression, communication, and signification. Three texts, in fact, work together in performance: the spoken text, the action text, and the subtext. Whereas the *spoken text,* or dialogue, is what the characters say to each other (or to the audience) during the play, the *action text*—whether scripted by the playwright or created by the director, the actors, or both—is the physical language of the play: the gestures and movements that significantly shape our understanding of the story. In highly conventionalized theater cultures, such as those of classical India and Japan, the actors' movements and gestures become intricate languages in their own right, signifying to an audience that understands their meaning specific relationships, emotions, and attitudes. But directors and actors of all eras have used the action text as a way of communicating meaning, even when the effect of such gestures and movements may be to undermine the sentiments expressed in the spoken text (as when the villain of nineteenth-century melodrama winks at the audience while professing his sincerity to an onstage character). *Subtext* consists of the unspoken thoughts, feelings, and intentions of the characters that underlie and prompt the action and spoken texts. The relationship between the subtext and its manifestation in word and action is as variable in the theater as it is in life. Sometimes language and gesture express the inner life directly and fully. "Language most shows the man; speak that I may see thee," wrote BEN JONSON in a prose collection published shortly after his death. But as *VOLPONE* (1606) and other plays by Jonson demonstrate, drama concerns itself more frequently with the discrepancy between private intention and public expression. Characters hide their meanings from others (and occasionally from themselves), feign indifference when they feel love, say only part of what they mean, pursue their designs under the unsuspecting eyes of those they interact with. Even silence—the choice not to speak—plays an important role in conveying contextual meaning.

The dynamic interplay of these three texts—and their interaction with set design, lighting, and the other elements of production—creates the depth and complexity of live theater. When we speak of an actor's interpretation of a role, or a director's concept for a production, we are thinking about the myriad choices that artists make, using these intersecting texts, to develop fully realized characters and to communicate with the audience through the play and its performance. The key word here is "interpretation," for the dramatic text as it exists on its own is fundamentally incomplete, suspended between possible realizations. Because plays are designed for performance, they depend on the activities of actors, directors, designers, stage managers, musicians, and the other theatrical practitioners who have served in different periods to usher them into life. And every choice that is made by these practitioners helps to realize, or interpret, the play in light of its possible range of meanings. Because the combinations of such choices are infinite, no two productions of a play are ever the same, and a great work of dramatic art has an endless capacity to surprise us with new experiences and insights whenever it is performed.

Because reading drama can and should resemble the process of actual production, you should approach the dramatic text as if you were a theater professional. Instead of reading a play to discern preexisting meanings, look for the places where a role, a scene, or a verbal exchange may be performed in different ways, and make choices as to how such components might be interpreted in the theater of your mind. What happens if an actor dwells on certain words in a speech as opposed to others? Where might he or she pause when delivering the lines, and what would be the effect of such vocal punctuation? What subtextual meanings do you see behind words and actions, and how might your actors bring them out? Consider the other elements of production as well. How would you light a production of your play, and what would be the effect of your decisions? How do the meaning and dynamics of a scene change if you focus your light on certain characters rather than others? What costumes do you imagine for your actors, and what would these tell us about the characters they play? Where would you position actors on the stage, and how would they move in relation to each other? Is the stage busy or relatively still during individual scenes? In those plays that lack detailed set descriptions, what theatrical environment do you envision for the action that takes place? Conversely, with plays that have extensive directions, what specific fixtures and objects might you choose to realize the desired effect? Although some dramatists have indicated that they expect their directions be followed exactly in production, would you want to modify the given directions in any way, either to accommodate different kinds of stages or to offer a more radical vision of the play and its dramatic possibilities? As you imagine your play in the theater, you can also consider how much—if any—of the direction provided by the playwright to employ, and what possible impact on an audience such changes in direction might have. Finally, what stage might you choose for a production of your play: a traditional stage, with the audience seated directly in front of the action (the proscenium stage, for instance), or a different stage arrangement, such as one in which the audience is seated on three sides (i.e., "in the round")? How do the meanings and implications of your play change when the spectators are so close to the actors and can see each other as they look at the stage?

Though reading a play in this way does not require extensive familiarity with the theater, your ability to appreciate the theatrical possibilities of a given play will be greatly enriched by the experience of seeing plays performed onstage. Go to the theater when you can; immerse yourself in the moment when the audience grows quiet, the actors enter, and the stage is taken over by a spectacle that is illusory but feels, in its most powerful moments, more real than life itself. And while attending the theater will enhance your reading of dramatic texts, the reverse is also true. Readers who imagine the theater as part of their reading become more informed and responsive audience members, actively aware of the choices the artists have made in interpreting dramatic texts and better able to evaluate their effectiveness. One of the many pleasures of reading drama is measuring your interpretation against actual performances of the play, and comparing those individual performances with each other. Like the aficionados of other arts, you may develop, over a lifetime, your own repertoire of remembered performances and texts. And as you deepen your awareness of the relationship between what is written and what takes place onstage, you may fall under the spell of drama, which—whether enacted in the theater or in your own mind—is timeless yet always new.

THE PLAYS

SOPHOCLES

ca. 496–406 B.C.E.

A GENERATION younger than Aeschylus, Sophocles is often regarded as the most accomplished author of Greek tragedy. He was certainly the most successful. Up to twenty-four victories at the Dionysus festival in Athens are recorded for him (in contrast to thirteen for Aeschylus and five for EURIPIDES), and it is said that he never finished lower than second. Aristotle, the first philosopher to write an extended work on Greek tragedy, singled out Sophocles' *OEDIPUS THE KING* as a model of what tragedy should look like. Ever since its first performance, *Oedipus the King* has stirred audiences, eliciting fear and pity for the protagonist who, without any bad intent, is caught in a string of misdeeds. Among all extant Greek tragedies, *Oedipus the King* is the best known and most often adapted. Its influence was expanded further in the twentieth century when Sigmund Freud coined the term "Oedipus complex," based in part on his interpretation of Sophocles' play, to describe one of his core psychological theories. Cultural anthropologists have used the play to explain features shared in different societies. Indeed, Sophocles' play has evoked strong responses, including censorship, in audiences across centuries and cultures. There can be no doubt that the story of the son who unwittingly kills his father and marries his mother touches a raw nerve, even today.

Although only scant information is available about Sophocles' life, we know that he was born into a wealthy family of Colonus and that he occupied some of the highest political positions in Athens. He served as treasurer of the Delian League, a network of allied and dependent states built by Athens after its victory over the Persians. Moreover, together with Pericles, the famed leader of Athens, he commanded the Athenian fleet in its campaign against Samos. Toward the end of his life, he became a proboulos, are of ten advisors endowed with special powers of governance. During his adult life, Sophocles watched Athens evolve from a small city-state to the greatest empire of the region, projecting its power far into Persia. The last decades of his life were dominated by a second war—the Peloponnesian War with a rival Greek city-state, Sparta. Sophocles died at the age of ninety as a respected and admired citizen and civic leader, a few years before the Peloponnesian War would end in the final defeat of Athens and the demise of its empire.

Sophocles launched his career as a playwright in 468 B.C.E., when he won his first victory at the Dionysus festival in Athens by defeating the acknowledged master of tragedy, Aeschylus. He was enormously productive, writing more than one hundred plays, although only seven have been preserved: *Ajax* (ca. 450), *Antigone* (ca. 441), *Oedipus the King* (ca. 428), *Electra* (ca. 419), *The Trachian Women* (ca. 413), *Philoctetes* (ca. 409), and *Oedipus at Colonus* (ca. 406), as well as one comical satyr play, *The Trackers* (date unknown). Sophocles shaped the course of theater not only through his plays but also through his theatrical innovations. The philosopher Aristotle praised Sophocles for having established new techniques of scene painting; for having introduced a third actor (hitherto, only two actors had been permitted), thereby significantly expanding the possibilities for interaction among individual characters; and for having enlarged the tragic chorus from twelve to fifteen. At the same time, Sophocles accorded the chorus less room in his plays than the older playwright Aeschylus had done, foregrounding instead the conflicts among individual characters. As a consequence, his plays are much closer to the form of contemporary drama than any previous Greek tragedies extant.

Like his predecessor Aeschylus and his younger contemporary Euripides, Sophocles took the material for his plays from Greek myth. However, he used this material in his own distinct manner. Sophocles placed much more emphasis than did Aeschylus on turning the individual characters into complex, three-dimensional humans with conflicting motives and passions. One example is his version of the Electra myth—the sole myth whose dramatic adaptations by all three major Greek tragedians survive (though different playwrights often treated the same myth). Comparing Sophocles' version with Aeschylus's, *The Libation Bearers* (the middle part of the *Oresteia* trilogy; see the headnote on Aeschylus, above) is particularly instructive. Sophocles' version is much more dynamic, and it shifts emphasis from Orestes' act of matricide to the solitary suffering of his sister, Electra. Sophocles also uses much more suspense, postponing and drawing out the recognition scenes as long as possible, even though the audience was of course familiar with the basic outlines of the plot.

Emphasizing the individual was an innovation that allowed for a more nuanced form of characterization. But it also had a cultural and political dimension. The very structure of Greek tragedy—with individual characters, often the rulers, engaging in conflict with a chorus, usually composed of elders or representative citizens—dramatized for the Athenian audience the political history of their own city. During the emergence of Athenian tragedy, Athens had gone from autocratic rule to a democracy that involved a growing number of male citizens in the political process. The rule of the one versus the rule of the many was therefore a topic of immense political importance. Sophocles' tragedies, depicting complex individuals, thus reflected the struggle over the new political form of democracy.

Of all the characters Sophocles used to populate his plays, none fascinated him more than Oedipus, a tragic figure perfectly suited to Sophocles' interest in conflicted persons. From one perspective, the myth of Oedipus is that of an individual doomed by outside forces. The son of the king and queen of Thebes, Oedipus is condemned to death to avoid the terrible prediction of an oracle that he would kill his father. But a servant takes pity on the child, and the young Oedipus is simply cast out. He grows up in the city of Corinth, ignorant of his true parents, and as an adult he returns to Thebes, unwittingly killing his father at a crossroads after having been provoked by one of the attendants. The next set piece of the myth is the encounter with the Sphinx, which is holding the city in her thrall. Oedipus submits to her test, correctly answering the riddle. Hailed as liberator of Thebes, he now marries the widowed queen and becomes a good ruler. It is only when a pestilence devastates the city and the oracle declares the murderer of the late king to be still at large that Oedipus turns to the crime and begins a methodical manhunt that constitutes most of the play. Only gradually does the truth come out, and Oedipus must finally recognize himself as the murderer he has been hunting. He blinds himself and submits to a life in exile, enduring perpetual wandering until he finds a final resting place near Athens.

Sophocles first treated the Oedipus myth with an early play about Oedipus's daughter *Antigone;* he then returned to the myth in his middle period with *Oedipus the*

King. Toward the end of his life, he felt himself drawn to the figure of Oedipus once more, composing his very last play, *Oedipus at Colonus,* on the aging Oedipus. Rather than being conceived as interrelated, the three Oedipus plays are unconnected works, each exemplary in its own way. *Antigone* is the starkest example of a tragedy depicting an unsolvable conflict between two equally legitimate moral values and positions. Bound by the ties of kinship, Antigone insists on burying her brother even though he had betrayed the city of Thebes. In doing so, she violates the law, for Creon, king of Thebes, had decreed that those who attacked the city in the war of the Seven against Thebes (the topic and title of an extant play by Aeschylus) should not receive the privilege of a proper burial. The tragedy depicts the cruel logic by which these two positions must collide, destroying the two antagonists in the process. *Oedipus at Colonus,* by contrast, is an example of Sophocles' late style. Containing almost no external action, it depicts the old, blinded Oedipus searching for a final resting place, which is finally granted to him by the liberal city of Athens. It is a ruminative and meditative play about an Oedipus reconciled to his fate and looking for a place to die.

Oedipus the King—composed seventeen years after *Antigone* and ten years before *Oedipus at Colonus*—is Sophocles' most haunting play about the Oedipus myth, and for many it is among the most haunting plays of all time. Its power arises in part from its extraordinary structure and form. In a bold move that distinguishes this play from most other Greek tragedies, Sophocles set the entire action of the play in its past, thus presenting onstage a gradual revelation of events—conveyed by speeches and dialogue—that happened long before the onstage "present." The past dominates the lives of the characters, holding them firmly in its grip.

Oedipus ponders the riddle of the Sphinx in this detail from a painted Greek *kylix*, or drinking cup.

The emphasis on the revelation of the past also means that *Oedipus the King* directs attention mostly to the realm of language rather than to the action presented on the stage. At the beginning of the play, King Oedipus has consulted the oracle at Delphi, seeking a way to halt the plague devastating the city. The oracle declares that the reason for the pestilence is the continued presence in Thebes of the murderer of the former king, Laius, who must be cast out. Oedipus is most eager to find the murderer and to expel him. As various witnesses and messengers are brought before him, the play turns into a veritable detective story—a search for traces and clues of a past crime through the cross-examination of witnesses and the careful interpretation of various prophecies and oracles. Oedipus leaps at this challenge, not only because his own rule and power depend on his success but also because he is supremely confident in his skill at untangling puzzles and riddles. As the foreign visitor who freed Thebes from the clutches of the Sphinx by solving its famous riddle, Oedipus had previously demonstrated his talent for sharp and analytical thinking. And because he owes his current position as venerated tyrant of Thebes to this skillful feat, his pride in his intellect seems warranted. Faced with a new threat to his adopted home, he is ready to exercise his skill again, once again deciphering riddles to free the city from its plight.

This time, however, things are different. Despite his self-confidence, he has in fact become something of a riddle himself. The whole play revolves around this paradox: on the one hand Oedipus is the ideal ruler, a patient and responsive king who speaks to his people directly and listens intently to their pleas; but on the other hand, he is the very pestilence that has ruined the city. Oedipus is a riddle or puzzle in another sense as well: by having unwittingly killed his father and married his mother, he becomes, as the chorus points out repeatedly, both son and husband and, to the offspring of this incestuous union, both father and sibling. These are paradoxes Oedipus cannot fathom or solve; they are the web spun around him, leading to the final, cruel revelation at the end of the play.

The riddle of a person who is both husband and son, brother and father is ultimately based on kinship. Kinship is central to Greek mythology, with its family curses passed down from parents to children. In *Oedipus the King* this theme is pursued to its extreme. In its largest dimensions, kinship helps distinguish between citizens and foreigners. Oedipus had come to Thebes as a voluntary exile, fleeing the couple whom he thought were his real parents in the city of Corinth in order to escape the prophecy that he would kill his father and marry his mother. Only at the end of the play, as part of its tragic turn, does it become clear that he is in fact a citizen of Thebes, son of the late King Laius and his wife (and now Oedipus's wife), Jocasta. Oedipus is thus doubly ignorant: he knows neither what city-state he belongs to nor who his kin are. This, precisely, is his crime, or his failure, and for this he is punished.

Dominated by messengers, reports, rumors, oracles, and prophecies, *Oedipus the King* is also unusually rich in puns and plays on names. Oedipus is named after his swollen (*oidos*) foot, an injury caused when he was cast out by his parents in their attempt to thwart the prophecy attached to their child. But his name also contains the word *oida,* which means "I know." The play is full of references to and echoes of both meanings, punning on the word for swelling and the concept of knowledge as well as its opposite, ignorance. The most famous metaphor for the play's attention to knowledge and ignorance is light. From the beginning, Oedipus vows to shed light on the mysterious murder of the former king and insists that he will force the obscure truth out into the open, no matter at what cost. Well into the play, his wife begins to fathom the grim reality of his identity and begs him to halt his single-minded search for his own past. But Oedipus wants nothing to remain hidden and does not stop until he has brought the bitter truth into the bright daylight. Given the role of light and darkness played in the entire tragedy, it is only fitting that Oedipus would punish himself not only with exile but also with blinding, so that he may no longer set eyes on the terrible deeds he has done. That the blind seer Tiresias has been right all along underscores the play's singular fixation on this one assemblage of images and metaphors.

Oedipus the King, with its pestilence and foreign ruler, is also embedded in the cultural and political history of Athens. The historian Thucydides famously described the plague that devastated Athens during the Peloponnesian War, which the plague in Thebes inevitably brings to mind. The play is also remarkable in its attention to medical language, registering the emergence of medicine as a specialized discipline in the fifth century. Finally, it should be remembered that the play was performed before Athenian audiences, which would naturally compare their own city to Thebes. This point is brought home in Sophocles' last play, *Oedipus at Colonus,* where the magnanimous Athenians protect the outcast Oedipus, thus gratifying the Athenian audience at the expense of their rival.

Modern audiences have been disturbed that Oedipus is punished for a deed he had not intended and which he had in fact done everything to avoid. But Oedipus is not merely a victim of fate. For one thing, he is overconfident in his own powers, in his ability to protect the city and to excise its pestilence. We see him pass rash judgment on those who want the truth to remain hidden in order to protect themselves and Oedipus. Yet he is not an unfair ruler. Rather, the play is a meditation on the concept of luck, *tuchē,* so central to Greek tragedy and morality. Oedipus had been an extraordinarily lucky man, as he himself admits. But he is revealed to be the unluckiest of all. That forces larger than human powers dominate these characters' lives is no reason to absolve them from responsibility and moral judgment, however. Indeed, Oedipus takes responsibility for all of it—for his actions, for his changing luck, for what he did not know, and also for what he had to learn.

Few plays have provoked the imagination and conscience of audiences as powerfully as this one, and few have inspired as many adaptations and interpretations. Julius Caesar wrote a version of *Oedipus the King,* as did the Roman playwright Seneca. A celebrated version by the French playwright Corneille (1659) was followed by that of the Enlightenment philosopher and playwright Voltaire (1718). The twentieth century brought an influential adaptation by Jean Cocteau (1934). *Oedipus the King* has also been set to music by Carl Orff (1959) and filmed by the influential Italian filmmaker Pier Paulo Pasolini (1967). Numerous performances and interpretations of Sophocles' play have ensured that the story of a man who killed his father and married his mother still captures our fears today.

In the end, however, what ensured the power of this play across centuries may not be its various adaptations or its focus on incest, a taboo across cultures and eras. Incest was in fact only one element in Sophocles' campaign to use the theater in a way that was startlingly new at the time: namely, as a vehicle for truth. The play depicts an uncompromising, even self-destructive, search for truth at all cost. Everything else—the well-being of Jocasta, of Creon, and of Oedipus himself—is ignored. If you want the truth, the play says, you must be ready to sacrifice everything for it. Rarely has a play formulated this fundamental insight and shown its consequences with greater clarity than does Sophocles' unique and radical tragedy.

M.P.

Oedipus the King[1]

CHARACTERS

OEDIPUS, king of Thebes
A PRIEST of Zeus
CREON, brother of Jocasta
A CHORUS of Theban citizens and their LEADER
TIRESIAS, a blind prophet
JOCASTA, the queen, wife of Oedipus
A MESSENGER from Corinth
A SHEPHERD
A MESSENGER from inside the palace
ANTIGONE, ISMENE, daughters of Oedipus and Jocasta
GUARDS and attendants
PRIESTS of Thebes

[TIME AND SCENE: *The royal house of Thebes.*[2] *Double doors dominate the façade; a stone altar stands at the center of the stage.*

Many years have passed since OEDIPUS *solved the riddle of the Sphinx*[3] *and ascended the throne of Thebes, and now a plague has struck the city. A procession of*

1. Translated by Robert Fagles.
2. Capital city of the region of Boeotia, in east-central Greece, famed throughout the ancient world for the seven gates in its fortifications.
3. A monster that had terrorized Thebes as long as no one could answer her riddle: "What walks on four feet in the morning, two at noon, and three in the evening?" When Oedipus correctly answered "Man," the monster killed herself, and Oedipus was rewarded with both the Theban kingship and the hand of Thebes' queen, Jocasta, in marriage.

priests enters; suppliants, broken and despondent, they carry branches wound in wool and lay them on the altar.

The doors open. Guards assemble. OEDIPUS *comes forward, majestic but for a telltale limp, and slowly views the condition of his people.*]

OEDIPUS Oh my children, the new blood of ancient Thebes,
why are you here? Huddling at my altar,
praying before me, your branches wound in wool.[4]
Our city reeks with the smoke of burning incense,
rings with cries for the Healer[5] and wailing for the dead.
I thought it wrong, my children, to hear the truth
from others, messengers. Here I am myself—
you all know me, the world knows my fame:
I am Oedipus.
[*Helping a* PRIEST *to his feet.*]
Speak up, old man. Your years,
your dignity—you should speak for the others.
Why here and kneeling, what preys upon you so?
Some sudden fear? some strong desire?
You can trust me. I am ready to help,
I'll do anything. I would be blind to misery
not to pity my people kneeling at my feet.

PRIEST Oh Oedipus, king of the land, our greatest power!
You see us before you now, men of all ages
clinging to your altars. Here are boys,
still too weak to fly from the nest,
and here the old, bowed down with the years,
the holy ones—a priest of Zeus[6] myself—and here
the picked, unmarried men, the young hope of Thebes.
And all the rest, your great family gathers now,
branches wreathed, massing in the squares,
kneeling before the two temples of queen Athena
or the river-shrine where the embers glow and die
and Apollo sees the future in the ashes.[7]
Our city—
look around you, see with your own eyes—
our ship pitches wildly, cannot lift her head
from the depths, the red waves of death . . .
Thebes is dying. A blight on the fresh crops
and the rich pastures, cattle sicken and die,
and the women die in labor, children stillborn,
and the plague, the fiery god of fever hurls down
on the city, his lightning slashing through us—
raging plague in all its vengeance, devastating

4. Emblems of supplication, laid on the altar and then taken up again after the suppliant's request is granted.
5. Apollo, god of medicine as well as light and prophecy.
6. Ruler of the Greek gods.
7. That is, the ashes of sacrificed animals: the priests of Apollo divined the future through the patterns found in them. *Athena*: goddess of wisdom and war.

the house of Cadmus![8] And black Death luxuriates
in the raw, wailing miseries of Thebes.
Now we pray to you. You cannot equal the gods,
your children know that, bending at your altar.
But we do rate you first of men,
both in the common crises of our lives
and face-to-face encounters with the gods.
You freed us from the Sphinx, you came to Thebes
and cut us loose from the bloody tribute we had paid
that harsh, brutal singer. We taught you nothing,
no skill, no extra knowledge, still you triumphed.
A god was with you, so they say, and we believe it—
you lifted up our lives.
So now again,
Oedipus, king, we bend to you, your power—
we implore you, all of us on our knees:
find us strength, rescue! Perhaps you've heard
the voice of a god or something from other men,
Oedipus . . . what do you know?
The man of experience—you see it every day—
his plans will work in a crisis, his first of all.

Act now—we beg you, best of men, raise up our city!
Act, defend yourself, your former glory!
Your country calls you savior now
for your zeal, your action years ago.
Never let us remember of your reign:
you helped us stand, only to fall once more.
Oh raise up our city, set us on our feet.
The omens were good that day you brought us joy—
be the same man today!
Rule our land, you know you have the power,
but rule a land of the living, not a wasteland.
Ship and towered city are nothing, stripped of men
alive within it, living all as one.

OEDIPUS
My children,
I pity you. I see—how could I fail to see
what longings bring you here? Well I know
you are sick to death, all of you,
but sick as you are, not one is sick as I.
Your pain strikes each of you alone, each
in the confines of himself, no other. But my spirit
grieves for the city, for myself and all of you.
I wasn't asleep, dreaming. You haven't wakened me—
I've wept through the nights, you must know that,
groping, laboring over many paths of thought.

8. The mythical founder of Thebes.

After a painful search I found one cure:
I acted at once. I sent Creon,
my wife's own brother, to Delphi[9]—
Apollo the Prophet's oracle—to learn
what I might do or say to save our city.

Today's the day. When I count the days gone by
it torments me . . . what is he doing?
Strange, he's late, he's gone too long.
But once he returns, then, then I'll be a traitor
if I do not do all the god makes clear.

PRIEST Timely words. The men over there
are signaling—Creon's just arriving.

OEDIPUS [*Sighting* CREON, *then turning to the altar.*]
Lord Apollo,
let him come with a lucky word of rescue,
shining like his eyes!

PRIEST Welcome news, I think—he's crowned, look,
and the laurel wreath is bright with berries.[1]

OEDIPUS We'll soon see. He's close enough to hear—

[*Enter* CREON *from the side; his face is shaded with a wreath.*]

Creon, prince, my kinsman, what do you bring us?
What message from the god?

CREON Good news.
I tell you even the hardest things to bear,
if they should turn out well, all would be well.

OEDIPUS Of course, but what were the god's *words*? There's no hope
and nothing to fear in what you've said so far.

CREON If you want my report in the presence of these . . .

[*Pointing to the priests while drawing* OEDIPUS *toward the palace.*]

I'm ready now, or we might go inside.

OEDIPUS Speak out,
speak to us all. I grieve for these, my people,
far more than I fear for my own life.

CREON Very well,
I will tell you what I heard from the god.
Apollo commands us—he was quite clear—
"Drive the corruption from the land,
don't harbor it any longer, past all cure,
don't nurse it in your soil—root it out!"

OEDIPUS How can we cleanse ourselves—what rites?
What's the source of the trouble?

CREON Banish the man, or pay back blood with blood.

9. Site of the shrine on the slope of Mount Parnassus, in central Greece, where Apollo prophesies through his priestess. *Creon:* a direct descendant of Cadmus, Thebes' founder; it was Creon who offered to share the Theban throne with anyone who could solve the riddle of the Sphinx.

1. The laurel crown is a sign that Creon bears good news.

Murder sets the plague-storm on the city.

OEDIPUS Whose murder?
Whose fate does Apollo bring to light?

CREON Our leader,
my lord, was once a man named Laius,[2]
before you came and put us straight on course.

OEDIPUS I know—
or so I've heard. I never saw the man myself.

CREON Well, he was killed, and Apollo commands us now—
he could not be more clear,
"Pay the killers back—whoever is responsible."

OEDIPUS Where on earth are they? Where to find it now,
the trail of the ancient guilt so hard to trace?

CREON "Here in Thebes," he said.
Whatever is sought for can be caught, you know,
whatever is neglected slips away.

OEDIPUS But where,
in the palace, the fields or foreign soil,
where did Laius meet his bloody death?

CREON He went to consult an oracle, Apollo said,
and he set out and never came home again.

OEDIPUS No messenger, no fellow-traveler saw what happened?
Someone to cross-examine?

CREON No,
they were all killed but one. He escaped,
terrified, he could tell us nothing clearly,
nothing of what he saw—just one thing.

OEDIPUS What's that?
one thing could hold the key to it all,
a small beginning give us grounds for hope.

CREON He said thieves attacked them—a whole band,
not single-handed, cut King Laius down.

OEDIPUS A thief,
so daring, so wild, he'd kill a king? Impossible,
unless conspirators paid him off in Thebes.

CREON We suspected as much. But with Laius dead
no leader appeared to help us in our troubles.

OEDIPUS Trouble? Your *king* was murdered—royal blood!
What stopped you from tracking down the killer
then and there?

CREON The singing, riddling Sphinx.
She . . . persuaded us to let the mystery go
and concentrate on what lay at our feet.

OEDIPUS No,
I'll start again—I'll bring it all to light myself!
Apollo is right, and so are you, Creon,

2. Former king of Thebes and husband of Jocasta; he was on his way to Delphi to consult the oracle of Apollo when he was killed.

to turn our attention back to the murdered man.
Now you have *me* to fight for you, you'll see:
I am the land's avenger by all rights,
and Apollo's champion too.
But not to assist some distant kinsman, no,
for my own sake I'll rid us of this corruption.
Whoever killed the king may decide to kill me too,
with the same violent hand—by avenging Laius
I defend myself.

[*To the priests.*]

Quickly, my children.
Up from the steps, take up your branches now.

[*To the guards.*]

One of you summon the city here before us,
tell them I'll do everything. God help us,
we will see our triumph—or our fall.

[OEDIPUS *and* CREON *enter the palace, followed by the guards.*]

PRIEST Rise, my sons. The kindness we came for
Oedipus volunteers himself.
Apollo has sent his word, his oracle—
Come down, Apollo, save us, stop the plague.

[*The priests rise, remove their branches and exit to the side. Enter a* CHORUS, *the citizens of Thebes, who have not heard the news that* CREON *brings. They march around the altar, chanting.*]

CHORUS Zeus!
Great welcome voice of Zeus,[3] what do you bring?
What word from the gold vaults of Delphi
comes to brilliant Thebes? Racked with terror—
terror shakes my heart
and I cry your wild cries, Apollo, Healer of Delos[4]
I worship you in dread . . . what now, what is your price?
some new sacrifice? some ancient rite from the past
come round again each spring?—
what will you bring to birth?
Tell me, child of golden Hope
warm voice that never dies!

You are the first I call, daughter of Zeus
deathless Athena—I call your sister Artemis,[5]
heart of the market place enthroned in glory,
guardian of our earth—
I call Apollo, Archer astride the thunderheads of heaven—
O triple shield against death, shine before me now!
If ever, once in the past, you stopped some ruin

3. That is, Apollo, who could speak for Zeus, his father.
4. Apollo's birthplace, an island in the Aegean Sea that was central to his cult.
5. Goddess of the moon and the hunt; twin sister of Apollo.

launched against our walls
    you hurled the flame of pain
far, far from Thebes—you gods
  come now, come down once more!
                    No, no
the miseries numberless, grief on grief, no end—
too much to bear, we are all dying
O my people . . .
  Thebes like a great army dying
and there is no sword of thought to save us, no
and the fruits of our famous earth, they will not ripen
no and the women cannot scream their pangs to birth—
screams for the Healer, children dead in the womb
    and life on life goes down
      you can watch them go
  like seabirds winging west, outracing the day's fire
down the horizon, irresistibly
    streaking on to the shores of Evening
                    Death
so many deaths, numberless deaths on deaths, no end—
Thebes is dying, look, her children
stripped of pity . . .
  generations strewn on the ground
unburied, unwept, the dead spreading death
and the young wives and gray-haired mothers with them
cling to the altars, trailing in from all over the city—
Thebes, city of death, one long cortege
    and the suffering rises
      wails for mercy rise
  and the wild hymn for the Healer blazes out
clashing with our sobs our cries of mourning—
  O golden daughter of god, send rescue
  radiant as the kindness in your eyes!

Drive him back!—the fever, the god of death
    that raging god of war[6]
not armored in bronze, not shielded now, he burns me,
battle cries in the onslaught burning on—
O rout him from our borders!
Sail him, blast him out to the Sea-queen's chamber
      the black Atlantic gulfs
  or the northern harbor, death to all
where the Thracian[7] surf comes crashing.
Now what the night spares he comes by day and kills—
the god of death.

6. Ares, son of Zeus and Hera, the god of savage warfare.
7. Ares was associated with Thrace, northeast of Greece, whose inhabitants the Greeks viewed as savage. *Sea-queen:* Amphitrite, consort of Poseidon, god of the sea.

O lord of the stormcloud,
you who twirl the lightning, Zeus, Father,
thunder Death to nothing!

Apollo, lord of the light, I beg you—
whip your longbow's golden cord
showering arrows on our enemies—shafts of power
champions strong before us rushing on!

Artemis, Huntress,
torches flaring over the eastern ridges—
ride Death down in pain!

God of the headdress gleaming gold, I cry to you—
your name and ours are one, Dionysus—
come with your face aflame with wine
your raving women's[8] cries
your army on the march! Come with the lightning
come with torches blazing, eyes ablaze with glory!
Burn that god of death[9] that all gods hate!

[OEDIPUS *enters from the palace to address the* CHORUS, *as if addressing the entire city of Thebes.*]

OEDIPUS You pray to the gods? Let me grant your prayers.
Come, listen to me—do what the plague demands:
you'll find relief and lift your head from the depths.
I will speak out now as a stranger to the story,[1]
a stranger to the crime. If I'd been present then,
there would have been no mystery, no long hunt
without a clue in hand. So now, counted
a native Theban years after the murder,
to all of Thebes I make this proclamation:
if any one of you knows who murdered Laius,
the son of Labdacus, I order him to reveal
the whole truth to me. Nothing to fear,
even if he must denounce himself,
let him speak up
and so escape the brunt of the charge—
he will suffer no unbearable punishment,
nothing worse than exile, totally unharmed.

[OEDIPUS *pauses, waiting for a reply.*]

Next,
if anyone knows the murderer is a stranger,
a man from alien soil, come, speak up.
I will give him a handsome reward, and lay up
gratitude in my heart for him besides.

8. The Maenads—frenzied women who worship Dionysus, the god of wine and of drama. He is identified with Thebes (see line 239) because his mother was Semele, a Theban princess.

9. That is, Ares.

1. Oedipus was raised in Corinth, a Greek city-state south of Thebes.

[*Silence again, no reply.*]
But if you keep silent, if anyone panicking,
trying to shield himself or friend or kin,
rejects my offer, then hear what I will do.
I order you, every citizen of the state
where I hold throne and power: banish this man—
whoever he may be—never shelter him, never
speak a word to him, never make him partner
to your prayers, your victims burned to the gods.
Never let the holy water touch his hands
Drive him out, each of you, from every home.
He is the plague, the heart of our corruption,
as Apollo's oracle has just revealed to me.
So I honor my obligations:
I fight for the god and for the murdered man.

Now my curse on the murderer. Whoever he is,
a lone man unknown in his crime
or one among many, let that man drag out
his life in agony, step by painful step—
I curse myself as well . . . if by any chance
he proves to be an intimate of our house,
here at my hearth, with my full knowledge,
may the curse I just called down on him strike me!

These are your orders: perform them to the last.
I command you, for my sake, for Apollo's, for this country
blasted root and branch by the angry heavens.
Even if god had never urged you on to act,
how could you leave the crime uncleansed so long?
A man so noble—your king, brought down in blood—
you should have searched. But I am the king now,
I hold the throne that he held then, possess his bed
and a wife who shares our seed[2] . . . why, our seed
might be the same, children born of the same mother
might have created blood-bonds between us
if his hope of offspring hadn't met disaster—
but fate swooped at his head and cut him short.
So I will fight for him as if he were my father,
stop at nothing, search the world
to lay my hands on the man who shed his blood,
the son of Labdacus descended of Polydorus,
Cadmus of old and Agenor, founder of the line:[3]
their power and mine are one.
Oh dear gods,
my curse on those who disobey these orders!

2. Jocasta, queen of Thebes, was the widow of Laius.
3. Here Oedipus traces the lineage of his predecessor, King Laius, back to Cadmus, the city's founder, and Agenor, father of Cadmus.

Let no crops grow out of the earth for them—
shrivel their women, kill their sons,
burn them to nothing in this plague
that hits us now, or something even worse.
But you, loyal men of Thebes who approve my actions,
may our champion, Justice, may all the gods
be with us, fight beside us to the end!

LEADER In the grip of your curse, my king, I swear
I'm not the murderer, I cannot point him out.
As for the search, Apollo pressed it on us—
he should name the killer.

OEDIPUS Quite right,
but to force the gods to act against their will—
no man has the power.

LEADER Then if I might mention
the next best thing . . .

OEDIPUS The third best too—
don't hold back, say it.

LEADER I still believe . . .
Lord Tiresias[4] sees with the eyes of Lord Apollo.
Anyone searching for the truth, my king,
might learn it from the prophet, clear as day.

OEDIPUS I've not been slow with that. On Creon's cue
I sent the escorts, twice, within the hour.
I'm surprised he isn't here.

LEADER We need him—
without him we have nothing but old, useless rumors.

OEDIPUS Which rumors? I'll search out every word.

LEADER Laius was killed, they say, by certain travelers.

OEDIPUS I know—but no one can find the murderer.

LEADER If the man has a trace of fear in him
he won't stay silent long,
not with your curses ringing in his ears.

OEDIPUS He didn't flinch at murder,
he'll never flinch at words.

[*Enter* TIRESIAS, *the blind prophet, led by a boy with escorts in attendance. He remains at a distance.*]

LEADER Here is the one who will convict him, look,
they bring him on at last, the seer, the man of god.
The truth lives inside him, him alone.

OEDIPUS O Tiresias,
master of all the mysteries of our life,
all you teach and all you dare not tell,
signs in the heavens, signs that walk the earth!
Blind as you are, you can feel all the more
what sickness haunts our city. You, my lord,
are the one shield, the one savior we can find.

4. The blind prophet of Thebes.

We asked Apollo—perhaps the messengers
haven't told you—he sent his answer back:
"Relief from the plague can only come one way.
Uncover the murderers of Laius,
put them to death or drive them into exile."
So I beg you, grudge us nothing now, no voice,
no message plucked from the birds, the embers
or the other mantic ways within your grasp.
Rescue yourself, your city, rescue me—
rescue everything infected by the dead.
We are in your hands. For a man to help others
with all his gifts and native strength:
that is the noblest work.

TIRESIAS How terrible—to see the truth
when the truth is only pain to him who sees!
I knew it well, but I put it from my mind,
else I never would have come.

OEDIPUS What's this? Why so grim, so dire?

TIRESIAS Just send me home. You bear your burdens,
I'll bear mine. It's better that way,
please believe me.

OEDIPUS Strange response . . . unlawful,
unfriendly too to the state that bred and reared you—
you withhold the word of god.

TIRESIAS I fail to see
that your own words are so well-timed.
I'd rather not have the same thing said of me . . .

OEDIPUS For the love of god, don't turn away,
not if you know something. We beg you,
all of us on our knees.

TIRESIAS None of you knows—
and I will never reveal my dreadful secrets,
not to say your own.

OEDIPUS What? You know and you won't tell?
You're bent on betraying us, destroying Thebes?

TIRESIAS I'd rather not cause pain for you or me.
So why this . . . useless interrogation?
You'll get nothing from me.

OEDIPUS Nothing! You,
you scum of the earth, you'd enrage a heart of stone!
You won't talk? Nothing moves you?
Out with it, once and for all!

TIRESIAS You criticize my temper . . . unaware
of the one *you* live with, you revile me.

OEDIPUS Who could restrain his anger hearing you?
What outrage—you spurn the city!

TIRESIAS What will come will come.
Even if I shroud it all in silence.

OEDIPUS What will come? You're bound to *tell* me that.

TIRESIAS I'll say no more. Do as you like, build your anger

to whatever pitch you please, rage your worst—

OEDIPUS Oh I'll let loose, I have such fury in me—
now I see it all. You helped hatch the plot,
you did the work, yes, short of killing him
with your own hands—and given eyes I'd say
you did the killing single-handed!

TIRESIAS Is that so!
I charge you, then, submit to that decree
you just laid down: from this day onward
speak to no one, not these citizens, not myself.
You are the curse, the corruption of the land!

OEDIPUS You, shameless—
aren't you appalled to start up such a story?
You think you can get away with this?

TIRESIAS I have already.
The truth with all its power lives inside me.

OEDIPUS Who primed you for this? Not your prophet's trade.

TIRESIAS You did, you forced me, twisted it out of me.

OEDIPUS What? Say it again—I'll understand it better.

TIRESIAS Didn't you understand, just now?
Or are you tempting me to talk?

OEDIPUS No, I can't say I grasped your meaning.
Out with it, again!

TIRESIAS I say you are the murderer you hunt.

OEDIPUS That obscenity, twice—by god, you'll pay.

TIRESIAS Shall I say more, so you can really rage?

OEDIPUS Much as you want. Your words are nothing—futile.

TIRESIAS You cannot imagine . . . I tell you,
you and your loved ones live together in infamy,
you cannot see how far you've gone in guilt.

OEDIPUS You think you can keep this up and never suffer?

TIRESIAS Indeed, if the truth has any power.

OEDIPUS It does
but not for you, old man. You've lost your power,
stone-blind, stone-deaf—senses, eyes blind as stone!

TIRESIAS I pity you, flinging at me the very insults
each man here will fling at you so soon.

OEDIPUS Blind,
lost in the night, endless night that cursed you!
You can't hurt me or anyone else who sees the light—
you can never touch me.

TIRESIAS True, it is not your fate
to fall at my hands. Apollo is quite enough,
and he will take some pains to work this out.

OEDIPUS Creon! Is this conspiracy his or yours?

TIRESIAS Creon is not your downfall, no, you are your own.

OEDIPUS O power—
wealth and empire, skill outstripping skill
in the heady rivalries of life,
what envy lurks inside you! Just for this,

the crown the city gave me—I never sought it,
they laid it in my hands—for this alone, Creon,
the soul of trust, my loyal friend from the start
steals against me . . . so hungry to overthrow me
he sets this wizard on me, this scheming quack,
this fortune-teller peddling lies, eyes peeled
for his own profit—seer blind in his craft!

Come here, you pious fraud. Tell me,
when did you ever prove yourself a prophet?
When the Sphinx, that chanting Fury kept her deathwatch here,
why silent then, not a word to set our people free?
There was a riddle, not for some passer-by to solve[5]—
it cried out for a prophet. Where were you?
Did you rise to the crisis? Not a word,
you and your birds, your gods—nothing.
No, but I came by, Oedipus the ignorant,
I stopped the Sphinx! With no help from the birds,
the flight of my own intelligence hit the mark.

And this is the man you'd try to overthrow?
You think you'll stand by Creon when he's king?
You and the great mastermind—
you'll pay in tears, I promise you, for this,
this witch-hunt. If you didn't look so senile
the lash would teach you what your scheming means!

LEADER I would suggest his words were spoken in anger,
Oedipus . . . yours too, and it isn't what we need.
The best solution to the oracle, the riddle
posed by god—we should look for that.

TIRESIAS You are the king no doubt, but in one respect,
at least, I am your equal: the right to reply.
I claim that privilege too.
I am not your slave. I serve Apollo.
I don't need Creon to speak for me in public.
So,
you mock my blindness? Let me tell you this.
You with your precious eyes,
you're blind to the corruption of your life,
to the house you live in, those you live with—
who *are* your parents? Do you know? All unknowing
you are the scourge of your own flesh and blood,
the dead below the earth and the living here above,
and the double lash of your mother and your father's curse
will whip you from this land one day, their footfall
treading you down in terror, darkness shrouding
your eyes that now can see the light!

5. Oedipus was on his way to Apollo's oracle at Delphi when he came upon the Sphinx.

Soon, soon
you'll scream aloud—what haven won't reverberate?
What rock of Cithaeron[6] won't scream back in echo?
That day you learn the truth about your marriage,
the wedding-march that sang you into your halls,
the lusty voyage home to the fatal harbor!
And a crowd of other horrors you'd never dream
will level you with yourself and all your children.

There. Now smear us with insults—Creon, myself,
and every word I've said. No man will ever
be rooted from the earth as brutally as you.

OEDIPUS Enough! Such filth from him? Insufferable—
what, still alive? Get out—
faster, back where you came from—vanish!

TIRESIAS I would never have come if you hadn't called me here.

OEDIPUS If I thought you would blurt out such absurdities,
you'd have died waiting before I'd had you summoned.

TIRESIAS Absurd, am I! To you, not to your parents:
the ones who bore you found me sane enough.

OEDIPUS Parents—who? Wait . . . who is my father?

TIRESIAS This day will bring your birth and your destruction.

OEDIPUS Riddles—all you can say are riddles, murk and darkness.

TIRESIAS Ah, but aren't you the best man alive at solving riddles?

OEDIPUS Mock me for that, go on, and you'll reveal my greatness.

TIRESIAS Your great good fortune, true, it was your ruin.

OEDIPUS Not if I saved the city—what do I care?

TIRESIAS Well then, I'll be going.
[*To his attendant.*]
Take me home, boy.

OEDIPUS Yes, take him away. You're a nuisance here.
Out of the way, the irritation's gone.
[*Turning his back on* TIRESIAS, *moving toward the palace.*]

TIRESIAS I will go,
once I have said what I came here to say.
I'll never shrink from the anger in your eyes—
you can't destroy me. Listen to me closely:
the man you've sought so long, proclaiming,
cursing up and down, the murderer of Laius—
he is here. A stranger,
you may think, who lives among you,
he soon will be revealed a native Theban
but he will take no joy in the revelation.
Blind who now has eyes, beggar who now is rich,
he will grope his way toward a foreign soil,
a stick tapping before him step by step.
[OEDIPUS *enters the palace.*]

6. The mountain range, south of Thebes, where the infant Oedipus was abandoned.

Revealed at last, brother and father both
to the children he embraces, to his mother
son and husband both—he sowed the loins
his father sowed, he spilled his father's blood!
Go in and reflect on that, solve that.
And if you find I've lied
from this day onward call the prophet blind.

[TIRESIAS *and the boy exit to the side.*]

CHORUS Who—
who is the man the voice of god denounces
resounding out of the rocky gorge of Delphi?
The horror too dark to tell,
whose ruthless bloody hands have done the work?
His time has come to fly
to outrace the stallions of the storm
his feet a streak of speed—
Cased in armor, Apollo son of the Father
lunges on him, lightning-bolts afire!
And the grim unerring Furies[7]
closing for the kill.
Look,
the word of god has just come blazing
flashing off Parnassus'[8] snowy heights!
That man who left no trace—
after him, hunt him down with all our strength!
Now under bristling timber
up through rocks and caves he stalks
like the wild mountain bull—
cut off from men, each step an agony, frenzied, racing blind
but he cannot outrace the dread voices of Delphi
ringing out of the heart of Earth,
the dark wings beating around him shrieking doom
the doom that never dies, the terror—
The skilled prophet scans the birds and shatters me with terror!
I can't accept him, can't deny him, don't know what to say,
I'm lost, and the wings of dark foreboding beating—
I cannot see what's come, what's still to come . . .
and what could breed a blood feud between
Laius' house and the son of Polybus?[9]
I know of nothing, not in the past and not now,
no charge to bring against our king, no cause
to attack his fame that rings throughout Thebes—
not without proof—not for the ghost of Laius,
not to avenge a murder gone without a trace.

7. Monstrous female personifications of vengeance.
8. Site of Delphi, where the oracular shrine was a deep cave or chasm (see lines 546–47).
9. A reference to the rivalry between the cities of Thebes (formerly ruled by King Laius) and Corinth (ruled by Polybus, Oedipus's adoptive father).

Zeus and Apollo know, they know, the great masters
of all the dark and depth of human life.
But whether a mere man can know the truth,
whether a seer can fathom more than I—
there is no test, no certain proof
though matching skill for skill
a man can outstrip a rival. No, not till I see
these charges proved will I side with his accusers.
We saw him then, when the she-hawk[1] swept against him,
saw with our own eyes his skill, his brilliant triumph—
there was the test—he was the joy of Thebes!
Never will I convict my king, never in my heart.

[*Enter* CREON *from the side.*]

CREON My fellow-citizens, I hear King Oedipus
levels terrible charges at me. I had to come.
I resent it deeply. If, in the present crisis
he thinks he suffers any abuse from me,
anything I've done or said that offers him
the slightest injury, why, I've no desire
to linger out this life, my reputation in ruins.
The damage I'd face from such an accusation
is nothing simple. No, there's nothing worse:
branded a traitor in the city, a traitor
to all of you and my good friends.

LEADER True,
but a slur might have been forced out of him,
by anger perhaps, not any firm conviction.

CREON The charge was made in public, wasn't it?
I put the prophet up to spreading lies?

LEADER Such things were said . . .
I don't know with what intent, if any.

CREON Was his glance steady, his mind right
when the charge was brought against me?

LEADER I really couldn't say. I never look
to judge the ones in power.

[*The doors open.* OEDIPUS *enters.*]

Wait,
here's Oedipus now.

OEDIPUS You—here? You have the gall
to show your face before the palace gates?
You, plotting to kill me, kill the king—
I see it all, the marauding thief himself
scheming to steal my crown and power!
Tell me,
in god's name, what did you take me for,
coward or fool, when you spun out your plot?

1. That is, the Sphinx, which had the paws of a lion, the tail of a serpent, and the wings of an eagle.

Your treachery—you think I'd never detect it
creeping against me in the dark? Or sensing it,
not defend myself? Aren't you the fool,
you and your high adventure. Lacking numbers,
powerful friends, out for the big game of empire—
you need riches, armies to bring that quarry down!

CREON Are you quite finished? It's your turn to listen
for just as long as you've . . . instructed me.
Hear me out, then judge me on the facts.

OEDIPUS You've a wicked way with words, Creon,
but I'll be slow to learn—from you.
I find you a menace, a great burden to me.

CREON Just one thing, hear me out in this.

OEDIPUS Just one thing,
don't tell *me* you're not the enemy, the traitor.

CREON Look, if you think crude, mindless stubbornness
such a gift, you've lost your sense of balance.

OEDIPUS If you think you can abuse a kinsman,
then escape the penalty, you're insane.

CREON Fair enough, I grant you. But this injury
you say I've done you, what is it?

OEDIPUS Did you induce me, yes or no,
to send for that sanctimonious prophet?

CREON I did. And I'd do the same again.

OEDIPUS All right then, tell me, how long is it now
since Laius . . .

CREON Laius—what did *he* do?

OEDIPUS Vanished,
swept from sight, murdered in his tracks.

CREON The count of the years would run you far back . . .

OEDIPUS And that far back, was the prophet at his trade?

CREON Skilled as he is today, and just as honored.

OEDIPUS Did he ever refer to me then, at that time?

CREON No,
never, at least, when I was in his presence.

OEDIPUS But you did investigate the murder, didn't you?

CREON We did our best, of course, discovered nothing.

OEDIPUS But the great seer never accused me then—why not?

CREON I don't know. And when I don't, *I* keep quiet.

OEDIPUS You do know this, you'd tell it too—
if you had a shred of decency.

CREON What?
If I know, I won't hold back.

OEDIPUS Simply this:
if the two of you had never put heads together,
we would never have heard about *my* killing Laius.

CREON If that's what he says . . . well, you know best.
But now I have a right to learn from you
as you just learned from me.

OEDIPUS Learn your fill,
you never will convict me of the murder.
CREON Tell me, you're married to my sister, aren't you?
OEDIPUS A genuine discovery—there's no denying that.
CREON And you rule the land with her, with equal power?
OEDIPUS She receives from me whatever she desires.
CREON And I am the third, all of us are equals?
OEDIPUS Yes, and it's there you show your stripes—
you betray a kinsman.
CREON Not at all.
Not if you see things calmly, rationally,
as I do. Look at it this way first:
who in his right mind would rather rule
and live in anxiety than sleep in peace?
Particularly if he enjoys the same authority.
Not I, I'm not the man to yearn for kingship,
not with a king's power in my hands. Who would?
No one with any sense of self-control.
Now, as it is, you offer me all I need,
not a fear in the world. But if I wore the crown . . .
there'd be many painful duties to perform,
hardly to my taste.
How could kingship
please me more than influence, power
without a qualm? I'm not that deluded yet,
to reach for anything but privilege outright,
profit free and clear.
Now all men sing my praises, all salute me,
now all who request your favors curry mine.
I am their best hope: success rests in me.
Why give up that, I ask you, and borrow trouble?
A man of sense, someone who sees things clearly
would never resort to treason.
No, I've no lust for conspiracy in me,
nor could I ever suffer one who does.

Do you want proof? Go to Delphi yourself,
examine the oracle and see if I've reported
the message word-for-word. This too:
if you detect that I and the clairvoyant
have plotted anything in common, arrest me,
execute me. Not on the strength of one vote,
two in this case, mine as well as yours.
But don't convict me on sheer unverified surmise.
How wrong it is to take the good for bad,
purely at random, or take the bad for good.
But reject a friend, a kinsman? I would as soon
tear out the life within us, priceless life itself.
You'll learn this well, without fail, in time.

Time alone can bring the just man to light—
the criminal you can spot in one short day.

LEADER Good advice,
my lord, for anyone who wants to avoid disaster.
Those who jump to conclusions may go wrong.

OEDIPUS When my enemy moves against me quickly,
plots in secret, I move quickly too, I must,
I plot and pay him back. Relax my guard a moment,
waiting his next move—he wins his objective,
I lose mine.

CREON What do you want?
You want me banished?

OEDIPUS No, I want you dead.

CREON Just to show how ugly a grudge can . . .

OEDIPUS So,
still stubborn? you don't think I'm serious?

CREON I think you're insane.

OEDIPUS Quite sane—in my behalf.

CREON Not just as much in mine?

OEDIPUS You—my mortal enemy?

CREON What if you're wholly wrong?

OEDIPUS No matter—I must rule.

CREON Not if you rule unjustly.

OEDIPUS Hear him, Thebes, my city!

CREON My city too, not yours alone!

LEADER Please, my lords.

[*Enter* JOCASTA *from the palace*.]

Look, Jocasta's coming,
and just in time too. With her help
you must put this fighting of yours to rest.

JOCASTA Have you no sense? Poor misguided men,
such shouting—why this public outburst?
Aren't you ashamed, with the land so sick,
to stir up private quarrels?

[*To* OEDIPUS.]

Into the palace now. And Creon, you go home.
Why make such a furor over nothing?

CREON My sister, it's dreadful . . . Oedipus, your husband,
he's bent on a choice of punishments for me,
banishment from the fatherland or death.

OEDIPUS Precisely. I caught him in the act, Jocasta,
plotting, about to stab me in the back.

CREON Never—curse me, let me die and be damned
if I've done you any wrong you charge me with.

JOCASTA Oh god, believe it, Oedipus,
honor the solemn oath he swears to heaven.
Do it for me, for the sake of all your people.

[*The* CHORUS *begins to chant*.]

CHORUS Believe it, be sensible
give way, my king, I beg you!
OEDIPUS What do you want from me, concessions?
CHORUS Respect him—he's been no fool in the past
and now he's strong with the oath he swears to god.
OEDIPUS You know what you're asking?
CHORUS I do.
OEDIPUS Then out with it!
CHORUS The man's your friend, your kin, he's under oath—
don't cast him out, disgraced
branded with guilt on the strength of hearsay only.
OEDIPUS Know full well, if that is what you want
you want me dead or banished from the land.
CHORUS Never—
no, by the blazing Sun, first god of the heavens!
Stripped of the gods, stripped of loved ones,
let me die by inches if that ever crossed my mind.
But the heart inside me sickens, dies as the land dies
and now on top of the old griefs you pile this,
your fury—both of you!
OEDIPUS Then let him go,
even if it does lead to my ruin, my death
or my disgrace, driven from Thebes for life.
It's you, not him I pity—your words move me.
He, wherever he goes, my hate goes with him.
CREON Look at you, sullen in yielding, brutal in your rage—
you'll go too far. It's perfect justice:
natures like yours are hardest on themselves.
OEDIPUS Then leave me alone—get out!
CREON I'm going.
You're wrong, so wrong. These men know I'm right.
[*Exit to the side. The* CHORUS *turns to* JOCASTA.]
CHORUS Why do you hesitate, my lady
why not help him in?
JOCASTA Tell me what's happened first.
CHORUS Loose, ignorant talk started dark suspicions
and a sense of injustice cut deeply too.
JOCASTA On both sides?
CHORUS Oh yes.
JOCASTA What did they say?
CHORUS Enough, please, enough! The land's so racked already
or so it seems to me . . .
End the trouble here, just where they left it.
OEDIPUS You see what comes of your good intentions now?
And all because you tried to blunt my anger.
CHORUS My king,
I've said it once, I'll say it time and again—
I'd be insane, you know it,
senseless, ever to turn my back on you.
You who set our beloved land—storm-tossed, shattered—

straight on course. Now again, good helmsman,
steer us through the storm!

[*The* CHORUS *draws away, leaving* OEDIPUS *and* JOCASTA *side by side.*]

JOCASTA For the love of god,
Oedipus, tell me too, what is it?
Why this rage? You're so unbending.

OEDIPUS I will tell you. I respect you, Jocasta,
much more than these . . .

[*Glancing at the* CHORUS.]

Creon's to blame, Creon schemes against me.

JOCASTA Tell me clearly, how did the quarrel start?

OEDIPUS He says *I* murdered Laius—I am guilty.

JOCASTA How does he know? Some secret knowledge
or simple hearsay?

OEDIPUS Oh, he sent his prophet in
to do his dirty work. You know Creon,
Creon keeps his own lips clean.

JOCASTA A prophet?
Well then, free yourself of every charge!
Listen to me and learn some peace of mind:
no skill in the world,
nothing human can penetrate the future.
Here is proof, quick and to the point.

An oracle came to Laius one fine day
(I won't say from Apollo himself
but his underlings, his priests) and it said
that doom would strike him down at the hands of a son,
our son, to be born of our own flesh and blood. But Laius,
so the report goes at least, was killed by strangers,
thieves, at a place where three roads meet . . . my son—
he wasn't three days old and the boy's father
fastened his ankles, had a henchman fling him away
on a barren, trackless mountain.
There, you see?
Apollo brought neither thing to pass. My baby
no more murdered his father than Laius suffered—
his wildest fear—death at his own son's hands.
That's how the seers and all their revelations
mapped out the future. Brush them from your mind.
Whatever the god needs and seeks
he'll bring to light himself, with ease.

OEDIPUS Strange,
hearing you just now . . . my mind wandered,
my thoughts racing back and forth.

JOCASTA What do you mean? Why so anxious, startled?

OEDIPUS I thought I heard you say that Laius
was cut down at a place where three roads meet.

JOCASTA That was the story. It hasn't died out yet.

OEDIPUS Where did this thing happen? Be precise.

JOCASTA A place called Phocis, where two branching roads,
one from Daulia,[2] one from Delphi,
come together—a crossroads.

OEDIPUS When? How long ago?

JOCASTA The heralds no sooner reported Laius dead
than you appeared and they hailed you king of Thebes.

OEDIPUS My god, my god—what have you planned to do to me?

JOCASTA What, Oedipus? What haunts you so?

OEDIPUS Not yet.
Laius—how did he look? Describe him.
Had he reached his prime?

JOCASTA He was swarthy,
and the gray had just begun to streak his temples,
and his build . . . wasn't far from yours.

OEDIPUS Oh no no,
I think I've just called down a dreadful curse
upon myself—I simply didn't know!

JOCASTA What are you saying? I shudder to look at you.

OEDIPUS I have a terrible fear the blind seer can see.
I'll know in a moment. One thing more—

JOCASTA Anything,
afraid as I am—ask, I'll answer, all I can.

OEDIPUS Did he go with a light or heavy escort,
several men-at-arms, like a lord, a king?

JOCASTA There were five in the party, a herald among them,
and a single wagon carrying Laius.

OEDIPUS Ai—
now I can see it all, clear as day.
Who told you all this at the time, Jocasta?

JOCASTA A servant who reached home, the lone survivor.

OEDIPUS So, could he still be in the palace—even now?

JOCASTA No indeed. Soon as he returned from the scene
and saw you on the throne with Laius dead and gone,
he knelt and clutched my hand, pleading with me
to send him into the hinterlands, to pasture,
far as possible, out of sight of Thebes.
I sent him away. Slave though he was,
he'd earned that favor—and much more.

OEDIPUS Can we bring him back, quickly?

JOCASTA Easily. Why do you want him so?

OEDIPUS I'm afraid,
Jocasta, I have said too much already.
That man—I've got to see him.

JOCASTA Then he'll come.
But even I have a right, I'd like to think,
to know what's torturing you, my lord.

2. A Boeotian town not far from Thebes. *Phocis:* the region where Delphi is located, west of Boeotia.

OEDIPUS And so you shall—I can hold nothing back from you,
now I've reached this pitch of dark foreboding.
Who means more to me than you? Tell me,
whom would I turn toward but you
as I go through all this?

My father was Polybus, king of Corinth.
My mother, a Dorian,[3] Merope. And I was held
the prince of the realm among the people there,
till something struck me out of nowhere,
something strange . . . worth remarking perhaps,
hardly worth the anxiety I gave it.
Some man at a banquet who had drunk too much
shouted out—he was far gone, mind you—
that I am not my father's son. Fighting words!
I barely restrained myself that day
but early the next I went to mother and father,
questioned them closely, and they were enraged
at the accusation and the fool who let it fly.
So as for my parents I was satisfied,
but still this thing kept gnawing at me,
the slander spread—I had to make my move.
And so,
unknown to mother and father I set out for Delphi,
and the god Apollo spurned me, sent me away
denied the facts I came for,
but first he flashed before my eyes a future
great with pain, terror, disaster—I can hear him cry,
"You are fated to couple with your mother, you will bring
a breed of children into the light no man can bear to see—
you will kill your father, the one who gave you life!"
I heard all that and ran. I abandoned Corinth,
from that day on I gauged its landfall only
by the stars, running, always running
toward some place where I would never see
the shame of all those oracles come true.
And as I fled I reached that very spot
where the great king, you say, met his death.

Now, Jocasta, I will tell you all.
Making my way toward this triple crossroad
I began to see a herald, then a brace of colts
drawing a wagon, and mounted on the bench . . . a man,
just as you've described him, coming face-to-face,
and the one in the lead and the old man himself
were about to thrust me off the road—brute force—
and the one shouldering me aside, the driver,
I strike him in anger!—and the old man, watching me

3. From Doris, a region of central Greece.

coming up along his wheels—he brings down
his prod, two prongs straight at my head!
I paid him back with interest!
Short work, by god—with one blow of the staff
in this right hand I knock him out of his high seat,
roll him out of the wagon, sprawling headlong—
I killed them all—every mother's son!

Oh, but if there is any blood-tie
between Laius and this stranger . . .
what man alive more miserable than I?
More hated by the gods? *I* am the man
no alien, no citizen welcomes to his house,
law forbids it—not a word to me in public,
driven out of every hearth and home.
And all these curses I—no one but I
brought down these piling curses on myself!
And you, his wife, I've touched your body with these,
the hands that killed your husband cover you with blood.

Wasn't I born for torment? Look me in the eyes!
I am abomination—heart and soul!
I must be exiled, and even in exile
never see my parents, never set foot
on native ground again. Else I am doomed
to couple with my mother and cut my father down . . .
Polybus who reared me, gave me life.
But why, why?
Wouldn't a man of judgment say—and wouldn't he be right—
some savage power has brought this down upon my head?

Oh no, not that, you pure and awesome gods,
never let me see that day! Let me slip
from the world of men, vanish without a trace
before I see myself stained with such corruption,
stained to the heart.

LEADER My lord, you fill our hearts with fear.
But at least until you question the witness,
do take hope.

OEDIPUS Exactly. He is my last hope—
I am waiting for the shepherd. He is crucial.

JOCASTA And once he appears, what then? Why so urgent?

OEDIPUS I will tell you. If it turns out that his story
matches yours, I've escaped the worst.

JOCASTA What did I say? What struck you so?

OEDIPUS You said *thieves*—
he told you a whole band of them murdered Laius.
So, if he still holds to the same number,
I cannot be the killer. One can't equal many.
But if he refers to one man, one alone,

clearly the scales come down on me:
I am guilty.

JOCASTA Impossible. Trust me,
I told you precisely what he said,
and he can't retract it now;
the whole city heard it, not just I.
And even if he should vary his first report
by one man more or less, still, my lord,
he could never make the murder of Laius
truly fit the prophecy. Apollo was explicit:
my son was doomed to kill my husband . . . my son,
poor defenseless thing, he never had a chance
to kill his father. They destroyed him first.

So much for prophecy. It's neither here nor there.
From this day on, I wouldn't look right or left.

OEDIPUS True, true. Still, that shepherd,
someone fetch him—now!

JOCASTA I'll send at once. But do let's go inside.
I'd never displease you, least of all in this.

[OEDIPUS *and* JOCASTA *enter the palace.*]

CHORUS Destiny guide me always
Destiny find me filled with reverence
pure in word and deed.
Great laws tower above us, reared on high
born for the brilliant vault of heaven—
Olympian Sky their only father,[4]
nothing mortal, no man gave them birth,
their memory deathless, never lost in sleep:
within them lives a mighty god, the god does not grow old.

Pride breeds the tyrant
violent pride, gorging, crammed to bursting
with all that is overripe and rich with ruin—
clawing up to the heights, headlong pride
crashes down the abyss—sheer doom!
No footing helps, all foothold lost and gone.
But the healthy strife that makes the city strong—
I pray that god will never end that wrestling:
god, my champion, I will never let you go.

But if any man comes striding, high and mighty
in all he says and does,
no fear of justice, no reverence
for the temples of the gods—
let a rough doom tear him down,
repay his pride, breakneck, ruinous pride!

4. Mount Olympus in Thessaly, in northern Greece, was believed to be the home of the gods.

If he cannot reap his profits fairly
cannot restrain himself from outrage—
mad, laying hands on the holy things untouchable!

Can such a man, so desperate, still boast
he can save his life from the flashing bolts of god?
If all such violence goes with honor now
why join the sacred dance?

Never again will I go reverent to Delphi,
the inviolate heart of Earth
or Apollo's ancient oracle at Abae
or Olympia[5] of the fires—
unless these prophecies all come true
for all mankind to point toward in wonder.
King of kings, if you deserve your titles
Zeus, remember, never forget!
You and your deathless, everlasting reign.

They are dying, the old oracles sent to Laius,
now our masters strike them off the rolls.
Nowhere Apollo's golden glory now—
the gods, the gods go down.

[*Enter* JOCASTA *from the palace, carrying a suppliant's branch wound in wool.*]

JOCASTA Lords of the realm,[6] it occurred to me,
just now, to visit the temples of the gods,
so I have my branch in hand and incense too.

Oedipus is beside himself. Racked with anguish,
no longer a man of sense, he won't admit
the latest prophecies are hollow as the old—
he's at the mercy of every passing voice
if the voice tells of terror.
I urge him gently, nothing seems to help,
so I turn to you, Apollo, you are nearest.

[*Placing her branch on the altar, while an old herdsman enters from the side, not the one just summoned by the King but an unexpected* MESSENGER *from Corinth.*]

I come with prayers and offerings . . . I beg you,
cleanse us, set us free of defilement!
Look at us, passengers in the grip of fear,
watching the pilot of the vessel go to pieces.

MESSENGER [*Approaching* JOCASTA *and the* CHORUS.]
Strangers, please, I wonder if you could lead us

5. Site in the western Peloponnesus of a major temple of Zeus (location of the quadrennial Olympic games). *Abae:* a town in Phocis, whose oracle of Apollo was older than that at Delphi.
6. That is, the chorus.

to the palace of the king . . . I think it's Oedipus.
Better, the man himself—you know where he is?

LEADER This is his palace, stranger. He's inside.
But here is his queen, his wife and mother
of his children.

MESSENGER Blessings on you, noble queen,
queen of Oedipus crowned with all your family—
blessings on you always!

JOCASTA And the same to you, stranger, you deserve it . . .
such a greeting. But what have you come for?
Have you brought us news?

MESSENGER Wonderful news—
for the house, my lady, for your husband too.

JOCASTA Really, what? Who sent you?

MESSENGER Corinth.
I'll give you the message in a moment.
You'll be glad of it—how could you help it?—
though it costs a little sorrow in the bargain.

JOCASTA What can it be, with such a double edge?

MESSENGER The people there, they want to make your Oedipus
king of Corinth, so they're saying now.

JOCASTA Why? Isn't old Polybus still in power?

MESSENGER No more. Death has got him in the tomb.

JOCASTA What are you saying? Polybus, dead?—dead?

MESSENGER If not,
if I'm not telling the truth, strike me dead too.

JOCASTA [*To a servant.*] Quickly, go to your master, tell him this!
You prophecies of the gods, where are you now?
This is the man that Oedipus feared for years,
he fled him, not to kill him—and now he's dead,
quite by chance, a normal, natural death,
not murdered by his son.

OEDIPUS [*Emerging from the palace.*]
Dearest,
what now? Why call me from the palace?

JOCASTA [*Bringing the* MESSENGER *closer.*]
Listen to *him,* see for yourself what all
those awful prophecies of god have come to.

OEDIPUS And who is he? What can he have for me?

JOCASTA He's from Corinth, he's come to tell you
your father is no more—Polybus—he's dead!

OEDIPUS [*Wheeling on the* MESSENGER.]
What? Let me have it from your lips.

MESSENGER Well,
if that's what you want first, then here it is:
Abae is a city in central Greece.
Make no mistake, Polybus is dead and gone.

OEDIPUS How—murder? sickness?—what? what killed him?

MESSENGER A light tip of the scales can put old bones to rest.

OEDIPUS Sickness then—poor man, it wore him down.
MESSENGER That,
and the long count of years he'd measured out.
OEDIPUS So!
Jocasta, why, why look to the Prophet's hearth,
the fires of the future? Why scan the birds
that scream above our heads? They winged me on
to the murder of my father, did they? That was my doom?
Well look, he's dead and buried, hidden under the earth,
and here I am in Thebes, I never put hand to sword—
unless some longing for me wasted him away,
then in a sense you'd say I caused his death.
But now, all those prophecies I feared—Polybus
packs them off to sleep with him in hell!
They're nothing, worthless.
JOCASTA There.
Didn't I tell you from the start?
OEDIPUS So you did. I was lost in fear.
JOCASTA No more, sweep it from your mind forever.
OEDIPUS But my mother's bed, surely I must fear—
JOCASTA Fear?
What should a man fear? It's all chance,
chance rules our lives. Not a man on earth
can see a day ahead, groping through the dark.
Better to live at random, best we can.
And as for this marriage with your mother—
have no fear. Many a man before you,
in his dreams, has shared his mother's bed.
Take such things for shadows, nothing at all—
Live, Oedipus,
as if there's no tomorrow!
OEDIPUS Brave words,
and you'd persuade me if mother weren't alive.
But mother lives, so for all your reassurances
I live in fear, I must.
JOCASTA But your father's death,
that, at least, is a great blessing, joy to the eyes!
OEDIPUS Great, I know . . . but I fear *her*—she's still alive.
MESSENGER Wait, who is this woman, makes you so afraid?
OEDIPUS Merope, old man. The wife of Polybus.
MESSENGER The queen? What's there to fear in her?
OEDIPUS A dreadful prophecy, stranger, sent by the gods.
MESSENGER Tell me, could you? Unless it's forbidden
other ears to hear.
OEDIPUS Not at all.
Apollo told me once—it is my fate—
I must make love with my own mother,
shed my father's blood with my own hands.
So for years I've given Corinth a wide berth,

and it's been my good fortune too. But still,
to see one's parents and look into their eyes
is the greatest joy I know.

MESSENGER You're afraid of that?
That kept you out of Corinth?

OEDIPUS My *father*, old man—
so I wouldn't kill my father.

MESSENGER So that's it.
Well then, seeing I came with such good will, my king,
why don't I rid you of that old worry now?

OEDIPUS What a rich reward you'd have for that!

MESSENGER What do you think I came for, majesty?
So you'd come home and I'd be better off.

OEDIPUS Never, I will never go near my parents.

MESSENGER My boy, it's clear, you don't know what you're doing.

OEDIPUS What do you mean, old man? For god's sake, explain.

MESSENGER If you ran from *them*, always dodging home . . .

OEDIPUS Always, terrified Apollo's oracle might come true—

MESSENGER And you'd be covered with guilt, from both your parents.

OEDIPUS That's right, old man, that fear is always with me.

MESSENGER Don't you know? You've really nothing to fear.

OEDIPUS But why? If I'm their son—Merope, Polybus?

MESSENGER Polybus was nothing to you, that's why, not in blood.

OEDIPUS What are you saying—Polybus was not my father?

MESSENGER No more than I am. He and I are equals.

OEDIPUS My father—
how can my father equal nothing? You're nothing to me!

MESSENGER Neither was he, no more your father than I am.

OEDIPUS Then why did he call me his son?

MESSENGER You were a gift,
years ago—know for a fact he took you
from my hands.

OEDIPUS No, from another's hands?
Then how could he love me so? He loved me, deeply . . .

MESSENGER True, and his early years without a child
made him love you all the more.

OEDIPUS And you, did you . . .
buy me? find me by accident?

MESSENGER I stumbled on you,
down the woody flanks of Mount Cithaeron.

OEDIPUS So close,
what were you doing here, just passing through?

MESSENGER Watching over my flocks, grazing them on the slopes.

OEDIPUS A herdsman, were you? A vagabond, scraping for wages?

MESSENGER Your savior too, my son, in your worst hour.

OEDIPUS Oh—
when you picked me up, was I in pain? What exactly?

MESSENGER Your ankles . . . they tell the story. Look at them.

OEDIPUS Why remind me of that, that old affliction?

MESSENGER Your ankles were pinned together. I set you free.
OEDIPUS That dreadful mark—I've had it from the cradle.
MESSENGER And you got your name from that misfortune too,
the name's still with you.[7]
OEDIPUS Dear god, who did it?—
mother? father? Tell me.
MESSENGER I don't know.
The one who gave you to me, he'd know more.
OEDIPUS What? You took me from someone else?
You didn't find me yourself?
MESSENGER No sir,
another shepherd passed you on to me.
OEDIPUS Who? Do you know? Describe him.
MESSENGER He called himself a servant of . . .
if I remember rightly—Laius.

[JOCASTA *turns sharply.*]

OEDIPUS The king of the land who ruled here long ago?
MESSENGER That's the one. That herdsman was *his* man.
OEDIPUS Is he still alive? Can I see him?
MESSENGER They'd know best, the people of these parts.

[OEDIPUS *and the* MESSENGER *turn to the* CHORUS.]

OEDIPUS Does anyone know that herdsman,
the one he mentioned? Anyone seen him
in the fields, in the city? Out with it!
The time has come to reveal this once for all.
LEADER I think he's the very shepherd you wanted to see,
a moment ago. But the queen, Jocasta,
she's the one to say.
OEDIPUS Jocasta,
you remember the man we just sent for?
Is *that* the one he means?
JOCASTA That man . . .
why ask? Old shepherd, talk, empty nonsense,
don't give it another thought, don't even think—
OEDIPUS What—give up now, with a clue like this?
Fail to solve the mystery of my birth?
Not for all the world!
JOCASTA Stop—in the name of god,
if you love your own life, call off this search!
My suffering is enough.
OEDIPUS Courage!
Even if my mother turns out to be a slave,
and I a slave, three generations back,
you would not seem common.
JOCASTA Oh no,
listen to me, I beg you, don't do this.
OEDIPUS Listen to you? No more. I must know it all,
must see the truth at last.

7. "Oedipus" literally means "swollen foot."

JOCASTA No, please—
for your sake—I want the best for you!
OEDIPUS Your best is more than I can bear.
JOCASTA You're doomed—
may you never fathom who you are!
OEDIPUS [*To a servant.*] Hurry, fetch me the herdsman, now!
Leave her to glory in her royal birth.
JOCASTA Aieeeeee—
man of agony—
that is the only name I have for you,
that, no other—ever, ever, ever!
[*Flinging through the palace doors. A long, tense silence follows.*]
LEADER Where's she gone, Oedipus?
Rushing off, such wild grief . . .
I'm afraid that from this silence
something monstrous may come bursting forth.
OEDIPUS Let it burst! Whatever will, whatever must!
I must know my birth, no matter how common
it may be—I must see my origins face-to-face.
She perhaps, she with her woman's pride
may well be mortified by my birth,
but I, I count myself the son of Chance,
the great goddess, giver of all good things—
I'll never see myself disgraced. She is my mother!
And the moons have marked me out, my blood-brothers,
one moon on the wane, the next moon great with power.
That is my blood, my nature—I will never betray it,
never fail to search and learn my birth!
CHORUS Yes—if I am a true prophet
if I can grasp the truth,
by the boundless skies of Olympus,
at the full moon of tomorrow, Mount Cithaeron
you will know how Oedipus glories in you—
you, his birthplace, nurse, his mountain-mother!
And we will sing you, dancing out your praise—
you lift our monarch's heart!
Apollo, Apollo, god of the wild cry
may our dancing please you!
Oedipus—
son, dear child, who bore you?
Who of the nymphs who seem to live forever
mated with Pan,[8] the mountain-striding Father?
Who was your mother? who, some bride of Apollo
the god who loves the pastures spreading toward the sun?
Or was it Hermes,[9] king of the lightning ridges?
Or Dionysus, lord of frenzy, lord of the barren peaks—

8. Son of Hermes and a nymph; the god of woods and pastures and the companion of Dionysus. *Nymphs*: female nature spirits, long-lived but not immortal.

9. Greek god of boundaries and travelers, Zeus's messenger and the gods' herald; like Dionysus, he was associated with wild places, especially mountains.

did he seize you in his hands, dearest of all his lucky finds?—
found by the nymphs, their warm eyes dancing, gift
to the lord who loves them dancing out his joy!

[OEDIPUS *strains to see a figure coming from the distance. Attended by palace guards, an old* SHEPHERD *enters slowly, reluctant to approach the King.*]

OEDIPUS I never met the man, my friends . . . still,
if I had to guess, I'd say that's the shepherd,
the very one we've looked for all along.
Brothers in old age, two of a kind,
he and our guest here. At any rate
the ones who bring him in are my own men,
I recognize them.

[*Turning to the* LEADER.]

But you know more than I,
you should, you've seen the man before.

LEADER I know him, definitely. One of Laius' men,
a trusty shepherd, if there ever was one.

OEDIPUS You, I ask you first, stranger,
you from Corinth—is this the one you mean?

MESSENGER You're looking at him. He's your man.

OEDIPUS [*To the* SHEPHERD.] You, old man, come over here—
look at me. Answer all my questions.
Did you ever serve King Laius?

SHEPHERD So I did . . .
a slave, not bought on the block though,
born and reared in the palace.

OEDIPUS Your duties, your kind of work?

SHEPHERD Herding the flocks, the better part of my life.

OEDIPUS Where, mostly? Where did you do your grazing?

SHEPHERD Well,
Cithaeron sometimes, or the foothills round about.

OEDIPUS This man—you know him? ever see him there?

SHEPHERD [*Confused, glancing from the* MESSENGER *to the King.*]
Doing what?—what man do you mean?

OEDIPUS [*Pointing to the* MESSENGER.] This one here—ever have
dealings with him?

SHEPHERD Not so I could say, but give me a chance,
my memory's bad . . .

MESSENGER No wonder he doesn't know me, master.
But let me refresh his memory for him.
I'm sure he recalls old times we had
on the slopes of Mount Cithaeron;
he and I, grazing our flocks, he with two
and I with one—we both struck up together,
three whole seasons, six months at a stretch
from spring to the rising of Arcturus[1] in the fall,

1. One of the brightest stars in the northern sky; its "rising" before dawn in September is a sign of summer's end.

then with winter coming on I'd drive my herds
to my own pens, and back he'd go with his
to Laius' folds.

[*To the* SHEPHERD.]

Now that's how it was,
wasn't it—yes or no?

SHEPHERD Yes, I suppose . . .
it's all so long ago.

MESSENGER Come, tell me,
you gave me a child back then, a boy, remember?
A little fellow to rear, my very own.

SHEPHERD What? Why rake up that again?

MESSENGER Look, here he is, my fine old friend—
the same man who was just a baby then.

SHEPHERD Damn you, shut your mouth—quiet!

OEDIPUS Don't lash out at him, old man—
you need lashing more than he does.

SHEPHERD Why,
master, majesty—what have I done wrong?

OEDIPUS You won't answer his question about the boy.

SHEPHERD He's talking nonsense, wasting his breath.

OEDIPUS So, you won't talk willingly—
then you'll talk with pain.

[*The guards seize the* SHEPHERD.]

SHEPHERD No, dear god, don't torture an old man!

OEDIPUS Twist his arms back, quickly!

SHEPHERD God help us, why?—
what more do you need to know?

OEDIPUS Did you give him that child? He's asking.

SHEPHERD I did . . . I wish to god I'd died that day.

OEDIPUS You've got your wish if you don't tell the truth.

SHEPHERD The more I tell, the worse the death I'll die.

OEDIPUS Our friend here wants to stretch things out, does he?

[*Motioning to his men for torture.*]

SHEPHERD No, no, I gave it to him—I just said so.

OEDIPUS Where did you get it? Your house? Someone else's?

SHEPHERD It wasn't mine, no, I got it from . . . someone.

OEDIPUS Which one of them?

[*Looking at the citizens.*]

OEDIPUS Whose house?

SHEPHERD No—
god's sake, master, no more questions!

OEDIPUS You're a dead man if I have to ask again.

SHEPHERD Then—the child came from the house . . . of Laius.

OEDIPUS A slave? or born of his own blood?

SHEPHERD Oh no,
I'm right at the edge, the horrible truth—I've got to say it!

OEDIPUS And I'm at the edge of hearing horrors, yes, but I must hear!

SHEPHERD All right! His son, they said it was—his son!
But the one inside, your wife,
she'd tell it best.
OEDIPUS My wife—
she gave it to you?
SHEPHERD Yes, yes, my king.
OEDIPUS Why, what for?
SHEPHERD To kill it.
OEDIPUS Her own child,
how could she?
SHEPHERD She was afraid—
frightening prophecies.
OEDIPUS What?
SHEPHERD They said—
he'd kill his parents.
OEDIPUS But you gave him to this old man—why?
SHEPHERD I pitied the little baby, master,
hoped he'd take him off to his own country,
far away, but he saved him for this, this fate.
If you are the man he says you are, believe me,
you were born for pain.
OEDIPUS O god—
all come true, all burst to light!
O light—now let me look my last on you!
I stand revealed at last—
cursed in my birth, cursed in marriage,
cursed in the lives I cut down with these hands!

[*Rushing through the doors with a great cry. The Corinthian* MESSENGER, *the* SHEPHERD *and attendants exit slowly to the side.*]

CHORUS O the generations of men
the dying generations—adding the total
of all your lives I find they come to nothing . . .
does there exist, is there a man on earth
who seizes more joy than just a dream, a vision?
And the vision no sooner dawns than dies
blazing into oblivion.
You are my great example, you, your life
your destiny, Oedipus, man of misery—
I count no man blest.

You outranged all men!
Bending your bow to the breaking-point
you captured priceless glory, O dear god,
and the Sphinx came crashing down,
the virgin, claws hooked
like a bird of omen singing, shrieking death—
like a fortress reared in the face of death
you rose and saved our land.

From that day on we called you king
we crowned you with honors, Oedipus, towering over all—
mighty king of the seven gates of Thebes.

But now to hear your story—is there a man more agonized?
More wed to pain and frenzy? Not a man on earth,
the joy of your life ground down to nothing
O Oedipus, name for the ages—
one and the same wide harbor served you
son and father both
son and father came to rest in the same bridal chamber.
How, how could the furrows your father plowed
bear you, your agony, harrowing on
in silence O so long?

But now for all your power
Time, all-seeing Time has dragged you to the light,
judged your marriage monstrous from the start—
the son and the father tangling, both one—
O child of Laius, would to god
I'd never seen you, never never!
Now I weep like a man who wails the dead
and the dirge comes pouring forth with all my heart!
I tell you the truth, you gave me life
my breath leapt up in you
and now you bring down night upon my eyes.

[*Enter a* MESSENGER *from the palace.*]

MESSENGER Men of Thebes, always first in honor,
what horrors you will hear, what you will see,
what a heavy weight of sorrow you will shoulder . . .
if you are true to your birth, if you still have
some feeling for the royal house of Thebes.
I tell you neither the waters of the Danube
nor the Nile[2] can wash this palace clean.
Such things it hides, it soon will bring to light—
terrible things, and none done blindly now,
all done with a will. The pains
we inflict upon ourselves hurt most of all.

LEADER God knows we have pains enough already.
What can you add to them?

MESSENGER The queen is dead.

LEADER Poor lady—how?

MESSENGER By her own hand. But you are spared the worst,
you never had to watch . . . I saw it all,
and with all the memory that's in me
you will learn what that poor woman suffered.

2. The Greek original reads "Phasis," a river in Asia Minor; like the Danube, Europe's second-longest river, it empties into the Black Sea.

Once she'd broken in through the gates,
dashing past us, frantic, whipped to fury,
ripping her hair out with both hands—
straight to her rooms she rushed, flinging herself
across the bridal-bed, doors slamming behind her—
once inside, she wailed for Laius, dead so long,
remembering how she bore his child long ago,
the life that rose up to destroy him, leaving
its mother to mother living creatures
with the very son she'd borne.
Oh how she wept, mourning the marriage-bed
where she let loose that double brood—monsters—
husband by her husband, children by her child.
And then—
but how she died is more than I can say. Suddenly
Oedipus burst in, screaming, he stunned us so
we couldn't watch her agony to the end,
our eyes were fixed on him. Circling
like a maddened beast, stalking, here, there,
crying out to us—
Give him a sword. His wife,
no wife, his mother, where can he find the mother earth
that cropped two crops at once, himself and all his children?
He was raging—one of the dark powers pointing the way,
none of us mortals crowding around him, no,
with a great shattering cry—someone, something leading him on—
he hurled at the twin doors and bending the bolts back
out of their sockets, crashed through the chamber.
And there we saw the woman hanging by the neck,
cradled high in a woven noose, spinning,
swinging back and forth. And when he saw her,
giving a low, wrenching sob that broke our hearts,
slipping the halter from her throat, he eased her down,
in a slow embrace he laid her down, poor thing . . .
then, what came next, what horror we beheld!

He rips off her brooches, the long gold pins
holding her robes—and lifting them high,
looking straight up into the points,
he digs them down the sockets of his eyes, crying, "You,
you'll see no more the pain I suffered, all the pain I caused!
Too long you looked on the ones you never should have seen,
blind to the ones you longed to see, to know! Blind
from this hour on! Blind in the darkness—blind!"
His voice like a dirge, rising, over and over
raising the pins, raking them down his eyes.
And at each stroke blood spurts from the roots,
splashing his beard, a swirl of it, nerves and clots—
black hail of blood pulsing, gushing down.

These are the griefs that burst upon them both,
coupling man and woman. The joy they had so lately,
the fortune of their old ancestral house
was deep joy indeed. Now, in this one day,
wailing, madness and doom, death, disgrace
all the griefs in the world that you can name,
all are theirs forever.

LEADER Oh poor man, the misery—
has he any rest from pain now?

[A voice within, in torment.]

MESSENGER He's shouting,
"Loose the bolts, someone, show me to all of Thebes!
My father's murderer, my mother's—"
No, I can't repeat it, it's unholy.
Now he'll tear himself from his native earth,
not linger, curse the house with his own curse.
But he needs strength, and a guide to lead him on.
This is sickness more than he can bear.

[The palace doors open.]

Look,
he'll show you himself. The great doors are opening—
you are about to see a sight, a horror
even his mortal enemy would pity.

[Enter OEDIPUS, blinded, led by a boy. He stands at the palace steps, as if surveying his people once again.]

CHORUS O the terror—
the suffering, for all the world to see,
the worst terror that ever met my eyes.
What madness swept over you? What god,
what dark power leapt beyond all bounds,
beyond belief, to crush your wretched life?—
godforsaken, cursed by the gods!
I pity you but I can't bear to look.
I've much to ask, so much to learn,
so much fascinates my eyes,
but you . . . I shudder at the sight.

OEDIPUS Oh, Ohh—
the agony! I am agony—
where am I going? where on earth?
where does all this agony hurl me?
where's my voice?—
winging, swept away on a dark tide—
My destiny, my dark power, what a leap you made!

CHORUS To the depths of terror, too dark to hear, to see.

OEDIPUS Dark, horror of darkness
my darkness, drowning, swirling around me
crashing wave on wave—unspeakable, irresistible
headwind, fatal harbor! Oh again,
the misery, all at once, over and over

the stabbing daggers, stab of memory
raking me insane.

CHORUS No wonder you suffer
twice over, the pain of your wounds,
the lasting grief of pain.

OEDIPUS Dear friend, still here?
Standing by me, still with a care for me,
the blind man? Such compassion,
loyal to the last. Oh it's you,
I know you're here, dark as it is
I'd know you anywhere, your voice—
it's yours, clearly yours.

CHORUS Dreadful, what you've done . . .
how could you bear it, gouging out your eyes?
What superhuman power drove you on?

OEDIPUS Apollo, friends, Apollo—
he ordained my agonies—these, my pains on pains!
But the hand that struck my eyes was mine,
mine alone—no one else—
I did it all myself!
What good were eyes to me?
Nothing I could see could bring me joy.

CHORUS No, no, exactly as you say.

OEDIPUS What can I ever see?
What love, what call of the heart
can touch my ears with joy? Nothing, friends.
Take me away, far, far from Thebes,
quickly, cast me away, my friends—
this great murderous ruin, this man cursed to heaven,
the man the deathless gods hate most of all!

CHORUS Pitiful, you suffer so, you understand so much . . .
I wish you'd never known.

OEDIPUS Die, die—
whoever he was that day in the wilds
who cut my ankles free of the ruthless pins,
he pulled me clear of death, he saved my life
for this, this kindness—
Curse him, kill him!
If I'd died then, I'd never have dragged myself,
my loved ones through such hell.

CHORUS Oh if only . . . would to god.

OEDIPUS I'd never have come to this,
my father's murderer—never been branded
mother's husband, all men see me now! Now,
loathed by the gods, son of the mother I defiled
coupling in my father's bed, spawning lives in the loins
that spawned my wretched life. What grief can crown this grief?
It's mine alone, my destiny—I am Oedipus!

CHORUS How can I say you've chosen for the best?
Better to die than be alive and blind.

OEDIPUS What I did was best—don't lecture me,
no more advice. I, with *my* eyes,
how could I look my father in the eyes
when I go down to death? Or mother, so abused . . .
I have done such things to the two of them,
crimes too huge for hanging.
Worse yet,
the sight of my children, born as they were born,
how could I long to look into their eyes?
No, not with these eyes of mine, never.
Not this city either, her high towers,
the sacred glittering images of her gods—
I am misery! I, her best son, reared
as no other son of Thebes was ever reared,
I've stripped myself, I gave the command myself.
All men must cast away the great blasphemer,
the curse now brought to light by the gods,
the son of Laius—I, my father's son!

Now I've exposed my guilt, horrendous guilt,
could I train a level glance on you, my countrymen?
Impossible! No, if I could just block off my ears,
the springs of hearing, I would stop at nothing—
I'd wall up my loathsome body like a prison,
blind to the sound of life, not just the sight.
Oblivion—what a blessing . . .
for the mind to dwell a world away from pain.

O Cithaeron, why did you give me shelter?
Why didn't you take me, crush my life out on the spot?
I'd never have revealed my birth to all mankind.
O Polybus, Corinth, the old house of my fathers,
so I believed—what a handsome prince you raised—
under the skin, what sickness to the core.
Look at me! Born of outrage, outrage to the core.
O triple roads—it all comes back, the secret,
dark ravine, and the oaks closing in
where the three roads join . . .
You drank my father's blood, my own blood
spilled by my own hands—you still remember me?
What things you saw me do? Then I came here
and did them all once more!
Marriages! O marriage,
you gave me birth, and once you brought me into the world
you brought my sperm rising back, springing to light
fathers, brothers, sons—one murderous breed—
brides, wives, mothers. The blackest things
a man can do, I have done them all!
No more—
it's wrong to name what's wrong to do. Quickly,

for the love of god, hide me somewhere,
kill me, hurl me into the sea
where you can never look on me again.

[*Beckoning to the* CHORUS *as they shrink away.*]

Closer,
it's all right. Touch the man of grief.
Do. Don't be afraid. My troubles are mine
and I am the only man alive who can sustain them.

[*Enter* CREON *from the palace, attended by palace guards.*]

LEADER Put your requests to Creon. Here he is,
just when we need him. He'll have a plan, he'll act.
Now that he's the sole defense of the country
in your place.

OEDIPUS Oh no, what can I say to him?
How can I ever hope to win his trust?
I wronged him so, just now, in every way.
You must see that—I was so wrong, so wrong.

CREON I haven't come to mock you, Oedipus,
or to criticize your former failings.

[*Turning to the guards.*]

You there,
have you lost all respect for human feelings?
At least revere the Sun, the holy fire
that keeps us all alive. Never expose a thing
of guilt and holy dread so great it appalls
the earth, the rain from heaven, the light of day!
Get him into the halls—quickly as you can.
Piety demands no less. Kindred alone
should see a kinsman's shame. This is obscene.

OEDIPUS Please, in god's name . . . you wipe my fears away,
coming so generously to me, the worst of men.
Do one thing more, for your sake, not mine.

CREON What do you want? Why so insistent?

OEDIPUS Drive me out of the land at once, far from sight,
where I can never hear a human voice.

CREON I'd have done that already, I promise you.
First I wanted the god to clarify my duties.

OEDIPUS The god? His command was clear, every word:
death for the father-killer, the curse—
he said destroy me!

CREON So he did. Still, in such a crisis
it's better to ask precisely what to do.

OEDIPUS So miserable—
you'd consult the god about a man like me?

CREON By all means. And this time, I assume,
even you will obey the god's decrees.

OEDIPUS I will,
I will. And you, I command you—I beg you . . .
the woman inside, bury her as you see fit.

It's the only decent thing,
to give your own the last rites. As for me,
never condemn the city of my fathers
to house my body, not while I'm alive, no,
let me live on the mountains, on Cithaeron,
my favorite haunt, I have made it famous.
Mother and father marked out that rock
to be my everlasting tomb—buried alive.
Let me die there, where they tried to kill me.

Oh but this I know: no sickness can destroy me,
nothing can. I would never have been saved
from death—I have been saved
for something great and terrible, something strange.
Well let my destiny come and take me on its way!
About my children, Creon, the boys at least,
don't burden yourself. They're men,
wherever they go, they'll find the means to live.
But my two daughters, my poor helpless girls,
clustering at our table, never without me
hovering near them . . . whatever I touched,
they always had their share. Take care of them,
I beg you. Wait, better—permit me, would you?
Just to touch them with my hands and take
our fill of tears. Please . . . my king.
Grant it, with all your noble heart.
If I could hold them, just once, I'd think
I had them with me, like the early days
when I could see their eyes.

[ANTIGONE *and* ISMENE, *two small children, are led in from the palace by a nurse.*]

What's that
O god! Do I really hear you sobbing?—
my two children. Creon, you've pitied me?
Sent me my darling girls, my own flesh and blood!
Am I right?

CREON Yes, it's my doing.
I know the joy they gave you all these years,
the joy you must feel now.

OEDIPUS Bless you, Creon!
May god watch over you for this kindness,
better than he ever guarded me.

Children, where are you?

Here, come quickly—

[*Groping for* ANTIGONE *and* ISMENE, *who approach their father cautiously, then embrace him.*]

Come to these hands of mine,
your brother's hands, your own father's hands
that served his once bright eyes so well—
that made them blind. Seeing nothing, children,

knowing nothing, I became your father,
I fathered you in the soil that gave me life.
How I weep for you—I cannot see you now . . .
just thinking of all your days to come, the bitterness,
the life that rough mankind will thrust upon you.
Where are the pubic gatherings you can join,
the banquets of the clans? Home you'll come,
in tears, cut off from the sight of it all,
the brilliant rites unfinished.
And when you reach perfection, ripe for marriage,
who will he be, my dear ones? Risking all
to shoulder the curse that weighs down my parents,
yes and you too—that wounds us all together.
What more misery could you want?
Your father killed his father, sowed his mother,
one, one and the selfsame womb sprang you—
he cropped the very roots of his existence.

Such disgrace, and you must bear it all!
Who will marry you then? Not a man on earth.
Your doom is clear: you'll wither away to nothing,
single, without a child.

[*Turning to* CREON.]

Oh Creon,
you are the only father they have now . . .
we who brought them into the world
are gone, both gone at a stroke—
Don't let them go begging, abandoned,
men without men. Your own flesh and blood!
Never bring them down to the level of my pains.
Pity them. Look at them, so young, so vulnerable,
shorn of everything—you're their only hope.
Promise me, noble Creon, touch my hand!

[*Reaching toward* CREON, *who draws back.*]

You, little ones, if you were old enough
to understand, there is much I'd tell you.
Now, as it is, I'd have you say a prayer.
Pray for life, my children,
live where you are free to grow and season.
Pray god you find a better life than mine,
the father who begot you.

CREON Enough.
You've wept enough. Into the palace now.

OEDIPUS I must, but I find it very hard.

CREON Time is the great healer, you will see.

OEDIPUS I am going—you know on what condition?

CREON Tell me. I'm listening.

OEDIPUS Drive me out of Thebes, in exile.

CREON Not I. Only the gods can give you that.

OEDIPUS Surely the gods hate me so much—
CREON You'll get your wish at once.
OEDIPUS You consent?
CREON I try to say what I mean; it's my habit.
OEDIPUS Then take me away. It's time.
CREON Come along, let go of the children.
OEDIPUS No—
don't take them away from me, not now! No no no!

[*Clutching his daughters as the guards wrench them loose and take them through the palace doors.*]

CREON Still the king, the master of all things?
No more: here your power ends.
None of your power follows you though life.

[*Exit* OEDIPUS *and* CREON *to the palace. The* CHORUS *comes forward to address the audience directly.*]

CHORUS People of Thebes, my countrymen, look on Oedipus.
He solved the famous riddle with his brilliance,
he rose to power, a man beyond all power.
Who could behold his greatness without envy?
Now what a black sea of terror has overwhelmed him.
Now as we keep our watch and wait the final day,
count no man happy till he dies, free of pain at last.

[*Exit in procession.*]

ARISTOPHANES

ca. 450–ca. 385 B.C.E.

COMEDY (a word derived from the Greek *kōmōidia*, "song of the *kōmos*," or band of revelers) officially joined its predecessor, tragedy, as part of the dramatic competitions in Athens in the fifth century B.C.E., first at the City Dionysia (ca. 486) and then at the Lenaea (ca. 442). While scholars estimate that several hundred plays that we now categorize as "Old Comedy" may have been produced at the festivals in the fifth century B.C.E. alone, only eleven relatively complete texts by Aristophanes remain to provide evidence of this important form of classical theater. Aristophanes' track record of success as a dramatist, with at least six first-place and four second-place awards in the competitions, may account in part for the preservation of his comedies across the centuries. Exuding energy and wit, his plays career from the depths of vulgarity to the heights of poetic sophistication. Although in some eras he has been faulted for the inconsistencies in his narratives and the implausibility of his scenarios, Aristophanes more recently has regained critical favor for his nuanced interplay of theme and action. LYSISTRATA stands out in this regard and has attracted sustained interest since the early twentieth century for its focus on women's roles at times of war.

Born in a region near Athens, Aristophanes appears to have been a landowner and also a political representative to the Athenian Council of 500, the group that helped establish the government's agenda. Plato's *Symposium* (ca. 384 B.C.E.) depicts Aristophanes as fitting in with the social and intellectual elite of Athens, and his plays certainly reflect familiarity with Attic politics and culture. Aristophanes is believed to have written more than forty plays, the first of which was produced in 427 B.C.E. and the last around 386 B.C.E. These works reflect the comparative freedom of expression granted to the comic playwrights of the era and are known for their pointed political critique, their frank sexuality, and their close engagement with the myths and social conventions of Attic culture. They blend the fantastic and the quotidian, often making the impossible seem plausible—as do the anthropomorphized choruses in *The Birds* (Dionysia, 414) and *The Frogs* (Lenaea, 405).

Produced at the Lenaea in 411, *Lysistrata* dealt directly with recent events in the Peloponnesian War, by then a twenty-year struggle between Athens (and its island and mainland dependencies) and Sparta (and its allies). The war would continue until 404, when the ultimate defeat of Athens' navy led to the end of its empire. This conflict spanned much of Aristophanes' career and recurred thematically in many of his plays. In *Lysistrata*, he was responding specifically to the disastrous loss of the

Athenian fleet in 413 at Sicily and its aftermath, including the appointment by the Athenian government of a board of executive councillors called "Probouloi" who could act quickly and could officially manage the city-state's finances without being subject to the usual democratic process.

With the men of Athens and Sparta at war, Aristophanes depicts the ongoing conflict's impact on the daily lives of others, especially women and the elderly men left in charge of the government. Lysistrata, an Athenian woman, decides that the best way to bring the hostilities to a quick end is for the women to refuse to have sex with the warriors. Calling together the women on both sides of the war, she persuades them to leave their homes and, in the case of the Athenians, to occupy the Acropolis—the main meeting place and market of Athens, as well as the site of the city's treasury. In this way, Lysistrata believes, the women will gain control over both the financial and the human resources integral to the war effort, forcing a declaration of peace and the return to the communities of domestic order, tranquillity, and economic security.

The dramatic structure of *Lysistrata* exemplifies the standard form of Old Comedy. The opening scene, or prologue, introduces us to the central concerns of the play: in this instance, the sex-strike plot for which the work is most remembered. During the entrance (*parados*) of the chorus, Aristophanes chooses to divide the standard group of twenty-four into two halves—twelve old men and twelve old women—whose antagonism contributes both to the humor of the work and to its themes of domestic and political upheaval; moreover, the *parados* sets up the grounds for the debate, or *agōn,* to follow. This rhetorical contest between Lysistrata and the Commissioner of Public Safety, a satiric portrait of one of the Probouloi, reflects the spirit of formal competition that pervaded classical Greek culture; it also enables Aristophanes to expand the scope of the play to incorporate additional social and political issues, including Lysistrata's heartfelt depiction of women's grief at the loss of their sons in war. In such moments, we see that Aristophanes distinguishes his title character from his satiric portraits of other figures, possibly because he modeled her on Lysimache, priestess of Athena Polias, the most important of such positions in Athenian religious culture. The *parabasis,* or interlude, that follows the *agōn* again showcases the chorus and provides a transition to the series of episodes that will resolve the action. Notable among these is the highly comic scene with the Athenian couple Myrrhine and Kinesias that bawdily demonstrates, through the oversized, erect phallus the latter sports, the effectiveness of the women's deprivation tactics.

At such a great remove from the classical era, audiences and readers today may find both the structure and style of ancient comedy challenging. Moreover, although we have some general knowledge of how these plays were performed, we lack the specific understanding necessary to envision them with historical authenticity. We know, for example, that the plays combined spoken verse, recitative (verse declaimed rhythmically), and song; music and dance also contributed significantly to the overall theatrical effect. Our uncertainty about the exact nature of any of these performative elements has frustrated some interpreters of *Lysistrata,* but others have capitalized on it to create exciting and innovative productions. The absence of stage directions, the corruptions in ancient manuscripts, and lingering doubts about the exact meaning of topical references or allusions all complicate the work of translators and scholars, but they also extend the range of possibilities for contemporary performances.

Despite the gaps in our knowledge about Greek comedy generally and *Lysistrata* specifically, we know enough to recognize that some aspects of the play that seem strange to us would have been considered routine, or at least not unusual, to fifth-century Athenians. First, because the City Dionysia and the Lenaea were both civic and religious festivals, replete with ritual sacrifices to the gods in addition to the theatrical competition, the mingling of religious and political themes in *Lysistrata* not only would have been highly appropriate for the festival context but also would have mirrored the tenor of Athenian daily life. Second, although the frank representation of sexuality, especially the prominence of the phallus, might strike some contempo-

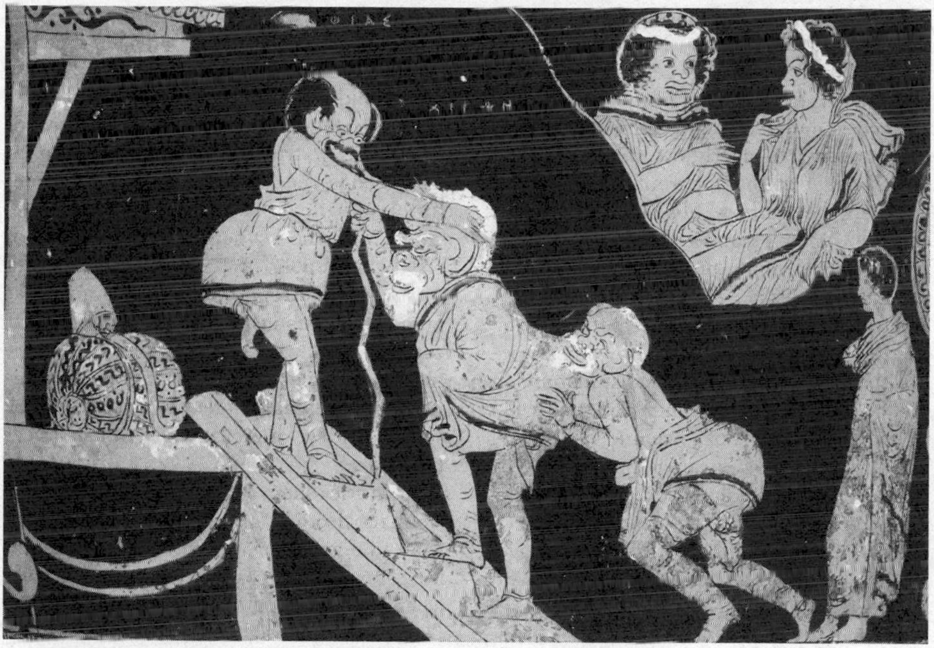

This detail from a painted bell-krater (large wine bowl) dating from the fourth century B.C.E. shows three actors performing in a comedy about the centaur Cheiron.

rary readers as antithetical to a religious ceremony, it was perfectly in keeping with Greek cultural traditions; such explicitness is even less surprising if we consider that comedy most likely is partly rooted in the rituals of cults that honored the fertility gods Dionysus and Demeter (among other deities). Finally, the play's sexually explicit banter and innuendo would have been matched by equally explicit costumery—not only the phalluses padded to indicate various degrees of erection but also the stuffed bodysuit worn by the character Reconciliation, overemphasizing the proportions of the female anatomy to render them visible to a large outdoor audience. *Lysistrata* thus illustrates vividly how comic writers perceptively capture, often through exaggeration, distinctive cultural practices as well as individuals' foibles.

An awareness of this connection between comedy and its original context is especially important to a clear understanding of the central role of female characters in *Lysistrata*. Although *Lysistrata* is believed to be the first Western comedy featuring a female heroine and incorporating varied images of women's lives and attributes, we should also remember that this title character and all the other women in the play would have been portrayed by male performers, in a society in which the activities of well-off women were circumscribed and revolved exclusively around the home. Only male citizens participated in public endeavors, and Lysistrata's entry into the public sphere, although appearing potentially realistic to contemporary readers and audiences, should be seen in its Greek context as fantastical—as implausible as choruses of singing and dancing birds and frogs. Thus we should not interpret the play as proto-feminist, or as a critique of the "separate spheres" ideology that informed classical Greek society. Indeed, Lysistrata wants nothing more than to restore the status quo, with all citizens—male and female—returning to their established roles.

The implausibilities and inconsistencies in Aristophanes' dramaturgy have proven alienating to some contemporary readers and audiences, who are more comfortable with the conventions of dramatic realism that have dominated the theater since the nineteenth century. Yet if we can keep in mind that ideas about narrative cohesion and realistic action—our notions of what makes a play "good"—are themselves historical constructs, we may better appreciate Aristophanes' shifts between, for example, the farcical sex-strike plot of the *parados* and the *agōn*'s more serious treatment of financial concerns. Similarly, we might suspend our disbelief at the apparent contradiction between the warriors' absence from home and the women's plan to deny them sex.

More importantly, our openness to these unique qualities of Aristophanic dramaturgy may enable us to discern the metaphors he used to structure his fantasy of women's political intervention. First, the disjunctions in the "logical" flow of dramatic action parallel the war's disruption of civic and family life. The two-pronged strategy proposed by Lysistrata—withholding sex and blocking access to state funds—also helps make evident the foundational elements of marriage: the sexual relationship between husband and wife, and the economic transactions that similarly support the home environment. Lysistrata then works to establish the links between the women's world and the state, describing how domestic management mirrors core elements of governmental practices. Aristophanes further develops these associations through the implied staging, which visually ties these domestic and civic worlds together. We assume that Lysistrata and her friend Calonike first encounter each other outside their homes, but soon the central door in the *scaenae frons* (the wooden stage building used for entrances and exits) is also serving as the entrance to the Acropolis. Later, Myrrhine transforms the space just outside the Acropolis into a bedroom, furthering the linkage, and the play concludes with the women's hosting a banquet on the Acropolis to celebrate the peace. Aristophanes' utopian vision of harmony at home and abroad thus shapes a comedy that could at best work to influence the state's future strategies or at least temporarily divert an Athenian audience otherwise consumed by its increasingly grim political prospects.

Centuries later, Aristophanes' concept of women's leading the initiative for peace spurred a group of women actors to launch the *Lysistrata* Project, a global protest against the United States' invasion of Iraq. On March 3, 2003, artists around the world held more than 1,000 public readings of the play in fifty-nine countries to voice their opposition to this military action. That these artists and their audiences saw such relevance in a work almost 2,500 years old expresses volumes about the ongoing power of theater to speak of and to humanity.

J.E.G.

Lysistrata[1]

CHARACTERS

LYSISTRATA, CALONIKE, MYRRHINE — Athenian women
LAMPITO, a Spartan woman
A BOEOTIAN WOMAN
A CORINTHIAN WOMAN
COMMISSIONER OF PUBLIC SAFETY
KINESIAS, husband of Myrrhine
SPARTAN HERALD AND ENVOYS
CHORUS OF ATHENIAN MEN
CHORUS OF ATHENIAN WOMEN
A BABY
A NURSE

1. Translated by Nicholas Ruddall.

MUTE CHARACTERS

ATHENIAN WOMEN
ISMENIA, a Theban woman
KORINTHIAN WOMAN
SPARTAN WOMEN
SKYTHIAN GIRL, Lysistrata's slave
MAGISTRATE'S SLAVES
SKYTHIAN POLICEMEN
OLD WOMEN, allies of Lysistrata
MANES, Kinesias' slave
SPARTAN DELEGATES
SPARTAN SLAVES, with the Spartan delegation
ATHENIAN DELEGATES
RECONCILIATION
DOORKEEPER

CHORUS

OLD ATHENIAN MEN (twelve)
OLD ATHENIAN WOMEN (twelve)

Prologue

[SCENE: *A neighborhood street in Athens, after dawn. The stage-building has a large central door and two smaller, flanking doors. From one of these* LYSISTRATA *emerges and looks expectantly up and down the street.*]

LYSISTRATA [*pacing*] Women! [*to audience*] Tell them there's an orgy going on, or a party for Pan,[2] or a fertility rite, and everything stops. You can't get through the streets. Women everywhere with their tambourines. But today there's not one woman here. Sorry! Here's someone. It's my next-door neighbor. Good morning, Calonike![3]

CALONIKE Same to you, Lysistrata.[4] But what's the matter? Don't squidge your face up like that, darling. Looking daggers doesn't suit you.

LYSISTRATA I am on fire. Right down to the bone. I'm furious. And all because of us women. You know what our husbands say. They say we're sly, deceitful, always . . .

CALONIKE They're right, too.

LYSISTRATA We promised to meet today to plan something devastatingly important. And what happens? They stay in bed.

CALONIKE Oh, they'll be along, my sweet. It's so hard to get out of the house. We have to bend over backwards for our husbands, wake the maid, wash the baby, feed the baby, put the baby to bed.

LYSISTRATA But there are other things far far more important.

CALONIKE Is that why you're calling the meeting, Lysistrata? How big a thing is this?

LYSISTRATA It's big.

CALONIKE And thick?

LYSISTRATA Massive. It's big enough for all of us.

CALONIKE Then why aren't they here?

LYSISTRATA If THAT'S what was up, they'd be here. No, Calonike, this is something I've been tossing around for the last few nights. I couldn't get any sleep.

2. Goat footed god of woods and pastures, often worshipped with Dionysos, the god of wine and fertility.

3. A name meaning "beautiful victory."

4. A name meaning "disbander of armies."

CALONIKE Sounds good to me! Was it good?

LYSISTRATA So good that. . . . The hope and salvation of Greece depend upon us women.

CALONIKE On us? Bye-bye, Greece.

LYSISTRATA We must make the decisions on national and international affairs. Take the Spartan question. Are you for peace or annihilation?

CALONIKE Annihilation every time.

LYSISTRATA And the same for the Boeotians?[5]

CALONIKE *Yes*! . . . Wait a minute. NO!! They have marvelous pickled eels[6] in that part of the country.

LYSISTRATA As for Athens. . . . It could happen to us . . . but I can't bring myself to say it. But listen, if all the women came here, from Boeotia, from Sparta, from the rest of the Peloponnese, we could save the entire country.

CALONIKE Us? Do you really think *we* could do something practical? All we are good for is sitting in front of the mirror, all primped and flowered in our exquisite little negligees and those chic little oriental slippers.

LYSISTRATA Exactly! Those are the weapons that will save us—perfumes and rouge, slippers and slips, and those see-through negligees.

CALONIKE Save us? What do you mean?

LYSISTRATA The result will be that the men will never raise their spears again. . . .

CALONIKE Then I'll have my best dress sent to the cleaners. . . .

LYSISTRATA Nor shoulder their shields . . .

CALONIKE And slip into that little negligee . . .

LYSISTRATA Nor unsheathe their swords . . .

CALONIKE And buy me a pair of those oriental slippers.

LYSISTRATA Then wasn't it essential for the women to be here?

CALONIKE Be here? They should have flown like the wind.

LYSISTRATA Listen, darling, you know what they're like. They're real Athenians: never do today what you can put off till tomorrow. But no one came from the coast, nor from Salamis[7] either.

CALONIKE Don't worry about them. They'll be here. They'd do anything for a good ride.

LYSISTRATA And where are the Acharnian women? I thought they'd be here first, after all they've had to put up with in this awful war.[8]

CALONIKE I saw Theogenes' wife as I was leaving. She was flying over here . . . high as a kite already. But look, hey, here's a few coming now. And some more over there. Marvelous. Marvelous. Where are they from?

LYSISTRATA Pisa, I think.

CALONIKE Smells like it.

MYRRHINE Are we late, Lysistrata? Well, why don't you answer?

LYSISTRATA I am very upset, Myrrhine.[9] You are so late when the matter is so important.

MYRRHINE I couldn't find my girdle in the dark. [*still pouting*] What's so important?

5. That is, Thebans in Boeotia, northwest of Athens. Sparta and Boeotia were Athens's main opponents in the Peloponnesian War.

6. A delicacy native to Boeotia.

7. An island in the Aegean Sea near Athens.

8. Acharnae was a district less than ten miles north of Athens that supplied the Athenian alliance with a vast number of fighting men.

9. A name meaning "myrtle," which was also a slang term for the volva.

CALONIKE Hold on a minute. She'll tell you everything when the Spartans and Boeotians get here.

MYRRHINE That's all right with me. . . . Here's Lampito coming for a start.

LYSISTRATA Welcome, Lampito, you Spartan beauty, you.

CALONIKE What a healthy complexion!

WOMAN Throbbing with life.

2ND WOMAN Ripe as a melon!

3RD WOMAN She could strangle a bull.

LAMPITO By golly, I think I could. I do my exercises every day—a few pushups every morning before breakfast.[1]

LYSISTRATA What a nice pair of titties!

LAMPITO Keep your hands to yourself. What do you think I am? A sacred cow?

LYSISTRATA And who is this other little girl? Where is she from?

LAMPITO She's an aristocratic young lady from Boeotia.

LYSISTRATA Ah, "Boeotia of the fertile plain."

CALONIKE [*lifting her robe*] Looks as if someone's been mowing the grass.

LYSISTRATA And who is this?

LAMPITO She is from Corinth.[2] Her family is very big back there.

CALONIKE She's pretty big back here.

LAMPITO All right. Let's get down to business. Who was it called this meeting?

LYSISTRATA I did.

LAMPITO Well, then tell us what you have in mind.

MYRRHINE Yes, tell us, sweetie, what's so important?

LYSISTRATA I'll answer you both in a minute. But first I want to ask a little question.

MYRRHINE Go right ahead.

LYSISTRATA Do you or do you not crave to have your husbands, the fathers of your children, home beside you? I know that all your husbands are abroad.

CALONIKE My husband's been gone for the last five months up in the mountains of Thrace.[3]

MYRRHINE Mine's been in Pylos[4] for seven.

LAMPITO My man's no sooner rotated out of the line than he's plugged back in. There's no discharge in this war.

LYSISTRATA And you can't find a lover anywhere. Not even synthetics. Ever since those Milesians revolted[5] and cut off the leather trade, you can't find one of those eight-inch do-it-yourself kits anywhere in town. So . . . if I can provide a plan that would bring an end to this war, I take it that I can count on your support.

CALONIKE YOU can count on me, and if it's money you need I'd pawn the shift off my back—then we could all go out and get smashed.

MYRRHINE I'm with you all the way. Even if they take me and split me up the middle and filet me like a mackerel.

1. Spartan women, unlike their counterparts elsewhere, received an education similar to that of men, including physical training. *By golly*: throughout the play, Aristophanes caricatures the Doric dialect of the Spartans, which differed notably from the Attic-Ionic Greek of the Athenians.

2. A city-state in the northern Peloponnesos; like Sparta and Thebes, a rival of Athens.

3. A region in northeastern Greece allied with Athens. Many battles were fought there during the war.

4. A district in the southern Peloponnesos, occupied by the Athenians since 425 B.C.E.

5. Miletus, a city-state on the coast of Asia Minor, revolted from Athens in 412 B.C.E.

LAMPITO Me, too! I'd climb the highest mountain in Sparta if I could just set my eyes on peace again.

LYSISTRATA All right, then, I'll tell you. There is no need to keep it a secret any longer. Sisters, women of Greece, if we have any hopes of forcing our husbands to negotiate peace, we must resort to total abstinence.

CALONIKE From what?

MYRRHINE Yes, what?

LYSISTRATA You'll do it?

CALONIKE Of course we will, even if it kills us.

LYSISTRATA Very well, then. We must resort to total abstinence from . . . the Prick. Why are you turning away? Where are you going? Hey! Why all this mooching and shaking of heads? [*mock tragic*] Why so pale? Whence these tears? Will you do it or won't you? Well, what are you going to do?

CALONIKE I just couldn't do it. On with the war!

MYRRHINE Me neither. On with the war!

ALL ON WITH THE WAR!

LYSISTRATA Is that all you have to say, my little mackerel? Two minutes ago you were ready to be split up the middle.

CALONIKE Got any other ideas? Think of something else. Anything. Look, I'd walk through fire if you told me to, but to give up the the . . . thing. . . . Uh uh. There's nothing like it, Lysistrata.

LYSISTRATA [*to the Corinthian and the Boeotian*] What about you, and you?

CORINTHIAN I'd be quite willing to walk through fire.

BOEOTIAN Me, too. Any fire around?

LYSISTRATA Whores, the whole lot of you! It's no wonder they write tragedies about us. You're a bunch of Phaedras,[6] that's all you are. You'd jump into bed with anyone. But you, my Spartan friend, if you, just you, join me in this, we can still salvage my plan. Give me your vote.

LAMPITO It's pretty tough, by golly, for girls to sleep without their dickies, but I'm with you. We need peace so badly.

LYSISTRATA Oh, you darling! The only woman worthy of the name.

CALONIKE Well, suppose we did . . . well, as far as possible, abstain from . . . what you said—God forbid. Could something like that bring peace any sooner?

LYSISTRATA Good God, of course. All we have to do is lounge around with the right amount of makeup on, maybe a flimsy slip, or nothing at all, and we just slink by them, perfumed and powdered and shaved smooth in all the right places. . . . Wham! Up they'll go. Lusting for a quick lay. But we won't go near them. Total abstinence. I wouldn't be surprised if they stopped the war within a week.

LAMPITO It could work. Menelaus dropped his sword when he saw Helen all nekked.[7]

CALONIKE [*to* LYSISTRATA] Wait a minute, buddy. What if they just walk away?

LYSISTRATA Then we'll just have to take things into our own hands.

6. Wife of Theseus, the legendary founder of Athens; she fell in love with Theseus's son, Hippolytus.

7. At the end of the Trojan War, after the Greeks had captured Troy, Menelaos, King of Sparta, was about to kill his wife, Helen, for adultery when he was overcome by her beauty.

CALONIKE There's nothing like the real thing.

BOEOTIAN What if they grab us and drag us off to the bedroom?

LAMPITO Hold on to the door.

CORINTHIAN What if they beat us?

LYSISTRATA You can give in. But don't enjoy it. Be nasty about it. It's no fun for them when it's no fun for you. It's not copulation without cooperation.

MYRRHINE I suppose it's all right if the *both* of you agree to this.

LAMPITO You can be sure of one thing: we Spartan women will make our men do exactly as they're told. But this lot in Athens! You'll never convince these fighting cocks.

LYSISTRATA We'll take care of it. I know how to make them listen.

LAMPITO I just don't see how you can make them do it. After all, they have a fleet in the harbor and money in the Acropolis.[8]

LYSISTRATA That's all taken care of. We're taking over the Acropolis today. The older women are up there already pretending to be holding a sacrifice. They're just waiting until we reach an agreement. As soon as we do, they seize the Acropolis.

LAMPITO I am very impressed. That's an excellent plan.

LYSISTRATA Then what are we waiting for? All we have to do now is swear a solemn oath.

CALONIKE You make the oath, we'll swear to it.

LYSISTRATA Excellent. This is it. Lampito, give me your shield. No, put it on the ground. Not that way up. Turn it over. Now, has anyone got any spare entrails of lamb?

CALONIKE What kind of ceremony is this, Lysistrata?

LYSISTRATA [*scratching her head*] Well, I think it's worked before. Aeschylus used it in the *Seven Against Thebes*.[9] They slaughtered a sheep and swore on a shield . . . I think.

CALONIKE But you can't make an oath about peace on a shield. That would be ridiculous.

LYSISTRATA Then what do you suggest?

CALONIKE How about a big white stallion?

LYSISTRATA Anyone got a spare one?

CALONIKE I never thought of that.

LYSISTRATA We're wasting time.

MYRRHINE I know. First we get an enormous bowl. Then we put it on the ground [*to* LAMPITO] the right way up. Then we proceed to slaughter a gallon or two of good red wine and swear that . . . we won't dilute it with water.[1]

BOEOTIAN I like that oath.

LYSISTRATA Bring the bowl and the wine.

CALONIKE Oooh! Girls! What an enormous bowl! It gives me a thrill just to touch it.

LYSISTRATA Set it down and place your hands reverently upon this blessed offering to the Gods. [*They raise the wine skin.*] O Goddess in Heaven . . .

8. A high, rocky plateau looming over Athens on which stood the Parthenon, a temple to the goddess Athena that also served as the city's treasury.

9. Aeschylus's *Seven Against Thebes* (467 B.C.E.), in which a band of seven captains swear an oath to help Polynices forcibly remove his brother, Eteocles, from the Theban throne.

1. Greeks viewed drinking wine mixed with water as a sign of refinement; the preference of women for undiluted wine was a comic stereotype.

ALL O Goddess in Heaven . . .

LYSISTRATA Our Mistress Persuasion . . .

ALL Our Mistress Persuasion . . .

LYSISTRATA And thou, O hallowed skin . . .

ALL And thou, O hallowed skin . . .

LYSISTRATA Hear our prayer.

ALL Hear our prayer.

MYRRHINE [*jumping up and down*] Oooh! Look at the blood! Look at the blood!

CALONIKE Excellent bouquet.

MYRRHINE Let me swear first.

CALONIKE No, me! Gimme the BOWL!

MYRRHINE Choose you for it! . . . [*They proceed to play a children's game to see who goes first.*]

LYSISTRATA Lampito, all of you women, come place your right hands on the cup and repeat after me, in order . . . I WILL HAVE NOTHING TO DO WITH HUSBAND OR LOVER.

CALONIKE I will have nothing to do with husband or lover.

LYSISTRATA EVEN THOUGH HE COME TO ME WITH A HARD ON. [*pause*] Go on, say it.

CALONIKE Even though he come to me with a hard on. Ooohhh! Lysistrata, I can't go on with this!

LYSISTRATA I SHALL REMAIN AT HOME UNMOUNTED.

MYRRHINE I shall remain at home unmounted.

LYSISTRATA IN MY THINNEST SAFFRON SILK.

MYRRHINE In my thinnest saffron silk.

LYSISTRATA SO THAT HE MAY BECOME . . .

MYRRHINE So that he may become . . .

LYSISTRATA AS STIFF AS A BOARD.

MYRRHINE [*also forcing herself to say it*] As stiff as a board.

LYSISTRATA I WILL NOT GIVE MYSELF . . .

LAMPITO I will not give myself . . .

LYSISTRATA WILLINGLY TO MY HUSBAND.

LAMPITO Willingly to my husband.

LYSISTRATA AND IF HE TAKES ME BY FORCE . . .

LAMPITO And if he takes me by force . . .

LYSISTRATA I SHALL RESIST HIM AND LIE ABSOLUTELY STILL.

LAMPITO [*also with difficulty*] I shall resist him and lie absolutely still.

LYSISTRATA I SHALL NOT LIFT MY SLIPPERS TO THE CEILING.

BOEOTIAN I shall not lift my slippers to the ceiling.

LYSISTRATA I SHALL NEVER ASSUME AN ANIMAL POSTURE.

CORINTHIAN I shall never assume an animal posture.

LYSISTRATA AND IF I KEEP THIS OATH LET ME DRINK FROM THIS BOWL. [*By this time the five main women have turned their backs on the ceremony, but when they hear this last phrase they rush back and shout together.*]

ALL AND IF I KEEP THIS OATH LET ME DRINK FROM THIS BOWL!

LYSISTRATA BUT IF I SLIP OR FALTER, LET MY BOWL BE FILLED WITH WATER.

ALL [*much quieter*] But if I slip or falter, let my bowl be filled with water.

LYSISTRATA You have all sworn?

CALONIKE We have. [*She indicates to the women who all shout together.*]

ALL Aah, men.

LYSISTRATA Well, then, I'll make the sacrifice.

CALONIKE Not too much now. We want to *stay* friends now, don't we? [*The women gather round and drink. Loud cries backstage.*]

LAMPITO What's all the commotion?

LYSISTRATA Just what I told you. The women have seized the Acropolis. The Treasury is OURS. Lampito, rush back to Sparta, get everything in order back there. Leave these girls here as hostages. Leave the rest to us. Girls, into the Acropolis! Shut the gates! Ram the bolts in tight!

CALONIKE What about the men? Won't they send reinforcements?

LYSISTRATA That's no problem. Leave them to me. Whether they come with fire or threats and an army, NOTHING will make me open these gates, except on my terms.

CALONIKE We'll show them. If they're going to call us dirty names, we might as well deserve them.

CHORUS OF OLD MEN [*the parts are designated I through VII*]

Before the doors of the Acropolis. The men are carrying lighted torches and a battering ram.

MAN I Forward march, Draces, me boy, forget your backs, lads. I know these logs are green and heavy. But to it, boys, to it!

MAN II What a life! There's this to be said for longevity, you get to see things you never thought you'd see.

MAN III Hey, Strymodorus, hey! I never thought I'd live to see our women, dammit, seize the citadel.

MAN IV We gave them everything they needed: food, clothing, and a punch in the mouth. Who'd have thought they'd have barred the doors—all . . . the subversive whores!

MAN I Now, Philourgos, get a move on! To the Acropolis on the double!
We'll pile up the logs in a great big heap,
And set them on fire while they're fast asleep.
We'll try them for treason. We'll cook their goose. And the first to go will by Ly—, Ly— [*remembering*] Lycon's wife. . . .

MAN V They're not going to make a fool out of me. No, sir! Cleomenes[2] tried it fifty years ago, the stinking old fool!

MAN VI Oh, we could sniff *him* out all right. He never took a bath for six long years. We flushed that Spartan out of there.

MAN VII Oh, that was a siege, my friends. Shields to the left of us, shields to the right. I slept like a baby.

MAN I So what should we do when *women*, of all things, women (whom God and Euripides hate) *women* try the same trick? If we fail to dispose of these hags, I'll turn in the medals I won at *Marathon*.[3]

ALL Move your feet and tote that load

2. A Spartan king who, while attempting to aid one Athenian faction, briefly occupied the Acropolis in 508 B.C.E.

3. Plain about 25 miles north of Athens, where the Athenians defeated a large invading Persian army in 490 B.C.E. *Euripides*: tragedian typically portrayed by Aristophanes as misogynist.

Just a few more yards of Acropolis road.
Up the step and onto the porch
Drop your burdens and apply the torch!

MAN II Damn this smoke.

ALL [*mass coughing and rubbing of eyes*]
We've come to aid the goddess,
We'll save her come what may,
For if the women stay inside,
They'll keep us from our pay.

MAN II Damn this smoke!

MAN I Well, thanks be to God, we made it. The fire is bright and burning. Here's my plan of attack. First we'll take a torch, light it in the fire, and then use it as a battering ram. . . . No, that wouldn't work. Well, if they don't listen to us and throw open the gates, we'll set fire to the woodwork and smoke them out. Damn this smoke! At ease, men. There's a logistical problem here. What we really need is an army of foreign advisers to take over the siege. All right, men, light the sacred fire. "Victory sits on our helm!"

ALL BURN THE BITCHES WHO CAPTURED THE CAPITOL. DEATH TO THE WOMEN, VICTORY FOR MEN!

CHORUS OF OLD WOMEN [*parts designated as for the Old Men*]

WOMAN I Come on, girls, I smell fire and smoke. There's a conflagration here.
Whack those rumps and lift those knees!

WOMAN II Fly, fly, Nikodike,
Before they scorch poor Calonike.

WOMAN III Watch out, lady, they'll burn your drawers. These damned old men with their stupid laws.

WOMAN IV But maybe, maybe, I've come too late—
The well this morning was in such a state.
Women everywhere drawing water.

WOMAN I We'll put out the fire and stop the slaughter.
We heard a rumor down by the well
That some old graybeards (on their way to Hell)
Had carried some wood and started a fire.
You know what that is? It's their funeral pyre.

WOMAN V They threatened to burn these glorious ladies,
But we'll smash them first right down to Hades.[4]

ALL We've come to aid the goddess,
We'll save her come what may,
The men must never get inside,
We'll keep them from their pay.

WOMAN II [*she has been grabbed by one of the old men*]
Help!! Leave me go, you dog!

WOMAN I Leave her alone, you simpering corpse.

MAN I I wouldn't have believed it—an army of women in the Acropolis.

WOMAN I You scum, you lowest of the low. Male hags, rag bags.

MAN II This is a sight I never thought to see. A swarm of women buzzing around the Acropolis.

4. The mythological realm of the dead.

WOMAN II You're so scared, you'll dirty your pants. But you ain't seen nothing yet.

MAN III [*stamps his foot*] I will *not* be talked back to by a woman! [*indicating man next to him*] Pick up a log, Phaedrias, and crown her cranium.

WOMAN I Down with your pots, girls, we'll need both hands in a minute.

MAN I Give them the old one-two to the jaw, boys, that'll shut 'em up.

WOMAN III Come on, then. Free shot! [*offers her jaw and one man advances*] Want a kick in the balls? [*He scurries back.*]

MAN IV I'll smash you to pieces with this stick.

WOMAN IV You just lay a finger on her and you'll never lay anything else again.

MAN IV Oh yeah?

WOMEN ALL Yeah.

MAN V Drop dead.

WOMAN V I'll rattle your ribs and ravage your rump.

MEN ALL Euripides! You're right!

MAN VI "Women are a curse," he said.

WOMAN I Okay, girls, position your pots. [*They circle the men who bunch together holding their torches in front of them during the following interchange.*]

MAN VII Why the water, you whoremaster's daughter?

WOMAN VI Why the fire, you walking graveyard? [*turns to the other women, giggling*] It's his funeral pyre!

MAN I I brought this fire to ignite a pyre and barbecue your friends.

WOMAN VII I brought this water to put out your fire. What do you think of that?

MAN II You'll put out my fire?

WOMAN VII You're not as dumb as you look.

MAN III Watch it, granny, or I'll fire your fanny.

WOMAN VI If you've got any soap, I'll give you a bath.

MAN VI A bath for me? You slut, you.

WOMAN VII He hasn't used soap since his wedding night!

MAN V Watch your lip.

WOMAN VII My lips are free to say what they like.

MAN I Burn, lads, burn.

WOMAN I Soak, girls, soak. [*Music stops.*]

MEN ALL Arrrgh!

WOMAN I Was it too cold? [*The women threaten to pour again.*]

MEN ALL Stop it. Stop it.

WOMAN II I'm just watering the garden. Maybe you'll sprout a leaf.

MAN II [*chattering*] I-I-I'm f-f-f-reezing.

WOMAN II Sorry to have cooled you off, we thought you were in heat. [*The men sit down bedraggled, the women move aside.*]

[*Enter Commissioner and four policemen.*]

COMMISSIONER Fire, eh? Females again. Spontaneous combustion of lust. Suspected as much. Rubadubdubbing. Incessant, incontinent whining for wine, ululating for Adonis[5] from the rooftops. Heard it all before. And they

5. The cult of Adonis, which had come to Athens relatively recently from the east, was especially favored by women.

do it in the damned parliament! Remember that debate on the Sicilian question? That knucklehead Demostratus rose to propose a naval task force for Sicily. His wife, writhing on the rooftop, stopped him in the middle: "Adonis, oh woe for Adonis." Demostratus, taking his cue from his wife, outshouted her: "A military goddamn draft! Enlist the whole island." She came back at him: "Oh, gnash your teeth and beat your breasts for Adonis." And so, Demostratus—that profane pimple, that son of a boil—rammed his goddamn program through. That's what women are good for: a complete disaster.[6]

MAN I Save your breath for actual crimes, Commissioner. Look what's happened to us. Insolence, insults, insufferable effrontery, and apart from that, they've soaked us. It looks as though we pissed in our tunics.

COMMISSIONER By Poseidon,[7] that liquid deity, you got what you deserved. It's all our own fault. We taught them all they know. We are the forgers of fornication. We sowed in them sexual license and now we reap rebellion. You see a husband go into a jeweler's: "Look," he'll say, "remember the necklace you made for my wife? Well, she was having a bit of a ball last night, dancing around, you know, and the prong slipped out of the hole. I've got to go out of town for a few days. Do me a favor, if you've got time. Slip over to the house tonight and put the prong in the hole for her." Someone else will go to the cobbler's—young, but no apprentice, a strong fellow with a great long tool—and say to him: "One of my wife's new sandals is a bit tight. It pinches her right on the pinkie. Could you drop by about lunch time and give it a stretch?" [*shrugs*] What do you expect? This is what happens. . . . [*indicates doors of Acropolis*] Take my own case. I'm the Commissioner for Public Safety. I've got men to pay. I need the money and look what happens. The women have shut *me* out of the public treasury. [*taking command*] All right, men. On your feet. Take up that log over there. Form a line. Get a move on. You can get drunk later. I'll give you a hand. [*They ram the gates without success. After three tries, as they are stepping back,* LYSISTRATA *opens the door.* CALONIKE *and* MYRRHINE *accompany her*.]

LYSISTRATA Put that thing down! I'm coming out of my own free will. What we want here is not bolts and bars and locks, but common sense.

COMMISSIONER Sense? Common sense? You . . . you . . . you . . . Where's a policeman? Arrest her! Tie her hands behind her back.

LYSISTRATA [*who is carrying wool on a spindle or a knitting needle*] By Artemis, goddess of the hunt, if he touches me, you'll be dropping one man from your payroll. [LYSISTRATA *jabs him*.]

COMMISSIONER What's this? Retreat? Get back in there. Grab her, the two of you.

MYRRHINE [*holding a large chamber pot*] By Artemis, goddess of the dew, if you lay a hand on her, I'll kick the shit out of you.

COMMISSIONER Shit? Disgusting. Arrest her for using obscene language.

CALONIKE [*carrying a lamp*] By Artemis, goddess of light, if you lay a finger on her, you'll need a doctor.

COMMISSIONER Apprehend that woman. Get her, NOW!

6. The Commissioner is referring to a disastrous expedition launched in 415 B.C.E. against Syracuse, on the island of Sicily. Demostratus was one of the proponents of the failed attack.

7. Greek god of the sea.

BOEOTIAN [*from the roof, with a broom*] By Artemis, goddess of witchcraft, if you go near her, I'll break your head open.

COMMISSIONER Good God, what a mess. Athens' finest disgraced! Defeated by a gaggle of girls. Close ranks, men! On your marks, get set, CHARGE!

LYSISTRATA [*holds her hand up and they stop*] Hold it! We've got four battalions of fully equipped infantry women back there.

COMMISSIONER Go inside and disarm them.

LYSISTRATA [*gives a loud whistle and women crowd the bottlenecks and the doorway with brooms, pots and pans, etc.*] Attack! Destroy them, you sifters of flour and beaters of eggs, you pressers of garlic, you dough girls, you bar maids, you market militia. Scratch them and tear them, bite and kick. Fall back, don't strip the enemy—the day is ours. [*The policemen are overpowered.*]

COMMISSIONER [*in tears*] Another glorious military victory for Athens!

LYSISTRATA What did you think we were? There's not an ounce of servility in us. A woman scorned is something to be reckoned with. You underestimated the capacity of freeborn women.

COMMISSIONER Capacity? I sure as hell did. You'd cause a drought in the saloons if they let you in.

MAN I Your honor, there's no use talking to animals. I know you're a civil servant, but don't overdo it.

MAN II Didn't we tell you? They gave us a public bath, fully dressed, without any soap.

WOMAN I What did you expect, sonny? You made the first move—we made the second. Try it again and you'll get another black eye. [*flute*] We are really sweet little stay-at-homes by nature, all sweetness and light, good little virgins, perfect dolls. [*They all rock to and fro coyly.*] But if you stick your finger in a hornet's nest, you're going to get stung.

MEN ALL [*and drums—they beat their feet rhythmically on the ground*]

Oh Zeus, oh Zeus.
Of all the beasts that thou has wrought,
What monster's worse than woman?
Who shall encompass with his thought
Their endless crimes? Let me tell you . . . no man!

They've seized the heights, the rock, the shrine.
But to what end I know not.
There must be *reasons* for the crime [*to audience*]
Do you know why? [*pause*] I thought not.

MAN I Scrutinize those women. *Assess* their re*butt*als.

MAN II 'Twould be culpable negligence not to probe this affair to the bottom.

COMMISSIONER [*as if before a jury*] My first question is this, gentlemen of the . . . What possible motive could you have had in seizing the Treasury?

LYSISTRATA We wanted to keep the money. *No money, no war*.

COMMISSIONER You think that money is the cause of the war?

LYSISTRATA Money is the cause of all our problems. Why did Peisander[8]

8. Athenian politician, often attacked in comedy for corruption. Soon after the first performance of *Lysistrata*, Peisander joined an oligarchic faction that seized power, with widespread violence and confiscations. By 410 B.C.E., democracy was restored.

seize the state? Money. Why the coup? Money. But there will be no more excuses. They'll not get another penny.

COMMISSIONER Then what do you propose to do?

LYSISTRATA Control the Treasury.

COMMISSIONER Control the Treasury?

LYSISTRATA Control the Treasury. National economics and home economics—they're one and the same.

COMMISSIONER No, they're not.

LYSISTRATA Why do you say so?

COMMISSIONER The national economy is for the war effort.

LYSISTRATA Who needs the war effort?

COMMISSIONER How can we protect the city?

LYSISTRATA Leave that to us.

ALL MEN You?

ALL WOMEN Us.

COMMISSIONER God save us.

LYSISTRATA Leave that to us.

COMMISSIONER Subversive nonsense!

LYSISTRATA Why get so upset? There's no stopping us now.

COMMISSIONER It's a downright crime.

LYSISTRATA We *must* save you.

COMMISSIONER [*pouting*] What if I don't want to be saved?

LYSISTRATA All the more reason to.

COMMISSIONER Might I ask where you got these ideas of war and peace?

LYSISTRATA If you'll allow me, I'll tell you.

COMMISSIONER Out with it then, or I'll . . .

LYSISTRATA Relax and put your hands down.

COMMISSIONER I can't help myself. You make me so damned angry.

CALONIKE Watch it.

COMMISSIONER Watch it yourself, you old wind bag.

LYSISTRATA Because of our natural self-restraint, we women have tolerated you men ever since this war began. We tolerated you and kept our thoughts to ourselves. (You never let us utter a peep, anyway.) But that does not mean that we were happy with you. We knew you all too well. Very often, in the evening, at suppertime, we would listen to you talk of some enormously important decision you had made. Deep down inside all we felt was pain, but we would force a smile and ask, "How was the assembly today, dear? Did you get to talk about peace?" And my husband would answer, "None of your business. Shut up!" And I would shut up.

CALONIKE I wouldn't have.

COMMISSIONER I'd have shut your mouth for you.

LYSISTRATA But then we would find out that you had passed a more disgusting resolution, and I would ask you, "Darling, how did you manage to do something so absolutely stupid?" And my husband would glare at me and threaten to slap my face if I did not attend to the distaff side of things. And then he'd always quote Homer: "The men must see to the fighting."

COMMISSIONER Well done. Well done.

LYSISTRATA What do you mean? Not to let us advise against your idiocy was bad enough, but then again we'd actually hear you out in public saying things like, "Who can we draft? There's not a man left in the country."

Someone else would say, "Quite right, not a man left. Pity." And so we women got together and decided to save Greece. There was no time to lose. Therefore, you keep quiet for a change and listen to us. For we have valuable advice to give this country. If you'll listen, we'll put you back on your feet again.

COMMISSIONER You'll do what? I'm not going to put up with this. I'm not going . . .

LYSISTRATA SILENCE!

COMMISSIONER I categorically decline to be silent for a woman. Women wear hats.[9]

LYSISTRATA If that's what is bothering you, try one on and shut up! [*puts one on him*]

CALONIKE Here's a spindle.

MYRRHINE And a basket of wool.

CALONIKE Go on home. There's a sweetheart. Put on your girdle, wind your wool, and mind the beans don't boil over.

LYSISTRATA "THE WOMEN MUST SEE TO THE FIGHTING."

WOMAN I Get ready, girls, to dance and sing, it's time to help our friends.

WOMEN ALL This is a dance that I know well,
My knees shall crack,
Wobble and creak I may, but hell!
I'm ready to attack.
Valor and grace march on ahead,
Love prods us from behind.
Our slogan is "Deny the Bed"
Our purpose: "Save mankind."

WOMAN I Women, remember your mothers and their mothers before them. What thorns they were in the side of the state. Sting them, Sisters, goad them into submission. You're in full sail.

LYSISTRATA [*in solemn prayer*]
O Eros of the sweet breath
O Aphrodite, Cyprian Queen,[1]
Breathe the softness of perfume
Upon our breast and thighs.
Tighten and tauten our husbands till they stand erect.
In all of Greece
We shall be called the Peacemakers.

COMMISSIONER How will you do that?

LYSISTRATA First we shall make the marketplace off limits to all weapon-crazy soldiers in town.

THEBAN WOMAN Aphrodite, be praised! Off the streets—and into the bedrooms.

LYSISTRATA Nowadays there are soldiers in every grocery and pottery shop, clanking around armed to the teeth, like Bacchantes[2] in heat.

COMMISSIONER Of course, of course, of course. A hero is always prepared.

9. Or, rather, a head covering. Respectable women in Athens wore veils in public, visual reminders that they were to be modest, circumspect, and subservient to men.

1. Aphrodite, goddess of love and beauty, sometimes claimed to have been born on or near Cyprus. *Eros*: god of desire and fertility.

2. Female followers of Dionysus.

LYSISTRATA I suppose he is. But it does look stupid buying sardines in a full suit of armor.

CALONIKE I saw a captain in the market the other day, all curls and grease—you know the type. He was drinking pea soup out of his helmet!

MYRRHINE Then there was this huge lunk from Thrace[3] swinging his spear around his head and scaring the woman at the fruit stall. She ran away, she was so scared—and he stole all her figs.

COMMISSIONER Beside the point, beside the point. Things are in a tangle. How can *you* set them straight?

LYSISTRATA Simple.

COMMISSIONER Explain.

LYSISTRATA Do you know anything about weaving? Say the wool gets tangled. We lift it up, like this, and work out the knots by winding it this way and that, up and down, on the spindles. That's how we'll unravel the war. We'll send our envoys this way and that, up and down, all over Greece.

COMMISSIONER Wool? Spindles? Are you out of your mind? War is a serious business.

LYSISTRATA If you had any sense, you'd learn a lesson from women's work.

COMMISSIONER Prove it.

LYSISTRATA The first thing we have to do is give the wool a good wash, get the dirt out of the fleece. We beat out the musk and pick out the hickies. Do the same for the city. Lambast the loafers and discard the dodgers. Then our spoiled wool—that's like your job-hunting sycophants—sack the spongers, decapitate the dabblers. But toss together into the wool basket the good aliens, the allies, the strangers, and begin spinning them into a ball. The colonies are loose threads; pick up the ends and gather them in. Wind them all into one, make a great bobbin of yarn, and weave, without bias or seam, a garment of government fit for the people.

COMMISSIONER It's all very well this weaving and bobbing—when you have absolutely no earthly idea what a war means.

LYSISTRATA You disgusting excuse for a man! The pain of giving birth was only our first pain. You took our boys and sent *them to their deaths in Sicily*.

COMMISSIONER Quiet! I beg you, let that memory lie still.

LYSISTRATA And now, when youth and beauty are still with us and our blood is hot, you take our husbands away, and we sleep alone. That's bad enough for us married women. But I pity the virgins growing old, alone in their beds.

COMMISSIONER Well, men grow old too, you know.

LYSISTRATA But it's not the same. A soldier's discharged, bald as a coot he may be, and . . . zap! he marries a nymphette. But a woman only has one summer, and when that has slipped by, she can spend her days and her years consulting oracles and fortune tellers, but they'll never send her a husband.

COMMISSIONER [*preening himself and offering his service*] But if a man can . . . er . . . rise to the occasion. . . .

LYSISTRATA Rise? Rise? Lie down and die. [*They attack him.*] Go buy a coffin. I'll bake a funeral cake. Here, take this garland. [winds wool around him]

3. A region to the northeast of the Greek peninsula, corresponding to modern day Bulgaria, northeastern Greece, and northwestern Turkey. Thracians were reputed to be fierce warriors.

MYRRHINE [*empties chamber pot*] Accept this token of our grief.

CALONIKE And a final garland for the dead. [*bangs him on the head with the lamp*]

LYSISTRATA What are you waiting for? The boats afloat? Charon's waiting, you're holding up the boat for hell.

COMMISSIONER This is scandalous—maltreatment of a public official—maltreatment of ME! [*departing*] I must show my fellow commissioners what you have done. I'm soaked.

LYSISTRATA We should have given him the last rites. Come back tomorrow, Commissioner, we'll lay you out.

MAN I Arise, ye men of Athens, fight for your freedom. Now. [*They take off their cloaks.*]

MEN ALL There's something rotten in the state of Athens.
An ominous aroma of constitutional rot.
My nose can smell a radical dissenter,
An anarchist, tyrannous, feminist plot.

The Spartans are behind it.
They must have masterminded
This anarchist, tyrannous, feminist plot.

MAN II And *Cleisthenes*,[4] our local queen, *he's* the double agent.

MEN ALL So fight them, stop them, hold them, Brothers.
They're our wives, our sisters, our mothers.
They've sold us out; the streets are teeming with women of all ages.
Shall we stand by and let them confiscate our wages?

MAN I Should *women* tell soldiers what to do? *Women* drilling us about our helmets and shields. *Women*, can you believe it, telling us to trust the nice little Spartans and put our heads in the mouth of the wolf. Tyranny, that's what it is. But not over me! I'll use their own weapon against them. With knife under cloak I'll take my post in the marketplace beside the statues of our national heroes—Harmodius, and Aristogiton,[5] and Me. Striking an epic pose, so, with full approval of the gods above. Pow, here's a punch in the jaw.

WOMAN I Your mommy won't recognize you when you get home. [*They take off their cloaks.*] Okay, girls, take it off, take it all off. Now listen to me, *audience*, and fathom what we say. We women love this country, too. It isn't only you.

WOMEN ALL When I was seven and sweet and young,
I carried flowers for the gods.
At ten years old, I danced and sung,
And then in saffron robes I walked, the bearer of the holy basket.
And then to cap this proud progression
I led the whole procession at Athena's celebration.
A virgin beauty, proud of her nation.

WOMAN II So don't you think I want to do all I can for Athens? I'm giving Athens the best advice she ever had. Don't I pay taxes to the state? Yes, I

4. A contemporary of Aristophanes, frequently ridiculed in his plays as effeminate.

5. Known and memorialized as the Tyrannicides, these two historical figures were considered martyrs for the cause of Athenian democracy.

pay them in baby boys. And what do you contribute, you impotent scum? Absolutely nothing. All our revenue gone, rifled. And not a penny out of your pockets. Well, then? Can you cough up an answer to that? So you're the ones who better watch out or—pow, here's a punch in the jaw.

MEN ALL Their native respect for our manhood is small
And keeps getting smaller. Let's bottle their gall.
The man who won't battle has no balls at all.

Let's loosen our belts and tighten our fists.
We'll show them our manhood and what they have missed.

A century back we soared to the heights
And beat vile tyranny down.[6]
'Tis time again to show our strength
And win us world renown.

MAN I Give them an inch and they'll take a mile. They'll be building ships next and planning new battles.

MAN II Maybe they want to get involved in the cavalry. They like a good ride. Just pop down to the temple, you'll see paintings of Amazons[7] wrestling with all those men.

MAN III So watch it, ladies, or we'll put you in your place—in the stocks.

WOMEN ALL The beast in me is fit for a brawl.
Just rile me a bit and I'll kick down the wall.
You'll bawl to your friends that you've no balls at all.

Let's loosen our belts and give 'em a sniff
Of feminine fury and not just a whiff.

Tangle with me and you'll get cramps.
I'll break your neck, you aging Gramps,
I'll scramble your eggs
And bake your beans.
Between my legs
You'll see such scenes
That never in your life did you think you'd see.
I'm tough—that's me.

WOMAN II If Lampito is on my side and Ismenia, you can go to hell. Pass a law. Pass seven. Make a reputation for yourself, worse than the one you've got now.

WOMAN III I wanted one of those Boeotian eels for a party yesterday. Couldn't get one anywhere. Why? You'd outlawed the eels.

WOMAN II Brilliant.

WOMAN III So watch it, bring your neck over here and I'll break it! [*They chase the men off the stage.*]

Several days have elapsed.

6. The reference here is to the overthrow of the Peisistratid tyranny in 510 B.C.E., and its replacement with democratic institutions.
7. A fresco in the temple of Theseus by the painter Mikon depicted Athenians fighting Amazons, a nation of warrior women believed to live on the southeastern shore of the Black Sea.

WOMAN I [*mock tragic*] Mistress, queen of this our subtle scheme, why does thou come forth thus sorrowful?

LYSISTRATA Oh, wickedness of women! The female mind doth sap my soul and set my feet a-pacing.

WOMAN I What dost thou say? What dost thou say?

LYSISTRATA The truth! The truth!

WOMAN I What woe is this? Declare to us your friends.

LYSISTRATA 'Tis a shame to utter, a pain to keep unsaid.

WOMAN I Conceal not the affliction which is ours.

LYSISTRATA [*breaking the mock tragedy*] Okay! We wanna get laid! That's the long and short of it.

WOMAN I Oh, my god.

LYSISTRATA No, not by God. It's men they want. MEN! I can't keep them away from men. They're all trying to get out of here. I saw one just five minutes ago crawling out through the sewerhole over in Pan's Cave.[8] And there was another one swinging down on a rope and tackle. Last night I saw a woman mount a sparrow, all ready to go off and join a whorehouse, but luckily I grabbed her by the hair. And all the excuses you'd ever want to hear to get out and go home. Here's one now. Hey, you, where do you think you're going?

WOMAN I I'll be right back, I promise you. Just let me give it a good stretch on the bed.

LYSISTRATA No stretching. No bedding. And no going nowhere.

WOMAN I But my wool will be ruined.

LYSISTRATA Tough. Get back in there.

WOMAN II What a shame. What a shame. I'm so *worried* about my flax. I left it at home, poor thing, totally unstripped.

LYSISTRATA She's worried about her flax. Get inside.

WOMAN II But I *will* come back, I swear. I'll just strip it, pluck a few fibers, and be right back.

LYSISTRATA No stripping, no plucking. Get back in there. Once you let one do it, they'll all want to.

WOMAN III O goddess of childbirth, let me not deliver in this sacred precinct.

LYSISTRATA What nonsense is this?

WOMAN III My contractions have started.

LYSISTRATA Contractions? You weren't even pregnant yesterday.

WOMAN III But I am today. Isn't it exciting? Quick, I must go home and get a midwife.

LYSISTRATA What are you talking about? What's this hard lump you've got?

WOMAN III [*coyly*] A little baby boy.

LYSISTRATA This? It's hollow. And sounds like it's made of brass. Come off it. Drop it. It's Athena's helmet. You took it off the statue. Pregnant! You . . .

WOMAN III I am *so* pregnant.

LYSISTRATA Then what's the helmet for?

WOMAN III If my little chickie's born here, in the Acropolis, I'll pop him inside like a little birdie's nest.

8. A cave on the Acropolis containing a shrine to Pan, the goat-footed god of woods, pastures, and wild places.

LYSISTRATA Get out of here. I'll call you when we've given your helmet a name.

WOMAN III But I can't stay in the Acropolis. Last night I dreamed I saw the sacred snake.[9]

WOMAN II And the owls[1] up there! I can't sleep a wink.

LYSISTRATA Stop lying to me. What you want is your men. But don't think *they* don't want you. Their nights are hard, I can tell you. If you can last a little longer, we shall win. The oracle says so.

WOMAN II Oracle, what oracle? Tell us.

LYSISTRATA This is what it says:

When swallows shall the hoopoe[2] shun
And spurn his hot desire,
Zeus will perfect what they've begun
And set the lower higher.

WOMAN I That means we'll have to do it on top of them.

LYSISTRATA But if the swallows shall fall out
And take the hoopoe's bait,
A curse must mark their hour of doubt
And infamy seal their fate.

WOMAN III There's nothing obscure about *that* oracle. Yeech.

LYSISTRATA Come, let's not give in to our desires. Let's go back in. We could never live down the disgrace of betraying the oracle. Come back inside.

CHORUS OF MEN

MEN ALL Now,
I have a little story
That I heard when I was a boy,
How
The huntsman, bold Melanion, was once a harried quarry.
The women in town, tracked him down, and badgered him to marry.
Melanion knew the cornered male eventually cohabits:
Assessing the odds, he took to the woods, and lived by trapping rabbits.
He remained a virgin, long sustained by rabbit meat and hate,
And never returned, but ever remained an absolute celibate.
Melanion is our ideal; his loathing makes us free.
Our constant aim is the gem-like flame of his misogyny.

MAN IV Gimme a kiss, hag face.

WOMAN IV Want an onion in your eye?

MAN IV How about a kick?

WOMAN IV What a thatch! What a jungle.

MEN ALL It's a sign of manhood!

CHORUS OF WOMEN

WOMEN ALL Now,
I will tell you a story
To counter your Melanion,

9. The snake sacred to Athena, believed to live in the foundations of the Erechtheum (a temple on the north side of the Acropolis), which had never been seen.

1. Birds sacred to Athena.

2. A bird known for its erectile crest.

How
Timon,[3] the noted local grump, spent his life in a rage,
A cantankerous hairy lump, the bane of the men of his age.
When random contracts overtaxed him, he didn't stop to pack,
But loaded curses on the male of the species, left town, and never came back.
Timon, you see, was a misanthrope in a properly narrow sense.
His spleen was vented only on *men*; *we* were his dearest friends.

WOMAN V How about a punch in the mouth?

MAN V I'm not afraid of you.

WOMAN V How about a kick?

MAN V She showed me her mantrap.

WOMEN ALL It's a sign of womanhood.

LYSISTRATA Quick, quick. Everyone. Over here!

WOMAN I What's all the fuss about?

LYSISTRATA It's a man, a real man, simply bulging with love. O, Aphrodite, goddess, show us the right road.

WOMAN II Where is he?

LYSISTRATA Over there on the steps.

WOMAN III You're right, you're right. But who is he?

LYSISTRATA Do any of you know him?

MYRRHINE It's my husband, Kinesias.[4]

LYSISTRATA Your duty is clear. Tease him and taunt him. Forbid it and flaunt it. Do everything except the one thing we swore we wouldn't.

MYRRHINE Don't worry, leave him to me.

LYSISTRATA I'll help you get him started. I'll stay here. The rest of you get back in.

KINESIAS Oh God, oh my God, it's agony. Hyperextension! The rack and the rod.

LYSISTRATA Who goes there? Who penetrates our positions?

KINESIAS Me.

LYSISTRATA A man?

KINESIAS Can't you see?

LYSISTRATA Then get right out of here.

KINESIAS Who are you to be throwing me out?

LYSISTRATA The watch guard.

KINESIAS Officer, please, by all the gods, bring Myrrhine out here.

LYSISTRATA Myrrhine? And who, sir, are you?

KINESIAS Name's Kinesias. My friends call me Humper. I'm her husband.

LYSISTRATA Oh, I beg your pardon. Of course. We're glad to see you. I've heard so much about you. Myrrhine, the sweetheart, is always talking about Kinesias. Never nibbles an egg or sucks a fig without saying, "Here's to Kinesias."

KINESIAS Is that the truth?

LYSISTRATA It is. When we're discussing men, she always says, "Compared with Kinesias, the rest have nothing."

KINESIAS BRING HER OUT HERE.

3. A legendary misanthrope; nowhere else is he depicted as a friend to women.

4. Common Greek name; in this play, also a sexual pun on the Greek verb *kinein*, "to move, to arouse."

LYSISTRATA And what do I get out of it?

KINESIAS You see how it is. I'll raise whatever I can. How about *this*?

LYSISTRATA I'll give her a call.

KINESIAS Hurry, hurry. She left our house and happiness went with her. Now I live with pain in an empty home, eating that awful tasteless food. IT'S HARD!

MYRRHINE Oh, I do love him, I'm mad about him. But he doesn't want my love. Please don't make me see him.

KINESIAS Myrrhine, Myrrhine, darling. What do you mean, not love you? Come down here.

MYRRHINE Down there? Certainly not.

KINESIAS It's me, Myrrhine. I'm begging you. Please come down.

MYRRHINE I don't see why you're begging me. You don't need me.

KINESIAS Not need you? I'm at the end of my rope.

MYRRHINE I'm leaving.

KINESIAS No, wait. For the sake of the child. Hey you little . . . call your mother.

BABY Mama, Mama.

KINESIAS Haven't you any feeling? He hasn't been washed and fed for a week.

MYRRHINE Oh, my baby, your father is so cruel to you.

KINESIAS Then come down and get him.

MYRRHINE Oh, all right. Motherhood! I'll have to come. I've got no choice.

KINESIAS She looks younger and prettier. And when she's mad like that and her eyes flash, I just go crazy with desire.

MYRRHINE Sweet babykins, with such a nasty daddy. Give mommy a kiss. Num num num num num.

KINESIAS You should be ashamed of yourself, letting those women lead you around. Why do you do these things? It's bad for both of us.

MYRRHINE Keep your hands off me.

KINESIAS Our house is a disaster.

MYRRHINE I don't care.

KINESIAS But your weaving is in a mess—the loom is full of chickens.

MYRRHINE I don't give a damn.

KINESIAS And the holy rites of Aphrodite? Think how long that's been. Come on, darling, let's go home.

MYRRHINE I absolutely refuse—unless you agree to a truce to end the war.

KINESIAS All right, then. All right, then, we'll stop the war.

MYRRHINE If you do it, I'll do it. For the time being, I've sworn off.

KINESIAS Lie down for just a minute.

MYRRHINE Stop it! No! But that doesn't mean that I don't love you.

KINESIAS I know you do, darling Myrrhine. So LIE DOWN.

MYRRHINE Don't be disgusting. In front of the baby?

KINESIAS Of course not. Take this thing home, nurse. Well, darling, we're rid of the kid. Let's go to bed.

MYRRHINE Where does one do this sort of thing?

KINESIAS Where? Pan's Cave will be perfect.

MYRRHINE But what about my purification after we do it? I need it to get back in.

KINESIAS Sponge off in the pool next door.

MYRRHINE I did swear an oath, you know. Should I perjure myself?

KINESIAS Forget the oath. I'll take the consequences.

MYRRHINE I'll go get us a bed.

KINESIAS No! No bed. The ground's good enough for us.

MYRRHINE *You*, on the dirty ground? Darling, I'd never let you.

KINESIAS Oh, she loves me, she really must love me.

MYRRHINE Here's the bed. Now get into bed while I undress. Oh dear! There's no mattress.

KINESIAS I don't want a mattress.

MYRRHINE You can't sleep without a mattress.

KINESIAS Give me a kiss, then.

MYRRHINE [*bites his neck*] There.

KINESIAS Ow! Come back quick. Hurry.

MYRRHINE Here's the mattress. Now, into bed while I undress. Wait a minute. I forgot the pillow.

KINESIAS I don't want a pillow!

MYRRHINE I know, but *I* do.

KINESIAS I'll burst, God knows, I'll burst.

MYRRHINE There we are. Ups-a-daisy.

KINESIAS So we are, so we are. Come here, my little jewel box.

MYRRHINE Just taking off my girdle. Don't break your promise: no cheating about the peace.

KINESIAS I swear to God. I'll die first.

MYRRHINE Just look, there isn't a sheet.

KINESIAS I don't want a sheet. I want to get laid.

MYRRHINE You'll get what you want. I'll be right back.

KINESIAS The woman will kill me with her pillows and sheets.

MYRRHINE Here we are. Get up.

KINESIAS Up? I've been up for weeks.

MYRRHINE Would you like a dash of perfume?

KINESIAS No, I damn well would not.

MYRRHINE Well, you're damn well going to get some anyway.

KINESIAS Dear Zeus, Lord, I don't ask for much. But please make her spill the bottle.

MYRRHINE Hold out your hand like a good boy. Rub it right in.

KINESIAS Damn it, it smells terrible. It's turning me off, not on.

MYRRHINE Silly me. I brought the wrong bottle. This is the Rhodian brand.[5]

KINESIAS It's fine, it's lovely, leave it alone.

MYRRHINE No trouble at all! Now, don't go away.

KINESIAS Goddamn the man who invented perfume.

MYRRHINE Here, try this bottle.

KINESIAS No, you try mine. Come to bed, you witch. . . . And don't bring me anything else.

MYRRHINE That's the last thing you're getting. Let me just take my shoes off. Incidentally, you will remember to vote for the truce.

KINESIAS I'll think it over! [MYRRHINE *runs away*.] God in heaven, she's gone. She's left me standing, stiff as a board. [*mock tragedy, to his phallus*] We're left alone, abandoned by the most beautiful woman in the world! There's

5. From the Aegean island of Rhodes.

the rub. To a nunnery, come? [*breaking the mock tragedy*] I know a marvelous little brothel down the street. . . .

CHORUS OF OLD MEN

MEN ALL [*mock tragedy*]
Alas for the woes of man, alas.
She hath brought you to a pretty pass.
Split, heart. Proud spirit, crack,
Sag, flesh, and cock, go slack.

MAN VI Your morning lay.

MAN VII Has gone astray.

KINESIAS O Zeus, reduce the throbs, the throes.

MAN I Friend, 'twas she that brought you to this state,
That hag, that bag, that reprobate.

KINESIAS [*departing*] No, curse not my light of love, my dove, my sweet.

MEN ALL Sweet? Oh blessed Zeus who rul'st the sky,
Snatch these women up on high,
Spin them all into one great ball
And then from the heavens let them fall.
Down they'll come, the pretty dears,
And split themselves on our thick spears.

[*enter* SPARTAN *HERALD*]

SPARTAN Excuse me, could you direct me to the Central Committee? I have something to show them.

COMMISSIONER Are you a man or a fertility symbol?

SPARTAN I refuse to answer that question. I, sir, am an official herald from Sparta, and I have come to talk about an armistice.

COMMISSIONER Then, why are you carrying that spear under your cloak?

SPARTAN That, sir, is not a spear.

COMMISSIONER Then take the cucumber out of your pocket.

SPARTAN You, sir, are out of your mind.

COMMISSIONER You have a hernia, maybe?

SPARTAN I have business to attend to.

COMMISSIONER Well, something's up, I can see that. And I don't like it.

SPARTAN Sir, I resent this.

COMMISSIONER I see that. But what *is* it?

SPARTAN It's a rod of office. I told you I am an official herald from Sparta.

COMMISSIONER That's some rod of office. But tell me, how are things in Sparta?

SPARTAN Hard, sir, hard. We're at a standstill. Can't seem to think of anything but women.

COMMISSIONER That certainly is a coincidence. Tell me, who do you think is behind this? Has Pan put a jinx on you?

SPARTAN Pan? Good God, no. . . . It's Lampito and her little nudie girl friends. They won't let anyone near them.

COMMISSIONER How are you handling it?

SPARTAN We're going out of our minds, if you want to know the truth. Everyone's walking around hunched over like this, like men carrying candles in a gale. The women have sworn that they will have nothing to do with us until we make a treaty.

COMMISSIONER I know. There's a general uprising all over Greece. But go back to Sparta, see that they send an armistice delegation. I'll work on things on this end. I can safely say that I too am a man of good standing. They'll listen to me.

SPARTAN You're a man after my own heart, sir. I thank you.

MAN I The female of the species is deadlier than the male. An animal is all she is, a creature without shame.

WOMAN I Then why do you fight us? Why do you attack? We might have been your partners, and worked behind your back.

MAN II I'll never stop hating you.

WOMAN II As you wish, but please get dressed. You look so stupid. Come on, get into your cloak. [*Women all dress their counterparts.*]

MAN III Thank you. I must admit I stripped it off in anger.

WOMAN III That's better. Now you look like a man again. Why have you been so unpleasant?

WOMAN IV Look, there's an insect in your eye. Shall I take it out?

MAN IV So that's what it was, a damn mosquito. Yes, please take it out.

WOMAN V I will, but please learn to behave, and you must treat us better.

WOMAN VI Good God, what a size! A veritable monster. A dragonfly.

MAN VI Oh, what a relief, your kindness pleases. But now you've unplugged me, here come the tears.

WOMAN VI I'll dry your tears, though I can't say why. You've behaved so badly.

WOMEN ALL And now, one little kiss!

MEN ALL No you don't.

WOMEN ALL Yes we will.

MEN ALL Just one. [*they kiss*]

MAN I How you get around us! There never was a truer saying!

MEN ALL Impossible to live with you; impossible without.

WOMAN I Then let us sign a mutual treaty. And never again will we raise a voice or hand in anger. Let's make a single chorus and celebrate our joy.

JOINT CHORUS ALL

Let it never be said
That my tongue is malicious.
Both by word and by deed
We shall be noble and gracious.

MAN I There's misery enough.

WOMAN I There's misery enough.

CHORUS ALL [*to audience*]

Is there anyone here who would like a small loan?
My purse is crammed—as you'll soon find –
And you needn't pay me back till peace gets signed.

We've organized a dinner for some playboys from Carystos.[6]
A lovely soup, a piglet roasted brown,
And then for all of you, some wine to wash it down.

MAN I You're all coming, I hope.

WOMAN I Bring the children.

6. A small town on the Aegean island of Euboea, north of Athens; an ally of Athens.

CHORUS ALL
But take a bath and then come over.
Walk right up, as if you owned the place.
I'm sure you'll never grudge it, if
you find you cannot budge it, if
the door is BOLTED IN YOUR FACE.

MAN I Look at this lot! It's the commissioners from Sparta. Look at the way they're walking. Gentlemen, welcome to Athens. How is life in Sparta?

SPARTAN I Do we have to tell you? Can't you see what a state we're in?

MAN II Well, I'll be damned, a disaster area.

SPARTAN II It's beyond belief. But come, gentlemen, call in your commissioners and let's talk about peace.

MAN III It's the same here at Athens. None of the men can bear to wear anything below the waist. It's a kind of pelvic paralysis. [*Enter* COMMISSIONER *and* KINESIAS.]

COMMISSIONER Somebody call Lysistrata. It looks like we're all in the same state.

SPARTAN I It's a dreadful situation. Do you feel a certain strain in the morning? What do you do about it?

KINESIAS I do, sir, and I take whatever is handy. But a few more days and Cleisthenes had better watch himself.

COMMISSIONER Could I give you a bit of advice? Try and hide your condition. You know what they did to those statues of Hermes.[7] Once bitten, twice shy.

SPARTANS I AND II [*covering their phalluses*] Thank you very much!

KINESIAS Anyway, welcome, gentlemen—despite the seriousness of the situation.

SPARTAN I It could be worse. If those Hermes choppers had seen us, they might have taken us down a peg or two.

COMMISSIONER Let's get down to details. Men of Sparta, what is your proposal?

SPARTAN II We propose to consider peace.

COMMISSIONER Excellent. That is also our intention. Call Lysistrata. There will be no peace without her.

SPARTAN I Call Lysis—anybody, only hurry.

KINESIAS There's no need to call. Here she is. She must have heard us talking.

MAN I Hail, Lysistrata, most virile of women. Now in your hour of greatness you must be terrible in your might.

MAN II Be tender.

MAN III Be lofty.

MAN IV Be lowbrow.

MAN V Be severe.

MAN VI Be demure.

WOMAN I You hold the leading statesmen of this land
In the palm of your beautiful hand.
We entrust to you our common fate. It is yours
to decide the future of Greece.

7. A reference to an act of vandalism by unknown individuals who, just before the great expedition was to leave for Sicily (in 415 B.C.E.), broke the erect phalluses off statues of Hermes. These representations of the messenger god, the patron of travelers, stood outside houses and public buildings throughout the city.

LYSISTRATA That will not be difficult (unless you start taking each other to bed—but I'd soon find out about that). Where's Reconciliation? [RECONCILIATION—*a scantily clad woman—enters.*] No, dear, not like our husbands—be a gentlewoman. If they refuse their hands, take 'em by the handle. Now do the same for the Athenians. Take anything they've got to offer. Stand there, please. And you over here. Now all of you listen to me. I am only a woman, I know. But I've a mind—and not a bad one. I was born with it. And I listened to my father and my elders. My education was not entirely worthless. Well, now that I've got you here, I intend to give you hell. At festivals, in Pan-Hellenic harmony, like true blood brothers, you share the self-same basin of holy water. You share altars all over Greece—Thermopylae, Olympia, Delphi.[8] But now when Persia sits by and waits, you men go raiding through the country from both sides. Greek killing Greek. That is my first point.

ATHENIAN Let me get at you, you lovely thing, you.

LYSISTRATA Men of Sparta, I direct these remarks to you. Have you forgotten that Pericleides came from your country once to ask our help? I can see him now, his grey face, his somber gown. Messene was up in arms against you. You needed an army. And Kimon took out four thousand troops from Athens—an army which saved the state of Sparta.[9] Yet every spring now, you come and decimate our crops.

ATHENIAN The Spartans are clearly in the wrong.

SPARTAN I We were wrong, but that's the prettiest behind I ever saw.

LYSISTRATA And you, Athenians, do you think I've nothing to say to you? Have you forgotten how the Spartans saved us in our hour of need? Their army destroyed the Thessalians and Hippias and his friends.[1] That was Sparta and only Sparta that saved Athens from slavery.

SPARTAN I What a figure of speech!

ATHENIAN What a conjunction!

LYSISTRATA Then why are we fighting? After all this mutual assistance in the past?

SPARTAN I We are ready, madam. First, that place you have in the rear.

LYSISTRATA What place?

SPARTAN I I mean the region of Pylos, ma'am.

COMMISSIONER Not a chance, by God.

LYSISTRATA Give it to them.

COMMISSIONER But what shall we have to bargain with?

LYSISTRATA Ask for something else in exchange.

8. Sites revered by all Greeks. Thermopylae, in central Greece, was the site of the Spartans' heroic stand against the Persians in 480 B.C.E.; Olympia, on the Peloponnesian Peninsula, was the site of the quadrennially-held Olympic Games; Delphi, in central Greece, was the site of the most important oracle of Apollo.

9. Kimon, an Athenian general and statesman, sent aid to Sparta in 464 B.C.E. after a devastating earthquake was followed by a rebellion of Spartan serfs. (Lysistrata fails to add that the Spartans abruptly sent the Athenians away, an affront to Athenian pride that resulted in Kimon's exile.)

1. The Spartans came to the aid of Athenian democrats and expelled the tyrant Hippias in 510 B.C.E. (Again, Lysistrata leaves out the acrimonious end of the story—the Spartans later attempt to overthrow the democracy.) *Thessalians:* from Thessaly, in northern Greece.

COMMISSIONER All right. [*using* RECONCILIATION *as a map*] We'll give you Pylos in the rear, if you give us . . . the twin peaks . . . the Corinthian Delta . . . and the Legs of Megara.

SPARTAN I My government objects.

LYSISTRATA Overruled. What's a pair of legs?

KINESIAS I feel an urgent desire to plow a few furrows.

SPARTAN II A little fertilizer first, before I sow my seed.

LYSISTRATA The country life is yours once you've made peace. If you are serious, consult your respective leaders and your allies.

ATHENIAN What do you mean, allies? We have here a mutual problem of postponed copulation. WE ARE WASTING TIME.

SPARTAN I My government agrees. [*general rejoicing*]

LYSISTRATA Then attend to your purification and we, the women, will entertain you in the citadel and treat you to all the delights of a home-cooked banquet. You'll exchange your oaths and pledge your faith, and every man will take his wife and depart for home. [*she exits*]

KINESIAS Let's get it over with.

SPARTAN I Lead the way.

KINESIAS Come on, let's go, hurry. [*All exit.*]

CHORUS OF WOMEN

WOMEN ALL [*during song they throw nuts to the audience*]

I'm so happy at the way things went.
I'm feeling quite lightheaded.
I'll hand to you whatever you want,
Whatever you want, whatever you want.
Embroidery fine and ornaments bright,
Delight of young girls in the prime of their life.
Come over to my house and sample my wine.
It's there for the taking; the drinking is free,
Yes, come over to my house
(But you'll find nothing there),
Bring all of the family, all your kids and your aunts,
I'll feed you and stuff you and go the whole hog,
But don't come too close, we've got a big savage dog.

CHORUS OF MEN

MAN I Come on, let me in.

COMMISSIONER [*opens the door; he is holding a torch*] Move along there now. Get a move on. I'd burn your ass for you if it wasn't such an old joke. But I refuse to do it. [*looks at audience*] All right, if that's what you want. . . .

MEN ALL We shall not be moved.

COMMISSIONER Get away from here. The gentlemen from Sparta are just coming back from dinner.

SPARTAN II I must say, I've never seen such a spread.

COMMISSIONER Those Spartans were absolutely marvelous. And why not? A sober man is a fool. Men of Athens, mark my words, the only good ambassador is a drunken ambassador. When in Sparta we're sober—they make speeches, we shut our ears. It's useless. But today we made music together. It was harmony and peace in there. [*sees the chorus*] Get out of here.

SPARTAN 1 I beg you, madam, would you play for us upon your flute? We would like to sing a song in honor of Athens. [MEN'S CHORUS *remove their masks and join him.*]

MEN ALL Memory . . . Send me . . . Your Muse . . . Who Knows . . . Our glory . . . Knows Athens . . . Tell the story . . . At Artemisium . . . Like gods they stampeded . . . the hulks of the Medes . . . And Leonidas[2] . . . leading us . . . and flowed . . . down our cheeks . . . to our knees below . . . The Persians there . . . like the sands of the sea . . . Hither, huntress . . . virgin, goddess . . . tracker, slayer . . . to our truce! . . . Hold us ever . . . fast together . . . bring our pledges . . . love and increase . . . wean us from the fox's wiles . . . Hither, huntress . . . Virgin, hither . . .

LYSISTRATA Now all is well, all is well. Spartans, take your wives. Athenians, take your wives. Live in union, in conjugal bliss. May we never again make wars in the world.

DOUBLE CHORUS
Start the chorus dancing,
Summon all the graces,
Artemis, dance, dance Phoebus, Lord of Dancing, dance.
Call on Bacchus, whirl the Thyrsus, dance Lady Hera,[3] dance.
Call the flashing fiery Zeus,
Call the gods, call all the gods,
Dance for the dearest bringer of peace, glorious Aphrodite.

Ai Ai Ai Ai
Leap for victory.

Ai Ai Ai Ai
Hail Hail Hail.

LYSISTRATA Spartan, sing for us again.
SPARTAN 1 From Taygetos, from Taygetos,
Spartan muse, come down,
Sing to the lord Apollo
Who rules Amyklai Town.[4]
Dance for Leda's twins, dance for Helen of Troy,[5]
Dance for the girls and the joy of the whirls of their curls
And the joy of their feet as they prance.
Leap like a deer and sing; Glory Athena, glory Athena, glory Athena,
Peace, peace, peace, peace, peace.

2. Spartan king and general who led the small band against the Persians (the Medes) at Thermopylae in 480 B.C.E.; at the same time, an indecisive naval battle took place nearby at Cape Artemisium.
3. Goddess of marriage and childbirth, wife of Zeus.
4. Site south of Sparta, and a major shrine to Apollo.
5. Leda, mythological queen of Sparta and mother of Castor and Pollux (the twins) and Helen of Troy, whose abduction by Paris brought about the Trojan War.

EURIPIDES

ca. 480–406 B.C.E.

THE last of the three important Greek tragedians, Euripides was also the most daring innovator of the classical stage. His startling and powerful plays quickly made him one of the most successful playwrights of Athens, a rival to the older and more established Aeschylus and SOPHOCLES, and after his death, his fame continued to grow. Euripides managed to push the drama he had inherited to new extremes and to inaugurate a new form of tragedy, one attuned to a growing skepticism toward inherited truths. Although still based on mythic figures and events, Euripides' tragedies treat gods and heroes with suspicion, making them more human, exposing their frailties, and bringing them closer to everyday reality. Euripides' skepticism spoke not only to contemporaries but to later audiences. While some commentators, particularly in the nineteenth and twentieth centuries, celebrated Euripides as the great modernizer of tragedy, others blamed him for its demise—most famously the nineteenth-century philosopher Friedrich Nietzsche, who accused Euripides of having killed tragedy. But no matter whether one wishes to praise Euripides as innovator or fault him for excessive irreverence, there can be no doubt that he changed the course of drama, leaving an imprint on the form of tragedy that can be felt even today.

Although born into a wealthy family, Euripides did not participate in public life. He began to write tragedies when he was eighteen, but did not win first prize at the Dionysia until he was around forty years old. Even though his tragedies found a following in Athens, they also made him enemies, who objected to his irreverent depiction of the gods. Probably because of the growing influence of these enemies, at an advanced age Euripides emigrated to Macedonia at the invitation of its king, Archelaus, and died there one year later. He won only four prizes at Athens during his lifetime, but the posthumous performance of his last play, *THE BACCHAE*, gained him a fifth; and soon his popularity was to surpass that of all other Greek tragedians.

Euripides' popularity was due to a number of innovations. The most important is that his tragedies are much more realistic than those of his predecessors, both in their depiction of character and in their language. Expanding on the changes introduced by Sophocles, his older contemporary, Euripides further reduced the importance of the chorus, placing more emphasis on dramatic interaction and confrontation. Doing so enabled him to make his plots more complicated and his characterization more nuanced. In part to bring his complex plots to a final conclusion, Euripides often relied on the *deus ex machina* (literally, "god from a machine"), the conventional recourse to a god brought onto the stage by means of a crane at the end of the play to intervene in hopeless situations, to resolve dilemmas, and to deal out punishment. Shortly after Euripides' death, ARISTOPHANES' comedy *The Frogs* (405 B.C.E.) shows Euripides in competition with the first master of tragedy, Aeschylus. Even though Aeschylus finally wins, because his language and topics are weightier than those of Euripides, Aristophanes acknowledges Euripides' greater skill in developing plots and his more realistic approach.

Through a series of historical accidents, Euripides' is the largest existing corpus of plays of any Greek playwright. A number of his plays, like other Greek tragedies, survived through acting copies, which in turn became the basis for the collection of Greek tragedy at the Library of Alexandria during the second century B.C.E. But we are fortunate to have as well a portion of what may have been Euripides' collected works in alphabetical order: plays beginning with the Greek letters epsilon, eta, iota, or kappa.

Even a cursory look at Euripides' plays shows both the variety of his styles and his most typical techniques. His version of *Electra,* for example, was conceived in direct competition with Aeschylus's treatment and probably also with Sophocles'. Of the three, Euripides' *Orestes* is the least heroic by far and most prone to hesitation and doubt. All the characters are drawn more realistically; they are more rooted in common, everyday reality, even though the play is still set in the mythical past. Euripides' *Helen* follows the same pattern. Based on a common variant of the myth, according to which Helen resided in Egypt during the Trojan War while her double—created by the gods—caused all the trouble in Troy, Euripides' *Helen* depicts the secret arrival of Menelaus in Egypt, clad in rags and unimpressive in many other ways as well. Another innovation is also visible in this play: it ends not tragically but with the happy escape of Menelaus and Helen. Tragedy here becomes romance.

Euripides made tragedy more realistic, more concerned with individual character, and more flexible in its endings. But this approach did not render his tragedies less stark or brutal. On the contrary, he created some of the most extreme situations and events ever depicted on the Greek stage. He became notorious for treatments of sensational subject matter—such as the doomed passion of a woman for her stepson (in *Hippolytus*), or the murder of two children by their own mother in a desperate act of revenge on their father (in *Medea*)—that often culminated in lurid violence. Euripides was never one to compromise, and he constantly sought to find new avenues to take and new areas to explore even if they seemed to go against custom and common decency.

The play that is without question his masterpiece, that indeed is one of the most powerful plays ever written, perfectly exemplifies all those traits: *The Bacchae*. It ends abruptly with a *deus ex machina,* Dionysus, who is hauled onto the stage by means of a crane to punish most of the characters still alive. The play culminates with the dismemberment of Pentheus by his temporarily deluded mother—an extreme turn of events even by Euripides' standards. Euripides wrote this play in exile and never saw it performed. In fact, he may not have meant it for immediate performance, although it exploited the existing possibilities of the Greek stage with ingenuity. In any case, it proved to be an immediate success when his son, also a playwright, staged it, together with *Iphigenia at Aulis* and the now lost *Alcmeon in Corinth,* in Athens.

Even though the concluding violence in *The Bacchae* is shocking, the play is also much more reflective, argumentative, and intellectual than the tragedies of previous playwrights. It is based on an opposition not only between two figures, Dionysus and Pentheus, but also between two philosophical positions, two conceptions of religion, and two views of political organization. Dionysus approaches the city from Asia as a figure whose natural habitat is the mountains, not the Greek city; Pentheus, in turn, wants to guard the Greek city or polis, the bastion of Greek civilization and political organization, and therefore attempts to keep this outsider and his cult from gaining a foothold in

Two bacchae tear Pentheus apart in this detail from a Greek vase-painting.

Thebes. Pentheus sees the foreign, rural cult of Dionysus as a threat to the urban order he has sworn to uphold, while Dionysus demands that his cult be established in the city alongside the existing ones. Pentheus thinks of himself as masculine and of Dionysus as effeminate, of his own clothes as proper and of Dionysus' garb as improper. In basing his play on a single opposition, Euripides was probably influenced by a new cast of traveling intellectuals, called sophists, who taught rhetoric and argument to enable citizens to represent themselves more effectively in court (Plato would soon criticize these early philosophers as being interested only in rhetorical prowess and not in truth, causing the term *sophist* to acquire the pejorative meaning it retains today). These philosophers left their mark on the language of Euripides, whose arguments are often constructed around reversals, subtle distinctions, and counterintuitive conclusions.

Although *The Bacchae* is in many ways typical of Euripides' style, it is also a unique play, a late work in which the playwright looks back over his long dramatic career, reflecting on his style and choices—and perhaps offering a response to contemporaries who criticized his portraits of gods and heroes as lacking in proper respect. While his previous plays were notorious in this regard, *The Bacchae* turns irreverence itself into the predominant theme: Pentheus, king of Thebes, refuses to recognize Dionysus as a god and Dionysus therefore seeks to prove his divinity. The entire play is devoted to furnishing this proof; and once Dionysus is revealed as a god at the end, Pentheus and the entire city of Thebes are punished for their doubt.

One reason for the extraordinary power of this play is Euripides' use of theatrical techniques, particularly masks and disguises. Greek actors had always worn masks and costumes, but Euripides turned these props into central dramatic elements. Dionysus is the main protagonist throughout the play, but he appears always disguised in various costumes, shapes, and forms. For Euripides, Dionysus becomes an ever-changing character who is impossible to pin down. The play uses many pseudonyms to refer to the god, who thus remains, until the end, incognito.

The different names serve to conceal the true identity of Dionysus, for the secrets of his cult must be carefully guarded. The Dionysus cult is a cult of initiates, and the chorus of followers refuse to divulge any of its secrets to Pentheus, who is eager to find out its true nature but is always thwarted. The play carefully leaves open several options. Though Pentheus believes that Dionysus drives the groups of reveling women into a sexual frenzy, the messengers sent to spy on them witness no sexual acts, and instead tell of natural miracles and a life led in a strange harmony with nature. Euripides here makes good use of another convention of Greek tragedy: rather than showing these events directly to the audience, he evokes them before the audience through messengers and reporters—through language, not performance. In this way, the play keeps the audience in the same position as Pentheus, guessing what really goes on in the secret rituals devoted to the god. The task of guarding the secrets of the Dionysus cult had to be respected even by Euripides. According to some sources, however, Euripides may have gotten into trouble with members of the Dionysus cult, who felt that despite his precautions he had revealed too much about the most secretive of Greek rituals.

Whether Euripides successfully hid the secrets from his original audience or inadvertently revealed some of them, these mysterious rituals are more or less shielded from the eyes of the audience. The traces of the Dionysian ritual that we can discern from the play are evoked by signs and shapes, such as the special costumes worn by Dionysus's followers or their distinctive staffs, and not by language or action. Costuming and dress thus play a central role in *The Bacchae,* from the very beginning of the play—which presents two revered older men, Cadmus and Tiresias, dressed in the distinctive feminine garments of the Dionysus cult, on their way to the mountains to participate in the rituals—to its conclusion, in which Pentheus himself dons the despised woman's attire to spy on the Bacchae in order to finally discover what they do.

This detail from a Greek amphora (two-handled jar) shows two devotees of Dionysus presenting him with an animal offering.

Because of its attention to external shapes, appearances, masks, disguises, and props, *The Bacchae* is also a play about the theater itself. Chiefly, it is a play about seeing and being seen. The bloody climax of the play, when Pentheus is torn to pieces by the Bacchae, is brought about by his desire to watch the revelers engage in their secret ritual. His desire to see is simply too strong; he is even ready to don the Bacchic dress for the purpose. Watching is precisely the primary activity of the theater audience—the Greek word for theater, *theatron*, identifies it as a place for seeing. Thus, every time the play's action turns on costumes, disguises, acting, and watching, the audience is invited to think about the theater, and about itself.

The Bacchae also signals that it is not only a tragedy but also a tragedy about tragedy through its devotion to Dionysus, the god of theater. Greek tragedy first emerged as part of the Dionysus ritual, and all Greek tragedies were performed as part of the City Dionysia, a festival devoted to Dionysus. The central question of the play, whether Dionysus will be given his due, is therefore also the question of whether theater will be given its due. *The Bacchae* in addition concerns the origin of the theater more specifically, as it explores the relation between theater and ritual, in particular ritual sacrifice. The word *tragedy* comes from the Greek *tragoidia*, which means "goat song," presumably to accompany animal sacrifice, the killing of a goat or a scapegoat. Ritual sacrifice is precisely what happens in *The Bacchae*: Pentheus is ritually ripped to pieces by the Bacchae, including his mother, who are acting under the delusion that they are killing an animal. To be sure, ritual sacrifice is a punishment for Pentheus's misdeeds, but it also serves as a reminder of theater's dark origins. In this sense, too, *The Bacchae* is a characteristic late work, an occasion for the aging playwright to present a searching examination of his chosen art form, the theater.

At the same time that *The Bacchae* reaches far back into the history and prehistory of tragedy, it is also responding to the cultural changes of contemporary Athens. Over the course of the fifth century, Athens had experienced an unprecedented rise in power, developing from a minor city-state to a sea-based empire dominating the Aegean and stretching east into Asia Minor and west to Sicily. Imperialism turned Athens into one of the most international of cities, with citizens of dependent or allied states living alongside Greeks. This new diversity undoubtedly contributed to the intellectual brilliance of the city—many of the philosophers, for example, were not originally from Athens—but it also forced traditional Greek culture to adapt to new customs and ways of life. This change forms the cultural background for *The Bacchae,* which presents the Dionysus cult as a specifically Asian and foreign cult whose acceptance in the Greek city of Thebes is anything but an easy matter.

In addition to being foreign, Dionysus worship was rural. Pentheus is suspicious of the cult because it incites the women of Thebes to leave the ordered space of the city, which is under his firm control, and to revel instead in the mountains over which he has no dominion. Finally, the Dionysus cult was also a cult that appealed to the lower orders of Greece, not the elite. This division, too, is part of the texture of the play, which pits Pentheus against an unruly mass, represented by the chorus. The chorus of Greek tragedy had always, implicitly and explicitly, represented the people against the individual ruler, and in *The Bacchae,* Euripides uses this convention to great effect and to present a warning: if the ruler disregards the many, they will tear him to shreds. Like many other plays set in the rival city of Thebes, *The Bacchae* also served to gratify the democratic audience of Athens, which had long accepted the Dionysus cult and had made it part of the city's civic and religious life. Euripides essentially congratulates Athens for having been more open-minded than Pentheus's Thebes.

The unusual construction of *The Bacchae,* simultaneously archaic and modern, philosophical and ritualistic, political and religious, has intrigued audiences from its first performance on. The play underwent a remarkable revival in the twentieth century, when playwrights and scholars developed a new interest in the ritualistic origins of theater. In recent decades, many leading playwrights and directors have produced versions of the *The Bacchae,* including the Nigerian Nobel Prize winner WOLE SOYINKA, whose adaptation (1973) emphasizes the multicultural dimension of the play, and the American playwright Charles L. Mee. Among contemporary U.S. directors who have tackled the play is Richard Schechner, whose production, *Dionysus in 69* (1968), was a central event for experimental theater in the 1960s. In 1978 the Japanese director Tadashi Suzuki created a compelling adaptation, mixing Japanese acting traditions with Western techniques.

These varied interpreters were drawn to Euripides because he had turned Greek tragedy into a form that reflected the political and cultural conflicts of his age. By bringing these conflicts to the fore, Euripides created plays that could be more easily adapted to new and different conflicts. Indeed, often no adaptation was necessary. The central conflicts depicted in his plays—attitudes toward the gods, responses to foreign influences, relations between the sexes—are as pressing and pertinent today as they were in the fifth century B.C.E. His contemporaries saw Euripides as modern, innovative, and daring, and he has remained so ever since. M.P.

The Bacchae[1]

CHARACTERS

DIONYSUS (also called Bromius, Evius, and Bacchus)
CHORUS of Asian Bacchae (followers of DIONYSUS)
TEIRESIAS
CADMUS
PENTHEUS
ATTENDANT
FIRST MESSENGER
SECOND MESSENGER
AGAVE
CORYPHAEUS (chorus leader)

[SCENE: *Before the royal palace at Thebes. On the left is the way to Cithaeron; on the right, to the city. In the center of the orchestra stands, still smoking, the vine-covered tomb of Semele, mother of Dionysus.*[2]

Enter DIONYSUS. *He is of soft, even effeminate, appearance. His face is beardless; he is dressed in a fawn-skin and carries a thyrsus (i.e., a stalk of fennel tipped with ivy leaves). On his head he wears a wreath of ivy, and his long blond curls ripple down over his shoulders. Throughout the play he wears a smiling mask.*]

DIONYSUS I am Dionysus, the son of Zeus,
come back to Thebes, this land where I was born.
My mother was Cadmus' daughter, Semele by name,

1. Translated by William Arrowsmith.
2. Greek god of wine and fertility, patron of agriculture and theater. *Cithaeron:* a mountain sacred to Dionysus, between Thebes (to the north) and Athens (to the southeast).

midwived by fire, delivered by the lightning's
blast.[3]
And here I stand, a god incognito,
disguised as man, beside the stream of Dirce[4]
and the waters of Ismenus. There before the palace
I see my lightning-married mother's grave,
and there upon the ruins of her shattered house
the living fire of Zeus still smolders on
in deathless witness of Hera's violence and rage
against my mother. But Cadmus wins my praise:
he has made this tomb a shrine, sacred to my mother.
It was I who screened her grave with the green
of the clustering vine.
Far behind me lie
those golden-rivered lands, Lydia and Phrygia,[5]
where my journeying began. Overland I went,
across the steppes of Persia where the sun strikes hotly
down, through Bactrian fastness and the grim waste
of Media.[6] Thence to rich Arabia I came;
and so, along all Asia's swarming littoral
of towered cities where Greeks and foreign nations,
mingling, live, my progress made. There
I taught my dances to the feet of living men,
establishing my mysteries and rites
that I might be revealed on earth for what I am:
a god.
And thence to Thebes.
This city, first
in Hellas,[7] now shrills and echoes to my women's cries,
their ecstasy of joy. Here in Thebes
I bound the fawn-skin to the women's flesh and armed
their hands with shafts of ivy.[8] For I have come
to refute that slander spoken by my mother's sisters—
those who least had right to slander her.
They said that Dionysus was no son of Zeus,
but Semele had slept beside a man in love
and fathered off her shame on Zeus—a fraud, they sneered,
contrived by Cadmus to protect his daughter's name.
They said she lied, and Zeus in anger at that lie
blasted her with lightning.

3. After Semele had been impregnated by Zeus, the king of the gods, the jealous Hera (his wife and sister) tricked her into asking Zeus to come to her as a god. His thunderbolts killed her, but he saved Dionysus (see lines 101–12). *Cadmus:* founder of Thebes.

4. Wife of Lycus, king of Thebes, and a devotee of Dionysus; she turned into a spring that feeds Thebes' river, the Ismenus.

5. Areas in Asia Minor (present-day Anatolia in Turkey). From the earliest times, Dionysus was viewed by the Greeks as a foreigner from the East.

6. A country of south Asia, corresponding to much of modern Iran and Iraq. *Bactrian fastness:* a remote, mountainous region of present-day Afghanistan.

7. Greece.

8. The thyrsi (staffs made of fennel stalks, tipped with pinecones and wound with ivy and grape vines) that, together with deerskin clothes, distinguished the members of the Dionysus cult.

Because of that offense
I have stung them with frenzy, hounded them from home
up to the mountains where they wander, crazed of mind,
and compelled to wear my orgies' livery.
Every woman in Thebes—but the women only—
I drove from home, mad. There they sit,
rich and poor alike, even the daughters of Cadmus,
beneath the silver firs on the roofless rocks.
Like it or not, this city must learn its lesson:
it lacks initiation in my mysteries;
that I shall vindicate my mother Semele
and stand revealed to mortal eyes as the god
she bore to Zeus.
Cadmus the king has abdicated,
leaving his throne and power to his grandson Pentheus;
who now revolts against divinity, in *me*;
thrusts *me* from his offerings; forgets *my* name
in his prayers. Therefore I shall *prove* to him
and every man in Thebes that I am god
indeed. And when my worship is established here,
and all is well, then I shall go my way
and be revealed to other men in other lands.
But if the men of Thebes attempt to force
my Bacchae from the mountainside by threat of arms,
I shall marshal my Maenads[9] and take the field.
To these ends I have laid my deity aside
and go disguised as man.

[*He wheels and calls offstage.*]

On, my women,
women who worship me, women whom I led
out of Asia where Tmolus[1] heaves its rampart
over Lydia!
On, comrades of my progress here!
Come, and with your native Phrygian drum—
Rhea's drum[2] and mine—pound at the palace doors
of Pentheus! Let the city of Thebes behold you,
while I return among Cithaeron's forest glens
where my Bacchae wait and join their whirling dances.

[*Exit* DIONYSUS *as the* CHORUS *of Asian Bacchae comes dancing in from the right. They are dressed in fawn-skins, crowned with ivy, and carry thyrsi, timbrels, and flutes.*]

CHORUS Out of the land of Asia,
down from holy Tmolus,
speeding the service of god,

9. Another name for the Bacchae, the group of ecstatic women following Dionysus.
1. A mountain range in Asia Minor (see lines 498–99).
2. Rhea, daughter of the sky god Uranus and mother of Zeus, was worshipped with tambourines and drums.

for Bromius[3] we come!
Hard are the labors of god;
hard, but his service is sweet.
Sweet to serve, sweet to cry:
Bacchus! *Evohé!*[4]
—You on the streets!
—You on the roads!
—Make way!
—Let every mouth be hushed. Let no ill-omened words
profane your tongues.
—Make way! Fall back!
—Hush.
—For now I raise the old, old hymn to Dionysus.

—Blessèd, blessèd are those who know the mysteries of god.
—Blessèd is he who hallows his life in the worship of god,
he whom the spirit of god possesseth, who is one
with those who belong to the holy body of god.
—Blessèd are the dancers and those who are purified,
who dance on the hill in the holy dance of god.
—Blessèd are they who keep the rite of Cybele[5] the Mother.
—Blessèd are the thyrsus-bearers, those who wield in their hands
the holy wand of god.
—Blessèd are those who wear the crown of the ivy of god.
—Blessèd, blessèd are they: Dionysus is their god!

—On, Bacchae, on, you Bacchae,
bear your god in triumph home!
Bear on the god, son of god,
escort your Dionysus home!
Bear him down from Phrygian hill,
attend him through the streets of Hellas!

—So his mother bore him once
in labor bitter; lightning-struck,
forced by fire that flared from Zeus,
consumed, she died, untimely torn,
in childbed dead by blow of light!
Of light the son was born!

—Zeus it was who saved his son;
with speed outrunning mortal eye,
bore him to a private place,
bound the boy with clasps of gold;

3. Another name for Dionysus (literally, "noisy").
4. A cry of joy.
5. Goddess of the earth, identified by the Greeks with Rhea, her worship spread from Phrygia, where she was said to have taught Dionysus the mysteries.

in his thigh as in a womb,
concealed his son from Hera's eyes.

—And when the weaving Fates fulfilled the time,
the bull-horned[6] god was born of Zeus. In joy
he crowned his son, set serpents on his head—
wherefrom, in piety, descends to us
the Maenad's writhing crown, her *chevelure*[7] of snakes.

—O Thebes, nurse of Semele,
crown your hair with ivy!
Grow green with bryony!
Redden with berries! O city,
with boughs of oak and fir,
come dance the dance of god!
Fringe your skins of dappled fawn
with tufts of twisted wool!
Handle with holy care
the violent wand of god!
And let the dance begin!
He is Bromius who runs
to the mountain!
to the mountain!
where the throng of women waits,
driven from shuttle and loom,
possessed by Dionysus!

—And I praise the holies of Crete,
the caves of the dancing Curetes,[8]
there where Zeus was born,
where helmed in triple tier
around the primal drum
the Corybantes[9] danced. They,
they were the first of all
whose whirling feet kept time
to the strict beat of the taut hide
and the squeal of the wailing flute.
Then from them to Rhea's hands
the holy drum was handed down;
but, stolen by the raving Satyrs,[1]
fell at last to me and now
accompanies the dance
which every other year

6. An epithet of Dionysus. *Fates:* three goddesses who spin, measure, and cut the threads of destiny.
7. Hair (French).
8. Divinities who protected the infant Zeus. *Crete:* largest Greek island, whose Minoan civilization was the cultural center of the Aegean before the rise of mainland Greece; it was characterized by goddess worship.
9. Dancing votaries of the goddess Cybele, with whom the Curetes are often identified.
1. Male attendants of Dionysus, creatures of the forest whose appetites for wine and sex are boundless.

celebrates your name:
Dionysus!

—He is sweet upon the mountains. He drops to the earth
from the running packs.
He wears the holy fawn-skin. He hunts the wild goat
and kills it.
He delights in the raw flesh.
He runs to the mountains of Phrygia, to the mountains
of Lydia he runs!
He is Bromius who leads us! *Evohé!*

—With milk the earth flows! It flows with wine!
It runs with the nectar of bees!

—Like frankincense in its fragrance
is the blaze of the torch he bears.
Flames float out from his trailing wand
as he runs, as he dances,
kindling the stragglers,
spurring with cries,
and his long curls stream to the wind!

—And he cries, as they cry, *Evohé!*—
On, Bacchae!
On, Bacchae!
Follow, glory of golden Tmolus,
hymning god
with a rumble of drums,
with a cry, *Evohé!* to the Evian god,[2]
with a cry of Phrygian cries,
when the holy flute like honey plays
the sacred song of those who go
to the mountain!
to the mountain!

—Then, in ecstasy, like a colt by its grazing mother,
the Bacchante[3] runs with flying feet, she leaps!

[*The* CHORUS *remains grouped in two semicircles about the orchestra as* TEIRESIAS[4] *makes his entrance. He is incongruously dressed in the bacchant's fawn-skin and is crowned with ivy. Old and blind, he uses his thyrsus to tap his way.*]

TEIRESIAS Ho there, who keeps the gates?
Summon Cadmus—
Cadmus, Agenor's son, the stranger from Sidon[5]
who built the towers of our Thebes.

2. That is, Dionysus (*Euios* is another of his names).
3. A female worshipper of Dionysus; a Maenad.
4. The blind prophet, adviser to Cadmus.
5. Major port city of Phoenicia (present-day Lebanon).

Go, someone.
Say Teiresias wants him. He will know what errand
brings me, that agreement, age with age, we made
to deck our wands, to dress in skins of fawn
and crown our heads with ivy.

[*Enter* CADMUS *from the palace. Dressed in Dionysiac costume and bent almost double with age, he is an incongruous and pathetic figure.*]

CADMUS My old friend,
I knew it must be you when I heard your summons.
For there's a wisdom in his voice that makes
the man of wisdom known.
But here I am,
dressed in the costume of the god, prepared to go.
Insofar as we are able, Teiresias, we must
do honor to this god, for he was born
my daughter's son, who has been revealed to men,
the god, Dionysus.
Where shall we go, where
shall we tread the dance, tossing our white heads
in the dances of god?
Expound to me, Teiresias.
For in such matters you are wise.
Surely
I could dance night and day, untiringly
beating the earth with my thyrsus! And how sweet it is
to forget my old age.

TEIRESIAS It is the same with me.
I too feel young, young enough to dance.

CADMUS Good. Shall we take our chariots to the mountain?

TEIRESIAS Walking would be better. It shows more honor
to the god.

CADMUS So be it. I shall lead, my old age
conducting yours.

TEIRESIAS The god will guide us there
with no effort on our part.

CADMUS Are we the only men
who will dance for Bacchus?

TEIRESIAS They are all blind.
Only we can see.

CADMUS But we delay too long.
Here, take my arm.

TEIRESIAS Link my hand in yours.

CADMUS I am a man, nothing more. I do not scoff
at heaven.

TEIRESIAS We do not trifle with divinity.
No, we are the heirs of customs and traditions
hallowed by age and handed down to us
by our fathers. No quibbling logic can topple *them*,
whatever subtleties this clever age invents.

People may say: "Aren't you ashamed? At your age,
going dancing, wreathing your head with ivy?"
Well, I am *not* ashamed. Did the god declare
that just the young or just the old should dance?
No, he desires his honor from all mankind.
He wants no one excluded from his worship.

CADMUS Because you cannot see, Teiresias, let me be
interpreter for you this once. Here comes
the man to whom I left my throne, Echion's son,
Pentheus, hastening toward the palace. He seems
excited and disturbed. Yes, listen to him.

[*Enter* PENTHEUS *from the right. He is a young man of athletic build, dressed in traditional Greek dress; like* DIONYSUS, *he is beardless. He enters excitedly, talking to the attendants who accompany him.*]

PENTHEUS I happened to be away, out of the city,
but reports reached me of some strange mischief here,
stories of our women leaving home to frisk
in mock ecstasies among the thickets on the mountain,
dancing in honor of the latest divinity,
a certain Dionysus, whoever he may be!
In their midst stand bowls brimming with wine.
And then, one by one, the women wander off
to hidden nooks where they serve the lusts of men.
Priestesses of Bacchus they claim they are,
but it's really Aphrodite[6] they adore.
I have captured some of them; my jailers
have locked them away in the safety of our prison.
Those who run at large shall be hunted down
out of the mountains like the animals they are—
yes, my own mother Agave, and Ino
and Autonoë, the mother of Actaeon.[7]
In no time at all I shall have them trapped
in iron nets and stop this obscene disorder.
I am also told a foreigner has come to Thebes
from Lydia, one of those charlatan magicians,
with long yellow curls smelling of perfumes,
with flushed cheeks and the spells of Aphrodite
in his eyes. His days and nights he spends
with women and girls, dangling before them the joys
of initiation in his mysteries.
But let me bring him underneath that roof
and I'll stop his pounding with his wand and tossing
his head. By god, I'll have his head cut off!
And *this* is the man who claims that Dionysus
is a god and was sewn into the thigh of Zeus,

6. Goddess of love.
7. Theban hero who saw the goddess Artemis naked while she bathed; as punishment, she turned him into a stag and he was killed by his own dogs (see lines 362–67). His mother, like Agave and Ino, was a daughter of Cadmus.

when, in point of fact, that same blast of lightning
consumed him and his mother both for her lie
that she had lain with Zeus in love. Whoever
this stranger is, aren't such impostures,
such unruliness, worthy of hanging?

[*For the first time he sees* TEIRESIAS *and* CADMUS *in their Dionysiac costumes.*]

What!
But this is incredible! Teiresias the seer
tricked out in a dappled fawn-skin!
And *you*,
you, my own grandfather, playing at the bacchant
with a wand!
Sir, I shrink to see your old age
so foolish. Shake that ivy off, grandfather!
Now drop that wand. Drop it, I say.

[*He wheels on* TEIRESIAS.]

Aha,
I see: this is *your* doing, Teiresias.
Yes, you want still another god revealed to men
so you can pocket the profits from burnt offerings
and bird-watching.[8] By heaven, only your age
restrains me now from sending you to prison
with those Bacchic women for importing here to Thebes
these filthy mysteries. When once you see
the glint of wine shining at the feasts of women,
then you may be sure the festival is rotten.

CORYPHAEUS What blasphemy! Stranger, have you no respect
for heaven? For Cadmus who sowed the dragon teeth?[9]
Will the son of Echion disgrace his house?

TEIRESIAS Give a wise man an honest brief to plead
and his eloquence is no remarkable achievement.
But you are glib; your phrases come rolling out
smoothly on the tongue, as though your words were wise
instead of foolish. The man whose glibness flows
from his conceit of speech declares the thing he is:
a worthless and a stupid citizen.
I tell you,
this god whom you ridicule shall someday have
enormous power and prestige throughout Hellas.
Mankind, young man, possesses two supreme blessings.
First of these is the goddess Demeter,[1] or Earth—
whichever name you choose to call her by.
It was she who gave to man his nourishment of grain.

8. An ancient method of divination.
9. After choosing a place to found his city, Cadmus killed the dragon of Ares, which was guarding a nearby spring. He then sowed the dragon's teeth, which turned into warriors said to be the ancestors of the Theban aristocracy.
1. Goddess of grain and fertility, a sister of Zeus.

But after her there came the son of Semele,
who matched her present by inventing liquid wine
as his gift to man. For filled with that good gift,
suffering mankind forgets its grief; from it
comes sleep; with it oblivion of the troubles
of the day. There is no other medicine
for misery. And when we pour libations
to the gods, we pour the god of wine himself
that through his intercession man may win
the favor of heaven.
You sneer, do you, at that story
that Dionysus was sewed into the thigh of Zeus?
Let me teach you what that really means. When Zeus
rescued from the thunderbolt his infant son,
he brought him to Olympus. Hera, however,
plotted at heart to hurl the child from heaven.
Like the god he is, Zeus countered her. Breaking off
a tiny fragment of that ether which surrounds the world,
he molded from it a dummy Dionysus.
This he *showed* to Hera, but with time men garbled
the word and said that Dionysus had been *sewed*
into the thigh of Zeus. This was their story,
whereas, in fact, Zeus *showed* the dummy to Hera
and gave it as a hostage for his son.
Moreover,
this is a god of prophecy. His worshippers,
like madmen, are endowed with mantic powers.
For when the god enters the body of a man
he fills him with the breath of prophecy.
Besides,
he has usurped even the functions of warlike Ares.[2]
Thus, at times, you see an army mustered under arms
stricken with panic before it lifts a spear.
This panic comes from Dionysus.
Someday
you shall even see him bounding with his torches
among the crags at Delphi,[3] leaping the pastures
that stretch between the peaks, whirling and waving
his thyrsus: great throughout Hellas.
Mark my words,
Pentheus. Do not be so certain that power
is what matters in the life of man; do not mistake
for wisdom the fantasies of your sick mind.
Welcome the god to Thebes; crown your head;
pour him libations and join his revels.
Dionysus does not, I admit, *compel* a woman
to be chaste. Always and in every case

2. Greek god of war, especially savage warfare and bloodlust.

3. Site, northwest of Thebes, where Apollo's principal oracle is located.

it is her character and nature that keeps
a woman chaste. But even in the rites of Dionysus,
the chaste woman will not be corrupted.
Think:
you are pleased when men stand outside your doors
and the city glorifies the name of Pentheus.
And so the god: he too delights in glory.
But Cadmus and I, whom you ridicule, will crown
our heads with ivy and join the dances of the god—
an ancient foolish pair perhaps, but dance
we must. Nothing you have said would make me
change my mind or flout the will of heaven.
You are mad, grievously mad, beyond the power
of any drugs to cure, for you are drugged
with madness.

CORYPHAEUS Apollo[4] would approve your words.
Wisely you honor Bromius: a great god.

CADMUS My boy,
Teiresias advises well. Your home is here
with us, with our customs and traditions, not
outside, alone. Your mind is distracted now,
and what you think is sheer delirium.
Even if this Dionysus is no god,
as you assert, persuade yourself that he is.
The fiction is a noble one, for Semele will seem
to be the mother of a god, and this confers
no small distinction on our family.
You saw
that dreadful death your cousin Actaeon died
when those man-eating hounds he had raised himself
savaged him and tore his body limb from limb
because he boasted that his prowess in the hunt surpassed
the skill of Artemis.[5]
Do not let his fate be yours.
Here, let me wreathe your head with leaves of ivy.
Then come with us and glorify the god.

PENTHEUS Take your hands off me! Go worship your Bacchus,
but do not wipe your madness off on me.
By god, I'll make him pay, the man who taught you
this folly of yours.

[*He turns to his attendants.*]

Go, someone, this instant,
to the place where this prophet prophesies.
Pry it up with crowbars, heave it over,
upside down; demolish everything you see.
Throw his fillets out to wind and weather.

4. Son of Zeus and god of light, healing, and prophecy.

5. Apollo's twin sister, the goddess of the hunt.

That will provoke him more than anything.
As for the rest of you, go and scour the city
for that effeminate stranger, the man who infects our women
with this strange disease and pollutes our beds.
And when you take him, clap him in chains
and march him here. He shall die as he deserves—
by being stoned to death. He shall come to rue
his merrymaking here in Thebes.

[*Exeunt*[6] *attendants.*]

TEIRESIAS Reckless fool,
you do not know the consequences of your words.
You talked madness before, but this is raving
lunacy!
Cadmus, let us go and pray
for this raving fool and for this city too,
pray to the god that no awful vengeance strike
from heaven.
Take your staff and follow me.
Support me with your hands, and I shall help you too
lest we stumble and fall, a sight of shame,
two old men together.
But go we must,
acknowledging the service that we owe to god,
Bacchus, the son of Zeus.
And yet take care
lest someday your house repent of Pentheus
in its sufferings. I speak not prophecy
but fact. The words of fools finish in folly.

[*Exeunt* TEIRESIAS *and* CADMUS. PENTHEUS *retires into the palace.*]

CHORUS —Holiness, queen of heaven,
Holiness on golden wing
who hover over earth,
do you hear what Pentheus says?
Do you hear his blasphemy
against the prince of the blessèd,
the god of garlands and banquets,
Bromius, Semele's son?
These blessings he gave:
laughter to the flute
and the loosing of cares
when the shining wine is spilled
at the feast of the gods,
and the wine-bowl casts its sleep
on feasters crowned with ivy.

—A tongue without reins,
defiance, unwisdom—
their end is disaster.

6. Exit (Latin, "they go out").

But the life of quiet good,
the wisdom that accepts—
these abide unshaken,
preserving, sustaining
the houses of men.
Far in the air of heaven,
the sons of heaven live.
But they watch the lives of men.
And what passes for wisdom is not;
unwise are those who aspire,
who outrange the limits of man.
Briefly, we live. Briefly,
then die. Wherefore, I say,
he who hunts a glory, he who tracks
some boundless, superhuman dream,
may lose his harvest here and now
and garner death. Such men are mad,
their counsels evil.

—O let me come to Cyprus,
island of Aphrodite,
homes of the loves that cast
their spells on the hearts of men!
Or Paphos[7] where the hundred-
mouthed barbarian river
brings ripeness without rain!
To Pieria, haunt of the Muses,
and the holy hill of Olympus![8]
O Bromius, leader, god of joy,
Bromius, take me there!
There the lovely Graces[9] go,
and there Desire, and there
the right is mine to worship
as I please.

—The deity, the son of Zeus,
in feast, in festival, delights.
He loves the goddess Peace,
generous of good,
preserver of the young.
To rich and poor he gives
the simple gift of wine,
the gladness of the grape.
But him who scoffs he hates,
and him who mocks his life,

7. City on the island of Cyprus that was the site of one of Aphrodite's most important cults.
8. The highest mountain in Greece, located in Pieria (an area of Thessaly, in northern Greece), was believed to be the home of the gods. *Muses:* nine daughters of Memory and Zeus who preside over the arts and all intellectual pursuits.
9. Daughters of Zeus, the personifications of beauty and grace.

the happiness of those
for whom the day is blessed
but doubly blessed the night;
whose simple wisdom shuns the thoughts
of proud, uncommon men and all
their god-encroaching dreams.
But what the common people do,
the things that simple men believe,
I too believe and do.

[*As* PENTHEUS *reappears from the palace, enter from the left several attendants leading* DIONYSUS *captive.*]

ATTENDANT Pentheus, here we are; not empty-handed either.
We captured the quarry you sent us out to catch.
But our prey here was tame: refused to run
or hide, held out his hands as willing as you please,
completely unafraid. His ruddy cheeks were flushed
as though with wine, and he stood there smiling,
making no objection when we roped his hands
and marched him here. It made me feel ashamed.
"Listen, stranger," I said, "I am not to blame.
We act under orders from Pentheus. He ordered
your arrest."
As for those women you clapped in chains
and sent to the dungeon, they're gone, clean away,
went skipping off to the fields crying on their god
Bromius. The chains on their legs snapped apart
by themselves. Untouched by any human hand,
the doors swung wide, opening of their own accord.
Sir, this stranger who has come to Thebes is full
of many miracles. I know no more than that.
The rest is your affair.

PENTHEUS Untie his hands.
We have him in our net. He may be quick,
but he cannot escape us now, I think.

[*While the servants untie* DIONYSUS' *hands,* PENTHEUS *attentively scrutinizes his prisoner. Then the servants step back, leaving* PENTHEUS *and* DIONYSUS *face to face.*]

So,
you *are* attractive, stranger, at least to women—
which explains, I think, your presence here in Thebes.
Your curls are long. You do not wrestle,[1] I take it.
And what fair skin you have—you must take care of it—
no daylight complexion; no, it comes from the night
when you hunt Aphrodite with your beauty.
Now then,
who are you and from where?

DIONYSUS It is nothing
to boast of and easily told. You have heard, I suppose,

1. Wrestlers customarily cut their hair short to deny their opponents an easy handhold.

of Mount Tmolus and her flowers?

PENTHEUS I know the place.
It rings the city of Sardis.

DIONYSUS I come from there.
My country is Lydia.

PENTHEUS Who is this god whose worship
you have imported into Hellas?

DIONYSUS Dionysus, the son of Zeus.
He initiated me.

PENTHEUS You have some local Zeus
who spawns new gods?

DIONYSUS He is the same as yours—
the Zeus who married Semele.

PENTHEUS How did you see him?
In a dream or face to face?

DIONYSUS Face to face.
He gave me his rites.

PENTHEUS What form do they take,
these mysteries of yours?

DIONYSUS It is forbidden
to tell the uninitiate.

PENTHEUS Tell me the benefits
that those who know your mysteries enjoy.

DIONYSUS I am forbidden to say. But they are worth knowing.

PENTHEUS Your answers are designed to make me curious.

DIONYSUS No:
our mysteries abhor an unbelieving man.

PENTHEUS You say you saw the god. What form did he assume?

DIONYSUS Whatever form he wished. The choice was his,
not mine.

PENTHEUS You evade the question.

DIONYSUS Talk sense to a fool
and he calls you foolish.

PENTHEUS Have you introduced your rites
in other cities too? Or is Thebes the first?

DIONYSUS Foreigners everywhere now dance for Dionysus.

PENTHEUS They are more ignorant than Greeks.

DIONYSUS In this matter
they are not. Customs differ.

PENTHEUS Do you hold your rites
during the day or night?

DIONYSUS Mostly by night.
The darkness is well suited to devotion.

PENTHEUS Better suited to lechery and seducing women.

DIONYSUS You can find debauchery by daylight too.

PENTHEUS You shall regret these clever answers.

DIONYSUS And you,
your stupid blasphemies.

PENTHEUS What a bold bacchant!
You wrestle well—when it comes to words.

DIONYSUS Tell me,
what punishment do you propose?
PENTHEUS First of all,
I shall cut off your girlish curls.
DIONYSUS My hair is holy.
My curls belong to god.
[PENTHEUS *shears away the god's curls.*]
PENTHEUS Second, you will surrender
your wand.
DIONYSUS *You* take it. It belongs to Dionysus.
[PENTHEUS *takes the thyrsus.*]
PENTHEUS Last, I shall place you under guard and confine you
in the palace.
DIONYSUS The god himself will set me free
whenever I wish.
PENTHEUS You will be with your women in prison
when you call on him for help.
DIONYSUS He is here now
and sees what I endure from you.
PENTHEUS Where is he?
I cannot see him.
DIONYSUS With me. Your blasphemies
have made you blind.
PENTHEUS [*to attendants*] Seize him. He is mocking me
and Thebes.
DIONYSUS I give you sober warning, fools:
place no chains on *me*.
PENTHEUS But *I* say: chain him.
And I am the stronger here.
DIONYSUS You do not know
the limits of your strength. You do not know
what you do. You do not know who you are.
PENTHEUS I am Pentheus, the son of Echion and Agave.
DIONYSUS Pentheus: you shall repent that name.
PENTHEUS Off with him.
Chain his hands; lock him in the stables by the palace.
Since he desires the darkness, give him what he wants.
Let him dance down there in the dark.
[*As the attendants bind* DIONYSUS' *hands, the* CHORUS *beats on its drums with increasing agitation as though to emphasize the sacrilege.*]
As for these women,
your accomplices in making trouble here,
I shall have them sold as slaves or put to work
at my looms. That will silence their drums.
[*Exit* PENTHEUS.]
DIONYSUS I go,
though not to suffer, since that cannot be.
But Dionysus whom you outrage by your acts,
who you deny is god, will call you to account.

When you set chains on me, you manacle the god.

[*Exeunt attendants with* DIONYSUS *captive.*]

CHORUS —O Dirce, holy river,
child of Achelöus' water,[2]
yours the springs that welcomed once
divinity, the son of Zeus!
For Zeus the father snatched his son
from deathless flame, crying:
Dithyrambus,[3] *come!*
Enter my male womb.
I name you Bacchus and to Thebes
proclaim you by that name.
But now, O blessèd Dirce,
you banish me when to your banks I come,
crowned with ivy, bringing revels.
O Dirce, why am I rejected?
By the clustered grapes I swear,
by Dionysus' wine,
someday you shall come to know
the name of *Bromius!*

—With fury, with fury, he rages,
Pentheus, son of Echion,
born of the breed of Earth,
spawned by the dragon, whelped by Earth!
Inhuman, a rabid beast,
a giant in wildness raging,
storming, defying the children of heaven.
He has threatened me with bonds
though my body is bound to god.
He cages my comrades with chains;
he has cast them in prison darkness.
O lord, son of Zeus, do you see?
O Dionysus, do you see
how in shackles we are held
unbreakably, in the bonds of oppressors?
Descend from Olympus, lord!
Come, whirl your wand of gold
and quell with death this beast of blood
whose violence abuses man and god
outrageously.

—O lord, where do you wave your wand
among the running companies of god?

2. The largest river in Greece; its presiding deity, Achelöus, is the chief of all the river deities, including Dirce (see line 6 with note).

3. That is, Dionysus. Dionysus was worshipped with exuberant choral lyrics called dithyrambs, a form of poetry incorporated early into Greek drama.

There on Nysa,[4] mother of beasts?
There on the ridges of Corycia?[5]
Or there among the forests of Olympus
where Orpheus[6] fingered his lyre
and mustered with music the trees,
mustered the wilderness beasts?
O Pieria, you are blessed!
Evius honors you. He comes to dance,
bringing his Bacchae, fording the race
where Axios runs, bringing his Maenads
whirling over Lydias,[7]
generous father of rivers
and famed for his lovely waters
that fatten a land of good horses.

[*Thunder and lightning. The earth trembles. The* CHORUS *is crazed with fear.*]

DIONYSUS [*from within*] Ho!
Hear me! Ho, Bacchae!
Ho, Bacchae! Hear my cry!

CHORUS Who cries?
Who calls me with that cry
of Evius? Where are you, lord?

DIONYSUS Ho! Again I cry—
the son of Zeus and Semele!

CHORUS O lord, lord Bromius!
Bromius, come to us now!

DIONYSUS *Let the earthquake come! Shatter the floor of the world!*

CHORUS —Look there, how the palace of Pentheus totters.
—Look, the palace is collapsing!
—Dionysus is within. Adore him!
—We adore him!
—Look there!
—Above the pillars, how the great stones
gape and crack!
—Listen. Bromius cries his victory!

DIONYSUS *Launch the blazing thunderbolt of god! O lightnings,*
come! Consume with flame the palace of Pentheus!

[*A burst of lightning flares across the façade of the palace and tongues of flame spurt up from the tomb of Semele. Then a great crash of thunder.*]

CHORUS Ah,
look how the fire leaps up
on the holy tomb of Semele,
the flame of Zeus of Thunders,
his lightnings, still alive,

4. A mythical mountain in Egypt or Ethiopia reputed to be the place where the infant Dionysus was raised (and the source of his name, interpreted as "Zeus of Nysa").

5. A cave on Mount Parnassus named for the nymph of a nearby spring.

6. In classical mythology, the greatest poet and singer, whose music not only entranced animals and humans but also made rocks and trees dance.

7. A river in Macedonia (northern Greece). *Axios:* a river ("race") in Macedonia and Paionia.

blazing where they fell!
Down, Maenads,
fall to the ground in awe! He walks
among the ruins he has made!
He has brought the high house low!
He comes, our god, the son of Zeus!

[The CHORUS *falls to the ground in oriental fashion, bowing their heads in the direction of the palace. A hush; then* DIONYSUS *appears, lightly picking his way among the rubble. Calm and smiling still, he speaks to the* CHORUS *with a solicitude approaching banter.]*

DIONYSUS What, women of Asia? Were you so overcome with fright
you fell to the ground? I think then you must have seen
how Bacchus jostled the palace of Pentheus. But come, rise.
Do not be afraid.

CORYPHAEUS O greatest light of our holy revels,
how glad I am to see your face! Without you I was lost.

DIONYSUS Did you despair when they led me away to cast me down
in the darkness of Pentheus' prison?

CORYPHAEUS What else could I do?
Where would I turn for help if something happened to you?
But how did you escape that godless man?

DIONYSUS With ease.
No effort was required.

CORYPHAEUS But the manacles on your wrists?

DIONYSUS There I, in turn, humiliated him, outrage for outrage.
He seemed to think that he was chaining me but never once
so much as touched my hands. He fed on his desires.
Inside the stable he intended as my jail, instead of me,
he found a bull and tried to rope its knees and hooves.
He was panting desperately, biting his lips with his teeth,
his whole body drenched with sweat, while I sat nearby,
quietly watching. But at that moment Bacchus came,
shook the palace and touched his mother's grave with tongues
of fire. Imagining the palace was in flames,
Pentheus went rushing here and there, shouting to his slaves
to bring him water. Every hand was put to work: in vain.
Then, afraid I might escape, he suddenly stopped short,
drew his sword and rushed to the palace. There, it seems,
Bromius had made a shape, a phantom which resembled me,
within the court. Bursting in, Pentheus thrust and stabbed
at that thing of gleaming air as though he thought it me.
And then, once again, the god humiliated him.
He razed the palace to the ground where it lies, shattered
in utter ruin—his reward for my imprisonment.
At that bitter sight, Pentheus dropped his sword, exhausted
by the struggle. A man, a man, and nothing more,
yet he presumed to wage a war with god.
For my part,
I left the palace quietly and made my way outside.
For Pentheus I care nothing.

But judging from the sound
of tramping feet inside the court, I think our man
will soon be here. What, I wonder, will he have to say?
But let him bluster. I shall not be touched to rage.
Wise men know constraint: our passions are controlled.

[*Enter* PENTHEUS, *stamping heavily, from the ruined palace.*]

PENTHEUS But this is mortifying. That stranger, that man
I clapped in irons, has escaped.

[*He catches sight of* DIONYSUS.]

What! *You?*
Well, what do you have to say for yourself?
How did you escape? Answer me.

DIONYSUS Your anger
walks too heavily. Tread lightly here.

PENTHEUS *How did you escape?*

DIONYSUS Don't you remember?
Someone, I said, would set me free.

PENTHEUS Someone?
But who? Who is this mysterious someone?

DIONYSUS [He who makes the grape grow its clusters
for mankind.][8]

PENTHEUS A splendid contribution, that.

DIONYSUS You disparage the gift that is his chiefest glory.

PENTHEUS [If I catch him here, he will not escape my anger.]
I shall order every gate in every tower
to be bolted tight.

DIONYSUS And so? Could not a god
hurdle your city walls?

PENTHEUS You are clever—very—
but not where it counts.

DIONYSUS Where it counts the most,
there I *am* clever.

[*Enter a* MESSENGER, *a herdsman from Mount Cithaeron.*]

But hear this messenger
who brings you news from the mountain of Cithaeron.
We shall remain where we are. Do not fear:
we will not run away.

MESSENGER Pentheus, king of Thebes,
I come from Cithaeron where the gleaming flakes of snow
fall on and on forever—

PENTHEUS Get to the point.
What is your message, man?

MESSENGER Sir, I have seen
the holy Maenads, the women who ran barefoot
and crazy from the city, and I wanted to report
to you and Thebes what weird fantastic things,
what miracles and more than miracles,

8. In this passage, the Greek text, as well as the attribution of some lines, is uncertain.

these women do. But may I speak freely
in my own way and words, or make it short?
I fear the harsh impatience of your nature, sire,
too kingly and too quick to anger.

PENTHEUS Speak freely.
You have my promise: I shall not punish you.
Displeasure with a man who speaks the truth is wrong.
However, the more terrible this tale of yours,
that much more terrible will be the punishment
I impose upon that man who taught our womenfolk
this strange new magic.

MESSENGER About that hour
when the sun lets loose its light to warm the earth,
our grazing herds of cows had just begun to climb
the path along the mountain ridge. Suddenly
I saw three companies of dancing women,
one led by Autonoë, the second captained
by your mother Agave, while Ino led the third.
There they lay in the deep sleep of exhaustion,
some resting on boughs of fir, others sleeping
where they fell, here and there among the oak leaves—
but all modestly and soberly, not, as you think,
drunk with wine, nor wandering, led astray
by the music of the flute, to hunt their Aphrodite
through the woods.
But your mother heard the lowing
of our hornèd herds, and springing to her feet,
gave a great cry to waken them from sleep.
And they too, rubbing the bloom of soft sleep
from their eyes, rose up lightly and straight—
a lovely sight to see: all as one,
the old women and the young and the unmarried girls.
First they let their hair fall loose, down
over their shoulders, and those whose straps had slipped
fastened their skins of fawn with writhing snakes
that licked their cheeks. Breasts swollen with milk,
new mothers who had left their babies behind at home
nestled gazelles and young wolves in their arms,
suckling them. Then they crowned their hair with leaves,
ivy and oak and flowering bryony. One woman
struck her thyrsus against a rock and a fountain
of cool water came bubbling up. Another drove
her fennel in the ground, and where it struck the earth,
at the touch of god, a spring of wine poured out.
Those who wanted milk scratched at the soil
with bare fingers and the white milk came welling up.
Pure honey spurted, streaming, from their wands.
If you had been there and seen these wonders for yourself,
you would have gone down on your knees and prayed
to the god you now deny.

We cowherds and shepherds
gathered in small groups, wondering and arguing
among ourselves at these fantastic things,
the awful miracles those women did.
But then a city fellow with the knack of words
rose to his feet and said: "All you who live
upon the pastures of the mountain, what do you say?
Shall we earn a little favor with King Pentheus
by hunting his mother Agave out of the revels?"
Falling in with his suggestion, we withdrew
and set ourselves in ambush, hidden by the leaves
among the undergrowth. Then at a signal
all the Bacchae whirled their wands for the revels
to begin. With one voice they cried aloud:
"*O Iacchus!*[9] *Son of Zeus!*" "*O Bromius!*" they cried
until the beasts and all the mountain seemed
wild with divinity. And when they ran,
everything ran with them.
It happened, however,
that Agave ran near the ambush where I lay
concealed. Leaping up, I tried to seize her,
but she gave a cry: "Hounds who run with me,
men are hunting us down! Follow, follow me!
Use your wands for weapons."
At this we fled
and barely missed being torn to pieces by the women.
Unarmed, they swooped down upon the herds of cattle
grazing there on the green of the meadow. And then
you could have seen a single woman with bare hands
tear a fat calf, still bellowing with fright,
in two, while others clawed the heifers to pieces.
There were ribs and cloven hooves scattered everywhere,
and scraps smeared with blood hung from the fir trees.
And bulls, their raging fury gathered in their horns,
lowered their heads to charge, then fell, stumbling
to the earth, pulled down by hordes of women
and stripped of flesh and skin more quickly, sire,
than you could blink your royal eyes. Then,
carried up by their own speed, they flew like birds
across the spreading fields along Asopus'[1] stream
where most of all the ground is good for harvesting.
Like invaders they swooped on Hysiae
and on Erythrae[2] in the foothills of Cithaeron.
Everything in sight they pillaged and destroyed.
They snatched the children from their homes. And when
they piled their plunder on their backs, it stayed in place,

9. Another epithet for Dionysus.
1. A river of Boeotia, the region surrounding Thebes.
2. Like Hysiae, a town in Boeotia, south of Thebes.

untied. Nothing, neither bronze nor iron,
fell to the dark earth. Flames flickered
in their curls and did not burn them. Then the villagers,
furious at what the women did, took to arms.
And *there*, sire, was something terrible to see.
For the men's spears were pointed and sharp, and yet
drew no blood, whereas the wands the women threw
inflicted wounds. And then the men *ran*,
routed by women! Some god, I say, was with them.
The Bacchae then returned where they had started,
by the springs the god had made, and washed their hands
while the snakes licked away the drops of blood
that dabbled their cheeks.
Whoever this god may be,
sire, welcome him to Thebes. For he is great
in many other ways as well. It was he,
or so they say, who gave to mortal men
the gift of lovely wine by which our suffering
is stopped. And if there is no god of wine,
there is no love, no Aphrodite either,
nor other pleasure left to men.
[*Exit* MESSENGER.]

CORYPHAEUS I tremble
to speak the words of freedom before the tyrant.
But let the truth be told: there is no god
greater than Dionysus.

PENTHEUS Like a blazing fire
this Bacchic violence spreads. It comes too close.
We are disgraced, humiliated in the eyes
of Hellas. This is no time for hesitation.
[*He turns to an attendant.*]
You there. Go down quickly to the Electran gates[3]
and order out all heavy-armored infantry;
call up the fastest troops among our cavalry,
the mobile squadrons and the archers. We march
against the Bacchae! Affairs are out of hand
when we tamely endure such conduct in our women.
[*Exit attendant.*]

DIONYSUS Pentheus, you do not hear, or else you disregard
my words of warning. You have done me wrong,
and yet, in spite of that, I warn you once
again: do not take arms against a god.
Stay quiet here. Bromius will not let you
drive his women from their revels on the mountain.

PENTHEUS Don't you lecture me. You escaped from prison.
Or shall I punish you again?

DIONYSUS If I were you,

3. One of the seven gates in the fortified wall surrounding the city of Thebes.

I would offer him a sacrifice, not rage
and kick against necessity, a man defying
god.

PENTHEUS I shall give your god the sacrifice
that he deserves. His victims will be his women.
I shall make a great slaughter in the woods of Cithaeron.

DIONYSUS You will all be routed, shamefully defeated,
when their wands of ivy turn back your shields of bronze.

PENTHEUS It is hopeless to wrestle with this man.
Nothing on earth will make him hold his tongue.

DIONYSUS Friend,
you can still save the situation.

PENTHEUS How?
By accepting orders from my own slaves?

DIONYSUS No.
I undertake to lead the women back to Thebes.
Without bloodshed.

PENTHEUS This is some trap.

DIONYSUS A trap?
How so, if I save you by my own devices?

PENTHEUS I know.
You and they have conspired to establish your rites
forever.

DIONYSUS True, I *have* conspired—with god.

PENTHEUS Bring my armor, someone. And *you* stop talking.

[PENTHEUS *strides toward the left, but when he is almost offstage,* DIONYSUS *calls imperiously to him.*]

DIONYSUS *Wait!*
Would you like to *see* their revels on the mountain?

PENTHEUS I would pay a great sum to see that sight.

DIONYSUS Why are you so passionately curious?

PENTHEUS Of course
I'd be sorry to see them drunk—

DIONYSUS But for all your sorrow,
you'd like very much to see them?

PENTHEUS Yes, very much.
I could crouch beneath the fir trees, out of sight.

DIONYSUS But if you try to hide, they may track you down.

PENTHEUS Your point is well taken. I will go openly.

DIONYSUS Shall I lead you there now? Are you ready to go?

PENTHEUS The sooner the better. The loss of even a moment
would be disappointing now.

DIONYSUS First, however,
you must dress yourself in women's clothes.

PENTHEUS *What?*
You want *me*, a man, to wear a woman's dress. But why?

DIONYSUS If they knew you were a man, they would kill you instantly.

PENTHEUS True. You are an old hand at cunning, I see.

DIONYSUS Dionysus taught me everything I know.

PENTHEUS Your advice is to the point. What I fail to see
is what we do.

DIONYSUS I shall go inside with you
and help you dress.

PENTHEUS Dress? In a *woman's* dress,
you mean? I would die of shame.

DIONYSUS Very well.
Then you no longer hanker to see the Maenads?

PENTHEUS What is this costume I must wear?

DIONYSUS On your head
I shall set a wig with long curls.

PENTHEUS And then?

DIONYSUS Next, robes to your feet and a net for your hair.

PENTHEUS Yes? Go on.

DIONYSUS Then a thyrsus for your hand
and a skin of dappled fawn.

PENTHEUS I could not bear it.
I *cannot* bring myself to dress in women's clothes.

DIONYSUS Then you must fight the Bacchae. That means bloodshed.

PENTHEUS Right. First we must go and reconnoiter.

DIONYSUS Surely a wiser course than that of hunting bad
with worse.

PENTHEUS But how can we pass through the city
without being seen?

DIONYSUS We shall take deserted streets.
I will lead the way.

PENTHEUS Any way you like,
provided those women of Bacchus don't jeer at me.
First, however, I shall ponder your advice,
whether to go or not.

DIONYSUS Do as you please.
I am ready, whatever you decide.

PENTHEUS Yes.
Either I shall march with my army to the mountain
or act on your advice.

[*Exit* PENTHEUS *into the palace.*]

DIONYSUS Women, our prey now thrashes
in the net we threw. He shall see the Bacchae
and pay the price with death.
O Dionysus,
now action rests with you. And you are near.
Punish this man. But first distract his wits;
bewilder him with madness. For sane of mind
this man would never wear a woman's dress;
but obsess his soul and he will not refuse.
After those threats with which he was so fierce,
I want him made the laughingstock of Thebes,
paraded through the streets, a woman.
Now

I shall go and costume Pentheus in the clothes
which he must wear to Hades[4] when he dies, butchered
by the hands of his mother. He shall come to know
Dionysus, son of Zeus, consummate god,
most terrible, and yet most gentle, to mankind.

[*Exit* DIONYSUS *into the palace.*]

CHORUS —When shall I dance once more
with bare feet the all-night dances,
tossing my head for joy
in the damp air, in the dew,
as a running fawn might frisk
for the green joy of the wide fields,
free from fear of the hunt,
free from the circling beaters
and the nets of woven mesh
and the hunters hallooing on
their yelping packs? And then, hard pressed,
she sprints with the quickness of wind,
bounding over the marsh, leaping
to frisk, leaping for joy,
gay with the green of the leaves,
to dance for joy in the forest,
to dance where the darkness is deepest,
where no man is.

—What is wisdom? What gift of the gods
is held in honor like this:
to hold your hand victorious
over the heads of those you hate?
Honor is precious forever.

—Slow but unmistakable
the might of the gods moves on.
It punishes that man,
infatuate of soul
and hardened in his pride,
who disregards the gods.
The gods are crafty:
they lie in ambush
a long step of time
to hunt the unholy.
Beyond the old beliefs,
no thought, no act shall go.
Small, small is the cost
to believe in this:
whatever is god is strong;
whatever long time has sanctioned,

4. The Greek underworld, the abode of the dead.

that is a law forever;
the law tradition makes
is the law of nature.
—What is wisdom? What gift of the gods
is held in honor like this:
to hold your hand victorious
over the heads of those you hate?
Honor is precious forever.

—Blessèd is he who escapes a storm at sea,
who comes home to his harbor.
—Blessèd is he who emerges from under affliction.
—In various ways one man outraces another in the
race for wealth and power.
—Ten thousand men posses ten thousand hopes.
—A few bear fruit in happiness; the others go awry.
—But he who garners day by day the good of life,
he is happiest. Blessèd is he.

[*Re-enter* DIONYSUS *from the palace. At the threshold he turns and calls back to* PENTHEUS.]

DIONYSUS Pentheus, if you are still so curious to see
forbidden sights, so bent on evil still,
come out. Let us see you in your woman's dress,
disguised in Maenad clothes so you may go and spy
upon your mother and her company.

[*Enter* PENTHEUS *from the palace. He wears a long linen dress which partially conceals his fawn-skin. He carries a thyrsus in his hand; on his head he wears a wig with long blond curls bound by a snood. He is dazed and completely in the power of the god who has now passed him.*]

Why,
you look exactly like one of the daughters of Cadmus.

PENTHEUS I seem to see two suns blazing in the heavens.
And now two Thebes, two cities, and each
with seven gates.[5] And you—you are a bull
who walks before me there. Horns have sprouted
from your head. Have you always been a beast?
But now I see a bull.

DIONYSUS It is the god you see.
Though hostile formerly, he now declares a truce
and goes with us. You see what you could not
when you were blind.

PENTHEUS [*coyly primping*] Do I look like anyone?
Like Ino or my mother Agave?

DIONYSUS So much alike
I almost might be seeing one of them. But look:
one of your curls has come loose from under the snood
where I tucked it.

PENTHEUS It must have worked loose

5. Thebes was famed throughout the ancient world for the seven gates in the fortifications surrounding the city.

when I was dancing for joy and shaking my head.
DIONYSUS Then let me be your maid and tuck it back.
Hold still.
PENTHEUS Arrange it. I am in your hands
completely.
[DIONYSUS *tucks the curl back under the snood.*]
DIONYSUS And now your strap has slipped. Yes,
and your robe hangs askew at the ankles.
PENTHEUS [*bending backward to look*] I think so.
At least on my right leg. But on the left the hem
lies straight.
DIONYSUS You will think me the best of friends
when you see to your surprise how chaste the Bacchae are.
PENTHEUS But to be a real Bacchante, should I hold
the wand in my right hand? Or this way?
DIONYSUS No.
In your right hand. And raise it as you raise
your right foot. I commend your change of heart.
PENTHEUS Could I lift Cithaeron up, do you think?
Shoulder the cliffs, Bacchae and all?
DIONYSUS If you wanted.
Your mind was once unsound, but now you think
as sane men do.
PENTHEUS Should we take crowbars with us?
Or should I put my shoulder to the cliffs
and heave them up?
DIONYSUS What? And destroy the haunts
of the nymphs, the holy groves where Pan[6] plays
his woodland pipe?
PENTHEUS You are right. In any case,
women should not be mastered by brute strength.
I will hide myself beneath the firs instead.
DIONYSUS You will find all the ambush you deserve,
creeping up to spy on the Maenads.
PENTHEUS Think.
I can see them already, there among the bushes,
mating like birds, caught in the toils of love.
DIONYSUS Exactly. This is your mission: you go to watch.
You may surprise them—or they may surprise you.
PENTHEUS Then lead me through the very heart of Thebes,
since I, alone of all this city, dare to go.
DIONYSUS You and you alone will suffer for your city.
A great ordeal awaits you. But you are worthy
of your fate. I shall lead you safely there;
someone else shall bring you back.
PENTHEUS Yes, my mother.
DIONYSUS An example to all men.
PENTHEUS It is for that I go.

6. The god of wild places and pastures, with horns and goat's feet; he joined together reeds of different lengths to invent the panpipe.

DIONYSUS You will be carried home—
PENTHEUS O luxury!
DIONYSUS cradled in your mother's arms.
PENTHEUS You will spoil me.
DIONYSUS I *mean* to spoil you.
PENTHEUS I go to my reward.
DIONYSUS You are an extraordinary young man, and you go
to an extraordinary experience. You shall win
a glory towering to heaven and usurping
god's.

[*Exit* PENTHEUS.]

Agave and you daughters of Cadmus,
reach out your hands! I bring this young man
to a great ordeal. The victor? Bromius.
Bromius—and I. The rest the event shall show.

[*Exit* DIONYSUS.]

CHORUS —Run to the mountain, fleet hounds of madness!
Run, run to the revels of Cadmus' daughters!
Sting them against the man in women's clothes,
the madman who spies on the Maenads, who peers
from behind the rocks, who spies from a vantage!
His mother shall see him first. She will cry
to the Maenads: "Who is this spy who has come
to the mountains to peer at the mountain-revels
of the women of Thebes? What bore him, Bacchae?
This man was born of no woman. Some lioness
gave him birth, some one of the Libyan gorgons!"[7]

—O Justice, principle of order, spirit of custom,
come! Be manifest; reveal yourself with a sword!
Stab through the throat that godless man,
the mocker who goes, flouting custom and outraging god!
O Justice, stab the evil earth-born spawn of Echion!

—Uncontrollable, the unbeliever goes,
in spitting rage, rebellious and amok,
madly assaulting the mysteries of god,
profaning the rites of the mother of god.
Against the unassailable he runs, with rage
obsessed. Headlong he runs to death.
For death the gods exact, curbing by that bit
the mouths of men. They humble us with death
that we remember what we are who are not god,
but men. We run to death. Wherefore, I say,
accept, accept:
humility is wise; humility is blest.

7. Medusa and her two sisters, snake-haired monsters who turned to stone all who looked at them. In some traditions, Gorgons were savage female warriors living in Libya.

But what the world calls wise I do not want.
Elsewhere the chase. I hunt another game,
those great, those manifest, those certain goals,
achieving which, our mortal lives are blest.
Let these things be the quarry of my chase:
purity; humility; an unrebellious soul,
accepting all. Let me go the customary way,
the timeless, honored, beaten path of those who walk
with reverence and awe beneath the sons of heaven.

—O Justice, principle of order, spirit of custom,
come! Be manifest; reveal yourself with a sword!
Stab through the throat that godless man,
the mocker who goes, flouting custom and outraging god!
O Justice, destroy the evil earth-born spawn of Echion!

—O Dionysus, reveal yourself a bull! Be manifest,
a snake with darting heads, a lion breathing fire!
O Bacchus, come! Come with your smile!
Cast your noose about this man who hunts
your Bacchae! Bring him down, trampled
underfoot by the murderous herd of your Maenads!

[*Enter a* MESSENGER *from Cithaeron.*]

MESSENGER How prosperous in Hellas these halls once were,
this house founded by Cadmus, the stranger from Sidon
who sowed the dragon seed in the land of the snake!
I am a slave and nothing more, yet even so
I mourn the fortunes of this fallen house.

CORYPHAEUS What is it?
Is there news of the Bacchae?

MESSENGER This is my news:
Pentheus, the son of Echion, is dead.

CORYPHAEUS All hail to Bromius! Our god is a great god!

MESSENGER What is this you say, women? You dare to rejoice
at these disasters which destroy this house?

CORYPHAEUS I am no Greek. I hail my god
in my own way. No longer need I
shrink with fear of prison.

MESSENGER If you suppose this city is so short of men—

CORYPHAEUS Dionysus, Dionysus, not Thebes,
has power over me.

MESSENGER Your feelings might be forgiven, then. But this,
this exultation in disaster—it is not right.

CORYPHAEUS Tell us how the mocker died.
How was he killed?

MESSENGER There were three of us in all: Pentheus and I,
attending my master, and that stranger who volunteered
his services as guide. Leaving behind us
the last outlying farms of Thebes, we forded
the Asopus and struck into the barren scrubland

of Cithaeron.
There in a grassy glen we halted,
unmoving, silent, without a word,
so we might see but not be seen. From the vantage,
in a hollow cut from the sheer rock of the cliffs,
a place where water ran and the pines grew dense
with shade, we saw the Maenads sitting, their hands
busily moving at their happy tasks. Some
wound the stalks of their tattered wands with tendrils
of fresh ivy; others, frisking like fillies
newly freed from the painted bridles, chanted
in Bacchic songs, responsively.
But Pentheus—
unhappy man—could not quite see the companies
of women. "Stranger," he said, "from where I stand,
I cannot see these counterfeited Maenads.
But if I climbed that towering fir that overhangs
the banks, then I could see their shameless orgies
better."
And now the stranger worked a miracle.
Reaching for the highest branch of a great fir,
he bent it down, down, down to the dark earth,
till it was curved the way a taut bow bends
or like a rim of wood when forced about the circle
of a wheel. Like that he forced that mountain fir
down to the ground. No mortal could have done it.
Then he seated Pentheus at the highest tip
and with his hands let the trunk rise straightly up,
slowly and gently, lest it throw its rider.
And the tree rose, towering to heaven, with my master
huddled at the top. And now the Maenads saw him
more clearly than he saw them. But barely had they seen,
when the stranger vanished and there came a great voice
out of heaven—Dionysus', it must have been—
crying: "Women, I bring you the man who has mocked
at you and me and at our holy mysteries.
Take vengeance upon him." And as he spoke
a flash of awful fire bound earth and heaven.
The high air hushed, and along the forest glen
the leaves hung still; you could hear no cry of beasts.
The Bacchae heard that voice but missed its words,
and leaping up, they stared, peering everywhere.
Again that voice. And now they knew his cry,
the clear command of god. And breaking loose
like startled doves, through grove and torrent,
over jagged rocks, they flew, their feet maddened
by the breath of god. And when they saw my master
perching in his tree, they climbed a great stone
that towered opposite his perch and showered him

with stones and javelins of fir, while the others
hurled their wands. And yet they missed their target,
poor Pentheus in his perch, barely out of reach
of their eager hands, treed, unable to escape.
Finally they splintered branches from the oaks
and with those bars of wood tried to lever up the tree
by prying at the roots. But every effort failed.
Then Agave cried out: "Maenads, make a circle
about the trunk and grip it with your hands.
Unless we take this climbing beast, he will reveal
the secrets of the god." With that, thousands of hands
tore the fir tree from the earth, and down, down
from his high perch fell Pentheus, tumbling
to the ground, sobbing and screaming as he fell,
for he knew his end was near. His own mother,
like a priestess with her victim, fell upon him
first. But snatching off his wig and snood
so she would recognize his face, he touched her cheeks,
screaming, "*No, no, Mother! I am Pentheus,*
your own son, the child you bore to Echion!
Pity me, spare me, Mother! I have done a wrong,
but do not kill your own son for my offense."
But she was foaming at the mouth, and her crazed eyes
rolling with frenzy. She was mad, stark mad,
possessed by Bacchus. Ignoring his cries of pity,
she seized his left arm at the wrist; then, planting
her foot upon his chest, she pulled, wrenching away
the arm at the shoulder—not by her own strength,
for the god had put inhuman power in her hands.
Ino, meanwhile, on the other side, was scratching off
his flesh. Then Autonoë and the whole horde
of Bacchae swarmed upon him. Shouts everywhere,
he screaming with what little breath was left,
they shrieking in triumph. One tore off an arm,
another a foot still warm in its shoe. His ribs
were clawed clean of flesh and every hand
was smeared with blood as they played ball with scraps
of Pentheus' body.
The pitiful remains lie scattered,
one piece among the sharp rocks, others
lying lost among the leaves in the depths
of the forest. His mother, picking up his head,
impaled it on her wand. She seems to think it is
some mountain lion's head which she carries in triumph
through the thick of Cithaeron. Leaving her sisters
at the Maenad dances, she is coming here, gloating
over her grisly prize. She calls upon Bacchus:
he is her "fellow-huntsman," "comrade of the chase,
crowned with victory." But all the victory

she carries home is her own grief.
Now,
before Agave returns, let me leave
this scene of sorrow. Humility,
a sense of reverence before the sons of heaven—
of all the prizes that a mortal man might win,
these, I say, are wisest; these are best.

[*Exit* MESSENGER.]

CHORUS —We dance to the glory of Bacchus!
We dance to the death of Pentheus,
the death of the spawn of the dragon!
He dressed in woman's dress;
he took the lovely thyrsus;
it waved him down to death,
led by a bull to Hades.
Hail, Bacchae! Hail, women of Thebes!
Your victory is fair, fair the prize,
this famous prize of grief!
Glorious the game! To fold your child
in your arms, streaming with his blood!

CORYPHAEUS But look: there comes Pentheus' mother, Agave,
running wild-eyed toward the palace.
—Welcome,
welcome to the reveling band of the god of joy!

[*Enter* AGAVE *with other Bacchantes. She is covered with blood and carries the head of* PENTHEUS *impaled upon her thyrsus.*]

AGAVE Bacchae of Asia—

CHORUS Speak, speak.

AGAVE We bring this branch to the palace,
this fresh-cut spray from the mountains.
Happy was the hunting.

CHORUS I see.
I welcome our fellow-reveler of god.

AGAVE The whelp of a wild mountain lion,
and snared by me without a noose.
Look, look at the prize I bring.

CHORUS Where was he caught?

AGAVE On Cithaeron—

CHORUS On Cithaeron?

AGAVE Our prize was killed.

CHORUS Who killed him?

AGAVE I struck him first.
The Maenads call me "Agave the blest."

CHORUS And then?

AGAVE Cadmus'—

CHORUS Cadmus'?

AGAVE Daughters.
After me, they reached the prey.
After me. Happy was the hunting.

CHORUS Happy indeed.

AGAVE Then share my glory,
share the feast.

CHORUS Share, unhappy woman?

AGAVE See, the whelp is young and tender.
Beneath the soft mane of its hair,
the down is blooming on the cheeks.

CHORUS With that mane he *looks* a beast.

AGAVE Our god is wise. Cunningly, cleverly,
Bacchus the hunter lashed the Maenads
against his prey.

CHORUS Our king is a hunter.

AGAVE You praise me now?

CHORUS I praise you.

AGAVE The men of Thebes—

CHORUS And Pentheus, your son?

AGAVE Will praise his mother. She caught
a great quarry, this lion's cub.

CHORUS Extraordinary catch.

AGAVE Extraordinary skill.

CHORUS You are proud?

AGAVE Proud and happy.
I have won the trophy of the chase,
a great prize, manifest to all.

CORYPHAEUS Then, poor woman, show the citizens of Thebes
this great prize, this trophy you have won
in the hunt.

[AGAVE *proudly exhibits her thyrsus with the head of* PENTHEUS *impaled upon the point.*]

AGAVE You citizens of this towered city,
men of Thebes, behold the trophy of your women's
hunting! *This* is the quarry of our chase, taken
not with nets nor spears of bronze but by the white
and delicate hands of women. What are they worth,
your boastings now and all that uselessness
your armor is, since we, with our bare hands,
captured this quarry and tore its bleeding body
limb from limb?

—But where is my father Cadmus?
He should come. And my son. Where is Pentheus?
Fetch him. I will have him set his ladder up
against the wall and, there upon the beam,
nail the head of this wild lion I have killed
as a trophy of my hunt.

[*Enter* CADMUS, *followed by attendants who bear upon a bier the dismembered body of* PENTHEUS.]

CADMUS Follow me, attendants.
Bear your dreadful burden in and set it down,
there before the palace.

[*The attendants set down the bier.*]

This was Pentheus
whose body, after long and weary searchings
I painfully assembled from Cithaeron's glens
where it lay, scattered in shreds, dismembered
throughout the forest, no two pieces
in a single place.
Old Teiresias and I
had returned to Thebes from the orgies on the mountain
before I learned of this atrocious crime
my daughters did. And so I hurried back
to the mountain to recover the body of this boy
murdered by the Maenads. There among the oaks
I found Aristaeus'[8] wife, the mother of Actaeon,
Autonoë, and with her Ino, both
still stung with madness. But Agave, they said,
was on her way to Thebes, still possessed.
And what they said was true, for there she is,
and not a happy sight.

AGAVE Now, Father,
yours can be the proudest boast of living men.
For you are now the father of the bravest daughters
in the world. All of your daughters are brave,
but I above the rest. I have left my shuttle
at the loom; I raised my sight to higher things—
to hunting animals with my bare hands.
You see?
Here in my hands I hold the quarry of my chase,
a trophy for our house. Take it, Father, take it.
Glory in my kill and invite your friends to share
the feast of triumph. For you are blest, Father,
by this great deed I have done.

CADMUS This is a grief
so great it knows no size. I cannot look.
This is the awful murder your hands have done.
This, *this* is the noble victim you have slaughtered
to the gods. And to share a feast like this
you now invite all Thebes and me?
O gods,
how terribly I pity you and then myself.
Justly—too, too justly—has lord Bromius,
this god of our own blood, destroyed us all,
every one.

AGAVE How scowling and crabbed is old age
in men. I hope my son takes after his mother

8. Son of Apollo; he was worshipped as a protector of flocks and olive trees, and he taught beekeeping to mortals.

and wins, as she has done, the laurels of the chase
when he goes hunting with the younger men of Thebes.
But all my son can do is quarrel with god.
He should be scolded, Father, and you are the one
who should scold him. Yes, someone call him out
so he can see his mother's triumph.

CADMUS Enough. No more.
When you realize the horror you have done,
you shall suffer terribly. But if with luck
your present madness lasts until you die,
you will seem to have, not having, happiness.

AGAVE Why do you reproach me? Is there something wrong?

CADMUS First raise your eyes to the heavens.

AGAVE There.
But why?

CADMUS Does it look the same as it did before?
Or has it changed?

AGAVE It seems—somehow—clearer,
brighter than it was before.

CADMUS Do you still feel
the same flurry inside you?

AGAVE The same—flurry?
No, I feel—somehow—calmer. I feel as though
my mind were somehow—changing.

CADMUS Can you still hear me?
Can you answer clearly?

AGAVE No. I have forgotten
what we were saying, Father.

CADMUS Who was your husband?

AGAVE Echion—a man, they said, born of the dragon seed.

CADMUS What was the name of the child you bore your husband?

AGAVE Pentheus.

CADMUS And whose head do you hold in your hands?

AGAVE [*averting her eyes*] A lion's head—or so the hunters told me.

CADMUS Look directly at it. Just a quick glance.

AGAVE What is it? What am I holding in my hands?

CADMUS Look more closely still. Study it carefully.

AGAVE *No!* O gods, I see the greatest grief there is.

CADMUS Does it look like a lion now?

AGAVE No, no. It is—
Pentheus' head—I hold—

CADMUS And mourned by me
before you ever knew.

AGAVE But *who* killed him?
Why am *I* holding him?

CADMUS O savage truth,
what a time to come!

AGAVE For god's sake, speak.
My heart is beating with terror.

CADMUS *You* killed him.
You and your sisters.

AGAVE But where was he killed?
Here at home? Where?

CADMUS He was killed on Cithaeron,
there where the hounds tore Actaeon to pieces.

AGAVE But why? Why had Pentheus gone to Cithaeron?

CADMUS He went to your revels to mock the god.

AGAVE But *we*—
what were we doing on the mountain?

CADMUS You were mad.
The whole city was possessed.

AGAVE Now, now I see:
Dionysus has destroyed us all.

CADMUS You outraged him.
You denied that he was truly god.

AGAVE Father,
where is my poor boy's body now?

CADMUS There it is.
I gathered the pieces with great difficulty.

AGAVE Is his body entire? Has he been laid out well?

CADMUS [All but the head. The rest is mutilated
horribly.]

AGAVE But why should Pentheus suffer for my crime?

CADMUS He, like you, blasphemed the god. And so
the god has brought us all to ruin at one blow,
you, your sisters, and this boy. All our house
the god has utterly destroyed and, with it,
me. For I have no sons left, no male heir;
and I have lived only to see this boy,
this branch of your own body, most horribly
and foully killed.

[*He turns and addresses the corpse.*]

—To you my house looked up.
Child, you were the stay of my house; you were
my daughter's son. Of you this city stood in awe.
No one who once had seen your face dared outrage
the old man, or if he did, you punished him.
Now I must go, a banished and dishonored man—
I, Cadmus the great, who sowed the soldiery
of Thebes and harvested a great harvest. My son,
dearest to me of all men—for even dead,
I count you still the man I love the most—
never again will your hand touch my chin;
no more, child, will you hug me and call me
"Grandfather" and say, "Who is wronging you?
Does anyone trouble you or vex your heart, old man?
Tell me, Grandfather, and I will punish him."
No, now there is grief for me; the mourning

for you; pity for your mother; and for her sisters,
sorrow.
If there is still any mortal man
who despises or defies the gods, let him look
on this boy's death and believe in the gods.

CORYPHAEUS Cadmus, I pity you. Your daughter's son
has died as he deserved, and yet his death
bears hard on you.

*[At this point there is a break in the manuscript of nearly fifty lines. The following speeches of Agave and Coryphaeus and the first part of Dionysus' speech have been conjecturally reconstructed from fragments and later material which made use of the Bacchae. Lines which can plausibly be assigned to the lacuna are otherwise not indicated. My own inventions are designed, not to complete the speeches, but to effect a transition between the fragments, and are bracketed.—*TRANS.]

AGAVE O Father, now you can see
how everything has changed. I am in anguish now,
tormented, who walked in triumph minutes past,
exulting in my kill. And that prize I carried home
with such pride was my own curse. Upon these hands
I bear the curse of my son's blood. How then
with these accursed hands may I touch his body?
How can I, accursed with such a curse, hold him
to my breast? O gods, what dirge can I sing
[that there might be] a dirge [for every]
broken limb?
. . . .
Where is a shroud to cover up his corpse?
O my child, what hands will give you proper care
unless with my own hands I lift my curse?

[She lifts up one of PENTHEUS' *limbs and asks the help of* CADMUS *in piecing the body together. She mourns each piece separately before replacing it on the bier.]*

Come, Father. We must restore his head
to this unhappy boy. As best we can, we shall make
him whole again.
—O dearest, dearest face!
Pretty boyish mouth! Now with this veil
I shroud your head, gathering with loving care
these mangled bloody limbs, this flesh I brought
to birth.
. . . .

CORYPHAEUS Let this scene teach those [who see these things:
Dionysus is the son] of Zeus.

[Above the palace DIONYSUS *appears in epiphany.]*

DIONYSUS [I am Dionysus,
the son of Zeus, returned to Thebes, revealed,
a god to men.] But the men [of Thebes] blasphemed me.
They slandered me; they said I came of mortal man,

and not content with speaking blasphemies,
[they dared to threaten my person with violence.]
These crimes this people whom I cherished well
did from malice to their benefactor. Therefore,
I now disclose the sufferings in store for them.
Like [enemies], they shall be driven from this city
to other lands; there, submitting to the yoke
of slavery, they shall wear out wretched lives,
captives of war, enduring much indignity.

[*He turns to the corpse of* PENTHEUS.]

This man has found the death which he deserved,
torn to pieces among the jagged rocks.
You are my witnesses: he came with outrage;
he attempted to chain my hands, abusing me
[and doing what he should least of all have done.]
And therefore he has rightly perished by the hands
of those who should the least of all have murdered him.
What he suffers, he suffers justly.
Upon you,
Agave, and on your sisters I pronounce this doom:
you shall leave this city in expiation
of the murder you have done. You are unclean,
and it would be a sacrilege that murderers
should remain at peace beside the graves [of those
whom they have killed].

[*He turns to* CADMUS.]

. . . .

Next I shall disclose the trials
which await this man. You, Cadmus, shall be changed
to a serpent, and your wife, the child of Ares,
immortal Harmonia, shall undergo your doom,
a serpent too. With her, it is your fate
to go a journey in a car drawn on by oxen,
leading behind you a great barbarian host.
For thus decrees the oracle of Zeus.
With a host so huge its numbers cannot be counted,
you shall ravage many cities; but when your army
plunders the shrine of Apollo, its homecoming
shall be perilous and hard. Yet in the end
the god Ares shall save Harmonia and you
and bring you both to live among the blest.
So say I, born of no mortal father,
Dionysus, true son of Zeus. If then,
when you would not, you had muzzled your madness,
you should have an ally now in the son of Zeus.

CADMUS We implore you, Dionysus. We have done wrong.
DIONYSUS Too late. When there was time, you did not know me.
CADMUS We have learned. But your sentence is too harsh.
DIONYSUS I am a god. I was blasphemed by you.

CADMUS Gods should be exempt from human passions.
DIONYSUS Long ago my father Zeus ordained these things.
AGAVE It is fated, Father. We must go.
DIONYSUS Why then delay?
For you must go.
CADMUS Child, to what a dreadful end
have we all come, you and your wretched sisters
and my unhappy self. An old man, I must go
to live a stranger among barbarian peoples, doomed
to lead against Hellas a motley foreign army.
Transformed to serpents, I and my wife,
Harmonia, the child of Ares, we must captain
spearsmen against the tombs and shrines of Hellas.
Never shall my sufferings end; not even
over Acheron[9] shall I have peace.
AGAVE [*embracing* CADMUS] O Father,
to be banished, to live without you!
CADMUS Poor child,
like a white swan warding its weak old father,
why do you clasp those white arms about my neck?
AGAVE But banished! Where shall I go?
CADMUS I do not know,
my child. Your father can no longer help you.
AGAVE Farewell, my home! City, farewell.
O bridal bed, banished I go,
in misery, I leave you now.
CADMUS Go, poor child, seek shelter in Aristaeus' house.
AGAVE I pity you, Father.
CADMUS And I pity you, my child,
and I grieve for your poor sisters. I pity them.
AGAVE Terribly has Dionysus brought
disaster down upon this house.
DIONYSUS I was terribly blasphemed,
my name dishonored in Thebes.
AGAVE Farewell, Father.
CADMUS Farewell to you, unhappy child.
Fare well. But you shall find your faring hard.
[*Exit* CADMUS.]
AGAVE Lead me, guides, where my sisters wait,
poor sisters of my exile. Let me go
where I shall never see Cithaeron more,
where that accursed hill may not see me,
where I shall find no trace of thyrsus!
That I leave to other Bacchae.
[*Exit* AGAVE *with attendants.*]
CHORUS The gods have many shapes.
The gods bring many things

9. That is, in death; Acheron is one of the rivers of the underworld.

to their accomplishment.
And what was most expected
has not been accomplished.
But god has found his way
for what no man expected.

So ends the play.

HROTSVIT OF GANDERSHEIM

935?–1002?

Hrotsvit, a canoness in the tenth-century abbey of Gandersheim, in north-central Germany, lays claim to several significant firsts in the history of Western literature. She is the first known Christian dramatist, the first Saxon poet, and the first female historian of Europe. Her plays are the first performable plays of the Middle Ages, and her epic poems are the only extant Latin epics composed by a woman. Her sophisticated output has been a puzzle and anomaly for literary scholars and historians for centuries, and opinions about the works have often been shaped by an unwillingness to acknowledge that a medieval woman could possibly know as much or write with as much skill as Hrotsvit did. Only during the last decades of the twentieth century were Hrotsvit's achievements given the sort of attention that they deserve; and even now, there is much that we don't know and can't fully appreciate about this remarkable woman.

What little we do know of Hrotsvit's life comes from clues in her own writing. Scholars suspect that she was born around 935. Although nothing is certain about her activities before she entered the abbey at Gandersheim in 955, we can say a few things confidently about the nature of her education and religious service once she chose to live in that Christian community. First, she would have had access to many classical Latin texts. During the medieval period, the major centers of learning in Europe were the monastic and cathedral schools, whose libraries amassed major collections of philosophical and theological writings. The Benedictine nunnery at Gandersheim was one of the most prominent of these centers. Such libraries collected manuscripts drawn not only from the Christian era but also from the classical Roman era that had preceded it. Because early Christian theologians believed that the pagan Latin texts were useful preparation for the more difficult challenge of reading Holy Scripture in Latin, students in monastic settings had access to much of the classical canon as well as to writings on church doctrine and biblical texts. Judging from clues in her own writings, it appears that Hrotsvit read Virgil, Ovid, and Terence among classical authors; she was also familiar with such early Christian philosophers as Augustine and Boethius. She was particularly well versed in saints' lives—the hagiographic texts that underlie many of her legends and dramas.

We also assume that Hrotsvit, like most canonesses who entered Gandersheim and other monasteries, was of noble birth. We know that she joined the community at about the same time that Gerberga II, a niece of Otto I (the German king and Holy Roman Emperor), came to the monastery. In her writings, Hrotsvit credits Gerberga with much of her education. This connection to one of the most powerful families in Saxony suggests that either before or during her years at Gandersheim, Hrotsvit may have spent time at court, which would have given her further access to broad cultural influences.

Hrotsvit's oeuvre remained completely unknown to scholars for nearly five hundred years after her death; then, in 1494, the German humanist Conrad Celtis found what is now known as the Emmeram-Munich Codex, which he published in 1501. While German scholars, in a spirit of cultural nationalism, were quick to embrace Hrotsvit, critics elsewhere found her writing so advanced compared to other manuscripts from that period that they questioned its authenticity. In 1867, the Viennese scholar Joseph von Aschbach asserted that Celtis had forged the codex,

The frontispiece for the first printed edition of Hrotsvit's complete works, published in 1501. In the image, Hrotsvit presents her book to Otto I, while Otto's niece (and Hrotsvit's friend) Gerberga II looks on.

arguing that no medieval woman could possibly have possessed Hrotsvit's knowledge of either the world or of classical literature. Aschbach's theories have subsequently been definitively refuted by the discovery of additional copies of Hrotsvit's writing, in their original Latin as well as in early vernacular translation. But the confirmation of the legitimacy of her oeuvre—which comprises eight verse legends; six plays in rhymed, rhythmic prose; two verse epics; and a short poem—has not resolved fundamental questions, particularly in the case of the plays, surrounding their genesis or historical significance.

Although we cannot definitively date Hrotsvit's work, most recent scholarship posits that she was at the height of her creative powers from 965 to 975. Scholars believe she began writing legends based on saints' lives soon after her arrival at the abbey, and her collection of plays followed. If these assumptions are true, then she may well have written her dramas at about the same time that the *Quem quaeritis* (Whom do you seek?) trope came to be added to the Easter Mass. This precursor to full-fledged medieval liturgical drama consisted of a short series of simple questions and answers between an angel and the women who come to Christ's tomb following the resurrection, sung by two halves of a church choir. Hrotsvit's work could thus predate the first extant mystery plays, or dramas based on scriptural incidents, by about seventy-five years. This revised history would then throw into question the long-held theory about how drama "reemerged" in the West after the end of the classical era.

In the standard explanation, dramatic arts declined precipitously after the collapse of Rome—essentially lying dormant for six centuries, only to be reborn in the tenth century. This rebirth was the product of growing theatricality in the rituals of the Catholic Mass, starting with the *Quem quaeritis* trope. Liturgical drama eventually broke free of the confines of the Mass, evolving into the mystery cycles that were sponsored and performed by professional guilds. From that point, scholars have generally believed, it was merely a matter of time before the drama would fully reflower, as it eventually did during the Renaissance.

Hrotsvit's dramas disrupt the prevailing narrative of medieval theater history because her plays are much more sophisticated than the rudimentary seed from which the revived Western drama was traditionally thought to have grown. In addition, the plays of Hrotsvit, which the playwright herself describes as imitations of the Roman comic dramatist Terence, demonstrate a continuity between classical and medieval theater, not the revival of a dead form.

Even among scholars who recognize that Hrotsvit's work complicates the standard history, there is considerable disagreement about the influence of her plays on medieval drama generally. Some have characterized Hrotsvit's work as an "isolated experiment," or a mere "literary exercise," implying that her plays were neither widely known nor intended for performance. While the discovery of copies of her manuscripts in different locations suggests that her works were known within the Christian community in Europe and thus could indeed have had some impact on medieval drama, the current evidence allows no more than conjecture about what, and how extensive, that impact might have been. Whether her plays were works of theater or just literary exercises has proven a more vexing question. We cannot conclude from the form of these six works that they were composed for theatrical performance. Like Seneca's plays in late antiquity, Hrotsvit's plays may simply have been examples of closet drama—pieces never staged, or never intended to be staged. But regardless of Hrotsvit's intentions, the plays themselves are undeniably theatrical, and can be performed.

The extent of Hrotsvit's understanding of theatrical performance is difficult to gauge, as many historians believe that Europeans in the tenth century had little knowledge of classical stage practice. In this era, written dialogues with speech prefixes (sometimes names of real people) were considered valuable pedagogical tools, but it is unclear whether they were meant to be read silently or aloud. Nor is it certain that such texts that we now understand to be dramatic or theatrical were distinguished from others in any way. Some scholars have speculated that dialogues may have been read aloud, either by a single person or by a number voicing the different "characters," with the suggested action silently dramatized by a mime, but there is little evidence to support or disprove this theory. What we can say is that of all of Hrotsvit's plays, *Dulcitius* most strongly suggests its author's sense of performance. For this reason, it has emerged as a crucial text for historians seeking to explore the possible conjunction of dialogue and action in medieval drama.

Further complicating our interpretation of Hrotsvit's intentions is the self-deprecating tone of the prefaces and epistles that introduce many of her works. Initially, Hrotsvit's own prose was taken as evidence of her negligibility as a writer, but scholars have more recently acknowledged that it simply adheres to a common medieval Christian convention that gives God, not the writer, credit for whatever genius might be found in the work. A better clue to her sense of self and of her earthly mission may reside in the Latin nom de plume she adopted: Clamor Validus Gandeshemensis, or "the strong voice of Gandersheim." Perhaps, like some modern critics, she saw her own strength in a bold and daring design in her writings that was unmatched by any efforts of her contemporaries, either in literature or visual art. Or perhaps she was thinking that representing wise, strong, and virtuous Christian women in texts to be shared within communities like her own would have the power to transform cultural stereotypes.

In the preface to her dramas, Hrotsvit explains her goals, declaring a debt to and a quarrel with the Latin playwright Terence:

> Many Catholics one may find, and we are also guilty of charges of this kind, who for the beauty of their eloquent style, prefer the use of pagan guile to the usefulness of Sacred Scripture. There are also others, who, devoted to sacred reading and scorning the works of other pagans, yet frequently read Terence's fiction, and as they delight in the sweetness of his style and diction, they are stained by learning of wicked things in his depiction. Therefore I, the strong voice of Gandersheim, have not refused to imitate him in writing whom others laud in reading, so that in that selfsame form of composition in which the shameless acts of lascivious women were phrased the laudable chastity of sacred virgins may be praised within the limits of my little talent.

From this brief statement, Hrotsvit's plan is clear: she will revise Terence for Christendom. While borrowing his compositional style, she will correct his misogynistic portrayal of women and instead promote images of female virtue and chastity.

Although critics are divided about the extent and nature of Hrotsvit's debt to Terence, they generally agree that *Dulcitius* is the most Terentian of her plays. The influence of classical comedy may be seen in the play's lighter moments, such as the scene in which the Roman governor Dulcitius makes a lunge at pots and pans, thinking they are the young Christian virgins whom he wishes to ravish, ends up with soot all over his face, and is then mistaken for a demon. Comparisons can likewise be made between Terence's use of established classical character types, such as bombastic fathers, and Hrotsvit's adaptation of them as Roman figures of authority. We may also observe a shared predilection for love conflicts as plot devices, and such motifs as scheming and disguise figuring in the works of both dramatists. Some critics, however, argue that these resemblances are isolated parallels, and that the spirit and content of Hrotsvit's plays much more thoroughly reflect medieval sensibilities. In their view, the comic scene and the conflicts between typed characters illustrate the use of Christian symbolism, as Hrotsvit pits the pagan forces of evil against the blessedness of Christian virtue and martyrdom.

Another illustration from the 1501 edition showing the virgins Agape (love), Chionia (purity), and Hirena (peace) being burned alive.

Hrotsvit is remarkably faithful in *Dulcitius* to her source material, which is taken from the *Acta Sanctorum* (*Acts of the Saints*), a sixty-eight-volume compendium of exemplary tales of Christian saints' lives. The story that serves as the basis for *Dulcitius* describes the martyrdom of the holy virgins Agape (love), Chionia (purity), and Hirene (peace), all put to death by order of the Roman emperor Diocletian in Thessalonica in the year 290. In her careful schema, Hrotsvit opposes the idealized women to the pagan male authorities Dulcitius (who represents lust), Diocletian (arrogance), and Sissinus (cruelty). The virgins' death at the hands of torturers ensures their Christian salvation, while their pagan persecutors secure eternal damnation—made literal by Dulcitius's representation as the soot-faced devil—for their evil deeds. Like Christ, the women are tempted to abandon their religious beliefs and sense of mission, but they resist. They withstand torture and death, thereby overpowering their male aggressors, whom they show to be impotent in the face of Christian faith. Through these trials, Hrotsvit throws into question the image of women as the weaker sex. Moreover, by celebrating female chastity she strongly links women not with Eve—the dominant association—but with the idealized Virgin Mary.

These themes of female fortitude and faith recur in Hrotsvit's other dramas, *Gallicanus, Calimachus, Abraham, Pafnutius,* and especially *Sapientia,* her last drama, which also depicts the martyrdom of three young virgins. The works not only were thematically innovative but also reflected an astounding facility with Latin rhetorical structures, including *stichomythia,* the use of alternating lines of dialogue to dramatize a dispute. By including doxologies (short hymns of praise to God) at the close of most of her works and in other ways, Hrotsvit demonstrated her clear understanding of the role her works might play in the broader arena of Christian education, as well as her knowledge of the liturgy. And her skill at characterization remains unprecedented in early medieval dramaturgy.

While scholars may never be able fully to determine how Hrotsvit's work may have influenced the development of the medieval drama, her growing significance in the modern period is indisputable. Her plays have been translated and performed steadily from the late nineteenth century forward. Especially noteworthy is the 1914 production of *Pafnutius* in London by the Pioneer Players, which showcased the talents of three prominent women of the Edwardian theater. Edith Craig directed, using the English translation of Christabel Marshall (under the pseudonym Christopher St. John), and the performance featured the legendary actor Ellen Terry in the role of the Nun. The study of Hrotsvit's plays from the mid-twentieth century onward has forced scholars both to carefully reexamine foundational assumptions in theater history and to reconsider dismissive attitudes toward women's writing throughout the Western tradition. The rediscovery of other medieval women authors—most notably the twelfth-century dramatist and musician/composer Hildegard of Bingen, writer of the earliest extant liturgical morality play, *Ordo virtutum*—will surely help fuel this important critical dialogue.

J.E.G.

The Martyrdom of the Holy Virgins Agape, Chionia, and Hirena[1]

DULCITIUS

CHARACTERS

DIOCLETIAN, a Roman emperor
AGAPE, a holy virgin
CHIONIA, a holy virgin
HIRENA, a holy virgin
DULCITIUS, a Roman governor
DULCITIUS'S WIFE
SISSINUS, a Roman count
SOLDIERS
GUARDS

1. Translated by Katharina M. Wilson.

The martyrdom of the holy virgins Agape, Chionia, and Hirena whom, in the silence of the night, Governor Dulcitius secretly visited, desiring to delight in their embrace.[2] *But as soon as he entered, he became demented and kissed and hugged the pots and pans, mistaking them for the girls until his face and his clothes were soiled with disgusting black dirt. Afterward Count Sissinus, acting on orders, was given the girls so he might put them to tortures. He, too, was deluded miraculously but finally ordered that Agape and Chionia be burnt and Hirena be slain by an arrow.*

DIOCLETIAN[3] The renown of your free and noble descent and the brightness of your beauty demand that you be married to one of the foremost men of my court. This will be done according to our command if you deny Christ and comply by bringing offerings to our gods.

AGAPE Be free of care, don't trouble yourself to prepare our wedding because we cannot be compelled under any duress to betray Christ's holy name, which we must confess, nor to stain our virginity.

DIOCLETIAN What madness possesses you? What rage drives you three?

AGAPE What signs of our madness do you see?

DIOCLETIAN An obvious and great display.

AGAPE In what way?

DIOCLETIAN Chiefly in that renouncing the practices of ancient religion you follow the useless, newfangled ways of the Christian superstition.

AGAPE Heedlessly you offend the majesty of the omnipotent God. That is dangerous . . .

DIOCLETIAN Dangerous to whom?

AGAPE To you and to the state you rule.

DIOCLETIAN She is mad; remove the fool!

CHIONIA My sister is not mad; she rightly reprehended your folly.

DIOCLETIAN She rages even more madly; remove her from our sight and arraign the third girl.

HIRENA You will find the third, too, a rebel and resisting you forever.

DIOCLETIAN Hirena, although you are younger in birth, be greater in worth!

HIRENA Show me, I pray, how?

DIOCLETIAN Bow your neck to the gods, set an example for your sisters, and be the cause for their freedom!

HIRENA Let those worship idols, Sire, who wish to incur God's ire. But I won't defile my head, anointed with royal unguent by debasing myself at the idols' feet.

DIOCLETIAN The worship of gods brings no dishonor but great honor.

HIRENA And what dishonor is more disgraceful, what disgrace is any more shameful than when a slave is venerated as a master?

DIOCLETIAN I don't ask you to worship slaves but the mighty gods of princes and greats.

HIRENA Is he not anyone's slave who, for a price, is up for sale?

2. The story of the martyrdom of the holy virgins in 290 C.E. derives from the *Acta Sanctorum* (*Acts of the Saints*), an encyclopedia of the saints recognized by the Roman Catholic Church. The virgins' Greek names mean Love, Purity, and Peace, respectively. Although there was an actual Dulcitius, a Roman military leader who in 369 C.E. was appointed *Dux Britanniarum* (commander of Britain; Latin), he lived nearly a century after the events depicted in the play. Hrotsvit may have chosen the name simply for the irony of its link to the Latin *dulcis*, which means "sweet, charming."

3. Gaius Aurelius Valerius Diocletianus (ca. 245–316 C.E.), Roman emperor from 284 to 305 C.E. He was zealous in the persecution of Christians.

DIOCLETIAN For her speech so brazen, to the tortures she must be taken.

HIRENA This is just what we hope for, this is what we desire, that for the love of Christ through tortures we may expire.

DIOCLETIAN Let these insolent girls who defy our decrees and words be put in chains and kept in the squalor of prison until Governor Dulcitius can examine them.[4]

*

DULCITIUS Bring forth, soldiers, the girls whom you hold sequestered.

SOLDIERS Here they are whom you requested.

DULCITIUS Wonderful, indeed, how beautiful, how graceful, how admirable these little girls are!

SOLDIERS Yes, they are perfectly lovely.

DULCITIUS I am captivated by their beauty.

SOLDIERS That is understandable.

DULCITIUS To draw them to my heart, I am eager.

SOLDIERS Your success will be meager.

DULCITIUS Why?

SOLDIERS Because they are firm in faith.

DULCITIUS What if I sway them by flattery?

SOLDIERS They will despise it utterly.

DULCITIUS What if with tortures I frighten them?

SOLDIERS Little will it matter to them.

DULCITIUS Then what should be done, I wonder?

SOLDIERS Carefully you should ponder.

DULCITIUS Place them under guard in the inner room of the pantry, where they keep the servants' pots.

SOLDIERS Why in that particular spot?

DULCITIUS So that I may visit them often at my leisure.

SOLDIERS At your pleasure.

DULCITIUS What do the captives do at this time of night?

SOLDIERS Hymns they recite.

DULCITIUS Let us go near.

SOLDIERS From afar we hear their tinkling little voices clear.

DULCITIUS Stand guard before the door with your lantern but I will enter and satisfy myself in their longed-for embrace.

SOLDIERS Enter. We will guard this place.

*

AGAPE What is that noise outside the door?

HIRENA That wretched Dulcitius coming to the fore.

CHIONIA May God protect us!

AGAPE Amen.

CHIONIA What is the meaning of this clash of the pots and the pans?

HIRENA I will check. Come here, please, and look through the crack!

AGAPE What is going on?

HIRENA Look, the fool, the madman base, he thinks he is enjoying our embrace.

AGAPE What is he doing?

4. The asterisks have been added by the translator to denote changes in locale or the passage of time; Hrotsvit's extant manuscripts contain no such scene divisions.

HIRENA Into his lap he pulls the utensils, he embraces the pots and the pans, giving them tender kisses.

CHIONIA Ridiculous!

HIRENA His face, his hands, his clothes, are so soiled, so filthy, that with all the soot that clings to him, he looks like an Ethiopian.

AGAPE It is only right that he should appear in body the way he is in his mind: possessed by the Devil.

HIRENA Wait! He prepares to leave. Let us watch how he is greeted, and how he is treated by the soldiers who wait for him.

*

SOLDIERS Who is coming out? A demon without doubt. Or rather, the Devil himself is he; let us flee!

DULCITIUS Soldiers, where are you taking yourselves in flight? Stay! Wait! Escort me home with your light!

SOLDIERS The voice is our master's tone but the look the Devil's own. Let us not stay! Let us run away; the apparition will slay us!

DULCITIUS I will go to the palace and complain, and reveal to the whole court the insults I had to sustain.

*

DULCITIUS Guards, let me into the palace; I must have a private audience.

GUARDS Who is this vile and detestable monster covered in torn and despicable rags? Let us beat him, from the steps let us sweep him; he must not be allowed to enter.

DULCITIUS Alas, alas, what has happened? Am I not dressed in splendid garments? Don't I look neat and clean? Yet anyone who looks at my mien loathes me as a foul monster. To my wife I shall return, and from her learn what has happened. But there is my spouse, with disheveled hair she leaves the house, and the whole household follows her in tears.

WIFE Alas, alas, my Lord Dulcitius, what has happened to you? You are not sane; the Christians have made a laughingstock out of you.

DULCITIUS Now I know at last. I owe this mockery to their witchcraft.

WIFE What upsets me so, what makes me more sad, is that you were ignorant of all that happened to you.

DULCITIUS I command that those insolent girls be led forth, and that they be publicly stripped of all their clothes, so that they experience similar mockery in retaliation for ours.

*

SOLDIERS We labor in vain; we sweat without gain. Behold, their garments stick to their virginal bodies like skin, and he who urged us to strip them snores in his seat, and he cannot be awakened from his sleep. Let us go to the Emperor and report what has happened.

*

DIOCLETIAN It grieves me very much to hear that Governor Dulcitius has been so greatly deluded, so greatly insulted, so utterly humiliated. But these vile young women shall not boast with impunity of having made a mockery of our gods and those who worship them. I shall direct Count Sissinus to take due vengeance.

*

SISSINUS Soldiers, where are those insolent girls who are to be tortured?

SOLDIERS They are kept in prison.

SISSINUS Leave Hirena there, bring the others here.

SOLDIERS Why do you except the one?

SISSINUS Sparing her youth. Perchance, she may be converted easier, if she is not intimidated by her sisters' presence.

SOLDIERS That makes sense.

*

SOLDIERS Here are the girls whose presence you requested.

SISSINUS Agape and Chionia, give heed, and to my council accede!

AGAPE We will not give heed.

SISSINUS Bring offerings to the gods.

AGAPE We bring offerings of praise forever to the true Father eternal, and to His Son co-eternal, and also to the Holy Spirit.

SISSINUS This is not what I bid, but on pain of penalty prohibit.

AGAPE You cannot prohibit it; neither shall we ever sacrifice to demons.

SISSINUS Cease this hardness of heart, and make your offerings. But if you persist, then I shall insist that you be killed according to the Emperor's orders.

CHIONIA It is only proper that you should obey the orders of your Emperor, whose decrees we disdain, as you know. For if you wait and try to spare us, then you could be rightfully killed.

SISSINUS Soldiers, do not delay, take these blaspheming girls away, and throw them alive into the flames.

SOLDIERS We shall instantly build the pyre you asked for, and we will cast these girls into the raging fire, and thus we'll put an end to these insults at last.

AGAPE O Lord, nothing is impossible for Thee; even the fire forgets its nature and obeys Thee; but we are weary of delay; therefore, dissolve the earthly bonds that hold our souls, we pray, so that as our earthly bodies die, our souls may sing your praise in Heaven.

*

SOLDIERS Oh, marvel, oh stupendous miracle! Behold their souls are no longer bound to their bodies, yet no traces of injury can be found; neither their hair, nor their clothes are burnt by the fire, and their bodies are not at all harmed by the pyre.

SISSINUS Bring forth Hirena.

*

SOLDIERS Here she is.

SISSINUS Hirena, tremble at the deaths of your sisters and fear to perish according to their example.

HIRENA I hope to follow their example and expire, so with them in Heaven eternal joy I may acquire.

SISSINUS Give in, give in to my persuasion.

HIRENA I will never yield to evil persuasion.

SISSINUS If you don't yield, I shall not give you a quick and easy death, but multiply your sufferings.

HIRENA The more cruelly I am tortured, the more gloriously I'll be exalted.

SISSINUS You fear no tortures, no pain? What you abhor, I shall ordain.

HIRENA Whatever punishment you design, I will escape with help Divine.

SISSINUS To a brothel you will be consigned, where your body will be shamefully defiled.

HIRENA It is better that the body be dirtied with any stain than that the soul be polluted with idolatry.

SISSINUS If you are so polluted in the company of harlots, you can no longer be counted among the virginal choir.

HIRENA Lust deserves punishment, but forced compliance the crown. With neither is one considered guilty, unless the soul consents freely.

SISSINUS In vain have I spared her, in vain have I pitied her youth.

SOLDIERS We knew this before; for on no possible score can she be moved to adore our gods, nor can she be broken by terror.

SISSINUS I shall spare her no longer.

SOLDIERS Rightly you ponder.

SISSINUS Seize her without mercy, drag her with cruelty, and take her in dishonor to the brothel.

HIRENA They will not do it.

SISSINUS Who can prohibit it?

HIRENA He whose foresight rules the world.

SISSINUS I shall see . . .

HIRENA Sooner than you wish, it will be.

SISSINUS Soldiers, be not afraid of what this blaspheming girl has said.

SOLDIERS We are not afraid, but eagerly follow what you bade.

*

SISSINUS Who are those approaching? How similar they are to the men to whom we gave Hirena just then. They are the same. Why are you returning so fast? Why so out of breath, I ask?

SOLDIERS You are the one for whom we look.

SISSINUS Where is she whom you just took?

SOLDIERS On the peak of the mountain.

SISSINUS Which one?

SOLDIERS The one close by.

SISSINUS Oh you idiots, dull and blind. You have completely lost your mind!

SOLDIERS Why do you accuse us, why do you abuse us, why do you threaten us with menacing voice and face?

SISSINUS May the gods destroy you!

SOLDIERS What have we committed? What harm have we done? How have we transgressed against your orders?

SISSINUS Have I not given the orders that you should take that rebel against the gods to a brothel?

SOLDIERS Yes, so you did command, and we were eager to fulfill your demand, but two strangers intercepted us saying that you sent them to us to lead Hirena to the mountain's peak.

SISSINUS That's new to me.

SOLDIERS We can see.

SISSINUS What were they like?

SOLDIERS Splendidly dressed and an awe-inspiring sight.

SISSINUS Did you follow?

SOLDIERS We did so.

SISSINUS What did they do?

SOLDIERS They placed themselves on Hirena's left and right, and told us to be forthright and not to hide from you what happened.

SISSINUS I see a sole recourse, that I should mount my horse and seek out those who so freely made sport with us.

*

SISSINUS Hmm, I don't know what to do. I am bewildered by the witchcraft of these Christians. I keep going around the mountain and keep finding this track but I neither know how to proceed nor how to find my way back.

SOLDIERS We are all deluded by some intrigue; we are afflicted with a great fatigue; if you allow this insane person to stay alive, then neither you nor we shall survive.

SISSINUS Anyone among you, I don't care which, string a bow, and shoot an arrow, and kill that witch!

SOLDIERS Rightly so.

HIRENA Wretched Sissinus, blush for shame, and proclaim your miserable defeat because without the help of weapons, you cannot overcome a tender little virgin as your foe.

SISSINUS Whatever the shame that may be mine, I will bear it more easily now because I know for certain that you will die.

HIRENA This is the greatest joy I can conceive, but for you this is a cause to grieve, because you shall be damned in Tartarus[5] for your cruelty, while I shall receive the martyr's palm and the crown of virginity; thus I will enter the heavenly bridal chamber of the Eternal King, to whom are all honor and glory in all eternity.

5. In Greek and Roman mythology, a realm of punishment and torment beneath the underworld; in the Christian context of *Dulcitius*, Tartarus refers to hell.

GUAN HANQING

ca. 1245–ca. 1322

HAILED as the most original pioneer of the form of dramatic theater called *zaju* (Northern variety drama), Guan Hanqing holds a position similar to that of SHAKESPEARE: a prolific writer during a pivotal historical era whose writings have been accorded unrivaled cultural status. While the critical reputations of his contemporaries have waxed and waned over the centuries, Guan's literary and theatrical standing remains unchallenged even today. Chinese critics and audiences alike have praised his works for their sympathetic portrayals of ordinary human life and suffering, their skillful balance of realism and dramatic poetry, and their remarkably powerful women characters. These qualities are exemplified in *Dou E Yuan*—literally *Injustice to Dou E*, but sometimes (as here) published in English as *SNOW IN MIDSUMMER*, the title of a well-known later adaptation—which remains one of the best-loved of Guan's *zaju* plays. In the centuries since it was written it has become one of the most frequently performed and adapted works in Chinese theater.

Guan was born in the mid-thirteenth century and lived out his life in the northern district of Yen-ching, which in 1267 became Kublai Khan's "great capital," Ta-tu, on the site of modern-day Beijing. He began writing around 1260 and did not stop until his death in the late thirteenth or early fourteenth century. His long career spanned the entire period of Kublai Khan's reign as Khan from 1260 to 1294 and as first ruler of the Mongol (or Yuan) dynasty (1271–1368). Official court records of the time make no specific reference to Guan, suggesting that he did not hold an official post there. Though this may at first seem surprising, given his celebrity as a respected writer, playwrights were rarely granted positions at court under Kublai Khan. It is also unlikely that Guan had sympathetic ties with the old Han Chinese aristocracy. He would never have known the court of the Song dynasty (960–1279), which the Mongol khans overthrew; and during his lifetime, north China under Kublai Khan was relatively peaceful and prosperous. A more probable explanation is that Guan favored more mundane pleasures over those of the court. Because Guan lived in a physician's household (where he himself may have worked as a practicing physician), he was protected from mandatory public service and taxation and enjoyed considerable freedom to live as he pleased. Indeed, he was known as the "Playboy of the Grand Capital" and focused his attention on gambling, drinking, and romance. By all accounts, he preferred the teahouse to the palace and would rather spend time with public entertainers and their commoner clientele than with courtly entertainers and their aristocratic patrons.

Although the performance traditions and techniques of Chinese theater have developed and changed considerably since the fourteenth century, Chinese still tend to view *zaju* plays as their "classical" drama, a corpus of works of higher poetic and literary quality than the drama of other eras. This lofty status is even more remarkable when we consider that there are more than three millennia of recorded theater history in China prior to the Yuan era. Accounts from court histories of the first millennium B.C.E. describe early theatrical performances in the time of the mythical King Yu Shun (2300–2205 B.C.E.). According to the scholars of the East Zhou dynasty (770–256 B.C.E.), theatrical rituals and musical performances occurred in China from the Shang dynasty (1760–1066 B.C.E.) onward. Imperial patronage during the first millennium B.C.E. supported jesters, puppeteers, storytellers, and other theatrical entertainers; Chinese actors today trace their art back to these various performative traditions, as well as to the famous Pear Orchard Conservatory, China's first known academy of music, which was established during the Tang dynasty (618–907 C.E.). Building on the various theatrical and musical forms that preceded them, early *zaju* of the Song dynasty in northern China arranged acrobatics, musical performances, and other entertainments around a short theatrical sketch, usually of a satirical nature. The growing popularity of theatrical entertainments coincided with the emergence of a vibrant middle class. To meet the increased demand for staged performances, numerous permanent theaters were built, some of them in the form of grand entertainment venues similar to today's film megaplexes.

This long tradition of performing arts in China might have been abruptly cut short had the Han intellectuals at the center of power during the Song dynasty held theatrical entertainments in high esteem, for the Mongol khans were keen to reject the cultural values of their predecessors and to keep the Han Chinese out of court. They therefore dismantled many crucial Chinese institutions after their conquest, casting many artists and intellectuals—who favored literary and philosophical pursuits dedicated to elucidating and expanding on the Confucian classics—out of positions of power and respect. Theatrical entertainers, who had enjoyed little respect from the Han elite, actually found their fortunes improved under Mongol rule: because they were officially classified with skilled technicians, they were protected from some of the more brutal state policies that affected intellectuals previously rewarded during the Song dynasty. It was the genius of Guan Hanqing and his contemporaries to take this cultural opportunity to transform the dramatic elements from various theatrical traditions, including early *zaju,* into cohesive dramatic texts—into a new form of *zaju* drama—much as the first great Greek theater artists, Thespis and Aeschylus, crafted tragedies from the looser frameworks of Dionysian rituals. As a result, during the Yuan dynasty *zaju* performances finally became high culture, and their scripts gained new literary respectability.

Guan's most admired *zaju* play, *Dou E Yuan,* concerns Dou E, who as a seven-year-old girl is given by her father, a poor Confucian scholar, to the widow Cai as payment for a debt. Ten years later, Dou E marries Cai's son but soon finds herself a widow. When another debtor, Doctor Lu, attempts to strangle Cai instead of repaying what he owes, she is rescued by Old Zhang and his son Donkey, who seek to marry the women. Dou E refuses Donkey's proposal out of loyalty to her dead husband, and the spurned suitor attempts to poison Cai, believing that the older woman's death will force Dou E to accept him. When instead Old Zhang drinks the poisoned soup and dies, Donkey accuses Dou E of murder and presents her with the choice of marrying him or going to court. Taken before the Prefect and beaten, Dou E maintains her innocence; but to spare her mother-in-law a beating, she falsely confesses to the crime and is sentenced to death. Dou E promises that her death will be followed by several signs that she has suffered an injustice, including a snowfall during the hottest part of the summer.

The ghost of Dou E appears to her father in this woodblock illustration from a Ming Dynasty publication of *Snow in Midsummer.*

Three years after her execution, her father returns as a court-appointed judicial official. Dou E's ghost appears to him, and when he hears her story he vows to avenge the wrong done to her.

Snow in Midsummer consists of four sequences of song sets (marked here as acts), each of which—as in Yuan *zaju* generally—contains about a dozen songs or verse passages connected by prose dialogue and action. In keeping with the dramatic convention of Yuan *zaju*, one major character—in this case, Dou E—sings the most morally and emotionally sympathetic lines of the play in lyric poetry. The other characters convey their feelings and opinions in various forms of spoken verse, while those passages whose principal function is to advance the story are spoken in simple prose. Because the Yuan stage had no formal scenery and minimal props, Guan's play relies heavily on language to underscore onstage movements, the passage of time, and the arc of its dramatic action. Characters identify and reidentify themselves, repeatedly recounting the events that have taken place. For example, Act 2 opens with an actor declaring: "I am Dr. Lu. I lured Mistress Cai outside the town and was just going to strangle her when two men rescued her. Today I am opening shop. I wonder who will turn up." This technique creates a story that is as much narrative as dramatic, and the sketch of past and present acquires an almost ceremonial clarity of presentation. It is the outline of moral illustration, but it is also the outline of a tragedy at once individual, social, and—in the face of death—cosmological.

Unifying these levels of meaning is the play's concern with justice in human affairs. *Snow in Midsummer* belongs to the popular genre of Chinese crime and detective fiction known in the sixteenth century as *kung-an*. *Zaju* plays written in this mode involve the commission of a crime and its prosecution under the legal system of the period. Within the courtroom, a judge or clerk ultimately solves the crime and dispenses justice. In almost all "courtroom" plays, the crime is murder, and the conflict is presented as a metaphysical struggle between good and evil. *Snow in Midsummer* also falls into a more specialized category: the "judgment-reversal" *zaju*, in which the verdict of a first judge is discovered to be erroneous and overturned by a second judge. The main points of interest in this subgenre are the difference between the corrupt judge and the honest judge and the process by which the latter undoes the damage caused by the former. Any Yuan courtroom play requires a villain, and the judgment-reversal plays call for two: the person who actually commits the crime and the dishonest judge. In *Snow in Midsummer* and other plays of this type, the victim is initially given a choice between a private and court settlement. The victim always chooses the court, confident that justice will prevail, but is proved terribly wrong. So it plays out in *Snow in Midsummer,* as the Prefect completes the cycle of injustice by sentencing Dou E to death.

The notion of justice portrayed in courtroom *zaju* is broadly in accordance with the principles of Confucius (551–479 B.C.E.), a philosopher whose teachings on government, justice, social relationships, and individual ethical conduct exerted a powerful influence on Chinese thought and literature for millennia. During the Song dynasty, which preceded the Mongol occupation, the *Analects* and other writings of the *Ru* philosophical school that Confucius founded were required study for those, like Dou E's father, who took the imperial civil service examinations. The principles of Confucianism—loyalty, proper observance of ritual, duty, justice, and benevolence—permeated every aspect of Chinese intellectual and cultural life. In the area of social relationships, Confucius stressed that cruelty should be redressed with justice, and all Yuan courtroom dramas, including *Snow in Midsummer,* meet that requirement in their conclusions. The judgment-reversal plays portray an especially stark imbalance in what a Confucian would view as the just equilibrium of human society, an imbalance epitomized in the disgraceful figure of the first judge and set right by his replacement in the second trial. From a Confucian perspective, the results are morally satisfying: the social, natural, and divine order is restored and an injustice redressed. Guan complicates these moral polarities that underlie Confucian thought and conventional judgment-reversal drama, however. In *Snow in Midsummer,* the second judge—Dou E's father—is not simply the inverse of the first judge. His methods appear no less brutal than those of his predecessor, and his powers of investigation little better. Moreover, it takes the otherworldly intercession of Dou E's ghost for her father even to pay attention to the case, and he discovers nothing that she does not explain to him.

Confucian principles also underlie the play's characterizations, though here, too, Guan's dramatic writing imbues Confucian models with human realism and complexity. Confucianism places a high value on filial duty and piety, for instance, and Dou E is clearly motivated by duty to her father (and, later, Cai). Yet rather than being a Confucian archetype, she is clearly an individual, motivated by passion and subject to historical social conditions. Throughout the play, she is the victim of misfortune and exploitation, and the social dimensions of her life's sorrows are recapitulated several times throughout the play, first by Cai and later with more personal bitterness by herself. The young widow's fierce denunciation of Cai's acceptance of a husband is fueled at least partly by her knowledge that fate has denied her the pleasures and protections of marriage. Medieval Chinese women were often powerless in the face of male desires, as demonstrated in the play by Cai's inability to fend off Zhang's advances despite her economic independence. Unmarried women and widows were especially vulnerable to such abuses, and Dou E's calamities are closely related to her status as a woman without a husband.

The personal difficulties of widowhood, of course, do not obscure the fact that Dou E acts at every turn in accordance with Confucian family values. Given the bitterness of her attack on Cai's inappropriate marriage, her willingness to sacrifice herself for her adoptive mother in court is stunning. But what appears in the abstract to be a noble act in the name of filial piety can also be understood as a welcome release from the tribulations of a miserable life. Similarly, while the miracles granted by Heaven at Dou E's execution and the circumstances of her return as a ghost to demand justice frame her story as a divine restoration of the natural Confucian order, the dramatic emphasis is on the final appeal from a daughter to her father to redress her personal tragedy. Justice may triumph at the end of *Snow in Midsummer,* but Guan's play remains haunted by Dou E's earlier protest and lament, sung before her execution:

The good are poor, and die before their time;
The wicked are rich, and live to a great old age.
The gods are afraid of the mighty and bully the weak;
They let evil take its course.
Ah, Earth! You will not distinguish good from bad,
And, Heaven! You let me suffer this injustice!
Tears pour down my cheeks in vain!

By calling into question Confucian notions of divine justice, lines such as these challenge the certainties of Confucian belief. Indeed, Dou E's redemption at the conclusion of the play seems as much a product of her will, indomitable even after death, as it is of heavenly or earthly justice.

Later adaptations of *Dou E Yuan* by the literati of the Ming dynasty (1368–1644) altered the work in ways that deepened its adherence to Confucian thought. But Guan's original play, which appealed to a wider, populist audience, emphasizes the ordinary passions and frustrations of Dou E and the other characters. Thus Dou E, who might be seen as a universal representation of conservative Confucian moral values, is at the same time a compellingly individual character, forceful in personality and articulate in her protests against the injustice she faces. Such complexity has led critics to variously interpret *Snow in Midsummer* as a Chinese tragedy, a piece of historical social realism, a parable of Confucian justice, and a proto-feminist work.

EVAN DARWIN WINET

Snow in Midsummer[1]

CHARACTERS

MISTRESS CAI, a widow
DOU TIANZHANG, a poor scholar, later a government inspector
DOU E, Dou Tianzhang's daughter DUANYUN
DOCTOR LU
OLD ZHANG
DONKEY, his son
PREFECT
ATTENDANT
The OFFICER in charge of executions
EXECUTIONER

Act 1

[*Enter* MISTRESS CAI.]

MRS. CAI A flower may blossom again,
But youth never returns.

I am Mistress Cai of Chuzhou.[2] There were three of us in my family; but unluckily my husband died, leaving me just one son who is eight years old. We live together, mother and son, and are quite well off. A scholar named Dou of Shanyang Prefecture borrowed five taels[3] of silver from me last year. Now the interest and capital come to ten taels,[4] and I've asked several times for the money; but Mr. Dou cannot pay it. He has a daughter, and I've a good mind to make her my daughter-in-law;[5] then he won't have to pay back the ten taels. Mr. Dou chose today as a lucky day, and is bringing the girl to me; so I won't ask him to pay me back, but wait for him at home. He should be here soon.

[*Enter* DOU TIANZHANG, *leading his daughter* DUANYUN.]

DOU I am master of all the learning in the world,
But my fate is worse than that of other men.

My name is Dou Tianzhang, and the home of my ancestors is Chang-an.[6] I have studied the classics since I was a child and read a good deal; but

1. Translated by Yang Xianyi and Gladys Yang.
2. A city in Anhui province, southeast China. In the original Chinese, Cai identifies herself here as an older woman with a humble term meaning "mother-in-law."
3. Chinese unit of weight, slightly more than an English ounce. *Scholar:* the original Chinese term here was used during the Tang dynasty (618–907 C.E.) to specify one who had passed the state examination to become a civil servant; later, under the Sung (907–1279) and Yuan (1271–1368) dynasties, it referred more generally to a scholar or candidate for the examination. *Shanyang Prefecture:* an administrative subdivision of Liaoning province in northeast China.
4. An interest rate that doubles the original loan is outrageously usurious, a recurring theme in the play.
5. It was customary for a family to take in a girl, usually from a poor family, to raise as a future daughter-in-law. Before marriage, she would be referred to as a "child-daughter-in-law" (in this translation, "child-bride").
6. Several times the capital of ancient China. Dou Tianzhang identifies himself humbly here with a traditional self-reference for a young man.

I haven't yet taken the examinations.[7] Unfortunately my wife has died, leaving me this only daughter, Duanyun. She lost her mother when she was three, and now she is seven. Living from hand to mouth, I moved to Shanyang Prefecture in Chuzhou and took lodgings here. There is a widow in this town named Cai, who lives alone with her son and is fairly well off, and as I had no money for traveling I borrowed five taels from her. Now, with the interest, I owe her ten taels; but though she has asked several times for the money, I haven't been able to pay her. And recently she has sent to say she would like my daughter to marry her son. Since the spring examinations will soon be starting, I should be going to the capital; but I have no money for the road. So I am forced to take Duanyun to Widow Cai as her future daughter-in-law. I'm not marrying my daughter but selling her! For this means the widow will cancel my debt and give me some cash for my journey. This is all I can hope for. Ah, child, your father does this against his will! While talking to myself I've reached her door. Mistress Cai! Are you at home?

[*Enter* MISTRESS CAI.]

MRS. CAI So it's Mr. Dou! Come in, please. I've been waiting for you.

[*They greet each other.*]

DOU I've brought you my daughter, ma'am, not to be your daughter-in-law—that would be asking too much—but to serve you day and night. I must be going to take the examination. I hope you will look after her.

MRS. CAI Well, you owed me ten taels including interest. Here is your promissory note back and another two taels for your journey. I hope you don't think it too little.

DOU Thank you, ma'am! Instead of asking for what I owe you, you have given me money for the road. Some day I shall repay your kindness in full. My daughter is a foolish child. Please take care of her, ma'am, for my sake.

MRS. CAI Don't worry, Mr. Dou. I shall look after your daughter as if she were my own.

DOU [*kneeling to her*] If the child deserves a beating, ma'am, for my sake just scold her! And if she deserves a scolding, for my sake speak gently to her! As for you, Duanyun, this isn't like at home, where your father used to put up with your whims. If you're naughty here, you'll be beaten and cursed. When shall I see you again, child? [*He sighs.*]

I drum sadly on my sheath;
I have studied the Confucian classics;
My unhappy wife died young,
And now I am parted from my only daughter.

[*Exit.*]

MRS. CAI Now Mr. Dou has left me his daughter, and gone to the capital for the examination. I must see to the house.

[*Exeunt.*[8]]

[*Enter* DOCTOR LU.]

7. That is, the state examinations to demonstrate literary proficiency; successful candidates were admitted to the civil bureaucracy, a primary means of climbing the social ladder. *The classics:* the works of Confucius (551–449 B.C.E.), which were the basis of a Chinese classical education.

8. They exit (Latin).

DOCTOR I diagnose all diseases with care,
And prescribe as the Herbal[9] dictates;
But I cannot bring dead men back to life,
And the live ones I treat often die.[1]

I am Doctor Lu. I own a drug shop[2] here. I've borrowed ten taels of silver from Mistress Cai of this town, and with interest now owe her twenty taels. She keeps coming for the money; but I haven't got it. If she doesn't come back, so much the better. If she does, I have a plan. I'll sit in my shop now, and wait to see who turns up.

[*Enter* MISTRESS CAI.]

MRS. CAI I am Mistress Cai. Thirteen years ago Mr. Dou Tianzhang left his daughter Duanyun with me to marry my son, and I changed her name to Dou E. But after their marriage my son died, so now she's a widow. That was nearly three years ago, and she'll soon be out of mourning.[3] I've told her that I'm going to town to collect a debt from Doctor Lu. Now I've reached his house. Is Doctor Lu in?

DOCTOR Yes, ma'am, come in.

MRS. CAI You've kept my money for a long time, doctor. You must pay me back

DOCTOR I've no money at home, ma'am. If you'll come with me to the village, I'll get money for you.

MRS. CAI Very well. I'll go with you.

[*They start walking.*]

DOCTOR Now we are outside the city. Here's a good spot, with no one about. Why not do it here? I've got the rope ready. Who's that calling you, ma'am?

MRS. CAI Where?

[*The* DOCTOR *strangles the widow with the rope. Enter* OLD ZHANG *and his son* DONKEY. *As they rush forward the* DOCTOR *takes to his heels.* OLD ZHANG *revives* MISTRESS CAI.]

DONKEY It's an old woman, dad, nearly strangled to death.

ZHANG Hey, you! Who are you? What's your name? Why did that fellow try to strangle you?

MRS. CAI My name is Cai and I live in town with my widowed daughter-in-law. Doctor Lu owes me twenty taels so he lured me here and tried to strangle me. If not for you and this young man,[4] it would have been all up with me!

DONKEY Did you hear that, dad? She has a daughter-in-law at home! Suppose you take her as your wife and I take the daughter-in-law? Propose it to her, dad!

ZHANG Hey, widow! You've no husband and I've no wife. How about the two of us getting married?

MRS. CAI What an idea! I shall give you a handsome sum of money to thank you.

DONKEY So you refuse! I'd better strangle you after all.

MRS. CAI Wait! Let me think a moment, brother!

9. An early Chinese pharmaceutical treatise.
1. Some translators interpret these ambiguous lines to mean "I uselessly treat the dead, and kill the living."
2. That is, a pharmacy, where raw medicinal herbs are sold.
3. That is, Dou E has faithfully observed the protocols of widowhood and will soon be able to stop wearing mourning clothes (and thus will become eligible for remarriage).
4. Mrs. Cai uses a courteous form of address that literally means "older brother."

DONKEY What do you need to think for? You take my dad, and I'll take your daughter-in-law.

MRS. CAI [*aside*] If I don't agree he'll strangle me! [*To them.*] Very well. Come home with me, both of you.

DONKEY Let's go.

[*Exeunt.*]

[*Enter* DOU E.]

DOU E I am Duanyun,[5] and my home was in Chuzhou. When I was three I lost my mother; and when I was seven I had to leave my father, for he sent me to Mistress Cai as her son's child-bride, and she changed my name to Dou E. At seventeen I married; but unluckily my husband died three years ago. Now I am twenty. There is a Doctor Lu in town who owes my mother-in-law twenty taels including interest; and though she has asked him several times for the money, he hasn't paid her back. She's gone today to try to collect the debt. Ah, when shall I escape from my misery?

My heart is full of grief,
I have suffered for so many years!
Morning or evening it is all the same:
From dawn to dusk I can neither eat nor sleep,
Racked by sad dreams at night, sad thoughts by day,
Unending sorrow which I cannot banish,
Unceasing reasons for fresh misery.
Wretchedness makes me weep, grief makes me frown;

Will this never come to an end?

Is it my fate to be wretched all my life?
Who else knows grief like mine?
For my sorrow, like flowing water, never ceases.
At three I lost my mother, at seven was torn from my father;
Then the life of the husband I married was cut short;
So my mother-in-law and I are left as widows,
With no one to care for us or see to our needs.
Did I burn too little incense in my last life[6]
That my marriage was unlucky?
We should all do good betimes;
So I mourn for my husband and serve my mother-in-law,
Obedient to all her bidding.

My mother-in-law has been gone a long time to collect that debt. What can be keeping her?

[*Enter* MISTRESS CAI *with* OLD ZHANG *and* DONKEY.]

MRS. CAI Wait here at the door while I go in.

DONKEY All right, mother. Go in and tell her her husband is at the door.

[MISTRESS CAI *sees* DOU E.]

DOU E So you're back, mother. Have you had a meal?

MRS. CAI [*crying*] Ah, poor child! How am I going to break this to you?

DOU E I see her in floods of tears,

5. Dou E identifies herself with a humble self-reference for a young woman.

6. A reference to the Buddhist belief in karma, the doctrine that one's actions determine one's destiny in future incarnations.

Hiding some grief in her heart;
Greeting her quickly, I beg her to tell me the reason.

MRS. CAI How can I say this?

DOU E She's shilly-shallying and looks ashamed.
What has upset you, mother? Why are you crying?

MRS. CAI When I asked Doctor Lu for the silver, he lured me outside the town, then tried to strangle me; but an old man called Zhang and his son Donkey saved my life. Now Old Zhang is going to marry me: that's why I'm upset.

DOU E That would never do, mother! Please think again! We're not short of money. Besides, you are growing old—how can you take another husband?

MRS. CAI Child, I couldn't do anything else!

DOU E Mother, listen to me!
What will become of you
If you choose a day and solemnize a wedding?[7]
Now your hair is as white as snow,
How can you wear the bright silk veil of a bride?
No wonder they say it is hard to keep women at home,[8]
If at sixty, when all thought of love should be over,
You've forgotten your former husband,
And taken a fancy to another man!
This will make others split their sides with laughter!
Yes, split their sides with laughter!
Like the widow who fanned her husband's tomb,
You're no tender bamboo shoot, no tender shoot.
How can you paint your eyebrows and remarry?
Your husband left you his property,
Made provision for the future,
For daily food and a good livelihood,
So that you and your son could remain beholden to no one,
And live to a ripe old age.
Did he go to such trouble for nothing?

MRS. CAI Since it has come to this, I think you'd better take a husband too, and today can be the wedding day.

DOU E You take a husband if you must. I won't!

MRS. CAI The date is fixed, and they are already here.

DONKEY Now we shall marry into their family. Our hats are brushed as good as new, and have narrow brims like bridegrooms'! Good! Fine!

DOU E Stand back, you fellows!
Women should not believe all men say;
Such a marriage could not last.
Where did she find this old yokel,
And this other ruffian here?
Have you no feeling left for the dead?
You must think this over again.
Your husband worked in different cities and counties
To amass a well-earned fortune, and lack nothing.

7. That is, by burning incense in ancestral halls.
8. According to a Chinese proverb, "A grown girl is not to be kept at home; if you try, you only make an enemy out of her."

How can you let his estate go to Donkey Zhang?
He tilled the land, but others are reaping the harvest.

[*Exit.*]

ZHANG [*to* MRS. CAI] Let us go and drink, ma'am.

[*Exeunt.*]

DONKEY Dou E refuses to have me, but I shan't let her get away: she will have to be my wife. Now I'll drink with my old man! [*Exit.*]

Act 2

[*Enter* DOCTOR LU.]

DOCTOR I am Doctor Lu. I lured Mistress Cai outside the town and was just going to strangle her when two men rescued her. Today I am opening shop. I wonder who will turn up.

[*Enter* DONKEY.]

DONKEY I am Donkey Zhang. Dou E still refuses to marry me. Now the old woman is ill, I'm going to poison her; for once the old one is dead, the young one will have to be my wife.[9] Ah, here is a drug shop. Doctor! I want a drug!

DOCTOR What drug do you want?

DONKEY I want some poison.

DOCTOR Who dares sell you poison? How can you ask such a thing?

DONKEY You won't let me have it then?

DOCTOR I won't. What are you going to do about it?

DONKEY [*seizing him*] Fine! Fine! Aren't you the man who tried to murder Mistress Cai? Do you think I don't recognize you? I'll take you to court.

DOCTOR [*in panic*] Let me go, brother! I've got it! I've got it!

[*Gives him the poison.*]

DONKEY Now that I've got the poison, I'm going home.

[*Exit.*]

DOCTOR So that man who came to buy poison was one of the men who rescued the widow. Since I've given him poison, he may get me into further trouble later. I'd better close my shop and go to Zhuozhou[1] to sell drugs.

[*Exit.*]

[*Enter* MISTRESS CAI, *supported by* OLD ZHANG *and* DONKEY.]

ZHANG I came to Mistress Cai's house hoping to be her second husband. Who would have thought that the widow would fall ill? I am really too unlucky. If there's anything you fancy to eat, ma'am, just let me know.

MRS. CAI I'd like some mutton tripe soup.

ZHANG Son, go and tell Dou E to make some mutton tripe soup for her mother-in-law.

DONKEY Dou E! Your mother-in-law wants some mutton tripe soup. Look sharp about it!

[*Enter* DOU E.]

DOU E I am Dou E. My mother-in-law is unwell and wants some mutton tripe soup, so I've made her some. When you think of it, some women are too fickle!

She wants to lie with a husband all her life,

9. That is, social and economic necessity will force Dou E to accept him as a husband.

1. A city in Hebei province, northeastern China.

Unwilling to sleep alone;
First she married one, and now she has picked another.
Some women never speak of household matters,
But pick up all the gossip,
Describe their husbands' adventures,
And are always up to some low tricks themselves.
Is there one like Lady Zhuo[2] who stooped to serve in a tavern?
Or like Meng Guang[3] who showed such respect to her husband?
The women today are different:
You can neither tell their character from their speech,
Nor judge them by their actions.
They're all of them faithless, all run after new lovers;
And before their husband's graves are dry
They set aside their mourning for new clothes.
Where is the woman whose tears for her husband
Caused the Great Wall to crumble?[4]
Where is she who left her washing
And drowned herself in the stream?[5]
Where is she who changed into stone
Through longing for her husband?[6]
How shameful that women today are so unfaithful,
So few of them are chaste, so many wanton!
All, all are gone, those virtuous women of old;
For wives will not cleave to their husbands!

Now the soup is ready. I had better take it in.

DONKEY Let me take it to her. [*He takes the bowl.*] This hasn't much flavor. Bring some salt and vinegar.

[DOU E *goes out.* DONKEY *puts poison in the soup.* DOU E *comes back.*]

DOU E Here are the salt and vinegar.

DONKEY Put some in.

DOU E You say that it lacks salt and vinegar,
Adding these will improve the flavor.
I hope my mother will be better soon,
And the soup will serve as a cordial.
Then the three of you can live happily together.

ZHANG Son, is the soup ready?

2. Zhuo Wenjun, the daughter of a rich man, who eloped with Sima Xiangru (179–117 B.C.E.), a famous Han Dynasty scholar. Since they were poor, they kept a small tavern in Chengdu where she served as barmaid [translator's note].

3. Wife of Liang Hung of the Later Han dynasty. She showed her respect and love for her husband by raising the dinner tray as high as her eyebrows when she brought it to him.

4. According to a folktale, Meng Jiang-nu's husband, a conscript laborer, died while building the Great Wall during the reign of the First Emperor of Qin. She went to the wall to find her missing husband, and wept so bitterly that part of it collapsed, revealing his dead body.

5. During the Spring and Autumn Period (770–475 B.C.E.), Wu Zixu, a minister of Chu, fled to Wu. He came upon a woman doing her laundry by a river, who fed him and then drowned herself in the river—both to prove that she would not betray him to his pursuers and because she had compromised her chastity by taking in a man who was a stranger.

6. A reference to a legend about a faithful wife who, during her husband's absence from home, climbed a hill every day to watch for his return. Finally she turned into a boulder, which was called *wang-fu shi* (watching-for-husband stone).

DONKEY Here it is. Take it.

ZHANG [*taking the soup*] Have some soup, ma'am.

MRS. CAI I am sorry to give you so much trouble. You have some first.

ZHANG Won't you try it?

MRS. CAI No, I want *you* to drink it first.

[OLD ZHANG *drinks the soup.*]

DOU E One says: "Won't you try it?"
The other says: "You have it!"
What a shameful way to talk!
How can I help being angry?
The new couple is in transports;
Forgetting her first husband,
She listens to this new man's lightest word.
Now her heart is like a willow seed in the breeze,
Not steadfast as a rock.
Old love is nothing to new love:
She wants to live with this new man forever,
Without a thought for the other man far away.

ZHANG Why has this soup made me dizzy?

[*He falls to the ground.*]

MRS. CAI Why should you feel unwell after that soup? [*Panic-stricken.*] Take a grip on yourself, old man! Don't give up so easily! [*Wails.*]

DOU E It's no use grieving for him;
All mortal men must die when their time is up.
Some fall ill, some meet with accidents;
Some catch a chill, some are struck down by heat;
Some die of hunger, surfeit, or overwork;
But every death has its cause,
Human life is ruled by fate,[7]
And no man can control it,
For our span of life is predestined.
He has been here a few days only;
He is not of your family,
And he never sent you wedding gifts:
Sheep, wine, silk, or money.
For a time you stayed together,
But now he is dead and gone!
I am not an unfilial daughter,
But I fear what the neighbors may say;
So stop your moaning and wailing:
He is not the man you married as a girl.

[OLD ZHANG *dies.*]

MRS. CAI What shall we do? He's dead!

DOU E He's no relation—I have no tears for him.
There's no need to be so overcome with grief,
Or to cry so bitterly and lose your head!

7. Human affairs are subject to the authority of Heaven and Earth, which is often invoked in this play when human judgment falters.

DONKEY Fine! You've poisoned my father! What are you going to do about it?

MRS. CAI Child, you had better marry him now.

DOU E How can you say such a thing, mother?
This fellow forced my mother-in-law to keep him;
Now he's poisoned his father,
But whom does he think he can frighten?

MRS. CAI You'd better marry him, child.

DOU E A horse can't have two saddles;[8]
I was your son's wife when he was alive,
Yet now you are urging me to marry again.
This is unthinkable!

DONKEY Dou E, you murdered my old man. Do you want to settle this in private or settle it in public?

DOU E What do you mean?

DONKEY If you want it settled in public, I'll drag you to the court, and you'll have to confess to the murder of my father! If you want it settled in private, agree to be my wife. Then I'll let you off.

DOU E I am innocent. I'll go with you to the prefect.[9]

[DONKEY *drags* DOU E *and* MISTRESS CAI *out.*]

Act 3

[*Enter the* PREFECT *with an* ATTENDANT.]

PREFECT I am a hard-working official;
I make money out of my lawsuits;
But when my superiors come to investigate,
I pretend to be ill and stay at home in bed.
I am prefect of Chuzhou. This morning I am holding court.
Attendant, summon the court!

[*The* ATTENDANT *gives a shout.*]

[*Enter* DONKEY, *dragging in* DOU E *and* MISTRESS CAI.]

DONKEY I want to lodge a charge.

ATTENDANT Come over here.

[DONKEY *and* DOU E *kneel to the* PREFECT, *who kneels to them.*][1]

PREFECT [*kneeling*] Please rise.

ATTENDANT Your Honor, this is a citizen who's come to ask for justice. Why should you kneel to him?

PREFECT Why? Because such citizens are food and clothes to me!

[*The* ATTENDANT *assents.*]

PREFECT Which of you is the plaintiff, which the defendant? Out with the truth now!

DONKEY I am the plaintiff. I accuse this young woman, Dou E, of poisoning my father with soup. Let justice be done, Your Honor!

PREFECT Who poisoned the soup?

DOU E Not I!

8. A proverb meaning that a wife cannot serve two husbands.

9. The presiding judicial magistrate.

1. A stylized self-presenting gesture of humility that is appropriate for Donkey and Dou E, but ironic for a prefect.

MRS. CAI Not I!

DONKEY Not I!

PREFECT If none of you did it, I wonder if I could have done it?

DOU E Your Honor is as discerning as a mirror,
And can see my innermost thoughts.
There was nothing wrong with the soup,
I know nothing about the poison;
He made a pretence of tasting it,
Then his father drank it and fell down dead.
It is not that I want to deny my guilt in court;
But I cannot confess to a crime I have not committed!

PREFECT Low characters are like that: they'll only confess when put to torture. Attendant! Bring the bastinado to beat her.

[*The* ATTENDANT *beats* DOU E. *Three times she faints and he has to sprinkle her with water to bring her round.*]

DOU E This terrible beating is more than I can bear.
You brought this on yourself, mother. Why complain?
May all women in the world who marry again
Be warned by me!
Why are they shouting so fiercely?
I groan with pain;
I come to myself, then faint away again.
A thousand strokes: I am streaming with blood!
At each blow from the bastinado
My blood spurts out and my skin is torn from my flesh;
My spirit takes flight in fear,
Approaching the nether regions.[2]
Who knows the bitterness in my heart?
It was not I who poisoned the old man;
I beg Your Honor to find out the truth!

PREFECT Will you confess now?

DOU E I swear it was not I who put in the poison.

PREFECT In that case, beat the old woman.

DOU E [*hastily*] Stop, stop! Don't beat my mother-in-law! Rather than that, I'll say I poisoned the old man.

PREFECT Fasten her in the cangue[3] and throw her into the gaol for the condemned. Tomorrow she shall be taken to the market-place to be executed.

MRS. CAI [*weeping*] Dou E, my child! It's because of me you are losing your life. Oh, this will be the death of me!

DOU E When I am a headless ghost, unjustly killed,
Do you think I will spare that scoundrel?
Men cannot be deceived for ever,
And Heaven will see this injustice.
I struggled as hard as I could, but now I am helpless;
I was forced to confess that I poisoned the old man;
How could I let you be beaten, mother?
How could I save you except by dying myself?

[*She is led off.*]

2. That is, nearing death.
3. A frame used to confine the neck and hands in a portable pillory or stocks.

DONKEY If she's to be killed tomorrow, I'll hang around.

[*Exit.*]

MRS. CAI Poor child! Tomorrow she will be killed in the market-place. This will be the death of me! [*Exit.*]

PREFECT Tomorrow Dou E will be executed. Today's work is done. Bring me my horse; I am going home to drink.

[*Exeunt.*]

[*Enter the* OFFICER *in charge.*]

OFFICER I am the officer in charge of executions. Today we are putting a criminal to death. We must stand guard at the end of the road, to see that no one comes through.

[*Enter the* ATTENDANTS. *They beat the drum and the gong three times; then the* EXECUTIONER *enters, sharpens his sword and waves a flag.* DOU E *is led on in a cangue. The gong and drum are beaten.*]

EXECUTIONER Get a move on! Let no one pass this way.

DOU E Through no fault of mine I am called a criminal,
And condemned to be beheaded—
I cry out to Heaven and Earth of this injustice!
I reproach both Earth and Heaven
For they would not save me.
The sun and moon give light by day and by night,
Mountains and rivers watch over the world of men;
Yet Heaven cannot tell the innocent from the guilty;
And confuses the wicked with the good!
The good are poor, and die before their time;
The wicked are rich, and live to a great old age.
The gods are afraid of the mighty and bully the weak;
They let evil take its course.
Ah, Earth! you will not distinguish good from bad,
And, Heaven! you let me suffer this injustice!
Tears pour down my cheeks in vain!

EXECUTIONER Get a move on! We are late.

DOU E The cangue round my neck makes me stagger this way and that,
And I'm jostled backward and forward by the crowd.
Will you do me a favor, brother?

EXECUTIONER What do you want?

DOU E If you take me the front way, I shall bear you a grudge;
If you take me the back way, I shall die content.
Please do not think me willful!

EXECUTIONER Now that you're going to the execution ground, are there any relatives you want to see?

DOU E I am going to die. What relatives do I need?

EXECUTIONER Why did you ask me just now to take you the back way?

DOU E Please don't go by the front street, brother,
But take me by the back street.
The other way my mother-in-law might see me.

EXECUTIONER You can't escape death, so why worry if she sees you?

DOU E If my mother-in-law were to see me in chains being led to the execution ground—
She would burst with indignation!

She would burst with indignation!
Please grant me this comfort, brother, before I die!

[*Enter* MISTRESS CAI.]

MRS. CAI Ah, Heaven! Isn't that my daughter-in-law? This will be the death of me!

EXECUTIONER Stand back, old woman!

DOU E Let her come closer so that I can say a few words to her.

EXECUTIONER Hey, old woman! Come here. Your daughter-in-law wants to speak to you.

MRS. CAI Poor child! This will be the death of me!

DOU E Mother, when you were unwell and asked for mutton tripe soup, I prepared some for you. Donkey Zhang made me fetch more salt and vinegar so that he could poison the soup, and then told me to give it to you. He didn't know his old man would drink it. Donkey Zhang poisoned the soup to kill you, so that he could force me to be his wife. He never thought his father would die instead. To take revenge, he dragged me to court. Because I didn't want you to suffer, I had to confess to murder, and now I am going to be killed. In future, mother, if you have gruel to spare, give me half a bowl; and if you have paper money to spare, burn some for me, for the sake of your dead son![4]

Take pity on one who is dying an unjust death;
Take pity on one whose head will be struck from her body;
Take pity on one who has worked with you in your home;
Take pity on one who has neither mother nor father;
Take pity on one who has served you all these years;
And at festivals offer my spirit a bowl of cold gruel.

MRS. CAI [*weeping*] Don't worry. Ah, this will be the death of me!

DOU E Burn some paper coins to my headless corpse,
For the sake of your dead son.
We wail and complain to Heaven:
There is no justice! Dou E is wrongly slain!

EXECUTIONER Now then, old woman, stand back! The time has come.

[DOU E *kneels, and the* EXECUTIONER *removes the cangue from her neck.*]

DOU E I want to say three things, officer. If you will let me, I shall die content. I want a clean mat and a white silk streamer twelve feet long to hang on the flagpole. When the sword strikes off my head, not a drop of my warm blood will stain the ground. It will all fly up instead to the white silk streamer. This is the hottest time of summer, sir. If injustice has indeed been done, three feet of snow will cover my dead body. Then this district will suffer from drought for three whole years.

EXECUTIONER Be quiet! What a thing to say!

[*The* EXECUTIONER *waves his flag.*]

DOU E A dumb woman was blamed for poisoning herself;
A buffalo is whipped while it toils for its master.

EXECUTIONER Why is it suddenly so overcast? It is snowing!

[*He prays to Heaven.*]

4. By the time of the play's composition, the ancient Chinese custom of offering burnt sacrifices for the newly dead had been superseded by the burning of paper symbols of worldly wealth—coins, livestock, luxury goods, etc.—to help ensure prosperity in the afterlife.

DOU E Once Zou Yan[5] caused frost to appear
Now snow will show the injustice done to me!

[*The* EXECUTIONER *beheads her, and the* ATTENDANT *sees to her body.*]

EXECUTIONER A fine stroke! Now let us go and have a drink.

[*The* ATTENDANTS *assent, and carry the body off.*]

Act 4

[*Enter* DOU TIANZHANG.][6]

DOU I am Dou Tianzhang. It is thirteen years since I left my child Duanyun. I went to the capital, passed the examination and was made a counsellor.[7] And because I am able, just, and upright, the emperor appointed me Inspector of the Huai River Area.[8] I have traveled from place to place investigating cases, and I have the sword of authority and golden tally[9] so that I can punish corrupt officials without first reporting to the throne. My heart is torn between grief and happiness. I am glad because I am a high official responsible for seeing that justice is done. I am sad, though, because when Duanyun was seven I gave her to Mistress Cai; and after I became an official and sent for news of the widow to Chuzhou, the neighbors said she had moved away—to what place they did not know—and there has been no word since. I have wept for my child till my eyes are dim and my hair is white. Now I have come south of the Huai River, and am wondering why this district has had no rain for three years. I shall rest in the district office, boy. Tell the local officers they need not call today. I shall see them early tomorrow.

SERVANT [*calling out*] The officers and secretaries are not to call on His Excellency today. He will see them early tomorrow.

DOU Tell the secretaries of the different departments to send all their cases here for my inspection. I shall study some under the lamp.

[*The* SERVANT *brings him the files.*]

DOU Light the lamp for me. You have been working hard, and you may rest now. But come when I call you.

[*The* SERVANT *lights the lamp and leaves.*]

DOU I shall go through a few cases. Here is one concerning Dou E, who poisoned her father-in-law. Curious that the first culprit's surname should be the same as mine! To murder one's father-in-law is one of the unpardonable crimes;[1] so it seems there are lawless elements among my clan. Since this

5. A loyal official serving the prince of Yan during the Warring States period (475 221 B.C.E.). When the prince imprisoned him on the strength of an enemy's accusation, Zou Yan cried out to heaven, which exhibited displeasure by bringing frost in midsummer.

6. His new status is indicated by a cap and a sash. He is accompanied by his servant (a role that would be played as a clown).

7. Specifically, a counsellor for state affairs in the Imperial Secretariat.

8. That is, a provincial surveillance commissioner for two adjacent judicial circuits north of the Yangtze River: one to the west of the Huai River, and the other to the east of the Huai River.

9. Symbols of authority, given by the emperor. The sword empowered the receiver to deliver the death penalty without the usual mandatory review by a central authority (an extraordinary sanction); the golden tablet was worn by high-ranking Yuan officials.

1. The Criminal Law Section in the *History of Yuan* lists ten unpardonable crimes: to contemplate rebellion, to contemplate a greatly subversive act, to contemplate treason, to commit a detestable or subversive act (Dou E's crime), to lack moral rules, to be extremely disrespectful, to lack filial piety, to abuse one for whom one would be obliged to mourn, to behave unrighteously, and to commit incest.

case has been dealt with, I need not read it. I'll put it at the bottom of the pile and look at another. Wait, I suddenly feel drowsy. I suppose I am growing old, and am tired after traveling. I will take a short nap on the desk. [*He sleeps.*]

[*Enter* DOU E*'s ghost.*]

DOU E Day after day I weep in the underworld,[2]
Waiting impatiently for my revenge.
I pace on slowly in darkness,
Then am borne along by the whirlwind;
Enveloped by mist I come swiftly in ghostly form.

[*She looks about her.*] Now the door-gods[3] will not let me pass. I am the daughter of Inspector Dou. Though I died unjustly, my father does not know it; so I have come to visit him in his dreams.

[*She enters the room and weeps.*]

DOU [*shedding tears*] Duanyun, my child! Where have you been?

[DOU E*'s spirit leaves,*[4] *and* DOU *wakes up.*]

How odd! I fell asleep and dreamed that I saw my daughter coming towards me; but where is she now? Let me go on with these cases.

[DOU E*'s spirit enters and makes the lamp burn low.*]

Strange! I was just going to read a case when the light flickered and dimmed. My servant is asleep; I must trim the wick myself. [*As he trims the lamp,* DOU E*'s spirit rearranges the file.*] Now the light is brighter, I can read again. "This concerns the criminal Dou E, who poisoned her father-in-law." Strange! I read this case first, and put it under the others. How has it come to the top? Since this case has already been dealt with let me put it at the bottom again and study a different one. [*Once more* DOU E*'s spirit makes the lamp burn low.*] Strange! Why is the light flickering again? I must trim it once more. [*As* DOU *trims the light,* DOU E*'s spirit once more turns over the file.*] Now the lamp is brighter, I can read another case. "This concerns the criminal Dou E, who poisoned her father-in-law." How extraordinary! I definitely put this at the bottom of the pile just before I trimmed the lamp. How has it come to the top again? Can there be ghosts in this office? Well, ghost or no ghost, an injustice must have been done. Let me put this underneath and read another. [DOU E*'s spirit makes the lamp burn low again.*] Strange! The lamp is flickering again. Can there actually be a ghost here tampering with it? I'll trim it once more. [*As he trims the wick,* DOU E*'s spirit comes up to him and he sees her. He strikes his sword on the desk.*] Ah, there's the ghost! I warn you, I am the emperor's inspector of justice. If you come near, I'll cut you in two. Hey, boy! How can you sleep so soundly? Get up at once! Ghosts! Ghosts! This is terrifying!

DOU E Fear is making him lose his head;
The sound of my weeping has frightened him more than ever.
Here, Dou Tianzhang, my old father,
Will you let your daughter Dou E bow to you?

DOU You say I am your father, ghost, and offer to bow to me as my daughter. Aren't you mistaken? My daughter's name is Duanyun. When she was

2. That is, she weeps at "the Home-gazing Terrace" to which, according to Chinese folklore, the dead ascend in order to watch their families in the human world.
3. At New Year's, pictures of the gods of the left and right doors are hung to ward off spirits.
4. A "false exit," as it is known in classical Chinese theater: the actor turns his or her back toward the audience to indicate an absence, and then simply turns around again to "reenter."

seven she was given to Mistress Cai as a child-bride. You call yourself by a different name, Dou E. How can you be my child?

DOU E After you gave me to Mistress Cai, father, she changed my name to Dou E.

DOU So you say you are my child Duanyun. Let me ask you this: Are you the woman accused of murdering her father-in-law and executed?

DOU E I am.

DOU Hush, girl! I've wept for you till my eyes grew dim, and worried for you till my hair turned white. How did you come to be condemned for this most heinous of crimes? I am a high official now, whose duty it is to see that justice is done. I have come here to investigate cases and discover corrupt officials. You are my child, but you are guilty of the worst crime of all. If I could not control you, how can I control others? When I married you to the widow's son, I expected you to observe the Three Duties and Four Virtues.[5] The Three Duties are obedience to your father before marriage, obedience to your husband after marriage, and obedience to your son after your husband's death. The Four Virtues are to serve your parents-in-law, to show respect to your husband, to remain on good terms with your sisters-in-law, and to live in peace with your neighbors. But regardless of your duties, you have committed the gravest crime of all! The proverb says: Look before you leap, or you may be sorry too late. For three generations no son of our clan has broken the law; for five generations no daughter has married again. As a married woman, you should have studied propriety and morality; but instead you perpetrated the most terrible crime. You have disgraced our ancestors and injured my good name. Tell me the whole truth at once, and nothing but the truth! If you utter one false word, I shall send you to the tutelary god; then your spirit will never re-enter human form, but remain a hungry ghost forever in the shades.[6]

DOU E Don't be so angry, father. Don't threaten me like an angry wolf or tiger! Let me explain this to you. At three, I lost my mother; at seven, I was parted from my father, when you sent me to Mistress Cai as her future daughter-in-law, and my name was changed to Dou E. At seventeen, I married; but unhappily two years later my husband died, and I stayed as a widow with my mother-in-law. In Chuzhou there lived a certain Doctor Lu, who owed my mother-in-law twenty taels of silver. One day when she went to ask him for the money, he lured her outside the town and tried to strangle her; but Donkey Zhang and his father came by and saved her life. Old Zhang asked: "Whom do you have in your family, ma'am?" My mother-in-law said: "No one but a widowed daughter-in-law." Old Zhang said: "In that case, I will marry you. What do you say?" When my mother-in-law refused, the two men said: "If you don't agree, we shall strangle you again!" So she was frightened into marrying him. Donkey tried to seduce me several times, but I always resisted him. One day my mother-in-law was unwell and wanted some mutton tripe soup. When I prepared it, Donkey told me to let him taste it. "It's good," he said. "But there's not enough salt and vinegar."

5. Fundamental Confucian principles. For a gentleman, the Three Duties are to cultivate nonviolence and gravity of bearing, to serve the truth, and to speak only what is worthy and just; the Four Virtues are sincerity, benevolence, filial piety, and propriety.

6. In Chinese folklore, ghosts are restless souls that wander forever in a perpetual state of unfulfilled desire. *To the tutelary god:* that is, to the temple of the city's guardian god.

When I went to fetch more, he secretly poisoned the soup and told me to take it to her. But my mother-in-law gave it to Old Zhang. Then blood spurted from the old man's mouth, nose, ears and eyes, and he died. At that Donkey said, "Dou E, you poisoned my father. Do you want to settle this in public or in private?" "What do you mean?" I asked. "If you want it settled in public," he said, "I shall take the case to court, and you will pay for my father's death with your life. If you want it settled in private, then be my wife." "A good horse won't have two saddles," I told him. "A good woman won't remarry. For three generations no son of our clan has broken the law; for five generations no daughter has married again. I'd rather die than be your wife. I am innocent. I'll go to court with you." Then he dragged me before the prefect. I was tried again and again, stripped and tortured; but I would rather have died than make a false confession. When the prefect saw that I wouldn't confess, he threatened to have my mother-in-law tortured; and because she was too old to stand the torture, I made a false confession. Then they took me to the execution ground to kill me. I made three vows before my death. First, I asked for a twelve-foot white silk streamer and swore that, if I was innocent, when the sword struck off my head no drop of my blood would stain the ground—it would all fly up to the streamer. Next I vowed that, though it was midsummer, Heaven would send down three feet of snow to cover my body. Last, I vowed that this district would suffer three years' drought. All these vows have come true, because of the crime against me.

I complained not to any official but to Heaven,
For I could not express the injustice that was done me;
And to save my mother from torture
I confessed to a crime of which I was innocent,
And remained true to my dead husband.
Three feet of snow fell on my corpse;
My hot blood gushed to the white silk streamer;
Zou Yan called down frost,
And snow showed the injustice done me.
Your child committed no crime,
But suffered a great wrong:
For resisting seduction I was executed!
I would not disgrace my clan, so I lost my life!
Day after day in the shades
My spirit mourns alone.
You are sent by the emperor with authority;
Consider this case and this man's wickedness;
Cut him in pieces and avenge my wrong!

DOU [*weeping*] Ah, my wrongly slain daughter, how this wrings my heart! Let me ask you this: Is it because of you that this district has suffered for three years from drought?

DOU E It is.

DOU So! This reminds me of a story. In the Han Dynasty[7] there was a virtuous widow whose mother-in-law hanged herself, and whose sister-in-law accused her of murdering the old woman. The governor of Donge[8] had her

7. 206 B.C.E.–220 C.E.

8. Unclear reference; Shih Chung-wen translates this title instead as the governor of Tung-hai, or the prefect of the East Sea.

executed, but because of her unjust death there was no rain in that district for three years. When Lord Yu came to investigate, he saw the dead woman's ghost carrying a plea and weeping before the hall; and after he changed the verdict, killed a bull, and sacrificed at her grave there was a great downpour of rain. This case is rather similar to that. Tomorrow I shall right this wrong for you.

I bow my white head in sorrow
Over the innocent girl who was wrongly slain.
Now dawn is breaking, you had better leave me;
Tomorrow I shall set right this miscarriage of justice.

DOU E [*bowing*] With sharp sword of authority and tally of gold,
You will kill all evil and corrupt officials,
To serve your sovereign and relieve the people!

[*She turns back.*] There's one thing I nearly forgot, father. My mother-in-law is old now, and has no one to look after her.

DOU This is dutiful, my child.

DOU E I ask my father to care for my mother-in-law,
For she is growing old. My father now
Will reopen my case and change the unjust verdict.

[*Exit.*]

DOU Dawn is breaking. Call the local officers, and all those concerned in the case of Dou E.

SERVANT Yes, Your Excellency.

[*The* PREFECT, MISTRESS CAI, DONKEY ZHANG *and* DOCTOR LU *are sent in. They kneel before* DOU.]

DOU Mistress Cai, do you recognize me?

MRS. CAI No, Your Excellency.

DOU I am Dou Tianzhang. Listen, all of you, to the verdict! Donkey Zhang murdered his father and blackmailed good citizens. He shall be executed in public. Let him be taken to the marketplace to be killed. The prefect passed a wrong sentence. He shall be given one hundred strokes and have his name struck off the official list.[9] Doctor Lu is guilty of selling poison. Let him be beheaded in the marketplace. Mistress Cai shall be lodged in my house. The wrong sentence passed on Dou E shall be rescinded.

Let the Donkey be killed in public,
The prefect dismissed from office;
Then let us offer a great sacrifice
So that my daughter's spirit may go to heaven.

9. That is, he will never again be eligible for government employment; hence, he will never be able to improve his social standing.

ZEAMI MOTOKIYO

1363–1443

Among the numerous theatrical forms and dramatic genres developed in Japan, none has been more revered than the stately yet elusive noh theater that became a high art form in the fourteenth century. While kabuki theater would later dazzle the senses with extravagant costumes, acrobatic movements, and elaborate scenic effects, noh achieved its dramatic and theatrical effects through understatement, ritualistic gesture, and a poetic conception of language, character, and the stage. In the evolution of noh from earlier forms of theater to a courtly entertainment of the samurai, or warrior, class, Zeami Motokiyo is a celebrated and central figure. Actor, head of an acting troupe, and playwright, Zeami refined the art of noh into a theatrical form combining songs, dance, music, and poetry. During his long and productive career, Zeami articulated the aesthetics of this newly crafted art and its performance in a series of treatises that rank among the world's most important works of dramatic theory.

Born in 1363, Zeami was the son of Kanami Kiyotsugu (1333–1384), who was an accomplished actor and playwright and the head of an acting troupe specializing in *sarugaku* (or *sarugaku noh*, as the theatrical form was then called). In 1374, Kanami and his eleven-year-old son performed at the Imakumano Shrine in Kyoto, the imperial capital of medieval Japan. As the result of this performance they won the patronage of the young shogun (or military ruler) Ashikaga Yoshimitsu (1358–1408), who, as part of his successful attempt to enhance his legitimacy, aided the arts as the earlier nobility had always done. With Yoshimitsu's support and with the benefit of a highly cultured audience, Kanami brought a number of innovations to *sarugaku* that furthered its development into the sophisticated art we recognize as noh.

His son became a favorite of the shogun, serving him as both artist and companion/lover, and upon Kanami's death the young Zeami took over as head of his father's troupe. Consolidating and extending his father's theatrical innovations, Zeami became one of the noh theater's most accomplished actors, playwrights, and theorists. In a number of studies—including *Fushikadensho* (*Teachings on Style and the Flower*, 1400–02), *Shikado* (*The True Path to the Flower*, 1420), and *Nosakusho* (*On Writing Noh Plays*, 1423)—Zeami discussed the origins of noh and its defining features, the intricacies of acting, and the principles of noh composition. About fifty plays are now ascribed to him, including some that are extensive revisions of earlier texts, and the greatest of these—such plays as *Komachi at Sekidera* and ATSUMORI—stand as crowning achievements in the canon of noh drama. With the death of Yoshimitsu in 1408, however, Zeami lost his privileged position at court; and though he continued to act and write for the noh theater, the shoguns who followed Yoshimitsu extended their patronage to other individuals and rival theatrical traditions. In 1422 Zeami passed the leadership of his acting troupe to his eldest son, Motomosa, and became a Buddhist monk. Greater disappointment and hardship awaited him. Under the shogun Yoshinori, who assumed power in 1429, Zeami and Motomosa were relieved of their official responsibilities; and in 1434 Zeami was banished to the remote island of Sado, where he composed *Kintōsho* (*Book of the Golden Island*) about his exile. When he returned—most likely following the general amnesty declared after the assassination of Yoshinori in 1441—he probably lived until his death at eighty in the care of his son-in-law and artistic successor Komparu Zenchiko (1405–ca. 1470).

In his theoretical and dramatic writings Zeami completed the development of noh from its roots in folk theater to a performance form marked by narrative concentration and verbal intensity. Whereas his father had conceived of noh through the aesthetics of imitation, Zeami took the form in a poetic direction. Drawing their plots from myth, legend, and history, Zeami's plays are dense in their allusions to poetry, court and military narratives, religious tales, and other established forms of Japanese and Chinese literature. But Zeami's poetic conception of noh went well beyond literary citation. Expanding traditional poetic techniques from verbal devices into theatrical ones, Zeami combined poetry, music, movement, and stage effects into a poetry for all the senses. Crafted with a jeweler's precision, many of his plays exemplify the ideal of *yūgen*—elegant, mysterious beauty—that was central to Zeami's aesthetic treatises. In Zeami's earliest writing, *yūgen* refers to the achievement of refinement in movement, bearing, and action—especially when such accomplishments involve unexpected grace or beauty. But over the course of Zeami's career the term acquired deeper, more elusive meanings that reflect the spiritual vision of Buddhism, including Zen, which was introduced to Japan at the end of the twelfth century and became popular with the samurai class. In this sense, *yūgen* arises from an awareness of the transitoriness of the world; it reflects both the ephemerality of material phenomena and the timelessness of the reality that underlies them.

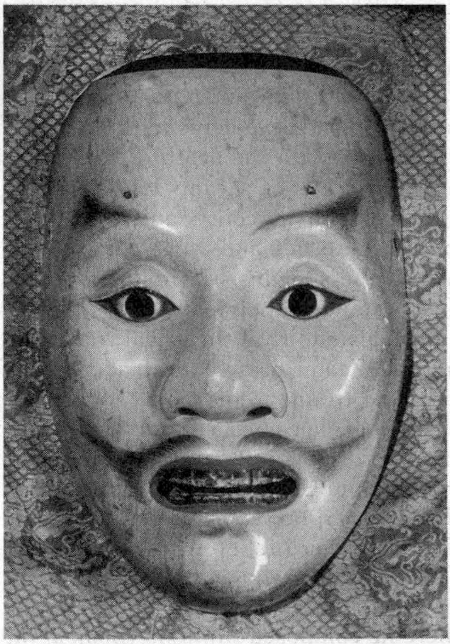

This noh mask, dating from the late fourteenth century, depicts a samurai character.

Zeami's greatest plays achieve the quality of *yūgen* not by concentrating on plot or personality but by presenting ideas and emotions, emphasizing spiritual and aesthetic concerns, and depicting the texture of existence, which unlike life, extends beyond the grave. One of his strategies for attaining this perspective on life was to feature ghosts as his leading characters. These ghosts are not seen through the eyes of the living, as they are in SHAKESPEARE's *Hamlet* and elsewhere in Western drama; rather, life in all its intensity is recalled and re-created by the ghosts themselves in evocative, highly poetic acts of memory. Not surprisingly, many of Zeami's most powerful characters were the ghosts of members of the military class for whom he so often performed. These "ghost-of-warrior plays" (*shura mono*), a form that Zeami largely introduced, constitute the second of five categories of plays that came to be performed in sequence as part of a formal noh program. The others are deity plays (*waki nō*); woman or "wig" plays (*kazura mono*); miscellaneous plays, including those about madness (*kyōran mono*) and those about individuals alive in the dramatic present (*genzai mono*); and plays featuring a supernatural being or demon (*kiri nō*). In *Atsumori*, one of the finest of these ghost-of-warrior plays, Zeami established a powerful counterpoint between the past as a site of heroic action and the dramatic present as a site of recollection, transcendent awareness, and reconciliation.

Taira Atsumori, a young warrior who died bravely in battle, had already been the subject of numerous Japanese tales and plays. Zeami's source for *Atsumori* was *The*

Tale of the Heike, a fictionalized narrative of the civil wars between supporters of the Taira clan (also called the Heike) and the Minamoto clan (also called the Genji) in the late twelfth century. In its most popular, fourteenth-century version, *The Tale of the Heike* was recited by players of the *biwa* (a kind of lute) who roamed the countryside. In this account, the fleeing Atsumori turns back to face the challenge of the mature Kumagae; they struggle, and Kumagae emerges victorious only to realize that his opponent is a youth his own son's age. Kumagae wishes to spare Atsumori, but because his own troops are fast approaching, he has no choice but to behead Atsumori quickly to save him further suffering and, sometime after the battle, take religious vows and pray for Atsumori's soul. The dramatic potentials of this story are legion, and some of them are developed at length in an eighteenth-century puppet play titled *The Chronicle of the Battle of Ichinotani,* which depicts the conflicts of love and duty. In the puppet play, duty wins: the social structure is outwardly affirmed, although the cost is Kumagae's sacrifice of his own son in place of Atsumori.

Zeami, however, was interested in neither the drama of physical battle nor the tension between love and duty. In his play, Atsumori's ghost appears some years after his death and confronts Kumagae, who has become the monk Renshō. In this ghost-of-warrior play, dramatic conflict is minimized; very little happens. The military events recorded in *The Tale of the Heike* are presented not only through brief sections of dramatic reenactment but through recited narration and stylized dance. Like the twenty-three-year rule of the Heike themselves, these events exist—to quote one of Zeami's most resonant lines—"in the space of a dream." But less, in this case, is more. The absence of extended external action in *Atsumori* makes possible a deeper exploration of time, self-knowledge, and the fleetingness of human life. Through his focus on interior experience, emotion, and reflection, Zeami creates a play of poignant beauty.

In keeping with his source, Zeami depicts Atsumori as both a brave warrior and an artist—an accomplished flutist. He also compares him with the ninth-century poet Ariwara no Yukihira and the fictional

Taira Atsumori, as depicted by the nineteenth-century painter Kikuchi Yosai.

shining prince of *The Tale of Genji,* both of whom were exiled at Suma, the noh play's setting. Like other ghost-of-warrior plays by Zeami, *Atsumori* aids in legitimizing the ruling class by helping to create and propagate the figure of the military aristocrat as both cultural and military hero, excelling in aesthetic creativity and sensibility as well as in military skills and virtues. At the same time, the play acknowledges the stature of the lower classes (within the text the grass cutters, but also the lowly actors) by arguing that humble people may also possess artistic talent. An effective parallel is drawn between the grass cutters in act 1 and the Taira clansmen in act 2. *Atsumori* directly advocates a social message: don't envy your superiors or despise your inferiors, for in this topsy-turvy world, those at the top may end up at the bottom and vice versa. It also expresses the classic Buddhist concept of nondualism: opposites are equivalents; enemies indeed are friends.

In medieval Japanese thought, which was deeply influenced both by the teachings of Buddhism and by the Japanese religion known as Shinto or "the way of the gods," human passions and desires do not cease with one's death. Ghosts continue to interact with living beings, usually because of some attachment to life that interferes with the attainment of enlightenment. The structure of Zeami's ghost plays reflects these assumptions. A priest (played by the secondary actor, who is called the *waki*) travels to a well-known place, where he meets and questions a local inhabitant (the main actor, or *shite*). The local figure describes a famous person connected with the place, hints that he is indeed that person, and disappears. In the second act, the ghost of the famous person (played by the recostumed *shite*) appears in his or her earthly form and presents crucial moments of that life. As dawn breaks the phantom disappears, often requesting that the traveler pray for his or her soul.

From its opening lines—"Awake to awareness, the world's but a dream, / . . . one may cast it aside—is this what is Real?"—the play sets up a complex relationship between reality and dream. The priest Renshō has cast aside secular life, but he is still attached to this illusory world through his desire to assuage his guilt over killing Atsumori by praying for his dead enemy's soul. Thus his good works bind him to life as an unenlightened being. Atsumori, whose ghost enters in act 2, is dead; however, he too exists in an unenlightened state, returning to earth "To clear the karma left from this waking world"—that is, to wash away the sins he committed while alive. When Renshō encounters Atsumori's ghost, he assumes that he must be dreaming. Atsumori puts Renshō's assumption into question by explaining that one gains nothing by distinguishing between dream and reality. Life is a dream and dreams are real, for both states are illusory and must be transcended. This transcendence is enlightenment, the state that both Atsumori and Renshō are seeking. They do not explicitly achieve it at the end of the play; all that is promised is the hope "that in the end they will be reborn together / on a single lotus petal" in paradise.

Shortly after the *shite,* garbed as a grass cutter, enters the stage, one of Ariwara no Yukihira's poems, written when the poet was exiled at Suma Bay, is quoted and expanded upon:

"If anyone should ask after me,
my reply would speak of lonely grief
here at Suma Bay
where brine drips from seaweed."
Should anyone learn who I am,
. . . .
then I too would have a friend.

Here Zeami employs a strategy successfully used in many of his plays, presenting the basic plot of the play in an early lyric passage; that is, the action of the poem becomes the action of the play. The speaker of the poem (the grass cutter) is living at Suma Bay; someone (the priest Renshō) comes to ask after him, and Atsumori's ghost (in its "true" form in act 2) replies by describing how the Taira clan passed dismal days on the Suma seacoast. Moreover, once the visitor Renshō learns Atsumori's identity, the two become friends "in Buddha's Law." By ascribing Yukihira's poem to Atsumori and incorporating its delivery, the play not only serves as a requiem for the souls of the warriors but also legitimizes the social status of the warrior class by identifying them with earlier noble exiles at Suma.

One other notable characteristic of this noh play, which it shares with the *Tale of the Heike,* is Atsumori's love of music. His return to the Taira encampment to retrieve his precious flute caused him to lose the opportunity to board one of the fleeing Taira ships and leads directly to his death. In act 1, Renshō hears and admires the flute playing of the grass cutter, just as Kumagae had heard and admired Atsumori's flute playing from the opposing military camp the night before their fatal encounter. In act 2, the lyrical tone of that earlier evening is presented through a gentle, medium-tempo dance—an unusual choice for a warrior play, but well-suited to this play's depiction of Atsumori as a cultured man. It is especially appropriate because the dance is performed to strains of flute music. Immediately after this graceful dance, the play turns to a more forceful enactment of the brave Atsumori's death in battle. Whereas most of the text is chanted in the melodic mode, a musical style associated with feminine and aristocratic characters, the battle scene at the play's conclusion is chanted in the dynamic mode, a style associated with warriors and ferocious characters. This deeply musical quality makes *Atsumori* one of Zeami's most elegant ghost-of-warrior plays.

Today noh is almost always performed on a special stage or a facsimile of it placed over a different structure. The noh stage is now most often a roofed area within an auditorium, with the audience seated at stage right and in front of it. A curtained bridgeway leads from far stage right to the main stage, a 19-foot square with a small back area for the attendants and instrumentalists; the chorus is at stage left. Backstage to the left is a small door through which the chorus and attendants enter and exit, and minor characters killed in the course of the play exit. All noh plays are accompanied by a flute and two or three drums, and much of the text (including lines attributed to the main character) is chanted by the chorus. The music is scripted and all movements are minutely choreographed. There is no

Contemporary performances of noh continue to retain traditional staging and costuming, as this woodcut image of a performance at the Kasuga Shrine, circa 1980, shows.

need for a director; the performers each learn their roles individually and the *shite* chooses any variations to the standard text and performance practices. One or two stage props may be present, although *Atsumori* uses none; otherwise there is no scenery. Museum-quality costumes and masks provide visual interest, and the actors manipulate fans, bundles of grass (for the grass cutters), swords (for warriors), and other hand props appropriate to the characters. A two-act noh play requires a minimum of three actors. The *shite* represents the main character, usually in two different forms, and the *waki* represents a priest or secondary male figure. Both of these actors may describe the scenery or the action as well as speak the lines of their character. In the interlude between acts, a *kyōgen* (or comic actor) often retells the story behind the play in more colloquial language (usually that of the eighteenth century) both to clarify the plot for the audience and to give the *shite* time to change his costume. All roles are traditionally played by male actors, although one occasionally sees women on the professional stage today, and both in its early days and in modern times female groups have performed noh. The texts of noh are relatively short, but most plays take about one and a half hours to perform.

Noh plays, especially Zeami's, became a focus of attention in the West in the early twentieth century. They were admired by such poets as Ezra Pound and W. B. Yeats, who were drawn to the poetic concentration and formal beauty of noh theater, and such modern stage designers as Edward Gordon Craig. Since that time, noh drama has continued to influence a wide variety of poets, playwrights, performers, filmmakers, and theater theorists. In Japan noh has been performed without interruption by professional and amateur actors, but its audience has changed over time. In 1879 Japanese diplomats entertained the former American president Ulysses S. Grant with a noh performance, and Tokyo audiences in the early twenty-first century include many hip young Japanese. From noh's early days amateurs have learned to chant, dance, and perform it; the texts have been illustrated in a number of artistic styles; and beginning in early modern times, excerpts from noh texts were taught in the schools. The texts' many allusions and quotations, part of the cultural currency of the medieval elite, have been explained in detail over the centuries, and high school courses on Japanese literature now rely on heavily annotated texts.

KAREN BRAZELL

Atsumori[1]

CHARACTERS

SHITE,[2] in act 1, a grass cutter without a mask; in act 2, the masked ghost of Atsumori

COMPANIONS, two or three other maskless grass cutters

WAKI,[3] Renshō (or Rensei), the priestly name of Kumagae (or Kumagai) no Jirō Naozane, the man who killed Atsumori in battle

KYŌGEN,[4] a local man

1. Translated by Karen Brazell.
2. Principal actor and character; protagonist.
3. Supporting actor and character (often a traveling priest).
4. Comic actor who performed in noh drama during the interlude between acts.

CHORUS of eight or ten members seated at stage left
Musicians with a flute and two hand drums seated at the back of the stage
Two attendants seated at the back of the stage, stage right of instruments

Act 1

[To the music of the hand drums and the flute, the WAKI, *dressed as a priest, enters the bridgeway*[5] *and moves slowly to back stage right, turns to face the pine tree painted on the back wall of the stage, and chants in the melodic mode.]*

WAKI Awake to awareness, the world's but a dream,
awake to awareness, the world's but a dream,
one may cast it aside—is this what is Real?[6]

CHORUS Awake to awareness, the world's but a dream,
one may cast it aside—is this what is Real?

[Intoned speech with no accompaniment; the WAKI *faces front.]*

WAKI I am Kumagae no Jirō Naozane, a resident of Musashi, who has renounced this world and taken the priestly name Renshō. I did this because of the deep remorse I felt at having killed Atsumori. Now I am going to Ichinotani[7] to pray for the repose of his soul.

[He continues to face front, chanting in the melodic mode with drum accompaniment.]

WAKI Departing the capital as clouds part
departing the capital as clouds part,
the moon too travels southward,
a small wheel rolling toward
Yodo; Yamazaki soon passed;
then the ponds of Koya, Ikuta River,

[Takes a few steps to indicate travel.]

Suma Bay, where "waves surge beside us";[8]
at Ichinotani I have arrived,

[Takes a few steps to indicate his arrival.]

I have arrived at Ichinotani.

How quickly I've reached Ichinotani in the province of Tsu. Scenes from the past come to mind as if present. [*Hands together in a prayer gesture*] Hail, Amida[9] Buddha. [*Turns slightly to the right*] What's that? I hear the

5. *Hashigakari,* the narrow passageway from which characters enter and exit the noh stage.
6. Here, the *waki* questions whether simply taking religious vows is enough to enable one to attain enlightenment.
7. The place on the Japan Sea, near Suma, where Kumagae killed Atsumori (in present-day Kobe). *Musashi*: province in eastern Japan that contains Tokyo. In the following passage Kumagae lists some of the intervening locations.
8. The first of many phrases in this play taken from the "Suma" chapter of *The Tale of Genji,* a classic 11th-century work attributed to Murasaki Shikibu (ca. 973–ca. 1031), a Japanese noblewoman.
9. A major manifestation of Buddha, in whose Pure Land the characters at the end of the play hope to achieve rebirth.

sound of a flute coming from that high meadow. I think I'll wait for the flutist and ask him to tell me something about this place.

[*The* SHITE *and two or three* COMPANIONS *costumed as humble grass cutters enter along the bridgeway. They are unmasked, and each carries a bamboo pole with grass attached. They proceed to the front of the stage and form two lines perpendicular to the front and facing each other.*]

SHITE and COMPANIONS The grass cutter's flute adds its voice,
the grass cutter's flute adds its voice
to the wind blowing over the meadows.

[*The* SHITE *faces front.*]

SHITE The "man who cuts grass on that hill"[1] makes his way
through the fields
in the gathering dusk; it's time to go home.

SHITE and COMPANIONS [*facing each other again*]
Was his way home, too, beside the Suma Sea?
How limited the path we tread
entering the hills, returning to the shore;
how miserable the lowly lives we lead.

"If anyone should ask after me,
my reply would speak of lonely grief
here at Suma Bay
where brine drips from seaweed."[2]
Should anyone learn who I am,

[*Brief instrumental interlude.*]

should anyone learn who I am,
then I, too, would have a friend.
Such wretched seafolk we've become that
"even dear ones are grown estranged."[3]

We live our lives, such as they are,
yielding to misery, we exhaust our days,

[*The* SHITE *goes to the shite spot*[4] *while the* COMPANIONS *line up in front of the* CHORUS.]

yielding to misery, we exhaust our days,

[*The* WAKI *stands at the waki spot*[5], *faces the* SHITE, *and speaks.*]

WAKI Hello there! There's something I'd like to ask you grass cutters.
SHITE Are you speaking to us? What is it you want?
WAKI Was one of you playing the flute just now?
SHITE Yes. One of us was playing.

1. This is a line from a poem by the poet Hitomaro (ca. 662–710), in which the speaker asks that the grass not be cut so that it can serve as feed for the horse of a lover whose arrival is expected.
2. A poem by the well-known poet Ariwara no Narihira (825–880).
3. An allusion to the preface to the *Kokinshū*, the early 10th-century anthology in which Ariwara's poem was first anthologized; it states that even close friends desert those who fall in status.
4. The spot on the noh stage closest to the passageway, where the *shite* often stands.
5. The place at front stage left of the noh stage where the *waki* usually stands or sits.

WAKI It was exquisite! And all the more exquisite because such music is not expected from men in your position.

SHITE You say it's unexpected from men in our position. People should neither envy superiors nor despise inferiors, or so it is said.

COMPANIONS [*chanting*] "Foresters' songs, shepherds' pipes"[6] is a set phrase;
grass cutters' flutes and woodsmen's songs

SHITE and COMPANIONS are well-known topics in poetry;
bamboo flutes have widespread fame.
Do not think it strange.

[*Song in the melodic mode to quiet drum accompaniment.*]

WAKI Indeed there is sense in what you say.
Those "foresters' songs and shepherds' pipes"

SHITE are the flutes of grass cutters

WAKI and the songs of woodsmen

SHITE "passing through this bitter world, a melody"[7]

WAKI to sing

SHITE to dance,

WAKI to blow,

SHITE to play.

CHORUS We lead our lives

[*The* SHITE *faces front and spreads his arms.*]

guided by discerning hearts that fancy,

[*Brief instrumental interlude; the* WAKI *sits at the waki spot.*]

guided by discerning hearts that fancy
bamboo flutes: Tender Branch, Broken Cicada,
such names as these are numerous.[8]

The flute the grass cutter plays
also has a name:
know it as Green Leaf.
At water's edge near Sumiyoshi

[*The* SHITE *circles the stage to the left, and the three* COMPANIONS *quietly exit up the bridgeway.*]

one would find Korean flutes;[9]
here at Suma one might say
seafolk play Charred Stick,
seafolk play Charred Stick.[1]

[*Intoned speech, no accompaniment.*]

6. Quoted from a poem written in Chinese by the Japanese poet Ki no Tadana (959–999): "When the sun sets on mountain roads / the sounds of foresters' songs and shepherds' pipes fill the ear. / When the birds return to valley nests / the tints of bamboo smoke and pine mist obstruct the vision." "Grass cutters" and "woodsmen" are Japanese references.

7. A phrase used in a medieval song/dance form (*kusemai*) called "Traveling to the West" to describe the songs of female entertainers.

8. Flutes and other valuable instruments were often named. According to *The Tale of the Heike,* Tender Branch was the flute Atsumori carried with him to his death; other sources give the name Green Leaf.

9. Used in court music. *Sumiyoshi*: a port frequented by ships from Korea, in present-day Osaka.

1. That is, burned wood to gain salt from brine. There is a reference in a 13th-century anthology of short tales (*Jikkinshō*) to a flute called Charred Head.

WAKI How strange. All the other grass cutters have left, yet you remain. Why is that?

SHITE Even you ask why? Drawn by the power of your voice above the evening waves, I have come to request ten Hail Amidas. Say them for me, please.

WAKI Ten Hail Amidas is an easy thing to grant. For whom should I pray?

SHITE To be honest, I am related to Atsumori.

WAKI You're related, you say? How nostalgic that makes me,

SHITE he says, putting his palms together [*clasps his rosary between his hands*], Hail, Amida Buddha.

SHITE [*The* SHITE *kneels, and they chant together*] "Should I attain enlightenment, no being in all the world

WAKI who calls my name shall be cast aside."[2]

[*The* SHITE *looks at the* WAKI *and lowers his hands.*]

CHORUS Please cast me not aside.
Though a single cry should suffice,
each day, each night, you pray.
How fortunate I am, my name

[*Looking down, he stands and then goes toward the shite spot.*]

unspoken, yet clear, at dawn and at dusk too
you hold services for the soul of one

[*He turns and looks intently at the* WAKI.]

whose name is mine, he says
as his figure fades from sight,

[*Facing front, he spreads his arms to indicate his disappearance.*]

as his figure fades from sight.

[*He walks quietly up the bridgeway and out under the raised curtain.*]

Kyōgen Interlude

[*The* KYŌGEN, *who has entered inconspicuously and seated himself at the back of the bridgeway, now rises and moves to the shite spot.*]

KYŌGEN I am a person who lives at Suma Bay. Today I've come to amuse myself by watching the boats go by. Hm! There's a priest I've never seen before. Where are you from?

WAKI I'm a priest from the capital. Do you live nearby?

KYŌGEN Yes, indeed I do.

WAKI Then please come over here. I've something I'd like to ask you.

KYŌGEN [*Goes to center stage and sits*] Certainly. What is it you want to know?

WAKI It's a bit unusual. I've heard that this is the harbor where the battle between the Heike and the Genji[3] was fought. Could you please tell me what you know about the death of the Heike nobleman Atsumori?

KYŌGEN That's certainly an unexpected request. Those of us who live around here don't know much about such things; however, since you've come out

2. Quoted from a passage in a basic sutra of Pure Land Buddhism that describes meditations centering on Amida Buddha.
3. That is, the Battle of Ichinotani (1184), late in the Genpei War, which pitted the Taira clan (the Heike) against the Minamoto clan (the Genji) in a struggle over imperial succession.

of your way to inquire, what can I do? I don't really know much, but I'll tell what I've heard.

WAKI Thank you.

KYŌGEN Sometime in the autumn of Jūei 2 [1183] when the Heike were forced from the capital by Kiso Yoshinaka, they retreated to this spot. However, the Genji, dividing their sixty thousand cavalry into two groups, attacked fiercely from both left and right. The Heike fled, scattering here and there. Among them was the young Atsumori, son of Tsunemori, chief of the Office of Palace Repairs. Atsumori had reached the shore, intending to board a ship, only to realize that he had left his precious flute, known as Little Branch, in the main camp. Not wanting it to fall into enemy hands, he went back to fetch it.

Upon retrieving his flute, Atsumori raced again to the shore, only to discover that all the boats, the imperial barque and the troopships, had already put out to sea. Atsumori's horse was strong, so he urged it into the sea. Just then, however, a resident of Musashi Province, Kumagae no Jirō Naozane, beckoned Atsumori with his fan, and he turned back to face this enemy. They fought in the waves, then grappled on the shore, finally falling from their horses. Kumagae, who was unusually strong, managed to come out on top and was about to cut off Atsumori's head when he glimpsed the face beneath the helmet. He saw the powdered brow and blackened teeth of a youth of fifteen or sixteen.[4]

"A pity! What an elegant warrior. If only I could spare him." He looked around. Doi and Kajiwara were fast approaching with a dozen other warriors.

"I would like to spare you," he explained, "however, as you can see, a group of my allies is almost upon us. I will kill you and then pray for your soul." Thus he took Atsumori's head.

Examining the corpse, he found a flute in a brocade bag. When he made his presentation before the general, people remarked on how cultivated the dead man must have been. Even among the nobility, few would concern themselves with a flute in such a crisis. The victors' armored sleeves were dampened by their tears. Eventually the youth was identified as Atsumori, the young son of Tsunemori.

Kumagae is said to have retired from the world to pray for Atsumori's enlightenment. Since he didn't spare Atsumori when he might have, this seems like a pack of lies to me. If that Kumagae should come here, we would kill him to prove our loyalty to Atsumori.

That's about all that I've heard. Why do you ask me about it? It seems a bit strange.

WAKI You were kind to tell me this tale. Why should I conceal anything? I was Kumagae no Jirō Naozane. Now I have become a priest and taken the name Renshō. I have come here to pray for the repose of Atsumori's soul.

KYŌGEN What! You're that lord Kumagae? Unwittingly I've told you these things. Please forgive me. A force for good is said to be a force for evil too. Maybe it works both ways. I hope that you will pray for Atsumori's soul.

WAKI Don't be upset. I have come only to pray for his soul. I would like to remain a while and read some efficacious sutras. I shall pray diligently.

4. His use of cosmetics identifies the youth as a member of an aristocratic family.

KYŌGEN If that's the case, I can give you lodging.
WAKI Thank you. That would be helpful.
KYŌGEN At your service.

[*He goes to the bridgeway and sits. After the* SHITE *has made his entrance, the* KYŌGEN *walks quietly up the bridgeway.*]

Act 2

[*Chanted in the melodic mode as he kneels at front stage left.*]

WAKI Spreading dew-drenched grass to make a bed,
spreading dew-drenched grass to make a bed,
now that the sun has set and night fallen
I'll pray to Amida that Atsumori
may yet achieve enlightenment, that he
may yet achieve enlightenment, I'll pray.

[*The* SHITE, *now costumed as the warrior Atsumori, enters to instrumental music and stands at backstage right facing front.*]

SHITE "Back and forth to Awaji plovers
fly; their cries awaken one
who guards the pass at Suma."[5]
What is your name?

[*Sung with the* SHITE *standing at the shite spot and the* WAKI *sitting at the waki spot.*]

SHITE Look here, Renshō,
Atsumori has arrived.
WAKI How very strange!
Beating on the gong, performing holy rites,
I have not had a moment to doze, and yet
Atsumori appears before me.
Surely this must be a dream.
SHITE Why need it be a dream?
To clear the karma left from this waking world
I make my appearance here.
WAKI This can't be. It's said,
"A single Hail Amida erases countless sins."
I've offered ceaseless prayers
to clear away all sinful hindrances.
What karma can remain from this rough sea of life,
SHITE so deep my sins, please wash them away,
WAKI and in doing so, my own salvation seek.
SHITE Your prayers affecting both our future lives—
WAKI once enemies
SHITE now instead
WAKI in Buddha's Law
SHITE made friends [*takes a step toward the* WAKI].

[*The* SHITE *spreads his arms facing front; the melodic song matches the accompanying drum rhythms.*]

5. Quoted from an early 12th-century poem by Minamoto Kanemasa (d. 1112). In the "Suma" chapter of *The Tale of Genji,* too, the cries of plovers awaken the exiled hero.

CHORUS Now I see!
"Cast aside an evil friend,

[*The* SHITE *points at the* WAKI *with his left hand and moves toward him.*]

beckon near an enemy who's good";

[*The* SHITE *flips his sleeve over his left arm and stares intently at the* WAKI.]

that refers to you!
How fortunate, how very fortunate!

[*Changing the mood, the* SHITE *circles left to the shite spot.*]

And now, with my confessional tale
let us while the night away,
let us while the night away.

[*The* SHITE *goes to center stage and sits on a stool provided by the stage attendant. The song is elaborately embellished.*]

Spring blossoms mounting tips of trees
inspire ascent toward enlightenment;
the autumn moon sinking to ocean's depths
symbolizes grace descending to mankind

[*All remain seated.*]

SHITE Even though the clan put forth new sprouts,
kinsmen branching out in all directions,
CHORUS "our glory was that of the short-lived rose of sharon."[6]
How difficult to find encouragement toward good—
good hard flintstones engender sparks
whose lights are gone before one knew they were—
the lives of humans flash by like this.
SHITE Yet those high up inflict pain on people down below;
those living lives of luxury are unaware of arrogance.

[*The* SHITE *stands and dances during the following segment sung in the melodic mode with the drum accompaniment. The flute enters midway.*]

CHORUS It happened that the Heike
ruled the world some twenty years,
truly a fleeting generation,
passed in the space of a dream.
"That famous autumn, leaves"[7]

[*Moves forward slightly.*]

lured by "winds from the four directions,"[8]
scattered here and there in leaflike

[*Moves his fan in a sweeping gesture and looks to the right.*]

6. A paraphrase of the second line of a well-known couplet by the Chinese poet Po Chu-i (772–846): "The pine has a thousand years, yet in the end, it dies: / the rose of sharon a single day to enjoy its glory."
7. An allusion to the Kakuichi version of *The Tale of the Heike*: "Now it is evident to every eye that adversity and happiness follow identical paths, that prosperity and decline are like a flip of the hand. Who of us could but feel pity? Once in the past they flourished like springtime blossoms; now in the present they fall like autumn leaves." *A fleeting generation*: an allusion to the Nagato version of *The Tale of the Heike*: "A generation used to last thirty-three years, but now it's only twenty-one."
8. The first of nine phrases in this section listed by Yoshimoto Nijō (Zeami's poetry mentor) as phrases that one should quote from the "Suma" chapter of *The Tale of Genji*.

boats bobbing on the waves, we sleep,
not even in our dreams returning home—
"caged birds longing for cloudy realms,
ranks of homing geese broken, scattered,"[9]
uncertain skies, aimless travel gowns tied

[*Looks up at the sky and circles left.*]

and layered sunsets, moonrises, months, a year
journeys by, returns to spring
here at Ichinotani secluded for a while
here at Suma Shore we live.

SHITE From the hills behind, winds roar down

[*Opens his fan and raises it before his face.*]

CHORUS to coastal fields keenly cold
our boats draw up, no day or night without
the cries of plovers,
our sleeves too

[*Twirls his sleeve over his arm to make a pillow and kneels.*]

dampened by the waves that
drench our rocky pillows,
in seaside shacks we huddle together
befriended only by Suma folk—
bent like wind-bent pines on the strands

[*Circles left to the shite spot.*]

of evening smoke rising from the fires—

[*Waving his fan in his left hand, the* SHITE *moves forward.*]

brushwood, it's called,

[*Holding out his fan parallel to the floor.*]

this stuff piled up to sleep upon.
Our worries, too, pile up in rustic Suma,
where we're forced to play out our lives

[*Pointing his fan to the right, he looks up.*]

becoming simple Suma folk—

[*Circles to the left.*]

such is our clan's fate; how forlorn we are!

[*Stops at backstage center.*]

[*The chanting changes from the melodic to the dynamic mode.*]

SHITE And then, on the night of the sixth day of the second month,
Tsunemori, my father, gathered us together
to enjoy ourselves with song and dance.

WAKI And your entertainment that night,
the elegant flute music from your encampment,
was clearly heard by us on the opposing side.

9. More phrases from the Kakuichi version of *The Tale of the Heike*, where they refer to a Heike clansman, Shigehira, who was captured by the Genji: "Perhaps his thoughts, fretful as caged birds longing for the sky, find themselves afloat on the southern seas, a thought miles from home. Perhaps his feelings are as sad as those of a lone goose headed homeward, separated from his fellows."

SHITE It was indeed Atsumori,
awaiting the end, his bamboo flute
WAKI accompanying a variety of
SHITE ballads and songs,
WAKI many voices
[The SHITE *circles right to the shite spot.]*
CHORUS arise, creating steady cadences.
[Medium tempo dance. The SHITE *performs a sprightly yet elegant dance to the music of the flute and hand drums. This dance, unusual in a warrior play, emphasizes Atsumori's artistic sensitivity. The context also foregrounds the flute music, which is the normal accompaniment to the dance.]*
SHITE *[Raising his fan]* And so it is,
the royal barque sets forth
[The dynamic song becomes strongly rhythmical, matching the steady beats of the drums.]
CHORUS and all the members of the clan
[The SHITE *stamps his feet.]*
board their ships to sail.
[Making a sweeping point with his fan, he turns to the right.]
Not wanting to be late
[Goes to the front of the stage.]
Atsumori races to the shore;
the royal barque and troopships, too,
have already put out to sea.
[Raises his fan over his head and looks out into the distance.]
SHITE It's hopeless! Reining in his horse
[Mimes pulling on the reins with his left hand.]
amidst the breakers, he stands bewildered.
[Waves his fan to indicate agitation.]
CHORUS At that very moment
[The SHITE *stamps his feet.]*
from behind comes
[He turns and faces the bridgeway.]
Kumagae no Jirō Naozane.
"Don't flee!"
[Hurries to the shite spot.]
he shouts and charges.
Atsumori too
[Moves quickly to center front.]
turns about his horse, and
[Mimes reining in his horse and races backstage.]
in the breakers they draw swords
[Mimes drawing a sword (represented by his fan) and goes to the front right corner.]
and exchange blows, twice, thrice,
[Strikes with his fan.]

they are seen to strike;
on horseback they grapple,
[*Wraps his arms around himself.*]
then fall onto the wave-swept shore,
[*Twirls around and kneels.*]
one atop the other; finally
struck down, Atsumori dies;
[*Points his fan at his head and looks down.*]
the wheel of fate turns, and they meet.
[*Stands, goes to center back, and draws his sword.*]
"The enemy's right here!"
[*Hurries toward the* WAKI.]
he cries and is about to strike.
[*Raises his sword to strike.*]
Returning good for evil,
[*Kneels.*]
the priest performs services and prays
[*Stands and returns to backstage.*]
that in the end they will be reborn together
[*Spreads his arms, moves toward the* WAKI *again, and drops his sword.*]
on a single lotus petal,
[*Circles to the front right corner.*]
and Renshō the priest
is an enemy no more.
[*Returns to the shite spot.*]
Please pray for my soul,
[*Makes a prayer gesture toward the* WAKI.]
please pray for my soul.
[*Turns to face the bridgeway and performs closing stamps;*
then exits slowly.]

EVERYMAN

ca. 1510

Everyman, the most widely read and frequently produced play written in English before the Elizabethan age, forms part of the tradition of morality drama that flourished in England during the fifteenth and early sixteenth centuries. A play about sin, repentance, and death, it reflects the religious and moral worldview of the late Middle Ages. Appearing at the turn of the sixteenth century, however, *Everyman* is also a transitional play in the history of English dramatic literature. As one of the first plays to be published in England, *Everyman* owes much of its popularity during its time to a new reading public that emerged after the invention of the printing press by the German Johannes Gutenberg around 1450. Such a readership had been unavailable to the dramatists of earlier centuries, whose plays were available only in manuscript. In addition, while this drama of Everyman's final reckoning reflects the theology of orthodox Catholicism, its insistence on certain doctrinal points suggests an awareness of the burgeoning reform movement that would profoundly divide Christian Europe during the Protestant Reformation. The allegorical structure of *Everyman* and other morality plays—in which characters, objects, and actions represent abstract concepts or principles in a narrative that conveys a moral lesson—provided English playwrights with a useful framework for examining these and other social and philosophical issues in the turbulent years that followed.

Everyman survives in four different editions, two of them incomplete, which appeared between 1510 and 1535. No manuscript of the play exists. The play bears close similarities to an earlier Dutch play titled *Elckerlijc*, which was written by a Petrus Diesthemius, or Peter from the [Flemish city of] Diest, frequently identified as the theologian and Carthusian priest Peter of Doorlandt. *Elckerlijc* was printed in 1495 in Delft; it was subsequently published in Antwerp, where it was awarded first prize at a *landjuweel*, or rhetorical contest. For a number of decades scholars argued over which play came first, but the weight of recent evidence—textual and otherwise—has established beyond reasonable doubt that the English *Everyman* was a translation of the Dutch original. As A. C. Cawley points out, Antwerp was an important printing center at the turn of the sixteenth century, regularly publishing English translations of books originally written in Dutch for sale in the English market. In London, foreign printers enjoyed privileges not granted to their domestic counterparts and were frequently accorded royal patronage. One of these printers, a Norman named Richard Pynson, published the first extant edition of *Everyman*; though we do not know the identity of the translator, we can infer the play's popularity from the number of surviving editions.

It has become a critical commonplace that while *Everyman* is the most famous of English morality plays, it is in many ways the least typical. In earlier moralities, such as *The Castle of Perseverence* (ca. 1405–25) and *Mankind* (ca. 1465–70), figures representing Virtue and Vice contend for the soul of humankind in often elaborate allegorical settings rife with incident and encounter. Moral conflict in these plays is frequently dramatized through comic horseplay, as the Vice figures demonstrate the distractions posed by earthly temptation. By focusing on words over action, in contrast, *Everyman* concentrates on the closing moments of life and on the moral crisis that occurs when Death calls the sinner to account. As Everyman undergoes his final journey, learning that the earthly things in which he had put

This woodcut from the fifteenth-century *Ars moriendi* shows Moriens, at the end of his struggle with earthly temptations, being welcomed into paradise.

his faith will fail him in his hour of extremity and that the path to salvation lies through good deeds and repentance, the distractions of earthly temptation and the diversions of horseplay are relegated to the past. No Vice figures prance across the stage in *Everyman;* instead, the play's moral allegory unfolds with a simplicity verging on parable. This theatrical asceticism may owe something to its sources, for scholars have determined that one of *Everyman*'s core narrative elements—the testing of friends in an hour of need—is Buddhist rather than Western in origin. This story was introduced to medieval Europe through the eleventh-century Greek text *Barlaam and Josaphat,* a collection of Christianized tales from the East.

In its focus on mortality, *Everyman* reflects a broader literary and social preoccupation with death in the fifteenth century. In his 1924 study *The Waning of the Middle Ages,* Johan Huizinga wrote: "No other epoch has laid so much stress as the expiring Middle Ages on the thought of death." *Memento mori* (remember that you must die) was a regular theme in the sermons of mendicant preachers since the thirteenth century, and its lesson resonated in a Europe that lost one-third of its population to the Black Death in the mid-1300s. Personifications of Death were common in fifteenth-century woodcuts, and the spectacle of Death choosing his victims indiscriminately from all stations of life formed the subject of the Dance of Death (or *Dunse Macabre*), a dramatic form that originated in Germany and was performed in England in the fifteenth century. Of even greater relevance to *Everyman* were the treatises on the art of holy dying or *Ars moriendi,* widely known throughout Europe in the 1400s. The *Ars moriendi* dealt with the process of death and the techniques (meditations, prayers, questions) that would help one die in a state of holiness. Particular attention was given to the temptations that threaten to divert the virtuous mind at the hour of death: heresy, despair, rage, spiritual pride, and an attachment to the things of the world. This last temptation, elaborated in William Caxton's 1490 translation (from a French work) *The Art and Craft to Know Well to Die*—"the over-great occupation of outward things and temporal, as toward his wife his children and his friends carnal, toward his riches or toward other things which he hath most loved in his life"—finds particularly strong echoes in *Everyman.* To find strength in the face of death, the dying individual is instructed to meditate on the death of Christ.

Like Moriens (literally, "The Dying One"), the protagonist at the center of the *Ars moriendi,* Everyman stands as the representative of a broader humanity that must come to terms with the inevitability of death and the impermanence of earthly life. The Messenger's speech that opens the play underscores the identification between Everyman on stage and Everyman in the audience—"Here shall you see how fellowship and jollity, / Both strength, pleasure, and beauty, / Will fade from thee as flower in May." God's speech, which follows it, extends this allegorical identification. As V. A. Kolve has noted, Everyman is spoken of as both singular and plural in number in God's opening speech: as a consequence of this linguistic slippage, "We are implicated collectively as well as individually." Like Death's victims in the Dance of Death, the character Everyman is caught unawares by calls of mortality and judgment. Immersed in a life of pleasure and possessions, he has elevated the temporal order over the spiritual; and as he embarks on this final journey, or "pilgrimage," he must revalue his life according to its higher moral law. *Everyman*'s many references to "reckoning" and to rendering "account," which recall the parable of the talents in Matthew 25. 14–30, emphasize the need for spiritual industry and proper discernment of what is transitory and what is eternal.

As he prepares to undertake Death's journey, Everyman seeks the company and support of his friends, kindred, and material possessions from which he derived pleasure in more carefree days. That Fellowship, Kindred, Cousin, and Goods abandon him in his hour of greatest need despite their earlier promises never to forsake him comes as no surprise to the audience; their departures are both inevitable and accompanied by a certain humor, as when Cousin protests that he cannot accompany Everyman because he has a cramp in his toe. The popular sayings that Everyman repeats in soliciting their help—"For it is said ever among / That money maketh all right that is wrong," for instance—are shown to be empty. When Everyman turns to his Good Deeds, he finds her willing to accompany him but too enfeebled by his sins to rise from the ground and do so. His encounter with her is a turning point both in the play's narrative and in his theological development, for he learns the steps by which he may render his spiritual account clean and adequate. He is introduced to Knowledge, whose name denoted a number of related understandings to the play's medieval audience: knowledge of God, acknowledgment of sin, and an awareness of its remedies. Knowledge, in turn, introduces him to Confession, who instructs him in contrition and encourages him to punish his offending flesh with the scourge of Penance. When Everyman has purified himself through these penitential acts, Good Deeds rises from the ground, restored, to accompany him on the remainder of his pilgrimage. The morally rejuvenated Everyman is also joined on his final pilgrimage by four "persons of great might": Discretion, Strength, Beauty, and Five-Wits (the personification of the five physical senses). Unlike Everyman's unreliable earlier companions, who signify the attachments of the external world, the allegorical figures

Frontispiece of the 1528–29 edition of *Everyman* printed by John Skot.

in this last group represent the individual's personal attributes redeemed by grace.

Before he reaches his grave Everyman departs to receive the sacraments of Holy Communion and extreme unction, or last rites, and his brief exit affords Knowledge and Five-Wits the opportunity for an extended digression on the importance of priesthood. Because they administer the seven sacraments, these two insist, priests stand even "above angels in degree." Though some priests violate their divine responsibilities, priesthood offers the only "remedy we find under God." The emphasis on sacraments is important to the play's doctrinal foundations, for in Roman Catholic belief and observance, they represent the vehicles by which God's grace is manifested in human life. Everyman has expressed contrition for his sins, but it is not until he receives the sacraments that his reconciliation with God is complete.

The closing sequence, in which Everyman meets his death and is received into heaven, achieves a surprisingly emotional effect in a play that is otherwise marked by the contemplative distance and processional formality of allegory. As Everyman stands before his grave—so weak he "may not stand"—he is successively abandoned by Beauty, Strength, Discretion, and Five-Wits. Unlike his earlier abandonment by his companions and worldly goods, which this scene mirrors, this last-minute departure comes as something of a jolt to the play's audience as well to as its protagonist. Although Strength may promise Everyman that "we will not from you go / Till ye have done this voyage long," the support of Everyman's attributes and faculties necessarily but painfully fail at the moment of death. Even Knowledge, whose support proved crucial to Everyman's transition into a state of grace, must abandon the dying individual in the end. When Everyman exclaims "O all thing faileth save God alone," he expresses the anguish that marks the loss of these deeply personal companions. But this anguish also affirms a faith in the constancy embodied in God's promise of salvation. Accompanied by Good Deeds, his lone companion into the afterlife, Everyman echoes Christ's dying words: "*In manus tuas . . . commendo spiritum meum*" ("Into thy hands I commend my spirit"; Luke 23.46). As reward for his moral regeneration he is welcomed by an Angel to heaven and eternal life. His reckoning, which was earlier described as "blotted and blind," is now "crystal clear."

The epilogue of *Everyman,* which is delivered by a theological Doctor, underscores the play's moral lesson: "And he that hath his account whole and sound, / High in heaven he shall be crowned." As he redirects the play's attention from Everyman on stage to Everyman in the audience—"Ye hearers"—he reminds us that this play about dying right is equally, in the end, about the importance of living right. Like other visual and literary works in the *memento mori* tradition, *Everyman* seeks to impress upon its audience an awareness of life's impermanence, an ability to discern the eternal in the midst of the transitory, and a commitment to live life as if every day might be one's last.

No evidence has survived concerning sixteenth-century performances of *Everyman;* indeed, there is no record of performance before the nineteenth century.

Because the title page of the 1528–29 edition of the play printed by John Skot (upon which the present text is based) opens with the words "HERE BEGINNETH A TREATISE . . . IN MANNER OF A MORAL PLAY," some critics have concluded that—in contrast with its Dutch counterpart, for which performance records exist—*Everyman* was translated and printed primarily for a reading public. But while the number of editions in which it appeared supports the claim that *Everyman* had a wide readership, the play's success in twentieth-century theaters, churches, and schools attests to its theatrical qualities, and the simplicity of its theatrical requirements encourages the belief that it was known to audiences as well as readers.

Whether *Everyman* was performed outdoors, like the earlier English moralities, or indoors, like the Tudor interludes it also resembles, is open to conjecture, and the absence of stage directions from the printed text makes precise reconstruction of a sixteenth-century performance impossible. But some of the play's central theatrical features are evident from textual indications, and others can be inferred from contemporary theatrical practice. The play's setting observes the dual structure characteristic of other medieval drama, in which a localized structure (or *sedes*) is contrasted with an unlocalized acting area (or *platea*). The House of Salvation—Confession's abode—looms over the action of *Everyman* as the site of the allegorical protagonist's pivotal transformations. As Cawley suggests, it is reasonable to assume that this structure had a battlement height from which God addresses sinful humanity at the start of the play and into which Everyman's soul is received at its conclusion. Placement of Everyman's grave in front of this structure would allow Everyman to exit his grave and ascend to heaven with requisite speed. Distinguished as they are by their initial immobility, both Goods and Good Deeds no doubt require their own acting areas. The text of *Everyman* provides evidence of additional theatrical elements. Props, while few in number, figure prominently in the play's dramatic and theological action: Everyman's account book, the penitential scourge, the crucifix that Everyman presents after receiving the sacraments. Costume also contributes to the play's meaning. Everyman, who is dressed "gaily" at the beginning of the play, exchanges these clothes for a penitential robe in the play's second half. He certainly would not have been the only character whose allegorical significance is marked by dress: if productions of *Everyman* followed Tudor theatrical practice, its costumes would have been vividly emblematic—most notably in the case of Death, whose representation would have drawn from an extensive repertoire of medieval woodcuts and other illustrations.

The history of Everyman's emergence in our own time as a classic of the early English theater is almost as striking as the play itself. After several centuries' absence from the stage, *Everyman* became the first medieval play to appear on the modern stage in July 1901, when William Poel, founder of the Elizabethan Stage Society, mounted a production of this supposedly "primitive" drama in the courtyard of a former London monastery. The production was an immediate sensation: by the following season it had reached the commercial theaters, and it subsequently toured abroad. An observation by one of the play's initial reviewers suggests both the success of Poel's production and the power that *Everyman* must have held for its Tudor audience as well: "In the open air in a courtyard and enclosed with antiquated buildings with no distinction of lighting to differentiate between performers and auditors . . . the essential human vitality of the whole thing was what most strongly appeared."

S.G.

Everyman[1]

CHARACTERS

MESSENGER	KNOWLEDGE
GOD	CONFESSION
DEATH	BEAUTY
EVERYMAN	STRENGTH
FELLOWSHIP	DISCRETION
KINDRED	FIVE-WITS
COUSIN	ANGEL
GOODS	DOCTOR
GOOD DEEDS	

HERE BEGINNETH A TREATISE HOW THE HIGH FATHER OF HEAVEN SENDETH DEATH TO SUMMON EVERY CREATURE TO COME AND GIVE ACCOUNT OF THEIR LIVES IN THIS WORLD, AND IS IN MANNER OF A MORAL PLAY.

[*Enter* MESSENGER.]

MESSENGER I pray you all give your audience,
And hear this matter with reverence,
By figure° a moral play. *In its form*
The Summoning of Everyman called it is,
That of our lives and ending shows
How transitory we be all day.° *always*
The matter is wonder precious,
But the intent of it is more gracious
And sweet to bear away.
The story saith: Man, in the beginning
Look well, and take good heed to the ending,
Be you never so gay.
You think sin in the beginning full sweet,
Which in the end causeth the soul to weep,
When the body lieth in clay.
Here shall you see how fellowship and jollity,
Both strength, pleasure, and beauty,
Will fade from thee as flower in May.
For ye shall hear how our Heaven-King
Calleth Everyman to a general reckoning.
Give audience and hear what he doth say.

[*Exit* MESSENGER.—*Enter* GOD.]

1. The text is based on the earliest printing of the play (no manuscript is known) by John Skot, about 1530, as reproduced by W. W. Greg (1904). The spelling has been modernized except where modernization would spoil the rhyme, and modern punctuation has been added. The stage directions have been amplified.

GOD I perceive, here in my majesty,
How that all creatures be to me unkind,[2]
Living without dread in worldly prosperity.
Of ghostly sight[3] the people be so blind,
Drowned in sin, they know me not for their God.
In worldly riches is all their mind:
They fear not of my righteousness the sharp rod;
My law that I showed when I for them died
They forget clean, and shedding of my blood red.
I hanged between two,[4] it cannot be denied:
To get them life I suffered to be dead.
I healed their feet, with thorns hurt was my head.
I could do no more than I did, truly—
And now I see the people do clean forsake me.
They use the seven deadly sins damnable,
As pride, coveitise,° wrath, and lechery[5] *covetousness*
Now in the world be made commendable.
And thus they leave of angels the heavenly company.
Every man liveth so after his own pleasure,
And yet of their life they be nothing sure.
I see the more that I them forbear,
The worse they be from year to year:
All that liveth appaireth° fast. *degenerates*
Therefore I will, in all the haste,
Have a reckoning of every man's person.
For, and° I leave the people thus alone *if*
In their life and wicked tempests,
Verily they will become much worse than beasts;
For now one would by envy another up eat.
Charity do they all clean forgeet.
I hoped well that every man
In my glory should make his mansion,° *dwelling place*
And thereto I had them all elect.° *chosen*
But now I see, like traitors deject,° *debased*
They thank me not for the pleasure that I to° them meant, *for*
Nor yet for their being that I them have lent.
I proffered the people great multitude of mercy,
And few there be that asketh it heartily.° *sincerely*
They be so cumbered° with worldly riches *encumbered*
That needs on them I must do justice—
On every man living without fear.
Where art thou, Death, thou mighty messenger?
[*Enter* DEATH.]
DEATH Almighty God, I am here at your will,
Your commandment to fulfill.
GOD Go thou to Everyman,

2. Lacking in natural filial affection or duty.
3. In spiritual vision.
4. That is, the two thieves between whom Jesus was crucified.
5. The other deadly sins are gluttony, sloth, and envy.

And show him, in my name,
A pilgrimage he must on him take,
Which he in no wise may escape;
And that he bring with him a sure reckoning
Without delay or any tarrying.
DEATH Lord, I will in the world go run over all,° *throughout*
And cruelly° out-search both great and small. *rigorously*
[*Exit* GOD.]
Everyman will I beset that liveth beastly
Out of God's laws, and dreadeth not folly.
He that loveth riches I will strike with my dart,
His sight to blind, and from heaven to depart° *cut off*
Except that Almsdeeds be his good friend—
In hell for to dwell, world without end.
Lo, yonder I see Everyman walking:
Full little he thinketh on my coming;
His mind is on fleshly lusts and his treasure,
And great pain it shall cause him to endure
Before the Lord, Heaven-King.
[*Enter* EVERYMAN.]
Everyman, stand still! Whither art thou going
Thus gaily? Hast thou thy Maker forgeet?° *forgotten*
EVERYMAN Why askest thou?
Why wouldest thou weet?° *know*
DEATH Yea, sir, I will show you:
In great haste I am sent to thee
From God out of his majesty.
EVERYMAN What! sent to me?
DEATH Yea, certainly.
Though thou have forgot him here,
He thinketh on thee in the heavenly sphere,
As, ere we depart, thou shalt know.
EVERYMAN What desireth God of me?
DEATH That shall I show thee:
A reckoning he will needs have
Without any longer respite.
EVERYMAN To give a reckoning longer leisure I crave.
This blind° matter troubleth my wit.° *obscure / understanding*
DEATH On thee thou must take a long journay:
Therefore thy book of count° with thee thou bring, *accounts*
For turn again thou cannot by no way.
And look thou be sure of thy reckoning,
For before God thou shalt answer and shew
Thy many bad deeds and good but a few—
How thou hast spent thy life and in what wise,
Before the Chief Lord of Paradise.
Have ado that we were in that way,[6]
For weet thou well thou shalt make none attornay.[7]

6. That is, let's get going.
7. No one (your) advocate.

EVERYMAN Full unready I am such reckoning to give.
I know thee not. What messenger art thou?
DEATH I am Death that no man dreadeth,[8]
For every man I 'rest,° and no man spareth; *arrest*
For it is God's commandment
That all to me should be obedient.
EVERYMAN O Death, thou comest when I had thee least in mind.
In thy power it lieth me to save:
Yet of my good° will I give thee, if thou will be kind, *goods*
Yea, a thousand pound shalt thou have—
And defer this matter till another day.
DEATH Everyman, it may not be, by no way.
I set nought by[9] gold, silver, nor riches,
Nor by pope, emperor, king, duke, nor princes,
For, and° I would receive gifts great, *if*
All the world I might get.
But my custom is clean contrary:
I give thee no respite. Come hence and not tarry!
EVERYMAN Alas, shall I have no longer respite?
I may say Death giveth no warning.
To think on thee it maketh my heart sick,
For all unready is my book of reckoning.
But twelve year and I might have a biding,[1]
My counting-book I would make so clear
That my reckoning I should not need to fear.
Wherefore, Death, I pray thee, for God's mercy,
Spare me till I be provided of remedy.
DEATH Thee availeth not to cry, weep, and pray;
But haste thee lightly° that thou were gone that journay *quickly*
And prove° thy friends, if thou can. *put to the test*
For weet° thou well the tide° abideth no man, *know / time*
And in the world each living creature
For Adam's sin must die of nature.[2]
EVERYMAN Death, if I should this pilgrimage take
And my reckoning surely make,
Show me, for saint° charity, *holy*
Should I not come again shortly?
DEATH No, Everyman. And thou be once there,
Thou mayst never more come here,
Trust me verily.
EVERYMAN O gracious God in the high seat celestial,
Have mercy on me in this most need!
Shall I have company from this vale terrestrial
Of mine acquaintance that way me to lead?
DEATH Yea, if any be so hardy
That would go with thee and bear thee company.
Hie thee that thou were gone[3] to God's magnificence,

8. Who is afraid of no man.
9. I set no store by.
1. If I might have a respite for twelve years.
2. In the course of nature.
3. Hurry up and go.

Thy reckoning to give before his presence.
What, weenest° thou thy life is given thee, *suppose*
And thy worldly goods also?
EVERYMAN I had weened so, verily.
DEATH Nay, nay, it was but lent thee.
For as soon as thou art go,° *gone*
Another a while shall have it and then go therefro,
Even as thou hast done.
Everyman, thou art mad! Thou hast thy wits° five, *senses*
And here on earth will not amend thy live![4]
For suddenly I do come.
EVERYMAN O wretched caitiff!° Whither shall I flee *unfortunate wretch*
That I might 'scape this endless sorrow?
Now, gentle Death, spare me till tomorrow,
That I may amend me
With good advisement.[5]
DEATH Nay, thereto I will not consent,
Nor no man will I respite,
But to the heart suddenly I shall smite,
Without any advisement.
And now out of thy sight I will me hie:
See thou make thee ready shortly,
For thou mayst say this is the day
That no man living may 'scape away.
[*Exit* DEATH.]
EVERYMAN Alas, I may well weep with sighs deep:
Now have I no manner of company
To help me in my journey and me to keep.° *protect*
And also my writing° is full unready— *account*
How shall I do now for to excuse me?
I would to God I had never be geet!° *been born*
To my soul a full great profit it had be.
For now I fear pains huge and great.
The time passeth: Lord, help, that all wrought!
For though I mourn, it availeth nought.
The day passeth and is almost ago:° *gone*
I wot° not well what for to do. *know*
To whom were I best my complaint to make?
What and° I to Fellowship thereof spake, *if*
And showed him of this sudden chance?
For in him is all mine affiance,° *trust*
We have in the world so many a day
Be good friends in sport and play.
I see him yonder, certainly.
I trust that he will bear me company.
Therefore to him will I speak to ease my sorrow.
[*Enter* FELLOWSHIP.]

4. In your life.
5. With proper reflection.

Well met, good Fellowship, and good morrow!
FELLOWSHIP Everyman, good morrow, by this day!
Sir, why lookest thou so piteously?
If anything be amiss, I pray thee me say,
That I may help to remedy.
EVERYMAN Yea, good Fellowship, yea:
I am in great jeopardy.
FELLOWSHIP My true friend, show to me your mind.
I will not forsake thee to my life's end
In the way of good company.
EVERYMAN That was well spoken, and lovingly!
FELLOWSHIP Sir, I must needs know your heaviness.° *sorrow*
I have pity to see you in any distress.
If any have you wronged, ye shall revenged be,
Though I on the ground be slain for thee,
Though that I know before that I should die.
EVERYMAN Verily, Fellowship, gramercy.° *many thanks*
FELLOWSHIP Tush! by thy thanks I set not a stree.° *straw*
Show me your grief and say no more.
EVERYMAN If I my heart should to you break,° *open*
And then you to turn your mind fro me,
And would not me comfort when ye hear me speak,
Then should I ten times sorrier be.
FELLOWSHIP Sir, I say as I will do, indeed.
EVERYMAN Then be you a good friend at need.
I have found you true herebefore.
FELLOWSHIP And so ye shall evermore.
For, in faith, and° thou go to hell, *if*
I will not forsake thee by the way.
EVERYMAN Ye speak like a good friend. I believe you well.
I shall deserve° it, and° I may. *repay / if*
FELLOWSHIP I speak of no deserving, by this day!
For he that will say and nothing do
Is not worthy with good company to go.
Therefore show me the grief of your mind,
As to your friend most loving and kind.
EVERYMAN I shall show you how it is:
Commanded I am to go a journay,
A long way, hard and dangerous,
And give a strait° count,° without delay, *strict / account*
Before the high judge Adonai.[6]
Wherefore I pray you bear me company,
As ye have promised, in this journay.
FELLOWSHIP This is matter indeed! Promise is duty—
But, and° I should take such a voyage on me, *if*
I know it well, it should be to my pain.
Also it maketh me afeard, certain.
But let us take counsel here, as well as we can—

6. A Hebrew name for God.

For your words would fear° a strong man. *frighten*
EVERYMAN Why, ye said if I had need,
Ye would me never forsake, quick ne° dead, *alive nor*
Though it were to hell, truly.
FELLOWSHIP So I said, certainly,
But such pleasures° be set aside, the sooth° to say. *pleasantries / truth*
And also, if we took such a journay,
When should we again come?
EVERYMAN Nay, never again, till the day of doom.[7]
FELLOWSHIP In faith, then will not I come there!
Who hath you these tidings brought?
EVERYMAN Indeed, Death was with me here.
FELLOWSHIP Now by God that all hath bought,° *redeemed*
If Death were the messenger,
For no man that is living today
I will not go that loath° journay— *loathsome*
Not for the father that begat me!
EVERYMAN Ye promised otherwise, pardie.° *by God*
FELLOWSHIP I wot well I said so, truly.
And yet, if thou wilt eat and drink and make good cheer,
Or haunt to women the lusty company,[8]
I would not forsake you while the day is clear,
Trust me verily!
EVERYMAN Yea, thereto ye would be ready—
To go to mirth, solace,° and play: *enjoyment*
Your mind to folly will sooner apply° *attend*
Than to bear me company in my long journay.
FELLOWSHIP Now in good faith, I will not that way.
But, and° thou will murder or any man kill, *if*
In that I will help thee with a good will.
EVERYMAN O that is simple° advice, indeed! *foolish*
Gentle fellow, help me in my necessity:
We have loved long, and now I need—
And now, gentle Fellowship, remember me!
FELLOWSHIP Whether ye have loved me or no,
By Saint John, I will not with thee go!
EVERYMAN Yet I pray thee take the labor and do so much for me,
To bring me forward,° for saint charity, *escort me*
And comfort me till I come without° the town. *outside*
FELLOWSHIP Nay, and° thou would give me a new gown, *even if*
I will not a foot with thee go.
But, and° thou had tarried, I would not have left thee so. *if*
And as° now, God speed thee in thy journay! *as for*
For from thee I will depart as fast as I may.
EVERYMAN Whither away, Fellowship? Will thou forsake me?
FELLOWSHIP Yea, by my fay!° To God I betake° thee. *faith / commend*
EVERYMAN Farewell, good Fellowship! For thee my heart is sore.
Adieu forever—I shall see thee no more.

7. That is, Judgment Day.

8. Or frequent the lusty company of women.

FELLOWSHIP In faith, Everyman, farewell now at the ending:
For you I will remember that parting is mourning.
[*Exit* FELLOWSHIP.]

EVERYMAN Alack, shall we thus depart° indeed— *part*
Ah, Lady,[9] help!—without any more comfort?
Lo, Fellowship forsaketh me in my most need!
For help in this world whither shall I resort?
Fellowship herebefore with me would merry make,
And now little sorrow for me doth he take.
It is said, "In prosperity men friends may find
Which in adversity be full unkind."
Now whither for succor shall I flee,
Sith° that Fellowship hath forsaken me? *Since*
To my kinsmen I will, truly,
Praying them to help me in my necessity.
I believe that they will do so,
For kind will creep where it may not go.[1]
I will go 'say°—for yonder I see them— *assay, try*
Where° be ye now my friends and kinsmen. *Whether*
[*Enter* KINDRED *and* COUSIN.]

KINDRED Here be we now at your commandment:
Cousin, I pray you show us your intent
In any wise, and not spare.

COUSIN Yea, Everyman, and to us declare
If ye be disposed to go anywhither.
For, weet° you well, we will live and die togither. *know*

KINDRED In wealth and woe we will with you hold,
For over his kin a man may be bold.[2]

EVERYMAN Gramercy, my friends and kinsmen kind.
Now shall I show you the grief of my mind.
I was commanded by a messenger
That is a high king's chief officer:
He bade me go a pilgrimage, to my pain—
And I know well I shall never come again.
Also I must give a reckoning strait,° *strict*
For I have a great enemy that hath me in wait,[3]
Which intendeth me to hinder.

KINDRED What account is that which ye must render?
That would I know.

EVERYMAN Of all my works I must show
How I have lived and my days spent;
Also of ill deeds that I have used
In my time sith life was me lent,
And of all virtues that I have refused.
Therefore I pray you go thither with me

9. The Virgin Mary.
1. For kinship will crawl where it cannot walk (proverbial); that is, kinsmen will find a way to help each other no matter what the circumstance.
2. That is, for a man may count on his kinsmen.
3. That is, Satan, who lies in wait for me.

To help me make mine account, for saint charity.
COUSIN What, to go thither? Is that the matter?
Nay, Everyman, I had liefer° fast° bread and water *rather / fast on*
All this five year and more!
EVERYMAN Alas, that ever I was bore!° *born*
For now shall I never be merry
If that you forsake me.
KINDRED Ah, sir, what? Ye be a merry man:
Take good heart to you and make no moan.
But one thing I warn you, by Saint Anne,[4]
As for me, ye shall go alone.
EVERYMAN My Cousin, will you not with me go?
COUSIN No, by Our Lady! I have the cramp in my toe:
Trust not to me. For, so God me speed,
I will deceive° you in your most need. *betray*
KINDRED It availeth you not us to 'tice.° *entice*
Ye shall have my maid with all my heart:
She loveth to go to feasts, there to be nice,° *wanton*
And to dance, and abroad to start.[5]
I will give her leave to help you in that journey,
If that you and she may agree.
EVERYMAN Now show me the very effect° of your mind: *tenor*
Will you go with me or abide behind?
KINDRED Abide behind? Yea, that will I and I may!
Therefore farewell till another day.
[*Exit* KINDRED.]
EVERYMAN How should I be merry or glad?
For fair promises men to me make,
But when I have most need they me forsake.
I am deceived. That maketh me sad.
COUSIN Cousin Everyman, farewell now,
For verily I will not go with you;
Also of mine own an unready reckoning
I have to account—therefore I make tarrying.° *stay behind*
Now God keep thee, for now I go.
[*Exit* COUSIN.]
EVERYMAN Ah, Jesus, is all come hereto?° *to this*
Lo, fair words maketh fools fain:° *glad*
They promise and nothing will do, certain.
My kinsmen promised me faithfully
For to abide with me steadfastly,
And now fast away do they flee.
Even so Fellowship promised me.
What friend were best me of to provide?[6]
I lose my time here longer to abide.
Yet in my mind a thing there is:

4. The mother of the Virgin Mary.
5. And to run around.
6. To provide myself with.

All my life I have loved riches;
If that my Good° now help me might, *Goods*
He would make my heart full light.
I will speak to him in this distress.
Where art thou, my Goods and riches?
GOODS [*within*] Who calleth me? Everyman? What, hast thou haste?
I lie here in corners, trussed and piled so high,
And in chests I am locked so fast—
Also sacked in bags—thou mayst see with thine eye
I cannot stir, in packs low where I lie.
What would ye have? Lightly° me say. *Quickly*
EVERYMAN Come hither, Good, in all the haste thou may,
For of counsel I must desire thee.
[*Enter* GOODS.]
GOODS Sir, and° ye in the world have sorrow or adversity, *if*
That can I help you to remedy shortly.
EVERYMAN It is another disease° that grieveth me: *trouble*
In this world it is not, I tell thee so.
I am sent for another way to go,
To give a strait count general
Before the highest Jupiter° of all. *God*
And all my life I have had joy and pleasure in thee:
Therefore I pray thee go with me,
For, peradventure, thou mayst before God Almighty
My reckoning help to clean and purify.
For it is said ever among[7]
That money maketh all right that is wrong.
GOODS Nay, Everyman, I sing another song:
I follow no man in such voyages.
For, and° I went with thee, *if*
Thou shouldest fare much the worse for me;
For because on me thou did set thy mind,
Thy reckoning I have made blotted and blind,° *illegible*
That thine account thou cannot make truly—
And that hast thou for the love of me.
EVERYMAN That would grieve me full sore
When I should come to that fearful answer.
Up, let us go thither together.
GOODS Nay, not so, I am too brittle, I may not endure.
I will follow no man one foot, be ye sure.
EVERYMAN Alas, I have thee loved and had great pleasure
All my life-days on good and treasure.
GOODS That is to thy damnation, without leasing,[8]
For my love is contrary to the love everlasting.
But if thou had me loved moderately during,[9]
As to the poor to give part of me,
Then shouldest thou not in this dolor° be, *distress*

7. For it is commonly said.
8. Without a lie (i.e., truly).
9. That is, during your lifetime.

Nor in this great sorrow and care.
EVERYMAN Lo, now was I deceived ere I was ware,
And all I may wite° misspending of time. *blame on*
GOODS What, weenest° thou that I am thine? *suppose*
EVERYMAN I had weened so.
GOODS Nay, Everyman, I say no.
As for a while I was lent thee;
A season thou hast had me in prosperity.
My condition° is man's soul to kill; *nature*
If I save one, a thousand I do spill.° *destroy*
Weenest thou that I will follow thee?
Nay, from this world, not verily.
EVERYMAN I had weened otherwise.
GOODS Therefore to thy soul Good is a thief;
For when thou art dead, this is my guise°— *custom*
Another to deceive in the same wise
As I have done thee, and all to his soul's repreef.° *shame*
EVERYMAN O false Good, cursed thou be,
Thou traitor to God, that hast deceived me
And caught me in thy snare!
GOODS Marry, thou brought thyself in care,[1]
Whereof I am glad:
I must needs laugh, I cannot be sad.
EVERYMAN Ah, Good, thou hast had long my heartly° love; *heartfelt*
I gave thee that which should be the Lord's above.
But wilt thou not go with me, indeed?
I pray thee truth to say.
GOODS No, so God me speed!
Therefore farewell and have good day.
[*Exit* GOODS.]
EVERYMAN Oh, to whom shall I make my moan
For to go with me in that heavy° journey? *sorrowful*
First Fellowship said he would with me gone:° *go*
His words were very pleasant and gay,
But afterward he left me alone.
Then spake I to my kinsmen, all in despair,
And also they gave me words fair—
They lacked no fair speaking,
But all forsake me in the ending.
Then went I to my Goods that I loved best,
In hope to have comfort; but there had I least
For my Goods sharply did me tell
That he bringeth many into hell.
Then of myself I was ashamed,
And so I am worthy to be blamed:
Thus may I well myself hate.
Of whom shall I now counsel take?

1. That is, you brought sorrow on yourself.

I think that I shall never speed
Till that I go to my Good Deed.
But alas, she is so weak
That she can neither go° nor speak. *walk*
Yet will I venture° on her now. *gamble*
My Good Deeds, where be you?

GOOD DEEDS [*speaking from the ground*] Here I lie, cold in the ground:
Thy sins hath me sore bound
That I cannot stear.° *stir*

EVERYMAN O Good Deeds, I stand in fear:
I must you pray of counsel,
For help now should come right well.[2]

GOOD DEEDS Everyman, I have understanding
That ye be summoned, account to make,
Before Messiah of Jer'salem King.
And you do by me,[3] that journey with you will I take.

EVERYMAN Therefore I come to you my moan to make:
I pray you that ye will go with me.

GOOD DEEDS I would full fain,° but I cannot stand, verily. *gladly*

EVERYMAN Why, is there anything on you fall?° *fallen*

GOOD DEEDS Yea, sir, I may thank you of all:
If ye had perfectly cheered me,
Your book of count full ready had be.

[GOOD DEEDS *shows him the account book.*]

Look, the books of your works and deeds eke,° *also*
As how they lie under the feet,
To your soul's heaviness.° *distress*

EVERYMAN Our Lord Jesus help me!
For one letter here I cannot see.

GOOD DEEDS There is a blind° reckoning in time of distress![4] *illegible*

EVERYMAN Good Deeds, I pray you help me in this need,
Or else I am forever damned indeed.
Therefore help me to make reckoning
Before the Redeemer of all thing
That King is and was and ever shall.

GOOD DEEDS Everyman, I am sorry of° your fall *for*
And fain would help you and° I were able. *if*

EVERYMAN Good Deeds, your counsel I pray you give me.

GOOD DEEDS That shall I do verily,
Though that on my feet I may not go;
I have a sister that shall with you also,
Called Knowledge, which shall with you abide
To help you to make that dreadful reckoning.

[*Enter* KNOWLEDGE.]

KNOWLEDGE Everyman, I will go with thee and be thy guide,
In thy most need to go by thy side.

2. For help would be most welcome now.
3. If you do as I advise.
4. That is, for the sinful person, the book of reckoning is hard to read in the hour of distress.

EVERYMAN In good condition I am now in everything,
And am whole content with this good thing,
Thanked be God my Creator.
GOOD DEEDS And when she hath brought you there
Where thou shalt heal thee of thy smart,° *pain*
Then go you with your reckoning and your Good Deeds together
For to make you joyful at heart
Before the blessed Trinity.[5]
EVERYMAN My Good Deeds, gramercy!
I am well content, certainly,
With your words sweet.
KNOWLEDGE Now go we together lovingly
To Confession, that cleansing river.
EVERYMAN For joy I weep—I would we were there!
But I pray you give me cognition,° *knowledge*
Where dwelleth that holy man Confession?
KNOWLEDGE In the House of Salvation:
We shall find him in that place,
That shall us comfort, by God's grace.

[KNOWLEDGE *leads* EVERYMAN *to* CONFESSION.]

Lo, this is Confession: kneel down and ask mercy,
For he is in good conceit° with God Almighty. *esteem*
EVERYMAN [*kneeling*] O glorious fountain that all
uncleanness doth clarify,° *purify*
Wash from me the spots of vice unclean,
That on me no sin may be seen.
I come with Knowledge for my redemption,
Redempt° with heart and full contrition, *Redeemed*
For I am commanded a pilgrimage to take
And great accounts before God to make.
Now I pray you, Shrift,° mother of Salvation, *Confession*
Help my Good Deeds for my piteous exclamation.
CONFESSION I know your sorrow well, Everyman:
Because with Knowledge ye come to me,
I will you comfort as well as I can,
And a precious jewel I will give thee,
Called Penance, voider° of adversity. *expeller*
Therewith shall your body chastised be—
With abstinence and perseverance in God's service.
Here shall you receive that scourge of me,
Which is penance strong that ye must endure,
To remember thy Saviour was scourged for thee
With sharp scourges, and suffered it patiently.
So must thou ere thou 'scape that painful pilgrimage.
Knowledge, keep° him in this voyage, *guard*
And by that time Good Deeds will be with thee.
But in any wise be secure° of mercy— *certain*
For your time draweth fast—and ye will saved be.

5. That is, God as existing in three persons: the Father, Son, and Holy Spirit.

Ask God mercy and he will grant, truly.
When with the scourge of penance man doth him° bind, *himself*
The oil of forgiveness then shall he find.
EVERYMAN Thanked be God for his gracious work,
For now I will my penance begin.
This hath rejoiced and lighted my heart,
Though the knots be painful and hard within.[6]
KNOWLEDGE Everyman, look your penance that ye fulfill,
What pain that ever it to you be;
And Knowledge shall give you counsel at will
How your account ye shall make clearly.
EVERYMAN O eternal God, O heavenly figure,
O way of righteousness, O goodly vision,
Which descended down in a virgin pure
Because he would every man redeem,
Which Adam forfeited by his disobedience;
O blessed Godhead, elect and high Divine,° *divinity*
Forgive my grievous offense!
Here I cry thee mercy in this presence:[7]
O ghostly Treasure, O Ransomer and Redeemer,
Of all the world Hope and Conduiter,° *Conductor, Guide*
Mirror of joy, Foundator° of mercy, *Founder*
Which enlumineth° heaven and earth thereby, *illuminates*
Hear my clamorous complaint, though it late be;
Receive my prayers, of thy benignity.
Though I be a sinner most abominable,
Yet let my name be written in Moses' table.[8]
O Mary, pray to the Maker of all thing° *things*
Me for to help at my ending,
And save me from the power of my enemy,
For Death assaileth me strongly.
And Lady, that I may by mean of thy prayer
Of your Son's glory to be partner—
By the means of his passion I it crave.
I beseech you help my soul to save.
Knowledge, give me the scourge of penance:
My flesh therewith shall give acquittance.° *satisfaction for sins*
I will now begin, if God give me grace.
KNOWLEDGE Everyman, God give you time and space!° *opportunity*
Thus I bequeath you in the hands of our Saviour:
Now may you make your reckoning sure.
EVERYMAN In the name of the Holy Trinity
My body sore punished shall be:
Take this, body, for the sin of the flesh!
Also° thou delightest to go gay and fresh,° *As / finely dressed*

6. Though the knots (of the scourge) are hard and painful to my senses.
7. That is, in the presence of Knowledge and Confession.
8. That is, the tablets that God gave Moses on Mount Sinai on which the Ten Commandments were written. In the Middle Ages these tablets were associated with baptism and penance.

And in the way of damnation thou did me bring,
Therefore suffer now strokes of punishing!
Now of penance I will wade the water clear,
To save me from purgatory, that sharp fire.

GOOD DEEDS I thank God, now can I walk and go,
And am delivered of my sickness and woe.
Therefore with Everyman I will go, and not spare:
His good works I will help him to declare.

KNOWLEDGE Now, Everyman, be merry and glad:
Your Good Deeds cometh now, ye may not be sad.
Now is your Good Deeds whole and sound,
Going° upright upon the ground. *Walking*

EVERYMAN My heart is light, and shall be evermore.
Now will I smite faster than I did before.

GOOD DEEDS Everyman, pilgrim, my special friend,
Blessed be thou without end!
For thee is preparate° the eternal glory. *prepared*
Ye have me made whole and sound
Therefore I will bide by thee in every stound.° *trial*

EVERYMAN Welcome, my Good Deeds! Now I hear thy voice,
I weep for very sweetness of love.

KNOWLEDGE Be no more sad, but ever rejoice:
God seeth thy living in his throne above.
Put on this garment to thy behove,° *advantage*
Which is wet with your tears—
Or else before God you may it miss
When ye to your journey's end come shall.

EVERYMAN Gentle Knowledge, what do ye it call?

KNOWLEDGE It is a garment of sorrow;
From pain it will you borrow:° *protect*
Contrition it is
That getteth forgiveness;
It pleaseth God passing° well. *exceedingly*

GOOD DEEDS Everyman, will you wear it for your heal?° *well-being*

EVERYMAN Now blessed be Jesu, Mary's son,
For now have I on true contrition.
And let us go now without tarrying.
Good Deeds, have we clear our reckoning?

GOOD DEEDS Yea, indeed, I have it here.

EVERYMAN Then I trust we need not fear.
Now friends, let us not part in twain.

KNOWLEDGE Nay, Everyman, that will we not, certain.

GOOD DEEDS Yet must thou lead with thee
Three persons of great might.

EVERYMAN Who should they be?

GOOD DEEDS Discretion and Strength they hight,° *are called*
And thy Beauty may not abide behind.

KNOWLEDGE Also ye must call to mind
Your Five-Wits° as for your counselors. *senses*

GOOD DEEDS You must have them ready at all hours.

EVERYMAN How shall I get them hither?
KNOWLEDGE You must call them all togither,
And they will be here incontinent.° *immediately*
EVERYMAN My friends, come hither and be present,
Discretion, Strength, my Five-Wits, and Beauty!
[*They enter.*]
BEAUTY Here at your will we be all ready.
What will ye that we should do?
GOOD DEEDS That ye would with Everyman go
And help him in his pilgrimage.
Advise you:° will ye with him or not in that voyage? *Consider*
STRENGTH We will bring him all thither,
To his help and comfort, ye may believe me.
DISCRETION So will we go with him all togither.
EVERYMAN Almighty God, loved° might thou be! *praised*
I give thee laud that I have hither brought
Strength, Discretion, Beauty, and Five-Wits—lack I nought—
And my Good Deeds, with Knowledge clear,
All be in my company at my will here:
I desire no more to my business.
STRENGTH And I, Strength, will by you stand in distress,
Though thou would in battle fight on the ground.
FIVE-WITS And though it were through the world round,
We will not depart for sweet ne sour.
BEAUTY No more will I, until death's hour,
Whatsoever thereof befall.
DISCRETION Everyman, advise you first of all:
Go with a good advisement° and deliberation. *reflection*
We all give you virtuous° monition° *confident / prediction*
That all shall be well.
EVERYMAN My friends, hearken what I will tell;
I pray God reward you in his heaven-sphere;
Now hearken all that be here,
For I will make my testament,
Here before you all present:
In alms half my good° I will give with my hands twain, *goods*
In the way of charity with good intent;
And the other half, still° shall remain, *which still*
I 'queath° to be returned there° it ought to be. *bequeath / where*
This I do in despite of the fiend of hell,
To go quit out of his perel,
Ever after and this day.[9]
KNOWLEDGE Everyman, hearken what I say:
Go to Priesthood, I you advise,
And receive of him, in any wise,° *at all costs*
The holy sacrament and ointment[1] togither;

9. To be free of his power today and ever after.
1. The Eucharist (see line 724) and extreme unction (anointing of the sick).

Then shortly see ye turn again hither:
We will all abide you here.

FIVE-WITS Yea, Everyman, hie you that ye ready were.
There is no emperor, king, duke, ne baron,
That of God hath commission
As hath the least priest in the world being:
For of the blessed sacraments pure and bening° *benign*
He beareth the keys,[2] and thereof hath the cure° *care*
For man's redemption—it is ever sure—
Which God for our souls' medicine
Gave us out of his heart with great pine,° *suffering*
Here in this transitory life for thee and me.
The blessed sacraments seven there be:
Baptism, confirmation, with priesthood° good, *ordination*
And the sacrament of God's precious flesh and blood,
Marriage, the holy extreme unction, and penance:
These seven be good to have in remembrance,
Gracious sacraments of high divinity.

EVERYMAN Fain° would I receive that holy body, *Gladly*
And meekly to my ghostly° father I will go. *spiritual*

FIVE-WITS Everyman, that is the best that ye can do:
God will you to salvation bring.
For priesthood exceedeth all other thing:° *things*
To us Holy Scripture they do teach,
And converteth man from sin, heaven to reach;
God hath to them more power given
Than to any angel that is in heaven.
With five words[3] he may consecrate
God's body in flesh and blood to make,
And handleth his Maker between his hands.
The priest bindeth and unbindeth all bands,[4]
Both in earth and in heaven.
Thou ministers° all the sacraments seven; *administers*
Though we kiss thy feet, thou were worthy;
Thou art surgeon that cureth sin deadly;
No remedy we find under God
But all° only priesthood. *Except*
Everyman, God gave priests that dignity
And setteth them in his stead among us to be.
Thus be they above angels in degree.

[*Exit* EVERYMAN.]

KNOWLEDGE If priests be good, it is so, surely.
But when Jesu hanged on the cross with great smart,° *pain*
There he gave out of his blessed heart
The same sacrament in great torment,
He sold them not to us, that Lord omnipotent:

2. Spiritual power or authority. See Matthew 16.19.
3. *Hoc est enim corpus meum* ("For this is my body"; Latin), words for the consecration of bread in the Roman Catholic liturgy.
4. Bonds (of sin). See Matthew 16.19.

Therefore Saint Peter the Apostle doth say
That Jesu's curse hath all they
Which God their Saviour do buy or sell[5]
Or they for any money do take or tell.[6]
Sinful priests giveth the sinners example bad:
Their children sitteth by other men's fires, I have heard;[7]
And some haunteth women's company
With unclean life, as lusts of lechery.
These be with sin made blind.

FIVE-WITS　I trust to God no such may we find.
Therefore let us priesthood honor,
And follow their doctrine for our souls' succor.
We be their sheep and they shepherds be
By whom we all be kept in surety.
Peace, for yonder I see Everyman come,
Which hath made true satisfaction.

GOOD DEEDS　Methink it is he indeed.

[*Re-enter* EVERYMAN.]

EVERYMAN　Now Jesu be your alder speed![8]
I have received the sacrament for my redemption,
And then mine extreme unction.
Blessed be all they that counseled me to take it!
And now, friends, let us go without longer respite.
I thank God that ye have tarried so long.
Now set each of you on this rood° your hond°　　*cross / hand*
And shortly follow me:
I go before there I would be.[9] God be our guide!

STRENGTH　Everyman, we will not from you go
Till ye have done this voyage long.

DISCRETION　I, Discretion, will bide by you also.

KNOWLEDGE　And though this pilgrimage be never so strong,°　　*wearisome*
I will never part you fro.

STRENGTH　Everyman, I will be as sure by thee
As ever I did by Judas Maccabee.[1]

EVERYMAN　Alas, I am so faint I may not stand—
My limbs under me doth fold!
Friends, let us not turn again to this land,
Not for all the world's gold.
For into this cave must I creep
And turn to earth, and there to sleep.

BEAUTY　What, into this grave, alas?

EVERYMAN　Yea, there shall ye consume,° more and lass.[2]　　*decay*

BEAUTY　And what, should I smother here?

5. An allusion to simony, the buying or selling of sacraments, sacred objects, or ecclesiastical offices. See Acts 8.18–21.
6. Or who for (any sacrament) take or pay money. *Tell:* to count out.
7. That is, they have illegitimate children.
8. Now may Jesus favor you all.
9. I lead (the way to) where I wish to be.
1. The leader of the Jews in their successful revolt against the Syrians in the 2nd century B.C.E.
2. More and less (i.e., all of you).

EVERYMAN Yea, by my faith, and nevermore appear.
In this world live no more we shall,
But in heaven before the highest Lord of all.
BEAUTY I cross out all this![3] Adieu, by Saint John—
I take my tape in my lap and am gone.[4]
EVERYMAN What, Beauty, whither will ye?
BEAUTY Peace, I am deaf—I look not behind me,
Not and° thou wouldest give me all the gold in thy chest. *if*
[*Exit* BEAUTY.]
EVERYMAN Alas, whereto may I trust?
Beauty goeth fast away fro me—
She promised with me to live and die!
STRENGTH Everyman, I will thee also forsake and deny.
Thy game liketh° me not at all. *pleases*
EVERYMAN Why then, ye will forsake me all?
Sweet Strength, tarry a little space.° *while*
STRENGTH Nay, sir, by the rood of grace,
I will hie me from thee fast,
Though thou weep till thy heart tobrast.° *break into pieces*
EVERYMAN Ye would ever bide by me, ye said.
STRENGTH Yea, I have you far enough conveyed!
Ye be old enough, I understand,
Your pilgrimage to take on hand:[5]
I repent me that I hither came.
EVERYMAN Strength, you to displease I am to blame,[6]
Yet promise is debt, this ye well wot.° *know*
STRENGTH In faith, I care not:
Thou art but a fool to complain;
You spend your speech and waste your brain.
Go, thrust thee into the ground.
[*Exit* STRENGTH.]
EVERYMAN I had weened° surer I should you have found. *supposed*
He that trusteth in his Strength
She him deceiveth at the length.
Both Strength and Beauty forsaketh me—
Yet they promised me fair and lovingly.
DISCRETION Everyman, I will after Strength be gone:
As for me, I will leave you alone.
EVERYMAN Why Discretion, will ye forsake me?
DISCRETION Yea, in faith, I will go from thee.
For when Strength goeth before,
I follow after evermore.
EVERYMAN Yet I pray thee, for the love of the Trinity,
Look in my grave once piteously.

3. I cancel all this (i.e., my promise to stay with you).
4. I'll gather up my knitting or spinning and be on my way (proverbial).
5. To take responsibility for your own pilgrimage.
6. I am to blame for displeasing you.

DISCRETION Nay, so nigh° will I not come. *near*
Farewell everyone!
[*Exit* DISCRETION.]
EVERYMAN O all thing faileth save God alone—
Beauty, Strength, and Discretion.
For when Death bloweth his blast
They all run fro me full fast.
FIVE-WITS Everyman, my leave now of thee I take.
I will follow the other, for here I thee forsake.
EVERYMAN Alas, then may I wail and weep,
For I took you for my best friend.
FIVE-WITS I will no longer thee keep.° *watch over*
Now farewell, and there an end!
[*Exit* FIVE-WITS.]
EVERYMAN O Jesu, help, all hath forsaken me!
GOOD DEEDS Nay, Everyman, I will bide with thee:
I will not forsake thee indeed;
Thou shalt find me a good friend at need.
EVERYMAN Gramercy, Good Deeds! Now may I true friends see.
They have forsaken me every one—
I loved them better than my Good Deeds alone.
Knowledge, will ye forsake me also?
KNOWLEDGE Yea, Everyman, when ye to Death shall go,
But not yet, for no manner of danger.
EVERYMAN Gramercy, Knowledge, with all my heart!
KNOWLEDGE Nay, yet will I not from hence depart
Till I see where ye shall become.[7]
EVERYMAN Methink, alas, that I must be gone
To make my reckoning and my debts pay,
For I see my time is nigh spent away.
Take example, all ye that this do hear or see,
How they that I best loved do forsake me,
Except my Good Deeds that bideth truly.
GOOD DEEDS All earthly things is but vanity.
Beauty, Strength, and Discretion do man forsake,
Foolish friends and kinsmen that fair spake—
All fleeth save Good Deeds, and that am I.
EVERYMAN Have mercy on me, God most mighty,
And stand by me, thou mother and maid, holy Mary!
GOOD DEEDS Fear not: I will speak for thee.
EVERYMAN Here I cry God mercy!
GOOD DEEDS Short° our end, and 'minish° our pain. *Shorten / diminish*
Let us go, and never come again.
EVERYMAN Into thy hands, Lord, my soul I commend:
Receive it, Lord, that it be not lost.
As thou me boughtest,° so me defend, *redeemed*
And save me from the fiend's boast,

7. What shall become of you.

That I may appear with that blessed host
That shall be saved at the day of doom.
In manus tuas, of mights most,
Forever *commendo spiritum meum.*[8]

[EVERYMAN *and* GOOD DEEDS *descend into the grave.*]

KNOWLEDGE Now hath he suffered that° we all shall endure, *that which*
The Good Deeds shall make all sure.
Now hath he made ending,
Methinketh that I hear angels sing
And make great joy and melody
Where Everyman's soul received shall be.

ANGEL [*within*] Come, excellent elect° spouse to Jesu![9] *chosen*
Here above thou shalt go
Because of thy singular virtue.
Now the soul is taken the body fro,
Thy reckoning is crystal clear:
Now shalt thou into the heavenly sphere—
Unto the which all ye shall come
That liveth well before the day of doom.

[*Enter* DOCTOR.[1]]

DOCTOR This moral men may have in mind:
Ye hearers, take it of worth,° old and young, *prize it highly*
And forsake Pride, for he deceiveth you in the end.
And remember Beauty, Five-Wits, Strength, and Discretion,
They all at the last do Everyman forsake,
Save° his Good Deeds there doth he take— *Only*
But beware, for and° they be small, *if*
Before God he hath no help at all—
None excuse may be there for Everyman.
Alas, how shall he do than?° *then*
For after death amends may no man make,
For then mercy and pity doth him forsake.
If his reckoning be not clear when he doth come,
God will say, *"Ite, maledicti, in ignem eternum!"*[2]
And he that hath his account whole and sound,
High in heaven he shall be crowned,
Unto which place God bring us all thither,
That we may live body and soul togither.
Thereto help, the Trinity!
Amen, say ye, for saint° charity. *holy*

8. Into thy hands, greatest of powers, I commend my spirit forever; the Latin directly quotes the last words of Jesus on the cross, according to Luke 23.46 (in the Vulgate).
9. Marriage was a common medieval metaphor for the soul's union with Christ.
1. A doctor of theology.
2. Go, ye cursed, into everlasting fire (slightly misquoting Matthew 25.41).

CHRISTOPHER MARLOWE

1564–1593

A LANDMARK event in the development of the Faust myth, Christopher Marlowe's *DOCTOR FAUSTUS* also served, at its moment of production (ca. 1590–93), as a legend of its own time. The play's representation of a consummate scholar's embrace of necromancy (or black magic) to gain a "world of profit and delight," the sale of his soul to the devil, and the consequent loss of both body and soul placed it at the heart of the age's religious controversies and debates. However, Marlowe's casting of his protagonist in the role of a Renaissance *magus*—a blend of scientist, physician, dabbler in the occult, and seeker of spiritual truths—also evoked that age's fascination with gaining mastery over the material world, probing the secrets of nature, and extending human experience to the frontiers of the globe. At a time when Spanish ships were returning from the Americas freighted down with gold and silver, travelers on new trade routes to the East were bringing back daily reports of exotic places and people, and great wealth was being created that could serve new tastes and desires, Marlowe's audience would understandably be drawn to a scholar born of "parents base of stock" who decided to employ forbidden means to realize his most extravagant dreams and ambitions.

Born the son of a shoemaker in 1564 in the cathedral city of Canterbury, Christopher Marlowe could surely be compared to such a character. Unlike most sons of tradesmen, who could at best expect to follow in their fathers' footsteps after a few years of schooling, Marlowe not only attended the King's School, having won a place set aside for gifted children of the poor, but was also awarded a prestigious scholarship to study at Corpus Christi College, Cambridge, where he joined a mix of the wealthiest and most "forward wits" of his time. Marlowe took up residence there in December 1580, earned his B.A. in 1584, and, despite notable unexplained absences, received his M.A. in 1587 at the special urging of Queen Elizabeth's Privy Council for having "done her Majesty good service . . . in matters touching the benefit of his country." This "service" almost surely involved spying on English Catholics in France on behalf of the Elizabethan secret service. Yet the very same year he received his M.A., Marlowe also emerged as the author of *Tamburlaine the Great*—one of the most successful, provocative, and influential plays to be performed on the Elizabethan stage.

Although Marlowe was one of several Cambridge graduates to turn their study of the classics, and their painstaking emulation of Latin verse forms, to positive artistic and commercial advantage in London, he was the first to make the leap from mannered imitation to the creation of an English blank-verse line answerable to the challenges of public playhouse performance. In *Tamburlaine,* Marlowe dramatizes the rise to unlimited worldly power of a former shepherd, who struts across the stage celebrating his successive triumphs with conquering looks and words, unconstrained by any moral misgiving or religious qualm. Urged on by the "strong enchantments" of what BEN JONSON would later call Marlowe's "mighty line," the London audience clamored for more; and Marlowe supplied it in an equally successful sequel to *Tamburlaine,* with Edward Alleyn, the leading actor of the time, again playing the featured role. Marlowe would go on to write four more plays—*The Jew of Malta, Edward II, Doctor Faustus,* and *The Massacre at Paris*—each one of which could have earned him the early death that in fact befell him had he directly identified himself with the pronouncements and professions of his protagonists: a "bottle-nosed" Jew bent on murder and mayhem; a lovesick English monarch, willing to trade his kingdom in order to "frolic" with his male lover; a renowned scholar who sells his soul to the devil; and a ruthless Machiavellian Catholic responsible for fomenting the notorious St. Bartholomew's Day massacre of French Protestants in 1572. Uncertain as the chronology of these plays' composition is, their intention to court controversy could not be clearer.

The Tragicall Hiſtory of the Life and Death of Doctor Fauſtus.

Written by Ch. Marklin.

LONDON,
Printed for *John Wright*, and are to be ſold at his ſhop without Newgate, at the [illegible] of the Bible. 1616.

Title page of the 1616 B-text of *Doctor Faustus.*

A study in mystery and contradiction from first to last, this remarkably gifted, mercurial poet-playwright—who was accounted "the Muses' darling" soon after his death—would meet his end in the town of Deptford on the evening of May 29, 1593, when one Ingram Frizer plunged a knife into his forehead. Marlowe was in the company of the same shady customers—debtors, money brokers, intriguers, spies—with whom he had been consorting for some time. No one knows whether Frizer acted in drunkenness, in self-defense, or in furtherance of a well-laid plan, or if Marlowe was a victim of his own violent temperament or scandalous opinions. Those opinions, including his supposed denial of Christ's divinity, had prompted the Privy Council on May 18 to issue a warrant for Marlowe's arrest. Nine days later, they featured prominently in a deposition from Richard Baines, another of Marlowe's suspect companions, claiming that Marlowe had denied Christ's divinity and made other blasphemous statements. The clock appears to have been counting down for Marlowe much as it did in the last minutes of Doctor Faustus's life, though a number of scholars argue that his former sponsors on the Privy Council are far more likely to have been responsible for his demise than the devil or despair.

Tempting as it is to bring Marlowe's notorious life and death to bear on that of his most famous protagonist, *Doctor Faustus* diverged considerably from the unerringly heterodox direction he pursued in his other plays. In a seeming departure from the "atheist lecture" he was reported to have delivered, Marlowe had Faustus entertain a series of grandiose fantasies only to bring the full weight of the medieval Christian cosmos—with its angels and devils whispering messages of mercy and despair in the wavering soul's ear—down upon the magus's head for daring to do "more than heavenly power permits." And he did so by situating Faustus within the framework of a medieval morality play presided over by a Chorus that influences the audience's impressions of Faustus from first to last, conflating Faustus's daring with the foolhardiness of the mythical Icarus and the presumption of Lucifer in the very first speech of the play. The plot, as Marlowe's Chorus proclaims it, could not be simpler. A brilliant scholar becomes so "swoll'n" with pride at his attainments that "Nothing so sweet as magic is to him, / Which he prefers before [what should be] his chiefest bliss." The stages of Faustus's conversion to the black arts are detailed in the play's first act, and almost immediately consummated in his first transactions with Lucifer's agent, Mephistopheles. The rest of the play dramatizes how little Faustus receives in return for his investment and how fiercely he strives to repent before the clock runs out on the twenty-four years of pleasure he has bargained for and Mephistopheles comes to claim him.

The dramatic foreshortening of Faustus's necromantic career is much more pronounced in the 1604 A-text of *Doctor Faustus* (reprinted here) than it is in the considerably longer 1616 B-text. Since neither version was published during Marlowe's lifetime, neither has the kind of authority scholars look for in making determinations about authorship. But since the disproportionate number of tricks and other comic business found in the B-text are symptomatic of the additions that the theatrical impresario Philip Henslowe commissioned after Marlowe's death, most scholars believe that the A-text is closer to the author's intentions. Like most cinematic remakes, the B-text lacks both the bite and integrity of its supposed original, which often bears the imprint of a dramatist composing in the white heat of artistic concentration. Marlowe seems to have written the haunting postscript—*"Terminat hora diem, terminat Author opus"* ("The hour ends the day, the author ends his work")—to his career-defining play just as the clock struck twelve.

Marlowe's comparatively orthodox treatment of his subject matter likely owes much to the critical tone taken toward Faustus's exploits by his source, *The History of the Damnable Life and Deserved Death of Doctor John Faustus,* a recent English translation (ca. 1589–92) of what has come to be known as the *Faustbook,* which was first published in German in 1587. However, Marlowe also took pains to transform the itinerant magician of his English and German sources into a universally accomplished scholar who makes the tragically momentous decision to risk everything to achieve godlike power. Marlowe signals at every turn the fatal (and foolish) mistakes Faustus makes. Indeed, nature itself rebels against Faustus's bargain, as when his blood congeals and refuses to flow long enough to allow him to deed his body and soul to Lucifer. In the end Faustus attempts to revolt against his devil's reckoning and tries to repent, but he is bullied back into submission by Mephistopheles. He concludes that his transgressions have rendered him unforgivable, forever incapable of sincerely asking for, much less receiving, God's saving grace.

Doctor Faustus is a study in paradox and contradiction, the product not only of colliding medieval and early modern worldviews but of competing religious professions and doctrinal debates. Though a strong case has been made for Calvinism—with its strict division of humanity into the elect and the damned—as the religious system of belief that informs Faustus's conception of himself as unredeemable and of God as vengeful and remote, the play presents a shifting array of religious signs and markers, making it difficult to determine which specific Christian ordering of nature presides over the scholar's fall. Faustus is, for example, told by Mephistopheles in the space of eight lines that hell lies "Within the bowels of these elements, / Where we are tortured and remain forever," as well as that "Hell hath no limits, nor is circumscribed / In one self place, for where we are is hell / And where hell is must we ever be." He is subsequently invited by Lucifer himself to view hell, as if it were a geographically demarcated place on a tour map. To delight his mind, he's even given a command performance of a parade of the seven deadly sins: a standard piece of the medieval theological and iconographic repertory that had fallen out of fashion by Marlowe's time. Other seeming contradictions present themselves with a devilishly deadly irony that the savvy Faustus should have anticipated from the very first appearance of the devil at his door when summoned, an indication that the worlds of good and evil, heaven and hell, angels on one side and demons on the other are both intact and fixed in opposition to one another. This dichotomy is clearly exemplified when Mephistopheles denies Faustus's seemingly modest request for a wife, claiming that "marriage is but a ceremonial toy"; what he really means is that marriage has a sacramental status that places it beyond the pale of the devil's control or authority.

Ironically, given the price he has paid for it, the twenty-four years of Faustus's supernatural power turn out to be uneventful, even tedious. For someone who dreamed of becoming "great emperor of the world," Faustus spends a disproportionate amount of time conjuring spirits, playing jokes, and trading quips. The end of the play finds him in the same place as its beginning: at home in Wittenberg with his servant Wagner and his fellow scholars. Whereas Robin, the clownish but practical fool, says he would never bargain his soul for a joint of lamb unless it were well roasted, Faustus appears to have traded "eternal joy" for a banquet that never gets served, much less eaten. In the end he finds himself alone, facing the ultimate penalty laid out in his signed agreement. Imagine the last hour of Faustus's life, abbreviated in Marlowe's play to the time it takes an actor to speak 58 lines—no more than two or three minutes. In a play in which so much else is rendered uncertain or ambiguous, death and damnation are facts that Faustus knows will arrive on schedule. The penalty for his life has been set: "the clock will strike; / The devil will come, and Faustus must be damned." Faustus tries to hope, tries to make time stop and the planets "stand still," tries to beg Christ for mercy. He asks the earth to "gape" so that he may run into it, asks that his body dissolve "like a foggy mist" into the clouds, and imagines his soul transmigrating into that of "some brutish beast," or metamorphosing "into little waterdrops / [That] fall into the ocean, ne'er [to] be found." All to no avail. God "bends his ireful brows," the devil pulls him down, and his last expedient, a promise to burn his books, falls on deaf ears. If it is true that there is nothing like the prospect of death to concentrate the mind, then it may well be said that nothing in dramatic literature concentrates the mind on the imminence of death as intensely as does the last scene of *Doctor Faustus.*

Yet what sin has Faustus committed that he must be damned? Is it pride, the deadliest of the seven deadly sins? Is it the unforgivable sin of despair, which prevents an individual from harboring any hope of redemption? Or is it Faustus's conviction that he has been singled out as one of the reprobate who, unlike the "elect," can do nothing to make himself worthy of God's grace? Apart from playing several crude practical jokes and asking Mephistopheles to torment the Old Man (who apparently has been sent on a mission of mercy from God), Faustus does nothing in the course of the drama to harm others; and on his last night on earth, he appears to be well-loved and regarded by those who know him best, Wagner and his students. Could (or should) God have made Faustus stronger, more capable of resisting the temptations and power of the devil? Or has God spoken through the words and ministrations of the Good Angel and Old Man, and given Faustus as much of a chance to redeem himself as he gives anyone?

As Faustus is spirited offstage by Mephistopheles and his crew of devils at the end of the play, it may well seem that the odds have worked against Faustus from the start and that while conscientiously cultivating his damnation, he has gotten precious little help or protection from on high. Indeed, the last image of God provided by Faustus is of a punishing, wrathful deity to whom he desperately pleads, "My God, my God, look not so fierce on me!" Faustus, the foolish, deluded, profoundly overmatched victim, as opposed to the arrogant, overreaching Faustus of the play's first two acts, is the final version of the character we see before the Chorus reenters to shut off controversy with the authority of a slammed door:

Cut is the branch that might have
grown full straight,
And burnèd is Apollo's laurel bough
That sometime grew within this
learnèd man.
Faustus is gone. Regard his hellish fall,
Whose fiendful fortune may exhort
the wise
Only to wonder at unlawful things,
Whose deepness doth entice such
forward wits
To practice more than heavenly
power permits.

A branch that might have grown straight has been cut, a laurel bough bespeaking divinely appointed inspiration has been burned, and the fault is Faustus's own for failing to take advantage of "learning's golden gifts." A hard verdict, no doubt, but one that may, in retrospect, remind us of another "Muses' darling" cut down in his prime.

THOMAS CARTELLI

The Tragical History of Doctor Faustus

CHARACTERS

The CHORUS
Doctor John FAUSTUS
WAGNER, his servant
The GOOD ANGEL
The EVIL ANGEL
VALDES, CORNELIUS } famous magicians
Three SCHOLARS
MEPHISTOPHELES
ROBIN, the clown, a stableman
Devils
RAFE, a stableman, another clown
LUCIFER
Beelzebub
PRIDE, COVETOUSNESS, WRATH, ENVY, GLUTTONY, SLOTH, LECHERY } the Seven Deadly Sins
The POPE
The Cardinal of LORRAINE
FRIARS
A VINTNER
The EMPEROR of Germany, Charles V
A KNIGHT
Attendants
Alexander the Great, His paramour } spirits
A HORSE-COURSER
The DUKE of Vanholt
The DUCHESS of Vanholt
Helen of Troy, a spirit
An OLD MAN

SCENE: *Doctor Faustus's study at Wittenberg, and on his travels.*

Prologue

[*Enter* CHORUS.]

CHORUS Not marching now in fields of Trasimene,[1]
Where Mars° did mate° the Carthaginians, *Roman god of war / defeat*
Nor sporting in the dalliance of love

1. The lake in Italy where the Carthaginian general Hannibal destroyed two Roman legions in 217 B.C.E.

In courts of kings where state is overturned,
Nor in the pomp of proud audacious deeds,
Intends our muse to vaunt his heavenly verse.[2]
Only this, gentlemen: we must perform
The form of Faustus' fortunes, good or bad.
To patient judgments we appeal our plaud,° *seek approval*
And speak for Faustus in his infancy.
Now is he born, his parents base of stock,
In Germany, within a town called Rhode.
Of riper years to Wittenberg he went,
Whereas° his kinsmen chiefly brought him up. *Where*
So soon he profits in divinity,
The fruitful plot of scholarism graced,
That shortly he was graced with doctor's name,
Excelling all whose sweet delight disputes
In heavenly matters of theology;
Till, swoll'n with cunning° of a self-conceit, *learning; cleverness*
His waxen wings did mount above his reach,[3]
And, melting, heavens conspired his overthrow.
For, falling to a devilish exercise,
And glutted more with learning's golden gifts,
He surfeits upon cursèd necromancy;
Nothing so sweet as magic is to him,
Which he prefers before his chiefest bliss.[4]
And this the man that in his study sits. [*Exit.*]

1.1

[*Enter* FAUSTUS *in his study.*]

FAUSTUS Settle thy studies, Faustus, and begin
To sound the depth of that° thou wilt profess. *that which*
Having commenced, be a divine in show,[5]
Yet level at the end° of every art, *aim at the goal*
And live and die in Aristotle's works.
Sweet *Analytics*,[6] 'tis thou hast ravished me!
[*He reads.*] *"Bene disserere est finis logices."*[7]
Is to dispute well logic's chiefest end?
Affords this art no greater miracle?
Then read no more; thou hast attained the end.
A greater subject fitteth Faustus' wit.
Bid *On kai me on*[8] farewell. Galen,[9] come!
Seeing *ubi desinit philosophus, ibi incipit medicus*,[1]

2. "Our muse" appears to refer to Marlowe himself, with the preceding lines alluding to earlier plays of his, including *Edward II* and the first and second parts of *Tamburlaine the Great*. The reference to a play about Hannibal remains obscure.
3. An allusion to the mythological figure Icarus, whose "waxen wings" (devised by his father, Daedalus), melted when he flew too close to the sun.
4. That is, the hope of salvation.
5. A theologian in appearance.
6. Two of the treatises on logic by the Greek philosopher Aristotle (384–322 B.C.E.) are the *Prior Analytics* and the *Posterior Analytics*.
7. Quoted (Latin) from Peter Ramus's *Dialectica* (1576), and translated in the following line.
8. Being and not being (Greek).
9. Greek physician (129–ca. 199 C.E.), the standard authority on medicine for centuries.
1. Where the philosopher ends, there the physician begins (Latin).

Be a physician, Faustus. Heap up gold,
And be eternized° for some wondrous cure. *made forever famous*
[*He reads.*] "*Summum bonum medicinae sanitas*":[2]
"The end of physic° is our body's health." *medicine*
Why, Faustus, hast thou not attained that end?
Is not thy common talk sound aphorisms?° *established wisdom*
Are not thy bills° hung up as monuments, *prescriptions*
Whereby whole cities have escaped the plague
And thousand desp'rate maladies been eased?
Yet art thou still but Faustus, and a man.
Wouldst thou make man to live eternally,
Or, being dead, raise them to life again,
Then this profession were to be esteemed.
Physic, farewell. Where is Justinian?[3]
[*He reads.*] "*Si una eademque res legatur duobus,*
Alter rem, alter valorem rei,"[4] etc.
A pretty° case of paltry legacies! *petty*
[*He reads.*] "*Exhaereditare filium non potest pater nisi*[5]—"
Such is the subject of the Institute
And universal body of the church.° *canon law*
His study fits a mercenary drudge
Who aims at nothing but external trash—
Too servile and illiberal° for me. *ungentlemanly*
When all is done, divinity is best.
Jerome's Bible,[6] Faustus, view it well.
[*He reads.*] "*Stipendium peccati mors est.*"° Ha! *(see Romans 6.23)*
"*Stipendium,*" etc.
"The reward of sin is death." That's hard.
[*He reads.*] "*Si peccasse negamus, fallimur,*
Et nulla est in nobis veritas."° *(see 1 John 1.8)*
"If we say that we have no sin,
We deceive ourselves, and there's no truth in us."
Why then belike we must sin,
And so consequently die.
Ay, we must die an everlasting death.
What doctrine call you this? Che serà, serà,° *(Spanish)*
"What will be, shall be"? Divinity, adieu!
[*He picks up a book of magic.*]
These metaphysics° of magicians *This occult lore*
And necromantic books are heavenly,
Lines, circles, signs, letters, and characters°— *astrological signs*
Ay, these are those that Faustus most desires.
Oh, what a world of profit and delight,
Of power, of honor, of omnipotence

2. An Aristotelian claim (see *Nicomachean Ethics* 1.7, 1097a).
3. Roman emperor (r. 527–565 C.E.); he codified Roman law in a series of publications, including the *Institutes* (533), the textbook quoted below.
4. If one thing is willed to two persons, one gets the thing, the other the value of the thing (Latin).
5. A father cannot disinherit his son unless (Latin).
6. The Latin (or Vulgate) version of the Bible, translated by Saint Jerome (ca. 347–419/420 C.E.).

Is promised to the studious artisan!° — *cultivator of the arts*
All things that move between the quiet° poles — *unmoving*
Shall be at my command. Emperors and kings
Are but obeyed in their several provinces,
Nor can they raise the wind or rend the clouds;
But his dominion that exceeds° in this — *excels*
Stretcheth as far as doth the mind of man.
A sound magician is a mighty god.
Here, Faustus, try° thy brains to gain a deity.° — *test / godhood*
[*Calling*] Wagner!

[*Enter* WAGNER.]

Commend me to my dearest friends,
The German Valdes and Cornelius.
Request them earnestly to visit me.

WAGNER I will, sir. [*Exit.*]

FAUSTUS Their conference will be a greater help to me
Than all my labors, plod I ne'er so fast.

[*Enter the* GOOD ANGEL *and the* EVIL ANGEL.]

GOOD ANGEL O Faustus, lay that damnèd book aside
And gaze not on it, lest it tempt thy soul
And heap God's heavy wrath upon thy head!
Read, read the Scriptures. That° is blasphemy. — *(the book of magic)*

EVIL ANGEL Go forward, Faustus, in that famous art
Wherein all nature's treasury is contained.
Be thou on earth as Jove° is in the sky, — *Jupiter (i.e., God)*
Lord and commander of these elements.

[*Exeunt*° ANGELS.] — *They exit (Latin)*

FAUSTUS How am I glutted with conceit° of this! — *the idea*
Shall I make spirits fetch me what I please,
Resolve me of° all ambiguities, — *Free me from*
Perform what desperate° enterprise I will? — *reckless*
I'll have them fly to India° for gold, — *the Indies*
Ransack the ocean for orient pearl,
And search all corners of the newfound world° — *(i.e., America)*
For pleasant fruits and princely delicates.° — *delicacies*
I'll have them read° me strange philosophy — *teach*
And tell the secrets of all foreign kings.
I'll have them wall all Germany with brass
And make swift Rhine circle fair Wittenberg.
I'll have them fill the public schools° with silk, — *university lecture halls*
Wherewith the students shall be bravely° clad. — *smartly*
I'll levy soldiers with the coin they bring
And chase the Prince of Parma[7] from our land,
And reign sole king of all our provinces;
Yea, stranger engines° for the brunt° of war — *machines / assault*
Than was the fiery keel at Antwerp's bridge[8]

7. The Spanish governor-general in the Netherlands from 1579 to 1592 and commander of the Spanish Armada in 1588.

8. Those defending Antwerp against the Spanish in 1585 used a fireship to destroy Parma's bridge over the Scheldt River.

I'll make my servile spirits to invent.
Come, German Valdes and Cornelius,
And make me blest with your sage conference!
[*Enter* VALDES *and* CORNELIUS.]
Valdes, sweet Valdes, and Cornelius,
Know that your words have won me at the last
To practice magic and concealèd arts.
Yet not your words only, but mine own fantasy,
That will receive no object,° for my head *other idea; objection*
But° ruminates on necromantic skill. *Only*
Philosophy is odious and obscure;
Both law and physic are for petty wits;
Divinity is basest of the three,
Unpleasant, harsh, contemptible, and vile.
'Tis magic, magic that hath ravished me.
Then, gentle° friends, aid me in this attempt, *wellborn*
And I, that have with concise syllogisms
Graveled° the pastors of the German church *Floored, confounded*
And made the flow'ring pride of Wittenberg
Swarm to my problems° as the infernal spirits *disputations, lectures*
On sweet Musaeus when he came to hell,[9]
Will be as cunning as Agrippa[1] was,
Whose shadows° made all Europe honor him. *spirits*

VALDES Faustus, these books, thy wit, and our experience
Shall make all nations to canonize us.
As Indian Moors[2] obey their Spanish lords,
So shall the subjects° of every element *servant-spirits*
Be always serviceable to us three.
Like lions shall they guard us when we please,
Like Almaine rutters° with their horsemen's staves,° *German cavalry / lances*
Or Lapland giants, trotting by our sides;
Sometimes like women, or unwedded maids,
Shadowing more beauty in their airy° brows *heavenly*
Than in the white breasts of the Queen of Love.° *Venus*
From Venice shall they drag huge argosies,° *large merchant ships*
And from America the golden fleece[3]
That yearly stuffs old Philip's treasury,
If learnèd Faustus will be resolute.

FAUSTUS Valdes, as resolute am I in this
As thou to live. Therefore object it not.° *do not object*

CORNELIUS The miracles that magic will perform
Will make thee vow to study nothing else.

9. Marlowe is apparently confusing the mythical poet Musaeus (described as standing in the midst of a large number of spirits in the underworld; Virgil, *Aeneid* 6.666–68) with his predecessor Orpheus, who descended to Hades in an unsuccessful attempt to retrieve his dead wife, Eurydice.

1. Henry Cornelius Agrippa (1486–1535), famous German physician and alchemist.

2. That is, the indigenous residents of the Americas, such as the Aztecs of Mexico and Incas of Peru.

3. That is, the huge amounts of gold the Spanish were transporting over the Atlantic to the king of Spain, Philip II (r. 1556–98). In classical mythology, a literal golden fleece was the object of the quest by Jason and the Argonauts.

He that is grounded in astrology,
Enriched with tongues,° well seen° in minerals, *languages / versed*
Hath all the principles magic doth require.
Then doubt not, Faustus, but to be renowned
And more frequented° for this mystery° *resorted to / art*
Than heretofore the Delphian oracle.[4]
The spirits tell me they can dry the sea
And fetch the treasure of all foreign wrecks—
Ay, all the wealth that our forefathers hid
Within the massy entrails of the earth.
Then tell me, Faustus, what shall we three want?° *lack*

FAUSTUS Nothing, Cornelius. Oh, this cheers my soul!
Come, show me some demonstrations magical,
That I may conjure in some lusty° grove *pleasant*
And have these joys in full possession.

VALDES Then haste thee to some solitary grove,
And bear wise Bacon's and Albanus' works,[5]
The Hebrew Psalter, and New Testament;
And whatsoever else is requisite
We will inform thee ere our conference cease.

CORNELIUS Valdes, first let him know the words of art,° *magical incantations*
And then, all other ceremonies learned,
Faustus may try his cunning by himself.

VALDES First I'll instruct thee in the rudiments,
And then wilt thou be perfecter than I.

FAUSTUS Then come and dine with me, and after meat° *food*
We'll canvass every quiddity° thereof, *scrutinize every detail*
For ere I sleep I'll try what I can do.
This night I'll conjure, though I die therefore. [*Exeunt.*]

1.2

[*Enter two* SCHOLARS.]

FIRST SCHOLAR I wonder what's become of Faustus, that was wont to make our schools ring with *"sic probo."*° *I prove it thus (Latin)*

SECOND SCHOLAR That shall we know, for see, here comes his boy.° *servant*

[*Enter* WAGNER *carrying wine.*]

FIRST SCHOLAR How now, sirrah,[6] where's thy master?

WAGNER God in heaven knows.

SECOND SCHOLAR Why, dost not thou know?

WAGNER Yes, I know, but that follows not.

FIRST SCHOLAR Go to, sirrah! Leave your jesting, and tell us where he is.

WAGNER That follows not necessary by force of argument

4. Apollo's shrine at Delphi, in lower central Greece, was the site of the most authoritative oracle in the ancient world.

5. The English scientist Roger Bacon (ca. 1220–1292) and the Italian physician Pietro d'Abano (ca. 1250–1316) were both philosophers accused of heresy and black magic.

6. A form of address to male social inferiors.

that you, being licentiate,° should stand upon't. There — *advanced scholars*
fore, acknowledge your error, and be attentive.
SECOND SCHOLAR Why, didst thou not say thou knew'st?
WAGNER Have you any witness on't?
FIRST SCHOLAR Yes, sirrah, I heard you.
WAGNER Ask my fellow if I be a thief.
SECOND SCHOLAR Well, you will not tell us.
WAGNER Yes, sir, I will tell you. Yet if you were not dunces,
you would never ask me such a question. For is not he
corpus naturale?° And is not that *mobile*? Then, where — *a natural body (Latin)*
fore should you ask me such a question? But that I
am° by nature phlegmatic,[7] slow to wrath, and prone to — *Were I not*
lechery—to love, I would say—it were not for you to
come within forty foot of the place of execution,° — *dining room; gallows*
although I do not doubt to see you both hanged
the next sessions.° Thus, having triumphed over you, — *sitting of the court*
I will set my countenance like a precisian° and begin to — *Puritan*
speak thus: Truly, my dear brethren, my master is
within at dinner with Valdes and Cornelius, as this
wine, if it could speak, it would inform Your Worships.
And so the Lord bless you, preserve you, and keep you,
my dear brethren, my dear brethren. [*Exit.*]
FIRST SCHOLAR Nay, then, I fear he is fall'n into that
damned art for which they two are infamous through the
world.
SECOND SCHOLAR Were he a stranger, and not allied° to me, — *a companion*
yet should I grieve for him. But come, let us go and in-
form the rector,° and see if he, by his grave counsel, can — *head of the university*
reclaim him.
FIRST SCHOLAR Oh, but I fear me nothing can reclaim him.
SECOND SCHOLAR Yet let us try what we can do. [*Exeunt.*]

1.3

[*Enter* FAUSTUS *to conjure.*]

FAUSTUS Now that the gloomy shadow of the earth,
Longing to view Orion's drizzling look,[8]
Leaps from th'Antarctic world unto the sky
And dims the welkin° with her pitchy breath, — *sky*
Faustus, begin thine incantations,
And try if devils will obey thy hest,° — *behest, command*
Seeing thou hast prayed and sacrificed to them.
Within this circle is Jehovah's name,
Forward and backward anagrammatized,
The breviated names of holy saints,
Figures of every adjunct to the heavens,

7. Sluggish or dull. According to early modern accounts of human emotion, imbalances in the four bodily humors (fluids)—black bile (melancholic), blood (sanguine), yellow bile (choleric), and phlegm—determined one's personality.

8. Because in the Northern Hemisphere the constellation Orion rises in November, it was associated with winter storms.

And characters of signs° and erring stars° *the zodiac / planets*
By which the spirits are enforced to rise.
Then fear not, Faustus, but be resolute,
And try the uttermost magic can perform.
Sint mihi dei Acherontis propitii! Valeat numen triplex Jehovae! Ignei, aerii, aquatici, terreni, spiritus, salvete! Orientis princeps Lucifer, Beelzebub, inferni ardentis monarcha, et Demogorgon, propitiamus vos, ut appareat et surgat Mephistopheles. Quid tu moraris? Per Jehovam, Gehennam, et consecratam aquam quam nunc spargo, signumque crucis quod nunc facio, et per vota nostra, ipse nunc surgat nobis dicatus Mephistopheles![9]

[FAUSTUS *sprinkles holy water and makes a sign of the cross.*]

[*Enter a devil* (MEPHISTOPHELES).]

I charge thee to return and change thy shape.
Thou art too ugly to attend on me.
Go, and return an old Franciscan friar;
That holy shape becomes a devil best.

[*Exit devil* (MEPHISTOPHELES).]

I see there's virtue° in my heavenly words. *power*
Who would not be proficient in this art?
How pliant is this Mephistopheles,
Full of obedience and humility!
Such is the force of magic and my spells.
Now, Faustus, thou art conjurer laureate,
That canst command great Mephistopheles.
Quin redis, Mephistopheles, fratris imagine![1]

[*Enter* MEPHISTOPHELES *dressed as a friar.*]

MEPHISTOPHELES Now, Faustus, what wouldst thou have me do?
FAUSTUS I charge thee wait upon me whilst I live,
To do whatever Faustus shall command,
Be it to make the moon drop from her sphere
Or the ocean to overwhelm the world.
MEPHISTOPHELES I am a servant to great Lucifer
And may not follow thee without his leave.
No more than he commands must we perform.
FAUSTUS Did not he charge thee to appear to me?
MEPHISTOPHELES No, I came now hither of mine own accord.
FAUSTUS Did not my conjuring speeches raise thee? Speak.
MEPHISTOPHELES That was the cause, but yet *per accidens*.° *incidentally* (*Latin*)
For when we hear one rack° the name of God, *torture, tear*

9. May the gods of Acheron be propitious to me. Away with the threefold godhead of Jehovah! Hail, spirits of fire, air, water, and earth! Lucifer, Prince of the East, Beelzebub, monarch of burning hell, and Demogorgon, we invoke you, that Mephistopheles may appear and rise. Why do you delay? By Jehovah, Gehenna, and the holy water that I now sprinkle, by the sign of the cross that I now make, and by our vows, may Mephistopheles himself, invoked by us, now rise! (Latin). *Acheron*: a river of the underworld. *Beelzebub, Demogorgon:* devils. *Gehenna*: hell.

1. Why not return in the image of a friar, Mephistopheles! (Latin).

Abjure the Scriptures and his Savior Christ,
We fly in hope to get his glorious soul,
Nor will we come unless he use such means
Whereby he is in danger to be damned.
Therefore, the shortest cut for conjuring
Is stoutly to abjure the Trinity[2]
And pray devoutly to the prince of hell.

FAUSTUS So Faustus hath
Already done, and holds this principle:
There is no chief but only Beelzebub,
To whom Faustus doth dedicate himself.
This word "damnation" terrifies not him,
For he confounds hell in Elysium.[3]
His ghost be with the old philosophers![4]
But leaving these vain trifles of men's souls,
Tell me what is that Lucifer thy lord?

MEPHISTOPHELES Archregent and commander of all spirits.

FAUSTUS Was not that Lucifer an angel once?

MEPHISTOPHELES Yes, Faustus, and most dearly loved of God.

FAUSTUS How comes it then that he is prince of devils?

MEPHISTOPHELES Oh, by aspiring pride and insolence,
For which God threw him from the face of heaven.

FAUSTUS And what are you that live with Lucifer?

MEPHISTOPHELES Unhappy spirits that fell with Lucifer,
Conspired against our God with Lucifer,
And are forever damned with Lucifer.

FAUSTUS Where are you damned?

MEPHISTOPHELES In hell.

FAUSTUS How comes it then that thou art out of hell?

MEPHISTOPHELES Why, this is hell, nor am I out of it.
Think'st thou that I, who saw the face of God
And tasted the eternal joys of heaven,
Am not tormented with ten thousand hells
In being deprived of everlasting bliss?
O Faustus, leave these frivolous demands,
Which strike a terror to my fainting soul!

FAUSTUS What, is great Mephistopheles so passionate
For being deprived of the joys of heaven?
Learn thou of° Faustus manly fortitude, *from*
And scorn those joys thou never shalt possess.
Go bear these tidings to great Lucifer:
Seeing Faustus hath incurred eternal death
By desp'rate thoughts against Jove's deity,
Say he surrenders up to him his soul,
So° he will spare him four-and-twenty years, *Provided that*
Letting him live in all voluptuousness,
Having thee ever to attend on me,

2. That is, God as existing in three persons: the Father, the Son, and the Holy Spirit.
3. He conflates the Christian Hell with the Elysian fields, the abode of the blessed in the underworld in Greek and Roman mythology.
4. That is, pre-Christian philosophers.

To give me whatsoever I shall ask,
To tell me whatsoever I demand,
To slay mine enemies and aid my friends,
And always be obedient to my will.
Go and return to mighty Lucifer,
And meet me in my study at midnight,
And then resolve me of° thy master's mind. *explain to me*

MEPHISTOPHELES I will, Faustus. [*Exit.*]

FAUSTUS Had I as many souls as there be stars,
I'd give them all for Mephistopheles.
By him I'll be great emperor of the world
And make a bridge through the moving air
To pass the ocean with a band of men;
I'll join the hills that bind° the Afric shore *surround, encircle*
And make that land continent to° Spain, *contiguous with*
And both contributory to my crown.
The emp'ror shall not live but by my leave,
Nor any potentate of Germany.
Now that I have obtained what I desire,
I'll live in speculation° of this art *comtemplation*
Till Mephistopheles return again. [*Exit.*]

1.4

[*Enter* WAGNER *and* ROBIN *the clown.*]

WAGNER Sirrah boy, come hither.

ROBIN How, "boy"? 'Swounds,° "boy"! I hope you have seen many boys with such pickedevants° as I have. "Boy," quotha?[5] *By God's wounds (oath)* *pointed beards*

WAGNER Tell me, sirrah, hast thou any comings in?° *income*

ROBIN Ay, and goings out[6] too, you may see else.

WAGNER Alas, poor slave,° see how poverty jesteth in his nakedness! The villain is bare and out of service,[7] and so hungry that I know he would give his soul to the devil for a shoulder of mutton, though it were blood raw. *rogue, servant*

ROBIN How? My soul to the devil for a shoulder of mutton, though 'twere blood raw? Not so, good friend. By'r Lady,[8] I had need have it well roasted, and good sauce to it, if I pay so dear.

WAGNER Well, wilt thou serve me, and I'll make thee go like *Qui mihi discipulus*?[9]

ROBIN How, in verse?

WAGNER No, sirrah, in beaten silk and stavesacre.[1]

ROBIN How, how, knave's acre?[2] [*Aside*] Ay, I thought that

5. That is, "You call *me* 'boy'?"
6. Expenses (with a possible reference to what can be seen through Robin's tattered clothing).
7. The wretch is poor and unemployed.
8. By our Lady—that is, the Virgin Mary (an oath).
9. You who are my pupil (Latin).
1. In embroidered silk anointed with larkspur (whose seeds were used to make a delousing concoction).
2. The name of a poor, narrow street in London.

was all the land his father left him. [*To* WAGNER] Do ye
hear? I would be sorry to rob you of your living.

WAGNER Sirrah, I say in stavesacre.

ROBIN Oho, oho, "stavesacre"! Why then, belike,° if I were — *probably*
your man,° I should be full of vermin. — *servant*

WAGNER So thou shalt, whether thou be'st with me or
no. But, sirrah, leave your jesting, and bind° yourself — *apprentice*
presently° unto me for seven years, or I'll turn all the lice — *now*
about thee into familiars,[3] and they shall tear thee in
pieces.

ROBIN Do you hear, sir? You may save that labor. They are
too familiar with me already. 'Swounds, they are as bold
with my flesh as if they had paid for my meat and drink.

WAGNER Well, do you hear, sirrah? [*Offering money*] Hold,
take these guilders.° — *Dutch coins*

ROBIN Gridirons?° What be they? — *Griddles*

WAGNER Why, French crowns.° — *coins*

ROBIN Mass,° but for the name of French crowns a man were — *By the Mass (oath)*
as good have as many English counters.[4] And what should I
do with these?

WAGNER Why now, sirrah, thou art at an hour's warning° — *notice*
whensoever or wheresoever the devil shall fetch thee.

ROBIN No, no, here, take your gridirons again.

[*He attempts to return the money.*]

WAGNER Truly, I'll none of them.

ROBIN Truly, but you shall.

WAGNER [*to the audience*] Bear witness I gave them him.

ROBIN Bear witness I gave them you again.

WAGNER Well, I will cause two devils presently to fetch
thee away. [*Calling*] Balioll and Belcher!

ROBIN Let your Balio and your Belcher come here and I'll
knock them. They were never so knocked since they
were devils. Say I should kill one of them, what would
folks say? "Do ye see yonder tall° fellow in the round — *valiant*
slop?° He has killed the devil." So I should be called "Kill — *baggy breeches*
devil" all the parish over.

[*Enter two devils, and* ROBIN *the clown runs up and down crying.*]

WAGNER Balioll and Belcher! Spirits, away!

[*Exeunt devils.*]

ROBIN What, are they gone? A vengeance on them! They
have vile long nails. There was a he-devil and a she-
devil. I'll tell you how you shall know them:° all he-devils — *tell them apart*
has horns,[5] and all she-devils has clefts° and cloven feet. — *cleft hooves; vulvas*

WAGNER Well, sirrah, follow me.

ROBIN But do you hear? If I should serve you, would you
teach me to raise up Banios and Belcheos?

3. Attendant evil spirits, which take the shape of animals.

4. Valueless tokens used in computation and exchange.

5. Devils' horns; cuckolds' horns.

WAGNER I will teach thee to turn thyself to anything, to a dog, or a cat, or a mouse, or a rat, or anything.

ROBIN How? A Christian fellow to a dog or a cat, a mouse or a rat? No, no, sir. If you turn me into anything, let it be in the likeness of a little, pretty, frisking flea, that I may be here and there and everywhere. Oh, I'll tickle the pretty wenches' plackets!° I'll be amongst them, i'faith! *slits in petticoats*

WAGNER Well, sirrah, come.

ROBIN But do you hear, Wagner?

WAGNER How? [*Calling*] Balioll and Belcher!

ROBIN Oh, Lord, I pray sir, let Banio and Belcher go sleep.

WAGNER Villain, call me Master Wagner, and let thy left eye be diametarily° fixed upon my right heel, with *quasi vestigiis nostris insistere*.[6] [*Exit.*] *diametrically*

ROBIN God forgive me, he speaks Dutch fustian.° Well, I'll follow him, I'll serve him, that's flat.° [*Exit.*] *bombast* / *for certain*

2.1

[*Enter* FAUSTUS *in his study.*]

FAUSTUS Now, Faustus, must thou needs be damned,
And canst thou not be saved.
What boots° it then to think of God or heaven? *avails*
Away with such vain fancies, and despair!
Despair in God and trust in Beelzebub.
Now go not backward. No, Faustus, be resolute.
Why waverest thou? Oh, something soundeth in mine ears:
"Abjure this magic, turn to God again!"
Ay, and Faustus will turn to God again.
To God? He loves thee not.
The god thou servest is thine own appetite,
Wherein is fixed the love of Beelzebub.
To him I'll build an altar and a church,
And offer lukewarm blood of newborn babes.

[*Enter* GOOD ANGEL *and* EVIL ANGEL.]

GOOD ANGEL Sweet Faustus, leave that execrable art.

FAUSTUS Contrition, prayer, repentance—what of them?

GOOD ANGEL Oh, they are means to bring thee unto heaven.

EVIL ANGEL Rather illusions, fruits of lunacy,
That makes men foolish that do trust them most.

GOOD ANGEL Sweet Faustus, think of heaven and heavenly things!

EVIL ANGEL No, Faustus, think of honor and wealth.

[*Exeunt* ANGELS.]

FAUSTUS Of wealth?
Why, the seigniory of Emden° shall be mine. *(port in north Germany)*
When Mephistopheles shall stand by me,
What god can hurt thee, Faustus? Thou art safe;
Cast° no more doubts. Come, Mephistopheles, *Entertain*
And bring glad tidings from great Lucifer.

6. As if to walk in our (my) footsteps (Latin).

Is't not midnight? Come, Mephistopheles!
Veni, veni,° *Mephistophile!* — *Come, come (Latin)*
[*Enter* MEPHISTOPHELES.]
Now tell, what says Lucifer, thy lord?
MEPHISTOPHELES That I shall wait on Faustus whilst he lives,
So° he will buy my service with his soul. — *Provided that*
FAUSTUS Already Faustus hath hazarded that for thee.
MEPHISTOPHELES But, Faustus, thou must bequeath it solemnly
And write a deed of gift with thine own blood,
For that security° craves great Lucifer. — *guarantee*
If thou deny it, I will back to hell.
FAUSTUS Stay, Mephistopheles, and tell me, what good Will
my soul do thy lord?
MEPHISTOPHELES Enlarge his kingdom.
FAUSTUS Is that the reason he tempts us thus?
MEPHISTOPHELES *Solamen miseris socios habuisse doloris.*[7]
FAUSTUS Have you any pain, that tortures° others? — *you who torture*
MEPHISTOPHELES As great as have the human souls of men.
But tell me, Faustus, shall I have thy soul?
And I will be thy slave, and wait on thee,
And give thee more than thou hast wit to ask.
FAUSTUS Ay, Mephistopheles, I give it thee.
MEPHISTOPHELES Then stab thine arm courageously,
And bind thy soul that at some certain day
Great Lucifer may claim it as his own,
And then be thou as great as Lucifer.
FAUSTUS [*cutting his arm*] Lo, Mephistopheles, for love of thee
I cut mine arm, and with my proper° blood — *own*
Assure my soul to be great Lucifer's,
Chief lord and regent of perpetual night.
View here the blood that trickles from mine arm,
And let it be propitious for my wish.
MEPHISTOPHELES But, Faustus, thou must
Write it in manner of a deed of gift.
FAUSTUS Ay, so I will. [*He writes.*] But Mephistopheles,
My blood congeals, and I can write no more.
MEPHISTOPHELES I'll fetch thee fire to dissolve it straight.° — *immediately*
[*Exit.*]
FAUSTUS What might the staying of my blood portend?
Is it unwilling I should write this bill?° — *legal document*
Why streams it not, that I may write afresh?
"Faustus gives to thee his soul"—ah, there it stayed!
Why shouldst thou not? Is not thy soul thine own?
Then write again: "Faustus gives to thee his soul."
[*Enter* MEPHISTOPHELES *with a chafer*° *of coals.*] — *chafing dish*
MEPHISTOPHELES Here's fire. Come, Faustus, set it on.
FAUSTUS So. Now the blood begins to clear again.
Now will I make an end immediately. [*He writes.*]

7. It is a comfort to the wretched to have companions in their sorrows (i.e., misery loves company; Latin).

MEPHISTOPHELES [*aside*] Oh, what will not I do to obtain his soul?
FAUSTUS *Consummatum est.*[8] This bill is ended,
And Faustus hath bequeathed his soul to Lucifer.
But what is this inscription on mine arm?
"*Homo, fuge!*"° Whither should I fly? *Flee, o man! (Latin)*
If unto God, he'll throw thee down to hell.—
My senses are deceived; here's nothing writ.—
I see it plain. Here in this place is writ
"*Homo, fuge!*" Yet shall not Faustus fly.
MEPHISTOPHELES [*aside*] I'll fetch him somewhat° to delight his mind. [*Exit.*] *something*

[*Enter* MEPHISTOPHELES *with devils, giving crowns and rich apparel to* FAUSTUS, *and dance and then depart.*]

FAUSTUS Speak, Mephistopheles. What means this show?
MEPHISTOPHELES Nothing, Faustus, but to delight thy mind withal° *with*
And to show thee what magic can perform.
FAUSTUS But may I raise up spirits when I please?
MEPHISTOPHELES Ay, Faustus, and do greater things than these.
FAUSTUS Then there's enough for° a thousand souls. *to pay for*
Here, Mephistopheles, receive this scroll,
A deed of gift of body and of soul—
But yet conditionally that thou perform
All articles prescribed between us both.
MEPHISTOPHELES Faustus, I swear by hell and Lucifer
To effect all promises between us made.
FAUSTUS Then hear me read them.
"On these conditions following:

First, that Faustus may be a spirit in form and substance.

Secondly, that Mephistopheles shall be his servant, and at his command.

Thirdly, that Mephistopheles shall do for him and bring him whatsoever.° *anything at all*

Fourthly, that he shall be in his chamber or house invisible.

Lastly, that he shall appear to the said John Faustus at all times in what form or shape soever he please.

I, John Faustus of Wittenberg, Doctor, by these presents° do give both body and soul to Lucifer, Prince of the East, and his minister Mephistopheles; and furthermore grant unto them that, four-and-twenty years being expired, the articles above written inviolate,° full power to fetch or carry the said John Faustus, body and soul, flesh, blood, or goods, into their habitation wheresoever. *this document* *not violated*

By me, John Faustus."

MEPHISTOPHELES Speak, Faustus. Do you deliver this as your deed?
FAUSTUS [*giving the deed*] Ay. Take it, and the devil give thee good on't.
MEPHISTOPHELES Now, Faustus, ask what thou wilt.

8. It is finished (Latin), the last words of Jesus on the cross, according to John 19.30 (Vulgate).

FAUSTUS First will I question with thee about hell.
Tell me, where is the place that men call hell?
MEPHISTOPHELES Under the heavens.
FAUSTUS Ay, but whereabout?
MEPHISTOPHELES Within the bowels of these elements,
Where we are tortured and remain forever.
Hell hath no limits, nor is circumscribed
In one self° place, for where we are is hell, *one and the same*
And where hell is must we ever be.
And, to conclude, when all the world dissolves,
And every creature shall be purified,
All places shall be hell that is not heaven.
FAUSTUS Come, I think hell's a fable.
MEPHISTOPHELES Ay, think so still, till experience change thy mind.
FAUSTUS Why, think'st thou then that Faustus shall be damned?
MEPHISTOPHELES Ay, of necessity, for here's the scroll
Wherein thou hast given thy soul to Lucifer.
FAUSTUS Ay, and body too. But what of that?
Think'st thou that Faustus is so fond° *foolish*
To imagine that after this life there is any pain?
Tush, these are trifles and mere old wives' tales.
MEPHISTOPHELES But, Faustus, I am an instance to prove the contrary,
For I am damned and am now in hell.
FAUSTUS How? Now in hell? Nay, an° this be hell, *if*
I'll willingly be damned here. What? Walking, disputing, etc.? But leaving off this, let me have a wife, the fairest maid in Germany, for I am wanton and lascivious and cannot live without a wife.
MEPHISTOPHELES How, a wife? I prithee, Faustus, talk not of a wife.
FAUSTUS Nay, sweet Mephistopheles, fetch me one, for I will have one.
MEPHISTOPHELES Well, thou wilt have one. Sit there till I come. I'll fetch thee a wife, in the devil's name. [*Exit.*]

[*Enter* MEPHISTOPHELES *with a devil dressed like a woman, with fireworks.*]

MEPHISTOPHELES Tell, Faustus, how dost thou like thy wife?
FAUSTUS A plague on her for a hot whore!
MEPHISTOPHELES Tut, Faustus, marriage is but a ceremonial toy.° *amusement*
If thou lovest me, think no more of it. [*Exit devil.*]
I'll cull thee out the fairest courtesans
And bring them ev'ry morning to thy bed.
She whom thine eye shall like thy heart shall have,
Be she as chaste as was Penelope,
As wise as Saba,[9] or as beautiful

9. The queen of Sheba, who greatly admired Solomon's wisdom (Kings 10.1–9). *Penelope:* the wife of Odysseus and in classical myth a model of faithfulness.

As was bright Lucifer before his fall.
[*Presenting a book*] Hold, take this book. Peruse it thoroughly.
The iterating° of these lines brings gold; *repeating, reciting*
The framing° of this circle on the ground *inscribing*
Brings whirlwinds, tempests, thunder, and lightning.
Pronounce this thrice devoutly to thyself,
And men in armor shall appear to thee,
Ready to execute what thou desir'st.

FAUSTUS Thanks, Mephistopheles. Yet fain° would I have a book wherein I might behold all spells and incantations, that I might raise up spirits when I please. *gladly*

MEPHISTOPHELES Here they are in this book.

[*There turn to them.*]

FAUSTUS Now would I have a book where I might see all characters° and planets of the heavens, that I might know their motions and dispositions. *astrological symbols*

MEPHISTOPHELES Here they are too. [*Turn to them.*]

FAUSTUS Nay, let me have one book more—and then I have done—wherein I might see all plants, herbs, and trees that grow upon the earth.

MEPHISTOPHELES Here they be. [*Turn to them.*]

FAUSTUS Oh, thou art deceived.

MEPHISTOPHELES Tut, I warrant thee. [*Exeunt.*]

2.2

[*Enter* ROBIN *the ostler° with a book in his hand.*] *stable boy*

ROBIN Oh, this is admirable! Here I ha' stol'n one of Doctor Faustus' conjuring books, and, i'faith, I mean to search some circles[1] for my own use. Now will I make all the maidens in our parish dance at my pleasure stark naked before me, and so by that means I shall see more than e'er I felt or saw yet.

[*Enter* RAFE, *calling* ROBIN.]

RAFE Robin, prithee, come away. There's a gentleman tarries to have his horse, and he would have his things[2] rubbed and made clean; he keeps such a chafing with my mistress about it, and she has sent me to look thee out.° Prithee, come away. *look for you*

ROBIN Keep out, keep out, or else you are blown up, you are dismembered, Rafe! Keep out, for I am about a roaring piece of work.

RAFE Come, what dost thou with that same book?° Thou canst not read? *that book there*

ROBIN Yes, my master and mistress shall find that I can read—he for his forehead, she for her private study.[3] She's born to bear with me,[4] or else my art fails.

1. Conjuring circles; vaginas.
2. His leather riding gear (with sexual suggestion).
3. That is, in sex with her, which will put a cuckold's horns on his forehead.
4. Put up with me; support my body in sex; bear my child.

RAFE Why, Robin, what book is that?

ROBIN What book? Why the most intolerable[5] book for conjuring that e'er was invented by any brimstone devil.

RAFE Canst thou conjure with it?

ROBIN I can do all these things easily with it: first, I can make thee drunk with hippocras° at any tavern in Europe for nothing. That's one of my conjuring works. (*spiced wine*)

RAFE Our Master Parson says that's nothing.

ROBIN True, Rafe; and more, Rafe, if thou hast any mind to° Nan Spit,[6] our kitchen maid, then turn her and wind her to thy own use as often as thou wilt, and at midnight. (*any liking for*)

RAFE Oh, brave,° Robin! Shall I have Nan Spit, and to mine own use? On that condition I'll feed thy devil with horse-bread° as long as he lives, of free cost. (*splendid*) (*horse feed, fodder*)

ROBIN No more, sweet Rafe. Let's go and make clean our boots, which lie foul upon our hands, and then to our conjuring, in the devil's name. [*Exeunt.*]

2.3

[*Enter* FAUSTUS *in his study, and* MEPHISTOPHELES.]

FAUSTUS When I behold the heavens, then I repent
And curse thee, wicked Mephistopheles,
Because thou hast deprived me of those joys.

MEPHISTOPHELES Why, Faustus,
Think'st thou heaven is such a glorious thing?
I tell thee, 'tis not half so fair as thou
Or any man that breathes on earth.

FAUSTUS How provest thou that?

MEPHISTOPHELES It was made for man; therefore is man
more excellent.

FAUSTUS If it were made for man, 'twas made for me.
I will renounce this magic and repent.

[*Enter* GOOD ANGEL *and* EVIL ANGEL.]

GOOD ANGEL Faustus, repent yet, God will pity thee.

EVIL ANGEL Thou art a spirit. God cannot pity thee.

FAUSTUS Who buzzeth in mine ears I am a spirit?
Be I a devil,[7] yet God may pity me;
Ay, God will pity me if I repent.

EVIL ANGEL Ay, but Faustus never shall repent.

[*Exeunt* ANGELS.]

FAUSTUS My heart's so hardened I cannot repent.
Scarce can I name salvation, faith, or heaven
But fearful echoes thunders in mine ears:
"Faustus, thou art damned!" Then swords and knives,
Poison, guns, halters° and envenomed steel° (*nooses / swords*)

5. Malapropism for "incomparable."
6. Named for the spit on which cooking meat is turned.
7. A notoriously ambiguous phrase, which may mean "Even if I *am* a devil" or "Even if I *were* a devil."

Are laid before me to dispatch myself;
And long ere this I should have slain myself
Had not sweet pleasure conquered deep despair.
Have not I made blind Homer sing to me
Of Alexander's love and Oenone's death?[8]
And hath not he that built the walls of Thebes
With ravishing sound of his melodious harp[9]
Made music with my Mephistopheles?
Why should I die, then, or basely despair?
I am resolved Faustus shall ne'er repent.
Come, Mephistopheles, let us dispute again
And argue of divine astrology.
Tell me, are there many heavens above the moon?
Are all celestial bodies but one globe,
As is the substance of this centric earth?[1]

MEPHISTOPHELES As are the elements, such are the spheres,
Mutually folded in each others' orb;
And, Faustus, all jointly move upon one axletree,° *axle, pole*
Whose terminine° is termed the world's wide pole. *limit*
Nor are the names of Saturn, Mars, or Jupiter
Feigned, but are erring stars.° *wandering planets*

FAUSTUS But tell me, have they all one motion, both *situ et tempore?*° *in space and time (Latin)*

MEPHISTOPHELES All jointly move from east to west in four-and-twenty hours upon the poles of the world, but differ in their motion upon the poles of the zodiac.° *i.e., along the zodiac*

FAUSTUS Tush, these slender trifles Wagner can decide.
Hath Mephistopheles no greater skill?
Who knows not the double motion of the planets?
The first is finished in a natural day,
The second thus, as Saturn in thirty years, Jupiter in twelve, Mars in four,° *(in fact, two)* the Sun, Venus, and Mercury in a year, the moon in twenty-eight days. Tush, these are freshmen's suppositions.° *arguing points* But tell me, hath every sphere a dominion or intelligentia?° *controlling spirit*

MEPHISTOPHELES Ay.

FAUSTUS How many heavens or spheres are there?

MEPHISTOPHELES Nine: the seven planets, the firmament, and the empyreal° *highest* heaven.

FAUSTUS Well, resolve me in this question: why have we not conjunctions, oppositions, aspects, eclipses all at one time,° *at regular intervals* but in some years we have more, in some less?

MEPHISTOPHELES *Per inaequalem motum respectu totius.*[2]

8. The story of the love of Paris (Alexander) for Helen, whom the Greeks waged the Trojan War to retrieve, forms the backdrop of Homer's *Iliad;* and Oenone, the daughter of a river god who was Paris's first love, killed herself after his death.

9. In Greek mythology Amphion, a son of Zeus, was famous for his musical talent; after he became king of Thebes, he built the city walls by playing his lyre to move their stones.

1. That is, this earth at the center of the universe (the Ptolemaic view).

2. Because of unequal motion in respect to the whole (Latin).

FAUSTUS Well, I am answered. Tell me who made the world.
MEPHISTOPHELES I will not.
FAUSTUS Sweet Mephistopheles, tell me.
MEPHISTOPHELES Move° me not, for I will not tell thee. *Anger*
FAUSTUS Villain, have I not bound thee to tell me anything?
MEPHISTOPHELES Ay, that is not against our kingdom, but this is. Think thou on hell, Faustus, for thou art damned.
FAUSTUS Think, Faustus, upon God, that made the world.
MEPHISTOPHELES Remember this.° [*Exit.*] *You will pay for this*
FAUSTUS Ay, go, accursèd spirit, to ugly hell!
'Tis thou hast damned distressèd Faustus' soul.
Is't not too late?

[*Enter* GOOD ANGEL *and* EVIL ANGEL.]

EVIL ANGEL Too late.
GOOD ANGEL Never too late, if Faustus can repent.
EVIL ANGEL If thou repent, devils shall tear thee in pieces.
GOOD ANGEL Repent, and they shall never raze thy skin.

[*Exeunt* ANGELS.]

FAUSTUS Ah, Christ, my Savior,
Seek to save distressèd Faustus' soul!

[*Enter* LUCIFER, BEELZEBUB, *and* MEPHISTOPHELES.]

LUCIFER Christ cannot save thy soul, for he is just.
There's none but I have int'rest in the same.
FAUSTUS Oh, who art thou that look'st so terrible?
LUCIFER I am Lucifer,
And this is my companion prince in hell.
FAUSTUS O Faustus, they are come to fetch away thy soul!
LUCIFER We come to tell thee thou dost injure us.
Thou talk'st of Christ, contrary to thy promise.
Thou shouldst not think of God. Think of the devil,
And of his dame,[3] too.
FAUSTUS Nor will I henceforth. Pardon me in this,
And Faustus vows never to look to heaven,
Never to name God or to pray to him,
To burn his Scriptures, slay his ministers,
And make my spirits pull his churches down.
LUCIFER Do so, and we will highly gratify° thee. Faustus, we are come from hell to show thee some pastime. Sit down, and thou shalt see all the Seven Deadly Sins appear in their proper° shapes. *reward, satisfy* / *own*
FAUSTUS That sight will be as pleasing unto me as Paradise was to Adam the first day of his creation.
LUCIFER Talk not of Paradise nor creation, but mark this show. Talk of the devil, and nothing else.—Come away!

[FAUSTUS *sits.*]

[*Enter the Seven Deadly Sins.*]

3. Dam, wife. Witchcraft manuals attribute to the devil (Lucifer) many sexual partners and, occasionally, a long-term female consort or wife.

Now, Faustus, examine them of° their several° names and dispositions. *about / different*

FAUSTUS What art thou, the first?

PRIDE I am Pride. I disdain to have any parents. I am like to Ovid's flea:[4] I can creep into every corner of a wench. Sometimes like a periwig I sit upon her brow, or like a fan of feathers I kiss her lips. Indeed I do. What do I not? But fie, what a scent is here! I'll not speak another word except° the ground were perfumed and covered with cloth of arras.° *unless* *rich tapestry*

FAUSTUS What art thou, the second?

COVETOUSNESS I am Covetousness, begotten of an old churl in an old leathern bag;° and might I have my wish, I would desire that this house and all the people in it were turned to gold, that I might lock you up in my good chest. O my sweet gold! *money bag*

FAUSTUS What art thou, the third?

WRATH I am Wrath. I had neither father nor mother. I leaped out of a lion's mouth when I was scarce half an hour old, and ever since I have run up and down the world with this case of rapiers,° wounding myself when I had nobody to fight withal.° I was born in hell, and look to it,° for some of you shall be my father. *pair of swords* *with* *be advised*

FAUSTUS What art thou, the fourth?

ENVY I am Envy, begotten of a chimney sweeper and an oyster-wife.° I cannot read, and therefore wish all books were burnt. I am lean with seeing others eat. Oh, that there would come a famine through all the world, that all might die, and I live alone! Then thou shouldst see how fat I would be. But must thou sit and I stand? Come down, with a vengeance!° *oyster seller* *with a curse (on you)*

FAUSTUS Away, envious rascal!—What are thou, the fifth?

GLUTTONY Who, I, sir? I am Gluttony. My parents are all dead, and the devil a penny° they have left me but a bare pension, and that is thirty meals a day, and ten bevers°—a small trifle to suffice nature.° Oh, I come of a royal parentage. My grandfather was a gammon of bacon,° my grandmother a hogshead° of claret wine. My godfathers these: Peter Pickle-herring° and Martin Martlemas-beef.[5] Oh, but jolly gentlewoman, and well beloved in every good town and city; her name was Mistress Margery March-beer.° Now, Faustus, thou hast heard all my progeny, wilt thou bid me to supper? *not even a penny* *snacks / bodily nature* *ham / large cask* *pickled herring* *strong beer*

FAUSTUS No, I'll see thee hanged. Thou wilt eat up all my victuals.

4. The medieval "Elegy of a Flea" was wrongly attributed to the Roman poet Ovid (43 B.C.E.–17 C.E.).

5. Beef slaughtered on the Feast of St. Martin (November 11).

GLUTTONY Then the devil choke thee!

FAUSTUS Choke thyself, glutton!—What art thou, the sixth?

SLOTH I am Sloth. I was begotten on a sunny bank, where I have lain ever since, and you have done me great injury to bring me from thence. Let me be carried thither again by Gluttony and Lechery. I'll not speak another word for a king's ransom.

FAUSTUS What are you, Mistress Minx, the seventh and last?

LECHERY Who, I, sir? I am one that loves an inch of raw mutton better than an ell of fried stockfish,[6] and the first letter of my name begins with lechery.

LUCIFER Away, to hell, to hell! [*Exeunt the Sins.*]
Now, Faustus, how dost thou like this?

FAUSTUS Oh, this feeds my soul!

LUCIFER Tut, Faustus, in hell is all manner of delight.

FAUSTUS Oh, might I see hell and return again, how happy were I then!

LUCIFER Thou shalt. I will send for thee at midnight. [*He presents a book.*] In meantime, take this book. Peruse it throughly,° and thou shalt turn thyself into what shape thou wilt. *thoroughly*

FAUSTUS [*taking the book*] Great thanks, mighty Lucifer.
This will I keep as chary° as my life. *carefully*

LUCIFER Farewell, Faustus, and think on the devil.

FAUSTUS Farewell, great Lucifer. Come, Mephistopheles.

[*Exeunt omnes*° FAUSTUS *and* MEPHISTOPHELES *by one way,* LUCIFER *and* BEELZEBUB *by another.*] *all (Latin)*

3. Chorus

[*Enter* WAGNER *solus.*°] *alone (Latin)*

WAGNER Learnèd Faustus,
To know the secrets of astronomy
Graven° in the book of Jove's high firmament, *Engraved*
Did mount himself to scale Olympus'[7] top,
Being seated in a chariot burning bright
Drawn by the strength of yoky° dragons' necks. *yoked*
He now is gone to prove° cosmography, *make trial of*
And, as I guess, will first arrive at Rome
To see the Pope and manner of his court
And take some part of° holy Peter's feast[8] *in*
That to this day is highly solemnized. [*Exit* WAGNER.]

6. One who prefers raw meat to dried cod—that is, hot sex to cold chastity.
7. A mountain in northern Greece and, in classical mythology, the home of the gods.
8. In the Roman Catholic Church, the main feast (or festival) of St. Peter and St Paul takes place on June 29.

3.1

[*Enter* FAUSTUS *and* MEPHISTOPHELES.]

FAUSTUS Having now, my good Mephistopheles
Passed with delight the stately town of Trier° *(in western Germany)*
Environed round with airy mountaintops,
With walls of flint and deep intrenchèd lakes° *moats*
Not to be won by any conquering prince;
From Paris next, coasting° the realm of France, *skirting*
We saw the river Maine fall into Rhine,
Whose banks are set with groves of fruitful vines.
Then up to Naples, rich Campania,
Whose buildings, fair and gorgeous to the eye,
The streets straight forth° and paved with finest brick, *perfectly straight*
Quarters the town in four equivalents.
There saw we learned Maro's[9] golden tomb,
The way he cut an English mile in length
Thorough° a rock of stone in one night's space[1] *through*
From thence to Venice, Padua, and the rest,
In midst of which a sumptuous temple[2] stands
That threats° the stars with her aspiring top. *threatens, challenges*
Thus hitherto hath Faustus spent his time.
But tell me now, what resting place is this?
Hast thou, as erst° I did command, *earlier*
Conducted me within the walls of Rome?

MEPHISTOPHELES Faustus, I have. And because° we will not be unprovided, I have taken up His Holiness's privy° chamber for our use. *in order that* *private*

FAUSTUS I hope His Holiness will bid us welcome.

MEPHISTOPHELES Tut, 'tis no matter, man. We'll be bold with his good cheer.
And now, my Faustus, that thou mayst perceive
What Rome containeth to delight thee with,
Know that this city stands upon seven hills
That underprops the groundwork of the same.
Just° through the midst runs flowing Tiber's stream, *Right*
With winding banks that cut it in two parts,
Over the which four stately bridges lean,
That makes safe passage to each part of Rome.
Upon the bridge called Ponte Angelo
Erected is a castle passing° strong, *surpassingly*
Within whose walls such store of ordnance are,
And double cannons, framed° of carvèd brass *made*
As match the days within one complete year[3]

9. The Roman poet Virgil (70–19 B.C.E.), whose full name was Publius Vergilius Maro.
1. This tunnel through volcanic tufa, about a half mile long, was probably constructed in the 1st century C.E.; in the Middle Ages, it was credited to Virgil and his magic.
2. That is, St. Mark's Basilica in Venice, consecrated in 1094.
3. That is, there are 365 cannons.

Besides the gates and high pyramides° — *obelisks*
Which Julius Caesar[4] brought from Africa.

FAUSTUS Now, by the kingdoms of infernal rule,
Of Styx, Acheron, and the fiery lake
Of ever-burning Phlegethon[5] I swear
That I do long to see the monuments
And situation of bright splendent Rome.
Come, therefore, let's away!

MEPHISTOPHELES Nay, Faustus, stay. I know you'd fain see the Pope
And take some part of holy Peter's feast,
Where thou shalt see a troupe of bald-pate friars
Whose *summum bonum*° is in belly cheer. — *highest good (Latin)*

FAUSTUS Well, I am content to compass° then some sport, — *devise*
And by their folly make us merriment.
Then charm° me, that I may be invisible, to do what I please unseen of any whilst, stay in Rome. — *put a spell on*

MEPHISTOPHELES [*placing a robe on* FAUSTUS] So, Faustus, now do what thou wilt, thou shalt not be discerned.

[*Sound a sennet.° Enter the* POPE *and the Cardinal of* LORRAINE *to the banquet, with* FRIARS *attending.*] — *trumpet call*

POPE My lord of Lorraine, will't please you draw near?

FAUSTUS Fall to, and the devil choke you an you spare.° — *if you hold back*

POPE How now, who's that which spake?—Friars, look about.

[*Some* FRIARS *attempt to search.*]

FRIAR Here's nobody, if it like° Your Holiness. — *please*

POPE [*presenting a dish*] My lord, here is a dainty dish was° sent me from the Bishop of Milan. — *that was*

FAUSTUS [*snatching it*] I thank you, sir.

POPE How now, who's that which snatched the meat from me? Will no man look? [*Some* FRIARS *search about.*] My lord, this dish was sent me from the Cardinal of Florence.

FAUSTUS [*snatching the dish*] You say true. I'll ha't.

POPE What, again?—My lord, I'll drink to Your Grace.

FAUSTUS [*snatching the cup*] I'll pledge Your Grace.

LORRAINE My lord, it may be some ghost, newly crept out of purgatory, come to beg a pardon of Your Holiness.

POPE It may be so.—Friars, prepare a dirge to lay° the fury of this ghost.—Once again, my lord, fall to.° — *allay* — *partake of the feast*

[*The* POPE *crosseth himself.*]

FAUSTUS What, are you crossing of yourself?
Well, use that trick no more, I would advise you.

[*The* POPE *crosses himself again.*]

4. During the civil war precipitated by Caesar (100–44 B.C.E.), the Roman general fought in Egypt and Africa; however, the first ruler to bring Egyptian obelisks to Rome was his successor, Augustus.

5. A river of fire in the classical underworld; Styx and Acheron are also rivers in Hades.

Well, there's a second time. Aware° the third, I give you fair warning. *Beware*

[*The* POPE *crosses himself again, and* FAUSTUS *hits him a box of the ear, and they all* (*except* FAUSTUS *and* MEPHISTOPHELES) *run away.*]

Come on, Mephistopheles. What shall we do?

MEPHISTOPHELES Nay, I know not. We shall be cursed with bell, book, and candle.[6]

FAUSTUS How? Bell, book, and candle, candle, book, and bell, Forward and backward, to curse Faustus to hell. Anon you shall hear a hog grunt, a calf bleat, and an ass bray, Because it is Saint Peter's holy day.

[*Enter all the* FRIARS *to sing the dirge.*]

FRIAR Come, brethren, let's about our business with good devotion.

[*The* FRIARS *sing this.*]

Cursèd be he that stole away His Holiness's meat from the table.

Maledicat Dominus![7]

Cursèd be he that struck His Holiness a blow on the face.

Maledicat Dominus!

Cursèd be he that took° Friar Sandelo a blow on the pate.° *gave / head*

Maledicat Dominus!

Cursèd be he that disturbeth our holy dirge.

Maledicat Dominus!

Cursèd be he that took away His Holiness's wine.

Maledicat Dominus!

Et omnes sancti.[8] Amen.

[FAUSTUS *and* MEPHISTOPHELES *beat the* FRIARS, *and fling fireworks among them, and so exeunt.*]

3.2

[*Enter* ROBIN *with a conjuring book and* RAFE *with a silver goblet.*]

ROBIN Come, Rafe, did not I tell thee we were forever made by this Doctor Faustus' book? *Ecce signum.*° Here's a simple purchase° for horse-keepers! Our horses shall eat no hay[9] as long as this lasts. *Behold the proof (Latin)* *acquisition*

[*Enter the* VINTNER.°] *innkeeper*

RAFE But, Robin, here comes the Vintner.

ROBIN Hush, I'll gull° him supernaturally.—Drawer,° I hope all is paid. God be with you. Come, Rafe. [*They start to go.*] *trick / Bartender*

VINTNER [*to* ROBIN] Soft,° sir, a word with you. I must yet have a goblet paid from you ere you go. *Wait*

6. A form of excommunication that involved ringing a bell, closing a holy book, and snuffing out a candle.

7. May the Lord curse him! (Latin).

8. And all the saints (Latin); that is, may all the saints curse him too.

9. That is, they will eat like kings.

ROBIN I, a goblet? Rafe, I, a goblet? I scorn you, and you are but a etc.[1] I, a goblet? Search me.

VINTNER I mean so, sir, with your favor.° *permission*

[*The* VINTNER *searches* ROBIN.]

ROBIN How say you now?

VINTNER I must say somewhat° to your fellow.—You, sir. *something*

RAFE Me, sir? Me, sir? Search your fill.

[*He tosses the goblet to* ROBIN; *then the* VINTNER *searches* RAFE.]

Now, sir, you may be ashamed to burden honest men with a matter of truth.° *question of honesty*

VINTNER Well, t'one of you hath this goblet about you.

ROBIN You lie, drawer, 'tis afore° me. Sirrah, you, I'll teach ye to impeach° honest men. Stand by. I'll scour° you for a goblet. Stand aside, you had best, I charge you in the name of Beelzebub. [*He tosses the goblet to* RAFE.] [*Aside to* RAFE] Look to the goblet, Rafe. *in front of* *accuse / beat*

VINTNER What mean you, sirrah?

ROBIN I'll tell you what I mean. [*He reads.*] "*Sanctobulorum Periphrasticon!*"°—Nay, I'll tickle you, Vintner. [*Aside to Rafe*] Look to the goblet, Rafe.—"*Polypragmos Belseborams framanto pacostiphos tostu Mephistopheles!*" etc.° *(Latin gibberish)* *(Latin gibberish)*

[*Enter to them* MEPHISTOPHELES.]

[*Exit the* VINTNER, *running.*]

MEPHISTOPHELES Monarch of hell, under whose black survey
Great potentates do kneel with awful° fear, *awe-filled*
Upon whose altars thousand souls do lie,
How am I vexèd with these villains' charms!° *spells*
From Constantinople am I hither come
Only for pleasure of these damnèd slaves.

ROBIN How, from Constantinople? You have had a great journey. Will you take sixpence in your purse to pay for your supper and be gone?

MEPHISTOPHELES Well, villains, for your presumption I transform thee [*to* ROBIN] into an ape, and thee [*to* RAFE] into a dog. And so, begone!

[*They are transformed in shape.*]

[*Exit* MEPHISTOPHELES.]

ROBIN How, into an ape? That's brave.° I'll have fine sport with the boys; I'll get nuts and apples enough. *excellent*

RAFE And I must be a dog.

ROBIN I'faith, thy head will never be out of the pottage° pot. *porridge*

[*Exeunt.*]

1. "Etc." signals a moment of improvisation.

4. Chorus

[*Enter* CHORUS.]

CHORUS When Faustus had with pleasure ta'en the view
Of rarest things and royal courts of kings,
He stayed his course° and so returnèd home, *stopped traveling*
Where such as bear his absence but with grief—
I mean his friends and nearest companions—
Did gratulate° his safety with kind words. *rejoice at*
And in their conference of what befell,
Touching° his journey through the world and air, *Regarding*
They put forth questions of astrology,
Which Faustus answered with such learnèd skill
As° they admired and wondered at his wit. *That*
Now is his fame spread forth in every land.
Amongst the rest the Emperor[2] is one,
Carolus the Fifth, at whose palace now
Faustus is feasted 'mongst his noblemen.
What there he did in trial° of his art° *demonstration / skill*
I leave untold, your eyes shall see performed. [*Exit.*]

4.1

[*Enter* EMPEROR, FAUSTUS, MEPHISTOPHELES, *and a* KNIGHT, *with attendants.*]

EMPEROR Master Doctor Faustus, I have heard strange° report of thy knowledge in the black art—how that none in my empire, nor in the whole world, can compare with thee for the rare effects of magic. They say thou hast a familiar spirit by whom thou canst accomplish what thou list.° This, therefore, is my request: that thou let me see some proof of thy skill, that mine eyes may be witnesses to confirm what mine ears have heard reported. And here I swear to thee, by the honor of mine imperial crown, that whatever thou dost, thou shalt be no ways prejudiced or endamaged. *unusual, wondrous* *desire, want*

KNIGHT [*aside*] I'faith, he looks much like a conjurer.° *(ironic)*

FAUSTUS My gracious sovereign, though I must confess myself far inferior to the report men have published,° and nothing answerable° to the honor of Your Imperial Majesty, yet, for that° love and duty binds me thereunto, I am content to do whatsoever Your Majesty shall command me. *spread abroad* *suitable* *because*

EMPEROR Then, Doctor Faustus, mark what I shall say.
As I was sometime° solitary set *recently*
Within my closet,° sundry thoughts arose *private room*
About the honor of mine ancestors—
How they had won by prowess such exploits,
Got such riches, subdued so many kingdoms
As we that do succeed or they that shall

2. Charles (Carolus) V (1500–1558), king of Spain (r. 1516–56) and emperor of the Holy Roman Empire (r. 1519–56).

Hereafter possess our throne shall,
I fear me, never attain to that degree
Of high renown and great authority.
Amongst which kings is Alexander the Great,[3]
Chief spectacle of the world's preeminence,
The bright shining of whose glorious acts
Lightens the world with his reflecting beams—
As° when I hear but motion° made of him, *so that / mention*
It grieves my soul I never saw the man.
If, therefore, thou by cunning of thine art
Canst raise this man from hollow vaults below
Where lies entombed this famous conqueror,
And bring with him his beauteous paramour,
Both in their right shapes, gesture, and attire
They used to wear during their time of life,
Thou shalt both satisfy my just desire
And give me cause to praise thee whilst I live.

FAUSTUS My gracious lord, I am ready to accomplish your request, so far forth as by art and power of my spirit I am able to perform.

KNIGHT [*aside*] I'faith, that's just nothing at all.

FAUSTUS But if it like° Your Grace, it is not in my ability to present before your eyes the true substantial bodies of those two deceased princes, which long since are consumed to dust. *please*

KNIGHT [*aside*] Ay, marry,° Master Doctor, now there's a sign of grace in you, when you will confess the truth. *by Mary (an oath)*

FAUSTUS But such spirits as can lively° resemble Alexander and his paramour shall appear before Your Grace in that manner that they best lived in, in their most flourishing estate—which I doubt not shall sufficiently content Your Imperial Majesty. *in a lifelike manner*

EMPEROR Go to,° Master Doctor. Let me see them presently.° *Proceed / at once*

KNIGHT Do you hear, Master Doctor? You bring Alexander and his paramour before the Emperor?

FAUSTUS How then, sir?

KNIGHT I'faith, that's as true as Diana[4] turned me to a stag.

FAUSTUS No, sir, but when Actaeon died,[5] he left the horns for you. [*Aside to* MEPHISTOPHELES] Mephistopheles, begone!

[*Exit* MEPHISTOPHELES.]

KNIGHT Nay, an you go to conjuring,° I'll be gone. *if you play mere tricks*

[*Exit* KNIGHT.]

FAUSTUS [*aside*] I'll meet with° you anon for interrupting me so.—Here they are, my gracious lord. *get even with*

[*Enter* MEPHISTOPHELES *with Alexander and his paramour.*]

3. Alexander III of Macedon (356–323 B.C.E.); the greatest of all Greek generals, he unified Greece and conquered much of Asia.
4. The Roman huntress goddess (the Greek Artemis).
5. Because Acteon saw the goddess naked, Artemis/Diana turned him into a stag, and he was torn to pieces by his own dogs.

EMPEROR Master Doctor, I heard this lady while she lived had a wart or mole in her neck. How shall I know whether it be so or no?

FAUSTUS Your Highness may boldly go and see.

[*The* EMPEROR *makes an inspection, and then exit Alexander with his paramour.*]

EMPEROR Sure these are no spirits, but the true substantial bodies of those two deceased princes.

FAUSTUS Will't please Your Highness now to send for the knight that was so pleasant° with me here of late? *humorous*

EMPEROR One of you call him forth.

[*An attendant goes to summon the* KNIGHT.]

[*Enter the* KNIGHT *with a pair of horns on his head.*]

How now, Sir Knight? Why, I had thought thou hadst been a bachelor, but now I see thou hast a wife, that not only gives thee horns but makes thee wear them.[6] Feel on thy head.

KNIGHT [*to* FAUSTUS] Thou damnèd wretch and execrable dog,
Bred in the concave° of some monstrous rock, *hollow*
How dar'st thou thus abuse a gentleman?
Villain, I say, undo what thou hast done.

FAUSTUS Oh, not so fast, sir. There's no haste but good.° *Don't be too hasty* Are you remembered° *Do you remember* how you crossed me in my conference with the Emperor? I think I have met with you for it.

EMPEROR Good Master Doctor, at my entreaty release him. He hath done penance sufficient.

FAUSTUS My gracious lord, not so much for the injury° *insult* he offered me here in your presence as to delight you with some mirth hath Faustus worthily requited this injurious knight; which being all I desire, I am content to release him of his horns.—And, Sir Knight, hereafter speak well of scholars. [*Aside to* MEPHISTOPHELES] Mephistopheles, transform him straight.° *at once* [*The horns are removed.*] Now, my good lord, having done my duty, I humbly take my leave.

EMPEROR Farewell, Master Doctor. Yet, ere you go,
Expect from me a bounteous reward.

[*Exeunt* EMPEROR, KNIGHT, *and attendants.*]

FAUSTUS Now, Mephistopheles, the restless course
That time doth run with calm and silent foot,
Short'ning my days and thread of vital life,
Calls for the payment of my latest° years. *last, final*
Therefore, sweet Mephistopheles, let us make haste
To Wittenberg.

MEPHISTOPHELES What, will you go on horseback or on foot?

FAUSTUS Nay, till I am past this fair and pleasant green,
I'll walk on foot.

[*Enter a* HORSE-COURSER.[7]]

6. Cuckolds were traditionally represented as wearing horns.

7. A horse dealer (stereotypically a shrewd or dishonest bargainer).

HORSE-COURSER I have been all this day seeking one Master Fustian.° Mass,° see where he is.—God save you, Master Doctor. *Bombast / By the Mass*

FAUSTUS What, Horse-courser! You are well met.[8]

HORSE-COURSER [*offering money*] Do you hear, sir? I have brought you forty dollars for your horse.

FAUSTUS I cannot sell him so. If thou lik'st him for fifty, take him.

HORSE-COURSER Alas, sir, I have no more. [*To* MEPHISTOPHELES] I pray you, speak for me.

MEPHISTOPHELES [*to* FAUSTUS] I pray you, let him have him. He is an honest fellow, and he has a great charge,° neither wife nor child. *financial burden*

FAUSTUS Well, come, give me your money. [*He takes the money.*] My boy° will deliver him to you. But I must tell you one thing before you have him: ride him not into the water, at any hand.° *servant* / *on any account*

HORSE-COURSER Why, sir, will he not drink of all waters?[9]

FAUSTUS Oh, yes, he will drink of all waters. But ride him not into the water. Ride him over hedge, or ditch, or where thou wilt, but not into the water.

HORSE-COURSER Well, sir. [*Aside*] Now am I made man forever! I'll not leave my horse for forty. If he had but the quality of hey, ding, ding, hey, ding, ding, I'd make a brave living on him; he has a buttock as slick as an eel.[1] [*To* FAUSTUS] Well, good-bye, sir. Your boy will deliver him me? But hark ye, sir: if my horse be sick or ill at ease, if I bring his water[2] to you, you'll tell me what it is?

FAUSTUS Away, you villain! What, dost think I am a horse doctor?

[*Exit* HORSE-COURSER.]

What art thou, Faustus, but a man condemned to die?
Thy fatal time doth draw to final end.
Despair doth drive distrust unto my thoughts.
Confound° these passions with a quiet sleep. *Allay, alleviate*
Tush! Christ did call the thief upon the cross;[3]
Then rest thee, Faustus, quiet in conceit.° *in thought*

[FAUSTUS *sleeps in his chair.*]

[*Enter* HORSE-COURSER *all wet, crying.*]

HORSE-COURSER Alas, alas! "Doctor" Fustian, quotha!° Mass, Doctor Lopus[4] was never such a doctor. He's given me a purgation, he's purged me of forty dollars. I shall never see them more. But yet, like an ass as I was, I would not *indeed*

8. An expression of greeting.
9. That is, go anywhere (proverbial).
1. That is, he is sleek and well-formed. *Hey, ding, ding*: a virile quality (to generate stud fees).
2. That is, his urine (to diagnose the illness).
3. Jesus said to the thief who feared the judgment of God, "Verily I say unto thee, Today shalt thou be with me in paradise" (Luke 23.43).
4. Roderigo Lopez (ca. 1525–1594), Queen Elizabeth's private physician; a Portuguese Jew, he was implicated in a plot to poison her and executed.

be ruled by him, for he bade me I should ride him into no
water. Now I, thinking my horse had had some rare
quality that he would not have had me known of, I, like
a venturous youth, rid him into the deep pond at the
town's end. I was no sooner in the middle of the pond
but my horse vanished away and I sat upon a bottle° of — *bundle*
hay, never so near drowning in my life. But I'll seek out
my doctor and have my forty dollars again, or I'll make it
the dearest horse! Oh, yonder is his snippersnapper.°— — *mouthy fellow*
Do you hear? You, hey-pass,[5] where's your master?

MEPHISTOPHELES Why, sir, what would you? You cannot speak with him.

HORSE-COURSER But I will speak with him.

MEPHISTOPHELES Why, he's fast asleep. Come some other time.

HORSE-COURSER I'll speak with him now, or I'll break his glass windows° about his ears. — *eyeglasses*

MEPHISTOPHELES I tell thee he has not slept this eight nights.

HORSE-COURSER An° he have not slept this eight weeks, I'll speak with him. — *Even if*

MEPHISTOPHELES See where he is, fast asleep.

HORSE-COURSER Ay, this is he.—God save ye, Master Doctor. Master Doctor, Master Doctor Fustian! Forty dollars, forty dollars for a bottle of hay!

MEPHISTOPHELES Why, thou see'st he hears thee not.

HORSE-COURSER [*hollers in his ear*] So-ho, ho! So-ho, ho! No? Will you not wake? I'll make you wake ere I go.

[*The* HORSE-COURSER *pulls him by the leg, and pulls it away.*]

Alas, I am undone! What shall I do?

FAUSTUS Oh, my leg, my leg! Help, Mephistopheles! Call the officers! My leg, my leg!

MEPHISTOPHELES [*seizing the* HORSE-COURSER] Come, villain, to the constable.

HORSE-COURSER Oh, Lord, sir, let me go, and I'll give you forty dollars more.

MEPHISTOPHELES Where be they?

HORSE-COURSER I have none about me. Come to my hostry° and I'll give them you. — *hostelry, inn*

MEPHISTOPHELES Begone, quickly. [HORSE-COURSER *runs away.*]

FAUSTUS What, is he gone? Farewell, he!° Faustus has his leg again, and the Horse-courser, I take it, a bottle of hay for his labor. Well, this trick shall cost him forty dollars more. — *Good riddance to him*

[*Enter* WAGNER.]

How now, Wagner, what's the news with thee?

WAGNER Sir, the Duke of Vanholt° doth earnestly entreat your company. — *Anhalt (in Germany)*

5. An exclamation of conjurors or jugglers commanding objects to move.

FAUSTUS The Duke of Vanholt! An honorable gentleman, to whom I must be no niggard of° my cunning.° Come, Mephistopheles, let's away to him. [*Exeunt.*] *unsparing with / skill*

4.2

[*Enter* FAUSTUS *with Mephistopheles. Enter to them the* DUKE *of Vanholt and the pregnant* DUCHESS. *The* DUKE *speaks.*]

DUKE Believe me, Master Doctor, this merriment hath much pleased me.

FAUSTUS My gracious lord, I am glad it contents you so well.—But it may be, madam, you take no delight in this. I have heard that great-bellied women do long for some dainties or other. What is it, madam? Tell me, and you shall have it.

DUCHESS Thanks, good Master Doctor. And, for° I see your courteous intent to pleasure me, I will not hide from you the thing my heart desires. And were it now summer, as it is January and the dead time of the winter, I would desire no better meat° than a dish of ripe grapes. *because* / *food*

FAUSTUS Alas, madam, that's nothing. [*Aside to* MEPHISTOPHELES] Mephistopheles, begone! [*Exit* MEPHISTOPHELES.] Were it a greater thing than this, so° it would content you, you should have it. *provided that*

[*Enter* MEPHISTOPHELES *with the grapes.*]

Here they be, madam. Will't please you taste on them?

[*The* DUCHESS *tastes the grapes.*]

DUKE Believe me, Master Doctor, this makes me wonder above the rest, that, being in the dead time of winter and in the month of January, how you should come by these grapes.

FAUSTUS If it like Your Grace, the year is divided into two circles over the whole world, that when it is here winter with us, in the contrary circle it is summer with them, as in India, Saba,[6] and farther countries in the East; and by means of a swift spirit that I have, I had them brought hither, as ye see.—How do you like them, madam? Be they good?

DUCHESS Believe me, Master Doctor, they be the best grapes that e'er I tasted in my life before.

FAUSTUS I am glad they content you so, madam.

DUKE Come, madam, let us in,
Where you must well reward this learnèd man
For the great kindness he hath showed to you.

DUCHESS And so I will, my lord, and whilst I live
Rest beholding° for this courtesy. *Remain beholden*

FAUSTUS I humbly thank Your Grace.

DUKE Come, Master Doctor, follow us and receive your reward.

[*Exeunt.*]

6. Sheba, an ancient kingdom on the Red Sea.

5.1

[*Enter* WAGNER *solus.*]

WAGNER I think my master means to die shortly,
For he hath given to me all his goods.
And yet methinks if that death were near
He would not banquet and carouse and swill
Amongst the students, as even now he doth,
Who are at supper with such belly-cheer
As Wagner ne'er beheld in all his life.
See where they come. Belike° the feast is ended. [*Exit.*] *Apparently*

[*Enter* FAUSTUS *with two or three* SCHOLARS *and* MEPHISTOPHELES.]

FIRST SCHOLAR Master Doctor Faustus, since our conference about fair ladies—which was the beautifull'st in all the world—we have determined with° ourselves that *among* Helen of Greece was the admirablest lady that ever lived. Therefore, Master Doctor, if you will do us that favor as to let us see that peerless dame of Greece, whom all the world admires for majesty, we should think ourselves much beholding unto you.

FAUSTUS Gentlemen,
For that° I know your friendship is unfeigned, *Because*
And Faustus' custom is not to deny
The just requests of those that wish him well,
You shall behold that peerless dame of Greece,
No otherways° for pomp and majesty *otherwise*
Than when Sir Paris crossed the seas with her
And brought the spoils to rich Dardania.° *Troy*
Be silent then, for danger is in words.

[*Music sounds and Helen led in by* MEPHISTOPHELES *passeth over the stage.*]

SECOND SCHOLAR Too simple is my wit to tell her praise,
Whom all the world admires for majesty.

THIRD SCHOLAR No marvel though the angry Greeks pursued° *avenged*
With ten years' war the rape° of such a queen, *abduction*
Whose heavenly beauty passeth all compare.° *comparison*

FIRST SCHOLAR Since we have seen the pride of nature's works
And only paragon of excellence,

[*Enter an* OLD MAN.]

Let us depart; and for this glorious deed
Happy and blest be Faustus evermore!

FAUSTUS Gentlemen, farewell. The same I wish to you.

[*Exeunt* SCHOLARS.]

OLD MAN Ah, Doctor Faustus, that I might prevail
To guide thy steps unto the way of life,
By which sweet path thou mayst attain the goal
That shall conduct thee to celestial rest!
Break heart, drop blood, and mingle it with tears—

Tears falling from repentant heaviness
Of thy most vile and loathsome filthiness,
The stench whereof corrupts the inward soul
With such flagitious° crimes of heinous sins *wicked*
As no commiseration may expel
But mercy, Faustus, of thy Savior sweet,
Whose blood alone must wash away thy guilt.

FAUSTUS Where art thou, Faustus? Wretch, what hast thou done?
Damned art thou, Faustus, damned! Despair and die!
Hell calls for right, and with a roaring voice
Says, "Faustus, come! Thine hour is come."

[MEPHISTOPHELES *gives him a dagger.*]

And Faustus will come to do thee right.

[FAUSTUS *prepares to stab himself.*]

OLD MAN Ah, stay, good Faustus, stay thy desperate steps!
I see an angel hovers o'er thy head,
And with a vial full of precious grace
Offers to pour the same into thy soul.
Then call for mercy and avoid despair.

FAUSTUS Ah, my sweet friend, I feel thy words
To comfort my distressèd soul.
Leave me awhile to ponder on my sins.

OLD MAN I go, sweet Faustus, but with heavy cheer,° *frame of mind*
Fearing the ruin of thy hopeless soul. [*Exit.*]

FAUSTUS Accursèd Faustus, where is mercy now?
I do repent, and yet I do despair.
Hell strives with grace for conquest in my breast.
What shall I do to shun the snares of death?

MEPHISTOPHELES Thou traitor, Faustus, I arrest thy soul
For disobedience to my sovereign lord.
Revolt,° or I'll in piecemeal tear thy flesh. *Recant, turn back*

FAUSTUS Sweet Mephistopheles, entreat thy lord
To pardon my unjust presumption,
And with my blood again I will confirm
My former vow I made to Lucifer.

MEPHISTOPHELES Do it then quickly, with unfeignèd heart,
Lest greater danger do attend thy drift.

[FAUSTUS *cuts his arm and writes with his blood.*]

FAUSTUS Torment, sweet friend, that base and crooked age° *old man*
That durst dissuade me from thy Lucifer,
With greatest torments that our hell affords.

MEPHISTOPHELES His faith is great. I cannot touch his soul.
But what I may afflict his body with
I will attempt, which is but little worth.

FAUSTUS One thing, good servant, let me crave of thee
To glut the longing of my heart's desire:
That I might have unto° my paramour *as*
That heavenly Helen which I saw of late,
Whose sweet embracings may extinguish clean° *entirely*

These thoughts that do dissuade me from my vow,
And keep mine oath I made to Lucifer.

MEPHISTOPHELES Faustus, this, or what else thou shalt desire,
Shall be performed in twinkling of an eye.

[*Enter Helen brought in by* MEPHISTOPHELES.]

FAUSTUS Was this the face that launched a thousand ships
And burnt the topless° towers of Ilium?° *immensely high / Troy*
Sweet Helen, make me immortal with a kiss. [*They kiss.*]
Her lips sucks forth my soul. See where it flies!
Come, Helen, come, give me my soul again.

[*They kiss again.*]

Here will I dwell, for heaven be in these lips,
And all is dross° that is not Helena. *impurity; rubbish*

[*Enter* OLD MAN.]

I will be Paris, and for love of thee
Instead of Troy shall Wittenberg be sacked,
And I will combat with weak Menelaus,[7]
And wear thy colors° on my plumèd crest. *emblems, device*
Yea, I will wound Achilles in the heel[8]
And then return to Helen for a kiss.
Oh, thou art fairer than the evening air,
Clad in the beauty of a thousand stars.
Brighter art thou than flaming Jupiter
When he appeared to hapless Semele,[9]
More lovely than the monarch of the sky
In wanton Arethusa's azured° arms;[1] *sky-blue*
And none but thou shalt be my paramour.

[*Exeunt* FAUSTUS *and Helen, with* MEPHISTOPHELES.]

OLD MAN Accursèd Faustus, miserable man,
That from thy soul exclud'st the grace of heaven
And fliest the throne of His tribunal seat!

[*Enter the devils with* MEPHISTOPHELES. *They menace the* OLD MAN.]

Satan begins to sift me with his pride.
As in this furnace God shall try my faith,
My faith, vile hell, shall triumph over thee.
Ambitious fiends, see how the heavens smiles
At your repulse and laughs your state to scorn!
Hence, hell! For hence I fly unto my God. [*Exeunt.*]

7. King of Sparta and Helen's cuckolded husband.

8. According to one legend, the mother of the Greek hero Achilles dipped her infant son into the river Styx, rendering him invulnerable except for the heel by which she held him. At Troy, he was fatally wounded by an arrow shot by Paris.

9. When Zeus (Roman Jupiter) complied with Semele's wish that he appear to her as he did to his wife, the goddess Hera, she was consumed by lightning.

1. The nymph Arethusa, an attendant of the virgin goddess Artemis, fled the sexual advances of the river god Alpheus (not Jupiter, monarch of the sky). When she was transformed by the goddess into a stream, the river god sought to mingle his waters with hers.

5.2

[*Enter* FAUSTUS *with the* SCHOLARS.]

FAUSTUS Ah, gentlemen!

FIRST SCHOLAR What ails Faustus?

FAUSTUS Ah, my sweet chamber-fellow! Had I lived with thee, then had I lived still, but now I die eternally. Look, comes he not? Comes he not?

[*The* SCHOLARS *speak among themselves.*]

SECOND SCHOLAR What means Faustus?

THIRD SCHOLAR Belike he is grown into some sickness by being oversolitary.

FIRST SCHOLAR If it be so, we'll have physicians to cure him. [*To* FAUSTUS] 'Tis but a surfeit.° Never fear, man. *excessive indulgence*

FAUSTUS A surfeit of deadly sin that hath damned both body and soul.

SECOND SCHOLAR Yet, Faustus, look up to heaven. Remember God's mercies are infinite.

FAUSTUS But Faustus' offense can ne'er be pardoned. The serpent that tempted Eve° may be saved, but not Faustus. *(see Gen. 3.1–6)* Ah, gentlemen, hear me with patience, and tremble not at my speeches. Though my heart pants and quivers to remember that I have been a student here these thirty years, oh, would I had never seen Wittenberg, never read book! And what wonders I have done, all Germany can witness, yea, all the world, for which Faustus hath lost both Germany and the world, yea, heaven itself—heaven, the seat of God, the throne of the blessed, the kingdom of joy—and must remain in hell forever. Hell, ah, hell forever! Sweet friends, what shall become of Faustus, being in hell forever?

THIRD SCHOLAR Yet, Faustus, call on God.

FAUSTUS On God, whom Faustus hath abjured? On God, whom Faustus hath blasphemed? Ah, my God, I would weep, but the devil draws in my tears. Gush forth blood instead of tears! Yea, life and soul! Oh, he stays my tongue! I would lift up my hands, but see, they hold them, they hold them!

ALL [THE SCHOLARS] Who, Faustus?

FAUSTUS Lucifer and Mephistopheles. Ah, gentlemen! I gave them my soul for my cunning.

ALL [THE SCHOLARS] God forbid!

FAUSTUS God forbade it indeed, but Faustus hath done it. For vain pleasure of four-and-twenty years hath Faustus lost eternal joy and felicity. I writ them a bill with mine own blood. The date is expired, the time will come, and he will fetch me.

FIRST SCHOLAR Why did not Faustus tell us of this before, that divines might have prayed for thee?

FAUSTUS Oft have I thought to have done so, but the devil threatened to tear me in pieces if I named God, to fetch both body and soul if I once gave ear to divinity. And now 'tis too late. Gentlemen, away, lest you perish with me.

SECOND SCHOLAR Oh, what shall we do to save Faustus?

FAUSTUS Talk not of me, but save yourselves and depart.

THIRD SCHOLAR God will strengthen me. I will stay with Faustus.

FIRST SCHOLAR [*to the* THIRD SCHOLAR] Tempt not° God, sweet friend, but let us into the next room and there pray for him. *Don't presumptuously test*

FAUSTUS Ay, pray for me, pray for me! And what noise soever ye hear, come not unto me, for nothing can rescue me.

SECOND SCHOLAR Pray thou, and we will pray that God may have mercy upon thee.

FAUSTUS Gentlemen, farewell. If I live till morning, I'll visit you; if not, Faustus is gone to hell.

ALL [THE SCHOLARS] Faustus, farewell!

[*Exeunt* SCHOLARS. *The clock strikes eleven.*]

FAUSTUS Ah, Faustus,
Now hast thou but one bare hour to live,
And then thou must be damned perpetually.
Stand still, you ever-moving spheres of heaven,
That time may cease and midnight never come!
Fair Nature's eye,° rise, rise again, and make *i.e., the sun*
Perpetual day; or let this hour be but
A year, a month, a week, a natural day,
That Faustus may repent and save his soul!
O lente, lente currite noctis equi![2]
The stars move still; time runs; the clock will strike;
The devil will come, and Faustus must be damned.
Oh, I'll leap up to my God! Who pulls me down?
See, see where Christ's blood streams in the firmament!
One drop would save my soul, half a drop. Ah, my Christ!
Ah, rend not my heart for naming of my Christ!
Yet will I call on him. Oh, spare me, Lucifer!
Where is it now? 'Tis gone; and see where God
Stretcheth out his arm and bends his ireful brows!
Mountains and hills, come, come and fall on me,
And hide me from the heavy wrath of God!
No, no!
Then will I headlong run into the earth.
Earth, gape! Oh, no, it will not harbor me.
You stars that reigned at my nativity,
Whose influence hath allotted death and hell,
Now draw up Faustus like a foggy mist
Into the entrails of yon laboring cloud,
That when you vomit forth into the air,° *hurl a thunderbolt*
My limbs may issue from your smoky mouths,
So that my soul may but ascend to heaven.

[*The watch strikes.*]

2. Oh, run slowly, slowly, horses of the night! (Latin; slightly misquoted from Ovid, *Amores* 1.13.40).

Ah, half the hour is past!
'Twill all be past anon.
O God,
If thou wilt not have mercy on my soul,
Yet for Christ's sake, whose blood hath ransomed me,
Impose some end to my incessant pain.
Let Faustus live in hell a thousand years,
A hundred thousand, and at last be saved!
Oh, no end is limited to damnèd souls.
Why wert thou not a creature wanting° soul? *lacking a*
Or why is this immortal that thou hast?
Ah, Pythagoras' metempsychosis,[3] were that true,
This soul should fly from me and I be changed
Unto some brutish beast.
All beasts are happy, for, when they die,
Their souls are soon dissolved in elements;
But mine must live still° to be plagued in hell. *always*
Curst be the parents that engendered me!
No, Faustus, curse thyself. Curse Lucifer,
That hath deprived thee of the joys of heaven.

[*The clock striketh twelve.*]

Oh, it strikes, it strikes! Now, body, turn to air,
Or Lucifer will bear thee quick° to hell. *alive*

[*Thunder and lightning.*]

O soul, be changed into little waterdrops,
And fall into the ocean, ne'er be found!
My God, my God, look not so fierce on me!

[*Enter* LUCIFER, MEPHISTOPHELES, *and other devils.*]

Adders and serpents, let me breathe awhile!
Ugly hell, gape not. Come not, Lucifer!
I'll burn my books. Ah, Mephistopheles!

[*The devils exeunt with him.*]

Epilogue

[*Enter* CHORUS.]

CHORUS Cut is the branch that might have grown full straight,
And burnèd is Apollo's laurel bough[4]
That sometime° grew within this learnèd man. *formerly*
Faustus is gone. Regard his hellish fall,
Whose fiendful fortune may exhort the wise

3. The passage of the soul at death into another body (human or animal), a theory espoused by the Greek philosopher Pythagoras (6th c. B.C.E.).

4. The laurel, sacred to Apollo, the god of wisdom, is associated with poetry and victory.

Only to wonder at[5] unlawful things,
Whose deepness doth entice such forward° wits *daring, presumptuous*
To practice more than heavenly power permits. [*Exit.*]

Terminat hora diem; terminat author opus.[6]

5. That is, to wonder at without partaking of.
6. The hour ends the day; the author ends his work (Latin).

WILLIAM SHAKESPEARE

1564–1616

"HE was not of an age, but for all time"—so wrote BEN JONSON, William Shakespeare's contemporary and rival playwright, in a commendatory poem included in the first collected edition of Shakespeare's plays, the so-called First Folio (published in 1623). Almost 400 years later, these words must seem prophetic to us. Shakespeare's plays and poetry have been translated into every conceivable language, his plays have been performed on stages the world over, and his influence on generations of writers and poets, on popular culture and media, and on the English language itself has been incalculable. What accounts for Shakespeare's enormous and lasting success? Is it the rich density and complexity of his verse, his keen insight into human nature, or his talent for capturing in words the energies, hopes, and anxieties of his time? One factor stands out above all others: from his earliest plays—the farcical *Comedy of Errors* (1589–93), the sprawling historical tetralogy about the English Wars of the Roses (1589–94), and the bloody Roman tragedy *Titus Andronicus* (1589–91)—Shakespeare demonstrated an unfailing sense of theater, both its ability to hold an audience and its power as a medium for social and psychological exploration. Shakespeare's plays have remained at the center of the theatrical repertoire through periods of changing dramatic tastes, and they have adapted themselves to different cultures and theatrical traditions. The success of such contemporary Hollywood movies as Kenneth Branagh's *Henry V* (1989), Baz Luhrmann's *Romeo+Juliet* (1996), Richard Loncraine's *Richard III* (1995), and Josh Madden's *Shakespeare in Love* (1998)—the Oscar-winning film about Shakespeare's life—demonstrates how fully this man of the theater has been embraced by new audiences and media.

William Shakespeare was born in 1564 in the small market town of Stratford-upon-Avon, to a glove maker named John Shakespeare and Mary Arden, a member of a distinguished Warwickshire family. Though a commoner and a craftsman, John Shakespeare must have been an ambitious man. He acquired real estate and held a series of increasingly important positions in local government, culminating in the office of bailiff (mayor) in 1569. Companies of traveling actors visited Stratford on a number of occasions during William's childhood, and it is almost certain that the young Shakespeare, perhaps because of his father's standing in the community, witnessed his first dramatic performances in the town's Guild Hall. The young boy's imagination may have been sparked by Corpus Christi or morality plays, or by early Tudor humanist plays, all of which left traces of influence in Shakespeare's dramas. In the late 1570s, however, when William was six years old, his father's financial and political fortunes took a steep downward turn, and the coat of arms for which he had applied, and which would have granted him the appellation of "gentleman," was held up (until William paid the remaining balance on the application in 1596).

It is likely that William Shakespeare attended Stratford's grammar school, where Latin and the classics were taught. He married at the age of eighteen. His bride, Anne Hathaway, was his senior by some eight years. Their first child, Susanna, was born in May 1583, about six months after the wedding. Two more children, the twins Judith and Hamnet, were born in 1585. After that the picture of Shakespeare's activities gets murky. There are apocryphal stories about him working as a schoolmaster, a lawyer's aide, a sailor, and a soldier, but there is no firm evidence to support any of them. A traveling company of actors, the Earl of Leicester's Men (which later was to become the Lord Chamberlain's Men), came through Stratford in 1587. It is tempting to imagine that the young Shakespeare, taken with the acting craft, found employment with them and accompanied them back to London, where he was to make his fortune as a dramatist. Unfortunately there is nothing in the historical record to validate such musings.

The next thing we know for certain is that Shakespeare was a working playwright in London by 1592. The rival dramatist Robert Greene refers to him in that year as an "upstart crow" and parodies a line from Shakespeare's early history play *Henry VI, Part 3*. Around 1594, Shakespeare joined the Lord Chamberlain's Men (the same troupe that had visited Stratford in 1587). Shakespeare was to stay with the Lord Chamberlain's Men, renamed the King's Men in 1603 when King James I assumed patronage over the company, until his retirement from the theater and return to Stratford around 1613. The Lord Chamberlain's Men had been the proud owners of the first permanent London playhouse, the Theatre, located in the district of Shoreditch—just northeast of the city walls and outside the jurisdiction of the city fathers, whose Puritan leanings made them aggressive opponents of stage plays. Following a financial dispute with their landlord, the Lord Chamberlain's Men pulled down their playhouse and reassembled it on the south bank of the river Thames; they named their new home, which opened for business in 1599, the Globe. It is in this theater that the comedy ***TWELFTH NIGHT, OR WHAT YOU WILL*** and ***THE TRAGEDY OF HAMLET, PRINCE OF DENMARK***, both anthologized here, were first presented to the public.

The conditions of performance at the Globe theater differed substantially from those on today's stages. First, all performances had to take place during daytime, as they were illuminated only by the sunlight pouring in through the open roof. The stage, a rectangular wooden scaffold some 5.5 feet high and believed to have measured roughly 43 feet wide by 27 feet deep, did not have a proscenium arch (as many stages do today), was covered by a roof, and protruded into the audience area of the theater known as the pit. The underside of the stage's roof, which was painted with the signs of the zodiac and was referred to as "the heavens," gave some protection to the actors during bad weather, a comfort not afforded to the "groundlings" who stood packed in the pit, exposed to the elements. Customers who paid more had seats in the covered, multitiered galleries surrounding the pit and the stage. The stage itself had a gallery above (which was used for such occasions as Romeo and Juliet's "balcony" scene), as well as a small inner stage or discovery space (used, for example, to reveal Miranda and Ferdinand playing chess in Shakespeare's late play *The Tempest*). The stage also had a trapdoor that could serve as the exit into hell (as in CHRISTOPHER MARLOWE'S *Doctor Faustus*) or as the point of entry for the ghost of Hamlet's father. With "the heavens" above and the netherworld below, Shakespeare's Globe symbolically encompassed the entire cosmos within the "wooden O" (*Henry V*) that was the theater. The manner of performance itself was in some ways deeply symbolic in that the

A detail from Claes Jansz Visscher's engraved panorama of London, *Londinum Florentissima Britanniae Urbs* (1616). The Globe theater is in the center foreground.

actors did not employ elaborate scenery or complicated special effects to create a sense of realism, though they did don sumptuous costumes.

Audiences of Shakespeare's *Hamlet*, for instance, were asked to accept that the Ghost appeared on the castle walls "in the dead waste and middle of the night," while the actor before them stood on a wooden stage, surrounded by spectators, on a bright, sunny afternoon. What is more, a prohibition against the appearance of female actors on the stage (which was not repealed until shortly after the restoration of the monarchy in 1660) meant that all female roles were acted by boys. Whether such cross-dressing undermined the "realism" of the performance, or exactly how Elizabethan audiences experienced it, is a matter of some controversy. More than anything, however, it is fair to say that actors relied heavily on Shakespeare's amazingly rich and allusive language to spark the imagination and hold the attention of their paying spectators.

HAMLET

By the time Shakespeare wrote *The Tragedy of Hamlet, Prince of Denmark* (1600–1601) he had reached the height of his powers as a dramatist. During the 1590s, Shakespeare had written a sonnet sequence, carefully crafted narrative poems, and a number of highly successful comedies, tragedies, and history plays, including *The Taming of the Shrew* (1592), *Richard II* (1595), *Romeo and Juliet* (1595), *A Midsummer Night's Dream* (1594–96), *The Merchant of Venice* (1596–97), *Henry IV, Part 1* (1596–97), *Henry V* (1598–99), *Julius Caesar* (1599), *Much Ado about Nothing* (1598), and *As You Like It* (1599–1600). With the composition of *Hamlet* he initiated a period of less than ten years during which he composed his greatest tragedies. Among these, *Hamlet* has probably captivated our interest the most; for more than four centuries, its titular hero has been a magnetic figure for actors, critics, and audiences alike. The Romantic poet Samuel Taylor Coleridge so deeply admired Hamlet's courage, skill, and ability for abstract and rational thought that he proclaimed, "I have a smack of Hamlet myself." Hamlet has been hailed not only as the quintessential Renaissance courtier and prince, but also as the first literary character who is like us: that is, one who dramatizes what Harold Bloom calls the "internalization of the self" so strikingly that it rivals or even exceeds the complex inner life we encounter in the thought of such early modern giants as Martin Luther, Desiderius Erasmus, and Michel de Montaigne. For some, Hamlet has become such an iconic figure that he has outgrown the play in which he appears. Whether or not this is true, many of us find ourselves attracted to and fascinated by Hamlet, even though we seem so far to have been unable to "pluck out the heart of [his] mystery."

Composed near the end of Elizabeth I's reign, *Hamlet* tells a story that is not original with Shakespeare. It may be based on a number of sources, the so-called *Ur-Hamlet* (a play that no longer exists), Saxo Grammaticus's *Historia Danica* (1180–1208), and François de Belleforest's *Histories Tragiques* (1576, a French translation of Grammaticus) chief among them. Although Shakespeare's play differs in many significant aspects from Grammaticus's narrative history, there are also similarities that appear too striking to be accidental. Grammaticus's account describes a fratricide (which, as in *Hamlet*, is also a regicide), an incestuous marriage, feigned madness (Hamlet's "antic disposition"), a spying courtier, the use of a woman (*Hamlet*'s Ophelia) as a lure, and a voyage to England.

A number of these elements are also vital to a group of Elizabethan revenge

Frontispiece illustration for Christiern Pedersen's 1514 edition of Saxo Grammaticus's *Historia Danica*.

plays to which *Hamlet* certainly belongs, and which includes Thomas Kyd's *The Spanish Tragedy* and works by John Webster, Thomas Middleton, John Marston, and others. Harkening back to the "tragedies of blood" created by the Roman playwright Seneca, Elizabethan revenge plays typically contain an act of murder that cannot be redressed by the authorities (usually because the highest authority in the play is complicit in the crime), an appearance of a ghost who demands just revenge (usually from a son or father), madness (feigned or actual), a great deal of intrigue, a hesitation or delay on the part of the avenger, and a set of actions that leads to the death of the murderer but simultaneously contaminates the avenger and typically results in his death. Shakespeare's *Hamlet* certainly puts most of these elements on display, but it handles them creatively in ways that enrich the genre and deeply complicate our understanding of the play.

The question of Hamlet's "delay" has long vexed critics and audiences. Why does Hamlet not simply kill Claudius after his initial meeting with his father's ghost? Hamlet is adamant that the specter is a trustworthy, "honest ghost," and he surely seems to have opportunities to kill Claudius. Yet considerable time passes, and Hamlet neither slays his uncle nor develops a plan to do so. The truth is that, like the critics who have tried to solve the riddle of his delay, Hamlet himself seems confused and perturbed by his inaction. Watching with admiration and bewilderment an impromptu performance of the fall of Troy by a troupe of traveling players who visit Elsinore, Hamlet wonders why it is that an actor can muster such intense passion in acting out a fiction—for "What's Hecuba to him, or he to Hecuba, / That he should weep for her?"—while he, who has a real "cue for passion," does nothing, "not for a king / Upon whose property and most dear life / A damned defeat was made." Hamlet never provides us with a satisfactory answer to his own question, which is all the more puzzling given that he despises Claudius and would not for a moment regret his death. Even when Hamlet appears to settle on a course of action by putting on "The Murder of Gonzago" to "catch the conscience of the King," his actions appear erratic and confused. This play-within-a-play sequence, as devised by Hamlet, has attracted critical interest as a prime example of metatheatricality, a dramaturgical device in which a play's characters take on various theatrical functions. In this scene, as well as in the "nunnery" scene with Ophelia, Hamlet embodies both directorial and playwriting roles in his orchestration of others' words and actions. Yet these scenes also demonstrate that actors and directors cannot completely control their audiences' reactions. While watching a loose reenactment of the murder of King Hamlet, Claudius does have a response that could be construed as guilt, but his calling an abrupt halt to the performance occurs not when the king is killed by a brother but when Lucianus, his nephew, pours poison into the sleeping king's ear. We may expect that Hamlet will now finally "sweep to [his] revenge," but instead he answers a summons from his mother. When, on his way to Gertrude's chambers, he comes upon Claudius at prayer, he fails to seize this opportunity to dispatch the king and instead takes his anger out on his mother in an unstoppable flood of words.

The depth and subtlety of Hamlet's trauma over the revenge question stand in sharp contrast with Shakespeare's handling of two other young princes, Laertes and Fortinbras, who also suffer the loss of a father. Fortinbras's father was killed in single combat by Hamlet's father before the start of the play, and Laertes' father, Polonius, is stabbed to death by Hamlet. Neither Fortinbras nor Laertes lacks the necessary passion for swift vengeance. In the first scene, we hear that Fortinbras is readying a military invasion of Denmark, and when Laertes learns of his father's death he rushes back from France to kill whoever is responsible, even if it turns out to be the King Claudius. "That drop of blood that's calm proclaims me bastard," Laertes says, suggesting that avenging a father's death is an instinctive act for an honorable son. Such an act requires no deliberation or concern for consequences, and it is this reckless liberty that Hamlet longs for but, as a result of his self-reflective nature, is unable to achieve.

Yet Hamlet finds it impossible to be more like Laertes or Fortinbras, and it is precisely in his inability to be a one-dimensional man of action that we encounter the depth and complexity of his character. He lacks the passion and singleness of purpose to act on his father's command. Maybe it is because he perceives too great a disjunction between the straightforwardness of the Ghost's call for justice and the widespread disorder and corruption that render Denmark an "unweeded garden / That grows to seed." Maybe Hamlet realizes that killing Claudius would be nothing more than an isolated and ambiguous act of revenge in a fundamentally unjust world. But whatever his reasons, Hamlet's inability to balance the Ghost's command with the corrupt world of Elsinore is precisely what intensifies and expands the inner life of his character. His inability to live in and accept the world as he finds it drives him inward, rendering him significantly more introspective and self-conscious, and therefore more

A young noblewoman, from Jost Amman's *Im Frauwenzimmer* (1586).

recognizably modern, than other characters who walked across the Elizabethan public stage. It is as if the character of Hamlet allows Shakespeare to explore recesses of the human mind of which other poets and dramatists had at best only been dimly aware.

But the depth of Hamlet's interiority, insofar as it is promoted by his frustration over not killing the king, comes at a heavy price. When the play comes to a close, not only Claudius but also Gertrude, Rosencrantz, Guildenstern, Laertes, Polonius, Ophelia, and Hamlet himself are dead, and one could argue that the swift execution of justice on Claudius by Hamlet in the first act would have saved the lives of all of them. The madness and death of Ophelia are particularly distressing to audiences because the young woman is wholly a victim of others' machinations, including those of Hamlet.

Ophelia's plight and the gender dynamics that shape it draw attention to the limited number of options aristocratic young women had available to them in the early modern period. During her premarriage days, Ophelia would have been expected to guard her reputation and chastity zealously, to be an obedient daughter to her father and an obedient sister to her brother. Her identity in Danish aristocratic society is defined largely in relation to the men in her life, and in terms of her exchangeability on the marriage market. As limiting as this life trajectory may seem to us, it was a reality for most aristocratic women of the time, and Ophelia apparently does not possess the inner strength to resist this model (as some of Shakespeare's other heroines attempt to do). What is more, it is the vital responsibility of the men who control Ophelia's destiny to facilitate her transition from one position to the next. Laertes' strong admonition to Ophelia to rebuff Hamlet's courtship reflects his guardianship of his sister's chastity as well as his recognition of the importance of her purity to the state. In practical terms, Laertes is guarding his sister's reputation; yet his action also hinders her transition from the role of sister and daughter to that of wife. Her father, Polonius, is equally anxious about Hamlet's intentions, and he forbids her from seeing Hamlet any further. Claudius, who, like Elizabeth I, has a fundamental interest in shaping aristocratic marriages, completely fails in his role as kingly guardian of one of his noble subjects when he goes along with Polonius's plan to use Ophelia as a pawn in a spying game to learn more about the cause of Hamlet's odd behavior. None of the men show any concern for how their words and actions destroy Ophelia's future in Danish society.

Hamlet also contributes significantly to Ophelia's anguish when he elects to inflict his "antic disposition" on her. The genuine distress that this performance causes Ophelia seems of no concern to Hamlet. Betrayed by her father, brother, king, and potential husband, there is literally nothing for Ophelia to *be* anymore. The "nunnery" to which a cruel Hamlet tries to consign her at one point might be a socially acceptable choice for Ophelia, but the option is never pursued.

Critics have long argued over whether Ophelia's madness speech gives us clues that she and Hamlet might have consummated their relationship. While her song about love betrayed and loss of maidenhead (4.5) need not imply physical consummation, her emotional and psychological commitment to a life with Hamlet is so complete that she is unable to imagine or reconstitute another role for herself in the world of Elsinore, whether she is physically a virgin or not. The dismantling of Ophelia's identity has led to the dissolution of her psychological coherence, and it results, following a cruel logic, in the loss of her very being in death.

It is possible that Hamlet's dying endorsement of the Norwegian warrior Prince Fortinbras as Denmark's new ruler is an acknowledgment that action, even reckless and violent action, is preferable to Hamlet's own propensity for delay and indecision. The rise of Fortinbras can be read as a return to power of Hamlet's father, a return of the feudal warrior-king. It functions as a rejection not only of the Machiavellian Claudius but also of Hamlet himself; indeed, it is difficult to imagine Hamlet as an effective ruler, given his style of decision making. But even so, despite the human cost associated with Hamlet's delay, it is precisely this delay, and more specifically Hamlet's anxious pondering of its meaning, that yields us a character of uncommon psychological depth, self-scrutiny, and complexity.

TWELFTH NIGHT

Twelfth Night, or What You Will (1600–1601) is one of Shakespeare's most provocative, captivating, and complex romantic comedies, and yet it appears to be the last that he composed in this form. Around 1601, at the height of his dramatic powers, Shakespeare entered an artistic phase that produced his so-called problem plays (or "dark comedies") and his mature tragedies, including *Hamlet*. The explanations of why Shakespeare abandoned romantic comedy at this time are necessarily speculative, but it appears likely that the dramatist was growing increasingly dissatisfied with the form's inability to accommodate the complexities of real life. In the midst of its festive spirit, *Twelfth Night* reveals the beginning of this dissatisfaction.

We know that *Twelfth Night* was performed at the Inns of Court (the residences in London of the city's legal societies) on the occasion of Candlemas Day, February 2, 1602. A witness to the performance noted a similarity between *Twelfth Night* and one of the mistaken-identity farces of the Roman playwright Plautus (which had also influenced an earlier Shakespeare play, *The Comedy of Errors*). The year 1602 marks the earliest *recorded* performance of the play, but it is possible that Shakespeare's acting company, the Lord Chamberlain's Men, had already staged it at the Globe. It has been suggested that a performance took place in 1601 at the court of Queen Elizabeth to coincide with the visit to England of the duke of Bracciano, Don Virginio Orsino. But as tempting as it is to tease out possible analogies between *Twelfth Night*'s Duke Orsino and the historical Don Virginio Orsino, there is no indication that Shakespeare wrote *Twelfth*

Night or any of his plays for special court occasions.

Twelfth Night—which is based on Barnabe Riche's story "Of Apolonius and Silla" (1581) and, indirectly, on the anonymous Italian comedy *Gl'Ingannati* (1537)—offers a compelling tale of look-alike twins separated by shipwreck. Characterized by a festive atmosphere and a preoccupation with love, romantic comedies exhibit a drive toward social unity, marriage, and happiness. Typically, Shakespeare starts his romantic comedies by presenting us with a group of young, single men and women who are eligible for marriage but who encounter obstacles to the fulfillment of their personal desires. What is more, the obstacles stand in the way not only of personal happiness but, more importantly, of socially acceptable unions that enable the orderly reproduction of existing social classes and family structures (both of which are of vital concern to the genre of romantic comedy). The impediment can take a variety of forms, including obstructionist parents, an antagonist who wishes the lovers ill, misguided desire, grief over the loss of a loved one, or fear of the opposite sex. The middle acts of romantic comedies are commonly taken up with the younger generation's clumsy but sometimes endearing attempts to overcome these obstacles, an endeavor in which they ultimately succeed, though sometimes only because of good fortune, outside aid from their elders, or supernatural intervention. The resolution of the story's dramatic conflicts is generally harmonious, mostly satisfying (to the characters as well as the audience), and life-affirming. *Twelfth Night*—perhaps reflecting the growing strain between realism and romance in

The King Drinks (ca. 1640), by David Teniers the Younger, depicts a popular ritual associated with Twelfth Night throughout Europe: the person who finds a dried bean in his serving of the "Three Kings cake" is pronounced king for the evening.

Shakespearean comedy—withholds some of that satisfaction and admits disturbances to that harmony.

Shakespeare signals his interest in the social energies associated with those disturbances in the title of his play. Loosely connected to the Roman festival of Saturnalia—which marked the winter solstice with feasting, revelry, playful disrespect for authority, and sensual indulgences—"twelfth night," also known as Epiphany, marks the end of the holiday season that lasts from Christmas through January 6. The carnivalesque spirit that prevailed during these days was sometimes channeled into ritualized lampoonings of Elizabethan civil and church authorities. The Feast of Fools and such figures as the Boy Bishop, the Lords of Misrule, and the Boy King inverted the established social order and allowed ordinary men and women to release (in a controlled fashion) any resentments and hostilities that might have accrued from living and working in an oppressive, hierarchical society with sharp divisions between the haves and have nots. Although Shakespeare neither mentions "twelfth night" in the body of his text nor dramatizes any of the popular rituals associated with it, the play is permeated on all levels with a carnivalesque spirit and energy that produces significant upheaval and reversal in the traditional social order.

The second part of the play's title—*What You Will*—connects the theme of disorder through *mis*directed desire more specifically to individual events and characters. According to the *Oxford English Dictionary,* the word *will* can mean "desire, wish, [or] longing," with a sexual connotation. Virtually all the characters in the play engage in forms of desire that conflict for one reason or another with the established social order and therefore impede the proper and orderly reproduction of the play's social structure, which is an essential element of a successful romantic comedy.

The hard-drinking Sir Toby Belch and the professional jester Feste, whose name implies festivity and who declares himself to be a deliberate "corrupter of words," are of course the most obvious representatives of a type of Saturnalian disorder; but the aristocrats themselves, because they insist on following their "will" or desire, appear equally at odds with the normative social order. Duke Orsino, for instance, wallows in an obsessive and self-indulgent love for the Countess Olivia, even though we quickly gather that she will never have him. His misdirected desire prevents him from marrying and producing an heir, thereby putting the processes of generational renewal and social reproduction as well as the future governance of Illyria, in limbo. Olivia, in turn, decides to mourn her recently deceased brother and father for the uncommonly long period of seven years, thus endangering the future of her estate and blocking the timely reproduction of the aristocratic class of Illyria. She further complicates things by unwittingly falling in love with an unobtainable partner, a woman named Viola who has disguised herself as a man (named Cesario). Viola herself falls in love with her employer, Duke Orsino, but her male disguise makes it impossible for her to pursue her desire in overt ways. Adding to the confusion, Toby and Maria (Olivia's gentlewoman) trick Malvolio into believing that Olivia is in love with him, prompting the sour but ambitious steward who dreams of becoming "Count Malvolio" to behave ridiculously and upend the very principles of decorum and propriety he is supposed to uphold. Sir Andrew Aguecheek, a foolish knight who spends his time in the company of Sir Toby, also has his heart set on the Countess Olivia, but it becomes clear almost immediately that he has no chance of winning her. His desire is fruitless; all he is good for is paying Toby's liquor bills. Antonio the sea captain, who saves Viola's twin brother Sebastian after the shipwreck, has very strong, homoerotic feelings for Sebastian, but the latter does not seem interested in reciprocating, giving rise to another instance of misdirected desire within a comic world where heterosexuality is the norm.

The expectation—created by the genre of romantic comedy—is that disorder gives way to order and harmony by play's end. These are ordinarily achieved by a repositioning of characters to their proper place within the social fabric of the play, either by confirming their proper social rank or gender or by having them enter into socially acceptable marriages. *Twelfth Night* certainly attempts to achieve such harmony through a repositioning of characters, but the effort is not entirely successful—a failure that is surely deliberate. On the surface, matters appear resolved. Viola is reunited with her look-alike twin brother, Sebastian. Viola's female gender is confirmed, and she will become Orsino's wife. The Countess Olivia realizes that she inadvertently fell for another woman, but this mistake is rectified when she equally inadvertently marries Sebastian (whom she believes to be Cesario at the time the couple exchanges their vows). Even the riotous Toby appears to leave behind his self-indulgent ways when he enters into a union with the sensible Maria. After all the disorder, it appears that the ruling class of Illyria may be settling down to a calmer family life and the business of biological and social reproduction.

But when we look just below its surface, we recognize that this newfound harmony may be only superficial. Olivia is now married to a man she has known for only a few hours, and their compatibility could well become an issue later. What is more, Olivia's same-sex desire for Viola cannot have magically evaporated. When Orsino describes Cesario's physical appearance, he stresses "his" feminine qualities: "Diane's lip / Is not more smooth and rubious; thy small pipe / Is as the maiden's organ, shrill and sound, / And all is semblative a woman's part." In other words, you sound like a woman, you look like a woman, and you resemble a woman in every way. Because the part of Viola was played by a boy actor in Shakespeare's theater, there is no doubt that the "woman's part" could have been removed from the performance. A boy could simply act as a boy would. But Shakespeare appears determined that Olivia shall fall madly in love with a character whose "woman's part" breaks through the masculine disguise. No matter how surprised Olivia is when she finally learns that Cesario is a woman, we cannot discount that she fell in love with "him" in part because of those female qualities. Sebastian tries to explain to Olivia what has transpired saying "lady, you have been mistook. / But nature to her bias drew in that. / You would have been contracted to a maid." Sebastian's metaphor is taken from

Two Young Men (ca. 1590), by Crispin van den Broeck.

the game of bowls, which was played with a ball with an off-center weight that made it curve from a straight path. These lines are generally interpreted as intended to quiet fears of Olivia's homoeroticism by suggesting that "nature" redirected her affections from Cesario to Sebastian. But if we take "that" to refer to what is "mistook," then nature's "bias" in fact drew Olivia to her mistake, to another woman.

An element of homoeroticism also remains part of the Orsino-Viola relationship. Viola's female gender has been verbally established at the time that Orsino proposes marriage, but Viola never removes her masculine disguise, meaning that we are visually presented with a union between two men. No doubt Viola will soon again don her "maiden weeds," but who is to say that Orsino will not one day remember the time he fell in love with "her," and ask, "Would you like to try on again those breeches and doublet you used to wear?" This question and the broader issue of how these couples will fare in the future are not openly addressed amid the festiveness of the play's conclusion, but they are implied or encouraged by the "o'erhasty marriage[s]"—to borrow a phrase from *Hamlet*.

We may not care very much that the marriage between Toby and Maria is equally hasty and unprepared for, nor may we feel very sorry that the foolish Sir Andrew is left without a mate at play's end, but we may be disturbed by Illyria's inability to find a place for Captain Antonio. Elizabethan culture strongly disapproved of sodomy, but writers often idealized male-male friendship, especially between aristocratic males, and described it in passionate and erotic language. We cannot be certain that Antonio is what we would today call a homosexual, but his complete devotion to Sebastian leaves him without an obvious partner when Sebastian marries. Yet Shakespeare makes it clear that Antonio does not deserve to be excluded from a newly harmonious Illyrian society. Antonio is a thoroughly noble and admirable character who unselfishly risks his life for Sebastian (and Viola) on more than one occasion. If anything, Shakespeare gives us reason to lament that a character as worthy as Antonio cannot find a place for himself within the society's social structure. It is as if in 1601 or 1602, when Shakespeare writes *Twelfth Night,* he no longer feels that the comedic resolution—which calls for heterosexual marriages—can adequately contain the complexities of human desire and social reality. And even the marriages that do occur seem somehow less plausible than we would want them to be. Of course it would be misleading to suggest that Shakespeare's earlier romantic comedies tie up all the loose ends neatly—they do not—but *Twelfth Night* seems to anticipate the even more problematic endings of his "dark comedies" to follow.

Audiences may be less troubled by the fate of Olivia's steward Malvolio, who, like Antonio and Andrew, is left unintegrated into the play's multiple unions, but his vow to "be revenged on the whole pack of you" strikes a jarring note at play's end. Such a tone does not seem to fit the supposedly conciliatory spirit of comedy. There is no doubt that Malvolio is an unpleasant person, and his rigid opposition to the spirit of carnival embraced by Toby, Andrew, and Maria make him a killjoy, but we cannot forget that he is ultimately only doing the bidding of his employer, the Countess Olivia. To an English audience living in a class-based society, it may indeed have seemed mad for the commoner Malvolio to think he could marry a countess; but such marriages were becoming increasingly common in Shakespeare's time, as many aristocratic families could not sustain themselves and their estates in the new economy and wealthy merchants and traders were increasingly willing to part with vast sums of money for the privilege of marrying into the upper class. Audiences may have disliked Malvolio as a man, but his ambition may well have been their fantasy.

The trend toward a darker, more pessimistic view of life, glimpsed at in *Twelfth Night* and fully realized in *Hamlet,* becomes increasingly persistent in the plays written in the first decade of the seventeenth century. Critics have speculated that the death of Shakespeare's father in 1601 may have led the playwright to contemplate his own mortality. The "problem" plays *Troilus and Cressida* (1602), *Measure for Measure* (1603), and *All's Well That Ends Well* (1604–05) contain elements of such earlier romantic comedies as *A Midsummer Night's Dream, Much Ado about Nothing,* and *As You Like It,* but they do not offer the same satisfying, life-affirming resolutions as those prior plays. The writing of *Hamlet* marks the beginning of a period in which Shakespeare wrote his greatest tragedies: *Othello* (1603–04), *King Lear* (1605), *Macbeth* (1606), and *Anthony and Cleopatra* (1606). In the final years of his career as a playwright, Shakespeare wrote four plays that are listed among the comedies in the First Folio but are more commonly referred to today as "romances": *Pericles* (1607–08), *Cymbeline* (1609–10), *The Winter's Tale* (1609), and *The Tempest* (1610–11). As we might expect from an aging author who harbors no illusions about the ways of the world yet is not without hope, these final plays tackle some of the same issues that dominate the tragedies—family crisis, destructive jealousy, political betrayal—but they rely on magical or miraculous interventions to produce endings that, while not unequivocally happy, avoid outright tragedy. In their self-conscious allusions to characters and dramatic situations from earlier in Shakespeare's career, these late plays reveal a playwright, on the eve of his retirement from the theater, looking back over his own artistic achievement and recombining elements from it in new, often magical configurations. Indeed, many critics have seen Prospero—the magician who stage-manages the events and transformations of *The Tempest*—as a figure of Shakespeare himself. In Prospero's decision to "abjure" his "rough magic" at the play's end, audiences, readers, and scholars have sometimes seen Shakespeare's farewell to his own dramatic art and to the stage—"this insubstantial pageant"—that he brought to life with such dazzling power. It is a measure of this power that centuries later, his plays continue to define the theater he took as his own.

IVO KAMPS

TEXTUAL NOTE FOR *HAMLET*

The earliest versions of Shakespeare's *Hamlet* exist in three printed forms: a quarto dated 1603, another quarto dated 1604, and the text printed in the First Folio of 1623. The consensus is that the 1603 text (known as Q1) is what scholars call a "bad quarto." It is most likely a reconstruction based on the memories of one or more of the actors who performed in the play. For that reason it may give us valuable insights into stage directions, and it may also offer accurate versions of speeches as delivered by the particular actor(s) in question, but it tends to be unreliable in most other ways. The second quarto is probably based on Shakespeare's own manuscript or on a scribal version of that manuscript. The Folio text is presumably based on a promptbook (a version of the play authorized for performance by the Master of the Revels, the government's censor). The promptbook, rather than the author's manuscript, was the basis for the play's performance, and therefore the version of the play that Shakespeare's audiences actually witnessed.

The survival of the second quarto (Q2) and the First Folio (F1) texts creates a dilemma for today's editors of Shakespeare's text. While the two texts are identical in many respects, they are also different in important ways. F1 deletes about 230 lines that appear in Q2, but F1 adds 83 different lines that are not present in Q2. F1, for instance, does not have Hamlet's famous final soliloquy, "How all occasions do inform against me." The crux, of course, lies in the reasons that account for the differences between the two texts. Are these differences the product of interventions by actors or by the printer, or do they represent Shakespeare's own revision of the play? Textual scholars have offered a range of answers to this question, but none is conclusive.

What is more, we have to decide what

our objective is in editing the play: do we want to get as close as possible to the Shakespearean "original," or do we want to reconstruct the text as it was performed in Shakespeare's theater in his time? If we seek the former, we should focus on Q2 as our primary text; if we want the theater-based text, we must turn to F1.

The dominant trend in twentieth-century textual scholarship was to privilege Q2 (the text closest to Shakespeare's manuscript or "foul" papers) and to supplement Q2 with those passages from F1 that do not appear in Q2. The resulting conflated text therefore differs from both Q2 and F1; and, though Shakespeare may have penned every line in it, it is not a text of *Hamlet* as Shakespeare conceived it, or as his contemporary audiences saw it. Stanley Wells and Gary Taylor broke with this tradition in 1986 when they published the Oxford edition of Shakespeare's plays. Wells and Taylor held that Shakespeare was a man of the theater who well understood that whatever script he wrote would be altered in rehearsal and performance. In other words, they conceived of Shakespeare's text not as fixed but as fluid, adjusted to suit the needs of the company. Wells and Taylor consequently based their Oxford edition on F1 and declined to include almost all the lines (some 230) that appear only in Q2.

In 1997, Norton published an edition of Shakespeare's plays with Stephen Greenblatt as general editor. Greenblatt did not return to the quartos and folio to construct a new text of *Hamlet*; instead, he based his text on Wells and Taylor's 1986 edition. Greenblatt, however, did not leave Wells and Taylor's text of *Hamlet* unchanged. He restored the omitted passages from Q2 and thereby produced a text similar to that in the standard college editions of David Bevington and G. Blakemore Evans. In an apparent effort to acknowledge that he was undoing Wells and Taylor's departure from the editorial tradition, Greenblatt printed the reintroduced passages from Q2 in italics.

The current edition consists of Greenblatt's Norton text (based on the Wells-Taylor edition) and preserves the passages from Q2 added by Greenblatt. Following Greenblatt's practice, the passages from Q2 are printed in italics, and footnotes remind the reader of their source.

The explanatory notes and the introduction to this edition of the play are new.

TEXTUAL NOTE FOR *TWELFTH NIGHT*

The text of *Twelfth Night* on which this edition is based is the one that appears in *The Norton Shakespeare* (ed. Stephen Greenblatt), but with a new introduction and new explanatory notes. The *Norton Shakespeare* text, in turn, is taken from the Oxford edition of Shakespeare's plays (1986), edited by Stanley Wells and Gary Taylor. The text of *Twelfth Night* that lies behind all three texts is the First Folio text of 1623.

The Tragedy of Hamlet, Prince of Denmark

THE PERSONS OF THE PLAY

GHOST of Hamlet, the late King of Denmark
KING CLAUDIUS, his brother
QUEEN GERTRUDE of Denmark, widow of King Hamlet, now wife of Claudius
Prince HAMLET, son of King Hamlet and Queen Gertrude
POLONIUS, a lord
LAERTES, son of Polonius
OPHELIA, daughter of Polonius
REYNALDO, servant of Polonius
HORATIO, ROSENCRANTZ, GUILDENSTERN } friends of Prince Hamlet
FRANCISCO, BARNARDO, MARCELLUS } soldiers
VALTEMAND, CORNELIUS, OSRIC, GENTLEMEN } courtiers
A SAILOR
Two CLOWNS, a gravedigger and his companion
A PRIEST
FORTINBRAS, Prince of Norway
A CAPTAIN in his army
AMBASSADORS from England
PLAYERS, who play the parts of the PROLOGUE, PLAYER KING, PLAYER QUEEN, and LUCIANUS, in *The Mousetrap*
Lords, messengers, attendants, guards, soldiers, followers of Laertes, sailors

1.1

Enter BARNARDO *and* FRANCISCO, *two sentinels [at several° doors]* — *separate*

BARNARDO Who's there?
FRANCISCO Nay, answer me.[1] Stand and unfold yourself.° — *make yourself known*
BARNARDO Long live the King!
FRANCISCO Barnardo?
BARNARDO He.
FRANCISCO You come most carefully° upon your hour. — *precisely*
BARNARDO 'Tis now struck twelve. Get thee to bed, Francisco.
FRANCISCO For this relief much thanks. 'Tis bitter cold,
And I am sick at heart.
BARNARDO Have you had quiet guard?
FRANCISCO Not a mouse stirring.
BARNARDO Well, good night.
If you do meet Horatio and Marcellus,
The rivals° of my watch, bid them make haste. — *partners*

1.1 Location: A guard platform on the battlements of Elsinore Castle in Denmark.
1. As the sentry on duty, Francisco has the right to challenge anyone who approaches.

Enter HORATIO *and* MARCELLUS

FRANCISCO I think I hear them.—Stand! Who's there?
HORATIO Friends to this ground.° *i.e., this country*
MARCELLUS And liegemen to the Dane.° *the Danish King*
FRANCISCO Give° you good night. *May God give*
MARCELLUS O farewell, honest soldier. Who hath relieved you?
FRANCISCO Barnardo has my place. Give you good night. *Exit*
MARCELLUS Holla, Barnardo!
BARNARDO Say—what, is Horatio there?
HORATIO A piece of him.[2]
BARNARDO Welcome, Horatio. Welcome, good Marcellus.
MARCELLUS What, has this thing appeared again tonight?
BARNARDO I have seen nothing.
MARCELLUS Horatio says 'tis but our fantasy,
And will not let belief take hold of him
Touching° this dreaded sight twice seen of° us. *Regarding / by*
Therefore I have entreated him along
With us to watch the minutes of this night,
That if again this apparition come
He may approve° our eyes and speak to it.[3] *confirm*
HORATIO Tush, tush, 'twill not appear.
BARNARDO Sit down a while,
And let us once again assail your ears,
That are so fortified against our story,
What we two nights have seen.
HORATIO Well, sit we down,
And let us hear Barnardo speak of this.
BARNARDO Last night of all,
When yon same star that's westward from the pole° *the North Star*
Had made his° course t'illume that part of heaven *its*
Where now it burns, Marcellus and myself,
The bell then beating one—

Enter the GHOST [*in complete armour, holding a truncheon, with his beaver° up*] *visor*

MARCELLUS Peace, break thee off. Look where it comes again.
BARNARDO In the same figure like the King that's dead.
MARCELLUS [*to* HORATIO] Thou art a scholar—speak to it, Horatio.
BARNARDO Looks it not like the King?—Mark it, Horatio.
HORATIO Most like. It harrows me with fear and wonder.
BARNARDO It would° be spoke to. *wants to*
MARCELLUS Question it, Horatio.
HORATIO [*to the* GHOST] What art thou that usurp'st[4] this time of night,
Together with that fair and warlike form

2. Horatio may mean that the only part of him that is visible in the dark is the hand he offers in greeting.

3. It was popularly held that a ghost could not speak unless spoken to. Marcellus thinks that Horatio, a man of learning, is the appropriate person to address the ghost (see line 40).

4. As a creature belonging to another realm, the ghost has entered the natural world and seized a shape belonging to the King of Denmark.

In which the majesty of buried Denmark[5]
Did sometimes° march? By heaven, I charge thee speak. *formerly*
MARCELLUS It is offended.
BARNARDO See, it stalks away.
HORATIO [*to the* GHOST] Stay, speak, speak, I charge thee speak.
Exit GHOST
MARCELLUS 'Tis gone, and will not answer.
BARNARDO How now, Horatio? You tremble and look pale.
Is not this something more than fantasy?
What think you on't?° *of it*
HORATIO Before my God, I might not this believe
Without the sensible° and true avouch° *sensory / guarantee*
Of mine own eyes.
MARCELLUS Is it not like the King?
HORATIO As thou art to thyself.
Such was the very armour he had on
When he th'ambitious Norway° combated. *King of Norway*
So frowned he once when in an angry parley° *discussion*
He smote the sledded Polacks[6] on the ice.
'Tis strange.
MARCELLUS Thus twice before, and just at this dead hour,
With martial stalk hath he gone by our watch.
HORATIO In what particular thought to work[7] I know not,
But in the gross and scope of my opinion[8]
This bodes some strange eruption° to our state. *disturbance*
MARCELLUS Good now,° sit down, and tell me, he that knows, *(an entreaty; "Please")*
Why this same strict and most observant watch
So nightly toils the subject of the land,[9]
And why such daily cast° of brazen cannon, *production*
And foreign mart° for implements of war, *trade*
Why such impress° of shipwrights, whose sore task *forced service*
Does not divide the Sunday from the week:
What might be toward° that this sweaty haste *imminent*
Doth make the night joint-labourer with the day,
Who is't that can inform me?
HORATIO That can I—
At least the whisper goes so: our last king,
Whose image even but now appeared to us,
Was as you know by Fortinbras of Norway,
Thereto pricked° on by a most emulate° pride, *urged / competitive*
Dared to the combat; in which our valiant Hamlet[1]—
For so this side of our known world esteemed him—
Did slay this Fortinbras, who by a sealed compact° *contract, agreement*
Well ratified by law and heraldry° *heraldic law*

5. That is, the recently deceased King of Denmark.
6. Poles (who traveled by sled).
7. Exactly how to comprehend this.
8. But in the general sense of my opinion (in contrast with my "particular thought" [line 66]).
9. Causes the subjects of this country to toil.
1. That is, the recently deceased king, not the young prince.

Did forfeit with his life all those his lands
Which he stood seized on[2] to the conqueror;
Against the which a moiety competent° — *un equal portion*
Was gagèd° by our King, which had returned° — *pledged / would have*
To the inheritance° of Fortinbras — *possession*
Had he been vanquisher, as by the same cov'nant
And carriage of the article designed° — *drawn up*
His fell to Hamlet. Now sir, young Fortinbras,[3]
Of unimprovèd° mettle hot and full, — *untested, unrestrained*
Hath in the skirts° of Norway here and there — *outlying territories*
Sharked up a list[4] of landless resolutes
For food and diet to some enterprise
That hath a stomach in't,° which is no other— — *appetite for it*
And it doth well° appear unto our state— — *clearly*
But to recover of us by strong hand
And terms compulsative° those foresaid lands — *compulsory*
So by his father lost. And this, I take it,
Is the main motive of our preparations,
The source of this our watch, and the chief head° — *source*
Of this post-haste and rummage° in the land.[5] — *turmoil*

BARNARDO *I think it be no other but e'en so.*
Well may it sort° that this portentous figure — *be fitting*
Comes armèd through our watch so like the king
That was and is the question° of these wars. — *cause*

HORATIO *A mote it is to trouble the mind's eye.*
In the most high and palmy° state of Rome, — *triumphant*
A little ere the mightiest Julius[6] fell,
The graves stood tenantless, and the sheeted° dead — *shrouded*
Did squeak and gibber in the Roman streets
At stars with trains of fire,[7] and dews of blood,
Disasters[8] in the sun; and the moist star,° — *the moon*
Upon whose influence Neptune's empire stands,[9]
Was sick almost to doomsday with eclipse.[1]
And even the like precurse° of feared events, — *precursor*
As harbingers° preceding still° the fates, — *heralds / always*
And prologue to the omen[2] coming on,
Have heaven and earth together demonstrated
Unto our climature° and countrymen. — *region*

Enter the GHOST [*as before.*]

2. Which he held in possession.
3. Son of the slain King of Norway.
4. Hastily and indiscriminately collected a band.
5. The lines that follow (106.1–106.18) appear in Q2 but are omitted from F1. See textual note in the introduction.
6. Julius Caesar (100–44 B.C.E.), Roman general and statesman, stabbed to death by a band of conspirators.
7. That is, comets, traditionally seen as ominous portents.
8. Signs of ill omen.
9. The seas depend (as by the currents and tides). *Neptune:* Roman god of the sea.
1. In 1598, England witnessed both solar and lunar eclipses. Many believed that the Second Coming and Final Judgment were close at hand, citing prophesies in the biblical Book of Revelation (6.12) of the sun "as black as dark sackcloth" and the moon "like blood."
2. Usually, an "omen" is a sign that presages of a future good or evil event, but here it appears to refer to the event itself.

But soft,° behold—lo where it comes again! *be quiet*
I'll cross[3] it though it blast° me.—Stay, illusion. *injure; curse*
[*The* GHOST] *spreads his arms.*
If thou hast any sound or use of voice,
Speak to me.
If there be any good thing to be done
That may to thee do ease and grace to me,
Speak to me.
If thou art privy to thy country's fate
Which happily° foreknowing may avoid, *perhaps*
O speak!
Or if thou hast uphoarded° in thy life *heaped up*
Extorted treasure in the womb of earth—
For which, they say, you spirits oft walk in death—
The cock crows
Speak of it, stay and speak.—Stop it, Marcellus.

MARCELLUS Shall I strike at it with my partisan?° *long-handled spear*

HORATIO Do, if it will not stand.

BARNARDO 'Tis here.

HORATIO 'Tis here.

Exit GHOST

MARCELLUS 'Tis gone.
We do it wrong, being so majestical,
To offer it the show of violence,
For it is as the air invulnerable,
And our vain blows malicious mockery.° *pretended violence*

BARNARDO It was about to speak when the cock crew.

HORATIO And then it started like a guilty thing
Upon a fearful summons. I have heard
The cock, that is the trumpet to the morn,
Doth with his lofty and shrill-sounding throat
Awake the god of day,° and at his warning, *the sun god Apollo*
Whether in sea or fire, in earth or air,
Th'extravagant and erring[4] spirit hies° *hastens*
To his confine;° and of the truth herein *territory*
This present object° made probation.° *sight / proof*

MARCELLUS It faded on the crowing of the cock.
Some say that ever 'gainst° that season comes *just before*
Wherein our saviour's birth is celebrated
The bird of dawning singeth all night long;
And then, they say, no spirit can walk abroad,
The nights are wholesome; then no planets strike,° *exert evil influence*
No fairy takes,° nor witch hath power to charm, *bewitches*
So hallowed and so gracious° is the time. *full of grace, blessed*

HORATIO So have I heard, and do in part believe it.
But look, the morn in russet mantle clad

3. Encounter; also, make the sign of cross (as a defense against its potentially evil power).

4. That is, wandering outside of its proper boundaries.

Walks o'er the dew of yon high eastern hill.
Break we our watch up, and by my advice
Let us impart what we have seen tonight
Unto young Hamlet; for upon my life,
This spirit, dumb to us, will° speak to him. *wishes to*
Do you consent we shall acquaint him with it,
As needful in our loves,[5] fitting our duty?

MARCELLUS Let's do't, I pray; and I this morning know
Where we shall find him most conveniently. *Exeunt°* *(They) exit (Latin)*

1.2

Flourish. Enter CLAUDIUS, *King of Denmark,* GERTRUDE *the Queen, [members of the] Council, [such] as* POLONIUS, *his son* LAERTES *and [daughter]* OPHELIA, *[Prince]* HAMLET *[dressed in black], cum aliis°* *with others (Latin)*

KING CLAUDIUS Though yet of Hamlet our[6] dear brother's death
The memory be green, and that it us befitted
To bear our hearts in grief and our whole kingdom
To be contracted in one brow of woe,
Yet so far hath discretion fought with nature[7]
That we with wisest sorrow think on him
Together with remembrance of ourselves.
Therefore our sometime° sister, now our queen, *former*
Th'imperial jointress° of this warlike state, *joint owner*
Have we as 'twere with a defeated joy,
With one auspicious° and one dropping° eye, *joyful / tearful*
With mirth in funeral and with dirge in marriage,
In equal scale weighing delight and dole,° *sorrow*
Taken to wife. Nor have we herein barred
Your better wisdoms, which have freely gone
With this affair along. For all, our thanks.
Now follows that you know° young Fortinbras, *be informed that*
Holding a weak supposal° of our worth, *estimation*
Or thinking by our late dear brother's death
Our state to be disjoint and out of frame,° *order*
Co-leaguèd° with the dream of his advantage, *Coupled*
He hath not failed to pester us with message
Importing° the surrender of those lands *Regarding*
Lost by his father, with all bonds° of law, *binding terms*
To our most valiant brother. So much for him.

Enter VALTEMAND *and* CORNELIUS

Now for ourself, and for this time of meeting,
Thus much the business is: we have here writ
To Norway, uncle of young Fortinbras—
Who, impotent and bed-rid, scarcely hears
Of this his nephew's purpose—to suppress

5. As necessitated by the love we bear him.
1.2 Location: The castle.
6. My (Claudius often uses the royal "we").
7. Natural inclination (to mourn the dead king).

His further gait° herein, in that the levies, *course*
The lists, and full proportions are all made
Out of his subject;[8] and we here dispatch
You, good Cornelius, and you, Valtemand,
For bearers of this greeting to old Norway,
Giving to you no further personal power
To business with the King more than the scope
Of these dilated° articles allow. *detailed*
Farewell, and let your haste commend your duty.[9]

VALTEMAND In that and all things will we show our duty.

KING CLAUDIUS We doubt it nothing,° heartily farewell. *not at all*

Exeunt VALTEMAND *and* CORNELIUS

And now, Laertes, what's the news with you?
You told us of some suit. What is't, Laertes?
You cannot speak of reason to the Dane[1]
And lose your voice.° What wouldst thou beg, Laertes, *i.e., waste your words*
That shall not be my offer, not thy asking?[2]
The head is not more native[3] to the heart,
The hand more instrumental to the mouth,
Than is the throne of Denmark to thy father.
What wouldst thou have, Laertes?

LAERTES Dread my° lord, *My revered*
Your leave° and favour° to return to France, *consent / approval*
From whence though willingly I came to Denmark
To show my duty in your coronation,
Yet now I must confess, that duty done,
My thoughts and wishes bend again towards France
And bow them to your gracious leave and pardon.° *permission to depart*

KING CLAUDIUS Have you your father's leave? What says Polonius?

POLONIUS He hath, my lord, wrung from me my slow leave
By laboursome petition, and at last
Upon his will° I sealed my hard° consent. *wish / grudging*
I do beseech you give him leave to go.

KING CLAUDIUS Take thy fair hour,[4] Laertes. Time be thine,
And thy best graces spend it at thy will.
But now, my cousin[5] Hamlet, and my son—

HAMLET A little more than kin and less than kind[6]

KING CLAUDIUS How is it that the clouds still hang on you?

HAMLET Not so, my lord, I am too much i'th' sun.[7]

QUEEN GERTRUDE Good Hamlet, cast thy nightly colour[8] off,

8. That is, because the expenses and troops are drawn from his subjects.
9. Let your haste in this matter be worthy of your duty (to Denmark).
1. The King of Denmark; that is, Claudius himself.
2. That I will not grant you before you even ask it.
3. Closely and naturally related (an allusion to the "body politic").
4. Seize the moment (of your youth).
5. Kinsman (a term used for relatives more distant than one's brother or sister).
6. As Claudius's stepson, Hamlet is now more than "kin"; but because he is Claudius's nephew he is also less than "kind" (son). Hamlet is also punning that he feels less than kindly toward Claudius.
7. In the sunlight of Claudius's favor (with a pun on "son").
8. His melancholy behavior as well as his black mourning attire.

And let thine eye look like a friend on Denmark.
Do not for ever with thy vailèd° lids *downcast*
Seek for thy noble father in the dust.
Thou know'st 'tis common—all that lives must die,
Passing through nature to eternity.
HAMLET Ay, madam, it is common.[9]
QUEEN GERTRUDE If it be,
Why seems it so particular° with thee? *personal, special*
HAMLET Seems, madam? Nay, it *is*. I know not 'seems'.
'Tis not alone my inky cloak, good-mother,° *stepmother*
Nor customary suits of solemn black,
Nor windy suspiration° of forced breath, *sighing*
No, nor the fruitful° river in the eye, *productive (of tears)*
Nor the dejected haviour° of the visage, *expression*
Together with all forms, moods, shows of grief
That can denote me truly. These indeed 'seem',
For they are actions that a man might play;
But I have that within which passeth show—
These but the trappings and the suits of woe.
KING CLAUDIUS 'Tis sweet and commendable in your nature, Hamlet,
To give these mourning duties to your father;
But you must know your father lost a father;
That father lost, lost his; and the survivor bound
In filial obligation for some term
To do obsequious sorrow.[1] But to persever
In obstinate condolement° is a course *lamentation*
Of impious stubbornness, 'tis unmanly grief,
It shows a will most incorrect to° heaven, *defiant of*
A heart unfortified, a mind impatient,
An understanding simple° and unschooled; *childish, ignorant*
For what we know must be, and is as common
As any the most vulgar thing to sense,[2]
Why should we in our peevish opposition
Take it to heart? Fie, 'tis a fault to heaven,
A fault against the dead, a fault to nature,
To reason most absurd, whose common theme
Is death of fathers, and who still° hath cried *always*
From the first corpse[3] till he that died today,
'This must be so'. We pray you throw to earth
This unprevailing° woe, and think of us *ineffective*
As of a father; for let the world take note
You are the most immediate° to our throne, *next in succession*
And with no less nobility of love
Than that which dearest father bears his son

9. Generally true; Hamlet may also be implying that it is vulgar.
1. To mourn in a manner appropriate to funeral rites.
2. As common as any of the ordinary things we perceive through our senses.
3. An infelicitous reference to the biblical character Abel, who, like Hamlet's father, was killed by his brother.

Do I impart towards you. For your intent
In going back to school in Wittenberg,[4]
It is most retrograde° to our desire, *contrary*
And we beseech you bend you° to remain *submit yourself*
Here in the cheer and comfort of our eye,
Our chiefest courtier, cousin, and our son.

QUEEN GERTRUDE Let not thy mother lose her prayers, Hamlet.
I pray thee stay with us, go not to Wittenberg.

HAMLET I shall in all my best obey you, madam.

KING CLAUDIUS Why, 'tis a loving and a fair reply.
Be as ourself in Denmark. [*To* GERTRUDE] Madam, come.
This gentle and unforced accord of Hamlet
Sits smiling to° my heart; in grace° whereof, *Pleases / honor*
No jocund health that Denmark° drinks today *the King of Denmark*
But the great cannon to the clouds shall tell,° *proclaim, sound*
And the King's rouse[5] the heavens shall bruit° again, *loudly sound*
Re-speaking earthly thunder. Come, away.

Flourish. Exeunt all but HAMLET

HAMLET O that this too too solid[6] flesh would melt,
Thaw, and resolve° itself into a dew, *dissolve*
Or that the Everlasting had not fixed
His canon° 'gainst self-slaughter! O God, O God, *law*
How weary, stale, flat, and unprofitable
Seem to me all the uses° of this world! *employments; customs*
Fie on't, ah fie, fie! 'Tis an unweeded garden
That grows to seed; things rank and gross in nature
Possess it merely.° That it should come to this— *utterly*
But two months dead—nay, not so much, not two—
So excellent a king, that was to this° *(Claudius)*
Hyperion to a satyr,[7] so loving to my mother
That he might not beteem° the winds of heaven *permit*
Visit her face too roughly! Heaven and earth,
Must I remember? Why, she would hang on him
As if increase of appetite had grown
By what it fed on, and yet within a month—
Let me not think on't; frailty, thy name is woman—
A little month, or ere° those shoes were old *before*
With which she followed my poor father's body,
Like Niobe, all tears,[8] why she, even she—
O God, a beast that wants discourse of reason[9]
Would have mourned longer!—married with mine uncle,
My father's brother, but no more like my father

4. A university town in Germany.
5. A bout of drinking or a toast.
6. Instead of "solid," Q1 has "sallied," which is probably an obsolete form of "sullied": contaminated, soiled, polluted.
7. In classical myth, a woodland creature part man and part goat, known for lechery and love of wine. *Hyperion:* the sun god (a Titan).
8. In Greek myth, Niobe wept so ceaselessly for her children, killed by the gods Apollo and Artemis to punish her for boasting, that she was turned into a stone from which water endlessly flows.
9. That is, that lacks the capacity to reason.

Than I to Hercules;[1] within a month,
Ere yet the salt of most unrighteous° tears — *hypocritical*
Had left the flushing° of her gallèd° eyes, — *redness / inflamed*
She married. O most wicked speed, to post° — *hasten*
With such dexterity° to incestuous sheets![2] — *nimbleness, eagerness*
It is not, nor it cannot come to good.
But break,° my heart, for I must hold my tongue. — *stop*

Enter HORATIO, MARCELLUS, *and* BARNARDO

HORATIO Hail to your lordship.
HAMLET I am glad to see you well.
Horatio—or I do forget myself.
HORATIO The same, my lord, and your poor servant ever.
HAMLET Sir, my good friend; I'll change° that name with you. — *exchange*
And what make you from[3] Wittenberg, Horatio?—
Marcellus.
MARCELLUS My good lord.
HAMLET I am very glad to see you. [*To* BARNARDO] Good even, sir.—
But what in faith make you from Wittenberg?
HORATIO A truant disposition,° good my lord. — *desire to play truant*
HAMLET I would not have your enemy say so,
Nor shall you do mine ear that violence
To make it truster of your own report
Against yourself. I know you are no truant.
But what is your affair in Elsinore?
We'll teach you to drink deep ere you depart.
HORATIO My lord, I came to see your father's funeral.
HAMLET I prithee do not mock me, fellow-student;
I think it was to see my mother's wedding.
HORATIO Indeed, my lord, it followed hard upon.° — *soon after*
HAMLET Thrift, thrift, Horatio. The funeral baked meats
Did coldly° furnish forth the marriage tables. — *when cold*
Would I had met my dearest° foe in heaven — *most bitter*
Ere I had ever seen that day, Horatio.
My father—methinks I see my father.
HORATIO O where, my lord?
HAMLET In my mind's eye, Horatio.
HORATIO I saw him once. A° was a goodly king. — *He*
HAMLET A was a man. Take him for all in all,
I shall not look upon his like again.
HORATIO My lord, I think I saw him yesternight.
HAMLET Saw? Who?
HORATIO My lord, the King your father.
HAMLET The King my father?
HORATIO Season your admiration[4] for a while
With an attent° ear till I may deliver, — *attentive*

1. In classical mythology, the greatest of all heroes.
2. Both the Catholic Church and the Church of England condemned as incest the marriage between a man and his deceased brother's wife.
3. That is, what are you doing away from.
4. Temper your astonishment.

Upon the witness of these gentlemen,
This marvel to you.

HAMLET For God's love let me hear!

HORATIO Two nights together had these gentlemen,
Marcellus and Barnardo, on their watch,
In the dead waste and middle of the night,
Been thus encountered. A figure like your father,
Armed at all points° exactly, cap-à-pie,[5] *in every detail*
Appears before them, and with solemn march
Goes slow and stately by them. Thrice he walked
By their oppressed and fear-surprisèd eyes
Within his truncheon's length, whilst they distilled° *melted*
Almost to jelly with the act° of fear *effect*
Stand dumb and speak not to him. This to me
In dreadful secrecy impart they did,
And I with them the third night kept the watch,
Where, as they had delivered, both in time,
Form of the thing, each word made true and good,
The apparition comes. I knew your father;
These hands are not more like.[6]

HAMLET But where was this?

MARCELLUS My lord, upon the platform where we watched.

HAMLET Did you not speak to it?

HORATIO My lord, I did,
But answer made it none; yet once methought
It lifted up it° head and did address *its*
Itself to motion like as it would speak,[7]
But even° then the morning cock crew loud, *just*
And at the sound it shrunk in haste away
And vanished from our sight.

HAMLET 'Tis very strange.

HORATIO As I do live, my honoured lord, 'tis true,
And we did think it writ down° in our duty *stipulated*
To let you know of it.

HAMLET Indeed, indeed, sirs; but this troubles me.—
Hold you the watch tonight?

BARNARDO *and* MARCELLUS We do, my lord.

HAMLET Armed, say you?

BARNARDO *and* MARCELLUS Armed, my lord.

HAMLET From top to toe?

BARNARDO *and* MARCELLUS My lord, from head to foot.

HAMLET Then saw you not his face.

HORATIO O yes, my lord, he wore his beaver up.

HAMLET What° looked he? Frowningly? *How*

HORATIO A countenance more
In sorrow than in anger.

5. Head to foot (French).
6. That is, my hands resemble each other as much as the apparition resembled your father.
7. That is, it made a gesture as if it wanted to speak.

HAMLET Pale or red?
HORATIO Nay, very pale.
HAMLET And fixed his eyes upon you?
HORATIO Most constantly.
HAMLET I would I had been there.
HORATIO It would have much amazed you.
HAMLET Very like, very like. Stayed it long?
HORATIO While one with moderate haste might tell° a hundred. *count to*
BARNARDO *and* MARCELLUS Longer, longer.
HORATIO Not when I saw't.
HAMLET His beard was grizzly,° no? *gray*
HORATIO It was as I have seen it in his life,
A sable silvered.[8]
HAMLET I'll watch tonight. Perchance
'Twill walk again.
HORATIO I warrant° you it will. *guarantee*
HAMLET If it assume my noble father's person
I'll speak to it though hell itself should gape
And bid me hold my peace. I pray you all,
If you have hitherto concealed this sight,
Let it be treble[9] in your silence still,
And whatsoever else shall hap° tonight, *happen*
Give it an understanding but no tongue.
I will requite your loves. So fare ye well.
Upon the platform 'twixt eleven and twelve
I'll visit you.
ALL THREE Our duty to your honour.
HAMLET Your love, as mine to you. Farewell.
Exeunt [*all but* HAMLET]
My father's spirit in arms! All is not well.
I doubt° some foul play. Would the night were come. *suspect*
Till then, sit still, my soul. Foul deeds will rise,
Though all the earth o'erwhelm them, to men's eyes. *Exit*

1.3

Enter LAERTES *and* OPHELIA, *his sister*

LAERTES My necessaries are inbarqued.° Farewell. *aboard ship*
And, sister, as the winds give benefit
And convoy is assistant,[1] do not sleep
But let me hear from you.
OPHELIA Do you doubt that?
LAERTES For Hamlet and the trifling of his favour,
Hold it a fashion and a toy in blood,[2]
A violet in the youth of primy nature,
Forward° not permanent, sweet not lasting, *Precocious*

8. Black and gray (or white).
9. Triply. Q2 reads "tenable" (held close).
1.3 Location: Polonius's rooms in the castle.
1. That is, a means of transport is available.
2. That is, consider it a passing enthusiasm and an amorous flirtation.

The perfume and suppliance° of a minute, *diversion*
No more.
OPHELIA No more but so?
LAERTES Think it no more.
For nature crescent° does not grow alone *growing*
In thews° and bulk, but as his temple° waxes *muscles / body*
The inward service° of the mind and soul *duty*
Grows wide withal.° Perhaps he loves you now, *along with it*
And now no soil° nor cautel° doth besmirch *blemish / trickery*
The virtue of his will;° but you must fear, *desires*
His greatness weighed,° his will is not his own, *considered*
For he himself is subject to his birth.
He may not, as unvalued persons° do, *commoners*
Carve for himself,[3] for on his choice depends
The sanity° and health of the whole state; *well-being*
And therefore must his choice be circumscribed
Unto the voice° and yielding° of that body[4] *vote / consent*
Whereof he is the head. Then if he says he loves you,
It fits° your wisdom so far to believe it *befits*
As he in his peculiar sect and force[5]
May give his saying deed,[6] which is no further
Than the main° voice of Denmark goes withal. *general*
Then weigh what loss your honour may sustain
If with too credent° ear you list° his songs, *credulous / listen to*
Or lose your heart, or your chaste treasure open
To his unmastered° importunity. *unrestrained*
Fear it, Ophelia, fear it, my dear sister,
And keep within the rear of your affection,[7]
Out of the shot° and danger of desire. *range*
The chariest° maid is prodigal enough *most circumspect*
If she unmask her beauty to the moon.[8]
Virtue itself scapes not calumnious strokes.
The canker galls the infants[9] of the spring
Too oft before their buttons be disclosed,° *are open*
And in the morn and liquid dew of youth
Contagious blastments° are most imminent. *blights*
Be wary then; best safety lies in fear;
Youth to itself rebels, though none else near.
OPHELIA I shall th'effect of this good lesson keep
As watchman to my heart; but, good my brother,
Do not, as some ungracious° pastors do, *graceless; ungodly*
Show me the steep and thorny way to heaven
Whilst like a puffed° and reckless libertine *bloated, proud*

3. That is, choose for himself.
4. The body politic, the state.
5. His particular rank and power.
6. That is, may turn his words into actions.
7. That is, stay behind the front line of your feelings (a military metaphor).
8. The moon (identified in classical mythology with the virgin huntress goddess Artemis / Diana) here symbolizes chastity.
9. That is, the cankerworm damages the young plants.

Himself the primrose path of dalliance treads
And recks° not his own rede.° *heeds / advice*
LAERTES O fear me not.° *don't worry about me*

Enter POLONIUS

I stay too long—but here my father comes.
A double blessing is a double grace;
Occasion smiles upon a second leave.[1]
POLONIUS Yet here, Laertes? Aboard, aboard, for shame!
The wind sits in the shoulder° of your sail, *billow*
And you are stayed° for. There—my blessing with thee, *waited*
And these few precepts in thy memory
See thou character.° Give thy thoughts no tongue, *inscribe*
Nor any unproportioned° thought his act. *disorderly*
Be thou familiar° but by no means vulgar.[2] *friendly*
The friends thou hast, and their adoption tried,[3]
Grapple them to thy soul with hoops of steel,
But do not dull thy palm with entertainment[4]
Of each new-hatched unfledged comrade. Beware
Of entrance to a quarrel, but being in,
Bear't° that th'opposèd may beware of thee. *Handle it so*
Give every man thine ear but few thy voice.
Take each man's censure,° but reserve thy judgement. *opinion*
Costly thy habit° as thy purse can buy, *clothing*
But not expressed in fancy;° rich not gaudy; *frivolous fashion*
For the apparel oft proclaims the man,
And they in France of the best rank and station
Are of all most select and generous chief in that.[5]
Neither a borrower nor a lender be,
For loan oft loses both itself and friend,
And borrowing dulls the edge of husbandry.° *thrift*
This above all—to thine own self be true,
And it must follow, as the night the day,
Thou canst not then be false to any man.
Farewell—my blessing season° this in thee. *ripen, mature*
LAERTES Most humbly do I take my leave, my lord.
POLONIUS The time invites you. Go; your servants tend.° *await*
LAERTES Farewell, Ophelia, and remember well
What I have said to you.
OPHELIA 'Tis in my memory locked,
And you yourself shall keep the key of it.
LAERTES Farewell. *Exit*
POLONIUS What is't, Ophelia, he hath said to you?
OPHELIA So please you, something touching the Lord Hamlet.
POLONIUS Marry,[6] well bethought.

1. That is, it is a happy opportunity that affords a second farewell.
2. Indiscriminate in friendship.
3. Their friendship tested.
4. That is, do not make the palm of your hand callous by shaking the hand.
5. The nobles of France are first in displaying their rank through their fine apparel.
6. By the Virgin Mary (a mild oath).

'Tis told me he hath very oft of late
Given private time to you, and you yourself
Have of your audience° been most free and bounteous. *attention*
If it be so—as so 'tis put on° me, *to*
And that in way of caution—I must tell you
You do not understand yourself so clearly
As it behoves my daughter and your honour.
What is between you? Give me up the truth.

OPHELIA He hath, my lord, of late made many tenders° *offers*
Of his affection to me.

POLONIUS Affection, pooh! You speak like a green girl
Unsifted° in such perilous circumstance. *Inexperienced*
Do you believe his 'tenders' as you call them?

OPHELIA I do not know, my lord, what I should think.

POLONIUS Marry, I'll teach you: think yourself a baby
That you have ta'en his tenders for true pay,
Which are not sterling.° Tender° yourself more dearly, *genuine / Price*
Or—not to crack the wind of the poor phrase,
Running it thus—you'll tender me a fool.[7]

OPHELIA My lord, he hath importuned me with love
In honourable fashion—

POLONIUS Ay, fashion you may call it. Go to,[8] go to.

OPHELIA And hath given countenance° to his speech, my lord, *authority*
With all the vows of heaven.

POLONIUS Ay, springes° to catch woodcocks.[9] I do know *snares*
When the blood burns how prodigal° the soul *generously; wastefully*
Lends the tongue vows. These blazes, daughter,
Giving more light than heat, extinct° in both *extinguished*
Even in their promise as it is a-making,
You must not take for fire. From this time, daughter,
Be somewhat scanter of your maiden presence.
Set your entreatments at a higher rate
Than a command to parley.[1] For Lord Hamlet,
Believe so much in° him, that he is young, *about*
And with a larger tether may he walk
Than may be given you. In few,° Ophelia, *short*
Do not believe his vows, for they are brokers,° *go-betweens*
Not of the dye which their investments[2] show,
But mere imploratators° of unholy suits, *implorers*
Breathing° like sanctified and pious bawds *Whispering*
The better to beguile. This is for all—
I would not, in plain terms, from this time forth
Have you so slander° any moment leisure *disgrace*

7. You will make me look like a fool; you will present me with a grandchild ("fool" was often used as a synonym for "child"). *Crack . . . thus:* wear out the phrase by overusing it.
8. Come now (i.e., "don't be so naïve"). *Fashion:* flattery resulting from a passing and youthful fancy (see line 6).
9. Proverbially stupid birds.
1. That is, value your favors more highly than to grant every request for an interview.
2. Clerical vestments (i.e., they are not what they seem).

As to give words or talk with the Lord Hamlet.
Look to't, I charge you. Come your ways.° *Come along*
OPHELIA I shall obey, my lord. *Exeunt*

1.4

Enter [Prince] HAMLET, HORATIO, *and* MARCELLUS

HAMLET The air bites shrewdly,° it is very cold. *sharply*
HORATIO It is a nipping and an eager° air. *biting*
HAMLET What hour now?
HORATIO I think it lacks of twelve.
MARCELLUS No, it is struck.
HORATIO Indeed? I heard it not. Then it draws near the season° *time*
Wherein the spirit held his wont° to walk. *was accustomed*
A flourish of trumpets, and two pieces [of ordnance] goes off
What does this mean, my lord?
HAMLET The King doth wake tonight and takes his rouse,° *drinks*
Keeps wassail, and the swagg'ring upspring reels,[3]
And as he drains his draughts of Rhenish° down *Rhine wine*
The kettle-drum and trumpet thus bray out
The triumph of his pledge.[4]
HORATIO Is it a custom?
HAMLET Ay, marry is't,
And to my mind, though I am native here
And to the manner° born, it is a custom *custom*
More honoured in the breach than the observance.[5]
This heavy-headed revel east and west
Makes us traduced and taxed of° other nations. *criticized by*
They clepe° us drunkards, and with swinish phrase° *call / calling us pigs*
Soil our addition;° and indeed it takes *reputation*
From our achievements, though performed at height,° *most excellently*
The pith° and marrow of our attribute.° *heart / reputation*
So, oft it chances in particular men
That, for some vicious mole of nature[6] in them—
As in their birth,° wherein they are not guilty, *Inherited at birth*
Since nature cannot choose his° origin, *its*
By the o'ergrowth of some complexion,[7]
Oft breaking down the pales° and forts of reason, *fences, boundaries*
Or by some habit that too much o'erleavens
The form of plausive manners[8]—that these men,
Carrying, I say, the stamp of one defect,
Being nature's livery or fortune's star,[9]

1.4 Location: The battlements of the castle.
3. Staggers through a vigorous dance. *Wassail:* carousal, health drinking.
4. The triumph of his toast (achieved by emptying his cup at a single draught).
5. Lines 18.1 through 18.22 appear in Q2 but are omitted from F1.
6. A blemish in some men's nature that leads to vice.
7. That is, by the domination of one of the four humors, thought to determine character: black bile was held responsible for a melancholy disposition; blood, sanguine; yellow bile, choleric; and phlegm, phlegmatic.
8. That is, exerts its negative influence over pleasing manners (as too much leavening can ruin a batch of bread dough).
9. Either by a defect in their nature or the influence of ill fortune.

His virtues else° be they as pure as grace, — *other virtues*
As infinite as man may undergo,° — *sustain*
Shall in the general censure° take corruption — *public opinion*
From that particular fault. The dram of evil[1]
Doth all the noble substance over-daub° — *smear over*
To his own scandal.° — *disgrace*

Enter GHOST [*as before*]

HORATIO Look, my lord, it comes.
HAMLET Angels and ministers of grace defend us!
Be thou a spirit of health or goblin° damned, — *demon*
Bring with thee airs from heaven or blasts[2] from hell,
Be thy intents wicked or charitable,
Thou com'st in such a questionable° shape — *question-provoking*
That I will speak to thee. I'll call thee Hamlet,
King, father, royal Dane. O answer me!
Let me not burst in ignorance, but tell
Why thy canonized° bones, hearsèd° in death, — *sanctified / coffined*
Have burst their cerements,° why the sepulchre — *grave clothes*
Wherein we saw thee quietly enurned° — *entombed*
Hath oped his ponderous and marble jaws
To cast thee up again. What may this mean,
That thou, dead corpse, again in complete steel,° — *full armor*
Revisitst thus the glimpses of the moon,° — *shimmering moonlight*
Making night hideous, and we fools of nature[3]
So horridly to shake our disposition° — *state of mind*
With thoughts beyond the reaches of our souls?
Say, why is this? Wherefore? What should we do?

GHOST *beckons* HAMLET

HORATIO It beckons you to go away with it
As if it some impartment° did desire — *communication*
To you alone.
MARCELLUS [*to* HAMLET] Look with what courteous action
It wafts° you to a more removèd ground. — *waves, beckons*
But do not go with it.
HORATIO [*to* HAMLET] No, by no means.
HAMLET It will not speak. Then will I follow it.
HORATIO Do not, my lord.
HAMLET Why, what should be the fear?
I do not set my life at a pin's fee,° — *the worth of a pin*
And for my soul, what can it do to that,
Being a thing immortal as itself?

[GHOST *beckons* HAMLET]

It waves me forth again. I'll follow it.
HORATIO What if it tempt you toward the flood,° my lord, — *sea*

1. Minuscule amount of evil, punning on "evil" and "eale," or yeast (see line 18.13).
2. Foul, malignant airs that spreads infection. *Airs:* wholesome breezes.
3. Accustomed to the natural order of things (and therefore shaken by supernatural phenomena).

Or to the dreadful summit of the cliff
That beetles o'er° his base into the sea, *overhangs*
And there assume some other horrible form
Which might deprive your sovereignty of reason[4]
And draw you into madness? Think of it.[5]
The very place puts toys of desperation,° *desperate fancies*
Without more motive, into every brain
That looks so many fathoms to the sea
And hears it roar beneath.

[GHOST *beckons* HAMLET]

HAMLET It wafts me still. [*To* GHOST] Go on, I'll follow thee.
MARCELLUS You shall not go, my lord.
HAMLET Hold off your hand.
HORATIO Be ruled. You shall not go.
HAMLET My fate cries out,
And makes each petty artere° in this body *artery; sinew*
As hardy as the Nemean lion's[6] nerve.

[GHOST *beckons* HAMLET]

Still am I called. Unhand me, gentlemen.
By heav'n, I'll make a ghost of him that lets° me. *hinders*
I say, away! [*To* GHOST] Go on, I'll follow thee.

Exeunt GHOST *and* HAMLET

HORATIO He waxes desperate with imagination.
MARCELLUS Let's follow. 'Tis not fit thus to obey him.
HORATIO Have after.° To what issue° will this come? *Go on / end*
MARCELLUS Something is rotten in the state of Denmark.
HORATIO Heaven will direct it.° *(the outcome)*
MARCELLUS Nay, let's follow him. *Exeunt*

1.5

Enter GHOST, *and* [*Prince*] HAMLET [*following*]

HAMLET Whither wilt thou lead me? Speak. I'll go no further.
GHOST Mark me.
HAMLET I will.
GHOST My hour is almost come
When I to sulph'rous and tormenting flames
Must render up myself.
HAMLET Alas, poor ghost!
GHOST Pity me not, but lend thy serious hearing
To what I shall unfold.
HAMLET Speak, I am bound to hear.
GHOST So art thou to revenge when thou shalt hear.
HAMLET What?
GHOST I am thy father's spirit,

4. Deprive reason of its sovereignty over your mind.
5. Lines 55.1 through 55.4 appear in Q2 but not in F1.
6. In classical mythology, a lion whose skin was impervious to weapons; killing it was the first of Hercules' twelve labors.
1.5 Location: The battlements of the castle.

Doomed for a certain term to walk the night,
And for the day confined to fast° in fires — *do penance*
Till the foul crimes done in my days of nature° — *my natural life*
Are burnt and purged away.[7] But that I am forbid
To tell the secrets of my prison-house
I could a tale unfold whose lightest word
Would harrow up thy soul, freeze thy young blood,
Make thy two eyes like stars start from their spheres,
Thy knotty and combinèd locks to part,
And each particular hair to stand on end
Like quills upon the fretful porcupine.
But this eternal blazon[8] must not be
To ears of flesh and blood. List,° Hamlet, list, O list! — *Listen*
If thou didst ever thy dear father love—

HAMLET O God!

GHOST Revenge his foul and most unnatural murder.

HAMLET Murder?

GHOST Murder most foul, as in the best it is,
But this most foul, strange, and unnatural.

HAMLET Haste, haste me to know it, that[9] with wings as swift
As meditation or the thoughts of love
May sweep to my revenge.

GHOST I find thee apt,
And duller shouldst thou be than the fat° weed — *gross*
That rots itself in ease on Lethe wharf[1]
Wouldst thou not stir in this. Now, Hamlet, hear.
'Tis given out that, sleeping in mine orchard,° — *garden*
A serpent stung me. So the whole ear of Denmark
Is by a forgèd process° of my death — *false account*
Rankly abused.° But know, thou noble youth, — *deceived*
The serpent that did sting thy father's life
Now wears his crown.

HAMLET O my prophetic soul! Mine uncle?

GHOST Ay, that incestuous, that adulterate° beast, — *adulterous*
With witchcraft of his wit, with traitorous gifts°— — *talents*
O wicked wit and gifts, that have the power
So to seduce!—won to his shameful lust
The will of my most seeming-virtuous queen.
O Hamlet, what a falling off was there!—
From me, whose love was of that dignity
That it went hand-in-hand even with the vow
I made to her in marriage, and to decline
Upon a wretch whose natural gifts were poor
To° those of mine. — *Compared to*
But virtue, as it never will be moved,

7. A description that suggests purgatory, the place, mainly associated with Catholicism, where the dead expiate their sins by suffering.
8. Revelation of eternal things.
9. So that I; "I," missing in F1, is supplied in Q2.
1. The bank of Lethe, the river in the classical underworld whose waters cause forgetfulness. *Rots . . . ease:* decays in passive growth.

Though lewdness court it in a shape of heaven,
So lust, though to a radiant angel linked,
Will sate itself in a celestial bed,
And prey on garbage.
But soft,° methinks I scent the morning's air. *wait*
Brief let me be. Sleeping within mine orchard,
My custom always in the afternoon,
Upon my secure hour thy uncle stole
With juice of cursèd hebenon[2] in a vial,
And in the porches° of mine ears did pour *entrances*
The leperous distilment,° whose effect *extracted essence*
Holds such an enmity with blood of man
That swift as quicksilver it courses through
The natural gates and alleys of the body,
And with a sudden vigour it doth posset° *curdle*
And curd, like eager° droppings into milk, *sour, acid*
The thin and wholesome blood. So did it mine;
And a most instant tetter barked about,[3]
Most lazar-like,° with vile and loathsome crust, *like a leper*
All my smooth body.
Thus was I, sleeping, by a brother's hand
Of life, of crown, of queen at once dispatched,° *dispossessed*
Cut off even in the blossoms of my sin,[4]
Unhouseled, disappointed, unaneled,[5]
No reck'ning made, but sent to my account
With all my imperfections on my head.
O horrible, O horrible, most horrible!
If thou hast nature° in thee, bear it not. *natural feeling*
Let not the royal bed of Denmark be
A couch for luxury° and damnèd incest. *lust*
But howsoever thou pursuest this act,
Taint not thy mind,[6] nor let thy soul contrive
Against thy mother aught.° Leave her to heaven, *anything whatsoever*
And to those thorns that in her bosom lodge
To prick and sting her. Fare thee well at once.
The glow-worm shows the matin° to be near, *morning*
And gins° to pale his uneffectual fire. *begins*
Adieu, adieu, Hamlet. Remember me. *Exit*

HAMLET O all you host of heaven! O earth! What else?
And shall I couple° hell? O fie! Hold, hold, my heart, *add*
And you, my sinews, grow not instant old,
But bear me stiffly up. Remember thee?
Ay, thou poor ghost, while memory holds a seat

2. A poison; possibly a confusion for "henbane," a plant with poisonous properties.
3. That is, a pustular eruption of the skin ("tetter") covered the body as bark covers a tree.
4. That is, before there was an opportunity to confess and repent sins.
5. Without the Eucharist ("unhouseled"); unprepared ("disappointed"), because unconfessed and unrepentant; and without receiving extreme unction or anointing ("unaneled").
6. Do not become corrupted yourself.

In this distracted globe.[7] Remember thee?
Yea, from the table° of my memory *tablet*
I'll wipe away all trivial fond° records, *foolish*
All saws of books, all forms, all pressures past,[8]
That youth and observation copied there,
And thy commandment all alone shall live
Within the book and volume of my brain
Unmixed with baser matter. Yes, yes, by heaven.
O most pernicious woman!
O villain, villain, smiling, damnèd villain!
My tables,° *writing tablets*
My tables—meet° it is I set it down *fitting*
That one may smile and smile and be a villain.
At least I'm sure it may be so in Denmark.
[*He writes*]
So, uncle, there you are. Now to my word:[9]
It is 'Adieu, adieu, remember me'.
I have sworn't.

HORATIO *and* MARCELLUS [*within*] My lord, my lord.

Enter HORATIO *and* MARCELLUS

MARCELLUS [*calling*] Lord Hamlet!
HORATIO Heaven secure him.
HAMLET So be it.
HORATIO [*calling*] Illo,[1] ho, ho, my lord.
HAMLET Hillo, ho, ho, boy; come, bird, come.
MARCELLUS How is't, my noble lord?
HORATIO [*to* HAMLET] What news, my lord?
HAMLET O wonderful!° *astonishing*
HORATIO Good my lord, tell it.
HAMLET No, you'll reveal it.
HORATIO Not I, my lord, by heaven.
MARCELLUS Nor I, my lord.
HAMLET How say you then, would heart of man once think it?
But you'll be secret?
HORATIO *and* MARCELLUS Ay, by heav'n, my lord.
HAMLET There's ne'er a villain dwelling in all Denmark
But he's an arrant° knave. *out-and-out*
HORATIO There needs no ghost, my lord, come from the grave
To tell us this.
HAMLET Why, right, you are i'th' right,
And so without more circumstance° at all *ceremony*
I hold it fit that we shake hands and part,
You as your business and desires shall point you—
For every man has business and desire,
Such as it is—and for mine own poor part,

7. Troubled earth; perhaps, confused head; also perhaps a reference to the Globe theater in which *Hamlet* was performed.
8. That is, all wise sayings from books, all shape or customs, all past impressions.
9. Perhaps, watchword; or the ghost's command; or oath.
1. A falconer's cry to his hawk.

Look you, I'll go pray.
HORATIO These are but wild and whirling words, my lord.
HAMLET I'm sorry they offend you, heartily,
Yes, faith, heartily.
HORATIO There's no offence, my lord.
HAMLET Yes, by Saint Patrick, but there is, Horatio,
And much offence, too. Touching this vision here,
It is an honest° ghost, that let me tell you. *truthful, reliable*
For your desire to know what is between us,
O'ermaster't as you may. And now, good friends,
As you are friends, scholars, and soldiers,
Give me one poor request.
HORATIO What is't, my lord? We will.
HAMLET Never make known what you have seen tonight.
HORATIO *and* MARCELLUS My lord, we will not.
HAMLET Nay, but swear't.
HORATIO In faith, my lord, not I.[2]
MARCELLUS Nor I, my lord, in faith.
HAMLET Upon my sword.
MARCELLUS We have sworn, my lord, already.
HAMLET Indeed, upon my sword, indeed.
GHOST *cries under the stage*
GHOST Swear.
HAMLET Ah ha, boy, sayst thou so? Art thou there, truepenny?°— *honest fellow*
Come on. You hear this fellow in the cellarage.
Consent to swear.
HORATIO Propose the oath, my lord.
HAMLET Never to speak of this that you have seen,
Swear by my sword.
GHOST [*under the stage*] Swear.
[*They swear*]
HAMLET *Hic et ubique?*[3] Then we'll shift our ground. —
Come hither, gentlemen,
And lay your hands again upon my sword.
Never to speak of this that you have heard,
Swear by my sword.
GHOST [*under the stage*] Swear.
[*They swear*]
HAMLET Well said, old mole. Canst work i'th' earth so fast?
A worthy pioneer.°—Once more remove,° good friends. *miner / move*
HORATIO O day and night, but this is wondrous strange!
HAMLET And therefore as a stranger give it welcome.[4]
There are more things in heaven and earth, Horatio,
Than are dreamt of in our philosophy.[5] But come,

2. Indeed, I will not reveal it.
3. Here and everywhere (Latin).
4. That is, welcome it with the courtesy due to a stranger.
5. Natural philosophy (i.e., science).

Here as before, never, so help you mercy,
How strange or odd soe'er I bear myself—
As I perchance hereafter shall think meet
To put an antic disposition on[6]—
That you at such time seeing me never shall,
With arms encumbered° thus, or this headshake, *folded*
Or by pronouncing of some doubtful° phrase *ambiguous*
As 'Well, we know' or 'We could an if° we would', *if only*
Or 'If we list° to speak', or 'There be, an if they might',[7] *liked*
Or such ambiguous giving out, to note
That you know aught° of me—this not to do, *anything*
So grace and mercy at your most need help you, swear.

GHOST [*under the stage*] Swear.

[*They swear*]

HAMLET Rest, rest, perturbèd spirit.—So, gentlemen,
With all my love I do commend me to you,
And what so poor a man as Hamlet is
May do t'express his love and friending° to you, *friendship*
God willing, shall not lack.° Let us go in together, *be deficient*
And still° your fingers on your lips, I pray. *always*
The time is out of joint.° O cursèd spite *in complete disorder*
That ever I was born to set it right!
Nay, come, let's go together.[8] *Exeunt*

2.1

Enter old POLONIUS *with his man* REYNALDO

POLONIUS Give him this money and these notes, Reynaldo.

REYNALDO I will, my lord.

POLONIUS You shall do marv'lous wisely, good Reynaldo,
Before you visit him to make enquire
Of his behaviour.

REYNALDO My lord, I did intend it.

POLONIUS Marry, well said, very well said. Look you, sir,
Enquire me° first what Danskers° are in Paris, *for me / Danes*
And how, and who, what means,° and where they keep,° *means of income* / *reside*
What company, at what expense; and finding
By this encompassment and drift of question[9]
That they do know my son, come you more nearer
Than your particular demands will touch it.[1]
Take you,° as 'twere, some distant knowledge of him, *Pretend*
As thus: 'I know his father and his friends,
And in part him'—do you mark this, Reynaldo?

REYNALDO Ay, very well, my lord.

6. To behave fantastically, to act like a madman.
7. There are those who would say this or that if they could so do safely.
8. Hamlet tells the others to depart with him (rather than to follow him, as befitting his rank).
2.1 Location: Polonius's rooms in the castle.
9. By this roundabout manner of questioning.
1. You will come nearer to the truth than if you make direct inquiries.

POLONIUS 'And in part him, but', you may say, 'not well,
But if't be he I mean, he's very wild,
Addicted so and so'; and there put on him° *accuse him of*
What forgeries[2] you please—marry, none so rank° *heinous*
As may dishonour him, take heed of that
But, sir, such wanton,° wild, and usual slips *unrestrained*
As are companions noted and most known
To youth and liberty.
REYNALDO As gaming, my lord?
POLONIUS Ay, or drinking, fencing, swearing,
Quarrelling, drabbing°—you may go so far. *whoring*
REYNALDO My lord, that would dishonour him.
POLONIUS Faith, no, as you may season° it in the charge. *moderate*
You must not put another scandal on him,
That he is open° to incontinency.° *given to / sexual excess*
That's not my meaning—but breathe his faults so quaintly° *delicately*
That they may seem the taints of liberty,[3]
The flash and outbreak of a fiery mind,
A savageness in unreclaimèd° blood, *untamed*
Of general assault.[4]
REYNALDO But, my good lord—
POLONIUS Wherefore° should you do this? *Why*
REYNALDO Ay, my lord.
I would know that.
POLONIUS Marry, sir, here's my drift,
And I believe it is a fetch of warrant:° *justifiable deception*
You laying these slight sullies on my son,
As 'twere a thing a little soiled i'th' working,[5]
Mark you, your party° in converse, him you would sound,° *partner / sound out*
Having° ever seen in the prenominate crimes[6] *If he has*
The youth you breathe of guilty, be assured
He closes with° you in this consequence:[7] *discloses to*
'Good sir', or so, or 'friend', or 'gentleman',
According to the phrase° and the addition[8] *expression*
Of man and country.
REYNALDO Very good, my lord.
POLONIUS And then, sir, does a° this—a does— *he*
what was I about to say? By the mass,° I was about to say *(a mild oath)*
something. Where did I leave?
REYNALDO At 'closes in the consequence', at 'friend,
Or so', and 'gentleman'.
POLONIUS At 'closes in the consequence'—ay, marry,
He closes with you thus: 'I know the gentleman,
I saw him yesterday'—or t'other day,
Or then, or then—'with such and such, and, as you say,

2. False accusations.
3. The blemishes that result from freedom without discipline.
4. To which all young men are prone.
5. Shopworn (i.e., slightly soiled while coming to maturity).
6. Aforementioned transgressions.
7. In the following manner
8. Title; customary style of address.

There was a° gaming, there o'ertook in 's rouse, — *he*
There falling out° at tennis', or perchance — *quarreling*
'I saw him enter such a house of sale',
Videlicet,° a brothel, or so forth. See you now, — *That is to say (Latin)*
Your bait of falsehood takes this carp of truth;
And thus do we of wisdom and of reach° — *understanding*
With windlasses and with assays of bias[9]
By indirections find directions out.[1]
So, by my former° lecture and advice, — *previous*
Shall you my son. You have me,° have you not? — *have my meaning*

REYNALDO My lord, I have.
POLONIUS God b'wi' ye. Fare ye well.
REYNALDO Good my lord.
POLONIUS Observe his inclination in° yourself. — *for*
REYNALDO I shall, my lord.
POLONIUS And let him ply° his music. — *practice*
REYNALDO Well, my lord.

Enter OPHELIA

POLONIUS Farewell. *Exit* REYNALDO
How now, Ophelia, what's the matter?
OPHELIA Alas, my lord, I have been so affrighted.
POLONIUS With what, i'th' name of God?
OPHELIA My lord, as I was sewing in my chamber,
Lord Hamlet, with his doublet all unbraced,° — *his jacket unlaced*
No hat upon his head, his stockings fouled,
Ungartered, and down-gyvèd to his ankle,[2]
Pale as his shirt, his knees knocking each other,
And with a look so piteous in purport
As if he had been loosèd out of hell
To speak of horrors, he comes before me.
POLONIUS Mad for thy love?
OPHELIA My lord, I do not know,
But truly I do fear it.
POLONIUS What said he?
OPHELIA He took me by the wrist and held me hard,
Then goes he to the length of all his arm,
And with his other hand thus o'er his brow
He falls to such perusal of my face
As a° would draw it. Long stayed he so. — *As if he*
At last, a little shaking of mine arm,
And thrice his head thus waving up and down,
He raised a sigh so piteous and profound
That it did seem to shatter all his bulk° — *body*
And end his being. That done, he lets me go,
And, with his head over his shoulder turned,
He seemed to find his way without his eyes,

9. That is, indirect efforts: a "windlass" is a roundabout approach to intercept the game in hunting; "bias" is the curve taken by the ball toward its target in the game of bowls.

1. That is, by indirect means find out the truth.

2. Fallen down around his ankles like shackles (gyves).

For out o' doors he went without their help,
And to the last bended their light[3] on me.
POLONIUS Come, go with me. I will go seek the King.
This is the very ecstasy° of love, *insanity*
Whose violent property fordoes° itself *destroys*
And leads the will to desperate undertakings
As oft as any passion under heaven
That does afflict our natures. I am sorry—
What, have you given him any hard words of late?
OPHELIA No, my good lord, but as you did command
I did repel his letters and denied
His access to me.
POLONIUS That hath made him mad.
I am sorry that with better speed and judgement
I had not quoted° him. I feared he did but trifle *observed*
And meant to wreck thee. But beshrew my jealousy![4]
By heaven, it is as proper to our age
To cast beyond ourselves[5] in our opinions
As it is common for the younger sort
To lack discretion. Come, go we to the King.
This must be known, which, being kept close,° might move *secret*
More grief to hide than hate to utter love.[6] *Exeunt*

2.2

Flourish. Enter KING [CLAUDIUS] *and* QUEEN [GERTRUDE],
ROSENCRANTZ *and* GUILDENSTERN, *cum aliis*° *with others (Latin)*

KING CLAUDIUS Welcome, dear Rosencrantz and Guildenstern.
Moreover° that we much did long to see you, *Besides*
The need we have to use you did provoke
Our hasty sending.° Something have you heard *summons*
Of Hamlet's transformation—so I call it,
Since not th'exterior nor the inward man
Resembles that° it was. What it should be, *what*
More than his father's death, that thus hath put him
So much from th'understanding of himself,
I cannot deem of.° I entreat you both *judge*
That, being of so young days° brought up with him, *from childhood*
And since so neighboured to[7] his youth and humour,° *disposition*
That you vouchsafe your rest° here in our court *agree to remain*
Some little time, so by your companies
To draw him on to pleasures, and to gather,
So much as from occasions° you may glean, *opportunities*
Whether aught to us unknown afflicts him thus
That, opened,° lies within our remedy. *if revealed*

3. That is, the light that eyes were thought to emit.
4. Curse my suspicious nature. *Wreck thee:* take your virginity
5. Go too far (by way of caution). *Proper to our age:* i.e., characteristic of men of Polonius's own (advanced) age.
6. That is, might cause more grief if kept secret than it would incur hatred (or disapproval) if revealed.
2.2 Location: A stateroom in the castle.
7. Familiar with.

QUEEN GERTRUDE Good gentlemen, he hath much talked of you,
And sure I am two men there is not living
To whom he more adheres.° If it will please you *is more attached*
To show us so much gentry° and good will *courtesy*
As to expend your time with us a while
For the supply and profit[8] of our hope,
Your visitation shall receive such thanks
As fits a king's remembrance.

ROSENCRANTZ Both your majesties
Might, by the sovereign power you have of° us, *over*
Put your dread° pleasures more into command *revered*
Than to entreaty.

GUILDENSTERN But we both obey,
And here give up ourselves in the full bent° *to our utmost*
To lay our service freely at your feet
To be commanded.

KING CLAUDIUS Thanks, Rosencrantz and gentle Guildenstern.

QUEEN GERTRUDE Thanks, Guildenstern and gentle Rosencrantz.
And I beseech you instantly to visit
My too-much changèd son.—Go, some of ye,
And bring the gentlemen where Hamlet is.

GUILDENSTERN Heavens make our presence and our practices° *doings; stratagems*
Pleasant and helpful to him.

QUEEN GERTRUDE Ay, amen!

Exeunt ROSENCRANTZ *and* GUILDENSTERN [*with others*]

Enter POLONIUS

POLONIUS Th'ambassadors from Norway, my good lord,
Are joyfully returned.

KING CLAUDIUS Thou still° hast been the father of good news. *always*

POLONIUS Have I, my lord? Assure you, my good liege,
I hold my duty, as I hold my soul,
Both to my God and to my gracious King.
And I do think—or else this brain of mine
Hunts not the trail of policy° so sure *statecraft*
As it hath used to do—that I have found
The very cause of Hamlet's lunacy.

KING CLAUDIUS O speak of that, that I do long to hear!

POLONIUS Give first admittance to th'ambassadors.
My news shall be the fruit° to that great feast. *dessert*

KING CLAUDIUS Thyself do grace to them, and bring them in.

[*Exit* POLONIUS]

He tells me, my sweet queen, that he hath found
The head° and source of all your son's distemper. *chief reason; source*

QUEEN GERTRUDE I doubt° it is no other but the main°— *suspect / main cause*
His father's death and our o'er-hasty marriage.

KING CLAUDIUS Well, we shall sift him.° *question (Polonius)*

8. Support and advancement.

Enter POLONIUS, VALTEMAND, *and* CORNELIUS

Welcome, my good friends.
Say, Valtemand, what from our brother° Norway? *fellow monarch*

VALTEMAND Most fair return of greetings and desires.° *good wishes*
Upon our first[9] he sent out to suppress
His nephew's levies, which to him appeared
To be a preparation 'gainst the Polack;° *the King of Poland*
But better looked into, he truly found
It was against your highness; whereat grieved
That so his sickness, age, and impotence
Was falsely borne in hand,[1] sends out arrests
On Fortinbras,[2] which he, in brief, obeys,
Receives rebuke from Norway, and, in fine,° *conclusion*
Makes vow before his uncle never more
To give th'essay of arms[3] against your majesty;
Whereon old Norway, overcome with joy,
Gives him three thousand crowns in annual fee° *payment*
And his commission to employ those soldiers
So levied as before, against the Polack,
With an entreaty herein further shown,
[*He gives a letter to* CLAUDIUS]
That it might please you to give quiet pass
Through your dominions for his enterprise
On such regards of safety and allowance[4]
As therein are set down.

KING CLAUDIUS It likes° us well, *pleases*
And at our more considered time[5] we'll read,
Answer, and think upon this business.
Meantime we thank you for your well took labour.
Go to your rest; at night we'll feast together.
Most welcome home.

Exeunt [VALTEMAND *and* CORNELIUS]

POLONIUS This business is very well ended.
My liege, and madam, to expostulate° *reason earnestly*
What majesty should be, what duty is,
Why day is day, night night, and time is time,
Were nothing but to waste night, day, and time.
Therefore, since brevity is the soul of wit,° *wisdom*
And tediousness the limbs and outward flourishes,° *rhetorical flourishes*
I will be brief. Your noble son is mad—
'Mad' call I it, for to define true madness,
What is't but to be nothing else but mad?
But let that go.

QUEEN GERTRUDE More matter with less art.° *rhetorical art*

9. When we first broached the matter (of young Fortinbras's military preparations).
1. That is, was deceitfully taken advantage of.
2. Orders to Fortinbras to stop his military action against Denmark.
3. To undertake military action.
4. With such safeguards and stipulations.
5. A convenient time for further consideration.

POLONIUS Madam, I swear I use no art at all.
That he is mad, 'tis true; 'tis true 'tis pity,
And pity 'tis 'tis true—a foolish figure,° *figure of speech*
But farewell it,° for I will use no art. *to it*
Mad let us grant him, then; and now remains
That we find out the cause of this effect—
Or rather say 'the cause of this *defect*',
For this effect defective comes by cause.[6]
Thus it remains, and the remainder thus.
Perpend.° *Consider*
I have a daughter—have whilst she is mine°— *until she marries*
Who in her duty and obedience, mark,
Hath given me this. Now gather and surmise.

[*He reads a*] *letter*

'To the celestial and my soul's idol, the most beautified° *beautiful*
Ophelia'— that's an ill phrase, a vile phrase, 'beautified'
is a vile phrase. But you shall hear—'these° in her excel- *these letters*
lent white bosom,[7] these'.

QUEEN GERTRUDE Came this from Hamlet to her?

POLONIUS Good madam, stay° a while. I will be faithful.° *wait / read faithfully*
'Doubt thou the stars are fire,
Doubt that the sun doth move,
Doubt° truth to be a liar, *Suspect*
But never doubt I love.
O dear Ophelia, I am ill at these numbers.[8] I have not art
to reckon my groans.[9] But that I love thee best, O most best,
believe it. Adieu.
Thine evermore, most dear lady, whilst this
machine is° to him, *body belongs*
Hamlet.'
This in obedience hath my daughter showed me,
And more above° hath his solicitings, *moreover*
As they fell out° by time, by means, and place, *came to pass*
All given to mine ear.

KING CLAUDIUS But how hath she
Received his love?

POLONIUS What do you think of me?

KING CLAUDIUS As of a man faithful and honourable.

POLONIUS I would fain° prove so. But what might you think, *gladly*
When I had seen this hot love on the wing,
As I perceived it—I must tell you that—
Before my daughter told me, what might you,
Or my dear majesty your queen here, think,
If I had played the desk or table-book,[1]
Or given my heart a winking° mute and dumb, *closing of the eyes*
Or looked upon this love with idle sight—

6. That is, this effect, which in Hamlet is a defect (i.e., his madness), has a cause.
7. Where love letters should be kept.
8. Bad at writing verses.
9. Count my groans (in metrical verse).
1. That is, if I had kept this knowledge secret.

What might you think? No, I went round° to work, *straightaway*
And my young mistress thus I did bespeak:° *address*
'Lord Hamlet is a prince out of thy star.[2]
This must not be'. And then I precepts gave her,
That she should lock herself from his resort,° *company*
Admit no messengers, receive no tokens;
Which done, she took the fruits of my advice,
And he, repulsèd—a short tale to make—
Fell into a sadness, then into a fast,
Thence to a watch,° thence into a weakness, *insomnia*
Thence to a lightness,° and, by this declension,° *light-headedness / decline*
Into the madness wherein now he raves,
And all we° wail for. *of us*

KING CLAUDIUS [*to* GERTRUDE] Do you think 'tis this?

QUEEN GERTRUDE It may be; very likely.

POLONIUS Hath there been such a time—I'd fain know that—
That I have positively said ''Tis so'
When it proved otherwise?

KING CLAUDIUS Not that I know.

POLONIUS [*touching his head, then his shoulder*]
Take this from this if this be otherwise.
If circumstances lead me I will find
Where truth is hid, though it were hid indeed
Within the centre.[3]

KING CLAUDIUS How may we try° it further? *test*

POLONIUS You know sometimes he walks four hours together
Here in the lobby.

QUEEN GERTRUDE So he does indeed.

POLONIUS At such a time I'll loose my daughter to him.
[*To* CLAUDIUS] Be you and I behind an arras° then. *a hanging tapestry*
Mark the encounter. If he love her not,
And be not from his reason fall'n thereon,° *for that reason*
Let me be no assistant for a state,
But keep a farm and carters.° *cart drivers*

KING CLAUDIUS We will try it.

Enter [*Prince*] HAMLET, [*madly attired,*] *reading on a book*

QUEEN GERTRUDE But look where sadly the poor wretch comes reading.

POLONIUS Away, I do beseech you both, away.
I'll board him presently.[4] O give me leave.

Exit KING *and* QUEEN

How does my good Lord Hamlet?

HAMLET Well, God-'a'-mercy.[5]

POLONIUS Do you know me, my lord?

HAMLET Excellent, excellent well. You're a fishmonger.

POLONIUS Not I, my lord.

HAMLET Then I would you were so honest a man.

POLONIUS Honest, my lord?

2. Above your sphere (a reference to the concentric spheres of the Ptolemaic universe).
3. The center of the earth (which, in the Ptolemaic system, is also the center of the universe).
4. I'll approach him immediately.
5. God have mercy (on you); a courteous response to a greeting.

HAMLET Ay, sir. To be honest, as this world goes, is to be one man picked out of ten thousand.

POLONIUS That's very true, my lord.

HAMLET For if the sun breed maggots in a dead dog, being a good kissing carrion[6]—have you a daughter?

POLONIUS I have, my lord.

HAMLET Let her not walk i'th' sun. Conception[7] is a blessing, but not as your daughter may conceive. Friend, look to't.°

be careful about that

POLONIUS [*aside*] How say you by that? Still harping on my daughter. Yet he knew me not at first—a° said I was a fishmonger. A is far gone, far gone, and truly, in my youth I suffered much extremity for love, very near this. I'll speak to him again.—What do you read, my lord?

he

HAMLET Words, words, words.

POLONIUS What is the matter,[8] my lord?

HAMLET Between who?

POLONIUS I mean the matter you read, my lord.

HAMLET Slanders, sir; for the satirical slave° says here that old men have grey beards, that their faces are wrinkled, their eyes purging° thick amber° or plum-tree gum, and that they have a plentiful lack of wit,° together with most weak hams.° All which, sir, though I most powerfully and potently believe, yet I hold it not honesty° to have it thus set down; for you yourself, sir, should be old as I am—if, like a crab, you could go backward.

rogue
discharging / resin
intelligence
thighs
proper, honorable

POLONIUS [*aside*] Though this be madness, yet there is method in't.—Will you walk out of the air,[9] my lord?

HAMLET Into my grave.

POLONIUS Indeed, that is out o'th' air. [*Aside*] How pregnant° sometimes his replies are! A happiness° that often madness hits on, which reason and sanity could not so prosperously° be delivered of. I will leave him, and suddenly° contrive the means of meeting between him and my daughter.—My lord, I will take my leave of you.

full of meaning / An aptness
successfully
right away

HAMLET You cannot, sir, take from me anything that I will more willingly part withal°—except my life, my life, my life.

with

POLONIUS [*going*] Fare you well, my lord.

HAMLET These tedious old fools!

Enter GUILDENSTERN *and* ROSENCRANTZ

POLONIUS You go to seek the Lord Hamlet. There he is.

ROSENCRANTZ God save you, sir.

GUILDENSTERN [*to* POLONIUS] Mine honoured lord.

[*Exit* POLONIUS]

6. Flesh good enough for the sun to "kiss." "Carrion" most often refers to a dead carcass, but it can also refer contemptuously to living flesh, with a sexual connotation.

7. The power to form ideas; pregnancy. *Let . . . sun:* have her avoid public spaces; keep her away from me (with a pun on "sun"/"son," and the use of the sun as an emblem of royalty).

8. Subject (but Hamlet takes it as a conflict between two parties).

9. Fresh air was thought harmful to the sick.

ROSENCRANTZ [*to* HAMLET] My most dear lord.

HAMLET My ex'llent good friends. How dost thou, Guildenstern? Ah, Rosencrantz—good lads, how do ye both?

ROSENCRANTZ As the indifferent children° of the earth. *ordinary men*

GUILDENSTERN Happy° in that we are not over-happy, *Fortunate*
On Fortune's cap we are not the very button.° *top*

HAMLET Nor the soles of her shoe?

ROSENCRANTZ Neither, my lord.

HAMLET Then you live about her waist, or in the middle of her favour?

GUILDENSTERN Faith, her privates[1] we.

HAMLET In the secret parts of Fortune? O, most true, she is a strumpet.° What's the news? *whore*

ROSENCRANTZ None, my lord, but that the world's grown honest.

HAMLET Then is doomsday near. But your news is not true. Let me question more in particular. What have you, my good friends, deserved at the hands of Fortune that she sends you to prison hither?

GUILDENSTERN Prison, my lord?

HAMLET Denmark's a prison.

ROSENCRANTZ Then is the world one.

HAMLET A goodly° one, in which there are many confines,° *spacious; fine / cells*
wards, and dungeons, Denmark being one o'th' worst.

ROSENCRANTZ We think not so, my lord.

HAMLET Why, then 'tis none to you, for there is nothing either good or bad but thinking makes it so. To me it is a prison.

ROSENCRANTZ Why, then your ambition makes it one;[2] 'tis too narrow for your mind.

HAMLET O God, I could be bounded in a nutshell and count myself a king of infinite space, were it not that I have bad dreams.

GUILDENSTERN Which dreams indeed are ambition; for the very substance of the ambitious is merely the shadow of a dream.

HAMLET A dream itself is but a shadow.

ROSENCRANTZ Truly, and I hold ambition of so airy and light a quality that it is but a shadow's shadow.

HAMLET Then are our beggars bodies, and our monarchs and outstretched heroes the beggars' shadows.[3] Shall we to th' court? For, by my fay,° I cannot reason. *faith*

ROSENCRANTZ *and* GUILDENSTERN We'll wait upon you.° *come with you*

HAMLET No such matter.° I will not sort° you with the *Absolutely not / class*
rest of my servants, for, to speak to you like an honest

1. Private parts; close friends; ordinary subjects (without title or office).
2. Rosencrantz assumes that Hamlet thinks of Denmark as a prison because he did not succeed to his father's throne.
3. That is, then it follows that beggars have bodies (because they have no ambitions), and kings and heroes, whose ambitions are extreme and stretched out, have none; and their shadows must therefore be the shadows of beggars.

man, I am most dreadfully attended.° But in the beaten way[4] of friendship, what make you at° Elsinore? — *waited upon* / *brings you to*

ROSENCRANTZ To visit you, my lord, no other occasion.

HAMLET Beggar that I am, I am even poor in thanks, but I thank you; and sure, dear friends, my thanks are too dear a half-penny.[5] Were you not sent for? Is it your own inclining? Is it a free° visitation? Come, deal justly with me. Come, come. Nay, speak. — *voluntary*

GUILDENSTERN What should we say, my lord?

HAMLET Why, anything—but to th' purpose. You were sent for, and there is a kind of confession in your looks which your modesties have[6] not craft enough to colour.° I know the good King and Queen have sent for you. — *conceal*

ROSENCRANTZ To what end, my lord?

HAMLET That you must teach me. But let me conjure° you by the rights of our fellowship, by the consonancy° of our youth, by the obligation of our ever-preserved love, and by what more dear a better proposer could charge you withal,° be even° and direct with me whether you were sent for or no. — *implore* / *concord, friendship* / *besides / honest*

ROSENCRANTZ [*to* GUILDENSTERN] What say you?

HAMLET Nay then, I have an eye of° you—if you love me, hold not off.° — *on* / *speak freely*

GUILDENSTERN My lord, we were sent for.

HAMLET I will tell you why. So shall my anticipation prevent your discovery,[7] and your secrecy to the King and Queen moult no feather.° I have of late—but wherefore I know not—lost all my mirth, forgone all custom of° exercise, and indeed it goes so heavily with my disposition that this goodly frame,° the earth, seems to me a sterile promontory. This most excellent canopy the air, look you, this brave o'erhanging,[8] this majestical roof fretted° with golden fire—why, it appears no other thing to me than a foul and pestilent congregation of vapours. What a piece of work° is a man! How noble in reason, how infinite in faculty,° in form and moving how express[9] and admirable, in action how like an angel, in apprehension how like a god—the beauty of the world, the paragon of animals! And yet to me what is this quintessence[1] of dust? Man delights not me—no, nor woman neither, though by your smiling you seem to say so. — *i.e., remain intact* / *customary* / *structure* / *decorated* / *masterpiece* / *natural aptitude*

4. Well-worn, familiar way.
5. That is, too expensively priced at a half-penny (i.e., my gratitude is of little worth).
6. Your personal integrity has.
7. Your having to betray the confidence (of the king and queen).
8. This splendid overhang; that is, the roof or "heavens" overhanging the Elizabethan stage, decorated with stars or the signs of the zodiac. Q2 reads: "this brave o'erhanging firmament."
9. Well framed, well designed.
1. The most essential part of a substance; literally, the "fifth essence" of which the heavenly bodies were supposedly composed, thought to be actually latent in the four elements (air, water, earth, fire).

ROSENCRANTZ My lord, there was no such stuff in my thoughts.

HAMLET Why did you laugh, then, when I said 'Man delights not me'?

ROSENCRANTZ To think, my lord, if you delight not in man what lenten entertainment[2] the players shall receive from you. We coted them° on the way, and hither are they coming to offer you service. *passed them by*

HAMLET He that plays the King shall be welcome; his majesty shall have tribute of me. The adventurous Knight shall use his foil and target,[3] the Lover shall not sigh gratis,° the Humorous Man shall end his part in peace,[4] the Clown shall make those laugh whose lungs are tickled o'th' sear,[5] and the Lady shall say her mind freely, or the blank verse shall halt for't.[6] What players are they? *without payment*

ROSENCRANTZ Even those you were wont to take delight in, the tragedians° of the city. *actors*

HAMLET How chances it they travel? Their residence[7] both in reputation and profit was better both ways.

ROSENCRANTZ I think their inhibition[8] comes by the means of the late innovation.[9]

HAMLET Do they hold the same estimation° they did when I was in the city? Are they so followed? *good reputation*

ROSENCRANTZ No, indeed, they are not.

HAMLET How comes it? Do they grow rusty?

ROSENCRANTZ Nay, their endeavour keeps° in the wonted° pace. But there is, sir, an eyrie° of children, little eyases,[1] that cry out on the top of question[2] and are most tyrannically° clapped for't. These are now the fashion, and so berattle° the common stages[3]—so they call them—that many wearing rapiers are afraid of goose-quills,[4] and dare scarce come thither. *continues / customary* *a nest* *outrageously* *rattle, shake*

2. Meager reception (with an allusion to the prohibition of plays during Lent).
3. Sword and shield.
4. That is, the man who is governed by one of the four humors shall be allowed to play his part without interruption. (The "Humorous Man," the "adventurous Knight," and the other figures mentioned in this speech are stock characters in Elizabethan plays.)
5. Easily made to laugh; literally, with a loose gunlock catch (i.e., hair-triggered).
6. That is, she shall be allowed to speak her mind (without censoring her words?), or else her blank verse (unrhymed iambic pentameter) will not scan properly.
7. That is, residence in the city, presumably in their permanent theater.
8. Ban on the performance of stage plays (perhaps a reference to a Privy Council order of 1600 limiting performances to two a week, in only two theaters.
9. If "the late innovation" means "recent political insurrection," then this could refer to a ban on stage plays possibly resulting from the performance of *Richard II* during the earl of Essex's rebellion in 1601 against Elizabeth I. "Innovation" may also refer to the emergence of the very popular company of boy actors that performed at the private Blackfriars theater and provided stiff competition for the adult companies (see lines 333ff.).
1. Young hawks (a reference to the Children of the Chapel, who began acting at Blackfriars in 1600).
2. Yelp out their speeches in high-pitched voices.
3. Public theaters (as opposed to the private theater of Blackfriars).
4. Pens (of satirical playwrights).

HAMLET What, are they children? Who maintains 'em? How are they escoted?[5] Will they pursue the quality° no longer than they can sing?° Will they not say afterwards, if they should grow themselves to common players—as it is like° most will, if their means° are not better—their writers do them wrong to make them exclaim against their own succession?°

(acting) profession / *until their voices change* / *likely / financial means* / *professional future*

ROSENCRANTZ Faith, there has been much to-do on both sides, and the nation° holds it no sin to tarre° them to controversy There was for a while no money bid for argument° unless the poet and the player went to cuffs in the question.[6]

populace / incite / *the plot of the play*

HAMLET Is't possible?

GUILDENSTERN O, there has been much throwing about of brains.[7]

HAMLET Do the boys carry it away?°

win

ROSENCRANTZ Ay, that they do, my lord, Hercules and his load too.[8]

HAMLET It is not strange; for mine uncle is King of Denmark, and those that would make mows° at him while my father lived give twenty, forty, an hundred ducats apiece for his picture in little.° 'Sblood,[9] there is something in this more than natural, if philosophy could find it out.

derisive grimaces / *miniature*

A flourish for the PLAYERS

GUILDENSTERN There are the players.

HAMLET Gentlemen, you are welcome to Elsinore. Your hands, come. Th'appurtenance° of welcome is fashion and ceremony. Let me comply with you in the garb,[1] lest my extent° to the players—which, I tell you, must show fairly° outward—should more appear like entertainment° than yours.°

accessory / *what I show* / *plainly* / *more welcoming / to you*

[*He shakes hands with them*]

You are welcome. But my uncle-father and aunt-mother are deceived.

GUILDENSTERN In what, my dear lord?

HAMLET I am but mad north-north-west;[2] when the wind is southerly, I know a hawk from a handsaw.[3]

Enter POLONIUS

POLONIUS Well be with you, gentlemen.

5. Supported financially.
6. Got into a fight (literally, came to blows) over the issue at hand, or in the text of the play.
7. A great battle of wits, insults.
8. As one of his twelve labors, Hercules held up the world for Atlas. The children do better; they carry Hercules and the world, too (with an allusion to the Globe playhouse, which had Hercules carrying the world as its sign).
9. By God's blood (a common oath).
1. Use courteous action with you in the appropriate fashion (by shaking hands).
2. That is, I am mad only when the wind blows from the north-northwest; or, I am only a little bit mad (because the north-northwesterly direction on a compass is only a little bit removed from true north).
3. That is, one tool from another (a "hawk" is a pickaxe in addition to being a bird of prey).

HAMLET [*aside*] Hark you, Guildenstern, and you too—at each ear a hearer—that great baby you see there is not yet out of his swathing-clouts.° *swaddling clothes*

ROSENCRANTZ [*aside*] Haply° he's the second time come to them, for they say an old man is twice° a child. *Perhaps* / *for the second time*

HAMLET [*aside*] I will prophesy he comes to tell me of the players. Mark it.—You say right, sir, for o' Monday morning, 'twas so indeed.

POLONIUS My lord, I have news to tell you.

HAMLET My lord, I have news to tell you. When Roscius[4] was an actor in Rome—

POLONIUS The actors are come hither, my lord.

HAMLET Buzz, buzz.° *(a response to old news)*

POLONIUS Upon mine honour—

HAMLET Then came each actor on his ass.

POLONIUS The best actors in the world, either for tragedy, comedy, history, pastoral, pastorical-comical, historical-pastoral, tragical-historical, tragical-comical-historical-pastoral, scene individable or poem unlimited.[5] Seneca cannot be too heavy, nor Plautus too light.[6] For the law of writ and the liberty,[7] these are the only men.

HAMLET O Jephthah, judge of Israel,[8] what a treasure hadst thou!

POLONIUS What a treasure had he, my lord?

HAMLET Why,
'One fair daughter and no more,
The which he lovèd passing° well'. *surpassing*

POLONIUS [*aside*] Still on my daughter.

HAMLET Am I not i'th' right, old Jephthah?

POLONIUS If you call me Jephthah, my lord, I have a daughter that I love passing well.

HAMLET Nay, that follows not.

POLONIUS What follows then, my lord?

HAMLET Why
'As by lot° *chance*
God wot',° *knows*
and then you know
'It came to pass
As most like° it was'— *likely*
the first row° of the pious chanson° will show you more, *stanza / song*
for look where my abridgements[9] come.

4. Quintus Roscius Gallus (d. ca. 62 B.C.E.), a famous Roman actor.
5. That is, scenes and plays that observe the unities of time, place, and action (individable) and those that ignore them (unlimited).
6. Lucius Annaeus Seneca (ca. 4 B.C.E.–65 C.E.), Roman writer of tragedy and philosophy; Titus Macchius Plautus (ca. 254–184 B.C.E.), Roman writer of comedies.
7. For plays that are written according to the rules and those that are not.
8. Title of a popular ballad (quoted by Hamlet in later lines). Jephthah vowed that if he defeated the Ammonites, he would sacrifice the first living thing that met him on his return home—which was his daughter (Judges 11.30–40).
9. Those who interrupt me; also, entertainments.

Enter four or five PLAYERS

You're welcome, masters, welcome all.—I am glad to see
thee well.—Welcome, good friends.—O, my old friend!
Thy face is valanced[1] since I saw thee last. Com'st thou
to beard° me in Denmark?—What, my young lady and — *oppose (with pun)*
mistress.[2] By'r Lady, your ladyship is nearer heaven
than when I saw you last by the altitude of a chopine.° — *i.e., a thick cork sole*
Pray God your voice, like a piece of uncurrent gold, be
not cracked within the ring.[3]—Masters, you are all welcome. We'll e'en to't° like French falc'ners, fly at any thing — *go at it*
we see.[4] We'll have a speech straight.° Come, give us a — *immediately*
taste of your quality.° Come, a passionate speech. — *abilities*

FIRST PLAYER What speech, my good lord?

HAMLET I heard thee speak me a speech once, but it was
never acted, or, if it was, not above once; for the play, I
remember, pleased not the million. 'Twas caviare to the
general.° But it was—as I received it, and others whose — *common people*
judgements in such matters cried in the top of° mine— — *superseded*
an excellent play, well digested° in the scenes, set down — *shaped*
with as much modesty° as cunning. I remember one — *restraint*
said there was no sallets[5] in the lines to make the matter
savoury, nor no matter in the phrase that might indict
the author of affectation, but called it an honest
method, as wholesome as sweet, and by very much more
handsome than fine.[6] One speech in it I chiefly loved,
'twas Aeneas' tale to Dido, and thereabout of it especially
where he speaks of Priam's slaughter.[7] If it live in your
memory, begin at this line—let me see, let me see:
'The rugged° Pyrrhus, like th'Hyrcanian beast'[8]— — *savage*
'tis not so. It begins with Pyrrhus—
'The rugged Pyrrhus, he whose sable° arms, — *black*
Black as his purpose, did the night resemble
When he lay couchèd° in the ominous horse,[9] — *hidden*
Hath now this dread and black complexion° smeared — *appearance*
With heraldry° more dismal. Head to foot — *heraldic colors*
Now is he total gules,° horridly tricked° — *red / sketched*
With blood of fathers, mothers, daughters, sons,
Baked and impasted with° the parching° streets, — *encrusted by / blazing*
That lend a tyrannous and damnèd light

1. Fringed (with facial hair).
2. The boy who played female characters.
3. That is, your voice is still suitable for acting female roles. Coins that were clipped (cracked) so deeply around the edges (to obtain small amounts of metal) that the circle around the monarch's head was broken were "uncurrent" (no longer legal tender).
4. That is, undertake anything, no matter how difficult and without much forethought.
5. Literally, salads, something mixed or savory; that is, spicy or vulgar words.
6. More graceful than ostentatious.
7. In book 2 of Virgil's *Aeneid* (19 B.C.E.), the Trojan Aeneas tells Dido, queen of Carthage, stories of the fall of Troy, including the death of its king, Priam.
8. The tiger (the region of Hyrcania in the Caucasus was associated in the *Aeneid* with tigers). *Pyrrhus:* the son of the Greek warrior Achilles, who came to Troy to avenge his father's death.
9. The wooden horse within which Greek soldiers hid to gain entry into Troy.

To their vile murders. Roasted in wrath and fire,
And thus o'er-sizèd[1] with coagulate gore,
With eyes like carbuncles[2] the hellish Pyrrhus
Old grandsire Priam seeks.'
So, proceed you.

POLONIUS Fore God, my lord, well spoken, with good accent and good discretion.

FIRST PLAYER 'Anon° he finds him, *Soon*
Striking too short at Greeks. His antique sword,
Rebellious to his arm, lies where it falls,
Repugnant° to command. Unequal match, *Resistant*
Pyrrhus at Priam drives, in rage strikes wide;
But with the whiff and wind of his fell° sword *fierce; deadly*
Th'unnervèd° father falls. Then senseless Ilium,[3] *unmanned*
Seeming to feel his blow, with flaming top
Stoops to his° base, and with a hideous crash *its*
Takes prisoner Pyrrhus' ear. For lo, his sword,
Which was declining° on the milky° head *descending / white*
Of reverend Priam, seemed i'th' air to stick.
So, as a painted tyrant,[4] Pyrrhus stood,
And, like a neutral to his will and matter,[5]
Did nothing.
But as we often see against° some storm *before*
A silence in the heavens, the rack° stand still, *mass of clouds*
The bold winds speechless, and the orb° below *sphere (earth)*
As hush as death, anon the dreadful thunder
Doth rend the region:° so, after Pyrrhus' pause, *sky*
A rousèd vengeance sets him new a-work;
And never did the Cyclops'[6] hammers fall
On Mars his armour, forged for proof eterne,[7]
With less remorse° than Pyrrhus' bleeding sword *pity*
Now falls on Priam.
Out, out, thou strumpet Fortune! All you gods,
In general synod, take away her power,
Break all the spokes and fellies from her wheel,[8]
And bowl the round nave° down the hill of heaven,[9] *hub*
As low as to the fiends!'

POLONIUS This is too long.

HAMLET It shall to the barber's, with your beard. [*To* FIRST PLAYER] Prithee, say on. He's for a jig[1] or a tale of bawdry, or he sleeps. Say on, come to Hecuba.[2]

1. Covered with size, a glutinous substance used to prepare a porous surface for painting.
2. Red jewels believed to shine in the dark.
3. The citadel of Troy.
4. That is, as a tyrant in a painting, unable to move.
5. As one indifferent to his intention and circumstance.
6. In classical mythology, one-eyed giants who forged weapons for the gods.
7. To be eternally impenetrable. *Mars his:* Mars's (the Roman god of war).
8. The goddess Fortune is often pictured with a wheel whose turning controls human fate. *Fellies:* segments of the wheel's rim.
9. Perhaps Mount Olympus, by tradition the home of the classical gods.
1. A comic song and dance (usually performed at the end of a play).
2. The wife of Priam, queen of Troy.

FIRST PLAYER 'But who, O who had seen the mobbled° queen'— *muffled*
HAMLET 'The mobbled queen'?
POLONIUS That's good; 'mobbled queen' is good.
FIRST PLAYER 'Run barefoot up and down, threat'ning the flames
With bisson rheum;° a clout° upon that head *blinding tears / cloth*
Where late the diadem stood, and for a robe,
About her lank and all o'er-teemèd[3] loins,
A blanket in th'alarm of fear caught up—
Who this had seen, with tongue in venom steeped,
'Gainst Fortune's state° would treason have pronounced. *rule*
But if the gods themselves did see her then,
When she saw Pyrrhus make malicious sport
In mincing with his sword her husband's limbs,
The instant burst of clamour that she made—
Unless things mortal move them not at all—
Would have made milch° the burning eyes of heaven, *moist*
And passion° in the gods.' *strong emotion*

POLONIUS Look whe'er° he has not turned his colour, and has tears in 's eyes. [*To* FIRST PLAYER] Prithee, no more. *whether*

HAMLET [*to* FIRST PLAYER] 'Tis well. I'll have thee speak out the rest soon. [*To* POLONIUS] Good my lord, will you see the players well bestowed?° Do ye hear?—let them be well used,° for they are the abstracts° and brief chronicles of the time. After your death you were better have a bad epitaph than their ill report while you live. *lodged* *treated / summaries*

POLONIUS My lord, I will use them according to their desert.

HAMLET God's bodykins,[4] man, much better. Use every man after° his desert, and who should scape whipping? Use them after your own honour and dignity—the less they deserve, the more merit is in your bounty. Take them in. *according to*

POLONIUS [*to* PLAYERS] Come, sirs. *Exit*

HAMLET [*to* PLAYERS] Follow him, friends. We'll hear a play tomorrow. Dost thou hear me, old friend? Can you play the murder of Gonzago?

PLAYERS Ay, my lord.

HAMLET We'll ha't° tomorrow night. You could for a need° study a speech of some dozen or sixteen lines which I would set down and insert in't, could ye not? *have it* *if necessary*

PLAYERS Ay, my lord.

HAMLET Very well. Follow that lord, and look you mock him not. *Exeunt* PLAYERS
My good friends, I'll leave you till night. You are welcome to Elsinore.

ROSENCRANTZ Good my lord.

3. Worn out with bearing children (more than a dozen, according to traditional accounts).

4. By God's little body (a mild oath).

HAMLET Ay, so. God b'wi'-ye. *Exeunt* [*all but*] HAMLET
Now I am alone.
O, what a rogue and peasant slave am I!
Is it not monstrous that this player here,
But° in a fiction, in a dream of passion, *Merely*
Could force his soul so to his whole conceit[5]
That from her° working all his visage wanned,° *(his soul's) / grew pale*
Tears in his eyes, distraction in 's aspect,
A broken voice, and his whole function° suiting *all his gestures*
With forms to his conceit?° And all for nothing. *imagination*
For Hecuba!
What's Hecuba to him, or he to Hecuba,
That he should weep for her? What would he do
Had he the motive and the cue for passion
That I have? He would drown the stage with tears,
And cleave the general ear[6] with horrid speech,
Make mad the guilty and appal the free,° *innocent*
Confound the ignorant, and amaze° indeed *perplex*
The very faculty of eyes and ears. Yet I,
A dull and muddy-mettled° rascal, peak° *dull-spirited / mope*
Like John-a-dreams,[7] unpregnant of° my cause, *not quickened by*
And can say nothing—no, not for a king
Upon whose property[8] and most dear life
A damned defeat[9] was made. Am I a coward?
Who calls me villain, breaks my pate° across, *head*
Plucks off my beard and blows it in my face,
Tweaks me by th' nose, gives me the lie i'th' throat
As deep as to the lungs?[1] Who does me this?
Ha? 'Swounds,° I should take it; for it cannot be *By God's wounds (an oath)*
But I am pigeon-livered and lack gall[2]
To make oppression bitter, or ere this
I should 'a' fatted all the region kites[3]
With this slave's offal. Bloody, bawdy villain!
Remorseless, treacherous, lecherous, kindles° villain! *unnatural*
O, vengeance!—
Why, what an ass am I? Ay, sure, this is most brave,° *splendid*
That I, the son of the dear murderèd,[4]
Prompted to my revenge by heaven and hell,
Must, like a whore, unpack my heart with words
And fall a-cursing like a very drab,° *whore*
A scullion!° Fie upon't, foh!—About,[5] my brain. *kitchen servant*
I have heard that guilty creatures sitting at a play
Have by the very cunning° of the scene *artfulness*

5. That is, could conform his very being to the character he was playing.
6. The ears of all who heard him.
7. A proverbial name for a dreamy fellow.
8. Crown and queen; also, Claudius's essential character qualities.
9. A destructive crime worthy of damnation.

1. Calls me an egregious liar.
2. Pigeons or doves were thought to be mild because they did not to secrete gall (believed to cause anger).
3. All the kites (birds of prey) in the air.
4. Q2 reads "A dear father murdered."
5. Get going; turn about.

Been struck so to the soul that presently° *instantly*
They have proclaimed their malefactions;
For murder, though it have no tongue, will speak
With most miraculous organ. I'll have these players
Play something like the murder of my father
Before mine uncle. I'll observe his looks,
I'll tent° him to the quick. If a° but blench, *probe / he*
I know my course. The spirit that I have seen
May be the devil, and the devil hath power
T'assume a pleasing shape; yea, and perhaps,
Out of my weakness and my melancholy—
As he is very potent with such spirits[6]—
Abuses° me to damn me. I'll have grounds *Tricks*
More relative° than this. The play's the thing *pertinent*
Wherein I'll catch the conscience of the King. *Exit*

3.1

Enter KING [CLAUDIUS], QUEEN [GERTRUDE], POLONIUS, OPHELIA, ROSENCRANTZ, GUILDENSTERN, *and lords*

KING CLAUDIUS [*to* ROSENCRANTZ *and* GUILDENSTERN]
And can you by no drift of circumstance[7]
Get from him why he puts on this confusion,
Grating so harshly all his days of quiet
With turbulent and dangerous lunacy?

ROSENCRANTZ He does confess he feels himself distracted,
But from what cause a° will by no means speak. *he*

GUILDENSTERN Nor do we find him forward° to be sounded,° *willing / questioned*
But with a crafty madness keeps aloof
When we would bring him on to some confession
Of his true state.

QUEEN GERTRUDE Did he receive you well?

ROSENCRANTZ Most like a gentleman.

GUILDENSTERN But with much forcing of his disposition.° *mood*

ROSENCRANTZ Niggard of question,[8] but of° our demands *to*
Most free in his reply.

QUEEN GERTRUDE Did you assay° him *try to win*
To any pastime?

ROSENCRANTZ Madam, it so fell out that certain players
We o'er-raught° on the way. Of these we told him, *overtook*
And there did seem in him a kind of joy
To hear of it. They are about the court,
And, as I think, they have already order
This night to play before him.

POLONIUS 'Tis most true,
And he beseeched me to entreat your majesties
To hear and see the matter.

6. It was thought that those given to melancholy and despair were more easily manipulated by the devil.

3.1 Location: The castle.

7. By no carefully directed conversation.

8. Sparing of conversation.

KING CLAUDIUS With all my heart; and it doth much content me
To hear him so inclined.—Good gentlemen,
Give him a further edge,° and drive his purpose on *encouragement*
To these delights.

ROSENCRANTZ We shall, my lord.

Exeunt ROSENCRANTZ *and* GUILDENSTERN

KING CLAUDIUS Sweet Gertrude, leave us too,
For we have closely° sent for Hamlet hither, *privately*
That he, as 'twere by accident, may here
Affront° Ophelia. *Meet*
Her father and myself, lawful espials,° *spies*
Will so bestow ourselves that, seeing unseen,
We may of their encounter frankly judge,
And gather by him, as he is behaved,
If't be th'affliction of his love or no
That thus he suffers for.

QUEEN GERTRUDE I shall obey you.
And for your part, Ophelia, I do wish
That your good beauties be the happy cause
Of Hamlet's wildness; so shall I hope your virtues
Will bring him to his wonted° way again, *usual*
To both your honours.

OPHELIA Madam, I wish it may.

[*Exit* GERTRUDE]

POLONIUS Ophelia, walk you here.—Gracious,° so please you, *Your Grace*
We will bestow ourselves.—Read on this book,
That show of such an exercise[9] may colour
Your loneliness.[1] We are oft to blame in this:
'Tis too much proved° that with devotion's visage *too often made plain*
And pious action we do sugar o'er
The devil himself.

KING CLAUDIUS O, 'tis too true.
[*Aside*] How smart° a lash that speech doth give my conscience. *stinging*
The harlot's cheek, beautied with plast'ring° art, *cosmetic*
Is not more ugly to° the thing that helps it[2] *compared to*
Than is my deed to my most painted word.
O heavy burden!

POLONIUS I hear him coming. Let's withdraw, my lord.

Exeunt [CLAUDIUS *and* POLONIUS]

Enter [*Prince*] HAMLET

HAMLET To be, or not to be; that is the question:
Whether 'tis nobler in the mind to suffer
The slings and arrows of outrageous fortune,
Or to take arms against a sea of troubles,
And, by opposing, end them. To die, to sleep—
No more, and by a sleep to say we end

9. Act of devotion (the book is a prayer book).

1. That is, may give a credible appearance to your solitude.

2. That is, the cosmetic.

The heartache and the thousand natural shocks
That flesh is heir to—'tis a consummation° *final ending*
Devoutly to be wished. To die, to sleep.
To sleep, perchance to dream. Ay, there's the rub,[3]
For in that sleep of death what dreams may come
When we have shuffled° off this mortal coil° *cast / turmoil; flesh*
Must give us pause. There's the respect° *consideration*
That makes calamity of so long life.° *so long-lived*
For who would bear the whips and scorns of time,
Th'oppressor's wrong, the proud man's contumely,° *insolent abuse*
The pangs of disprized° love, the law's delay, *unvalued*
The insolence of office,[4] and the spurns° *insults*
That patient merit of th'unworthy takes,[5]
When he himself might his quietus make[6]
With a bare bodkin?° Who would these fardels° bear, *dagger / burdens*
To grunt and sweat under a weary life,
But that the dread of something after death,
The undiscovered country from whose bourn° *boundary*
No traveller returns, puzzles° the will, *perplexes*
And makes us rather bear those ills we have
Than fly to others that we know not of?
Thus conscience° does make cowards of us all, *moral judgment; knowledge*
And thus the native hue° of resolution *natural (sanguine) color*
Is sicklied o'er with the pale cast° of thought, *tinge, shade*
And enterprises of great pith[7] and moment° *importance*
With this regard° their currents° turn awry, *respect / courses*
And lose the name of action. Soft you, now,
The fair Ophelia!—Nymph, in thy orisons° *prayers*
Be all my sins remembered.

OPHELIA Good my lord,
How does your honour for this many a day?

HAMLET I humbly thank you, well, well, well.

OPHELIA My lord, I have remembrances of yours
That I have longèd long to redeliver.
I pray you now receive them.

HAMLET No, no, I never gave you aught.

OPHELIA My honoured lord, you know right well you did,
And with them words of so sweet breath composed
As made the things more rich. Their perfume lost,
Take these again; for to the noble mind
Rich gifts wax° poor when givers prove unkind. *grow*
There, my lord.

HAMLET Ha, ha? Are you honest?° *chaste; truthful*

OPHELIA My lord.

HAMLET Are you fair?

3. In the game of bowls, an obstacle that hinders or diverts a bowl from its intended course.
4. That is, of officeholders; bureaucrats.
5. That is, that the worthy have to endure patiently from the unworthy.
6. Gain his discharge—here, death. Paid-off debts were marked *quietus est*, "he is quit" (Latin).
7. Profundity. Q2 has "pitch," meaning "height" (as of a falcon's flight).

OPHELIA What means your lordship?

HAMLET That if you be honest and fair, your honesty should admit no discourse to° your beauty.

conversation with

OPHELIA Could beauty, my lord, have better commerce° than with honesty?

dealings

HAMLET Ay, truly, for the power of beauty will sooner transform honesty from what it is to a bawd than the force of honesty can translate beauty into his° likeness. This was sometime a paradox, but now the time° gives it proof. I did love you once.

its / *the present time*

OPHELIA Indeed, my lord, you made me believe so.

HAMLET You should not have believed me, for virtue cannot so inoculate our old stock but we shall relish of it.[8] I loved you not.

OPHELIA I was the more deceived.

HAMLET Get thee to a nunnery.[9] Why wouldst thou be a breeder of sinners? I am myself indifferent honest,° but yet I could accuse me of such things that it were better my mother had not borne me. I am very proud, revengeful, ambitious, with more offences at my beck° than I have thoughts to put them in, imagination to give them shape, or time to act them in. What should such fellows as I do crawling between heaven and earth? We are arrant° knaves, all. Believe none of us. Go thy ways to a nunnery. Where's your father?

reasonably virtuous / *command* / *out-and-out*

OPHELIA At home, my lord.

HAMLET Let the doors be shut upon him, that he may play the fool nowhere but in 's own house. Farewell.

OPHELIA O help him, you sweet heavens!

HAMLET If thou dost marry, I'll give thee this plague for thy dowry: be thou as chaste as ice, as pure as snow, thou shalt not escape calumny. Get thee to a nunnery, go, farewell. Or if thou wilt needs marry, marry a fool; for wise men know well enough what monsters[1] you° make of them. To a nunnery, go, and quickly, too. Farewell.

you women

OPHELIA O heavenly powers, restore him!

HAMLET I have heard of your paintings, too, well enough. God hath given you one face, and you make yourselves another. You jig, you amble, and you lisp,° and nickname God's creatures,[2] and make your wantonness your ignorance.[3] Go to, I'll no more on't.° It hath made me mad. I say we will have no more marriages. Those that are married already—all but one—shall live. The rest shall keep as they are. To a nunnery, go. *Exit*

speak affectedly / *of it*

8. That is, we will always taste ("relish") our original sin because a graft of virtue, no matter how strong in us, is unable to overcome it (a metaphor from horticulture).

9. A convent (requiring Ophelia to take a vow of chastity); also, in slang, a brothel.

1. Cuckolds, who were said to grow horns on their forehead.

2. That is, as if the true names of God's creatures are not good enough.

3. Excuse your illicit and seductive behavior as ignorance.

OPHELIA O what a noble mind is here o'erthrown!
The courtier's, soldier's, scholar's eye, tongue, sword,
Th'expectancy and rose of the fair state,
The glass° of fashion and the mould of form,[4] *mirror image*
Th'observed of all observers, quite, quite, down!
And I, of ladies most deject and wretched,
That sucked the honey of his music vows,
Now see that noble and most sovereign reason
Like sweet bells jangled out of tune and harsh;
That unmatched form and feature of blown° youth *in full bloom*
Blasted° with ecstasy.° O woe is me, *Blighted / madness*
T'have seen what I have seen, see what I see!

Enter KING [CLAUDIUS] *and* POLONIUS

KING CLAUDIUS Love? His affections° do not that way tend, *feelings*
Nor what he spake, though it lacked form a little,
Was not like madness. There's something in his soul
O'er which his melancholy sits on brood,
And I do doubt° the hatch and the disclose° *fear / disclosure*
Will be some danger; which to prevent
I have in quick determination
Thus set it down:° he shall with speed to England *determined it*
For the demand of our neglected tribute.[5]
Haply the seas and countries different,
With variable objects,[6] shall expel
This something-settled° matter in his heart, *somewhat established*
Whereon his brains still° beating puts him thus *always*
From fashion of himself.[7] What think you on't?
POLONIUS It shall do well. But yet do I believe
The origin and commencement of this grief
Sprung from neglected° love.—How now, Ophelia? *unrequited*
You need not tell us what Lord Hamlet said;
We heard it all.—My lord, do as you please,
But, if you hold it fit, after the play
Let his queen mother all alone entreat him
To show his griefs. Let her be round° with him, *frank*
And I'll be placed, so please you, in the ear° *within earshot*
Of all their conference. If she find him not,[8]
To England send him, or confine him where
Your wisdom best shall think.
KING CLAUDIUS It shall be so.
Madness in great ones° must not unwatched go. *Exeunt* *those of high rank*

3.2

Enter [*Prince*] HAMLET *and two or three of the* PLAYERS

HAMLET Speak the speech, I pray you, as I pronounced it to you—trippingly on the tongue; but if you mouth it,[9] as

4. The pattern of courtly decorum.
5. Between 886 and 1066, considerable parts of England were under Danish control.
6. With various (new) objects of interest.
7. Puts him out of his normal conduct.
8. If she fails to uncover the truth.
3.2 Location: A room in the castle.
9. If you speak in a pompously oratorical style.

many of your players do, I had as lief° [soon] the town-crier had spoke my lines. Nor do not saw the air too much with your hand, thus, but use all gently; for in the very torrent, tempest, and as I may say the whirlwind of your passion, you must acquire and beget a temperance that may give it smoothness. O, it offends me to the soul to hear a robustious,° periwig-pated° [bombastic / wig-wearing] fellow tear a passion to tatters, to very rags, to split the ears of the groundlings,[1] who for the most part are capable of° [able to understand] nothing but inexplicable dumb shows[2] and noise. I would have such a fellow whipped for o'erdoing Termagant. It out-Herods Herod.[3] Pray you avoid it.

A PLAYER I warrant your honour.[4]

HAMLET Be not too tame, neither; but let your own discretion be your tutor. Suit the action to the word, the word to the action, with this special observance: that you o'erstep not the modesty° [moderation] of nature. For anything so overdone is from° [contrary to] the purpose of playing, whose end, both at the first and now, was and is to hold as 'twere the mirror up to nature, to show virtue her own feature, scorn her own image, and the very age and body of the time his form and pressure.[5] Now this overdone, or come tardy off,° though it make the unskilful° [done poorly / ignorant] laugh, cannot but make the judicious grieve; the censure of the which one[6] must in your allowance o'erweigh a whole theatre of others. O, there be players that I have seen play, and heard others praise, and that highly, not to speak it profanely, that neither having the accent of Christians nor the gait of Christian, pagan, nor no man, have so strutted and bellowed that I have thought some of nature's journeymen[7] had made men, and not made them well, they imitated humanity so abominably.

A PLAYER I hope we have reformed that indifferently° [tolerably] with us, sir.

HAMLET O, reform it altogether. And let those that play your clowns speak no more than is set down for them; for there be of° them that will themselves laugh to set on° [some of / provoke] some quantity of barren° [witless] spectators to laugh too, though in the mean time some necessary question of the play be then to be considered. That's villainous, and shows a most pitiful ambition in the fool that uses it. Go make you ready.

Exeunt PLAYERS

1. Those who paid the least to see plays; they stood in the yard of the theater (in front of the stage).
2. Pantomime episodes that perform the plot of the next scene (see 3.2.129ff.).
3. The Herod of the New Testament was portrayed in medieval mystery plays as a raging tyrant. *Termagant:* an imaginary deity, presented in mystery plays as a violent and raging character worshipped by Muslims.
4. I promise your lordship (that we will avoid it).
5. That is, a play shows the imprint of the truth of the present time in the same way that a stamp imprints itself on wax.
6. The judgment of even one of them (the judicious).
7. Hirelings, not yet masters of their trade.

Enter POLONIUS, GUILDENSTERN, *and* ROSENCRANTZ

[*To* POLONIUS] How now, my lord? Will the King hear
this piece of work?

POLONIUS And the Queen too, and that presently.° *immediately*

HAMLET Bid the players make haste. *Exit* POLONIUS
Will you two help to hasten them?

ROSENCRANTZ *and* GUILDENSTERN We will, my lord. *Exeunt*

HAMLET What ho, Horatio!

Enter HORATIO

HORATIO Here, sweet lord, at your service.

HAMLET Horatio, thou art e'en as just° a man *honest; well-balanced*
As e'er my conversation coped withal.[8]

HORATIO O my dear lord—

HAMLET Nay, do not think I flatter;
For what advancement may I hope from thee,
That no revenue hast but thy good spirits
To feed and clothe thee? Why should the poor be flattered?
No, let the candied° tongue lick absurd pomp, *flattering*
And crook the pregnant° hinges of the knee *ready (to bend)*
Where thrift may follow feigning.[9] Dost thou hear?—
Since my dear soul was mistress of her choice[1]
And could of° men distinguish, her election *between*
Hath sealed° thee for herself; for thou hast been *set a mark on; claimed*
As one in suff'ring all that suffers nothing,
A man that Fortune's buffets and rewards
Hath ta'en with equal thanks; and blest are those
Whose blood° and judgement are so well commingled *passions*
That they are not a pipe for Fortune's finger
To sound what stop[2] she please. Give me that man
That is not passion's slave, and I will wear him
In my heart's core, ay, in my heart of heart,
As I do thee. Something too much of this.
There is a play tonight before the King.
One scene of it comes near the circumstance
Which I have told thee of my father's death.
I prithee, when thou seest that act afoot,
Even with the very comment of thy soul[3]
Observe mine uncle. If his occulted° guilt *hidden*
Do not itself unkennel in one speech,
It is a damnèd ghost that we have seen,
And my imaginations are as foul
As Vulcan's stithy.[4] Give him heedful note,
For I mine eyes will rivet to his face,
And after, we will both our judgements join
To censure of his seeming.[5]

HORATIO Well, my lord.

8. As ever I encountered in my dealings ("conversation") with people.
9. Where profit may result from flattery.
1. Was able to discriminate.
2. Finger hole in a wind instrument.
3. With your most acute critical faculty.
4. Blacksmith's shop. Vulcan was the Roman god of fire and metalworking.
5. To judge his appearance or reaction.

If a° steal aught the whilst this play is playing — *he*
And scape detecting, I will pay the theft.

Enter trumpets and kettle drums. Sound a flourish

HAMLET They are coming to the play. I must be idle.° — *unoccupied; incoherent*
Get you a place.

Danish march. Enter KING [CLAUDIUS], QUEEN [GERTRUDE], POLONIUS, OPHELIA, ROSENCRANTZ, GUILDENSTERN, *and other lords attendant, with* [*the* KING'*s*] *guard carrying torches*

KING CLAUDIUS How fares[6] our cousin° Hamlet? — *kinsman*
HAMLET Excellent, i'faith, of the chameleon's dish. I eat the air,[7] promise-crammed. You cannot feed capons[8] so.
KING CLAUDIUS I have nothing with this answer, Hamlet. These words are not mine.
HAMLET No, nor mine now. [*To* POLONIUS] My lord, you played once i'th' university, you say.
POLONIUS That I did, my lord, and was accounted a good actor.
HAMLET And what did you enact?
POLONIUS I did enact Julius Caesar. I was killed i'th' Capitol. Brutus killed me.
HAMLET It was a brute part of him to kill so capital a calf° there.—Be the players ready? — *fool*
ROSENCRANTZ Ay, my lord, they stay° upon your patience. — *wait*
QUEEN GERTRUDE Come hither, my good Hamlet. Sit by me.
HAMLET No, good-mother,° here's mettle more attractive.[9] — *stepmother*
[*He sits by* OPHELIA]
POLONIUS [*aside*] O ho, do you mark that?
HAMLET [*to* OPHELIA] Lady, shall I lie in your lap?
OPHELIA No, my lord.
HAMLET I mean my head upon your lap?
OPHELIA Ay, my lord.
HAMLET Do you think I meant country matters?[1]
OPHELIA I think nothing, my lord.
HAMLET That's a fair thought to lie between maids' legs.
OPHELIA What is, my lord?
HAMLET No thing.
OPHELIA You are merry, my lord.
HAMLET Who, I?
OPHELIA Ay, my lord.
HAMLET O God, your only jig-maker![2] What should a man do but be merry? For look you how cheerfully my mother looks, and my father died within 's° two hours. — *these*

6. Does. *Fare* also means "food" or "to feed," a meaning on which Hamlet plays in his response.
7. Chameleons were believed to feed on air.
8. Castrated roosters, fattened or "crammed" for eating; also, dull men. *Promise-crammed:* possibly a reference to Claudius's promise that Hamlet will succeed to the throne (1.2.109, 3.2.322–23), perhaps with a play on "air"/"heir."
9. Metal (also "temperament") with greater magnetic powers.
1. Vulgar doings (with a pun on "cunt"). The sexual puns continue with "nothing" (vagina) and "thing" (penis).
2. The performer or creator of a farcical song and dance, frequently performed right after the end of a play. *Only:* peerless, best.

OPHELIA Nay, 'tis twice two months, my lord.

HAMLET So long? Nay then, let the devil wear black, for I'll have a suit of sables.[3] O heavens, die two months ago and not forgotten yet! Then there's hope a great man's memory may outlive his life half a year. But, by'r Lady, a° *he* must build churches then, or else shall a suffer not thinking on,[4] with the hobby-horse,[5] whose epitaph is 'For O, for O, the hobby-horse is forgot.'

Hautboys° play. The dumb show enters. Enter a KING *and a* QUEEN *very lovingly, the* QUEEN *embracing him. She kneels and makes show of protestation unto him. He takes her up and declines his head upon her neck. He lays him down upon a bank of flowers. She, seeing him asleep, leaves him. Anon comes in a fellow, takes off his crown, kisses it, and pours poison in the King's ears, and exits. The* QUEEN *returns, finds the* KING *dead, and makes passionate action. The poisoner, with some two or three mutes,° comes in again, seeming to lament with her. The dead body is carried away. The poisoner woos the* QUEEN *with gifts. She seems loath and unwilling a while, but in the end accepts his love. Exeunt* [*the* PLAYERS]

°*Oboes* °*nonspeaking actors*

OPHELIA What means this, my lord?

HAMLET Marry, this is miching *malhecho*.[6] That means mischief.

OPHELIA Belike this show imports the argument° of the play. *plot*

Enter PROLOGUE

HAMLET We shall know by this fellow. The players cannot keep counsel,° they'll tell all. *a secret*

OPHELIA Will a° tell us what this show meant? *he*

HAMLET Ay, or any show that you'll show him. Be not you ashamed to show, he'll not shame to tell you what it means.

OPHELIA You are naught,° you are naught. I'll mark the play. *indecent*

PROLOGUE For us and for our tragedy
Here stooping to your clemency,
We beg your hearing patiently. [*Exit*]

HAMLET Is this a prologue, or the posy of a ring?[7]

OPHELIA 'Tis brief, my lord.

HAMLET As woman's love.

Enter the [PLAYER] KING *and his* QUEEN

PLAYER KING Full thirty times hath Phoebus' cart[8] gone round
Neptune's salt wash and Tellus' orbèd ground,[9]

3. A suit trimmed with (black) sable fur (not an appropriate garment for a mourner).
4. Endure not being thought of.
5. The performer in morris dances and May Day festivities who wore the figure of a horse (also called a hobbyhorse) around his waist. The "epitaph" for the hobbyhorse—which disapproving Puritans sought to ban—is probably a line from a song.
6. Sneaking misdeed ('*malhecho*' is Spanish).
7. The motto inscribed in a ring.
8. The chariot of the sun god Apollo (i.e., the sun).
9. Tellus is the Roman goddess of the earth ("orbèd ground"); Neptune is the Roman god of the sea.

And thirty dozen moons with borrowed° sheen *reflected*
About the world have times twelve thirties been
Since love our hearts and Hymen° did our hands *god of marriage*
Unite commutual in most sacred bands.

PLAYER QUEEN So many journeys may the sun and moon
Make us again count o'er ere love be done.
But woe is me, you are so sick of late,
So far from cheer and from your former state,
That I distrust° you. Yet, though I distrust, *am worried about*
Discomfort° you my lord it nothing must. *Disturb*
For women's fear and love holds quantity,° *are of equal proportion*
In neither aught, or in extremity.[1]
Now what my love is, proof° hath made you know, *experience*
And as my love is sized,° my fear is so.[2] *proportioned*
Where love is great, the littlest doubts are fear;
Where little fears grow great, great love grows there.

PLAYER KING Faith, I must leave thee, love, and shortly too.
My operant° powers their functions leave° to do, *active / cease*
And thou shalt live in this fair world behind,
Honoured, beloved; and haply° one as kind *perhaps*
For husband shalt thou—

PLAYER QUEEN O, confound° the rest! *bring to nought*
Such love must needs be treason in my breast.
In second husband let me be accurst;
None wed the second but who killed the first.

HAMLET Wormwood,[3] wormwood.

PLAYER QUEEN The instances° that second marriage move° *reasons / motivate*
Are base respects of thrift,° but none of love. *desires for profit*
A second time I kill my husband dead
When second husband kisses me in bed.

PLAYER KING I do believe you think what now you speak;
But what we do determine oft we break.
Purpose is but the slave to memory,[4]
Of violent birth but poor validity,° *durability*
Which now like fruit unripe sticks on the tree,
But fall unshaken when they mellow be.
Most necessary 'tis that we forget
To pay ourselves what to ourselves is debt.[5]
What to ourselves in passion we propose,
The passion ending, doth the purpose lose.
The violence of either grief or joy
Their own enactures with themselves destroy.[6]
Where joy most revels, grief doth most lament;
Grief joys, joy grieves, on slender accident.[7]
This world is not for aye,° nor 'tis not strange *always*

1. Either not existing at all or extremely strong.
2. The next two lines (161.1–2) appear in Q2 but not in F1.
3. A proverbially bitter-tasting plant whose oil was used in medicine.
4. That is, (carrying out) an intention depends on memory.
5. That is, it is natural that we forget the promises that we made to ourselves.
6. Extreme grief or joy destroy themselves in their fulfillment.
7. Because of a small, unanticipated event.

That even our loves should with our fortunes change;
For 'tis a question left us yet to prove
Whether love lead fortune or else fortune love.
The great man down, you mark his favourite flies;
The poor advanced° makes friends of enemies. *promoted*
And hitherto° doth love on fortune tend,° *thus far / attend*
For who not needs shall never lack a friend,
And who in want a hollow friend doth try° *test*
Directly seasons him° his enemy. *trains him (to be)*
But orderly to end where I begun,
Our wills and fates do so contrary run
That our devices still° are overthrown; *our plans always*
Our thoughts are ours, their ends° none of our own. *outcomes*
So think thou wilt no second husband wed;
But die thy thoughts when thy first lord is dead.

PLAYER QUEEN Nor earth to me give food, nor heaven light,
Sport and repose lock from me day and night,[8]
To desperation turn my trust and hope;
An anchor's cheer in prison be my scope.[9]
Each opposite[1] that blanks° the face of joy *makes pale*
Meet what I would have well and it destroy,
Both here and hence pursue me lasting strife
If, once a widow, ever I be wife.

HAMLET If she should break it now!

PLAYER KING [*to* PLAYER QUEEN]
'Tis deeply sworn. Sweet, leave me here a while.
My spirits grow dull, and fain° I would beguile *gladly*
The tedious day with sleep.

PLAYER QUEEN Sleep rock thy brain,
And never come mischance between us twain.

[PLAYER KING] *sleeps. Exit* [PLAYER QUEEN]

HAMLET [*to* GERTRUDE] Madam, how like you this play?

QUEEN GERTRUDE The lady protests too much, methinks.

HAMLET O, but she'll keep her word.

KING CLAUDIUS Have you heard the argument?° Is there no offence in't? *plot*

HAMLET No, no, they do but jest, poison in jest. No offence i'th' world.

KING CLAUDIUS What do you call the play?

HAMLET *The Mousetrap*. Marry, how? Tropically.[2] This play is the image of a murder done in Vienna. Gonzago is the Duke's name, his wife Baptista. You shall see anon. 'Tis a knavish piece of work; but what o' that? Your majesty, and we that have free° souls, it touches° us not. Let the galled jade wince, our withers are unwrung.[3] *innocent / concerns*

8. The next two lines (206.1–206.2) appear only in Q2, not in F1.
9. The extent of my happiness. *An anchor's cheer*: a hermit's (anchorite's) fare.
1. Each adverse event.
2. Figuratively (i.e., as a trope).
3. Let the inferior horse ("jade") whose hide is sore from chafing wince, our shoulders (literally, the portion of the horse's back between the shoulder blades) are not rubbed sore ("unwrung").

Enter [PLAYER] LUCIANUS

This is one Lucianus, nephew to the King.

OPHELIA You are as good as a chorus,[4] my lord.

HAMLET I could interpret between you and your love if I could see the puppets dallying.[5]

OPHELIA You are keen,° my lord, you are keen. *sharp-witted*

HAMLET It would cost you a groaning to take off mine edge.[6]

OPHELIA Still better, and worse.[7]

HAMLET So you mis-take your husbands.[8] [*To* LUCIANUS] Begin, murderer. Pox, leave thy damnable faces[9] and begin. Come: 'the croaking raven doth bellow for revenge'.[1]

PLAYER LUCIANUS Thoughts black, hands apt, drugs fit,
and time agreeing,
Confederate° season, else no creature seeing; *Conniving*
Thou mixture rank° of midnight weeds collected, *foul*
With Hecate's ban[2] thrice blasted, thrice infected,
Thy natural magic and dire property° *quality*
On wholesome life usurp immediately.

[*He*] *pours the poison in* [*the* PLAYER KING'*s*] *ears*

HAMLET A° poisons him i'th' garden for 's estate.° His name's Gonzago. The story is extant, and writ in choice Italian. You shall see anon how the murderer gets the love of Gonzago's wife. *He / state, kingdom*

OPHELIA The King rises.

HAMLET What, frighted with false fire?[3]

QUEEN GERTRUDE [*to* CLAUDIUS] How fares my lord?

POLONIUS Give o'er° the play. *Stop*

KING CLAUDIUS Give me some light. Away.

COURTIERS Lights, lights, lights!

Exeunt all but HAMLET *and* HORATIO

HAMLET Why, let the stricken deer go weep,[4]
The hart ungallèd° play, *unwounded*
For some must watch,° while some must sleep, *stay awake*
So runs the world away.[5]
Would not this, sir, and a forest of feathers,[6] if the rest of my fortunes turn Turk[7] with me, with two Provençal

4. A character (named "Chorus") who describes or interprets the action of the play (see Shakespeare's *Henry V* and *Romeo and Juliet*).
5. Flirting. In a puppet show, the actor who narrates the dialogue was known as the "interpreter."
6. To satisfy my sexual desire (Hamlet puns on "keen" as "sexually aroused") leading to "groaning" in sexual intercourse, childbirth, or both.
7. More sharp-witted and less well-mannered.
8. So you take husbands under false pretenses ("for better and for worse") and subsequently betray them.
9. Facial expressions. *Pox:* here, an expression of impatience.
1. Misquoted from the anonymous *The True Tragedy of Richard III* (ca. 1591).
2. Curse of Hecate, Greek goddess of childbirth and later witchcraft.
3. The discharge of blank cartridges.
4. A deer was thought to weep when mortally hurt. Lines 257–60 are probably from a lost ballad.
5. That's the way things go (in the world).
6. Plumes, often worn by Elizabethan actors on stage. *This:* the play just performed.
7. Become a renegade (literally, convert to Islam).

roses on my razed shoes,[8] get me a fellowship in a cry of players,[9] sir?

HORATIO Half a share.

HAMLET A whole one, I.

For thou dost know, O Damon[1] dear,
This realm dismantled° was — *stripped*
Of Jove[2] himself, and now reigns here
A very, very—pajock.[3]

HORATIO You might have rhymed.

HAMLET O good Horatio, I'll take the Ghost's word for a thousand pound. Didst perceive?

HORATIO Very well, my lord.

HAMLET Upon the talk of the pois'ning?

HORATIO I did very well note him.

Enter ROSENCRANTZ *and* GUILDENSTERN

HAMLET Ah ha! Come, some music, come, the recorders,
For if the King like not the comedy,
Why then, belike he likes it not, pardie.° — *by God; indeed*
Come, some music.

GUILDENSTERN Good my lord, vouchsafe me a word with you.

HAMLET Sir, a whole history.

GUILDENSTERN The King, sir—

HAMLET Ay, sir, what of him?

GUILDENSTERN Is in his retirement° marvellous distempered. — *withdrawal*

HAMLET With drink, sir?

GUILDENSTERN No, my lord, rather with choler.[4]

HAMLET Your wisdom should show itself more richer° to signify this to his doctor, for for me to put him to his purgation[5] would perhaps plunge him into far more choler. — *of greater value*

GUILDENSTERN Good my lord, put your discourse into some frame,° and start° not so wildly from my affair. — *order / leap away*

HAMLET I am tame, sir. Pronounce.

GUILDENSTERN The Queen your mother, in most great affliction of spirit, hath sent me to you.

HAMLET You are welcome.

GUILDENSTERN Nay, good my lord, this courtesy is not of the right breed.° If it shall please you to make me a wholesome° answer, I will do your mother's commandment; if not, your pardon° and my return shall be the end of my business. — *kind* / *sane; beneficial* / *permission to depart*

HAMLET Sir, I cannot.

GUILDENSTERN What, my lord?

8. Shoes with decorative slashes. *Provençal roses:* rosettes of ribbon (resembling French roses).

9. Part ownership in a theatrical company (literally, a pack of players).

1. A figure in Greek mythology, legendary for his friendship with Pythias.

2. Jupiter, the king of the Roman gods.

3. Peacock (here used as a term of contempt.). "Pajock" appears in the place of the expected rhyme word, "ass."

4. Anger; also, a bilious disorder requiring the attentions of a physician (the meaning to which Hamlet responds).

5. Bloodletting; spiritual purging.

HAMLET Make you a wholesome answer. My wit's diseased. But, sir, such answers as I can make, you shall command; or rather, as you say, my mother. Therefore no more, but to the matter. My mother, you say?

ROSENCRANTZ Then thus she says: your behaviour hath struck her into amazement and admiration.° *astonishment*

HAMLET O wonderful son, that can so astonish a mother! But is there no sequel at the heels of this mother's admiration?

ROSENCRANTZ She desires to speak with you in her closet° ere you go to bed. *private chamber*

HAMLET We shall obey, were she ten times our mother. Have you any further trade with us?

ROSENCRANTZ My lord, you once did love me.

HAMLET So I do still, by these pickers and stealers.[6]

ROSENCRANTZ Good my lord, what is your cause of distemper? You do freely° bar the door of your own liberty if you deny your griefs to your friend. *of your own accord*

HAMLET Sir, I lack advancement.

ROSENCRANTZ How can that be when you have the voice of the King himself for your succession in Denmark?

HAMLET Ay, but 'while the grass grows . . .'[7]—the proverb is something° musty. *somewhat*

Enter one with a recorder

O, the recorder. Let me see. [*To* ROSENCRANTZ *and* GUILDENSTERN, *taking them aside*] To withdraw° with you, why do you go about to recover the wind[8] of me as if you would drive me into a toil?° *speak privately* *trap*

GUILDENSTERN O my lord, if my duty be too bold, my love is too unmannerly.[9]

HAMLET I do not well understand that. Will you play upon this pipe?° *(the recorder)*

GUILDENSTERN My lord, I cannot.

HAMLET I pray you.

GUILDENSTERN Believe me, I cannot.

HAMLET I do beseech you.

GUILDENSTERN I know no touch of it, my lord.

HAMLET 'Tis as easy as lying. Govern these ventages° with your fingers and thumb, give it breath with your mouth, and it will discourse most excellent music. Look you, these are the stops. *finger holes*

GUILDENSTERN But these cannot I command to any utterance of harmony. I have not the skill.

HAMLET Why, look you now, how unworthy a thing you make of me! You would play upon me, you would seem to

6. Hands. (The catechism in the Book of Common Prayer contains the promise "to keep my hands from picking and stealing.")

7. "While the grass grows, the horse starves." Hamlet means that he may not live long enough to gain the crown of Denmark.

8. Move to the windward side (as would a hunter, to prevent his prey from smelling his approach).

9. That is, if I am too presumptuous (with you) it is only because of my love (for you).

know my stops, you would pluck out the heart of my mystery, you would sound me[1] from my lowest note to the top of my compass;° and there is much music, excellent voice in this little organ,° yet cannot you make it speak. 'Sblood, do you think I am easier to be played on than a pipe? Call me what instrument you will, though you can fret[2] me, you cannot play upon me. *range (of musical pitch)* *musical instrument*

Enter POLONIUS

God bless you, sir.

POLONIUS My lord, the Queen would speak with you, and presently.° *immediately*

HAMLET Do you see yonder cloud that's almost in shape of a camel?

POLONIUS By th' mass, and 'tis: like a camel, indeed.

HAMLET Methinks it is like a weasel.

POLONIUS It is backed like a weasel.

HAMLET Or like a whale.

POLONIUS Very like a whale.

HAMLET Then will I come to my mother by and by.° [*Aside*] They fool me to the top of my bent.[3] [*To* POLONIUS] I will come by and by. *right away*

POLONIUS I will say so.

HAMLET 'By and by' is easily said. *Exit* [POLONIUS]

Leave me, friends. [*Exeunt* ROSENCRANTZ *and* GUILDENSTERN]

'Tis now the very witching time of night,
When churchyards yawn, and hell itself breathes out
Contagion to this world. Now could I drink hot blood,
And do such bitter business as the day
Would quake to look on. Soft, now to my mother.
O heart, lose not thy nature!° Let not ever *natural affection*
The soul of Nero[4] enter this firm° bosom. *resolute*
Let me be cruel, not unnatural.
I will speak daggers to her, but use none.
My tongue and soul in this be hypocrites[5]—
How in my words somever she be shent,[6]
To give them seals[7] never my soul consent. *Exit*

3.3

Enter KING [CLAUDIUS], ROSENCRANTZ, *and* GUILDENSTERN.

KING CLAUDIUS I like him not, nor stands it safe with us
To let his madness range. Therefore prepare you.
I your commission will forthwith dispatch,° *prepare*
And he to England shall along with you.

1. Ascertain my depth; play on me.
2. Vex. Also, to furnish with frets, the bars on the fingerboard of stringed instruments that regulate the fingering.
3. They make me play the madman to the limits of my skill.
4. The Roman emperor Nero (r. 54–68 C.E.) murdered his mother, Agrippina.
5. That is, let my words and appearance misleadingly suggest that I mean to do her violence.
6. However my words put her to shame.
7. To validate them with actions.
3.3 Location: The castle.

The terms of our estate° may not endure — *My position as king*
Hazard so dangerous as doth hourly grow
Out of his lunacies.

GUILDENSTERN We will ourselves provide.
Most holy and religious fear° it is — *care*
To keep those many many bodies safe
That live and feed upon your majesty.

ROSENCRANTZ The single and peculiar° life is bound — *individual and private*
With all the strength and armour of the mind
To keep itself from noyance;° but much more — *harm*
That spirit upon whose weal° depends and rests — *well-being*
The lives of many. The cease° of majesty — *decease*
Dies not alone, but like a gulf° doth draw — *whirlpool*
What's near it with it. It is a massy° wheel[8] — *massive*
Fixed on the summit of the highest mount,
To whose huge spokes ten thousand lesser things
Are mortised° and adjoined, which° when it falls — *attached / so that*
Each small annexment, petty consequence,
Attends° the boist'rous ruin. Never alone — *Accompanies*
Did the King sigh, but with a general groan.

KING CLAUDIUS Arm you,° I pray you, to this speedy voyage, — *Prepare yourself*
For we will fetters put upon this fear
Which now goes too free-footed.

ROSENCRANTZ *and* GUILDENSTERN We will haste us.

Exeunt [*both*]

Enter POLONIUS

POLONIUS My lord, he's going to his mother's closet.
Behind the arras° I'll convey myself — *wall tapestry*
To hear the process.° I'll warrant she'll tax him home.[9] — *proceedings*
And, as you said—and wisely was it said—
'Tis meet° that some more audience than a mother, — *proper*
Since nature makes them partial, should o'erhear
The speech of vantage.[1] Fare you well, my liege.
I'll call upon you ere you go to bed,
And tell you what I know.

KING CLAUDIUS Thanks, dear my lord.

Exit [POLONIUS]

O, my offence is rank! It smells to heaven.
It hath the primal eldest curse[2] upon't,
A brother's murder. Pray can I not.
Though inclination be as sharp as will,[3]
My stronger guilt defeats my strong intent,
And like a man to double business bound[4]
I stand in pause where I shall first begin,

8. That is, Fortune's wheel (usually depicted with the king at its top).
9. Scold him sternly.
1. To (our) profit or benefit.
2. The curse God put on Cain for committing the first murder, of his brother, Abel (Genesis 4.11–12).
3. Though my desire is as strong as my resolve.
4. That is, committed to divergent goals.

And both neglect. What if this cursèd hand
Were thicker than itself with brother's blood,[5]
Is there not rain enough in the sweet heavens
To wash it white as snow? Whereto serves mercy
But to confront the visage of offence?[6]
And what's in prayer but this twofold force,
To be forestallèd° ere we come to fall, *prevented (from sinning)*
Or pardoned being down? Then I'll look up.
My fault is past—but O, what form of prayer
Can serve my turn? 'Forgive me my foul murder'?
That cannot be, since I am still possessed
Of those effects for which I did the murder—
My crown, mine own ambition, and my queen.
May one be pardoned and retain th'offence?
In the corrupted currents of this world
Offence's gilded° hand may shove by justice, *bribing*
And oft 'tis seen the wicked prize[7] itself
Buys out the law. But 'tis not so above.
There is no shuffling,° there the action lies *evasive conduct*
In his° true nature,[8] and we ourselves compelled *its*
Even to the teeth and forehead of° our faults *face to face with*
To give in evidence.[9] What then? What rests?° *remains*
Try what repentance can. What can it not?
Yet what can it when one cannot repent?
O wretched state, O bosom black as death,
O limèd[1] soul that, struggling to be free,
Art more engaged!° Help, angels! Make assay.° *restricted / an attempt*
Bow, stubborn knees; and heart with strings of steel,
Be soft as sinews of the new-born babe.
All may be well.

[*He kneels.*]

Enter [*Prince*] HAMLET [*behind him*]

HAMLET Now might I do it pat,° now a° is praying, *readily / he*
And now I'll do't,

[*He draws his sword*]

and so a goes to heaven,
And so am I revenged. That would be scanned.[2]
A villain kills my father, and for that
I, his sole son, do this same villain send
To heaven.
O, this is hire and salary, not revenge!
A took my father grossly, full of bread,[3]

5. What if this hand had on it a layer of blood thicker than the hand itself.
6. That is, what function does mercy have other than to confront sin face to face?
7. The fruits of wickedness.
8. The deed (literally, the legal proceeding) is truly revealed.
9. To testify. Unlike in an English court, in heaven one is compelled to give evidence against oneself.
1. Caught as with birdlime, a sticky substance used for snaring birds.
2. That needs to be examined.
3. In full enjoyment of worldly pleasures. "Behold, this was the iniquity of thy sister Sodom, pride, fullness of bread, and abundance of idleness was in her and in her daughters" (Ezekiel 16.49).

With all his crimes broad blown,[4] as flush° as May; *lusty, lively*
And how his audit° stands, who knows save heaven? *account*
But in our circumstance and course of thought[5]
'Tis heavy with him. And am I then revenged
To take him in the purging of his soul,
When he is fit and seasoned° for his passage? *suitably prepared*
No.

[*He sheathes his sword*]

Up, sword, and know thou a more horrid hint.° *occasion*
When he is drunk asleep, or in his rage,
Or in th'incestuous pleasure of his bed,
At gaming, swearing, or about some act
That has no relish° of salvation in't, *linge*
Then trip him that his heels may kick at heaven,
And that his soul may be as damned and black
As hell whereto it goes. My mother stays.° *awaits*
This physic[6] but prolongs thy sickly days. *Exit*

KING CLAUDIUS My words fly up, my thoughts remain below.
Words without thoughts never to heaven go. *Exit*

3.4

Enter QUEEN GERTRUDE *and* POLONIUS

POLONIUS A° will come straight.° Look you lay home to him.[7] *He / right away*
Tell him his pranks have been too broad° to bear with, *unrestrained; indecent*
And that your grace hath screened and stood between
Much heat° and him. I'll silence me e'en here. *anger*
Pray you be round° with him. *blunt*

HAMLET (*within*) Mother, mother, mother!

QUEEN GERTRUDE I'll warr'nt you. Fear° me not. Withdraw; I hear him coming. *Doubt*

[POLONIUS *hides behind the arras.*]

Enter [*Prince*] HAMLET

HAMLET Now, mother, what's the matter?

QUEEN GERTRUDE Hamlet, thou hast thy father° much offended. *(stepfather, Claudius)*

HAMLET Mother, you have my father° much offended. *(old Hamlet)*

QUEEN GERTRUDE Come, come, you answer with an idle° tongue. *foolish*

HAMLET Go, go, you question with a wicked tongue.

QUEEN GERTRUDE Why, how now,° Hamlet? *what's this*

HAMLET What's the matter now?

QUEEN GERTRUDE Have you forgot me?[8]

HAMLET No, by the rood,° not so. *cross (of Christ)*
You are the Queen, your husband's brother's wife.
But—would you were not so—you are my mother.

QUEEN GERTRUDE Nay, then, I'll set those to you that can speak.[9]

4. With all his sins in full bloom.
5. That is, in the context of our limited understanding here on earth.
6. Medicine (i.e., both Hamlet's delay in revenging and Claudius's prayer).
3.4 Location: The Queen's private chamber.
7. Be sure you admonish him ("lay" means "thrust").
8. Have you forgotten to whom you are speaking?
9. That is, who can speak to someone as ill-mannered as you.

HAMLET Come, come, and sit you down. You shall not budge.
You go not till I set you up a glass° *mirror*
Where you may see the inmost part of you.
QUEEN GERTRUDE What wilt thou do? Thou wilt not murder me?
Help, help, ho!
POLONIUS [*behind the arras*] What ho! Help, help, help!
HAMLET How now, a rat? Dead for a ducat, dead.[1]
[*He thrusts his sword through the arras.*] *Kills* POLONIUS
POLONIUS O, I am slain!
QUEEN GERTRUDE [*to* HAMLET] O me, what hast thou done?
HAMLET Nay, I know not. Is it the King?
QUEEN GERTRUDE O, what a rash and bloody deed is this!
HAMLET A bloody deed—almost as bad, good-mother,° *stepmother*
As kill a king and marry with his brother.
QUEEN GERTRUDE As kill a king?
HAMLET Ay, lady, 'twas my word.
[*To* POLONIUS] Thou wretched, rash, intruding fool, farewell.
I took thee for thy better.° Take thy fortune. *(i.e., Claudius)*
Thou find'st to be too busy° is some danger.— *prying*
Leave wringing of your hands. Peace, sit you down,
And let me wring your heart; for so I shall
If it be made of penetrable stuff,
If damnèd custom° have not brassed[2] it so *habitual sinfulness*
That it is proof and bulwark against sense.[3]
QUEEN GERTRUDE What have I done, that thou dar'st wag thy tongue
In noise so rude against me?
HAMLET Such an act
That blurs the grace and blush of modesty,
Calls virtue hypocrite, takes off the rose[4]
From the fair forehead of an innocent love
And sets a blister there,[5] makes marriage vows
As false as dicers' oaths—O, such a deed
As from the body of contraction° plucks *the marriage contract*
The very soul, and sweet religion makes
A rhapsody[6] of words. Heaven's face doth glow,° *blush*
Yea, this solidity and compound mass[7]
With tristful° visage, as against the doom,[8] *sorrowful*
Is thought-sick at the act.
QUEEN GERTRUDE Ay me, what act,
That roars so loud and thunders in the index?[9]
HAMLET Look here upon this picture, and on this,
The counterfeit presentment° of two brothers. *painted representation*
See what a grace was seated on this brow—
Hyperion's curls, the front° of Jove himself, *brow*

1. I'll wager a ducat he is dead; or, I'll kill him for a ducat.
2. Brazened, hardened.
3. Armed and fortified against natural feeling.
4. The emblem of ideal love.
5. Prostitutes were branded on the forehead.
6. A disconnected string.
7. The earth itself (a compound of the four elements believed to constitute all matter).
8. As if doomsday were at hand.
9. Table of contents; preface.

An eye like Mars, to threaten or command,
A station° like the herald Mercury[1] — *stance*
New lighted° on a heaven-kissing hill; — *Newly alighted*
A combination and a form indeed
Where every god did seem to set his seal° — *to authenticate*
To give the world assurance of a man.
This *was* your husband. Look you now what follows.
Here *is* your husband, like a mildewed ear° — *eur of grain*
Blasting° his wholesome brother. Have you eyes? — *Infecting*
Could you on this fair mountain leave° to feed, — *cease*
And batten on this moor?[2] Ha, have you eyes?
You cannot call it love, for at your age
The heyday in the blood° is tame, it's humble, — *sexual desire*
And waits upon° the judgement; and what judgement — *Is subservient to*
Would step from this to this?[3]
Sense[4] sure you have,
Else could you not have motion;° but sure that sense — *locomotion*
Is apoplexed,° for madness would not err, — *paralyzed*
Nor sense to ecstasy° was ne'er so thralled — *madness*
But it reserved some quantity of choice
To serve in such a difference.[5] What devil was't
That thus hath cozened you at hoodman-blind?° — *blindman's buff*
Eyes without feeling, feeling without sight,
Ears without hands or eyes, smelling sans all,[6]
Or but a sickly part of one true sense
Could not so mope.° — *be so stupefied*
What devil was't
That thus hath cozened you at hood-man blind?
O shame, where is thy blush? Rebellious hell,
If thou canst mutine° in a matron's bones, — *mutiny*
To flaming youth let virtue be as wax
And melt in her° own fire. Proclaim no shame — *(youth's)*
When the compulsive ardour gives the charge,° — *orders the attack*
Since frost itself as actively doth burn,
And reason panders will.[7]

QUEEN GERTRUDE O Hamlet, speak no more!
Thou turn'st mine eyes into my very soul,
And there I see such black and grainèd° spots — *ingrained*
As will not leave their tinct.° — *color*

HAMLET Nay, but to live
In the rank sweat of an enseamèd° bed, — *a greasy*
Stewed[8] in corruption, honeying and making love

1. The winged messenger of the Roman gods.
2. Gorge yourself on this barren wasteland.
3. With the exception of a part of line 73.6 and 73.7, lines 73.1–73.11 appear in Q2 but not in F1.
4. Perception through the five senses (sight, smell, hearing, taste, and touch).
5. That is, the difference between Hamlet's father and Claudius.
6. Without the other senses.
7. When mature passion ("frost") burns as intensely as does youthful passion, and when reason, which is supposed to counsel the will with restraint, instead acts as a pimp to desire.
8. Boiled (with a pun on *stew,* meaning "brothel").

Over the nasty sty—

QUEEN GERTRUDE O, speak to me no more!
These words like daggers enter in mine ears.
No more, sweet Hamlet.

HAMLET A murderer and a villain,
A slave that is not twenti'th part the tithe° *tenth part*
Of your precedent° lord, a vice[9] of kings, *former*
A cutpurse° of the empire and the rule, *pickpocket*
That from a shelf the precious diadem stole
And put it in his pocket—

QUEEN GERTRUDE No more.

HAMLET A king of shreds and patches[1]—

Enter GHOST *in his nightgown*[2]

Save me and hover o'er me with your wings,
You heavenly guards! [*To* GHOST] What would you, gracious figure?

QUEEN GERTRUDE Alas, he's mad.

HAMLET [*to* GHOST] Do you not come your tardy son to chide,
That, lapsed in time and passion,[3] lets go by
Th'important° acting of your dread command? *urgent*
O, say!

GHOST Do not forget. This visitation
Is but to whet thy almost blunted purpose.
But look, amazement° on thy mother sits. *bewilderment*
O, step between her and her fighting° soul. *struggling, conflicted*
Conceit° in weakest bodies strongest works. *Imagination*
Speak to her, Hamlet.

HAMLET How is it with you, lady?

QUEEN GERTRUDE Alas, how is't with you,
That you do bend your eye on vacancy,
And with th'incorporal° air do hold discourse? *immaterial*
Forth at your eyes your spirits wildly peep,
And, as the sleeping soldiers in th'alarm,° *call to arms*
Your bedded hair, like life in excrements,[4]
Start up and stand on end. O gentle son,
Upon the heat and flame of thy distemper° *disordered mind*
Sprinkle cool patience! Whereon do you look?

HAMLET On him, on him. Look you how pale he glares.
His form and cause conjoined,[5] preaching to stones,
Would make them capable.° [*To* GHOST] Do not look upon me, *receptive*
Lest with this piteous action you convert° *turn aside*
My stern effects.° Then what I have to do *purpose*
Will want true colour—tears perchance for blood.[6]

QUEEN GERTRUDE To whom do you speak this?

9. The comic character in a morality play presenting a vice.
1. The multicolored outfit of the vice character.
2. The "nightgown" appears only in the stage directions to Q1 (the bad quarto) and Q2, not in F1.
3. Having allowed time to elapse and my passion (for revenge) to cool.
4. In outgrowths (such as hair and nails). *Bedded:* laid flat.
5. His appearance joined with his purpose for appearing.
6. That is, then my purpose (i.e., revenge) will lack true passion or motivation; I will instead produce colorless tears and not shed red blood.

HAMLET Do you see nothing there?
QUEEN GERTRUDE Nothing at all, yet all that is I see.
HAMLET Nor did you nothing hear?
QUEEN GERTRUDE No, nothing but ourselves.
HAMLET Why, look you there. Look how it steals away.
My father, in his habit as he lived.[7]
Look where he goes even now out at the portal.
Exit GHOST
QUEEN GERTRUDE This is the very coinage of your brain.
This bodiless creation ecstasy
Is very cunning in.[8]
HAMLET Ecstasy?
My pulse as yours doth temperately keep time,
And makes as healthful music. It is not madness
That I have uttered. Bring me to the test,
And I the matter will reword,° which madness *repeat verbatim*
Would gambol° from. Mother, for love of grace *leap away*
Lay not a flattering unction[9] to your soul
That not your trespass but my madness speaks.
It will but skin° and film the ulcerous place *thinly cover*
Whilst rank corruption, mining° all within, *undermining*
Infects unseen. Confess yourself to heaven;
Repent what's past, avoid what is to come,
And do not spread the compost o'er the weeds
To make them ranker. Forgive me this my virtue,° *my virtuous entreaty*
For in the fatness° of these pursy° times *grossness / fat*
Virtue itself of vice must pardon beg,
Yea, curb° and woo for leave° to do him good. *bow / permission*
QUEEN GERTRUDE O Hamlet, thou hast cleft my heart in twain!
HAMLET O, throw away the worser part of it,
And live the purer with the other half!
Good night—but go not to mine uncle's bed.
Assume° a virtue if you have it not.[1] *Act out*
That monster custom, who all sense doth eat,
Of habits devilish, is angel yet in this:
That to the use° of actions fair and good *habit*
He likewise gives a frock or livery
That aptly° is put on. Refrain tonight, *fittingly*
And that shall lend a kind of easiness
To the next abstinence, the next more easy—
For use almost can change the stamp of nature—
And either in° the devil, or throw him out *let in*
With wondrous potency.
Refrain tonight,
And that shall lend a kind of easiness

7. In his typical attire and appearance as if (or when) he lived.
8. Madness is especially crafty in the creation of hallucinations like this.
9. An ointment that appears to heal (by lessening or removing discomfort) but does not cure the disease.
1. Lines 155.1 through 155.10 appear in Q2 but not in F1.

To the next abstinence. Once more, good night;
And when you are desirous to be blest,
I'll blessing beg of you. For this same lord,° *(Polonius)*
I do repent. But heaven hath pleased it so
To punish me with this, and this with me,
That I must be their scourge and minister.[2]
I will bestow° him, and will answer well[3] *dispose of*
The death I gave him. So, again, good night.
I must be cruel only to be kind.
Thus bad begins, and worse remains behind.

QUEEN GERTRUDE What shall I do?

HAMLET Not this, by no means, that I bid you do:
Let the bloat° King tempt you again to bed, *bloated*
Pinch wanton on your cheek, call you his mouse,
And let him for a pair of reechy° kisses, *filthy*
Or paddling° in your neck with his damned fingers, *playing fondly*
Make you to ravel° all this matter out, *unwind (i.e., reveal)*
That I essentially am not in madness,
But mad in craft.° 'Twere good you let him know, *by design*
For who that's but° a queen, fair, sober, wise, *only*
Would from a paddock,° from a bat, a gib,° *toad / tomcat*
Such dear concernings° hide? Who would do so? *important matters*
No, in despite of sense and secrecy,
Unpeg the basket on the house's top,
Let the birds fly, and, like the famous ape,
To try conclusions° in the basket creep, *To experiment*
And break your own neck down.[4]

QUEEN GERTRUDE Be thou assured, if words be made of breath,
And breath of life, I have no life to breathe
What thou hast said to me.

HAMLET I must to England.
You know that?

QUEEN GERTRUDE Alack, I had forgot.
'Tis so concluded on.[5]

HAMLET *There's letters sealed, and my two schoolfellows—*
Whom I will trust as I will adders fanged—
They bear the mandate, they must sweep my way
And marshal me to knavery.[6] Let it work,
For 'tis the sport to have the engineer[7]
Hoised with his own petard;[8] and't shall go hard

2. "Scourge" and "minister" were sometimes used interchangeably to refer to one who punishes sin on God's behalf. "Scourge" is also applied to tyrants, who may still be serving God's justice when they kill, but who appear to contaminate or condemn themselves in the process because they kill cruelly or for personal reasons. God's "minister," by contrast, acts as God's servant and does not become an independent agent of revenge.

3. Assume responsibility for.

4. In a story now lost, an ape apparently enters a cage on top of a house that has been opened (unpegged), allowing birds to escape. The ape falls to its death, perhaps because it tries to fly.

5. The lines 189.1 through 189.9 appear in Q2 but not in F1.

6. Prepare the way for me and lead me into a trap.

7. The designer of military devices.

8. Blown up by his own explosive.

But I will delve one yard below their mines° — *military tunnels*
And blow them at the moon. O, 'tis most sweet
When in one line two crafts directly meet.[9]

HAMLET — This man shall set me packing.
I'll lug the guts into the neighbour room.
Mother, good night indeed. This counsellor
Is now most still, most secret, and most grave,
Who was in life a foolish prating knave.—
Come, sir, to draw toward an end with you.[1]—
Good night, mother. *Exit, tugging in* POLONIUS

4.1

Enter KING CLAUDIUS *to* QUEEN GERTRUDE

KING CLAUDIUS — There's matter in these sighs, these profound heaves;
You must translate. 'Tis fit we understand them.
Where is your son?

QUEEN GERTRUDE — *Bestow this place on us a little while*[2]

Exeunt [ROSENCRANTZ *and* GUILDENSTERN]

Ah, my good lord, what have I seen tonight!

KING CLAUDIUS — What, Gertrude? How does Hamlet?

QUEEN GERTRUDE — Mad as the sea and wind when both contend
Which is the mightier. In his lawless fit,
Behind the arras hearing something stir,
He whips his rapier out and cries 'A rat, a rat!',
And in his brainish apprehension° kills — *headstrong delusion*
The unseen good old man.

KING CLAUDIUS — O heavy deed!
It had been so with us° had we been there. — *me (the royal "we")*
His liberty is full of threats to all—
To you yourself, to us, to everyone.
Alas, how shall this bloody deed be answered?° — *explained satisfactorily*
It will be laid to° us, whose providence° — *blamed on / foresight*
Should have kept short,° restrained, and out of haunt[3] — *controlled*
This mad young man. But so much was our love,
We would not understand what was most fit,
But, like the owner° of a foul disease, — *carrier*
To keep it from divulging,° let it feed — *being known*
Even on the pith° of life. Where is he gone? — *vital substance*

QUEEN GERTRUDE — To draw apart the body he hath killed,
O'er whom—his very madness, like some ore° — *vein of gold*
Among a mineral° of metals base, — *mine*
Shows itself pure—a° weeps for what is done. — *he*

KING CLAUDIUS — O Gertrude, come away!
The sun no sooner shall the mountains touch
But we will ship him hence; and this vile deed
We must with all our majesty and skill

9. When two cunning plots come together.
1. To conclude matters between us (with a pun on "draw," pull).

4.1 Location: The castle.
2. Line 3.1 appears in Q2 but not in F1.
3. Away from places frequented by others.

Both countenance° and excuse.—Ho, Guildenstern! *authorize*

Enter ROSENCRANTZ *and* GUILDENSTERN

Friends both, go join you with some further aid.
Hamlet in madness hath Polonius slain,
And from his mother's closet hath he dragged him.
Go seek him out, speak fair, and bring the body
Into the chapel. I pray you haste in this.

Exeunt [ROSENCRANTZ *and* GUILDENSTERN]

Come, Gertrude, we'll call up our wisest friends
To let them know both what we mean to do
And what's untimely done.[4]
So envious slander,[5]
Whose whisper o'er the world's diameter,° *whole extent*
As level as the cannon to his blank,[6]
Transports his poisoned shot, may miss our name
And hit the woundless° air. *invulnerable*
O, come away!
My soul is full of discord and dismay. *Exeunt*

4.2

Enter [*Prince*] HAMLET

HAMLET Safely stowed.

ROSENCRANTZ *and* GUILDENSTERN (*within*) Hamlet, Lord Hamlet!

HAMLET What noise? Who calls on Hamlet?

Enter ROSENCRANTZ *and* GUILDENSTERN

O, here they come.

ROSENCRANTZ What have you done, my lord, with the dead body?

HAMLET Compounded° it with dust, whereto 'tis kin. *United*

ROSENCRANTZ Tell us where 'tis, that we may take it thence
And bear it to the chapel.

HAMLET Do not believe it.

ROSENCRANTZ Believe what?

HAMLET That I can keep your counsel and not mine own.[7] Besides, to be demanded of° a sponge—what replication° should be made by the son of a king? *questioned by / reply*

ROSENCRANTZ Take you me for a sponge, my lord?

HAMLET Ay, sir, that soaks up the King's countenance,° his rewards, his authorities. But such officers do the King best service in the end. He keeps them, like an ape an apple in the corner of his jaw, first mouthed to be last swallowed. When he needs what you have gleaned, it is but squeezing you, and, sponge, you shall be dry again. *favor*

4. Lines 39.1 through 39.5 are in Q2 but not in F1.

5. The phrase "So envious slander" is supplied by earlier editors because half a verse line is missing from Q2.

6. As straight as the cannon to its target (i.e., point-blank).

4.2 Location: The scene continues.

7. That I can follow your advice ("counsel") and keep my secret ("counsel").

ROSENCRANTZ I understand you not, my lord.
HAMLET I am glad of it. A knavish speech sleeps in° a foolish ear. *is meaningless in*
ROSENCRANTZ My lord, you must tell us where the body is, and go with us to the King.
HAMLET The body is with the King, but the King is not with the body.[8] The King is a thing—
GUILDENSTERN A thing, my lord?
HAMLET Of nothing. Bring me to him. Hide fox, and all after.[9]
[*Exit running, pursued by the others*]

4.3

Enter KING [CLAUDIUS][1]

KING CLAUDIUS I have sent to seek him, and to find the body.
How dangerous is it that this man goes loose!
Yet must not we put the strong law on him.
He's loved of° the distracted° multitude, *by / fickle*
Who like not in their judgement but their eyes,[2]
And where 'tis so, th'offender's scourge° is weighed, *punishment*
But never the offence. To bear° all smooth and even, *manage*
This sudden sending him away must seem
Deliberate pause.[3] Diseases desperate grown
By desperate appliance° are relieved, *remedy*
Or not at all.

Enter ROSENCRANTZ

How now, what hath befall'n?
ROSENCRANTZ Where the dead body is bestowed, my lord,
We cannot get from him.
KING CLAUDIUS But where is he?
ROSENCRANTZ Without, my lord, guarded to know your pleasure.
KING CLAUDIUS Bring him before us.
ROSENCRANTZ Ho, Guildenstern! Bring in my lord.

Enter [*Prince*] HAMLET *and* GUILDENSTERN

KING CLAUDIUS Now, Hamlet, where's Polonius?
HAMLET At supper.
KING CLAUDIUS At supper? Where?
HAMLET Not where he eats, but where a° is eaten. A certain convocation of politic[4] worms are e'en° at him. Your worm is your only emperor for diet.[5] We fat all creatures else° to fat us, and we fat ourselves for maggots. Your fat *he / now / other than ourselves*

8. The theory of "the king's two bodies" distinguished the monarch's mortal body from the sacred and eternal body of his royal office.
9. A cry from a version of the children's game of hide-and-seek.
4.3 Location: The scene continues.
1. Q2 reads "Enter King, and two or three."
2. Who judge not with their rational faculties but by outward appearance.
3. A carefully considered decision (to interrupt the action).
4. Crafty; skilled in statecraft.
5. Food; perhaps also a pun on the Diet (council) at the German city of Worms in 1521, at which the reform-minded theologian Martin Luther, in the presence of Emperor Charles V, was condemned for religious heresy.

king and your lean beggar is but variable service°—two dishes, but to one table. That's the end. *different courses*

KING CLAUDIUS Alas, alas!

HAMLET A man may fish with the worm that hath eat of a king, and eat of the fish that hath fed of that worm.

KING CLAUDIUS What dost thou mean by this?

HAMLET Nothing but to show you how a king may go a progress[6] through the guts of a beggar.

KING CLAUDIUS Where is Polonius?

HAMLET In heaven. Send thither to see. If your messenger find him not there, seek him i'th' other place yourself. But indeed, if you find him not this month, you shall nose him as you go up the stairs into the lobby.

KING CLAUDIUS [*to* ROSENCRANTZ] Go seek him there.

HAMLET [*to* ROSENCRANTZ] A will stay till ye come.

[*Exit* ROSENCRANTZ]

KING CLAUDIUS Hamlet, this deed of thine, for thine especial safety—
Which we do tender° as we dearly grieve *value*
For that which thou hast done—must send thee hence
With fiery quickness. Therefore prepare thyself.
The barque is ready, and the wind at help,
Th'associates tend,° and everything is bent° *companions wait / ready*
For England.

HAMLET For England?

KING CLAUDIUS Ay, Hamlet.

HAMLET Good.

KING CLAUDIUS So is it if thou knew'st our purposes.

HAMLET I see a cherub[7] that sees them. But come, for England. Farewell, dear mother.

KING CLAUDIUS Thy loving father, Hamlet.

HAMLET My mother. Father and mother is man and wife, man and wife is one flesh,[8] and so my mother. Come, for England. *Exit*

KING CLAUDIUS [*to* GUILDENSTERN] Follow him at foot.° Tempt *at his heels*
him with speed aboard.
Delay it not. I'll have him hence tonight.
Away, for everything is sealed and done
That else leans° on th'affair. Pray you, make haste. *bears*

[*Exit* GUILDENSTERN]

And, England,[9] if my love thou hold'st at aught° *at any value*
As my great power thereof may give thee sense,[1]
Since yet thy cicatrice° looks raw and red *scar*

6. On a state journey made by a royal or noble.

7. A member of the second-highest rank in the angelic hierachy, associated by the early Catholic Church with divine knowledge.

8. A reference to the biblical injunction that "a man . . . shall cleave unto his wife: and they shall be one flesh" (Genesis 2.24).

9. King of England.

1. That is, as my great power may give you reason to value my love.

After the Danish sword, and thy free awe[2]
Pays homage to us— thou mayst not coldly set° *regard with indifference*
Our sovereign process,° which imports at full,[3] *royal command*
By letters conjuring° to that effect, *appealing earnesty*
The present° death of Hamlet. Do it, England, *immediate*
For like the hectic° in my blood he rages, *consumptive fever*
And thou must cure me. Till I know 'tis done,
Howe'er my haps,° my joys were ne'er begun. *Exit* *fortunes*

4.4

Enter FORTINBRAS *with a drum and his army over the stage*

FORTINBRAS Go, captain, from me greet the Danish king.
Tell him that by his licence° Fortinbras *permission*
Claims the conveyance of° a promised march *escort*
Over his kingdom. You know the rendezvous.
If that his majesty would aught with us,
We shall express our duty in his eye,° *presence*
And let him know so.
CAPTAIN I will do't, my lord. [*Exit*]
FORTINBRAS Go safely on. *Exeunt* [*marching*][4]

Enter [*Prince*] HAMLET, ROSENCRANTZ, [GUILDENSTERN,] *etc.*

HAMLET [*to the* CAPTAIN] *Good sir, whose powers° are these?* *forces*
CAPTAIN *They are of Norway, sir.*
HAMLET *How purposed, sir, I pray you?*
CAPTAIN *Against some part of Poland.*
HAMLET *Who commands them, sir?*
CAPTAIN *The nephew to old Norway, Fortinbras.*
HAMLET *Goes it against the main° of Poland, sir,* *the main part*
Or for some frontier?
CAPTAIN *Truly to speak, and with no addition,°* *exaggeration*
We go to gain a little patch of ground
That hath in it no profit but the name.
To pay five ducats, five, I would not farm° it, *lease*
Nor will it yield to Norway or the Pole
A ranker rate,° should it be sold in fee.° *higher return / outright*
HAMLET *Why then, the Polack never will defend it.*
CAPTAIN *Yes, it is already garrisoned.*
HAMLET *Two thousand souls and twenty thousand ducats*
Will now debate the question of this straw.° *trifling matter*
This is th'imposthume° of much wealth and peace, *abscess*
That inward breaks and shows no cause without° *on the outside*
Why the man dies. I humbly thank you, sir.
CAPTAIN *God buy° you, sir.* [*Exit*] *be with*
ROSENCRANTZ *Will't please you go, my lord?*
HAMLET *I'll be with you straight. Go a little before*
[*Exeunt all but* HAMLET]

2. Voluntary show of reverence.
3. Communicates in detailed instructions.
4.4 Location: The Danish coast.
4. In Q2 the captain does not exit, and the conversation continues. Lines 9.1–9.56 appear in Q2 but not in F1.

How all occasions do inform against° me — accuse
And spur my dull revenge! What is a man
If his chief good and market° of his time — profit
Be but to sleep and feed?—a beast, no more.
Sure, he that made us with such large discourse,° — powers of reasoning
Looking before and after,[5] gave us not
That capability° and god-like reason — intelligence
To fust° in us unused. Now whether it be — become moldy
Bestial oblivion,[6] or some craven scruple° — cowardly qualm
Of° thinking too precisely on th'event— — From
A thought which, quartered, hath but one part wisdom
And ever three parts coward—I do not know
Why yet I live to say 'This thing's to do',
Sith° I have cause, and will, and strength, and means, — Since
To do't. Examples gross° as earth exhort me, — obvious
Witness this army of such mass and charge,° — expense
Led by a delicate and tender° prince, — skillful and young
Whose spirit with divine ambition puffed° — swollen
Makes mouths at the invisible event,[7]
Exposing what is mortal and unsure
To all that fortune, death, and danger dare,
Even for an eggshell. Rightly to be great
Is not to stir without great argument,
But greatly to find quarrel in a straw
When honour's at the stake.[8] How stand I, then,
That have a father killed, a mother stained,
Excitements of° my reason and my blood, — Events that excite
And let all sleep while, to my shame, I see
The imminent death of twenty thousand men
That, for a fantasy and trick° of fame, — trifle; sham
Go to their graves like beds, fight for a plot
Whereon the numbers cannot try the cause,[9]
Which is not tomb enough and continent° — container
To hide the slain. O, from this time forth
My thoughts be bloody or be nothing worth! Exit

4.5

Enter QUEEN GERTRUDE *and* HORATIO

QUEEN GERTRUDE I will not speak with her.
HORATIO She is importunate,
Indeed distraught. Her mood will needs be pitied.
QUEEN GERTRUDE What would she have?
HORATIO She speaks much of her father, says she hears
There's tricks° i'th' world, and hems, and beats her heart,° — dishonesty / breast

5. With an understanding of the past and the future.

6. Animal-like forgetfulness.

7. Makes disdainful faces at unforeseeable consequences.

8. That is, to be truly great is not to start a war without outstanding reasons, but nobly ("greatly") to find conflict in a trifling matter when honor hangs in the balance.

9. That is, not large enough for the armies to fight on.

4.5 Location: A public room in the castle.

Spurns enviously at straws,[1] speaks things in doubt° *obscurely*
That carry but half sense. Her speech is nothing,
Yet the unshapèd use° of it doth move *confused manner*
The hearers to collection.° They aim° at it, *inference / guess*
And botch° the words up fit to their own thoughts, *patch*
Which,° as her winks and nods and gestures yield them, *(i.e., the words)*
Indeed would make one think there might be thought,
Though nothing sure, yet much unhappily.

QUEEN GERTRUDE 'Twere good she were spoken with, for she may strew
Dangerous conjectures in ill-breeding minds.
Let her come in.

[HORATIO *withdraws to admit* OPHELIA]

QUEEN GERTRUDE To my sick soul, as sin's true nature is,
Each toy° seems prologue to some great amiss.° *trifle / misfortune*
So full of artless jealousy° is guilt, *crude suspicion*
It spills itself in fearing to be spilt.

Enter OPHELIA *distracted, playing on a lute, and her hair down, singing*[2]

OPHELIA Where is the beauteous majesty of Denmark?

QUEEN GERTRUDE How now, Ophelia?

OPHELIA (*sings*) How should I your true love know
From another one?—
By his cockle hat and staff,
And his sandal shoon.[3]

QUEEN GERTRUDE Alas, sweet lady, what imports° this song? *means*

OPHELIA Say you? Nay, pray you, mark.° *listen*
(*Song*) He is dead and gone, lady,
He is dead and gone.
At his head a grass-green turf,
At his heels a stone.

QUEEN GERTRUDE Nay, but Ophelia—

OPHELIA Pray you, mark.
(*Song*) White his shroud as the mountain snow—

Enter KING [CLAUDIUS]

QUEEN GERTRUDE Alas, look here, my lord.

OPHELIA (*Song*) Larded° with sweet flowers, *Bedecked*
Which bewept to the grave did—not[4]—go
With true-love showers.° *tears*

KING CLAUDIUS How do ye, pretty lady?

OPHELIA Well, God'ield° you. They say the owl was a baker's daughter.[5] Lord, we know what we are, but know not what we may be. God be at your table! *God yield (repay)*

1. Takes offense angrily at trifles.
2. F1's stage direction reads "Enter Ophelia distracted." The additions here are taken from Q1, which is probably based on the recollections of one or more actors who took part in an actual performance of the play.
3. The "sandal shoon" (shoes) and the "cockle hat" were typical attributes of a pilgrim (the cockleshell was attached to the hats of those who had returned from the shrine of St. James in Compostella, Spain).
4. The insertion of "not" interrupts the meter and changes the expected meaning.
5. In an old folktale, a baker's daughter who gave ungenerously when Christ asked for bread was turned into an owl. In Wales, the owl's cry was thought to signify an unmarried girl's loss of virginity.

KING CLAUDIUS [*to* GERTRUDE] Conceit° upon her father. *Morbid thoughts*

OPHELIA Pray you, let's have no words of this, but when they ask you what it means, say you this.

(Song) Tomorrow is Saint Valentine's day,[6]
All in the morning betime,° *early*
And I a maid at your window
To be your Valentine.
Then up he rose, and donned his clothes,
And dupped° the chamber door; *opened*
Let in the maid, that out a maid° *a virgin*
Never departed more.

KING CLAUDIUS Pretty Ophelia—

OPHELIA Indeed, la? Without an oath, I'll make an end on't.° *of it*

(Song) By Gis,° and by Saint Charity,[7] *Jesus*
Alack, and fie for shame!
Young men will do't° if they come to't, *i.e., have sex*
By Cock,[8] they are to blame.
Quoth she 'Before you tumbled me,
You promised me to wed.'
So would I 'a' done, by yonder sun,
An° thou hadst not come to my bed. *If*

KING CLAUDIUS [*to* GERTRUDE] How long hath she been thus?

OPHELIA I hope all will be well. We must be patient. But I cannot choose but weep to think they should lay him i'th' cold ground. My brother shall know of it. And so I thank you for your good counsel. Come, my coach! Good night, ladies, good night, sweet ladies, good night, good night. *Exit*

KING CLAUDIUS [*to* HORATIO] Follow her close. Give her good watch, I pray you. [*Exit* HORATIO]
O, this is the poison of deep grief! It springs
All from her father's death. O Gertrude, Gertrude,
When sorrows come they come not single spies,° *scouts*
But in battalions. First, her father slain;
Next, your son gone, and he most violent author
Of his own just remove; the people muddied,° *confused*
Thick and unwholesome in their thoughts and whispers
For good Polonius' death; and we have done but greenly° *foolishly*
In hugger-mugger° to inter him; poor Ophelia *Secretly*
Divided from herself and her fair judgement,
Without the which we are pictures or mere beasts;
Last, and as much containing° as all these, *as pertinent*
Her brother is in secret come from France,
Feeds on this wonder, keeps himself in clouds,[9]
And wants° not buzzers° to infect his ear *lacks / rumormongers*
With pestilent speeches of his father's death;
Wherein necessity, of matter beggared,° *lacking facts*

6. The song hints at the notion that the first girl seen by a man on Valentine's day will be his true love.

7. That is, Holy Charity (not an actual saint).

8. A common corruption of "God" in mild oaths (with an obvious pun on "penis").

9. Obscure, hidden; or, perhaps, in clouds of suspicion.

Will nothing stick our persons to arraign
In ear and ear.[1] O my dear Gertrude, this,
Like to a murd'ring-piece,[2] in many places
Gives me superfluous[3] death.

A noise within

QUEEN GERTRUDE Alack, what noise is this?

KING CLAUDIUS Where is my Switzers?[4] Let them guard the door.

Enter a MESSENGER

What is the matter?

MESSENGER Save yourself, my lord.
The ocean, overpeering of his list,[5]
Eats not the flats with more impetuous[6] haste
Than young Laertes, in a riotous head,° *armed force*
O'erbears your officers. The rabble call him lord,
And, as the world were now but[7] to begin,
Antiquity forgot, custom not known,
The ratifiers and props of every word,[8]
They cry 'Choose we! Laertes shall be king.'
Caps, hands, and tongues applaud it to the clouds,
'Laertes shall be king, Laertes king.'

QUEEN GERTRUDE How cheerfully on the false trail they cry![9]

A noise within

O, this is counter,[1] you false Danish dogs!

KING CLAUDIUS The doors are broke.

Enter LAERTES *with [his* FOLLOWERS *at the door]*

LAERTES Where is the King?—Sirs, stand you all without.

ALL HIS FOLLOWERS No, let's come in.

LAERTES I pray you, give me leave.

ALL HIS FOLLOWERS We will, we will.

LAERTES I thank you. Keep the door. [*Exeunt* FOLLOWERS]
O thou vile king,
Give me my father.

QUEEN GERTRUDE Calmly, good Laertes.

LAERTES That drop of blood that's calm proclaims me bastard,
Cries cuckold to my father, brands the harlot
Even here between the chaste unsmirchèd brow
Of my true mother.

KING CLAUDIUS What is the cause, Laertes,
That thy rebellion looks so giant-like?—
Let him go, Gertrude. Do not fear our° person. *fear for my*
There's such divinity doth hedge° a king *protect*

1. That is, will not fail to accuse me in every ear.
2. A cannon that scattered its shot.
3. Superfluous because one death would be enough.
4. Swiss mercenaries (employed as royal guards at a number of European courts).
5. Rising above its shore (boundary).
6. Spelled "impitious" (without pity, violently) in Q2 and "impittious" in F1.
7. That is, as if the world were only now beginning.
8. The ancient traditions and customs, which ratify the meaning of every word, have been forgotten (by the rabble).
9. That is, as if they were hounds baying after their prey.
1. Following the trail of game in the reverse (here, the wrong) direction.

That treason can but peep to what it would,[2]
Acts little of his° will.—Tell me, Laertes, *its*
Why thou art thus incensed.—Let him go, Gertrude.—
Speak, man.
LAERTES Where is my father?
KING CLAUDIUS Dead.
QUEEN GERTRUDE [*to* LAERTES] But not by him.
KING CLAUDIUS Let him demand his fill.
LAERTES How came he dead? I'll not be juggled with.° *deceived*
To hell, allegiance! Vows to the blackest devil!
Conscience and grace to the profoundest pit!
I dare damnation. To this point I stand,[3]
That both the worlds I give to negligence,[4]
Let come what comes. Only I'll be revenged
Most throughly° for my father. *thoroughly*
KING CLAUDIUS Who shall stay° you? *stop*
LAERTES My will, not all the world;
And for my means, I'll husband them so well
They shall go far with little.
KING CLAUDIUS Good Laertes,
If you desire to know the certainty
Of your dear father's death, is't writ in your revenge
That, sweepstake,[5] you will draw° both friend and foe, *take from*
Winner and loser?
LAERTES None but his enemies.
KING CLAUDIUS Will you know them then?
LAERTES To his good friends thus wide I'll ope my arms,
And, like the kind life-rend'ring pelican,
Repast them with my blood.[6]
KING CLAUDIUS Why, now you speak
Like a good child and a true gentleman.
That I am guiltless of your father's death,
And am most sensibly° in grief for it, *intensely*
It shall as level° to your judgement pierce *plain*
As day does to your eye.

A noise within

VOICES [*within*] Let her come in.
LAERTES How now, what noise is that?

Enter OPHELIA [*as before*]

O heat dry up my brains![7] Tears seven times salt
Burn out the sense and virtue° of mine eye! *power*

2. That is, that treason can only glimpse at what it would like to do.
3. This I insist on.
4. That I do not care about the consequences in this world or the one after death.
5. Indiscriminately (literally, taking all the stakes in a game of chance).
6. The pelican mother was thought to feed ("repast") its young with blood from a wound she pecked in her own breast.
7. According to the humoral theory of physiology, the brain was a cold and moist organ. In this line and the next, Laertes expresses the wish that his rational and sensory abilities perish so that he would not have to bear witness to Ophelia's madness.

By heaven, thy madness shall be paid by weight
Till our scale turns the beam.[8] O rose of May,
Dear maid, kind sister, sweet Ophelia!
O heavens, is't possible a young maid's wits
Should be as mortal as an old man's life?
Nature is fine in love, and where 'tis fine
It sends some precious instance of itself
After the thing it loves.[9]

OPHELIA (*Song*) They bore him barefaced on the bier,
Hey non nony, nony, hey nony,
And on his grave rained many a tear—
Fare you well, my dove.

LAERTES Hadst thou thy wits and didst persuade° revenge, *argue for*
It could not move thus.

OPHELIA You must sing 'Down, a-down',[1] and you, 'Call him a down-a'. O, how the wheel[2] becomes it! It is the false steward that stole his master's daughter.

LAERTES This nothing's more than matter.[3]

OPHELIA There's rosemary, that's for remembrance. Pray, love, remember. And there is pansies; that's for thoughts.[4]

LAERTES A document° in madness—thoughts and remembrance fitted.° *lesson* / *conferred fittingly*

OPHELIA There's fennel for you, and columbines.[5] There's rue for you, and here's some for me. We may call it herb-grace o' Sundays. O, you must wear your rue with a difference.[6] There's a daisy. I would give you some violets,[7] but they withered all when my father died. They say a° made a good end. *he*

(*Song*) For bonny sweet Robin is all my joy.

LAERTES Thought and affliction, passion,° hell itself *suffering*
She turns to favour° and to prettiness. *grace*

OPHELIA (*Song*) And will a not come again,
And will a not come again?
No, no, he is dead,
Go to thy death-bed,
He never will come again.

8. The image is of the scales of justice, in which madness will be outweighed by vengeance.
9. Perhaps alluding to the Neoplatonic notion that love refined and etherealized human nature, sending part of that purified nature after its object, Laertes suggests that Ophelia loved her father so much that she sent part of her nature (her sanity) after him when he died.
1. A common refrain in popular ballads.
2. Refrain; possibly also a reference to Fortune's wheel.
3. That is, this nonsense means more than coherent speech does.
4. Rosemary was thought to strengthen memory, and it was commonly associated with remembrance at weddings and at funerals. Pansies symbolize love; Ophelia puns on *pensées* (thoughts; French), from which the flower's name derives.
5. Fennel signifies flattery; columbine was known for its horned shape and here may signify cuckoldry. Rue (an aromatic herb) suggests regret and repentance.
6. Perhaps Ophelia means that she and the recipient (the King or Queen?) of the imaginary rue have different reasons for wearing it.
7. The daisy may signify dissembling or faithlessness; the violets, faithfulness.

His beard as white as snow,
All flaxen° was his poll.° *white / head*
He is gone, he is gone,
And we cast away moan.
God 'a' mercy on his soul.
And of all Christian souls, I pray God. God b'wi' ye.
Exeunt OPHELIA [*and* GERTRUDE]

LAERTES Do you see this, O God?

KING CLAUDIUS Laertes, I must commune with° your grief, *share in*
Or you deny me right. Go but apart,
Make choice of whom° your wisest friends you will, *whichever of*
And they shall hear and judge 'twixt you and me.
If by direct or by collateral° hand *indirect*
They find us touched,° we will our kingdom give, *touched with guilt*
Our crown, our life, and all that we call ours,
To you in satisfaction.° But if not, *compensation*
Be you content to lend your patience to us,
And we shall jointly labour with your soul
To give it due content.

LAERTES Let this be so.
His means of death, his obscure burial—
No trophy,° sword, nor hatchment[8] o'er his bones, *memorial*
No noble rite nor formal ostentation°— *display, ceremony*
Cry to be heard, as 'twere from heaven to earth,
That I must call't in question.

KING CLAUDIUS So you shall;
And where th'offence is, let the great axe fall.
I pray you go with me. *Exeunt*

4.6

Enter HORATIO *with* [*a* SERVANT]

HORATIO What are they that would speak with me?

SERVANT Sailors, sir. They say they have letters for you.

HORATIO Let them come in. [*Exit* SERVANT]
I do not know from what part of the world
I should be greeted if not from Lord Hamlet.

Enter SAILOR[S]

A SAILOR God bless you, sir.

HORATIO Let him bless thee too.

A SAILOR A° shall, sir, an't° please him. There's a letter for you, sir. It comes from th'ambassador that was bound for England—if your name be Horatio, as I am let to know it is. *He / if it*

HORATIO (*reads*) 'Horatio, when thou shalt have over-looked° this, give these fellows some means° to the King. They have letters for him. Ere we were two days *read* *access*

8. A square or lozenge-shaped tablet exhibiting the armorial bearings of the deceased.
4.6 Location: The castle.

old at sea, a pirate of very warlike appointment° gave us chase. Finding ourselves too slow of sail, we put on a compelled valour, and in the grapple I boarded them. On the instant they got clear of our ship, so I alone became their prisoner. They have dealt with me like thieves of mercy; but they knew what they did:[9] I am to do a good turn for them. Let the King have the letters I have sent, and repair° thou to me with as much haste as thou wouldst fly° death. I have words to speak in thine ear will make thee dumb, yet are they much too light for the bore of the matter.[1] These good fellows will bring thee where I am. Rosencrantz and Guildenstern hold their course for England. Of them I have much to tell thee. Farewell.

appointment: *equipment*; *repair*: *come*; *fly*: *flee*

He that thou knowest thine,
Hamlet.'

Come, I will give you way° for these your letters, *a means of delivery*
And do't the speedier that you may direct me
To him from whom you brought them. *Exeunt*

4.7

Enter KING [CLAUDIUS] *and* LAERTES

KING CLAUDIUS Now must your conscience my acquittance seal,[2]
And you must put me in your heart for friend,
Sith° you have heard, and with a knowing ear, *Since*
That he which hath your noble father slain
Pursued my life.

LAERTES It well appears. But tell me
Why you proceeded not against these feats,° *acts*
So crimeful and so capital° in nature, *punishable by death*
As by your safety, wisdom, all things else,
You mainly° were stirred up. *greatly*

KING CLAUDIUS O, for two special reasons,
Which may to you perhaps seem much unsinewed,° *very feeble*
And yet to me they're strong. The Queen his mother
Lives almost by his looks; and for myself—
My virtue or my plague, be it either which—
She's so conjunctive° to my life and soul *closely joined*
That, as the star moves not but in his sphere,[3]
I could not but by her. The other motive
Why to a public count° I might not go *accounting*
Is the great love the general gender° bear him, *common people*
Who, dipping all his faults in their affection,

9. That is, the pirates showed mercy to Hamlet with the expectation of some reward or compensation. *Thieves of mercy*: merciful thieves.
1. A firearms metaphor: the caliber or importance ("bore") of this subject ("the matter") requires more than the light-gauge shot ("words") Hamlet has at his disposal.
4.7 Location: The castle.
2. That is, your conscience must confirm my innocence.
3. According to Ptolemaic astronomy, planets (stars) circled around the earth, each confined to a specific sphere.

Would, like the spring that turneth wood to stone,[4]
Convert his guilts to graces; so that my arrows,
Too slightly timbered° for so loud° a wind, *light / strong*
Would have reverted to my bow again,
And not where I had aimed them.

LAERTES And so have I a noble father lost,
A sister driven into desp'rate terms,° *circumstances*
Who has, if praises may go back again,[5]
Stood challenger, on mount, of all the age
For her perfections.[6] But my revenge will come.

KING CLAUDIUS Break not your sleeps for that. You must not think
That we are made of stuff so flat and dull° *tame and spiritless*
That we can let our beard be shook with danger,[7]
And think it pastime. You shortly shall hear more.
I loved your father, and we love ourself.
And that, I hope, will teach you to imagine—

Enter a MESSENGER *with letters*

How now? What news?

MESSENGER Letters, my lord, from Hamlet.
This to your majesty; this to the Queen.

KING CLAUDIUS From Hamlet? Who brought them?

MESSENGER Sailors, my lord, they say. I saw them not.
They were given me by Claudio. He received them.

KING CLAUDIUS Laertes, you shall hear them.—Leave us.

Exit MESSENGER

[*Reads*] 'High and mighty, you shall know I am set naked° on your kingdom. Tomorrow shall I beg leave to see your kingly eyes, when I shall, first asking your pardon,° thereunto recount th'occasions of my sudden and more strange return. *destitute; defenseless* / *permission*

Hamlet.'

What should this mean? Are all the rest come back?
Or is it some abuse,° and no such thing? *trickery*

LAERTES Know you the hand?

KING CLAUDIUS 'Tis Hamlet's character.° *handwriting*
'Naked'—and in a postscript here he says
'Alone'. Can you advise me?

LAERTES I'm lost in it, my lord. But let him come.
It warms the very sickness in my heart
That I shall live and tell him to his teeth,
'Thus diddest thou'.

KING CLAUDIUS If it be so, Laertes—
As how should it be so, how otherwise?[8]—

4. The spring whose water contains so much lime that it petrifies fallen branches or exposed roots.
5. May refer to the past (i.e., to Ophelia's former virtues).
6. Challenged the world, in the sight of all ("on mount"), to match her virtues.
7. That I will let myself be affronted by someone powerful.
8. That is, how can Hamlet have returned (despite the order for his execution), but how else to explain the letter?

Will you be ruled by me?
LAERTES If so° you'll not o'errule me to a peace. *Provided that*
KING CLAUDIUS To thine own peace. If he be now returned,
As checking at[9] his voyage, and that° he means *if*
No more to undertake it, I will work him
To an exploit, now ripe in my device,° *planning*
Under the which he shall not choose but fall;
And for his death no wind of blame shall breathe;
But even his mother shall uncharge° the practice° *not accuse / scheme*
And call it accident.[1]
LAERTES *My lord, I will be ruled,*
The rather if you could devise it so
That I might be the organ.° *instrument*
KING CLAUDIUS *It falls right.*
You have been talked of, since your travel, much,
And that in Hamlet's hearing, for a quality
Wherein they say you shine. Your sum of parts° *abilities combined*
Did not together pluck such envy from him
As did that one, and that, in my regard,
Of the unworthiest siege.° *lowest rank*
LAERTES *What part is that, my lord?*
KING CLAUDIUS *A very ribbon in the cap of youth,*
Yet needful too, for youth no less becomes° *is suited by*
The light and careless livery that it wears
Than settled age his sables° and his weeds° *furred gowns / garments*
Importing health and graveness.° *seriousness, sobriety*
Some two months since° *ago*
Here was a gentleman of Normandy.
I've seen myself, and served against, the French,
And they can well° on horseback; but this gallant *are skilled*
Had witchcraft in't. He grew into his seat,
And to such wondrous doing brought his horse
As had he been incorpsed and demi-natured[2]
With the brave beast. So far he passed my thought
That I in forgery of shapes and tricks[3]
Come short of what he did.
LAERTES A Norman was't?
KING CLAUDIUS A Norman.
LAERTES Upon my life, Lamord.
KING CLAUDIUS The very same.
LAERTES I know him well. He is the brooch° indeed, *ornament*
And gem, of all the nation.
KING CLAUDIUS He made confession° of you, *acknowledgment*
And gave you such a masterly report
For art and exercise in your defence,

9. Turning away from (as a falcon abandons the prey it was sent to pursue).

1. Lines 66.1 through 66.14 appear in Q2 but not in F1.

2. As if he had been made into one body and had half the nature (like a centaur).

3. That my ability to imagine his maneuvers and feats of skill.

And for your rapier most especially,
That he cried out 'twould be a sight indeed
If one could match you.[4]
Th'escrimers° of their nation — fencers
He swore had neither motion, guard, nor eye
If you opposed them.
Sir, this report of his
Did Hamlet so envenom with his envy
That he could nothing do but wish and beg
Your sudden° coming o'er to play° with him. — prompt / fence
Now, out of this—

LAERTES What out of this, my lord?

KING CLAUDIUS Laertes, was your father dear to you?
Or are you like the painting of a sorrow,
A face without a heart?

LAERTES Why ask you this?

KING CLAUDIUS Not that I think you did not love your father,
But that I know love is begun by time,° — by circumstances
And that I see, in passages of proof,° — actual instances
Time qualifies° the spark and fire of it.[5] — tempers
There lives within the very flame of love
A kind of wick or snuff[6] that will abate it,
And nothing is at a like° goodness still,° — an identical / always
For goodness, growing to a plurisy,[7]
Dies in his own too much.[8] That we would do
We should do when we would, for this 'would' changes,
And hath abatements° and delays as many — decreases
As there are tongues, are hands, are accidents;° — occurrences
And then this 'should' is like a spendthrift's sigh,
That hurts by easing.[9] But to the quick° of th'ulcer— — life, core
Hamlet comes back. What would you undertake
To show yourself your father's son in deed
More than in words?

LAERTES To cut his throat i'th' church.

KING CLAUDIUS No place indeed should murder sanctuarize.[1]
Revenge should have no bounds. But, good Laertes,
Will you do this?—keep close within your chamber.
Hamlet returned shall know you are come home.
We'll put on° those shall praise your excellence, — encourage
And set a double varnish on the fame
The Frenchman gave you; bring you, in fine,° together, — conclusion
And wager on your heads. He, being remiss,° — inattentive
Most generous,° and free from all contriving, — noble in nature

4. Lines 84.1 through 84.3 appear in Q2 but not in F1.
5. Lines 95.1 through 95.10 appear in Q2 but not in F1.
6. The burned part of the wick (which must be removed to allow the candle to burn brightly).
7. An excess (the inflammatory lung disease pleurisy was believed to be caused by an excess of humors).
8. Of its own overabundance.
9. Each sigh was believed to cost a drop of blood.
1. Shield a murderer from punishment. In England, criminals who took refuge in a church were protected from arrest for all crimes except sacrilege and treason.

Will not peruse the foils; so that with ease,
Or with a little shuffling, you may choose
A sword unbated,° and, in a pass of practice,[2] *unblunted*
Requite him for your father.

LAERTES I will do't,
And for that purpose I'll anoint my sword.
I bought an unction° of a mountebank° *ointment / quack doctor*
So mortal that, but dip a knife in it,
Where it draws blood no cataplasm° so rare, *poultice*
Collected from all simples° that have virtue° *herbs / healing powers*
Under the moon,[3] can save the thing from death
That is but scratched withal.° I'll touch my point *with it*
With this contagion, that if I gall° him slightly, *wound*
It may be death.

KING CLAUDIUS Let's further think of this;
Weigh what convenience both of time and means
May fit us to our shape.[4] If this should fail,
And that our drift look° through our bad performance, *purpose become visible*
'Twere better not essayed.° Therefore this project *attempted*
Should have a back or second° that might hold *back up position*
If this should blast in proof.[5] Soft, let me see.
We'll make a solemn wager on your cunnings° . . . *skills*
I ha't! When in your motion° you are hot and dry— *exercise*
As make your bouts more violent to that end—
And that he calls for drink, I'll have prepared him
A chalice for the nonce,° whereon but sipping, *occasion*
If he by chance escape your venomed stuck,° *thrust*
Our purpose may hold there.—

Enter QUEEN [GERTRUDE]

How now, sweet Queen?

QUEEN GERTRUDE One woe doth tread upon another's heel,
So fast they follow. Your sister's drowned, Laertes.

LAERTES Drowned? O, where?

QUEEN GERTRUDE There is a willow[6] grows aslant a brook
That shows his hoar° leaves in the glassy stream. *gray; white*
Therewith fantastic garlands did she make
Of crow-flowers, nettles, daisies, and long purples,° *purple orchids*
That liberal° shepherds give a grosser[7] name, *free-spoken*
But our cold° maids do dead men's fingers call them. *chaste*
There on the pendent boughs her crownet° weeds *made into a crown*
Clamb'ring to hang,[8] an envious sliver° broke, *a malicious branch*
When down the weedy trophies and herself
Fell in the weeping brook. Her clothes spread wide,

2. With a treacherous sword thrust.
3. Herbs picked by moonlight were believed to be especially potent.
4. May make us ready for the roles we will assume (in our plan).
5. Should blow up in our faces (like a cannon).
6. The willow is an emblem of forsaken love and of mourning.
7. More lewd (eg., "priest's-pintle" [penis]; "dog's cullions" [testicles])
8. Forsaken lovers were said to hang garlands in willow trees.

And mermaid-like a while they bore her up;
Which time she chanted snatches of old tunes,
As one incapable° of her own distress, *unaware*
Or like a creature native and endued° *adopted*
Unto that element. But long it could not be
Till that her garments, heavy with their drink,
Pulled the poor wretch from her melodious lay° *song*
To muddy death.

LAERTES Alas, then is she drowned.

QUEEN GERTRUDE Drowned, drowned.

LAERTES Too much of water hast thou, poor Ophelia,
And therefore I forbid my tears. But yet
It is our trick;° nature her custom holds, *natural tendency*
Let shame say what it will.

[*He weeps*]

When these are gone,
The woman will be out.[9] Adieu, my lord.
I have a speech of fire that fain° would blaze, *eagerly*
But that this folly douts° it. *Exit* *extinguishes*

KING CLAUDIUS Let's follow, Gertrude.
How much I had to do to calm his rage!
Now fear I this will give it start again;
Therefore let's follow. *Exeunt*

5.1

Enter two CLOWNS[1] *carrying a spade and a pickaxe*

FIRST CLOWN Is she to be buried in Christian burial that wilfully seeks her own salvation?[2]

SECOND CLOWN I tell thee she is, and therefore make her grave straight.° The coroner hath sat on her, and finds it Christian burial.[3] *immediately*

FIRST CLOWN How can that be unless she drowned herself in her own defence?

SECOND CLOWN Why, 'tis found so.

FIRST CLOWN It must be *se offendendo*,[4] it cannot be else; for here lies the point: if I drown myself wittingly, it argues an act; and an act hath three branches: it is to act, to do, and to perform. Argal[5] she drowned herself wittingly.

SECOND CLOWN Nay, but hear you, Goodman Delver.° *Master Digger*

9. That is, when I am done crying the woman in me will also be gone.

5.1 Location: A chruch yard.

1. Men from the country, rustics.

2. Possibly a mistake for "damnation"; suicide was considered a mortal sin that disqualified one from a "Christian burial" in consecrated ground. Or the clown may be suggesting that Ophelia is speeding her "salvation" by going to her reward "wilfully" rather than by waiting for nature to take its course.

3. The coroner has investigated the case of her death and concluded that it merits a Christian burial (i.e., that her drowning was not a suicide).

4. In self-offense; an error for the Latin legal phrase *se defendendo*, "[killing] in self-defense."

5. A corruption of the Latin *ergo* (therefore).

FIRST CLOWN Give me leave. Here lies the water—good. Here stands the man—good. If the man go to this water and drown himself, it is, will he nill he,° he goes. Mark you that. But if the water come to him and drown him, he drowns not himself; argal he that is not guilty of his own death shortens not his own life.

willy-nilly

SECOND CLOWN But is this law?

FIRST CLOWN Ay, marry, is't: coroner's quest° law.

inquest

SECOND CLOWN Will you ha' the truth on't? If this had not been a gentlewoman, she should have been buried out o' Christian burial.

FIRST CLOWN Why, there thou sayst,° and the more pity that great folk should have count'nance° in this world to drown or hang themselves more than their even° Christian. Come, my spade. There is no ancient gentlemen but gardeners, ditchers, and gravemakers; they hold up° Adam's profession.

that's right
privilege
fellow
continue in

[FIRST CLOWN *digs*]

SECOND CLOWN Was he a gentleman?

FIRST CLOWN A° was the first that ever bore arms.[6]

He

SECOND CLOWN Why, he had none.

FIRST CLOWN What, art a heathen? How dost thou understand the Scripture? The Scripture says Adam digged. Could he dig without arms? I'll put another question to thee. If thou answerest me not to the purpose, confess thyself[7]—

SECOND CLOWN Go to.[8]

FIRST CLOWN What is he that builds stronger than either the mason, the shipwright, or the carpenter?

SECOND CLOWN The gallows-maker; for that frame° outlives a thousand tenants.

structure

FIRST CLOWN I like thy wit well, in good faith. The gallows does well.° But how does it well? It does well to those that do ill. Now thou dost ill to say the gallows is built stronger than the church, argal the gallows may do well to thee. To't again, come.

is a good answer

SECOND CLOWN 'Who builds stronger than a mason, a shipwright, or a carpenter?'

FIRST CLOWN Ay, tell me that, and unyoke.[9]

SECOND CLOWN Marry,° now I can tell.

By the Virgin Mary

FIRST CLOWN To't.

SECOND CLOWN Mass,° I cannot tell.

By the Mass

Enter [Prince] HAMLET *and* HORATIO *afar off*

6. Was given the heraldic insignia that entitled a man to call himself a "gentleman" (punning on "arms" meaning "limbs").
7. Proverbial: "Confess thyself and be hanged."
8. An exclamation of impatience.
9. Cease (your joking), as an ox stops working at the end of the day when unyoked.

FIRST CLOWN Cudgel thy brains no more about it, for your dull ass will not mend° his pace with beating; and when you are asked this question next, say 'a grave-maker'; the houses that he makes lasts till doomsday. Go, get thee to Johan.[1] Fetch me a stoup° of liquor.
quicken / *flagon*

[*Exit* SECOND CLOWN]

(*Sings*) In youth when I did love, did love,
Methought it was very sweet
To contract°-O-the time for-a-my behove,° *shorten / advantage*
O methought there-a-was nothing-a-meet.[2]

HAMLET Has this fellow no feeling of his business that a sings at grave-making?

HORATIO Custom hath made it in him a property of easiness.[3]

HAMLET 'Tis e'en so; the hand of little employment hath the daintier sense.[4]

FIRST CLOWN (*sings*) But age with his stealing steps
Hath caught me in his clutch,
And hath shipped me intil the land,° *into the earth*
As if I had never been such.[5]

[*He throws up a skull*]

HAMLET That skull had a tongue in it and could sing once. How the knave jowls° it to th' ground as if 'twere Cain's jawbone, that did the first murder! This might be the pate of a politician° which this ass o'er-offices,[6] one that would circumvent God, might it not?
dashes / *schemer*

HORATIO It might, my lord.

HAMLET Or of a courtier, which could say 'Good morrow, sweet lord. How dost thou, good lord?' This might be my lord such a one, that praised my lord such a one's horse when a° meant to beg it, might it not?
he

HORATIO Ay, my lord.

HAMLET Why, e'en so, and now my lady Worm's, chapless,° and knocked about the mazard° with a sexton's spade. Here's fine revolution, an we had the trick[7] to see't. Did these bones cost no more the breeding but to play at loggats with 'em?[8] Mine ache to think on't.
without a lower jaw / head

1. The reference to "Johan" is unclear; editors have variously suggested that it is the name of an alehouse or an alehouse keeper, or have changed "to Johan" to "in."
2. That is, nothing so suitable. The clown's song is a garbled version of lines from Lord Thomas Vaux's poem "The Aged Lover Renounceth Love," which appears in *Tottel's Miscellany* (1557).
3. Something he can do easily, without emotional distress.
4. Is more sensitive (because it is not calloused).
5. Perhaps, been such in youth.
6. Lords it over (as if he were of superior rank).
7. If we had the ability. *Revolution*: a turning of Fortune's wheel.
8. That is, did these bones mature for no other purpose than to be used in loggats (a game played by throwing sticks as closely as possible to a stake)?

FIRST CLOWN *(sings)* A pickaxe and a spade, a spade,
For and° a shrouding-sheet;
O, a pit of clay for to be made
For such a guest is meet.

And also

[*He throws up another skull*]

HAMLET There's another. Why might not that be the skull of a lawyer? Where be his quiddits° now, his quillets,° his cases, his tenures,° and his tricks? Why does he suffer this rude knave now to knock him about the sconce° with a dirty shovel, and will not tell him of his action of battery?° H'm! This fellow might be in 's time a great buyer of land, with his statutes, his recognizances, his fines, his double vouchers, his recoveries.[9] Is this the fine° of his fines and the recovery° of his recoveries, to have his fine° pate full of fine dirt? Will his vouchers vouch° him no more of his purchases, and double ones too, than the length and breadth of a pair of indentures?° The very conveyances° of his lands will hardly lie in this box;° and must th'inheritor° himself have no more, ha?

subtleties / *quibbles / property titles* / *head* / *prosecution for assault* / *end / profit* / *excellent* / *assure* / *contracts / deeds* / *coffin / owner*

HORATIO Not a jot more, my lord.

HAMLET Is not parchment made of sheepskins?

HORATIO Ay, my lord, and of calf-skins too.

HAMLET They are sheep and calves° that seek out assurance[1] in that. I will speak to this fellow. [*To the* FIRST CLOWN] Whose grave's this, sirrah?[2]

simpletons and dolts

FIRST CLOWN Mine, sir.
(Sings) O, a pit of clay for to be made
For such a guest is meet.

HAMLET I think it be thine indeed, for thou liest in't.

FIRST CLOWN You lie out on't, sir, and therefore it is not yours. For my part, I do not lie in't, and yet it is mine.

HAMLET Thou dost lie in't, to be in't and say 'tis thine. 'Tis for the dead, not for the quick;° therefore thou liest.

living

FIRST CLOWN 'Tis a quick° lie, sir, 'twill away again from me to you.

lively

HAMLET What man dost thou dig it for?

FIRST CLOWN For no man, sir.

HAMLET What woman, then?

FIRST CLOWN For none, neither.

HAMLET Who is to be buried in't?

FIRST CLOWN One that was a woman, sir; but, rest her soul, she's dead.

9. All legal terms: "statutes" and "recognizances" are documents in which portions of land or properties were pledged as surety in a contractual agreement; "double vouchers" are summons of two persons into court to attest to the title to a property; "recoveries" are processes by which an entailed estate is transferred from one party to another.

1. Who seek security (in legal documents).

2. Term of address to a social inferior.

HAMLET How absolute° the knave is! We must speak by the card,[3] or equivocation will undo us. By the Lord, Horatio, these three years I have taken note of it. The age is grown so picked° that the toe of the peasant comes so near the heel of the courtier he galls his kibe.° [*To the* FIRST CLOWN] How long hast thou been a grave-maker? *precise, literal* *refined* *chafes his heel*

FIRST CLOWN Of all the days i'th' year I came to't that day that our last King Hamlet o'ercame Fortinbras.

HAMLET How long is that since?

FIRST CLOWN Cannot you tell that? Every fool can tell that. It was the very day that young Hamlet was born—he that was mad and sent into England.

HAMLET Ay, marry, why was he sent into England?

FIRST CLOWN Why, because a° was mad. A shall recover his wits there; or if a do not, 'tis no great matter there. *he*

HAMLET Why?

FIRST CLOWN 'Twill not be seen in him there. There the men are as mad as he.

HAMLET How came he mad?

FIRST CLOWN Very strangely, they say.

HAMLET How strangely?

FIRST CLOWN Faith, e'en with losing his wits.

HAMLET Upon what ground?° *For what reason*

FIRST CLOWN Why, here in Denmark. I have been sexton here, man and boy, thirty years.

HAMLET How long will a man lie i'th' earth ere he rot?

FIRST CLOWN I'faith, if a be not rotten before a die—as we have many pocky[4] corpses nowadays, that will scarce hold the laying in[5]—a will last you some eight year or nine year. A tanner will last you nine year.

HAMLET Why he more than another?

FIRST CLOWN Why, sir, his hide is so tanned with his trade that a will keep out water a great while, and your water is a sore decayer of your whoreson[6] dead body. Here's a skull, now. This skull has lain in the earth three-and-twenty years.

HAMLET Whose was it?

FIRST CLOWN A whoreson mad fellow's it was. Whose do you think it was?

HAMLET Nay, I know not.

FIRST CLOWN A pestilence on him for a mad rogue—a poured a flagon of Rhenish° on my head once! This same skull, sir, was Yorick's skull, the King's jester. *Rhine wine*

3. With utmost clarity (Hamlet may be referring to the mariner's card, on which were marked the points of a compass).
4. Infected with the pox (a term that usually referred to syphilis).
5. That is, that will scarcely hold together during the burial ceremony.
6. Vile (a general term of contempt).

HAMLET This?

FIRST CLOWN E'en that.

HAMLET Let me see.

[*He takes the skull*]

Alas, poor Yorick. I knew him, Horatio—a fellow of infinite jest, of most excellent fancy. He hath borne me on his back a thousand times; and now, how abhorred my imagination is! My gorge rises at it. Here hung those lips that I have kissed I know not how oft. Where be your gibes now, your gambols, your songs, your flashes of merriment that were wont to set the table on a roar? Not one now to mock your own grinning? Quite chop-fallen?[7] Now get you to my lady's chamber and tell her, let her paint° an inch thick, to this favour° she must come. Make her laugh at that. Prithee, Horatio, tell me one thing.

wear makeup/ appearance

HORATIO What's that, my lord?

HAMLET Dost thou think Alexander[8] looked o' this fashion i'th' earth?

HORATIO E'en so.

HAMLET And smelt so? Pah!

[*He throws the skull down*]

HORATIO E'en so, my lord.

HAMLET To what base uses we may return, Horatio! Why may not imagination trace the noble dust of Alexander till a find it stopping a bung-hole?

HORATIO 'Twere to consider too curiously° to consider so. *minutely*

HAMLET No, faith, not a jot; but to follow him thither with modesty° enough, and likelihood to lead it, as thus: Alexander died, Alexander was buried, Alexander returneth into dust, the dust is earth, of earth we make loam,[9] and why of that loam whereto he was converted might they not stop a beer-barrel?

moderation

Imperial Caesar, dead and turned to clay,
Might stop a hole to keep the wind away.
O, that that earth which kept the world in awe
Should patch a wall t'expel the winter's flaw!° *gust of wind*
But soft, but soft; aside.

[HAMLET *and* HORATIO *stand aside*.] *Enter* KING [CLAUDIUS], QUEEN [GERTRUDE], LAERTES, *and a coffin, with* [*a* PRIEST *and*] *lords attendant*

Here comes the King,
The Queen, the courtiers—who is that they follow,
And with such maimèd rites?[1] This doth betoken

7. Dejected; with lower jaw fallen away.

8. Alexander the Great (356–323 B.C.E.), King of Macedon, who conquered a great empire.

9. A mixture of clay, sand, and other materials, used to make bricks and plaster.

1. A curtailed ceremony (rather than an elaborate court funeral).

The corpse they follow did with desp'rate hand
Fordo it° own life. 'Twas of some estate.° *Destroy its / rank*
Couch we° a while, and mark. *Let us hide*

LAERTES What ceremony else?

HAMLET [*aside to* HORATIO] That is Laertes, a very noble youth. Mark.

LAERTES What ceremony else?

PRIEST Her obsequies have been as far enlarged
As we have warrantise.° Her death was doubtful,[2] *authority*
And but that great command o'ersways the order[3]
She should in ground unsanctified have lodged
Till the last trumpet.° For° charitable prayers, *Judgment Day / Instead of*
Shards, flints, and pebbles should be thrown on her,
Yet here she is allowed her virgin rites,
Her maiden strewments,° and the bringing home *strewn flowers*
Of bell and burial.[4]

LAERTES Must there no more be done?

PRIEST No more be done.
We should profane the service of the dead
To sing sage° requiem and such rest to her *solemn*
As to peace-parted° souls. *peacefully departed*

LAERTES Lay her i'th' earth,
And from her fair and unpolluted flesh
May violets spring. I tell thee, churlish priest,
A minist'ring angel shall my sister be
When thou liest howling.° *(in hell)*

HAMLET [*aside*] What, the fair Ophelia!

QUEEN GERTRUDE [*scattering flowers*] Sweets to the sweet. Farewell.
I hoped thou shouldst have been my Hamlet's wife.
I thought thy bride-bed to have decked, sweet maid,
And not t'have strewed thy grave.

LAERTES O, treble woe
Fall ten times treble on that cursèd head
Whose wicked deed thy most ingenious sense° *keen intellect*
Deprived thee of!—Hold off the earth a while,
Till I have caught her once more in mine arms.

[LAERTES] *leaps into the grave*

Now pile your dust upon the quick and dead
Till of this flat a mountain you have made
To o'ertop old Pelion,[5] or the skyish head
Of blue Olympus.

HAMLET [*coming forward*] What is he whose grief
Bears such an emphasis, whose phrase° of sorrow *particular expression*

2. Questionable (because it may have been a suicide.)
3. If the power of the court had not overruled church practice.
4. The burial procession and interment to the sound of church bells.
5. The highest mountain of a range in Thessaly, in northern Greece; in Greek mythology, the Titans piled Mount Ossa on Pelion in an attempt to scale Mount Olympus and defeat the gods.

Conjures the wand'ring stars° and makes them stand *planets*
Like wonder-wounded° hearers? This is I, *awestruck*
Hamlet the Dane.[6]

HAMLET *leaps in after* LAERTES

LAERTES The devil take thy soul.
HAMLET Thou pray'st not well.
I prithee take thy fingers from my throat,
For though I am not splenative° and rash, *hot-tempered*
Yet have I something in me dangerous,
Which let thy wiseness fear. Away thy hand.
KING CLAUDIUS [*to* LORDS] Pluck them asunder.
QUEEN GERTRUDE Hamlet, Hamlet!
ALL THE LORDS Gentlemen!
HORATIO [*to* HAMLET] Good my lord, be quiet.
HAMLET Why, I will fight with him upon this theme
Until my eyelids will no longer wag.° *blink*
QUEEN GERTRUDE O my son, what theme?
HAMLET I loved Ophelia. Forty thousand brothers
Could not, with all their quantity of love,
Make up my sum.—What wilt thou do for her?
KING CLAUDIUS O, he is mad, Laertes.
QUEEN GERTRUDE [*to* LAERTES] For love of God, forbear him.° *leave him alone*
HAMLET [*to* LAERTES] 'Swounds,° show me what thou'lt do. *By God's wounds*
Woot° weep, woot fight, woot fast, woot tear thyself, *Wilt thou*
Woot drink up eisel,° eat a crocodile? *vinegar*
I'll do't. Dost thou come here to whine,
To outface me with leaping in her grave?
Be buried quick° with her, and so will I. *alive*
And if thou prate of mountains, let them throw
Millions of acres on us, till our ground,
Singeing his pate against the burning zone,[7]
Make Ossa like a wart. Nay, an° thou'lt mouth,° *if / rant, rage*
I'll rant as well as thou.
KING CLAUDIUS [*to* LAERTES] This is mere madness,
And thus a while the fit will work on him.
Anon,° as patient as the female dove *Soon*
When that her golden couplets[8] are disclosed,° *hatched*
His silence will sit drooping.
HAMLET [*to* LAERTES] Hear you, sir,
What is the reason that you use me thus?
I loved you ever. But it is no matter.
Let Hercules himself do what he may,
The cat will mew, and dog will have his day.[9] *Exit*

6. The title normally given to the King of Denmark.
7. In the Ptolemaic system, the sphere of the sun.
8. Two yellow chicks.
9. That is, even if mighty Hercules were to stand in the way, each will do what he must.

KING CLAUDIUS I pray you, good Horatio, wait upon° him. *accompany*
[*Exit*] HORATIO
[*To* LAERTES] Strengthen your patience in° our last night's speech. *with*
We'll put the matter to the present push.°— *to immediate trial*
Good Gertrude, set some watch over your son.—
This grave shall have a living° monument. *lasting*
An hour of quiet shortly shall we see;
Till then, in patience our proceeding be. *Exeunt*

5.2

Enter [*Prince*] HAMLET *and* HORATIO.

HAMLET So much for this, sir. Now, let me see, the other.° *other matter*
You do remember all the circumstance?
HORATIO Remember it, my lord!
HAMLET Sir, in my heart there was a kind of fighting
That would not let me sleep. Methought I lay
Worse than the mutines in the bilboes.[1] Rashly°— *Impulsively*
And praised be rashness for it: let us know° *acknowledge*
Our indiscretion sometime serves us well
When our dear plots do pall,° and that should teach us *weaken*
There's a divinity that shapes our ends,
Rough-hew° them how we will— *Roughly form*
HORATIO That is most certain.
HAMLET Up from my cabin,
My sea-gown scarfed about me in the dark,
Groped I to find out them, had my desire,
Fingered° their packet, and in fine° withdrew *Filched / finally*
To mine own room again, making so bold,
My fears forgetting manners, to unseal
Their grand commission; where I found, Horatio—
O royal knavery!—an exact command,
Larded° with many several° sorts of reasons *Enriched / different*
Importing° Denmark's health, and England's, too, *Relating to*
With ho! such bugs and goblins in my life,[2]
That on the supervise,° no leisure bated,° *reading / delay permitted*
No, not to stay° the grinding of the axe, *await*
My head should be struck off.
HORATIO Is't possible?
HAMLET [*giving it to him*] Here's the commission. Read it at more leisure.
But wilt thou hear me how I did proceed?
HORATIO I beseech you.
HAMLET Being thus benetted round with villainies—
Ere I could make a prologue to my brains,
They had begun the play[3]—I sat me down,

5.2 Location: Stateroom in the castle.
1. The mutineers in the shackles.
2. Such things to be dreaded if I were allowed to live. *Bugs:* bugbears.
3. That is, Hamlet began to devise a plan before he consciously intended to do so.

Devised a new commission, wrote it fair.[4]
I once did hold it, as our statists° do, *statesmen, politicians*
A baseness° to write fair, and laboured much *lower-class skill*
How to forget that learning; but, sir, now
It did me yeoman's service.° Wilt thou know *served me well*
Th'effect of what I wrote?

HORATIO Ay, good my lord.

HAMLET An earnest conjuration° from the King, *request*
As England was his faithful tributary,
As love between them like the palm should flourish,
As peace should still her wheaten garland[5] wear
And stand a comma° 'tween their amities, *link*
And many such like 'as'es of great charge,[6]
That on the view and know of these contents,
Without debatement further more or less,
He should the bearers put to sudden death,
Not shriving-time[7] allowed.

HORATIO How was this sealed?

HAMLET Why, even in that was heaven ordinant.° *guiding*
I had my father's signet in my purse,
Which was the model of that Danish seal;
Folded the writ up in the form of th'other,
Subscribed° it, gave't th'impression,[8] placed it safely, *Signed*
The changeling[9] never known. Now the next day
Was our sea-fight; and what to this was sequent° *subsequent*
Thou know'st already.

HORATIO So Guildenstern and Rosencrantz go to't.

HAMLET Why, man, they did make love to this employment.
They are not near my conscience. Their defeat° *destruction*
Doth by their own insinuation° grow. *interference*
'Tis dangerous when the baser nature comes
Between the pass and fell incensèd points
Of mighty opposites.[1]

HORATIO Why, what a king is this!

HAMLET Does it not, think'st thee, stand me now upon[2]—
He that hath killed my king and whored my mother,
Popped in between th'election[3] and my hopes,
Thrown out his angle° for my proper° life, *fishing hook / own*
And with such coz'nage°—is't not perfect conscience *deceit*
To quit° him with this arm? And is't not to be damned *repay*

4. That is, in the clear handwriting of the clerks who prepared official documents.
5. A symbol of agricultural prosperity and peace.
6. Important clauses beginning with "as" (with a pun on "asses").
7. No time for confession and absolution (as ordinarily granted to the condemned).
8. Imprinted the seal in wax.
9. The substituted letter (literally, an elf child substituted for a human child by fairies).
1. Between the thrust and fiercely angry rapiers ("points") of mighty adversaries.
2. Rest incumbent on me.
3. In Denmark, the king was elected.

To let this canker° of our nature come — *spreading sore; cancer*
In° further evil? — *Into*
HORATIO It must be shortly known to him from England
What is the issue° of the business there. — *outcome*
HAMLET It will be short. The interim's mine,
And a man's life's no more than to say 'one'.[4]
But I am very sorry, good Horatio,
That to Laertes I forgot myself;
For by the image° of my cause I see — *reflection*
The portraiture of his. I'll court his favours.
But sure, the bravery° of his grief did put me — *bravado*
Into a tow'ring passion.
HORATIO Peace, who comes here?

Enter young OSRIC, *a courtier* [*taking off his hat*]

OSRIC Your lordship is right welcome back to Denmark.
HAMLET I humbly thank you, sir. [*To* HORATIO] Dost know this water-fly?
HORATIO No, my good lord.
HAMLET Thy state is the more gracious,° for 'tis a vice to know him. He hath much land, and fertile. Let a beast be lord of beasts, and his crib shall stand at the king's mess.[5] 'Tis a chuff,° but, as I say, spacious in the possession of dirt. — *blessed*; *boor*
OSRIC Sweet lord, if your friendship were at leisure I should impart a thing to you from his majesty.
HAMLET I will receive it, sir, with all diligence of spirit.
Put your bonnet° to his right use; 'tis for the head. — *hat*
OSRIC I thank your lordship, 'tis very hot.
HAMLET No, believe me, 'tis very cold. The wind is northerly.
OSRIC It is indifferent° cold, my lord, indeed. — *somewhat*
HAMLET Methinks it is very sultry and hot for my complexion.° — *constitution*
OSRIC Exceedingly, my lord. It is very sultry, as 'twere— I cannot tell how. But, my lord, his majesty bade me signify to you that a° has laid a great wager on your head. Sir, this is the matter. — *he*
HAMLET I beseech you, remember.[6]
OSRIC Nay, good my lord, for mine ease, in good faith.[7]
Sir here is newly come to court Laertes, believe me, an absolute gentleman, full of most excellent

4. That is, life lasts no longer than it takes to count to "one."
5. A man of wealth and property (possessing many herds) shall find himself at the king's table, even if he is no better than his animals. *Crib:* feed box, manger.
6. That is, remember your courtesy (i.e., put your hat back on).
7. Lines 106.1 through 106.38 appear in Q2 but not in F1.

differences,° of very soft society and great showing.[8] *superior qualities*
Indeed, to speak feelingly° of him, he is the card° or *discerningly / map*
calendar of gentry,[9] *for you shall find in him the*
continent of what part[1] *a gentleman would see.*

HAMLET *Sir, his definement suffers no perdition in*
you,[2] *though I know to divide him inventorially°* *by way of inventory*
would dizzy th'arithmetic of memory, and yet but yaw
neither in respect of his quick sail.[3] *But in the verity*
of extolment,° I take him to be a soul of great article,[4] *future praise*
and his infusion° of such dearth° and rareness as, *inborn essence / dearness*
to make true diction° of him, his semblable° is his *to speak truly / likeness*
mirror, and who else would trace him his umbrage,
nothing more.[5]

OSRIC *Your lordship speaks most infallibly of him.*

HAMLET *The concernancy,° sir? Why do we wrap the* *relevance*
gentleman in our more rawer breath?° *words*

OSRIC *Sir?*

HORATIO *Is't not possible to understand in another*
tongue? You will to't, sir, rarely.[6]

HAMLET *What imports the nomination° of this gentle-* *mention*
man?

OSRIC *Of Laertes?*

HORATIO [*aside to* HAMLET] *His purse is empty already;*
all 's golden words are spent.

HAMLET [*to* OSRIC] *Of him, sir.*

OSRIC *I know you are not ignorant—*

HAMLET *I would you did, sir; yet, in faith, if you did it*
would not much approve° me. Well, sir? *recommend*

OSRIC *You are not ignorant of what excellence Laertes*
is.

HAMLET *I dare not confess that, lest I should compare*
with him in excellence.[7] *But to know a man well*
were to know himself.

OSRIC *I mean, sir, for his weapon. But in the impu-*
tation laid on him by them, in his meed° he's *merit*
unfellowed.° *unequaled*

8. Of pleasing manners and noble appearance.

9. That is, the model of gentlemanly behavior. *Calendar:* guide, register.

1. Embodiment of all qualities. ("Continent" continues the geographical metaphor begun in line 106.4.)

2. He loses nothing in your definition of him. Hamlet mimics Osric's affected style of speech to acknowledge that Osric's description does Laertes justice.

3. Still mocking Osric's mode of speech, Hamlet employs a nautical metaphor: any such tediously verbose attempt to list all of Laertes' virtues would tend to swerve ("yaw") off course in comparison with Laertes' rapid forward motion ("quick sail").

4. Of great moment.

5. That is, anyone who imitates him becomes only his shadow, nothing more.

6. That is, is it not possible to understand your own (Osric's) manner of speech when spoken by another (Hamlet)? You can if you will try, sir, splendidly.

7. That is, I dare not confirm his excellence, because I would have to assert my own equal excellence to recognize his.

Sir, you are not ignorant of what excellence Laertes is at his weapon.

HAMLET What's his weapon?

OSRIC Rapier and dagger.

HAMLET That's two of his weapons. But well.

OSRIC The King, sir, hath wagered with him six Barbary horses, against the which he imponed,° as I take it, six French rapiers and poniards, with their assigns[8] as girdle, hanger[9], or so. Three of the carriages, in faith, are very dear to fancy,° very responsive to the hilts, most delicate° carriages, and of very liberal conceit.°

wagered
beautifully made
charming
elaborate design

HAMLET What call you the carriages?[1]

HORATIO [*aside to* HAMLET] *I know you must be edified by the margin[2] ere you had done.*

OSRIC The carriages, sir, are the hangers.

HAMLET The phrase would be more germane to the matter if we could carry cannon by our sides.[3] I would it might be hangers till then. But on: six Barbary horses against six French swords, their assigns, and three liberal-conceited carriages—that's the French bet against the Danish. Why is this 'imponed', as you call it?

OSRIC The King, sir, hath laid,° sir, that in a dozen passes between you and him he shall not exceed you three hits.[4] He hath on't twelve for nine,[5] and it would come to immediate trial if your lordship would vouchsafe the answer.°

wagered
accept the challenge

HAMLET How if I answer no?

OSRIC I mean, my lord, the opposition of your person in trial.

HAMLET Sir, I will walk here in the hall. If it please his majesty, 'tis the breathing time of day[6] with me. Let the foils be brought; the gentleman willing, an° the King hold his purpose, I will win for him an I can. If not, I'll gain nothing but my shame and the odd hits.

if

OSRIC Shall I re-deliver you e'en so?

HAMLET To this effect, sir; after what flourish your nature will.

8. With their paraphernalia ("assigns"), such as sword belt ("girdle") and the loop or strap on a sword belt from which the sword was hung (often richly ornamented).
9. A pretentious way of saying "hangers."
1. Lines 119.1 and 119.2 appear in Q2 but not in F1.
2. That is, by a gloss, as in the margin of a book.
3. Hamlet refers to a gun carriage (the wheeled frame on which a cannon is mounted).
4. That is, the King has wagered that in twelve bouts Laertes will outscore Hamlet by no more than three hits.
5. The meaning of this phrase is unclear. Perhaps Osric is saying that in the twelve bouts Laertes must score twelve hits against Hamlet's nine to win.
6. That is, the time for exercise.

OSRIC I commend my duty° to your lordship. *offer my service*

HAMLET Yours, yours. [*Exit* OSRIC]

He does well to commend° it himself; there are no tongues else for 's turn.[7] *recommend*

HORATIO This lapwing runs away with the shell on his head.[8]

HAMLET A did comply with his dug[9] before a sucked it. Thus has he—and many more of the same bevy that I know the drossy° age dotes on—only got the tune of the time and outward habit of encounter,[1] a kind of yeasty collection° which carries them through and through the most fanned and winnowed opinions;[2] and do but blow them to their trial, the bubbles are out.[3] *worthless* *set of frothy phrases*

Enter a LORD

LORD [*to* HAMLET] *My lord, his majesty commended him to you by young Osric, who brings back to him that you attend him in the hall. He sends to know if your pleasure hold to play with Laertes, or that you will take longer time.*

HAMLET *I am constant to my purposes; they follow the King's pleasure. If his fitness speaks, mine is ready,[4] now or whensoever, provided I be so able as now.*

LORD *The King and Queen and all are coming down.*

HAMLET *In happy time.[5]*

LORD *The Queen desires you to use some gentle entertainment to Laertes[6] before you fall to play.*

HAMLET *She well instructs me.* [*Exit* LORD]

HORATIO *You will lose, my lord.*

HORATIO You will lose this wager, my lord.

HAMLET I do not think so. Since he went into France, I have been in continual practice. I shall win at the odds.° But thou wouldst not think how all here about my heart—but it is no matter. *(see 5.2.123–25)*

HORATIO Nay, good my lord—

HAMLET It is but foolery, but it is such a kind of gain-giving° as would perhaps trouble a woman. *misgiving*

7. That is, no one else will do it for him.

8. Elizabethans frequently alluded to the notion that the newly hatched plover lapwing (plover) runs from the nest with its shell on its head. The suggestion here is that Osric has finally replaced his bonnet. Also, his gait may resemble the lapwing's wavering flight.

9. He did bow politely to his mother's breast.

1. The style of speech ("tune") of the time and the conventions ("habit") of polite social intercourse.

2. The most well-aired and well-sifted opinions.

3. Put them to the test ("blow them") and their ignorance will be exposed (the "bubbles" will burst). Lines 155.1 through 155.14 appear in Q2 but not in F1. In Q2 these lines replace Horatio's "You will lose this wager, my lord."

4. That is, if this is a good time for him, it is also for me.

5. At an opportune time (a polite phrase).

6. To receive Laertes with some sign of respect or courtesy.

HORATIO If your mind dislike anything, obey it. I will forestall their repair° hither, and say you are not fit. *arrival*

HAMLET Not a whit. We defy augury. There's a special providence in the fall of a sparrow.[7] If it be now, 'tis not to come. If it be not to come, it will be now. If it be not now, yet it will come. The readiness is all. Since no man has aught of what he leaves, what is't to leave betimes?[8]

Enter KING [CLAUDIUS], QUEEN [GERTRUDE], LAERTES, *and lords, with* [OSRIC *and*] *other attendants with trumpets, drums, cushions, foils, and gauntlets; a table, and flagons of wine on it*

KING CLAUDIUS Come, Hamlet, come, and take this hand from me.

HAMLET [*to* LAERTES] Give me your pardon, sir. I've done you wrong;
But pardon't as you are a gentleman.
This presence° knows, *royal assembly*
And you must needs have heard, how I am punished
With sore distraction. What I have done
That might your nature, honour, and exception° *displeasure*
Roughly awake, I here proclaim was madness.
Was't Hamlet wronged Laertes? Never Hamlet.
If Hamlet from himself be ta'en away,
And when he's not himself does wrong Laertes,
Then Hamlet does it not, Hamlet denies it.
Who does it then? His madness. If't be so,
Hamlet is of the faction that is wronged.
His madness is poor Hamlet's enemy.
Sir, in this audience
Let my disclaiming from° a purposed evil *disavowing any part in*
Free me so far in your most generous thoughts
That I have shot mine arrow o'er the house
And hurt my brother.[9]

LAERTES I am satisfied in nature,[1]
Whose motive in this case should stir me most
To my revenge. But in my terms of honour
I stand aloof, and will no reconcilement
Till by some elder masters of known honour
I have a voice° and precedent of peace *authoritative declaration*
To keep my name ungored;° but till that time *unblemished*
I do receive your offered love like love,
And will not wrong it.

7. Elizabethans distinguished between general providence (God's overarching plan for human history) and special providence (God's guidance in particular events, such as the fall of a single sparrow, which, according to Matthew 10.29, shall not happen without God's knowledge).

8. That is, because no man truly owns what he leaves behind (i.e., earthly possessions), what does it matter if he leaves this world early?

9. F1 has "mother" instead of "brother."

1. That is, according to natural personal feeling.

HAMLET I do embrace it freely,
And will this brothers' wager frankly° play.— *freely*
[*To attendants*] Give us the foils. Come on.
LAERTES [*to attendants*] Come, one for me.
HAMLET I'll be your foil,[2] Laertes. In mine ignorance
Your skill shall, like a star i'th' darkest night,
Stick° fiery off indeed. *Stand out; thrust*
LAERTES You mock me, sir.
HAMLET No, by this hand.
KING CLAUDIUS Give them the foils, young Osric. Cousin Hamlet,
You know the wager?
HAMLET Very well, my lord.
Your grace hath laid the odds o'th' weaker side.
KING CLAUDIUS I do not fear it; I have seen you both.
But since he is bettered,° we have therefore odds.[3] *favored*
LAERTES [*taking a foil*] This is too heavy; let me see another.
HAMLET [*taking a foil*] This likes° me well. These foils have all *pleases*
a° length? *the same*
OSRIC Ay, my good lord.

[HAMLET *and* LAERTES] *prepare to play*

KING CLAUDIUS [*to attendants*] Set me the stoups° of wine upon *flagons*
that table.
If Hamlet give the first or second hit,
Or quit in answer of the third exchange,[4]
Let all the battlements their ordnance fire.
The King shall drink to Hamlet's better breath,° *improved energy*
And in the cup an union° shall he throw *a pearl*
Richer than that which four successive kings
In Denmark's crown have worn. Give me the cups,
And let the kettle° to the trumpet speak, *kettledrum*
The trumpet to the cannoneer without,
The cannons to the heavens, the heaven to earth,
'Now the King drinks to Hamlet'.

Trumpets the while [*he drinks*]

Come, begin.
And you, the judges, bear a wary eye.
HAMLET [*to* LAERTES] Come on, sir.
LAERTES Come, my lord.

They play

HAMLET One.
LAERTES No.
HAMLET [*to* OSRIC] Judgement.

2. Flattering contrast (from the metal foil placed under a gem to add to its brilliance), with a pun on fencing foils.
3. That is, I have arranged the terms in your favor (referring to Hamlet's advantage of three hits).
4. Repay ("quit") Laertes with a hit in the third bout (presumably having lost the first two).

OSRIC A hit, a very palpable hit.

LAERTES Well, again.

KING CLAUDIUS Stay.° Give me drink. Hamlet, this pearl is thine. *Stop*
Here's to thy health.—

Drum [and] trumpets sound, and shot goes off

Give him the cup.

HAMLET I'll play this bout first. Set it by a while.—
Come.

They play again

Another hit. What say you?

LAERTES A touch, a touch, I do confess.

KING CLAUDIUS Our son shall win.

QUEEN GERTRUDE He's fat° and scant of breath.— *sweaty; out of shape / handkerchief*
Here, Hamlet, take my napkin.° Rub thy brows.
The Queen carouses° to thy fortune, Hamlet. *drinks a toast*

HAMLET Good madam.

KING CLAUDIUS Gertrude, do not drink.

QUEEN GERTRUDE I will, my lord, I pray you pardon me.

She drinks [then offers the cup to HAMLET*]*

KING CLAUDIUS [*aside*] It is the poisoned cup; it is too late.

HAMLET I dare not drink yet, madam; by and by.

QUEEN GERTRUDE [*to* HAMLET] Come, let me wipe thy face.

LAERTES [*aside to* CLAUDIUS] My lord, I'll hit him now.

KING CLAUDIUS [*aside to* LAERTES] I do not think't.

LAERTES [*aside*] And yet 'tis almost 'gainst my conscience.

HAMLET Come for the third, Laertes, you but dally.
I pray you pass° with your best violence. *thrust*
I am afeard you make a wanton of me.[5]

LAERTES Say you so? Come on.

[They] play

OSRIC Nothing neither way.

LAERTES [*to* HAMLET] Have at you now!

[LAERTES *wounds* HAMLET.] *In scuffling, they change rapiers [and* HAMLET *wounds* LAERTES*]*

KING CLAUDIUS [*to attendants*] Part them, they are incensed.

HAMLET [*to* LAERTES] Nay, come again.

[*The* QUEEN *falls down*[6]]

OSRIC Look to the Queen there, ho!

HORATIO They bleed on both sides. [*To* HAMLET] How is't, my lord?

OSRIC How is't, Laertes?

LAERTES Why, as a woodcock[7] to mine own springe,° Osric. *trap*
I am justly killed with mine own treachery.

HAMLET How does the Queen?

KING CLAUDIUS She swoons to see them bleed.

QUEEN GERTRUDE No, no, the drink, the drink! O my dear Hamlet,

5. You play with me as if I were a spoiled child.

6. This stage direction and the one at line 266 are taken from Q1.

7. A proverbially stupid bird.

The drink, the drink—I am poisoned. [*She dies*]

HAMLET O villainy! Ho! Let the door be locked! [*Exit* OSRIC]
Treachery, seek it out.

LAERTES It is here, Hamlet. Hamlet, thou art slain.
No med'cine in the world can do thee good.
In thee there is not half an hour of life.
The treacherous instrument is in thy hand,
Unbated° and envenomed. The foul practice *Not blunted*
Hath turned itself on me. Lo, here I lie,
Never to rise again. Thy mother's poisoned.
I can no more. The King, the King's to blame.

HAMLET The point envenomed too? Then, venom, to thy work.
[*He*] *hurts* KING [CLAUDIUS]

ALL THE COURTIERS Treason, treason!

KING CLAUDIUS O yet defend me, friends! I am but hurt.

HAMLET Here, thou incestuous, murd'rous, damnèd Dane,
Drink off this potion. Is thy union[8] here?
Follow my mother. KING [CLAUDIUS] *dies*

LAERTES He is justly served.
It is a poison tempered° by himself. *mixed*
Exchange forgiveness with me, noble Hamlet.
Mine and my father's death come not upon thee,[9]
Nor thine on me. LAERTES *dies*

HAMLET Heaven make thee free of it! I follow thee.
I am dead, Horatio. Wretched Queen, adieu!
You that look pale and tremble at this chance,
That are but mutes° or audience to this act, *silent witnesses*
Had I but time—as this fell sergeant[1] Death
Is strict in his arrest—O, I could tell you—
But let it be. Horatio, I am dead,
Thou liv'st. Report me and my cause aright
To the unsatisfied.

HORATIO Never believe it.
I am more an antique Roman than a Dane.[2]
Here's yet some liquor left.

HAMLET As thou'rt a man,
Give me the cup. Let go. By heaven, I'll ha't.
O God, Horatio, what a wounded name,
Things standing thus unknown, shall live behind me!
If thou didst ever hold me in thy heart,
Absent thee from felicity a while,
And in this harsh world draw thy breath in pain
To tell my story.
March afar off, and shout within
What warlike noise is this?

Enter OSRIC

8. Pearl (with a pun on "marriage").
9. That is, you are not responsible for our deaths.
1. This dread sheriff's officer.
2. The ancient Romans (unlike the Christian Danes) viewed suicide as sometimes honorable.

OSRIC Young Fortinbras, with conquest come from Poland,
To th'ambassadors of England gives
This warlike volley.° *military salute*

HAMLET O, I die, Horatio!
The potent poison quite o'ercrows° my spirit. *triumphs over*
I cannot live to hear the news from England,
But I do prophesy th'election lights
On Fortinbras. He has my dying voice.° *vote*
So tell him, with th'occurrents,° more and less, *events*
Which have solicited.[3] The rest is silence.
O, O, O, O! HAMLET *dies*

HORATIO Now cracks a noble heart. Good night, sweet prince,
And flights of angels sing thee to thy rest.—
Why does the drum come hither?

Enter FORTINBRAS *with the English* AMBASSADORS, *with drumme[r], colours, and attendants*

FORTINBRAS Where is this sight?

HORATIO What is it ye would see?
If aught of woe or wonder, cease your search.

FORTINBRAS This quarry cries on havoc.[4] O proud death,
What feast is toward° in thine eternal cell *in preparation*
That thou so many princes at a shot
So bloodily hast struck!

AMBASSADOR The sight is dismal,
And our affairs from England come too late.
The ears are senseless that should give us hearing
To tell him° his commandment is fulfilled, *(Claudius)*
That Rosencrantz and Guildenstern are dead.
Where should we have our thanks?

HORATIO Not from his mouth,
Had it th'ability of life to thank you.
He never gave commandment for their death.
But since so jump° upon this bloody question° *immediately / quarrel*
You from the Polack wars, and you from England,
Are here arrived, give order that these bodies
High on a stage be placèd to the view;
And let me speak to th' yet unknowing world
How these things came about. So shall you hear
Of carnal, bloody, and unnatural acts,
Of accidental judgements,° casual° slaughters, *retributions / chance*
Of deaths put on° by cunning and forced cause; *instigated*
And, in this upshot, purposes mistook
Fall'n on th'inventors' heads. All this can I
Truly deliver.

FORTINBRAS Let us haste to hear it,
And call the noblest to the audience.

3. Incited (this sentence seems to be incomplete, possibly broken off as Hamlet realizes he is about to die).

4. This heap of game ("quarry") proclaims a massacre.

For me, with sorrow I embrace my fortune.
I have some rights of memory° in this kingdom, *unforgotten*
Which now to claim my vantage° doth invite me. *favorable opportunity*

HORATIO Of that I shall have also cause to speak,
And from his mouth whose voice will draw on more.[5]
But let this same be presently performed,
Even whiles men's minds are wild, lest more mischance
On° plots and errors happen. *On top of*

FORTINBRAS Let four captains
Bear Hamlet like a soldier to the stage,
For he was likely, had he been put on,[6]
To have proved most royally; and for his passage,
The soldiers' music and the rites of war
Speak loudly for him.
Take up the body. Such a sight as this
Becomes the field,[7] but here shows° much amiss. *appears*
Go, bid the soldiers shoot.

[*Exeunt, marching* [*with the bodies*]; *after the which, a peal of ordnance are shot off*]

5. Whose vote will draw more votes (in Fortinbras's favor).

6. Put to the test (as King of Denmark).

7. Is fitting for a battlefield.

Twelfth Night
or, *What You Will*

THE PERSONS OF THE PLAY

ORSINO, Duke of Illyria
VALENTINE } attending on Orsino
CURIO } attending on Orsino
FIRST OFFICER
SECOND OFFICER
VIOLA, a lady, later disguised as Cesario
A CAPTAIN
SEBASTIAN, her twin brother
ANTONIO, another sea-captain
OLIVIA, a Countess
MARIA, her waiting-gentlewoman
SIR TOBY Belch, Olivia's kinsman
SIR ANDREW Aguecheek, companion of Sir Toby
MALVOLIO, Olivia's steward
FABIAN, a member of Olivia's household
FESTE the clown, her jester
A PRIEST
A SERVANT of Olivia
Musicians, sailors, lords, attendants

1.1

Music. Enter ORSINO *Duke of Illyria,*[1] CURIO, *and other lords.*

ORSINO If music be the food of love, play on,
Give me excess of it that, surfeiting,
The appetite may sicken and so die.
That strain° again, it had a dying fall.° *(of music) / cadence*
O, it came o'er my ear like the sweet sound
That breathes upon a bank of violets,
Stealing and giving odour. Enough, no more,
'Tis not so sweet now as it was before.
[*Music ceases*]
O spirit of love, how quick and fresh[2] art thou
That, notwithstanding thy capacity
Receiveth as the sea,° naught enters there, *without limit*
Of what validity° and pitch[3] so e'er, *value*
But falls into abatement° and low price *decreased value*
Even in a minute! So full of shapes° is fancy° *fanciful forms / love*
That it alone is high fantastical.[4]
CURIO Will you go hunt, my lord?
ORSINO What, Curio?
CURIO The hart.
ORSINO Why so I do, the noblest that I have.[5]

1.1 Location: Orsino's palace.
1. An imaginary dukedom on the eastern coast of the Adriatic Sea.
2. Lively and eager to devour.
3. High worth (in falconry, "pitch" is the highest point in a hawk's flight).
4. That is, love reigns supreme in the imagination of the lover.
5. Orsino puns on "hart" and "heart."

O, when mine eyes did see Olivia first
Methought she purged the air of pestilence;[6]
That instant was I turned into a hart,
And my desires, like fell° and cruel hounds, *fierce*
E'er since pursue me.[7]

Enter VALENTINE

How now, what news from her?

VALENTINE So please my lord, I might not be admitted,° *was not granted entry*
But from her handmaid do return this answer:
The element itself till seven years' heat[8]
Shall not behold her face at ample° view, *full*
But like a cloistress° she will veilèd walk *nun*
And water once a day her chamber round
With eye-offending brine°—all this to season° *salty tears / preserve*
A brother's dead love,[9] which she would keep fresh
And lasting in her sad remembrance.

ORSINO O, she that hath a heart of that fine frame[1]
To pay this debt of love but to a° brother, *to a mere*
How will she love when the rich golden shaft[2]
Hath killed the flock of all affections else° *all other feelings*
That live in her—when liver, brain, and heart,[3]
These sovereign thrones, are all supplied, and filled
Her sweet perfections[4] with one self° king! *one and the same*
Away before me to sweet beds of flowers.
Love-thoughts lie rich when canopied with bowers.

Exeunt° *They exit (Latin)*

1.2

Enter VIOLA, *a* CAPTAIN, *and sailors*

VIOLA What country, friends, is this?

CAPTAIN This is Illyria, lady.

VIOLA And what should I do in Illyria?
My brother, he is in Elysium.[5]
Perchance° he is not drowned. What think you sailors? *Perhaps*

CAPTAIN It is perchance° that you yourself were saved. *by chance*

VIOLA O my poor brother!—and so perchance may he be.

CAPTAIN True, madam, and to comfort you with chance,° *that possibility*
Assure yourself, after our ship did split,° *break up*
When you and those poor number savèd with you
Hung on our driving boat,[6] I saw your brother,

6. Any fatal epidemic disease.
7. Orsino compares himself to Actaeon, a hunter in classical mythology who was turned into a stag and torn apart by his own dogs after he saw the goddess Diana (Artemis) bathing naked.
8. The sky ("element") itself for seven hot summers.
9. That is, her love for her dead brother.
1. Such excellent construction.
2. The arrow of Cupid, Roman god of love.
3. In the Renaissance, the liver, brain, and heart were often identified as the seats of, respectively, love, the rational soul, and feeling or emotion.
4. And her sweet perfections are filled.
1.2 Location: The coast of Illyria.
5. In classical mythology, the abode of the blessed after death.
6. Our boat being driven before the wind.

Most provident in peril, bind himself—
Courage and hope both teaching him the practice—
To a strong mast that lived° upon the sea, *floated*
Where, like Arion[7] on the dolphin's back,
I saw him hold acquaintance with the waves[8]
So long as I could see.
VIOLA [*giving money*] For saying so, there's gold.
Mine own escape unfoldeth to° my hope, *discloses*
Whereto thy speech serves for authority,° *corroboration*
The like° of him. Know'st thou this country? *The same (news)*
CAPTAIN Ay, madam, well, for I was bred and born
Not three hours' travel from this very place.
VIOLA Who governs here?
CAPTAIN A noble duke, in nature
As in name.
VIOLA What is his name?
CAPTAIN Orsino.
VIOLA Orsino. I have heard my father name him.
He was a bachelor then.
CAPTAIN And so is now, or was so very late,° *recently*
For but a month ago I went from hence,
And then 'twas fresh in murmur°—as, you know, *rumor*
What great ones do the less will prattle of—
That he did seek the love of fair Olivia.
VIOLA What's she?
CAPTAIN A virtuous maid, the daughter of a count
That died some twelvemonth since, then leaving her
In the protection of his son, her brother,
Who shortly° also died, for whose dear love, *Shortly thereafter*
They say, she hath abjured the sight
And company of men.
VIOLA O that I served that lady,
And might not be delivered° to the world *made known*
Till I had made mine own occasion mellow,° *ripe (to be known)*
What my estate° is. *rank, social position*
CAPTAIN That were hard to compass,° *achieve*
Because she will admit no kind of suit,° *petition*
No, not the Duke's.
VIOLA There is a fair behaviour[9] in thee, captain,
And though that nature with a beauteous wall
Doth oft close in pollution,[1] yet of thee
I will believe thou hast a mind that suits
With this thy fair and outward character.
I pray thee—and I'll pay thee bounteously—
Conceal me what I am, and be my aid

7. Greek poet and singer (late 7th c. B.C.E.). According to legend, to avoid being murdered by pirates, he jumped into the sea and was rescued by dolphins enchanted by his music.

8. That is, stay above water.

9. Manner of conduct; external appearance.

1. Though nature often conceals a person's inward corruption with outward beauty.

For such disguise as haply° shall become *possibly*
The form of my intent.[2] I'll serve this duke.
Thou shalt present me as an eunuch[3] to him.
It may be worth thy pains,° for I can sing, *troubles*
And speak to him in many sorts of music
That will allow me very worth his service.[4]
What else may hap, to time I will commit.
Only shape thou thy silence to my wit.° *plan*

CAPTAIN Be you his eunuch, and your mute° I'll be. *silent servant*
When my tongue blabs, then let mine eyes not see.

VIOLA I thank thee. Lead me on. *Exeunt*

1.3

Enter SIR TOBY [*Belch*] *and* MARIA[5]

SIR TOBY What a plague° means my niece to take the death of her brother thus? I am sure care's an enemy to life. *(an oath)*

MARIA By my troth, Sir Toby, you must come in earlier o' nights. Your cousin,° my lady, takes great exceptions to your ill hours. *kinswoman*

SIR TOBY Why, let her except, before excepted.[6]

MARIA Ay, but you must confine yourself within the modest limits of order.

SIR TOBY Confine? I'll confine myself no finer[7] than I am. These clothes are good enough to drink in, and so be these boots too; an° they be not, let them hang themselves in their own straps. *if*

MARIA That quaffing and drinking will undo you. I heard my lady talk of it yesterday, and of a foolish knight that you brought in one night here to be her wooer.

SIR TOBY Who, Sir Andrew Aguecheek?[8]

MARIA Ay, he.

SIR TOBY He's as tall[9] a man as any's in Illyria.

MARIA What's that to th' purpose?

SIR TOBY Why, he has three thousand ducats a year.

MARIA Ay, but he'll have but a year in all these ducats.[1] He's a very fool, and a prodigal.

SIR TOBY Fie that you'll say so! He plays o'th' viol-de-gamboys,[2] and speaks three or four languages word for word without book,° and hath all the good gifts of nature. *from memory*

2. The outward appearance of my plan.
3. A castrato, a male soprano.
4. That will prove me very worthy to serve him.
1.3 Location: The Countess Olivia's residence.
5. Usually pronounced "Ma-RYE-uh."
6. A play on a Latin legal phrase (*exceptis excipiendis*) meaning "with the necessary exceptions having been made." Thus Toby sidesteps Olivia's criticism.
7. A pun: he will dress ('confine') himself neither more strictly (because of his girth) nor more elegantly.
8. Usually pronounced "AY-gyoo-cheek."
9. Brave (Maria understands the word in its usual modern sense).
1. That is, he will spend his money in a year.
2. The viola da gamba, a bowed stringed instrument played while held between the legs (as is the modern cello).

MARIA He hath indeed, almost natural,[3] for besides that he's a fool, he's a great quarreller, and but that he hath the gift° of a coward to allay the gust° he hath in quarrelling, 'tis thought among the prudent he would quickly have the gift of a grave. *talent / relish*

SIR TOBY By this hand, they are scoundrels and substractors° that say so of him. Who are they? *i.e., detractors*

MARIA They that add, moreover, he's drunk nightly in your company.

SIR TOBY With drinking healths to my niece. I'll drink to her as long as there is a passage in my throat and drink in Illyria. He's a coward and a coistrel° that will not drink to my niece till his brains turn o'th' toe, like a parish top.[4] What wench, *Castiliano, vulgo,*[5] for here comes Sir Andrew Agueface.[6] *horse groom; knave*

Enter SIR ANDREW *[Aguecheek]*

SIR ANDREW Sir Toby Belch! How now, Sir Toby Belch?

SIR TOBY Sweet Sir Andrew.

SIR ANDREW [*to* MARIA] Bless you, fair shrew.[7]

MARIA And you too, sir.

SIR TOBY Accost, Sir Andrew, accost.[8]

SIR ANDREW What's that?

SIR TOBY My niece's chambermaid.° *lady-in-waiting*

SIR ANDREW Good Mistress Accost, I desire better acquaintance.

MARIA My name is Mary, sir.

SIR ANDREW Good Mistress-Mary Accost.

SIR TOBY You mistake, knight. 'Accost' is front her, board her, woo her, assail[9] her.

SIR ANDREW By my troth, I would not undertake[1] her in this company.° Is that the meaning of 'accost'? *this audience*

MARIA Fare you well, gentlemen.

SIR TOBY An° thou let part so, Sir Andrew, would thou mightst never draw sword again.[2] *If*

SIR ANDREW An you part so, mistress, I would I might never draw sword again. Fair lady, do you think you have fools in hand?° *are dealing with fools*

MARIA Sir, I have not you by th' hand.

SIR ANDREW Marry,[3] but you shall have, and here's my hand.

3. Naturally deficient in intellect. (Idiots were called "naturals.")
4. A large top that parishioners could whip into spinning, for their entertainment and exercise.
5. The meaning of this phrase is unknown; perhaps "speak of the devil," because Castilians were considered devilish.
6. With a face pale and thin, as if he were suffering from the cold stage of an ague.
7. A woman given to scolding; here, probably used in a benign and playful sense.
8. Greet (Maria), possibly with a kiss as was Elizabethan fashion.
9. A series of terms with nautical meanings, beginning with "accost, or sail alongside; (which is also a meaning of "board"). *Front:* meet face-to-face; *board:* make advances to; *assail*: make trial of, woo.
1. Attempt her (with sexual implication).
2. That is, to part with her in this fashion is unworthy of a knight (but also with sexual implication).
3. By the Virgin Mary (a mild oath).

MARIA [*taking his hand*] Now sir, thought is free.[4] I pray you, bring your hand to th' buttery-bar,[5] and let it drink.

SIR ANDREW Wherefore,° sweetheart? What's your metaphor? *Why*

MARIA It's dry,[6] sir.

SIR ANDREW Why, I think so. I am not such an ass but I can keep my hand dry.[7] But what's your jest?

MARIA A dry jest,[8] sir.

SIR ANDREW Are you full of them?

MARIA Ay, sir, I have them at my fingers' ends.[9] Marry, now I let go your hand I am barren.° *Exit* *(of jokes)*

SIR TOBY O knight, thou lackest° a cup of canary.[1] When did I see thee so put down?[2] *are in need of*

SIR ANDREW Never in your life, I think, unless you see canary put me down.° Methinks sometimes I have no more wit than a Christian° or an ordinary man has; but I am a great eater of beef,[3] and I believe that does harm to my wit. *lay me low* *an ordinary human*

SIR TOBY No question.

SIR ANDREW An I thought that, I'd forswear it. I'll ride home tomorrow, Sir Toby.

SIR TOBY *Pourquoi,°* my dear knight? *Why (French)*

SIR ANDREW What is 'Pourquoi'? Do, or not do? I would I had bestowed that time in the tongues[4] that I have in fencing, dancing, and bear-baiting. O, had I but followed the arts!° *i.e., liberal arts*

SIR TOBY Then hadst thou had an excellent head of hair.

SIR ANDREW Why, would that have mended° my hair? *improved*

SIR TOBY Past question, for thou seest it will not curl by nature.

SIR ANDREW But it becomes me well enough, does't not?

SIR TOBY Excellent, it hangs like flax on a distaff,[5] and I hope to see a housewife take thee between her legs and spin it off.[6]

SIR ANDREW Faith,° I'll home tomorrow, Sir Toby. Your niece will not be seen, or if she be, it's four to one she'll none of me. The Count[7] himself here hard by° woos her. *By my faith* *(a mild oath)* *nearby*

4. I may think whatever I like (proverbial).
5. The ledge on top of the half-door to the buttery, a storeroom for liquor and provisions, over which such items were served.
6. Unproductive of its intended meaning. Dryness of the palm of Sir Andrew's hand (which Maria is holding) is also a sign of sexual impotence.
7. A reference to the proverb "fools have wit enough to keep themselves out of the rain."
8. A joke about dryness; a joke that displays a dry or sharp wit; a joke that partially fails because of Sir Andrew's obtuseness.
9. Ready at hand; she also refers to Sir Andrew, whom she holds at her fingers' ends.
1. A sweet wine (originally from the Canary Islands).
2. Defeated verbally, made a fool of.
3. Eating too much beef was believed to lower intelligence.
4. The study of languages; Sir Toby answers as if he had meant (curling) tongs.
5. A staff that holds the wool or flax being spun into thread.
6. That is, remove his hair both by using it as if it were flax to be spun and by infecting him with venereal disease (which will result in baldness). One meaning of "housewife" (huswife) is prostitute.
7. That is, Duke Orsino (sometimes referred to as "Count" in the play).

SIR TOBY She'll none o'th' Count. She'll not match above her degree,° neither in estate,° years, nor wit, I have heard her swear't. Tut, there's life in't,[8] man. *social rank / status*

SIR ANDREW I'll stay a month longer. I am a fellow o'th' strangest mind i'th' world. I delight in masques and revels sometimes altogether.

SIR TOBY Art thou good at these kickshawses,[9] knight?

SIR ANDREW As any man in Illyria, whatsoever he be, under the degree of my betters; and yet I will not compare with an old man.° *expert*

SIR TOBY What is thy excellence in a galliard,[1] knight?

SIR ANDREW Faith, I can cut a caper.[2]

SIR TOBY And I can cut the mutton° to't. *cooked sheep; whore*

SIR ANDREW And I think I have the back-trick[3] simply as strong as any man in Illyria.

SIR TOBY Wherefore are these things hid? Wherefore have these gifts a curtain[4] before 'em? Are they like to take dust, like Mistress Mall's[5] picture? Why dost thou not go to church in a galliard, and come home in a coranto?[6] My very walk should be a jig. I would not so much as make water but in a cinquepace.[7] What dost thou mean? Is it a world to hide virtues in? I did think by the excellent constitution of thy leg it was formed under the star of a galliard.[8]

SIR ANDREW Ay, 'tis strong, and it does indifferent° well in a divers-coloured stock.° Shall we set about some revels? *reasonably* / *multicolored* / *stockings*

SIR TOBY What shall we do else—were we not born under Taurus?[9]

SIR ANDREW Taurus? That's sides and heart.

SIR TOBY No, sir, it is legs and thighs: let me see thee caper.
[SIR ANDREW *capers*]
Ha, higher! Ha ha, excellent. *Exeunt*

1.4

Enter VALENTINE, *and* VIOLA [*as Cesario*] *in man's attire*

VALENTINE If the Duke continue these favours towards you, Cesario, you are like to be much advanced. He hath known you but three days, and already you are no stranger.

8. Where there's life, there's hope (proverbial).
9. Trifles (from the French *quelque chose*).
1. A quick, lively dance in triple time.
2. Dance or leap in a frolicsome way. Also, capers (the buds or berries of a plant used as a condiment) were employed in mutton sauces.
3. Backward step in the galliard.
4. Paintings were sometimes hidden behind curtains to protect them from dust and sunlight.
5. "Mall" was a nickname for "Mary." It has been suggested that this is a reference to Queen Elizabeth's lady-in-waiting, Mary Fitton, who was pregnant with Sir William Knollys's illegitimate child at the time Shakespeare wrote *Twelfth Night*.
6. A "running dance" (*courante*) of French origin.
7. A galliard-like dance, whose steps were regulated by the number five.
8. That is, under a star conducive to dancing.
9. The second sign of the zodiac, the Bull, was associated with the neck and the throat, and, less commonly, with the legs and thighs, but never with the sides and the heart (as Sir Andrew suggests).
1.4 Location: Orsino's palace.

VIOLA You either fear his humour° or my negligence, that you call in question the continuance of his love. Is he inconstant, sir, in his favours? *changeable mood*

VALENTINE No, believe me.

Enter DUKE, CURIO, and attendants

VIOLA I thank you. Here comes the Count.
ORSINO Who saw Cesario, ho?
VIOLA On your attendance,° my lord, here. *At your service*
ORSINO [*to* CURIO *and attendants*] Stand you a while aloof.° *to the side*
[*To* VIOLA] Cesario,
Thou know'st no less but all.° I have unclasped *i.e., everything*
To thee the book even of my secret soul.
Therefore, good youth, address thy gait unto her,° *go to (Olivia)*
Be not denied access, stand at her doors,
And tell them there thy fixèd foot shall grow° *take root*
Till thou have audience.
VIOLA Sure, my noble lord,
If she be so abandoned to her sorrow
As it is spoke, she never will admit me.
ORSINO Be clamorous, and leap all civil bounds,[1]
Rather than make unprofited° return. *unsuccessful*
VIOLA Say I do speak with her, my lord, what then?
ORSINO O then unfold the passion of my love,
Surprise her with discourse of my dear faith.[2]
It shall become thee well to act my woes—
She will attend it better in thy youth
Than in a nuncio's° of more grave aspect.° *messenger's / appearance*
VIOLA I think not so, my lord.
ORSINO Dear lad, believe it;
For they shall yet belie thy happy years
That say thou art a man. Diana's lip
Is not more smooth and rubious;° thy small pipe° *ruby red / treble voice*
Is as the maiden's organ, shrill and sound,° *clear*
And all is semblative° a woman's part. *similar to*
I know thy constellation[3] is right apt
For this affair. [*To* CURIO *and attendants*] Some four or five attend him.
All if you will, for I myself am best
When least in company. [*To* VIOLA] Prosper well in this
And thou shalt live as freely as thy lord,
To call his fortunes thine.
VIOLA I'll do my best
To woo your lady—[*aside*] yet a barful strife[4]—
Whoe'er I woo, myself would be his wife. *Exeunt*

1. Exceed the norms of courtesy.
2. Take her unawares with speech of my heartfelt love.
3. That is, your nature (as determined by the stars).
4. A task full of hindrances.

1.5

Enter MARIA, *and* [FESTE,[5] *the*] *clown*

MARIA Nay, either tell me where thou hast been or I will not open my lips so wide as a bristle may enter in° way of thy excuse. My lady will hang thee for thy absence. *by*

FESTE Let her hang me. He that is well hanged[6] in this world needs to fear no colours.[7]

MARIA Make that good.° *Explain that*

FESTE He shall see none to fear.

MARIA A good lenten[8] answer. I can tell thee where that saying was born, of 'I fear no colours'.

FESTE Where, good Mistress Mary?

MARIA In the wars, and that may you be bold to say in your foolery.

FESTE Well, God give them wisdom that have it; and those that are fools, let them use their talents.[9]

MARIA Yet you will be hanged for being so long absent, or to be turned away°—is not that as good as a hanging to you? *dismissed*

FESTE Many a good hanging[1] prevents a bad marriage, and for turning away, let summer bear it out.[2]

MARIA You are resolute then?

FESTE Not so neither, but I am resolved on two points.° *issues; laces*

MARIA That if one break, the other will hold; or if both break, your gaskins° fall. *wide breeches*

FESTE Apt, in good faith, very apt. Well, go thy way. If Sir Toby would leave drinking thou wert as witty a piece of Eve's flesh° as any in Illyria.[3] *a woman*

MARIA Peace, you rogue, no more o' that. Here comes my lady. Make your excuse wisely, you were best.° [*Exit*] *it would be best for you*

Enter Lady OLIVIA, *with* MALVOLIO[4] [*and attendants*]

FESTE [*aside*] Wit,° an't° be thy will, put me into good fooling! Those wits that think they have thee do very oft prove fools, and I that am sure I lack thee may pass for a wise man. For what says Quinapalus?[5]—'Better a witty fool than a foolish wit.' [*To* OLIVIA] God bless thee, lady. *Intelligence / if it*

OLIVIA [*to attendants*] Take the fool away.

FESTE Do you not hear, fellows? Take away the lady.

1.5 Location: Olivia's residence.
5. Usually pronounced "FESS-tee."
6. Hanged to death. Feste also implies that he is "well hung" (i.e., well-endowed sexually), a trait regularly attributed to fools (as supposed to accompany mental deficiency).
7. Fear no foe (literally, military flags); punning on "collars," the hangman's noose.
8. Lean or meager (i.e., appropriate to Lent).
9. Abilities, with a punning allusion to the parable of the talents (coins) in Matthew 25.14–30.

1. A reference to both capital punishment and sexual endowment.
2. That is, let mild weather make it bearable (for the newly homeless).
3. Feste appears to say that Toby is as likely to give up drinking as Maria is to be witty.
4. Usually pronounced "Mal-VOE-lee-o" (a name meaning "ill will").
5. An invented philosopher whose wisdom Feste pretends to quote.

OLIVIA Go to[6] you're a dry° fool. I'll no more of you. Besides, you grow dishonest.[7] *dull*

FESTE Two faults, madonna,° that drink and good counsel will amend, for give the dry fool drink, then is the fool not dry; bid the dishonest man mend° himself : if he mend, he is no longer dishonest; if he cannot, let the botcher° mend him. Anything that's mended is but patched. Virtue that transgresses is but patched with sin, and sin that amends is but patched with virtue.[8] If that this simple syllogism will serve, so. If it will not, what remedy? As there is no true cuckold but calamity, so beauty's a flower.[9] The lady bade take away the fool, therefore I say again, take her away. *my lady (Italian)* *reform* *mender of old clothes*

OLIVIA Sir, I bade them take away you.

FESTE Misprision[1] in the highest degree! Lady, '*Cucullus non facit monachum*'[2]—that's as much to say as I wear not motley[3] in my brain. Good madonna, give me leave to prove you a fool.

OLIVIA Can you do it?

FESTE Dexteriously,° good madonna. *Dexterously*

OLIVIA Make your proof.

FESTE I must catechize you for it, madonna. Good my mouse° of virtue, answer me. *(term of endearment)*

OLIVIA Well, sir, for want of other idleness° I'll bide° your proof. *diversion / await*

FESTE Good madonna, why mournest thou?

OLIVIA Good fool, for my brother's death.

FESTE I think his soul is in hell, madonna.

OLIVIA I know his soul is in heaven, fool.

FESTE The more fool, madonna, to mourn for your brother's soul, being in heaven. Take away the fool, gentlemen.

OLIVIA What think you of this fool, Malvolio? Doth he not mend?[4]

MALVOLIO Yes, and shall do till the pangs of death shake him. Infirmity, that decays the wise, doth ever make the better fool.

FESTE God send you, sir, a speedy infirmity for the better increasing your folly. Sir Toby will be sworn that I am no fox, but he will not pass his word for twopence that you are no fool.

OLIVIA How say you to that, Malvolio?

MALVOLIO I marvel your ladyship takes delight in such a barren rascal. I saw him put down[5] the other day with an

6. An expression of impatience.
7. Unreliable (because unaccountably absent from the house).
8. In this passage, Feste caricatures formal logic (the syllogism).
9. That is, the cuckold is the misfortune that Olivia has wed, to which she must be unfaithful so that her beauty can bloom and find love (before it fades).

1. Misunderstanding; wrongful arrest.
2. The cowl does not make the monk (Latin proverb).
3. The multicolored tunic of professional jesters.
4. Improve (by becoming more entertaining); Malvolio takes the improvement to lie in becoming more foolish.
5. Defeated in a battle of wits.

ordinary fool that has no more brain than a stone. Look you now, he's out of his guard° already. Unless you laugh and minister occasion[6] to him, he is gagged. I protest I take these wise men that crow so at these set kind of fools no better than the fools' zanies.[7] *defenseless*

OLIVIA O, you are sick of° self-love, Malvolio, and taste with a distempered° appetite. To be generous, guiltless, and of free° disposition is to take those things for birdbolts[8] that you deem cannon bullets. There is no slander in an allowed fool, though he do nothing but rail; nor no railing in a known discreet man, though he do nothing but reprove. *from* *unhealthy* *magnanimous*

FESTE Now Mercury indue thee with leasing,[9] for thou speakest well of fools.

Enter MARIA

MARIA Madam, there is at the gate a young gentleman much desires to speak with you.

OLIVIA From the Count Orsino, is it?

MARIA I know not, madam. 'Tis a fair young man, and well attended.

OLIVIA Who of my people hold him in delay?

MARIA Sir Toby, madam, your kinsman.

OLIVIA Fetch him off, I pray you, he speaks nothing but madman.° Fie on him. Go you, Malvolio. If it be a suit from the Count, I am sick, or not at home—what you will to dismiss it. *madman's speech*

Exit MALVOLIO

Now you see, sir, how your fooling grows old, and people dislike it.

FESTE Thou hast spoke for us, madonna, as if thy eldest son should be a fool, whose skull Jove[1] cram with brains, for—here he comes—

Enter SIR TOBY

one of thy kin has a most weak *pia mater*.[2]

OLIVIA By mine honour, half-drunk. What is he at the gate, cousin?° *kinsman*

SIR TOBY A gentleman.

OLIVIA A gentleman? What gentleman?

SIR TOBY 'Tis a gentleman here. [*He belches*] A plague o' these pickle herring! [*To* FESTE] How now, sot?° *fool, drunkard*

FESTE Good Sir Toby.

OLIVIA Cousin, cousin, how have you come so early by this lethargy?

6. Provide opportunity.
7. The subordinate fools who imitate the main comic performers ("zany" is a term from the Italian commedia dell'arte). *Set*: deliberate, artificial.
8. Blunt-headed arrows for shooting birds.
9. That is, may Mercury, the Roman god of traders, thieves, and tricksters, grant you the gift of lying.
1. Jupiter, the king of the Roman gods.
2. The brain (literally, the membrane enclosing it; "tender mother," in Latin).

SIR TOBY Lechery? I defy lechery. There's one° at the gate. *someone*

OLIVIA Ay, marry, what is he?

SIR TOBY Let him be the devil an° he will, I care not. Give me faith,[3] say I. Well, it's all one. [*Exit*] *if*

OLIVIA What's a drunken man like, fool?

FESTE Like a drowned man, a fool, and a madman—one draught above heat[4] makes him a fool, the second mads him, and a third drowns him.

OLIVIA Go thou and seek the coroner, and let him sit o'° my coz,° for he's in the third degree of drink, he's drowned. Go look after him. *hold an inquest on* / *cousin (Toby)*

FESTE He is but mad yet, madonna, and the fool shall look to the madman. [*Exit*]

Enter MALVOLIO

MALVOLIO Madam, yon young fellow swears he will speak with you. I told him you were sick—he takes on him to understand so much, and therefore comes to speak with you. I told him you were asleep—he seems to have a foreknowledge of that too, and therefore comes to speak with you. What is to be said to him, lady? He's fortified against any denial.

OLIVIA Tell him he shall not speak with me.

MALVOLIO He's been told so, and he says he'll stand at your door like a sheriff's post,[5] and be the supporter to a bench, but he'll speak with you.

OLIVIA What kind o' man is he?

MALVOLIO Why, of mankind.

OLIVIA What manner of man?

MALVOLIO Of very ill manner: he'll speak with you, will you or no.

OLIVIA Of what personage° and years is he? *appearance*

MALVOLIO Not yet old enough for a man, nor young enough for a boy; as a squash[6] is before 'tis a peascod, or a codling° when 'tis almost an apple. 'Tis with him in standing water[7] between boy and man. He is very well-favoured,° and he speaks very shrewishly.° One would think his mother's milk were scarce out of him. *unripe apple* / *handsome* / *like a woman*

OLIVIA Let him approach. Call in my gentlewoman.

MALVOLIO Gentlewoman, my lady calls. *Exit*

Enter MARIA

OLIVIA Give me my veil. Come, throw it o'er my face.
We'll once more hear Orsino's embassy.° *ambassador's message*

Enter VIOLA [*as Cesario*]

VIOLA The honourable lady of the house, which is she?

OLIVIA Speak to me, I shall answer for her. Your will.

3. That is, faith to resist the devil.
4. One more drink than it takes to make him feel warm.
5. The painted post outside the sheriff's office to which proclamations were affixed.
6. An unripe pea pod.
7. The time between the incoming and outgoing tides.

VIOLA Most radiant, exquisite, and unmatchable beauty— I pray you, tell me if this be the lady of the house, for I never saw her. I would be loath to cast away° my speech, for besides that it is excellently well penned, I have taken great pains to con° it. Good beauties, let me sustain° no scorn; I am very 'countable,° even to the least sinister usage.[8]

waste · *memorize / endure* · *sensitive*

OLIVIA Whence came you, sir?

VIOLA I can say little more than I have studied,° and that question's out of my part. Good gentle one, give me modest° assurance if you be the lady of the house, that I may proceed in my speech.

committed to memory · *reasonable*

OLIVIA Are you a comedian?°

an actor

VIOLA No, my profound heart;[9] and yet—by the very fangs of malice I swear—I am not that I play.° Are you the lady of the house?

what I act

OLIVIA If I do not usurp° myself, I am.

impersonate

VIOLA Most certain if you are she you do usurp yourself, for what is yours to bestow is not yours to reserve.[1] But this is from° my commission.° I will on with my speech in your praise, and then show you the heart of my message.

beyond / instructions

OLIVIA Come to what is important in't, I forgive you° the praise.

excuse you from reciting

VIOLA Alas, I took great pains to study it, and 'tis poetical.

OLIVIA It is the more like to be feigned, I pray you keep it in. I heard you were saucy at my gates, and allowed your approach rather to wonder at you than to hear you. If you be not mad, be gone. If you have reason, be brief. 'Tis not that time of moon with me to make one in so skipping a dialogue.[2]

MARIA Will you hoist sail, sir? Here lies your way.

VIOLA No, good swabber, I am to hull[3] here a little longer. [*To* OLIVIA] Some mollification for your giant,[4] sweet lady. Tell me your mind, I am a messenger.

OLIVIA Sure, you have some hideous matter to deliver when the courtesy[5] of it is so fearful. Speak your office.°

commission

VIOLA It alone concerns your ear. I bring no overture° of war, no taxation of homage.[6] I hold the olive° in my hand. My words are as full of peace as matter.°

declaration · *olive branch* · *meaning*

OLIVIA Yet you began rudely. What are you? What would you?

VIOLA The rudeness that hath appeared in me have I learned from my entertainment.° What I am and what I

reception

8. The smallest discourtesy.
9. My most wise lady.
1. That is, a woman usurps a husband's rightful role if she bestows herself not on a man but on herself (by "reserving" herself).
2. That is, I am not so under the moon's influence (literally, so lunatic) that I am willing to participate in such a fantastic conversation.
3. Lie at anchor, with furled sails. *Swabber:* one who mops the decks of a ship.
4. Maria, who is small of stature, is here mockingly identified as one of the giants who protected ladies in medieval romances.
5. The courteous preamble.
6. Demand for payment of tribute.

would are as secret as maidenhead;° to your ears, divinity; to any others', profanation. *virginity*

OLIVIA [*to* MARIA *and attendants*] Give us the place alone, we will hear this divinity.° [*Exeunt* MARIA *and attendants*] Now sir, what is your text?[7] *religious discourse*

VIOLA Most sweet lady—

OLIVIA A comfortable° doctrine, and much may be said of it. Where lies your text? *comforting*

VIOLA In Orsino's bosom.

OLIVIA In his bosom? In what chapter of his bosom?

VIOLA To answer by the method,° in the first of his heart. *in the same style*

OLIVIA O, I have read it. It is heresy. Have you no more to say?

VIOLA Good madam, let me see your face.

OLIVIA Have you any commission from your lord to negotiate with my face? You are now out of° your text. But we will draw the curtain and show you the picture. *straying from*

[*She unveils*]

Look you, sir, such a one I was this present.[8] Is't not well done?

VIOLA Excellently done, if God did all.[9]

OLIVIA 'Tis in grain,° sir, 'twill endure wind and weather. *It is dyed fast*

VIOLA 'Tis beauty truly blent,° whose red and white *blended*
Nature's own sweet and cunning° hand laid on. *skillful*
Lady, you are the cruell'st she° alive *woman*
If you will lead these graces to the grave
And leave the world no copy.[1]

OLIVIA O sir, I will not be so hard-hearted. I will give out divers schedules° of my beauty. It shall be inventoried and every particle and utensil labelled[2] to my will, as, *item,* two lips, indifferent° red; *item,* two grey eyes, with lids to them; *item,* one neck, one chin, and so forth. Were you sent hither to praise° me? *inventory* *moderately* *appraise*

VIOLA I see you what you are, you are too proud,
But if° you were the devil, you are fair. *even if*
My lord and master loves you. O, such love
Could be but recompensed though[3] you were crowned
The nonpareil of beauty.° *An unsurpassed beauty*

OLIVIA How does he love me?

VIOLA With adorations, fertile° tears, *plentiful*
With groans that thunder love, with sighs of fire.[4]

OLIVIA Your lord does know my mind, I cannot love him.
Yet I suppose him virtuous, know him noble,

7. That is, the passage on which "Cesario's" sermon will expound.
8. That is, this is a current ("present") likeness of me (as though she were revealing a portrait of herself).
9. If it is your natural face, without cosmetics.
1. That is, no child; Olivia, however, takes "copy" to mean "written record."
2. Every individual part and article described and added as a codicil.
3. Should be equally returned even if.
4. The "tears," "groans," and "sighs of fire" are all clichés of romantic melancholy, fashionable in Elizabethan sonnet writing.

Of great estate, of fresh and stainless youth,
In voices well divulged,° free,° learned, and valiant, *well spoken of / noble*
And in dimension and the shape of nature° *physical appearance*
A gracious° person; but yet I cannot love him. *An attractive*
He might have took his answer long ago.

VIOLA If I did love you in° my master's flame,° *with / passion*
With such a suff'ring, such a deadly° life, *deathlike*
In your denial I would find no sense,
I would not understand it.

OLIVIA Why, what would you?

VIOLA Make me a willow[5] cabin at your gate
And call upon my soul° within the house, *(i.e., Olivia)*
Write loyal cantons° of contemnèd° love, *songs / despised*
And sing them loud even in the dead of night;
Halloo° your name to the reverberate° hills, *Shout / echoing*
And make the babbling gossip of the air[6]
Cry out 'Olivia!' O, you should not rest
Between the elements of air and earth
But you should pity me.

OLIVIA You might do much.
What is your parentage?

VIOLA Above my fortunes,[7] yet my state° is well. *social standing*
I am a gentleman.

OLIVIA Get you to your lord.
I cannot love him. Let him send no more,
Unless, perchance, you come to me again
To tell me how he takes it. Fare you well.
I thank you for your pains. [*Offering a purse*] Spend
this for me.

VIOLA I am no fee'd post,° lady. Keep your purse. *hired messenger*
My master, not myself, lacks recompense.
Love make his heart of flint that you shall love,[8]
And let your fervour, like my master's, be
Placed in contempt. Farewell, fair cruelty. *Exit*

OLIVIA 'What is your parentage?'
'Above my fortunes, yet my state is well.
I am a gentleman.' I'll be sworn thou art.
Thy tongue, thy face, thy limbs, actions, and spirit
Do give thee five-fold blazon.[9] Not too fast. Soft,° soft— *Wait*
Unless the master were the man.° How now? *servant*
Even so quickly may one catch the plague?
Methinks I feel this youth's perfections
With an invisible and subtle stealth
To creep in at mine eyes. Well, let it be.
What ho, Malvolio.

5. The willow was a symbol of grief for unrequited love.

6. Echo, in classical mythology. In love with but rejected by Narcissus, the nymph Echo was eventually reduced to nothing but a voice.

7. My (current) circumstances.

8. That is, may love harden the heart of the man you fall in love with.

9. That is, your natural attributes—tongue, face, limbs, etc.—proclaim you a gentleman as well as any coat of arms would.

Enter MALVOLIO

MALVOLIO Here, madam, at your service.
OLIVIA Run after that same peevish messenger
The County's° man. He left this ring behind him, *Count's (i.e., Duke's)*
Would I° or not. Tell him I'll none of it. *Whether I wished it*
Desire him not to flatter with° his lord, *encourage*
Nor hold him up with hopes. I am not for him.
If that the youth will come this way tomorrow,
I'll give him reasons for't. Hie thee,° Malvolio. *Hurry*
MALVOLIO Madam, I will. *Exit [at one door]*
OLIVIA I do I know not what, and fear to find
Mine eye too great a flatterer for my mind.[1]
Fate, show thy force. Ourselves we do not owe.° *own*
What is decreed must be; and be this so.
[Exit at another door]

2.1

Enter ANTONIO *and* SEBASTIAN

ANTONIO Will you stay no longer, nor will° you not that I go with you? *wish*

SEBASTIAN By your patience, no. My stars shine darkly over me. The malignancy of my fate[2] might perhaps distemper° yours, therefore I shall crave of you your leave that I may bear my evils alone. It were a bad recompense for your love to lay any of them on you. *disturb; infect*

ANTONIO Let me yet know of you whither you are bound.

SEBASTIAN No, sooth,° sir. My determinate° voyage is mere extravagancy.° But I perceive in you so excellent a touch of modesty° that you will not extort from me what I am willing to keep in. Therefore it charges me in manners° the rather to express myself. You must know of me then, Antonio, my name is Sebastian, which I called Roderigo. My father was that Sebastian of Messaline[3] whom I know you have heard of. He left behind him myself and a sister, both born in an hour.° If the heavens had been pleased, would we had so ended. But you, sir, altered that, for some hour before you took me from the breach° of the sea was my sister drowned. *truly / determined-on* *aimless meandering* *civility; reserve* *in courteous fashion* *in the same hour* *surf*

ANTONIO Alas the day!

SEBASTIAN A lady, sir, though it was said she much resembled me, was yet of many accounted beautiful. But though I could not with such estimable wonder° over-far believe that, yet thus far I will boldly publish° her: she bore a mind that envy° could not but call fair. She is drowned already, sir, with salt water, though I seem to drown her remembrance again with more. *appreciative judgment* *declare* *envy itself; the envious*

1. That is, my eye has seduced my reason.
2.1 Location: Somewhere near the Illyrian coast.
2. The malevolent influence of the stars (which shape my future); "malignancy" also has its medical sense.
3. Possibly Messina (in Sicily) or Massila (modern-day Marseille), or a fictional town.

ANTONIO Pardon me, sir, your bad entertainment.[4]

SEBASTIAN O good Antonio, forgive me your trouble.[5]

ANTONIO If you will not murder me° for my love, let me be your servant. *cause my death*

SEBASTIAN If you will not undo what you have done—that is, kill him whom you have recovered°—desire it not. Fare ye well at once. My bosom is full of kindness,° and I am yet° so near the manners of my mother that upon the least occasion more mine eyes will tell tales of me.[6] I am bound to the Count Orsino's court. Farewell. *Exit* *rescued* *tender feelings* *still*

ANTONIO The gentleness of all the gods go with thee!
I have many enemies in Orsino's court,
Else would I very shortly see thee there.
But come what may, I do adore thee so
That danger shall seem sport, and I will go. *Exit*

2.2

Enter VIOLA *as Cesario, and* MALVOLIO *at several° doors* *different*

MALVOLIO Were not you ev'n° now with the Countess Olivia? *just*

VIOLA Even now, sir, on° a moderate pace, I have since arrived but hither.° *at* *traveled only this far*

MALVOLIO [*offering a ring*] She returns this ring to you, sir. You might have saved me my pains to have taken it away yourself. She adds, moreover, that you should put your lord into a desperate assurance° she will none of him. And one thing more: that you be never so hardy° to come again in his affairs, unless it be to report your lord's taking of this.[7] Receive it so. *hopeless certainty* *bold*

VIOLA She took the ring of me.[8] I'll none of it.

MALVOLIO Come, sir, you peevishly threw it to her, and her will is it should be so returned.
[*He throws the ring down*]
If it be worth stooping for, there it lies, in your eye;° if not, be it his that finds it. *Exit* *within your view*

VIOLA [*picking up the ring*] I left no ring with her.
What means this lady?
Fortune forbid my outside° have not charmed her. *outward appearance*
She made good view of me,° indeed so much *examined me closely*
That straight methought her eyes had lost° her tongue, *had made her lose*
For she did speak in starts, distractedly.
She loves me, sure. The cunning of her passion
Invites me in° this churlish messenger. *by means of*
None of my lord's ring! Why, he sent her none.

4. That is, the inadequate hospitality I have offered you.
5. The trouble I have put you through (by being your guest).
6. That is, my tears will betray my feelings.
2.2 Location: Somewhere between Olivia's estate and Orsino's palace.
7. Reaction to Olivia's rejection.
8. From me (Viola plays along with Olivia's story).

I am the man.[9] If it be so—as 'tis—
Poor lady, she were better love a dream!
Disguise, I see thou art a wickedness
Wherein the pregnant° enemy° does much. *resourceful / (Satan)*
How easy is it for the proper false[1]
In women's waxen hearts to set their forms![2]
Alas, our frailty is the cause, not we,
For such as we are made of, such we be.[3]
How will this fadge?° My master loves her dearly, *turn out*
And I, poor monster,[4] fond° as much on him, *dote*
And she, mistaken, seems to dote on me.
What will become of this? As I am man,
My state is desperate for my master's love.
As I am woman, now, alas the day,
What thriftless° sighs shall poor Olivia breathe! *unprofitable*
O time, thou must untangle this, not I.
It is too hard a knot for me t'untie. [*Exit*]

2.3

Enter SIR TOBY *and* SIR ANDREW

SIR TOBY Approach, Sir Andrew. Not to be abed after midnight is to be up betimes,° and *diliculo surgere*,[5] thou knowest. *early*

SIR ANDREW Nay, by my troth,° I know not; but I know to be up late is to be up late. *by my faith (a mild oath)*

SIR TOBY A false conclusion. I hate it as an unfilled can.° To be up after midnight and to go to bed then is early; so that to go to bed after midnight is to go to bed betimes. Does not our lives consist of the four elements?[6] *drinking vessel, tankard*

SIR ANDREW Faith, so they say, but I think it rather consists of eating and drinking.

SIR TOBY Thou'rt a scholar; let us therefore eat and drink. Marian, I say, a stoup° of wine. *drinking vessel*

Enter [FESTE, *the*] *clown*

SIR ANDREW Here comes the fool, i'faith.

FESTE How now, my hearts. Did you never see the picture of 'we three'?[7]

SIR TOBY Welcome, ass. Now let's have a catch.° *sing a round*

SIR ANDREW By my troth, the fool has an excellent breast.° I had rather than forty shillings I had such a leg,° and so sweet a breath to sing, as the fool has. In sooth, thou wast in very gracious fooling last night, when thou spokest of *voice* *(for dancing)*

9. That is, the man of Olivia's affections.
1. Men who are handsome and duplicitous.
2. To make strong impressions in women's soft hearts (the seat of their passions).
3. That is, we are frail because we are made of frail flesh.
4. That is, both a man and a woman.
2.3 Location: Olivia's house.
5. An abbreviated form of the Latin phrase *Diluculo surgere saluberrimum est* (To rise at dawn is most healthful).
6. The four elements—fire, water, earth, and air—thought to constitute all matter.
7. A picture, inscribed "we three," of two fools or ass heads, the third being the viewer.

Pigrogromitus, of the Vapians passing the equinoctial of Queubus.[8] 'Twas very good, i'faith. I sent thee sixpence for thy leman.° Hadst it? *sweetheart*

FESTE I did impeticos thy gratility;[9] for Malvolio's nose is no whipstock.° My lady has a white hand, and the Myrmidons[1] are no bottle-ale houses.° *whip handle* / *low-class taverns*

SIR ANDREW Excellent! Why, this is the best fooling, when all is done. Now a song.

SIR TOBY [*to* FESTE] Come on, there is sixpence for you. Let's have a song.

SIR ANDREW [*to* FESTE] There's a testril[2] of me, too. If one knight give a—

FESTE Would you have a love-song, or a song of good° life? *virtuous*

SIR TOBY A love song, a love-song.

SIR ANDREW Ay, ay. I care not for good life.

FESTE (*sings*) O mistress mine, where are you roaming?
O stay and hear, your true love's coming,
That can sing both high and low.
Trip° no further, pretty sweeting. *Go*
Journeys end in lovers meeting,
Every wise man's son doth know.

SIR ANDREW Excellent good, i'faith.

SIR TOBY Good, good.

FESTE What is love? 'Tis not hereafter,
Present mirth hath present laughter.
What's to come is still° unsure. *always*
In delay there lies no plenty,
Then come kiss me, sweet and twenty.[3]
Youth's a stuff will not endure.

SIR ANDREW A mellifluous voice, as I am true knight.

SIR TOBY A contagious breath.[4]

SIR ANDREW Very sweet and contagious, i'faith.

SIR TOBY To hear by the nose, it is dulcet in contagion.[5] But shall we make the welkin° dance indeed? Shall we rouse the night-owl in a catch that will draw three souls out of one weaver?[6] Shall we do that? *heavens*

SIR ANDREW An° you love me, let's do't. I am dog° at a catch. *If / expert*

FESTE By'r Lady, sir, and some dogs will catch well.

SIR ANDREW Most certain. Let our catch be 'Thou knave'.

FESTE 'Hold thy peace, thou knave', knight. I shall be constrained in't to call thee knave, knight.

8. Examples of Feste's mock learning.
9. That is, impetticoat (pocket) your gratuity (a small tip).
1. Followers of the Greek warrior Achilles at Troy; here, possibly the name of a tavern (the obscurity of Feste's meaning is probably intentional).
2. That is, a tester, a sixpence coin.
3. Sweet and twenty more times sweet.
4. A catchy voice; also, foul or infectious breath.
5. If we heard with our noses, the sound would be sweetly infectious.
6. Weavers, commonly associated with the singing of psalms, would presumably be resistant to most simple catches. Music was believed able to draw the soul from the body.

SIR ANDREW 'Tis not the first time I have constrained one to call me knave. Begin, fool. It begins 'Hold thy peace'.

FESTE I shall never begin if I hold my peace.

SIR ANDREW Good, i'faith. Come, begin.

[They sing the] catch.

Enter MARIA

MARIA What a caterwauling do you keep here! If my lady have not called up her steward Malvolio and bid him turn you out of doors, never trust me.

SIR TOBY My lady's a Cathayan,[7] we are politicians,° Malvolio's a Peg-o'-Ramsey, and 'Three merry men be we'.[8] Am not I consanguineous?[9] Am I not of her blood? Tilly-vally°—'lady'! 'There dwelt a man in Babylon, lady, lady.'[1] [*connivers*; *Fiddlesticks*]

FESTE Beshrew me,° the knight's in admirable fooling. [*Curse me (a mild oath)*]

SIR ANDREW Ay, he does well enough if he be disposed, and so do I, too. He does it with a better grace, but I do it more natural.[2]

SIR TOBY 'O' the twelfth day of December'[3]—

MARIA For the love o' God, peace.

Enter MALVOLIO

MALVOLIO My masters, are you mad? Or what are you? Have you no wit,° manners, nor honesty,° but to gabble like tinkers at this time of night? Do ye make an alehouse of my lady's house, that ye squeak out your coziers'° catches without any mitigation or remorse° of voice? Is there no respect of place, persons, nor time in you? [*sense / decency*; *cobblers'*; *intermission*]

SIR TOBY We did keep time, sir, in our catches. Sneck up!° [*Go hang yourself*]

MALVOLIO Sir Toby, I must be round° with you. My lady bade me tell you that though she harbours you as her kinsman she's nothing allied° to your disorders. If you can separate yourself and your misdemeanours you are welcome to the house. If not, an° it would please you to take leave of her she is very willing to bid you farewell. [*direct*; *no kin*; *if*]

SIR TOBY 'Farewell, dear heart, since I must needs be gone.'[4]

MARIA Nay, good Sir Toby.

FESTE 'His eyes do show his days are almost done.'

MALVOLIO Is't even so?

SIR TOBY 'But I will never die.'

FESTE 'Sir Toby, there you lie.'

MALVOLIO This is much credit to you.

SIR TOBY 'Shall I bid him go?'

FESTE 'What an if you do?'

SIR TOBY 'Shall I bid him go, and spare not?'

FESTE 'O no, no, no, no, you dare not.'

7. Chinese; but also a slang term for "cheat."
8. A line from an old song. *Peg-o'-Ramsey:* a character in a popular ballad (here used scornfully).
9. That is, a blood relative of Olivia.
1. The first line ("There dwelt a man in Babylon") and the refrain ("Lady, lady") of the ballad "Constant Susanna."
2. Effortlessly; "natural" also means "idiot."
3. Probably the first line of another ballad.
4. A line from the ballad "Corydon's Farewell to Phyllis."

SIR TOBY Out o' tune, sir, ye lie. [*To* MALVOLIO] Art° any more than a steward? Dost thou think because thou art virtuous there shall be no more cakes and ale?[5] *Are you*

FESTE Yes, by Saint Anne, and ginger[6] shall be hot i'th' mouth, too.

SIR TOBY Thou'rt i'th' right. [*To* MALVOLIO] Go, sir, rub your chain with crumbs.[7] [*To* MARIA] A stoup of wine, Maria.

MALVOLIO Mistress Mary, if you prized my lady's favour at anything more than contempt you would not give means° for this uncivil rule.° She shall know of it, by this hand. *Exit* *drink / uncivilized behavior*

MARIA Go shake your ears.° *(i.e., your ass's ears)*

SIR ANDREW 'Twere as good a deed as to drink when a man's a-hungry to challenge him the field° and then to break promise with him, and make a fool of him. *to a duel*

SIR TOBY Do't, knight. I'll write thee a challenge, or I'll deliver thy indignation to him by word of mouth.

MARIA Sweet Sir Toby, be patient for tonight. Since the youth of the Count's was today with my lady she is much out of quiet. For Monsieur Malvolio, let me alone with him. If I do not gull him into a nayword and make him a common recreation,[8] do not think I have wit enough to lie straight in my bed. I know I can do it.

SIR TOBY Possess° us, possess us, tell us something of him. *Inform*

MARIA Marry, sir, sometimes he is a kind of puritan.[9]

SIR ANDREW O, if I thought that I'd beat him like a dog.

SIR TOBY What, for being a puritan? Thy exquisite° reason, dear knight. *ingenious*

SIR ANDREW I have no exquisite reason for't, but I have reason good enough.

MARIA The dev'l a puritan that he is, or anything constantly but a time-pleaser,° an affectioned° ass that cons state without book[1] and utters it by great swathes;° the best persuaded of himself,[2] so crammed, as he thinks, with excellencies, that it is his grounds of faith° that all that look on him love him; and on that vice in him will my revenge find notable cause to work. *flatterer / affected* *in long stretches* *unyielding belief*

SIR TOBY What wilt thou do?

MARIA I will drop in his way some obscure epistles of love, wherein by the colour of his beard, the shape of his leg, the manner of his gait, the expressure° of his eye, fore- *expression*

5. That is, good things. Cakes and ale were often served at church fairs, a practice frowned on by the Puritans (with whom Malvolio is associated by Maria in line 123, below).

6. A root used to flavor drinks such as ale. *Saint Anne:* mother of the Virgin Mary (the veneration of whom was offensive to Puritans).

7. That is, mind your own business (literally, "go shine your steward's chain").

8. One who provides recreation or entertainment for all (by becoming a laughingstock). *Nayword:* a byword (for "gull" or "fool").

9. That is, he is puritanical in his strictness and moral conduct (though not necessarily a member of a Puritan sect).

1. Memorizes high-flown language.

2. Having the highest opinion of himself.

head, and complexion,° he shall find himself most feelingly personated.° I can write very like my lady your niece; on a forgotten matter we can hardly make distinction of our hands.° *appearance* / *represented* / *handwriting*

SIR TOBY Excellent, I smell a device.° *scheme, plot*

SIR ANDREW I have't in my nose too.

SIR TOBY He shall think by the letters that thou wilt drop that they come from my niece, and that she's in love with him.

MARIA My purpose is indeed a horse of that colour.

SIR ANDREW And your horse now would make him an ass.

MARIA Ass° I doubt not. *(punning on "as")*

SIR ANDREW O, 'twill be admirable.

MARIA Sport° royal, I warrant you. I know my physic° will work with him. I will plant you two—and let the fool a third—where he shall find the letter. Observe his make construction° of it. For this night, to bed, and dream on the event.° Farewell. *Exit* *Amusement* / *medicine* / *interpretation* / *outcome*

SIR TOBY Good night, Penthesilea.[3]

SIR ANDREW Before me,[4] she's a good wench.

SIR TOBY She's a beagle true bred, and one that adores me. What o' that?

SIR ANDREW I was adored once, too.

SIR TOBY Let's to bed, knight. Thou hadst need send for more money.

SIR ANDREW If I cannot recover° your niece, I am a foul way out.° *win* / *at a financial loss*

SIR TOBY Send for money, knight. If thou hast her not i'th' end, call me cut.[5]

SIR ANDREW If I do not, never trust me, take it how you will.

SIR TOBY Come, come, I'll go burn some sack,° 'tis too late to go to bed now. Come knight, come knight. *Exeunt*[6] *warm some Spanish wine*

2.4

Enter Duke, VIOLA *[as Cesario],* CURIO, *and others*

ORSINO Give me some music. Now good morrow,° friends. *morning*
Now good Cesario, but° that piece of song, *(give us) just*
That old and antic° song we heard last night. *quaint*
Methought it did relieve my passion° much, *suffering*
More than light airs and recollected° terms *studied; practiced*
Of these most brisk and giddy-pacèd times.
Come, but one verse.

CURIO He is not here, so please your lordship, that should sing it.

3. Queen of the Amazons (another playful allusion to Maria's small size).
4. A play on the common oath "before God."
5. Dock-tailed, as a workhorse; also, slang term for a gelding.
6. Feste appears to have exited the scene earlier; he has no lines after line 108.
2.4 Location: Orsino's palace.

ORSINO Who was it?
CURIO Feste the jester, my lord, a fool that the lady Olivia's father took much delight in. He is about the house.
ORSINO Seek him out, and play the tune the while.
[*Exit* CURIO]
Music plays
[*To* VIOLA] Come hither, boy. If ever thou shalt love,
In the sweet pangs of it remember me;
For such as I am, all true lovers are,
Unstaid° and skittish in all motions° else   *Unsteady / emotions*
Save in the constant image of the creature
That is beloved. How dost thou like this tune?
VIOLA It gives a very echo to the seat
Where love is throned.°   *(i.e., the heart)*
ORSINO Thou dost speak masterly.°   *masterfully*
My life upon't, young though thou art thine eye
Hath stayed upon some favour° that it loves.   *face*
Hath it not, boy?
VIOLA A little, by your favour.°   *leave; face*
ORSINO What kind of woman is't?
VIOLA Of your complexion.
ORSINO She is not worth thee then. What years, i'faith?
VIOLA About your years, my lord.
ORSINO Too old, by heaven. Let still° the woman take   *always*
An elder than herself. So wears she° to him;   *she slowly adapts*
So sways she level° in her husband's heart.   *she holds steady*
For, boy, however we do praise ourselves,
Our fancies° are more giddy and unfirm,   *affections*
More longing, wavering, sooner lost and worn,°   *spent, exhausted*
Than women's are.
VIOLA I think° it well, my lord.   *believe*
ORSINO Then let thy love be younger than thyself,
Or thy affection cannot hold the bent;°   *remain steady*
For women are as roses, whose fair flower
Being once displayed; doth fall that very hour.
VIOLA And so they are. Alas that they are so:
To die even° when they to perfection grow.   *just*
Enter CURIO *and* [FESTE, *the*] *clown*
ORSINO [*to* FESTE] O fellow, come, the song we had last night.
Mark it, Cesario, it is old and plain.
The spinsters,° and the knitters in the sun,   *spinners*
And the free° maids that weave their thread with bones,[7]   *carefree*
Do use° to chant it. It is silly sooth,   *Are accustomed*
And dallies with° the innocence of love,   *lingers lovingly on*
Like the old age.[8]

7. Use bone bobbins (to weave "bone lace").

8. As in the good old days.

FESTE Are you ready, sir?

ORSINO I prithee, sing.

Music

FESTE [*sings*] Come away,° come away death, — *hither*
And in sad cypress[9] let me be laid.
Fie away, fie away breath,
I am slain by a fair cruel maid.
My shroud of white, stuck all with yew,° — *yew sprigs*
O prepare it.
My part of death no one so true
Did share it.[1]
Not a flower, not a flower sweet
On my black coffin let there be strewn.
Not a friend, not a friend greet
My poor corpse, where my bones shall be thrown.
A thousand thousand sighs to save,
Lay me O where
Sad true lover never find my grave,
To weep there.

ORSINO [*giving money*] There's for thy pains.° — *efforts*

FESTE No pains, sir. I take pleasure in singing, sir.

ORSINO I'll pay thy pleasure then.

FESTE Truly, sir, and pleasure will be paid,[2] one time or another.

ORSINO Give me now leave to leave° thee. — *permission to dismiss*

FESTE Now the melancholy god[3] protect thee, and the tailor make thy doublet° of changeable taffeta,[4] for thy mind is a very opal.[5] I would have men of such constancy put to sea, that their business might be everything, and their intent° everywhere, for that's it that always makes a good voyage of nothing.[6] Farewell. *Exit* — *jacket*; *destination*

ORSINO Let all the rest give place:° — *leave us*

[*Exeunt* CURIO *and others*]

Once more, Cesario,
Get thee to yon same sovereign cruelty.
Tell her my love, more noble than the world,
Prizes not quantity of dirty lands.
The parts° that fortune hath bestowed upon her — *rank and riches*
Tell her I hold as giddily° as fortune; — *lightly*
But 'tis that miracle and queen of gems° — *(i.e., her beauty)*

9. A coffin made of cypress wood, or a bier covered with cypress boughs. The cypress, like the yew (line 55), symbolized mourning and death.

1. That is, no one died so true to love as I.

2. That is, pleasure must be paid for (proverbial).

3. Saturn, the god and planet associated by astrology with melancholy.

4. A thin silk, whose color appears to change when viewed from different perspectives.

5. An iridescent gemstone, that appears to change color when viewed from different perspectives.

6. That is, an aimless sea voyage is a good experience for the fickle lover because he has no specific goal.

That nature pranks° her in attracts my soul. *dresses*
VIOLA But if she cannot love you, sir?
ORSINO I cannot be so answered.
VIOLA Sooth,° but you must. *In truth*
Say that some lady, as perhaps there is,
Hath for your love as great a pang of heart
As you have for Olivia. You cannot love her.
You tell her so. Must she not then be answered?
ORSINO There is no woman's sides
Can bide° the beating of so strong a passion *endure*
As love doth give my heart; no woman's heart
So big, to hold so much. They lack retention.° *capacity, constancy*
Alas, their love may be called appetite,
No motion of the liver, but the palate,[7]
That suffer surfeit, cloyment,° and revolt.° *satiety / revulsion*
But mine is all as hungry as the sea,
And can digest as much. Make no compare
Between that love a woman can bear me
And that I owe° Olivia. *have for*
VIOLA Ay, but I know—
ORSINO What dost thou know?
VIOLA Too well what love women to men may owe.
In faith, they are as true of heart as we.
My father had a daughter loved a man
As it might be, perhaps, were I a woman
I should your lordship.
ORSINO And what's her history?
VIOLA A blank, my lord. She never told her love,
But let concealment, like a worm i'th' bud,
Feed on her damask° cheek. She pined in thought, *pink and white*
And with a green and yellow[8] melancholy
She sat like patience on a monument,[9]
Smiling at grief. Was not this love indeed?
We men may say more, swear more, but indeed
Our shows are more than will;[1] for still° we prove *always*
Much in our vows, but little in our love.
ORSINO But died thy sister of her love, my boy?
VIOLA I am all the daughters of my father's house,
And all the brothers too; and yet I know not.
Sir, shall I to this lady?
ORSINO Ay, that's the theme,
To her in haste. Give her this jewel. Say
My love can give no place, bide no denay.° *cannot abide denial*
Exeunt [*severally*]

7. That is, their love originates not in the liver (the seat of real, lasting love) but in the palate (and thus is a matter of casual taste).
8. Pale and sallow in complexion.
9. That is, like a sculpted figure of Patience atop a gravestone.
1. Our displays of passion are greater than the love we feel.

2.5

Enter SIR TOBY, SIR ANDREW, *and* FABIAN

SIR TOBY Come thy ways,° Signor Fabian. *Come along*

FABIAN Nay, I'll come. If I lose a scruple° of this sport let me be boiled to death with melancholy.[2] *the least bit*

SIR TOBY Wouldst thou not be glad to have the niggardly rascally sheep-biter[3] come by some notable shame?

FABIAN I would exult, man. You know he brought me out o' favour with my lady about a bear-baiting[4] here.

SIR TOBY To anger him we'll have the bear again, and we will fool° him black and blue, shall we not, Sir Andrew? *mock*

SIR ANDREW An° we do not, it is pity of our lives. *If*

Enter MARIA [*with a letter*]

SIR TOBY Here comes the little villain. How now, my metal of India?[5]

MARIA Get ye all three into the box-tree.° Malvolio's coming down this walk. He has been yonder i' the sun practising behaviour to his own shadow this half-hour. Observe him, for the love of mockery, for I know this letter will make a contemplative[6] idiot of him. Close,° in the name of jesting! *boxwood hedge* / *Hide*

[*The men hide.* MARIA *places the letter*]

Lie thou there, for here comes the trout that must be caught with tickling.[7] *Exit*

Enter MALVOLIO

MALVOLIO 'Tis but fortune, all is fortune. Maria once told me she did affect° me, and I have heard herself come thus near, that should she fancy° it should be one of my complexion. Besides, she uses me with a more exalted respect than anyone else that follows her. What should I think on't? *(Olivia) was fond of* / *fall in love*

SIR TOBY Here's an overweening rogue.

FABIAN O, peace! Contemplation makes a rare turkeycock of him—how he jets° under his advanced° plumes! *struts / pulled up*

SIR ANDREW 'Slight,° I could so beat the rogue. *By God's light (an oath)*

SIR TOBY Peace, I say.

MALVOLIO To be Count Malvolio!

SIR TOBY Ah, rogue.

SIR ANDREW Pistol him, pistol him.

SIR TOBY Peace, peace.

2.5 Location: Olivia's garden.

2. In the humoral theory of physiology, melancholy was a cold humor, caused by a preponderance of bile, on which "boiled" may pun.

3. A sneaking fellow (literally, a dog that bites sheep); also, a whoremonger (someone who chases after "mutton" or whores).

4. A pursuit frowned on by Puritans.

5. Gold (implying that Maria is worth her weight in gold).

6. Meditative (a word with religious overtones).

7. That is, flattery; trout can be caught by gently stroking beneath them until they back into one's hand.

MALVOLIO There is example° for't: the Lady of the Strachey married the yeoman of the wardrobe[8] *precedent*

SIR ANDREW Fie on him, Jezebel.[9]

FABIAN O peace, now he's deeply in. Look how imagination blows him.° *puffs him up*

MALVOLIO Having been three months married to her, sitting in my state°— *chair of state*

SIR TOBY O for a stone-bow[1] to hit him in the eye!

MALVOLIO Calling my officers° about me, in my branched[2] velvet gown, having come from a day-bed° where I have left Olivia sleeping— *household staff* *sofa*

SIR TOBY Fire and brimstone!

FABIAN O peace, peace.

MALVOLIO And then to have the humour of state[3] and—after a demure travel of regard,[4] telling them I know my place, as I would they should do theirs—to ask for my kinsman Toby.

SIR TOBY Bolts and shackles!

FABIAN O peace, peace, peace, now, now.

MALVOLIO Seven of my people with an obedient start make out° for him. I frown the while, and perchance wind up my watch, or play with my—[*touching his chain*] some rich jewel.[5] Toby approaches; curtsies° there to me. *go forth* *bows*

SIR TOBY Shall this fellow live?

FABIAN Though our silence be drawn from us with cars,[6] yet peace.

MALVOLIO I extend my hand to him thus, quenching my familiar° smile with an austere regard of control— *friendly*

SIR TOBY And does not Toby take° you a blow o' the lips, then? *give*

MALVOLIO Saying 'Cousin Toby, my fortunes, having cast me on your niece, give me this prerogative of speech'—

SIR TOBY What, what!

MALVOLIO 'You must amend your drunkenness.'

SIR TOBY Out, scab.

FABIAN Nay, patience, or we break the sinews of our plot.

MALVOLIO 'Besides, you waste the treasure of your time with a foolish knight'—

SIR ANDREW That's me, I warrant you.

MALVOLIO 'One Sir Andrew.'

SIR ANDREW I knew 'twas I, for many do call me fool.

8. The person in charge of the linen and clothing in a wealthy household (this Lady has not been identified).
9. A proud, immoral woman (from the wife of King Ahab of Israel; see especially 1 Kings 21).
1. A crossbow used to shoot stones.
2. Embroidered in a figured pattern.
3. To adopt the manner of the great.
4. Casting my eye about the room with proper gravity.
5. Malvolio probably begins to say "my chain" (the symbol of his rank as steward in the household), but then remembers that as Olivia's husband he will have replaced it with a more appropriate ornament, a jewel.
6. That is, by torture (a prisoner might be tied to two carts, or "cars," which then pulled in opposite directions).

MALVOLIO [*seeing the letter*] What employment° have we here? [business]

FABIAN Now is the woodcock near the gin.[7]

SIR TOBY O peace, and the spirit of humours intimate[8] reading aloud to him.

MALVOLIO [*taking up the letter*] By my life, this is my lady's hand. These be her very c's, her u's, and her t's,[9] and thus makes she her great P's. It is in contempt of° question her hand. [beyond]

SIR ANDREW Her c's, her u's, and her t's? Why that?

MALVOLIO [*reads*] 'To the unknown beloved, this, and my good wishes.' Her very phrases! [*Opening the letter*] By your leave, wax°—soft,° and the impressure her Lucrece,[1] with which she uses to seal—'tis my lady. To whom should this be? [sealing wax / wait]

FABIAN This wins him, liver[2] and all.

MALVOLIO
'Jove knows I love,
But who?
Lips do not move,
No man must know.'

'No man must know.' What follows? The numbers° altered. 'No man must know.' If this should be thee, Malvolio? [meter]

SIR TOBY Marry, hang thee, brock.[3]

MALVOLIO
'I may command where I adore,
But silence like a Lucrece knife
With bloodless stroke my heart doth gore.
M.O.A.I. doth sway my life.'

FABIAN A fustian° riddle. [pompous]

SIR TOBY Excellent wench, say I.

MALVOLIO 'M.O.A.I. doth sway my life.' Nay, but first let me see, let me see, let me see.

FABIAN What dish o' poison has she dressed° him! [prepared for]

SIR TOBY And with what wing the staniel checks at it![4]

MALVOLIO 'I may command where I adore.' Why, she may command me. I serve her, she is my lady. Why, this is evident to any formal capacity.[5] There is no obstruction° in this. And the end—what should that alphabetical position° portend? If I could make that resemble some thing in me. Softly—'M.O.A.I.' [difficulty] [ordering of letters]

SIR TOBY O ay, make up that, he is now at a cold scent.

FABIAN Sowter will cry upon't for all this, though it be as rank as a fox.[6]

7. Snare. The woodcock is a proverbially stupid and easily caught bird.
8. May the spirit of whimsy suggest.
9. Malvolio unwittingly spells "cut," slang for the vagina.
1. The image of Lucretia, the Roman model of chastity (who stabbed herself to death after being raped), was printed in the wax.
2. The seat of love (see 1.1.36n).
3. Badger, conventionally labeled "stinky"; so, dirty fellow, skunk.
4. That is, with what speed does this inferior hawk fly after it.
5. Normal understanding.
6. "Sowter" (the name of a hound) will cry out when it loses the scent of its quarry, even though that scent is as strong ("rank") as a fox's.

MALVOLIO 'M.' Malvolio—'M'—why, that begins my name.

FABIAN Did not I say he would work it out? The cur is excellent at faults.[7]

MALVOLIO 'M.' But then there is no consonancy in the sequel.[8] That suffers under probation.° 'A' should follow, *close scrutiny*
but 'O' does.

FABIAN And 'O'[9] shall end, I hope.

SIR TOBY Ay, or I'll cudgel him, and make him cry 'O!'

MALVOLIO And then 'I' comes behind.

FABIAN Ay, an° you had any eye behind you you might see *if*
more detraction° at your heels than fortunes before you. *defamation*

MALVOLIO 'M.O.A.I.' This simulation° is not as the former; *riddle*
and yet to crush° this a little, it would bow[1] to me, for *force*
every one of these letters are in my name. Soft, here follows prose: 'If this fall into thy hand, revolve.° In my stars° *consider / fortunes*
I am above thee, but be not afraid of greatness. Some are born great, some achieve greatness, and some have greatness thrust upon 'em. Thy fates open their hands,° *offer their bounty*
let thy blood and spirit embrace them, and to inure° *accustom likely*
thyself to what thou art like° to be, cast thy humble slough,[2] and appear fresh. Be opposite° with a kinsman, *contrary,*
surly with servants. Let thy tongue tang arguments of *quarrelsome*
state;[3] put thyself into the trick of singularity.° She thus *act eccentrically*
advises thee that sighs for thee. Remember who commended thy yellow stockings, and wished to see thee ever cross-gartered.[4] I say remember, go to,° thou art made *get going*
if thou desirest to be so; if not, let me see thee a steward still, the fellow of servants, and not worthy to touch Fortune's fingers. Farewell. She that would alter services[5] with thee,

The Fortunate-Unhappy.'

Daylight and champaign discovers[6] not more. This is open.° I will be proud, I will read politic° authors, I will *clear / political*
baffle° Sir Toby, I will wash off gross acquaintance,[7] I will *disgrace*
be point-device the very man.[8] I do not now fool myself, to let imagination jade° me; for every reason excites to this, *trick*
that my lady loves me. She did commend my yellow stockings of late, she did praise my leg, being cross-gartered, and in this she manifests herself to my love, and with a kind of injunction drives me to these habits° of her *this attire*
liking. I thank my stars, I am happy. I will be strange,° *aloof*

7. That is, good at following his quarry (literally, excellent at lost scents, or "faults").
8. No pattern to the letters that follow.
9. That is, the hangman's noose (perhaps also a cry of pain or lamentation).
1. Yield (its meaning).
2. Cast off your humble deportment, as a snake sheds (sloughs) its old skin.
3. Let your tongue ring loudly with arguments about politics or statecraft.
4. The fashion (possibly outmoded by the time of the play) of wearing the garters so that in front they pass above as well as below the knee.
5. Exchange places (of mistress and servant).
6. Open country reveals.
7. Rid myself of acquaintances of low social rank.
8. That is, I will become, to the smallest detail, the man described in the letter.

stout,° in yellow stockings, and cross-gartered, even with the swiftness of putting on. Jove and my stars be praised. Here is yet a postscript. 'Thou canst not choose but know who I am. If thou entertainest° my love, let it appear in thy smiling, thy smiles become thee well. Therefore in my presence still° smile, dear my sweet, I prithee.' Jove, I thank thee. I will smile, I will do everything that thou wilt have me. *Exit*

proud · *accept* · *always*

[SIR TOBY, SIR ANDREW, *and* FABIAN *come from hiding*]

FABIAN I will not give my part of this sport for a pension of thousands to be paid from the Sophy.° *Shah of Persia*

SIR TOBY I could marry this wench for this device.

SIR ANDREW So could I, too.

SIR TOBY And ask no other dowry with her but such another jest.

Enter MARIA

SIR ANDREW Nor I neither.

FABIAN Here comes my noble gull-catcher.° *fool catcher*

SIR TOBY [*to* MARIA] Wilt thou set thy foot o' my neck?[9]

SIR ANDREW [*to* MARIA] Or o' mine either?

SIR TOBY [*to* MARIA] Shall I play° my freedom at tray-trip,[1] and become thy bondslave? *gamble*

SIR ANDREW [*to* MARIA] I'faith, or I either?

SIR TOBY [*to* MARIA] Why, thou hast put him in such a dream that when the image of it leaves him, he must run mad.

MARIA Nay, but say true, does it work upon him?

SIR TOBY Like aqua vitae° with a midwife. *strong liquor*

MARIA If you will then see the fruits of the sport, mark his first approach before my lady. He will come to her in yellow stockings, and 'tis a colour she abhors, and cross-gartered, a fashion she detests; and he will smile upon her, which will now be so unsuitable to her disposition, being addicted to a melancholy as she is, that it cannot but turn him into a notable contempt.[2] If you will see it, follow me.

SIR TOBY To the gates of Tartar,[3] thou most excellent devil of wit.

SIR ANDREW I'll make one,° too. *Exeunt* *go along*

3.1

Enter VIOLA [*as Cesario*] *and* [FESTE, *the*] *clown* [*with pipe and tabor*]° *small drum*

VIOLA Save° thee, friend, and thy music. Dost thou live by thy tabor? *God save*

FESTE No, sir, I live by° the church. *near*

9. An act symbolizing a conquerer's triumph.
1. A game of dice, in which three (trey) was a winning roll.
2. A notable object of contempt.
3. Tartarus (that part of the classical underworld where the wicked were punished).
3.1 Location: Olivia's garden.

VIOLA Art thou a churchman?° *clergyman*

FESTE No such matter, sir. I do live by the church for I do live at my house, and my house doth stand by the church.

VIOLA So thou mayst say the king lies by[4] a beggar if a beggar dwell near him, or the church stands° by thy tabor if thy tabor stand by the church. *is maintained*

FESTE You have said, sir. To see this age!—A sentence° is but a cheverel° glove to a good wit, how quickly the wrong side may be turned outward. *saying* *kidskin*

VIOLA Nay, that's certain. They that dally nicely° with words may quickly make them wanton.[5] *play cleverly*

FESTE I would therefore my sister had had no name, sir.

VIOLA Why, man?

FESTE Why, sir, her name's a word, and to dally with that word might make my sister wanton. But indeed, words are very rascals since bonds[6] disgraced them.

VIOLA Thy reason, man?

FESTE Troth, sir, I can yield you none without words, and words are grown so false I am loath to prove reason with them.

VIOLA I warrant thou art a merry fellow, and carest for nothing.

FESTE Not so, sir, I do care for something; but in my conscience, sir, I do not care for you. If that be to care for nothing, sir, I would it would make you invisible.

VIOLA Art not thou the Lady Olivia's fool?

FESTE No indeed, sir, the Lady Olivia has no folly, she will keep no fool, sir, till she be married, and fools are as like husbands as pilchards are to herrings—the husband's the bigger. I am indeed not her fool, but her corrupter of words.

VIOLA I saw thee late° at the Count Orsino's. *recently*

FESTE Foolery, sir, does walk about the orb[7] like the sun, it shines everywhere. I would be sorry, sir, but° the fool should be as oft with your master as with my mistress. I think I saw your wisdom[8] there. *unless*

VIOLA Nay, an thou pass upon me,[9] I'll no more with thee. [*Giving money*] Hold, there's expenses for thee.

FESTE Now Jove in his next commodity° of hair send thee a beard. *parcel, supply*

VIOLA By my troth I'll tell thee, I am almost sick° for one, though I would not have it grow on *my* chin. Is thy lady within? *eager; lovesick*

FESTE Would not a pair of these° have bred,° sir? *(coins) / multiplied*

4. Dwells near; also, lies with sexually.
5. Equivocal; also, lewd.
6. Written contracts, which replaced a man's simple promise. Feste puns on the meaning "fetters."
7. The earth (around which, in the Ptolemaic system, all heavenly bodies orbited).
8. "Your wisdom" is a form of address, here sarcastic.
9. If you attack me (literally, make a fencing pass at me).

VIOLA Yes, being kept together and put to use.[1]
FESTE I would play Lord Pandarus[2] of Phrygia, sir, to bring a Cressida to this Troilus.
VIOLA [*giving money*] I understand you, sir, 'tis well begged.
FESTE The matter I hope is not great, sir; begging but a beggar—Cressida was a beggar.[3] My lady is within, sir. I will conster° to them whence you come. Who you are and what you would are out of my welkin°—I might say 'element', but the word is overworn. *Exit*

explain / *sky; air* / *(an element)*

VIOLA This fellow is wise enough to play the fool,
And to do that well craves° a kind of wit.° — *requires / intelligence*
He must observe their mood on whom he jests,
The quality° of persons, and the time, — *social rank; character*
And, like the haggard,° check at every feather[4] — *wild hawk*
That comes before his eye. This is a practice° — *skill*
As full of labour as a wise man's art,
For folly that he wisely shows is fit,° — *appropriate*
But wise men, folly-fall'n, quite taint their wit.[5]

Enter SIR TOBY *and* [SIR] ANDREW

SIR TOBY Save you, gentleman.
VIOLA And you, sir.
SIR ANDREW *Dieu vous garde, monsieur.*[6]
VIOLA *Et vous aussi, votre serviteur.*[7]
SIR ANDREW I hope, sir, you are, and I am yours.
SIR TOBY Will you encounter° the house? My niece is desirous you should enter if your trade be to her. — *approach; enter*
VIOLA I am bound to° your niece, sir: I mean she is the list° of my voyage. — *for* / *limit, destination*
SIR TOBY Taste° your legs, sir, put them to motion. — *Try, test*
VIOLA My legs do better understand° me, sir, than I understand what you mean by bidding me taste my legs. — *stand under*
SIR TOBY I mean to go, sir, to enter.
VIOLA I will answer you with gait and entrance.[8]

Enter OLIVIA, *and* [MARIA, *her*] *gentlewoman*

But we are prevented.° [*To* OLIVIA] Most excellent accomplished lady, the heavens rain odours on you. — *anticipated*
SIR ANDREW [*to* SIR TOBY] That youth's a rare° courtier; 'rain odours'—well. — *an excellent*
VIOLA My matter hath no voice,° lady, but to your own most pregnant° and vouchsafed[9] ear. — *must not be spoken* / *receptive*
SIR ANDREW [*to* SIR TOBY] 'Odours', 'pregnant', and 'vouchsafed'—I'll get 'em all three all ready.° — *committed to memory*

1. Invested; lent out at interest.
2. The go-between in the love story of Troilus and Cressida. Feste will bring two coins together, as Pandarus would lovers, and have them reproduce.
3. In Robert Henryson's version of the story, *Testament of Cresseid* (though not in Shakespeare's own *Troilus and Cressida*), Cressida becomes a leprous beggar.
4. Fly after every bird.
5. That is, wise men, having fallen into folly, tarnish their innate intelligence or wisdom.
6. God protect you, sir (French).
7. And you, also; (I am) your servant (French).
8. Going and entering, with a pun on "gate."
9. Graciously offered.

OLIVIA Let the garden door be shut, and leave me to my
hearing. [*Exeunt* SIR TOBY, SIR ANDREW, *and* MARIA]
Give me your hand, sir.
VIOLA My duty, madam, and most humble service.
OLIVIA What is your name?
VIOLA Cesario is your servant's name, fair princess.
OLIVIA My servant, sir? 'Twas never merry world
Since lowly feigning was called compliment.[1]
You're servant to the Count Orsino, youth.
VIOLA And he is yours, and his must needs be yours.
Your servant's servant is *your* servant, madam.
OLIVIA For° him, I think not on him. For his thoughts, *As for*
Would they were blanks rather than filled with me.
VIOLA Madam, I come to whet your gentle thoughts
On his behalf.
OLIVIA O by your leave,[2] I pray you.
I bade you never speak again of him;
But would you undertake another suit,
I had rather hear you to solicit that
Than music from the spheres.[3]
VIOLA Dear lady—
OLIVIA Give me leave, beseech you. I did send,
After the last enchantment you did here,
A ring in chase of you. So did I abuse° *dishonor*
Myself, my servant, and I fear me you.
Under your hard construction must I sit,[4]
To force° that on you in a shameful cunning *For forcing*
Which you knew none of yours. What might you think?
Have you not set mine honour at the stake
And baited it with all th'unmuzzled thoughts[5]
That tyrannous heart can think? To one of your receiving° *perceptiveness*
Enough is shown. A cypress,[6] not a bosom,
Hides my heart. So let me hear you speak.
VIOLA I pity you.
OLIVIA That's a degree to° love. *step toward*
VIOLA No, not a grece,° for 'tis a vulgar proof° *step / common experience*
That very oft we pity enemies.
OLIVIA Why then, methinks 'tis time to smile again.[7]
O world, how apt° the poor are to be proud! *ready*
If one should be a prey, how much the better
To fall before the lion than the wolf![8]

1. That is, the world has not been a happy place since flattery came to be called courtesy.
2. Permit me to interrupt (a courteous expression, as is "give me leave," line 107).
3. In the Ptolemaic system, the planets and other heavenly bodies were thought to be affixed to concentric spheres, whose turning made glorious music inaudible to human ears.
4. I must be judged harshly by you.
5. An allusion to bearbaiting, in which a bear is chained to a stake and attacked by hungry dogs.
6. A piece of light, transparent material, often used (when black) for mourning.
7. That is, to leave melancholy behind (because we are not enemies).
8. That is, to fall before a noble foe like Orsino, rather than unyielding Cesario.

Clock strikes

The clock upbraids me with the waste of time.
Be not afraid, good youth, I will not have you;
And yet when wit and youth is come to harvest
Your wife is like to reap a proper° man. *handsome; worthy*
There lies your way, due west.

VIOLA Then westward ho![9]
Grace and good disposition° attend your ladyship. *frame of mind*
You'll nothing, madam, to my lord by me?

OLIVIA Stay. I prithee tell me what thou think'st of me.

VIOLA That you do think you are not what you are.

OLIVIA If I think so, I think the same of you.[1]

VIOLA Then think you right, I am not what I am.

OLIVIA I would you were as I would have you be.

VIOLA Would it be better, madam, than I am?
I wish it might, for now I am your fool.[2]

OLIVIA [*aside*] O, what a deal of scorn looks beautiful
In the contempt and anger of his lip!
A murd'rous guilt shows not itself more soon
Than love that would seem hid. Love's night is noon.[3]
[*To* VIOLA] Cesario, by the roses of the spring,
By maidhood, honour, truth, and everything,
I love thee so that, maugre° all thy pride, *despite*
Nor° wit nor reason can my passion hide. *Neither*
Do not extort thy reasons from this clause,
For that I woo, thou therefore hast no cause.[4]
But rather reason thus with reason fetter:[5]
Love sought is good, but given unsought, is better.

VIOLA By innocence I swear, and by my youth,
I have one heart, one bosom, and one truth,
And that no woman has, nor never none
Shall mistress be of it save I alone.
And so adieu, good madam. Never more
Will I my master's tears to you deplore.° *lament*

OLIVIA Yet come again, for thou perhaps mayst move
That heart which now abhors, to like his love.

Exeunt [*severally*]

3.2

Enter SIR TOBY, SIR ANDREW, *and* FABIAN

SIR ANDREW No, faith, I'll not stay a jot longer.

SIR TOBY Thy reason, dear venom,° give thy reason. *venomous one*

9. The cry of Thames boatmen as they depart from London toward Westminster.
1. Here, apparently rebuffed by "Cesario," Olivia switches back to the polite "you" after having used the familiar "thou" (line 133).
2. That is, you made a fool of me.
3. That is, love shines out brightly at all times.
4. That is, do not extract reasons from what I have just said to argue that because ("for that") I woo, you need not reciprocate my love.
5. But instead restrain your reasoning with the following reason.
3.2 Location: Olivia's house.

FABIAN You must needs yield your reason, Sir Andrew.
SIR ANDREW Marry, I saw your niece do more favours to
the Count's servingman than ever she bestowed upon
me. I saw't i'th' orchard.° *garden*
SIR TOBY Did she see thee the while, old boy? Tell me that.
SIR ANDREW As plain as I see you now.
FABIAN This was a great argument° of love in her toward *proof*
you.
SIR ANDREW 'Slight, will you make an ass o' me?
FABIAN I will prove it legitimate, sir, upon the oaths of
judgement and reason.
SIR TOBY And they have been grand-jurymen[6] since before
Noah was a sailor.
FABIAN She did show favour to the youth in your sight
only to exasperate you, to awake your dormouse[7] valour,
to put fire in your heart and brimstone° in your liver. You *heat*
should then have accosted her, and with some excellent
jests, fire-new from the mint, you should have banged
the youth into dumbness. This was looked for at your
hand, and this was balked.[8] The double gilt° of this oppor- *gold plating*
tunity you let time wash off, and you are now sailed into
the north of my lady's opinion,[9] where you will hang like
an icicle on a Dutchman's[1] beard unless you do redeem
it by some laudable attempt either of valour or policy.° *crafty device*
SIR ANDREW An't° be any way, it must be with valour, for *If it*
policy I hate. I had as lie° be a Brownist as a politician.[2] *soon*
SIR TOBY Why then, build me thy fortunes upon the basis of valour. Challenge me° the Count's youth to fight *for me*
with him, hurt him in eleven places. My niece shall
take note of it; and assure thyself, there is no love-
broker° in the world can more prevail in man's commen- *go-between*
dation with woman than report of valour.
FABIAN There is no way but this, Sir Andrew.
SIR ANDREW Will either of you bear me a challenge to him?
SIR TOBY Go, write it in a martial hand, be curst° and *abusive*
brief. It is no matter how witty so it be eloquent and
full of invention.° Taunt him with the licence of ink.[3] If *imagination*
thou 'thou'st' him[4] some thrice, it shall not be amiss, and
as many lies as will lie in thy sheet of paper, although the
sheet were big enough for the bed of Ware,[5] in England,
set 'em down, go about it. Let there be gall enough in

6. Experts at evaluating evidence.
7. Sleeping (dormice are small rodents known for their long periods of hibernation).
8. This opportunity was ignored.
9. That is, out of the warmth of her favor.
1. An allusion to the Dutch Arctic explorer Willem Barents (ca. 1550–1597), who made several attempts to discover a navigable passage to the East along the northern coast of Russia.
2. An intriguer. *Brownist:* a follower of the Puritan sect founded by Robert Browne (ca. 1550–1633).
3. With the freedom that writing allows (when compared to conversation).
4. That is, address him discourteously (to use the familiar "thou" to a relative stranger was an insult).
5. A famous bedstead built in 1590, almost 11 feet square (twice the normal size of beds of the period).

thy ink; though thou write with a goose-pen,[6] no matter. About it.° *Get on with it*

SIR ANDREW Where shall I find you?

SIR TOBY We'll call thee at the cubiculo.° Go. *little chamber*

Exit SIR ANDREW

FABIAN This is a dear manikin° to you, Sir Toby. *puppet*

SIR TOBY I have been dear° to him, lad, some two thousand strong or so. *costly*

FABIAN We shall have a rare letter from him; but you'll not deliver't.

SIR TOBY Never trust me then; and by all means stir on the youth to an answer. I think oxen and wain-ropes° cannot hale° them together. For Andrew, if he were opened and you find so much blood in his liver[7] as will clog° the foot of a flea, I'll eat the rest of th'anatomy.° *wagon ropes* / *pull* / *burden* / *cadaver*

FABIAN And his opposite,° the youth, bears in his visage no great presage of cruelty. *rival*

Enter MARIA

SIR TOBY Look where the youngest wren of nine[8] comes.

MARIA If you desire the spleen,[9] and will laugh yourselves into stitches, follow me. Yon gull° Malvolio is turned heathen, a very renegado,[1] for there is no Christian that means to be saved by believing rightly can ever believe such impossible passages of grossness.[2] He's in yellow stockings. *dupe*

SIR TOBY And cross-gartered?

MARIA Most villainously,° like a pedant° that keeps a school i'th' church.[3] I have dogged him like his murderer. He does obey every point of the letter that I dropped to betray him. He does smile his face into more lines than is in the new map with the augmentation of the Indies.[4] You have not seen such a thing as 'tis. I can hardly forbear hurling things at him. I know my lady will strike him. If she do, he'll smile, and take't for a great favour. *atrociously / teacher*

SIR TOBY Come bring us, bring us where he is. *Exeunt*

3.3

Enter SEBASTIAN *and* ANTONIO

SEBASTIAN I would not by my will have troubled you,
But since you make your pleasure of your pains
I will no further chide you.

6. A quill pen made from the feather of a goose, a proverbially foolish bird. *Gall:* an ingredient of ink; bitterness, acrimony.
7. Cowards were believed to have little or no blood in their liver.
8. The smallest wren in a nest of nine; that is, the smallest of the small.
9. Thought to be the seat of immoderate laughter.
1. Renegade (Spanish); apostate.
2. Such obvious absurdities (as the planted letter contains; see 2.5).
3. The practice of holding classes in church buildings was disappearing in Shakespeare's time.
4. Possibly a reference to a new map (published ca. 1599) that showed the earth's surface crisscrossed by rhumb lines and that was "augmented" with recent discoveries in both the Americas and the East Indies.
3.3 Location: A street.

ANTONIO I could not stay behind you. My desire,
More sharp than filèd steel, did spur me forth,
And not all° love to see you— though so much *not entirely (out of)*
As might have drawn one to a longer voyage—
But jealousy° what might befall your travel, *anxiety about*
Being skilless in° these parts, which to a stranger, *unfamiliar with*
Unguided and unfriended, often prove
Rough and unhospitable. My willing love
The rather° by these arguments of fear *All the more*
Set forth in your pursuit.

SEBASTIAN My kind Antonio,
I can no other answer make but thanks,
And thanks; and ever oft° good turns *very often*
Are shuffled off° with such uncurrent[5] pay. *shrugged off*
But were my worth as is my conscience° firm, *awareness of my debt*
You should find better dealing. What's to do?
Shall we go see the relics° of this town? *antiquities, memorials*

ANTONIO Tomorrow, sir. Best first go see your lodging.

SEBASTIAN I am not weary, and 'tis long to night.
I pray you let us satisfy our eyes
With the memorials and the things of fame
That do renown this city.

ANTONIO Would you'd pardon me.
I do not without danger walk these streets.
Once in a sea-fight 'gainst the Count his° galleys *(the Count's)*
I did some service, of such note indeed
That were I ta'en here it would scarce be answered.[6]

SEBASTIAN Belike° you slew great number of his people. *Perhaps*

ANTONIO Th'offence is not of such a bloody nature,
Albeit the quality° of the time and quarrel *circumstances*
Might well have given us bloody argument.° *reason for bloodshed*
It might have since been answered in repaying
What we took from them, which for traffic's° sake *trade's*
Most of our city did. Only myself stood out,° *refused to go along*
For which if I be latched° in this place *captured*
I shall pay dear.

SEBASTIAN Do not then walk too open.

ANTONIO It doth not fit° me. Hold, sir, here's my purse. *is not fitting for*
In the south suburbs at the Elephant° *(an inn)*
Is best to lodge. I will bespeak our diet° *order our food*
Whiles you beguile° the time and feed your knowledge *pass*
With viewing of the town. There shall you have me.

SEBASTIAN Why I your purse?

ANTONIO Haply° your eye shall light upon some toy° *Perhaps / trifle*
You have desire to purchase; and your store° *supply of money*
I think is not for idle markets,[7] sir.

SEBASTIAN I'll be your purse-bearer, and leave you
For an hour.

5. No longer current; that is, worthless.

6. That is, it would be hard for me to defend myself or make reparations.

7. Sufficient to buy unnecessary luxuries.

ANTONIO To th' Elephant.

SEBASTIAN I do remember.

Exeunt [severally]

3.4

Enter OLIVIA *and* MARIA

OLIVIA [*aside*] I have sent after him, he says he'll come.
How shall I feast him? What bestow of° him? — *on*
For youth is bought more oft than begged or borrowed.
I speak too loud.
[*To* MARIA] Where's Malvolio? He is sad° and civil,° — *serious / respectful*
And suits well for a servant with my fortunes.
Where is Malvolio?

MARIA He's coming, madam, but in very strange manner. He is sure possessed,[8] madam.

OLIVIA Why, what's the matter? Does he rave?

MARIA No, madam, he does nothing but smile. Your ladyship were best to have some guard about you if he come, for sure the man is tainted in's° wits. — *in his*

OLIVIA Go call him hither. *[Exit* MARIA*]*
I am as mad as he,
If sad and merry madness equal be.

Enter MALVOLIO *[cross-gartered and wearing yellow stockings, with* MARIA*]*

How now, Malvolio?

MALVOLIO Sweet lady, ho, ho!

OLIVIA Smil'st thou? I sent for thee upon a sad occasion.° — *serious matter*

MALVOLIO Sad, lady? I could be sad. This does make some obstruction in the blood, this cross-gartering, but what of that? If it please the eye of one, it is with me as the very true sonnet° 'Please one, and please all'.[9] — *short poem; song*

OLIVIA Why, how dost thou, man? What is the matter with thee?

MALVOLIO Not black in my mind, though yellow in my legs.[1] It did come to his hands, and commands shall be executed. I think we do know the sweet roman hand.[2]

OLIVIA Wilt thou go to bed,[3] Malvolio?

MALVOLIO [*kissing his hand*] To bed? 'Ay, sweetheart, and I'll come to thee.'[4]

OLIVIA God comfort thee. Why dost thou smile so, and kiss thy hand so oft?

MARIA How do you, Malvolio?

3.4 Location: Olivia's garden.

8. That is, insane; possession by a demon or the devil was a common explanation for madness.

9. That is, "If I please you, then I please everyone I care to please" (a line from a popular ballad).

1. Black indicated melancholy; yellow, both jealousy and choler.

2. The Italian-style handwriting then coming into use.

3. That is, to cure your madness with sleep.

4. A line from a popular song.

MALVOLIO At your request?—yes, nightingales answer daws.[5]

MARIA Why appear you with this ridiculous boldness before my lady?

MALVOLIO 'Be not afraid of greatness'—'twas well writ.

OLIVIA What meanest thou by that, Malvolio?

MALVOLIO 'Some are born great'—

OLIVIA Ha?

MALVOLIO 'Some achieve greatness'—

OLIVIA What sayst thou?

MALVOLIO 'And some have greatness thrust upon them.'

OLIVIA Heaven restore thee.

MALVOLIO 'Remember who commended thy yellow stockings'—

OLIVIA 'Thy yellow stockings'?

MALVOLIO 'And wished to see thee cross-gartered.'

OLIVIA 'Cross-gartered'?

MALVOLIO 'Go to, thou art made, if thou desirest to be so.'

OLIVIA Am I made?

MALVOLIO 'If not, let me see thee a servant still.'

OLIVIA Why, this is very midsummer madness.[6]

Enter a SERVANT

SERVANT Madam, the young gentleman of the Count Orsino's is returned. I could hardly entreat him back. He attends° your ladyship's pleasure. *awaits*

OLIVIA I'll come to him. [*Exit* SERVANT]
Good Maria, let this fellow be looked to. Where's my cousin Toby? Let some of my people have a special care of him, I would not have him miscarry° for the half of my dowry. *come to harm*

Exeunt [OLIVIA *and* MARIA, *severally*]

MALVOLIO O ho, do you come near° me now? No worse man than Sir Toby to look to me. This concurs directly with the letter, she sends him on purpose, that I may appear stubborn to him, for she incites me to that in the letter. 'Cast thy humble slough,' says she, 'be opposite with a kinsman, surly with servants, let thy tongue tang arguments of state, put thyself into the trick of singularity', and consequently° sets down the manner how, as a sad face, a reverend carriage, a slow tongue,° in the habit° of some sir of note,° and so forth. I have limed her,[7] but it is Jove's doing, and Jove make me thankful. And when she went away now, 'let this fellow be looked to'. Fellow![8]—not 'Malvolio', nor after my degree, but 'fellow'. Why, everything adheres together that no dram of a scruple, *understand* / *thereafter* / *deliberate speech* / *clothing* / *a gentleman*

5. That is, should I answer you? A nightingale (whose song is proverbially beautiful) does not respond to a crow.

6. The midsummer moon was thought to cause insanity.

7. Caught her, like a bird trapped by sticky birdlime spread on a branch.

8. Malvolio gives "fellow" the meaning (unintended by Olivia) "consort" or "counterpart."

no scruple of a scruple,[9] no obstacle, no incredulous° or unsafe circumstance—what can be said?—nothing that can be can come between me and the full prospect of my hopes. Well, Jove, not I, is the doer of this, and he is to be thanked. *incredible*

Enter [SIR] TOBY, FABIAN, *and* MARIA

SIR TOBY Which way is he, in the name of sanctity?° If all the devils of hell be drawn in little,° and Legion[1] himself possessed him, yet I'll speak to him. *of all that is sacred* / *in miniature*

FABIAN Here he is, here he is. [*To* MALVOLIO] How is't with you, sir? How is't with you, man?

MALVOLIO Go off, I discard you. Let me enjoy my private.° Go off. *privacy*

MARIA Lo, how hollow° the fiend speaks within him. Did not I tell you? Sir Toby, my lady prays you to have a care of him. *resoundingly*

MALVOLIO Aha, does she so?

SIR TOBY Go to, go to. Peace, peace, we must deal gently with him. Let me alone.° How do you, Malvolio? How is't with you? What, man, defy the devil. Consider, he's an enemy to mankind. *Leave him to me*

MALVOLIO Do you know what you say?

MARIA La° you, an° you speak ill of the devil, how he takes it at heart. Pray God he be not bewitched. *Look / if*

FABIAN Carry his water to th' wise woman.[2]

MARIA Marry, and it shall be done tomorrow morning, if I live. My lady would not lose him for more than I'll say.

MALVOLIO How now, mistress?

MARIA O Lord!

SIR TOBY Prithee hold thy peace, this is not the way. Do you not see you move° him? Let me alone with him. *excite; anger*

FABIAN No way but gentleness, gently, gently. The fiend is rough,° and will not be roughly used. *violent*

SIR TOBY Why how now, my bawcock?[3] How dost thou, chuck?° *chick (endearment)*

MALVOLIO Sir!

SIR TOBY Ay, biddy,° come with me. What man, 'tis not for gravity to play at cherry-pit[4] with Satan. Hang him, foul collier.[5] *hen, chicken*

MARIA Get him to say his prayers. Good Sir Toby, get him to pray.

MALVOLIO My prayers, minx?° *insolent girl*

MARIA No, I warrant you, he will not hear of godliness.

9. That is, no bit of doubt; as apothecaries' weights, a dram is 60 grains and a scruple is one-third of a dram.
1. The name of an "unclean spirit" exorcized by Jesus (Mark 5.8–9).
2. The female healer, herbalist. *Water:* urine (used to diagnose illness).
3. Fine fellow (from the French *beau coq,* "fine bird").
4. It is not fitting for a dignified man to play a children's game (pitching cherry stones into a small hole).
5. Coal miner or carrier (the devil was commonly portrayed as pitch black).

MALVOLIO Go hang yourselves, all. You are idle° shallow things, I am not of your element.° You shall know more hereafter. *Exit*

foolish / social sphere

SIR TOBY Is't possible?

FABIAN If this were played upon a stage, now, I could condemn it as an improbable fiction.

SIR TOBY His very genius° hath taken the infection of the device,° man.

spirit; soul / scheme

MARIA Nay, pursue him now, lest the device take air and taint.[6]

FABIAN Why, we shall make him mad indeed.

MARIA The house will be the quieter.

SIR TOBY Come, we'll have him in a dark room and bound.[7] My niece is already in the belief that he's mad. We may carry it thus for our pleasure and his penance till our very pastime, tired out of breath, prompt us to have mercy on him, at which time we will bring the device to the bar[8] and crown thee for a finder of madmen. But see, but see.

Enter SIR ANDREW [*with a paper*]

FABIAN More matter for a May morning.[9]

SIR ANDREW Here's the challenge, read it. I warrant there's vinegar and pepper in't.

FABIAN Is't so saucy?

SIR ANDREW Ay—is't? I warrant him. Do but read.

SIR TOBY Give me.

[*Reads*] 'Youth, whatsoever thou art, thou art but a scurvy fellow.'

FABIAN Good, and valiant.

SIR TOBY 'Wonder not, nor admire° not in thy mind why I do call thee so, for I will show thee no reason for't.'

marvel

FABIAN A good note, that keeps you from the blow of the law.[1]

SIR TOBY 'Thou comest to the Lady Olivia, and in my sight she uses thee kindly; but thou liest in thy throat,° that is not the matter I challenge thee for.'

deeply, egregiously

FABIAN Very brief, and to exceeding good sense [*aside*] -less.

SIR TOBY 'I will waylay thee going home, where if it be thy chance to kill me'—

FABIAN Good.

SIR TOBY 'Thou killest me like a rogue and a villain.'

FABIAN Still you keep o'th' windy side[2] of the law—good.

SIR TOBY 'Fare thee well, and God have mercy upon one of our souls. He may have mercy upon mine, but my hope is better, and so look to thyself.

6. Be exposed to the effects of the air (i.e., become public knowledge) and therefore spoil.
7. A standard treatment of the insane.
8. That is, the bar of judgment; to a court.
9. Entertainment for May Day (i.e., a holiday)

1. That safeguards you from legal action (for slander or disturbing the peace).
2. To windward and thus out of the reach of the law.

Thy friend as thou usest him, and thy sworn enemy,
Andrew Aguecheek.'
If this letter move° him not, his legs cannot. I'll give't him.

incite

MARIA You may have very fit occasion for't. He is now in some commerce° with my lady, and will by and by depart.

dealings

SIR TOBY Go, Sir Andrew. Scout me° for him at the corner of the orchard like a bum-baily.[3] So soon as ever thou seest him, draw, and as thou drawest, swear horrible, for it comes to pass oft that a terrible oath, with a swaggering accent sharply twanged off, gives manhood more approbation° than ever proof° itself would have earned him. Away.

Look out

confirmation / demonstration; deed

SIR ANDREW Nay, let me alone for swearing.[4] *Exit*

SIR TOBY Now will not I deliver his letter, for the behaviour of the young gentleman gives him out to be of good capacity° and breeding. His employment between his lord and my niece confirms no less. Therefore this letter, being so excellently ignorant, will breed no terror in the youth. He will find it comes from a clodpoll.° But, sir, I will deliver his challenge by word of mouth, set upon Aguecheek a notable report of valour, and drive the gentleman—as I know his youth will aptly receive it[5]—into a most hideous° opinion of his rage, skill, fury, and impetuosity. This will so fright them both that they will kill one another by the look, like cockatrices.[6]

ability

blockhead

terrifying

Enter OLIVIA, *and* VIOLA [*as Cesario*]

FABIAN Here he comes with your niece. Give them way° till he take leave, and presently° after him.

Stay out of their way

immediately go

SIR TOBY I will meditate the while upon some horrid message for a challenge. [*Exeunt* SIR TOBY, FABIAN, *and* MARIA]

OLIVIA I have said too much unto a heart of stone,
And laid mine honour too unchary[7] out.
There's something in me that reproves my fault,
But such a headstrong potent fault it is
That it but mocks reproof.

VIOLA With the same 'haviour
That your passion bears goes on my master's griefs.[8]

OLIVIA [*giving a jewel*] Here, wear this jewel[9] for me, 'tis my picture—
Refuse it not, it hath no tongue to vex you—
And I beseech you come again tomorrow.
What shall you ask of me that I'll deny,
That honour, saved, may upon asking give?[1]

3. A contemptuous term for a bailiff, an officer charged with making arrests.
4. That is, I am unsurpassed at swearing.
5. That is, his inexperience will cause him to believe the report of Sir Andrew's valor.
6. Basilisks, mythical monsters that killed with a look.
7. Risked my honor too incautiously.
8. With the same behavior that marks your passion, my master's griefs persist.
9. That is, a jeweled locket.
1. That honor, uncompromised, may give when asked.

VIOLA Nothing but this: your true love for my master.
OLIVIA How with mine honour may I give him that
Which I have given to you?
VIOLA I will acquit you.[2]
OLIVIA Well, come again tomorrow. Fare thee well.
A fiend like thee might bear my soul to hell. *Exit*

Enter [SIR] TOBY *and* FABIAN

SIR TOBY Gentleman, God save thee.

VIOLA And you, sir.

SIR TOBY That defence thou hast, betake thee to't. Of what nature the wrongs are thou hast done him, I know not, but thy intercepter, full of despite,° bloody as the hunter,[3] attends° thee at the orchard end. Dismount thy tuck,° be yare° in thy preparation, for thy assailant is quick, skilful, and deadly.

defiance / *awaits* / *Draw your rapier* / *quick*

VIOLA You mistake, sir, I am sure no man hath any quarrel to° me. My remembrance° is very free and clear from any image of offence done to any man.

with / *memory*

SIR TOBY You'll find it otherwise, I assure you. Therefore, if you hold your life at any price, betake you to your guard, for your opposite° hath in him what youth, strength, skill, and wrath can furnish man withal.°

opponent / *with*

VIOLA I pray you, sir, what is he?

SIR TOBY He is knight dubbed with unhatched[4] rapier and on carpet consideration,[5] but he is a devil in private brawl. Souls and bodies hath he divorced three, and his incensement at this moment is so implacable that satisfaction can be none but by pangs of death and sepulchre. Hob nob[6] is his word,° give't or take't.

motto

VIOLA I will return again into the house and desire some conduct° of the lady. I am no fighter. I have heard of some kind of men that put quarrels purposely on others, to taste° their valour. Belike° this is a man of that quirk.

protective escort / *test* / *Perhaps*

SIR TOBY Sir, no. His indignation derives itself out of a very competent° injury, therefore get you on, and give him his desire. Back you shall not to the house unless you undertake that° with me which with as much safety you might answer him. Therefore on, or strip your sword stark naked, for meddle° you must, that's certain, or forswear to wear iron about you.[7]

sufficient / *(a duel)* / *fight a duel*

VIOLA This is as uncivil as strange. I beseech you do me this courteous office, as to know of° the knight what my offence to him is. It is something of my negligence, nothing of my purpose.

from

2. Release you (from your promise to me).
3. Bloodthirsty as a hunting dog, or a huntsman.
4. Unhatched (because unused in battle).
5. "Carpet knights" won their titles not in battle but in the carpeted ease of the court.
6. Have or have not; that is, give it or take it, or kill or be killed.
7. Or give up your right to wear a sword.

SIR TOBY I will do so. Signor Fabian, stay you by this gentleman till my return. *Exit*

VIOLA Pray you, sir, do you know of this matter?

FABIAN I know the knight is incensed against you even to a mortal arbitrement,° but nothing of the circumstance more.

arbitrement: fight to the death

VIOLA I beseech you, what manner of man is he?

FABIAN Nothing of that wonderful promise to read° him by his form° as you are like to find him in the proof of his valour. He is indeed, sir, the most skilful, bloody, and fatal opposite that you could possibly have found in any part of Illyria. Will you° walk towards him, I will make your peace with him if I can.

read: judge; form: appearance; Will you: If you will

VIOLA I shall be much bound to you for't. I am one that had rather go with Sir Priest than Sir Knight—I care not who knows so much of my mettle.° *Exeunt*

mettle: temperament; courage

Enter [SIR] TOBY *and* [SIR] ANDREW

SIR TOBY Why, man, he's a very devil, I have not seen such a virago.° I had a pass[8] with him, rapier, scabbard, and all, and he gives me the stuck-in[9] with such a mortal motion that it is inevitable, and on the answer,° he pays you as surely as your feet hits the ground they step on. They say he has been fencer to the Sophy.°

virago: female warrior; answer: return hit; Sophy: Shah of Persia

SIR ANDREW Pox on't, I'll not meddle with him.

SIR TOBY Ay, but he will not now be pacified, Fabian can scarce hold him yonder.

SIR ANDREW Plague on't, an° I thought he had been valiant and so cunning in fence I'd have seen him damned ere I'd have challenged him. Let him let the matter slip and I'll give him my horse, grey Capulet.

an: if

SIR TOBY I'll make the motion.° Stand here, make a good show on't—this shall end without the perdition of souls.° [*Aside*] Marry, I'll ride your horse as well as I ride you.

motion: offer; perdition of souls: loss of lives

Enter FABIAN, *and* VIOLA [*as Cesario*]

[*Aside to* FABIAN] I have his horse to take up° the quarrel, I have persuaded him the youth's a devil.

take up: settle

FABIAN [*aside to* SIR TOBY] He is as horribly conceited[1] of him, and pants and looks pale as if a bear were at his heels.

SIR TOBY [*to* VIOLA] There's no remedy, sir, he will fight with you for's° oath' sake. Marry, he hath better bethought him of his quarrel, and he finds that now scarce to be worth talking of. Therefore draw for the supportance of his vow,[2] he protests° he will not hurt you.

for's: for his; protests: solemnly declares

VIOLA [*aside*] Pray God defend me. A little thing[3] would make me tell them how much I lack of a man.

FABIAN [*to* SIR ANDREW] Give ground if you see him furious.

8. Bout of fencing.
9. The stoccado, a thrust or stab (from the Italian *stoccata*).
1. He has as horrifying a conception of him.
2. So that he may keep his oath.
3. Possibly a sexual innuendo.

SIR TOBY Come, Sir Andrew, there's no remedy, the gentleman will for his honour's sake have one bout with you, he cannot by the duello° avoid it, but he has promised me, as he is a gentleman and a soldier, he will not hurt you. Come on, to't. *code of duelling*

SIR ANDREW Pray God he keep his oath.

Enter ANTONIO

VIOLA I do assure you 'tis against my will.

[SIR ANDREW *and* VIOLA *draw their swords*]

ANTONIO [*drawing his sword, to* SIR ANDREW] Put up your sword. If this young gentleman
Have done offence, I take the fault on me.
If you offend him, I for him defy you.

SIR TOBY You, sir? Why, what are you?

ANTONIO One, sir, that for his love dares yet do more
Than you have heard him brag to you he will.

SIR TOBY [*drawing his sword*] Nay, if you be an undertaker,[4] I am for° you. *i.e., will fight*

Enter OFFICERS

FABIAN O, good Sir Toby, hold. Here come the officers.

SIR TOBY [*to* ANTONIO] I'll be with you anon.

VIOLA [*to* SIR ANDREW] Pray, sir, put your sword up if you please.

SIR ANDREW Marry will I, sir, and for that° I promised you I'll be as good as my word. He° will bear you easily, and reins well. *that which* *(Capulet, line 272)*

[SIR ANDREW *and* VIOLA *put up their swords*]

FIRST OFFICER This is the man, do thy office.

SECOND OFFICER Antonio, I arrest thee at the suit of Count Orsino.

ANTONIO You do mistake me, sir.

FIRST OFFICER No, sir, no jot. I know your favour° well, *face*
Though now you have no seacap on your head.
[*To* SECOND OFFICER] Take him away, he knows I know him well.

ANTONIO I must obey. [*To* VIOLA] This comes with seeking you.
But there's no remedy, I shall answer it.° *defend myself*
What will you do now my necessity
Makes me to ask you for my purse? It grieves me
Much more for what I cannot do for you
Than what befalls myself. You stand amazed,
But be of comfort.

SECOND OFFICER Come, sir, away.

ANTONIO [*to* VIOLA] I must entreat of you some of that money.

VIOLA What money, sir?

4. One who takes up a challenge.

For the fair kindness you have showed me here,
And part° being prompted by your present trouble, *partly*
Out of my lean and low ability
I'll lend you something. My having is not much.
I'll make division of my present° with you. *i.e., what I now have*
Hold, [*offering money*] there's half my coffer.° *funds*

ANTONIO Will you deny me now?
Is't possible that my deserts to you
Can lack persuasion?[5] Do not tempt my misery,
Lest that it make me so unsound° a man *weak*
As to upbraid you with those kindnesses
That I have done for you.

VIOLA I know of none,
Nor know I you by voice, or any feature.
I hate ingratitude more in a man
Than lying, vainness, babbling drunkenness,
Or any taint of vice whose strong corruption
Inhabits our frail blood.

ANTONIO O heavens themselves!

SECOND OFFICER Come, sir, I pray you go.

ANTONIO Let me speak a little. This youth that you see here
I snatched one half out of the jaws of death,
Relieved him with such sanctity° of love, *purity*
And to his image,[6] which methought did promise
Most venerable worth,[7] did I devotion.

FIRST OFFICER What's that to us? The time goes by, away.

ANTONIO But O, how vile an idol proves this god!
Thou hast, Sebastian, done good feature shame.° *shamed physical beauty*
In nature there's no blemish but the mind.
None can be called deformed but the unkind.
Virtue is beauty, but the beauteous evil
Are empty trunks o'er-flourished[8] by the devil.

FIRST OFFICER The man grows mad, away with him. Come,
come, sir.

ANTONIO Lead me on. *Exit* [*with* OFFICERS]

VIOLA [*aside*] Methinks his words do from such passion fly
That he believes himself. So do not I.[9]
Prove true, imagination, O prove true,
That I, dear brother, be now ta'en for you!

SIR TOBY Come hither, knight. Come hither, Fabian. We'll
whisper o'er a couplet or two of most sage saws.° *sayings*

[*They stand aside*]

VIOLA He named Sebastian. I my brother know
Yet living in my glass.° Even such and so *mirror*
In favour° was my brother, and he went *appearance*

5. Is it possible that my former acts of kindness toward you cannot persuade you?
6. Outward appearance; also, a religious icon.
7. Which appeared to me worthy of veneration.
8. Chests (or bodies) elaborately decorated.
9. That is, I cannot quite dare to believe what these words suggest to me.

Still° in this fashion, colour, ornament, *Always*
For him I imitate. O, if it prove,
Tempests are kind, and salt waves fresh in love! *Exit*

SIR TOBY [*to* SIR ANDREW] A very dishonest,° paltry boy, *disgraceful* and more a coward than a hare. His dishonesty appears in leaving his friend here in necessity, and denying him; and for his cowardship, ask Fabian.

FABIAN A coward, a most devout coward, religious in it.

SIR ANDREW 'Slid,° I'll after him again, and beat him. *By God's eyelid (an oath)*

SIR TOBY Do, cuff him soundly, but never draw thy sword.

SIR ANDREW An° I do not— [*Exit*] *If*

FABIAN Come, let's see the event.° *outcome*

SIR TOBY I dare lay any money 'twill be nothing yet.° *after all*

Exeunt

4.1

Enter SEBASTIAN *and* [FESTE, *the*] *clown*

FESTE Will you° make me believe that I am not sent for you? *Are you attempting to*

SEBASTIAN Go to, go to, thou art a foolish fellow,
Let me be clear° of thee. *free*

FESTE Well held out,° i'faith! No, I do not know you, nor *continued* I am not sent to you by my lady to bid you come speak with her, nor your name is not Master Cesario, nor this is not my nose, neither. Nothing that is so, is so.

SEBASTIAN I prithee vent° thy folly somewhere else, *air, utter*
Thou know'st not me.

FESTE Vent my folly! He has heard that word of some great man, and now applies it to a fool. Vent my folly— I am afraid this great lubber° the world will prove a cockney.° I *lout / effeminate fop* prithee now ungird thy strangeness,[1] and tell me what I shall 'vent' to my lady? Shall I 'vent' to her that thou art coming?

SEBASTIAN I prithee, foolish Greek,° depart from me. *buffoon*
There's money for thee. If you tarry longer
I shall give worse payment.

FESTE By my troth, thou hast an open hand. These wise men that give fools money get themselves a good report,° *reputation* after fourteen years' purchase.[2]

Enter [SIR] ANDREW, [SIR] TOBY, *and* FABIAN

SIR ANDREW [*to* SEBASTIAN] Now, sir, have I met you again?
[*Striking him*] There's for you.

SEBASTIAN [*striking* SIR ANDREW *with his dagger*] Why, there's for thee, and there, and there.
Are all the people mad?

4.1 Location: Somewhere near Olivia's house.
1. Drop the pretence that you are a stranger.
2. That is, at too high a price (a piece of land was usually valued at twelve times its annual rent).

SIR TOBY [*to* SEBASTIAN, *holding him back*] Hold, sir, or I'll throw your dagger o'er the house.

FESTE This will I tell my lady straight,° I would not be in some of your coats for twopence. [*Exit*] — *immediately*

SIR TOBY Come on, sir, hold.

SIR ANDREW Nay, let him alone, I'll go another way to work with him. I'll have an action of battery° against him if there be any law in Illyria. Though I struck him first, yet it's no matter for that. — *charges of assault*

SEBASTIAN Let go thy hand.

SIR TOBY Come, sir, I will not let you go. Come, my young soldier, put up your iron. You are well fleshed.° Come on. — *experienced in combat*

SEBASTIAN [*freeing himself*] I will be free from thee. What wouldst thou now?
If thou dar'st tempt me further, draw thy sword.

SIR TOBY What, what? Nay then, I must have an ounce or two of this malapert° blood from you. — *impudent*

[SIR TOBY *and* SEBASTIAN *draw their swords.*]

Enter OLIVIA

OLIVIA Hold, Toby, on thy life I charge thee hold.

SIR TOBY Madam.

OLIVIA Will it be ever thus? Ungracious wretch,
Fit for the mountains and the barbarous caves,
Where manners ne'er were preached—out of my sight!
Be not offended, dear Cesario.
[*To* SIR TOBY] Rudesby,° be gone. — *Ruffian*

[*Exeunt* SIR TOBY, SIR ANDREW, *and* FABIAN]

I prithee, gentle friend,
Let thy fair wisdom, not thy passion sway
In this uncivil and unjust extent° — *attack*
Against thy peace. Go with me to my house,
And hear thou there how many fruitless pranks
This ruffian hath botched up,° that thou thereby — *badly put together*
Mayst smile at this. Thou shalt not choose but go.
Do not deny. Beshrew° his soul for me, — *Curse*
He started one poor heart of mine in thee.[3]

SEBASTIAN What relish° is in this? How runs the stream? — *taste; meaning*
Or° I am mad, or else this is a dream. — *Either*
Let fancy° still my sense in Lethe[4] steep. — *imagination*
If it be thus to dream, still° let me sleep. — *always*

OLIVIA Nay, come, I prithee, would thou'dst be ruled by me.

SEBASTIAN Madam, I will.

OLIVIA O, say so, and so be. *Exeunt*

3. That is, he has frightened my heart, which I have given to you. Because "start" (to force from a hiding place) is also a hunting term, there may be a pun on "heart" and "hart."

4. The river of forgetfulness in the classical underworld.

4.2

Enter MARIA [*carrying a gown and false beard, and* FESTE, *the*] *clown*

MARIA Nay, I prithee put on this gown and this beard, make
him believe thou art Sir Topas[5] the curate. Do it quickly.
I'll call Sir Toby the whilst.° *Exit* *in the meantime*

FESTE Well, I'll put it on, and I will dissemble° myself in't, *disguise*
and I would I were the first that ever dissembled° in such *deceived*
a gown.

[*He disguises himself*]

I am not tall° enough to become the function well,[6] nor *stout*
lean enough to be thought a good student,° but to be said° *(of divinity) / known as*
'an honest man and a good housekeeper'° goes as fairly as[7] *household manager*
to say 'careful man and a great scholar'. The competitors° *My partners*
enter.

Enter [SIR] TOBY [*and* MARIA]

SIR TOBY Jove bless thee, Master Parson.

FESTE *Bonos dies,* Sir Toby, for, as the old hermit of
Prague,[8] that never saw pen and ink, very wittily said to
a niece of King Gorboduc,[9] 'That that is, is.' So I, being
Master Parson, am Master Parson; for what is 'that' but
'that', and 'is' but 'is'?

SIR TOBY To him, Sir Topas.

FESTE What ho, I say, peace in this prison.

SIR TOBY The knave counterfeits well—a good knave.

MALVOLIO *within*

MALVOLIO Who calls there?

FESTE Sir Topas the curate, who comes to visit Malvolio
the lunatic.

MALVOLIO Sir Topas, Sir Topas, good Sir Topas, go to my
lady.

FESTE Out, hyperbolical° fiend,[1] how vexest thou this man! *ranting*
Talkest thou nothing but of ladies?

SIR TOBY Well said, Master Parson.

MALVOLIO Sir Topas, never was man thus wronged. Good
Sir Topas, do not think I am mad. They have laid me
here in hideous darkness.

FESTE Fie, thou dishonest Satan—I call thee by the most
modest° terms, for I am one of those gentle ones that will *mildest*
use the devil himself with courtesy. Sayst thou that house° *room*
is dark?

MALVOLIO As hell, Sir Topas.

4.2 Location: Olivia's house.
5. Perhaps an allusion to Chaucer's burlesque knight of the "Rime of Sir Topas" in *The Canterbury Tales.* Also, the semiprecious stone topaz was thought to cure a variety of ailments, including madness.
6. To grace the role of priest (priests were stereotypically fat, and students underfed).
7. Sounds as good as.
8. Probably another of Feste's invented authorities. *Bonos dies:* good day (corruption of Latin *bonus dies*).
9. Legendary king of ancient Britain.
1. Feste addresses the devil that supposedly possesses Malvolio.

FESTE Why, it hath bay windows transparent as barricadoes,[2] and the clerestories° toward the south-north are as lustrous as ebony,[3] and yet complainest thou of obstruction?

windows in the upper wall

MALVOLIO I am not mad, Sir Topas; I say to you this house is dark.

FESTE Madman, thou errest. I say there is no darkness but ignorance, in which thou art more puzzled than the Egyptians in their fog.[4]

MALVOLIO I say this house is as dark as ignorance, though ignorance were as dark as hell; and I say there was never man thus abused. I am no more mad than you are. Make the trial of it in any constant question.°

rational discourse

FESTE What is the opinion of Pythagoras[5] concerning wildfowl?

MALVOLIO That the soul of our grandam might haply° inhabit a bird.

perhaps

FESTE What thinkest thou of his opinion?

MALVOLIO I think nobly of the soul, and no way approve his opinion.

FESTE Fare thee well. Remain thou still in darkness. Thou shalt hold th'opinion of Pythagoras ere I will allow of thy wits,° and fear to kill a woodcock[6] lest thou dispossess the soul of thy grandam. Fare thee well.

certify your sanity

MALVOLIO Sir Topas, Sir Topas!

SIR TOBY My most exquisite Sir Topas.

FESTE Nay, I am for all waters.[7]

MARIA Thou mightst have done this without thy beard and gown, he sees thee not.

SIR TOBY [*to* FESTE] To him in thine own voice, and bring me word how thou findest him. I would we were well rid of this knavery. If he may be conveniently delivered,° I would he were, for I am now so far in offence with my niece that I cannot pursue with any safety this sport to the upshot.° [*To* MARIA] Come by and by to my chamber.

set free

conclusion

Exit [*with* MARIA]

FESTE [*sings*][8] 'Hey Robin, jolly Robin,
Tell me how thy lady does.'

MALVOLIO Fool!

FESTE 'My lady is unkind, pardie.'[9]

MALVOLIO Fool!

FESTE 'Alas, why is she so?'

MALVOLIO Fool, I say!

2. As barricades (that is, not transparent at all).
3. A hard wood that is a dull black (that is, not at all "lustrous," or bright).
4. One of the biblical plagues was a "darkness over the land of Egypt" (see Exodus 10.21–23).
5. Greek philosopher (6th c. B.C.E.), well-known for his belief in the transmigration of souls between living things.
6. A proverbially stupid bird.
7. I can sail any sea (i.e., I am able to handle all situations).
8. Feste's sung lines are fragments of an old song.
9. Certainly, indeed (from the French *pardieu*, "by God").

FESTE 'She loves another.'
Who calls, ha?

MALVOLIO Good fool, as ever thou wilt deserve well at my hand, help me to a candle and pen, ink, and paper. As I am a gentleman, I will live to be thankful to thee for't.

FESTE Master Malvolio?

MALVOLIO Ay, good fool.

FESTE Alas, sir, how fell you besides° your five wits?[1] *out of*

MALVOLIO Fool, there was never man so notoriously° *outrageously* abused. I am as well in my wits, fool, as thou art.

FESTE But° as well? *Only* Then you are mad indeed, if you be no better in your wits than a fool.

MALVOLIO They have here propertied me,[2] keep me in darkness, send ministers to me, asses, and do all they can to face me[3] out of my wits.

FESTE Advise you° what you say, the minister is here. *Be careful* [*As Sir Topas*] Malvolio, Malvolio, thy wits the heavens restore. Endeavour thyself to sleep, and leave thy vain bibble-babble.

MALVOLIO Sir Topas.

FESTE [*as Sir Topas*] Maintain no words with him, good fellow. [*As himself*] Who I, sir? Not I, sir. God b'wi' you,° good *God be with you* Sir Topas. [*As Sir Topas*] Marry, amen. [*As himself*] I will, sir, I will.

MALVOLIO Fool, fool, fool, I say.

FESTE Alas, sir, be patient. What say you, sir? I am shent° *reproved* for speaking to you.

MALVOLIO Good fool, help me to some light and some paper. I tell thee I am as well in my wits as any man in Illyria.

FESTE Well-a-day° that you were, sir. *Alas*

MALVOLIO By this hand, I am. Good fool, some ink, paper, and light, and convey what I will set down to my lady. It shall advantage thee more than ever the bearing of letter did.

FESTE I will help you to't. But tell me true, are you not mad indeed, or do you but counterfeit?

MALVOLIO Believe me, I am not, I tell thee true.

FESTE Nay, I'll ne'er believe a madman till I see his brains. I will fetch you light, and paper, and ink.

MALVOLIO Fool, I'll requite it in the highest degree. I prithee, be gone.

FESTE
I am gone, sir,
And anon, sir,
I'll be with you again,
In a trice,
Like to the old Vice,[4]

1. The five wits are common sense, fantasy, memory, judgment, and imagination.
2. Treated me like a piece of property.
3. Falsely portray me as.
4. A stock comic character in morality plays and interludes.

Your need to sustain,
Who with dagger of lath
In his rage and his wrath
Cries 'Aha,' to the devil,
Like a mad lad,
'Pare thy nails, dad,
Adieu, goodman[5] devil.' *Exit*

4.3

Enter SEBASTIAN

SEBASTIAN This is the air, that is the glorious sun.
This pearl she gave me, I do feel't and see't,
And though 'tis wonder that enwraps me thus,
Yet 'tis not madness. Where's Antonio then?
I could not find him at the Elephant,
Yet there he was,° and there I found this credit,° *he had been / report*
That he did range° the town to seek me out. *wander*
His counsel now might do me golden service,
For though my soul disputes well with my sense[6]
That this may be some error but no madness,
Yet doth this accident and flood of fortune
So far exceed all instance,° all discourse,° *precedent / reason*
That I am ready to distrust mine eyes
And wrangle with my reason that persuades me
To any other trust° but that I am mad, *conviction*
Or else the lady's mad. Yet if 'twere so
She could not sway° her house, command her followers, *rule*
Take and give back affairs and their dispatch[7]
With such a smooth, discreet, and stable bearing
As I perceive she does. There's something in't
That is deceivable.° But here the lady comes. *deceptive*

Enter OLIVIA *and* PRIEST

OLIVIA Blame not this haste of mine. If you mean well
Now go with me, and with this holy man,
Into the chantry by.° There before him, *nearby private chapel*
And underneath that consecrated roof,
Plight me the full assurance of your faith,[8]
That my most jealous° and too doubtful soul *anxious*
May live at peace. He shall conceal it
Whiles° you are willing it shall come to note,° *Until / become public*
What° time we will our celebration keep *At which*
According to my birth.° What do you say? *social rank*

SEBASTIAN I'll follow this good man, and go with you,
And having sworn truth, ever will be true.

5. A vague title of dignity for one of low social rank.
4.3 Location: Olivia's garden.
6. My reason agrees with my other senses.
7. That is, receive reports on household matters and issue orders for their management.
8. That is, enter into a betrothal (a binding contract), to be followed with a marriage ceremony at a later date (lines 30–31).

OLIVIA Then lead the way, good father, and heavens so shine
That they may fairly note° this act of mine. *Exeunt* — *look favorably on*

5.1

Enter [FESTE, *the*] *clown and* FABIAN

FABIAN Now, as thou lovest me, let me see his letter.
FESTE Good Master Fabian, grant me another request.
FABIAN Anything.
FESTE Do not desire to see this letter.
FABIAN This is to give a dog, and in recompense desire my dog again.[9]

Enter Duke, VIOLA [*as Cesario*], CURIO, *and lords*

ORSINO Belong you to the Lady Olivia, friends?
FESTE Ay, sir, we are some of her trappings.° — *ornaments; i.e., entourage*
ORSINO I know thee well. How dost thou, my good fellow?
FESTE Truly, sir, the better for my foes and the worse for my friends.
ORSINO Just the contrary—the better for thy friends.
FESTE No, sir, the worse.
ORSINO How can that be?
FESTE Marry, sir, they praise me, and make an ass of me.[1] Now my foes tell me plainly I am an ass, so that by my foes, sir, I profit in the knowledge of myself, and by my friends I am abused;° so that, conclusions to be as kisses, if your four negatives make your two affirmatives,[2] why then the worse for my friends and the better for my foes. — *misled*
ORSINO Why, this is excellent.
FESTE By my troth, sir, no, though it please you to be one of my friends.
ORSINO [*giving money*] Thou shalt not be the worse for me. There's gold.
FESTE But° that it would be double-dealing,[3] sir, I would you could make it another. — *Except for the fact*
ORSINO O, you give me ill counsel.
FESTE Put your grace in your pocket,[4] sir, for this once, and let your flesh and blood obey it.
ORSINO Well, I will be so much a sinner to° be a double-dealer. — *as to*
[*Giving money*] There's another.
FESTE *Primo, secundo, tertio*[5] is a good play,° and the old — *game*

5.1 Location: Near Olivia's house.

9. Perhaps a reference to a story about Elizabeth I, related in the diary of John Manningham (ca. 1575–1622): the queen asked for a dog from a man named Dr. Bullein; granted a request in return, he asked for the dog back.

1. That is, they flatter me into thinking better of myself than I deserve, which makes me look foolish.

2. That is, because a grammatical double negative is a positive, a woman who says "no, no, no, no" in response to a request for kisses is really saying "yes, yes."

3. Duplicity (because he is asking for a double donation).

4. That is, pocket up your virtue; also, let your grace (the proper address to a duke) reach into your purse (to bring out an additional coin).

5. First, second, third (Latin).

saying is 'The third pays for all'.[6] The triplex,° sir, is a good tripping measure, or the bells of Saint Bennet,[7] sir, may put you in mind—'one, two, three'. *triple time in music*

ORSINO You can fool no more money out of me at this throw.° If you will let your lady know I am here to speak with her, and bring her along with you, it may awake my bounty° further. *(of the dice)* *generosity*

FESTE Marry, sir, lullaby to your bounty till I come again. I go, sir, but I would not have you to think that my desire of having is the sin of covetousness. But as you say, sir, let your bounty take a nap, I will awake it anon. *Exit*

Enter ANTONIO *and* OFFICERS

VIOLA Here comes the man, sir, that did rescue me.

ORSINO That face of his I do remember well,
Yet when I saw it last it was besmeared
As black as Vulcan[8] in the smoke of war.
A baubling° vessel was he captain of, *paltry*
For shallow draught and bulk unprizable,[9]
With which such scatheful° grapple did he make *destructive*
With the most noble bottom° of our fleet *ship*
That very envy and the tongue of loss[1]
Cried fame and honour on him. What's the matter?

FIRST OFFICER Orsino, this is that Antonio
That took the *Phoenix* and her freight from Candy,° *Candia, capital of Crete*
And this is he that did the *Tiger* board
When your young nephew Titus lost his leg.
Here in the streets, desperate of shame and state,[2]
In private brabble° did we apprehend him. *brawl*

VIOLA He did me kindness, sir, drew on my side,[3]
But in conclusion put strange speech upon° me. *spoke strangely to*
I know not what 'twas but distraction.° *except madness*

ORSINO [*to* ANTONIO] Notable° pirate, thou salt-water thief, *Notorious*
What foolish boldness brought thee to their mercies
Whom thou in terms so bloody and so dear° *costly*
Hast made thine enemies?

ANTONIO Orsino, noble sir,
Be pleased that I shake off these names you give me.
Antonio never yet was thief or pirate,
Though, I confess, on base° and ground enough *foundation*
Orsino's enemy. A witchcraft drew me hither.
That most ingrateful boy there by your side
From the rude sea's enraged and foamy mouth

6. The third time is the charm.
7. Perhaps the church of St. Bennet Hithe, located across the Thames from the Globe theater.
8. Roman god of fire and metalworking.
9. That is, of no value as a prize because of its shallow draft (the depth of water required to float it) and small size.
1. The voices of the losers. *Very envy:* even the envious, his enemies.
2. That is, without regard for his honor or safety (as a wanted man).
3. Drew his sword on my behalf.

Did I redeem. A wreck° past hope he was. *castaway*
His life I gave him, and did thereto add
My love without retention° or restraint, *reservation*
All his in dedication.° For his sake *dedicated to him*
Did I expose myself, pure° for his love, *purely*
Into the danger of this adverse° town, *hostile*
Drew to defend him when he was beset,
Where being apprehended, his false cunning—
Not meaning to partake with me in danger—
Taught him to face me out of his acquaintance,[4]
And grew a twenty years' removèd thing
While one would wink,[5] denied me mine own purse,
Which I had recommended° to his use *committed*
Not half an hour before.

VIOLA How can this be?

ORSINO When came he to this town?

ANTONIO Today, my lord, and for three months before,
No int'rim, not a minute's vacancy,° *interval*
Both day and night did we keep company.

Enter OLIVIA *and attendants*

ORSINO Here comes the Countess. Now heaven walks on earth.
But for thee, fellow—fellow, thy words are madness.
Three months this youth hath tended upon me.
But more of that anon. Take him aside.

OLIVIA What would my lord, but that[6] he may not have,
Wherein Olivia may seem serviceable?° *be of service*
Cesario, you do not keep promise with me.

VIOLA Madam—

ORSINO Gracious Olivia—

OLIVIA What do you say, Cesario? Good my lord—

VIOLA My lord would speak, my duty hushes me.

OLIVIA If it be aught° to the old tune, my lord, *anything*
It is as fat and fulsome° to mine ear *gross and repugnant*
As howling after music.

ORSINO Still so cruel?

OLIVIA Still so constant, lord.

ORSINO What, to perverseness? You uncivil lady,
To whose ingrate and unauspicious[7] altars
My soul the faithfull'st off 'rings hath breathed out
That e'er devotion tendered—what shall I do?

OLIVIA Even what it please my lord that shall become° him. *befit*

ORSINO Why should I not, had I the heart to do it,
Like to th' Egyptian thief, at point of death
Kill what I love[8]—a savage jealousy

4. To shamelessly deny knowing me.
5. In the time it takes to blink.
6. Except that (my love) which.
7. Ungrateful and unfavorable.
8. In Heliodorus's prose romance *Ethiopica* (3rd c. C.E.; translated from Greek into English in 1569), an Egyptian robber named Thyamis tries to kill Chariclea (his captive, with whom he has fallen in love) when they are attacked by a larger band of robbers.

That sometime savours nobly.° But hear me this: *has nobility in it*
Since you to non-regardance° cast my faith, *neglect*
And that I partly know the instrument
That screws° me from my true place in your favour, *forces*
Live you the marble-breasted tyrant still.
But this your minion,° whom I know you love, *favorite*
And whom, by heaven I swear, I tender° dearly, *regard*
Him will I tear out of that cruel eye
Where he sits crownèd in his master's spite.[9]
[*To* VIOLA] Come, boy, with me. My thoughts are ripe in mischief.
I'll sacrifice the lamb that I do love
To spite a raven's heart within a dove.

VIOLA And I most jocund,° apt,° and willingly *happily / readily*
To do you rest a thousand deaths would die.

OLIVIA Where goes Cesario?

VIOLA After him I love
More than I love these eyes, more than my life,
More by all mores° than e'er I shall love wife. *(such) comparisons*
If I do feign, you witnesses above,
Punish my life for tainting of my love.

OLIVIA Ay me detested,° how am I beguiled! *rejected*

VIOLA Who does beguile you? Who does do you wrong?

OLIVIA Hast thou forgot thyself ? Is it so long?
Call forth the holy father. [*Exit an attendant*]

ORSINO [*to* VIOLA] Come, away.

OLIVIA Whither, my lord? Cesario, husband, stay.

ORSINO Husband?

OLIVIA Ay, husband. Can he that deny?

ORSINO [*to* VIOLA] Her husband, sirrah?[1]

VIOLA No, my lord, not I.

OLIVIA Alas, it is the baseness of thy fear
That makes thee strangle thy propriety.[2]
Fear not, Cesario, take thy fortunes up,
Be that° thou know'st thou art, and then thou art *that which*
As great as that° thou fear'st. *he whom (i.e., Orsino)*

Enter PRIEST

O welcome, father.
Father, I charge thee by thy reverence
Here to unfold—though lately we intended
To keep in darkness what occasion° now *necessity*
Reveals before 'tis ripe—what thou dost know
Hath newly° passed between this youth and me. *recently*

PRIEST A contract of eternal bond of love,
Confirmed by mutual joinder° of your hands, *joining*
Attested by the holy close° of lips, *meeting*

9. Notwithstanding the opposition of his master.
1. Customary form of address to a male social inferior.
2. That is, kill your own identity (as my husband).

Strengthened by interchangement of your rings,
And all the ceremony of this compact
Sealed in my function,[3] by my testimony;
Since when, my watch hath told me, toward my grave
I have travelled but two hours.

ORSINO [*to* VIOLA] O thou dissembling cub, what wilt thou be
When time hath sowed a grizzle on thy case?[4]
Or will not else thy craft° so quickly grow — *cunning*
That thine own trip shall be thine overthrow?[5]
Farewell, and take her, but direct thy feet
Where thou and I henceforth may never meet.

VIOLA My lord, I do protest.

OLIVIA O, do not swear!
Hold little° faith, though thou hast too much fear. — *Keep a little*

Enter SIR ANDREW

SIR ANDREW For the love of God, a surgeon—send one presently° to Sir Toby. — *immediately*

OLIVIA What's the matter?

SIR ANDREW He's broke° my head across, and has given Sir Toby a bloody coxcomb,[6] too. For the love of God, your help! I had rather than forty pound I were at home. — *cut*

OLIVIA Who has done this, Sir Andrew?

SIR ANDREW The Count's gentleman, one Cesario. We took him for a coward, but he's the very devil incardinate.° — *(incarnate)*

ORSINO My gentleman, Cesario?

SIR ANDREW 'Od's lifelings,[7] here he is. [*To* VIOLA] You broke my head for nothing, and that that I did I was set on to do't by Sir Toby.

VIOLA Why do you speak to me? I never hurt you.
You drew your sword upon me without cause,
But I bespake you fair,[8] and hurt you not.

Enter [SIR] TOBY *and* [FESTE, *the*] *clown*

SIR ANDREW If a bloody coxcomb be a hurt you have hurt me. I think you set nothing by° a bloody coxcomb. Here comes Sir Toby, halting.° You shall hear more; but if° he had not been in drink he would have tickled° you other gates° than he did. — *think nothing of* / *limping / if only* / *chastised* / *otherwise*

ORSINO [*to* SIR TOBY] How now, gentleman? How is't with you?

SIR TOBY That's all one,° he's hurt me, and there's th'end on't. — *irrelevant*
[*To* FESTE] Sot,° didst see Dick Surgeon, sot? — *Fool, drunkard*

FESTE O, he's drunk, Sir Toby, an hour agone. His eyes were set° at eight i'th' morning. — *closed*

3. That is, ratified by my priestly authority.
4. Gray hairs on your hide.
5. That your attempt to take down another shall be your own downfall ("trip" is a wrestling term).
6. Head; also, a fool's hat, which resembles the crest of a cock.
7. By God's little lives (an oath).
8. I spoke to you with all courtesy.

SIR TOBY Then he's a rogue, and a passy-measures pavan.[9]
I hate a drunken rogue.

OLIVIA Away with him! Who hath made this havoc with them?

SIR ANDREW I'll help you, Sir Toby, because we'll be dressed[1] together.

SIR TOBY Will *you* help—an ass-head, and a coxcomb,° and a knave; a thin-faced knave, a gull?° — *fool*; *dupe*

OLIVIA Get him to bed, and let his hurt be looked to.

[*Exeunt* SIR TOBY, SIR ANDREW, FESTE, *and* FABIAN]

Enter SEBASTIAN

SEBASTIAN [*to* OLIVIA] I am sorry, madam, I have hurt your kinsman,
But had it been the brother of my blood
I must have done no less with wit and safety.[2]
You throw a strange regard upon me,[3] and by that
I do perceive it hath offended you.
Pardon me, sweet one, even for the vows
We made each other but so late ago.

ORSINO One face, one voice, one habit, and two persons,
A natural perspective,[4] that is and is not.° — *(an illusion)*

SEBASTIAN Antonio! O, my dear Antonio,
How have the hours racked and tortured me
Since I have lost thee!

ANTONIO Sebastian are you?

SEBASTIAN Fear'st thou that,° Antonio? — *Do you doubt that*

ANTONIO How have you made division of yourself?
An apple cleft in two is not more twin
Than these two creatures. Which is Sebastian?

OLIVIA Most wonderful!° — *amazing*

SEBASTIAN [*seeing* VIOLA] Do I stand there? I never had a brother,
Nor can there be that deity° in my nature — *divine power*
Of here and everywhere.° I had a sister, — *omnipresence*
Whom the blind° waves and surges have devoured. — *indiscriminate*
Of charity,° what kin are you to me? — *Kindly (tell me)*
What countryman? What name? What parentage?

VIOLA Of Messaline. Sebastian was my father.
Such a Sebastian was my brother, too.
So went he suited° to his watery tomb. — *dressed; in appearance*
If spirits can assume both form and suit
You come to fright us.

SEBASTIAN A spirit I am indeed,
But am in that dimension grossly clad

9. A slow, stately dance of Italian origin (*passamezzo*). Sir Toby may think that its swaying movements resemble the unsteadiness of a drunk.
1. We'll have our wounds tended to.
2. With reasonable prudence for my own safety.
3. That is, you look at me as if I were a stranger.
4. An optical illusion produced by nature (and not by a mirror).

Which from the womb I did participate.[5]
Were you a woman, as the rest goes even,[6]
I should my tears let fall upon your cheek
And say 'Thrice welcome, drownèd Viola.'

VIOLA My father had a mole upon his brow.

SEBASTIAN And so had mine.

VIOLA And died that day when Viola from her birth
Had numbered thirteen years.

SEBASTIAN O, that record is lively[7] in my soul.
He finishèd indeed his mortal act
That day that made my sister thirteen years.

VIOLA If nothing lets° to make us happy both *[prevents]*
But this my masculine usurped attire,
Do not embrace me till each circumstance
Of place, time, fortune do cohere and jump° *[agree]*
That I am Viola, which to confirm
I'll bring you to a captain in this town
Where lie my maiden weeds,° by whose gentle help *[clothes]*
I was preserved to serve this noble count.
All the occurrence of my fortune[8] since
Hath been between° this lady and this lord. *[as messenger between]*

SEBASTIAN [*to* OLIVIA] So comes it, lady, you have been mistook,
But nature to her bias drew in that.[9]
You would have been contracted° to a maid, *[betrothed]*
Nor are you therein, by my life, deceived.
You are betrothed both to a maid and man.[1]

ORSINO [*to* OLIVIA] Be not amazed. Right noble is his blood.
If this be so, as yet the glass seems true,[2]
I shall have share in this most happy wreck.° *[fortunate shipwreck]*
[*To* VIOLA] Boy, thou hast said to me a thousand times
Thou never shouldst love woman like to me.° *[as much as (you love) me]*

VIOLA And all those sayings will I overswear,° *[swear again]*
And all those swearings keep as true in soul
As doth that orbèd continent the fire[3]
That severs day from night.

ORSINO Give me thy hand,
And let me see thee in thy woman's weeds.

VIOLA The captain that did bring me first on shore
Hath my maid's garments. He upon some action° *[legal charge]*
Is now in durance,° at Malvolio's suit, *[prison]*
A gentleman and follower of my lady's.

5. That is, I am a spirit, yes, but one, like all humans, dressed in flesh from the time I was in the womb.
6. As everything else indicates.
7. The memory of that is vivid.
8. That is, all that has happened to me.
9. That is, but nature caused you to swerve to me in that matter. (The image is from the game of bowls, played with a weighted ball that curves from a straight path.)
1. That is, a man who is a virgin.
2. That is, the "natural perspective" (of line 216) continues to seem real.
3. That is, as the sun's sphere contains the fire.

OLIVIA He shall enlarge° him. Fetch Malvolio hither— *release*
And yet, alas, now I remember me,
They say, poor gentleman, he's much distraught.

Enter [FESTE, *the*] *clown with a letter, and* FABIAN

A most extracting frenzy° of mine own *distracting madness*
From my remembrance clearly banished his.° *his madness*
How does he, sirrah?

FESTE Truly, madam, he holds Beelzebub at the stave's end[4] as well as a man in his case may do. He's here writ a letter to you. I should have given't you today morning. But as a madman's epistles are no gospels,[5] so it skills° not much when they are delivered. *matters*

OLIVIA Open't and read it.

FESTE Look then to be well edified when the fool delivers° the madman. [*Reads*] 'By the Lord, madam'— *speaks the words of*

OLIVIA How now, art thou mad?

FESTE No, madam, I do but read madness. An° your ladyship will have it as it ought to be you must allow vox.[6] *If*

OLIVIA Prithee, read i'thy right wits.

FESTE So I do, madonna, but to read his right wits[7] is to read thus. Therefore perpend,° my princess, and give ear. *pay attention*

OLIVIA [*to* FABIAN] Read it you, sirrah.

[FESTE *gives the letter to* FABIAN]

FABIAN (*reads*) 'By the Lord, madam, you wrong me, and the world shall know it. Though you have put me into darkness and given your drunken cousin rule over me, yet have I the benefit of my senses as well as your ladyship. I have your own letter that induced me to the semblance I put on, with the which I doubt not but to do myself much right or you much shame. Think of me as you please. I leave my duty[8] a little unthought of, and speak out of my injury.

The madly-used Malvolio.

OLIVIA Did he write this?

FESTE Ay, madam.

ORSINO This savours not much of distraction.° *madness*

OLIVIA See him delivered,° Fabian, bring him hither. *released*
My lord, so please you—these things further thought on—
To think me as well a sister as a wife,[9]
One day shall crown th'alliance on't,[1] so please you,
Here at my house and at my proper cost.° *own expense*

ORSINO Madam, I am most apt° t'embrace your offer. *ready*
[*To* VIOLA] Your master quits° you, and for your service done him *releases*

4. Keeps the devil at a distance (proverbial).
5. The letters of a madman are not to be taken as gospel truths.
6. The voice (Latin); Feste is using a voice he thinks appropriate for a madman.
7. To read his state of mind correctly.
8. The duty I owe you (as your servant).
9. That is, think of me as favorably as your sister-in-law as you would have had I been your wife.
1. That is, be the occasion of the two marriages that will cement this new relationship.

So much against the mettle° of your sex, — *temperament*
So far beneath your soft and tender breeding,
And since you called me master for so long,
Here is my hand. You shall from this time be
Your master's mistress.

OLIVIA [*to* VIOLA] A sister, you are she.

Enter MALVOLIO

ORSINO Is this the madman?

OLIVIA Ay, my lord, this same.
How now, Malvolio?

MALVOLIO Madam, you have done me wrong,
Notorious wrong.

OLIVIA Have I, Malvolio? No.

MALVOLIO [*showing a letter*] Lady, you have. Pray you peruse
that letter.
You must not now deny it is your hand.° — *handwriting*
Write from° it if you can, in hand or phrase, — *differently from*
Or say 'tis not your seal, not your invention.° — *composition*
You can say none of this. Well, grant it then,
And tell me in the modesty of honour[2]
Why you have given me such clear lights° of favour, — *signs*
Bade me come smiling and cross-gartered to you,
To put on yellow stockings, and to frown
Upon Sir Toby and the lighter° people, — *lesser*
And acting° this in an obedient hope, — *after doing*
Why have you suffered me to be imprisoned,
Kept in a dark house, visited by the priest,
And made the most notorious geck° and gull — *fool*
That e'er invention° played on? Tell me why? — *trickery*

OLIVIA Alas, Malvolio, this is not my writing,
Though I confess much like the character,° — *(my) handwriting*
But out of question, 'tis Maria's hand.
And now I do bethink me, it was she
First told me thou wast mad; then cam'st° in smiling, — *you came*
And in such forms which here were presupposed
Upon thee in the letter. Prithee be content;
This practice° hath most shrewdly passed° upon thee, — *trick / cleverly played*
But when we know the grounds and authors of it
Thou shalt be both the plaintiff and the judge
Of thine own cause.

FABIAN Good madam, hear me speak,
And let no quarrel nor no brawl to come
Taint the condition of this present hour,
Which I have wondered at. In hope it shall not,
Most freely I confess myself and Toby
Set this device against Malvolio here
Upon some stubborn and uncourteous parts
We had conceived against him.[3] Maria writ

2. As an honorable person would.
3. That is, because of some rude and uncivil qualities that we discerned in him and held against him.

The letter, at Sir Toby's great importance,° *importuning*
In recompense whereof he hath married her.
How with a sportful malice it was followed° *carried through*
May rather pluck on° laughter than revenge *encourage*
If that the injuries be justly weighed
That have on both sides passed.

OLIVIA [*to* MALVOLIO] Alas, poor fool, how have they baffled° thee! *disgraced*

FESTE Why, 'Some are born great, some achieve greatness, and some have greatness thrown upon them.' I was one, sir, in this interlude,° one Sir Topas, sir; but that's all one. 'By the Lord, fool, I am not mad'—but do you remember, 'Madam, why laugh you at such a barren rascal, an° you smile not, he's gagged'—and thus the whirligig° of time brings in his revenges. *comedy* *if / spinning top*

MALVOLIO I'll be revenged on the whole pack of you. [*Exit*]

OLIVIA He hath been most notoriously abused.

ORSINO Pursue him, and entreat him to a peace.
He hath not told us of the captain yet. [*Exit one or more*]
When that is known, and golden time convents,° *suits*
A solemn combination shall be made
Of our dear souls. Meantime, sweet sister,
We will not part from hence.° Cesario, come— *here (Olivia's house)*
For so you shall be while you are a man;
But when in other habits you are seen,
Orsino's mistress, and his fancy's° queen. *imagination's; love's*

Exeunt [*all but* FESTE]

FESTE (*sings*) When that I was and a little tiny boy,
With hey, ho, the wind and the rain,
A foolish thing was but a toy,
For the rain it raineth every day.

But when I came to man's estate,
With hey, ho, the wind and the rain,
'Gainst knaves and thieves men shut their gate,
For the rain it raineth every day.

But when I came, alas, to wive,
With hey, ho, the wind and the rain,
By swaggering° could I never thrive, *blustering, bullying*
For the rain it raineth every day.

But when I came unto my beds,
With hey, ho, the wind and the rain,
With tosspots° still had drunken heads, *drunkards*
For the rain it raineth every day.

A great while ago the world begun,
With hey, ho, the wind and the rain,
But that's all one, our play is done,
And we'll strive to please you every day. *Exit*

MOLIÈRE (JEAN-BAPTISTE POQUELIN)

1621?–1673

FRANCE'S greatest comic dramatist, Molière (born Jean-Baptiste Poquelin) has remained, since the seventeenth century, among the world's most frequently produced and widely studied playwrights. An actor, a director, and a manager as well, Molière was a consummate man of the theater, completely dedicated to art; his thirty-year career coincided with, and significantly contributed to, the flowering of French dramaturgy. A contemporary of the renowned tragic dramatists Pierre Corneille (1606–1684) and Jean Racine (1639–1699), Molière joined his colleagues in catapulting the French theater to European prominence. Under the leadership of Louis XIV (r. 1643–1715), whose appreciation for and support of the arts defined his reign, France emerged at the cultural vanguard in the baroque era, setting standards for dramatic composition and production that lasted until the advent of modernism.

Born into a family of bourgeois artisan merchants, Jean-Baptiste was baptized on January 15, 1622. His father, Jean Poquelin, and mother, Marie Cressé, worked in the bedding trade, and in 1631 Jean was named *tapissier ordinaire du roi,* a royal appointment that involved caring for the king's furniture. Their gain in economic security and prestige enabled them to send their son to the Collège de Clermont, the most fashionable school in Paris at the time. This Jesuit institution introduced Jean-Baptiste to a study of the humanities, which included classical languages and literatures, rhetoric, theology, and philosophy. Very probably he acted in Latin comedies and tragedies as part of his education; the works of the Roman comic dramatists PLAUTUS and Terence, replete with narratives of frustrated young lovers, overbearing parents, and cunning slaves, clearly informed his development as a writer. He likely also saw the popular folk theater of the day.

When Jean-Baptiste reached age fifteen, Jean Poquelin conveyed his royal appointment to his son, securing for the youth a solid future in the family trade. Though the young man may have accompanied the king in this capacity on a military campaign in 1642, he apparently continued his studies, including a new focus in law. In any case, in 1643 Jean-Baptiste's career took a novel and decisive turn. In exchange for 630 livres from his father, he gave up his royal office and with a small group of colleagues formed the Illustre Théâtre. The creation of the company benefited the actors in a number of ways: they gained control of their employment, the profits, and the kinds of work produced, as they moved away from older dramatic traditions. About a year later, Jean-Baptiste assumed the stage name Molière.

A drawing of the fifteen-year-old Louis XIV—also known as the "Sun King"—as Apollo in *Le ballet royal de la nuit.*

It was a challenging time to embark on a theatrical career. Elsewhere in Europe, dramatic writing had already blossomed in the Renaissance, but France lagged behind. Theatrical activity there in the early decades of the seventeenth century consisted mainly of productions of scripts from other countries as well as the lively Italian farces performed in the streets of Paris and in the provinces. A native variant of this latter tradition had also developed after liturgical drama was secularized in the late medieval period. Equally popular were the traveling companies specializing in the Italian commedia dell'arte, with its repertoire of stock characters, familiar plots, and improvised comic business called *lazzi* that surmounted the language barrier. We can trace the direct impact of all these traditions on a play like TARTUFFE (1664–69), one of Molière's greatest and most controversial comedies.

Just a decade before the founding of the Illustre Théâtre, the shape of French literature had been transformed by the establishment of the French Academy (*Académie Française*), under the sponsorship of the influential minister Cardinal Richelieu. The Academy created rules for the composition of French literature and national standards for literary taste. Drawing on Aristotle's *Poetics,* the Academy emphasized the importance of adhering to the unities of time, place, and action for the drama and stressed that tragedy should depict the lives of kings and the aristocracy, while comedy should portray those of lower social status. Under the Academy's direction, verse drama prevailed. The twelve-syllable line called the *alexandrine* dominated French dramaturgy, and Molière frequently utilized the rhyming couplets that were standard for his era. (The translation of *Tartuffe* included here renders the couplets in the pentameter line more natural in English.) The Academy also established that plausibility (*vraisemblance*) and propriety (*bienséance*) should inform all dramatic writing. Many of Molière's works display the tension between his efforts to conform to these rules and his appreciation of the bawdier farce traditions that had proven so popular with the audiences he now sought to attract. He also recognized that his plays had to somehow acknowledge and win the king's invaluable ongoing patronage.

Before he could pen the masterpieces that define his theatrical legacy, Molière and his colleagues struggled for more than a decade just to make ends meet. Finding it impossible to pay its bills in Paris, the Illustre Théâtre survived for almost fifteen years by touring the provinces. During this period, the company members honed their skills as actors, and Molière began to compose some short, comic plays for the group to perform before their main productions—for the most part, tragic dramas from the emerging French repertoire. His first full-length work, *L'Étourdi* (*The Blockhead*), based on a commedia scenario, dates from about 1655. The troupe returned to Paris in 1658, under the patronage of the king's brother; the successful production of Molière's *Les Précieuses ridicules* (*The Affected Young Ladies*) the following year secured their standing both at court and with the Parisian public. In 1660, the king granted them the right to perform at the Palais Royal theater. New challenges soon arose, however. Beginning with his companion pieces *L'École des maris* and *L'École des femmes* (*The School for Husbands* and *The School for Wives*, 1661–62), Molière repeatedly found himself embroiled in public controversy, as his comedies assailed the mores and exposed the foibles of Parisian society. Yet these disputes pale in comparison to the religious furor that erupted over *Tartuffe*.

The Protestant reform movement that had swept over much of Europe during the sixteenth century had little affect on France owing mainly to the Catholic Church's brutal suppression of the Protestant Huguenots, which began with the St. Bartholomew's Day Massacre in 1572. Henry IV's Edict of Nantes, issued in 1598, officially ended France's half century of religious wars and placed the country firmly within the control of a moderate but decidedly Catholic monarchy. Although Catholic rule by Molière's time was more tolerant than the bloody repression that had preceded it, the church's oversight of many aspects of French life remained largely unchecked throughout the seventeenth century. At the same time, a wide range of ideological positions existed within French Catholicism, from the strict asceticism of the Jansenists to the more worldly open-mindedness of the Christian humanists to the scholastics' focus on doctrine. Adding to this sometimes fractious mix were religious organizations such as the Compagnie du Saint-Sacrement (Society of the Blessed Sacrament), whose members—many powerful laypeople among them—combined charitable work with efforts to enforce a strict moral code. Such internal frictions did not affect the church's hostility to the theater, especially the profession of acting; its opposition had been strong since the late Middle Ages. Because the church viewed theatrical representation, or pretense to another identity, as inherently sinful, actors lived under the constant threat of excommunication. Indeed, because Molière died suddenly—within hours after coughing up blood while performing in his *Le Malade imaginaire* (*The Imaginary Invalid*, 1673)—as an unrepentant actor he was denied a full Christian burial.

Even Louis XIV had to approach such matters carefully. Far from devout, he nevertheless recognized the enormous political power of the clergy in his country. Within his own household, he had to deal with the exacting religious strictures of his mother, the Dowager Queen Anne d'Autriche—a model, scholars believe, for Mme Pernelle, *Tartuffe*'s overbearing mother figure. Yet the king, like Molière, well understood that some individuals used declarations of faith for personal gain; with royal acquiescence or perhaps even encouragement, Molière could expose their hypocrisy and turn the tables on those who defamed his profession. In *Tartuffe,* the vices long attributed to the theater are ascribed to the character who would have been among the theater's most vocal opponents: Tartuffe himself.

Molière quickly establishes the conflict that will dominate the play's action. The well-to-do but gullible Monsieur Orgon and his domineering mother have fallen under the influence of Monsieur Tartuffe, a man who pretends to great humility, self-sacrifice, and religious devotion. Orgon takes Tartuffe into his home and begins to treat him as his most valued relation. Although Orgon's wife and children see through Tartuffe, they cannot convince Orgon or his mother of the pretense. Events take a more serious turn when Orgon decides to marry his daughter to the hypocrite rather than the man to whom she is betrothed, Valère. This decision in turn threatens the happiness of his son Damis, who is engaged to Valère's sister. Indeed, Orgon endangers the well-being of his entire family by entrusting Tartuffe with secret information and even his property. Ultimately, through the efforts of his resourceful wife Elmire and the intervention of the king, Tartuffe's true nature is revealed, and the family is saved from disaster.

Molièristes have long argued inconclusively about whether the playwright based the figure of Tartuffe on any particular individual or on features of any specific Catholic faction. Just as plausibly, Tartuffe may be a composite portrait drawn from Molière's keen observations of false devotion. Realistic yet indeterminate, the characterization incensed a number of religious leaders, precisely because its subtle inclusion of elements of many different groups' ideologies enabled it to be interpreted as an attack on widely disparate religious individuals and their affiliations. As Molière noted in a letter to the king in 1667,

> The men whom I depict in my comedy [*Tartuffe*] . . . know how to display all of their aims in the most favorable light; yet, no matter how pious they may seem, it is surely not the interests of God which stir them; they have proven this often enough in the comedies they have allowed to be performed hundreds of times without making the least objection. Those plays attacked only piety and religion, for which they care very little; but this play attacks and makes fun of them, and that is what they cannot bear.

Already in 1664, after the king—clearly under pressure from religious leaders or powerful members of the Compagnie du Saint-Sacrement—had banned the play following its initial performance, Molière was warning Louis XIV that "the Tartuffes have skillfully gained Your Majesty's favor, and the models [i.e., the religious hypocrites] have succeeded in eliminating the copy [i.e., the play]." In both letters, Molière tried to alert the king to the connections between what was represented in the play itself and what was going on at court and in Parisian society, and to persuade him to allow the play to be staged once again.

Complicating our understanding of these issues and the elements of the play that initially spawned the controversy is the script's history: only the last of its three different versions still exists. On May 12, 1664, at the request of Louis XIV, Molière presented at Versailles a new three-act play titled *Tartuffe ou L'Hypocrite*. While we will never know how closely the final play corresponds to this first performance, many scholars believe that it contained what in our text are acts 1, 3, and 4—those scenes focusing on Tartuffe and his increasing dominance in Orgon's household. Over the next five years, Molière would make numerous attempts to have the ban on *Tartuffe* lifted; to appease his opponents, he also significantly revised and expanded the play. Molière hints in his second letter to the king that Tartuffe was originally costumed as a cleric, but that he was attired later as a lay figure, with long hair and lace on his clothing. In the second version Molière also changed the character's name to Panulphe, making him a sword-carrying man of the world. But these alterations satisfied no one, and Molière subsequently dropped them. In his preface to the final version, Molière explains that in revising the play, he had

> used all the art and skill that I could to distinguish clearly the character of the hypocrite from that of the truly devout man. For that purpose I used two whole acts to prepare the appearance of my scoundrel. Never is there a moment's doubt about his character; he is known at once from the qualities I have given him; and from one end of the play to the other, he does not say a word, he does not perform an action which does not depict to the audience the character of a wicked man.

Finally, in February 1669, the king acceded to the playwright's requests, allowing the work now titled *Tartuffe ou L'Imposteur* to be performed in public. The reason for his change of heart remains a mystery, but scholars believe that the death of the dowager queen may have removed one major obstacle; other likely factors were Molière's revisions and his persuasive arguments that by exposing and ridiculing hypocrisy, the comedy could benefit the public. Audiences responded with wild enthusiasm; *Tartuffe* became the most popular play of its era and beyond, with more than 2,000 performances at the Comédie Française, the French national theater, between 1680 and 1900.

One of the keys to the work's success is its timelessness: the bourgeois family narrative of generational conflict and endangered love relationships transcends the play's origins in the specific religious and political context of the 1660s. *Tartuffe* weaves together time-honored characters and plot elements, popular since the heyday of Roman comedy, with enduring concerns

Frontispiece of a 1682 printing of *Tartuffe, ou L'Imposteur.*

about the law, justice, leadership, and the relationship between the family and the state.

To be sure, the second act, with its extended quarrel between Mariane and her lover Valère over their true feelings for each other, and the fifth act, with its whirlwind of events leading up to the ultimately happy ending, may at first strike some as tacked on and having little relation to the play's central concern—Tartuffe and his duplicitous nature. Yet a common theme of illusion versus reality ties the marriage plot to the revelation of Tartuffe's deceptions. Just as the lovers must work through their false assumptions to rediscover the truth of their mutual devotion, so Orgon and his mother must be made to see Tartuffe for who he really is. In addition, Mariane's understanding of her father's control of her marital destiny resonates with other questions of power and appropriate social behavior in the play. Orgon rules the home as the king rules the state; Orgon must learn from his monarch how to exercise that authority wisely. Tartuffe thus emerges as a threat not only to the family of Orgon but also to the entire kingdom.

Molière builds his resolution around the political trope "*L'état, c'est moi*" (I am the state), which equates monarch and realm. The somewhat fantastical denouement—which some scholars have called a "rex ex machina" on the model of the classical deus ex machina—certainly stretches the limits of verisimilitude, or *vraisemblance*. But as an extended tribute to Louis XIV, the ending did realize the Academy's principle of propriety (*bienséance*) and appears to have contributed to the work's ultimate success. Molière, here as in many of his plays, walks a fine line between following the dictates of the French Academy and realizing his own dramatic goals. His calculated decision to acknowledge the king's beneficence within *Tartuffe,* as well as to represent an idealized monarchy, provides a space that also enables him to remind Louis XIV of how to best deploy royal power to the benefit of all France.

Molière continued to explore the issues of hypocrisy, authority, and benevolence in many of his later works, including *Dom Juan, ou le Festin de pierre* (*Dom Juan, or the Feast with the Statue,* 1665), *Le Misanthrope* (1666), and *Le Bourgeois gentilhomme* (*The Bourgeois Gentleman,* 1670). Written for actors by an actor, the plays have sparked some of the theater's most legendary performances and productions. And because the timelessness of his themes ensures their timeliness across the ages, Molière's comedies have continued to serve as vehicles for social commentary. Since the seventeenth century, directors have repeatedly found these works able to critique the present moment and to reveal the vagaries and varieties of human behavior. J.E.G.

Tartuffe[1]

CHARACTERS

MADAME PERNELLE, mother of Orgon
ORGON, husband of Elmire
ELMIRE, wife of Orgon
DAMIS, son of Orgon
MARIANE, daughter of Orgon
VALÈRE, fiancé of Mariane
CLÉANTE, brother-in-law of Orgon
TARTUFFE,[2] a religious hypocrite
DORINE, lady's maid to Mariane
MONSIEUR LOYAL, a bailiff
THE EXEMPT, an officer of the king
FLIPOTE, lady's maid to Madame Pernelle
LAURENT, a servant of Tartuffe

1. Versification by Constance Congdon, from a translation by Virginia Scott.
2. The name Tartuffe is similar both to the Italian word *tartufo,* meaning "truffle," and to the French word for truffle, *truffe,* from which is derived the French verb *truffer*—one meaning of which in Molière's day was "to deceive or cheat."

The scene is Paris, in ORGON'S *house.*

1.1

[MADAME PERNELLE, FLIPOTE, ELMIRE, MARIANE, DORINE, DAMIS, CLÉANTE]

MADAME PERNELLE[3] Flipote, come on! My visit here is through!
ELMIRE You walk so fast I can't keep up with you!
MADAME PERNELLE Then stop! That's your last step! Don't take another.
After all, I'm just your husband's mother.
ELMIRE And, as his wife, I have to see you out—
Agreed? Now, what is this about?
MADAME PERNELLE I cannot bear the way this house is run—
As if I don't know how things should be done!
No one even thinks about my pleasure,
And, if I ask, I'm served at someone's leisure.
It's obvious—the values here aren't good
Or everyone would treat me as they should.
The Lord of Misrule here has his dominion—
DORINE But—
MADAME PERNELLE See? A servant with an opinion.
You're the former nanny, nothing more.
Were I in charge here, you'd be out the door.
DAMIS If—
MADAME PERNELLE —You—be quiet. Now let Grandma spell
Her special word for you: "F-O-O-L."
Oh yes! Your dear grandmother tells you that,
Just as I told my son, "Your son's a brat.
He won't become a drunkard or a thief,
And yet, he'll be a lifetime full of grief."
MARIANE I think—
MADAME PERNELLE —Oh, don't do that, my dear grandchild.
You'll hurt your brain. You think that we're beguiled
By your quietude, you fragile flower,
But as they say, still waters do run sour.
ELMIRE But Mother—
MADAME PERNELLE —Daughter-in-law, please take this well—
Behavior such as yours leads straight to hell.
You spend money like it grows on trees
Then wear it on your back in clothes like these.
Are you a princess? No? You're dressed like one!
One wonders whom you dress for—not my son.
Look to these children whom you have corrupted
When their mama's life was interrupted.
She spun in her grave when you were wed;
She's still a better mother, even dead.
CLÉANTE Madame, I do insist—
MADAME PERNELLE —You do? On what?

3. The role of Madame Pernelle was originally played by a male actor, a practice that was already a comic convention in Molière's time.

That we live life as you do, caring not
For morals? I hear each time you give that speech
Your sister memorizing what you teach.
I'd slam the door on you. Forgive my frankness.
That is how I am! And it is thankless.

DAMIS Tartuffe would, from the bottom of his heart,
If he had one, thank you.

MADAME PERNELLE Oh, now you start.
Grandson, it's "Monsieur Tartuffe" to you.
And he's a man who should be listened to.
If you provoke him with ungodly chat,
I will not tolerate it, and that's that.

DAMIS Yet I should tolerate this trickster who
Has become the voice we answer to.
And I'm to be as quiet as a mouse
About this tyrant's power in our house?
All the fun things lately we have planned,
We couldn't do. And why? Because they're banned—

DORINE By him! Anything we take pleasure in
Suddenly becomes a mortal sin.

MADAME PERNELLE Then "he's here just in time" is what I say!
Don't you see? He's showing you the way
To heaven! Yes! So follow where he leads!
My son knows he is just what this house needs.

DAMIS Now Grandmother, listen. Not Father, not you,
No one can make me follow this man who
Rules this house, yet came here as a peasant.
I'll put him in his place. It won't be pleasant.

DORINE When he came here he wasn't wearing shoes.
But he's no village saint—it's all a ruse.
There was no vow of poverty—he's poor!
And he was just some beggar at the door
Whom we should have tossed. He's a disaster!
To think this street bum now plays the master.

MADAME PERNELLE May God have mercy on me. You're all blind.
A nobler, kinder man you'll never find.

DORINE So you think he's a saint. That's what he wants.
But he's a hypocrite and merely flaunts
This so-called godliness.

MADAME PERNELLE Will you be quiet!?

DORINE And that man of his—I just don't buy it—
He's supposed to be his servant? No.
They're in cahoots, I bet.

MADAME PERNELLE How would you know?
When, clearly, you don't understand, in fact,
How a servant is supposed to act?
This holy man you think of as uncouth,
Tries to help by telling you the truth
About yourself. But you can't hear it.
He knows what heaven wants and that you fear it.

DORINE So "heaven" hates these visits by our friends?
I see! And that's why Tartuffe's gone to any ends
To ruin our fun? But it is he who's zealous
About "privacy"—and why? He's jealous.
You can't miss it, whenever men come near—
He's lusting for our own Madame Elmire.

MADAME PERNELLE Since you, Dorine, have never understood
Your place, or the concepts of "should"
And "should not," one can't expect you to see
Tartuffe's awareness of propriety.
When these men visit, they bring noise and more—
Valets and servants planted at the door,
Carriages and horses, constant chatter.
What must the neighbors think? These things matter.
Is something going on? Well, I hope not.
You know you're being talked about a lot.

CLÉANTE Really, Madame, you think you can prevent
Gossip? When most human beings are bent
On rumormongering and defamation,
And gathering or faking information
To make us all look bad—what can we do?
The fools who gossip don't care what is true.
You would force the whole world to be quiet?
Impossible! And each new lie—deny it?
Who in the world would want to live that way?
Let's live our lives. Let gossips have their say.

DORINE It's our neighbor, Daphne. I just know it.
They don't like us. It's obvious—they show it
In the way they watch us—she and her mate.
I've seen them squinting at us, through their gate.
It's true—those whose private conduct is the worst
Will mow each other down to be the first
To weave some tale of lust, so hearts are broken
Out of a simple kiss that's just a token
Between friends—just friends and nothing more.
See—those whose trysts are kept behind a door
Yet everyone finds out? Well, then, they need
New stories for the gossip mill to feed
To all who'll listen. So they must repaint
The deeds of others, hoping that a taint
Will color others' lives in darker tone
And, by this process, lighten up their own.

MADAME PERNELLE Daphne and her mate are not the point.
But when Orante says things are out of joint,
There's a problem. She's a person who
Prays every day and should be listened to.
She condemns the mob that visits here.

DORINE This good woman shouldn't live so near
Those, like us, who run a bawdy house.
I hear she lives as quiet as a mouse—

Devout, though. Everyone applauds her zeal.
She needed that when age stole her appeal.
Her passion is policing—it's her duty
And compensation for her loss of beauty.
She's a reluctant prude. And now, her art,
Once used so well to win a lover's heart,
Is gone. Her eyes, that used to flash with lust,
Are steely from her piety. She must
Have seen that it's too late to be a wife,
And so she lives a plain and pious life.
This is a strategy of old coquettes.
It's how they manage once the world forgets
Them. First, they wallow in a dark depression,
Then see no recourse but in the profession
Of a prude. They criticize the lives of everyone.
They censure everything, and pardon none.
It's envy. Pleasures that they are denied
By time and age, now, they just can't abide.

MADAME PERNELLE You do go on and on. [*To* ELMIRE] My dear Elmire,
This is all your doing. It's so clear
Because you let a servant give advice.
Just be aware—I'm tired of being nice.
It's obvious to anyone with eyes
That what my son has done is more than wise
In welcoming this man who's so devout;
His very presence casts the devils out.
Or most of them—that's why I hope you hear him.
And I advise all of you to stay near him.
You need his protection and advice.
Your casual attention won't suffice.
It's heaven sent him here to fill a need,
To save you from yourselves—oh yes, indeed.
These visits from your friends you seem to want—
Listen to yourselves! So nonchalant!
As if no evil lurks in these events.
As if you're blind to what Satan invents.
And dances! What are those but food for slander!
It's to the worst desires these parties pander.
I ask you now, what purpose do they serve?
Where gossip's passed around like an hors-d'oeuvre.
A thousand cackling hens, busy with what?
It takes a lot of noise to cover smut.
It truly is the tower of Babylon,[4]
Where people babble on and on and on.
Ah! Case in point—there stands Monsieur Cléante,

4. That is, the biblical Tower of Babel (the Hebrew equivalent of the Akkadian Bab-ilu, or Babylon—a name explained by the similar sounding but unrelated Hebrew verb *balal,* "confuse"), described in Genesis 11.1–9; to prevent it from being constructed and reaching heaven, God scattered all the people and confused their language, creating many tongues where there had been only one.

Sniggering and eyeing me askant,
As if this has nothing to do with him,
And nothing that he does would God condemn.
And so, Elmire, my dear, I say farewell.
Till when? When it is a fine day in hell.
Farewell, all of you. When I pass through that door,
You won't have me to laugh at anymore.
Flipote! Wake up! Have you heard nothing I have said?
I'll march you home and beat you till you're dead.
March, slut, march.

1.2[5]

[DORINE, CLÉANTE]

CLÉANTE I'm staying here. She's scary,
That old lady—
DORINE I know why you're wary.
Shall I call her back to hear you say,
"That *old* lady"? That would make her day.
CLÉANTE She's lost her mind, she's—now we have the proof—
Head over heels in love with whom? Tartuffe.
DORINE So here's what's worse and weird—so is her son.
What's more—it's obvious to everyone.
Before Tartuffe and he became entwined,
Orgon once ruled this house in his right mind.
In the troubled times,[6] he backed the prince,
And that took courage. We haven't seen it since.
He is intoxicated with Tartuffe—
A potion that exceeds a hundred proof.
It's put him in a trance, this devil's brew.
And so he worships this imposter who
He calls "brother" and loves more than one—
This charlatan—more than daughter, wife, son.
This charlatan hears all our master's dreams,
And all his secrets. Every thought, it seems,
Is poured out to Tartuffe, like he's his priest!
You'd think they'd see the heresy, at least.
Orgon caresses him, embraces him, and shows
More love for him than any mistress knows.
Come for a meal and who has the best seat?
Whose preferences determine what we eat?
Tartuffe consumes enough for six, is praised,
And to his health is every goblet raised,
While on his plate are piled the choicest bites.

5. In classical French drama, a new scene begins whenever a character enters or leaves the stage, even if the action continues without interruption; this convention has become known as "French scenes." Characters remaining onstage are listed; others from the previous scene can be assumed to have exited.

6. That is, during the Fronde (literally, "sling"; 1648–53), a civil war that took place while France was being ruled by a regent for Louis XIV—"the prince" whom Orgon supported—as various factions of the nobility sought to limit the growing authority of the monarchy.

Then when he belches, our master delights
In that and shouts, "God bless you!" to the beast,
As if Tartuffe's the reason for the feast.
Did I mention the quoting of each word,
As if it's the most brilliant thing we've heard?
And, oh, the miracles Tartuffe creates!
The prophecies! We write while he dictates.
All that's ridiculous. But what's evil
Is seeing the deception and upheaval
Of the master and everything he owns.
He hands him money. They're not even loans—
He's giving it away. It's gone too far.
To watch Tartuffe play him like a guitar!
And this Laurent, his man, found some lace.
Shredded it and threw it in my face.
He'd found it pressed inside *The Lives of Saints*,[7]
I thought we'd have to put him in restraints.
"To put the devil's finery beside
The words and lives of saintly souls who died—
Is action of satanical transgression!"
And so, of course, I hurried to confession.

1.3

[ELMIRE, MARIANE, DAMIS, CLÉANTE, DORINE]

ELMIRE [*to* CLÉANTE] Lucky you, you stayed. Yes, there was more,
And more preaching from Grandma, at the door.
My husband's coming! I didn't catch his eye.
I'll wait for him upstairs. Cléante, good-bye.
CLÉANTE I'll see you soon. I'll wait here below,
Take just a second for a brief hello.
DAMIS While you have him, say something for me?
My sister needs for Father to agree
To her marriage with Valère, as planned.
Tartuffe opposes it and will demand
That Father break his word, and that's not fair;
Then I can't wed the sister of Valère.
Listening only to Tartuffe's voice,
He'd break four hearts at once—
DORINE He's here.

1.4

[ORGON, CLÉANTE, DORINE]

ORGON Rejoice!
I'm back.
CLÉANTE I'm glad to see you, but I'm on my way.
Just stayed to say hello.
ORGON No more to say?
Dorine! Come back! And Cléante, why the hurry?

7. A text (*Flos Sanctorum*, 1599–1601) by the Spanish Jesuit Pedro de Ribadeneyra, available in French translation by 1646.

Indulge me for a moment. You know I worry.
I've been gone two days! There's news to tell.
Now don't hold back. Has everyone been well?
DORINE Not quite. There was that headache Madame had
The day you left. Well, it got really bad.
She had a fever—
ORGON And Tartuffe?
DORINE He's fine—
Rosy-nosed and red-cheeked, drinking your wine.
ORGON Poor man!
DORINE And then, Madame became unable
To eat a single morsel at the table.
ORGON Ah, and Tartuffe?
DORINE He sat within her sight,
Not holding back, he ate with great delight,
A brace of partridge, and a leg of mutton.
In fact, he ate so much, he popped a button.
ORGON Poor man!
DORINE That night until the next sunrise,
Your poor wife couldn't even close her eyes.
What a fever! Oh, how she did suffer!
I don't see how that night could have been rougher.
We watched her all night long, worried and weepy.
ORGON Ah, and Tartuffe?
DORINE At dinner he grew sleepy.
After such a meal, it's not surprising.
He slept through the night, not once arising.
ORGON Poor man!
DORINE At last won over by our pleading,
Madame agreed to undergo a bleeding.[8]
And this, we think, has saved her from the grave.
ORGON Ah, and Tartuffe?
DORINE Oh, he was very brave.
To make up for the blood Madame had lost
Tartuffe slurped down red wine, all at your cost.
ORGON Poor man!
DORINE Since then, they've both been fine, although
Madame needs me. I'll go and let her know
How anxious you have been about her health,
And that you prize it more than all your wealth.

1.5

[ORGON, CLÉANTE]

CLÉANTE You know that girl was laughing in your face.
I fear I'll make you angry, but in case
There is a chance you'll listen, I will try
To say that you are laughable and why.
I've never known of something so capricious

8. Bloodletting (whether by leeches or other means), for centuries a standard medical treatment for a wide range of diseases.

As letting this man do just as he wishes
In your home and to your family.
You brought him here, relieved his poverty,
And, in return—

ORGON Now you listen to me!
You're just my brother-in-law, Cléante. Quite!
You don't know this man. And don't deny it!

CLÉANTE I don't know him, yes, that may be so,
But men like him are not so rare, you know.

ORGON If you only could know him as I do,
You would be his true disciple, too.
The universe, your ecstasy would span.
This is a man . . . who . . . ha! . . . well, such a man.
Behold him. Let him teach you profound peace.
When first we met, I felt my troubles cease.
Yes, I was changed after I talked with him.
I saw my wants and needs as just a whim!
Everything that's written, all that's sung,
The world, and you and me, well, it's all dung!
Yes, it's crap! And isn't that a wonder!
The real world—it's just some spell we're under!
He's taught me to love nothing and no one!
Mother, father, wife, daughter, son—
They could die right now, I'd feel no pain.

CLÉANTE What feelings you've developed, how humane.

ORGON You just don't see him in the way I do,
But if you did, you'd feel what I feel, too.
Every day he came to church and knelt,
And from his groans, I knew just what he felt.
Those sounds he made from deep inside his soul,
Were fed by piety he could not control.
Of the congregation, who could ignore
The way he humbly bowed and kissed the floor?
And when they tried to turn away their eyes,
His fervent prayers to heaven and deep sighs
Made them witness his deep spiritual pain.
Then something happened I can't quite explain.
I rose to leave—he quickly went before
To give me holy water at the door.
He knew what I needed, so he blessed me.
I found his acolyte, he'd so impressed me,
To ask who he was and there I learned
About his poverty and how he spurned
The riches of this world. And when I tried
To give him gifts, in modesty, he cried,
"That is too much," he'd say, "A half would do."
Then gave a portion back, with much ado.
"I am not worthy. I do not deserve
Your gifts or pity. I am here to serve
The will of heaven, that and nothing more."

Then takes the gift and shares it with the poor.
So heaven spoke to me inside my head.
"Just bring him home with you" is what it said
And so I did. And ever since he came,
My home's a happy one. I also claim
A moral home, a house that's free of sin,
Tartuffe's on watch—he won't let any in.
His interest in my wife is reassuring,
She's innocent of course, but so alluring,
He tells me whom she sees and what she does.
He's more jealous than I ever was.
It's for my honor that he's so concerned.
His righteous anger's all for me, I've learned,
To the point that just the other day,
A flea annoyed him as he tried to pray,
Then he rebuked himself, as if he'd willed it—
His excessive anger when he killed it.

CLÉANTE Orgon, listen. You're out of your mind.
Or you're mocking me. Or both combined.
How can you speak such nonsense without blinking?

ORGON I smell an atheist! It's that freethinking!
Such nonsense is the bane of your existence.
And that explains your damnable resistance.
Ten times over, I've tried to save your soul
From your corrupted mind. That's still my goal.

CLÉANTE You have been corrupted by your friends,
You know of whom I speak. Your thought depends
On people who are blind and want to spread it
Like some horrid flu, and, yes, I dread it.
I'm no atheist. I see things clearly.
And what I see is loud lip service, merely,
To make exhibitionists seem devout.
Forgive me, but a prayer is not a shout.
Yet those who don't adore these charlatans
Are seen as faithless heathens by your friends.
It's as if you think you'd never find
Reason and the sacred intertwined.
You think I'm afraid of retribution?
Heaven sees my heart and their pollution.
So we should be the slaves of sanctimony?
Monkey see, monkey do, monkey phony.
The true believers we should emulate
Are not the ones who groan and lay prostrate.
And yet you see no problem in the notion
Of hypocrisy as deep devotion.
You see as one the genuine and the spurious.
You'd extend this to your money? I'm just curious.
In your business dealings, I'd submit,
You'd not confuse the gold with counterfeit.
Men are strangely made, I'd have to say.

They're burdened with their reason, till one day,
They free themselves with such force that they spoil
The noblest of things for which they toil.
Because they must go to extremes. It's a flaw.
Just a word in passing, Brother-in-law.

ORGON Oh, you are the wisest man alive, so
You know everything there is to know.
You are the one enlightened man, the sage.
You are Cato the Elder[9] of our age.
Next to you, all men are dumb as cows.

CLÉANTE I'm not the wisest man, as you espouse,
Nor do I know—what—all there is to know?
But I do know, Orgon, that quid pro quo
Does not apply at all to "false" and "true,"
And I would never trust a person who
Cannot tell them apart. See, I revere
Everyone whose worship is sincere.
Nothing is more noble or more beautiful
Than fervor that is holy, not just dutiful.
So nothing is more odious to me
Than the display of specious piety
Which I see in every charlatan
Who tries to pass for a true holy man.
Religious passion worn as a facade
Abuses what's sacred and mocks God.
These men who take what's sacred and most holy
And use it as their trade, for money, solely,
With downcast looks and great affected cries,
Who suck in true believers with their lies,
Who ceaselessly will preach and then demand
"Give up the world!" and then, by sleight of hand,
End up sitting pretty at the court,
The best in lodging and new clothes to sport.
If you're their enemy, then heaven hates you.
That's their claim when one of them berates you.
They'll say you've sinned. You'll find yourself removed
And wondering if you'll be approved
For anything, at all, ever again.
Because so heinous was this fictional "sin."
When these men are angry, they're the worst,
There's no place to hide, you're really cursed.
They use what we call righteous as their sword,
To coldly murder in the name of the Lord.
But next to these imposters faking belief,
The devotion of the true is a relief.
Our century has put before our eyes
Glorious examples we can prize.

9. Roman statesman and author (234–149 B.C.E.), famous as a stern moralist devoted to traditional Roman ideals of honor, courage, and simplicity.

Look at Ariston, and look at Periandre,
Oronte, Alcidamas, Polydore, Clitandre:[1]
Not one points out his own morality,
Instead they speak of their mortality.
They don't form cabals,[2] they don't have factions,
They don't censure other people's actions.
They see the flagrant pride in such correction
And know that humans can't achieve perfection.
They know this of themselves and yet their lives
Good faith, good works, all good, epitomize.
They don't exhibit zeal that's more intense
Than heaven shows us in its own defense.
They'd never claim a knowledge that's divine
And yet they live in virtue's own design.
They concentrate their hatred on the sin,
And when the sinner grieves, invite him in.
They leave to others the arrogance of speech.
Instead they practice what others only preach.
These are the men who show us how to live.
Their lives, the best example I can give.
These are my men, the ones whom I would follow.
Your man and his life, honestly, are hollow.
I believe you praise him quite sincerely,
I also think you'll pay for this quite dearly.
He's a fraud, this man whom you adore.

ORGON Oh, you've stopped talking. Is there any more?
CLEANTE No.
ORGON I am your servant, sir.
CLÉANTE No! wait!
There's one more thing—no more debate—
I want to change the subject, if I might.
I heard that you said the other night,
To Valère, he'd be your son-in-law.
ORGON I did.
CLÉANTE And set the date?
ORGON Yes.
CLÉANTE Did you withdraw?
ORGON I did.
CLÉANTE You're putting off the wedding? Why?
ORGON Don't know.
CLÉANTE There's more?
ORGON Perhaps.
CLÉANTE Again I'll try:
You would break your word?
ORGON I couldn't say.
CLÉANTE Then, Orgon, why did you change the day?

1. Made-up names.
2. A possible allusion to the Compagnie de Saint-Sacrement, a tightly knit group of prominent French citizens known for public works as well as strict morality; they were pejoratively referred to as the *cabale*.

ORGON Who knows?
CLÉANTE But we need to know, don't we now?
Is there a reason you would break your vow?
ORGON That depends.
CLÉANTE On what? Orgon, what is it?
Valère was the reason for my visit.
ORGON Who knows? Who knows?
CLÉANTE So there's some mystery there?
ORGON Heaven knows.
CLÉANTE It does? And now, Valère—
May he know, too?
ORGON Can't say.
CLÉANTE But, dear Orgon,
We have no information to go on.
We need to know—
ORGON What heaven wants, I'll do.
CLÉANTE Is that your final answer? Then I'm through.
But your pledge to Valère? You'll stand by it?
ORGON Good-bye.

[ORGON *exits.*]

CLÉANTE More patience, yes, I should try it.
I let him get to me. Now I confess
I fear the worst for Valère's happiness.

2.1

[ORGON, MARIANE]

ORGON Mariane.
MARIANE Father.
ORGON Come. Now. Talk with me.
MARIANE Why are you looking everywhere?
ORGON To see
If everyone is minding their own business.
So. Child, I've always loved your gentleness.
MARIANE And for your love, I'm grateful, Father dear.
ORGON Well said. And so to prove that you're sincere,
And worthy of my love, you have the task
Of doing for me anything I ask.
MARIANE Then my obedience will be my proof.
ORGON Good. What do you think of our guest, Tartuffe?
MARIANE Who, me?
ORGON Yes, you. Watch what you say right now.
MARIANE Then, Father, I will say what you allow.
ORGON Wise words, Daughter. So this is what you say:
"He is a perfect man in every way;
In body and soul, I find him divine."
And then you say, "Please Father, make him mine."
Huh?
MARIANE Huh?
ORGON Yes?
MARIANE I heard . . .

ORGON Yes.
MARIANE What did you say?
Who is this perfect man in every way,
Whom in body and soul I find divine
And ask of you, "Please, Father, make him mine?"
ORGON Tartuffe.
MARIANE All that I've said, I now amend
Because you wouldn't want me to pretend.
ORGON Absolutely not—that's so misguided.
Have it be the truth, then. It's decided.
MARIANE What?! Father, you want—
ORGON Yes, my dear, I do—
To join in marriage my Tartuffe and you.
And since I have—

2.2

[DORINE, ORGON, MARIANE]

ORGON Dorine, I know you're there!
Any secrets in this house you don't share?
DORINE "Marriage"—I think, yes, I heard a rumor,
Someone's failed attempt at grotesque humor,
So when I heard the story, I said, "No!
Preposterous! Absurd! It can't be so."
ORGON Oh, you find it preposterous? And why?
DORINE It's so outrageous, it must be a lie.
ORGON Yet it's the truth and you will believe it.
DORINE Yet as a joke is how I must receive it.
ORGON But it's a story that will soon come true.
DORINE A fantasy!
ORGON I'm getting tired of you.
Mariane, it's not a joke—
DORINE Says he,
Laughing up his sleeve for all to see.
ORGON I'm telling you—
DORINE —more make-believe for fun.
It's very good—you're fooling everyone.
ORGON You have made me really angry now.
DORINE I see the awful truth across your brow.
How can a man who looks as wise as you
Be such a fool to want—
ORGON What can I do
About a servant with a mouth like that?
The liberties you take! Decorum you laugh at!
I'm not happy with you—
DORINE Oh sir, don't frown.
A smile is just a frown turned upside down.
Be happy, sir, because you've shared your scheme,
Even though it's just a crazy dream.
Because, dear sir, your daughter is not meant
For this zealot—she's too innocent.

She'd be alarmed by his robust desire
And question heaven's sanction of this fire
And then the gossip! Your friends will talk a lot,
Because you're a man of wealth and he is not.
Could it be your reasoning has a flaw—
Choosing a beggar for a son-in-law?

ORGON You, shut up! If he has nothing now
Admire that, as if it were his vow,
This poverty. His property was lost
Because he would not pay the deadly cost
Of daily duties nibbling life away,
Leaving him with hardly time to pray.
The grandeur in his life comes from devotion
To the eternal, thus his great emotion.
And at those moments, I can plainly see
What my special task has come to be:
To end the embarrassment he feels
And the sorrow he so nobly conceals
Of the loss of his ancestral domain.
With my money, I can end his pain.
I'll raise him up to be, because I can,
With my help, again, a gentleman.

DORINE So he's a gentleman. Does that seem vain?
Then what about this piety and pain?
Those with "domains" are those of noble birth.
A holy man's domain is not on earth.
It seems to me a holy man of merit
Wouldn't brag of what he might inherit—
Even gifts in heaven, he won't mention.
To live a humble life is his intention.
Yet he wants something back? That's just ambition
To feed his pride. Is that a holy mission?
You seem upset. Is it something I said?
I'll shut up. We'll talk of her instead.
Look at this girl, your daughter, your own blood.
How will her honor fare covered with mud?
Think of his age. So from the night they're wed,
Bliss, if there is any, leaves the marriage bed,
And she'll be tied unto this elderly person.
Her dedication to fidelity will worsen
And soon he will sprout horns,[3] your holy man,
And no one will be happy. If I can
Have another word, I'd like to say
Old men and young girls are married every day,
And the young girls stray, but who's to blame
For the loss of honor and good name?
The father, who proceeds to pick a mate,
Blindly, though it's someone she may hate,

3. The traditional sign of the cuckold.

Bears the sins the daughter may commit,
Imperiling his soul because of it.
If you do this, I vow you'll hear the bell,
As you die, summoning you to hell.

ORGON You think that you can teach me how to live.

DORINE If you'd just heed the lessons that I give.

ORGON Can heaven tell me why I still endure
This woman's ramblings? Yet, of this I'm sure,
I know what's best for you—I'm your father.
I gave you to Valère, without a bother.
But I hear he gambles and what's more,
He thinks things that a Christian would abhor.
It's from free thinking that all evils stem.
No wonder, then, at church, I don't see him.

DORINE Should he race there, if he only knew
Which Mass you might attend, and be on view?
He could wait at the door with holy water.

ORGON Go away. I'm talking to my daughter.
Think, my child, he is heaven's favorite!
And age in marriage? It can flavor it,
A sweet comfit suffused with deep, deep pleasure.
You will be loving, faithful, and will treasure
Every single moment—two turtledoves—
Next to heaven, the only thing he loves.
And he will be the only one for you.
No arguments or quarrels. You'll be true.
Like two innocent children, you will thrive,
In heaven's light, thrilled to be alive.
And as a woman, surely you must know
Wives mold husbands, like making pies from dough.

DORINE Four and twenty cuckolds baked in a pie.

ORGON Ugh! What a thing to say!

DORINE Oh, really, why?
He's destined to be cheated on, it's true.
You know he'd always question her virtue.

ORGON Quiet! Just be quiet. I command it!

DORINE I'll do just that, because you do demand it!
But your best interests—I will protect them.

ORGON Too kind of you. Be quiet and neglect them.

DORINE If I weren't fond of you—

ORGON —Don't want you to

DORINE I will be fond of you in spite of you.

ORGON Don't!

DORINE But your honor is so dear to me,
How can you expose yourself to mockery?

ORGON Will you never be quiet!

DORINE Oh, dear sir,
I can't let you do this thing to her,
It's against my conscience—

ORGON You vicious asp!

DORINE Sometimes the things you call me make me gasp.
And anger, sir, is not a pious trait.
ORGON It's your fault, girl! You make me irate!
I am livid! Why won't you be quiet!
DORINE I will. For you, I'm going to try it.
But I'll be thinking.
ORGON Fine. Now, Mariane,
You have to trust—your father's a wise man.
I have thought a lot about this mating.
I've weighed the options—
DORINE It's infuriating
Not to be able to speak.
ORGON And so
I'll say this. Of up and coming men I know,
He's not one of them, no money in the bank,
Not handsome.
DORINE That's the truth. Arf! Arf! Be frank.
He's a dog!
ORGON He has manly traits.
And other gifts.
DORINE And who will blame the fates
For failure of this marriage made in hell?
And whose fault will it be? Not hard to tell.
Since everyone you know will see the truth:
You gave away your daughter to Tartuffe.
If I were in her place, I'd guarantee
No man would live the night who dared force me
Into a marriage that I didn't want.
There would be war with no hope of détente.
ORGON I asked for silence. This is what I get?
DORINE You said not to talk to *you*. Did you forget?
ORGON What do you call what you are doing now?
DORINE Talking to myself.
ORGON You insolent cow!
I'll wait for you to say just one more word.
I'm waiting . . .

[ORGON *prepares to give* DORINE *a smack but each time he looks over at her, she stands silent and still.*]

Just ignore her. Look at me.
I've chosen you a husband who would be,
If rated, placed among the highest ranks.
[*To* DORINE] Why don't you talk?
DORINE Don't feel like it, thanks.
ORGON I'm watching you.
DORINE Do you think I'm a fool?
ORGON I realize that you may think me cruel.
But here's the thing, child, I will be obeyed,
And this marriage, child, will not be delayed.
DORINE [*running from* ORGON, DORINE *throws a line to* MARIANE]
You'll be a joke with Tartuffe as a spouse.

[ORGON *tries to slap her but misses.*]

ORGON What we have is a plague in our own house!
It's her fault that I'm in the state I'm in,
So furious, I might commit a sin.
She'll drive me to murder. Or to curse.
I need fresh air before my mood gets worse. [ORGON *exits.*]

2.3

[DORINE, MARIANE]

DORINE Tell me, have you lost the power of speech?
I'm forced to play your role and it's a reach.
How can you sit there with nothing to say
Watching him tossing your whole life away?
MARIANE Against my father, what am I to do?
DORINE You want out of this marriage scheme, don't you?
MARIANE Yes.
DORINE Tell him no one can command a heart.
That when you marry, you will have no part
Of anyone unless he pleases you.
And tell your father, with no more ado,
That you will marry for yourself, not him,
And that you won't obey his iron whim.
Since he finds Tartuffe to be such a catch,
He can marry him himself. There's a match.
MARIANE You know that fathers have such sway
Over our lives that I've nothing to say.
I've never had the strength.
DORINE Let's think. All right?
Didn't Valère propose the other night?
Do you or don't you love Valère?
MARIANE You know the answer, Dorine—that's unfair.
Just talking about it tears me apart.
I've said a hundred times, he has my heart.
I'm wild about him. I know. And I've told you.
DORINE But how am I to know, for sure, that's true?
MARIANE Because I told you. And yet you doubt it?
See me blushing when I speak about it?
DORINE So you do love him?
MARIANE Yes, with all my might.
DORINE He loves you just as much?
MARIANE I think that's right.
DORINE And it's to the altar you're both heading?
MARIANE Yes.
DORINE So what about this other wedding?
MARIANE I'll kill myself. That's what I've decided.
DORINE What a great solution you've provided!
To get out of trouble, you plan to die!
Immediately? Or sometime, by and by?
MARIANE Oh, really, Dorine, you're not my friend,
Unsympathetic—

DORINE I'm at my wit's end,
Talking to you whose answer is dying,
Who, in a crisis, just gives up trying.
MARIANE What do you want of me, then?
DORINE Come alive!
Love needs a resolute heart to survive.
MARIANE In my love for Valère, I'm resolute.
But the next step is his.
DORINE And so, you're mute?
MARIANE What can I say? It's the job of Valère,
His duty, before I go anywhere,
To deal with my father—
DORINE —Then, you'll stay.
"Orgon was born bizarre" is what some say.
It there were doubts before, we have this proof—
He is head over heels for his Tartuffe,
And breaks off a marriage that he arranged.
Valère's at fault if your father's deranged?
MARIANE But my refusal will be seen as pride
And, worse, contempt. And I have to hide
My feelings for Valère, I must not show
That I'm in love at all. If people know,
Then all the modesty my sex is heir to
Will be gone. There's more: how can I bear to
Not be a proper daughter to my father?
DORINE No, no, of course not. God forbid we bother
The way the world sees you. What people see,
What other people think of us, should be
Our first concern. Besides, I see the truth:
You really want to be Madame Tartuffe.
What was I thinking, urging opposition
To Monsieur Tartuffe! This proposition,
To merge with him—he's such a catch!
In fact, for you, he's just the perfect match.
He's much respected, everywhere he goes.
And his ruddy complexion nearly glows.
And as his wife, imagine the delight
Of being near him, every day and night.
And vital? Oh, my dear, you won't want more.
MARIANE Oh, heaven help me!
DORINE How your soul will soar,
Savoring this marriage down to the last drop,
With such a handsome—
MARIANE All right! You can stop!
Just help me. Please. And tell me there's a way
To save me. I'll do whatever you say.
DORINE Each daughter must choose always to say yes
To what her father wants, no more and no less.
If he wants to give her an ape to marry,
Then she must do it, without a query.

But it's a happy fate! What is this frown?
You'll go by wagon to his little town,
Eager cousins, uncles, aunts will greet you
And will call you "sister" when they meet you,
Because you're family now. Don't look so grim.
You will so adore chatting with them.
Welcomed by the local high society,
You'll be expected to maintain propriety
And sit straight, or try to, in the folding chair
They offer you, and never, ever stare
At the wardrobe of the bailiff's wife
Because you'll see her every day for life.[4]
Let's not forget the village carnival!
Where you'll be dancing at a lavish ball
To a bagpipe orchestra of locals,
An organ grinder's monkey doing vocals—
And your husband—

MARIANE —Dorine, I beg you, please,
Help me. Should I get down here on my knees?

DORINE Can't help you.

MARIANE Please, Dorine, I'm begging you!

DORINE And you deserve this man.

MARIANE That just not true!

DORINE Oh yes? What changed?

MARIANE My darling Dorine . . .

DORINE No.

MARIANE You can't be this mean.
I love Valère. I told you and it's true.

DORINE Who's that? Oh. No, Tartuffe's the one for you.

MARIANE You've always been completely on my side.

DORINE No more. I sentence you to be Tartuffified!

MARIANE It seems my fate has not the power to move you,
So I'll seek my solace and remove to
A private place for me in my despair.
To end the misery that brought me here.

[MARIANE *starts to exit.*]

DORINE Wait! Wait! Come back! Please don't go out that door.
I'll help you. I'm not angry anymore.

MARIANE If I am forced into this martyrdom,
You see, I'll have to die, Dorine.

DORINE Oh come,
Give up this torment. Look at me—I swear.
We'll find a way. Look, here's your love, Valère.

[DORINE *moves to the side of the stage.*]

4. Dorine's description reflects the stereotypes associated with rural pretensions to culture.

2.4

[VALÈRE, MARIANE, DORINE]

VALÈRE So I've just heard some news that's news to me,
And very fine news it is, do you agree?
MARIANE What?
VALÈRE You have plans for marriage I didn't know.
You're going to marry Tartuffe. Is this so?
MARIANE My father has that notion, it is true.
VALÈRE Madame, your father promised—
MARIANE —me to you?
He changed his mind, announced this change to me,
Just minutes ago . . .
VALÈRE Quite seriously?
MARIANE It's his wish that I should marry this man.
VALÈRE And what do you think of your father's plan?
MARIANE I don't know.
VALÈRE Honest words—better than lies.
You don't know?
MARIANE No.
VALÈRE No?
MARIANE What do you advise?
VALÈRE I advise you to . . . marry Tartuffe. Tonight.
MARIANE You advise me to . . .
VALÈRE Yes.
MARIANE Really?
VALÈRE That's right.
Consider it. It's an obvious choice.
MARIANE I'll follow your suggestion and rejoice.
VALÈRE I'm sure that you can follow it with ease.
MARIANE Just as you gave it. It will be a breeze.
VALÈRE Just to please you was my sole intent.
MARIANE To please you, I'll do it and be content.
DORINE I can't wait to see what happens next.
VALÈRE And this is love to you? I am perplexed.
Was it a sham when you—
MARIANE That's in the past
Because you said so honestly and fast
That I should take the one bestowed on me.
I'm nothing but obedient, you see,
So, yes, I'll take him. That's my declaration,
Since that's your advice and expectation.
VALÈRE I see, you're using me as an excuse,
Any pretext, so you can cut me loose.
You didn't think I'd notice—I'd be blind
To the fact that you'd made up your mind?
MARINE How true. Well said.
VALÈRE And so it's plain to see,
Your heart never felt a true love for me.

MARIANE If you want to, you may think that is true.
It's clear this thought has great appeal for you.
VALÈRE If I want? I will, but I'm offended
To my very soul. But your turn's ended,
And I can win this game we're playing at:
I've someone else in mind.
MARIANE I don't doubt that.
Your good points—
VALÈRE Oh, let's leave them out of this.
I've very few—in fact, I am remiss.
I must be. Right? You've made that clear to me.
But I know someone, hearing that I'm free,
To make up for my loss, will eagerly consent.
MARIANE The loss is not that bad. You'll be content
With your new choice, replacement, if you will.
VALÈRE I will. And I'll remain contented still,
In knowing you're as happy as I am.
A woman tells a man her love's a sham.
The man's been fooled and his honor blighted.
He can't deny his love is unrequited,
Then he forgets this woman totally,
And if he can't, pretends, because, you see,
It is ignoble conduct and weak, too,
Loving someone who does not love you.
MARIANE What a fine, noble sentiment to heed.
VALÈRE And every man upholds it as his creed.
What? You expect me to keep on forever
Loving you after you blithely sever
The bond between us, watching as you go
Into another's arms and not bestow
This heart you've cast away upon someone
Who might welcome—
MARIANE I wish it were done.
That's exactly what I want, you see.
VALÈRE That's what you want?
MARIANE Yes.
VALÈRE Then let it be.
I'll grant your wish.
MARIANE Please do.
VALÈRE Just don't forget,
Whose fault it was when you, filled with regret,
Realize that you forced me out the door.
MARIANE True.
VALÈRE You've set the example and what's more,
I'll match you with my own hardness of heart.
You won't see me again, if I depart.
MARIANE That's good!
[VALÈRE *goes to exit, but when he gets to the door, he returns.*]

VALÈRE What?
MARIANE What?
VALÈRE You said . . . ?
MARIANE Nothing at all.
VALÈRE Well, I'll be on my way, then.
[*He goes, stops.*]
Did you call?
MARIANE Me? You must be dreaming.
VALÈRE I'll go away.
Good-bye, then.
MARIANE Good-bye.
DORINE I am here to say,
You both are idiots! What's this about?
I left you two alone to fight it out,
To see how far you'd go. You're quite a pair
In matching tit for tat— Hold on, Valère!
Where are you going?
VALÈRE What, Dorine? You spoke?
DORINE Come here.
VALÈRE I'm upset and will not provoke
This lady. Do not try to change my mind.
I'm doing what she wants.
DORINE You are so blind.
Just stop.
VALÈRE No. It's settled.
DORINE Oh, is that so?
MARIANE He can't stand to look at me, I know.
He wants to go away, so please let him.
No, I shall leave so I can forget him.
DORINE Where are you going?
MARIANE Leave me alone.
DORINE Come back here at once.
MARIANE No. Even that tone
Won't bring me. I'm not a child, you see.
VALÈRE She's tortured by the very sight of me.
It's better that I free her from her pain.
DORINE What more proof do you need? You are insane!
Now stop this nonsense! Come here both of you.
VALÈRE To what purpose?
MARIANE What are you trying to do?
DORINE Bring you two together! And end this fight.
It's so stupid! Yes?
VALÈRE No. It wasn't right
The way she spoke to me. Didn't you hear?
DORINE Your voices are still ringing in my ear.
MARIANE The way he treated me—you didn't see?
DORINE Saw and heard it all. Now listen to me.
The only thing she wants, Valère, is you.
I can attest to that right now. It's true.

And Mariane, he wants you for his wife,
And only you. On that I'll stake my life.

MARIANE He told me to be someone else's bride!

VALÈRE She asked for my advice and I replied!

DORINE You're both impossible. What can I do?
Give your hand—

VALÈRE What for?

DORINE Come on, you.
Now yours, Mariane—don't make me shout.
Come on!

MARIANE All right. But what is this about?

DORINE Here. Take each other's hand and make a link.
You love each other better than you think.

VALÈRE Mademoiselle, this is your hand I took,
You think you could give me a friendly look?

[MARIANE *peeks at* VALÈRE *and smiles.*]

DORINE It's true. Lovers are not completely sane.

VALÈRE Mariane, haven't I good reason to complain?
Be honest. Wasn't it a wicked ploy?
To say—

MARIANE You think I told you that with joy?
And you confronted me.

DORINE Another time.
This marriage to Tartuffe would be a crime,
We have to stop it.

MARIANE So, what can we do?
Tell us.

DORINE All sorts of things involving you.
It's all nonsense and your father's joking.
But if you play along, say, without choking,
And give your consent, for the time being,
He'll take the pressure off, thereby freeing
All of us to find a workable plan
To keep you from a marriage with this man.
Then you can find a reason every day
To postpone the wedding, in this way:
One day you're sick and that can take a week.
Another day you're better but can't speak,
And we all know you have to say "I do,"
Or the marriage isn't legal. And that's true.
Now bad omens—would he have his daughter
Married when she's dreamt of stagnant water,
Or broken a mirror or seen the dead?
He may not care and say it's in your head,
But you will be distraught in your delusion,
And require bed rest and seclusion.
I do know this—if we want to succeed,
You can't be seen together. [*To* VALÈRE] With all speed,
Go, and gather all your friends right now,

Have them insist that Orgon keep his vow.
Social pressure helps. Then to her brother.
All of us will work on her stepmother.
Let's go.

VALÈRE Whatever happens, can you see?
My greatest hope is in your love for me.

MARIANE Though I don't know just what Father will do,
I do know I belong only to you.

VALÈRE You put my heart at ease! I swear I will . . .

DORINE It seems that lovers' tongues are never still.
Out, I tell you.

VALÈRE [*taking a step and returning*] One last—

DORINE No more chat!
You go out this way, yes, and you go that.

3.1

[DAMIS, DORINE]

DAMIS May lightning strike me dead, right here and now,
Call me a villain, if I break this vow:
Forces of heaven or earth won't make me sway
From this my—

DORINE Let's not get carried away.
Your father only said what he intends
To happen. The real event depends
On many things and something's bound to slip,
Between this horrid cup and his tight lip.

DAMIS That this conceited fool Father brought here
Has plans? Well, they'll be ended—do not fear.

DORINE Now stop that! Forget him. Leave him alone.
Leave him to your stepmother. He is prone,
This Tartuffe, to indulge her every whim.
So let her use her power over him.
It does seem pretty clear he's soft on her,
Pray God that's true. And if he will concur
That this wedding your father wants is bad,
That's good. But he might want it, too, the cad.
She's sent for him so she can sound him out
On this marriage you're furious about,
Discover what he feels and tell him clearly
If he persists that it will cost him dearly.
It seems he can't be seen while he's at prayers,
So I have my own vigil by the stairs
Where his valet says he will soon appear.
Do leave right now, and I'll wait for him here.

DAMIS I'll stay to vouch for what was seen and heard.

DORINE They must be alone.

DAMIS I won't say a word.

DORINE Oh, right. I know what you are like. Just go.
You'll spoil everything, believe me, I know.
Out!

DAMIS I promise I won't get upset.

[DORINE *pinches* DAMIS *as she used to do when he was a child.*]

Ow!

DORINE Do as I say. Get out of here right *now!*

3.2

[TARTUFFE, LAURENT, DORINE]

TARTUFFE [*noticing* DORINE] Laurent, lock up my scourge and hair shirt,[5] too.
And pray that our Lord's grace will shine on you.
If anyone wants me, I've gone to share
My alms at prison with the inmates there.

DORINE What a fake! What an imposter! What a sleaze!

TARTUFFE What do you want?

DORINE To say—

TARTUFFE [*taking a handkerchief from his pocket*] Good heavens, please,
Do take this handkerchief before you speak.

DORINE What for?

TARTUFFE Cover your bust. The flesh is weak.
Souls are forever damaged by such sights,
When sinful thoughts begin their evil flights.

DORINE It seems temptation makes a meal of you—
To turn you on, a glimpse of flesh will do.
Inside your heart, a furnace must be housed.
For me, I'm not so easily aroused.
I could see you naked, head to toe—
Never be tempted once, and this I know.

TARTUFFE Please! Stop! And if you're planning to resume
This kind of talk, I'll leave the room.

DORINE If someone is to go, let it be me.
Yes, I can't wait to leave your company.
Madame is coming down from her salon,
And wants to talk to you, if you'll hang on.

TARTUFFE Of course. Most willingly.

DORINE [*aside*] Look at him melt.
I'm right. I always knew that's how he felt.

TARTUFFE Is she coming soon?

DORINE You want me to leave?
Yes, here she is in person, I believe.

3.3

[ELMIRE, TARTUFFE]

TARTUFFE Ah, may heaven in all its goodness give
Eternal health to you each day you live,
Bless your soul and body, and may it grant
The prayerful wishes of this supplicant.

5. Implements to mortify his flesh (penitential practices of religious ascetics).

ELMIRE Yes. Thank you for that godly wish, and please,
Let's sit down so we can talk with ease.
TARTUFFE Are you recovered from your illness now?
ELMIRE My fever disappeared, I don't know how.
TARTUFFE My small prayers, I'm sure, had not the power,
Though I was on my knees many an hour.
Each fervent prayer wrenched from my simple soul
Was made with your recovery as its goal.
ELMIRE I find your zeal a little disconcerting.
TARTUFFE I can't enjoy my health if you are hurting.
Your health's true worth, I can't begin to tell.
I'd give mine up, in fact, to make you well.
ELMIRE Though you stretch Christian charity too far,
Your thoughts are kind, however strange they are.
TARTUFFE You merit more, that's in my humble view.
ELMIRE I need a private space to talk to you.
I think that this will do—what do you say?
TARTUFFE Excellent choice. And this is a sweet day,
To find myself here tête-à-tête with you,
That I've begged heaven for this, yes, is true,
And now it's granted to my great relief.
ELMIRE Although our conversation will be brief,
Please open up your heart and tell me all.
You must hide nothing now, however small.
TARTUFFE I long to show you my entire soul,
My need for truth I can barely control.
I'll take this time, also, to clear the air—
The criticisms I have brought to bear
Around the visits that your charms attract,
Were never aimed at you or how you act,
But rather were my own transports of zeal,
Which carried me away with how I feel,
Consumed by impulses, though always pure,
Nevertheless, intense in how—
ELMIRE I'm sure
That my salvation is your only care.
TARTUFFE [*grasping her fingertips*] Yes, you're right, and so my fervor there—
ELMIRE Ouch! You're squeezing too hard.
TARTUFFE —comes from this zeal . . .
I didn't mean to squeeze. How does this feel?
[*He puts his hand on* ELMIRE*'s knee.*]
ELMIRE Your hand—what is it doing . . . ?
TARTUFFE So tender,
The fabric of your dress, a sweet surrender
Under my hand—
ELMIRE I'm quite ticklish. Please, don't.
[*She moves her chair back, and* TARTUFFE *moves his forward.*]
TARTUFFE I want to touch this lace—don't fret, I won't.
It's marvelous! I so admire the trade
Of making lace. Don't tell me you're afraid.

ELMIRE What? No. But getting back to business now,
It seems my husband plans to break a vow
And offer you his daughter. Is this true?
TARTUFFE He mentioned it, but I must say to you,
The wondrous gifts that catch my zealous eye,
I see quite near in bounteous supply.
ELMIRE Not earthly things for which you would atone.
TARTUFFE My chest does not contain a heart of stone.
ELMIRE Well, I believe your eyes follow your soul,
And your desires have heaven as their goal.
TARTUFFE The love that to eternal beauty binds us
Doesn't stint when temporal beauty finds us.
Our senses can as easily be charmed
When by an earthly work we are disarmed.
You are a rare beauty, without a flaw,
And in your presence, I'm aroused with awe
But for the Author of All Nature, so,
My heart has ardent feelings, even though
I feared them at first, questioning their source.
Had I been ambushed by some evil force?
I felt that I must hide from this temptation:
You. My feelings threatened my salvation.
Yes, I found this sinful and distressing,
Until I saw your beauty as a blessing!
So now my passion never can be wrong,
And, thus, my virtue stays intact and strong.
That is how I'm here in supplication,
Offering my heart in celebration
Of the audacious truth that I love you,
That only you can make this wish come true,
That through your grace, my offering's received,
And accepted, and that I have achieved
Salvation of a sort, and by your grace,
I could be content in this low place.
It all depends on you, at your behest—
Am I to be tormented or be blest?
You are my welfare, solace, and my hope,
But, whatever your decision, I will cope.
Will I be happy? I'll rely on you.
If you want me to be wretched, that's fine, too.
ELMIRE Well, what a declaration! How gallant!
But I'm surprised you want the things you want.
It seems your heart could use a talking to—
It's living in the chest of someone who
Proclaims to be pious—
TARTUFFE —And so I am.
My piety's a true thing—not a sham,
But I'm no less a man, so when I find
Myself with you, I quickly lose my mind.
My heart is captured and, with it, my thought.

Yet since I know the cause, I'm not distraught.
Words like these from me must be alarming,
But it is your beauty that's so charming,
I cannot help myself, I am undone.
And I'm no angel, nor could I be one.
If my confession earns your condemnation,
Then blame your glance for the annihilation
Of my command of this: my inmost being.
A surrender of my soul is what you're seeing.
Your eyes blaze with more than human splendor,
And that first look had the effect to render
Powerless the bastions of my heart.
No fasting, tears or prayers, no pious art
Could shield my soul from your celestial gaze
Which I will worship till the End of Days.[6]
A thousand times my eyes, my sighs have told
The truth that's in my heart. Now I am bold,
Encouraged by your presence, so I say,
With my true voice, will this be the day
You condescend to my poor supplication,
Offered up with devout admiration,
And save my soul by granting this request:
Accept this love I've lovingly confessed?
Your honor has, of course, all my protection,
And you can trust my absolute discretion.
For those men that all the women die for,
Love's a game whose object is a high score.
Although they promise not to talk, they will.
They need to boast of their superior skill,
Receive no favors not as soon revealed,
Exposing what they vowed would be concealed.
And in the end, this love is overpriced,
When a woman's honor's sacrificed.
But men like me burn with a silent flame,
Our secrets safe, our loves we never name,
Because our reputations are our wealth.
When we transgress, it's with the utmost stealth.
Your honor's safe as my hand in a glove,
So I can offer, free from scandal, love,
And pleasure without fear of intervention.

ELMIRE Your sophistry does not hide your intention.
In fact, you know, it makes it all too clear.
What if, through me, my husband were to hear
About this love for me you now confess
Which shatters the ideals you profess?
How would your friendship fare, then, I wonder?

TARTUFFE It's your beauty cast this spell I suffer under.
I'm made of flesh, like you, like all mankind.

6. That is, the final days before human history ends and the Kingdom of God is established.

And since your soul is pure, you will be kind,
And not judge me harshly for my brashness
In speaking of my love in all its rashness.
I beg you to forgive me my offense,
I plead your perfect face as my defense.

ELMIRE Some might take offense at your confession,
But I will show a definite discretion,
And keep my husband in the dark about
These sinful feelings for me that you spout.
But I want something from you in return:
There's a promised marriage, you will learn,
That supersedes my husband's recent plan—
The marriage of Valère and Mariane.
This marriage you will openly support,
Without a single quibble, and, in short,
Renounce the unjust power of a man
Who'd give his own daughter, Mariane,
To another when she's promised to Valère.
In return, my silence—

3.4

[ELMIRE, DAMIS, TARTUFFE]

DAMIS [*jumping out from where he had been hiding*]
—Hold it right there!
No, no! You're done. All this will be revealed.
I heard each word. And as I was concealed,
Something besides your infamy came clear:
Heaven in its great wisdom brought me here,
To witness and then give my father proof
Of the hypocrisy of his Tartuffe,
This so-called saint anointed from above.
Speaking to my father's wife of love!

ELMIRE Damis, there is a lesson to be learned,
And there is my forgiveness to be earned.
I promised him. Don't make me take it back.
It's not my nature to see as an attack
Such foolishness as this, or see the need
To tell my husband of the trivial deed.

DAMIS So, you have your reasons, but I have mine.
To grant this fool forgiveness? I decline.
To want to spare him is a mockery,
Because he's more than foolish, can't you see?
This fanatic in his insolent pride,
Brought chaos to my house, and would divide
Me and my father—unforgivable!
What's more, he's made my life unlivable,
As he undermines two true love affairs,
Mine and Valère's sister, my sister and Valère's!
Father must hear the truth about this man.
Heaven helped me—I must do what I can

To use this chance. I'd deserve to lose it,
If I dropped it now and didn't use it.
ELMIRE Damis—
DAMIS No, please, I have to follow through.
I've never felt as happy as I do
Right now. And don't try to dissuade me—
I'll have my revenge. If you forbade me,
I'd still do it, so you don't have to bother.
I'll finish this for good. Here comes my father.

3.5

[ORGON, DAMIS, TARTUFFE, ELMIRE]

DAMIS Father! You have arrived. Let's celebrate!
I have a tale that I'd like to relate.
It happened here and right before my eyes,
I offer it to you—as a surprise!
For all your love, you have been repaid
With duplicity. You have been betrayed
By your dear friend here, whom I just surprised
Making verbal love, I quickly surmised,
To your wife. Yes, this is how he shows you
How he honors you—he thinks he knows you.
But as your son, I know you much better—
You demand respect down to the letter.
Madame, unflappable and so discreet,
Would keep this secret, never to repeat.
But, as your son, my feelings are too strong,
And to be silent is to do you wrong.
ELMIRE One learns to spurn without being unkind,
And how to spare a husband's peace of mind.
Although I understood just what he meant,
My honor wasn't touched by this event.
That's how I feel. And you would have, Damis,
Said nothing, if you had listened to me.

3.6

[ORGON, DAMIS, TARTUFFE]

ORGON Good heavens! What he said? Can it be true?
TARTUFFE Yes, my brother, I'm wicked through and through.
The most miserable of sinners, I.
Filled with iniquity, I should just die.
Each moment of my life's so dirty, soiled,
Whatever I come near is quickly spoiled.
I'm nothing but a heap of filth and crime.
I'd name my sins, but we don't have the time.
And I see that heaven, to punish me,
Has mortified my soul quite publicly.
What punishment I get, however great,
I well deserve so I'll accept my fate.
Defend myself? I'd face my own contempt,

If I thought that were something I'd attempt.
What you've heard here, surely, you abhor,
So chase me like a criminal from your door.
Don't hold back your rage, please, let it flame,
For I deserve to burn, in my great shame.

ORGON [*to* DAMIS] Traitor! And how dare you even try
To tarnish this man's virtue with a lie?

DAMIS What? This hypocrite pretends to be contrite
And you believe him over me?

ORGON That's spite!
And shut your mouth!

TARTUFFE No, let him have his say.
And don't accuse him. Don't send him away.
Believe his story—why be on my side?
You don't know what motives I may hide.
Why give me so much loyalty and love?
Do you know what I am capable of?
My brother, you have total trust in me,
And think I'm good because of what you see?
No, no, by my appearance you're deceived,
And what I say you think must be believed.
Well, believe this—I have no worth at all.
The world sees me as worthy, yet I fall
Far below. Sin is so insidious.
[*To* DAMIS] Dear son, do treat me as perfidious,
Infamous, lost, a murderer, a thief.
Speak on, because my sins, beyond belief,
Can bring this shameful sinner to his knees,
In humble, paltry effort to appease.

ORGON [*to* TARTUFFE] Brother, there is no need . . .
[*To* DAMIS] Will you relent?

DAMIS He has seduced you!

ORGON Can't you take a hint?
Be quiet! [*To* TARTUFFE] Brother, please get up. [*To* DAMIS] Ingrate!

DAMIS But father, this man

ORGON —whom you denigrate.

DAMIS But you should—

ORGON Quiet!

DAMIS But I saw and heard—

ORGON I'll slap you if you say another word.

TARTUFFE In the name of God, don't be that way.
Brother, I'd rather suffer, come what may,
Than have this boy receive what's meant for me.

ORGON [*to* DAMIS] Heathen!

TARTUFFE Please! I beg of you on bended knee.

ORGON [*to* DAMIS] Wretch! See his goodness?!

DAMIS But—

ORGON No!

DAMIS But—

ORGON Be still!
And not another word from you until

You admit the truth. It's plain to see
Although you thought that I would never be
Aware and know your motives, yet I do.
You all hate him. And I saw today, you,
Wife, servants—everyone beneath my roof—
Are trying everything to force Tartuffe
Out of my house—this holy man, my friend.
The more you try to banish him and end
Our sacred brotherhood, the more secure
His place is. I have never been more sure
Of anyone. I give him as his bride
My daughter. If that hurts the family pride,
Then good. It needs humbling. You understand?

DAMIS You're going to force her to accept his hand?

ORGON Yes, traitor, and this evening. You know why?
To infuriate you. Yes, I defy
You all. I am master and you'll obey.
And you, you ingrate, now I'll make you pay
For your abuse of him—kneel on the floor,
And beg his pardon, or go out the door.

DAMIS Me? Kneel and ask the pardon of this fraud?

ORGON What? You refuse? Someone get me a rod!
A stick! Something! [*To* TARTUFFE] Don't hold me.
[*To* DAMIS] Here's your whack!
Out of my house and don't ever come back!

DAMIS Yes, I'll leave, but—

ORGON Get out of my sight!
I disinherit you, you traitor, you're a blight
On this house. And you'll get nothing now
From me, except my curse!

3.7

[ORGON, TARTUFFE]

ORGON You have my vow,
He'll never more question your honesty.

TARTUFFE [*to heaven*] Forgive him for the pain he's given me.
[*To* ORGON] How I suffer. If you could only see
What I go through when they disparage me.

ORGON Oh no!

TARTUFFE The ingratitude, even in thought,
Tortures my soul so much, it leaves me fraught
With inner pain. My heart's stopped. I'm near death,
I can barely speak now. Where is my breath?

ORGON [*running in tears to the door through which he chased* DAMIS]
You demon! I held back, you little snot
I should have struck you dead right on the spot!
[*To* TARTUFFE] Get up, Brother. Don't worry anymore.

TARTUFFE Let us end these troubles, Brother, I implore.
For the discord I have caused, I deeply grieve,
So for the good of all, I'll take my leave.

ORGON What? Are you joking? No!
TARTUFFE They hate me here.
It pains me when I see them fill your ear
With suspicions.
ORGON But that doesn't matter.
I don't listen.
TARTUFFE That persistent chatter
You now ignore, one day you'll listen to.
Repetition of a lie can make it true.
ORGON No, my brother. Never.
TARTUFFE A man's wife
Can so mislead his soul and ruin his life.
ORGON No, no.
TARTUFFE Brother, let me, by leaving here,
Remove any cause for doubt or fear.
ORGON No, no. You will stay. My soul is at stake.
TARTUFFE Well, then, a hefty penance I must make.
I'll mortify myself, unless . . .
ORGON No need!
TARTUFFE Then we will never speak of it, agreed?
But the question of your honor still remains,
And with that I'll take particular pains
To prevent rumors. My absence, my defense—
I'll never see your wife again, and hence—
ORGON No. You spend every hour with her you want,
And be seen with her. I want you to flaunt,
In front of them, this friendship with my wife.
And I know how to really turn the knife
I'll make you my heir, my only one,
Yes, you will be my son-in-law and son.[7]
A good and faithful friend means more to me
Than any member of my family.
Will you accept this gift that I propose?
TARTUFFE Whatever heaven wants I can't oppose.
ORGON Poor man! A contract's what we need to write.
And let all the envious burst with spite.

4.1

[CLÉANTE, TARTUFFE]

CLÉANTE Yes, everyone is talking and each word
Diminishes your glory, rest assured.
Though your name's tainted with scandal and shame,
I'm glad I ran across you, all the same,
Because I need to share with you my view
On this disaster clearly caused by you.
Damis, let's say for now, was so misguided,
He spoke before he thought. But you decided

7. In fact, French laws governing inheritance would have made such a change extremely difficult to accomplish.

To just sit back and watch him be exiled
From his own father's house. Were he a child,
Then, really, would you dare to treat him so?
Shouldn't you forgive him, not make him go?
However, if there's vengeance in your heart,
And you act on it, tell me what's the part
That's Christian in that? And are you so base,
You'd let a son fall from his father's grace?
Give God your anger as an offering,
Bring peace and forgive all for everything.

TARTUFFE I'd do just that, if it were up to me.
I blame him for nothing, don't you see?
I've pardoned him already. That's my way.
And I'm not bitter, but have this to say:
Heaven's best interests will have been served,
When wrongdoers have got what they deserved.
In fact, if he returns here, I would leave,
Because God knows what people might believe.
Faking forgiveness to manipulate
My accuser, silencing the hate
He has for me could be seen as my goal.
When I would only wish to save his soul.
What he said to me, though unforgivable,
I give unto God to make life livable.

CLÉANTE To this conclusion, sir, I have arrived:
Your excuses could not be more contrived.
Just how did you come by the opinion
Heaven's business is in your dominion,
Judging who is guilty and who is not?
Taking revenge is heaven's task, I thought.
And if you're under heaven's sovereignty,
What human verdict would you ever be
The least bit moved by. No, you wouldn't care—
Judging other's lives is so unfair.
Heaven seems to say "live and let live,"
And our task, I believe, is to forgive.

TARTUFFE I said I've pardoned him. I take such pains
To do exactly what heaven ordains.
But after his attack on me, it's clear,
Heaven does not ordain that he live here.

CLÉANTE Does it ordain, sir, that you nod and smile,
When taking what is not yours, all the while?
On this inheritance you have no claim
And yet you think it's yours. Have you no shame?

TARTUFFE That this gift was, in any way, received
Out of self-interest, would not be believed
By anyone who knows me well. They'd say,
"The world's wealth, to him, holds no sway."
I am not dazzled by gold nor its glitter,
So lack of wealth has never made me bitter.

If I take this present from the father,
The source of all this folderol and bother,
I am saving, so everyone understands,
This wealth from falling into the wrong hands.
Waste of wealth and property's a crime,
And that is what would happen at this time.
But I would use it as part of my plan:
For glory of heaven, and the good of man.

CLÉANTE Well, sir, I think these small fears that plague you,
In fact, may cause the rightful heir to sue.
Why trouble yourself, sir—couldn't you just
Let him own his property, if he must?
Let others say his property's misused
By him, rather than have yourself accused
Of taking it from its rightful owner.
Wouldn't a pious man be a donor
Of property? Unless there is a verse
Or proverb about how you fill your purse
With what's not yours, at all, in any part.
And if heaven has put into your heart
This obstacle to living with Damis,
The honorable thing, you must agree,
As well as, certainly, the most discreet,
Is pack your bags and, quickly, just retreat.
To have the son of the house chased away,
Because a guest objects, is a sad day.
Leaving now would show your decency,
Sir . . .

TARTUFFE Yes. Well, it is half after three;
Pious duties consume this time of day,
You will excuse my hurrying away.

CLÉANTE Ah!

4.2

[ELMIRE, MARIANE, DORINE, CLÉANTE]

DORINE Please, come to the aid of Mariane.
She's suffering because her father's plan
To force this marriage, impossible to bear,
Has pushed her from distress into despair.
Her father's on his way here. Do your best,
Turn him around. Use subtlety, protest,
Whatever way will work to change his mind.

4.3

[ORGON, ELMIRE, MARIANE, CLÉANTE, DORINE]

ORGON Ah! Here's everyone I wanted to find!
[*To* MARIANE] This document I have here in my hand
Will make you very happy, understand?

MARIANE Father, in the name of heaven, I plead

To all that's good and kind in you, concede
Paternal power, just in this sense:
Free me from my vows of obedience.
Enforcing that inflexible law today
Will force me to confess each time I pray
My deep resentment of my obligation.
I know, father, that I am your creation,
That you're the one who's given life to me.
Why would you now fill it with misery?
If you destroy my hopes for the one man
I've dared to love by trying now to ban
Our union, then I'm kneeling to implore,
Don't give me to a man whom I abhor.
To you, Father, I make this supplication.
Don't drive me to some act of desperation,
By ruling me simply because you can.

ORGON [*feeling himself touched*] Be strong! Human weakness shames a man!

MARIANE Your affection for him doesn't bother me—
Let it erupt, give him your property,
And if that's not enough, then give him mine.
Any claim on it, I do now decline.
But in this gifting, don't give him my life.
If I must wed, then I will be God's wife,
In a convent, until my days are done.

ORGON Ah! So you will be a holy, cloistered nun,
Because your father thwarts your love affair.
Get up! The more disgust you have to bear,
The more of heaven's treasure you will earn.
And the heaven will bless you in return.
Through this marriage, you'll mortify your senses.
Don't bother me with any more pretenses.

DORINE But . . . !

ORGON Quiet, you! I see you standing there.
Don't speak a single world! don't even dare!

CLÉANTE If you permit, I'd like to say a word . . .

ORGON Brother, the best advice the world has heard
Is yours—its reasoning, hard to ignore.
But I refuse to hear it anymore.

ELMIRE [*to* ORGON] And now, I wonder, have you lost your mind?
Your love for this one man has made you blind.
Can you stand there and say you don't believe
A word we've said? That we're here to deceive?

ORGON Excuse me—I believe in what I see.
You, indulging my bad son, agree
To back him up in this terrible prank,
Accusing my dear friend of something rank.
You should be livid if what you claim took place,
And yet this look of calm is on your face.

ELMIRE Because a man says he's in love with me,
I'm to respond with heavy artillery?

I laugh at these unwanted propositions.
Mirth will quell most ardent ambitions.
Why make a fuss over an indiscretion?
My honor's safe and in my possession.
You say I'm calm? Well, that's my constancy—
It won't need a defense, or clemency.
I know I'll never be a vicious prude
Who always seems to hear men being rude,
And then defends her honor tooth and claw,
Still snarling, even as the men withdraw.
From honor like that heaven preserve me,
If that's what you want, you don't deserve me.
Besides, you're the one who has been betrayed.

ORGON I see through this trick that's being played.

ELMIRE How can you be so dim? I am amazed
How you can hear these sins and stay unfazed.
But what if I could show you what he does?

ORGON Show?

ELMIRE Yes.

ORGON A fiction!

ELMIRE No, the truth because
I am quite certain I can find a way
To show you in the fullest light of day . . .

ORGON Fairy tales!

ELMIRE Come on, at least answer me.
I've given up expecting you to be
My advocate. What have you got to lose,
By hiding somewhere, anyplace you choose,
And see for yourself. And then we can
Hear what you say about your holy man.

ORGON Then I'll say nothing because it cannot be.

ELMIRE Enough. I'm tired. You'll see what you see.
I'm not a liar, though I've been accused.
The time is now and I won't be refused.
You'll be a witness. And we can stop our rants.

ORGON All right! I call your bluff, Miss Smarty Pants.

ELMIRE [*to* DORINE] Tell Tartuffe to come.

DORINE Watch out. He's clever.
Men like him are caught, well, almost never.

ELMIRE Narcissism is a great deceiver,
And he has lots of that. He's a believer
In his charisma. [*To* CLÉANTE and MARIANE] Leave us for a bit.

4.4

[ELMIRE, ORGON]

ELMIRE See this table? Good. Get under it.

ORGON What!

ELMIRE You are hiding. Get under there and stay.

ORGON Under the table?

ELMIRE: Just do as I say.

I have a plan, but for it to succeed,
You must be hidden. So are we agreed?
You want to know? I'm ready to divulge it.

ORGON This fantasy of yours—I'll indulge it.
But then I want to lay this thing to rest.

ELMIRE Oh, that'll happen. Because he'll fail the test.
You see, I'm going to have a conversation
I'd never have—just as an illustration
Of how this hypocrite behaved with me.
So don't be scandalized. I must be free
To flirt. Clearly, that's what it's going to take
To prove to you your holy man's a fake.
I'm going to lead him on, to lift his mask,
Seem to agree to anything he'll ask,
Pretend to respond to his advances.
It's for you I'm taking all these chances.
I'll stop as soon as you have seen enough;
I hope that comes before he calls my bluff.
His plans for me must be circumvented,
His passion's strong enough to be demented,
So the moment you're convinced, you let me know
That I've revealed the fraud I said I'd show.
Stop him so I won't have a minute more
Exposure to your friend, this lecherous boor.
You're in control. I'm sure I'll be all right.
And . . . here he comes—so hush, stay out of sight.

4.5

[TARTUFFE, ELMIRE, ORGON (*under the table*)]

TARTUFFE I'm told you want to have a word with me.

ELMIRE Yes. I have a secret but I'm not free
To speak. Close that door, have a look around,
We certainly do not want to be found
The way we were just as Damis appeared.
I was terrified for you and as I feared,
He was irate. You saw how hard I tried
To calm him down and keep him pacified.
I was so upset; I never had the thought
"Deny it all," which might have helped a lot,
But as it turns out, we've nothing to fear.
My husband's not upset, it would appear.
Things are good, to heaven I defer,
Because they're even better than they were.
I have to say I'm quite amazed, in fact,
His good opinion of you is intact.
To clear the air and quiet every tongue,
And to kill any gossip that's begun—
You could've pushed me over with a feather—
He wants us to spend all our time together!
That's why, with no fear of a critical stare,

I can be here with you or anywhere.
Most important, I am completely free
To show my ardor for you, finally.

TARTUFFE Ardor? This is a sudden change of tone
From the last time we found ourselves alone.

ELMIRE If thinking I was turning you away
Has made you angry, all that I can say
Is that you do not know a woman's heart!
Protecting our virtue keeps us apart,
And makes us seem aloof, and even cold.
But cooler outside, inside the more bold.
When love overcomes us, we are ashamed,
Because we fear that we might be defamed.
We must protect our honor—not allow
Our love to show. I fear that even now,
In this confession, you'll think ill of me.
But now I've spoken, and I hope you see
My ardor that is there. Why would I sit
And listen to you? Why would I permit
Your talk of love, unless I had a notion
Just like yours, and with the same emotion?
And when Damis found us, didn't I try
To quiet him? And did you wonder why,
In speaking of Mariane's marriage deal,
I not only asked you, I made an appeal
That you turn it down? What was I doing?
Making sure I'd be the one you'd be wooing.

TARTUFFE It is extremely sweet, without a doubt,
To watch your lips as loving words spill out.
Abundant honey there for me to drink,
But I have doubts. I cannot help but think,
"Does she tell the truth, or does she lie,
To get me to break off this marriage tie?
Is all this ardor something she could fake,
And just an act for her stepdaughter's sake?"
So many questions, yet I want to trust.
But need to know the truth, in fact, I must.
Pleasing you, Elmire, is my main task,
And happiness, and so I have to ask
To sample this deep ardor felt for me
Right here and now, in blissful ecstasy.

ELMIRE [*coughing to alert* ORGON]
You want to spend this passion instantly?
I've been opening my heart consistently,
But for you, it's not enough, this sharing.
Yet for a woman, it is very daring.
So why can't you be happy with a taste,
Instead of the whole meal consumed in haste?

TARTUFFE We dare not hope, all those of us who don't
Deserve a thing. And so it is I won't

Be satisfied with words. I'll always doubt,
Assume my fortune's taken the wrong route
On its way to me. And that is why
I don't believe in anything till I
Have touched, partaken until satisfied.

ELMIRE So suddenly, your love can't be denied.
It wants complete dominion over me,
And what it wants, it wants violently.
I know I'm flustered, I know I'm out of breath—
Your power over me could be the death
Of my reason. Does this seem right to you?
To use my weakness against me, just to
Conquer? No one's gallant anymore.
I invite you in. You break down the door.

TARTUFFE If your passion for me isn't a pretense,
Then why deny me its best evidence?

ELMIRE But, heaven, sir, that place that you address
So often, would judge us both if we transgress.

TARTUFFE That's all that's in the way of my desires?
These judgments heaven makes of what transpires?
All you fear is heaven's bad opinion.

ELMIRE But I am made to fear its dominion.

TARTUFFE And I know how to exorcise these fears.
To sin is not as bad as it appears
If, and stay with me on this, one can think
That in some cases, heaven gives a wink

[*It is a scoundrel speaking.*][8]

When it comes to certain needs of men
Who can remain upright but only when
There is a pure intention. So you see,
If you just let yourself be led by me,
You'll have no worries, and I can enjoy
You. And you, me. Because we will employ
This way of thinking—a real science
And a secret, thus, with your compliance,
Fulfilling my desires without fear,
Is easy now, so let it happen here.

[ELMIRE *coughs.*]

That cough, Madame, is bad.

ELMIRE I'm in such pain.

TARTUFFE A piece of licorice might ease the strain.

ELMIRE [*directed to* ORGON] This cold I have is very obstinate.
It stubbornly holds on. I can't shake it.

TARTUFFE That's most annoying.

ELMIRE More than I can say.

TARTUFFE Let's get back to finding you a way,
Finally, to get around your scruples:

8. This stage direction, inserted by Molière himself, supports the playwright's assertion that he took pains to demonstrate Tartuffe's true nature.

Secrecy—I'm one of its best pupils
And practitioners. Responsibility
For any evil—you can put on me.
I will answer up to heaven if I must,
And give a good accounting you can trust.
There'll be no sins for which we must atone,
'Cause evil exists only when it's known.
Adam and Eve were public in their fall.
To sin in private is not to sin at all.

ELMIRE [*after coughing again*] Obviously, I must give in to you,
Because, it seems, you are a person who
Refuses to believe anything I say.
Live testimony only can convey
The truth of passion here, no more, no less.
That it should go that far, I must confess,
Is such a pity. But I'll cross the line,
And give myself to you. I won't decline
Your offer, sir, to vanquish me right here.
But let me make one point extremely clear:
If there's a moral judgment to be made,
If anyone here feels the least betrayed,
Then none of that will be my fault. Instead,
The sin weighs twice as heavy on your head.
You forced me to this brash extremity.

TARTUFFE Yes, yes, I will take all the sin on me.

ELMIRE Open the door and check because I fear
My husband—just look—might be somewhere near.

TARTUFFE What does it matter if he comes or goes?
The secret is, I lead him by the nose.
He's urged me to spend all my time with you.
So let him see—he won't believe it's true.

ELMIRE Go out and look around. Indulge my whim.
Look everywhere and carefully for him.

4.6

[ORGON, ELMIRE]

ORGON [*coming out from under the table*]
I swear that is the most abominable man!
How will I bear this? I don't think I can.
I'm stupefied!

ELMIRE What? Out so soon? No, no.
You can't be serious. There's more to go.
Get back under there. You can't be too sure.
It's never good relying on conjecture.

ORGON That kind of wickedness comes straight from hell.

ELMIRE You've turned against this man you know so well?
Good lord, be sure the evidence is strong
Before you are convinced. You might be wrong.

[*She steps in front of* ORGON.]

4.7

[TARTUFFE, ELMIRE, ORGON]

TARTUFFE Yes, all is well; there's no one to be found,
And I was thorough when I looked around.
To my delight, my rapture, at last . . .

ORGON [*stopping him*] Just stop a minute there! You move too fast!
Delight and rapture? Fulfilling desire?
Ah! Ah! You are a traitor and a liar!
Some holy man you are, to wreck my life,
Marry my daughter? Lust after my wife?
I've had my doubts about you, but kept quiet,
Waiting for you to slip and then deny it.
Well, now it's happened and I'm so relieved,
To stop pretending that I am deceived.

ELMIRE [*to* TARTUFFE] I don't approve of what I've done today,
But I needed to do it, anyway.

TARTUFFE What? You can't think . . .

ORGON No more words from you.
Get out of here, you. . . . You and I are through.

TARTUFFE But my intentions . . .

ORGON You still think I'm a dunce?
You shut your mouth and leave this house at once!

TARTUFFE You're the one to leave, you, acting like the master.
Now I'll make it known, the full disaster:
This house belongs to me, yes, all of it,
And I'll decide what's true, as I see fit.
You can't entrap me with demeaning tricks,
Yes, here's a situation you can't fix.
Here nothing happens without my consent.
You've offended heaven. You must repent.
But I know how to really punish you.
Those who harm me, they know not what they do.

4.8

[ELMIRE, ORGON]

ELMIRE What was that about? I mean, the latter.

ORGON I'm not sure, but it's no laughing matter.

ELMIRE Why?

ORGON I've made a mistake I now can see,
The deed I gave him is what troubles me.

ELMIRE The deed?

ORGON And something else. I am undone.
I think my troubles may have just begun.

ELMIRE What else?

ORGON You'll know it all. I have to race,
To see if a strongbox is in its place.

5.1

[ORGON, CLÉANTE]

CLÉANTE Where are you running to?
ORGON Who knows.
CLÉANTE Then wait.
It seems to me we should deliberate,
Meet, plan, and have some family talks.
ORGON I can't stop thinking about the damned box
More than anything, that's the loss I fear.
CLÉANTE What about this box makes it so dear?
ORGON I have a friend whom I felt sorry for,
Because he chose the wrong side in the war;[9]
Before he fled, he brought it to me,
This locked box. He didn't leave a key.
He told me it has papers, this doomed friend,
On which his life and property depend.
CLÉANTE Are you saying you gave the box away?
ORGON Yes, that's true, that's what I'm trying to say.
I was afraid that I would have to lie,
If I were confronted. That is why
I went to my betrayer and confessed
And he, in turn, told me it would be best
If I gave him the box, to keep, in case
Someone were to ask me to my face
About it all, and I might lie and then,
In doing so, commit a venial sin.[1]
CLÉANTE As far as I can see, this is a mess,
And with a lot of damage to assess.
This secret that you told, this deed you gave,
Make the situation hard to save.
He's holding all the cards, your holy man,
Because you gave them to him. If you can,
Restrain yourself a bit and stay away.
That would be best. And do watch what you say.
ORGON What? With his wicked heart and corrupt soul,
Yet I'm to keep my rage under control?
Yes, me who took him in, right off the street?
Damn all holy men! They're filled with deceit!
I now renounce them all, down to the man,
And I'll treat them worse than Satan can.
CLÉANTE Listen to yourself! You're over the top,
Getting carried away again. Just stop.
"Moderation." Is that a word you know?
I think you've learned it, but then off you go,

9. That is, he opposed Louis in the Fronde (see 1.2.11 and note). Although Orgon supported the king, this act left him open to the charge of being a traitor to the throne—a capital offense.

1. Because Tartuffe had possession of the box, Orgon could deny that he had it without lying. A venial (or "pardonable") sin is relatively minor.

Always ignoring the strength in reason,
Flinging yourself from loyalty to treason.
Why can't you just admit that you were swayed
By the fake piety that man displayed?
But no. Rather than change your ways, you turned
Like that. [*Snaps fingers*] Attacking holy men who've earned
The right to stand among the true believers.
So now all holy men are base deceivers?
Instead of just admitting your delusion,
"They're all like that!" you say—brilliant conclusion.
Why trust reason, when you have emotion?
You've implied there is no true devotion.
Freethinkers are the ones who hold that view,
And yet, you don't agree with them, do you?
You judge a man as good without real proof.
Appearances can lie—witness: Tartuffe.
If your respect is something to be prized,
Don't toss it away to those disguised
In a cloak of piety and virtue.
Don't you see how deeply they can hurt you?
Look for simple goodness—it does exist.
And just watch for imposters in our midst,
With this in mind, try not to be unjust
To true believers, sin on the side of trust.

5.2

[DAMIS, ORGON, CLÉANTE]

DAMIS Father, what? I can't believe it's true,
That scoundrel has the gall to threaten you?
And use the things you gave him in his case
'Gainst you? To throw you out? I'll break his face.
ORGON My son, I'm in more pain than you can see.
DAMIS I'll break both his legs. Leave it to me.
We must not bend under his insolence.
I'll finish this business, punish his offense,
I'll murder him and do it with such joy.
CLÉANTE Damis, you're talking like a little boy,
Tantrums head the list of your main flaws.
We live in modern times, with things called "laws."
Murder is illegal. At least for us.

5.3

[MADAME PERNELLE, MARIANE, ELMIRE, DORINE,
DAMIS, ORGON, CLÉANTE]

MADAME PERNELLE It's unbelievable! Preposterous!
ORGON Believe it. I've seen it with my own eyes.
He returned kindness with deceit and lies.
I took in a man, miserable and poor,
Brought him home, gave him the key to my door,

I loaded him with favors every day,
To him, my daughter, I just gave away,
My house, my wealth, a locked box from a friend.
But to what depths this devil would descend.
This betrayer, this abomination,
Who had the gall to preach about temptation,
And know in his black heart he'd woo my wife,
Seduce her! Yes! And then to steal my life,
Using my property, which I transferred to him,
I know, I know—it was a stupid whim.
He wants to ruin me, chase me from my door,
He wants me as he was, abject and poor.

DORINE Poor man!

MADAME PERNELLE I don't believe a word, my son,
This isn't something that he could have done.

ORGON What?

MADAME PERNELLE Holy men always arouse envy.

ORGON Mother, what are you trying to say to me?

MADAME PERNELLE That you live rather strangely in this house;
He's hated here, especially by your spouse.

ORGON What has this got to do with what I said?

MADAME PERNELLE Heaven knows, I've beat into your head:
"In this world, virtue is mocked forever;
Envious men may die, but envy never."

ORGON How does that apply to what's happened here?

MADAME PERNELLE Someone made up some lies; it's all too clear.

ORGON But I saw it myself, you understand.

MADAME PERNELLE "Whoever spreads slander has a soiled hand."

ORGON You'll make me, Mother, say something not nice.
I saw it for myself; I've told you twice.

MADAME PERNELLE "No one can trust what gossips have to say,
Yet they'll be with us until Judgment Day."

ORGON You're talking total nonsense, Mother!
I said I saw him, this man I called Brother!
I saw him with my wife, with these two eyes.
The word is "saw," past tense of "see." These "lies"
That you misnamed are just the truth.
I saw my wife almost beneath Tartuffe.

MADAME PERNELLE Oh, is that all? Appearances deceive.
What we think we see, we then believe.

ORGON I'm getting angry.

MADAME PERNELLE False suspicions, see?
We are subject to them, occasionally,
Good deeds can be seen as something other.

ORGON So I'm to see this as a good thing, Mother,
A man trying to kiss my wife?

MADAME PERNELLE You must.
Because, to be quite certain you are just,
You should wait until you're very, very sure
And not rely on faulty conjecture.

ORGON Goddammit! You would have me wait until . . . ?
And just be quiet while he has his fill,
Right before my very eyes, Mother, he'd—

MADAME PERNELLE I can't believe that he would do this "deed"
Of which he's been accused. There is no way.
His soul is pure.

ORGON I don't know what to say!
Mother!

DORINE Just deserts, for what you put us through.
You thought we lied, now she thinks that of you.

CLÉANTE Why are we wasting time with all of this?
We're standing on the edge of the abyss.
This man is dangerous! He has a plan!

DAMIS How could he hurt us? I don't think he can.

ELMIRE He won't get far, complaining to the law—
You'll tell the truth, and he'll have to withdraw.

CLÉANTE Don't count on it; trust me, he'll find a way
To use these weapons you gave him today.
He has legal documents, and the deed.
To kick us out, just what else does he need?
And if he's doubted, there are many ways
To trap you in a wicked legal maze.
You give a snake his venom, nice and quick,
And after that you poke him with a stick?

ORGON I know. But what was I supposed to do?
Emotions got the best of me, it's true.

CLÉANTE If we could placate him, just for a while,
And somehow get the deed back with a smile.

ELMIRE Had I known we had all this to lose,
I never would have gone through with my ruse.
I would've—

[*A knock on the door.*]

ORGON What does that man want? You go find out.
But I don't want to know what it's about.

5.4

[MONSIEUR LOYAL, MADAME PERNELLE, ORGON, DAMIS, MARIANE, DORINE, ELMIRE, CLÉANTE]

MONSIEUR LOYAL [*to* DORINE] Dear sister, hello. Please, I beg of you,
Your master is the one I must speak to.

DORINE He's not receiving visitors today.

MONSIEUR LOYAL I bring good news so don't send me away.
My goal in coming is not to displease;
I'm here to put your master's mind at ease.

DORINE And you are . . . who?

MONSIEUR LOYAL Just say that I have come
For his own good and with a message from
Monsieur Tartuffe.

DORINE [*to* ORGON] It's a soft-spoken man,

Who says he's here to do just what he can
To ease your mind. Tartuffe sent him.

CLÉANTE Let's see
What he might want.

ORGON Oh, what's my strategy?
He's come to reconcile us, I just know.

CLÉANTE Your strategy? Don't let your anger show,
For heaven's sake. And listen for a truce.

MONSIEUR LOYAL My greetings, sir. I'm here to be of use.

ORGON Just what I thought. His language is benign.
For the prospect of peace, a hopeful sign.

MONSIEUR LOYAL Your family's dear to me, I hope you know.
I served your father many years ago.

ORGON I humbly beg your pardon, to my shame,
I don't know you, nor do I know your name.

MONSIEUR LOYAL My name's Loyal. I'm Norman by descent.
My job of bailiff is what pays my rent.
Thanks be to heaven, it's been forty years
I've done my duty free of doubts or fear.
That you invited me in, I can report,
When I serve you with this writ from the court.

ORGON What? You're here . . .

MONSIEUR LOYAL No upsetting outbursts, please.
It's just a warrant saying we can seize,
Not me, of course, but this Monsieur Tartuffe—
Your house and land as his. Here is the proof.
I have the contract here. You must vacate
These premises. Please, now, don't be irate.
Just gather up your things now, and make way
For this man, without hindrance or delay.

ORGON Me? Leave my house?

MONSIEUR LOYAL That's right, sir, out the door.
This house, at present, as I've said before,
Belongs to good Monsieur Tartuffe, you see,
He's lord and master of this property
By virtue of this contract I hold right here.
Is that not your signature? It's quite clear.

DAMIS He's so rude, I do almost admire him.

MONSIEUR LOYAL Excuse me. Is it possible to fire him?
My business is with you, a man of reason,
Who knows resisting would be seen as treason.
You understand that I must be permitted
To execute the orders as committed.

DAMIS I'll execute him, Father, to be sure.
His long black nightgown won't make him secure.

MONSIEUR LOYAL He's your son! I thought he was a servant.
Control the boy. His attitude's too fervent,
His anger is a bone of contention—
Throw him out, or I will have to mention
His name in this, my official report.

DORINE "Loyal" is loyal only to the court.
MONSIEUR LOYAL I have respect for all God-fearing men,
So instantly I knew I'd come here when
I heard your name attached to this assignment.
I knew you'd want a bailiff with refinement.
I'm here for you, just to accommodate,
To make removal something you won't hate.
Now, if I hadn't come, then you would find
You got a bailiff who would be less kind.
ORGON I'm sorry, I don't see the kindness in
An eviction order.
MONSIEUR LOYAL Let me begin:
I'm giving you time. I won't carry out
This order you are so upset about.
I've come only to spend the night with you,
With my men, who will be coming through.
All ten of them, as quiet as a mouse.
Oh, you must give me the keys to the house.
We won't disturb you. You will have your rest—
You need a full night's sleep—that's always best.
There'll be no scandal, secrets won't be bared;
Tomorrow morning you must be prepared,
To pack your things, down to the smallest plate,
And cup, and then these premises vacate.
You'll have helpers; the men I chose are strong,
And they'll have this house empty before long.
I can't think of who would treat you better
And still enforce the law down to the letter,
Just later with the letter is my gift.
So, no resistance. And there'll be no rift.
ORGON From that which I still have, I'd give this hour,
One hundred coins of gold to have the power
To sock this bailiff with a punch as great
As any man in this world could create.
CLÉANTE That's enough. Let's not make it worse.
DAMIS The nerve
Of him. Let's see what my right fist can serve.
DORINE Mister Loyal, you have a fine, broad back,
And if I had a stick, you'd hear it crack.
MONSIEUR LOYAL Words like that are punishable, my love—
Be careful when a push becomes a shove.
CLÉANTE Oh, come on, there's no reason to postpone,
Just serve your writ and then leave us alone.
MONSIEUR LOYAL May heaven keep you, till we meet again!
ORGON And strangle you, and him who sent you in!

5.5

[ORGON, CLÉANTE, MARIANE, ELMIRE, MADAME PERNELLE, DORINE, DAMIS]

ORGON Well, Mother, look at this writ. Here is proof
Of treachery supreme by your Tartuffe.
Don't jump to judgment—that's what you admonished.
MADAME PERNELLE I'm overwhelmed, I'm utterly astonished.
DORINE I hear you blaming him and that's just wrong.
You'll see his good intentions before long.
"Just love thy neighbor" is here on this writ,
Between the lines, you see him saying it.
Because men are corrupted by their wealth.
Out of concern for your spiritual health,
He's taking, with a pure motivation,
Everything that keeps you from salvation.
ORGON Aren't you sick of hearing "Quiet!" from me?
CLÉANTE Thoughts of what to do now? And quickly?
ELMIRE Once we show the plans of that ingrate,
His trickery can't get him this estate.
As soon as they see his disloyalty,
He'll be denied, I hope, this property.

5.6

[VALÈRE, ORGON, CLÉANTE, ELMIRE, MARIANE, *etc.*]

VALÈRE I hate to ruin your day—I have bad news.
Danger's coming. There's no time to lose.
A good friend, quite good, as it turns out,
Discovered something you must know about,
Something at the court that's happening now.
That swindler—sorry, if you will allow,
That holy faker—has gone to the king,
Accusing you of almost everything.
But here's the worst: he says that you have failed
Your duty as a subject, which entailed
The keeping of a strongbox so well hidden,
That you could deny knowledge, if bidden,
Of a traitor's whereabouts. What's more,
That holy fraud will come right through that door,
Accusing you. You can't do anything.
He had this box and gave it to the king.
So there's an order out for your arrest!
And evidently, it's the king's behest,
That Tartuffe come, so justice can be done.
CLÉANTE Well, there it is, at last, the smoking gun.
He can claim this house, at the very least.
ORGON The man is nothing but a vicious beast.
VALÈRE You must leave now, and I will help you hide.
Here's ten thousand in gold. My carriage is outside.
When a storm is bearing down on you

Running is the best thing one can do.
I have a place where both of us can stay.
ORGON My boy, I owe you more than I can say.
I pray to heaven that, before too long,
I can pay you back and right the wrong
I've done to you. [*To* ELMIRE] Good-bye. Take care, my dear.
CLÉANTE We'll plan. You go while the way is still clear.

5.7

[THE EXEMPT, TARTUFFE, VALÈRE, ORGON, ELMIRE, MARIANE, DORINE, *etc.*[2]]

TARTUFFE Easy, just a minute, you move too fast.
Your cowardice, dear sir, is unsurpassed.
What I have to say is uncontested.
Simply put, I'm having you arrested.
ORGON You villain, you traitor, your lechery
Is second only to your treachery.
And you arrest me—that's the crowning blow.
TARTUFFE Suffering for heaven is all I know,
So revile me. It's all for heaven's sake.
CLÉANTE Why does he persist when we know it's fake?
DAMIS He's mocking heaven. What a loathsome beast.
TARTUFFE Get mad—I'm not bothered in the least.
It is my duty, what I'm doing here.
MARIANE You really think that if you persevere
In this lie, you'll keep your reputation?
TARTUFFE My honor is safeguarded by my station,
As I am on a mission from the king.
ORGON You dog, have you forgotten everything?
Who picked you up from total poverty?
TARTUFFE I know that there were things you did for me.
My duty to our monarch is what stifles
Memory, so your past gifts are trifles.
My obligations to him are so rife,
That I would give up family, friends, and life.
ELMIRE Fraud!
DORINE Now there's a lie that beats everything,
His pretended reverence for our king!
CLÉANTE This "duty to our monarch," as you say,
Why didn't it come up before today?
You had the box, you lived here for some time,
To say the least, and yet this crime
That you reported—why then did you wait?
Orgon caught you about to desecrate
The holy bonds of marriage with his wife.
Suddenly, your obligations are so "rife"
To our dear king, that you're here to turn in

2. Molière himself added "etc." to the list of speaking characters. Thus Laurent and Flipote may return to the stage for this final scene.

Your former friend and "brother" and begin
To move into his house, a gift, but look,
Why would you accept gifts from a crook?

TARTUFFE [*to* THE EXEMPT] Save me from this whining! I have had my fill!
Do execute your orders, if you will.

THE EXEMPT I will. I've waited much too long for that.
I had to let you have your little chat.
It confirmed the facts our monarch knew,
That's why, Tartuffe, I am arresting you.[3]

TARTUFFE Who, me?

THE EXEMPT Yes, you.

TARTUFFE You're putting me in jail?

THE EXEMPT Immediately. And there will be no bail.
[*To* ORGON] You may compose yourself now, sir, because
We're fortunate in leadership and laws.
We have a king who sees into men's hearts,
And cannot be deceived, so he imparts
Great wisdom, and a talent for discernment.
Thus frauds are guaranteed a quick internment.
Our Prince of Reason sees things as they are,
So hypocrites do not get very far.
But saintly men and the truly devout,
He cherishes and has no doubts about.
This man could not begin to fool the king
Who can defend himself against the sting
Of much more subtle predators. And thus,
When this craven pretender came to us,
Demanding justice and accusing you,
He betrayed himself. Our king could view
The baseness lurking in his coward's heart.
Evil like that can set a man apart.
And so divine justice nodded her head,
The king did not believe a word he said.
It was soon confirmed, he has a crime
For every sin, but why squander the time
To list them or the aliases he used.
For the king, it's enough that he abused
Your friendship and your faith. And though we knew
Each accusation of his was untrue,
Our monarch himself, wanting to know
Just how far this imposter planned to go,
Had me wait to find this out, then pounce,
Arrest this criminal, quickly denounce
The man and all his lies. And now, the king
Orders delivered to you, everything
This scoundrel took, the deed, all documents,
This locked box of yours and all its contents,

3. In his capacity as officer of the king, The Exempt becomes both Louis's representative and his surrogate.

And nullifies the contract giving away
Your property, effective today.
And finally, our monarch wants to end
Your worries about aiding your old friend
Before he went into exile because,
In that same way, and in spite of the laws,
You openly defended our king's right
To his throne. And you were prepared to fight.
From his heart, and because it makes good sense
That a good deed deserves a recompense,
He pardons you. And wanted me to add:
He remembers good longer than the bad.

DORINE May heaven be praised!

MADAME PERNELLE I am so relieved.

ELMIRE A happy ending!

MARIANE Can it be believed?

ORGON [*to* TARTUFFE] Now then, you traitor . . .

CLÉANTE Stop that, Brother, please.
You're sinking to his level. Don't appease
His expectations of mankind. His fate
Is misery. But it's never too late
To take another path, and feel remorse.
So let's wish, rather, he will change his course,
And turn his back upon his life of vice,
Embrace the good and know it will suffice.
We've all seen the wisdom of this great king,
Whom we should go and thank for everything.

ORGON Yes, and well said. So come along with me,
To thank him for his generosity.
And then once that glorious task is done,
We'll come back here for yet another one—
I mean a wedding for which we'll prepare,
To give my daughter to the good Valère.

APHRA BEHN

1640?–1689

In her famous essay on women's writing, *A Room of One's Own* (1929), Virginia Woolf opines, "All women together ought to let flowers fall upon the tomb of Aphra Behn . . . , for it was she who earned them the right to speak their minds." As one of the first professional woman writers, Behn personifies for Woolf the struggles and triumphs attendant on living solely by one's pen. Yet the phenomenon of Behn as a professional writer, and the discovery of the circumstances that spawned her theatrical and literary career, initially drew more attention than her prodigious output itself. Indeed, even for Woolf, Behn's financial achievement "outweighs anything that she actually wrote." Ironically, Behn's unique professional status long allowed critics to dismiss her work as that of a hack and, more pointedly, of an immodest woman. Alexander Pope's notorious observation that Behn "fairly puts all characters to bed" reinforced the presumption that her dramas reflected personal licentiousness. Only in recent decades has her writing received a thorough analysis. That thoughtful reconsideration has established her importance as a Restoration dramatist and theater theorist, as a poet, and as a progenitor of the English novel.

Indisputably, the scarcity of concrete facts about her life combined with persistent insinuations of "irregular" behavior, including stories of her having spied for the English Crown, continues to tantalize us about Behn. No records exist to confirm her birth, but most biographers believe she was born in 1640, in the vicinity of Canterbury, to parents (possibly named Johnson) of uncertain social position. The biographer Angeline Goreau argues that the sophistication of Behn's writing, even in her earliest works, suggests a level of education available only to women of the gentry and higher social orders. Perhaps more significantly, we can see clear textual evidence in *THE ROVER* (1677) and elsewhere of Behn's keen understanding of class positions and their pervasive social impact. Moreover, as a child of a Royalist family, growing up in the periods of the English Civil War (1642–49) and the Commonwealth (1649–60), she developed an acute sensitivity to her country's shifting tides of power. Political concerns, and a sense of political commitment, underlie much of her dramaturgy.

It appears that in 1663 Aphra and her family embarked on a voyage to the then British colony of Surinam, where her father may have been assigned to a government post or may have hoped to profit as a planter. He died during the journey, however, and the surviving family members left

Surinam in early 1664. Yet the brief stay made a strong impression; Aphra's observations of plantation life and the practices of slavery inform her best-known novel, *Oroonoko* (1688). Upon her return to England, she apparently married one Mr. Behn, who may have been a merchant. Some biographers conjecture that he soon died in the plague that swept London in 1664 to 1666, leaving her without financial support; others believe that the marriage was fictitious, created by Behn to provide herself social legitimacy.

During her time in Surinam, Aphra had met William Scot, whose father, Thomas Scot, had been executed for his role in the regicide of Charles I. Although the nature of their relationship is unknown, it seems likely that William introduced Aphra to the world of political intrigue, which would soon involve her directly. In 1666, Behn probably became a spy for the restored Charles II, traveling to Antwerp to reconnect with William Scot, who was living there in exile and was probably an informant in the Anglo-Dutch War. Behn, like many in government service at the time, quickly fell into financial distress when promised payments failed to materialize. When she returned to England in 1667, she was seriously in debt and was briefly held in debtor's prison. This experience of privation marked her indelibly, and the precarious financial status of women in Restoration society became one of her dominant concerns. Yet her time in Antwerp had also persuaded her of her self-sufficiency, even in dangerous and male-dominated arenas. In the preface to her late play *The Lucky Chance* (1687), she openly connected her creativity to her understanding of the masculine sphere in which she worked, claiming privilege "for my Masculine Part the Poet in me."

After her release from jail, Behn decided to embark on a career as a professional playwright. In September 1670, her first piece, *The Forced Marriage,* premiered at Lincoln's Inn Fields and ran for six nights—a solid performance record for the period. Behn followed with *The Amorous Prince* (1671), *The Dutch Lover* (1673), *Abdelazer* (1676), *The Town Fop* (1676), *The Debauchee* (later attributed to her, 1677), and, in March 1677, the first part of *The Rover*.

Over the next twelve years, Behn's output included approximately a dozen more plays (attributions remain conjectural for some, produced anonymously), including the second part of *The Rover* (1681), numerous translations, several volumes of verse, the proto-novelistic *Love Letters between a Nobleman and His Sister,* and the fictional prose works *Oroonoko* and *The Fair Jilt*. Two other plays and several other fictional works appeared posthumously. Behn died in April 1689, shortly after the coronation of William and Mary, and is buried in Westminster Abbey.

That Behn could maintain even a meager livelihood in the professional theater for more than twenty years clearly indicates that she was a popular dramatist. The reasons aren't hard to imagine. What is true of mass culture today was equally valid for the Restoration: though some degree of novelty may be welcome, the public enjoys entertainment forms that it already knows well. Behn had a quick wit and a ready hand at adaptation and translation, and she used these skills to create new plays that incorporated themes, dramatic structures, character types, and plot devices that had already proven their stageworthiness.

The closure of the theaters from 1642 to 1660 by the Puritan government had severely impeded but could not altogether quash the ongoing development of the English drama, which had flourished in the Renaissance. When Thomas Killigrew and Sir William Davenant received patents from Charles II to operate London's two licensed theaters, they looked to published drama, especially by WILLIAM SHAKESPEARE, Ben Jonson, and Francis Beaumont and John Fletcher, to remount. These revivals, as well as adaptations of established works and of closet dramas written during the interregnum (the time between the beheading of Charles I in 1649 and the restoration of the monarchy in 1660), constituted most of the early Restoration stage repertoire. The new dramas that had immediately preceded the Commonwealth period, such as the comedies of James Shirley, provided further inspiration for aspiring Restoration dramatists.

The Rover may be best understood within these complex political and theatrical contexts. Following common dramatic practice, Behn decided to adapt a lengthy unproduced work by Killigrew, written in 1654 and published a decade later, titled *Thomaso, or, The Wanderer*. By refashioning characters, streamlining action, and highlighting plot elements from *Thomaso* that she suspected would please her audience, Behn created in *The Rover* a play that could also carry her distinctive themes. Her subtle revisions of well-established patterns of stage dialogue and character types, which had been codified over the preceding decade through the dramas of Sir George Etherege, John Dryden, and William Wycherley, among others, enabled her both to develop these themes and to build upon her growing theatrical reputation.

Behn's first strategic choice in adapting *Thomaso* was to change its setting. She moves the action from the time of the Spanish Inquisition to the more recent past—the period of Royalist exile—and places her characters in Naples during the carnival season of revelry that precedes Lent. After the murder of Charles I, his son Prince Charles fled England, as did a good number of his supporters, who feared persecution under the Puritan regime. That Cromwell then confiscated many of the Royalists' estates may account for the impecunious state of characters like the "rover" Willmore, whose seaboard travels also associate him with the Prince. As the Royalists' friend Blunt avows, "I thank my stars I had more grace than to forfeit my estate by cavaliering." But he also admits that supporting his friends "is a greater crime to my conscience, gentlemen, than to the commonwealth."

Behn depicts the adventures of a band of these traveling Englishmen (her subtitle is "The Banished Cavaliers"), led by the rakish Willmore and his more earnest friend Belvile. They encounter the local women "of quality," Hellena, Florinda, and Valeria, as well as prostitutes, especially the courtesan Angellica. Although the setting is foreign and somewhat exotic, the narrative arc is traditional, centering on which of the characters will marry and how those relationships will be solidified. Behn thus brings together conventions from both the drama of intrigue and romantic comedy. She retains the swashbuckling flavor of Killigrew's Spanish setting and peppers her action with lively swordplay between rivals for the favors of Angellica and protectors of the honor of the chaste Florinda. By removing the

"Venetian" masquerades, such as the one pictured here that was held in Ranelagh Gardens, London, in April of 1749, were quite popular in England during the late seventeenth and early eighteenth centuries.

drama from a court setting, moreover, she participates in the Restoration theater's shift of focus away from the aristocracy and toward those in the growing middle ranks of society. By interweaving dramatic forms and broadening the range of characters, Behn can explore issues of class and gender frankly while simultaneously confirming her loyalty to the returned monarch and his supporters.

From the medieval era forward, Western literature has depicted the carnival season preceding Lent as a time of culturally sanctioned upheaval, when rigid social structures are briefly relaxed. Behn dramatizes just such a moment in *The Rover,* as the aristocratic young women of Naples disguise themselves and escape their sequestered home environment to join the revelry, where they meet the English cavaliers. Behn must have seen a direct link between her carnival setting and Restoration culture writ large, given their shared predilections for masking, posturing, and sexual license; we may assume that audiences for *The Rover* grasped these connections through such devices as the thinly disguised characterization of the libertine John Wilmot, earl of Rochester, as her libertine Willmore. At the same time, however, Behn demonstrates that even within the freedoms offered by masquerade, women remained subject to male power and assumed sexual privilege. Behn's viewers may also have perceived the metatheatrical quality of the play, as she repeatedly calls our attention to the donning of a series of costumes by Hellena, Florinda, and Valeria, as well as to the highly staged yet ignominious duping of Blunt by the conniving Lucetta.

Behn signals her focus on the female characters from her opening scene, which introduces us to Florinda and her sister Hellena. We are privy to the sisters' exchanges about Florinda's multiple suitors and Hellena's desire to find a man and to avoid having to become a nun: "I'm resolved to provide myself this Carnival, if there be e'er a handsome proper fellow of my humour above ground, though I ask first." Behn contrasts the sisters through their attitudes toward sexuality. While Hellena is willing to transcend traditional feminine passivity by "ask[ing] first," Florinda is the more conventional romantic heroine. We learn that Florinda has previously been rescued in Pamplona from the "licensed lust of common soldiers" by her admirer, Captain Belvile, but she will face three more threats of sexual assault before she is safely united with him. She must also outwit her brother Pedro and her father, each of whom has arranged for her marriage to an eligible, but undesired, suitor. The feistier Hellena soon develops an attraction for the rake Willmore, but finds she must plot to secure his complete attention and fidelity.

Through the play's opening dialogue, Behn establishes the competing tensions that will shape her comedy: between women's desire to make their own matrimonial choices and men's assumption of that privilege, between women's interest in reciprocal enjoyment of sex and men's single-minded lust, between women's financial dependence on men and their wish to gain some control over their economic future. Behn deploys the familiar trope of marriage and money central to Restoration comedy, but refocuses it by realistically depicting the social and financial constraints affecting the female characters. The introduction of the courtesan Angellica Bianca and the "jilting wench" Lucetta, who play important roles in the play's examination of women's economic status, also enables Behn to explore the traditional depiction of women as either virgins or whores and to question the relationship of these opposing roles to the exchange economy she portrays.

Restoration comedy frequently critiqued marriages based solely on economic convenience, but Behn portrays the emotional and personal costs of such arrangements to women with real poignancy. Women of the era were legally considered the property of their fathers until, through the dowry system, they became the property of their husbands, who thereby gained complete control of their wealth and their person. Arranged marriages thus served to protect and enhance family fortunes. As Behn's contemporary Margaret Cavendish, duchess of Newcastle, once remarked, "Daughters are to be accounted but as Movable Goods or Furniture that wear out." In the opening scene of *The Rover,* Florinda implores her brother not to "follow the ill customs of our country and make a slave of his sister" by marrying her to a man she hates.

Where Behn departs from Restoration dramatic convention is in overtly connecting the financial networks of marriage and prostitution—especially in the absence of true affection. When Willmore tries to convince Angellica to favor him sexually for the sake of desire alone, chastising her, "Poor as I am I would not sell myself, / No, not to gain your charming high-prized person," Angellica exposes his hypocrisy:

> Pray tell me, sir, are not you guilty of the same mercenary crime? When a lady is proposed to you for a wife, you never ask how fair, discreet, or virtuous she is, but what's her fortune; which, if but small, you cry "She will not do my business," and basely leave her, though she languish for you. Say, is not this as poor?

That Hellena and Florinda both possess fortunes, enhancing their suitability for marriage to the impecunious but noble cavaliers, underscores this irony. Behn does not attempt to overcome the power of dramatic (and moral) convention by disrupting the inevitable union of the "gay couple" Hellena and Willmore with a serious relationship between Willmore and Angellica. But she does, through the amorous triangulation of these three characters, resist typical structures of jealousy and opposition between women. Indeed, throughout the play, Behn provides multiple instances of women joining

Eleanor "Nell" Gwynn, mistress of Charles II and one of the first English actresses.

forces to achieve their economic and amatory goals.

However, a darker corollary to these associations among the play's women emerges from the male characters' repeated inability to distinguish between prostitutes and women "of quality." Blunt, after being tricked out of his belongings by Lucetta, whom he erroneously assumed was a lady of elevated social standing, displays open hostility to the female sex as a whole. For Blunt, virgins and whores are "as much one as t'other," and his plan to rape Florinda blatantly displays male sexuality as the exercise of power over women: "Cruel? Yes, I will kiss and beat thee all over, kiss and see thee all over; thou shalt lie with me, too, not that I care for the enjoyment, but to let thee see I have ta'en deliberated malice to thee, and will be revenged on one whore for the sins of another." Behn makes clear that no woman is immune to the potential for sexual violation in the carnivalesque culture she depicts.

In his rage, Blunt calls attention to the pretense he associates with prostitution, designating all whores "dissembling witches." He describes Florinda's tale of persecution by a group of unknown men she encounters while trying to flee to Belvile as if it were a performance—a calculated impersonation of the damsel in distress designed to fool him yet again. Such gestures point toward Behn's understanding of the increasingly complex interplay of women and theatricality in the Restoration. Behn's own entry into the theater as a playwright coincided with the appearance of the first professional English actresses. The display of women on stage quickly became associated with prostitution, a linkage made notorious by the actress Nell Gwynn, who was Charles II's mistress. But Behn realized that her own self-promotion, required of her as a playwright, drew a similar judgment; she very possibly retained the name Angellica Bianca from Killigrew and treated the character more sympathetically because she perceived that the courtesan character and she had much in common.

By deftly balancing sympathetic portraits of female characters with their frank display—particularly of Hellena, costumed in the breeches that allowed for more of the actress's body to be revealed—Behn calculatedly negotiated her position in the Restoration playhouse. She recognized that she could interject her own perspectives on women's lives as long as she also worked within established theatrical practices that appealed to the male patrons of the stage. Her combination of comic action, witty dialogue, bravado, romantic suspense, and titillation succeeded theatrically well into the eighteenth century. *The Rover* remained a regular part of the repertoire throughout the first half of that century and returned to popularity late in the twentieth, demonstrating its worth not only as an exemplar of Restoration drama but also as successful and timeless stage comedy.

J.E.G.

The Rover
or, *The Banished Cavaliers*[1]

Prologue

Wits, like physicians, never can agree,
When of a different society.
And Rabel's drops[2] were never more cried down
By all the learned doctors of the town,
Than a new play whose author is unknown.[3]
Nor can those doctors with more malice sue
(And powerful purses) the dissenting few,
Than those, with an insulting pride, do rail
At all who are not of their own cabal.° *clique*
If a young poet hit your humour° right, *mood*
You judge him then out of revenge and spite.
So amongst men there are ridiculous elves,
Who monkeys hate for being too like themselves.
So that the reason of the grand debate
Why wit so oft is damned when good plays take,
Is that you censure as you love, or hate.
Thus like a learned conclave poets sit,
Catholic° judges both of sense and wit, *Universal*
And damn or save as they themselves think fit.
Yet those who to others' faults are so severe,
Are not so perfect but themselves may err.
Some write correct, indeed, but then the whole
(Bating° their own dull stuff i'th' play) is stole: *Excepting*
As bees do suck from flowers their honeydew,
So they rob others striving to please you.
Some write their characters genteel and fine,
But then they do so toil for every line,
That what to you does easy seem, and plain,
Is the hard issue of their laboring brain.
And some th'effects of all their pains, we see,
Is but to mimic good extempore.° *improvisation*
Others, by long converse about the town,
Have wit enough to write a lewd lampoon,
But their chief skill lies in a bawdy song.
In short, the only wit that's now in fashion,
Is but the gleanings of good conversation.
As for the author of this coming play,

1. The Royalist supporters of Charles I; as many went into exile during the English Civil War and interregnum of 1642–60, often their estates were confiscated by Oliver Cromwell.

2. A well-known patent medicine.

3. *The Rover* was initially produced and published anonymously.

I asked him[4] what he thought fit I should say
In thanks for your good company today:
He called me fool, and said it was well known
You came not here for our sakes, but your own.
New plays are stuffed with wits and with deboches,° *debauchees*
That crowd and sweat like cits in May-Day coaches.[5]

WRITTEN BY A PERSON OF QUALITY

CHARACTERS

DON ANTONIO, the Viceroy's son
DON PEDRO, a noble Spaniard, his friend
BELVILE, an English colonel in love with Florinda
WILLMORE, the Rover
FREDERICK, an English gentleman, and friend to Belvile and Blunt
BLUNT, an English country gentleman
STEPHANO, servant to Don Pedro
PHILIPPO, Lucetta's gallant
SANCHO, pimp to Lucetta
BISKEY and SEBASTIAN, two bravos° to Angellica *hired ruffians, henchmen*
OFFICER and SOLDIERS
DIEGO, Page to Don Antonio
FLORINDA, sister to Don Pedro
HELLENA, a gay young woman designed for[6] a nun, and sister to Florinda
VALERIA, a kinswoman to Florinda
ANGELLICA BIANCA, a famous courtesan
MORETTA, her woman
CALLIS, governess to Florinda and Hellena
LUCETTA, a jilting wench
SERVANTS, OTHER MASQUERADERS, MEN AND WOMEN

THE SCENE: *Naples, in Carnival time.*[7]

1.1

[SCENE: *A chamber.*]

[*Enter* FLORINDA *and* HELLENA.]

FLORINDA What an impertinent thing is a young girl bred in a nunnery! How full of questions! Prithee no more, Hellena; I have told thee more than thou understand'st already.

HELLENA The more's my grief. I would fain° know as much as you, which makes me so inquisitive; nor is't enough I know you're a lover, unless you tell me too who 'tis you sigh for. *gladly*

4. Behn used the masculine pronoun so that playgoers would not dismiss this work as written by a woman.
5. It was customary to ride around Hyde Park in coaches on May Day. *Cits:* urban males, but not gentlemen (slang).
6. That is, designated (by her family) to become.
7. The period of festival before the fasting and prayer of Lent, commonly celebrated in Roman Catholic countries.

FLORINDA When you're a lover I'll think you fit for a secret of that nature.

HELLENA 'Tis true, I never was a lover yet, but I begin to have a shrewd guess what 'tis to be so, and fancy it very pretty to sigh, and sing, and blush, and wish, and dream and wish, and long and wish to see the man, and when I do, look pale and tremble, just as you did when my brother brought home the fine English colonel to see you. What do you call him? Don Belvile?

FLORINDA Fie, Hellena.

HELLENA That blush betrays you. I am sure 'tis so. Or is it Don Antonio the Viceroy's son? Or perhaps the rich old Don Vincentio, whom my father designs you for a husband? Why do you blush again?

FLORINDA With indignation; and how near soever my father thinks I am to marrying that hated object, I shall let him see I understand better what's due to my beauty, birth, and fortune, and more to my soul, than to obey those unjust commands.

HELLENA Now hang me, if I don't love thee for that dear disobedience. I love mischief strangely, as most of our sex do who are come to love nothing else. But tell me, dear Florinda, don't you love that fine *Anglese*?° For I vow, next to loving him myself, 'twill please me most that you do so, for he is so gay and so handsome.

Englishman (Italian)

FLORINDA Hellena, a maid designed for a nun ought not to be so curious in a discourse of love.

HELLENA And dost thou think that ever I'll be a nun? Or at least till° I'm so old I'm fit for nothing else? Faith no, sister; and that which makes me long to know whether you love Belvile, is because I hope he has some mad companion or other that will spoil my devotion. Nay, I'm resolved to provide myself this Carnival, if there be e'er a handsome proper fellow of my humour above ground, though I ask first.

before

FLORINDA Prithee be not so wild.

HELLENA Now you have provided yourself of a man you take no care of poor me. Prithee tell me, what dost thou see about me that is unfit for love? Have I not a world of youth? A humour gay? A beauty passable? A vigor desirable? Well shaped? Clean limbed? Sweet breathed? And sense enough to know how all these ought to be employed to the best advantage? Yes, I do and will; therefore lay aside your hopes of my fortune by my being a devote,° and tell me how you came acquainted with this Belvile. For I perceive you knew him before he came to Naples.

nun

FLORINDA Yes, I knew him at the siege of Pamplona;[8] he was then a colonel of French horse, who when the

8. The capital of the Spanish province of Navarre, which was several times attacked by the French during the Thirty Years War (1618–48) waged throughout Europe.

town was ransacked, nobly treated my brother and myself, preserving us from all insolences. And I must own, besides great obligations, I have I know not what that pleads kindly for him about my heart, and will suffer no other to enter. But see, my brother.

[*Enter* DON PEDRO, STEPHANO *with a masking habit,*° *and* CALLIS.] — masquerade costume

PEDRO Good morrow, sister. Pray when saw you your lover Don Vincentio?

FLORINDA I know not, sir. Callis, when was he here? For I consider it so little I know not when it was.

PEDRO I have a command from my father here to tell you you ought not to despise him, a man of so vast a fortune, and such a passion for you. —Stephano, my things.

[*Puts on his masking habit.*]

FLORINDA A passion for me? 'Tis more than e'er I saw, or he had a desire should be known. I hate Vincentio, sir, and I would not have a man so dear to me as my brother follow the ill customs of our country and make a slave of his sister. And, sir, my father's will I'm sure you may divert.

PEDRO I know not how dear I am to you, but I wish only to be ranked in your esteem equal with the English colonel Belvile. Why do you frown and blush? Is there any guilt belongs to the name of that cavalier?

FLORINDA I'll not deny I value Belvile. When I was exposed to such dangers as the licensed lust of common soldiers threatened, when rage and conquest flew through the city, then Belvile, this criminal for my sake, threw himself into all dangers to save my honor. And will you not allow him my esteem?

PEDRO Yes, pay him what you will in honor, but you must consider Don Vincentio's fortune, and the jointure[9] he'll make you.

FLORINDA Let him consider my youth, beauty, and fortune, which ought not to be thrown away on his age and jointure.

PEDRO 'Tis true, he's not so young and fine a gentleman as that Belvile. But what jewels will that cavalier present you with. Those of his eyes and heart?

HELLENA And are not those better than any Don Vincentio has brought from the Indies?

PEDRO Why, how now! Has your nunnery breeding taught you to understand the value of hearts and eyes?

HELLENA Better than to believe Vincentio's deserve value from any woman. He may perhaps increase her bags,° but not her family. — wealth

PEDRO This is fine! Go! Up to your devotion! You are not designed for the conversation of lovers.

9. The property promised to a wife at marriage in the event of her husband's death.

HELLENA [*aside*] Nor saints yet a while, I hope. —Is't not enough you make a nun of me, but you must cast my sister away too, exposing her to a worse confinement than a religious life?

PEDRO The girl's mad! It is a confinement to be carried into the country to an ancient villa belonging to the family of the Vincentios these five hundred years, and have no other prospect° (*view*) than that pleasing one of seeing all her own that meets her eyes: a fine air, large fields, and gardens where she may walk and gather flowers?

HELLENA When, by moonlight? For I am sure she dares not encounter with the heat of the sun; that were a task only for Don Vincentio and his Indian breeding, who loves it in the dog days.[1] And if these be her daily divertissements,° (*amusements*) what are those of the night? To lie in a wide moth-eaten bedchamber with furniture in fashion in the reign of King Sancho the First;[2] the bed, that which his forefathers lived and died in.

PEDRO Very well.

HELLENA This apartment, new furbished and fitted out for the young wife, he out of freedom makes his dressing room; and being a frugal and a jealous coxcomb,° (*fool*) instead of a valet to uncase° (*undress*) his feeble carcass, he desires you to do that office. Signs of favor, I'll assure you, and such as you must not hope for unless your woman be out of the way.

PEDRO Have you done yet?

HELLENA That honor being past, the giant stretches itself, yawns and sighs a belch or two loud as a musket, throws himself into bed, and expects° (*waits for*) you in his foul sheets; and ere you can get yourself undressed, calls you with a snore or two. And are not these fine blessings to a young lady?

PEDRO Have you done yet?

HELLENA And this man you must kiss, nay you must kiss none but him too, and nuzzle through his beard to find his lips. And this you must submit to for threescore years, and all for a jointure.

PEDRO For all your character of Don Vincentio, she is as like to marry him as she was before.

HELLENA Marry Don Vincentio! Hang me, such a wedlock would be worse than adultery with another man. I had rather see her in the *Hostel de Dieu*,[3] to waste her youth there in vows, and be a handmaid to lazars° (*lepers*) and cripples, than to lose it in such a marriage.

PEDRO You have considered, sister, that Belvile has no

1. The hottest part of summer, when Sirius (the Dog Star) rises. *Indian breeding*: birth in the West Indies.

2. King of Pamplona (Navarre) in the 10th century

3. A charitable hospital operated by a religious order.

fortune to bring you to; banished his country, despised at home, and pitied abroad.

HELLENA What then? The Viceroy's son is better than that old Sir Fifty. Don Vincentio! Don Indian! He thinks he's trading to Gambo[4] still, and would barter himself—that bell and bauble—for your youth and fortune.

PEDRO Callis, take her hence and lock her up all this Carnival, and at Lent she shall begin her everlasting penance in a monastery.

HELLENA I care not; I had rather be a nun than be obliged to marry as you would have me if I were designed for't.

PEDRO Do not fear the blessing of that choice. You shall be a nun.

HELLENA [*aside*] Shall I so? You may chance to be mistaken in my way of devotion. A nun! Yes, I am like to make a fine nun! I have an excellent humour for a grate![5] No, I'll have a saint of my own to pray to shortly, if I like any that dares venture on me.

PEDRO Callis, make it your business to watch this wildcat. —As for you, Florinda, I've only tried° you all this while and urged my father's will; but mine is that you would love Antonio: he is brave and young, and all that can complete the happiness of a gallant maid. This absence of my father will give us opportunity to free you from Vincentio by marrying here, which you must do tomorrow. *tested*

FLORINDA Tomorrow!

PEDRO Tomorrow, or 'twill be too late. 'Tis not my friendship to Antonio which makes me urge this, but love to thee and hatred to Vincentio; therefore resolve upon tomorrow.

FLORINDA Sir, I shall strive to do as shall become your sister.

PEDRO I'll both believe and trust you. Adieu.

[*Exeunt*° PEDRO *and* STEPHANO.] *They exit (Latin)*

HELLENA As becomes his sister! That is to be as resolved your way as he is his.

[HELLENA *goes to* CALLIS.]

FLORINDA I ne'er till now perceived my ruin near.
I've no defence against Antonio's love,
For he has all the advantages of nature,
The moving arguments of youth and fortune.

HELLENA But hark you, Callis, you will not be so cruel to lock me up indeed, will you?

CALLIS I must obey the commands I have. Besides, do you consider what a life you are going to lead?

HELLENA Yes, Callis, that of a nun; and till then I'll be indebted a world of prayers to you if you'll let me now see what I never did, the divertissements of a Carnival.

4. The British colony of Gambia in West Africa, a center of the slave trade.

5. The framework of bars on a convent's doors and windows, separating nuns from the secular world.

CALLIS What, go in masquerade? 'Twill be a fine farewell to the world, I take it. Pray what would you do there?

HELLENA That which all the world does, as I am told: be as mad as the rest and take all innocent freedoms. Sister, you'll go too, will you not? Come, prithee be not sad. We'll outwit twenty brothers if you'll be ruled by me. Come, put off this dull humour with your clothes, and assume one as gay and as fantastic as the dress my cousin Valeria and I have provided, and let's ramble.

FLORINDA Callis, will you give us leave to go?

CALLIS [*aside*] I have a youthful itch of going myself.— Madam, if I thought your brother might not know it, and I might wait on you; for by my troth I'll not trust young girls alone.

FLORINDA Thou seest my brother's gone already, and thou shalt attend and watch us.

[*Enter* STEPHANO.]

STEPHANO Madam, the habits° are come, and your cousin Valeria is dressed and stays for you. (*costumes*)

FLORINDA [*aside*] 'Tis well. I'll write a note, and if I chance to see Belvile and want an opportunity to speak to him, that shall let him know what I've resolved in favor of him.

HELLENA Come, let's in and dress us.

[*Exeunt.*]

1.2

[SCENE: *A long street.*]

[*Enter* BELVILE, *melancholy;* BLUNT *and* FREDERICK.]

FREDERICK Why, what the devil ails the colonel, in a time when all the world is gay, to look like mere° Lent thus? (*pure*) Hadst thou been long enough in Naples to have been in love, I should have sworn some such judgment had befallen thee.

BELVILE No, I have made no new amours since I came to Naples.

FREDERICK You have left none behind you in Paris?

BELVILE Neither.

FREDERICK I cannot divine the cause then, unless the old cause, the want of money.

BLUNT And another old cause, the want of a wench. Would not that revive you?

BELVILE You are mistaken, Ned.

BLUNT Nay, 'adsheartlikins,° then thou'rt past cure. (*God's little heart (oath)*)

FREDERICK I have found it out: thou hast renewed thy acquaintance with the lady that cost thee so many sighs at the siege of Pamplona—pox on't,° what d'ye call her—her brother's a noble Spaniard, nephew to the dead general. (*(an oath)*)

Florinda. Ay, Florinda. And will nothing serve thy turn but that damned virtuous woman, whom on my conscience thou lov'st in spite too, because thou seest little or no possibility of gaining her.

BELVILE Thou art mistaken; I have int'rest enough in that lovely virgin's heart to make me proud and vain, were it not abated by the severity of a brother, who, perceiving my happiness—

FREDERICK Has civilly forbid thee the house?

BELVILE 'Tis so, to make way for a powerful rival, the Viceroy's son, who has the advantage of me in being a man of fortune, a Spaniard, and her brother's friend; which gives him liberty to make his court, whilst I have recourse only to letters and distant looks from her window, which are as soft and kind as those which heaven sends down on penitents.

BLUNT Heyday! 'Adsheartlikins, simile! By this light the man is quite spoiled. Fred, what the devil are we made of that we cannot be thus concerned for a wench? 'Adsheartlikins, our Cupids[6] are like the cooks of the camp: they can roast or boil a woman, but they have none of the fine tricks to set 'em off; no hogoes° to make the sauce pleasant and the stomach sharp. *savory relishes*

FREDERICK I dare swear I have had a hundred as young, kind, and handsome as this Florinda; and dogs eat me if they were not as troublesome to me i'th' morning as they were welcome o'er night.

BLUNT And yet I warrant he would not touch another woman if he might have her for nothing.

BELVILE That's thy joy, a cheap whore.

BLUNT Why, 'adsheartlikins, I love a frank soul. When did you ever hear of an honest woman that took a man's money? I warrant 'em good ones. But gentlemen, you may be free; you have been kept so poor with parliaments and protectors that the little stock you have is not worth preserving. But I thank my stars I had more grace than to forfeit my estate by cavaliering.[7]

BELVILE Methinks only following the court should be sufficient to entitle 'em to that.

BLUNT 'Adsheartlikins, they know I follow it to do it no good, unless they pick a hole in my coat for lending you money now and then, which is a greater crime to my conscience, gentlemen, than to the commonwealth.

[*Enter* WILLMORE.]

6. Cupid is the Roman god of love, often depicted as winged; his arrows cause their target to fall in love.

7. The estates of many Royalists (i.e., Cavaliers) were confiscated by Oliver Cromwell's government following the Parliamentarian victory in the English Civil War. The official title of the country's leader during that period was Lord Protector of the Commonwealth.

WILLMORE Ha! Dear Belvile! Noble colonel!

BELVILE Willmore! Welcome ashore, my dear rover! What happy wind blew us this good fortune?

WILLMORE Let me salute my dear Fred, and then command me. —How is't, honest lad?

FREDERICK Faith, sir, the old compliment, infinitely the better to see my dear mad Willmore again. Prithee, why camest thou ashore? And where's the Prince?[8]

WILLMORE He's well, and reigns still lord of the wat'ry element. I must aboard again within a day or two, and my business ashore was only to enjoy myself a little this Carnival.

BELVILE Pray know our new friend, sir; he's but bashful, a raw traveler, but honest, stout, and one of us.

[*Embraces* BLUNT.]

WILLMORE That you esteem him gives him an int'rest here.

BLUNT Your servant, sir.

WILLMORE But well, faith, I'm glad to meet you again in a warm climate, where the kind sun has its godlike power still over the wine and women. Love and mirth are my business in Naples, and if I mistake not the place, here's an excellent market for chapmen° of my humour. *merchants*

BELVILE See, here be those kind merchants of love you look for.

[*Enter several men in masking habits, some playing on music, others dancing after; women dressed like courtesans, with papers pinned on their breasts, and baskets of flowers in their hands.*]

BLUNT 'Adsheartlikins, what have we here?

FREDERICK Now the game begins.

WILLMORE Fine pretty creatures! May a stranger have leave to look and love? What's here? "Roses for every month"? [*Reads the papers.*]

BLUNT Roses for every month? What means that?

BELVILE They are, or would have you think they're courtesans, who here in Naples are to be hired by the month.

WILLMORE Kind and obliging to inform us, pray where do these roses grow? I would fain plant some of 'em in a bed of mine.

WOMAN Beware such roses, sir.

WILLMORE A pox of fear: I'll be baked with thee between a pair of sheets, and that's thy proper still;[9] so I might but strew such roses over me and under me. Fair one, would you would give me leave to gather at your bush this idle month; I would go near to make somebody smell of it all the year after.

8. The exiled son of Charles I, soon to be crowned Charles II (1630–1685; r. 1660–85).

9. That is, apparatus for distilling rose petals to make perfume.

BELVILE And thou hast need of such a remedy, for thou stink'st of tar and ropes' ends like a dock or pesthouse.[1]

[*The* WOMAN *puts herself into the hands of a man and exeunt.*]

WILLMORE Nay, nay, you shall not leave me so.

BELVILE By all means use no violence here.

WILLMORE Death!° Just as I was going to be damnably in love, to have her led off! I could pluck that rose out of his hand, and even kiss the bed the bush grew in. — *God's death (an oath)*

FREDERICK No friend to love like a long voyage at sea.

BLUNT Except a nunnery,° Fred. — *convent; brothel*

WILLMORE Death! But will they not be kind? Quickly be kind? Thou know'st I'm no tame sigher, but a rampant lion of the forest.

[*Advances from the farther end of the scenes two men dressed all over with horns*[2] *of several sorts, making grimaces at one another, with papers pinned on their backs.*]

BELVILE Oh the fantastical rogues, how they're dressed! 'Tis a satire against the whole sex.

WILLMORE Is this a fruit that grows in this warm country?

BELVILE Yes, 'tis pretty to see these Italians start, swell, and stab at the word *cuckold*, and yet stumble at horns on every threshold.

WILLMORE See what's on their back. [*Reads.*] "Flowers of every night." Ah, rogue! And more sweet than roses of every month! This is a gardener of Adam's own breeding.[3]

[*They dance.*]

BELVILE What think you of these grave people? Is a wake in Essex[4] half so mad or extravagant?

WILLMORE I like their sober grave way; 'tis a kind of legal authorized fornication, where the men are not chid for't, nor the women despised, as amongst our dull English. Even the monsieurs want that part of good manners.

BELVILE But here in Italy, a monsieur is the humblest best-bred gentleman: duels are so baffled by bravos° that an age shows not one but between a Frenchman and a hangman, who is as much too hard for him on the Piazza as they are for a Dutchman on the New Bridge.[5] But see, another crew. — *hired ruffians*

[*Enter* FLORINDA, HELLENA, *and* VALERIA, *dressed like gipsies;* CALLIS *and* STEPHANO, LUCETTA, PHILIPPO *and* SANCHO *in masquerade.*]

1. A hospital for victims of the plague.
2. The symbol of a cuckold.
3. An allusion to the Garden of Eden.
4. The location of Blunt's home in rural southeastern England (see also 2.1).
5. Nieuwerbrug (New Bridge), in southern Holland, was attacked by the French in the Third Anglo-Dutch War (1672–74)—an anachronistic reference, as the play is set before 1660.

HELLENA Sister, there's your Englishman, and with him a handsome proper fellow. I'll to him, and instead of telling him his fortune, try my own.

WILLMORE Gipsies, on my life. Sure these will prattle if a man cross their hands. [*Goes to* HELLENA.] —Dear, pretty, and, I hope, young devil, will you tell an amorous stranger what luck he's like to have?

HELLENA Have a care how you venture with me, sir, lest I pick your pocket, which will more vex your English humor than an Italian fortune will please you.

WILLMORE How the devil cam'st thou to know my country and humor?

HELLENA The first I guess by a certain forward impudence, which does not displease me at this time; and the loss of your money will vex you because I hope you have but very little to lose.

WILLMORE Egad, child, thou'rt i'th' right; it is so little I dare not offer it thee for a kindness. But cannot you divine what other things of more value I have about me that I would more willingly part with?

HELLENA Indeed no, that's the business of a witch, and I am but a gipsy yet. Yet without looking in your hand, I have a parlous guess 'tis some foolish heart you mean, an inconstant English heart, as little worth stealing as your purse.

WILLMORE Nay, then thou dost deal with the devil, that's certain. Thou hast guessed as right as if thou hadst been one of that number it has languished for. I find you'll be better acquainted with it, nor can you take it in a better time; for I am come from sea, child, and Venus not being propitious to me in her own element,[6] I have a world of love in store. Would you would be good-natured and take some on't off my hands.

HELLENA Why, I could be inclined that way, but for a foolish vow I am going to make to die a maid.

WILLMORE Then thou art damned without redemption, and as I am a good Christian, I ought in charity to divert so wicked a design. Therefore prithee, dear creature, let me know quickly when and where I shall begin to set a helping hand to so good a work.

HELLENA If you should prevail with my tender heart, as I begin to fear you will, for you have horrible loving eyes, there will be difficulty in't that you'll hardly° undergo for my sake.
with hardship

WILLMORE Faith, child, I have been bred in dangers, and wear a sword that has been employed in a worse cause than for a handsome kind woman. Name the danger; let it be anything but a long siege, and I'll undertake it.

6. Venus, the Roman goddess of love, was born from the sea foam off the island of Cythera.

HELLENA Can you storm?

WILLMORE Oh, most furiously.

HELLENA What think you of a nunnery wall? For he that wins me must gain that first.

WILLMORE A nun! Oh, now I love thee for't! There's no sinner like a young saint. Nay, now there's no denying me; the old law had no curse to a woman like dying a maid: witness Jeptha's daughter.[7]

HELLENA A very good text this, if well handled; and I perceive, Father Captain, you would impose no severe penance on her who were inclined to console herself before she took orders.° *became a nun*

WILLMORE If she be young and handsome.

HELLENA Ay, there's it. But if she be not—

WILLMORE By this hand, child, I have an implicit faith, and dare venture on° *dare to approach* thee with all faults. Besides, 'tis more meritorious to leave the world when thou hast tasted and proved the pleasure on't. Then 'twill be a virtue in thee, which now will be pure ignorance.

HELLENA I perceive, good Father Captain, you design only to make me fit for heaven. But if, on the contrary, you should quite divert me from it, and bring me back to the world again, I should have a new man to seek, I find. And what a grief that will be; for when I begin, I fancy I shall love like anything; I never tried yet.

WILLMORE Egad, and that's kind! Prithee, dear creature, give me credit for a heart, for faith, I'm a very honest fellow. Oh, I long to come first to the banquet of love! And such a swinging° *hearty* appetite I bring. Oh, I'm impatient. Thy lodging, sweetheart, thy lodging, or I'm a dead man!

HELLENA Why must we be either guilty of fornication or murder if we converse with you men? And is there no difference between leave to love me, and leave to lie with me?

WILLMORE Faith, child, they were made to go together.

LUCETTA [*pointing to* BLUNT] Are you sure this is the man?

SANCHO When did I mistake your game?

LUCETTA This is a stranger, I know by his gazing; if he be brisk he'll venture to follow me, and then, if I understand my trade, he's mine. He's English, too, and they say that's a sort of good-natured loving people, and have generally so kind an opinion of themselves that a woman with any wit may flatter 'em into any sort of fool she pleases.

[*She often passes by* BLUNT *and gazes on him; he struts and cocks, and walks and gazes on her.*]

BLUNT 'Tis so, she is taken; I have beauties which my false glass° *mirror* at home did not discover.° *reveal*

7. Sacrificed by Jephthah to fulfill his vow to God, after she was allowed two months to "bewail [her] virginity" (see Judges 11.30–39).

FLORINDA [*aside*] This woman watches me so, I shall get no opportunity to discover myself to him, and so miss the intent of my coming. —[*To* BELVILE.] But as I was saying, sir, by this line you should be a lover.

[*Looking in his hand.*]

BELVILE I thought how right you guessed: all men are in love, or pretend to be so. Come, let me go; I'm weary of this fooling.

[*Walks away.*]

FLORINDA I will not, sir, till you have confessed whether the passion that you have vowed Florinda be true or false.

[*She holds him; he strives to get from her.*]

BELVILE Florinda!

[*Turns quick towards her.*]

FLORINDA Softly.

BELVILE Thou hast nam'd one will fix me here forever.

FLORINDA She'll be disappointed then, who expects you this night at the garden gate. And if you fail not, as— [*Looks on* CALLIS, *who observes 'em.*] Let me see the other hand—you will go near to do, she vows to die or make you happy.

BELVILE What canst thou mean?

FLORINDA That which I say. Farewell.

[*Offers*° *to go.*] *Attempts*

BELVILE Oh charming sybil,° stay; complete that joy which as it is will turn into distraction! Where must I be? At the garden gate? I know it. At night, you say? I'll sooner forfeit heaven than disobey. *prophetess*

[*Enter* DON PEDRO *and other maskers, and pass over the stage.*]

CALLIS Madam, your brother's here.

FLORINDA Take this to instruct you farther.

[*Gives him a letter, and goes off.*]

FREDERICK Have a care, sir, what you promise; this may be a trap laid by her brother to ruin you.

BELVILE Do not disturb my happiness with doubts.

[*Opens the letter.*]

WILLMORE My dear pretty creature, a thousand blessings on thee! Still in this habit, you say? And after dinner at this place?

HELLENA Yes, if you will swear to keep your heart and not bestow it between this and that.

WILLMORE By all the little gods of love, I swear; I'll leave it with you, and if you run away with it, those deities of justice will revenge me.

[*Exeunt all the women except* LUCETTA.]

FREDERICK Do you know the hand?° *handwriting*

BELVILE 'Tis Florinda's. All blessings fall upon the virtuous maid.

FREDERICK Nay, no idolatry; a sober sacrifice I'll allow you.

BELVILE Oh friends, the welcom'st news! The softest° letter! Nay, you shall all see it! And could you now be serious, I might be made the happiest man the sun shines on! *most tender*

WILLMORE The reason of this mighty joy?

BELVILE See how kindly she invites me to deliver her from the threatened violence of her brother. Will you not assist me?

WILLMORE I know not what thou mean'st, but I'll make one at any mischief where a woman's concerned. But she'll be grateful to us for the favor, will she not?

BELVILE How mean you?

WILLMORE How should I mean? Thou know'st there's but one way for a woman to oblige me.

BELVILE Do not profane; the maid is nicely virtuous.

WILLMORE Who, pox, then she's fit for nothing but a husband. Let her e'en go, colonel.

FREDERICK Peace, she's the colonel's mistress, sir.

WILLMORE Let her be the devil; if she be thy mistress, I'll serve her. Name the way.

BELVILE Read here this postscript.

[*Gives him a letter.*]

WILLMORE [*reads*] "At ten at night, at the garden gate, of which, if I cannot get the key, I will contrive a way over the wall. Come attended with a friend or two."—Kind heart, if we three cannot weave a string to let her down a garden wall, 'twere pity but the hangman wove one for us all.

FREDERICK Let her alone for that; your woman's wit, your fair kind woman, will out-trick a broker or a Jew, and contrive like a Jesuit in chains.[8] But see, Ned Blunt is stolen out after the lure of a damsel.

[*Exeunt* BLUNT *and* LUCETTA.]

BELVILE So, he'll scarce find his way home again unless we get him cried by the bellman° in the market place. And 'twould sound prettily: "A lost English boy of thirty." *town crier*

FREDERICK I hope 'tis some common crafty sinner, one that will fit him. It may be she'll sell him for Peru:[9] the rogue's sturdy, and would work well in a mine. At least I hope she'll dress him for our mirth, cheat him of all, then have him well-favoredly banged,° and turned out at midnight. *beaten*

WILLMORE Prithee what humor is he of, that you wish him so well?

BELVILE Why, of an English elder brother's humour: educated in a nursery, with a maid to tend him till fifteen, and lies with his grandmother till he's of age; one that

8. A description that rests on stereotypes of Jews as cheating bargainers and Jesuits as equivocal and deceptive in argument.

9. That is, sell him for slave labor in the mines of Peru, then a Spanish colony.

knows no pleasure beyond riding to the next fair, or going up to London with his right worshipful father in parliament time, wearing gay clothes, or making honorable love to his lady mother's laundry maid; gets drunk at a hunting match, and ten to one then gives some proofs of his prowess. A pox upon him, he's our banker, and has all our cash about him; and if he fail, we are all broke.

FREDERICK Oh, let him alone for that matter; he's of a damned stingy quality that will secure our stock. I know not in what danger it were indeed if the jilt should pretend she's in love with him, for 'tis a kind believing coxcomb; otherwise, if he part with more than a piece of eight,° geld him—for which offer he may chance to be beaten if she be a whore of the first rank. *Spanish dollar*

BELVILE Nay, the rogue will not be easily beaten; he's stout enough. Perhaps if they talk beyond his capacity he may chance to exercise his courage upon some of them, else I'm sure they'll find it as difficult to beat as to please him.

WILLMORE 'Tis a lucky devil to light upon so kind a wench!

FREDERICK Thou hadst a great deal of talk with thy little gipsy; couldst thou do no good upon her? For mine was hardhearted.

WILLMORE Hang her, she was some damned honest person of quality, I'm sure, she was so very free and witty. If her face be but answerable to her wit and humor, I would be bound to constancy this month to gain her. In the meantime, have you made no kind acquaintance since you came to town? You do not use to be honest so long, gentlemen.

FREDERICK Faith, love has kept us honest: we have been all fir'd with a beauty newly come to town, the famous Paduana° Angellica Bianca. *woman from Padua*

WILLMORE What, the mistress of the dead Spanish general?

BELVILE Yes, she's now the only ador'd beauty of all the youth in Naples, who put on all their charms to appear lovely in her sight: their coaches, liveries, and themselves all gay as on a monarch's birthday to attract the eyes of this fair charmer, while she has the pleasure to behold all languish for her that see her.

FREDERICK 'Tis pretty to see with how much love the men regard her, and how much envy the women.

WILLMORE What gallant has she?

BELVILE None; she's exposed to sale, and four days in the week she's yours, for so much a month.

WILLMORE The very thought of it quenches all manner of fire in me. Yet prithee, let's see her.

BELVILE Let's first to dinner, and after that we'll pass the day as you please. But at night ye must all be at my devotion.

WILLMORE I will not fail you.

[*Exeunt.*]

2.1

[SCENE: *The long street.*]

[*Enter* BELVILE *and* FREDERICK *in masking habits, and* WILLMORE *in his own clothes, with a vizard° in his hand.*] *mask*

WILLMORE But why thus disguised and muzzled?

BELVILE Because whatever extravagances we commit in these faces, our own may not be obliged to answer 'em.

WILLMORE I should have changed my eternal buff,° too; but no matter, my little gipsy would not have found me out then. For if she should change hers, it is impossible I should know her unless I should hear her prattle. A pox on't, I cannot get her out of my head. Pray heaven, if ever I do see her again, she prove damnably ugly, that I may fortify myself against her tongue. *habitual military jacket*

BELVILE Have a care of love, for o' my conscience she was not of a quality to give thee any hopes.

WILLMORE Pox on 'em, why do they draw a man in then? She has played with my heart so, that 'twill never lie still till I have met with some kind wench that will play the game out with me. Oh, for my arms full of soft, white, kind woman—such as I fancy Angellica.

BELVILE This is her house, if you were but in stock° to get admittance. They have not dined yet; I perceive the picture is not out. *possessed of capital*

[*Enter* BLUNT.]

WILLMORE I long to see the shadow of the fair substance; a man may gaze on that for nothing.

BLUNT Colonel, thy hand. And thine, Fred. I have been an ass, a deluded fool, a very coxcomb from my birth till this hour, and heartily repent my little faith.

BELVILE What the devil's the matter with thee, Ned?

BLUNT Oh, such a mistress, Fred! Such a girl!

WILLMORE Ha! Where?

FREDERICK Ay, where?

BLUNT So fond, so amorous, so toying,° and so fine! And all for sheer love, ye rogue! Oh, how she looked and kissed! And soothed my heart from my bosom! I cannot think I was awake, and yet methinks I see and feel her charms still. Fred, try if she have not left the taste of her balmy kisses upon my lips. *flirting*

[*Kisses him.*]

BELVILE Ha! Ha! Ha!

WILLMORE Death, man, where is she?

BLUNT What a dog was I to stay in dull England so long! How have I laughed at the colonel when he sighed for love! But now the little archer° has revenged him! And by this one dart I can guess at all his joys, which then I took *i.e., Cupid* for fancies, mere dreams and fables. Well, I'm resolved to sell all in Essex and plant here forever.

BELVILE What a blessing 'tis, thou hast a mistress thou dar'st boast of; for I know thy humour is rather to have a proclaimed clap° than a secret amour. *gonorrhea*

WILLMORE Dost know her name?

BLUNT Her name? No, 'adsheartlikins. What care I for names? She's fair, young, brisk and kind, even to ravishment! And what a pox care I for knowing her by any other title?

WILLMORE Didst give her anything?

BLUNT Give her? Ha! Ha! Ha! Why, she's a person of quality. That's a good one! Give her? 'Adsheartlikins, dost think such creatures are to be bought? Or are we provided for such a purchase? Give her, quoth ye? Why, she presented me with this bracelet for the toy of a diamond I used to wear. No, gentlemen, Ned Blunt is not everybody. She expects me again tonight.

WILLMORE Egad, that's well; we'll all go.

BLUNT Not a soul! No, gentlemen, you are wits; I am a dull country rogue, I.

FREDERICK Well, sir, for all your person of quality, I shall be very glad to understand your purse be secure; 'tis our whole estate at present, which we are loath to hazard in one bottom.[1] Come sir, unlade.° *unload*

BLUNT Take the necessary trifle useless now to me, that am beloved by such a gentlewoman. 'Adsheartlikins, money! Here, take mine too.

FREDERICK No, keep that to be cozened,° that we may laugh. *tricked, cheated*

WILLMORE Cozened? Death! Would I could meet with one that would cozen me of all the love I could spare tonight.

FREDERICK Pox, 'tis some common whore, upon my life.

BLUNT A whore? Yes, with such clothes, such jewels, such a house, such furniture, and so attended! A whore!

BELVILE Why yes, sir, they are whores, though they'll neither entertain you with drinking, swearing, or bawdry; are whores in all those gay clothes and right jewels; are whores with those great houses richly furnished with velvet beds, store of plate,° handsome attendance, and fine coaches; are whores, and arrant° ones. *silver or gold utensils* *thorough; notorious*

WILLMORE Pox on't, where do these fine whores live?

BELVILE Where no rogues in office, ycleped° constables, dare give 'em laws, nor the wine-inspired bullies of the town break their windows; yet they are whores though this Essex calf° believe 'em persons of quality. *called* *fool*

BLUNT 'Adsheartlikins, y'are all fools. There are things about this Essex calf that shall take with the ladies, beyond all your wit and parts. This shape and size, gentlemen, are

1. In the hold of one ship; that is, in a single location.

not to be despised; my waist, too, tolerably long, with other inviting signs that shall be nameless.

WILLMORE Egad, I believe he may have met with some person of quality that may be kind to him.

BELVILE Dost thou perceive any such tempting things about him that should make a fine woman, and of quality, pick him out from all mankind to throw away her youth and beauty upon; nay, and her dear heart, too? No, no, Angellica has raised the price too high.

WILLMORE May she languish for mankind till she die, and be damned for that one sin alone.

[*Enter two* BRAVOS *and hang up a great picture of* ANGELLICA*'s against the balcony, and two little ones at each side of the door.*]

BELVILE See there the fair sign to the inn where a man may lodge that's fool enough to give her price.

[WILLMORE *gazes on the picture.*]

BLUNT 'Adsheartlikins, gentlemen, what's this?

BELVILE A famous courtesan, that's to be sold.

BLUNT How? To be sold? Nay, then I have nothing to say to her. Sold? What impudence is practiced in this country; with what order and decency whoring's established here by virtue of the Inquisition![2] Come, let's be gone; I'm sure we're no chapmen for this commodity.

FREDERICK Thou art none, I'm sure, unless thou couldst have her in thy bed at a price of a coach in the street.

WILLMORE How wondrous fair she is! A thousand crowns a month? By heaven, as many kingdoms were too little! A plague of this poverty, of which I ne'er complain but when it hinders my approach to beauty which virtue ne'er could purchase.

[*Turns from the picture.*]

BLUNT What's this? [*Reads.*] "A thousand crowns a month"! 'Adsheartlikins, here's a sum! Sure 'tis a mistake. —[*To one of the* BRAVOS.] Hark you, friend, does she take or give so much by the month?

FREDERICK A thousand crowns! Why, 'tis a portion° for the Infanta![3] *dowry*

BLUNT Hark ye, friends, won't she trust?

BRAVO This is a trade, sir, that cannot live by credit.

[*Enter* DON PEDRO *in masquerade, followed by* STEPHANO.]

BELVILE See, here's more company; let's walk off a while.

[*Exeunt English;* PEDRO *reads.*]

PEDRO Fetch me a thousand crowns; I never wished to buy this beauty at an easier rate. [*Passes off.*°] *Departs*

2. A Roman Catholic tribunal set up to combat heresy.

3. The daughter of the king of Spain.

[*Enter* ANGELLICA *and* MORETTA *in the balcony, and draw a silk curtain.*]

ANGELLICA Prithee, what said those fellows to thee?

BRAVO Madam, the first were admirers of beauty only, but no purchasers; they were merry with your price and picture, laughed at the sum, and so passed off.

ANGELLICA No matter, I'm not displeased with their rallying; their wonder feeds my vanity, and he that wishes but° to buy gives me more pride than he that gives my price can make my pleasure. *only wishes*

BRAVO Madam, the last I knew through all his disguises to be Don Pedro, nephew to the general, and who was with him in Pamplona.

ANGELLICA Don Pedro? My old gallant's nephew? When his uncle died he left him a vast sum of money; it is he who was so in love with me at Padua, and who used to make the general so jealous.

MORETTA Is this he that used to prance before our window, and take such care to show himself an amorous ass? If I am not mistaken, he is the likeliest man to give your price.

ANGELLICA The man is brave and generous, but of a humour so uneasy and inconstant that the victory over his heart is as soon lost as won; a slave that can add little to the triumph of the conqueror. But inconstancy's the sin of all mankind, therefore I'm resolved that nothing but gold shall charm my heart.

MORETTA I'm glad on't; 'tis only interest that women of our profession ought to consider, though I wonder what has kept you from that general disease of our sex so long; I mean, that of being in love.

ANGELLICA A kind but sullen star under which I had the happiness to be born. Yet I have had no time for love; the bravest and noblest of mankind have purchased my favors at so dear a rate, as if no coin but gold were current with our trade. But here's Don Pedro again; fetch me my lute, for 'tis for him or Don Antonio the Viceroy's son that I have spread my nets.

[*Enter at one door* DON PEDRO, STEPHANO; DON ANTONIO *and* DIEGO *(his page) at the other door, with people following him in masquerade, anticly° attired, some with music. They both go up to the picture.*] *bizarrely*

ANTONIO A thousand crowns! Had not the painter flattered her, I should not think it dear.

PEDRO Flattered her? By heaven, he cannot. I have seen the original, nor is there one charm here more than adorns her face and eyes; all this soft and sweet, with a certain languishing air that no artist can represent.

ANTONIO What I heard of her beauty before had fired my soul, but this confirmation of it has blown it to a flame.

PEDRO Ha!

DIEGO Sir, I have known you throw away a thousand crowns on a worse face, and though y'are near your marriage, you may venture a little love here; Florinda will not miss it.

PEDRO [*aside*] Ha! Florinda! Sure 'tis Antonio.

ANTONIO Florinda! Name not those distant joys; there's not one thought of her will check my passion here.

PEDRO [*aside*] Florinda scorned! [*A noise of a lute above.*] And all my hopes defeated of the possession of Angelica! [ANTONIO *gazes up.*] Her injuries, by heaven, he shall not boast of!

[*Song to a lute above.*]

SONG

I

When Damon first began to love
He languished in a soft desire,
And knew not how the gods to move,
To lessen or increase his fire.
For Caelia in her charming eyes
Wore all love's sweets, and all his cruelties.

II

But as beneath a shade he lay,
Weaving of flowers for Caelia's hair,
She chanced to lead her flock that way,
And saw the am'rous shepherd there.
She gazed around upon the place,
And saw the grove, resembling night,
To all the joys of love invite,
Whilst guilty smiles and blushes dressed her face.
At this the bashful youth all transport grew,
And with kind force he taught the virgin how
To yield what all his sighs could never do.

[ANGELLICA *throws open the curtains and bows to* ANTONIO, *who pulls off his vizard and bows and blows up kisses.* PEDRO, *unseen, looks in's face.*]

ANTONIO By heaven, she's charming fair!

PEDRO [*aside*] 'Tis he, the false Antonio!

ANTONIO [*to a bravo*] Friend, where must I pay my off'ring of love?
My thousand crowns I mean.

PEDRO That off'ring I have designed to make,
And yours will come too late.

ANTONIO Prithee begone; I shall grow angry else,
And then thou art not safe.

PEDRO My anger may be fatal, sir, as yours,
And he that enters here may prove this truth.

ANTONIO I know not who thou art, but I am sure thou'rt worth my killing, for aiming at Angellica.

[*They draw and fight.*]

[*Enter* WILLMORE *and* BLUNT, *who draw and part 'em.*]

BLUNT 'Adsheartlikins, here's fine doings.

WILLMORE Tilting for the wench, I'm sure. Nay, gad, if that would win her I have as good a sword as the best of ye. Put up,° put up, and take another time and place, for this is designed for lovers only. *Sheathe (your swords)*

[*They all put up.*]

PEDRO We are prevented; dare you meet me tomorrow on the Molo?° *pier*
For I've a title to a better quarrel,
That of Florinda, in whose credulous heart
Thou'st made an int'rest, and destroyed my hopes.

ANTONIO Dare! I'll meet thee there as early as the day.

PEDRO We will come thus disguised, that whosoever chance to get the better, he may escape unknown.

ANTONIO It shall be so.

[*Exeunt* PEDRO *and* STEPHANO.]

—Who should this rival be? Unless the English colonel, of whom I've often heard Don Pedro speak. It must be he, and time he were removed who lays a claim to all my happiness.

[WILLMORE, *having gazed all this while on the picture, pulls down a little one.*]

WILLMORE This posture's loose and negligent;
The sight on't would beget a warm desire
In souls whom impotence and age had chilled.
This must along with me.

BRAVO What means this rudeness, sir? Restore the picture.

ANTONIO Ha! Rudeness committed to the fair Angellica! —
Restore the picture, sir.

WILLMORE Indeed I will not, sir.

ANTONIO By heaven, but you shall.

WILLMORE Nay, do not show your sword; if you do, by this dear beauty, I will show mine too.

ANTONIO What right can you pretend to't?

WILLMORE That of possession, which I will maintain. You, perhaps, have a thousand crowns to give for the original.

ANTONIO No matter, sir, you shall restore the picture.

ANGELLICA Oh, Moretta, what's the matter?

[ANGELLICA *and* MORETTA *above.*]

ANTONIO Or leave your life behind.

WILLMORE Death! You lie; I will do neither.

[*They fight. The Spaniards join with* ANTONIO, BLUNT *laying on° like mad.*] *vigorously attacking*

ANGELLICA Hold, I command you, if for me you fight.

[*They leave off and bow.*]

WILLMORE [*aside*] How heavenly fair she is! Ah, plague of her price!

ANGELLICA You sir, in buff, you that appear a soldier, that first began this insolence—

WILLMORE 'Tis true, I did so, if you call it insolence for a man to preserve himself. I saw your charming picture and was wounded; quite through my soul each pointed beauty ran; and wanting a thousand crowns to procure my remedy, I laid this little picture to my bosom, which, if you cannot allow me, I'll resign.

ANGELLICA No, you may keep the trifle.

ANTONIO You shall first ask me leave, and this.

[*Fight again as before.*]

[*Enter* BELVILE *and* FREDERICK, *who join with the English.*]

ANGELLICA Hold! Will you ruin me? —Biskey! Sebastian! Part 'em!

[*The Spaniards are beaten off.*]

MORETTA Oh, madam, we're undone. A pox upon that rude fellow; he's set on to ruin us. We shall never see good days again till all these fighting poor rogues are sent to the galleys.

[*Enter* BELVILE, BLUNT, FREDERICK, *and* WILLMORE *with's shirt bloody.*]

BLUNT 'Adsheartlikins, beat me at this sport and I'll ne'er wear sword more.

BELVILE [*to* WILLMORE] The devil's in thee for a mad fellow; thou art always one at an unlucky adventure. Come, let's be gone whilst we're safe, and remember these are Spaniards, a sort of people that know how to revenge an affront.

FREDERICK You bleed! I hope you are not wounded.

WILLMORE Not much. A plague on your dons;° if they fight no better they'll ne'er recover Flanders.[4] What the devil wasn't to them that I took down the picture? *Spaniards*

BLUNT Took it! 'Adsheartlikins, we'll have the great one too; 'tis ours by conquest. Prithee help me up and I'll pull it down.

ANGELLICA [*to* WILLMORE] Stay, sir, and ere you affront me farther let me know how you durst commit this outrage. To you I speak, sir, for you appear a gentleman.

WILLMORE To me, madam? —Gentlemen, your servant.[5]

[BELVILE *stays him.*]

BELVILE Is the devil in thee? Dost know the danger of ent'ring the house of an incensed courtesan?

WILLMORE I thank you for your care, but there are other

4. The Low Countries, which largely revolted from Spanish rule in the 16th century.

5. That is, "I am your servant," a polite leave-taking.

matters in hand, there are, though we have no great temptation. Death! Let me go!

FREDERICK Yes, to your lodging if you will, but not in here. Damn these gay harlots; by this hand I'll have as sound and handsome a whore for a patacoon.[6] Death, man, she'll murder thee!

WILLMORE Oh, fear me not. Shall I not venture where a beauty calls? A lovely charming beauty! For fear of danger? When, by heaven, there's none so great as to long for her whilst I want money to purchase her.

FREDERICK Therefore 'tis loss of time unless you had the thousand crowns to pay.

WILLMORE It may be she may give a favor; at least I shall have the pleasure of saluting° her when I enter and when I depart. *kissing*

BELVILE Pox, she'll as soon lie with thee as kiss thee, and sooner stab than do either. You shall not go.

ANGELLICA Fear not, sir, all I have to wound with is my eyes.

BLUNT Let him go. 'Adsheartlikins, I believe the gentlewoman means well.

BELVILE Well, take thy fortune; we'll expect you in the next street. Farewell, fool, farewell.

WILLMORE 'Bye, colonel. [*Goes in.*]

FREDERICK The rogue's stark mad for a wench.

[*Exeunt.*]

2.2

[SCENE: *A fine chamber.*]

[*Enter* WILLMORE, ANGELLICA, *and* MORETTA.]

ANGELLICA Insolent sir, how durst you pull down my picture?

WILLMORE Rather, how durst you set it up to tempt poor am'rous mortals with so much excellence, which I find you have but too well consulted by the unmerciful price you set upon't. Is all this heaven of beauty shown to move despair in those that cannot buy? And can you think th'effects of that despair should be less extravagant than I have shown?

ANGELLICA I sent for you to ask my pardon, sir, not to aggravate your crime. I thought I should have seen you at my feet imploring it.

WILLMORE You are deceived. I came to rail at you, and rail such truths too, as shall let you see the vanity of that pride which taught you how to set such price on sin. For such it is whilst that which is love's due is meanly bartered for.

ANGELLICA Ha! Ha! Ha! Alas, good captain, what pity 'tis your edifying doctrine will do no good upon me.

6. A Portuguese and Spanish coin of relatively little value.

Moretta, fetch the gentleman a glass, and let him survey himself to see what charms he has. —[*Aside, in a soft tone.*] And guess my business.

MORETTA He knows himself of old: I believe those breeches and he have been acquainted ever since he was beaten at Worcester.[7]

ANGELLICA Nay, do not abuse the poor creature.

MORETTA Good weatherbeaten corporal, will you march off? We have no need of your doctrine, though you have of our charity. But at present we have no scraps; we can afford no kindness for God's sake. In fine,° sirrah,[8] the price is too high i'th' mouth for you, therefore troop,° I say. *In conclusion* *be off*

WILLMORE Here, good forewoman of the shop, serve me and I'll be gone.

[*Offers money.*]

MORETTA Keep it to pay your laundress; your linen stinks of the gun room. For here's no selling by retail.

WILLMORE Thou hast sold plenty of thy stale ware at a cheap rate.

MORETTA Ay, the more silly kind heart I, but this is an age wherein beauty is at higher rates. In fine, you know the price of this.

WILLMORE I grant you 'tis here set down, a thousand crowns a month. Pray, how much may come to my share for a pistole?° Bawd, take your black lead and sum it up, that I may have a pistole's worth of this vain gay thing, and I'll trouble you no more. *a gold coin*

MORETTA Pox on him, he'll fret me to death! Abominable fellow, I tell thee we only sell by the whole piece.

WILLMORE 'Tis very hard, the whole cargo or nothing. Faith, madam, my stock will not reach it; I cannot be your chapman. Yet I have countrymen in town, merchants of love like me; I'll see if they'll put in for a share. We cannot lose much by it, and what we have no use for, we'll sell upon the Friday's mart at "Who gives more?" —I am studying, madam, how to purchase you, though at present I am unprovided of money.

ANGELLICA [*aside*] Sure this from any other man would anger me; nor shall he know the conquest he has made. —Poor angry man, how I despise this railing.

WILLMORE Yes, I am poor. But I'm a gentleman,
And one that scorns this baseness which you practice.
Poor as I am I would not sell myself,
No, not to gain your charming high-prized person.
Though I admire you strangely for your beauty,

7. The site of Cromwell's 1651 defeat of Prince Charles in the final battle of the English Civil War.

8. A form of address to male social inferiors, and thus here indicating contempt.

Yet I contemn° your mind. *scorn, despise*
And yet I would at any rate enjoy you;
At your own rate; but cannot. See here
The only sum I can command on earth:
I know not where to eat when this is gone.
Yet such a slave I am to love and beauty
This last reserve I'll sacrifice to enjoy you.
Nay, do not frown, I know you're to be bought,
And would be bought by me. By me,
For a meaning trifling sum, if I could pay it down.
Which happy knowledge I will still repeat,
And lay it to my heart: it has a virtue in't,
And soon will cure those wounds your eyes have made.
And yet, there's something so divinely powerful there—
Nay, I will gaze, to let you see my strength.

[*Holds her, looks on her, and pauses and sighs.*]

By heav'n, bright creature, I would not for the world
Thy fame° were half so fair as is thy face. *reputation*

[*Turns her away from him.*]

ANGELLICA [*aside*] His words go through me to the very soul.—
If you have nothing else to say to me—

WILLMORE Yes, you shall hear how infamous you are—
For which I do not hate thee—
But that secures my heart, and all the flames it feels
Are but so many lusts:
I know it by their sudden bold intrusion.
The fire's impatient and betrays; 'tis false.
For had it been the purer flame of love,
I should have pined and languished at your feet,
Ere found the impudence to have discovered it.
I now dare stand your scorn and your denial.

MORETTA [*aside*] Sure she's bewitched, that she can stand thus tamely and hear his saucy railing. —Sirrah, will you be gone?

ANGELLICA [*to* MORETTA] How dare you take this liberty! Withdraw! —Pray tell me, sir, are not you guilty of the same mercenary crime? When a lady is proposed to you for a wife, you never ask how fair, discreet, or virtuous she is, but what's her fortune; which, if but small, you cry "She will not do my business," and basely leave her, though she languish for you. Say, is not this as poor?

WILLMORE It is a barbarous custom, which I will scorn to defend in our sex, and do despise in yours.

ANGELLICA Thou'rt a brave° fellow! Put up thy gold, and know, *fine, handsome*
That were thy fortune as large as is thy soul,
Thou shouldst not buy my love.
Couldst thou forget those mean effects of vanity
Which set me out to sale,

And as a lover prize my yielding joys.
Canst thou believe they'll be entirely thine,
Without considering they were mercenary?

WILLMORE I cannot tell, I must bethink me first.
[*Aside*.] Ha! Death, I'm going to believe her.

ANGELLICA Prithee confirm that faith, or if thou canst not,
Flatter me a little: 'twill please me from thy mouth.

WILLMORE [*aside*] Curse on thy charming tongue! Dost thou return
My feigned contempt with so much subtlety?—
Thou'st found the easiest way into my heart,
Though I yet know that all thou say'st is false.
[*Turning from her in rage.*]

ANGELLICA By all that's good, 'tis real;
I never loved before, though oft a mistress.
Shall my first vows be slighted?

WILLMORE [*aside*] What can she mean?

ANGELLICA [*in an angry tone*] I find you cannot credit me.

WILLMORE I know you take me for an errant ass,
An ass that may be soothed into belief,
And then be used at pleasure;
But, madam, I have been so often cheated
By prejured, soft, deluding hypocrites,
That I've no faith left for the cozening sex,
Especially for women of your trade.

ANGELLICA The low esteem you have of me perhaps
May bring my heart again:
For I have pride that yet surmounts my love.
[*She turns with pride; he holds her.*]

WILLMORE Throw off this pride, this enemy to bliss,
And show the power of love: 'tis with those arms
I can be only vanquished, made a slave.

ANGELLICA Is all my mighty expectation vanished?
No, I will not hear thee talk; thou hast a charm
In every word that draws my heart away,
And all the thousand trophies I designed
Thou hast undone. Why art thou soft?
Thy looks are bravely rough, and meant for war.
Couldst thou not storm on still?
I then perhaps had been as free as thou.

WILLMORE [*aside*] Death, how she throws her fire about my soul!—
Take heed, fair creature, how you raise my hopes,
Which once assumed pretends to all dominion:
There's not a joy thou hast in store
I shall not then command.
For which I'll pay you back my soul, my life!
Come, let's begin th'account this happy minute!

ANGELLICA And will you pay me then the price I ask?

WILLMORE Oh, why dost thou draw me from an awful° worship, *awe-filled*
By showing thou art no divinity.

Conceal the fiend, and show me all the angel!
Keep me but ignorant, and I'll be devout
And pay my vows forever at this shrine.

[*Kneels and kisses her hand.*]

ANGELLICA The pay I mean is but thy love for mine.
Can you give that?

WILLMORE Entirely. Come, let's withdraw where I'll renew my vows, and breathe 'em with such ardor thou shalt not doubt my zeal.

ANGELLICA Thou hast a power too strong to be resisted.

[*Exeunt* WILLMORE *and* ANGELLICA.]

MORETTA Now my curse go with you! Is all our project fallen to this? To love the only enemy to our trade? Nay, to love such a shameroon,° a very beggar; nay, a pirate beggar, whose business is to rifle and be gone; a no-purchase, no-pay tatterdemalion, and English picaroon;° a rogue that fights for daily drink, and takes a pride in being loyally lousy? Oh, I could curse now, if I durst. This is the fate of most whores.

phony, deceiver

rogue; pirate

Trophies, which from believing fops we win,
Are spoils to those who cozen us again. [*Exit.*]

3.1

[SCENE: *A street.*]

[*Enter* FLORINDA, VALERIA, HELLENA, *in antic different dresses from what they were in before;* CALLIS *attending.*]

FLORINDA I wonder what should make my brother in so ill a humor? I hope he has not found out our ramble this morning.

HELLENA No, if he had, we should have heard on't at both ears, and have been mewed up° this afternoon, which I would not for the world should have happened. Hey ho, I'm as sad as a lover's lute.

pent up, confined

VALERIA Well, methinks we have learnt this trade of gipsies as readily as if we had been bred upon the road to Loretto;[9] and yet I did so fumble when I told the stranger his fortune that I was afraid I should have told my own and yours by mistake. But methinks Hellena has been very serious ever since.

FLORINDA I would give my garters she were in love, to be revenged upon her for abusing me. How is't, Hellena?

HELLENA Ah, would I had never seen my mad monsieur. And yet, for all your laughing, I am not in love. And yet

9. An Italian town near the Adriatic coast; it is the site of a shrine of the Virgin Mary visited by many pilgrims.

this small acquaintance, o' my conscience, will never out of my head.

VALERIA Ha! Ha! Ha! I laugh to think how thou art fitted with a lover, a fellow that I warrant loves every new face he sees.

HELLENA Hum, he has not kept his word with me here, and may be taken up. That thought is not very pleasant to me. What the deuce should this be now that I feel?

VALERIA What is't like?

HELLENA Nay, the Lord knows, but if I should be hanged I cannot choose but be angry and afraid when I think that mad fellow should be in love with anybody but me. What to think of myself I know not: would I could meet with some true damned gipsy, that I might know my fortune.

VALERIA Know it! Why there's nothing so easy: thou wilt love this wand'ring inconstant till thou find'st thyself hanged about his neck, and then be as mad to get free again.

FLORINDA Yes, Valeria, we shall see her bestride his baggage horse and follow him to the campaign.

HELLENA So, so, now you are provided for there's no care taken of poor me. But since you have set my heart a-wishing, I am resolved to know for what; I will not die of the pip,[1] so I will not.

FLORINDA Art thou mad to talk so? Who will like thee well enough to have thee, that hears what a mad wench thou art?

HELLENA Like me? I don't intend every he that likes me shall have me, but he that I like. I should have stayed in the nunnery still if I had liked my lady abbess as well as she liked me. No, I came thence not, as my wise brother imagines, to take an eternal farewell of the world, but to love and to be beloved; and I will be beloved, or I'll get one of your men, so I will.

VALERIA Am I put into the number of lovers?

HELLENA You? Why, coz,[2] I know thou'rt too good-natured to leave us in any design; thou wouldst venture a cast° though thou comest off a loser, especially with such a gamester. I observe your man, and your willing ear incline that way; and if you are not a lover, 'tis an art soon learnt—that I find. [*Sighs.*]

i.e., roll the dice

FLORINDA I wonder how you learnt to love so easily. I had a thousand charms to meet my eyes and ears ere I could yield, and 'twas the knowledge of Belvile's merit, not the surprising person, took my soul. Thou art too rash, to give a heart at first sight.

HELLENA Hang your considering lover! I never thought

1. A vague, catchall term for human diseases; here, heartache or depression.

2. Cousin, an affectionate term for any relative outside the speaker's immediate family.

beyond the fancy that 'twas a very pretty, idle, silly kind of pleasure to pass one's time with: to write little soft nonsensical billets,° and with great difficulty and danger receive answers in which I shall have my beauty praised, my wit admired, though little or none, and have the vanity and power to know I am desirable. Then I have the more inclination that way because I am to be a nun, and so shall not be suspected to have any such earthly thoughts about me; but when I walk thus—and sigh thus—they'll think my mind's upon my monastery, and cry, "How happy 'tis she's so resolved." But not a word of man.

brief notes

FLORINDA What a mad creature's this!

HELLENA I'll warrant, if my brother hears either of you sigh, he cries gravely, "I fear you have the indiscretion to be in love, but take heed of the honor of our house, and your own unspotted fame"; and so he conjures on till he has laid the soft-winged god in your hearts, or broke the bird's nest. But see, here comes your lover, but where's my inconstant? Let's step aside, and we may learn something. [*Go aside.*]

[*Enter* BELVILE, FREDERICK, *and* BLUNT.]

BELVILE What means this! The picture's taken in.

BLUNT It may be the wench is good natured, and will be kind gratis. Your friend's a proper handsome fellow.

BELVILE I rather think she has cut his throat and is fled; I am mad he should throw himself into dangers. Pox on't, I shall want him, too, at night. Let's knock and ask for him.

HELLENA My heart goes a-pit, a-pat, for fear 'tis my man they talk of.

[*Knock;* MORETTA *above.*]

MORETTA What would you have?

BELVILE Tell the stranger that entered here about two hours ago that his friends stay here for him.

MORETTA A curse upon him for Moretta: would he were at the devil!
But he's coming to you.

[*Enter* WILLMORE.]

HELLENA Ay, ay 'tis he. Oh, how this vexes me!

BELVILE And how and how, dear lad, has fortune smiled?
Are we to break her windows, or raise up altars to her, hah?

WILLMORE Does not my fortune sit triumphant on my brow? Dost not see the little wanton god there all gay and smiling? Have I not an air about my face and eyes that distinguish me from the crowd of common lovers? By heaven, Cupid's quiver has not half so many darts as her eyes! Oh, such a *bona roba!*[3] To sleep in her arms is lying *in fresco,*° all perfumed air about me.

in fresh air (Italian)

3. Courtesan; literally, "good stuff" (*buonaroba*, Italian).

HELLENA [*aside*] Here's fine encouragement for me to fool on!

WILLMORE Hark'ee, where didst thou purchase that rich Canary[4] we drank today? Tell me, that I may adore the spigot and sacrifice to the butt. The juice was divine; into which I must dip my rosary, and then bless all things that I would have bold or fortunate.

BELVILE Well, sir, let's go take a bottle and hear the story of your success.

FREDERICK Would not French wine do better?

WILLMORE Damn the hungry balderdash! Cheerful sack[5] has a generous virtue in't inspiring a successful confidence, gives eloquence to the tongue and vigor to the soul, and has in a few hours completed all my hopes and wishes! There's nothing left to raise a new desire in me. Come, let's be gay and wanton. And, gentlemen, study; study what you want, for here are friends that will supply gentlemen. [*Jingles gold.*] Hark what a charming sound they make! 'Tis the he and the she gold whilst here, and shall beget new pleasures every moment.

BLUNT But hark'ee, sir, you are not married, are you?

WILLMORE All the honey of matrimony but none of the sting, friend.

BLUNT 'Adsheartlikins, thou'rt a fortunate rogue!

WILLMORE I am so, sir: let these inform you! Ha, how sweetly they chime! Pox of poverty: it makes a man a slave, makes wit and honor sneak. My soul grew lean and rusty for want of credit.

BLUNT 'Adsheartlikins, this I like well; it looks like my lucky bargain! Oh, how I long for the approach of my squire, that is to conduct me to her house again. Why, here's two provided for!

FREDERICK By this light, y'are happy men.

BLUNT Fortune is pleased to smile on us, gentlemen, to smile on us.

[*Enter* SANCHO *and pulls down* BLUNT *by the sleeve; they go aside.*]

SANCHO Sir, my lady expects you. She has removed all that might oppose your will and pleasure, and is impatient till you come.

BLUNT Sir, I'll attend you. —Oh the happiest rogue! I'll take no leave, lest they either dog me or stay me.

[*Exit with* SANCHO.]

BELVILE But then the little gipsy is forgot?

WILLMORE A mischief on thee for putting her into my

4. A sweet wine from the Canary Islands.
5. A dry white wine from Spain and the Canary Islands.

thoughts! I had quite forgot her else, and this night's debauch had drunk her quite down.

HELLENA Had it so, good captain! [*Claps him on the back.*]

WILLMORE [*aside*] Ha! I hope she did not hear me!

HELLENA What, afraid of such a champion?

WILLMORE Oh, you're a fine lady of your word, are you not? To make a man languish a whole day—

HELLENA In tedious search of me.

WILLMORE Egad, child, thou'rt in the right. Hadst thou seen what a melancholy dog I have been ever since I was a lover, how I have walked the streets like a Capuchin,° *Franciscan monk* with my hands in my sleeves—faith, sweetheart, thou wouldst pity me.

HELLENA [*aside*] Now if I should be hanged I can't be angry with him, he dissembles so heartily.—Alas, good captain, what pains you have taken; now were I ungrateful not to reward so true a servant.

WILLMORE Poor soul, that's kindly said; I see thou barest a conscience. Come then, for a beginning show me thy dear face.

HELLENA I'm afraid, my small acquaintance, you have been staying that swinging stomach you boasted of this morning. I then remember my little collation° *light meal* would have gone down with you without the sauce of a handsome face. Is your stomach so queasy now?

WILLMORE Faith, long fasting, child, spoils a man's appetite. Yet if you durst treat, I could so lay about me° still— *i.e., eat heartily*

HELLENA And would you fall to before a priest says grace?

WILLMORE Oh fie, fie, what an old out-of-fashioned thing hast thou named? Thou couldst not dash me more out of countenance shouldst thou show me an ugly face.

[*Whilst he is seemingly courting* HELLENA, *enter* ANGELLICA, MORETTA, BISKEY, *and* SEBASTIAN, *all in masquerade.* ANGELLICA *sees* WILLMORE *and stares.*]

ANGELLICA Heavens, 'tis he! And passionately fond to see another woman!

MORETTA What could you less expect from such a swaggerer?

ANGELLICA Expect? As much as I paid him: a heart entire,
Which I had pride enough to think when'er I gave,
It would have raised the man above the vulgar,
Made him all soul, and that all soft and constant.

HELLENA You see, captain, how willing I am to be friends with you, till time and ill luck make us lovers; and ask you the question first rather than put your modesty to the blush by asking me. For alas, I know you captains are such strict men, and such severe observers of your vows to chastity, that 'twill be hard to prevail with your tender conscience to marry a young willing maid.

WILLMORE Do not abuse me, for fear I should take thee at thy word and marry thee indeed, which I'm sure will be revenge sufficient.

HELLENA O' my conscience, that will be our destiny, because we are both of one humor: I am as inconstant as you, for I have considered, captain, that a handsome woman has a great deal to do whilst her face is good. For then is our harvesttime to gather friends, and should I in these days of my youth catch a fit of foolish constancy, I were undone: 'tis loitering by daylight in our great journey. Therefore, I declare I'll allow but one year for love, one year for indifference, and one year for hate; and then go hang yourself, for I profess myself the gay, the kind, and the inconstant. The devil's in't if this won't please you!

WILLMORE Oh, most damnably. I have a heart with a hole quite through it too; no prison mine, to keep a mistress in.

ANGELLICA [*aside*] Perjured man! How I believe thee now!

HELLENA Well, I see our business as well as humors are alike: yours to cozen as many maids as will trust you, and I as many men as have faith. See if I have not as desperate a lying look as you can have for the heart of you. [*Pulls off her vizard; he starts.*] How do you like it, captain?

WILLMORE Like it! By heaven, I never saw so much beauty! Oh, the charms of those sprightly black eyes! That strangely fair face, full of smiles and dimples! Those soft round melting cherry lips and small even white teeth! Not to be expressed, but silently adored! [*She replaces her mask.*] Oh, one look more, and strike me dumb, or I shall repeat nothing else till I'm mad.

[*He seems to court her to pull off her vizard; she refuses.*]

ANGELLICA I can endure no more. Nor is it fit to interrupt him, for if I do, my jealousy has so destroyed my reason I shall undo° him. Therefore I'll retire, and you, Sebastian [*to one of her bravos*], follow that woman and learn who 'tis; while you [*to the other bravo*] tell the fugitive I would speak to him instantly. [*Exit.*] *destroy*

[*This while* FLORINDA *is talking to* BELVILE, *who stands sullenly;* FREDERICK *courting* VALERIA.]

VALERIA [*to* BELVILE] Prithee, dear stranger, be not so sullen, for though you have lost your love you see my friend frankly offers you hers to play with in the meantime.

BELVILE Faith, madam, I am sorry I can't play at her game.

FREDERICK [*to* VALERIA] Pray leave your intercession and mind your own affair. They'll better agree apart: he's a modest sigher in company, but alone no woman 'scapes him.

FLORINDA [*aside*] Sure he does but rally.° Yet, if it should be true? I'll tempt him farther. —Believe me, noble stranger, I'm no common mistress. And for a little proof *banter* on't, wear this jewel. Nay, take it, sir, 'tis right, and bills of exchange may sometimes miscarry.

BELVILE Madam, why am I chose out of all mankind to be the object of your bounty?

VALERIA There's another civil question asked.

FREDERICK [*aside*] Pox of 's modesty; it spoils his own markets and hinders mine.

FLORINDA Sir, from my window I have often seen you, and women of my quality have so few opportunities for love that we ought to lose none.

FREDERICK [*to* VALERIA] Ay, this is something! Here's a woman! When shall I be blest with so much kindness from your fair mouth? —[*Aside to* BELVILE.] Take the jewel, fool!

BELVILE You tempt me strangely, madam, every way—

FLORINDA [*aside*] So, if I find him false, my whole repose is gone.

BELVILE And but for a vow I've made to a very fair lady, this goodness had subdued me.

FREDERICK [*aside to* BELVILE] Pox on't, be kind, in pity to me be kind. For I am to thrive here but as you treat her friend.

HELLENA Tell me what you did in yonder house, and I'll unmask.

WILLMORE Yonder house? Oh, I went to a– -to– why, there's a friend of mine lives there.

HELLENA What, a she or a he friend?

WILLMORE A man, upon honor, a man. A she friend? No, no, madam, you have done my business, I thank you.

HELLENA And was't your man friend that had more darts in's eyes than Cupid carries in's whole budget° of arrows? *quiver*

WILLMORE So—

HELLENA "Ah, such a *bona roba!* To be in her arms is lying *in fresco,* all perfumed air about me." Was this your man friend too?

WILLMORE So—

HELLENA That gave you the he and the she gold, that begets young pleasures?

WILLMORE Well, well, madam, then you can see there are ladies in the world that will not be cruel. There are, madam, there are.

HELLENA And there be men, too, as fine, wild, inconstant fellows as yourself. There be, captain, there be, if you go to that now. Therefore, I'm resolved—

WILLMORE Oh!

HELLENA To see your face no more—

WILLMORE Oh!

HELLENA Till tomorrow.

WILLMORE Egad, you frighted me.

HELLENA Nor then neither, unless you'll swear never to see that lady more.

WILLMORE See her! Why, never to think of womankind again.

HELLENA Kneel, and swear.

[*Kneels; she gives him her hand.*]

WILLMORE I do, never to think, to see, to love, nor lie, with any but thyself.

HELLENA Kiss the book.

WILLMORE Oh, most religiously. [*Kisses her hand.*]

HELLENA Now what a wicked creature am I, to damn a proper fellow.

CALLIS [*to* FLORINDA] Madam, I'll stay no longer: 'tis e'en dark.

FLORINDA [*to* BELVILE] However, sir, I'll leave this with you, that when I'm gone you may repent the opportunity you have lost by your modesty.

[*Gives him the jewel, which is her picture, and exit. He gazes after her.*]

WILLMORE [*to* HELLENA] 'Twill be an age till tomorrow, and till then I will most impatiently expect you. Adieu, my dear pretty angel.

[*Exeunt all the women.*]

BELVILE Ha! Florinda's picture! 'Twas she herself. What a dull dog was I! I would have given the world for one minute's discourse with her.

FREDERICK This comes of your modesty. Ah, pox o' your vow; 'twas ten to one but we had lost the jewel by't.

BELVILE Willmore, the blessed'st opportunity lost! Florinda, friends, Florinda!

WILLMORE Ah, rogue! Such black eyes! Such a face! Such a mouth! Such teeth! And so much wit!

BELVILE All, all, and a thousand charms besides.

WILLMORE Why, dost thou know her?

BEVILE Know her! Ay, ay, and a pox take me with all my heart for being so modest.

WILLMORE But hark'ee, friend of mine, are you my rival? And have I been only beating the bush all this while?

BELVILE I understand thee not. I'm mad! See here—

[*Shows the picture.*]

WILLMORE Ha! Whose picture's this? 'Tis a fine wench!

FREDERICK The colonel's mistress, sir.

WILLMORE Oh, oh, here. [*Gives the picture back.*] I thought't had been another prize. Come, come, a bottle will set thee right again.

BELVILE I am content to try, and by that time 'twill be late enough for our design.

WILLMORE Agreed.

Love does all day the soul's great empire keep,
But wine at night lulls the soft god asleep.

[*Exeunt.*]

3.2

[SCENE: LUCETTA's *house.*]

[*Enter* BLUNT *and* LUCETTA *with a light.*]

LUCETTA Now we are safe and free: no fears of the coming home of my old jealous husband, which made me a little thoughtful° when you came in first. But now love is all the business of my soul. *preoccupied*

BLUNT I am transported!—[*Aside.*] Pox on't, that I had but some fine things to say to her, such as lovers use. I was a fool not to learn of° Fred a little by heart before I came. Something I must say. —'Adsheartlikins, sweet soul, I am not used to compliment, but I'm an honest gentleman, and thy humble servant. *from*

LUCETTA I have nothing to pay for so great a favor, but such a love as cannot but be great, since at first sight of that sweet face and shape it made me your absolute captive.

BLUNT [*aside*] Kind heart, how prettily she talks! Egad, I'll show her husband a Spanish trick: send him out of the world and marry her; she's damnably in love with me, and will ne'er mind settlements,[6] and so there's that saved.

LUCETTA Well, sir, I'll go and undress me, and be with you instantly.

BLUNT Make haste then, for 'adsheartlikins, dear soul, thou canst not guess at the pain of a longing lover when his joys are drawn within the compass of a few minutes.

LUCETTA You speak my sense, and I'll make haste to prove it.

[*Exit.*]

BLUNT 'Tis a rare girl, and this one night's enjoyment with her will be worth all the days I ever passed in Essex. Would she would go with me into England, though to say truth, there's plenty of whores already. But a pox on 'em, they are such mercenary prodigal whores that they want such a one as this, that's free and generous, to give 'em good examples. Why, what a house she has, how rich and fine!

[*Enter* SANCHO.]

SANCHO Sir, my lady has sent me to conduct you to her chamber.

BLUNT Sir, I shall be proud to follow.—[*Aside.*] Here's one of her servants too; 'adsheartlikins, by this garb and gravity he might be a justice of peace in Essex, and is but a pimp here.

[*Exeunt.*]

6. Property secured for a wife at marriage.

3.3

[SCENE: *The scene changes to a chamber with an alcove bed in't, a table, etc.;* LUCETTA *in bed.*]

[*Enter* SANCHO *and* BLUNT, *who takes the candle of* SANCHO *at the door.*]

SANCHO Sir, my commission reaches no farther.

BLUNT Sir, I'll excuse your compliment.

[*Exit* SANCHO.]

—What, in bed, my sweet mistress?

LUCETTA You see, I still outdo you in kindness.

BLUNT And thou shalt see what haste I'll make to quit scores. Oh, the luckiest rogue!

[*He undresses himself.*]

LUCETTA Should you be false or cruel now—

BLUNT False! 'Adsheartlikins, what dost thou take me for, a Jew? An insensible heathen? A pox of thy old jealous husband: an° he were dead, egad, sweet soul, it should be none of my fault if I did not marry thee.

if

LUCETTA It never should be mine.

BLUNT Good soul! I'm the fortunatest dog!

LUCETTA Are you not undressed yet?

BLUNT As much as my impatience will permit.

[*Goes toward the bed in his shirt, drawers, etc.*]

LUCETTA Hold, sir, put out the light; it may betray us else.

BLUNT Anything; I need no other light but that of thine eyes.—[*Aside.*] 'Adsheartlikins, there I think I had it.

[*Puts out the candle; the bed descends; he gropes about to find it.*]

Why, why, where am I got? What, not yet? Where are you, sweetest? —Ah, the rogue's silent now. A pretty love-trick this; how she'll laugh at me anon! —You need not, my dear rogue, you need not! I'm all on fire already; come, come, now call me, in pity.—Sure I'm enchanted! I have been round the chamber, and can find neither woman nor bed. I locked the door; I'm sure she cannot go that way, or if she could, the bed could not. —Enough, enough, my pretty wanton; do not carry the jest too far! [*Lights on a trap, and is let down.*] —Ha! Betrayed! Dogs! Rogues! Pimps! Help! Help!

[*Enter* LUCETTA, PHILLIPO, *and* SANCHO *with a light.*]

PHILLIPO Ha! Ha! Ha! He's dispatched finely.

LUCETTA Now, sir, had I been coy, we had missed of this booty.

PHILLIPO Nay, when I saw 'twas a substantial fool, I was mollified. But when you dote upon a serenading coxcomb, upon a face, fine clothes, and a lute, it makes me rage.

LUCETTA You know I was never guilty of that folly, my dear Phillipo, but with yourself. But come, let's see what we have got by this.

PHILLIPO A rich coat; sword and hat; these breeches, too, are well lined! See here, a gold watch! A purse—Ha! Gold! At least two hundred pistoles! A bunch of diamond rings, and one with the family arms! A gold box, with a medal of his king, and his lady mother's picture! These were sacred relics, believe me. See, the waistband of his breeches have a mine of gold—old queen Bess's![7] We have a quarrel to her ever since eighty-eight,[8] and may therefore justify the theft: the Inquisition might have committed it.

LUCETTA See, a bracelet of bowed gold! These his sisters tied about his arm at parting. But well, for all this, I fear his being a stranger may make a noise and hinder our trade with them hereafter.

PHILLIPO That's our security: he is not only a stranger to us, but to the country too. The common shore° into, which he is descended thou know'st, conducts him into another street, which this light will hinder him from ever finding again. He knows neither your name, nor that of the street where your house is; nay, nor the way to his own lodgings. *sewer*

LUCETTA And art thou not an unmerciful rogue, not to afford him one night for all this? I should not have been such a Jew.

PHILLIPO Blame me not, Lucetta, to keep as much of thee as I can to myself. Come, that thought makes me wanton; let's to bed. —Sancho, lock up these.

This is the fleece which fools do bear,
Designed for witty men to shear.

[*Exeunt.*]

3.4

[SCENE: *The scene changes, and discovers* BLUNT *creeping out of a common shore; his face, etc., all dirty.*]

BLUNT [*climbing up*] Oh, Lord, I am got out at last, and, which is a miracle, without a clue.[9] And now to damning and cursing! But if that would ease me, where shall I begin? With my fortune, myself, or the quean° that cozened me? What a dog was I to believe in woman! Oh, coxcomb! Ignorant conceited coxcomb! To fancy she could be enamored with my person! At first sight enamored! Oh, I'm a cursed puppy! 'Tis plain, fool was writ upon my forehead! She perceived it; saw the Essex calf there. For what allurements could there be in this countenance, which I can endure because I'm acquainted with it. Ohdull, silly dog, to be thus soothed into a cozening! Had *whore*

7. Queen Elizabeth I of England (r. 1558–1603).
8. That is, 1588, when the Spanish Armada was defeated by the English navy.
9. A ball of thread used to guide one's way out of a maze.

I been drunk, I might fondly have credited the young quean; but as I was in my right wits to be thus cheated, confirms it: I am a dull believing English country fop. But my comrades! Death and the devil, there's the worst of all! Then a ballad will be sung tomorrow on the Prado,° to a lousy tune of the enchanted squire and the annihilated damsel. But Fred—that rogue—and the colonel will abuse me beyond all Christian patience. Had she left me my clothes, I have a bill of exchange at home would have saved my credit. But now all hope is taken from me. Well, I'll home, if I can find the way, with this consolation: that I am not the first kind believing coxcomb; but there are, gallants, many such good natures amongst ye. *fashionable promenade*

And though you've better arts to hide your follies,
'Adsheartlikins, y'are all as arrant cullies.° [*Exit.*] *dupes*

3.5

[SCENE: *The garden in the night.*]

[*Enter* FLORINDA *in an undress, with a key and a little box.*]

FLORINDA Well, thus far I'm in my way to happiness. I have got myself free from Callis; my brother too, I find by yonder light, is got into his cabinet,° and thinks not of me; I have by good fortune got the key of the garden back door. I'll open it to prevent Belvile's knocking: a little noise will now alarm my brother. Now am I as fearful as a young thief. [*Unlocks the door.*] Hark! What noise is that? Oh, 'twas the wind that played amongst the boughs. Belvile stays long, methinks; it's time. Stay, for fear of a surprise,° I'll hide these jewels in yonder jasmine. *small private room* *sudden attack*

[*She goes to lay down the box.*]

[*Enter* WILLMORE, *drunk.*]

WILLMORE What the devil is become of these fellows Belvile and Frederick? They promised to stay at the next corner for me, but who the devil knows the corner of a full moon? Now, whereabouts am I? Ha, what have we here? A garden! A very convenient place to sleep in. Ha! What has God sent us here? A female! By this light, a woman! I'm a dog if it be not a very wench!

FLORINDA He's come! Ha! Who's there?

WILLMORE Sweet soul, let me salute thy shoestring.

FLORINDA [*aside*] 'Tis not my Belvile. Good heavens, I know him not!—Who are you, and from whence come you?

WILLMORE Prithee, prithee, child, not so many hard questions! Let it suffice I am here, child. Come, come kiss me.

FLORINDA Good gods! What luck is mine?

WILLMORE Only good luck, child, parlous° good luck. Come hither. —[*Aside.*] 'Tis a delicate shining wench. By this hand, she's perfumed, and smells like any nosegay. —[*To* FLORINDA.] Prithee, dear soul, let's not play the fool and lose time—precious time. For as Gad shall save me, I'm as honest a fellow as breathes, though I'm a little disguised° at present. Come, I say. Why, thou mayst be free with me: I'll be very secret. I'll not boast who 'twas obliged me, not I; for hang me if I know thy name.

extremely

drunk

FLORINDA Heavens! What a filthy beast is this!

WILLMORE I am so, and thou ought'st the sooner to lie with me for that reason. For look you, child, there will be no sin in't, because 'twas neither designed nor premeditated: 'tis pure accident on both sides. That's a certain thing now. Indeed, should I make love to you, and you vow fidelity, and swear and lie till you believed and yielded—that were to make it wilful fornication, the crying sin of the nation. Thou art, therefore, as thou art a good Christian, obliged in conscience to deny me nothing. Now, come be kind without any more idle prating.

[*He seizes her by the arm.*]

FLORINDA Oh, I am ruined! Wicked man, unhand me!

WILLMORE Wicked? Egad, child, a judge, were he young and vigorous, and saw those eyes of thine, would know 'twas they gave the first blow, the first provocation. Come, prithee let's lose no time, I say. This is a fine convenient place.

FLORINDA Sir, let me go, I conjure° you, or I'll call out.

beseech

WILLMORE Ay, ay, you were best to call witness to see how finely you treat me. Do!

FLORINDA I'll cry murder, rape, or anything, if you do not instantly let me go!

WILLMORE A rape! Come, come, you lie, you baggage,° you lie. What! I'll warrant you would fain° have the world believe now that you are not so forward as I. No, not you. Why at this time of night was your cobweb door set open, dear spider, but to catch flies? Ha! Come, or I shall be damnably angry. Why, what a coil° is here!

whore
gladly

fuss

FLORINDA Sir, can you think—

WILLMORE That you would do't for nothing? Oh, oh, I find what you would be at. Look here, here's a pistole for you. Here's a work indeed! Here, take it, I say!

FLORINDA For heaven's sake, sir, as you're a gentleman—

WILLMORE So now, now, she would be wheedling me for more! What, you will not take it then? You are resolved you will not? Come, come, take it or I'll put it up again, for look ye, I never give more. Why, how now, mistress, are you so high i'th' mouth a pistole won't down with you? Ha! Why, what a work's here! In good time! Come, no struggling to be gone. But an° y'are good at a dumb wrestle, I'm for ye. Look ye, I'm for ye. *if*

[*She struggles with him.*]

[*Enter* BELVILE *and* FREDERICK.]

BELVILE The door is open. A pox of this mad fellow! I'm angry that we've lost him; I durst have sworn he had followed us.

FREDERICK But you were so hasty, colonel, to be gone.

FLORINDA Help! Help! Murder! Help! Oh, I am ruined!

BELVILE Ha! Sure that's Florinda's voice! [*Comes up to them.*] A man! —Villain, let go that lady!

[*A noise;* WILLMORE *turns and draws;* FREDERICK *interposes.*]

FLORINDA Belvile! Heavens! My brother too is coming, and 'twill be impossible to escape. Belvile, I conjure you to walk under my chamber window, from whence I'll give you some instructions what to do. This rude man has undone us. [*Exit.*]

WILLMORE Belvile!

[*Enter* PEDRO, STEPHANO, *and other servants, with lights.*]

PEDRO I'm betrayed! Run, Stephano, and see if Florinda be safe.

[*Exit* STEPHANO.]

[*They fight, and* PEDRO'S *party beats 'em out.*]

—So, whoe'er they be, all is not well. I'll to Florinda's chamber.

[*Going out, meets* STEPHANO.]

STEPHANO You need not, sir: the poor lady's fast asleep, and thinks no harm. I would not awake her, sir, for fear of frighting her with your danger.

PEDRO I'm glad she's there. —Rascals, how came the garden door open?

STEPHANO That question comes too late, sir. Some of my fellow servants masquerading, I'll warrant.

PEDRO Masquerading! A lewd custom to debauch our youth! There's something more in this than I imagine.

[*Exeunt.*]

3.6

[SCENE: *Scene changes to the street.*]

[*Enter* BELVILE *in rage,* FREDERICK *holding him,* WILLMORE *melancholy.*]

WILLMORE Why, how the devil should I know Florinda?

BELVILE Ah, plague of your ignorance! If it had not been Florinda, must you be a beast? A brute? A senseless swine?

WILLMORE Well, sir, you see I am endued with patience: I can bear. Though egad, y'are very free with me, methinks. I was in good hopes the quarrel would have been on my side, for so uncivilly interrupting me.

BELVILE Peace, brute, whilst thou'rt safe. Oh, I'm distracted!

WILLMORE Nay, nay, I'm an unlucky dog, that's certain.

BELVILE Ah, curse upon the star that ruled my birth, or whatsoever other influence that makes me still so wretched.

WILLMORE Thou break'st my heart with these complaints. There is no star in fault, no influence but sack, the cursed sack I drunk.

FREDERICK Why, how the devil came you so drunk?

WILLMORE Why, how the devil came you so sober?

BELVILE A curse upon his thin skull, he was always beforehand that way.

FREDERICK Prithee, dear colonel, forgive him; he's sorry for his fault.

BELVILE He's always so after he has done a mischief. A plague on all such brutes!

WILLMORE By this light, I took her for an errant harlot.

BELVILE Damn your debauched opinion! Tell me, sot, hadst thou so much sense and light about thee to distinguish her woman, and couldst not see something about her face and person to strike an awful reverence into thy soul?

WILLMORE Faith no, I considered her as mere a woman as I could wish.

BELVILE 'Sdeath, I have no patience. Draw, or I'll kill you!

WILLMORE Let that alone till tomorrow, and if I set not all right again, use your pleasure.

BELVILE Tomorrow! Damn it,
The spiteful light will lead me to no happiness.
Tomorrow is Antonio's, and perhaps
Guides him to my undoing. Oh, that I could meet
This rival, this powerful fortunate!

WILLMORE What then?

BELVILE Let thy own reason, or my rage, instruct thee.

WILLMORE I shall be finely informed then, no doubt. Hear me, colonel, hear me; show me the man and I'll do his business.

BELVILE I know him no more than thou, or if I did I should not need thy aid.

WILLMORE This you say is Angellica's house; I promised the kind baggage to lie with her tonight.

[*Offers to go in.*]

[*Enter* ANTONIO *and* DIEGO. ANTONIO *knocks on the hilt of's sword.*]

ANTONIO You paid the thousand crowns I directed?

DIEGO To the lady's old woman, sir, I did.

WILLMORE Who the devil have we here?

BELVILE I'll now plant myself under Florinda's window, and if I find no comfort there, I'll die.

[*Exeunt* BELVILE *and* FREDERICK.]

[*Enter* MORETTA.]

MORETTA Page?

DIEGO Here's my lord.

WILLMORE How is this? A picaroon° going to board my frigate?— Here's one chase gun[1] for you! *pirate*

[*Drawing his sword, justles* ANTONIO, *who turns and draws. They fight;* ANTONIO *falls.*]

MORETTA Oh, bless us! We're all undone!

[*Runs in and shuts the door.*]

DIEGO Help! Murder!

[BELVILE *returns at the noise of fighting.*]

BELVILE Ha! The mad rogue's engaged in some unlucky adventure again.

[*Enter two or three* MASQUERADERS.]

MASQUERADER Ha! A man killed!

WILLMORE How, a man killed? Then I'll go home to sleep.

[*Puts up*° *and reels out. Exeunt* MASQUERADERS *another way.*] *Sheathes his sword*

BELVILE Who should it be? Pray heaven the rogue is safe, for all my quarrel to him.

[*As* BELVILE *is groping about, enter an* OFFICER *and six* SOLDIERS.]

SOLDIER Who's there?

OFFICER So, here's one dispatched. Secure the murderer.

BELVILE Do not mistake my charity for murder! I came to his assistance!

[*Soldiers seize on* BELVILE.]

OFFICER That shall be tried, sir. St. Jago![2] Swords drawn in the Carnival time!

[*Goes to* ANTONIO.]

ANTONIO Thy hand, prithee.

OFFICER Ha! Don Antonio! Look well to the villain there. —How is it, sir?

ANTONIO I'm hurt.

BELVILE Has my humanity made me a criminal?

OFFICER Away with him!

BELVILE What a curst chance is this!

[*Exeunt soldiers with* BELVILE.]

ANTONIO [*aside*] This is the man that has set upon me twice. —[*To the officer.*] Carry him to my apartment till you have farther orders from me.

[*Exit* ANTONIO, *led.*]

1. A cannon mounted at a port in the bow or stern of a ship.

2. St. James, revered in Spain (where, according to tradition, he preached and his body was brought).

4.1

[SCENE: *A fine room.*]

[*Discovers* BELVILE *as by dark alone.*]

BELVILE When shall I be weary of railing on fortune, who is resolved never to turn with smiles upon me? Two such defeats in one night none but the devil and that mad rogue could have contrived to have plagued me with. I am here a prisoner. But where, heaven knows. And if there be murder done, I can soon decide the fate of a stranger in a nation without mercy. Yet this is nothing to the torture my soul bows with when I think of losing my fair, my dear Florinda. Hark, my door opens. A light! A man, and seems of quality. Armed, too! Now shall I die like a dog, without defense.

[*Enter* ANTONIO *in a nightgown, with a light; his arm in a scarf, and a sword under his arm. He sets the candle on the table.*]

ANTONIO Sir, I come to know what injuries I have done you, that could provoke you to so mean an action as to attack me basely without allowing time for my defense?

BELVILE Sir, for a man in my circumstances to plead innocence would look like fear. But view me well, and you will find no marks of coward on me, nor anything that betrays that brutality you accuse me with.

ANTONIO In vain, sir, you impose upon my sense. You are not only he who drew on me last night, but yesterday before the same house, that of Angellica. Yet there is something in your face and mien that makes me wish I were mistaken.

BELVILE I own I fought today in the defense of a friend of mine with whom you, if you're the same, and your party were first engaged. Perhaps you think this crime enough to kill me, but if you do, I cannot fear you'll do it basely.

ANTONIO No sir, I'll make you fit for a defense with this.

[*Gives him the sword.*]

BELVILE This gallantry surprises me, nor know I how to use this present, sir, against a man so brave.

ANTONIO You shall not need. For know, I come to snatch you from a danger that is decreed against you: perhaps your life, or long imprisonment. And 'twas with so much courage you offended, I cannot see you punished.

BELVILE How shall I pay this generosity?

ANTONIO It had been safer to have killed another than have attempted me. To show your danger, sir, I'll let you know my quality: and 'tis the Viceroy's son whom you have wounded.

BELVILE The Viceroy's son! —[*Aside.*] Death and confusion! Was this plague reserved to complete all the rest? Obliged by him, the man of all the world I would destroy!

ANTONIO You seem disordered, sir.

BELVILE Yes, trust me, I am, and 'tis with pain that man receives such bounties who wants° the power to pay 'em back again. *lacks*

ANTONIO To gallant spirits 'tis indeed uneasy, but you may quickly overpay me, sir.

BELVILE [*aside*] Then I am well. Kind heaven, but set us even, that I may fight with him and keep my honor safe. —Oh, I'm impatient, sir, to be discounting° the mighty debt I owe you. Command me quickly. *reducing*

ANTONIO I have a quarrel with a rival, sir, about the maid we love.

BELVILE [*aside*] Death, 'tis Florinda he means! That thought destroys my reason, and I shall kill him.

ANTONIO My rival, sir, is one has all the virtues man can boast of—

BELVILE [*aside*] Death, who should this be?

ANTONIO He challenged me to meet him on the Molo as soon as day appeared, but last night's quarrel has made my arm unfit to guide a sword.

BELVILE I apprehend you, sir. You'd have me kill the man that lays a claim to the maid you speak of. I'll do't. I'll fly to do't!

ANTONIO Sir, do you know her?

BELVILE No, sir, but 'tis enough she is admired by you.

ANTONIO Sir, I shall rob you of the glory on't, for you must fight under my name and dress.

BELVILE That opinion must be strangely obliging that makes you think I can personate the brave Antonio, whom I can but strive to imitate.

ANTONIO You say too much to my advantage. Come, sir, the day appears that calls you forth. Within, sir, is the habit. [*Exit* ANTONIO.]

BELVILE Fantastic fortune, thou deceitful light,
That cheats the wearied traveler by night,
Though on a precipice each step you tread,
I am resolved to follow where you lead. [*Exit.*]

4.2

[SCENE: *The Molo.*]

[*Enter* FLORINDA *and* CALLIS *in masks, with* STEPHANO.]

FLORINDA [*aside*] I'm dying with my fears: Belvile's not coming as I expected under my window makes me believe that all those fears are true.—Canst thou not tell with whom my brother fights?

STEPHANO No, madam, they were both in masquerade. I was by when they challenged one another, and they had decided the quarrel then, but were prevented by some cavaliers; which made 'em put it off till now. But I am sure 'tis about you they fight.

FLORINDA [*aside*] Nay, then, 'tis with Belvile, for what other lover have I that dares fight for me except Antonio, and he is too much in favor with my brother. If it be he, for whom shall I direct my prayers to heaven?

STEPHANO Madam, I must leave you, for if my master see me, I shall be hanged for being your conductor. I escaped narrowly for the excuse I made for you last night i'th' garden.

FLORINDA And I'll reward thee for't. Prithee, no more.

[*Exit* STEPHANO.]

[*Enter* DON PEDRO *in his masking habit.*]

PEDRO Antonio's late today; the place will fill, and we may be prevented.

[*Walks about.*]

FLORINDA [*aside*] Antonio? Sure I heard amiss.

PEDRO But who will not excuse a happy lover
When soft fair arms confine the yielding neck,
And the kind whisper languishingly breathes
"Must you be gone so soon?"
Sure I had dwelt forever on her bosom—
But stay, he's here.

[*Enter* BELVILE *dressed in Antonio's clothes.*]

FLORINDA [*aside*] 'Tis not Belvile; half my fears are vanished.

PEDRO Antonio!

BELVILE [*aside*] This must be he.—You're early, sir; I do not use° to be outdone this way. *am not accustomed*

PEDRO The wretched, sir, are watchful, and 'tis enough you've the advantage of me in Angellica.

BELVILE [*aside*] Angellica! Or° I've mistook my man, or else Antonio! Can he forget his interest in Florinda and fight for common prize? *Either*

PEDRO Come, sir, you know our terms.

BELVILE [*aside*] By heaven, not I. —No talking; I am ready, sir.

[*Offers to fight;* FLORINDA *runs in.*]

FLORINDA [*to* BELVILE] Oh, hold! Whoe'er you be, I do conjure you hold! If you strike here, I die!

PEDRO Florinda!

BELVILE Florinda imploring for my rival!

PEDRO Away; this kindness is unseasonable.

[*Puts her by; they fight; she runs in just as* BELVILE *disarms* PEDRO.]

FLORINDA Who are you, sir, that dares deny my prayers?

BELVILE Thy prayers destroy him; if thou wouldst preserve him, do that thou'rt unacquainted with, and curse him.

[*She holds him.*]

FLORINDA By all you hold most dear, by her you love,
I do conjure you, touch him not.

BELVILE By her I love?
See, I obey, and at your feet resign
The useless trophy of my victory.

[*Lays his sword at her feet.*]

PEDRO Antonio, you've done enough to prove you love Florinda.

BELVILE Love Florinda! Does heaven love adoration, prayer, or penitence? Love her? Here, sir, your sword again.

[*Snatches up the sword and gives it to him.*]

Upon this truth I'll fight my life away.

PEDRO No, you've redeemed my sister, and my friendship.

[*He gives him* FLORINDA, *and pulls off his vizard to show his face, and puts it on again.*]

BELVILE Don Pedro!

PEDRO Can you resign your claims to other women, and give your heart entirely to Florinda?

BELVILE Entire, as dying saints' confessions are!
I can delay my happiness no longer:
This minute let me make Florinda mine.

PEDRO This minute let it be. No time so proper: this night my father will arrive from Rome, and possibly may hinder what we purpose.

FLORINDA Oh, heavens! This minute?

[*Enter masqueraders and pass over.*]

BELVILE Oh, do not ruin me!

PEDRO The place begins to fill, and that we may not be observed, do you walk off to St. Peter's church, where I will meet you and conclude your happiness.

BELVILE I'll meet you there. —[*Aside.*] If there be no more saints' churches in Naples.

FLORINDA Oh, stay, sir, and recall your hasty doom!
Alas, I have not yet prepared my heart
To entertain so strange a guest.

PEDRO Away; this silly modesty is assumed too late.

BELVILE Heaven, madam, what do you do?

FLORINDA Do? Despise the man that lays a tyrant's claim
To what he ought to conquer by submission.

BELVILE You do not know me. Move a little this way.

[*Draws her aside.*]

FLORINDA Yes, you may force me even to the altar,
But not the holy man that offers° there *worships*
Shall force me to be thine.

[PEDRO *talks to* CALLIS *this while.*]

BELVILE Oh, do not lose so blest an opportunity!

[*Pulls off his vizard.*]

See, 'tis your Belvile, not Antonio,
Whom your mistaken scorn and anger ruins.

FLORINDA Belvile!
Where was my soul it could not meet thy voice,
And take this knowledge in.

[*As they are talking, enter* WILLMORE, *finely dressed, and* FREDERICK.]

WILLMORE No intelligence? No news of Belvile yet? Well, I am the most unlucky rascal in nature. Ha! Am I deceived, or is it he? Look, Fred! 'Tis he, my dear Belvile!

[*Runs and embraces him;* BELVILE'S *vizard falls out on's hand.*]

BELVILE Hell and confusion seize thee!

PEDRO Ha! Belvile! I beg your pardon, sir.

[*Takes* FLORINDA *from him.*]

BELVILE Nay, touch her not. She's mine by conquest, sir;
I won her by my sword.

WILLMORE Didst thou so? And egad, child, we'll keep her by the sword.

[*Draws on* PEDRO; BELVILE *goes between.*]

BELVILE Stand off!
Thou'rt so profanely lewd, so curst by heaven,
All quarrels thou espousest must be fatal.

WILLMORE Nay, an° you be so hot, my valor's coy, *if*
And shall be courted when you want it next.

[*Puts up his sword.*]

BELVILE [*to* PEDRO] You know I ought to claim a victor's right,
But you're the brother to divine Florinda,
To whom I'm such a slave. To purchase her
I durst not hurt the man she holds so dear.

PEDRO 'Twas by Antonio's, not by Belvile's sword
This question should have been decided, sir.
I must confess much to your bravery's due,
Both now and when I met you last in arms;
But I am nicely punctual° in my word, *punctilious*
As men of honor ought, and beg your pardon:
For this mistake another time shall clear.

[*Aside to* FLORINDA *as they are going out*]

—This was some plot between you and Belvile,
But I'll prevent you.

[*Exeunt* PEDRO *and* FLORINDA.]

[BELVILE *looks after her and begins to walk up and down in rage.*]

WILLMORE Do not be modest now and lose the woman.
But if we shall fetch her back so—

BELVILE Do not speak to me!

WILLMORE Not speak to you? Egad, I'll speak to you, and will be answered, too.

BELVILE Will you, sir?

WILLMORE I know I've done some mischief, but I'm so dull a puppy that I'm the son of a whore if I know how or where. Prithee inform my understanding.

BELVILE Leave me, I say, and leave me instantly!

WILLMORE I will not leave you in this humor, nor till I know my crime.

BELVILE Death, I'll tell you, sir—

[*Draws and runs at* WILLMORE; *he runs out,* BELVILE *after him,* FREDERICK *interposes.*]

[*Enter* ANGELLICA, MORETTA, *and* SEBASTIAN.]

ANGELLICA Ha! Sebastian, is that not Willmore? Haste! haste and bring him back.

[*Exit* SEBASTIAN.]

FREDERICK [*aside*] The colonel's mad: I never saw him thus before. I'll after 'em lest he do some mischief, for I am sure Willmore will not draw on him. [*Exit.*]

ANGELLICA I am all rage! My first desires defeated!
For one for aught he knows that has no
Other merit than her quality,
Her being Don Pedro's sister. He loves her!
I know 'tis so. Dull, dull, insensible,
He will not see me now, though oft invited,
And broke his word last night. False perjured man!
He that but yesterday fought for my favors,
And would have made his life a sacrifice
To've gained one night with me,
Must now be hired and courted to my arms.

MORETTA I told you what would come on't, but Moretta's an old doting fool. Why did you give him five hundred crowns, but to set himself out for other lovers? You should have kept him poor if you had meant to have had any good from him.

ANGELLICA Oh, name not such mean trifles! Had I given him all
My youth has earned from sin,
I had not lost a thought nor sigh upon't.
But I have given him my eternal rest,
My whole repose, my future joys, my heart!
My virgin heart, Moretta! Oh, 'tis gone!

MORETTA Curse on him, here he comes. How fine she has made him, too.

[*Enter* WILLMORE *and* SEBASTIAN; ANGELLICA *turns and walks away.*]

WILLMORE How now, turned shadow?
Fly when I pursue, and follow when I fly?

[*Sings.*]

Stay, gentle shadow of my dove,
And tell me ere I go,

Whether the substance may not prove
A fleeting thing like you.

[*As she turns she looks on him.*]

There's a soft kind look remaining yet.

ANGELLICA Well, sir, you may be gay: all happiness, all joys pursue you still. Fortune's your slave, and gives you every hour choice of new hearts and beauties, till you are cloyed with the repeated bliss which others vainly languish for. But know, false man, that I shall be revenged.

[*Turns away in rage.*]

WILLMORE So, gad, there are of those faint-hearted lovers, whom such a sharp lesson next their hearts would make as impotent as fourscore.° Pox o' this whining; my business is to laugh and love. A pox on't, I hate your sullen lover: a man shall lose as much time to put you in humor now as would serve to gain a new woman.

as an 80-year-old man

ANGELLICA I scorn to cool that fire I cannot raise,
Or do the drudgery of your virtuous mistress.

WILLMORE A virtuous mistress? Death, what a thing thou hast found out for me! Why, what the devil should I do with a virtuous woman, a sort of ill-natured creatures that take a pride to torment a lover. Virtue is but an infirmity in woman, a disease that renders even the handsome ungrateful; whilst the ill-favored, for want of solicitations and address, only fancy themselves so. I have lain with a woman of quality who has all the while been railing at whores.

ANGELLICA I will not answer for your mistress's virtue,
Though she be young enough to know no guilt;
And I could wish you would persuade my heart
'Twas the two hundred thousand crowns you courted.

WILLMORE Two hundred thousand crowns! What story's this? What trick? What woman, ha?

ANGELLICA How strange you make it. Have you forgot the creature you entertained on the Piazzo last night?

WILLMORE [*aside*] Ha! My gipsy worth two hundred thousand crowns! Oh, how I long to be with her! Pox, I knew she was of quality.

ANGELLICA False man! I see my ruin in thy face.
How many vows you breathed upon my bosom
Never to be unjust. Have you forgot so soon?

WILLMORE Faith, no; I was just coming to repeat 'em. But here's a humor indeed would make a man a saint. —[*Aside.*] Would she would be angry enough to leave me, and command me not to wait on her.

[*Enter* HELLENA *dressed in man's clothes.*]

HELLENA This must be Angellica: I know it by her mumping° matron here. Ay, ay, 'tis she. My mad captain's with her, too, for all his swearing. How this unconstant humor makes me love him! —Pray, good grave gentlewoman, is not this Angellica?

grimacing

MORETTA My too young sir, it is. —[*Aside.*] I hope 'tis one from Don Antonio.

[*Goes to* ANGELLICA.]

HELLENA [*aside*] Well, something I'll do to vex him for this.

ANGELLICA I will not speak with him. Am I in humor to receive a lover?

WILLMORE Not speak with him? Why, I'll be gone, and wait your idler minutes. Can I show less obedience to the thing I love so fondly?

[*Offers to go.*]

ANGELLICA A fine excuse this! Stay—

WILLMORE And hinder your advantage? Should I repay your bounties so ungratefully?

ANGELLICA [*to* HELLENA] Come hither, boy. —[*To* WILLMORE.]
That I may let you see
How much above the advantages you name
I prize one minute's joy with you.

WILLMORE [*impatient to be gone*] Oh, you destroy me with this endearment.—[*Aside.*] Death, how shall I get away?—Madam, 'twill not be fit I should be seen with you. Besides, it will not be convenient. And I've a friend—that's dangerously sick.

ANGELLICA I see you're impatient. Yet you shall stay.

WILLMORE [*aside*] And miss my assignation with my gipsy.

[*Walks about impatiently;* MORETTA *brings* HELLENA, *who addresses herself to* ANGELLICA.]

HELLENA Madam,
You'll hardly pardon my intrusion
When you shall know my business,
And I'm too young to tell my tale with art;
But there must be a wondrous store of goodness
Where so much beauty dwells.

ANGELLICA A pretty advocate, whoever sent thee.
Prithee proceed.
[*To* WILLMORE, *who is stealing off.*]
—Nay, sir, you shall not go.

WILLMORE [*aside*] Then I shall lose my dear gipsy forever.
Pox on't, she stays me out of spite.

HELLENA I am related to a lady, madam,
Young, rich, and nobly born, but has the fate
To be in love with a young English gentleman.
Strangely she loves him, at first sight she loved him,
But did adore him when she heard him speak;
For he, she said, had charms in every word
That failed not to surprise, to wound and conquer.

WILLMORE [*aside*] Ha! Egad, I hope this concerns me.

ANGELLICA [*aside*] 'Tis my false man he means. Would he were gone:
This praise will raise his pride, and ruin me.

[*To* WILLMORE.] —Well,
Since you are so impatient to be gone,
I will release you, sir.

WILLMORE [*aside*] Nay, then I'm sure 'twas me he spoke of: this cannot be the effects of kindness in her. —No, Madam, I've considered better on't, and will not give you cause of jealousy.

ANGELLICA But sir, I've business that—

WILLMORE This shall not do; I know 'tis but to try me.

ANGELLICA Well, to your story, boy. —[*Aside*]. Though 'twill undo me.

HELLENA With this addition to his other beauties,
He won her unresisting tender heart.
He vowed, and sighed, and swore he loved her dearly;
And she believed the cunning flatterer,
And thought herself the happiest maid alive.
Today was the appointed time by both
To consummate their bliss:
The virgin, altar, and the priest were dressed;
And whilst she languished for th'expected bridegroom,
She heard he paid his broken vows to you.

WILLMORE [*aside*] So, this is some dear rogue that's in love with me, and this way lets me know it. Or, if it be not me, she means someone whose place I may supply.

ANGELLICA Now I perceive
The cause of thy impatience to be gone,
And all the business of this glorious dress.

WILLMORE Damn the young prater; I know not what he means.

HELLENA Madam,
In your fair eyes I read too much concern
To tell my farther business.

ANGELLICA Prithee, sweet youth, talk on: thou mayst perhaps
Raise here a storm that may undo my passion,
And then I'll grant thee anything.

HELLENA Madam, 'tis to entreat you (oh unreasonable)
You would not see this stranger.
For if you do, she vows you are undone;
Though nature never made a man so excellent,
And sure he 'ad been a god, but for inconstancy.

WILLMORE [*aside*] Ah, rogue, how finely he's instructed! 'Tis plain, some woman that has seen me *en passant*.° *in passing (French)*

ANGELLICA Oh, I shall burst with jealousy! Do you know the man you speak of?

HELLENA Yes, madam, he used to be in buff and scarlet.

ANGELLICA [*to* WILLMORE] Thou false as hell, what canst thou say to this?

WILLMORE By heaven—

ANGELLICA Hold, do not damn thyself—

HELLENA Nor hope to be believed.

[*He walks about; they follow.*]

ANGELLICA Oh perjured man!
Is't thus you pay my generous passion back?

HELLENA Why would you, sir, abuse my lady's faith?

ANGELLICA And use me so unhumanely.

HELLENA A maid so young, so innocent—

WILLMORE Ah, young devil!

ANGELLICA Dost thou not know thy life is in my power?

HELLENA Or think my lady cannot be revenged?

WILLMORE [*aside*] So, so, the storm comes finely on.

ANGELLICA Now thou art silent: guilt has struck thee dumb.
Oh, hadst thou still been so, I'd lived in safety.

[*She turns away and weeps.*]

WILLMORE [*aside to* HELLENA] Sweetheart, the lady's name and house—quickly! I'm impatient to be with her.

[*Looks toward* ANGELLICA *to watch her turning, and as she comes towards them he meets her.*]

HELLENA [*aside*] So, now is he for another woman.

WILLMORE The impudent'st young thing in nature: I cannot persuade him out of his error, madam.

ANGELLICA I know he's in the right; yet thou'st a tongue
That would persuade him to deny his faith.

[*In rage walks away.*]

WILLMORE [*said softly to* HELLENA] Her name, her name, dear boy!

HELLENA Have you forgot it, sir?

WILLMORE [*aside*] Oh, I perceive he's not to know I am a stranger to his lady. —Yes, yes, I do know, but I have forgot the—[ANGELLICA *turns.*] —By heaven, such early confidence I never saw.

ANGELLICA Did I not charge you with this mistress, sir?
Which you denied, though I beheld your perjury.
This little generosity of thine has rendered back my heart. [*Walks away.*]

WILLMORE [*to* HELLENA] So, you have made sweet work here, my little mischief. Look your lady be kind and good-natured now, or I shall have but a cursed bargain on't. [ANGELLICA *turns toward them.*] —The rogue's bred up to mischief; art thou so great a fool to credit him?

ANGELLICA Yes, I do, and you in vain impose upon me.
Come hither, boy. Is not this he you spake of?

HELLENA I think it is. I cannot swear, but I vow he has just such another lying lover's look.

[HELLENA *looks in his face; he gazes on her.*]

WILLMORE [*aside*] Ha! Do I not know that face? By heaven, my little gipsy! What a dull dog was I: had I but looked that way I'd known her. Are all my hopes of a new woman banished?—Egad, if I do not fit° thee for this, hang me. —[To ANGELLICA.] Madam, I have found out the plot. *punish*

HELLENA [*aside*] Oh lord, what does he say? Am I discovered now?

WILLMORE Do you see this young spark here?

HELLENA [*aside*] He'll tell her who I am.

WILLMORE Who do you think this is?

HELLENA [*aside*] Ay, ay, he does know me. —Nay, dear captain, I am undone if you discover me.

WILLMORE Nay, nay, no cogging°; she shall know what a precious mistress I have. *deceit; wheedling*

HELLENA Will you be such a devil?

WILLMORE Nay, nay, I'll teach you to spoil sport you will not make. — This small ambassador comes not from a person of quality, as you imagine and he says, but from a very errant° gipsy: the talking'st, prating'st, canting'st little animal thou ever saw'st. *good-for-nothing*

ANGELLICA What news you tell me, that's the thing I mean.

HELLENA [*aside*] Would I were well off the place! If ever I go a-captain-hunting again—

WILLMORE Mean that thing? That gipsy thing? Thou mayst as well be jealous of thy monkey or parrot as of her. A German motion° were worth a dozen of her, and a dream were a better enjoyment— a creature of a constitution fitter for heaven than man. *puppet*

HELLENA [*aside*] Though I'm sure he lies, yet this vexes me.

ANGELLICA You are mistaken: she's a Spanish woman made up of no such dull materials.

WILLMORE Materials? Egad, an she be made of any that will either dispense or admit of love, I'll be bound to continence.

HELLENA [*aside to him*] Unreasonable man, do you think so?

WILLMORE You may return, my little brazen head, and tell your lady, that till she be handsome enough to be beloved, or I dull enough to be religious, there will be small hopes of me.

ANGELLICA Did you not promise, then, to marry her?

WILLMORE Not I, by heaven.

ANGELLICA You cannot undeceive my fears and torments, till you have vowed you will not marry her.

HELLENA [*aside*] If he swears that, he'll be revenged on me indeed for all my rogueries.

ANGELLICA I know what arguments you'll bring against me: fortune and honor.

WILLMORE Honor! I tell you, I hate it in your sex; and those that fancy themselves possessed of that foppery are the most impertinently troublesome of all womankind,

and will transgress nine commandments to keep one.[3]
And to satisfy your jealousy, I swear—

HELLENA [*aside to him*] Oh, no swearing, dear captain.

WILLMORE If it were possible I should ever be inclined to marry, it should be some kind young sinner: one that has generosity enough to give a favor handsomely to one that can ask it discreetly, one that has wit enough to manage an intrigue of love. Oh, how civil such a wench is to a man that does her the honor to marry her.

ANGELLICA By heaven, there's no faith in anything he says.

[*Enter* SEBASTIAN.]

SEBASTIAN Madam, Don Antonio—

ANGELLICA Come hither.

HELLENA [*aside*] Ha! Antonio! He may be coming hither, and he'll certainly discover me. I'll therefore retire without a ceremony. [*Exit* HELLENA.]

ANGELLICA I'll see him. Get my coach ready.

SEBASTIAN It waits you, madam.

WILLMORE [*aside*] This is lucky. —What, madam, now I may be gone and leave you to the enjoyment of my rival?

ANGELLICA Dull man, that canst not see how ill, how poor,
That false dissimulation looks. Be gone,
And never let me see thy cozening face again,
Lest I relapse and kill thee.

WILLMORE Yes, you can spare me now. Farewell, till you're in better humor. —[*Aside.*] I'm glad of this release. Now for my gipsy:
For though to worse we change, yet still we find
New joys, new charms, in a new miss that's kind.

[*Exit* WILLMORE.]

ANGELLICA He's gone, and in this ague of my soul
The shivering fit returns.
Oh, with what willing haste he took his leave,
As if the longed-for minute were arrived
Of some blest assignation.
In vain I have consulted all my charms,
In vain this beauty prized, in vain believed
My eyes could kindle any lasting fires;
I had forgot my name, my infamy,
And the reproach that honor lays on those
That dare pretend a sober passion here.
Nice° reputation, though it leave behind *Strict in conduct*
More virtues than inhabit where that dwells,
Yet that once gone, those virtues shine no more.
Then since I am not fit to be beloved,

3. That is, the commandment forbidding adultery (Exodus 20.14; Deuteronomy 5.18).

I am resolved to think on a revenge
On him that soothed° me thus to my undoing. *flattered*

[*Exeunt.*]

4.3

[SCENE: *A street.*]

[*Enter* FLORINDA *and* VALERIA *in habits different from what they have been seen in.*]

FLORINDA We're happily escaped, and yet I tremble still.

VALERIA A lover, and fear? Why, I am but half an one, and yet I have courage for any attempt. Would Hellena were here: I would fain have had her as deep in this mischief as we; she'll fare but ill else, I doubt.

FLORINDA She pretended a visit to the Augustine nuns; but I believe some other design carried her out; pray heaven we light on her. Prithee, what didst do with Callis?

VALERIA When I saw no reason would do good on her, I followed her into the wardrobe,° and as she was looking for something in a great chest, I toppled her in by the heels, snatched the key of the apartment where you were confined, locked her in, and left her bawling for help. *dressing room*

FLORINDA 'Tis well you resolve to follow my fortunes, for thou darest never appear at home again after such an action.

VALERIA That's according as the young stranger and I shall agree. But to our business. I delivered your note to Belvile when I got out under pretense of going to Mass. I found him at his lodging, and believe me it came seasonably, for never was man in so desperate a condition. I told him of your resolution of making your escape today if your brother would be absent long enough to permit you; if not, to die rather than be Antonio's.

FLORINDA Thou should'st have told him I was confined to my chamber upon my brother's suspicion that the business on the Molo was a plot laid between him and I.

VALERIA I said all this, and told him your brother was now gone to his devotion; and he resolves to visit every church till he find him, and not only undeceive him in that, but caress him so as shall delay his return home.

FLORINDA Oh heavens! He's here, and Belvile with him, too.

[*They put on their vizards.*]

[*Enter* DON PEDRO, BELVILE, WILLMORE; BELVILE *and* DON PEDRO *seeming in serious discourse.*]

VALERIA Walk boldly by them, and I'll come at a distance, lest he suspect us.

[*She walks by them and looks back on them.*]

WILLMORE Ha! A woman, and of excellent mien!

PEDRO She throws a kind look back on you.

WILLMORE Death, 'tis a likely wench, and that kind look shall not be cast away. I'll follow her.

BELVILE Prithee do not.

WILLMORE Do not? By heavens, to the antipodies,[4] with such an invitation.

[*She goes out, and* WILLMORE *follows her.*]

BELVILE 'Tis a mad fellow for a wench.

[*Enter* FREDERICK.]

FREDERICK Oh, colonel, such news!

BELVILE Prithee what?

FREDERICK News that will make you laugh in spite of fortune.

BELVILE What, Blunt has had some damned trick put upon him? Cheated, banged, or clapped?[5]

FREDERICK Cheated, sir, rarely° cheated of all but his shirt and drawers; the unconscionable whore too turned him out before consummation, so that, traversing the streets at midnight, the watch found him in this *fresco* and conducted him home. By heaven, 'tis such a sight, and yet I durst as well been hanged as laughed at him or pity him: he beats all that do but ask him a question, and is in such an humour.

superbly

PEDRO Who is't has met with this ill usage, sir?

BELVILE A friend of ours whom you must see for mirth's sake. — [*Aside.*] I'll employ him to give Florinda time for an escape.

PEDRO What is he?

BELVILE A young countryman of ours, one that has been educated at so plentiful a rate he yet ne'er knew the want of money; and 'twill be a great jest to see how simply he'll look without it. For my part, I'll lend him none: and the rogue know not how to put on a borrowing face and ask first, I'll let him see how good 'tis to play our parts whilst I play his. Prithee, Fred, do you go home and keep him in that posture till we come.

[*Exeunt.*]

[*Enter* FLORINDA *from the farther end of the scene, looking behind her.*]

FLORINDA I am followed still. Ha! My brother too advancing this way! Good heavens defend me from being seen by him! [*She goes off.*]

[*Enter* WILLMORE, *and after him* VALERIA, *at a little distance.*]

WILLMORE Ah, there she sails! She looks back as she were willing to be boarded; I'll warrant her prize.°

a ship legally captured

[*He goes out,* VALERIA *following.*]

4. The opposite side of the earth.

5. Infected with the clap (gonorrhea).

[*Enter* HELLENA, *just as he goes out, with a page.*]

HELLENA Ha, is not that my captain that has a woman in chase? 'Tis not Angellica.—Boy, follow those people at a distance, and bring me an account where they go in.

[*Exit page.*]

—I'll find his haunts, and plague him everywhere. Ha! My brother!

[BELVILE, WILLMORE, PEDRO *cross the stage;* HELLENA *runs off.*]

4.4

[SCENE: *Scene changes to another street.*]

[*Enter* FLORINDA.]

FLORINDA What shall I do? My brother now pursues me. Will no kind power protect me from his tyranny? Ha! Here's a door open; I'll venture in, since nothing can be worse than to fall into his hands. My life and honor are at stake, and my necessity has no choice. [*She goes in.*]

[*Enter* VALERIA, *and* HELLENA'S PAGE *peeping after* FLORINDA.]

PAGE Here she went in; I shall remember this house.

[*Exit boy.*]

VALERIA This is Belvile's lodging; she's gone in as readily as if she knew it. Ha! Here's that mad fellow again; I dare not venture in. I'll watch my opportunity.

[*Goes aside.*]

[*Enter* WILLMORE, *gazing about him.*]

WILLMORE I have lost her hereabouts. Pox on't, she must not 'scape me so. [*Goes out.*]

4.5

[SCENE: *Scene changes to* BLUNT'S *chamber, discovers him sitting on a couch in his shirt and drawers, reading.*]

BLUNT So, now my mind's a little at peace, since I have resolved revenge. A pox on this tailor, though, for not bringing home the clothes I bespoke.° And a pox of all poor cavaliers: a man can never keep a spare suit for 'em, and I shall have these rogues come in and find me naked, and then I'm undone. But I'm resolved to arm myself: the rascals shall not insult over me too much. [*Puts on an old rusty sword and buff belt.*] Now, how like a morris dancer[6] I am equipped! A fine ladylike whore to cheat me thus without affording me a kindness for my money! A pox light on her, I shall never be reconciled to

ordered

6. That is, costumed in white, like an English folk dancer.

the sex more; she has made me as faithless as a physician, as uncharitable as a churchman, and as ill-natured as a poet. Oh, how I'll use all womankind hereafter! What would I give to have one of 'em within my reach now! Any mortal thing in petticoats, kind fortune, send me, and I'll forgive thy last night's malice. —Here's a cursed book, too—a warning to all young travelers—that can instruct me how to prevent such mischiefs now 'tis too late. Well, 'tis a rare convenient thing to read a little now and then, as well as hawk and hunt.

[*Sits down again and reads.*]

[*Enter to him* FLORINDA.]

FLORINDA This house is haunted, sure: 'tis well furnished, and no living thing inhabits it. Ha! A man! Heavens, how he's attired! Sure 'tis some rope dancer,° or fencing master. I tremble now for fear, and yet I must venture now to speak to him. —Sir, if I may not interrupt your meditations— *tightrope walker*

[*He starts up and gazes.*]

BLUNT Ha, what's here? Are my wishes granted? And is not that a she creature? 'Adsheartlikins, 'tis. —What wretched thing art thou, ha?

FLORINDA Charitable sir, you've told yourself already what I am: a very wretched maid, forced by a strange unlucky accident to seek a safety here, and must be ruined if you do not grant it.

BLUNT Ruined! Is there any ruin so inevitable as that which now threatens thee? Dost thou know, miserable woman, into what den of mischiefs thou art fallen; what abyss of confusion, ha? Dost not see something in my looks that frights thy guilty soul, and makes thee wish to change that shape of woman for any humble animal, or devil? For those were safer for thee, and less mischievous.

FLORINDA Alas, what mean you, sir? I must confess, your looks have something in 'em makes me fear, but I beseech you, as you seem a gentleman, pity a harmless virgin that takes your house for sanctuary.

BLUNT Talk on, talk on; and weep, too, till my faith return. Do, flatter me out of my senses again. A harmless virgin with a pox; as much one as t'other, 'adsheartlikins. Why, what the devil, can I not be safe in my house for you, not in my chamber? Nay, not even being naked too cannot secure me? This is an impudence greater than has invaded me yet. Come, no resistance.

[*Pulls her rudely.*]

FLORINDA Dare you be so cruel?

BLUNT Cruel? 'Adsheartlikins, as a galley slave, or a Spanish whore. Cruel? Yes, I will kiss and beat thee all over, kiss and see thee all over; thou shalt lie with me too, not that I care for the enjoyment, but to let thee see I have ta'en deliberated malice to thee, and will be revenged on one whore for the sins of another. I will smile and deceive thee; flatter thee, and beat thee; embrace thee and rob thee, as she did me; fawn on thee, and strip thee stark naked; then hang thee out at my window by the heels, with a paper of scurvy verses fastened to thy breast in praise of damnable women. Come, come, along.

FLORINDA Alas, sir, must I be sacrificed for the crimes of the most infamous of my sex? I never understood the sins you name.

BLUNT Do, persuade the fool you love him, or that one of you can be just or honest; tell me I was not an easy coxcomb, or any strange impossible tale: it will be believed sooner than thy false showers or protestations. A generation of damned hypocrites! To flatter my very clothes from my back! Dissembling witches! Are these the returns you make an honest gentleman that trusts, believes, and loves you? But if I be not even with you—Come along, or I shall—

[*Pulls her again.*]

[*Enter* FREDERICK.]

FREDERICK Ha, what's here to do?

BLUNT 'Adsheartlikins, Fred, I am glad thou art come, to be a witness of my dire revenge.

FREDERICK What's this, a person of quality too, who is upon the ramble to supply the defects of some grave impotent husband?

BLUNT No, this has another pretense: some very unfortunate accident brought her hither, to save a life pursued by I know not who or why, and forced to take sanctuary here at fool's haven. 'Adsheartlikins, to me of all mankind for protection? Is the ass to be cajoled again, think ye? No, young one, no prayers or tears shall mitigate my rage; therefore prepare for both my pleasures of enjoyment and revenge. For I am resolved to make up my loss here on thy body: I'll take it out in kindness and in beating.

FREDERICK Now, mistress of mine, what do you think of this?

FLORINDA I think he will not, dares not be so barbarous.

FREDERICK Have a care, Blunt, she fetched a deep sigh; she is enamoured with thy shirt and drawers. She'll strip thee even of that; there are of her calling such unconscionable baggages and such dexterous thieves, they'll flay a man and he shall ne'er miss his skin till he feels the cold. There was a countryman of ours robbed of a row of teeth whilst he was a-sleeping, which the jilt made him buy again when he waked. You see, lady, how little reason we have to trust you.

BLUNT 'Adsheartlikins, why this is most abominable!

FLORINDA Some such devils there may be, but by all that's holy, I am none such. I entered here to save a life in danger.

BLUNT For no goodness, I'll warrant her.

FREDERICK Faith, damsel, you had e'en confessed the plain truth, for we are fellows not to be caught twice in the same trap. Look on that wreck: a tight vessel when he set out of haven, well trimmed and laden. And see how a female picaroon of this island of rogues has shattered him, and canst thou hope for any mercy?

BLUNT No, no, gentlewoman, come along; 'adsheartlikins, we must be better acquainted.—We'll both lie with her, and then let me alone to bang° her. *beat*

FREDERICK I'm ready to serve you in matters of revenge that has a double pleasure in't.

BLUNT Well said.—You hear, little one, how you are condemned by public vote to the bed within; there's no resisting your destiny, sweetheart.

[*Pulls her.*]

FLORINDA Stay, sir. I have seen you with Belvile, an English cavalier. For his sake, use me kindly. You know him, sir.

BLUNT Belvile? Why yes, sweeting, we do know Belvile, and wish he were with us now. He's a cormorant[7] at whore and bacon: he'd have a limb or two of thee, my virgin pullet. But 'tis no matter; we'll leave him the bones to pick.

FLORINDA Sir, if you have any esteem for that Belvile, I conjure you to treat me with more gentleness; he'll thank you for the justice.

FREDERICK Hark'ee, Blunt, I doubt° we are mistaken in this matter. *fear*

FLORINDA Sir, if you find me not worth Belvile's care, use me as you please. And that you may think I merit better treatment than you threaten, pray take this present.

[*Gives him a ring; he looks on it.*]

BLUNT Hum, a diamond! Why, 'tis a wonderful virtue now that lies in this ring, a mollifying virtue. 'Adsheartlikins, there's more persuasive rhetoric in't than all her sex can utter.

FREDERICK I begin to suspect something, and 'twould anger us vilely to be trussed up for a rape upon a maid of quality, when we only believe we ruffle[8] a harlot.

BLUNT Thou art a credulous fellow, but 'adsheartlikins, I have no faith yet. Why, my saint prattled as parlously° as this does; she gave me a bracelet, too, a devil on her! But I sent my man to sell it today for necessaries, and it proved as counterfeit as her vows of love. *excessively*

7. That is, he is insatiably greedy; cormorants are voracious seabirds.

8. Handle with rude familiarity.

FREDERICK However, let it reprieve her till we see Belvile.

BLUNT That's hard, yet I will grant it.

[*Enter a* SERVANT.]

SERVANT Oh, sir, the colonel is just come in with his new friend and a Spaniard of quality, and talks of having you to dinner with 'em.

BLUNT 'Adsheartlikins, I'm undone! I would not see 'em for the world. Hark'ee, Fred, lock up the wench in your chamber.

FREDERICK Fear nothing, madam: whate'er he threatens, you are safe whilst in my hands.

[*Exeunt* FREDERICK *and* FLORINDA.]

BLUNT And sirrah, upon your life, say I am not at home, or that I'm asleep, or—or—anything. Away; I'll prevent their coming this way.

[*Locks the door, and exeunt.*]

5.1

[SCENE: BLUNT's *chamber.*]

[*After a great knocking as at his chamber door, enter* BLUNT *softly crossing the stage, in his shirt and drawers as before.*]

VOICES [*call within*] Ned! Ned Blunt! Ned Blunt!

BLUNT The rogues are up in arms. 'Adsheartlikins, this villainous Frederick has betrayed me: they have heard of my blessed fortune.

VOICES [*and knocking within*] Ned Blunt! Ned! Ned!

BELVILE [*within*] Why, he's dead, sir, without dispute dead; he has not been seen today. Let's break open the door. Here, boy—

BLUNT Ha, break open the door? 'Adsheartlikins, that mad fellow will be as good as his word.

BELVILE [*within*] Boy, bring something to force the door.

[*A great noise within, at the door again.*]

BLUNT So, now must I speak in my own defense; I'll try what rhetoric will do.—Hold, hold! What do you mean, gentlemen, what do you mean?

BELVILE [*within*] Oh, rogue, art alive? Prithee open the door and convince us.

BLUNT Yes, I am alive, gentlemen, but at present a little busy.

BELVILE [*within*] How, Blunt grown a man of business? Come, come, open and let's see this miracle.

BLUNT No, no, no, no, gentlemen, 'tis no great business. But—I am—at—my devotion. 'Adsheartlikins, will you not allow a man time to pray?

BELVILE [*within*] Turned religious? A greater wonder than the first! Therefore open quickly, or we shall unhinge, we shall.

BLUNT [*aside*] This won't do.—Why hark'ee, colonel, to tell you the truth, I am about a necessary affair of life: I have a wench with me. You apprehend me?—The devil's in't if they be so uncivil as to disturb me now.

WILLMORE [*within*] How, a wench? Nay then, we must enter and partake. No resistance. Unless it be your lady of quality, and then we'll keep our distance.

BLUNT So, the business is out,

WILLMORE [*within*] Come, come, lend's more hands to the door. Now heave, all together. [*Breaks open the door.*] So, well done, my boys.

[*Enter* BELVILE *and his* PAGE, WILLMORE, FREDERICK, *and* PEDRO. BLUNT *looks simply,*° *they all laugh at him; he lays his hand on his sword, and comes up to* WILLMORE.] *foolish*

BLUNT Hark'ee, sir, laugh out your laugh quickly, d'ye hear, and be gone. I shall spoil your sport else, 'adsheartlikins, sir, I shall. The jest has been carried on too long.—[*Aside.*] A plague upon my tailor!

WILLMORE 'Sdeath, how the whore has dressed him! Faith, sir, I'm sorry.

BLUNT Are you so, sir? Keep't to yourself then, sir, I advise you, d'ye hear, for I can as little endure your pity as his mirth.

[*Lays his hand on's sword.*]

BELVILE Indeed, Willmore, thou wert a little too rough with Ned Blunt's mistress. Call a person of quality whore, and one so young, so handsome, and so eloquent? Ha, ha, he.

BLUNT Hark'ee, sir, you know me, and know I can be angry. Have a care, for 'adsheartlikins, I can fight, too, I can, sir. Do you mark me? No more.

BELVILE Why so peevish, good Ned? Some disappointments, I'll warrant. What, did the jealous count, her husband, return just in the nick?

BLUNT Or the devil, sir. [*They laugh.*] D'ye laugh? Look ye settle me a good sober countenance, and that quickly, too, or you shall know Ned Blunt is not—

BELVILE Not everybody, we know that.

BLUNT Not an ass to be laughed at, sir.

WILLMORE Unconscionable sinner! To bring a lover so near his happiness—a vigorous passionate lover—and then not only cheat him of his movables,° but his very desires, too. *personal property*

BELVILE Ah, sir, a mistress is a trifle with Blunt; he'll have a dozen the next time he looks abroad. His eyes have charms not to be resisted; there needs no more than to expose that taking person to the view of the fair, and he leads 'em all in triumph.

PEDRO Sir, though I'm a stranger to you, I am ashamed at the rudeness of my nation; and could you learn who did it, would assist you to make an example of 'em.

BLUNT Why ay, there's one speaks sense now, and handsomely. And let me tell you, gentlemen, I should not have showed myself like a jack pudding° thus to have made you mirth, but that I have revenge within my power. For know, I have got into my possession a female, who had better have fallen under any curse than the ruin I design her. 'Adsheartlikins, she assaulted me here in my own lodgings, and had doubtless committed a rape upon me, had not this sword defended me. *clown, buffoon*

FREDERICK I know not that, but o' my conscience thou had ravished her, had she not redeemed herself with a ring. Let's see't, Blunt.

[*Blunt shows the ring.*]

BELVILE [*aside*] Ha! The ring I gave Florinda when we exchanged our vows!—Hark'ee, Blunt—

[*Goes to whisper to him.*]

WILLMORE No whispering, good colonel, there's a woman in the case. No whispering.

BELVILE [*aside to* BLUNT] Hark'ee, fool, be advised, and conceal both the ring and the story for your reputation's sake. Do not let people know what despised cullies we English are; to be cheated and abused by one whore, and another rather bribe thee than be kind to thee, is an infamy to our nation.

WILLMORE Come, come, where's the wench? We'll see her; let her be what she will, we'll see her.

PEDRO Ay, ay, let us see her. I can soon discover whether she be of quality, or for your diversion.

BLUNT She's in Fred's custody.

WILLMORE Come, come, the key—

[*To* FREDERICK, *who gives him the key; they are going.*]

BELVILE [*aside*] Death, what shall I do?—Stay, gentlemen.—[*Aside.*] Yet if I hinder 'em, I shall discover all.—Hold, let's go one at once. Give me the key.

WILLMORE Nay, hold there, colonel, I'll go first.

FREDERICK Nay, no dispute, Ned and I have the propriety° of her. *right of possession*

WILLMORE Damn propriety! Then we'll draw cuts.° [BELVILE *goes to whisper* WILLMORE.] Nay, no corruption, good colonel. Come, the longest sword carries her. *draw lots*

[*They all draw, forgetting* DON PEDRO, *being a Spaniard, had the longest.*[9]]

BLUNT I yield up my interest to you, gentlemen, and that will be revenge sufficient.

9. The English commonly fought with a shorter sword than the Spanish.

WILLMORE [*to* PEDRO] The wench is yours. —[*Aside.*] Pox of his Toledo,[1] I had forgot that.

FREDERICK Come, sir, I'll conduct you to the lady.

[*Exeunt* FREDERICK *and* PEDRO.]

BELVILE [*aside*] To hinder him will certainly discover her. —Dost know, dull beast, what mischief thou hast done?

[WILLMORE *walking up and down, out of humor.*]

WILLMORE Ay, ay, to trust our fortune to lots! A devil on't, 'twas madness, that's the truth on't.

BELVILE Oh, intolerable sot—

[*Enter* FLORINDA *running, masked,* PEDRO *after her;* WILLMORE *gazing round her.*]

FLORINDA [*aside*] Good heaven defend me from discovery!

PEDRO 'Tis but in vain to fly me; you're fallen to my lot.

BELVILE [*aside*] Sure she's undiscovered yet, but now I fear there is no way to bring her off.° *rescue her*

WILLMORE [*aside*] Why, what a pox, is not this my woman, the same I followed but now?

[PEDRO *talking to* FLORINDA, *who walks up and down.*]

PEDRO As if I did not know ye, and your business here.

FLORINDA [*aside*] Good heaven, I fear he does indeed!

PEDRO Come, pray be kind; I know you meant to be so when you entered here, for these are proper gentlemen.

WILLMORE But sir, perhaps the lady will not be imposed upon: she'll choose her man.

PEDRO I am better bred than not to leave her choice free.

[*Enter* VALERIA, *and is surprised at sight of* DON PEDRO.]

VALERIA [*aside*] Don Pedro here! There's no avoiding him.

FLORINDA [*aside*] Valeria! Then I'm undone.

VALERIA [*to* PEDRO, *running to him*] Oh, I have found you, sir! The strangest accident—if I had breath—to tell it.

PEDRO Speak! Is Florinda safe? Hellena well?

VALERIA Ay, ay, sir. Florinda is safe. —[*Aside.*] From any fears of you.

PEDRO Why, where's Florinda? Speak!

VALERIA Ay, where indeed, sir; I wish I could inform you. But to hold you no longer in doubt—

FLORINDA [*aside*] Oh, what will she say?

VALERIA She's fled away in the habit—of one of her pages, sir. But Callis thinks you may retrieve her yet, if you make haste away. She'll tell you, sir, the rest. —[*Aside.*] If you can find her out.

PEDRO Dishonorable girl, she has undone my aim. —[*To* BELVILE.] Sir, you see my necessity of leaving you, and I hope you'll pardon it. My sister, I know, will make her flight to you; and if she do, I shall expect she should be rendered back.

1. A sword made in Toledo, a city in Spain famous for the quality of its steel blades.

BELVILE I shall consult my love and honor, sir.

[*Exit* PEDRO.]

FLORINDA [*to* VALERIA] My dear preserver, let me embrace thee.

WILLMORE What the devil's all this?

BLUNT Mystery, by this light.

VALERIA Come, come, make haste and get yourselves married quickly, for your brother will return again.

BELVILE I'm so surprised with fears and joys, so amazed to find you here in safety, I can scarce persuade my heart into a faith of what I see.

WILLMORE Hark'ee, colonel, is this that mistress who has cost you so many sighs, and me so many quarrels with you?

BELVILE It is. —[*To* FLORINDA.] Pray give him the honor of your hand.

WILLMORE Thus it must be received, then. [*Kneels and kisses her hand.*] And with it give your pardon, too.

FLORINDA The friend to Belvile may command me anything.

WILLMORE [*aside*] Death, would I might; 'tis a surprising beauty.

BELVILE Boy, run and fetch a father° instantly. *priest*

[*Exit* BOY.]

FREDERICK So, now do I stand like a dog, and have not a syllable to plead my own cause with. By this hand, madam, I was never thoroughly confounded before, nor shall I ever more dare look up with confidence, till you are pleased to pardon me.

FLORINDA Sir, I'll be reconciled to you on one condition: that you'll follow the example of your friend in marrying a maid that does not hate you, and whose fortune, I believe, will not be unwelcome to you.

FREDERICK Madam, had I° no inclinations that way, I should obey your kind commands. *even if I had*

BELVILE Who, Fred marry? He has so few inclinations for womankind that had he been possessed of paradise he might have continued there to this day, if no crime but love could have disinherited him.

FREDERICK Oh, I do not use to boast of my intrigues.

BELVILE Boast! Why, thou dost nothing but boast. And I dare swear, wert thou as innocent from the sin of the grape as thou art from the apple,[2] thou might'st yet claim that right in Eden which our first parents lost by too much loving.

FREDERICK I wish this lady would think me so modest a man.

2. That is, the fruit of the tree of knowledge; the disobedience of Adam and Eve in eating it (not "too much loving") led to their expulsion from Eden (Genesis 2.15–17, 3.1–24).

VALERIA She would be sorry then, and not like you half so well. And I should be loath to break my word with you, which was, that if your friend and mine agreed, it should be a match between you and I.

[*She gives him her hand.*]

FREDERICK Bear witness, colonel, 'tis a bargain.

[*Kisses her hand.*]

BLUNT [*to* FLORINDA] I have a pardon to beg, too; but 'adsheartlikins, I am so out of countenance° that I'm a dog if I can say anything to purpose. *abashed*

FLORINDA Sir, I heartily forgive you all.

BLUNT That's nobly said, sweet lady.—Belvile, prithee present her her ring again, for I find I have not courage to approach her myself.

[*Gives him the ring; he gives it to* FLORINDA.]

[*Enter* BOY.]

BOY Sir, I have brought the father that you sent for.

[*Exit* BOY.]

BELVILE 'Tis well. And now, my dear Florinda, let's fly to complete that mighty joy we have so long wished and sighed for.—Come, Fred, you'll follow?

FREDERICK Your example, sir, 'twas ever my ambition in war, and must be so in love.

WILLMORE And must not I see this juggling° knot tied? *cheating, deceptive*

BELVILE No, thou shalt do us better service and be our guard, lest Don Pedro's sudden return interrupt the ceremony.

WILLMORE Content; I'll secure this pass.

[*Exeunt* BELVILE, FLORINDA, FREDERICK, *and* VALERIA.]

[*Enter* BOY.]

BOY [*to* WILLMORE] Sir, there's a lady without would speak to you.

WILLMORE Conduct her in; I dare not quit my post.

BOY [*to* BLUNT] And sir, your tailor waits you in your chamber.

BLUNT Some comfort yet: I shall not dance naked at the wedding.

[*Exeunt* BLUNT *and* BOY.]

[*Enter again the* BOY, *conducting in* ANGELLICA *in a masking habit and a vizard.* WILLMORE *runs to her.*]

WILLMORE [*aside*] This can be none but my pretty gipsy.—Oh, I see you can follow as well as fly. Come, confess thyself the most malicious devil in nature; you think you have done my business with Angellica—

ANGELLICA Stand off, base villain!

[*She draws a pistol and holds it to his breast.*]

WILLMORE Ha, 'tis not she! Who art thou, and what's thy business?

ANGELLICA One thou hast injured, and who comes to kill thee for't.

WILLMORE What the devil canst thou mean?

ANGELLICA By all my hopes to kill thee—

[*Holds still the pistol to his breast; he going back, she following still.*]

WILLMORE Prithee, on what acquaintance? For I know thee not.

ANGELLICA Behold this face so lost to thy remembrance,

[*Pulls off her vizard.*]

And then call all thy sins about thy soul,
And let 'em die with thee.

WILLMORE Angellica!

ANGELLICA Yes, traitor! Does not thy guilty blood run shivering through thy veins? Hast thou no horror at this sight, that tells thee thou hast not long to boast thy shameful conquest?

WILLMORE Faith, no, child. My blood keeps its old ebbs and flows still, and that usual heat too, that could oblige thee with a kindness, had I but opportunity.

ANGELLICA Devil! Dost wanton with my pain? Have at thy heart!

WILLMORE Hold, dear virago![o] Hold thy hand a little; I am not now at leisure to be killed. Hold and hear me. —[*Aside.*] Death, I think she's in earnest.

[o] *warrior woman*

ANGELLICA [*aside, turning from him*] Oh, if I take not heed, my coward heart will leave me to his mercy. — What have you, sir, to say? —But should I hear thee, thoud'st talk away all that is brave about me, and I have vowed thy death by all that's sacred.

[*Follows him with the pistol to his breast.*]

WILLMORE Why then, there's an end of a proper handsome fellow, that might 'a lived to have done good service yet. That's all I can say to't.

ANGELLICA [*pausingly*] Yet—I would give thee time for—penitence.

WILLMORE Faith, child, I thank God I have ever took care to lead a good, sober, hopeful life, and am of a religion that teaches me to believe I shall depart in peace.

ANGELLICA So will the devil! Tell me,
How many poor believing fools thou hast undone?
How many hearts thou hast betrayed to ruin?
Yet these are little mischiefs to the ills
Thou'st taught mine to commit: thou'st taught it love.

WILLMORE Egad, 'twas shrewdly hurt the while.

ANGELLICA Love, that has robbed it of its unconcern,
Of all that pride that taught me how to value it.
And in its room
A mean submissive passion was conveyed,

That made me humbly bow, which I ne'er did
To anything but heaven.
Thou, perjured man, didst this; and with thy oaths,
Which on thy knees thou didst devoutly make,
Softened my yielding heart, and then I was a slave.
Yet still had been content to've worn my chains,
Worn 'em with vanity and joy forever,
Hadst thou not broke those vows that put them on.
'Twas then I was undone.

[*All this while follows him with the pistol to his breast.*]

WILLMORE Broke my vows? Why, where hast thou lived? Amongst the gods? For I never heard of mortal man that has not broke a thousand vows.

ANGELLICA Oh, impudence!

WILLMORE Angellica, that beauty has been too long tempting, not to have made a thousand lovers languish; who, in the amorous fever, no doubt have sworn like me. Did they all die in that faith, still adoring? I do not think they did.

ANGELLICA No, faithless man; had I repaid their vows, as I did thine, I would have killed the ingrateful that had abandoned me.

WILLMORE This old general has quite spoiled thee: nothing makes a woman so vain as being flattered. Your old lover ever supplies the defects of age with intolerable dotage, vast charge, and that which you call constancy; and attributing all this to your own merits, you domineer, and throw your favors in's teeth, upbraiding him still with the defects of age, and cuckold him as often as he deceives your expectations. But the gay, young, brisk lover, that brings his equal fires, and can give you dart for dart, he'll be as nice° as you sometimes. *wanton*

ANGELLICA All this thou'st made me know, for which I hate thee.
Had I remained in innocent security,
I should have thought all men were born my slaves,
And worn my power like lightning in my eyes,
To have destroyed at pleasure when offended.
But when love held the mirror, the undeceiving glass
Reflected all the weakness of my soul, and made me know
My richest treasure being lost, my honor,
All the remaining spoil could not be worth
The conqueror's care or value.
Oh, how I fell, like a long-worshiped idol,
Discovering all the cheat.
Would not the incense and rich sacrifice
Which blind devotion offered at my altars
Have fallen to thee?
Why wouldst thou then destroy my fancied power?

WILLMORE By heaven, thou'rt brave, and I admire thee strangely.° *to an exceptional degree*

I wish I were that dull, that constant thing
Which thou wouldst have, and nature never meant me.
I must, like cheerful birds, sing in all groves,
And perch on every bough,
Billing the next kind she that flies to meet me;
Yet, after all, could build my nest with thee,
Thither repairing when I'd loved my round,
And still reserve a tributary flame.
To gain your credit, I'll pay you back your charity,
And be obliged for nothing but for love.

[*Offers her a purse of gold.*]

ANGELLICA Oh, that thou wert in earnest!
So mean a thought of me
Would turn my rage to scorn, and I should pity thee,
And give thee leave to live;
Which for the public safety of our sex,
And my own private injuries, I dare not do.
Prepare— [*Follows still, as before.*]
I will no more be tempted with replies.

WILLMORE Sure—

ANGELLICA Another word will damn thee! I've heard thee talk too long.

[*She follows him with the pistol ready to shoot; he retires, still amazed. Enter* DON ANTONIO, *his arm in a scarf, and lays hold on the pistol.*]

ANTONIO Ha! Angellica!

ANGELLICA Antonio! What devil brought thee hither?

ANTONIO Love and curiosity, seeing your coach at door. Let me disarm you of this unbecoming instrument of death. [*Takes away the pistol.*] Amongst the number of your slaves was there not one worthy the honor to have fought your quarrel? —[*To* WILLMORE.] Who are you, sir, that are so very wretched to merit death from her?

WILLMORE One, sir, that could have made a better end of an amorous quarrel without you, than with you.

ANTONIO Sure 'tis some rival. Ha! The very man took down her picture yesterday; the very same that set on me last night! Blessed opportunity—

[*Offers to shoot him.*]

ANGELLICA Hold, you're mistaken, sir.

ANTONIO By heavens, the very same!—Sir, what pretensions have you to this lady?

WILLMORE Sir, I do not use° to be examined, and am ill at all disputes but this— *am not accustomed*

[*Draws;* ANTONIO *offers to shoot.*]

ANGELLICA [*to* WILLMORE] Oh, hold! You see he's armed with certain death.
—And you, Antonio, I command you hold,

By all the passion you've so lately vowed me.

[*Enter* DON PEDRO, *sees* ANTONIO, *and stays.*]

PEDRO [*aside*] Ha! Antonio! And Angellica!

ANTONIO When I refuse obedience to your will,
May you destroy me with your mortal hate.
By all that's holy, I adore you so,
That even my rival, who has charms enough
To make him fall a victim to my jealousy,
Shall live; nay, and have leave to love on still.

PEDRO [*aside*] What's this I hear?

ANGELLICA [*pointing to* WILLMORE] Ah thus, 'twas thus he talked, and I believed.
Antonio, yesterday
I'd not have sold my interest in his heart
For all the sword has won and lost in battle.
—But now, to show my utmost of contempt,
I give thee life; which, if thou wouldst preserve,
Live where my eyes may never see thee more.
Live to undo someone whose soul may prove
So bravely constant to revenge my love.

[*Goes out.* ANTONIO *follows, but* PEDRO *pulls him back.*]

PEDRO Antonio, stay.

ANTONIO Don Pedro!

PEDRO What coward fear was that prevented thee from meeting me this morning on the Molo?

ANTONIO Meet thee?

PEDRO Yes, me; I was the man that dared thee to't.

ANTONIO Hast thou so often seen me fight in war, to find no better cause to excuse my absence? I sent my sword and one to do thee right, finding myself uncapable to use a sword.

PEDRO But 'twas Florinda's quarrel that we fought, and you, to show how little you esteemed her, sent me your rival, giving him your interest. But I have found the cause of this affront, and when I meet you fit for the dispute, I'll tell you my resentment.

ANTONIO I shall be ready, sir, ere long, to do you reason. [*Exit* ANTONIO.]

PEDRO If I could find Florinda, now whilst my anger's high, I think I should be kind, and give her to Belvile in revenge.

WILLMORE Faith, sir, I know not what you would do, but I believe the priest within has been so kind.

PEDRO How? My sister married?

WILLMORE I hope by this time he is, and bedded too, or he has not my longings about him.

PEDRO Dares he do this? Does he not fear my power?

WILLMORE Faith, not at all; if you will go in and thank him for the favor he has done your sister, so; if not, sir, my power's greater in this house than yours: I have a damned surly crew here that will keep you till the next tide, and then clap you on board for prize.° My ship lies but a league off the Molo, and we shall show your donship a damned Tramontana[3] rover's trick.

as a captive of

[*Enter* BELVILE.]

BELVILE This rogue's in some new mischief. Ha! Pedro returned!

PEDRO Colonel Belvile, I hear you have married my sister.

BELVILE You have heard truth then, sir.

PEDRO Have I so? Then, sir, I wish you joy.

BELVILE How?

PEDRO By this embrace I do, and I am glad on't.

BELVILE Are you in earnest?

PEDRO By our long friendship and my obligations to thee, I am; the sudden change I'll give you reasons for anon. Come, lead me to my sister, that she may know I now approve her choice.

[*Exit* BELVILE *with* PEDRO.]

[WILLMORE *goes to follow them. Enter* HELLENA, *as before in boy's clothes, and pulls him back.*]

WILLMORE Ha! My gipsy! Now a thousand blessings on thee for this kindness. Egad, child, I was e'en in despair of ever seeing thee again; my friends are all provided for within, each man his kind woman.

HELLENA Ha! I thought they had served me some such trick!

WILLMORE And I was e'en resolved to go aboard, and condemn myself to my lone cabin, and the thoughts of thee.

HELLENA And could you have left me behind? Would you have been so ill natured?

WILLMORE Why, 'twould have broke my heart, child. But since we are met again, I defy foul weather to part us.

HELLENA And would you be a faithful friend now, if a maid should trust you?

WILLMORE For a friend I cannot promise: thou art of a form so excellent, a face and humour too good for cold dull friendship. I am parlously afraid of being in love, child; and you have not forgotten how severely you have used me?

HELLENA That's all one; such usage you must still look for: to find out all your haunts, to rail at you to all that love you, till I have made you love only me in your own defense, because nobody else will love you.

WILLMORE But hast thou no better quality to recommend thyself by?

3. Barbarous (literally, "north wind" in Italian—i.e., across the mountains).

HELLENA Faith, none, captain. Why, 'twill be the greater charity to take me for thy mistress. I am a lone child, a kind of orphan lover; and why I should die a maid, and in a captain's hands too, I do not understand.

WILLMORE Egad, I was never clawed away with broadsides from any female before. Thou hast one virtue I adore—good nature. I hate a coy demure mistress, she's as troublesome as a colt; I'll break none. No, give me a mad mistress when mewed,° and in flying, one I dare trust upon the wing, that whilst she's kind will come to the lure. *confined (as a hawk)*

HELLENA Nay, as kind as you will, good captain, whilst it lasts. But let's lose no time.

WILLMORE My time's as precious to me as thine can be. Therefore, dear creature, since we are so well agreed, let's retire to my chamber; and if ever thou wert treated with such savory love! Come, my bed's prepared for such a guest all clean and sweet as thy fair self. I love to steal a dish and a bottle with a friend, and hate long graces. Come, let's retire and fall to.

HELLENA 'Tis but getting my consent, and the business is soon done. Let but old gaffer Hymen[4] and his priest say amen to't, and I dare lay my mother's daughter by as proper a fellow as your father's son, without fear or blushing.

WILLMORE Hold, hold, no bug° words, child. Priest and Hymen? Prithee add a hangman to 'em to make up the consort. No, no, we'll have no vows but love, child, nor witness but the lover: the kind deity enjoins naught but love and enjoy. Hymen and priest wait still upon portion and jointure; love and beauty have their own ceremonies. Marriage is as certain a bane to love as lending money is to friendship. I'll neither ask nor give a vow, though I could be content to turn gipsy and become a left-handed bridegroom[5] to have the pleasure of working that great miracle of making a maid a mother, if you durst venture. 'Tis upse° gipsy that, and if I miss I'll lose my labor. *terrifying* / *in the manner of*

HELLENA And if you do not lose, what shall I get? A cradle full of noise and mischief, with a pack of repentance at my back? Can you teach me to weave incle° to pass my time with? 'Tis upse gipsy that, too. *linen thread*

WILLMORE I can teach thee to weave a true love's knot better.

HELLENA So can my dog.

WILLMORE Well, I see we are both upon our guards, and I see there's no way to conquer good nature but by yielding. Here, give me thy hand: one kiss, and I am thine.

4. The classical god of marriage, usually represented not as an old man ("gaffer") but as youthful.

5. That is, a "bridegroom" in a wedding not properly solemnized and thus not fully legal.

HELLENA One kiss! How like my page he speaks! I am resolved you shall have none, for asking such a sneaking sum. He that will be satisfied with one kiss will never die of that longing. Good friend single-kiss, is all your talking come to this? A kiss, a caudle![6] Farewell, captain single-kiss.

[*Going out; he stays her.*]

WILLMORE Nay, if we part so, let me die like a bird upon a bough, at the sheriff's charge. By heaven, both the Indies shall not buy thee from me. I adore thy humour and will marry thee, and we are so of one humour it must be a bargain. Give me thy hand. [*Kisses her hand.*] And now let the blind ones, love and fortune, do their worst.

HELLENA Why, god-a-mercy, captain!

WILLMORE But hark'ee: the bargain is now made, but is it not fit we should know each other's names, that when we have reason to curse one another hereafter, and people ask me who 'tis I give to the devil, I may at least be able to tell what family you came of?

HELLENA Good reason, captain; and where I have cause, as I doubt not but I shall have plentiful, that I may know at whom to throw my—blessings, I beseech ye your name.

WILLMORE I am called Robert the Constant.

HELLENA A very fine name! Pray was it your faulkner° or butler that christened you? Do they not use to whistle when they call you? *hawk keeper*

WILLMORE I hope you have a better, that a man may name without crossing himself—you are so merry with mine.

HELLENA I am called Hellena the Inconstant.

[*Enter* PEDRO, BELVILE, FLORINDA, FREDERICK, VALERIA.]

PEDRO Ha! Hellena!

FLORINDA Hellena!

HELLENA The very same. Ha! My brother! Now, captain, show your love and courage; stand to your arms and defend me bravely, or I am lost forever.

PEDRO What's this I hear? False girl, how came you hither, and what's your business? Speak!

[*Goes roughly to her.*]

WILLMORE Hold off, sir; you have leave to parley° only. *speak; negotiate*

[*Puts himself between.*]

HELLENA I had e'en as good tell it, as you guess it. Faith, brother, my business is the same with all living creatures of my age: to love and be beloved—and here's the man.

PEDRO Perfidious maid, hast thou deceived me too; deceived thyself and heaven?

HELLENA 'Tis time enough to make my peace with that. Be you but kind, let me alone with heaven.

6. A warm drink (of thin gruel mixed with ale or wine) for an invalid, given especially to women after childbirth.

PEDRO Belvile, I did not expect this false play from you. Was't not enough you'd gain Florinda, which I pardoned, but your lewd friends too must be enriched with the spoils of a noble family?

BELVILE Faith, sir, I am as much surprised at this as you can be. Yet, sir, my friends are gentlemen, and ought to be esteemed for their misfortunes, since they have the glory to suffer with the best of men and kings. 'Tis true, he's a rover of fortune, yet a prince aboard his little wooden world.

PEDRO What's this to the maintenance of a woman of her birth and quality?

WILLMORE Faith, sir, I can boast of nothing but a sword which does me right where'er I come, and has defended a worse cause than a woman's; and since I loved her before I either knew her birth or name, I must pursue my resolution and marry her.

PEDRO And is all your holy intent of becoming a nun debauched into a desire of man?

HELLENA Why, I have considered the matter, brother, and find the three hundred thousand crowns my uncle left me, and you cannot keep from me, will be better laid out in love than in religion, and turn to as good an account. Let most voices carry it: for heaven or the captain?

ALL CRY A captain! A captain!

HELLENA Look ye, sir, 'tis a clear case.

PEDRO Oh, I am mad! —[*Aside.*] If I refuse, my life's in danger. —Come, there's one motive induces me. Take her; I shall now be free from fears of her honor. Guard it you now, if you can; I have been a slave to't long enough.

[*Gives her to him.*]

WILLMORE Faith, sir, I am of a nation that are of opinion a woman's honor is not worth guarding when she has a mind to part with it.

HELLENA Well said, captain.

PEDRO [*to* VALERIA] This was your plot, mistress, but I hope you have married one that will revenge my quarrel to you.

VALERIA There's no altering destiny, sir.

PEDRO Sooner than a woman's will; therefore I forgive you all, and wish you may get my father's pardon as easily, which I fear.

[*Enter* BLUNT *dressed in a Spanish habit, looking very ridiculously; his* MAN *adjusting his band.*°] *collar*

MAN 'Tis very well, sir.

BLUNT Well, sir! 'Adsheartlikins, I tell you 'tis damnable ill, sir. A Spanish habit! Good Lord! Could the devil and my tailor devise no other punishment for me but the mode of a nation I abominate?

BELVILE What's the matter, Ned?

BLUNT Pray view me round, and judge.

[*Turns round.*]

BELVILE I must confess thou art a kind of an odd figure.

BLUNT In a Spanish habit with a vengeance! I had rather be in the Inquisition for Judaism than in this doublet and breeches; a pillory were an easy collar to this, three handfuls high; and these shoes, too, are worse than the stocks, with the sole an inch shorter than my foot. In fine, gentlemen, methinks I look like a bag of bays[7] stuffed full of fool's flesh.

BELVILE Methinks 'tis well, and makes thee look e'en cavalier. Come, sir, settle your face and salute our friends. Lady—

BLUNT [*to* HELLENA] Ha! Sayst thou so, my little rover? Lady, if you be one, give me leave to kiss your hand, and tell you, 'adsheartlikins, for all I look so, I am your humble servant. A pox of my Spanish habit!

[*Music is heard to play.*]

WILLMORE Hark! What's this?

[*Enter* BOY.]

BOY Sir, as the custom is, the gay people in masquerade, who make every man's house their own, are coming up.

[*Enter several men and women in masking habits, with music; they put themselves in order and dance.*]

BLUNT 'Adsheartlikins, would 'twere lawful to pull off their false faces, that I might see if my doxy° were not amongst 'em. *prostitute*

BELVILE [*to the maskers*] Ladies and gentlemen, since you are come so *a propos*,° you must take a small collation with us. *opportunely (French)*

WILLMORE [*to* HELLENA] Whilst we'll to the good man within, who stays to give us a cast of his office.[8] Have you no trembling at the near approach?

HELLENA No more than you have in an engagement or a tempest.

WILLMORE Egad, thou'rt a brave girl, and I admire thy love and courage.

Lead on; no other dangers they can dread,
Who venture in the storms o'th' marriage bed.

[*Exeunt.*]

7. Perhaps "baize," a thick cloth; or perhaps a bag containing bay leaves, used in cooking.
8. A taste of his customary function.

Epilogue

The banished cavaliers! A roving blade!
A popish carnival! A masquerade!
The devil's in't if this will please the nation
In these our blessed times of reformation,
When conventickling[9] is so much in fashion.
And yet—
That mutinous tribe less factions do beget,
Than your continual differing in wit.
Your judgment's, as your passion's, a disease:
Nor° muse nor miss your appetite can please; *Neither*
You're grown as nice° as queasy consciences, *fastidious*
Whose each convulsion, when the spirit moves,
Damns everything that maggot° disapproves. *capricious person*
With canting rule you would the stage refine,
And to dull method all our sense confine.
With th'insolence of commonwealths you rule,
Where each gay fop and politic grave fool
On monarch wit impose, without control.
As for the last, who seldom sees a play,
Unless it be the old Blackfriars[1] way;
Shaking his empty noddle o'er bamboo,° *cane*
He cries, "Good faith, these plays will never do!
Ah, sir, in my young days, what lofty wit,
What high-strained scenes of fighting there were writ.
These are slight airy toys. But tell me, pray,
What has the House of Commons done today?"
Then shows his politics, to let you see
Of state affairs he'll judge as notably
As he can do of wit and poetry.
The younger sparks, who hither do resort,
Cry,
"Pox o' your genteel things! Give us more sport!
Damn me, I'm sure 'twill never please the court."
Such fops are never pleased, unless the play
Be stuffed with fools as brisk° and dull as they. *pert*
Such might the half-crown spare, and in a glass° *mirror*
At home behold a more accomplished ass.
Where they may set their cravats, wigs, and faces,
And practice all their buffoonry grimaces:
See how this huff becomes, this damny,° stare, *damn me!*
Which they at home may act because they dare,
But must with prudent caution do elsewhere.
Oh that our Nokes, or Tony Lee,[2] could show
A fop but half so much to th' life as you.

9. Holding meetings of religious nonconformists.
1. A London theater that closed in 1642, at the onset of the English Civil War.
2. James Nokes (1642–1696) and Anthony Leigh (d. 1692), popular comic actors of the 1670s who often appeared together.

Postscript

This play had been sooner in print, but for a report about the town (made by some either very malicious or very ignorant) that 'twas *Thomaso*[3] altered; which made the booksellers fear some trouble from the proprietor of that admirable play, which indeed has wit enough to stock a poet, and is not to be pieced or mended by any but the excellent author himself. That I have stolen some hints from it, may be a proof that I valued it more than to pretend to alter it, had I the dexterity of some poets, who are not more expert in stealing than in the art of concealing, and who even that way outdo the Spartan boys.[4] I might have appropriated all to myself; but I, vainly proud of my judgment, hang out the sign of Angellica (the only stolen object) to give notice where a great part of the wit dwelt; though if the *Play of the Novella*[5] were as well worth remembering as *Thomaso*, they might (bating the name) have as well said I took it from thence. I will only say the plot and business (not to boast on't) is my own; as for the words and characters, I leave the reader to judge and compare 'em with *Thomaso*, to whom I recommend the great entertainment of reading it. Though had this succeeded ill, I should have had no need of imploring that justice from the critics, who are naturally so kind to any that pretend to usurp their dominion, especially of our sex:[6] they would doubtless have given me the whole honor on't. Therefore I will only say in English what the famous Virgil[7] does in Latin: I make verses, and others have the fame.

Finis

3. The 1654 play by Thomas Killigrew on which *The Rover* is largely based.
4. In ancient Sparta, boys were deliberately underfed so that they would learn to steal food; but if caught, they were disgraced.
5. The 1632 play by Richard Brome that inspired some elements of *The Rover*.
6. This acknowledgment of female authorship did not appear in the first issue of the first quarto or in some copies of the second issue.
7. Roman poet (70–19 B.C.E.), author of the *Aeneid;* according to the Roman grammarian Donatus (4th c. C.E.), a couplet he wrote anonymously in praise of the emperor Augustus was claimed by another.

SOR JUANA INÉS DE LA CRUZ

1648–1695

CONSIDERED the last great writer of the Spanish Golden Age, Sor Juana Inés de la Cruz was also deemed the first feminist in the New World by early twentieth-century critics who had rediscovered her work. This remarkable seventeenth-century Mexican author penned hundreds of poems, more than a dozen carol sequences for use in church services, and twenty-seven plays, including religious dramas (*autos sacramentales*), comedies, farces, and *loas*—short dramatic pieces that either preceded full-length works or were performed on their own at religious or court celebrations. Although Sor Juana may be best known for the controversial theological essay *Carta atenagórica* (*Letter Worthy of Athena*) and its defense, *La Respuesta* (*The Answer*), written toward the end of her career, her critical reputation rests on other works as well. These include *Primero sueño* (*First Dream*), a 975-stanza poem considered the most important philosophical verse of the Golden Age, and EL DIVINO NARCISO (*THE DIVINE NARCISSUS*), an *auto sacramental* that reflects Sor Juana's deep engagements with baroque dramaturgy, Ovidian mythology, and Christian allegory. The *loa* to this drama reveals with great clarity both Sor Juana's sophisticated understanding of gender roles within a highly structured Catholic culture and her prescient sensitivity to the impact of Spanish colonialism in the New World.

Juana Inés de Asbaje y Ramírez de Santillana was born in Nepantla, near Mexico City. Her father, Pedro Manuel de Asbaje y Vargas Machuca, was a Basque military officer, and her mother, Isabel Ramírez, helped manage the family's lands while raising six children. Juana spent her childhood years in the home of her maternal grandfather, whose extensive library provided her initial education. She states that she learned to read at age three, and she supposedly wrote her first *loa* at age eight. She claims that she unsuccessfully pleaded with her mother to allow her to dress as a boy so that she could attend school in Mexico City, but she was soon sent there to live with her aunt and uncle—a move that enabled her to learn Latin and, more importantly, to come to the attention of the Spanish viceroy and his wife, who in short order brought her to live at court. A great favorite of the vicereine, Juana composed much of her early verse in honor of her benefactor. At the request of the viceroy, who was eager to showcase the prodigy, Juana agreed to be examined by forty scholars, representing all branches of learning. According to an early biography by Father Diego Calleja, a Jesuit priest, Juana triumphed during this examination: "in the manner that a royal galleon might fend off the attacks of small canoes, so did Juana extricate herself from the questions, arguments, and objections these many men, each in his speciality, directed to her."

Juana spent five years as a lady-in-waiting at court, and then decided to enter the convent of Santa Paula in 1668. She made this choice, she explained later, because of her unwillingness to marry, the only other suitable option for a woman of her class at that time. Juana understood that as a married woman, she would have little say in her day-to-day activities, and most probably would have to devote herself exclusively to her family. Though convent life was highly structured and restricted in some ways, it also afforded her time and space to continue her studies and writing. In 1690, Sor Juana drafted a critique of a well-known sermon by the Jesuit Antonio Vieyra on Christ's greatest gift to humanity. The document came to the attention of Don Manuel Fernández de Santa Cruz, bishop of Puebla, and without her knowledge he had the essay published under the title *Carta atenagórica*. He sent her a copy but appended a strong rejoinder, under the pseudonym Sor Filotea de la Cruz, that criticized her entrance into the arena of theological discourse and urged her to focus on forms of devotion more appropriate for a woman. In response, she wrote her famous *La Respuesta*. This essay, although unpublished in her lifetime, provides much of the biographical information we have on Sor Juana. It also serves more broadly as a defense of women's right to education, culture, and independence of thought that was unprecedented for its time.

The Answer proved to be Sor Juana's last major work. In 1695, while nursing others at the convent, she contracted the plague that had swept through their community; she died on April 17. Aware of the controversies surrounding her writing, critics have subsequently combed her verse, plays, and essays in an attempt to gain a fuller understanding of Sor Juana both as an individual and as a seventeenth-century woman attempting to find self-fulfillment and self-expression under Spanish colonial and ecclesiastical rule. Her literary works in particular have been scrutinized for the light they might shed on her theological beliefs and her discomfort—veiled though it was—with the rigid structures that shaped her life.

In *The Divine Narcissus*, for example, we find some of the same themes that Sor Juana later incorporated in the more personal *Answer*—in particular, the significance of secular writing to an understanding of scripture. Yet to employ her dramas and verse only as a lens through which to read her essays or understand her as an individual would be to undervalue and misrepresent these works' importance to the Golden Age and to Hispanic culture. Indeed, a focus on the plays themselves reveals her remarkable sensitivity to and skill in deploying the range of dramaturgical styles and conventions that flourished in the era. Sor Juana's dramatic works delighted audiences at court as well as at public festivals and display equal ease in engaging with religious and with secular themes.

The sheer volume of her writing in one form, the *loa*, suggests Sor Juana's special affinity for this kind of drama; the eighteen *loas* she composed during her career represent two-thirds of her total dramatic output. *Loa*, like the English word *laud*, is derived from the Latin *laus* (praise), and the form arose in a context of praise for audience or locale. Originally a monologue that served as a prelude to a comedy, the *loa* evolved during the sixteenth century into a short, highly stylized drama with multiple characters, frequently on allegorical themes. In keeping with baroque conventions, *loas* reflect considerable metric variety and elaborate wordplay (often difficult to capture in translation), as well as vivid imagery. All the leading Golden Age playwrights wrote *loas*, and it is reasonable to hypothesize that Sor Juana's pieces were influenced by their published works, especially those of Pedro Calderón de la Barca (1600–1681), whose style of intellectual allegory she appears to have embraced. The *loas* that accompanied the *autos sacramentales* also bolstered Spain's efforts in the Counter-Reformation. Because these short plays emphasized traditional religious values and teachings, they helped oppose the tide of religious and political reform sweeping across other parts of Europe. The insularity of Spain during this period shielded its artistry from the influence of other cultures, and religious drama in particular survived longer in the Spanish empire than in other regions where supporters of the Reformation strongly opposed such practices.

We can trace the lineage of the *autos* themselves back to medieval liturgical drama. In Spain, the springtime celebration of the feast of Corpus Christi had, since the thirteenth century, included such theatrical elements as processions and performances on *carros*—that is, traveling stages on which actors sang, danced, and recited. In reaction to the Reformation, the Catholic Church urged that this celebration be refined and returned to its religious roots. In New Spain (as Spain's imperial holdings in Latin America were then called), such celebrations date to the 1530s. Records note that a Calderónian *auto* was translated into Nahuatl, one of the native Indian languages spoken in the Mexico City area, and that Mexican colonial authors' *autos* were produced in other native Indian languages and in Spanish. Documentation from the era is incomplete, however, and it is unclear whether Sor Juana's *autos* were performed in Mexico. Historians speculate that she was encouraged to begin writing more regularly in the form in 1687 when the vicereine learned that pieces by dramatists other than Calderón might be produced in Madrid. The *loa* to *The Divine Narcissus* supports this theory, as it ends by briefly noting that the piece is suitable for audiences in Madrid as well as in New Spain. It may indeed have been performed in Madrid in 1689, after the vicereine's return to Spain, but we know with certainty only that the play was published there in 1690.

In keeping with the festival theme, *autos sacramentales* all consider in some way humanity's redemption through the Eucharist—the body and blood of Christ. *The Divine Narcissus* focuses on Christ's death as the foundation for this sacrament, using an Ovidian myth of transformation as an allegory of Jesus' crucifixion and resurrection. As the translator Patricia Peters observes, this *auto* is "a lovely pastoral drama of redemption, framed by a remarkable reflection on the plight of the Aztecs under the scourge of Spanish colonization."

Its colonial frame provides, within the

A human sacrifice in honor of the Aztec god Huitzilopoxtli, as depicted in the early-seventeenth-century *Codex Magliabecchi*.

eucharistic context, the core thematic link between *loa* and *auto* in *The Divine Narcissus:* the *loa* explicitly pits the native Indian rulers, Occident and his consort America, as well as their Aztec traditions, against the Spanish conqueror Zeal and lady Religion, in a battle for both political and religious dominance. Yet labels as critical or direct as Peters's "plight" or "scourge" are found nowhere in the *loa* itself. As a nun writing during the Inquisition, Sor Juana would have been acutely aware that heresy or opposition to the Catholic Church could not be overtly expressed. Moreover, her loyalty to the vicereine would have made inconceivable any blatant critique of the Spanish government or Spain's imperial mission, which was inextricable from Counter-Reformation ideology. But as a *criolla*—a Mexican-born woman of Spanish ancestry—Sor Juana may have felt considerable ambivalence about Spain's treatment of the native peoples among whom she lived. Sor Juana thus may have written her *loas* in part to assist Spanish audiences

This image by the Flemish Protestant engraver Theodore de Bry is an illustration for a Latin translation of Bartolomeo de las Casas's *A Brief Account of the Destruction of the Indies,* published in 1598 (the original was published in 1552). Together with de las Casas's textual account, de Bry's engravings cemented European opinion about Spanish conquistadores' appalling conduct in the Americas.

in understanding the Indians and their beliefs, even as she appears to embrace the necessity of the Aztec conversion to Catholicism that provides the arc of the drama. From her poems, we know that Sor Juana understood and used Nahuatl and other native dialects; and the language and tone of the speeches of the Aztecs in the *loa* imbue these characters with a dignity not found in the conquistador Zeal. Her knowledge of and respect for native culture emerges through her use of an Aztec song and dance, the *tocotín,* in the *loa*'s opening scene, as well as through her engagement with the Indian myths and religious practices that ultimately provide the grounds for intercultural communication. Sor Juana invokes as a bridging figure the "great God of the Seeds," Huitzilopoxtli, who was also the Aztec god of war and of the sun and required the blood of sacrificial victims to protect his people. The Aztecs were said to mix seeds and grain with the victims' blood to form a life-size statue of the god, which was then shot with arrows until it toppled, at which time participants in the ritual broke up and ate small bits of the figure. The rite was called "God is eaten." In highlighting the similarity of this ceremony to the Eucharist, Sor Juana demonstrates why this myth suits the *auto sacramental* so perfectly.

Yet the violence endemic to both Aztec ritual and Spanish colonialism lends the play a dark center. Historians believe that Sor Juana accepted the concept of the "just war," as articulated by Thomas Aquinas, which rationalized Christian crusaders' attacks on "sinful" non-Christians' bloody practices. The play, however, clearly endorses only female Religion's verbal, intellectual means of conversion, rejecting the violent methods of Zeal and his soldiers. The *loa*'s final lines, in which all characters acknowledge and worship "the great God of Seeds," are ambiguous, as they might be seen as a subversive endorsement of the native beliefs that Occident and America both insist cannot be shaken.

Like her medieval predecessor HROTSVIT, the "strong voice" of Gandersheim, Sor Juana was a remarkable and singular strong voice for her time. Frequently labeled "the Tenth Muse," in the poetic tradition of Sappho and of her American contemporary Anne Bradstreet, Sor Juana has become a cultural icon in Mexico, memorialized on both the 1,000 peso coin and the 200 peso bill. A model for women writers and a critical link in the creation of Western female literary and theatrical traditions, Sor Juana nevertheless emerges as exceptional within her culture and her time, a figure who throws into relief the multiple forces against which she struggled to achieve her unique place in history. J.E.G.

The Loa for the Auto Sacramental of The Divine Narcissus
An Allegory[1]

CHARACTERS

OCCIDENT
AMERICA
ZEAL
RELIGION
MUSIC[2]
MUSICIANS
SOLDIERS

Scene 1

[*Enter* OCCIDENT, *a gallant-looking Aztec, wearing a crown. By his side is* AMERICA, *an Aztec woman of poised self-possession. They are dressed in the* mantas *and* huipiles *worn for singing a* tocotin.[3] *They seat themselves on two chairs. On each side, Aztec men and women dance with feathers and rattles in their hands, as is customary for those doing this dance. While they dance,* MUSIC *sings.*]

MUSIC O, Noble Mexicans,
whose ancient ancestry
comes forth from the clear light
and brilliance of the Sun,
since this, of all the year,
is your most happy feast
in which you venerate

1. Translated by Patricia A. Peters and Reneé Domeier, O.S.B.
2. Probably an unintentional omission in the cast list by Sor Juana. The copy text of 1725, which Alfonso Méndez Plancarte used as the basis for his definitive edition, does not distinguish between Music as a character and the Musicians who perform during the play.
3. An Aztec song and dance. *Mantas:* men's garments similar to ponchos. *Huipiles:* women's garments similar to ponchos, but not open on the sides.

your greatest deity,
come and adorn yourselves
with vestments of your rank;
let your holy fervor be
made one with jubilation;
and celebrate in festive pomp
the great God of the Seeds![4]

Since the abundance of
our native fields and farms
is owed to him alone
who gives fertility,
then offer him your thanks,
for it is right and just
to give from what has grown,
the first of the new fruits.
From your own veins, draw out
and give, without reserve,
the best blood, mixed with seed,
so that his cult be served,
and celebrate in festive pomp,
the great God of the Seeds!

[OCCIDENT *and* AMERICA *rise, and* MUSIC *ceases singing.*]

OCCIDENT Of all the deities to whom
our rites demand I bend my knee—
among two thousand gods or more
who dwell within this royal city
and who require the sacrifice
of human victims still entreating
for life until their blood is drawn
and gushes forth from hearts still beating
and bowels still pulsing—I declare,
among all these, (it bears repeating),
whose ceremonies we observe,
the greatest is, surpassing all
this pantheon's immensity,
the great God of the Seeds.

AMERICA And you are right, since he alone
daily sustains our monarchy
because our lives depend on his
providing crops abundantly;
and since he gives us graciously
the gift from which all gifts proceed,
our fields rich with golden maize,
the source of life through daily bread,
we render him our highest praise.
Then how will it improve our lives
if rich America abounds

4. Huitzilopoxtli, the Aztec god of war and the sun.

in gold from mines whose smoke deprives
the fields of their fertility
and with their clouds of filthy soot
will not allow the crops to grow
which blossom now so fruitfully
from seeded earth? Moreover, his
protection of our people far
exceeds our daily food and drink,
the body's sustenance. Indeed,
he feeds us with his very flesh
(first purified of every stain).
We eat his body, drink his blood,
and by this sacred meal are freed
and cleansed from all that is profane,
and thus, he purifies our soul.
And now, attentive to his rites,
together let us all proclaim:

[*They* (OCCIDENT, AMERICA, *Dancers, and* MUSIC) *sing.*]

we celebrate in festive pomp, the great God of the Seeds!

[*They exit dancing.*]

Scene 2

[*Enter Christian* RELIGION *as a Spanish lady,* ZEAL *as a Captain General in armor, and Spanish soldiers.*]

RELIGION How, being Zeal, can you suppress
the flames of righteous Christian wrath
when here before your very eyes
idolatry, so blind with pride,
adores, with superstitious rites,
an idol, leaving your own bride,
the holy faith of Christ, disgraced?

ZEAL Religion, trouble not your mind
or grieve my failure to attack,
complaining that my love is slack,
for now the sword I wear is bared,
its hilt in hand, clasped ready and
my arm raised high to take revenge.
Please stand aside and deign to wait
till I requite your grievances.

[*Enter* OCCIDENT *and* AMERICA *dancing, and accompanied by* MUSIC, *who enters from the other side.*]

MUSIC And celebrate in festive pomp,
the great God of the Seeds!

ZEAL Here they come! I will confront them.

RELIGION And I, in peace, will also go
(before your fury lays them low)
for justice must with mercy kiss;
I shall invite them to arise
from superstitious depths to faith.

ZEAL Let us approach while they are still
absorbed in their lewd rituals.
MUSIC And celebrate in festive pomp,
the great God of the Seeds!

[ZEAL *and* RELIGION *cross the stage.*]

RELIGION Great Occident, most powerful;
America, so beautiful
and rich; you live in poverty
amid the treasures of your land.
Abandon this irreverent cult
with which the demon has waylaid you.
Open your eyes! Follow the path
that leads straightforwardly to truth,
to which my love yearns to persuade you.
OCCIDENT Who are these unknown people, so
intrusive in my sight, who dare
to stop us in our ecstasy?
Heaven forbid such infamy!
AMERICA Who are these nations, never seen,
that wish, by force, to pit themselves
against my ancient power supreme?
OCCIDENT Oh, you alien beauty fair;
oh, pilgrim woman from afar,
who comes to interrupt my prayer,
please speak and tell me who you are.
RELIGION Christian Religion is my name,
and I intend that all this realm
will make obeisance unto me.
OCCIDENT An impossible concession!
AMERICA Yours is but a mad obsession!
OCCIDENT You will meet with swift repression.
AMERICA Pay no attention; she is mad!
Let us go on with our procession.
MUSIC *and all* [*Aztecs on stage*] And celebrate in festive pomp,
the great God of the Seeds!
ZEAL How is this, barbarous Occident?
Can it be, sightless Idolatry,
that you insult Religion,
the spouse I cherish tenderly?
Abomination fills your cup
and overruns the brim, but see
that God will not permit you to
continue drinking down delight,
and I am sent to deal your doom.
OCCIDENT And who are you who frightens all
who only look upon your face?
ZEAL I am Zeal. Does that surprise you?
Take heed! For when your excesses
bring disgrace to fair Religion,

then will Zeal arise to vengeance;
for insolence I will chastise you.
I am the minister of God,
Who, growing weary with the sight
of overreaching tyrannies
so sinful that they reach the height
of error, practiced many years,
has sent me forth to penalize you.
And thus, these military hosts,
with flashing thunderbolts of steel,
the ministers of His great wrath,
are sent, His anger to reveal.

OCCIDENT What god? What sin? What tyranny?
What punishment do you foresee?
Your reasons make no sense to me,
nor can I make the slightest guess
who you might be with your insistence
on tolerating no resistance,
impeding us with rash persistence
from lawful worship as we sing.

MUSIC And celebrate with festive pomp,
the great God of the Seeds!

AMERICA Madman, blind, and barbarous,
with mystifying messages
you try to mar our calm and peace,
destroying the tranquility
that we enjoy. Your plots must cease,
unless, of course, you wish to be
reduced to ashes, whose existence
even the winds will never sense.
[*To* OCCIDENT] And you, my spouse, and your cohort,
close off your hearing and your sight
to all their words; refuse to heed
their fantasies of zealous might;
proceed to carry out your rite.
Do not concede to insolence
from foreigners intent to dull
our ritual's magnificence.

MUSIC And celebrate with festive pomp,
the great God of the Seeds!

ZEAL Since our initial offering
of peaceful terms you held so cheap,
the dire alternative of war,
I guarantee, you'll count more dear.
Take up your arms! To war! To war!

[*Drums and trumpets sound.*]

OCCIDENT What miscarriages of justice
has heaven sent against me?
What are these weapons, blazing fire,

before my unbelieving eyes?
Get ready, guards! Aim well, my troops,
Your arrows at this enemy!

AMERICA What lightning bolts does heaven send
to lay me low? What molten balls
of burning lead so fiercely rain?
What centaurs[5] crush with monstrous force
and cause my people such great pain?

[*Within*]

To arms! To arms! War! War!

[*Drums and trumpets sound.*]

Long life to Spain! Long live her king!

[*The battle begins. Indians enter through one door and flee through another with the Spanish pursuing at their heels. From backstage,* OCCIDENT *backs away from* RELIGION *and* AMERICA *retreats before* ZEAL*'s onslaught.*]

Scene 3

RELIGION Give up, arrogant Occident!

OCCIDENT I must bow to your aggression,
but not before your arguments.

ZEAL Die, impudent America!

RELIGION Desist! Do not give her to Death;
her life is of some worth to us.

ZEAL How can you now defend this maid
who has so much offended you?

RELIGION America has been subdued
because your valor won the strife,
but now my mercy intervenes
in order to preserve her life.
It was your part to conquer her
by force with military might;
mine is to gently make her yield,
persuading her by reason's light.

ZEAL But you have seen the stubbornness
with which these blind ones still abhor
your creed; is it not better far
that they all die?

RELIGION Good Zeal, restrain
your justice, and do not kill them.
My gentle disposition deigns
to forbear vengeance and forgive.
I want them to convert and live.

AMERICA If your petition for my life
and show of Christian charity

5. That is, mounted troops, who—to the people of the New World, who had not seen horses before—might well seem to resemble the half-human, half-horse creatures of Greek mythology.

are motivated by the hope
that you, at last, will conquer me,
defeating my integrity
with verbal steel where bullets failed,
then you are sadly self-deceived.
A weeping captive, I may mourn
for liberty, yet my will grows
beyond these bonds; my heart is free,
and I will worship my own gods!

OCCIDENT Forced to surrender to your power,
I have admitted my defeat,
but still it must be clearly said
that violence cannot devour
my will, nor force constrain its right.
Although in grief, I now lament,
a prisoner, your cruel might
has limits. You cannot prevent
my saying here within my heart
I worship the great God of Seeds!

Scene 4

RELIGION Wait! What you perceive as force
is not coercion, but affection.
What god is this that you adore?

OCCIDENT The great God of the Seeds
who causes fields to bring forth fruit.
To him the lofty heavens bow;
to him the rains obedience give;
and when, at last, he cleanses us
from stains of sin, then he invites
us to the meal that he prepares.
Consider whether you could find
a god more generous and good
who blesses more abundantly
than he whom I describe to you.

RELIGION [*aside*] O God, help me! What images,
what dark designs, what shadowings
of truths most sacred to our Faith
do these lies seek to imitate?
O false, sly, and deceitful snake!
O asp, with sting so venomous!
O hydra,[6] that from seven mouths
pours noxious poisons, every one
a passage to oblivion!
To what extent, with this façade,
do you intend maliciously
to mock the mysteries of God?

6. In Greek mythology, a monstrous water snake that lived in a swamp; it had many heads, which grew back as quickly as they were cut off, and its breath was poisonous.

Mock on! For with your own deceit,
if God empowers my mind and tongue,
I'll argue and impose defeat.

AMERICA Why do you find yourself perplexed?
Do you not see there is no god
other than ours who verifies
with countless blessings his great works?

RELIGION In doctrinal disputes, I hold
with the apostle Paul, for when
he preached to the Athenians
and found they had a harsh decree
imposing death on anyone
who tried to introduce new gods,
since he had noticed they were free
to worship at a certain shrine,
an altar to "the Unknown God,"
he said to them, "This Lord of mine
is no new god, but one unknown
that you have worshipped in this place,
and it is He my voice proclaims."[7]
And thus I—

[OCCIDENT *and* AMERICA *whisper to each other.*]

Listen, Occident!
and hear me, blind Idolatry!
For all your happiness depends
on listening attentively.

These miracles that you recount,
these prodigies that you suggest,
these apparitions and these rays
of light in superstition dressed
are glimpsed but darkly through a veil.
These portents you exaggerate,
attributing to your false gods
effects that you insinuate,
but wrongly so, for all these works
proceed from our true God alone,
and of His Wisdom come to birth.
Then if the soil richly yields,
and if the fields bud and bloom,
if fruits increase and multiply,
if seeds mature in earth's dark womb,
if rains pour forth from leaden sky,
all is the work of His right hand;
for neither the arm that tills the soil
nor rains that fertilize the land
nor warmth that calls life from the tomb
of winter's death can make plants grow;
for they lack reproductive power

7. See Acts 17.22–31.

if Providence does not concur,
by breathing into each of them
a vegetative soul.
AMERICA That might be so;
then tell me, is this God so kind—
this deity whom you describe—
that I might touch Him with my hands,
these very hands that carefully
create the idol, here before you,
an image made from seeds of earth
and innocent, pure human blood
shed only for this sacred rite?
RELIGION Although the Essence of Divinity
is boundless and invisible,
because already It has been
eternally united with
our nature, He resembles us
so much in our humanity
that He permits unworthy priests
to take Him in their humble hands.[8]
AMERICA In this, at least, we are agreed,
for to my God no human hands
are so unstained that they deserve
to touch Him; nonetheless, He gives
this honor graciously to those
who serve Him with their priestly lives.
No others dare to touch the God,
nor in the sanctuary stand.
ZEAL A reverence most worthily
directed to the one true God!
OCCIDENT Whatever else you claim, now tell
me this: Is yours a God composed
of human blood, an offering
of sacrifice, and in Himself
does He combine with bloody death
the life-sustaining seeds of earth?
RELIGION As I have said, His boundless
Majesty is insubstantial,
but in the Holy Sacrifice
of Mass, His blessed humanity
is placed unbloody under the
appearances of bread, which comes
from seeds of wheat and is transformed
into His Body and His Blood;[9]
and this most holy Blood of Christ,
contained within a sacred cup,

8. That is, holding the bread and wine while delivering Holy Communion.
9. In the Eucharist.

is verily the offering
most innocent, unstained, and pure
that on the altar of the cross
was the redemption of the world.

AMERICA Such miracles, unknown to us,
make me desire to believe;
but would the God that you reveal
offer Himself so lovingly
transformed for me into a meal
as does the god that I adore?

RELIGION In truth, He does. For this alone
His Wisdom came upon the earth
to dwell among all humankind.

AMERICA And so that I can be convinced,
may I not see this Deity?

OCCIDENT And so that I can be made free
of old beliefs that shackle me?

RELIGION Yes, you will see when you are bathed
in crystal waters from the font
of baptism.

OCCIDENT And well I know,
in preparation to attend
a banquet, I must bathe, or else
our ancient custom I offend.

ZEAL Your vain ablutions will not do
the cleansing that your stains require.

OCCIDENT Then what?

RELIGION There is a sacrament
of living waters, which can cleanse
and purify you of your sins.

AMERICA Because you deluge my poor mind
with concepts of theology,
I've just begun to understand;
there is much more I want to see,
and my desire to know is now
by holy inspiration led.

OCCIDENT And I desire more keenly still
to know about the life and death
of the God you say is in the bread.

RELIGION Then come along with me, and I
shall make for you a metaphor,
a concept clothed in rhetoric
so colorful that what I show
to you, your eyes will clearly see;
for now I know that you require
objects of sight instead of words,
by which faith whispers in your ears
too deaf to hear. I understand,
for you necessity demands

that through the eyes faith find her way
to her reception in your hearts.
OCCIDENT Exactly so. I do prefer
to see the things you would impart.

Scene 5

RELIGION Then come.
ZEAL Religion, answer me:
what metaphor will you employ
to represent these mysteries?
RELIGION An *auto*[1] will make visible
through allegory images
of what America must learn
and Occident implores to know
about the questions that now burn
within him so.
ZEAL What will you call
this play in allegory cast?
RELIGION *Divine Narcissus*,[2] let it be,
because if that unhappy maid
adored an idol which disguised
in such strange symbols the attempt
the demon made to counterfeit
the great and lofty mystery
of the most Blessed Eucharist,
then there were also, I surmise,
among more ancient pagans hints
of such high marvels symbolized.
ZEAL Where will your drama be performed?
RELIGION In the crown city of Madrid,
which is the center of the Faith,
the seat of Catholic majesty,[3]
to whom the Indies owe their best
beneficence, the blessed gift
of Holy Writ, the Gospel light
illuminating all the West.
ZEAL That you should write in Mexico
for royal patrons don't you see
to be an impropriety?

1. A short play on a spiritual or religious subject, popular in Spain from medieval times up to the middle of the 18th century.
2. In Greek mythology, a beautiful youth who loved none who became enamored of him. As Ovid told the story (*Metamorphoses* 3.344–510; ca. 10 B.C.E.), the nymph Echo faded to nothing but a voice because he rejected her; after another whom he scorned prayed for vengeance, Narcissus fell in love with his own image, wasted away, and after death was turned into the flower that bears his name.
3. At the time during which this *loa* is set, Madrid was both home to the Spanish court and the seat of the Holy Roman Empire; Charles I, king of Spain (1500–1558; r. 1516–56) was also Holy Roman Emperor (as Charles V; r. 1519–56).

RELIGION Is it beyond imagination
that something made in one location
can in another be of use?
Furthermore, my writing it
comes, not of whimsical caprice,
but from my vowed obedience
to do what seems beyond my reach.
Well, then, this work, however rough
and little polished it might be,
results from my obedience,
and not from any arrogance.

ZEAL Then answer me, Religion, how
(before you leave the matter now)
will you respond when you are chid
for loading the whole Indies on
a stage to transport to Madrid?

RELIGION The purpose of my play can be
none other than to glorify
the Eucharistic Mystery;
and since the cast of characters
are no more than abstractions which
depict the theme with clarity,
then surely no one should object
if they are taken to Madrid;
distance can never hinder thought
with persons of intelligence,
nor seas impede exchange of sense.

ZEAL Then, prostrate at his royal feet,
beneath whose strength two worlds are joined,
we beg for pardon of the King;

RELIGION and from her eminence, the Queen;[4]

AMERICA whose sovereign and anointed feet
the humble Indies bow to kiss;

ZEAL and from the Royal High Council;

RELIGION and from the ladies, who bring light
into their hemisphere;

AMERICA and from
their poets, I most humbly beg
forgiveness for my crude attempt,
desiring with these awkward lines
to represent the Mystery.

OCCIDENT Let's go, for anxiously I long to see
exactly how this God of yours
will give Himself as food to me.

[AMERICA, OCCIDENT, *and* ZEAL *sing:*]

The Indies know
and do concede
who is the true

4. Isabella of Portugal (1503–1539), who married Charles I (see note 3, above) in 1526.

God of the Seeds.
In loving tears
which joy prolongs
we gladly sing
our happy songs.

ALL Blest be the day
when I could see
and worship the
great God of Seeds.

[*They all exit, dancing and singing.*]

AUGUST STRINDBERG

1849–1912

When scholars try to decide who invented modern drama, their arguments focus on two Scandinavian playwrights: the Norwegian HENRIK IBSEN and the Swede Johan August Strindberg. Ibsen is the more classical writer of the two: his plays are tightly constructed, formally controlled, and carefully paced. Strindberg, by contrast, is a modernist rebel: his plays are flights of fancy, manifestations of a wild imagination that created characters engaged in a perpetual struggle of wills and desires. Strindberg refused to have anything to do with inherited forms of drama. Instead, he reinvented drama from scratch. In order to find new models for his plays, he turned to the most unlikely places. He read contemporary philosophy—for example, the German philosopher Friedrich Nietzsche. He explored the logic of dreams. He studied Eastern religions such as Hinduism. At the same time, he made a name for himself as a painter and wrote a voluminous geographical and cultural history of Sweden as well as a large number of essays, pamphlets, and books on a great variety of subjects, including the occult, magic, and science. Strindberg's career was littered with ill-conceived and quixotic projects, such as his attempts to synthesize gold, which nearly cost him his sanity. Even more disturbing, and notorious, were his anti-Semitic pamphlets and his attacks on the women's rights movement. But somehow out of this volatile life and mind emerged a number of modernism's most compelling and revolutionary plays.

Strindberg was born into a lower-middle-class family, but his mother had been a servant. The stigma attached to this parentage, which Strindberg captured and exaggerated in his first autobiographical novel, *The Son of a Servant* (1886), continued to haunt him to the end of his life. So did his lack of economic resources. He was financially dependent on his friends as early as his student days in Upsala, and even after he had established himself as a writer he could barely make ends meet. His precarious finances forced him to give up his university studies and take jobs as a teacher and also, briefly, as an actor. Eventually he landed a somewhat more secure position as a librarian, which allowed him enough free time to start his career as a writer. But the uneventful and quiet periods in Strindberg's life were few, in part because of his difficult relations with women. His first marriage—to Siri von Essen, an independent and freethinking Finnish aristocrat—lasted for seven tumultuous years and became the subject of his autobiographical novel *A Madman's Defense*

(1888). At the same time, his professional life was in almost as much turmoil. Some of his early plays were staged with relative success, but Strindberg felt attacked by critics and ignored by the theater establishment, a sense that persisted throughout his life. This perceived lack of appreciation was also why he left Sweden in 1883, beginning a long self-imposed exile in France, Germany, Switzerland, and Denmark, interrupted only briefly by returns home.

Many of Strindberg's best-known plays, including *The Father* (1887) and *MISS JULIE* (1888), were first produced outside Sweden, where he first achieved fame as a dramatist. Most of the important influences on Strindberg were likewise European. He engaged in a long correspondence with the influential Danish critic and philosopher Georg Brandes and had less extensive exchanges with Friedrich Nietzsche and Émile Zola. While living in Berlin, he met the director Max Reinhardt, who produced several of Strindberg's plays to great acclaim. Strindberg made friends, but he had a greater talent for making enemies, and he often broke with friends and supporters for no good reason. One of the targets of Strindberg's ire was Ibsen, the older and more established of the two Scandinavian playwrights.

Even though Strindberg had been a professed atheist for much of his life, in the 1890s he increasingly turned to religion, occultism, and pseudo-science. This period also coincided with the end of his volatile second marriage, to Frida Uhl, an Austrian writer. In 1895, after separating from her, he found himself in desolate circumstances in Paris and stopped writing literature entirely. Instead, he spent his scant funds purchasing chemical equipment with which he attempted to produce gold. Paranoid delusions, illness, and failed experiments, together with the mystical writings of Emanuel Swedenborg (1688–1772), fueled his mental instability. The autobiographical *Inferno* (ca. 1898) and his *Occult Diary* (written 1896–1908) sadly testify to this physical and mental decline. In 1897, when he was close to fifty years old, he finally returned permanently to Sweden.

Upon his return to Sweden, Strindberg started to write plays again, but in a very different mode. Whereas his earlier plays had concentrated on single events and encounters, these new, symbolist and expressionist plays, including *The Road to Damascus* (1898) and *The Dream Play* (1901), unfold in loosely connected scenes and episodes. Characters are fluid and shifting, mysterious encounters lead to unforeseen consequences, and the dialogue is infused with religious figures and expressions. These later plays—which also include his so-called chamber plays, among them *The Ghost Sonata* (1907) and *The Pelican* (1907)—revolve around suffering, sin, and redemption. Back in Stockholm Strindberg had also gotten married a third time, to Harriet Bosse, an actress much younger than he. But this marriage was brief, and Strindberg spent his last years alone, in a modest apartment in Stockholm known as the Blue Tower. He never became popular, but in the last years of his life he achieved something of a literary reputation. Although he failed to win the Nobel Prize in Literature—one of the five prizes endowed by the final bequest of the Swedish chemist and armaments manufacturer Alfred Nobel, first awarded in 1901—he was finally honored with a state pension and a so-called Anti-Nobel Prize, a large sum raised by national subscription, one year before his death.

Miss Julie belongs to Strindberg's naturalist period, which also includes *The Father* and *Creditors* (1889). Naturalist drama was a rebellion against the bombastic history plays of Romanticism, the simplistic division between good and evil characters in melodrama, and the neatly constructed drawing-room comedies that flourished in the middle of the century. Naturalism, by contrast, privileged contemporary, and particularly lower-class, settings, which had rarely been seen on the stage except for comic effect. Strindberg's naturalist plays are interested in class differences, especially their effect on the relations between men and women. Like his autobiographical novels and short stories, Strindberg's naturalist plays depict the sexes as engaged in an all-out war. Whether vampires or degenerate creatures, women are always seeking the subjection of men. *The Father* pushes such irrational misogyny to an extreme: it portrays a man who, surrounded by his wife, daughter, mother-in-law, and old nurse, is slowly but surely being driven mad by these vengeful women; finally, he collapses dead in the arms of his nurse. The dramatist's autobiographical novels, as well as his letters and essays, suggest that Strindberg experienced his own marriages as similarly assaultive. But in his plays, at least, he was able to treat his own bitter experiences and paranoid obsessions with more detachment, thereby turning them into more compelling artistic forms.

Miss Julie strives for verisimilitude in its form. The play, confined to a single setting and one long act, represents a single, continuous action that lasts precisely as long as the play itself; it thus strictly obeys the neo-Aristotelian unities of time, place, and action. It is set not in some elaborate drawing room but in the kitchen of an estate, the domain of a cook and her apparent fiancé, another servant in the house in which a count lives with his daughter. Though its opening scene depicts the two servants, the play soon turns to its primary interest: the relation between the emancipated and freethinking mistress of the house, Miss Julie, and the ambitious, virile valet, Jean. The play describes a simple dramatic arc. At first Miss Julie has the upper hand. She flirts with her servant and finally persuades him to dance with her. After a sexual encounter, the dynamics change: now the servant is the dominant one. The play shows in detail the shifting power balance as Jean suggests to Miss Julie that they flee together and fantasizes about setting up a hotel in Italy. But nothing comes of the plan: they are trapped in the kitchen and trapped by their deed. Miss Julie finds herself in the hands of a power-hungry but volatile man, and by the end of the play she has lost her social position and her honor, and has nowhere to turn.

As is to be expected from a self-declared opponent of the New Woman such as Strindberg, Miss Julie does not fare well in this play precisely because she is too emancipated. In keeping with naturalist doctrine, her stance is caused by her parents' corrupting influence; one sign of their moral failings is their initial refusal to be lawfully wedded. Her mother's descent into adultery and arson also helps explain the transformation of the seemingly self-confident and articulate mistress into a moral wreck. Nowhere is Strindberg's reactionary view on marriage and emancipation clearer than in the backstory of Miss Julie, which serves to justify her ultimate downfall. Like many other naturalists, Strindberg was deeply influenced by "social Darwinists," who misapplied evolutionary theory to explain and justify social inequities; here, bad parentage necessarily dooms her. Such plots of social rising and falling are common in naturalist novels and plays alike.

Even though the emancipated aristocrat Miss Julie may in some ways be reminiscent of Strindberg's first wife, the play itself is based not on his own marriage but rather on an account Strindberg had heard of a servant who ended up dominating his former mistress both sexually and socially. In Strindberg's moral universe, the degenerate aristocrat must ultimately be brought down, just as the servant Jean, of humble birth but possessing a forceful will, must rise. The relation between Miss Julie and

Siri von Essen, Strindberg's first wife and the first to play the lead role in the 1889 production of *Miss Julie* at the Scandinavian Experimental Theater.

Jean, couched in a language of dominance, servitude, and struggle, is indebted to Nietzsche, especially those aspects of his philosophy that now seem most troubling.

All the characters in *Miss Julie* are measured in terms of their power and their will to dominate others, but the backdrop of their struggle for dominance is a fixed class structure. Even though in the second part of the play Jean presents himself as the strong servant who will triumph over his mistress, he wavers between arrogance and submission, falling into the latter attitude especially toward Miss Julie's absent father. Throughout the play, the count's return is expected and with it the resumption of Jean's duties, epitomized in the task of polishing his master's shoes. Miss Julie, too, fears the return of her father, who has wholly rejected his former liberal attitudes and now rules sternly and justly, conforming to Strindberg's own conservative ideal. The battle between Jean and Miss Julie is waged in the oppressive atmosphere of the servants' quarters, a setting that underscores the constant threat of retribution. Despite Strindberg's belief in social Darwinism and the survival of the stronger, the determining power of social class can never be entirely overcome in *Miss Julie*: the play and its protagonist remain mired in class resentment. Jean may despise Miss Julie and manage to bring her into his power, but part of him remains a servant.

The oscillation between dominance and subservience within an individual is part of the theory of characterization that Strindberg articulates in his famous preface to the play. He rejects the traditional stage characters, who often manifest a single dominant trait—such stock figures as the hapless victim, the scheming villain, and the trusted friend. Clear motivations and distinct types may be useful in the construction of plots, but in Strindberg's view they fail to represent the conflicted and shifting forces that actually drive human action. Like modernist novelists such as James Joyce and Virginia Woolf, Strindberg wanted to replicate the irregular workings of the human mind. While other naturalists placed great emphasis on external detail of costume and dialect, Strindberg was more interested in interiority and psychology. His characters change their minds constantly; and when they express their thoughts, they are allowed to be inconsistent, shifting, and inarticulate. Strindberg also insisted on abolishing many of the artificial aspects of stagecraft, including painted scenes, makeup, unnatural lighting effects such as those caused by footlights, and the practice of playing to the audience. At the same time, he made no attempt to do away with all elements of theatrical artifice. Even in his naturalist plays, he included theatrical set pieces such as dance, music, and ballet. They often take the place of crowd scenes, which Strindberg did not believe could be staged naturalistically in the theater. He thus pragmatically opted for established theatrical techniques when necessary.

Miss Julie has remained a central play in the canon of modern drama. Early productions were mounted in Copenhagen, Berlin, and, most famously, Paris at André Antoine's Théâtre Libre in 1893, a production that confirmed Strindberg's standing as a leading naturalist playwright. In Sweden, the play was not produced until 1906, when it was staged at the Intima Teater. Upon his return to Sweden, Strindberg had founded this theater with the director August Falck, and many of his late chamber plays were written for it. Decorated in green and white draperies, with a bust of Strindberg in the small foyer, the Intima Teater was in fact modeled on Antoine's Théâtre Libre. But even though Strindberg had control over this theater, he was never entirely content with its productions of his plays. The quality of the acting was mixed, and the theater was under constant financial strain. In 1910 it had to be closed for good. Despite his efforts, Strindberg thus never found a company that could adequately translate his theories and plays into theatrical reality. And not until shortly before his death did he receive the enthusiastic support from the press, publishers, and the theatergoing public that had eluded him for decades.

Strindberg's life was a struggle against the world and against himself. His plays, likewise, are full of struggles among characters, even as they fight for a new type of drama. While Strindberg's struggles were mostly destructive in his life, they were immensely productive in his art. His plays never take anything for granted, and in each play he sought to invent drama anew. In the process, he first created an unusual form of naturalism; then, in his later work, he pioneered what would be known as expressionism—plays full of enigmatic characters, religious language, and episodic plots. But neither label can entirely capture the essence of Strindberg's plays, which are among the most personal and singular in the history of modern drama. Even though readers today are, if anything, more shocked than his contemporaries at his racist, misogynist, and strange religious opinions, Strindberg's unusual plays have continued to compel generations of readers, theatergoers, and critics, and his varied and rich work remains one of the pillars of modern drama. M.P.

Miss Julie[1]

Preface

Like the arts in general, the theater has for a long time seemed to me a *Biblia Pauperum*,[2] a picture Bible for those who cannot read, and the playwright merely a lay preacher who hawks the latest ideals in popular form, so popular that the middle classes—the bulk of the audiences—can grasp them without racking their brains too much. That explains why the theater has always been an elementary school for youngsters and the half-educated, and for women, who still retain a primitive capacity for deceiving themselves and for letting themselves be deceived, that is, for succumbing to illusions and responding hypnotically to the suggestions of the author. Consequently, now that the rudimentary and undeveloped mental processes that operate in the realm of fantasy appear to be evolving to the level of reflection, research, and experimentation, I believe that the theater, like religion, is about to be replaced as a dying institution for whose enjoyment we lack the necessary qualifications. Support for my view is provided by the theater crisis through which all of Europe is now passing, and still more by the fact that in those highly cultured lands which have produced the finest minds of our time—England and Germany—the drama is dead, as for the most part are the other fine arts.

Other countries, however, have thought to create a new drama by filling the old forms with new contents. But since there has not been enough time to popularize the new ideas, the public cannot understand them. And in the second place, controversy has so stirred up the public that they can no longer look on with a pure and dispassionate interest, especially when they see their most cherished ideals assailed or hear an applauding or booing majority openly exercise its tyrannical power, as can happen in the theater. And in the third place, since the new forms for the new ideas have not been created, the new wine has burst the old bottles.

In the play that follows I have not tried to accomplish anything new—that is impossible. I have only tried to modernize the form to satisfy what I believe up-to-date people expect and demand of this art. And with that in mind I have seized upon—or let myself be seized by—a theme that may be said to lie outside current party strife, since the question of being on the way up or on the way down the social ladder, of

1. Translated by Evert Sprinchorn.

2. Bible of the Poor (Latin).

being on the top or on the bottom, superior or inferior, man or woman, is, has been, and will be of perennial interest. When I took this theme from real life—I heard about it a few years ago and it made a deep impression on me—I thought it would be a suitable subject for a tragedy, since it still strikes us as tragic to see a happily favored individual go down in defeat, and even more so to see an entire family line die out. But perhaps a time will come when we shall be so highly developed and so enlightened that we can look with indifference upon the brutal, cynical, and heartless spectacle that life offers us, a time when we shall have laid aside those inferior and unreliable mechanical apparatuses called emotions, which will become superfluous and even harmful as our mental organs develop. The fact that my heroine wins sympathy is due entirely to the fact that we are still too weak to overcome the fear that the same fate might overtake us. The extremely sensitive viewer will of course not be satisfied with mere expressions of sympathy, and the man who believes in progress will demand that certain positive actions be taken for getting rid of the evil, a kind of program, in other words. But in the first place absolute evil does not exist. The decline of one family is the making of another, which now gets its chance to rise. This alternate rising and falling provides one of life's greatest pleasures, for happiness is, after all, relative. As for the man who has a program for changing the disagreeable circumstance that the hawk eats the chicken and that lice eat up the hawk, I should like to ask him why it should be changed. Life is not prearranged with such idiotic mathematical precision that only the larger gets to eat the smaller. Just as frequently the bee destroys the lion (in Aesop's[3] fable)—or at least drives him wild.

If my tragedy makes most people feel sad, that is their fault. When we get to be as strong as the first French Revolutionists were, we shall be perfectly content and happy to watch the forests being cleared of rotting, superannuated trees that have stood too long in the way of others with just as much right to grow and flourish for a while—as content as we are when we see an incurably ill man finally die.

Recently my tragedy *The Father*[4] was censured for being too unpleasant—as if one wanted merry tragedies. "The joy of life" is now the slogan of the day. Theater managers send out orders for nothing but farces, as if the joy of living lay in behaving like a clown and in depicting people as if they were afflicted with St. Vitus's dance[5] or congenital idiocy. I find the joy of living in the fierce and ruthless battles of life, and my pleasure comes from learning something, from being taught something. That is why I have chosen for my play an unusual but instructive case, an exception, in other words—but an important exception of the kind that proves the rule—a choice of subject that I know will offend all lovers of the conventional. The next thing that will bother simple minds is that the motivation for the action is not simple and that the point of view is not single. Usually an event in life—and this is a fairly new discovery—is the result of a whole series of more or less deep-rooted causes. The spectator, however, generally chooses the one that puts the least strain on his mind or reflects most credit on his insight. Consider a case of suicide. "Business failure," says the merchant. "Unhappy love," say the women. "Physical illness," says the sick man. "Lost hopes," says the down-and-out. But it may be that the reason lay in all of these or in none of them, and that the suicide hid his real reason behind a completely different one that would reflect greater glory on his memory.

I have motivated the tragic fate of Miss Julie with an abundance of circumstances: her mother's basic instincts, her father's improper bringing-up of the girl, her own inborn nature, and her fiancé's sway over her weak and degenerate mind. Further and

3. Greek storyteller (early 6th c. B.C.E.), known especially for his moralizing animal fables (Strindberg is here apparently thinking of "The Gnat and the Lion").

4. Published one year earlier, in 1887.

5. Chorea, a disease characterized by involuntary spasmodic movements.

more immediately: the festive atmosphere of Midsummer Eve, her father's absence, her period, her preoccupation with animals, the erotic excitement of the dance, the long summer twilight, the highly aphrodisiac influence of flowers, and finally chance itself, which drives two people together in an out-of-the-way room, plus the boldness of the aroused man.

As one can see, I have not been entirely the physiologist, not been obsessively psychological, not traced everything to her mother's heredity, not found the sole cause in her period, not attributed everything to our "immoral times," and not simply preached a moral lesson. Lacking a priest, I have let the cook handle that.

I am proud to say that this complicated way of looking at things is in tune with the times. And if others have anticipated me in this, I am proud that I am not alone in my paradoxes, as all new discoveries are called. And no one can say this time that I am being one-sided.

As far as the drawing of characters is concerned, I have made the people in my play fairly "characterless" for the following reasons. In the course of time the word *character* has acquired many meanings. Originally it probably meant the dominant and fundamental trait in the soul complex and was confused with temperament. Later the middle class used it to mean an automaton. An individual who once and for all had found his own true nature or adapted himself to a certain role in life, who in fact had ceased to grow, was called a man of character, while the man who was constantly developing, who, like a skillful sailor on the currents of life, did not sail with close-tied sheets but who fell off before the wind in order to luff again, was called a man of no character—derogatorily of course, since he was so difficult to keep track of, to pin down and pigeonhole. This middle-class conception of a fixed character was transferred to the stage, where the middle class has always ruled. A character there came to mean someone who was always one and the same, always drunk, always joking, always melancholy, and who needed to be characterized only by some physical defect such as a club foot, a wooden leg, or a red nose, or by the repetition of some such phrase as, "That's capital," or "Barkis is willin'."[6] This uncomplicated way of viewing people is still to be found in the great Molière. Harpagon[7] is nothing but a miser, although Harpagon could have been both a miser and an exceptional financier, a fine father, and a good citizen. Worse still, his "defect" is extremely advantageous to his son-in-law and his daughter, who will be his heirs and who therefore should not find fault with him, even if they do have to wait a while to jump into bed together. So I do not believe in simple stage characters. And the summary judgments that writers pass on people—he is stupid, this one is brutal, that one is jealous, this one is stingy, and so on—should not pass unchallenged by the naturalists who know how complicated the soul is and who realize that vice has a reverse side very much like virtue.

Since the persons in my play are modern characters, living in a transitional era more hectic and hysterical than the previous one at least, I have depicted them as more unstable, as torn and divided, a mixture of the old and the new. Nor does it seem improbable to me that modern ideas might also have seeped down through newspapers and kitchen talk to the level of the servants. Consequently the valet may belch forth from his inherited slave soul certain modern ideas. And if there are those who find it wrong to allow people in a modern drama to talk Darwin and who recommend the practice of Shakespeare to our attention, may I remind them that the gravedigger in *Hamlet* talks the then-fashionable philosophy of Giordano Bruno

6. A phrase repeated by Mr. Barkis, a character in Charles Dickens's *David Copperfield* (1849–50), to indicate his desire to marry Clara Peggotty; that novel, like many other works by Dickens, was successfully adapted to the stage.

7. The protagonist in *The Miser* (1668), a play by the French dramatist Molière (1622–1673).

(Bacon's philosophy),[8] which is even more improbable, seeing that the means of spreading ideas were fewer then than now. And besides, the fact of the matter is that Darwinism has always existed, ever since Moses' history of creation[9] from the lower animals up to man, but it was not until recently that we discovered it and formulized it.

My souls—or characters—are conglomerations from various stages of culture, past and present, walking scrapbooks, shreds of human lives, tatters torn from old rags that were once Sunday best—hodgepodges just like the human soul. I have even supplied a little source history into the bargain by letting the weaker steal and repeat words of the stronger, letting them get ideas (suggestions as they are called) from one another, from the environment (the songbird's blood), and from objects (the razor). I have also arranged for *Gedankenübertragung*[1] through an inanimate medium to take place (the count's boots, the servant's bell). And I have even made use of "waking suggestions" (a variation of hypnotic suggestion), which have by now been so popularized that they cannot arouse ridicule or skepticism as they would have done in Mesmer's[2] time.

I say Miss Julie is a modern character not because the man-hating half-woman has not always existed but because she has now been brought out into the open, has taken the stage, and is making a noise about herself. Victim of a superstition (one that has seized even stronger minds) that woman, that stunted form of human being, standing with man, the lord of creation, the creator of culture, is meant to be the equal of man or could ever possibly be, she involves herself in an absurd struggle with him in which she falls. Absurd because a stunted form, subject to the laws of propagation, will always be born stunted and can never catch up with the one who has the lead. As follows: A (the man) and B (the woman) start from the same point C, A with a speed of let us say 100 and B with a speed of 60. When will B overtake A? Answer: never. Neither with the help of equal education or equal voting rights—nor by universal disarmament and temperance societies—any more than two parallel lines can ever meet. The half-woman is a type that forces itself on others, selling itself for power, medals, recognition, diplomas, as formerly it sold itself for money. It represents degeneration. It is not a strong species for it does not maintain itself, but unfortunately it propagates its misery in the following generation. Degenerate men unconsciously select their mates from among these half-women, so that they breed and spread, producing creatures of indeterminate sex to whom life is a torture, but who fortunately are overcome eventually either by a hostile reality, or by the uncontrolled breaking loose of their repressed instincts, or else by their frustration in not being able to compete with the male sex. It is a tragic type, offering us the spectacle of a desperate fight against nature; a tragic legacy of romanticism, which is now being dissipated by naturalism—a movement that seeks only happiness, and for that strong and healthy species are required.

Miss Julie, however, is also a vestige of the old warrior nobility that is now being superseded by a new nobility of nerve and brain. She is a victim of the disorder produced within a family by a mother's "crime," of the mistakes of a whole generation gone wrong, of circumstances, of her own defective constitution—all of which put together is equivalent to the fate or universal law of the ancients. The naturalists have banished

8. Perhaps a reference to the extreme logical precision of the gravedigger's wordplay in Shakespeare's *Hamlet* (1600–01), 5.1. Francis Bacon (1561–1626), an English philosopher and essayist, promoted the use of the inductive method of modern science; Bruno (1548–1600), an Italian philosopher, challenged dogmatism (he was burned at the stake for heresy). The major idea of the English naturalist Charles Darwin (1809–1882)—the theory of evolution through natural selection, or Darwinism—was gaining wider acceptance at the end of the 19th century.

9. That is, the account given in Genesis, whose authorship was traditionally ascribed to Moses.

1. Telepathy (German).

2. Franz Anton Mesmer (1734–1815), German physician who devised a therapeutic technique, based on "animal magnetism," that was developed into hypnosis.

guilt along with God, but the consequences of an act—punishment, imprisonment, or the fear of it—cannot be banished for the simple reason that they remain whether or not the naturalist dismisses the case from his court. Those sitting on the sidelines can easily afford to be lenient; but what of the injured parties? And even if her father were compelled to forgo taking his revenge, Miss Julie would take vengeance on herself, as she does in the play, because of that inherited or acquired sense of honor that has been transmitted to the upper classes from—well, where does it come from? From the age of barbarism, from the first Aryans,[3] from the chivalry of the Middle Ages. And a very fine code it was, but now inimical to the survival of the race. It is the aristocrat's form of hara-kiri, a law of conscience that bids the Japanese to slice his own stomach when someone else dishonors him. The same sort of thing survives, slightly modified, in that exclusive prerogative of the aristocracy, the duel. (Example: the husband challenges his wife's lover to a duel; the lover shoots the husband and runs off with the wife. Result: the husband has saved his *honor* but lost his wife.) Hence the servant Jean lives on; but not Miss Julie, who cannot live without honor. The advantage that the slave has over his master is that he has not committed himself to this defeatist principle. In all of us Aryans there is enough of the nobleman, or of the Don Quixote,[4] to make us sympathize with the man who takes his own life after having dishonored himself by shameful deeds. And we are all of us aristocrats enough to be distressed at the sight of a great man lying like a dead hulk ready for the scrap pile, even, I suppose, if he were to raise himself up again and redeem himself by honorable deeds.

The servant Jean is the beginning of a new species in which noticeable differentiation has already taken place. He began as a child of a poor worker and is now evolving through self-education into a future gentleman of the upper classes. He is quick to learn, has highly developed senses (smell, taste, sight), and a keen appreciation of beauty. He has already come up in the world, for he is strong enough not to hesitate to make use of other people. He is already a stranger to his old friends, whom he despises as reminders of past stages in his development, and whom he fears and avoids because they know his secrets, guess his intentions, look with envy on his rise and with joyful expectation toward his fall. Hence his character is unformed and divided. He wavers between an admiration of high positions and a hatred of the men who occupy them. He is an aristocrat—he says so himself—familiar with the ins and outs of good society. He is polished on the outside, but coarse underneath. He wears his frock coat with elegance but offers no guarantee that he keeps his body clean.

Although he respects Miss Julie, he is afraid of Christine, because she knows his innermost secrets. Yet he is sufficiently hard-hearted not to let the events of the night upset his plans for the future. Possessing both the coarseness of the slave and the toughmindedness of the born ruler, he can look at blood without fainting, shake off bad luck like water, and take calamity by the horns. Consequently he will escape from the battle unwounded, probably ending up as proprietor of a hotel. And if he himself does not get to be a Rumanian count, his son will doubtless go to college and possibly end up as a government official.

Now his observations about life as the lower classes see it, from below, are well worth listening to—that is, they are whenever he is telling the truth, which is not too often, because he is more likely to say what is advantageous to him than what is true. When Miss Julie supposes that everyone in the lower classes must feel greatly oppressed by the weight of the classes above, Jean naturally agrees with her since he wants to win her sympathy. But he promptly takes it all back when he finds it expedient to separate himself from the mob.

3. Hypothetical ancient speakers of Indo-European, progenitors of European (especially the Germanic) peoples.

4. The eponymous hero of Miguel de Cervantes's novel (1605, 1615), here invoked as a symbol of unflagging devotion to chivalric ideals.

Apart from the fact that Jean is coming up in the world, he is also superior to Miss Julie in that he is a man. In the sexual sphere, he is the aristocrat. He has the strength of the male, more highly developed senses, and the ability to take the initiative. His inferiority is merely the result of his social environment, which is only temporary and which he will probably slough off along with his livery.

His slave nature expresses itself in his awe of the count (the boots) and his religious superstitions. But he is awed by the count mainly because the count occupies the place he wants most in life; and this awe is still there even after he has won the daughter of the house and seen how empty that beautiful shell was.

I do not believe that any love in the "higher" sense can be born from the union of two such different souls; so I have let Miss Julie's love be refashioned in her imagination as a love that protects and purifies, and I have let Jean imagine that even his love might have a chance to grow under other social circumstances. For I suppose love is very much like the hyacinth that must strike roots deep in the dark earth *before* it can produce a vigorous blossom. Here it shoots up, bursts into bloom, and turns to seed all at once. Such plants can only be short-lived.

Christine—finally to get to her—is a female slave, spineless and phlegmatic after years spent at the kitchen stove, bovinely unconscious of her own hypocrisy, and with a full quota of moral and religious notions that serve as scapegoats and cloaks for her sins—which a stronger soul does not require since he is able either to carry the burden of his own sins or to rationalize them out of existence. She attends church regularly where she deftly unloads unto Jesus her household thefts and picks up from him another load of innocence. She is only a secondary character, and I have deliberately done no more than sketch her in—just as I treated the country doctor and parish priest in *The Father* where I only wanted to draw ordinary everyday people such as most country doctors and parsons are. That some have found my minor characters one-dimensional is due to the fact that ordinary people while at work are to a certain extent one-dimensional and do lack an independent existence, showing only one side of themselves in the performance of their duties. And as long as the audience does not feel it needs to see them from different angles, my abstract sketches will pass muster.

Now as far as the dialogue is concerned, I have broken somewhat with tradition in refusing to make my characters into interlocutors who ask stupid questions to elicit witty answers. I have avoided the symmetrical and mathematical design of the artfully constructed French dialogue and have let minds work as irregularly as they do in real life, where no subject is quite exhausted before another mind engages at random some cog in the conversation and governs it for a while. My dialogue wanders here and there, gathers material in the first scenes which is later picked up, repeated, reworked, developed, and expanded like the theme in a piece of music.

The action of the play poses no problem. Since it really involves only two people, I have limited myself to these two, introducing only one minor character, the cook, and keeping the unhappy spirit of the father brooding over the action as a whole. I have chosen this course because I have noticed that what interests people most nowadays is the psychological action. Our inveterately curious souls are no longer content to see a thing happen; we want to see how it happens. We want to see the strings, look at the machinery, examine the double-bottom drawer, put on the magic ring to find the hidden seam, look in the deck for the marked cards.

In treating the subject this way I have had in mind the case-history novels of the Goncourt brothers,[5] which appeal to me more than anything else in modern literature.

As far as play construction is concerned, I have made a stab at getting rid of act divisions. I was afraid that the spectator's declining susceptibility to illusion might not carry him through the intermission, when he would have time to think about what

5. Edmond de Goncourt (1822–1896) and Jules de Goncourt (1830–1870), coauthors of six novels set in 18th-century France.

he has seen and to escape the suggestive influence of the author-hypnotist. I figure my play lasts about ninety minutes. Since one can listen to a lecture, a sermon, or a political debate for that long or even longer, I have convinced myself that a play should not exhaust an audience in that length of time. As early as 1872 in one of my first attempts at the drama, *The Outlaw,* I tried out this concentrated form, although with little success. I had finished the work in five acts when I noticed the disjointed and disturbing effect it produced. I burned it, and from the ashes there arose a single, complete reworked act of fifty pages that would run for less than an hour. Although this play form is not completely new, it seems to be my special property and has a good chance of gaining favor with the public when tastes change. My hope is to educate a public to sit through a full evening's show in one act. But this whole question must first be probed more deeply. In the meantime, in order to establish resting places for the audience and the actors without destroying the illusion, I have made use of three arts that belong to the drama: the monologue, the pantomime, and the ballet, all of which were part of classic tragedy, the monody having become the monologue and the choral dance, the ballet.

The realists have banished the monologue from the stage as implausible. But if I can motivate it, I make it plausible, and I can then use it to my advantage. Now it is certainly plausible for a speaker to pace the floor and read his speech aloud to himself. It is plausible for an actor to practice his part aloud, for a child to talk to her cat, a mother to babble to her baby, an old lady to chatter to her parrot, and a sleeping man to talk in his sleep. And in order to give the actor a chance to work on his own for once and for a moment not be obliged to follow the author's directions, I have not written out the monologues in detail but simply outlined them. Since it makes very little difference what is said while asleep, or to the parrot or the cat, inasmuch as it does not affect the main action, a gifted player who is in the midst of the situation and mood of the play can probably improvise the monologue better than the author, who cannot estimate ahead of time how much may be said and for how long before the illusion is broken.

Some theaters in Italy have, as we know, returned to the art of improvisation[6] and have thereby trained actors who are truly inventive—without, however, violating the intentions of the author. This seems to be a step in the right direction and possibly the beginning of a new, fertile form of art that will be genuinely *creative*.

In places where the monologue cannot be properly motivated, I have resorted to pantomime. Here I have given the actor even more freedom to be creative and win honor on his own. Nevertheless, not to try the audience beyond its limits, I have relied on music—well motivated by the Midsummer Eve dance—to exercise its hypnotic powers during the pantomime scene. I beg the music director to select his tunes with great care, so that associations foreign to the mood of the play will not be produced by reminders of popular operattas or current dance numbers or by folk music of interest only to ethnologists.

The ballet that I have introduced cannot be replaced by a so-called crowd scene. Such scenes are always badly acted, with a pack of babbling fools taking advantage of the occasion to "gag it up," thereby destroying the illusion. Inasmuch as country people do not improvise their taunts but make use of material already to hand by giving it a double meaning, I have not composed an original lampoon but have made use of a little-known round dance that I noted down in the Stockholm district. The words do not fit the situation exactly, which is what I intended, since the slave in his cunning (that is, weakness) never attacks directly. At any rate, let us have no comedians in this serious story and no obscene smirking over an affair that nails the lid on a family coffin.

As far as the scenery is concerned, I have borrowed from impressionistic painting the idea of asymmetrical and open composition, and I believe that I have thereby

6. That is, the commedia dell'arte, which relies on improvisation by stock characters along conventional plotlines.

gained something in the way of greater illusion. Because the audience cannot see the whole room and all the furniture, they will have to surmise what's missing; that is, their imagination will be stimulated to fill in the rest of the picture. I have gained something else by this: I have avoided those tiresome exits through doors. Stage doors are made of canvas and rock at the slightest touch. They cannot even be used to indicate the wrath of an angry father who storms out of the house after a bad dinner, slamming the door behind him "so that the whole house shakes." (In the theater it sways and billows.) Furthermore, I have confined the action to one set, both to give the characters a chance to become part and parcel of their environment and to cut down on scenic extravagance. If there is only one set, one has a right to expect it to be as realistic as possible. Yet nothing is more difficult than to make a room look like a room, however easy it may be for the scene painter to create waterfalls and erupting volcanos. I suppose we shall have to put up with walls made of canvas, but isn't it about time that we stopped painting shelves and pots and pans on the canvas? There are so many other conventions in the theater that we are told to accept in good faith that we should be spared the strain of believing in painted saucepans.

I have placed the backdrop and the table at an angle to force the actors to play face to face or in half profile when they are seated opposite each other at the table. In a production of *Aida*[7] I saw a flat placed at such an angle, which led the eye out in an unfamiliar perspective. Nor did it look as if it had been set that way simply to be different or to avoid those monotonous right angles.

Another desirable innovation would be the removal of the footlights. I understand that the purpose of lighting from below is to make the actors look more full in the face. But may I ask why all actors should have full faces? Doesn't this kind of lighting wipe out many of the finer features in the lower part of the face, especially around the jaws? Doesn't it distort the shape of the nose and throw false shadows above the eyes? If not, it certainly does something else: it hurts the actor's eyes. The footlights hit the retina at an angle from which it is usually shielded (except in sailors who must look at the sunlight reflected in the water), and the result is the loss of any effective play of the eyes. All one ever sees on stage are goggle-eyed glances sideways at the boxes or upward at the balcony, with only the whites of the eyes being visible in the latter case. And this probably also accounts for that tiresome fluttering of the eyelashes that the female performers are particularly guilty of. If an actor nowadays wants to express something with his eyes, he can only do it looking right at the audience, in which case he makes direct contact with someone outside the proscenium arch—a bad habit known, justifiably or not, as "saying hello to friends."

I should think that the use of sufficiently strong side lights (through the use of reflectors or something like them) would provide the actor with a new asset: an increased range of expression made possible by the play of the eyes, the most expressive part of the face.

I have scarcely any illusions about getting actors to play for the audience and not directly at them, although this should be the goal. Nor do I dream of ever seeing an actor play through all of an important scene with his back to the audience. But is it too much to hope that crucial scenes could be played where the author indicated and not in front of the prompter's box as if they were duets demanding applause? I am not calling for a revolution, only for some small changes. I am well aware that transforming the stage into a real room with the fourth wall missing and with some of the furniture placed with backs to the auditorium would only upset the audience, at least for the present.

If I bring up the subject of makeup, it is not because I dare hope to be heeded by the ladies, who would rather be beautiful than truthful. But the male actor might do well to consider if it is an advantage to paint his face with character lines that remain

7. An Italian opera by Giuseppe Verdi (1871), set in ancient Egypt.

there like a mask. Let us imagine an actor who pencils in with soot a few lines between his eyes to indicate great anger, and let us suppose that in that permanently enraged state he finds he has to smile on a certain line. Imagine the horrible grimace! And how can the old character actor wrinkle his brows in anger when his false bald pate is as smooth as a billiard ball?

In a modern psychological drama, in which every tremor of the soul should be reflected more by facial expressions than by gestures and grunts, it would probably be most sensible to experiment with strong side lighting on a small stage, using actors without any makeup or a minimum of it.

And then, if we could get rid of the visible orchestra with its disturbing lights and the faces turned toward the public; if the auditorium floor could be raised so that the spectator's eyes are not level with the actor's knees; if we could get rid of the proscenium boxes and their occupants, arriving giggling and drunk from their dinners; and if we could have it dark in the auditorium during the performance; and if, above everything else, we could have a *small* stage and an *intimate* auditorium—then possibly a new drama might arise and at least one theater become a refuge for cultured audiences. While we are waiting for such a theater, we shall have to write for the dramatic stockpile and prepare the repertory that one day shall come.

Here is my attempt. If I have failed, there is still time to try again!

CHARACTERS

MISS JULIE, twenty-five years old
JEAN, valet, thirty years old
CHRISTINE, cook, thirty-five years old
THE CHORUS, a party of country folk

The scene is a country estate in Sweden.

The time: A Midsummer Night in the 1880s. The hours after midnight, June 24, St. John the Baptist's Day.

The Set

The scene is the kitchen of the estate belonging to the count, MISS JULIE's *father. It is a large kitchen, situated along with the servants' quarters in the basement of the manor house. The side walls and the ceiling of the kitchen are masked by the tormentors*[8] *and borders of the set. The rear wall runs obliquely upstage from the left. On this wall to the left are two shelves with pots and pans of copper, iron, and pewter. The shelves are decorated with goffered*[9] *paper. A little to the right can be seen three-fourths of a deep arched entry with two glass doors, and through them can be seen a fountain with a statue of a cupid,*[1] *lilac bushes in bloom, and the tops of some Lombardy poplars.*

From the left of the stage the corner of a large, Dutch-tile kitchen stove protrudes with part of the hood showing.

Projecting from the right side of the stage is one end of the servants' dining table of white pine, with a few chairs around it.

The stove is decorated with branches of birch leaves; the floor is strewn with juniper twigs.

On the end of the table is a large Japanese spice jar filled with lilacs.

8. Curtains or doors on the sides of a stage set that hide the wings from the view of the audience.

9. Embossed to produce patterns of raised figures.

1. A representation of the Roman god of love.

An icebox, a sink, a washbasin.

Over the door a big old-fashioned bell; and to the left of the door the gaping mouth of a speaking tube.[2]

[CHRISTINE *is standing at the stove, frying something in a pan. She is wearing a light-colored cotton dress and an apron.*]

[JEAN *enters, dressed in livery and carrying a pair of high-top boots with spurs. He sets them where they are clearly visible.*]

JEAN What a night! She's wild again! Miss Julie's absolutely wild!

CHRISTINE You sure took your time getting back!

JEAN I took the count down to the station, and on my way back, I passed the barn and went in for a dance. And there was Miss Julie leading the dance with the game warden. Then she noticed me. And she ran right into my arms and chose me for the ladies' waltz. And she's been dancing ever since like—like I don't know what. Wild, I tell you, absolutely wild!

CHRISTINE That's nothing new. But she's been worse than ever during the last two weeks, ever since her engagement was broken off.

JEAN Yes. I never did hear all there was to that. He was a good man, too, even if he wasn't rich. Well, they've got such crazy ideas. [*He sits down at the end of the table.*] Tell me, isn't it strange that a young girl like her—all right, young woman—prefers to stay home here with the servants rather than go with her father to visit her relatives?

CHRISTINE I suppose she's ashamed to face them after that fiasco with her young man.

JEAN No doubt. He wouldn't take any nonsense from her. Do you know what happened, Christine? I saw the whole thing. Of course, I didn't let on.

CHRISTINE You were there? I don't believe it.

JEAN Well, I was. They were in the stable yard one evening—and she was training him, that's what she called it. Do you know what? She was making him jump over her riding whip—training him like a dog. He jumped over twice, and she whipped him both times. But the third time, he grabbed the whip from her, [scratched her face with it—long scratch on her left cheek;][3] then broke it in a thousand pieces—and walked off.

CHRISTINE I don't believe it! What do you know!

JEAN Yes, that put an end to that affair. —What have you got for me that's really good, Christine?

CHRISTINE [*serving him from the frying pan*] Just a little bit of kidney. Cut it from the veal roast.

JEAN [*smelling it*] Wonderful! One of my special *délices!*[4] [*Feeling the plate*] Hey, you didn't warm the plate!

CHRISTINE You're more fussy than the count himself when you set your mind to it. [*She rumples his hair affectionately.*]

JEAN [*irritated*] Cut it out! Don't muss up my hair. You know how particular I am!

2. A hollow pipe connecting two cones, used in businesses and upper-class homes in the 19th century for communicating over distances.

3. The passage in brackets was deleted in Strindberg's manuscript, probably by Strindberg himself [translator's note].

4. Pleasures, delights (French).

CHRISTINE Oh, don't get mad. Can I help it if I like you?

[JEAN *eats.* CHRISTINE *gets out a bottle of beer.*]

JEAN Beer on Midsummer Eve! No thank you! I've got something much better than that. [*He opens a drawer in the table and takes out a bottle of red wine with a gold seal.*] Do you see that? Gold Seal. Now give me a glass.

[*She hands him a tumbler.*]

—No, a wineglass of course. This has to be drunk properly. No water.

CHRISTINE [*goes back to the stove and puts on a small saucepan*] Lord help the woman who gets you for a husband. You're an old fussbudget!

JEAN Talk, talk! You'd consider yourself lucky if you got yourself a man as good as me. It hasn't done you any harm to have people think I'm your fiancé. [*He tastes the wine.*] Very good. Excellent. But warmed just a little too little. [*Warming the glass in his hands*] We bought this in Dijon. Four francs a liter, unbottled—and the tax on top of that. . . . What on earth are you cooking? It stinks like hell!

CHRISTINE Some damn mess that Miss Julie wants for her Diana, that damn dog of hers.

JEAN You should watch your language, Christine. . . . Why do you have to stand in front of the stove on a holiday, cooking for that mutt? Is it sick?

CHRISTINE Oh, she's sick, all right! She sneaked out to the gatekeeper's pug and—got herself in a fix. And you know Miss Julie, she can't stand anything like that.

JEAN She's too stuck-up in some ways and not proud enough in others. Just like her mother. The countess felt right at home in the kitchen or down in the barn with the cows, but when she went driving, one horse wasn't enough for her, she had to have a pair. Her sleeves were always dirty, but her buttons had the royal crown on them. As for Miss Julie, she doesn't give a hoot in hell how she looks and acts. I mean, she's not really refined, not really. Just now, down at the barn, she grabbed the game warden right from under Anna's eyes and asked him to dance. You wouldn't see anybody in our class behaving like that. But that's what happens when the gentry try to act like the common people—they become common! . . . However, I'll say one thing for her: she *is* beautiful! Statuesque! Ah, those shoulders—those—and so forth, and so forth!

CHRISTINE Oh, don't exaggerate. Clara tells me all about her, and Clara dresses her.

JEAN Clara, pooh! You women are always jealous of each other. I've been out riding with her. . . . And how she can dance . . . !

CHRISTINE Listen, Jean, you *are* going to dance with me, aren't you, when I'm finished here?

JEAN Certainly! Of course I am.

CHRISTINE Promise?

JEAN Promise! Listen—if I say I'm going to do a thing, I do it. . . . Christine, I thank you for a delicious meal. Superb! [*He shoves the cork back into the bottle.*]

[MISS JULIE *appears in the entry, talking to someone outside.*]

MISS JULIE I'll be right back. Don't wait for me.

[JEAN *slips the bottle into the table drawer quickly and rises respectfully.* MISS JULIE *comes in and crosses over to* CHRISTINE, *who is at the stove.*]

MISS JULIE Did you get it ready?

[CHRISTINE *signals that* JEAN *is present.*]

JEAN [*polite and charming*] Are you ladies sharing secrets?

MISS JULIE [*flipping her handkerchief in his face*] Don't be nosy!

JEAN Oh, that smells good! Violets.

MISS JULIE [*flirting with him*] Don't be impudent! And don't tell me you're an expert on perfumes, too. I love the way you dance!—No, mustn't look! Go away!

JEAN [*cocky but pleasant*] What are the ladies cooking up? A witches' brew for Midsummer Eve? So they can tell the future?[5] Read what's in the cards for them, and see who they'll marry?

MISS JULIE [*curtly*] You'd have to have good eyes to see that. [*To* CHRISTINE] Pour it into a small bottle, and seal it tight. . . . Jean, come and dance a schottische[6] with me.

JEAN [*hesitating*] I hope you don't think I'm being rude, but I've already promised this dance to Christine.

MISS JULIE She can always find someone. Isn't that so, Christine? You don't mind if I borrow Jean for a minute, do you?

CHRISTINE It ain't up to me. If Miss Julie is gracious enough to invite you, it ain't right for you to say no, Jean. You go on, and thank her for the honor.

JEAN Frankly, Miss Julie, I don't want to hurt your feelings, but I wonder if it's wise—I mean for you to dance twice in a row with the same partner. Especially since the people around here love to talk.

MISS JULIE [*bridling*] What do you mean? What kind of talk? What are you trying to say?

JEAN [*retreating*] I wish you wouldn't misunderstand me, Miss Julie. It just doesn't look right for you to prefer one of your servants to the others who are hoping for the same unusual honor.

MISS JULIE Prefer! What an idea! I'm really surprised. I, the mistress of the house, am good enough to come to their dance, and when I feel like dancing, I want to dance with someone who knows how to lead. After all I don't want to look ridiculous.

JEAN As you wish, Miss Julie. I am at your orders.

MISS JULIE [*gently*] Don't take it as an order. Tonight we're all just having a good time. There's no question of rank. Now give me your arm. —Don't worry, Christine. I won't run off with your boyfriend.

[JEAN *gives her his arm and leads her out.*]

Pantomime Scene

This should be played as if the actress were actually alone. She turns her back on the audience when she feels like it; she does not look out into the auditorium; she does not rush through the scene as if afraid the audience will grow impatient.

CHRISTINE ***alone. In the distance the sound of the violins playing the schottische.*** CHRISTINE, ***humming in time with the music, cleans up after*** JEAN, ***washes the dishes, dries them, and puts them away in a cupboard. Then she takes off her apron, takes a little mir-***

5. In Swedish folklore, Midsummer Eve is a time of fortune-telling.

6. Literally, "Scottish" (German), a country dance similar to the polka.

ror from one of the table drawers, and leans it against the jar of lilacs on the table. She lights a tallow candle, heats a curling iron, and curls the bangs on her forehead. Then she goes to the doorway and stands listening to the music. She comes back to the table and finds the handkerchief that MISS JULIE *left behind. She smells it, spreads it out, and then, as if lost in thought, stretches it, smooths it out, and folds it in four.*

[JEAN *enters alone.*]

JEAN Wild! I told you she was wild! You should have seen the way she was dancing. Everyone was peeking at her from behind the doors and laughing at her. What's the matter with her, Christine?

CHRISTINE You might know it's her monthlies, Jean. She always acts peculiar then. . . . Well, are you going to dance with me?

JEAN You're not mad at me because I broke my promise?

CHRISTINE Of course not. Not for a little thing like that, you know that. I know my place.

JEAN [*grabs her around the waist*] You're a sensible girl, Christine. You're going to make somebody a good wife—

[MISS JULIE, *coming in, sees them together. She is unpleasantly surprised.*]

MISS JULIE [*with forced gaiety*] Well, aren't you the gallant beau—running away from your partner!

JEAN On the contrary, Miss Julie. As you can see, I've hurried back to the partner I deserted.

MISS JULIE [*changing tack*] You know, you're the best dancer I've met. —Why are you wearing livery on a holiday? Take it off at once.

JEAN I'd have to ask you to leave for a minute. My black coat is hanging right here—[*He moves to the right and points.*]

MISS JULIE You're not embarrassed because I'm here, are you? Just to change your coat? Go in your room and come right back again. Or else stay here and I'll turn my back.

JEAN If you'll excuse me, Miss Julie.

[*He goes off to the right. His arm can be seen as he changes his coat.*]

MISS JULIE [*to* CHRISTINE] Tell me something, Christine. Is Jean your fiancé? He acts so familiar with you.

CHRISTINE Fiancé? I suppose so. At least we say we are.

MISS JULIE What do you mean?

CHRISTINE Well, Miss Julie, you have had fiancés yourself, and you know—

MISS JULIE But we were properly engaged—!

CHRISTINE I know, but did anything come of it?

[JEAN *comes back, wearing a black cutaway coat and derby.*]

MISS JULIE *Très gentil, monsieur Jean! Très gentil!*

JEAN *Vous voulez plaisanter, madame.*

MISS JULIE *Et vous voulez parler français!*[7] Where did you learn to speak French?

JEAN In Switzerland. I was *sommelier*[8] in one of the biggest hotels in Lucerne.

MISS JULIE My! but you look quite the gentleman in that coat! *Charmant!*[9]

[*She sits down at the table.*]

7. "Very nice, Mister Jean! Very nice!" "You are trying to flatter me, madam." "And you are trying to speak French!" (French).

8. Wine steward.

9. Charming (French).

JEAN Flatterer!

MISS JULIE [*stiffening*] Who said I was flattering you?

JEAN My natural modesty would not allow me to presume that you were paying sincere compliments to someone like me, and therefore I could only assume that you were exaggerating, which, in this case, means flattering me.

MISS JULIE You certainly have a way with words. Where did you learn to talk like that? Seeing plays?

JEAN And other places. You don't think I stayed in the house for six years when I was a valet in Stockholm, do you?

MISS JULIE I thought you were born in this district. Weren't you?

JEAN My father worked as a farmhand on the district attorney's estate, next door to yours. I used to see you when you were little. Of course you didn't notice me.

MISS JULIE Did you really?

JEAN Yes. I remember one time in particular—. But I can't tell you about that!

MISS JULIE Of course you can. . . . Oh, come on. Just this once—for me.

JEAN No. No, I really couldn't. Not now. Some other time maybe.

MISS JULIE Some other time? That means never. What's the harm in telling me now?

JEAN There's no harm. I just don't feel like it. —Look at her.

[*He nods at* CHRISTINE, *who has fallen asleep in a chair by the stove.*]

MISS JULIE Won't she make somebody a pretty wife! I'll bet she snores, too.

JEAN No, she doesn't. But she talks in her sleep.

MISS JULIE [*archly*] Now how could you know she talks in her sleep?

JEAN [*coolly*] I've heard her . . .

[*Pause. They look at each other.*]

MISS JULIE Why don't you sit down?

JEAN I wouldn't take the liberty in your presence.

MISS JULIE Not even if I ordered you?

JEAN Of course I'd obey.

MISS JULIE Well then: sit down. —Wait a minute. Could you get me something to drink?

JEAN I don't know what there is in the icebox. Only beer, I suppose.

MISS JULIE Only beer?! I have simple tastes. I prefer beer to wine.

[JEAN *takes a bottle of beer from the icebox and opens it. He looks in the cupboard for a glass and a plate, and serves her.*]

JEAN At your service, *mademoiselle.*[1]

MISS JULIE Thank you. What about you?

JEAN I'm not much of a beer-drinker, thank you, but if it's your wish—

MISS JULIE My wish! I should think a gentleman would want to keep his lady company.

JEAN A point well taken! [*He opens another bottle and takes a glass.*]

MISS JULIE Now drink a toast to me!

[JEAN *hesitates.*]

You're not shy, are you? A big, strong man like you?

[*Playfully,* JEAN *kneels and raises his glass in mock gallantry.*]

1. Miss (French).

JEAN To my lady's health!

MISS JULIE Bravo! Now you have to kiss my shoe, too. Then you will have hit it off perfectly.

[**JEAN** *hesitates, then boldly grasps her foot and touches it lightly with his lips.*]

Superb! You should have been an actor.

JEAN [*rising*] This has got to stop, Miss Julie! Someone might come in and see us.

MISS JULIE So what?

JEAN People would talk, that's what! If you knew how their tongues were wagging out there just a few minutes ago!

MISS JULIE What did they say? Tell me. Sit down and tell me.

JEAN I don't want to hurt your feelings. . . . They used expressions that—that hinted at certain—you know what I mean. You're not a child. And when they see a woman drinking, alone with a man—and a servant at that—in the middle of the night—well . . .

MISS JULIE Well what?! Besides, we're not alone. Christine is here.

JEAN Sleeping!

MISS JULIE I'll wake her up. [*She goes over to* **CHRISTINE**.] Christine! Are you asleep? [**CHRISTINE** *babbles in her sleep.*] Christine! —My, how sound she sleeps!

CHRISTINE [*talking in her sleep*] Count's boots are brushed . . . put on the coffee . . . right away, right away, right . . . mm—mm . . . poofff . . .

[**MISS JULIE** *shakes* **CHRISTINE**.]

MISS JULIE Wake up, will you!

JEAN [*sternly*] Let her alone! Let her sleep!

MISS JULIE [*sharply*] What?

JEAN She's been standing over the stove all day. She's worn out when night comes. Anyone asleep is entitled to some consideration.

MISS JULIE [*changing her tone*] That's a very kind thought. It does you credit, Jean. You're right, of course. [*She offers* **JEAN** *her hand.*] Now come on out and pick some lilacs for me.

[*During the following,* **CHRISTINE** *wakes up and, drunk with sleep, shuffles off to the right to go to bed. A polka can be heard in the distance.*]

JEAN With you, Miss Julie?

MISS JULIE Yes, with me.

JEAN That's no good. Absolutely not.

MISS JULIE I don't know what you're thinking. Aren't you letting your imagination run away with you?

JEAN No. Other people are.

MISS JULIE How? Imagining that I'm—*verliebt*[2] with a servant?

JEAN I'm not conceited, but it's been known to happen. And to these people nothing's sacred.

MISS JULIE "These people!" Why, I do believe you're an aristocrat!

JEAN Yes, I am.

MISS JULIE I'm climbing down—

JEAN Don't climb down, Miss Julie! Take my advice. No one will believe that you climbed down deliberately. They'll say you fell.

2. In love (German).

MISS JULIE I have a higher opinion of these people than you do. Let's see who's right! Come on! [*She gives him a long, steady look.*]

JEAN You know, you're very strange.

MISS JULIE Perhaps. But then so are you. . . . Besides, everything is strange. Life, people, everything. It's all scum, drifting and drifting on the water until it sinks—drowns. There's a dream I have every now and then. It's coming back to me now. I'm sitting on top of a pillar. I've climbed up it somehow and I don't know how to get back down. When I look down I get dizzy. I have to get down but I don't have the courage to jump. I can't hold on much longer and I want to fall; but I don't fall. I know I won't have any peace until I get down; no rest until I get down, down on the ground. And if I ever got down on the ground, I'd want to go farther down, right down into the earth. . . . Have you ever felt anything like that?

JEAN Never! I used to dream that I'm lying under a tall tree in a dark woods. I want to get up, up to the very top, to look out over the bright landscape with the sun shining on it, to rob the bird's nest up there with the golden eggs in it. And I climb and I climb, but the trunk is so thick, and so smooth, and it's such a long way to that first branch. But I know that if I could just reach that first branch, I'd go right to the top as if on a ladder. I've never reached it yet, but someday I will—even if only in my dreams.

MISS JULIE Here I am talking about dreams with you. Come out with me. Only into the park a way. [*She offers him her arm, and they start to go.*]

JEAN Let's sleep on nine midsummer flowers, Miss Julie, and then our dreams will come true![3]

[MISS JULIE *and* JEAN *suddenly turn around in the doorway.* JEAN *is holding his hand over one eye.*]

MISS JULIE You've caught something in your eye. Let me see.

JEAN It's nothing. Just a bit of dust. It'll go away.

MISS JULIE The sleeve of my dress must have grazed your eye. Sit down and I'll help you. [*She takes him by the arm and sits him down. She takes his head and leans it back. With the corner of her handkerchief she tries to get out the bit of dust.*] Now sit still, absolutely still. [*She slaps his hand.*] Do as you're told. Why, I believe you're trembling—a big, strong man like you. [*She feels his biceps.*] With such big arms!

JEAN [*warningly*] Miss Julie!

MISS JULIE Yes, *Monsieur Jean?*

JEAN *Attention! Je ne suis qu'un homme!*[4]

MISS JULIE Sit still, I tell you! . . . There now! It's out. Kiss my hand and thank me!

JEAN [*rising to his feet.*] Listen to me, Miss Julie—Christine has gone to bed! —Listen to me, I tell you!

MISS JULIE Kiss my hand first!

JEAN Listen to me!

MISS JULIE Kiss my hand first!

JEAN All right. But you'll have no one to blame but yourself.

3. A girl would pick in silence on Midsummer Eve nine different sorts of flowers, make a bouquet of them, and place them under her pillow. The man who appeared in her dreams would be the man she would marry [translator's note].

4. Be careful! I am just a man! (French).

MISS JULIE For what?

JEAN For what! Are you twenty-five years old and still a child? Don't you know it's dangerous to play with fire?

MISS JULIE Not for me, I'm insured!

JEAN [*boldly*] Oh, no, you're not! And even if you are, there's inflammable stuff next door.

MISS JULIE Meaning you?

JEAN Yes. Not just because it's me, but because I'm young and—

MISS JULIE And irresistibly handsome? What incredible conceit! A Don Juan, maybe! Or a Joseph![5] Yes, bless my soul, that's it: you're a Joseph!

JEAN You think so?

MISS JULIE I'm almost afraid so!

[JEAN *boldly steps up to her, grabs her around the waist, tries to kiss her. She slaps his face.*]

None of that!

JEAN More games? Or are you serious?

MISS JULIE I'm serious.

JEAN Then you must have been serious a moment ago, too! You take your games too seriously; that's dangerous. Well, I'm tired of your games, and if you'll excuse me, I'll return to my work. [*Takes up the boots and starts to brush them.*] The count will be wanting his boots on time, and it's long past midnight.

MISS JULIE Put those boots down.

JEAN No! This is my job. It's what I'm here for. I never undertook to be your playmate. That's something I could never be. I consider myself too good for that.

MISS JULIE You are proud.

JEAN In some ways. Not in others.

MISS JULIE Have you ever been in love?

JEAN We don't use that word around here. But I've hankered after some girls, if that's what you mean. . . . I even got sick once because I couldn't have the one I wanted—really sick, like the princes in the Arabian Nights[6]—who couldn't eat or drink for love.

MISS JULIE Who was she?

[JEAN *does not reply.*]

Who was the girl?

JEAN You can't get that out of me.

MISS JULIE Even if I ask you as an equal—ask you—as a friend? . . . Who was she?

JEAN You.

MISS JULIE [*sitting down*] How—amusing . . .

JEAN Yes, maybe so. Ridiculous. . . . That's why I didn't want to tell you about it before. Want to hear the whole story? . . . Have you any idea what

5. In the Bible, a son of Jacob: after Joseph was sold into slavery by his brothers, his good looks led his master's wife to make sexual advances toward him; when he refused her, she falsely accused him of rape (Genesis 39.6–18). *Don Juan:* the legendary Spanish seducer of women, whose story is told in a number of European dramas and in Mozart's opera *Don Giovanni* (1787).

6. *The Thousand and One Nights,* a collection of ancient tales in Arabic, arranged in its present form in the 15th century.

you and your people look like from down below? Of course not. Like hawks or eagles, that's what: you hardly ever see their backs because they're always soaring so high up. I lived with seven brothers and sisters—and a pig—out on the wasteland where there wasn't even a tree growing. But from my window I could see the wall of the count's garden with the apple trees sticking up over it. That was the Garden of Eden for me, and there were many angry angels with flaming swords standing guard over it.[7] But in spite of them, I and the other boys found a way to the Tree of Life. . . . How contemptible, that's what you're thinking.

MISS JULIE For stealing apples? All boys do that.

JEAN That's what you say now. All the same, you think me contemptible. Never mind. One day I went with my mother into this paradise to weed the onion beds. Next to the vegetable garden stood a Turkish pavilion, shaded by jasmine and hung all over with honeysuckle. I couldn't imagine what it was used for; I only knew I had never seen such a beautiful building. People went in, and came out again. And then one day the door was left open. I sneaked in. The walls were covered with portraits of kings and emperors, and the windows had red curtains with tassels on them. —Recognize it? Yes, the count's private privy. . . . I— [*He breaks off a lilac and holds it under* MISS JULIE*'s nose.*] I had never been inside a castle, never seen anything besides the church. This was more beautiful. And no matter what I tried to think about, my thoughts always came back—to that little pavilion. And little by little there arose in me a desire to experience just for once the whole pleasure of—. *Enfin,*[8] I sneaked in, looked about, and marveled. And just then I heard someone coming! There was only one way out—for the upper-class people. But for me there was one more—a lower one.[9] And I had no other choice but to take it. [MISS JULIE, *who has taken the lilac from* JEAN, *lets it fall to the table.*] Then I began to run like mad, plunging through the raspberry bushes, plowing through the strawberry patches, and came up on the rose terrace. And there I caught sight of a pink dress and a pair of white stockings. You! I crawled under—well, you can imagine what it was like—under thistles that pricked me and wet dirt that stank to high heaven. And all the while I could see you walking among the roses. I said to myself, "If it's true that a thief can enter heaven and be with the angels,[1] isn't it strange that a poor man's child here on God's green earth can't enter the count's park and play with the count's daughter."

MISS JULIE [*sentimentally*] Do you think all poor children have felt that way?

JEAN [*hesitatingly at first, then with mounting conviction*] If all poor ch—? Yes—yes, naturally. Of course!

MISS JULIE It must be terrible to be poor.

JEAN [*with exaggerated intensity*] Oh, Miss Julie! You don't know! A dog can lie on the sofa with its mistress; a horse can have its nose stroked by the hand of a countess; but a servant—! [*Changing his tone*] Of course, now and then you meet somebody with guts enough to work his way up in the world, but how often? —Anyway, you know what I did afterward? I threw myself into the millstream with all my clothes on. Got fished out and spanked. But the following Sunday, when Pa and everybody else in the house went to visit

7. See Genesis 3.24.

8. Finally (French).

9. That is, through the pit or trench under the outhouse.

1. According to 1 Corinthians 6.9–10, the thief cannot enter heaven.

Grandma, I arranged things so I'd be left behind. Then I washed myself all over with soap and warm water, put on my best clothes, and went off to church—just to see you there once more. I saw you, and then I went home determined to die. But I wanted to die beautifully and comfortably, without pain. I remembered some stories I had heard about how fatal it was to sleep under an elderberry bush. And we had a big one that had just blossomed out. I stripped it of every leaf and blossom it had and made a bed of them in a bin of oats. Have you ever noticed how smooth oats are? As smooth to the touch as human skin. . . . So I pulled the lid of the bin shut and closed my eyes. Fell asleep. And when they woke me I was really very sick. However, I didn't die, as you can see. —What was I trying to prove? I don't know. There was no hope of winning you. It was just that you were a symbol of the absolute hopelessness of my ever getting out of the class I was born in.

MISS JULIE You know, you have a real gift for telling stories. Did you go to school?

JEAN A little. But I've read a lot of novels and gone to the theater. And I've also listened to educated people talk. That way I learned the most.

MISS JULIE You mean to tell me you stand around listening to what we're saying!

JEAN Certainly! And I've heard an awful lot, I can tell you—sitting on the coachman's seat or rowing the boat. One time I heard you and a girlfriend talking—

MISS JULIE Really? . . . And just what did you hear?

JEAN Well, now, I don't know if I can repeat it. I can tell you I was a little amazed. I couldn't imagine where you had learned such words. Maybe at bottom there isn't such a big difference as you might think, between people and people.

MISS JULIE How vulgar! At least people in my class don't behave like you when we're engaged.

JEAN [*looking her in the eye*] Are you sure? —Come on now, it's no use playing the innocent with me.

MISS JULIE He was a beast. The man I offered my love was a beast.

JEAN That's what you all say—afterward.

MISS JULIE All?

JEAN I'd say so. I've heard the same expression used several times before in similar circumstances.

MISS JULIE What kind of circumstances?

JEAN The kind we're talking about. I remember the last time I—

MISS JULIE [*rising*] That's enough! I don't want to hear any more.

JEAN How strange! Neither did she! . . . Well, now if you'll excuse me, I'll go to bed.

MISS JULIE [*softly*] Go to bed on Midsummer Eve?

JEAN That's right. Dancing with that crowd up there really doesn't amuse me.

MISS JULIE Jean, get the key to the boathouse and row me out on the lake. I want to see the sun come up.

JEAN Do you think that's wise?

MISS JULIE You sound as if you were worried about your reputation.

JEAN Why not? I don't particularly care to be made ridiculous, or to be kicked out without a recommendation just when I'm trying to establish myself. Besides, I have a certain obligation to Christine.

MISS JULIE Oh, I see. It's Christine now.

JEAN Yes, but I'm thinking of you, too. Take my advice, Miss Julie. Go up to your room.

MISS JULIE When did you start giving me orders?

JEAN Just this once. For your own sake! Please! It's very late. You're so tired, you're drunk; you don't know what you're doing. Go to bed, Miss Julie. —Besides, if my ears aren't deceiving me, they're coming this way, looking for me. If they find us here together, you're done for!

THE CHORUS [*is heard coming nearer, singing*]

Said Jill to Jack, "Soil needs a tilling."
Tri-di-ri-di-ralla, tri-di-ri-di-ra.
Said Jack to Jill, "Time's a-spilling."
Tri-di-ri-di-ralla-la.
Said Jill to Jack, "Gold's a-hoarding."
Tri-di-ri-di-ralla, tri-di-ri-di-ra.
Said Jack to Jill, "Tell not my lording."
Tri-di-ri-di-ralla-la.
Said Jill to Jack, "Hair is for plaiting."
Tri-di-ri-di-ralla, tri-di-ri-di-ra.
"But Jill for Jack is not waiting."
Tri-di-ri-di-ralla-la![2]

MISS JULIE I know these people. I love them just as they love me. Let them come. You'll see.

JEAN Oh, no, Miss Julie, they don't love you! They take the food you give them, but they spit on it as soon as your back is turned. Believe me! Just listen to them. Listen to what they're singing. —No, you'd better not listen.

MISS JULIE [*listening*] What are they singing?

JEAN A nasty song—about you and me!

MISS JULIE How disgusting! Oh, what cowardly, sneaking—

JEAN That's what the mob always is—cowards! You can't fight them; you can only run away.

MISS JULIE Run away? Where? There's no way out of here. And we can't go in to Christine.

JEAN What about my room? What do you say? Rules don't count in a situation like this. You can trust me. —You said, let's be friends. Remember? Well, I'm your friend—your true, devoted, respectful friend.

MISS JULIE But suppose—suppose they looked for you there?

JEAN I'll bolt the door. If they try to break it down, I'll shoot. Come, Miss Julie! [*On his knees*] Please, Miss Julie!

MISS JULIE [*meaningfully*] You promise me that you won't—

JEAN I swear to you!

[MISS JULIE *goes out quickly to the right. Jean follows her impetuously.*]

The Ballet

The country people enter in festive costumes, with flowers in their hats. The fiddler is in the lead. A keg of small beer and a little keg of liquor, decorated with greenery, are set up on the table. Glasses are brought out. They all drink. Then they form a circle and sing

2. A peasants' folk song.

"Said Jill to Jack," dancing the round dance as they sing. At the end of the dance, they all leave singing.

MISS JULIE *comes in alone; looks at the devastated kitchen; clasps her hands together; then takes out a powder puff and powders her face.* JEAN *enters. He is in high spirits.*

JEAN You see! You heard them, didn't you? You've got to admit it's impossible to stay here.

MISS JULIE No, I don't. But even if I did, what could we do?

JEAN Go away, travel, get away from here!

MISS JULIE Travel? Yes—but where?

JEAN Switzerland, the Italian lakes. You've never been there?

MISS JULIE No. Is it beautiful?

JEAN Eternal summer, oranges, laurel trees, ah . . . !

MISS JULIE What do we do when we get there?

JEAN I'll set up a hotel—a first-class hotel with a first-class clientele.

MISS JULIE Hotel?

JEAN I tell you that's the life! Always new faces, new languages. Not a minute to think about yourself or worry about your nerves. No looking for something to do. The work keeps you busy. Day and night the bells ring, the trains whistle, the buses come and go. And all the while the money comes rolling in. I tell you it's the life!

MISS JULIE Yes, that's the life. But what about me?

JEAN The mistress of the whole place, the star of the establishment! With your looks—and your personality—it can't fail. It's perfect! You'll sit in the office like a queen, setting your slaves in motion by pressing an electric button. The guests will file before your throne and timidly lay their treasures on your table. You can't imagine how people tremble when you shove a bill in their face! I'll salt the bills and you'll sugar them with your prettiest smile. Come on, let's get away from here—[*He takes a timetable from his pocket.*]—right away—the next train! We'll be in Malmö at six-thirty, Hamburg eight-forty in the morning; Frankfurt to Basel in one day, and to Como[3] by way of the Gotthard tunnel in—let me see—three days! Three days!

MISS JULIE You make it sound so wonderful. But, Jean, you have to give me strength. Tell me you love me. Come and put your arms around me.

JEAN [*hesitates*] I want to . . . but I don't dare. Not anymore, not in this house. I do love you—without a shadow of a doubt. How can you doubt that, Miss Julie?

MISS JULIE [*shyly, very becomingly*] You don't have to be formal with me, Jean. You can call me Julie. There aren't any barriers between us now. Call me Julie.

JEAN [*agonized*] I can't! There are still barriers between us, Miss Julie, as long as we stay in this house! There's the past, there's the count. I've never met anyone I feel so much respect for. I've only got to see his gloves lying on a table and I shrivel up. I only have to hear that bell ring and I shy like a frightened horse. I only have to look at his boots standing there so stiff and proud and I feel my spine bending. [*He kicks the boots.*] Superstitions, prejudices that they've drilled into us since we were children! But they can be forgotten just as easily! Just get us to another country where they have a republic!

3. A city on the southwest end of Lake Como, in northern Italy; Jean outlines the journey there from Sweden through Germany and Switzerland.

They'll crawl on their hands and knees when they see my uniform. On their hands and knees, I tell you! But not me! Oh, no. I'm not made for crawling. I've got guts, backbone. And once I grab that first branch, you just watch me climb. I may be a valet now, but next year I'll be owning property; in ten years, I'll be living off my investments. Then I'll go to Rumania, get myself some decorations, and maybe—notice I only say maybe—end up as a count!

MISS JULIE How wonderful, wonderful.

JEAN Listen, in Rumania you can buy titles. You'll be a countess after all. My countess.

MISS JULIE But I'm not interested in that. I'm leaving all that behind. Tell me you love me, Jean, or else—or else what difference does it make what I am?

JEAN I'll tell you a thousand times—but later! Not now. And not here. Above all, let's keep our feelings out of this or we'll make a mess of everything. We have to look at this thing calmly and coolly, like sensible people. [*He takes out a cigar, clips the end, and lights it.*] Now you sit there and I'll sit here, and we'll talk as if nothing had happened.

MISS JULIE [*in anguish*] My God, what are you? Don't you have any feelings?

JEAN Feelings? Nobody's got more feelings than I have. But I've learned to control them.

MISS JULIE A few minutes ago you were kissing my shoe—and now—!

JEAN [*harshly*] That was a few minutes ago. We've got other things to think about now!

MISS JULIE Don't speak to me like that, Jean!

JEAN I'm just trying to be sensible. We've been stupid once; let's not be stupid again. Your father might be back at any moment, and we've got to decide our future before then. —Now what do you think about my plans? Do you approve or don't you?

MISS JULIE I don't see anything wrong with them. Except one thing. For a big undertaking like that, you'd need a lot of capital. Have you got it?

JEAN [*chewing on his cigar*] Have I got it? Of course I have. I've got my knowledge of the business, my vast experience, my familiarity with languages. That's capital that counts for something, let me tell you.

MISS JULIE You can't even buy the railway tickets with it.

JEAN That's true. That's why I need a backer—someone to put up the money.

MISS JULIE Where can you find him on a moment's notice?

JEAN You'll find him—if you want to be my partner.

MISS JULIE I can't. And I don't have a penny to my name.

[*Pause.*]

JEAN Then you can forget the whole thing.

MISS JULIE Forget—?

JEAN And things will stay just the way they are.

MISS JULIE Do you think I'm going to live under the same roof with you as your mistress? Do you think I'm going to have people sneering at me behind my back? How do you think I'll ever be able to look my father in the face after this? No, no! Take me away from here, Jean—the shame, the humiliation. . . . What have I done? Oh, my God, my God! What have I done! [*She bursts into tears.*]

JEAN Now don't start singing that tune. It won't work. What have you done that's so awful? You're not the first.

MISS JULIE [*crying hysterically*] Now you think me contemptible—I'm falling, falling!

JEAN Fall down to me, and I'll lift you up again!

MISS JULIE What awful hold did you have over me? What drove me to you? The weak to the strong? The falling to the rising! Or maybe it was love? Love? This? You don't know what love is!

JEAN Want to bet? Did you think I was a virgin?

MISS JULIE You're coarse—vulgar! The things you say, the things you think!

JEAN That's the way I was brought up. It's the way I am! Now don't get hysterical. And don't play the fine lady with me. We're eating off the same platter now. . . . That's better. Come over here and be a good girl and I'll treat you to something special. [*He opens the table drawer and takes out the wine bottle. He pours the wine into two used glasses.*]

MISS JULIE Where did you get that wine?

JEAN From the wine cellar.

MISS JULIE My father's burgundy!

JEAN Should be good enough for his son-in-law.

MISS JULIE I was drinking beer and you—!

JEAN Shows I have better taste than you.

MISS JULIE Thief!

JEAN You going to squeal on me?

MISS JULIE Oh, God! Partner in crime with a petty house thief! I must have been drunk; I must have been walking in my sleep. Midsummer Night! Night of innocent games—

JEAN Yes, very innocent!

MISS JULIE [*pacing up and down*] Is there anyone here on earth as miserable as I am?

JEAN Why be miserable? Look at the conquest you've made! Think of poor Christine in there. Don't you think she's got any feelings?

MISS JULIE I thought so a while ago; I don't now. A servant's a servant—

JEAN And a whore's a whore!

MISS JULIE [*falls to her knees and clasps her hands together*] Oh, God in heaven, put an end to my worthless life! Lift me out of this awful filth I'm sinking in! Save me! Save me!

JEAN I feel sorry for you, I have to admit it. When I was lying in the onion beds, looking up at you on the rose terrace, I—I'm telling you the truth now—I had the same dirty thoughts that all boys have.

MISS JULIE And you said you wanted to die for me!

JEAN In the oat bin? That was only a story.

MISS JULIE A lie, you mean.

JEAN [*getting sleepy*] Practically. I think I read it in a paper about a chimney sweep who curled up in a wood-bin with some lilacs because they were going to arrest him for nonsupport of his child.

MISS JULIE Now I see you as you really are.

JEAN What did you expect me to do? It's always the fancy talk that gets the women.

MISS JULIE You dog!

JEAN You bitch!

MISS JULIE Well, now you've seen the eagle's back—

JEAN Wasn't exactly its back—!

MISS JULIE I was going to be the window dressing for your hotel—!

JEAN And I the hotel—!

MISS JULIE Sitting at the desk, attracting your customers, padding your bills—!

JEAN I could manage that myself—!

MISS JULIE How can a human soul be so dirty and filthy?

JEAN Then why don't you clean it up?

MISS JULIE You lackey! You shoeshine boy! Stand up when I talk to you!

JEAN You lackey lover! You bootblack's tramp! Shut your mouth and get out of here! Who do you think you are telling me I'm coarse? I've never seen anybody in my class behave as crudely as you did tonight. Have you ever seen any of the girls around here grab at a man like you did? Do you think any of the girls of my class would throw themselves at a man like that? I've never seen the like of it except in animals and prostitutes!

MISS JULIE [*crushed*] That's right! Hit me! Walk all over me! It's all I deserve. I'm rotten. But help me! Help me to get out of this—if there is any way out for me!

JEAN [*less harsh*] I'd be doing myself an injustice if I didn't admit that part of the credit for this seduction belongs to me. But do you think a person in my position would have dared to look twice at you if you hadn't asked for it? I'm still amazed—

MISS JULIE And still proud.

JEAN Why not? But I've got to confess the victory was a little too easy to give me any real thrill.

MISS JULIE Go on, hit me again!

JEAN [*standing up*] No. . . . I'm sorry I said that. I never hit a person who's down, especially a woman. I can't deny that, in one way, it was good to find out that what I saw glittering up above was only fool's gold, to see that the eagle's back was as gray as its belly, that the smooth cheek was just powder, and that there could be dirt under the manicured nails, that the handkerchief was soiled even though it smelled of perfume. But, in another way, it hurts to find that everything I was striving for wasn't very high above me after all, wasn't even real. It hurts me to see you sink far lower than your own cook. Hurts, like seeing the last flowers cut to pieces by the autumn rains and turned to muck.

MISS JULIE You talk as if you already stood high above me.

JEAN Well, don't I? Don't forget I could make you a countess but you can never make me a count.

MISS JULIE I have a father for a count. You can never have that!

JEAN True. But I might father my own counts—that is, if—

MISS JULIE You're a thief! I'm not!

JEAN There are worse things than being a thief. A lot worse. And besides, when I take a position in a house, I consider myself a member of the family—in a way, like a child in the house. It's no crime for a child to steal a few ripe cherries when they're falling off the trees, is it? [*He begins to feel passionate again.*] Miss Julie, you're a beautiful woman, much too good for the likes of me. You got carried away by your emotions and now you want to cover up your mistake by telling yourself that you love me. You don't love me. Maybe you were attracted by my looks—in which case your kind of love is no better than mine. But I could never be satisfied to be just an animal for you, and I could never make you love me.

MISS JULIE How do you know that for sure?

JEAN You mean there's a chance? I could love you, there's no doubt about that. You're beautiful, you're refined—[*He goes up to her and takes her hand.*]—educated, lovable when you want to be, and once you set a man's heart on fire, I'll bet it burns forever. [*He puts his arm around her waist.*] You're like hot wine with strong spices. One of your kisses is enough to—

[*He attempts to lead her out, but she rather reluctantly breaks away from him.*]

MISS JULIE Let me go. You don't get me that way.

JEAN Then how? Not by petting you and not with pretty words, not by planning for the future, not by saving you from humiliation! Then how, tell me how?

MISS JULIE How? How? I don't know how! I don't know at all! —I hate you like I hate rats, but I can't get away from you.

JEAN Then come away with me!

MISS JULIE [*pulling herself together*] Away? Yes, we'll go away! —But I'm so tired. Pour me a glass of wine, will you?

[JEAN *pours the wine,* MISS JULIE *looks at her watch.*]

Let's talk first. We still have a little time. [*She empties the glass of wine and holds it out for more.*]

JEAN Don't overdo it. You'll get drunk.

MISS JULIE What difference does it make?

JEAN What difference? It looks cheap. —What did you want to say to me?

MISS JULIE We're going to run away together, right? But we'll talk first—that is, I'll talk. So far you've done all the talking. You've told me your life, now I'll tell you mine. That way we'll know each other through and through before we become . . . traveling companions.

JEAN Wait a minute. Are you sure you won't regret this afterward—surrendering your secrets to me?

MISS JULIE I thought you were my friend.

JEAN I am—sometimes. Just don't count on it.

MISS JULIE You don't mean that. Anyway, everybody knows my secrets. —My mother's parents were very ordinary people, just commoners. She was brought up, according to the theories of her time, to believe in equality, the independence of women, and all that. And she had a strong aversion to marriage. When my father proposed to her, she swore she would never become his wife but that she might possibly consent to become his mistress. So he told her he didn't want to see the woman he loved enjoy less respect than he did. But she said she didn't care what the world thought—and he, believing that he couldn't live without her, accepted her conditions. That did it. From then on he was cut off from his old circle of friends and left without anything to do in the house, which couldn't have kept him occupied anyway. Then I came into the world—against my mother's wishes, as far as I can make out. My mother decided to bring me up as a nature child. And on top of that I had to learn everything a boy learns, so I could be living proof that women were just as good as men. I had to wear boy's clothes, learn to handle horses—but not to milk the cows! Girls did that! I was made to groom the horses and harness them, and learn farming and go hunting—I even had to learn how to slaughter the animals. It was disgusting. Awful! And on the estate all the men were set to doing women's chores, and the women to doing men's work—with the result that the whole place fell to pieces, and we became the local laughing-stock. Finally, my father must have come out of his trance. He rebelled, and everything was changed according to his wishes. They got married—very quietly. Then my mother got sick. I don't know what kind of sickness it was, but she often had convulsions, and she would hide herself in the attic or in the garden, and sometimes she would stay out all night. Then there occurred that big fire you've heard about. The house, the stables, the cowsheds, all burned down—and under very peculiar circumstances that led one to suspect arson. You see, the accident occurred the day after the insurance expired, and the premiums on the new policy, which my father had sent in, were delayed through the messenger's carelessness, and didn't arrive in time. [*She refills her glass and drinks.*]

JEAN You've had enough.

MISS JULIE Who cares! —We were left without a penny to our name. We had to sleep in the carriages. My father didn't know where to turn for money to rebuild the house. Then Mother suggested to him that he might try to borrow money from an old friend of hers, who owned a brick factory not far from here. Father took out a loan, but there wasn't any interest charged, which surprised him. So the place was rebuilt. [*She drinks some more.*] Do you know who set fire to the place?

JEAN Your honorable mother!

MISS JULIE Do you know who the brick manufacturer was?

JEAN Your mother's lover?

MISS JULIE Do you know whose money it was?

JEAN Let me think a minute. . . . No, I give up.

MISS JULIE It was my mother's!

JEAN The count's, you mean. Or was there a marriage settlement?[4]

MISS JULIE There wasn't a settlement. My mother had a little money of her own which she didn't want under my father's control, so she invested it with her—friend.

JEAN Who pinched it!

MISS JULIE Right! He kept it for himself. Well, my father found out what happened. But he couldn't go to court, couldn't pay his wife's lover, couldn't prove that it was his wife's money. That was how my mother got her revenge because he had taken control of the house. He was on the verge of shooting himself. There was even a rumor that he tried and failed. But somehow he took a new lease on life and he forced my mother to pay for her mistakes. Can you imagine what those five years were like for me? I loved my father, but I took my mother's side because I didn't know the whole story. She had taught me to hate all men—I'm sure you've heard how she hated men—and I swore to her that I'd never be slave to any man.

JEAN You got engaged to the attorney, didn't you?

MISS JULIE Only to make him my slave.

JEAN I guess he didn't go for that, did he?

MISS JULIE Oh, he wanted to well enough. I didn't give him the chance. I got bored with him.

JEAN Yes, so I noticed—in the stable yard.

4. An agreement, made before a marriage, to transfer some property to the wife.

MISS JULIE What did you notice?

JEAN I saw how he —. [Still see it on your cheek.

MISS JULIE What!

JEAN The stripe on your cheek.][5] He broke it off.

MISS JULIE It's a lie! I broke it off! Did he tell you that? He's beneath contempt!

JEAN Come on now, as bad as that? So you hate men, hm?

MISS JULIE Yes, I do. . . . Most of the time. But sometimes, when I can't help myself—oh . . . [*She shudders in disgust.*]

JEAN Then you hate me, too?

MISS JULIE You have no idea how much! I'd like to see you killed like an animal—

JEAN Like when you're caught having sex with an animal: you get two years at hard labor and the animal is killed. Right?

MISS JULIE Right.

JEAN But there's no one to catch us—and *no animal!*—So what are we going to do?

MISS JULIE Go away from here.

JEAN To torture ourselves to death?

MISS JULIE No. To enjoy ourselves for a day or two, or a week, for as long as we can—and then—to die —

JEAN Die? That's stupid! I've got a better idea: start a hotel!

MISS JULIE [*continuing without hearing* JEAN] —on the shores of Lake Como, where the sun is always shining, where the laurels bloom at Christmas, and the golden oranges glow on the trees.

JEAN Lake Como is a stinking wet hole, and the only oranges I saw there were on the fruit stands. But it's a good tourist spot with a lot of villas and cottages that are rented out to lovers. Now there's a profitable business. You know why? They rent the villa for the whole season, but they leave after three weeks.

MISS JULIE [*naively*] Why after only three weeks?

JEAN Because that's about as long as they can stand each other. Why else? But they still have to pay the rent. You see? Then you rent it out again to another couple, and so on. There's no shortage of love—even if it doesn't last very long.

MISS JULIE Then you don't want to die with me?

JEAN I don't want to die at all! I enjoy life too much. And moreover, I consider taking your own life a sin against the Providence that gave us life.

MISS JULIE You believe in God? You?

JEAN Yes, certainly I do! I go to church every other Sunday—. Honestly, I've had enough of this talk. I'm going to bed.

MISS JULIE Really? You think you're going to get off that easy? Don't you know that a man owes something to the woman he's dishonored?

JEAN [*takes out his purse and throws a silver coin on the table*] There you are. I don't want to owe anybody anything.

MISS JULIE [*pretending not to notice*] Do you know what the law says—?

JEAN Lucky for you the law says nothing about women who seduce men!

MISS JULIE [*as before*] What else can we do but go away from here, get married, and get divorced?

5. The passage in brackets was deleted in Strindberg's manuscript, probably by Strindberg himself [translator's note].

JEAN Suppose I refuse to enter into this *mésalliance?*[6]

MISS JULIE *Mésalliance?*

JEAN For me! I've got better ancestors than you. I don't have a female arsonist in my family.

MISS JULIE You can't prove that.

JEAN You can't prove the opposite—because we don't have any family records—except in the police files. But I've read the whole history of your family in that peerage book in the drawing room. Do you know who the founder of your family line was? A miller—who let his wife sleep with the king one night during the Danish war.[7] I don't have any ancestors like that. I don't have any ancestors at all! But I can become an ancestor myself.

MISS JULIE This is what I get for baring my heart and soul to someone too low to understand, for sacrificing the honor of my family—

JEAN Dishonor! —I warned you, remember? Drinking makes one talk, and talking's bad.

MISS JULIE Oh, how sorry I am! . . . If only it had never happened! . . . If only you at least loved me!

JEAN For the last time—what do you want me to do? Cry? Jump over your whip? Kiss you? Lure you to Lake Como for three weeks and then—? What am I supposed to do? What do you want? I've had more than I can take. This is what I get for involving myself with women. . . . Miss Julie, I can see that you're unhappy; I know that you're suffering; but I simply cannot understand you. My people don't behave like this. We don't hate each other. We make love for the fun of it, when we can get any time off from our work. But we don't have time for it all day and all night like you do. If you ask me, you're sick, Miss Julie. Your mother's mind was affected, you know. There are whole counties affected with pietism. That was your mother's trouble—pietism. It's spreading like the plague.

MISS JULIE You can be understanding, Jean. You're talking to me like a human being now.

JEAN Well, be human yourself. You spit on me, but you don't let me wipe it off—on you.

MISS JULIE Help me, Jean. Help me. Tell me what I should do, that's all—which way to go.

JEAN For Christ's sake, if only I knew myself!

MISS JULIE I've been crazy—I've been out of my mind—but does that mean there's no way out for me?

JEAN Stay here as if nothing had happened. Nobody knows anything.

MISS JULIE Impossible! Everybody who works here knows. Christine knows.

JEAN They don't know a thing. Anyhow they'd never believe it.

MISS JULIE [*slowly, significantly*] But . . . it might happen again.

JEAN That's true!

MISS JULIE And one time there might be . . . consequences.

JEAN [*stunned*] Consequences!! What on earth have I been thinking of! You're right. There's only one thing to do: get away from here! Immediately!

6. Literally, "misalliance" (French), an ill-advised marriage.
7. That is, the war begun by Denmark in 1657 that ended with the Treaty of Copenhagen (1660), which restored to Sweden its southern provinces.

I can't go with you—that would give the whole game away. You'll have to go by yourself. Somewhere—I don't care where!

MISS JULIE By myself? Where? —Oh, no, Jean, I can't. I can't!

JEAN You've got to! Before the count comes back. You know as well as I do what will happen if you stay here. After one mistake, you figure you might as well go on—the damage is already done. Then you get more and more careless until—finally you're exposed. I tell you, you've got to get out of the country. Afterward you can write to the count and tell him everything—leaving me out, of course. He'd never figure it was me. He wouldn't even let himself think it was me.

MISS JULIE I'll go—if you'll come with me!

JEAN Lady, are you out of your mind? "Miss Julie elopes with her footman." The day after tomorrow it would be in all the papers. The count would never live it down.

MISS JULIE I can't go away. I can't stay. Help me. I'm so tired, so awfully tired. . . . Tell me what to do. Order me. Start me going. I can't think anymore, can't move anymore . . .

JEAN Now do you realize how weak you all are? What gives you the right to go strutting around with your noses in the air as if you owned the world? All right, I'll give you your orders. Go up and get dressed. Get some traveling money. And come back down here.

MISS JULIE [*almost in a whisper*] Come up with me!

JEAN To your room? . . . You're going crazy again! [*He hesitates a moment.*] No! No! Go! Right now! [*He takes her hand and leads her out.*]

MISS JULIE [*as she is leaving*] Don't be so harsh, Jean.

JEAN Orders always sound harsh. You've never had to take them.

[JEAN, *left alone, heaves a sigh of relief and sits down at the table. He takes out a notebook and a pencil and begins to calculate, counting aloud now and then. The pantomime continues until* CHRISTINE *enters, dressed for church, and carrying* JEAN'*s white tie and shirtfront in her hand.*]

CHRISTINE Lord in Heaven, what a mess! What on earth have you been doing?

JEAN It was Miss Julie. She dragged the whole crowd in here. You must have been sleeping awfully sound if you didn't hear anything.

CHRISTINE I slept like a log.

JEAN You already dressed for church?

CHRISTINE Yes, indeed. Don't you remember you promised to go to communion with me today?

JEAN Oh, yes. Of course, I remember. I see you've brought my things. All right. Come on, put it on me. [*He sits down, and* CHRISTINE *starts to put the white tie and shirtfront on him. Pause.*]

JEAN [*yawning*] What's the lesson for today?

CHRISTINE The beheading of John the Baptist, what else? It's Midsummer. It's his feast day.

JEAN My God, that will go on forever. —Hey, you're choking me! . . . Oh, I'm so sleepy, so sleepy.

CHRISTINE What were you doing up all night? You look green in the face.

JEAN I've been sitting here talking with Miss Julie.

CHRISTINE That girl! She doesn't know how to behave herself!

[*Pause.*]

JEAN Tell me something, Christine . . .

CHRISTINE Well, what?

JEAN Isn't it strange when you think about it? Her, I mean.

CHRISTINE What's so strange?

JEAN Everything!

[*Pause.* CHRISTINE *looks at the half-empty glasses on the table.*]

CHRISTINE Have you been drinking with her?

JEAN Yes!

CHRISTINE Shame on you! —Look me in the eyes! You haven't . . . ?

JEAN Yes!

CHRISTINE Is it possible? Is it really possible?

JEAN [*thinking about it*] Yes. It is.

CHRISTINE Oh, how disgusting! I could never have believed anything like this would happen! No. No. This is too much!

JEAN Don't tell me you're jealous of her?

CHRISTINE No, not of her. If it had been Clara—or Sophie—I would have scratched your eyes out! But her—? That's different. I don't know why. . . . But it's still disgusting!

JEAN You're not mad at her?

CHRISTINE No. Mad at you. You were mean and cruel to do a thing like that, very mean. The poor girl! . . . Let me tell you, I'm not going to stay in this house a moment longer, not when I can't have any respect for my employers.

JEAN Why do you want to respect them?

CHRISTINE Don't try to be smart. You don't want to work for people who behave like pigs, do you? Well, do you? If you ask me, you'd be lowering yourself by doing that.

JEAN Oh, I don't know. I think it's rather comforting to find out that they're not one damn bit better than we are.

CHRISTINE Well, I don't. If they're not any better, there's no point in us trying to be like them. —And think of the count. Think of all the sorrows he's been through in his time. My God! I won't stay in this house any longer. . . . Imagine! You, of all people! If it had been the attorney fellow; if it had been somebody respectable—

JEAN Now just a minute—!

CHRISTINE Oh, you're all right in your own way. But there's a big difference between one class and another. You can't deny that. —No, this is something I can never get over. She was so proud, and so sarcastic about men, you'd never believe she'd go and throw herself at one. And at someone like you! And she was going to have Diana shot because the poor thing ran after the gatekeeper's mongrel! —Well, I tell you, I've had enough! I'm not going to stay here any longer. When my term's up, I'm leaving.

JEAN Then what'll you do?

CHRISTINE Well, since you brought it up, it's about time that you got yourself a decent place, if we're going to get married.

JEAN Why should I go looking for another place? I could never get a job like this if I'm married.

CHRISTINE Well, I know that! But you could get a job as a porter, or maybe try to get a government job as a caretaker somewhere. A square deal and a square meal, that's what you get from the government—and a pension for the wife and children.

JEAN [*wryly*] Fine, fine! But I'm not the kind of guy who thinks about dying for his wife and children this early in the game. Let me tell you, I've got slightly bigger plans than that.

CHRISTINE Plans! Ha! What about your obligations? You'd better start giving them a little thought!

JEAN Don't start nagging me about obligations! I know what I have to do without you telling me. [*He hears a sound upstairs.*] Anyhow, we'll have plenty of chance to talk about this later. You just go and get yourself ready, and we'll be off to church.

CHRISTINE Who is that walking around up there?

JEAN I don't know. Clara, I suppose. Who else?

CHRISTINE [*starting to leave*] It can't be the count, can it? Could he have come back without anybody hearing him?

JEAN [*frightened*] The count? No, it can't be. He would have rung.

CHRISTINE [*leaving*] God help us! I've never heard the like of this.

[*The sun has now risen and strikes the tops of the trees in the park. As the scene progresses, the light shifts gradually until it is shining very obliquely through the windows.* JEAN *goes to the door and signals.* MISS JULIE *enters, dressed for travel, and carrying a small birdcage, covered with a towel. She sets the cage down on a chair.*]

MISS JULIE I'm ready now.

JEAN Shh! Christine's awake.

MISS JULIE [*extremely tense and nervous during the following*] Did she suspect anything?

JEAN She doesn't know a thing. —My God, what happened to you?

MISS JULIE What do you mean? Do I look so strange?

JEAN You're white as a ghost, and you've—excuse me—you've got dirt on your face.

MISS JULIE Let me wash it off. [*She goes over to the washbasin and washes her face and hands.*] There! Do you have a towel? . . . Oh, look, the sun's coming up!

JEAN That breaks the magic spell!

MISS JULIE Yes, we were spellbound last night, weren't we? Midsummer madness . . . Jean, listen to me! Come with me. I've got the money!

JEAN [*suspiciously*] Enough?

MISS JULIE Enough for a start. Come with me, Jean. I can't travel alone today. Midsummer Day on a stifling hot train, packed in with crowds of people, all staring at me—stopping at every station when I want to be flying. I can't, Jean, I can't! . . . And everything will remind me of the past. Midsummer Day when I was a child and the church was decorated with leaves—birch leaves and lilacs . . . the table spread for dinner with friends and relatives . . . and after dinner, dancing in the park, with flowers and games. Oh, no matter how far you travel, the memories tag right along in the baggage car . . . and the regrets and the remorse.

JEAN All right, I'll go with you! But it's got to be now—before it's too late! This very instant!

MISS JULIE Hurry and get dressed! [*She picks up the birdcage.*]

JEAN No baggage! It would give us away.

MISS JULIE Nothing. Only what we can take to our seats.

JEAN [*as he gets his hat*] What in the devil have you got there? What is that?

MISS JULIE It's only my canary. I can't leave it behind.

JEAN A canary! My God, do you expect us to carry a birdcage around with us? You're crazy. Put that cage down!

MISS JULIE It's the only thing I'm taking with me from my home—the only living thing who loves me since Diana was unfaithful to me! Don't be cruel, Jean. Let me take it with me.

JEAN I told you to put that cage down! —And don't talk so loud. Christine can hear us.

MISS JULIE No, I won't leave it with a stranger. I won't. I'd rather have you kill it.

JEAN Give it here, the little pest. I'll wring its neck.

MISS JULIE Oh, don't hurt it. Don't—. No, I can't do it!

JEAN Don't worry, I can. Give it here.

[MISS JULIE *takes the bird out of the cage and kisses it.*]

MISS JULIE Oh, my little Serena, must you die and leave your mistress?

JEAN You don't have to make a scene of it. It's a question of your whole life and future. You're wasting time!

[JEAN *grabs the canary from her, carries it to the chopping block, and picks up a meat cleaver.* MISS JULIE *turns away.*]

You should have learned how to kill chickens instead of shooting revolvers—[*He brings the cleaver down.*]—then a drop of blood wouldn't make you faint.

MISS JULIE [*screaming*] Kill me too! Kill me! You can kill an innocent creature without turning a hair—then kill me. Oh, how I hate you! I loathe you! There's blood between us. I curse the moment I first laid eyes on you! I curse the moment I was conceived in my mother's womb.

JEAN What good does your cursing do? Let's get out of here!

MISS JULIE [*approaches the chopping block, drawn to it against her will*]. No, I don't want to go yet. I can't. —I have to see. —Shh! [*She listens but keeps her eyes fastened on the chopping block and cleaver.*] You don't think I can stand the sight of blood, do you? You think I'm so weak, don't you? Oh, how I'd love to see your blood, your brains on that chopping block. I'd love to see the whole of your sex swimming in a sea of blood just like that. I could drink blood out of your skull. Use your chest as a foot bath, dip my toes in your guts! I could eat your heart roasted whole! —You think I'm weak! You think I loved you because my womb hungered for your semen. You think I want to carry your brood under my heart and feed it with my blood? Bear your child and take your name? —Come to think of it, what is your name? I've never even heard your last name. I'll bet you don't have one. I'd be Mrs. Doorman or Madame Garbageman. You dog with *my* name on your collar—you lackey with *my* initials on your buttons! Do you think I'm going to share you with my cook and fight over you with my maid?! Ohh! —You think I'm a coward who's going to run away! No, I'm going to stay—come hell or high water. My father will come home—find his desk broken into—his money gone. He'll ring—on that bell—two rings for the valet. And then he'll send for the sheriff—and I'll tell him everything. Everything! Oh, what a relief it'll be to have it all over . . . over and done with . . . if only it will be over. . . . He'll have a stroke and die . . . and there'll be an end to all of us. There'll be peace . . . and quiet . . . forever. . . . The coat of arms will be broken on his coffin; the count's line will be extinct—while the valet's breed will continue in an orphanage, win triumphs in the gutter, and end in jail!

[CHRISTINE *enters, dressed for church and with a hymnbook in her hand.* MISS JULIE *rushes over to her and throws herself into her arms as if seeking protection.*]

MISS JULIE Help me, Christine! Protect me against this man!

CHRISTINE [*cold and unmoved*] This is a fine way to behave on a holy day! [*She sees the chopping block.*] Just look at the mess you've made there! How do you explain that? And what's all this shouting and screaming about?

MISS JULIE Christine, you're a woman, you're my friend! I warn you, watch out for this—this monster!

JEAN [*feeling awkward*] If you ladies are going to talk, you won't want me around. I think I'll go and shave. [*He slips out to the right.*]

MISS JULIE You've got to understand, Christine! You've got to listen to me!

CHRISTINE No, I don't. I don't understand this kind of shenanigans at all. Where do you think you're going dressed like that? And Jean with his hat on? —Well? —Well?

MISS JULIE Listen to me, Christine! If you'll just listen to me, I'll tell you everything.

CHRISTINE I don't want to know anything.

MISS JULIE You've got to listen to me—!

CHRISTINE What about? About your stupid behavior with Jean? I tell you that doesn't bother me at all, because it's none of my business. But if you have any silly idea about talking him into skipping out with you, I'll soon put a stop to that.

MISS JULIE [*extremely tense*] Christine, please don't get upset. Listen to me. I can't stay here, and Jean can't stay here. So you see, we have to go away.

CHRISTINE Hm, hm, hm.

MISS JULIE [*suddenly brightening up*] Wait! I've got an idea! Why couldn't all three of us go away together?—out of the country—to Switzerland—and start a hotel? I've got the money, you see. Jean and I would be responsible for the whole affair—and Christine, you could run the kitchen, I thought. Doesn't that sound wonderful! Say you'll come, Christine, then everything will be settled. Say you will! Please! [*She throws her arms around* CHRISTINE *and pats her.*]

CHRISTINE [*remaining aloof and unmoved*] Hm. Hm.

MISS JULIE [*presto tempo*[8]] You've never been traveling, Christine. You have to get out and see the world. You can't imagine how wonderful it is to travel by train—constantly new faces, new countries. We'll go to Hamburg, and stop over to look at the zoo—it's famous, has everything—you'll love that. And we'll go to the theater and the opera. And then when we get to Munich, we'll go to the museums, Christine. They have Rubenses and Raphaels there—those great painters, you know. Of course you've heard about Munich where King Ludwig[9] lived—you know, the king who went mad. And then we can go and see his castles—they're just like the ones you read about in fairy tales. And from there it's just a short trip to Switzerland—with the

8. Quick time (Italian), a musical direction.

9. King Ludwig II of Bavaria (1845–1886; r. 1864–86), known as "the Fairy-Tale King," built several extravagant palaces—most famously Neuschwanstein, the so-called Cinderella castle; he was declared insane in 1886. Peter Paul Rubens (1577–1640) was a Flemish baroque painter; Raphael (Raffaello Sanzio, 1483–1520), a master of the Italian Renaissance.

Alps. Think of the Alps, Christine, covered with snow in the middle of summer. And oranges grow there, and laurel trees that are green the whole year round—

[JEAN *can be seen in the wings at the right, sharpening his straight razor on a strop held between his teeth and his left hand. He listens to* MISS JULIE *with a satisfied expression on his face, now and then nodding approvingly.* MISS JULIE *continues tempo prestissimo.*[1]]

—and that's where we'll get a hotel. I'll sit at the desk while Jean stands at the door and receives the guests, goes out shopping, writes the letters. What a life that will be! The train whistle blowing, then the bus arriving, then a bell ringing upstairs, then the bell in the restaurant rings—and I'll be making out the bills—and I know just how much to salt them—you can't imagine how timid tourists are when you shove a bill in their face! —And you, Christine, you'll run the whole kitchen—there'll be no standing at the stove for you—of course not. If you're going to talk to the people, you'll have to dress. And with your looks—I'm not trying to flatter you, Christine—you'll run off with some man one fine day—a rich Englishman, that's who it'll be, they're so easy to—[*Slowing down*]—to catch. —Then we'll all be rich. —We'll build a villa on Lake Como. —Maybe it does rain there sometimes, but—[*More and more lifelessly*]—the sun has to shine sometimes, too—even if it looks cloudy. —And—then . . . or else we can always travel some more—and come back . . . [*Pause*]—here . . . or somewhere else . . .

CHRISTINE Do you really believe a word of that yourself, Miss Julie?

MISS JULIE [*completely beaten*] Do I believe a word of it myself?

CHRISTINE Do you?

MISS JULIE [*exhausted*] I don't know. I don't believe anything anymore. [*She sinks down on the bench and lays her head between her arms on the table.*] Nothing. Nothing at all.

CHRISTINE [*turns to the right and faces* JEAN] So! You were planning to run away, were you?

JEAN [*taken aback, lays his razor down on the table*] We weren't exactly going to run away! Don't exaggerate. You heard Miss Julie's plans. Even if she's tired now after being up all night, her plans are perfectly practical.

CHRISTINE Well, just listen to you! Did you really think you could get me to cook for that little—!

JEAN [*sharply*] You keep a respectful tongue in your mouth when you talk to your mistress! Understand?

CHRISTINE Mistress!

JEAN Yes, mistress!

CHRISTINE Well of all the—! I don't have to listen—

JEAN Yes, you do! You need to listen more and blabber less. Miss Julie is your mistress. Don't you forget that! And if you're going to despise her for what she did, you ought to despise yourself for the same reason.

CHRISTINE I've always held myself high enough to—

JEAN High enough to make you look down on others!

CHRISTINE —enough to keep from lowering myself beneath my station. Don't you dare say that the count's cook has ever had anything to do with the stable groom or the swineherd. Don't you dare!

1. At a very rapid tempo (Italian).

JEAN Yes, you got yourself a decent man. Lucky you!

CHRISTINE What kind of a decent man is it who sells the oats from the count's stables?

JEAN Listen to who's talking! You get the gravy on the groceries and take bribes from the butcher!

CHRISTINE How dare you say a thing like that!

JEAN And you say you can't respect your employers. You of all people! You!

CHRISTINE Are you going to church or aren't you? You need a good sermon after your great exploits.

JEAN No, I'm not going to church! Go yourself. Go tell God how bad you are.

CHRISTINE Yes, I'll do just that. And I'll come back with enough forgiveness for your sins, too. Our Redeemer suffered and died on the cross for all our sins, and if we come to Him in faith and with a penitent heart, He will take all our sins upon Himself.

JEAN Rake-offs[2] included?

MISS JULIE Do you really believe that, Christine?

CHRISTINE With all my heart, as sure as I'm standing here. It was the faith I was born into, and I've held on to it since I was a little girl, Miss Julie. Where sin aboundeth, there grace aboundeth also.[3]

MISS JULIE If I had your faith, Christine, if only—

CHRISTINE But you see, that's something you can't have without God's special grace. And it is not granted to everyone to receive it.

MISS JULIE Then who receives it?

CHRISTINE That's the secret of the workings of grace, Miss Julie, and God is no respecter of persons. With Him the last shall be first[4]—

MISS JULIE In that case, he does have respect for the last, doesn't he?

CHRISTINE [*continuing*] —and it is easier for a camel to go through the eye of a needle than for a rich man to enter the kingdom of God.[5] That's how things are, Miss Julie. I'm going to leave now—alone. And on my way out I'm going to tell the stable boy not to let any horses out, in case anyone has any ideas about leaving before the count comes home. Goodbye.

[*She leaves.*]

JEAN She's a devil in skirts!—All because of a canary!

MISS JULIE [*listlessly*] Never mind the canary. . . . Do you see any way out of this, any end to it?

JEAN [*after thinking for a moment*] No.

MISS JULIE What would you do if you were in my place?

JEAN In your place? Let me think. . . . An aristocrat, a woman, and—fallen. . . . I don't know. —Or maybe I do.

MISS JULIE [*picks up the razor and makes a gesture with it*] Like this?

JEAN Yes. But I wouldn't do it, you understand. That's the difference between us.

MISS JULIE Because you're a man and I'm a woman? What difference does that make?

JEAN Just the difference that there is—between a man and a woman.

2. Cuts; money or goods skimmed off the top.
3. Romans 5.20.
4. Matthew 19.30, 20.16; Luke 13.30; Mark 10.31.
5. Matthew 19.24.

MISS JULIE [*holding the razor in her hand*] I want to! But I can't do it. My father couldn't do it either, that time when he should have.

JEAN No, he was right not to. He had to get his revenge first.

MISS JULIE And now my mother is getting her revenge again through me.

JEAN Didn't you ever love your father, Miss Julie?

MISS JULIE Yes, enormously. But I must have hated him too. I must have hated him without knowing it. It was he who brought me up to despise my own sex, to be half woman and half man. Who's to blame for what has happened? My father, my mother, myself? Myself? I don't have a self that's my own. I don't have a single thought I didn't get from my father, not an emotion I didn't get from my mother. And that last idea—about all people being equal—I got that from him, my fiancé. That's why I say he's beneath contempt. How can it be my own fault? Put the blame on Jesus, like Christine does? I'm too proud to do that—and too intelligent, thanks to what my father taught me. . . . A rich man can't get into heaven? That's a lie. But at least Christine, who's got money in the savings bank, won't get in. . . . Who's to blame? What difference does it make who's to blame? I'm still the one who has to bear the guilt, suffer the consequences—

JEAN Yes, but—

[*The bell rings sharply twice.* MISS JULIE *jumps up.* JEAN *changes his coat.*]

JEAN The count's back! What if Christine—[*He goes to the speaking tube, taps on it, and listens.*]

MISS JULIE Has he looked in his desk yet?

JEAN This is Jean, sir! [*Listens. The audience cannot hear what the count says.*] Yes, sir! [*Listens.*] Yes, sir! Yes, as soon as I can. [*Listens.*] Yes, at once, sir! [*Listens.*] Very good, sir! In half an hour.

MISS JULIE [*trembling with anxiety*] What did he say? For God's sake, what did he say?

JEAN He ordered his boots and his coffee in half an hour.

MISS JULIE Half an hour then! . . . Oh, I'm so tired. I can't bring myself to do anything. Can't repent, can't run away, can't stay, can't live . . . can't die. Help me, Jean. Command me, and I'll obey like a dog. Do me this last favor. Save my honor, save his name. You know what I ought to do but can't force myself to do. Let me use your willpower. You command me and I'll obey.

JEAN I don't know—. I can't either, not now. I don't know why. It's as if this coat made me—I can't give you orders in this. And now, after the count has spoken to me, I—I can't really explain it—but—I've got the backbone of a damned lackey! If the count came down here now and ordered me to cut my throat, I'd do it on the spot.

MISS JULIE Then pretend you're him. Pretend I'm you. You were such a good actor just a while ago, when you were kneeling before me. You were the aristocrat then. Or else—have you been to the theater and seen a hypnotist?

[JEAN *nods.*]

He says to his subject, "Take this broom!" and he takes it. He says, "Now sweep!" and he sweeps.

JEAN The person has to be asleep!

MISS JULIE [*ecstatic, transported*] I'm already asleep. The whole room has turned to smoke. You seem like an iron stove, a stove that looks like a man in black with a high hat. Your eyes are glowing like fading coals in a dying fire. Your face is a white smudge, like ashes.

[*The sun is now shining in on the floor and falls on* JEAN.]

It's so good and warm—[*She rubs her hands together as if warming them at a fire.*]—and so bright—and so peaceful.

JEAN [*takes the razor and puts it in her hand*] There's the broom. Go now, when the sun is up—out into the barn—and—[*He whispers in her ear.*]

MISS JULIE [*waking up*] Thanks! I'm going to get my rest. But tell me one thing. Tell me that the first can also receive the gift of grace. Tell me that, even if you don't believe it.

JEAN The first? I can't tell you that. —Wait a moment, Miss Julie. I know what I can tell you. You're no longer one of the first. You're one of—the last.

MISS JULIE That's true! I'm one of the last. I am the very last! —Oh! —Now I can't go! Tell me just once more, tell me to go!

JEAN Now I can't either. I can't!

MISS JULIE And the first shall be the last . . .

JEAN Don't think—don't think! You're taking all my strength from me. You're making me a coward. . . . What?! I thought I saw the bell move. No. . . . Let me stuff some paper in it. —Afraid of a bell! But it isn't just a bell. There's somebody behind it. A hand that makes it move. And there's something that makes the hand move. —Stop your ears, that's it, stop your ears! But it only rings louder. Rings louder and louder until you answer it. And then it's too late. Then the sheriff comes—and then—[*There are two sharp rings on the bell.* JEAN *gives a start, then straightens himself up.*] It's horrible! But there's no other way for it to end. —Go!

[MISS JULIE *walks resolutely out through the door.*]

HENRIK IBSEN

1828–1906

WRITING in an era when the theater had become a second-rate occupation, with most gifted writers turning instead to novels or poetry, Henrik Johan Ibsen restored to drama its prestige and relevance. During the nineteenth century, the invention of new theatrical machinery and techniques had turned theater into spectacle. Producers spent their time and money on special effects, dazzling audiences with lighting, horses, or even sea battles to add to—and sometimes replace—the appeal of popular actors. Nineteenth-century theater was in some ways comparable to present-day Hollywood and its focus on blockbuster action movies filled with special effects and big-name stars. Ibsen showed Europe that drama could be more than just spectacle: it could be an art form addressing the most serious moral and social questions of the time. The theatergoing public was first shocked, and later thrilled, to have controversial figures and themes presented on the stage, in plays that relied not on special effects but on carefully drawn characters and well-constructed dramatic situations. Honing his dramatic technique over half a century, Ibsen almost single-handedly brought a new seriousness to drama, and in doing so he won enduring acclaim as the originator of modern drama.

Ibsen achieved his unparalleled success against all odds. He was born in Skien, a small town in Norway, far removed from the cultural centers of Europe both physically and linguistically. When Ibsen left his provincial home at the age of fifteen, he was apprenticed to a pharmacist for more than six years, during that time he began to write occasional pieces, including his first play, *Catiline* (written 1848–49). Only at the age of twenty-two was he able to free himself from his apprenticeship—as well as from a liaison with a maid that had resulted in an illegitimate child—and move to the capital, Christiania (now Oslo), to study for the university entrance exam, which he failed. His efforts as a dramatist were better received, as one of his plays—the one-act *The Burial Mound* (1850)—was performed. The true beginning of his career occurred several years later, however, when he moved to Bergen to take his first job in the theater. After a few years spent learning the craft, he assumed positions of greater responsibility—as artistic director and dramatist—at a theater back in Christiania, where in 1857 he also married and had another child. By the time Ibsen was thirty-five, the foundation for his subsequent success as a dramatist had been laid.

While working at the theaters in Bergen and Christiania, Ibsen got to know the standard dramatic form of the time, the so-called well-made play (a literal translation of the French *pièce bien-fait*). Popularized by the French playwrights Victorien Sardou (1831–1908) and Augustin-Eugène Scribe (1791–1861), well-made plays were formulaic dramas focused less on well-developed characters than on complicated plots and well-timed confrontations. They offered fast-moving action, intrigues, alliances, and sudden revelations. Immensely popular at the time, the genre was also attacked by proponents of modern drama for favoring cheap suspense and empty entertainment over social relevance and meaningful art.

Ibsen's own drama can be viewed as an evolving series of reactions to the well-made play, beginning with *Brand* (1866) and *Peer Gynt* (1867)—the two plays that established him throughout Europe as a writer of significance. They mark Ibsen's rejection not only of the well-made play but of the theater as such, for they were "dramatic poems"—plays written exclusively to be read, not performed. All the rules that governed stage action, the rules of the well-made play, could thus be ignored entirely. Both plays were built around a single character on a singular and willful mission. *Brand* is the more tragic of the two; it presents a fanatical preacher who seeks to impose an uncompromising religion on his small parish high up in the Norwegian mountains, demanding increasingly large sacrifices of his congregants and of himself until he finally dies in utter isolation. In *Peer Gynt*, the protagonist's quest is cast in a more satirical form. The adventures of the title character, a notorious liar, take him from the fairy-tale realm of the Norwegian mountain trolls to the Moroccan desert and then back to Norway, where he dies not as a hero but as a mediocrity, even in his sinning. Drawing on literary models such as Goethe's *Faust* (1808, 1832) and Byron's *Don Juan* (1819–24), *Peer Gynt* freely mixes fantasy and reality, conjuring mountain trolls, mad German philosophers, and the devil himself.

By the time he wrote *Brand* and *Peer Gynt,* Ibsen had left Norway. He would spend twenty-seven years on the Continent, mostly in Italy and Germany, before returning to his homeland in 1891, at the age of sixty-three. Exile became the condition in which he thrived and from which he suffered. After *Brand* and *Peer Gynt* had secured his reputation, Ibsen started writing for the stage once more, but in an entirely different style. Whereas his earliest dramas had dealt with Norway's history, he now chose to write, once and for all, about the contemporary world he knew best—namely, the contemporary Norwegian middle class—in prose, not verse. His single purpose was to lay bare the ugly reality behind the facade of middle-class respectability, to expose the lies of bourgeois characters and indeed of bourgeois society as a whole. The five plays of this period—*The Pillars of Society* (1877), *A Doll House* (1879), *Ghosts* (1881), *An Enemy of the People* (1882), and *The Wild Duck* (1884)—made Ibsen notorious throughout Europe and established him as an author of shock, confrontation, and revolt: in short, as a modern. With these plays, Ibsen struck a nerve and secured his place in the pantheon of world drama.

The main cause of audiences' consternation also explains why these plays are now seen as the beginning of modern drama: they introduced realism, long established in the novel, to the theater. Using idiomatic language, Ibsen created a drama devoted to unveiling hidden motives and past misdeeds so that the truth would shine forth on the stage. In this way, Ibsen campaigned not only against a theater of special effects but also against a theater of convention. Realism, for Ibsen, required a theater of emotional and moral truth, a theater centered on understanding the subjective experience and objective conditions of modern life.

After winning fame and some infamy with his realist plays, Ibsen changed course once more as he attempted to write modern versions of Greek tragedy. In this last phase of his career, he managed to give definite shape to the tragedy of modern middle-class life. ***HEDDA GABLER*** (1890) is the most compelling and famous of the plays from this period, but it shares many features with the others—*Rosmersholm* (1886), *Lady from the Sea* (1888), *The Master Builder* (1892), *Little Eyolf* (1894), *John Gabriel Borkman* (1896), and

When We Dead Awaken (1899). All are set in the same bourgeois milieu as his realist plays, but they are less concerned with social deceptions and pretense. Instead, they are interested in the bourgeois characters themselves, presented as complex figures with hidden yearnings and fantasies that take them outside of the constricted worlds in which they live.

The title character of *Hedda Gabler* is the daughter of a general; she has married an aspiring scholar (Tesman) waiting for his university post. As the play begins, upon the couple's return from their honeymoon, we see almost immediately that the marriage is an unequal, and unsettled, one. Tesman is eager to start his new life and he is clearly proud of his beautiful wife. Hedda, by contrast, is dismissive of both his affectionate tone and his values. She snubs him, is impatient, abruptly changes the topic of conversation, and sulks. The class difference between the upper-middle-class Hedda and lower-middle-class Tesman is starkly drawn, as the collision between Hedda's and Tesman's respective classes, expectations, and attitudes occurs in and in fact centers on the bourgeois home. Like many of Ibsen's late plays, the home in *Hedda Gabler* bears and reveals the contradictions of bourgeois life. While Tesman thinks he has provided an ideal house, his wife from the bottom of her heart despises it and the life it offers. Gradually we learn that Hedda married Tesman and encouraged his purchase of the house only out of boredom and because she felt that her time and options were running out. But now she finds herself trapped in her marriage, and in the house.

Inger Munch, Sister of the Artist, by Edvard Munch (1892).

For that reason, Ibsen has Hedda focus her scorn on the house and its furnishings, as the play revolves around what they represent: class and taste. Hedda Gabler demands a new piano, because her old one does not "fit in" with the "other things" in this house and expects to have horses so that she can keep up the lifestyle to which she is accustomed. At the same time, she despises those objects associated with Tesman and his class—the déclassé hat of one of his aunts and his old and worn slippers, which his other aunt has hand embroidered. She admires the remnants of her former life, preserved in the towering portrait of the general and his set of pistols. Tesman's scholarly area is the handicrafts of the Middle Ages. What he does not see is that around him a battle is occurring over a different set of objects, which become the game pieces in a struggle of two classes and two wills.

Hedda Gabler, bored and without a function except to bear children—a thought she rejects with horror—manipulates everyone around her in order to exert control. Her coaxing Tesman to get a house he cannot afford is just the beginning. Hedda is equally calculating in her dealings with the other characters, from Tesman's aunt to Løvborg and his companion, Mrs. Elvsted, whom she knew as a schoolgirl. She gets them to do her bidding through force, lies, flattery, and utter ruthlessness. As the play progresses, we find her destroying careers and lives without blinking an eye; she lacks any moral compass beyond her own will. Although her actions at times seem to have some motive, they more often have no apparent goal. Hedda seems to value power as an end in itself.

The main victim of Hedda's plotting is Tesman's rival, Løvborg, who not only has published a well-received history of civilization but has just completed a book about the future. At an earlier moment in his career, Ibsen might have shown interest in the content of Løvborg's ideas, as he had done in examining the idealist drive for truth in *The Wild Duck,* for example, or in discussing marriage in *A Doll House*; here, the ideas are reduced to their container, Løvberg's manuscript, which becomes a central plot device—lost, found, and finally burned. Ibsen had learned from the well-made play how to weave objects and characters into suspenseful plots. But these props also convey something important about those who possess them: they are multifaceted devices that take on a life of their own.

Hedda may be a manipulator, but she is a manipulator with a vision. She is driven by her hunger for a more fulfilling, ideal, and beautiful life. She fantasizes about acts of heroism and beauty, which she tries to bring about by assigning roles to the people around her as if she were the director of a play. Hedda shares her desire for a better life with many tragic characters of Ibsen's later plays, characters who cannot rid themselves of the chains that bind them to their houses, their objects, their habits, their class, and their past. The architect Solness falls from the tower of his final house in the play *The Master Builder* and the sculptor Rubek, in *When We Dead Awaken,* climbs higher and higher into the dangerous mountains with his former love only to be killed by an avalanche. Ibsen's attitude toward his characters' desire for beauty is ambivalent. On the one hand, he sympathizes with them—even the cold-hearted Hedda Gabler. On the other hand, his plays show that the single-minded desire to achieve an ideal life wreaks destruction. Hedda Gabler's vision is an escape fantasy, the stuff of historical and idealist plays of the kind Ibsen had written in his youth. Ibsen perceived and understood both the desire for ideals and their destructive effects.

Ibsen is a dramatist of singular importance in part because he has consistently inspired the most important actors and directors. In England, Ibsen initially owed his influence to GEORGE BERNARD SHAW and William Archer, writers who led what some have called the Ibsen campaign. Shaw's defense of Ibsen against the scornful reception given his drama in the popular press and Archer's translations and productions of Ibsen's plays turned the Norwegian into the most important figure in British modern drama. Directors and playwrights elsewhere soon championed Ibsen as well. André Antoine, whose Théâtre Libre had pioneered a naturalist style of acting and design, played Oswald in *Ghosts* in 1890,

Elizabeth Robins as Hedda. Robins was the first actress to play Hedda in English, at the Vaudeville Theatre in London in 1891.

and the influential Russian director Konstantin Stanislavski, whose Moscow Art Theater promoted an acting style based on authentic emotional responses, played Doctor Stockman in *An Enemy of the People* in 1900. Ibsen's later plays, including *Hedda Gabler*, attracted a different set of directors, more interested in symbolism and poetry than in naturalism and truth. Aurélien Lugné-Poe, who had attacked realist drama and instead pioneered a symbolist theater full of ominous allusions and hieratic moods, staged *Rosmersholm* (1893) and *The Master Builder* (1894) in Paris, and directors interested in surrealism and suggestive stagecraft, such as Ingmar Bergman, have continued to be attracted first and foremost to Ibsen's late plays.

Ibsen is acknowledged as a founder of modern drama, but his place in theater history is full of enigmas and contradictions. He started his career with historical dramas that were typical nineteenth-century fare, yet became the herald of modern drama. Rather than simply rejecting the dramatic techniques of his time, he transformed them into a drama that seemed new, shocking, and modern to his audience. He received the most attention for his realist plays, but later turned realism in a more poetic and symbolist direction. In the end, Ibsen created a dramatic oeuvre of unparalleled variety and complexity. His plays could be many things to many people, viewed as stirring manifestos against social injustice or modern tragedies of striking poetic and dramatic force. This versatility, more than anything else, is responsible for Ibsen's having remained one of the most popular dramatists of all time. Today, he ranks second only after SHAKESPEARE as the world's most-performed playwright, a position that testifies to Ibsen's dramatic art: shocking and novel when it was first presented to audiences, it has stood the test of time.

M.P.

Hedda Gabler[1]

CHARACTERS

GEORGE TESMAN, research fellow in cultural history
HEDDA TESMAN, his wife
MISS JULIANA TESMAN, his aunt
MRS. ELVSTED
JUDGE BRACK
EILERT LØVBORG
BERTA, the TESMANS' maid

The action takes place in TESMAN'S *residence in the fashionable part of town.*

Act 1

[*A large, attractively furnished drawing room, decorated in dark colors. In the rear wall, a wide doorway with curtains drawn back. The doorway opens into a smaller room in the same style as the drawing room. In the right wall of the front room, a folding door that leads to the hall. In the left wall opposite, a glass door, with curtains similarly drawn back. Through the panes one can see part of an overhanging veranda and trees in autumn colors. In the foreground is an oval table with tablecloth and chairs around it. By the right wall, a wide, dark porcelain stove, a high-backed armchair, a cushioned footstool, and two taborets. In the right-hand corner, a settee with a small round table in front. Nearer, on the left and slightly out from the wall, a piano. On either side of the doorway in back, étagères with terra-cotta and majolica ornaments. Against the back wall of the inner room, a sofa, a table, and a couple of chairs can be seen. Above this sofa hangs a portrait of a handsome, elderly man in a general's uniform. Over the table, a hanging lamp with an opalescent glass shade. A number of bouquets of flowers are placed about the drawing room in vases and glasses. Others lie on the tables. The floors in both rooms are covered with thick carpets. Morning light. The sun shines in through the glass door.*

MISS JULIANA TESMAN, *wearing a hat and carrying a parasol, comes in from the hall, followed by* BERTA, *who holds a bouquet wrapped in paper.* MISS TESMAN *is a lady around sixty-five with a kind and good-natured look, nicely but simply dressed in a gray tailored suit.* BERTA *is a maid somewhat past middle age, with a plain and rather provincial appearance.*]

MISS TESMAN [*stops close by the door, listens, and says softly*] Goodness, I don't think they're even up yet!

BERTA [*also softly*] That's just what I said, Miss Juliana. Remember how late the steamer got in last night. Yes, and afterward! My gracious, how much the young bride had to unpack before she could get to bed.

MISS TESMAN Well, then—let them enjoy a good rest. But they must have some of this fresh morning air when they do come down. [*She goes to the glass door and opens it wide.*]

1. Translated by Rolf Fjelde.

BERTA [*by the table, perplexed, with the bouquet in her hand*] I swear there isn't a bit of space left. I think I'll have to put it here, miss. [*Places the bouquet on the piano.*]

MISS TESMAN So now you have a new mistress, Berta dear. Lord knows it was misery for me to give you up.

BERTA [*on the verge of tears*] And for me, miss! What can I say? All those many blessed years I've been in your service, you and Miss Rina.

MISS TESMAN We must take it calmly, Berta. There's really nothing else to do. George needs you here in this house, you know that. You've looked after him since he was a little boy.

BERTA Yes, but miss, I'm all the time thinking of her, lying at home. Poor thing—completely helpless. And with that new maid! She'll never take proper care of an invalid, that one.

MISS TESMAN Oh, I'll manage to teach her. And most of it, you know, I'll do myself. So you mustn't be worrying over my poor sister.

BERTA Well, but there's something else too, miss. I'm really so afraid I won't please the young mistress.

MISS TESMAN Oh, well—there might be something or other at first—

BERTA Because she's so very particular.

MISS TESMAN Well, of course. General Gabler's daughter. What a life she had in the general's day! Remember seeing her out with her father—how she'd go galloping past in that long black riding outfit, with a feather in her hat?

BERTA Oh yes—I remember! But I never would have dreamed then that she and George Tesman would make a match of it.

MISS TESMAN Nor I either. But now, Berta—before I forget: from now on, you mustn't say George Tesman. You must call him Doctor Tesman.

BERTA Yes, the young mistress said the same thing—last night, right after they came in the door. Is that true then, miss?

MISS TESMAN Yes, absolutely. Think of it, Berta—they gave him his doctor's degree. Abroad, that is—on this trip, you know. I hadn't heard one word about it, till he told me down on the pier.

BERTA Well, he's clever enough to be anything. But I never thought he'd go in for curing people.

MISS TESMAN No, he wasn't made that kind of doctor. [*Nods significantly.*] But as a matter of fact, you may soon now have something still greater to call him.

BERTA Oh, really! What's that, miss?

MISS TESMAN [*smiling*] Hm, wouldn't you like to know! [*Moved*] Ah, dear God—if only my poor brother could look up from his grave and see what his little boy has become! [*Glancing about*] But what's this, Berta? Why, you've taken all the slipcovers off the furniture—?

BERTA Madam told me to. She doesn't like covers on chairs, she said.

MISS TESMAN Are they going to make this their regular living room, then?

BERTA It seems so—with her. For his part—the doctor—he said nothing.

[GEORGE TESMAN *enters the inner room from the right, singing to himself and carrying an empty, unstrapped suitcase. He is a youngish-looking man of thirty-three, medium sized, with an open, round, cheerful face, blond hair and beard. He wears glasses and is somewhat carelessly dressed in comfortable lounging clothes.*]

MISS TESMAN Good morning, good morning, George!

TESMAN [*in the doorway*] Aunt Julie! Dear Aunt Julie! [*Goes over and warmly shakes her hand.*] Way out here—so early in the day—uh?

MISS TESMAN Yes, you know I simply had to look in on you a moment.

TESMAN And that without a decent night's sleep.

MISS TESMAN Oh, that's nothing at all to me.

TESMAN Well, then you did get home all right from the pier? Uh?

MISS TESMAN Why, of course I did—thank goodness. Judge Brack was good enough to see me right to my door.

TESMAN We were sorry we couldn't drive you up. But you saw for yourself—Hedda had all those boxes to bring along.

MISS TESMAN Yes, that was quite something, the number of boxes she had.

BERTA [*to* TESMAN] Should I go in and ask Mrs. Tesman if there's anything I can help her with?

TESMAN No, thanks, Berta—don't bother. She said she'd ring if she needed anything.

BERTA [*going off toward the right*] All right.

TESMAN But wait now—you can take this suitcase with you.

BERTA [*taking it*] I'll put it away in the attic. [*She goes out by the hall door.*]

TESMAN Just think, Aunt Julie—I had that whole suitcase stuffed full of notes. You just can't imagine all I've managed to find, rummaging through archives. Marvelous old documents that nobody knew existed—

MISS TESMAN Yes, you've really not wasted any time on your wedding trip, George.

TESMAN I certainly haven't. But do take your hat off, Auntie. Here—let me help you—uh?

MISS TESMAN [*as he does so*] Goodness—this is exactly as if you were still back at home with us.

TESMAN [*turning the hat in his hand and studying it from all sides*] My—what elegant hats you go in for!

MISS TESMAN I bought that for Hedda's sake.

TESMAN For Hedda's sake? Uh?

MISS TESMAN Yes, so Hedda wouldn't feel ashamed of me if we walked down the street together.

TESMAN [*patting her cheek*] You think of everything, Aunt Julie! [*Laying the hat on a chair by the table*] Sh—look, suppose we sit down on the sofa and have a little chat till Hedda comes. [*They settle themselves. She puts her parasol on the corner of the sofa.*]

MISS TESMAN [*takes both of his hands and gazes at him*] How wonderful it is having you here, right before my eyes again, George! You—dear Jochum's own boy!

TESMAN And for me too, to see you again, Aunt Julie! You, who've been father and mother to me both.

MISS TESMAN Yes, I'm sure you'll always keep a place in your heart for your old aunts.

TESMAN But Auntie Rina—hm? Isn't she any better?

MISS TESMAN Oh no—we can hardly expect that she'll ever be better, poor thing. She lies there, just as she has all these years. May God let me keep her a little while longer! Because otherwise, George, I don't know what I'd do with my life. The more so now, when I don't have you to look after.

TESMAN [*patting her on the back*] There, there, there—

MISS TESMAN [*suddenly changing her tone*] No, but to think of it, that now you're a married man! And that it was *you* who carried off Hedda Gabler. The beautiful Hedda Gabler! Imagine! She, who always had so many admirers!

TESMAN [*hums a little and smiles complacently*] Yes, I rather suspect I have several friends who'd like to trade places with me.

MISS TESMAN And then to have such a wedding trip! Five—almost six months—

TESMAN Well, remember, I used it for research, too. All those libraries I had to check—and so many books to read!

MISS TESMAN Yes, no doubt. [*More confidentially; lowering her voice*] But now listen, George—isn't there something—something special you have to tell me?

TESMAN From the trip?

MISS TESMAN Yes.

TESMAN No, I can't think of anything beyond what I wrote in my letters. I got my doctor's degree down there—but I told you that yesterday.

MISS TESMAN Yes, of course. But I mean—whether you have any kind of—expectations—?

TESMAN Expectations?

MISS TESMAN My goodness, George—I'm your old aunt!

TESMAN Why, naturally I have expectations.

MISS TESMAN Ah!

TESMAN I have every expectation in the world of becoming a professor shortly.

MISS TESMAN Oh, a professor, yes—

TESMAN Or I might as well say, I'm sure of it. But, Aunt Julie—you know that perfectly well yourself.

MISS TESMAN [*with a little laugh*] That's right, so I do. [*Changing the subject*] But we were talking about your trip. It must have cost a terrible amount of money.

TESMAN Well, that big fellowship, you know—it took us a good part of the way.

MISS TESMAN But I don't see how you could stretch it enough for two.

TESMAN No, that's not so easy to see—uh?

MISS TESMAN And especially traveling with a lady. For I hear tell that's much more expensive.

TESMAN Yes, of course—it's a bit more expensive. But Hedda just had to have that trip. She *had* to. There was nothing else to be done.

MISS TESMAN No, no, I guess not. A honeymoon abroad seems to be the thing nowadays. But tell me—have you had a good look around your house?

TESMAN You can bet I have! I've been up since daybreak.

MISS TESMAN And how does it strike you, all in all?

TESMAN First-rate! Absolutely first-rate! Only, I don't know what we'll do with the two empty rooms between the back parlor and Hedda's bedroom.

MISS TESMAN [*laughing again*] Oh, my dear George, I think you can use them—as time goes on.

TESMAN Yes, you're quite right about that, Aunt Julie! In time, as I build up my library—uh?

MISS TESMAN Of course, my dear boy. It was your library I meant.

TESMAN I'm happiest now for Hedda's sake. Before we were engaged, she used to say so many times there was no place she'd rather live than here, in Secretary Falk's town house.

MISS TESMAN Yes, and then to have it come on the market just after you'd sailed.

TESMAN We really have had luck, haven't we?

MISS TESMAN But expensive, George dear! You'll find it expensive, all this here.

TESMAN [*looks at her, somewhat crestfallen*] Yes, I suppose I will.

MISS TESMAN Oh, Lord, yes!

TESMAN How much do you think? Approximately? Hm?

MISS TESMAN It's impossible to say till the bills are all in.

TESMAN Well, fortunately Judge Brack has gotten me quite easy terms. That's what he wrote Hedda.

MISS TESMAN Don't worry yourself about that, dear. I've also put up security to cover the carpets and furniture.

TESMAN Security? Aunt Julie, dear—you? What kind of security could *you* give?

MISS TESMAN I took out a mortgage on our pension.

TESMAN [*jumping up*] What! On your—and Auntie Rina's pension!

MISS TESMAN I saw nothing else to do.

TESMAN [*standing in front of her*] But you're out of your mind, Aunt Julie! That pension—it's all Aunt Rina and you have to live on.

MISS TESMAN Now, now—don't make so much of it. It's only a formality; Judge Brack said so. He was good enough to arrange the whole thing for me. Just a formality, he said.

TESMAN That's all well enough. But still—

MISS TESMAN You'll be drawing your own salary now. And, good gracious, if we have to lay out a bit, just now at the start—why, it's no more than a pleasure for us.

TESMAN Oh, Aunt Julie—you never get tired of making sacrifices for me!

MISS TESMAN [*rises and places her hands on his shoulders*] What other joy do I have in this world than smoothing the path for you, my dear boy? You, without father or mother to turn to. And now we've come to the goal, George! Things may have looked black at times; but now, thank heaven, you've made it.

TESMAN Yes, it's remarkable, really, how everything's turned out for the best.

MISS TESMAN Yes—and those who stood against you—who wanted to bar your way—they've gone down. They've fallen, George. The one most dangerous to you—he fell farthest. And he's lying there now, in the bed he made—poor, misguided creature.

TESMAN Have you heard any news of Eilert? I mean, since I went away.

MISS TESMAN Only that he's supposed to have brought out a new book.

TESMAN What's that? Eilert Løvborg? Just recently, uh?

MISS TESMAN So they say. But considering everything, it can hardly amount to much. Ah, but when *your* new book comes out—it'll be a different story, George! What will it be about?

TESMAN It's going to treat the domestic handicrafts of Brabant[2] in the Middle Ages.

MISS TESMAN Just imagine—that you can write about things like that!

TESMAN Actually, the book may take quite a while yet. I have this tremendous collection of material to put in order, you know.

MISS TESMAN Yes, collecting and ordering—you do that so well. You're not my brother's son for nothing.

TESMAN I look forward so much to getting started. Especially now, with a comfortable home of my own to work in.

MISS TESMAN And most of all, dear, now that you've won her, the wife of your heart.

TESMAN [*embracing her*] Yes, yes, Aunt Julie! Hedda—that's the most beautiful part of it all! [*Glancing toward the doorway*] But I think she's coming—uh?

[HEDDA *enters from the left through the inner room. She is a woman of twenty-nine. Her face and figure show breeding and distinction; her complexion is pallid and opaque. Her steel gray eyes express a cool, unruffled calm. Her hair is an attractive medium brown, but not particularly abundant. She wears a tasteful, rather loose-fitting gown.*]

MISS TESMAN [*going to meet* HEDDA] Good morning, Hedda dear—how good to see you!

HEDDA [*holding out her hand*] Good morning, my dear Miss Tesman! Calling so early? This *is* kind of you.

MISS TESMAN [*slightly embarrassed*] Well—did the bride sleep well in her new home?

HEDDA Oh yes, thanks. Quite adequately.

TESMAN Adequately! Oh, I like that, Hedda! You were sleeping like a stone when I got up.

HEDDA Fortunately. But of course one has to grow accustomed to anything new, Miss Tesman—little by little. [*Looking toward the left*] Oh! That maid has left the door open—and the sunlight's just flooding in.

MISS TESMAN [*going toward the door*] Well, we can close it.

HEDDA No, no—don't! [*To* TESMAN] There, dear, draw the curtains. It gives a softer light.

TESMAN [*by the glass door*] All right—all right. Look, Hedda—now you have shade and fresh air both.

HEDDA Yes, we really need some fresh air here, with all these piles of flowers— But—won't you sit down, Miss Tesman?

MISS TESMAN Oh no, thank you. Now that I know that everything's fine—thank goodness—I will have to run along home. My sister's lying there waiting, poor thing.

TESMAN Give her my very, very best, won't you? And say I'll be looking in on her later today.

MISS TESMAN Oh, you can be sure I will. But what do you know, George—[*Searching in her bag*]—I nearly forgot. I have something here for you.

TESMAN What's that, Aunt Julie? Hm?

MISS TESMAN [*brings out a flat package wrapped in newspaper and hands it to him*] There, dear. Look.

2. A province of central Belgium.

TESMAN [*opening it*] Oh, my—you kept them for me, Aunt Julie! Hedda! That's really touching! Uh!

HEDDA [*by the étagère on the right*] Yes, dear, what is it?

TESMAN My old bedroom slippers! My slippers!

HEDDA Oh yes. I remember how often you spoke of them during the trip.

TESMAN Yes, I missed them terribly. [*Going over to her*] Now you can see them, Hedda!

HEDDA [*moves toward the stove*] Thanks, but I really don't care to.

TESMAN [*following her*] Imagine—Auntie Rina lay and embroidered them, sick as she was. Oh, you couldn't believe how many memories are bound up in them.

HEDDA [*at the table*] But not for me.

MISS TESMAN I think Hedda is right, George.

TESMAN Yes, but I only thought, now that she's part of the family—

HEDDA [*interrupting*] We're never going to manage with this maid, Tesman.

MISS TESMAN Not manage with Berta?

TESMAN But dear—why do you say that? Uh?

HEDDA [*pointing*] See there! She's left her old hat lying out on a chair.

TESMAN [*shocked; dropping the slippers*] But Hedda—!

HEDDA Suppose someone came in and saw it.

TESMAN Hedda—that's Aunt Julie's hat!

HEDDA Really?

MISS TESMAN [*picking it up*] That's right, it's mine. And what's more, it certainly is not old—Mrs. Tesman.

HEDDA I really hadn't looked closely at it, Miss Tesman.

MISS TESMAN [*putting on the hat*] It's actually the first time I've had it on. The very first time.

TESMAN And it's lovely, too. Most attractive!

MISS TESMAN Oh, it's hardly all that, George. [*Looks about.*] My parasol—? Ah, here. [*Takes it.*] For that's mine too. [*Murmurs.*] Not Berta's.

TESMAN New hat and new parasol! Just imagine, Hedda!

HEDDA Quite charming, really.

TESMAN Yes, aren't they, uh? But Auntie, take a good look at Hedda before you leave. See how charming *she* is!

MISS TESMAN But George dear, there's nothing new in that. Hedda's been lovely all her life. [*She nods and starts out, right.*]

TESMAN [*following her*] But have you noticed how plump and buxom she's grown? How much she's filled out on the trip?

HEDDA [*crossing the room*] Oh, do be quiet—!

MISS TESMAN [*who has stopped and turned*] Filled out?

TESMAN Of course, you can't see it so well when she has that dressing gown on. But I, who have the opportunity to—

HEDDA [*by the glass door, impatiently*] Oh, you have no opportunity for anything!

TESMAN It must have been the mountain air, down in the Tyrol[3]—

HEDDA [*brusquely interrupting*] I'm exactly as I was when I left.

TESMAN Yes, that's your claim. But you certainly are not. Auntie, don't you agree?

3. A region of the eastern Alps, mainly in western Austria but partly in northern Italy.

MISS TESMAN [*gazing at her with folded hands*] Hedda is lovely—lovely—lovely. [*Goes up to her, takes her head in both hands, bends it down and kisses her hair.*] God bless and keep Hedda Tesman—for George's sake.

HEDDA [*gently freeing herself*] Oh—! Let me go.

MISS TESMAN [*with quiet feeling*] I won't let a day go by without looking in on you two.

TESMAN Yes, please do that, Aunt Julie! Uh?

MISS TESMAN Good-bye—good-bye!

[*She goes out by the hall door.* TESMAN *accompanies her, leaving the door half open. He can be heard reiterating his greetings to Aunt Rina and his thanks for the slippers. At the same time,* HEDDA *moves about the room, raising her arms and clenching her fists as if in a frenzy. Then she flings back the curtains from the glass door and stands there, looking out. A moment later* TESMAN *comes back, closing the door after him.*]

TESMAN [*retrieving the slippers from the floor*] What are you standing and looking at, Hedda?

HEDDA [*again calm and controlled*] I'm just looking at the leaves—they're so yellow—and so withered.

TESMAN [*wraps up the slippers and puts them on the table*] Yes, well, we're into September now.

HEDDA [*once more restless*] Yes, to think—that already we're in—in September.

TESMAN Didn't Aunt Julie seem a bit strange? A little—almost formal? What do you suppose was bothering her? Hm?

HEDDA I hardly know her at all. Isn't that how she usually is?

TESMAN No, not like this, today.

HEDDA [*leaving the glass door*] Do you think this thing with the hat upset her?

TESMAN Oh, not very much. A little, just at the moment, perhaps—

HEDDA But really, what kind of manners has she—to go throwing her hat about in a drawing room! It's just not proper.

TESMAN Well, you can be sure Aunt Julie won't do it again.

HEDDA Anyhow, I'll manage to smooth it over with her.

TESMAN Yes, Hedda dear, I wish you would!

HEDDA When you go in to see them later on, you might ask her out for the evening.

TESMAN Yes, I'll do that. And there's something else you could do that would make her terribly happy.

HEDDA Oh?

TESMAN If only you could bring yourself to speak to her warmly, by her first name. For my sake, Hedda? Uh?

HEDDA No, no—don't ask me to do that. I told you this once before. I'll try to call her "Aunt."[4] That should be enough.

TESMAN Oh, all right. I was only thinking, now that you belong to the family—

HEDDA Hm—I really don't know— [*She crosses the room to the doorway.*]

4. In the original Norwegian text, Tesman has just asked his wife to address his aunt with the familiar *du* (thou), used only by intimate friends and family, rather than with the formal *De* (you). Hedda refuses, but suggests the compromise of calling her "Aunt."

TESMAN [*after a pause*] Is something the matter, Hedda? Uh?

HEDDA I'm just looking at my old piano. It doesn't really fit in with all these other things.

TESMAN With the first salary I draw, we can see about trading it in on a new one.

HEDDA No, not traded in. I don't want to part with it. We can put it there, in the inner room, and get another here in its place. When there's a chance, I mean.

TESMAN [*slightly cast down*] Yes, we could do that, of course.

HEDDA [*picks up the bouquet from the piano*] These flowers weren't here when we got in last night.

TESMAN Aunt Julie must have brought them for you.

HEDDA [*examining the bouquet*] A visiting card. [*Takes it out and reads it.*] "Will stop back later today." Can you guess who this is from?

TESMAN No. Who? Hm?

HEDDA It says "Mrs. Elvsted."

TESMAN No, really? Sheriff Elvsted's wife. Miss Rysing, she used to be.

HEDDA Exactly. The one with the irritating hair that she was always showing off. An old flame of yours, I've heard.

TESMAN [*laughing*] Oh, that wasn't for long. And it was before I knew you, Hedda. But imagine—that she's here in town.

HEDDA It's odd that she calls on us. I've hardly seen her since we were in school.

TESMAN Yes, I haven't seen her either—since God knows when. I wonder how she can stand living in such an out-of-the-way place. Hm?

HEDDA [*thinks a moment, then bursts out*] But wait—isn't it somewhere up in those parts that he—that Eilert Løvborg lives?

TESMAN Yes, it's someplace right around there.

[BERTA *enters by the hall door.*]

BERTA She's back again, ma'am—that lady who stopped by and left the flowers an hour ago. [*Pointing*] The ones you have in your hand, ma'am.

HEDDA Oh, is she? Good. Would you ask her to come in.

[BERTA *opens the door for* MRS. ELVSTED *and goes out.* MRS. ELVSTED *is a slender woman with soft, pretty features. Her eyes are light blue, large, round, and somewhat prominent, with a startled, questioning look. Her hair is remarkably light, almost a white-gold, and unusually abundant and wavy. She is a couple of years younger than* HEDDA. *She wears a dark visiting dress, tasteful, but not quite in the latest fashion.*]

HEDDA [*going to greet her warmly*] Good morning, my dear Mrs. Elvsted. How delightful to see you again!

MRS. ELVSTED [*nervously; struggling to control herself*] Yes, it's a very long time since we last met.

TESMAN [*gives her his hand*] Or since *we* met, uh?

HEDDA Thank you for your beautiful flowers—

MRS. ELVSTED Oh, that's nothing—I would have come straight out here yesterday afternoon, but then I heard you weren't at home—

TESMAN Have you just now come to town? Uh?

MRS. ELVSTED I got in yesterday toward noon. Oh, I was in desperation when I heard that you weren't at home.

HEDDA Desperation! Why?

TESMAN But my dear Mrs. Rysing—Mrs. Elvsted, I mean—

HEDDA You're not in some kind of trouble?

MRS. ELVSTED Yes, I am. And I don't know another living soul down here I can turn to.

HEDDA [*putting the bouquet down on the table*] Come, then—let's sit here on the sofa—

MRS. ELVSTED Oh, I can't sit down. I'm really too much on edge!

HEDDA Why, of course you can. Come here.

[*She draws* MRS. ELVSTED *down on the sofa and sits beside her.*]

TESMAN Well? What is it, Mrs. Elvsted?

HEDDA Has anything particular happened at home?

MRS. ELVSTED Yes, that's both it—and not it. Oh, I do want so much that you don't misunderstand me—

HEDDA But then the best thing, Mrs. Elvsted, is simply to speak your mind.

TESMAN Because I suppose that's why you've come. Hm?

MRS. ELVSTED Oh yes, that's why. Well, then, I have to tell you—if you don't already know—that Eilert Løvborg's also in town.

HEDDA Løvborg—!

TESMAN What! Is Eilert Løvborg back! Just think, Hedda!

HEDDA Good Lord, I can hear.

MRS. ELVSTED He's been back all of a week's time now. A whole week—in this dangerous town! Alone! With all the bad company that's around.

HEDDA But my dear Mrs. Elvsted, what does *he* have to do with you?

MRS. ELVSTED [*glances anxiously at her and says quickly*] He was the children's tutor.

HEDDA Your children's?

MRS. ELVSTED My husband's. I have none.

HEDDA Your stepchildren's, then.

MRS. ELVSTED Yes.

TESMAN [*somewhat hesitantly*] But was he—I don't know quite how to put it—was he sufficiently—responsible in his habits for such a job? Uh?

MRS. ELVSTED In these last two years, there wasn't a word to be said against him.

TESMAN Not a word? Just think of that, Hedda!

HEDDA I heard it.

MRS. ELVSTED Not even a murmur, I can assure you! Nothing. But anyway—now that I know he's here—in this big city—and with so much money in his hands—then I'm just frightened to death for him.

TESMAN But why didn't he stay up there where he was? With you and your husband? Uh?

MRS. ELVSTED After the book came out, he just couldn't rest content with us.

TESMAN Yes, that's right—Aunt Julie was saying he'd published a new book.

MRS. ELVSTED Yes, a great new book, on the course of civilization—in all its stages. It's been out two weeks. And now it's been bought and read so much—and it's made a tremendous stir—

TESMAN Has it really? It must be something he's had lying around from his better days.

MRS. ELVSTED Years back, you mean?

TESMAN I suppose.

MRS. ELVSTED No, he's written it all up there with us. Now—in this last year.

TESMAN That's marvelous to hear. Hedda! Just imagine!

MRS ELVSTED Yes, if only it can go on like this!

HEDDA Have you seen him here in town?

MRS. ELVSTED No, not yet. I had such trouble finding out his address. But this morning I got it at last.

HEDDA [*looks searchingly at her*] I must say it seems rather odd of your husband—

MRS. ELVSTED [*with a nervous start*] Of my husband—! What?

HEDDA To send you to town on this sort of errand. Not to come and look after his friend himself.

MRS. ELVSTED No, no, my husband hasn't the time for that. And then I had—some shopping to do.

HEDDA [*with a slight smile*] Oh, that's different.

MRS. ELVSTED [*getting up quickly and uneasily*] I beg you, please, Mr. Tesman—be good to Eilert Løvborg if he comes to you. And he will, I'm sure. You know—you were such good friends in the old days. And you're both doing the same kind of work. The same type of research—from what I can gather.

TESMAN We were once, at any rate.

MRS. ELVSTED Yes, and that's why I'm asking you, please—you too—to keep an eye on him. Oh, you will do that, Mr. Tesman—promise me that?

TESMAN I'll be only too glad to, Mrs. Rysing—

HEDDA Elvsted.

TESMAN I'll certainly do everything in my power for Eilert. You can depend on that.

MRS. ELVSTED Oh, how terribly kind of you! [*Pressing his hands*] Many, many thanks! [*Frightened*] He means so much to my husband, you know.

HEDDA [*rising*] You ought to write him, dear. He might not come by on his own.

TESMAN Yes, that probably would be the best, Hedda? Hm?

HEDDA And the sooner the better. Right now, I'd say.

MRS. ELVSTED [*imploringly*] Oh yes, if you could!

TESMAN I'll write him this very moment. Have you got his address, Mrs.—Mrs. Elvsted?

MRS. ELVSTED Yes. [*Takes a slip of paper from her pocket and hands it to him.*] Here it is.

TESMAN Good, good. Then I'll go in— [*Looking about*] But wait—my slippers? Ah! Here. [*Takes the package and starts to leave.*]

HEDDA Write him a really warm, friendly letter. Nice and long, too.

TESMAN Don't worry, I will.

MRS. ELVSTED But please, not a word that I asked you to!

TESMAN No, that goes without saying. Uh? [*Leaves by the inner room, to the right.*]

HEDDA [*goes over to* MRS. ELVSTED, *smiles, and speaks softly*] How's that! Now we've killed two birds with one stone.

MRS. ELVSTED What do you mean?

HEDDA Didn't you see that I wanted him out of the room?

MRS. ELVSTED Yes, to write the letter—

HEDDA But also to talk with you alone.

MRS. ELVSTED [*confused*] About this same thing?

HEDDA Precisely.

MRS. ELVSTED [*upset*] But Mrs. Tesman, there's nothing more to say! Nothing!

HEDDA Oh yes, but there is. There's a great deal more—I can see that. Come, sit here—and let's speak openly now, the two of us. [*She forces* MRS. ELVSTED *down into the armchair by the stove and sits on one of the taborets.*]

MRS. ELVSTED [*anxiously glancing at her watch*] But Mrs. Tesman, dear—I was just planning to leave.

HEDDA Oh, you can't be in such a rush— Now! Tell me a little about how things are going at home.

MRS. ELVSTED Oh, that's the last thing I'd ever want to discuss.

HEDDA But with me, dear—? After all, we were in school together.

MRS. ELVSTED Yes, but you were a class ahead of me. Oh, I was terribly afraid of you then!

HEDDA Afraid of me?

MRS. ELVSTED Yes, terribly. Because whenever we met on the stairs, you'd always pull my hair.

HEDDA Did I really?

MRS. ELVSTED Yes, and once you said you would burn it off.

HEDDA Oh, that was just foolish talk, you know.

MRS. ELVSTED Yes, but I was so stupid then. And, anyway, since then—we've drifted so far—far apart from each other. We've moved in such different circles.

HEDDA Well, let's try now to come closer again. Listen, at school we were quite good friends, and we called each other by our first names[5]—

MRS. ELVSTED No, I'm sure you're mistaken.

HEDDA Oh, I couldn't be! I remember it clearly. And that's why we have to be perfectly open, just as we were. [*Moves the stool nearer* MRS. ELVSTED.] There now! [*Kissing her cheek*] You have to call me Hedda.

MRS. ELVSTED [*pressing and patting her hands*] Oh, you're so good and kind—! It's not at all what I'm used to.

HEDDA There, there! And I'm going to call you my own dear Thora.

MRS. ELVSTED My name is Thea.

HEDDA Oh yes, of course. I meant Thea. [*Looks at her compassionately.*] So you're not much used to goodness or kindness, Thea? In your own home?

MRS. ELVSTED If only I had a home! But I don't. I never have.

HEDDA [*glances quickly at her*] I thought it had to be something like that.

MRS. ELVSTED [*gazing helplessly into space*] Yes—yes—yes.

HEDDA I can't quite remember now—but wasn't it as a housekeeper that you first came up to the Elvsteds?

MRS. ELVSTED Actually as a governess. But his wife—his first wife—she was an invalid and mostly kept to her bed. So I had to take care of the house too.

HEDDA But finally you became mistress of the house yourself.

MRS. ELVSTED [*heavily*] Yes, I did.

HEDDA Let me see—about how long ago was that?

MRS. ELVSTED That I was married?

5. In the original Norwegian text, Hedda claims that they used to address each other with the familiar *du*. Not used to this level of intimacy, Mrs. Elvsted will slip back into the formal *De* before adopting *du*.

HEDDA Yes.

MRS. ELVSTED It's five years now.

HEDDA That's right. It must be.

MRS. ELVSTED Oh, these five years—! Or the last two or three, anyway. Oh, if you only knew, Mrs. Tesman—

HEDDA [*gives her hand a little slap*] Mrs. Tesman! Now, Thea!

MRS. ELVSTED I'm sorry; I'll try— Yes, if you could only understand—Hedda—

HEDDA [*casually*] Eilert Løvborg has lived up there about three years too, hasn't he?

MRS. ELVSTED [*looks at her doubtfully*] Eilert Løvborg? Yes—he has.

HEDDA Had you already known him here in town?

MRS. ELVSTED Hardly at all. Well, I mean—by name, of course.

HEDDA But up there—I suppose he'd visit you both?

MRS. ELVSTED Yes, he came to see us every day. He was tutoring the children, you know. Because, in the long run, I couldn't do it all myself.

HEDDA No, that's obvious. And your husband—? I suppose he often has to be away?

MRS. ELVSTED Yes, you can imagine, as sheriff, how much traveling he does around in the district.

HEDDA [*leaning against the chair arm*] Thea—my poor, sweet Thea—now you must tell me everything—just as it is.

MRS. ELVSTED Well, then you have to ask the questions.

HEDDA What sort of man is your husband, Thea? I mean—you know—to be with. Is he good to you?

MRS. ELVSTED [*evasively*] He believes he does everything for the best.

HEDDA I only think he must be much too old for you. More than twenty years older, isn't he?

MRS. ELVSTED [*irritated*] That's true. Along with everything else. I just can't stand him! We haven't a single thought in common. Nothing at all—he and I.

HEDDA But doesn't he care for you all the same—in his own way?

MRS. ELVSTED Oh, I don't know what he feels. I'm no more than useful to him. And then it doesn't cost much to keep me. I'm inexpensive.

HEDDA That's stupid of you.

MRS. ELVSTED [*shaking her head*] It can't be otherwise. Not with him. He really doesn't care for anyone but himself—and maybe a little for the children.

HEDDA And for Eilert Løvborg, Thea.

MRS. ELVSTED [*looking at her*] Eilert Løvborg! Why do you think so?

HEDDA But my dear—it seems to me, when he sends you all the way into town to look after him— [*Smiles almost imperceptibly.*] Besides, it's what you told my husband.

MRS. ELVSTED [*with a little nervous shudder*] Really? Yes, I suppose I did. [*In a quiet outburst*] No—I might as well tell you here and now! It's bound to come out in time.

HEDDA But my dear Thea—?

MRS. ELVSTED All right, then! My husband never knew I was coming here.

HEDDA What! Your husband never knew—

MRS. ELVSTED Of course not. Anyway, he wasn't at home. Off traveling somewhere. Oh, I couldn't bear it any longer, Hedda. It was impossible! I would have been so alone up there now.

HEDDA Well? What then?

MRS. ELVSTED So I packed a few of my things together—the barest necessities—without saying a word. And I slipped away from the house.

HEDDA Right then and there?

MRS. ELVSTED Yes, and took the train straight into town.

HEDDA But my dearest girl—that you could dare to do such a thing!

MRS. ELVSTED [*rising and walking about the room*] What else could I possibly do!

HEDDA But what do you think your husband will say when you go back home?

MRS. ELVSTED [*by the table, looking at her*] Back to *him?*

HEDDA Yes, of course.

MRS. ELVSTED I'll never go back to him.

HEDDA [*rising and approaching her*] You mean you've left, in dead earnest, for good?

MRS. ELVSTED Yes. There didn't seem anything else to do.

HEDDA But—to go away so openly.

MRS. ELVSTED Oh, you can't keep a thing like that secret.

HEDDA But what do you think people will say about you, Thea?

MRS. ELVSTED God knows they'll say what they please. [*Sitting wearily and sadly on the sofa*] I only did what I had to do.

HEDDA [*after a short silence*] What do you plan on now? What kind of work?

MRS. ELVSTED I don't know yet. I only know I have to live here, where Eilert Løvborg is—if I'm going to live at all.

HEDDA [*moves a chair over from the table, sits beside her, and strokes her hands*] Thea dear—how did this—this friendship—between you and Eilert Løvborg come about?

MRS. ELVSTED Oh, it happened little by little. I got some kind of power, almost, over him.

HEDDA Really?

MRS. ELVSTED He gave up his old habits. Not because I'd asked him to. I never dared do that. But he could tell they upset me, and so he dropped them.

HEDDA [*hiding an involuntary, scornful smile*] My dear little Thea—just as they say—you rehabilitated him.

MRS. ELVSTED Well, he says so, at any rate. And he—on his part—he's made a real human being out of me. Taught me to think—and understand so many things.

HEDDA You mean he tutored you also?

MRS. ELVSTED No, not exactly. But he'd talk to me—talk endlessly on about one thing after another. And then came the wonderful, happy time when I could share in his work! When I could help him!

HEDDA Could you really?

MRS. ELVSTED Yes! Whenever he wrote anything, we'd always work on it together.

HEDDA Like two true companions.

MRS. ELVSTED [*eagerly*] Companions! You know, Hedda—that's what he said too! Oh, I ought to feel so happy—but I can't. I just don't know if it's going to last.

HEDDA You're no more sure of him than that?

MRS. ELVSTED [*despondently*] There's a woman's shadow between Eilert Løvborg and me.

HEDDA [*looks at her intently*] Who could that be?

MRS. ELVSTED I don't know. Someone out of his—his past. Someone he's really never forgotten.

HEDDA What has he said—about this!

MRS. ELVSTED It's only once—and just vaguely—that he touched on it.

HEDDA Well! And what did he say!

MRS. ELVSTED He said that when they broke off she was going to shoot him with a pistol.

HEDDA [*with cold constraint*] That's nonsense! Nobody behaves that way around here.

MRS. ELVSTED No. And that's why I think it must have been that redheaded singer that at one time he—

HEDDA Yes, quite likely.

MRS. ELVSTED I remember they used to say about her that she carried loaded weapons.

HEDDA Ah—then of course it must have been her.

MRS. ELVSTED [*wringing her hands*] But you know what, Hedda—I've heard that this singer—that she's in town again! Oh, it has me out of my mind—

HEDDA [*glancing toward the inner room*] Shh! Tesman's coming. [*Gets up and whispers.*] Thea—keep all this just between us.

MRS. ELVSTED [*jumping up*] Oh yes! In heaven's name—!

[GEORGE TESMAN, *with a letter in his hand, enters from the right through the inner room.*]

TESMAN There, now—the letter's signed and sealed.

HEDDA That's fine. I think Mrs. Elvsted was just leaving. Wait a minute. I'll go with you to the garden gate.

TESMAN Hedda, dear—could Berta maybe look after this?

HEDDA [*taking the letter*] I'll tell her to.

[BERTA *enters from the hall.*]

BERTA Judge Brack is here and says he'd like to greet you and the Doctor, ma'am.

HEDDA Yes, ask Judge Brack to come in. And, here—put this letter in the mail.

BERTA [*takes the letter*] Yes, ma'am.

[*She opens the door for* JUDGE BRACK *and goes out.* BRACK *is a man of forty-five, thickset, yet well-built, with supple movements. His face is roundish, with a distinguished profile. His hair is short, still mostly black, and carefully groomed. His eyes are bright and lively. Thick eyebrows; a mustache to match, with neatly clipped ends. He wears a trimly tailored walking suit, a bit too youthful for his age. Uses a monocle, which he now and then lets fall.*]

JUDGE BRACK [*hat in hand, bowing*] May one dare to call so early?

HEDDA Of course one may.

TESMAN [*shakes his hand*] You're always welcome here. [*Introducing him*] Judge Brack—Miss Rysing—

HEDDA Ah—!

BRACK [*bowing*] I'm delighted.

HEDDA [*looks at him and laughs*] It's really a treat to see you by daylight, Judge!

BRACK You find me—changed?

HEDDA Yes. A bit younger, I think.

BRACK Thank you, most kindly.

TESMAN But what do you say for Hedda, uh? Doesn't she look flourishing? She's actually—

HEDDA Oh, leave me out of it! You might thank Judge Brack for all the trouble he's gone to—

BRACK Nonsense—it was a pleasure—

HEDDA Yes, you're a true friend. But here's Thea, standing here, aching to get away. Excuse me, Judge; I'll be right back.

[*Mutual good-byes.* MRS. ELVSTED *and* HEDDA *go out by the hall door.*]

BRACK So—is your wife fairly well satisfied, then—?

TESMAN Yes, we can't thank you enough. Of course—I gather there's some rearrangement called for here and there. And one or two things are lacking. We still have to buy a few minor items.

BRACK Really?

TESMAN But that's nothing for you to worry about. Hedda said she'd pick up those things herself. Why don't we sit down, hm?

BRACK Thanks. Just for a moment. [*Sits by the table.*] There's something I'd like to discuss with you, Tesman.

TESMAN What? Oh, I understand! [*Sitting*] It's the serious part of the banquet we're coming to, uh?

BRACK Oh, as far as money matters go, there's no great rush—though I must say I wish we'd managed things a bit more economically.

TESMAN But that was completely impossible! Think about Hedda, Judge! You, who know her so well—I simply couldn't have her live like a grocer's wife.

BRACK No, no—that's the trouble, exactly.

TESMAN And then—fortunately—it can't be long before I get my appointment.

BRACK Well, you know—these things can often hang fire.

TESMAN Have you heard something further? Hm?

BRACK Nothing really definite— [*Changing the subject*] But incidentally—I do have one piece of news for you.

TESMAN Well?

BRACK Your old friend Eilert Løvborg is back in town.

TESMAN I already know.

BRACK Oh? How did you hear?

TESMAN She told me. The lady that left with Hedda.

BRACK I see. What was her name again? I didn't quite catch it—

TESMAN Mrs. Elvsted.

BRACK Aha—Sheriff Elvsted's wife. Yes—it's up near them he's been staying.

TESMAN And, just think—what a pleasure to hear that he's completely stable again!

BRACK Yes, that's what they claim.

TESMAN And that he's published a new book, uh?

BRACK Oh yes!

TESMAN And it's created quite a sensation.

BRACK An extraordinary sensation.

TESMAN Just imagine—isn't that marvelous? He, with his remarkable talents—I was so very afraid that he'd really gone down for good.

BRACK That's what everyone thought.

TESMAN But I've no idea what he'll find to do now. How on earth can he ever make a living? Hm?

[*During the last words,* HEDDA *comes in by the hall door.*]

HEDDA [*to* BRACK, *laughing, with a touch of scorn*] Tesman always goes around worrying about how people are going to make a living.

TESMAN My Lord—it's poor Eilert Løvborg we're talking of, dear.

HEDDA [*glancing quickly at him*] Oh, really? [*Sits in the armchair by the stove and asks casually.*] What's the matter with him?

TESMAN Well—he must have run through his inheritance long ago. And he can't write a new book every year. Uh? So I was asking, really, what's going to become of him.

BRACK Perhaps I can shed some light on that.

TESMAN Oh?

BRACK You must remember that he does have relatives with a great deal of influence.

TESMAN Yes, but they've washed their hands of him altogether.

BRACK They used to call him the family's white hope.

TESMAN They used to, yes! But he spoiled all that himself.

HEDDA Who knows? [*With a slight smile*] He's been rehabilitated up at the Elvsteds—

BRACK And then this book that he's published—

TESMAN Oh, well, let's hope they really help him some way or other. I just now wrote to him. Hedda dear, I asked him out here this evening.

BRACK But my dear fellow, you're coming to my stag party this evening. You promised down on the pier last night.

HEDDA Had you forgotten, Tesman?

TESMAN Yes, I absolutely had.

BRACK For that matter, you can rest assured that he'd never come.

TESMAN What makes you say that, hm?

BRACK [*hesitating, rising and leaning on the back of the chair*] My dear Tesman—and you too, Mrs. Tesman—I can't, in all conscience, let you go on without knowing something that—that—

TESMAN Something involving Eilert—?

BRACK Both you and him.

TESMAN But my dear Judge, then tell us!

BRACK You must be prepared that your appointment may not come through as quickly as you've wished or expected.

TESMAN [*jumping up nervously*] Has something gone wrong? Uh?

BRACK It may turn out that there'll have to be a competition for the post—

TESMAN A competition! Imagine, Hedda!

HEDDA [*leaning farther back in the chair*] Ah, there—you see!

TESMAN But with whom! You can't mean—?

BRACK Yes, exactly. With Eilert Løvborg.

TESMAN [*striking his hands together*] No, no—that's completely unthinkable! It's impossible! Uh?

BRACK Hm—but it may come about, all the same.

TESMAN No, but, Judge Brack—that would just be incredibly inconsiderate toward me! [*Waving his arms*] Yes, because—you know—I'm a married man! We married on my prospects, Hedda and I. We went into debt. And even borrowed money from Aunt Julie. Because that job—my Lord, it was as good as promised to me, uh?

BRACK Easy now—I'm sure you'll get the appointment. But you will have to compete for it.

HEDDA [*motionless in the armchair*] Just think, Tesman—it will be like a kind of championship match.

TESMAN But Hedda dearest, how can you take it so calmly!

HEDDA [*as before*] I'm not the least bit calm. I can't wait to see how it turns out.

BRACK In any case, Mrs. Tesman, it's well that you know now how things stand. I mean—with respect to those little purchases I hear you've been threatening to make.

HEDDA This business can't change anything.

BRACK I see! Well, that's another matter. Good-bye. [*To* TESMAN] When I take my afternoon walk, I'll stop by and fetch you.

TESMAN Oh yes, please do—I don't know where I'm at.

HEDDA [*leaning back and reaching out her hand*] Good-bye, Judge. And come again soon.

BRACK Many thanks. Good-bye now.

TESMAN [*accompanying him to the door*] Good-bye, Judge! You really must excuse me—

[BRACK *goes out by the hall door.*]

TESMAN [*pacing about the room*] Oh, Hedda—one should never go off and lose oneself in dreams, uh?

HEDDA [*looks at him and smiles*] Do *you* do *that?*

TESMAN No use denying it. It was living in dreams to go and get married and set up house on nothing but expectations.

HEDDA Perhaps you're right about that.

TESMAN Well, at least we have our comfortable home, Hedda! The home that we always wanted. That we both fell in love with, I could almost say. Hm?

HEDDA [*rising slowly and wearily*] It was part of our bargain that we'd live in society—that we'd keep a great house—

TESMAN Yes of course—how I'd looked forward to that! Imagine—seeing you as a hostess—in our own select circle of friends! Yes, yes—well, for a while, we two will just have to get on by ourselves, Hedda. Perhaps have Aunt Julie here now and then. Oh, you—for you I wanted to have things so—so utterly different—!

HEDDA Naturally this means I can't have a butler now.

TESMAN Oh no—I'm sorry, a butler—we can't even talk about that, you know.

HEDDA And the riding horse I was going to have—

TESMAN [*appalled*] Riding horse!

HEDDA I suppose I can't think of that anymore.

TESMAN Good Lord, no—that's obvious!

HEDDA [*crossing the room*] Well, at least I have one thing left to amuse myself with.

TESMAN [*beaming*] Ah, thank heaven for that! What is it, Hedda? Uh?

HEDDA [*in the center doorway, looking at him with veiled scorn*] My pistols, George.

TESMAN [*in fright*] Your pistols!

HEDDA [*her eyes cold*] General Gabler's pistols.

[*She goes through the inner room and out to the left.*]

TESMAN [*runs to the center doorway and calls after her*] No, for heaven's sake, Hedda darling—don't touch those dangerous things! For my sake, Hedda! Uh?

Act 2

[*The rooms at the* TESMANS', *same as in the first act, except that the piano has been moved out, and an elegant little writing table with a bookcase put in its place. A smaller table stands by the sofa to the left. Most of the flowers have been removed.* MRS. ELVSTED's *bouquet stands on the large table in the foreground. It is afternoon.*

HEDDA, *dressed to receive callers, is alone in the room. She stands by the open glass door, loading a revolver. The match to it lies in an open pistol case on the writing table.*]

HEDDA [*looking down into the garden and calling*] Good to see you again, Judge!

BRACK [*heard from below, at a distance*] Likewise, Mrs. Tesman!

HEDDA [*raises the pistol and aims*] And now, Judge, I'm going to shoot you!

BRACK [*shouting from below*] No-no-no! Don't point that thing at me!

HEDDA That's what comes of sneaking in the back way. [*She fires.*]

BRACK [*nearer*] Are you out of your mind—!

HEDDA Oh, dear—I didn't hit you, did I?

BRACK [*still outside*] Just stop this nonsense!

HEDDA All right, you can come in, Judge.

[JUDGE BRACK, *dressed for a stag party, enters through the glass door. He carries a light overcoat on his arm.*]

BRACK Good God! Are you still playing such games? What are you shooting at?

HEDDA Oh, I was just shooting into the sky.

BRACK [*gently taking the pistol out of her hand*] Permit me. [*Looks at it.*] Ah, this one—I know it well. [*Glancing around*] Where's the case? Ah, here. [*Puts the pistol away and shuts the case.*] We'll have no more of that kind of fun today.

HEDDA Well, what in heaven's name do you want me to do with myself?

BRACK You haven't had any visitors?

HEDDA [*closing the glass door*] Not a single one. All of our set are still in the country, I guess.

BRACK And Tesman isn't home either?

HEDDA [*at the writing table, putting the pistol case away in a drawer*] No. Right after lunch he ran over to his aunts. He didn't expect you so soon.

BRACK Hm— I should have realized. That was stupid of me.

HEDDA [*turning her head and looking at him*] Why stupid?

BRACK Because in that case I would have stopped by a little bit—earlier.

HEDDA [*crossing the room*] Well, you'd have found no one here then at all. I've been up in my room dressing since lunch.

BRACK And there's not the least little crack in the door we could have conferred through.

HEDDA You forgot to arrange it.

BRACK Also stupid of me.

HEDDA Well, we'll just have to settle down here—and wait. Tesman won't be back for a while.

BRACK Don't worry, I can be patient.

[HEDDA *sits in the corner of the sofa.* BRACK *lays his coat over the back of the nearest chair and sits down, keeping his hat in his hand. A short pause. They look at each other.*]

HEDDA Well?

BRACK [*in the same tone*] Well?

HEDDA I spoke first.

BRACK [*leaning slightly forward*] Then let's have a nice little cozy chat, Mrs. Hedda.[6]

HEDDA [*leaning farther back on the sofa*] Doesn't it seem like a whole eternity since the last time we talked together? Oh, a few words last night and this morning—but they don't count.

BRACK You mean, like this—between ourselves? Just the two of us?

HEDDA Well, more or less.

BRACK There wasn't a day that I didn't wish you were home again.

HEDDA And I was wishing exactly the same.

BRACK You? Really, Mrs. Hedda? And I thought you were having such a marvelous time on this trip.

HEDDA Oh, you can imagine!

BRACK But that's what Tesman always wrote.

HEDDA Oh, him! There's nothing he likes better than grubbing around in libraries and copying out old parchments, or whatever you call them.

BRACK [*with a touch of malice*] But after all, it's his calling in life. In good part, anyway.

HEDDA Yes, that's true. So there's nothing wrong with it— But what about *me!* Oh, Judge, you don't know—I've been so dreadfully bored.

BRACK [*sympathetically*] You really mean that? In all seriousness?

HEDDA Well, you can understand—! To go for a whole six months without meeting a soul who knew the least bit about our circle. No one that one could talk to about our kind of things.

BRACK Ah, yes—I think that would bother me too.

HEDDA But then the most unbearable thing of all—

BRACK What?

HEDDA To be everlastingly together with—with one and the same person—

BRACK [*nodding in agreement*] Morning, noon, and night—yes. At every conceivable hour.

HEDDA I said "everlastingly."

BRACK All right. But with our good friend Tesman, I really should have thought—

HEDDA My dear Judge, Tesman is—a specialist.

BRACK Undeniably.

HEDDA And specialists aren't at all amusing to travel with. Not in the long run, anyway.

6. Although Brack uses the playful "Mrs. Hedda" when they are alone, in Ibsen's original Norwegian text he addresses her with the formal *De* throughout the play.

BRACK Not even—the specialist that one *loves?*

HEDDA Ugh—don't use that syrupy word!

BRACK [*startled*] What's that, Mrs. Hedda!

HEDDA [*half laughing, half annoyed*] Well, just try it yourself! Try listening to the history of civilization morning, noon, and—

BRACK Everlastingly.

HEDDA Yes! Yes! And then all this business about domestic crafts in the Middle Ages—! That really is just too revolting!

BRACK [*looks searchingly at her*] But tell me—I can't see how it ever came about that—? Hm—

HEDDA That George Tesman and I could make a match?

BRACK All right, let's put it that way.

HEDDA Good Lord, does it seem so remarkable?

BRACK Well, yes—and no, Mrs. Hedda.

HEDDA I really had danced myself out, Judge. My time was up. [*With a slight shudder*] Ugh! No, I don't want to say that. Or think it, either.

BRACK You certainly have no reason to.

HEDDA Oh—reasons— [*Watching him carefully*] And George Tesman—he is, after all, a thoroughly acceptable choice.

BRACK Acceptable and dependable, beyond a doubt.

HEDDA And I don't find anything especially ridiculous about him. Do you?

BRACK Ridiculous? No-o-o, I wouldn't say that.

HEDDA Hm. Anyway, he works incredibly hard on his research! There's every chance that, in time, he could still make a name for himself.

BRACK [*looking at her with some uncertainty*] I thought you believed, like everyone else, that he was going to be quite famous some day.

HEDDA [*wearily*] Yes, so I did. And then when he kept pressing and pleading to be allowed to take care of me—I didn't see why I ought to resist.

BRACK No. From that point of view, of course not—

HEDDA It was certainly more than my other admirers were willing to do for me, Judge.

BRACK [*laughing*] Well, I can't exactly answer for all the others. But as far as I'm concerned, you know that I've always cherished a—a certain respect for the marriage bond. Generally speaking, that is.

HEDDA [*bantering*] Oh, I never really held out any hopes for *you.*

BRACK All I want is to have a warm circle of intimate friends, where I can be of use one way or another, with the freedom to come and go as—as a trusted friend—

HEDDA Of the man of the house, you mean?

BRACK [*with a bow*] Frankly—I prefer the lady. But the man, too, of course, in his place. That kind of—let's say, triangular arrangement—you can't imagine how satisfying it can be all around.

HEDDA Yes, I must say I longed for some third person so many times on that trip. Oh—those endless tête-à-têtes in railway compartments—!

BRACK Fortunately the wedding trip's over now.

HEDDA [*shaking her head*] The trip will go on—and on. I've only come to one stop on the line.

BRACK Well, then what you do is jump out—and stretch yourself a little, Mrs. Hedda.

HEDDA I'll never jump out.

BRACK Never?

HEDDA No. Because there's always someone on the platform who—

BRACK [*with a laugh*] Who looks at your legs, is that it?

HEDDA Precisely.

BRACK Yes, but after all—

HEDDA [*with a disdainful gesture*] I'm not interested. I'd rather keep my seat—right here, where I am. Tête-à-tête.

BRACK Well, but suppose a third person came on board and joined the couple.

HEDDA Ah! That's entirely different.

BRACK A trusted friend, who understands—

HEDDA And can talk about all kinds of lively things—

BRACK Who's not in the least a specialist.

HEDDA [*with an audible sigh*] Yes, that would be a relief.

BRACK [*hearing the front door open and glancing toward it*] The triangle is complete.

HEDDA [*lowering her voice*] And the train goes on.

[GEORGE TESMAN, *in a gray walking suit and a soft felt hat, enters from the hall. He has a good number of unbound books under his arm and in his pockets.*]

TESMAN [*going up to the table by the corner settee*] Phew! Let me tell you, that's hot work—carrying all these. [*Setting the books down*] I'm actually sweating, Hedda. And what's this—you're already here, Judge? Hm? Berta didn't tell me.

BRACK [*rising*] I came in through the garden.

HEDDA What are all these books you've gotten?

TESMAN [*stands leafing through them*] They're new publications in my special field. I absolutely need them.

HEDDA Your special field?

BRACK Of course. Books in his special field, Mrs. Tesman.

[BRACK *and* HEDDA *exchange a knowing smile.*]

HEDDA You need still more books in your special field?

TESMAN Hedda, my dear, it's impossible ever to have too many. You have to keep up with what's written and published.

HEDDA Oh, I suppose so.

TESMAN [*searching among the books*] And look—I picked up Eilert Løvborg's new book too. [*Offering it to her*] Maybe you'd like to have a look at it? Uh?

HEDDA No, thank you. Or—well, perhaps later.

TESMAN I skimmed through some of it on the way home.

BRACK Well, what do you think of it—as a specialist?

TESMAN I think it's amazing how well it holds up. He's never written like this before. [*Gathers up the books.*] But I'll take these into the study now I can't wait to cut the pages—![7] And then I better dress up a bit. [*To* BRACK] We don't have to rush right off, do we? Hm?

BRACK No, not at all. There's ample time.

7. When books are published, four or eight pages are usually printed on one sheet, which is subsequently folded to properly order the leaves; formerly, books were often sold with the outer edges of the folded pages left uncut.

TESMAN Ah, then I'll be at my leisure. [*Starts out with the books, but pauses and turns in the doorway.*] Oh, incidentally, Hedda—Aunt Julie won't be by to see you this evening.

HEDDA She won't? I suppose it's that business with the hat?

TESMAN Not at all. How can you think that of Aunt Julie? Imagine—! No, it's Auntie Rina—she's very ill.

HEDDA She always is.

TESMAN Yes, but today she really took a turn for the worse.

HEDDA Well, then it's only sensible for her sister to stay with her. I'll have to bear with it.

TESMAN But you can't imagine how delighted Aunt Julie was all the same—because you'd filled out so nicely on the trip!

HEDDA [*under her breath; rising*] Oh, these eternal aunts!

TESMAN What?

HEDDA [*going over to the glass door*] Nothing.

TESMAN All right, then. [*He goes through the inner room and out, right.*]

BRACK What were you saying about a hat?

HEDDA Oh, it's something that happened with Miss Tesman this morning. She'd put her hat down over there on the chair. [*Looks at him and smiles.*] And I pretended I thought it was the maid's.

BRACK [*shaking his head*] But my dear Mrs. Hedda, how could you do that! Hurt that nice old lady!

HEDDA [*nervously, pacing the room*] Well, it's—these things come over me, just like that, suddenly. And I can't hold back. [*Throws herself down in the armchair by the stove.*] Oh, I don't know myself how to explain it.

BRACK [*behind the armchair*] You're not really happy—that's the heart of it.

HEDDA [*gazing straight ahead*] And I don't know why I ought to be—happy. Or maybe you can tell me why?

BRACK Yes—among other things, because you've gotten just the home you've always wanted.

HEDDA [*looks up at him and laughs*] You believe that story too?

BRACK You mean there's nothing to it?

HEDDA Oh yes—there's something to it.

BRACK Well?

HEDDA There's this much to it, that I used Tesman as my escort home from parties last summer—

BRACK Unfortunately—I was headed quite a different way.

HEDDA How true. Yes, you went several different ways last summer.

BRACK [*laughing*] For shame, Mrs. Hedda! Well—so you and Tesman—?

HEDDA Yes, so one evening we walked by this place. And Tesman, poor thing, was writhing in torment, because he couldn't find anything to say. And I felt sorry for a man of such learning—

BRACK [*smiling skeptically*] Did you? Hm—

HEDDA No, I honestly did. And so—just to help him off the hook—I came out with some rash remark about this lovely house being where I'd always wanted to live.

BRACK No more than that?

HEDDA No more that evening.

BRACK But afterward?

HEDDA Yes, my rashness had its consequences, Judge.

BRACK I'm afraid our rashness all too often does, Mrs. Hedda.

HEDDA Thanks! But don't you see, it was this passion for the old Falk mansion that drew George Tesman and me together! It was nothing more than that, that brought on our engagement and the marriage and the wedding trip and everything else. Oh yes, Judge—I was going to say, you make your bed and then you lie in it.

BRACK But that's priceless! So actually you couldn't care less about all this?

HEDDA God knows, not in the least.

BRACK But even now? Now that we've got it furnished a bit cosier for you here?

HEDDA Ugh—all the rooms seem to smell of lavender and dried roses. But maybe that scent was brought in by Aunt Julie.

BRACK [*laughing*] No, I think it's a bequest from the late Mrs. Falk.

HEDDA Yes, there's something in it of the odor of death. It's like a corsage—the day after the dance. [*Folds her hands behind her neck, leans back in her chair, and looks at him.*] Oh, my dear Judge—you can't imagine how horribly I'm going to bore myself here.

BRACK But couldn't you find some goal in life to work toward? Others do, Mrs. Hedda.

HEDDA A goal—that would really absorb me?

BRACK Yes, preferably.

HEDDA God only knows what that could be. I often wonder if— [*Breaks off.*] But that's impossible too.

BRACK Who knows? Tell me.

HEDDA I was thinking—if I could get Tesman to go into politics.

BRACK [*laughing*] Tesman! No, I can promise you—politics is absolutely out of his line.

HEDDA No, I can believe you. But even so, I wonder if I could get him into it?

BRACK Well, what satisfaction would you have in that, if he can't succeed? Why push him in that direction?

HEDDA Because, I've told you, I'm bored! [*After a pause*] Then you think it's really out of the question that he could ever be a cabinet minister?

BRACK Hm—you see, Mrs. Hedda—to be anything like that, he'd have to be fairly wealthy to start with.

HEDDA [*rising impatiently*] Yes, there it is! It's this tight little world I've stumbled into— [*Crossing the room*] That's what makes life so miserable! So utterly ludicrous! Because that's what it *is*.

BRACK I'd say the fault lies elsewhere.

HEDDA Where?

BRACK You've never experienced anything that's really stirred you.

HEDDA Anything serious, you mean.

BRACK Well, you can call it that, if you like. But now perhaps it's on the way.

HEDDA [*tossing her head*] Oh, you mean all the fuss over that wretched professorship! But that's Tesman's problem. I'm not going to give it a single thought.

BRACK No, that isn't—ah, never mind. But suppose you were to be confronted now by what—in rather elegant language—is called your most solemn responsibility. [*Smiling*] A new responsibility, Mrs. Hedda.

HEDDA [*angrily*] Be quiet! You'll never see me like that!

BRACK [*delicately*] We'll discuss it again in a year's time—at the latest.

HEDDA [*curtly*] I have no talent for such things, Judge. I won't have responsibilities!

BRACK Don't you think you've a talent for what almost every woman finds the most meaningful—

HEDDA [*over by the glass door*] Oh, I told you, be quiet! I often think I have talent for only one thing in life.

BRACK [*moving closer*] And what, may I ask, is that?

HEDDA [*stands looking out*] Boring myself to death. And that's the truth. [*Turns, looks toward the inner room, and laughs.*] See what I mean! Here comes the professor.

BRACK [*in a low tone of warning*] Ah-ah-ah, Mrs. Hedda!

[GEORGE TESMAN, *dressed for the party, with hat and gloves in hand, enters from the right through the inner room.*]

TESMAN Hedda—there's been no word from Eilert Løvborg, has there? Hm?

HEDDA No.

TESMAN Well, he's bound to be here soon then. You'll see.

BRACK You really believe he'll come?

TESMAN Yes, I'm almost positive of it. Because I'm sure they're nothing but rumors, what you told us this morning.

BRACK Oh?

TESMAN Yes. At least Aunt Julie said she couldn't for the world believe that he'd stand in my way again. Can you imagine that!

BRACK So, then everything's well and good.

TESMAN [*putting his hat with the gloves inside on a chair to the right*] Yes, but I really would like to wait for him as long as possible.

BRACK We have plenty of time for that. There's no one due at my place till seven or half past.

TESMAN Why, then we can keep Hedda company for a while. And see what turns up. Uh?

HEDDA [*taking* BRACK's *hat and coat over to the settee*] And if worst comes to worst, Mr. Løvborg can sit and talk with me.

BRACK [*trying to take his things himself*] Ah, please, Mrs. Tesman—! What do you mean by "worst," in this case?

HEDDA If he won't go with you and Tesman.

TESMAN [*looks doubtfully at her*] But Hedda dear—is it quite right that he stays with you here? Uh? Remember that Aunt Julie isn't coming.

HEDDA No, but Mrs. Elvsted is. The three of us can have tea together.

TESMAN Oh, well, that's all right.

BRACK [*smiling*] And that might be the soundest plan for him too.

HEDDA Why?

BRACK Well, really, Mrs. Tesman, you've made enough pointed remarks about my little bachelor parties. You've always said they're only fit for men of the strictest principles.

HEDDA But Mr. Løvborg is surely a man of principle now. After all, a reformed sinner—

[BERTA *appears at the hall door.*]

BERTA Ma'am, there's a gentleman here who'd like to see you—

HEDDA Yes, show him in.

TESMAN [*softly*] I'm sure it's him! Just think!

[EILERT LØVBORG *enters from the hall. He is lean and gaunt, the same age as* TESMAN, *but looks older and somewhat run-down. His hair and beard are dark brown, his face long and pale, but with reddish patches over the cheekbones. He is dressed in a trim black suit, quite new, and holds dark gloves and a top hat in his hand. He hesitates by the door and bows abruptly. He seems somewhat embarrassed.*]

TESMAN [*crosses over and shakes his hand*] Ah, my dear Eilert—so at last we meet again!

EILERT LØVBORG [*speaking in a hushed voice*] Thanks for your letter, George! [*Approaching* HEDDA] May I shake hands with you too, Mrs. Tesman?

HEDDA [*taking his hand*] So glad to see you, Mr. Løvborg. [*Gesturing with her hand*] I don't know if you two gentlemen—?

LØVBORG [*bowing slightly*] Judge Brack, I believe.

BRACK [*reciprocating*] Of course. It's been some years—

TESMAN [*to* LØVBORG, *with his hands on his shoulders*] And now, Eilert, make yourself at home, completely! Right, Hedda? I hear you'll be settling down here in town again? Uh?

LØVBORG I plan to.

TESMAN Well, that makes sense. Listen—I just got hold of your new book. But I really haven't had time to read it yet.

LØVBORG You can save yourself the bother.

TESMAN Why? What do you mean?

LØVBORG There's very little to it.

TESMAN Imagine—you can say that!

BRACK But it's won such high praise, I hear.

LØVBORG That's exactly what I wanted. So I wrote a book that everyone could agree with.

BRACK Very sound.

TESMAN Yes, but my dear Eilert—!

LØVBORG Because now I want to build up my position again—and try to make a fresh start.

TESMAN [*somewhat distressed*] Yes, that is what you want, I suppose. Uh?

LØVBORG [*smiling, puts down his hat and takes a packet wrapped in brown paper out of his coat pocket*] But when this comes out—George Tesman—you'll have to read it. Because this is the real book—the one that speaks for my true self.

TESMAN Oh, really? What sort of book is that?

LØVBORG It's the sequel.

TESMAN Sequel? To what?

LØVBORG To the book.

TESMAN The one just out?

LØVBORG Of course.

TESMAN Yes, but my dear Eilert—that comes right down to our own time!

LØVBORG Yes, it does. And this one deals with the future.

TESMAN The future! But good Lord, there's nothing we know about that!

LØVBORG True. But there are one or two things worth saying about it all the same. [*Opens the packet.*] Here, take a look—

TESMAN But that's not your handwriting.

LØVBORG I dictated it. [*Paging through the manuscript*] It's divided into two sections. The first is about the forces shaping the civilization of the future.

And the second part, here—[*Paging further on*] suggests what lines of development it's likely to take.

TESMAN How extraordinary! It never would have occurred to me to write about anything like that.

HEDDA [*at the glass door, drumming on the pane*] Hm—no, of course not.

LØVBORG [*puts the manuscript back in its wrapping and lays it on the table*] I brought it along because I thought I might read you a bit of it this evening.

TESMAN Ah, that's very good of you, Eilert; but this evening— [*Glancing at* BRACK] I'm really not sure that it's possible—

LØVBORG Well, some other time, then. There's no hurry.

BRACK I should explain, Mr. Løvborg—there's a little party at my place tonight. Mostly for Tesman, you understand.

LØVBORG [*looking for his hat*] Ah—then I won't stay—

BRACK No, listen—won't you give me the pleasure of having you join us?

LØVBORG [*sharply and decisively*] No, I can't. Thanks very much.

BRACK Oh, nonsense! Do that. We'll be a small, select group. And you can bet we'll have it "lively," as Mrs. Hed—Mrs. Tesman says.

LØVBORG I don't doubt it. But nevertheless—

BRACK You could bring your manuscript with you and read it to Tesman there, at my place. I have plenty of rooms.

TESMAN Why, of course, Eilert—you could do that, couldn't you? Uh?

HEDDA [*intervening*] But dear, if Mr. Løvborg simply doesn't want to! I'm sure Mr. Løvborg would much prefer to settle down here and have supper with me.

LØVBORG [*looking at her*] With you, Mrs. Tesman!

HEDDA And with Mrs. Elvsted.

LØVBORG Ah. [*Casually*] I saw her a moment this afternoon.

HEDDA Oh, did you? Well, she'll be here soon. So it's almost essential for you to stay, Mr. Løvborg. Otherwise, she'll have no one to see her home.

LØVBORG That's true. Yes, thank you, Mrs. Tesman—I'll be staying, then.

HEDDA Then let me just tell the maid—

[*She goes to the hall door and rings.* BERTA *enters.* HEDDA *talks to her quietly and points toward the inner room.* BERTA *nods and goes out again.*]

TESMAN [*at the same time, to* LØVBORG] Tell me, Eilert—is it this new material—about the future—that you're going to be lecturing on?

LØVBORG Yes.

TESMAN Because I heard at the bookstore that you'll be giving a lecture series here this autumn.

LØVBORG I intend to. I hope you won't be offended, Tesman.

TESMAN Why, of course not! But—?

LØVBORG I can easily understand that it makes things rather difficult for you.

TESMAN [*dispiritedly*] Oh, I could hardly expect that for my sake you'd—

LØVBORG But I'm going to wait till you have your appointment.

TESMAN You'll wait! Yes, but—but—you're not competing for it, then? Uh?

LØVBORG No. I only want to win in the eyes of the world.

TESMAN But, my Lord—then Aunt Julie was right after all! Oh yes—I knew it all along! Hedda! Can you imagine—Eilert Løvborg won't stand in our way!

HEDDA [*brusquely*] Our way? Leave me out of it.

[*She goes up toward the inner room where* BERTA *is putting a tray with decanters and glasses on the table.* HEDDA *nods her approval and comes back again.* BERTA *goes out.*]

TESMAN [*at the same time*] But you, Judge—what do you say to all this? Uh?

BRACK Well, I'd say that victory and honor—hm—after all, they're very sweet—

TESMAN Yes, of course. But still—

HEDDA [*regarding* TESMAN *with a cold smile*] You look as if you'd been struck by lightning.

TESMAN Yes—something like it—I guess—

BRACK That's because a thunderstorm just passed over us, Mrs. Tesman.

HEDDA [*pointing toward the inner room*] Won't you gentlemen please help yourselves to a glass of cold punch?

BRACK [*looking at his watch*] A parting cup? That's not such a bad idea.

TESMAN Marvelous, Hedda! Simply marvelous! The way I feel now, with this weight off my mind—

HEDDA Please, Mr. Løvborg, you too,

LØVBORG [*with a gesture of refusal*] No, thank you. Not for me.

BRACK Good Lord, cold punch—it isn't poison, you know.

LØVBORG Perhaps not for everyone.

HEDDA I'll keep Mr. Løvborg company a while.

TESMAN All right, Hedda dear, you do that.

[*He and* BRACK *go into the inner room, sit down, drink punch, smoke cigarettes, and talk animatedly during the following.* LØVBORG *remains standing by the stove.* HEDDA *goes to the writing table.*]

HEDDA [*slightly raising her voice*] I can show you some photographs, if you like. Tesman and I traveled through the Tyrol on our way home.

[*She brings over an album and lays it on the table by the sofa, seating herself in the farthest corner.* EILERT LØVBORG *comes closer, stops, and looks at her. Then he takes a chair and sits down on her left, his back toward the inner room.*]

HEDDA [*opening the album*] You see this view of the mountains, Mr. Løvborg. That's the Ortler group. Tesman's labeled them underneath. Here it is: "The Ortler group, near Meran."[8]

LØVBORG [*whose eyes have never left her, speaking in a low, soft voice*] Hedda—Gabler!

HEDDA [*with a quick glance at him*] Ah! Shh!

LØVBORG [*repeating softly*] Hedda Gabler!

HEDDA [*looks at the album*] Yes, I used to be called that. In those days—when we two knew each other.

LØVBORG And from now on—for the rest of my life—I have to teach myself not to say Hedda Gabler.

HEDDA [*turning the pages*] Yes, you have to. And I think you ought to start practicing it. The sooner the better, I'd say.

LØVBORG [*resentment in his voice*] Hedda Gabler married? And to George Tesman!

8. Merano, a district in northeastern Italy on the southern slope of the Alps.

HEDDA Yes—that's how it goes.

LØVBORG Oh, Hedda, Hedda—how could you throw yourself away like that![9]

HEDDA [*looks at him sharply*] All right—no more of that!

LØVBORG What do you mean?

[TESMAN *comes in and over to the sofa.*]

HEDDA [*hears him coming and says casually*] And this one, Mr. Løvborg, was taken from the Val d'Ampezzo.[1] Just look at the peaks of those mountains. [*Looks warmly up at* TESMAN.] Now what were those marvelous mountains called, dear?

TESMAN Let me see. Oh, those are the Dolomites.

HEDDA Why, of course! Those are the Dolomites, Mr. Løvborg.

TESMAN Hedda dear—I only wanted to ask if we shouldn't bring in some punch anyway. At least for you, hm?

HEDDA Yes, thank you. And a couple of *petits fours*, please.

TESMAN No cigarettes?

HEDDA No.

TESMAN Right.

[*He goes through the inner room and out to the right.* BRACK *remains sitting inside, keeping his eye from time to time on* HEDDA *and* LØVBORG.]

LØVBORG [*softly, as before*] Answer me, Hedda—how could you go and do such a thing?

HEDDA [*apparently immersed in the album*] If you keep on saying Hedda like that to me, I won't talk to you.

LØVBORG Can't I say Hedda even when we're alone?

HEDDA No. You can think it, but you mustn't say it like that.

LØVBORG Ah, I understand. It offends your—love for George Tesman.

HEDDA [*glances at him and smiles*] Love? You *are* absurd!

LØVBORG Then you don't love him!

HEDDA I don't expect to be unfaithful, either. I'm not having any of that!

LØVBORG Hedda, just answer me one thing—

HEDDA Shh!

[TESMAN, *carrying a tray, enters from the inner room.*]

TESMAN Look out! Here come the goodies. [*He sets the tray on the table.*]

HEDDA Why do you do the serving?

TESMAN [*filling the glasses*] Because I think it's such fun to wait on you, Hedda.

HEDDA But now you've poured out two glasses. And you know Mr. Løvborg doesn't want—

TESMAN Well, but Mrs. Elvsted will be along soon.

HEDDA Yes, that's right—Mrs. Elvsted—

TESMAN Had you forgotten her? Uh?

HEDDA We've been so caught up in these. [*Showing him a picture*] Do you remember this little village?

9. When addressing Hedda, Løvborg uses the familiar *du* in the first part of this scene; here, he reverts to the formal *De*. However, he calls her by her first name throughout. Hedda, by contrast, addresses him as "Mr. Løvborg" and uses only the formal *De*.

1. A valley in northern Italy in the Dolomites, a section of the Tyrolean Alps.

TESMAN Oh, that's the one just below the Brenner Pass![2] It was there that we stayed overnight—

HEDDA And met all those lively summer people.

TESMAN Yes, that's the place. Just think—if we could have had *you* with us, Eilert! My! [*He goes back and sits beside* BRACK.]

LØVBORG Answer me just one thing, Hedda—

HEDDA Yes?

LØVBORG Was there no love with respect to me, either? Not a spark—not one glimmer of love at all?

HEDDA I wonder, really, was there? To me it was as if we were two true companions—two very close friends. [*Smiling*] You, especially, were so open with me.

LØVBORG You wanted it that way.

HEDDA When I look back on it now, there was really something beautiful and fascinating—and daring, it seems to me, about—about our secret closeness—our companionship that no one, not a soul, suspected.

LØVBORG Yes, Hedda, that's true! Wasn't there? When I'd come over to your father's in the afternoon—and the general sat by the window reading his papers—with his back to us—

HEDDA And we'd sit on the corner sofa—

LØVBORG Always with the same illustrated magazine in front of us—

HEDDA Yes, for the lack of an album.

LØVBORG Yes, Hedda—and the confessions I used to make—telling you things about myself that no one else knew of then. About the way I'd go out, the drinking, the madness that went on day and night, for days at a time. Ah, what power was it in you, Hedda, that made me tell you such things?

HEDDA You think it was some kind of power in me?

LØVBORG How else can I explain it? And all those—those devious questions you asked me—

HEDDA That you understood so remarkably well—

LØVBORG To think you could sit there and ask such questions! So boldly.

HEDDA Deviously, please.

LØVBORG Yes, but boldly, all the same. Interrogating me about—all that kind of thing!

HEDDA And to think you could answer, Mr. Løvborg.

LØVBORG Yes, that's exactly what I don't understand—now, looking back. But tell me, Hedda—the root of that bond between us, wasn't it love? Didn't you feel, on your part, as if you wanted to cleanse and absolve me—when I brought those confessions to you? Wasn't that it?

HEDDA No, not quite.

LØVBORG What made you do it, then?

HEDDA Do you find it so very surprising that a young girl—if there's no chance of anyone knowing—

LØVBORG Yes?

HEDDA That she'd like some glimpse of a world that—

LØVBORG That—?

HEDDA That she's forbidden to know anything about.

2. One of the main passes in the Alps, between Austria and Italy.

LØVBORG So that was it?

HEDDA Partly. Partly that, I guess.

LØVBORG Companionship in a thirst for life. But why, then, couldn't it have gone on?

HEDDA But that was your fault.

LØVBORG You broke it off.

HEDDA Yes, when that closeness of ours threatened to grow more serious. Shame on you, Eilert Løvborg! How could you violate my trust when I'd been so—so bold with my friendship?

LØVBORG [*clenching his fists*] Oh, why didn't you do what you said! Why didn't you shoot me down!

HEDDA I'm—much too afraid of scandal.

LØVBORG Yes, Hedda, you're a coward at heart.

HEDDA A terrible coward. [*Changing her tone*] But that was lucky for you. And now you're so nicely consoled at the Elvsteds'.

LØVBORG I know what Thea's been telling you.

HEDDA And perhaps you've been telling her all about us?

LØVBORG Not a word. She's too stupid for that sort of thing.

HEDDA Stupid?

LØVBORG When it comes to those things, she's stupid.

HEDDA And I'm a coward. [*Leans closer, without looking him in the eyes, and speaks softly.*] But there *is* something now that I can tell you.

LØVBORG [*intently*] What?

HEDDA When I didn't dare shoot you—

LØVBORG Yes?

HEDDA That wasn't my worst cowardice—that night.

LØVBORG [*looks at her a moment, understands, and whispers passionately*] Oh, Hedda! Hedda Gabler! Now I begin to see it, the hidden reason why we've been so close! You and I—![3] It was the hunger for *life* in you—

HEDDA [*quietly, with a sharp glance*] Careful! That's no way to think!

[*It has begun to grow dark. The hall door is opened from without by* BERTA.]

HEDDA [*clapping the album shut and calling out with a smile*] Well, at last! Thea dear—please come in!

[MRS. ELVSTED *enters from the hall. She is in evening dress. The door is closed behind her.*]

HEDDA [*on the sofa, stretching her arms out toward her*] Thea, my sweet—I thought you were never coming!

[*In passing,* MRS. ELVSTED *exchanges light greetings with the gentlemen in the inner room, then comes over to the table and extends her hand to* HEDDA. LØVBORG *has gotten up. He and* MRS. ELVSTED *greet each other with a silent nod.*]

MRS. ELVSTED Perhaps I ought to go in and talk a bit with your husband?

HEDDA Oh, nonsense. Let them be. They're leaving soon.

MRS. ELVSTED They're leaving?

HEDDA Yes, for a drinking party.

MRS. ELVSTED [*quickly, to* LØVBORG] But you're not?

3. Here Løvborg reverts to the familiar *du* while Hedda continues to address him with the formal *De*.

LØVBORG No.

HEDDA Mr. Løvborg—is staying with us.

MRS. ELVSTED [*taking a chair, about to sit down beside him*] Oh, it's so good to be here!

HEDDA No, no, Thea dear! Not there! You have to come over here by me. I want to be in the middle.

MRS. ELVSTED Any way you please.

[*She goes around the table and sits on the sofa to* HEDDA'S *right.* LØVBORG *resumes his seat.*]

LØVBORG [*after a brief pause, to* HEDDA] Isn't she lovely to look at?

HEDDA [*lightly stroking her hair*] Only to look at?

LØVBORG Yes. Because we two—she and I—we really *are* true companions. We trust each other completely. We can talk things out together without any reservations—

HEDDA Never anything devious, Mr. Løvborg?

LØVBORG Well—

MRS. ELVSTED [*quietly, leaning close to* HEDDA] Oh, Hedda, you don't know how happy I am! Just think—he says that I've inspired him.

HEDDA [*regarding her with a smile*] Really, dear; did he say that?

LØVBORG And then the courage she has, Mrs. Tesman, when it's put to the test.

MRS. ELVSTED Good heavens, me! Courage!

LØVBORG Enormous courage—where I'm concerned.

HEDDA Yes, courage—yes! If one only had that.

LØVBORG Then what?

HEDDA Then life might still be bearable. [*Suddenly changing her tone*] But now, Thea dearest—you really must have a nice glass of cold punch.

MRS. ELVSTED No, thank you. I never drink that sort of thing.

HEDDA Well, then you, Mr. Løvborg.

LØVBORG Thanks, not for me either.

MRS. ELVSTED No, not for him either!

HEDDA [*looking intently at him*] But if I insist?

LØVBORG Makes no difference.

HEDDA [*with a laugh*] Poor me, then I have no power over you at all?

LØVBORG Not in that area.

HEDDA But seriously, I think you ought to, all the same. For your own sake.

MRS. ELVSTED But Hedda—!

LØVBORG Why do you think so?

HEDDA Or, to be more exact, for others' sakes.

LØVBORG Oh?

HEDDA Otherwise, people might get the idea that you're not very bold at heart. That you're not really sure of yourself at all.

MRS. ELVSTED [*softly*] Oh, Hedda, don't—!

LØVBORG People can think whatever they like, for all I care.

MRS. ELVSTED [*happily*] Yes, that's right!

HEDDA I saw it so clearly in Judge Brack a moment ago.

LØVBORG What did you see?

HEDDA The contempt in his smile when you didn't dare join them for a drink

LØVBORG Didn't dare! Obviously I'd rather stay here and talk with you.

MRS. ELVSTED That's only reasonable, Hedda.

HEDDA But how could the judge know that? And besides, I noticed him smile and glance at Tesman when you couldn't bring yourself to go to their wretched little party.

LØVBORG Couldn't! Are you saying I couldn't?

HEDDA I'm not. But that's the way Judge Brack sees it.

LØVBORG All right, let him.

HEDDA Then you won't go along?

LØVBORG I'm staying here with you and Thea.

MRS. ELVSTED Yes, Hedda—you can be sure he is!

HEDDA [*smiles and nods approvingly at* LØVBORG] I see. Firm as a rock. True to principle, to the end of time. There, that's what a man ought to be! [*Turning to* MRS. ELVSTED *and patting her*] Well, now, didn't I tell you that, when you came here so distraught this morning—

LØVBORG [*surprised*] Distraught?

MRS. ELVSTED [*terrified*] Hedda—! But Hedda—!

HEDDA Can't you see for yourself? There's no need at all for your going around so deathly afraid that— [*Changing her tone*] There! Now we can all enjoy ourselves!

LØVBORG [*shaken*] What is all this, Mrs. Tesman?

MRS. ELVSTED Oh, God, oh, God, Hedda! What are you saying! What are you doing!

HEDDA Not so loud. That disgusting judge is watching you.

LØVBORG So deathly afraid? For my sake?

MRS. ELVSTED [*in a low moan*] Oh, Hedda, you've made me so miserable!

LØVBORG [*looks intently at her a moment, his face drawn*] So that's how completely you trusted me.

MRS. ELVSTED [*imploringly*] Oh, my dearest—if you'll only listen—!

LØVBORG [*takes one of the glasses of punch, raises it, and says in a low, hoarse voice*] Your health, Thea! [*He empties the glass, puts it down, and takes the other.*]

MRS. ELVSTED [*softly*] Oh, Hedda, Hedda—how could you want such a thing!

HEDDA Want it? I? Are you crazy?

LØVBORG And your health too, Mrs. Tesman. Thanks for the truth. Long live truth! [*Drains the glass and starts to refill it.*]

HEDDA [*laying her hand on his arm*] All right—no more for now. Remember, you're going to a party.

MRS. ELVSTED No, no, no!

HEDDA Shh! They're watching you.

LØVBORG [*putting down his glass*] Now, Thea—tell me honestly—

MRS. ELVSTED Yes!

LØVBORG Did your husband know that you followed me?

MRS. ELVSTED [*wringing her hands*] Oh, Hedda—listen to him!

LØVBORG Did you have it arranged, you and he, that you should come down into town and spy on me? Or maybe he got you to do it himself? Ah, yes—I'm sure he needed me back in the office! Or maybe he missed my hand at cards?

MRS. ELVSTED [*softly, in anguish*] Oh, Eilert, Eilert—!

LØVBORG [*seizing his glass to fill it*] Skoal to the old sheriff, too!

HEDDA [*stopping him*] That's enough. Don't forget, you're giving a reading for Tesman.

LØVBORG [*calmly, setting down his glass*] That was stupid of me, Thea. I mean, taking it like this. Don't be angry at me, my dearest. You'll see—you and all the others—that if I stumbled and fell—I'm back on my feet again now! With your help, Thea.

MRS. ELVSTED [*radiant with joy*] Oh, thank God—!

[BRACK, *in the meantime, has looked at his watch. He and* TESMAN *stand up and enter the drawing room.*]

BRACK [*takes his hat and overcoat*] Well, Mrs. Tesman, our time is up.

HEDDA I suppose it is.

LØVBORG [*rising*] Mine too, Judge.

MRS. ELVSTED [*softly pleading*] Oh, Eilert—don't!

HEDDA [*pinching her arm*] They can hear you!

MRS. ELVSTED [*with a small cry*] Ow!

LØVBORG [*to* BRACK] You were kind enough to ask me along.

BRACK Oh, then you *are* coming, after all?

LØVBORG Yes, thank you.

BRACK I'm delighted—

LØVBORG [*putting the packet back in his pocket, to* TESMAN] I'd like to show you one or two things before I turn this in.

TESMAN Just think—how exciting! But Hedda dear, how will Mrs. Elvsted get home? Uh?

HEDDA Oh, we'll hit on something.

LØVBORG [*glancing toward the ladies*] Mrs. Elvsted? Don't worry, I'll stop back and fetch her. [*Coming nearer*] Say about ten o'clock, Mrs. Tesman? Will that do?

HEDDA Yes. That will do very nicely.

TESMAN Well, then everything's all set. But you mustn't expect *me* that early, Hedda.

HEDDA Dear, you stay as long—just as long as you like.

MRS. ELVSTED [*with suppressed anxiety*] Mr. Løvborg—I'll be waiting here till you come.

LØVBORG [*his hat in his hand*] Yes, I understand.

BRACK So, gentlemen—the excursion train is leaving! I hope it's going to be lively, as a certain fair lady puts it.

HEDDA Ah, if only that fair lady could be there, invisible—

BRACK Why invisible?

HEDDA To hear a little of your unadulterated liveliness, Judge.

BRACK [*laughs*] I wouldn't advise the fair lady to try.

TESMAN [*also laughing*] Oh, Hedda, that's a good one! Just imagine!

BRACK Well, good night. Good night, ladies.

LØVBORG [*bowing*] About ten o'clock, then.

[BRACK, LØVBORG, *and* TESMAN *go out the hall door. At the same time,* BERTA *enters from the inner room with a lighted lamp, which she sets on the drawing room table, then goes out the same way.*]

MRS. ELVSTED [*having risen, moving restlessly about the room*] Hedda—Hedda—what's going to come of all this?

HEDDA At ten o'clock—he'll be here. I can see him now—with vine leaves in his hair[4]—fiery and bold—

MRS. ELVSTED Oh, how good that would be!

4. That is, adorned like Dionysus, the Greek god of wine, whose worship is associated with mad frenzy (his rites were called orgies) and with the origins of Greek tragedy.

HEDDA And then, you'll see—he'll be back in control of himself. He'll be a free man, then, for the rest of his days.

MRS. ELVSTED Oh, God—if only he comes as you see him now!

HEDDA He'll come back like that, and no other way! [*Gets up and goes closer.*] Go on and doubt him as much as you like. *I* believe in him. And now we'll find out—

MRS. ELVSTED There's something behind what you're doing, Hedda.

HEDDA Yes, there is. For once in my life, I want to have power over a human being.

MRS. ELVSTED But don't you have that?

HEDDA I don't have it. I've never had it.

MRS. ELVSTED Not with your husband?

HEDDA Yes, what a bargain *that* was! Oh, if you only could understand how poor I am. And you're allowed to be so rich! [*Passionately throws her arms about her.*] I think I'll burn your hair off, after all!

MRS. ELVSTED Let go! Let me go! I'm afraid of you, Hedda!

BERTA [*in the doorway to the inner room*] Supper's waiting in the dining room, ma'am.

HEDDA All right, we're coming.

MRS. ELVSTED No, no, no! I'd rather go home alone! Right away—now!

HEDDA Nonsense! First you're going to have tea, you little fool. And then—ten o'clock—Eilert Løvborg comes—with vine leaves in his hair.

[*She drags* MRS. ELVSTED, *almost by force, toward the doorway.*]

Act 3

[*The same rooms at the* TESMANS'. *The curtains are drawn across the doorway to the inner room, and also across the glass door. The lamp, shaded and turned down low, is burning on the table. The door to the stove stands open; the fire has nearly gone out.*

MRS. ELVSTED, *wrapped in a large shawl, with her feet up on a footstool, lies back in the armchair close by the stove.* HEDDA, *fully dressed, is asleep on the sofa, with a blanket over her. After a pause,* MRS. ELVSTED *suddenly sits straight up in the chair, listening tensely. Then she sinks wearily back again.*]

MRS. ELVSTED [*in a low moan*] Not yet—oh, God—oh, God—not yet!

[BERTA *slips in cautiously by the hall door. She holds a letter in her hand.*]

MRS. ELVSTED [*turns and whispers anxiously*] Yes? Has anyone come?

BERTA [*softly*] Yes, a girl just now stopped by with this letter.

MRS. ELVSTED [*quickly, reaching out her hand*] A letter! Give it to me!

BERTA No, it's for the Doctor, ma'am.

MRS. ELVSTED Oh.

BERTA It was Miss Tesman's maid that brought it. I'll leave it here on the table.

MRS. ELVSTED Yes, do.

BERTA [*putting the letter down*] I think I'd best put out the lamp. It's smoking.

MRS. ELVSTED Yes, put it out. It'll be daylight soon.

BERTA [*does so*] It's broad daylight already, ma'am.

MRS. ELVSTED It's daylight! And still no one's come—!

BERTA Oh, mercy—I knew it would go like this.

MRS. ELVSTED You knew?

BERTA Yes, when I saw that a certain gentleman was back here in town—and that he went off with them. We've heard plenty about that gentleman over the years.

MRS. ELVSTED Don't talk so loud. You'll wake Mrs. Tesman.

BERTA [*looks toward the sofa and sighs*] Goodness me—yes, let her sleep, poor thing. Should I put a bit more on the fire?

MRS. ELVSTED Thanks, not for me.

BERTA All right. [*She goes quietly out the hall door.*]

HEDDA [*wakes as the door shuts and looks up*] What's that?

MRS. ELVSTED It was just the maid—

HEDDA [*glancing about*] In here—? Oh yes, I remember now. [*Sits up on the sofa, stretches, and rubs her eyes.*] What time is it, Thea?

MRS. ELVSTED [*looking at her watch*] It's after seven.

HEDDA When did Tesman get in?

MRS. ELVSTED He isn't back.

HEDDA Not back yet?

MRS. ELVSTED [*getting up*] No one's come in.

HEDDA And we sat here and waited up for them till four o'clock

MRS. ELVSTED [*wringing her hands*] And *how* I've waited for him!

HEDDA [*yawns, and speaks with her hand in front of her mouth*] Oh, dear—we could have saved ourselves the trouble.

MRS. ELVSTED Did you get any sleep?

HEDDA Oh yes. I slept quite well, I think. Didn't you?

MRS. ELVSTED No, not at all. I couldn't, Hedda! It was just impossible.

HEDDA [*rising and going toward her*] There, there, now! There's nothing to worry about. It's not hard to guess what happened.

MRS. ELVSTED Oh, what? Tell me!

HEDDA Well, it's clear that the party must have gone on till all hours—

MRS. ELVSTED Oh, Lord, yes—it must have. But even so—

HEDDA And then, of course, Tesman didn't want to come home and make a commotion in the middle of the night. [*Laughs.*] Probably didn't care to show himself, either—so full of his party spirits.

MRS. ELVSTED But where else could he have gone?

HEDDA He must have gone up to his aunts' to sleep. They keep his old room ready.

MRS. ELVSTED No, he can't be with them. Because he just now got a letter from Miss Tesman. It's over there.

HEDDA Oh? [*Looking at the address*] Yes, that's Aunt Julie's handwriting, all right. Well, then he must have stayed over at Judge Brack's. And Eilert Løvborg—he's sitting with vine leaves in his hair, reading away.

MRS. ELVSTED Oh, Hedda, you say these things, and you really don't believe them at all.

HEDDA You're such a little fool, Thea.

MRS. ELVSTED That's true; I guess I am.

HEDDA And you really look dead tired.

MRS. ELVSTED Yes, I feel dead tired.

HEDDA Well, you just do as I say, then. Go in my room and stretch out on the bed for a while.

MRS. ELVSTED No, no—I still wouldn't get any sleep.

HEDDA Why, of course you would.

MRS. ELVSTED Well, but your husband's sure to be home now soon. And I've got to know right away—

HEDDA I'll call you the moment he comes.

MRS. ELVSTED Yes? Promise me, Hedda?

HEDDA You can count on it. Just go and get some sleep.

MRS. ELVSTED Thanks. I'll try. [*She goes out through the inner room.*]

[HEDDA *goes over to the glass door and draws the curtains back. Bright daylight streams into the room. She goes over to the writing table, takes out a small hand mirror, regards herself and arranges her hair. She then goes to the hall door and presses the bell. After a moment,* BERTA *enters.*]

BERTA Did you want something, ma'am?

HEDDA Yes, you can build up the fire. I'm freezing in here.

BERTA Why, my goodness—we'll have it warm in no time. [*She rakes the embers together and puts some wood on, then stops and listens.*] There's the front doorbell, ma'am.

HEDDA Go see who it is. I'll take care of the stove.

BERTA It'll be burning soon. [*She goes out the hall door.*]

[HEDDA *kneels on the footstool and lays more wood on the fire. After a moment,* GEORGE TESMAN *comes in from the hall. He looks tired and rather serious. He tiptoes toward the doorway to the inner room and is about to slip through the curtains.*]

HEDDA [*at the stove, without looking up*] Good morning.

TESMAN [*turns*] Hedda! [*Approaching her*] But what on earth—! You're up so early? Uh?

HEDDA Yes, I'm up quite early today.

TESMAN And I was so sure you were still in bed sleeping. Isn't that something, Hedda!

HEDDA Not so loud. Mrs. Elvsted's resting in my room.

TESMAN Was Mrs. Elvsted here all night?

HEDDA Well, no one returned to take her home.

TESMAN No, I guess that's right.

HEDDA [*shuts the door to the stove and gets up*] So—did you enjoy your party?

TESMAN Were you worried about me? Hm?

HEDDA No, that never occurred to me. I just asked if you'd had a good time.

TESMAN Oh yes, I really did, for once. But more at the beginning, I'd say—when Eilert read to me out of his book. We got there more than an hour too soon—imagine! And Brack had so much to get ready. But then Eilert read to me.

HEDDA [*sitting at the right-hand side of the table*] Well? Tell me about it—

TESMAN [*sitting on a footstool by the stove*] Really, Hedda—you can't imagine what a book that's going to be! I do believe it's one of the most remarkable things ever written. Just think!

HEDDA Yes, yes, I don't care about that—

TESMAN But I have to make a confession, Hedda. When he'd finished reading—I had such a nasty feeling—

HEDDA Nasty?

TESMAN I found myself envying Eilert, that he was able to write such a book. Can you imagine, Hedda!

HEDDA Oh yes, I can imagine!

TESMAN And then how sad to see—that with all his gifts—he's still quite irreclaimable.

HEDDA Don't you mean that he has more courage to live than the others?

TESMAN Good Lord, no—I mean, he simply can't take his pleasures in moderation.

HEDDA Well, what happened then—at the end?

TESMAN I suppose I'd have to say it turned into an orgy, Hedda.

HEDDA Were there vine leaves in his hair?

TESMAN Vine leaves? Not that I noticed. But he gave a long, muddled speech in honor of the woman who'd inspired his work. Yes, that was his phrase for it.

HEDDA Did he give her name?

TESMAN No, he didn't. But it seems to me it has to be Mrs. Elvsted. Wait and see!

HEDDA Oh? Where did you leave him?

TESMAN On the way here. We broke up—the last of us—all together. And Brack came along with us too, to get a little fresh air. And then we did want to make sure that Eilert got home safe. Because he really had a load on, you know.

HEDDA He must have.

TESMAN But here's the curious part of it, Hedda. Or perhaps I should say, the distressing part. Oh, I'm almost ashamed to speak of it—for Eilert's sake—

HEDDA Yes, go on—

TESMAN Well, as we were walking toward town, you see, I happened to drop back a little behind the others. Only for a minute or two—you follow me?

HEDDA Yes, yes, so—?

TESMAN And then when I was catching up with the rest of them, what do you think I found on the sidewalk? Uh?

HEDDA Oh, how should I know!

TESMAN You mustn't breathe a word to anyone, Hedda—you hear me? Promise me that, for Eilert's sake. [*Takes a manila envelope out of his coat pocket.*] Just think—I found this.

HEDDA Isn't that what he had with him yesterday?

TESMAN That's right. It's the whole of his precious, irreplaceable manuscript. And he went and lost it—without even noticing. Can you imagine, Hedda! How distressing—

HEDDA But why didn't you give it right back to him?

TESMAN No, I didn't dare do that—in the state he was in—

HEDDA And you didn't tell any of the others you'd found it?

TESMAN Of course not. I'd never do that, you know—for Eilert's sake.

HEDDA Then there's no one who knows you have Eilert Løvborg's manuscript?

TESMAN No. And no one must ever know, either.

HEDDA What did you say to him afterwards?

TESMAN I had no chance at all to speak with him. As soon as we reached the edge of town, he and a couple of others got away from us and disappeared. Imagine!

HEDDA Oh? I expect they saw him home.

TESMAN Yes, they probably did, I suppose. And also Brack went home.

HEDDA And where've you been carrying on since then?

TESMAM Well, I and some of the others—we were invited up by one of the fellows and had morning coffee at his place. Or a post-midnight snack, maybe—uh? But as soon as I've had a little rest—and given poor Eilert time to sleep it off, then I've got to take this back to him.

HEDDA [*reaching out for the envelope*] No—don't give it back! Not yet, I mean. Let me read it first.

TESMAN Hedda dearest, no. My Lord, I can't do that.

HEDDA You can't?

TESMAN No. Why, you can just imagine the anguish he'll feel when he wakes up and misses the manuscript. He hasn't any copy of it, you know. He told me that himself.

HEDDA [*looks searchingly at him*] Can't such a work be rewritten? I mean, over again?

TESMAN Oh, I don't see how it could. Because the inspiration, you know—

HEDDA Yes, yes—that's the thing, I suppose. [*Casually*] Oh, by the way—there's a letter for you.

TESMAN No, really—?

HEDDA [*handing it to him*] It came early this morning.

TESMAN Dear, from Aunt Julie! What could that be? [*Sets the envelope on the other taboret, opens the letter, skims through it, and springs to his feet.*] Oh, Hedda—she says poor Auntie Rina's dying!

HEDDA It's no more than we've been expecting.

TESMAN And if I want to see her one last time, I've got to hurry. I'll have to hop right over.

HEDDA [*suppressing a smile*] Hop?

TESMAN Oh, Hedda dearest, if you could only bring yourself to come with me! Think of it!

HEDDA [*rises and dismisses the thought wearily*] No, no, don't ask me to do such things. I don't want to look on sickness and death. I want to be free of everything ugly.

TESMAN Yes, all right, then— [*Dashing about*] My hat—? My overcoat—? Oh, in the hall—I do hope I'm not there too late, Hedda! Hm?

HEDDA Oh, if you just hop to it—

[BERTA *appears at the hall door.*]

BERTA Judge Brack's outside, asking if he might stop in.

TESMAN At a time like this! No, I can't possibly see him now.

HEDDA But I can. [*To* BERTA] Ask the judge to come in.

[BERTA *goes out.*]

HEDDA [*quickly, in a whisper*] Tesman, the manuscript! [*She snatches it from the taboret.*]

TESMAN Yes, give it here!

HEDDA No, no, I'll keep it till you're back.

[*She moves over to the writing table and slips it in the bookcase.* TESMAN *stands flustered, unable to get his gloves on.* BRACK *enters from the hall.*]

HEDDA Well, aren't you the early bird.

BRACK Yes, wouldn't you say so? [*To* TESMAN] Are you off and away too?

TESMAN Yes, I absolutely have to get over to my aunts'. Just think—the invalid one, she's dying.

BRACK Good Lord, she is? But then you mustn't let me detain you. Not at a moment like this—

TESMAN Yes, I really must run— Good-bye! Good-bye!

[*He goes hurriedly out the hall door.*]

HEDDA It would seem you had quite a time of it last night, Judge.

BRACK I've not been out of my clothes yet, Mrs. Hedda.

HEDDA Not you, either?

BRACK No, as you can see. But what's Tesman been telling you about our night's adventures?

HEDDA Oh, some tedious tale. Something about stopping up somewhere for coffee.

BRACK Yes, I know all about the coffee party. Eilert Løvborg wasn't with them, I expect?

HEDDA No, they'd already taken him home.

BRACK Tesman, as well.

HEDDA No, but he said some others had.

BRACK [*smiles*] George Tesman is really a simple soul, Mrs. Hedda.

HEDDA God knows he's that. But was there something else that went on?

BRACK Oh, you might say so.

HEDDA Well, now! Let's sit down, Judge; you'll talk more easily then.

[*She sits at the left-hand side of the table, with* BRACK *at the long side, near her.*]

HEDDA So?

BRACK I had particular reasons for keeping track of my guests—or, I should say, certain of my guests, last night.

HEDDA And among them Eilert Løvborg, perhaps?

BRACK To be frank—yes.

HEDDA Now you really have me curious—

BRACK You know where he and a couple of the others spent the rest of the night, Mrs. Hedda?

HEDDA Tell me—if it's fit to be told.

BRACK Oh, it's very much fit to be told. Well, it seems they showed up at a quite animated soirée.

HEDDA Of the lively sort.

BRACK Of the liveliest.

HEDDA Do go on, Judge—

BRACK Løvborg, and the others also, had advance invitations. I knew all about it. But Løvborg had begged off, because now, of course, he was supposed to have become a new man, as you know.

HEDDA Up at the Elvsteds', yes. But he went anyway?

BRACK Well, you see, Mrs. Hedda—unfortunately the spirit moved him up at my place last evening—

HEDDA Yes, I hear that he *was* inspired there.

BRACK To a very powerful degree, I'd say. Well, so his mind turned to other things, that's clear. We males, sad to say—we're not always so true to principle as we ought to be.

HEDDA Oh, I'm sure you're an exception, Judge. But what about Løvborg—?

BRACK Well, to cut it short—the result was that he wound up in Mademoiselle Diana's parlors.

HEDDA Mademoiselle Diana's?

BRACK It was Mademoiselle Diana who was holding the soirée. For a select circle of lady friends and admirers.

HEDDA Is she a redhaired woman?

BRACK Precisely.

HEDDA Sort of a—singer?

BRACK Oh yes—she's that too. And also a mighty huntress—of men,[5] Mrs. Hedda. You've undoubtedly heard about her. Løvborg was one of her ruling favorites—back there in his palmy days.

HEDDA And how did all this end?

BRACK Less amicably, it seems. She gave him a most tender welcoming, with open arms, but before long she'd taken to fists.

HEDDA Against Løvborg?

BRACK That's right. He accused her or her friends of having robbed him. He claimed that his wallet was missing—along with some other things. In short, he must have made a frightful scene.

HEDDA And what did it come to?

BRACK It came to a regular free-for-all, the men and the women both. Luckily the police finally got there.

HEDDA The police too?

BRACK Yes. But it's likely to prove an expensive little romp for Eilert Løvborg. That crazy fool.

HEDDA So?

BRACK He apparently made violent resistance. Struck one of the officers on the side of the head and ripped his coat. So they took him along to the station house.

HEDDA Where did you hear all this?

BRACK From the police themselves.

HEDDA [*gazing straight ahead*] So that's how it went. Then he had no vine leaves in his hair.

BRACK Vine leaves, Mrs. Hedda?

HEDDA [*changing her tone*] But tell me, Judge—just why do you go around like this, spying on Eilert Løvborg?

BRACK In the first place, it's hardly a matter of no concern to me, if it's brought out during the investigation that he'd come direct from my house.

HEDDA There'll be an investigation—?

BRACK Naturally. Anyway, that takes care of itself. But I felt that as a friend of the family I owed you and Tesman a full account of his nocturnal exploits.

HEDDA Why, exactly?

BRACK Well, because I have a strong suspicion that he'll try to use you as a kind of screen.

HEDDA Oh, how could you ever think such a thing!

BRACK Good Lord—we're really not blind, Mrs. Hedda. You'll see! This Mrs. Elvsted, she won't be going home now so quickly.

HEDDA Well, even supposing there were something between them, there are plenty of other places where they could meet.

BRACK Not one single home. From now on, every decent house will be closed to Eilert Løvborg.

5. Diana was the Roman virgin goddess of the hunt.

HEDDA So mine ought to be too, is that what you mean?

BRACK Yes. I'll admit I'd find it more than annoying if that gentleman were to have free access here. If he came like an intruder, an irrelevancy, forcing his way into—

HEDDA Into the triangle?

BRACK Precisely. It would almost be like turning me out of my home.

HEDDA [*looks at him with a smile*] I see. The one cock of the walk—that's what you want to be.

BRACK [*nodding slowly and lowering his voice*] Yes, that's what I want to be. And that's what I'll fight for—with every means at my disposal.

HEDDA [*her smile vanishing*] You can be a dangerous person, can't you—in a tight corner.

BRACK Do you think so?

HEDDA Yes, now I'm beginning to think so. And I'm thoroughly grateful—that you have no kind of hold over me.

BRACK [*with an ambiguous laugh*] Ah, yes, Mrs. Hedda—perhaps you're right about that. If I had, then who knows just what I might do?

HEDDA Now you listen here, Judge! That sounds too much like a threat.

BRACK [*rising*] Oh, nothing of the kind! A triangle, after all—is best fortified and defended by volunteers.

HEDDA There we're agreed.

BRACK Well, now that I've said all I have to say, I'd better get back to town. Good-bye, Mrs. Hedda. [*He goes toward the glass door.*]

HEDDA [*rising*] Are you going through the garden?

BRACK Yes, I find it's shorter.

HEDDA Yes, and then it's the back way, too.

BRACK How true. I have nothing against back ways. At certain times they can be rather piquant.

HEDDA You mean, when somebody's sharpshooting?

BRACK [*in the doorway, laughing*] Oh, people don't shoot their tame roosters!

HEDDA [*also laughing*] I guess not. Not when there's only one—

[*Still laughing, they nod good-bye to each other. He goes. She shuts the door after him, then stands for a moment, quite serious, looking out. She then goes over and glances through the curtains to the inner room. Moves to the writing table, takes* LØVBORG'S *envelope from the bookcase, and is about to page through it, when* BERTA'S *voice is heard loudly in the hall.* HEDDA *turns and listens. She hurriedly locks the envelope in the drawer and lays the key on the desk.* EILERT LØVBORG, *with his overcoat on and his hat in his hand, throws open the hall door. He looks confused and excited.*]

LØVBORG [*turned toward the hall*] And I'm telling you, I have to go in! I will, you hear me! [*He shuts the door, turns, sees* HEDDA, *immediately gains control of himself and bows.*]

HEDDA [*at the writing table*] Well, Mr. Løvborg, it's late to call for Thea.

LØVBORG Or rather early to call on you. You must forgive me.

HEDDA How did you know she was still with me?

LØVBORG. They said at her lodgings that she'd been out all night.

HEDDA [*goes to the center table*] Did you notice anything in their faces when they said that?

LØVBORG [*looking at her inquiringly*] Notice anything?

HEDDA I mean, did it look like they had their own thoughts on the matter?

LØVBORG [*suddenly understanding*] Oh yes, that's true! I'm dragging her down with me! Actually, I didn't notice anything. Tesman—I don't suppose he's up yet?

HEDDA No, I don't think so.

LØVBORG When did he get in?

HEDDA Very late.

LØVBORG Did he tell you anything?

HEDDA Well, I heard you'd had a high time of it out at Judge Brack's.

LØVBORG Anything else?

HEDDA No, I don't think so. As a matter of fact, I was terrible sleepy—

[MRS. ELVSTED *comes in through the curtains to the inner room.*]

MRS. ELVSTED [*running toward him*] Oh, Eilert! At last—!

LØVBORG Yes, at last. And too late.

MRS. ELVSTED [*looking anxiously at him*] What's too late?

LØVBORG Everything's too late now. It's over with me.

MRS. ELVSTED Oh no, no—don't say that!

LØVBORG You'll say the same thing when you've heard—

MRS. ELVSTED I won't hear anything!

HEDDA Maybe you'd prefer to talk with her alone. I can leave.

LØVBORG No, stay—you too. Please.

MRS. ELVSTED But I tell you, I don't want to hear anything!

LØVBORG It's nothing about last night.

MRS. ELVSTED What is it, then—?

LØVBORG It's simply this, that from now on, we separate.

MRS. ELVSTED Separate!

HEDDA [*involuntarily*] I knew it!

LØVBORG Because I have no more use for you, Thea.

MRS. ELVSTED And you can stand there and say that! No more use for me! Then I'm not going to help you now, as I have? We're not going to go on working together?

LØVBORG I have no plans for any more work.

MRS. ELVSTED [*in desperation*] Then what will I do with my life?

LØVBORG You must try to go on living as if you'd never known me.

MRS. ELVSTED But I can't do that!

LØVBORG You must try to, Thea. You'll have to go home again—

MRS. ELVSTED [*in a fury of protest*] Never! No! Where you are, that's where I want to be! I won't be driven away like this! I'm going to stay right here—and be together with you when the book comes out.

HEDDA [*in a tense whisper*] Ah, yes—the book!

LØVBORG [*looks at her*] My book and Thea's—for that's what it is.

MRS. ELVSTED Yes, that's what I feel it is. And that's why I have the right, as well, to be with you when it comes out. I want to see you covered with honor and respect again. And the joy—I want to share the joy of it with you too.

LØVBORG Thea—our book's never coming out.

HEDDA Ah!

MRS. ELVSTED Never coming out!

LØVBORG *Can* never come out.

MRS. ELVSTED [*with anguished foreboding*] Eilert—what have you done with the manuscript?

HEDDA [*watching him intently*] Yes, the manuscript—?

MRS. ELVSTED Where is it!

LØVBORG Oh, Thea—don't ask me that.

MRS. ELVSTED Yes, yes, I have to know. I've got a right to know, this minute!

LØVBORG The manuscript—well, you see—I tore the manuscript into a thousand pieces.

MRS. ELVSTED [*screams*] Oh no, no—!

HEDDA [*involuntarily*] But that just isn't—!

LØVBORG [*looks at her*] Isn't so, you think?

HEDDA [*composing herself*] All right. Of course; if you say it yourself. But it sounds so incredible—

LØVBORG It's true, all the same.

MRS. ELVSTED [*wringing her hands*] Oh, God—oh, God, Hedda—to tear his own work to bits!

LØVBORG I've torn my own life to bits. So why not tear up my life's work as well—

MRS. ELVSTED And you did this thing last night!

LØVBORG Yes, you heard me. In a thousand pieces. And scattered them into the fjord. Far out. At least there, there's clean salt water. Let them drift out to sea—drift with the tide and the wind. And after a while, they'll sink. Deeper and deeper. As I will, Thea.

MRS. ELVSTED Do you know, Eilert, this thing you've done with the book—for the rest of my life it will seem to me as if you'd killed a little child.

LØVBORG You're right. It was like murdering a child.

MRS. ELVSTED But how could you do it—! It was my child too.

HEDDA [*almost inaudible*] Ah, the child—

MRS. ELVSTED [*breathes heavily*] Then it *is* all over. Yes, yes, I'm going now, Hedda.

HEDDA But you're not leaving town, are you?

MRS. ELVSTED Oh, I don't know myself what I'll do. Everything's dark for me now. [*She goes out the hall door.*]

HEDDA [*stands waiting a moment*] You're not going to take her home, then, Mr. Løvborg?

LØVBORG I? Through the streets? So people could see that she'd been with me?

HEDDA I don't know what else may have happened last night. But is it so completely irredeemable?

LØVBORG It won't just end with last night—I know that well enough. But the thing is, I've lost all desire for that kind of life. I don't want to start it again, not now. It's the courage and daring for life—that's what she's broken in me.

HEDDA [*staring straight ahead*] To think that pretty little fool could have a man's fate in her hands. [*Looks at him.*] But still, how could you treat her so heartlessly?

LØVBORG Oh, don't say it was heartless!

HEDDA To go ahead and destroy what's filled her whole being for months and years! That's not heartless?

LØVBORG To you, Hedda—I can tell the truth.

HEDDA The truth?

LØVBORG Promise me first—give me your word that what I tell you now, you'll never let Thea know.

HEDDA You have my word.

LØVBORG Good. I can tell you, then, that what I said here just now isn't true.

HEDDA About the manuscript?

LØVBORG Yes. I didn't tear it up—or throw it in the fjord.

HEDDA No, but—where is it, then?

LØVBORG I've destroyed it all the same, Hedda. Utterly destroyed it.

HEDDA I don't understand.

LØVBORG Thea said that what I've done, for her was like killing a child.

HEDDA Yes—that's what she said.

LØVBORG But killing his child—that's not the worst thing a father can do.

HEDDA *That's* not the worst?

LØVBORG No. I wanted to spare Thea the worst.

HEDDA And what's that—the worst?

LØVBORG Suppose now, Hedda, that a man—in the early morning hours, say—after a wild, drunken night, comes home to his child's mother and says: "Listen—I've been out to this place and that—here and there. And I had our child with me. In this place and that. And I lost the child. Just lost it. God only knows what hands it's come into. Or who's got hold of it."

HEDDA Well—but when all's said and done—it was only a book—

LØVBORG Thea's pure soul was in that book.

HEDDA Yes, I understand.

LØVBORG Well, then you can understand that for her and me there's no future possible any more.

HEDDA What do you intend to do?

LØVBORG Nothing. Just put an end to it all. The sooner the better.

HEDDA [*coming a step closer*] Eilert Løvborg—listen to me. Couldn't you arrange that—that it's done beautifully?

LØVBORG Beautifully? [*Smiles.*] With vine leaves in my hair, as you used to dream in the old days—

HEDDA No. I don't believe in vine leaves any more. But beautifully, all the same. For this once—! Good-bye! You must go now—and never come here again.

LØVBORG Good-bye, then. And give my best to George Tesman. [*He turns to leave.*]

HEDDA No. wait. I want you to have a souvenir from me.

[*She goes to the writing desk and opens the drawer and the pistol case, then comes back to* LØVBORG *with one of the pistols.*]

LØVBORG [*looks at her*] That? Is that the souvenir?

HEDDA [*nods slowly*] Do you recognize it? It was aimed at you once.

LØVBORG You should have used it then.

HEDDA Here! Use it now.

LØVBORG [*puts the pistol in his breast pocket*] Thanks.

HEDDA And beautifully, Eilert Løvborg. Promise me that!

LØVBORG Good-bye, Hedda Gabler.

[*He goes out the hall door.* HEDDA *listens a moment at the door. Then she goes over to the writing table, takes out the envelope with the manuscript, glances inside, pulls some of the sheets half out and looks at them. She then goes over to the armchair by the stove and sits, with the envelope in her lap. After a moment, she opens the stove door, then brings out the manuscript.*]

HEDDA [*throwing some of the sheets into the fire and whispering to herself*] Now I'm burning your child, Thea! You, with your curly hair! [*Throwing another sheaf in the stove*] Your child and Eilert Løvborg's. [*Throwing in the rest*] Now I'm burning—I'm burning the child.

Act 4

[*The same rooms at the* TESMANS'. *It is evening. The drawing room is in darkness. The inner room is lit by the hanging lamp over the table. The curtains are drawn across the glass door.* HEDDA, *dressed in black, is pacing back and forth in the dark room. She then enters the inner room, moving out of sight toward the left. Several chords are heard on the piano. She comes in view again, returning into the drawing room.* BERTA *enters from the right through the inner room with a lighted lamp, which she puts on the table in front of the settee in the drawing room. Her eyes are red from crying, and she has black ribbons on her cap.*[6] *She goes quietly and discreetly out to the right.* HEDDA *moves to the glass door, lifts the curtains aside slightly, and gazes out into the darkness.*

Shortly after, MISS TESMAN, *in mourning, with a hat and veil, comes in from the hall.* HEDDA *goes toward her, extending her hand.*]

MISS TESMAN Well, Hedda, here I am, all dressed in mourning. My poor sister's ordeal is finally over.

HEDDA As you see, I've already heard. Tesman sent me a note.

MISS TESMAN Yes, he promised he would. But all the same I thought that, to Hedda—here in the house of life—I ought to bear the news of death myself.

HEDDA That was very kind of you.

MISS TESMAN Ah, Rina ought not to have passed on just now. This is no time for grief in Hedda's house.

HEDDA [*changing the subject*] She had a peaceful death, then, Miss Tesman?

MISS TESMAN Oh, she went so calmly, so beautifully. And so inexpressibly happy that she could see George once again. And say good bye to him properly. Is it possible that he's still not home?

HEDDA No, he wrote that I shouldn't expect him too early. But won't you sit down?

MISS TESMAN No, thank you, my dear—blessed Hedda. I'd love to, but I have so little time. I want to see her dressed and made ready as best as I can. She should go to her grave looking her finest.

HEDDA Can't I help you with something?

MISS TESMAN Oh, you mustn't think of it. This is nothing for Hedda Tesman to put her hands to. Or let her thoughts dwell on, either. Not at a time like this, no.

HEDDA Ah, thoughts—they're not so easy to control—

MISS TESMAN [*continuing*] Well, there's life for you. At my house now we'll be sewing a shroud for Rina. And here, too, there'll be sewing soon, I imagine. But a far different kind, praise God!

[GEORGE TESMAN *enters from the hall.*]

6. Worn to signify mourning.

HEDDA Well, at last! It's about time.

TESMAN Are you here, Aunt Julie? With Hedda? Think of that!

MISS TESMAN I was just this minute leaving, dear boy. Well, did you get done all you promised you would?

TESMAN No, I'm really afraid I've forgotten half. I'll have to run over and see you tomorrow. My brain's completely in a whirl today. I can't keep my thoughts together.

MISS TESMAN But George dear, you mustn't take it that way.

TESMAN Oh? Well, how should I, then?

MISS TESMAN You should rejoice in your grief. Rejoice in everything that's happened, as I do.

TESMAN Oh yes, of course. You're thinking of Auntie Rina.

HEDDA It's going to be lonely for you, Miss Tesman.

MISS TESMAN For the first few days, yes. But it won't be for long, I hope. I won't let dear Rina's little room stand empty.

TESMAN No? Who would you want to have in it? Hm?

MISS TESMAN Oh, there's always some poor invalid in need of care and attention.

HEDDA Would you really take another burden like that on yourself?

MISS TESMAN Burden! Mercy on you, child—it's been no burden for me.

HEDDA But now, with a stranger—

MISS TESMAN Oh, you soon make friends with an invalid. And I do so much need someone to live for—I, too. Well, thank God, in this house as well, there soon ought to be work that an old aunt can turn her hand to.

HEDDA Oh, forget about us—

TESMAN Yes, think how pleasant it could be for the three of us if—

HEDDA If—?

TESMAN [*uneasily*] Oh, nothing. It'll all take care of itself. Let's hope so. Uh?

MISS TESMAN Ah, yes. Well, I expect you two have things to talk about. [*Smiles.*] And perhaps Hedda has something to tell you, George. Goodbye. I'll have to get home now to Rina. [*Turning at the door*] Goodness me, how strange! Now Rina's both with me and with poor dear Jochum as well.

TESMAN Yes, imagine that, Aunt Julie! Hm?

[MISS TESMAN *goes out the hall door.*]

HEDDA [*follows* TESMAN *with a cold, probing look*] I almost think you feel this death more than she.

TESMAN Oh, it's not just Auntie Rina's death. It's Eilert who has me worried.

HEDDA [*quickly*] Any news about him?

TESMAN I stopped up at his place this afternoon, thinking to tell him that the manuscript was safe.

HEDDA Well? Didn't you see him then?

TESMAN No, he wasn't home. But afterward I met Mrs. Elvsted, and she said he'd been here early this morning.

HEDDA Yes, right after you left.

TESMAN And apparently he said he'd torn his manuscript up. Uh?

HEDDA Yes, he claimed that he had.

TESMAN But good Lord, then he must have been completely demented! Well, then I guess you didn't dare give it back to him, Hedda, did you?

HEDDA No, he didn't get it.

TESMAN But you did tell him we had it, I suppose?

HEDDA No. [*Quickly*] Did you tell Mrs. Elvsted anything?

TESMAN No, I thought I'd better not. But you should have said something to him. Just think, if he goes off in desperation and does himself some harm! Give me the manuscript, Hedda! I'm taking it back to him right away. Where do you have it?

HEDDA [*cold and impassive, leaning against the armchair*] I don't have it anymore.

TESMAN You don't have it! What on earth do you mean by that?

HEDDA I burned it—the whole thing.

TESMAN [*with a start of terror*] Burned it! Burned Eilert Løvborg's manuscript!

HEDDA Stop shouting. The maid could hear you.

TESMAN Burned it! But my God in heaven—! No, no, no—that's impossible!

HEDDA Yes, but it's true, all the same.

TESMAN But do you realize what you've done, Hedda! It's illegal disposition of lost property. Just think! Yes, you can ask Judge Brack; he'll tell you.

HEDDA It would be wiser not mentioning this—either to the judge or to anyone else.

TESMAN But how could you go and do such an incredible thing! Whatever put it into your head? What got into you, anyway? Answer me! Well?

HEDDA [*suppressing an almost imperceptible smile*] I did it for your sake, George.

TESMAN For my sake!

HEDDA When you came home this morning and told about how he'd read to you—

TESMAN Yes, yes, then what?

HEDDA Then you confessed that you envied him this book.

TESMAN Good Lord, I didn't mean it literally.

HEDDA Never mind. I still couldn't bear the thought that anyone should eclipse you.

TESMAN [*in an outburst of mingled doubt and joy*] Hedda—is this true, what you say? Yes, but—but—I never dreamed you could show your love like this. Imagine!

HEDDA Well, then it's best you know that—that I'm going to— [*Impatiently, breaking off*] No, no—you ask your Aunt Julie. She's the one who can tell you.

TESMAN Oh, I'm beginning to understand you, Hedda! [*Claps his hands together.*] Good heavens, no! Is it actually *that*? Can it be? Uh?

HEDDA Don't shout so. The maid can hear you.

TESMAN The maid! Oh, Hedda, you're priceless, really! The maid—but that's Berta! Why, I'll go out and tell her myself.

HEDDA [*clenching her fists in despair*] Oh, I'll die—I'll die of all this!

TESMAN Of what, Hedda? Uh?

HEDDA Of all these—absurdities—George.

TESMAN Absurdities? What's about my being so happy? Well, all right—I guess there's no point in my saying anything to Berta.

HEDDA Oh, go ahead—why not that, too?

TESMAN No, no, not yet. But Aunt Julie will have to hear. And then, that you've started to call me George, too! Imagine! Oh, Aunt Julie will be so glad—so glad!

HEDDA When she hears that I burned Eilert Løvborg's book—for your sake?

TESMAN Well, as far as that goes—this thing with the book—of course, no one's to know about that. But that you have a love that burns for me, Hedda—Aunt Julie can certainly share in that! You know, I wonder, really, if things such as this are common among young wives? Hm?

HEDDA I think you should ask Aunt Julie about that, too.

TESMAN Yes, I'll do it definitely, when I have the chance. [*Again looks distressed and preoccupied.*] No, but—but the manuscript! My Lord, it's just terrible to think about poor Eilert.

[MRS. ELVSTED, *dressed as on her first visit, with hat and coat, comes in the hall door.*]

MRS. ELVSTED [*greets them hurriedly and speaks in agitation*] Oh, Hedda dear, don't be annoyed that I'm back again.

HEDDA Has something happened, Thea?

TESMAN Something with Eilert Løvborg? Uh?

MRS. ELVSTED Yes, I'm so terribly afraid he's met with an accident.

HEDDA [*seizing her arm*] Ah—you think so!

TESMAN But, Mrs. Elvsted, where did you get that idea?

MRS. ELVSTED Well, because I heard them speaking of him at the boardinghouse, just as I came in. Oh, there are the most incredible rumors about him in town today.

TESMAN Yes, you know, I heard them too! And yet I could swear that he went right home to bed last night. Imagine!

HEDDA Well—what did they say at the boardinghouse?

MRS. ELVSTED Oh, I couldn't get anything clearly. They either didn't know much themselves, or else—They stopped talking when they saw me. And I didn't dare to ask.

TESMAN [*restlessly moving about*] Let's hope—let's hope you misunderstood them, Mrs. Elvsted!

MRS. ELVSTED No, no, I'm sure they were talking of him. And then I heard them say something or other about the hospital, or—

TESMAN The hospital!

HEDDA No—but that's impossible!

MRS. ELVSTED Oh, I'm so deathly afraid for him now. And later I went up to his lodging to ask about him.

HEDDA But was that very wise to do, Thea?

MRS. ELVSTED What else could I do? I couldn't bear the uncertainty any longer.

TESMAN But didn't you find him there either? Hm?

MRS. ELVSTED No. And no one had any word of him. He hadn't been in since yesterday afternoon, they said.

TESMAN Yesterday! Imagine them saying that!

MRS. ELVSTED I think there can only be one reason—something terrible must have happened to him!

TESMAN Hedda dear—suppose I went over and made a few inquiries—?

HEDDA No, no—don't you get mixed up in this business.

[JUDGE BRACK, *with hat in hand, enters from the hall,* BERTA *letting him in and shutting the door after him. He looks grave and bows silently.*]

TESMAN Oh, is that you, Judge? Uh?

BRACK Yes, it's imperative that I see you this evening.

TESMAN I can see that you've heard the news from Aunt Julie.

BRACK Among other things, yes.

TESMAN It's sad, isn't it? Uh?

BRACK Well, my dear Tesman, that depends on how you look at it.

TESMAN [*eyes him doubtfully*] Has anything else happened?

BRACK Yes, as a matter of fact.

HEDDA [*intently*] Something distressing, Judge?

BRACK Again, that depends on how you look at it, Mrs. Tesman.

MRS. ELVSTED [*in an uncontrollable outburst*] Oh, it's something about Eilert Løvborg!

BRACK [*glancing at her*] Now how did you hit upon that, Mrs. Elvsted? Have you, perhaps, heard something already—?

MRS. ELVSTED [*in confusion*] No, no, nothing like that—but—

TESMAN Oh, for heaven's sake, tell us!

BRACK [*with a shrug*] Well—I'm sorry, but—Eilert Løvborg's been taken to the hospital. He's dying.

MRS. ELVSTED [*crying out*] Oh, God, oh, God—!

TESMAN To the hospital! And dying!

HEDDA [*involuntarily*] All so soon—!

MRS. ELVSTED [*wailing*] And we parted in anger, Hedda!

HEDDA [*in a whisper*] Thea—be careful, Thea!

MRS. ELVSTED [*ignoring her*] I have to see him! I have to see him alive!

BRACK No use, Mrs. Elvsted. No one's allowed in to see him.

MRS. ELVSTED Oh, but tell me, at least, what happened to him! What is it?

TESMAN Don't tell me he tried to—! Uh?

HEDDA Yes, he did, I'm sure of it.

TESMAN Hedda—how can you say—!

BRACK [*his eyes steadily on her*] Unhappily, you've guessed exactly right, Mrs. Tesman.

MRS. ELVSTED Oh, how horrible!

TESMAN Did it himself! Imagine!

HEDDA Shot himself!

BRACK Again, exactly right, Mrs. Tesman.

MRS. ELVSTED [*trying to control herself*] When did it happen, Mr. Brack?

BRACK This afternoon. Between three and four.

TESMAN But good Lord—where did he do it, then? Hm?

BRACK [*hesitating slightly*] Where? Why—in his room, I suppose.

MRS. ELVSTED No, that can't be right. I was there between six and seven

BRACK Well, somewhere else, then. I don't know exactly. I only know he was found like that. Shot—in the chest.

MRS. ELVSTED What a horrible thought! That he should end that way!

HEDDA [*to* BRACK] In the chest, you say.

BRACK Yes—I told you.

HEDDA Not the temple?

BRACK In the chest, Mrs. Tesman.

HEDDA Well—well, the chest is just as good.

BRACK Why, Mrs. Tesman?

HEDDA [*evasively*] Oh, nothing—never mind.

TESMAN And the wound is critical, you say? Uh?

BRACK The wound is absolutely fatal. Most likely, it's over already.

MRS. ELVSTED Yes, yes, I can feel that it is! It's over! All over! Oh, Hedda—!

TESMAN But tell me now—how did you learn about this?

BRACK [*brusquely*] One of the police. Someone I had to talk to.

HEDDA [*in a clear, bold voice*] At last, something truly done!

TESMAN [*shocked*] My God, what are you saying, Hedda!

HEDDA I'm saying there's beauty in all this.

BRACK Hm, Mrs. Tesman—

TESMAN Beauty! What an idea!

MRS. ELVSTED Oh, Hedda, how can you talk about beauty in such a thing?

HEDDA Eilert Løvborg's settled accounts with himself. He's had the courage to do what—what had to be done.

MRS. ELVSTED Don't you believe it! It never happened like that. When he did this, he was in a delirium!

TESMAN In despair, you mean.

HEDDA No, he wasn't. I'm certain of that.

MRS. ELVSTED But he was! In delirium! The way he was when he tore up our book.

BRACK [*startled*] The book? His manuscript, you mean? He tore it up?

MRS. ELVSTED Yes. Last night.

TESMAN [*in a low whisper*] Oh, Hedda, we'll never come clear of all this.

BRACK Hm, that's very strange.

TESMAN [*walking about the room*] To think Eilert could be gone like that! And then not to have left behind the one thing that could have made his name live on.

MRS. ELVSTED Oh, if it could only be put together again!

TESMAN Yes, imagine if that were possible! I don't know what I wouldn't give—

MRS. ELVSTED Perhaps it can, Mr. Tesman.

TESMAN What do you mean?

MRS. ELVSTED [*searching in the pockets of her dress*] Look here. I've kept all these notes that he used to dictate from.

HEDDA [*coming a step closer*] Ah—!

TESMAN You've kept them, Mrs. Elvsted! Uh?

MRS. ELVSTED Yes, here they are. I took them along when I left home. And they've stayed right here in my pocket—

TESMAN Oh, let me look!

MRS. ELVSTED [*hands him a sheaf of small papers*] But they're in such a mess. All mixed up.

TESMAN But just think, if we could decipher them, even so! Maybe the two of us could help each other—

MRS. ELVSTED Oh yes! At least, we could try—

TESMAN We can do it! We *must!* I'll give my whole life to this!

HEDDA You, George? Your life?

TESMAN Yes. Or, let's say, all the time I can spare. My own research will have to wait. You can understand, Hedda. Hm! It's something I owe to Eilert's memory.

HEDDA Perhaps.

TESMAN And so, my dear Mrs. Elvsted, let's pull ourselves together. Good Lord, there's no use brooding over what's gone by. Uh? We must try to compose our thoughts as much as we can, in order that—

MRS. ELVSTED Yes, yes, Mr. Tesman, I'll do the best I can.

TESMAN Come on, then. Let's look over these notes right away. Where shall we sit? Here? No, in there, in the back room. Excuse us, Judge. You come with me, Mrs. Elvsted.

MRS. ELVSTED Dear God—if only we can do this!

[TESMAN *and* MRS. ELVSTED *go into the inner room. She takes off her hat and coat. They both sit at the table under the hanging lamp and become totally immersed in examining the papers.* HEDDA *goes toward the stove and sits in the armchair. After a moment,* BRACK *goes over by her.*]

HEDDA [*her voice lowered*] Ah, Judge—what a liberation it is, this act of Eilert Løvborg's.

BRACK Liberation, Mrs. Hedda? Well, yes, for him; you could certainly say he's been liberated—

HEDDA I mean for me. It's liberating to know that there can still actually be a free and courageous action in this world. Something that shimmers with spontaneous beauty.

BRACK [*smiling*] Hm— my dear Mrs. Hedda—

HEDDA Oh, I already know what you're going to say. Because you're a kind of specialist too, you know, just like— Oh, well!

BRACK [*looking fixedly at her*] Eilert Løvborg meant more to you than you're willing to admit, perhaps even to yourself. Or am I wrong about that?

HEDDA I won't answer that sort of question. I simply know that Eilert Løvborg's had the courage to live life after his own mind. And now—this last great act, filled with beauty! That he had the strength and the will to break away from the banquet of life—so young.

BRACK It grieves me, Mrs. Hedda—but I'm afraid I have to disburden you of this beautiful illusion.

HEDDA Illusion?

BRACK One that, in any case, you'd soon be deprived of.

HEDDA And what's that?

BRACK He didn't shoot himself—of his own free will.

HEDDA He didn't—!

BRACK No. This whole affair didn't go off quite the way I described it.

HEDDA [*in suspense*] You've hidden something? What is it?

BRACK For poor Mrs. Elvsted's sake, I did a little editing here and there.

HEDDA Where?

BRACK First, the fact that he's already dead.

HEDDA In the hospital?

BRACK Yes. Without regaining consciousness.

HEDDA What else did you hide?

BRACK That the incident didn't occur in his room.

HEDDA Well, that's rather unimportant.

BRACK Not entirely. Suppose I were to tell you that Eilert Løvborg was found shot in—in Mademoiselle Diana's boudoir.

HEDDA [*half rises, then sinks back again*] That's impossible, Judge! He wouldn't have gone there again today!

BRACK He was there this afternoon. He went there, demanding something he said they'd stolen from him. Kept raving about a lost child—

HEDDA Ah—so that was it—

BRACK I thought perhaps that might be his manuscript. But, I hear now, he destroyed that himself. So it must have been his wallet.

HEDDA I suppose so. Then, there—that's where they found him.

BRACK Yes, there. With a discharged pistol in his breast pocket. The bullet had wounded him fatally.

HEDDA In the chest—yes.

BRACK No—in the stomach—more or less.

HEDDA [*stares up at him with a look of revulsion*] That too! What is it, this—this curse—that everything I touch turns ridiculous and vile?

BRACK There's something else, Mrs. Hedda. Another ugly aspect to the case.

HEDDA What's that?

BRACK The pistol he was carrying—

HEDDA [*breathlessly*] Well! What about it!

BRACK He must have stolen it.

HEDDA [*springs up*] Stolen! That's not true! He didn't!

BRACK It seems impossible otherwise. He must have stolen it—shh!

[TESMAN *and* MRS. ELVSTED *have gotten up from the table in the inner room and come into the drawing room.*]

TESMAN [*with both hands full of papers*] Hedda dear—it's nearly impossible to see in there under that overhead lamp. You know?

HEDDA Yes, I know.

TESMAN Do you think it would be all right if we used your table for a while? Hm?

HEDDA Yes, I don't mind. [*Quickly*] Wait! No, let me clear it off first.

TESMAN Oh, don't bother, Hedda. There's plenty of room.

HEDDA No, no, let me just clear it off, can't you? I'll put all this in by the piano. There!

[*She has pulled out an object covered with sheet music from under the bookcase, adds more music to it, and carries the whole thing into the inner room and off left.* TESMAN *puts the scraps of paper on the writing table and moves the lamp over from the corner table. He and* MRS. ELVSTED *sit down and go on with their work.* HEDDA *comes back.*]

HEDDA [*behind* MRS. ELVSTED'*s chair, gently ruffling her hair*] Well, my sweet little Thea—how is it going with Eilert Løvborg's monument?

MRS. ELVSTED [*looking despondently up at her*] Oh, dear—it's going to be terribly hard to set these in order.

TESMAN It's got to be done. There's just no alternative. Besides, setting other people's papers in order—it's exactly what I can do best.

[HEDDA *goes over by the stove and sits on one of the taborets.* BRACK *stands over her, leaning on the armchair.*]

HEDDA [*whispering*] What did you say about the pistol?

BRACK [*softly*] That he must have stolen it.

HEDDA Why, necessarily, that?

BRACK Because every other explanation would seem impossible, Mrs. Hedda.

HEDDA I see.

BRACK [*glancing at her*] Of course, Eilert Løvborg was here this morning. Wasn't he?

HEDDA Yes.

BRACK Were you alone with him?

HEDDA Yes, briefly.

BRACK Did you leave the room while he was here?

HEDDA No.

BRACK Consider. You didn't leave, even for a moment.

HEDDA Well, yes, perhaps, just for a moment—into the hall.

BRACK And where did you have your pistol case?

HEDDA I had it put away in—

BRACK Yes, Mrs. Hedda?

HEDDA It was lying over there, on the writing table.

BRACK Have you looked since to see if both pistols are there?

HEDDA No.

BRACK No need to. I saw the pistol. Løvborg had it on him. I knew it immediately, from yesterday. And other days too.

HEDDA Do you have it, maybe?

BRACK No, the police have it.

HEDDA What will they do with it?

BRACK Try to trace it to the owner.

HEDDA Do you think they'll succeed?

BRACK [*bending over her and whispering*] No, Hedda Gabler—as long as I keep quiet.

HEDDA [*looking at him anxiously*] And if you don't keep quiet—then what?

BRACK [*with a shrug*] Counsel could always claim that the pistol was stolen.

HEDDA [*decisively*] I'd rather die!

BRACK [*smiling*] People *say* such things. But they don't *do* them.

HEDDA [*without answering*] And what, then, if the pistol wasn't stolen. And they found the owner. What would happen?

BRACK Well, Hedda—there'd be a scandal.

HEDDA A scandal!

BRACK A scandal, yes—the kind you're so deathly afraid of. Naturally, you'd appear in court—you and Mademoiselle Diana. She'd have to explain how the whole thing occurred. Whether it was an accident or homicide. Was he trying to pull the pistol out of his pocket to threaten her? Is that why it went off? Or had she torn the pistol out of his hand, shot him, and slipped it back in his pocket again? It's rather like her to do that, you know. She's a solid piece of work, this Mademoiselle Diana.

HEDDA But all that sordid business is no concern of mine.

BRACK No. But you'll have to answer the question: why did you give Eilert Løvborg the pistol? And what conclusions will people draw from the fact that you did give it to him?

HEDDA [*her head sinking*] That's true. I hadn't thought of that.

BRACK Well, luckily there's no danger, as long as I keep quiet.

HEDDA So I'm in your power, Judge. You have your hold over me from now on.

BRACK [*whispers more softly*] My dearest Hedda—believe me—I won't abuse my position.

HEDDA All the same, I'm in your power. Tied to your will and desire. Not free. Not free, then! [*Rises angrily.*] No—I can't bear the thought of it. Never!

BRACK [*looks at her half mockingly*] One usually manages to adjust to the inevitable.

HEDDA [*returning his look*] Yes, perhaps so. [*She goes over to the writing table. Suppressing an involuntary smile, she imitates* TESMAN'S *intonation.*] Well? Getting on with it, George? Uh?

TESMAN Goodness knows, dear. It's going to mean months and months of work, in any case.

HEDDA [*as before*] Imagine that! [*Runs her hand lightly through* MRS. ELVSTED'S *hair.*] Don't you find it strange, Thea? Here you are, sitting now beside Tesman—just as you used to sit with Eilert Løvborg.

MRS. ELVSTED Oh, if I could only inspire your husband in the same way.

HEDDA Oh, that will surely come—in time.

TESMAN Yes, you know what, Hedda—I really think I'm beginning to feel something of the kind. But you go back and sit with Judge Brack.

HEDDA Is there nothing the two of you can use me for here?

TESMAN No, nothing in the world. [*Turning his head*] From now on, Judge, you'll have to be good enough to keep Hedda company.

BRACK [*with a glance at* HEDDA] I'll take the greatest pleasure in that.

HEDDA Thanks. But I'm tired this evening. I want to rest a while in there on the sofa.

TESMAN Yes, do that, dear. Uh?

[HEDDA *goes into the inner room, pulling the curtains closed after her. Short pause. Suddenly she is heard playing a wild dance melody on the piano.*]

MRS. ELVSTED [*starting up from her chair*] Oh—what's that?

TESMAN [*running to the center doorway*] But Hedda dearest—don't go playing dance music tonight! Think of Auntie Rina! And Eilert, too!

HEDDA [*putting her head out between the curtains*] And Auntie Julie. And all the rest of them. From now on I'll be quiet. [*She closes the curtains again.*]

TESMAN [*at the writing table*] She can't feel very happy seeing us do this melancholy work. You know what, Mrs. Elvsted—you must move in with Aunt Julie. Then I can come over evenings. And then we can sit and work *there*. Uh?

MRS. ELVSTED Yes, perhaps that would be best—

HEDDA [*from the inner room*] I can hear everything you say, Tesman. But what will I do evenings over here?

TESMAN [*leafing through the notes*] Oh, I'm sure Judge Brack will be good enough to stop by and see you.

BRACK [*in the armchair, calling out gaily*] Gladly, every blessed evening, Mrs. Tesman! We'll have great times here together, the two of us!

HEDDA [*in a clear, ringing voice*] Yes, don't you hope so, Judge? You, the one cock of the walk—

[*A shot is heard within.* TESMAN, MRS. ELVSTED, *and* BRACK *start from their chairs.*]

TESMAN Oh, now she's fooling with those pistols again.

[*He throws the curtains back and runs in.* MRS. ELVSTED *follows.* HEDDA *lies, lifeless, stretched out on the sofa. Confusion and cries.* BERTA *comes in, bewildered, from the right.*]

TESMAN [*shrieking to* BRACK] Shot herself! Shot herself in the temple! Can you imagine!

BRACK [*in the armchair, prostrated*] But good God! People don't *do* such things!

OSCAR WILDE

1854–1900

OSCAR Wilde cut a remarkable figure within the literary, cultural, and theatrical worlds of late nineteenth-century Britain. Dandy, man of letters, public speaker, proponent of aestheticism (the movement championing "Art for Art's Sake"), and prolific author of poetry, fiction, essays, children's stories, criticism, and drama, he entertained London high society with his epigrammatic wit even as he flouted some of the most deeply held values of late-Victorian society. His 1890 novel, *The Picture of Dorian Gray,* scandalized many of its readers with its decadence and perceived amorality, and his society comedies of the early 1890s both entertained and satirized their West End audience. Something of an outsider by virtue of his Irishness and homosexuality, he fashioned a distinctly modern form of celebrity that challenged the norms of Victorian respectability. But Wilde's position in the society of his day was, it turned out, a precarious one. In 1895, even as two of his dramas played on the West End, he was convicted and imprisoned on the charge of "gross indecency" after three sensational trials that represent, to this day, a landmark in the public perception of homosexuality. "I'll be a poet, a writer, a dramatist," he wrote to a friend before leaving Oxford University in 1878. "Somehow or other, I'll be famous, and if not famous, notorious." One of the most accomplished writers for the theater in fin de siècle London, Oscar Wilde became, in the end, his own greatest drama.

Oscar Fingal O'Flahertie Wills Wilde was born in Dublin on October 16, 1854, to William Wilde, an eye and ear surgeon, and the former Jane Francesca Elgee, who wrote Irish Nationalist poetry under the pseudonym "Speranza." After graduating from Portora Royal School in Enniskillen, he attended Trinity College, Dublin, where he distinguished himself as a student of the classics; he won a number of awards, including the prestigious Berkeley Prize for Greek. In 1874 he was awarded a scholarship to Magdalen College, Oxford, which he attended for the next four years. Wilde later referred to two great turning points in his life: "the first when my father sent me to Oxford, the second when Society sent me to prison." At Oxford Wilde studied with John Ruskin and Walter Pater, two leading scholars of aesthetics. Pater exerted the most lasting influence on the young Irishman. In his recently published *Studies in the History of the Renaissance* (1873), Pater celebrated "poetic passion, the desire for beauty, and the love of art for art's sake." Wilde, who had been attracted to aestheticism even before he arrived in Oxford, adopted the movement's beliefs, manners, and poses. He wore his hair long, dressed flamboyantly, and decorated his room in the aesthetic mode, with such accessories as lilies (associated with the Pre-Raphaelite painters) and studiously artistic furnishings. "I find it harder and harder every day to live up to my blue china," he famously stated, and the mannered self-consciousness of such sentiments would make him one of England's most visible aesthetes. During this time Wilde also wrote many of the poems that would appear in an 1881 collection of verse.

When Wilde moved from Oxford to London in 1878, he quickly established himself in high society through his brilliant conversation and wit. Within two years the newspaper *Punch* was regularly caricaturing him as a figurehead of the aesthetic movement, and in 1881 W. S. Gilbert and Sir Arthur Sullivan's comic opera *Patience* satirized aestheticism through the "perfectly precious" Wilde-like character Bunthorne. When the producer of *Patience* took the opera on tour in the United States and Canada the following year, Wilde accompanied the production as a lecturer and representative aesthete. Wilde traveled from coast to coast; met Ulysses S. Grant, Walt Whitman, and other prominent Americans; and registered his impressions of the New World in such epigrams as this: "When good Americans die they go to Paris; when bad Americans die they stay in America." Back in England, Wilde toured the British Isles as lecturer, worked as a journalist and book reviewer, and assumed the editorship of *Woman's World*, a popular late-Victorian periodical. In 1884 Wilde married Constance Mary Lloyd, with whom he had two sons over the next two years. But while Wilde continued to entertain the fashionable society of London with his witty conversation, and while his marriage established a degree of social respectability, he was known for little beyond being a celebrity. That began to change in 1888 with the publication of *The Happy Prince and Other Tales*, the first of two collections of original fairy tales. Over the next seven years, Wilde published a collection of critical essays (which included "The Artist as Critic" [1890]); two additional collections of stories; *The Picture of Dorian Gray*, his novel about a hedonistic aristocrat that shocked the Victorian public; and his five major plays.

An avid theatergoer since his college days and a friend of such theater luminaries as the actresses Lillie Langtry and Sarah Bernhardt, Wilde first tried his hand at drama with *Vera; or, The Nihilists* and *The Duchess of Padua*, which were written in the early 1880s and given short runs in New York. In 1891 Wilde agreed to write a social comedy for George Alexander, manager of the St. James's Theatre, and it was this play that would catapult him to the forefront of the London theater scene. *Lady Windermere's Fan*, produced in 1892, uses the narrative frame of the "problem play"—a nineteenth-century dramatic genre that dealt with controversial social issues—but deploys provocative social commentary and witty epigram to undermine the comfortable moral conclusions that plays in this genre frequently adopted. The play was widely popular, and the attention it received was intensified by Wilde himself, who strolled onstage, cigarette in hand, to greet the opening night applause and congratulated the audience for thinking as highly of his play as he did. *Lady Windermere's Fan* was followed by three more extremely successful social comedies: *A Woman of No Importance* (1893), *An Ideal Husband* (1895), and—Wilde's greatest play—*THE IMPORTANCE OF BEING EARNEST* (1895). *Salomé*, which Wilde wrote in 1891, dramatized the love of Salomé, Herodias's daughter, for John the Baptist (or Iokanaan) and her incantatory dance with his severed head. Deeply influenced by the symbolist drama of Stéphane Mallarmé (1842–1898) and Maurice Maeterlinck (1862–1949), *Salomé* was refused production by the Lord Chamberlain, who invoked a centuries-old law that prohibited the theatrical depiction of biblical figures. Wilde's poetic tragedy would not be seen on the English stage until after the playwright's death.

But even as Wilde was establishing himself as London's leading literary figure, the elements of his precipitous change in fortune were being set in place. In 1891 he met Lord Alfred Douglas, third son of the ninth marquess of Queensberry, and the two became inseparable. It is not clear when Wilde first became involved in homosexual relationships, but by the 1890s he was leading an active hidden life in London and

Wilde and his lover, Lord Alfred Douglas, in 1893.

abroad. The antagonism of Douglas's father toward what he understood to be a scandalous connection came to a head in February 1895 when Queensberry delivered a card to the London club of which Wilde was a member with the inscription "To Oscar Wilde, posing Somdomite [*sic*]." Wilde took out a warrant charging Queensberry with criminal libel, and in April the case went to trial. When Queensberry presented a list of male prostitutes who would testify concerning Wilde's illegal activities, however, Wilde withdrew the prosecution and the marquess was acquitted. Wilde, who was quickly arrested, now found himself the defendant, and after two trials (the first ended with a hung jury), he was sentenced to two years' hard labor for homosexual conduct. Over the next twenty-four months he suffered the misery and deprivations of the Victorian prison system. Initially allowed only a Bible, hymnbook, and prayerbook, he was eventually able to obtain other books and writing materials. Under these somewhat more lenient conditions he wrote *De Profundis* (published in part in 1905; unexpurgated, in 1962), a book-length letter to Douglas that included a meditation on his own life and fate. When Wilde was released from prison in May 1897, he left for France and never again set foot in England. In 1898 Wilde published *The Ballad of Reading Gaol*—inspired by his experience in prison—but his career as a writer was effectively over. He died in Paris on November 30, 1900, at the age of forty-six.

In *De Profundis,* which became his own eulogy, Wilde summed up what he felt to be the nature of his contribution to the cultural and philosophical life of his times:

> I made art a philosophy, and philosophy an art: I altered the minds of men and the colors of things: there was nothing I said or did that did not make people wonder: I took the drama, the most objective form known to art, and made it as personal a mode of expression as the lyric or the sonnet, at the same time that I widened its range and enriched its characterization. . . . I treated Art as the supreme reality, and life as a mere mode of fiction: I awoke the imagination of my century so that it created myth and legend around me: I summed up all systems in a phrase, and all existence in an epigram.

Wilde's conception of art resists both the moral seriousness of much nineteenth-century literature and what he considered to be the Philistine tendencies of the Victorian middle and upper classes. Writing that "all art is quite useless," he sought to dissociate artistic creation from traditional notions of social usefulness and moral edification. The result of this creative principle was a sophisticated manipulation of literary and social form. Indeed, Wilde became one of his age's most visible celebrities by also serving as its most clever critic. Even as his writing detailed the rituals and conventions of Victorian high society, Wilde subverted the hierarchy of values that structured this world.

Nowhere is this transgressive impulse more evident than in the famous Wildean epigrams, which invert traditional platitudes through clever turns of phrase. Take one example: "Ignorance is like a delicate exotic fruit; touch it and the bloom is gone." The immediate effect of such a remark is studied frivolity: as Algernon says of another epigram, similarly found in *The Importance of Being Earnest*, "It is perfectly phrased! and quite as true as any observation in civilized life should be." At the same time, the line offers a pointed commentary on those segments of the British upper class who value privilege over education. Wilde's plays draw on the manners tradition of social comedy, but in their boundary-assaulting wit they bear more than passing kinship to the more explicitly political drama of his fellow Irishman GEORGE BERNARD SHAW.

The Importance of Being Earnest, which opened to widespread acclaim at the St. James's Theatre on February 14, 1895, is the epitome of Wilde's subversive mode of playwriting. Its philosophy, as Wilde defined it, is straightforward: "That we should treat all the trivial things of life seriously, and all the serious things of life with sincere and studied triviality." Unlike Wilde's earlier comedies, which borrowed the situations and plot devices of contemporary popular drama and were occasionally marred by the uneasy blend of melodrama and wit, *The Importance of Being Earnest* embraces the logic of a thoroughly stylized world in which action borders on farce, epigram rules the day, and even the butler speaks with exceptional propriety. Its world is ruthlessly superficial—"In matters of grave importance," Gwendolen insists, "style, not sincerity is the vital thing"—and its irreverent wit satirizes the institutions and ideals of Victorian society: marriage, religion, gender roles, family, the class system, colonialism, English country living, science, education, romantic idealism, and (of course) earnestness, the habit of taking oneself and one's cherished beliefs quite seriously.

Algernon and Jack, the play's central male characters, pursue a life of leisure and pleasure untroubled by the codes of respectability and responsibility that govern the society around them. Wilde's audience would have recognized them as "dandies" within a nineteenth-century tradition of mannered individualism that included the

Allan Aynesworth as Algernon and George Alexander as Jack in the original 1895 production of *The Importance of Being Earnest*.

fashionable man-about-town Beau Brummell (1778–1840). The dandy, as Alan Sinfield observes, rejected the middle-class values of work and purity through a display of "conspicuous idleness, moral skepticism, and effeminacy." As much an attitude toward life as a manner and style of dress, dandyism called attention to its originality even as it embraced the outward forms of aristocratic society. Unlike Wilde's earlier comedies, which introduce dandy characters in conventional social settings, *The Importance of Being Earnest* presents a world in which wit, pleasure, and studied superficiality are the moral norm. It is a world of erased distinctions and inverted expectations, where smoking is as good an occupation for a man as any other and the most important thing to do in a moment of crisis is eat a muffin in the proper manner. Even Lady Bracknell, that most formidable representative of British social propriety, carries the observance of appearance and form to a dandiacal level of irreverence: "To lose one parent may be regarded as a misfortune—to lose *both* seems like carelessness."

In "The Critic as Artist" Wilde wrote: "Man is least himself when he talks in his own person. Give him a mask, and he will tell you the truth." Few characters in The Importance of Being Earnest are what they appear. Jack Worthing takes on his alter ego, Ernest, when he slips away to the city to see his nonexistent brother, and Algernon assumes the same name when he visits Cecily on the pretense of visiting his imaginary friend Bunbury. Gwendolen hides the secret of her romance with Jack from her mother, Cecily creates an imaginary engagement, and Lady Bracknell's authoritarian manner hides the fact that she married into her social position from decidedly nonaristocratic origins. Even Lane, the butler, and Miss Prism, the governess, have their secrets. In a play that pivots on the question of who one is, "Bunburying" becomes a metaphor for more fundamental shifts of identity. As Neil Sammells points out, *The Importance of Being Earnest* is obsessed with public and private documents—letters, diaries, birth certificates, Army Lists, novels—and with "their fallibility as a means of establishing 'authenticity,' whether of person or incident." But in "an age of surfaces" (the phrase belongs to Lady Bracknell), such categories as truth and identity remain elusive, caught in the play of social conventions and outward forms. The play on the word "Earnest" in the comedy's title reflects a society where who one is may hinge on a name, and where Sincerity is the stepchild of Accident. "It is a terrible thing," Jack laments, "for a man to find out suddenly that all his life he has been speaking nothing but the truth."

In the end, Victorian earnestness had its revenge, and for those who know the playwright's biography it is hard not to view Wilde's final comedy in light of the events that followed shortly upon its premiere. When Wilde was arrested after the first trial, his name was taken off the billboards for *The Ideal Husband* and *The Importance of Being Earnest,* and in view of the author's sudden notoriety the two productions were soon canceled. The Bunburying in which Wilde's protagonists engage must have felt, to many in his audience, uncomfortably close to the secret life of which he was accused and for which he was convicted. In fact, the connections are more than coincidental. As recent scholars have demonstrated, Wilde wove a series of homosexual allusions within the play: in addition to its other meanings, for instance, *earnest* was a Victorian code word for homosexual. But though *The Importance of Being Earnest* engages and is framed by the trenchant realities of late-nineteenth-century society, its strategy of taking seriousness lightly and lightness seriously ensures that its world maintains the studied refinement for which Wilde strove. Dandyism, Wilde wrote, "is the assertion of the absolute modernity of beauty." What dominates this greatest of nineteenth-century comedies—"written by a butterfly for butterflies" (as Wilde wrote a friend)—is the power of wit, satire, and unscrupulous elegance.

S.G.

The Importance of Being Earnest
A Trivial Comedy for Serious People

CHARACTERS

JOHN WORTHING, J.P.[1]
ALGERNON MONCRIEFF
REV. CANON CHASUBLE, D.D.[2]
MERRIMAN, butler
LANE, manservant
LADY BRACKNELL
HON. GWENDOLEN FAIRFAX
CECILY CARDEW
MISS PRISM, governess

Time
The Present.

First Act

[SCENE: *Morning-room in Algernon's flat in Half Moon Street.*[3] *The room is luxuriously and artistically furnished. The sound of a piano is heard in the adjoining room.*]

[LANE *is arranging afternoon tea on the table, and after the music has ceased,* ALGERNON *enters.*]

ALGERNON Did you hear what I was playing, Lane?

LANE I didn't think it polite to listen, sir.

ALGERNON I'm sorry for that, for your sake. I don't play accurately—anyone can play accurately—but I play with wonderful expression. As far as the piano is concerned, sentiment is my forte. I keep science for Life.

LANE Yes, sir.

ALGERNON And, speaking of the science of Life, have you got the cucumber sandwiches cut for Lady Bracknell?

LANE Yes, sir. [*Hands them on a salver.*]

ALGERNON [*inspects them, takes two, and sits down on the sofa*] Oh! . . . by the way, Lane, I see from your book that on Thursday night, when Lord Shoreham and Mr Worthing were dining with me, eight bottles of champagne are entered as having been consumed.

LANE Yes, sir; eight bottles and a pint.

ALGERNON Why is it that at a bachelor's establishment the servants invariably drink the champagne? I ask merely for information.

LANE I attribute it to the superior quality of the wine, sir. I have often observed that in married households the champagne is rarely of a first-rate brand.

ALGERNON Good Heavens! Is marriage so demoralizing as that?

LANE I believe it *is* a very pleasant state, sir. I have had very little experience of it myself up to the present. I have only been married once. That was in consequence of a misunderstanding between myself and a young person.

1. Justice of the Peace.
2. Doctor of Divinity.
3. Located off Piccadilly Street in Mayfair, a fashionable district of London's West End.

Morning-room: an informal room for receiving morning visitors. Later visitors would be received in the more formal drawing room.

ALGERNON [*languidly*] I don't know that I am much interested in your family life, Lane.

LANE No, sir; it is not a very interesting subject. I never think of it myself.

ALGERNON Very natural, I am sure. That will do, Lane, thank you.

LANE Thank you, sir. [LANE *goes out.*]

ALGERNON Lane's views on marriage seem somewhat lax. Really, if the lower orders don't set us a good example, what on earth is the use of them? They seem, as a class, to have absolutely no sense of moral responsibility.

[*Enter* LANE.]

LANE Mr Ernest Worthing.

[*Enter* JACK.] [LANE *goes out.*]

ALGERNON How are you, my dear Ernest? What brings you up to town?

JACK Oh, pleasure, pleasure! What else should bring one anywhere? Eating as usual, I see, Algy!

ALGERNON [*stiffly*] I believe it is customary in good society to take some slight refreshment at five o'clock. Where have you been since last Thursday?

JACK [*sitting down on the sofa*] In the country.

ALGERNON What on earth do you do there?

JACK [*pulling off his gloves*] When one is in town one amuses oneself. When one is in the country one amuses other people. It is excessively boring.

ALGERNON And who are the people you amuse?

JACK [*airily*] Oh, neighbours, neighbours.

ALGERNON Got nice neighbours in your part of Shropshire?[4]

JACK Perfectly horrid! Never speak to one of them.

ALGERNON How immensely you must amuse them! [*Goes over and takes sandwich.*] By the way, Shropshire is your county, is it not?

JACK Eh? Shropshire? Yes, of course. Hallo! Why all these cups? Why cucumber sandwiches? Why such reckless extravagance in one so young? Who is coming to tea?

ALGERNON Oh! merely Aunt Augusta and Gwendolen.

JACK How perfectly delightful!

ALGERNON Yes, that is all very well; but I am afraid Aunt Augusta won't quite approve of your being here.

JACK May I ask why?

ALGERNON My dear fellow, the way you flirt with Gwendolen is perfectly disgraceful. It is almost as bad as the way Gwendolen flirts with you.

JACK I am in love with Gwendolen. I have come up to town expressly to propose to her.

ALGERNON I thought you had come up for pleasure? . . . I call that business.

JACK How utterly unromantic you are!

ALGERNON I really don't see anything romantic in proposing. It is very romantic to be in love. But there is nothing romantic about a definite proposal. Why, one may be accepted. One usually is, I believe. Then the excitement is all over. The very essence of romance is uncertainty. If ever I get married, I'll certainly try to forget the fact.

4. A county of England in the west Midlands, adjoining the Welsh border (about 150 miles northwest of London).

JACK I have no doubt about that, dear Algy. The Divorce Court was specially invented for people whose memories are so curiously constituted.

ALGERNON Oh! there is no use speculating on that subject. Divorces are made in Heaven——[JACK *puts out his hand to take a sandwich.* ALGERNON *at once interferes.*] Please don't touch the cucumber sandwiches. They are ordered specially for Aunt Augusta. [*Takes one and eats it.*]

JACK Well, you have been eating them all the time.

ALGERNON That is quite a different matter. She is my aunt. [*Takes plate from below.*] Have some bread and butter. The bread and butter is for Gwendolen. Gwendolen is devoted to bread and butter.

JACK [*advancing to table and helping himself*] And very good bread and butter it is too.

ALGERNON Well, my dear fellow, you need not eat as if you were going to eat it all. You behave as if you were married to her already. You are not married to her already, and I don't think you ever will be.

JACK Why on earth do you say that?

ALGERNON Well, in the first place girls never marry the men they flirt with. Girls don't think it right.

JACK Oh, that is nonsense!

ALGERNON It isn't. It is a great truth. It accounts for the extraordinary number of bachelors that one sees all over the place. In the second place, I don't give my consent.

JACK Your consent!

ALGERNON My dear fellow, Gwendolen is my first cousin. And before I allow you to marry her, you will have to clear up the whole question of Cecily. [*Rings bell.*]

JACK Cecily! What on earth do you mean? What do you mean, Algy, by Cecily? I don't know anyone of the name of Cecily.

[*Enter* LANE.]

ALGERNON Bring me that cigarette case Mr Worthing left in the smoking-room the last time he dined here.

LANE Yes, sir. [LANE *goes out.*]

JACK Do you mean to say you have had my cigarette case all this time? I wish to goodness you had let me know. I have been writing frantic letters to Scotland Yard[5] about it. I was very nearly offering a large reward.

ALGERNON Well, I wish you would offer one. I happen to be more than usually hard up.

JACK There is no good offering a large reward now that the thing is found.

[*Enter* LANE *with the cigarette case on a salver.* ALGERNON *takes it at once.* LANE *goes out.*]

ALGERNON I think that is rather mean of you, Ernest, I must say. [*Opens case and examines it.*] However, it makes no matter, for, now that I look at the inscription inside, I find that the thing isn't yours after all.

JACK Of course it's mine. [*Moving to him*] You have seen me with it a hundred times, and you have no right whatsoever to read what is written inside. It is a very ungentlemanly thing to read a private cigarette case.

5. The headquarters of the London Metropolitan Police Force.

ALGERNON Oh! it is absurd to have a hard-and-fast rule about what one should read and what one shouldn't. More than half of modern culture depends on what one shouldn't read.

JACK I am quite aware of the fact, and I don't propose to discuss modern culture. It isn't the sort of thing one should talk of in private. I simply want my cigarette case back.

ALGERNON Yes; but this isn't your cigarette case. This cigarette case is a present from someone of the name of Cecily, and you said you didn't know anyone of that name.

JACK Well, if you want to know, Cecily happens to be my aunt.

ALGERNON Your aunt!

JACK Yes. Charming old lady she is, too. Lives at Tunbridge Wells.[6] Just give it back to me, Algy.

ALGERNON [*retreating to back of sofa*] But why does she call herself little Cecily if she is your aunt and lives at Tunbridge Wells. [*Reading*] 'From little Cecily with her fondest love.'

JACK [*moving to sofa and kneeling upon it*] My dear fellow, what on earth is there in that? Some aunts are tall, some aunts are not tall. That is a matter that surely an aunt may be allowed to decide for herself. You seem to think that every aunt should be exactly like your aunt! That is absurd! For Heaven's sake give me back my cigarette case. [*Follows* ALGERNON *round the room.*]

ALGERNON Yes. But why does your aunt call you her uncle? 'From little Cecily, with her fondest love to her dear Uncle Jack.' There is no objection, I admit, to an aunt being a small aunt, but why an aunt, no matter what her size may be, should call her own nephew her uncle, I can't quite make out. Besides, your name isn't Jack at all; it is Ernest.

JACK It isn't Ernest; it's Jack.

ALGERNON You have always told me it was Ernest. I have introduced you to everyone as Ernest. You answer to the name of Ernest. You look as if your name was Ernest. You are the most earnest looking person I ever saw in my life. It is perfectly absurd your saying that your name isn't Ernest. It's on your cards. Here is one of them. [*Taking it from case*] 'Mr Ernest Worthing, B. 4, The Albany.'[7] I'll keep this as a proof that your name is Ernest if ever you attempt to deny it to me, or to Gwendolen, or to anyone else. [*Puts the card in his pocket.*]

JACK Well, my name is Ernest in town and Jack in the country, and the cigarette case was given to me in the country.

ALGERNON Yes, but that does not account for the fact that your small Aunt Cecily, who lives at Tunbridge Wells, calls you her dear uncle. Come, old boy, you had much better have the thing out at once.

JACK My dear Algy, you talk exactly as if you were a dentist. It is very vulgar to talk like a dentist when one isn't a dentist. It produces a false impression.

ALGERNON Well, that is exactly what dentists always do. Now, go on! Tell me the whole thing. I may mention that I have always suspected you of being a confirmed and secret Bunburyist, and I am quite sure of it now.

JACK Bunburyist? What on earth do you mean by a Bunburyist?

ALGERNON I'll reveal to you the meaning of that incomparable expression as soon as you are kind enough to inform me why you are Ernest in town and Jack in the country.

6. A fashionable spa town in Kent, about 30 miles southeast of London.

7. Popular bachelors' quarters near Piccadilly Street, in central London.

JACK Well, produce my cigarette case first.

ALGERNON Here it is. [*Hands cigarette case.*] Now produce your explanation, and pray make it improbable. [*Sits on sofa.*]

JACK My dear fellow, there is nothing improbable about my explanation at all. In fact it's perfectly ordinary. Old Mr Thomas Cardew, who adopted me when I was a little boy, made me in his will guardian to his grand-daughter, Miss Cecily Cardew. Cecily who addresses me as her uncle from motives of respect that you could not possibly appreciate, lives at my place in the country under the charge of her admirable governess, Miss Prism.

ALGERNON Where is that place in the country, by the way?

JACK That is nothing to you, dear boy. You are not going to be invited. . . . I may tell you candidly that the place is not in Shropshire.

ALGERNON I suspected that, my dear fellow! I have Bunburyed all over Shropshire on two separate occasions. Now, go on. Why are you Ernest in town and Jack in the country?

JACK My dear Algy, I don't know whether you will be able to understand my real motives. You are hardly serious enough. When one is placed in the position of guardian, one has to adopt a very high moral tone on all subjects. It's one's duty to do so. And as a high moral tone can hardly be said to conduce very much to either one's health or one's happiness, in order to get up to town I have always pretended to have a younger brother of the name of Ernest, who lives in the Albany, and gets into the most dreadful scrapes. That, my dear Algy, is the whole truth pure and simple.

ALGERNON The truth is rarely pure and never simple. Modern life would be very tedious if it were either, and modern literature a complete impossibility!

JACK That wouldn't be at all a bad thing.

ALGERNON Literary criticism is not your forte, my dear fellow. Don't try it. You should leave that to people who haven't been at a University. They do it so well in the daily papers. What you really are is a Bunburyist. I was quite right in saying you were a Bunburyist. You are one of the most advanced Bunburyists I know.

JACK What on earth do you mean?

ALGERNON You have invented a very useful younger brother called Ernest, in order that you may be able to come up to town as often as you like. I have invented an invaluable permanent invalid called Bunbury, in order that I may be able to go down into the country whenever I choose. Bunbury is perfectly invaluable. If it wasn't for Bunbury's extraordinary bad health, for instance, I wouldn't be able to dine with you at Willis's[8] tonight, for I have been really engaged to Aunt Augusta for more than a week.

JACK I haven't asked you to dine with me anywhere tonight.

ALGERNON I know. You are absurdly careless about sending out invitations. It is very foolish of you. Nothing annoys people so much as not receiving invitations.

JACK You had much better dine with your Aunt Augusta.

ALGERNON I haven't the smallest intention of doing anything of the kind. To begin with, I dined there on Monday, and once a week is quite enough to dine with one's own relations. In the second place, whenever I do dine

8. A fashionable restaurant on King Street, near Piccadilly, frequented by Wilde and his companion Alfred Lord Douglas.

there I am always treated as a member of the family, and sent down[9] with either no woman at all, or two. In the third place, I know perfectly well whom she will place me next to, tonight. She will place me next Mary Farquhar, who always flirts with her own husband across the dinner-table. That is not very pleasant. Indeed, it is not even decent . . . and that sort of thing is enormously on the increase. The amount of women in London who flirt with their own husbands is perfectly scandalous. It looks so bad. It is simply washing one's clean linen in public. Besides, now that I know you to be a confirmed Bunburyist I naturally want to talk to you about Bunburying. I want to tell you the rules.

JACK I'm not a Bunburyist at all. If Gwendolen accepts me, I am going to kill my brother, indeed I think I'll kill him in any case. Cecily is a little too much interested in him. It is rather a bore. So I am going to get rid of Ernest. And I strongly advise you to do the same with Mr . . . with your invalid friend who has the absurd name.

ALGERNON Nothing will induce me to part with Bunbury, and if you ever get married, which seems to me extremely problematic, you will be very glad to know Bunbury. A man who marries without knowing Bunbury has a very tedious time of it.

JACK That is nonsense. If I marry a charming girl like Gwendolen, and she is the only girl I ever saw in my life that I would marry, I certainly won't want to know Bunbury.

ALGERNON Then your wife will. You don't seem to realize, that in married life three is company and two is none.

JACK [*sententiously*] That, my dear young friend, is the theory that the corrupt French Drama[1] has been propounding for the last fifty years.

ALGERNON Yes; and that the happy English home has proved in half the time.

JACK For heaven's sake, don't try to be cynical. It's perfectly easy to be cynical.

ALGERNON My dear fellow, it isn't easy to be anything nowadays. There's such a lot of beastly competition about. [*The sound of an electric bell is heard.*] Ah! that must be Aunt Augusta. Only relatives, or creditors, ever ring in that Wagnerian[2] manner. Now, if I get her out of the way for ten minutes, so that you can have an opportunity for proposing to Gwendolen, may I dine with you tonight at Willis's?

JACK I suppose so, if you want to.

ALGERNON Yes, but you must be serious about it. I hate people who are not serious about meals. It is so shallow of them.

[*Enter* LANE.]

LANE Lady Bracknell and Miss Fairfax.

[ALGERNON *goes forward to meet them. Enter* LADY BRACKNELL *and* GWENDOLEN.]

LADY BRACKNELL Good afternoon, dear Algernon, I hope you are behaving very well.

ALGERNON I'm feeling very well, Aunt Augusta.

9. Directed to accompany someone to dinner. Victorian dinner guests would gather upstairs in the drawing room, and then gentlemen would escort ladies to the dining room in arranged couples.

1. Because its plots frequently involved adultery and infidelity, French drama was often viewed by the English as immoral.

2. Loud and imposing, like the operas of the German composer Richard Wagner (1813–1883).

LADY BRACKNELL That's not quite the same thing. In fact the two things rarely go together. [*Sees* JACK *and bows to him with icy coldness.*]

ALGERNON [*to* GWENDOLEN] Dear me, you are smart![3]

GWENDOLEN I am always smart! Aren't I, Mr Worthing?

JACK You're quite perfect, Miss Fairfax.

GWENDOLEN Oh! I hope I am not that. It would leave no room for developments, and I intend to develop in many directions. [GWENDOLEN *and* JACK *sit down together in the corner.*]

LADY BRACKNELL I'm sorry if we are a little late, Algernon, but I was obliged to call on dear Lady Harbury. I hadn't been there since her poor husband's death. I never saw a woman so altered; she looks quite twenty years younger. And now I'll have a cup of tea, and one of those nice cucumber sandwiches you promised me.

ALGERNON Certainly, Aunt Augusta. [*Goes over to tea-table.*]

LADY BRACKNELL Won't you come and sit here, Gwendolen?

GWENDOLEN Thanks, mamma, I'm quite comfortable where I am.

ALGERNON [*picking up empty plate in horror*] Good heavens! Lane! Why are there no cucumber sandwiches? I ordered them specially.

LANE [*gravely*] There were no cucumbers in the market this morning, sir. I went down twice.

ALGERNON No cucumbers!

LANE No, sir. Not even for ready money.[4]

ALGERNON That will do, Lane, thank you.

LANE Thank you, sir. [*Goes out.*]

ALGERNON I am greatly distressed, Aunt Augusta, about there being no cucumbers, not even for ready money.

LADY BRACKNELL It really makes no matter, Algernon. I had some crumpets with Lady Harbury, who seems to me to be living entirely for pleasure now.

ALGERNON I hear her hair has turned quite gold from grief.

LADY BRACKNELL It certainly has changed its colour. From what cause I, of course, cannot say. [ALGERNON *crosses and hands tea.*] Thank you. I've quite a treat for you tonight, Algernon. I am going to send you down with Mary Farquhar. She is such a nice woman, and so attentive to her husband. It's delightful to watch them.

ALGERNON I am afraid, Aunt Augusta, I shall have to give up the pleasure of dining with you tonight after all.

LADY BRACKNELL [*frowning*] I hope not, Algernon. It would put my table completely out.[5] Your uncle would have to dine upstairs. Fortunately he is accustomed to that.

ALGERNON It is a great bore, and, I need hardly say, a terrible disappointment to me, but the fact is I have just had a telegram to say that my poor friend Bunbury is very ill again. [*Exchanges glances with* JACK.] They seem to think I should be with him.

LADY BRACKNELL It is very strange. This Mr Bunbury seems to suffer from curiously bad health.

ALGERNON Yes; poor Bunbury is a dreadful invalid.

3. Neatly stylish in appearance.

4. Immediate cash payment (the well-off often bought goods on credit).

5. That is, ruin the seating arrangement, which was always carefully planned to balance male and female guests.

LADY BRACKNELL Well, I must say, Algernon, that I think it is high time that Mr Bunbury made up his mind whether he was going to live or to die. This shilly-shallying with the question is absurd. Nor do I in any way approve of the modern sympathy with invalids. I consider it morbid. Illness of any kind is hardly a thing to be encouraged in others. Health is the primary duty of life. I am always telling that to your poor uncle, but he never seems to take much notice . . . as far as any improvement in his ailments goes. I should be much obliged if you would ask Mr Bunbury, from me, to be kind enough not to have a relapse on Saturday, for I rely on you to arrange my music for me. It is my last reception, and one wants something that will encourage conversation, particularly at the end of the season[6] when everyone has practically said whatever they had to say, which, in most cases, was probably not much.

ALGERNON I'll speak to Bunbury, Aunt Augusta, if he is still conscious, and I think I can promise you he'll be all right by Saturday. Of course the music is a great difficulty. You see, if one plays good music, people don't listen, and if one plays bad music people don't talk. But I'll run over the programme I've drawn out, if you will kindly come into the next room for a moment.

LADY BRACKNELL Thank you, Algernon. It is very thoughtful of you. [*Rising, and following* ALGERNON] I'm sure the programme will be delightful, after a few expurgations. French songs I cannot possibly allow. People always seem to think that they are improper, and either look shocked, which is vulgar, or laugh, which is worse. But German sounds a thoroughly respectable language, and indeed, I believe is so. Gwendolen, you will accompany me.

GWENDOLEN Certainly, mamma.

[LADY BRACKNELL *and* ALGERNON *go into the music-room*, GWENDOLEN *remains behind.*]

JACK Charming day it has been, Miss Fairfax.

GWENDOLEN Pray don't talk to me about the weather, Mr Worthing. Whenever people talk to me about the weather, I always feel quite certain that they mean something else. And that makes me so nervous.

JACK I do mean something else.

GWENDOLEN I thought so. In fact, I am never wrong.

JACK And I would like to be allowed to take advantage of Lady Bracknell's temporary absence . . .

GWENDOLEN I would certainly advise you to do so. Mamma has a way of coming back suddenly into a room that I have often had to speak to her about.

JACK [*nervously*] Miss Fairfax, ever since I met you I have admired you more than any girl . . . I have ever met since . . . I met you.

GWENDOLEN Yes, I am quite aware of the fact. And I often wish that in public, at any rate, you had been more demonstrative. For me you have always had an irresistible fascination. Even before I met you I was far from indifferent to you. [JACK *looks at her in amazement.*] We live, as I hope you know, Mr Worthing, in an age of ideals. The fact is constantly mentioned in the more expensive monthly magazines, and has reached the provincial pulpits I am told: and my ideal has always been to love some one of the name of Ernest. There is something in that name that inspires absolute

6. That is, the social season in London, which began in May and lasted through July; during this time fashionable society attended balls, dinners, and other entertainments.

confidence. The moment Algernon first mentioned to me that he had a friend called Ernest, I knew I was destined to love you.

JACK You really love me, Gwendolen?

GWENDOLEN Passionately!

JACK Darling! You don't know how happy you've made me.

GWENDOLEN My own Ernest!

JACK But you don't really mean to say that you couldn't love me if my name wasn't Ernest?

GWENDOLEN But your name is Ernest.

JACK Yes, I know it is. But supposing it was something else? Do you mean to say you couldn't love me then?

GWENDOLEN [*glibly*] Ah! that is clearly a metaphysical speculation, and like most metaphysical speculations has very little reference at all to the actual facts of real life, as we know them.

JACK Personally, darling, to speak quite candidly, I don't much care about the name of Ernest . . . I don't think the name suits me at all.

GWENDOLEN It suits you perfectly. It is a divine name. It has a music of its own. It produces vibrations.

JACK Well, really, Gwendolen, I must say that I think there are lots of other much nicer names. I think Jack, for instance, a charming name.

GWENDOLEN Jack? . . . No, there is very little music in the name Jack, if any at all, indeed. It does not thrill. It produces absolutely no vibrations. . . . I have known several Jacks, and they all, without exception, were more than usually plain. Besides, Jack is a notorious domesticity[7] for John! And I pity any woman who is married to a man called John. She would probably never be allowed to know the entrancing pleasure of a single moment's solitude. The only really safe name is Ernest.

JACK Gwendolen, I must get christened at once—I mean we must get married at once. There is no time to be lost.

GWENDOLEN Married, Mr Worthing?

JACK [*astounded*] Well . . . surely. You know that I love you, and you led me to believe, Miss Fairfax, that you were not absolutely indifferent to me.

GWENDOLEN I adore you. But you haven't proposed to me yet. Nothing has been said at all about marriage. The subject has not even been touched on.

JACK Well . . . may I propose to you now?

GWENDOLEN I think it would be an admirable opportunity. And to spare you any possible disappointment, Mr Worthing, I think it only fair to tell you quite frankly beforehand that I am fully determined to accept you.

JACK Gwendolen!

GWENDOLEN Yes, Mr Worthing, what have you got to say to me?

JACK You know what I have got to say to you.

GWENDOLEN Yes, but you don't say it.

JACK Gwendolen, will you marry me? [*Goes on his knees.*]

GWENDOLEN Of course I will, darling. How long you have been about it! I am afraid you have had very little experience in how to propose.

JACK My own one, I have never loved anyone in the world but you.

GWENDOLEN Yes, but men often propose for practice. I know my brother Gerald does. All my girl-friends tell me so. What wonderfully blue eyes you

7. A domestic or familiar expression.

have, Ernest! They are quite, quite, blue. I hope you will always look at me just like that, especially when there are other people present.

[*Enter* LADY BRACKNELL.]

LADY BRACKNELL Mr Worthing! Rise, sir, from this semi-recumbent posture. It is most indecorous.

GWENDOLEN Mamma! [*He tries to rise; she restrains him.*] I must beg you to retire. This is no place for you. Besides, Mr Worthing has not quite finished yet.

LADY BRACKNELL Finished what, may I ask?

GWENDOLEN I am engaged to Mr Worthing, mamma. [*They rise together.*]

LADY BRACKNELL Pardon me, you are not engaged to anyone. When you do become engaged to some one, I, or your father, should his health permit him, will inform you of the fact. An engagement should come on a young girl as a surprise, pleasant or unpleasant, as the case may be. It is hardly a matter that she could be allowed to arrange for herself. . . . And now I have a few questions to put to you, Mr Worthing. While I am making these inquiries, you, Gwendolen, will wait for me below in the carriage.

GWENDOLEN [*reproachfully*] Mamma!

GWENDOLEN In the carriage, Gwendolen! [GWENDOLEN *goes to the door. She and* JACK *blow kisses to each other behind* LADY BRACKNELL*'s back.* LADY BRACKNELL *looks vaguely about as if she could not understand what the noise was. Finally turns round.*] Gwendolen, the carriage!

GWENDOLEN Yes, mamma. [*Goes out, looking back at* JACK.]

LADY BRACKNELL [*sitting down*] You can take a seat, Mr Worthing.

[*Looks in her pocket for note-book and pencil.*]

JACK Thank you, Lady Bracknell, I prefer standing.

LADY BRACKNELL [*pencil and note-book in hand*] I feel bound to tell you that you are not down on my list of eligible young men, although I have the same list as the dear Duchess of Bolton has. We work together, in fact. However, I am quite ready to enter your name, should your answers be what a really affectionate mother requires. Do you smoke?

JACK Well, yes, I must admit I smoke.

LADY BRACKNELL I am glad to hear it. A man should always have an occupation of some kind. There are far too many idle men in London as it is. How old are you?

JACK Twenty-nine.

LADY BRACKNELL A very good age to be married at. I have always been of opinion that a man who desires to get married should know either everything or nothing. Which do you know?

JACK [*after some hesitation*] I know nothing, Lady Bracknell.

LADY BRACKNELL I am pleased to hear it. I do not approve of anything that tampers with natural ignorance. Ignorance is like a delicate exotic fruit; touch it and the bloom is gone. The whole theory of modern education is radically unsound. Fortunately in England, at any rate, education produces no effect whatsoever. If it did, it would prove a serious danger to the upper classes, and probably lead to acts of violence in Grosvenor Square.[8] What is your income?

8. A Mayfair neighborhood east of Speakers' Corner in Hyde Park.

JACK Between seven and eight thousand[9] a year.

LADY BRACKNELL [*makes a note in her book*] In land, or in investments?

JACK In investments, chiefly.

LADY BRACKNELL That is satisfactory. What between the duties expected of one during one's lifetime, and the duties exacted from one after one's death,[1] land has ceased to be either a profit or a pleasure. It gives one position, and prevents one from keeping it up. That's all that can be said about land.

JACK I have a country house with some land, of course, attached to it, about fifteen hundred acres, I believe; but I don't depend on that for my real income. In fact, as far as I can make out, the poachers are the only people who make anything out of it.

LADY BRACKNELL A country house! How many bedrooms? Well, that point can be cleared up afterwards. You have a town house, I hope? A girl with a simple, unspoiled nature, like Gwendolen, could hardly be expected to reside in the country.

JACK Well, I own a house in Belgrave Square,[2] but it is let by the year to Lady Bloxham. Of course, I can get it back whenever I like, at six months' notice.

LADY BRACKNELL Lady Bloxham? I don't know her.

JACK Oh, she goes about very little. She is a lady considerably advanced in years.

LADY BRACKNELL Ah, nowadays that is no guarantee of respectability of character. What number in Belgrave Square?

JACK 149.

LADY BRACKNELL [*shaking her head*] The unfashionable side. I thought there was something. However, that could easily be altered.

JACK Do you mean the fashion, or the side?

LADY BRACKNELL [*sternly*] Both, if necessary, I presume. What are your politics?

JACK Well, I am afraid I really have none. I am a Liberal Unionist.[3]

LADY BRACKNELL Oh, they count as Tories. They dine with us. Or come in the evening, at any rate. Now to minor matters. Are your parents living?

JACK I have lost both my parents.

LADY BRACKNELL Both? To lose one parent may be regarded as a misfortune—to lose *both* seems like carelessness. Who was your father? He was evidently a man of some wealth. Was he born in what the Radical papers call the purple of commerce, or did he rise from the ranks of the aristocracy?

JACK I am afraid I really don't know. The fact is, Lady Bracknell, I said I had lost my parents. It would be nearer the truth to say that my parents seem to have lost me . . . I don't actually know who I am by birth. I was . . . well, I was found.

LADY BRACKNELL Found!

JACK The late Mr Thomas Cardew, an old gentleman of a very charitable and kindly disposition, found me, and gave me the name of Worthing, because

9. That is £7,000 to £8,000, roughly equivalent to $1 million today.

1. That is, inheritance taxes, a play on the secondary meaning of "duties."

2. The center of Belgravia, a fashionable neighborhood just west of Buckingham Palace.

3. The Liberal Unionists were a splinter group of the Liberal Party that joined with the Conservatives (known as the Tories) to defeat William Gladstone's Home Rule Bill of 1886, which would have granted political autonomy to Ireland.

he happened to have a first-class ticket for Worthing in his pocket at the time. Worthing is a place in Sussex.[4] It is a seaside resort.

LADY BRACKNELL Where did the charitable gentleman who had a first-class ticket for this seaside resort find you?

JACK [*gravely*] In a hand-bag.

LADY BRACKNELL A hand-bag?

JACK [*very seriously*] Yes, Lady Bracknell. I was in a hand-bag—a somewhat large, black leather hand-bag, with handles to it—an ordinary hand-bag in fact.

LADY BRACKNELL In what locality did this Mr James, or Thomas, Cardew come across this ordinary hand-bag?

JACK In the cloak-room at Victoria Station.[5] It was given to him in mistake for his own.

LADY BRACKNELL The cloak-room at Victoria Station?

JACK Yes. The Brighton line.[6]

LADY BRACKNELL The line is immaterial. Mr Worthing, I confess I feel somewhat bewildered by what you have just told me. To be born, or at any rate bred, in a hand-bag, whether it had handles or not, seems to me to display a contempt for the ordinary decencies of family life that reminds one of the worst excesses of the French Revolution. And I presume you know what that unfortunate movement led to? As for the particular locality in which the hand-bag was found, a cloak-room at a railway station might serve to conceal a social indiscretion—has probably, indeed, been used for that purpose before now—but it could hardly be regarded as an assured basis for a recognized position in good society.

JACK May I ask you then what you would advise me to do? I need hardly say I would do anything in the world to ensure Gwendolen's happiness.

LADY BRACKNELL I would strongly advise you, Mr Worthing, to try and acquire some relations as soon as possible, and to make a definite effort to produce at any rate one parent, of either sex, before the season is quite over.

JACK Well, I don't see how I could possibly manage to do that. I can produce the hand-bag at any moment. It is in my dressing-room at home. I really think that should satisfy you, Lady Bracknell.

LADY BRACKNELL Me, sir! What has it to do with me? You can hardly imagine that I and Lord Bracknell would dream of allowing our only daughter—a girl brought up with the utmost care—to marry into a cloak-room, and form an alliance with a parcel? Good morning, Mr Worthing!

[LADY BRACKNELL *sweeps out in majestic indignation.*]

JACK Good morning! [ALGERNON, *from the other room, strikes up the Wedding March.*[7] JACK *looks perfectly furious, and goes to the door.*] For goodness' sake don't play that ghastly tune, Algy! How idiotic you are!

[*The music stops, and* ALGERNON *enters cheerily.*]

4. Wilde, who frequently named characters after places, wrote *The Importance of Being Earnest* while vacationing with his family in the coastal town of Worthing. Sussex is a county south of London.

5. One of London's main rail stations, located in Belgravia.

6. The rail line to Brighton, a popular seaside resort in Sussex on England's south coast.

7. The recessional often played at weddings, from Felix Mendelssohn's *A Midsummer Night's Dream* (1842).

ALGERNON Didn't it go off all right, old boy? You don't mean to say Gwendolen refused you? I know it is a way she has. She is always refusing people. I think it is most ill-natured of her.

JACK Oh, Gwendolen is as right as a trivet.[8] As far as she is concerned, we are engaged. Her mother is perfectly unbearable. Never met such a Gorgon[9] . . . I don't really know what a Gorgon is like, but I am quite sure that Lady Bracknell is one. In any case, she is a monster, without being a myth, which is rather unfair . . . I beg your pardon, Algy, I suppose I shouldn't talk about your own aunt in that way before you.

ALGERNON My dear boy, I love hearing my relations abused. It is the only thing that makes me put up with them at all. Relations are simply a tedious pack of people, who haven't got the remotest knowledge of how to live, nor the smallest instinct about when to die.

JACK Oh, that is nonsense!

ALGERNON It isn't!

JACK Well, I won't argue about the matter. You always want to argue about things.

ALGERNON That is exactly what things were originally made for.

JACK Upon my word, if I thought that, I'd shoot myself . . . [*A pause*] You don't think there is any chance of Gwendolen becoming like her mother in about a hundred and fifty years, do you Algy?

ALGERNON All women become like their mothers. That is their tragedy. No man does. That's his.

JACK Is that clever?

ALGERNON It is perfectly phrased! and quite as true as any observation in civilized life should be.

JACK I am sick to death of cleverness. Everybody is clever nowadays. You can't go anywhere without meeting clever people. The thing has become an absolute public nuisance. I wish to goodness we had a few fools left.

ALGERNON We have.

JACK I should extremely like to meet them. What do they talk about?

ALGERNON The fools? Oh! about the clever people, of course.

JACK What fools!

ALGERNON By the way, did you tell Gwendolen the truth about your being Ernest in town, and Jack in the country?

JACK [*in a very patronizing manner*] My dear fellow, the truth isn't quite the sort of thing one tells to a nice sweet refined girl. What extraordinary ideas you have about the way to behave to a woman!

ALGERNON The only way to behave to a woman is to make love to her,[1] if she is pretty, and to someone else if she is plain.

JACK Oh, that is nonsense.

ALGERNON What about your brother? What about the profligate Ernest?

JACK Oh, before the end of the week I shall have got rid of him. I'll say he died in Paris of apoplexy. Lots of people die of apoplexy, quite suddenly, don't they?

ALGERNON Yes, but it's hereditary, my dear fellow. It's a sort of thing that runs in families. You had much better say a severe chill.

8. Proverbial expression for steadiness; a trivet is a three-footed stand used to support cooking vessels over a fire.

9. In Greek mythology, one of three snake-haired sisters, the sight of whom turned all who looked at them to stone.

1. That is, flirt with her, court her.

JACK You are sure a severe chill isn't hereditary, or anything of that kind?

ALGERNON Of course it isn't!

JACK Very well, then. My poor brother Ernest is carried off suddenly in Paris, by a severe chill. That gets rid of him.

ALGERNON But I thought you said that . . . Miss Cardew was a little too much interested in your poor brother Ernest? Won't she feel his loss a good deal?

JACK Oh, that is all right. Cecily is not a silly romantic girl, I am glad to say. She has got a capital appetite, goes on long walks, and pays no attention at all to her lessons.

ALGERNON I would rather like to see Cecily.

JACK I will take very good care you never do. She is excessively pretty, and she is only just eighteen.

ALGERNON Have you told Gwendolen yet that you have an excessively pretty ward who is only just eighteen?

JACK Oh! one doesn't blurt these things out to people. Cecily and Gwendolen are perfectly certain to be extremely great friends. I'll bet you anything you like that half an hour after they have met, they will be calling each other sister.

ALGERNON Women only do that when they have called each other a lot of other things first. Now, my dear boy, if we want to get a good table at Willis's, we really must go and dress. Do you know it is nearly seven?

JACK [*irritably*] Oh! it always is nearly seven.

ALGERNON Well, I'm hungry.

JACK I never knew you when you weren't. . . .

ALGERNON What shall we do after dinner? Go to a theatre?

JACK Oh no! I loathe listening.

ALGERNON Well, let us go to the Club?[2]

JACK Oh, no! I hate talking.

ALGERNON Well, we might trot round to the Empire[3] at ten?

JACK Oh no! I can't bear looking at things. It is so silly.

ALGERNON Well, what shall we do?

JACK Nothing!

ALGERNON It is awfully hard work doing nothing. However, I don't mind hard work where there is no definite object of any kind.

[*Enter* LANE.]

LANE Miss Fairfax.

[*Enter* GWENDOLEN. LANE *goes out.*]

ALGERNON Gwendolen, upon my word!

GWENDOLEN Algy, kindly turn your back. I have something very particular to say to Mr Worthing.

ALGERNON Really, Gwendolen, I don't think I can allow this at all.

GWENDOLEN Algy, you always adopt a strictly immoral attitude towards life. You are not quite old enough to do that.

[ALGERNON *retires to the fireplace.*]

2. Any one of a number of exclusive, members-only clubs for men.

3. The Empire Theatre of Varieties, a well-known music hall in Leicester Square, a center of entertainments in London's West End.

JACK My own darling!

GWENDOLEN Ernest, we may never be married. From the expression on mamma's face I fear we never shall. Few parents nowadays pay any regard to what their children say to them. The old-fashioned respect for the young is fast dying out. Whatever influence I ever had over mamma, I lost at the age of three. But although she may prevent us from becoming man and wife, and I may marry someone else, and marry often, nothing that she can possibly do can alter my eternal devotion to you.

JACK Dear Gwendolen!

GWENDOLEN The story of your romantic origin, as related to me by mamma, with unpleasing comments, has naturally stirred the deeper fibres of my nature. Your Christian name has an irresistible fascination. The simplicity of your character makes you exquisitely incomprehensible to me. Your town address at the Albany I have. What is your address in the country?

JACK The Manor House, Woolton, Hertfordshire.[4]

[ALGERNON, *who has been carefully listening, smiles to himself, and writes the address on his shirt-cuff. Then picks up the Railway Guide.*]

GWENDOLEN There is a good postal service, I suppose? It may be necessary to do something desperate. That of course will require serious consideration. I will communicate with you daily.

JACK My own one!

GWENDOLEN How long do you remain in town?

JACK Till Monday.

GWENDOLEN Good! Algy, you may turn round now.

ALGERNON Thanks, I've turned round already.

GWENDOLEN You may also ring the bell.

JACK You will let me see you to your carriage, my own darling?

GWENDOLEN Certainly.

JACK [*to* LANE, *who now enters*] I will see Miss Fairfax out.

LANE Yes, sir.

[JACK *and* GWENDOLEN *go off.*]

[LANE *presents several letters on a salver to Algernon. It is to be surmised that they are bills, as* ALGERNON, *after looking at the envelopes, tears them up.*]

ALGERNON A glass of sherry, Lane.

LANE Yes, sir.

ALGERNON Tomorrow, Lane, I'm going Bunburying.

LANE Yes, sir.

ALGERNON I shall probably not be back till Monday. You can put up my dress clothes, my smoking jacket,[5] and all the Bunbury suits . . .

LANE Yes, sir. [*Handing sherry*]

ALGERNON I hope tomorrow will be a fine day, Lane.

LANE It never is, sir.

ALGERNON Lane, you're a perfect pessimist.

LANE I do my best to give satisfaction, sir.

[*Enter* JACK. LANE *goes off.*]

4. A rural county just northeast of London.

5. A loose-fitting casual jacket worn at home, usually in the evening. *Put up:* pack.

JACK There's a sensible, intellectual girl! the only girl I ever cared for in my life. [ALGERNON *is laughing immoderately.*] What on earth are you so amused at?

ALGERNON Oh, I'm a little anxious about poor Bunbury, that is all.

JACK If you don't take care, your friend Bunbury will get you into a serious scrape some day.

ALGERNON I love scrapes. They are the only things that are never serious.

JACK Oh, that's nonsense, Algy. You never talk anything but nonsense.

ALGERNON Nobody ever does.

[JACK *looks indignantly at him, and leaves the room.* ALGERNON *lights a cigarette, reads his shirt-cuff, and smiles.*]

Act Drop.[6]

Second Act

[SCENE: *Garden at the Manor House. A flight of gray stone steps leads up to the house. The garden, an old-fashioned one, full of roses. Time of year, July. Basket chairs, and a table covered with books, are set under a large yew tree.*]

[MISS PRISM *discovered seated at the table.* CECILY *is at the back watering flowers.*]

MISS PRISM [*calling*] Cecily, Cecily! Surely such a utilitarian occupation as the watering of flowers is rather Moulton's duty[7] than yours? Especially at a moment when intellectual pleasures await you. Your German grammar is on the table. Pray open it at page fifteen. We will repeat yesterday's lesson.

CECILY [*coming over very slowly*] But I don't like German. It isn't at all a becoming language. I know perfectly well that I look quite plain after my German lesson.

MISS PRISM Child, you know how anxious your guardian is that you should improve yourself in every way. He laid particular stress on your German, as he was leaving for town yesterday. Indeed, he always lays stress on your German when he is leaving for town.

CECILY Dear Uncle Jack is so very serious! Sometimes he is so serious that I think he cannot be quite well.

MISS PRISM [*drawing herself up*] Your guardian enjoys the best of health, and his gravity of demeanour is especially to be commended in one so comparatively young as he is. I know no one who has a higher sense of duty and responsibility.

CECILY I suppose that is why he often looks a little bored when we three are together.

MISS PRISM Cecily! I am surprised at you. Mr Worthing has many troubles in his life. Idle merriment and triviality would be out of place in his conversation. You must remember his constant anxiety about that unfortunate young man his brother.

CECILY I wish Uncle Jack would allow that unfortunate young man, his brother, to come down here sometimes. We might have a good influence over him, Miss Prism. I am sure you certainly would. You know German,

6. The painted curtain lowered to indicate divisions between acts or scenes.

7. The gardener Moulton appears in Wilde's earlier, four-act version of the play.

and geology, and things of that kind influence a man very much. [CECILY *begins to write in her diary.*]

MISS PRISM [*shaking her head*] I do not think that even I could produce any effect on a character that according to his own brother's admission is irretrievably weak and vacillating. Indeed I am not sure that I would desire to reclaim him. I am not in favour of this modern mania for turning bad people into good people at a moment's notice. As a man sows so let him reap.[8] You must put away your diary, Cecily. I really don't see why you should keep a diary at all.

CECILY I keep a diary in order to enter the wonderful secrets of my life. If I didn't write them down I should probably forget all about them.

MISS PRISM Memory, my dear Cecily, is the diary that we all carry about with us.

CECILY Yes, but it usually chronicles the things that have never happened, and couldn't possibly have happened. I believe that Memory is responsible for nearly all the three-volume novels that Mudie[9] sends us.

MISS PRISM Do not speak slightingly of the three-volume novel, Cecily. I wrote one myself in earlier days.

CECILY Did you really, Miss Prism? How wonderfully clever you are! I hope it did not end happily? I don't like novels that end happily. They depress me so much.

MISS PRISM The good ended happily, and the bad unhappily. That is what Fiction means.

CECILY I suppose so. But it seems very unfair. And was your novel ever published?

MISS PRISM Alas! no. The manuscript unfortunately was abandoned. I use the word in the sense of lost or mislaid.[1] To your work, child, these speculations are profitless.

CECILY [*smiling*] But I see dear Dr Chasuble coming up through the garden.

MISS PRISM [*rising and advancing*] Dr Chasuble! This is indeed a pleasure.

[*Enter* CANON CHASUBLE.]

CHASUBLE And how are we this morning? Miss Prism, you are, I trust, well?

CECILY Miss Prism has just been complaining of a slight headache. I think it would do her so much good to have a short stroll with you in the Park, Dr Chasuble.

MISS PRISM Cecily, I have not mentioned anything about a headache.

CECILY No, dear Miss Prism, I know that, but I felt instinctively that you had a headache. Indeed I was thinking about that, and not about my German lesson, when the Rector came in.

CHASUBLE I hope Cecily, you are not inattentive.

CECILY Oh, I am afraid I am.

CHASUBLE That is strange. Were I fortunate enough to be Miss Prism's pupil, I would hang upon her lips. [MISS PRISM *glares.*] I spoke metaphorically.—My

8. A New Testament proverb: "Be not deceived; God is not mocked: for whatsoever a man soweth, that shall he also reap" (Galatians 6.7).

9. Charles Edward Mudie (1818–1890), an English publisher who in 1842 founded a lending library that charged subscribers to borrow books; most Victorian fiction was published in three volumes (a practice that benefited for-fee libraries).

1. That is, not in the sense of "licentious" or "unrestrained."

metaphor was drawn from bees.[2] Ahem! Mr Worthing I suppose, has not returned from town yet?

MISS PRISM We do not expect him till Monday afternoon.

CHASUBLE Ah yes, he usually likes to spend his Sunday in London. He is not one of those whose sole aim is enjoyment, as, by all accounts, that unfortunate young man his brother seems to be. But I must not disturb Egeria and her pupil any longer.

MISS PRISM Egeria? My name is Lætitia,[3] Doctor.

CHASUBLE [*bowing*] A classical allusion merely, drawn from the Pagan authors. I shall see you both no doubt at Evensong?[4]

MISS PRISM I think, dear Doctor, I will have a stroll with you. I find I have a headache after all, and a walk might do it good.

CHASUBLE With pleasure, Miss Prism, with pleasure. We might go as far as the schools and back.

MISS PRISM That would be delightful. Cecily, you will read your Political Economy in my absence. The chapter on the Fall of the Rupee[5] you may omit. It is somewhat too sensational. Even these metallic problems have their melodramatic side. [*Goes down the garden with* DR CHASUBLE.]

CECILY [*picks up books and throws them back on table*] Horrid Political Economy! Horrid Geography! Horrid, horrid German!

[*Enter* MERRIMAN *with a card on a salver.*]

MERRIMAN Mr Ernest Worthing has just driven over from the station. He has brought his luggage with him.

CECILY [*takes the card and reads it*] 'Mr Ernest Worthing, B.4 The Albany, W.' Uncle Jack's brother! Did you tell him Mr Worthing was in town?

MERRIMAN Yes, Miss. He seemed very much disappointed. I mentioned that you and Miss Prism were in the garden. He said he was anxious to speak to you privately for a moment.

CECILY Ask Mr Ernest Worthing to come here. I suppose you had better talk to the housekeeper about a room for him.

MERRIMAN Yes, Miss. [MERRIMAN *goes off.*]

CECILY I have never met any really wicked person before. I feel rather frightened. I am so afraid he will look just like everyone else.

[*Enter* ALGERNON, *very gay and debonnair.*]

He does!

ALGERNON [*raising his hat*] You are my little cousin Cecily, I'm sure.

CECILY You are under some strange mistake. I am not little. In fact, I believe I am more than usually tall for my age. [ALGERNON *is rather taken aback.*] But I am your cousin Cecily. You, I see from your card, are Uncle Jack's brother, my cousin Ernest, my wicked cousin Ernest.

ALGERNON Oh! I am not really wicked at all, cousin Cecily. You mustn't think that I am wicked.

2. A reference to the honey of Miss Prism's instruction.

3. A Latin name (literally, "beauty, grace, joy"). *Egeria:* in Roman mythology, one of the Camenae (prophetic nymphs), said to have counseled Numa Pompilius, the legendary second king of Rome; thus, any female adviser or patron.

4. Evening church services.

5. India's currency had been declining in value for a number of years. *Political Economy:* that is, an economics textbook.

CECILY If you are not, then you have certainly been deceiving us all in a very inexcusable manner. I hope you have not been leading a double life, pretending to be wicked and being really good all the time. That would be hypocrisy.

ALGERNON [*looks at her in amazement*] Oh! Of course I have been rather reckless.

CECILY I am glad to hear it.

ALGERNON In fact, now you mention the subject, I have been very bad in my own small way.

CECILY I don't think you should be so proud of that, although I am sure it must have been very pleasant.

ALGERNON It is much pleasanter being here with you.

CECILY I can't understand how you are here at all. Uncle Jack won't be back till Monday afternoon.

ALGERNON That is a great disappointment. I am obliged to go up by the first train on Monday morning. I have a business appointment that I am anxious . . . to miss.

CECILY Couldn't you miss it anywhere but in London?

ALGERNON No: the appointment is in London.

CECILY Well, I know, of course, how important it is not to keep a business engagement, if one wants to retain any sense of the beauty of life, but still I think you had better wait till Uncle Jack arrives. I know he wants to speak to you about your emigrating.

ALGERNON About my what?

CECILY Your emigrating. He has gone up to buy your outfit.

ALGERNON I certainly wouldn't let Jack buy my outfit. He has no taste in neckties at all.

CECILY I don't think you will require neckties. Uncle Jack is sending you to Australia.[6]

ALGERNON Australia! I'd sooner die.

CECILY Well, he said at dinner on Wednesday night, that you would have to choose between this world, the next world, and Australia.

ALGERNON Oh, well! The accounts I have received of Australia and the next world, are not particularly encouraging. This world is good enough for me, cousin Cecily.

CECILY Yes, but are you good enough for it?

ALGERNON I'm afraid I'm not that. That is why I want you to reform me. You might make that your mission, if you don't mind, cousin Cecily.

CECILY I'm afraid I've no time, this afternoon.

ALGERNON Well, would you mind my reforming myself this afternoon?

CECILY It is rather Quixotic[7] of you. But I think you should try.

ALGERNON I will. I feel better already.

CECILY You are looking a little worse.

ALGERNON That is because I am hungry.

CECILY How thoughtless of me. I should have remembered that when one is going to lead an entirely new life, one requires regular and wholesome meals. Won't you come in?

6. While Australia was no longer a penal colony in Wilde's day, it was still widely seen as a place where disreputable family members might be sent.

7. Impulsively idealistic, like the hero of Miguel de Cervantes's *Don Quixote* (1605, 1615).

ALGERNON Thank you. Might I have a buttonhole[8] first? I never have any appetite unless I have a buttonhole first.

CECILY A Maréchal Niel?[9] [*Picks up scissors.*]

ALGERNON No, I'd sooner have a pink rose.

CECILY Why? [*Cuts a flower.*]

ALGERNON Because you are like a pink rose, Cousin Cecily.

CECILY I don't think it can be right for you to talk to me like that. Miss Prism never says such things to me.

ALGERNON Then Miss Prism is a short-sighted old lady. [CECILY *puts the rose in his buttonhole.*] You are the prettiest girl I ever saw.

CECILY Miss Prism says that all good looks are a snare.

ALGERNON They are a snare that every sensible man would like to be caught in.

CECILY Oh! I don't think I would care to catch a sensible man. I shouldn't know what to talk to him about.

[*They pass into the house.* MISS PRISM *and* DR CHASUBLE *return.*]

MISS PRISM You are too much alone, dear Dr Chasuble. You should get married. A misanthrope I can understand—a womanthrope, never!

CHASUBLE [*with a scholar's shudder*] Believe me, I do not deserve so neologistic a phrase.[1] The precept as well as the practice of the Primitive Church was distinctly against matrimony.[2]

MISS PRISM [*sententiously*] That is obviously the reason why the Primitive Church has not lasted up to the present day. And you do not seem to realize, dear Doctor, that by persistently remaining single, a man converts himself into a permanent public temptation. Men should be more careful; this very celibacy leads weaker vessels astray.

CHASUBLE But is a man not equally attractive when married?

MISS PRISM No married man is ever attractive except to his wife.

CHASUBLE And often, I've been told, not even to her.

MISS PRISM That depends on the intellectual sympathies of the woman. Maturity can always be depended on. Ripeness can be trusted. Young women are green.[3] [DR CHASUBLE *starts.*] I spoke horticulturally. My metaphor was drawn from fruits. But where is Cecily?

CHASUBLE Perhaps she followed us to the schools.

[*Enter* JACK *slowly from the back of the garden. He is dressed in the deepest mourning, with crape hat-band*[4] *and black gloves.*]

MISS PRISM Mr Worthing!

CHASUBLE Mr Worthing?

MISS PRISM This is indeed a surprise. We did not look for you till Monday afternoon.

8. A flower worn in the lapel of a man's jacket.

9. A fragrant yellow rose, developed in France and first grown in England in 1864; it was named after Adolphe Niel, marshal of France under Napoleon III.

1. Chasuble is pained by the illogical coinage "womanthrope," which mixes Old English and Greek roots.

2. That is, the marriage of clergy (permitted in the Church of England). *The Primitive Church*: the Early Christian church. As his comment on celibacy indicates, the High Church Anglicanism practiced by Chasuble—whose name evokes a vestment worn during services—saw itself as maintaining that tradition.

3. Unripe, and thus inexperienced, easily deceived; understood by Chasuble as suffering from greensickness, an anemic condition found especially in adolescent girls and long believed to be caused by celibacy.

4. A band of crepe material, worn to signify mourning.

JACK [*shakes* MISS PRISM'*s hand in a tragic manner*] I have returned sooner than I expected. Dr Chasuble, I hope you are well?

CHASUBLE Dear Mr Worthing, I trust this garb of woe does not betoken some terrible calamity?

JACK My brother.

MISS PRISM More shameful debts and extravagance?

CHASUBLE Still leading his life of pleasure?

JACK [*shaking his head*] Dead!

CHASUBLE Your brother Ernest dead?

JACK Quite dead.

MISS PRISM What a lesson for him! I trust he will profit by it.

CHASUBLE Mr Worthing, I offer you my sincere condolence. You have at least the consolation of knowing that you were always the most generous and forgiving of brothers.

JACK Poor Ernest! He had many faults, but it is a sad, sad blow.

CHASUBLE Very sad indeed. Were you with him at the end?

JACK No. He died abroad; in Paris, in fact. I had a telegram last night from the manager of the Grand Hotel.[5]

CHASUBLE Was the cause of death mentioned?

JACK A severe chill, it seems.

MISS PRISM As a man sows, so shall he reap.

CHASUBLE [*raising his hand*] Charity, dear Miss Prism, charity! None of us are perfect. I myself am peculiarly susceptible to draughts. Will the interment take place here?

JACK No. He seemed to have expressed a desire to be buried in Paris.

CHASUBLE In Paris! [*Shakes his head.*] I fear that hardly points to any very serious state of mind at the last. You would no doubt wish me to make some slight allusion to this tragic domestic affliction next Sunday. [JACK *presses his hand convulsively.*] My sermon on the meaning of the manna in the wilderness[6] can be adapted to almost any occasion, joyful, or, as in the present case, distressing. [*All sigh.*] I have preached it at harvest celebrations, christenings, confirmations, on days of humiliation and festal days. The last time I delivered it was in the Cathedral, as a charity sermon on behalf of the Society for the Prevention of Discontent among the Upper Orders. The Bishop, who was present, was much struck by some of the analogies I drew.

JACK Ah! that reminds me, you mentioned christenings I think, Dr Chasuble? I suppose you know how to christen all right? [DR CHASUBLE *looks astounded.*] I mean, of course, you are continually christening, aren't you?

MISS PRISM It is, I regret to say, one of the Rector's most constant duties in this parish. I have often spoken to the poorer classes on the subject. But they don't seem to know what thrift is.

CHASUBLE But is there any particular infant in whom you are interested, Mr Worthing? Your brother was, I believe, unmarried, was he not?

JACK Oh, yes.

MISS PRISM [*bitterly*] People who live entirely for pleasure usually are.

5. A luxurious Paris hotel.
6 The food said to have miraculously fallen from heaven for the hungry Israelites when they wandered in the wilderness (Exodus 16).

JACK But it is not for any child, dear Doctor. I am very fond of children. No! the fact is, I would like to be christened myself, this afternoon, if you have nothing better to do.

CHASUBLE But surely, Mr Worthing, you have been christened already?

JACK I don't remember anything about it.

CHASUBLE But have you any grave doubts on the subject?

JACK I certainly intend to have. Of course I don't know if the thing would bother you in any way, or if you think I am a little too old now.

CHASUBLE Not at all. The sprinkling, and, indeed, the immersion of adults is a perfectly canonical practice.

JACK Immersion!

CHASUBLE You need have no apprehensions. Sprinkling is all that is necessary, or indeed I think advisable. Our weather is so changeable. At what hour would you wish the ceremony performed?

JACK Oh, I might trot round about five if that would suit you.

CHASUBLE Perfectly, perfectly! In fact I have two similar ceremonies to perform at that time. A case of twins that occurred recently in one of the outlying cottages on your own estate. Poor Jenkins the carter, a most hard-working man.

JACK Oh! I don't see much fun in being christened along with other babies. It would be childish. Would half-past five do?

CHASUBLE Admirably! Admirably! [*Takes out watch.*] And now, dear Mr Worthing, I will not intrude any longer into a house of sorrow. I would merely beg you not to be too much bowed down by grief. What seem to us bitter trials are often blessings in disguise.

MISS PRISM This seems to me a blessing of an extremely obvious kind.

[*Enter* CECILY *from the house.*]

CECILY Uncle Jack! Oh, I am pleased to see you back. But what horrid clothes you have got on! Do go and change them.

MISS PRISM Cecily!

CHASUBLE My child! my child!

[CECILY *goes towards* JACK; *he kisses her brow in a melancholy manner.*]

CECILY What is the matter, Uncle Jack? Do look happy! You look as if you had toothache, and I have got such a surprise for you. Who do you think is in the dining-room? Your brother!

JACK Who?

CECILY Your brother Ernest. He arrived about half an hour ago.

JACK What nonsense! I haven't got a brother.

CECILY Oh, don't say that. However badly he may have behaved to you in the past he is still your brother. You couldn't be so heartless as to disown him. I'll tell him to come out. And you will shake hands with him, won't you, Uncle Jack? [*Runs back into the house.*]

CHASUBLE These are very joyful tidings.

MISS PRISM After we had all been resigned to his loss, his sudden return seems to me peculiarly distressing.

JACK My brother is in the dining-room? I don't know what it all means. I think it is perfectly absurd.

[*Enter* ALGERNON *and* CECILY *hand in hand. They come slowly up to* JACK.]

JACK Good heavens! [*Motions* ALGERNON *away.*]

ALGERNON Brother John, I have come down from town to tell you that I am very sorry for all the trouble I have given you, and that I intend to lead a better life in the future.

[JACK *glares at him and does not take his hand.*]

CECILY Uncle Jack, you are not going to refuse your own brother's hand?

JACK Nothing will induce me to take his hand. I think his coming down here disgraceful. He knows perfectly well why.

CECILY Uncle Jack, do be nice. There is some good in everyone. Ernest has just been telling me about his poor invalid friend Mr Bunbury whom he goes to visit so often. And surely there must be much good in one who is kind to an invalid, and leaves the pleasures of London to sit by a bed of pain.

JACK Oh! he has been talking about Bunbury has he?

CECILY Yes, he has told me all about poor Mr Bunbury, and his terrible state of health.

JACK Bunbury! Well, I won't have him talk to you about Bunbury or about anything else. It is enough to drive one perfectly frantic.

ALGERNON Of course I admit that the faults were all on my side. But I must say that I think that Brother John's coldness to me is peculiarly painful. I expected a more enthusiastic welcome, especially considering it is the first time I have come here.

CECILY Uncle Jack, if you don't shake hands with Ernest I will never forgive you.

JACK Never forgive me?

CECILY Never, never, never!

JACK Well, this is the last time I shall ever do it. [*Shakes hands with* ALGERNON *and glares.*]

CHASUBLE It's pleasant, is it not, to see so perfect a reconciliation? I think we might leave the two brothers together.

MISS PRISM Cecily, you will come with us.

CECILY Certainly, Miss Prism. My little task of reconciliation is over.

CHASUBLE You have done a beautiful action today, dear child.

MISS PRISM We must not be premature in our judgments.

CECILY I feel very happy.

[*They all go off.*]

JACK You young scoundrel, Algy, you must get out of this place as soon as possible. I don't allow any Bunburying here.

[*Enter* MERRIMAN.]

MERRIMAN I have put Mr Ernest's things in the room next to yours, sir. I suppose that is all right?

JACK What?

MERRIMAN Mr Ernest's luggage, sir. I have unpacked it and put it in the room next to your own.

JACK His luggage?

MERRIMAN Yes, sir. Three portmanteaus, a dressing-case,[7] two hat-boxes, and a large luncheon-basket.

ALGERNON I am afraid I can't stay more than a week this time.

7. A case for toiletries.

JACK Merriman, order the dog-cart[8] at once. Mr Ernest has been suddenly called back to town.

MERRIMAN Yes, sir. [*Goes back into the house.*]

ALGERNON What a fearful liar you are, Jack. I have not been called back to town at all.

JACK Yes, you have.

ALGERNON I haven't heard anyone call me.

JACK Your duty as a gentleman calls you back.

ALGERNON My duty as a gentleman has never interfered with my pleasures in the smallest degree.

JACK I can quite understand that.

ALGERNON Well, Cecily is a darling.

JACK You are not to talk of Miss Cardew like that. I don't like it.

ALGERNON Well, I don't like your clothes. You look perfectly ridiculous in them. Why on earth don't you go up and change? It is perfectly childish to be in deep mourning for a man who is actually staying for a whole week with you in your house as a guest. I call it grotesque.

JACK You are certainly not staying with me for a whole week as a guest or anything else. You have got to leave . . . by the four-five train.

ALGERNON I certainly won't leave you so long as you are in mourning. It would be most unfriendly. If I were in mourning you would stay with me, I suppose. I should think it very unkind if you didn't.

JACK Well, will you go if I change my clothes?

ALGERNON Yes, if you are not too long. I never saw anybody take so long to dress, and with such little result.

JACK Well, at any rate, that is better than being always over-dressed as you are.

ALGERNON If I am occasionally a little over-dressed, I make up for it by being always immensely over-educated.

JACK Your vanity is ridiculous, your conduct an outrage, and your presence in my garden utterly absurd. However, you have got to catch the four-five, and I hope you will have a pleasant journey back to town. This Bunburying, as you call it, has not been a great success for you. [*Goes into the house.*]

ALGERNON I think it has been a great success. I'm in love with Cecily, and that is everything.

[*Enter* CECILY *at the back of the garden. She picks up the can and begins to water the flowers.*]

But I must see her before I go, and make arrangements for another Bunbury. Ah, there she is.

CECILY Oh, I merely came back to water the roses. I thought you were with Uncle Jack.

ALGERNON He's gone to order the dog-cart for me.

CECILY Oh, is he going to take you for a nice drive?

ALGERNON He's going to send me away.

CECILY Then have we got to part?

ALGERNON I am afraid so. It's a painful parting.

CECILY It is always painful to part from people whom one has known for a very brief space of time. The absence of old friends one can endure with

8. A light, two-wheeled open carriage, originally designed with a small rear compartment to hold sportsmen's dogs.

equanimity. But even a momentary separation from anyone to whom one has just been introduced is almost unbearable.

ALGERNON Thank you.

[*Enter* MERRIMAN.]

MERRIMAN The dog-cart is at the door, sir.

[ALGERNON *looks appealingly at* CECILY.]

CECILY It can wait, Merriman . . . for . . . five minutes.

MERRIMAN Yes, Miss. [*Exit* MERRIMAN.]

ALGERNON I hope, Cecily, I shall not offend you if I state quite frankly and openly that you seem to me to be in every way the visible personification of absolute perfection.

CECILY I think your frankness does you great credit, Ernest. If you will allow me I will copy your remarks into my diary. [*Goes over to table and begins writing in diary.*]

ALGERNON Do you really keep a diary? I'd give anything to look at it. May I?

CECILY Oh no. [*Puts her hand over it.*] You see, it is simply a very young girl's record of her own thoughts and impressions, and consequently meant for publication. When it appears in volume form I hope you will order a copy. But pray, Ernest, don't stop. I delight in taking down from dictation. I have reached 'absolute perfection'. You can go on. I am quite ready for more.

ALGERNON [*somewhat taken aback*] Ahem! Ahem!

CECILY Oh, don't cough, Ernest. When one is dictating one should speak fluently and not cough. Besides, I don't know how to spell a cough. [*Writes as* ALGERNON *speaks.*]

ALGERNON [*speaking very rapidly*] Cecily, ever since I first looked upon your wonderful and incomparable beauty, I have dared to love you wildly, passionately, devotedly, hopelessly.

CECILY I don't think that you should tell me that you love me wildly, passionately, devotedly, hopelessly. Hopelessly doesn't seem to make much sense, does it?

ALGERNON Cecily!

[*Enter* MERRIMAN.]

MERRIMAN The dog-cart is waiting, sir.

ALGERNON Tell it to come round next week, at the same hour.

MERRIMAN [*looks at* CECILY, *who makes no sign*] Yes, sir. [MERRIMAN *retires.*]

CECILY Uncle Jack would be very much annoyed if he knew you were staying on till next week, at the same hour.

ALGERNON Oh, I don't care about Jack. I don't care for anybody in the whole world but you. I love you, Cecily. You will marry me, won't you?

CECILY You silly boy! Of course. Why, we have been engaged for the last three months.

ALGERNON For the last three months?

CECILY Yes, it will be exactly three months on Thursday.

ALGERNON But how did we become engaged?

CECILY Well, ever since dear Uncle Jack first confessed to us that he had a younger brother who was very wicked and bad, you of course have formed the chief topic of conversation between myself and Miss Prism. And of course a man who is much talked about is always very attractive. One feels there must be something in him after all. I daresay it was foolish of me, but I fell in love with you, Ernest.

ALGERNON Darling! And when was the engagement actually settled?

CECILY On the 14th of February last.[9] Worn out by your entire ignorance of my existence, I determined to end the matter one way or the other, and after a long struggle with myself I accepted you under this dear old tree here. The next day I bought this little ring in your name, and this is the little bangle with the true lovers' knot I promised you always to wear.

ALGERNON Did I give you this? It's very pretty, isn't it?

CECILY Yes, you've wonderfully good taste, Ernest. It's the excuse I've always given for your leading such a bad life. And this is the box in which I keep all your dear letters. [*Kneels at table, opens box, and produces letters tied up with blue ribbon.*]

ALGERNON My letters! But my own sweet Cecily, I have never written you any letters.

CECILY You need hardly remind me of that, Ernest. I remember only too well that I was forced to write your letters for you. I wrote always three times a week, and sometimes oftener.

ALGERNON Oh, do let me read them, Cecily?

CECILY Oh, I couldn't possibly. They would make you far too conceited. [*Replaces box.*] The three you wrote me after I had broken off the engagement are so beautiful, and so badly spelled, that even now I can hardly read them without crying a little.

ALGERNON But was our engagement ever broken off?

CECILY Of course it was. On the 22nd of last March. You can see the entry if you like. [*Shows diary.*] 'Today I broke off my engagement with Ernest. I feel it is better to do so. The weather still continues charming.'

ALGERNON But why on earth did you break it off? What had I done? I had done nothing at all. Cecily, I am very much hurt indeed to hear you broke it off. Particularly when the weather was so charming.

CECILY It would hardly have been a really serious engagement if it hadn't been broken off at least once. But I forgave you before the week was out.

ALGERNON [*crossing to her, and kneeling*] What a perfect angel you are, Cecily.

CECILY You dear romantic boy. [*He kisses her, she puts her fingers through his hair.*] I hope your hair curls naturally, does it?

ALGERNON Yes, darling, with a little help from others.

CECILY I am so glad.

ALGERNON You'll never break off our engagement again, Cecily?

CECILY I don't think I could break it off now that I have actually met you. Besides, of course, there is the question of your name.

ALGERNON Yes, of course. [*Nervously*]

CECILY You must not laugh at me, darling, but it had always been a girlish dream of mine to love some one whose name was Ernest. [ALGERNON *rises*, CECILY *also.*] There is something in that name that seems to inspire absolute confidence. I pity any poor married woman whose husband is not called Ernest.

ALGERNON But, my dear child, do you mean to say you could not love me if I had some other name?

CECILY But what name?

9. Valentine's Day, also the date when *The Importance of Being Earnest* premiered at St. James's Theatre in 1895.

ALGERNON Oh, any name you like—Algernon—for instance . . .

CECILY But I don't like the name of Algernon.

ALGERNON Well, my own dear, sweet, loving little darling, I really can't see why you should object to the name of Algernon. It is not at all a bad name. In fact, it is rather an aristocratic name. Half of the chaps who get into the Bankruptcy Court are called Algernon. But seriously, Cecily . . . [*Moving to her*] . . . if my name was Algy, couldn't you love me?

CECILY [*rising*] I might respect you, Ernest, I might admire your character, but I fear that I should not be able to give you my undivided attention.

ALGERNON Ahem! Cecily! [*Picking up hat*] Your Rector here is, I suppose, thoroughly experienced in the practice of all the rites and ceremonials of the Church?

CECILY Oh yes. Dr Chasuble is a most learned man. He has never written a single book, so you can imagine how much he knows.

ALGERNON I must see him at once on a most important christening—I mean on most important business.

CECILY Oh!

ALGERNON I shan't be away more than half an hour.

CECILY Considering that we have been engaged since February the 14th, and that I only met you today for the first time, I think it is rather hard that you should leave me for so long a period as half an hour. Couldn't you make it twenty minutes?

ALGERNON I'll be back in no time. [*Kisses her and rushes down the garden.*]

CECILY What an impetuous boy he is! I like his hair so much. I must enter his proposal in my diary.

[*Enter* MERRIMAN.]

MERRIMAN A Miss Fairfax has just called to see Mr Worthing. On very important business Miss Fairfax states.

CECILY Isn't Mr Worthing in his library?

MERRIMAN Mr Worthing went over in the direction of the Rectory some time ago.

CECILY Pray ask the lady to come out here; Mr Worthing is sure to be back soon. And you can bring tea.

MERRIMAN Yes, Miss. [*Goes out.*]

CECILY Miss Fairfax! I suppose one of the many good elderly women who are associated with Uncle Jack in some of his philanthropic work in London. I don't quite like women who are interested in philanthropic work. I think it is so forward of them.

[*Enter* MERRIMAN.]

MERRIMAN Miss Fairfax.

[*Enter* GWENDOLEN.] [*Exit* MERRIMAN.]

CECILY [*advancing to meet her*] Pray let me introduce myself to you. My name is Cecily Cardew.

GWENDOLEN Cecily Cardew? [*Moving to her and shaking hands*] What a very sweet name! Something tells me that we are going to be great friends. I like you already more than I can say. My first impressions of people are never wrong.

CECILY How nice of you to like me so much after we have known each other such a comparatively short time. Pray sit down.

GWENDOLEN [*still standing up*] I may call you Cecily, may I not?

CECILY With pleasure!

GWENDOLEN And you will always call me Gwendolen, won't you.

CECILY If you wish.

GWENDOLEN Then that is all quite settled, is it not?

CECILY I hope so.

[*A pause. They both sit down together.*]

GWENDOLEN Perhaps this might be a favourable opportunity for my mentioning who I am. My father is Lord Bracknell. You have never heard of papa, I suppose?

CECILY I don't think so.

GWENDOLEN Outside the family circle, papa, I am glad to say, is entirely unknown. I think that is quite as it should be. The home seems to me to be the proper sphere for the man.[1] And certainly once a man begins to neglect his domestic duties he becomes painfully effeminate, does he not? And I don't like that. It makes men so very attractive. Cecily, mamma, whose views on education are remarkably strict, has brought me up to be extremely short-sighted; it is part of her system; so do you mind my looking at you through my glasses?

CECILY Oh! not at all, Gwendolen. I am very fond of being looked at.

GWENDOLEN [*after examining* CECILY *carefully through a lorgnette*] You are here on a short visit I suppose.

CECILY Oh no! I live here.

GWENDOLEN [*severely*] Really? Your mother, no doubt, or some female relative of advanced years, resides here also?

CECILY Oh no! I have no mother, nor, in fact, any relations.

GWENDOLEN Indeed?

CECILY My dear guardian, with the assistance of Miss Prism, has the arduous task of looking after me.

GWENDOLEN Your guardian?

CECILY Yes, I am Mr Worthing's ward.

GWENDOLEN Oh! It is strange he never mentioned to me that he had a ward. How secretive of him! He grows more interesting hourly. I am not sure, however, that the news inspires me with feelings of unmixed delight. [*Rising and going to her*] I am very fond of you, Cecily; I have liked you ever since I met you! But I am bound to state that now that I know that you are Mr Worthing's ward, I cannot help expressing a wish you were—well just a little older than you seem to be—and not quite so very alluring in appearance. In fact, if I may speak candidly——

CECILY Pray do! I think that whenever one has anything unpleasant to say, one should always be quite candid.

GWENDOLEN Well, to speak with perfect candour, Cecily, I wish that you were fully forty-two, and more than usually plain for your age. Ernest has a strong upright nature. He is the very soul of truth and honour. Disloyalty would be as impossible to him as deception. But even men of the noblest possible moral character are extremely susceptible to the influence of the physical charms of others. Modern, no less than Ancient History, supplies

1. The 19th-century doctrine of separate spheres divided life into two domains: public (male) and private (female).

us with many most painful examples of what I refer to. If it were not so, indeed, History would be quite unreadable.

CECILY I beg your pardon, Gwendolen, did you say Ernest?

GWENDOLEN Yes.

CECILY Oh, but it is not Mr Ernest Worthing who is my guardian. It is his brother—his elder brother.

GWENDOLEN [*sitting down again*] Ernest never mentioned to me that he had a brother.

CECILY I am sorry to say they have not been on good terms for a long time.

GWENDOLEN Ah! that accounts for it. And now that I think of it I have never heard any man mention his brother. The subject seems distasteful to most men. Cecily, you have lifted a load from my mind. I was growing almost anxious. It would have been terrible if any cloud had come across a friendship like ours, would it not? Of course you are quite, quite sure that it is not Mr Ernest Worthing who is your guardian?

CECILY Quite sure. [*A pause*] In fact, I am going to be his.

GWENDOLEN [*enquiringly*] I beg your pardon?

CECILY [*rather shy and confidingly*] Dearest Gwendolen, there is no reason why I should make a secret of it to you. Our little county newspaper is sure to chronicle the fact next week. Mr Ernest Worthing and I are engaged to be married.

GWENDOLEN [*quite politely, rising*] My darling Cecily, I think there must be some slight error. Mr Ernest Worthing is engaged to me. The announcement will appear in the 'Morning Post'[2] on Saturday at the latest.

CECILY [*very politely, rising*] I am afraid you must be under some misconception. Ernest proposed to me exactly ten minutes ago. [*Shows diary.*]

GWENDOLEN [*examines diary through her lorgnette carefully*] It is certainly very curious, for he asked me to be his wife yesterday afternoon at 5.30. If you would care to verify the incident, pray do so. [*Produces diary of her own.*] I never travel without my diary. One should always have something sensational to read in the train. I am so sorry, dear Cecily, if it is any disappointment to you, but I am afraid *I* have the prior claim.

CECILY It would distress me more than I can tell you, dear Gwendolen, if it caused you any mental or physical anguish, but I feel bound to point out that since Ernest proposed to you he clearly has changed his mind.

GWENDOLEN [*meditatively*] If the poor fellow has been entrapped into any foolish promise I shall consider it my duty to rescue him at once, and with a firm hand.

CECILY [*thoughtfully and sadly*] Whatever unfortunate entanglement my dear boy may have got into, I will never reproach him with it after we are married.

GWENDOLEN Do you allude to me, Miss Cardew, as an entanglement? You are presumptuous. On an occasion of this kind it becomes more than a moral duty to speak one's mind. It becomes a pleasure.

CECILY Do you suggest, Miss Fairfax, that I entrapped Ernest into an engagement? How dare you? This is no time for wearing the shallow mask of manners. When I see a spade I call it a spade.

GWENDOLEN [*satirically*] I am glad to say that I have never seen a spade. It is obvious that our social spheres have been widely different.

2. The London *Morning Post,* a conservative daily newspaper.

[*Enter* MERRIMAN, *followed by the footman. He carries a salver, table cloth, and plate stand.* CECILY *is about to retort. The presence of the servants exercises a restraining influence, under which both girls chafe.*]

MERRIMAN Shall I lay tea here as usual, Miss?

CECILY [*sternly, in a calm voice*] Yes, as usual.

[MERRIMAN *begins to clear table and lay cloth. A long pause.* CECILY *and* GWENDOLEN *glare at each other.*]

GWENDOLEN Are there many interesting walks in the vicinity, Miss Cardew?

CECILY Oh! yes! a great many. From the top of one of the hills quite close one can see five counties.

GWENDOLEN Five counties! I don't think I should like that. I hate crowds.

CECILY [*sweetly*] I suppose that is why you live in town?

[GWENDOLEN *bites her lip, and beats her foot nervously with her parasol.*]

GWENDOLEN [*looking round*] Quite a well-kept garden this is, Miss Cardew.

CECILY So glad you like it, Miss Fairfax.

GWENDOLEN I had no idea there were any flowers in the country.

CECILY Oh, flowers are as common here, Miss Fairfax, as people are in London.

GWENDOLEN Personally, I cannot understand how anybody manages to exist in the country, if anybody who is anybody does. The country always bores me to death.

CECILY Ah! This is what the newspapers call agricultural depression,[3] is it not? I believe the aristocracy are suffering very much from it just at present. It is almost an epidemic amongst them, I have been told. May I offer you some tea, Miss Fairfax?

GWENDOLEN [*with elaborate politeness*] Thank you. [*Aside*] Detestable girl! But I require tea!

CECILY [*sweetly*] Sugar?

GWENDOLEN [*superciliously*] No, thank you. Sugar is not fashionable any more.

[CECILY *looks angrily at her, takes up the tongs and puts four lumps of sugar into the cup.*]

CECILY [*severely*] Cake or bread and butter?

GWENDOLEN [*in a bored manner*] Bread and butter, please. Cake is rarely seen at the best houses nowadays.

CECILY [*cuts a very large slice of cake, and puts it on the tray*] Hand that to Miss Fairfax.

[MERRIMAN *does so, and goes out with footman.* GWENDOLEN *drinks the tea and makes a grimace. Puts down cup at once, reaches out her hand to the bread and butter, looks at it, and finds it is cake. Rises in indignation.*]

GWENDOLEN You have filled my tea with lumps of sugar, and though I asked most distinctly for bread and butter, you have given me cake. I am known for the gentleness of my disposition, and the extraordinary sweetness of my nature, but I warn you, Miss Cardew, you may go too far.

CECILY [*rising*] To save my poor, innocent, trusting boy from the machinations of any other girl there are no lengths to which I would not go.

3. British agriculture had been in an economic slump since the 1870s.

GWENDOLEN From the moment I saw you I distrusted you. I felt that you were false and deceitful. I am never deceived in such matters. My first impressions of people are invariably right.

CECILY It seems to me, Miss Fairfax, that I am trespassing on your valuable time. No doubt you have many other calls of a similar character to make in the neighbourhood.

[*Enter* JACK.]

GWENDOLEN [*catching sight of him*] Ernest! My own Ernest!

JACK Gwendolen! Darling! [*Offers*[4] *to kiss her.*]

GWENDOLEN [*drawing back*] A moment! May I ask if you are engaged to be married to this young lady? [*Points to* CECILY.]

JACK [*laughing*] To dear little Cecily! Of course not! What could have put such an idea into your pretty little head?

GWENDOLEN Thank you. You may! [*Offers her cheek.*]

CECILY [*very sweetly*] I knew there must be some misunderstanding, Miss Fairfax. The gentleman whose arm is at present round your waist is my dear guardian, Mr John Worthing.

GWENDOLEN I beg your pardon?

CECILY This is Uncle Jack.

GWENDOLEN [*receding*] Jack! Oh!

[*Enter* ALGERNON.]

CECILY Here is Ernest.

ALGERNON [*goes straight over to* CECILY *without noticing anyone else*] My own love! [*Offers to kiss her.*]

CECILY [*drawing back*] A moment, Ernest! May I ask you—are you engaged to be married to this young lady?

ALGERNON [*looking round*] To what young lady? Good heavens! Gwendolen!

CECILY Yes, to good heavens, Gwendolen, I mean to Gwendolen.

ALGERNON [*laughing*] Of course not! What could have put such an idea into your pretty little head?

CECILY Thank you. [*Presenting her cheek to be kissed*] You may.

[ALGERNON *kisses her.*]

GWENDOLEN I felt there was some slight error, Miss Cardew. The gentleman who is now embracing you is my cousin, Mr Algernon Moncrieff.

CECILY [*breaking away from* ALGERNON] Algernon Moncrieff! Oh!

[*The two girls move towards each other and put their arms round each other's waists as if for protection.*]

CECILY Are you called Algernon?

ALGERNON I cannot deny it.

CECILY Oh!

GWENDOLEN Is your name really John?

JACK [*standing rather proudly*] I could deny it if I liked. I could deny anything if I liked. But my name certainly is John. It has been John for years.

CECILY [*to* GWENDOLEN] A gross deception has been practised on both of us.

GWENDOLEN My poor wounded Cecily!

CECILY My sweet wronged Gwendolen!

GWENDOLEN [*slowly and seriously*] You will call me sister, will you not?

4. Attempts.

[*They embrace.* JACK *and* ALGERNON *groan and walk up and down.*]

CECILY [*rather brightly*] There is just one question I would like to be allowed to ask my guardian.

GWENDOLEN An admirable idea! Mr Worthing, there is just one question I would like to be permitted to put to you. Where is your brother Ernest? We are both engaged to be married to your brother Ernest, so it is a matter of some importance to us to know where your brother Ernest is at present.

JACK [*slowly and hesitatingly*] Gwendolen—Cecily—it is very painful for me to be forced to speak the truth. It is the first time in my life that I have ever been reduced to such a painful position, and I am really quite inexperienced in doing anything of the kind. However I will tell you quite frankly that I have no brother Ernest. I have no brother at all. I never had a brother in my life, and I certainly have not the smallest intention of ever having one in the future.

CECILY [*surprised*] No brother at all?

JACK [*cheerily*] None!

GWENDOLEN [*severely*] Had you never a brother of any kind?

JACK [*pleasantly*] Never. Not even of any kind.

GWENDOLEN I am afraid it is quite clear, Cecily, that neither of us is engaged to be married to anyone.

CECILY It is not a very pleasant position for a young girl suddenly to find herself in. Is it?

GWENDOLEN Let us go into the house. They will hardly venture to come after us there.

CECILY No, men are so cowardly, aren't they?

[*They retire into the house with scornful looks.*]

JACK This ghastly state of things is what you call Bunburying, I suppose?

ALGERNON Yes, and a perfectly wonderful Bunbury it is. The most wonderful Bunbury I have ever had in my life.

JACK Well, you've no right whatsoever to Bunbury here.

ALGERNON That is absurd. One has a right to Bunbury anywhere one chooses. Every serious Bunburyist knows that.

JACK Serious Bunburyist! Good heavens!

ALGERNON Well, one must be serious about something, if one wants to have any amusement in life. I happen to be serious about Bunburying. What on earth you are serious about I haven't got the remotest idea. About everything, I should fancy. You have such an absolutely trivial nature.

JACK Well, the only small satisfaction I have in the whole of this wretched business is that your friend Bunbury is quite exploded. You won't be able to run down to the country quite so often as you used to do, dear Algy. And a very good thing too.

ALGERNON Your brother is a little off colour,[5] isn't he, dear Jack? You won't be able to disappear to London quite so frequently as your wicked custom was. And not a bad thing either.

JACK As for your conduct towards Miss Cardew, I must say that your taking in a sweet, simple, innocent girl like that is quite inexcusable. To say nothing of the fact that she is my ward.

5. That is, in poor health.

ALGERNON I can see no possible defence at all for your deceiving a brilliant, clever, thoroughly experienced young lady like Miss Fairfax. To say nothing of the fact that she is my cousin.

JACK I wanted to be engaged to Gwendolen, that is all. I love her.

ALGERNON Well, I simply wanted to be engaged to Cecily. I adore her.

JACK There is certainly no chance of your marrying Miss Cardew.

ALGERNON I don't think there is much likelihood, Jack, of you and Miss Fairfax being united.

JACK Well, that is no business of yours.

ALGERNON If it was my business, I wouldn't talk about it. [*Begins to eat muffins.*] It is very vulgar to talk about one's business. Only people like stock-brokers do that, and then merely at dinner parties.

JACK How you can sit there, calmly eating muffins when we are in this horrible trouble, I can't make out. You seem to me to be perfectly heartless.

ALGERNON Well, I can't eat muffins in an agitated manner. The butter would probably get on my cuffs. One should always eat muffins quite calmly. It is the only way to eat them.

JACK I say it's perfectly heartless your eating muffins at all, under the circumstances.

ALGERNON When I am in trouble, eating is the only thing that consoles me. Indeed, when I am in really great trouble, as anyone who knows me intimately will tell you, I refuse everything except food and drink. At the present moment I am eating muffins because I am unhappy. Besides, I am particularly fond of muffins. [*Rising*]

JACK [*rising*] Well, that is no reason why you should eat them all in that greedy way. [*Takes muffins from* ALGERNON.]

ALGERNON [*offering tea-cake*] I wish you would have tea-cake instead. I don't like tea-cake.

JACK Good heavens! I suppose a man may eat his own muffins in his own garden.

ALGERNON But you have just said it was perfectly heartless to eat muffins.

JACK I said it was perfectly heartless of you, under the circumstances. That is a very different thing.

ALGERNON That may be. But the muffins are the same. [*He seizes the muffin-dish from* JACK.]

JACK Algy, I wish to goodness you would go.

ALGERNON You can't possibly ask me to go without having some dinner. It's absurd. I never go without my dinner. No one ever does, except vegetarians and people like that. Besides I have just made arrangements with Dr Chasuble to be christened at a quarter to six under the name of Ernest.

JACK My dear fellow, the sooner you give up that nonsense the better. I made arrangements this morning with Dr Chasuble to be christened myself at 5.30, and I naturally will take the name of Ernest. Gwendolen would wish it. We can't both be christened Ernest. It's absurd. Besides, I have a perfect right to be christened if I like. There is no evidence at all that I ever have been christened by anybody. I should think it extremely probable I never was, and so does Dr Chasuble. It is entirely different in your case. You have been christened already.

ALGERNON Yes, but I have not been christened for years.

JACK Yes, but you have been christened. That is the important thing.

ALGERNON Quite so. So I know my constitution can stand it. If you are not quite sure about your ever having been christened, I must say I think it rather dangerous your venturing on it now. It might make you very unwell. You can hardly have forgotten that someone very closely connected with you was very nearly carried off this week in Paris by a severe chill.

JACK Yes, but you said yourself that a severe chill was not hereditary.

ALGERNON It usen't to be, I know—but I daresay it is now. Science is always making wonderful improvements in things.

JACK [*picking up the muffin-dish*] Oh, that is nonsense; you are always talking nonsense.

ALGERNON Jack, you are at the muffins again! I wish you wouldn't. There are only two left. [*Takes them.*] I told you I was particularly fond of muffins.

JACK But I hate tea-cake.

ALGERNON Why on earth then do you allow tea-cake to be served up for your guests? What ideas you have of hospitality!

JACK Algernon! I have already told you to go. I don't want you here. Why don't you go!

ALGERNON I haven't quite finished my tea yet! and there is still one muffin left.

[JACK *groans, and sinks into a chair.* ALGERNON *still continues eating.*]

Act Drop.

Third Act

[SCENE: *Morning room at the Manor House.*]

[GWENDOLEN *and* CECILY *are at the window, looking out into the garden.*]

GWENDOLEN The fact that they did not follow us at once into the house, as anyone else would have done, seems to me to show that they have some sense of shame left.

CECILY They have been eating muffins. That looks like repentance.

GWENDOLEN [*after a pause*] They don't seem to notice us at all. Couldn't you cough?

CECILY But I haven't got a cough.

GWENDOLEN They're looking at us. What effrontery!

CECILY They're approaching. That's very forward of them.

GWENDOLEN Let us preserve a dignified silence.

CECILY Certainly. It's the only thing to do now.

[*Enter* JACK *followed by* ALGERNON. *They whistle some dreadful popular air from a British Opera.*[6]]

GWENDOLEN This dignified silence seems to produce an unpleasant effect

CECILY A most distasteful one,

GWENDOLEN But we will not be the first to speak.

CECILY Certainly not.

GWENDOLEN Mr Worthing, I have something very particular to ask you. Much depends on your reply.

6. Possibly a reference to the comic operas of W. S. Gilbert (1836–1911) and Sir Arthur Sullivan (1842–1900), whose 1881 *Patience* satirized Wilde and the aesthetic movement.

CECILY Gwendolen, your common sense is invaluable. Mr Moncrieff, kindly answer me the following question. Why did you pretend to be my guardian's brother?

ALGERNON In order that I might have an opportunity of meeting you.

CECILY [*to* GWENDOLEN] That certainly seems a satisfactory explanation, does it not?

GWENDOLEN Yes, dear, if you can believe him.

CECILY I don't. But that does not affect the wonderful beauty of his answer.

GWENDOLEN True. In matters of grave importance, style, not sincerity is the vital thing. Mr Worthing, what explanation can you offer to me for pretending to have a brother? Was it in order that you might have an opportunity of coming up to town to see me as often as possible?

JACK Can you doubt it, Miss Fairfax?

GWENDOLEN I have the gravest doubts upon the subject. But I intend to crush them. This is not the moment for German scepticism.[7] [*Moving to* CECILY] Their explanations appear to be quite satisfactory, especially Mr Worthing's. That seems to me to have the stamp of truth upon it.

CECILY I am more than content with what Mr Moncrieff said. His voice alone inspires one with absolute credulity.

GWENDOLEN Then you think we should forgive them?

CECILY Yes. I mean no.

GWENDOLEN True! I had forgotten. There are principles at stake that one cannot surrender. Which of us should tell them? The task is not a pleasant one.

CECILY Could we not both speak at the same time?

GWENDOLEN An excellent idea! I nearly always speak at the same time as other people. Will you take the time from me?

CECILY Certainly.

[GWENDOLEN *beats time with uplifted finger.*]

GWENDOLEN and CECILY [*speaking together*] Your Christian names are still an insuperable barrier. That is all!

JACK and ALGERNON [*speaking together*] Our Christian names! Is that all? But we are going to be christened this afternoon.

GWENDOLEN [*to* JACK] For my sake you are prepared to do this terrible thing?

JACK I am.

CECILY [*to* ALGERNON] To please me you are ready to face this fearful ordeal?

ALGERNON I am!

GWENDOLEN How absurd to talk of the equality of the sexes! Where questions of self-sacrifice are concerned, men are infinitely beyond us.

JACK We are. [*Clasps hands with* ALGERNON.]

CECILY They have moments of physical courage of which we women know absolutely nothing.

GWENDOLEN [*to* JACK] Darling!

ALGERNON [*to* CECILY] Darling! [*They fall into each other's arms.*]

[*Enter* MERRIMAN. *When he enters he coughs loudly, seeing the situation.*]

7. German biblical scholars of the 19th century were notorious among the British for their skepticism toward scriptural authority and claims of divine revelation.

MERRIMAN Ahem! Ahem! Lady Bracknell!

JACK Good heavens!

[*Enter* LADY BRACKNELL. *The couples separate in alarm.*]

[*Exit* MERRIMAN.]

LADY BRACKNELL Gwendolen! What does this mean?

GWENDOLEN Merely that I am engaged to be married to Mr Worthing, mamma.

LADY BRACKNELL Come here. Sit down. Sit down immediately. Hesitation of any kind is a sign of mental decay in the young, of physical weakness in the old. [*Turns to* JACK.] Apprised, sir, of my daughter's sudden flight by her trusty maid, whose confidence I purchased by means of a small coin, I followed her at once by a luggage train.[8] Her unhappy father is, I am glad to say, under the impression that she is attending a more than usually lengthy lecture by the University Extension Scheme[9] on the Influence of a permanent income on Thought. I do not propose to undeceive him. Indeed I have never undeceived him on any question. I would consider it wrong. But of course, you will clearly understand that all communication between yourself and my daughter must cease immediately from this moment. On this point, as indeed on all points, I am firm.

JACK I am engaged to be married to Gwendolen, Lady Bracknell!

LADY BRACKNELL You are nothing of the kind, sir. And now, as regards Algernon! . . . Algernon!

ALGERNON Yes, Aunt Augusta.

LADY BRACKNELL May I ask if it is in this house that your invalid friend Mr Bunbury resides?

ALGERNON [*stammering*] Oh! No! Bunbury doesn't live here. Bunbury is somewhere else at present. In fact, Bunbury is dead.

LADY BRACKNELL Dead! When did Mr Bunbury die? His death must have been extremely sudden.

ALGERNON [*airily*] Oh! I killed Bunbury this afternoon. I mean poor Bunbury died this afternoon.

LADY BRACKNELL What did he die of?

ALGERNON Bunbury? Oh, he was quite exploded.

LADY BRACKNELL Exploded! Was he the victim of a revolutionary outrage? I was not aware that Mr Bunbury was interested in social legislation. If so, he is well punished for his morbidity.

ALGERNON My dear Aunt Augusta, I mean he was found out! The doctors found out that Bunbury could not live, that is what I mean—so Bunbury died.

LADY BRACKNELL He seems to have had great confidence in the opinion of his physicians. I am glad, however, that he made up his mind at the last to some definite course of action, and acted under proper medical advice. And now that we have finally got rid of this Mr Bunbury, may I ask, Mr Worthing, who is that young person whose hand my nephew Algernon is now holding in what seems to me a peculiarly unnecessary manner?

JACK That lady is Miss Cecily Cardew, my ward.

[LADY BRACKNELL *bows coldly to* CECILY.]

8. Freight train.

9. An extramural education program in which university instructors delivered lectures to students not pursuing regular degrees.

ALGERNON I am engaged to be married to Cecily, Aunt Augusta.

LADY BRACKNELL I beg your pardon?

CECILY Mr Moncrieff and I are engaged to be married, Lady Bracknell.

LADY BRACKNELL [*with a shiver, crossing to the sofa and sitting down*] I do not know whether there is anything peculiarly exciting in the air of this particular part of Hertfordshire, but the number of engagements that go on seems to me considerably above the proper average that statistics have laid down for our guidance. I think some preliminary enquiry on my part would not be out of place. Mr Worthing, is Miss Cardew at all connected with any of the larger railway stations in London? I merely desire information. Until yesterday I had no idea that there were any families or persons whose origin was a Terminus.[1]

[JACK *looks perfectly furious, but restrains himself.*]

JACK [*in a clear, cold voice*] Miss Cardew is the granddaughter of the late Mr Thomas Cardew of 149, Belgrave Square, S.W.; Gervase Park, Dorking, Surrey; and the Sporran, Fifeshire, N.B.[2]

LADY BRACKNELL That sounds not unsatisfactory. Three addresses always inspire confidence, even in tradesmen. But what proof have I of their authenticity?

JACK I have carefully preserved the Court Guides[3] of the period. They are open to your inspection, Lady Bracknell.

LADY BRACKNELL [*grimly*] I have known strange errors in that publication.

JACK Miss Cardew's family solicitors are Messrs[4] Markby, Markby, and Markby.

LADY BRACKNELL Markby, Markby, and Markby? A firm of the very highest position in their profession. Indeed I am told that one of the Mr Markbys is occasionally to be seen at dinner parties. So far I am satisfied.

JACK [*very irritably*] How extremely kind of you, Lady Bracknell! I have also in my possession, you will be pleased to hear, certificates of Miss Cardew's birth, baptism, whooping cough, registration, vaccination, confirmation, and the measles; both the German and the English variety.[5]

LADY BRACKNELL Ah! A life crowded with incident, I see; though perhaps somewhat too exciting for a young girl. I am not myself in favour of premature experiences. [*Rises, looks at her watch.*] Gwendolen! the time approaches for our departure. We have not a moment to lose. As a matter of form, Mr Worthing, I had better ask you if Miss Cardew has any little fortune?

JACK Oh! about a hundred and thirty thousand pounds in the Funds.[6] That is all. Goodbye, Lady Bracknell. So pleased to have seen you.

LADY BRACKNELL [*sitting down again*] A moment, Mr Worthing. A hundred and thirty thousand pounds! And in the Funds! Miss Cardew seems to me

1. The station at the end of a railway line.
2. That is, with residences in Belgravia, in a county south of London, and in Scotland ("North Britain").
3. Annual publications listing the names and addresses of those presented at court—that is, the British nobility, gentry, and anyone else of social importance.
4. The plural of "Mister." *Solicitors:* British lawyers who advise and represent clients, but do not argue cases in court.
5. That is, both rubeola and rubella.
6. Interest-bearing government bonds—and a considerable fortune (roughly equivalent to $20 million today).

a most attractive young lady, now that I look at her. Few girls of the present day have any really solid qualities, any of the qualities that last, and improve with time. We live, I regret to say, in an age of surfaces. [*To* CECILY] Come over here, dear. [CECILY *goes across.*] Pretty child! your dress is sadly simple, and your hair seems almost as Nature might have left it. But we can soon alter all that. A thoroughly experienced French maid produces a really marvellous result in a very brief space of time. I remember recommending one to young Lady Lancing, and after three months her own husband did not know her.

JACK [*aside*] And after six months nobody knew her.[7]

LADY BRACKNELL [*glares at* JACK *for a few moments. Then bends, with a practised smile, to* CECILY] Kindly turn round, sweet child. [CECILY *turns completely round.*] No, the side view is what I want. [CECILY *presents her profile.*] Yes, quite as I expected. There are distinct social possibilities in your profile. The two weak points in our age are its want of principle and its want of profile. The chin a little higher, dear. Style largely depends on the way the chin is worn. They are worn very high, just at present. Algernon!

ALGERNON Yes, Aunt Augusta!

LADY BRACKNELL There are distinct social possibilities in Miss Cardew's profile.

ALGERNON Cecily is the sweetest, dearest, prettiest girl in the whole world. And I don't care twopence about social possibilities.

LADY BRACKNELL Never speak disrespectfully of Society, Algernon. Only people who can't get into it do that. [*To* CECILY] Dear child, of course you know that Algernon has nothing but his debts to depend upon. But I do not approve of mercenary marriages. When I married Lord Bracknell I had no fortune of any kind. But I never dreamed for a moment of allowing that to stand in my way. Well, I suppose I must give my consent.

ALGERNON Thank you, Aunt Augusta.

LADY BRACKNELL Cecily, you may kiss me!

CECILY [*kisses her*] Thank you, Lady Bracknell.

LADY BRACKNELL You may also address me as Aunt Augusta for the future.

CECILY Thank you, Aunt Augusta.

LADY BRACKNELL The marriage, I think, had better take place quite soon.

ALGERNON Thank you, Aunt Augusta.

CECILY Thank you, Aunt Augusta.

LADY BRACKNELL To speak frankly, I am not in favour of long engagements. They give people the opportunity of finding out each other's character before marriage, which I think is never advisable.

JACK I beg your pardon for interrupting you, Lady Bracknell, but this engagement is quite out of the question. I am Miss Cardew's guardian, and she cannot marry without my consent until she comes of age. That consent I absolutely decline to give.

LADY BRACKNELL Upon what grounds may I ask? Algernon is an extremely, I may almost say an ostentatiously, eligible young man. He has nothing, but he looks everything. What more can one desire?

JACK It pains me very much to have to speak frankly to you, Lady Bracknell, about your nephew, but the fact is that I do not approve at all of his moral character. I suspect him of being untruthful.

7. Acknowledged her socially (i.e., her behavior had become scandalous).

[ALGERNON *and* CECILY *look at him in indignant amazement.*]

LADY BRACKNELL Untruthful! My nephew Algernon? Impossible! He is an Oxonian.[8]

JACK I fear there can be no possible doubt about the matter. This afternoon, during my temporary absence in London on an important question of romance, he obtained admission to my house by means of the false pretence of being my brother. Under an assumed name he drank, I've just been informed by my butler, an entire pint bottle of my Perrier-Jouet, Brut, '89;[9] a wine I was specially reserving for myself. Continuing his disgraceful deception, he succeeded in the course of the afternoon in alienating the affections of my only ward. He subsequently stayed to tea, and devoured every single muffin. And what makes his conduct all the more heartless is, that he was perfectly well aware from the first that I have no brother, that I never had a brother, and that I don't intend to have a brother, not even of any kind. I distinctly told him so myself yesterday afternoon.

LADY BRACKNELL Ahem! Mr Worthing, after careful consideration I have decided entirely to overlook my nephew's conduct to you.

JACK That is very generous of you, Lady Bracknell. My own decision, however, is unalterable. I decline to give my consent.

LADY BRACKNELL [*to* CECILY] Come here, sweet child. [CECILY *goes over.*] How old are you, dear?

CECILY Well, I am really only eighteen, but I always admit to twenty when I go to evening parties.

LADY BRACKNELL You are perfectly right in making some slight alteration. Indeed, no woman should ever be quite accurate about her age. It looks so calculating. . . . [*In a meditative manner*] Eighteen, but admitting to twenty at evening parties. Well, it will not be very long before you are of age and free from the restraints of tutelage. So I don't think your guardian's consent is, after all, a matter of any importance.

JACK Pray excuse me, Lady Bracknell, for interrupting you again, but it is only fair to tell you that according to the terms of her grandfather's will Miss Cardew does not come legally of age till she is thirty-five.

LADY BRACKNELL That does not seem to me to be a grave objection. Thirty-five is a very attractive age. London society is full of women of the very highest birth who have, of their own free choice, remained thirty-five for years. Lady Dumbleton is an instance in point. To my own knowledge she has been thirty-five ever since she arrived at the age of forty, which was many years ago now. I see no reason why our dear Cecily should not be even still more attractive at the age you mention than she is at present. There will be a large accumulation of property.

CECILY Algy, could you wait for me till I was thirty-five?

ALGERNON Of course I could, Cecily. You know I could.

CECILY Yes, I felt it instinctively, but I couldn't wait all that time. I hate waiting even five minutes for anybody. It always makes me rather cross. I am not punctual myself, I know, but I do like punctuality in others, and waiting, even to be married, is quite out of the question.

ALGERNON Then what is to be done, Cecily?

CECILY I don't know, Mr Moncrieff.

8. A student at or graduate of Oxford University.

9. A particularly fine vintage of dry champagne.

LADY BRACKNELL My dear Mr Worthing, as Miss Cardew states positively that she cannot wait till she is thirty five—a remark which I am bound to say seems to me to show a somewhat impatient nature—I would beg of you to reconsider your decision.

JACK But my dear Lady Bracknell, the matter is entirely in your own hands. The moment you consent to my marriage with Gwendolen, I will most gladly allow your nephew to form an alliance with my ward.

LADY BRACKNELL [*rising and drawing herself up*] You must be quite aware that what you propose is out of the question.

JACK Then a passionate celibacy is all that any of us can look forward to.

LADY BRACKNELL That is not the destiny I propose for Gwendolen. Algernon, of course, can choose for himself. [*Pulls out her watch.*] Come, dear; [GWENDOLEN *rises.*] we have already missed five, if not six, trains. To miss any more might expose us to comment on the platform.

[*Enter* DR CHASUBLE.]

CHASUBLE Everything is quite ready for the christenings.

LADY BRACKNELL The christenings, sir! Is not that somewhat premature?

CHASUBLE [*looking rather puzzled, and pointing to* JACK *and* ALGERNON] Both these gentlemen have expressed a desire for immediate baptism.

LADY BRACKNELL At their age? The idea is grotesque and irreligious! Algernon, I forbid you to be baptized. I will not hear of such excesses. Lord Bracknell would be highly displeased if he learned that that was the way in which you wasted your time and money.

CHASUBLE Am I to understand then that there are to be no christenings at all this afternoon?

JACK I don't think that, as things are now, it would be of much practical value to either of us, Dr Chasuble.

CHASUBLE I am grieved to hear such sentiments from you, Mr Worthing. They savour of the heretical views of the Anabaptists,[1] views that I have completely refuted in four of my unpublished sermons. However, as your present mood seems to be one peculiarly secular, I will return to the church at once. Indeed, I have just been informed by the pew-opener[2] that for the last hour and a half Miss Prism has been waiting for me in the vestry.

LADY BRACKNELL [*starting*] Miss Prism! Did I hear you mention a Miss Prism?

CHASUBLE Yes, Lady Bracknell. I am on my way to join her.

LADY BRACKNELL Pray allow me to detain you for a moment. This matter may prove to be one of vital importance to Lord Bracknell and myself. Is this Miss Prism a female of repellent aspect, remotely connected with education?

CHASUBLE [*somewhat indignantly*] She is the most cultivated of ladies, and the very picture of respectability.

LADY BRACKNELL It is obviously the same person. May I ask what position she holds in your household?

1. Members of a radical Protestant sect, established in Germany in the 16th century, that advocated the baptism only of adult believers (*Anabaptist* literally means "one who baptizes over again"); the label was sometimes applied pejoratively to Baptists or to others who rejected Anglican doctrine.

2. An usher who unlocked the private pews provided by many churches.

CHASUBLE [*severely*] I am a celibate, madam.

JACK [*interposing*] Miss Prism, Lady Bracknell, has been for the last three years Miss Cardew's esteemed governess and valued companion.

LADY BRACKNELL In spite of what I hear of her, I must see her at once. Let her be sent for.

CHASUBLE [*looking off*] She approaches; she is nigh.

[*Enter* MISS PRISM *hurriedly.*]

MISS PRISM I was told you expected me in the vestry, dear Canon. I have been waiting for you there for an hour and three quarters. [*Catches sight of* LADY BRACKNELL *who has fixed her with a stony glare.* MISS PRISM *grows pale and quails. She looks anxiously round as if desirous to escape.*]

LADY BRACKNELL [*in a severe, judicial voice*] Prism! [MISS PRISM *bows her head in shame.*] Come here, Prism! [MISS PRISM *approaches in a humble manner.*] Prism! Where is that baby? [*General consternation. The* CANON *starts back in horror.* ALGERNON *and* JACK *pretend to be anxious to shield* CECILY *and* GWENDOLEN *from hearing the details of a terrible public scandal.*] Twenty-eight years ago, Prism, you left Lord Bracknell's house, Number 104, Upper Grosvenor Street, in charge of a perambulator[3] that contained a baby, of the male sex. You never returned. A few weeks later, through the elaborate investigations of the Metropolitan police, the perambulator was discovered at midnight, standing by itself in a remote corner of Bayswater.[4] It contained the manuscript of a three-volume novel of more than usually revolting sentimentality. [MISS PRISM *starts in involuntary indignation.*] But the baby was not there! [*Everyone looks at* MISS PRISM.] Prism! Where is that baby? [*A pause.*]

MISS PRISM Lady Bracknell, I admit with shame that I do not know. I only wish I did. The plain facts of the case are these. On the morning of the day you mention, a day that is for ever branded on my memory, I prepared as usual to take the baby out in its perambulator. I had also with me a somewhat old, but capacious hand-bag in which I had intended to place the manuscript of a work of fiction that I had written during my few unoccupied hours. In a moment of mental abstraction, for which I never can forgive myself, I deposited the manuscript in the bassinette, and placed the baby in the hand-bag.

JACK [*who has been listening attentively*] But where did you deposit the hand-bag?

MISS PRISM Do not ask me, Mr Worthing.

JACK Miss Prism, this is a matter of no small importance to me. I insist on knowing where you deposited the hand-bag that contained that infant.

MISS PRISM I left it in the cloak-room of one of the larger railway stations in London.

JACK What railway station?

MISS PRISM [*quite crushed*] Victoria. The Brighton line. [*Sinks into a chair.*]

JACK I must retire to my room for a moment. Gwendolen, wait here for me.

GWENDOLEN If you are not too long, I will wait here for you all my life.

[*Exit* JACK *in great excitement.*]

3. Baby carriage (pram).

4. A fashionable residential area of west London, north of Kensington Gardens.

CHASUBLE What do you think this means, Lady Bracknell?

LADY BRACKNELL I dare not even suspect, Dr Chasuble. I need hardly tell you that in families of high position strange coincidences are not supposed to occur. They are hardly considered the thing.

[Noises heard overhead as if someone was throwing trunks about. Everyone looks up.]

CECILY Uncle Jack seems strangely agitated.

CHASUBLE Your guardian has a very emotional nature.

LADY BRACKNELL This noise is extremely unpleasant. It sounds as if he was having an argument. I dislike arguments of any kind. They are always vulgar, and often convincing.

CHASUBLE *[looking up]* It has stopped now. *[The noise is redoubled.]*

LADY BRACKNELL I wish he would arrive at some conclusion.

GWENDOLEN This suspense is terrible. I hope it will last.

[Enter JACK *with a hand-bag of black leather in his hand.]*

JACK *[rushing over to* MISS PRISM*]* Is this the hand-bag, Miss Prism? Examine it carefully before you speak. The happiness of more than one life depends on your answer.

MISS PRISM *[calmly]* It seems to be mine. Yes, here is the injury it received through the upsetting of a Gower Street omnibus[5] in younger and happier days. Here is the stain on the lining caused by the explosion of a temperance beverage, an incident that occurred at Leamington.[6] And here, on the lock, are my initials. I had forgotten that in an extravagant mood I had had them placed there. The bag is undoubtedly mine. I am delighted to have it so unexpectedly restored to me. It has been a great inconvenience being without it all these years.

JACK *[in a pathetic voice]* Miss Prism, more is restored to you than this hand-bag. I was the baby you placed in it.

MISS PRISM *[amazed]* You?

JACK *[embracing her]* Yes . . . mother!

MISS PRISM *[recoiling in indignant astonishment]* Mr Worthing! I am unmarried!

JACK Unmarried! I do not deny that is a serious blow. But after all, who has the right to cast a stone[7] against one who has suffered? Cannot repentance wipe out an act of folly? Why should there be one law for men, and another for women. Mother, I forgive you. *[Tries to embrace her again.]*

MISS PRISM *[still more indignant]* Mr Worthing, there is some error. *[Pointing to* LADY BRACKNELL*]* There is the lady who can tell you who you really are.

JACK *[after a pause]* Lady Bracknell, I hate to seem inquisitive, but would you kindly inform me who I am?

LADY BRACKNELL I am afraid that the news I have to give you will not altogether please you. You are the son of my poor sister, Mrs Moncrieff, and consequently Algernon's elder brother.

5. Public carriage (bus). *Gower Street*: a street in the Bloomsbury section of central London (where the University of London and the British Museum are located).

6. Royal Leamington Spa, in Warwickshire, about 100 miles northwest of London. *Temperance beverage*: in the 1890s, carbonated soda drinks were marketed as wholesome alternatives to alcohol.

7. That is, condemn a sinner—in the phrase's original context, a woman caught committing adultery (see John 8.7).

JACK Algy's elder brother! Then I have a brother after all. I knew I had a brother! I always said I had a brother! Cecily—how could you have ever doubted that I had a brother. [*Seizes hold of* ALGERNON.] Dr Chasuble, my unfortunate brother. Miss Prism, my unfortunate brother. Gwendolen, my unfortunate brother. Algy, you young scoundrel, you will have to treat me with more respect in the future. You have never behaved to me like a brother in all your life.

ALGERNON Well, not till today, old boy, I admit. I did my best, however, though I was out of practice. [*Shakes hands.*]

GWENDOLEN [*to* JACK] My own! But what own are you? What is your Christian name, now that you have become someone else?

JACK Good heavens! . . . I had quite forgotten that point. Your decision on the subject of my name is irrevocable, I suppose?

GWENDOLEN I never change, except in my affections.

CECILY What a noble nature you have, Gwendolen!

JACK Then the question had better be cleared up at once. Aunt Augusta, a moment. At the time when Miss Prism left me in the hand-bag, had I been christened already?

LADY BRACKNELL Every luxury that money could buy, including christening, had been lavished on you by your fond and doting parents.

JACK Then I was christened! That is settled. Now, what name was I given? Let me know the worst.

LADY BRACKNELL Being the eldest son you were naturally christened after your father.

JACK [*irritably*] Yes, but what was my father's Christian name?

LADY BRACKNELL [*meditatively*] I cannot at the present moment recall what the General's Christian name was. But I have no doubt he had one. He was eccentric, I admit. But only in later years. And that was the result of the Indian climate, and marriage, and indigestion, and other things of that kind.

JACK Algy! Can't you recollect what our father's Christian name was?

ALGERNON My dear boy, we were never even on speaking terms. He died before I was a year old.

JACK His name would appear in the Army Lists[8] of the period, I suppose, Aunt Augusta?

LADY BRACKNELL The General was essentially a man of peace, except in his domestic life. But I have no doubt his name would appear in any military directory.

JACK The Army Lists of the last forty years are here. These delightful records should have been my constant study. [*Rushes to bookcase and tears the books out.*] M. Generals . . . Mallam, Maxbohm, Magley, what ghastly names they have—Markby, Migsby, Mobbs, Moncrieff! Lieutenant 1840, Captain, Lieutenant-Colonel, Colonel, General 1869, Christian names, Ernest John. [*Puts book very quietly down and speaks quite calmly.*] I always told you, Gwendolen, my name was Ernest, didn't I? Well, it is Ernest after all. I mean it naturally is Ernest.

LADY BRACKNELL Yes, I remember now that the General was called Ernest. I knew I had some particular reason for disliking the name.

8. The official lists of all the commissioned officers in the army.

GWENDOLEN Ernest! My own Ernest! I felt from the first that you could have no other name!

JACK Gwendolen, it is a terrible thing for a man to find out suddenly that all his life he has been speaking nothing but the truth. Can you forgive me?

GWENDOLEN I can. For I feel that you are sure to change.

JACK My own one!

CHASUBLE [*to* MISS PRISM] Lætitia! [*Embraces her.*]

MISS PRISM [*enthusiastically*] Frederick! At last!

ALGERNON Cecily! [*Embraces her.*] At last!

JACK Gwendolen! [*Embraces her.*] At last!

LADY BRACKNELL My nephew, you seem to be displaying signs of triviality.

JACK On the contrary, Aunt Augusta, I've now realized for the first time in my life the vital Importance of Being Earnest.

Tableau.[9]

Curtain.

9. That is, a tableau vivant: having characters freeze in a final pose as the curtain fell was a vogue in 19th-century theater.

ANTON CHEKHOV

1860–1904

ANTON Chekhov, who died four years after the dawn of the new century, casts a long shadow over the history of modern theater. The greatest dramatist the Russian stage has ever seen, he stands as a central figure in the emergence of twentieth-century drama. At first glance, Chekhov may seem an unlikely candidate for this historical role. Inheriting a tradition of Russian fiction that included such literary monuments as Fyodor Dostoevsky's novel *Crime and Punishment* (1866) and Leo Tolstoy's *War and Peace* (1865–89), Chekhov achieved his initial literary reputation through the writing of novellas and short stories rather than drama. Of the dozen and a half plays that he wrote, the majority are comic one acts, and those on which his reputation chiefly rests—*The Seagull*, *Uncle Vanya*, *The Three Sisters*, and THE CHERRY ORCHARD—are only four in number and were written relatively late in his career. In Chekhov's case, though, numbers are misleading, for the dramatic terrain that these plays opened up proved so innovative that their influence can be felt more than a century after his death. Rewriting the aesthetic of theatrical realism through a drama of understatement, indirection, and psychological nuance, Chekhov's major plays offer a new vision of the relationship between theater and everyday life.

Chekhov was born on January 17, 1860, in Taganrog, a small seaport on the Sea of Azov (a northern arm of the Black Sea) in southern Russia. His father was a merchant and his paternal grandfather a serf who had purchased his freedom and that of his family in 1841. Only one generation removed from serfdom, Chekhov remained acutely aware of his background: in an autobiographical letter to his friend and publisher Alexei Suvorin in 1889, he described an imaginary character who, after squeezing the slave blood out of himself "drop by drop," awakes one day to find that "the blood coursing through his veins is no longer that of a slave but that of a real human being." After attending local schools, he graduated in 1879 with a scholarship for university study. Chekhov's father had moved the rest of his family to Moscow three years earlier in order to escape debtor's prison, and when Anton joined them he enrolled at the Moscow University School of Medicine, from which he earned a degree at the age of twenty-four. Although Chekhov soon gave up private practice to focus on writing, his medical training remained an essential part of his personal and professional identity. "Medicine is my lawful wife and literature is my mistress," he later commented. "When I get tired of one I go to the other." He continued to treat patients, often for free, and he demonstrated a lifelong interest in matters of public health. During the famine and cholera epidemic of 1892–93, he served as head of a district sanitary committee and treated many of the epidemic's poorest victims.

Chekhov began writing in his teens. He edited a school newspaper and, encouraged by his older brothers, wrote humorous anecdotes and sketches. By the time he graduated from medical school, he was publishing comic sketches, parodies, dialogues, and short stories in small-press periodicals. As the popularity of his fiction grew, Chekhov's stories began appearing in more established periodicals and newspapers, and in 1884 he published his first collection of short stories, *Fairy Tales of Melpomene*. Dmitri Grigorovich, a leading short-story writer and a prominent figure in Russia's literary establishment, praised Chekhov as the most talented writer of his generation; the young writer's accomplishment was given official recognition when his second collection of stories, *In the Twilight,* was awarded the Pushkin Prize by the Imperial Academy of Science in 1888. Although Chekhov attempted unsuccessfully to write a novel, he was attracted—and his artistic temperament was suited—to more condensed fictional forms. Focusing on the particularities of character, social class, and setting while maintaining the authorial objectivity for which he became renowned, he developed the short story into a vehicle of unprecedented psychological complexity and acute social observation. His finest stories—such as "Ward No. 6" (1892), "My Life" (1896), and "Peasants" (1897)—are considered masterpieces of the genre.

Chekhov's interest in the theater also developed at an early age. As a schoolboy, he participated in amateur theatrical skits with his siblings (he had four brothers and one sister), and he and his friends saw professional plays at the Taganrog theater. In his late teens he composed two plays that have not survived, a one-act farce and a full-length drama titled "Fatherlessness," and during his first two years of medical school he produced a cumbersome four-act drama that may have been a reworked version of the latter play. Though he subsequently destroyed this play, a copy was discovered after his death and has been published under the title *Platonov.* Chekhov's first theatrical production did not occur until 1887, when *Ivanov,* a play about a bored and disillusioned landowner, premiered in Moscow to critical and popular acclaim. It was followed in 1889 by *The Wood Demon,* a full-length comedy, and by a series of one-act comedies that Chekhov wrote between 1887 and 1901. Conceived in the tradition of vaudeville farce, these "airy trifles" (as Chekhov called them) were little more than curtain-raisers, though *The Bear* (1888) proved popular throughout Russia and *The Proposal* (1889) entertained a St. Petersburg audience that included Czar Alexander III.

A gap of five years separates this early drama from the earliest of the four mature plays that figure so prominently in the history of modern drama. In 1895, Chekhov wrote *The Seagull,* a play about art, disappointed love, and the psychology of survival. Set, like his other major plays, on a provincial Russian estate, it explores the shifting relationships in a quartet of central characters: Arkádina, an aging actress; her son Tréplev, an avant-garde writer; Trigórin, an established novelist; and Nína, a young actress whose aspirations, hardships, and disappointments identify her with a seagull that Tréplev has shot. At the play's premiere in St. Petersburg on October 17, 1896, the audience responded so negatively that Chekhov fled the auditorium during the second act and vowed never to write another play. However, when Konstantin Stanislavsky and Vladimir Nemirovich-Danchenko, founders of the newly formed Moscow Art Theatre, revived *The Seagull* two years later, the play proved so popular that the theater company adopted its title bird as their emblem. With Stanislavsky as director, the MAT staged the Moscow premieres of Chekhov's remaining plays: *Uncle Vanya,* a reworked version of *The Wood Demon*, in 1899; *The Three Sisters* in 1901; and *The Cherry Orchard* in 1904. Six months after *The Cherry Orchard* opened, Chekhov died of tuberculosis at the age of forty-four.

The innovations of dramaturgy and stagecraft in these plays are both subtle and wide-ranging. Late nineteenth-century Russian theater was dominated by farce and melodrama, genres that relied on stock characters and heightened dramatic incident. Reacting against these theatrical conventions, Chekhov insisted that drama imitate the textures, issues, and actions of everyday life and that its characters reflect the complexity of human experience. In a statement of his artistic principles, Chekhov wrote:

> The demand is made that the hero and heroine should be dramatically effective. But in life people do not shoot themselves, or hang themselves, or fall in love, or deliver themselves of clever sayings every minute. They spend most of their time eating, drinking, running after women or men, talking nonsense. It is therefore necessary that this should be shown on the stage. A play ought to be written in which the people should come and go, dine, talk of the weather, or play cards, not because the author wants it but because that is what happens in real life. Life on the stage should be as it really is, and the people, too, should be as they are and not on stilts.

In order to accomplish this objective, Chekhov reduced the importance of traditional dramatic climaxes by minimizing their impact or eliminating them altogether. His characters resist dramatic stereotype, and the stage they occupy generates multiple points of attention rather than central protagonists and antagonists. These characters talk, do ordinary things, and are defined more by the actions they don't take than those they do. In keeping with Chekhov's belief that a dramatist's job is not to judge the characters created but to present them in the light of dispassionate observation, his plays give little evidence of their author's point of view. The result is a drama of understatement, indirection, and nuance, where action and emotion lie beneath the words. Chekhov famously observed: "People are having a meal, just having a meal, but at the same time their happiness is being created, or their lives are being destroyed."

The Cherry Orchard is one of the finest examples of Chekhov's "drama of the undramatic" (in the critic Richard Gilman's phrase). Its plot hinges on the fate of the Ranyévskaya estate, famed for its beautiful cherry orchard but no longer able to support its occupants or their privileged lifestyle. Its threatened sale is the stuff of French "mortgage melodramas," which often hinged on the possible or actual loss of property at the hands of a villainous manipulator; but the climactic event of Chekhov's play—the auction at which the estate is sold—occurs offstage, and its outcome is recounted after the fact. In a similar undermining of expectations, the participants in this crisis do not fit the moral categories of conventional melodrama. Liubóv (Madame Ranyévskaya) and her brother Gáyev, who cling to their childhood memories of the orchard, lose the estate through a mixture of paralysis and fecklessness, not victimization; indeed, their inaction in the face of the imminent loss of their property is the play's most sustained narrative thread. For his part, Lopákhin—the former serf who eventually buys the estate—is a far cry from the stock villain of melodrama. He urges Liubóv and Gáyev to sell the orchard as a way of saving the estate, and in the giddiness of having bought the property he speaks movingly (if somewhat thoughtlessly) about his social transformation. In terms of dramatic technique, the moment in act 3 when he delivers this speech is a rare example in Chekhov's play of a character's dominating the stage and claiming attention. The rest of the time characters engage in conversation with each other, sometimes listening, sometimes not. In keeping with its muted sphere of action, *The Cherry Orchard* opens with the arrival of characters and ends with their departure.

Chekhov wrote *The Cherry Orchard* while living as a semi-invalid in Yalta, and its composition was long and difficult. Yet the play is the most comic of his mature dramas. In September 1903 he wrote to his wife, Olga Knipper, who would play the role of Madame Ranyévskaya, "My play . . . hasn't turned out as a drama, but as a comedy, at times almost a farce." Subtitling his play "A Comedy in Four Acts," Chekhov insisted on this view of the play throughout its rehearsals and found himself in frequent disagreement with his director, Stanislavsky, who considered the play a tragedy and accentuated the atmosphere

The Moscow Art Theater's original 1904 production of *The Cherry Orchard*, directed by Constantin Stanislavsky. Stanislavsky, who performed the role of Gayev in this production, is on the far left, gesturing toward the bookcase.

of pathos and loss. In Chekhov's hands, comedy is central to the play's mixture of tones. In addition to the obvious moments of slapstick—Liubóv's adopted daughter Várya swings a stick at the accountant Yepikhódov in anger but hits Lopákhin instead, while "the eternal student" Trofímov falls noisily down the stairs after an argument with Liubóv—Chekhov employs comedy as a vehicle of irony and distance. His use of comedy is particularly evident in those moments when the physical world intrudes on private emotion and in those tics and mannerisms that signal a character's self-absorption. When the governess Carlotta laments that she doesn't own a birth certificate at the start of the play's second act—"Where I'm from . . . who I am . . . no idea"—the painful undertones of her meditation are deflected when she reaches into her pocket and absent-mindedly takes a bite out of a cucumber pickle. And when Gáyev plays his imaginary billiards game or delivers an oration to the family bookcase, these humorous moments measure the extent to which he, like all the play's characters, inhabits a world of his own.

The problem in Stanislavsky's "tearful" direction of *The Cherry Orchard,* in other words, was that he sought to reveal the play's emotions through overt gesture rather than through the ironic counterpoint of surface activity and emotional undercurrents. In Chekhovian drama the weight of emotion lies in what is not said, as when the forced gaiety of the ball in act 3 is undercut by the audience's awareness that the auction is taking place offstage. And few scenes in all of Chekhov's plays hold the emotional power of Várya's exchange with Lopákhin near the play's end, when the two exchange small talk while failing to address the life-deciding issue that hangs over them.

As elsewhere in Chekhov's writing, individual psychology in *The Cherry Orchard* is deeply embedded within the social, economic, and political landscape of turn-of-the-century Russia. In the sale of the Ranyévskaya estate, Chekhov dramatizes the historical eclipse of the landowning class that had formed the historical pillar of feudal Russia. Semyónov-Píshchik, a neighboring landowner, must borrow money from Liubóv to meet his financial needs, and he pays her back only after selling the rights to extract the white clay that has been discovered on his property. In Lopákhin's plan to cut down the cherry orchard and build vacation homes we feel the emerging class of others, like him, who have grown prosperous through acquired wealth. Social mobility defines *The Cherry Orchard,* and as the contrasting destinies of Chekhov's central characters demonstrate, this mobility extends in both directions. Beyond the circle of property and money, of course, is the vast number of Russia's poor and uneducated. Firs, the family's aging house servant, recalls the emancipation of the serfs in 1861, and Chekhov's play provides ample evidence of

Chekhov's home in Melikhovo, Russia, where he and his family lived from 1892 to 1899.

the poverty and social dislocation that this class has had to endure. Indigent peasants have been staying in the old servants' quarters, and a homeless man intrudes upon the pastoral quiet of act 2. The student Trofímov addresses this poverty and its history in a speech to Liubóv's daughter Ánya: "Your grandfather, and his father, and his father's fathers, they *owned* the people who slaved away for them all over this estate, and now the voices and faces of human beings hide behind every cherry in the orchard, every leaf, every tree trunk." Envisioning a future of happiness and social justice, he calls on Ánya to devote her life to working in the cause of human progress. "This whole country is our orchard," he proclaims, widening the scope of the play's issues to include czarist Russia as a whole.

In view of subsequent Russian history—in 1917 the Communist-led Russian Revolution overthrew Czar Nicholas II and proclaimed an era of social equality—Trofímov's speeches in act 2 have sometimes been taken as Chekhov's own call for transformative social change. Not surprisingly, Soviet productions of *The Cherry Orchard* made Trofímov the herald of a new revolutionary order. To be sure, Chekhov's Trofímov articulates the revolutionary sentiment that had gained increasing force in Russia by the turn of the century. Universities were major sites of antigovernment agitation, and (as Chekhov indicated in a letter to his wife) Trofímov's extended career as a graduate student reflects the fact that he has been expelled more than once for political reasons. At the same time, though Trofímov's rhetoric is stirring, his vision of a future that will redeem the present resembles the beautiful dreams that other Chekhov characters use to escape the drabness and disappointment of their lives. Trofímov does little to translate language into action, and this character who likes the sound of his own voice cuts a somewhat ridiculous figure at times. The optimism of his predictions exist in ironic counterpoint with the present, just as the historical evolution represented by change in *The Cherry Orchard* coexists with the painfulness of individual loss. To push the tone of *The Cherry Orchard* in one direction at the expense of another—to stress its resignation or its desire for something better, its comedy or its tears—is to deny the multiple perspectives that Chekhov so masterfully calls into play.

S.G.

The Cherry Orchard
A Comedy in Four Acts[1]

CHARACTERS

LIUBÓV RANYÉVSKAYA [Lyúba, Liúba Andréyevna], who owns the estate
ÁNYA, her daughter, seventeen years old
VÁRYA, her adopted daughter, twenty-four years old
LEONÍD GÁYEV [Lonya, Lyónya Andréyich], Liubóv's brother
YERMOLÁI LOPÁKHIN [Yermolái Alexéyich], a businessman
PÉTYA TROFÍMOV, a graduate student
BORÍS SEMYÓNOV-PÍSHCHIK, who owns land in the neighborhood
CARLOTTA, the governess
SEMYÓN YEPIKHÓDOV, an accountant
DUNYÁSHA [Avdótya Fyódorovna, Dunyáhsa Kozoyédov], the maid
FIRS, the butler, eighty-seven years old
YÁSHA, the valet
A HOMELESS MAN
The STATIONMASTER
The POSTMASTER
Guests, servants

The action takes place on Ranyévskaya's estate.

Act 1

[*A room they still call the nursery. A side door leads to* ÁNYA'S *room. Almost dawn; the sun is about to rise. It's May; the cherry orchard is already in bloom, but there's a chill in the air. The windows are shut. Enter* DUNYÁSHA *with a lamp, and* LOPÁKHIN *with a book in his hand.*]

LOPÁKHIN The train's finally in, thank God. What time is it?

DUNYÁSHA Almost two. [*She blows out the lamp.*] It's getting light.

LOPÁKHIN How late is the train this time? Must be at least two hours. [*He yawns and stretches.*] That was dumb. I came over on purpose just to meet them at the station, and then I fell asleep. Sat right here and fell asleep. Too bad. You should have woke me up.

DUNYÁSHA I thought you already left. [*She listens.*] Listen, that must be them.

LOPÁKHIN [*he listens*] No, they still have the luggage to get, and all that. [*Pause*] She's been away five years now; no telling how she's changed. She was always a good person. Very gentle, never caused a fuss. I remember one time when I was a kid, fifteen or so, they had my old man working in the store down by the village, and he hit me, hard, right in the face; my nose started to bleed. And we had to come up here to make a delivery or something; he was still drunk. And Liubóv Andréyevna—she wasn't much older than I was, kind of thin—she brought me inside the house, right into the nursery here, and washed the blood off my face for me. "Don't cry," she told me. "Don't cry, poor boy; you'll live long enough to get married." [*Pause*] Poor boy . . . Well, my father was poor, but take a look at me now,

1. Translated by Paul Schmidt.

all dressed up, brand-new suit and tan shoes. Silk purse out of a sow's ear, I guess . . . I'm rich now, got lots of money, but when you think about it, I guess I'm still a poor boy from the country. [*He flips the pages of the book.*] I tried reading this book, couldn't figure out a word it said. Put me to sleep.

[*Pause.*]

DUNYÁSHA The dogs were barking all night long; they know their mistress is coming home.

LOPÁKHIN Don't be silly.

DUNYÁSHA I'm so excited I'm shaking. I may faint.

LOPÁKHIN You're getting too full of yourself, Dunyásha. Look at you, all dressed up like that, and that hairdo. You watch out for that. You got to remember who you are.

[*Enter* YEPIKHÓDOV *with a bunch of flowers; he wears a jacket and tie and brightly polished boots, which squeak loudly. As he comes in, he drops the flowers.*]

YEPIKHÓDOV [*picking up the flowers*] Here. The gardener sent these over; he said put them on the dining room table. [*He gives the flowers to* DUNYÁSHA.]

LOPÁKHIN And bring me a beer.

DUNYÁSHA Right away.

[*She goes out.*]

YEPIKHÓDOV It's freezing this morning—it must be in the thirties—and the cherry blossoms are out already. I cannot abide the climate here. [*He sighs.*] I never have abided it, ever. [*Beat*][2] Yermolái Alexéyich, would you examinate something for me, please? Day before yesterday I bought myself a new pair of boots, and listen to them squeak, will you? I just cannot endear it. Do you know anything I can put on them?

LOPÁKHIN Will you shut up? You drive me crazy.

YEPIKHÓDOV Every day something awful happens to me. It's like a habit. But I don't complain. I just try to keep smiling.

[*Enter* DUNYÁSHA; *she brings* LOPÁKHIN *a beer.*]

YEPIKHÓDOV I'm going. [*He bumps into a chair, which falls over.*] You see? [*He seems proud of it.*] You see what I was referring about? Excuse my expressivity, but what a concurrence. It's almost uncanny, isn't it?

[*He leaves.*]

DUNYÁSHA You know what? That Yepikhódov proposed to me!

LOPÁKHIN Oh?

DUNYÁSHA I just don't know what to think. He's kind of nice. . . . He's a real quiet boy, but then he opens his mouth, and you can't ever understand what he's talking about. I mean, it sounds nice, but it just doesn't make any sense. I do like him, though. Kind of. And he's crazy about me. It's funny, you know, every day something awful happens to him. People around here call him Double Trouble.

LOPÁKHIN [*he listens*] That must be them.

DUNYÁSHA It's them! Oh, I don't know what's the matter with me! I feel so funny; I'm cold all over.

LOPÁKHIN It really is them this time. Let's go; we should be there at the door. You think she'll recognize me? It's been five years.

2. Pause.

DUNYÁSHA [*excited*] Oh, my God! I'm going to faint! I think I'm going to faint!

[*The sound of two carriages outside the house.* LOPÁKHIN *and* DUNYÁSHA *hurry out. The stage is empty. The sound outside gets louder.* FIRS, *leaning heavily on his cane, crosses the room, heading for the door; he wears an old-fashioned butler's livery and a top hat; he says something to himself, but you can't make out the words. The offstage noise and bustle increases. A voice: "Here we are . . . this way." Enter* LIUBÓV ANDRÉYEVNA, ÁNYA, *and* CARLOTTA, *dressed in traveling clothes.* VÁRYA *wears an overcoat, and a kerchief on her head.* GÁYEV, SEMYÓNOV-PÍSHCHIK, LOPÁKHIN, DUNYÁSHA *with a bundle and an umbrella, Servants with the luggage—all pass across the stage.*]

ÁNYA Here we are. Oh, Mama, do you remember this room?

LIUBÓV ANDRÉYEVNA The nursery!

VÁRYA It's freezing; my hands are like ice. We kept your room exactly as you left it, Mama. The white and lavender one.

LIUBÓV ANDRÉYEVNA The nursery! Oh, this house, this beautiful house! I slept in this room when I was a child. . . . [*She weeps.*] And I feel like a child again! [*She hugs* GÁYEV, VÁRYA, *then* GÁYEV *again.*] And Várya hasn't changed at all—still looks like a nun! And Dunyásha dear! Of course I remember you! [*She hugs* DUNYÁSHA.]

GÁYEV The train was two hours late. What kind of efficiency is that? Eh?

CARLOTTA And my dog loves nuts.

SEMYÓNOV-PÍSHCHIK Really! I don't believe it!

[*Everyone leaves, except* ÁNYA *and* DUNYÁSHA.]

DUNYÁSHA We've been up all night, waiting. . . . [*She takes* ÁNYA*'s coat and hat.*]

ÁNYA I've been up for four nights now. . . . I didn't sleep the whole trip. And now I'm freezing.

DUNYÁSHA When you went away it was still winter, it was snowing, and now look! Oh, sweetie, you're back! [*She laughs and hugs Ánya.*] I've been up all night, waiting to see you. Sweetheart, I just can't wait—I've got to tell you what happened. I can't wait another minute!

ÁNYA [*wearily*] Now what?

DUNYÁSHA Yepikhódov proposed the day after Easter! He wants to marry me!

ÁNYA That's all you ever think about. . . . [*She fixes her hair.*] I lost all my hairpins. . . .

DUNYÁSHA I just don't know what to do about him. He really, really loves me!

ÁNYA [*looking through the door to her room*] My own room, just as if I'd never left. I'm back home! Tomorrow I'll get up and go for a walk in the orchard. I just wish I could get some sleep. I didn't sleep the whole trip, I was so worried.

DUNYÁSHA Pétya's here. He got here day before yesterday.

ÁNYA [*joyfully*] Pétya!

DUNYÁSHA He's staying out in the barn. Said he didn't want to bother anybody. [*She looks at her watch.*] He told me to get him up, but Várya said not to. You let him sleep, she said.

[*Enter* VÁRYA. *She has a big bunch of keys attached to her belt.*]

VÁRYA Dunyásha, go get the coffee. Mama wants her coffee.

DUNYÁSHA Oh, I forgot!

[*She goes out.*]

VÁRYA You're back. Thank God! You're home again! [*She embraces Ánya.*] My angel is home again! My beautiful darling!

ÁNYA You won't believe what I've been through!

VÁRYA I can imagine.

ÁNYA I left just before Easter; it was cold. Carlotta never shut up the whole trip; she kept doing those silly tricks of hers. I don't know why you had to stick me with her.

VÁRYA Darling, you couldn't go all that way by yourself! You're only seventeen!

ÁNYA We got to Paris, it was cold and snowy, and my French is just awful! Mama was living in this fifth-floor apartment, we had to walk up, we get there and there's all these French people, some old priest reading some book, and it was crowded, and everybody was smoking these awful cigarettes—and I felt so sorry for Mama, I just threw my arms around her and couldn't let go. And she was so glad to see me, she cried—

VÁRYA [*almost crying*] I know, I know . . .

ÁNYA And she sold the villa in Mentón,[3] and the money was already gone, all of it! And I spent everything you gave me for the trip; I haven't got a thing left. And Mama still doesn't understand! We have dinner at the train station, and she orders the most expensive things on the menu, and then she tips the waiters a ruble[4] each! And Carlotta does the same! And Yásha expects the same treatment—he's just awful. You know, Yásha, that flunky of Mama's—he came back with us.

VÁRYA I saw him, the lazy good-for-nothing.

ÁNYA So what happened? Did you get the interest paid?

VÁRYA With what?

ÁNYA Oh, my God, my God . . .

VÁRYA The place goes up for sale in August.

ÁNYA Oh, my God.

[LOPÁKHIN *sticks his head in the doorway and makes a mooing sound, then goes away.*]

VÁRYA Oh, that man! I'd like to—[*She shakes her fist.*]

ÁNYA [*she hugs her*] Várya, did he propose yet? [VÁRYA *shakes her head no.*] But you know he loves you! Why don't the two of you just sit down and be honest with each other? What are you waiting for?

VÁRYA I don't think anything will ever come of it. He's always so busy, he never has time for me. He just isn't interested! It's hard for me when I see him, but I don't care anymore. Everybody talks about us getting married, people even congratulate me, but there's nothing. . . . I mean, it's all just a dream. [*A change of tone*] Oh, you've got a new pin, a little bee. . . .

ÁNYA [*with a sigh*] I know. Mama bought it for me. [*She goes into her room and starts to giggle, like a little girl.*] You know what? In Paris I went for a ride in a balloon!

VÁRYA Oh, darling, you're back! My angel is home again!

3. A resort town on the French Mediterranean coast.

4. Roughly equivalent to $20 today.

[DUNYÁSHA *comes in, carrying a tray with coffee things, and begins setting them out on the table.* VÁRYA *stands at the doorway and talks to* ÁNYA *in the other room.*]

You know, dear, I spend the livelong day trying to keep this house going, and all I do is dream. I want to see you married off to somebody rich, then I can rest easy. And I think then I'll go away by myself, maybe live in a convent, or just go traveling: Kiev, Moscow . . . spend all my time making visits to churches. I'd start walking and just go and go and go. That would be heaven!

ÁNYA Listen to the birds in the orchard! What time is it?

VÁRYA It must be almost three. You should get some sleep, darling. [*She goes into* ÁNYA'*s room.*] Yes, that would be heaven!

[*Enter* YÁSHA *with a suitcase and a lap robe. He walks with an affected manner.*]

YÁSHA I beg pardon! May I intrude?

DUNYÁSHA I didn't even recognize you, Yásha. You got so different there in France.

YÁSHA *I'm* sorry—who are you exactly?

DUNYÁSHA When you left, I wasn't any higher than this. [*She holds her hand a distance from the floor.*] I'm Dunyásha. You know, Dunyásha Kozoyédov. Don't you remember me?

YÁSHA Well! You sure turned out cute, didn't you? [*He looks around carefully, then grabs and kisses her; she screams and drops a saucer;* YÁSHA *leaves in a hurry.*]

VÁRYA [*at the door, annoyed*] Now what happened?

DUNYÁSHA [*almost in tears*] I broke a saucer.

VÁRYA [*ironically*] Well, isn't that lucky!

ÁNYA [*entering*] Somebody should let Mama know Pétya's here.

VÁRYA I told them to let him sleep.

ÁNYA [*lost in thought*] Father died six years ago, and a month later our little brother, Grísha, drowned. Sweet boy, he was only seven. And Mama couldn't face it, that's why she went away, just went away and never looked back. [*Shivers.*] And I understand exactly how she felt. I wish she knew that.

[*Pause.*]

And Pétya Trofímov was Grísha's tutor. He might remind her . . .

[*Enter* FIRS *in his old-fashioned butler's livery. He crosses to the table and begins looking over the coffee things.*]

FIRS The missus will have her breakfast here. [*He puts on a pair of white gloves.*] Is the coffee ready? [*To* DUNYÁSHA, *crossly*] Where's the cream? Go get the cream!

DUNYÁSHA Oh, my God, I'm sorry. . . .

[*Hurries off.*]

FIRS [*he starts fussing with the coffee things*] Young flibbertigibbet . . . [*He mumbles to himself.*] They're all back from Paris. . . . In the old days they went to Paris too . . . had to go the whole way in a horse and buggy. [*He laughs.*]

VÁRYA Firs, what are you talking about?

FIRS Beg pardon? [*Joyfully*] The missus is home! Going to see her at last! Now I can die happy. . . . [*He starts to cry with joy.*]

[*Enter* LIUBÓV, GÁYEV, LOPÁKHIN, *and* SEMYÓNOV-PÍSHCHIK, *who wears a crumpled linen suit. As* GÁYEV *enters, he gestures as if he were making a billiard shot.*]

LIUBÓV ANDRÉYEVNA How did it go? I'm trying to remember. . . . Yellow ball in the side pocket! Bank shot off the corner!

GÁYEV And right down the middle! Oh, sister, sister, just think . . . when you and I were little we used to sleep in this room, and now I'm almost fifty-one! Strange, isn't it?

LOPÁKHIN Time sure passes. . . .

GÁYEV [*beat*] Say again?

LOPÁKHIN I said, time sure passes.

GÁYEV [*looking at* LOPÁKHIN] Who's wearing that cheap cologne?

ÁNYA I'm going to bed. Good night, Mama. [*She kisses her mother.*]

LIUBÓV ANDRÉYEVNA Oh, my darling little girl, my baby! Are you glad you're home? I still can't quite believe I'm here.

ÁNYA Good night, Uncle.

GÁYEV [*he kisses her*] God bless you, dear. You're getting to look so much like your mother! Liúba, she looks just like you when you were her age. She really does.

[ÁNYA *says good night to* LOPÁKHIN *and* PÍSHCHIK, *goes into her room, and closes the door behind her.*]

LIUBÓV ANDRÉYEVNA She's tired to death.

PÍSHCHIK Well, that's such a long trip!

VÁRYA Gentlemen, please. It's almost three; time you were going.

LIUBÓV ANDRÉYEVNA [*laughs*] You're the same as ever, Várya. [*Hugs and kisses her.*] Just let me have my coffee, then we'll all be going.

[FIRS *puts a pillow beneath her feet.*]

Thank you, dear. I've really gotten addicted to coffee; I drink it day and night. You old darling, you! Thank you.

VÁRYA I'll just go make sure they've got everything unloaded.

[*Goes out.*]

LIUBÓV ANDRÉYEVNA I can't believe I'm really here! [*Laughs.*] I feel like jumping up and waving my arms in the air! [*Covers her face with her hands.*] It's still like a dream. I love this country, really I do, I adore it. I started to cry every time I looked out the train windows. [*Almost in tears*] But I do need my coffee! Thank you, Firs, thank you, darling. I'm so glad you're still alive.

FIRS Day before yesterday.

GÁYEV He doesn't hear too well anymore.

LOPÁKHIN Time for me to go. I have to leave for Hárkov[5] at five. I'm really disappointed; I was looking forward to seeing you, have a chance to talk. . . . You look wonderful, just the way you always did.

PÍSHCHIK [*breathes hard*] Better than she always did. That Paris outfit. . . . She makes me feel young again!

LOPÁKHIN Your brother here thinks I'm crude, calls me a money grubber. That doesn't bother me; he can call me whatever he wants. I just hope you'll trust me the way you used to, look at me the way you used to. . . . My

5. That is, Kharkov, the second-largest city in Ukraine (then part of the Russian Empire).

God, my father slaved for your father and grandfather, my whole family worked for yours; but you, you treated me different. You did so much for me I forgot about all that. Fact is, I . . . I love you like you were family . . . more, even.

LIUBÓV ANDRÉYEVNA I can't sit still; I'm just not in the mood! [*Gets up excitedly, moves about the room.*] I'm so happy I could die! I know I sound stupid—go ahead, laugh. . . . Dear old bookcase. . . . [*Kisses the bookcase.*] My little desk . . .

GÁYEV Did I tell you Nanny died while you were away?

LIUBÓV ANDRÉYEVNA [*sits back down and drinks her coffee*] Yes, you wrote me. God rest her.

GÁYEV Stásy died too. And Petrúsha Kosói quit and moved into town; he works at the police station. [*Takes out a little box of hard candies and puts one in his mouth.*]

PÍSHCHIK Dáshenka—you remember Dáshenka? My daughter? Anyway, she sends her regards. . . .

LOPÁKHIN Well, I'd like to give you some very good news. [*Looks at his watch.*] Afraid there's no time to talk now, though; I've got to go. Well, just to make it short, you know you haven't kept up the mortgage payments on your place here. So now they foreclosed and your estate is up for sale. At auction. They set a date already, August twenty-second, but don't you worry, you can rest easy. We can take care of this—I've got a great idea. Now listen, here's how it works: your place here is fifteen miles from town, and it's only a short drive from the train station. All you've got to do is clear out the old cherry orchard, plus that land down by the river, and subdivide! You lease the plots, build vacation homes, and I swear that'll bring you in twenty-five thousand[6] a year, maybe more.

GÁYEV What an outrageous thing to say!

LIUBÓV ANDRÉYEVNA Excuse me . . . Excuse me, I don't think I quite understand. . . .

LOPÁKHIN You'll get at least twenty-five hundred an acre! And if you start advertising right away, I swear to God come this fall you won't have a single plot left. You see what I'm saying? Your troubles are over! Congratulations! The location is terrific; the river's a real selling point. Only thing is, you've got to start clearing right away. Get rid of all the old buildings. This house, for instance, will have to go. You can't get people to live in a barn like this anymore. And you'll have to cut down that old cherry orchard.

LIUBÓV ANDRÉYEVNA Cut down the cherry orchard? My dear man, you don't understand! Our cherry orchard is a landmark! It's famous for miles around!

LOPÁKHIN The only thing famous about it is how big it is. You only get cherries every two years, and even then you can't get rid of them. Nobody buys them. It's just not a commercial crop.

GÁYEV Our cherry orchard is mentioned in the encyclopedia![7]

LOPÁKHIN [*looks at his watch*] We have to think of something to do and then do it. Otherwise the cherry orchard will be sold at auction on August twenty-second, this house and all the land with it. Make up your minds!

6. Roughly equivalent to $500,000 today (all references to money are in rubles).

7. Probably a reference to the *Great Russian Encyclopedic Dictionary* (1890–1906), an authoritative 86-volume reference work published by F. A. Brockhaus and I. A. Efron.

Believe me, I've thought this through; there isn't any other way to do it. There just isn't.

FIRS Back in the old days, forty, fifty years ago, they used to make dried cherries, pickled cherries, preserved cherries, cherry jam, and sometimes—

GÁYEV Oh, Firs, just shut up.

FIRS —sometimes they sent them off to Moscow by the wagonload. People paid a lot for them! Back then the dried cherries were soft and juicy and sweet, and they smelled just lovely; back then they knew how to fix them. . . .

LIUBÓV ANDRÉYEVNA Does anybody know how to fix them nowadays?

FIRS Nope. They all forgot.

PÍSHCHIK Tell us about Paris. What was it like? Did you eat frogs?

LIUBÓV ANDRÉYEVNA I ate crocodiles.

PÍSHCHIK Crocodiles? Really! I don't believe it!

LOPÁKHIN You see, it used to be out here in the country there were only landlords and poor farmers, but now all of a sudden there are summer people moving in; they want vacation homes. Every town you can name is surrounded by them—it's the coming thing. In twenty years they'll expand and multiply! Right now maybe they're only places to relax on the weekend, but I bet you eventually people will put down roots out here, they'll create neighborhoods, and then your cherry orchard will blossom and bear fruit once again—and even bring in a profit!

GÁYEV [*indignantly*] That's outrageous!

[*Enter* VÁRYA *and* YÁSHA.]

VÁRYA Mama, a couple of telegrams came for you. [*Takes a key and opens the old bookcase; the lock creaks.*] Here they are.

LIUBÓV ANDRÉYEVNA They're from Paris. [*She tears them up without opening them.*] I'm through with Paris.

GÁYEV Liúba, have you any idea how old this bookcase is? Last week I pulled out the bottom drawer, and there was the date on the back, burned right into the wood. A hundred years! This bookcase is exactly a hundred years old! What do you say to that, eh? We should have a birthday celebration. Of course, it's an inanimate object, any way you look at it, but still, it's a . . . well, it's a . . . a bookcase.

PÍSHCHIK A hundred years old! Really! I don't believe it!

GÁYEV Yes, yes, it is. [*He caresses the bookcase.*] Dear old bookcase! Wonderful old bookcase! I rejoice in your existence. For a hundred years now you have borne the shining ideals of goodness and justice, a hundred years have not dimmed your silent summons to useful labor. To generations of our family [*Almost in tears*] you have offered courage, a belief in a better future, you have instructed us in ideals of goodness and social awareness. . . .

[*Pause.*]

LOPÁKHIN Right. Well . . .

LIUBÓV ANDRÉYEVNA Oh, Lonya, you're still the same as ever!

GÁYEV [*somewhat embarrassed*] Yellow ball in the side pocket! Bank shot off the center!

LOPÁKHIN Well, I've got to be off.

YÁSHA [*gives* LIUBÓV *a pillbox*] Isn't it perhaps time for your pills?

PÍSHCHIK No, no, no, dear lady! Never take medicine! Won't do any good! Won't do any harm either, though. Watch! [*Takes the pillbox, dumps the contents into his hand, puts them in his mouth, and swallows them with a swig of beer.*] There! All gone!

LIUBÓV ANDRÉYEVNA [*alarmed*] Are you out of your mind?

PÍSHCHIK I have just taken all your pills for you.

LOPÁKHIN What a glutton.

[*Everybody laughs.*]

FIRS He was here over the holidays, ate half a crock of pickles. . . . [*Mumbles.*]

LIUBÓV ANDRÉYEVNA What's he mumbling about?

VÁRYA He's been going on like that for the last three years. We're used to it by now.

YÁSHA He's getting senile.

[*Enter* CARLOTTA, *in a white dress with a lorgnette on a chain. She starts to cross the room.*]

LOPÁKHIN Oh, excuse me, Carlotta, I didn't get a chance to say hello yet. [*Tries to kiss her hand.*]

CARLOTTA [*takes her hand away*] I let you kiss my hand, first thing I know, you'll want to kiss my elbow, then my shoulder . . .

LOPÁKHIN This isn't my lucky day.

[*Everybody laughs.*]

Carlotta, show us a trick!

LIUBÓV ANDRÉYEVNA Yes, do, Carlotta—show us a trick!

CARLOTTA Not now. I'm off to bed.

[*Leaves.*]

LOPÁKHIN Well, I'll see you in three weeks. [*Kisses* LIUBÓV's *hand.*] Goodbye now. I've got to be off. [*To* GÁYEV] Goodbye. [*Hugs* PÍSHCHIK.] So long. [*Shakes hands with* VÁRYA, *then with* FIRS *and* YÁSHA.] I sort of hate to leave. [*To* LIUBÓV] Think over what I said about subdividing the place. You decide to do it, let me know, and I'll take care of everything. I'll get you a loan of fifty thousand. Think it over now, seriously.

VÁRYA [*angry*] Will you please just go?

LOPÁKHIN I'm going, I'm going.

[*Leaves.*]

GÁYEV What a bore. Oh, excuse me, *pardon*,[8] I forgot—that's Várya's boyfriend. He's going to marry our Várya.

VÁRYA Uncle, will you please not talk nonsense?

LIUBÓV ANDRÉYEVNA Oh, but Várya, that's wonderful! He's a fine man!

PÍSHCHIK One of the finest, in fact . . . the very, very finest . . . My Dáshenka always says . . . she says . . . she says a lot of things. [*Snores, but immediately wakes up.*] Dear lady, yes, always respected you, hmm. . . . You think you could lend me, say, two hundred and forty rubles? Mortgage payment, you know, due tomorrow . . .

VÁRYA [*terrified*] We can't; we don't have any!

LIUBÓV ANDRÉYEVNA I'm afraid that's the truth. We haven't any money.

PÍSHCHIK I'll get it somewhere. [*Laughs.*] I never give up hope. There was that time I thought I was finished, it was all over, and all of a sudden—boom!

8. Gáyev's interjection of the French word *pardon* (excuse me) is typical of the upper classes, who in pre-Soviet Russia spoke French as a second language.

The railroad cut across some of my land and paid me for it. You'll see, something will turn up tomorrow or the next day. Dáshenka will win two hundred thousand in the lottery; she just bought a ticket.

LIUBÓV ANDRÉYEVNA Well, the coffee's gone. We might as well go to bed.

FIRS [*takes out a clothes brush and brushes* GÁYEV'*s clothes; scolds him*] You've got on the wrong trousers again. What am I supposed to do with you?

VÁRYA [*softly*] Ánya's asleep. [*Quietly opens the window.*] The sun's coming up; it's not as cold as it was. Look, Mama, what wonderful trees! Smell the perfume! Oh, Lord! And the orioles are singing!

GÁYEV [*opens another window*] The whole orchard is white. You remember, Liúba? That long path, stretched out like a ribbon, on and on, the way it used to shine in the moonlight? You remember? You haven't forgotten?

LIUBÓV ANDRÉYEVNA Oh, my childhood! My innocence! I slept in this room, I could look out over the orchard, when I woke up in the morning I was happy, and it all looked exactly the same as this! Nothing has changed! [*Laughs delightedly.*] White, white, all white! My whole orchard is white! Autumn was dark and drizzly, and winter was cold, but now you're young again, flowering with happiness—the angels of heaven have never abandoned you. If only I could shake off this weight I've been carrying so long. If only I could forget my past!

GÁYEV Yes, and now they're selling the orchard to pay our debts. Strange, isn't it?

LIUBÓV ANDRÉYEVNA Look! There . . . in the orchard . . . it's Mother! In her white dress! [*Laughs delightedly.*] It's Mother!

GÁYEV Where?

VÁRYA Oh, Mama, for God's sake . . .

LIUBÓV ANDRÉYEVNA It's all right; I was just imagining things. There to the right, by the path to the summerhouse, that little white tree all bent over . . . it looked just like a woman.

[*Enter* TROFÍMOV. *He is dressed like a student and wears wire-rimmed glasses.*]

What a glorious orchard! All those white blossoms, and the blue sky—

TROFÍMOV Liubóv Andréyevna!

[*She turns to look at him.*]

I don't mean to disturb you; I just wanted to say hello. [*Shakes her hand warmly.*] They told me to wait until later, but I couldn't. . . .

[LIUBÓV *stares at him, bewildered.*]

VÁRYA It's Pétya Trofímov. . . .

TROFÍMOV Pétya Trofímov—I was your little boy Grísha's tutor. . . . Have I really changed all that much?

[LIUBÓV *embraces him and begins to weep softly.*]

GÁYEV [*embarrassed*] Liúba, that'll do, that'll do. . . .

VÁRYA [*weeps*] Oh, Pétya, I told you to wait till tomorrow.

LIUBÓV ANDRÉYEVNA Grísha . . . my little boy. Grísha . . . my son . . .

VÁRYA Oh, Mama, don't; it was God's will.

TROFÍMOV [*gently, almost in tears*] There, there . . .

LIUBÓV ANDRÉYEVNA [*weeps softly*] My little boy drowned, lost forever . . . Why? What for? My dear boy, why? [*Quiets down.*] Ánya's asleep, and here I am carrying on like this. . . . Pétya, what's happened to you? You used to be such a nice-looking boy. What happened? You look dreadful. You've gotten so old!

TROFÍMOV Some lady on the train called me a high-class tramp.

LIUBÓV ANDRÉYEVNA You were only a boy then, just out of high school, you were adorable, and now you've got glasses and you're losing your hair. And haven't you graduated yet? [*Goes to the door.*]

TROFÍMOV I suppose I'm what you'd call a permanent graduate student.

LIUBÓV ANDRÉYEVNA [*kisses* GÁYEV, *then* VÁRYA] Time for bed. You've gotten old too, Leoníd.

PÍSHCHIK [*follows* LIUBÓV] Time for bed, time to go . . . Ooh, my gout! I'd better stay the night. Now, dear, look, look . . . Liubóv Andréyevna, tomorrow morning I need . . . two hundred and forty rubles. . . .

GÁYEV He never gives up, does he?

PÍSHCHIK Two hundred and forty rubles; my mortgage payment due. . . .

LIUBÓV ANDRÉYEVNA Darling, I simply have no money.

PÍSHCHIK But, dear, I'll give it right back. . . . It's such a *trivial* amount. . . .

LIUBÓV ANDRÉYEVNA Oh, all right. Leoníd will get it for you. Leoníd, you give him the money.

GÁYEV I should give him money? That'll be the day.

LIUBÓV ANDRÉYEVNA We have to give it to him; he needs it. He'll give it back.

[*Exit* LIUBÓV, TROFÍMOV, PÍSHCHIK, *and* FIRS. GÁYEV, VÁRYA, *and* YÁSHA *remain.*]

GÁYEV She still thinks money grows on trees. [*To* YÁSHA] My good man, will you leave us, please? Go back to the barn, where you belong.

YÁSHA [*smiles*] Leoníd Andréyich, you're the same as you always were.

GÁYEV What say? [*To* VÁRYA] What did he just say?

VÁRYA [*to* YÁSHA] Your mother came in from the country to see you. She's been sitting in the kitchen for two days now, waiting.

YÁSHA Oh, for God's sake, can't she leave me alone?

VÁRYA You are really disgraceful!

YÁSHA That's all I need right now. Why couldn't she wait till tomorrow?

[*Goes out.*]

VÁRYA Mama hasn't changed; she's the same as she always was. If it were up to her, she'd give away everything.

GÁYEV Yes. . . . [*Pause*] Someone gets sick, you know, and the doctor tries one thing after another, that means there's no cure. I've been thinking and thinking, racking my brains, I come up with one thing, then another, but the truth is, none of them will work. It would be wonderful if somebody left us a lot of money, it would be wonderful if we could marry off Ánya to somebody with a lot of money, it would be wonderful if we could go see Ánya's godmother in Yároslavl,[9] try to borrow the money from her. She's very, very rich.

VÁRYA [*weeps*] If only God would help us!

GÁYEV Oh, stop crying. She's very, very rich, but she doesn't like us. Because in the first place, my sister married a mere lawyer instead of a man with a title. . . .

[ÁNYA *appears in the doorway.*]

9. A city on the Volga River, about 160 miles northeast of Moscow.

She married a lawyer, and then her behavior has not been—how shall I put it?—particularly exemplary. She's a lovely woman, goodhearted, charming, and of course she's my sister and I love her very much, and there are extenuating circumstances and such, but the fact is, she's what you'd have to call a . . . a loose woman. And she doesn't care who knows it; you can feel it in every move she makes.

VÁRYA [*whispers*] Ánya's here.

GÁYEV What say? [*Pause*] Funny, I must have gotten something in my eye: I can't see too well. . . . Did I tell you what happened Thursday, when I was at the county courthouse?

[ÁNYA *comes into the room.*]

VÁRYA Why aren't you asleep?

ÁNYA I tried. I couldn't sleep.

GÁYEV Kitten . . . [*Kisses* ÁNYA's *cheek, then her hands.*] My dear child . . . [*Almost in tears*] You're more than just my niece, you're my angel, you know that? You're my whole world, believe me, believe me. . . .

ÁNYA I believe you, Uncle. And I love you; we all love you. . . . But, Uncle dear, you should learn not to talk so much. The things you were saying just now about Mama, about your own sister . . . What were you saying all that for?

GÁYEV I know, I know. . . . [*Covers his face with her hand.*] It's awful, I know. My God, a few minutes ago I made a speech to a piece of furniture. . . . It was so stupid! The thing is, I never realize how stupid I sound until I'm done.

VÁRYA She's right, Uncle. You just have to learn to keep still, that's all.

ÁNYA If you do, you'll feel much better about yourself, you know you will. . . .

GÁYEV I will, I will, I promise. [*Kisses* ÁNYA's *and* VÁRYA's *hands.*] I'll keep still. Only right now I have to talk a little more. Business! On Thursday I was at the county courthouse; there was a group of us talking—just this and that—and it turns out I might be able to arrange a promissory note for enough money to pay off the mortgage.

VÁRYA If only God would help us!

GÁYEV I'm going in on Tuesday, I'll talk to them again. [*To* VÁRYA] Don't whine! [*To* ÁNYA] Your mother will talk to Lopákhin; he can't refuse to help her. And you, as soon as you're rested, you go to Yároslavl, go talk to your godmother. There. We'll be operating on three fronts at once; we're sure to succeed. We *will* pay off this mortgage, I know we will. . . . [*He pops a hard candy into his mouth.*] I swear by my honor, I swear by anything you want, the estate will not be sold! [*Excitedly*] I swear by my own happiness! Here, you have my hand on it. You may call me . . . dishonorable, call me anything you will, if I ever let this estate go on the auction block! I swear by my entire existence!

ÁNYA [*her calm mood has returned; she is happy*] You're so smart, Uncle! You're such a wonderful man! [*Hugs* GÁYEV.] Now I feel better! So much better! I'm happy again!

[*Enter* FIRS.]

FIRS [*reproachfully*] Leoníd Andréyich, why aren't you in bed, like decent God-fearing people?

GÁYEV I'm coming, I'm coming. You go to bed, Firs. I can get undressed by myself. All right, children, nighty-night. We can talk about the details tomorrow, now it's time for bed. [*Kisses* ÁNYA *and* VÁRYA.] I am a man of the eighties, you know. People don't think much of that era now, but I can tell you frankly that I have had the courage of my convictions and often had to pay the price.[1] But these local peasants all love me. You have to get to know them, that's all. You have to get to know them, and—

ÁNYA Uncle. You're at it again.

VÁRYA Just be quiet, Uncle.

FIRS [*angrily*] Leoníd Andréyich!

GÁYEV I'm coming, I'm coming. . . . Go to bed now. Yellow ball in the side pocket! Clean shot!

[*Goes out;* FIRS *follows him, limping.*]

ÁNYA I feel much better. I don't much want to go to Yároslavl, I don't like my godmother, but I feel better now. Thanks to Uncle [*Sits down.*]

VÁRYA We've got to get some sleep. I'm going to bed. Oh, there's something came up since you left. You know we've got all those old retired servants living out back—Paulina, old Karp, and the rest of them. And what happened, they started inviting people in to spend the night. Well, it's annoying, but I never said a thing. Then what happened was, they started telling everybody all they were getting to eat was beans. Because I was so cheap, you see. It was that old Karp was doing it. So I said to myself, All right, that's the way you want it, all right, just wait, and I sent for him [*Yawns*], and in he comes, so I say, Karp, you're such an idiot—[*Looks at* ÁNYA.] Ánya!

[*Pause.*]

She's asleep. [*Lifts* ÁNYA *by the arms.*] Come on, time for bed. . . . Come on, let's go. . . . [*Leads her off.*] My angel fell asleep! Come on. . . . [*They start out.*]

[*In the distance, beyond the orchard, a shepherd plays a pipe.* TROFÍMOV *enters, sees* ÁNYA *and* VÁRYA, *stops.*]

VÁRYA Shh! She's asleep. . . . Come on, darling, let's go. . . .

ÁNYA [*softly, half asleep*] I was so tired. . . . All those bells . . . Uncle dear . . . and Mama. Uncle and Mama.

VÁRYA Come on, darling, come on. . . .

[*They go off into* ÁNYA*'s room.*]

TROFÍMOV [*deeply moved*] My sunshine! My springtime!

Curtain.

Act 2

[*An open space. The overgrown ruin of an abandoned chapel. There is a well beside it and some large stones that must once have been grave markers. An old bench. Beyond, the road to the Gáyev estate. On one side a shadowy row of poplar trees; they mark the limits of the cherry orchard. A row of telegraph poles, and on the far distant horizon, on a clear day, you can just make out the city. It's late afternoon, almost sunset.* CARLOTTA, YÁSHA, *and* DUNYÁSHA *are sitting on the bench;* YEPIKHÓDOV *stands nearby, strumming his guitar; each seems lost in his own thoughts.* CARLOTTA *wears an old military cap and is adjusting the strap on a hunting rifle.*]

1. When Alexander III (1845–1894) became czar in 1881, he initiated a series of repressive measures designed to combat liberal and revolutionary elements in Russian society.

CARLOTTA [*meditatively*] I haven't got a birth certificate, so I don't know how old I really am. I just think of myself as young. When I was a little girl, Mama and my father used to travel around to fairs and put on shows, good ones. I did back flips, things like that. And after they died this German woman brought me up, taught me a few things. And that was it. Then I grew up and had to go to work. As a governess. Where I'm from . . . who I am . . . no idea. Who my parents were—maybe they weren't even married—no idea. [*Takes a large cucumber pickle out of her pocket and takes a bite.*] No idea at all.

[*Pause.*]

And I feel like talking all the time, but there's no one to talk to. No one.

YEPIKHÓDOV [*plays the guitar and sings*]

"What do I care for the rest of the world,
or care what it cares for me . . ."[2]

Very agreeable, playing a mandolin.

DUNYÁSHA That's not a mandolin, it's a guitar. [*Takes out a compact with a mirror and powders herself.*]

YEPIKHÓDOV When a man is madly in love, a guitar is a mandolin. [*Sings.*]

"As long as my heart is on fire with love,
and the one I love loves me."

[YÁSHA *sings harmony.*]

CARLOTTA Oof! You people sound like hyenas.

DUNYÁSHA But it must have been just lovely, being in Europe.

YÁSHA Oh, it was. Quite, quite lovely. I have to agree with you there. [*Yawns, then lights a cigar.*]

YEPIKHÓDOV That's understandable. In Europe, things have already come to a complex.

YÁSHA [*beat*] I suppose you could say that.

YEPIKHÓDOV I'm a true product of the educational system; I read all the time. All the right books too, but I have no chosen directive in life. For me, strictly speaking, it's live or shoot myself. That's why I always carry a loaded pistol. See? [*Takes out a revolver.*]

CARLOTTA All done. Time to go. [*Slings the rifle over her shoulder.*] You're a very smart man, Yepikhódov, and a very scary one. Ooh! The women must adore you. [*Starts off.*] They're all so dumb, these smart boys. Never anyone to talk to . . . Always alone, all by myself, no one to talk to . . . and I still don't know who I am. Or why. No idea.

[*Walks slowly off.*]

YEPIKHÓDOV I should explain, by the way, for the sake of expressivity, that fate has been, ah, *rigorous* to me. I am, strictly speaking, tempest-tossed. Always have been. Now, you may say to me, Oh, you're imagining things, but then why, when I wake up this morning—here's an example—and I look down, why is there this spider on my stomach? Detrimentally large too. [*Makes a circle with his two hands.*] Big as that. Or take a beer, let's say.

2. Words from a popular turn-of-the-century ballad.

I go to drink it, what do I see floating around in it? Something highly unappreciative, like a cockroach.

[*Pause.*]

Have you ever read Henry Thomas Buckle?[3]

[*Pause.*]

May I design to disturb you, Avdótya Fyódorovna, with something I have to say?

DUNYÁSHA So say it.

YEPIKHÓDOV Preferentially alone. [*Sighs.*]

DUNYÁSHA [*embarrassed*] All right. . . . Only first get me my wrap; it's by the kitchen door. It's getting kind of damp.

YEPIKHÓDOV Ah, I see. Yes, get the wrap, of course. Now I know what to do with my gun.

[*Takes his guitar and goes off, strumming.*]

YÁSHA Double Trouble. He's an idiot, if you ask me. [*Yawns.*]

DUNYÁSHA I hope to God he doesn't shoot himself.

[*Pause.*]

I get upset over every little thing anymore. Ever since I started working for them here, I've gotten used to their *lifestyle.* Just look at my hands. Look at how white they are, just like I was rich. I'm different now from like I was. I'm more delicate, I'm more sensitive; everything upsets me. . . . It's just awful how things upset me. So if you cheat on me, Yásha, I may just have a nervous breakdown.

YÁSHA [*kisses her*] Oh, you little cutie! Just remember, though: a girl has to watch her step. What I'm after is a *nice* girl.

DUNYÁSHA I really love you, Yásha, I really do. You're so smart, you know so many things. . . .

[*Pause.*]

YÁSHA [*yawns*] Yeah. . . . But my theory is, a girl says she loves you, she's not a nice girl.

[*Pause.*]

Nothing like smoking a cigar out here in the fresh air. . . . [*Listens.*] Somebody's coming. . . . It's them. . . .

[DUNYÁSHA *hugs him impulsively.*]

YÁSHA Go on back to the house. Go back the other way, make believe you've been swimming down by the river, so they don't think we've been . . . we've been getting together out here like this. I don't want them to think that.

DUNYÁSHA [*a little cough*] That cigar smoke is giving me a headache. . . .

[*Goes out.*]

[YÁSHA *sits beside the chapel wall. Enter* LIUBÓV, GÁYEV, *and* LOPÁKHIN.]

LOPÁKHIN You have to make up your mind one way or the other; time's running out. There's no argument left. You want to subdivide or don't you? Just give me an answer, one word, yes or no.

3. English historian (1821–1862), author of *History of Civilization in England* (1857–61), an unfinished attempt to present history as an exact science.

LIUBÓV ANDRÉYEVNA Who's been smoking those cheap cigars? [*Sits down.*]

GÁYEV Everything's so convenient, now that there's the railroad. We went into town just to have lunch. Yellow ball in the side pocket! What do you say—why don't we go back to the house, eh? Have ourselves a little game . . .

LIUBÓV ANDRÉYEVNA Let's wait till later.

LOPÁKHIN Just one word! [*Imploringly*] Why don't you give me an answer?

GÁYEV [*yawns*] To what?

LIUBÓV ANDRÉYEVNA [*rummages in her purse*] Yesterday I had a lot of money, today it's all gone. My poor Várya feeds us all on soup to economize, the poor old people get nothing but beans, and I just spend and spend. . . . [*Drops her purse; gold coins spill out.*] Oh, I've spilled everything. . . .

YÁSHA Here, allow me. [*Picks up the money.*]

LIUBÓV ANDRÉYEVNA Oh, please do, Yasha; thank you. And why I had to go into that town for lunch—that stupid restaurant of yours, those stupid musicians, those stupid tablecloths; they smelled of soap. . . . Why do we drink so much, Lyónya? And eat so much? Why do we talk so much? The whole time we were in the restaurant, you kept talking, and none of it made any sense. Talking about the seventies, about Symbolism.[4] And to who? The waiters! Talking about Symbolism to waiters!

LOPÁKHIN Yes.

GÁYEV [*makes a deprecating gesture*] I'm incorrigible, I suppose. . . . [*To* YÁSHA, *irritably*] What are *you* doing here? Why are you always underfoot every time I turn around?

YÁSHA [*laughs*] Because every time I hear your voice it makes me laugh.

GÁYEV Either he goes or I do!

LIUBÓV ANDRÉYEVNA Yásha, please . . . just go 'way, will you?

YÁSHA [*gives* LIUBÓV *her purse*] I'm going. Right now. [*Barely containing his laughter*] Right this very minute . . .

[*Goes out.*]

LOPÁKHIN You know who Derigánov is? You know how much money he has? You know he's planning to buy your property? They say he's coming to the auction himself.

LIUBÓV ANDRÉYEVNA Who told you that?

LOPÁKHIN Everybody in town knows about it.

GÁYEV The old lady in Yároslavl promised to send money. . . . But when, and how much, she didn't say.

LOPÁKHIN How much will she send? A hundred thousand? Two hundred?

LIUBÓV ANDRÉYEVNA Ten or fifteen thousand. And we're lucky to get that much.

LOPÁKHIN Excuse me, but you people . . . I have never met anyone so unbusinesslike, so impractical, so . . . so *crazy* as the pair of you! Somebody tells you flat out your land is about to be sold, you don't even seem to understand!

LIUBÓV ANDRÉYEVNA But what should we do? Just tell us what we should do!

4. A movement in literature and art that began in France in the last third of the 19th century; it emphasized the evocation of subjective emotion, via symbol and metaphor, rather than objective description, and it had its greatest influence in Russia in the 1880s. *The seventies:* a time of widespread populist agitation among Russia's peasant population.

LOPÁKHIN I tell you every day what you should do! Every day I come out here and say the same thing. The cherry orchard and the rest of the land has to be subdivided and developed for leisure homes, and it has to be done right away. The auction date is getting closer! Can't you understand? All you have to do is make up your mind to subdivide, you'll have more money than even you can spend! Your troubles will be over!

LIUBÓV ANDRÉYEVNA Subdivide, leisure homes . . . excuse me, but it's all so hopelessly vulgar.

GÁYEV I couldn't agree more.

LOPÁKHIN You people drive me crazy! Another minute, I'll be shouting my head off! Oh, I give up, I give up! Why do I even bother? [*To* GÁYEV] You're worse than an old lady!

GÁYEV What say?

LOPÁKHIN I said you're an old lady! [*Starts to leave.*]

LIUBÓV ANDRÉYEVNA [*fearfully*] No, no, no, please, my dear, don't go. Please. I'm sure we'll think of something.

LOPÁKHIN What's there to think of?

LIUBÓV ANDRÉYEVNA Please. Don't go. Things are easier when you're around. . . .

[*Pause.*]

I keep waiting for something to happen. It's as if the house were about to fall down around our ears or something. . . .

GÁYEV [*meditatively*] Yellow ball in the side pocket . . . Clean shot down the middle . . .

LIUBÓV ANDRÉYEVNA We're guilty of so many sins, I know—

LOPÁKHIN Sins? What are you talking about?

GÁYEV [*pops a hard candy into his mouth*] People say I've eaten up my entire inheritance in candy. [*Laughs.*]

LIUBÓV ANDRÉYEVNA All my sins . . . I've always wasted money, just thrown it away like a madwoman, and I married a man who never paid a bill in his life. He was an alcoholic; he drank himself to death—on champagne. And I was so unhappy I fell in love with another man, *unfortunately,* and had an affair with him, and that was when—that was the first thing, my first punishment, right down there, in the river, my little boy drowned, and I left, I went to France, I left and never wanted to come back, I never wanted to see that river again, I just closed my eyes and *ran,* forgot about everything, and that man followed me. He just wouldn't let up. And he was so mean to me, so cruel! I bought a villa in Mentón because he got sick while we were there, and for the next three years I never had a moment's peace, day or night. He tormented me from his sickbed. I could feel my soul dry up. And last year I couldn't afford the villa anymore, so I sold it and we moved to Paris, and once we were in Paris he took everything I had left and ran off with another woman, and I tried to kill myself. It was so stupid, and so shameful! Finally all I wanted was to come back home, to where I was born, to my daughter. [*Wipes away her tears.*] Oh, dear God, dear God, forgive me! Forgive me my sins! Don't punish me again! [*Takes a telegram from her purse.*] This came today, from Paris. . . . He says he's sorry, he wants me back. . . . [*Tears up the telegram.*] Where's [*Listens.*] . . . where's that music coming from?

GÁYEV That's our famous local orchestra. Those Jewish musicians, you remember? Four fiddles, a clarinet, and a double bass.

LIUBÓV ANDRÉYEVNA Are they still around? We should have them over some evening and throw a party.

LOPÁKHIN [*listens*] I don't hear anything. [*Sings to himself.*]

"Ooh-la-la . . .
Just a little bit of money
makes a lady very French . . ."

[*Laughs.*] I went to the theater last night, saw this musical. Very funny.

LIUBÓV ANDRÉYEVNA I doubt there was anything funny about it. You ought to stop going to see playacting and take a good look at your own reality. What a boring life you lead! And what uninteresting things you talk about.

LOPÁKHIN Well . . . yeah, there's some truth to that. It is a pretty dumb life we lead. . . .

[*Pause.*]

My father was a . . . he was a dirt farmer, an idiot, never understood me, never taught me anything, just got drunk and beat me up. With a stick. Fact is, I'm not much better myself. Never did well in school, my writing's terrible, I'm ashamed if anybody sees it. I write like a pig.

LIUBÓV ANDRÉYEVNA My dear man, you should get married.

LOPÁKHIN Yes. . . . Yes, I should.

LIUBÓV ANDRÉYEVNA And you should marry our Várya. She's a wonderful girl.

LOPÁKHIN She is.

LIUBÓV ANDRÉYEVNA Her people were quite ordinary, but she works like a dog, and the main thing is, she loves you. And you like her, I know you do. You always have.

LOPÁKHIN Look, I've got nothing against it. I . . . She's a wonderful girl.

[*Pause.*]

GÁYEV They offered me a position at the bank. Six thousand a year. Did I tell you?

LIUBÓV ANDRÉYEVNA Don't be silly! You stay right here where you belong.

[*Enter* FIRS, *carrying an overcoat.*]

FIRS Sir, sir, please put this on. It's getting damp.

GÁYEV [*puts it on*] Firs, you're getting to be a bore.

FIRS That so? Went out this morning, didn't even tell me. [*Tries to adjust* GÁYEV'S *clothes.*]

LIUBÓV ANDRÉYEVNA Poor Firs! You've gotten so old!

FIRS Beg pardon?

LOPÁKHIN She said you got very old!

FIRS I've lived a long time. They were trying to marry me off way back before your daddy was born. [*Laughs.*] By the time we got our freedom back,[5] I was already head butler. I had all the freedom I needed, so I stayed right here with the masters.

[*Pause.*]

I remember everybody got all excited about it, but they never even knew what they were getting excited about.

5 That is, 1861, when the serfs—feudal agricultural workers bound to their lord's land, who made up one-third of Russia's total population—were freed by Alexander II's Edict of Emancipation.

LOPÁKHIN Oh, sure, things were wonderful back in the good old days! They had the right to beat you if they wanted, remember?

FIRS [*doesn't hear*] That's right. Masters stood by the servants, servants stood by the masters. Nowadays it's all mixed up; you can't tell who's who.

GÁYEV Shut up, Firs. . . . I have to go into town tomorrow. A friend promised to introduce me to someone who might be able to arrange a loan. Some general.

LOPÁKHIN That's never going to work. Trust me, you won't get enough even for the interest payments.

LIUBÓV ANDRÉYEVNA He's imagining things. There's no general.

[*Enter* ÁNYA, VÁRYA, *and* TROFÍMOV.]

GÁYEV Here come our young people.

ÁNYA Mama's resting.

LIUBÓV ANDRÉYEVNA [*tenderly*] Here we are, dears, over here. [*Kisses* ÁNYA *and Várya.*] If you only knew how much I love you both. Come sit here by me . . . that's right.

[*They all sit down.*]

LOPÁKHIN Our permanent graduate student seems to spend all his time studying the ladies.

TROFÍMOV Mind your own business.

LOPÁKHIN Almost in his fifties, he's still in school.

TROFÍMOV Just stop the silly jokes, will you?

LOPÁKHIN Oh, the *scholar* is losing his temper!

TROFÍMOV Will you please just leave me alone?

LOPÁKHIN [*laughs*] Let me ask you a question: You look at me, what do you see?

TROFÍMOV When I look at you, Yermolái Alexéyich, what I see is a rich man. One who will soon be a millionaire. You are as necessary a part of the evolution of the species as the wild animal that eats up anything in its path.

[*Everybody laughs.*]

VÁRYA Forget biology, Pétya. You should stick to counting stars.

LIUBÓV ANDRÉYEVNA I want to hear more about what we were talking about last night.

TROFÍMOV What were we talking about?

GÁYEV About human dignity.

TROFÍMOV We talked about a lot last night, but we never got anywhere. You people talk about human dignity as if it were something mystical. I suppose it is, in a way, for you anyway, but when you really get down to it, what have humans got to be proud of? Biologically we're pretty minor specimens—besides which, the great majority of human beings are vulgar and unhappy and totally *un*dignified. We should stop patting ourselves on the back and get to work.

GÁYEV You still have to die.

TROFÍMOV Who says? Anyway, what does that mean, to die? Maybe we have a hundred senses, and all we lose when we die are the five we're familiar with, and the other ninety-five go on living.

LIUBÓV ANDRÉYEVNA Oh, Pétya, you're so smart!

LOPÁKHIN [*with irony*] Oh, yes, very.

TROFÍMOV Remember, human beings are constantly progressing, and their power keeps growing. Things that seem impossible to us nowadays, the day will come when they're not a problem at all, only we have to work toward that day. We have to seek out the truth. We don't do that, you know. Most of the people in this country aren't working toward anything. People I come in contact with—at the university, for instance—they're supposed to be educated, but they're not interested in the truth. They're not interested in much of anything, actually. They certainly don't *do* much. They call themselves intellectuals and think that gives them the right to look down on the rest of the world. They never read anything worthwhile, they're completely ignorant where science is concerned, they talk about art and they don't even know what it is they're talking about. They take themselves so seriously, they're full of theories and ideas, but just go look at the cities they live in. Miles and miles of slums, where people go hungry and where they live packed into unheated tenements full of cockroaches and garbage, and their lives are full of violence and immorality. So what are all the theories for? To keep people like us from seeing all that. Where are the day-care centers they talk so much about, and the literacy programs? It's all just talk. You go out to the parts of town where the poor people live, you can't find them. All you find is dirt and ignorance and crime. That's why I don't like all this talk, all these theories. Bothers me, makes me afraid. If that's all our talk is good for, we'd better just shut up.

LOPÁKHIN I get up at five and work from morning to night, and you know, my business involves a lot of money, my own and other people's, so I see lots of people, see what they're like. And you just try to get anything accomplished: you'll see how few decent, honest people there really are. Sometimes at night I can't sleep, and I think: Dear God, you gave us this beautiful earth to live on, these great forests, these wide fields, the broad horizons . . . by rights we should be giants.

LIUBÓV ANDRÉYEVNA What do you want giants for? The only good giants are in fairy tales. Real ones would scare you to death.

[*Upstage,* YEPIKHÓDOV *strolls by, playing his guitar.*]

[*Dreamily*] There goes Yepikhódov. . . .

ÁNYA [*dreamily*] There goes Yepikhódov. . . .

GÁYEV The sun, ladies and gentlemen, has just set.

TROFÍMOV Yes.

GÁYEV [*as if reciting a poem, but not too loud*] O wondrous nature, cast upon us your eternal rays, forever beautiful, forever indifferent. . . . Mother, we call you; life and death reside within you; you bring forth and lay waste—

VÁRYA [*pleading*] Uncle, please!

ÁNYA Uncle, you're doing it again.

TROFÍMOV We'd rather have the yellow ball in the side pocket.

GÁYEV Sorry, sorry. I'll keep still.

[*They all sit in silence. The only sound we hear is old* FIRS *mumbling. Suddenly a distant sound seems to fall from the sky, a sad sound, like a harp string breaking. It dies away.*]

LIUBÓV ANDRÉYEVNA What was that?

LOPÁKHIN Can't tell. Sounds like it could be an echo from a mine shaft. But it must be far away.

GÁYEV Or some kind of bird . . . like a heron.

TROFÍMOV Or an owl.

LIUBÓV ANDRÉYEVNA [*shivers*] Makes me nervous.

[*Pause.*]

FIRS It's like just before the trouble started. They heard an owl screech, and the kettle wouldn't stop whistling. . . .

GÁYEV Before what trouble?

FIRS The day we got our freedom back.

[*Pause.*]

LIUBÓV ANDRÉYEVNA My dears, it's getting dark; we should be going in. [*To* ÁNYA] You've got tears in your eyes, darling. What's the matter? [*Hugs* ÁNYA.]

ÁNYA Nothing, Mama. It's all right.

TROFÍMOV Someone's coming.

[*Enter a* HOMELESS MAN *in a white cap and an overcoat; he's slightly drunk.*]

HOMELESS MAN Can anyone please tell me, can I get to the train station this way?

GÁYEV Of course you can. Just follow this road.

HOMELESS MAN Much obliged. [*Bows.*] Wonderful weather we're having . . . [*Recites.*] "Behold one of the poor in spirit, just trying to inherit a little of the earth. . . ."[6] [*To* VÁRYA] Listen, you think you could spare some money for a hungry man?

[VÁRYA *is terrified; she screams.*]

LOPÁKHIN [*angrily*] Now hold on just a minute!

LIUBÓV ANDRÉYEVNA [*panicked*] Here . . . here . . . take this. [*Fumbles in her purse.*] Oh, I don't seem to have anything smaller. Here, take this. [*Gives him a gold piece.*]

HOMELESS MAN Very much obliged!

[*Goes out.*]

[*Everybody laughs.*]

VÁRYA Get me out of here! Oh, please get me out! Mama, how could you! We can't even feed the servants, and you go and give him a gold piece!

LIUBÓV ANDRÉYEVNA I know, darling, I'm just stupid about money. When we get home I'll give you whatever I've got left; you can take care of it. Yermolái Alexéyich, can you lend me some money?

LOPÁKHIN Of course.

LIUBÓV ANDRÉYEVNA My darlings, it really is time to go in. Várya dear, we've just gotten you engaged. Congratulations.

VÁRYA [*almost in tears*] Mama, that's nothing to joke about!

LOPÁKHIN Amelia, get thee to a nunnery![7]

GÁYEV Look how my hands shake. I don't know if I could play billiards anymore. . . .

6. An allusion to two of the beatitudes from Jesus' Sermon on the Mount: "Blessed are the poor in spirit, for theirs is the kingdom of heaven. . . . Blessed are the meek, for they shall inherit the earth" (Matthew 5.3, 5).

7. Hamlet's charge to Ophelia in Shakespeare's *Hamlet* (1600–01; 3.1.122). Lopákhin's next line also quotes Hamlet though he substitutes "horizons" for "orisons" 3.1.91–92).

LOPÁKHIN Nymph, in thy horizons be all my sins remembered!

LIUBÓV ANDRÉYEVNA Please, let's go. It's almost suppertime.

VÁRYA He scared me half to death. I can feel my heart pounding.

LOPÁKHIN But keep in mind, the cherry orchard is going to be sold. On August twenty-second! You hear what I'm saying? You've got to think about this! You've got to!

[*They all go off except* ÁNYA *and* TROFÍMOV.]

ÁNYA [*laughs*] I'm so glad that tramp scared Várya off. Now we can be alone.

TROFÍMOV Várya's afraid we're going to fall in love; that's why she never leaves us alone. She's so narrow-minded; she simply can't understand that we are above love. Our goal is to get rid of the silly illusions that keep us from being free and happy. We are moving forward, toward the future! Toward one bright star that burns ahead of us! Forward, friends! Come join us in our journey!

ÁNYA [*claps her hands*] Oh, you talk so beautifully!

[*Pause.*]

It's just heavenly out here today!

TROFÍMOV Yes, the weather's been really good lately.

ÁNYA I don't know what it is you've done to me, Pétya, but I don't love the cherry orchard anymore, not the way I used to. I used to think there was no place on earth like our orchard.

TROFÍMOV This whole country is our orchard. It's a big country and a beautiful one; it has lots of wonderful places in it.

[*Pause.*]

Just think, Ánya: your grandfather, and his father, and his father's fathers, they *owned* the people who slaved away for them all over this estate, and now the voices and faces of human beings hide behind every cherry in the orchard, every leaf, every tree trunk. Can't you see them? And hear them? And owning human beings has left its mark on all of you. Look at your mother and your uncle! They live off the labor of others, they always have, and they've never even noticed! They owe their entire lives to those other people, people they wouldn't even let walk through the front gate of their beloved cherry orchard! This whole country has fallen behind; it'll take us at least two hundred years to catch up. The thing is, we don't have any real sense of our own history; all we do is sit around and talk, talk, talk, then we feel depressed, so we go out and get drunk. If there's one thing that's clear to me, it's this: if we want to have any real life in the present, we have to do something to make up for our past, we have to get over it, and the only way to do that is to make sacrifices, get down to work, and work harder than we've ever worked before. Do you understand what I mean, Ánya?

ÁNYA The house we live in isn't our house anymore. It hasn't ever been, really. And I'll leave it all behind, I promise you I will.

TROFÍMOV Yes, you will! Throw away your house keys and go as far away as you can! You'll be free as the wind.

ÁNYA [*radiant*] I love the way you say things!

TROFÍMOV You have to understand me, Ánya. I'm not thirty yet, I'm still young; I may still be in school, but I've learned a lot. Winter comes, sometimes I get cold and hungry, or sick and upset, I don't have a cent to my name; things work out or they don't. . . . But no matter what, my heart and soul are always full of feelings, all kinds . . . I can't even explain them. And I feel happiness coming, Ánya, I can feel it, I can almost see it—

ÁNYA [*dreamily*] Look, the moon's rising.

[*The sound of* YEPIKHÓDOV'*s guitar, still playing the same mournful song. The moon rises. Somewhere beyond the poplar trees,* VÁRYA *can be heard calling.*]

VÁRYA [*off*] Anya! Ánya, where are you?

TROFÍMOV Yes, the moon is rising.

[*Pause.*]

It's happiness, that's what it is: it's rising, it's coming closer and closer, I can hear it. And even if we miss it, if we never find it, that's all right! Someone will!

VÁRYA [*off*] Ánya! Ánya, where are you?

TROFÍMOV [*angrily*] That Várya! Why won't she let us alone!

ÁNYA Don't let her bother you. Let's take a walk by the river. It's so nice there.

TROFÍMOV All right, let's go.

[*They leave. The stage is empty.*]

VÁRYA [*off*] Ánya! Ánya!

Curtain.

Act 3

[*A sitting room, separated from the ballroom in back by an archway. The chandeliers are lit. From the entrance hall comes the sounds of an orchestra, the Jewish musicians* GÁYEV *mentioned in Act 2. Evening. In the ballroom, everyone is dancing a grande ronde.* SEMYÓNOV-PÍSHCHIK'*s voice is heard calling the figures of the dance: "Promenade à une paire!"*[8] *The dancers dance through the sitting room in pairs in the following order:* PÍSHCHIK *and* CARLOTTA, TROFÍMOV *and* LIUBÓV ANDREYÉVNA, ÁNYA *and the* POSTMASTER, VÁRYA *and the* STATIONMASTER, *etc.* VÁRYA *is in tears, which she tries to wipe away as she dances. The final pair includes* DUNYÁSHA. *As the dancers return to the ballroom,* PÍSHCHIK *calls out: "Grande ronde, balancez!" and "Les cavaliers à genoux et remercier vos dames."*[9] FIRS *in his butler's uniform crosses the stage, carrying a seltzer bottle on a tray.* PÍSHCHIK *and* TROFÍMOV *come into the sitting room.*]

PÍSHCHIK I'm prone to strokes, already had two of 'em, I really shouldn't be dancing, but you know what they say: When in Rome. Besides, I'm really strong as a horse. Speaking of Romans, my father—what a joker he was—he used to claim our family was descended from the emperor Caligula's horse—you know, the one he made a senator?[1] [*Sits down.*] The only problem is we have no money. [*His head nods, he snores, then immediately wakes up.*] So the only thing I ever think about is money.

8. "Promenade with your partner!" (French).
9. "Large circle, swing with your arms!"; "Gentlemen, kneel down and thank your ladies" (French).
1. According to the Roman historian Suetonius, the emperor Caligula (r. 37–41 C.E.) considered making his favorite racehorse a consul; the version in popular lore is that he appointed the animal a senator.

TROFÍMOV Your father was right. You do look a little like a horse.

PÍSHCHIK Nothing wrong with horses. Wonderful animals. If I had one, I could sell it. . . .

[*From the adjacent billiard room come the sounds of a game.* VÁRYA *appears in the archway.*]

TROFÍMOV [*teases her*] Mrs. Lopákhin! Mrs. Lopákhin!

VÁRYA [*angrily*] High-class tramp!

TROFÍMOV Yes, I'm a high-class tramp, and I'm proud of it!

VÁRYA [*bitterly*] We've hired an orchestra! And what are we supposed to pay them with?

[*Goes out.*]

TROFÍMOV [*to* PÍSHCHIK] All the energy you've used trying to find money to pay your mortgage, if you'd spent that energy on something else, you could have moved the world.

PÍSHCHIK Nietzsche,[2] you know, the philosopher—a great thinker, Nietzsche, a man of genius, one of the great minds of the century—now Nietzsche, you know, says, in his memoirs, that counterfeit money's just as good as real. . . .

TROFÍMOV I didn't know you'd read Nietzsche.

PÍSHCHIK Well . . . actually, Dáshenka told me. And I'm desperate enough. I'm ready to start counterfeiting. I need three hundred and ten rubles, day after tomorrow. All I've got so far is a hundred and thirty. . . . [*He feels in his pockets anxiously.*] It's gone! My money's gone! [*Almost in tears*] I've lost my money! [*Joyfully*] Oh, here it is! It slipped down into the lining of my coat! God, I'm all in a sweat!

[*Enter* LIUBÓV *and* CARLOTTA.]

LIUBÓV ANDREYÉVNA [*she hums a dance tune*] Why is it taking so long? What's Leoníd doing all this time in town? He should be back by now. [*Calls to* DUNYÁSHA *in the ballroom.*] Dunyásha, tell the musicians they can take a break.

TROFÍMOV They probably postponed the auction.

LIUBÓV ANDREYÉVNA I suppose it was a mistake to hire an orchestra. Or to have a party in the first place. Oh, well . . . what difference does it make? [*Sits down and hums quietly.*]

CARLOTTA [*hands* PÍSHCHIK *a deck of cards*] Here's the deck. Pick a card, any card. . . . No, no, just think of one.

PÍSHCHIK All right, I'm thinking of one.

CARLOTTA Good. Now shuffle the deck. Very good. Now give it to me. Observe, my dear Píshchik! *Eins, zwei, drei!*[3] Now look in your jacket pocket, and you will find your card.

PÍSHCHIK [*takes a card from his jacket pocket*] That's it, the eight of spades! [*Amazed*] Really! I don't believe it!

CARLOTTA [*holds out the deck to* TROFÍMOV] Quick, what's the top card?

TROFÍMOV The top card? Oh . . . uh . . . the queen of spades.

CARLOTTA Correct! [*To* PÍSHCHIK] Now which card's on top?

PÍSHCHIK Ace of hearts!

2. Friedrich Nietzsche (1844–1900), German philosopher who was among the most influential of modern thinkers.

3. One, two, three! (German).

CARLOTTA Correct! [*Claps her hands, and the deck disappears.*] Well, isn't this a lovely day we're having?

[*A mysterious woman's voice answers; it seems to come from the floorboards: "A lovely day indeed. I couldn't agree more."*]

Whoever you are, I adore you!

[*The voice: "I adore you too!"*]

STATIONMASTER [*applauds*] Bravo! A lady ventriloquist!

PÍSHCHIK [*amazed*] Really! I don't believe it! Carlotta, you are amazing! I'm completely in love with you!

CARLOTTA In love? [*Shrugs her shoulders.*] What do you know about love? *Guter Mensch aber schlechter Musikant.*[4]

TROFÍMOV [*slaps* PÍSHCHIK *on the shoulder*] You're just an old horse!

CARLOTTA All right, everybody, watch closely! One more trick! [*Takes a lap robe from a chair.*] See, what a lovely blanket! I'm thinking of selling it. [*Shakes out the lap robe and holds it up.*] Who wants to buy?

PÍSHCHIK [*amazed*] Really! I don't believe it!

CARLOTTA *Eins, zwei, drei!* [*Quickly raises the lap robe.*]

[ÁNYA *appears behind the lap robe; she curtsies, runs to her mother and kisses her, then runs back into the ballroom. General applause and cries of delight.*]

LIUBÓV ANDREYÉVNA [*applauding*] Bravo! Bravo!

CARLOTTA Now one more! *Eins, zwei, drei!*

[*She raises the lap robe;* VÁRYA *appears; she takes a bow.*]

PÍSHCHIK Really! I don't believe it!

CARLOTTA That's all. The show is over.

[*Throws the lap robe to* PÍSHCHIK, *takes a bow, goes through the ballroom and out.*]

PÍSHCHIK [*goes after her*] Enchanting! What a woman! What a woman!

[*Goes out.*]

LIUBÓV ANDREYÉVNA Leoníd still isn't back from town yet. I don't understand what could be taking him so long! It's got to be all over by now: either the estate has been sold or they've postponed the auction. Why does he have to keep us in suspense like this?

VÁRYA [*tries to comfort her*] Uncle bought the estate, I'm sure he has.

TROFÍMOV [*ironically*] Oh, I'm sure.

VÁRYA Ánya's godmother sent him a power of attorney to buy the estate in her name; she agreed to take over the mortgage. She did it for Ánya. So God *has* helped us. Uncle has saved the estate.

LIUBÓV ANDREYÉVNA The old lady in Yároslavl sent us fifteen thousand to buy the place in her name—she doesn't trust us—but that's not even enough to pay the interest. [*Covers her face with her hands.*] My fate . . . my entire life . . . It's all being decided today.

TROFÍMOV [*teases* VÁRYA] Mrs. Lopákhin! Mrs. Lopákhin!

VÁRYA [*angrily*] And you're a permanent graduate student! Who's been suspended twice!

LIUBÓV ANDRÉYEVNA Don't get so angry, Várya; he's only teasing you. What's wrong with that? And what's wrong with Lopákhin? If you want to marry

4. A good man but a bad musician (German); that is, an incompetent.

him, do; he's a nice man. Interesting, even. If you don't want to marry him, don't; nobody's forcing you.

VÁRYA It's not a joking matter, Mama, believe me. I'm serious about him. He is a nice man, and I like him.

LIUBÓV ANDRÉYEVNA Then go ahead and marry him! I don't understand what you're waiting for!

VÁRYA Mama, I can't propose to him myself! For two years now everybody's been telling me to marry him, everybody, but he never mentions it. Or he jokes about it! Look, I understand, he's busy getting rich, he doesn't have time for me. Oh, if I had just a little money—I don't care how much, even a couple of hundred—I'd get out of here and go someplace far away. I'd go join a convent.

TROFÍMOV Now, there's an exalted idea!

VÁRYA [*to* TROFÍMOV] I thought students were supposed to be smart! [*Her tone softens; almost crying.*] Oh, Pétya, you used to be so nice-looking, and now you're getting old! [*To* LIUBÓV, *in a normal tone*] It's just that I need something to do all the time, Mama; it's the way I am. I can't sit around and do nothing.

[*Enter* YÁSHA.]

YÁSHA [*barely controlling his laughter*] Yepikhódov broke a billiard cue!

[*Goes out.*]

VÁRYA What is Yepikhódov doing here? Who asked him to come? And what's he doing playing billiards? I just don't understand these people. . . .

[*Goes out.*]

LIUBÓV ANDRÉYEVNA Pétya, don't tease her like that; you can see she's upset already.

TROFÍMOV Oh, she's such a busybody, always poking her nose into other people's business. She hasn't left Ánya and me alone the whole summer; she's afraid we're having a . . . an *affair.* What business is it of hers? Besides, it's not true. I'd never do anything so sordid. We're above love!

LIUBÓV ANDRÉYEVNA And I, I suppose, am beneath love. [*Upset*] Why isn't Leoníd back yet? I just want to know: has the estate been sold or not? The whole disaster seems so impossible to me, I don't know what to think, or do. . . . Oh, God, I'm losing my mind! I want to scream, or do something completely stupid . . . Help me, Pétya! Save me! Say something, say something!

TROFÍMOV Whether they sell it or not, does it make any difference really? You can't go back to the past. Everything here came to an end a long time ago. Try to calm down. You can't go on deceiving yourself; at least once in your life you have to look the truth straight in the eye.

LIUBÓV ANDRÉYEVNA What truth? You seem so sure what's truth and what isn't, but I'm not. I've lost any sense of it, I've lost sight of the truth. You're so sure of yourself, aren't you, so sure you have all the answers to everything, but darling, have you ever really had to live with one of your answers? You're too young. Of course *you* look into the future and see a brave new world, you don't expect any difficulties, but that's because you know nothing about life! Yes, you have more courage than my generation has, and better morals, and you're better educated, but for God's sake have a little sense of what it's like for me, and be easier on me. Pétya, I was born here! My parents lived here all their lives; so did my grandfather. I love this house! Without the cherry orchard my life makes no sense, and if you have to sell it, you might as well sell me with it. [*She embraces* TROFÍMOV *and kisses his forehead.*] And it was here my son drowned, you know that. . . . [*Weeps.*] Have some feeling for me, Pétya, you're such a good, sweet boy.

TROFÍMOV I pity you. [*Beat*] I do, from the bottom of my heart.

LIUBÓV ANDRÉYEVNA You should have said that differently, just a little differently. . . . [*Takes out her handkerchief; a telegram falls to the floor.*] You can't imagine how miserable I am today. All this noise, and every new sound makes me shake. I can't get away from it, but then when I'm alone in my room I can't stand the silence. Don't judge me, Pétya! I love you like one of my own family; I'd be very happy to see you and Ánya married, you know I would, only, darling, you must finish school first! You have *got* to graduate! You don't do anything except drift around from place to place—what kind of life is that? It's true, isn't it? Isn't that the truth? And we have to do something about that beard of yours; it's so scraggly. . . . [*Laughs.*] You've gotten so funny-looking!

TROFÍMOV [*picks up the telegram*] I have no desire to be good-looking.

LIUBÓV ANDRÉYEVNA The telegram's from Paris. I get a new one every day. One yesterday, now again today. That madman is sick again and in trouble. . . . He wants me to forgive him, he wants me back . . . and I suppose I should go back to Paris to be with him. Now see, Pétya, you're giving me that superior look, but darling, what am I supposed to do? He's sick, he's alone, he's unhappy, and who has he got to look after him? To give him his medicine and keep him out of trouble? And I love him—why do I have to pretend I don't, or not talk about it? I love him. That's just the way it is: I love him. I love him! He's a millstone around my neck, and he'll drown me with him, but he's *my* millstone! I love him and I can't live without him! [*Grabs* TROFÍMOV*'s hand.*] Don't judge me, Pétya, don't think badly of me, just don't say anything, please just don't say anything. . . .

TROFÍMOV [*almost in tears*] But for God's sake, you have to face the facts! He robbed you blind!

LIUBÓV ANDRÉYEVNA No, no, please, you mustn't say that, you mustn't—

TROFÍMOV He doesn't care a thing for you—you're the only person who doesn't seem to understand that! He's rotten!

LIUBÓV ANDRÉYEVNA [*gets angry but tries to control it*] And you, you're what? Twenty-six, twenty-seven? Listen to you: you sound like you'd never even graduated to long pants!

TROFÍMOV That's fine with me!

LIUBÓV ANDRÉYEVNA You're supposed to be a man; at your age you ought to know something about love. You ought to be in love yourself! [*Angrily*] Really! You think you're so smart, you're just a kid who doesn't know the first thing about it, you're probably a virgin, you're ridiculous, you're grotesque—

TROFÍMOV [*horrified*] What are you saying!

LIUBÓV ANDREYÉVNA "I'm above love!" You're not above love; you've just never gotten down to it! You're all wet, like Firs says. At your age, you ought to be sleeping with someone!

TROFÍMOV [*horrified*] What a terrible thing to say! That's terrible! [*He runs toward the ballroom, covering his ears.*] That's just horrible. . . . I can't listen to that; I'm leaving. [*Goes out, but reappears immediately.*] All is over between us!

[*Goes out into the entrance hall.*]

LIUBÓV ANDRÉYEVNA [*calls after him*] Pétya, wait a minute! Come back! I was just joking, Pétya, don't be so silly! Pétya!

[*A great clatter from the entrance hall; someone has fallen downstairs.* ÁNYA *and* VÁRYA *scream.*]

What happened?

[ÁNYA *and* VÁRYA *suddenly howl with laughter.*]

ÁNYA [*runs in, laughing*] Pétya just fell headfirst down the stairs!

[*Runs out.*]

LIUBÓV ANDRÉYEVNA Oh, what a silly boy!

[*The* STATIONMASTER *in the ballroom gets on a chair and begins declaiming the opening lines of "The Magdalen" by Alexei Tolstoy.*[5]]

STATIONMASTER "The splendid ballroom gleams with gold and candles,
a crowd of dancers whirls around the room;
and there apart, an empty glass beside her,
behold the fallen beauty, the lost, the doomed.

Her lavish gown and jewels make all eyes wonder,
her shameless glance bespeaks a life of sin;
young men and old cast longing glances at her—
see, how her fatal beauty draws them in!"

[*Everyone gathers to listen, but soon the orchestra returns and the strains of a waltz are heard from the entrance hall. The reading breaks off, and everybody begins to dance.* TROFÍMOV, ÁNYA, *and* VÁRYA *come in from the entrance hall.*]

LIUBÓV ANDRÉYEVNA Pétya . . . oh, darling, I'm so sorry. . . . You sweet thing, please forgive me. . . . Come on, let's dance. [*Dances with* TROFÍMOV.]

[ÁNYA *and* VÁRYA *dance together.* FIRS *enters, leans his walking stick against the side door.* YÁSHA *appears and stands watching the dancers.*]

YÁSHA What's the matter, pops?

FIRS I don't feel so good. The old days, we had a dance, we had generals and barons and admirals; nowadays we have to send out for the postmaster and the stationmaster. And they're none too eager to come, either. Oh, I'm getting old and feeble. The old master, their grandfather, anybody got sick, he used to dose 'em all with sealing wax. Didn't matter what they had, they all got sealing wax. I've been taking sealing wax myself now for nigh onto twenty years. Take some every day. That's probably why I'm still alive.

YÁSHA You're getting boring, pops. [*Yawns.*] Time for you to crawl off and die.

FIRS Oh, you . . . you young flibbertigibbet. [*Mumbles.*]

[TROFÍMOV *and* LIUBÓV *dance through the ballroom, into the sitting room.*]

5. Russian novelist, poet, and playwright (1817–1875), a distant relative of the more famous novelist Leo Tolstoy. "The Magdalen" is sometimes translated "The Sinful Woman" (a *magdalen* is a reformed prostitute).

LIUBÓV ANDRÉYEVNA *Merci.*[6] I need to sit down and rest a bit. . . . [*Sits.*] I'm so tired.

[*Enter* ÁNYA.]

ÁNYA [*upset*] There was a man in the kitchen just now, he said the cherry orchard's already been sold!

LIUBÓV ANDRÉYEVNA Who bought it?

ÁNYA He didn't say. And he's gone now. [*Dances with* TROFÍMOV; *they dance off across the ballroom.*]

YÁSHA That was just some old guy talking crazy. It wasn't anybody from around here.

FIRS And Leoníd Andréyich still isn't back. All he had on was his topcoat; you watch, he'll catch cold. He's all wet, that one.

LIUBÓV ANDRÉYEVNA I'll never live through this. Yásha, go out and see if anybody knows who bought it.

YÁSHA It was just some old guy. He left long ago. [*Laughs.*]

LIUBÓV ANDRÉYEVNA [*somewhat annoyed*] What are you laughing at? What's so funny?

YÁSHA That Yepikhódov. What a dope. Old Double Trouble.

LIUBÓV ANDRÉYEVNA Firs, suppose the estate is sold—where are you going to go?

FIRS I'll go wherever you tell me to.

LIUBÓV ANDRÉYEVNA What's the matter? Your face looks so funny. . . . Are you sick? You should go to bed.

FIRS Yes . . . [*Smirks.*] Yes, sure, go to bed, and then who'll take care of things? I'm the only one you've got.

YÁSHA Liubóv Andréyevna, there's a favor I have *got* to ask you; it's very important. If you go back to Paris, please take me with you. Please! You've got to! I positively cannot stay around here. [*Looks around, lowers his voice.*] You can see for yourself this place is hopeless. The whole country's a mess, nobody has any culture, it's boring, the food is lousy, and there's that old Firs drooling all over the place and talking like an idiot. Please, take me with you—you've just got to!

[*Enter* PÍSHCHIK.]

PÍSHCHIK Beautiful lady, what about a waltz? Just one little waltz! [LIUBÓV *crosses to him.*] You dazzler, you! And what about a loan, just one little loan, just a hundred and eighty, that's all I need. [*They begin to dance.*] Just a hundred and eighty . . .

[*They dance off into the ballroom.*]

YÁSHA [*sings to himself*] "Can't you see my heart is breaking . . ."

[*In the ballroom, a figure appears dressed in checkered trousers and a gray top hat, jumping and waving its arms. We hear shouts of "Bravo, Carlotta!"*]

DUNYÁSHA [*stops to powder her nose*] The missus told me to dance—there's too many gentlemen and not enough ladies—so I did, I've been dancing all night and my heart won't stop beating, and you know what, Firs? Just now, the postmaster, you know? He said something almost made me faint.

[*The orchestra stops playing.*]

6. Thank you (French).

FIRS What did he say?

DUNYÁSHA That I was like a flower. That's what he said.

YÁSHA [*yawns*] What does he know about it?

[*Goes out.*]

DUNYÁSHA Just like a flower. I'm a very romantic girl, really. I just adore that kind of talk.

FIRS You're out of your mind.

[*Enter* YEPIKHÓDOV.]

YEPIKHÓDOV [*to* DUNYÁSHA] Why are you deliberating not to notice me? You act as if I wasn't here, like I was a bug or something [*Sighs.*] Ah, life!

DUNYÁSHA Excuse me?

YEPIKHÓDOV Of course, you may be right. [*Sighs.*] But if you look at it, let's say, from a . . . a point of view, then you're the faulty one—excuse my expressivity—because you led me on. Into this predictament. Look at me! Every day something awful happens to me. It's like a habit. But I can look disaster in the face and keep smiling. You gave me your word, you know, and you even—

DUNYÁSHA Do you mind? Let's talk about it later. Right now I'd rather be left alone. With my dreams. [*Plays with a fan.*]

YEPIKHÓDOV Every day. Something awful. But all I do—excuse my expressivity—is try to keep smiling. Sometimes I even laugh.

[*Enter* VÁRYA *from the ballroom.*]

VÁRYA [*to* YEPIKHÓDOV] Are you still here? I thought I told you to go home. Really, you have no consideration. [*To* DUNYÁSHA] Dunyásha, go back to the kitchen! [*To* YEPIKHÓDOV] You come in here and start playing billiards, you break one of our cues, now you hang around in here as if we'd invited you.

YEPIKHÓDOV Excuse my expressivity, but you have no right to penalize me.

VÁRYA I'm not penalizing you, I'm telling you! All you do here is wander around and bump into the furniture. You're supposed to be working for us, and you don't do a thing. I don't know why we hired you in the first place.

YEPIKHÓDOV [*offended*] Whether I work or not or wander around or not or play billiards or not is none of your business! You do not have the know-it-all to make my estimation!

VÁRYA How dare you talk to me like that! [*In a rage*] How dare you! What do you mean, I don't have the know-it-all? You get yourself out of here right this minute! Right this minute!

YEPIKHÓDOV [*apprehensively*] I wish you wouldn't use language like that—

VÁRYA [*beside herself*] Get out of here right this minute! Out! [*He goes to the door; she follows him.*] Double Trouble! I don't want to see hide or hair of you, I don't want to lay eyes on you ever again! [YEPIKHÓDOV *goes out; from behind the door we hear him screech: "I'll call the police on you!"*] Oh, you coming back for more? [*Grabs the stick that* FIRS *has left by the door.*] Come on . . . Come on . . . Come on, I'll show you! All right, all right, you asked for it—[*Swings the stick; the door opens, and she hits* LOPÁKHIN *over the head as he enters.*]

LOPÁKHIN Thanks a lot.

VÁRYA [*still angry, sarcastic*] Oh, I'm so sorry!

LOPÁKHIN S'all right. Always appreciate a warm welcome.

VÁRYA I don't need appreciation. [*Walks off, then turns and asks gently.*] I didn't hurt you, did I?

LOPÁKHIN No, I'm fine. Just a whopping big lump, that's all.

[*Voices from the ballroom: "Lopákhin! Lopákhin's here! He's back! Lopákhin's back!" People crowd into the sitting room.*]

PÍSHCHIK The great man in person! [*Hugs* LOPÁKHIN.] Is that cognac I smell? It is! You've been celebrating! Well, so have we. Join the party!

LIUBÓV ANDRÉYEVNA It's you, Yermolái Alexéyich. Where have you been all this time? Where's Leoníd?

LOPÁKHIN He's coming; we took the same train.

LIUBÓV ANDRÉYEVNA What happened? Did they have the auction? Tell me!

LOPÁKHIN [*embarrassed, afraid to show his joy*] The auction was all over by four this afternoon, but we missed the train. We had to wait for the nine-thirty. [*Exhales heavily.*] Oof! My head is really spinning. . . .

[*Enter* GÁYEV; *he holds a wrapped package in one hand, wipes his eyes with the other.*]

LIUBÓV ANDRÉYEVNA Lyónya, what's the matter? Lyónya! [*Impatiently, beginning to cry*] For God's sake, what happened!

GÁYEV [*weeps and can't answer her; makes a despairing gesture with his free hand and turns to* FIRS] Here, take these . . . some anchovies . . . imported. I haven't eaten a thing all day. You have no idea what I've been through! [*The door to the billiard room is open; we hear the click of billiard balls and* YÁSHA*'s voice: "Seven ball in the left pocket!"* GÁYEV*'s expression changes; he stops crying.*] I'm all worn out. Firs, come help me get ready for bed.

[*Goes through the ballroom and out;* FIRS *follows him.*]

PÍSHCHIK What about the auction? Tell us what happened!

LIUBÓV ANDRÉYEVNA Is the cherry orchard sold?

LOPÁKHIN It's sold.

LIUBÓV ANDRÉYEVNA Who bought it?

LOPÁKHIN I did.

[*Pause.* LIUBÓV *is overcome; she would fall, if she weren't standing beside a table and the armchair.* VÁRYA *takes the keys from her belt, throws them on the floor, crosses the room, and goes out.*]

I did! I bought it! No, wait, don't go, please. I'm still a little mixed up about it, I can't talk yet. . . . [*Laughs.*] We get to the auction, and there's Derigánov, all ready and waiting. Leoníd Andréyich only had fifteen thousand, so right away Derigánov raises the bid to thirty, that's on top of the balance on the mortgage. So I see what he's up to, and I bid against him. Raise it to forty. He bids forty-five. I bid fifty-five. See, he was raising by five, and I double him, I raise him ten each time. Anyway, finally it's all over, and I got it! Ninety thousand plus the balance on the mortgage.[7] And now the cherry orchard is mine! Mine! [*A loud laugh*] My God, the cherry orchard belongs to me! Tell me I'm drunk, tell me it's all a dream, I'm making this up—[*Stomps on the floor.*] And don't anybody laugh! My God, if my father and my grandfather could be here now and see this, see *me*, their Yermolái, the boy they beat, who went barefoot in winter and never

7. The winning bid for the estate was equivalent to nearly $2 million today—about twice what Lopákhin had offered to lend Liubóv and her family to save the estate (act 1).

went to school, see how that poor boy just bought the most beautiful estate in the whole world! I bought the estate where my father and my grandfather slaved away their lives, where they wouldn't even let them in the kitchen! My God, I must be dreaming—I can't believe all this is happening! [*Picks up* VÁRYA*'s keys; smiles gently.*] See, she threw away her keys; she knows she isn't running the place anymore. . . . [*Jingles the keys.*] Well, that's all right.

[*The orchestra starts tuning up again.*]

That's it, let's have some music—come on, I want to hear it! Everybody come watch! Come on and watch what I do! I'm going to chop down every tree in that cherry orchard, every goddamn one of them, and then I'm going to develop that land! Watch me! I'm going to do something our children and grandchildren can be proud of! Come on, you musicians, play!

[*The orchestra begins to play.* LIUBÓV *curls up in the armchair and weeps bitterly.*]

LOPÁKHIN [*reproachfully*] Oh, why didn't you listen to me? You dear woman, you dear good woman, you can't ever go back to the past. [*With tears in his eyes*] Oh, if only we could change things, if only life were different, this unhappy, messy life . . .

PÍSHCHIK [*takes his arm; quietly*] She's crying. Come on, we'll go in the other room, leave her alone for a while. Come on. . . . [*Leads him into the ballroom.*]

LOPÁKHIN What's the matter? Tell the band to keep playing! Louder! [*Ironic*] It's my house now! The cherry orchard belongs to me! I can do what I want to! [*Bumps into a small table, almost knocking over a candlestick.*] Don't worry about that: I can pay for it! I can pay for everything!

[*Goes out with* PÍSHCHIK*.*]

[*The sitting room is empty except for* LIUBÓV*, who sits tightly clenched and weeping bitterly. The orchestra plays softly. Suddenly* ÁNYA *and* TROFÍMOV *enter.* ÁNYA *goes and kneels before her mother.* TROFÍMOV *remains by the archway.*]

ÁNYA Mama! Mama, you're crying. Mama dear, I love you, I'll take care of you. The cherry orchard is sold, it's gone now, that's the truth, Mama, that's the truth, but don't cry. You still have your life to lead, you're still a good person. . . . Come with me, Mama, we'll go away, someplace far away from here. We'll plant a new orchard, even better than this one, you'll see, Mama, you'll understand, and you'll feel a new kind of joy, like a light in your soul. . . . Let's go, Mama. Let's go!

Curtain.

Act 4

[*The same room as Act 1. The curtains have been taken down, the pictures are gone from the walls, and there are only a few pieces of furniture shoved into a corner, as if for sale. The place feels empty. By the doorway, a pile of trunks, suitcases, etc. The door on the right is open; we hear* ÁNYA *and* VÁRYA *talking in the room beyond.* LOPÁKHIN *stands waiting. Beside him,* YÁSHA *holds a tray of glasses filled with champagne. Through the door we see* YEPIKHÓDOV *in the front hall, fastening the straps on a trunk. The sound of murmured voices offstage; some of the local people have come to say goodbye.* GÁYEV*'s voice: "Thank you all, good people, thanks, thanks very much for coming."*]

YÁSHA It's some of these poor yokels, come to say goodbye. I'm of the opinion, you know, these people around here . . . ? They're okay, but they're . . . they're just a bunch of know-nothings.

[*The murmur of voices dies away.* LIUBÓV *and* GÁYEV *come in from the entrance hall; she has stopped crying, but she is shaking slightly, and her face is pale. She cannot speak.*]

GÁYEV You gave them all the money you had, Liúba. You can't do that! You can't do that anymore!

LIUBÓV ANDREYÉVNA I couldn't help it! I just couldn't help it!

[*They both go out.* LOPÁKHIN *follows them to the door.*]

LOPÁKHIN Wait, please. How about a little glass of champagne, just to celebrate? I forgot to bring some from town, but I got this one bottle at the station. It was all they had.

[*Pause.*]

No? What's the matter, don't you want any? [*Comes back from the door.*] If I'd known that, I wouldn't have bought it. I don't feel like any myself.

[YÁSHA *carefully puts the tray down on a chair.*]

Go on, Yásha, you might as well have one.

YÁSHA *Bon voyage!* And here's to the girls we leave behind! [*Drinks.*] This is not your real French champagne, I can tell.

LOPÁKHIN Cost me enough.

[*Pause.*]

It's cold as hell in here.

YÁSHA They figured they were going away today anyway—they decided not to heat the place. [*Laughs.*]

LOPÁKHIN What's with you?

YÁSHA I'm laughing because everything worked out just the way I wanted.

LOPÁKHIN It's October already, but the sun's out; it feels like summer. Good weather for home builders. [*Looks at his watch, then at the door.*] Listen, everybody, you got forty-six minutes till train time! And it's twenty minutes from here to the station, so you better get a move on.

[*Enter* TROFÍMOV *from outside; he's wearing an overcoat.*]

TROFÍMOV It must be time to go. The carts are here. Where the hell are my galoshes? I've lost them somewhere. [*At the door*] Ánya, where are my galoshes? I can't find them anyplace!

LOPÁKHIN I'm off to Hárkov. I'll be taking the same train as you. Off to Hárkov, spend the winter there. I've been hanging around here too long, doing nothing; I can't stand that. I got to keep working, otherwise I don't know what to do with my hands; if they're not doing something, they feel like they don't belong to me.

TROFÍMOV So. We're leaving, and you're going back to your useful labors in the real world.

LOPÁKHIN Have a glass of champagne.

TROFÍMOV No, thanks.

LOPÁKHIN So you're off to Moscow?

TROFÍMOV Yes. I'll go into town with them today, and then leave tomorrow for Moscow.

LOPÁKHIN Sure. I'll bet all those professors are waiting for you to show up, wouldn't want to start their lectures without you!

TROFÍMOV Mind your own business.

LOPÁKHIN How long you say you've been at that university?

TROFÍMOV Come on! Think up something new, will you? You're getting boring. [*Pokes around, looking for his galoshes.*] You know, we probably won't ever see each other again, so you mind my giving you a little advice? As a farewell present? Don't wave your arms around so much. Bad habit. And this development you're putting in out here—you think that's going to improve the world? You think your leisure home buyers are going to turn into yeoman farmers? That's a lot of arm waving too. Well, what the hell. I like you anyway. You've got nice hands. Gentle and sensitive. You could have been an artist. And you're like that inside too—gentle and sensitive.

LOPÁKHIN [*hugs him*] Goodbye, boy. Thanks for everything. Here, let me give you a little money. You may need it for the trip.

TROFÍMOV What for? I don't need money!

LOPÁKHIN What *for*? You don't have any!

TROFÍMOV I do too. Thanks all the same. I got paid for a translation I did. I have money right here in my pocket. [*Worried*] I just wish I could find my galoshes!

VÁRYA [*from the next room*] Here they are! The smelly things . . . [*Throws a pair of galoshes into the room.*]

TROFÍMOV What are you always getting mad for? Hmm . . . These aren't my galoshes.

LOPÁKHIN This past spring I planted a big crop of poppies. Three hundred acres. Sold the poppy seed, made forty thousand clear. And when those poppies were all in flower, what a picture that was! So look, I just made forty thousand, I can afford to loan you some money. Why turn up your nose at it? Because you think I'm just a dirt farmer?

TROFÍMOV So your father was a dirt farmer. Mine worked in a drugstore. What does that prove?

[LOPÁKHIN *takes out his wallet.*]

Forget it, forget it. Look, you could give me a couple of hundred thousand, I still wouldn't take it. I'm a free man. And you people, everything you think is so valuable, it doesn't mean a thing to me. I don't care whether you're rich or poor; you've got no power over me. I can do without you, I can go right on past you, because I am proud and I am strong. Humanity is moving onward, toward a higher truth and a higher happiness, higher than anyone can imagine. And I'm ahead of the rest!

LOPÁKHIN You think you'll ever get there?

TROFÍMOV I'll get there.

[*Pause.*]

I'll get there. Or I'll make sure the rest of them get there.

[*From the orchard comes the sound of axes; they've started chopping down the cherry trees.*]

LOPÁKHIN Well, boy, goodbye. Time to go. You and I don't see eye to eye, but life goes on anyway. Whenever I work real hard, round the clock practically, that clears my mind somehow, and for a minute I think maybe I know what we're all here for. But God, boy, think of the thousands of people in this country who don't know what they're doing or why they're doing it.

But . . . I guess that doesn't have much to do with the price of eggs. They told me Leoníd Andréyich got a job at the bank, six thousand a year. He won't last; he's too lazy.

ÁNYA [*at the door*] Mama asks you to please wait until she's gone before you start cutting down the orchard.

TROFÍMOV I agree. That isn't very tactful, you know.

[*Goes out into the front hall.*]

LOPÁKHIN All right, all right, I'll take care of it. God, these people . . .

[*Goes out after him.*]

ÁNYA Have they taken Firs to the nursing home?

YÁSHA I told them about it this morning. So I imagine they have.

ÁNYA [*to* YEPIKHÓDOV, *who crosses the room*] Yepikhódov, could you please go and make sure they've taken Firs to the nursing home?

YÁSHA [*offended*] I already told them this morning! Why keep asking?

YEPIKHÓDOV The aged Firs, in my ultimate opinion, is beyond nursing. They ought to take him to the cemetery. And I can only envy him. [*Sets a suitcase down on a cardboard hatbox and crushes it.*] There. Finally. Wouldn't you know.

[*Goes out.*]

YÁSHA [*snickers*] Old Double Trouble.

VÁRYA [*from the next room*] Have they taken Firs to the nursing home?

ÁNYA They took him this morning.

VÁRYA Then why didn't they take the letter for the doctor?

ÁNYA They must have forgotten. We'll have to send someone after them with it.

VÁRYA Where's Yásha? Tell him his mother is here; she wants to say goodbye.

YÁSHA [*with a dismissive gesture*] What a bore! Why can't she just leave me alone?

[DUNYÁSHA *has been drifting in and out, fussing with the baggage; now that she sees* YÁSHA *alone, she goes to him.*]

DUNYÁSHA Oh . . . oh, Yásha, why won't you even look at me? You're going away . . . you're leaving me behind. . . . [*Starts to cry and throws her arms around his neck.*]

YÁSHA What are you crying about? [*Drinks some champagne.*] Six days from now, I'll be back in Paris. Tomorrow we get on the express train, and we're off! And that's the last you'll ever see of me! I can't hardly believe it myself. *Vive la France!*[8] I can't live around here anymore; it's just not my kind of place. They're all so ignorant, and I can't stand that. [*Drinks more champagne.*] What are you crying about? If you'd been a nice girl, you wouldn't have anything to cry about.

DUNYÁSHA [*powders her nose in a mirror*] Don't forget to send me a letter from Paris. Because I loved you, Yásha, I really did. I'm a very sensitive person, Yásha, I really am—

YÁSHA Watch it, someone's coming. [*He starts fussing with the luggage, whistling quietly.*]

[*Enter* LIUBÓV, GÁYEV, ÁNYA, *and* CARLOTTA.]

8. Long live France! (French).

GÁYEV We should be going. We're already a little late. [*Looks at* YÁSHA.] Who smells like herring?

LIUBÓV ANDRÉYEVNA We've only got ten minutes; then we absolutely must start out. [*Glances around the room.*] Goodbye, house! Wonderful old house! Winter's almost here, and come spring you'll be gone. They'll tear you down. Think of everything these walls have seen! [*Kisses* ÁNYA *with great feeling.*] My treasure, look at you! You're radiant today! Your eyes are shining like diamonds! Are you happy? Really happy?

ÁNYA Oh, yes, Mama, really! We're starting a new life!

GÁYEV She's right —everything worked out extremely well. Before the cherry orchard was sold we were at our wit's end—remember how painful it was?—and now everything's finally settled, once and for all, no turning back, and see? We've all calmed down. We're even rather happy. I'm going to work at the bank, I'm about to become a financier! Yellow ball in the side pocket . . . And you look better than you have in a long time, Lyúba; you do, you know.

LIUBÓV ANDRÉYEVNA I know. My nerves have quieted down. You're quite right.

[*Someone holds out her hat and coat.*]

And I sleep much better now. Take my things, Yásha, will you? It's time to go. [*To* ÁNYA] Darling, we'll see each other soon enough. I'm off to Paris—I kept the money your godmother in Yároslavl sent to buy the estate. [*A hard laugh*] Thank God for the old lady! That ought to get me through the winter at least. . . .

ÁNYA And you'll come back soon, won't you? You promise? I'll study hard and get my diploma, and then I'll get a job and help you out. We can read together the way we used to, can't we? [*Kisses her mother's hands.*] We'll spend long autumn evenings together; we'll read lots of books and learn all about the wonderful new world of the future. . . . [*Dreamily*] Don't forget, Mama, you promised. . . .

LIUBÓV ANDRÉYEVNA I will, my angel, I promise. [*Embraces her.*]

[*Enter* LOPÁKHIN. CARLOTTA *hums a tune under her breath.*]

GÁYEV Carlotta must be happy; she's singing!

CARLOTTA [*picks up a bundle that looks like a baby in swaddling clothes*] Here's my little baby. Bye, bye, baby . . .

[*We hear a baby's voice: "Wah! Wah!"*]

Shh, baby, shh, shh . . . good little children don't cry. . . .

[*Again: "Wah! Wah!"*]

I feel so sorry for the poor thing. [*Hurls the bundle to the floor.*] You will find me a job, won't you? I can't go on like this anymore.

LOPÁKHIN Don't worry, Carlotta; we'll take care of you.

GÁYEV Everybody's just thrown us away. Várya's leaving. . . . All of a sudden we're useless.

CARLOTTA How can I live in that town of yours? There must be someplace I can go. . . . [*Hums.*] What difference does it make . . . ?

[*Enter* PÍSHCHIK.]

LOPÁKHIN Here comes the wonder boy.

PÍSHCHIK [*panting*] Ooh, give me a minute . . . I'm all worn out. Good morning, good morning, good morning. Could I get a drink of water?

GÁYEV [*sarcastic*] You're sure it isn't money you want? You'll all have to excuse me if I remove myself from the approaching negotiations.

[*Goes out.*]

PÍSHCHIK I'm so glad to see you all. . . . Dear lady . . . I've been a stranger, I know. [*To* LOPÁKHIN] And you're here too. Delighted, delighted, a man I admire, always have. . . . Here. Here. This is for you. [*Gives* LOPÁKHIN *money.*] Four hundred. And I still owe you eight hundred and forty.

LOPÁKHIN [*a bewildered shrug*] I must be dreaming. Where did you get money?

PÍSHCHIK Wait a minute; let me cool off. Well, it was an absolutely extraordinary thing. These Englishmen showed up, they poked around on my land, found some kind of white clay. . . . [*To* LIUBÓV] Here . . . Here's the four hundred. You've been so kind . . . so sweet . . . [*Gives her money.*] And you'll have the rest before you know it. [*Takes a drink of water.*] You know, there was a young man on the train just now, he was saying . . . there was this philosopher, he said, who wanted us all to jump off the roof. "Jump!" he said. "Jump!" That was his whole philosophy. [*Amazed*] Really! I don't believe it! Give me some more water. . . .

LOPÁKHIN What Englishmen are you talking about?

PÍSHCHIK I gave them a lease on the land, the place where the clay is, a twenty-four-year lease. And now excuse me, but I'm off. Lots of people to see, pay back what I owe. I owe money all over the place. [*Takes a drink of water.*] Well, I just wanted to say hello. I'll come by again on Thursday.

LIUBÓV ANDRÉYEVNA But we're leaving for town today. And tomorrow I'm going back to Paris.

PÍSHCHIK What? [*Astonished*] Leaving for town? Oh, my . . . Oh, of course; the furniture's gone. And all these trunks. I didn't realize. [*Almost in tears*] I didn't realize. Great thinkers, these English . . . God bless you all. And be happy. I didn't realize. Well, all things must come to an end. [*Kisses* LIUBÓV's *hand.*] I'll come to an end myself one of these days. And when I do, I want you all to say: "Semyónov-Píshchik . . . he was a good old horse. God bless him." Wonderful weather we're having. Yes. . . . [*Starts out, overcome with emotion, stops in the doorway and turns.*] Oh, by the way, Dáshenka says hello.

[*Goes out.*]

LIUBÓV ANDRÉYEVNA Now we can go. There are just two things still on my mind. The first is old Firs. [*Looks at her watch.*] We've still got five minutes. . . .

ÁNYA Mama, they took Firs to the nursing home this morning. Yásha took care of it.

LIUBÓV ANDRÉYEVNA . . . And then there's our Várya. She's used to getting up early and working around here all day long, and now she's . . . out of a job. Like a fish out of water. Poor thing—she's so nervous, she cries, she's losing weight . . .

[*Pause.*]

You know, Yermolái Alexéyich—well, of course you know—I'd always dreamed . . . always dreamed she'd marry you; you know we all think it's a wonderful idea. . . . [*Whispers to* ÁNYA, *who nods to* CARLOTTA; *they both leave.*] She loves you, you like her. . . . I don't know why, I just don't know why the two of you keep avoiding the issue. Really!

LOPÁKHIN I don't know why either. It's all a little funny. Well, I don't mind. If there's still time, I'll do it. . . . All right, *basta*,[9] let's just get it over with. But I don't know, I don't think I can propose without you—

LIUBÓV ANDRÉYEVNA Of course you can. All it takes is a minute. I'll send her right in. . . .

LOPÁKHIN We've even got some champagne all ready. [*Looks at the tray of empty glasses.*] Or at least we did. Somebody must have drunk it all up.

[YÁSHA *coughs.*]

Guzzled it down, I should say.

LIUBÓV ANDRÉYEVNA Wonderful! We'll leave you alone. Yásha, *allez!*[1] I'll go call her. [*At the door*] Várya, leave that alone; come here a minute, will you? Come on, dear!

[*Goes out with* YÁSHA.]

LOPÁKHIN [*looks at his watch*] Well . . .

[*Pause. A few stifled laughs and whispers behind the door. Finally* VÁRYA *enters.*]

VÁRYA [*examines the luggage; takes her time*] That's funny, I can't find them. . . .

LOPÁKHIN What are you looking for?

VÁRYA I packed them myself, and now I don't remember where.

[*Pause.*]

LOPÁKHIN What . . . ah . . . where are you off to, Várya?

VÁRYA Me? I'm going to work for the Ragúlins. I talked to them about it already; they need a housekeeper. And look after things, you know. . . .

LOPÁKHIN All the way over there? That's fifty miles away.

[*Pause.*]

Well, looks like this is the end of things around here. . . .

VÁRYA [*still examining the luggage*] Where are they . . . ? Or maybe I put them in the trunk. You're right: this is the end of things here. The end of one life—

LOPÁKHIN I'm going too. To Hárkov. Taking the same train, actually. I've got a million things waiting for me. I'm leaving Yepikhódov, though. Hired him to take charge here.

VÁRYA You hired *who?*

LOPÁKHIN Last year this time it was snowing already, remember? Today it's still sunny. Nice day. A little chilly, though . . . It was freezing this morning; must have been in the thirties.

VÁRYA I didn't notice.

[*Pause.*]

Anyway, the thermometer's broken.

[*Pause. A voice from outside calls: "Lopákhin!"*]

LOPÁKHIN [*as if he'd been waiting for the call*] I'm coming!

[*Goes out.*]

[VÁRYA *sits down on the floor, leans her head on a bundle of dresses, and cries. The door opens;* LIUBÓV *enters carefully.*]

LIUBÓV ANDRÉYEVNA Well?

[*Pause.*]

9. Enough (Italian).

1. Go on! (French).

We have to go.

VÁRYA [*already stopped crying, wipes her eyes*] Right, Mama, we have to go. I can get to the Ragúlins' today, if I don't miss the train.

LIUBÓV ANDRÉYEVNA Ánya, get your coat on.

[*Enter* ÁNYA, GÁYEV, CARLOTTA. GÁYEV *wears a winter overcoat. Servants and drivers come in to pick up the luggage.* YEPIKHÓDOV *directs the operation.*]

Well, we're ready to start.

ÁNYA [*joyfully*] Ready to start!

GÁYEV My dear friends, my very dear friends! On this occasion, this farewell to our beloved house, I cannot keep still. I feel I must say a few words to express the emotion that overwhelms me, overwhelms us all—

ÁNYA [*pleads*] Uncle, please!

VÁRYA That's enough, Uncle.

GÁYEV [*crushed*] All right . . . Yellow ball in the side pocket . . . I'll keep still.

[*Enter* TROFÍMOV, *then* LOPÁKHIN.]

TROFÍMOV Ladies and gentlemen, time to go! You'll be late!

LOPÁKHIN Yepikhódov, get my coat.

LIUBÓV ANDRÉYEVNA Let me stay a little minute longer. I never really noticed these walls before, or the ceilings. I want a last look, one last long look. . . .

GÁYEV I remember when I was six, I was watching out that window, right over there. It was a holy day, Trinity Sunday,[2] I think, and I saw Father on his way to church. . . .

LIUBÓV ANDRÉYEVNA Have we got everything?

LOPÁKHIN I guess so. [*To* YEPIKHÓDOV, *who helps him on with his coat*] You keep an eye on things, Yepikhódov.

YEPIKHÓDOV [*loud, businesslike tone*] You can count on me, Yermolái Alexéyich!

LOPÁKHIN Why are you talking like that all of a sudden?

YEPIKHÓDOV I just had a drink—water. . . . It went down the wrong way.

YÁSHA [*with contempt*] Dumb hick!

LIUBÓV ANDRÉYEVNA We're all going away. There won't be a soul left on the place. . . .

LOPÁKHIN But wait till you see what happens here come spring!

[VÁRYA *grabs an umbrella from the luggage, as if she were going to hit him.* LOPÁKHIN *pretends to be terrified.*]

VÁRYA Don't get excited. It was just a joke.

TROFÍMOV You've all got to get moving! It's time to go! You'll miss your train!

VÁRYA Here's your galoshes, Pétya, behind this suitcase. [*With tears in her eyes*] Smelly old things . . .

TROFÍMOV [*puts them on*] It's time to go!

GÁYEV [*deeply moved, afraid he'll start crying*] Yes, the train . . . mustn't miss the train . . . Yellow ball in the side pocket, white in the corner . . .

LIUBÓV ANDRÉYEVNA Let's go!

LOPÁKHIN Everybody here? Nobody left? [*Closes and locks the door, left.*] Got to lock up; I've got a few things stored here. All right, let's go!

2. A celebration of the Christian doctrine of the Trinity (the belief that the Father, Son, and Holy Spirit exist together in God); in Eastern Christianity it falls on Pentecost (seven weeks after Easter).

ÁNYA Goodbye, house! Goodbye, old life!

TROFÍMOV No, hello, new life!

[Goes out with Ánya.]

*[*VÁRYA *looks around the room again; she's not eager to go.* YÁSHA *goes out with* CARLOTTA *and her little dog.]*

LOPÁKHIN So. Until next spring. Come on, let's go, everybody. Goodbye!

*[*LIUBÓV *and* GÁYEV *are left alone. It's as if they'd been waiting for this moment. They throw their arms around each other and burst out crying, but try to keep the others outside from hearing.]*

GÁYEV *[in despair]* Oh, sister, sister . . .

LIUBÓV ANDRÉYEVNA Oh, my orchard, my beautiful orchard! My life, my youth, my happiness, goodbye! Goodbye! Goodbye!

*[*ÁNYA*'s voice, joyful: "Mama!"* TROFÍMOV*'s voice, joyful, excited: "Yoo-hoo!"]*

These walls, these windows, for the last time . . . And Mama loved this room . . .

GÁYEV Oh, sister, sister . . .

*[*ÁNYA*: "Mama!"* TROFÍMOV*: "Yoo-hoo!"]*

LIUBÓV ANDRÉYEVNA We're coming!

[They leave.]

[The stage is empty. We hear the sound of the door being locked, then the carriages as they drive away. It grows very quiet. In the silence, we hear the occasional sound of an ax chopping down the cherry trees, a mournful, lonely sound. Then we hear steps. Enter FIRS *from the door, right. He wears his usual butler's livery, but with bedroom slippers. He's very ill.]*

FIRS *[goes to the door, tries the handle]* Locked. They're gone. *[Sits on the sofa.]* They forgot about me. That's all right; I'll just sit here for a bit. . . . And Leoníd Andréyich probably forgot his winter coat. *[A worried sigh]* I should have looked. . . . He's still all wet, that one. . . . *[Mumbles something we can't make out.]* Well, it's all over now, and I never even had a life to live. . . . *[Lies back.]* I'll just lie here for a bit. . . . No strength left, nothing left, not a thing . . . Oh, you. You young flibbertigibbet. *[Lies there, no longer moving.]*

[In the distance we hear a sound that seems to come from the sky, a sad sound, like a string snapping. It dies away. Everything grows quiet. We can hear the occasional sound of an ax on a tree.]

Curtain.

GEORGE BERNARD SHAW

1856–1950

In the history of English drama, George Bernard Shaw stands second only to SHAKESPEARE as the playwright with the most profound influence on his own era and beyond. Winner of the Nobel Prize for Literature in 1925, Shaw was not only the most famous author of his time but also a highly regarded social critic, routinely sought after for his responses to world events and political issues. Although in the latter part of his career he was best known globally as a public intellectual, his theatrical writing was responsible for his place, long after his death in 1950, as one of the leading cultural forces of the twentieth century. Shaw's plays are still regularly revived and continue to strike audiences as relevant and compelling. This "timeliness" in his work in part reflects how little has changed at the very core of modern civilization over the past century; Shaw's tireless dissection of social ills as well as his insightful grasp of human motivations and foibles also enables his plays to speak to each generation anew. Yet the truthfulness and acuity of his vision would not matter much to audiences if the plays themselves were not such exemplars of theatrical craftsmanship. Shaw's ability to interweave captivating narratives and memorable characters with social critique and, above all, humor sets him apart in the pantheon of modern drama. *PYGMALION* (1913) is one of the most popular, and arguably among the very finest, of Shaw's comedies. Gently poking fun at the pretensions of the lower class, and the idiosyncrasies of the upper class, *Pygmalion* entrances us with fairy-tale transformations and the possibility of romance; at the same time, it exposes the very real economic and gender inequities that continue to plague our modern world.

Shaw was born in 1856 to an Irish Protestant family that had more aspirations to social position than their father's income—reduced by his alcoholism—could sustain. George Carr Shaw cut short his son's formal education at age fifteen and sent him to work to help support his mother and two older sisters. Shaw spent five years as a clerk in a land agency, experience he would later use in his first play, *Widowers' Houses* (1892), which considers the hypocrisies of slum landlords. Shaw's mother, Lucinda Elizabeth Gurly Shaw, a talented singer, focused much of her time and energy on her music and, apparently, on her voice teacher, George J. Vandeleur Lee, with whom she may have been romantically involved. In 1873, Shaw's mother followed Lee to London, taking her two daughters with her. Shaw joined them in 1876. His first employment there was as a ghostwriter of music reviews for Lee, and he parlayed what he learned into lifelong journalistic work as a music, art, theater, and social critic. But Shaw desired a literary career, and he drafted a novel, *Immaturity* (written 1879), that he hoped would establish him both professionally and financially. Over the next four years, he composed four additional novels, only one of which, *Cashel Byron's Profession* (1886; rev. ed., 1901), saw any real success.

In 1884, Shaw discovered the newly organized Fabian Society, a socialist organization named after the Roman general Fabius Cunctator (the Delayer); its guiding principle was the idea that the best way to accomplish political and social reform was through the calculated, gradual infiltration of established channels of power. In the late nineteenth century and into the first decades of the twentieth, the Fabian Society came to have increasing influence on English politics, attracting into its ranks some of the foremost figures of the era—including its leaders, Sidney and Beatrice Webb, and the novelist H. G. Wells. Through the Fabians Shaw also met Charlotte Payne Townshend, whom he married in 1898. Shaw's writing skills and lecturing acumen soon made him the most visible member of this elite group dedicated to the pursuit of what Shaw deemed its "Socialist and Democratic objects."

In 1890, Shaw began to draw together his passionate commitment to the arts and to socialism by delivering a series of lectures for the Society on HENRIK IBSEN, whose dramas had recently been translated into English by Shaw's friend William Archer. As these plays began to be produced on the London stage, they galvanized broader public debate, especially about marriage and the role of women in modern society. Shaw published his talks the following year as *The Quintessence of Ibsenism,* and his analysis of these pioneering works of the modern theater helped him discover his own vocation as a dramatist.

The timing of these events could not have been more auspicious. Shaw emerged as a playwright just as theatrical modernism was beginning to coalesce as a movement across Europe. Shaw championed the arrival of the "New Drama" in England, leading a theatrical revolution that sought to replace formulaic native melodrama and Continental well-made plays with works closely engaged with the pressing issues of the day. Shaw also quickly learned that humor was a highly effective vehicle for social critique, and he exploited its didactic potential throughout his career. A remarkably prolific author, Shaw generated new plays and essays annually through the early 1920s, and was still writing steadily through World War II.

Pygmalion brings together many of Shaw's lifelong concerns: class and economic structures, shifting gender roles, and England's global influence and power, among others. The play's opening scene, set in London's Covent Garden, provides an opportunity for Shaw to introduce a cross section of character types and ranks in English society. As members of the upper class search for taxis to take them home from an evening at the theater, a "poor girl," Eliza Doolittle, tries to earn her meager income selling bunches of flowers to the passersby. Henry Higgins, a professor of phonetics who frequents the area to study its range of English idioms, hears Eliza, whose Cockney speech interests him. Quite by accident, he also encounters an amateur linguist, Colonel Pickering, an expert in Indian dialects who has come to London to meet him, and Higgins invites Pickering to his home. Eliza overhears Higgins giving out his address, and she shows up the next day to ask Higgins to teach her "genteel" speech, so that she will be qualified to work in a flower shop instead of on the streets. Higgins bets Pickering that he can teach Eliza convincingly to speak as a member of the upper class and comport herself as a duchess. But what will it mean for Eliza to appear to be what she is not? What happens when one is removed from one's "natural" place in the social order? While in its plot *Pygmalion* echoes such tales as "The Ugly Duckling," Shaw's transformation narrative also reflects the real and pressing concerns faced by working-class women with severely limited financial options to improve their lives.

Shaw took his title from a classical myth, best known today in the version that appears in book 10 of Ovid's *Metamorphoses*. Pygmalion, "revolted by the many faults which nature has implanted in the female sex," carves a statue "lovelier than any woman born." He promptly falls in love with his creation, and prays to the goddess of love for a wife like his "ivory maid" (translation by Mary M. Innes). Venus brings the statue to life, and Pygmalion immediately marries and impregnates Galatea. Such stories of male construction of idealized womanhood pervade Western literature, and Shaw could have drawn on many versions of this myth, including W. S. Gilbert's theatrical extravaganza *Pygmalion and Galatea* (1871). Higgins's claim "I said I'd make a woman of you; and I have," coupled with his assertion (also in act 5) that he has "created this thing out of the squashed cabbage leaves of Covent Garden," indisputably connects him to this tradition. Shaw's rendition may also have been influenced by even darker variants of such tales, such as Mary Shelley's gothic novel *Frankenstein* (1818), which depicts the uncontrollability of creations once they are brought to life. Echoing Shelley's label for Frankenstein's monster, Higgins refers to Eliza as "the creature," ultimately damning his "own folly in having lavished hard-earned knowledge and the treasure of [his] regard" on her.

Shaw weaves together this creation myth with another equally powerful narrative, a tale of a girl magically transformed, as was Cinderella, from rags to riches. By asserting that he can make a "duchess" from a "draggle-tailed guttersnipe," Higgins presents himself as the modern-day fairy godfather who will provide Eliza with clothes fit for an ambassador's party and with rides in a taxi, almost as magical to her as a pumpkin coach. But here, too, Shaw introduces a darker tone by also depicting Higgins as the evil stepfather/witch out of a story like "Snow White," tempting Eliza with sweets and munching on an apple taken from the same dessert stand.

For audiences *Pygmalion*'s enduring appeal clearly lies in part in the teasingly undefined and unresolved relationship of Higgins and Eliza. Shaw builds the comedy, which he subtitled a "A Romance in Five Acts," around Higgins's disavowals of romantic interest in Eliza as well as Eliza's need for "a little kindness" and her "right to be loved." Eliza maintains that "the sort of feeling" she wants from Higgins is not the same as that experienced by men such as the poor but aristocratic Freddy Eynsford Hill, who writes "sheets and sheets" of love letters to her. Shaw always insisted that his subtitle should suggest an older sense of the term *romance*—the sense in which it is

Left to right: Edmund Gurney as Alfred Doolittle, Stella Campbell as his daughter, Eliza Doolittle, and Herbert Beerbohm Tree as Professor Henry Higgins in the original 1914 production of *Pygmalion*.

applied to the late plays of Shakespeare, which similarly depict mythic transformations and adventures beyond the everyday. Nevertheless, the agonistic dynamic between Higgins and Eliza has struck many audiences and critics as the verbal equivalent of sexual foreplay, in the tradition of Beatrice and Benedick in Shakespeare's *Much Ado about Nothing* (ca. 1598), or Mirabel and Millimant in William Congreve's *The Way of the World* (1700). From the first production of *Pygmalion* forward, Shaw had to fight both actors' inclinations and audiences' expectations that the comedy end conventionally, in marriage. In that legendary first staging, Herbert Beerbohm Tree (Higgins) got around Shaw by tossing flowers to Stella Campbell (Eliza) right before the final curtain to signal the pair's ultimate union. Well aware of theatergoers' delight at this gesture, Tree told the irate Shaw, "My ending makes money; you ought to be grateful." Shaw responded, "Your ending is damnable: you ought to be shot."

The critical and theatrical controversy that erupted over the play's lack of narrative closure has perennially overshadowed explorations of other social and political issues raised in the play. It is certainly possible that Shaw perceived the amatory dynamic at work in *Pygmalion,* but actively sought to expose the darker realities behind such romantic fantasies. Shortly before Shaw conceived the play, the London periodical *Pall Mall Gazette* featured an exposé of white slavery that prompted a public debate over sexual predation and may have contributed to the drama's aura of barely disguised sexual threat. The journal's revelations of the sexual availability and vulnerability of young working-class women, and their exploitation by men in more economically privileged positions, would certainly have been familiar to Shaw's audiences. That Stella Campbell, for whom Shaw created the role of Eliza, was already known to audiences through her prior star turns in highly sexualized "fallen woman" roles, such as in Arthur Pinero's *The Second Mrs. Tanqueray* (1893), only complicated their perception of her and the reception of *Pygmalion*.

Shaw uses details of language—what he calls "phonetics"—to explore class boundaries and their potential malleability. He overtly links economics with dialect and grammar by suggesting that class position is culturally bound to speech. Through Higgins (whom Shaw partly modeled on Henry Sweet, a noted philologist he had met in 1880), Shaw states that the lower class's acquisition of "new speech"—by which he means what came to be known as Standard British English—can "fil[l] up the deepest gulf that separates class from class and soul from soul." He sets up this major arc of the play in act 1, when Higgins remarks: "You see this creature with her kerbstone English: the English that will keep her in the gutter to the end of her days. . . . [I]n three months I could pass that girl off as a duchess. . . . I could even get her a place as lady's maid or shop assistant, which requires better English." In Higgins's idealized vision, once the marker of lower-class status is removed from speech, individuals

Stella Campbell, for whom Shaw created the role of Eliza.

not only will be able to move upward through social ranks, they will also be able to realize their full potential economically, intellectually, and spiritually.

The juxtaposition of two branches of linguistic inquiry undertaken by Higgins and Pickering—one rooted in the British class system, the other emerging from its imperial endeavors—cannot be accidental. Shaw had already anonymously written the manifesto *Fabianism and the Empire* (1900) for the Fabian Society and had dramatized the familiar parallel of the British and Roman empires in *Caesar and Cleopatra* (written 1898). In *Pygmalion* Shaw demonstrates how language can be used either to perpetuate or to level social distinctions both at home and, by extension, in the colonies. He combines the established idea that British English should be the vehicle for the education and enculturation of colonized natives with social reformers' notions that Britain's underclass had much in common with its colonial "Others."

Shaw uses a streamlined version of the Elizabethan dramatic structure of main plot and comic subplot to develop his themes of language and class. Eliza's willing transfiguration through speech has its comic counterpart in her father's resistance to his removal from the legions of "the undeserving poor" and forced embrace of "middle class morality" when he unexpectedly receives a sizable legacy. The character of Alfred Doolittle owes much to earlier Victorian literature, especially the novels of Charles Dickens (1812–1870) and the dramas of T. W. Robertson (1829–1871), with their depictions of colorful laggards and other lowlifes. These Victorian characterological influences emerged in Shaw's earliest plays—including *Widowers' Houses,* which featured the rent collector Lickcheese; in *Pygmalion* Shaw more fully and pointedly uses Doolittle to expose the hypocrisy and pretensions of elevated class position through the resolutely unreformed dustman's lectures on "Moral Reform"—lectures that, under the terms of the will that irrevocably changes his social position, he must deliver.

Some critics have contrasted the "human" comedy of Eliza to the "social" comedy of her father, claiming that only the latter is about class. But Shaw's grounding in socialism was too thorough to allow him to separate an understanding of modern humanity from individuals' placement in a class system. Rather, through the triangulated relations of Eliza, Pickering, and Higgins, we come to realize that class position has both external markers and intrinsic qualities. Eliza learns that "apart from the things anyone can pick up (the dressing and the proper way of speaking, and so on), the difference between a lady and a flower girl is not how she behaves, but how shes treated." Henry's mother sees Eliza's transformation from still another perspective: the tension between the appearance of elevated class position and the economic realities of women's lives. Mrs. Higgins questions her son's having taught Eliza "the manners and habits that disqualify a fine lady from earning her own living without giving her a fine lady's income." Eliza pointedly comes to understand the price of class standing for women without independent means—the necessity of finding a husband in a society that still saw marriage as the only "profession" appropriate to real ladies. "I sold flowers. I didnt sell myself. Now youve made a lady of me I'm not fit to sell anything else."

Though Shaw's postscript spells out Eliza's later career in some detail, his play's intentionally ambiguous ending leaves unclear whether she will marry the impecunious Freddy Eynsford Hill, "as soon as hes able to support me," or teach phonetics. It could well be that the financial and emotional independence she craves if she "cant have kindness" proved too threatening to dramatize fully at that time. Tree's conventionally romantic gesture at the final curtain reassured his audiences—members of a society that could not yet accept women's suffrage and other struggles for human equality—that the social problems Shaw placed within the spotlight could be easily resolved. Yet the continued theatrical appeal of *Pygmalion* suggests that the issues Shaw depicts are with us still. Not only can we appreciate the value of complexity and indeterminacy, but such ambiguity may well affirm, better than any pat ending, the realities of our lives.

J.E.G.

Pygmalion
A Romance in Five Acts

CHARACTERS

CLARA EYNSFORD HILL	MRS. PEARCE
MRS. EYNSFORD HILL	ALFRED DOOLITTLE
FREDDY EYNSFORD HILL	MRS. HIGGINS
ELIZA DOOLITTLE	
COLONEL PICKERING	A PARLOR-MAID
HENRY HIGGINS	BYSTANDERS

Act 1

[*Covent Garden*[1] *at* 11.15 *p.m. Torrents of heavy summer rain. Cab whistles blowing frantically in all directions. Pedestrians running for shelter into the market and under the portico of St. Paul's Church, where there are already several people, among them a lady and her daughter in evening dress. They are all peering out gloomily at the rain, except one man with his back turned to the rest, who seems wholly preoccupied with a notebook in which he is writing busily.*

The church clock strikes the first quarter.]

THE DAUGHTER [*in the space between the central pillars, close to the one on her left*] I'm getting chilled to the bone. What can Freddy be doing all this time? Hes[2] been gone twenty minutes.

THE MOTHER [*on her daughter's right*] Not so long. But he ought to have got us a cab by this.

A BYSTANDER [*on the lady's right*] He wont get no cab not until half-past eleven, missus, when they come back after dropping their theatre fares.

THE MOTHER But we must have a cab. We cant stand here until half-past eleven. It's too bad.

THE BYSTANDER Well, it aint my fault, missus.

THE DAUGHTER If Freddy had a bit of gumption, he would have got one at the theatre door.

THE MOTHER What could he have done, poor boy?

THE DAUGHTER Other people got cabs. Why couldnt he?

[FREDDY *rushes in out of the rain from the Southampton Street side, and comes between them closing a dripping umbrella. He is a young man of twenty, in evening dress, very wet around the ankles.*]

THE DAUGHTER Well, havnt you got a cab?

FREDDY Theres not one to be had for love or money.

1. The site of London's main produce and flower market from the 1600s until 1974, in Westminster; also the site of major entertainment venues, including the Royal Opera House and the Drury Lane Theatre.

2. An example of one of the spelling reforms advocated by Shaw, who argued that the apostrophe was unnecessary in most contractions (he also insisted on dropping the final *e* from Shakespeare).

THE MOTHER Oh, Freddy, there must be one. You cant have tried.

THE DAUGHTER It's too tiresome. Do you expect us to go and get one ourselves?

FREDDY I tell you theyre all engaged. The rain was so sudden: nobody was prepared; and everybody had to take a cab. Ive been to Charing Cross one way and nearly to Ludgate Circus the other;[3] and they were all engaged.

THE MOTHER Did you try Trafalgar Square?[4]

FREDDY There wasnt one at Trafalgar Square.

THE DAUGHTER Did you try?

FREDDY I tried as far as Charing Cross Station. Did you expect me to walk to Hammersmith?[5]

THE DAUGHTER You havnt tried at all.

THE MOTHER You really are very helpless, Freddy. Go again; and dont come back until you have found a cab.

FREDDY I shall simply get soaked for nothing.

THE DAUGHTER And what about us? Are we to stay here all night in this draught, with next to nothing on. You selfish pig—

FREDDY Oh, very well: I'll go, I'll go.

[*He opens his umbrella and dashes off Strandwards,*[6] *but comes into collision with a flower girl, who is hurrying in for shelter, knocking her basket out of her hands. A blinding flash of lightning, followed instantly by a rattling peal of thunder, orchestrates the incident.*]

THE FLOWER GIRL Nah then, Freddy: look wh' y' gowin, deah.

FREDDY Sorry.

[*He rushes off.*]

THE FLOWER GIRL [*picking up her scattered flowers and replacing them in the basket*] Theres menners f' yer! Te-oo banches o voylets trod into the mad.

[*She sits down on the plinth of the column, sorting her flowers, on the lady's right. She is not at all an attractive person. She is perhaps eighteen, perhaps twenty, hardly older. She wears a little sailor hat of black straw that has long been exposed to the dust and soot of London and has seldom if ever been brushed. Her hair needs washing rather badly: its mousy color can hardly be natural. She wears a shoddy black coat that reaches nearly to her knees and is shaped to her waist. She has a brown skirt with a coarse apron. Her boots are much the worse for wear. She is no doubt as clean as she can afford to be; but compared to the ladies she is very dirty. Her features are no worse than theirs; but their condition leaves something to be desired; and she needs the services of a dentist.*]

THE MOTHER How do you know that my son's name is Freddy, pray?

THE FLOWER GIRL Ow, eez ye-ooa san, is e? Wal, fewd dan y' de-ooty bawmz a mather should, eed now bettern to spawl a pore gel's flahrzn than ran awy athaht[7] pyin. Will ye-oo py me f'them? [*Here, with apologies, this desperate*

3. Freddy has walked more than a half mile in different directions: first southwest to Charing Cross, the busy intersection of a number of major Westminster thoroughfares, and then east to Ludgate Circus, near the entrance to the old City of London.

4. A large plaza near Charing Cross.

5. The westernmost of the inner London boroughs, several miles beyond Charing Cross.

6. That is, toward the Strand, a street in Westminster south of Covent Garden where many theaters were located.

7. Without. *Fewd dan y' de-ooty bawmz*: if you'd done your duty by him.

attempt to represent her dialect without a phonetic alphabet must be abandoned as unintelligible outside London.][8]

THE DAUGHTER Do nothing of the sort, mother. The idea!

THE MOTHER Please allow me, Clara. Have you any pennies?

THE DAUGHTER No. I've nothing smaller than sixpence.[9]

THE FLOWER GIRL [*hopefully*] *I* can give you change for a tanner,[1] kind lady.

THE MOTHER [*to* CLARA] Give it to me. [CLARA *parts reluctantly.*] Now [*To the* GIRL] This is for your flowers.

THE FLOWER GIRL Thank you kindly, lady.

THE DAUGHTER Make her give you the change. These things are only a penny a bunch.

THE MOTHER Do hold your tongue, Clara. [*To the* GIRL] You can keep the change.

THE FLOWER GIRL Oh, thank you, lady.

THE MOTHER Now tell me how you know that young gentleman's name.

THE FLOWER GIRL I didnt.

THE MOTHER I heard you call him by it. Dont try to deceive me.

THE FLOWER GIRL [*protesting*] Whos trying to deceive you? I called him Freddy or Charlie same as you might yourself if you was talking to a stranger and wished to be pleasant. [*She sits down beside her basket.*]

THE DAUGHTER Sixpence thrown away! Really, mamma, you might have spared Freddy that. [*She retreats in disgust behind the pillar.*]

[*An elderly gentleman of the amiable military type rushes into shelter, and closes a dripping umbrella. He is in the same plight as* FREDDY, *very wet about the ankles. He is in evening dress, with a light overcoat. He takes the place left vacant by the daughter's retirement.*]

THE GENTLEMAN Phew!

THE MOTHER [*to the* GENTLEMAN] Oh, sir, is there any sign of its stopping?

THE GENTLEMAN I'm afraid not. It started worse than ever about two minutes ago. [*He goes to the plinth beside the flower girl; puts up his foot on it; and stoops to turn down his trouser ends.*]

THE MOTHER Oh, dear! [*She retires sadly and joins her daughter.*]

THE FLOWER GIRL [*taking advantage of the military gentleman's proximity to establish friendly relations with him*] If it's worse it's a sign it's nearly over. So cheer up, Captain; and buy a flower off a poor girl.

THE GENTLEMAN I'm sorry, I havnt any change.

THE FLOWER GIRL I can give you change, Captain.

THE GENTLEMAN For a sovereign?[2] Ive nothing less.

THE FLOWER GIRL Garn! Oh do buy a flower off me, Captain. I can change half-a-crown.[3] Take this for tuppence.[4]

8. Shaw's note.
9. That is, six pennies, roughly equivalent in value to $2 today. Before the decimalization of U.K. currency in 1971, the pound was worth twenty shillings, and each shilling was worth twelve pence.
1. Nickname for a sixpence coin.
2. A coin worth one pound, roughly equivalent to $80 today.
3. Go on!
4. Two pence (a single coin). *Half-a-crown:* a coin worth two and a half shillings, roughly equivalent to $10 today.

THE GENTLEMAN Now dont be troublesome: theres a good girl. [*Trying his pockets*] I really havnt any change—Stop: heres three hapence,[5] if thats any use to you. [*He retreats to the other pillar.*]

THE FLOWER GIRL [*disappointed, but thinking three halfpence better than nothing*] Thank you, sir.

THE BYSTANDER [*to the girl*] You be careful: give him a flower for it. Theres a bloke[6] here behind taking down every blessed word youre saying. [*All turn to the man who is taking notes.*]

THE FLOWER GIRL [*springing up terrified*] I aint done nothing wrong by speaking to the gentleman. Ive a right to sell flowers if I keep off the kerb.[7] [*Hysterically*] I'm a respectable girl: so help me, I never spoke to him except to ask him to buy a flower off me. [*General hubbub, mostly sympathetic to the* FLOWER GIRL, *but deprecating her excessive sensibility. Cries of* Dont start hollerin. Whos hurting you? Nobody's going to touch you. Whats the good of fussing? Steady on. Easy, easy, etc., *come from the elderly staid spectators, who pat her comfortingly. Less patient ones bid her shut her head,*[8] *or ask her roughly what is wrong with her. A remoter group, not knowing what the matter is, crowd in and increase the noise with question and answer:* Whats the row? What she do? Where is he? A tec[9] taking her down. What! him? Yes: him over there: Took money off the gentleman, etc. *The* FLOWER GIRL, *distraught and mobbed, breaks through them to the gentleman, crying wildly.*] Oh, sir, dont let him charge me. You dunno what it means to me. Theyll take away my character[1] and drive me on the streets for speaking to gentlemen. They—

THE NOTE TAKER [*coming forward on her right, the rest crowding after him*] There, there, there, there! whos hurting you, you silly girl? What do you take me for?

THE BYSTANDER It's all right: hes a gentleman: look at his boots. [*Explaining to the* NOTE TAKER] She thought you was a copper's nark, sir.

THE NOTE TAKER [*with quick interest*] Whats a copper's nark?

THE BYSTANDER [*inapt at definition*] It's a —well, it's a copper's nark, as you might say. What else would you call it? A sort of informer.

THE FLOWER GIRL [*still hysterical*] I take my Bible oath I never said a word—

THE NOTE TAKER [*overbearing but good-humored*] Oh, shut up, shut up. Do I look like a policeman?

THE FLOWER GIRL [*far from reassured*] Then what did you take down my words for? How do I know whether you took me down right? You just shew[2] me what youve wrote about me. [*The* NOTE TAKER *opens his book and holds it steadily under her nose, though the pressure of the mob trying to read it over his shoulders would upset a weaker man.*] Whats that? That aint proper writing. I cant read that.

THE NOTE TAKER I can. [*Reads, reproducing her pronunciation exactly.*] "Cheer ap, Keptin; n' baw ya flahr orf a pore gel."

5. Half-penny coins.
6. Man.
7. Curb.
8. That is, shut up.
9. Detective (slang).
1. Testimony about an employee's qualities, provided by the employer; more generally, reputation. A woman who lost her reputation, and who therefore was unable to find legal work, was in danger of being driven into prostitution ("on the streets").
2. Show.

THE FLOWER GIRL [*much distressed*] It's because I called him Captain. I meant no harm. [*To the* GENTLEMAN] Oh, sir, dont let him lay a charge agen[3] me for a word like that. You—

THE GENTLEMAN Charge! I make no charge. [*To the* NOTE TAKER] Really, sir, if you are a detective, you need not begin protecting me against molestation by young women until I ask you. Anybody could see that the girl meant no harm.

THE BYSTANDERS GENERALLY [*demonstrating against police espionage*] Course they could. What business is it of yours? You mind your own affairs. He wants promotion, he does. Taking down people's words! Girl never said a word to him. What harm if she did? Nice thing a girl cant shelter from the rain without being insulted, etc., etc., etc. [*She is conducted by the more sympathetic demonstrators back to her plinth, where she resumes her seat and struggles with her emotion.*]

THE BYSTANDER He aint a tec. Hes a blooming busybody: thats what he is. I tell you, look at his boots.

THE NOTE TAKER [*turning on him genially*] And how are all your people down at Selsey?[4]

THE BYSTANDER [*suspiciously*] Who told you my people come from Selsey?

THE NOTE TAKER Never you mind. They did. [*To the* GIRL] How do you come to be up so far east? You were born in Lisson Grove.[5]

THE FLOWER GIRL [*appalled*] Oh, what harm is there in my leaving Lisson Grove? It wasnt fit for a pig to live in; and I had to pay four-and-six[6] a week. [*In tears*] Oh, boo—hoo—oo—

THE NOTE TAKER Live where you like; but stop that noise.

THE GENTLEMAN [*to the* GIRL] Come, come! he cant touch you: you have a right to live where you please.

A SARCASTIC BYSTANDER [*thrusting himself between the* NOTE TAKER *and the* GENTLEMAN] Park Lane, for instance. Id like to go into the Housing Question[7] with you, I would.

THE FLOWER GIRL [*subsiding into a brooding melancholy over her basket, and talking very low-spiritedly to herself*] I'm a good girl, I am.

THE SARCASTIC BYSTANDER [*not attending to her*] Do you know where *I* come from?

THE NOTE TAKER [*promptly*] Hoxton.[8]

[*Titterings. Popular interest in the* NOTE TAKER*'s performance increases.*]

THE SARCASTIC ONE [*amazed*] Well, who said I didnt? Bly me![9] You know everything, you do.

THE FLOWER GIRL [*still nursing her sense of injury*] Aint no call to meddle with me, he aint.

3. Against.
4. A town on the coast of England, directly south of London.
5. A district of northwest London notorious in Shaw's day for slums, crime, and prostitution.
6. That is, four shillings and sixpence (the standard form of expressing amounts of these currencies).
7. The early twentieth-century debate over the need to provide adequate, affordable housing for the working classes. *Park Lane:* one of the most fashionable streets in London, about a mile west of Covent Garden.
8. A district of central London known for its theaters and music halls, as well as its overcrowding and slums.
9. That is, blimey, a shortened form of "gorblimey" (God blind me!), an exclamation of surprise.

THE BYSTANDER [*to her*] Of course he aint. Dont you stand it from him. [*To the* NOTE TAKER] See here: what call have you to know about people what never offered to meddle with you? Wheres your warrant?

SEVERAL BYSTANDERS [*encouraged by this seeming point of law*] Yes: wheres your warrant?

THE FLOWER GIRL Let him say what he likes. I dont want to have no truck with him.

THE BYSTANDER You take us for dirt under your feet, dont you? Catch you taking liberties with a gentleman!

THE SARCASTIC BYSTANDER Yes: tell him where he come from if you want to go fortune-telling.

THE NOTE TAKER Cheltenham, Harrow, Cambridge, and India.[1]

THE GENTLEMAN Quite right. [*Great laughter. Reaction in the* NOTE TAKER'S *favor. Exclamations of* He knows all about it. Told him proper. Hear him tell the toff[2] where he come from? etc.] May I ask, sir, do you do this for your living at a music hall?

THE NOTE TAKER Ive thought of that. Perhaps I shall some day.

[*The rain has stopped; and the persons on the outside of the crowd begin to drop off.*]

THE FLOWER GIRL [*resenting the reaction*] Hes no gentleman, he aint, to interfere with a poor girl.

THE DAUGHTER [*out of patience, pushing her way rudely to the front and displacing the* GENTLEMAN, *who politely retires to the other side of the pillar*] What on earth is Freddy doing? I shall get pneumonia if I stay in this draught any longer.

THE NOTE TAKER [*to himself, hastily making a note of her pronunciation of "monia"*] Earlscourt.[3]

THE DAUGHTER [*violently*] Will you please keep your impertinent remarks to yourself?

THE NOTE TAKER Did I say that out loud? I didnt mean to. I beg your pardon. Your mother's Epsom,[4] unmistakeably.

THE MOTHER [*advancing between her* DAUGHTER *and the* NOTE TAKER] How very curious! I was brought up in Largelady Park, near Epsom.

THE NOTE TAKER [*uproariously amused*] Ha! ha! What a devil of a name! Excuse me. [*To the* DAUGHTER] You want a cab, do you?

THE DAUGHTER Dont dare speak to me.

THE MOTHER Oh, please, please Clara. [*Her* DAUGHTER *repudiates her with an angry shrug and retires haughtily.*] We should be so grateful to you, sir, if you found us a cab. [*The* NOTE TAKER *produces a whistle.*] Oh, thank you. [*She joins her* DAUGHTER.]

[*The* NOTE TAKER *blows a piercing blast.*]

THE SARCASTIC BYSTANDER There! I knowed he was a plain-clothes copper.

1. In effect, a summary of the gentleman's life: born in Cheltenham, a town in Gloucestershire, west of London; educated first at Harrow, a prestigious private school for boys in a borough of London, and then at Cambridge University, in Cambridge; and finally embarked on a career in India, which, as a large part of the British Empire, required the services of many British army officers and administrators.

2. Slightly derogatory slang term for a well-dressed gentleman.

3. That is, Earls Court, a well-to-do section of west London.

4. A suburb on the western periphery of greater London, known for horseracing.

THE BYSTANDER That aint a police whistle: thats a sporting whistle.

THE FLOWER GIRL [*still preoccupied with her wounded feelings*] Hes no right to take away my character. My character is the same to me as any lady's.

THE NOTE TAKER I dont know whether youve noticed it; but the rain stopped about two minutes ago.

THE BYSTANDER So it has. Why didnt you say so before? and us losing our time listening to your silliness. [*He walks off towards the Strand.*]

THE SARCASTIC BYSTANDER I can tell where you come from. You come from Anwell. Go back there.

THE NOTE TAKER [*helpfully*] Hanwell.[5]

THE SARCASTIC BYSTANDER [*affecting great distinction of speech*] Thenk you, teacher. Haw haw! So long.

[*He touches his hat with mock respect and strolls off.*]

THE FLOWER GIRL Frightening people like that! How would he like it himself.

THE MOTHER It's quite fine now, Clara. We can walk to a motor bus. Come.

[*She gathers her skirts above her ankles and hurries off towards the Strand.*]

THE DAUGHTER But the cab—[*Her mother is out of hearing.*] Oh, how tiresome!

[*She follows angrily.*]

[*All the rest have gone except the* NOTE TAKER, *the* GENTLEMAN, *and the* FLOWER GIRL, *who sits arranging her basket, and still pitying herself in murmurs.*]

THE FLOWER GIRL Poor girl! Hard enough for her to live without being worrited and chivied.[6]

THE GENTLEMAN [*returning to his former place on the* NOTE TAKER*'s left*] How do you do it, if I may ask?

THE NOTE TAKER Simply phonetics. The science of speech. Thats my profession: also my hobby. Happy is the man who can make a living by his hobby! You can spot an Irishman or a Yorkshireman by his brogue. *I* can place any man within six miles. I can place him within two miles in London. Sometimes within two streets.

THE FLOWER GIRL Ought to be ashamed of himself, unmanly coward!

THE GENTLEMAN But is there a living in that?

THE NOTE TAKER Oh yes. Quite a fat one. This is an age of upstarts. Men begin in Kentish Town with £80 a year, and end in Park Lane with a hundred thousand.[7] They want to drop Kentish Town; but they give themselves away every time they open their mouths. Now I can teach them—

THE FLOWER GIRL Let him mind his own business and leave a poor girl—

THE NOTE TAKER [*explosively*] Woman: cease this detestable boohooing instantly; or else seek the shelter of some other place of worship.

THE FLOWER GIRL [*with feeble defiance*] Ive a right to be here if I like, same as you.

5. Dropped *hs* are typical of Cockney pronunciation. Hanwell, a working-class precinct of western London, contained a lunatic asylum founded in 1831.

6. That is, worried and hounded.

7. That is, men rise from grim working-class beginnings (Kentish Town is in northwest London) to become millionaires.

THE NOTE TAKER A woman who utters such depressing and disgusting sounds has no right to be anywhere—no right to live. Remember that you are a human being with a soul and the divine gift of articulate speech: that your native language is the language of Shakespear and Milton and The Bible;[8] and dont sit there crooning like a bilious pigeon.

THE FLOWER GIRL [*quite overwhelmed, and looking up at him in mingled wonder and deprecation without daring to raise her head*] Ah-ah-ah-ow-ow-ow-oo!

THE NOTE TAKER [*whipping out his book*] Heavens! what a sound! [*He writes; then holds out the book and reads, reproducing her vowels exactly.*] Ah-ah-ah-ow-ow-ow-oo!

THE FLOWER GIRL [*tickled by the performance, and laughing in spite of herself*] Garn!

THE NOTE TAKER You see this creature with her kerbstone English: the English that will keep her in the gutter to the end of her days. Well, sir, in three months I could pass that girl off as a duchess at an ambassador's garden party. I could even get her a place as lady's maid or shop assistant, which requires better English. Thats the sort of thing I do for commercial millionaires. And on the profits of it I do genuine scientific work in phonetics, and a little as a poet on Miltonic lines.

THE GENTLEMAN I am myself a student of Indian dialects; and—

THE NOTE TAKER [*eagerly*] Are you? Do you know Colonel Pickering, the author of Spoken Sanscrit?

THE GENTLEMAN I am Colonel Pickering. Who are you?

THE NOTE TAKER Henry Higgins, author of Higgins's Universal Alphabet.

PICKERING [*with enthusiasm*] I came from India to meet you.

HIGGINS I was going to India to meet you.

PICKERING Where do you live?

HIGGINS 27A Wimpole Street.[9] Come and see me tomorrow.

PICKERING I'm at the Carlton.[1] Come with me now and lets have a jaw over some supper.

HIGGINS Right you are.

THE FLOWER GIRL [*to* PICKERING, *as he passes her*] Buy a flower, kind gentleman. I'm short for my lodging.

PICKERING I really havnt any change. I'm sorry.

[*He goes away.*]

HIGGINS [*shocked at girl's mendacity*] Liar. You said you could change half-a-crown.

THE FLOWER GIRL [*rising in desperation*] You ought to be stuffed with nails, you ought. [*Flinging the basket at his feet*] Take the whole blooming basket for sixpence.

[*The church clock strikes the second quarter.*]

8. Three of the greatest literary influences on the English language: the playwright William Shakespeare (1564–1616), the poet John Milton (1608–1674), and the translation of the Bible commissioned by King James (1611).

9. A street in Westminster; its most famous resident was Elizabeth Barrett, who eloped with Robert Browning from her family's home at 50 Wimpole St. in 1846.

1. An elegant London hotel on Haymarket, near Piccadilly Circus.

HIGGINS [*hearing in it the voice of God, rebuking him for his Pharisaic*[2] *want of charity to the poor girl*] A reminder.

[*He raises his hat solemnly; then throws a handful of money into the basket and follows Pickering.*]

THE FLOWER GIRL [*picking up a half-crown*] Ah-ow-ooh! [*Picking up a couple of florins*] Aaah-ow-ooh! [*Picking up several coins*] Aaaaaah-ow-ooh! [*Picking up a half-sovereign*][3] Aaaaaaaaaaaah-ow-ooh!!!

FREDDY [*springing out of a taxicab*] Got one at last. Hallo! [*To the* GIRL] Where are the two ladies that were here?

THE FLOWER GIRL They walked to the bus when the rain stopped.

FREDDY And left me with a cab on my hands. Damnation!

THE FLOWER GIRL [*with grandeur*] Never you mind, young man. I'm going home in a taxi. [*She sails off to the cab. The driver puts his hand behind him and holds the door firmly shut against her. Quite understanding his mistrust, she shews him her handful of money.*] Eightpence aint no object to me, Charlie. [*He grins and opens the door.*] Angel Court, Drury Lane,[4] round the corner of Micklejohn's oil shop. Lets see how fast you can make her hop it.[5] [*She gets in and pulls the door to with a slam as the taxicab starts.*]

FREDDY Well, I'm dashed![6]

Act 2

[*Next day at 11 a.m. Higgins's laboratory in Wimpole Street. It is a room on the first floor, looking on the street, and was meant for the drawing-room. The double doors are in the middle of the back wall; and persons entering find in the corner to their right two tall file cabinets at right angles to one another against the walls. In this corner stands a flat writing-table, on which are a phonograph, a laryngoscope,*[7] *a row of tiny organ pipes with a bellows, a set of lamp chimneys for singeing flames with burners attached to a gas plug in the wall by an indiarubber tube, several tuning-forks of different sizes, a life-size image of half a human head, showing in section the vocal organs, and a box containing a supply of wax cylinders for the phonograph.*

Further down the room, on the same side, is a fireplace, with a comfortable leather-covered easy-chair at the side of the hearth nearest the door, and a coal-scuttle. There is a clock on the mantelpiece. Between the fireplace and the phonograph table is a stand for newspapers.

On the other side of the central door, to the left of the visitor, is a cabinet of shallow drawers. On it is a telephone and the telephone directory. The corner beyond, and most of the side wall, is occupied by a grand piano, with the keyboard at the end furthest from the door, and a bench for the player extending the full length of the keyboard. On the piano is a dessert dish heaped with fruit and sweets, mostly chocolates.

The middle of the room is clear. Besides the easy-chair, the piano bench, and two chairs at the phonograph table, there is one stray chair. It stands near the fireplace. On the walls, engravings; mostly Piranesis[8] *and mezzotint portraits. No paintings.*

2. That is, self-righteous and hypocritical, like the Pharisees as depicted in The New Testament.
3. A half-pound coin. *Florins:* two-shilling coins.
4. A street close to Covent Garden; once fashionable, by the nineteenth century it became one of London's worst slums.
5. Go away quickly.
6. That is, "I'll be damned!"
7. An instrument for examining the larynx, invented in the mid-19th century.
8. Reproductions of works by Giovanni Battista Piranesi (1720–1778), an Italian printmaker known for his depictions of classical and contemporary Roman sites.

PICKERING *is seated at the table, putting down some cards and a tuning-fork which he has been using.* HIGGINS *is standing up near him, closing two or three file drawers which are hanging out. He appears in the morning light as a robust, vital, appetizing sort of man of forty or thereabouts, dressed in a professional-looking black frock-coat with a white linen collar and black silk tie. He is of the energetic, scientific type, heartily, even violently interested in everything that can be studied as a scientific subject, and careless about himself and other people, including their feelings. He is, in fact, but for his years and size, rather like a very impetuous baby "taking notice"*[9] *eagerly and loudly, and requiring almost as much watching to keep him out of unintended mischief. His manner varies from genial bullying when he is in a good humor to stormy petulance when anything goes wrong; but he is so entirely frank and void of malice that he remains likeable even in his least reasonable moments.*]

HIGGINS [*as he shuts the last drawer*] Well, I think thats the whole show.

PICKERING It's really amazing. I havnt taken half of it in, you know.

HIGGINS Would you like to go over any of it again?

PICKERING [*rising and coming to the fireplace, where he plants himself with his back to the fire*] No, thank you; not now. I'm quite done up for this morning.

HIGGINS [*following him, and standing beside him on his left*] Tired of listening to sounds?

PICKERING Yes. It's a fearful strain. I rather fancied myself because I can pronounce twenty-four distinct vowel sounds; but your hundred and thirty beat me. I cant hear a bit of difference between most of them.

HIGGINS [*chuckling, and going over to the piano to eat sweets*] Oh, that comes with practice. You hear no difference at first; but you keep on listening, and presently you find theyre all as different as A from B. [MRS. PEARCE *looks in: she is* HIGGINS*'s housekeeper.*] Whats the matter?

MRS. PEARCE [*hesitating, evidently perplexed*] A young woman wants to see you, sir.

HIGGINS A young woman! What does she want?

MRS. PEARCE Well, sir, she says youll be glad to see her when you know what shes come about. Shes quite a common girl, sir. Very common indeed. I should have sent her away, only I thought perhaps you wanted her to talk into your machines. I hope Ive not done wrong; but really you see such queer people sometimes—youll excuse me, I'm sure, sir

HIGGINS Oh, thats all right, Mrs. Pearce. Has she an interesting accent?

MRS. PEARCE Oh, something dreadful, sir, really. I dont know how you can take an interest in it.

HIGGINS [*to* PICKERING] Lets have her up. Shew her up, Mrs. Pearce. [*He rushes across to his working table and picks out a cylinder to use on the phonograph.*]

MRS. PEARCE [*only half resigned to it*] Very well, sir. It's for you to say.

[*She goes downstairs.*]

HIGGINS This is rather a bit of luck. I'll shew you how I make records. We'll set her talking; and I'll take it down first in Bell's Visible Speech, then in

9. Showing signs of intelligent observation (a phrase used specifically of babies).

broad Romic,[1] and then we'll get her on the phonograph so that you can turn her on as often as you like with the written transcript before you.

MRS. PEARCE [*returning*] This is the young woman, sir.

[*The* FLOWER GIRL *enters in state. She has a hat with three ostrich feathers, orange, sky-blue, and red. She has a nearly clean apron, and the shoddy coat has been tidied a little. The pathos of this deplorable figure, with its innocent vanity and consequential air, touches* PICKERING, *who has already straightened himself in the presence of* MRS. PEARCE. *But as to* HIGGINS, *the only distinction he makes between men and women is that when he is neither bullying nor exclaiming to the heavens against some featherweight cross, he coaxes women as a child coaxes its nurse when it wants to get anything out of her.*]

HIGGINS [*brusquely, recognizing her with unconcealed disappointment, and at once, babylike, making an intolerable grievance of it*] Why, this is the girl I jotted down last night. Shes no use: Ive got all the records I want of the Lisson Grove lingo; and I'm not going to waste another cylinder on it. [*To the* GIRL] Be off with you: I dont want you.

THE FLOWER GIRL Dont you be so saucy. You aint heard what I come for yet. [*To* MRS. PEARCE, *who is waiting at the door for further instruction*] Did you tell him I come in a taxi?

MRS. PEARCE Nonsense, girl! what do you think a gentleman like Mr. Higgins cares what you came in?

THE FLOWER GIRL Oh, we are proud! He aint above giving lessons, not him: I heard him say so. Well, I aint come here to ask for any compliment; and if my money's not good enough I can go elsewhere.

HIGGINS Good enough for what?

THE FLOWER GIRL Good enough for ye-oo. Now you know, dont you? I'm come to have lessons, I am. And to pay for em too: make no mistake.

HIGGINS [*stupent*][2] Well ! ! ! [*Recovering his breath with a gasp*] What do you expect me to say to you?

THE FLOWER GIRL Well, if you was a gentleman, you might ask me to sit down, I think. Dont I tell you I'm bringing you business?

HIGGINS Pickering: shall we ask this baggage to sit down or shall we throw her out of the window?

THE FLOWER GIRL [*running away in terror to the piano, where she turns at bay*] Ah-ah-ah-ow-ow-ow-oo! [*Wounded and whimpering*] I wont be called a baggage when Ive offered to pay like any lady.

[*Motionless, the two men stare at her from the other side of the room, amazed.*]

PICKERING [*gently*] What is it you want, my girl?

1. The system of phonetic notation—a precursor of the International Phonetic Alphabet (IPA) used today—devised by Henry Sweet (1845–1912), a linguist on whose career Shaw drew in creating Higgins and who defined a "broad" transcription as less detailed (and less scientific) than a narrow one. *Bell's Visible Speech:* a system of notation created a decade earlier than Sweet's by the educator Alexander Melville Bell (1819–1905), the father of the inventor Alexander Graham Bell; it attempts to represent the position of the vocal organs as individual sounds are produced.

2. In a state of stupefied amazement.

THE FLOWER GIRL I want to be a lady in a flower shop stead of selling at the corner of Tottenham Court Road.[3] But they wont take me unless I can talk more genteel. He said he could teach me. Well, here I am ready to pay him—not asking any favor—and he treats me as if I was dirt.

MRS. PEARCE How can you be such a foolish ignorant girl as to think you could afford to pay Mr. Higgins?

THE FLOWER GIRL Why shouldnt I? I know what lessons cost as well as you do; and I'm ready to pay.

HIGGINS How much?

THE FLOWER GIRL [*coming back to him, triumphant*] Now youre talking! I thought youd come off it when you saw a chance of getting back a bit of what you chucked at me last night. [*Confidentially*] Youd had a drop in,[4] hadnt you?

HIGGINS [*peremptorily*] Sit down.

THE FLOWER GIRL Oh, if youre going to make a compliment of it—

HIGGINS [*thundering at her*] Sit down.

MRS. PEARCE [*severely*] Sit down, girl. Do as youre told. [*She places the stray chair near the hearthrug between* HIGGINS *and* PICKERING, *and stands behind it waiting for the girl to sit down.*]

THE FLOWER GIRL Ah-ah-ah-ow-ow-oo! [*She stands, half rebellious, half bewildered.*]

PICKERING [*very courteous*] Wont you sit down?

THE FLOWER GIRL [*coyly*] Dont mind if I do. [*She sits down.* PICKERING *returns to the hearthrug.*]

HIGGINS Whats your name?

THE FLOWER GIRL Liza Doolittle.

HIGGINS [*declaiming gravely*]
Eliza, Elizabeth, Betsy and Bess,
They went to the woods to get a birds nes':

PICKERING They found a nest with four eggs in it:

HIGGINS They took one apiece, and left three in it.

They laugh heartily at their own wit.

LIZA Oh, dont be silly.

MRS. PEARCE You mustnt speak to the gentleman like that.

LIZA Well, why wont he speak sensible to me?

HIGGINS Come back to business. How much do you propose to pay me for the lessons?

LIZA Oh, I know whats right. A lady friend of mine gets French lessons for eighteenpence an hour from a real French gentleman. Well, you wouldnt have the face to ask me the same for teaching me my own language as you would for French; so I wont give more than a shilling. Take it or leave it.

HIGGINS [*walking up and down the room, rattling his keys and his cash in his pockets*] You know, Pickering, if you consider a shilling, not as a simple shilling, but as a percentage of this girl's income, it works out as fully equivalent to sixty or seventy guineas[5] from a millionaire.

3. A busy central London shopping street, within a half mile of Covent Garden.

4. That is, you'd had something to drink.

5. Roughly equivalent to $6,000 today; a guinea is a gold coin worth twenty-one shillings.

PICKERING How so?

HIGGINS Figure it out. A millionaire has about £150 a day. She earns about half-a-crown.

LIZA [*haughtily*] Who told you I only—

HIGGINS [*continuing*] She offers me two-fifths of her day's income for a lesson. Two-fifths of a millionaire's income for a day would be somewhere about £60. It's handsome. By George, it's enormous! it's the biggest offer I ever had.

LIZA [*rising, terrified*] Sixty pounds! What are you talking about? I never offered you sixty pounds. Where would I get—

HIGGINS Hold your tongue.

LIZA [*weeping*] But I aint got sixty pounds. Oh—

MRS. PEARCE Dont cry, you silly girl. Sit down. Nobody is going to touch your money.

HIGGINS Somebody is going to touch you, with a broomstick, if you dont stop snivelling. Sit down.

LIZA [*obeying slowly*] Ah-ah-ah-ow-oo-o! One would think you was my father.

HIGGINS If I decide to teach you, I'll be worse than two fathers to you. Here! [*He offers her his silk handkerchief.*]

LIZA Whats this for?

HIGGINS To wipe your eyes. To wipe any part of your face that feels moist. Remember: thats your handkerchief; and thats your sleeve. Dont mistake the one for the other if you wish to become a lady in a shop.

[LIZA, *utterly bewildered, stares helplessly at him.*]

MRS. PEARCE It's no use talking to her like that, Mr. Higgins: she doesnt understand you. Besides, youre quite wrong: she doesnt do it that way at all. [*She takes the handkerchief.*]

LIZA [*snatching it*] Here! You give me that handkerchief. He give it to me, not to you.

PICKERING [*laughing*] He did. I think it must be regarded as her property, Mrs. Pearce.

MRS. PEARCE [*resigning herself*] Serve you right, Mr. Higgins.

PICKERING Higgins: I'm interested. What about the ambassador's garden party? I'll say youre the greatest teacher alive if you make that good. I'll bet you all the expenses of the experiment you cant do it. And I'll pay for the lessons.

LIZA Oh, you are real good. Thank you, Captain.

HIGGINS [*tempted, looking at her*] It's almost irresistible. Shes so deliciously low—so horribly dirty—

LIZA [*protesting extremely*] Ah-ah-ah-ah-ow-ow-oo-oo!!! I aint dirty: I washed my face and hands afore I come, I did.

PICKERING Youre certainly not going to turn her head with flattery, Higgins.

MRS. PEARCE [*uneasy*] Oh, dont say that, sir: theres more ways than one of turning a girl's head; and nobody can do it better than Mr. Higgins, though he may not always mean it. I do hope, sir, you wont encourage him to do anything foolish.

HIGGINS [*becoming excited as the idea grows on him*] What is life but a series of inspired follies? The difficulty is to find them to do. Never lose a chance: it doesnt come every day. I shall make a duchess of this draggle-tailed guttersnipe.

LIZA [*strongly deprecating this view of her*] Ah-ah-ah-ow-ow-oo!

HIGGINS [*carried away*] Yes: in six months—in three if she has a good ear and a quick tongue—I'll take her anywhere and pass her off as anything. We'll start today: now! this moment! Take her away and clean her, Mrs. Pearce. Monkey Brand,[6] if it wont come off any other way. Is there a good fire in the kitchen?

MRS. PEARCE [*protesting*] Yes; but—

HIGGINS [*storming on*] Take all her clothes off and burn them. Ring up Whiteley[7] or somebody for new ones. Wrap her up in brown paper til they come.

LIZA Youre no gentleman, youre not, to talk of such things. I'm a good girl, I am; and I know what the like of you are, I do.

HIGGINS We want none of your Lisson Grove prudery here, young woman. Youve got to learn to behave like a duchess. Take her away, Mrs. Pearce. If she gives you any trouble wallop her.

LIZA [*springing up and running between* PICKERING *and* MRS. PEARCE *for protection*] No! I'll call the police, I will.

MRS. PEARCE But Ive no place to put her.

HIGGINS Put her in the dustbin.

LIZA Ah-ah-ah-ow-ow-oo!

PICKERING Oh come, Higgins! be reasonable.

MRS. PEARCE [*resolutely*] You must be reasonable, Mr. Higgins: really you must. You cant walk over everybody like this.

[HIGGINS, *thus scolded, subsides. The hurricane is succeeded by a zephyr of amiable surprise.*]

HIGGINS [*with professional exquisiteness of modulation*] I walk over everybody! My dear Mrs. Pearce, my dear Pickering, I never had the slightest intention of walking over anyone. All I propose is that we should be kind to this poor girl. We must help her to prepare and fit herself for her new station in life. If I did not express myself clearly it was because I did not wish to hurt her delicacy, or yours.

[LIZA, *reassured, steals back to her chair.*]

MRS. PEARCE [*to* PICKERING] Well, did you ever hear anything like that, sir?

PICKERING [*laughing heartily*] Never, Mrs. Pearce: never.

HIGGINS [*patiently*] Whats the matter?

MRS. PEARCE Well, the matter is, sir, that you cant take a girl up like that as if you were picking up a pebble on the beach.

HIGGINS Why not?

MRS. PEARCE Why not! But you dont know anything about her. What about her parents? She may be married.

LIZA Garn!

HIGGINS There! As the girl very properly says, Garn! Married indeed! Dont you know that a woman of that class looks a worn out drudge of fifty a year after shes married.

LIZA Whood marry me?

HIGGINS [*suddenly resorting to the most thrillingly beautiful low tones in his best elocutionary style*] By George, Eliza, the streets will be strewn with

6. A popular brand of scouring soap.

7. A large department store in London.

the bodies of men shooting themselves for your sake before Ive done with you.

MRS. PEARCE Nonsense, sir. You mustnt talk like that to her.

LIZA [*rising and squaring herself determinedly*] I'm going away. He's off his chump, he is. I dont want no balmies[8] teaching me.

HIGGINS [*wounded in his tenderest point by her insensibility to his elocution*] Oh, indeed! I'm mad, am I? Very well, Mrs. Pearce: you neednt order the new clothes for her. Throw her out.

LIZA [*whimpering*] Nah-ow. You got no right to touch me.

MRS. PEARCE You see now what comes of being saucy. [*Indicating the door*] This way, please.

LIZA [*almost in tears*] I didnt want no clothes. I wouldnt have taken them. [*She throws away the handkerchief.*] I can buy my own clothes.

HIGGINS [*deftly retrieving the handkerchief and intercepting her on her reluctant way to the door*] Youre an ungrateful wicked girl. This is my return for offering to take you out of the gutter and dress you beautifully and make a lady of you.

MRS. PEARCE Stop, Mr. Higgins. I wont allow it. It's you that are wicked. Go home to your parents, girl; and tell them to take better care of you.

LIZA I aint got no parents. They told me I was big enough to earn my own living and turned me out.

MRS. PEARCE Wheres your mother?

LIZA I aint got no mother. Her that turned me out was my sixth stepmother. But I done without them. And I'm a good girl, I am.

HIGGINS Very well, then, what on earth is all this fuss about? The girl doesnt belong to anybody—is no use to anybody but me. [*He goes to* MRS. PEARCE *and begins coaxing.*] You can adopt her, Mrs. Pearce: I'm sure a daughter would be a great amusement to you. Now dont make any more fuss. Take her downstairs; and—

MRS. PEARCE But whats to become of her? Is she to be paid anything? Do be sensible, sir.

HIGGINS Oh, pay her whatever is necessary: put it down in the housekeeping book. [*Impatiently*] What on earth will she want with money? She'll have her food and her clothes. She'll only drink if you give her money.

LIZA [*turning on him*] Oh you are a brute. It's a lie: nobody ever saw the sign of liquor on me. [*She goes back to her chair and plants herself there defiantly.*]

PICKERING [*in good-humored remonstrance*] Does it occur to you, Higgins, that the girl has some feelings?

HIGGINS [*looking critically at her*] Oh no, I dont think so. Not any feelings that we need bother about. [*Cheerily*] Have you, Eliza?

LIZA I got my feelings same as anyone else.

HIGGINS [*to* PICKERING, *reflectively*] You see the difficulty?

PICKERING Eh? What difficulty?

HIGGINS To get her to talk grammar. The mere pronunciation is easy enough.

LIZA I dont want to talk grammar. I want to talk like a lady.

8. Crazies, madmen (slang). *Off his chump:* out of his senses (*chump* is slang for "head").

MRS. PEARCE Will you please keep to the point, Mr. Higgins. I want to know on what terms the girl is to be here. Is she to have any wages? And what is to become of her when youve finished your teaching? You must look ahead a little.

HIGGINS [*impatiently*] Whats to become of her if I leave her in the gutter? Tell me that, Mrs. Pearce.

MRS. PEARCE Thats her own business, not yours, Mr. Higgins.

HIGGINS Well, when Ive done with her, we can throw her back into the gutter; and then it will be her own business again; so thats all right.

LIZA Oh, youve no feeling heart in you: you dont care for nothing but yourself. [*She rises and takes the floor resolutely.*] Here! Ive had enough of this. I'm going. [*Making for the door*] You ought to be ashamed of yourself, you ought.

HIGGINS [*snatching a chocolate cream from the piano, his eyes suddenly beginning to twinkle with mischief*] Have some chocolates, Eliza.

LIZA [*halting, tempted*] How do I know what might be in them? Ive heard of girls being drugged by the like of you.

[HIGGINS *whips out his penknife; cuts a chocolate in two; puts one half into his mouth and bolts it; and offers her the other half.*]

HIGGINS Pledge of good faith, Eliza. I eat one half: you eat the other. [LIZA *opens her mouth to retort: he pops the half chocolate into it.*] You shall have boxes of them, barrels of them, every day. You shall live on them. Eh?

LIZA [*who has disposed of the chocolate after being nearly choked by it*] I wouldnt have ate it, only I'm too ladylike to take it out of my mouth.

HIGGINS Listen, Eliza. I think you said you came in a taxi.

LIZA Well, what if I did? Ive as good a right to take a taxi as anyone else.

HIGGINS You have, Eliza; and in future you shall have as many taxis as you want. You shall go up and down and round the town in a taxi every day. Think of that, Eliza.

MRS. PEARCE Mr. Higgins: youre tempting the girl. It's not right. She should think of the future.

HIGGINS At her age! Nonsense! Time enough to think of the future when you havnt any future to think of. No, Eliza: do as this lady does: think of other people's futures; but never think of your own. Think of chocolates, and taxis, and gold, and diamonds.

LIZA No: I dont want no gold and no diamonds. I'm a good girl, I am. [*She sits down again, with an attempt at dignity.*]

HIGGINS You shall remain so, Eliza, under the care of Mrs. Pearce. And you shall marry an officer in the Guards, with a beautiful moustache: the son of a marquis, who will disinherit him for marrying you, but will relent when he sees your beauty and goodness—

PICKERING Excuse me, Higgins; but I really must interfere. Mrs. Pearce is quite right. If this girl is to put herself in your hands for six months for an experiment in teaching, she must understand thoroughly what shes doing.

HIGGINS How can she? Shes incapable of understanding anything. Besides, do any of us understand what we are doing? If we did, would we ever do it?

PICKERING Very clever, Higgins; but not sound sense. [*To* ELIZA] Miss Doolittle—

LIZA [*overwhelmed*] Ah-ah-ow-oo!

HIGGINS There! Thats all you get out of Eliza. Ah-ah-ow-oo! No use explaining. As a military man you ought to know that. Give her her orders: thats what she wants. Eliza: you are to live here for the next six months, learning how to speak beautifully, like a lady in a florist's shop. If youre good and do whatever youre told, you shall sleep in a proper bedroom, and have lots to eat, and money to buy chocolates and take rides in taxis. If youre naughty and idle you will sleep in the back kitchen among the black beetles, and be walloped by Mrs. Pearce with a broomstick. At the end of six months you shall go to Buckingham Palace in a carriage, beautifully dressed. If the King finds out youre not a lady, you will be taken by the police to the Tower of London, where your head will be cut off as a warning to other presumptuous flower girls. If you are not found out, you shall have a present of seven-and-sixpence to start life with as a lady in a shop. If you refuse this offer you will be a most ungrateful and wicked girl; and the angels will weep for you. [*To* PICKERING] Now are you satisfied, Pickering? [*To* MRS. PEARCE] Can I put it more plainly and fairly, Mrs. Pearce?

MRS. PEARCE [*patiently*] I think youd better let me speak to the girl properly in private. I dont know that I can take charge of her or consent to the arrangement at all. Of course I know you dont mean her any harm; but when you get what you call interested in people's accents, you never think or care what may happen to them or you. Come with me, Eliza.

HIGGINS Thats all right. Thank you, Mrs. Pearce. Bundle her off to the bathroom.

LIZA [*rising reluctantly and suspiciously*] Youre a great bully, you are. I wont stay here if I dont like. I wont let nobody wallop me. I never asked to go to Bucknam Palace, I didnt. I was never in trouble with the police, not me. I'm a good girl—

MRS. PEARCE Dont answer back, girl. You dont understand the gentleman. Come with me. [*She leads the way to the door, and holds it open for* ELIZA.]

LIZA [*as she goes out*] Well, what I say is right. I wont go near the king, not if I'm going to have my head cut off. If I'd known what I was letting myself in for, I wouldnt have come here. I always been a good girl; and I never offered to say a word to him; and I dont owe him nothing; and I dont care; and I wont be put upon; and I have my feelings the same as anyone else—

[MRS. PEARCE *shuts the door; and* ELIZA'S *plaints are no longer audible.* PICKERING *comes from the hearth to the chair and sits astride it with his arms on the back.*]

PICKERING Excuse the straight question, Higgins. Are you a man of good character where women are concerned?

HIGGINS [*moodily*] Have you ever met a man of good character where women are concerned?

PICKERING Yes: very frequently.

HIGGINS [*dogmatically, lifting himself on his hands to the level of the piano, and sitting on it with a bounce*] Well, I havnt. I find that the moment I let a woman make friends with me, she becomes jealous, exacting, suspicious, and a damned nuisance. I find that the moment I let myself make friends with a woman, I become selfish and tyrannical. Women upset everything. When you let them into your life, you find that the woman is driving at one thing and youre driving at another.

PICKERING At what, for example?

HIGGINS [*coming off the piano restlessly*] Oh, Lord knows! I suppose the woman wants to live her own life; and the man wants to live his; and each tries to drag the other on to the wrong track. One wants to go north and the other south; and the result is that both have to go east, though they both hate the east wind. [*He sits down on the bench at the keyboard.*] So here I am, a confirmed old bachelor, and likely to remain so.

PICKERING [*rising and standing over him gravely*] Come, Higgins! You know what I mean. If I'm to be in this business I shall feel responsible for that girl. I hope it's understood that no advantage is to be taken of her position.

HIGGINS What! That thing! Sacred, I assure you. [*Rising to explain*] You see, she'll be a pupil; and teaching would be impossible unless pupils were sacred. Ive taught scores of American millionairesses how to speak English: the best looking women in the world. I'm seasoned. They might as well be blocks of wood. *I* might as well be a block of wood. It's—

[MRS. PEARCE *opens the door. She has* ELIZA'*s hat in her hand.* PICKERING *retires to the easy-chair at the hearth and sits down.*]

HIGGINS [*eagerly*] Well, Mrs. Pearce: is it all right?

MRS. PEARCE [*at the door*] I just wish to trouble you with a word, if I may, Mr. Higgins.

HIGGINS Yes, certainly. Come in. [*She comes forward.*] Dont burn that, Mrs. Pearce. I'll keep it as a curiosity. [*He takes the hat.*]

MRS. PEARCE Handle it carefully, sir, please. I had to promise her not to burn it; but I had better put it in the oven for a while.

HIGGINS [*putting it down hastily on the piano*] Oh! thank you. Well, what have you to say to me?

PICKERING Am I in the way?

MRS. PEARCE Not at all, sir. Mr. Higgins: will you please be very particular what you say before the girl?

HIGGINS [*sternly*] Of course. I'm always particular about what I say. Why do you say this to me?

MRS. PEARCE [*unmoved*] No, sir: youre not at all particular when youve mislaid anything or when you get a little impatient. Now it doesnt matter before me: I'm used to it. But you really must not swear before the girl.

HIGGINS [*indignantly*] I swear! [*Most emphatically*] I never swear. I detest the habit. What the devil do you mean?

MRS. PEARCE [*stolidly*] Thats what I mean, sir. You swear a great deal too much. I dont mind your damning and blasting, and what the devil and where the devil and who the devil—

HIGGINS Mrs. Pearce: this language from your lips! Really!

MRS. PEARCE [*not to be put off*] —but there is a certain word I must ask you not to use. The girl has just used it herself because the bath was too hot. It begins with the same letter as bath.[9] She knows no better: she learnt it at her mother's knee. But she must not hear it from your lips

HIGGINS [*loftily*] I cannot charge myself with having ever uttered it, Mrs. Pearce. [*She looks at him steadfastly. He adds, hiding an uneasy conscience with a judicial air.*] Except perhaps in a moment of extreme and justifiable excitement.

MRS. PEARCE Only this morning, sir, you applied it to your boots, to the butter, and to the brown bread.

HIGGINS Oh, that! Mere alliteration, Mrs. Pearce, natural to a poet

9. That is, "bloody," a colloquial intensifier that came to be considered highly offensive and profane (folk etymology linked it to the oath "God's blood!").

MRS. PEARCE Well, sir, whatever you choose to call it, I beg you not to let the girl hear you repeat it.

HIGGINS Oh, very well, very well. Is that all?

MRS. PEARCE No, sir. We shall have to be very particular with this girl as to personal cleanliness.

HIGGINS Certainly. Quite right. Most important.

MRS. PEARCE I mean not to be slovenly about her dress or untidy in leaving things about.

HIGGINS [*going to her solemnly*] Just so. I intended to call your attention to that. [*He passes on to* PICKERING, *who is enjoying the conversation immensely.*] It is these little things that matter, Pickering. Take care of the pence and the pounds will take care of themselves is as true of personal habits as of money. [*He comes to anchor on the hearthrug, with the air of a man in an unassailable position.*]

MRS. PEARCE Yes, sir. Then might I ask you not to come down to breakfast in your dressing-gown, or at any rate not to use it as a napkin to the extent you do, sir. And if you would be so good as not to eat everything off the same plate, and to remember not to put the porridge saucepan out of your hand on the clean tablecloth, it would be a better example to the girl. You know you nearly choked yourself with a fishbone in the jam only last week.

HIGGINS [*rounded from the hearthrug and drifting back to the piano*] I may do these things sometimes in absence of mind; but surely I dont do them habitually. [*Angrily*] By the way: my dressing-gown smells most damnably of benzine.[1]

MRS. PEARCE No doubt it does, Mr. Higgins. But if you will wipe your fingers—

HIGGINS [*yelling*] Oh very well, very well: I'll wipe them in my hair in future.

MRS. PEARCE I hope youre not offended, Mr. Higgins.

HIGGINS [*shocked at finding himself thought capable of an unamiable sentiment*] Not at all, not at all. Youre quite right, Mrs. Pearce: I shall be particularly careful before the girl. Is that all?

MRS. PEARCE No, sir. Might she use some of those Japanese dresses you brought from abroad? I really cant put her back into her old things.

HIGGINS Certainly. Anything you like. Is that all?

MRS. PEARCE Thank you, sir. Thats all. [*She goes out.*]

HIGGINS You know, Pickering, that woman has the most extraordinary ideas about me. Here I am, a shy, diffident sort of man. Ive never been able to feel really grown-up and tremendous, like other chaps. And yet shes firmly persuaded that I'm an arbitrary overbearing bossing kind of person. I cant account for it.

[MRS. PEARCE *returns.*]

MRS. PEARCE If you please, sir, the trouble's beginning already. Theres a dustman[2] downstairs, Alfred Doolittle, wants to see you. He says you have his daughter here.

PICKERING [*rising*] Phew! I say! [*He retreats to the hearthrug.*]

HIGGINS [*promptly*] Send the blackguard up.

MRS. PEARCE Oh, very well, sir. [*She goes out.*]

PICKERING He may not be a blackguard, Higgins.

HIGGINS Nonsense. Of course hes a blackguard.

1. A solvent used to remove grease spots. 2. Garbage collector.

PICKERING Whether he is or not, I'm afraid we shall have some trouble with him.

HIGGINS [*confidently*] Oh no: I think not. If theres any trouble he shall have it with me, not I with him. And we are sure to get something interesting out of him.

PICKERING About the girl?

HIGGINS No. I mean his dialect.

PICKERING Oh!

MRS. PEARCE [*at the door*] Doolittle, sir. [*She admits* DOOLITTLE *and retires.*]

[ALFRED DOOLITTLE *is an elderly but vigorous dustman, clad in the costume of his profession, including a hat with a back brim covering his neck and shoulders. He has well marked and rather interesting features, and seems equally free from fear and conscience. He has a remarkably expressive voice, the result of a habit of giving vent to his feelings without reserve. His present pose is that of wounded honor and stern resolution.*]

DOOLITTLE [*at the door, uncertain which of the two gentlemen is his man*] Professor Higgins?

HIGGINS Here. Good morning. Sit down.

DOOLITTLE Morning, Governor. [*He sits down magisterially.*] I come about a very serious matter, Governor.

HIGGINS [*to* PICKERING] Brought up in Hounslow.[3] Mother Welsh, I should think. [DOOLITTLE *opens his mouth, amazed.* HIGGINS *continues.*] What do you want, Doolittle?

DOOLITTLE [*menacingly*] I want my daughter: thats what I want. See?

HIGGINS Of course you do. Youre her father, arnt you? You dont suppose anyone else wants her, do you? I'm glad to see you have some spark of family feeling left. Shes upstairs. Take her away at once.

DOOLITTLE [*rising, fearfully taken aback*] What!

HIGGINS Take her away. Do you suppose I'm going to keep your daughter for you?

DOOLITTLE [*remonstrating*] Now, now, look here, Governor. Is this reasonable? Is it fairity[4] to take advantage of a man like this? The girl belongs to me. You got her. Where do I come in? [*He sits down again.*]

HIGGINS Your daughter had the audacity to come to my house and ask me to teach her how to speak properly so that she could get a place in a flowershop. This gentleman and my housekeeper have been here all the time. [*Bullying him*] How dare you come here and attempt to blackmail me? You sent her here on purpose.

DOOLITTLE [*protesting*] No, Governor.

HIGGINS You must have. How else could you possibly know that she is here?

DOOLITTLE Dont take a man up like that, Governor.

HIGGINS The police shall take you up. This is a plant—a plot to extort money by threats. I shall telephone for the police. [*He goes resolutely to the telephone and opens the directory.*]

DOOLITTLE Have I asked you for a brass farthing?[5] I leave it to the gentleman here: have I said a word about money?

3. A working-class suburb west of central London.

4. Fair (Doolittle's fanciful coinage).

5. An expression equivalent to "one red cent"; a farthing is one quarter of a penny, and "brass" here is emphatic.

HIGGINS [*throwing the book aside and marching down on* DOOLITTLE *with a poser*] What else did you come for?

DOOLITTLE [*sweetly*] Well, what would a man come for? Be human, Governor.

HIGGINS [*disarmed*] Alfred: did you put her up to it?

DOOLITTLE So help me, Governor, I never did. I take my Bible oath I aint seen the girl these two months past.

HIGGINS Then how did you know she was here?

DOOLITTLE [*"most musical, most melancholy"*[6]] I'll tell you, Governor, if youll only let me get a word in. I'm willing to tell you. I'm wanting to tell you. I'm waiting to tell you.

HIGGINS Pickering: this chap has a certain natural gift of rhetoric. Observe the rhythm of his native wood-notes wild.[7] "I'm willing to tell you: I'm wanting to tell you: I'm waiting to tell you." Sentimental rhetoric! thats the Welsh strain in him. It also accounts for his mendacity and dishonesty.

PICKERING Oh, please, Higgins: I'm west country[8] myself. [*To* DOOLITTLE] How did you know the girl was here if you didnt send her?

DOOLITTLE It was like this, Governor. The girl took a boy in the taxi to give him a jaunt. Son of her landlady, he is. He hung about on the chance of her giving him another ride home. Well, she sent him back for her luggage when she heard you was willing for her to stop here. I met the boy at the corner of Long Acre and Endell Street.

HIGGINS Public house.[9] Yes?

DOOLITTLE The poor man's club, Governor: why shouldnt I?

PICKERING Do let him tell his story, Higgins.

DOOLITTLE He told me what was up. And I ask you, what was my feelings and my duty as a father? I says to the boy, "You bring me the luggage," I says—

PICKERING Why didnt you go for it yourself?

DOOLITTLE Landlady wouldnt have trusted me with it, Governor. Shes that kind of woman: you know. I had to give the boy a penny afore he trusted me with it, the little swine. I brought it to her just to oblige you like, and make myself agreeable. Thats all.

HIGGINS How much luggage?

DOOLITTLE Musical instrument, Governor. A few pictures, a trifle of jewelry, and a bird-cage. She said she didnt want no clothes. What was I to think from that, Governor? I ask you as a parent what was I to think?

HIGGINGS So you came to rescue her from worse than death, eh?

DOOLITTLE [*appreciatively: relieved at being so well understood*] Just so, Governor. Thats right.

PICKERING But why did you bring her luggage if you intended to take her away?

DOOLITTLE Have I said a word about taking her away? Have I now?

HIGGINS [*determinedly*] Youre going to take her away, double quick. [*He crosses to the hearth and rings the bell.*]

6. From John Milton's poem "Il Penseroso" (ca. 1631), line 62.

7. A quotation from Milton's "L'Allegro" (ca. 1631), line 134; in the poem (a companion piece to "Il Penseroso"), the phrase refers to Shakespeare.

8. The southwestern counties of England—Somerset, Dorset, Devon, and Cornwall. The inhabitants of Cornwall and Wales are connected by their related languages, and the English long regarded (and often denigrated) them as separate cultural groups.

9. That is, a pub.

DOOLITTLE [*rising*] No, Governor. Dont say that. I'm not the man to stand in my girl's light. Heres a carcer opening for her, as you might say; and—

[MRS. PEARCE *opens the door and awaits orders.*]

HIGGINS Mrs. Pearce: this is Eliza's father. He has come to take her away. Give her to him. [*He goes back to the piano, with an air of washing his hands of the whole affair.*]

DOOLITTLE No. This is a misunderstanding. Listen here—

MRS. PEARCE He cant take her away, Mr. Higgins: how can he? You told me to burn her clothes.

DOOLITTLE Thats right. I cant carry the girl through the streets like a blooming monkey, can I? I put it to you.

HIGGINS You have put it to me that you want your daughter. Take your daughter. If she has no clothes go out and buy her some.

DOOLITTLE [*desperate*] Wheres the clothes she come in? Did I burn them or did your missus here?

MRS. PEARCE I am the housekeeper, if you please. I have sent for some clothes for your girl. When they come you can take her away. You can wait in the kitchen. This way, please.

[DOOLITTLE, *much troubled, accompanies her to the door; then hesitates; finally turns confidentially to* HIGGINS.]

DOOLITTLE Listen here, Governor. You and me is men of the world, aint we?

HIGGINS Oh! Men of the world, are we? Youd better go, Mrs. Pearce.

MRS. PEARCE I think so, indeed, sir.

[*She goes, with dignity.*]

PICKERING The floor is yours, Mr. Doolittle.

DOOLITTLE [*to* PICKERING] I thank you, Governor. [*To* HIGGINS, *who takes refuge on the piano bench, a little overwhelmed by the proximity of his visitor; for* DOOLITTLE *has a professional flavor of dust about him*] Well, the truth is, Ive taken a sort of fancy to you, Governor; and if you want the girl, I'm not so set on having her back home again but what I might be open to an arrangement. Regarded in the light of a young woman, shes a fine handsome girl. As a daughter shes not worth her keep; and so I tell you straight. All I ask is my rights as a father; and youre the last man alive to expect me to let her go for nothing; for I can see youre one of the straight sort, Governor. Well, whats a five pound note to you? And whats Eliza to me? [*He returns to his chair and sits down judicially.*]

PICKERING I think you ought to know, Doolittle, that Mr. Higgins's intentions are entirely honorable.

DOOLITTLE Course they are, Governor. If I thought they wasnt, Id ask fifty.

HIGGINS [*revolted*] Do you mean to say, you callous rascal, that you would sell your daughter for £50?

DOOLITTLE Not in a general way I wouldnt; but to oblige a gentleman like you I'd do a good deal, I do assure you.

PICKERING Have you no morals, man?

DOOLITTLE [*unabashed*] Cant afford them, Governor. Neither could you if you was as poor as me. Not that I mean any harm, you know. But if Liza is going to have a bit out of this, why not me too?

HIGGINS [*troubled*] I dont know what to do, Pickering. There can be no question that as a matter of morals it's a positive crime to give this chap a farthing. And yet I feel a sort of rough justice in his claim.

DOOLITTLE Thats it, Governor. Thats all I say. A father's heart, as it were.

PICKERING Well, I know the feeling; but really it seems hardly right—

DOOLITTLE Dont say that, Governor. Dont look at it that way. What am I, Governors both? I ask you, what am I? I'm one of the undeserving poor: thats what I am. Think of what that means to a man. It means that hes up agen[1] middle class morality all the time. If theres anything going, and I put in for a bit of it, it's always the same story: "Youre undeserving; so you cant have it." But my needs is as great as the most deserving widow's that ever got money out of six different charities in one week for the death of the same husband. I dont need less than a deserving man: I need more. I dont eat less hearty than him; and I drink a lot more. I want a bit of amusement, cause I'm a thinking man. I want cheerfulness and a song and a band when I feel low. Well, they charge me just the same for everything as they charge the deserving. What is middle class morality? Just an excuse for never giving me anything. Therefore, I ask you, as two gentlemen, not to play that game on me. I'm playing straight with you. I aint pretending to be deserving. I'm undeserving; and I mean to go on being undeserving. I like it; and thats the truth. Will you take advantage of a man's nature to do him out of the price of his own daughter what hes brought up and fed and clothed by the sweat of his brow until shes growed big enough to be interesting to you two gentlemen? Is five pounds unreasonable? I put it to you; and I leave it to you.

HIGGINS [*rising, and going over to* PICKERING] Pickering: if we were to take this man in hand for three months, he could choose between a seat in the Cabinet and a popular pulpit in Wales.

PICKERING What do you say to that, Doolittle?

DOOLITTLE Not me, Governor, thank you kindly. Ive heard all the preachers and all the prime ministers—for I'm a thinking man and game for politics or religion or social reform same as all the other amusements—and I tell you it's a dog's life anyway you look at it. Undeserving poverty is my line. Taking one station in society with another, it's—it's—well, it's the only one that has any ginger in it, to my taste.

HIGGINS I suppose we must give him a fiver.

PICKERING He'll make a bad use of it, I'm afraid.

DOOLITTLE Not me, Governor, so help me I wont. Dont you be afraid that I'll save it and spare it and live idle on it. There wont be a penny of it left by Monday: I'll have to go to work same as if I'd never had it. It wont pauperize me, you bet. Just one good spree for myself and the missus, giving pleasure to ourselves and employment to others, and satisfaction to you to think it's not been throwed away. You couldnt spend it better.

HIGGINS [*taking out his pocket book and coming between* DOOLITTLE *and the piano*] This is irresistible. Lets give him ten. [*He offers two notes to the dustman.*]

DOOLITTLE No, Governor. She wouldnt have the heart to spend ten; and perhaps I shouldnt neither. Ten pounds is a lot of money: it makes a man feel prudent like: and then good-bye to happiness. You give me what I ask you, Governor: not a penny more, and not a penny less.

PICKERING Why dont you marry that missus of yours? I rather draw the line at encouraging that sort of immorality.

1. Against.

DOOLITTLE Tell her so, Governor: tell her so. *I'm* willing. It's me that suffers by it. Ive no hold on her. I got to be agreeable to her. I got to give her presents. I got to buy her clothes something sinful. I'm a slave to that woman, Governor, just because I'm not her lawful husband. And she knows it too. Catch her marrying me! Take my advice, Governor: marry Eliza while shes young and dont know no better. If you dont youll be sorry for it after. If you do, she'll be sorry for it after; but better you than her, because youre a man, and shes only a woman and dont know how to be happy anyhow.

HIGGINS Pickering: if we listen to this man another minute, we shall have no convictions left. [*To* DOOLITTLE] Five pounds I think you said.

DOOLITTLE Thank you kindly, Governor.

HIGGINS Youre sure you wont take ten?

DOOLITTLE Not now. Another time, Governor.

HIGGINS [*handing him a five-pound note*] Here you are.

DOOLITTLE Thank you, Governor. Good morning.

[*He hurries to the door, anxious to get away with his booty. When he opens it he is confronted with a dainty and exquisitely clean young Japanese lady in a simple blue cotton kimono printed cunningly with small white jasmine blossoms.* MRS. PEARCE *is with her. He gets out of her way deferentially and apologizes.*]

Beg pardon, miss.

THE JAPANESE LADY Garn! Dont you know your own daughter?

DOOLITTLE, HIGGINS, PICKERING } *exclaiming simultaneously* {
DOOLITTLE: Bly me! it's Eliza!
HIGGINS: Whats that! This!
PICKERING: By Jove!

LIZA Dont I look silly?

HIGGINS Silly?

MRS. PEARCE [*at the door*] Now, Mr. Higgins, please dont say anything to make the girl conceited about herself.

HIGGINS [*conscientiously*] Oh! Quite right, Mrs. Pearce. [*To* ELIZA] Yes: damned silly.

MRS. PEARCE Please, sir.

HIGGINS [*correcting himself*] I mean extremely silly.

LIZA I should look all right with my hat on. [*She takes up her hat; puts it on; and walks across the room to the fireplace with a fashionable air.*]

HIGGINS A new fashion, by George! And it ought to look horrible!

DOOLITTLE [*with fatherly pride*] Well, I never thought she'd clean up as good looking as that, Governor. Shes a credit to me, aint she?

LIZA I tell you, it's easy to clean up here. Hot and cold water on tap, just as much as you like, there is. Woolly towels, there is; and a towel horse[2] so hot, it burns your fingers. Soft brushes to scrub yourself, and a wooden bowl of soap smelling like primroses. Now I know why ladies is so clean. Washing's a treat for them. Wish they saw what it is for the like of me!

HIGGINS I'm glad the bath-room met with your approval.

LIZA It didnt: not all of it; and I dont care who hears me say it. Mrs. Pearce knows.

HIGGINS What was wrong, Mrs. Pearce?

MRS. PEARCE [*blandly*] Oh, nothing, sir. It doesnt matter.

2. A towel rack, in this case apparently a metal pipe filled with hot water (usually such racks were made of wood).

LIZA I had a good mind to break it. I didnt know which way to look. But I hung a towel over it, I did.

HIGGINS Over what?

MRS. PEARCE Over the looking-glass, sir.

HIGGINS Doolittle: you have brought your daughter up too strictly.

DOOLITTLE Me! I never brought her up at all, except to give her a lick of a strap now and again. Dont put it on me, Governor. She aint accustomed to it, you see: thats all. But she'll soon pick up your free-and-easy ways.

LIZA I'm a good girl, I am; and I wont pick up no free and easy ways.

HIGGINS Eliza: if you say again that youre a good girl, your father shall take you home.

LIZA Not him. You dont know my father. All he come here for was to touch you for some money to get drunk on.

DOOLITTLE Well, what else would I want money for? To put into the plate in church, I suppose. [*She puts out her tongue at him. He is so incensed by this that* PICKERING *presently finds it necessary to step between them.*] Dont you give me none of your lip; and dont let me hear you giving this gentleman any of it neither, or youll hear from me about it. See?

HIGGINS Have you any further advice to give her before you go, Doolittle? Your blessing, for instance.

DOOLITTLE No, Governor: I aint such a mug[3] as to put up my children to all I know myself. Hard enough to hold them in without that. If you want Eliza's mind improved, Governor, you do it yourself with a strap. So long, gentlemen. [*He turns to go.*]

HIGGINS [*impressively*] Stop. Youll come regularly to see your daughter. It's your duty, you know. My brother is a clergyman; and he could help you in your talks with her.

DOOLITTLE [*evasively*] Certainly. I'll come, Governor. Not just this week, because I have a job at a distance. But later on you may depend on me. Afternoon, gentlemen. Afternoon, maam.

[*He takes off his hat to* MRS. PEARCE, *who disdains the salutation and goes out. He winks at* HIGGINS, *thinking him probably a fellow-sufferer from* MRS. PEARCE'*s difficult disposition, and follows her.*]

LIZA Dont you believe the old liar. He'd as soon you set a bull-dog on him as a clergyman. You wont see him again in a hurry.

HIGGINS I dont want to, Eliza. Do you?

LIZA Not me. I dont want never to see him again, I dont. Hes a disgrace to me, he is, collecting dust, instead of working at his trade.

PICKERING What is his trade, Eliza?

LIZA Talking money out of other people's pockets into his own. His proper trade's a navvy;[4] and he works at it sometimes too—for exercise—and earns good money at it. Aint you going to call me Miss Doolittle any more?

PICKERING I beg your pardon, Miss Doolittle. It was a slip of the tongue.

LIZA Oh, I dont mind; only it sounded so genteel. I should just like to take a taxi to the corner of Tottenham Court Road and get out there and tell it to wait for me, just to put the girls in their place a bit. I wouldnt speak to them, you know.

PICKERING Better wait til we get you something really fashionable.

3. Fool.

4. An unskilled laborer who digs earth.

HIGGINS Besides, you shouldnt cut[5] your old friends now that you have risen in the world. Thats what we call snobbery.

LIZA You dont call the like of them my friends now, I should hope. Theyve took it out of me often enough with their ridicule when they had the chance; and now I mean to get a bit of my own back. But if I'm to have fashionable clothes, I'll wait. I should like to have some. Mrs. Pearce says youre going to give me some to wear in bed at night different to what I wear in the daytime; but it do seem a waste of money when you could get something to shew. Besides, I never could fancy changing into cold things on a winter night

MRS. PEARCE [*coming back*] Now, Eliza. The new things have come for you to try on.

LIZA Ah-ow-oo-ooh!

[*She rushes out.*]

MRS. PEARCE [*following her*] Oh, dont rush about like that, girl.

[*She shuts the door behind her.*]

HIGGINS Pickering: we have taken on a stiff job.

PICKERING [*with conviction*] Higgins: we have.

Act 3

[*It is* MRS. HIGGINS'*s at-home day.*[6] *Nobody has yet arrived. Her drawing-room, in a flat on Chelsea Embankment,*[7] *has three windows looking on the river; and the ceiling is not so lofty as it would be in an older house of the same pretension. The windows are open, giving access to a balcony with flowers in pots. If you stand with your face to the windows, you have the fireplace on your left and the door in the right-hand wall close to the corner nearest the windows.*

MRS. HIGGINS *was brought up on Morris and Burne Jones,*[8] *and her room, which is very unlike her son's room in Wimpole Street, is not crowded with furniture and little tables and nicknacks. In the middle of the room there is a big ottoman; and this, with the carpet, the Morris wall-papers, and the Morris chintz windows curtains and brocade covers of the ottoman and its cushions, supply all the ornament, and are much too handsome to be hidden by odds and ends of useless things. A few good oil-paintings from the exhibitions in the Grosvenor Gallery thirty years ago (the Burne Jones, not the Whistler side of them)*[9] *are on the walls. The only landscape is a Cecil Lawson on the scale of a Rubens.*[1] *There is a portrait of* MRS. HIGGINS *as she was when she defied fashion in her youth in one of the beautiful Rossettian*[2] *costumes which, when caricatured by people*

5. Break off acquaintance with; pretend not to know.
6. In middle- and upper-class society, a set time each week for receiving visitors.
7. A roadway along the north bank of the Thames in central London, developed in the late 19th century with residences for the well-to-do.
8. Two highly influential Victorian artists and designers, who were friends and colleagues. William Morris (1834–1896), associated with the Pre Raphaelites, was one of the founders of the Arts and Crafts movement and is especially well-known for his wallpaper and fabric designs; Edward Burne-Jones (1833–1898), known for his medieval-style paintings, came under the influence of the Pre-Raphaelites at about the same time as Morris.
9. An allusion to an 1877 exhibition; the painting by the American artist James McNeill Whistler (1834–1903) was so severely attacked in a review by John Ruskin (who praised Burne-Jones's work) that Whistler sued for libel.
1. Peter Paul Rubens (1577–1640), a Flemish artist identified with the baroque style and known for very large paintings. Lawson (1851–1882), an English landscape painter whose early works included a number of studies of Chelsea.
2. In the style of Dante Gabriel Rossetti (1828–1882), an English poet and painter who was a founding member of the Pre Raphaelite Brotherhood; many of his works depict idealized, sensuous women in flowing garments.

who did not understand, let to the absurdities of popular estheticism in the eighteen-seventies.

In the corner diagonally opposite the door MRS. HIGGINS, *now over sixty and long past taking the trouble to dress out of the fashion, sits writing at an elegantly simple writing-table with a bell button within reach of her hand. There is a Chippendale*[3] *chair further back in the room between her and the window nearest her side. At the other side of the room, further forward, is an Elizabethan chair roughly carved in the taste of Inigo Jones.*[4] *On the same side a piano in a decorated case. The corner between the fireplace and the window is occupied by a divan cushioned in Morris chintz.*

It is between four and five in the afternoon.

The door is opened violently; and Higgins enters with his hat on.]

MRS. HIGGINS [*dismayed*] Henry! [*Scolding him*] What are you doing here today? It is my at-home day: you promised not to come. [*As he bends to kiss her, she takes his hat off, and presents it to him.*]

HIGGINS Oh bother! [*He throws the hat down on the table.*]

MRS. HIGGINS Go home at once.

HIGGINS [*kissing her*] I know, mother. I came on purpose.

MRS. HIGGINS But you mustnt. I'm serious, Henry. You offend all my friends: they stop coming whenever they meet you.

HIGGINS Nonsense! I know I have no small talk; but people dont mind. [*He sits on the settee.*]

MRS. HIGGINS Oh! dont they? Small talk indeed! What about your large talk? Really, dear, you mustnt stay.

HIGGINS I must. Ive a job for you. A phonetic job.

MRS. HIGGINS No use, dear. I'm sorry; but I cant get round your vowels; and though I like to get pretty postcards in your patent shorthand, I always have to read the copies in ordinary writing you so thoughtfully send me.

HIGGINS Well, this isnt a phonetic job.

MRS. HIGGINS You said it was.

HIGGINS Not your part of it. Ive picked up a girl.

MRS. HIGGINS Does that mean that some girl has picked you up?

HIGGINS Not at all. I dont mean a love affair.

MRS. HIGGINS What a pity!

HIGGINS Why?

MRS. HIGGINS Well, you never fall in love with anyone under forty-five. When will you discover that there are some rather nice-looking young women about?

HIGGINS Oh, I cant be bothered with young women. My idea of a loveable woman is something as like you as possible. I shall never get into the way of seriously liking young women: some habits lie too deep to be changed. [*Rising abruptly and walking about, jingling his money and his keys in his trouser pockets*] Besides, theyre all idiots.

MRS. HIGGINS Do you know what you would do if you really loved me, Henry?

HIGGINS Oh bother! What? Marry, I suppose?

MRS. HIGGINS No. Stop fidgeting and take your hands out of your pockets. [*With a gesture of despair, he obeys and sits down again.*] Thats a good boy. Now tell me about the girl.

3. A popular 18th-century furniture style, graceful and often ornate; it was named for the English cabinetmaker Thomas Chippendale (1718–1779).

4. The founder of English classical architecture (1573–1652); he designed stage sets as well as buildings.

HIGGINS Shes coming to see you.

MRS. HIGGINS I dont remember asking her.

HIGGINS You didnt. *I* asked her. If youd known her you wouldnt have asked her.

MRS. HIGGINS Indeed! Why?

HIGGINS Well, it's like this. Shes a common flower girl. I picked her off the kerbstone.

MRS. HIGGINS And invited her to my at-home!

HIGGINS [*rising and coming to her to coax her*] Oh, thatll be all right. Ive taught her to speak properly; and she has strict orders as to her behavior. Shes to keep to two subjects: the weather and everybody's health—Fine day and How do you do, you know—and not to let herself go on things in general. That will be safe.

MRS. HIGGINS Safe! To talk about our health! about our insides! perhaps about our outsides! How could you be so silly, Henry?

HIGGINS [*impatiently*] Well, she must talk about something. [*He controls himself and sits down again.*] Oh, she'll be all right: dont you fuss. Pickering is in it with me. Ive a sort of bet on that I'll pass her off as a duchess in six months. I started on her some months ago; and shes getting on like a house on fire. I shall win my bet. She has a quick ear; and shes been easier to teach than my middle-class pupils because shes had to learn a complete new language. She talks English almost as you talk French.

MRS. HIGGINS Thats satisfactory, at all events.

HIGGINS Well, it is and it isnt.

MRS. HIGGINS What does that mean?

HIGGINS You see, Ive got her pronunciation all right; but you have to consider not only how a girl pronounces, but what she pronounces; and thats where—

[*They are interrupted by the* PARLOR-MAID, *announcing guests.*]

THE PARLOR-MAID Mrs. and Miss Fynsford Hill.

[*She withdraws.*]

HIGGINS Oh Lord! [*He rises; snatches his hat from the table; and makes for the door; but before he reaches it his mother introduces him.*]

[MRS. *and* MISS EYNSFORD HILL *are the mother and daughter who sheltered from the rain in Covent Garden. The mother is well bred, quiet, and has the habitual anxiety of straitened means. The daughter has acquired a gay air of being very much at home in society: the bravado of genteel poverty.*]

MRS. EYNSFORD HILL [*to* MRS. HIGGINS] How do you do? [*They shake hands.*]

MISS EYNSFORD HILL How d'you do? [*She shakes.*]

MRS. HIGGINS [*introducing*] My son Henry.

MRS. EYNSFORD HILL Your celebrated son! I have so longed to meet you, Professor Higgins.

HIGGINS [*glumly, making no movement in her direction*] Delighted. [*He backs against the piano and bows brusquely.*]

MISS EYNSFORD HILL [*going to him with confident familiarity*] How do you do?

HIGGINS [*staring at her*] Ive seen you before somewhere. I havnt the ghost of a notion where; but Ive heard your voice. [*Drearily*] It doesnt matter. Youd better sit down.

MRS. HIGGINS I'm sorry to say that my celebrated son has no manners. You mustnt mind him.

MISS EYNSFORD HILL [*gaily*] I dont. [*She sits in the Elizabethan chair.*]

MRS. EYNSFORD HILL [*a little bewildered*] Not at all. [*She sits on the ottoman between her daughter and* MRS. HIGGINS, *who has turned her chair away from the writing-table.*]

HIGGINS Oh, have I been rude? I didnt mean to be.

[*He goes to the central window, through which, with his back to the company, he contemplates the river and the flowers in Battersea Park on the opposite bank as if they were a frozen desert.*]

[*The* PARLOR-MAID *returns, ushering in* PICKERING.]

THE PARLOR-MAID Colonel Pickering.

[*She withdraws.*]

PICKERING How do you do, Mrs. Higgins?

MRS. HIGGINS So glad youve come. Do you know Mrs. Eynsford Hill—Miss Eynsford Hill? [*Exchange of bows. The* COLONEL *brings the Chippendale chair a little forward between* MRS. HILL *and* MRS. HIGGINS, *and sits down.*]

PICKERING Has Henry told you what weve come for?

HIGGINS [*over his shoulder*] We were interrupted: damn it!

MRS. HIGGINS Oh Henry, Henry, really!

MRS. EYNSFORD HILL [*half rising*] Are we in the way?

MRS. HIGGINS [*rising and making her sit down again*] No, no. You couldnt have come more fortunately: we want you to meet a friend of ours.

HIGGINS [*turning hopefully*] Yes, by George! We want two or three people. Youll do as well as anybody else.

[*The* PARLOR-MAID *returns, ushering* FREDDY.]

THE PARLOR-MAID Mr. Eynsford Hill.

HIGGINS [*almost audibly, past endurance*] God of Heaven! another of them.

FREDDY [*shaking hands with* MRS. HIGGINS] Ahdedo?[5]

MRS. HIGGINS Very good of you to come. [*Introducing*] Colonel Pickering.

FREDDY [*bowing*] Ahdedo?

MRS. HIGGINS I dont think you know my son, Professor Higgins.

FREDDY [*going to Higgins*] Ahdedo?

HIGGINS [*looking at him much as if he were a pickpocket*] I'll take my oath Ive met you before somewhere. Where was it?

FREDDY I dont think so.

HIGGINS [*resignedly*] It dont matter, anyhow. Sit down.

[*He shakes* FREDDY'*s hand, and almost slings him on the ottoman with his face to the windows; then comes round to the other side of it.*]

HIGGINS Well, here we are, anyhow! [*He sits down on the ottoman next* MRS. EYNSFORD HILL, *on her left.*] And now, what the devil are we going to talk about until Eliza comes?

MRS. HIGGINS Henry: you are the life and soul of the Royal Society's[6] soirées; but really youre rather trying on more commonplace occasions.

HIGGINS Am I? Very sorry. [*Beaming suddenly*] I suppose I am, you know. [*Uproariously*] Ha, ha!

5. That is, "How do you do?"

6. An independent academy of science in the United Kingdom (formally named in its 1663 charter "The Royal Society of London for Improving Natural Knowledge").

MISS EYNSFORD HILL [*who considers* HIGGINS *quite eligible matrimonially*] I sympathize. *I* havnt any small talk. If people would only be frank and say what they really think!

HIGGINS [*relapsing into gloom*] Lord forbid!

MRS. EYNSFORD HILL [*taking up her daughter's cue*] But why?

HIGGINS What they think they ought to think is bad enough, Lord knows; but what they really think would break up the whole show. Do you suppose it would be really agreeable if I were to come out now with what *I* really think?

MISS EYNSFORD HILL [*gaily*] Is it so very cynical?

HIGGINS Cynical! Who the dickens said it was cynical? I mean it wouldnt be decent.

MRS. EYNSFORD HILL [*seriously*] Oh! I'm sure you dont mean that, Mr. Higgins.

HIGGINS You see, we're all savages, more or less. We're supposed to be civilized and cultured—to know all about poetry and philosophy and art and science, and so on; but how many of us know even the meanings of these names? [*To* MISS HILL] What do you know of poetry? [*To* MRS. HILL] What do you know of science? [*Indicating* FREDDY] What does he know of art or science or anything else? What the devil do you imagine I know of philosophy?

MRS. HIGGINS [*warningly*] Or of manners, Henry?

THE PARLOR-MAID [*opening the door*] Miss Doolittle. [*She withdraws.*]

HIGGINS [*rising hastily and running to* MRS. HIGGINS] Here she is, mother. [*He stands on tiptoe and makes signs over his mother's head to* ELIZA *to indicate to her which lady is her hostess.*]

[ELIZA, *who is exquisitely dressed, produces an impression of such remarkable distinction and beauty as she enters that they all rise, quite fluttered. Guided by* HIGGINS*'s signals, she comes to* MRS. HIGGINS *with studied grace.*]

LIZA [*speaking with pedantic correctness of pronunciation and great beauty of tone*] How do you do, Mrs. Higgins? [*She gasps slightly in making sure of the H in Higgins, but is quite successful.*] Mr. Higgins told me I might come.

MRS. HIGGINS [*cordially*] Quite right: I'm very glad indeed to see you.

PICKERING How do you do, Miss Doolittle?

LIZA [*shaking hands with him*] Colonel Pickering, is it not?

MRS. EYNSFORD HILL I feel sure we have met before, Miss Doolittle. I remember your eyes.

LIZA How do you do? [*She sits down on the ottoman gracefully in the place just left vacant by* HIGGINS.]

MRS. EYNSFORD HILL [*introducing*] My daughter Clara.

LIZA How do you do?

CLARA [*impulsively*] How do you do? [*She sits down on the ottoman beside* ELIZA, *devouring her with her eyes.*]

FREDDY [*coming to their side of the ottoman*] Ive certainly had the pleasure.

MRS. EYNSFORD HILL [*introducing*] My son Freddy.

LIZA How do you do?

[FREDDY *bows and sits down in the Elizabethan chair, infatuated.*]

HIGGINS [*suddenly*] By George, yes: it all comes back to me! [*They stare at him.*] Covent Garden! [*Lamentably*] What a damned thing!

MRS. HIGGINS Henry, please! [*He is about to sit on the edge of the table.*] Dont sit on my writing-table: youll break it.

HIGGINS [*sulkily*] Sorry.

[He goes to the divan, stumbling into the fender[7] *and over the fire-irons on his way; extricating himself with muttered imprecations; and finishing his disastrous journey by throwing himself so impatiently on the divan that he almost breaks it. Mrs. Higgins looks at him, but controls herself and says nothing.]*

[A long and painful pause ensues.]

MRS. HIGGINS [*at last, conversationally*] Will it rain, do you think?

LIZA The shallow depression in the west of these islands is likely to move slowly in an easterly direction. There are no indications of any great change in the barometrical situation.

FREDDY Ha! ha! how awfully funny!

LIZA What is wrong with that, young man? I bet I got it right.

FREDDY Killing!

MRS. EYNSFORD HILL I'm sure I hope it wont turn cold. Theres so much influenza about. It runs right through our whole family regularly every spring.

LIZA [*darkly*] My aunt died of influenza: so they said.

MRS. EYNSFORD HILL [*clicks her tongue sympathetically*] !!!

LIZA [*in the same tragic tone*] But it's my belief they done the old woman in.

MRS. HIGGINS [*puzzled*] Done her in?

LIZA Y-e-e-e-es, Lord love you! Why should she die of influenza? She come through diphtheria right enough the year before. I saw her with my own eyes. Fairly blue with it, she was. They all thought she was dead; but my father he kept ladling gin down her throat til she came to so sudden that she bit the bowl off the spoon.

MRS. EYNSFORD HILL [*startled*] Dear me!

LIZA [*piling up the indictment*] What call would a woman with that strength in her have to die of influenza? What become of her new straw hat that should have come to me? Somebody pinched it; and what I say is, them as pinched it done her in.

MRS. EYNSFORD HILL What does doing her in mean?

HIGGINS [*hastily*] Oh, thats the new small talk. To do a person in means to kill them.

MRS. EYNSFORD HILL [*to* ELIZA, *horrified*] You surely dont believe that your aunt was killed?

LIZA Do I not! Them she lived with would have killed her for a hat-pin, let alone a hat.

MRS. EYNSFORD HILL But it cant have been right for your father to pour spirits down her throat like that. It might have killed her.

LIZA Not her. Gin was mother's milk to her. Besides, he'd poured so much down his own throat that he knew the good of it.

MRS. EYNSFORD HILL Do you mean that he drank?

LIZA Drank! My word! Something chronic.

MRS. EYNSFORD HILL How dreadful for you!

LIZA Not a bit. It never did him no harm what I could see. But then he did not keep it up regular. [*Cheerfully*] On the burst,[8] as you might say, from time to time. And always more agreeable when he had a drop in. When he was out of work, my mother used to give him fourpence and tell him to go

7. A low metal fire screen.

8. A bout of drunkenness; a binge.

out and not come back until he'd drunk himself cheerful and loving-like. Theres lots of women has to make their husbands drunk to make them fit to live with. [*Now quite at her ease*] You see, it's like this. If a man has a bit of a conscience, it always takes him when he's sober; and then it makes him low-spirited. A drop of booze just takes that off and makes him happy. [*To* FREDDY, *who is in convulsions of suppressed laughter*] Here! what are you sniggering at?

FREDDY The new small talk. You do it so awfully well.

LIZA If I was doing it proper, what was you laughing at? [*To* HIGGINS] Have I said anything I oughtnt?

MRS. HIGGINS [*interposing*] Not at all, Miss Doolittle.

LIZA Well, thats a mercy, anyhow. [*Expansively*] What I always say is—

HIGGINS [*rising and looking at his watch*] Ahem!

LIZA [*looking round at him; taking the hint; and rising*] Well: I must go. [*They all rise.* FREDDY *goes to the door.*] So pleased to have met you. Good-bye. [*She shakes hands with* MRS. HIGGINS.]

MRS. HIGGINS. Good-bye.

LIZA Good-bye, Colonel Pickering.

PICKERING Good-bye, Miss Doolittle. [*They shake hands.*]

LIZA [*nodding to the others*] Good-bye, all.

FREDDY [*opening the door for her*] Are you walking across the Park, Miss Doolittle? If so—

LIZA Walk! Not bloody likely. [*Sensation*] I am going in a taxi. [*She goes out.*]

[PICKERING *gasps and sits down.* FREDDY *goes out on the balcony to catch another glimpse of* ELIZA.]

MRS. EYNSFORD HILL [*suffering from shock*] Well, I really cant get used to the new ways.

CLARA [*throwing herself discontentedly into the Elizabethan chair*] Oh, it's all right, mamma, quite right. People will think we never go anywhere or see anybody if you are so old-fashioned.

MRS. EYNSFORD HILL I daresay I am very old-fashioned; but I do hope you wont begin using that expression, Clara. I have got accustomed to hear you talking about men as rotters, and calling everything filthy and beastly; though I do think it horrible and unladylike. But this last is really too much. Dont you think so, Colonel Pickering?

PICKERING Dont ask me. Ive been away in India for several years; and manners have changed so much that I sometimes dont know whether I'm at a respectable dinner-table or in a ship's forecastle.

CLARA It's all a matter of habit. Theres no right or wrong in it. Nobody means anything by it. And it's so quaint, and gives such a smart emphasis to things that are not in themselves very witty. I find the new small talk delightful and quite innocent.

MRS. EYNSFORD HILL [*rising*] Well, after that, I think it's time for us to go.

[PICKERING *and* HIGGINS *rise.*]

CLARA [*rising*] Oh yes: we have three at-homes to go to still. Good-bye, Mrs. Higgins. Good-bye, Colonel Pickering. Good-bye, Professor Higgins.

HIGGINS [*coming grimly at her from the divan, and accompanying her to the door*] Good-bye. Be sure you try on that small talk at the three at-homes. Dont be nervous about it. Pitch it in strong.

CLARA [*all smiles*] I will. Good-bye. Such nonsense, all this early Victorian prudery!

HIGGINS [*tempting her*] Such damned nonsense!

CLARA Such bloody nonsense!

MRS. EYNSFORD HILL [*convulsively*] Clara!

CLARA. Ha! ha!

[*She goes out radiant, conscious of being thoroughly up to date, and is heard descending the stairs in a stream of silvery laughter.*]

FREDDY [*to the heavens at large*] Well, I ask you—[*He gives it up, and comes to* MRS. HIGGINS]. Good-bye.

MRS. HIGGINS [*shaking hands*] Good-bye. Would you like to meet Miss Doolittle again?

FREDDY [*eagerly*] Yes, I should, most awfully.

MRS. HIGGINS Well, you know my days.

FREDDY Yes. Thanks awfully. Good-bye. [*He goes out.*]

MRS. EYNSFORD HILL Good-bye, Mr. Higgins.

HIGGINS Good-bye. Good-bye.

MRS. EYNSFORD HILL [*to* PICKERING] It's no use. I shall never be able to bring myself to use that word.

PICKERING Dont. It's not compulsory, you know. Youll get on quite well without it.

MRS. EYNSFORD HILL Only, Clara is so down on me if I am not positively reeking with the latest slang. Good-bye.

PICKERING Good-bye. [*They shake hands.*]

MRS. EYNSFORD HILL [*to* MRS. HIGGINS] You mustnt mind Clara. [PICKERING, *catching from her lowered tone that this is not meant for him to hear, discreetly joins* HIGGINS *at the window.*] We're so poor! and she gets so few parties, poor child! She doesnt quite know. [MRS. HIGGINS, *seeing that her eyes are moist, takes her hand sympathetically and goes with her to the door.*] But the boy is nice. Dont you think so?

MRS. HIGGINS Oh, quite nice. I shall always be delighted to see him.

MRS. EYNSFORD HILL Thank you, dear. Good-bye.

[*She goes out.*]

HIGGINS [*eagerly*] Well? Is Eliza presentable? [*He swoops on his mother and drags her to the ottoman, where she sits down in* ELIZA's *place with her son on her left.*]

[PICKERING *returns to his chair on her right.*]

MRS. HIGGINS You silly boy, of course shes not presentable. Shes a triumph of your art and of her dressmaker's; but if you suppose for a moment that she doesnt give herself away in every sentence she utters, you must be perfectly cracked about[9] her.

PICKERING But dont you think something might be done? I mean something to eliminate the sanguinary element[1] from her conversation.

MRS. HIGGINS Not as long as she is in Henry's hands.

HIGGINS [*aggrieved*] Do you mean that my language is improper?

MRS. HIGGINS No, dearest: it would be quite proper—say on a canal barge; but it would not be proper for her at a garden party.

HIGGINS [*deeply injured*] Well I must say—

9. Infatuated with.

1. That is, the word "bloody."

PICKERING [*interrupting him*] Come, Higgins: you must learn to know yourself. I havnt heard such language as yours since we used to review the volunteers[2] in Hyde Park twenty years ago.

HIGGINS [*sulkily*] Oh, well, if you say so, I suppose I dont always talk like a bishop.

MRS. HIGGINS [*quieting* HENRY *with a touch*] Colonel Pickering: will you tell me what is the exact state of things in Wimpole Street?

PICKERING [*cheerfully: as if this completely changed the subject*] Well, I have come to live there with Henry. We work together at my Indian Dialects; and we think it more convenient—

MRS. HIGGINS Quite so. I know all about that: it's an excellent arrangement. But where does this girl live?

HIGGINS With us, of course. Where would she live?

MRS. HIGGINS But on what terms? Is she a servant? If not, what is she?

PICKERING [*slowly*] I think I know what you mean, Mrs. Higgins.

HIGGINS Well, dash me if *I* do! Ive had to work at the girl every day for months to get her to her present pitch. Besides, shes useful. She knows where my things are, and remembers my appointments and so forth.

MRS. HIGGINS How does your housekeeper get on with her?

HIGGINS Mrs. Pearce? Oh, shes jolly glad to get so much taken off her hands; for before Eliza came, she used to have to find things and remind me of my appointments. But shes got some silly bee in her bonnet about Eliza. She keeps saying "You dont think, sir": doesnt she, Pick?

PICKERING Yes: thats the formula. "You dont think, sir." Thats the end of every conversation about Eliza.

HIGGINS As if I ever stop thinking about the girl and her confounded vowels and consonants. I'm worn out, thinking about her, and watching her lips and her teeth and her tongue, not to mention her soul, which is the quaintest of the lot.

MRS. HIGGINS You certainly are a pretty pair of babies, playing with your live doll.

HIGGINS Playing! The hardest job I ever tackled: make no mistake about that, mother. But you have no idea how frightfully interesting it is to take a human being and change her into a quite different human being by creating a new speech for her. It's filling up the deepest gulf that separates class from class and soul from soul.

PICKERING [*drawing his chair closer to* MRS. HIGGINS *and bending over to her eagerly*] Yes: it's enormously interesting. I assure you, Mrs. Higgins, we take Eliza very seriously. Every week—every day almost—there is some new change. [*Closer again*] We keep records of every stage—dozens of gramophone disks and photographs—

HIGGINS [*assailing her at the other ear*] Yes, by George: it's the most absorbing experiment I ever tackled. She regularly fills our lives up; doesnt she, Pick?

PICKERING We're always talking Eliza.

HIGGINS Teaching Eliza.

PICKERING Dressing Eliza.

MRS. HIGGINS What!

HIGGINS Inventing new Elizas.

2. Inspect the troops. Hyde Park, a large park in central London northwest of Buckingham Palace, was frequently used for large-scale military reviews in the 19th century.

HIGGINS [*speaking together*] You know, she has the most extraordinary quickness of ear:
PICKERING I assure you, my dear Mrs. Higgins, that girl
HIGGINS just like a parrot. Ive tried her with every
PICKERING is a genius. She can play the piano quite beautifully.
HIGGINS possible sort of sound that a human being can make—
PICKERING We have taken her to classical concerts and to music
HIGGINS Continental dialects, African dialects, Hottentot
PICKERING halls; and it's all the same to her: she plays everything
HIGGINS clicks,[3] things it took me years to get hold of; and
PICKERING she hears right off when she comes home, whether it's
HIGGINS she picks them up like a shot, right away, as if she had
PICKERING Beethoven and Brahms or Lehar and Lionel Monckton;[4]
HIGGINS been at it all her life.
PICKERING though six months ago, she'd never as much as touched a piano—

MRS. HIGGINS [*putting her fingers in her ears, as they are by this time shouting one another down with an intolerable noise*] Sh-sh-sh—sh! [*They stop.*]

PICKERING I beg your pardon. [*He draws his chair back apologetically.*]

HIGGINS Sorry. When Pickering starts shouting nobody can get a word in edgeways.

MRS. HIGGINS Be quiet, Henry. Colonel Pickering: dont you realize that when Eliza walked into Wimpole Street, something walked in with her?

PICKERING Her father did. But Henry soon got rid of him.

MRS. HIGGINS It would have been more to the point if her mother had. But as her mother didnt something else did.

PICKERING But what?

MRS. HIGGINS [*unconsciously dating herself by the word*] A problem.

PICKERING Oh, I see. The problem of how to pass her off as a lady.

HIGGINS I'll solve that problem. Ive half solved it already.

MRS. HIGGINS No, you two infinitely stupid male creatures: the problem of what is to be done with her afterwards.

HIGGINS I dont see anything in that. She can go her own way, with all the advantages I have given her.

MRS. HIGGINS The advantages of that poor woman who was here just now! The manners and habits that disqualify a fine lady from earning her own living without giving her a fine lady's income! Is that what you mean?

3. *Hottentot clicks:* implosive consonant sounds used in a number of languages of southern Africa.

4. Examples of composers featured in classical concerts—the Germans Ludwig van Beethoven (1770–1827) and Johannes Brahms (1833–1897)—and those celebrated for more popular fare, the Hungarian Franz Lehár (1870–1948), known for his operettas, and the English Lionel Monckton (1861–1924), who wrote many hit songs for musical theater.

PICKERING [*indulgently, being rather bored*] Oh, that will be all right, Mrs. Higgins. [*He rises to go.*]

HIGGINS [*rising also*] We'll find her some light employment.

PICKERING Shes happy enough. Dont you worry about her. Good-bye. [*He shakes hands as if he were consoling a frightened child, and makes for the door.*]

HIGGINS Anyhow, theres no good bothering now. The things done. Good-bye, mother. [*He kisses her, and follows* PICKERING.]

PICKERING [*turning for a final consolation*] There are plenty of openings. We'll do whats right. Good-bye.

HIGGINS [*to* PICKERING *as they go out together*] Let's take her to the Shakespear exhibition at Earls Court.

PICKERING Yes: lets. Her remarks will be delicious.

HIGGINS She'll mimic all the people for us when we get home.

PICKERING Ripping.

[*Both are heard laughing as they go downstairs.*]

MRS. HIGGINS [*rises with an impatient bounce, and returns to her work at the writing-table. She sweeps a litter of disarranged papers out of her way; snatches a sheet of paper from her stationery case; and tries resolutely to write. At the third line she gives it up; flings down her pen; grips the table angrily and exclaims.*] Oh, men! men!! men!!!

Act 4

[*The Wimpole Street laboratory. Midnight. Nobody in the room. The clock on the mantelpiece strikes twelve. The fire is not alight: it is a summer night.*

Presently HIGGINS *and* PICKERING *are heard on the stairs.*]

HIGGINS [*calling down to* PICKERING] I say, Pick: lock up, will you. I shant be going out again.

PICKERING Right. Can Mrs. Pearce go to bed? We dont want anything more, do we?

HIGGINS Lord, no!

[ELIZA *opens the door and is seen on the lighted landing in opera cloak, brilliant evening dress, and diamonds, with fan, flowers, and all accessories. She comes to the hearth, and switches on the electric lights there. She is tired: her pallor contrasts strongly with her dark eyes and hair; and her expression is almost tragic. She takes off her cloak; puts her fan and flowers on the piano; and sits down on the bench, brooding and silent.* HIGGINS, *in evening dress, with overcoat and hat, comes in, carrying a smoking jacket*[5] *which he has picked up downstairs. He takes off the hat and overcoat; throws them carelessly on the newspaper stand; disposes of his coat in the same way; puts on the smoking jacket; and throws himself wearily into the easy-chair at the hearth.* PICKERING *similarly attired, comes in. He also takes off his hat and overcoat, and is about to throw them on* HIGGINS*'s when he hesitates.*]

PICKERING I say: Mrs. Pearce will row[6] if we leave these things lying about in the drawing-room.

5. A casual jacket worn at home, usually in the evening.

6. That is, start a quarrel.

HIGGINS Oh, chuck them over the bannisters into the hall. She'll find them there in the morning and put them away all right. She'll think we were drunk.

PICKERING We are, slightly. Are there any letters?

HIGGINS I didnt look. [PICKERING *takes the overcoats and hats and goes downstairs. Higgins begins half singing half yawning an air from La Fanciulla del Golden West.*[7] *Suddenly he stops and exclaims*] I wonder where the devil my slippers are!

[ELIZA *looks at him darkly; then rises suddenly and leaves the room.*]

[HIGGINS *yawns again, and resumes his song.*]

[PICKERING *returns, with the contents of the letter-box in his hand.*]

PICKERING Only circulars, and this coroneted billet-doux[8] for you. [*He throws the circulars into the fender, and posts himself on the hearthrug, with his back to the grate.*]

HIGGINS [*glancing at the billet-doux*] Money-lender. [*He throws the letter after the circulars.*]

[ELIZA *returns with a pair of large down-at-heel slippers. She places them on the carpet before* HIGGINS, *and sits as before without a word.*]

HIGGINS [*yawning again*] Oh Lord! What an evening! What a crew! What a silly tomfoollery! [*He raises his shoe to unlace it, and catches sight of the slippers. He stops unlacing and looks at them as if they had appeared there of their own accord.*] Oh! theyre there, are they?

PICKERING [*stretching himself*] Well, I feel a bit tired. It's been a long day. The garden party, a dinner party, and the opera! Rather too much of a good thing. But youve won your bet, Higgins. Eliza did the trick, and something to spare, eh?

HIGGINS [*fervently*] Thank God it's over!

[ELIZA *flinches violently; but they take no notice of her; and she recovers herself and sits stonily as before.*]

PICKERING Were you nervous at the garden party? *I* was. Eliza didnt seem a bit nervous.

HIGGINS Oh, she wasnt nervous. I knew she'd be all right. No: it's the strain of putting the job through all these months that has told on me. It was interesting enough at first, while we were at the phonetics; but after that I got deadly sick of it. If I hadnt backed myself to do it I should have chucked the whole thing up two months ago. It was a silly notion: the whole thing has been a bore.

PICKERING Oh come! the garden party was frightfully exciting. My heart began beating like anything.

HIGGINS Yes, for the first three minutes. But when I saw we were going to win hands down, I felt like a bear in a cage, hanging about doing nothing. The dinner was worse: sitting gorging there for over an hour, with nobody but a damned fool of a fashionable woman to talk to! I tell you, Pickering, never again for me. No more artificial duchesses. The whole thing has been simple purgatory.

PICKERING Youve never been broken in properly to the social routine. [*Strolling over to the piano*] I rather enjoy dipping into it occasionally

7. That is, *La Fanciulla del West* (*The Girl of the Golden West,* 1910), an opera by Giacomo Puccini.

8. A love letter on fine stationery (coronets signify nobility).

myself: it makes me feel young again. Anyhow, it was a great success: an immense success. I was quite frightened once or twice because Eliza was doing it so well. You see, lots of the real people cant do it at all: theyre such fools that they think style comes by nature to people in their position; and so they never learn. Theres always something professional about doing a thing superlatively well.

HIGGINS Yes: thats what drives me mad: the silly people dont know their own silly business. [*Rising*] However, it's over and done with; and now I can go to bed at last without dreading tomorrow.

[ELIZA'*s beauty becomes murderous.*]

PICKERING I think I shall turn in too. Still, it's been a great occasion: a triumph for you. Good-night.

[*He goes.*]

HIGGINS [*following him*] Good-night. [*Over his shoulder, at the door*] Put out the lights, Eliza; and tell Mrs. Pearce not to make coffee for me in the morning: I'll take tea.

[*He goes out.*]

[ELIZA *tries to control herself and feel indifferent as she rises and walks across to the hearth to switch off the lights. By the time she gets there she is on the point of screaming. She sits down in* HIGGINS'*s chair and holds on hard to the arms. Finally she gives way and flings herself furiously on the floor raging.*]

HIGGINS [*in despairing wrath outside*] What the devil have I done with my slippers? [*He appears at the door.*]

LIZA [*snatching up the slippers, and hurling them at him one after the other with all her force*] There are your slippers. And there. Take your slippers; and may you never have a day's luck with them!

HIGGINS [*astounded*] What on earth—! [*He comes to her.*] Whats the matter? Get up. [*He pulls her up.*] Anything wrong?

LIZA [*breathless*] Nothing wrong—with you. Ive won your bet for you, havnt I? That enough for you. *I* dont matter, I suppose.

HIGGINS You won my bet! You! Presumptuous insect! *I* won it. What did you throw those slippers at me for?

LIZA Because I wanted to smash your face. I'd like to kill you, you selfish brute. Why didnt you leave me where you picked me out of—in the gutter? You thank God it's all over, and that now you can throw me back again there, do you? [*She crisps*[9] *her fingers frantically.*]

HIGGINS [*looking at her in cool wonder*] The creature is nervous, after all.

LIZA [*gives a suffocated scream of fury, and instinctively darts her nails at his face*] !!

HIGGINS [*catching her wrists*] Ah! would you? Claws in, you cat. How dare you shew your temper to me? Sit down and be quiet. [*He throws her roughly into the easy-chair.*]

LIZA [*crushed by superior strength and weight*] Whats to become of me? Whats to become of me?

HIGGINS How the devil do I know whats to become of you? What does it matter what becomes of you?

9. Curls.

LIZA You dont care. I know you dont care. You wouldnt care if I was dead. I'm nothing to you—not so much as them slippers.

HIGGINS [*thundering*] Those slippers.

LIZA [*with bitter submission*] Those slippers. I didnt think it made any difference now.

[*A pause.* ELIZA *hopeless and crushed.* HIGGINS *a little uneasy.*]

HIGGINS [*in his loftiest manner*] Why have you begun going on like this? May I ask whether you complain of your treatment here?

LIZA No.

HIGGINS Has anybody behaved badly to you? Colonel Pickering? Mrs. Pearce? Any of the servants?

LIZA No.

HIGGINS I presume you dont pretend that *I* have treated you badly.

LIZA No.

HIGGINS I am glad to hear it. [*He moderates his tone.*] Perhaps youre tired after the strain of the day. Will you have a glass of champagne? [*He moves towards the door.*]

LIZA No. [*Recollecting her manners*] Thank you.

HIGGINS [*good-humored again*] This has been coming on you for some days. I suppose it was natural for you to be anxious about the garden party. But thats all over now. [*He pats her kindly on the shoulder. She writhes.*] Theres nothing more to worry about.

LIZA No. Nothing more for you to worry about. [*She suddenly rises and gets away from him by going to the piano bench, where she sits and hides her face.*] Oh God! I wish I was dead.

HIGGINS [*staring after her in sincere surprise*] Why? in heaven's name, why? [*Reasonably, going to her*] Listen to me, Eliza. All this irritation is purely subjective.

LIZA I dont understand. I'm too ignorant.

HIGGINS It's only imagination. Low spirits and nothing else. Nobody's hurting you. Nothing's wrong. You go to bed like a good girl and sleep it off. Have a little cry and say your prayers: that will make you comfortable.

LIZA I heard your prayers. "Thank God it's all over!"

HIGGINS [*impatiently*] Well, dont you thank God it's all over? Now you are free and can do what you like.

LIZA [*pulling herself together in desperation*] What am I fit for? What have you left me fit for? Where am I to go? What am I to do? Whats to become of me?

HIGGINS [*enlightened, but not at all impressed*] Oh, thats whats worrying you, is it? [*He thrusts his hands into his pockets, and walks about in his usual manner, rattling the contents of his pockets, as if condescending to a trivial subject out of pure kindness.*] I shouldnt bother about it if I were you. I should imagine you wont have much difficulty in settling yourself somewhere or other, though I hadnt quite realized that you were going away. [*She looks quickly at him: he does not look at her, but examines the dessert stand on the piano and decides that he will eat an apple.*] You might marry, you know. [*He bites a large piece out of the apple, and munches it noisily.*] You see, Eliza, all men are not confirmed old bachelors like me and the Colonel. Most men are the marrying sort (poor devils!); and youre not bad-looking; it's quite a pleasure to look at you sometimes—not now, of course, because youre crying and looking as ugly as the very devil; but when youre all right and quite yourself, youre what I should call attractive. That is, to the people in the marrying line, you understand. You go to bed and have a good nice rest; and then get up and look at yourself in the glass; and you wont feel so cheap.

[ELIZA *again looks at him, speechless, and does not stir.*]

[*The look is quite lost on him: he eats his apple with a dreamy expression of happiness, as it is quite a good one.*]

HIGGINS [*a genial afterthought occurring to him*] I daresay my mother could find some chap or other who would do very well.

LIZA We were above that at the corner of Tottenham Court Road.

HIGGINS [*waking up*] What do you mean?

LIZA I sold flowers. I didnt sell myself. Now youve made a lady of me I'm not fit to sell anything else. I wish youd left me where you found me.

HIGGINS [*slinging the core of the apple decisively into the grate*] Tosh, Eliza. Dont you insult human relations by dragging all this cant about buying and selling into it. You neednt marry the fellow if you dont like him.

LIZA What else am I to do?

HIGGINS Oh, lots of things. What about your old idea of a florist's shop? Pickering could set you up in one: hes lots of money. [*Chuckling*] He'll have to pay for all those togs you have been wearing today; and that, with the hire of the jewellery, will make a big hole in two hundred pounds. Why, six months ago you would have thought it the millennium to have a flower shop of your own. Come! youll be all right. I must clear off to bed: I'm devilish sleepy. By the way, I came down for something: I forget what it was.

LIZA Your slippers.

HIGGINS Oh yes, of course. You shied them at me. [*He picks them up, and is going out when she rises and speaks to him.*]

LIZA Before you go, sir—

HIGGINS [*dropping the slippers in his surprise at her calling him Sir*] Eh?

LIZA Do my clothes belong to me or to Colonel Pickering?

HIGGINS [*coming back into the room as if her question were the very climax of unreason*] What the devil use would they be to Pickering?

LIZA He might want them for the next girl you pick up to experiment on.

HIGGINS [*shocked and hurt*] Is that the way you feel towards us?

LIZA I dont want to hear anything more about that. All I want to know is whether anything belongs to me. My own clothes were burnt.

HIGGINS But what does it matter? Why need you start bothering about that in the middle of the night?

LIZA I want to know what I may take away with me. I dont want to be accused of stealing.

HIGGINS [*now deeply wounded*] Stealing! You shouldnt have said that, Eliza. That shews a want of feeling.

LIZA I'm sorry. I'm only a common ignorant girl; and in my station I have to be careful. There cant be any feelings between the like of you and the like of me. Please will you tell me what belongs to me and what doesn't?

HIGGINS [*very sulky*] You may take the whole damned houseful if you like. Except the jewels. Theyre hired. Will that satisfy you? [*He turns on his heel and is about to go in extreme dudgeon.*]

LIZA [*drinking in his emotion like nectar, and nagging him to provoke a further supply*] Stop, please. [*She takes off her jewels.*] Will you take these to your room and keep them safe? I dont want to run the risk of their being missing.

HIGGINS [*furious*] Hand them over. [*She puts them into his hands.*] If these belonged to me instead of to the jeweler, I'd ram them down your ungrateful throat. [*He perfunctorily thrusts them into his pockets, unconsciously decorating himself with the protruding ends of the chains.*]

LIZA [*taking a ring off*] This ring isnt the jeweler's: it's the one you bought me in Brighton.[1] I dont want it now. [*Higgins dashes the ring violently into the fireplace, and turns on her so threateningly that she crouches over the piano with her hands over her face, and exclaims.*] Don't you hit me.

HIGGINS Hit you! You infamous creature, how dare you accuse me of such a thing? It is you who have hit me. You have wounded me to the heart.

LIZA [*thrilling with hidden joy*] I'm glad. Ive got a little of my own back, anyhow.

HIGGINS [*with dignity, in his finest professional style*] You have caused me to lose my temper: a thing that has hardly ever happend to me before. I prefer to say nothing more tonight. I am going to bed.

LIZA [*pertly*] Youd better leave a note for Mrs. Pearce about the coffee; for she wont be told by me.

HIGGINS [*formally*] Damn Mrs. Pearce; and damn the coffee; and damn you; and damn my own folly in having lavished hard-earned knowledge and the treasure of my regard and intimacy on a heartless guttersnipe.

[*He goes out with impressive decorum, and spoils it by slamming the door savagely.*]

[ELIZA *smiles for the first time; expresses her feelings by a wild pantomime in which an imitation of* HIGGINS*'s exit is confused with her own triumph; and finally goes down on her knees on the hearthrug to look for the ring.*]

Act 5

[*Mrs.* HIGGINS*'s drawing-room. She is at her writing-table as before. The* PARLOR-MAID *comes in.*]

THE PARLOR-MAID [*at the door*] Mr. Henry, mam, is downstairs with Colonel Pickering.

MRS. HIGGINS Well, shew them up.

THE PARLOR-MAID Theyre using the telephone, mam. Telephoning to the police, I think.

MRS. HIGGINS What!

THE PARLOR-MAID [*coming further in and lowering her voice*] Mr. Henry's in a state, mam. I thought I'd better tell you.

MRS. HIGGINS If you had told me that Mr. Henry was not in a state it would have been more surprising. Tell them to come up when theyve finished with the police. I suppose hes lost something.

THE PARLOR-MAID Yes, mam. [*Going*]

MRS. HIGGINS Go upstairs and tell Miss Doolittle that Mr. Henry and the Colonel are here. Ask her not to come down till I send for her.

THE PARLOR-MAID Yes, mam.

[HIGGINS *bursts in. He is, as the* PARLOR-MAID *has said, in a state.*]

1. A seaside resort on the English Channel, about 50 miles south of London.

HIGGINS Look here, mother: heres a confounded thing!

MRS. HIGGINS Yes, dear. Good-morning. [*He checks his impatience and kisses her, whilst the* PARLOR-MAID *goes out.*] What is it?

HIGGINS Eliza's bolted.

MRS. HIGGINS [*calmly continuing her writing*] You must have frightened her.

HIGGINS Frightened her! nonsense! She was left last night, as usual, to turn out the lights and all that; and instead of going to bed she changed her clothes and went right off: her bed wasnt slept in. She came in a cab for her things before seven this morning; and that fool Mrs. Pearce let her have them without telling me a word about it. What am I to do?

MRS. HIGGINS Do without, I'm afraid, Henry. The girl has a perfect right to leave if she chooses.

HIGGINS [*wandering distractedly across the room*] But I cant find anything. I dont know what appointments Ive got. I'm— [PICKERING *comes in.* MRS. HIGGINS *puts down her pen and turns away from the writing-table.*]

PICKERING [*shaking hands*] Good-morning, Mrs. Higgins. Has Henry told you? [*He sits down on the ottoman.*]

HIGGINS What does that ass of an inspector say? Have you offered a reward?

MRS. HIGGINS [*rising in indignant amazement*] You dont mean to say you have set the police after Eliza?

HIGGINS Of course. What are the police for? What else could we do? [*He sits in the Elizabethan chair.*]

PICKERING The inspector made a lot of difficulties. I really think he suspected us of some improper purpose.

MRS. HIGGINS Well, of course he did. What right have you to go to the police and give the girl's name as if she were a thief, or a lost umbrella, or something? Really! [*She sits down again, deeply vexed.*]

HIGGINS But we want to find her.

PICKERING We cant let her go like this, you know, Mrs. Higgins. What were we to do?

MRS. HIGGINS You have no more sense, either of you, than two children. Why—

[*The* PARLOR-MAID *comes in and breaks off the conversation.*]

THE PARLOR-MAID Mr. Henry: a gentleman wants to see you very particular. Hes been sent on from Wimpole Street.

HIGGINS Oh, bother! I cant see anyone now. Who is it?

THE PARLOR-MAID A Mr. Doolittle, sir.

PICKERING Doolittle! Do you mean the dustman?

THE PARLOR-MAID Dustman! Oh no, sir: a gentleman.

HIGGINS [*springing up excitedly*] By George, Pick, it's some relative of hers that shes gone to. Somebody we know nothing about. [*To the* PARLOR-MAID] Send him up, quick.

THE PARLOR-MAID Yes, sir.

[*She goes.*]

HIGGINS [*eagerly, going to his mother*] Genteel relatives! now we shall hear something. [*He sits down in the Chippendale chair.*]

MRS. HIGGINS Do you know any of her people?

PICKERING Only her father: the fellow we told you about.

THE PARLOR-MAID [*announcing*] Mr. Doolittle.

[*She withdraws.*]

[DOOLITTLE *enters. He is brilliantly dressed in a new fashionable frock-coat, with white waistcoat and grey trousers. A flower in his buttonhole, a dazzling silk hat, and patent leather shoes complete the effect. He is too concerned with the business he has come on to notice* MRS. HIGGINS. *He walks straight to* HIGGINS, *and accosts him with vehement reproach.*]

DOOLITTLE [*indicating his own person*] See here! Do you see this? You done this.

HIGGINS Done what, man?

DOOLITTLE This, I tell you. Look at it. Look at this hat. Look at this coat.

PICKERING Has Eliza been buying you clothes?

DOOLITTLE Eliza! not she. Not half. Why would she buy me clothes?

MRS. HIGGINS Good-morning, Mr. Doolittle. Wont you sit down?

DOOLITTLE [*taken aback as he becomes conscious that he has forgotten his hostess*] Asking your pardon, maam. [*He approaches her and shakes her proffered hand.*] Thank you. [*He sits down on the ottoman, on Pickering's right.*] I am that full of what has happened to me that I cant think of anything else.

HIGGINS What the dickens has happened to you?

DOOLITTLE I shouldnt mind if it had only happened to me: anything might happen to anybody and nobody to blame but Providence, as you might say. But this is something that you done to me: yes, you, Henry Higgins.

HIGGINS Have you found Eliza? Thats the point.

DOOLITTLE Have you lost her?

HIGGINS Yes.

DOOLITTLE You have all the luck, you have. I aint found her; but she'll find me quick enough now after what you done to me.

MRS. HIGGINS But what has my son done to you, Mr. Doolittle?

DOOLITTLE Done to me! Ruined me. Destroyed my happiness. Tied me up and delivered me into the hands of middle class morality.

HIGGINS [*rising intolerantly and standing over Doolittle*] Youre raving. Youre drunk. Youre mad. I gave you five pounds. After that I had two conversations with you, at half-a-crown an hour. Ive never seen you since.

DOOLITTLE Oh! Drunk! am I? Mad! am I? Tell me this. Did you or did you not write a letter to an old blighter in America that was giving five millions to found Moral Reform Societies all over the world, and that wanted you to invent a universal language for him?

HIGGINS What! Ezra D. Wannafeller![2] Hes dead. [*He sits down again carelessly.*]

DOOLITTLE Yes: hes dead; and I'm done for. Now did you or did you not write a letter to him to say that the most original moralist at present in England, to the best of your knowledge, was Alfred Doolittle, a common dustman.

HIGGINS Oh, after your last visit I remember making some silly joke of the kind.

DOOLITTLE Ah! you may well call it a silly joke. It put the lid on me right enough. Just give him the chance he wanted to shew that Americans is not like us: that they recognize and respect merit in every class of life, however humble. Them words is in his blooming will, in which, Henry Higgins, thanks to your silly joking, he leaves me a share in his Pre-digested Cheese

2. Shaw conflates the names of two actual American millionaires, the merchant John Wanamaker (1838–1922) and the industrialist John D. Rockefeller (1839–1937).

Trust worth three thousand a year[3] on condition that I lecture for his Wannafeller Moral Reform World League as often as they ask me up to six times a year.

HIGGINS The devil he does! Whew! [*Brightening suddenly*] What a lark!

PICKERING A safe thing for you, Doolittle. They wont ask you twice.

DOOLITTLE It aint the lecturing I mind. I'll lecture them blue in the face, I will, and not turn a hair. It's making a gentleman of me that I object to. Who asked him to make a gentleman of me? I was happy. I was free. I touched pretty nigh everybody for money when I wanted it, same as I touched you, Henry Higgins. Now I am worrited; tied neck and heels; and everybody touches me for money. It's a fine thing for you, says my solicitor. Is it? says I. You mean it's a good thing for you, I says. When I was a poor man and had a solicitor once when they found a pram in the dust cart, he got me off, and got shut of[4] me and got me shut of him as quick as he could. Same with the doctors: used to shove me out of the hospital before I could hardly stand on my legs, and nothing to pay. Now they finds out that I'm not a healthy man and cant live unless they looks after me twice a day. In the house I'm not let do a hand's turn for myself: somebody else must do it and touch me for it. A year ago I hadnt a relative in the world except two or three that wouldnt speak to me. Now Ive fifty, and not a decent week's wages among the lot of them. I have to live for others and not for myself: thats middle class morality. You talk of losing Eliza. Dont you be anxious: I bet shes on my doorstep by this: she that could support herself easy by selling flowers if I wasnt respectable. And the next one to touch me will be you, Henry Higgins. I'll have to learn to speak middle class language from you, instead of speaking proper English. Thats where youll come in; and I daresay thats what you done it for.

MRS. HIGGINS But, my dear Mr. Doolittle, you need not suffer all this if you are really in earnest. Nobody can force you to accept this bequest. You can repudiate it. Isnt that so, Colonel Pickering?

PICKERING I believe so.

DOOLITTLE [*softening his manner in deference to her sex*] Thats the tragedy of it, maam. It's easy to say chuck it; but I havent the nerve. Which of us has? We're all intimidated. Intimidated, maam: thats what we are. What is there for me if I chuck it but the workhouse in my old age? I have to dye my hair[5] already to keep my job as a dustman. If I was one of the deserving poor, and had put by a bit, I could chuck it; but then why should I, acause[6] the deserving poor might as well be millionaires for all the happiness they ever has. They dont know what happiness is. But I, as one of the undeserving poor, have nothing between me and the pauper's uniform but this here blasted three thousand a year that shoves me into the middle class. (Excuse the expression, maam: youd use it yourself if you had my provocation.) Theyve got you every way you turn: it's a choice between the Skilly of the workhouse and the Char Bydis of the middle class;[7] and I havnt the nerve

3. Roughly equivalent to $250,000 today.
4. Rid of.
5. That is, to keep from being fired because of his advancing age (no laws prevented such firing).
6. Because.
7. That is, between two equal dangers. In Greek mythology, Scylla and Charybdis are two monsters (who become a rock and whirlpool, respectively) that endanger sailors between Sicily and Italy.

for the workhouse. Intimidated: thats what I am. Broke. Bought up. Happier men than me will call for my dust, and touch me for their tip; and I'll look on helpless, and envy them. And thats what your son has brought me to. [*He is overcome by emotion.*]

MRS. HIGGINS Well, I'm very glad youre not going to do anything foolish, Mr. Doolittle. For this solves the problem of Eliza's future. You can provide for her now.

DOOLITTLE [*with melancholy resignation*] Yes, maam: I'm expected to provide for everyone now, out of three thousand a year.

HIGGINS [*jumping up*] Nonsense! he cant provide for her. He shant provide for her. She doesnt belong to him. I paid him five pounds for her. Doolittle: either youre an honest man or a rogue.

DOOLITTLE [*tolerantly*] A little of both, Henry, like the rest of us: a little of both.

HIGGINS Well, you took that money for the girl; and you have no right to take her as well.

MRS. HIGGINS Henry: dont be absurd. If you really want to know where Eliza is, she is upstairs.

HIGGINS [*amazed*] Upstairs!!! Then I shall jolly soon fetch her downstairs. [*He makes resolutely for the door.*]

MRS. HIGGINS [*rising and following him*] Be quiet, Henry. Sit down.

HIGGINS I—

MRS. HIGGINS Sit down, dear; and listen to me.

HIGGINS Oh very well, very well, very well. [*He throws himself ungraciously on the ottoman, with his face towards the windows.*] But I think you might have told me this half an hour ago.

MRS. HIGGINS Eliza came to me this morning. She passed the night partly walking about in a rage, partly trying to throw herself into the river and being afraid to, and partly in the Carlton Hotel. She told me of the brutal way you two treated her.

HIGGINS [*bounding up again*] What!

PICKERING [*rising also*] My dear Mrs. Higgins, shes been telling you stories. We didnt treat her brutally. We hardly said a word to her; and we parted on particularly good terms. [*Turning on* HIGGINS] Higgins: did you bully her after I went to bed?

HIGGINS Just the other way about. She threw my slippers in my face. She behaved in the most outrageous way. I never gave her the slightest provocation. The slippers came bang into my face the moment I entered the room—before I had uttered a word. And used perfectly awful language.

PICKERING [*astonished*] But why? What did we do to her?

MRS. HIGGINS I think I know pretty well what you did. The girl is naturally rather affectionate, I think. Isnt she, Mr. Doolittle?

DOOLITTLE Very tender-hearted, maam. Takes after me.

MRS. HIGGINS Just so. She had become attached to you both. She worked very hard for you, Henry! I dont think you quite realize what anything in the nature of brain work means to a girl like that. Well, it seems that when the great day of trial came, and she did this wonderful thing for you without making a single mistake, you two sat there and never said a word to her, but talked together of how glad you were that it was all over and how you had been bored with the whole thing. And then you were surprised because she threw your slippers at you! *I* should have thrown the fire-irons at you.

HIGGINS We said nothing except that we were tired and wanted to go to bed. Did we, Pick?

PICKERING [*shrugging his shoulders*] That was all.

MRS. HIGGINS [*ironically*] Quite sure?

PICKERING Absolutely. Really, that was all.

MRS. HIGGINS You didn't thank her, or pet her, or admire her, or tell her how splendid she'd been.

HIGGINS [*impatiently*] But she knew all about that. We didnt make speeches to her, if thats what you mean.

PICKERING [*conscience stricken*] Perhaps we were a little inconsiderate. Is she very angry?

MRS. HIGGINS [*returning to her place at the writing-table*] Well, I'm afraid she wont go back to Wimpole Street, especially now that Mr. Doolittle is able to keep up the position you have thrust on her; but she says she is quite willing to meet you on friendly terms and to let bygones be bygones.

HIGGINS [*furious*] Is she, by George? Ho!

MRS. HIGGINS If you promise to behave yourself, Henry, I'll ask her to come down. If not, go home; for you have taken up quite enough of my time.

HIGGINS Oh, all right. Very well. Pick: you behave yourself. Let us put on our best Sunday manners for this creature that we picked out of the mud. [*He flings himself sulkily into the Elizabethan chair.*]

DOOLITTLE [*remonstrating*] Now, now, Henry Higgins! have some consideration for my feelings as a middle class man.

MRS. HIGGINS Remember your promise, Henry. [*She presses the bell-button on the writing-table.*] Mr. Doolittle: will you be so good as to step out on the balcony for a moment. I dont want Eliza to have the shock of your news until she has made it up with these two gentlemen. Would you mind?

DOOLITTLE As you wish, lady. Anything to help Henry to keep her off my hands.

[*He disappears through the window.*]

[*The* PARLOR-MAID *answers the bell.* PICKERING *sits down in Doolittle's place.*]

MRS. HIGGINS Ask Miss Doolittle to come down, please.

THE PARLOR-MAID Yes, mam. [*She goes out.*]

MRS. HIGGINS Now, Henry: be good.

HIGGINS I am behaving myself perfectly.

PICKERING He is doing his best, Mrs. Higgins.

[*A pause.* HIGGINS *throws back his head; stretches out his legs; and begins to whistle.*]

MRS. HIGGINS Henry, dearest, you dont look at all nice in that attitude.

HIGGINS [*pulling himself together*] I was not trying to look nice, mother.

MRS. HIGGINS It doesnt matter, dear. I only wanted to make you speak.

HIGGINS Why?

MRS. HIGGINS Because you cant speak and whistle at the same time.

[HIGGINS *groans. Another very trying pause.*]

HIGGINS [*springing up, out of patience*] Where the devil is that girl? Are we to wait here all day?

[ELIZA *enters, sunny, self-possessed, and giving a staggeringly convincing exhibition of ease of manner. She carries a little work-basket, and is very much at home.* PICKERING *is too much taken aback to rise.*]

LIZA How do you do, Professor Higgins? Are you quite well?

HIGGINS [*choking*] Am I— [*He can say no more*].

LIZA But of course you are: you are never ill. So glad to see you again, Colonel Pickering. [*He rises hastily; and they shake hands.*] Quite chilly this morning, isnt it? [*She sits down on his left. He sits beside her.*]

HIGGINS Dont you dare try this game on me. I taught it to you; and it doesnt take me in. Get up and come home; and dont be a fool.

[ELIZA *takes a piece of needlework from her basket, and begins to stitch at it, without taking the least notice of this outburst.*]

MRS. HIGGINS Very nicely put, indeed, Henry. No woman could resist such an invitation.

HIGGINS You let her alone, mother. Let her speak for herself. You will jolly soon see whether she has an idea that I havnt put into her head or a word that I havnt put into her mouth. I tell you I have created this thing out of the squashed cabbage leaves of Covent Garden; and now she pretends to play the fine lady with me.

MRS. HIGGINS [*placidly*] Yes, dear; but youll sit down, wont you?

[HIGGINS *sits down again, savagely.*]

LIZA [*to* PICKERING, *taking no apparent notice of* HIGGINS, *and working away deftly*] Will you drop me altogether now that the experiment is over, Colonel Pickering?

PICKERING Oh dont. You mustnt think of it as an experiment. It shocks me, somehow.

LIZA Oh, I'm only a squashed cabbage leaf—

PICKERING [*impulsively*] No.

LIZA [*continuing quietly*] —but I owe so much to you that I should be very unhappy if you forgot me.

PICKERING It's very kind of you to say so, Miss Doolittle.

LIZA It's not because you paid for my dresses. I know you are generous to everybody with money. But it was from you that I learnt really nice manners; and that is what makes one a lady, isnt it? You see it was so very difficult for me with the example of Professor Higgins always before me. I was brought up to be just like him, unable to control myself, and using bad language on the slightest provocation. And I should never have known that ladies and gentlemen didnt behave like that if you hadnt been there.

HIGGINS Well!!

PICKERING Oh, thats only his way, you know. He doesnt mean it.

LIZA Oh, *I* didnt mean it either, when I was a flower girl. It was only my way. But you see I did it; and thats what makes the difference after all.

PICKERING No doubt. Still, he taught you to speak; and I couldnt have done that, you know.

LIZA [*trivially*] Of course: that is his profession.

HIGGINS Damnation!

LIZA [*continuing*] It was just like learning to dance in the fashionable way: there was nothing more than that in it. But do you know what began my real education?

PICKERING What?

LIZA [*stopping her work for a moment*] Your calling me Miss Doolittle that day when I first came to Wimpole Street. That was the beginning of self-respect for me. [*She resumes her stitching.*] And there were a hundred little things you never noticed, because they came naturally to you. Things about standing up and taking off your hat and opening door—

PICKERING Oh, that was nothing.

LIZA Yes: things that shewed you thought and felt about me as if I were something better than a scullery-maid; though of course I know you would have been just the same to a scullery-maid if she had been let in the drawing-room. You never took off your boots in the dining room when I was there.

PICKERING You mustnt mind that. Higgins takes off his boots all over the place.

LIZA I know. I am not blaming him. It is his way, isnt it? But it made such a difference to me that you didnt do it. You see, really and truly, apart from the things anyone can pick up (the dressing and the proper way of speaking, and so on), the difference between a lady and a flower girl is not how she behaves, but how shes treated. I shall always be a flower girl to Professor Higgins, because he always treats me as a flower girl, and always will; but I know I can be a lady to you, because you always treat me as a lady, and always will.

MRS. HIGGINS Please dont grind your teeth, Henry.

PICKERING Well, this is really very nice of you, Miss Doolittle.

LIZA I should like you to call me Eliza, now, if you would.

PICKERING Thank you. Eliza, of course.

LIZA And I should like Professor Higgins to call me Miss Doolittle.

HIGGINS I'll see you damned first.

MRS. HIGGINS Henry! Henry!

PICKERING [*laughing*] Why dont you slang back[8] at him? Dont stand it. It would do him a lot of good.

LIZA I cant. I could have done it once; but now I cant go back to it. Last night, when I was wandering about, a girl spoke to me; and I tried to get back into the old way with her; but it was no use. You told me, you know, that when a child is brought to a foreign country, it picks up the language in a few weeks, and forgets its own. Well, I am a child in your country. I have forgotten my own language, and can speak nothing but yours. Thats the real break-off with the corner of Tottenham Court Road. Leaving Wimpole Street finishes it.

PICKERING [*much alarmed*] Oh! but youre coming back to Wimpole Street, arnt you? Youll forgive Higgins?

HIGGINS [*rising*] Forgive! Will she, by George! Let her go. Let her find out how she can get on without us. She will relapse into the gutter in three weeks without me at her elbow.

[DOOLITTLE *appears at the centre window. With a look of dignified reproach at* HIGGINS, *he comes slowly and silently to his daughter, who, with her back to the window, is unconscious of his approach.*]

PICKERING Hes incorrigible, Eliza. You wont relapse, will you?

8. That is, respond with equal abuse.

LIZA No: Not now. Never again. I have learnt my lesson. I dont believe I could utter one of the old sounds if I tried. [DOOLITTLE *touches her on her left shoulder. She drops her work, losing her self-possession utterly at the spectacle of her father's splendor.*] A-a-a-a-a-ah-ow-ooh!

HIGGINS [*with a crow of triumph*] Aha! Just so. A-a-a-a-ahowooh! A-a-a-a-ahowooh! A-a-a-a-ahowooh! Victory! Victory! [*He throws himself on the divan, folding his arms, and spraddling arrogantly.*]

DOOLITTLE Can you blame the girl? Dont look at me like that, Eliza. It aint my fault. Ive come into some money.

LIZA You must have touched a millionaire this time, dad.

DOOLITTLE I have. But I'm dressed something special today. I'm going to St. George's,[9] Hanover Square. Your stepmother is going to marry me.

LIZA [*angrily*] Youre going to let yourself down to marry that low common woman!

PICKERING [*quietly*] He ought to, Eliza. [*To* DOOLITTLE] Why has she changed her mind?

DOOLITTLE [*sadly*] Intimidated, Governor. Intimidated. Middle class morality claims its victim. Wont you put on your hat, Liza, and come and see me turned off?

LIZA If the Colonel says I must, I—I'll [*Almost sobbing*] I'll demean myself. And get insulted for my pains, like enough.

DOOLITTLE Dont be afraid: she never comes to words with anyone now, poor woman! respectability has broke all the spirit out of her.

PICKERING [*squeezing* ELIZA'*s elbow gently*] Be kind to them, Eliza. Make the best of it.

LIZA [*forcing a little smile for him through her vexation*] Oh well, just to shew theres no ill feeling. I'll be back in a moment. [*She goes out.*]

DOOLITTLE [*sitting down beside* PICKERING] I feel uncommon nervous about the ceremony, Colonel. I wish youd come and see me through it.

PICKERING But youve been through it before, man. You were married to Eliza's mother.

DOOLITTLE Who told you that, Colonel?

PICKERING Well, nobody told me. But I concluded—naturally—

DOOLITTLE No: that aint the natural way, Colonel: it's only the middle class way. My way was always the undeserving way. But dont say nothing to Eliza. She dont know: I always had a delicacy about telling her.

PICKERING Quite right. We'll leave it so, if you dont mind.

DOOLITTLE And youll come to the church, Colonel, and put me through straight?

PICKERING With pleasure. As far as a bachelor can.

MRS. HIGGINS May I come, Mr. Doolittle? I should be very sorry to miss your wedding.

DOOLITTLE I should indeed be honored by your condescension,[1] maam; and my poor old woman would take it as a tremenjous compliment. Shes been very low, thinking of the happy days that are no more.

MRS. HIGGINS [*rising*] I'll order the carriage and get ready. [*The men rise, except* HIGGINS.] I shant be more than fifteen minutes. [*As she goes to the*

9. A church in Mayfair, a fashionable area of Westminster.

1. Here, courteous disregard of differences in rank (without the negative connotation common in today's usage).

door ELIZA *comes in, hatted and buttoning her gloves.*] I'm going to the church to see your father married, Eliza. You had better come in the brougham[2] with me. Colonel Pickering can go on with the bridegroom.

[MRS. HIGGINS *goes out.* ELIZA *comes to the middle of the room between the centre window and the ottoman.* PICKERING *joins her.*]

DOOLITTLE Bridegroom! What a word! It makes a man realize his position, somehow. [*He takes up his hat and goes towards the door.*]

PICKERING Before I go, Eliza, do forgive him and come back to us.

LIZA I dont think papa would allow me. Would you, dad?

DOOLITTLE [*sad but magnanimous*] They played you off very cunning, Eliza, them two sportsmen. If it had been only one of them, you could have nailed him. But you see, there was two; and one of them chaperoned the other, as you might say. [*To* PICKERING] It was artful of you, Colonel; but I bear no malice: I should have done the same myself. I been the victim of one woman after another all my life; and I dont grudge you two getting the better of Eliza. I shant interfere. It's time for us to go, Colonel. So long, Henry. See you in St. George's, Eliza.

[*He goes out.*]

PICKERING [*coaxing*] Do stay with us, Eliza.

[*He follows* DOOLITTLE.]

[ELIZA *goes out on the balcony to avoid being alone with* HIGGINS. *He rises and joins her there. She immediately comes back into the room and makes for the door; but he goes along the balcony quickly and gets his back to the door before she reaches it.*]

HIGGINS Well, Eliza, youve had a bit of your own back, as you call it. Have you had enough? and are you going to be reasonable? Or do you want any more?

LIZA You want me back only to pick up your slippers and put up with your tempers and fetch and carry for you.

HIGGINS I havnt said I wanted you back at all.

LIZA Oh, indeed. Then what are we talking about?

HIGGINS About you, not about me. If you come back I shall treat you just as I have always treated you. I cant change my nature; and I dont intend to change my manners. My manners are exactly the same as Colonel Pickering's.

LIZA Thats not true. He treats a flower girl as if she was a duchess.

HIGGINS And I treat a duchess as if she was a flower girl.

LIZA I see. [*She turns away composedly, and sits on the ottoman, facing the window.*] The same to everybody.

HIGGINS Just so.

LIZA Like father.

HIGGINS [*grinning, a little taken down*[3]] Without accepting the comparison at all points, Eliza, it's quite true that your father is not a snob, and that he will be quite at home in any station of life to which his eccentric destiny may call him. [*Seriously*] The great secret, Eliza, is not having bad manners or good manners or any other particular sort of manners, but having the

2. A one-horse closed carriage, which holds two or four.

3. Humbled.

same manner for all human souls: in short, behaving as if you were in Heaven, where there are no third-class carriages, and one soul is as good as another.

LIZA Amen. You are a born preacher.

HIGGINS [*irritated*] The question is not whether I treat you rudely, but whether you ever heard me treat anyone else better.

LIZA [*with sudden sincerity*] I dont care how you treat me. I dont mind your swearing at me. I dont mind a black eye: Ive had one before this. But [*Standing up and facing him*] I wont be passed over.[4]

HIGGINS Then get out of my way; for I wont stop for you. You talk about me as if I were a motor bus.

LIZA So you are a motor bus: all bounce and go, and no consideration for anyone. But I can do without you: dont think I cant.

HIGGINS I know you can. I told you you could.

LIZA [*wounded, getting away from him to the other side of the ottoman with her face to the hearth*] I know you did, you brute. You wanted to get rid of me.

HIGGINS Liar.

LIZA Thank you. [*She sits down with dignity.*]

HIGGINS You never asked yourself, I suppose, whether *I* could do without you.

LIZA [*earnestly*] Dont you try to get round me.[5] Youll have to do without me.

HIGGINS [*arrogant*] I can do without anybody. I have my own soul: my own spark of divine fire. But [*With sudden humility*] I shall miss you, Eliza. [*He sits down near her on the ottoman.*] I have learnt something from your idiotic notions: I confess that humbly and gratefully. And I have grown accustomed to your voice and appearance. I like them, rather.

LIZA Well, you have both of them on your gramophone and in your book of photographs. When you feel lonely without me, you can turn the machine on. It's got no feelings to hurt.

HIGGINS I cant turn your soul on. Leave me those feelings; and you can take away the voice and the face. They are not you.

LIZA Oh, you are a devil. You can twist the heart in a girl as easy as some could twist her arms to hurt her. Mrs. Pearce warned me. Time and again she has wanted to leave you; and you always got round her at the last minute. And you dont care a bit for her. And you dont care a bit for me.

HIGGINS I care for life, for humanity; and you are a part of it that has come my way and been built into my house. What more can you or anyone ask?

LIZA I wont care for anybody that doesnt care for me.

HIGGINS Commercial principles, Eliza. Like [*Reproducing her Covent Garden pronunciation with professional exactness*] s'yollin voylets [selling violets], isnt it?

LIZA Dont sneer at me. It's mean to sneer at me.

HIGGINS I have never sneered in my life. Sneering doesnt become either the human face or the human soul. I am expressing my righteous contempt for Commercialism. I dont and wont trade in affection. You call me a brute because you couldnt buy a claim on me by fetching my slippers and finding my spectacles. You were a fool: I think a woman fetching a man's slippers is a disgusting sight: did I ever fetch your slippers? I think a good deal more

4. Ignored.

5. That is, don't try to deceive or outsmart me.

of you for throwing them in my face. No use slaving for me and then saying you want to be cared for: who cares for a slave? If you come back, come back for the sake of good fellowship; for youll get nothing else. Youve had a thousand times as much out of me as I have out of you; and if you dare to set up your little dog's tricks of fetching and carrying slippers against my creation of a Duchess Eliza, I'll slam the door in your silly face.

LIZA What did you do it for if you didnt care for me?

HIGGINS [*heartily*] Why, because it was my job.

LIZA You never thought of the trouble it would make for me.

HIGGINS Would the world ever have been made if its maker had been afraid of making trouble? Making life means making trouble. Theres only one way of escaping trouble; and thats killing things. Cowards, you notice, are always shrieking to have troublesome people killed.

LIZA I'm no preacher: I dont notice things like that. I notice that you dont notice me.

HIGGINS [*jumping up and walking about intolerantly*] Eliza: youre an idiot. I waste the treasures of my Miltonic mind by spreading them before you. Once for all, understand that I go my way and do my work without caring twopence what happens to either of us. I am not intimidated, like your father and your stepmother. So you can come back or go to the devil: which you please.

LIZA What am I to come back for?

HIGGINS [*bouncing up on his knees on the ottoman and leaning over it to her*] For the fun of it. Thats why I took you on.

LIZA [*with averted face*] And you may throw me out tomorrow if I dont do everything you want me to?

HIGGINS Yes; and you may walk out tomorrow if I dont do everything you want me to.

LIZA And live with my stepmother?

HIGGINS Yes, or sell flowers.

LIZA Oh! if I only could go back to my flower basket! I should be independent of both you and father and all the world! Why did you take my independence from me? Why did I give it up? I'm a slave now, for all my fine clothes.

HIGGINS Not a bit. I'll adopt you as my daughter and settle money on you if you like. Or would you rather marry Pickering?

LIZA [*looking fiercely round at him*] I wouldnt marry you if you asked me; and youre nearer my age than what he is.

HIGGINS [*gently*] Than he is: not "than what he is."

LIZA [*losing her temper and rising*] I'll talk as I like. Youre not my teacher now.

HIGGINS [*reflectively*] I dont suppose Pickering would, though. Hes as confirmed an old bachelor as I am.

LIZA Thats not what I want; and dont you think it. Ive always had chaps enough wanting me that way. Freddy Hill writes to me twice and three times a day,[6] sheets and sheets.

6. At the time, most places in England had two or three mail deliveries daily, and London had even more.

HIGGINS [*disagreeably surprised*] Damn his impudence! [*He recoils and finds himself sitting on his heels.*]

LIZA He has a right to if he likes, poor lad. And he does love me.

HIGGINS [*getting off the ottoman*] You have no right to encourage him.

LIZA Every girl has a right to be loved.

HIGGINS What! By fools like that?

LIZA Freddy's not a fool. And if hes weak and poor and wants me, may be hed make me happier than my betters that bully me and dont want me.

HIGGINS Can he make anything of you? Thats the point.

LIZA Perhaps I could make something of him. But I never thought of us making anything of one another; and you never think of anything else. I only want to be natural.

HIGGINS In short, you want me to be as infatuated about you as Freddy? Is that it?

LIZA No I dont. Thats not the sort of feeling I want from you. And dont you be too sure of yourself or of me. I could have been a bad girl if I'd liked. Ive seen more of some things than you, for all your learning. Girls like me can drag gentlemen down to make love to[7] them easy enough. And they wish each other dead the next minute.

HIGGINS Of course they do. Then what in thunder are we quarrelling about?

LIZA [*much troubled*] I want a little kindness. I know I'm a common ignorant girl, and you a book-learned gentleman; but I'm not dirt under your feet. What I done [*Correcting herself*] what I did was not for the dresses and the taxis: I did it because we were pleasant together and I come—came—to care for you; not to want you to make love to me, and not forgetting the difference between us, but more friendly like.

HIGGINS Well, of course. Thats just how I feel. And how Pickering feels. Eliza: youre a fool.

LIZA Thats not a proper answer to give me. [*She sinks on the chair at the writing-table in tears.*]

HIGGINS It's all youll get until you stop being a common idiot. If youre going to be a lady, youll have to give up feeling neglected if the men you know dont spend half their time snivelling over you and the other half giving you black eyes. If you cant stand the coldness of my sort of life, and the strain of it, go back to the gutter. Work til you are more a brute than a human being; and then cuddle and squabble and drink til you fall asleep. Oh, it's a fine life, the life of the gutter. It's real: it's warm: it's violent: you can feel it through the thickest skin: you can taste it and smell it without any training or any work. Not like Science and Literature and Classical Music and Philosophy and Art. You find me cold, unfeeling, selfish, dont you? Very well: be off with you to the sort of people you like. Marry some sentimental hog or other with lots of money, and a thick pair of lips to kiss you with and a thick pair of boots to kick you with. If you cant appreciate what youve got, youd better get what you can appreciate.

LIZA [*desperate*] Oh, you are a cruel tyrant. I cant talk to you: you turn everything against me: I'm always in the wrong. But you know very well all the time that youre nothing but a bully. You know I cant go back to the gutter, as you call it, and that I have no real friends in the world but you and

7. To pay amorous attention to, to court.

the Colonel. You know well I couldnt bear to live with a low common man after you two; and it's wicked and cruel of you to insult me by pretending I could. You think I must go back to Wimpole Street because I have nowhere else to go but father's. But dont you be too sure that you have me under your feet to be trampled on and talked down. I'll marry Freddy, I will, as soon as hes able to support me.

HIGGINS [*sitting down beside her*] Rubbish! you shall marry an ambassador. You shall marry the Governor-General of India or the Lord-Lieutenant of Ireland, or somebody who wants a deputy-queen. I'm not going to have my masterpiece thrown away on Freddy.

LIZA You think I like you to say that. But I havnt forgot what you said a minute ago; and I wont be coaxed round as if I was a baby or a puppy. If I cant have kindness, I'll have independence.

HIGGINS Independence? Thats middle class blasphemy. We are all dependent on one another, every soul of us on earth.

LIZA [*rising determinedly*] I'll let you see whether I'm dependent on you. If you can preach, I can teach. I'll go and be a teacher.

HIGGINS Whatll you teach, in heaven's name?

LIZA What you taught me. I'll teach phonetics.

HIGGINS Ha! Ha! Ha!

LIZA I'll offer myself as an assistant to Professor Nepean.

HIGGINS [*rising in a fury*] What! That impostor! that humbug! that toadying ignoramus! Teach him my methods! my discoveries! You take one step in his direction and I'll wring your neck. [*He lays hands on her.*] Do you hear?

LIZA [*defiantly non-resistant*] Wring away. What do I care? I knew youd strike me some day. [*He lets her go, stamping with rage at having forgotten himself, and recoils so hastily that he stumbles back into his seat on the ottoman.*] Aha! Now I know how to deal with you. What a fool I was not to think of it before! You cant take away the knowledge you gave me. You said I had a finer ear than you. And I can be civil and kind to people, which is more than you can. Aha! Thats done[8] you, Henry Higgins, it has. Now I dont care that [*Snapping her fingers*] for your bullying and your big talk. I'll advertize it in the papers that your duchess is only a flower girl that you taught, and that she'll teach anybody to be a duchess just the same in six months for a thousand guineas. Oh, when I think of myself crawling under your feet and being trampled on and called names, when all the time I had only to lift up my finger to be as good as you, I could just kick myself.

HIGGINS [*wondering at her*] You damned impudent slut, you! But it's better than snivelling; better than fetching slippers and finding spectacles, isnt it? [*Rising*] By George, Eliza, I said I'd make a woman of you; and I have. I like you like this.

LIZA Yes: you turn round and make up to me now that I'm not afraid of you, and can do without you.

HIGGINS Of course I do, you little fool. Five minutes ago you were like a millstone round my neck. Now youre a tower of strength: a consort[9] battleship. You and I and Pickering will be three old bachelors together instead of only two men and a silly girl.

8. Defeated.

9. A ship sailing in company with another.

[MRS. HIGGINS *returns, dressed for the wedding.* ELIZA *instantly becomes cool and elegant.*]

MRS. HIGGINS The carriage is waiting, Eliza. Are you ready?

LIZA Quite. Is the Professor coming?

MRS. HIGGINS Certainly not. He cant behave himself in church. He makes remarks out loud all the time on the clergyman's pronunciation.

LIZA Then I shall not see you again, Professor. Good-bye. [*She goes to the door.*]

MRS. HIGGINS [*coming to* HIGGINS] Good-bye, dear.

HIGGINS Good-bye, mother. [*He is about to kiss her, when he recollects something.*] Oh, by the way, Eliza, order a ham and a Stilton cheese, will you? And buy me a pair of reindeer gloves, number eights, and a tie to match that new suit of mine, at Eale & Binman's. You can choose the color. [*His cheerful, careless, vigorous voice shows that he is incorrigible.*]

LIZA [*disdainfully*] Buy them yourself.

[*She sweeps out.*]

MRS. HIGGINS I'm afraid youve spoiled that girl, Henry. But never mind, dear: I'll buy you the tie and gloves.

HIGGINS [*sunnily*] Oh, dont bother. She'll buy em all right enough. Good-bye.

[*They kiss.* MRS. HIGGINS *runs out.* HIGGINS, *left alone, rattles his cash in his pocket; chuckles; and disports himself in a highly self-satisfied manner.*]

* * * * *

The rest of the story need not be shown in action, and indeed, would hardly need telling if our imaginations were not so enfeebled by their lazy dependence on the ready-mades and reach-me-downs of the ragshop[1] in which Romance keeps its stock of "happy endings" to misfit all stories. Now, the history of Eliza Doolittle, though called a romance because of the transfiguration it records seems exceedingly improbable, is common enough. Such transfigurations have been achieved by hundreds of resolutely ambitious young women since Nell Gwynne[2] set them the example by playing queens and fascinating kings in the theatre in which she began by selling oranges. Nevertheless, people in all directions have assumed, for no other reason than that she became the heroine of a romance, that she must have married the hero of it. This is unbearable, not only because her little drama, if acted on such a thoughtless assumption, must be spoiled, but because the true sequel is patent to anyone with a sense of human nature in general, and of feminine instinct in particular.

Eliza, in telling Higgins she would not marry him if he asked her, was not coquetting: she was announcing a well-considered decision. When a bachelor interests, and dominates, and teaches, and becomes important to a spinster, as Higgins with Eliza, she always, if she has character enough to be capable of it, considers very seriously indeed whether she will play for becoming that bachelor's wife, especially if he is so little interested in marriage that a determined and devoted woman might capture him if she set herself resolutely to do it.

1. That is, a shop selling cheap mass-produced and secondhand clothing ("ready-mades and reach-me-downs").

2. Eleanor Gwynn (1650–1687), one of the first prominent English actresses and a mistress of King Charles II.

Her decision will depend a good deal on whether she is really free to choose; and that, again, will depend on her age and income. If she is at the end of her youth, and has no security for her livelihood, she will marry him because she must marry anybody who will provide for her. But at Eliza's age a good-looking girl does not feel that pressure: she feels free to pick and choose. She is therefore guided by her instinct in the matter. Eliza's instinct tells her not to marry Higgins. It does not tell her to give him up. It is not in the slightest doubt as to his remaining one of the strongest personal interests in her life. It would be very sorely strained if there was another woman likely to supplant her with him. But as she feels sure of him on that last point, she has no doubt at all as to her course, and would not have any, even if the difference of twenty years in age, which seems so great to youth, did not exist between them.

As our own instincts are not appealed to by her conclusion, let us see whether we cannot discover some reason in it. When Higgins excused his indifference to young women on the ground that they had an irresistible rival in his mother, he gave the clue to his inveterate old-bachelordom. The case is uncommon only to the extent that remarkable mothers are uncommon. If an imaginative boy has a sufficiently rich mother who has intelligence, personal grace, dignity of character without harshness, and a cultivated sense of the best art of her time to enable her to make her house beautiful, she sets a standard for him against which very few women can struggle, besides effecting for him a disengagement of his affections, his sense of beauty, and his idealism from his specifically sexual impulses. This makes him a standing puzzle to the huge number of uncultivated people who have been brought up in tasteless homes by commonplace or disagreeable parents, and to whom, consequently, literature, painting, sculpture, music, and affectionate personal relations come as modes of sex if they come at all. The word passion means nothing else to them; and that Higgins could have a passion for phonetics and idealize his mother instead of Eliza, would seem to them absurd and unnatural. Nevertheless, when we look round and see that hardly anyone is too ugly or disagreeable to find a wife or a husband if he or she wants one, whilst many old maids and bachelors are above the average in quality and culture, we cannot help suspecting that the disentanglement of sex from the associations with which it is so commonly confused, a disentanglement which persons of genius achieve by sheer intellectual analysis, is sometimes produced or aided by parental fascination.

Now, though Eliza was incapable of thus explaining to herself Higgins's formidable powers of resistance to the charm that prostrated Freddy at the first glance, she was instinctively aware that she could never obtain a complete grip of him, or come between him and his mother (the first necessity of the married woman). To put it shortly, she knew that for some mysterious reason he had not the makings of a married man in him, according to her conception of a husband as one to whom she would be his nearest and fondest and warmest interest. Even had there been no mother-rival, she would still have refused to accept an interest in herself that was secondary to philosophic interests. Had Mrs. Higgins died, there would still have been Milton and the Universal Alphabet. Landor's[3] remark that to those who have the greatest power of loving, love is a secondary affair, would not have recommended Landor to

3. The English poet Walter Savage Landor (1775–1864); in "Roger Ascham and the Lady Jane Grey," in *Imaginary Conversations of Literary Men and Statesmen* (1824), he wrote, "Love is a secondary passion in those who love most, a primary in those who love least."

Eliza. Put that along with her resentment of Higgins's domineering superiority, and her mistrust of his coaxing cleverness in getting round her and evading her wrath when he had gone too far with his impetuous bullying, and you will see that Eliza's instinct had good grounds for warning her not to marry her Pygmalion.

And now, whom did Eliza marry? For if Higgins was a predestinate old bachelor, she was most certainly not a predestinate old maid. Well, that can be told very shortly to those who have not guessed it from the indications she has herself given them.

Almost immediately after Eliza is stung into proclaiming her considered determination not to marry Higgins, she mentions the fact that young Mr. Frederick Eynsford Hill is pouring out his love for her daily through the post. Now Freddy is young, practically twenty years younger than Higgins: he is a gentleman (or, as Eliza would qualify him, a toff), and speaks like one; he is nicely dressed, is treated by the Colonel as an equal, loves her unaffectedly, and is not her master, nor ever likely to dominate her in spite of his advantage of social standing. Eliza has no use for the foolish romantic tradition that all women love to be mastered, if not actually bullied and beaten. "When you go to women," says Nietzsche, "take your whip with you."[4] Sensible despots have never confined that precaution to women: they have taken their whips with them when they have dealt with men, and been slavishly idealized by the men over whom they have flourished the whip much more than by women. No doubt there are slavish women as well as slavish men; and women, like men, admire those that are stronger than themselves. But to admire a strong person and to live under that strong person's thumb are two different things. The weak may not be admired and hero-worshipped; but they are by no means disliked or shunned; and they never seem to have the least difficulty in marrying people who are too good for them. They may fail in emergencies; but life is not one long emergency: it is mostly a string of situations for which no exceptional strength is needed, and with which even rather weak people can cope if they have a stronger partner to help them out. Accordingly, it is a truth everywhere in evidence that strong people, masculine or feminine, not only do not marry stronger people, but do not shew any preference for them in selecting their friends. When a lion meets another with a louder roar "the first lion thinks the last a bore."[5] The man or woman who feels strong enough for two, seeks for every other quality in a partner than strength.

The converse is also true. Weak people want to marry strong people who do not frighten them too much; and this often leads them to make the mistake we describe metaphorically as "biting off more than they can chew." They want too much for too little; and when the bargain is unreasonable beyond all bearing, the union becomes impossible: it ends in the weaker party being either discarded or borne as a cross, which is worse. People who are not only weak, but silly or obtuse as well, are often in these difficulties.

This being the state of human affairs, what is Eliza fairly sure to do when she is placed between Freddy and Higgins? Will she look forward to a lifetime

4. Spoken by a fictional old woman in *Thus Spoke Zarathustra* (1883), by the German philosopher Friedrich Nietzsche (1844–1900).

5. Shaw slightly misquotes the popular comic opera *Bombastes Furioso* (1810), by English dramatist William Barnes Rhodes: "So have I heard on Afric's burning shore / Another lion give a grievous roar; / And the first lion thought the last a bore."

of fetching Higgins's slippers or to a lifetime of Freddy fetching hers? There can be no doubt about the answer. Unless Freddy is biologically repulsive to her, and Higgins biologically attractive to a degree that overwhelms all her other instincts, she will, if she marries either of them, marry Freddy.

And that is just what Eliza did.

Complications ensued; but they were economic, not romantic. Freddy had no money and no occupation. His mother's jointure, a last relic of the opulence of Largelady Park, had enabled her to struggle along in Earlscourt with an air of gentility, but not to procure any serious secondary education for her children, much less give the boy a profession. A clerkship at thirty shillings a week was beneath Freddy's dignity, and extremely distasteful to him besides. His prospects consisted of a hope that if he kept up appearances somebody would do something for him. The something appeared vaguely to his imagination as a private secretaryship or a sinecure of some sort. To his mother it perhaps appeared as a marriage to some lady of means who could not resist her boy's niceness. Fancy her feelings when he married a flower girl who had become déclassée under extraordinary circumstances which were now notorious!

It is true that Eliza's situation did not seem wholly ineligible. Her father, though formerly a dustman, and now fantastically disclassed, had become extremely popular in the smartest society by a social talent which triumphed over every prejudice and every disadvantage. Rejected by the middle class, which he loathed, he had shot up at once into the highest circles by his wit, his dustmanship (which he carried like a banner), and his Nietzschean transcendence of good and evil.[6] At intimate ducal dinners he sat on the right hand of the Duchess; and in country houses he smoked in the pantry and was made much of by the butler when he was not feeding in the dining-room and being consulted by cabinet ministers. But he found it almost as hard to do all this on four thousand a year as Mrs. Eynsford Hill to live in Earlscourt on an income so pitiably smaller that I have not the heart to disclose its exact figure. He absolutely refused to add the last straw to his burden by contributing to Eliza's support.

Thus Freddy and Eliza, now Mr. and Mrs. Eynsford Hill, would have spent a penniless honeymoon but for a wedding present of £500[7] from the Colonel to Eliza. It lasted a long time because Freddy did not know how to spend money, never having had any to spend, and Eliza, socially trained by a pair of old bachelors, wore her clothes as long as they held together and looked pretty, without the least regard to their being many months out of fashion. Still, £500 will not last two young people for ever; and they both knew, and Eliza felt as well, that they must shift for themselves in the end. She could quarter herself on Wimpole Street because it had come to be her home; but she was quite aware that she ought not to quarter Freddy there, and that it would not be good for his character if she did.

Not that the Wimpole Street bachelors objected. When she consulted them, Higgins declined to be bothered about her housing problem when that solution was so simple. Eliza's desire to have Freddy in the house with her seemed of no more importance than if she had wanted an extra piece of bedroom furniture. Pleas as to Freddy's character, and the moral obligation on

6. A well-known work by Nietzsche is titled *Beyond Good and Evil* (1886).

7. Roughly equivalent to $40,000 today.

him to earn his own living, were lost on Higgins. He denied that Freddy had any character, and declared that if he tried to do any useful work some competent person would have the trouble of undoing it: a procedure involving a net loss to the community; and great unhappiness to Freddy himself, who was obviously intended by Nature for such light work as amusing Eliza, which, Higgins declared, was a much more useful and honorable occupation than working in the city.[8] When Eliza referred again to her project of teaching phonetics, Higgins abated not a jot of his violent opposition to it. He said she was not within ten years of being qualified to meddle with his pet subject; and as it was evident that the Colonel agreed with him, she felt she could not go against them in this grave matter, and that she had no right, without Higgins's consent, to exploit the knowledge he had given her; for his knowledge seemed to her as much his private property as his watch: Eliza was no communist. Besides, she was superstitiously devoted to them both, more entirely and frankly after her marriage than before it.

It was the Colonel who finally solved the problem, which had cost him much perplexed cogitation. He one day asked Eliza, rather shyly, whether she had quite given up her notion of keeping a flower shop. She replied that she had thought of it, but had put it out of her head, because the Colonel had said, that day at Mrs. Higgins's, that it would never do. The Colonel confessed that when he said that, he had not quite recovered from the dazzling impression of the day before. They broke the matter to Higgins that evening. The sole comment vouchsafed by him very nearly led to a serious quarrel with Eliza. It was to the effect that she would have in Freddy an ideal errand boy.

Freddy himself was next sounded on the subject. He said he had been thinking of a shop himself; though it had presented itself to his pennilessness as a small place in which Eliza should sell tobacco at one counter whilst he sold newspapers at the opposite one. But he agreed that it would be extraordinarily jolly to go early every morning with Eliza to Covent Garden and buy flowers on the scene of their first meeting: a sentiment which earned him many kisses from his wife. He added that he had always been afraid to propose anything of the sort, because Clara would make an awful row about a step that must damage her matrimonial chances, and his mother could not be expected to like it after clinging for so many years to that step of the social ladder on which retail trade is impossible.

This difficulty was removed by an event highly unexpected by Freddy's mother. Clara, in the course of her incursions into those artistic circles which were the highest within her reach, discovered that her conversational qualifications were expected to include a grounding in the novels of Mr. H. G. Wells.[9] She borrowed them in various directions so energetically that she swallowed them all within two months. The result was a conversion of a kind quite common today. A modern Acts of the Apostles would fill fifty whole Bibles if anyone were capable of writing it.

Poor Clara, who appeared to Higgins and his mother as a disagreeable and ridiculous person, and to her own mother as in some inexplicable way a social failure, had never seen herself in either light; for, though to some extent

8. That is, working in London's finance district.
9. The English writer Herbert George Wells (1866–1946), a prominent member of the socialist Fabian Society and the author not only of science-fiction novels such as *The War of the Worlds* (1898) but also novels of social criticism such as *Tono-Bungay* (1908).

ridiculed and mimicked in West Kensington[1] like everybody else there, she was accepted as a rational and normal—or shall we say inevitable?—sort of human being. At worst they called her The Pusher;[2] but to them no more than to herself had it ever occurred that she was pushing the air, and pushing it in a wrong direction. Still, she was not happy. She was growing desperate. Her one asset, the fact that her mother was what the Epsom greengrocer called a carriage lady had no exchange value, apparently. It had prevented her from getting educated, because the only education she could have afforded was education with the Earlscourt greengrocer's daughter. It had led her to seek the society of her mother's class; and that class simply would not have her, because she was much poorer than the greengrocer, and, far from being able to afford a maid,[3] could not afford even a housemaid, and had to scrape along at home with an illiberally treated general servant. Under such circumstances nothing could give her an air of being a genuine product of Largelady Park. And yet its tradition made her regard a marriage with anyone within her reach as an unbearable humiliation. Commercial people and professional people in a small way were odious to her. She ran after painters and novelists; but she did not charm them; and her bold attempts to pick up and practise artistic and literary talk irritated them. She was, in short, an utter failure, an ignorant, incompetent, pretentious, unwelcome, penniless, useless little snob; and though she did not admit these disqualifications (for nobody ever faces unpleasant truths of this kind until the possibility of a way out dawns on them) she felt their effects too keenly to be satisfied with her position.

Clara had a startling eyeopener when, on being suddenly wakened to enthusiasm by a girl of her own age who dazzled her and produced in her a gushing desire to take her for a model, and gain her friendship, she discovered that this exquisite apparition had graduated from the gutter in a few months' time. It shook her so violently, that when Mr. H. G. Wells lifted her on the point of his puissant pen, and placed her at the angle of view from which the life she was leading and the society to which she clung appeared in its true relation to real human needs and worthy social structure, he effected a conversion and a conviction of sin comparable to the most sensational feats of General Booth or Gypsy Smith.[4] Clara's snobbery went bang. Life suddenly began to move with her. Without knowing how or why, she began to make friends and enemies. Some of the acquaintances to whom she had been a tedious or indifferent or ridiculous affliction, dropped her: others became cordial. To her amazement she found that some "quite nice" people were saturated with Wells, and that this accessibility to ideas was the secret of their niceness. People she had thought deeply religious, and had tried to conciliate on that tack with disastrous results, suddenly took an interest in her, and revealed a hostility to conventional religion which she had never conceived possible except among the most desperate characters. They made her read Galsworthy;[5] and Galsworthy exposed the vanity of Largelady Park and finished her. It exasperated her to think that the dungeon in which she had languished for so

1. An area of London at the western edge of the inner suburbs.
2. That is, The Social Climber.
3. A personal attendant, as distinct from a general servant who does housework.
4. That is, feats of religious conversion. William Booth (1829–1912), a Methodist revivalist, founded the Salvation Army; Rodney Smith (1860–1947), briefly a captain in the Salvation Army, became an internationally renowned evangelist.
5. John Galsworthy (1867–1933), an English playwright and novelist whose writings cast a realistic and critical light on the upper middle class.

many unhappy years had been unlocked all the time, and that the impulses she had so carefully struggled with and stifled for the sake of keeping well with society, were precisely those by which alone she could have come into any sort of sincere human contact. In the radiance of these discoveries, and the tumult of their reaction, she made a fool of herself as freely and conspicuously as when she so rashly adopted Eliza's expletive in Mrs. Higgins's drawing-room; for the new-born Wellsian had to find her bearings almost as ridiculously as a baby; but nobody hates a baby for its ineptitudes, or thinks the worse of it for trying to eat the matches; and Clara lost no friends by her follies. They laughed at her to her face this time; and she had to defend herself and fight it out as best she could.

When Freddy paid a visit to Earlscourt (which he never did when he could possibly help it) to make the desolating announcement that he and his Eliza were thinking of blackening the Largelady scutcheon[6] by opening a shop, he found the little household already convulsed by a prior announcement from Clara that she also was going to work in an old furniture shop in Dover Street, which had been started by a fellow Wellsian. This appointment Clara owed, after all, to her old social accomplishment of Push. She had made up her mind that, cost what it might, she would see Mr. Wells in the flesh; and she had achieved her end at a garden party. She had better luck than so rash an enterprise deserved. Mr. Wells came up to her expectations. Age had not withered him, nor could custom stale his infinite variety in half an hour.[7] His pleasant neatness and compactness, his small hands and feet, his teeming ready brain, his unaffected accessibility, and a certain fine apprehensiveness which stamped him as susceptible from his topmost hair to his tipmost toe, proved irresistible. Clara talked of nothing else for weeks and weeks afterwards. And as she happened to talk to the lady of the furniture shop, and that lady also desired above all things to know Mr. Wells and sell pretty things to him, she offered Clara a job on the chance of achieving that end through her.

And so it came about that Eliza's luck held, and the expected opposition to the flower shop melted away. The shop is in the arcade of a railway station not very far from the Victoria and Albert Museum; and if you live in that neighborhood you may go there any day and buy a buttonhole[8] from Eliza.

Now here is a last opportunity for romance. Would you not like to be assured that the shop was an immense success, thanks to Eliza's charms and her early business experience in Covent Garden? Alas! the truth is the truth: the shop did not pay for a long time, simply because Eliza and her Freddy did not know how to keep it. True, Eliza had not to begin at the very beginning: she knew the names and prices of the cheaper flowers; and her elation was unbounded when she found that Freddy, like all youths educated at cheap, pretentious, and thoroughly inefficient schools, knew a little Latin. It was very little, but enough to make him appear to her a Porson or Bentley,[9] and to put him at his ease with botanical nomenclature. Unfortunately he knew nothing else; and Eliza, though she could count money up to eighteen shillings or so, and had acquired a certain familiarity with the language of

6. Reputation (literally, a heraldic shield).
7. An allusion to the description of Cleopatra in Shakespeare's *Antony and Cleopatra* (1606–07): "Age cannot wither her, nor custom stale / Her infinite variety" (2.2.240–41).
8. A flower worn in the buttonhole of a lapel.
9. A great classicist, such as the English scholars Richard Porson (1759–1808) and Richard Bentley (1662–1742).

Milton from her struggles to qualify herself for winning Higgins's bet, could not write out a bill without utterly disgracing the establishment. Freddy's power of stating in Latin that Balbus built a wall and that Gaul was divided into three parts[1] did not carry with it the slightest knowledge of accounts or business: Colonel Pickering had to explain to him what a cheque book and a bank account meant. And the pair were by no means easily teachable. Freddy backed up Eliza in her obstinate refusal to believe that they could save money by engaging a bookkeeper with some knowledge of the business. How, they argued, could you possibly save money by going to extra expense when you already could not make both ends meet? But the Colonel, after making the ends meet over and over again, at last gently insisted; and Eliza, humbled to the dust by having to beg from him so often, and stung by the uproarious derision of Higgins, to whom the notion of Freddy succeeding at anything was a joke that never palled, grasped the fact that business, like phonetics, has to be learned.

On the piteous spectacle of the pair spending their evenings in shorthand schools and polytechnic classes, learning bookkeeping and typewriting with incipient junior clerks, male and female, from the elementary schools, let me not dwell. There were even classes at the London School of Economics, and a humble personal appeal to the director of that institution to recommend a course bearing on the flower business. He, being a humorist, explained to them the method of the celebrated Dickensian essay on Chinese Metaphysics by the gentleman who read an article on China and an article on Metaphysics and combined the information.[2] He suggested that they should combine the London School with Kew Gardens. Eliza, to whom the procedure of the Dickensian gentleman seemed perfectly correct (as in fact it was) and not in the least funny (which was only her ignorance) took his advice with entire gravity. But the effort that cost her the deepest humiliation was a request to Higgins, whose pet artistic fancy, next to Milton's verse, was caligraphy, and who himself wrote a most beautiful Italian hand, that he would teach her to write. He declared that she was congenitally incapable of forming a single letter worthy of the least of Milton's words; but she persisted; and again he suddenly threw himself into the task of teaching her with a combination of stormy intensity, concentrated patience, and occasional bursts of interesting disquisition on the beauty and nobility, the august mission and destiny, of human handwriting. Eliza ended by acquiring an extremely uncommercial script which was a positive extension of her personal beauty, and spending three times as much on stationery as anyone else because certain qualities and shapes of paper became indispensable to her. She could not even address an envelope in the usual way because it made the margins all wrong.

Their commercial school days were a period of disgrace and despair for the young couple. They seemed to be learning nothing about flower shops. At last they gave it up as hopeless, and shook the dust of the shorthand schools, and the polytechnics, and the London School of Economics from their feet for ever. Besides, the business was in some mysterious way beginning to take care of itself. They had somehow forgotten their objections to employing other people. They came to the conclusion that their own way was the best,

1. Phrases from standard Latin exercise books (the second is the opening of Caesar's *Gallic War* [ca. 50 B.C.E.]).

2. An allusion to *The Pickwick Papers* (1836–37), a novel by Charles Dickens.

and that they had really a remarkable talent for business. The Colonel, who had been compelled for some years to keep a sufficient sum on current account at his bankers to make up their deficits, found that the provision was unnecessary: the young people were prospering. It is true that there was not quite fair play between them and their competitors in trade. Their week-ends in the country cost them nothing, and saved them the price of their Sunday dinners; for the motor car was the Colonel's; and he and Higgins paid the hotel bills. Mr. F. Hill, florist and greengrocer (they soon discovered that there was money in asparagus; and asparagus led to other vegetables), had an air which stamped the business as classy; and in private life he was still Frederick Eynsford Hill, Esquire. Not that there was any swank about him: nobody but Eliza knew that he had been christened Frederick Challoner. Eliza herself swanked like anything.

That is all. That is how it has turned out. It is astonishing how much Eliza still manages to meddle in the housekeeping at Wimpole Street in spite of the shop and her own family. And it is notable that though she never nags her husband, and frankly loves the Colonel as if she were his favorite daughter, she has never got out of the habit of nagging Higgins that was established on the fatal night when she won his bet for him. She snaps his head off on the faintest provocation, or on none. He no longer dares to tease her by assuming an abysmal inferiority of Freddy's mind to his own. He storms and bullies and derides; but she stands up to him so ruthlessly that the Colonel has to ask her from time to time to be kinder to Higgins; and it is the only request of his that brings a mulish expression into her face. Nothing but some emergency or calamity great enough to break down all likes and dislikes, and throw them both back on their common humanity—and may they be spared any such trial!—will ever alter this. She knows that Higgins does not need her, just as her father did not need her. The very scrupulousness with which he told her that day that he had become used to having her there, and dependent on her for all sorts of little services, and that he should miss her if she went away (it would never have occurred to Freddy or the Colonel to say anything of the sort) deepens her inner certainty that she is "no more to him than them slippers," yet she has a sense, too, that his indifference is deeper than the infatuation of commoner souls. She is immensely interested in him. She has even secret mischievous moments in which she wishes she could get him alone, on a desert island, away from all ties and with nobody else in the world to consider, and just drag him off his pedestal and see him making love like any common man. We all have private imaginations of that sort. But when it comes to business, to the life that she really leads as distinguished from the life of dreams and fancies, she likes Freddy and she likes the Colonel; and she does not like Higgins and Mr. Doolittle. Galatea never does quite like Pygmalion: his relation to her is too godlike to be altogether agreeable.[3]

3. In classical mythology, Pygmalion was a legendary king of Cyprus who fell in love with an ivory statue of a woman that he had carved. In answer to his prayers, Aphrodite (called Venus by the Romans), the goddess of love, gave it life and they married; the most familiar version of the story is found in Ovid, *Metamorphoses* (ca. 10 C.E.), 10.243–97.

SUSAN GLASPELL

1876–1948

The rediscovery of Susan Glaspell's writing by feminist critics and theater artists has, over the past few decades, exposed new generations of readers and audiences to this groundbreaking American playwright, novelist, and short story author, who received the Pulitzer Prize for drama in 1931. Glaspell came of age in the late nineteenth century, during the heyday of the "local color" movement in American literature. Works in this tradition—such as those of Glaspell's fellow Davenport, Iowa, resident Alice French (writing as Octave Thanet, 1850–1934)—celebrated regional American life and exposed its idiosyncrasies. By the early twentieth century, however, writers were increasingly focusing on the cultural, economic, and political differences growing between the country's burgeoning urban centers and its established rural locales. Glaspell and her contemporaries felt compelled to share with the nation their large and probing questions about American beliefs, values, and goals. In their creative endeavors, they framed these questions through the lenses of the Progressive era and their modern age, most notably the recent discoveries about human psychology. Glaspell's writing—especially her plays—reflects her keen engagement with the pressing issues of her day: how to foster a democratic and equitable society, what to think about the evolving roles of men and women, and how to honor the nation's founding principles while embracing the spirit of modernism. Artists like Glaspell were also engaged in formal experimentation, and their works reveal a sense of creative excitement as they sought new ways, structurally and aesthetically, to represent these cogent contemporary themes. Glaspell's 1916 play *Trifles* has emerged as a canonical text precisely because it exemplifies these intertwining artistic and social goals within American modernism.

Like many American modernists, Glaspell grew up in the nation's heartland. Her father, Elmer Glaspell, was a feed dealer; her mother, born Alice Keating, had been a schoolteacher before her marriage. Glaspell began her career as a journalist, writing a society column for her local paper before leaving home to attend Drake University. After graduation, she secured a post with the *Des Moines Daily News* as a statehouse and legislative reporter, but after two years, she decided to devote herself to fiction. She quickly had success writing short stories, which she placed in such national magazines as *McClure's* and *Harper's*. Following in the local-color tradition, Glaspell based many of her narratives on her experiences growing up in and around Davenport. But she interlaced these intimate portraits of midwestern life with the sharper edge of social critique that epitomizes her evolution as a Progressive and modernist artist. She published her first novel in 1909 and her second in 1911, as she continued to write short fiction. Following her marriage to George Cram "Jig" Cook in 1913, she and her new husband moved to Greenwich Village, as did many other young writers and artists of their generation. They were drawn to New York's bohemian lifestyle and creative freedom, which they felt were unattainable in the Midwest.

During this early twentieth-century moment, a growing number of American modernists recognized the potential of the stage to convey vivid images of life in the contemporary United States and, even more importantly, to engage audiences directly with larger social concerns. Eschewing the commercial theater and its devotion to profit-making entertainment, they sought to create a new kind of theater that would foster the development of a distinctly American culture. As a co-founder of the influential Provincetown Players—the company originally based in Provincetown, Massachusetts, that first produced the work of Eugene O'Neill during summer vacations—Glaspell played a central role in this movement. With Cook and other friends and colleagues such as John Reed, Djuna Barnes, Edna St. Vincent Millay, Theodore Dreiser, and Wallace Stevens, Glaspell participated in establishing a national theater dedicated to artistically innovative and political drama reflecting the explosive arrival of modernism in the United States.

For financial, practical, and philosophical reasons, most of the works produced by the Provincetown Players in their early years were one acts. Having been influenced by a U.S. tour of what was still called the Irish Players—the group founded in 1899 by the poet William Butler Yeats, Lady Gregory, and others that in 1904 became the Abbey Theatre—Cook believed that their repertoire of one-act plays had great impact as both artistic and nationalist creations, and he encouraged the Provincetown dramatists to use this form. Glaspell wrote eleven plays, seven of which were one acts (two written with Cook), for the Provincetown group between 1915 and 1922. Glaspell and Cook then departed from New York for Greece, leaving the Provincetown Players to reconfigure themselves under others' leadership. After Cook died unexpectedly in 1924, Glaspell chose to return to their home on Cape Cod rather than renew her life in the bohemian Greenwich Village milieu. She also chose to return to her first creative form, fiction, producing six new novels and a children's tale. Glaspell did not abandon the theater however. With her new companion Norman Matson, with whom she lived until 1932, Glaspell wrote *The Comic Artist* (1927); soon thereafter she composed *Alison's House* (1930), based on the life and family of Emily Dickinson, for which she won the Pulitzer Prize. From 1936 to 1938 she lived in Chicago, serving as the director of the Midwest Play Bureau of the Federal Theater Project. Glaspell wrote one additional play, *Springs Eternal* (written 1944), which was neither published nor produced. She died in Provincetown in 1948.

Glaspell's first play, *Trifles,* was quickly identified by critics as an exemplar of one-act dramaturgy, and it was soon both widely produced and anthologized. Although Glaspell had initially conceived the piece as another short story, her husband persuaded her to write it first as a play; its short story version, "A Jury of Her Peers," was equally praised on its publication the following year. *Trifles* established Glaspell as a dramatist of real power; like all her short dramatic pieces, it displays her skill at constructing tight plots and using distinctive images in the service of theme. Like her American modernist contemporaries, Glaspell experimented freely with the various "isms" that defined the period, including realism, symbolism, and expressionism, often combining these approaches to achieve a specific thematic or stylistic effect. She demonstrated the effectiveness of both comedy and tragedy as vehicles for social critique. And she capitalized on the power of live theater to examine issues of particular concern to women, placing female characters and their struggles at the center of her dramaturgy. *The Outside* (1917), set in a lifesaving station on Cape Cod, epitomizes her method of integrating the symbolism of her setting with the play's action, as she portrays characters literally and figuratively in need of salvation. Such one acts as *Woman's Honor* (1918) showcase Glaspell's gifts as a comic playwright, particularly her ability to depict the foibles of all her characters equally, as she introduces a group of allegorical women responding to what they take to be a demonstration of chivalry. This even-handedness in her dramaturgical technique gives her plays a sense of balance, which is especially important when her theme is politically charged. Her ability to represent differing ideological perspectives is clearly displayed in *Inheritors* (1921), a full-length play that explores the Espionage Act (1917) and the Sedition Act (1918), which were intended to silence opposition to U.S. involvement in World War I. Other longer dramas, such as her highly regarded *The Verge* (1921), feature Glaspell's engagement with questions of gender identity and feminist consciousness, as well as stylistic experimentation with realism and expressionism. Though some earlier critics faulted Glaspell for what they perceived as inconsistencies in style or thematic focus, more recently this variety and breadth have been championed as integral to the modernist movement in America and its willingness to engage with many facets of contemporary life.

Between December 1900 and April 1901, while working as a journalist, Glaspell had written a series of articles on the murder case that became the genesis for *Trifles:* the story of an Iowa farmer named Hossack whose wife was accused of killing him with an axe, and her subsequent trial and conviction. Glaspell transformed the details disclosed in the trial into a dramatic work of remarkable power, economy, and artistry. *Trifles* is set in the kitchen of "the now abandoned farmhouse" of John and Minnie Wright. We soon learn that shortly after the murder, a neighbor, Lewis Hale, discovered John strangled in his bed upstairs and Minnie dazedly rocking in her kitchen. With the body removed and the accused wife in jail, the play opens with the arrival of Hale; the sheriff, Henry Peters; and the county prosecutor, George Henderson, to inspect the crime scene. The wives of the sheriff and the neighbor, Mrs. Peters and Mrs. Hale, remain in the kitchen area to collect a few things Minnie has requested from prison. Glaspell's choice to identify them only by their married names underscores the traditional assumption that women have significance only through their relation to their husbands. Once the men leave the room, however, the women begin to explore the domestic space on their own. As they interact with the stage environment, the two women discover clues to the couple's personalities, as well as potential evidence in the case. Despite their absence from the scene, Minnie and John Wright become

The Hossack family in front of their farmhouse, ca. 1892.

The 1916 production of *Trifles* by the Washington Square Players at the Comedy Theater. Pictured, from left to right, are Marjorie Vonnegut (Mrs. Peters), Elinor M. Cox (Mrs. Hale), John King (Lewis Hale), Arthur E. Hohl (Henry Peters), and T. W. Gibson (George Henderson).

vivid figures for us via the dialogue and actions of Mrs. Hale and Mrs. Peters. Glaspell's technique of building a plot around these absent centers is a hallmark of her dramaturgy, recurring in *Bernice* (1919) and *Alison's House,* among other plays. This device enables her to show that identity is as much constructed as innate. Moreover, it creates a distance between the audience and these characters that thwarts identification, thus making it possible for theatergoers to see them and their reported actions from multiple points of view. The irony that Glaspell emphasizes throughout the play (and in its very title) is the inconsequentiality—to the men who are empowered to solve the crime—of the domestic details these women embrace. The "trifles" of women's lives and work that the men dismiss hold great significance for the women who understand how to read their import empathically. Although the women do not really know each other at the beginning of the play, they come to find they have much in common, just as they do with the absent Minnie. Recognizing a sense of responsibility for and community with this other woman, Mrs. Hale exclaims: "I might have known she needed help! I know how things can be—for women. . . . We all go through the same things—it's all just a different kind of the same thing."

By reversing the narrative conventions that place men at the center of a plot as figures of power and knowledge, Glaspell guides her audience toward the recognition that different perspectives and values are essential to appreciate women's lives. The short story's title, "A Jury of Her Peers," adds another layer of irony by highlighting the impossibility of a woman facing such a jury at a time when women were systematically denied the right to be jurors. In effect, Mrs. Peters and Mrs. Hale (played by Glaspell in the first production) try Minnie Wright in an alternative venue, using a process that reveals details of her experience and possible motives—aspects of the case that the men's investigation will never discover. While Minnie's ultimate fate is left unresolved at the play's end, we sense that these women have come to their own verdict, one that exonerates Minnie and makes the audience wonder who in the couple was the victim.

Part of the ongoing appeal of *Trifles* surely stems from its reliance on the conventions of the murder mystery. Glaspell capitalized on the growing interest in this form of narrative, a genre that was popularized first in the United States by Edgar Allan Poe (1809–1849) and that gained an even wider readership with the Sherlock Holmes stories of England's Arthur Conan Doyle (1859–1930). Like many writers of mysteries, Glaspell uses amateur detectives—the two women—who turn out to be more perceptive than the male experts investigating the case. Glaspell involves her audience in the process of discovery and deduction intrinsic to the form. Her employment of the mystery genre thus advances her feminist agenda: all members of the audience, regardless of sex, come to understand each piece of the puzzle through the perspectives of the women sleuths as they grapple with the evidence. As feminist critics point out, Glaspell's play teaches its viewers to see as women, to resist the conventions that have dominated the Western theater since its inception.

Glaspell's deft layering of imagery, her poignant representation of her midwestern locale, and the specificity of her characterizations and dialect in such a brief work all point to her mastery of the one-act form and her significance as an American dramatist. During her period of greatest productivity, she was considered by many to be one of the country's two most important dramatists—O'Neill being the other. The prominent cultural critic Ludwig Lewisohn wrote in 1932, "Susan Glaspell was followed by Eugene O'Neill. The rest was silence; the rest is silence still." Though recent critical attention has focused on Glaspell primarily as a feminist writer, her dramatic work reflects a number of compelling aesthetic and political concerns. She made important contributions to the development of American modernism, and her writing reflects a forceful commitment to the country's foundational principles of democracy and personal liberty. For those wishing to grasp essential nuances of our cultural and political heritage, Susan Glaspell provides eloquent renditions of our nation a century ago. J.E.G.

Trifles

A Play in One Act

CHARACTERS

GEORGE HENDERSON, county attorney
HENRY PETERS, sheriff
LEWIS HALE, a neighboring farmer
MRS. PETERS
MRS. HALE

SCENE: *The kitchen in the now abandoned farmhouse of* JOHN WRIGHT, *a gloomy kitchen, and left without having been put in order—unwashed pans under the sink, a loaf of bread outside the breadbox, a dish towel on the table—other signs of incompleted work.*

[*At the rear the outer door opens and the* SHERIFF *comes in followed by the* COUNTY ATTORNEY *and* HALE. *The* SHERIFF *and* HALE *are men in middle life, the* COUNTY ATTORNEY *is a young man; all are much bundled up and go at once to the stove. They are followed by the two women—the* SHERIFF'S *wife first; she is a slight wiry woman, a thin nervous face.* MRS. HALE *is larger and would ordinarily be called more comfortable*[1] *looking, but she is disturbed now and looks fearfully about as she enters. The women have come in slowly, and stand close together near the door.*]

COUNTY ATTORNEY [*rubbing his hands*] This feels good. Come up to the fire, ladies.

MRS. PETERS [*after taking a step forward*] I'm not—cold.

SHERIFF [*unbuttoning his overcoat and stepping away from the stove as if to mark the beginning of official business*] Now, Mr. Hale, before we move things about, you explain to Mr. Henderson just what you saw when you came here yesterday morning.

COUNTY ATTORNEY By the way, has anything been moved? Are things just as you left them yesterday?

SHERIFF [*looking about*] It's just the same. When it dropped below zero last night I thought I'd better send Frank out this morning to make a fire for us—no use getting pneumonia with a big case on, but I told him not to touch anything except the stove—and you know Frank.

COUNTY ATTORNEY Somebody should have been left here yesterday.

SHERIFF Oh—yesterday. When I had to send Frank to Morris Center for that man who went crazy—I want you to know I had my hands full yesterday. I knew you could get back from Omaha by today and as long as I went over everything here myself—

COUNTY ATTORNEY Well, Mr. Hale, tell just what happened when you came here yesterday morning.

HALE Harry and I had started to town with a load of potatoes. We came along the road from my place and as I got here I said, "I'm going to see if I can't get John Wright to go in with me on a party telephone."[2] I spoke to Wright about it once before and he put me off, saying folks talked too much anyway, and all he asked was peace and quiet—I guess you know about how much he talked himself; but I thought maybe if I went to the house and talked about it before his wife, though I said to Harry that I didn't know as what his wife wanted made much difference to John—

COUNTY ATTORNEY Let's talk about that later, Mr. Hale. I do want to talk about that, but tell now just what happened when you got to the house.

HALE I didn't hear or see anything; I knocked at the door, and still it was all quiet inside. I knew they must be up, it was past eight o'clock. So I knocked again, and I thought I heard somebody say, "Come in." I wasn't sure, I'm not sure yet, but I opened the door—this door [*indicating the door by which the two women are still standing*] and there in that rocker—[*pointing to it*] sat Mrs. Wright.

[*They all look at the rocker.*]

COUNTY ATTORNEY What—was she doing?

HALE She was rockin' back and forth. She had her apron in her hand and was kind of—pleating it.

COUNTY ATTORNEY And how did she—look?

1. That is, appearing more relaxed.
2. That is, a single telephone line shared by two or four households.

HALE Well, she looked queer.

COUNTY ATTORNEY How do you mean—queer?

HALE Well, as if she didn't know what she was going to do next. And kind of done up.[3]

COUNTY ATTORNEY How did she seem to feel about your coming?

HALE Why, I don't think she minded—one way or other. She didn't pay much attention. I said, "How do, Mrs. Wright, it's cold, ain't it?" And she said, "Is it?"—and went on kind of pleating at her apron. Well, I was surprised; she didn't ask me to come up to the stove, or to set down, but just sat there, not even looking at me, so I said, "I want to see John." And then she— laughed. I guess you would call it a laugh. I thought of Harry and the team outside, so I said a little sharp: "Can't I see John?" "No," she says, kind o' dull like. "Ain't he home?" says I. "Yes," says she, "he's home." "Then why can't I see him?" I asked her, out of patience. "'Cause he's dead," says she. *"Dead?"* says I. She just nodded her head, not getting a bit excited, but rockin' back and forth. "Why—where is he?" says I, not knowing what to say. She just pointed upstairs—like that [*himself pointing to the room above*]. I got up, with the idea of going up there. I walked from there to here—then I says, "Why, what did he die of?" "He died of a rope round his neck," says she, and just went on pleatin' at her apron. Well, I went out and called Harry. I thought I might—need help. We went upstairs and there he was lyin'—

COUNTY ATTORNEY I think I'd rather have you go into that upstairs, where you can point it all out. Just go on now with the rest of the story.

HALE Well, my first thought was to get that rope off. It looked . . . [*Stops, his face twitches.*] . . . but Harry, he went up to him, and he said, "No, he's dead all right, and we'd better not touch anything." So we went back down stairs. She was still sitting that same way. "Has anybody been notified?" I asked. "No," says she, unconcerned. "Who did this, Mrs. Wright?" said Harry. He said it business-like—and she stopped pleatin' of her apron. "I don't know," she says. "You don't *know?*" says Harry. "No," says she. "Weren't you sleepin' in the bed with him?" says Harry. "Yes," says she, "but I was on the inside." "Somebody slipped a rope round his neck and strangled him and you didn't wake up?" says Harry. "I didn't wake up," she said after him. We must 'a looked as if we didn't see how that could be, for after a minute she said, "I sleep sound." Harry was going to ask her more questions but I said maybe we ought to let her tell her story first to the coroner, or the sheriff, so Harry went fast as he could to Rivers' place, where there's a telephone.

COUNTY ATTORNEY And what did Mrs. Wright do when she knew that you had gone for the coroner?

HALE She moved from that chair to this one over here [*pointing to a small chair in the corner*] and just sat there with her hands held together and looking down. I got a feeling that I ought to make come conversation, so I said I had come in to see if John wanted to put in a telephone, and at that she started to laugh, and then she stopped and looked at me—scared. [*The* COUNTY ATTORNEY, *who has had his notebook out, makes a note.*] I dunno, maybe it wasn't scared. I wouldn't like to say it was. Soon Harry got back,

3. Worn out.

and then Dr. Lloyd came, and you, Mr. Peters, and so I guess that's all I know that you don't.

COUNTY ATTORNEY [*looking around*] I guess we'll go upstairs first—and then out to the barn and around there. [*To the* SHERIFF] You're convinced that there was nothing important here—nothing that would point to any motive.

SHERIFF Nothing here but kitchen things.

[*The* COUNTY ATTORNEY, *after again looking around the kitchen, opens the door of a cupboard closet. He gets up on a chair and looks on a shelf. Pulls his hand away, sticky.*]

COUNTY ATTORNEY Here's a nice mess.

[*The women draw nearer.*]

MRS. PETERS [*to the other woman*] Oh, her fruit; it did freeze. [*To the* LAWYER] She worried about that when it turned so cold. She said the fire'd go out and her jars would break.

SHERIFF Well, can you beat the women! Held for murder and worryin' about her preserves.

COUNTY ATTORNEY I guess before we're through she may have something more serious than preserves to worry about.

HALE Well, women are used to worrying over trifles.

[*The two women move a little closer together.*]

COUNTY ATTORNEY [*with the gallantry of a young politician*] And yet, for all their worries, what would we do without the ladies? [*The women do not unbend. He goes to the sink, takes a dipperful of water from the pail and pouring it into a basin, washes his hands. Starts to wipe them on the roller towel, turns it for a cleaner place.*] Dirty towels! [*Kicks his foot against the pans under the sink.*] Not much of a housekeeper, would you say, ladies?

MRS. HALE [*stiffly*] There's a great deal of work to be done on a farm.

COUNTY ATTORNEY To be sure. And yet [*with a little bow to her*] I know there are some Dickson county farmhouses which do not have such roller towels.

[*He gives it a pull to expose its full length again.*]

MRS. HALE Those towels get dirty awful quick. Men's hands aren't always as clean as they might be.

COUNTY ATTORNEY Ah, loyal to your sex, I see. But you and Mrs. Wright were neighbors. I suppose you were friends, too.

MRS. HALE [*shaking her head*] I've not seen much of her of late years. I've not been in this house—it's more than a year.

COUNTY ATTORNEY And why was that? You didn't like her?

MRS. HALE I liked her all well enough. Farmers' wives have their hands full, Mr. Henderson. And then—

COUNTY ATTORNEY Yes—?

MRS. HALE [*looking about*] It never seemed a very cheerful place.

COUNTY ATTORNEY No—it's not cheerful. I shouldn't say she had the homemaking instinct.

MRS. HALE Well, I don't know as Wright had, either.

COUNTY ATTORNEY You mean that they didn't get on very well?

MRS. HALE No, I don't mean anything. But I don't think a place'd be any cheerfuller for John Wright's being in it.

COUNTY ATTORNEY I'd like to talk more of that a little later. I want to get the lay of things upstairs now.

[He goes to the left, where three steps lead to a stair door.]

SHERIFF I suppose anything Mrs. Peters does'll be all right. She was to take in some clothes for her, you know, and a few little things. We left in such a hurry yesterday.

COUNTY ATTORNEY Yes, but I would like to see what you take, Mrs. Peters, and keep an eye out for anything that might be of use to us.

MRS. PETERS Yes, Mr. Henderson.

[The women listen to the men's steps on the stairs, then look about the kitchen.]

MRS. HALE I'd hate to have men coming into my kitchen, snooping around and criticising.

[She arranges the pans under sink which the LAWYER *had shoved out of place.]*

MRS. PETERS Of course it's no more than their duty.

MRS. HALE Duty's all right, but I guess that deputy sheriff that came out to make the fire might have got a little of this on. [*Gives the roller towel a pull.*] Wish I'd thought of that sooner. Seems mean to talk about her for not having things slicked up when she had to come away in such a hurry.

MRS. PETERS [*who has gone to a small table in the left rear corner of the room, and lifted one end of a towel that covers a pan*] She had bread set.

[Stands still.]

MRS. HALE [*Eyes fixed on a loaf of bread beside the bread box, which is on a low shelf at the other side of the room. Moves slowly toward it.*] She was going to put this in there. [*Picks up loaf, then abruptly drops it. In a manner of returning to familiar things.*] It's a shame about her fruit. I wonder if it's all gone. [*Gets up on the chair and looks.*] I think there's some here that's all right, Mrs. Peters. Yes—here; [*holding it toward the window*] this is cherries, too. [*Looking again*] I declare I believe that's the only one. [*Gets down, bottle in her hand. Goes to the sink and wipes it off on the outside.*] She'll feel awful bad after all her hard work in the hot weather. I remember the afternoon I put up my cherries last summer.

[She puts the bottle on the big kitchen table, center of the room. With a sigh, is about to sit down in the rocking chair. Before she is seated realizes what chair it is; with a slow look at it, steps back. The chair which she has touched rocks back and forth.]

MRS. PETERS Well, I must get those things from the front room closet. [*She goes to the door at the right, but after looking into the other room, steps back.*] You coming with me, Mrs. Hale? You could help me carry them.

[They go in the other room; reappear, MRS. PETERS *carrying a dress and skirt,* MRS. HALE *following with a pair of shoes.]*

MRS. PETERS My, it's cold in there.

[She puts the clothes on the big table, and hurries to the stove.]

MRS. HALE [*examining the skirt*] Wright was close.[4] I think maybe that's why she kept so much to herself. She didn't even belong to the Ladies Aid. I suppose she felt she couldn't do her part, and then you don't enjoy things when you feel shabby. She used to wear pretty clothes and be lively, when

4. Stingy.

she was Minnie Foster, one of the town girls singing in the choir. But that—oh, that was thirty years ago. This all you was to take in?

MRS. PETERS She said she wanted an apron. Funny thing to want, for there isn't much to get you dirty in jail, goodness knows. But I suppose just to make her feel more natural. She said they was in the top drawer in this cupboard. Yes, here. And then her little shawl that always hung behind the door. [*Opens stair door and looks.*] Yes, here it is.

[*Quickly shuts door leading upstairs.*]

MRS. HALE [*abruptly moving toward her*] Mrs. Peters?

MRS. PETERS Yes, Mrs. Hale?

MRS. HALE Do you think she did it?

MRS. PETERS [*in a frightened voice*] Oh, I don't know.

MRS. HALE Well, I don't think she did. Asking for an apron and her little shawl. Worrying about her fruit.

MRS. PETERS [*starts to speak, glances up, where footsteps are heard in the room above. In a low voice*] Mr. Peters says it looks bad for her. Mr. Henderson is awful sarcastic in a speech and he'll make fun of her sayin' she didn't wake up.

MRS. HALE Well, I guess John Wright didn't wake when they was slipping that rope under his neck.

MRS. PETERS No, it's strange. It must have been done awful crafty and still. They say it was such a—funny way to kill a man, rigging it all up like that.

MRS. HALE That's just what Mr. Hale said. There was a gun in the house. He says that's what he can't understand.

MRS. PETERS Mr. Henderson said coming out that what was needed for the case was a motive; something to show anger, or—sudden feeling.

MRS. HALE [*who is standing by the table*] Well, I don't see any signs of anger around here. [*She puts her hand on the dish towel which lies on the table, stands looking down at table, one half of which is clean, the other half messy.*] It's wiped to here. [*Makes a move as if to finish work, then turns and looks at loaf of bread outside the breadbox. Drops towel. In that voice of coming back to familiar things*] Wonder how they are finding things upstairs. I hope she had it a little more red-up[5] up there. You know, it seems kind of *sneaking*. Locking her up in town and then coming out here and trying to get her own house to turn against her!

MRS. PETERS But Mrs. Hale, the law is the law.

MRS. HALE I s'pose 'tis. [*Unbuttoning her coat*] Better loosen up your things, Mrs. Peters. You won't feel them when you go out.

[MRS. PETERS *takes off her fur tippet, goes to hang it on hook at back of room, stands looking at the under part of the small corner table.*]

MRS. PETERS She was piecing a quilt.

[*She brings the large sewing basket and they look at the bright pieces.*]

MRS. HALE It's log cabin pattern. Pretty, isn't it? I wonder if she was goin' to quilt it or just knot it?

[*Footsteps have been heard coming down the stairs. The* SHERIFF *enters followed by* HALE *and the* COUNTY ATTORNEY.]

SHERIFF They wonder if she was going to quilt it or just knot it!

5. Tidied up.

[*The men laugh, the women look abashed.*]

COUNTY ATTORNEY [*rubbing his hands over the stove*] Frank's fire didn't do much up there, did it? Well, let's go out to the barn and get that cleared up.

[*The men go outside.*]

MRS. HALE [*resentfully*] I don't know as there's anything so strange, our takin' up our time with little things while we're waiting for them to get the evidence. [*She sits down at the big table smoothing out a block with decision.*] I don't see as it's anything to laugh about.

MRS. PETERS [*apologetically*] Of course they've got awful important things on their minds.

[*Pulls up a chair and joins* MRS. HALE *at the table.*]

MRS. HALE [*examining another block*] Mrs. Peters, look at this one. Here, this is the one she was working on, and look at the sewing! All the rest of it has been so nice and even. And look at this! It's all over the place! Why, it looks as if she didn't know what she was about!

[*After she has said this they look at each other, then start to glance back at the door. After an instant* MRS. HALE *has pulled at a knot and ripped the sewing.*]

MRS. PETERS Oh, what are you doing, Mrs. Hale?

MRS. HALE [*mildly*] Just pulling out a stitch or two that's not sewed very good. [*Threading a needle*] Bad sewing always made me fidgety.

MRS. PETERS [*nervously*] I don't think we ought to touch things.

MRS. HALE I'll just finish up this end. [*Suddenly stopping and leaning forward*] Mrs. Peters?

MRS. PETERS Yes, Mrs. Hale?

MRS. HALE What do you suppose she was so nervous about?

MRS. PETERS Oh—I don't know. I don't know as she was nervous. I sometimes sew awful queer when I'm just tired. [MRS. HALE *starts to say something, looks at* MRS. PETERS, *then goes on sewing.*] Well I must get these things wrapped up. They may be through sooner than we think. [*Putting apron and other things together*] I wonder where I can find a piece of paper, and string.

MRS. HALE In that cupboard, maybe.

MRS. PETERS [*looking in cupboard*] Why, here's a bird-cage. [*Holds it up.*] Did she have a bird, Mrs. Hale?

MRS. HALE Why, I don't know whether she did or not—I've not been here for so long. There was a man around last year selling canaries cheap, but I don't know as she took one; maybe she did. She used to sing real pretty herself.

MRS. PETERS [*glancing around*] Seems funny to think of a bird here. But she must have had one, or why would she have a cage? I wonder what happened to it.

MRS. HALE I s'pose maybe the cat got it.

MRS. PETERS No, she didn't have a cat. She's got that feeling some people have about cats—being afraid of them. My cat got in her room and she was real upset and asked me to take it out.

MRS. HALE My sister Bessie was like that. Queer, ain't it?

MRS. PETERS [*examining the cage*] Why, look at this door. It's broke. One hinge is pulled apart.

MRS. HALE [*looking too*] Looks as if someone must have been rough with it.

MRS. PETERS Why, yes.

[*She brings the cage forward and puts it on the table.*]

MRS. HALE I wish if they're going to find any evidence they'd be about it. I don't like this place.

MRS. PETERS But I'm awful glad you came with me, Mrs. Hale. It would be lonesome for me sitting here alone.

MRS. HALE It would, wouldn't it? [*Dropping her sewing*] But I tell you what I do wish, Mrs. Peters. I wish I had come over sometimes when *she* was here. I—[*looking around the room*]—wish I had.

MRS. PETERS But of course you were awful busy, Mrs. Hale—your house and your children.

MRS. HALE I could've come. I stayed away because it weren't cheerful—and that's why I ought to have come. I—I've never liked this place. Maybe because it's down in a hollow and you don't see the road. I dunno what it is, but it's a lonesome place and always was. I wish I had come over to see Minnie Foster sometimes. I can see now—[*Shakes her head.*]

MRS. PETERS Well, you mustn't reproach yourself, Mrs. Hale. Somehow we just don't see how it is with other folks until—something comes up.

MRS. HALE Not having children makes less work—but it makes a quiet house, and Wright out to work all day, and no company when he did come in. Did you know John Wright, Mrs. Peters?

MRS. PETERS Not to know him; I've seen him in town. They say he was a good man.

MRS. HALE Yes—good; he didn't drink, and kept his word as well as most, I guess, and paid his debts. But he was a hard man, Mrs. Peters. Just to pass the time of day with him— [*Shivers.*] Like a raw wind that gets to the bone. [*Pauses, her eye falling on the cage.*] I should think she would 'a wanted a bird. But what do you suppose went with it?

MRS. PETERS I don't know, unless it got sick and died.

[*She reaches over and swings the broken door, swings it again, both women watch it.*]

MRS. HALE You weren't raised round here, were you? [MRS. PETERS *shakes her head.*] You didn't know—her?

MRS. PETERS Not till they brought her yesterday.

MRS. HALE She—come to think of it, she was kind of like a bird herself—real sweet and pretty, but kind of timid and—fluttery. How—she—did—change. [*Silence; then as if struck by a happy thought and relieved to get back to everyday things.*] Tell you what, Mrs. Peters, why don't you take the quilt in with you? It might take up her mind.

MRS. PETERS Why, I think that's a real nice idea, Mrs. Hale. There couldn't possibly be any objection to it, could there? Now, just what would I take? I wonder if her patches are in here—and her things.

[*They look in the sewing basket.*]

MRS. HALE Here's some red. I expect this has got sewing things in it. [*Brings out a fancy box.*] What a pretty box. Looks like something somebody would give you. Maybe her scissors are in here. [*Opens box. Suddenly puts her hand to her nose.*] Why — [MRS. PETERS *bends nearer, then turns her face away.*] There's something wrapped up in this piece of silk.

MRS. PETERS Why, this isn't her scissors.

MRS. HALE [*lifting the silk*] Oh, Mrs. Peters—it's—

[MRS. PETERS *bends closer.*]

MRS. PETERS It's the bird.

MRS. HALE [*jumping up*] But, Mrs. Peters—look at it! Its neck! Look at its neck! It's all—other side *to*.[6]

MRS. PETERS Somebody—wrung—its—neck.

[*Their eyes meet. A look of growing comprehension, of horror, Steps are heard outside.* MRS. HALE *slips box under quilt pieces, and sinks into her chair. Enter* SHERIFF *and* COUNTY ATTORNEY. MRS. PETERS *rises.*]

COUNTY ATTORNEY [*as one turning from serious things to little pleasantries*] Well, ladies, have you decided whether she was going to quilt it or knot it?

MRS. PETERS We think she was going to—knot it.

COUNTY ATTORNEY Well, that's interesting, I'm sure. [*Seeing the birdcage*] Has the bird flown?

MRS. HALE [*putting more quilt pieces over the box*] We think the—cat got it.

COUNTY ATTORNEY [*preoccupied*] Is there a cat?

[MRS. HALE *glances in a quick covert way at* MRS. PETERS.]

MRS. PETERS Well, not *now*. They're superstitious, you know. They leave.

COUNTY ATTORNEY [*to* SHERIFF PETERS, *continuing an interrupted conversation*] No sign at all of anyone having come from the outside. Their own rope. Now let's go up again and go over it piece by piece. [*They start upstairs.*] It would have to have been someone who knew just the—

[MRS. PETERS *sits down. The two women sit there not looking at one another, but as if peering into something and at the same time holding back. When they talk now it is in the manner of feeling their way over strange ground, as if afraid of what they are saying, but as if they cannot help saying it.*]

MRS. HALE She liked the bird. She was going to bury it in that pretty box.

MRS. PETERS [*in a whisper*] When I was a girl—my kitten—there was a boy took a hatchet, and before my eyes—and before I could get there—[*covers her face an instant*] If they hadn't held me back I would have—[*catches herself, looks upstairs where steps are heard, falters weakly.*]—hurt him.

MRS. HALE [*with a slow look around her*] I wonder how it would seem never to have had any children around. [*Pause*] No, Wright wouldn't like the bird—a thing that sang. She used to sing. He killed that, too.

MRS. PETERS [*moving uneasily*] We don't know who killed the bird.

MRS. HALE I knew John Wright.

MRS. PETERS It was an awful thing was done in this house that night, Mrs. Hale. Killing a man while he slept, slipping a rope around his neck that choked the life out of him.

MRS. HALE His neck. Choked the life out of him.

[*Her hand goes out and rests on the birdcage.*]

MRS. PETERS [*with rising voice*] We don't know who killed him. We don't *know*.

MRS. HALE [*her own feeling not interrupted*] If there'd been years and years of nothing, then a bird to sing to you, it would be awful—still, after the bird was still.

MRS. PETERS [*something within her speaking*] I know what stillness is. When we homesteaded in Dakota, and my first baby died—after he was two years old, and me with no other then—

6. Twisted around.

MRS. HALE [*moving*] How soon do you suppose they'll be through, looking for the evidence?

MRS. PETERS I know what stillness is. [*Pulling herself back*] The law has got to punish crime, Mrs. Hale.

MRS. HALE [*not as if answering that*] I wish you'd seen Minnie Foster when she wore a white dress with blue ribbons and stood up there in the choir and sang. [*A look around the room*] Oh, I *wish* I'd come over here once in a while! That was a crime! That was a crime! Who's going to punish that?

MRS. PETERS [*looking upstairs*] We mustn't—take on.

MRS. HALE I might have known she needed help! I know how things can be—for women. I tell you, it's queer, Mrs. Peters. We live close together and we live far apart. We all go through the same things—it's all just a different kind of the same thing. [*Brushes her eyes, noticing the bottle of fruit, reaches out for it.*] If I was you I wouldn't tell her her fruit was gone. Tell her it *ain't*. Tell her it's all right. Take this in to prove it to her. She—she may never know whether it was broke or not.

MRS. PETERS [*Takes the bottle, looks about for something to wrap it in; takes petticoat from the clothes brought from the other room, very nervously begins winding this around the bottle. In a false voice.*] My, it's a good thing the men couldn't hear us. Wouldn't they just laugh! Getting all stirred up over a little thing like a—dead canary. As if that could have anything to do with—with—wouldn't they *laugh!*

[*The men are heard coming down stairs.*]

MRS. HALE [*under her breath*] Maybe they would—maybe they wouldn't.

COUNTY ATTORNEY No, Peters, it's all perfectly clear except a reason for doing it. But you know juries when it comes to women. If there was some definite thing. Something to show—something to make a story about—a thing that would connect up with this strange way of doing it—

[*The women's eyes meet for an instant. Enter* HALE *from outer door.*]

HALE Well, I've got the team around. Pretty cold out there.

COUNTY ATTORNEY I'm going to stay here a while by myself. [*To the* SHERIFF] You can send Frank out for me, can't you? I want to go over everything. I'm not satisfied that we can't do better.

SHERIFF Do you want to see what Mrs. Peters is going to take in?

[*The* LAWYER *goes to the table, picks up the apron, laughs.*]

COUNTY ATTORNEY Oh, I guess they're not very dangerous things the ladies have picked out. [*Moves a few things about, disturbing the quilt pieces which cover the box. Steps back.*] No, Mrs. Peters doesn't need supervising. For that matter, a sheriff's wife is married to the law. Ever think of it that way, Mrs. Peters?

MRS. PETERS Not—just that way.

SHERIFF [*chuckling*] Married to the law. [*Moves toward the other room.*] I just want you to come in here a minute, George. We ought to take a look at these windows.

COUNTY ATTORNEY [*scoffingly*] Oh, windows!

SHERIFF We'll be right out, Mr. Hale.

[HALE *goes outside. The* SHERIFF *follows the* COUNTY ATTORNEY *into the other room. Then* MRS. HALE *rises, hands tight together, looking intensely at* MRS. PETERS, *whose eyes make a slow turn, finally meeting* MRS.

HALE'S. *A moment* MRS. HALE *holds her, then her own eyes point the way to where the box is concealed. Suddenly* MRS. PETERS *throws back quilt pieces and tries to put the box in the bag she is wearing. It is too big. She opens box, starts to take bird out, cannot touch it, goes to pieces, stands there helpless. Sound of a knob turning in the other room.* MRS. HALE *snatches the box and puts it in the pocket of her big coat. Enter* COUNTY ATTORNEY *and* SHERIFF.]

COUNTY ATTORNEY [*facetiously*] Well, Henry, at least we found out that she was not going to quilt it. She was going to—what is it you call it, ladies?

MRS. HALE [*her hand against her pocket*] We call it—knot it, Mr. Henderson.

Curtain.

LUIGI PIRANDELLO

1867–1937

When Pirandello received the Nobel Prize in Literature in 1934, at the age of sixty-seven, he was widely known as the author of intricate philosophical comedies. One in particular, *SIX CHARACTERS IN SEARCH OF AN AUTHOR* (1921), had catapulted him onto the international scene in the early 1920s, leading to acclaimed performances all over Europe and the Americas. Like his contemporaries GEORGE BERNARD SHAW for the English-speaking world and Maurice Maeterlinck for the French-speaking world, Pirandello became the Italian representative of the New Drama. Pirandello's worldwide success occurred relatively late in his life, at the end of a busy writing career that included hundreds of short stories, dozens of early plays, and a handful of novels as well as essays, a dissertation in linguistics, and several film scripts. Outside Italy, however, Pirandello's name remained tied to the invention of a new, intellectual drama thriving on arguments, paradoxes, and inversions. These plays, of which *Six Characters* is the best known, apply their wit to the theater itself, turning actors, directors, and dramatic authors into the material from which to fashion outrageous plots and far fetched conceits. Somehow, Pirandello managed to transform himself from an author of local and rather traditional novellas and plays into the most fashionable and advanced European dramatist of his age.

Luigi Pirandello was born into a nineteenth century Sicily where a small landowning class lorded over impoverished peasants. It was a society with many lingering feudal structures and a deeply traditional literature and culture to go with it. Pirandello himself was rather fortunate, since his father was quite wealthy and was therefore capable of financing Pirandello's studies in Rome, his doctorate at the University of Bonn, and his early career as a writer. Despite his cosmopolitan education, however, Pirandello did not reject the social values of Sicily and agreed to an arranged marriage to Antonietta Portulano, the daughter of one of his father's business partners, whom he barely knew. His marriage of 1894, business interests, the sulphur mine—these were the pillars of Pirandello's life. But they did not last. His father's fortune and his wife's dowry were heavily invested in a mine that was flooded in 1903, and everything was lost. In the meantime, Pirandello had began teaching at a women's college in Rome, an occupation he continued until his international breakthrough in the early twenties. Just as the economic foundations of his life crumbled, so did the personal ones. His wife was subject to increasingly pathological fits of jealousy and other delusional behavior, and Pirandello retired more and more from social life, maintaining his three children and suffering from an untenable domestic arrangement until Antonietta was eventually committed to a mental institution in 1914.

In the early twentieth century, Pirandello withdrew from life, but he also became a prolific writer of short stories, with which he supplemented his teacher's income. Over the years, he perfected his command of the genre and reissued selected short stories in a collection, *Novellas for a Year* (15 vols., 1922–37), that still enjoys great popularity in Italy. Pirandello's later mastery of drama can be traced back to these works. Like drama, the short story is a genre that requires economy and constraint and is often built around very few scenes and exchanges. Pirandello would frequently recycle his short stories in his dramas, including *Six Characters*.

The world in which Pirandello had grown up had fallen to pieces, but it continued to make itself felt in his literary work. His short stories, novels, and plays often revolve around closed family structures made insufferable by arranged marriages, jealousy, and betrayal. They are set in deeply patriarchal worlds in which women are seen as mothers, virgins, or whores. Even when Pirandello shows the extent to which these roles lead to pathologies, he held onto them to the end. His acclaimed comedies, such as *Six Characters* and *Henry IV* (1922), with their plays-within-the-play, philosophizing characters, and modern structures, contain under their surface the traditional plots of marriage and fertility, jealousy and adultery that are premised on the most traditional of family roles. Pirandello could never quite let go of Sicily—even during his time in Germany, when he studied philology and philosophy at Bonn, he chose as his dissertation subject the Sicilian dialects of his home region.

A similar fascination with Sicily also prompted Pirandello to turn from the short story to drama. After having become acquainted with a Sicilian dialect theater group headed by the charismatic Angelo Musco, Pirandello started writing dialect plays of high passion and melodrama. It was a traditionalist and provincial beginning for the future modern dramatist, but it gave him a first taste of the pleasures of the theater, which would come to full fruition in his most successful plays. Musco's group acted in a style reminiscent of the commedia dell'arte, the tradition of improvised theater based on fixed types that are often accentuated with masks. Pirandello continued to use this technique later in his career: for example, in *Six Characters*, where a number of actors wear such masks. Indeed, it was Carlo Goldoni (1707–1793), the playwright most closely associated with commedia dell'arte, rather than HENRIK IBSEN, Shaw, or any of the other modern dramatists, who was Pirandello's favorite playwright. Pirandello's best and bestknown dialect play, *Liolà* (1916), whose plot is taken entirely from the first chapters of his novel *The Late Mattia Pascal* (1904), is representative of this phase of his work in that it revolves around fertility, adultery, and the necessity of producing an heir. Yet all these subjects are presented in a particular form of comedy. In a long essay written to qualify for his teaching position, Pirandello had defined humor as the collision of ideals and harsh reality, as a sentiment of contradiction, as a moment when one position merges with its opposite, and as an art of quick reversals and inversions. This theory of humor underlies much of Pirandello's later drama.

Despite some considerable success in the theater, however, Pirandello still viewed it as a secondary art form. He put actors in the same category as illustrators of novels or translators—merely necessary but lamentable vehicles for bringing works of literature to the public. But over time, he became more interested in theatrical representation as well as in modernist forms of literature and drama. The first of his modernist plays, *It Is So! (If You Think So)* (1917), introduced the philosophizing *raisonneur*—a character that comments on the main action of the play, expressing skepticism about the truth of appearances. More important than the validity of this skepticism as a philosophical position is its close relation to Pirandello's theory of humor, which is premised on sudden reversals and quick changes from one appearance to the next. Many of his later plays, including *Six Characters, Henry IV*, and *Each in His Own Way* (1923), exploit philosophical relativism as a vehicle for a comedy, and they often rely on the figure of the *raisonneur*. Because of the prominence of this figure in many of his plays, Pirandello's works are sometimes considered too theoretical or intellectual, too dependent on words and conceits. But in his most successful plays, Pirandello manages to draw these explanatory figures into the action, exposing their own blindness, missteps, and mistakes. After decades of writing more or less realistic literature set in Sicily and Rome, Pirandello found that the theater formed the perfect setting and subject matter for his art.

The best-known and most cunning of these plays about theater is *Six Characters*. Here Pirandello highlights the difference between the fixed dramatic text and its ever-changing performances by staging a conflict between two groups: a set of characters and the actors who want to impersonate these characters according to the traditions and rules of theatrical representation. Even though the characters are putatively searching for an author who will write down their story, that story already exists within them. The real conflict breaks out not over how to transform these characters into a play but over how to bring the story that they represent onto the stage. The title, in this sense, is a misnomer, one that can be explained by the history of the play's composition; like many of Pirandello's dramas, it originated as a short story. In fact, it originated as three short stories, all of which featured "characters" appearing before an author and demanding to be turned into literature: "Character" (1906), "A Character's Tragedy" (1911), and "Interview of Characters" (1915). But once this conceit is transported to the theater, characters and actors engage in a struggle over the question of what it means to stage a play. While the characters demand absolute fidelity to their story, the director and the actors recast that story into one suitable for the theater. They simplify the plot, reduce the number of scenes, and do everything necessary for an audience to be able to follow the play.

Having characters appear on stage as characters and not as full-fledged persons creates a number of interesting problems and conundrums, which Pirandello exploits to the full. Since the story is enclosed inside these characters, they have to tell their story to the director and the actors so that it can be brought to the stage. Most of the narration is done by the father, another version of Pirandello's *raisonneur* figure; he also explains the predicament of the actors, who are caught in their roles and hope to find release through an author. Far from being detached observers, however, these characters, including the father, are fully immersed in their story and therefore lack the capacity to tell it coherently and succinctly. Every time they begin to narrate what happened and how it happened, they "fall into character," as the common theatrical idiom has it—that is, they stop narrating and start feeling and enacting their plight. Indeed, they are entirely trapped inside their story and are forced to live it over and over again. It is only at the very end of the play, after many conflicts between characters and actors, that the audience can surmise that story's contours.

But living the story is one thing, playing it is another. While the characters *feel* their passions, the actors need to *represent* them. The director and the actors in this play argue directly against the common critique of acting as falsifying the author's intentions (a position Pirandello himself had maintained early in his career)—or, more precisely, they prove the necessity of such falsifications in the interest of art. *Six Characters* is thus essentially a play about acting, about theater, about the rules and integrity of theatrical representation. As eccentric and unusual as this piece of metatheater may be, the actual story inside the characters is strikingly traditional. It is precisely the kind of story that had populated Pirandello's earlier works, featuring an adulterous affair, a separation between husband and wife, the threat of incest, and rivalries between stepsiblings, as well as hatred and shame. *Six Characters* is metatheater, but metatheater with a traditional, melodramatic core.

The difference between the unchanging eternal play to which the characters are tied and its variations every time they relive it on the stage was something Pirandello had absorbed from the Italian critic Adriano Tilgher. Tilgher supplied Pirandello with an aesthetic philosophy, borrowed from such theorists as Henri Bergson (1859–1941) and Friedrich Nietzsche (1844–1900), according to which life is a perpetual chaos onto which the human mind seeks to impose order and form. Art, in Tilgher's view, is the highest imposition of form onto life, connecting the ever-changing with eternal and ideal forms. Pirandello realized that this difference between eternal works of art and ever-changing life corresponded directly to

Benito Mussolini in *The Yellow Caesar* (1941), an Italian fascist propaganda film.

the relation between a fixed literary text and its ever-new performances through live actors. This insight was put into practice most brilliantly in Pirandello's plays about the theater. Some of these metatheatrical pieces—*Six Characters, Each in His Own Way*, and *Tonight We Improvise* (1930)—actually take place in the theater, but many others that draw on the same aesthetic theory do not.

Six Characters, and Pirandello's metatheater more generally, has a more sinister, political side, which is often ignored: it supplied the language in which Pirandello formulated his strong and unwavering allegiance to Benito Mussolini and Italian fascism. Pirandello favored a powerful leader who could stand above the chaos of democratic multiplicity and lead the country with a strong and fatherly hand. In Mussolini he got precisely the leader he was looking for. He met Mussolini in 1923 and immediately began to heap praise on him in the right-wing press, in the precise terms of his aesthetic doctrine—namely, as a strong leader capable of imposing onto the chaos of the nation a single and eternal form. Pirandello thus envisioned Mussolini as the artist of the Italian nation. The playwright who often declared that his art had nothing to do with his politics here treated politics as if it were nothing but an extension of art.

Pirandello's antidemocratic and profascist sympathies were not isolated moments of enthusiasm but were deeply felt. Indeed, he made his strongest gesture of support for fascism at a time of the movement's greatest weakness, after fascist supporters had brutally murdered a socialist member of parliament, Giacomo Matteotti. Rather than being outraged at this level of brutality, as many otherwise sympathetic to fascism were, Pirandello publicly declared his allegiance to the National Fascist Party and finally applied for membership. This political dimension may also account for a somewhat puzzling aspect of Pirandello's work: its violence. Even and especially his most philosophical and metatheatrical plays end with acts of extreme violence; *Six Characters*, for instance, culminates in two sudden deaths, one a suicide. This unexpectedly violent turn in an otherwise talkative and intellectual play corresponds structurally to the fascist doctrine of action: talking is what democracy practices in parliament and it must be ended by pure and bloody acts. It is as if Pirandello felt that his verbose and witty plays likewise needed to be concluded with bloodshed, so that mere talking could stop and real action could start.

In addition to Pirandello's genuine attraction to fascism, there was also a mercenary element to his relationship with Mussolini—he hoped that the fascist leader would establish a national theater and place him in charge of it. After his success with *Six Characters,* which received multiple stagings by Europe's most innovative directors, Pirandello founded a theater of his own, the Teatro d'Arte. Although Mussolini never gave sufficient funds to satisfy Pirandello's ambitious plans for a national theater, he supplied enough to enable Pirandello's theater company to tour Europe and the Americas with *Six Characters* and other plays, thereby functioning, as Pirandello never tired of telling Mussolini, as cultural ambassadors for fascist Italy. These tours also exposed Pirandello to Europe's most innovative directors, such as the Russian Nikolai Evreinov and the Austrian Max Reinhardt, who had perfected new forms of spectacular theater. Indeed, one of Pirandello's last pieces of metatheater set in a theater, *Tonight We Improvise,* contains a parody of Max Reinhardt as a director disrespectful of the playwright and interested only in creating spectacles.

It was during his own work as director and producer that Pirandello in 1925 met the young actress Marta Abba, whom he fell in love with and continued to adore for the rest of his life. It was for her that he wrote his final plays, all of which feature strong female protagonists, such as the utopian *The New Colony* (1928) or his last play, *The Mountain Giants* (1937), a metatheatrical work that features a group of actors and magicians living in a remote mountain region. After a tumultuous life of personal tragedy, political entanglement, and artistic fame, Pirandello ended with a eulogy to the art that he had first rejected but that turned out to be his calling: the theater.

M.P.

Six Characters in Search of an Author[1]

CHARACTERS OF THE PLAY-IN-THE-MAKING

The FATHER
The MOTHER
The SON, aged 22
The STEPDAUGHTER, 18
The BOY, 14
The LITTLE GIRL, 4
(these two last do not speak)
Then, called into being:
MADAM PACE

ACTORS IN THE COMPANY

The DIRECTOR (DIRETTORE-CAPOCOMICO)[2]
LEADING LADY
LEADING MAN
SECOND ACTRESS
INGENUE
JUVENILE LEAD
Other actors and actresses
STAGE MANAGER
PROMPTER
PROPERTY MAN
TECHNICIAN
Director's SECRETARY
STAGE DOOR MAN
STAGE CREW

1. Translated by Eric Bentley.
2. Pirandello here combines the modern 20th-century role of director (*direttore* in Italian) with the older position of actor-manager (or "chief actor," *capocomico* in Italian), who fulfilled the function of supervising a theatrical production.

THE PLACE: *The stage of a playhouse.*[3]

When the audience arrives in the theater, the curtain is raised; and the stage, as normally in the daytime, is without wings or scenery and almost completely dark and empty. From the beginning we are to receive the impression of an unrehearsed performance.

Two stairways, left and right respectively, connect the stage with the auditorium.

Onstage the dome of the prompter's box[4] *has been placed on one side of the box itself. On the other side, at the front of the stage, a small table and an armchair with its back to the audience, for the* DIRETTORE-CAPOCOMICO [DIRECTOR].

Two other small tables of different sizes with several chairs around them have also been placed at the front of the stage, ready as needed for the rehearsal. Other chairs here and there, left and right, for the actors, and at the back, a piano, on one side and almost hidden.

As soon as the houselights dim, the TECHNICIAN *is seen entering at the door onstage. He is wearing a blue shirt, and a tool bag hangs from his belt. From a corner at the back he takes several stage braces,*[5] *then arranges them on the floor downstage, and kneels down to hammer some nails in. At the sound of the hammering, the* STAGE MANAGER *comes running from the door that leads to the dressing rooms.*

STAGE MANAGER Oh! What are you doing?

TECHNICIAN What am I doing? Hammering.

STAGE MANAGER At this hour? [*He looks at the clock.*] It's ten-thirty already. The Director will be here any moment. For the rehearsal.

TECHNICIAN I gotta have time to work, too, see.

STAGE MANAGER You will have. But not now.

TECHNICIAN When?

STAGE MANAGER Not during rehearsal hours. Now move along, take all this stuff away, and let me set the stage for the second act of, um, *The Game of Role Playing.*[6]

[*Muttering, grumbling, the* TECHNICIAN *picks up the stage braces and goes away. Meanwhile, from the door onstage, the* ACTORS OF THE COMPANY *start coming in, both men and women, one at a time at first, then in twos, at random, nine or ten of them, the number one would expect as the cast in rehearsals of Pirandello's play "The Game of Role Playing," which is the order of the day. They enter, greet the* STAGE MANAGER *and each other, all saying good-morning to all. Several go to their dressing rooms. Others, among them the* PROMPTER, *who has a copy of the script rolled up under his arm, stay onstage, waiting for the* DIRECTOR *to begin the rehearsal. Meanwhile, either seated in conversational groups, or*

3. The play has neither acts nor scenes. The performance should be interrupted twice; first—without any lowering of the curtain—when the Director and the chief among the Characters retire to put the scenario together and the Actors leave the stage; second when the Technician lets the curtain down by mistake [Pirandello's note].

4. A box in the apron or on the side of a stage, opening toward the actors, that houses someone with a script (sitting below the stage) who is ready to prompt the actors when they forget their lines.

5. Braces used to support a stage set from behind.

6. *Il Gioco delle Parti* (1918), a stage adaptation of Pirandello's own novella.

standing, they exchange a few words among themselves. One lights a cigarette, one complains about the part he has been assigned, one reads aloud to his companions items of news from a theater journal. It would be well if both the Actresses and the Actors wore rather gay and brightly colored clothes and if this first improvised scene [scena a soggetto] *combined vivacity with naturalness. At a certain point, one of the actors can sit down at the piano and strike up a dance tune. The younger actors and actresses start dancing.*]

STAGE MANAGER [*clapping his hands to call them to order*] All right, that's enough of that. The Director's here.

[*The noise and the dancing stop at once. The Actors turn and look toward the auditorium from the door of which the* DIRECTOR *is now seen coming. A bowler hat on his head, a walking stick under his arm, and a big cigar in his mouth, he walks down the aisle and, greeted by the Actors, goes onstage by one of the two stairways. The* SECRETARY *hands him his mail: several newspapers and a script in a wrapper.*]

DIRECTOR Letters?

SECRETARY None. That's all the mail there is.

DIRECTOR [*handing him the script*] Take this to my room. [*Then, looking around and addressing himself to the* STAGE MANAGER] We can't see each other in here. Want to give us a little light?

STAGE MANAGER OK.

[*He goes to give the order, and shortly afterward, the whole left side of the stage where the Actors are is lit by a vivid white light. Meanwhile, the* PROMPTER *has taken up his position in his box. He uses a small lamp and has the script open in front of him.*]

DIRECTOR [*clapping his hands*] Very well, let's start. [*To the* STAGE MANAGER] Someone missing?

STAGE MANAGER The Leading Lady.

DIRECTOR As usual! [*He looks at the clock.*] We're ten minutes late already. Fine her for that, would you, please? Then she'll learn to be on time.

[*He has not completed his rebuke when the voice of the* LEADING LADY *is heard from the back of the auditorium.*]

LEADING LADY No, no, for heaven's sake! I'm here! I'm here! [*She is dressed all in white with a big, impudent hat on her head and a cute little dog in her arms. She runs down the aisle and climbs one of the sets of stairs in great haste.*]

DIRECTOR You've sworn an oath always to keep people waiting.

LEADING LADY You must excuse me. Just couldn't find a taxi. But you haven't even begun, I see. And I'm not on right away. [*Then, calling the* STAGE MANAGER *by name, and handing the little dog over to him*] Would you please shut him in my dressing room?

DIRECTOR [*grumbling*] And the little dog to boot! As if there weren't enough dogs around here. [*He claps his hands again and turns to the* PROMPTER.] Now then, the second act of *The Game of Role Playing*. [*As he sits down in his armchair*] Quiet, gentlemen. Who's onstage?

[*The Actresses and Actors clear the front of the stage and go and sit on one side, except for the three who will start the rehearsal and the* LEADING LADY *who, disregarding the* DIRECTOR's *request, sits herself down at one of the two small tables.*]

DIRECTOR [*to the* LEADING LADY] You're in this scene, are you?

LEADING LADY Me? No, no.

DIRECTOR [*irritated*] Then how about getting up, for Heaven's sake?

[*The* LEADING LADY *rises and goes and sits beside the other Actors who have already gone to one side.*]

DIRECTOR [*to the* PROMPTER] Start, start.

PROMPTER [*reading from the script*] "In the house of Leone Gala. A strange room, combined study and dining room."

DIRECTOR [*turning to the* STAGE MANAGER] We'll use the red room.

STAGE MANAGER [*making a note on a piece of paper*] Red room. Very good.

PROMPTER [*continuing to read from the script*] "The table is set and the desk has books and papers on it. Shelves with books on them, and cupboards with lavish tableware. Door in the rear through which one goes to Leone's bedroom. Side door on the left through which one goes to the kitchen. The main entrance is on the right."

DIRECTOR [*rising and pointing*] All right, now listen carefully. That's the main door. This is the way to the kitchen. [*Addressing himself to the Actor playing the part of Socrates*] You will come on and go out on this side. [*To the* STAGE MANAGER] The compass at the back. And curtains. [*He sits down again.*]

STAGE MANAGER [*making a note*] Very good.

PROMPTER [*reading as before*] "Scene One. Leone Gala, Guido Venanzi, Filippo called Socrates." [*To the* DIRECTOR] Am I supposed to read the stage directions, too?

DIRECTOR Yes, yes, yes! I've told you that a hundred times!

PROMPTER [*reading as before*] "At the rise of the curtain, Leone Gala, wearing a chef's hat and apron, is intent on beating an egg in a saucepan with a wooden spoon. Filippo, also dressed as a cook, is beating another egg. Guido Venanzi, seated, is listening."

LEADING ACTOR [*to the* DIRECTOR] Excuse me, but do I really have to wear a chef's hat?

DIRECTOR [*annoyed by this observation*] I should say so! It's in the script. [*And he points at it.*]

LEADING ACTOR But it's ridiculous, if I may say so.

DIRECTOR [*leaping to his feet, furious*] "Ridiculous, ridiculous!" What do you want me to do? We never get a good play from France any more, so we're reduced to producing plays by Pirandello, a fine man and all that, but neither the actors, the critics, nor the audience are ever happy with his plays, and if you ask me, he does it all on purpose. [*The Actors laugh. And now he rises and coming over to the* LEADING ACTOR *shouts.*] A cook's hat, yes, my dear man! And you beat eggs. And you think you have nothing more on your hands than the beating of eggs? Guess again. You symbolize the shell of those eggs. [*The Actors resume their laughing, and start making ironical comments among themselves.*] Silence! And pay attention while I explain. [*Again addressing himself to the* LEADING ACTOR] Yes, the shell: that is to say, the empty *form* of reason without the *content* of instinct, which is blind. You are reason, and your wife is instinct in the game of role playing. You play the part assigned you, and you're your own puppet—of your own free will. Understand?

LEADING ACTOR [*extending his arms, palms upward*] Me? No.

DIRECTOR [*returning to his place*] Nor do I. Let's go on. Wait and see what I do with the ending. [*In a confidential tone*] I suggest you face three-quarters front. Otherwise, what with the abstruseness of the dialogue, and an audience that can't hear you, good-bye play! [*Again clapping*] Now, again, order! Let's go.

PROMPTER Excuse me, sir, may I put the top back on the prompter's box? There's rather a draft.

DIRECTOR Yes, yes, do that.

[*The* STAGE DOOR MAN *has entered the auditorium in the meanwhile, his braided cap on his head. Proceeding down the aisle, he goes up onstage to announce to the* DIRECTOR *the arrival of the Six Characters, who have also entered the auditorium, and have started following him at a certain distance, a little lost and perplexed, looking around them.*

Whoever is going to try and translate this play into scenic terms must take all possible measures not *to let these Six Characters get confused with the Actors of the Company. Placing both groups correctly, in accordance with the stage directions, once the Six are onstage, will certainly help, as will lighting the two groups in contrasting colors. But the most suitable and effective means to be suggested here is the use of special masks for the Characters: masks specially made of material which doesn't go limp when sweaty and yet masks which are not too heavy for the Actors wearing them, cut out and worked over so they leave eyes, nostrils, and mouth free. This will also bring out the inner significance of the play. The Characters in fact should not be presented as ghosts but as created realities, unchanging constructs of the imagination, and therefore more solidly real than the Actors with their fluid naturalness. The masks will help to give the impression of figures constructed by art, each one unchangeably fixed in the expression of its own fundamental sentiment, thus:*

remorse *in the case of the* FATHER; revenge *in the case of the* STEPDAUGHTER; disdain *in the case of the* SON; grief *in the case of the* MOTHER, *who should have wax tears fixed in the rings under her eyes and on her cheeks, as with the sculpted and painted images of the* mater dolorosa[7] *in church. Their clothes should be of special material and design, without extravagance, with rigid, full folds like a statue, in short not suggesting a material you might buy at any store in town, cut out and tailored at any dressmaker's.*

The FATHER *is a man of about fifty, hair thin at the temples, but not bald, thick mustache coiled round a still youthful mouth that is often open in an uncertain, pointless smile. Pale, most notably on his broad forehead: blue eyes, oval, very clear and piercing; dark jacket and light trousers: at times gentle and smooth, at times he has hard, harsh outbursts.*

The MOTHER *seems scared and crushed by an intolerable weight of shame and self-abasement. Wearing a thick black crepe widow's veil, she is modestly dressed in black, and when she lifts the veil, the face does not show signs of suffering, and yet seems made of wax. Her eyes are always on the ground.*

The STEPDAUGHTER, *eighteen, is impudent, almost insolent. Very beautiful, and also in mourning, but mourning of a showy elegance. She shows contempt for the timid, afflicted, almost humiliated manner of her little brother, rather a mess of a* BOY, *fourteen, also dressed in black, but a lively tenderness for her little sister, a* LITTLE GIRL *of around four, dressed in white with a black silk sash round her waist.*

7. Grieving mother (Latin); specifically, Mary, mother of Jesus, grieving over the body of her dead son.

The SON, *twenty-two, tall, almost rigid with contained disdain for the* FATHER *and supercilious indifference toward the* MOTHER, *wears a mauve topcoat and a long green scarf wound round his neck.*]

STAGE DOOR MAN [*beret in hand*] Excuse me, your honor.

DIRECTOR [*rudely jumping on him*] What is it now?

STAGE DOOR MAN [*timidly*] There are some people here asking for you.

[*The* DIRECTOR *and the Actors turn in astonishment to look down into the auditorium.*]

DIRECTOR [*furious again*] But I'm rehearsing here! And you know perfectly well no one can come in during rehearsal! [*Turning again toward the house*] Who are these people? What do they want?

THE FATHER [*stepping forward, followed by the others, to one of the two little stairways to the stage*] We're here in search of an author.

DIRECTOR [*half angry, half astounded*] An author? What author?

FATHER Any author, sir.

DIRECTOR There's no author here at all. It's not a new play we're rehearsing.

STEPDAUGHTER [*very vivaciously as she rushes up the stairs*] Then so much the better, sir! *We* can be your new play!

ONE OF THE ACTORS [*among the racy comments and laughs of the others*] Did you hear that?

FATHER [*following the* STEPDAUGHTER *onstage*] Certainly, but if the author's not here . . . [*To the* DIRECTOR] Unless *you'd* like to be the author?

[*The* MOTHER, *holding the* LITTLE GIRL *by the hand, and the* BOY *climb the first steps of the stairway and remain there waiting. The* SON *stays morosely below.*]

DIRECTOR Is this your idea of a joke?

FATHER Heavens, no! Oh, sir, on the contrary: we bring you a painful drama.

STEPDAUGHTER We can make your fortune for you.

DIRECTOR Do me a favor, and leave. We have no time to waste on madmen.

FATHER [*wounded, smoothly*] Oh, sir, you surely know that life is full of infinite absurdities which, brazenly enough, do not need to appear probable, because they're true.

DIRECTOR What in God's name are you saying?

FATHER I'm saying it can actually be considered madness, sir, to force oneself to do the opposite: that is, to give probability to things so they will seem true. But permit me to observe that, if this is madness, it is also the *raison d'être* of your profession.

[*The Actors become agitated and indignant.*]

DIRECTOR [*rising and looking him over*] It is, is it? It seems to you an affair for madmen, our profession?

FATHER Well, to make something seem true which is not true . . . without any need, sir: just for fun . . . Isn't it your job to give life onstage to creatures of fantasy?

DIRECTOR [*immediately, making himself spokesman for the growing indignation of his Actors*] Let me tell you something, my good sir. The actor's profession is a very noble one. If, as things go nowadays, our new playwrights give us nothing but stupid plays, with puppets in them instead of men, it is our boast, I'd have you know, to have given life—on these very boards—to immortal works of art.

[*Satisfied, the Actors approve and applaud their* DIRECTOR.]

FATHER [*interrupting and bearing down hard*] Exactly! That's just it. You have created living beings—*more* alive than those that breathe and wear clothes! Less real, perhaps; but more true! We agree completely!

[*The Actors look at each other, astounded.*]

DIRECTOR What? You were saying just now . . .

FATHER No, no, don't misunderstand me. You shouted that you hadn't time to waste on madmen. So I wanted to tell you that no one knows better than you that Nature employs the human imagination to carry her work of creation on to a higher plane!

DIRECTOR All right, all right. But what are you getting at, exactly?

FATHER Nothing, sir. I only wanted to show that one may be born to this life in many modes, in many forms: as tree, as rock, water or butterfly . . . or woman. And that . . . characters are born too.

DIRECTOR [*his amazement ironically feigned*] And you—with these companions of yours—were born a character?

FATHER Right, sir. And alive, as you see.

[*The* DIRECTOR *and the Actors burst out laughing as at a joke.*]

FATHER [*wounded*] I'm sorry to hear you laugh, because, I repeat, we carry a painful drama within us, as you all might deduce from the sight of that lady there, veiled in black.

[*As he says this, he gives his hand to the* MOTHER *to help her up the last steps and, still holding her by the hand, he leads her with a certain tragic solemnity to the other side of the stage, which is suddenly bathed in fantastic light. The* LITTLE GIRL *and the* BOY *follow the* MOTHER*; then the* SON, *who stands on one side at the back; then the* STEPDAUGHTER *who also detaches herself from the others—downstage and leaning against the proscenium arch. At first astonished at this development, then overcome with admiration, the Actors now burst into applause as at a show performed for their benefit.*]

DIRECTOR [*bowled over at first, then indignant*] Oh, stop this! Silence please! [*Then, turning to the Characters*] And you, leave! Get out of here! [*To the* STAGE MANAGER] For God's sake, get them out!

STAGE MANAGER [*stepping forward but then stopping, as if held back by a strange dismay*] Go! Go!

FATHER [*to the* DIRECTOR] No, look, we, um—

DIRECTOR [*shouting*] I tell you we've got to work!

LEADING MAN It's not right to fool around like this . . .

FATHER [*resolute, stepping forward*] I'm amazed at your incredulity! You're accustomed to seeing the created characters of an author spring to life, aren't you, right here on this stage, the one confronting the other? Perhaps the trouble is there's no script *there* [*Pointing to the* PROMPTER'S *box*] with us in it?

STEPDAUGHTER [*going right up to the* DIRECTOR, *smiling, coquettish*] Believe me, we really are six characters, sir. Very interesting ones at that. But lost. Adrift.

FATHER [*brushing her aside*] Very well: lost, adrift. [*Going right on*] In the sense, that is, that the author who created us, made us live, did not wish, or simply and materially was not able, to place us in the world of art. And that was a real crime, sir, because whoever has the luck to be born a living character can also laugh at death. He will never die! The man will die, the writer, the instrument of creation; the creature will never die! And to have eternal life it doesn't even take extraordinary gifts, nor the performance of miracles. Who was Sancho Panza? Who was Don Abbondio?[8] But they live forever because, as live germs, they have the luck to find a fertile matrix, an imagination which knew how to raise and nourish them, make them live through all eternity!

DIRECTOR That's all well and good. But what do you people want here?

FATHER We want to live, sir.

DIRECTOR [*ironically*] Through all eternity?

FATHER No, sir. But for a moment at least. In you.

AN ACTOR Well, well, well!

LEADING LADY They want to live in us.

JUVENILE LEAD [*pointing to the* STEPDAUGHTER] Well, I've no objection, so long as I get that one.

FATHER Now look, look. The play is still in the making. [*To the* DIRECTOR] But if you wish, and your actors wish, we can make it right away. Acting in concert.

LEADING MAN [*annoyed*] Concert? We don't put on concerts! We do plays, dramas, comedies!

FATHER Very good. That's why we came.

DIRECTOR Well, where's the script?

FATHER Inside us, sir. [*The Actors laugh.*] The drama is inside us. It *is* us. And we're impatient to perform it. According to the dictates of the passion within us.

STEPDAUGHTER [*scornful, with treacherous grace, deliberate impudence*] My passion—if you only knew, sir! My passion—for him! [*She points to the* FATHER *and makes as if to embrace him but then breaks into a strident laugh.*]

FATHER [*an angry interjection*] You keep out of this now. And please don't laugh that way!

STEPDAUGHTER No? Then, ladies and gentlemen, permit me. A two months' orphan, I shall dance and sing for you all. Watch how! [*She mischievously starts to sing "Beware of Chu Chin Chow" by Dave Stamper, reduced to fox-trot or slow one-step by Francis Salabert:[9] the first verse, accompanied by a step or two of dancing. While she sings and dances, the Actors, especially the young ones, as if drawn by some strange fascination, move toward her and half raise their hands as if to take hold of her. She runs away and when the Actors burst into applause she just stands there, remote, abstracted, while the* DIRECTOR *protests.*]

ACTORS and ACTRESSES [*laughing and clapping*] Brava![1] Fine! Splendid!

DIRECTOR [*annoyed*] Silence! What do you think this is, a night spot? [*Taking the* FATHER *a step or two to one side, with a certain amount of consternation*] Tell me something. Is she crazy?

8. A rural priest in Alessandro Manzoni's novel *I Promessi sposi* (*The Betrothed*, 1825–27). *Sancho Panza:* the servant and companion of the title character in Miguel de Cervantes' novel *Don Quixote* (1605, 1615).

9. A French music publisher (1884–1946); his company released numerous recordings of dance music in the 1920s and 1930s. "Beware of Chu Chin Chow" (1917), with music by Dave Stamper (1883–1963) and words by Gene Buck and Charles Wilmott, was a popular novelty song.

1. An Italian exclamation of approval, used when applauding a woman (as *bravo* is used of a man).

FATHER Crazy? Of course not. It's much worse than that.

STEPDAUGHTER [*running over at once to the* DIRECTOR] Worse! Worse! Not crazy but worse! Just listen: I'll play it for you right now, this drama, and at a certain point you'll see me—when this dear little thing—[*She takes the* LITTLE GIRL *who is beside the* MOTHER *by the hand and leads her to the* DIRECTOR.]—isn't she darling? [*Takes her in her arms and kisses her.*] Sweetie! Sweetie! [*Puts her down again and adds with almost involuntary emotion.*] Well, when God suddenly takes this little sweetheart away from her poor mother, and that idiot there—[*Thrusting the* BOY *forward, rudely seizing him by a sleeve*] does the stupidest of things, like the nitwit that he is, [*With a shove she drives him back toward the* MOTHER] then you will see me take to my heels. Yes, ladies and gentlemen, take to my heels! I can hardly wait for that moment. For after what happened between him and me—[*She points to the* FATHER *with a horrible wink.*] something very intimate, you understand—I can't stay in such company any longer, witnessing the anguish of our mother on account of that fool there—[*She points to the* SON.] Just look at him, look at him!—how indifferent, how frozen, because he is the legitimate son, that's what he is, full of contempt for me, for him [*the* BOY], and for that little creature [*the* LITTLE GIRL], because we three are bastards, d'you see? Bastards. [*Goes to the* MOTHER *and embraces her.*] And this poor mother, the common mother of us all, he—well, he doesn't want to acknowledge her as *his* mother too, and he looks down on her, that's what he does, looks on her as only the mother of us three bastards, the wretch! [*She says this rapidly in a state of extreme excitement. Her voice swells to the word: "bastards!" and descends again to the final "wretch," almost spitting it out.*]

MOTHER [*to the* DIRECTOR, *with infinite anguish*] In the name of these two small children, sir, I implore you . . . [*She grows faint and sways.*] Oh, heavens . . .

FATHER [*rushing over to support her with almost all the Actors, who are astonished and scared*] Please! Please, a chair, a chair for this poor widow!

ACTORS [*rushing over*] —Is it true then?—She's *really* fainting?

DIRECTOR A chair!

[*One of the Actors proffers a chair. The others stand around, ready to help. The* MOTHER, *seated, tries to stop the* FATHER *from lifting the veil that hides her face.*]

FATHER [*to the* DIRECTOR] Look at her, look at her . . .

MOTHER Heavens, no, stop it!

FATHER Let them see you. [*He lifts her veil.*]

MOTHER [*rising and covering her face with her hands, desperate*] Oh, sir, please stop this man from carrying out his plan. It's horrible for me!

DIRECTOR [*surprised, stunned*] I don't know where we're at! What's this all about? [*To the* FATHER] Is this your wife?

FATHER [*at once*] Yes, sir, my wife.

DIRECTOR Then how is she a widow, if you're alive?

[*The Actors relieve their astonishment in a loud burst of laughter.*]

FATHER [*wounded, with bitter resentment*] Don't laugh! Don't laugh like that! Please! Just that is her drama, sir. She had another man. Another man who should be here!

MOTHER [*with a shout*] No! No!

STEPDAUGHTER He had the good luck to die. Two months ago, as I told you. We're still in mourning as you see.

FATHER But he's absent, you see, not just because he's dead. He's absent—take a look at her, sir, and you will understand at once!—Her drama wasn't in the love of two men for whom she was incapable of feeling anything—except maybe a little gratitude [not to me, but to him]—She is not a woman, she is a mother!—And her drama—a powerful one, very powerful—is in fact all in those four children which she bore to her two men.

MOTHER *My* men? Have you the gall to say I wanted two men? It was him, sir. He forced the other man on me. Compelled—yes, compelled—me to go off with him!

STEPDAUGHTER [*cutting in, roused*] It's not true!

MOTHER [*astounded*] How d'you mean, not true?

STEPDAUGHTER It's not true! It's not true!

MOTHER And what can you know about it?

STEPDAUGHTER It's not true. [*To the* DIRECTOR] Don't believe it. Know why she says it? For his sake. [*Pointing to the* SON] His indifference tortures her, destroys her. She wants him to believe that, if she abandoned him when he was two, it was because he [*the* FATHER] compelled her to.

MOTHER [*with violence*] He did compel me, he did compel me, as God is my witness! [*To the* DIRECTOR] Ask him if that isn't true. [*Her husband*] Make him tell him. [*The* SON] She couldn't know anything about it.

STEPDAUGHTER With my father, while he lived, I know you were always happy and content. Deny it if you can.

MOTHER I don't deny it, I don't . . .

STEPDAUGHTER He loved you, he cared for you! [*To the* BOY, *with rage*] Isn't that so? Say it! Why don't you speak, you dope?

MOTHER Leave the poor boy alone. Why d'you want to make me out ungrateful, daughter? I have no wish to offend your father! I told him [*the* FATHER] I didn't abandon my son and my home for my own pleasure. It wasn't my fault.

FATHER That's true, sir. It was mine.

[*Pause.*]

LEADING MAN [*to his companions*] What a show!

LEADING LADY And *they* put it on—for us.

JUVENILE LEAD Quite a change!

DIRECTOR [*who is now beginning to get very interested*] Let's listen to this, let's listen! [*And saying this, he goes down one of the stairways into the auditorium, and stands in front of the stage, as if to receive a spectator's impression of the show.*]

SON [*without moving from his position, cold, quiet, ironic*] Oh yes, you can now listen to the philosophy lecture. He will tell you about the Demon of Experiment.

FATHER You are a cynical idiot, as I've told you a hundred times. [*To the* DIRECTOR, *now in the auditorium*] He mocks me, sir, on account of that phrase I found to excuse myself with.

SON [*contemptuously*] Phrases!

FATHER Phrases! Phrases! As if they were not a comfort to everyone: in the face of some unexplained fact, in the face of an evil that eats into us, to find a word that says nothing but at least quiets us down!

STEPDAUGHTER Quiets our guilt feelings too. That above all.

FATHER Our guilt feelings? Not so. I have never quieted my guilt feelings with words alone.

STEPDAUGHTER It took a little money as well, didn't it, it took a little dough! The hundred lire[2] he was going to pay me, ladies and gentlemen!

[*Movement of horror among the Actors.*]

SON [*with contempt toward the* STEPDAUGHTER] That's filthy.

STEPDAUGHTER Filthy? The dough was there. In a small pale blue envelope on the mahogany table in the room behind the shop. Madam Pace's [*she pronounces it "Pah-chay"*] shop. One of those Madams who lure us poor girls from good families into their *ateliers* under the pretext of selling *Robes et Manteaux*.[3]

SON And with those hundred lire he was going to pay she has bought the right to tyrannize over us all. Only it so happens—I'd have you know—that he never actually incurred the debt.

STEPDAUGHTER Oh, oh, but we were really going to it, I assure you! [*She bursts out laughing.*]

MOTHER [*rising in protest*] Shame, daughter! Shame!

STEPDAUGHTER [*quickly*] Shame? It's my revenge! I am frantic, sir, frantic to live it, live that scene! The room . . . here's the shop window with the coats in it; there's the bed-sofa; the mirror; a screen; and in front of the window the little mahogany table with the hundred lire in the pale blue envelope. I can see it. I could take it. But you men should turn away now: I'm almost naked. I don't blush anymore. It's he that blushes now. [*Points to the* FATHER.] But I assure you he was very pale, very pale, at that moment. [*To the* DIRECTOR] You must believe me, sir.

DIRECTOR You lost me some time ago.

FATHER Of course! Getting it thrown at you like that! Restore a little order, sir, and let *me* speak. And never mind this ferocious girl. She's trying to heap opprobrium on me by withholding the relevant explanations!

STEPDAUGHTER This is no place for long-winded narratives!

FATHER I said—explanations.

STEPDAUGHTER Oh, certainly. Those that suit your turn.

[*At this point, the* DIRECTOR *returns to the stage to restore order.*]

FATHER But that's the whole root of the evil. Words. Each of us has, inside him, a world of things—to everyone, his world of things. And how can we understand each other, sir, if, in the words I speak, I put the sense and value of things as they are inside me, whereas the man who hears them inevitably receives them in the sense and with the value they have for him, the sense and value of the world inside him? We think we understand each other but we never do. Consider: the compassion, all the compassion I feel for this woman [*the* MOTHER] has been received by her as the most ferocious of cruelties!

MOTHER You ran me out of the house.

FATHER Hear that? Ran her out. It *seemed to her* that I ran her out.

MOTHER You can talk; I can't . . . But, look, sir, after he married me . . . and who knows why he did? I was poor, of humble birth . . .

2. Equivalent to about $50 today.
3. Dressing gowns and coats (French). *Ateliers:* workshops (French).

FATHER And that's why I married you for your . . . humility. I loved you for it, believing . . . [*He breaks off, seeing her gestured denials; seeing the impossibility of making himself understood by her, he opens his arms wide in a gesture of despair, and turns to the* DIRECTOR.] See that? She says No. It's scarifying, isn't it, sir, scarifying, this deafness of hers, this mental deafness! She has a heart, oh yes, where her children are concerned! But she's deaf, deaf in the brain, deaf, sir, to the point of desperation!

STEPDAUGHTER [*to the* DIRECTOR] All right, but now make him tell you what his intelligence has ever done for us.

FATHER If we could only foresee all the evil that can result from the good we believe we're doing!

[*At this point, the* LEADING LADY, *who has been on hot coals seeing the* LEADING MAN *flirt with the* STEPDAUGHTER, *steps forward and asks of the* DIRECTOR:]

LEADING LADY Excuse me, is the rehearsal continuing?

DIRECTOR Yes, of course! But let me listen a moment.

JUVENILE LEAD This is something quite new.

INGENUE Very interesting!

LEADING LADY If that sort of thing interests you. [*And she darts a look at the* LEADING MAN.]

DIRECTOR [*to the* FATHER] But you must give us *clear* explanations. [*He goes and sits down.*]

FATHER Right. Yes. Listen. There was a man working for me. A poor man. As my secretary. Very devoted to me. Understood *her* [*the* MOTHER] very well. There was mutual understanding between them. Nothing wrong in it. They thought no harm at all. Nothing off-color about it. No, no, he knew his place, as she did. They didn't do anything wrong. Didn't even think it.

STEPDAUGHTER So he thought it *for* them. And did it.

FATHER It's not true! I wanted to do them some good. And myself too, oh yes, I admit. I'd got to this point, sir: I couldn't say a word to either of them but they would exchange a significant look. The one would consult the eyes of the other, asking how what I had said should be taken, if they didn't want to put me in a rage. That sufficed, you will understand, to keep me continually in a rage, in a state of unbearable exasperation.

DIRECTOR Excuse me, why didn't you fire him, this secretary?

FATHER Good question! That's what I did do, sir. But then I had to see that poor woman remain in my house, a lost soul. Like an animal without a master that one takes pity on and carries home.

MOTHER No, no, it's—

FATHER [*at once, turning to her to get it in first*] Your son? Right?

MOTHER He'd already snatched my son from me.

FATHER But not from cruelty. Just so he'd grow up strong and healthy. In touch with the soil.

STEPDAUGHTER [*pointing at the latter, ironic*] And just look at him!

FATHER [*at once*] Uh? Is it also my fault if he then grew up this way? I sent him to a wet nurse, sir, in the country, a peasant woman. I didn't find her [*the* MOTHER] strong enough, despite her humble origin. I'd married her for similar reasons, as I said. All nonsense maybe, but there we are. I always had these confounded aspirations toward a certain solidity, toward what is morally sound. [*Here the* STEPDAUGHTER *bursts out laughing*.] Make her stop that! It's unbearable!

DIRECTOR Stop it. I can't hear, for Heaven's sake!

[*Suddenly, again, as the* DIRECTOR *rebukes her, she is withdrawn and remote, her laughter cut off in the middle. The* DIRECTOR *goes down again from the stage to get an impression of the scene*.]

FATHER I couldn't bear to be with that woman anymore. [*Points to the* MOTHER] Not so much, believe me, because she irritated me, and even made me feel physically ill, as because of the pain—a veritable anguish that I felt on her account.

MOTHER And he sent me away!

FATHER. Well provided for. And to that man. Yes, sir. So she could be free of me.

MOTHER And so *he* could be free.

FATHER That, too. I admit it. And much evil resulted. But I intended good. And more for her than for me, I swear it! [*He folds his arms across his chest. Then, suddenly, turning to the* MOTHER] I never lost sight of you, never lost sight of you till, from one day to the next, unbeknown to me, he carried you off to another town. He noticed I was interested in her, you see, but that was silly, because my interest was absolutely pure, absolutely without ulterior motive. The interest I took in her new family, as it grew up, had an unbelievable tenderness to it. Even she should bear witness to that! [*He points to the* STEPDAUGHTER.]

STEPDAUGHTER Oh, very much so! I was a little sweetie. Pigtails over my shoulders. Panties coming down a little bit below my skirt. A little sweetie. He would see me coming out of school, at the gate. He would come and see me as I grew up . . .

FATHER This is outrageous. You're betraying me!

STEPDAUGHTER I'm not! What do you mean?

FATHER Outrageous. Outrageous. [*Immediately, still excited, he continues in a tone of explanation, to the* DIRECTOR.] My house, sir, when she had left it, at once seemed empty. [*Points to the* MOTHER.] She was an incubus. But she filled my house for me. Left alone, I wandered through these rooms like a fly without a head. This fellow here [*the* SON] was raised away from home. Somehow, when he got back, he didn't seem mine anymore. Without a mother between me and him, he grew up on his own, apart, without any relationship to me, emotional or intellectual. And then—strange, sir, but true—first I grew curious, then I was gradually attracted toward *her* family, which I had brought into being. The thought of *this* family began to fill the void around me. I had to—really had to—believe she was at peace, absorbed in the simplest cares of life, lucky to be away and far removed from the complicated torments of my spirit. And to have proof of this, I would go and see that little girl at the school gate.

STEPDAUGHTER Correct! He followed me home, smiled at me and, when I was home, waved to me, like this! I would open my eyes wide and look at him suspiciously. I didn't know who it was. I told mother. And she guessed right away it was him. [*The* MOTHER *nods*.] At first she didn't want to send me back to school for several days. When I did go, I saw him again at the gate—the clown!—with a brown paper bag in his hand. He came up to me, caressed me, and took from the bag a lovely big Florentine straw hat with a ring of little May roses round it—for me!

DIRECTOR You're making too long a story of this.

SON [*contemptuously*] Story is right! Fiction! Literature!

FATHER Literature? This is life, sir. Passion!

DIRECTOR Maybe! But not actable!

FATHER I agree. This is all preliminary. I wouldn't *want* you to act it. As you see, in fact, she [*the* STEPDAUGHTER] is no longer that little girl with pigtails—

STEPDAUGHTER —and the panties showing below her skirt!

FATHER The drama comes now, sir. Novel, complex—

STEPDAUGHTER [*gloomy, fierce, steps forward*] —What my father's death meant for us was—

FATHER [*not giving her time to continue*] —poverty, sir. They returned, unbeknownst to me. She's so thickheaded. [*Pointing to the* MOTHER] It's true she can hardly write herself, but she could have had her daughter write, or her son, telling me they were in need!

MOTHER But, sir, how could I have guessed he felt the way he did?

FATHER Which is just where you always went wrong. You could never guess how I felt about anything!

MOTHER After so many years of separation, with all that had happened . . .

FATHER And is it my fault if that fellow carried you off as he did? [*Turning to the* DIRECTOR] From one day to the next, as I say. He'd found some job someplace. I couldn't even trace them. Necessarily, then, my interest dwindled, with the years. The drama breaks out, sir, unforeseen and violent, at their return. When I, alas, was impelled by the misery of my still-living flesh . . . Oh, and what misery that is for a man who is alone, who has not wanted to form debasing relationships, not yet old enough to do without a woman, and no longer young enough to go and look for one without shame! Misery? It's horror, horror, because no woman can give him love anymore.—Knowing this, one should go without! Well, sir, on the outside, when other people are watching, each man is clothed in dignity: but, on the inside, he knows what unconfessable things are going on within him. One gives way, gives way to temptation, to rise again, right afterward, of course, in a great hurry to put our dignity together again, complete, solid, a stone on a grave that hides and buries from our eyes every sign of our shame and even the very memory of it! It's like that with everybody. Only the courage to say it is lacking—to say certain things.

STEPDAUGHTER The courage to do them, though—everybody's got that.

FATHER Everybody. But in secret. That's why it takes more courage to say them. A man only has to say them and it's all over: he's labeled a cynic. But, sir, he isn't! He's just like everybody else. Better! He's better because he's not afraid to reveal, by the light of intelligence, the red stain of shame, there, in the human beast, which closes its eyes to it. Woman—yes, woman—what is she like, actually? She looks at us, inviting, tantalizing. You take hold of her. She's no sooner in your arms than she shuts her eyes. It is the sign of her submission. The sign with which she tells the man: Blind yourself for I am blind.

STEPDAUGHTER How about when she no longer keeps them shut? When she no longer feels the need to hide the red stain of shame from herself by closing her eyes, and instead, her eyes now dry and impassive, sees the shame of the man, who has blinded himself even without love? They make me vomit, all those intellectual elaborations, this philosophy that begins by revealing the beast and then goes on to excuse it and save its soul . . . I can't bear to hear about it! Because when a man feels obliged to *reduce* life this way, reduce it all to "the beast," throwing overboard every vestige of the truly human, every aspiration after chastity, all feelings of purity, of the ideal, of duties, of modesty, of shame, then nothing is more contemptible, more nauseating than his wretched guilt feelings! Crocodile tears!

DIRECTOR Let's get to the facts, to the facts! This is just discussion.

FATHER Very well. But a fact is like a sack. When it's empty, it won't stand up. To make it stand up you must first pour into it the reasons and feelings by which it exists. I couldn't know that—when that man died and they returned here in poverty—she went out to work as a dressmaker to support the children, nor that the person she went to work for was that . . . that Madam Pace!

STEPDAUGHTER A high-class dressmaker, if you'd all like to know! To all appearances, she serves fine ladies, but then she arranges things so that the fine ladies serve *her* . . . without prejudice to ladies not so fine!

MOTHER Believe me, sir, I never had the slightest suspicion that that old witch hired me because she had her eye on my daughter . . .

STEPDAUGHTER Poor mama! Do you know, sir, what the woman did when I brought her my mother's work? She would point out to me the material she'd ruined by giving it to my mother to sew. And she deducted for that, she deducted. And so, you understand, *I* paid, while that poor creature thought she was making sacrifices for me and those two by sewing, even at night, Madam Pace's material!

[*Indignant movements and exclamations from the Actors.*]

DIRECTOR [*without pause*] And there, one day, you met—

STEPDAUGHTER [*pointing to the* FATHER] —him, him, yes sir! An old client! Now there's a scene for you to put on! Superb!

FATHER Interrupted by her—the mother—

STEPDAUGHTER [*without pause, treacherously*] —almost in time!—

FATHER [*shouting*] No, no, *in* time! Because, luckily, I recognized the girl in time. And I took them all back, sir, into my home. Now try to visualize my situation and hers, the one confronting the other—she as you see her now, myself unable to look her in the face anymore.

STEPDAUGHTER It's too absurd! But—afterward—was it possible for me to be a modest little miss, virtuous and well-bred, in accordance with those confounded aspirations toward a certain solidity, toward what is morally sound?

FATHER And therein lies the drama, sir, as far as I'm concerned: in my awareness that each of us thinks of himself as *one* but that, well, it's not true, each of us is many, oh so many, sir, according to the possibilities of being that are in us. We are one thing for this person, another for that! Already *two* utterly different things! And with it all, the illusion of being always one thing for all men, and always this one thing in every single action. It's not true! Not true! We realize as much when, by some unfortunate chance, in one or another of our acts, we find ourselves suspended, hooked. We see, I mean, that we are not wholly in that act, and that therefore it would be abominably unjust to judge us by that act alone, to hold us suspended, hooked, in the pillory, our whole life long, as if our life were summed up in that act! Now do you understand this girl's treachery? She surprised me in a place, in an act, in which she should never have had to know me—I couldn't be that way for her. And she wants to give me a reality such as I could never had expected I would have to assume for her, the reality of a fleeting moment, a shameful one, in my life! This, sir, this is what I feel most strongly. And you will see that the drama will derive tremendous value from this. But now add the situation of the others! His . . . [*He points to the* SON.]

SON [*shrugging contemptuously*] Leave me out of this! It's none of my business.

FATHER What? None of your business?

SON None. And I *want* to be left out. I wasn't made to be one of you, and you know it.

STEPDAUGHTER We're common, aren't we?—And he's so refined.—But from time to time I give him a hard, contemptuous look, and he looks down at the ground. You may have noticed that, sir. He looks down at the ground. For he knows the wrong he's done me.

SON [*hardly looking at her*] Me?

STEPDAUGHTER You! You! I'm on the streets because of you! [*A movement of horror from the Actors*] Did you or did you not, by your attitude, deny us—I won't say the intimacy of home but even the hospitality which puts guests at their ease? We were the intruders, coming to invade the kingdom of your legitimacy! I'd like to have you see, sir, certain little scenes between just him and me! He says I tyrannized over them all. But it was entirely because of his attitude that I started to exploit the situation he calls filthy, a situation which had brought me into his home with my mother, who is also *his* mother, *as its mistress!*

SON [*coming slowly forward*] They can't lose, sir, three against one, an easy game. But figure to yourself a son, sitting quietly at home, who one fine day sees a young woman arrive, an impudent type with her nose in the air, asking for his father, with whom she has heaven knows what business; and then he sees her return, in the same style, accompanied by that little girl over there; and finally he sees her treat his father—who can say why?—in a very ambiguous and cool manner, demanding money, in a tone that takes for granted that he *has* to give it, has to, is obligated—

FATHER —but I *am* obligated: it's for your mother!

SON How would I know? When, sir, [*To the* DIRECTOR] have I ever seen her? When have I ever heard her spoken of? One day I see her arrive with her [*the* STEPDAUGHTER], with that boy, with that little girl. They say to me: "It's your mother too, know that?" I manage to figure out from her carryings-on [*Pointing at the* STEPDAUGHTER] why they arrived in our home from one day to the next . . . What I'm feeling and experiencing I can't put into words, and wouldn't want to. I wouldn't want to confess it, even to myself. It cannot therefore result in any action on my part. You can see that. Believe me, sir, I'm a character that, dramatically speaking, remains unrealized. I'm out of place in their company. So please leave me out of it all!

FATHER What? But it's just because you're so—

SON [*in violent exasperation*] —I'm so what? How would *you* know? When did you ever care about me?

FATHER *Touché! Touché!* But isn't even that a dramatic situation? This withdrawnness of yours, so cruel to me, and to your mother who, on her return home is seeing you almost for the first time, a grown man she doesn't recognize, though she knows you're her son . . . [*Pointing out the* MOTHER *to the* DIRECTOR] Just look at her, she's crying.

STEPDAUGHTER [*angrily, stamping her foot*] Like the fool she is!

FATHER [*pointing her out to the* DIRECTOR] And she can't abide him, you know. [*Again referring to the* SON]—He says it's none of his business. The truth is he's almost the pivot of the action. Look at that little boy, clinging to his mother all the time, scared, humiliated . . . It's all because of *him* [*the* SON]. Perhaps the most painful situation of all is that little boy's: he feels alien, more than all the others, and the poor little thing is so mortified, so anguished at being taken into our home—out of charity, as it were . . . [*Confidentially*] He's just like his father: humble, doesn't say anything . . .

DIRECTOR He won't fit anyway. You've no idea what a nuisance children are onstage.

FATHER But he wouldn't be a nuisance for long. Nor would the little girl, no, she's the first to go . . .

DIRECTOR Very good, yes! The whole thing interests me very much indeed. I have a hunch, a definite hunch, that there's material here for a fine play!

STEPDAUGHTER [*trying to inject herself*] With a character like me in it!

FATHER [*pushing her to one side in his anxiety to know what the* DIRECTOR *will decide*] You be quiet!

DIRECTOR [*going right on, ignoring the interruption*] Yes, it's new stuff . . .

FATHER Very new!

DIRECTOR You had some gall, though, to come and throw it at me this way . . .

FATHER Well, you see, sir, born as we are to the stage . . .

DIRECTOR You're amateurs, are you?

FATHER No. I say: "born to the stage" because . . .

DIRECTOR Oh, come on, you must have done some acting!

FATHER No, no, sir, only as every man acts the part assigned to him—by himself or others—in this life. In me you see passion itself, which—in almost all people, as it rises—invariably becomes a bit theatrical . . .

DIRECTOR Well, never mind! Never mind about that!—You see, my dear sir, without the author . . . I could direct you to an author . . .

FATHER No, no, look: you be the author!

DIRECTOR Me? What are you talking about?

FATHER Yes, you. You. Why not?

DIRECTOR Because I've never been an author, that's why not!

FATHER Couldn't you be one now, hm? There's nothing to it. Everyone's doing it. And your job is made all the easier by the fact that you have us—here—alive—right in front of your nose!

DIRECTOR It wouldn't be enough.

FATHER Not enough? Seeing us live our own drama . . .

DIRECTOR I know, but you always need someone to write it!

FATHER No. Just someone to take it down, maybe, since you have us here—in action—scene by scene. It'll be enough if we piece together a rough sketch for you, then you can rehearse it.

DIRECTOR [*tempted, goes up onstage again*] Well, I'm almost, almost tempted . . . Just for kicks . . . We could actually rehearse . . .

FATHER Of course you could! What scenes you'll see emerge! I can list them for you right away.

DIRECTOR I'm tempted . . . I'm tempted . . . Let's give it a try . . . Come to my office. [*Turns to the Actors.*] Take a break, will you? But don't go away. We'll be back in fifteen or twenty minutes. [*To the* FATHER] Let's see what we can do . . . Maybe we can get something very extraordinary out of all this . . .

FATHER We certainly can. Wouldn't it be better to take *them* along? [*He points to the Characters.*]

DIRECTOR Yes, let them all come. [*Starts going off, then comes back to address the Actors.*] Now don't forget. Everyone on time. Fifteen minutes.

[DIRECTOR *and Six Characters cross the stage and disappear. The Actors stay there and look at one another in amazement.*]

LEADING MAN Is he serious? What's he going to do?

JUVENILE This is outright insanity.

A THIRD ACTOR We have to improvise a drama right off the bat?

JUVENILE LEAD That's right. Like Commedia dell'Arte.[4]

LEADING LADY Well, if he thinks *I'm* going to lend myself to that sort of thing . . .

INGENUE Count me out.

A FOURTH ACTOR [*alluding to the Characters*] I'd like to know who those people are.

THE THIRD ACTOR Who would they be? Madmen or crooks!

JUVENILE LEAD And he's going to pay attention to them?

INGENUE Carried away by vanity! Wants to be an author now . . .

LEADING MAN It's out of this world. If this is what the theater is coming to, my friends . . .

A FIFTH ACTOR I think it's rather fun.

THE THIRD ACTOR Well! We shall see. We shall see. [*And chatting thus among themselves, the Actors leave the stage, some using the little door at the back, others returning to their dressing rooms.*]

The curtain remains raised. The performance is interrupted by a twenty-minute intermission.

Bells ring. The performance is resumed.

[*From dressing rooms, from the door, and also from the house, the Actors, the* STAGE MANAGER, *the* TECHNICIAN, *the* PROMPTER, *the* PROPERTY MAN *return to the stage; at the same time the* DIRECTOR *and the Six Characters emerge from the office.*

As soon as the house lights are out, the stage lighting is as before.]

DIRECTOR Let's go, everybody! Is everyone here? Quiet! We're beginning. [*Calls the* TECHNICIAN *by name.*]

4. A traditional form of Italian comedy featuring stock characters, some in masks, who improvise dialogue.

TECHNICIAN Here!

DIRECTOR Set the stage for the parlor scene. Two wings and a backdrop with a door in it will do, quickly please!

[The TECHNICIAN *at once runs to do the job, and does it while the* DIRECTOR *works things out with the* STAGE MANAGER, *the* PROPERTY MAN, *the* PROMPTER, *and the Actors. This indication of a set consists of two wings, a drop with a door in it, all in pink and gold stripes.]*

DIRECTOR *[to the* PROPERTY MAN*]* See if we have some sort of bed-sofa in the prop room.

PROPERTY MAN Yes, sir, there's the green one.

STEPDAUGHTER No, no, not green! It was yellow, flowered, plush, and very big. Extremely comfortable.

PROPERTY MAN Well, we have nothing like that.

DIRECTOR But it doesn't matter. Bring the one you have.

STEPDAUGHTER Doesn't matter? Madam Pace's famous chaise longue!

DIRECTOR This is just for rehearsal. Please don't meddle! *[To the* STAGE MANAGER*]* See if we have a display case—long and rather narrow.

STEPDAUGHTER The table, the little mahogany table for the pale blue envelope!

STAGE MANAGER *[to the* DIRECTOR*]* There's the small one. Gilded.

DIRECTOR All right. Get that one.

FATHER A large mirror.

STEPDAUGHTER And the screen. A screen, please, or what'll I do?

STAGE MANAGER Yes, ma'am, we have lots of screens, don't worry.

DIRECTOR *[to the* STEPDAUGHTER*]* A few coat hangers?

STEPDAUGHTER A great many, yes.

DIRECTOR *[to the* STAGE MANAGER*]* See how many we've got, and have them brought on.

STAGE MANAGER Right, sir, I'll see to it.

[The STAGE MANAGER *also hurries to do his job and while the* DIRECTOR *goes on talking with the* PROMPTER *and then with the Characters and the Actors, has the furniture carried on by stagehands and arranges it as he thinks fit.]*

DIRECTOR *[to the* PROMPTER*]* Meanwhile you can get into position. Look: this is the outline of the scenes, act by act. *[He gives him several sheets of paper.]* You'll have to be a bit of a virtuoso today.

PROMPTER Shorthand?

DIRECTOR *[pleasantly surprised]* Oh, good! You know shorthand?

PROMPTER I may not know prompting, but shorthand . . . *[Turning to a stagehand]* Get me some paper from my room—quite a lot—all you can find!

[The stagehand runs off and returns a little later with a wad of paper which he gives to the PROMPTER.*]*

DIRECTOR *[going right on, to the* PROMPTER*]* Follow the scenes line by line as we play them, and try to pin down the speeches, at least the most important ones. *[Then, turning to the Actors]* Clear the stage please, everyone! Yes, come over to this side and pay close attention. *[He indicates the left.]*

LEADING LADY Excuse me but—

DIRECTOR *[forestalling]* There'll be no improvising, don't fret.

LEADING MAN Then what are we to do?

DIRECTOR Nothing. For now, just stop, look, and listen. Afterward you'll be given written parts. Right now we'll rehearse. As best we can. With them doing the rehearsing for us. *[He points to the Characters.]*

FATHER [*amid all the confusion onstage, as if he'd fallen from the clouds*] *We're* rehearsing? How d'you mean?

DIRECTOR Yes, for them. You rehearse for them. [*Indicates the Actors.*]

FATHER But if we are the characters . . .

DIRECTOR All right, you're characters, but, my dear sir, characters don't perform here, actors perform here. The characters are there, in the script [*He points to the* PROMPTER*'s box.*]—when there *is* a script!

FATHER Exactly! Since there isn't, and you gentlemen have the luck to have them right here, alive in front of you, those characters . . .

DIRECTOR Oh, great! Want to do it all yourselves? Appear before the public, do the acting yourselves?

FATHER Of course. Just as we are.

DIRECTOR [*ironically*] I'll bet you'd put on a splendid show!

LEADING MAN Then what's the use of staying?

DIRECTOR [*without irony, to the Characters*] Don't run away with the idea that you can act! That's laughable . . . [*And in fact the Actors laugh.*] Hear that? They're laughing. [*Coming back to the point*] I was forgetting. I must cast the show. It's quite easy. It casts itself. [*To the* SECOND ACTRESS] You, ma'am, will play the Mother. [*To the* FATHER] You'll have to find her a name.

FATHER Amalia, sir.

DIRECTOR But that's this lady's real name. We wouldn't want to call her by her real name!

FATHER Why not? If that is her name . . . But of course, if it's to be this lady . . . [*He indicates the* SECOND ACTRESS *with a vague gesture.*] To me *she* [*the* MOTHER] is Amalia. But suit yourself . . . [*He is getting more and more confused.*] I don't know what to tell you . . . I'm beginning to . . . oh, I don't know . . . to find my own words ringing false, they sound different somehow.

DIRECTOR Don't bother about that, just don't bother about it. We can always find the right sound. As for the name, if you say Amalia, Amalia it shall be; or we'll find another. For now, we'll designate the characters thus: [*To the* JUVENILE LEAD] You're the Son. [*To the* LEADING LADY] You, ma'am, are of course the Stepdaughter.

STEPDAUGHTER [*excitedly*] What, what? That one there is me? [*She bursts out laughing.*]

DIRECTOR [*mad*] What is there to laugh at?

LEADING LADY [*aroused*] No one has ever dared laugh at me! I insist on respect—or I quit!

STEPDAUGHTER But, excuse me, I'm not laughing at you.

DIRECTOR [*to the* STEPDAUGHTER] You should consider yourself honored to be played by . . .

LEADING LADY [*without pause, contemptuously*] —"That one there!"

STEPDAUGHTER But I wasn't speaking of you, believe me. I was speaking of me. I don't see me in you, that's all. I don't know why . . . I guess you're just not like me!

FATHER That's it, exactly, my dear sir! What is *expressed* in us . . .

DIRECTOR Expression, expression! You think that's your business? Not at all!

FATHER Well, but what *we* express . . .

DIRECTOR But you don't. You don't express. You provide us with raw material. The actors give it body and face, voice and gesture. They've given expression to much loftier material, let me tell you. Yours is on such a small scale that, if it stands up onstage at all, the credit, believe me, should all go to my actors.

FATHER I don't dare contradict you, sir, but it's terribly painful for us who are as you see us—with these bodies, these faces—

DIRECTOR [*cutting in, out of patience*] —that's where makeup comes in, my dear sir, for whatever concerns the face, the remedy is makeup!

FATHER Yes. But the voice, gesture—

DIRECTOR Oh, for Heaven's sake! You can't exist here! Here the actor acts you, and that's that!

FATHER I understand, sir. But now perhaps I begin to guess also why our author who saw us, alive as we are, did not want to put us onstage. I don't want to offend your actors. God forbid! But I feel that seeing myself acted . . . I don't know by whom . . .

LEADING MAN [*rising with dignity and coming over, followed by the gay young Actresses who laugh*] By me, if you've no objection.

FATHER [*humble, smooth*] I'm very honored, sir. [*He bows.*] But however much art and willpower the gentleman puts into absorbing me into himself . . . [*He is bewildered now.*]

LEADING MAN Finish. Finish.

[*The Actresses laugh.*]

FATHER Well, the performance he will give, even forcing himself with makeup to resemble me, well, with that figure [*All the Actors laugh.*] he can hardly play me as I am. I shall rather be—even apart from the face—what he interprets me to be, as he feels I am—if he feels I am anything—and not as I feel myself inside myself. And it seems to me that whoever is called upon to judge us should take this into account.

DIRECTOR So now you're thinking of what the critics will say? And I was still listening! Let the critics say what they want. We will concentrate on putting on your play! [*He walks away a little, and looks around.*] Come on, come on. Is the set ready? [*To the Actors and the Characters*] Don't clutter up the stage, I want to be able to see! [*He goes down from the stage.*] Let's not lose any more time! [*To the* STEPDAUGHTER] Does the set seem pretty good to you?

STEPDAUGHTER Oh! But I can't recognize it!

DIRECTOR Oh my God, don't tell me we should reconstruct Madam Pace's back room for you! [*To the* FATHER] Didn't you say a parlor with flowered wallpaper?

FATHER Yes, sir. White.

DIRECTOR It's not white. Stripes. But it doesn't matter. As for furniture we're in pretty good shape. That little table—bring it forward a bit! [*Stagehands do this. To the* PROPERTY MAN] Meanwhile you get an envelope, possibly a light blue one, and give it to the gentleman. [*Indicating the* FATHER]

PROPERTY MAN A letter envelope?

DIRECTOR and FATHER Yes, a letter envelope.

PROPERTY MAN I'll be right back.

[*He exits.*]

DIRECTOR Come on, come on. It's the young lady's scene first. [*The* LEADING LADY *comes forward.*] No, no, wait. I said the young lady. [*Indicating the* STEPDAUGHTER] You will just watch—

STEPDAUGHTER [*adding, without pause*] —watch me live it!

LEADING LADY [*resenting this*] I'll know how to live it too, don't worry, once I put myself in the role!

DIRECTOR [*raising his hands to his head*] Please! No more chatter! Now, scene one. The Young Lady with Madam Pace. Oh, and how about this Madam Pace? [*Bewildered, looking around him, he climbs back onstage.*]

FATHER She isn't with us, sir.

DIRECTOR Then what do we do?

FATHER But she's alive. She's alive too.

DIRECTOR Fine. But where?

FATHER I'll tell you. [*Turning to the Actresses*] If you ladies will do me the favor of giving me your hats for a moment.

THE ACTRESSES [*surprised a little, laughing a little, in chorus*] —What?—Our hats?—What does he say?—Why?—Oh, dear!

DIRECTOR What are you going to do with the ladies' hats?

[*The Actors laugh.*]

FATHER Oh, nothing. Just put them on these coathooks for a minute. And would some of you be so kind as to take your coats off too?

ACTORS [*as before*] Their coats too?—And then?—He's nuts!

AN ACTRESS OR TWO [*as above*] —But why?—Just the coats?

FATHER Just so they can be hung there for a moment. Do me this favor. Will you?

ACTRESSES [*taking their hats off, and one or two of them their coats, too, continuing to laugh, and going to hang the hats here and there on the coathooks*] —Well, why not?—There!—This is getting to be really funny!—Are we to put them on display?

FATHER Exactly! That's just right, ma'am: on display!

DIRECTOR May one inquire *why* you are doing this?

FATHER Yes, sir. If we set the stage better, who knows but she may come to us, drawn by the objects of her trade . . . [*Inviting them to look toward the entrance at the back*] Look! Look!

[*The entrance at the back opens, and* MADAM PACE *walks a few paces downstage, a hag of enormous fatness with a pompous wig of carrot-colored wool and a fiery red rose on one side of it,* à l'espagnole,[5] *heavily made up, dressed with gauche elegance in garish red silk, a feathered fan in one hand and the other hand raised to hold a lighted cigarette between two fingers. At the sight of this apparition, the* DIRECTOR *and the Actors at once dash off the stage with a yell of terror, rushing down the stairs and making as if to flee up the aisle. The* STEPDAUGHTER, *on the other hand runs to* MADAM PACE*—deferentially, as to her boss.*]

STEPDAUGHTER [*running to her*] Here she is, here she is!

FATHER [*beaming*] It's she! What did I tell you? Here she is!

DIRECTOR [*overcoming his first astonishment, and incensed now*] What tricks are these?

[*The next four speeches are more or less simultaneous.*]

LEADING MAN What goes on around here?

JUVENILE LEAD Where on earth did she come from?

INGENUE They must have been holding her in reserve.

5. Spanish-style (French).

LEADING LADY Hocus pocus! Hocus pocus!

FATHER [*dominating these protests*] Excuse me, though! Why, actually, would you want to destroy this prodigy in the name of vulgar truth, this miracle of a reality that is born of the stage itself—called into being by the stage, drawn here by the stage, and shaped by the stage—and which has more right to live on the stage than you have because it is much truer? Which of you actresses will later re-create Madam Pace? This lady *is* Madam Pace. You must admit that the actress who re-creates her will be less true than this lady—who is Madam Pace. Look: my daughter recognized her, and went right over to her. Stand and watch the scene!

[*Hesitantly, the* DIRECTOR *and the Actors climb back onstage. But the scene between the* STEPDAUGHTER *and* MADAM PACE *has begun during the protest of the Actors and the* FATHER*'s answer: sotto voce,*[6] *very quietly, in short naturally—as would never be possible on a stage. When, called to order by the* FATHER, *the Actors turn again to watch, they hear* MADAM PACE, *who has just placed her hand under the* STEPDAUGHTER*'s chin in order to raise her head, talk unintelligibly. After trying to hear for a moment, they just give up.*]

DIRECTOR Well?

LEADING MAN What's she saying?

LEADING LADY One can't hear a thing.

JUVENILE LEAD Louder!

STEPDAUGHTER [*leaving* MADAM PACE, *who smiles a priceless smile, and walking down toward the Actors*] Louder, huh? How d'you mean: louder? These aren't things that can be said louder. *I* was able to say them loudly—to shame him [*Indicating the* FATHER]—that was my revenge. For Madam, it's different, my friends: it would mean—jail.

DIRECTOR Oh my God! It's like that, is it? But, my dear young lady, in the theater one must be heard. And even we couldn't hear you, right here on the stage. How about an audience out front? There's a scene to be done. And anyway you *can* speak loudly—it's just between yourselves, we won't be standing here listening like now. Pretend you're alone. In a room. The back room of the shop. No one can hear you. [*The* STEPDAUGHTER *charmingly and with a mischievous smile tells him No with a repeated movement of the finger.*] Why not?

STEPDAUGHTER [*sotto voce, mysteriously*] There's someone who'll hear if she [MADAM PACE] speaks loudly.

DIRECTOR [*in consternation*] Is someone else going to pop up now?

[*The Actors make as if to quit the stage again.*]

FATHER No, no, sir. She means me. I'm to be there—behind the door—waiting. And Madam knows. So if you'll excuse me. I must be ready for my entrance. [*He starts to move.*]

DIRECTOR [*stopping him*] No, wait. We must respect the exigencies of the theater. Before you get ready—

STEPDAUGHTER [*interrupting him*] Let's get on with it! I tell you I'm dying with desire to live it, to live that scene! If he's ready, I'm more than ready!

DIRECTOR [*shouting*] But first we have to get that scene out of you and her! [*Indicating* MADAM PACE] Do you follow me?

6. Under the voice (Italian); that is, spoken very softly, under the breath.

STEPDAUGHTER Oh dear, oh dear, she was telling me things you already know—that my mother's work had been badly done once again, the material is ruined, and I'm going to have to bear with her if I want her to go on helping us in our misery.

MADAM PACE [*coming forward with a great air of importance*] Sí, sí, señor, porque yo[7] no want profit. No advantage, no.

DIRECTOR [*almost scared*] What, what? She talks like *that?!*

[*All the Actors loudly burst out laughing.*]

STEPDAUGHTER [*also laughing*] Yes, sir, she talks like that—halfway between Spanish and English—very funny, isn't it?

MADAM PACE Now that is not good manners, no, that you laugh at me! Yo hablo[8] the English as good I can, señor!

DIRECTOR And it *is* good! Yes! Do talk that way, ma'am! It's a surefire effect! There couldn't be anything better to, um, soften the crudity of the situation! Do talk that way! It's fine!

STEPDAUGHTER Fine! Of course! To have certain propositions put to you in a lingo like that. Surefire, isn't it? Because, sir, it seems almost a joke. When I hear there's "an old señor" who wants to "have good time conmigo,"[9] I start to laugh—don't I, Madam Pace?

MADAM PACE Old, viejo, no. Viejito—leetle beet old, sí, darling? Better like that: if he no give you fun, he bring you prudencia.[1]

MOTHER [*jumping up, to the stupefaction and consternation of all the Actors, who had been taking no notice of her, and who now respond to her shouts with a start and, smiling, try to restrain her, because she has grabbed* MADAM PACE*'s wig and thrown it on the floor*] Witch! Witch! Murderess! My daughter!

STEPDAUGHTER [*running over to restrain her* MOTHER] No, no, mama, no, please!

FATHER [*running over too at the same time*] Calm down, calm down! Sit here.

MOTHER Then send that woman away!

STEPDAUGHTER [*to the* DIRECTOR, *who also has run over*] It's not possible, not possible that my mother should be here!

FATHER [*also to the* DIRECTOR] They can't be together. That's why, you see, the woman wasn't with us when we came. Their being together would spoil it, you understand.

DIRECTOR It doesn't matter, doesn't matter at all. This is just a preliminary sketch. Everything helps. However confusing the elements, I'll piece them together somehow. [*Turning to the* MOTHER *and sitting her down again in her place*] Come along, come along, ma'am, calm down: sit down again.

STEPDAUGHTER [*who meanwhile has moved center stage again. Turning to* MADAM PACE] All right, let's go!

MADAM PACE Ah, no! No thank you! Yo aquí no do nada[2] with your mother present.

STEPDAUGHTER Oh, come on! Bring in that old señor who wants to have

7. Yes, yes, yes, Mister, because I . . . (Spanish). In Pirandello's original Italian text, Madam Pace mixes Spanish and Italian.

8. I speak (Spanish).

9. With me (Spanish).

1. Care, caution (Spanish).

2. I do nothing here (Spanish and English).

good time conmigo! [*Turning imperiously to all the others*] Yes, we've got to have it, this scene!—Come on, let's go! [*To* MADAM PACE] You may leave.

MADAM PACE Ah sí, I go, I go, go seguramente[3] . . . [*She makes her exit furiously, putting her wig back on, and looking haughtily at the Actors who applaud mockingly.*]

STEPDAUGHTER [*to the* FATHER] And you can make your entrance. No need to go out and come in again. Come here. Pretend, you're already in. Right. Now I'm here with bowed head, modest, huh? Let's go! Speak up! With a different voice, the voice of someone just in off the street: "Hello, miss."

DIRECTOR [*by this time out front again*] Now look: are you directing this, or am I? [*To the* FATHER *who looks undecided and perplexed.*] Do it, yes. Go to the back. Don't leave the stage, though. And then come forward.

[*The* FATHER *does it, almost dismayed. Very pale; but already clothed in the reality of his created life, he smiles as he approaches from the back, as if still alien to the drama which will break upon him. The Actors now pay attention to the scene which is beginning.*]

DIRECTOR [*softly, in haste, to the* PROMPTER *in the box*] And you, be ready now, ready to write!

THE SCENE

FATHER [*coming forward, with a different voice*] Hello, miss.

STEPDAUGHTER [*with bowed head and contained disgust*] Hello.

FATHER [*scrutinizing her under her hat which almost hides her face and noting that she is very young, exclaims, almost to himself, a little out of complaisance and a little out of fear of compromising himself in a risky adventure*] Oh . . . —Well, I was thinking, it wouldn't be the first time, hm? The first time you came here.

STEPDAUGHTER [*as above*] No, sir.

FATHER You've been here other times? [*And when the* STEPDAUGHTER *nods*] More than once? [*He waits a moment for her to answer, then again scrutinizes her under her hat; smiles; then says*] Well then, hm . . . it shouldn't any longer be so . . . May I take this hat off for you?

STEPDAUGHTER [*without pause, to forestall him, not now containing her disgust*] No, sir, *I* will take it off! [*And she does so in haste, convulsed.*]

[*The* MOTHER, *watching the scene with the* SON *and with the two others, smaller and more her own, who are close to her all the time, forming a group at the opposite side of the stage from the Actors, is on tenterhooks as she follows the words and actions of* FATHER *and* STEPDAUGHTER *with varied expression: grief, disdain, anxiety, horror, now hiding her face, now emitting a moan.*]

MOTHER Oh God! My God!

FATHER [*is momentarily turned to stone by the moaning; then he reassumes the previous tone*] Now give it to me: I'll hang it up for you. [*He takes the hat from her hands.*] But I could wish for a little hat worthier of such a dear, lovely little head! Would you like to help me choose one? From the many Madam has?—You wouldn't?

INGENUE [*interrupting*] Oh now, come on, those are *our* hats!

3. Certainly (Spanish).

DIRECTOR [*without pause, very angry*] Silence, for Heaven's sake, don't try to be funny!—This is the stage. [*Turning back to the* STEPDAUGHTER] Would you begin again, please?

STEPDAUGHTER [*beginning again*] No, thank you, sir.

FATHER Oh, come on now, don't say no. Accept one from me. To please me . . . There are some lovely ones you know. And we would make Madam happy. Why else does she put them on display?

STEPDAUGHTER No, no, sir, look: I wouldn't even be able to wear it.

FATHER You mean because of what the family would think when they saw you come home with a new hat on? Think nothing of it. Know how to handle that? What to tell them at home?

STEPDAUGHTER [*breaking out, at the end of her rope*] But that's not why, sir. I couldn't wear it because I'm . . . as you see me. You might surely have noticed! [*Points to her black attire.*]

FATHER In mourning, yes. Excuse me. It's true: I do see it. I beg your pardon. I'm absolutely mortified, believe me.

STEPDAUGHTER [*forcing herself and plucking up courage to conquer her contempt and nausea*] Enough! Enough! It's for me to thank you, it is not for you to be mortified or afflicted. Please pay no more attention to what I said. Even for me, you understand . . . [*She forces herself to smile and adds*] I need to forget I am dressed like this.

DIRECTOR [*interrupting, addressing himself to the* PROMPTER *in his box, and going up onstage again*] Wait! Wait! Don't write. Leave that last sentence out, leave it out! [*Turning to the* FATHER *and* STEPDAUGHTER] It's going very well indeed. [*Then to the* FATHER *alone*] This is where you go into the part we prepared. [*To the Actors*] Enchanting, that little hat scene, don't you agree?

STEPDAUGHTER Oh, but the best is just coming. Why aren't we continuing?

DIRECTOR Patience one moment. [*Again addressing himself to the Actors*] Needs rather delicate handling, of course . . .

LEADING MAN —With a certain *ease*—

LEADING LADY Obviously. But there's nothing to it. [*To the* LEADING MAN] We can rehearse it at once, can't we?

LEADING MAN As far as I'm . . . Very well, I'll go out and make my entrance. [*And he does go out by the back door, ready to reenter.*]

DIRECTOR [*to the* LEADING LADY] And so, look, your scene with that Madam Pace is over. I'll write it up later. You are standing . . . Hey, where are you going?

LEADING LADY Wait. I'm putting my hat back on . . . [*She does so, taking the hat from the hook.*]

DIRECTOR Oh yes, good.—Now, you're standing here with your head bowed.

STEPDAUGHTER [*amused*] But she's not wearing black!

LEADING LADY *I shall* wear black! And I'll carry it better than you!

DIRECTOR [*to the* STEPDAUGHTER] Keep quiet, please! Just watch. You can learn something. [*Claps his hands.*] Get going, get going! The entrance! [*And he goes back out front to get an impression of the stage.*]

[*The door at the back opens, and the* LEADING MAN *comes forward, with the relaxed, waggish manner of an elderly Don Juan.*[4] *From the first*

4. That is, a great lover or seducer of women (from the legendary Spaniard of that name).

speeches, the performance of the scene by the Actors is quite a different thing, without, however, having any element of parody in it—rather, it seems corrected, set to rights. Naturally, the STEPDAUGHTER *and the* FATHER, *being quite unable to recognize themselves in this* LEADING LADY *and* LEADING MAN *but hearing them speak their own words express in various ways, now with gestures, now with smiles, now with open protests, their surprise, their wonderment, their suffering, etc., as will be seen forthwith.*

The PROMPTER*'s voice is clearly heard from the box.*]

LEADING MAN Hello, miss.

FATHER [*without pause, unable to contain himself*] No, no!

[*The* STEPDAUGHTER, *seeing how the* LEADING MAN *makes his entrance, has burst out laughing.*]

DIRECTOR [*coming from the proscenium, furious*] Silence here! And stop that laughing at once! We can't go ahead till it stops.

STEPDAUGHTER [*coming from the proscenium*] How can I help it? This lady [*the* LEADING LADY] just stands there. If she's supposed to be me, let me tell you that if anyone said hello to me in that manner and that tone of voice, I'd burst out laughing just as I actually did!

FATHER [*coming forward a little too*] That's right . . . the manner, the tone . . .

DIRECTOR Manner! Tone! Stand to one side now, and let me see the rehearsal.

LEADING MAN [*coming forward*] If I'm to play an old man entering a house of ill—

DIRECTOR Oh, pay no attention, please. Just begin again. It was going fine. [*Waiting for the Actor to resume*] Now then . . .

LEADING MAN Hello, miss.

LEADING LADY Hello.

LEADING MAN [*re-creating the* FATHER*'s gesture of scrutinizing her under her hat, but then expressing very distinctly first the complaisance and then the fear*] Oh . . . Well . . . I was thinking it wouldn't be the first time, I hope . . .

FATHER [*unable to help correcting him*] Not "I hope." "Would it?" "Would it?"

DIRECTOR He says: "would it?" A question.

LEADING MAN [*pointing to the* PROMPTER] I heard: "I hope."

DIRECTOR Same thing! "Would it." Or: "I hope." Continue, continue.—Now, maybe a bit less affected . . . Look, I'll do it for you. Watch me . . . [*Returns to the stage, then repeats the bit since the entrance*]—Hello, miss.

LEADING LADY Hello.

DIRECTOR Oh, well . . . I was thinking . . . [*Turning to the* LEADING MAN *to have him note how he has looked at the* LEADING LADY *under her hat*] Surprise . . . fear and complaisance. [*Then, going on, and turning to the* LEADING LADY] It wouldn't be the first time, would it? The first time you came here. [*Again turning to the* LEADING MAN *with an inquiring look*] Clear? [*To the* LEADING LADY] Then you say: No, sir. [*Back to the* LEADING MAN] How shall I put it? Plasticity! [*Goes back out front.*]

LEADING LADY No, sir.

LEADING MAN You came here other times? More than once?

DIRECTOR No, no, wait. [*Indicating the* LEADING LADY] First let her nod. "You came here other times?"

[*The* LEADING LADY *raises her head a little, closes her eyes painfully as if in disgust, then nods twice at the word "Down" from the* DIRECTOR.]

STEPDAUGHTER [*involuntarily*] Oh, my God! [*And she at once puts her hand on her mouth to keep the laughter in.*]

DIRECTOR [*turning round*] What is it?

STEPDAUGHTER [*without pause*] Nothing, nothing.

DIRECTOR [*to the* LEADING MAN That's your cue. Go straight on.

LEADING MAN More than once? Well then, hm . . . it shouldn't any longer be so . . . May I take this little hat off for you?

[*The* LEADING MAN *says this last speech in such a tone and accompanies it with such a gesture that the* STEPDAUGHTER, *her hands on her mouth, much as she wants to hold herself in, cannot contain her laughter, which comes bursting out through her fingers irresistibly and very loud.*]

LEADING LADY [*returning to her place, enraged*] Now look, I'm not going to be made a clown of by that person!

LEADING MAN Nor am I. Let's stop.

DIRECTOR [*to the* STEPDAUGHTER, *roaring*] Stop it! Stop it!

STEPDAUGHTER Yes, yes. Forgive me, forgive me . . .

DIRECTOR You have no manners! You're presumptuous! So there!

FATHER [*seeking to intervene*] That's true, yes, that's true, sir, but forgive . . .

DIRECTOR [*onstage again*] Forgive nothing! It's disgusting!

FATHER Yes, sir. But believe me, it has such a strange effect—

DIRECTOR Strange? Strange? What's strange about it?

FATHER I admire your actors, sir, I really admire them, this gentleman [LEADING MAN] and that lady [LEADING LADY] but assuredly . . . well, they're not us . . .

DIRECTOR So what? How *could* they be you, if they're the actors?

FATHER Exactly, the actors! And they play our parts well, both of them. But of course, to us, they seem something else—that tries to be the same but simply isn't!

DIRECTOR How d'you mean: isn't? What is it then?

FATHER Something that . . . becomes theirs. And stops being ours.

DIRECTOR Necessarily! I explained that to you!

FATHER Yes. I understand, I do under—

DIRECTOR Then that will be enough! [*Turning to the Actors*] We'll be rehearsing by ourselves as we usually do. Rehearsing with authors present has always been hell, in my experience. There's no satisfying them. [*Turning to the* FATHER and the STEPDAUGHTER] Come along then. Let's resume. And let's hope you find it possible not to laugh this time.

STEPDAUGHTER Oh, no, I won't be laughing this time around. My big moment comes up now. Don't worry!

DIRECTOR Very well, when she says: "Please pay no more attention to what I said . . . Even for me—you understand . . ." [*Turning to the* FATHER] You'll have to cut right in with: "I understand, oh yes, I understand . . ." and ask her right away—

STEPDAUGHTER [*interrupting*] Oh? Ask me what?

DIRECTOR —why she is in mourning.

STEPDAUGHTER No, no, look: when I told him I needed to forget I was dressed like this, do you know what his answer was? "Oh, good! Then let's take that little dress right off, shall we?"

DIRECTOR Great! Terrific! It'll knock 'em right out of their seats!

STEPDAUGHTER But it's the truth.

DIRECTOR Truth, is it? Well, well, well. This is the theater! Our motto is: truth up to a certain point!

STEPDAUGHTER Then what would you propose?

DIRECTOR You'll see. You'll see it. Just leave me alone.

STEPDAUGHTER Certainly not. From my nausea—from all the reasons one more cruel than another why I am what I am, why I am "that one there"—you'd like to cook up some romantic, sentimental concoction, wouldn't you? He asks me why I'm in mourning, and I tell him, through my tears, that Papa died two months ago! No, my dear sir! He has to say what he did say: "Then let's take that little dress right off, shall we?" And I, with my two-months mourning in my heart, went back there—you see? behind that screen—and—my fingers quivering with shame, with loathing—I took off my dress, took off my corset . . .

DIRECTOR [*running his hands through his hair*] Good God, what are you saying?

STEPDAUGHTER [*shouting frantically*] The truth, sir, the truth!

DIRECTOR Well, yes, of course, that must be the truth . . . and I quite understand your horror, young lady. Would you try to understand that all that is impossible *on the stage*?

STEPDAUGHTER Impossible? Then, thanks very much, I'm leaving.

DIRECTOR No, no, look . . .

STEPDAUGHTER I'm leaving, I'm leaving! You went in that room, you two, didn't you, and figured out "what is possible on the stage"? Thanks very much. I see it all. He wants to skip to the point where he can act out his [*Exaggerating*] spiritual travail! But I want to play *my* drama. Mine!

DIRECTOR [*annoyed, and shrugging haughtily*] Oh well, *your* drama. This is not just your drama, if I may say so. How about the drama of the others? His drama [*the* FATHER], hers [*the* MOTHER]? We can't let one character hog the limelight, just taking the whole stage over, and overshadowing all the others! Everything must be placed within the frame of one harmonious picture! We must perform only what is performable! I know as well as you do that each of us has a whole life of his own inside him and would like to bring it all out. But the difficult thing is this: to bring out only as much as is needed—in relation to the others—and in this to *imply* all the rest, *suggest* what remains inside! Oh, it would be nice if every character could come down to the footlights and tell the audience just what is brewing inside him—in a fine monologue or, if you will, a lecture! [*Good-natured, conciliatory*] Miss, you will have to *contain yourself*. And it will be in your interest. It could make a bad impression—let me warn you—this tearing fury, this desperate disgust—since, if I may say so, you confessed having been with others at Madam Pace's—before him—more than once!

STEPDAUGHTER [*lowering her head, pausing to recollect, a deeper note in her voice*] It's true. But to me the others are also *him*, all of them equally!

DIRECTOR [*not getting it*] The others? How d'you mean?

STEPDAUGHTER People "go wrong." And wrong follows on the heels of wrong. Who is responsible, if not whoever it was who first brought them down? Isn't that always the case? And for me that is him. Even before I was born. Look at him, and see if it isn't so.

DIRECTOR Very good. And if he has so much to feel guilty about, can't you appreciate how it must weigh him down? So let's at least permit him to act it out.

STEPDAUGHTER And how, may I ask, how could he act out all that "noble" guilt, all those so "moral" torments, if you propose to spare him the horror of one day finding in his arms—after having bade her take off the black clothes that marked her recent loss—a woman now, and already gone wrong—that little girl, sir, that little girl whom he used to go watch coming out of school?

[*She says these last words in a voice trembling with emotion. The* MOTHER, *hearing her say this, overcome with uncontrollable anguish, which comes out first in suffocated moans and subsequently bursts out in bitter weeping. The emotion takes hold of everyone. Long pause.*]

STEPDAUGHTER [*as soon as the* MOTHER *gives signs of calming down, somber, determined*] We're just among ourselves now. Still unknown to the public. Tomorrow you will make of us the show you have in mind. You will put it together in your way. But would you like to really see—our drama? Have it explode—the real thing?

DIRECTOR Of course. Nothing I'd like better. And I'll use as much of it as I possibly can!

STEPDAUGHTER Very well. Have this Mother here go out.

MOTHER [*ceasing to weep, with a loud cry*] No, no! Don't allow this, don't allow it!

DIRECTOR I only want to take a look, ma'am.

MOTHER I can't, I just can't!

DIRECTOR But if it's already happened? Excuse me but I just don't get it.

MOTHER No, no, it's happening now. It's always happening. My torment is not a pretense! I am alive and present—always, in every moment of my torment—it keeps renewing itself, it too is alive and always present. But those two little ones over there—have you heard them speak? They cannot speak, sir, not anymore! They still keep clinging to me—to keep my torment alive and present. For themselves they don't exist, don't exist any longer. And she [*the* STEPDAUGHTER], she just fled, ran away from me, she's lost, lost . . . . If I see her before me now, it's for the same reason: to renew the torment, keep it always alive and present forever—the torment I've suffered on her account too—forever!

FATHER [*solemn*] The eternal moment, sir, as I told you. She [*the* STEPDAUGHTER] is here to catch me, fix me, hold me there in the pillory, hanging there forever, hooked, in that single fleeting shameful moment of my life! She cannot give it up. And, actually, sir, *you* cannot spare me.

DIRECTOR But I didn't say I wouldn't use that. On the contrary, it will be the nucleus of the whole first act. To the point where she [*the* MOTHER] surprises you.

FATHER Yes, exactly. Because that is the sentence passed upon me: all our passion which has to culminate in her [*the* MOTHER*'s*] final cry!

STEPDAUGHTER It still rings in my ears. It's driven me out of my mind, that cry!—You can present me as you wish, sir, it doesn't matter. Even dressed. As long as at least my arms—just my arms—are bare. Because it was like this. [*She goes to the* FATHER *and rests her head on his chest.*] I was standing like this with my head on his chest and my arms round his neck like this. Then I saw something throbbing right here on my arm. A vein. Then, as if it was just this living vein that disgusted me, I jammed my eyes shut, like this, d'you see? and buried my head on his chest. [*Turning to the* MOTHER] Scream, scream, mama! [*Buries her head on the* FATHER'S *chest and with her shoulders raised as if to avoid hearing the scream she adds in a voice stifled with torment.*] Scream as you screamed then!

MOTHER [*rushing forward to part them*] No! My daughter! My daughter! [*Having pulled her from him*] Brute! Brute! It's my daughter, don't you see—my daughter!

DIRECTOR [*the outburst having sent him reeling to the footlights, while the Actors show dismay*] Fine! Splendid! And now: curtain, curtain!

FATHER [*running to him, convulsed*] Right! Yes! Because that, sir, is how it actually was!

DIRECTOR [*in admiration and conviction*] Yes, yes, of course! Curtain! Curtain!

[*Hearing this repeated cry of the* DIRECTOR, *the* TECHNICIAN *lets down the curtain, trapping the* DIRECTOR *and the* FATHER *between curtain and footlights.*]

DIRECTOR [*looking up, with raised arms*] What an idiot! I say Curtain, meaning that's how the act should end, and they let down the actual curtain! [*He lifts a corner of the curtain so he can get back onstage. To the* FATHER] Yes, yes, fine, splendid! Absolutely surefire! Has to end that way. I can vouch for the first act. [*Goes behind the curtain with the* FATHER.]

[*When the curtain rises we see that the stagehands have struck that first "indication of a set," and have put onstage in its stead a small garden fountain. On one side of the stage, the Actors are sitting in a row, and on the other are the Characters. The* DIRECTOR *is standing in the middle of the stage, in the act of meditating with one hand, fist clenched, on his mouth.*]

DIRECTOR [*shrugging after a short pause*] Yes, well then, let's get to the second act. Just leave it to me as we agreed beforehand and everything will be all right.

STEPDAUGHTER Our entrance into his house [*the* FATHER] in spite of him [*the* SON].

DIRECTOR [*losing patience*] Very well. But leave it all to me, I say.

STEPDAUGHTER In spite of him. Just let that be clear.

MOTHER [*shaking her head from her corner*] For all the good that's come out of it . . .

STEPDAUGHTER [*turning quickly on her*] It doesn't matter. The more damage to us, the more guilt feelings for him.

DIRECTOR [*still out of patience*] I understand, I understand. All this will be taken into account, especially at the beginning. Rest assured.

MOTHER [*supplicatingly*] Do make them understand, I beg you, sir, for my conscience' sake, for I tried in every possible way—

STEPDAUGHTER [*continuing her* MOTHER'S *speech, contemptuously*] To placate me, to advise me not to give him trouble. [*To the* DIRECTOR] Do what she wants, do it because it's true. I enjoy the whole thing very much because, look: the more she plays the suppliant and tries to gain entrance into his heart, the more he holds himself aloof: he's an absentee! How I relish this!

DIRECTOR We want to get going—on the second act, don't we?

STEPDAUGHTER I won't say another word. But to play it all in the garden, as you want to, won't be possible.

DIRECTOR Why won't it be possible?

STEPDAUGHTER Because he [*the* SON] stays shut up in his room, on his own. Then again we need the house for the part about this poor bewildered little boy, as I told you.

DIRECTOR Quite right. But on the other hand, we can't change the scenery in view of the audience three or four times in one act, nor can we stick up signs—

LEADING MAN They used to at one time . . .

DIRECTOR Yes, when the audiences were about as mature as that little girl.

LEADING LADY They got the illusion more easily.

FATHER [*suddenly, rising*] The illusion, please don't say illusion! Don't use that word! It's especially cruel to us.

DIRECTOR [*astonished*] And why, if I may ask?

FATHER Oh yes, cruel, cruel! You should understand that.

DIRECTOR What word would you have us use anyway? The illusion of creating here for our spectators—

LEADING MAN —By our performance—

DIRECTOR —the illusion of a reality.

FATHER I understand, sir, but perhaps you do not understand us. Because, you see, for you and for your actors all this—quite rightly—is a game—

LEADING LADY [*indignantly interrupting*] Game! We are not children, sir. We act in earnest.

FATHER I don't deny it. I just mean the game of your art which, as this gentleman rightly says, must provide a perfect illusion of reality.

DIRECTOR Yes, exactly.

FATHER But consider this. We [*He quickly indicates himself and the other five Characters.*], we have no reality outside this illusion.

DIRECTOR [*astonished, looking at his Actors who remain bewildered and lost*] And that means?

FATHER [*after observing them briefly, with a pale smile*] Just that, ladies and gentlemen. How should we have any other reality? What for you is an illusion, to be created, is for us our unique reality. [*Short pause. He takes several short steps toward the* DIRECTOR, *and adds*] But not for us alone, of course. Think a moment. [*He looks into his eyes.*] Can you tell me who you are? [*And he stands there pointing his first finger at him.*]

DIRECTOR [*upset, with a half-smile*] How do you mean, who I am? I am I.

FATHER And if I told you that wasn't true because you are me?

DIRECTOR I would reply that you are out of your mind. [*The Actors laugh.*]

FATHER You are right to laugh: because this is a game. [*To the* DIRECTOR] And you can object that it's only in a game that that gentleman there [LEADING MAN], who is himself, must be me, who am *myself*. I've caught you in a trap, do you see that?

[*Actors start laughing again.*]

DIRECTOR [*annoyed*] You said all this before. Why repeat it?

FATHER I won't—I didn't intend to say that. I'm inviting you to emerge from this game. [*He looks at the* LEADING LADY *as if to forestall what she might say.*] This game of art which you are accustomed to play here with your actors. Let me again ask quite seriously: Who are you?

DIRECTOR [*turning to the Actors, amazed and at the same time irritated*] The gall of this fellow! Calls himself a character and comes here to ask me who I am!

FATHER [*dignified, but not haughty*] A character, sir, can always ask a man who he is. Because a character really has his own life, marked with his own characteristics, by virtue of which he is always someone. Whereas, a man—I'm not speaking of you now—*a man* can be no one.

DIRECTOR Oh sure. But you are asking me! And I am the manager, understand?

FATHER [*quite softly with mellifluous modesty*] Only in order to know, sir, if you as you now are see yourself . . . for example, at a distance in time. Do you see the man you once were, with all the illusions you had then, with everything, inside you and outside, as it seemed then—as it was then for you?—Well sir, thinking back to those illusions which you don't have anymore, to all those things which no longer seem to be what at one time they were for you, don't you feel, not just the boards of this stage, but the very earth beneath slipping away from you? For will not all that you feel yourself to be now, your whole reality of today, as it is now, inevitably seem an illusion tomorrow?

DIRECTOR [*who has not followed exactly, but has been staggered by the plausibilities of the argument*] Well, well, what do you want to prove?

FATHER Oh nothing, sir. I just wanted to make you see that if *we* [*pointing again at himself and the other Characters*] have no reality outside of illusion, it would be well if you should distrust your reality because, though you breathe it and touch it today, it is destined like that of yesterday to stand revealed to you tomorrow as illusion.

DIRECTOR [*deciding to mock him*] Oh splendid! And you'll be telling me next that you and this play that you have come to perform for me are truer and more real than I am.

FATHER [*quite seriously*] There can be no doubt of that, sir.

DIRECTOR Really?

FATHER I thought you had understood that from the start.

DIRECTOR More real than me?

FATHER If your reality can change overnight . . .

DIRECTOR Of course it can, it changes all the time, like everyone else's.

FATHER [*with a cry*] But ours does not, sir. You see, that is the difference. It does not change, it cannot ever change or be otherwise because it is already fixed, it is what is, just that, forever—a terrible thing, sir!—an immutable reality. You should shudder to come near us.

DIRECTOR [*suddenly struck by a new idea, he steps in front of the* FATHER] I should like to know, however, when anyone ever saw a character get out of his part and set about expounding and explicating it, delivering lectures on it. Can you tell me? I have never seen anything like that.

FATHER You have never seen it, sir, because authors generally hide the travail of their creations. When characters are alive and turn up, living, before their author, all that author does is follow the words and gestures which they propose to him. He has to want them to be as they themselves want to be. Woe betide him if he doesn't! When a character is born, he at once acquires such an independence, even of his own author, that the whole world can imagine him in innumerable situations other than those the author thought to place him in. At times he acquires a meaning that the author never dreamt of giving him.

DIRECTOR Certainly, I know that.

FATHER Then why all this astonishment at us? Imagine what a misfortune it is for a character such as I described to you—given life in the imagination of an author who then wished to deny him life—and tell me frankly: isn't such a character, given life and left without life, isn't he right to set about doing just what we are doing now as we stand here before you, after having done just the same—for a very long time, believe me—before *him,* trying to persuade him, trying to push him . . . I would appear before him sometimes, sometimes she [*looks at* STEPDAUGHTER] would go to him, sometimes that poor mother . . .

STEPDAUGHTER [*coming forward as if in a trance*] It's true. I too went there, sir, to tempt him, many times, in the melancholy of that study of his, at the twilight hour, when he would sit stretched out in his armchair, unable to make up his mind to switch the light on, and letting the evening shadows invade the room, knowing that these shadows were alive with us and that we were coming to tempt him . . . [*As if she saw herself still in that study and felt only annoyance at the presence of all of these Actors*] Oh, if only you would all go away! Leave us alone! My mother there with her son—I with this little girl—the boy there always alone—then I with him [*the* FATHER]—then I by myself, I by myself . . . in those shadows. [*Suddenly she jumps up as if she wished to take hold of herself in the vision she has of herself lighting up the shadows and alive.*] Ah, my life! What scenes, what scenes we went there to propose to him: I, I tempted him more than the others.

FATHER Right, but perhaps that was the trouble: you insisted too much. You thought you could seduce him.

STEPDAUGHTER Nonsense. He wanted me that way. [*She comes up to the* DIRECTOR *to tell him as in confidence.*] If you ask me, sir, it was because he was so depressed, or because he despised the theater the public knows and wants . . .

DIRECTOR Let's continue. Let's continue, for heaven's sake. Enough theories, I'd like some facts. Give me some facts.

STEPDAUGHTER It seems to me that we have already given you more facts than you can handle—with our entry into his [*the* FATHER*'s*] house! You said you couldn't change the scene every five minutes or start hanging signs.

DIRECTOR Nor can we, of course not, we have to combine the scenes and group them in one simultaneous close-knit action. Not your idea at all. You'd like to see your brother come home from school and wander through the house like a ghost, hiding behind the doors, and brooding on a plan which—how did you put it—?

STEPDAUGHTER —shrivels him up, sir, completely shrivels him up, sir.

DIRECTOR "Shrivels!" What a word! All right then: his growth was stunted except for his eyes. Is that what you said?

STEPDAUGHTER Yes, sir. Just look at him. [*She points him out next to the* MOTHER.]

DIRECTOR Good girl. And then at the same time you want this little girl to be playing in the garden, dead to the world. Now, the boy in the house, the girl in the garden, is that possible?

STEPDAUGHTER Happy in the sunshine! Yes, that is my only reward, her pleasure, her joy in that garden! After the misery, the squalor of a horrible room where we slept, all four of us, she with me: just think, of the horror of my contaminated body next to hers! She held me tight, oh so tight with her loving innocent little arms! In the garden she would run and take my hand as soon as she saw me. She did not see the big flowers, she ran around looking for the teeny ones and wanted to show them to me, oh the joy of it!

[*Saying this and tortured by the memory she breaks into prolonged desperate sobbing, dropping her head onto her arms which are spread out on the work table. Everyone is overcome by her emotion. The* DIRECTOR *goes to her almost paternally and says to comfort her*]

DIRECTOR We'll do the garden. We'll do the garden, don't worry, and you'll be very happy about it. We'll bring all the scenes together in the garden. [*Calling a* STAGEHAND *by name*] Hey, drop me a couple of trees, will you, two small cypress trees, here in front of the fountain.

[*Two small cypress trees are seen descending from the flies.*[5] *A* STAGEHAND *runs on to secure them with nails and a couple of braces.*]

DIRECTOR [*to the* STEPDAUGHTER] Something to go on with anyway. Gives us an idea. [*Again calling the* STAGEHAND *by name*] Hey, give me a bit of sky

STAGEHAND [*from above*] What?

DIRECTOR Bit of sky, a backcloth, to go behind that fountain. [*A white backdrop is seen descending from the flies.*] Not white, I said sky. It doesn't matter, leave it, I'll take care of it. [*Shouting*] Hey, Electrician, put these lights out. Let's have a bit of atmosphere, lunar atmosphere, blue background, and give me a blue spot on that backcloth. That's right. That's enough. [*At his command a mysterious lunar scene is created which induces the Actors to talk and move as they would on an evening in the garden beneath the moon.*] [*To* STEPDAUGHTER] You see? And now instead of hiding behind doors in the house the boy could move around here in the garden and hide behind trees. But it will be difficult, you know, to find a little girl to play the scene where she shows you the flowers. [*Turning to the* BOY] Come down this way a bit. Let's see how this can be worked out. [*And when the* BOY *doesn't move*] Come on, come on. [*Then dragging him forward he tries to make him hold his head up but it falls down again every time.*] Oh dear, another problem, this boy . . . What *is* it? . . . My God, he'll have to say something . . . [*He goes up to him, puts a hand on his shoulder and leads him behind one of the tree drops.*] Come on. Come on. Let me see. You can hide a bit here . . . Like this . . . You can stick your head out a bit to look . . . [*He goes to one side to see the effect. The* BOY *has scarcely run through the actions when the Actors are deeply affected; and they remain quite overwhelmed.*] Ah! Fine! Splendid! [*He turns again to the* STEPDAUGHTER.] If the little girl surprises him looking out and runs over to him, don't you think she might drag a few words out of him too?

STEPDAUGHTER [*jumping to her feet*] Don't expect him to speak while *he's* here. [*She points to the* SON.] You have to send *him* away first.

5. The space over the stage from which scenery and equipment can be lowered.

SON [*going resolutely toward one of the two stairways*] Suits me. Glad to go. Nothing I want more.

DIRECTOR [*immediately calling him*] No. Where are you going? Wait.

[*The* MOTHER *rises, deeply moved, in anguish at the thought that he is really going. She instinctively raises her arms as if to halt him, yet without moving away from her position.*]

SON [*arriving at the footlights, where the* DIRECTOR *stops him*] I have absolutely nothing to do here. So let me go please. Just let me go.

DIRECTOR How do you mean, you have nothing to do?

STEPDAUGHTER [*placidly, with irony*] Don't hold him! He won't go.

FATHER He has to play the terrible scene in the garden with his mother.

SON [*unhesitating, resolute, proud*] I play nothing. I said so from the start. [*To the* DIRECTOR] Let me go.

STEPDAUGHTER [*running to the* DIRECTOR *to get him to lower his arms so that he is no longer holding the* SON *back*] Let him go. [*Then turning to the* SON *as soon as the* DIRECTOR *has let him go*] Very well, go. [*The* SON *is all set to move toward the stairs but, as if held by some occult power, he cannot go down the steps. While the Actors are both astounded and deeply troubled, he moves slowly across the footlights straight to the other stairway. But having arrived there he remains poised for the descent but unable to descend. The* STEPDAUGHTER, *who has followed him with her eyes in an attitude of defiance, bursts out laughing.*] He can't, you see. He can't. He has to stay here, has to. Bound by a chain, indissolubly. But if I who do take flight, sir, when that happens which has to happen, and precisely because of the hatred I feel for him, precisely so as not to see him again—very well, if *I* am still here and can bear the sight of him and his company—you can imagine whether *he* can go away. He who really must, must remain here with that fine father of his and that mother there who no longer has any other children. [*Turning again to the* MOTHER] Come on, Mother, come on. [*Turning again to the* DIRECTOR *and pointing to the* MOTHER] Look, she got up to hold him back. [*To the* MOTHER, *as if exerting a magical power over her*] Come. Come . . . [*Then to the* DIRECTOR] You can imagine how little she wants to display her love in front of your actors. But so great is her desire to get at him that—look, you see—she is even prepared to live her scene.

[*In fact the* MOTHER *has approached and no sooner has the* STEPDAUGHTER *spoken her last words than she spreads her arms to signify consent.*]

SON [*without pause*] But *I* am not, *I* am not. If I cannot go I will stay here, but I repeat: I will play nothing.

FATHER [*to the* DIRECTOR, *enraged*] You can force him, sir.

SON No one can force me.

FATHER I will force you.

STEPDAUGHTER Wait, wait. First the little girl must be at the fountain. [*She runs to take the* LITTLE GIRL, *drops on her knees in front of her, takes her little face in her hands.*] My poor little darling, you look bewildered with those lovely big eyes of yours. Who knows where you think you are? We are on a stage my dear. What is a stage? It is a place where you play at being serious, a place for playacting, where we will now playact. But seriously! For real! You too . . . [*She embraces her, presses her to her bosom, and rocks her a little.*] Oh, little darling, little darling, what an ugly play you will enact! What a horrible thing has been planned for you, the garden, the fountain . . . All pretense, of course, that's the trouble, my sweet, everything is make-believe here, but perhaps for you, my child, a make-believe fountain is nicer than a real one for playing in, hmm? It will be a game for the others, but not for you, alas, because you are real, my darling, and are actually playing in a fountain that is real, beautiful, big, green with many bamboo plants reflected in it and giving it shade. Many, many ducklings can swim in it, breaking the shade to bits. You want to take hold of one of these ducklings . . . [*With a shout that fills everyone with dismay*] No! No, my Rosetta! Your mother is not looking after you because of that beast of a son. A thousand devils are loose in my head . . . and *he* . . . [*She leaves the* LITTLE GIRL *and turns with her usual hostility to the* BOY.] And what are you doing here, always looking like a beggar child? It will be your fault too if this little girl drowns—with all your standing around like that. As if I hadn't paid for everybody when I got you all into this house. [*Grabbing one of his arms to force him to take a hand out of his pocket*] What have you got there? What are you hiding? Let's see this hand. [*Tears his hand out of his pocket, and to the horror of everyone discovers that it holds a small revolver. She looks at it for a moment as if satisfied and then says*] Ah! Where did you get that and how? [*And as the* BOY *in his confusion, with his eyes staring and vacant all the time, does not answer her*] Idiot, if I were you I wouldn't have killed myself, I would have killed one of those two—or both of them—the father and the son! [*She hides him behind the small cypress tree from which he had been looking out, and she takes the* LITTLE GIRL *and hides her in the fountain, having her lie down in it in such a way as to be quite hidden. Finally, the* STEPDAUGHTER *goes down on her knees with her face in her hands, which are resting on the rim of the fountain.*]

DIRECTOR Splendid! [*Turning to the* SON] And at the same time . . .

SON [*with contempt*] And at the same time, nothing. It is not true, sir. There was never any scene between me and her. [*He points to the* MOTHER.] Let her tell you herself how it was.

[*Meanwhile the* SECOND ACTRESS *and the* JUVENILE LEAD *have detached themselves from the group of Actors. The former has started to observe the* MOTHER, *who is opposite her, very closely. And the other has started to observe the* SON. *Both are planning how they will re-create the roles.*]

MOTHER Yes, it is true, sir. I had gone to his room.

SON My room, did you hear that? Not the garden.

DIRECTOR That is of no importance. We have to rearrange the action, I told you that.

SON [*noticing that the* JUVENILE LEAD *is observing him*] What do *you* want?

JUVENILE LEAD Nothing. I am observing you.

SON [*turning to the other side where the* SECOND ACTRESS *is*] Ah, and here we have you to re-create the role, eh? [*He points to the* MOTHER.]

DIRECTOR Exactly, exactly. You should be grateful, it seems to me, for the attention they are giving you.

SON Oh yes, thank you. But you still haven't understood that you cannot do this drama. We are not inside you, not in the least, and your actors are looking at us from the outside. Do you think it's possible for us to live before a mirror which, not content to freeze us in the fixed image it provides of our expression, also throws back at us an unrecognizable grimace purporting to be ourselves?

FATHER That is true. That is true. You must see that.

DIRECTOR [*to the* JUVENILE LEAD *and the* SECOND ACTRESS] Very well, get away from here.

SON No good. I won't cooperate.

DIRECTOR Just be quiet a minute and let me hear your mother. [*To the* MOTHER] Well? You went into his room?

MOTHER Yes sir, into his room. I was at the end of my tether. I wanted to pour out all of the anguish which was oppressing me. But as soon as he saw me come in—

SON —There was no scene. I went away. I went away so there would be no scene. Because I have never made scenes, never, understand?

MOTHER That's true. That's how it was. Yes.

DIRECTOR But now there's got to be a scene between you and him. It is indispensable.

MOTHER As for me, sir, I am ready. If only you could find some way to have me speak to him for one moment, to have me say what is in my heart.

FATHER [*going right up to the* SON, *very violent*] You will do it! For your mother! For your mother!

SON [*more decisively than ever*] I will do nothing!

FATHER [*grabbing him by the chest and shaking him*] By God, you will obey! Can't you hear how she is talking to you? Aren't you her son?

SON [*grabbing his* FATHER] No! No! Once and for all let's have done with it!

[*General agitation. The* MOTHER, *terrified, tries to get between them to separate them.*]

MOTHER [*as before*] Please, please!

FATHER [*without letting go of the* SON] You must obey, you must obey!

SON [*wrestling with his* FATHER *and in the end throwing him to the ground beside the little stairway, to the horror of everyone*] What's this frenzy that's taken hold of you? To show your shame and ours to everyone? Have you no restraint? I won't cooperate, I won't cooperate! And that is how I interpret the wishes of the man who did not choose to put us onstage.

DIRECTOR But you came here.

SON [*pointing to his* FATHER] He came here—not me!

DIRECTOR But aren't you here too?

SON It was he who wanted to come, dragging the rest of us with him, and then getting together with you to plot not only what really happened, but also—as if that did not suffice—*what did not happen*.

DIRECTOR Then tell me. Tell me what did happen. Just tell me. You came out of your room without saying a thing?

SON [*after a moment of hesitation*] Without saying a thing. In order not to make a scene.

DIRECTOR [*driving him on*] Very well, and then, what did you do then?

SON [*while everyone looks on in anguished attention, he moves a few steps on the front part of the stage*] Nothing . . . crossing the garden . . . [*He stops, gloomy, withdrawn.*]

DIRECTOR [*always driving him on to speak, impressed by his reticence*] Very well, crossing the garden?

SON [*desperate, hiding his face with one arm*] Why do you want to make me say it, sir? It is horrible.

[*The* MOTHER *trembles all over, and stifles groans, looking toward the fountain.*]

DIRECTOR [*softly, noticing this look of hers, turning to the* SON, *with growing apprehension*] The little girl?

SON [*looking out into the auditorium*] Over there—in the fountain . . .

FATHER [*on the ground, pointing compassionately toward the* MOTHER] And she followed him, sir.

DIRECTOR [*to the* SON, *anxiously*] And then you . . .

SON [*slowly, looking straight ahead all the time*] I ran out. I started to fish her out . . . but all of a sudden I stopped. Behind those trees I saw something that froze me: the boy, the boy was standing there, quite still. There was madness in the eyes. He was looking at his drowned sister in the fountain. [*The* STEPDAUGHTER, *who has been bent over the fountain, hiding the* LITTLE GIRL, *is sobbing desperately, like an echo from the bottom. Pause.*] I started to approach and then . . .

[*From behind the trees where the* BOY *has been hiding, a revolver shot rings out.*]

MOTHER [*running up with a tormented shout, accompanied by the* SON *and all the Actors in a general tumult*] Son! My son! [*And then amid the hubbub and the disconnected shouts of the others*] Help! Help!

DIRECTOR [*amid the shouting, trying to clear a space while the* BOY *is lifted by his head and feet and carried away behind the backcloth*] Is he wounded, is he wounded, really?

[*Everyone except the* DIRECTOR *and the* FATHER, *who has remained on the ground beside the steps, has disappeared behind the backcloth which has served for a sky, where they can still be heard for a while whispering anxiously. Then from one side and the other of this curtain, the Actors come back onstage.*]

LEADING LADY [*reentering from the right, very much upset*] He's dead! Poor boy! He's dead! What a terrible thing!

LEADING MAN [*reentering from the left, laughing*] How do you mean, dead? Fiction, fiction, one doesn't believe such things.

OTHER ACTORS [*on the right*] Fiction? Reality! Reality! He is dead!

OTHER ACTORS [*on the left*] No! Fiction! Fiction!

FATHER [*rising, and crying out to them*] Fiction indeed! Reality, reality, gentlemen, reality! [*Desperate, he too disappears at the back.*]

DIRECTOR [*at the end of his rope*] Fiction! Reality! To hell with all of you! Lights, lights, lights! [*At a single stroke the whole stage and auditorium is flooded with very bright light. The* DIRECTOR *breathes again, as if freed from an incubus, and they all look each other in the eyes, bewildered and lost.*] Things like this don't happen to me, they've made me lose a whole day. [*He looks at his watch.*] Go, you can all go. What could we do now anyway? It is too late to pick up the rehearsal where we left off. See you this evening. [*As soon as the Actors have gone he talks to the* ELECTRICIAN *by name.*] Hey, Electrician, lights out. [*He has hardly said the words when the theater is plunged for a moment into complete darkness.*] Hey, for God's sake, leave me at least one light! I like to see where I am going!

[*Immediately, from behind the backcloth, as if the wrong switch had been pulled, a green light comes on which projects the silhouettes, clear-cut and large, of the Characters, minus the* BOY *and the* LITTLE GIRL. *Seeing the silhouettes, the* DIRECTOR, *terrified, rushes from the stage. At the same time the light behind the backcloth goes out and the stage is again lit in nocturnal blue as before.*

Slowly, from the right side of the curtain, the SON *comes forward first, followed by the* MOTHER *with her arms stretched out toward him; then from the left side, the* FATHER. *They stop in the middle of the stage and stay there as if in a trance. Last of all from the right, the* STEPDAUGHTER *comes out and runs toward the two stairways. She stops on the first step, to look for a moment at the other three, and then breaks into a harsh laugh before throwing herself down the steps; she runs down the aisle between the rows of seats; she stops one more time and again laughs, looking at the three who are still onstage; she disappears from the auditorium, and from the lobby her laughter is still heard. Shortly thereafter the curtain falls.*]

LANGSTON HUGHES

1902–1967

LANGSTON Hughes, who made his name as a writer during the Harlem Renaissance of the 1920s, is widely considered one of the leading African American literary figures of the twentieth century. The author of novels, short stories, autobiographies, nonfiction, screenplays, and translations, he is best known for his poetry, which expressed the aspirations and painful realities of African American life in a language that drew on the rhythms of jazz, the blues, and African American vernacular. Perhaps because of his fame as a poet, Hughes's importance as a dramatist has, until recently, been overlooked. But between 1920 and his death in 1967, Hughes wrote nearly seventy plays for theater, radio, and television; pageants; musicals; and operas. The Broadway version of his play *Mulatto* (1935) ran for more performances than any previous play by an African American playwright. Arguably, no African American dramatist worked more deliberately—and across a wider range of theatrical forms and genres—to explore the social, psychological, and cultural experience of twentieth-century African Americans.

Like the Harlem Renaissance itself, Langston Hughes's early life was shaped by a variety of forces: the Jim Crow legal and social practices of a United States that still practiced racial segregation, a demographic shift that brought tens of thousands of black Americans to northern cities in the early and mid-twentieth century, and the international sensibility that characterized modernism as a cultural movement. Hughes was born on February 1, 1902, in Joplin, Missouri. His childhood was marked by frequent moves and family instability. His father, James, who could not take the Oklahoma bar exam because he was black, abandoned the family when Hughes was five and moved to Mexico, where his race did not prevent him from practicing law. Hughes lived for much of his childhood with his maternal grandmother in Lawrence, Kansas; after she died in 1915, he joined his mother, who had remarried, and they eventually settled in Cleveland. At an integrated high school there he was named editor of the yearbook and class poet during his senior year.

Upon graduating from high school, Hughes spent a year with his father in Mexico, and during that time he made plans to attend Columbia University. In September 1921, he arrived in New York. That year, his poems appeared in two periodicals of the National Association for the Advancement of Colored People (NAACP)—*The Brownie's Book,* a magazine for children, and *The Crisis,* the organization's chief publication. One of these poems, "The Negro Speaks of Rivers," was to become one of the most anthologized of all twentieth-century American poems. Hughes enrolled as a freshman at Columbia but dropped out after a year in order to support himself and to take greater advantage of the life and culture that surrounded him in Harlem. After working at a variety of jobs, he determined to see the world by sea. Long fascinated by the idea of Africa as an ancestral home, in 1923 he embarked on a freighter headed to the West Coast of Africa. He visited a number of ports from Senegal to Angola, and then spent ten months living and working in Paris. Back in the United States and with his reputation growing as one of the leading young African American writers, he published his first collection of poems (*The Weary Blues* [1926]); earned a bachelor's degree from Lincoln University, a historically black college in Pennsylvania; and grew close to such leading figures of the Harlem Renaissance as Countee Cullen, Wallace Thurman, and Zora Neale Hurston. But while Harlem would remain his spiritual and physical home until his death, he never abandoned the wandering life that he had known since childhood. Beginning in the early 1930s he traveled to Cuba, Haiti, the Soviet Union (where he lived for a year), China, Japan, and Mexico.

The Harlem that Hughes embraced in the 1920s was the center of a growing social, economic, political, and cultural self-consciousness on the part of black America. As its population rose from 50,000 to 300,000 in the years 1914–30, Harlem became the symbol of the "New Negro Renaissance," as it was often called. Books were written by and about African Americans, the politics of black nationalism were debated in an emerging black press, and a vogue for things "Negro" was evident in the popularity of jazz, such dances as the Charleston, *Shuffle Along* (1921) and other musicals, and the careers of such entertainers as Josephine Baker and Paul Robeson. Later scholars have debated the nature and scope of the Harlem Renaissance; as some have pointed out, a number of its participants lived outside New York; the emergence of a black self-consciousness was evident before the end of World War I and continued well after the Depression; and the prominence of its activities and personalities did not alter the fact that (in Hughes's own words) "[t]he ordinary Negroes hadn't heard of the Negro Renaissance. And if they had, it hadn't raised their wages any." That said, in the years 1910–40 black writers, thinkers, and artists enjoyed unprecedented opportunities and a cultural visibility that African Americans have only recently surpassed.

Drama and the theater played an important part in the Harlem Renaissance. Faced with the popularity of "black" plays by white playwrights (most importantly, Ridgely Torrence's *Three Plays for a Negro Theater* [1917] and Eugene O'Neill's *The Emperor Jones* [1920]) and the enormous success of *Shuffle Along* (written by African Americans but with a cartoonist plot that relied on racial stereotypes), black cultural figures called for a drama grounded in the experiences of African Americans themselves. In 1916, W. E. B. Du Bois predicted "the slow growth of a new folk drama built around the actual experience of Negro American life." And in 1924 he wrote: "No greater mine of dramatic material ever lay ready for the great artist's hands than the situation of men of Negro blood in modern America." During the 1920s, the NAACP instituted a commission on drama, the periodicals *Crisis* and *Opportunity* (published by the Urban League) offered awards for playwriting, and the first anthologies of plays by African American writers appeared in the 1920s and 1930s, collecting the works of such dramatists as Angelina Weld Grimké, Willis Richardson, Theophilus Lewis, and Georgia Douglas Johnson. In keeping with Du Bois's dictum that a "real Negro theater" should be "in a Negro neighborhood near the mass of ordinary Negro people," a number of black theater groups—with Du Bois's own Krigwa Players prominent among them—were established between 1920 and 1930.

Hughes's first attempt at playwriting was a short children's play titled *The Gold Piece*, which was published in 1921. His next attempt—*Mulatto: A Tragedy of the Deep South*, written in the summer of 1930—would establish his reputation in the theater. An exploration of the theme of the tragic mulatto, or person of mixed-race ancestry, *Mulatto* takes place on a Georgia plantation whose white owner has had several children with his black housekeeper, who has been his mistress for thirty years. In defiance of the arrangements that his parents have made in order to live as a family while maintaining the South's racial hierarchies, Robert, the youngest of these children, asserts his right to public recognition as his father's son. In the end, Robert kills his father during a violent struggle, takes his life to avoid a mob seeking his death, and leaves his mother to question the racial contradictions that have defined her life. A production of *Mulatto* opened in 1935 on Broadway, where it ran for more than a year before touring the country for two additional seasons, but the play was altered by its producer, who made its plot even more sensationalistic by adding an attempted rape scene and introducing other changes.

In this and other plays Hughes explored a variety of dramatic styles and genres. A great deal of politically and socially engaged drama was produced in the 1930s, and Hughes wrote explicitly political plays about such issues as a farmworkers' strike in California and the notorious case of the "Scottsboro Boys," the 1931 trial in Alabama of nine black youths falsely accused of rape. But despite his interests in agitprop theater, his talents as a playwright led him more frequently toward a tradition of folk realism. In 1930 Hughes collaborated with Zora Neale Hurston on *Mule Bone: A Comedy of Negro Life*, which employed folk material that Hurston had collected (because the two quarreled over authorship, *Mule Bone* was not produced until 1991). Hughes's first urban comedy, *Little Ham* (1936), features Hamlet Jones, a diminutive shoe shiner and lady's man in late 1920s Harlem, and a cast of other vividly drawn characters. *Simply Heavenly* (1957), which is also set in Harlem, showcases Jesse B. Semple ("Simple"), a humorous character first introduced by Hughes in a popular series of sketches that began appearing in the *Chicago Defender* in 1943. Other plays revealed Hughes's interest in the role of music in black society and culture. *Tambourines to Glory* (1963), for instance—a "folk ballad in stage form"—incorporates the rhythms of gospel hymns and spirituals in its tale of duplicity and goodness within a storefront church.

None of Hughes's plays is richer in its mix of genres and tones than *SOUL GONE HOME*, a one-act "tragi-comedy" that Hughes wrote in January 1936 for the Gilpin Players of Cleveland. This dramatized confrontation between a mother and her dead son was not performed then, however, perhaps (as Hughes's biographer Faith Berry speculates) because Hughes's own mother was ill with cancer and would recognize the play's unresolved mother-son conflict. *Soul Gone Home* was published in the July 1937 issue of *One Act Play* magazine, has been performed a number of times since then, and was produced as an opera by Ulysses Kay in 1951. Scholars and critics have been alternately bewildered and intrigued by this brief play, which mixes naturalism and surrealism, comedy and the tragic, in the sardonic darkness of Hughes's urban fantasy.

The title *Soul Gone Home* evokes the lyrical emotionalism of a gospel hymn, but the play itself refuses such sentimentality. The play opens in a "bare, ugly, dirty" tenement room in an unnamed northern city, where a Mother kneels weeping beside

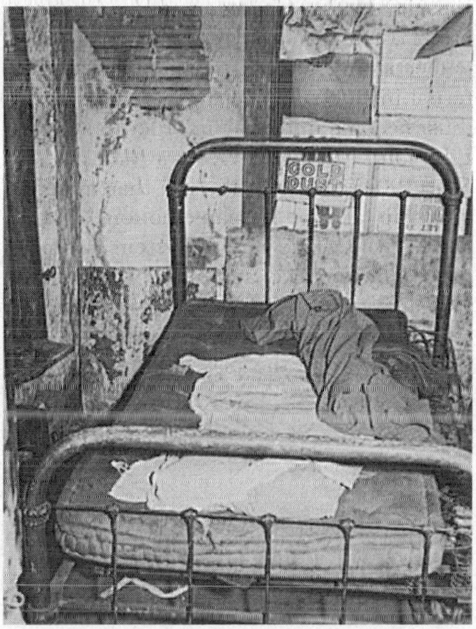

"Room in rooming house for negroes. Chicago, Illinois" (1941). Photo by Russell Lee.

the body of her Son lying on a cot. The Mother's grief is simulated, Hughes's directions indicate, and the action that follows deepens this discrepancy between the ideal of the sorrowing mother and the realities of family relationships in this harsh urban setting. When Ronnie, her son, rises from the dead, he charges her with neglect: "You been a hell of a mama!" Having seen his life for what it was during his brief stay in the spirit world, Ronnie accuses his mother, who earns her living as a prostitute, of letting him grow up in the streets, putting him to work selling newspapers as soon as he could walk, and contributing to the tuberculosis that killed him by failing to feed him properly. For her part, his mother accuses him of ingratitude, of causing her pain at birth, and of failing to earn his keep. Like his, her speech is distinguished by its darkly comic streetwise vernacular: "Well, damn your hide, you ain't even decent dead." But while *Soul Gone Home* portrays an intimate landscape of incrimination and failure, its condemnation is directed toward a racially unjust society that forces the black urban poor to pit love against survival. Even Ronnie must acknowledge that his mother's claim not to have enough money to buy him milk and eggs was valid. Like BERTOLT BRECHT's antiwar play *Mother Courage and Her Children* (1941), Hughes's play dramatizes a social and economic system in which normal maternal instincts are a luxury for those who must become unfeeling in order to survive. Like John Millington Synge's *Riders to the Sea* (1904), it shows the toll that material hardship takes on human emotion.

The white face of this system is represented by the two ambulance attendants who arrive in the play's closing moments to take Ronnie's body to the undertaker. For the first time in the play, mother and son act in unison. When the men enter the room, they are met by the spectacle of a grieving mother weeping "hysterically." As it was in the play's opening moments, the scene of grief is a performance, this time for a white America that is denied access to the lives of those it marginalizes. Like the country beyond it, the tenement room is a theater with forestages and backstages, and its inhabitants are actors to their outside audience. The final image of *Soul Gone Home* is of the Mother, now alone, powdering (or whitening) her face in a mirror in order to attract that evening's customers. In a play so deeply engaged with questions of simulation and role-playing, race may be the most pervasive performance of all.

Hughes stressed on several occasions that *Soul Gone Home* should be performed with attention to its comedy. In reference to the operatic version of the play he wrote: "[I]t is NOT a heavy tragic sentimental play. . . . There should be as many laughs as possible in the way the SON's part is written and played—otherwise the tragi-comedy will not come through, and it will be merely an over sentimental and unpleasantly grim piece." He added: "[B]oth of [the characters] are hard-boiled marginal people, slum-shocked products of the rip tides of life." By playing sentimentality against itself and bringing humor to such painful subjects, Hughes allows the play's ironies and outrages to be experienced in jarring, unsettling ways. And by crossing the boundaries separating realism from nonrealistic dramatic modes, he incorporates in social commentary the surreal, the self-consciously theatrical, and the macabre. It is a short distance from *Soul Gone Home* to the more recent plays of Amiri Baraka, AUGUST WILSON, and SUZAN-LORI PARKS.

S.G.

Soul Gone Home

CHARACTERS

THE MOTHER
THE SON
TWO MEN

Night.

[*A tenement room, bare, ugly, dirty. An unshaded electric-light bulb. In the middle of the room a cot on which the body of a* NEGRO YOUTH *is lying. His hands are folded across his chest. There are pennies on his eyes.*[1] *He is a soul gone home.*

As the curtain rises, his MOTHER, *a large, middle-aged woman in a red sweater, kneels weeping beside the cot, loudly simulating grief.*]

MOTHER Oh, Gawd! Oh, Lawd! Why did you take my son from me? Oh, Gawd, why did you do it? He was all I had! Oh, Lawd, what am I gonna do? [*Looking at the dead boy and stroking his head*] Oh, son! Oh, Ronnie! Oh, my boy, speak to me! Ronnie, say something to me! Son, why don't you talk to your mother? Can't you see she's bowed down in sorrow? Son, speak to me, just a word! Come back from the spirit world and speak to me! Ronnie, come back from the dead and speak to your mother!

SON [*lying there dead as a doornail. Speaking loudly*] I wish I wasn't dead, so I *could* speak to you. You been a hell of a mama!

MOTHER [*falling back from the cot in astonishment, but still on her knees*] Ronnie! Ronnie! What's that you say? What you sayin' to your mother? [*Wild-eyed*] Is you done opened your mouth and spoke to me?

SON I said you a hell of a mama!

MOTHER [*rising suddenly and backing away, screaming loudly*] Awo-ooo-o! Ronnie, that ain't you talkin'!

SON Yes, it is me talkin', too! I say you been a no-good mama.

MOTHER What for you talkin' to me like that, Ronnie? You ain't never said nothin' like that to me before.

SON I know it, but I'm dead now—and I can say what I want to say. [*Stirring*] You done called on me to talk, ain't you? Lemme take these pennies off my eyes so I can see. [*He takes the coins off his eyes, throws them across the room, and sits up in bed. He is a very dark boy in a torn white shirt. He looks hard at his mother.*] Mama, you know you ain't done me right.

MOTHER What you mean, I ain't done you right? [*She is rooted in horror.*] What you mean, huh?

SON You know what I mean.

1. In the 18th and 19th centuries, African Americans often put coins on the eyes of the dead to keep them closed and, in accordance with West African folk tradition, provide the deceased with money to pay for the journey to the spirit world.

MOTHER No, I don't neither. [*Trembling violently*] What you mean comin' back to haunt your poor old mother? Ronnie, what does you mean?

SON [*leaning forward*] I'll tell you just what I mean! You been a bad mother to me.

MOTHER Shame! Shame! Shame, talkin' to your mama that away. Damn it! Shame! I'll slap your face. [*She starts toward him, but he rolls his big white eyes at her, and she backs away.*] Me, what borned you! Me, what suffered the pains o' death to bring you into this world! Me, what raised you up, what washed your dirty didies.[2] [*Sorrowfully*] And now I'm left here mighty nigh prostrate 'cause you gone from me! Ronnie, what you mean talkin' to *me* like that—what brought you into this world?

SON You never did feed me good, that's what I mean! Who wants to come into the world hongry, and go out the same way?

MOTHER What you mean hongry? When I had money, ain't I fed you?

SON [*Sullenly*] Most of the time you ain't had no money.

MOTHER 'Twarn't my fault then.

SON 'Twarnt *my* fault then.

MOTHER [*defensively*] You always was so weak and sickly, you couldn't earn nothin' sellin' papers.

SON I know it.

MOTHER You never was no use to me.

SON So you just lemme grow up in the street, and I ain't had no manners nor morals, neither.

MOTHER Manners and morals? Ronnie, where'd you learn all them big words?

SON I learnt 'em just now in the spirit-world.

MOTHER [*coming nearer*] But you ain't been dead no more'n an hour.

SON That's long enough to learn a lot.

MOTHER Well, what else did you find out?

SON I found out you was a hell of a mama puttin' me out in the cold to sell papers soon as I could even walk.

MOTHER What? You little liar!

SON If I'm lyin', I'm dyin'! And lettin' me grow up all bowlegged and stunted from undernourishment.

MOTHER Under-nurse-mint?

SON Undernourishment. You heard what the doctor said last week?

MOTHER Naw, what'd he say?

SON He said I was dyin' o' undernourishment, that's what he said. He said I had TB 'cause I didn't have enough to eat never when I were a child. And he said I couldn't get well, nohow eating nothin' but beans ever since I been sick. Said I needed milk and eggs. And you said you ain't got no money for milk and eggs, which I know you ain't. [*Gently*] We never had no money, mama, not even since you took up hustlin' on the streets.

MOTHER Son, money ain't everything.

SON Naw, but when you got TB you have to have milk and eggs.

MOTHER [*advancing sentimentally*] Anyhow, I love you, Ronnie!

SON [*rudely*] Sure you love me—but here I am dead.

MOTHER [*angrily*] Well, damn your hide, you ain't even decent dead. If you was, you wouldn't be sittin' there jawin' at your mother when she's sheddin' every tear she's got for you tonight.

2. Diapers.

SON First time you ever did cry for me, far as I know.

MOTHER 'Tain't! You's a liar! I cried when I borned you—you was such a big child—ten pounds.

SON Then *I* did the cryin' after that, I reckon.

MOTHER [*proudly*] Sure, I could of let you die, but I didn't. Naw, I kept you with me—off and on. And I lost the chance to marry many a good man, too—if it weren't for you. No man wants to take care o' nobody else's child. [*Self-pityingly*] You been a burden to me, Randolph.

SON [*angrily*] What did you have me for then, in the first place?

MOTHER How could I help havin' you, you little bastard? Your father ruint me—and you's the result. And I been worried with you for sixteen years. [*Disgustedly*] Now, just when you get big enough to work and do me some good, you have to go and die.

SON I sure am dead!

MOTHER But you ain't decent dead! Here you come back to haunt your poor old mama, and spoil her cryin' spell, and spoil the mournin'. [*There is the noise of an ambulance gong outside. The* MOTHER *goes to the window and looks down into the street. Turns to* SON.] Ronnie, lay down quick! Here comes the city's ambulance to take you to the undertaker's. Don't let them white men see you dead, sitting up here quarrelin' with your mother. Lay down and fold your hands back like I had 'em.

SON [*passing his hand across his head*] All right, but gimme that comb yonder and my stocking cap. I don't want to go out of here with my hair standin' straight up in front, even if I is dead. [*The* MOTHER *hands him a comb and his stocking cap. The* SON *combs his hair and puts the cap on. Noise of men coming up the stairs.*]

MOTHER Hurry up, Ronnie, they'll be here in no time.

SON Aw, they got another flight to come yet. Don't rush me, ma!

MOTHER Yes, but I got to put these pennies back on your eyes, boy! [*She searches in a corner for the coins as her* SON *lies down and folds his hands, stiff in death. She finds the coins and puts them nervously on his eyes, watching the door meanwhile. A knock.*] Come in.

[*Enter two* MEN *in the white coats of city health employees.*]

MAN Somebody sent for us to get the body of Ronnie Bailey? Third floor, apartment five.

MOTHER Yes, sir, here he is! [*Weeping loudly*] He's my boy! Oh, Lawd, he's done left me! Oh, Lawdy, he's done gone home! His soul's gone home! Oh, what am I gonna do? Mister! Mister! Mister, the Lawd's done took him home! [*As the* MEN *unfold the stretchers, she continues to weep hysterically. They place the boy's thin body on the stretchers and cover it with a rubber cloth. Each man takes his end of the stretchers. Silently, they walk out the door as the* MOTHER *wails.*] Oh, my son! Oh, my boy! Come back, come back, come back! Ronnie, come back! [*One loud scream as the door closes*] Awo-ooo-o!

[*As the footsteps of the men die down on the stairs, the* MOTHER *becomes suddenly quiet. She goes to a broken mirror and begins to rouge and powder her face. In the street the ambulance gong sounds fainter and fainter in the distance. The* MOTHER *takes down an old fur coat from a nail and puts it on. Before she leaves, she smooths back the quilts on the cot from which the dead boy has been removed. She looks into the mirror again, and once more whitens her face with powder. She dons a red hat. From a handbag she takes a cigarette, lights it, and walks slowly out the door. At the door she switches off the light. The hallway is dimly illuminated. She turns before closing the door, looks back into the room, and speaks.*]

MOTHER Tomorrow, Ronnie, I'll buy you some flowers—if I can pick up a dollar tonight. You was a hell of a no-good son, I swear!

Curtain.

BERTOLT BRECHT

1898–1956

ARGUABLY the most influential dramatist of the twentieth century, Bertolt Brecht developed and popularized a provocative form of theater that has changed the course of theater history. Through dozens of plays and adaptations, elaborate theories of acting, and a whole new approach to theatrical performance, Brecht touched every aspect of theater making and imposed on it his distinct style and method. Collaborating with leading musicians, writers, actors, and designers, such as the composers Kurt Weill and Hanns Eisler, the writer Elisabeth Hauptmann, the actor Helene Weigel (Brecht's wife), and the designer Caspar Neher, Brecht sought to combine these different arts into a new and jarring theatrical experience. He was also intrigued by radio and film, the newest media at the time, and sought to transform the theater in their light, making sure that it would remain "up to date," as he liked to put it. Brecht wanted to create new theater fit for an age dominated by science and progress. The product also of an intensely felt political and social vision, Brecht's reform sought above all to change the relation between theater and its audience, seeking to instill in the audience a critical and analytical attitude. The lasting impact of his work can be measured by the fact that the adjective *Brechtian* has long ceased to refer to Brecht's particular reforms and practices, and often stands for much modernist theater in general.

Born in the city of Augsburg in southern Germany, Brecht studied philosophy and medicine in Munich; but in 1924, he left Munich in order to work with Max Reinhardt, the acclaimed director of the Deutsches Theater in Berlin. By that time, he had already won some recognition with a number of plays, including *Baal* (1922), *Drums in the Night* (1922), and *In the Jungle of Cities* (1923; 1927). Influenced by the episodic structures and jagged style of German expressionist playwrights such as Ernst Toller (1893–1939) and Georg Kaiser (1878–1945), these plays are set in a world whose social fabric has broken down; even the language spoken by the characters is ruptured, shifting abruptly from colloquial speech to abstract metaphysical and religious terms, never resting in a single, stable idiom.

In the course of the 1920s, Brecht gradually moved away from the topics and the characteristic language of his early expressionist plays, although he retained their episodic structure. Increasingly, his theater became a vehicle for understanding, analyzing, and criticizing the social world. *Man Equals Man* (1926) is a good example of this change, focused as it is on the analysis of a single problem: the transformation of a porter, Galy Gay, into a cold-blooded soldier, or rather into a "human fighting machine," as the play puts it. A similar purpose of critical analysis informs *The Rise and Fall of the City of Mahagonny* (1927; 1930), which identifies different forms of greed and consumption in a capitalist Sodom and Gomorrah. Brecht's greatest success during this period was *The Threepenny Opera* (1928), inspired by John Gay's *Beggar's Opera* (1728). *The Threepenny Opera* depicts a reality as cold as that of *Mahagonny:* the criminal underworld of London, where the king of the beggars, Peachum, and a crook, Macheath, fight for Peachum's daughter. This criminal sphere itself is not the main object of critique, however; instead, it functions as a metaphor for the criminality of capitalism. Though never a member of the Communist Party, Brecht shared with Marxist intellectuals an interest in power relations, and he sought to expose, through his plays, the hidden mechanisms of exploitation. Theater for him had become part of the struggle for a better society.

Even though the subject matter of Brecht's plays had grown more sober during the 1920s, their form and style remained exuberant. *Man Equals Man*, *Mahagonny*, and *The Threepenny Opera*—as well as many subsequent works, including *THE GOOD WOMAN OF SETZUAN* (1943)—were conceived as musical plays. In some cases, the music has come to overshadow the plays themselves. The popularity of *The Threepenny Opera*, perhaps the most entertaining work of them all, was due mostly to Kurt Weill's catchy songs; the best known is "Mack the Knife," which hit the top of the American charts after being recorded in the 1950s by Louis Armstrong and by Bobby Darin. On stage, however, Brecht did not so much use the conventions of musical theater as transform them. Rather than being smoothly integrated into these plays, the music was deliberately set apart. The same was true of the other elements of performance—dialogue, acting, set design. Brecht called this technique the "separation of the elements"; it was an attempt to use the different components of performance in such a way that they would interrupt one another rather than work in unison. Brecht and his collaborators thought of the resulting productions as antioperas: operas whose components had been pulled apart and put back together in a new and startling manner.

The result was the *Verfremdungseffekt* or the "estrangement effect," the attempt to "make strange" the entire experience of watching theater (an alternate translation sometimes used, "alienation effect," misleadingly implies an alienation from nature rather than the defamiliarization emphasized by Brecht). This was the heart of the theory of drama that made Brecht famous. Instead of enchanting the audience through well-integrated, harmonious spectacles, Brecht and his collaborators meant to disentangle the different sensory experiences associated with music, acting, scene design, language, and suspenseful plots and to set them against one another. Ultimately, they envisioned estrangement as the foundation of a new relation between theatrical performance and the audience, aimed at making the audience pause, examine, reflect, and criticize—that is, to look at the performance as if from a distance. Brecht once compared this attitude to that displayed by spectators at a boxing match or a similar sporting event; such audiences examine the skill of the players, appreciating their strategies and techniques from a critical distance, rather than being drawn unreflectively into a simulated world.

The technique of estrangement also extended to acting. Whereas traditionally the actor was supposed to inhabit the role completely, Brecht wanted his actors to remind the audience that they were only playing, that they were pretending to be another person for the duration of the performance. Put in the language of the theater, this meant that actor and role were to be clearly distinguished. Accomplishing this separation was a difficult task, but Brecht helped the actors by often having them speak about the character they are impersonating in the third person—commenting on the role as if from the outside. To illustrate his ideal of estranged acting, Brecht used the example of a courtroom in which witnesses are asked to demonstrate to the jury how a particular accident occurred. They take on different roles, Brecht explains, and go through the action, but do not seek to become completely absorbed in their performance. They never lose sight of their specific purpose. To encourage playgoers to shift their attention from the "what" (what happened) to the "how" (how did it happen), Brecht often gave away the plot at the beginning of each scene, sometimes writing a brief summary on a half-curtain. The audience (the "jury") was meant to analyze the events depicted on stage, focusing on how they had taken place and how they could be altered, rather than be engrossed by the suspense.

The final dimension of estrangement Brecht employed was geographic. Many of his plays are set in non-European locales: America (*Jungle of Cities; Mahagonny; St. Joan of the Stockyards* [1932]), South Asia (*Man Equals Man*), China (*The Good Woman of Setzuan*), Japan (*The Yea Sayer* [1930]). Brecht's goal here was not to represent, as accurately as possible, these different cultures. Instead he used settings that were foreign (to his German audience) to facilitate a distanced, analytical attitude toward the events depicted on stage, rather than one complicated by familiar investments and opinions. At the same time, however, Brecht was genuinely influenced by the tradition of Chinese acting and by the Japanese noh theater; his play *The Yea Sayer,* for example, is based on the noh play *Taniko* (fifteenth century).

The geographic displacement of the plays was mirrored by Brecht's later life. Fearing rise of National Socialism, he fled first to Denmark in 1933 and then to the United States in 1941, where he tried and mostly failed to produce his plays or make a living by writing Hollywood screenplays. In 1947, as the McCarthyite anticommunist witch hunts began, Brecht was called before the House Un-American Activities Committee (HUAC); he left the United States directly after the harrowing experience, going first to Switzerland and then, in 1949, to East Germany, where he built the Berliner Ensemble into one of the premier theaters of the world. It was during the years in exile that he wrote not only some of his best-known plays, including *Mother Courage* (1941), *The Life of Galileo Galilei* (1943), and *The Good Woman of Setzuan,* but also his adaptation of Aeschylus's *Antigone* (1948; his other famous adaptation, of SHAKESPEARE's *Coriolanus,* was written and left incomplete in 1952). In his last years, Brecht withdrew from the public eye, though he was accompanied, as he had been throughout his life, not only by his wife, Helene Weigel, but also by a number of lovers; indeed, many of his plays were collaborations with lovers (especially Elisabeth Hauptmann). He died in East Berlin in 1956, having become the most important cultural representative of socialist East Germany.

The Good Woman of Setzuan, written between 1930 and 1942 but not published until 1953, combines many of Brecht's characteristic techniques. It is set in a remote locale, the Chinese province of Sichuan (spelled "Sezuan" by Brecht and "Setzuan" in the following translation). A prelude, interludes, and the play's scenes are organized episodically and not into a tightly constructed plot; the play is also scattered with songs, written by Paul Dessau, that interrupt the flow of the action. In accordance with Brecht's theory

Brecht and Elizabeth Hauptmann working, Berlin, 1927.

of acting, actors address the audience directly, commenting on the action and explaining their problems and thus destroying any illusion of realism. Brecht worked on this play over a long period of time—precisely the period in which he formulated the tenets of his theory of estrangement. It therefore became the chief representative of estranged theater, or what Brecht himself preferred to call "epic theater."

Like many of Brecht's plays, *The Good Woman of Setzuan* presents a relatively simple dilemma: the inability of the female protagonist, Shen Te, to be good in the world as it is. Brecht even uses a didactic genre, the parable, to drive this point home: three gods visit Setzuan in order to find a single good person. The only good person they can find, the only one to offer them shelter, is the prostitute Shen Te, whom they reward by giving her a considerable sum of money. They then leave her to her own devices, urging her only to remain good. Doing so, however, is not all that easy. Shen Te uses the money to buy a tobacco store. As a good person, she soon begins taking in all kinds of people in need and distributing food to the poor, until finally the tobacco store itself is in danger of failing. It is at this point that she calls on the services of Shui Ta, her hard-nosed cousin, to keep her business afloat. Immediately, Shui Ta cuts down on Shen Te's philanthropy, and thus restores her business to a sound economic footing. Therein lies the play's central concern: being a good person and getting by in this world are mutually incompatible goals.

The play presents this point through an intriguing variation on the estrangement technique—Shen Te and Shui Ta are the same person and are played by the same actor. The device is revealed to the audience relatively early, when the change in costume occurs in front of the spectators' eyes; yet all but one of the other characters on the stage remain in the dark.

The 1957 Berliner Ensemble production of *The Good Person of Szechwan*.

Brecht thereby ensures that the audience has more information at its disposal than the characters and can thus observe their motivations and actions. No attention is wasted on a state of suspense, trying to discover this identity (the "what"); the focus instead is entirely on understanding why Shen Te depends on Shui Ta. Brecht employs a split character to show not psychological conflict but social conflict.

Another source of dramatic conflict is the demand made by the gods that Shen Te must be good, which fails to take into account whether she can afford goodness. The state of the world, the fact that the world as it is does not allow a person be good and survive, does not concern them. This discrepancy between the world and the gods is mediated by a man named Wong, a water carrier. No angel himself, Wong knows what this world requires and how it forces those who live in it to behave. At the same time, he honors the gods, striving to please them as best he can, even as he recognizes the impossibility of their demands. He seeks shelter for them and tries to hide most people's indifference toward them. He is a figure of compromise and attempts to mediate the clash between the gods and the harsh realities of the world—with limited success.

Fueling this clash is not just the gods' disinterest in the world but ultimately their ignorance of it. Wong first recognizes them because their very appearance bears no traces of labor; they are creatures of leisure who know nothing of the world's hard realities; their conception of goodness is merely a lofty ideal. In particular, the gods refuse to interfere in the area of economics, assuming instead that morality and economics have nothing to do with one another. They cling to Shen Te's goodness without recognizing that it depends on the constant interventions of her harder self, of which the gods disapprove. By revealing to the audience that Shui Ta is just the other side of Shen Te, Brecht constructs a disjunction between the audience and the gods of which only the audience is aware. The gods are thus in a position of ignorance and the audience, of knowledge.

Like Brecht's other didactic plays, *The Good Woman of Setzuan* does not offer, or preach, a particular solution to the dilemma it presents, such as a socialist society or a new conception of goodness. What it does do, however, is suggest a problem or a set of contradictions, here between the conception of goodness imposed by the gods and the (economic) requisites of the world. It is clear that such a contradiction offers two lines of attack: to get rid of the gods or to get rid of the economic system that does not allow for goodness.

These two consequences are suggested throughout, but they come to the fore in the final scene, which is a trial. Now the contradictions on which the entire play is built are brought into the open: the audience, both onstage and offstage, has to make up its mind. Indeed, trial scenes can be found frequently in Brecht's works, for they offer an opportunity to expose false morals, false laws, and other abuses. At the same time, trial scenes resonate with Brecht's ideal audience: an audience willing to make its own judgments and to come to its own conclusions.

Brecht's theater shaped many of the most important theater makers of the twentieth century, including the German experimental writers Heiner Müller and Peter Weiss, the British feminist playwright CARYL CHURCHILL, and the Brazilian political dramatist Augusto Boal. That they, despite their enormous differences, all refer to Brecht as their primary influence testifies to the long and varied impact he has had on contemporary theater the world over. This unparalleled influence was due to Brecht's ability to institute a coherent theater reform in every dimension of performance, a reform that other artists could then adopt, alter, or rebel against. But despite all his fame, Brecht did not achieve—or at least he did not fully achieve—his ultimate end: namely, to transform the theater from a vehicle of entertainment into a vehicle of critical thought. His legacy is thus an ambiguous one: he single-handedly changed the course of theater history, and yet this change fell short of his grand goal.

M.P.

The Good Woman of Setzuan[1]

CHARACTERS

WONG, *a water seller*
THREE GODS
SHEN TE, *a prostitute, later a shopkeeper*
MRS. SHIN, *former owner of Shen Te's shop*
A family of eight (HUSBAND, WIFE, BROTHER, SISTER-IN-LAW, GRANDFATHER, NEPHEW, NIECE, BOY)
An UNEMPLOYED MAN
A CARPENTER
MRS. MI TZU, *Shen Te's landlady*
Mr. SHUI TA
YANG SUN, *an unemployed pilot, later a factory manager*
An OLD WHORE
A POLICEMAN
An OLD MAN
An OLD WOMAN, *his wife*
Mr. SHU FU, *a barber*
MRS. YANG, *mother of Yang Sun*
GENTLEMEN, VOICES, PRIEST, WAITER, *children (three), etc.*

Prologue

At the gates of the half-Westernized city of Setzuan. Evening. WONG *the water seller*[2] *introduces himself to the audience.*

WONG I sell water here in the city of Setzuan. It isn't easy. When water is scarce, I have long distances to go in search of it, and when it is plentiful, I have no income. But in our part of the world there is nothing unusual about poverty. Many people think only the gods can save the situation. And I hear from a cattle merchant—who travels a lot—that some of the highest gods are on their way here at this very moment. Informed sources have it that heaven is quite disturbed at all the complaining. I've been coming out here to the city gates for three days now to bid these gods welcome. I want to be the first to greet them. What about those fellows over there? No, no, they *work*. And that one there has ink on his fingers, he's no god, he must be a clerk from the cement factory. *Those* two are another story. They look as though they'd like to beat you. But gods don't need to beat you, do they? [THREE GODS *appear*.] What about those three? Old-fashioned clothes—dust on their feet—they *must* be gods! [*He throws himself at their feet.*] Do with me what you will, illustrious ones!

FIRST GOD [*With an ear trumpet.*] Ah! [*He is pleased.*] So we were expected?

WONG [*Giving them water.*] Oh, yes. And I *knew* you'd come.

FIRST GOD We need somewhere to stay the night. You know of a place?

1. Translated by Eric Bentley.
2. The "city of Setzuan" is Chengdu, the capital of Sichuan (Setzuan), a province in Western China. However, the Chinese setting of this play is drawn largely from Brecht's imagination, not from historical or geographical fact.

WONG The whole town is at your service, illustrious ones! What sort of a place would you like?

[*The* GODS *eye each other.*]

FIRST GOD Just try the first house you come to, my son.

WONG That would be Mr. Fo's place.

FIRST GOD Mr. Fo.

WONG One moment! [*He knocks at the first house.*]

VOICE FROM MR. FO'S No!

[WONG *returns a little nervously.*]

WONG It's too bad. Mr. Fo isn't in. And his servants don't dare do a thing without his consent. He'll have a fit when he finds out who they turned away, won't he?

FIRST GOD [*Smiling.*] He will, won't he?

WONG One moment! The next house is Mr. Cheng's. Won't he be thrilled!

FIRST GOD Mr. Cheng

[WONG *knocks.*]

VOICE FROM MR. CHENG'S Keep your gods. We have our own troubles!

WONG [*Back with the* GODS.] Mr. Cheng is very sorry, but he has a houseful of relations. I think some of them are a bad lot, and naturally, he wouldn't like you to see them.

THIRD GOD Are we so terrible?

WONG Well, only with bad people, of course. Everyone knows the province of Kwan is always having floods.

SECOND GOD Really? How's that?

WONG Why, because they're so irreligious.

SECOND GOD Rubbish. It's because they neglected the dam.

FIRST GOD [*To* SECOND.] Sh! [*To* WONG.] You're still in hopes, aren't you, my son?

WONG Certainly. All Setzuan is competing for the honor! What happened up to now is pure coincidence. I'll be back. [*He walks away, but then stands undecided.*]

SECOND GOD What did I tell you?

THIRD GOD It *could* be pure coincidence.

SECOND GOD The same coincidence in Shun, Kwan, and Setzuan? People just aren't religious any more, let's face the fact. Our mission has failed!

FIRST GOD Oh come, we might run into a good person any minute.

THIRD GOD How did the resolution read? [*Unrolling a scroll and reading from it.*] "The word can stay as it is if enough people are found [*At the word "found" he unrolls it a little more*] living lives worthy of human beings." Good people, that is. Well, what about this water seller himself? *He's* good, or I'm very much mistaken.

SECOND GOD You're very much mistaken. When he gave us a drink, I had the impression there was something odd about the cup. Well, look! [*He shows the cup to the* FIRST GOD.]

FIRST GOD A false bottom!

SECOND GOD The man is a swindler.

FIRST GOD Very well, count *him* out. That's one man among millions. And as a matter of fact, we only need one on *our* side. These atheists are saying, "The world must be changed because no one can *be* good and *stay* good." No one, eh? I say: let us find one—just one—and we have those fellows where we want them!

THIRD GOD [*To* WONG.] Water seller, is it so hard to find a place to stay?

WONG Nothing could be easier. It's just me. I don't go about it right.

THIRD GOD Really?

[*He returns to the others. A* GENTLEMAN *passes by.*]

WONG Oh dear, they're catching on. [*He accosts the* GENTLEMAN.] Excuse the intrusion, dear sir, but three gods have just turned up. Three of the very highest. They need a place for the night. Seize this rare opportunity—to have real gods as your guests!

GENTLEMAN [*laughing*] A new way of finding free rooms for a gang of crooks. [*Exit* GENTLEMAN.]

WONG [*shouting at him.*] Godless rascal! Have you no religion, gentlemen of Setzuan? [*Pause*]. Patience, illustrious ones! [*Pause.*] There's only one person left. Shen Te, the prostitute. She *can't* say no. [*Calls up to a window.*] Shen Te!

[SHEN TE *opens the shutters and looks out.*]

WONG Shen Te, it's Wong. *They're* here, and nobody wants them. Will you take them?

SHEN TE Oh, no, Wong, I'm expecting a gentleman.

WONG Can't you forget about him for tonight?

SHEN TE The rent has to be paid by tomorrow or I'll be out on the street.

WONG This is no time for calculation, Shen Te.

SHEN TE Stomachs rumble even on the Emperor's birthday, Wong.

WONG Setzuan is one big dung hill!

SHEN TE Oh, very well! I'll hide till my gentleman has come and gone. Then I'll take them. [*She disappears.*]

WONG They mustn't see her gentleman or they'll know what she is.

FIRST GOD [*Who hasn't heard any of this.*] I think it's hopeless.

[*They approach* WONG.]

WONG [*Jumping, as he finds them behind him.*] A room has been found, illustrious ones! [*He wipes sweat off his brow.*]

SECOND GOD Oh, good.

THIRD GOD Let's see it.

WONG [*Nervously.*] Just a minute. It has to be tidied up a bit.

THIRD GOD Then we'll sit down here and wait.

WONG [*Still more nervous.*] No, no! [*Holding himself back.*] Too much traffic, you know.

THIRD GOD [*With a smile.*] Of course, if you *want* us to move.

[*They retire a little. They sit on a doorstep.* WONG *sits on the ground.*]

WONG [*After a deep breath.*] You'll be staying with a single girl—the finest human being in Setzuan!

THIRD GOD That's nice.

WONG [*To the audience.*] They gave me such a look when I picked up my cup just now.

THIRD GOD You're worn out, Wong.

WONG A little, maybe.

FIRST GOD Do people here have a hard time of it?

WONG The good ones do.

FIRST GOD What about yourself!

WONG You mean I'm not good. That's true. And I don't have an easy time either!

[During this dialogue, a GENTLEMAN *has turned up in front of Shen Te's House, and has whistled several times. Each time* WONG *has given a start.]*

THIRD GOD *[To* WONG, *softly.]* Psst! I think he's gone now.

WONG *[Confused and surprised.]* Ye-e-es.

[The GENTLEMAN *has left now, and* SHEN TE *has come down to the street.]*

SHEN TE *[softly.]* Wong!

[Getting no answer, she goes off down the street. WONG *arrives just too late, forgetting his carrying pole.]*

WONG *[Softly.]* Shen Te! Shen Te! *[To himself.]* So she's gone off to earn the rent. Oh dear, I can't go to the gods *again* with no room to offer them. Having failed in the service of the gods, I shall run to my den in the sewer pipe down by the river and hide from their sight!

[He rushes off. SHEN TE *returns, looking for him, but finding the* GODS. *She stops in confusion.]*

SHEN TE You are the illustrious ones? My name is Shen Te. It would please me very much if my simple room could be of use to you.

THIRD GOD Where is the water seller, Miss . . . Shen Te?

SHEN TE I missed him, somehow.

FIRST GOD Oh, he probably thought you weren't coming, and was afraid of telling us.

THIRD GOD *[Picking up the carrying pole.]* We'll leave this with you. He'll be needing it.

[Led by SHEN TE, *they go into the house. It grows dark, then light. Dawn. Again escorted by* SHEN TE, *who leads them through the half-light with a little lamp, the* GODS *take their leave.]*

FIRST GOD Thank you, thank you, dear Shen Te, for your elegant hospitality! We shall not forget! And give our thanks to the water seller—he showed us a good human being.

SHEN TE Oh, *I'm* not good. Let me tell you something: when Wong asked me to put you up, I hesitated.

FIRST GOD It's all right to hesitate if you then go ahead! And in giving us that room you did much more than you knew. You proved that good people still exist, a point that has been disputed of late—even in heaven. Farewell!

SECOND GOD Farewell!

THIRD GOD Farewell!

SHEN TE Stop, illustrious ones! I'm not sure you're right. I'd like to be good, it's true, but there's the rent to pay. And that's not all: I sell myself for a living. Even so I can't make ends meet, there's too much competition. I'd like to honor my father and mother and speak nothing but the truth and not covet my neighbor's house. I should love to stay with one man. But how? How is it done? Even breaking a few of your commandments, I can hardly manage.

FIRST GOD *[Clearing his throat.]* These thoughts are but, um, the misgivings of an unusually good woman!

THIRD GOD Good-bye, Shen Te! Give our regards to the water seller!

SECOND GOD And above all: be good! Farewell!

FIRST GOD Farewell!

THIRD GOD Farewell!

[They start to wave good-bye.]

SHEN TE But everything is so expensive, I don't feel sure I can do it!

SECOND GOD That's not in our sphere. We never meddle with economics.

THIRD GOD One moment. [*They stop.*] Isn't it true she might do better if she had more money?

SECOND GOD Come, come! How could we ever account for it Up Above?

FIRST GOD Oh, there are ways. [*They put their heads together and confer in dumb show. To* SHEN TE, *with embarrassment.*] As you say you can't pay your rent, well, um, we're not paupers, so of course we *insist* on paying for our room. [*Awkwardly thrusting money into her hands.*] There! [*Quickly.*] But don't tell anyone! The incident is open to misinterpretation.

SECOND GOD It certainly is!

FIRST GOD [*Defensively.*] But there's no law against it! It was never decreed that a god mustn't pay hotel bills!

[*The* GODS *leave.*]

1

A small tobacco shop. The shop is not as yet completely furnished and hasn't started doing business.

SHEN TE [*To the audience.*] It's three days now since the gods left. When they said they wanted to pay for the room, I looked down at my hand, and there was more than a thousand silver dollars! I bought a tobacco shop with the money, and moved in yesterday. I don't own the building, of course, but I can pay the rent, and I hope to do a lot of good here. Beginning with Mrs. Shin, who's just coming across the square with her pot. She had the shop before me, and yesterday she dropped in to ask for rice for her children. [*Enter* MRS. SHIN. *Both women bow.*] How do you do, Mrs. Shin.

MRS. SHIN How do you do, Miss Shen Te. You like your new home?

SHEN TE Indeed, yes. Did your children have a good night?

MRS. SHIN In that hovel? The youngest is coughing already.

SHEN TE Oh, dear!

MRS. SHIN You're going to learn a thing or two in these slums.

SHEN TE Slums? That's not what you said when you sold me the shop!

MRS. SHIN Now don't start nagging! Robbing me and my innocent children of their home and then calling it a slum! That's the limit!

[*She weeps.*]

SHEN TE [*Tactfully.*] I'll get your rice.

MRS. SHIN And a little cash while you're at it.

SHEN TE I'm afraid I haven't sold anything yet.

MRS. SHIN [*Screeching.*] I've got to have it. Strip the clothes from my back and then cut my throat, will you? I know what I'll do: I'll dump my children on your doorstep! [*She snatches the pot out of* SHEN TE's *hands.*]

SHEN TE Please don't be angry. You'll spill the rice.

[*Enter an elderly* HUSBAND *and* WIFE *with their shabbily dressed* NEPHEW.]

WIFE Shen Te, dear! You've come into money, they tell me. And we haven't a roof over our heads! A tobacco shop. We had one too. But it's gone. Could we spend the night here, do you think?

NEPHEW [*Appraising the shop.*] Not bad!

WIFE He's our nephew. We're inseparable!

MRS. SHIN And who are these . . . ladies and gentlemen?

SHEN TE They put me up when I first came in from the country. [*To the audience.*] Of course, when my small purse was empty, they put me out on the street, and they may be afraid I'll do the same to them [*To the newcomers, kindly.*] Come in, and welcome, though I've only one little room for you—it's behind the shop.

HUSBAND That'll do. Don't worry.

WIFE [*Bringing* SHEN TE *some tea.*] We'll stay over here, so we won't be in your way. Did you make it a tobacco shop in memory of your first real home? We can certainly give you a hint or two! That's one reason we came.

MRS. SHIN [*To* SHEN TE.] Very nice! As long as you have a few customers too!

HUSBAND Sh! A customer!

[*Enter an* UNEMPLOYED MAN, *in rags.*]

UNEMPLOYED MAN Excuse me. I'm unemployed.

[MRS. SHIN *laughs.*]

SHEN TE Can I help you?

UNEMPLOYED MAN Have you any damaged cigarettes? I thought there might be some damage when you're unpacking.

WIFE What nerve, begging for tobacco! [*Rhetorically.*] Why don't they ask for bread?

UNEMPLOYED MAN Bread is expensive. One cigarette butt and I'll be a new man.

SHEN TE [*Giving him cigarettes.*] That's very important—to be a new man. You'll be my first customer and bring me luck.

[*The* UNEMPLOYED MAN *quickly lights a cigarette, inhales, and goes off, coughing.*]

WIFE Was that right, Shen Te, dear?

MRS. SHIN If this is the opening of a shop, you can hold the closing at the end of the week.

HUSBAND I bet he had money on him.

SHEN TE Oh, no, he said he hadn't!

NEPHEW How d'you know he wasn't lying?

SHEN TE [*Angrily.*] How do you know he was?

WIFE [*Wagging her head.*] You're too good, Shen Te, dear. If you're going to keep this shop, you'll have to learn to say no.

HUSBAND Tell them the place isn't yours to dispose of. Belongs to . . . some relative who insists on all accounts being strictly in order . . .

MRS. SHIN That's right! What do you think you are—a philanthropist?

SHEN TE [*Laughing.*] Very well, suppose I ask you for my rice back, Mrs. Shin?

WIFE [*Combatively, at* MRS. SHIN.] So that's *her* rice?

[*Enter the* CARPENTER, *a small man.*]

MRS. SHIN [*Who, at the sight of him, starts to hurry away.*] See you tomorrow, Miss Shen Te! [*Exit* MRS. SHIN.]

CARPENTER Mrs. Shin, it's you I want!

WIFE [*To* SHEN TE.] Has she some claim on you?

SHEN TE She's hungry. That's a claim.

CARPENTER Are you the new tenant? And filling up the shelves already? Well, they're not yours till they're paid for, ma'am. I'm the carpenter, so I should know.

SHEN TE I took the shop "furnishings included."

CARPENTER You're in league with that Mrs. Shin, of course. All right. I demand my hundred silver dollars.

SHEN TE I'm afraid I haven't got a hundred silver dollars.

CARPENTER Then you'll find it. Or I'll have you arrested.

WIFE [*Whispering to* SHEN TE.] That relative: make it a cousin.

SHEN TE Can't it wait till next month?

CARPENTER No!

SHEN TE Be a little patient, Mr. Carpenter, I can't settle all claims at once.

CARPENTER Who's patient with me? [*He grabs a shelf from the wall.*] Pay up—or I take the shelves back!

WIFE Shen Te! Dear! Why don't you let your . . . cousin settle this affair? [*To* CARPENTER.] Put your claim in writing. Shen Te's cousin will see you get paid.

CARPENTER [*Derisively.*] Cousin, eh?

HUSBAND Cousin, yes.

CARPENTER I know these cousins!

NEPHEW Don't be silly. He's a personal friend of mine.

HUSBAND What a man! Sharp as a razor!

CARPENTER All right. I'll put my claim in writing. [*Puts shelf on floor, sits on it, writes out bill.*]

WIFE [*To* SHEN TE.] He'd tear the dress off your back to get his shelves. Never recognize a claim! That's my motto.

SHEN TE He's done a job, and wants something in return. It's shameful that I can't give it to him. What will the gods say?

HUSBAND You did your bit when you took *us* in.

[*Enter the* BROTHER, *limping, and the* SISTER-IN-LAW, *pregnant.*]

BROTHER [*To* HUSBAND *and* WIFE.] So this is where you're hiding out! There's family feeling for you! Leaving us on the corner!

WIFE [*Embarrassed, to* SHEN TE.] It's my brother and his wife. [*To them.*] Now stop grumbling, and sit quietly in that corner. [*To* SHEN TE.] It can't be helped. She's in her fifth month.

SHEN TE Oh yes. Welcome!

WIFE [*To the couple.*] Say thank you. [*They mutter something.*] The cups are there. [*To* SHEN TE.] Lucky you bought this shop when you did!

SHEN TE [*Laughing and bringing tea.*] Lucky indeed!

[*Enter* MRS. MI TZU, *the landlady.*]

MRS. MI TZU Miss Shen Te? I am Mrs. Mi Tzu, your landlady. I hope our relationship will be a happy one. I like to think I give my tenants modern, personalized service. Here is your lease. [*To the others, as* SHEN TE *reads the lease.*] There's nothing like the opening of a little shop, is there? A moment of true beauty! [*She is looking around.*] Not very much on the shelves, of course. But everything in the gods' good time! Where are your references, Miss Shen Te?

SHEN TE Do I *have* to have references?

MRS. MI TZU After all, I haven't a notion who you are!

HUSBAND Oh, *we'd* be glad to vouch for Miss Shen Te! We'd go through fire for her!

MRS. MI TZU And who may *you* be?

HUSBAND [*Stammering.*] Ma Fu, tobacco dealer.

MRS. MI TZU Where is your shop, Mr. . . . Ma Fu?

HUSBAND Well, um, I haven't got a shop—I've just sold it.

MRS. MI TZU I see. [*To* SHEN TE.] Is there no one else that knows you?

WIFE [*Whispering to* SHEN TE.] Your cousin! Your cousin!

MRS. MI TZU This is a respectable house, Miss Shen Te. I never sign a lease without certain assurances.

SHEN TE [*Slowly, her eyes downcast.*] I have . . . a cousin.

MRS. MI TZU On the square? Let's go over and see him. What does he do?

SHEN TE [*As before.*] He lives . . . in another city.

WIFE [*Prompting.*] Didn't you say he was in Shung?

SHEN TE That's right. Shung.

HUSBAND [*Prompting.*] I had his name on the tip of my tongue, Mr. . . .

SHEN TE [*With an effort.*] Mr. . . . Shui . . . Ta.

HUSBAND That's it! Tall, skinny fellow!

SHEN TE Shui Ta!

NEPHEW [*To* CARPENTER.] *You* were in touch with him, weren't you? About the shelves?

CARPENTER [*Surlily.*] Give him this bill. [*He hands it over.*] I'll be back in the morning. [*Exit* CARPENTER.]

NEPHEW [*Calling after him, but with his eyes on* MRS. MI TZU.] Don't worry! Mr. Shui Ta pays on the nail!

MRS. MI TZU [*Looking closely at* SHEN TE.] I'll be happy to make his acquaintance, Miss Shen Te. [*Exit* MRS. MI TZU.]

[*Pause.*]

WIFE By tomorrow morning she'll know more about you than you do yourself.

SISTER-IN-LAW [*To* NEPHEW.] This thing isn't built to last.

[*Enter* GRANDFATHER.]

WIFE It's Grandfather! [*To* SHEN TE.] Such a good old soul!

[*The* BOY *enters.*]

BOY [*Over his shoulder.*] Here they are!

WIFE And the boy, how he's grown! But he always could eat enough for ten.

[*Enter the* NIECE.]

WIFE [*To* SHEN TE.] Our little niece from the country. There are more of us now than in your time. The less we had, the more there were of us; the more there were of us, the less we had. Give me the key. We must protect ourselves from unwanted guests. [*She takes the key and locks the door.*] Just make yourself at home. I'll light the little lamp.

NEPHEW [*A big joke.*] I hope her cousin doesn't drop in tonight! The strict Mr. Shui Ta!

[SISTER-IN-LAW *laughs.*]

BROTHER [*Reaching for a cigarette.*] One cigarette more or less . . .

HUSBAND One cigarette more or less.

[*They pile into the cigarettes. The* BROTHER *hands a jug of wine round.*]

NEPHEW Mr. Shui Ta'll pay for it!

GRANDFATHER [*Gravely, to* SHEN TE.] How do you do?

[SHEN TE, *a little taken aback by the belatedness of the greeting, bows. She has the carpenter's bill in one hand, the landlady's lease in the other.*]

WIFE How about a bit of a song? To keep Shen Te's spirits up?

NEPHEW Good idea. Grandfather: you start!

SONG OF THE SMOKE

GRANDFATHER

I used to think (before old age beset me)
That brains could fill the pantry of the poor.
But where did all my cerebration get me?
I'm just as hungry as I was before.
So what's the use?
See the smoke float free
Into ever colder coldness!
It's the same with me

HUSBAND

The straight and narrow path leads to disaster
And so the crooked path I tried to tread.
That got me to disaster even faster.
(They say we shall be happy when we're dead.)
So what's the use?
See the smoke float free
Into ever colder coldness!
It's the same with me

NIECE

You older people, full of expectation,
At any moment now you'll walk the plank!
The future's for the younger generation!
Yes, even if that future is a blank.
So what's the use?
See the smoke float free
Into ever colder coldness!
It's the same with me.

NEPHEW [*To the* BROTHER.] Where'd you get that wine?

SISTER-IN-LAW [*Answering for the* BROTHER.] He pawned the sack of tobacco.

HUSBAND [*Stepping in.*] What? That tobacco was all we had to fall back on! You pig!

BROTHER *You'd* call a man a pig because your wife was frigid! Did you refuse to drink it?

[*They fight. The shelves fall over.*]

SHEN TE [*Imploringly.*] Oh don't! Don't break everything! Take it, take it all, but don't destroy a gift from the gods!

WIFE [*Disparagingly.*] This shop isn't big enough. I should never have mentioned it to Uncle and the others. When *they* arrive, it's going to be disgustingly overcrowded.

SISTER-IN-LAW And did you hear our gracious hostess? She cools off quick!

[*Voices outside. Knocking at the door.*]

UNCLE'S VOICE Open the door!

WIFE Uncle? Is that you, Uncle?

UNCLE'S VOICE Certainly, it's me. Auntie says to tell you she'll have the children here in ten minutes.

WIFE [*To* SHEN TE.] I'll have to let him in.

SHEN TE [*Who scarcely hears her.*]

The little lifeboat is swiftly sent down
Too many men too greedily
Hold on to it as they drown.

1a

Wong's den in a sewer pipe.

WONG [*Crouching there.*] All quiet! It's four days now since I left the city. The gods passed this way on the second day. I heard their steps on the bridge over there. They must be a long way off by this time, so I'm safe. [*Breathing a sigh of relief, he curls up and goes to sleep. In his dream the pipe becomes transparent, and the* GODS *appear. Raising an arm, as if in self-defense.*] I know, I know, illustrious ones! I found no one to give you a room—not in all Setzuan! There, it's out. Please continue on your way!

FIRST GOD [*Mildly.*] But you did find someone. Someone who took us in for the night, watched over us in our sleep, and in the early morning lighted us down to the street with a lamp.

WONG It was . . . Shen Te that took you in?

THIRD GOD Who else?

WONG And I ran away! "She isn't coming," I thought, "she just can't afford it."

GODS [*Singing.*]

O you feeble, well-intentioned, and yet feeble chap
Where there's need the fellow thinks there is no goodness!
When there's danger he thinks courage starts to ebb away!
Some people only see the seamy side!
What hasty judgment! What premature desperation!

WONG I'm *very* ashamed, illustrious ones.

FIRST GOD Do us a favor, water seller. Go back to Setzuan. Find Shen Te, and give us a report on her. We hear that she's come into a little money. Show interest in her goodness—for no one can be good for long if goodness is not in demand. Meanwhile we shall continue the search, and find other good people. After which, the idle chatter about the impossibility of goodness will stop!

[*The* GODS *vanish.*]

2

A knocking.

WIFE Shen Te! Someone at the door. Where is she anyway?

NEPHEW She must be getting the breakfast. Mr. Shui Ta will pay for it.

[*The* WIFE *laughs and shuffles to the door. Enter Mr.* SHUI TA *and the* CARPENTER.]

WIFE Who is it?

SHUI TA I am Miss Shen Te's cousin.

WIFE What??

SHUI TA My name is Shui Ta.

WIFE Her cousin?

NEPHEW Her cousin?

NIECE But that was a joke. She hasn't got a cousin.

HUSBAND So early in the morning?

BROTHER What's all the noise?

SISTER-IN-LAW This fellow says he's her cousin.

BROTHER Tell him to prove it.

NEPHEW Right. If you're Shen Te's cousin, prove it by getting the breakfast.

SHUI TA [*Whose regime begins as he puts out the lamp to save oil; loudly, to all present, asleep or awake.*] Would you all please get dressed! Customers will be coming! I wish to open my shop!

HUSBAND *Your* shop? Doesn't it belong to our good friend Shen Te?

[SHUI TA *shakes his head.*]

SISTER-IN-LAW So we've been cheated. Where *is* the little liar?

SHUI TA Miss Shen Te has been delayed. She wishes me to tell you there will be nothing she can do—now I am here.

WIFE [*Bowled over.*] I thought she was good!

NEPHEW Do you have to believe *him*?

HUSBAND I don't.

NEPHEW Then do something.

HUSBAND Certainly! I'll send out a search party at once. You, you, you, and you, go out and look for Shen Te. [*As the* GRANDFATHER *rises and makes for the door*] Not you, Grandfather, you and I will hold the fort.

SHUI TA You won't find Miss Shen Te. She has suspended her hospitable activity for an unlimited period. There are too many of you. She asked me to say: this is a tobacco shop, not a gold mine.

HUSBAND Shen Te never said a thing like that. Boy, food! There's a bakery on the corner. Stuff your shirt full when they're not looking!

SISTER-IN-LAW Don't overlook the raspberry tarts.

HUSBAND And don't let the policeman see you.

[*The* BOY *leaves.*]

SHUI TA Don't you depend on this shop now? Then why give it a bad name by stealing from the bakery?

NEPHEW Don't listen to him. Let's find Shen Te. She'll give him a piece of her mind.

SISTER-IN-LAW Don't forget to leave us some breakfast.

[BROTHER, SISTER-IN-LAW *and* NEPHEW *leave.*]

SHUI TA [*To the* CARPENTER.] You see, Mr. Carpenter, nothing has changed since the poet, eleven hundred years ago, penned these lines:

> A governor was asked what was needed
> To save the freezing people in the city.
> He replied:
> "A blanket ten thousand feet long
> To cover the city and all its suburbs."

[*He starts to tidy up the shop.*]

CARPENTER Your cousin owes me money. I've got witnesses. For the shelves.

SHUI TA Yes, I have your bill. [*He takes it out of his pocket.*] Isn't a hundred silver dollars rather a lot?

CARPENTER No deductions! I have a wife and children.

SHUI TA How many children?

CARPENTER Three.

SHUI TA I'll make you an offer. Twenty silver dollars.

[*The* HUSBAND *laughs.*]

CARPENTER You're crazy. Those shelves are real walnut.

SHUI TA Very well, Take them away.

CARPENTER What?

SHUI TA They cost too much. Please take them away.

WIFE Not bad! [*And she, too, is laughing.*]

CARPENTER [*A little bewildered.*] Call Shen Te, someone! [*To* SHUI TA.] She's good!

SHUI TA Certainly. She's ruined.

CARPENTER [*Provoked into taking some of the shelves.*] All right, you can keep your tobacco on the floor.

SHUI TA [*to the* HUSBAND.] Help him with the shelves.

HUSBAND [*Grins and carries one shelf over to the door where the* CARPENTER *now is.*] Good-bye, shelves!

CARPENTER [*To the* HUSBAND.] You dog! You want my family to starve?

SHUI TA I repeat my offer. I have no desire to keep my tobacco on the floor. Twenty silver dollars.

CARPENTER [*With desperate aggressiveness.*] One hundred!

[SHUI TA *shows indifference, looks through the window. The* HUSBAND *picks up several shelves.*]

CARPENTER [*To* HUSBAND.] You needn't smash them against the doorpost, you idiot! [*To* SHUI TA.] These shelves were made to measure. They're no use anywhere else!

SHUI TA Precisely.

[*The* WIFE *squeals with pleasure.*]

CARPENTER [*Giving up, sullenly.*] Take the shelves. Pay what you want to pay.

SHUI TA [*Smoothly.*] Twenty silver dollars.

[*He places two large coins on the table. The* CARPENTER *picks them up.*]

HUSBAND [*Brings the shelves back in.*] And quite enough too!

CARPENTER [*Slinking off.*] Quite enough to get drunk on.

HUSBAND [*Happily.*] Well, we got rid of *him*!

WIFE [*Weeping with fun, gives a rendition of the dialogue just spoken.*] "Real walnut," says he. "Very well, take them away," says his lordship. "I have three children," says he. "Twenty silver dollars," says his lordship. "They're no use anywhere else," says he. "Pre-cisely," said his lordship! [*She dissolves into shrieks of merriment.*]

SHUI TA And now: go!

HUSBAND What's that?

SHUI TA You're thieves, parasites. I'm giving you this chance. Go!

HUSBAND [*Summoning all his ancestral dignity.*] That sort deserves no answer. Besides, one should never shout on an empty stomach.

WIFE Where's that boy?

SHUI TA Exactly. The boy. I want no stolen goods in this shop. [*Very loudly.*] I strongly advise you to leave! [*But they remain seated, noses in the air. Quietly.*] As you wish. [SHUI TA *goes to the door. A* POLICEMAN *appears.* SHUI TA *bows.*] I am addressing the officer in charge of this precinct?

POLICEMAN That's right, Mr., um, what was the name, sir?

SHUI TA Mr. Shui Ta.

POLICEMAN Yes, of course, sir.

[*They exchange a smile.*]

SHUI TA Nice weather we're having.

POLICEMAN A little on the warm side, sir.

SHUI TA Oh, a little on the warm side.

HUSBAND [*Whispering to the* WIFE.] If he keeps it up till the boy's back, we're done for. [*Tries to signal* SHUI TA.]

SHUI TA [*Ignoring the signal.*] Weather, of course, is one thing indoors, another out on the dusty street!

POLICEMAN Oh, quite another, sir!

WIFE [*To the* HUSBAND.] It's all right as long as he's standing in the doorway—the boy will see him.

SHUI TA Step inside for a moment! It's quite cool indoors. My cousin and I have just opened the place. And we attach the greatest importance to being on good terms with the, um, authorities.

POLICEMAN [*Entering.*] Thank you, Mr. Shui Ta. It *is* cool!

HUSBAND [*Whispering to the* WIFE.] And now the boy *won't* see him.

SHUI TA [*Showing* HUSBAND *and* WIFE *to the* POLICEMAN.] Visitors, I think my cousin knows them. They were just leaving.

HUSBAND [*Defeated.*] Ye-e-es, we were . . . just leaving.

SHUI TA I'll tell my cousin you couldn't wait.

[*Noise from the street. Shouts of "Stop, Thief!"*]

POLICEMAN What's that?

[*The* BOY *is in the doorway with cakes and buns and rolls spilling out of his shirt. The* WIFE *signals desperately to him to leave. He gets the idea.*]

POLICEMAN No, you don't. [*He grabs the* BOY *by the collar.*] Where's all this from?

BOY [*Vaguely pointing.*] Down the street.

POLICEMAN [*Grimly.*] So that's it. [*Prepares to arrest the* BOY.]

WIFE [*Stepping in.*] And *we* knew nothing about it. [*To the* BOY.] Nasty little thief!

POLICEMAN [*Dryly.*] Can you clarify the situation, Mr. Shui Ta?

[SHUI TA *is silent.*]

POLICEMAN [*Who understands silence.*] Aha. You're all coming with me—to the station.

SHUI TA I can hardly say how sorry I am that *my* establishment . . .

WIFE Oh, he saw the boy leave not ten minutes ago!

SHUI TA And to conceal the theft asked a policeman in?

POLICEMAN Don't listen to her, Mr. Shui Ta, I'll be happy to relieve you of their presence one and all! [*To all three.*] Out!

[*He drives them before him.*]

GRANDFATHER [*Leaving last, gravely.*] Good morning!

POLICEMAN Good morning!

[SHUI TA, *left alone, continues to tidy up.* MRS. MI TZU *breezes in.*]

MRS. MI TZU *You're* her cousin, are you? Then have the goodness to explain what all this means—police dragging people from a respectable house! By what right does your Miss Shen Te turn my property into a house of assignation?—Well, as you see, I know all!

SHUI TA Yes. My cousin has the worst possible reputation: that of being poor.

MRS. MI TZU No sentimental rubbish, Mr. Shui Ta. Your cousin was a common . . .

SHUI TA Pauper. Let's use the uglier word.

MRS. MI TZU I'm speaking of her conduct, not her earnings. But there must have *been* earnings, or how did she buy all this? Several elderly gentlemen took care of it, I suppose. I repeat: this is a respectable house! I have tenants who prefer not to live under the same roof with such a person.

SHUI TA [*Quietly.*] How much do you want?

MRS. MI TZU [*He is ahead of her now.*] I beg your pardon.

SHUI TA To reassure yourself. To reassure your tenants. How much will it cost?

MRS. MI TZU You're a cool customer.

SHUI TA [*Picking up the lease.*] The rent is high. [*He reads on.*] I assume it's payable by the month?

MRS. MI TZU Not in her case.

SHUI TA [*Looking up.*] What?

MRS. MI TZU Six months' rent payable in advance. Two hundred silver dollars.

SHUI TA Six . . . ! Sheer usury! And where am I to find it?

MRS. MI TZU You should have thought of that before.

SHUI TA Have you no heart, Mrs. Mi Tzu? It's true Shen Te acted foolishly, being kind to all those people, but she'll improve with time. I'll see to it she does. She'll work her fingers to the bone to pay her rent, and all the time be as quiet as a mouse, as humble as a fly.

MRS. MI TZU Her social background . . .

SHUI TA Out of the depths! She came out of the depths! And before she'll go back there, she'll work, sacrifice, shrink from nothing. . . . Such a tenant is worth her weight in gold, Mrs. Mi Tzu.

MRS. MI TZU It's silver we were talking about, Mr. Shui Ta. Two hundred silver dollars or . . .

[*Enter the* POLICEMAN.]

POLICEMAN Am I intruding, Mr. Shui Ta?

MRS. MI TZU This tobacco shop is well known to the police, I see.

POLICEMAN Mr. Shui Ta has done us a service, Mrs. Mi Tzu. I am here to present our official felicitations!

MRS. MI TZU That means less than nothing to me, sir. Mr. Shui Ta, all I can say is: I hope your cousin will find my terms acceptable. Good day, gentlemen. [*Exit.*]

SHUI TA Good day, ma'am.

[*Pause.*]

POLICEMAN Mrs. Mi Tzu a bit of a stumbling block, sir?

SHUI TA She wants six months' rent in advance.

POLICEMAN And you haven't got it, eh? [SHUI TA *is silent.*] But surely you can get it, sir? A man like you?

SHUI TA What about a woman like Shen Te?

POLICEMAN You're not staying, sir?

SHUI TA No, and I won't be back. Do you smoke?

POLICEMAN [*Taking two cigars, and placing them both in his pocket.*] Thank you, sir—I see your point, Miss Shen Te—let's mince no words—Miss Shen Te lived by selling herself. "What else could she have done?" you ask.

"How else was she to pay the rent?" True. But the fact remains, Mr. Shui Ta, it is not respectable. Why not? A very deep question. But, in the first place, love—love isn't bought and sold like cigars, Mr. Shui Ta. In the second place, it isn't respectable to go waltzing off with someone that's paying his way, so to speak—it must be for love! Thirdly and lastly, as the proverb has it: not for a handful of rice but for love! [*Pause. He is thinking hard.*] "Well," you may say, "and what good is all this wisdom if the milk's already spilt?" Miss Shen Te is what she is. Is *where* she is. We have to face the fact that if she doesn't get hold of six months' rent pronto, she'll be back on the streets. The question then as I see it—everything in this world is a matter of opinion—the question as I see it is: *how* is she to get hold of this rent? How? Mr. Shui Ta: I don't know. [*Pause.*] I take that back, sir. It's just come to me. A husband. We must find her a husband!

[*Enter a little* OLD WOMAN.]

OLD WOMAN A good cheap cigar for my husband, we'll have been married forty years tomorrow and we're having a little celebration.

SHUI TA Forty years? And you still want to celebrate?

OLD WOMAN As much as we can afford to. We have the carpet shop across the square. We'll be good neighbors, I hope?

SHUI TA I hope so too.

POLICEMAN [*Who keeps making discoveries.*] Mr. Shui Ta, you know what we need? We need capital. And how do we acquire capital? We get married.

SHUI TA [*To* OLD WOMAN.] I'm afraid I've been pestering this gentleman with my personal worries.

POLICEMAN [*Lyrically.*] We can't pay six months' rent, so what do we do? We marry money.

SHUI TA That might not be easy.

POLICEMAN Oh, I don't know. She's a good match. Has a nice, growing business. [*To the* OLD WOMAN.] What do you think?

OLD WOMAN [*Undecided.*] Well—

POLICEMAN Should she put an ad in the paper?

OLD WOMAN [*Not eager to commit herself.*] Well, if *she* agrees—

POLICEMAN I'll write it for her. *You* lend us a hand, and *we* write an ad for you! [*He chuckles away to himself, takes out his notebook, wets the stump of a pencil between his lips, and writes away.*]

SHUI TA [*Slowly.*] Not a bad idea.

POLICEMAN "What . . . *respectable* . . . man . . . with small capital . . . widower . . . not excluded . . . desires . . . marriage . . . into flourishing . . . tobacco shop?" And now let's add: "Am . . . pretty . . ." No! . . . "Prepossessing appearance."

SHUI TA If you don't think that's an exaggeration?

OLD WOMAN Oh, not a bit. I've seen her.

[*The* POLICEMAN *tears the page out of his notebook, and hands it over to* SHUI TA.]

SHUI TA [*With horror in his voice.*] How much luck we need to keep our heads above water! How many ideas! How many friends! [*To the* POLICEMAN.] Thank you, sir, I think I see my way clear.

3

Evening in the municipal park. Noise of a plane overhead. YANG SUN, *a young man in rags, is following the plane with his eyes: one can tell that the machine is describing a curve above the park.* YANG SUN *then takes a rope out of his pocket, looking anxiously about him as he does so. He moves toward a large willow. Enter two prostitutes, one old, the other the* NIECE *whom we have already met.*

NIECE Hello. Coming with me?

YANG SUN [*Taken aback.*] If you'd like to buy me a dinner.

OLD WHORE Buy you a dinner! [*To the* NIECE.] Oh, we know him—it's the unemployed pilot. Waste no time on him!

NIECE But he's the only man left in the park. And it's going to rain.

OLD WHORE Oh, how do you know?

[*And they pass by.* YANG SUN *again looks about him, again takes his rope, and this time throws it round a branch of the willow tree. Again he is interrupted. It is the two prostitutes returning—and in such a hurry they don't notice him.*]

NIECE It's going to pour!

[*Enter* SHEN TE.]

OLD WHORE There's that *gorgon* Shen Te! That *drove* your family out into the cold!

NIECE It wasn't her. It was that cousin of hers. She offered to pay for the cakes. I've nothing against her.

OLD WHORE I have, though. [*So that* SHEN TE *can hear.*] Now where could the little lady be off to? She may be rich now but that won't stop her snatching our young men, will it?

SHEN TE I'm going to the tearoom by the pond.

NIECE Is it true what they say? You're marrying a widower—with three children?

SHEN TE Yes. I'm just going to see him.

YANG SUN [*His patience at breaking point.*] Move on there! This is a park, not a whorehouse!

OLD WHORE Shut your mouth!

[*But the two prostitutes leave.*]

YANG SUN Even in the farthest corner of the park, even when it's raining, you can't get rid of them! [*He spits.*]

SHEN TE [*Overhearing this.*] And what right have you to scold them? [*But at this point she sees the rope.*] Oh!

YANG SUN Well, what are you staring at?

SHEN TE That rope. What is it for?

YANG SUN Think! Think! I haven't a penny. Even if I had, I wouldn't spend it on you. I'd buy a drink of water.

[*The rain starts.*]

SHEN TE [*Still looking at the rope.*] What is the rope for? You mustn't!

YANG SUN What's it to you? Clear out!

SHEN TE [*Irrelevantly.*] It's raining.

YANG SUN Well, don't try to come under this tree.

SHEN TE Oh, no. [*She stays in the rain.*]

YANG SUN Now go away. [*Pause.*] For one thing, I don't like your looks, you're bowlegged.

SHEN TE [*Indignantly.*] That's not true!

YANG SUN Well, don't show 'em to me. Look, it's raining. You better come under this tree.

[*Slowly, she takes shelter under the tree.*]

SHEN TE Why did you want to do it?

YANG SUN You really want to know? [*Pause.*] To get rid of you! [*Pause.*] You know what a flyer is?

SHEN TE Oh yes, I've met a lot of pilots. At the tearoom.

YANG SUN You call *them* flyers? Think they know what a machine is? Just 'cause they have leather helmets? They gave the airfield director a bribe, that's the way *those* fellows got up in the air! Try one of them out sometime. "Go up to two thousand feet," tell him, "then let it fall, then pick it up again with a flick of the wrist at the last moment." Know what he'll say to that? "It's not in my contract." Then again, there's the landing problem. It's like landing on your own backside. It's no different, planes are human. Those fools don't understand. [*Pause.*] And I'm the biggest fool for reading the book on flying in the Peking[3] school and skipping the page where it says: "We've got enough flyers and we don't need you." I'm a mail pilot with no mail. You understand that?

SHEN TE [*Shyly.*] Yes, I do.

YANG SUN No, you don't. You'd never understand that.

SHEN TE When we were little we had a crane with a broken wing. He made friends with us and was very good-natured about our jokes. He would strut along behind us and call out to stop us going too fast for him. But every spring and autumn when the cranes flew over the villages in great swarms, he got quite restless. [*Pause.*] I understand that.

[*She bursts out crying.*]

YANG SUN Don't!

SHEN TE [*Quieting down.*] No.

YANG SUN It's bad for the complexion.

SHEN TE [*Sniffing.*] I've stopped.

[*She dries her tears on her big sleeve. Leaning against the tree, but not looking at her, he reaches for her face.*]

YANG SUN You can't even wipe your own face. [*He is wiping it for her with his handkerchief. Pause.*]

SHEN TE [*Still sobbing.*] I don't know *anything*!

YANG SUN You interrupted me! What for?

SHEN TE It's such a rainy day. You only wanted to do . . . *that* because it's such a rainy day. [*To the audience.*]

In our country
The evenings should never be somber
High bridges over rivers
The gray hour between night and morning
And the long, long winter:
Such things are dangerous
For, with all the misery,

3. That is, Beijing, the capital of China.

A very little is enough
And men throw away an unbearable life.

[*Pause.*]

YANG SUN Talk about yourself for a change.

SHEN TE What about me? I have a shop.

YANG SUN [*Incredulous.*] You have a shop, have you? Never thought of walking the streets?

SHEN TE I did walk the streets. Now I have a shop.

YANG SUN [*Ironically.*] A gift of the gods, I suppose!

SHEN TE How did you know?

YANG SUN [*Even more ironical.*] One fine evening the gods turned up saying: here's some money!

SHEN TE [*Quickly.*] One fine morning.

YANG SUN [*Fed up.*] This isn't much of an entertainment.

[*Pause.*]

SHEN TE I can play the zither a little. [*Pause.*] And I can mimic men. [*Pause.*] I got the shop, so the first thing I did was to give my zither away. I can be as stupid as a fish now, I said to myself, and it won't matter.

I'm rich now, I said
I walk alone, I sleep alone
For a whole year, I said
I'll have nothing to do with a man.

YANG SUN And now you're marrying one! The one at the tearoom by the pond?

[SHEN TE *is silent.*]

YANG SUN What do you know about love?

SHEN TE Everything.

YANG SUN Nothing. [*Pause.*] Or d'you just mean you enjoyed it?

SHEN TE No.

YANG SUN [*Again without turning to look at her, he strokes her cheek with his hand.*] You like that?

SHEN TE Yes.

YANG SUN [*Breaking off.*] You're easily satisfied, I must say. [*Pause.*] What a town!

SHEN TE You have no friends?

YANG SUN [*Defensively.*] Yes, I have! [*Change of tone.*] But they don't want to hear I'm still unemployed. "What?" they ask. "Is there still water in the sea?" You have friends?

SHEN TE [*Hesitating.*] Just a . . . cousin.

YANG SUN Watch him carefully.

SHEN TE He only came once. Then he went away. He won't be back. [YANG SUN *is looking away.*] But to be without hope, they say, is to be without goodness!

[*Pause.*]

YANG SUN Go on talking. A voice is a voice.

SHEN TE Once, when I was a little girl, I fell, with a load of brushwood. An old man picked me up. He gave me a penny too. Isn't it funny how people who don't have very much like to give some of it away? They must like to show what they can do, and how could they show it better than by being kind? Being wicked is just like being clumsy. When we sing a song, or build a machine, or plant some rice, we're being kind. You're kind.

FIRST GOD [*Sententiously.*] A prudent gardener works miracles on the smallest plot.

WONG She hands out rice every morning. That eats up half her earnings.

FIRST GOD [*A little disappointed.*] Well, as a beginning . . .

WONG They call her the Angel of the Slums—whatever the carpenter may say!

FIRST GOD What's this? A carpenter speaks ill of her?

WONG Oh, he only says her shelves weren't paid for in full.

SECOND GOD [*Who has a bad cold and can't pronounce his n's and m's.*] What's this? Not paying a carpenter? Why was that?

WONG I suppose she didn't have the money.

SECOND GOD [*Severely.*] One pays what one owes, that's in our book of rules! First the letter of the law, then the spirit.

WONG But it wasn't Shen Te, illustrious ones, it was her cousin. She called *him* in to help.

SECOND GOD Then her cousin must never darken her threshold again!

WONG Very well, illustrious ones! But in fairness to Shen Te, let me say that her cousin is a businessman.

FIRST GOD Perhaps we should inquire what is customary? I find business quite unintelligible. But everybody's doing it. Business! Did the Seven Good Kings do business? Did Kung the Just[4] sell fish?

SECOND GOD In any case, such a thing must not occur again!

[*The* GODS *start to leave.*]

THIRD GOD Forgive us for taking this tone with you, Wong, we haven't been getting enough sleep. The rich recommend us to the poor, and the poor tell us they haven't enough room.

SECOND GOD Feeble, feeble, the best of them!

FIRST GOD No great deeds! No heroic daring!

THIRD GOD On such a *small* scale!

SECOND GOD Sincere, yes, but what is actually *achieved*?

[*One can no longer hear them.*]

WONG [*Calling after them.*] I've thought of something, illustrious ones: Perhaps you shouldn't ask—too—much—all—at—once!

4

The square in front of Shen Te's tobacco shop. Besides Shen Te's place, two other shops are seen: the carpet shop and a barber's. Morning. Outside Shen Te's the GRANDFATHER, *the* SISTER-IN-LAW, *the* UNEMPLOYED MAN, *and* MRS. SHIN *stand waiting.*

SISTER-IN-LAW She's been out all night again.

MRS. SHIN No sooner did we get rid of that crazy cousin of hers than Shen Te herself starts carrying on! Maybe she does give us an ounce of rice now and then, but can you depend on her? Can you depend on her?

[*Loud voices from the barber's.*]

VOICE OF SHU FU What are you doing in my shop? Get out—at once!

4. K'ung Futzu (Master K'ung), the Chinese philosopher better known by his latinized name, Confucius (551–497 B.C.E.). *Seven Good Kings*: rulers of the first historical dynasty of China (traditionally dated ca. 1766–ca. 1122 B.C.E.), whom the Confucian scholar Mencius called "sage worthies."

VOICE OF WONG But sir. They all let me sell . . .

[WONG *comes staggering out of the barber's shop pursued by Mr.* SHU FU, *the barber, a fat man carrying a heavy curling iron.*]

SHU FU Get out, I said! Pestering my customers with your slimy old water! Get out! Take your cup!

[*He holds out the cup.* WONG *reaches out for it. Mr.* SHU FU *strikes his hand with the curling iron, which is hot.* WONG *howls.*]

SHU FU You had it coming my man!

[*Puffing, he returns to his shop. The* UNEMPLOYED MAN *picks up the cup and gives it to* WONG.]

UNEMPLOYED MAN You can report that to the police.

WONG My hand! It's smashed up!

UNEMPLOYED MAN Any bones broken?

WONG I can't move my fingers.

UNEMPLOYED MAN Sit down. I'll put some water on it.

[WONG *sits.*]

MRS. SHIN The water won't cost you anything.

SISTER-IN-LAW You might have got a bandage from Miss Shen Te till she took to staying out all night. It's a scandal.

MRS. SHIN [*Despondently.*] If you ask me, she's forgotten we ever existed!

[*Enter* SHEN TE *down the street, with a dish of rice.*]

SHEN TE [*To the audience.*] How wonderful to see Setzuan in the early morning! I always used to stay in bed with my dirty blanket over my head afraid to wake up. This morning I saw the newspapers being delivered by little boys, the streets being washed by strong men, and fresh vegetables coming in from the country on ox carts. It's a long walk from where Yang Sun lives, but I feel lighter at every step. They say you walk on air when you're in love, but it's even better walking on the rough earth, on the hard cement. In the early morning, the old city looks like a great heap of rubbish! Nice, though, with all its little lights. And the sky so pink, so transparent, before the dust comes and muddies it! What a lot you miss if you never see your city rising from its slumbers like an honest old craftsman pumping his lungs full of air and reaching for his tools, as the poet says! [*Cheerfully, to her waiting guests.*] Good morning, everyone, here's your rice! [*Distributing the rice, she comes upon* WONG.] Good morning, Wong, I'm quite lightheaded today. On my way over, I looked at myself in all the shop windows. I'd love to be beautiful.

[*She slips into the carpet shop. Mr.* SHU FU *has just emerged from his shop.*]

SHU FU [*To the audience.*] It surprises me how beautiful Miss Shen Te is looking today! I never gave her a passing thought before. But now I've been gazing upon her comely form for exactly three minutes! I begin to suspect I am in love with her. She is overpoweringly attractive! [*Crossly, to* WONG.] Be off with you rascal!

[*He returns to his shop.* SHEN TE *comes back out of the carpet shop with the* OLD MAN, *its proprietor, and his wife—whom we have already met—the* OLD WOMAN. SHEN TE *is wearing a shawl. The* OLD MAN *is holding up a looking glass for her.*]

OLD WOMAN Isn't it lovely? We'll give you a reduction because there's a little hole in it.

SHEN TE [*Looking at another shawl on the old woman's arm.*] The other one's nice too.

OLD WOMAN [*Smiling.*] Too bad there's no hole in that!

SHEN TE That's right. My shop doesn't make very much.

OLD WOMAN And your deeds eat it all up! Be more careful, my dear . . .

SHEN TE [*Trying on the shawl with the hole.*] Just now, I'm lightheaded! Does the color suit me?

OLD WOMAN You'd better ask a man.

SHEN TE [*To the* OLD MAN.] Does the color suit me?

OLD MAN You'd better ask your young friend.

SHEN TE I'd like to have your opinion.

OLD MAN It suits you very well. But wear it this way: the dull side out.

[SHEN TE *pays up.*]

OLD WOMAN If you decide you don't like it, you can exchange it. [*She pulls* SHEN TE *to one side.*] Has he got money?

SHEN TE [*With a laugh*] Yang Sun? Oh, no.

OLD WOMAN Then how're you going to pay your rent?

SHEN TE I'd forgotten about that.

OLD WOMAN And next Monday is the first of the month! Miss Shen Te, I've got something to say to you. After we [*Indicating her husband.*] got to know you, we had our doubts about that marriage ad. We thought it would be better if you'd let *us* help you. Out of our savings. We reckon we could lend you two hundred silver dollars. We don't need anything in writing—you could pledge us your tobacco stock.

SHEN TE You're prepared to lend money to a person like me?

OLD WOMAN It's folks like you that need it. We'd think twice about lending anything to your cousin.

OLD MAN [*Coming up.*] All settled, my dear?

SHEN TE I wish the gods could have heard what your wife was just saying, Mr. Ma. They're looking for good people who're happy—and helping me makes you happy because you know it was love that got me into difficulties!

[*The old couple smile knowingly at each other.*]

OLD MAN And here's the money, Miss Shen Te.

[*He hands her an envelope.* SHEN TE *takes it. She bows. They bow back. They return to their shop.*]

SHEN TE [*Holding up her envelope.*] Look, Wong, here's six months' rent! Don't you believe in miracles now? And how do you like my new shawl?

WONG For the young fellow I saw you with in the park?

[SHEN TE *nods.*]

MRS. SHIN Never mind all that. It's time you took a look at this hand!

SHEN TE Have you hurt your hand?

MRS. SHIN That barber smashed it with his hot curling iron. Right in front of our eyes.

SHEN TE [*Shocked at herself.*] And I never noticed! We must get you to a doctor this minute or who knows what will happen?

UNEMPLOYED MAN It's not a doctor he should see, it's a judge. He can ask for compensation. The barber's filthy rich.

WONG You think I have a chance?

MRS. SHIN [*With relish.*] If it's really good and smashed. But is it?

WONG I think so. It's very swollen. Could I get a pension?

MRS. SHIN You'd need a witness.

WONG Well, you all saw it. You could all testify.

[*He looks round. The* UNEMPLOYED MAN, *the* GRANDFATHER, *and the* SISTER-IN-LAW *are all sitting against the wall of the shop eating rice. Their concentration on eating is complete.*]

SHEN TE [*To* MRS. SHIN.] You saw it yourself.

MRS. SHIN I want nothing to do with the police. It's against my principles.

SHEN TE [*To* SISTER-IN-LAW.] What about you?

SISTER-IN-LAW Me? I wasn't looking.

SHEN TE [*To the* GRANDFATHER, *coaxingly.*] Grandfather, *you'll* testify, won't you?

SISTER-IN-LAW And a lot of good that will do. He's simple-minded.

SHEN TE [*To the* UNEMPLOYED MAN.] You seem to be the only witness left.

UNEMPLOYED MAN My testimony would only hurt him. I've been picked up twice for begging.

SHEN TE

Your brother is assaulted, and you shut your eyes?
He is hit, cries out in pain, and you are silent?
The beast prowls, chooses and seizes his victim, and you say:
"Because we showed no displeasure, he has spared us."
If no one present will be a witness, I will. I'll say *I* saw it.

MRS. SHIN [*Solemnly.*] The name for that is perjury.

WONG I don't know if I can accept that. Though maybe I'll have to. [*Looking at his hand.*] Is it swollen enough, do you think? The swelling's not going down.

UNEMPLOYED MAN No, no, the swelling's holding up well.

WONG Yes. It's *more* swollen if anything. Maybe my wrist is broken after all. I'd better see a judge at once.

[*Holding his hand very carefully, and fixing his eyes on it, he runs off.* MRS. SHIN *goes quickly into the barber's shop.*]

UNEMPLOYED MAN [*Seeing her.*] She is getting on the right side of Mr. Shu Fu.

SISTER-IN-LAW You and I can't change the world, Shen Te.

SHEN TE Go away! Go away all of you! [*The* UNEMPLOYED MAN , *the* SISTER-IN-LAW , *and the* GRANDFATHER *stalk off, eating and sulking. To the audience.*]

They've stopped answering
They stay put
They do as they're told
They don't care
Nothing can make them look up
But the smell of food.

[*Enter* MRS. YANG, *Yang Sun's mother, out of breath.*]

MRS. YANG Miss Shen Te. My son has told me everything. I am Mrs. Yang, Sun's mother. Just think. He's got an offer. Of a job as a pilot. A letter has just come. From the director of the airfield in Peking!

SHEN TE So he can fly again! Isn't that wonderful!

MRS. YANG [*Less breathlessly all the time.*] They won't give him the job for nothing. They want five hundred silver dollars.

SHEN TE We can't let money stand in his way, Mrs. Yang!

MRS. YANG If only you could help him out!

SHEN TE I have the shop. I can try! [*She embraces* MRS. YANG.] I happen to have two hundred with me now. Take it. [*She gives her the old couple's money.*] It was a loan but they said I could repay it with my tobacco stock.

MRS. YANG And they were calling Sun the Dead Pilot of Setzuan! A friend in need!

SHEN TE We must find another three hundred.

MRS. YANG How?

SHEN TE Let me think. [*Slowly.*] I know someone who can help. I didn't want to call on his services again, he's hard and cunning. But a flyer must fly. And I'll make this the last time.

[*Distant sound of a plane.*]

MRS. YANG If the man you mentioned can do it . . . Oh, look, there's the morning mail plane, heading for Peking!

SHEN TE The pilot can see us, let's wave!

[*They wave. The noise of the engine is louder.*]

MRS. YANG You know that pilot up there?

SHEN TE Wave, Mrs. Yang! I know the pilot who will be up there. He gave up hope. But he'll do it now. One man to raise himself above the misery, above us all. [*To the audience.*]

Yang Sun, my lover:
Braving the storms
In company with the clouds
Crossing the heavens
And bringing to friends in faraway lands
The friendly mail!

4a

In front of the inner curtain. Enter SHEN TE *, carrying Shui Ta's mask. She sings.*

THE SONG OF DEFENSELESSNESS

In our country
A useful man needs luck
Only if he finds strong backers
Can he prove himself useful.
The good can't defend themselves and
Even the gods are defenseless.

Oh, why don't the gods have their own ammunition
And launch against badness their own expedition
Enthroning the good and preventing sedition
And bringing the world to a peaceful condition?

Oh, why don't the gods do the buying and selling
Injustice forbidding, starvation dispelling
Give bread to each city and joy to each dwelling?
Oh, why don't the gods do the buying and selling?

[*She puts on Shui Ta's mask and sings in his voice.*]

You can only help one of your luckless brothers
By trampling down a dozen others.

Why is it the gods do not feel indignation
And come down in fury to end exploitation
Defeat all defeat and forbid desperation
Refusing to tolerate such toleration?

Why is it?

5

Shen Te's tobacco shop. Behind the counter, Mr. SHUI TA, *reading the paper.* MRS. SHIN *is cleaning up. She talks and he takes no notice.*

MRS. SHIN And when certain rumors get about, what *happens* to a little place like this? It goes to pot. *I* know. So, if you want my advice, Mr. Shui Ta, find out just what has been going on between Miss Shen Te and that Yang Sun from Yellow Street. And remember: a certain interest in Miss Shen Te has been expressed by the barber next door, a man with twelve houses and only one wife,[5] who, for that matter, is likely to drop off at any time. A certain interest has been expressed. He was even inquiring about her means and, if *that* doesn't prove a man is getting serious, what would?

[*Still getting no response, she leaves with her bucket.*]

YANG SUN'S VOICE Is that Miss Shen Te's tobacco shop?

MRS. SHIN'S VOICE Yes, it is, but it's Mr. Shui Ta who's here today.

[SHUI TA *runs to the mirror with the short, light steps of* SHEN TE, *and is just about to start primping, when he realizes his mistake, and turns away, with a short laugh. Enter* YANG SUN. MRS. SHIN *enters behind him and slips into the back room to eavesdrop.*]

YANG SUN I am Yang Sun. [SHUI TA *bows.*] Is Shen Te in?

SHUI TA No.

YANG SUN I guess you know our relationship? [*He is inspecting the stock.*] Quite a place! And I thought she was just talking big. I'll be flying again, all right. [*He takes a cigar, solicits and receives a light from* SHUI TA.] You think we can squeeze the other three hundred out of the tobacco stock?

SHUI TA May I ask if it is your intention to sell at once?

YANG SUN It was decent of her to come out with the two hundred but they aren't much use with the other three hundred still missing.

SHUI TA Shen Te was overhasty promising so much. She might have to sell the shop itself to raise it. Haste, they say, is the wind that blows the house down.

YANG SUN Oh, she isn't a girl to keep a man waiting. For one thing or the other, if you take my meaning.

SHUI TA I take your meaning

YANG SUN [*Leering.*] Uh, huh.

SHUI TA Would you explain what the five hundred silver dollars are for?

YANG SUN Want to sound me out? Very well. The director of the Peking airfield is a friend of mine from flying school. I give him five hundred: he gets me the job.

5. Ancient Chinese law permitted a man to have more than one wife.

SHUI TA The price is high.

YANG SUN Not as these things go. He'll have to fire one of the present pilots—for negligence. Only the man he has in mind isn't negligent. Not easy, you understand. You needn't mention that part of it to Shen Te.

SHUI TA [*Looking intently at* YANG SUN.] Mr. Yang Sun, you are asking my cousin to give up her possessions, leave her friends, and place her entire fate in your hands. I presume you intend to marry her?

YANG SUN I'd be prepared to.

[*Slight pause.*]

SHUI TA Those two hundred silver dollars would pay the rent here for six months. If you were Shen Te wouldn't you be tempted to continue in business?

YANG SUN What? Can you imagine Yang Sun the flyer behind a counter? [*In an oily voice.*] "A strong cigar or a mild one, worthy sir?" Not in this century!

SHUI TA My cousin wishes to follow the promptings of her heart, and, from her own point of view, she may even have what is called the right to love. Accordingly, she has commissioned me to help you to this post. There is nothing here that I am not empowered to turn immediately into cash. Mrs. Mi Tzu, the landlady, will advise me about the sale.

[*Enter* MRS. MI TZU.]

MRS. MI TZU Good morning, Mr. Shui Ta, you wish to see me about the rent? As you know it falls due the day after tomorrow.

SHUI TA Circumstances have changed, Mrs. Mi Tzu: my cousin is getting married. Her future husband here, Mr. Yang Sun, will be taking her to Peking. I am interested in selling the tobacco stock.

MRS. MI TZU How much are you asking, Mr. Shui Ta?

YANG SUN Three hundred sil—

SHUI TA Five hundred silver dollars.

MRS. MI TZU How much did she pay for it, Mr. Shui Ta?

SHUI TA A thousand. And very little has been sold.

MRS. MI TZU She was robbed. But I'll make you a special offer if you'll promise to be out by the day after tomorrow. Three hundred silver dollars.

YANG SUN [*Shrugging.*] Take it, man, take it.

SHUI TA It is not enough.

YANG SUN Why not? Why not? Certainly, it's enough.

SHUI TA Five hundred silver dollars.

YANG SUN But why? We only need three!

SHUI TA [*To* MRS. MI TZU.] Excuse me. [*Takes* YANG SUN *on one side.*] The tobacco stock is pledged to the old couple who gave my cousin the two hundred.

YANG SUN Is it in writing?

SHUI TA No.

YANG SUN [*To* MRS. MI TZU.] Three hundred will do.

MRS. MI TZU Of course, I need an assurance that Miss Shen Te is not in debt.

YANG SUN Mr. Shui Ta?

SHUI TA She is not in debt.

YANG SUN When can you let us have the money?

MRS. MI TZU The day after tomorrow. And remember: I'm doing this because I have a soft spot in my heart for young lovers! [*Exit.*]

YANG SUN [*Calling after her.*] Boxes, jars and sacks—three hundred for the lot and the pain's over! [*To* SHUI TA.] Where else can we raise money by the day after tomorrow?

SHUI TA Nowhere. Haven't you enough for the trip and the first few weeks?

YANG SUN Oh, certainly.

SHUI TA How much, exactly.

YANG SUN Oh, I'll dig it up, even if I have to steal it.

SHUI TA I see.

YANG SUN Well, don't fall off the roof. I'll get to Peking somehow.

SHUI TA Two people can't travel for nothing.

YANG SUN [*Not giving* SHUI TA *a chance to answer.*] I'm leaving *her* behind. No millstones round *my* neck!

SHUI TA Oh.

YANG SUN Don't look at me like that!

SHUI TA How precisely is my cousin to live?

YANG SUN Oh, you'll think of something.

SHUI TA A small request, Mr. Yang Sun. Leave the two hundred silver dollars here until you can show me two tickets for Peking.

YANG SUN You learn to mind your own business, Mr. Shui Ta.

SHUI TA I'm afraid Miss Shen Te may not wish to sell the shop when she discovers that . . .

YANG SUN You don't know women. She'll want to. Even then.

SHUI TA [*A slight outburst.*] She is a human being, sir! And not devoid of common sense!

YANG SUN Shen Te is a woman: she *is* devoid of common sense. I only have to lay my hand on her shoulder, and church bells ring.

SHUI TA [*With difficulty.*] Mr. Yang Sun!

YANG SUN Mr. Shui Whatever-it-is!

SHUI TA My cousin is devoted to you . . . because . . .

YANG SUN Because I have my hands on her breasts. Give me a cigar. [*He takes one for himself, stuffs a few more in his pocket, then changes his mind and takes the whole box.*] Tell her I'll marry her, then bring me the three hundred. Or let her bring it. One or the other. [*Exit.*]

MRS. SHIN [*Sticking her head out of the back room.*] Well, he has your cousin under his thumb, and doesn't care if all Yellow Street knows it!

SHUI TA [*Crying out.*] I've lost my shop! And he doesn't love me! [*He runs berserk through the room, repeating these lines incoherently Then stops suddenly, and addresses* MRS. SHIN.] Mrs. Shin, you grew up in the gutter, like me. Are we lacking in hardness? I doubt it. If you steal a penny from me, I'll take you by the throat till you spit it out! You'd do the same to me. The times are bad, this city is hell, but we're like ants, we keep coming, up and up the walls, however smooth! Till bad luck comes. Being in love, for in stance. One weakness is enough, and love is the deadliest.

MRS. SHIN [*Emerging from the back room.*] You should have a little talk with Mr. Shu Fu, the barber. He's a real gentleman and just the thing for your cousin. [*She runs off.*]

SHUI TA

A caress becomes a stranglehold
A sigh of love turns to a cry of fear

Why are there vultures circling in the air?
A girl is going to meet her lover.

[SHUI TA *sits down and Mr.* SHU FU *enters with* MRS. SHIN.]

SHUI TA Mr. Shu Fu?

SHU FU Mr. Shui Ta.

[*They both bow.*]

SHUI TA I am told that you have expressed a certain interest in my cousin Shen Te. Let me set aside all propriety and confess: she is at this moment in grave danger.

SHU FU Oh, dear!

SHUI TA She has lost her shop, Mr. Shu Fu.

SHU FU The charm of Miss Shen Te, Mr. Shui Ta, derives from the goodness, not of her shop, but of her heart. Men call her the Angel of the Slums.

SHUI TA Yet her goodness has cost her two hundred silver dollars in a single day: we must put a stop to it.

SHU FU Permit me to differ, Mr. Shui Ta. Let us, rather, open wide the gates to such goodness! Every morning, with pleasure tinged by affection, I watch her charitable ministrations. For they are hungry, and she giveth them to eat! Four of them, to be precise. Why only four? I ask. Why not four hundred? I hear she has been seeking shelter for the homeless. What about my humble cabins behind the cattle run? They are at her disposal. And so forth. And so on. Mr. Shui Ta, do you think Miss Shen Te could be persuaded to listen to certain ideas of mine? Ideas like these?

SHUI TA Mr. Shu Fu, she would be honored.

[*Enter* WONG *and the* POLICEMAN. *Mr.* SHU FU *turns abruptly away and studies the shelves.*]

WONG Is Miss Shen Te here?

SHUI TA No.

WONG I am Wong the water seller. You are Mr. Shui Ta?

SHUI TA I am.

WONG I am a friend of Shen Te's.

SHUI TA An intimate friend, I hear.

WONG [*To the* POLICEMAN.] You see? [*To* SHUI TA.] It's because of my hand.

POLICEMAN He hurt his hand, sir, that's a fact.

SHUI TA [*Quickly.*] You need a sling, I see. [*He takes a shawl from the back room, and throws it to* WONG.]

WONG But that's her new shawl!

SHUI TA She has no more use for it.

WONG But she bought it to please someone!

SHUI TA It happens to be no longer necessary.

WONG [*Making the sling.*] She is my only witness.

POLICEMAN Mr. Shui Ta, your cousin is supposed to have seen the barber hit the water seller with a curling iron.

SHUI TA I'm afraid my cousin was not present at the time

WONG But she was, sir! Just ask her! Isn't she in?

SHUI TA [*Gravely.*] Mr. Wong, my cousin has her own troubles. You wouldn't wish her to add to them by committing perjury?

WONG But it was she that told me to go to the judge!

SHUI TA Was the judge supposed to heal your hand?

[Mr. SHU FU *turns quickly around.* SHUI TA *bows to* SHU FU, *and vice versa.*]

WONG [*Taking the sling off, and putting it back.*] I see how it is.

POLICEMAN Well, I'll be on my way. [*To* WONG.] And you be careful. If Mr. Shu Fu wasn't a man who tempers justice with mercy, as the saying is, you'd be in jail for libel. Be off with you!

[*Exit* WONG *followed by* POLICEMAN.]

SHUI TA Profound apologies, Mr. Shu Fu.

SHU FU Not at all, Mr. Shui Ta. [*Pointing to the shawl.*] The episode is over?

SHUI TA It may take her time to recover. There are some fresh wounds.

SHU FU We shall be discreet. Delicate. A short vacation could be arranged . . .

SHUI TA First of course, you and she would have to talk things over.

SHU FU At a small supper in a small, but high-class, restaurant.

SHUI TA I'll go and find her. [*Exit into back room.*]

MRS. SHIN [*Sticking her head in again.*] Time for congratulations, Mr. Shu Fu?

SHU FU Ah, Mrs. Shin! Please inform Miss Shen Te's guests they may take shelter in the cabins behind the cattle run!

[MRS. SHIN *nods, grinning.*]

SHU FU [*To the audience.*] Well? What do you think of me, ladies and gentlemen? What could a man do more? Could he be less selfish? More farsighted? A small supper in a small but . . . Does that bring rather vulgar and clumsy thoughts into your mind? Ts, ts, ts. Nothing of the sort will occur. She won't even be touched. Not even accidentally while passing the salt. An exchange of ideas only. Over the flowers on the table—white chrysanthemums, by the way [*He writes down a note of this.*]—yes, over the white chrysanthemums, two young souls will . . . shall I say "find each other"? We shall NOT exploit the misfortune of others. Understanding? Yes. An offer of assistance? Certainly. But quietly. Almost inaudibly. Perhaps with a single glance. A glance that could also—mean more.

MRS. SHIN [*Coming forward.*] Everything under control, Mr. Shu Fu?

SHU FU Oh, Mrs. Shin, what do you know about this worthless rascal Yang Sun?

MRS. SHIN Why, he's the most worthless rascal . . .

SHU FU Is he really? You're sure? [*As she opens her mouth.*] From now on, he doesn't exist! Can't be found anywhere!

[*Enter* YANG SUN.]

YANG SUN What's been going on here?

MRS. SHIN Shall I call Mr. Shui Ta, Mr. Shu Fu? He wouldn't want strangers in here!

SHU FU Mr. Shui Ta is in conference with Miss Shen Te. Not to be disturbed!

YANG SUN Shen Te here? I didn't see her come in. What kind of conference?

SHU FU [*Not letting him enter the back room.*] Patience, dear sir! And if by chance I have an inkling who you are, pray take note that Miss Shen Te and I are about to announce our engagement.

YANG SUN What?

MRS. SHIN You didn't expect that, did you?

[YANG SUN *is trying to push past the barber into the back room when* SHEN TE *comes out.*]

SHU FU My dear Shen Te, ten thousand apologies! Perhaps you . . .

YANG SUN What is it, Shen Te? Have you gone crazy?

SHEN TE [*Breathless.*] My cousin and Mr. Shu Fu have come to an understanding. They wish me to hear Mr. Shu Fu's plans for helping the poor.

YANG SUN Your cousin wants to part us.

SHEN TE Yes.

YANG SUN And you've agreed to it?

SHEN TE Yes.

YANG SUN They told you I was bad. [SHEN TE *is silent.*] And suppose I am. Does that make me need you less? I'm low, Shen Te, I have no money, I don't do the right thing but at least I put up a fight! [*He is near her now, and speaks in an undertone.*] Have you no eyes? Look at him. Have you forgotten already?

SHEN TE No.

YANG SUN How it was raining?

SHEN TE No.

YANG SUN How you cut me down from the willow tree? Bought me water? Promised me money to fly with?

SHEN TE [*Shakily.*] Yang Sun, what do you want?

YANG SUN I want you to come with me

SHEN TE [*In a small voice.*] Forgive me, Mr. Shu Fu, I want to go with Mr. Yang Sun.

YANG SUN We're lovers, you know. Give me the key to the shop. [SHEN TE *takes the key from around her neck.* YANG SUN *puts it on the counter. To* MRS. SHIN.] Leave it under the mat when you're through. Let's go, Shen Te.

SHU FU But this is rape! Mr. Shui Ta!!

YANG SUN [*To* SHEN TE.] Tell him not to shout.

SHEN TE Please don't shout for my cousin, Mr. Shu Fu. He doesn't agree with me, I know, but he's wrong. [*To the audience.*]

I want to go with the man I love
I don't want to count the cost
I don't want to consider if it's wise
I don't want to know if he loves me
I want to go with the man I love.

YANG SUN That's the spirit.

[*And the couple leave.*]

5a

In front of the inner curtain. SHEN TE *in her wedding clothes, on the way to her wedding.*

SHEN TE Something terrible has happened. As I left the shop with Yang Sun, I found the old carpet dealer's wife waiting on the street, trembling all over. She told me her husband had taken to his bed—sick with all the worry and excitement over the two hundred silver dollars they lent me. She said it would be best if I gave it back now. Of course, I had to say I would. She said she couldn't quite trust my cousin Shui Ta or even my fiancé, Yang Sun. There were tears in her eyes. With my emotions in an uproar, I threw myself into Yang Sun's arms, I couldn't resist him. The things he'd said to Shui Ta had taught Shen Te nothing. Sinking into his arms, I said to myself:

To let no one perish, not even oneself
To fill everyone with happiness, even oneself
Is so good

How could I have forgotten those two old people? Yang Sun swept me away like a small hurricane. But he's not a bad man, and he loves me. He'd rather work in the cement factory than owe his flying to a crime. Though, of course, flying *is* a great passion with Sun. Now, on the way to my wedding, I waver between fear and joy.

6

The "private dining room" on the upper floor of a cheap restaurant in a poor section of town. With SHEN TE: *the* GRANDFATHER, *the* SISTER-IN-LAW, *the* NIECE, MRS. SHIN, *the* UNEMPLOYED MAN. *In a corner, alone, a* PRIEST.[6] *A* WAITER *pouring wine. Downstage,* YANG SUN *talking to his mother. He wears a dinner jacket.*

YANG SUN Bad news, Mamma. She came right out and told me she can't sell the shop for me. Some idiot is bringing a claim because he lent her the two hundred she gave you.

MRS. YANG What did you say? Of course, you can't marry her now.

YANG SUN It's no use saying anything to *her*. I've sent for her cousin, Mr. Shui Ta. He said there was nothing in writing.

MRS. YANG Good idea. I'll go out and look for him. Keep an eye on things.

[*Exit* MRS. YANG. SHEN TE *has been pouring wine.*]

SHEN TE [*To the audience, pitcher in hand.*] I wasn't mistaken in him. He's bearing up well. Though it must have been an awful blow—giving up flying. I do love him so. [*Calling across the room to him.*] Sun, you haven't drunk a toast with the bride!

YANG SUN What do we drink to?

SHEN TE Why, to the future!

YANG SUN When the bridegroom's dinner jacket won't be a hired one!

SHEN TE But when the bride's dress will still get rained on sometimes!

YANG SUN To everything we ever wished for!

SHEN TE May all our dreams come true!

[*They drink.*]

YANG SUN [*With loud conviviality.*] And now, friends, before the wedding gets under way, I have to ask the bride a few questions. I've no idea what kind of a wife she'll make, and it worries me. [*Wheeling on* SHEN TE.] For example. Can you make five cups of tea with three tea leaves?

SHEN TE No.

YANG SUN So I won't be getting very much tea. Can you sleep on a straw mattress the size of that book? [*He points to the large volume the* PRIEST *is reading.*]

SHEN TE The two of us?

YANG SUN The one of you.

SHEN TE In that case, no.

YANG SUN What a wife! I'm shocked!

[*While the audience is laughing, his mother returns. With a shrug of her shoulders, she tells* SUN *the expected guest hasn't arrived. The* PRIEST *shuts the book with a bang, and makes for the door.*]

6. A Buddhist monk or priest.

MRS. YANG Where are *you* off to? It's only a matter of minutes.

PRIEST [*Watch in hand.*] Time goes on, Mrs. Yang, and I've another wedding to attend to. Also a funeral.

MRS. YANG [*Irately.*] D'you think we planned it this way? I was hoping to manage with one pitcher of wine, and we've run through two already. [*Points to empty pitcher. Loudly.*] My dear Shen Te, I don't know where your cousin can be keeping himself!

SHEN TE My cousin?!

MRS. YANG Certainly. I'm old-fashioned enough to think such a close relative should attend the wedding.

SHEN TE Oh, Sun, is it the three hundred silver dollars?

YANG SUN [*Not looking her in the eye.*] Are you deaf? Mother says she's old-fashioned. And I say I'm considerate. We'll wait another fifteen minutes.

HUSBAND Another fifteen minutes.

MRS. YANG [*Addressing the company.*] Now you all know, don't you, that my son is getting a job as a mail pilot?

SISTER-IN-LAW In Peking, too, isn't it?

MRS. YANG In Peking, too! The two of us are moving to Peking!

SHEN TE Sun, tell your mother Peking is out of the question now.

YANG SUN Your cousin'll tell her. If he agrees. I don't agree.

SHEN TE [*Amazed, and dismayed.*] Sun!

YANG SUN I hate this godforsaken Setzuan. What people! Know what they look like when I half close my eyes? Horses! Whinnying, fretting, stamping, screwing their necks up! [*Loudly.*] And what is it the thunder says? They are su-per-flu-ous! [*He hammers out the syllables.*] They've run their last race! They can go trample themselves to death! [*Pause.*] I've got to get out of here.

SHEN TE But I've promised the money to the old couple.

YANG SUN And since you always do the wrong thing, it's lucky your cousin's coming. Have another drink.

SHEN TE [*Quietly.*] My cousin can't be coming.

YANG SUN How d'you mean?

SHEN TE My cousin can't be where I am.

YANG SUN Quite a conundrum!

SHEN TE [*Desperately.*] Sun, I'm the one that loves you. Not my cousin. He was thinking of the job in Peking when he promised you the old couple's money—

YANG SUN Right. And that's why he's bringing the three hundred silver dollars. Here—to my wedding.

SHEN TE He is not bringing the three hundred silver dollars.

YANG SUN Huh? What makes you think that?

SHEN TE [*Looking into his eyes.*] He says you only bought one ticket to Peking.

[*Short pause.*]

YANG SUN That was yesterday. [*He pulls two tickets part way out of his inside pocket, making her look under his coat.*] Two tickets. I don't want Mother to know. She'll get left behind. I sold her furniture to buy these tickets, so you see . . .

SHEN TE But what's to become of the old couple?

YANG SUN What's to become of me? Have another drink. Or do you believe in moderation? If I drink, I fly again. And if you drink, you may learn to understand me.

SHEN TE You want to fly. But I can't help you.

YANG SUN "Here's a plane, my darling—but it's only got one wing!"

[*The* WAITER *enters.*]

WAITER Mrs. Yang!

MRS. YANG Yes?

WAITER Another pitcher of wine, ma'um?

MRS. YANG We have enough, thanks. Drinking makes me sweat.

WAITER Would you mind paying, ma'am?

MRS. YANG [*To everyone.*] Just be patient a few moments longer, everyone, Mr. Shui Ta is on his way over! [*To the* WAITER.] Don't be a spoilsport.

WAITER I can't let you leave till you've paid your bill, ma'am.

MRS. YANG But they know me here!

WAITER That's just it.

PRIEST [*Ponderously getting up.*] I humbly take my leave. [*And he does.*]

MRS. YANG [*To the others, desperately.*] Stay where you are, everybody! The priest says he'll be back in two minutes!

YANG SUN It's no good Mamma. Ladies and gentlemen, Mr. Shui Ta still hasn't arrived and the priest has gone home. We won't detain you any longer.

[*They are leaving now*]

GRANDFATHER [*In the doorway, having forgotten to put his glass down.*] To the bride! [*He drinks, puts down the glass, and follows the others.*]

[*Pause.*]

SHEN TE Shall I go too?

YANG SUN You? Aren't you the bride? Isn't this your wedding? [*He drags her across the room, tearing her wedding dress.*] If we can wait, you can wait. Mother calls me her falcon. She wants to see me in the clouds. But I think it may be St. Nevercome's Day before she'll go to the door and see my plane thunder by. [*Pause. He pretends the guests are still present.*] Why such a lull in the conversation, ladies and gentlemen? Don't you like it here? The ceremony is only slightly postponed—because an important guest is expected at any moment. Also because the bride doesn't know what love is. While we're waiting, the bridegroom will sing a little song. [*He does so.*]

THE SONG OF ST. NEVERCOME'S DAY

On a certain day, as is generally known,
 One and all will be shouting: Hooray, hooray!
For the beggar maid's son has a solid-gold throne
 And the day is St. Nevercome's Day
On St. Nevercome's, Nevercome's, Nevercome's Day
 He'll sit on his solid-gold throne

Oh, hooray, hooray! That day goodness will pay!
 That day badness will cost you your head!
And merit and money will smile and be funny
 While exchanging salt and bread

On St. Nevercome's, Nevercome's, Nevercome's Day
While exchanging salt and bread

And the grass, oh, the grass will look down at the sky
And the pebbles will roll up the stream
And all men will be good without batting an eye
They will make of our earth a dream
On St. Nevercome's, Nevercome's, Nevercome's Day
They will make of our earth a dream

And as for me, that's the day I shall be
A flyer and one of the best
Unemployed man, you will have work to do
Washerwoman, you'll get your rest
On St. Nevercome's, Nevercome's, Nevercome's Day
Washerwoman, you'll get your rest

MRS. YANG It looks like he's not coming.

[*The three of them sit looking at the door.*]

6a

Wong's den. The sewer pipe is again transparent and again the GODS *appear to* WONG *in a dream.*

WONG I'm so glad you've come, illustrious ones. It's Shen Te. She's in great trouble from following the rule about loving thy neighbor. Perhaps she's *too* good for this world!

FIRST GOD Nonsense! You are eaten up by lice and doubts!

WONG Forgive me, illustrious one, I only meant you might deign to intervene.

FIRST GOD Out of the question! My colleague here intervened in some squabble or other only yesterday. [*He points to the* THIRD GOD, *who has a black eye.*] The results are before us!

WONG She had to call on her cousin again. But not even he could help. I'm afraid the shop is done for.

THIRD GOD [*A little concerned.*] Perhaps we should help after all?

FIRST GOD The gods help those that help themselves.

WONG What if we *can't* help ourselves, illustrious ones?

[*Slight pause.*]

SECOND GOD Try, anyway! Suffering ennobles!

FIRST GOD Our faith in Shen Te is unshaken!

THIRD GOD We certainly haven't found any *other* good people. You can see where we spend our nights from the straw on our clothes.

WONG You might help her find her way by—

FIRST GOD The good man finds his own way here below!

SECOND GOD The good woman too.

FIRST GOD The heavier the burden, the greater her strength!

THIRD GOD We're only onlookers, you know.

FIRST GOD And everything will be all right in the end, O ye of little faith!

[*They are gradually disappearing through these last lines.*]

7

The yard behind Shen Te's shop. A few articles of furniture on a cart. SHEN TE *and* MRS. SHIN *are taking the washing off the line.*

MRS. SHIN If you ask me, you should fight tooth and nail to keep the shop.

SHEN TE How can I? I have to sell the tobacco to pay back the two hundred silver dollars today.

MRS. SHIN No husband, no tobacco, no house and home! What are you going to live on?

SHEN TE I can work. I can sort tobacco.

MRS. SHIN Hey, look, Mr. Shui Ta's trousers! He must have left here stark naked!

SHEN TE Oh, he may have another pair, Mrs. Shin.

MRS. SHIN But if he's gone for good as you say, why has he left his pants behind?

SHEN TE Maybe he's thrown them away.

MRS. SHIN Can I take them?

SHEN TE Oh, no.

[*Enter Mr.* SHU FU, *running.*]

SHU FU Not a word! Total silence! I know all. You have sacrificed your own love and happiness so as not to hurt a dear old couple who had put their trust in you! Not in vain does this district—for all its malevolent tongues—call you the Angel of the Slums! That young man couldn't rise to your level, so you left him. And now, when I see you closing up the little shop, that veritable haven of rest for the multitude, well, I cannot, I cannot let it pass. Morning after morning I have stood watching in the doorway not unmoved—while you graciously handed out rice to the wretched. Is that never to happen again? Is the good woman of Setzuan to disappear? If only you would allow *me* to assist you! Now don't say anything! No assurances, no exclamations of gratitude! [*He has taken out his checkbook.*] Here! A blank check. [*He places it on the cart.*] Just my signature. Fill it out as you wish. Any sum in the world. I herewith retire from the scene, quietly, unobtrusively, making no claims, on tiptoe, full of veneration, absolutely selflessly . . . [*He has gone.*]

MRS. SHIN Well! You're saved. There's always some idiot of a man. . . . Now hurry! Put down a thousand silver dollars and let me fly to the bank before he comes to his senses.

SHEN TE I can pay you for the washing without any check.

MRS. SHIN What? You're not going to cash it just because you might have to marry him? Are you crazy? Men like him *want* to be led by the nose! Are you still thinking of that flyer? All Yellow Street knows how he treated you!

SHEN TE

When I heard his cunning laugh, I was afraid
But when I saw the holes in his shoes, I loved him dearly.

MRS. SHIN Defending that good-for-nothing after all that's happened!

SHEN TE [*Staggering as she holds some of the washing.*] Oh!

MRS. SHIN [*Taking the washing from her, dryly.*] So you feel dizzy when you stretch and bend? There couldn't be a little visitor on the way? If that's it, you can forget Mr. Shu Fu's blank check: it wasn't meant for a christening present!

[*She goes to the back with a basket. Shen Te's eyes follow* MRS. SHIN *for a moment. Then she looks down at her own body, feels her stomach, and a great joy comes into her eyes.*]

SHEN TE O joy! A new human being is on the way. The world awaits him. In the cities the people say: he's got to be reckoned with, this new human being! [*She imagines a little boy to be present, and introduces him to the audience.*] This is my son, the well-known flyer!

Say: Welcome
To the conqueror of unknown mountains and unreachable regions
Who brings us our mail across the impassable deserts!

[*She leads him up and down by the hand.*]

Take a look at the world, my son. That's a tree. Tree, yes. Say: "Hello, tree!" And bow. Like this. [*She bows.*] Now you know each other. And, look, here comes the water seller. He's a friend, give him your hand. A cup of fresh water for my little son, please. Yes, it *is* a warm day. [*Handing the cup.*] Oh dear, a policeman, we'll have to make a circle round *him*. Perhaps we can pick a few cherries over there in the rich Mr. Pung's garden. But we mustn't be seen. You want cherries? Just like children with fathers. No, no, you can't go straight at them like that. Don't pull. We must learn to be reasonable. Well, have it your own way. [*She has let him make for the cherries.*] Can you reach? Where to put them? Your mouth is the best place. [*She tries one herself.*] Mmm, they're good. But the policeman, we must run! [*They run.*] Yes, back to the street. Calm now, so no one will notice us. [*Walking the street with her child, she sings.*]

Once a plum—'twas in Japan—
Made a conquest of a man
But the man's turn soon did come
For he gobbled up the plum

[*Enter* WONG, *with a child by the hand. He coughs.*]

SHEN TE Wong!

WONG It's about the carpenter, Shen Te. He's lost his shop, and he's been drinking. His children are on the streets. This is one. Can you help?

SHEN TE [*To the child.*] Come here, little man. [*Takes him down to the footlights. To the audience.*]

You there! A man is asking you for shelter!
A man of tomorrow says: what about today?
His friend the conqueror, whom you know,
Is his advocate!

[*To* WONG.] He can live in Mr. Shu Fu's cabins. I may have to go there myself. I'm going to have a baby. That's a secret—don't tell Yang Sun—we'd only be in his way. Can you find the carpenter for me?

WONG I knew you'd think of something. [*To the child.*] Good-bye, son, I'm going for your father.

SHEN TE What about your hand, Wong? I wanted to help, but my cousin . . .

WONG Oh, I can get along with one hand, don't worry. [*He shows how he can handle his pole with his left hand alone.*]

SHEN TE But your right hand! Look, take this cart, sell everything that's on it, and go to the doctor with the money . . .

WONG She's still good. But first I'll bring the carpenter. I'll pick up the cart when I get back [*Exit* WONG.]

SHEN TE [*To the child.*] Sit down over here, son, till your father comes.

[*The child sits crosslegged on the ground. Enter the* HUSBAND *and* WIFE, *each dragging a large, full sack.*]

WIFE [*Furtively.*] You're alone, Shen Te, dear?

[SHEN TE *nods. The* WIFE *beckons to the* NEPHEW *offstage. He comes on with another sack.*]

WIFE Your cousin's away? [SHEN TE *nods.*] He's not coming back?

SHEN TE No. I'm giving up the shop.

WIFE That's why we're here. We want to know if we can leave these things in your new home. Will you do us this favor?

SHEN TE Why, yes, I'd be glad to.

HUSBAND [*Cryptically.*] And if anyone asks about them, say they're yours.

SHEN TE Would anyone ask?

WIFE [*With a glance back at her husband.*] Oh, someone might. The police, for instance. They don't seem to like us. Where can we put it?

SHEN TE Well, I'd rather not get in any more trouble . . .

WIFE Listen to her! The good woman of Setzuan!

[SHEN TE *is silent.*]

HUSBAND There's enough tobacco in those sacks to give us a new start in life. We could have our own tobacco factory!

SHEN TE [*Slowly.*] You'll have to put them in the back room

[*The sacks are taken offstage, while the child is alone. Shyly glancing about him, he goes to the garbage can, starts playing with the contents, and eating some of the scraps. The others return.*]

WIFE We're counting on you, Shen Te!

SHEN TE Yes. [*She sees the child and is shocked.*]

HUSBAND We'll see you in Mr. Shu Fu's cabins.

NEPHEW The day after tomorrow.

SHEN TE Yes. Now, go. Go! I'm not feeling well.

[*Exeunt all three, virtually pushed off.*]

He is eating the refuse in the garbage can!
Only look at his little gray mouth!

[*Pause. Music.*]

As this is the world *my* son will enter
I will study to defend him.
To be good to you, my son,
I shall be a tigress to all others
If I have to.
And I shall have to.

[*She starts to go*]

One more time, then. I hope really the last.

[*Exit* SHEN TE, *taking Shui Ta's trousers.* MRS. SHIN *enters and watches her with marked interest. Enter the* SISTER-IN-LAW *and the* GRANDFATHER.]

SISTER-IN-LAW So it's true, the shop has closed down. And the furniture's in the back yard. It's the end of the road!

MRS. SHIN [*Pompously.*] The fruit of high living, selfishness, and sensuality! Down the primrose path to Mr. Shu Fu's cabins—with you!

SISTER-IN-LAW Cabins? Rat holes! He gave them to us because his soap supplies only went moldy there!

[*Enter the* UNEMPLOYED MAN.]

UNEMPLOYED MAN Shen Te is moving?

SISTER-IN-LAW Yes. She was sneaking away.

MRS. SHIN She's ashamed of herself, and no wonder!

UNEMPLOYED MAN Tell her to call Mr. Shui Ta or she's done for this time!

SISTER-IN-LAW Tell her to call Mr. Shui Ta or *we're* done for this time!

[*Enter* WONG *and* CARPENTER, *the latter with a child on each hand.*]

CARPENTER So we'll have a roof over our heads for a change!

MRS. SHIN Roof? Whose roof?

CARPENTER Mr. Shu Fu's cabins. And we have little Feng to thank for it. [*Feng, we find, is the name of the child already there; his father now takes him. To the other two.*] Bow to your little brother, you two!

[*The* CARPENTER *and the two new arrivals bow to Feng. Enter* SHUI TA.]

UNEMPLOYED MAN Sst! Mr. Shui Ta!

[*Pause.*]

SHUI TA And what is this crowd here for, may I ask?

WONG How do you do, Mr. Shui Ta. This is the carpenter. Miss Shen Te promised him space in Mr. Shu Fu's cabins.

SHUI TA That will not be possible.

CARPENTER We can't go there after all?

SHUI TA All the space is needed for other purposes.

SISTER-IN-LAW You mean we have to get out? But we've got nowhere to go.

SHUI TA Miss Shen Te finds it possible to provide employment. If the proposition interests you, you may stay in the cabins.

SISTER-IN-LAW [*With distaste.*] You mean *work*? Work for Miss Shen Te?

SHUI TA Making tobacco, yes. There are three bales here already. Would you like to get them?

SISTER-IN-LAW [*Trying to bluster.*] We have our own tobacco! We were in the tobacco business before you were born!

SHUI TA [*To the* CARPENTER *and the* UNEMPLOYED MAN] You *don't* have your own tobacco. What about you?

[*The* CARPENTER *and the* UNEMPLOYED MAN *get the point, and go for the sacks. Enter* MRS. MI TZU.]

MRS. MI TZU Mr. Shui Ta? I've brought you your three hundred silver dollars.

SHUI TA I'll sign your lease instead. I've decided not to sell.

MRS. MI TZU What? You don't need the money for that flyer?

SHUI TA No.

MRS. MI TZU And you can pay six months' rent?

SHUI TA [*Takes the barber's blank check from the cart and fills it out.*] Here is a check for ten thousand silver dollars. On Mr. Shu Fu's account. Look. [*He shows her the signature on the check.*] Your six months' rent will be in your hands by seven this evening. And now, if you'll excuse me.

MRS. MI TZU So it's Mr. Shu Fu now. The flyer has been given his walking papers. These modern girls! In my day they'd have said she was flighty. That poor, deserted Mr. Yang Sun!

[*Exit* MRS. MI TZU. *The* CARPENTER *and the* UNEMPLOYED MAN *drag the three sacks back on the stage.*]

CARPENTER [*To* SHUI TA.] I don't know why I'm doing this for you.

SHUI TA Perhaps your children want to eat, Mr. Carpenter.

SISTER-IN-LAW [*Catching sight of the sacks.*] Was my brother-in-law here?

MRS. SHIN Yes, he was.

SISTER-IN-LAW I thought as much. I know those sacks! That's our tobacco!

SHUI TA Really? I thought it came from my back room! Shall we consult the police on the point?

SISTER-IN-LAW [*Defeated.*] No.

SHUI TA Perhaps you will show me the way to Mr. Shu Fu's cabins?

[*Taking Feng by the hand,* SHUI TA *goes off, followed by the* CARPENTER *and his two older children, the* SISTER-IN-LAW, *the* GRANDFATHER, *and the* UNEMPLOYED MAN. *Each of the last three drags a sack. Enter* OLD MAN *and* OLD WOMAN.]

MRS. SHIN A pair of pants—missing from the clothes line one minute—and next minute on the honorable backside of Mr. Shui Ta.

OLD WOMAN We thought Miss Shen Te was here.

MRS. SHIN [*Preoccupied.*] Well, she's not.

OLD MAN There was something she was going to give us.

WONG She was going to help me too. [*Looking at his hand.*] It'll be too late soon. But she'll be back. This cousin has never stayed long.

MRS. SHIN [*Approaching a conclusion.*] No, he hasn't, has he?

7a

The Sewer Pipe: WONG *asleep. In his dream, he tells the* GODS *his fears. The* GODS *seem tired from all their travels. They stop for a moment and look over their shoulders at the water seller.*

WONG Illustrious ones. I've been having a bad dream. Our beloved Shen Te was in great distress in the rushes down by the river—the spot where the bodies of suicides are washed up. She kept staggering and holding her head down as if she was carrying something and it was dragging her down into the mud. When I called out to her, she said she had to take your Book of Rules[7] to the other side, and not get it wet, or the ink would all come off. You had talked to her about the virtues, you know, the time she gave you shelter in Setzuan.

THIRD GOD Well, but what do you suggest, my dear Wong?

WONG Maybe a little relaxation of the rules, Benevolent One, in view of the bad times.

THIRD GOD As for instance?

WONG Well, um, good-will, for instance, might do instead of love?

THIRD GOD I'm afraid that would create new problems.

WONG Or, instead of justice, good sportsmanship?

THIRD GOD That would only mean more work.

WONG Instead of honor, outward propriety?

THIRD GOD Still more work! No, no! The rules will have to stand, my dear Wong!

[*Wearily shaking their heads, all three journey on.*]

7. Reference to neo-Confucianist commentator's rigid and prescriptive interpretation of Confucius's *Analects*, especially regarding the role of women.

8

Shui Ta's tobacco factory in Shu Fu's cabins. Huddled together behind bars, several families, mostly women and children. Among these people the SISTER-IN-LAW, *the* GRANDFATHER, *the* CARPENTER, *and his three children. Enter* MRS. YANG *followed by* YANG SUN.

MRS. YANG [*To the audience.*] There's something I just *have* to tell you: strength and wisdom are wonderful things. The strong and wise Mr. Shui Ta has transformed my son from a dissipated good-for-nothing into a model citizen. As you may have heard, Mr. Shui Ta opened a small tobacco factory near the cattle runs. It flourished. Three months ago—I shall never forget it—I asked for an appointment, and Mr. Shui Ta agree to see us—me and my son. I can see him now as he came through the door to meet us. . . .

[*Enter* SHUI TA, *from a door.*]

SHUI TA What can I do for you, Mrs. Yang?

MRS. YANG This morning the police came to the house. We find you've brought an action for breach of promise of marriage. In the name of Shen Te. You also claim that Sun came by two hundred silver dollars by improper means.

SHUI TA That is correct.

MRS. YANG Mr. Shui Ta, the money's all gone. When the Peking job didn't materialize, he ran through it all in three days. I know he's a good-for-nothing. He sold my furniture. He was moving to Peking without me. Miss Shen Te thought highly of him at one time.

SHUI TA What do *you* say, Mr. Yang Sun?

YANG SUN The money's gone.

SHUI TA [*To* MRS. YANG.] Mrs. Yang, in consideration of my cousin's incomprehensible weakness for your son, I am prepared to give him another chance. He can have a job—here. The two hundred silver dollars will be taken out of his wages.

YANG SUN So it's the factory or jail?

SHUI TA Take your choice.

YANG SUN May I speak with Shen Te?

SHUI TA You may not.

[*Pause.*]

YANG SUN [*Sullenly.*] Show me where to go.

MRS. YANG Mr. Shui Ta, you are kindness itself: the gods will reward you! [*To* YANG SUN.] And honest work will make a man of you, my boy. [YANG SUN *follows* SHUI TA *into the factory.* MRS. YANG *comes down again to the footlights.*] Actually, honest work didn't agree with him—at first. And he got no opportunity to distinguish himself till—in the third week—when the wages were being paid . . .

[SHUI TA *has a bag of money. Standing next to his foreman—the former* UNEMPLOYED MAN—*he counts out the wages. It is Yang Sun's turn.*]

UNEMPLOYED MAN [*Reading.*] Carpenter, six silver dollars. Yang Sun, six silver dollars.

YANG SUN [*Quietly.*] Excuse me, sir. I don't think it can be more than five. May I see? [*He takes the foreman's list.*] It says six working days. But that's a mistake, sir. I took a day off for court business. And I won't take what I haven't earned, however miserable the pay is!

UNEMPLOYED MAN Yang Sun. Five silver dollars. [*To* SHUI TA.] A rare case, Mr. Shui Ta!

SHUI TA How is it the book says six when it should say five?

UNEMPLOYED MAN I must've made a mistake, Mr. Shui Ta. [*With a look at* YANG SUN.] It won't happen again.

SHUI TA [*Taking* YANG SUN *aside.*] You don't hold back, do you? You give your all to the firm. You're even honest. Do the foreman's mistakes always favor the workers?

YANG SUN He does have . . . friends.

SHUI TA Thank you. May I offer you any little recompense?

YANG SUN Give me a trial period of one week, and I'll prove my intelligence is worth more to you than my strength.

MRS. YANG [*Still down at the footlights.*] Fighting words, fighting words! That evening, I said to Sun: "If you're a flyer, then fly, my falcon! Rise in the world!" And he got to be foreman. Yes, in Mr. Shui Ta's tobacco factory, he worked real miracles.

[*We see* YANG SUN *with his legs apart standing behind the workers, who are handing along a basket of raw tobacco above their heads.*]

YANG SUN Faster! Faster! You, there, d'you think you can just stand around, now you're not foreman any more? It'll be your job to lead us in song. Sing!

[UNEMPLOYED MAN *starts singing. The others join in the refrain.*]

SONG OF THE EIGHTH ELEPHANT

Chang had seven elephants—all much the same—
  But then there was Little Brother
The seven, they were wild, Little Brother, he was tame
  And to guard them Chang chose Little Brother
    Run faster!
    Mr. Chang has a forest park
    Which must be cleared before tonight
    And already it's growing dark!

When the seven elephants cleared that forest park
  Mr. Chang rode high on Little Brother
While the seven toiled and moiled till dark
  On his big behind sat Little Brother
    Dig faster!
    Mr. Chang has a forest park
    Which must be cleared before tonight
    And already it's growing dark!

And the seven elephants worked many an hour
  Till none of them could work another
Old Chang, he looked sour, on the seven he did glower
  But gave a pound of rice to Little Brother
    What was that?
    Mr. Chang has a forest park
    Which must be cleared before tonight
    And already it's growing dark!

And the seven elephants hadn't any tusks
The one that had the tusks was Little Brother
Seven are no match for one, if the one has a gun!
How old Chang did laugh at Little Brother!
Keep on digging!
Mr. Chang has a forest park
Which must be cleared before tonight
And already it's growing dark!

[*Smoking a cigar,* SHUI TA *strolls by.* YANG SUN, *laughing, has joined in the refrain of the third stanza and speeded up the tempo of the last stanza by clapping his hands.*]

MRS. YANG And that's why I say: strength and wisdom are wonderful things. It took the strong and wise Mr. Shui Ta to bring out the best in Yang Sun. A real superior man is like a bell. If you ring it, it rings, and if you don't, it don't, as the saying is.[8]

9

Shen Te's shop, now an office with club chairs and fine carpets. It is raining. SHUI TA, *now fat, is just dismissing the* OLD MAN *and* OLD WOMAN. MRS. SHIN, *in obviously new clothes, looks on, smirking.*

SHUI TA No! I CANNOT tell you when we expect her back.

OLD WOMAN The two hundred silver dollars came today. In an envelope. There was no letter, but it must be from Shen Te. We want to write and thank her. May we have her address?

SHUI TA I'm afraid I haven't got it.

OLD MAN [*Pulling Old Woman's sleeve.*] Let's be going.

OLD WOMAN She's got to come back some time!

[*They move off, uncertainly, worried.* SHUI TA *bows.*]

MRS. SHIN They lost the carpet shop because they couldn't pay their taxes. The money arrived too late.

SHUI TA They could have come to me.

MRS. SHIN People don't like coming to you.

SHUI TA [*Sits suddenly, one hand to his head.*] I'm dizzy.

MRS. SHIN After all, you *are* in your seventh month. But old Mrs. Shin will be there in your hour of trial! [*She cackles feebly.*]

SHUI TA [*In a stifled voice.*] Can I count on that?

MRS. SHIN We all have our price, and mine won't be too high for the great Mr. Shui Ta! [*She opens Shui Ta's collar.*]

SHUI TA It's for the child's sake. All of this.

MRS. SHIN "All for the child," of course.

SHUI TA I'm so fat. People must notice.

MRS. SHIN Oh no, they think it's 'cause you're rich.

SHIU TA [*More feelingly.*] What will happen to the child?

MRS. SHIN You ask that nine times a day. Why, it'll have the best that money can buy!

SHUI TA He must never see Shui Ta.

MRS. SHIN Oh, no. Always Shen Te.

8. A saying by the Chinese philosopher Mo-tzu (470–391 B.C.E.).

SHUI TA What about the neighbors? There are rumors, aren't there?

MRS. SHIN As long as Mr. Shu Fu doesn't find out, there's nothing to worry about. Drink this.

[*Enter* YANG SUN *in a smart business suit, and carrying a businessman's briefcase.* SHUI TA *is more or less in Mrs. Shin's arms.*]

YANG SUN [*Surprised.*] I guess I'm in the way.

SHUI TA [*Ignoring this, rises with an effort.*] Till tomorrow, Mrs. Shin.

[MRS. SHIN *leaves with a smile, putting her new gloves.*]

YANG SUN Gloves now! She couldn't be fleecing you? And since when did *you* have a private life? [*Taking a paper from the briefcase.*] You haven't been at your best lately, and things are getting out of hand. The police want to close us down. They say that at the most they can only permit twice the lawful number of workers.

SHUI TA [*Evasively.*] The cabins are quite good enough.

YANG SUN For the workers maybe, not for the tobacco. They're too damp. We must take over some of Mrs. Mi Tzu's buildings.

SHUI TA Her price is double what I can pay.

YANG SUN Not unconditionally. If she has me to stroke her knees she'll come down.

SHUI TA I'll never agree to that.

YANG SUN What's wrong? Is it the rain? You get so irritable whenever it rains.

SHUI TA Never! I will never . . .

YANG SUN Mrs. Mi Tzu'll be here in five minutes. *You* fix it. And Shu Fu will be with her. . . . What's all that noise?

[*During the above dialogue,* WONG *is heard offstage, calling:* "The good Shen Te, where is she? Which of you has seen Shen Te, good people? Where is Shen Te?" *A knock. Enter* WONG.]

WONG Mr. Shui Ta, I've come to ask when Miss Shen Te will be back, it's six months now. . . . There are rumors. People say something's happened to her.

SHUI TA I'm busy. Come back next week.

WONG [*Excited.*] In the morning there was always rice on her doorstep—for the needy. It's been there again lately!

SHUI TA And what do people conclude from this?

WONG That Shen Te is still in Setzuan! She's been . . . [*He breaks off.*]

SHUI TA She's been what? Mr. Wong, if you're Shen Te's friend, talk a little less about her, that's my advice to you.

WONG I don't want your advice! Before she disappeared, Miss Shen Te told me something very important—she's pregnant!

YANG SUN What? What was that?

SHUI TA [*Quickly.*] The man is lying.

WONG A good woman isn't so easily forgotten, Mr. Shui Ta.

[*He leaves.* SHUI TA *goes quickly into the back room.*]

YANG SUN [*To the audience.*] Shen Te pregnant? So that's why. Her cousin sent her away, so I wouldn't get wind of it. I have a son, a Yang appears on the scene, and what happens? Mother and child vanish into thin air! That scoundrel, that unspeakable . . . [*The sound of sobbing is heard from the back room.*] What was that? Someone sobbing? Who was it? Mr. Shui Ta the Tobacco King doesn't weep his heart out. And where does the rice come from that's on the doorstep in the morning? [SHUI TA *returns. He goes to the door and looks out into the rain.*] Where is she?

SHUI TA Sh! It's nine o'clock. But the rain's so heavy, you can't hear a thing.

YANG SUN What do you want to hear?

SHUI TA The mail plane.

YANG SUN What?!

SHUI TA I've been told *you* wanted to fly at one time. Is that all forgotten?

YANG SUN Flying mail is night work. I prefer the daytime. And the firm is very dear to me—after all it belongs to my ex-fiancée, even if she's not around. And she's not, is she?

SHUI TA What do you mean by that?

YANG SUN Oh, well, let's say I haven't altogether—lost interest.

SHUI TA My cousin might like to know that.

YANG SUN I might not be indifferent—if I found she was being kept under lock and key.

SHUI TA By whom?

YANG SUN By you.

SHUI TA What could you do about it?

YANG SUN I could submit for discussion—my position in the firm.

SHUI TA You are now my manager. In return for a more . . . appropriate position, you might agree to drop the inquiry into your ex-fiancée's whereabouts?

YANG SUN I might.

SHUI TA What position *would* be more appropriate?

YANG SUN The one at the top.

SHUI TA My own? [*Silence.*] And if I preferred to throw you out on your neck?

YANG SUN I'd come back on my feet. With suitable escort.

SHUI TA The police?

YANG SUN The police.

SHUI TA And when the police found no one?

YANG SUN I might ask them not to overlook the back room. [*Ending the pretense.*] In short, Mr. Shui Ta, my interest in this young woman has not been officially terminated. I should like to see more of her. [*Into Shui Ta's face.*] Besides, she's pregnant and needs a friend. [*He moves to the door.*] I shall talk about it with the water seller.

[*Exit.* SHUI TA *is rigid for a moment, then he quickly goes into the back room. He returns with Shen Te's belongings: underwear, etc. He takes a long look at the shawl of the previous scene. He then wraps the things in a bundle, which, upon hearing a noise, he hides under the table. Enter* MRS. MI TZU *and Mr.* SHU FU. *They put away their umbrellas and galoshes.*]

MRS. MI TZU I thought your manager was here, Mr. Shui Ta. He combines charm with business in a way that can only be to the advantage of all of us.

SHU FU You sent for us, Mr. Shui Ta?

SHUI TA The factory is in trouble.

SHU FU It always is.

SHUI TA The police are threatening to close us down unless I can show that the extension of our facilities is imminent.

SHU FU Mr. Shui Ta, I'm sick and tired of your constantly expanding projects. I place cabins at your cousin's disposal; you make a factory of them. I hand your cousin a check; you present it. Your cousin disappears; you find the cabins too small and start talking of yet more—

SHUI TA Mr. Shu Fu, I'm authorized to inform you that Miss Shen Te's return is now imminent.

SHU FU Imminent? It's becoming his favorite word.

MRS. MI TZU Yes, what does it mean?

SHUI TA Mrs. Mi Tzu, I can pay you exactly half what you asked for your buildings. Are you ready to inform the police that I am taking them over?

MRS. MI TZU Certainly, if I can take over your manager.

SHU FU What?

MRS. MI TZU He's so efficient.

SHUI TA I'm afraid I need Mr. Yang Sun.

MRS. MI TZU So do I.

SHUI TA He will call on you tomorrow.

SHU FU So much the better. With Shen Te likely to turn up at any moment, the presence of that young man is hardly in good taste.

SHUI TA So we have reached a settlement. In what was once the good Shen Te's little shop we are laying the foundations for the great Mr. Shui Ta's twelve magnificent super tobacco markets. You will bear in mind that though they call me the Tobacco King of Setzuan, it is my cousin's interests that have been served . . .

VOICES [*Off.*] The police, the police! Going to the tobacco shop! Something must have happened!

[*Enter* YANG SUN, WONG, *and the* POLICEMAN.]

POLICEMAN Quiet there, quiet, quiet! [*They quiet down.*] I'm sorry, Mr. Shui Ta, but there's a report that you've been depriving Miss Shen Te of her freedom. Not that I believe all I hear, but the whole city's in an uproar.

SHUI TA That's a lie.

POLICEMAN Mr. Yang Sun has testified that he heard someone sobbing in the back room.

SHU FU Mrs. Mi Tzu and myself will testify that no one here has been sobbing.

MRS. MI TZU We have been quietly smoking our cigars.

POLICEMAN Mr. Shui Ta, I'm afraid I shall have to take a look at that room. [*He does so. The room is empty.*] No one there, of course, sir.

YANG SUN But I heard sobbing. What's that?

[*He finds the clothes.*]

WONG Those are Shen Te's things. [*To crowd.*] Shen Te's clothes are here!

VOICES [*Off, in sequence.*] Shen Te's clothes!
—They've been found under the table!
—Body of murdered girl still missing!
—Tobacco King suspected!

POLICEMAN Mr. Shui Ta, unless you can tell us where the girl is, I'll have to ask you to come along.

SHUI TA I do not know.

POLICEMAN I can't say how sorry I am, Mr. Shui Ta. [*He shows him the door.*]

SHUI TA Everything will be cleared up in no time. There are still judges in Setzuan.

YANG SUN I heard sobbing!

9a

Wong's den. For the last time, the GODS *appear to the water seller in his dream. They have changed and show signs of a long journey, extreme fatigue, and plenty of mishaps. The* FIRST *no longer has a hat; the* THIRD *has lost a leg; all three are barefoot.*

WONG Illustrious ones, at last you're here. Shen Te's been gone for months and today her cousin's been arrested. They think he murdered her to get the shop. But I had a dream and in this dream Shen Te said her cousin was keeping her prisoner. You must find her for us, illustrious ones!

FIRST GOD We've found very few good people anywhere, and even they didn't keep it up. Shen Te is still the only one that stayed good.

SECOND GOD If she *has* stayed good.

WONG Certainly she has. But she's vanished.

FIRST GOD That's the last straw. All is lost!

SECOND GOD A little moderation, dear colleague!

FIRST GOD [*Plaintively.*] What's the good of moderation now? If she can't be found, we'll have to resign! The world is a terrible place! Nothing but misery, vulgarity, and waste! Even the countryside isn't what it used to be. The trees are getting their heads chopped off by telephone wires, and there's such a noise from all the gunfire, and I can't stand those heavy clouds of smoke, and—

THIRD GOD The place is absolutely unlivable! Good intentions bring people to the brink of the abyss, and good deeds push them over the edge. I'm afraid our book of rules is destined for the scrap heap—

SECOND GOD It's people! They're a worthless lot!

THIRD GOD The world is too cold!

SECOND GOD It's people! They're too weak!

FIRST GOD Dignity, dear colleagues, dignity! Never despair! As for this world, didn't we agree that we only have to find one human being who can stand the place? Well, we found her. True, we lost her again. We must find her again, that's all! And at once!

[*They disappear.*]

10

Courtroom. Groups: SHU FU *and* MRS. MI TZU; YANG SUN *and* MRS. YANG; WONG, *the* CARPENTER, *the* GRANDFATHER, *the* NIECE, *the* OLD MAN, *the* OLD WOMAN; MRS. SHIN, *the* POLICEMAN; *the* UNEMPLOYED MAN, *the* SISTER-IN-LAW.

OLD MAN So much power isn't good for one man.

UNEMPLOYED MAN And he's going to open twelve super tobacco markets!

WIFE One of the judges is a friend of Mr. Shu Fu's.

SISTER-IN-LAW Another one accepted a present from Mr. Shui Ta only last night. A great fat goose.

OLD WOMAN [*To* WONG] And Shen Te is nowhere to be found.

WONG Only the gods will ever know the truth.

POLICEMAN Order in the court! My lords the judges!

[*Enter the* THREE GODS *in judges' robes. We overhear their conversation as they pass along the footlights to their bench.*]

THIRD GOD We'll never get away with it, our certificates were so badly forged.

SECOND GOD My predecessor's "sudden indigestion" will certainly cause comment.

FIRST GOD But he *had* just eaten a whole goose.

UNEMPLOYED MAN Look at that! *New* judges.

WONG New judges. And what good ones!

[*The* THIRD GOD *hears this, and turns to smile at* WONG. *The* GODS *sit. The* FIRST GOD *beats on the bench with his gavel. The* POLICEMAN *brings in* SHUI TA, *who walks with lordly steps. He is whistled*[9] *at.*]

POLICEMAN [*To* SHUI TA.] Be prepared for a surprise. The judges have been changed.

[SHUI TA *turns quickly round, looks at them, and staggers.*]

NIECE What's the matter now?

WIFE The great Tobacco King nearly fainted.

HUSBAND Yes, as soon as he saw the new judges.

WONG Does *he* know who they are?

[SHUI TA *picks himself up, and the proceedings open.*]

FIRST GOD Defendant Shui Ta, you are accused of doing away with your cousin Shen Te in order to take possession of her business. Do you plead guilty or not guilty?

SHUI TA Not guilty, my lord.

FIRST GOD [*Thumbing through the documents of the case.*] The first witness is the policeman. I shall ask him to tell us something of the respective reputations of Miss Shen Te and Mr. Shui Ta.

POLICEMAN Miss Shen Te was a young lady who aimed to please, my lord. She liked to live and let live, as the saying goes. Mr. Shui Ta, on the other hand, is a man of principle. Though the generosity of Miss Shen Te forced him at times to abandon half measures, unlike the girl he was always on the side of the law, my lord. One time, he even unmasked a gang of thieves to whom his too trustful cousin had given shelter. The evidence, in short, my lord, proves that Mr. Shui Ta was *incapable* of the crime of which he stands accused!

FIRST GOD I see. And are there others who could testify along, shall we say, the same lines?

[SHU FU *rises.*]

POLICEMAN [*Whispering to* GODS.] Mr. Shu Fu—a very important person.

FIRST GOD [*Inviting him to speak.*] Mr. Shu Fu!

SHU FU Mr. Shui Ta is a businessman, my lord. Need I say more?

FIRST GOD Yes.

SHU FU Very well, I will. He is Vice President of the Council of Commerce and is about to be elected a Justice of the Peace. [*He returns to his seat.* MRS. MI TZU *rises.*]

WONG Elected! *He* gave him the job!

[*With a gesture the* FIRST GOD *asks who* MRS. MI TZU *is.*]

POLICEMAN Another very important person. Mrs. Mi Tzu.

FIRST GOD [*Inviting her to speak.*] Mrs. Mi Tzu!

MRS. MI TZU My lord, as Chairman of the Committee on Social Work, I wish to call attention to just a couple of eloquent facts: Mr. Shui Ta not only has

9. Hissed.

erected a model factory with model housing in our city, he is a regular contributor to our home for the disabled. [*She returns to her seat.*]

POLICEMAN [*Whispering.*] And she's a great friend of the judge that ate the goose!

FIRST GOD [*To the* POLICEMAN.] Oh, thank you. What next? [*To the Court, genially.*] Oh, yes. We should find out if any of the evidence is less favorable to the defendant.

[WONG, *the* CARPENTER, *the* OLD MAN, *the* OLD WOMAN, *the* UNEMPLOYED MAN, *the* SISTER-IN-LAW, *and the* NIECE *come forward.*]

POLICEMAN [*Whispering.*] Just the riffraff, my lord.

FIRST GOD [*Addressing the "riffraff."*] Well, um, riffraff—do you know anything of the defendant, Mr. Shui Ta?

WONG Too much, my lord.

UNEMPLOYED MAN What don't we know, my lord.

CARPENTER He ruined us.

SISTER-IN-LAW He's a cheat.

NIECE Liar.

WIFE Thief.

BOY Blackmailer.

BROTHER Murderer.

FIRST GOD Thank you. We should now let the defendant state his point of view.

SHUI TA I only came on the scene when Shen Te was in danger of losing what I had understood was a gift from the gods. Because I did the filthy jobs which someone had to do, they hate me. My activities were restricted to the minimum, my lord.

SISTER-IN-LAW He had us arrested!

SHUI TA Certainly. You stole from the bakery!

SISTER-IN-LAW Such concern for the bakery! You didn't want the shop for yourself, I suppose!

SHUI TA I didn't want the shop overrun with parasites.

SISTER-IN-LAW We had nowhere else to go.

SHUI TA There were too many of you.

WONG What about this old couple: Were *they* parasites?

OLD MAN We lost our shop because of you!

OLD WOMAN And we gave your cousin money!

SHUI TA My cousin's fiancé was a flyer. The money had to go to *him*.

WONG Did you care whether he flew or not? Did you care whether she married him or not? You wanted her to marry someone else!

[*He points to* SHU FU.]

SHUI TA The flyer unexpectedly turned out to be a scoundrel.

YANG SUN [*Jumping up.*] Which was the reason you made him your manager?

SHUI TA Later on he improved.

WONG And when he improved, you sold him to her? [*He points out* MRS. MI TZU.]

SHUI TA She wouldn't let me have her premises unless she had him to stroke her knees!

MRS. MI TZU What? The man's a pathological liar. [*To him.*] Don't mention my property to me as long as you live! Murderer! [*She rustles off, in high dudgeon.*]

YANG SUN [*Pushing in.*] My lord, I wish to speak for the defendant.

SISTER-IN-LAW Naturally. He's your employer.

UNEMPLOYED MAN And the worst slave driver in the country.

MRS. YANG That's a lie! My lord, Mr. Shui Ta is a great man. He . . .

YANG SUN He's this and he's that, but he is not a murderer, my lord. Just fifteen minutes before his arrest I heard Shen Te's voice in his own back room.

FIRST GOD Oh? Tell us more!

YANG SUN I heard sobbing, my lord!

FIRST GOD But lots of women sob, we've been finding.

YANG SUN Could I fail to recognize her voice?

SHU FU No, you made her sob so often yourself, young man!

YANG SUN Yes. But I also made her happy. Till he [*Pointing at* SHUI TA.] decided to sell her to you!

SHUI TA Because you didn't love her.

WONG Oh, no: it was for the money, my lord!

SHUI TA And what was the money for, my lord? For the poor! And for Shen Te so she could go on being good!

WONG For the poor? That he sent to his sweatshops? And why didn't you let Shen Te be good when you signed the big check?

SHUI TA For the child's sake, my lord.

CARPENTER What about *my* children? What did he do about them?

[SHUI TA *is silent.*]

WONG The shop was to be a fountain of goodness. That was the gods' idea. You came and spoiled it!

SHUI TA If I hadn't, it would have run dry!

MRS. SHIN There's a lot in that, my lord.

WONG What have you done with the good Shen Te, bad man? She *was* good, my lords, she was, I swear it! [*He raises his hand in an oath.*]

THIRD GOD What's happened to your hand, water seller?

WONG [*Pointing to* SHUI TA.] It's all his fault, my lord, *she* was going to send me to a doctor— [*To* SHUI TA.] You were her worst enemy!

SHUI TA I was her only friend!

WONG Where is she then? Tell us where your good friend is!

[*The excitement of this exchange has run through the whole crowd.*]

ALL Yes, where is she? Where is Shen Te? [*Etc.*]

SHUI TA Shen Te . . . had to go.

WONG Where? Where to?

SHUI TA I cannot tell you! I cannot tell you!

ALL Why? Why did she have to go away? [*Etc.*]

WONG [*Into the din with the first words, but talking on beyond the others.*] Why not, why not? Why did she have to go away?

SHUI TA [*Shouting.*] Because you'd all have torn her to shreds, that's why! My lords, I have a request. Clear the court! When only the judges remain, I will make a confession.

ALL [*Except* WONG, *who is silent, struck by the new turn of events.*] So he's guilty? He's confessing! [*Etc.*]

FIRST GOD [*Using the gavel.*] Clear the court!

POLICEMAN Clear the court!

WONG Mr. Shui Ta has met his match this time.

MRS. SHIN [*With a gesture toward the judges.*] You're in for a little surprise.
[*The court is cleared. Silence.*]

SHUI TA Illustrious ones!

[*The* GODS *look at each other, not quite believing their ears.*]

SHUI TA Yes, I recognize you!

SECOND GOD [*Taking matters in hand, sternly.*] What have you done with our good woman of Setzuan?

SHUI TA I have a terrible confession to make: I am she! [*He takes off his mask, and tears away his clothes.* SHEN TE *stands there.*]

SECOND GOD Shen Te!

SHEN TE Shen Te, yes. Shui Ta *and* Shen Te. Both.

Your injunction
To be good and yet to live
Was a thunderbolt:
It has torn me in two
I can't tell how it was
But to be good to others
And myself at the same time
I could not do it
Your world is not an easy one, illustrious ones!
When we extend our hand to a beggar, he tears it off for us
When we help the lost, we are lost ourselves
And so
Since not to eat is to die
Who can long refuse to be bad?
As I lay prostrate beneath the weight of good intentions
Ruin stared me in the face
It was when I was unjust that I ate good meat
And hobnobbed with the mighty
Why?
Why are bad deeds rewarded?
Good ones punished?
I enjoyed giving
I truly wished to be the Angel of the Slums
But washed by a foster-mother in the water of the gutter
I developed a sharp eye
The time came when pity was a thorn in my side
And, later, when kind words turned to ashes in my mouth
And anger took over
I became a wolf
Find me guilty, then, illustrious ones,
But know:
All that I have done I did
To help my neighbor
To love my lover
And to keep my little one from want
For your great, godly deeds, I was too poor, too small.

[*Pause.*]

FIRST GOD [*Shocked.*] Don't go on making yourself miserable, Shen Te! We're overjoyed to have found you!

SHEN TE I'm telling you I'm the bad man who committed all those crimes!

FIRST GOD [*Using—or failing to use—his ear trumpet.*] The good woman who did all those good deeds?

SHEN TE Yes, but the bad man too!

FIRST GOD [*As if something had dawned.*] Unfortunate coincidences! Heartless neighbors!

THIRD GOD [*Shouting in his ear.*] But how is she to continue?

FIRST GOD Continue? Well, she's a strong, healthy girl . . .

SECOND GOD You didn't hear what she said!

FIRST GOD I heard every word! She is confused, that's all! [*He begins to bluster.*] And what about this book of rules—we can't renounce our rules, can we? [*More quietly.*] Should the world be changed? How? By whom? The world should *not* be changed! [*At a sign from him, the lights turn pink, and music plays.*]

And now the hour of parting is at hand.
Dost thou behold, Shen Te, yon fleecy cloud?
It is our chariot. At a sign from me
'Twill come and take us back from whence we came
Above the azure vault and silver stars. . . .

SHEN TE No! Don't go, illustrious ones!

FIRST GOD

Our cloud has landed now in yonder field
From which it will transport us back to heaven.
Farewell, Shen Te, let not thy courage fail thee. . . .

[*Exeunt* GODS.]

SHEN TE What about the old couple? They've lost their shop! What about the water seller and his hand? And I've got to defend myself against the barber, because I don't love him! And against Sun, because I do love him! How? How?

[*Shen Te's eyes follow the* GODS *as they are imagined to step into a cloud, which rises and moves forward over the orchestra and up beyond the balcony.*]

FIRST GOD [*From on high.*] We have faith in you, Shen Te!

SHEN TE There'll be a child. And he'll have to be fed. I can't stay here. Where shall I go?

FIRST GOD Continue to be good, good woman of Setzuan!

SHEN TE I need my bad cousin!

FIRST GOD But not very often!

SHEN TE Once a week at least!

FIRST GOD Once a month will be quite enough!

SHEN TE [*Shrieking.*] No, no! Help!

[*But the cloud continues to recede as the* GODS *sing.*]

VALEDICTORY HYMN

What rapture, oh, it is to know
A good thing when you see it
And having seen a good thing, oh,
What rapture 'tis to flee it

Be good, sweet maid of Setzuan
Let Shui Ta be clever
Departing, we forget the man
Remember your endeavor

Because through all the length of days
Her goodness faileth never
Sing hallelujah! Make Shen Te's
Good name live on forever!

SHEN TE Help!

Epilogue

You're thinking, aren't you, that this is no right
Conclusion to the play you've seen tonight?
After a tale, exotic, fabulous,
A nasty ending was slipped up on us.
We feel deflated too. We too are nettled
To see the curtain down and nothing settled.
How could a better ending be arranged?
Could one change people? Can the world be changed?
Would new gods do the trick? Will atheism?
Moral rearmament? Materialism?
It is for you to find a way, my friends,
To help good men arrive at happy ends.
You write the happy ending to the play!
There must, there must, there's got to be a way!

TENNESSEE WILLIAMS

1911–1983

WHEN Tennessee Williams's play *The Glass Menagerie* premiered in 1944, American drama found itself at a crossroads. Eugene O'Neill, whose plays helped establish the American theater as a serious artistic medium, had been absent from the stage since 1934, and the drama of social protest that dominated the 1930s was eclipsed by the outbreak of World War II. American society was undergoing a transition, as traditional values and institutions were shaken by the mid-twentieth century's accelerating economic and social transformations. In this theatrical and social climate, the plays of Williams and ARTHUR MILLER restored the centrality of theater to the nation's cultural life. But whereas Miller's *All My Sons* (1947) and *Death of a Salesman* (1949) concentrated on the ethical conflicts of individuals and society, Williams's drama explored the deeper (and often darker) regions of America's psyche: the psychological fault lines between convention and romantic individualism; the dynamics of sexuality, violence, and alienation; and the place of art and the artist's visionary temperament in a society seen as increasingly hostile to the imagination. Drawn to characters who cling to failing illusions—outsiders who have difficulty fitting in the modern world—Williams pioneered a lyrical dramatic style that confronted but also transcended the harsh realities of contemporary life. In plays such as *The Glass Menagerie*, A STREETCAR NAMED DESIRE (1947), and *Cat on a Hot Tin Roof* (1955), the clash of cultures, generations, and psyches is marked by a lyricism reminiscent of the works of ANTON CHEKHOV (1860–1904) and Federico García Lorca (1898–1936). After Williams's death, the playwright David Mamet called these plays "the greatest dramatic poetry in the American language."

Williams was, before all else, a Southern writer; like his fellow twentieth-century authors William Faulkner, Eudora Welty, and Flannery O'Connor, he explored the region's self-defining myths and codes of behavior, its changing economy, and its multiple—often conflicting—cultures. The playwright was born Thomas Lanier Williams III on March 26, 1911, in Columbus, Mississippi, to Edwina Dakin Williams, the daughter of an Episcopal minister, and Cornelius Coffin Williams, a shoe salesman from east Tennessee. (The playwright would later change his first name to Tennessee in recognition of his paternal ancestors.) Although he suffered a near-fatal bout of diphtheria at the age of five that kept him out of school, his childhood in Mississippi was an idyllic one. But the idyll ended in 1918 when his father moved the family to St. Louis to take a managerial position at the International Shoe Company. Living in what he later recalled as "a perpetually dim little apartment in a wilderness of identical brick and concrete structures with no grass and no trees nearer than the park," mocked by other children for their southern accents, Williams and his sister Rose (with whom he was very close) found themselves isolated and unhappy in this harsh urban setting. The situation at home was hardly better: his parents quarreled frequently, and his relationship with his father was strained.

Williams began writing at the age of twelve and saw his first article published in a popular magazine at the age of sixteen. He attended the University of Missouri from 1929 to 1932 and majored in journalism, but his father withdrew him from college after he failed a mandatory ROTC course. For the next several years, he worked at his father's company while writing stories at night. Williams eventually attended Washington University in St. Louis and the University of Iowa, where he earned a B.A. in English in 1938. During these years Williams turned his attention to playwriting. A year after his first play—a farce about sailors titled *Cairo! Shanghai! Bombay!*—was produced in a backyard theater in 1935, Williams became involved with the Mummers, a semiprofessional St. Louis theater group specializing in plays of social protest. The country was in the throes of the Depression, and the theater had become an outlet for expressing social and political discontent. Clifford Odets's *Waiting for Lefty* took the theater world by storm in 1935, and the Federal Theatre Project (part of the New Deal's Works Progress Administration) was popularizing the multimedia "Living Newspaper" format as a way of commenting on poverty and other social issues. Reflecting this theatrical climate, Williams's drama during these years was socially and politically engaged. In 1937 the Mummers produced *Candles to the Sun*, a play about Alabama coal miners, and *Fugitive Kind*, which explored the hardships of Depression America through a group of characters living in a St. Louis flophouse. Williams also completed *Not About Nightingales*, a play about prison conditions that he had started at the University of Iowa; the Mummers considered this play, but it would not be produced until 1998.

Buoyed by the local success of these plays, Williams submitted three works to a playwriting competition sponsored by the Group Theater, one of the leading American theater companies of the 1930s. He also moved to New Orleans for two months, a city to which he would return throughout his career and to which he would later refer as his "spiritual home." Williams received a special prize from the Group Theater for a collection of one-act plays and subsequently won a Rockefeller Foundation fellowship, which he used to write *The Battle of Angels*. The Theater Guild of New York produced this play in Boston in 1940, but the production was condemned by spectators and critics.

Over the next four years Williams held a variety of jobs, including a two-month scriptwriting stint for MGM in Hollywood, and he worked on a number of other writing projects. One of these, a play titled *The Gentleman Caller*, would earn Williams the fame that had eluded him in Boston. Under the revised title *The Glass Menagerie*, this play opened in Chicago in December 1944. Response was initially lukewarm, but the glowing review by a prominent Chicago theater critic led to sold-out houses. After transferring to Broadway in March 1945, the play ran for 561 performances and won the New York Drama Critics' Circle Award for Best Play. Williams's most deeply autobiographical drama—its narrator, Tom Wingfield, is modeled on Williams himself, and his sister Laura is a portrait of Rose Williams—*The Glass Menagerie* was important to American theater (and to the playwright's subsequent career) as much for its technical and stylistic innovations as for its subject matter. Seeking to express the fluidity of memory in theatrical terms, Williams employs setting, music, and light in ways that blur the lines between realism and expressionism. The playwright's production notes to *The Glass Menagerie* call for "a new, plastic theatre which must take the place of the exhausted theatre of realistic conventions if the theatre is to resume vitality as a part of our culture." Such a theater must not escape reality; rather, the use of expressionistic and poetic devices allows fuller access to the truth. "[T]ruth, life, or reality," Williams wrote, "is an organic thing which the poetic imagination can represent or suggest, in essence, only through transformation, through changing into other forms than those which were merely present in appearance."

The success of *The Glass Menagerie* catapulted Williams to the forefront of public attention and generated a celebrity toward which he remained profoundly ambivalent. His reputation as one of America's leading dramatists was underscored by the success of his next play, *A Streetcar Named Desire*. Williams had conceived the play's outlines in the early 1940s and had written a number of early versions: *Blanche's Chair on the Moon, The Moth, The Primary Colors,* and *The Poker Night* were among the titles he tried. The completed *A Streetcar Named Desire* opened on December 3, 1947, at the Ethel Barrymore Theater in New York in a production directed by Elia Kazan. Starring a little-known actor, Marlon Brando, in the role of Stanley Kowalski, the play ran for 855 performances over the next two years and was awarded a Pulitzer Prize and the New York Drama Critics' Circle Award. The 1951 film version of *Streetcar* (also directed by Kazan) was equally celebrated. In addition to receiving a number of major revivals, *A Streetcar Named Desire* has been translated into nearly twenty-five languages and staged around the world.

During the decade and a half after *A Streetcar Named Desire,* Williams had a string of plays produced on Broadway: *The Rose Tattoo* (1951), *Camino Real* (1953), *Cat on a Hot Tin Roof* (1955, Pulitzer Prize), *Orpheus Descending* (1957), *Suddenly Last Summer* (1958), *Sweet Bird of Youth* (1959), and *The Night of the Iguana* (1961). Although Williams continued to write plays in the 1960s and 1970s—including *In the Bar of a Tokyo Hotel* (1969), *The Two-Character Play/Out Cry* (1967, 1971), *The Red Devil Battery Sign* (1975), and *Clothes for a Summer Hotel* (1980)—his dramatic work after *Night of the Iguana* failed to receive the acclaim of his earlier plays. Convinced for most of his life that he would die young, Tennessee Williams passed away at the age of seventy one on February 25, 1983.

A Streetcar Named Desire is set in the French Quarter of New Orleans, a city known for its international influences (French, Spanish, Caribbean) as well as its theatricalized ceremonies and celebrations

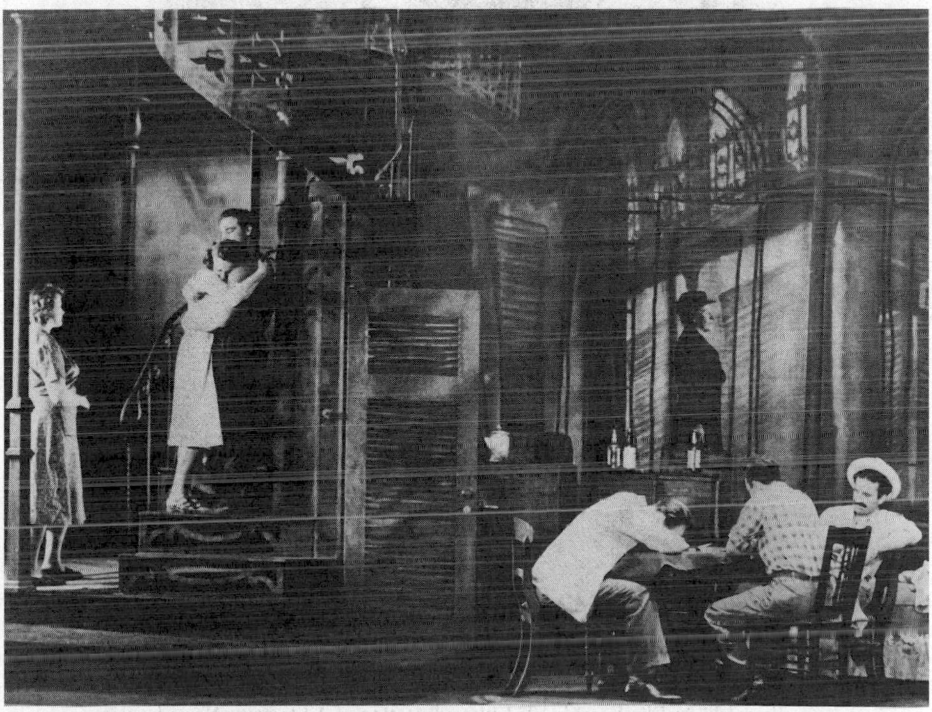

Final scene from the original 1947 Broadway production of *A Streetcar Named Desire*.

and its bohemian subculture. The play is full of references to the city's sites and institutions; indeed, the streetcar named Desire, which brings Blanche DuBois to her sister's apartment in the play's opening scene, did run through the French Quarter in the 1940s. At the same time, William's New Orleans is as much an atmosphere as an actual location. Like the blues music rising from a nearby bar, the turquoise evening sky that opens the play "invests the scene with a kind of lyricism and gracefully attenuates the atmosphere of decay." Throughout *A Streetcar Named Desire,* the play's setting embodies moods and states of mind, accentuating points of crisis and imbuing realism with expressionism's more subjective reach. The apartment of Stanley and Stella Kowalski reflects this shifting border between inside and outside. Obscured in darkness when the play's action takes place outside, it appears as an interior acting space when the lighting changes. Its back wall consists of a scrim (or see-through fabric), which appears solid when lit from the front but transparent when lit from behind, allowing a view of the alley beyond the apartment.

Reviewers and scholars who have written about *A Streetcar Named Desire* have focused, for the most part, on the characters of Stanley and Blanche. While such an emphasis risks obscuring the important roles of other characters (particularly Stella and Stanley's friend Mitch), the interaction between Stanley and Blanche represents one of the great *agones,* or dramatic conflicts, in Western drama. The two characters are, in many ways, dramatic antitheses. From his initial appearance, Stanley is defined by his rough manners, working-class pride, and sexual confidence. Polish American by birth, he inhabits a neighborhood defined by its relaxed—at times violent—behavior and its ethnic and racial mix. Stanley's is a male-centered world of poker nights, Jax beer, and sexual pleasure; as Williams writes in introducing the character, "Since earliest manhood the center of his being has been pleasure with women, the giving and taking of it, not with weak indulgence, dependently, but with the

Vivien Leigh as Blanche DuBois and Marlon Brando as Stanley Kowalski, in Elia Kazan's 1951 film adaptation of *A Streetcar Named Desire*.

power and pride of a richly feathered male bird among hens." Given to explosive outbursts but also a man of shrewdness and calculation, he defends his territory with a fierceness that masks an awareness of his own limitations. His charismatic yet threatening presence in Williams's play derives from the aggressive masculinity that he wears like a badge. In this mode of interacting with others he contrasts markedly with Mitch, a man of sensitivity and deep emotional attachments who lives with his mother.

Unlike Stanley, Blanche comes from a plantation world of landed wealth, breeding, and sexual decorum, a world (encapsulated in the plantation's name, Belle Reve—French for "beautiful dream") that was, in reality, already yielding in the 1940s to a newly industrializing South. With her white suit, bodice, and gloves, Blanche's mothlike appearance in the opening scene is incongruous with her urban surroundings. Whereas Stanley represents the vitality, dynamism, and swagger of a country emerging from World War II, Blanche represents more traditional ideals of culture, civilization, and manners. Yet even as Blanche articulates these ideals, the audience is aware that they have failed her. Belle Reve has been lost to the sexual appetites and financial improvidence of its inhabitants, and the history of decline and death that Blanche recounts is gothic in tone. Traumatized by the suicide of her homosexual husband years earlier, Blanche has led a life of promiscuity and fleeting encounters. As age begins to threaten her attractiveness, her efforts to maintain the southern belle image that she was raised to project grow more strained. Standing as the centerpiece of Williams's theatrical world, Blanche becomes stage manager in her own right, controlling the lighting by which she is seen and adding music, decorating the Kowalski apartment, and dressing herself and applying makeup in order to play the starring role in her interactions with others. "I don't want realism. I want magic!" she tells Mitch, and these words capture her increasingly desperate faith in the compensatory power of illusion. Her attempts to maintain this illusion and the accompanying struggle to hold together the different parts of her personality break down the lines between her subjective life and the ever more hostile surroundings in which she finds herself. Of all the characters, it is Blanche who is most closely linked to the expressionistic devices of *A Streetcar Named Desire*. In the play's early scenes she hears the Varsouviana polka that was playing the night her husband shot himself; and as the play progresses, the lighting and sound effects of the stage increasingly mirror her mental and emotional turmoil.

In the aftermath of Stanley's violent outburst at the poker night he hosts for his friends in scene 3, Blanche pleads with Stella to choose tenderness and civilization over the bestiality and violence that Stanley embodies: "*Don't—don't hang back with the brutes!*" By framing the choice of values so explicitly, Blanche seeks to triumph over Stanley in the battle for Stella's love and allegiance. But the claims presented by the characters engage the audience's sympathies as well. Though scholars and reviewers have often sided with Stanley or Blanche in their assessments of the play's central confrontation, such judgments violate the complex balances and counterpoints that Williams establishes. In their sympathies, audiences must come to terms with competing social and moral codes, and they must deal with the fact that Williams's character portrayals amplify and change as the play progresses. For his part, while Williams condemned what he called "the ravishment of the tender, the sensitive, the delicate, by the savage and brutal forces of modern society," his sympathies extended in both directions: "[Blanche] was broken on the rock of the world; I find her a sympathetic character, but I also find Stanley sympathetic."

With its exploration of traditional and contemporary gender roles and its juxtaposition of the old South with the new, *A Streetcar Named Desire* offers a powerful portrait of the changing social landscape of postwar America. In keeping with this achievement, its characters, actions, and lines of dialogue became potent cultural symbols in the decades that followed. Brando's Stanley—memorialized by the widely successful film adaptation—became an image of masculinity for a generation that also worshipped such male icons as John Wayne, Elvis Presley, and James Dean. Subsequent actors playing Stanley have had to work to free their role from this mesmerizing performance. But the figure of Blanche DuBois—introduced on stage by Jessica Tandy and popularized on screen by Vivien Leigh—may be more resonant in the latter half of the twentieth century and the early years of the twenty-first. Embodying the strains in female social roles during the supposed return to normalcy following World War II, Blanche serves as an image of the conflicted place of both women and men in a society in which expected ideals and behaviors no longer match the realities of contemporary gender relations. Like Stanley, she deals with the realities of desire—physical and emotional—that fly in the face of death itself. That she cannot control her journey on the streetcar named Desire says as much about the society she inhabits as it does her precarious psyche. Though the contemporary world is no longer that of postwar America, issues of sexuality remain pressing in both traditional and cosmopolitan societies. When the drag queen Prior Walters quotes Blanche in TONY KUSHNER's *Angels in America* (1991–92), he acknowledges the line between Williams's female protagonist—trapped between roles—and a more contemporary field of sexual identities. S.G.

A Streetcar Named Desire

And so it was I entered the broken world
To trace the visionary company of love, its voice
An instant in the wind (I know not whither hurled)
But not for long to hold each desperate choice.
"*The Broken Tower*" by *Hart Crane*[1]

CHARACTERS

BLANCHE
STELLA
STANLEY
MITCH
EUNICE
STEVE
PABLO
A NEGRO WOMAN
A DOCTOR
A NURSE
A YOUNG COLLECTOR
A MEXICAN WOMAN

Scene 1

The exterior of a two-story corner building on a street in New Orleans which is named Elysian Fields and runs between the L & N tracks[2] *and the river. The section is poor but,*

1. American poet (1899–1932); "The Broken Tower" was the last poem Crane wrote before committing suicide at the age of 32.
2. Tracks used by trains of the Louisville and Nashville Railroad—formerly a major freight and passenger company in the southeastern United States. *Elysian Fields:* a street just north of the French Quarter, the oldest neighborhood of New Orleans; also, in classical mythology, the abode of the blessed dead.

unlike corresponding sections in other American cities, it has a raffish charm. The houses are mostly white frame, weathered grey, with rickety outside stairs and galleries and quaintly ornamented gables. This building contains two flats, upstairs and down. Faded white stairs ascend to the entrances of both.

It is first dark of an evening early in May. The sky that shows around the dim white building is a peculiarly tender blue, almost a turquoise, which invests the scene with a kind of lyricism and gracefully attenuates the atmosphere of decay. You can almost feel the warm breath of the brown river beyond the river warehouses with their faint redolences of bananas and coffee. A corresponding air is evoked by the music of Negro entertainers at a barroom around the corner. In this part of New Orleans you are practically always just around the corner, or a few doors down the street, from a tinny piano being played with the infatuated fluency of brown fingers. This "blue piano" expresses the spirit of the life which goes on here.

Two women, one white and one colored, are taking the air on the steps of the building. The white woman is EUNICE, *who occupies the upstairs flat; the colored woman a neighbor, for New Orleans is a cosmopolitan city where there is a relatively warm and easy intermingling of races in the old part of town.*

Above the music of the "blue piano" the voices of people on the street can be heard overlapping.

[*Two men come around the corner,* STANLEY KOWALSKI *and* MITCH. *They are about twenty-eight or thirty years old, roughly dressed in blue denim work clothes.* STANLEY *carries his bowling jacket and a red-stained package from a butcher's. They stop at the foot of the steps.*]

STANLEY [*bellowing*] Hey, there! Stella, baby!

[STELLA *comes out on the first floor landing, a gentle young woman, about twenty-five, and of a background obviously quite different from her husband's.*]

STELLA [*mildly*] Don't holler at me like that. Hi, Mitch.

STANLEY Catch!

STELLA What?

STANLEY Meat!

[*He heaves the package at her. She cries out in protest but manages to catch it: then she laughs breathlessly. Her husband and his companion have already started back around the corner.*]

STELLA [*calling after him*] Stanley! Where are you going?

STANLEY Bowling!

STELLA Can I come watch?

STANLEY Come on.

[*He goes out.*]

STELLA Be over soon. [*To the white woman*] Hello, Eunice. How are you?

EUNICE I'm all right. Tell Steve to get him a poor boy's sandwich[3] 'cause nothing's left here.

[*They all laugh; the* COLORED WOMAN *does not stop.* STELLA *goes out.*]

COLORED WOMAN What was that package he th'ew at 'er? [*She rises from steps, laughing louder.*]

EUNICE You hush, now!

NEGRO WOMAN Catch *what!*

3. A po'boy, the Gulf Coast version of a submarine sandwich, featuring beef, shrimp, or other fillings in a hollowed-out loaf of French bread.

[*She continues to laugh.* BLANCHE *comes around the corner, carrying a valise. She looks at a slip of paper, then at the building, then again at the slip and again at the building. Her expression is one of shocked disbelief. Her appearace is incongruous to this setting. She is daintily dressed in a white suit with a fluffy bodice, necklace and earrings of pearl, white gloves and hat, looking as if she were arriving at a summer tea or cocktail party in the garden district.*[4] *She is about five years older than* STELLA. *Her delicate beauty must avoid a strong light. There is something about her uncertain manner, as well as her white clothes, that suggests a moth.*]

EUNICE [*finally*] What's the matter, honey? Are you lost?

BLANCHE [*with faintly hysterical humor*] They told me to take a streetcar named Desire, and then transfer to one called Cemeteries[5] and ride six blocks and get off at—Elysian Fields!

EUNICE That's where you are now.

BLANCHE At Elysian Fields?

EUNICE This here is Elysian Fields.

BLANCHE They mustn't have—understood—what number I wanted . . .

EUNICE What number you lookin' for?

[BLANCHE *wearily refers to the slip of paper.*]

BLANCHE Six thirty-two.

EUNICE You don't have to look no further.

BLANCHE [*uncomprehendingly*] I'm looking for my sister, Stella DuBois. I mean—Mrs. Stanley Kowalski.

EUNICE That's the party.—You just did miss her, though.

BLANCHE This—can this be—her home?

EUNICE She's got the downstairs here and I got the up.

BLANCHE Oh. She's—out?

EUNICE You noticed that bowling alley around the corner?

BLANCHE I'm—not sure I did.

EUNICE Well, that's where she's at, watchin' her husband bowl. [*There is a pause.*] You want to leave your suitcase here an' go find her?

BLANCHE No.

NEGRO WOMAN I'll go tell her you come.

BLANCHE Thanks.

NEGRO WOMAN You welcome.

[*She goes out.*]

EUNICE She wasn't expecting you?

BLANCHE No. No, not tonight.

EUNICE Well, why don't you just go in and make yourself at home till they get back.

BLANCHE How could I—do that?

EUNICE We own this place so I can let you in.

[*She gets up and opens the downstairs door. A light goes on behind the blind, turning it light blue.* BLANCHE *slowly follows her into the downstairs flat. The surrounding areas dim out as the interior is lighted.*]

4. An elegant New Orleans neighborhood known for its Greek Revival and Italianate architecture.

5. Streetcar routes in New Orleans at the time the play was written; the Desire line, which went through the French Quarter, was replaced by a bus in 1948.

[*Two rooms can be seen, not too clearly defined. The one first entered is primarily a kitchen but contains a folding bed to be used by* BLANCHE. *The room beyond this is a bedroom. Off this room is a narrow door to a bathroom.*]

EUNICE [*defensively, noticing* BLANCHE'*s look*] It's sort of messed up right now but when it's clean it's real sweet.

BLANCHE Is it?

EUNICE Uh-huh, I think so. So you're Stella's sister?

BLANCHE Yes. [*Wanting to get rid of her*] Thanks for letting me in.

EUNICE *Por nada,*[6] as the Mexicans say, *por nada!* Stella spoke of you.

BLANCHE Yes?

EUNICE I think she said you taught school.

BLANCHE Yes.

EUNICE And you're from Mississippi, huh?

BLANCHE Yes.

EUNICE She showed me a picture of your home-place, the plantation.

BLANCHE Belle Reve?[7]

EUNICE A great big place with white columns.

BLANCHE Yes . . .

EUNICE A place like that must be awful hard to keep up.

BLANCHE If you will excuse me, I'm just about to drop.

EUNICE Sure, honey. Why don't you set down?

BLANCHE What I meant was I'd like to be left alone.

EUNICE [*offended*] Aw. I'll make myself scarce, in that case.

BLANCHE I didn't mean to be rude, but—

EUNICE I'll drop by the bowling alley an' hustle her up.

[*She goes out the door.*]

[BLANCHE *sits in a chair very stiffly with her shoulders slightly hunched and her legs pressed close together and her hands tightly clutching her purse as if she were quite cold. After a while the blind look goes out of her eyes and she begins to look slowly around. A cat screeches. She catches her breath with a startled gesture. Suddenly she notices something in a half-opened closet. She springs up and crosses to it, and removes a whiskey bottle. She pours a half tumbler of whiskey and tosses it down. She carefully replaces the bottle and washes out the tumbler at the sink. Then she resumes her seat in front of the table.*]

BLANCHE [*faintly to herself*] I've got to keep hold of myself!

[STELLA *comes quickly around the corner of the building and runs to the door of the downstairs flat.*]

STELLA [*calling out joyfully*] *Blanche!*

[*For a moment they stare at each other. Then* BLANCHE *springs up and runs to her with a wild cry.*]

BLANCHE Stella, oh, Stella, Stella! Stella for Star![8]

[*She begins to speak with feverish vivacity as if she feared for either of them to stop and think. They catch each other in a spasmodic embrace.*]

BLANCHE Now, then, let me look at you. But don't you look at me, Stella, no, no, no, not till later, not till I've bathed and rested! And turn that over-light

6. It's nothing (Spanish).
7. Beautiful Dream (French).
8. *Stella* means "star" in Latin.

off! Turn that off! I won't be looked at in this merciless glare! [STELLA *laughs and complies.*] Come back here now! Oh, my baby! Stella! Stella for Star! [*She embraces her again.*] I thought you would never come back to this horrible place! What am I saying? I didn't mean to say that. I meant to be nice about it and say—Oh, what a convenient location and such—Ha-a-ha! Precious lamb! You haven't said a *word* to me.

STELLA You haven't given me a chance to, honey! [*She laughs, but her glance at* BLANCHE *is a little anxious.*]

BLANCHE Well, now you talk. Open your pretty mouth and talk while I look around for some liquor! I know you must have some liquor on the place! Where could it be, I wonder? Oh, I spy, I spy!

[*She rushes to the closet and removes the bottle; she is shaking all over and panting for breath as she tries to laugh. The bottle nearly slips from her grasp.*]

STELLA [*noticing*] Blanche, you sit down and let me pour the drinks. I don't know what we've got to mix with. Maybe a coke's[9] in the icebox. Look'n see, honey, while I'm—

BLANCHE No coke, honey, not with my nerves tonight! Where—where—where is—?

STELLA Stanley? Bowling! He loves it. They're having a—found some soda!—tournament . . .

BLANCHE Just water, baby, to chase it! Now don't get worried, your sister hasn't turned into a drunkard, she's just all shaken up and hot and tired and dirty! You sit down, now, and explain this place to me! What are you doing in a place like this?

STELLA Now, Blanche—

BLANCHE Oh, I'm not going to be hypocritical, I'm going to be honestly critical about it! Never, never, never in my worst dreams could I picture—Only Poe! Only Mr. Edgar Allan Poe!—could do it justice! Out there I suppose is the ghoul-haunted woodland of Weir![1] [*She laughs.*]

STELLA No, honey, those are the L & N tracks.

BLANCHE No, now seriously, putting joking aside. Why didn't you tell me, why didn't you write me, honey, why didn't you let me know?

STELLA [*carefully, pouring herself a drink*] Tell you what, Blanche?

BLANCHE Why, that you had to live in these conditions!

STELLA Aren't you being a little intense about it? It's not that bad at all! New Orleans isn't like other cities.

BLANCHE This has got nothing to do with New Orleans. You might as well say—forgive me, blessed baby! [*She suddenly stops short.*] The subject is closed!

STELLA [*a little drily*] Thanks.

[*During the pause,* BLANCHE *stares at her. She smiles at* BLANCHE.]

BLANCHE [*looking down at her glass, which shakes in her hand*] You're all I've got in the world, and you're not glad to see me!

STELLA [*sincerely*] Why, Blanche, you know that's not true.

BLANCHE No?—I'd forgotten how quiet you were.

9. In the South, *coke* is often used as a generic term for any soft drink.

1. The setting of the gothic ballad "Ulalume" (1847), by Poe, the American short story writer and poet (1809–1849).

STELLA You never did give me a chance to say much, Blanche. So I just got in the habit of being quiet around you.

BLANCHE [*vaguely*] A good habit to get into . . . [*Then, abruptly*] You haven't asked me how I happened to get away from the school before the spring term ended.

STELLA Well, I thought you'd volunteer that information—if you wanted to tell me.

BLANCHE You thought I'd been fired?

STELLA No, I—thought you might have—resigned . . .

BLANCHE I was so exhausted by all I'd been through my—nerves broke. [*Nervously tamping cigarette*] I was on the verge of—lunacy, almost! So Mr. Graves—Mr. Graves is the high school superintendent—he suggested I take a leave of absence. I couldn't put all of those details into the wire[2] . . . [*She drinks quickly.*] Oh, this buzzes right through me and feels so *good!*

STELLA Won't you have another?

BLANCHE No, one's my limit.

STELLA Sure?

BLANCHE You haven't said a word about my appearance.

STELLA You look just fine.

BLANCHE God love you for a liar! Daylight never exposed so total a ruin! But you—you've put on some weight, yes, you're just as plump as a little partridge! And it's so becoming to you!

STELLA Now, Blanche—

BLANCHE Yes, it is, it is or I wouldn't say it! You just have to watch around the hips a little. Stand up.

STELLA Not now.

BLANCHE You hear me? I said stand up! [STELLA *complies reluctantly.*] You messy child, you, you've spilt something on that pretty white lace collar! About your hair—you ought to have it cut in a feather bob with your dainty features. Stella, you have a maid, don't you?

STELLA No. With only two rooms it's—

BLANCHE What? *Two* rooms, did you say?

STELLA This one and— [*She is embarrassed.*]

BLANCHE The other one? [*She laughs sharply. There is an embarrassed silence.*] I am going to take just one little tiny nip more, sort of to put the stopper on, so to speak. . . . Then put the bottle away so I won't be tempted. [*She rises.*] I want you to look at *my* figure! [*She turns around.*] You know I haven't put on one ounce in ten years, Stella? I weigh what I weighed the summer you left Belle Reve. The summer Dad died and you left us . . .

STELLA [*a little wearily*] It's just incredible, Blanche, how well you're looking.

[*They both laugh uncomfortably.*]

BLANCHE But, Stella, there's only two rooms, I don't see where you're going to put me!

STELLA We're going to put you in here.

2. Telegram.

BLANCHE What kind of bed's this—one of those collapsible things? [*She sits on it.*]

STELLA Does it feel all right?

BLANCHE [*dubiously*] Wonderful, honey. I don't like a bed that gives much. But there's no door between the two rooms, and Stanley—will it be decent?

STELLA Stanley is Polish, you know.

BLANCHE Oh, yes. They're something like Irish, aren't they?

STELLA Well—

BLANCHE Only not so—highbrow? [*They both laugh again in the same way.*] I brought some nice clothes to meet all your lovely friends in.

STELLA I'm afraid you won't think they are lovely.

BLANCHE What are they like?

STELLA They're Stanley's friends.

BLANCHE Polacks?

STELLA They're a mixed lot, Blanche.

BLANCHE Heterogeneous—types?

STELLA Oh, yes. Yes, types is right!

BLANCHE Well—anyhow—I brought nice clothes and I'll wear them. I guess you're hoping I'll say I'll put up at a hotel, but I'm not going to put up at a hotel. I want to be *near* you, got to be *with* somebody, I *can't* be *alone!* Because—as you must have noticed—I'm—*not* very *well* . . . [*Her voice drops and her look is frightened.*]

STELLA You seem a little bit nervous or overwrought or something.

BLANCHE Will Stanley like me, or will I be just a visiting in-law, Stella? I couldn't stand that.

STELLA You'll get along fine together, if you'll just try not to—well—compare him with men that we went out with at home.

BLANCHE Is he so—different?

STELLA Yes. A different species.

BLANCHE In what way; what's he like?

STELLA Oh, you can't describe someone you're in love with! Here's a picture of him! [*She hands a photograph to* BLANCHE.]

BLANCHE An officer?

STELLA A Master Sergeant in the Engineers' Corps.[3] Those are decorations!

BLANCHE He had those on when you met him?

STELLA I assure you I wasn't just blinded by all the brass.

BLANCHE That's not what I—

STELLA But of course there were things to adjust myself to later on.

BLANCHE Such as his civilian background! [STELLA *laughs uncertainly.*] How did he take it when you said I was coming?

STELLA Oh, Stanley doesn't know yet.

BLANCHE [*frightened*] You—haven't told him?

STELLA He's on the road a good deal.

BLANCHE Oh. Travels?

STELLA Yes.

BLANCHE Good. I mean—isn't it?

3. A branch of the U.S. Army that provides construction and engineering services in support of combat soldiers and federal agencies.

STELLA [*half to herself*] I can hardly stand it when he is away for a night . . .

BLANCHE Why, Stella!

STELLA When he's away for a week I nearly go wild!

BLANCHE Gracious!

STELLA And when he comes back I cry on his lap like a baby . . . [*She smiles to herself.*]

BLANCHE I guess that is what is meant by being in love . . . [STELLA *looks up with a radiant smile.*] Stella—

STELLA What?

BLANCHE [*in an uneasy rush*] I haven't asked you the things you probably thought I was going to ask. And so I'll expect you to be understanding about what *I* have to tell *you.*

STELLA What, Blanche? [*Her face turns anxious.*]

BLANCHE Well, Stella—you're going to reproach me, I know that you're bound to reproach me—but before you do—take into consideration—you left! I stayed and struggled! You came to New Orleans and looked out for yourself! *I* stayed at *Belle Reve* and tried to hold it together! I'm not meaning this in any reproachful way, but *all* the burden descended on *my* shoulders.

STELLA The best I could do was make my own living, Blanche.

[*Blanche begins to shake again with intensity.*]

BLANCHE I know, I know. But you are the one that abandoned Belle Reve, not I! I stayed and fought for it, bled for it, almost died for it!

STELLA Stop this hysterical outburst and tell me what's happened? What do you mean fought and bled? What kind of—

BLANCHE I knew you would, Stella. I knew you would take this attitude about it!

STELLA About—what?—please!

BLANCHE [*slowly*] The loss—the loss . . .

STELLA Belle Reve? Lost, is it? No!

BLANCHE Yes, Stella.

[*They stare at each other across the yellow-checked linoleum of the table.* BLANCHE *slowly nods her head and* STELLA *looks slowly down at her hands folded on the table. The music of the "blue piano" grows louder.* BLANCHE *touches her handkerchief to her forehead.*]

STELLA But how did it go? What happened?

BLANCHE [*springing up*] You're a fine one to ask me how it went!

STELLA Blanche!

BLANCHE You're a fine one to sit there *accusing me* of it!

STELLA *Blanche!*

BLANCHE I, I, *I* took the blows in my face and my body! All of those deaths! The long parade to the graveyard! Father, Mother! Margaret, that dreadful way! So big with it, it couldn't be put in a coffin! But had to be burned like rubbish! You just came home in time for the funerals, Stella. And funerals are pretty compared to deaths. Funerals are quiet, but deaths— not always. Sometimes their breathing is hoarse, and sometimes it rattles, and sometimes they even cry out to you, "Don't let me go!" Even the old, sometimes, say, "Don't let me go." As if you were able to stop them! But funerals are quiet, with pretty flowers. And, oh, what gorgeous boxes they pack them away in! Unless you were there at the bed when they cried out, "Hold me!"

you'd never suspect there was the struggle for breath and bleeding. You didn't dream, but I saw! *Saw! Saw!* And now you sit there telling me with your eyes that I let the place go! How in hell do you think all that sickness and dying was paid for? Death is expensive, Miss Stella! And old Cousin Jessie's right after Margaret's, hers! Why, the Grim Reaper had put up his tent on our doorstep! . . . Stella. Belle Reve was his headquarters! Honey—that's how it slipped through my fingers! Which of them left us a fortune? Which of them left a cent of insurance even? Only poor Jessie—one hundred to pay for her coffin. That was all, Stella! And I with my pitiful salary at the school. Yes, accuse me! Sit there and stare at me, thinking I let the place go! *I* let the place go? Where were *you!* In bed with your—Polack!

STELLA [*springing*] Blanche! You be still! That's enough! [*She starts out.*]

BLANCHE Where are you going?

STELLA I'm going into the bathroom to wash my face.

BLANCHE Oh, Stella, Stella, you're crying!

STELLA Does that surprise you?

BLANCHE Forgive me—I didn't mean to—

[*The sound of men's voices is heard.* STELLA *goes into the bathroom, closing the door behind her. When the men appear, and* BLANCHE *realizes it must be* STANLEY *returning, she moves uncertainly from the bathroom door to the dressing table, looking apprehensively toward the front door.* STANLEY *enters, followed by* STEVE *and* MITCH. STANLEY *pauses near his door,* STEVE *by the foot of the spiral stair, and* MITCH *is slightly above and to the right of them, about to go out. As the men enter, we hear some of the following dialogue.*]

STANLEY Is that how he got it?

STEVE Sure that's how he got it. He hit the old weather-bird for 300 bucks on a six-number-ticket.[4]

MITCH Don't tell him those things; he'll believe it.

[MITCH *starts out.*]

STANLEY [*restraining* MITCH] Hey, Mitch—come back here.

[BLANCHE, *at the sound of voices, retires in the bedroom. She picks up* STANLEY'S *photo from dressing table, looks at it, puts it down. When* STANLEY *enters the apartment, she darts and hides behind the screen at the head of bed.*]

STEVE [*to* STANLEY *and* MITCH] Hey, are we playin' poker tomorrow?

STANLEY Sure—at Mitch's.

MITCH [*hearing this, returns quickly to the stair rail*] No—not at my place. My mother's still sick!

STANLEY Okay, at my place . . . [MITCH *starts out again.*] But you bring the beer!

[MITCH *pretends not to hear—calls out "Goodnight, all," and goes out, singing.*]

EUNICE [*heard from above*] Break it up down there! I made the spaghetti dish and ate it myself.

4. That is, he won $300 on a six-number lottery ticket. *Hit the old weather-bird:* got extraordinarily lucky (as one would have to be to shoot at and hit an ornamental weather vane, which traditionally was shaped like a rooster).

STEVE [*going upstairs*] I told you and phoned you we was playing. [*To the men*] Jax beer![5]

EUNICE You never phoned me once.

STEVE I told you at breakfast—and phoned you at lunch . . .

EUNICE Well, never mind about that. You just get yourself home here once in a while.

STEVE You want it in the papers?

[*More laughter and shouts of parting come from the men.* STANLEY *throws the screen door of the kitchen open and comes in. He is of medium height, about five feet eight or nine, and strongly, compactly built. Animal joy in his being is implicit in all his movements and attitudes. Since earliest manhood the center of his life has been pleasure with women, the giving and taking of it, not with weak indulgence, dependently, but with the power and pride of a richly feathered male bird among hens. Branching out from this complete and satisfying center are all the auxiliary channels of his life, such as his heartiness with men, his appreciation of rough humor, his love of good drink and food and games, his car, his radio, everything that is his, that bears his emblem of the gaudy seed-bearer. He sizes women up at a glance, with sexual classifications, crude images flashing into his mind and determining the way he smiles at them.*]

BLANCHE [*drawing involuntarily back from his stare*] You must be Stanley. I'm Blanche.

STANLEY Stella's sister?

BLANCHE Yes.

STANLEY H'lo. Where's the little woman?

BLANCHE In the bathroom.

STANLEY Oh. Didn't know you were coming in town.

BLANCHE I—uh—

STANLEY Where you from, Blanche?

BLANCHE Why, I—live in Laurel.[6]

[*He has crossed to the closet and removed the whiskey bottle.*]

STANLEY In Laurel, huh? Oh, yeah. Yeah, in Laurel, that's right. Not in my territory. Liquor goes fast in hot weather.

[*He holds the bottle to the light to observe its depletion.*]

Have a shot?

BLANCHE No, I—rarely touch it.

STANLEY Some people rarely touch it, but it touches them often.

BLANCHE [*faintly*] Ha-ha.

STANLEY My clothes're stickin' to me. Do you mind if I make myself comfortable? [*He starts to remove his shirt.*]

BLANCHE Please, please do.

STANLEY Be comfortable is my motto.

BLANCHE It's mine, too. It's hard to stay looking fresh. I haven't washed or even powdered my face and—here you are!

5. Made by the Jackson Brewing Company of New Orleans until 1974. The brewery sponsored a bowling team in nearby St. Charles.

6. A town in southeast Mississippi, about 135 miles from New Orleans.

STANLEY You know you can catch cold sitting around in damp things, especially when you been exercising hard like bowling is. You're a teacher, aren't you?

BLANCHE Yes.

STANLEY What do you teach, Blanche?

BLANCHE English.

STANLEY I never was a very good English student. How long you here for, Blanche?

BLANCHE I—don't know yet.

STANLEY You going to shack up here?

BLANCHE I thought I would if it's not inconvenient for you all.

STANLEY Good.

BLANCHE Traveling wears me out.

STANLEY Well, take it easy.

[*A cat screeches near the window.* BLANCHE *spring up.*]

BLANCHE What's that?

STANLEY Cats . . . Hey, Stella!

STELLA [*faintly, from the bathroom*] Yes, Stanley.

STANLEY Haven't fallen in, have you? [*He grins at* BLANCHE. *She tries unsuccessfully to smile back. There is a silence.*] I'm afraid I'll strike you as being the unrefined type. Stella's spoke of you a good deal. You were married once, weren't you?

[*The music of the polka rises up, faint in the distance.*]

BLANCHE Yes. When I was quite young.

STANLEY What happened?

BLANCHE The boy—the boy died. [*She sinks back down.*] I'm afraid I'm—going to be sick!

[*Her head falls on her arms.*]

Scene 2

It is six o'clock the following evening. BLANCHE *is bathing.* STELLA *is completing her toilette.* BLANCHE*'s dress, a flowered print, is laid out on* STELLA*'s bed.*

STANLEY *enters the kitchen from outside, leaving the door open on the perpetual "blue piano" around the corner.*

STANLEY What's all this monkey doings?

STELLA Oh, Stan! [*She jumps up and kisses him, which he accepts with lordly composure.*] I'm taking Blanche to Galatoire's[7] for supper and then to a show, because it's your poker night.

STANLEY How about my supper, huh? I'm not going to no Galatoire's for supper!

STELLA I put you a cold plate on ice.

STANLEY Well, isn't that just dandy!

STELLA I'm going to try to keep Blanche out till the party breaks up because I don't know how she would take it. So we'll go to one of the little places in the Quarter[8] afterward and you'd better give me some money.

STANLEY Where is she?

7. An elegant restaurant on Bourbon Street, specializing in French Creole cuisine.

8. The French Quarter.

STELLA She's soaking in a hot tub to quiet her nerves. She's terribly upset.

STANLEY Over what?

STELLA She's been through such an ordeal.

STANLEY Yeah?

STELLA Stan, we've—lost Belle Reve!

STANLEY The place in the country?

STELLA Yes.

STANLEY How?

STELLA [*vaguely*] Oh, it had to be—sacrificed or something. [*There is a pause while* STANLEY *considers.* STELLA *is changing into her dress.*] When she comes in be sure to say something nice about her appearance. And, oh! Don't mention the baby. I haven't said anything yet, I'm waiting until she gets in a quieter condition.

STANLEY [*ominously*] So?

STELLA And try to understand her and be nice to her, Stan.

BLANCHE [*singing in the bathroom*] "From the land of the sky blue water, They brought a captive maid!"[9]

STELLA She wasn't expecting to find us in such a small place. You see I'd tried to gloss things over a little in my letters.

STANLEY So?

STELLA And admire her dress and tell her she's looking wonderful. That's important with Blanche. Her little weakness!

STANLEY Yeah. I get the idea. Now let's skip back a little to where you said the country place was disposed of.

STELLA Oh!—yes . . .

STANLEY How about that? Let's have a few more details on that subjeck.

STELLA It's best not to talk much about it until she's calmed down.

STANLEY So that's the deal, huh? Sister Blanche cannot be annoyed with business details right now!

STELLA You saw how she was last night.

STANLEY Uh-hum, I saw how she was. Now let's have a gander at the bill of sale.

STELLA I haven't seen any.

STANLEY She didn't show you no papers, no deed of sale or nothing like that, huh?

STELLA It seems like it wasn't sold.

STANLEY Well, what in hell was it then, give away? To charity?

STELLA Shhh! She'll hear you.

STANLEY I don't care if she hears me. Let's see the papers!

STELLA There weren't any papers, she didn't show any papers, I don't care about papers.

STANLEY Have you ever heard of the Napoleonic code?[1]

STELLA No, Stanley, I haven't heard of the Napoleonic code and if I have, I don't see what it—

9. From "From the Land of the Sky-Blue Water" (1908), by Nelle Richmond Eberhart and Charles Wakefield Cadman, a song popularized by the Andrews Sisters in the late 1930s.

1. The civil law code established in France under Napoleon in 1804 and adopted by most other European countries. In 1808, after Louisiana had been purchased from France but before it became a state, it adopted a version of the Napoleonic code; all other U.S. states follow the British common law model.

STANLEY Let me enlighten you on a point or two, baby.

STELLA Yes?

STANLEY In the state of Louisiana we have the Napoleonic code according to which what belongs to the wife belongs to the husband and vice versa. For instance if I had a piece of property, or you had a piece of property—

STELLA My head is swimming!

STANLEY All right. I'll wait till she gets through soaking in a hot tub and then I'll inquire if *she* is acquainted with the Napoleonic code. It looks to me like you have been swindled, baby, and when you're swindled under the Napoleonic code I'm swindled *too.* And I don't like to be *swindled.*

STELLA There's plenty of time to ask her questions later but if you do now she'll go to pieces again. I don't understand what happened to Belle Reve but you don't know how ridiculous you are being when you suggest that my sister or I or anyone of our family could have perpetrated a swindle on anyone else.

STANLEY Then where's the money if the place was sold?

STELLA Not sold—*lost, lost!*

[*He stalks into bedroom, and she follows him.*]

Stanley!

[*He pulls open the wardrobe trunk standing in middle of room and jerks out an armful of dresses.*]

STANLEY Open your eyes to this stuff! You think she got them out of a teacher's pay?

STELLA Hush!

STANLEY Look at these feathers and furs that she come here to preen herself in! What's this here? A solid-gold dress, I believe! And this one! What is these here? Fox-pieces! [*He blows on them.*] Genuine fox fur-pieces, a half a mile long! Where are your fox-pieces, Stella? Bushy snow-white ones, no less! Where are your white fox-pieces?

STELLA Those are inexpensive summer furs that Blanche has had a long time.

STANLEY I got an acquaintance who deals in this sort of merchandise. I'll have him in here to appraise it. I'm willing to bet you there's thousands of dollars invested in this stuff here!

STELLA Don't be such an idiot, Stanley!

[*He hurls the furs to the day bed. Then he jerks open small drawer in the trunk and pulls up a fistful of costume jewelry.*]

STANLEY And what have we here? The treasure chest of a pirate!

STELLA Oh, Stanley!

STANLEY Pearls! Ropes of them! What is this sister of yours, a deep-sea diver? Bracelets of solid gold, too! Where are your pearls and gold bracelets?

STELLA Shhh! Be still, Stanley!

STANLEY And diamonds! A crown for an empress!

STELLA A rhinestone tiara she wore to a costume ball.

STANLEY What's rhinestone?

STELLA Next door to glass.

STANLEY Are you kidding? I have an acquaintance that works in a jewelry store. I'll have him in here to make an appraisal of this. Here's your plantation, or what was left of it, here!

STELLA You have no idea how stupid and horrid you're being! Now close that trunk before she comes out of the bathroom!

[*He kicks the trunk partly closed and sits on the kitchen table.*]

STANLEY The Kowalskis and the DuBoises have different notions.

STELLA [*angrily*] Indeed they have, thank heavens!—*I'm* going outside.

[*She snatches up her white hat and gloves and crosses to the outside door.*]

You come out with me while Blanche is getting dressed.

STANLEY Since when do you give me orders?

STELLA Are you going to stay here and insult her?

STANLEY You're damn tootin' I'm going to stay here.

[STELLA *goes out to the porch.* BLANCHE *comes out of the bathroom in a red satin robe.*]

BLANCHE [*airily*] Hello, Stanley! Here I am, all freshly bathed and scented, and feeling like a brand new human being!

[*He lights a cigarette.*]

STANLEY That's good.

BLANCHE [*drawing the curtains at the windows*] Excuse me while I slip on my pretty new dress!

STANLEY Go right ahead, Blanche.

[*She closes the drapes between the rooms.*]

BLANCHE I understand there's to be a little card party to which we ladies are cordially *not* invited!

STANLEY [*ominously*] Yeah?

[BLANCHE *throws off her robe and slips into a flowered print dress.*]

BLANCHE Where's Stella?

STANLEY Out on the porch.

BLANCHE I'm going to ask a favor of you in a moment.

STANLEY What could that be, I wonder?

BLANCHE Some buttons in back! You may enter!

[*He crosses through drapes with a smoldering look.*]

How do I look?

STANLEY You look all right.

BLANCHE Many thanks! Now the buttons!

STANLEY I can't do nothing with them.

BLANCHE You men with your big clumsy fingers. May I have a drag on your cig?

STANLEY Have one for yourself.

BLANCHE Why, thanks! . . . It looks like my trunk has exploded.

STANLEY Me an' Stella were helping you unpack.

BLANCHE Well, you certainly did a fast and thorough job of it!

STANLEY It looks like you raided some stylish shops in Paris.

BLANCHE Ha-ha! Yes—clothes are my passion!

STANLEY What does it cost for a string of fur-pieces like that?

BLANCHE Why, those were a tribute from an admirer of mine!

STANLEY He must have had a lot of—admiration!

BLANCHE Oh, in my youth I excited some admiration. But look at me now! [*She smiles at him radiantly.*] Would you think it possible that I was once considered to be—attractive?

STANLEY Your looks are okay.

BLANCHE I was fishing for a compliment, Stanley.

STANLEY I don't go in for that stuff.

BLANCHE What—stuff?

STANLEY Compliments to women about their looks. I never met a woman that didn't know if she was good-looking or not without being told, and some of them give themselves credit for more than they've got. I once went out with a doll who said to me, "I am the glamorous type, I am the glamorous type!" I said, "So what?"

BLANCHE And what did she say then?

STANLEY She didn't say nothing. That shut her up like a clam.

BLANCHE Did it end the romance?

STANLEY It ended the conversation—that was all. Some men are took in by this Hollywood glamor stuff and some men are not.

BLANCHE I'm sure you belong in the second category.

STANLEY That's right.

BLANCHE I cannot imagine any witch of a woman casting a spell over you.

STANLEY That's—right.

BLANCHE You're simple, straightforward and honest, a little bit on the primitive side I should think. To interest you a woman would have to— [*She pauses with an indefinite gesture.*]

STANLEY [*slowly*] Lay . . . her cards on the table.

BLANCHE [*smiling*] Well, I never cared for wishy-washy people. That was why, when you walked in here last night, I said to myself—"My sister has married a man!"—Of course that was all that I could tell about you.

STANLEY [*booming*] Now let's cut the re-bop![2]

BLANCHE [*pressing hands to her ears*] Ouuuuu!

STELLA [*calling from the steps*] Stanley! You come out here and let Blanche finish dressing!

BLANCHE I'm through dressing, honey.

STELLA Well, you come out, then.

STANLEY Your sister and I are having a little talk.

BLANCHE [*lightly*] Honey, do me a favor. Run to the drugstore and get me a lemon Coke with plenty of chipped ice in it!—Will you do that for me, sweetie?

STELLA [*uncertainly*] Yes.

[*She goes around the corner of the building.*]

BLANCHE The poor little thing was out there listening to us, and I have an idea she doesn't understand you as well as I do. . . . All right; now, Mr. Kowalski, let us proceed without any more double-talk. I'm ready to answer all questions. I've nothing to hide. What is it?

STANLEY There is such a thing in this state of Louisiana as the Napoleonic code, according to which whatever belongs to my wife is also mine—and vice versa.

BLANCHE My, but you have an impressive judicial air!

[*She sprays herself with her atomizer; then playfully sprays him with it. He seizes the atomizer and slams it down on the dresser. She throws back her head and laughs.*]

2. Nonsense (a variant of *bebop* or *bop,* the virtuosic jazz of the late 1940s and a term meaning "glib or deceptive talk").

STANLEY If I didn't know that you was my wife's sister I'd get ideas about you!

BLANCHE Such as what!

STANLEY Don't play so dumb. You know what!

BLANCHE [*she puts the atomizer on the table*] All right. Cards on the table. That suits me. [*She turns to* STANLEY.] I know I fib a good deal. After all, a woman's charm is fifty per cent illusion, but when a thing is important I tell the truth, and this is the truth: I haven't cheated my sister or you or anyone else as long as I have lived.

STANLEY Where's the papers? In the trunk?

BLANCHE Everything that I own is in that trunk.

[STANLEY *crosses to the trunk, shoves it roughly open and begins to open compartments.*]

BLANCHE What in the name of heaven are you thinking of! What's in the back of that little boy's mind of yours? That I am absconding with something, attempting some kind of treachery on my sister?—Let me do that! It will be faster and simpler . . . [*She crosses to the trunk and takes out a box.*] I keep my papers mostly in this tin box. [*She opens it.*]

STANLEY What's them underneath? [*He indicates another sheaf of paper.*]

BLANCHE These are love-letters, yellowing with antiquity, all from one boy. [*He snatches them up. She speaks fiercely.*] Give those back to me!

STANLEY I'll have a look at them first!

BLANCHE The touch of your hands insults them!

STANLEY Don't pull that stuff!

[*He rips off the ribbon and starts to examine them.* BLANCHE *snatches them from him, and they cascade to the floor.*]

BLANCHE Now that you've touched them I'll burn them!

STANLEY [*staring, baffled*] What in hell are they?

BLANCHE [*on the floor gathering them up*] Poems a dead boy wrote. I hurt him the way that you would like to hurt me, but you can't! I'm not young and vulnerable any more. But my young husband was and I– never mind about that! Just give them back to me!

STANLEY What do you mean by saying you'll have to burn them?

BLANCHE I'm sorry, I must have lost my head for a moment. Everyone has something he won't let others touch because of their—intimate nature . . .

[*She now seems faint with exhaustion and she sits down with the strong box and puts on a pair of glasses and goes methodically through a large stack of papers.*]

Ambler & Ambler. Hmmmmm. . . . Crabtree. . . . More Ambler & Ambler.

STANLEY What is Ambler & Ambler?

BLANCHE A firm that made loans on the place.

STANLEY Then it *was* lost on a mortgage?

BLANCHE [*touching her forehead*] That must've been what happened.

STANLEY I don't want no ifs, ands or buts! What's all the rest of them papers?

[*She hands him the entire box. He carries it to the table and starts to examine the papers.*]

BLANCHE [*picking up a large envelope containing more papers*] There are thousands of papers, stretching back over hundreds of years, affecting Belle Reve as, piece by piece, our improvident grandfathers and father and uncles and brothers exchanged the land for their epic fornications—to put it plainly! [*She removes her glasses with an exhausted laugh.*] The four-letter word deprived us of our plantation, till finally all that was left—and Stella can verify that!—was the house itself and about twenty acres of ground, including a graveyard, to which now all but Stella and I have retreated. [*She pours the contents of the envelope on the table.*] Here all of them are, all papers! I hereby endow you with them! Take them, peruse them—commit them to memory, even! I think it's wonderfully fitting that Belle Reve should finally be this bunch of old papers in your big, capable hands! . . . I wonder if Stella's come back with my lemon Coke . . . [*She leans back and closes her eyes.*]

STANLEY I have a lawyer acquaintance who will study these out.

BLANCHE Present them to him with a box of aspirin tablets.

STANLEY [*becoming somewhat sheepish*] You see, under the Napoleonic code—a man has to take an interest in his wife's affairs—especially now that she's going to have a baby.

[BLANCHE *opens her eyes. The "blue piano" sounds louder.*]

BLANCHE Stella? Stella going to have a baby? [*Dreamily*] I didn't know she was going to have a baby!

[*She gets up and crosses to the outside door.* STELLA *appears around the corner with a carton from the drugstore.*]

[STANLEY *goes into the bedroom with the envelope and the box.*]

[*The inner rooms fade to darkness and the outside wall of the house is visible.* BLANCHE *meets* STELLA *at the foot of the steps to the sidewalk.*]

BLANCHE Stella, Stella for Star! How lovely to have a baby! It's all right. Everything's all right.

STELLA I'm sorry he did that to you.

BLANCHE Oh, I guess he's just not the type that goes for jasmine perfume, but maybe he's what we need to mix with our blood now that we've lost Belle Reve. We thrashed it out. I feel a bit shaky, but I think I handled it nicely, I laughed and treated it all as a joke. [STEVE *and* PABLO *appear, carrying a case of beer.*] I called him a little boy and laughed and flirted. Yes, I was flirting with your husband! [*As the men approach*] The guests are gathering for the poker party. [*The two men pass between them, and enter the house.*] Which way do we go now, Stella—this way?

STELLA No, this way. [*She leads* BLANCHE *away.*]

BLANCHE [*laughing*] The blind are leading the blind![3]

[*A tamale* VENDOR *is heard calling.*]

VENDOR'S VOICE Red-hot!

Scene 3

The Poker Night[4]

There is a picture of Van Gogh's of a billiard-parlor at night.[5] *The kitchen now suggests that sort of lurid nocturnal brilliance, the raw colors of childhood's spectrum. Over the*

3. See Matthew 15.14: "And if the blind lead the blind, both shall fall into the ditch."
4. "The Poker Night" was Williams's working title for *A Streetcar Named Desire.*
5. *The Night Café* (1888), by the Dutch painter Vincent Van Gogh (1853–1890).

*yellow linoleum of the kitchen table hangs an electric bulb with a vivid green glass shade. The poker players —*STANLEY, STEVE, MITCH, *and* PABLO*—wear colored shirts, solid blue, a purple, a red-and-white check, a light green, and they are men at the peak of their physical manhood, as coarse and direct and powerful as the primary colors. There are vivid slices of watermelon on the table, whiskey bottles and glasses. The bedroom is relatively dim with only the light that spills between the portieres*[6] *and through the wide window on the street. For a moment, there is absorbed silence as a hand is dealt.*

STEVE Anything wild this deal?

PABLO One-eyed jacks are wild.

STEVE Give me two cards.

PABLO You, Mitch?

MITCH I'm out.

PABLO One.

MITCH Anyone want a shot?

STANLEY Yeah. Me.

PABLO Why don't somebody go to the Chinaman's and bring back a load of chop suey?

STANLEY When I'm losing you want to eat! Ante up! Openers? Openers! Get y'r ass off the table, Mitch. Nothing belongs on a poker table but cards, chips, and whiskey.

[*He lurches up and tosses some watermelon rinds to the floor.*]

MITCH Kind of on your high horse, ain't you?

STANLEY How many?

STEVE Give me three.

STANLEY One.

MITCH I'm out again. I oughta go home pretty soon.

STANLEY Shut up.

MITCH I gotta sick mother. She don't go to sleep until I come in at night.

STANLEY Then why don't you stay home with her?

MITCH She says to go out, so I go, but I don't enjoy it. All the while I keep wondering how she is.

STANLEY Aw, for the sake of Jesus, go home, then!

PABLO What've you got?

STEVE Spade flush.

MITCH You all are married. But I'll be alone when she goes—I'm going to the bathroom.

STANLEY Hurry back and we'll fix you a sugar-tit.[7]

MITCH Aw, go rut. [*He crosses through the bedroom into the bathroom.*]

STEVE [*dealing a hand*] Seven card stud. [*Telling his joke as he deals.*] This ole farmer is out in back of his house sittin' down th'owing corn to the chickens when all at once he hears a loud cackle and this young hen comes lickety split around the side of the house with the rooster right behind her and gaining on her fast.

STANLEY [*impatient with the story*] Deal!

STEVE But when the rooster catches sight of the farmer th'owing the corn he puts on the brakes and lets the hen get away and starts pecking corn. And the old farmer says, "Lord God, I hopes I never gits *that* hongry!"

6. Heavy curtains hung across a doorway.
7. A pacifier dipped in sugar.

[STEVE *and* PABLO *laugh. The sisters appear around the corner of the building.*]

STELLA The game is still going on.

BLANCHE How do I look?

STELLA Lovely, Blanche.

BLANCHE I feel so hot and frazzled. Wait till I powder before you open the door. Do I look done in?

STELLA Why no. You are as fresh as a daisy.

BLANCHE One that's been picked a few days.

[STELLA *opens the door and they enter.*]

STELLA Well, well, well. I see you boys are still at it!

STANLEY Where you been?

STELLA Blanche and I took in a show. Blanche, this is Mr. Gonzales and Mr. Hubbell.

BLANCHE Please don't get up.

STANLEY Nobody's going to get up, so don't be worried.

STELLA How much longer is this game going to continue?

STANLEY Till we get ready to quit.

BLANCHE Poker is so fascinating. Could I kibitz?

STANLEY You could not. Why don't you women go up and sit with Eunice?

STELLA Because it is nearly two-thirty. [BLANCHE *crosses into the bedroom and partially closes the portieres.*] Couldn't you call it quits after one more hand?

[*A chair scrapes.* STANLEY *gives a loud whack of his hand on her thigh.*]

STELLA [*sharply*] That's not fun, Stanley.

[*The men laugh.* STELLA *goes into the bedroom.*]

STELLA It makes me so mad when he does that in front of people.

BLANCHE I think I will bathe.

STELLA Again?

BLANCHE My nerves are in knots. Is the bathroom occupied?

STELLA I don't know.

[BLANCHE *knocks.* MITCH *opens the door and comes out, still wiping his hands on a towel.*]

BLANCHE Oh!—good evening.

MITCH Hello. [*He stares at her.*]

STELLA Blanche, this is Harold Mitchell. My sister, Blanche DuBois.

MITCH [*with awkward courtesy*] How do you do, Miss DuBois.

STELLA How is your mother now, Mitch?

MITCH About the same, thanks. She appreciated your sending over that custard.—Excuse me, please.

[*He crosses slowly back into the kitchen, glancing back at* BLANCHE *and coughing a little shyly. He realizes he still has the towel in his hands and with an embarrassed laugh hands it to* STELLA. BLANCHE *looks after him with a certain interest.*]

BLANCHE That one seems—superior to the others.

STELLA Yes, he is.

BLANCHE I thought he had a sort of sensitive look.

STELLA His mother is sick.

BLANCHE Is he married?

STELLA No.

BLANCHE Is he a wolf?

STELLA Why, Blanche! [BLANCHE *laughs.*] I don't think he would be.

BLANCHE What does—what does he do?

[*She is unbuttoning her blouse.*]

STELLA He's on the precision bench in the spare parts department. At the plant Stanley travels for.

BLANCHE Is that something much?

STELLA No. Stanley's the only one of his crowd that's likely to get anywhere.

BLANCHE What makes you think Stanley will?

STELLA Look at him.

BLANCHE I've looked at him.

STELLA Then you should know.

BLANCHE I'm sorry, but I haven't noticed the stamp of genius even on Stanley's forehead.

[*She takes off the blouse and stands in her pink silk brassiere and white skirt in the light through the portieres. The game has continued in undertones.*]

STELLA It isn't on his forehead and it isn't genius.

BLANCHE Oh. Well, what is it, and where? I would like to know.

STELLA It's a drive that he has. You're standing in the light, Blanche!

BLANCHE Oh, am I!

[*She moves out of the yellow streak of light. Stella has removed her dress and put on a light blue satin kimona.*[8]]

STELLA [*with girlish laughter*] You ought to see their wives.

BLANCHE [*laughingly*] I can imagine. Big, beefy things, I suppose.

STELLA You know that one upstairs? [*More laughter*] One time [*Laughing*] the plaster—[*Laughing*] cracked—

STANLEY You hens cut out that conversation in there!

STELLA You can't hear us.

STANLEY Well, you can hear me and I said to hush up!

STELLA This is my house and I'll talk as much as I want to!

BLANCHE Stella, don't start a row.

STELLA He's half drunk!—I'll be out in a minute.

[*She goes into the bathroom.* BLANCHE *rises and crosses leisurely to a small white radio and turns it on.*]

STANLEY Awright, Mitch, you in?

MITCH What? Oh!—No, I'm out!

[BLANCHE *moves back into the streak of light. She raises her arms and stretches, as she moves indolently back to the chair.*]

[*Rhumba music comes over the radio.* MITCH *rises at the table.*]

STANLEY Who turned that on in there?

BLANCHE I did. Do you mind?

STANLEY Turn it off!

STEVE Aw, let the girls have their music.

PABLO Sure, that's good, leave it on!

STEVE Sounds like Xavier Cugat![9]

8. Kimono.

9. The Cuban American bandleader (1900–1990) whose hits of the 1930s won him the nickname "Rhumba King."

[STANLEY *jumps up and, crossing to the radio, turns it off. He stops short at the sight of* BLANCHE *in the chair. She returns his look without flinching. Then he sits again at the poker table.*]

[*Two of the men have started arguing hotly.*]

STEVE I didn't hear you name it.

PABLO Didn't I name it, Mitch?

MITCH I wasn't listenin'.

PABLO What were you doing, then?

STANLEY He was looking through them drapes. [*He jumps up and jerks roughly at curtains to close them.*] Now deal the hand over again and let's play cards or quit. Some people get ants[1] when they win.

[MITCH *rises as* STANLEY *returns to his seat.*]

STANLEY [*yelling*] Sit down!

MITCH I'm going to the "head."[2] Deal me out.

PABLO Sure he's got ants now. Seven five-dollar bills in his pants pocket folded up tight as spitballs.

STEVE Tomorrow you'll see him at the cashier's window getting them changed into quarters.

STANLEY And when he goes home he'll deposit them one by one in a piggy bank his mother give him for Christmas. [*Dealing*] This game is Spit in the Ocean.

[MITCH *laughs uncomfortably and continues through the portieres. He stops just inside.*]

BLANCHE [*softly*] Hello! The Little Boys' Room is busy right now.

MITCH We've—been drinking beer.

BLANCHE I hate beer.

MITCH It's—a hot weather drink.

BLANCHE Oh, I don't think so; it always makes me warmer. Have you got any cigs? [*She has slipped on the dark red satin wrapper.*]

MITCH Sure.

BLANCHE What kind are they?

MITCH Luckies.

BLANCHE Oh, good. What a pretty case. Silver?

MITCH Yes. Yes; read the inscription.

BLANCHE Oh, is there an inscription? I can't make it out. [*He strikes a match and moves closer.*] Oh! [*Reading with feigned difficulty.*]

"And if God choose,
I shall but love thee better—after—death!"

Why, that's from my favorite sonnet by Mrs. Browning![3]

MITCH You know it?

BLANCHE Certainly I do!

MITCH There's a story connected with that inscription.

BLANCHE It sounds like a romance.

MITCH A pretty sad one.

1. Antsy.
2. Navy slang for a ship's toilet.
3. The English poet Elizabeth Barrett Browning (1806–1861). She is best known for her *Sonnets from the Portuguese* (1850), a sequence of love poems written before her marriage to Robert Browning; Blanche quotes from the most famous of them, Sonnet XLIII ("How do I love thee? Let me count the ways").

BLANCHE Oh?

MITCH The girl's dead now.

BLANCHE [*in a tone of deep sympathy*] *Oh!*

MITCH She knew she was dying when she give me this. A very strange girl, very sweet—very!

BLANCHE She must have been fond of you. Sick people have such deep, sincere attachments.

MITCH That's right, they certainly do.

BLANCHE Sorrow makes for sincerity, I think.

MITCH It sure brings it out in people.

BLANCHE The little there is belongs to people who have experienced some sorrow.

MITCH I believe you are right about that.

BLANCHE I'm positive that I am. Show me a person who hasn't known any sorrow and I'll show you a shuperficial—Listen to me! My tongue is a little—thick! You boys are responsible for it. The show let out at eleven and we couldn't come home on account of the poker game so we had to go somewhere and drink. I'm not accustomed to having more than one drink. Two is the limit—and *three!* [*She laughs.*] Tonight I had three.

STANLEY Mitch!

MITCH Deal me out. I'm talking to Miss—

BLANCHE DuBois.

MITCH Miss DuBois?

BLANCHE It's a French name. It means woods and Blanche means white, so the two together mean white woods. Like an orchard in spring! You can remember it by that.

MITCH You're French?

BLANCHE We are French by extraction. Our first American ancestors were French Huguenots.[4]

MITCH You are Stella's sister, are you not?

BLANCHE Yes, Stella is my precious little sister. I call her little in spite of the fact she's somewhat older than I. Just slightly. Less than a year. Will you do something for me?

MITCH Sure. What?

BLANCHE I bought this adorable little colored paper lantern at a Chinese shop on Bourbon.[5] Put it over the light bulb! Will you, please?

MITCH Be glad to.

BLANCHE I can't stand a naked light bulb, any more than I can a rude remark or a vulgar action.

MITCH [*adjusting the lantern*] I guess we strike you as being a pretty rough bunch.

BLANCHE I'm very adaptable—to circumstances.

MITCH Well, that's a good thing to be. You are visiting Stanley and Stella?

BLANCHE Stella hasn't been so well lately, and I came down to help her for a while. She's very run down.

4. French Protestants, repeatedly persecuted by the Catholic monarchy. Many Huguenots emigrated to the American colonies after Louis XIV's Edict of Fontainebleau declared Protestantism illegal in 1685.

5. Bourbon Street, the center of the French Quarter's nightlife.

MITCH You're not—?

BLANCHE Married? No, no. I'm an old maid schoolteacher!

MITCH You may teach school but you're certainly not an old maid.

BLANCHE Thank you, sir! I appreciate your gallantry!

MITCH So you are in the teaching profession?

BLANCHE Yes. Ah, yes . . .

MITCH Grade school or high school or—

STANLEY [*bellowing*] *Mitch!*

MITCH *Coming!*

BLANCHE Gracious, what lung-power! . . . I teach high school. In Laurel.

MITCH What do you teach? What subject?

BLANCHE Guess!

MITCH I bet you teach art or music? [BLANCHE *laughs delicately.*] Of course I could be wrong. You might teach arithmetic.

BLANCHE Never arithmetic, sir; never arithmetic! [*With a laugh*] I don't even know my multiplication tables! No, I have the misfortune of being an English instructor. I attempt to instill a bunch of bobby-soxers and drugstore Romeos with reverence for Hawthorne and Whitman and Poe![6]

MITCH I guess that some of them are more interested in other things.

BLANCHE How very right you are! Their literary heritage is not what most of them treasure above all else! But they're sweet things! And in the spring, it's touching to notice them making their first discovery of love! As if nobody had ever known it before!

[*The bathroom door opens and* STELLA *comes out.* BLANCHE *continues talking to* MITCH.]

Oh! Have you finished? Wait—I'll turn on the radio.

[*She turns the knobs on the radio and it begins to play "Wien, Wien, nur du allein."*[7] BLANCHE *waltzes to the music with romantic gestures.* MITCH *is delighted and moves in awkward imitation like a dancing bear.*]

[STANLEY *stalks fiercely through the portieres into the bedroom. He crosses to the small white radio and snatches it off the table. With a shouted oath, he tosses the instrument out the window.*]

STELLA *Drunk—drunk—animal thing, you!* [*She rushes through to the poker table.*] All of you—please go home! If any of you have one spark of decency in you—

BLANCHE [*wildly*] Stella, watch out, he's—

[STANLEY *charges after* STELLA.]

MEN [*feebly*] Take it easy, Stanley. Easy, fellow.—Let's all—

STELLA You lay your hands on me and I'll—

[*She backs out of sight. He advances and disappears. There is the sound of a blow.* STELLA *cries out.* BLANCHE *screams and runs into the kitchen.*

6. Classic American authors: Nathaniel Hawthorne (1804–1864), Walt Whitman (1819–1892), and Edgar Allan Poe. *Bobby-soxers and drugstore Romeos:* teenage boys and girls. "Bobby-soxer" was a term first applied to the girls in ankle socks who cried and swooned at Frank Sinatra's concerts in the early 1940s; and boys were "drugstore Romeos" because drugstores usually had soda fountains, where teenagers socialized.

7. "Vienna, Vienna, only you alone" (German); from the popular waltz "Wien, du Stadt meiner Träume" ("Vienna, You City of My Dreams," 1914), by the Austrian composer Rudolf Sieczynski.

The men rush forward and there is grappling and cursing. Something is overturned with a crash.]

BLANCHE [*shrilly*] My sister is going to have a baby!

MITCH This is terrible.

BLANCHE Lunacy, absolute lunacy!

MITCH Get him in here, men.

[STANLEY *is forced, pinioned by the two men, into the bedroom. He nearly throws them off. Then all at once he subsides and is limp in their grasp.*]

[*They speak quietly and lovingly to him and he leans his face on one of their shoulders.*]

STELLA [*in a high, unnatural voice, out of sight*] I want to go away, I want to go away!

MITCH Poker shouldn't be played in a house with women.

[BLANCHE *rushes into the bedroom.*]

BLANCHE I want my sister's clothes! We'll go to that woman's upstairs!

MITCH Where is the clothes?

BLANCHE [*opening the closet*] I've got them! [*She rushes through to* STELLA.] Stella, Stella, precious! Dear, dear little sister, don't be afraid!

[*With her arms around* STELLA, BLANCHE *guides her to the outside door and upstairs.*]

STANLEY [*dully*] What's the matter; what's happened?

MITCH You just blew your top, Stan.

PABLO He's okay, now.

STEVE Sure, my boy's okay!

MITCH Put him on the bed and get a wet towel.

PABLO I think coffee would do him a world of good, now.

STANLEY [*thickly*] I want water.

MITCH Put him under the shower!

[*The men talk quietly as they lead him to the bathroom.*]

STANLEY Let the rut go of me, you sons of bitches!

[*Sounds of blows are heard. The water goes on full tilt.*]

STEVE Let's get quick out of here!

[*They rush to the poker table and sweep up their winings on their way out.*]

MITCH [*sadly but firmly*] Poker should not be played in a house with women.

[*The door closes on them and the place is still. The Negro entertainers in the bar around the corner play "Paper Doll"*[8] *slow and blue. After a moment Stanley comes out of the bathroom dripping water and still in his clinging wet polka-dot drawers.*]

STANLEY Stella! [*There is a pause.*] My baby doll's left me!

[*He breaks into sobs. Then he goes to the phone and dials, still shuddering with sobs.*]

Eunice? I want my baby! [*He waits a moment; then he hangs up and dials again.*] Eunice! I'll keep on ringin' until I talk with my baby!

8. A song written by Johnny S. Black in 1915; the Mills Brothers' 1943 version was a huge hit.

[*An indistinguishable shrill voice is heard. He hurls phone to floor. Dissonant brass and piano sounds as the rooms dim out to darkness and the outer walls appear in the night light. The "blue piano" plays for a brief interval.*]

[*Finally,* STANLEY *stumbles half-dressed out to the porch and down the wooden steps to the pavement before the building. There he throws back his head like a baying hound and bellows his wife's name: "Stella! Stella, sweetheart! Stella!"*]

STANLEY Stell-*lahhhhh!*

EUNICE [*calling down from the door of her upper apartment*] Quit that howling out there an' go back to bed!

STANLEY I want my baby down here. Stella, Stella!

EUNICE She ain't comin' down so you quit! Or you'll git th' law on you!

STANLEY Stella!

EUNICE You can't beat on a woman an' then call 'er back! She won't come! And her goin' t' have a baby! . . . You stinker! You whelp of a Polack, you! I hope they do haul you in and turn the fire hose on you, same as the last time!

STANLEY [*humbly*] Eunice, I want my girl to come down with me!

EUNICE Hah! [*She slams her door.*]

STANLEY [*with heaven-splitting violence*] *STELL-LAHHHHH!*

[*The low-tone clarinet moans. The door upstairs opens again.* STELLA *slips down the rickety stairs in her robe. Her eyes are glistening with tears and her hair loose about her throat and shoulders. They stare at each other. Then they come together with low, animal moans. He falls to his knees on the steps and presses his face to her belly, curving a little with maternity. Her eyes go blind with tenderness as she catches his head and raises him level with her. He snatches the screen door open and lifts her off her feet and bears her into the dark flat.*]

[BLANCHE *comes out on the upper landing in her robe and slips fearfully down the steps.*]

BLANCHE Where is my little sister? Stella? Stella?

[*She stops before the dark entrance of her sister's flat. Then catches her breath as if struck. She rushes down to the walk before the house. She looks right and left as if for a sanctuary.*]

[*The music fades away.* MITCH *appears from around the corner.*]

MITCH Miss DuBois?

BLANCHE Oh!

MITCH All quiet on the Potomac[9] now?

BLANCHE She ran downstairs and went back in there with him.

MITCH Sure she did.

BLANCHE I'm terrified!

MITCH Ho-ho! There's nothing to be scared of. They're crazy about each other.

BLANCHE I'm not used to such—

MITCH Naw, it's a shame this had to happen when you just got here. But don't take it serious.

9. Because of the inaction of the Union general George McClellan in 1861–62, newspaper correspondents frequently reported "All quiet on the Potomac"; it became a bitter catchphrase, featured in ballads and a popular song.

BLANCHE Violence! Is so—

MITCH Set down on the steps and have a cigarette with me.

BLANCHE I'm not properly dressed.

MITCH That don't make no difference in the Quarter.

BLANCHE Such a pretty silver case.

MITCH I showed you the inscription, didn't I?

BLANCHE Yes. [*During the pause, she looks up at the sky.*] There's so much—so much confusion in the world . . . [*He coughs diffidently.*] Thank you for being so kind! I need kindness now.

Scene 4

It is early the following morning. There is a confusion of street cries like a choral chant.

STELLA *is lying down in the bedroom. Her face is serene in the early morning sunlight. One hand rests on her belly, rounding slightly with new maternity. From the other dangles a book of colored comics. Her eyes and lips have that almost narcotized tranquility that is in the faces of Eastern idols.*

The table is sloppy with remains of breakfast and the debris of the preceding night, and STANLEY'S *gaudy pyjamas lie across the threshold of the bathroom. The outside door is slightly ajar on a sky of summer brilliance.*

BLANCHE *appears at this door. She has spent a sleepless night and her appearance entirely contrasts with Stella's. She presses her knuckles nervously to her lips as she looks through the door, before entering.*

BLANCHE Stella?

STELLA [*stirring lazily*] Hmmh?

[BLANCHE *utters a moaning cry and runs into the bedroom, throwing herself down beside* STELLA *in a rush of hysterical tenderness.*]

BLANCHE Baby, my baby sister!

STELLA [*drawing away from her*] Blanche, what is the matter with you?

[BLANCHE *straightens up slowly and stands beside the bed looking down at her sister with knuckles pressed to her lips.*]

BLANCHE He's left?

STELLA Stan? Yes.

BLANCHE Will he be back?

STELLA He's gone to get the car greased. Why?

BLANCHE Why! I've been half crazy, Stella! When I found out you'd been insane enough to come back in here after what happened—I started to rush in after you!

STELLA I'm glad you didn't.

BLANCHE What were you thinking of? [STELLA *makes an indefinite gesture.*] Answer me! What? What?

STELLA Please, Blanche! Sit down and stop yelling.

BLANCHE All right, Stella. I will repeat the question quietly now. How could you come back in this place last night? Why, you must have slept with him!

[STELLA *gets up in a calm and leisurely way.*]

STELLA Blanche, I'd forgotten how excitable you are. You're making much too much fuss about this.

BLANCHE Am I?

STELLA Yes, you are, Blanche. I know how it must have seemed to you and I'm awful sorry it had to happen, but it wasn't anything as serious as you seem to take it. In the first place, when men are drinking and playing poker anything can happen. It's always a powder-keg. He didn't know what he was doing. . . . He was as good as a lamb when I came back and he's really very, very ashamed of himself.

BLANCHE And that—that makes it all right?

STELLA No, it isn't all right for anybody to make such a terrible row, but—people do sometimes. Stanley's always smashed things. Why, on our wedding night—soon as we came in here—he snatched off one of my slippers and rushed about the place smashing light bulbs with it.

BLANCHE He did—*what?*

STELLA He smashed all the light bulbs with the heel of my slipper! [*She laughs.*]

BLANCHE And you—you *let* him? Didn't *run,* didn't *scream?*

STELLA I was—sort of—thrilled by it. [*She waits for a moment.*] Eunice and you had breakfast?

BLANCHE Do you suppose I wanted any breakfast?

STELLA There's some coffee left on the stove.

BLANCHE You're so—matter-of-fact about it, Stella.

STELLA What other can I be? He's taken the radio to get it fixed. It didn't land on the pavement so only one tube[1] was smashed.

BLANCHE And you are standing there smiling!

STELLA What do you want me to do?

BLANCHE Pull yourself together and face the facts.

STELLA What are they, in your opinion?

BLANCHE In my opinion? You're married to a madman!

STELLA No!

BLANCHE Yes, you are, your fix is worse than mine is! Only you're not being sensible about it. I'm going to *do* something. Get hold of myself and make myself a new life!

STELLA Yes?

BLANCHE But you've given in. And that isn't right, you're not old! You can get out.

STELLA [*slowly and emphatically*] I'm not in anything I want to get out of.

BLANCHE [*incredulously*] What—Stella?

STELLA I said I am not in anything that I have a desire to get out of. Look at the mess in this room! And those empty bottles! They went through two cases last night! He promised this morning that he was going to quit having these poker parties, but you know how long such a promise is going to keep. Oh, well, it's his pleasure, like mine is movies and bridge. People have got to tolerate each other's habits, I guess.

BLANCHE I don't understand you. [STELLA *turns toward her.*] I don't understand your indifference. Is this a Chinese philosophy you've—cultivated?

STELLA Is what—what?

BLANCHE This—shuffling about and mumbling—'One tube smashed—beer bottles—mess in the kitchen!'—as if nothing out of the ordinary has happened! [STELLA *laughs uncertainly and picking up the broom, twirls it in her hands.*]

BLANCHE Are you deliberately shaking that thing in my face?

1. Vacuum tube (used in radios before the invention of transistors).

STELLA No.

BLANCHE Stop it. Let go of that broom. I won't have you cleaning up for him!

STELLA Then who's going to do it? Are you?

BLANCHE I? I!

STELLA No, I didn't think so.

BLANCHE Oh, let me think, if only my mind would function! We've got to get hold of some money, that's the way out!

STELLA I guess that money is always nice to get hold of.

BLANCHE Listen to me. I have an idea of some kind. [*Shakily she twists a cigarette into her holder.*] Do you remember Shep Huntleigh? [STELLA *shakes her head.*] Of course you remember Shep Huntleigh. I went out with him at college and wore his pin[2] for a while. Well—

STELLA Well?

BLANCHE I ran into him last winter. You know I went to Miami during the Christmas holidays?

STELLA No.

BLANCHE Well, I did. I took the trip as an investment, thinking I'd meet someone with a million dollars.

STELLA Did you?

BLANCHE Yes. I ran into Shep Huntleigh—I ran into him on Biscayne Boulevard, on Christmas Eve, about dusk . . . getting into his car—Cadillac convertible; must have been a block long!

STELLA I should think it would have been—inconvenient in traffic!

BLANCHE You've heard of oil wells?

STELLA Yes—remotely.

BLANCHE He has them, all over Texas. Texas is literally spouting gold in his pockets.

STELLA My, my.

BLANCHE Y'know how indifferent I am to money. I think of money in terms of what it does for you. But he could do it, he could certainly do it!

STELLA Do what, Blanche?

BLANCHE Why—set us up in a—shop!

STELLA What kind of a shop?

BLANCHE Oh, a—shop of some kind! He could do it with half what his wife throws away at the races.

STELLA He's married?

BLANCHE Honey, would I be here if the man weren't married? [STELLA *laughs a little.* BLANCHE *suddenly springs up and crosses to phone. She speaks shrilly.*] How do I get Western Union?[3]—Operator! Western Union!

STELLA That's a dial phone,[4] honey.

BLANCHE I can't dial, I'm too—

STELLA Just dial O.

BLANCHE O?

2. A fraternity pin, worn as a sign that a couple were "going steady."

3. The dominant American telegraph company for most of the twentieth century.

4. Though dial telephones came into use in the 1930s, in some parts of the country (rural Mississippi presumably among them) operators placed all calls for another decade or more.

STELLA Yes, "O" for Operator! [BLANCHE *considers a moment; then she puts the phone down.*]

BLANCHE Give me a pencil. Where is a slip of paper? I've got to write it down first—the message, I mean . . .

[*She goes to the dressing table, and grabs up a sheet of Kleenex and an eyebrow pencil for writing equipment.*]

Let me see now . . . [*She bites the pencil.*] 'Darling Shep. Sister and I in desperate situation.'

STELLA I beg your pardon!

BLANCHE 'Sister and I in desperate situation. Will explain details later. Would you be interested in—?' [*She bites the pencil again.*] 'Would you be—interested—in . . .' [*She smashes the pencil on the table and springs up.*] You never get anywhere with direct appeals!

STELLA [*with a laugh*] Don't be so ridiculous, darling!

BLANCHE But I'll think of something, I've *got* to think of—*some*thing! Don't, don't laugh at me, Stella! Please, please don't—I—I want you to look at the contents of my purse! Here's what's in it! [*She snatches her purse open.*] Sixty-five measly cents in coin of the realm!

STELLA [*crossing to bureau*] Stanley doesn't give me a regular allowance, he likes to pay bills himself, but—this morning he gave me ten dollars to smooth things over. You take five of it, Blanche, and I'll keep the rest.

BLANCHE Oh, no. No, Stella.

STELLA [*insisting*] I know how it helps your morale just having a little pocket money on you.

BLANCHE No, thank you—I'll take to the streets!

STELLA Talk sense! How did you happen to get so low on funds?

BLANCHE Money just goes—it goes places. [*She rubs her forehead.*] Sometime today I've got to get hold of a Bromo![5]

STELLA I'll fix you one now.

BLANCHE Not yet—I've got to keep thinking!

STELLA I wish you'd just let things go, at least for a—while . . .

BLANCHE Stella, I can't live with him! You can, he's your husband. But how could I stay here with him, after last night, with just those curtains between us?

STELLA Blanche, you saw him at his worst last night.

BLANCHE On the contrary, I saw him at his best! What such a man has to offer is animal force and he gave a wonderful exhibition of that! But the only way to live with such a man is to—go to bed with him! And that's your job—not mine!

STELLA After you've rested a little, you'll see it's going to work out. You don't have to worry about anything while you're here. I mean—expenses . . .

BLANCHE I have to plan for us both, to get us both—out!

STELLA You take it for granted that I am in something that I want to get out of.

BLANCHE I take it for granted that you still have sufficient memory of Belle Reve to find this place and these poker players impossible to live with.

STELLA Well, you're taking entirely too much for granted.

BLANCHE I can't believe you're in earnest.

5. Bromo-Seltzer, a headache remedy and antacid introduced in 1891; its effervescent granules are dissolved in water.

STELLA No?

BLANCHE I understand how it happened—a little. You saw him in uniform, an officer, not here but—

STELLA I'm not sure it would have made any difference where I saw him.

BLANCHE Now don't say it was one of those mysterious electric things between people! If you do I'll laugh in your face.

STELLA I am not going to say anything more at all about it!

BLANCHE All right, then, don't!

STELLA But there are things that happen between a man and a woman in the dark—that sort of make everything else seem—unimportant. [*Pause*]

BLANCHE What you are talking about is brutal desire—just—Desire!—the name of that rattletrap streetcar that bangs through the Quarter, up one old narrow street and down another . . .

STELLA Haven't you ever ridden on that streetcar?

BLANCHE It brought me here.—Where I'm not wanted and where I'm ashamed to be . . .

STELLA Then don't you think your superior attitude is a bit out of place?

BLANCHE I am not being or feeling at all superior, Stella. Believe me I'm not! It's just this. This is how I look at it. A man like that is someone to go out with—once—twice—three times when the devil is in you. But live with? Have a child by?

STELLA I have told you I love him.

BLANCHE Then I *tremble* for you! I just—*tremble* for you. . . .

STELLA I can't help your trembling if you insist on trembling!

[*There is a pause.*]

BLANCHE May I—speak—*plainly?*

STELLA Yes, do. Go ahead. As plainly as you want to.

[*Outside, a train approaches. They are silent till the noise subsides. They are both in the bedroom.*]

[*Under cover of the train's noise* STANLEY *enters from outside. He stands unseen by the women, holding some packages in his arms, and overhears their following conversation. He wears an undershirt and grease-stained seersucker pants.*]

BLANCHE Well—if you'll forgive me—he's *common!*

STELLA Why, yes, I suppose he is.

BLANCHE Suppose! You can't have forgotten that much of our bringing up, Stella, that you just *suppose* that any part of a gentleman's in his nature! *Not one particle, no!* Oh, if he was just—*ordinary!* Just *plain*—but good and wholesome, but—*no*. There's something downright—*bestial*—about him! You're hating me saying this, aren't you?

STELLA [*coldly*] Go on and say it all, Blanche.

BLANCHE He acts like an animal, has an animal's habits! Eats like one, moves like one, talks like one! There's even something—subhuman—something not quite to the stage of humanity yet! Yes, something—apelike about him, like one of those pictures I've seen in—anthropological studies! Thousands and thousands of years have passed him right by, and there he is—Stanley Kowalski—survivor of the Stone Age! Bearing the raw meat home from the kill in the jungle! And you—*you here*—*waiting* for him! Maybe he'll strike you or maybe grunt and kiss you! That is, if kisses have been discovered yet! Night falls and the other apes gather! There in the front of the cave, all grunting like him, and swilling and gnawing and hulking! His poker night!—you call it—this party of apes! Somebody growls—some creature snatches at something—the fight is on! *God!* Maybe we are a long way from being made in God's image, but Stella—my sister—there has been *some* progress since then! Such things as art—as poetry and music—such kinds of new light have come into the world since then! In some kinds of people some tenderer feelings have had some little beginning! That we have got to make *grow!* And *cling* to, and hold as our flag! In this dark march toward whatever it is we're approaching. . . . *Don't—don't hang back with the brutes!*

[*Another train passes outside.* STANLEY *hesitates, licking his lips. Then suddenly he turns stealthily about and withdraws through front door. The women are still unaware of his presence. When the train has passed he calls through the closed front door.*]

STANLEY Hey! Hey, Stella!

STELLA [*who has listened gravely to* BLANCHE] Stanley!

BLANCHE Stell, I—

[*But* STELLA *has gone to the front door.* STANLEY *enters casually with his packages.*]

STANLEY Hiyuh, Stella. Blanche back?

STELLA Yes, she's back.

STANLEY Hiyuh, Blanche. [*He grins at her.*]

STELLA You must've got under the car.

STANLEY Them darn mechanics at Fritz's don't know their ass fr'm—*Hey!*

[STELLA *has embraced him with both arms, fiercely, and full in the view of* BLANCHE. *He laughs and clasps her head to him. Over her head he grins through the curtains at* BLANCHE.]

[*As the lights fade away, with a lingering brightness on their embrace, the music of the "blue piano" and trumpet and drums is heard.*]

Scene 5

BLANCHE *is seated in the bedroom fanning herself with a palm leaf as she reads over a just-completed letter. Suddenly she bursts into a peal of laughter.* STELLA *is dressing in the bedroom.*

STELLA What are you laughing at, honey?

BLANCHE Myself, myself, for being such a liar! I'm writing a letter to Shep. [*She picks up the letter.*] "Darling Shep. I am spending the summer on the wing, making flying visits here and there. And who knows, perhaps I shall take a sudden notion to *swoop* down on *Dallas!* How would you feel about that? Ha-ha! [*She laughs nervously and brightly, touching her throat as if actually talking to Shep.*] Forewarned is forearmed, as they say!"—How does that sound?

STELLA Uh-huh . . .

BLANCHE [*going on nervously*] "Most of my sister's friends go north in the summer but some have homes on the Gulf and there has been a continued round of entertainments, teas, cocktails, and luncheons—"

[*A disturbance is heard upstairs at the Hubbells' apartment.*]

STELLA Eunice seems to be having some trouble with Steve.

[EUNICE'S *voice shouts in terrible wrath.*]

EUNICE I heard about you and that blonde!

STEVE That's a damn lie!

EUNICE You ain't pulling the wool over my eyes! I wouldn't mind if you'd stay down at the Four Deuces, but you always going up.

STEVE Who ever seen me up?

EUNICE I seen you chasing her 'round the balcony—I'm gonna call the vice squad!

STEVE Don't you throw that at me!

EUNICE [*shrieking*] You hit me! I'm gonna call the police!

[*A clatter of aluminum striking a wall is heard, followed by a man's angry roar, shouts and overturned furniture. There is a crash; then a relative hush.*]

BLANCHE [*brightly*] Did he *kill* her?

[EUNICE *appears on the steps in daemonic disorder.*]

STELLA No! She's coming downstairs.

EUNICE Call the police, I'm going to call the police! [*She rushes around the corner.*]

[*They laugh lightly.* STANLEY *comes around the corner in his green and scarlet silk bowling shirt. He trots up the steps and bangs into the kitchen.* BLANCHE *registers his entrance with nervous gestures.*]

STANLEY What's a matter with Eun-uss?

STELLA She and Steve had a row. Has she got the police?

STANLEY Naw. She's gettin' a drink.

STELLA That's much more practical!

[STEVE *comes down nursing a bruise on his forehead and looks in the door.*]

STEVE She here?

STANLEY Naw, naw. At the Four Deuces.

STEVE That rutting hunk! [*He looks around the corner a bit timidly, then turns with affected boldness and runs after her.*]

BLANCHE I must jot that down in my notebook. Ha-ha! I'm compiling a notebook of quaint little words and phrases I've picked up here.

STANLEY You won't pick up nothing here you ain't heard before.

BLANCHE Can I count on that?

STANLEY You can count on it up to five hundred.

BLANCHE That's a mighty high number. [*He jerks open the bureau drawer, slams it shut and throws shoes in a corner. At each noise* BLANCHE *winces slightly. Finally she speaks.*] What sign were you born under?

STANLEY [*while he is dressing*] Sign?

BLANCHE Astrological sign. I bet you were born under Aries. Aries people are forceful and dynamic. They dote on noise! They love to bang things around! You must have had lots of banging around in the army and now that you're out, you make up for it by treating inanimate objects with such a fury!

[STELLA *has been going in and out of closet during this scene. Now she pops her head out of the closet.*]

STELLA Stanley was born just five minutes after Christmas.

BLANCHE Capricorn—the Goat!

STANLEY What sign were *you* born under?

BLANCHE Oh, my birthday's next month, the fifteenth of September; that's under Virgo.

STANLEY What's Virgo?

BLANCHE Virgo is the Virgin.

STANLEY [*contemptuously*] *Hah!* [*He advances a little as he knots his tie.*] Say, do you happen to know somebody named Shaw?

[*Her face expresses a faint shock. She reaches for the cologne bottle and dampens her handkerchief as she answers carefully.*]

BLANCHE Why, everybody knows somebody named Shaw!

STANLEY Well, this somebody named Shaw is under the impression he met you in Laurel, but I figure he must have got you mixed up with some other party because this other party is someone he met at a hotel called the Flamingo.

[BLANCHE *laughs breathlessly as she touches the cologne-dampened handkerchief to her temples.*]

BLANCHE I'm afraid he does have me mixed up with this "other party." The Hotel Flamingo is not the sort of establishment I would dare to be seen in!

STANLEY You know of it?

BLANCHE Yes, I've seen it and smelled it.

STANLEY You must've got pretty close if you could smell it.

BLANCHE The odor of cheap perfume is penetrating.

STANLEY That stuff you use is expensive?

BLANCHE Twenty-five dollars an ounce! I'm nearly out. That's just a hint if you want to remember my birthday! [*She speaks lightly but her voice has a note of fear.*]

STANLEY Shaw must've got you mixed up. He goes in and out of Laurel all the time so he can check on it and clear up any mistake.

[*He turns away and crosses to the portieres.* BLANCHE *closes her eyes as if faint. Her hand trembles as she lifts the handkerchief again to her forehead.*]

[STEVE *and* EUNICE *come around corner.* STEVE*'s arm is around* EUNICE*'s shoulder and she is sobbing luxuriously and he is cooing love-words. There is a murmur of thunder as they go slowly upstairs in a tight embrace.*]

STANLEY [*to* STELLA] I'll wait for you at the Four Deuces!

STELLA Hey! Don't I rate one kiss?

STANLEY Not in front of your sister.

[*He goes out.* BLANCHE *rises from her chair. She seems faint; looks about her with an expression of almost panic.*]

BLANCHE Stella! What have you heard about me?

STELLA Huh?

BLANCHE What have people been telling you about me?

STELLA Telling?

BLANCHE You haven't heard any—unkind—gossip about me?

STELLA Why, no, Blanche, of course not!

BLANCHE Honey, there was—a good deal of talk in Laurel.

STELLA About *you*, Blanche?

BLANCHE I wasn't so good the last two years or so, after Belle Reve had started to slip through my fingers.

STELLA All of us do things we—

BLANCHE I never was hard or self-sufficient enough. When people are soft—soft people have got to shimmer and glow—they've got to put on soft colors, the colors of butterfly wings, and put a—paper lantern over the light. . . . It isn't enough to be soft. You've got to be soft *and attractive*. And I—I'm fading now! I don't know how much longer I can turn the trick.

[*The afternoon has faded to dusk.* STELLA *goes into the bedroom and turns on the light under the paper lantern. She holds a bottled soft drink in her hand.*]

BLANCHE Have you been listening to me?

STELLA I don't listen to you when you are being morbid! [*She advances with the bottled Coke.*]

BLANCHE [*with abrupt change to gaiety*] Is that Coke for me?

STELLA Not for anyone else!

BLANCHE Why, you precious thing, you! Is it just Coke?

STELLA [*turning*] You mean you want a shot in it!

BLANCHE Well, honey, a shot never does a Coke any harm! Let me! You mustn't wait on me!

STELLA I like to wait on you, Blanche. It makes it seem more like home. [*She goes into the kitchen, finds a glass and pours a shot of whiskey into it.*]

BLANCHE I have to admit I love to be waited on . . .

[*She rushes into the bedroom.* STELLA *goes to her with the glass.* BLANCHE *suddenly clutches* STELLA*'s free hand with a moaning sound and presses the hand to her lips.* STELLA *is embarrassed by her show of emotion.* BLANCHE *speaks in a choked voice.*]

You're—you're—so *good* to me! And I

STELLA Blanche.

BLANCHE I know, I won't! You hate me to talk sentimental! But honey, *believe* I feel things more than I *tell* you! I *won't* stay long! I won't, I *promise* I—

STELLA Blanche!

BLANCHE [*hysterically*] I won't, I promise, *I'll* go! Go *soon!* I will *really!* I *won't* hang around until he—throws me out . . .

STELLA Now will you stop talking foolish?

BLANCHE Yes, honey. Watch how you pour—that fizzy stuff foams over!

[BLANCHE *laughs shrilly and grabs the glass, but her hand shakes so it almost slips from her grasp.* STELLA *pours the Coke into the glass. It foams over and spills.* BLANCHE *gives a piercing cry.*]

STELLA [*shocked by the cry*] Heavens!

BLANCHE Right on my pretty white skirt!

STELLA Oh . . . Use my hanky. Blot gently.

BLANCHE [*slowly recovering*] I know—gently—gently . . .

STELLA Did it stain?

BLANCHE Not a bit. Ha-ha! Isn't that lucky? [*She sits down shakily, taking a grateful drink. She holds the glass in both hands and continues to laugh a little.*]

STELLA Why did you scream like that?

BLANCHE I don't know why I screamed! [*Continuing nervously*] Mitch—Mitch is coming at seven. I guess I am just feeling nervous about our relations. [*She begins to talk rapidly and breathlessly.*] He hasn't gotten a thing but a good-night kiss, that's all I have given him, Stella. I want his respect. And men don't want anything they get too easy. But on the other hand men lose interest quickly. Especially when the girl is over—thirty. They think a girl over thirty ought to—the vulgar term is—"put out." . . . And I—I'm not "putting out." Of course he—he doesn't know—I mean I haven't informed him—of my real age!

STELLA Why are you sensitive about your age?

BLANCHE Because of hard knocks my vanity's been given. What I mean is—he thinks I'm sort of—prim and proper, you know! [*She laughs out sharply.*] I want to *deceive* him enough to make him—want me . . .

STELLA Blanche, do you want *him?*

BLANCHE I want to *rest!* I want to breathe quietly again! Yes—I *want* Mitch . . . *very badly!* Just think! If it happens! I can leave here and not be anyone's problem . . .

[STANLEY *comes around the corner with a drink under his belt.*]

STANLEY [*bawling*] Hey, Steve! Hey, Eunice! Hey, Stella!

[*There are joyous calls from above. Trumpet and drums are heard from around the corner.*]

STELLA [*kissing* BLANCHE *impulsively*] It *will* happen!

BLANCHE [*doubtfully*] It will?

STELLA It *will!* [*She goes across into the kitchen, looking back at* BLANCHE.] It will, honey, *it will*. . . . But don't take another drink! [*Her voice catches as she goes out the door to meet her husband.*

[BLANCHE *sinks faintly back in her chair with her drink.* EUNICE *shrieks with laughter and runs down the steps.* STEVE *bounds after her with goat-like screeches and chases her around corner.* STANLEY *and* STELLA *twine arms as they follow, laughing.*]

[*Dusk settles deeper. The music from the Four Deuces is slow and blue.*]

BLANCHE Ah, me, ah, me, ah, me . . .

[*Her eyes fall shut and the palm leaf fan drops from her fingers. She slaps her hand on the chair arm a couple of times. There is a little glimmer of lightning about the building.*]

[*A* YOUNG MAN *comes along the street and rings the bell.*]

BLANCHE Come in.

[*The* YOUNG MAN *appears through the portieres. She regards him with interest.*]

BLANCHE Well, well! What can I do for *you?*

YOUNG MAN I'm collecting for *The Evening Star.*

BLANCHE I didn't know that stars took up collections.

YOUNG MAN It's the paper.

BLANCHE I know, I was joking—feebly! Will you—have a drink?

YOUNG MAN No, ma'am. No, thank you. I can't drink on the job.

BLANCHE Oh, well, now, let's see. . . . No, I don't have a dime! I'm not the lady of the house. I'm her sister from Mississippi. I'm one of those poor relations you've heard about.

YOUNG MAN That's all right. I'll drop by later. [*He starts to go out. She approaches a little.*]

BLANCHE Hey! [*He turns back shyly. She puts a cigarette in a long holder.*] Could you give me a light? [*She crosses toward him. They meet at the door between the two rooms.*]

YOUNG MAN Sure. [*He takes out a lighter.*] This doesn't always work.

BLANCHE It's temperamental? [*It flares.*] Ah!—thank you. [*He starts away again.*] Hey! [*He turns again, still more uncertainly. She goes close to him.*] Uh—what time is it?

YOUNG MAN Fifteen of seven, ma'am.

BLANCHE So late? Don't you just love these long rainy afternoons in New Orleans when an hour isn't just an hour—but a little piece of eternity dropped into your hands—and who knows what to do with it? [*She touches his shoulders.*] You—uh—didn't get wet in the rain?

YOUNG MAN No, ma'am. I stepped inside.

BLANCHE In a drugstore? And had a soda?

YOUNG MAN Uh-huh.

BLANCHE Chocolate?

YOUNG MAN No, ma'am. Cherry.

BLANCHE [*laughing*] Cherry!

YOUNG MAN A cherry soda.

BLANCHE You make my mouth water. [*She touches his cheek lightly, and smiles. Then she goes to the trunk.*]

YOUNG MAN Well, I'd better be going—

BLANCHE [*stopping him*] Young man!

[*He turns. She takes a large, gossamer scarf from the trunk and drapes it about her shoulders.*]

[*In the ensuing pause, the "blue piano" is heard. It continues through the rest of this scene and the opening of the next. The young man clears his throat and looks yearningly at the door.*]

Young man! Young, young, young man! Has anyone ever told you that you look like a young Prince out of the Arabian Nights?[6]

[*The* YOUNG MAN *laughs uncomfortably and stands like a bashful kid.* BLANCHE *speaks softly to him.*]

Well, you do, honey lamb! Come here. I want to kiss you, just once, softly and sweetly on your mouth!

[*Without waiting for him to accept, she crosses quickly to him and presses her lips to his.*]

Now run along, now, quickly! It would be nice to keep you, but I've got to be good—and keep my hands off children.

[*He stares at her a moment. She opens the door for him and blows a kiss at him as he goes down the steps with a dazed look. She stands there a little dreamily after he has disappeared. Then* MITCH *appears around the corner with a bunch of roses.*]

BLANCHE [*gaily*] Look who's coming! My Rosenkavalier! Bow to me first . . . now present them! *Ahhhh—Merciiii!*[7]

[*She looks at him over them, coquettishly pressing them to her lips. He beams at her self-consciously.*]

6. That is, *The Thousand and One Nights*, a collection of ancient tales in Arabic, arranged in its present form in the 15th century.

7. Thank you (French). *Rosenkavalier:* literally, "Knight of the Rose" (German), an allusion to Richard Strauss's romantic opera *Der Rosenkavalier* (1911).

Scene 6

It is about two A.M. *on the same evening. The outer wall of the building is visible.* BLANCHE *and* MITCH *come in. The utter exhaustion which only a neurasthenic personality*[8] *can know is evident in* BLANCHE*'s voice and manner.* MITCH *is stolid but depressed. They have probably been out to the amusement park on Lake Pontchartrain, for* MITCH *is bearing, upside down, a plaster statuette of Mae West,*[9] *the sort of prize won at shooting galleries and carnival games of chance.*

BLANCHE [*stopping lifelessly at the steps*] Well—

[MITCH *laughs uneasily.*]

Well . . .

MITCH I guess it must be pretty late—and you're tired.

BLANCHE Even the hot tamale man has deserted the street, and he hangs on till the end. [MITCH *laughs uneasily again.*] How will you get home?

MITCH I'll walk over to Bourbon and catch an owl-car.[1]

BLANCHE [*laughing grimly*] Is that streetcar named Desire still grinding along the tracks at this hour?

MITCH [*heavily*] I'm afraid you haven't gotten much fun out of this evening, Blanche.

BLANCHE I spoiled it for *you*.

MITCH No, you didn't, but I felt all the time that I wasn't giving you much—entertainment.

BLANCHE I simply couldn't rise to the occasion. That was all. I don't think I've ever tried so hard to be gay and made such a dismal mess of it. I get ten points for trying!—I *did* try.

MITCH Why did you try if you didn't feel like it, Blanche?

BLANCHE I was just obeying the law of nature.

MITCH Which law is that?

BLANCHE The one that says the lady must entertain the gentleman—or no dice! See if you can locate my door key in this purse. When I'm so tired my fingers are all thumbs!

MITCH [*rooting in her purse*] This it?

BLANCHE No, honey, that's the key to my trunk which I must soon be packing.

MITCH You mean you are leaving here soon?

BLANCHE I've outstayed my welcome.

MITCH This it?

[*The music fades away.*]

BLANCHE Eureka! Honey, you open the door while I take a last look at the sky. [*She leans on the porch rail. He opens the door and stands awkwardly behind her.*] I'm looking for the Pleiades, the Seven Sisters,[2] but these girls are not out tonight. Oh, yes they are, there they are! God bless them! All in

8. Someone suffering from neurasthenia, a psychological disorder characterized by nervous exhaustion. A common clinical diagnosis during the late 19th century, the term is no longer in scientific use.

9. An American actress of burlesque shows, stage, and screen (1893–1980), famous for her sexual double entendres. *Lake Pontchartrain:* the large, shallow lake immediately north of New Orleans.

1. A late-night streetcar (i.e., for "night owls").

2. In Greek mythology, the Pleiades are the seven daughters of Atlas who were changed into a cluster of stars in the constellation Taurus.

a bunch going home from their little bridge party. . . . Y' get the door open? Good boy! I guess you—want to go now . . .

[*He shuffles and coughs a little.*]

MITCH Can I—uh—kiss you—good night?

BLANCHE Why do you always ask me if you may?

MITCH I don't know whether you want me to or not.

BLANCHE Why should you be so doubtful?

MITCH That night when we parked by the lake and I kissed you, you—

BLANCHE Honey, it wasn't the kiss I objected to. I liked the kiss very much. It was the other little—familiarity—that I—felt obliged to—discourage. . . . I didn't resent it! Not a bit in the world! In fact, I was somewhat flattered that you—desired me! But, honey, you know as well as I do that a single girl, a girl alone in the world, has got to keep a firm hold on her emotions or she'll be lost!

MITCH [*solemnly*] Lost?

BLANCHE I guess you are used to girls that like to be lost. The kind that get lost immediately, on the first date!

MITCH I like you to be exactly the way that you are, because in all my—experience—I have never known anyone like you.

[BLANCHE *looks at him gravely; then she bursts into laughter and then claps a hand to her mouth.*]

MITCH Are you laughing at me?

BLANCHE No, honey. The lord and lady of the house have not yet returned, so come in. We'll have a nightcap. Let's leave the lights off. Shall we?

MITCH You just—do what you want to.

[BLANCHE *precedes him into the kitchen. The outer wall of the building disappears and the interiors of the two rooms can be dimly seen.*]

BLANCHE [*remaining in the first room*] The other room's more comfortable—go on in. This crashing around in the dark is my search for some liquor.

MITCH You want a drink?

BLANCHE I want *you* to have a drink! You have been so anxious and solemn all evening, and so have I; we have both been anxious and solemn and now for these few last remaining moments of our lives together—I want to create—*joie de vivre!*[3] I'm lighting a candle.

MITCH That's good.

BLANCHE We are going to be very Bohemian. We are going to pretend that we are sitting in a little artists' cafe on the Left Bank[4] in Paris! [*She lights a candle stub and puts it in a bottle.*] *Je suis la Dame aux Camellias! Vous êtes—Armand!*[5] Understand French?

MITCH [*heavily*] Naw. Naw, I—

3. Joy of life (French).
4. A neighborhood on the western ("left") bank of the river Seine, known for cultural and intellectual activities.
5. I am the Lady of the Camellias. You are—Armand! (French). The reference is to Alexandre Dumas's novel *La Dame aux camélias* (1848), the tragic story of Marguerite Gautier, a Parisian courtesan who falls in love with Armand Duval, a respectable member of middle-class society, and dies of consumption. Dumas's 1852 theatrical adaptation of this novel (often titled *Camille* in English) was highly popular with late 19th-century audiences.

BLANCHE *Voulez-vous couchez avec moi ce soir? Vous ne comprenez pas? Ah, quelle dommage!*[6] I mean it's a damned good thing. . . . I've found some liquor! Just enough for two shots without any dividends, honey . . .

MITCH [*heavily*] That's—good.

[*She enters the bedroom with the drinks and the candle.*]

BLANCHE Sit down! Why don't you take off your coat and loosen your collar?

MITCH I better leave it on.

BLANCHE No. I want you to be comfortable.

MITCH I am ashamed of the way I perspire. My shirt is sticking to me.

BLANCHE Perspiration is healthy. If people didn't perspire they would die in five minutes. [*She takes his coat from him.*] This is a nice coat. What kind of material is it?

MITCH They call that stuff alpaca.

BLANCHE Oh. Alpaca.

MITCH It's very light-weight alpaca.

BLANCHE Oh. Light-weight alpaca.

MITCH I don't like to wear a wash-coat[7] even in summer because I sweat through it.

BLANCHE Oh.

MITCH And it don't look neat on me. A man with a heavy build has got to be careful of what he puts on him so he don't look too clumsy.

BLANCHE You are not too heavy.

MITCH You don't think I am?

BLANCHE You are not the delicate type. You have a massive bone-structure and a very imposing physique.

MITCH Thank you. Last Christmas I was given a membership to the New Orleans Athletic Club.

BLANCHE Oh, good.

MITCH It was the finest present I ever was given. I work out there with the weights and I swim and I keep myself fit. When I started there, I was getting soft in the belly but now my belly is hard. It is so hard now that a man can punch me in the belly and it don't hurt me. Punch me! Go on! See? [*She pokes lightly at him.*]

BLANCHE Gracious. [*Her hand touches her chest.*]

MITCH Guess how much I weigh, Blanche?

BLANCHE Oh, I'd say in the vicinity of—one hundred and eighty?

MITCH Guess again.

BLANCHE Not that much?

MITCH No. More.

BLANCHE Well, you're a tall man and you can carry a good deal of weight without looking awkward.

MITCH I weigh two hundred and seven pounds and I'm six feet one and one half inches tall in my bare feet—without shoes on. And that is what I weigh stripped.

BLANCHE Oh, my goodness, me! It's awe-inspiring.

6. Would you like to go to bed with me tonight? You don't understand? Ah, what a shame! (French).

7. A light washable jacket, here made of a silky wool.

MITCH [*embarrassed*] My weight is not a very interesting subject to talk about. [*He hesitates for a moment.*] What's yours?

BLANCHE My weight?

MITCH Yes.

BLANCHE Guess!

MITCH Let me lift you.

BLANCHE Samson![8] Go on, lift me. [*He comes behind her and puts his hands on her waist and raises her lightly off the ground.*] Well?

MITCH You are light as a feather.

BLANCHE Ha-ha! [*He lowers her but keeps his hands on her waist.* BLANCHE *speaks with an affectation of demureness.*] You may release me now.

MITCH Huh?

BLANCHE [*gaily*] I said unhand me, sir. [*He fumblingly embraces her. Her voice sounds gently reproving.*] Now, Mitch. Just because Stanley and Stella aren't at home is no reason why you shouldn't behave like a gentleman.

MITCH Just give me a slap whenever I step out of bounds.

BLANCHE That won't be necessary. You're a natural gentleman, one of the very few that are left in the world. I don't want you to think that I am severe and old maid school-teacherish or anything like that. It's just—well—

MITCH Huh?

BLANCHE I guess it is just that I have—old-fashioned ideals! [*She rolls her eyes, knowing he cannot see her face.* MITCH *goes to the front door. There is a considerable silence between them.* BLANCHE *sighs and* MITCH *coughs self-consciously.*]

MITCH [*finally*] Where's Stanley and Stella tonight?

BLANCHE They have gone out. With Mr. and Mrs. Hubbell upstairs.

MITCH Where did they go?

BLANCHE I think they were planning to go to a midnight prevue at Loew's State.

MITCH We should all go out together some night.

BLANCHE No. That wouldn't be a good plan.

MITCH Why not?

BLANCHE You are an old friend of Stanley's?

MITCH We was together in the Two-forty-first.[9]

BLANCHE I guess he talks to you frankly?

MITCH Sure.

BLANCHE Has he talked to you about me?

MITCH Oh—not very much.

BLANCHE The way you say that, I suspect that he has.

MITCH No, he hasn't said much.

BLANCHE But what he *has* said. What would you say his attitude toward me was?

MITCH Why do you want to ask that?

BLANCHE Well—

MITCH Don't you get along with him?

BLANCHE What do you think?

MITCH I don't think he understands you.

8. An Israelite hero of great strength (see Judges 13–16).

9. The 241st Battalion of the Army Corps of Engineers.

BLANCHE That is putting it mildly. If it weren't for Stella about to have a baby, I wouldn't be able to endure things here.

MITCH He isn't—nice to you?

BLANCHE He is insufferably rude. Goes out of his way to offend me.

MITCH In what way, Blanche?

BLANCHE Why, in every conceivable way.

MITCH I'm surprised to hear that.

BLANCHE Are you?

MITCH Well, I—don't see how anybody could be rude to you.

BLANCHE It's really a pretty frightful situation. You see, there's no privacy here. There's just these portieres between the two rooms at night. He stalks through the rooms in his underwear at night. And I have to ask him to close the bathroom door. That sort of commonness isn't necessary. You probably wonder why I don't move out. Well, I'll tell you frankly. A teacher's salary is barely sufficient for her living expenses. I didn't save a penny last year and so I had to come here for the summer. That's why I have to put up with my sister's husband. And he has to put up with me, apparently so much against his wishes. . . . Surely he must have told you how much he hates me!

MITCH I don't think he hates you.

BLANCHE He hates me. Or why would he insult me? The first time I laid eyes on him I thought to myself, that man is my executioner! That man will destroy me, unless—

MITCH Blanche—

BLANCHE Yes, honey?

MITCH Can I ask you a question?

BLANCHE Yes. What?

MITCH How old are you?

[*She makes a nervous gesture.*]

BLANCHE Why do you want to know?

MITCH I talked to my mother about you and she said, "How old is Blanche?" And I wasn't able to tell her. [*There is another pause.*]

BLANCHE You talked to your mother about me?

MITCH Yes.

BLANCHE Why?

MITCH I told my mother how nice you were, and I liked you.

BLANCHE Were you sincere about that?

MITCH You know I was.

BLANCHE Why did your mother want to know my age?

MITCH Mother is sick.

BLANCHE I'm sorry to hear it. Badly?

MITCH She won't live long. Maybe just a few months.

BLANCHE Oh.

MITCH She worries because I'm not settled.

BLANCHE Oh.

MITCH She wants me to be settled down before she—[*His voice is hoarse and he clears his throat twice, shuffling nervously around with his hands in and out of his pockets.*]

BLANCHE You love her very much, don't you?

MITCH Yes.

BLANCHE I think you have a great capacity for devotion. You will be lonely when she passes on, won't you? [MITCH *clears his throat and nods.*] I understand what that is.

MITCH To be lonely?

BLANCHE I loved someone, too, and the person I loved I lost.

MITCH Dead? [*She crosses to the window and sits on the sill, looking out. She pours herself another drink.*] A man?

BLANCHE He was a boy, just a boy, when I was a very young girl. When I was sixteen, I made the discovery—love. All at once and much, much too completely. It was like you suddenly turned a blinding light on something that had always been half in shadow, that's how it struck the world for me. But I was unlucky. Deluded. There was something different about the boy, a nervousness, a softness and tenderness which wasn't like a man's, although he wasn't the least bit effeminate-looking—still—that thing was there. . . . He came to me for help. I didn't know that. I didn't find out anything till after our marriage when we'd run away and come back and all I knew was I'd failed him in some mysterious way and wasn't able to give the help he needed but couldn't speak of! He was in the quicksands and clutching at me—but I wasn't holding him out, I was slipping in with him! I didn't know that. I didn't know anything except I loved him unendurably but without being able to help him or help myself. Then I found out. In the worst of all possible ways. By coming suddenly into a room that I thought was empty—which wasn't empty, but had two people in it . . . the boy I had married and an older man who had been his friend for years . . .

[*A locomotive is heard approaching outside. She claps her hands to her ears and crouches over. The headlight of the locomotive glares into the room as it thunders past. As the noise recedes she straightens slowly and continues speaking.*]

Afterward we pretended that nothing had been discovered. Yes, the three of us drove out to Moon Lake Casino,[1] very drunk and laughing all the way.

[*Polka music sounds, in a minor key faint with distance.*]

We danced the Varsouviana![2] Suddenly in the middle of the dance the boy I had married broke away from me and ran out of the casino. A few moments later—a shot!

[*The polka stops abruptly*]

[BLANCHE *rises stiffly. Then, the polka resumes in a major key.*]

I ran out—all did!—all ran and gathered about the terrible thing at the edge of the lake! I couldn't get near for the crowding. Then somebody caught my arm. "Don't go any closer! Come back! You don't want to see!" See? See what! Then I heard voices say—Allan! Allan! The Grey boy! He'd stuck the revolver into his mouth, and fired—so that the back of his head had been—blown away!

[*She sways and covers her face.*]

It was because—on the dance floor—unable to stop myself—I'd suddenly said—"I saw! I know! You disgust me . . ." And then the searchlight which had been turned on the world was turned off again and never for one

1. A popular night spot and casino during the 1940s, located in Dundee, Mississippi.

2. A jaunty polka dance.

moment since has there been any light that's stronger than this—kitchen—candle . . .

[MITCH *gets up awkwardly and moves toward her a little. The polka music increases.* MITCH *stands beside her.*]

MITCH [*drawing her slowly into his arms*] You need somebody. And I need somebody, too. Could it be—you and me, Blanche?

[*She stares at him vacantly for a moment. Then with a soft cry huddles in his embrace. She makes a sobbing effort to speak but the words won't come. He kisses her forehead and her eyes and finally her lips. The polka tune fades out. Her breath is drawn and released in long, grateful sobs.*]

BLANCHE Sometimes—there's God—so quickly!

Scene 7

It is late afternoon in mid-September.

The portieres are open and a table is set for a birthday supper, with cake and flowers. STELLA *is completing the decorations as* STANLEY *comes in.*

STANLEY What's all this stuff for?

STELLA Honey, it's Blanche's birthday.

STANLEY She here?

STELLA In the bathroom.

STANLEY [*mimicking*] "Washing out some things"?

STELLA I reckon so.

STANLEY How long she been in there?

STELLA All afternoon.

STANLEY [*mimicking*] "Soaking in a hot tub"?

STELLA Yes.

STANLEY Temperature 100 on the nose, and she soaks herself in a hot tub.

STELLA She says it cools her off for the evening.

STANLEY And you run out an' get her cokes, I suppose? And serve 'em to Her Majesty in the tub? [STELLA *shrugs.*] Set down here a minute.

STELLA Stanley, I've got things to do.

STANLEY Set down! I've got th' dope on your big sister, Stella.

STELLA Stanley, stop picking on Blanche.

STANLEY That girl calls *me* common!

STELLA Lately you been doing all you can think of to rub her the wrong way, Stanley, and Blanche is sensitive and you've got to realize that Blanche and I grew up under very different circumstances than you did.

STANLEY So I been told. And told and told and told! You know she's been feeding us a pack of lies here?

STELLA No, I don't, and—

STANLEY Well, she has, however. But now the cat's out of the bag! I found out some things!

STELLA What—things?

STANLEY Things I already suspected. But now I got proof from the most reliable sources—which I have checked on!

[BLANCHE *is singing in the bathroom a saccharine popular ballad which is used contrapuntally with Stanley's speech.*]

STELLA [*to* STANLEY] Lower your voice!

STANLEY Some canary bird, huh!

STELLA Now please tell me quietly what you think you've found out about my sister.

STANLEY Lie Number One: All this squeamishness she puts on! You should just know the line she's been feeding to Mitch. He thought she had never been more than kissed by a fellow! But Sister Blanche is no lily! Ha-ha! Some lily she is!

STELLA What have you heard and who from?

STANLEY Our supply-man down at the plant has been going through Laurel for years and he knows all about her and everybody else in the town of Laurel knows all about her. She is as famous in Laurel as if she was the President of the United States, only she is not respected by any party! This supply-man stops at a hotel called the Flamingo.

BLANCHE [*singing blithely*]

"Say, it's only a paper moon, Sailing over a cardboard sea—But it
wouldn't be make-believe If you believed in me!"[3]

STELLA What about the—Flamingo?

STANLEY She stayed there, too.

STELLA My sister lived at Belle Reve.

STANLEY This is after the home-place had slipped through her lily-white fingers! She moved to the Flamingo! A second-class hotel which has the advantage of not interfering in the private social life of the personalities there! The Flamingo is used to all kinds of goings-on. But even the management of the Flamingo was impressed by Dame Blanche! In fact they was so impressed by Dame Blanche that they requested her to turn in her room key—for permanently! This happened a couple of weeks before she showed here.

BLANCHE [*singing*]

"It's a Barnum and Bailey world,[4] Just as phony as it can be—
But it wouldn't be make-believe If you believed in me!"

STELLA What—contemptible—lies!

STANLEY Sure, I can see how you would be upset by this. She pulled the wool over your eyes as much as Mitch's!

STELLA It's pure invention! There's not a word of truth in it and if I were a man and this creature had dared to invent such things in my presence—

BLANCHE [*singing*]

"Without your love,
It's a honky-tonk parade!
Without your love,
It's a melody played In a penny arcade . . ."

STANLEY Honey, I told you I thoroughly checked on these stories! Now wait till I finished. The trouble with Dame Blanche was that she couldn't put on her act any more in Laurel! They got wised up after two or three dates with her and then they quit, and she goes on to another, the same old line, same old act, same old hooey! But the town was too small for this to go on forever!

3. From "It's Only a Paper Moon" (lyrics by Yip Harburg and Billy Rose, music by Harold Arlen), used in the film *Take a Chance* (1933).

4. That is, a circus performance. P. T. Barnum (1810–1891) and James A. Bailey (1847–1906) merged their circuses in 1881.

And as time went by she became a town character. Regarded as not just different but downright loco—nuts.

[STELLA *draws back.*]

And for the last year or two she has been washed up like poison. That's why she's here this summer, visiting royalty, putting on all this act—because she's practically told by the mayor to get out of town! Yes, did you know there was an army camp near Laurel and your sister's was one of the places called "Out-of-Bounds"?

BLANCHE

"It's only a paper moon, Just as phony as it can be—
But it wouldn't be make-believe If you believed in me!"

STANLEY Well, so much for her being such a refined and particular type of girl. Which brings us to Lie Number Two.

STELLA I don't want to hear any more!

STANLEY She's not going back to teach school! In fact I am willing to bet you that she never had no idea of returning to Laurel! She didn't resign temporarily from the high school because of her nerves! No, siree, Bob! She didn't. They kicked her out of that high school before the spring term ended—and I hate to tell you the reason that step was taken! A seventeen-year-old boy—she'd gotten mixed up with!

BLANCHE

"It's a Barnum and Bailey world, Just as phony as it can be—"

[*In the bathroom the water goes on loud; little breathless cries and peals of laughter are heard as if a child were frolicking in the tub.*]

STELLA This is making me—sick!

STANLEY The boy's dad learned about it and got in touch with the high school superintendent. Boy, oh, boy, I'd like to have been in that office when Dame Blanche was called on the carpet! I'd like to have seen her trying to squirm out of that one! But they had her on the hook good and proper that time and she knew that the jig was all up! They told her she better move on to some fresh territory. Yep, it was practickly a town ordinance passed against her!

[*The bathroom door is opened and* BLANCHE *thrusts her head out, holding a towel about her hair.*]

BLANCHE Stella!

STELLA [*faintly*] Yes, Blanche?

BLANCHE Give me another bath-towel to dry my hair with. I've just washed it.

STELLA Yes, Blanche. [*She crosses in a dazed way from the kitchen to the bathroom door with a towel.*]

BLANCHE What's the matter, honey?

STELLA Matter? Why?

BLANCHE You have such a strange expression on your face!

STELLA Oh—[*She tries to laugh.*] I guess I'm a little tired!

BLANCHE Why don't you bathe, too, soon as I get out?

STANLEY [*calling from the kitchen*] How soon is that going to be?

BLANCHE Not so terribly long! Possess your soul in patience![5]

5. "In your patience possess ye your souls" (Luke 21.19).

STANLEY It's not my soul, it's my kidneys I'm worried about!

[BLANCHE *slams the door.* STANLEY *laughs harshly.* STELLA *comes slowly back into the kitchen.*]

STANLEY Well, what do you think of it?

STELLA I don't believe all of those stories and I think your supply-man was mean and rotten to tell them. It's possible that some of the things he said are partly true. There are things about my sister I don't approve of—things that caused sorrow at home. She was always—flighty!

STANLEY Flighty!

STELLA But when she was young, very young, she married a boy who wrote poetry. . . . He was extremely good-looking. I think Blanche didn't just love him but worshipped the ground he walked on! Adored him and thought him almost too fine to be human! But then she found out

STANLEY What?

STELLA This beautiful and talented young man was a degenerate. Didn't your supply-man give you that information?

STANLEY All we discussed was recent history. That must have been a pretty long time ago.

STELLA Yes, it was—a pretty long time ago . . .

[STANLEY *comes up and takes her by the shoulders rather gently. She gently withdraws from him. Automatically she starts sticking little pink candles in the birthday cake.*]

STANLEY How many candles you putting in that cake?

STELLA I'll stop at twenty-five.

STANLEY Is company expected?

STELLA We asked Mitch to come over for cake and ice-cream.

[STANLEY *looks a little uncomfortable. He lights a cigarette from the one he has just finished.*]

STANLEY I wouldn't be expecting Mitch over tonight.

[STELLA *pauses in her occupation with candles and looks slowly around at* STANLEY.]

STELLA *Why?*

STANLEY Mitch is a buddy of mine. We were in the same outfit together—Two-forty-first Engineers. We work in the same plant and now on the same bowling team. You think I could face him if—

STELLA Stanley Kowalski, did you—did you repeat what that—?

STANLEY You're goddam right I told him! I'd have that on my conscience the rest of my life if I knew all that stuff and let my best friend get caught!

STELLA Is Mitch through with her?

STANLEY Wouldn't you be if—?

STELLA I said, *Is Mitch through with her?*

[BLANCHE'*s voice is lifted again, serenely as a bell. She sings "But it wouldn't be make believe If you believed in me."*]

STANLEY No, I don't think he's necessarily through with her—just wised up!

STELLA Stanley, she thought Mitch was—going to—going to marry her. I was hoping so, too.

STANLEY Well, he's not going to marry her. Maybe he *was*, but he's not going to jump in a tank with a school of sharks—now! [*He rises.*] Blanche! Oh, Blanche! Can I please get in my bathroom? [*There is a pause.*]

BLANCHE Yes, indeed, sir! Can you wait one second while I dry?

STANLEY Having waited one hour I guess one second ought to pass in a hurry.

STELLA And she hasn't got her job? Well, what will she do!

STANLEY She's not stayin' here after Tuesday. You know that, don't you? Just to make sure I bought her ticket myself. A bus ticket?

STELLA In the first place, Blanche wouldn't go on a bus.

STANLEY She'll go on a bus and like it.

STELLA No, she won't, no, she won't, Stanley!

STANLEY *She'll go!* Period. P.S. She'll go *Tuesday!*

STELLA [*slowly*] What'll—she—do? What on earth will she—*do!*

STANLEY Her future is mapped out for her.

STELLA What do you mean?

[BLANCHE *sings.*]

STANLEY Hey, canary bird! Toots! Get *OUT* of the *BATHROOM!*

[*The bathroom door flies open and* BLANCHE *emerges with a gay peal of laughter, but as* STANLEY *crosses past her, a frightened look appears in her face, almost a look of panic. He doesn't look at her but slams the bathroom door shut as he goes in.*]

BLANCHE [*snatching up a hairbrush*] Oh, I feel so good after my long, hot bath, I feel so good and cool and—rested!

STELLA [*sadly and doubtfully from the kitchen*] Do you, Blanche?

BLANCHE [*brushing her hair vigorously*] Yes, I do, so refreshed! [*She tinkles her highball glass.*] A hot bath and a long, cold drink always give me a brand new outlook on life! [*She looks through the portieres at* STELLA, *standing between them, and slowly stops brushing.*] Something has happened!—What is it?

STELLA [*turning away quickly*] Why, nothing has happened, Blanche.

BLANCHE You're lying! Something has!

[*She stares fearfully at* STELLA, *who pretends to be busy at the table. The distant piano goes into a hectic breakdown.*]

Scene 8

Three-quarters of an hour later.

The view through the big windows is fading gradually into a still-golden dusk. A torch of sunlight blazes on the side of a big water-tank or oil-drum across the empty lot toward the business district which is now pierced by pinpoints of lighted windows or windows reflecting the sunset.

The three people are completing a dismal birthday supper. STANLEY *looks sullen.* STELLA *is embarrassed and sad.* BLANCHE *has a tight, artificial smile on her drawn face. There is a fourth place at the table which is left vacant.*

BLANCHE [*suddenly*] Stanley, tell us a joke, tell us a funny story to make us all laugh. I don't know what's the matter, we're all so solemn. Is it because I've been stood up by my beau?

[STELLA *laughs feebly.*]

It's the first time in my entire experience with men, and I've had a good deal of all sorts, that I've actually been stood up by anybody! Ha-ha! I don't know how to take it. . . . Tell us a funny little story, Stanley! Something to help us out.

STANLEY I didn't think you liked my stories, Blanche.

BLANCHE I like them when they're amusing but not indecent.

STANLEY I don't know any refined enough for your taste.

BLANCHE Then let me tell one.

STELLA Yes, you tell one, Blanche. You used to know lots of good stories.

[*The music fades.*]

BLANCHE Let me see, now. . . . I must run through my repertoire! Oh, yes—I love parrot stories! Do you all like parrot stories? Well, this one's about the old maid and the parrot. This old maid, she had a parrot that cursed a blue streak and knew more vulgar expressions than Mr. Kowalski!

STANLEY Huh.

BLANCHE And the only way to hush the parrot up was to put the cover back on its cage so it would think it was night and go back to sleep. Well, one morning the old maid had just uncovered the parrot for the day—when who should she see coming up the front walk but the preacher! Well, she rushed back to the parrot and slipped the cover back on the cage and then she let in the preacher. And the parrot was perfectly still, just as quiet as a mouse, but just as she was asking the preacher how much sugar he wanted in his coffee—the parrot broke the silence with a loud—[*She whistles.*]—and said—"God *damn*, but that was a short day!"

[*She throws back her head and laughs.* STELLA *also makes an ineffectual effort to seem amused.* STANLEY *pays no attention to the story but reaches way over the table to spear his fork into the remaining chop which he eats with his fingers.*]

BLANCHE Apparently Mr. Kowalski was not amused.

STELLA Mr. Kowalski is too busy making a pig of himself to think of anything else!

STANLEY That's right, baby.

STELLA Your face and your fingers are disgustingly greasy. Go and wash up and then help me clear the table.

[*He hurls a plate to the floor.*]

STANLEY That's how I'll clear the table! [*He seizes her arm.*] Don't ever talk that way to me! "Pig—Polack—disgusting—vulgar—greasy!"—them kind of words have been on your tongue and your sister's too much around here! What do you two think you are? A pair of queens? Remember what Huey Long said—"Every Man is a King!"[6] And I am the king around here, so don't forget it! [*He hurls a cup and saucer to the floor.*] My place is cleared! You want me to clear your places?

[STELLA *begins to cry weakly.* STANLEY *stalks out on the porch and lights a cigarette.*]

[*The Negro entertainers around the corner are heard.*]

BLANCHE What happened while I was bathing? What did he tell you, Stella?

STELLA Nothing, nothing, nothing!

BLANCHE I think he told you something about Mitch and me! You know why Mitch didn't come but you won't tell me! [STELLA *shakes her head helplessly.*] I'm going to call him!

STELLA I wouldn't call him, Blanche.

BLANCHE I am, I'm going to call him on the phone.

6. The slogan used by the populist Democrat Long (1893–1935) in his successful campaigns for governor of and then senator from Louisiana.

STELLA [*miserably*] I wish you wouldn't.

BLANCHE I intend to be given some explanation from someone!

[*She rushes to the phone in the bedroom.* STELLA *goes out on the porch and stares reproachfully at her husband. He grunts and turns away from her.*]

STELLA I hope you're pleased with your doings. I never had so much trouble swallowing food in my life, looking at that girl's face and the empty chair! [*She cries quietly.*]

BLANCHE [*at the phone*] Hello. Mr. Mitchell, please. . . . Oh. . . . I would like to leave a number if I may. Magnolia 9047. And say it's important to call. . . . Yes, very important. . . . Thank you. [*She remains by the phone with a lost, frightened look.*]

[STANLEY *turns slowly back toward his wife and takes her clumsily in his arms.*]

STANLEY Stell, it's gonna be all right after she goes and after you've had the baby. It's gonna be all right again between you and me the way that it was. You remember that way that it was? Them nights we had together? God, honey, it's gonna be sweet when we can make noise in the night the way that we used to and get the colored lights going with nobody's sister behind the curtains to hear us!

[*Their upstairs neighbors are heard in bellowing laughter at something.* STANLEY *chuckles.*]

Steve an' Eunice . . .

STELLA Come on back in. [*She returns to the kitchen and starts lighting the candles on the white cake.*] Blanche?

BLANCHE Yes. [*She returns from the bedroom to the table in the kitchen.*] Oh, those pretty, pretty little candles! Oh, don't burn them, Stella.

STELLA I certainly will.

[STANLEY *comes back in.*]

BLANCHE You ought to save them for baby's birthdays. Oh, I hope candles are going to glow in his life and I hope that his eyes are going to be like candles, like two blue candles lighted in a white cake!

STANLEY [*sitting down*] What poetry!

BLANCHE [*she pauses reflectively for a moment*] I shouldn't have called him.

STELLA There's lots of things could have happened.

BLANCHE There's no excuse for it, Stella. I don't have to put up with insults. I won't be taken for granted.

STANLEY Goddamn, it's hot in here with the steam from the bathroom.

BLANCHE I've said I was sorry three times. [*The piano fades out.*] I take hot baths for my nerves. Hydrotherapy, they call it. You healthy Polack, without a nerve in your body, of course you don't know what anxiety feels like!

STANLEY I am not a Polack. People from Poland are Poles, not Polacks. But what I am is a one-hundred-per-cent American, born and raised in the greatest country on earth and proud as hell of it, so don't ever call me a Polack.

[*The phone rings.* BLANCHE *rises expectantly.*]

BLANCHE Oh, that's for me, I'm sure.

STANLEY *I'm* not sure. Keep your seat. [*He crosses leisurely to phone.*] H'lo. Aw, yeh, hello, Mac.

[*He leans against wall, staring insultingly in at* BLANCHE. *She sinks back in her chair with a frightened look.* STELLA *leans over and touches her shoulder.*]

BLANCHE Oh, keep your hands off me, Stella. What is the matter with you? Why do you look at me with that pitying look?

STANLEY [*bawling*] QUIET IN THERE!—We've got a noisy woman on the place.—Go on, Mac. At Riley's? No, I don't wanta bowl at Riley's. I had a little trouble with Riley last week. I'm the team captain, ain't I? All right, then, we're not gonna bowl at Riley's, we're gonna bowl at the West Side or the Gala! All right, Mac. See you!

[*He hangs up and returns to the table.* BLANCHE *fiercely controls herself, drinking quickly from her tumbler of water. He doesn't look at her but reaches in a pocket. Then he speaks slowly and with false amiability.*]

Sister Blanche, I've got a little birthday remembrance for you.

BLANCHE Oh, have you, Stanley? I wasn't expecting any, I—I don't know why Stella wants to observe my birthday! I'd much rather forget it—when you—reach twenty-seven! Well—age is a subject that you'd prefer to—ignore!

STANLEY Twenty-seven?

BLANCHE [*quickly*] What is it? Is it for *me?*

[*He is holding a little envelope toward her.*]

STANLEY Yes, I hope you like it!

BLANCHE Why, why—Why, it's a—

STANLEY Ticket! Back to Laurel! On the Greyhound![7] Tuesday!

[*The Varsouviana music steals in softly and continues playing.* STELLA *rises abruptly and turns her back.* BLANCHE *tries to smile. Then she tries to laugh. Then she gives both up and springs from the table and runs into the next room. She clutches her throat and then runs into the bathroom. Coughing, gagging sounds are heard.*]

Well!

STELLA You didn't need to do that.

STANLEY Don't forget all that I took off her.

STELLA You needn't have been so cruel to someone alone as she is.

STANLEY Delicate piece she is.

STELLA She is. She was. You didn't know Blanche as a girl. Nobody, nobody, was tender and trusting as she was. But people like you abused her, and forced her to change.

[*He crosses into the bedroom, ripping off his shirt, and changes into a brilliant silk bowling shirt. She follows him.*]

Do you think you're going bowling now?

STANLEY Sure.

STELLA You're not going bowling. [*She catches hold of his shirt.*] Why did you do this to her?

STANLEY I done nothing to no one. Let go of my shirt. You've torn it.

STELLA I want to know why. Tell me why.

STANLEY When we first met, me and you, you thought I was common. How right you was, baby. I was common as dirt. You showed me the snapshot of

7. That is, the long-distance bus.

the place with the columns. I pulled you down off them columns and how you loved it, having them colored lights going! And wasn't we happy together, wasn't it all okay till she showed here?

[STELLA *makes a slight movement. Her look goes suddenly inward as if some interior voice had called her name. She begins a slow, shuffling progress from the bedroom to the kitchen, leaning and resting on the back of the chair and then on the edge of a table with a blind look and listening expression. Stanley, finishing with his shirt, is unaware of her reaction.*]

And wasn't we happy together? Wasn't it all okay? Till she showed here. Hoity-toity, describing me as an ape. [*He suddenly notices the change in* STELLA.] Hey, what is it, Stell? [*He crosses to her.*]

STELLA [*quietly*] Take me to the hospital.

[*He is with her now, supporting her with his arm, murmuring indistinguishably as they go outside.*]

Scene 9

A while later that evening. BLANCHE *is seated in a tense hunched position in a bedroom chair that she has recovered with diagonal green and white stripes. She has on her scarlet satin robe. On the table beside chair is a bottle of liquor and a glass. The rapid, feverish polka tune, the "Varsouviana," is heard. The music is in her mind; she is drinking to escape it and the sense of disaster closing in on her, and she seems to whisper the words of the song. An electric fan is turning back and forth across her.*

MITCH *comes around the corner in work clothes: blue denim shirt and pants. He is unshaven. He climbs the steps to the door and rings.* BLANCHE *is startled.*

BLANCHE Who is it, please?

MITCH [*hoarsely*] Me. Mitch.

[*The polka tune stops.*]

BLANCHE Mitch!—Just a minute.

[*She rushes about frantically, hiding the bottle in a closet, crouching at the mirror and dabbing her face with cologne and powder. She is so excited that her breath is audible as she dashes about. At last she rushes to the door in the kitchen and lets him in.*]

Mitch!—Y'know, I really shouldn't let you in after the treatment I have received from you this evening! So utterly uncavalier! But hello, beautiful!

[*She offers him her lips. He ignores it and pushes past her into the flat. She looks fearfully after him as he stalks into the bedroom.*]

My, my, what a cold shoulder! And such uncouth apparel! Why, you haven't even shaved! The unforgivable insult to a lady! But I forgive you. I forgive you because it's such a relief to see you. You've stopped that polka tune that I had caught in my head. Have you ever had anything caught in your head? No, of course you haven't, you dumb angel-puss, you'd never get anything awful caught in your head!

[*He stares at her while she follows him while she talks. It is obvious that he has had a few drinks on the way over.*]

MITCH Do we have to have that fan on?

BLANCHE No!

MITCH I don't like fans.

BLANCHE Then let's turn it off, honey. I'm not partial to them!

[*She presses the switch and the fan nods slowly off. She clears her throat uneasily as* MITCH *plumps himself down on the bed in the bedroom and lights a cigarette.*]

I don't know what there is to drink. I—haven't investigated.

MITCH I don't want Stan's liquor.

BLANCHE It isn't Stan's. Everything here isn't Stan's. Some things on the premises are actually mine! How is your mother? Isn't your mother well?

MITCH Why?

BLANCHE Something's the matter tonight, but never mind. I won't cross-examine the witness. I'll just—[*She touches her forehead vaguely. The polka tune starts up again.*]—pretend I don't notice anything different about you! That—music again . . .

MITCH What music?

BLANCHE The "Varsouviana"! The polka tune they were playing when Allan—Wait!

[*A distant revolver shot is heard.* BLANCHE *seems relieved.*]

There now, the shot! It always stops after that.

[*The polka music dies out again.*]

Yes, now it's stopped.

MITCH Are you boxed out of your mind?

BLANCHE I'll go and see what I can find in the way of—[*She crosses into the closet, pretending to search for the bottle.*] Oh, by the way, excuse me for not being dressed. But I'd practically given you up! Had you forgotten your invitation to supper?

MITCH I wasn't going to see you anymore.

BLANCHE Wait a minute. I can't hear what you're saying and you talk so little that when you do say something, I don't want to miss a single syllable of it. . . . What am I looking around here for? Oh, yes—liquor! We've had so much excitement around here this evening that I *am* boxed out of my mind! [*She pretends suddenly to find the bottle. He draws his foot up on the bed and stares at her contemptuously.*] Here's something, Southern Comfort![8] What is that, I wonder?

MITCH If you don't know, it must belong to Stan.

BLANCHE Take your foot off the bed. It has a light cover on it. Of course you boys don't notice things like that. I've done so much with this place since I've been here.

MITCH I bet you have.

BLANCHE You saw it before I came. Well, look at it now! This room is almost—dainty! I want to keep it that way. I wonder if this stuff ought to be mixed with something? Ummm, it's sweet, so sweet! It's terribly, terribly sweet! Why, it's a *liqueur*, I believe! Yes, that's what it *is*, a liqueur! [MITCH *grunts.*] I'm afraid you won't like it, but try it, and maybe you will.

MITCH I told you already I don't want none of his liquor and I mean it. You ought to lay off his liquor. He says you been lapping it up all summer like a wild cat!

BLANCHE What a fantastic statement! Fantastic of him to say it, fantastic of you to repeat it! I won't descend to the level of such cheap accusations to answer them, even!

8. A flavored whiskey liqueur.

MITCH Huh.

BLANCHE What's in your mind? I see something in your eyes!

MITCH [*getting up*] It's dark in here.

BLANCHE I like it dark. The dark is comforting to me.

MITCH I don't think I ever seen you in the light. [BLANCHE *laughs breathlessly.*] That's a fact!

BLANCHE Is it?

MITCH I've never seen you in the afternoon.

BLANCHE Whose fault is that?

MITCH You never want to go out in the afternoon.

BLANCHE Why, Mitch, you're at the plant in the afternoon!

MITCH Not Sunday afternoon. I've asked you to go out with me sometimes on Sundays but you always make an excuse. You never want to go out till after six and then it's always some place that's not lighted much.

BLANCHE There is some obscure meaning in this but I fail to catch it.

MITCH What it means is I've never had a real good look at you, Blanche. Let's turn the light on here.

BLANCHE [*fearfully*] Light? Which light? What for?

MITCH This one with the paper thing on it. [*He tears the paper lantern off the light bulb. She utters a frightened gasp.*]

BLANCHE What did you do that for?

MITCH So I can take a look at you good and plain!

BLANCHE Of course you don't really mean to be insulting!

MITCH No, just realistic.

BLANCHE I don't want realism. I want magic! [MITCH *laughs.*] Yes, yes, magic! I try to give that to people. I misrepresent things to them. I don't tell truth, I tell what *ought* to be truth. And if that is sinful, then let me be damned for it!—*Don't turn the light on!*

[MITCH *crosses to the switch. He turns the light on and stares at her. She cries out and covers her face. He turns the light off again.*]

MITCH [*slowly and bitterly*] I don't mind you being older than what I thought. But all the rest of it—Christ! That pitch about your ideals being so old-fashioned and all the malarkey that you've dished out all summer. Oh, I knew you weren't sixteen anymore. But I was a fool enough to believe you was straight.

BLANCHE Who told you I wasn't—"straight"? My loving brother-in-law. And you believed him.

MITCH I called him a liar at first. And then I checked on the story. First I asked our supply-man who travels through Laurel. And then I talked directly over long-distance to this merchant.

BLANCHE Who is this merchant?

MITCH Kiefaber.

BLANCHE The merchant Kiefaber of Laurel! I know the man. He whistled at me. I put him in his place. So now for revenge he makes up stories about me.

MITCH Three people, Kiefaber, Stanley, and Shaw, swore to them!

BLANCHE Rub-a-dub-dub, three men in a tub![9] And such a filthy tub!

9. A reference to the nursery rhyme.

MITCH Didn't you stay at a hotel called The Flamingo?

BLANCHE Flamingo? No! Tarantula was the name of it! I stayed at a hotel called The Tarantula Arms!

MITCH [*stupidly*] Tarantula?

BLANCHE Yes, a big spider! That's where I brought my victims. [*She pours herself another drink.*] Yes, I had many intimacies with strangers. After the death of Allan—intimacies with strangers was all I seemed able to fill my empty heart with. . . . I think it was panic, just panic, that drove me from one to another, hunting for some protection—here and there, in the most—unlikely places—even, at last, in a seventeen-year-old boy but—somebody wrote the superintendent about it—"This woman is morally unfit for her position!"

[*She throws back her head with convulsive, sobbing laughter. Then she repeats the statement, gasps, and drinks.*]

True? Yes, I suppose—unfit somehow—anyway. . . . So I came here. There was nowhere else I could go. I was played out. You know what played out is? My youth was suddenly gone up the water-spout, and—I met you. You said you needed somebody. Well, I needed somebody, too. I thanked God for you, because you seemed to be gentle—a cleft in the rock of the world that I could hide in! But I guess I was asking, hoping—too much! Kiefaber, Stanley, and Shaw have tied an old tin can to the tail of the kite.

[*There is a pause.* MITCH *stares at her dumbly.*]

MITCH You lied to me, Blanche.

BLANCHE Don't say I lied to you.

MITCH Lies, lies, inside and out, all lies.

BLANCHE Never inside, I didn't lie in my heart . . .

[*A vendor comes around the corner. She is a blind* MEXICAN WOMAN *in a dark shawl, carrying bunches of those gaudy tin flowers that lower-class Mexicans display at funerals and other festive occasions. She is calling barely audibly. Her figure is only faintly visible outside the building.*]

MEXICAN WOMAN Flores. Flores. Flores para los muertos.[1] Flores. Flores.

BLANCHE What? Oh! Somebody outside . . . [*She goes to the door, opens it and stares at the* MEXICAN WOMAN.]

MEXICAN WOMAN [*she is at the door and offers* BLANCHE *some of her flowers*] Flores? Flores para los muertos?

BLANCHE [*frightened*] No, no! Not now! Not now!

[*She darts back into the apartment, slamming the door.*]

MEXICAN WOMAN [*she turns away and starts to move down the street*] Flores para los muertos.

[*The polka tune fades in.*]

BLANCHE [*as if to herself*] Crumble and fade and—regrets—recriminations . . . "If you'd done this, it wouldn't've cost me that!"

MEXICAN WOMAN Corones[2] para los muertos. Corones . . .

BLANCHE Legacies! Huh. . . . And other things such as bloodstained pillow-slips—"Her linen needs changing"—"Yes, Mother. But couldn't we get a colored girl to do it?" No, we couldn't of course. Everything gone but the—

1. Flowers for the dead (Spanish).
2. Crowns (Spanish); wreaths of flowers.

MEXICAN WOMAN Flores.

BLANCHE Death—I used to sit here and she used to sit over there and death was as close as you are. . . . We didn't dare even admit we had ever heard of it!

MEXICAN WOMAN Flores para los muertos, flores—flores . . .

BLANCHE The opposite is desire. So do you wonder? How could you possibly wonder! Not far from Belle Reve, before we had lost Belle Reve, was a camp where they trained young soldiers. On Saturday nights they would go in town to get drunk—

MEXICAN WOMAN [*softly*] Corones . . .

BLANCHE —and on the way back they would stagger onto my lawn and call—"Blanche! Blanche!"—the deaf old lady remaining suspected nothing. But sometimes I slipped outside to answer their calls. . . . Later the paddy-wagon would gather them up like daisies . . . the long way home . . .

[*The* MEXICAN WOMAN *turns slowly and drifts back off with her soft mournful cries.* BLANCHE *goes to the dresser and leans forward on it. After a moment,* MITCH *rises and follows her purposefully. The polka music fades away. He places his hands on her waist and tries to turn her about.*]

BLANCHE What do you want?

MITCH [*fumbling to embrace her*] What I been missing all summer.

BLANCHE Then marry me, Mitch!

MITCH I don't think I want to marry you anymore.

BLANCHE No?

MITCH [*dropping his hands from her waist*] You're not clean enough to bring in the house with my mother.

BLANCHE Go away, then. [*He stares at her.*] Get out of here quick before I start screaming fire! [*Her throat is tightening with hysteria.*] Get out of here quick before I start screaming fire.

[*He still remains staring. She suddenly rushes to the big window with its pale blue square of the soft summer light and cries wildly.*]

Fire! Fire! Fire!

[*With a startled gasp,* MITCH *turns and goes out the outer door, clatters awkwardly down the steps and around the corner of the building.* BLANCHE *staggers back from the window and falls to her knees. The distant piano is slow and blue.*]

Scene 10

It is a few hours later that night.

BLANCHE *has been drinking fairly steadily since* MITCH *left. She has dragged her wardrobe trunk into the center of the bedroom. It hangs open with flowery dresses thrown across it. As the drinking and packing went on, a mood of hysterical exhilaration came into her and she has decked herself out in a somewhat soiled and crumpled white satin evening gown and a pair of scuffed silver slippers with brilliants*[3] *set in their heels.*

Now she is placing the rhinestone tiara on her head before the mirror of the dressing-table and murmuring excitedly as if to a group of spectral admirers.

BLANCHE How about taking a swim, a moonlight swim at the old rock quarry? If anyone's sober enough to drive a car! Ha-ha! Best way in the

3. Sparkling gems.

world to stop your head buzzing! Only you've got to be careful to dive where the deep pool is—if you hit a rock you don't come up till tomorrow. . . .

[*Tremblingly she lifts the hand mirror for a closer inspection. She catches her breath and slams the mirror face down with such violence that the glass cracks. She moans a little and attempts to rise.*]

[STANLEY *appears around the corner of the building. He still has on the vivid green silk bowling shirt. As he rounds the corner the honky-tonk music is heard. It continues softly throughout the scene.*]

[*He enters the kitchen, slamming the door. As he peers in at* BLANCHE, *he gives a low whistle. He has had a few drinks on the way and has brought some quart beer bottles home with him.*]

BLANCHE How is my sister?

STANLEY She is doing okay.

BLANCHE And how is the baby?

STANLEY [*grinning amiably*] The baby won't come before morning so they told me to go home and get a little shut-eye.

BLANCHE Does that mean we are to be alone in here?

STANLEY Yep. Just me and you, Blanche. Unless you got somebody hid under the bed. What've you got on those fine feathers for?

BLANCHE Oh, that's right. You left before my wire came.

STANLEY You got a wire?

BLANCHE I received a telegram from an old admirer of mine.

STANLEY Anything good?

BLANCHE I think so. An invitation.

STANLEY What to? A fireman's ball?

BLANCHE [*throwing back her head*] A cruise of the Caribbean on a yacht!

STANLEY Well, well. What do you know?

BLANCHE I have never been so surprised in my life.

STANLEY I guess not.

BLANCHE It came like a bolt from the blue!

STANLEY Who did you say it was from?

BLANCHE An old beau of mine.

STANLEY The one that give you the white fox-pieces?

BLANCHE Mr. Shep Huntleigh. I wore his ATO[4] pin my last year at college. I hadn't seen him again until last Christmas. I ran in to him on Biscayne Boulevard. Then—just now—this wire—inviting me on a cruise of the Caribbean! The problem is clothes. I tore into my trunk to see what I have that's suitable for the tropics!

STANLEY And come up with that—gorgeous—diamond—tiara?

BLANCHE This old relic? Ha-ha! It's only rhinestones.

STANLEY Gosh. I thought it was Tiffany diamonds.[5] [*He unbuttons his shirt.*]

BLANCHE Well, anyhow, I shall be entertained in style.

STANLEY Uh-huh. It goes to show, you never know what is coming.

BLANCHE Just when I thought my luck had begun to fail me—

STANLEY Into the picture pops this Miami millionaire.

BLANCHE This man is not from Miami. This man is from Dallas.

STANLEY This man is from Dallas?

4. The fraternity Alpha Tau Omega.
5. That is, diamonds from the famous jewelry store in New York.

BLANCHE Yes, this man is from Dallas where gold spouts out of the ground!

STANLEY Well, just so he's from somewhere! [*He starts removing his shirt.*]

BLANCHE Close the curtains before you undress any further.

STANLEY [*amiably*] This is all I'm going to undress right now. [*He rips the sack off a quart beer bottle.*] Seen a bottle-opener?

[*She moves slowly toward the dresser, where she stands with her hands knotted together.*]

I used to have a cousin who could open a beer bottle with his teeth. [*Pounding the bottle cap on the corner of table.*] That was his only accomplishment, all he could do—he was just a human bottle-opener. And then one time, at a wedding party, he broke his front teeth off! After that he was so ashamed of himself he used t' sneak out of the house when company came . . .

[*The bottle cap pops off and a geyser of foam shoots up.* STANLEY *laughs happily, holding up the bottle over his head.*]

Ha-ha! Rain from heaven! [*He extends the bottle toward her.*] Shall we bury the hatchet and make it a loving-cup? Huh?

BLANCHE No, thank you.

STANLEY Well, it's a red-letter night for us both. You having an oil millionaire and me having a baby.

[*He goes to the bureau in the bedroom and crouches to remove something from the bottom drawer.*]

BLANCHE [*drawing back*] What are you doing in here?

STANLEY Here's something I always break out on special occasions like this. The silk pyjamas I wore on my wedding night!

BLANCHE Oh.

STANLEY When the telephone rings and they say, "You've got a son!" I'll tear this off and wave it like a flag! [*He shakes out a brilliant pyjama coat.*] I guess we are both entitled to put on the dog.[6] [*He goes back to the kitchen with the coat over his arm.*]

BLANCHE When I think of how divine it is going to be to have such a thing as privacy once more—I could weep with joy!

STANLEY This millionaire from Dallas is not going to interfere with your privacy any?

BLANCHE It won't be the sort of thing you have in mind. This man is a gentleman and he respects me. [*Improvising feverishly.*] What he wants is my companionship. Having great wealth sometimes makes people lonely! A cultivated woman, a woman of intelligence and breeding, can enrich a man's life—immeasurably! I have those things to offer, and this doesn't take them away. Physical beauty is passing. A transitory possession. But beauty of the mind and richness of the spirit and tenderness of the heart—and I have all of those things—aren't taken away, but grow! Increase with the years! How strange that I should be called a destitute woman! When I have all of these treasures locked in my heart. [*A choked sob comes from her.*] I think of myself as a very, very rich woman! But I have been foolish—casting my pearls before swine![7]

STANLEY Swine, huh?

6. That is, put on uncharacteristic stylishness, show off.

7. An allusion to Jesus' Sermon on the Mount (Matthew 7.6).

BLANCHE Yes, swine! Swine! And I'm thinking not only of you but of your friend, Mr. Mitchell. He came to see me tonight. He dared to come here in his work clothes! And to repeat slander to me, vicious stories that he had gotten from you! I gave him his walking papers. . . .

STANLEY You did, huh?

BLANCHE But then he came back. He returned with a box of roses to beg my forgiveness! He implored my forgiveness. But some things are not forgivable. Deliberate cruelty is not forgivable. It is the one unforgivable thing in my opinion and it is the one thing of which I have never, never been guilty. And so I told him, I said to him, "Thank you," but it was foolish of me to think that we could ever adapt ourselves to each other. Our ways of life are too different. Our attitudes and our backgrounds are incompatible. We have to be realistic about such things So farewell, my friend! And let there be no hard feelings . . .

STANLEY Was this before or after the telegram came from the Texas oil millionaire?

BLANCHE What telegram? No! No, after! As a matter of fact, the wire came just as—

STANLEY As a matter of fact there wasn't no wire at all!

BLANCHE Oh, oh!

STANLEY There isn't no millionaire! And Mitch didn't come back with roses 'cause I know where he is—

BLANCHE Oh!

STANLEY There isn't a goddam thing but imagination!

BLANCHE Oh!

STANLEY And lies and conceit and tricks!

BLANCHE Oh!

STANLEY And look at yourself! Take a look at yourself in that worn out Mardi Gras[8] outfit, rented for fifty cents from some rag picker! And with the crazy crown on! What queen do you think you are?

BLANCHE Oh—God . . .

STANLEY I've been on to you from the start! Not once did you pull any wool over this boy's eyes! You come in here and sprinkle the place with powder and spray perfume and cover the lightbulb with a paper lantern, and lo and behold the place has turned into Egypt and you are the Queen of the Nile! Sitting on your throne and swilling down my liquor! I say—*Ha!—Ha!* Do you hear me? *Ha—ha—ha!* [*He walks into the bedroom.*]

BLANCHE Don't come in here!

[*Lurid reflections appear on the walls around* BLANCHE. *The shadows are of a grotesque and menacing form. She catches her breath, crosses to the phone and jiggles the hook.* STANLEY *goes into the bathroom and closes the door.*]

Operator, operator! Give me long-distance, please. . . . I want to get in touch with Mr. Shep Huntleigh of Dallas. He's so well known he doesn't require any address. Just ask anybody who—Wait!!—No, I couldn't find it

8. Fat Tuesday (French), or Shrove Tuesday, the final day before Lent, traditionally a time of penitence and prayer for Christians, begins. In many places it is celebrated with merrymaking and parades; the festivities are particularly famous and extensive in New Orleans.

right now. . . . Please understand, I—No! No, wait! . . . One moment! Someone is—Nothing! Hold on, please!

[*She sets the phone down and crosses warily into the kitchen. The night is filled with inhuman voices like cries in a jungle.*]

[*The shadows and lurid reflections move sinuously as flames along the wall spaces.*]

[*Through the back wall of the rooms, which have become transparent, can be seen the sidewalk. A prostitute has rolled*[9] *a drunkard. He pursues her along the walk, overtakes her and there is a struggle. A policeman's whistle breaks it up. The figures disappear.*]

[*Some moments later the* NEGRO WOMAN *appears around the corner with a sequined bag which the prostitute had dropped on the walk. She is rooting excitedly through it.*]

[BLANCHE *presses her knuckles to her lips and returns slowly to the phone. She speaks in a hoarse whisper.*]

BLANCHE Operator! Operator! Never mind long-distance. Get Western Union. There isn't time to be—Western—Western Union!

[*She waits anxiously.*]

Western Union? Yes! I—want to—Take down this message! "In desperate, desperate circumstances! Help me! Caught in a trap. Caught in—" *Oh!*

[*The bathroom door is thrown open and* STANLEY *comes out in the brilliant silk pyjamas. He grins at her as he knots the tasseled sash about his waist. She gasps and backs away from the phone. He stares at her for a count of ten. Then a clicking becomes audible from the telephone, steady and rasping.*]

STANLEY You left th' phone off th' hook.

[*He crosses to it deliberately and sets it back on the hook. After he has replaced it, he stares at her again, his mouth slowly curving into a grin, as he weaves between* BLANCHE *and the outer door.*]

[*The barely audible "blue piano" begins to drum up louder. The sound of it turns into the roar of an approaching locomotive.* BLANCHE *crouches, pressing her fists to her ears until it has gone by.*]

BLANCHE [*finally straightening*] Let me—let me get by you!

STANLEY Get by me? Sure. Go ahead. [*He moves back a pace in the doorway.*]

BLANCHE You—you stand over there! [*She indicates a further position.*]

STANLEY [*grinning*] You got plenty of room to walk by me now.

BLANCHE Not with you there! But I've got to get out somehow!

STANLEY You think I'll interfere with you? Ha-ha!

[*The "blue piano" goes softly. She turns confusedly and makes a faint gesture. The inhuman jungle voices rise up. He takes a step toward her, biting his tongue which protrudes between his lips.*]

STANLEY [*softly*] Come to think of it—maybe you wouldn't be bad to—interfere with . . .

[BLANCHE *moves backward through the door into the bedroom.*]

BLANCHE Stay back! Don't you come toward me another step or I'll—

STANLEY What?

9. Robbed (by going through the pockets of someone drunk, unconscious, or asleep).

BLANCHE Some awful thing will happen! It will!

STANLEY What are you putting on now?

[*They are now both inside the bedroom.*]

BLANCHE I warn you, don't, I'm in danger!

[*He takes another step. She smashes a bottle on the table and faces him, clutching the broken top.*]

STANLEY What did you do that for?

BLANCHE So I could twist the broken end in your face!

STANLEY I bet you would do that!

BLANCHE I would! I will if you—

STANLEY Oh! So you want some roughhouse! All right, let's have some roughhouse!

[*He springs toward her, overturning the table. She cries out and strikes at him with the bottle top but he catches her wrist.*]

Tiger—tiger! Drop the bottle-top! Drop it! We've had this date with each other from the beginning!

[*She moans. The bottle-top falls. She sinks to her knees. He picks up her inert figure and carries her to the bed. The hot trumpet and drums from the Four Deuces sound loudly.*]

Scene 11

It is some weeks later. STELLA *is packing* BLANCHE'S *things. Sound of water can be heard running in the bathroom.*

*The portieres are partly open on the poker players—*STANLEY, STEVE, MITCH, *and* PABLO*—who sit around the table in the kitchen. The atmosphere of the kitchen is now the same raw, lurid one of the disastrous poker night.*

The building is framed by the sky of turquoise. STELLA *has been crying as she arranges the flowery dresses in the open trunk.*

EUNICE *comes down the steps from her flat above and enters the kitchen. There is an outburst from the poker table.*

STANLEY Drew to an inside straight and made it, by God.

PABLO *Maldita sea tu suerto!*

STANLEY Put it in English, greaseball.

PABLO I am cursing your rutting luck.

STANLEY [*prodigiously elated*] You know what luck is? Luck is believing you're lucky. Take at Salerno.[1] I believed I was lucky. I figured that 4 out of 5 would not come through but I would . . . and I did. I put that down as a rule. To hold front position in this rat race you've got to believe you are lucky.

MITCH You . . . you . . . you. . . . Brag . . . brag . . . bull . . . bull.

[STELLA *goes into the bedroom and starts folding a dress.*]

STANLEY What's the matter with him?

EUNICE [*walking past the table*] I always did say that men are callous things with no feelings, but this does beat anything. Making pigs of yourselves. [*She comes through the portieres into the bedroom.*]

STANLEY What's the matter with her?

1. A city in southern Italy on the Gulf of Salerno, an important beachhead in the Allied invasion of Italy during World War II.

STELLA How is my baby?

EUNICE Sleeping like a little angel. Brought you some grapes. [*She puts them on a stool and lowers her voice.*] Blanche?

STELLA Bathing.

EUNICE How is she?

STELLA She wouldn't eat anything but asked for a drink.

EUNICE What did you tell her?

STELLA I—just told her that—we'd made arrangements for her to rest in the country. She's got it mixed in her mind with Shep Huntleigh.

[BLANCHE *opens the bathroom door slightly.*]

BLANCHE Stella.

STELLA Yes, Blanche?

BLANCHE If anyone calls while I'm bathing take the number and tell them I'll call right back.

STELLA Yes.

BLANCHE That cool yellow silk—the bouclé.[2] See if it's crushed. If it's not too crushed I'll wear it and on the lapel that silver and turquoise pin in the shape of a seahorse. You will find them in the heart-shaped box I keep my accessories in. And Stella . . . Try and locate a bunch of artificial violets in that box, too, to pin with the seahorse on the lapel of the jacket.

[*She closes the door.* STELLA *turns to* EUNICE.]

STELLA I don't know if I did the right thing.

EUNICE What else could you do?

STELLA I couldn't believe her story and go on living with Stanley.

EUNICE Don't ever believe it. Life has got to go on. No matter what happens, you've got to keep on going.

[*The bathroom door opens a little.*]

BLANCHE [*looking out*] Is the coast clear?

STELLA Yes, Blanche. [*To* EUNICE] Tell her how well she's looking.

BLANCHE Please close the curtains before I come out.

STELLA They're closed.

STANLEY —How many for you?

PABLO —Two.

STEVE —Three.

[BLANCHE *appears in the amber light of the door. She has a tragic radiance in her red satin robe following the sculptural lines of her body. The "Varsouviana" rises audibly as* BLANCHE *enters the bedroom.*]

BLANCHE [*with faintly hysterical vivacity*] I have just washed my hair.

STELLA Did you?

BLANCHE I'm not sure I got the soap out.

EUNICE Such fine hair!

BLANCHE [*accepting the compliment*] It's a problem. Didn't I get a call?

STELLA Who from, Blanche?

BLANCHE Shep Huntleigh . . .

STELLA Why, not yet, honey!

BLANCHE How strange! I—

2. A rough-textured fabric made of looped yarn.

[*At the sound of* BLANCHE'*s voice* MITCH'*s arm supporting his cards has sagged and his gaze is dissolved into space.* STANLEY *slaps him on the shoulder.*]

STANLEY Hey, Mitch, come to!

[*The sound of this new voice shocks* BLANCHE. *She makes a shocked gesture, forming his name with her lips.* STELLA *nods and looks quickly away.* BLANCHE *stands quite still for some moments—the silver-backed mirror in her hand and a look of sorrowful perplexity as though all human experience shows on her face.* BLANCHE *finally speaks but with sudden hysteria.*]

BLANCHE What's going on here?

[*She turns from* STELLA *to* EUNICE *and back to* STELLA. *Her rising voice penetrates the concentration of the game.* MITCH *ducks his head lower but* STANLEY *shoves back his chair as if about to rise.* STEVE *places a restraining hand on his arm.*]

BLANCHE [*continuing*] What's happened here? I want an explanation of what's happened here.

STELLA [*agonizingly*] Hush! Hush!

EUNICE Hush! Hush! Honey.

STELLA Please, Blanche.

BLANCHE Why are you looking at me like that? Is something wrong with me?

EUNICE You look wonderful, Blanche. Don't she look wonderful?

STELLA Yes.

EUNICE I understand you are going on a trip.

STELLA Yes, Blanche *is*. She's going on a vacation.

EUNICE I'm green with envy.

BLANCHE Help me, help me get dressed!

STELLA [*handing her dress*] Is this what you—

BLANCHE Yes, it will do! I'm anxious to get out of here—this place is a trap!

EUNICE What a pretty blue jacket.

STELLA It's lilac colored.

BLANCHE You're both mistaken. It's Della Robbia blue.[3] The blue of the robe in the old Madonna pictures. Are these grapes washed?

[*She fingers the bunch of grapes which* EUNICE *had brought in.*]

EUNICE Huh?

BLANCHE Washed, I said. Are they washed?

EUNICE They're from the French Market.[4]

BLANCHE That doesn't mean they've been washed. [*The cathedral bells chime.*] Those cathedral bells—they're the only clean thing in the Quarter. Well, I'm going now. I'm ready to go.

EUNICE [*whispering*] She's going to walk out before they get here.

STELLA Wait, Blanche.

BLANCHE I don't want to pass in front of those men.

EUNICE Then wait'll the game breaks up.

STELLA Sit down and . . .

3. The distinctive blue backgrounds of the reliefs made first by the Florentine sculptor Luca della Robbia (ca. 1400–1482), and then by his descendants. The color blue is symbolic of heaven and is associated with fidelity, chastity, and modesty.

4. A city market—partly open-air, partly enclosed—in the French Quarter, on the bank of the Mississippi, since 1791.

[BLANCHE *turns weakly, hesitantly about. She lets them push her into a chair.*]

BLANCHE I can smell the sea air. The rest of my time I'm going to spend on the sea. And when I die, I'm going to die on the sea. You know what I shall die of? [*She plucks a grape.*] I shall die of eating an unwashed grape one day out on the ocean. I will die—with my hand in the hand of some nice-looking ship's doctor, a very young one with a small blond mustache and a big silver watch. "Poor lady," they'll say, "the quinine[5] did her no good. That unwashed grape has transported her soul to heaven." [*The cathedral chimes are heard.*] And I'll be buried at sea sewn up in a clean white sack and dropped overboard—at noon—in the blaze of summer—and into an ocean as blue as [*Chimes again*] my first lover's eyes!

[*A* DOCTOR *and a* MATRON *have appeared around the corner of the building and climbed the steps to the porch. The gravity of their profession is exaggerated—the unmistakable aura of the state institution with its cynical detachment. The* DOCTOR *rings the doorbell. The murmur of the game is interrupted.*]

EUNICE [*whispering to* STELLA] That must be them.

[STELLA *presses her fists to her lips.*]

BLANCHE [*rising slowly*] What is it?

EUNICE [*affectedly casual*] Excuse me while I see who's at the door.

STELLA Yes.

[EUNICE *goes into the kitchen.*]

BLANCHE [*tensely*] I wonder if it's for me.

[*A whispered colloquy takes place at the door.*]

EUNICE [*returning, brightly*] Someone is calling for Blanche.

BLANCHE It *is* for me, then! [*She looks fearfully from one to the other and then to the portieres. The "Varsouviana" faintly plays.*] Is it the gentleman I was expecting from Dallas?

EUNICE I think it is, Blanche.

BLANCHE I'm not quite ready.

STELLA Ask him to wait outside.

BLANCHE I . . .

[EUNICE *goes back to the portieres. Drums sound very softly.*]

STELLA Everything packed?

BLANCHE My silver toilet articles are still out.

STELLA Ah!

EUNICE [*returning*] They're waiting in front of the house.

BLANCHE They! Who's "they"?

EUNICE There's a lady with him.

BLANCHE I cannot imagine who this "lady" could be! How is she dressed?

EUNICE Just—just a sort of a—plain-tailored outfit.

BLANCHE Possibly she's— [*Her voice dies out nervously.*]

STELLA Shall we go, Blanche?

BLANCHE Must we go through that room?

STELLA I will go with you.

BLANCHE How do I look?

5. A salt used to treat malaria and reduce fever.

STELLA Lovely.

EUNICE [*echoing*] Lovely.

[BLANCHE *moves fearfully to the portieres.* EUNICE *draws them open for her.* BLANCHE *goes into the kitchen.*]

BLANCHE [*to the men*] Please don't get up. I'm only passing through.

[*She crosses quickly to outside door.* STELLA *and* EUNICE *follow. The poker players stand awkwardly at the table—all except* MITCH, *who remains seated, looking down at the table.* BLANCHE *steps out on a small porch at the side of the door. She stops short and catches her breath.*]

DOCTOR How do you do?

BLANCHE You are not the gentleman I was expecting. [*She suddenly gasps and starts back up the steps. She stops by* STELLA, *who stands just outside the door, and speaks in a frightening whisper.*] That man isn't Shep Huntleigh.

[*The "Varsouviana" is playing distantly.*]

[STELLA *stares back at* BLANCHE. EUNICE *is holding* STELLA's *arm. There is a moment of silence—no sound but that of* STANLEY *steadily shuffling the cards.*]

[BLANCHE *catches her breath again and slips back into the flat. She enters the flat with a peculiar smile, her eyes wide and brilliant. As soon as her sister goes past her,* STELLA *closes her eyes and clenches her hands.* EUNICE *throws her arms comfortingly about her. Then she starts up to her flat.* BLANCHE *stops just inside the door.* MITCH *keeps staring down at his hands on the table, but the other men look at her curiously. At last she starts around the table toward the bedroom. As she does,* STANLEY *suddenly pushes back his chair and rises as if to block her way. The* MATRON *follows her into the flat.*]

STANLEY Did you forget something?

BLANCHE [*shrilly*] Yes! Yes, I forgot something!

[*She rushes past him into the bedroom. Lurid reflections appear on the walls in odd, sinuous shapes. The "Varsouviana" is filtered into a weird distortion, accompanied by the cries and noises of the jungle.* BLANCHE *seizes the back of a chair as if to defend herself.*]

STANLEY [*sotto voce*[6]] Doc, you better go in.

DOCTOR [*sotto voce, motioning to the* MATRON] Nurse, bring her out.

[*The* MATRON *advances on one side,* STANLEY *on the other. Divested of all the softer properties of womanhood, the* MATRON *is a peculiarly sinister figure in her severe dress. Her voice is bold and toneless as a fire-bell.*]

MATRON Hello, Blanche.

[*The greeting is echoed and re-echoed by other mysterious voices behind the walls, as if reverberated through a canyon of rock.*]

STANLEY She says that she forgot something.

[*The echo sounds in threatening whispers.*]

MATRON That's all right.

STANLEY What did you forget, Blanche?

BLANCHE I—I—

MATRON It don't matter. We can pick it up later.

STANLEY Sure. We can send it along with the trunk.

6. Under his breath, in an undertone (Italian).

BLANCHE [*retreating in panic*] I don't know you—I don't know you. I want to be—left alone—please!

MATRON Now, Blanche!

ECHOES [*rising and falling*] Now, Blanche—now, Blanche—now, Blanche!

STANLEY You left nothing here but spilt talcum and old empty perfume bottles—unless it's the paper lantern you want to take with you. You want the lantern?

[*He crosses to dressing table and seizes the paper lantern, tearing it off the light bulb, and extends it toward her. She cries out as if the lantern was herself. The* MATRON *steps boldly toward her. She screams and tries to break past the* MATRON. *All the men spring to their feet.* STELLA *runs out to the porch, with* EUNICE *following to comfort her, simultaneously with the confused voices of the men in the kitchen.* STELLA *rushes into* EUNICE*'s embrace on the porch.*]

STELLA Oh, my God, Eunice help me! Don't let them do that to her, don't let them hurt her! Oh, God, oh, please God, don't hurt her! What are they doing to her? What are they doing? [*She tries to break from* EUNICE*'s arms.*]

EUNICE No, honey, no, no, honey. Stay here. Don't go back in there. Stay with me and don't look.

STELLA What have I done to my sister? Oh, God, what have I done to my sister?

EUNICE You done the right thing, the only thing you could do. She couldn't stay here; there wasn't no other place for her to go.

[*While* STELLA *and* EUNICE *are speaking on the porch the voices of the men in the kitchen overlap them.* MITCH *has started toward the bedroom.* STANLEY *crosses to block him.* STANLEY *pushes him aside.* MITCH *lunges and strikes at* STANLEY. STANLEY *pushes* MITCH *back. Mitch collapses at the table, sobbing.*]

[*During the preceding scenes, the* MATRON *catches hold of* BLANCHE*'s arm and prevents her flight.* BLANCHE *turns wildly and scratches at the* MATRON. *The heavy woman pinions her arms.* BLANCHE *cries out hoarsely and slips to her knees.*]

MATRON These fingernails have to be trimmed. [*The* DOCTOR *comes into the room and she looks at him.*] Jacket,[7] Doctor?

DOCTOR Not unless necessary.

[*He takes off his hat and now he becomes personalized. The unhuman quality goes. His voice is gentle and reassuring as he crosses to* BLANCHE *and crouches in front of her. As he speaks her name, her terror subsides a little. The lurid reflections fade from the walls, the inhuman cries and noises die out and her own hoarse crying is calmed.*]

DOCTOR Miss DuBois.

[*She turns her face to him and stares at him with desperate pleading. He smiles; then he speaks to the* MATRON.]

It won't be necessary.

BLANCHE [*faintly*] Ask her to let go of me.

DOCTOR [*to the* MATRON] Let go.

[*The* MATRON *releases her.* BLANCHE *extends her hands toward the* DOCTOR. *He draws her up gently and supports her with his arm and leads her through the portieres.*]

7. Straitjacket.

BLANCHE [*holding tight to his arm*] Whoever you are—I have always depended on the kindness of strangers.

[*The poker players stand back as* BLANCHE *and the* DOCTOR *cross the kitchen to the front door. She allows him to lead her as if she were blind. As they go out on the porch,* STELLA *cries out her sister's name from where she is crouched a few steps up on the stairs.*]

STELLA Blanche! Blanche, Blanche!

[BLANCHE *walks on without turning, followed by the* DOCTOR *and the* MATRON. *They go around the corner of the building.*]

[EUNICE *descends to* STELLA *and places the child in her arms. It is wrapped in a pale blue blanket. Stella accepts the child, sobbingly.* EUNICE *continues downstairs and enters the kitchen where the men, except for* STANLEY, *are returning silently to their places about the table.* STANLEY *has gone out on the porch and stands at the foot of the steps looking at* STELLA.]

STANLEY [*a bit uncertainly*] Stella?

[*She sobs with inhuman abandon. There is something luxurious in her complete surrender to crying now that her sister is gone.*]

STANLEY [*voluptuously, soothingly*] Now, honey. Now, love. Now, now, love. [*He kneels beside her and his fingers find the opening of her blouse.*] Now, now, love. Now, love. . . .

[*The luxurious sobbing, the sensual murmur fade away under the swelling music of the "blue piano" and the muted trumpet.*]

STEVE This game is seven-card stud.

Curtain.

ARTHUR MILLER

1915–2005

In a career that lasted sixty-one years and garnered national and international acclaim, Arthur Miller established himself as one of the American theater's most visible and publicly engaged playwrights. He was born two years before the United States' entry into World War I, and his political and artistic convictions were forged in the crucible of national crisis: the Great Depression, World War II, McCarthyism. While Miller felt the impact of these turbulent years in very personal ways—like Eugene O'Neill and TENNESSEE WILLIAMS, he is a deeply autobiographical playwright—his plays situate the personal within social realms where the individual is defined as an ethical and moral agent. The son of an Eastern European Jewish immigrant, Miller grew up in a country struggling to come to terms with its national identity, with the social contracts that underlie this identity, and with the increasing tension between its various animating myths and ideologies. Following what the playwright called "the age-old tradition of theatre as a civic art," Miller's plays trace the fault lines running through social psyche of twentieth-century America.

In plays such as *DEATH OF A SALESMAN* (1949), Miller determined many of the directions that postwar American drama would follow. But the roots of his drama and the central experiences to which it gives form lie in the century's earlier decades. Miller was born in Manhattan on October 17, 1915, to Isadore Miller, a clothing manufacturer, and his wife, Augusta Barnett Miller. The family lived in an apartment on the edge of Harlem overlooking Central Park and enjoyed an affluent life during Miller's childhood. When his father's business failed in 1928, however, they were forced to move to a small house in Brooklyn. The stock market crash in 1929 and the Depression years that followed deepened the future playwright's awareness of the narrow line separating success and failure and the discrepancy between myth and reality in the American capitalist system. Attending high school in Brooklyn, Miller played on the football team but was an average student; for two years after he graduated he held a series of jobs, including deliveryman for his father and sales clerk in an auto parts warehouse in Manhattan. Having saved enough money to attend college, Miller applied and was accepted to the University of Michigan in 1934.

In Ann Arbor, Miller wrote for the school newspaper, majored in English, and began writing drama. He studied playwriting with the English professor Kenneth Rowe and became aware of Clifford Odets, the author of *Waiting for Lefty* (1935), and other dramatists who made the theater an instrument of social protest during the 1930s. His first two plays won the university's prestigious Avery Hopwood Award in drama in successive years, and he won the Theatre Guild Bureau of New Plays award in 1937. After graduating in June of that year, Miller went to New York to work with the Federal Theatre Project, which was established in 1935 to offer employment to promising young playwrights as part of the New Deal's Works Progress Administration. When the program was abolished by Congress in 1939, he worked in a series of jobs, sold a number of radio scripts, and published *Situation Normal* (1944), a work of military reportage, and *Focus* (1945), a novel dealing with anti-Semitism. At that time, he was living in Brooklyn Heights with his first wife, Mary Grace Slattery, and their two children.

Miller's emergence onto the New York theater scene came in November 1944, when his play *The Man Who Had All the Luck* was produced on Broadway. Although this production received some favorable notice, most reviews were negative and it closed after only four performances. Three more years would elapse before Miller found Broadway success with *All My Sons* (1947). This play—which is about Joe Keller, a manufacturer of airplane engines, and the disclosure that he had sold defective airplane parts that led to the death of twenty-one pilots and, indirectly, his eldest son—won the New York Drama Critics' Circle Award and was made into a movie in 1948. Its critical and financial success would pale, of course, next to the acclaim that greeted Miller's next play. After a brief preview run in Philadelphia, *Death of a Salesman* opened on February 10, 1949, at Broadway's Morosco Theater in a production directed by Elia Kazan (who had also directed *All My Sons*) and starring Lee J. Cobb as the aging salesman Willy Loman. Hailed by many reviewers as one of the finest plays to emerge in the American theater, *Salesman* won the Critics' Circle Award and the inaugural Pulitzer Prize for Drama. The play ran for 742 productions on Broadway, and by early 1950, eleven foreign productions had opened in Europe, South America, and Israel.

The success of *Salesman* catapulted Miller into the ranks of America's leading writers. But the country itself, growing increasingly obsessed with what it perceived as the Communist threat to its way of life, was undergoing a different kind of transformation. In response to the heightened paranoia of the postwar Red Scare, Miller wrote a play about the 1692 witch persecutions in Salem, Massachusetts. *The Crucible* (1953) is the story of John Proctor, a Salem individualist who struggles with questions of guilt, responsibility, and moral conduct as the witch hunt develops and he is accused. Miller himself was subpoenaed to appear before the House Un-American Activities Committee in June 1956; and while he was forthright in answering questions concerning his own brief involvement with so-called subversive organizations during the war, he, like Proctor, refused to provide the names of others who attended meetings of Communist writers. As a result, he was found guilty of contempt of Congress in May 1957, a conviction that was reversed the following year by the U.S. Court of Appeals.

In the decade after *The Crucible,* Miller wrote several important plays for the theater, including *A View from The Bridge* (1955), *After the Fall* (1964), and *Incident at Vichy* (1964). *After the Fall,* Miller's most autobiographical play, drew on the playwright's often troubled marriage (1956–61) with his second wife, the film star Marilyn Monroe. He married Inge Morath, an Austrian-born photographer, in 1962 (they had two children, and they remained together until Inge's death in 2002). After a four-year break from playwriting—during which he was appointed president of PEN, an international organization that fights censorship and other political pressures on writers—Miller returned to the theater in 1968 with *The Price,* which ran on Broadway for more than a year. But the American theater was changing, and in ways that proved less hospitable to Miller's drama of the individual, society, and the ethical life. Miller wrote a number of plays after *The Price*—including *The Creation of the World and Other Business* (1972), *The Archbishop's Ceiling* (1977), *The American Clock* (1980), *The Last Yankee* (1991; 1993), *The Ride Down Mt. Morgan* (1991), *Broken Glass* (1994),

The set, designed by Jo Mielziner, for the original 1949 Broadway production of *Death of a Salesman* at the Morosco Theater in New York.

Mr. Peters' Connections (1998), and *Resurrection Blues* (2002)—but these later works received a mixed reception from American reviewers.

Death of a Salesman is one of the most widely known and influential plays of the twentieth-century theater, and in its narrative techniques and stagecraft, it represents an important development in Miller's career. His preceding play, *All My Sons*, which hinges on the gradual revelation of past events, follows the cause-and-effect structure of discovery and consequence that he admired in the plays of HENRIK IBSEN. In *Salesman*, in contrast, the playwright sought to capture the lived experience of time, with its fluid boundaries between past and present, inner world and outer world. He wanted a play, he later wrote, that would "cut through time like a knife through a layer cake or a road through a mountain revealing its geologic layers, and instead of one incident in one time-frame succeeding another, display past and present concurrently, with neither one ever coming to a stop." Miller's initial image of the set was of a face as tall as the proscenium arch that would open up to reveal the inside of a man's head, a conception captured in his early working title: *The Inside of His Head*. But as the play developed—and as he incorporated the theatrical contributions of Kazan and the stage designer, Jo Mielziner—Miller abandoned such an expressionistic approach for the mode of subjective realism that Mielziner had pioneered in productions of Tennessee Williams's *A Glass Menagerie* (1945) and *A Streetcar Named Desire* (1947).

By drawing on realist stagecraft while simultaneously transcending it, subjective realism renders porous the boundaries between internal and external reality. *Death of a Salesman* takes place in the house and backyard of the Loman family in midcentury Brooklyn. Surrounding this area, marked by a harsh orange glow, loom the towering shapes of city buildings. The house itself, which creates an impression of fragility, is indicated only in outline, with imaginary walls, a one-dimensional roofline, and minimal furnishings. An apron that curves into the audience provides the setting for other city scenes and for Willy Loman's memories and imaginings. When the play's action takes place in the present, characters observe the conventions of realistic time and space, entering the house only through its doors. When the scene shifts to the past, however, characters walk through the imaginary walls as if they didn't exist. In keeping with Willy's memories of a more pastoral Brooklyn when the neighborhood was covered with elms, the surrounding buildings recede and the stage is lit with a pattern of leaves during those scenes when Willy relives his past.

Even before Miller wrote *Death of a Salesman* in the spring of 1948, the figure of the salesman occupied an important place in his life and imagination. His father had worked as a salesman for Miller's grandfather's company, traveling around the country selling coats, and two of his uncles—both of whom lived with their families in Brooklyn, where Miller visited them before his own family moved to the borough—were career salesmen. The traveling salesmen whom Miller knew embodied the entrepreneurial dreams and haunting failures that marked American capitalism. "[T]hese men lived like artists," Miller declared, "like actors whose product is first of all themselves, forever imagining triumphs in a world that either ignores them or denies their presence altogether." While working for his father in the early 1930s, Miller wrote a short story, "In Memoriam," that was based on a salesman in his father's business who had committed suicide by throwing himself in front of a New York elevated train.

In the twenty-four hours during which the play takes place, Willy Loman searches for some way of reconciling the aspirations that have shaped his life with what he fears is the failure of that life. More than sixty years old, he can no longer earn his keep as a traveling salesman, his sons have not fulfilled the dreams he held for them, and the contradictions that have defined his personality are becoming increasingly apparent. Faced with a desperate present, he seeks refuge in a past that is the product more of nostalgia than of accurate recall. The "remembered" scenes with his family a quarter century earlier, in which he basks in his sons' adoration, are clearly idealized, polished and buffed like his old car. The glow of this past is the glow of an America with a limitless panorama of opportunity and promise, a place where the sky's the limit and all things are possible for a man with personal magnetism. This America has roots in the nineteenth-century frontier: specifically, the American West, where Willy's father sold flutes with his family in a covered wagon, and the territories—Alaska and Africa—where his brother Ben earned a fortune. "[T]hat's the wonder, the wonder of this country," Willy rhapsodizes, "that a man can end with diamonds here on the basis of being liked!" These myths of individualism and success are epitomized in Dave Singleman, a salesman of the previous generation who, after a successful career spent crisscrossing the country, winning customers and making friends, dies "the death of a salesman"—in green velvet slippers in the smoking car of a train—and is fondly remembered by hundreds of salesmen and buyers at his funeral.

Willy holds fiercely to this entrepreneurial dream and all it entails—competition, consumerism, status, the marketing of oneself as a commodity—as if his faith in the American dream guaranteed him a place within it. His slogans about success and popularity are repeated like mantras. But the discrepancies between myth and reality, as well as the contradictions between different facets of the myth itself, create powerful ironies. Willy buys the refrigerator that has the "biggest ads" but finds it in constant need of repairs. He boasts of his popularity on the road—"I can park my car in any street in New England, and the cops protect it like their own"—but minutes later confides to his wife that prospective customers laugh at him behind his back. Willy champions his sons Biff and Happy over their neighbor Bernard, but it is the latter who achieves economic and social success. Once a promising high school football star, Biff drifts from job to job, compulsively stealing things in a self-destructive flight from himself. And the ironically named Happy, who works as an assistant manager, womanizes as a way of bolstering his self-image. Willy has tried to imbue his sons with the secrets of success, but what they inherit from him are the pathological undersides of the ethic he advocates.

To the director and drama critic Harold Clurman, *Death of a Salesman* represents a challenge to the American dream, or at least the capitalist version of it: "[S]ince the Civil War, and particularly since 1900, the American dream has become distorted by the dream of business success." From a Marxist perspective, Willy's tragedy reflects the logic of commodification, whereby the value of something is what it can sell for. Alienated from the work of his hands and the genuineness of relationships, this salesman is worth, in the end, only the dollar amount of the insurance policy on his life. Reacting to this component of Miller's critique, one right-wing publication called *Death of a Salesman* "a time bomb expertly placed under the edifice of Americanism." But Miller's attitude toward the capitalist culture that produced Willy Loman was ambivalent. As he himself pointed out, the most decent person in the play is Charley, a successful businessman, and the dreams that he and his son hold come to pass, as far as we can see. And while Biff Loman finds himself by rejecting his father's aspirations—"He had the wrong dreams"—Charley offers an alternative perspective: "A salesman is got to dream, boy. It comes with the territory."

The last words in *Salesman* belong to Linda Loman, and her presence underscores the centrality of family to Miller's tragedy. *Death of a Salesman* was written and produced in the years immediately after World War II, and its dramatic concerns reflect pressures on the institution of the family that mounted in the postwar United States: urbanization, the emergence (and increasing isolation) of the nuclear family, and a hardening of gender roles that would continue into the 1950s. Miller registers the impact of these forces on the relation-

Willy Loman (played by Lee Cobb, center) in a "memory" scene with his boys Happy (left; played by Cameron Mitchell) and Biff (right; played by Arthur Kennedy), from the 1949 Broadway production of *Death of a Salesman*.

ships within the Loman family, particularly those between fathers and sons. The sense of need that drives Willy—he confesses to feeling "kind of temporary about [him]self"—is linked to his having been abandoned by his father at an early age, and he turns to his brother Ben as a surrogate for that missing paternal presence. Looking to the generation ahead, he seeks to consolidate through his two sons what identity he does possess. Despite the heightened images of male accomplishment throughout the play—high school football hero, wilderness explorer, business tycoon, ladies' man—masculinity, for Miller, is a source of anxiety, and the struggles, exaggerations, and rule breaking in which Willy engages are compensations for his failure to live up to these images. Emphasizing this dynamic, feminist and other analysts have drawn attention to Linda's role within the play. Some critics view her as a source of Willy's problems, arguing that she fails to understand him, encourages him in self-deception or illusion, or interjects materialistic values of her own. Others see her as a source of strength, acting forcefully at a number of moments while trying to balance the claims of reality with her husband's need for self-esteem. In the eyes of one of the play's early reviewers, the single-mindedness of Linda's love holds the play together; more recently, a number of feminist critics have contended that her characterization is circumscribed by the roles available to her in the masculine value system that dominates Miller's play.

In a 1999 essay commemorating the play's fiftieth anniversary, Miller described what he considered to be the power of *Death of a Salesman:* "Being human—a father, mother, son—is something most of us fail at most of the time, and a little mercy is eminently in order given the societies we live in, which purport to be stable and sound as mountains when in fact they are all trembling in a fast wind blowing mindlessly around the earth." In countries as remote from postwar America as Communist China (where *Salesman* was produced to great acclaim in 1983), the play has spoken to the dreams and anxieties of the late twentieth- and early twenty-first-century world. Indeed, as national economies become part of an ever-expanding global capitalism—and developed nations deal with outsourced labor, international finance markets, and the loss of blue-collar jobs—its insistence on the dignity of the individual is as urgent as ever. S.G.

Death of a Salesman

CHARACTERS

WILLY LOMAN	UNCLE BEN
LINDA	HOWARD WAGNER
BIFF	JENNY
HAPPY	STANLEY
BERNARD	MISS FORSYTHE
THE WOMAN	LETTA
CHARLEY	

The action takes place in Willy Loman's house and yard and in various places he visits in the New York and Boston of today.

Act 1

A melody is heard, played upon a flute. It is small and fine, telling of grass and trees and the horizon. The curtain rises.

Before us is the Salesman's house. We are aware of towering, angular shapes behind it, surrounding it on all sides. Only the blue light of the sky falls upon the house and forestage; the surrounding area shows an angry glow of orange. As more light appears, we see a solid vault of apartment houses around the small, fragile-seeming home. An air of the dream clings to the place, a dream rising out of reality. The kitchen at center seems actual enough, for there is a kitchen table with three chairs, and a refrigerator. But no other fixtures are seen. At the back of the kitchen there is a draped entrance, which leads to the living room. To the right of the kitchen, on a level raised two feet, is a bedroom furnished only with a brass bedstead and a straight chair. On a shelf over the bed a silver athletic trophy stands. A window opens onto the apartment house at the side.

Behind the kitchen, on a level raised six and a half feet, is the boys' bedroom, at present barely visible. Two beds are dimly seen, and at the back of the room a dormer window. (This bedroom is above the unseen living room.) At the left a stairway curves up to it from the kitchen.

The entire setting is wholly, or, in some places, partially transparent. The roofline of the house is one-dimensional; under and over it we see the apartment buildings. Before the house lies an apron,[1] curving beyond the forestage into the orchestra. This forward area serves as the backyard as well as the locale of all WILLY's *imaginings and of his city scenes. Whenever the action is in the present the actors observe the imaginary wall-lines, entering the house only through its door at the left. But in the scenes of the past these boundaries are broken, and characters enter or leave a room by stepping "through" a wall onto the forestage.*

From the right, WILLY LOMAN, *the Salesman, enters, carrying two large sample cases. The flute plays on. He hears but is not aware of it. He is past sixty years of age, dressed quietly. Even as he crosses the stage to the doorway of the house, his exhaustion is apparent.*

1. The foremost part of the stage, in front of the proscenium arch.

He unlocks the door, comes into the kitchen, and thankfully lets his burden down, feeling the soreness of his palms. A word-sigh escapes his lips—it might be "Oh, boy, oh, boy." He closes the door, then carries his cases out into the living room, through the draped kitchen doorway.

LINDA, *his wife, has stirred in her bed at the right. She gets out and puts on a robe, listening. Most often jovial, she has developed an iron repression of her exceptions to Willy's behavior—she more than loves him, she admires him, as though his mercurial nature, his temper, his massive dreams and little cruelties, served her only as sharp reminders of the turbulent longings within him, longings which she shares but lacks the temperament to utter and follow to their end.*

LINDA [*hearing* WILLY *outside the bedroom, calls with some trepidation*] Willy!

WILLY It's all right. I came back.

LINDA Why? What happened? [*Slight pause*] Did something happen, Willy?

WILLY No, nothing happened.

LINDA You didn't smash the car, did you?

WILLY [*with casual irritation*] I said nothing happened. Didn't you hear me?

LINDA Don't you feel well?

WILLY I'm tired to the death. [*The flute has faded away. He sits on the bed beside her, a little numb.*] I couldn't make it. I just couldn't make it, Linda.

LINDA [*very carefully, delicately*] Where were you all day? You look terrible.

WILLY I got as far as a little above Yonkers. I stopped for a cup of coffee. Maybe it was the coffee.

LINDA What?

WILLY [*after a pause*] I suddenly couldn't drive anymore. The car kept going off onto the shoulder, y'know?

LINDA [*helpfully*] Oh. Maybe it was the steering again. I don't think Angelo knows the Studebaker.

WILLY No, it's me, it's me. Suddenly I realize I'm goin' sixty miles an hour and I don't remember the last five minutes. I'm—I can't seem to—keep my mind to it.

LINDA Maybe it's your glasses. You never went for your new glasses.

WILLY No, I see everything. I came back ten miles an hour. It took me nearly four hours from Yonkers.

LINDA [*resigned*] Well, you'll just have to take a rest, Willy, you can't continue this way.

WILLY I just got back from Florida.

LINDA But you didn't rest your mind. Your mind is overactive, and the mind is what counts, dear.

WILLY I'll start out in the morning. Maybe I'll feel better in the morning. [*She is taking off his shoes.*] These goddam arch supports are killing me.

LINDA Take an aspirin. Should I get you an aspirin? It'll soothe you.

WILLY [*with wonder*] I was driving along, you understand? And I was fine. I was even observing the scenery. You can imagine, me looking at scenery, on the road every week of my life. But it's so beautiful up there, Linda, the trees are so thick, and the sun is warm. I opened the windshield and just let the warm air bathe over me. And then all of a sudden I'm goin' off the road! I'm tellin' ya, I absolutely forgot I was driving. If I'd've gone the other way over the white line I might've killed somebody. So I went on again—and five minutes later I'm dreamin' again, and I nearly—[*He presses two fingers against his eyes.*] I have such thoughts, I have such strange thoughts.

LINDA Willy, dear. Talk to them again. There's no reason why you can't work in New York.

WILLY They don't need me in New York. I'm the New England man. I'm vital in New England.

LINDA But you're sixty years old. They can't expect you to keep traveling every week.

WILLY I'll have to send a wire to Portland. I'm supposed to see Brown and Morrison tomorrow morning at ten o'clock to show the line. Goddammit, I could sell them! [*He starts putting on his jacket.*]

LINDA [*taking the jacket from him*] Why don't you go down to the place tomorrow and tell Howard you've simply got to work in New York? You're too accommodating, dear.

WILLY If old man Wagner was alive I'd a been in charge of New York now! That man was a prince, he was a masterful man. But that boy of his, that Howard, he don't appreciate. When I went north the first time, the Wagner Company didn't know where New England was!

LINDA Why don't you tell those things to Howard, dear?

WILLY [*encouraged*] I will, I definitely will. Is there any cheese?

LINDA I'll make you a sandwich.

WILLY No, go to sleep. I'll take some milk. I'll be up right away. The boys in?

LINDA They're sleeping. Happy took Biff on a date tonight.

WILLY [*interested*] That so?

LINDA It was so nice to see them shaving together, one behind the other, in the bathroom. And going out together. You notice? The whole house smells of shaving lotion.

WILLY Figure it out. Work a lifetime to pay off a house. You finally own it, and there's nobody to live in it.

LINDA Well, dear, life is a casting off. It's always that way.

WILLY No, no, some people—some people accomplish something. Did Biff say anything after I went this morning?

LINDA You shouldn't have criticized him, Willy, especially after he just got off the train. You mustn't lose your temper with him.

WILLY When the hell did I lose my temper? I simply asked him if he was making any money. Is that a criticism?

LINDA But, dear, how could he make any money?

WILLY [*worried and angered*] There's such an undercurrent in him. He became a moody man. Did he apologize when I left this morning?

LINDA He was crestfallen, Willy. You know how he admires you. I think if he finds himself, then you'll both be happier and not fight any more.

WILLY How can he find himself on a farm? Is that a life? A farmhand? In the beginning, when he was young, I thought, well, a young man, it's good for him to tramp around, take a lot of different jobs. But it's more than ten years now and he has yet to make thirty-five dollars[2] a week!

LINDA He's finding himself, Willy.

WILLY Not finding yourself at the age of thirty-four is a disgrace!

LINDA Shh!

WILLY The trouble is he's lazy, goddammit!

2. The equivalent of about $325 in 2008.

LINDA Willy, please!

WILLY Biff is a lazy bum!

LINDA They're sleeping. Get something to eat. Go on down.

WILLY Why did he come home? I would like to know what brought him home.

LINDA I don't know. I think he's still lost, Willy. I think he's very lost.

WILLY Biff Loman is lost. In the greatest country in the world a young man with such—personal attractiveness, gets lost. And such a hard worker. There's one thing about Biff—he's not lazy.

LINDA Never.

WILLY [*with pity and resolve*] I'll see him in the morning; I'll have a nice talk with him. I'll get him a job selling. He could be big in no time. My God! Remember how they used to follow him around in high school? When he smiled at one of them their faces lit up. When he walked down the street . . . [*He loses himself in reminiscences.*]

LINDA [*trying to bring him out of it*] Willy, dear, I got a new kind of American-type cheese today. It's whipped.

WILLY Why do you get American when I like Swiss?

LINDA I just thought you'd like a change—

WILLY I don't want a change! I want Swiss cheese. Why am I always being contradicted?

LINDA [*with a covering laugh*] I thought it would be a surprise.

WILLY Why don't you open a window in here, for God's sake?

LINDA [*with infinite patience*] They're all open, dear.

WILLY The way they boxed us in here. Bricks and windows, windows and bricks.

LINDA We should've bought the land next door.

WILLY The street is lined with cars. There's not a breath of fresh air in the neighborhood. The grass don't grow anymore, you can't raise a carrot in the backyard. They should've had a law against apartment houses. Remember those two beautiful elm trees out there? When I and Biff hung the swing between them?

LINDA Yeah, like being a million miles from the city.

WILLY They should've arrested the builder for cutting those down. They massacred the neighborhood. [*Lost*] More and more I think of those days, Linda. This time of year it was lilac and wisteria. And then the peonies would come out, and the daffodils. What fragrance in this room!

LINDA Well, after all, people had to move somewhere.

WILLY No, there's more people now.

LINDA I don't think there's more people. I think—

WILLY There's more people! That's what's ruining this country! Population is getting out of control. The competition is maddening! Smell the stink from that apartment house! And another one on the other side . . . How can they whip cheese?

[*On* WILLY'*s last line,* BIFF *and* HAPPY *raise themselves up in their beds, listening.*]

LINDA Go down, try it. And be quiet.

WILLY [*turning to* LINDA, *guiltily*] You're not worried about me, are you, sweetheart?

BIFF What's the matter?

HAPPY Listen!

LINDA You've got too much on the ball to worry about.

WILLY You're my foundation and my support, Linda.

LINDA Just try to relax, dear. You make mountains out of molehills.

WILLY I won't fight with him anymore. If he wants to go back to Texas, let him go.

LINDA He'll find his way.

WILLY Sure. Certain men just don't get started till later in life. Like Thomas Edison, I think. Or B. F. Goodrich.[3] One of them was deaf. [*He starts for the bedroom doorway.*] I'll put my money on Biff.

LINDA And Willy—if it's warm Sunday we'll drive in the country. And we'll open the windshield, and take lunch.

WILLY No, the windshields don't open on the new cars.

LINDA But you opened it today.

WILLY Me? I didn't. [*He stops.*] Now isn't that peculiar! Isn't that a remarkable—[*He breaks off in amazement and fright as the flute is heard distantly.*]

LINDA What, darling?

WILLY That is the most remarkable thing.

LINDA What, dear?

WILLY I was thinking of the Chevvy. [*Slight pause*] Nineteen twenty-eight . . . when I had that red Chevvy—[*Breaks off.*] That funny? I coulda sworn I was driving that Chevvy today.

LINDA Well, that's nothing. Something must've reminded you.

WILLY Remarkable. Ts. Remember those days? The way Biff used to simonize[4] that car? The dealer refused to believe there was eighty thousand miles on it. [*He shakes his head.*] Heh! [*To* LINDA] Close your eyes, I'll be right up. [*He walks out of the bedroom.*]

HAPPY [*to* BIFF] Jesus, maybe he smashed up the car again!

LINDA [*calling after* WILLY] Be careful on the stairs, dear! The cheese is on the middle shelf! [*She turns, goes over to the bed, takes his jacket, and goes out of the bedroom.*]

[*Light has risen on the boys' room. Unseen,* WILLY *is heard talking to himself, "Eighty thousand miles," and a little laugh.* BIFF *gets out of bed, comes downstage a bit, and stands attentively.* BIFF *is two years older than his brother* HAPPY, *well built, but in these days bears a worn air and seems less self-assured. He has succeeded less, and his dreams are stronger and less acceptable than* HAPPY'S. HAPPY *is tall, powerfully made. Sexuality is like a visible color on him, or a scent that many women have discovered. He, like his brother, is lost, but in a different way, for he has never allowed himself to turn his face toward defeat and is thus more confused and hard-skinned, although seemingly more content.*]

HAPPY [*getting out of bed*] He's going to get his license taken away if he keeps that up. I'm getting nervous about him, y'know, Biff?

3. An American industrialist (1851–1888); his first investment venture into rubber manufacturing failed, but in 1870 he helped form the company that soon bore only his name. The legendary American inventor Edison (1847–1931) is most famous for creating the phonograph and the first commercially viable incandescent lightbulb; his rapid rise to success and early hearing loss are well-known chapters in his life story.

4. To polish (the Simoniz brand of car wax was first sold in 1935).

BIFF His eyes are going.

HAPPY No, I've driven with him. He sees all right. He just doesn't keep his mind on it. I drove into the city with him last week. He stops at a green light and then it turns red and he goes. [*He laughs.*]

BIFF Maybe he's color-blind.

HAPPY Pop? Why he's got the finest eye for color in the business. You know that.

BIFF [*sitting down on his bed*] I'm going to sleep.

HAPPY You're not still sour on Dad, are you, Biff?

BIFF He's all right, I guess.

WILLY [*underneath them, in the living room*] Yes, sir, eighty thousand miles—eighty-two thousand!

BIFF You smoking?

HAPPY [*holding out a pack of cigarettes*] Want one?

BIFF [*taking a cigarette*] I can never sleep when I smell it.

WILLY What a simonizing job, heh!

HAPPY [*with deep sentiment*] Funny, Biff, y'know? Us sleeping in here again? The old beds. [*He pats his bed affectionately.*] All the talk that went across those two beds, huh? Our whole lives.

BIFF Yeah. Lotta dreams and plans.

HAPPY [*with a deep and masculine laugh*] About five hundred women would like to know what was said in this room.

[*They share a soft laugh.*]

BIFF Remember that big Betsy something—what the hell was her name—over on Bushwick Avenue?[5]

HAPPY [*combing his hair*] With the collie dog!

BIFF That's the one. I got you in there, remember?

HAPPY Yeah, that was my first time—I think. Boy, there was a pig! [*They laugh, almost crudely.*] You taught me everything I know about women. Don't forget that.

BIFF I bet you forgot how bashful you used to be. Especially with girls.

HAPPY Oh, I still am, Biff.

BIFF Oh, go on.

HAPPY I just control it, that's all. I think I got less bashful and you got more so. What happened, Biff? Where's the old humor, the old confidence? [*He shakes* BIFF*'s knee.* BIFF *gets up and moves restlessly about the room.*] What's the matter?

BIFF Why does Dad mock me all the time?

HAPPY He's not mocking you, he—

BIFF Everything I say there's a twist of mockery on his face. I can't get near him.

HAPPY He just wants you to make good, that's all. I wanted to talk to you about Dad for a long time, Biff. Something's—happening to him. He—talks to himself.

BIFF I noticed that this morning. But he always mumbled.

HAPPY But not so noticeable. It got so embarrassing I sent him to Florida. And you know something? Most of the time he's talking to you.

BIFF What's he say about me?

5. A major thoroughfare in Brooklyn, New York.

HAPPY I can't make it out.

BIFF What's he say about me?

HAPPY I think the fact that you're not settled, that you're still kind of up in the air . . .

BIFF There's one or two other things depressing him, Happy.

HAPPY What do you mean?

BIFF Never mind. Just don't lay it all to me.

HAPPY But I think if you just got started—I mean—is there any future for you out there?

BIFF I tell ya, Hap, I don't know what the future is. I don't know—what I'm supposed to want.

HAPPY What do you mean?

BIFF Well, I spent six or seven years after high school trying to work myself up. Shipping clerk, salesman, business of one kind or another. And it's a measly manner of existence. To get on that subway on the hot mornings in summer. To devote your whole life to keeping stock, or making phone calls, or selling or buying. To suffer fifty weeks of the year for the sake of a two-week vacation, when all you really desire is to be outdoors, with your shirt off. And always to have to get ahead of the next fella. And still—that's how you build a future.

HAPPY Well, you really enjoy it on a farm? Are you content out there?

BIFF [*with rising agitation*] Hap, I've had twenty or thirty different kinds of jobs since I left home before the war, and it always turns out the same. I just realized it lately. In Nebraska when I herded cattle, and the Dakotas, and Arizona, and now in Texas. It's why I came home now, I guess, because I realized it. This farm I work on, it's spring there now, see? And they've got about fifteen new colts. There's nothing more inspiring or—beautiful than the sight of a mare and a new colt. And it's cool there now, see? Texas is cool now, and it's spring. And whenever spring comes to where I am, I suddenly get the feeling, my God, I'm not gettin' anywhere! What the hell am I doing, playing around with horses, twenty-eight dollars a week! I'm thirty-four years old, I oughta be makin' my future. That's when I come running home. And now, I get here, and I don't know what to do with myself. [*After a pause*] I've always made a point of not wasting my life, and every time I come back here I know that all I've done is to waste my life.

HAPPY You're a poet, you know that, Biff? You're a—you're an idealist!

BIFF No, I'm mixed up very bad. Maybe I oughta get married. Maybe I oughta get stuck into something. Maybe that's my trouble. I'm like a boy. I'm not married, I'm not in business, I just—I'm like a boy. Are you content, Hap? You're a success, aren't you? Are you content?

HAPPY Hell, no!

BIFF Why? You're making money, aren't you?

HAPPY [*moving about with energy, expressiveness*] All I can do now is wait for the merchandise manager to die. And suppose I get to be merchandise manager? He's a good friend of mine, and he just built a terrific estate on Long Island. And he lived there about two months and sold it, and now he's building another one. He can't enjoy it once it's finished. And I know that's just what I would do. I don't know what the hell I'm workin' for. Sometimes I sit in my apartment—all alone. And I think of the rent I'm paying. And it's crazy. But then, it's what I always wanted. My own apartment, a car, and plenty of women. And still, goddammit, I'm lonely.

BIFF [*with enthusiasm*] Listen, why don't you come out West with me?

HAPPY You and I, heh?

BIFF Sure, maybe we could buy a ranch. Raise cattle, use our muscles. Men built like we are should be working out in the open.

HAPPY [*avidly*] The Loman Brothers, heh?

BIFF [*with vast affection*] Sure, we'd be known all over the counties!

HAPPY [*enthralled*] That's what I dream about, Biff. Sometimes I want to just rip my clothes off in the middle of the store and outbox that goddam merchandise manager. I mean I can outbox, outrun, and outlift anybody in that store, and I have to take orders from those common, petty sons-of-bitches till I can't stand it anymore.

BIFF I'm tellin' you, kid, if you were with me I'd be happy out there.

HAPPY [*enthused*] See, Biff, everybody around me is so false that I'm constantly lowering my ideals . . .

BIFF Baby, together we'd stand up for one another, we'd have someone to trust.

HAPPY If I were around you—

BIFF Hap, the trouble is we weren't brought up to grub for money. I don't know how to do it.

HAPPY Neither can I!

BIFF Then let's go!

HAPPY The only thing is—what can you make out there?

BIFF But look at your friend. Builds an estate and then hasn't the peace of mind to live in it.

HAPPY Yeah, but when he walks into the store the waves part in front of him. That's fifty-two thousand dollars a year coming through the revolving door, and I got more in my pinky finger than he's got in his head.

BIFF Yeah, but you just said—

HAPPY I gotta show some of those pompous, self-important executives over there that Hap Loman can make the grade. I want to walk into the store the way he walks in. Then I'll go with you, Biff. We'll be together yet, I swear. But take those two we had tonight. Now weren't they gorgeous creatures?

BIFF Yeah, yeah, most gorgeous I've had in years.

HAPPY I get that anytime I want, Biff. Whenever I feel disgusted. The only trouble is, it gets like bowling or something. I just keep knockin' them over and it doesn't mean anything. You still run around a lot?

BIFF Naa. I'd like to find a girl—steady, somebody with substance.

HAPPY That's what I long for.

BIFF Go on! You'd never come home.

HAPPY I would! Somebody with character, with resistance! Like Mom, y'know? You're gonna call me a bastard when I tell you this. That girl Charlotte I was with tonight is engaged to be married in five weeks. [*He tries on his new hat*.]

BIFF No kiddin'!

HAPPY Sure, the guy's in line for the vice-presidency of the store. I don't know what gets into me, maybe I just have an overdeveloped sense of competition or something, but I went and ruined her, and furthermore I can't get rid of her. And he's the third executive I've done that to. Isn't that a crummy characteristic? And to top it all, I go to their weddings! [*Indignantly, but laughing*] Like I'm not supposed to take bribes. Manufacturers offer me a hundred-dollar bill now and then to throw an order their way. You know how honest I am, but it's like this girl, see. I hate myself for it. Because I don't want the girl, and, still, I take it and—I love it!

BIFF Let's go to sleep.

HAPPY I guess we didn't settle anything, heh?

BIFF I just got one idea that I think I'm going to try.

HAPPY What's that?

BIFF Remember Bill Oliver?

HAPPY Sure, Oliver is very big now. You want to work for him again?

BIFF No, but when I quit he said something to me. He put his arm on my shoulder, and he said, "Biff, if you ever need anything, come to me."

HAPPY I remember that. That sounds good.

BIFF I think I'll go to see him. If I could get ten thousand or even seven or eight thousand dollars I could buy a beautiful ranch.

HAPPY I bet he'd back you. 'Cause he thought highly of you, Biff. I mean, they all do. You're well liked, Biff. That's why I say to come back here, and we both have the apartment. And I'm tellin' you, Biff, any babe you want . . .

BIFF No, with a ranch I could do the work I like and still be something. I just wonder though. I wonder if Oliver still thinks I stole that carton of basketballs.

HAPPY Oh, he probably forgot that long ago. It's almost ten years. You're too sensitive. Anyway, he didn't really fire you.

BIFF Well, I think he was going to. I think that's why I quit. I was never sure whether he knew or not. I know he thought the world of me, though. I was the only one he'd let lock up the place.

WILLY [*below*] You gonna wash the engine, Biff?

HAPPY Shh!

[BIFF *looks at* HAPPY, *who is gazing down, listening.* WILLY *is mumbling in the parlor.*]

HAPPY You hear that?

[*They listen.* WILLY *laughs warmly.*]

BIFF [*growing angry*] Doesn't he know Mom can hear that?

WILLY Don't get your sweater dirty, Biff!

[*A look of pain crosses* BIFF*'s face.*]

HAPPY Isn't that terrible? Don't leave again, will you? You'll find a job here. You gotta stick around. I don't know what to do about him, it's getting embarrassing.

WILLY What a simonizing job!

BIFF Mom's hearing that!

WILLY No kiddin', Biff, you got a date? Wonderful!

HAPPY Go on to sleep. But talk to him in the morning, will you?

BIFF [*reluctantly getting into bed*] With her in the house. Brother!

HAPPY [*getting into bed*] I wish you'd have a good talk with him.

[*The light on their room begins to fade.*]

BIFF [*to himself in bed*] That selfish, stupid . . .

HAPPY Sh . . . Sleep, Biff.

[*Their light is out. Well before they have finished speaking,* WILLY*'s form is dimly seen below in the darkened kitchen. He opens the refrigerator, searches in there, and takes out a bottle of milk. The apartment houses are fading out, and the entire house and surroundings become covered with leaves. Music insinuates itself as the leaves appear.*]

WILLY Just wanna be careful with those girls, Biff, that's all. Don't make any promises. No promises of any kind. Because a girl, y'know, they always believe what you tell 'em, and you're very young, Biff, you're too young to be talking seriously to girls.

[*Light rises on the kitchen.* WILLY, *talking, shuts the refrigerator door and comes downstage to the kitchen table. He pours milk into a glass. He is totally immersed in himself, smiling faintly.*]

WILLY Too young entirely, Biff. You want to watch your schooling first. Then when you're all set, there'll be plenty of girls for a boy like you. [*He smiles broadly at a kitchen chair.*] That so? The girls pay for you? [*He laughs.*] Boy, you must really be makin' a hit.

[WILLY *is gradually addressing—physically—a point offstage, speaking through the wall of the kitchen, and his voice has been rising in volume to that of a normal conversation.*]

WILLY I been wondering why you polish the car so careful. Ha! Don't leave the hubcaps, boys. Get the chamois to the hubcaps. Happy, use newspaper on the windows, it's the easiest thing. Show him how to do it, Biff! You see, Happy? Pad it up, use it like a pad. That's it, that's it, good work. You're doin' all right, Hap. [*He pauses, then nods in approbation for a few seconds, then looks upward.*] Biff, first thing we gotta do when we get time is clip that big branch over the house. Afraid it's gonna fall in a storm and hit the roof. Tell you what. We get a rope and sling her around, and then we climb up there with a couple of saws and take her down. Soon as you finish the car, boys, I wanna see ya. I got a surprise for you, boys.

BIFF [*offstage*] Whatta ya got, Dad?

WILLY No, you finish first. Never leave a job till you're finished—remember that. [*Looking toward the "big trees"*] Biff, up in Albany I saw a beautiful hammock. I think I'll buy it next trip, and we'll hang it right between those two elms. Wouldn't that be something? Just swingin' there under those branches. Boy, that would be . . .

[YOUNG BIFF *and* YOUNG HAPPY *appear from the direction* WILLY *was addressing.* HAPPY *carries rags and a pail of water.* BIFF, *wearing a sweater with a block "S," carries a football.*]

BIFF [*pointing in the direction of the car offstage*] How's that, Pop, professional?

WILLY Terrific. Terrific job, boys. Good work, Biff.

HAPPY Where's the surprise, Pop?

WILLY In the back seat of the car.

HAPPY Boy! [*He runs off.*]

BIFF What is it, Dad? Tell me, what'd you buy?

WILLY [*laughing, cuffs him*] Never mind, something I want you to have.

BIFF [*turns and starts off*] What is it, Hap?

HAPPY [*offstage*] It's a punching bag!

BIFF Oh, Pop!

WILLY It's got Gene Tunney's[6] signature on it!

[HAPPY *runs onstage with a punching bag.*]

BIFF Gee, how'd you know we wanted a punching bag?

WILLY Well, it's the finest thing for the timing.

HAPPY [*lies down on his back and pedals with his feet*] I'm losing weight, you notice, Pop?

WILLY [*to* HAPPY] Jumping rope is good too.

BIFF Did you see the new football I got?

WILLY [*examining the ball*] Where'd you get a new ball?

BIFF The coach told me to practice my passing.

WILLY That so? And he gave you the ball, heh?

BIFF Well, I borrowed it from the locker room. [*He laughs confidentially.*]

WILLY [*laughing with him at the theft*] I want you to return that.

HAPPY I told you he wouldn't like it!

BIFF [*angrily*] Well, I'm bringing it back!

WILLY [*stopping the incipient argument, to* HAPPY] Sure, he's gotta practice with a regulation ball, doesn't he? [*To* BIFF] Coach'll probably congratulate you on your initiative!

BIFF Oh, he keeps congratulating my initiative all the time, Pop.

WILLY That's because he likes you. If somebody else took that ball there'd be an uproar. So what's the report, boys, what's the report?

BIFF Where'd you go this time, Dad? Gee, we were lonesome for you.

WILLY [*pleased, puts an arm around each boy and they come down to the apron*] Lonesome, heh?

BIFF Missed you every minute.

WILLY Don't say? Tell you a secret, boys. Don't breathe it to a soul. Someday I'll have my own business, and I'll never have to leave home anymore.

HAPPY Like Uncle Charley, heh?

WILLY Bigger than Uncle Charley! Because Charley is not—liked. He's liked, but he's not—well liked.

BIFF Where'd you go this time, Dad?

WILLY Well, I got on the road, and I went north to Providence. Met the Mayor.

BIFF The Mayor of Providence!

WILLY He was sitting in the hotel lobby.

BIFF What'd he say?

WILLY He said, "Morning!" And I said, "You got a fine city here, Mayor." And then he had coffee with me. And then I went to Waterbury. Waterbury is a fine city. Big clock city, the famous Waterbury clock. Sold a nice bill[7] there. And then Boston—Boston is the cradle of the Revolution. A fine city. And a couple of other towns in Mass., and on to Portland and Bangor and straight home!

BIFF Gee, I'd love to go with you sometime, Dad.

WILLY Soon as summer comes.

HAPPY Promise?

6. James Joseph Tunney (1897–1978), an American boxer who was undefeated world heavyweight champion, 1926–28.

7. That is, a bill of goods; a consignment of merchandise.

WILLY You and Hap and I, and I'll show you all the towns. America is full of beautiful towns and fine, upstanding people. And they know me, boys, they know me up and down New England. The finest people. And when I bring you fellas up, there'll be open sesame for all of us, 'cause one thing, boys: I have friends. I can park my car in any street in New England, and the cops protect it like their own. This summer, heh?

BIFF and HAPPY [*together*] Yeah! You bet!

WILLY We'll take our bathing suits.

HAPPY We'll carry your bags, Pop!

WILLY Oh, won't that be something! Me comin' into the Boston stores with you boys carryin' my bags. What a sensation!

[BIFF *is prancing around, practicing passing the ball.*]

WILLY You nervous, Biff, about the game?

BIFF Not if you're gonna be there.

WILLY What do they say about you in school, now that they made you captain?

HAPPY There's a crowd of girls behind him every time the classes change.

BIFF [*taking* WILLY*'s hand*] This Saturday, Pop, this Saturday—just for you, I'm going to break through for a touchdown.

HAPPY You're supposed to pass.

BIFF I'm takin' one play for Pop. You watch me, Pop, and when I take off my helmet, that means I'm breakin' out. Then you watch me crash through that line!

WILLY [*kisses* BIFF] Oh, wait'll I tell this in Boston!

[BERNARD *enters in knickers. He is younger than* BIFF, *earnest and loyal, a worried boy.*]

BERNARD Biff, where are you? You're supposed to study with me today.

WILLY Hey, looka Bernard. What're you lookin' so anemic about, Bernard?

BERNARD He's gotta study, Uncle Willy. He's got Regents[8] next week.

HAPPY [*tauntingly, spinning* BERNARD *around*] Let's box, Bernard!

BERNARD Biff! [*He gets away from* HAPPY.] Listen, Biff, I heard Mr. Birnbaum say that if you don't start studyin' math he's gonna flunk you, and you won't graduate. I heard him!

WILLY You better study with him, Biff. Go ahead now.

BERNARD I heard him!

BIFF Oh, Pop, you didn't see my sneakers! [*He holds up a foot for* WILLY *to look at.*]

WILLY Hey, that's a beautiful job of printing!

BERNARD [*wiping his glasses*] Just because he printed University of Virginia on his sneakers doesn't mean they've got to graduate him, Uncle Willy!

WILLY [*angrily*] What're you talking about? With scholarships to three universities they're gonna flunk him?

BERNARD But I heard Mr. Birnbaum say—

WILLY Don't be a pest, Bernard! [*To his boys*] What an anemic!

BERNARD Okay, I'm waiting for you in my house, Biff.

[BERNARD *goes off. The Lomans laugh.*]

8. That is, Regents examinations: tests in specific subject areas administered by the state of New York to all students in public high schools.

WILLY Bernard is not well liked, is he?

BIFF He's liked, but he's not well liked.

HAPPY That's right, Pop.

WILLY That's just what I mean. Bernard can get the best marks in school, y'understand, but when he gets out in the business world, y'understand, you are going to be five times ahead of him. That's why I thank Almighty God you're both built like Adonises.[9] Because the man who makes an appearance in the business world, the man who creates personal interest, is the man who gets ahead. Be liked and you will never want. You take me, for instance. I never have to wait in line to see a buyer. "Willy Loman is here!" That's all they have to know, and I go right through.

BIFF Did you knock them dead, Pop?

WILLY Knocked 'em cold in Providence, slaughtered 'em in Boston.

HAPPY [*on his back, pedaling again*] I'm losing weight, you notice, Pop?

[LINDA *enters, as of old, a ribbon in her hair, carrying a basket of washing.*]

LINDA [*with youthful energy*] Hello, dear!

WILLY Sweetheart!

LINDA How'd the Chevvy run?

WILLY Chevrolet, Linda, is the greatest car ever built. [*To the boys*] Since when do you let your mother carry wash up the stairs?

BIFF Grab hold there, boy!

HAPPY Where to, Mom?

LINDA Hang them up on the line. And you better go down to your friends, Biff. The cellar is full of boys. They don't know what to do with themselves.

BIFF Ah, when Pop comes home they can wait!

WILLY [*laughs appreciatively*] You better go down and tell them what to do, Biff.

BIFF I think I'll have them sweep out the furnace room.

WILLY Good work, Biff.

BIFF [*goes through wall-line of kitchen to doorway at back and calls down*] Fellas! Everybody sweep out the furnace room! I'll be right down!

VOICES All right! Okay, Biff.

BIFF George and Sam and Frank, come out back! We're hangin' up the wash! Come on, Hap, on the double! [*He and* HAPPY *carry out the basket.*]

LINDA The way they obey him!

WILLY Well, that's training, the training. I'm tellin' you, I was sellin' thousands and thousands, but I had to come home.

LINDA Oh, the whole block'll be at that game. Did you sell anything?

WILLY I did five hundred gross in Providence and seven hundred gross in Boston.

LINDA No! Wait a minute, I've got a pencil. [*She pulls pencil and paper out of her apron pocket.*] That makes your commission . . . Two hundred—my God! Two hundred and twelve dollars!

WILLY Well, I didn't figure it yet, but . . .

LINDA How much did you do?

WILLY Well, I—I did—about a hundred and eighty gross in Providence. Well, no—it came to—roughly two hundred gross on the whole trip.

9. In Greek mythology, Adonis was a beautiful youth.

LINDA [*without hesitation*] Two hundred gross. That's . . . [*She figures.*]

WILLY The trouble was that three of the stores were half closed for inventory in Boston. Otherwise I woulda broke records.

LINDA Well, it makes seventy dollars and some pennies. That's very good.

WILLY What do we owe?

LINDA Well, on the first there's sixteen dollars on the refrigerator—

WILLY Why sixteen?

LINDA Well, the fan belt broke, so it was a dollar eighty.

WILLY But it's brand new.

LINDA Well, the man said that's the way it is. Till they work themselves in, y'know.

[*They move through the wall-line into the kitchen.*]

WILLY I hope we didn't get stuck on that machine.

LINDA They got the biggest ads of any of them!

WILLY I know, it's a fine machine. What else?

LINDA Well, there's nine-sixty for the washing machine. And for the vacuum cleaner there's three and a half due on the fifteenth. Then the roof, you got twenty-one dollars remaining.

WILLY It don't leak, does it?

LINDA No, they did a wonderful job. Then you owe Frank for the carburetor.

WILLY I'm not going to pay that man! That goddam Chevrolet, they ought to prohibit the manufacture of that car!

LINDA Well, you owe him three and a half. And odds and ends, comes to around a hundred and twenty dollars by the fifteenth.

WILLY A hundred and twenty dollars! My God, if business don't pick up I don't know what I'm gonna do!

LINDA Well, next week you'll do better.

WILLY Oh, I'll knock 'em dead next week. I'll go to Hartford. I'm very well liked in Hartford. You know, the trouble is, Linda, people don't seem to take to me.

[*They move onto the forestage.*]

LINDA Oh, don't be foolish.

WILLY I know it when I walk in. They seem to laugh at me.

LINDA Why? Why would they laugh at you? Don't talk that way, Willy.

[WILLY *moves to the edge of the stage.* LINDA *goes into the kitchen and starts to darn stockings.*]

WILLY I don't know the reason for it, but they just pass me by. I'm not noticed.

LINDA But you're doing wonderful, dear. You're making seventy to a hundred dollars a week.

WILLY But I gotta be at it ten, twelve hours a day. Other men—I don't know—they do it easier. I don't know why—I can't stop myself—I talk too much. A man oughta come in with a few words. One thing about Charley. He's a man of few words, and they respect him.

LINDA You don't talk too much, you're just lively.

WILLY [*smiling*] Well, I figure, what the hell, life is short, a couple of jokes. [*To himself*] I joke too much! [*The smile goes.*]

LINDA Why? You're—

WILLY I'm fat. I'm very—foolish to look at, Linda. I didn't tell you, but Christmastime I happened to be calling on F. H. Stewart's, and a salesman

I know, as I was going in to see the buyer I heard him say something about—walrus. And I—I cracked him right across the face. I won't take that. I simply will not take that. But they do laugh at me. I know that.

LINDA Darling . . .

WILLY I gotta overcome it. I know I gotta overcome it. I'm not dressing to advantage, maybe.

LINDA Willy, darling, you're the handsomest man in the world—

WILLY Oh, no, Linda.

LINDA To me you are. [*Slight pause*] The handsomest.

[*From the darkness is heard the laughter of a woman.* WILLY *doesn't turn to it, but it continues through* LINDA*'s lines.*]

LINDA And the boys, Willy. Few men are idolized by their children the way you are.

[*Music is heard as behind a scrim, to the left of the house,* THE WOMAN, *dimly seen, is dressing.*]

WILLY [*with great feeling*] You're the best there is, Linda, you're a pal, you know that? On the road—on the road I want to grab you sometimes and just kiss the life outa you.

[*The laughter is loud now, and he moves into a brightening area at the left, where* THE WOMAN *has come from behind the scrim and is standing, putting on her hat, looking into a "mirror" and laughing.*]

WILLY 'Cause I get so lonely—especially when business is bad and there's nobody to talk to. I get the feeling that I'll never sell anything again, that I won't make a living for you, or a business, a business for the boys. [*He talks through* THE WOMAN*'s subsiding laughter;* THE WOMAN *primps at the "mirror."*] There's so much I want to make for—

THE WOMAN Me? You didn't make me, Willy. I picked you.

WILLY [*pleased*] You picked me?

THE WOMAN [*who is quite proper-looking,* WILLY*'s age*] I did. I've been sitting at that desk watching all the salesmen go by, day in, day out. But you've got such a sense of humor, and we do have such a good time together, don't we?

WILLY Sure, sure. [*He takes her in his arms.*] Why do you have to go now?

THE WOMAN It's two o'clock . . .

WILLY No, come on in! [*He pulls her.*]

THE WOMAN . . . my sisters'll be scandalized. When'll you be back?

WILLY Oh, two weeks about. Will you come up again?

THE WOMAN Sure thing. You do make me laugh. It's good for me. [*She squeezes his arm, kisses him.*] And I think you're a wonderful man.

WILLY You picked me, heh?

THE WOMAN Sure. Because you're so sweet. And such a kidder.

WILLY Well, I'll see you next time I'm in Boston.

THE WOMAN I'll put you right through to the buyers.

WILLY [*slapping her bottom*] Right. Well, bottoms up!

THE WOMAN [*slaps him gently and laughs*] You just kill me, Willy. [*He suddenly grabs her and kisses her roughly.*] You kill me. And thanks for the stockings. I love a lot of stockings. Well, good night.

WILLY Good night. And keep your pores open!

THE WOMAN Oh, Willy!

[THE WOMAN *bursts out laughing, and* LINDA*'s laughter blends in.* THE WOMAN *disappears into the dark. Now the area at the kitchen table brightens.* LINDA *is sitting where she was at the kitchen table, but now is mending a pair of her silk stockings.*]

LINDA You are, Willy. The handsomest man. You've got no reason to feel that—

WILLY [*coming out of* THE WOMAN*'s dimming area and going over to* LINDA] I'll make it all up to you, Linda, I'll—

LINDA There's nothing to make up, dear. You're doing fine, better than—

WILLY [*noticing her mending*] What's that?

LINDA Just mending my stockings. They're so expensive—

WILLY [*angrily, taking them from her*] I won't have you mending stockings in this house! Now throw them out!

[LINDA *puts the stockings in her pocket.*]

BERNARD [*entering on the run*] Where is he? If he doesn't study!

WILLY [*moving to the forestage, with great agitation*] You'll give him the answers!

BERNARD I do, but I can't on a Regents! That's a state exam! They're liable to arrest me!

WILLY Where is he? I'll whip him, I'll whip him!

LINDA And he'd better give back that football, Willy, it's not nice.

WILLY Biff! Where is he? Why is he taking everything?

LINDA He's too rough with the girls, Willy. All the mothers are afraid of him!

WILLY I'll whip him!

BERNARD He's driving the car without a license!

[THE WOMAN*'s laugh is heard.*]

WILLY Shut up!

LINDA All the mothers—

WILLY Shut up!

BERNARD [*backing quietly away and out*] Mr. Birnbaum says he's stuck up.

WILLY Get outa here!

BERNARD If he doesn't buckle down he'll flunk math! [*He goes off.*]

LINDA He's right, Willy, you've gotta—

WILLY [*exploding at her*] There's nothing the matter with him! You want him to be a worm like Bernard? He's got spirit, personality . . .

[*As he speaks,* LINDA*, almost in tears, exits into the living room.* WILLY *is alone in the kitchen, wilting and staring. The leaves are gone. It is night again, and the apartment houses look down from behind.*]

WILLY Loaded with it. Loaded! What is he stealing? He's giving it back, isn't he? Why is he stealing? What did I tell him? I never in my life told him anything but decent things.

[HAPPY *in pajamas has come down the stairs;* WILLY *suddenly becomes aware of* HAPPY*'s presence.*]

HAPPY Let's go now, come on.

WILLY [*sitting down at the kitchen table*] Huh! Why did she have to wax the floors herself? Everytime she waxes the floors she keels over. She knows that!

HAPPY Shh! Take it easy. What brought you back tonight?

WILLY I got an awful scare. Nearly hit a kid in Yonkers. God! Why didn't I go to Alaska with my brother Ben that time! Ben! That man was a genius, that man was success incarnate! What a mistake! He begged me to go.

HAPPY Well, there's no use in—

WILLY You guys! There was a man started with the clothes on his back and ended up with diamond mines!

HAPPY Boy, someday I'd like to know how he did it.

WILLY What's the mystery? The man knew what he wanted and went out and got it! Walked into a jungle, and comes out, the age of twenty-one, and he's rich! The world is an oyster, but you don't crack it open on a mattress!

HAPPY Pop, I told you I'm gonna retire you for life.

WILLY You'll retire me for life on seventy goddam dollars a week? And your women and your car and your apartment, and you'll retire me for life! Christ's sake, I couldn't get past Yonkers today! Where are you guys, where are you? The woods are burning! I can't drive a car!

[CHARLEY *has appeared in the doorway. He is a large man, slow of speech, laconic, immovable. In all he says, despite what he says, there is pity, and, now, trepidation. He has a robe over pajamas, slippers on his feet. He enters the kitchen.*]

CHARLEY Everything all right?

HAPPY Yeah, Charley, everything's . . .

WILLY What's the matter?

CHARLEY I heard some noise. I thought something happened. Can't we do something about the walls? You sneeze in here, and in my house hats blow off.

HAPPY Let's go to bed, Dad. Come on.

[CHARLEY *signals to* HAPPY *to go.*]

WILLY You go ahead, I'm not tired at the moment.

HAPPY [*to* WILLY] Take it easy, huh? [*He exits.*]

WILLY What're you doin' up?

CHARLEY [*sitting down at the kitchen table opposite* WILLY] Couldn't sleep good. I had a heartburn.

WILLY Well, you don't know how to eat.

CHARLEY I eat with my mouth.

WILLY No, you're ignorant. You gotta know about vitamins and things like that.

CHARLEY Come on, let's shoot. Tire you out a little.

WILLY [*hesitantly*] All right. You got cards?

CHARLEY [*taking a deck from his pocket*] Yeah, I got them. Someplace. What is it with those vitamins?

WILLY [*dealing*] They build up your bones. Chemistry.

CHARLEY Yeah, but there's no bones in a heartburn.

WILLY What are you talkin' about? Do you know the first thing about it?

CHARLEY Don't get insulted.

WILLY Don't talk about something you don't know anything about.

[*They are playing. Pause.*]

CHARLEY What're you doin' home?

WILLY A little trouble with the car.

CHARLEY Oh. [*Pause*] I'd like to take a trip to California.

WILLY Don't say.

CHARLEY You want a job?

WILLY I got a job, I told you that. [*After a slight pause*] What the hell are you offering me a job for?

CHARLEY Don't get insulted.

WILLY Don't insult me.

CHARLEY I don't see no sense in it. You don't have to go on this way.

WILLY I got a good job. [*Slight pause*] What do you keep comin' in here for?

CHARLEY You want me to go?

WILLY [*after a pause, withering*] I can't understand it. He's going back to Texas again. What the hell is that?

CHARLEY Let him go.

WILLY I got nothin' to give him, Charley, I'm clean, I'm clean.

CHARLEY He won't starve. None a them starve. Forget about him.

WILLY Then what have I got to remember?

CHARLEY You take it too hard. To hell with it. When a deposit bottle is broken you don't get your nickel back.

WILLY That's easy enough for you to say.

CHARLEY That ain't easy for me to say.

WILLY Did you see the ceiling I put up in the living room?

CHARLEY Yeah, that's a piece of work. To put up a ceiling is a mystery to me. How do you do it?

WILLY What's the difference?

CHARLEY Well, talk about it.

WILLY You gonna put up a ceiling?

CHARLEY How could I put up a ceiling?

WILLY Then what the hell are you bothering me for?

CHARLEY You're insulted again.

WILLY A man who can't handle tools is not a man. You're disgusting.

CHARLEY Don't call me disgusting. Willy.

[UNCLE BEN, *carrying a valise and an umbrella, enters the forestage from around the right corner of the house. He is a stolid man, in his sixties, with a mustache and an authoritative air. He is utterly certain of his destiny, and there is an aura of far places about him. He enters exactly as* WILLY *speaks.*]

WILLY I'm getting awfully tired, Ben.

[BEN'*s music is heard.* BEN *looks around at everything.*]

CHARLEY Good, keep playing; you'll sleep better. Did you call me Ben?

[BEN *looks at his watch.*]

WILLY That's funny. For a second there you reminded me of my brother Ben.

BEN I only have a few minutes. [*He strolls, inspecting the place.* WILLY *and* CHARLEY *continue playing.*]

CHARLEY You never heard from him again, heh? Since that time?

WILLY Didn't Linda tell you? Couple of weeks ago we got a letter from his wife in Africa. He died.

CHARLEY That so.

BEN [*chuckling*] So this is Brooklyn, eh?

CHARLEY Maybe you're in for some of his money.

WILLY Naa, he had seven sons. There's just one opportunity I had with that man . . .

BEN I must make a train, William. There are several properties I'm looking at in Alaska.

WILLY Sure, sure! If I'd gone with him to Alaska that time, everything would've been totally different.

CHARLEY Go on, you'd froze to death up there.

WILLY What're you talking about?

BEN Opportunity is tremendous in Alaska, William. Surprised you're not up there.

WILLY Sure, tremendous.

CHARLEY Heh?

WILLY There was the only man I ever met who knew the answers.

CHARLEY Who?

BEN How are you all?

WILLY [*taking a pot,*[1] *smiling*] Fine, fine.

CHARLEY Pretty sharp tonight.

BEN Is Mother living with you?

WILLY No, she died a long time ago.

CHARLEY Who?

BEN That's too bad. Fine specimen of a lady, Mother.

WILLY [*to Charley*] Heh?

BEN I'd hoped to see the old girl.

CHARLEY Who died?

BEN Heard anything from Father, have you?

WILLY [*unnerved*] What do you mean, who died?

CHARLEY [*taking a pot*] What're you talkin' about?

BEN [*looking at his watch*] William, it's half-past eight!

WILLY [*as though to dispel his confusion he angrily stops* CHARLEY's *hand*] That's my build![2]

CHARLEY I put the ace—

WILLY If you don't know how to play the game I'm not gonna throw my money away on you!

CHARLEY [*rising*] It was my ace, for God's sake!

WILLY I'm through, I'm through!

BEN When did Mother die?

WILLY Long ago. Since the beginning you never knew how to play cards.

CHARLEY [*picks up the cards and goes to the door*] All right! Next time I'll bring a deck with five aces.

WILLY I don't play that kind of game!

CHARLEY [*turning to him*] You ought to be ashamed of yourself!

WILLY Yeah?

CHARLEY Yeah! [*He goes out.*]

WILLY [*slamming the door after him*] Ignoramus!

BEN [*as* WILLY *comes toward him through the wall-line of the kitchen*] So you're William.

WILLY [*shaking* BEN's *hand*] Ben! I've been waiting for you so long! What's the answer? How did you do it?

BEN Oh, there's a story in that.

[LINDA *enters the forestage, as of old, carrying the wash basket.*]

LINDA Is this Ben?

BEN [*gallantly*] How do you do, my dear.

1. The bets at stake in a hand of casino, the card game they are playing.
2. Casino players must take in builds (cards that combine to form a declared total) to win.

LINDA Where've you been all these years? Willy's always wondered why you—

WILLY [*pulling* BEN *away from her impatiently*] Where is Dad? Didn't you follow him? How did you get started?

BEN Well, I don't know how much you remember.

WILLY Well, I was just a baby, of course, only three or four years old—

BEN Three years and eleven months.

WILLY What a memory, Ben!

BEN I have many enterprises, William, and I have never kept books.

WILLY I remember I was sitting under the wagon in—was it Nebraska?

BEN It was South Dakota, and I gave you a bunch of wild flowers.

WILLY I remember you walking away down some open road.

BEN [*laughing*] I was going to find Father in Alaska.

WILLY Where is he?

BEN At that age I had a very faulty view of geography, William. I discovered after a few days that I was heading due south, so instead of Alaska, I ended up in Africa.

LINDA Africa!

WILLY The Gold Coast![3]

BEN Principally diamond mines.

LINDA Diamond mines!

BEN Yes, my dear. But I've only a few minutes—

WILLY No! Boys! Boys! [YOUNG BIFF *and* HAPPY *appear.*] Listen to this. This is your Uncle Ben, a great man! Tell my boys, Ben!

BEN Why, boys, when I was seventeen I walked into the jungle, and when I was twenty-one I walked out. [*He laughs.*] And by God I was rich.

WILLY [*to the boys*] You see what I been talking about? The greatest things can happen!

BEN [*glancing at his watch*] I have an appointment in Ketchikan Tuesday week.[4]

WILLY No, Ben! Please tell about Dad. I want my boys to hear. I want them to know the kind of stock they spring from. All I remember is a man with a big beard, and I was in Mamma's lap, sitting around a fire, and some kind of high music.

BEN His flute. He played the flute.

WILLY Sure, the flute, that's right!

[*New music is heard, a high, rollicking tune.*]

BEN Father was a very great and a very wild-hearted man. We would start in Boston, and he'd toss the whole family into the wagon, and then he'd drive the team right across the country; through Ohio, and Indiana, Michigan, Illinois, and all the Western states. And we'd stop in the towns and sell the flutes that he'd made on the way. Great inventor, Father. With one gadget he made more in a week than a man like you could make in a lifetime.

WILLY That's just the way I'm bringing them up, Ben—rugged, well liked, all-around.

3. The region of West Africa that is now Ghana (still a British colony in 1949); industrial diamonds are one of its major exports.

4. That is, in Ketchikan, Alaska, one week from Tuesday.

BEN Yeah? [*To* BIFF] Hit that, boy—hard as you can. [*He pounds his stomach.*]

BIFF Oh, no, sir!

BEN [*taking boxing stance*] Come on, get to me! [*He laughs.*]

WILLY Go to it, Biff! Go ahead, show him!

BIFF Okay! [*He cocks his fists and starts in.*]

LINDA [*to* WILLY] Why must he fight, dear?

BEN [*sparring with* BIFF] Good boy! Good boy!

WILLY How's that, Ben, heh?

HAPPY Give him the left, Biff!

LINDA Why are you fighting?

BEN Good boy! [*Suddenly comes in, trips* BIFF, *and stands over him, the point of his umbrella poised over* BIFF*'s eye.*]

LINDA Look out, Biff!

BIFF Gee!

BEN [*patting* BIFF*'s knee*] Never fight fair with a stranger, boy. You'll never get out of the jungle that way. [*Taking* LINDA*'s hand and bowing*] It was an honor and a pleasure to meet you, Linda.

LINDA [*withdrawing her hand coldly, frightened*] Have a nice—trip.

BEN [*to* WILLY] And good luck with your—what do you do?

WILLY Selling.

BEN Yes. Well . . . [*He raises his hand in farewell to all.*]

WILLY No, Ben, I don't want you to think . . . [*He takes* BEN*'s arm to show him.*] It's Brooklyn, I know, but we hunt too.

BEN Really, now.

WILLY Oh, sure, there's snakes and rabbits and—that's why I moved out here. Why, Biff can fell any one of these trees in no time! Boys! Go right over to where they're building the apartment house and get some sand. We're gonna rebuild the entire front stoop right now! Watch this, Ben!

BIFF Yes, sir! On the double, Hap!

HAPPY [*as he and* BIFF *run off*] I lost weight, Pop, you notice?

[CHARLEY *enters in knickers, even before the boys are gone.*]

CHARLEY Listen, if they steal any more from that building the watchman'll put the cops on them!

LINDA [*to Willy*] Don't let Biff . . .

[BEN *laughs lustily.*]

WILLY You shoulda seen the lumber they brought home last week. At least a dozen six-by-tens worth all kinds a money.

CHARLEY Listen, if that watchman—

WILLY I gave them hell, understand. But I got a couple of fearless characters there.

CHARLEY Willy, the jails are full of fearless characters.

BEN [*clapping* WILLY *on the back, with a laugh at* CHARLEY] And the stock exchange, friend!

WILLY [*joining in Ben's laughter*] Where are the rest of your pants?

CHARLEY My wife bought them.

WILLY Now all you need is a golf club and you can go upstairs and go to sleep. [*To* BEN] Great athlete! Between him and his son Bernard they can't hammer a nail!

BERNARD [*rushing in*] The watchman's chasing Biff!

WILLY [*angrily*] Shut up! He's not stealing anything!

LINDA [*alarmed, hurrying off left*] Where is he? Biff, dear! [*She exits.*]

WILLY [*moving toward the left, away from* BEN] There's nothing wrong. What's the matter with you?

BEN Nervy boy. Good!

WILLY [*laughing*] Oh, nerves of iron, that Biff!

CHARLEY Don't know what it is. My New England man comes back and he's bleedin', they murdered him up there.

WILLY It's contacts, Charley, I got important contacts!

CHARLEY [*sarcastically*] Glad to hear it, Willy. Come in later, we'll shoot a little casino. I'll take some of your Portland money. [*He laughs at Willy and exits.*]

WILLY [*turning to* BEN] Business is bad, it's murderous. But not for me, of course.

BEN I'll stop by on my way back to Africa.

WILLY [*longingly*] Can't you stay a few days? You're just what I need, Ben, because I—I have a fine position here, but I—well, Dad left when I was such a baby and I never had a chance to talk to him and I still feel—kind of temporary about myself.

BEN I'll be late for my train.

[*They are at opposite ends of the stage.*]

WILLY Ben, my boys—can't we talk? They'd go into the jaws of hell for me, see, but I—

BEN William, you're being first-rate with your boys. Outstanding, manly chaps!

WILLY [*hanging on to his words*] Oh, Ben, that's good to hear! Because sometimes I'm afraid that I'm not teaching them the right kind of—Ben, how should I teach them?

BEN [*giving great weight to each word, and with a certain vicious audacity*] William, when I walked into the jungle, I was seventeen. When I walked out I was twenty-one. And, by God, I was rich! [*He goes off into the darkness around the right corner of the house.*]

WILLY . . . was rich! That's just the spirit I want to imbue them with! To walk into a jungle! I was right! I was right! I was right!

[BEN *is gone, but* WILLY *is still speaking to him as* LINDA, *in nightgown and robe, enters the kitchen, glances around for* WILLY, *then goes to the door of the house, looks out and sees him. Comes down to his left. He looks at her.*]

LINDA Willy, dear? Willy?

WILLY I was right!

LINDA Did you have some cheese? [*He can't answer.*] It's very late, darling. Come to bed, heh?

WILLY [*looking straight up*] Gotta break your neck to see a star in this yard.

LINDA You coming in?

WILLY Whatever happened to that diamond watch fob? Remember? When Ben came from Africa that time? Didn't he give me a watch fob with a diamond in it?

LINDA You pawned it, dear. Twelve, thirteen years ago. For Biff's radio correspondence course.

WILLY Gee, that was a beautiful thing. I'll take a walk.

LINDA But you're in your slippers.

WILLY [*starting to go around the house at the left*] I was right! I was! [*Half to* LINDA, *as he goes, shaking his head*] What a man! There was a man worth talking to. I was right!

LINDA [*calling after* WILLY] But in your slippers, Willy!

[WILLY *is almost gone when* BIFF, *in his pajamas, comes down the stairs and enters the kitchen.*]

BIFF What is he doing out there?

LINDA Sh!

BIFF God Almighty, Mom, how long has he been doing this?

LINDA Don't, he'll hear you.

BIFF What the hell is the matter with him?

LINDA It'll pass by morning.

BIFF Shouldn't we do anything?

LINDA Oh, my dear, you should do a lot of things, but there's nothing to do, so go to sleep.

[HAPPY *comes down the stair and sits on the steps.*]

HAPPY I never heard him so loud, Mom.

LINDA Well, come around more often; you'll hear him. [*She sits down at the table and mends the lining of* WILLY*'s jacket.*]

BIFF Why didn't you ever write me about this, Mom?

LINDA How would I write to you? For over three months you had no address.

BIFF I was on the move. But you know I thought of you all the time. You know that, don't you, pal?

LINDA I know, dear, I know. But he likes to have a letter. Just to know that there's still a possibility for better things.

BIFF He's not like this all the time, is he?

LINDA It's when you come home he's always the worst.

BIFF When I come home?

LINDA When you write you're coming, he's all smiles, and talks about the future, and—he's just wonderful. And then the closer you seem to come, the more shaky he gets, and then, by the time you get here, he's arguing, and he seems angry at you. I think it's just that maybe he can't bring himself to—to open up to you. Why are you so hateful to each other? Why is that?

BIFF [*evasively*] I'm not hateful, Mom.

LINDA But you no sooner come in the door than you're fighting!

BIFF I don't know why. I mean to change. I'm tryin', Mom, you understand?

LINDA Are you home to stay now?

BIFF I don't know. I want to look around, see what's doin'.

LINDA Biff, you can't look around all your life, can you?

BIFF I just can't take hold, Mom. I can't take hold of some kind of a life.

LINDA Biff, a man is not a bird, to come and go with the springtime.

BIFF Your hair . . . [*He touches her hair.*] Your hair got so gray.

LINDA Oh, it's been gray since you were in high school. I just stopped dyeing it, that's all.

BIFF Dye it again, will ya? I don't want my pal looking old. [*He smiles.*]

LINDA You're such a boy! You think you can go away for a year and . . . You've got to get it into your head now that one day you'll knock on this door and there'll be strange people here—

BIFF What are you talking about? You're not even sixty, Mom.

LINDA But what about your father?

BIFF [*lamely*] Well, I meant him too.

HAPPY He admires Pop.

LINDA Biff, dear, if you don't have any feeling for him, then you can't have any feeling for me.

BIFF Sure I can, Mom.

LINDA No. You can't just come to see me, because I love him. [*With a threat, but only a threat, of tears*] He's the dearest man in the world to me, and I won't have anyone making him feel unwanted and low and blue. You've got to make up your mind now, darling, there's no leeway any more. Either he's your father and you pay him that respect, or else you're not to come here. I know he's not easy to get along with—nobody knows that better than me—but . . .

WILLY [*from the left, with a laugh*] Hey, hey, Biffo!

BIFF [*starting to go out after* WILLY] What the hell is the matter with him? [HAPPY *stops him.*]

LINDA Don't—don't go near him!

BIFF Stop making excuses for him! He always, always wiped the floor with you. Never had an ounce of respect for you.

HAPPY He's always had respect for—

BIFF What the hell do you know about it?

HAPPY [*surlily*] Just don't call him crazy!

BIFF He's got no character—Charley wouldn't do this. Not in his own house—spewing out that vomit from his mind.

HAPPY Charley never had to cope with what he's got to.

BIFF People are worse off than Willy Loman. Believe me, I've seen them!

LINDA Then make Charley your father, Biff. You can't do that, can you? I don't say he's a great man. Willy Loman never made a lot of money. His name was never in the paper. He's not the finest character that ever lived. But he's a human being, and a terrible thing is happening to him. So attention must be paid. He's not to be allowed to fall into his grave like an old dog. Attention, attention must be finally paid to such a person. You called him crazy—

BIFF I didn't mean—

LINDA No, a lot of people think he's lost his—balance. But you don't have to be very smart to know what his trouble is. The man is exhausted.

HAPPY Sure!

LINDA A small man can be just as exhausted as a great man. He works for a company thirty-six years this March, opens up unheard-of territories to their trademark, and now in his old age they take his salary away.

HAPPY [*indignantly*] I didn't know that, Mom.

LINDA You never asked, my dear! Now that you get your spending money someplace else you don't trouble your mind with him.

HAPPY But I gave you money last—

LINDA Christmastime, fifty dollars! To fix the hot water it cost ninety-seven fifty! For five weeks he's been on straight commission, like a beginner, an unknown!

BIFF Those ungrateful bastards!

LINDA Are they any worse than his sons? When he brought them business, when he was young, they were glad to see him. But now his old friends, the old buyers that loved him so and always found some order to hand him in a pinch—they're all dead, retired. He used to be able to make six, seven calls a day in Boston. Now he takes his valises out of the car and puts them back and takes them out again and he's exhausted. Instead of walking he talks now. He drives seven hundred miles, and when he gets there no one knows him anymore, no one welcomes him. And what goes through a man's mind, driving seven hundred miles home without having earned a cent? Why shouldn't he talk to himself? Why? When he has to go to Charley and borrow fifty dollars a week and pretend to me that it's his pay? How long can that go on? How long? You see what I'm sitting here and waiting for? And you tell me he has no character? The man who never worked a day but for your benefit? When does he get the medal for that? Is this his reward—to turn around at the age of sixty-three and find his sons, who he loved better than his life, one a philandering bum—

HAPPY Mom!

LINDA That's all you are, my baby! [*To* BIFF] And you! What happened to the love you had for him? You were such pals! How you used to talk to him on the phone every night! How lonely he was till he could come home to you!

BIFF All right, Mom. I'll live here in my room, and I'll get a job. I'll keep away from him, that's all.

LINDA No, Biff. You can't stay here and fight all the time.

BIFF He threw me out of this house, remember that.

LINDA Why did he do that? I never knew why.

BIFF Because I know he's a fake and he doesn't like anybody around who knows!

LINDA Why a fake? In what way? What do you mean?

BIFF Just don't lay it all at my feet. It's between me and him—that's all I have to say. I'll chip in from now on. He'll settle for half my paycheck. He'll be all right. I'm going to bed. [*He starts for the stairs.*]

LINDA He won't be all right.

BIFF [*turning on the stairs, furiously*] I hate this city and I'll stay here. Now what do you want?

LINDA He's dying, Biff.

[HAPPY *turns quickly to her, shocked.*]

BIFF [*after a pause*] Why is he dying?

LINDA He's been trying to kill himself.

BIFF [*with great horror*] How?

LINDA I live from day to day.

BIFF What're you talking about?

LINDA Remember I wrote you that he smashed up the car again? In February?

BIFF Well?

LINDA The insurance inspector came. He said that they have evidence. That all these accidents in the last year—weren't—weren't—accidents.

HAPPY How can they tell that? That's a lie.

LINDA It seems there's a woman . . . [*She takes a breath as*]

BIFF [*sharply but contained*] What woman? }
LINDA [*simultaneously*] . . . and this woman . . . }

LINDA What?

BIFF Nothing. Go ahead.

LINDA What did you say?

BIFF Nothing. I just said what woman?

HAPPY What about her?

LINDA Well, it seems she was walking down the road and saw his car. She says that he wasn't driving fast at all, and that he didn't skid. She says he came to that little bridge, and then deliberately smashed into the railing, and it was only the shallowness of the water that saved him.

BIFF Oh, no, he probably just fell asleep again.

LINDA I don't think he fell asleep.

BIFF Why not?

LINDA Last month . . . [*With great difficulty*] Oh, boys, it's so hard to say a thing like this! He's just a big stupid man to you, but I tell you there's more good in him than in many other people. [*She chokes, wipes her eyes.*] I was looking for a fuse. The lights blew out, and I went down the cellar. And behind the fuse box—it happened to fall out—was a length of rubber pipe—just short.

HAPPY No kidding?

LINDA There's a little attachment on the end of it. I knew right away. And sure enough, on the bottom of the water heater there's a new little nipple on the gas pipe.

HAPPY [*angrily*] That—jerk.

BIFF Did you have it taken off?

LINDA I'm—I'm ashamed to. How can I mention it to him? Every day I go down and take away that little rubber pipe. But, when he comes home, I put it back where it was. How can I insult him that way? I don't know what to do. I live from day to day, boys. I tell you, I know every thought in his mind. It sounds so old-fashioned and silly, but I tell you he put his whole life into you and you've turned your backs on him. [*She is bent over in the chair, weeping, her face in her hands.*] Biff, I swear to God! Biff, his life is in your hands!

HAPPY [*to* BIFF] How do you like that damned fool!

BIFF [*kissing her*] All right, pal, all right. It's all settled now. I've been remiss. I know that, Mom. But now I'll stay, and I swear to you, I'll apply myself. [*Kneeling in front of her, in a fever of self-reproach*] It's just—you see, Mom, I don't fit in business. Not that I won't try. I'll try, and I'll make good.

HAPPY Sure you will. The trouble with you in business was you never tried to please people.

BIFF I know, I—

HAPPY Like when you worked for Harrison's. Bob Harrison said you were tops, and then you go and do some damn fool thing like whistling whole songs in the elevator like a comedian.

BIFF [*against* HAPPY] So what? I like to whistle sometimes.

HAPPY You don't raise a guy to a responsible job who whistles in the elevator!

LINDA Well, don't argue about it now.

HAPPY Like when you'd go off and swim in the middle of the day instead of taking the line around.

BIFF [*his resentment rising*] Well, don't you run off? You take off sometimes, don't you? On a nice summer day?

HAPPY Yeah, but I cover myself!

LINDA Boys!

HAPPY If I'm going to take a fade[5] the boss can call any number where I'm supposed to be and they'll swear to him that I just left. I'll tell you something that I hate to say, Biff, but in the business world some of them think you're crazy.

BIFF [*angered*] Screw the business world!

HAPPY All right, screw it! Great, but cover yourself!

LINDA Hap, Hap!

BIFF I don't care what they think! They've laughed at Dad for years, and you know why? Because we don't belong in this nuthouse of a city! We should be mixing cement on some open plain, or—or carpenters. A carpenter is allowed to whistle!

[WILLY *walks in from the entrance of the house, at left.*]

WILLY Even your grandfather was better than a carpenter. [*Pause. They watch him.*] You never grew up. Bernard does not whistle in the elevator, I assure you.

BIFF [*as though to laugh* WILLY *out of it*] Yeah, but you do, Pop.

WILLY I never in my life whistled in an elevator! And who in the business world thinks I'm crazy?

BIFF I didn't mean it like that, Pop. Now don't make a whole thing out of it, will ya?

WILLY Go back to the West! Be a carpenter, a cowboy, enjoy yourself!

LINDA Willy, he was just saying—

WILLY I heard what he said!

HAPPY [*trying to quiet* WILLY] Hey, Pop, come on now . . .

WILLY [*continuing over* HAPPY*'s line*] They laugh at me, heh? Go to Filene's, go to the Hub,[6] go to Slattery's, Boston. Call out the name Willy Loman and see what happens! Big shot!

BIFF All right, Pop.

WILLY Big!

BIFF All right!

WILLY Why do you always insult me?

BIFF I didn't say a word. [*To* LINDA] Did I say a word?

LINDA He didn't say anything, Willy.

WILLY [*going to the doorway of the living room*] All right, good night, good night.

LINDA Willy, dear, he just decided . . .

WILLY [*to* BIFF] If you get tired hanging around tomorrow, paint the ceiling I put up in the living room.

BIFF I'm leaving early tomorrow.

HAPPY He's going to see Bill Oliver, Pop.

WILLY [*interestedly*] Oliver? For what?

BIFF [*with reserve, but trying, trying*] He always said he'd stake me. I'd like to go into business, so maybe I can take him up on it.

LINDA Isn't that wonderful?

WILLY Don't interrupt. What's wonderful about it? There's fifty men in the City of New York who'd stake him. [*To* BIFF] Sporting goods?

5. Disappear.
6. Boston (label given the Massachusetts State House in 1858 by Oliver Wendell Holmes).

BIFF I guess so. I know something about it and—

WILLY He knows something about it! You know sporting goods better than Spalding,[7] for God's sake! How much is he giving you?

BIFF I don't know, I didn't even see him yet, but—

WILLY Then what're you talkin' about?

BIFF [*getting angry*] Well, all I said was I'm gonna see him, that's all!

WILLY [*turning away*] Ah, you're counting your chickens again.

BIFF [*starting left for the stairs*] Oh, Jesus, I'm going to sleep!

WILLY [*calling after him*] Don't curse in this house!

BIFF [*turning*] Since when did you get so clean?

HAPPY [*trying to stop them*] Wait a . . .

WILLY Don't use that language to me! I won't have it!

HAPPY [*grabbing* BIFF, *shouts*] Wait a minute! I got an idea. I got a feasible idea. Come here, Biff, let's talk this over now, let's talk some sense here. When I was down in Florida last time, I thought of a great idea to sell sporting goods. It just came back to me. You and I, Biff—we have a line, the Loman Line. We train a couple of weeks, and put on a couple of exhibitions, see?

WILLY That's an idea!

HAPPY Wait! We form two basketball teams, see? Two water-polo teams. We play each other. It's a million dollars' worth of publicity. Two brothers, see? The Loman Brothers. Displays in the Royal Palms—all the hotels. And banners over the ring and the basketball court: "Loman Brothers." Baby, we could sell sporting goods!

WILLY That is a one-million-dollar idea!

LINDA Marvelous!

BIFF I'm in great shape as far as that's concerned.

HAPPY And the beauty of it is, Biff, it wouldn't be like a business. We'd be out playin' ball again . . .

BIFF [*enthused*] Yeah, that's . . .

WILLY Million-dollar . . .

HAPPY And you wouldn't get fed up with it, Biff. It'd be the family again. There'd be the old honor, and comradeship, and if you wanted to go off for a swim or somethin'—well, you'd do it! Without some smart cooky gettin' up ahead of you!

WILLY Lick the world! You guys together could absolutely lick the civilized world.

BIFF I'll see Oliver tomorrow. Hap, if we could work that out . . .

LINDA Maybe things are beginning to—

WILLY [*wildly enthused, to* LINDA] Stop interrupting! [*To* BIFF] But don't wear sport jacket and slacks when you see Oliver.

BIFF No, I'll—

WILLY A business suit, and talk as little as possible, and don't crack any jokes.

BIFF He did like me. Always liked me.

LINDA He loved you!

7. The sporting goods company named after the American baseball star A. G. Spalding (1850–1915), who founded it.

WILLY [*to* LINDA] Will you stop! [*To* BIFF] Walk in very serious. You are not applying for a boy's job. Money is to pass. Be quiet, fine, and serious. Everybody likes a kidder, but nobody lends him money.

HAPPY I'll try to get some myself, Biff. I'm sure I can.

WILLY I see great things for you kids, I think your troubles are over. But remember, start big and you'll end big. Ask for fifteen. How much you gonna ask for?

BIFF Gee, I don't know—

WILLY And don't say "Gee." "Gee" is a boy's word. A man walking in for fifteen thousand dollars does not say "Gee!"

BIFF Ten, I think, would be top though.

WILLY Don't be so modest. You always started too low. Walk in with a big laugh. Don't look worried. Start off with a couple of your good stories to lighten things up. It's not what you say, it's how you say it—because personality always wins the day.

LINDA Oliver always thought the highest of him—

WILLY Will you let me talk?

BIFF Don't yell at her, Pop, will ya?

WILLY [*angrily*] I was talking, wasn't I?

BIFF I don't like you yelling at her all the time, and I'm tellin' you, that's all.

WILLY What're you, takin' over this house?

LINDA Willy—

WILLY [*turning on her*] Don't take his side all the time, goddammit!

BIFF [*furiously*] Stop yelling at her!

WILLY [*suddenly pulling on his cheek, beaten down, guilt ridden*] Give my best to Bill Oliver—he may remember me. [*He exits through the living room doorway.*]

LINDA [*her voice subdued*] What'd you have to start that for? [BIFF *turns away.*] You see how sweet he was as soon as you talked hopefully? [*She goes over to* BIFF.] Come up and say good night to him. Don't let him go to bed that way.

HAPPY Come on, Biff, let's buck him up.

LINDA Please, dear. Just say good night. It takes so little to make him happy. Come. [*She goes through the living room doorway, calling upstairs from within the living room.*] Your pajamas are hanging in the bathroom, Willy!

HAPPY [*looking toward where* LINDA *went out*] What a woman! They broke the mold when they made her. You know that, Biff?

BIFF He's off salary. My God, working on commission!

HAPPY Well, let's face it: he's no hot-shot selling man. Except that sometimes, you have to admit, he's a sweet personality.

BIFF [*deciding*] Lend me ten bucks, will ya? I want to buy some new ties.

HAPPY I'll take you to a place I know. Beautiful stuff. Wear one of my striped shirts tomorrow.

BIFF She got gray. Mom got awful old. Gee, I'm gonna go in to Oliver tomorrow and knock him for a—

HAPPY Come on up. Tell that to Dad. Let's give him a whirl. Come on.

BIFF [*steamed up*] You know, with ten thousand bucks, boy!

HAPPY [*as they go into the living room*] That's the talk, Biff, that's the first time I've heard the old confidence out of you! [*From within the living room, fading off*] You're gonna live with me, kid, and any babe you want just say the word . . . [*The last lines are hardly heard. They are mounting the stairs to their parents' bedroom.*]

LINDA [*entering her bedroom and addressing* WILLY, *who is in the bathroom. She is straightening the bed for him.*] Can you do anything about the shower? It drips.

WILLY [*from the bathroom*] All of a sudden everything falls to pieces! Goddam plumbing, oughta be sued, those people. I hardly finished putting it in and the thing . . . [*His words rumble off.*]

LINDA I'm just wondering if Oliver will remember him. You think he might?

WILLY [*coming out of the bathroom in his pajamas*] Remember him? What's the matter with you, you crazy? If he'd've stayed with Oliver he'd be on top by now! Wait'll Oliver gets a look at him. You don't know the average caliber any more. The average young man today—[*He is getting into bed.*]—is got a caliber of zero. Greatest thing in the world for him was to bum around.

[BIFF *and* HAPPY *enter the bedroom. Slight pause.*]

WILLY [*stops short, looking at* BIFF] Glad to hear it, boy.

HAPPY He wanted to say good night to you, sport.

WILLY [*to* BIFF] Yeah. Knock him dead, boy. What'd you want to tell me?

BIFF Just take it easy, Pop. Good night. [*He turns to go.*]

WILLY [*unable to resist*] And if anything falls off the desk while you're talking to him—like a package or something—don't you pick it up. They have office boys for that.

LINDA I'll make a big breakfast—

WILLY Will you let me finish? [*To* BIFF] Tell him you were in the business in the West. Not farm work.

BIFF All right, Dad.

LINDA I think everything—

WILLY [*going right through her speech*] And don't undersell yourself. No less than fifteen thousand dollars.

BIFF [*unable to bear him*] Okay. Good night, Mom. [*He starts moving.*]

WILLY Because you got a greatness in you, Biff, remember that. You got all kinds a greatness . . . [*He lies back, exhausted.* BIFF *walks out.*]

LINDA [*calling after Biff*] Sleep well, darling!

HAPPY I'm gonna get married, Mom. I wanted to tell you.

LINDA Go to sleep, dear.

HAPPY [*going*] I just wanted to tell you.

WILLY Keep up the good work. [HAPPY *exits.*] God . . . remember that Ebbets Field[8] game? The championship of the city?

LINDA Just rest. Should I sing to you?

WILLY Yeah. Sing to me. [LINDA *hums a soft lullaby.*] When that team came out—he was the tallest, remember?

LINDA Oh, yes. And in gold.

[BIFF *enters the darkened kitchen, takes a cigarette, and leaves the house. He comes downstage into a golden pool of light. He smokes, staring at the night.*]

8. Brooklyn's baseball stadium, home of the Dodgers before the team's move to Los Angeles in 1957. Football was also played there.

WILLY Like a young god. Hercules[9]—something like that. And the sun, the sun all around him. Remember how he waved to me? Right up from the field, with the representatives of three colleges standing by? And the buyers I brought, and the cheers when he came out—Loman, Loman, Loman! God Almighty, he'll be great yet. A star like that, magnificent, can never really fade away!

[The light on WILLY *is fading. The gas heater begins to glow through the kitchen wall, near the stairs, a blue flame beneath red coils.]*

LINDA *[timidly]* Willy dear, what has he got against you?

WILLY I'm so tired. Don't talk anymore.

*[*BIFF *slowly returns to the kitchen. He stops, stares toward the heater.]*

LINDA Will you ask Howard to let you work in New York?

WILLY First thing in the morning. Everything'll be all right.

*[*BIFF *reaches behind the heater and draws out a length of rubber tubing. He is horrified and turns his head toward* WILLY*'s room, still dimly lit, from which the strains of* LINDA*'s desperate but monotonous humming rise.]*

WILLY *[staring through the window into the moonlight]* Gee, look at the moon moving between the buildings!

*[*BIFF *wraps the tubing around his hand and quickly goes up the stairs.]*

Curtain.

Act 2

Music is heard, gay and bright. The curtain rises as the music fades away. WILLY, *in shirt sleeves, is sitting at the kitchen table, sipping coffee, his hat in his lap.* LINDA *is filling his cup when she can.*

WILLY Wonderful coffee. Meal in itself.

LINDA Can I make you some eggs?

WILLY No. Take a breath.

LINDA You look so rested, dear.

WILLY I slept like a dead one. First time in months. Imagine, sleeping till ten on a Tuesday morning. Boys left nice and early, heh?

LINDA They were out of here by eight o'clock.

WILLY Good work!

LINDA It was so thrilling to see them leaving together. I can't get over the shaving lotion in this house!

WILLY *[smiling]* Mmm—

LINDA Biff was very changed this morning. His whole attitude seemed to be hopeful. He couldn't wait to get downtown to see Oliver.

WILLY He's heading for a change. There's no question, there simply are certain men that take longer to get—solidified. How did he dress?

LINDA His blue suit. He's so handsome in that suit. He could be a—anything in that suit!

*[*WILLY *gets up from the table.* LINDA *holds his jacket for him.]*

WILLY There's no question, no question at all. Gee, on the way home tonight I'd like to buy some seeds.

9. In classical mythology, the greatest of all heroes (a son of Zeus, king of the gods, and the mortal Alcmene).

LINDA [*laughing*] That'd be wonderful. But not enough sun gets back there. Nothing'll grow anymore.

WILLY You wait, kid, before it's all over we're gonna get a little place out in the country, and I'll raise some vegetables, a couple of chickens . . .

LINDA You'll do it yet, dear.

[WILLY *walks out of his jacket.* LINDA *follows him.*]

WILLY And they'll get married, and come for a weekend. I'd build a little guest house. 'Cause I got so many fine tools, all I'd need would be a little lumber and some peace of mind.

LINDA [*joyfully*] I sewed the lining . . .

WILLY I could build two guest houses, so they'd both come. Did he decide how much he's going to ask Oliver for?

LINDA [*getting him into the jacket*] He didn't mention it, but I imagine ten or fifteen thousand. You going to talk to Howard today?

WILLY Yeah. I'll put it to him straight and simple. He'll just have to take me off the road.

LINDA And Willy, don't forget to ask for a little advance, because we've got the insurance premium. It's the grace period now.

WILLY That's a hundred . . . ?

LINDA A hundred and eight, sixty-eight. Because we're a little short again.

WILLY Why are we short?

LINDA Well, you had the motor job on the car . . .

WILLY That goddam Studebaker!

LINDA And you got one more payment on the refrigerator . . .

WILLY But it just broke again!

LINDA Well, it's old, dear.

WILLY I told you we should've bought a well-advertised machine. Charley bought a General Electric and it's twenty years old and it's still good, that son-of-a-bitch.

LINDA But, Willy—

WILLY Whoever heard of a Hastings refrigerator? Once in my life I would like to own something outright before it's broken! I'm always in a race with the junkyard! I just finished paying for the car and it's on its last legs. The refrigerator consumes belts like a goddam maniac. They time those things. They time them so when you finally paid for them, they're used up.

LINDA [*buttoning up his jacket as he unbuttons it*] All told, about two hundred dollars would carry us, dear. But that includes the last payment on the mortgage. After this payment, Willy, the house belongs to us.

WILLY It's twenty-five years!

LINDA Biff was nine years old when we bought it.

WILLY Well, that's a great thing. To weather a twenty-five year mortgage is—

LINDA It's an accomplishment.

WILLY All the cement, the lumber, the reconstruction I put in this house! There ain't a crack to be found in it anymore.

LINDA Well, it served its purpose.

WILLY What purpose? Some stranger'll come along, move in, and that's that. If only Biff would take this house, and raise a family . . . [*He starts to go.*] Good-by, I'm late.

LINDA [*suddenly remembering*] Oh, I forgot! You're supposed to meet them for dinner.

WILLY Me?

LINDA At Frank's Chop House on Forty-eighth near Sixth Avenue.

WILLY Is that so! How about you?

LINDA No, just the three of you. They're gonna blow you to a big meal![1]

WILLY Don't say! Who thought of that?

LINDA Biff came to me this morning, Willy, and he said, "Tell Dad, we want to blow him to a big meal." Be there six o'clock. You and your two boys are going to have dinner.

WILLY Gee whiz! That's really somethin'. I'm gonna knock Howard for a loop, kid. I'll get an advance, and I'll come home with a New York job. Goddammit, now I'm gonna do it!

LINDA Oh, that's the spirit, Willy!

WILLY I will never get behind a wheel the rest of my life!

LINDA It's changing, Willy, I can feel it changing!

WILLY Beyond a question. G'by, I'm late. [*He starts to go again.*]

LINDA [*calling after him as she runs to the kitchen table for a handkerchief*] You got your glasses?

WILLY [*feels for them, then comes back in*] Yeah, yeah, got my glasses.

LINDA [*giving him the handkerchief*] And a handkerchief.

WILLY Yeah, handkerchief.

LINDA And your saccharine?

WILLY Yeah, my saccharine.

LINDA Be careful on the subway stairs.

[*She kisses him, and a silk stocking is seen hanging from her hand.* WILLY *notices it.*]

WILLY Will you stop mending stockings? At least while I'm in the house. It gets me nervous. I can't tell you. Please.

[LINDA *hides the stocking in her hand as she follows* WILLY *across the forestage in front of the house.*]

LINDA Remember, Frank's Chop House.

WILLY [*passing the apron*] Maybe beets would grow out there.

LINDA [*laughing*] But you tried so many times.

WILLY Yeah. Well, don't work hard today. [*He disappears around the right corner of the house.*]

LINDA Be careful!

[*As* WILLY *vanishes, Linda waves to him. Suddenly the phone rings. She runs across the stage and into the kitchen and lifts it.*]

LINDA Hello? Oh, Biff! I'm so glad you called, I just . . . Yes, sure, I just told him. Yes, he'll be there for dinner at six o'clock, I didn't forget. Listen, I was just dying to tell you. You know that little rubber pipe I told you about? That he connected to the gas heater? I finally decided to go down the cellar this morning and take it away and destroy it. But it's gone! Imagine? He took it away himself, it isn't there! [*She listens*]. When? Oh, then you took it. Oh—nothing, it's just that I'd hoped he'd taken it away himself. Oh, I'm not worried, darling, because this morning he left in such high spirits, it was like the old days! I'm not afraid anymore. Did Mr. Oliver see you? . . . Well, you wait there then. And make a nice impression on him, darling.

1. That is, treat him to dinner, spending extravagantly on it.

Just don't perspire too much before you see him. And have a nice time with Dad. He may have big news too! . . . That's right, a New York job. And be sweet to him tonight, dear. Be loving to him. Because he's only a little boat looking for a harbor. [*She is trembling with sorrow and joy.*] Oh, that's wonderful, Biff, you'll save his life. Thanks, darling. Just put your arm around him when he comes into the restaurant. Give him a smile. That's the boy . . . Good-by, dear. . . . You got your comb? . . . That's fine. Good-by, Biff dear.

[*In the middle of her speech,* HOWARD WAGNER, *thirty-six, wheels in a small typewriter table on which is a wire-recording machine*[2] *and proceeds to plug it in. This is on the left forestage. Light slowly fades on* LINDA *as it rises on* HOWARD. HOWARD *is intent on threading the machine and only glances over his shoulder as* WILLY *appears.*]

WILLY Pst! Pst!

HOWARD Hello, Willy, come in.

WILLY Like to have a little talk with you, Howard.

HOWARD Sorry to keep you waiting. I'll be with you in a minute.

WILLY What's that, Howard?

HOWARD Didn't you ever see one of these? Wire recorder.

WILLY Oh. Can we talk a minute?

HOWARD Records things. Just got delivery yesterday. Been driving me crazy, the most terrific machine I ever saw in my life. I was up all night with it.

WILLY What do you do with it?

HOWARD I bought it for dictation, but you can do anything with it. Listen to this. I had it home last night. Listen to what I picked up. The first one is my daughter. Get this. [*He flicks the switch and "Roll out the Barrel"*[3] *is heard being whistled.*] Listen to that kid whistle.

WILLY That is lifelike, isn't it?

HOWARD Seven years old. Get that tone.

WILLY Ts, ts. Like to ask a little favor if you . . .

[*The whistling breaks off, and the voice of* HOWARD's *daughter is heard.*]

HIS DAUGHTER "Now you, Daddy."

HOWARD She's crazy for me! [*Again the same song is whistled.*] That's me! Ha! [*He winks.*]

WILLY You're very good!

[*The whistling breaks off again. The machine runs silent for a moment.*]

HOWARD Sh! Get this now, this is my son.

HIS SON "The capital of Alabama is Montgomery; the capital of Arizona is Phoenix; the capital of Arkansas is Little Rock; the capital of California is Sacramento . . ." [*And on, and on.*]

HOWARD [*holding up five fingers*] Five years old, Willy!

WILLY He'll make an announcer some day!

HIS SON [*continuing*] "The capital . . ."

HOWARD Get that—alphabetical order! [*The machine breaks off suddenly.*] Wait a minute. The maid kicked the plug out.

2. The earliest practical magnetic sound recording machine, first commercially available after World War II (soon made obsolete by the tape recorder).

3. "The Beer Barrel Polka" (music written 1927; English lyrics written 1939), a song that became very popular during World War II.

WILLY It certainly is a—

HOWARD Sh, for God's sake!

HIS SON "It's nine o'clock, Bulova watch time.[4] So I have to go to sleep."

WILLY That really is—

HOWARD Wait a minute! The next is my wife.

[*They wait.*]

HOWARD'S VOICE "Go on, say something." [*Pause*] "Well, you gonna talk?"

HIS WIFE "I can't think of anything."

HOWARD'S VOICE "Well, talk—it's turning."

HIS WIFE [*shyly, beaten*] "Hello." [*Silence*] "Oh, Howard, I can't talk into this . . ."

HOWARD [*snapping the machine off*] That was my wife.

WILLY That is a wonderful machine. Can we—

HOWARD I tell you, Willy, I'm gonna take my camera, and my bandsaw, and all my hobbies, and out they go. This is the most fascinating relaxation I ever found.

WILLY I think I'll get one myself.

HOWARD Sure, they're only a hundred and a half. You can't do without it. Supposing you wanna hear Jack Benny,[5] see? But you can't be at home at that hour. So you tell the maid to turn the radio on when Jack Benny comes on, and this automatically goes on with the radio . . .

WILLY And when you come home you . . .

HOWARD You can come home twelve o'clock, one o'clock, anytime you like, and you get yourself a Coke and sit yourself down, throw the switch, and there's Jack Benny's program in the middle of the night!

WILLY I'm definitely going to get one. Because lots of time I'm on the road, and I think to myself, what I must be missing on the radio!

HOWARD Don't you have a radio in the car?

WILLY Well, yeah, but who ever thinks of turning it on?

HOWARD Say, aren't you supposed to be in Boston?

WILLY That's what I want to talk to you about, Howard. You got a minute?

[*He draws a chair in from the wing.*]

HOWARD What happened? What're you doing here?

WILLY Well . . .

HOWARD You didn't crack up again, did you?

WILLY Oh, no. No . . .

HOWARD Geez, you had me worried there for a minute. What's the trouble?

WILLY Well, tell you the truth, Howard. I've come to the decision that I'd rather not travel any more.

HOWARD Not travel! Well, what'll you do?

WILLY Remember, Christmastime, when you had the party here? You said you'd try to think of some spot for me here in town.

HOWARD With us?

WILLY Well, sure.

HOWARD Oh, yeah, yeah. I remember. Well, I couldn't think of anything for you, Willy.

4. A phrase used for years in Bulova's radio advertisements, beginning in 1926.

5. American comedian and actor (Benjamin Kubelsky, 1894–1974), host of a popular comedy show on radio (1932–55) and television (1950–65).

WILLY I tell ya, Howard. The kids are all grown up, y'know. I don't need much anymore. If I could take home—well, sixty-five dollars a week, I could swing it.

HOWARD Yeah, but Willy, see I—

WILLY I tell ya why, Howard. Speaking frankly and between the two of us, y'know—I'm just a little tired.

HOWARD Oh, I could understand that, Willy. But you're a road man, Willy, and we do a road business. We've only got a half-dozen salesmen on the floor here.

WILLY God knows, Howard, I never asked a favor of any man. But I was with the firm when your father used to carry you in here in his arms.

HOWARD I know that, Willy, but—

WILLY Your father came to me the day you were born and asked me what I thought of the name of Howard, may he rest in peace.

HOWARD I appreciate that, Willy, but there just is no spot here for you. If I had a spot I'd slam you right in, but I just don't have a single solitary spot.

[*He looks for his lighter.* WILLY *has picked it up and gives it to him. Pause.*]

WILLY [*with increasing anger*] Howard, all I need to set my table is fifty dollars a week.

HOWARD But where am I going to put you, kid?

WILLY Look, it isn't a question of whether I can sell merchandise, is it?

HOWARD No, but it's a business, kid, and everybody's gotta pull his own weight.

WILLY [*desperately*] Just let me tell you a story, Howard—

HOWARD 'Cause you gotta admit, business is business.

WILLY [*angrily*] Business is definitely business, but just listen for a minute. You don't understand this. When I was a boy—eighteen, nineteen—I was already on the road. And there was a question in my mind as to whether selling had a future for me. Because in those days I had a yearning to go to Alaska. See, there were three gold strikes in one month in Alaska, and I felt like going out. Just for the ride, you might say.

HOWARD [*barely interested*] Don't say.

WILLY Oh, yeah, my father lived many years in Alaska. He was an adventurous man. We've got quite a little streak of self-reliance in our family. I thought I'd go out with my older brother and try to locate him, and maybe settle in the North with the old man. And I was almost decided to go, when I met a salesman in the Parker House.[6] His name was Dave Singleman. And he was eighty-four years old, and he'd drummed merchandise in thirty-one states. And old Dave, he'd go up to his room, y'understand, put on his green velvet slippers—I'll never forget—and pick up his phone and call the buyers, and without ever leaving his room, at the age of eighty-four, he made his living. And when I saw that, I realized that selling was the greatest career a man could want. 'Cause what could be more satisfying than to be able to go, at the age of eighty-four, into twenty or thirty different cities, and pick up a phone, and be remembered and loved and helped by so many different people? Do you know? when he died—and by the way

6. A venerable Boston luxury hotel.

he died the death of a salesman, in his green velvet slippers in the smoker[7] of the New York, New Haven and Hartford, going into Boston—when he died, hundreds of salesmen and buyers were at his funeral. Things were sad on a lotta trains for months after that. [*He stands up.* HOWARD *has not looked at him.*] In those days there was personality in it, Howard. There was respect, and comradeship, and gratitude in it. Today, it's all cut and dried, and there's no chance for bringing friendship to bear—or personality. You see what I mean? They don't know me anymore.

HOWARD [*moving away, to the right*] That's just the thing, Willy.

WILLY If I had forty dollars a week—that's all I'd need. Forty dollars, Howard.

HOWARD Kid, I can't take blood from a stone, I—

WILLY [*desperation is on him now*] Howard, the year Al Smith was nominated,[8] your father came to me and—

HOWARD [*starting to go off*] I've got to see some people, kid.

WILLY [*stopping him*] I'm talking about your father! There were promises made across this desk! You mustn't tell me you've got people to see—I put thirty-four years into this firm, Howard, and now I can't pay my insurance! You can't eat the orange and throw the peel away—a man is not a piece of fruit! [*After a pause*] Now pay attention. Your father—in 1928 I had a big year. I averaged a hundred and seventy dollars a week in commissions.

HOWARD [*impatiently*] Now, Willy, you never averaged—

WILLY [*banging his hand on the desk*] I averaged a hundred and seventy dollars a week in the year of 1928! And your father came to me—or rather, I was in the office here—it was right over this desk—and he put his hand on my shoulder—

HOWARD [*getting up*] You'll have to excuse me, Willy, I gotta see some people. Pull yourself together. [*Going out*] I'll be back in a little while.

[*On* HOWARD*'s exit, the light on his chair grows very bright and strange.*]

WILLY Pull myself together! What the hell did I say to him? My God, I was yelling at him! How could I! [WILLY *breaks off, staring at the light, which occupies the chair, animating it. He approaches this chair, standing across the desk from it.*] Frank, Frank, don't you remember what you told me that time? How you put your hand on my shoulder, and Frank . . . [*He leans on the desk and as he speaks the dead man's name he accidentally switches on the recorder, and instantly.*]

HOWARD'S SON ". . . of New York is Albany. The capital of Ohio is Cincinnati, the capital of Rhode Island is . . ." [*The recitation continues.*]

WILLY [*leaping away with fright, shouting*] Ha! Howard! Howard! Howard!

HOWARD [*rushing in*] What happened?

WILLY [*pointing at the machine, which continues nasally, childishly, with the capital cities*] Shut it off! Shut it off!

HOWARD [*pulling the plug out*] Look, Willy . . .

WILLY [*pressing his hands to his eyes*] I gotta get myself some coffee. I'll get some coffee . . .

[WILLY *starts to walk out.* HOWARD *stops him.*]

7. The smoking car on a train (Willy names the specific railroad).

8. That is, in 1928; Smith (1873–1944) was the Democratic Party's presidential nominee.

HOWARD [*rolling up the cord*] Willy, look . . .

WILLY I'll go to Boston.

HOWARD Willy, you can't go to Boston for us.

WILLY Why can't I go?

HOWARD I don't want you to represent us. I've been meaning to tell you for a long time now.

WILLY Howard, are you firing me?

HOWARD I think you need a good long rest, Willy.

WILLY Howard—

HOWARD And when you feel better, come back, and we'll see if we can work something out.

WILLY But I gotta earn money, Howard. I'm in no position to—

HOWARD Where are your sons? Why don't your sons give you a hand?

WILLY They're working on a very big deal.

HOWARD This is no time for false pride, Willy. You go to your sons and you tell them that you're tired. You've got two great boys, haven't you?

WILLY Oh, no question, no question, but in the meantime . . .

HOWARD Then that's that, heh?

WILLY All right, I'll go to Boston tomorrow.

HOWARD No, no.

WILLY I can't throw myself on my sons. I'm not a cripple!

HOWARD Look, kid, I'm busy this morning.

WILLY [*grasping* HOWARD*'s arm*] Howard, you've got to let me go to Boston!

HOWARD [*hard, keeping himself under control*] I've got a line of people to see this morning. Sit down, take five minutes, and pull yourself together, and then go home, will ya? I need the office, Willy. [*He starts to go, turns, remembering the recorder, starts to push off the table holding the recorder.*] Oh, yeah. Whenever you can this week, stop by and drop off the samples. You'll feel better, Willy, and then come back and we'll talk. Pull yourself together, kid, there's people outside.

[HOWARD *exits, pushing the table off left.* WILLY *stares into space, exhausted. Now the music is heard—*BEN*'s music—first distantly, then closer, closer. As* WILLY *speaks,* BEN *enters from the right. He carries valise and umbrella.*]

WILLY Oh, Ben, how did you do it? What is the answer? Did you wind up the Alaska deal already?

BEN Doesn't take much time if you know what you're doing. Just a short business trip. Boarding ship in an hour. Wanted to say good-by.

WILLY Ben, I've got to talk to you.

BEN [*glancing at his watch*] Haven't the time, William.

WILLY [*crossing the apron to Ben*] Ben, nothing's working out. I don't know what to do.

BEN Now, look here, William. I've bought timberland in Alaska and I need a man to look after things for me.

WILLY God, timberland! Me and my boys in those grand outdoors!

BEN You've a new continent at your doorstep, William. Get out of these cities, they're full of talk and time payments and courts of law. Screw on your fists and you can fight for a fortune up there.

WILLY Yes, yes! Linda, Linda!

[LINDA *enters as of old, with the wash.*]

LINDA Oh, you're back?

BEN I haven't much time.

WILLY No, wait! Linda, he's got a proposition for me in Alaska.

LINDA But you've got—[*To* BEN] He's got a beautiful job here.

WILLY But in Alaska, kid, I could—

LINDA You're doing well enough, Willy!

BEN [*to* LINDA] Enough for what, my dear?

LINDA [*frightened of* BEN *and angry at him*] Don't say those things to him! Enough to be happy right here, right now. [*To* WILLY, *while* BEN *laughs*] Why must everybody conquer the world? You're well liked, and the boys love you, and someday—[*To* BEN]—why, old man Wagner told him just the other day that if he keeps it up he'll be a member of the firm, didn't he, Willy?

WILLY Sure, sure. I am building something with this firm, Ben, and if a man is building something he must be on the right track, mustn't he?

BEN What are you building? Lay your hand on it. Where is it?

WILLY [*hesitantly*] That's true, Linda, there's nothing.

LINDA Why? [*To* BEN] There's a man eighty-four years old—

WILLY That's right, Ben, that's right. When I look at that man I say, what is there to worry about?

BEN Bah!

WILLY It's true, Ben. All he has to do is go into any city, pick up the phone, and he's making his living and you know why?

BEN [*picking up his valise*] I've got to go.

WILLY [*holding* BEN *back*] Look at this boy!

[BIFF, *in his high school sweater, enters carrying suitcase.* HAPPY *carries* BIFF*'s shoulder guards, gold helmet, and football pants.*]

WILLY Without a penny to his name, three great universities are begging for him, and from there the sky's the limit, because it's not what you do, Ben. It's who you know and the smile on your face! It's contacts, Ben, contacts! The whole wealth of Alaska passes over the lunch table at the Commodore Hotel, and that's the wonder, the wonder of this country, that a man can end with diamonds here on the basis of being liked! [*He turns to* BIFF.] And that's why when you get out on that field today it's important. Because thousands of people will be rooting for you and loving you. [*To* BEN, *who has again begun to leave*] And Ben! when he walks into a business office his name will sound out like a bell and all the doors will open to him! I've seen it, Ben, I've seen it a thousand times! You can't feel it with your hand like timber, but it's there!

BEN Good-by, William.

WILLY Ben, am I right? Don't you think I'm right? I value your advice.

BEN There's a new continent at your doorstep, William. You could walk out rich. Rich! [*He is gone.*]

WILLY We'll do it here, Ben! You hear me? We're gonna do it here!

[YOUNG BERNARD *rushes in. The gay music of the Boys is heard.*]

BERNARD Oh, gee, I was afraid you left already!

WILLY Why? What time is it?

BERNARD It's half-past one!

WILLY Well, come on, everybody! Ebbets Field next stop! Where's the pennants? [*He rushes through the wall-line of the kitchen and out into the living room.*]

LINDA [*to* BIFF] Did you pack fresh underwear?

BIFF [*who has been limbering up*] I want to go!

BERNARD Biff, I'm carrying your helmet, ain't I?

HAPPY No, I'm carrying the helmet.

BERNARD Oh, Biff, you promised me.

HAPPY I'm carrying the helmet.

BERNARD How am I going to get in the locker room?

LINDA Let him carry the shoulder guards. [*She puts her coat and hat on in the kitchen.*]

BERNARD Can I, Biff? 'Cause I told everybody I'm going to be in the locker room.

HAPPY In Ebbets Field it's the clubhouse.

BERNARD I meant the clubhouse. Biff!

HAPPY Biff!

BIFF [*grandly, after a slight pause*] Let him carry the shoulder guards.

HAPPY [*as he gives* BERNARD *the shoulder guards*] Stay close to us now.

[WILLY *rushes in with the pennants.*]

WILLY [*handing them out*] Everybody wave when Biff comes out on the field. [HAPPY *and* BERNARD *run off.*] You set now, boy?

[*The music has died away.*]

BIFF Ready to go, Pop. Every muscle is ready.

WILLY [*at the edge of the apron*] You realize what this means?

BIFF That's right, Pop.

WILLY [*feeling* BIFF*'s muscle*] You're comin' home this afternoon captain of the All-Scholastic Championship Team of the City of New York.

BIFF I got it, Pop. And remember, pal, when I take off my helmet, that touchdown is for you.

WILLY Let's go! [*He is starting out, with his arm around Biff, when* CHARLEY *enters, as of old, in knickers.*] I got no room for you, Charley.

CHARLEY Room? For what?

WILLY In the car.

CHARLEY You goin' for a ride? I wanted to shoot some casino.

WILLY [*furiously*] Casino! [*Incredulously*] Don't you realize what today is?

LINDA Oh, he knows, Willy. He's just kidding you.

WILLY That's nothing to kid about!

CHARLEY No. Linda, what's goin' on?

LINDA He's playing in Ebbets Field.

CHARLEY Baseball in this weather?

WILLY Don't talk to him. Come on, come on! [*He is pushing them out.*]

CHARLEY Wait a minute, didn't you hear the news?

WILLY What?

CHARLEY Don't you listen to the radio? Ebbets Field just blew up.

WILLY You go to hell! [CHARLEY *laughs. Pushing them out*] Come on, come on! We're late.

CHARLEY [*as they go*] Knock a homer, Biff, knock a homer!

WILLY [*the last to leave, turning to* CHARLEY] I don't think that was funny, Charley. This is the greatest day of his life.

CHARLEY Willy, when are you going to grow up?

WILLY Yeah, heh? When this game is over, Charley, you'll be laughing out of the other side of your face. They'll be calling him another Red Grange.[9] Twenty-five thousand a year.

CHARLEY [*kidding*] Is that so?

WILLY Yeah, that's so.

CHARLEY Well, then, I'm sorry, Willy. But tell me something.

WILLY What?

CHARLEY Who is Red Grange?

WILLY Put up your hands. Goddam you, put up your hands!

[CHARLEY, *chuckling, shakes his head and walks away, around the left corner of the stage.* WILLY *follows him. The music rises to a mocking frenzy.*]

WILLY Who the hell do you think you are, better than everybody else? You don't know everything, you big, ignorant, stupid . . . Put up your hands!

[*Light rises, on the right side of the forestage, on a small table in the reception room of* CHARLEY'S *office. Traffic sounds are heard.* BERNARD, *now mature, sits whistling to himself. A pair of tennis rackets and an overnight bag are on the floor beside him.*]

WILLY [*offstage*] What are you walking away for? Don't walk away! If you're going to say something say it to my face! I know you laugh at me behind my back. You'll laugh out of the other side of your goddam face after this game. Touchdown! Touchdown! Eighty thousand people! Touchdown! Right between the goal posts.

[BERNARD *is a quiet, earnest, but self-assured young man.* WILLY'S *voice is coming from right upstage now.* BERNARD *lowers his feet off the table and listens.* JENNY, *his father's secretary, enters.*]

JENNY [*distressed*] Say, Bernard, will you go out in the hall?

BERNARD What is that noise? Who is it?

JENNY Mr. Loman. He just got off the elevator.

BERNARD [*getting up*] Who's he arguing with?

JENNY Nobody. There's nobody with him. I can't deal with him any more, and your father gets all upset everytime he comes. I've got a lot of typing to do, and your father's waiting to sign it. Will you see him?

WILLY [*entering*] Touchdown! Touch—[*He sees* JENNY.] Jenny, Jenny, good to see you. How're ya? Workin'? Or still honest?

JENNY Fine. How've you been feeling?

WILLY Not much anymore, Jenny. Ha, ha! [*He is surprised to see the rackets.*]

BERNARD Hello, Uncle Willy.

WILLY [*almost shocked*] Bernard! Well, look who's here! [*He comes quickly, guiltily, to* BERNARD *and warmly shakes his hand.*]

BERNARD How are you? Good to see you.

WILLY What are you doing here?

BERNARD Oh, just stopped by to see Pop. Get off my feet till my train leaves. I'm going to Washington in a few minutes.

WILLY Is he in?

9. Harold Edward Grange (1903–1991), a football player who was a three-time All-American halfback at the University of Illinois (1923–25); after starting for the Chicago Bears, he became a sportscaster.

BERNARD Yes, he's in his office with the accountant. Sit down.

WILLY [*sitting down*] What're you going to do in Washington?

BERNARD Oh, just a case I've got there, Willy.

WILLY That so? [*Indicating the rackets*] You going to play tennis there?

BERNARD I'm staying with a friend who's got a court.

WILLY Don't say. His own tennis court. Must be fine people, I bet.

BERNARD They are, very nice. Dad tells me Biff's in town.

WILLY [*with a big smile*] Yeah, Biff's in. Working on a very big deal, Bernard.

BERNARD What's Biff doing?

WILLY Well, he's been doing very big things in the West. But he decided to establish himself here. Very big. We're having dinner. Did I hear your wife had a boy?

BERNARD That's right. Our second.

WILLY Two boys! What do you know!

BERNARD What kind of a deal has Biff got?

WILLY Well, Bill Oliver—very big sporting-goods man—he wants Biff very badly. Called him in from the West. Long distance, carte blanche, special deliveries. Your friends have their own private tennis court?

BERNARD You still with the old firm, Willy?

WILLY [*after a pause*] I'm—I'm overjoyed to see how you made the grade, Bernard, overjoyed. It's an encouraging thing to see a young man really—really—Looks very good for Biff—very—[*He breaks off, then*] Bernard—[*He is so full of emotion, he breaks off again.*]

BERNARD What is it, Willy?

WILLY [*small and alone*] What—what's the secret?

BERNARD What secret?

WILLY How—how did you? Why didn't he ever catch on?

BERNARD I wouldn't know that, Willy.

WILLY [*confidentially, desperately*] You were his friend, his boyhood friend. There's something I don't understand about it. His life ended after that Ebbets Field game. From the age of seventeen nothing good ever happened to him.

BERNARD He never trained himself for anything.

WILLY But he did, he did. After high school he took so many correspondence courses. Radio mechanics; television; God knows what, and never made the slightest mark.

BERNARD [*taking off his glasses*] Willy, do you want to talk candidly?

WILLY [*rising, faces* BERNARD] I regard you as a very brilliant man, Bernard. I value your advice.

BERNARD Oh, the hell with the advice, Willy. I couldn't advise you. There's just one thing I've always wanted to ask you. When he was supposed to graduate, and the math teacher flunked him—

WILLY Oh, that son-of-a-bitch ruined his life.

BERNARD Yeah, but, Willy, all he had to do was go to summer school and make up that subject.

WILLY That's right, that's right.

BERNARD Did you tell him not to go to summer school?

WILLY Me? I begged him to go. I ordered him to go!

BERNARD Then why wouldn't he go?

WILLY Why? Why! Bernard, that question has been trailing me like a ghost for the last fifteen years. He flunked the subject, and laid down and died like a hammer hit him!

BERNARD Take it easy, kid.

WILLY Let me talk to you—I got nobody to talk to. Bernard, Bernard, was it my fault? Y'see? It keeps going around in my mind, maybe I did something to him. I got nothing to give him.

BERNARD Don't take it so hard.

WILLY Why did he lay down? What is the story there? You were his friend!

BERNARD Willy, I remember, it was June, and our grades came out. And he'd flunked math.

WILLY That son-of-a-bitch!

BERNARD No, it wasn't right then. Biff just got very angry, I remember, and he was ready to enroll in summer school.

WILLY [*surprised*] He was?

BERNARD He wasn't beaten by it at all. But then, Willy, he disappeared from the block for almost a month. And I got the idea that he'd gone up to New England to see you. Did he have a talk with you then?

[WILLY *stares in silence.*]

BERNARD Willy?

WILLY [*with a strong edge of resentment in his voice*] Yeah, he came to Boston. What about it?

BERNARD Well, just that when he came back—I'll never forget this, it always mystifies me. Because I'd thought so well of Biff, even though he'd always taken advantage of me. I loved him, Willy, y'know? And he came back after that month and took his sneakers—remember those sneakers with "University of Virginia" printed on them? He was so proud of those, wore them every day. And he took them down in the cellar, and burned them up in the furnace. We had a fist fight. It lasted at least half an hour. Just the two of us, punching each other down the cellar, and crying right through it. I've often thought of how strange it was that I knew he'd given up his life. What happened in Boston, Willy?

[WILLY *looks at him as at an intruder.*]

BERNARD I just bring it up because you asked me.

WILLY [*angrily*] Nothing. What do you mean, "What happened?" What's that got to do with anything?

BERNARD Well, don't get sore.

WILLY What are you trying to do, blame it on me? If a boy lays down is that my fault?

BERNARD Now, Willy, don't get—

WILLY Well, don't—don't talk to me that way! What does that mean, "What happened?"

[CHARLEY *enters. He is in his vest, and he carries a bottle of bourbon.*]

CHARLEY Hey, you're going to miss that train. [*He waves the bottle.*]

BERNARD Yeah, I'm going. [*He takes the bottle.*] Thanks, Pop. [*He picks up his rackets and bag.*] Good-by, Willy, and don't worry about it. You know, "If at first you don't succeed . . ."

WILLY Yes, I believe in that.

BERNARD But sometimes, Willy, it's better for a man just to walk away.

WILLY Walk away?

BERNARD That's right.

WILLY But if you can't walk away?

BERNARD [*after a slight pause*] I guess that's when it's tough. [*Extending his hand*] Good-by, Willy.

WILLY [*shaking* BERNARD*'s hand*] Good-by, boy.

CHARLEY [*an arm on* BERNARD*'s shoulder*] How do you like this kid? Gonna argue a case in front of the Supreme Court.

BERNARD [*protesting*] Pop!

WILLY [*genuinely shocked, pained, and happy*] No! The Supreme Court!

BERNARD I gotta run. 'By, Dad!

CHARLEY Knock 'em dead, Bernard!

[BERNARD *goes off.*]

WILLY [*as* CHARLEY *takes out his wallet*] The Supreme Court! And he didn't even mention it!

CHARLEY [*counting out money on the desk*] He don't have to—he's gonna do it.

WILLY And you never told him what to do, did you? You never took any interest in him.

CHARLEY My salvation is that I never took any interest in anything. There's some money—fifty dollars. I got an accountant inside.

WILLY Charley, look . . . [*With difficulty*] I got my insurance to pay. If you can manage it—I need a hundred and ten dollars.

[CHARLEY *doesn't reply for a moment; merely stops moving.*]

WILLY I'd draw it from my bank but Linda would know, and I . . .

CHARLEY Sit down, Willy.

WILLY [*moving toward the chair*] I'm keeping an account of everything, remember. I'll pay every penny back. [*He sits.*]

CHARLEY Now listen to me, Willy.

WILLY I want you to know I appreciate . . .

CHARLEY [*sitting down on the table*] Willy, what're you doin'? What the hell is goin' on in your head?

WILLY Why? I'm simply . . .

CHARLEY I offered you a job. You can make fifty dollars a week. And I won't send you on the road.

WILLY I've got a job.

CHARLEY Without pay? What kind of a job is a job without pay? [*He rises.*] Now, look, kid, enough is enough. I'm no genius but I know when I'm being insulted.

WILLY Insulted!

CHARLEY Why don't you want to work for me?

WILLY What's the matter with you? I've got a job.

CHARLEY Then what're you walkin' in here every week for?

WILLY [*getting up*] Well, if you don't want me to walk in here—

CHARLEY I am offering you a job.

WILLY I don't want your goddam job!

CHARLEY When the hell are you going to grow up?

WILLY [*furiously*] You big ignoramus, if you say that to me again I'll rap you one! I don't care how big you are! [*He's ready to fight.*]

[*Pause.*]

CHARLEY [*kindly, going to him*] How much do you need, Willy?

WILLY Charley, I'm strapped, I'm strapped. I don't know what to do. I was just fired.

CHARLEY Howard fired you?

WILLY That snotnose. Imagine that? I named him. I named him Howard.

CHARLEY Willy, when're you gonna realize that them things don't mean anything? You named him Howard, but you can't sell that. The only thing you got in this world is what you can sell. And the funny thing is that you're a salesman, and you don't know that.

WILLY I've always tried to think otherwise, I guess. I always felt that if a man was impressive, and well liked, that nothing—

CHARLEY Why must everybody like you? Who liked J. P. Morgan?[1] Was he impressive? In a Turkish bath he'd look like a butcher. But with his pockets on he was very well liked. Now listen, Willy, I know you don't like me, and nobody can say I'm in love with you, but I'll give you a job because—just for the hell of it, put it that way. Now what do you say?

WILLY I—I just can't work for you, Charley.

CHARLEY What're you, jealous of me?

WILLY I can't work for you, that's all, don't ask me why.

CHARLEY [*angered, takes out more bills*] You been jealous of me all your life, you damned fool! Here, pay your insurance. [*He puts the money in* WILLY'S *hand.*]

WILLY I'm keeping strict accounts.

CHARLEY I've got some work to do. Take care of yourself. And pay your insurance.

WILLY [*moving to the right*] Funny, y'know? After all the highways, and the trains, and the appointments, and the years, you end up worth more dead than alive.

CHARLEY Willy, nobody's worth nothin' dead. [*After a slight pause*] Did you hear what I said?

[WILLY *stands still, dreaming.*]

CHARLEY Willy!

WILLY Apologize to Bernard for me when you see him. I didn't mean to argue with him. He's a fine boy. They're all fine boys, and they'll end up big—all of them. Someday they'll all play tennis together. Wish me luck, Charley. He saw Bill Oliver today.

CHARLEY Good luck.

WILLY [*on the verge of tears*] Charley, you're the only friend I got. Isn't that a remarkable thing? [*He goes out.*]

CHARLEY Jesus!

[CHARLEY *stares after him a moment and follows. All light blacks out. Suddenly raucous music is heard, and a red glow rises behind the screen at right.* STANLEY, *a young waiter, appears, carrying a table, followed by* HAPPY, *who is carrying two chairs.*]

STANLEY [*putting the table down*] That's all right, Mr. Loman, I can handle it myself. [*He turns and takes the chairs from* HAPPY *and places them at the table.*]

1. American financier, industrialist, and philanthropist (1837–1913); he amassed an enormous fortune.

HAPPY [*glancing around*] Oh, this is better.

STANLEY Sure, in the front there you're in the middle of all kinds a noise. Whenever you got a party, Mr. Loman, you just tell me and I'll put you back here. Y'know, there's a lotta people they don't like it private, because when they go out they like to see a lotta action around them because they're sick and tired to stay in the house by theirself. But I know you, you ain't from Hackensack.[2] You know what I mean?

HAPPY [*sitting down*] So how's it coming, Stanley?

STANLEY Ah, it's a dog's life. I only wish during the war they'd a took me in the Army. I coulda been dead by now.

HAPPY My brother's back, Stanley.

STANLEY Oh, he come back, heh? From the Far West.

HAPPY Yeah, big cattle man, my brother, so treat him right. And my father's coming too.

STANLEY Oh, your father too!

HAPPY You got a couple of nice lobsters?

STANLEY Hundred per cent, big.

HAPPY I want them with the claws.

STANLEY Don't worry, I don't give you no mice. [HAPPY *laughs.*] How about some wine? It'll put a head on the meal.

HAPPY No. You remember, Stanley, that recipe I brought you from overseas? With the champagne in it?

STANLEY Oh, yeah, sure. I still got it tacked up yet in the kitchen. But that'll have to cost a buck apiece anyways.

HAPPY That's all right.

STANLEY What'd you, hit a number[3] or somethin'?

HAPPY No, it's a little celebration. My brother is—I think he pulled off a big deal today. I think we're going into business together.

STANLEY Great! That's the best for you. Because a family business, you know what I mean?—that's the best.

HAPPY That's what I think.

STANLEY 'Cause what's the difference? Somebody steals? It's in the family. Know what I mean? [*Sotto voce*[4]] Like this bartender here. The boss is goin' crazy what kinda leak he's got in the cash register. You put it in but it don't come out.

HAPPY [*raising his head*] Sh!

STANLEY What?

HAPPY You notice I wasn't lookin' right or left, was I?

STANLEY No.

HAPPY And my eyes are closed.

STANLEY So what's the—?

HAPPY Strudel's comin'.

STANLEY [*catching on, looks around*] Ah, no, there's no—

[*He breaks off as a furred, lavishly dressed girl enters and sits at the next table. Both follow her with their eyes.*]

STANLEY Geez, how'd ya know?

2. A mainly working-class town in northern New Jersey, several miles from Manhattan.
3. That is, win in an illegal lottery.
4. Under the voice (Italian); that is, spoken very softly, under the breath.

HAPPY I got radar or something. [*Staring directly at her profile*] Oooooooo . . . Stanley.

STANLEY I think that's for you, Mr. Loman.

HAPPY Look at that mouth. Oh, God. And the binoculars.

STANLEY Geez, you got a life, Mr. Loman.

HAPPY Wait on her.

STANLEY [*going to the girl's table*] Would you like a menu, ma'am?

GIRL I'm expecting someone, but I'd like a—

HAPPY Why don't you bring her—excuse me, miss, do you mind? I sell champagne, and I'd like you to try my brand. Bring her a champagne, Stanley.

GIRL That's awfully nice of you.

HAPPY Don't mention it. It's all company money. [*He laughs.*]

GIRL That's a charming product to be selling, isn't it?

HAPPY Oh, gets to be like everything else. Selling is selling, y'know.

GIRL I suppose.

HAPPY You don't happen to sell, do you?

GIRL No, I don't sell.

HAPPY Would you object to a compliment from a stranger? You ought to be on a magazine cover.

GIRL [*looking at him a little archly*] I have been.

[STANLEY *comes in with a glass of champagne.*]

HAPPY What'd I say before, Stanley? You see? She's a cover girl.

STANLEY Oh, I could see, I could see.

HAPPY [*to the* GIRL] What magazine?

GIRL Oh, a lot of them. [*She takes the drink.*] Thank you.

HAPPY You know what they say in France, don't you? "Champagne is the drink of the complexion"—Hya, Biff!

[BIFF *has entered and sits with* HAPPY.]

BIFF Hello, kid. Sorry I'm late.

HAPPY I just got here. Uh, Miss—?

GIRL Forsythe.

HAPPY Miss Forsythe, this is my brother.

BIFF Is Dad here?

HAPPY His name is Biff. You might've heard of him. Great football player.

GIRL Really? What team?

HAPPY Are you familiar with football?

GIRL No, I'm afraid I'm not.

HAPPY Biff is quarterback with the New York Giants.

GIRL Well, that is nice, isn't it? [*She drinks.*]

HAPPY Good health.

GIRL I'm happy to meet you.

HAPPY That's my name. Hap. It's really Harold, but at West Point they called me Happy.

GIRL [*now really impressed*] Oh, I see. How do you do? [*She turns her profile.*]

BIFF Isn't Dad coming?

HAPPY You want her?

BIFF Oh, I could never make that.

HAPPY I remember the time that idea would never come into your head. Where's the old confidence, Biff?

BIFF I just saw Oliver—

HAPPY Wait a minute. I've got to see that old confidence again. Do you want her? She's on call.[5]

BIFF Oh, no. [*He turns to look at the* GIRL.]

HAPPY I'm telling you. Watch this. [*Turning to the* GIRL] Honey? [*She turns to him.*] Are you busy?

GIRL Well, I am . . . but I could make a phone call.

HAPPY Do that, will you, honey? And see if you can get a friend. We'll be here for a while. Biff is one of the greatest football players in the country.

GIRL [*standing up*] Well, I'm certainly happy to meet you.

HAPPY Come back soon.

GIRL I'll try.

HAPPY Don't try, honey, try hard.

[*The* GIRL *exits.* STANLEY *follows, shaking his head in bewildered admiration.*]

HAPPY Isn't that a shame now? A beautiful girl like that? That's why I can't get married. There's not a good woman in a thousand. New York is loaded with them, kid!

BIFF Hap, look—

HAPPY I told you she was on call!

BIFF [*strangely unnerved*] Cut it out, will ya? I want to say something to you.

HAPPY Did you see Oliver?

BIFF I saw him all right. Now look, I want to tell Dad a couple of things and I want you to help me.

HAPPY What? Is he going to back you?

BIFF Are you crazy? You're out of your goddam head, you know that?

HAPPY Why? What happened?

BIFF [*breathlessly*] I did a terrible thing today, Hap. It's been the strangest day I ever went through. I'm all numb, I swear.

HAPPY You mean he wouldn't see you?

BIFF Well, I waited six hours for him, see? All day. Kept sending my name in. Even tried to date his secretary so she'd get me to him, but no soap.

HAPPY Because you're not showin' the old confidence, Biff. He remembered you, didn't he?

BIFF [*stopping* HAPPY *with a gesture*] Finally, about five o'clock, he comes out. Didn't remember who I was or anything. I felt like such an idiot, Hap.

HAPPY Did you tell him my Florida idea?

BIFF He walked away. I saw him for one minute. I got so mad I could've torn the walls down! How the hell did I ever get the idea I was a salesman there? I even believed myself that I'd been a salesman for him! And then he gave me one look and—I realized what a ridiculous lie my whole life has been! We've been talking in a dream for fifteen years. I was a shipping clerk.

HAPPY What'd you do?

BIFF [*with great tension and wonder*] Well, he left, see. And the secretary went out. I was all alone in the waiting-room. I don't know what came over

5. That is, a call girl, a prostitute.

me, Hap. The next thing I know I'm in his office—paneled walls, everything. I can't explain it. I—Hap, I took his fountain pen.

HAPPY Geez, did he catch you?

BIFF I ran out. I ran down all eleven flights. I ran and ran and ran.

HAPPY That was an awful dumb—what'd you do that for?

BIFF [*agonized*] I don't know, I just—wanted to take something, I don't know. You gotta help me, Hap, I'm gonna tell Pop.

HAPPY You crazy? What for?

BIFF Hap, he's got to understand that I'm not the man somebody lends that kind of money to. He thinks I've been spiting him all these years and it's eating him up.

HAPPY That's just it. You tell him something nice.

BIFF I can't.

HAPPY Say you got a lunch date with Oliver tomorrow.

BIFF So what do I do tomorrow?

HAPPY You leave the house tomorrow and come back at night and say Oliver is thinking it over. And he thinks it over for a couple of weeks, and gradually it fades away and nobody's the worse.

BIFF But it'll go on forever!

HAPPY Dad is never so happy as when he's looking forward to something!

[WILLY *enters.*]

HAPPY Hello, scout!

WILLY Gee, I haven't been here in years!

[STANLEY *has followed* WILLY *in and sets a chair for him.* STANLEY *starts off but* HAPPY *stops him.*]

HAPPY Stanley!

[STANLEY *stands by, waiting for an order.*]

BIFF [*going to* WILLY *with guilt, as to an invalid*] Sit down, Pop. You want a drink?

WILLY Sure, I don't mind.

BIFF Let's get a load on.

WILLY You look worried.

BIFF N-no. [*To* STANLEY] Scotch all around. Make it doubles.

STANLEY Doubles, right. [*He goes.*]

WILLY You had a couple already, didn't you?

BIFF Just a couple, yeah.

WILLY Well, what happened, boy? [*Nodding affirmatively, with a smile*] Everything go all right?

BIFF [*takes a breath, then reaches out and grasps* WILLY'S *hand*] Pal . . . [*He is smiling bravely, and* WILLY *is smiling too.*] I had an experience today.

HAPPY Terrific, Pop.

WILLY That so? What happened?

BIFF [*high, slightly alcoholic, above the earth*] I'm going to tell you everything from first to last. It's been a strange day. [*Silence. He looks around, composes himself as best he can, but his breath keeps breaking the rhythm of his voice.*] I had to wait quite a while for him, and—

WILLY Oliver?

BIFF Yeah, Oliver. All day, as a matter of cold fact. And a lot of—instances—facts, Pop, facts about my life came back to me. Who was it, Pop? Who ever said I was a salesman with Oliver?

WILLY Well, you were.

BIFF No, Dad, I was a shipping clerk.

WILLY But you were practically—

BIFF [*with determination*] Dad, I don't know who said it first, but I was never a salesman for Bill Oliver.

WILLY What're you talking about?

BIFF Let's hold on to the facts tonight, Pop. We're not going to get anywhere bullin' around. I was a shipping clerk.

WILLY [*angrily*] All right, now listen to me—

BIFF Why don't you let me finish?

WILLY I'm not interested in stories about the past or any crap of that kind because the woods are burning, boys, you understand? There's a big blaze going on all around. I was fired today.

BIFF [*shocked*] How could you be?

WILLY I was fired, and I'm looking for a little good news to tell your mother, because the woman has waited and the woman has suffered. The gist of it is that I haven't got a story left in my head, Biff. So don't give me a lecture about facts and aspects. I am not interested. Now what've you got to say to me?

[STANLEY *enters with three drinks. They wait until he leaves.*]

WILLY Did you see Oliver?

BIFF Jesus, Dad!

WILLY You mean you didn't go up there?

HAPPY Sure he went up there.

BIFF I did. I—saw him. How could they fire you?

WILLY [*on the edge of his chair*] What kind of a welcome did he give you?

BIFF He won't even let you work on commission?

WILLY I'm out! [*Driving*] So tell me, he gave you a warm welcome?

HAPPY Sure, Pop, sure!

BIFF [*driven*] Well, it was kind of—

WILLY I was wondering if he'd remember you. [*To* HAPPY] Imagine, man doesn't see him for ten, twelve years and gives him that kind of a welcome!

HAPPY Damn right!

BIFF [*trying to return to the offensive*] Pop, look—

WILLY You know why he remembered you, don't you? Because you impressed him in those days.

BIFF Let's talk quietly and get this down to the facts, huh?

WILLY [*as though* BIFF *had been interrupting*] Well, what happened? It's great news, Biff. Did he take you into his office or'd you talk in the waiting room?

BIFF Well, he came in, see, and—

WILLY [*with a big smile*] What'd he say? Betcha he threw his arm around you.

BIFF Well, he kinda—

WILLY He's a fine man. [*To* HAPPY] Very hard man to see, y'know.

HAPPY [*agreeing*] Oh, I know.

WILLY [*to Biff*] Is that where you had the drinks?

BIFF Yeah, he gave me a couple of—no, no!

HAPPY [*cutting in*] He told him my Florida idea.

WILLY Don't interrupt. [*To* BIFF] How'd he react to the Florida idea?

BIFF Dad, will you give me a minute to explain?

WILLY I've been waiting for you to explain since I sat down here! What happened? He took you into his office and what?

BIFF Well—I talked. And—and he listened, see.

WILLY Famous for the way he listens, y'know. What was his answer?

BIFF His answer was—[*He breaks off, suddenly angry.*] Dad, you're not letting me tell you what I want to tell you!

WILLY [*accusing, angered*] You didn't see him, did you?

BIFF I did see him!

WILLY What'd you insult him or something? You insulted him, didn't you?

BIFF Listen, will you let me out of it, will you just let me out of it!

HAPPY What the hell!

WILLY Tell me what happened!

BIFF [*to* HAPPY] I can't talk to him!

[*A single trumpet note jars the ear. The light of green leaves stains the house, which holds the air of night and a dream.* YOUNG BERNARD *enters and knocks on the door of the house.*]

YOUNG BERNARD [*frantically*] Mrs. Loman, Mrs. Loman!

HAPPY Tell him what happened!

BIFF [*to* HAPPY] Shut up and leave me alone!

WILLY No, no! You had to go and flunk math!

BIFF What math? What're you talking about?

YOUNG BERNARD Mrs. Loman, Mrs. Loman!

[LINDA *appears in the house, as of old.*]

WILLY [*wildly*] Math, math, math!

BIFF Take it easy, Pop!

YOUNG BERNARD Mrs. Loman!

WILLY [*furiously*] If you hadn't flunked you'd've been set by now!

BIFF Now, look, I'm gonna tell you what happened, and you're going to listen to me.

YOUNG BERNARD Mrs. Loman!

BIFF I waited six hours—

HAPPY What the hell are you saying?

BIFF I kept sending in my name but he wouldn't see me. So finally he . . . [*He continues unheard as light fades low on the restaurant.*]

YOUNG BERNARD Biff flunked math!

LINDA No!

YOUNG BERNARD Birnbaum flunked him! They won't graduate him!

LINDA But they have to. He's gotta go to the university. Where is he? Biff! Biff!

YOUNG BERNARD No, he left. He went to Grand Central.[6]

LINDA Grand—You mean he went to Boston!

YOUNG BERNARD Is Uncle Willy in Boston?

LINDA Oh, maybe Willy can talk to the teacher. Oh, the poor, poor boy!

[*Light on house area snaps out.*]

BIFF [*at the table, now audible, holding up a gold fountain pen*] . . . so I'm washed up with Oliver, you understand? Are you listening to me?

6. Grand Central Terminal, one of New York City's two main railroad stations.

WILLY [*at a loss*] Yeah, sure. If you hadn't flunked—

BIFF Flunked what? What're you talking about?

WILLY Don't blame everything on me! I didn't flunk math—you did! What pen?

HAPPY That was awful dumb, Biff, a pen like that is worth—

WILLY [*seeing the pen for the first time*] You took Oliver's pen?

BIFF [*weakening*] Dad, I just explained it to you.

WILLY You stole Bill Oliver's fountain pen!

BIFF I didn't exactly steal it! That's just what I've been explaining to you!

HAPPY He had it in his hand and just then Oliver walked in, so he got nervous and stuck it in his pocket!

WILLY My God, Biff!

BIFF I never intended to do it, Dad!

OPERATOR'S VOICE Standish Arms, good evening!

WILLY [*shouting*] I'm not in my room!

BIFF [*frightened*] Dad, what's the matter? [*He and* HAPPY *stand up.*]

OPERATOR Ringing Mr. Loman for you!

WILLY I'm not there, stop it!

BIFF [*horrified, gets down on one knee before* WILLY] Dad, I'll make good, I'll make good. [WILLY *tries to get to his feet.* BIFF *holds him down.*] Sit down now.

WILLY No, you're no good, you're no good for anything.

BIFF I am, Dad, I'll find something else, you understand? Now don't worry about anything. [*He holds up* WILLY*'s face.*] Talk to me, Dad.

OPERATOR Mr. Loman does not answer. Shall I page him?

WILLY [*attempting to stand, as though to rush and silence the* OPERATOR] No, no, no!

HAPPY He'll strike something, Pop.

WILLY No, no . . .

BIFF [*desperately, standing over* WILLY] Pop, listen! Listen to me! I'm telling you something good. Oliver talked to his partner about the Florida idea. You listening? He—he talked to his partner, and he came to me . . . I'm going to be all right, you hear? Dad, listen to me, he said it was just a question of the amount!

WILLY Then you . . . got it?

HAPPY He's gonna be terrific, Pop!

WILLY [*trying to stand*] Then you got it, haven't you? You got it! You got it!

BIFF [*agonized, holds* WILLY *down*] No, no. Look, Pop. I'm supposed to have lunch with them tomorrow. I'm just telling you this so you'll know that I can still make an impression, Pop. And I'll make good somewhere, but I can't go tomorrow, see?

WILLY Why not? You simply—

BIFF But the pen, Pop!

WILLY You give it to him and tell him it was an oversight!

HAPPY Sure, have lunch tomorrow!

BIFF I can't say that—

WILLY You were doing a crosswood puzzle and accidentally used his pen!

BIFF Listen, kid, I took those balls years ago, now I walk in with his fountain pen? That clinches it, don't you see? I can't face him like that! I'll try elsewhere.

PAGE'S VOICE Paging Mr. Loman!

WILLY Don't you want to be anything?

BIFF Pop, how can I go back?

WILLY You don't want to be anything, is that what's behind it?

BIFF [*now angry at* WILLY *for not crediting his sympathy*] Don't take it that way! You think it was easy walking into that office after what I'd done to him? A team of horses couldn't have dragged me back to Bill Oliver!

WILLY Then why'd you go?

BIFF Why did I go? Why did I go! Look at you! Look at what's become of you!

[*Off left,* THE WOMAN *laughs.*]

WILLY Biff, you're going to go to that lunch tomorrow, or—

BIFF I can't go. I've got no appointment!

HAPPY Biff, for . . . !

WILLY Are you spiting me?

BIFF Don't take it that way! Goddammit!

WILLY [*strikes* BIFF *and falters away from the table*] You rotten little louse! Are you spiting me?

THE WOMAN Someone's at the door, Willy!

BIFF I'm no good, can't you see what I am?

HAPPY [*separating them*] Hey, you're in a restaurant! Now cut it out, both of you! [*The girls enter.*] Hello, girls, sit down.

[THE WOMAN *laughs, off left.*]

MISS FORSYTHE I guess we might as well. This is Letta.

THE WOMAN Willy, are you going to wake up?

BIFF [*ignoring* WILLY] How're ya, miss, sit down. What do you drink?

MISS FORSYTHE Letta might not be able to stay long.

LETTA I gotta get up very early tomorrow. I got jury duty. I'm so excited! Were you fellows ever on a jury?

BIFF No, but I been in front of them! [*The girls laugh.*] This is my father.

LETTA Isn't he cute? Sit down with us, Pop.

HAPPY Sit him down, Biff!

BIFF [*going to him*] Come on, slugger, drink us under the table. To hell with it! Come on, sit down, pal.

[*On* BIFF*'s last insistence,* WILLY *is about to sit.*]

THE WOMAN [*now urgently*] Willy, are you going to answer the door!

[THE WOMAN*'s call pulls* WILLY *back. He starts right, befuddled.*]

BIFF Hey, where are you going?

WILLY Open the door.

BIFF The door?

WILLY The washroom . . . the door . . . where's the door?

BIFF [*leading* WILLY *to the left*] Just go straight down.

[WILLY *moves left.*]

THE WOMAN Willy, Willy, are you going to get up, get up, get up, get up?

[WILLY *exits left.*]

LETTA I think it's sweet you bring your daddy along.

MISS FORSYTHE Oh, he isn't really your father!

BIFF [*at left, turning to her resentfully*] Miss Forsythe, you've just seen a prince walk by. A fine, troubled prince. A hard-working, unappreciated prince. A pal, you understand? A good companion. Always for his boys.

LETTA That's so sweet.

HAPPY Well, girls, what's the program? We're wasting time. Come on, Biff. Gather round. Where would you like to go?

BIFF Why don't you do something for him?

HAPPY Me!

BIFF Don't you give a damn for him, Hap?

HAPPY What're you talking about? I'm the one who—

BIFF I sense it, you don't give a good goddam about him. [*He takes the rolled-up hose from his pocket and puts it on the table in front of* HAPPY.] Look what I found in the cellar, for Christ's sake. How can you bear to let it go on?

HAPPY Me? Who goes away? Who runs off and—

BIFF Yeah, but he doesn't mean anything to you. You could help him—I can't! Don't you understand what I'm talking about? He's going to kill himself, don't you know that?

HAPPY Don't I know it! Me!

BIFF Hap, help him! Jesus . . . help him . . . Help me, help me, I can't bear to look at his face! [*Ready to weep, he hurries out, up right.*]

HAPPY [*starting after him*] Where are you going?

MISS FORSYTHE What's he so mad about?

HAPPY Come on, girls, we'll catch up with him.

MISS FORSYTHE [*as Happy pushes her out*] Say, I don't like that temper of his!

HAPPY He's just a little overstrung, he'll be all right!

WILLY [*off left, as* THE WOMAN *laughs*] Don't answer! Don't answer!

LETTA Don't you want to tell your father—

HAPPY No, that's not my father. He's just a guy. Come on, we'll catch Biff, and, honey, we're going to paint this town! Stanley, where's the check! Hey, Stanley!

[*They exit.* STANLEY *looks toward left.*]

STANLEY [*calling to* HAPPY *indignantly*] Mr. Loman! Mr. Loman!

[STANLEY *picks up a chair and follows them off. Knocking is heard off left.* THE WOMAN *enters, laughing.* WILLY *follows her. She is in a black slip; he is buttoning his shirt. Raw, sensuous music accompanies their speech.*]

WILLY Will you stop laughing? Will you stop?

THE WOMAN Aren't you going to answer the door? He'll wake the whole hotel.

WILLY I'm not expecting anybody.

THE WOMAN Whyn't you have another drink, honey, and stop being so damn self-centered?

WILLY I'm so lonely.

THE WOMAN You know you ruined me, Willy? From now on, whenever you come to the office, I'll see that you go right through to the buyers. No waiting at my desk anymore, Willy. You ruined me.

WILLY That's nice of you to say that.

THE WOMAN Gee, you are self-centered! Why so sad? You are the saddest, self-centeredest soul I ever did see-saw. [*She laughs. He kisses her.*] Come on inside, drummer[7] boy. It's silly to be dressing in the middle of the night. [*As knocking is heard*] Aren't you going to answer the door?

7. A commercial traveler, a salesman.

WILLY They're knocking on the wrong door.

THE WOMAN But I felt the knocking. And he heard us talking in here. Maybe the hotel's on fire!

WILLY [*his terror rising*] It's a mistake.

THE WOMAN Then tell him to go away!

WILLY There's nobody there.

THE WOMAN It's getting on my nerves, Willy. There's somebody standing out there and it's getting on my nerves!

WILLY [*pushing her away from him*] All right, stay in the bathroom here, and don't come out. I think there's a law in Massachusetts about it,[8] so don't come out. It may be that new room clerk. He looked very mean. So don't come out. It's a mistake, there's no fire.

[*The knocking is heard again. He takes a few steps away from her, and she vanishes into the wing. The light follows him, and now he is facing* YOUNG BIFF, *who carries a suitcase. Biff steps toward him. The music is gone.*]

BIFF Why didn't you answer?

WILLY Biff! What are you doing in Boston?

BIFF Why didn't you answer? I've been knocking for five minutes, I called you on the phone—

WILLY I just heard you. I was in the bathroom and had the door shut. Did anything happen home?

BIFF Dad—I let you down.

WILLY What do you mean?

BIFF Dad . . .

WILLY Biffo, what's this about? [*Putting his arm around* BIFF] Come on, let's go downstairs and get you a malted.

BIFF Dad, I flunked math.

WILLY Not for the term?

BIFF The term. I haven't got enough credits to graduate.

WILLY You mean to say Bernard wouldn't give you the answers?

BIFF He did, he tried, but I only got a sixty-one.

WILLY And they wouldn't give you four points?

BIFF Birnbaum refused absolutely. I begged him, Pop, but he won't give me those points. You gotta talk to him before they close the school. Because if he saw the kind of man you are, and you just talked to him in your way, I'm sure he'd come through for me. The class came right before practice, see, and I didn't go enough. Would you talk to him? He'd like you, Pop. You know the way you could talk.

WILLY You're on. We'll drive right back.

BIFF Oh, Dad, good work! I'm sure he'll change it for you!

WILLY Go downstairs and tell the clerk I'm checkin' out. Go right down.

BIFF Yes, sir! See, the reason he hates me, Pop—one day he was late for class so I got up at the blackboard and imitated him. I crossed my eyes and talked with a lithp.

WILLY [*laughing*] You did? The kids like it?

BIFF They nearly died laughing!

8. That is, adultery, which is a felony in Massachusetts, though this law was rarely enforced even in the 1940s.

WILLY Yeah? What'd you do?

BIFF The thquare root of thixthy twee is . . . [WILLY *bursts out laughing;* BIFF *joins him.*] And in the middle of it he walked in!

[WILLY *laughs and* THE WOMAN *joins in offstage.*]

WILLY [*without hesitation*] Hurry downstairs and—

BIFF Somebody in there?

WILLY No, that was next door.

[THE WOMAN *laughs offstage.*]

BIFF Somebody got in your bathroom!

WILLY No, it's the next room, there's a party—

THE WOMAN [*enters, laughing. She lisps this*] Can I come in? There's something in the bathtub, Willy, and it's moving!

[WILLY *looks at* BIFF, *who is staring open-mouthed and horrified at* THE WOMAN.]

WILLY Ah—you better go back to your room. They must be finished painting by now. They're painting her room so I let her take a shower here. Go back, go back . . . [*He pushes her.*]

THE WOMAN [*resisting*] But I've got to get dressed, Willy, I can't—

WILLY Get out of here! Go back, go back . . . [*Suddenly striving for the ordinary*] This is Miss Francis, Biff, she's a buyer. They're painting her room. Go back, Miss Francis, go back . . .

THE WOMAN But my clothes, I can't go out naked in the hall!

WILLY [*pushing her offstage*] Get outa here! Go back, go back!

[BIFF *slowly sits down on his suitcase as the argument continues offstage.*]

THE WOMAN Where's my stockings? You promised me stockings, Willy!

WILLY I have no stockings here!

THE WOMAN You had two boxes of size nine sheers for me, and I want them!

WILLY Here, for God's sake, will you get outa here!

THE WOMAN [*enters holding a box of stockings*] I just hope there's nobody in the hall. That's all I hope. [*To* BIFF] Are you football or baseball?

BIFF Football.

THE WOMAN [*angry, humiliated*] That's me too. G'night. [*She snatches her clothes from* WILLY, *and walks out.*]

WILLY [*after a pause*] Well, better get going. I want to get to the school first thing in the morning. Get my suits out of the closet. I'll get my valise. [BIFF *doesn't move.*] What's the matter? [BIFF *remains motionless, tears falling.*] She's a buyer. Buys for J. H. Simmons. She lives down the hall—they're painting. You don't imagine—[*He breaks off. After a pause*] Now listen, pal, she's just a buyer. She sees merchandise in her room and they have to keep it looking just so . . . [*Pause. Assuming command*] All right, get my suits. [BIFF *doesn't move.*] Now stop crying and do as I say. I gave you an order. Biff, I gave you an order! Is that what you do when I give you an order? How dare you cry! [*Putting his arm around Biff*] Now look, Biff, when you grow up you'll understand about these things. You mustn't—you mustn't overemphasize a thing like this. I'll see Birnbaum first thing in the morning.

BIFF Never mind.

WILLY [*getting down beside* BIFF] Never mind! He's going to give you those points. I'll see to it.

BIFF He wouldn't listen to you.

WILLY He certainly will listen to me. You need those points for the U. of Virginia.

BIFF I'm not going there.

WILLY Heh? If I can't get him to change that mark you'll make it up in summer school. You've got all summer to—

BIFF [*his weeping breaking from him*] Dad . . .

WILLY [*infected by it*] Oh, my boy . . .

BIFF Dad . . .

WILLY She's nothing to me, Biff. I was lonely, I was terribly lonely.

BIFF You—you gave her Mama's stockings! [*His tears break through and he rises to go.*]

WILLY [*grabbing for* BIFF] I gave you an order!

BIFF Don't touch me, you—liar!

WILLY Apologize for that!

BIFF You fake! You phony little fake! You fake! [*Overcome, he turns quickly and weeping fully goes out with his suitcase.* WILLY *is left on the floor on his knees.*]

WILLY I gave you an order! Biff, come back here or I'll beat you! Come back here! I'll whip you!

[STANLEY *comes quickly in from the right and stands in front of* WILLY.]

WILLY [*shouts at Stanley*] I gave you an order . . .

STANLEY Hey, let's pick it up, pick it up, Mr. Loman. [*He helps* WILLY *to his feet.*] Your boys left with the chippies.[9] They said they'll see you home.

[*A second waiter watches some distance away.*]

WILLY But we were supposed to have dinner together.

[*Music is heard,* WILLY*'s theme.*]

STANLEY Can you make it?

WILLY I'll—sure, I can make it. [*Suddenly concerned about his clothes*] Do I—I look all right?

STANLEY Sure, you look all right. [*He flicks a speck off* WILLY*'s lapel.*]

WILLY Here—here's a dollar.

STANLEY Oh, your son paid me. It's all right.

WILLY [*putting it in* STANLEY*'s hand*] No, take it. You're a good boy.

STANLEY Oh, no, you don't have to . . .

WILLY Here—here's some more, I don't need it anymore. [*After a slight pause*] Tell me—is there a seed store in the neighborhood?

STANLEY Seeds? You mean like to plant?

[*As* WILLY *turns,* STANLEY *slips the money back into his jacket pocket.*]

WILLY Yes. Carrots, peas . . .

STANLEY Well, there's hardware stores on Sixth Avenue, but it may be too late now.

WILLY [*anxiously*] Oh, I'd better hurry, I've got to get some seeds. [*He starts off to the right.*] I've got to get some seeds, right away. Nothing's planted. I don't have a thing in the ground.

[WILLY *hurries out as the light goes down.* STANLEY *moves over to the right after him, watches him off. The other waiter has been staring at* WILLY.]

9. Tramps, prostitutes.

STANLEY [*to the waiter*] Well, whatta you looking at?

[*The waiter picks up the chairs and moves off right.* STANLEY *takes the table and follows him. The light fades on this area. There is a long pause, the sound of the flute coming over. The light gradually rises on the kitchen, which is empty.* HAPPY *appears at the door of the house, followed by* BIFF. HAPPY *is carrying a large bunch of long-stemmed roses. He enters the kitchen, looks around for* LINDA. *Not seeing her, he turns to* BIFF, *who is just outside the house door, and makes a gesture with his hands, indicating "Not here, I guess." He looks into the living room and freezes. Inside, Linda, unseen, is seated,* WILLY'S *coat on her lap. She rises ominously and quietly and moves toward* HAPPY, *who backs up into the kitchen, afraid.*]

HAPPY Hey, what're you doing up? [LINDA *says nothing but moves toward him implacably.*] Where's Pop? [*He keeps backing to the right, and now* LINDA *is in full view in the doorway to the living room.*] Is he sleeping?

LINDA Where were you?

HAPPY [*trying to laugh it off*] We met two girls, Mom, very fine types. Here, we brought you some flowers. [*Offering them to her*] Put them in your room, Ma.

[*She knocks them to the floor at* BIFF'S *feet. He has now come inside and closed the door behind him. She stares at* BIFF, *silent.*]

HAPPY Now what'd you do that for? Mom, I want you to have some flowers—

LINDA [*cutting* HAPPY *off, violently to* BIFF] Don't you care whether he lives or dies?

HAPPY [*going to the stairs*] Come upstairs, Biff.

BIFF [*with a flare of disgust, to* HAPPY] Go away from me! [*To* LINDA] What do you mean, lives or dies? Nobody's dying around here, pal.

LINDA Get out of my sight! Get out of here!

BIFF I wanna see the boss.

LINDA You're not going near him!

BIFF Where is he? [*He moves into the living room and* LINDA *follows.*]

LINDA [*shouting after* BIFF] You invite him for dinner. He looks forward to it all day—[BIFF *appears in his parents' bedroom, looks around, and exits.*]—and then you desert him there. There's no stranger you'd do that to!

HAPPY Why? He had a swell time with us. Listen, when I—[LINDA *comes back into the kitchen.*]—desert him I hope I don't outlive the day!

LINDA Get out of here!

HAPPY Now look, Mom . . .

LINDA Did you have to go to women tonight? You and your lousy rotten whores!

[BIFF *reenters the kitchen.*]

HAPPY Mom, all we did was follow Biff around trying to cheer him up! [*To* BIFF] Boy, what a night you gave me!

LINDA Get out of here, both of you, and don't come back! I don't want you tormenting him anymore. Go on now, get your things together! [*To* BIFF] You can sleep in his apartment. [*She starts to pick up the flowers and stops herself.*] Pick up this stuff, I'm not your maid anymore. Pick it up, you bum, you!

[HAPPY *turns his back to her in refusal.* BIFF *slowly moves over and gets down on his knees, picking up the flowers.*]

LINDA You're a pair of animals! Not one, not another living soul would have had the cruelty to walk out on that man in a restaurant!

BIFF [*not looking at her*] Is that what he said?

LINDA He didn't have to say anything. He was so humiliated he nearly limped when he came in.

HAPPY But, Mom, he had a great time with us—

BIFF [*cutting him off violently*] Shut up!

[*Without another word,* HAPPY *goes upstairs.*]

LINDA You! You didn't even go in to see if he was all right!

BIFF [*still on the floor in front of* LINDA, *the flowers in his hand; with self-loathing*] No. Didn't. Didn't do a damned thing. How do you like that, heh? Left him babbling in a toilet.

LINDA You louse. You . . .

BIFF Now you hit it on the nose! [*He gets up, throws the flowers in the wastebasket.*] The scum of the earth, and you're looking at him!

LINDA Get out of here!

BIFF I gotta talk to the boss, Mom. Where is he?

LINDA You're not going near him. Get out of this house!

BIFF [*with absolute assurance, determination*] No. We're gonna have an abrupt conversation, him and me.

LINDA You're not talking to him!

[*Hammering is heard from outside the house, off right.* BIFF *turns toward the noise.*]

LINDA [*suddenly pleading*] Will you please leave him alone?

BIFF What's he doing out there?

LINDA He's planting the garden!

BIFF [*quietly*] Now? Oh, my God!

[BIFF *moves outside,* LINDA *following. The light dies down on them and comes up on the center of the apron as* WILLY *walks into it. He is carrying a flashlight, a hoe, and a handful of seed packets. He raps the top of the hoe sharply to fix it firmly, and then moves to the left, measuring off the distance with his foot. He holds the flashlight to look at the seed packets, reading off the instructions. He is in the blue of night.*]

WILLY Carrots . . . quarter-inch apart. Rows . . . one-foot rows. [*He measures it off.*] One foot. [*He puts down a package and measures off.*] Beets. [*He puts down another package and measures again.*] Lettuce. [*He reads the package, puts it down.*] One foot—[*He breaks off as* BEN *appears at the right and moves slowly down to him.*] What a proposition, ts, ts. Terrific, terrific. 'Cause she's suffered, Ben, the woman has suffered. You understand me? A man can't go out the way he came in, Ben, a man has got to add up to something. You can't, you can't—[BEN *moves toward him as though to interrupt.*] You gotta consider, now. Don't answer so quick. Remember, it's a guaranteed twenty-thousand-dollar proposition. Now look, Ben, I want you to go through the ins and outs of this thing with me. I've got nobody to talk to, Ben, and the woman has suffered, you hear me?

BEN [*standing still, considering*] What's the proposition?

WILLY It's twenty thousand dollars on the barrelhead. Guaranteed, gilt-edged, you understand?

BEN You don't want to make a fool of yourself. They might not honor the policy.

WILLY How can they dare refuse? Didn't I work like a coolie to meet every premium on the nose? And now they don't pay off? Impossible!

BEN It's called a cowardly thing, William.

WILLY Why? Does it take more guts to stand here the rest of my life ringing up a zero?

BEN [*yielding*] That's a point, William. [*He moves, thinking, turns.*] And twenty thousand—that *is* something one can feel with the hand, it is there.

WILLY [*now assured, with rising power*] Oh, Ben, that's the whole beauty of it! I see it like a diamond, shining in the dark, hard and rough, that I can pick up and touch in my hand. Not like—like an appointment! This would not be another damned-fool appointment, Ben, and it changes all the aspects. Because he thinks I'm nothing, see and so he spites me. But the funeral—[*Straightening up*] Ben, that funeral will be massive! They'll come from Maine, Massachusetts, Vermont, New Hampshire! All the old-timers with the strange license plates—that boy will be thunder-struck, Ben, because he never realized—I am known! Rhode Island, New York, New Jersey—I am known, Ben, and he'll see it with his eyes once and for all. He'll see what I am, Ben! He's in for a shock, that boy!

BEN [*coming down to the edge of the garden*] He'll call you a coward.

WILLY [*suddenly fearful*] No, that would be terrible.

BEN Yes. And a damned fool.

WILLY No, no, he mustn't, I won't have that! [*He is broken and desperate.*]

BEN He'll hate you, William.

[*The gay music of the Boys is heard.*]

WILLY Oh, Ben, how do we get back to all the great times? Used to be so full of light, and comradeship, the sleigh-riding in winter, and the ruddiness on his cheeks. And always some kind of good news coming up, always something nice coming up ahead. And never even let me carry the valises in the house, and simonizing, simonizing that little red car! Why, why can't I give him something and not have him hate me?

BEN Let me think about it. [*He glances at his watch.*] I still have a little time. Remarkable proposition, but you've got to be sure you're not making a fool of yourself.

[BEN *drifts off upstage and goes out of sight.* BIFF *comes down from the left.*]

WILLY [*suddenly conscious of* BIFF, *turns and looks up at him, then begins picking up the packages of seeds in confusion*] Where the hell is that seed? [*Indignantly*] You can't see nothing out here! They boxed in the whole goddam neighborhood!

BIFF There are people all around here. Don't you realize that?

WILLY I'm busy. Don't bother me.

BIFF [*taking the hoe from* WILLY] I'm saying good-by to you, Pop. [WILLY *looks at him, silent, unable to move.*] I'm not coming back anymore.

WILLY You're not going to see Oliver tomorrow?

BIFF I've got no appointment, Dad.

WILLY He put his arm around you, and you've got no appointment?

BIFF Pop, get this now, will you? Everytime I've left it's been a fight that sent me out of here. Today I realized something about myself and I tried to explain it to you and I—I think I'm just not smart enough to make any sense out of it for you. To hell with whose fault it is or anything like that. [*He takes* WILLY*'s arm.*] Let's just wrap it up, heh? Come on in, we'll tell Mom. [*He gently tries to pull* WILLY *to left.*]

WILLY [*frozen, immobile, with guilt in his voice*] No, I don't want to see her.

BIFF Come on! [*He pulls again, and* WILLY *tries to pull away.*]

WILLY [*highly nervous*] No, no, I don't want to see her.

BIFF [*tries to look into* WILLY*'s face, as if to find the answer there*] Why don't you want to see her?

WILLY [*more harshly now*] Don't bother me, will you?

BIFF What do you mean, you don't want to see her? You don't want them calling you yellow, do you? This isn't your fault; it's me, I'm a bum. Now come inside! [WILLY *strains to get away.*] Did you hear what I said to you?

[WILLY *pulls away and quickly goes by himself into the house.* BIFF *follows.*]

LINDA [*to* WILLY] Did you plant, dear?

BIFF [*at the door, to* LINDA] All right, we had it out. I'm going and I'm not writing anymore.

LINDA [*going to* WILLY *in the kitchen*] I think that's the best way, dear. 'Cause there's no use drawing it out, you'll just never get along.

[WILLY *doesn't respond.*]

BIFF People ask where I am and what I'm doing, you don't know, and you don't care. That way it'll be off your mind and you can start brightening up again. All right? That clears it, doesn't it? [WILLY *is silent, and* BIFF *goes to him.*] You gonna wish me luck, scout? [*He extends his hand.*] What do you say?

LINDA Shake his hand, Willy.

WILLY [*turning to her, seething with hurt*] There's no necessity to mention the pen at all, y'know.

BIFF [*gently*] I've got no appointment, Dad.

WILLY [*erupting fiercely*] He put his arm around . . . ?

BIFF Dad, you're never going to see what I am, so what's the use of arguing? If I strike oil I'll send you a check. Meantime forget I'm alive.

WILLY [*to* LINDA] Spite, see?

BIFF Shake hands, Dad.

WILLY Not my hand.

BIFF I was hoping not to go this way.

WILLY Well, this is the way you're going. Good-by.

[BIFF *looks at him a moment, then turns sharply and goes to the stairs.*]

WILLY [*stops him with*] May you rot in hell if you leave this house!

BIFF [*turning*] Exactly what is it that you want from me?

WILLY I want you to know, on the train, in the mountains, in the valleys, wherever you go, that you cut down your life for spite!

BIFF No, no.

WILLY Spite, spite, is the word of your undoing! And when you're down and out, remember what did it. When you're rotting somewhere beside the railroad tracks, remember, and don't you dare blame it on me!

BIFF I'm not blaming it on you!

WILLY I won't take the rap for this, you hear?

[HAPPY *comes down the stairs and stands on the bottom step, watching.*]

BIFF That's just what I'm telling you!

WILLY [*sinking into a chair at the table, with full accusation*] You're trying to put a knife in me—don't think I don't know what you're doing!

BIFF All right, phony! Then let's lay it on the line. [*He whips the rubber tube out of his pocket and puts it on the table.*]

HAPPY You crazy—

LINDA Biff! [*She moves to grab the hose, but* BIFF *holds it down with his hand.*]

BIFF Leave it there! Don't move it!

WILLY [*not looking at it*] What is that?

BIFF You know goddam well what that is.

WILLY [*caged, wanting to escape*] I never saw that.

BIFF You saw it. The mice didn't bring it into the cellar! What is this supposed to do, make a hero out of you? This supposed to make me sorry for you?

WILLY Never heard of it.

BIFF There'll be no pity for you, you hear it? No pity!

WILLY [*to* LINDA] You hear the spite!

BIFF No, you're going to hear the truth—what you are and what I am!

LINDA Stop it!

WILLY Spite!

HAPPY [*coming down toward* BIFF] You cut it now!

BIFF [*to* HAPPY] The man don't know who we are! The man is gonna know! [*To* WILLY] We never told the truth for ten minutes in this house!

HAPPY We always told the truth!

BIFF [*turning on him*] You big blow, are you the assistant buyer? You're one of the two assistants to the assistant, aren't you?

HAPPY Well, I'm practically—

BIFF You're practically full of it! We all are! And I'm through with it. [*To* WILLY] Now hear this, Willy, this is me.

WILLY I know you!

BIFF You know why I had no address for three months? I stole a suit in Kansas City and I was in jail. [*To* LINDA, *who is sobbing*] Stop crying. I'm through with it.

[LINDA *turns away from them, her hands covering her face.*]

WILLY I suppose that's my fault!

BIFF I stole myself out of every good job since high school!

WILLY And whose fault is that?

BIFF And I never got anywhere because you blew me so full of hot air I could never stand taking orders from anybody! That's whose fault it is!

WILLY I hear that!

LINDA Don't, Biff!

BIFF It's goddam time you heard that! I had to be boss big shot in two weeks, and I'm through with it!

WILLY Then hang yourself! For spite, hang yourself!

BIFF No! Nobody's hanging himself, Willy! I ran down eleven flights with a pen in my hand today. And suddenly I stopped, you hear me? And in the middle of that office building, do you hear this? I stopped in the middle of that building and I saw—the sky. I saw the things that I love in this world. The work and the food and time to sit and smoke. And I looked at the pen and said to myself, what the hell am I grabbing this for? Why am I trying to become what I don't want to be? What am I doing in an office, making a contemptuous, begging fool of myself, when all I want is out there, waiting for me the minute I say I know who I am! Why can't I say that, Willy? [*He tries to make* WILLY *face him, but* WILLY *pulls away and moves to the left.*]

WILLY [*with hatred, threateningly*] The door of your life is wide open!

BIFF Pop! I'm a dime a dozen, and so are you!

WILLY [*turning on him now in an uncontrolled outburst*] I am not a dime a dozen! I am Willy Loman, and you are Biff Loman!

[BIFF *starts for* WILLY, *but is blocked by* HAPPY. *In his fury,* BIFF *seems on the verge of attacking his father.*]

BIFF I am not a leader of men, Willy, and neither are you. You were never anything but a hard-working drummer who landed in the ash can like all the rest of them! I'm one dollar an hour, Willy! I tried seven states and couldn't raise it. A buck an hour! Do you gather my meaning? I'm not bringing home any prizes anymore, and you're going to stop waiting for me to bring them home!

WILLY [*directly to* BIFF] You vengeful, spiteful mut!

[BIFF *breaks from* HAPPY. WILLY, *in fright, starts up the stairs.* BIFF *grabs him.*]

BIFF [*at the peak of his fury*] Pop, I'm nothing! I'm nothing, Pop. Can't you understand that? There's no spite in it anymore. I'm just what I am, that's all.

[BIFF's *fury has spent itself, and he breaks down, sobbing, holding on to* WILLY, *who dumbly fumbles for* BIFF's *face.*]

WILLY [*astonished*] What're you doing? What're you doing? [*To* LINDA] Why is he crying?

BIFF [*crying, broken*] Will you let me go, for Christ's sake? Will you take that phony dream and burn it before something happens? [*Struggling to contain himself, he pulls away and moves to the stairs.*] I'll go in the morning. Put him—put him to bed. [*Exhausted,* BIFF *moves up the stairs to his room.*]

WILLY [*after a long pause, astonished, elevated*] Isn't that—isn't that remarkable? Biff—he likes me!

LINDA He loves you, Willy!

HAPPY [*deeply moved*] Always did, Pop.

WILLY Oh, Biff! [*Staring wildly*] He cried! Cried to me. [*He is choking with his love, and now cries out his promise*] That boy—that boy is going to be magnificent!

[BEN *appears in the light just outside the kitchen.*]

BEN Yes, outstanding, with twenty thousand behind him.

LINDA [*sensing the racing of his mind, fearfully, carefully*] Now come to bed, Willy. It's all settled now.

WILLY [*finding it difficult not to rush out of the house*] Yes, we'll sleep. Come on. Go to sleep, Hap.

BEN And it does take a great kind of a man to crack the jungle.

[*In accents of dread,* BEN's *idyllic music starts up.*]

HAPPY [*his arm around* LINDA] I'm getting married, Pop, don't forget it. I'm changing everything. I'm gonna run that department before the year is up. You'll see, Mom. [*He kisses her.*]

BEN The jungle is dark but full of diamonds, Willy.

[WILLY *turns, moves, listening to* BEN.]

LINDA Be good. You're both good boys, just act that way, that's all.

HAPPY Night, Pop. [*He goes upstairs.*]

LINDA [*to* WILLY] Come, dear.

BEN [*with greater force*] One must go in to fetch a diamond out.

WILLY [*to* LINDA, *as he moves slowly along the edge of the kitchen, toward the door*] I just want to get settled down, Linda. Let me sit alone for a little.

LINDA [*almost uttering her fear*] I want you upstairs.

WILLY [*taking her in his arms*] In a few minutes, Linda. I couldn't sleep right now. Go on, you look awful tired. [*He kisses her.*]

BEN Not like an appointment at all. A diamond is rough and hard to the touch.

WILLY Go on now. I'll be right up.

LINDA I think this is the only way, Willy.

WILLY Sure, it's the best thing.

BEN Best thing!

WILLY The only way. Everything is gonna be—go on, kid, get to bed. You look so tired.

LINDA Come right up.

WILLY Two minutes.

[LINDA *goes into the living room, then reappears in her bedroom.* WILLY *moves just outside the kitchen door.*]

WILLY Loves me. [*Wonderingly*] Always loved me. Isn't that a remarkable thing? Ben, he'll worship me for it!

BEN [*with promise*] It's dark there, but full of diamonds.

WILLY Can you imagine that magnificence with twenty thousand dollars in his pocket?

LINDA [*calling from her room*] Willy! Come up!

WILLY [*calling into the kitchen*] Yes! Yes. Coming! It's very smart, you realize that, don't you, sweetheart? Even Ben sees it. I gotta go, baby. 'By! 'By! [*Going over to Ben, almost dancing*] Imagine? When the mail comes he'll be ahead of Bernard again!

BEN A perfect proposition all around.

WILLY Did you see how he cried to me? Oh, if I could kiss him, Ben!

BEN Time, William, time!

WILLY Oh, Ben, I always knew one way or another we were gonna make it, Biff and I!

BEN [*looking at his watch*] The boat. We'll be late. [*He moves slowly off into the darkness.*]

WILLY [*elegiacally, turning to the house*] Now when you kick off, boy, I want a seventy-yard boot, and get right down the field under the ball, and when you hit, hit low and hit hard, because it's important, boy. [*He swings around and faces the audience.*] There's all kinds of important people in the stands, and the first thing you know . . . [*Suddenly realizing he is alone*] Ben! Ben, where do I . . . ? [*He makes a sudden movement of search.*] Ben, how do I . . . ?

LINDA [*calling*] Willy, you coming up?

WILLY [*uttering a gasp of fear, whirling about as if to quiet her*] Sh! [*He turns around as if to find his way; sounds, faces, voices, seem to be swarming in upon him and he flicks at them, crying*] Sh! Sh! [*Suddenly music, faint and *high, stops him. It rises in intensity, almost to an unbearable scream. He goes up and down on his toes, and rushes off around the house.*] Shhh!

LINDA Willy?

[*There is no answer.* LINDA *waits.* BIFF *gets up off his bed. He is still in his clothes.* HAPPY *sits up.* BIFF *stands listening.*]

LINDA [*with real fear*] Willy, answer me! Willy!

[*There is the sound of a car starting and moving away at full speed.*]

LINDA No!

BIFF [*rushing down the stairs*] Pop!

[*As the car speeds off, the music crashes down in a frenzy of sound, which becomes the soft pulsation of a single cello string.* BIFF *slowly returns to his bedroom. He and* HAPPY *gravely don their jackets.* LINDA *slowly walks out of her room. The music has developed into a dead march. The leaves of day are appearing over everything.* CHARLEY *and* BERNARD, *somberly dressed, appear and knock on the kitchen door.* BIFF *and* HAPPY *slowly descend the stairs to the kitchen as* CHARLEY *and* BERNARD *enter. All stop a moment when* LINDA, *in clothes of mourning, bearing a little bunch of roses, comes through the draped doorway into the kitchen. She goes to* CHARLEY *and takes his arm. Now all move toward the audience, through the wall-line of the kitchen. At the limit of the apron,* LINDA *lays down the flowers, kneels, and sits back on her heels. All stare down at the grave.*]

Requiem[1]

CHARLEY It's getting dark, Linda.

[LINDA *doesn't react. She stares at the grave.*]

BIFF How about it, Mom? Better get some rest, heh? They'll be closing the gate soon.

[LINDA *makes no move. Pause.*]

HAPPY [*deeply angered*] He had no right to do that. There was no necessity for it. We would've helped him.

CHARLEY [*grunting*] Hmmm.

BIFF Come along, Mom.

LINDA Why didn't anybody come?

CHARLEY It was a very nice funeral.

LINDA But where are all the people he knew? Maybe they blame him.

CHARLEY Naa. It's a rough world, Linda. They wouldn't blame him.

LINDA I can't understand it. At this time especially. First time in thirty-five years we were just about free and clear. He only needed a little salary. He was even finished with the dentist.

CHARLEY No man only needs a little salary.

LINDA I can't understand it.

BIFF There were a lot of nice days. When he'd come home from a trip; or on Sundays, making the stoop; finishing the cellar; putting on the new porch; when he built the extra bathroom; and put up the garage. You know something, Charley, there's more of him in that front stoop than in all the sales he ever made.

CHARLEY Yeah. He was a happy man with a batch of cement.

1. In Roman Catholicism, a special mass for the repose of departed souls; also, a musical setting for such a mass, and by extension any solemn dirge or chant for the dead.

LINDA He was so wonderful with his hands.

BIFF He had the wrong dreams. All, all, wrong.

HAPPY [*almost ready to fight* BIFF] Don't say that!

BIFF He never knew who he was.

CHARLEY [*stopping* HAPPY'S *movement and reply. To* BIFF] Nobody dast blame this man. You don't understand: Willy was a salesman. And for a salesman, there is no rock bottom to the life. He don't put a bolt to a nut, he don't tell you the law or give you medicine. He's a man way out there in the blue, riding on a smile and a shoeshine. And when they start not smiling back—that's an earthquake. And then you get yourself a couple of spots on your hat, and you're finished. Nobody dast blame this man. A salesman is got to dream, boy. It comes with the territory.

BIFF Charley, the man didn't know who he was.

HAPPY [*infuriated*] Don't say that!

BIFF Why don't you come with me, Happy?

HAPPY I'm not licked that easily. I'm staying right in this city, and I'm gonna beat this racket! [*He looks at* BIFF, *his chin set.*] The Loman Brothers!

BIFF I know who I am, kid.

HAPPY All right, boy. I'm gonna show you and everybody else that Willy Loman did not die in vain. He had a good dream. It's the only dream you can have—to come out number-one man. He fought it out here, and this is where I'm gonna win it for him.

BIFF [*with a hopeless glance at* HAPPY, *bends toward his mother*] Let's go, Mom.

LINDA I'll be with you in a minute. Go on, Charley. [*He hesitates.*] I want to, just for a minute. I never had a chance to say good-by.

[CHARLEY *moves away, followed by* HAPPY. BIFF *remains a slight distance up and left of* LINDA. *She sits there, summoning herself. The flute begins, not far away, playing behind her speech.*]

LINDA Forgive me, dear. I can't cry. I don't know what it is, but I can't cry. I don't understand it. Why did you ever do that? Help me, Willy, I can't cry. It seems to me that you're just on another trip. I keep expecting you. Willy, dear, I can't cry. Why did you do it? I search and search and I search, and I can't understand it, Willy. I made the last payment on the house today. Today, dear. And there'll be nobody home. [*A sob rises in her throat.*] We're free and clear. [*Sobbing more fully, released*] We're free. [BIFF *comes slowly toward her.*] We're free . . . We're free . . .

[BIFF *lifts her to her feet and moves out up right with her in his arms.* LINDA *sobs quietly.* BERNARD *and* CHARLEY *come together and follow them, followed by* HAPPY. *Only the music of the flute is left on the darkening stage as over the house the hard towers of the apartment buildings rise into sharp focus, and*]

The curtain falls.

TAWFIQ AL-HAKIM

1898–1987

COMMONLY regarded as the founder of modern Egyptian drama, Tawfiq al-Hakim is a towering literary figure in Egypt and the Arab world. His diverse literary output includes plays, short stories, poems, autobiographies, essays, and novels, but his reputation rests mostly on his dramatic work. Driven by what he called a "creative panic" to explore new artistic terrain and new modes of expression, al-Hakim continuously examined fresh perspectives and challenged the social and artistic status quo. Throughout his long life, al-Hakim was also involved in the intellectual and political ferment of his country, and by the 1980s, he was widely revered as a sage and elder statesman as well as one of the most prominent Arab writers. Produced domestically and internationally, such plays as *SONG OF DEATH* (1950), address the shifting cultural and political landscapes of twentieth-century Egypt and the broader Arab world.

Born to a rural upper-middle-class family, al-Hakim was pushed by his parents to become a lawyer. In 1920, he was sent to live with his uncles in Cairo to finish his undergraduate studies in law, but al-Hakim spent this unsupervised time attending plays and getting to know Cairo's theatrical community. Before long, he started writing musicals and farces—the most popular theatrical forms at that time—for the well-known 'Ukasha Brothers Troupe. Between 1920 and 1925, he wrote four plays: three of them were adaptations of French plays and the fourth, *al-Mar'ah al-Jadida* (*The Modern Woman,* 1923), was an original play inspired by the nascent feminist movement in Egypt. Though al-Hakim had assumed a pseudonym, hoping to avoid his parents' disapproval, they discovered his increasingly active participation in Cairo's theater world. After al-Hakim finished his *Licence en droit* (Bachelor's in Law) in 1925 at Cairo University, his father attempted to break his son's attachment to the theater by sending him to France to obtain a doctorate in law. But the move only encouraged the young playwright, for in Paris al-Hakim had the opportunity to attend the plays of such modern European dramatists as HENRIK IBSEN, Maurice Maeterlinck, GEORGE BERNARD SHAW, Jean Cocteau, and LUIGI PIRANDELLO. He found himself drawn to the intellectual content in these plays and to the craftsmanship of the European stage. Al-Hakim also read widely during this time in philosophy, poetry, and fiction. Among the writers who affected him deeply were Lope de Vega, Johann Wolfgang von Goethe, Edgar Allan Poe, Arthur Rimbaud, Friedrich Nietzsche, and Andre Gide. Al-Hakim's time in Paris profoundly expanded his aesthetic and creative consciousness,

The Opera House at Ezbekiah Garden, ca. 1930. This theater, built in the mid-nineteeth century at the height of European influence in Cairo, was one of the major venues for Egypt's cultural and economic elite prior to the socialist revolution of Gamal Abdel Nasser in 1952.

transforming him into a full-fledged writer and intellectual.

Realizing after a few years that his son was not going to earn his doctorate, al-Hakim's father summoned him back to Cairo and encouraged him to become a public prosecutor in the Egyptian provinces. Upon his return to Cairo in 1928, al-Hakim embarked on an important new stage in his playwriting career, as he ceased to collaborate with popular theater troupes. Determined that Arab theater not remain an ephemeral art form, al-Hakim set out to write serious plays that would help establish an Arab dramatic literary heritage. In choosing this path, he was consciously working against the long-held belief in Egypt and the Arab world more generally that theater was a popular form, not high literature, and that plays therefore need not be preserved for future generations or even published at all. Most of Egypt's theater producers were convinced that to achieve commercial success, they must stage popular drama, in colloquial language. At the same time, Egypt's cultural elite scorned any texts not written in classical Arabic, a language in which few were proficient; they viewed colloquial texts as beneath the dignity of the Arabic literary canon. Consequently, though theater was a vital part of popular culture, Egypt had no written dramatic literary tradition to speak of.

In choosing to write plays in a literary mode, al-Hakim thus filled a glaring gap in modern Arabic literature. His plays of the 1930s were inspired by history, Greek and Arab mythology, folklore, and religion and were written in the classical Arabic known as *Fusha:* they belonged to what he called the "theater of ideas" (or "theater of the mind"). Al-Hakim considered these plays—among them, *Ahl al-Kahf* (*People of the Cave,* 1933), *Shahrazad* (1934), *Praxagora* (1939; enlarged, 1954), *Pygmalion* (1942), *Sulayman al-Hakim* (*Solomon the Wise,* 1943), and *Al-Malik Udib* (*King Oedipus,* 1949)—works to be read, not staged; he insisted that they should be categorized as dramatic literature, not theatrical pieces.

The earliest of these plays, *People of the Cave,* was both a turning point in al-Hakim's career and a milestone in Egyptian and Arab drama. Based on a Christian tale retold in the Qur'an, *People of the Cave* tells the story of three Christian converts who seek refuge in a cave in order to escape the wrath of a brutal king who is persecuting converts. The three characters and a dog sleep there for three hundred years. When they rise from their long slumber, they realize that the world around them has changed. Overwhelmed by these changes and aware that they have become representatives of the past, the characters decide to retreat to the cave. Addressed to Egyptians unsure of how to respond to a rapidly changing modern world, al-Hakim's play suggests that if nations do not modernize, they perish. The intellectual content of this play (as well as others that al-Hakim wrote during the early 1930s) and the classical Arabic language in which it was written gained the approval of Egypt's literary and intellectual elite, who praised al-Hakim for winning drama a place in the canon of Arabic literature. In recognition of its importance, *People of the Cave* was the first play staged at Egypt's National Theater when it opened in 1935. Though the play's use of classical Arabic—and its division into four very long acts—guaranteed that *People of the Cave* would not appeal to a broad audience, it remains a touchstone in Egyptian cultural memory.

Al-Hakim continued to compose philosophy-steeped plays through the 1940s, but in the 1950s, he started to write in a more populist vein. This shift in al-Hakim's career was tied in part to political changes in the country. In 1952, a peaceful coup d'état led by Gamal Abdel Nasser transformed Egypt from a 150-year-old monarchy into a socialist republic. Nasser and his allies instituted educational and cultural reforms designed to publicize and promote the socialist principles of the new republic. Many Egyptian authors, including the novelist Naguib Mahfouz (who would win the Nobel Prize in Literature in 1988), supported Nasser's reforms and embraced a "social realist" style that reflected his ideology.

Under the leadership of the Ministry of Culture, those engaged in the performance arts turned away from the adaptations of Western plays, musicals, and farces that had dominated the pre-Nasser period and directed their efforts toward establishing a national literacy dramatic canon. While the National Theater continued to provide a venue for classic Arab plays and world classics in translation, additional theaters were built that featured other kinds of performance: the Puppet Theater for children's drama, the Pocket Theater for experimental drama, the Balloon Theater for ballet and folkloric dance, and the Modern Theater for contemporary texts. A number of new initiatives were also undertaken to support artists, such as artist-in-residence programs, and prizes were granted to honor excellence in the arts. Al-Hakim himself received two important playwriting awards in the 1950s.

During this decade of social and political reform, both Nasser's government and the creative community were mainly concerned with giving artistic expression to the lives of the masses. The young playwrights who emerged in the postrevolutionary period with the state's encouragement and financial support generally advocated commitment to social change. The dramas (and films) that they produced during this period focused on social issues, the family, and the place of the new postcolonial Egyptian in the world, and did so in a realist and naturalistic vein. Playwrights and intellectuals during the 1950s paid equal attention to the remaking of Egyptian theater arts and of Arab theater more generally. For most Egyptian intellectuals, this work of creating a uniquely Arab theater depended on their establishing a connection to the Arab past—a period of intellectual and cultural flowering that, they believed, was cut off by European colonialism. As part of this cultural effort, many playwrights, including al-Hakim, incorporated Arab history and folklore into their plays.

The issue of language played a central role in this nationalist project. Wanting both to reach a wide audience and to help shape the identity of Egyptian and Arab theater, al-Hakim realized that the longstanding dispute over the use of classical versus colloquial language in drama had to be resolved if Arab theater was to continue developing at all. His solution was a new stage language, which he called "the third language." He proposed that writers compose plays in a style that could both entertain and serve literature, accessible to the layperson as well as the intellectual; such a style could accommodate realist topics and express a variety of themes, including tragic ones. The language of these plays was similar to classical Arabic, or *Fusha,* but with some concessions to everyday speech. By writing in this modified version of *Fusha* rather than the local Egyptian dialect, al-Hakim also ensured that his plays could be understood in each of the twenty-two Standard Arabic–speaking countries that constitute the Arab world. Al-Hakim's approach could easily be adapted to Arabic's many local dialects, and by the 1960s, the period many consider the heyday of Arab drama, a number of other playwrights had taken it up.

In his introduction to *Masrah al-Mujtama* (*Theater of Social Themes,* 1950), a collection of short plays from this period that contains some of his most widely read and produced works, al-Hakim emphasizes that every play in the volume—even ones whose plots seem to be far-fetched—authentically reflects Egyptian social realities in the 1940s and 1950s. One central reality is the place of women in traditional Arab society. Three plays in the collection underscore women's power and represent female characters in nonstereotypical ways: *Urid Hadha'l-Rajul* (*I Want This Man*), *al-Na'iba al-Muhtarama* (*The Honorable Lady Member of Parliament*), and *Ughiniyyat al-Mawt* (*Song of Death*), which is included here. In keeping with the dictates of social realism, al-Hakim wished to depict the opportunities for education and work that became increasingly available to women during the 1940s and 1950s. Although feminist and other critics have taken issue with aspects of his representation of women—arguing, for instance, that these characters are given to irrationality and often pursue domestic bliss more avidly than independence—the works in this collection explore the social, familial, and psychological demands with which Arab women contend and the conflicting roles they have traditionally assumed.

No play of al-Hakim's more powerfully captures the pressures of tradition on women—and on Egyptian society as a whole—than *Song of Death*, whose well-crafted structure and poignant, tragic tone have won it praise as one of the finest modern Arabic plays. An unsparing critique of brutal village customs and the tyranny of traditional gender roles, *Song of Death* takes as its subject the long-standing peasant tradition of blood revenge. For centuries, cycles of blood revenge were the undisputed law of the land for country folk in Egypt, and since the beginning of the twentieth century, governments have combated the deeply ingrained belief that the murder of a family member should be punished privately, not by the state's justice

Egyptian president Gamal Abdel Nasser, mobbed by enthusiastic supporters in the early 1960s.

system. As a public prosecutor who had confronted this provincial mind-set directly, al-Hakim strongly believed that private vengeance was a barbaric and regressive custom—a tradition that had to end if society was to move forward. *Song of Death* was his attempt in dramatic form to address his professional and humanistic concerns about this destructive tradition.

Al-Hakim's play takes place in a peasant house in Upper Egypt, the region of the Nile Valley that stretches south of Cairo. Asakir, a widow, has spent seventeen years yearning for retribution for the death of her husband, murdered by a member of a rival family as part of a generations-long blood feud. As the play opens, she is awaiting the arrival of her son, Ilwan, who was sent away as a child and raised as a student at one of Cairo's oldest theology schools (housed in an ancient mosque), with the expectation that he will take the weapon with which his father was killed and exact vengeance. When Ilwan arrives and challenges the cycle of violence, maintaining that the law is more important, his refusal to meet traditional expectations precipitates an equally devastating tragedy, and Asakir must face the consequences of her commitment to retribution and family honor. *Song of Death* embeds its story of vengeance and loss in the images and remembered sounds of rural Egyptian life: a reference to walls painted in mud, the joyful trilling of women, ritual gestures.

Hard and single-minded, the figure of Asakir dominates the play. With "a memory that can never forget and a heart that cannot relent," she has put her implacable fantasy of revenge before maternal and other feelings. The events of the past have shaped her view of the world, but the hardness to which she has given herself also reflects the social role that she, as woman and mother, has been asked to assume. The deliberately masculine name Asakir (which means "soldiers" in Arabic) indicates that although she is a woman, she is expected to act as a man. In peasant societies, such as the one depicted in the play, masculinity has historically signified strength and status; thus, sons have been valued more than daughters. This power imbalance forces women to act in conformity with masculine ways—to teach their sons to be "men" and to inspire their daughters to become more like men (by giving them ruthless-sounding names, for instance). Women in such communities are responsible for upholding the laws of their village and passing them down to their children. As *Song of Death* illustrates, women also play central roles in preserving and defending family honor.

But such hardening comes with a price. What makes Asakir such a richly dramatic figure is the conflict between her consuming desire for vengeance and the emotional bond that connects her, despite her struggles to escape it, to her son, Ilwan. Asakir is portrayed as both nurturing and controlling, but her excessive determination to take revenge for her husband's murder turns her into a tragic figure: her single-minded focus on killing drives all tenderness from her motherly love, leaving her with nothing but hatred on her mind and in her heart. By upholding the code that requires sons to avenge their fathers, she places the imperatives of the past over life in the present. In the play's climactic scene, as her desires pull her in opposite directions, Asakir confronts the grim logic of her vengeance in a growing spectacle of loss.

Song of Death delves deeply into the particularities of Egyptian rural life and exposes universal human flaws, such as excessive hatred, adherence to illogical traditions, and the blindness caused by anger and pride. Its themes are as relevant to our contemporary world as to al-Hakim's Egypt in 1950. Because of its poignant message—its insistence on the need to put an end to violence between nations and to the cycles of grievance that perpetuate this violence—it continues to be staged by Arab directors. The local and universal layers of *Song of Death* suggest why al-Hakim's name remains synonymous with modern Arab theater, and why his concerns, vision, and tireless experimentation are still points of reference for emerging dramatic voices in the Arab world.

DINA AHMED AMIN

Song of Death[1]

CHARACTERS[2]

ASAKIR, a widowed peasant woman
MABRUKA, her sister-in-law
SIMEIDA, son of Mabruka
ILWAN, son of Asakir

[A peasant hut in an Upper Egyptian village.[3] ASAKIR *and* MABRUKA, *both dressed in black, are sitting near the entrance, with heads bowed in silence. Close by them a calf and a kid are seen eating herbage and dried clover. The whistle of a train is heard.]*

MABRUKA *[raising her head]* There's the train.

ASAKIR *[without moving]* Do you think he has come on it?

MABRUKA Didn't he say he would, in his letter? Sheikh[4] Isnawi, the schoolteacher, read it out for us yesterday.

ASAKIR Are you sure you've told no one at all that he's my son?

MABRUKA Do you think I've gone mad? Your son Ilwan died when he was a mere child of two. He was drowned in the sluice of the waterwheel.[5] The whole village knows that.

ASAKIR But *they* no longer believe it.

MABRUKA Who are "they"? The Tahawis?

ASAKIR Didn't your son Simeida tell you what he heard in the market the other day?

MABRUKA No. What did he hear?

ASAKIR He heard someone say to a group of people, "Either the Azizes have no more men left among them or else they're concealing a man in order to take revenge, a man closer to the victim then his nephew Simeida." And who but a man's own son can be any closer than his nephew?

MABRUKA Oh yes: Simeida told me about that. If it hadn't been for this rumor he would never have been able to hold up his head in the village.

ASAKIR Well, let them know now that the dead man's son is still alive. We've no fear for him now that he's a grown man. I'm not the one who is afraid now. It's them that fear keeps awake of a night. Hurry up, train, and bring him soon. I've waited a long time—seventeen years, I've counted them

1. Translated by Mustafa Badawi; revised by Andrew Parkin and Mahmoud Manzalaoui.

2. The characters' names in this play, like most Arabic names, have specific meanings: *Asakir*, "army of soldiers"; *Mabruka*, "blessed"; *Simeida*, "stiff" or "stonelike"; *Ilwan*, "transcendent" or "sublime."

3. That is, a village in the less populous southern region of Egypt, up the Nile River from Cairo.

4. An honorary title given to teachers in provincial religious schools (and to graduates of al-Azhar University). The local schoolteacher reads the letter to Asakir and Mabruka because they are illiterate.

5. An irrigation device.

hour by hour. Seventeen whole years and I've milked them out of Time's udders, drop after drop, with all the hard tugging you'd need if you were milking a cow that's far gone in her age.

MABRUKA [*listening to a far-off sound*] There's the train arrived in the station. He'll find my son Simeida waiting to meet him.

ASAKIR [*as if talking to herself*] That's right.

MABRUKA [*turning to her*] What's the matter with you, Asakir? You're trembling.

ASAKIR [*as if to herself*] Simeida's song will tell me.

MABRUKA Tell you?

ASAKIR That he's come.

MABRUKA Did you tell my son to sing as a sign that Ilwan was here?

ASAKIR Yes, as soon as they set foot across the village bounds.

MABRUKA Patience, Asakir. Be patient. The worst is over now.

ASAKIR It's not fear nor weakness that I'm feeling now.

MABRUKA The fearsome days have now gone. Gone forever, they are. I shan't ever forget the day when you hid your son Ilwan—and he a mere child of two then—hid him in the flour basket and carried him under cover of darkness out of the village. Took him all the way to Cairo, and gave him into the care of that kinsman of yours, the flour merchant who kept shop in the spice dealer's row near the mosque of our blessed Hussein.[6]

ASAKIR Bring him up as a butcher, I said to him. Let him learn to use the knife like a master.

MABRUKA But he never did as you asked him.

ASAKIR He did that! Soon as he was seven years old he placed him in a butcher's shop. But run away, he did, some time later.

MABRUKA And went into the Holy al-Azhar[7] as a student.

ASAKIR That's it. When I visited him last year I saw him in his gown and turban[8] looking most dignified. I said to him, "If only your father could have seen you looking like that, he'd have been mighty proud." But they didn't spare him to enjoy watching his son grow up.

MABRUKA Wouldn't it have been better if he'd stayed on in the butcher's shop?

ASAKIR What makes you say that, Mabruka?

MABRUKA I don't know. It's only a thought that came into my head.

ASKIR I reckon I know your thought.

MABRUKA What is it, then, Asakir?

ASAKIR It grieves you to see my son in gown and turban while yours goes on wearing his woolly skull cap and his smock.[9]

MABRUKA By the memory of the dear departed, I give you my oath, nothing of the kind was in my mind.

ASAKIR Why then don't you like Ilwan to be at the Holy al-Azhar?

MABRUKA I give you my oath, it isn't that I don't like it, it's just that I'm afraid . . .

6. That is, the ancient mosque and shrine of Hussein (also spelled al-Husayn, ca. 629–680), the grandson of the Prophet Muhammad, in the heart of old Cairo.

7. That is, Cairo's al-Azhar University; established in 975, it is one of the oldest universities in the world and a leading center for the study of Islam and the Arabic language.

8. Attire worn by students and graduates of al-Azhar, highly respected as clerics and scholars.

9. That is, wearing attire typical of peasants.

ASAKIR Afraid?

MABRUKA That he might not be such a master at wielding his knife.

ASAKIR Set your mind at rest, Mabruka. When you see Ilwan now, a full-grown man, you'll realize that he has the lean, strong-thewed arm of the Aziz family.

MABRUKA [*listening to the train whistle*] The train's moving out of the station now.

ASAKIR Let it go where it will, so long as it's brought us Ilwan to force the murderer's soul out of his body, and to leave him for the farm dogs in scattered gobbets of flesh.

MABRUKA What if he hasn't come?

ASAKIR Why do you say that, Mabruka?

MABRUKA I don't know. Just a feeling I've got.

ASAKIR What would stop him coming?

MABRUKA What would drive him to leave Cairo and the city life and the Holy al-Azhar and come to this—?

ASAKIR This is where he was born, where blood is calling out to him.

MABRUKA Our village is a long, long way away from Cairo! Can blood make itself heard as far as the cities?

ASAKIR Do you really think he hasn't come?

MABRUKA I know no more about it than you do.

ASAKIR And what about the letter that the schoolmaster read out to us?

MABRUKA Don't you recall his words: "I hope to come if my circumstances allow it." Who knows whether or not his circumstances have allowed it?

ASAKIR Don't dampen my spirits, Mabruka. Don't dash my hope. I've just heard the train whistle turning into trills[1] of joy in my heart, announcing that the end of this long mourning is near. Ilwan not come? What would become of me if that were true? And how much longer would I have to wait then?

MABRUKA The station isn't so far from here, nor the main road. If he'd arrived, Simeida would be singing now.

ASAKIR Perhaps they're taking their time, chatting. After all, they haven't seen each other for more than three years . . . since your son was in Cairo last during the Fair of the Blessed Hussein.[2]

MABRUKA If he'd come my son's heart would have brimmed over with joy and he'd have started his singing even before he'd reached the main road.

ASAKIR Perhaps he's forgotten to sing.

MABRUKA It's impossible: he can't forget.

ASAKIR [*listening*] I can hear no one singing.

MABRUKA [*listening*] Nor I neither.

ASAKIR [*continuing to listen*] There's no one singing, not even a shepherd lad. There's not a single creature singing, not even the owl over in the ruins. You're right, Mabruka. He hasn't come.

MABRUKA [*as if to herself*] My heart tells me things.

ASAKIR No, not yours—mine. Mine, that's as secret as the grave, as hard as rock, is now beginning to tell me things.

MABRUKA What things?

1. High-pitched sounds traditionally made by women to express joy on such happy occasions as weddings, pregnancy announcements, and the births of children.

2. In the Islamic world, fairs are popular festivals in honor of venerated religious figures.

ASAKIR Things that will happen.

MABRUKA Do tell me.

ASAKIR [*listening intently*] Hush! Listen, listen. Can you not hear, Mabruka? Can you not hear?

MABRUKA Simeida singing.

ASAKIR The heavens be thanked for that!

[*They listen for a while to* SIMEIDA*'s song, which grows increasingly clear.*]

SIMEIDA [*sings*]

O my dear one,
Your bitter voice accuses:
Repentance and excuses
Were all I ever gave!
You reproached me then the more,
And out of grief
My clothes
To shreds I tore.
When they told me of your father,
It was my silent shame
Which set unmanly cheeks aflame,
Where eyes ran dry
And made a desert of my face.

ASAKIR He's come, Ilwan is here! And now it's off with the shirt of my shame and on with my garment of honor.

MABRUKA And now we can hold the true rites[3] over the body of the dear one—and may he rest in peace.

ASAKIR And sacrifice to his spirit the kid and the calf.

MABRUKA O joy! O happiness! [*Makes as though to give out a loud trill.*]

ASAKIR [*restrains her*] Not now. Otherwise we'll be known to the world too early.

MABRUKA Your hours are numbered, Suwellam Tahawi![4]

[*A knock on the door.* ASAKIR *rushes to open it:* SIMEIDA *appears carrying a bag.*]

SIMEIDA I have brought you Sheikh Ilwan. [*Puts the bag on the floor and is soon followed in by* ILWAN.]

ASAKIR [*with open arms*] Ilwan, my son.

ILWAN [*kisses her head*] Mother.

ASAKIR [*to her son*] Say your greetings to your Aunt Mabruka.

ILWAN [*turns to* MABRUKA] Are you well, Aunt Mabruka?

MABRUKA You can see for yourself, Ilwan. You are our only hope now.

SIMEIDA Let us go home now, Mother.

MABRUKA Come. It's close now, Asakir—the hour of relief.

[MABRUKA *and* SIMEIDA *go out.*]

ASAKIR You must be hungry, Ilwan. I've a bowl of sour milk.

ILWAN Thank you, Mother. No, I'm not hungry. I had some hard-boiled eggs and some barley cake on the train.

3. By village custom, a person killed in a blood feud is not officially mourned until his family has avenged his death.

4. Either the man or the son of the man who killed Asakir's husband.

ASAKIR You'll be thirsty then?

ILWAN No, not thirsty either.

ASAKIR Of course you haven't come here for food or drink. You've come to eat of his flesh and drink of his blood.

ILWAN [*as if in a trance*] I have come here to do something truly great, Mother.

ASAKIR I know, I know, my son. Wait till I bring you something: something you've never set your eyes on before. [*Rushes to an inner room where she disappears for a while.*]

ILWAN [*casting a look around the room*] My eyes can still see animals and their droppings in your houses. The dirty water jar, firewood, and dried stalks of maize forming a shaky roof.

ASAKIR [*emerges from the inner room holding a saddlebag which she lays before her son*] Here. For seventeen years I have kept these things for you.

ILWAN [*looks at the saddlebag without moving*] What is this?

ASAKIR The saddlebag that your father's body was sent to me in, carried on his donkey. In this pouch I found his severed head, and in the other one the rest of his body, hacked to pieces. With his own knife they stabbed him to death—the knife he was carrying, then they put knife and body in the saddlebag. See, here is the knife. I left the blood on it until it's turned to rust as you can see. As for the donkey that brought me the body of your murdered father, tracing its steps back to this house by force of habit, with its head bowed down, as if it was grieving over its master—I couldn't keep it alive for you. It couldn't endure for all these years: it's died.

ILWAN Who did this?

ASAKIR Suweilam Tahawi.

ILWAN How do you know?

ASAKIR The whole village knows.

ILWAN I know you've told me that. You've told that name to me over and over again, whenever you came to visit me in Cairo. I was too young to think then or to argue. But now my reason needs to be satisfied. What's the evidence? Did the police ever look into the crime?

ASAKIR Look into the crime?

ILWAN Yes. What did you say to the Public Prosecutor?

ASAKIR Public Prosecutor? The shame of it! We say anything to the Public Prosecutor? We the Azizes do that? Did even the Tahawis ever do that?

ILWAN Didn't the Public Prosecutor ask you any questions?

ASAKIR Of course. But we said we knew nothing about the business, that we'd seen no corpse. Meantime we had buried your father in secret under cover of darkness.

ILWAN [*as if addressing himself*] So that we may exact requital with our own hands.

ASAKIR With the selfsame knife that stabbed your father.

ILWAN And the murderer?

ASAKIR Alive and hearty. There's not a saint or a holy man in the neighborhood but whose shrine I visited. I held on to the railings of their sanctuary, uncovered my head and heaped dust from their ground over my hair,[5] and

5. A traditional gesture of abasement and supplication.

I prayed to them to beseech our God for me that He might prolong the slayer's days until you, my son, should take his life—with your own hands.

ILWAN Are you sure, Mother, that he was the murderer?

ASAKIR We've no enemies beside the Tahawis.

ILWAN But how do you know it was Suweilam himself who did it?

ASAKIR Because he believed it was your father who'd murdered his father.

ILWAN And is that true? Did my father kill his father?

ASAKIR God alone knows.

ILWAN But what started this family feud in the first place?

ASAKIR I don't know. Nobody knows. It's something far gone in the past. All that we know is that there's always been blood spilt between us.

ILWAN The cause may well be that one of our calves happened to drink from a water-channel in a field that belonged to their ancestors!

ASAKIR God alone knows. As for us mortals, all that we know is that between the Azizes and Tahawis rivers of blood have flowed.

ILWAN Rivers that water neither crop nor fruit.

ASAKIR Rivers that stopped flowing only with the death of your father. And that because of your tender age. Years then went past dry as the thirsty season, and people whispered lies and false rumors, while I was writhing in the flames of my hidden anger, waiting for this hour. And now the hour has come, so get up, son, and put out my fire and slake my thirst for the blood of Suweilam Tahawi.

ILWAN Has this Suweilam Tahawi got a son?

ASAKIR Yes. Fourteen years old.

ILWAN So I have no more than another four or five years to live.

ASAKIR What is it you are saying?

ILWAN . . . Only until he grows strong enough to do to me what I am supposed to do to his father.

ASAKIR Do you fear for your life, Ilwan?

ILWAN And what about you, Mother? Do you fear for my life?

ASAKIR The Lord be my witness, how I fear for every hair on your head.

ILWAN You really care about my life, Mother?

ASAKIR Has my life any worth without yours? Or for that matter, the lives of all the Azizes? It's your life alone has made it possible for every one of us to live through the past seventeen years.

ILWAN [*bows his head*] I see.

ASAKIR How often we suffered shame and humiliation. But as soon as your image crossed our minds our energy would revive, our resolution would strengthen and we were united in the hope that we placed upon you.

ILWAN [*his head still bowed and as if talking to himself*] You certainly need my life.

ASAKIR Even your father's funeral waits for you, Ilwan. These sacrifices here are ready for the slaughter. My lamentation which I've been choking down in my throat all these years is waiting for you to set it free. My frock, which I've kept myself from tearing open all that time, is waiting for you,[6] too. Everything in our existence is dead. Stagnant. Looking to you to breathe life into it.

6. In Egyptian villages, the tearing of one's outer garments is a ritualized expression of extreme grief.

ILWAN Is this how life is breathed into you?

ASAKIR Yes, Ilwan. Bring the appointed hour closer. Be quick, for we've been waiting for it for so long.

ILWAN [*in wonder*] The appointed hour?

ASAKIR I've forgotten nothing. Even the stone to whet the rusty knife I've brought for you and hidden in this room.

ILWAN But how am I to know this Suweilam? I've never set eyes on him in the whole of my life.

ASAKIR Simeida will show you where to find him. He'll point him out to you.

ILWAN [*looks at his clothes*] Am I to commit this deed while I'm dressed in this way?

ASAKIR Take off those clothes. I've a cloak that belonged to your father. I've kept it for you. [*She turns to go into the inner room.*]

ILWAN [*stops her*] Just a minute, Mother. Why the hurry?

ASAKIR Every breath Suweilam draws while you are here is a gift which you are granting to him.

ILWAN And what harm is there in that?

ASAKIR It's taken from our breaths; it's drawn out of our well-being. Against our wishes we were forced to extend his life by as much as nearly brought us to the grave. Look at your mother, Ilwan. I was a young woman when your father died. But look what all those years have done to me. It is as if they were forty years, not seventeen. The sap of my youth has dried up and my bones have grown weak. All I have left is a memory that can never forget and a heart that cannot relent.

ILWAN [*as if to himself*] What a price it costs to avenge one's blood.

ASAKIR [*uncomprehending*] What did you say, Ilwan?

ILWAN I said that God the Mighty Avenger is merciful to us: He offers to relive us of this burden without any cost to us.

ASAKIR [*in a suspicious tone*] What do you mean?

ILWAN Nothing, Mother, nothing.

ASAKIR [*decisively*] Take off those clothes. I'll bring you the cloak and sharpen the knife for you myself.

ILWAN Isn't there a mosque nearby?

ASAKIR We've only a little chapel next to Sheikh Isnawi's schoolhouse.

ILWAN [*moving*] I'll go there and say my evening prayers.

ASAKIR At this hour?

ILWAN I think the sun is about to set.[7]

ASAKIR Do you want to be seen in the mosque by everyone in the village?

ILWAN That would be the best opportunity for my purpose.

ASAKIR [*stares him in the face*] Have you gone mad, Ilwan?

ILWAN It's most important for me to meet the villagers. Haven't I just told you that I have come to do something truly great?

ASAKIR [*as if mocking him*] I shouldn't imagine you'll want to reveal to the village the reason for your coming here?

ILWAN It's essential to let them all hear what I have to tell.

7. Every healthy adult Muslim is required to pray five times daily—at dawn, at midday, in late afternoon, at sunset, and at night before retiring—and it is better to pray in a mosque than alone.

ASAKIR Ilwan, my son! What is it that I hear you say? Are you serious? Are you in your right mind? What is it that you want to tell them?

ILWAN [*as if in a dream*] I'll tell them what I have come here to say. I have often thought about my village and its people, in spite of the long time I've been away from it. There, at al-Azhar, when the classes were over, we—the students, that is—we'd gather together and read the newspapers. And we'd think of the places we'd come from. We were very homesick. And we often worried about when our people in the countryside would be able to live like human beings, in clean houses where they wouldn't share their meals with animals. When the roofs of their houses would be something better than dry stalks of cotton and maize, and the walls painted with something better than mud and the droppings of their beasts. When the water pot would disappear and there would be clean piped water in the house. When electric lights would replace the oil lamp. Was that too much to ask for our people? Don't they have the same rights as others?

ASAKIR [*as if uncomprehending*] What is all this you're saying, Ilwan?

ILWAN This is what the people of the village ought to know. And those of us who were educated in Cairo—it's our duty to make them see and realize their human rights. It shouldn't be difficult for them to achieve this aim: if only they would unite, join hands, and co-operate. They ought to set up a council. Elect a council, that's it, from amongst themselves. And they could tax those who had money enough to pay. They'd form a team of able-bodied men to spend those long hours when there's nothing doing in making dykes and bridges and other constructive things. Not wasting time in squabbles and feuds. Why, if they worked together like that, if they would only make the effort, we'd make this a model village. And it would soon be an example for all the other villages in the country to follow.

ASAKIR You're talking the language of books. You can keep that for later. For when you have your evening talk with Sheikh Muhammad Isnawi. He can understand it—I can't. As for the present, there's something more important that we've to do, Ilwan.

ILWAN [*shocked*] What is it that's more important?

ASAKIR No. Don't go to the mosque to pray tonight. Else our plan might fail. Pray here tonight, if you wish to. Go and take off those clothes. I'll fetch water from the water pot for you to prepare for your prayers.[8] Put on the cloak and help me sharpen the knife.

ILWAN [*his head bowed, whispers*] Your mercy, O God, Your favor and forgiveness!

ASAKIR What are you saying, Ilwan?

ILWAN [*raises his head*] I am saying that I have come here only to make you see and realize what life is, to bring you life.

ASAKIR And that's exactly what we've been waiting for patiently for all these long nights. For seventeen years all the Azizes have been dead, waiting for your return to bring life back to them.

ILWAN [*whispers with his head bowed down*] God! What am I to do with these people?

ASAKIR What is wrong with you, Ilwan? You keep bowing your head. Come on. Get up. Don't waste any more time.

8 In Islam, ritual washing before prayer is obligatory.

ILWAN [*raises his head and takes courage*] Mother, I will not kill.

ASAKIR [*tries to conceal her distress*] What do I hear?

ILWAN I will not kill.

ASAKIR [*in a rough voice*] The blood of your father!

ILWAN It's you yourselves who left it spilt and wasted by hiding the crime from the government. It's up to the authorities to punish.

ASAKIR [*beside herself*] The blood of your father!

ILWAN My hand wasn't made to destroy a human being.

ASAKIR [*as if in a trance*] The blood of your father!

ILWAN [*alarmed at her condition*] Mother, Mother: what is the matter with you?

ASAKIR [*as if she can see nobody in front of her*] The blood of your father! Seventeen years. The blood of your father. Seventeen years . . . !

ILWAN Mother, calm yourself. Of course it's a shock to you. But you must realize that I could never be an assassin and use my knife on a man.

ASAKIR [*whispers as if out of her mind*] Seventeen years . . . Vengeance for your father's murder . . . Seventeen years . . .

ILWAN [*as if to himself*] Mother, I know that you've stood it patiently for so long. If only this patience and endurance of yours were given up to a useful cause you would perform miracles! But you must understand that I—

ASAKIR [*with a quaver in her throat*] The blood of your father!

ILWAN [*rushes towards her, alarmed*] Mother! Mother! Mother!

ASAKIR [*recovers awareness of her surroundings*] Who are you?

ILWAN Your son, Ilwan. Your son.

ASAKIR [*screams*] Son? *My* son? No, no! Never, never, never!

ILWAN [*astonished*] Mother!

ASAKIR I'm not your mother. I don't know you. No son has ever been born out of my womb. No son have I ever given birth to.

ILWAN [*pleading*] Please, Mother! Try to understand that I—

ASAKIR Out of my house . . . God's curse be upon you to the Day of Judgment. Out of my house.

ILWAN Mother!

ASAKIR [*screams*] Out of my house . . . or else I'll ask the help of our men to throw you out. We still have men. There are still men among the Azizes. But you—you're not one of them. Out of my house with you.

ILWAN [*picks up his bag*] I'll go to the station and go back to where I came from. And I'll pray to God that your disturbed soul may find peace, and that I may see you in Cairo soon to explain my way of looking at things, in quiet, far away from here. Goodbye, Mother.

[*He leaves. His mother remains motionless in her place. After a while,* SIMEIDA *enters, first putting his head round the door, then gently pushing it open.*]

SIMEIDA Was it you screaming, Aunt Asakir?

ASAKIR [*with determination: she is fully recovered now*] Come here, Simeida.

SIMEIDA [*looks round*] Where's Ilwan? Where's your son?

ASAKIR I have no son. I never bore a son.

SIMEIDA What are you saying, Aunt Asakir?

ASAKIR If I had a son he'd now be avenging his father's murder.

SIMEIDA Where has he gone?

ASAKIR To the station. On his way back to Cairo.

SIMEIDA My mother was right. As soon as she saw him just now, she said, as we were leaving, "That turbaned preacher will never kill Suweilam Tahawi."

ASAKIR I wish my womb had been torn to shreds before it brought such a son into the world!

SIMEIDA Don't upset yourself, Aunt. There are still men among the Azizes.

ASAKIR Our hope is now in you, Simeida.

SIMEIDA A nephew can stand in for a son.

ASAKIR But in this case the son's alive. It's his duty before anybody else, to avenge the shedding of his father's blood. He's alive. Alive. He's about amongst the living.

SIMEIDA Just try to tell yourself that he's dead.

ASAKIR I wish he had really died, drowned in the sluice of the waterwheel when he was a child. We would then never have had to wait all those years, writhing and roasting on the live coals of our pent-up anger, waiting to no purpose. I wish he had truly died. We would have been able to live honorably then, and not be wearing our garment of shame. But he is alive, and it has been broadcast in the market places and in the whole neighborhood that he is alive. Oh, the shame. The ignominy. The disgrace!

SIMEIDA Aunt, don't be so upset.

ASAKIR It's impossible not to be upset by a disgrace like this. Carrying such a shame, life will be impossible. How can I go on living in this village now that people know that I have a son like this. How many a mouth'll spit whenever his name is mentioned. From all directions the cry will be heard: "Cursed be the womb that brought him forth!" Yes, this womb [*striking her belly hard and wildly*]. A curse on this womb. All the women of the village will mock it: even the ugly, the dim-witted, the barren. This womb . . . this womb . . . this womb.

SIMEIDA [*tries to stop her*] Aunt Asakir, don't punish yourself so!

ASAKIR Fetch the knife, Simeida, fetch the knife, and rip it open.

SIMEIDA Have you gone mad?

ASAKIR [*screams*] Simeida: are you a man?

SIMEIDA [*looks at her intently*] What is it you want?

ASAKIR Stop your cousin's disgrace.

SIMEIDA Ilwan's?

ASAKIR And his mother's, your Aunt Asakir's. Prevent her shame.

SIMEIDA How?

ASAKIR [*takes the knife from the saddle bag*] Kill him with this knife.

SIMEIDA Kill who?

ASAKIR Ilwan. Dig this knife into his heart.

SIMEIDA I kill Ilwan? Your son?

ASAKIR Yes. Kill him. Send him to join the dead.

SIMEIDA Pull yourself together, Aunt.

ASAKIR Do this, Simeida . . . for my sake and for his!

SIMEIDA For his sake!

ASAKIR Yes. Better for him and better for me that it should be said he was killed, than for folk to say that he fled from his duty of avenging his father's murder.

SIMEIDA My own cousin!

ASAKIR If you're a man, Simeida, you must never let him bring shame upon the Azizes. Never again will you be able to carry yourself like a man. Men will whisper and laugh behind their hands at you and point at you in the marketplace, and say: "There goes no more than a woman and one who's given shelter to another mere woman, at that."

SIMEIDA [*to himself*] A woman!

ASAKIR If the Tahawis had such a son they'd never have let him live for an hour.

SIMEIDA [*to himself*] A woman—giving shelter to another woman!

ASAKIR Yes, that's so; that'll be you if you allow him to behave as he means to.

SIMEIDA [*stretches out his hand resolutely*] Give me the knife.

ASAKIR [*hands him the knife*] Here it is. But wait till I wash the dried blood and the rust off its blade.

SIMEIDA [*impatiently*] Give it to me, before he slips away by the evening train.

ASAKIR [*gives him the knife eagerly and forcefully*] Take it. Let his blood wash away the blood of his father that's dried upon the blade.

SIMEIDA [*goes off with the knife*] If I manage to kill him, you'll at hear my voice raised in song at the outskirts of the village, Aunt.

[*Exit quickly.* ASAKIR *remains alone, fixed to the spot like a statue, gazing motionless and absently. After a while,* MABRUKA *appears, carrying a water pitcher on her head.*]

MABRUKA [*puts down the pitcher*] I've brought some dried fish for Sheikh Ilwan.

ASAKIR [*turns to her slowly*] May your life be longer than his,[9] Mabruka.

MABRUKA Who are you talking about?

ASAKIR Ilwan.

MABRUKA Your son?

ASAKIR He's no longer mine; he belongs to the dust.

MABRUKA What are you saying, Asakir? I left him with you only a moment ago. Where is he?

ASAKIR Gone to the station on his way back to where he came from. Giving his back to the duty of avenging his father's murder.

MABRUKA [*her head bowed down*] Just as my heart has been telling me.

ASAKIR Your prophecy has come true, Mabruka.

MABRUKA If only he had never come.

ASAKIR Seventeen years we've been waiting.

MABRUKA Every year you used to say, "He's growing." You measured him by the handspan as if he were a shoot of maize. But then, when he grew tall and his cob was ripe, you stripped him, only to find that there was no grain on the cob.

ASAKIR It wouldn't have been such a disaster if he were no more than a bare cob. We never expected any material gain through him. We expected him to give us back our dignity—that was all. How proud I was of him, Mabruka, how often I boasted about him to you. I thought I'd brought forth the son who'd cleanse the stain off the honor of the family. And how

9. According to funeral etiquette throughout the Arab world, the blessing "May you live long after the departed one" is directed to the deceased family; the customary response is "May your life be longer than his."

has he turned out now? The very son I've given birth to, the son I took great care to hide like a treasure in a crock of clay—he's no more than a stain on our tree, like a blight overtaking a cotton plant. God's mercy be on your soul, my husband: they spilt your blood and it has not been avenged. I've given you a son who brings comfort to your enemies and makes them gloat.

MABRUKA Oh shame, shame on the Azizes!

ASAKIR If he stays alive. But before long he'll be buried in the earth.

MABRUKA [*turns round suddenly*] Where's Simeida?

[*The whistling of a train is heard.*]

ASAKIR [*listening intently*] Hush! There's the evening train entering the station.

MABRUKA Asakir, where's Simeida?

ASAKIR [*still listening intently*] Be quiet. Now, at this instant, at this very instant.

MABRUKA [*astonished*] What happens at this instant?

ASAKIR [*as if to herself*] Do you think the train has carried him off? Or has he been carried off by—

MABRUKA If he's gone to the station, as you say, he must have got on the train. All these curses you are heaping on his head will do no good.

ASAKIR Do you really think he has got on the train?

MABRUKA What could have stopped him?

ASAKIR [*slipping out the answer*] Simeida!

MABRUKA Simeida? Did he go after him to stop him leaving?

ASAKIR Yes.

MABRUKA When did he go?

ASAKIR A short while before you came.

MABRUKA I shouldn't think he could have overtaken him.

ASAKIR [*sighs in relief*] Do you really think so?

MABRUKA Unless he ran very fast.

[*The train whistle is heard again.*]

ASAKIR [*listens intently*] There, the train is leaving the station.

MABRUKA [*stares at her*] What's wrong with you, Asakir? Why have you gone so pale?

ASAKIR What does your heart tell you, Mabruka?

MABRUKA It tells me that he has gone.

ASAKIR Gone. Gone—where?

MABRUKA Where he came from.

ASAKIR What do you mean?

MABRUKA [*watches her*] Why is your breast heaving like that?

ASAKIR [*in a whisper, her eyes wandering*] Gone where he came from!

MABRUKA Do you still hope for some good from him?

ASAKIR No.

MABRUKA You must think of him as if he'd never been.

ASAKIR [*as if to herself*] Yes. His death is less shameful than his life.

MABRUKA And thank God that he's far away.

ASAKIR [*to herself*] Is he on the train now?

MABRUKA Who knows? Perhaps Simeida was able to catch him up and persuade him not to go: perhaps he'll bring him back now.

ASAKIR [*as if dreaming*] Bring him back now?

MABRUKA Why not? If Simeida ran really fast he wouldn't have missed the train.

ASAKIR [*whispers*] . . . Was able to catch him up . . .

MABRUKA And it may not be long before we see them coming back again together.

ASAKIR [*to herself*] No. This time Simeida will be coming alone.

MABRUKA [*watches her anxiously*] Your face, Asakir: it fills me with terror.

ASAKIR [*listens intently*] Hush! Listen! Listen! Can't you hear anything?

MABRUKA No. What do you want me to hear?

ASAKIR Singing.

MABRUKA No, I cannot hear any singing.

ASAKIR [*with relief*] Nor can I.

MABRUKA Did Simeida tell you he was going to sing?

ASAKIR [*to herself, anxiously*] Perhaps he hasn't reached the edge of the village yet.

MABRUKA I should imagine he has, by now.

ASAKIR [*breathing more freely*] And he is not singing!

MABRUKA Now the blood has come back to your cheeks.

ASAKIR [*whispers*] He hasn't caught him up.

MABRUKA You'd rather he didn't come back, Asakir, wouldn't you? You'd rather the train carried him away from this village. So would I. I'd much rather he returned to his Cairo, to his preachers and the other students. He doesn't belong to us, nor we to him. He's done well to leave us so soon, before the people of the village could meet him and get to know what we know about him. [ASAKIR *listens to a distant sound.*] You're not listening to me, Asakir. Don't you think I'm right?

ASAKIR [*in a rough, alarmed voice*] No, no, I can't hear anything!

MABRUKA [*listens*] It is Simeida singing. [*Turns, alarmed, to* ASAKIR, *whose eyes have glazed over.*] Asakir! Asakir! What's wrong? You scare me!

SIMEIDA [*outside, sings*]

O my dear one,
Your bitter voice accuses:
Repentance and excuses
Were all I ever gave!
You reproached me then the more,
And out of grief
My clothes
To shreds I tore.
When they told me of your father,
It was my silent shame
Which set unmanly cheeks aflame,
Where eyes ran dry
And made a desert of my face.

ASAKIR [*pulls herself together, to stop herself from collapsing, but lets slip a faint choking cry like a death rattle*] My son!

Curtain.

SAMUEL BECKETT

1906–1989

The career of Samuel Beckett, one of the modern period's most influential dramatists, bridges the most important artistic currents of the early and late twentieth century. A member of the novelist James Joyce's literary circle in Paris during the late 1920s and early 1930s, Beckett was one of the last of the high modernists, and his drama and fiction mark the twilight of a movement that produced such works as Joyce's *Ulysses* and T. S. Eliot's *The Waste Land* (both published in 1922). A writer who lived in France most of his life (and who often composed in French), he also continued a tradition of modern Irish playwriting that flourished in the plays of William Butler Yeats and John Millington Synge. Even as they are rooted in the past, however, Beckett's works opened paths for later twentieth-century writers. His trailblazing is particularly evident in the theater, whose boundaries Beckett's plays extended in radically individual ways. *WAITING FOR GODOT*, which premiered in Paris in 1953 and became a symbol of the crisis of meaning in post–World War II Europe, stands as the landmark play of contemporary drama. With its drama of non-action announcing the exhaustion of traditional dramatic structures, *Waiting for Godot*—like Beckett's other plays— inaugurated new theatrical possibilities for dramatists as diverse as Harold Pinter, Sam Shepard, Athol Fugard, and CARYL CHURCHILL.

Samuel Barclay Beckett was born in 1906 to an affluent Protestant family who lived in the Dublin suburb of Foxrock. His date of birth is listed on his birth certificate as May 13, though he was actually born on April 13 (Beckett relished the fact that this date coincided not only with Friday the thirteenth but also with Good Friday). Beckett was educated in Portora Royal School in County Fermanagh, the alma mater of his fellow Irish writer OSCAR WILDE, and Trinity College, Dublin, where he excelled as a student while studying Dante as well as English and French literature. Upon graduation, Beckett taught French in Belfast for two terms; he then was chosen to represent Trinity as *lecteur* in English at the Ecole Normale Supérieure in Paris, and he began this two year position in 1928. It was in Paris that Beckett met Joyce, who was at work on his final novel, *Finnegans Wake* (1939), and who became a powerful influence on the younger Irishman. Beckett's own career as a writer was launched with an essay on Joyce's work (published in 1929 as the lead essay in a collection of essays on *Finnegans Wake,* then known as *Work in Progress*) and a poetic parody of the seventeenth-century French philosopher Descartes titled *Whoroscope,* which was published in 1930. In

1930, Beckett also wrote a study of Marcel Proust, the French author whose novel *Remembrance of Things Past* (1913–27) explores questions of time, memory, and human consciousness that would prove central to Beckett's later writing.

After completing his term as *lecteur,* Beckett spent seven years living in Dublin, Paris, and London before returning to France for good in 1937. In addition to *Proust,* which appeared in 1931, these years saw the publication of a collection of short stories, *More Kicks Than Pricks* (1934), and the novel *Murphy* (1938). Twenty years after the end of World War I, war was on the horizon again; and when Germany invaded France in 1940 Beckett joined the French Resistance, typing and translating information concerning German troop movements. As a result of his activities he was forced to flee Paris in 1942; he spent the rest of the war in hiding in Roussillon, in the Vichy-controlled south of France, where he wrote the novel *Watt* (published in 1953).

The period immediately after World War II was, for Beckett, a time of enormous creativity. In fiction, Beckett wrote a trilogy that helped revolutionize the novel form: *Molloy* (1951), *Malone Dies* (1951), and *The Unnamable* (1953). Composed originally in French, then translated (primarily by Beckett) into English, these novels establish deeply self-referential narrative worlds; they explore the limits of fiction, as consciousness engages in an increasingly urgent struggle with the language in which it seeks to articulate itself. It was in part to escape the constrictions of language in these novels that Beckett turned to the stage. In 1948–49, between completing the second and third novels in his trilogy, Beckett wrote *En attendant Godot*—soon to be translated by the author himself as *Waiting for Godot*—"as a relaxation, to get away from the awful prose I was writing at the time." It was not his first play. *Eleuthéria,* a drawing room play that was written in January 1947 but never pub-

The cast and set of the original 1953 production of *Waiting for Godot* at the Théâtre de Babylone. From left to right, Jean Martin as Lucky, Lucien Raimbourg as Vladimir, Pierre Latour as Estragon, and Roger Blin (the director of the production) as Pozzo.

lished or produced during Beckett's lifetime, gave little indication of what he would achieve less than two years later. When *Godot* opened at the 230-seat Théâtre de Babylone in Paris on January 5, 1953, audiences were confronted by a radically new conception of drama. Over the course of two acts that mix vaudeville routines with metaphysical speculation, two tramps wait on a country road for a figure—referred to as Godot—who never arrives. *Waiting for Godot*, which ran for more than 100 performances, became an immediate cause célèbre, and critics struggled to come to terms with its reduced but undeniably powerful dramatic vision. Beckett's "tragicomedy" was soon produced in Berlin (1953), London (1955), and Miami (the United States premiere, 1956); in the decades since, it has received theatrical productions all over the world.

In the plays that followed *Godot*, Beckett continued his theatrical innovations as he explored the human predicament. The action of *Endgame* (1957), one of Beckett's most bleakly comic plays, is restricted to a room set against a postapocalyptic landscape; its characters, positioned like pieces in the terminal stage of a chess match, play out their diminished existence within a world that is winding down. *Krapp's Last Tape* (1958) explores the existence of the individual in time as its lone protagonist plays the recorded voices of his earlier selves. In *Happy Days* (1961), a woman buried in a mound up to her waist—then neck—plays with the objects and words that are all that is left of her world. *Play* (1963) offers one of Beckett's most arresting stage images: three characters, entombed up to their necks in urns, recount the details of a love triangle in alternating confessional fragments. In the late 1950s and early 1960s, he also wrote several plays for radio—including *All That Fall*, which was broadcast by the British Broadcasting Company in 1957—that allowed him to experiment with the staging of disembodied voices.

Following the principle that less is more, Beckett's drama from *Godot* to *Play* is increasingly minimalistic, with its characters progressively immobilized and its dialogue transformed into interiorized monologues. Through that process, this drama laid the foundation for his remarkable plays of the 1970s and 1980s, where character and setting are more radically reduced and even the human body is subject to fragmentation. The protagonist of *Not I* (1972) is a mouth: illuminated at a height of 8 feet above the stage floor, it narrates the disconnected pieces of a life that it refuses to acknowledge as its own. A companion play, *That Time* (1976), features a suspended head listening to the voices of intersecting memories. Inhabiting an increasingly spectral space, the figures who people these and other late Beckett plays—*Footfalls* (1976), *Rockaby* (1981), *Ohio Impromptu* (1981), and *What Where* (1983), to name some of the most prominent— encounter the voices of their own ghosted lives within a field of emptiness and silence. This deepening minimalism also characterizes Beckett's late plays for television, a medium whose dramatic possibilities first interested him in the 1960s. His television plays of the 1970s and 1980s—including *Ghost Trio* (1977), *. . . but the clouds . . .* (1977), and *Nacht und Träume* (1983)—exploit the medium's technical possibilities in order to achieve unearthly, and deeply lyrical, visual landscapes. By the 1970s, Beckett's dramatic writing—and his continuing work in fiction—had garnered an international reputation; he received the Nobel Prize in Literature in 1969, and he was revered as one of the greatest living writers until his death in 1989. Since then, his plays have continued to be produced around the world.

Waiting for Godot, the play that launched Beckett's career in the theater, reflects the intellectual and artistic climate of a Europe still recovering from the devastation of World War II. In the aftermath of the war's unprecedented horrors, a number of Continental dramatists rejected dramatic coherence and logic and the centuries-old tradition of rationality on which they stood. In 1961, the critic Martin Esslin coined the influential phrase "Theater of the Absurd" to describe the drama of Beckett, Eugène Ionesco, Jean Genet, and others. Philosophically akin to the writings of Albert Camus, Jean-Paul Sartre, and other existential philosophers who were writing about human existence in a world without meaning, the Theater of the Absurd, according to Esslin, sought to convey this human condition in nontraditional dramatic forms. In *The Myth of Sisyphus* (1942), Albert Camus wrote:

> A world that can be explained by reasoning, however faulty, is a familiar world. But in a universe that is suddenly deprived of illusions and of light, man feels a stranger. His is an irremediable exile, because he is deprived of memories of a lost homeland as much as he lacks the hope of a promised land to come. This divorce between man and his life, the actor and his setting, truly constitutes the feeling of Absurdity.

Playing out the implications of Camus' theatrical metaphor, Beckett dismantles the elements, or meaning structures, that have sustained and defined dramatic literature. In place of a plot that might organize onstage incidents in relation to each other and that generates movement toward a conclusion, *Waiting for Godot* is organized around activities—pacing, speaking, remembering, falling down—that refuse to cohere into a beginning, middle, and end. Instead of presenting dramatic action, Beckett dramatizes the condition of waiting, a quintessential non-action that depends on forces and events beyond the acting subject. Time, for its part, loses what claim it has to linearity and becomes disconnected and unknowable. The amount of time that elapses between acts 1 and 2 of *Godot* remains mysterious: the latter act seems to take place the next day, but the lone onstage tree has sprouted leaves—a change that suggests a longer temporal span—and neither Vladimir (Didi) nor Estragon (Gogo), the play's protagonists, can determine how much time has passed. The play's minimalist setting—"A country road. A tree."—is equally indeterminate. Unlike the coherent settings of such modern dramatists as HENRIK IBSEN or GEORGE BERNARD SHAW, Beckett's setting is a kind of nonplace. Uncongenial, not humanized in any way, it is obviously a stage, and an empty one at that. The world beyond the stage is even more frightening and unknown. The characters make references

The second act of *Waiting for Godot* in the 1961 Paris Odeon production. The tree was designed by Beckett's friend, the Italian sculptor Alberto Giacometti.

to more idyllic times and places—climbing the Eiffel Tower in the 1890s, grape harvesting near the Rhône—but it is barely conceivable that these realms could be continuous with the inert, radically reduced world the text describes.

Like all of Beckett's characters, Vladimir and Estragon try to understand this world and to come to terms with their own being (or nonbeing) as its inhabitants. Waiting for a figure whose arrival might give meaning to their lives, the two ponder their condition while devising strategies to pass the time. It is worth noting, in this regard, that the play's original French title—*En attendant Godot*—translates into English more accurately as "While waiting for Godot," a participial phrase that shifts attention from the act of waiting to what one does to kill time during that time of waiting. Didi and Gogo develop routines—putting on boots, engaging in crosstalk "canters," even (they fantasize) hanging themselves—that provide distractions from the tedium of waiting. Much of the crosstalk and many of the routines that these tramps devise recall vaudeville and music hall entertainment, clown performances, and the silent films of Charlie Chaplin; indeed, the many visual gags (pants falling down, pratfalls, exchanges of hats) of *Waiting for Godot* help explain why this play has attracted many of the theater's finest comic actors. But there is no mistaking either the urgency of the characters' attempts to distract themselves through such activities or the high stakes for these figures whose very reality and purpose elude their grasp. As Estragon says to Vladimir, "We always find something, eh Didi, to give us the impression we exist?" The absurdity of their predicament and the meaninglessness of their existence repeatedly interrupt their attempts at play, particularly at those times when language gives way to silence. In such moments, as Beckett wrote in his study of Proust, "the boredom of living is replaced by the suffering of being." After one particularly long silence, Vladimir's anguish is undisguisable: "Say something! . . . Say anything at all!"

The two tramps' greatest distraction in each of the two acts is the arrival and departure of Pozzo and Lucky, whose master-slave relationship is reflected in the rope that connects them. Pozzo, a former landowner, seeks to dominate the stage and those around him with oratorical declamations and physical assertions of power. The ironically named Lucky, his servant, carries his bags like a packhorse and submits to Pozzo's abuse. Lucky remains silent until commanded to "think" near the end of the first act, at which point he delivers a disjointed monologue consisting of quasi-philosophical and quasi-theological discourse, arcane and invented references, and sexual/scatological wordplay. This monologue, which teases the audience with fragmentary structures and half meanings amid its barrage of apparent nonsense, offers a mock-academic portrayal of an intellectual tradition whose religious and rational frameworks have imploded. The very notion of an originative thinking subject is undermined by Lucky's performance. His torrent of words issues forth—involuntarily, it seems—like water from a faucet, and it is turned off just as mechanically when Vladimir wrestles away his hat.

Pozzo and Lucky cross the stage in each act, moving on a linear course between unknown points. In this regard, they differ from Vladimir and Estragon, who return to the same point each evening, who mark the boundaries of their familiar space by marking the edges of the stage, and whose existence is one of familiarities and recurrences. Pozzo and Lucky undergo catastrophic changes between acts—Pozzo becomes blind, and Lucky loses the ability to speak—while the two tramps seem largely unchanged. Like the German drinking song that Vladimir sings to open it—in which a dog's death is recounted in an endlessly repeating narrative—the play's second act recapitulates many of the situations, actions, and changes of the first act. At the same time, it is not an exact repetition. The scholar Vivian Mercier may have characterized Godot, famously, as "a play in which nothing happens, twice," but the shape and feel of nothing assume different forms in the two acts. The second act is noticeably darker than the first, the comic efforts of its central figures more strained. Time for Didi and Gogo is a process of diminishment, in which "lessness" (to borrow a title from one of Beckett's late prose pieces) makes itself felt with increasing force. The carrot of act 1 is gone in act 2. Even memory seems to weaken between acts. The two characters labor to remember what happened in act 1, and the uncertainty that they confront renders their lives even more out of their control.

And what about Godot, the object of their waiting? Scholars have speculated on the origins of this name—Godeau is the name of an absent character in a Balzac novel, and *godillot* and *godasse* are French slang terms for "boot"—but whatever echoes the name may carry, the identity of this figure remains, in the end, unknowable. A frequent assumption by spectators, readers, and critics is that Godot represents the Christian God and that his absence marks the twentieth-century historical moment when the Age of Faith had passed and the idea of God no longer served, in the minds of leading artists and intellectuals, as the foundation of moral order. The play is filled, to be sure, with Christian references and allusions: Didi and Gogo speak of the two thieves who were crucified on either side of Jesus, and references to crucifixion, salvation, and other Christian motifs occur throughout. But the name "Godot" is not linguistically identical with "God"; and as Beckett himself noted, this resemblance is wholly absent from the text in French, the play's original language. Beckett also said that if he knew who Godot was, he would have said so in the play. In the absence of such direct identification, we can conclude little more than the following: Godot is that for which Didi and Gogo wait, the absent promise on which they pin their desires for meaningfulness and purpose. Does he really exist? Though his repeated failure to arrive may suggest that he doesn't, the entrance of a boy who brings a message from him at the end of each act undermines even this potential certainty. Beckett once stated, not surprisingly, that his favorite word was "perhaps."

Against their uncertainty and disappointment, the dignity of these two tramps lies in their insistence on keeping their appointment and their refusal to succumb to despair, close though they may come to it. They also have the presence of each other and their shared familiarity, which keeps them together even though they ask themselves, in moments of weariness, whether they should part. Finally, they have the consolation of language, which finds poetry in the most painful of recognitions: "Astride of a grave and a difficult birth. Down in the hole, lingeringly, the grave-digger puts on the forceps. We have time to grow old. The air is full of our cries." In its gritty lyricism and daringly innovative use of the stage, this most original of plays offers a theatrically rich portrayal of boredom, anguish, hope, and resiliency. In urging his London audience to see *Waiting for Godot,* Harold Hobson, one of the play's first English reviewers, captured its haunting power for a generation that had experienced nothing like it: "At the worst you will discover a curiosity, a four-leaved clover, a black tulip; at the best, something that will securely lodge in a corner of your mind for as long as you live."

S.G.

Waiting for Godot
A Tragicomedy in Two Acts[1]

CHARACTERS

ESTRAGON	POZZO
VLADIMIR	A BOY
LUCKY	

Act 1

A country road. A tree.
Evening.

[ESTRAGON, *sitting on a low mound, is trying to take off his boot. He pulls at it with both hands, panting. He gives up, exhausted, rests, tries again. As before.*]

[*Enter* VLADIMIR.]

ESTRAGON [*giving up again*] Nothing to be done.

VLADIMIR [*advancing with short, stiff strides, legs wide apart*] I'm beginning to come round to that opinion. All my life I've tried to put it from me, saying, Vladimir, be reasonable, you haven't yet tried everything. And I resumed the struggle. [*He broods, musing on the struggle. Turning to* ESTRAGON.] So there you are again.

ESTRAGON Am I?

VLADIMIR I'm glad to see you back. I thought you were gone for ever.

ESTRAGON Me too.

VLADIMIR Together again at last! We'll have to celebrate this. But how? [*He reflects.*] Get up till I embrace you.

ESTRAGON [*irritably*] Not now, not now.

VLADIMIR [*hurt, coldly*] May one enquire where His Highness spent the night?

ESTRAGON In a ditch.

VLADIMIR [*admiringly*] A ditch! Where?

ESTRAGON [*without gesture*] Over there.

VLADIMIR And they didn't beat you?

ESTRAGON Beat me? Certainly they beat me.

VLADIMIR The same lot as usual?

ESTRAGON The same? I don't know.

VLADIMIR When I think of it . . . all these years . . . but for me . . . where would you be . . . [*Decisively*] You'd be nothing more than a little heap of bones at the present minute, no doubt about it.

ESTRAGON And what of it?

1. Translated from the original French text by the author.

VLADIMIR [*gloomily*] It's too much for one man. [*Pause. Cheerfully.*] On the other hand what's the good of losing heart now, that's what I say. We should have thought of it a million years ago, in the nineties.[2]

ESTRAGON Ah stop blathering and help me off with this bloody thing.

VLADIMIR Hand in hand from the top of the Eiffel Tower, among the first. We were respectable in those days. Now it's too late. They wouldn't even let us up. [ESTRAGON *tears at his boot.*] What are you doing?

ESTRAGON Taking off my boot. Did that never happen to you?

VLADIMIR Boots must be taken off every day, I'm tired telling you that. Why don't you listen to me?

ESTRAGON [*feebly*] Help me!

VLADIMIR It hurts?

ESTRAGON [*angrily*] Hurts! He wants to know if it hurts!

VLADIMIR [*angrily*] No one ever suffers but you. I don't count. I'd like to hear what you'd say if you had what I have.

ESTRAGON It hurts?

VLADIMIR [*angrily*] Hurts! He wants to know if it hurts!

ESTRAGON [*pointing*] You might button it all the same.

VLADIMIR [*stooping*] True. [*He buttons his fly.*] Never neglect the little things of life.

ESTRAGON What do you expect, you always wait till the last moment.

VLADIMIR [*musingly*] The last moment . . . [*He meditates.*] Hope deferred maketh the something sick, who said that?[3]

ESTRAGON Why don't you help me?

VLADIMIR Sometimes I feel it coming all the same. Then I go all queer. [*He takes off his hat, peers inside it, feels about inside it, shakes it, puts it on again.*] How shall I say? Relieved and at the same time . . . [*He searches for the word.*] . . . appalled. [*With emphasis*] AP-PALLED. [*He takes off his hat again, peers inside it.*] Funny. [*He knocks on the crown as though to dislodge a foreign body, peers into it again, puts it on again.*] Nothing to be done. [ESTRAGON *with a supreme effort succeeds in pulling off his boot. He peers inside it, feels about inside it, turns it upside down, shakes it, looks on the ground to see if anything has fallen out, finds nothing, feels inside it again, staring sightlessly before him.*] Well?

ESTRAGON Nothing.

VLADIMIR Show.

ESTRAGON There's nothing to show.

VLADIMIR Try and put it on again.

ESTRAGON [*examining his foot*] I'll air it for a bit.

VLADIMIR There's man all over for you, blaming on his boots the faults of his feet. [*He takes off his hat again, peers inside it, feels about inside it, knocks on the crown, blows into it, puts it on again.*] This is getting alarming. [*Silence. Vladimir deep in thought, Estragon pulling at his toes.*] One of the thieves was saved.[4] [*Pause*] It's a reasonable percentage. [*Pause*] Gogo.

2. That is, the 1890s.

3. "Hope deferred maketh the heart sick: but when the desire cometh, it is a tree of life" (Proverbs 13.12).

4. That is, one of the two thieves crucified at the same time as Jesus. One of the Gospels describes one thief railing at him and the other asking to be remembered in heaven. To the second thief Jesus replied, "Verily I say unto thee, Today shalt thou be with me in paradise" (Luke 23.43).

ESTRAGON What?
VLADIMIR Suppose we repented.
ESTRAGON Repented what?
VLADIMIR Oh . . . [*He reflects.*] We wouldn't have to go into the details.
ESTRAGON Our being born?

[VLADIMIR *breaks into a hearty laugh which he immediately stifles, his hand pressed to his pubis, his face contorted.*]

VLADIMIR One daren't even laugh any more.
ESTRAGON Dreadful privation.
VLADIMIR Merely smile. [*He smiles suddenly from ear to ear, keeps smiling, ceases as suddenly.*] It's not the same thing. Nothing to be done. [*Pause*] Gogo.
ESTRAGON [*irritably*] What is it?
VLADIMIR Did you ever read the Bible?
ESTRAGON The Bible . . . [*He reflects.*] I must have taken a look at it.
VLADIMIR Do you remember the Gospels?
ESTRAGON I remember the maps of the Holy Land. Coloured they were. Very pretty. The Dead Sea[5] was pale blue. The very look of it made me thirsty. That's where we'll go, I used to say, that's where we'll go for our honeymoon. We'll swim. We'll be happy.
VLADIMIR You should have been a poet.
ESTRAGON I was. [*Gesture towards his rags*] Isn't that obvious?

[*Silence.*]

VLADIMIR Where was I . . . How's your foot?
ESTRAGON Swelling visibly.
VLADIMIR Ah yes, the two thieves. Do you remember the story?
ESTRAGON No.
VLADIMIR Shall I tell it to you?
ESTRAGON No.
VLADIMIR It'll pass the time. [*Pause*] Two thieves, crucified at the same time as our Saviour. One—
ESTRAGON Our what?
VLADIMIR Our Saviour. Two thieves. One is supposed to have been saved and the other . . . [*He searches for the contrary of saved.*] . . . damned.
ESTRAGON Saved from what?
VLADIMIR Hell.
ESTRAGON I'm going.

[*He does not move.*]

VLADIMIR And yet . . . [*Pause*] . . . how is it—this is not boring you I hope—how is it that of the four Evangelists only one speaks of a thief being saved. The four of them were there—or thereabouts—and only one speaks of a thief being saved. [*Pause*] Come on, Gogo, return the ball, can't you, once in a way?
ESTRAGON [*with exaggerated enthusiasm*] I find this really most extraordinarily interesting.

5. A salt lake, about 45 miles long and up to 10 miles wide, on the boundary between Israel and Jordan.

VLADIMIR One out of four. Of the other three two don't mention any thieves at all and the third says that both of them abused him.[6]

ESTRAGON Who?

VLADIMIR What?

ESTRAGON What's all this about? Abused who?

VLADIMIR The Saviour.

ESTRAGON Why?

VLADIMIR Because he wouldn't save them.

ESTRAGON From hell?

VLADIMIR Imbecile! From death.

ESTRAGON I thought you said hell.

VLADIMIR From death, from death.

ESTRAGON Well what of it?

VLADIMIR Then the two of them must have been damned.

ESTRAGON And why not?

VLADIMIR But one of the four says that one of the two was saved.

ESTRAGON Well? They don't agree and that's all there is to it.

VLADIMIR But all four were there. And only one speaks of a thief being saved. Why believe him rather than the others?

ESTRAGON Who believes him?

VLADIMIR Everybody. It's the only version they know.

ESTRAGON People are bloody ignorant apes.

[*He rises painfully, goes limping to extreme left, halts, gazes into distance off with his hand screening his eyes, turns, goes to extreme right, gazes into distance.* VLADIMIR *watches him, then goes and picks up the boot, peers into it, drops it hastily.*]

VLADIMIR Pah!

[*He spits.* ESTRAGON *moves to center, halts with his back to auditorium.*]

ESTRAGON Charming spot. [*He turns, advances to front, halts facing auditorium.*] Inspiring prospects. [*He turns to* VLADIMIR.] Let's go.

VLADIMIR We can't.

ESTRAGON Why not?

VLADIMIR We're waiting for Godot.

ESTRAGON [*despairingly*] Ah! [*Pause*] You're sure it was here?

VLADIMIR What?

ESTRAGON That we were to wait.

VLADIMIR He said by the tree. [*They look at the tree.*] Do you see any others?

ESTRAGON What is it?

VLADIMIR I don't know. A willow.[7]

ESTRAGON Where are the leaves?

VLADIMIR It must be dead.

ESTRAGON No more weeping.

VLADIMIR Or perhaps it's not the season.

ESTRAGON Looks to me more like a bush.

VLADIMIR A shrub.

ESTRAGON A bush.

6. See Matthew 27.44. Both Mark (15.27) and John (who calls them simply "two others"; 19.18) mention the thieves.

7. A tree associated with mourning.

VLADIMIR A—. What are you insinuating? That we've come to the wrong place?

ESTRAGON He should be here.

VLADIMIR He didn't say for sure he'd come.

ESTRAGON And if he doesn't come?

VLADIMIR We'll come back tomorrow.

ESTRAGON And then the day after tomorrow.

VLADIMIR Possibly.

ESTRAGON And so on.

VLADIMIR The point is—

ESTRAGON Until he comes.

VLADIMIR You're merciless.

ESTRAGON We came here yesterday.

VLADIMIR Ah no, there you're mistaken.

ESTRAGON What did we do yesterday?

VLADIMIR What did we do yesterday?

ESTRAGON Yes.

VLADIMIR Why . . . [*Angrily*] Nothing is certain when you're about.

ESTRAGON In my opinion we were here.

VLADIMIR [*looking round*] You recognize the place?

ESTRAGON I didn't say that.

VLADIMIR Well?

ESTRAGON That makes no difference.

VLADIMIR All the same . . . that tree . . . [*Turning towards auditorium*] that bog . . .

ESTRAGON You're sure it was this evening?

VLADIMIR What?

ESTRAGON That we were to wait.

VLADIMIR He said Saturday. [*Pause*] I think.

ESTRAGON You think.

VLADIMIR I must have made a note of it. [*He fumbles in his pockets, bursting with miscellaneous rubbish.*]

ESTRAGON [*very insidious*] But what Saturday? And is it Saturday? Is it not rather Sunday? [*Pause*] Or Monday? [*Pause*] Or Friday?

VLADIMIR [*looking wildly about him, as though the date was inscribed in the landscape*] It's not possible!

ESTRAGON Or Thursday?

VLADIMIR What'll we do?

ESTRAGON If he came yesterday and we weren't here you may be sure he won't come again today.

VLADIMIR But you say we were here yesterday.

ESTRAGON I may be mistaken. [*Pause*] Let's stop talking for a minute, do you mind?

VLADIMIR [*feebly*] All right. [ESTRAGON *sits down on the mound.* VLADIMIR *paces agitatedly to and fro, halting from time to time to gaze into distance off.* ESTRAGON *falls asleep.* VLADIMIR *halts finally before* ESTRAGON.] Gogo! . . . Gogo! . . . GOGO!

[ESTRAGON *wakes with a start.*]

ESTRAGON [*restored to the horror of his situation*] I was asleep! [*Despairingly*] Why will you never let me sleep?

VLADIMIR I felt lonely.

ESTRAGON I had a dream.

VLADIMIR Don't tell me!

ESTRAGON I dreamt that—

VLADIMIR DON'T TELL ME!

ESTRAGON [*gesture towards the universe*] This one is enough for you? [*Silence*] It's not nice of you, Didi. Who am I to tell my private nightmares to if I can't tell them to you?

VLADIMIR Let them remain private. You know I can't bear that.

ESTRAGON [*coldly*] There are times when I wonder if it wouldn't be better for us to part.

VLADIMIR You wouldn't go far.

ESTRAGON That would be too bad, really too bad. [*Pause*] Wouldn't it, Didi, be really too bad? [*Pause*] When you think of the beauty of the way. [*Pause*] And the goodness of the wayfarers. [*Pause. Wheedling.*] Wouldn't it, Didi?

VLADIMIR Calm yourself.

ESTRAGON [*voluptuously*] Calm . . . calm . . . The English say cawm. [*Pause*] You know the story of the Englishman in the brothel?

VLADIMIR Yes.

ESTRAGON Tell it to me.

VLADIMIR Ah stop it!

ESTRAGON An Englishman having drunk a little more than usual proceeds to a brothel. The bawd asks him if he wants a fair one, a dark one or a red-haired one. Go on.

VLADIMIR STOP IT!

[*Exit* VLADIMIR *hurriedly.* ESTRAGON *gets up and follows him as far as the limit of the stage. Gestures of* ESTRAGON *like those of a spectator encouraging a pugilist. Enter* VLADIMIR. *He brushes past* ESTRAGON, *crosses the stage with bowed head.* ESTRAGON *takes a step towards him, halts.*]

ESTRAGON [*gently*] You wanted to speak to me? [*Silence.* ESTRAGON *takes a step forward.*] You had something to say to me? [*Silence. Another step forward.*] Didi . . .

VLADIMIR [*without turning*] I've nothing to say to you.

ESTRAGON [*step forward*] You're angry? [*Silence. Step forward.*] Forgive me. [*Silence. Step forward.* ESTRAGON *lays his hand on* VLADIMIR*'s shoulder.*] Come, Didi. [*Silence*] Give me your hand. [VLADIMIR *half turns.*] Embrace me! [VLADIMIR *stiffens.*] Don't be stubborn! [VLADIMIR *softens. They embrace.* ESTRAGON *recoils.*] You stink of garlic!

VLADIMIR It's for the kidneys. [*Silence.* ESTRAGON *looks attentively at the tree.*] What do we do now?

ESTRAGON Wait.

VLADIMIR Yes, but while waiting.

ESTRAGON What about hanging ourselves?

VLADIMIR Hmm. It'd give us an erection.

ESTRAGON [*highly excited*] An erection!

VLADIMIR With all that follows. Where it[8] falls mandrakes grow. That's why they shriek when you pull them up. Did you not know that?

8. That is, semen. The mandrake, whose root sometimes splits in a way that resembles a man's body, was long believed to be inhabited by a demon (its shriek at being uprooted was said to be fatal). The idea that mandrakes grow from the semen of hanged men was widespread in Europe in the Middle Ages.

ESTRAGON Let's hang ourselves immediately!
VLADIMIR From a bough? [*They go towards the tree.*] I wouldn't trust it.
ESTRAGON We can always try.
VLADIMIR Go ahead.
ESTRAGON After you.
VLADIMIR No no, you first.
ESTRAGON Why me?
VLADIMIR You're lighter than I am.
ESTRAGON Just so!
VLADIMIR I don't understand.
ESTRAGON Use your intelligence, can't you?

[VLADIMIR *uses his intelligence.*]

VLADIMIR [*finally*] I remain in the dark.
ESTRAGON This is how it is. [*He reflects.*] The bough . . . the bough . . . [*Angrily*] Use your head, can't you?
VLADIMIR You're my only hope.
ESTRAGON [*with effort*] Gogo light—bough not break—Gogo dead. Didi heavy—bough break—Didi alone. Whereas—
VLADIMIR I hadn't thought of that.
ESTRAGON If it hangs you it'll hang anything.
VLADIMIR But am I heavier than you?
ESTRAGON So you tell me. I don't know. There's an even chance. Or nearly.
VLADIMIR Well? What do we do?
ESTRAGON Don't let's do anything. It's safer.
VLADIMIR Let's wait and see what he says.
ESTRAGON Who?
VLADIMIR Godot.
ESTRAGON Good idea.
VLADIMIR Let's wait till we know exactly how we stand.
ESTRAGON On the other hand it might be better to strike the iron before it freezes.[9]
VLADIMIR I'm curious to hear what he has to offer. Then we'll take it or leave it.
ESTRAGON What exactly did we ask him for?
VLADIMIR Were you not there?
ESTRAGON I can't have been listening.
VLADIMIR Oh . . . Nothing very definite.
ESTRAGON A kind of prayer.
VLADIMIR Precisely.
ESTRAGON A vague supplication.
VLADIMIR Exactly.
ESTRAGON And what did he reply?
VLADIMIR That he'd see.
ESTRAGON That he couldn't promise anything.
VLADIMIR That he'd have to think it over.
ESTRAGON In the quiet of his home.
VLADIMIR Consult his family.

9. A version of the proverb "Strike while the iron is hot," whose earliest attribution is to Publilius Syrus (1st c. B.C.E.).

ESTRAGON His friends.
VLADIMIR His agents.
ESTRAGON His correspondents.
VLADIMIR His books.
ESTRAGON His bank account.
VLADIMIR Before taking a decision.[1]
ESTRAGON It's the normal thing.
VLADIMIR Is it not?
ESTRAGON I think it is.
VLADIMIR I think so too.

[*Silence.*]

ESTRAGON [*anxious*] And we?
VLADIMIR I beg your pardon?
ESTRAGON I said, And we?
VLADIMIR I don't understand.
ESTRAGON Where do we come in?
VLADIMIR Come in?
ESTRAGON Take your time.
VLADIMIR Come in? On our hands and knees.
ESTRAGON As bad as that?
VLADIMIR Your Worship wishes to assert his prerogatives?
ESTRAGON We've no rights any more?

[*Laugh of* VLADIMIR, *stifled as before, less the smile.*]

VLADIMIR You'd make me laugh if it wasn't prohibited.
ESTRAGON We've lost our rights?
VLADIMIR [*distinctly*] We got rid of them.

[*Silence. They remain motionless, arms dangling, heads sunk, sagging at the knees.*]

ESTRAGON [*feebly*] We're not tied? [*Pause*] We're not—
VLADIMIR Listen!

[*They listen, grotesquely rigid.*]

ESTRAGON I hear nothing.
VLADIMIR Hsst! [*They listen.* ESTRAGON *loses his balance, almost falls. He clutches the arm of* VLADIMIR *who totters. They listen, huddled together.*] Nor I.

[*Sighs of relief. They relax and separate.*]

ESTRAGON You gave me a fright.
VLADIMIR I thought it was he.
ESTRAGON Who?
VLADIMIR Godot.
ESTRAGON Pah! The wind in the reeds.
VLADIMIR I could have sworn I heard shouts.
ESTRAGON And why would he shout?
VLADIMIR At his horse.

[*Silence.*]

ESTRAGON [*violently*] I'm hungry!
VLADIMIR Do you want a carrot?

1. That is, making a decision (a British idiom).

ESTRAGON Is that all there is?

VLADIMIR I might have some turnips.

ESTRAGON Give me a carrot. [VLADIMIR *rummages in his pockets, takes out a turnip and gives it to* ESTRAGON *who takes a bite out of it. Angrily.*] It's a turnip!

VLADIMIR Oh pardon! I could have sworn it was a carrot. [*He rummages again in his pockets, finds nothing but turnips.*] All that's turnips. [*He rummages.*] You must have eaten the last. [*He rummages.*] Wait, I have it. [*He brings out a carrot and gives it to* ESTRAGON.] There, dear fellow. [ESTRAGON *wipes the carrot on his sleeve and begins to eat it.*] Make it last, that's the end of them.

ESTRAGON [*chewing*] I asked you a question.

VLADIMIR Ah.

ESTRAGON Did you reply?

VLADIMIR How's the carrot?

ESTRAGON It's a carrot.

VLADIMIR So much the better, so much the better. [*Pause.*] What was it you wanted to know?

ESTRAGON I've forgotten. [*Chews.*] That's what annoys me. [*He looks at the carrot appreciatively, dangles it between finger and thumb.*] I'll never forget this carrot. [*He sucks the end of it meditatively.*] Ah yes, now I remember.

VLADIMIR Well?

ESTRAGON [*his mouth full, vacuously*] We're not tied?

VLADIMIR I don't hear a word you're saying.

ESTRAGON [*chews, swallows*] I'm asking you if we're tied.

VLADIMIR Tied?

ESTRAGON Ti-ed.

VLADIMIR How do you mean tied?

ESTRAGON Down.

VLADIMIR But to whom? By whom?

ESTRAGON To your man.

VLADIMIR To Godot? Tied to Godot! What an idea! No question of it. [*Pause*] For the moment

ESTRAGON His name is Godot?

VLADIMIR I think so.

ESTRAGON Fancy that. [*He raises what remains of the carrot by the stub of leaf, twirls it before his eyes.*] Funny, the more you eat the worse it gets.

VLADIMIR With me it's just the opposite.

ESTRAGON In other words?

VLADIMIR I get used to the muck as I go along.

ESTRAGON [*after prolonged reflection*] Is that the opposite?

VLADIMIR Question of temperament.

ESTRAGON Of character.

VLADIMIR Nothing you can do about it.

ESTRAGON No use struggling.

VLADIMIR One is what one is.

ESTRAGON No use wriggling.

VLADIMIR The essential doesn't change.

ESTRAGON Nothing to be done. [*He proffers the remains of the carrot to* VLADIMIR.] Like to finish it?

[*A terrible cry, close at hand.* ESTRAGON *drops the carrot. They remain motionless, then together make a sudden rush towards the wings.* ESTRAGON *stops halfway, runs back, picks up the carrot, stuffs it in his pocket, runs to rejoin* VLADIMIR *who is waiting for him, stops again, runs back, picks up his boot, runs to rejoin* VLADIMIR. *Huddled together, shoulders hunched, cringing away from the menace, they wait.*]

[*Enter* POZZO *and* LUCKY. POZZO *drives* LUCKY *by means of a rope passed round his neck, so that* LUCKY *is the first to enter, followed by the rope which is long enough to let him reach the middle of the stage before* POZZO *appears.* LUCKY *carries a heavy bag, a folding stool, a picnic basket and a greatcoat,* POZZO *a whip.*]

POZZO [*off*] On! [*Crack of whip.* POZZO *appears. They cross the stage.* LUCKY *passes before* VLADIMIR *and* ESTRAGON *and exit.* POZZO *at the sight of* VLADIMIR *and* ESTRAGON *stops short. The rope tautens.* POZZO *jerks at it violently.*] Back!

[*Noise of* LUCKY *falling with all his baggage.* VLADIMIR *and* ESTRAGON *turn towards him, half wishing half fearing to go to his assistance.* VLADIMIR *takes a step towards Lucky,* ESTRAGON *holds him back by the sleeve.*]

VLADIMIR Let me go!

ESTRAGON Stay where you are!

POZZO Be careful! He's wicked. [VLADIMIR *and* ESTRAGON *turn towards* POZZO.] With strangers.

ESTRAGON [*undertone*] Is that him?

VLADIMIR Who?

ESTRAGON [*trying to remember the name*] Er . . .

VLADIMIR Godot?

ESTRAGON Yes.

POZZO I present myself: Pozzo.

VLADIMIR [*to* ESTRAGON] Not at all!

ESTRAGON He said Godot.

VLADIMIR Not at all!

ESTRAGON [*timidly, to* POZZO] You're not Mr. Godot, Sir?

POZZO [*terrifying voice*] I am Pozzo! [*Silence*] Pozzo! [*Silence*] Does that name mean nothing to you? [*Silence*] I say does that name mean nothing to you?

[VLADIMIR *and* ESTRAGON *look at each other questioningly.*]

ESTRAGON [*pretending to search*] Bozzo . . . Bozzo . . .

VLADIMIR [*ditto*] Pozzo . . . Pozzo . . .

POZZO PPPOZZZO!

ESTRAGON Ah! Pozzo . . . let me see . . . Pozzo . . .

VLADIMIR Is it Pozzo or Bozzo?

ESTRAGON Pozzo . . . no . . . I'm afraid I . . . no . . . I don't seem to . . .

[POZZO *advances threateningly.*]

VLADIMIR [*conciliating*] I once knew a family called Cozzo. The mother had the clap.[2]

ESTRAGON [*hastily*] We're not from these parts, Sir.

POZZO [*halting*] You are human beings none the less. [*He puts on his glasses.*] As far as one can see. [*He takes off his glasses.*] Of the same species as my-

2. Gonorrhea (slang).

self. [*He bursts into an enormous laugh.*] Of the same species as Pozzo! Made in God's image!

VLADIMIR Well you see—

POZZO [*peremptory*] Who is Godot?

ESTRAGON Godot?

POZZO You took me for Godot.

VLADIMIR Oh no, Sir, not for an instant, Sir.

POZZO Who is he?

VLADIMIR Oh he's a . . . he's a kind of acquaintance.

ESTRAGON Nothing of the kind, we hardly know him.

VLADIMIR True . . . we don't know him very well . . . but all the same . . .

ESTRAGON Personally I wouldn't even know him if I saw him.

POZZO You took me for him.

ESTRAGON [*recoiling before* POZZO] That's to say . . . you understand . . . the dusk . . . the strain . . . waiting . . . I confess . . . I imagined . . . for a second . . .

POZZO Waiting? So you were waiting for him?

VLADIMIR Well you see—

POZZO Here? On my land?

VLADIMIR We didn't intend any harm.

ESTRAGON We meant well.

POZZO The road is free to all.

VLADIMIR That's how we looked at it.

POZZO It's a disgrace. But there you are.

ESTRAGON Nothing we can do about it.

POZZO [*with magnanimous gesture*] Let's say no more about it. [*He jerks the rope.*] Up pig! [*Pause*] Every time he drops he falls asleep. [*Jerks the rope.*] Up hog! [*Noise of* LUCKY *getting up and picking up his baggage.* POZZO *jerks the rope.*] Back! [*Enter* LUCKY *backwards.*] Stop! [LUCKY *stops.*] Turn! [LUCKY *turns. To* VLADIMIR *and* ESTRAGON, *affably.*] Gentlemen, I am happy to have met you. [*Before their incredulous expression*] Yes yes, sincerely happy. [*He jerks the rope.*] Closer! [LUCKY *advances.*] Stop! [LUCKY *stops.*] Yes, the road seems long when one journeys all alone for . . . [*He consults his watch.*] . . . yes . . . [*He calculates.*] . . . yes, six hours, that's right, six hours on end, and never a soul in sight. [*To* LUCKY] Coat! [LUCKY *puts down the bag, advances, gives the coat, goes back to his place, takes up the bag.*] Hold that! [POZZO *holds out the whip.* LUCKY *advances and, both his hands being occupied, takes the whip in his mouth, then goes back to his place.* POZZO *begins to put on his coat, stops.*] Coat! [LUCKY *puts down bag, basket and stool, advances, helps* POZZO *on with his coat, goes back to his place and takes up bag, basket and stool.*] Touch of autumn in the air this evening. [POZZO *finishes buttoning his coat, stoops, inspects himself, straightens up.*] Whip! [LUCKY *advances, stoops,* POZZO *snatches the whip from his mouth,* LUCKY *goes back to his place.*] Yes, gentlemen, I cannot go for long without the society of my likes [*He puts on his glasses and looks at the two likes.*] even when the likeness is an imperfect one. [*He takes off his glasses.*] Stool! [LUCKY *puts down bag and basket, advances, opens stool, puts it down, goes back to his place, takes up bag and basket.*] Closer! [LUCKY *puts down bag and basket, advances, moves stool, goes back to his place, takes up bag and basket.* POZZO *sits down, places the butt of his whip against* LUCKY*'s chest and pushes.*]

Back! [LUCKY *takes a step back.*] Further! [LUCKY *takes another step back.*] Stop! [LUCKY *stops. To* VLADIMIR *and* ESTRAGON.] That is why, with your permission, I propose to dally with you a moment, before I venture any further. Basket! [LUCKY *advances, gives the basket, goes back to his place.*] The fresh air stimulates the jaded appetite. [*He opens the basket, takes out a piece of chicken and a bottle of wine.*] Basket! [LUCKY *advances, picks up the basket and goes back to his place.*] Further! [LUCKY *takes a step back.*] He stinks. Happy days!

[*He drinks from the bottle, puts it down and begins to eat. Silence.* VLADIMIR *and* ESTRAGON, *cautiously at first, then more boldly, begin to circle about* LUCKY, *inspecting him up and down.* POZZO *eats his chicken voraciously, throwing away the bones after having sucked them.* LUCKY *sags slowly, until bag and basket touch the ground, then straightens up with a start and begins to sag again. Rhythm of one sleeping on his feet.*]

ESTRAGON What ails him?
VLADIMIR He looks tired.
ESTRAGON Why doesn't he put down his bags?
VLADIMIR How do I know? [*They close in on him.*] Careful!
ESTRAGON Say something to him.
VLADIMIR Look!
ESTRAGON What?
VLADIMIR [*pointing*] His neck!
ESTRAGON [*looking at the neck*] I see nothing.
VLADIMIR Here.

[ESTRAGON *goes over beside* VLADIMIR.]

ESTRAGON Oh I say!
VLADIMIR A running sore!
ESTRAGON It's the rope.
VLADIMIR It's the rubbing.
ESTRAGON It's inevitable.
VLADIMIR It's the knot.
ESTRAGON It's the chafing.

[*They resume their inspection, dwell on the face.*]

VLADIMIR [*grudgingly*] He's not bad looking.
ESTRAGON [*shrugging his shoulders, wry face*] Would you say so?
VLADIMIR A trifle effeminate.
ESTRAGON Look at the slobber.
VLADIMIR It's inevitable.
ESTRAGON Look at the slaver.[3]
VLADIMIR Perhaps he's a halfwit.
ESTRAGON A cretin.
VLADIMIR [*looking closer*] Looks like a goiter.
ESTRAGON [*ditto*] It's not certain.
VLADIMIR He's panting.
ESTRAGON It's inevitable.
VLADIMIR And his eyes!
ESTRAGON What about them?
VLADIMIR Goggling out of his head.

3. Saliva falling from the mouth.

ESTRAGON Looks at his last gasp to me.

VLADIMIR It's not certain. [*Pause*] Ask him a question.

ESTRAGON Would that be a good thing?

VLADIMIR What do we risk?

ESTRAGON [*timidly*] Mister . . .

VLADIMIR Louder.

ESTRAGON [*louder*] Mister . . .

POZZO Leave him in peace! [*They turn towards* POZZO *who, having finished eating, wipes his mouth with the back of his hand.*] Can't you see he wants to rest? Basket! [*He strikes a match and begins to light his pipe.* ESTRAGON *sees the chicken bones on the ground and stares at them greedily. As* LUCKY *does not move* POZZO *throws the match angrily away and jerks the rope.*] Basket! [LUCKY *starts, almost falls, recovers his senses, advances, puts the bottle in the basket and goes back to his place.* ESTRAGON *stares at the bones.* POZZO *strikes another match and lights his pipe.*] What can you expect, it's not his job. [*He pulls at his pipe, stretches out his legs.*] Ah! That's better.

ESTRAGON [*timidly*] Please Sir . . .

POZZO What is it, my good man?

ESTRAGON Er . . . you've finished with the . . . er . . . you don't need the . . . er . . . bones, Sir?

VLADIMIR [*scandalized*] You couldn't have waited?

POZZO No no, he does well to ask. Do I need the bones? [*He turns them over with the end of his whip.*] No, personally I do not need them any more. [ESTRAGON *takes a step towards the bones.*] But . . . [ESTRAGON *stops short.*] . . . but in theory the bones go to the carrier. He is therefore the one to ask. [ESTRAGON *turns towards* LUCKY, *hesitates.*] Go on, go on, don't be afraid, ask him, he'll tell you.

[ESTRAGON *goes towards* LUCKY, *stops before him.*]

ESTRAGON Mister . . . excuse me, Mister . . .

POZZO You're being spoken to, pig! Reply! [*To* ESTRAGON] Try him again.

ESTRAGON Excuse me, Mister, the bones, you won't be wanting the bones?

[LUCKY *looks long at* ESTRAGON.]

POZZO [*in raptures*] Mister! [LUCKY *bows his head.*] Reply! Do you want them or don't you? [*Silence of* LUCKY. *To* ESTRAGON.] They're yours. [ESTRAGON *makes a dart at the bones, picks them up and begins to gnaw them.*] I don't like it. I've never known him refuse a bone before. [*He looks anxiously at* LUCKY.] Nice business it'd be if he fell sick on me! [*He puffs at his pipe.*]

VLADIMIR [*exploding*] It's a scandal!

[*Silence. Flabbergasted,* ESTRAGON *stops gnawing, looks at* POZZO *and* VLADIMIR *in turn.* POZZO *outwardly calm.* VLADIMIR *embarrassed.*]

POZZO [*to* VLADIMIR] Are you alluding to anything in particular?

VLADIMIR [*stutteringly resolute*] To treat a man . . . [*Gesture towards* LUCKY] . . . like that . . . I think that . . . no . . . a human being . . . no . . . it's a scandal!

ESTRAGON [*not to be outdone*] A disgrace! [*He resumes his gnawing.*]

POZZO You are severe. [*To* VLADIMIR] What age are you, if it's not a rude question? [*Silence*] Sixty? Seventy? [*To* ESTRAGON] What age would you say he was?

ESTRAGON Eleven.

POZZO I am impertinent. [*He knocks out his pipe against the whip, gets up.*] I must be getting on. Thank you for your society. [*He reflects.*] Unless I smoke another pipe before I go. What do you say? [*They say nothing.*] Oh I'm only a small smoker, a very small smoker, I'm not in the habit of smoking two pipes one on top of the other, it makes [*Hand to heart, sighing*] my heart go pit-a-pat. [*Silence*] It's the nicotine, one absorbs it in spite of one's precautions. [*Sighs*] You know how it is. [*Silence*] But perhaps you don't smoke? Yes? No? It's of no importance. [*Silence*] But how am I to sit down now, without affectation, now that I have risen? Without appearing to—how shall I say—without appearing to falter. [*To* VLADIMIR] I beg your pardon? [*Silence*] Perhaps you didn't speak? [*Silence*] It's of no importance. Let me see . . . [*He reflects.*]

ESTRAGON Ah! That's better. [*He puts the bones in his pocket.*]

VLADIMIR Let's go.

ESTRAGON So soon?

POZZO One moment! [*He jerks the rope.*] Stool! [*He points with his whip.* LUCKY *moves the stool.*] More! There! [*He sits down.* LUCKY *goes back to his place.*] Done it! [*He fills his pipe.*]

VLADIMIR [*vehemently*] Let's go!

POZZO I hope I'm not driving you away. Wait a little longer, you'll never regret it.

ESTRAGON [*sensing charity*] We're in no hurry.

POZZO [*having lit his pipe*] The second is never so sweet . . . [*He takes the pipe out of his mouth, contemplates it.*] . . . as the first I mean. [*He puts the pipe back in his mouth.*] But it's sweet just the same.

VLADIMIR I'm going.

POZZO He can no longer endure my presence. I am perhaps not particularly human, but who cares? [*To* VLADIMIR] Think twice before you do anything rash. Suppose you go now while it is still day, for there is no denying it is still day. [*They all look up at the sky.*] Good. [*They stop looking at the sky.*] What happens in that case—[*He takes the pipe out of his mouth, examines it.*]—I'm out—[*He relights his pipe.*]—in that case—[*Puff*]—in that case—[*Puff*]—what happens in that case to your appointment with this . . . Godet . . . Godot . . . Godin . . . anyhow you see who I mean, who has your future in his hands . . . [*Pause*] . . . at least your immediate future?

VLADIMIR Who told you?

POZZO He speaks to me again! If this goes on much longer we'll soon be old friends.

ESTRAGON Why doesn't he put down his bags?

POZZO I too would be happy to meet him. The more people I meet the happier I become. From the meanest creature one departs wiser, richer, more conscious of one's blessings. Even you . . . [*He looks at them ostentatiously in turn to make it clear they are both meant.*] . . . even you, who knows, will have added to my store.

ESTRAGON Why doesn't he put down his bags?

POZZO But that would surprise me.

VLADIMIR You're being asked a question.

POZZO [*delighted*] A question! Who? What? A moment ago you were calling me Sir, in fear and trembling. Now you're asking me questions. No good will come of this!

VLADIMIR [*to* ESTRAGON] I think he's listening.
ESTRAGON [*circling about* LUCKY] What?
VLADIMIR You can ask him now. He's on the alert.
ESTRAGON Ask him what?
VLADIMIR Why he doesn't put down his bags.
ESTRAGON I wonder.
VLADIMIR Ask him, can't you?
POZZO [*who has followed these exchanges with anxious attention, fearing lest the question get lost*] You want to know why he doesn't put down his bags, as you call them.
VLADIMIR That's it.
POZZO [*to* ESTRAGON] You are sure you agree with that?
ESTRAGON He's puffing like a grampus.[4]
POZZO The answer is this. [*To* ESTRAGON] But stay still, I beg of you, you're making me nervous!
VLADIMIR Here.
ESTRAGON What is it?
VLADIMIR He's about to speak.

[ESTRAGON *goes over beside* VLADIMIR. *Motionless, side by side, they wait.*]

POZZO Good. Is everybody ready? Is everybody looking at me? [*He looks at* LUCKY, *jerks the rope.* LUCKY *raises his head.*] Will you look at me, pig! [LUCKY *looks at him.*] Good. [*He puts the pipe in his pocket, takes out a little vaporizer and sprays his throat, puts back the vaporizer in his pocket, clears his throat, spits, takes out the vaporizer again, sprays his throat again, puts back the vaporizer in his pocket.*] I am ready. Is everybody listening? Is everybody ready? [*He looks at them all in turn, jerks the rope.*] Hog! [LUCKY *raises his head.*] I don't like talking in a vacuum. Good. Let me see. [*He reflects.*]
ESTRAGON I'm going.
POZZO What was it exactly you wanted to know?
VLADIMIR Why he—
POZZO [*angrily*] Don't interrupt me! [*Pause. Calmer.*] If we all speak at once we'll never get anywhere. [*Pause.*] What was I saying? [*Pause. Louder.*] What was I saying?

[VLADIMIR *mimics one carrying a heavy burden.* POZZO *looks at him, puzzled.*]

ESTRAGON [*forcibly*] Bags. [*He points at* LUCKY.] Why? Always hold. [*He sags, panting.*] Never put down. [*He opens his hands, straightens up with relief.*] Why?
POZZO Ah! Why couldn't you say so before? Why he doesn't make himself comfortable? Let's try and get this clear. Has he not the right to? Certainly he has. It follows that he doesn't want to. There's reasoning for you. And why doesn't he want to? [*Pause*] Gentlemen, the reason is this.
VLADIMIR [*to* ESTRAGON] Make a note of this.
POZZO He wants to impress me, so that I'll keep him.
ESTRAGON What?
POZZO Perhaps I haven't got it quite right. He wants to mollify me, so that I'll give up the idea of parting with him. No, that's not exactly it either.

4. A variety of dolphin.

VLADIMIR You want to get rid of him?

POZZO He wants to cod[5] me, but he won't.

VLADIMIR You want to get rid of him?

POZZO He imagines that when I see how well he carries I'll be tempted to keep him on in that capacity.

ESTRAGON You've had enough of him?

POZZO In reality he carries like a pig. It's not his job.

VLADIMIR You want to get rid of him?

POZZO He imagines that when I see him indefatigable I'll regret my decision. Such is his miserable scheme. As though I were short of slaves! [*All three look at* LUCKY.] Atlas, son of Jupiter![6] [*Silence*] Well, that's that I think. Anything else?

[*Vaporizer.*]

VLADIMIR You want to get rid of him?

POZZO Remark that I might just as well have been in his shoes and he in mine. If chance had not willed otherwise. To each one his due.

VLADIMIR You waagerrim?

POZZO I beg your pardon?

VLADIMIR You want to get rid of him?

POZZO I do. But instead of driving him away as I might have done, I mean instead of simply kicking him out on his arse, in the goodness of my heart I am bringing him to the fair, where I hope to get a good price for him. The truth is you can't drive such creatures away. The best thing would be to kill them.

[LUCKY *weeps.*]

ESTRAGON He's crying!

POZZO Old dogs have more dignity. [*He proffers his handkerchief to* ESTRAGON.] Comfort him, since you pity him. [ESTRAGON *hesitates.*] Come on. [ESTRAGON *takes the handkerchief.*] Wipe away his tears, he'll feel less forsaken.

[ESTRAGON *hesitates.*]

VLADIMIR Here, give it to me, I'll do it.

[ESTRAGON *refuses to give the handkerchief. Childish gestures.*]

POZZO Make haste, before he stops. [ESTRAGON *approaches* LUCKY *and makes to wipe his eyes.* LUCKY *kicks him violently in the shins.* ESTRAGON *drops the handkerchief, recoils, staggers about the stage howling with pain.*] Hanky!

[LUCKY *puts down bag and basket, picks up handkerchief and gives it to* POZZO, *goes back to his place, picks up bag and basket.*]

ESTRAGON Oh the swine! [*He pulls up the leg of his trousers.*] He's crippled me!

POZZO I told you he didn't like strangers.

VLADIMIR [*to* ESTRAGON] Show. [ESTRAGON *shows his leg. To* POZZO, *angrily*] He's bleeding!

POZZO It's a good sign.

5. Play a joke on, tease; or, perhaps, a shortened version of *coddle*.

6. In classical mythology, Atlas's father was the Titan Iapetus, not Jupiter; as punishment for leading the Titans in their war against the Olympian gods, Atlas was condemned to hold the heavens on his shoulders.

ESTRAGON [*on one leg*] I'll never walk again!

VLADIMIR [*tenderly*] I'll carry you. [*Pause*] If necessary.

POZZO He's stopped crying. [*To* ESTRAGON] You have replaced him as it were. [*Lyrically*] The tears of the world are a constant quantity. For each one who begins to weep somewhere else another stops. The same is true of the laugh. [*He laughs.*] Let us not then speak ill of our generation, it is not any unhappier than its predecessors. [*Pause*] Let us not speak well of it either. [*Pause*] Let us not speak of it at all. [*Pause. Judiciously.*] It is true the population has increased.

VLADIMIR Try and walk.

[ESTRAGON *takes a few limping steps, stops before* LUCKY *and spits on him, then goes and sits down on the mound.*]

POZZO Guess who taught me all these beautiful things. [*Pause. Pointing to* LUCKY] My Lucky!

VLADIMIR [*looking at the sky*] Will night never come?

POZZO But for him all my thoughts, all my feelings, would have been of common things. [*Pause. With extraordinary vehemence.*] Professional worries! [*Calmer*] Beauty, grace, truth of the first water,[7] I knew they were all beyond me. So I took a knook.[8]

VLADIMIR [*startled from his inspection of the sky*] A knook?

POZZO That was nearly sixty years ago . . . [*He consults his watch.*] . . . yes, nearly sixty. [*Drawing himself up proudly*] You wouldn't think it to look at me, would you? Compared to him I look like a young man, no? [*Pause*] Hat! [LUCKY *puts down the basket and takes off his hat. His long white hair falls about his face. He puts his hat under his arm and picks up the basket.*] Now look. [POZZO *takes off his hat.*[9] *He is completely bald. He puts on his hat again.*] Did you see?

VLADIMIR And now you turn him away? Such an old and faithful servant!

ESTRAGON Swine!

[POZZO *more and more agitated.*]

VLADIMIR After having sucked all the good out of him you chuck him away like a . . . like a banana skin. Really . . .

POZZO [*groaning, clutching his head*] I can't bear it . . . any longer . . . the way he goes on . . . you've no idea . . . it's terrible . . . he must go . . . [*He waves his arms.*] . . . I'm going mad . . . [*He collapses, his head in his hands.*] . . . I can't bear it . . . any longer . . .

[*Silence. All look at* POZZO.]

VLADIMIR He can't bear it.

ESTRAGON Any longer.

VLADIMIR He's going mad.

ESTRAGON It's terrible.

VLADIMIR [*to* LUCKY] How dare you! It's abominable! Such a good master! Crucify him like that! After so many years! Really!

7. Of the highest quality (formerly, a technical term used of diamonds).

8. A coinage of Beckett's, possibly echoing *knut* (the Russian word for "whip"). In a passage from the original French version that Beckett did not include in his English translation, Pozzo expounds on the word to Vladimir as follows: "You are not from these parts. Are you so out of touch with the times? Years ago people used to have jesters. Now they have knouks. Those who are able to afford them."

9. All four wear bowlers [Beckett's note].

POZZO [*sobbing*] He used to be so kind . . . so helpful . . . and entertaining . . . my good angel . . . and now . . . he's killing me.

ESTRAGON [*to* VLADIMIR] Does he want to replace him?

VLADIMIR What?

ESTRAGON Does he want someone to take his place or not?

VLADIMIR I don't think so.

ESTRAGON What?

VLADIMIR I don't know.

ESTRAGON Ask him.

POZZO [*calmer*] Gentlemen, I don't know what came over me. Forgive me. Forget all I said. [*More and more his old self*] I don't remember exactly what it was, but you may be sure there wasn't a word of truth in it. [*Drawing himself up, striking his chest*] Do I look like a man that can be made to suffer? Frankly? [*He rummages in his pockets.*] What have I done with my pipe?

VLADIMIR Charming evening we're having.

ESTRAGON Unforgettable.

VLADIMIR And it's not over.

ESTRAGON Apparently not.

VLADIMIR It's only beginning.

ESTRAGON It's awful.

VLADIMIR Worse than the pantomime.

ESTRAGON The circus.

VLADIMIR The music-hall.

ESTRAGON The circus.

POZZO What can I have done with that briar?[1]

ESTRAGON He's a scream. He's lost his dudeen.[2] [*Laughs noisily.*]

VLADIMIR I'll be back. [*He hastens towards the wings.*]

ESTRAGON End of the corridor, on the left.

VLADIMIR Keep my seat. [*Exit* VLADIMIR.]

POZZO [*on the point of tears*] I've lost my Kapp and Peterson![3]

ESTRAGON [*convulsed with merriment*] He'll be the death of me!

POZZO You didn't see by any chance—. [*He misses* VLADIMIR.] Oh! He's gone! Without saying goodbye! How could he! He might have waited!

ESTRAGON He would have burst.

POZZO Oh! [*Pause*] Oh well then of course in that case . . .

ESTRAGON Come here.

POZZO What for?

ESTRAGON You'll see.

POZZO You want me to get up?

ESTRAGON Quick! [POZZO *gets up and goes over beside* ESTRAGON. ESTRAGON *points off.*] Look!

POZZO [*having put on his glasses*] Oh I say!

ESTRAGON It's all over.

1. That is, his pipe made from briar wood.
2. A short-stemmed clay tobacco pipe (Irish Gaelic).
3. A brand of pipe. Kapp and Peterson were Dublin's most renowned manufacturers and purveyors of smoking pipes and other tobacco products.

[*Enter* VLADIMIR, *somber. He shoulders* LUCKY *out of his way, kicks over the stool, comes and goes agitatedly.*]

POZZO He's not pleased.

ESTRAGON [*to* VLADIMIR] You missed a treat. Pity.

[VLADIMIR *halts, straightens the stool, comes and goes, calmer.*]

POZZO He subsides. [*Looking round*] Indeed all subsides. A great calm descends. [*Raising his hand*] Listen! Pan sleeps.[4]

VLADIMIR Will night never come?

[*All three look at the sky.*]

POZZO You don't feel like going until it does?

ESTRAGON Well you see—

POZZO Why it's very natural, very natural. I myself in your situation, if I had an appointment with a Godin . . . Godet . . . Godot . . . anyhow you see who I mean, I'd wait till it was black night before I gave up. [*He looks at the stool.*] I'd very much like to sit down, but I don't quite know how to go about it.

ESTRAGON Could I be of any help?

POZZO If you asked me perhaps.

ESTRAGON What?

POZZO If you asked me to sit down.

ESTRAGON Would that be a help?

POZZO I fancy so.

ESTRAGON Here we go. Be seated, Sir, I beg of you.

POZZO No no, I wouldn't think of it! [*Pause. Aside.*] Ask me again.

ESTRAGON Come come, take a seat I beseech you, you'll get pneumonia.

POZZO You really think so?

ESTRAGON Why it's absolutely certain.

POZZO No doubt you are right. [*He sits down.*] Done it again! [*Pause*] Thank you, dear fellow. [*He consults his watch.*] But I must really be getting along, if I am to observe my schedule.

VLADIMIR Time has stopped.

POZZO [*cuddling his watch to his ear*] Don't you believe it, Sir, don't you believe it. [*He puts his watch back in his pocket.*] Whatever you like, but not that.

ESTRAGON [*to* POZZO] Everything seems black to him today.

POZZO Except the firmament. [*He laughs, pleased with this witticism.*] But I see what it is, you are not from these parts, you don't know what our twilights can do. Shall I tell you? [*Silence.* ESTRAGON *is fiddling with his boot again,* VLADIMIR *with his hat.*] I can't refuse you. [*Vaporizer*] A little attention, if you please. [VLADIMIR *and* ESTRAGON *continue their fiddling,* LUCKY *is half asleep.* POZZO *cracks his whip feebly.*] What's the matter with this whip? [*He gets up and cracks it more vigorously, finally with success.* LUCKY *jumps.* VLADIMIR*'s hat,* ESTRAGON*'s boot,* LUCKY*'s hat, fall to the ground.* POZZO *throws down the whip.*] Worn out, this whip. [*He looks at* VLADIMIR *and* ESTRAGON.] What was I saying?

VLADIMIR Let's go.

4. Pan, the Greek god of pastures, flocks, and wild places, was said to sleep at noon; to accommodate him, all of nature fell quiet.

ESTRAGON But take the weight off your feet, I implore you, you'll catch your death.

POZZO True. [*He sits down. To* ESTRAGON.] What is your name?

ESTRAGON Adam.

POZZO [*who hasn't listened*] Ah yes! The night. [*He raises his head.*] But be a little more attentive, for pity's sake, otherwise we'll never get anywhere. [*He looks at the sky.*] Look! [*All look at the sky except* LUCKY *who is dozing off again.* POZZO *jerks the rope.*] Will you look at the sky, pig! [LUCKY *looks at the sky.*] Good, that's enough. [*They stop looking at the sky.*] What is there so extraordinary about it? Qua[5] sky. It is pale and luminous like any sky at this hour of the day. [*Pause*] In these latitudes. [*Pause*] When the weather is fine. [*Lyrical*] An hour ago [*He looks at his watch, prosaic.*] roughly [*Lyrical*] after having poured forth even since [*He hesitates, prosaic.*] say ten o'clock in the morning [*Lyrical*] tirelessly torrents of red and white light it begins to lose its effulgence, to grow pale [*Gesture of the two hands lapsing by stages*] pale, ever a little paler, a little paler until [*Dramatic pause, ample gesture of the two hands flung wide apart*] pppfff! finished! it comes to rest. But—[*Hand raised in admonition*]—but behind this veil of gentleness and peace night is charging [*Vibrantly*] and will burst upon us [*Snaps his fingers.*] pop! like that! [*His inspiration leaves him.*] just when we least expect it. [*Silence. Gloomily.*] That's how it is on this bitch of an earth.

[*Long silence.*]

ESTRAGON So long as one knows.

VLADIMIR One can bide one's time.

ESTRAGON One knows what to expect.

VLADIMIR No further need to worry.

ESTRAGON Simply wait.

VLADIMIR We're used to it. [*He picks up his hat, peers inside it, shakes it, puts it on.*]

POZZO How did you find me? [VLADIMIR *and* ESTRAGON *look at him blankly.*] Good? Fair? Middling? Poor? Positively bad?

VLADIMIR [*first to understand*] Oh very good, very very good.

POZZO [*to* ESTRAGON] And you, Sir?

ESTRAGON Oh tray bong, tray tray tray bong.[6]

POZZO [*fervently*] Bless you, gentlemen, bless you! [*Pause*] I have such need of encouragement! [*Pause*] I weakened a little towards the end, you didn't notice?

VLADIMIR Oh perhaps just a teeny weeny little bit.

ESTRAGON I thought it was intentional.

POZZO You see my memory is defective.

[*Silence.*]

ESTRAGON In the meantime nothing happens.

POZZO You find it tedious?

ESTRAGON Somewhat.

POZZO [*to* VLADIMIR] And you, Sir?

5. As (a term common in philosophical discourse).

6. "Oui! Tray bong!" (which plays on the French phrase *oui très bon*—"yes, very good") was the title of a late 19th-century song made popular in English music halls by Charles Chaplin Sr., father of the famous film actor.

VLADIMIR I've been better entertained.

[*Silence.* POZZO *struggles inwardly.*]

POZZO Gentlemen, you have been . . . civil to me.

ESTRAGON Not at all!

VLADIMIR What an idea!

POZZO Yes yes, you have been correct. So that I ask myself is there anything I can do in my turn for these honest fellows who are having such a dull, dull time.

ESTRAGON Even ten francs would be a help.

VLADIMIR We are not beggars!

POZZO Is there anything I can do, that's what I ask myself, to cheer them up? I have given them bones, I have talked to them about this and that, I have explained the twilight, admittedly. But is it enough, that's what tortures me, is it enough?

ESTRAGON Even five.

VLADIMIR [*to* ESTRAGON, *indignantly*] That's enough!

ESTRAGON I couldn't accept less.

POZZO Is it enough? No doubt. But I am liberal. It's my nature. This evening. So much the worse for me. [*He jerks the rope.* LUCKY *looks at him.*] For I shall suffer, no doubt about that. [*He picks up the whip.*] What do you prefer? Shall we have him dance, or sing, or recite, or think, or—

ESTRAGON Who?

POZZO Who! You know how to think, you two?

VLADIMIR He thinks?

POZZO Certainly. Aloud. He even used to think very prettily once, I could listen to him for hours. Now . . . [*He shudders.*] So much the worse for me. Well, would you like him to think something for us?

ESTRAGON I'd rather he'd dance, it'd be more fun.

POZZO Not necessarily.

ESTRAGON Wouldn't it, Didi, be more fun?

VLADIMIR I'd like well to hear him think.

ESTRAGON Perhaps he could dance first and think afterwards, if it isn't too much to ask him.

VLADIMIR [*to* POZZO] Would that be possible?

POZZO By all means, nothing simpler. It's the natural order. [*He laughs briefly.*]

VLADIMIR Then let him dance.

[*Silence.*]

POZZO Do you hear, hog?

ESTRAGON He never refuses?

POZZO He refused once. [*Silence*] Dance, misery!

[LUCKY *puts down bag and basket, advances towards front, turns to* POZZO. LUCKY *dances. He stops.*]

ESTRAGON Is that all?

POZZO Encore!

[LUCKY *executes the same movements, stops.*]

ESTRAGON Pooh! I'd do as well myself. [*He imitates* LUCKY, *almost falls.*] With a little practice.

POZZO He used to dance the farandole, the fling, the brawl, the jig, the fandango and even the hornpipe.[7] He capered. For joy. Now that's the best he can do. Do you know what he calls it?

ESTRAGON The Scapegoat's Agony.

VLADIMIR The Hard Stool.

POZZO The Net. He thinks he's entangled in a net.

VLADIMIR [*squirming like an aesthete*] There's something about it . . .

[LUCKY *makes to return to his burdens.*]

POZZO Woaa!

[LUCKY *stiffens.*]

ESTRAGON Tell us about the time he refused.

POZZO With pleasure, with pleasure. [*He fumbles in his pockets.*] Wait. [*He fumbles.*] What have I done with my spray? [*He fumbles.*] Well now isn't that . . . [*He looks up, consternation on his features. Faintly.*] I can't find my pulverizer![8]

ESTRAGON [*faintly*] My left lung is very weak! [*He coughs feebly. In ringing tones.*] But my right lung is as sound as a bell!

POZZO [*normal voice*] No matter! What was I saying. [*He ponders.*] Wait. [*Ponders.*] Well now isn't that . . . [*He raises his head.*] Help me!

ESTRAGON Wait!

VLADIMIR Wait!

POZZO Wait!

[*All three take off their hats simultaneously, press their hands to their foreheads, concentrate.*]

ESTRAGON [*triumphantly*] Ah!

VLADIMIR He has it.

POZZO [*impatient*] Well?

ESTRAGON Why doesn't he put down his bags?

VLADIMIR Rubbish!

POZZO Are you sure?

VLADIMIR Damn it haven't you already told us?

POZZO I've already told you?

ESTRAGON He's already told us?

VLADIMIR Anyway he has put them down.

ESTRAGON [*glance at Lucky*] So he has. And what of it?

VLADIMIR Since he has put down his bags it is impossible we should have asked why he does not do so.

POZZO Stoutly reasoned!

ESTRAGON And why has he put them down?

POZZO Answer us that.

VLADIMIR In order to dance.

ESTRAGON True!

POZZO True!

[*Silence. They put on their hats.*]

ESTRAGON Nothing happens, nobody comes, nobody goes, it's awful!

VLADIMIR [*to* POZZO] Tell him to think.

7. All energetic dances, associated (respectively) with Provence, the Scottish highlands, France, Ireland, Spain, and England.

8. That is, his vaporizer, mentioned earlier.

POZZO Give him his hat.

VLADIMIR His hat?

POZZO He can't think without his hat.

VLADIMIR [*to* ESTRAGON] Give him his hat.

ESTRAGON Me! After what he did to me! Never!

VLADIMIR I'll give it to him. [*He does not move.*]

ESTRAGON [*to* POZZO] Tell him to go and fetch it.

POZZO It's better to give it to him.

VLADIMIR I'll give it to him.

[*He picks up the hat and tenders it at arm's length to* LUCKY, *who does not move.*]

POZZO You must put it on his head.

ESTRAGON [*to* POZZO] Tell him to take it.

POZZO It's better to put it on his head.

VLADIMIR I'll put it on his head.

[*He goes round behind* LUCKY, *approaches him cautiously, puts the hat on his head and recoils smartly.* LUCKY *does not move. Silence.*]

ESTRAGON What's he waiting for?

POZZO Stand back! [VLADIMIR *and* ESTRAGON *move away from* LUCKY. POZZO *jerks the rope.* LUCKY *looks at* POZZO.] Think, pig! [*Pause.* LUCKY *begins to dance.*] Stop! [LUCKY *stops.*] Forward! [LUCKY *advances.*] Stop! [LUCKY *stops.*] Think!

[*Silence.*]

LUCKY On the other hand with regard to—

POZZO Stop! [LUCKY *stops.*] Back! [LUCKY *moves back.*] Stop! [LUCKY *stops.*] Turn! [LUCKY *turns towards auditorium.*] Think!

LUCKY Given the existence as uttered forth in the public works of Puncher and Wattmann[9] of a personal God quaquaquaqua with white beard quaquaquaqua outside time without extension who from the heights of divine apathia divine athambia divine aphasia[1] loves us dearly with some exceptions for reasons unknown but time will tell and

[VLADIMIR *and* ESTRAGON *all attention,* POZZO *dejected and*

suffers like the divine Miranda[2] with those who for reasons unknown but time will tell are plunged in torment plunged in fire whose fire flames if that continues and who can doubt it will fire the firmament that is to say blast hell to heaven so blue still and calm so calm with a calm which even though intermittent is better than nothing but not so fast and considering what is more that as a result of the labors left unfinished crowned by the Acacacacademy of Anthropopopometry of Essy-in-Possy[3] of

9. Fictitious academics, as are "Testew and Cunard," "Fartov and Belcher," "Steinweg and Peterman," and so on, below. Mixing quasi-philosophical discourse, arcane language, and sexual/scatological wordplay, this speech uses invented and altered proper names, technical terms, and allusions to create half-meanings amid apparent nonsense.

1. Of the three Greek words employed here—*apatheia* (freedom from emotion), *athambia* (freedom from fear or surprise), and *aphasia* (lack or loss of speech)—only the last is actually used in English.

2. The character in William Shakespeare's *The Tempest* (1611) who agonizes over a shipwreck she has witnessed: "O, I have sufferèd / With those that I saw suffer!" (1.2.5–6).

3. An echo of the Latin verbs *esse* (to be) and *posse* (to be able to). *Acacacacademy*: in several Romance languages, including French, *caca* is a child's word for excrement. *Anthropopopometry*: that is, anthropometry (the study of measurement of the human body)

disgusted.]

Testew and Cunard it is established beyond all doubt all other doubt than that which clings to the labors of men that as a

[VLADIMIR *and* ESTRAGON *begin to protest,* POZZO's *sufferings increase.*]

result of the labors unfinished of Testew and Cunard it is established as hereinafter but not so fast for reasons unknown that as a result of the public works of Puncher and Wattmann it is established beyond all doubt that in view of the labors of Fartov and Belcher left unfinished for reasons unknown of Testew and Cunard left unfinished it is established what many deny that man in Possy of Testew and Cunard that man in Essy that man in short that man in brief in spite of the strides of alimentation and defecation wastes and pines wastes and pines

[VLADIMIR *and* ESTRAGON *attentive again,* POZZO *more and more agitated and groaning.*]

and concurrently simultaneously what is more for reasons unknown in spite of the strides of physical culture the practice of sports such as tennis football running cycling swimming flying floating riding gliding conating camogie[4] skating tennis of all kinds dying flying sports of all sorts autumn summer winter winter tennis of all kinds hockey of all sorts penicillin and succedanea[5] in a word I resume flying gliding golf over nine and eighteen holes tennis of all sorts in a word for reasons unknown in Feckham Peckham Fulham Clapham[6] namely concurrently simultaneously what is more for reasons unknown but time will tell fades away I resume Fulham Clapham in a word the dead loss per head since the death of Bishop Berkeley[7] being to the tune of one inch four ounce per head approximately by and large more or less to the nearest decimal

[VLADIMIR *and* ESTRAGON *protest violently.* POZZO *jumps up, pulls on the rope. General outcry.* LUCKY *pulls on the rope, staggers, shouts his text. All three throw themselves*

good measure round figures stark naked in the stockinged feet in Connemara[8] in a word for reasons unknown no matter what matter the facts are there and considering what is more much more grave that in the light of the labors lost of Steinweg and Peterman it appears what is more much more grave that in the light the light the light of the labors lost of Steinweg and Peterman that in the plains in the mountains by the seas by the rivers running water running fire the air is the same and then the earth namely the air and then the earth in the great cold the great dark the air and the earth abode of stones in the great cold alas alas in the year of their Lord six hundred and something the air the earth the sea the earth abode of stones in the great deeps the great cold on sea on land and in the air I resume for reasons unknown in spite of the tennis the facts are there but time will tell I resume alas alas on on in short in fine on on abode of stones who can doubt it I resume but not so fast I resume the skull fading fading fading and concurrently simultaneously what is more for reasons

4. A Celtic team sport played with sticks and a ball (the women's version of hurling). *Conating:* desiring, attempting (Beckett's back-formation from *conation*).

5. Substitutes.

6. Three areas of south London, preceded by an obscene pun on them.

7. George Berkeley (1685–1753), Irish idealist philosopher and bishop in the Church of Ireland. Berkeley's theory, which held that the world exists only insofar as it is perceived by the senses, is summed up in his Latin dictum *Esse est percipi* (To be is to be perceived).

8. A region of Galway in western Ireland.

on LUCKY *who struggles and shouts his text.*] unknown in spite of the tennis on on the beard the flames the tears the stones so blue so calm alas alas on on the skull the skull the skull the skull in Connemara in spite of the tennis the labors abandoned left unfinished graver still abode of stones in a word I resume alas alas abandoned unfinished the skull the skull in Connemara in spite of the tennis the skull alas the stones Cunard [*Mêlée, final vociferations*] tennis . . . the stones . . . so calm . . . Cunard . . . unfinished . . .

POZZO His hat!

[VLADIMIR *seizes* LUCKY*'s hat. Silence of* LUCKY. *He falls. Silence. Panting of the victors.*]

ESTRAGON Avenged!

[VLADIMIR *examines the hat, peers inside it.*]

POZZO Give me that! [*He snatches the hat from* VLADIMIR, *throws it on the ground, tramples on it.*] There's an end to his thinking!

VLADIMIR But will he be able to walk?

POZZO Walk or crawl! [*He kicks* LUCKY.] Up pig!

ESTRAGON Perhaps he's dead.

VLADIMIR You'll kill him.

POZZO Up scum! [*He jerks the rope.*] Help me!

VLADIMIR How?

POZZO Raise him up!

[VLADIMIR *and* ESTRAGON *hoist* LUCKY *to his feet, support him an instant, then let him go. He falls.*]

ESTRAGON He's doing it on purpose!

POZZO You must hold him. [*Pause*] Come on, come on, raise him up.

ESTRAGON To hell with him!

VLADIMIR Come on, once more.

ESTRAGON What does he take us for?

[*They raise* LUCKY, *hold him up.*]

POZZO Don't let him go! [VLADIMIR *and* ESTRAGON *totter.*] Don't move! [POZZO *fetches bag and basket and brings them towards* LUCKY.] Hold him tight! [*He puts the bag in* LUCKY*'s hand.* LUCKY *drops it immediately.*] Don't let him go! [*He puts back the bag in* LUCKY*'s hand. Gradually, at the feel of the bag,* LUCKY *recovers his senses and his fingers finally close round the handle.*] Hold him tight! [*As before with basket*] Now! You can let him go. [VLADIMIR *and* ESTRAGON *move away from* LUCKY *who totters, reels, sags, but succeeds in remaining on his feet, bag and basket in his hands.* POZZO *steps back, cracks his whip.*] Forward! [LUCKY *totters forward.*] Back! [LUCKY *totters back.*] Turn! [LUCKY *turns.*] Done it! He can walk. [*Turning to* VLADIMIR *and* ESTRAGON] Thank you, gentlemen, and let me . . . [*He fumbles in his pockets*] . . . let me wish you . . . [*Fumbles.*] . . . wish you . . . [*Fumbles.*] . . . what have I done with my watch? [*Fumbles.*] A genuine half-hunter, gentlemen, with deadbeat escapement![9] [*Sobbing.*] Twas my granpa gave it to me! [*He searches on the ground,* VLADIMIR *and* ESTRAGON *likewise.* POZZO *turns over with his foot the remains of* LUCKY*'s hat.*] Well now isn't that just—

9. The mechanism in watches that regulates the movement of the hands, here "deadbeat" because it does not recoil. *Half-hunter:* a kind of pocket watch featuring a metal case with a small glass window through which the hands are visible.

VLADIMIR Perhaps it's in your fob.[1]

POZZO Wait! [*He doubles up in an attempt to apply his ear to his stomach, listens. Silence.*] I hear nothing. [*He beckons them to approach.* VLADIMIR *and* ESTRAGON *go over to him, bend over his stomach.*] Surely one should hear the tick-tick.

VLADIMIR Silence!

[*All listen, bent double.*]

ESTRAGON I hear something.

POZZO Where?

VLADIMIR It's the heart.

POZZO [*disappointed*] Damnation!

VLADIMIR Silence!

ESTRAGON Perhaps it has stopped.

[*They straighten up.*]

POZZO Which of you smells so bad?

ESTRAGON He has stinking breath and I have stinking feet.

POZZO I must go.

ESTRAGON And your half-hunter?

POZZO I must have left it at the manor.

[*Silence.*]

ESTRAGON Then adieu.

POZZO Adieu.

VLADIMIR Adieu.

POZZO Adieu.

[*Silence. No one moves.*]

VLADIMIR Adieu.

POZZO Adieu.

ESTRAGON Adieu.

[*Silence.*]

POZZO And thank you.

VLADIMIR Thank *you*.

POZZO Not at all.

ESTRAGON Yes yes.

POZZO No no.

VLADIMIR Yes yes.

ESTRAGON No no.

[*Silence.*]

POZZO I don't seem to be able . . . [*Long hesitation*] . . . to depart.

ESTRAGON Such is life.

[POZZO *turns, moves away from* LUCKY *towards the wings, paying out the rope as he goes.*]

VLADIMIR You're going the wrong way.

POZZO I need a running start. [*Having come to the end of the rope, i.e. off stage, he stops, turns and cries.*] Stand back! [VLADIMIR *and* ESTRAGON *stand back, look towards* POZZO. *Crack of whip.*] On! On!

1. A small pocket, originally in the waistband (also known as a "watch pocket").

ESTRAGON On!

VLADIMIR On!

[LUCKY *moves off.*]

POZZO Faster! [*He appears, crosses the stage preceded by* LUCKY. VLADIMIR *and* ESTRAGON *wave their hats. Exit* LUCKY.] On! On! [*On the point of disappearing in his turn he stops and turns. The rope tautens. Noise of* LUCKY *falling off.*] Stool! [VLADIMIR *fetches stool and gives it to* POZZO *who throws it to* LUCKY.] Adieu!

VLADIMIR }
ESTRAGON } [*waving*] Adieu! Adieu!

POZZO Up! Pig! [*Noise of* LUCKY *getting up.*] On! [*Exit* POZZO.] Faster! On! Adieu! Pig! Yip! Adieu!

[*Long silence.*]

VLADIMIR That passed the time.

ESTRAGON It would have passed in any case.

VLADIMIR Yes, but not so rapidly.

[*Pause.*]

ESTRAGON What do we do now?

VLADIMIR I don't know.

ESTRAGON Let's go.

VLADIMIR We can't.

ESTRAGON Why not?

VLADIMIR We're waiting for Godot.

ESTRAGON [*despairingly*] Ah!

[*Pause.*]

VLADIMIR How they've changed!

ESTRAGON Who?

VLADIMIR Those two.

ESTRAGON That's the idea, let's make a little conversation.

VLADIMIR Haven't they?

ESTRAGON What?

VLADIMIR Changed.

ESTRAGON Very likely. They all change. Only we can't.

VLADIMIR Likely! It's certain. Didn't you see them?

ESTRAGON I suppose I did. But I don't know them.

VLADIMIR Yes you do know them.

ESTRAGON No I don't know them.

VLADIMIR We know them, I tell you. You forget everything. [*Pause. To himself.*] Unless they're not the same . . .

ESTRAGON Why didn't they recognize us then?

VLADIMIR That means nothing. I too pretended not to recognize them. And then nobody ever recognizes us.

ESTRAGON Forget it. What we need—ow! [VLADIMIR *does not react.*] Ow!

VLADIMIR [*to himself*] Unless they're not the same . . .

ESTRAGON Didi! It's the other foot! [*He goes hobbling towards the mound.*]

VLADIMIR Unless they're not the same . . .

BOY [*off*] Mister!

[ESTRAGON *halts. Both look towards the voice.*]

ESTRAGON Off we go again.

VLADIMIR Approach, my child.

[*Enter* BOY, *timidly. He halts.*]

BOY Mister Albert . . . ?

VLADIMIR Yes.

ESTRAGON What do you want?

VLADIMIR Approach!

[*The* BOY *does not move.*]

ESTRAGON [*forcibly*] Approach when you're told, can't you?

[*The* BOY *advances timidly, halts.*]

VLADIMIR What is it?

BOY Mr. Godot . . .

VLADIMIR Obviously . . . [*Pause*] Approach.

ESTRAGON [*violently*] Will you approach! [*The* BOY *advances timidly.*] What kept you so late?

VLADIMIR You have a message from Mr. Godot?

BOY Yes Sir.

VLADIMIR Well, what is it?

ESTRAGON What kept you so late?

[*The* BOY *looks at them in turn, not knowing to which he should reply.*]

VLADIMIR [*to* ESTRAGON] Let him alone.

ESTRAGON [*violently*] You let me alone. [*Advancing, to the* BOY] Do you know what time it is?

BOY [*recoiling*] It's not my fault, Sir.

ESTRAGON And whose is it? Mine?

BOY I was afraid, Sir.

ESTRAGON Afraid of what? Of us? [*Pause*] Answer me!

VLADIMIR I know what it is, he was afraid of the others.

ESTRAGON How long have you been here?

BOY A good while, Sir.

VLADIMIR You were afraid of the whip?

BOY Yes Sir.

VLADIMIR The roars?

BOY Yes Sir.

VLADIMIR The two big men.

BOY Yes Sir.

VLADIMIR Do you know them?

BOY No Sir.

VLADIMIR Are you a native of these parts? [*Silence*] Do you belong to these parts?

BOY Yes Sir.

ESTRAGON That's all a pack of lies. [*Shaking the* BOY *by the arm*] Tell us the truth!

BOY [*trembling*] But it is the truth, Sir!

VLADIMIR Will you let him alone! What's the matter with you? [ESTRAGON *releases the* BOY, *moves away, covering his face with his hands.* VLADIMIR *and the* BOY *observe him.* ESTRAGON *drops his hands. His face is convulsed.*] What's the matter with you?

ESTRAGON I'm unhappy.

VLADIMIR Not really! Since when?

ESTRAGON I'd forgotten.

VLADIMIR Extraordinary the tricks that memory plays!

[ESTRAGON *tries to speak, renounces, limps to his place, sits down and begins to take off his boots. To* BOY]

Well?

BOY Mr. Godot—

VLADIMIR I've seen you before, haven't I?

BOY I don't know, Sir.

VLADIMIR You don't know me?

BOY No Sir.

VLADIMIR It wasn't you came yesterday?

BOY No Sir.

VLADIMIR This is your first time?

BOY Yes Sir.

[*Silence.*]

VLADIMIR Words words. [*Pause*] Speak.

BOY [*in a rush*] Mr. Godot told me to tell you he won't come this evening but surely tomorrow.

[*Silence.*]

VLADIMIR Is that all?

BOY Yes Sir.

[*Silence.*]

VLADIMIR You work for Mr. Godot?

BOY Yes Sir.

VLADIMIR What do you do?

BOY I mind the goats, Sir.

VLADIMIR Is he good to you?

BOY Yes Sir.

VLADIMIR He doesn't beat you?

BOY No Sir, not me.

VLADIMIR Whom does he beat?

BOY He beats my brother, Sir

VLADIMIR Ah, you have a brother?

BOY Yes Sir.

VLADIMIR What does he do?

BOY He minds the sheep, Sir.

VLADIMIR And why doesn't he beat you?

BOY I don't know, Sir.

VLADIMIR He must be fond of you.

BOY I don't know, Sir.

[*Silence.*]

VLADIMIR Does he give you enough to eat? [*The* BOY *hesitates.*] Does he feed you well?

BOY Fairly well, Sir.

VLADIMIR You're not unhappy? [*The* BOY *hesitates.*] Do you hear me?

BOY Yes Sir.

VLADIMIR Well?

BOY I don't know, Sir.

VLADIMIR You don't know if you're unhappy or not?

BOY No Sir.

VLADIMIR You're as bad as myself. [*Silence*] Where do you sleep?

BOY In the loft, Sir.

VLADIMIR With your brother?

BOY Yes Sir.

VLADIMIR In the hay?

BOY Yes Sir.

[*Silence.*]

VLADIMIR All right, you may go.

BOY What am I to tell Mr. Godot, Sir?

VLADIMIR Tell him . . . [*He hesitates.*] . . . tell him you saw us. [*Pause*] You did see us, didn't you?

BOY Yes Sir.

[*He steps back, hesitates, turns and exits running. The light suddenly fails. In a moment it is night. The moon rises at back, mounts in the sky, stands still, shedding a pale light on the scene.*]

VLADIMIR At last! [ESTRAGON *gets up and goes towards* VLADIMIR, *a boot in each hand. He puts them down at edge of stage, straightens and contemplates the moon.*] What are you doing?

ESTRAGON Pale for weariness.

VLADIMIR Eh?

ESTRAGON Of climbing heaven and gazing on the likes of us.

VLADIMIR Your boots, what are you doing with your boots?

ESTRAGON [*turning to look at the boots*] I'm leaving them there. [*Pause*] Another will come, just as . . . as . . . as me, but with smaller feet, and they'll make him happy.

VLADIMIR But you can't go barefoot!

ESTRAGON Christ did.

VLADIMIR Christ! What has Christ got to do with it? You're not going to compare yourself to Christ!

ESTRAGON All my life I've compared myself to him.

VLADIMIR But where he lived it was warm, it was dry!

ESTRAGON Yes. And they crucified quick.

[*Silence.*]

VLADIMIR We've nothing more to do here.

ESTRAGON Nor anywhere else.

VLADIMIR Ah Gogo, don't go on like that. Tomorrow everything will be better.

ESTRAGON How do you make that out?

VLADIMIR Did you not hear what the child said?

ESTRAGON No.

VLADIMIR He said that Godot was sure to come tomorrow. [*Pause*] What do you say to that?

ESTRAGON Then all we have to do is to wait on here.

VLADIMIR Are you mad? We must take cover. [*He takes* ESTRAGON *by the arm.*] Come on.

[*He draws* ESTRAGON *after him.* ESTRAGON *yields, then resists. They halt.*]

ESTRAGON [*looking at the tree*] Pity we haven't got a bit of rope.

VLADIMIR Come on. It's cold.

[*He draws* ESTRAGON *after him. As before.*]

ESTRAGON Remind me to bring a bit of rope tomorrow.
VLADIMIR Yes. Come on.
[*He draws him after him. As before.*]
ESTRAGON How long have we been together all the time now?
VLADIMIR I don't know. Fifty years maybe.
ESTRAGON Do you remember the day I threw myself into the Rhône?[2]
VLADIMIR We were grape harvesting.
ESTRAGON You fished me out.
VLADIMIR That's all dead and buried.
ESTRAGON My clothes dried in the sun.
VLADIMIR There's no good harking back on that. Come on.
[*He draws him after him. As before.*]
ESTRAGON Wait!
VLADIMIR I'm cold!
ESTRAGON Wait! [*He moves away from* VLADIMIR.] I sometimes wonder if we wouldn't have been better off alone, each one for himself. [*He crosses the stage and sits down on the mound.*] We weren't made for the same road.
VLADIMIR [*without anger*] It's not certain.
ESTRAGON No, nothing is certain.
[VLADIMIR *slowly crosses the stage and sits down beside* ESTRAGON.]
VLADIMIR We can still part, if you think it would be better.
ESTRAGON It's not worthwhile now.
[*Silence.*]
VLADIMIR No, it's not worthwhile now.
[*Silence.*]
ESTRAGON Well, shall we go?
VLADIMIR Yes, let's go.
[*They do not move.*]

Curtain.

Act 2

Next day. Same time.
Same place.

[ESTRAGON's *boots front center, heels together, toes splayed.* LUCKY's *hat at same place.*]

[*The tree has four or five leaves.*]

[*Enter* VLADIMIR *agitatedly. He halts and looks long at the tree, then suddenly begins to move feverishly about the stage. He halts before the boots, picks one up, examines it, sniffs it, manifests disgust, puts it back carefully. Comes and goes. Halts extreme right and gazes into distance off, shading his eyes with his hand. Comes and goes. Halts extreme left, as before. Comes and goes. Halts suddenly and begins to sing loudly.*]

VLADIMIR A dog came in—

2. A major river in southeastern France.

[*Having begun too high he stops, clears his throat, resumes.*]

A dog came in the kitchen
And stole a crust of bread.
Then cook up with a ladle
And beat him till he was dead.

Then all the dogs came running
And dug the dog a tomb—

[*He stops, broods, resumes.*]

Then all the dogs came running
And dug the dog a tomb
And wrote upon the tombstone
For the eyes of dogs to come:

A dog came in the kitchen
And stole a crust of bread.
Then cook up with a ladle
And beat him till he was dead.

Then all the dogs came running
And dug the dog a tomb—

[*He stops, broods, resumes.*]

Then all the dogs came running
And dug the dog a tomb—

[*He stops, broods. Softly.*]

And dug the dog a tomb . . .

[*He remains a moment silent and motionless, then begins to move feverishly about the stage. He halts before the tree, comes and goes, before the boots, comes and goes, halts extreme right, gazes into distance, extreme left, gazes into distance. Enter* ESTRAGON *right, barefoot, head bowed. He slowly crosses the stage.* VLADIMIR *turns and sees him.*]

VLADIMIR You again! [ESTRAGON *halts but does not raise his head.* VLADIMIR *goes towards him.*] Come here till I embrace you.

ESTRAGON Don't touch me!

[VLADIMIR *holds back, pained.*]

VLADIMIR Do you want me to go away? [*Pause*] Gogo! [*Pause.* VLADIMIR *observes him attentively.*] Did they beat you? [*Pause*] Gogo! [ESTRAGON *remains silent, head bowed.*] Where did you spend the night?

ESTRAGON Don't touch me! Don't question me! Don't speak to me! Stay with me!

VLADIMIR Did I ever leave you?

ESTRAGON You let me go.

VLADIMIR Look at me. [ESTRAGON *does not raise his head. Violently.*] Will you look at me!

[ESTRAGON *raises his head. They look long at each other, then suddenly embrace, clapping each other on the back. End of the embrace.* ESTRAGON, *no longer supported, almost falls.*]

ESTRAGON What a day!

VLADIMIR Who beat you? Tell me.

ESTRAGON Another day done with.

VLADIMIR Not yet.

ESTRAGON For me it's over and done with, no matter what happens. [*Silence*] I heard you singing.

VLADIMIR That's right, I remember.

ESTRAGON That finished me. I said to myself, He's all alone, he thinks I'm gone for ever, and he sings.

VLADIMIR One is not master of one's moods. All day I've felt in great form. [*Pause*] I didn't get up in the night, not once!

ESTRAGON [*sadly*] You see, you piss better when I'm not there.

VLADIMIR I missed you . . . and at the same time I was happy. Isn't that a queer thing?

ESTRAGON [*shocked*] Happy?

VLADIMIR Perhaps it's not quite the right word.

ESTRAGON And now?

VLADIMIR Now? . . . [*Joyous*] There you are again . . . [*Indifferent*] There we are again . . . [*Gloomy*] There I am again.

ESTRAGON You see, you feel worse when I'm with you. I feel better alone too.

VLADIMIR [*vexed*] Then why do you always come crawling back?

ESTRAGON I don't know.

VLADIMIR No, but I do. It's because you don't know how to defend yourself. I wouldn't have let them beat you.

ESTRAGON You couldn't have stopped them.

VLADIMIR Why not?

ESTRAGON There was ten of them.

VLADIMIR No, I mean before they beat you. I would have stopped you from doing whatever it was you were doing.

ESTRAGON I wasn't doing anything.

VLADIMIR Then why did they beat you?

ESTRAGON I don't know.

VLADIMIR Ah no, Gogo, the truth is there are things escape you that don't escape me, you must feel it yourself.

ESTRAGON I tell you I wasn't doing anything.

VLADIMIR Perhaps you weren't. But it's the way of doing it that counts, the way of doing it, if you want to go on living.

ESTRAGON I wasn't doing anything.

VLADIMIR You must be happy too, deep down, if you only knew it.

ESTRAGON Happy about what?

VLADIMIR To be back with me again.

ESTRAGON Would you say so?

VLADIMIR Say you are, even if it's not true.

ESTRAGON What am I to say?

VLADIMIR Say, I am happy.

ESTRAGON I am happy.

VLADIMIR So am I.

ESTRAGON So am I.

VLADIMIR We are happy.

ESTRAGON We are happy. [*Silence*] What do we do now, now that we are happy?

VLADIMIR Wait for Godot. [ESTRAGON *groans. Silence.*] Things have changed here since yesterday.

ESTRAGON And if he doesn't come.

VLADIMIR [*after a moment of bewilderment*] We'll see when the time comes. [*Pause*] I was saying that things have changed here since yesterday.

ESTRAGON Everything oozes.

VLADIMIR Look at the tree.

ESTRAGON It's never the same pus from one second to the next.

VLADIMIR The tree, look at the tree.

[ESTRAGON *looks at the tree.*]

ESTRAGON Was it not there yesterday?

VLADIMIR Yes of course it was there. Do you not remember? We nearly hanged ourselves from it. But you wouldn't. Do you not remember?

ESTRAGON You dreamt it.

VLADIMIR Is it possible you've forgotten already?

ESTRAGON That's the way I am. Either I forget immediately or I never forget.

VLADIMIR And Pozzo and Lucky, have you forgotten them too?

ESTRAGON Pozzo and Lucky?

VLADIMIR He's forgotten everything!

ESTRAGON I remember a lunatic who kicked the shins off me. Then he played the fool.

VLADIMIR That was Lucky.

ESTRAGON I remember that. But when was it?

VLADIMIR And his keeper, do you not remember him?

ESTRAGON He gave me a bone.

VLADIMIR That was Pozzo.

ESTRAGON And all that was yesterday, you say?

VLADIMIR Yes of course it was yesterday.

ESTRAGON And here where we are now?

VLADIMIR Where else do you think? Do you not recognize the place?

ESTRAGON [*suddenly furious*] Recognize! What is there to recognize? All my lousy life I've crawled about in the mud! And you talk to me about scenery! [*Looking wildly about him*] Look at this muckheap! I've never stirred from it!

VLADIMIR Calm yourself, calm yourself.

ESTRAGON You and your landscapes! Tell me about the worms!

VLADIMIR All the same, you can't tell me that this [*Gesture*] bears any resemblance to . . . [*He hesitates.*] . . . to the Mâcon country[3] for example. You can't deny there's a big difference.

ESTRAGON The Mâcon country! Who's talking to you about the Mâcon country?

VLADIMIR But you were there yourself, in the Mâcon country.

ESTRAGON No I was never in the Mâcon country! I've puked my puke of a life away here, I tell you! Here! In the Cackon country!

VLADIMIR But we were there together, I could swear to it! Picking grapes for a man called . . . [*He snaps his fingers.*] . . . can't think of the name of the

3. A wine-producing district in the Bourgogne region of east-central France.

man, at a place called . . . [*Snaps his fingers.*] . . . can't think of the name of the place, do you not remember?

ESTRAGON [*a little calmer*] It's possible. I didn't notice anything.

VLADIMIR But down there everything is red!

ESTRAGON [*exasperated*] I didn't notice anything, I tell you!

[*Silence.* VLADIMIR *sighs deeply.*]

VLADIMIR You're a hard man to get on with, Gogo.

ESTRAGON It'd be better if we parted.

VLADIMIR You always say that and you always come crawling back.

ESTRAGON The best thing would be to kill me, like the other.

VLADIMIR What other? [*Pause*] What other?

ESTRAGON Like billions of others.

VLADIMIR [*sententious*] To every man his little cross. [*He sighs.*] Till he dies. [*Afterthought*] And is forgotten.

ESTRAGON In the meantime let us try and converse calmly, since we are incapable of keeping silent.

VLADIMIR You're right, we're inexhaustible.

ESTRAGON It's so we won't think.

VLADIMIR We have that excuse.

ESTRAGON It's so we won't hear.

VLADIMIR We have our reasons.

ESTRAGON All the dead voices.

VLADIMIR They make a noise like wings.

ESTRAGON Like leaves.

VLADIMIR Like sand.

ESTRAGON Like leaves.

[*Silence.*]

VLADIMIR They all speak at once.

ESTRAGON Each one to itself.

[*Silence.*]

VLADIMIR Rather they whisper.

ESTRAGON They rustle.

VLADIMIR They murmur.

ESTRAGON They rustle.

[*Silence.*]

VLADIMIR What do they say?

ESTRAGON They talk about their lives.

VLADIMIR To have lived is not enough for them.

ESTRAGON They have to talk about it.

VLADIMIR To be dead is not enough for them.

ESTRAGON It is not sufficient.

[*Silence.*]

VLADIMIR They make a noise like feathers.

ESTRAGON Like leaves.

VLADIMIR Like ashes.

ESTRAGON Like leaves.

[*Long silence.*]

VLADIMIR Say something!

ESTRAGON I'm trying.

[*Long silence.*]

VLADIMIR [*in anguish*] Say anything at all!

ESTRAGON What do we do now?

VLADIMIR Wait for Godot.

ESTRAGON Ah!

[*Silence.*]

VLADIMIR This is awful!

ESTRAGON Sing something.

VLADIMIR No no! [*He reflects.*] We could start all over again perhaps.

ESTRAGON That should be easy.

VLADIMIR It's the start that's difficult.

ESTRAGON You can start from anything.

VLADIMIR Yes, but you have to decide.

ESTRAGON True.

[*Silence.*]

VLADIMIR Help me!

ESTRAGON I'm trying.

[*Silence.*]

VLADIMIR When you seek you hear.

ESTRAGON You do.

VLADIMIR That prevents you from finding.

ESTRAGON It does.

VLADIMIR That prevents you from thinking.

ESTRAGON You think all the same.

VLADIMIR No no, impossible.

ESTRAGON That's the idea, let's contradict each other.

VLADIMIR Impossible.

ESTRAGON You think so?

VLADIMIR We're in no danger of ever thinking any more.

ESTRAGON Then what are we complaining about?

VLADIMIR Thinking is not the worst.

ESTRAGON Perhaps not. But at least there's that.

VLADIMIR That what?

ESTRAGON That's the idea, let's ask each other questions.

VLADIMIR What do you mean, at least there's that?

ESTRAGON That much less misery.

VLADIMIR True.

ESTRAGON Well? If we gave thanks for our mercies?

VLADIMIR What is terrible is to *have* thought.

ESTRAGON But did that ever happen to us?

VLADIMIR Where are all these corpses from?

ESTRAGON These skeletons.

VLADIMIR Tell me that.

ESTRAGON True.

VLADIMIR We must have thought a little.

ESTRAGON At the very beginning.

VLADIMIR A charnel-house! A charnel-house![4]

4. A building or vault in which the bodies or bones of the dead are placed.

ESTRAGON You don't have to look.

VLADIMIR You can't help looking.

ESTRAGON True.

VLADIMIR Try as one may.

ESTRAGON I beg your pardon?

VLADIMIR Try as one may.

ESTRAGON We should turn resolutely towards Nature.

VLADIMIR We've tried that.

ESTRAGON True.

VLADIMIR Oh it's not the worst, I know.

ESTRAGON What?

VLADIMIR To have thought.

ESTRAGON Obviously.

VLADIMIR But we could have done without it.

ESTRAGON Que voulez-vous?[5]

VLADIMIR I beg your pardon?

ESTRAGON Que voulez-vous.

VLADIMIR Ah! que voulez-vous. Exactly.

[*Silence.*]

ESTRAGON That wasn't such a bad little canter.

VLADIMIR Yes, but now we'll have to find something else.

ESTRAGON Let me see. [*He takes off his hat, concentrates.*]

VLADIMIR Let me see. [*He takes off his hat, concentrates. Long silence.*] Ah! [*They put on their hats, relax.*]

ESTRAGON Well?

VLADIMIR What was I saying, we could go on from there.

ESTRAGON What were you saying when?

VLADIMIR At the very beginning.

ESTRAGON The very beginning of WHAT?

VLADIMIR This evening . . . I was saying . . . I was saying . . .

ESTRAGON I'm not a historian.

VLADIMIR Wait . . . we embraced . . . we were happy . . . happy . . . what do we do now that we're happy . . . go on waiting . . . waiting . . . let me think . . . it's coming . . . go on waiting . . . now that we're happy . . . let me see . . . ah! The tree!

ESTRAGON The tree?

VLADIMIR Do you not remember?

ESTRAGON I'm tired.

VLADIMIR Look at it.

[*They look at the tree.*]

ESTRAGON I see nothing.

VLADIMIR But yesterday evening it was all black and bare. And now it's covered with leaves.

ESTRAGON Leaves?

VLADIMIR In a single night.

ESTRAGON It must be the Spring.

VLADIMIR But in a single night!

5. What do you want? (French).

ESTRAGON I tell you we weren't here yesterday. Another of your nightmares.

VLADIMIR And where were we yesterday evening according to you?

ESTRAGON How would I know? In another compartment. There's no lack of void.

VLADIMIR [*sure of himself*] Good. We weren't here yesterday evening. Now what did we do yesterday evening?

ESTRAGON Do?

VLADIMIR Try and remember.

ESTRAGON Do . . . I suppose we blathered.

VLADIMIR [*controlling himself*] About what?

ESTRAGON Oh . . . this and that I suppose, nothing in particular. [*With assurance*] Yes, now I remember, yesterday evening we spent blathering about nothing in particular. That's been going on now for half a century.

VLADIMIR You don't remember any fact, any circumstance?

ESTRAGON [*weary*] Don't torment me, Didi.

VLADIMIR The sun. The moon. Do you not remember?

ESTRAGON They must have been there, as usual.

VLADIMIR You didn't notice anything out of the ordinary?

ESTRAGON Alas!

VLADIMIR And Pozzo? And Lucky?

ESTRAGON Pozzo?

VLADIMIR The bones.

ESTRAGON They were like fishbones.

VLADIMIR It was Pozzo gave them to you.

ESTRAGON I don't know.

VLADIMIR And the kick.

ESTRAGON That's right, someone gave me a kick.

VLADIMIR It was Lucky gave it to you.

ESTRAGON And all that was yesterday?

VLADIMIR Show your leg.

ESTRAGON Which?

VLADIMIR Both. Pull up your trousers. [ESTRAGON *gives a leg to* VLADIMIR, *staggers.* VLADIMIR *takes the leg. They stagger.*] Pull up your trousers.

ESTRAGON I can't.

[VLADIMIR *pulls up the trousers, looks at the leg, lets it go.* ESTRAGON *almost falls.*]

VLADIMIR The other. [ESTRAGON *gives the same leg.*] The other, pig! [ESTRAGON *gives the other leg. Triumphantly.*] There's the wound! Beginning to fester!

ESTRAGON And what about it?

VLADIMIR [*letting go the leg*] Where are your boots?

ESTRAGON I must have thrown them away.

VLADIMIR When?

ESTRAGON I don't know.

VLADIMIR Why?

ESTRAGON [*exasperated*] I don't know why I don't know!

VLADIMIR No, I mean why did you throw them away?

ESTRAGON [*exasperated*] Because they were hurting me!

VLADIMIR [*triumphantly, pointing to the boots*] There they are! [ESTRAGON *looks at the boots.*] At the very spot where you left them yesterday!

[ESTRAGON *goes towards the boots, inspects them closely.*]

ESTRAGON They're not mine.

VLADIMIR [*stupefied*] Not yours!

ESTRAGON Mine were black. These are brown.

VLADIMIR You're sure yours were black?

ESTRAGON Well they were a kind of grey.

VLADIMIR And these are brown. Show.

ESTRAGON [*picking up a boot*] Well they're a kind of green.

VLADIMIR Show. [ESTRAGON *hands him the boot.* VLADIMIR *inspects it, throws it down angrily.*] Well of all the—

ESTRAGON You see, all that's a lot of bloody—

VLADIMIR Ah! I see what it is. Yes, I see what's happened

ESTRAGON All that's a lot of bloody—

VLADIMIR It's elementary. Someone came and took yours and left you his.

ESTRAGON Why?

VLADIMIR His were too tight for him, so he took yours.

ESTRAGON But mine were too tight.

VLADIMIR For you. Not for him.

ESTRAGON [*having tried in vain to work it out*] I'm tired! [*Pause*] Let's go.

VLADIMIR We can't.

ESTRAGON Why not?

VLADIMIR We're waiting for Godot.

ESTRAGON Ah! [*Pause. Despairing*] What'll we do, what'll we do!

VLADIMIR There's nothing we can do.

ESTRAGON But I can't go on like this!

VLADIMIR Would you like a radish?

ESTRAGON Is that all there is?

VLADIMIR There are radishes and turnips.

ESTRAGON Are there no carrots?

VLADIMIR No. Anyway you overdo it with your carrots.

ESTRAGON Then give me a radish. [VLADIMIR *fumbles in his pockets, finds nothing but turnips, finally brings out a radish and hands it to* ESTRAGON *who examines it, sniffs it.*] It's black!

VLADIMIR It's a radish.

ESTRAGON I only like the pink ones, you know that!

VLADIMIR Then you don't want it?

ESTRAGON I only like the pink ones!

VLADIMIR Then give it back to me. [ESTRAGON *gives it back.*]

ESTRAGON I'll go and get a carrot. [*He does not move.*]

VLADIMIR This is becoming really insignificant.

ESTRAGON Not enough.

[*Silence.*]

VLADIMIR What about trying them.

ESTRAGON I've tried everything.

VLADIMIR No, I mean the boots.

ESTRAGON Would that be a good thing?

VLADIMIR It'd pass the time. [ESTRAGON *hesitates.*] I assure you, it'd be an occupation.

ESTRAGON A relaxation.

VLADIMIR A recreation.

ESTRAGON A relaxation.

VLADIMIR Try.

ESTRAGON You'll help me?

VLADIMIR I will of course.

ESTRAGON We don't manage too badly, eh Didi, between the two of us?

VLADIMIR Yes yes. Come on, we'll try the left first.

ESTRAGON We always find something, eh Didi, to give us the impression we exist?

VLADIMIR [*impatiently*] Yes yes, we're magicians. But let us persevere in what we have resolved, before we forget. [*He picks up a boot.*] Come on, give me your foot. [ESTRAGON *raises his foot.*] The other, hog! [ESTRAGON *raises the other foot.*] Higher! [*Wreathed together they stagger about the stage.* VLADIMIR *succeeds finally in getting on the boot.*] Try and walk. [ESTRAGON *walks.*] Well?

ESTRAGON It fits.

VLADIMIR [*taking string from his pocket*] We'll try and lace it.

ESTRAGON [*vehemently*] No no, no laces, no laces!

VLADIMIR You'll be sorry. Let's try the other. [*As before*] Well?

ESTRAGON [*grudgingly*] It fits too.

VLADIMIR They don't hurt you?

ESTRAGON Not yet.

VLADIMIR Then you can keep them.

ESTRAGON They're too big.

VLADIMIR Perhaps you'll have socks some day.

ESTRAGON True.

VLADIMIR Then you'll keep them?

ESTRAGON That's enough about these boots.

VLADIMIR Yes, but—

ESTRAGON [*violently*] Enough! [*Silence*] I suppose I might as well sit down. [*He looks for a place to sit down, then goes and sits down on the mound.*]

VLADIMIR That's where you were sitting yesterday evening.

ESTRAGON If I could only sleep.

VLADIMIR Yesterday you slept.

ESTRAGON I'll try. [*He resumes his foetal posture, his head between his knees.*]

VLADIMIR Wait. [*He goes over and sits down beside* ESTRAGON *and begins to sing in a loud voice.*]

> Bye bye bye bye
> Bye bye—

ESTRAGON [*looking up angrily*] Not so loud!

VLADIMIR [*softly*]

> Bye bye bye bye
> Bye bye bye bye
> Bye bye bye bye
> Bye bye . . .

[ESTRAGON *sleeps.* VLADIMIR *gets up softly, takes off his coat and lays it across* ESTRAGON*'s shoulders, then starts walking up and down, swinging* *his arms to keep himself warm.* ESTRAGON *wakes with a start, jumps up, casts about wildly.* VLADIMIR *returns to him, puts his arms round him.*]

There . . . there . . . Didi is there . . . don't be afraid . . .

ESTRAGON Ah!

VLADIMIR There . . . there . . . it's all over.

ESTRAGON I was falling—

VLADIMIR It's all over, it's all over.

ESTRAGON I was on top of a–

VLADIMIR Don't tell me! Come, we'll walk it off.

[*He takes* ESTRAGON *by the arm and walks him up and down until* ESTRAGON *refuses to go any further.*]

ESTRAGON That's enough. I'm tired.

VLADIMIR You'd rather be stuck there doing nothing?

ESTRAGON Yes.

VLADIMIR Please yourself.

[*He releases* ESTRAGON, *picks up his coat and puts it on.*]

ESTRAGON Let's go.

VLADIMIR We can't.

ESTRAGON Why not?

VLADIMIR We're waiting for Godot.

ESTRAGON Ah! [VLADIMIR *walks up and down.*] Can you not stay still?

VLADIMIR I'm cold.

ESTRAGON We came too soon.

VLADIMIR It's always at nightfall.

ESTRAGON But night doesn't fall.

VLADIMIR It'll fall all of a sudden, like yesterday.

ESTRAGON Then it'll be night.

VLADIMIR And we can go.

ESTRAGON Then it'll be day again. [*Pause. Despairing.*] What'll we do, what'll we do!

VLADIMIR [*halting, violently*] Will you stop whining! I've had about my bellyful of your lamentations!

ESTRAGON I'm going.

VLADIMIR [*seeing* LUCKY*'s hat*] Well!

ESTRAGON Farewell.

VLADIMIR Lucky's hat. [*He goes towards it.*] I've been here an hour and never saw it. [*Very pleased*] Fine!

ESTRAGON You'll never see me again.

VLADIMIR I knew it was the right place. Now our troubles are over. [*He picks up the hat, contemplates it, straightens it.*] Must have been a very fine hat. [*He puts it on in place of his own which he hands to* ESTRAGON.] Here.

ESTRAGON What?

VLADIMIR Hold that.

[ESTRAGON *takes* VLADIMIR*'s hat.* VLADIMIR *adjusts* LUCKY*'s hat on his head.* ESTRAGON *puts on* VLADIMIR*'s hat in place of his own which he hands to* VLADIMIR. VLADIMIR *takes* ESTRAGON*'s hat.* ESTRAGON *adjusts* VLADIMIR*'s hat on his head.* VLADIMIR *puts on* ESTRAGON*'s hat in place of* LUCKY*'s which he hands to* ESTRAGON. ESTRAGON *takes* LUCKY*'s hat.* VLADIMIR *adjusts* ESTRAGON*'s hat on his head.* ESTRAGON *puts on* LUCKY*'s* *hat in place of* VLADIMIR'S *which he hands to* VLADIMIR. VLADIMIR *takes his hat.* ESTRAGON *adjusts* LUCKY'S *hat on his head.* VLADIMIR *puts on his hat in place of* ESTRAGON'S *which he hands to* ESTRAGON. ESTRAGON *takes his hat.* VLADIMIR *adjusts his hat on his head.* ESTRAGON *puts on his hat in place of* LUCKY'S *which he hands to* VLADIMIR. VLADIMIR *takes* LUCKY'S *hat.* ESTRAGON *adjusts his hat on his head.* VLADIMIR *puts on* LUCKY'S *hat in place of his own which he hands to* ESTRAGON. ESTRAGON *takes* VLADIMIR'S *hat.* VLADIMIR *adjusts* LUCKY'S *hat on his head.* ESTRAGON *hands* VLADIMIR'S *hat back to* VLADIMIR *who takes it and hands it back to* ESTRAGON *who takes it and hands it back to* VLADIMIR *who takes it and throws it down.*]

How does it fit me?

ESTRAGON How would I know?

VLADIMIR No, but how do I look in it? [*He turns his head coquettishly to and fro, minces like a mannequin.*]

ESTRAGON Hideous.

VLADIMIR Yes, but not more so than usual?

ESTRAGON Neither more nor less.

VLADIMIR Then I can keep it. Mine irked me. [*Pause*] How shall I say? [*Pause*] It itched me. [*He takes off* LUCKY'S *hat, peers into it, shakes it, knocks on the crown, puts it on again.*]

ESTRAGON I'm going.

[*Silence.*]

VLADIMIR Will you not play?

ESTRAGON Play at what?

VLADIMIR We could play at Pozzo and Lucky.

ESTRAGON Never heard of it.

VLADIMIR I'll do Lucky, you do Pozzo. [*He imitates* LUCKY *sagging under the weight of his baggage.* ESTRAGON *looks at him with stupefaction.*] Go on.

ESTRAGON What am I to do?

VLADIMIR Curse me!

ESTRAGON [*after reflection*] Naughty!

VLADIMIR Stronger!

ESTRAGON Gonococcus! Spirochete![6]

[VLADIMIR *sways back and forth, doubled in two.*]

VLADIMIR Tell me to think.

ESTRAGON What?

VLADIMIR Say, Think, pig!

ESTRAGON Think, pig!

[*Silence.*]

VLADIMIR I can't!

ESTRAGON That's enough of that.

VLADIMIR Tell me to dance.

ESTRAGON I'm going.

VLADIMIR Dance, hog! [*He writhes. Exit* ESTRAGON *left, precipitately.*] I can't! [*He looks up, misses* ESTRAGON.] Gogo! [*He moves wildly about the stage. Enter* ESTRAGON *left, panting. He hastens towards* VLADIMIR, *falls into his arms.*] There you are again at last!

6. Bacteria that cause venereal diseases. The gonococcus bacterium is associated with gonorrhea; the spirochete, with syphilis as well as other diseases.

ESTRAGON I'm accursed!
VLADIMIR Where were you? I thought you were gone for ever.
ESTRAGON They're coming!
VLADIMIR Who?
ESTRAGON I don't know.
VLADIMIR How many?
ESTRAGON I don't know.
VLADIMIR [*triumphantly*] It's Godot! At last! Gogo! It's Godot! We're saved! Let's go and meet him! [*He drags* ESTRAGON *towards the wings.* ESTRAGON *resists, pulls himself free, exit right.*] Gogo! Come back! [VLADIMIR *runs to extreme left, scans the horizon. Enter* ESTRAGON *right, he hastens towards* VLADIMIR, *falls into his arms.*] There you are again again!
ESTRAGON I'm in hell!
VLADIMIR Where were you?
ESTRAGON They're coming there too!
VLADIMIR We're surrounded! [ESTRAGON *makes a rush towards back.*] Imbecile! There's no way out there. [*He takes* ESTRAGON *by the arm and drags him towards front. Gesture towards front.*] There! Not a soul in sight! Off you go! Quick! [*He pushes* ESTRAGON *towards auditorium.* ESTRAGON *recoils in horror.*] You won't? [*He contemplates auditorium.*] Well I can understand that. Wait till I see. [*He reflects.*] Your only hope left is to disappear.
ESTRAGON Where?
VLADIMIR Behind the tree. [ESTRAGON *hesitates.*] Quick! Behind the tree. [ESTRAGON *goes and crouches behind the tree, realizes he is not hidden, comes out from behind the tree.*] Decidedly this tree will not have been the slightest use to us.
ESTRAGON [*calmer*] I lost my head. Forgive me. It won't happen again. Tell me what to do.
VLADIMIR There's nothing to do.
ESTRAGON You go and stand there. [*He draws* VLADIMIR *to extreme right and places him with his back to the stage.*] There, don't move, and watch out. [VLADIMIR *scans horizon, screening his eyes with his hand.* ESTRAGON *runs and takes up same position extreme left. They turn their heads and look at each other.*] Back to back like in the good old days. [*They continue to look at each other for a moment, then resume their watch. Long silence.*] Do you see anything coming?
VLADIMIR [*turning his head.*] What?
ESTRAGON [*louder*] Do you see anything coming?
VLADIMIR No.
ESTRAGON Nor I.

[*They resume their watch. Silence.*]

VLADIMIR You must have had a vision.
ESTRAGON [*turning his head*] What?
VLADIMIR [*louder*] You must have had a vision.
ESTRAGON No need to shout!

[*They resume their watch. Silence.*]

VLADIMIR } ESTRAGON } [*turning simultaneously*] Do you—
VLADIMIR Oh pardon!
ESTRAGON Carry on.

VLADIMIR No no, after you.
ESTRAGON No no, you first.
VLADIMIR I interrupted you.
ESTRAGON On the contrary.
[*They glare at each other angrily.*]
VLADIMIR Ceremonious ape!
ESTRAGON Punctilious pig!
VLADIMIR Finish your phrase, I tell you!
ESTRAGON Finish your own!
[*Silence. They draw closer, halt.*]
VLADIMIR Moron!
ESTRAGON That's the idea, let's abuse each other.
[*They turn, move apart, turn again and face each other.*]
VLADIMIR Moron!
ESTRAGON Vermin!
VLADIMIR Abortion!
ESTRAGON Morpion![7]
VLADIMIR Sewer-rat!
ESTRAGON Curate!
VLADIMIR Cretin!
ESTRAGON [*with finality*] Crritic!
VLADIMIR Oh! [*He wilts, vanquished, and turns away.*]
ESTRAGON Now let's make it up.
VLADIMIR Gogo!
ESTRAGON Didi!
VLADIMIR Your hand!
ESTRAGON Take it!
VLADIMIR Come to my arms!
ESTRAGON Your arms?
VLADIMIR My breast!
ESTRAGON Off we go!
[*They embrace. They separate. Silence.*]
VLADIMIR How time flies when one has fun!
[*Silence.*]
ESTRAGON What do we do now?
VLADIMIR While waiting.
ESTRAGON While waiting.
[*Silence.*]
VLADIMIR We could do our exercises.
ESTRAGON Our movements.
VLADIMIR Our elevations.
ESTRAGON Our relaxations.
VLADIMIR Our elongations.
ESTRAGON Our relaxations.
VLADIMIR To warm us up.
ESTRAGON To calm us down.

7. Crab louse (a French word, obsolete in English).

VLADIMIR Off we go.

[VLADIMIR *hops from one foot to the other.* ESTRAGON *imitates him.*]

ESTRAGON [*stopping*] That's enough. I'm tired.

VLADIMIR [*stopping*] We're not in form. What about a little deep breathing?

ESTRAGON I'm tired breathing.

VLADIMIR You're right. [*Pause*] Let's just do the tree, for the balance.

ESTRAGON The tree?

[VLADIMIR *does the tree, staggering about on one leg.*]

VLADIMIR [*stopping*] Your turn.

[ESTRAGON *does the tree, staggers.*]

ESTRAGON Do you think God sees me?

VLADIMIR You must close your eyes.

[ESTRAGON *closes his eyes, staggers worse.*]

ESTRAGON [*stopping, brandishing his fists, at the top of his voice*] God have pity on me!

VLADIMIR [*vexed*] And me?

ESTRAGON On me! On me! Pity! On me!

[*Enter* POZZO *and* LUCKY. POZZO *is blind.* LUCKY *burdened as before. Rope as before, but much shorter, so that* POZZO *may follow more easily.* LUCKY *wearing a different hat. At the sight of* VLADIMIR *and* ESTRAGON *he stops short.* POZZO, *continuing on his way, bumps into him.*]

VLADIMIR Gogo!

POZZO [*clutching on to* LUCKY *who staggers*] What is it? Who is it?

[LUCKY *falls, drops everything and brings down* POZZO *with him. They lie helpless among the scattered baggage.*]

ESTRAGON Is it Godot?

VLADIMIR At last! [*He goes towards the heap.*] Reinforcements at last!

POZZO Help!

ESTRAGON Is it Godot?

VLADIMIR We were beginning to weaken. Now we're sure to see the evening out.

POZZO Help!

ESTRAGON Do you hear him?

VLADIMIR We are no longer alone, waiting for the night, waiting for Godot, waiting for . . . waiting. All evening we have struggled, unassisted. Now it's over. It's already tomorrow.

POZZO Help!

VLADIMIR Time flows again already. The sun will set, the moon rise, and we away . . . from here.

POZZO Pity!

VLADIMIR Poor Pozzo!

ESTRAGON I knew it was him.

VLADIMIR Who?

ESTRAGON Godot.

VLADIMIR But it's not Godot.

ESTRAGON It's not Godot?

VLADIMIR It's not Godot.

ESTRAGON Then who is it?

VLADIMIR It's Pozzo.

POZZO Here! Here! Help me up!

VLADIMIR He can't get up.

ESTRAGON Let's go.

VLADIMIR We can't.

ESTRAGON Why not?

VLADIMIR We're waiting for Godot.

ESTRAGON Ah!

VLADIMIR Perhaps he has another bone for you.

ESTRAGON Bone?

VLADIMIR Chicken. Do you not remember?

ESTRAGON It was him?

VLADIMIR Yes.

ESTRAGON Ask him.

VLADIMIR Perhaps we should help him first.

ESTRAGON To do what?

VLADIMIR To get up.

ESTRAGON He can't get up?

VLADIMIR He wants to get up.

ESTRAGON Then let him get up.

VLADIMIR He can't.

ESTRAGON Why not?

VLADIMIR I don't know.

[POZZO *writhes, groans, beats the ground with his fists.*]

ESTRAGON We should ask him for the bone first. Then if he refuses we'll leave him there.

VLADIMIR You mean we have him at our mercy?

ESTRAGON Yes.

VLADIMIR And that we should subordinate our good offices to certain conditions?

ESTRAGON What?

VLADIMIR That seems intelligent all right. But there's one thing I'm afraid of.

POZZO Help!

ESTRAGON What?

VLADIMIR That Lucky might get going all of a sudden. Then we'd be ballocksed.[8]

ESTRAGON Lucky?

VLADIMIR The one that went for you yesterday.

ESTRAGON I tell you there was ten of them.

VLADIMIR No, before that, the one that kicked you.

ESTRAGON Is he there?

VLADIMIR As large as life. [*Gesture towards* LUCKY.] For the moment he is inert. But he might run amuck any minute.

POZZO Help!

ESTRAGON And suppose we gave him a good beating the two of us?

VLADIMIR You mean if we fell on him in his sleep?

ESTRAGON Yes.

8. Ruined, screwed (slang).

VLADIMIR That seems a good idea all right. But could we do it? Is he really asleep? [*Pause*] No, the best would be to take advantage of Pozzo's calling for help—

POZZO Help!

VLADIMIR To help him—

ESTRAGON *We* help *him*?

VLADIMIR In anticipation of some tangible return.

ESTRAGON And suppose he—

VLADIMIR Let us not waste our time in idle discourse! [*Pause. Vehemently.*] Let us do something, while we have the chance! It is not every day that we are needed. Not indeed that we personally are needed. Others would meet the case equally well, if not better. To all mankind they were addressed, those cries for help still ringing in our ears! But at this place, at this moment of time, all mankind is us, whether we like it or not. Let us make the most of it, before it is too late! Let us represent worthily for once the foul brood to which a cruel fate consigned us! What do you say? [ESTRAGON *says nothing.*] It is true that when with folded arms we weigh the pros and cons we are no less a credit to our species. The tiger bounds to the help of his congeners[9] without the least reflexion, or else he slinks away into the depths of the thickets. But that is not the question. What are we doing here, *that* is the question. And we are blessed in this, that we happen to know the answer. Yes, in this immense confusion one thing alone is clear. We are waiting for Godot to come—

ESTRAGON Ah!

POZZO Help!

VLADIMIR Or for night to fall. [*Pause*] We have kept our appointment and that's an end to that. We are not saints, but we have kept our appointment. How many people can boast as much?

ESTRAGON Billions.

VLADIMIR You think so?

ESTRAGON I don't know.

VLADIMIR You may be right.

POZZO Help!

VLADIMIR All I know is that the hours are long, under these conditions, and constrain us to beguile them with proceedings which—how shall I say—which may at first sight seem reasonable, until they become a habit. You may say it is to prevent our reason from foundering. No doubt. But has it not long been straying in the night without end of the abyssal depths? That's what I sometimes wonder. You follow my reasoning?

ESTRAGON [*aphoristic for once*] We are all born mad. Some remain so.

POZZO Help! I'll pay you!

ESTRAGON How much?

POZZO One hundred francs!

ESTRAGON It's not enough.

VLADIMIR I wouldn't go so far as that.

ESTRAGON You think it's enough?

VLADIMIR No, I mean so far as to assert that I was weak in the head when I came into the world. But that is not the question.

9. Members of his class or kind.

POZZO Two hundred!

VLADIMIR We wait. We are bored. [*He throws up his hand.*] No, don't protest, we are bored to death, there's no denying it. Good. A diversion comes along and what do we do? We let it go to waste. Come, let's get to work! [*He advances towards the heap, stops in his stride.*] In an instant all will vanish and we'll be alone once more, in the midst of nothingness! [*He broods.*]

POZZO Two hundred!

VLADIMIR We're coming!

[*He tries to pull* POZZO *to his feet, fails, tries again, stumbles, falls, tries to get up, fails.*]

ESTRAGON What's the matter with you all?

VLADIMIR Help!

ESTRAGON I'm going.

VLADIMIR Don't leave me! They'll kill me!

POZZO Where am I?

VLADIMIR Gogo!

POZZO Help!

VLADIMIR Help!

ESTRAGON I'm going.

VLADIMIR Help me up first, then we'll go together.

ESTRAGON You promise?

VLADIMIR I swear it!

ESTRAGON And we'll never come back?

VLADIMIR Never!

ESTRAGON We'll go to the Pyrenees.[1]

VLADIMIR Wherever you like.

ESTRAGON I've always wanted to wander in the Pyrenees.

VLADIMIR You'll wander in them.

ESTRAGON [*recoiling*] Who farted?

VLADIMIR Pozzo.

POZZO Here! Here! Pity!

ESTRAGON It's revolting!

VLADIMIR Quick! Give me your hand!

ESTRAGON I'm going. [*Pause. Louder.*] I'm going.

VLADIMIR Well I suppose in the end I'll get up by myself. [*He tries, fails.*] In the fullness of time.

ESTRAGON What's the matter with you?

VLADIMIR Go to hell.

ESTRAGON Are you staying there?

VLADIMIR For the time being.

ESTRAGON Come on, get up, you'll catch a chill.

VLADIMIR Don't worry about me.

ESTRAGON Come on, Didi, don't be pig-headed!

[*He stretches out his hand which* VLADIMIR *makes haste to seize.*]

VLADIMIR Pull!

[ESTRAGON *pulls, stumbles, falls. Long silence.*]

1. The mountain range on the border between Spain and France, extending from the Atlantic Ocean to the Mediterranean Sea.

POZZO Help!

VLADIMIR We've arrived.

POZZO Who are you?

VLADIMIR We are men.

[*Silence.*]

ESTRAGON Sweet mother earth!

VLADIMIR Can you get up?

ESTRAGON I don't know.

VLADIMIR Try.

ESTRAGON Not now, not now.

[*Silence.*]

POZZO What happened?

VLADIMIR [*violently*] Will you stop it, you! Pest! He can think of nothing but himself!

ESTRAGON What about a little snooze?

VLADIMIR Did you hear him? He wants to know what happened!

ESTRAGON Don't mind him. Sleep.

[*Silence.*]

POZZO Pity! Pity!

ESTRAGON [*with a start*] What is it?

VLADIMIR Were you asleep?

ESTRAGON I must have been.

VLADIMIR It's this bastard Pozzo at it again.

ESTRAGON Make him stop it. Kick him in the crotch.

VLADIMIR [*striking Pozzo*] Will you stop it! Crablouse! [POZZO *extricates himself with cries of pain and crawls away. He stops, saws the air blindly, calling for help.* VLADIMIR, *propped on his elbow, observes his retreat.*] He's off! [POZZO *collapses.*] He's down!

ESTRAGON What do we do now?

VLADIMIR Perhaps I could crawl to him.

ESTRAGON Don't leave me!

VLADIMIR Or I could call to him.

ESTRAGON Yes, call to him.

VLADIMIR Pozzo! [*Silence*] Pozzo! [*Silence*] No reply.

ESTRAGON Together.

VLADIMIR }
ESTRAGON } Pozzo! Pozzo!

VLADIMIR He moved.

ESTRAGON Are you sure his name is Pozzo?

VLADIMIR [*alarmed*] Mr. Pozzo! Come back! We won't hurt you!

[*Silence.*]

ESTRAGON We might try him with other names.

VLADIMIR I'm afraid he's dying.

ESTRAGON It'd be amusing.

VLADIMIR What'd be amusing?

ESTRAGON To try him with other names, one after the other. It'd pass the time. And we'd be bound to hit on the right one sooner or later.

VLADIMIR I tell you his name is Pozzo.

ESTRAGON We'll soon see. [*He reflects.*] Abel! Abel!

POZZO Help!

ESTRAGON Got it in one!

VLADIMIR I begin to weary of this motif.

ESTRAGON Perhaps the other is called Cain.[2] Cain! Cain!

POZZO Help!

ESTRAGON He's all humanity. [*Silence*] Look at the little cloud.

VLADIMIR [*raising his eyes*] Where?

ESTRAGON There. In the zenith.[3]

VLADIMIR Well? [*Pause*] What is there so wonderful about it?

[*Silence.*]

ESTRAGON Let's pass on now to something else, do you mind?

VLADIMIR I was just going to suggest it.

ESTRAGON But to what?

VLADIMIR Ah!

[*Silence.*]

ESTRAGON Suppose we got up to begin with?

VLADIMIR No harm trying.

[*They get up.*]

ESTRAGON Child's play.

VLADIMIR Simple question of will-power.

ESTRAGON And now?

POZZO Help!

ESTRAGON Let's go.

VLADIMIR We can't.

ESTRAGON Why not?

VLADIMIR We're waiting for Godot.

ESTRAGON Ah! [*Despairing*] What'll we do, what'll we do!

POZZO Help!

VLADIMIR What about helping him?

ESTRAGON What does he want?

VLADIMIR He wants to get up.

ESTRAGON Then why doesn't he?

VLADIMIR He wants us to help him to get up.

ESTRAGON Then why don't we? What are we waiting for?

[*They help* POZZO *to his feet, let him go. He falls.*]

VLADIMIR We must hold him. [*They get him up again.* POZZO *says between them, his arms round their necks.*] Feeling better?

POZZO Who are you?

VLADIMIR Do you not recognize us?

POZZO I am blind.

[*Silence.*]

ESTRAGON Perhaps he can see into the future.

VLADIMIR Since when?

POZZO I used to have wonderful sight—but are you friends?

ESTRAGON [*laughing noisily*] He wants to know if we are friends!

2. In the Bible, the first murderer (a son of Adam and Eve); after Cain killed his brother Abel, God made him "a fugitive and a vagabond" (Genesis 4.12).

3. Literally, the point of the sky directly overhead.

VLADIMIR No, he means friends of his.

ESTRAGON Well?

VLADIMIR We've proved we are, by helping him.

ESTRAGON Exactly. Would we have helped him if we weren't his friends?

VLADIMIR Possibly.

ESTRAGON True.

VLADIMIR Don't let's quibble about that now.

POZZO You are not highwaymen?

ESTRAGON Highwaymen! Do we look like highwaymen?

VLADIMIR Damn it can't you see the man is blind!

ESTRAGON Damn it so he is. [*Pause*] So he says.

POZZO Don't leave me!

VLADIMIR No question of it.

ESTRAGON For the moment.

POZZO What time is it?

VLADIMIR [*inspecting the sky*] Seven o'clock . . . eight o'clock . . .

ESTRAGON That depends what time of year it is.

POZZO Is it evening?

[*Silence.* VLADIMIR *and* ESTRAGON *scrutinize the sunset.*]

ESTRAGON It's rising.

VLADIMIR Impossible.

ESTRAGON Perhaps it's the dawn.

VLADIMIR Don't be a fool. It's the west over there.

ESTRAGON How do you know?

POZZO [*anguished*] Is it evening?

VLADIMIR Anyway it hasn't moved.

ESTRAGON I tell you it's rising.

POZZO Why don't you answer me?

ESTRAGON Give us a chance.

VLADIMIR [*reassuring*] It's evening, Sir, it's evening, night is drawing nigh. My friend here would have me doubt it and I must confess he shook me for a moment. But it is not for nothing I have lived through this long day and I can assure you it is very near the end of its repertory. [*Pause*] How do you feel now?

ESTRAGON How much longer are we to cart him around. [*They half release him, catch him again as he falls.*] We are not caryatids![4]

VLADIMIR You were saying your sight used to be good, if I heard you right.

POZZO Wonderful! Wonderful, wonderful sight!

[*Silence.*]

ESTRAGON [*irritably*] Expand! Expand!

VLADIMIR Let him alone. Can't you see he's thinking of the days when he was happy. [*Pause*] *Memoria praeteritorum bonorum*[5]—that must be unpleasant.

ESTRAGON We wouldn't know.

VLADIMIR And it came on you all of a sudden?

POZZO Quite wonderful!

4. In architecture, draped female figures that act as supporting columns.

5. Memory of past goods (Latin); a phrase quoted from St. Thomas Aquinas, *Summa Theologica* (1269–73), 2.2.36.1.

VLADIMIR I'm asking you if it came on you all of a sudden.

POZZO I woke up one fine day as blind as Fortune.[6] [*Pause*] Sometimes I wonder if I'm not still asleep.

VLADIMIR And when was that?

POZZO I don't know.

VLADIMIR But no later than yesterday—

POZZO [*violently*] Don't question me! The blind have no notion of time. The things of time are hidden from them too.

VLADIMIR Well just fancy that! I could have sworn it was just the opposite.

ESTRAGON I'm going.

POZZO Where are we?

VLADIMIR I couldn't tell you.

POZZO It isn't by any chance the place known as the Board?[7]

VLADIMIR Never heard of it.

POZZO What is it like?

VLADIMIR [*looking round*] It's indescribable. It's like nothing. There's nothing. There's a tree.

POZZO Then it's not the Board.

ESTRAGON [*sagging*] Some diversion!

POZZO Where is my menial?

VLADIMIR He's about somewhere,

POZZO Why doesn't he answer when I call?

VLADIMIR I don't know. He seems to be sleeping. Perhaps he's dead.

POZZO What happened exactly?

ESTRAGON Exactly!

VLADIMIR The two of you slipped. [*Pause*] And fell.

POZZO Go and see is he hurt.

VLADIMIR We can't leave you.

POZZO You needn't both go.

VLADIMIR [*to* ESTRAGON] You go.

ESTRAGON After what he did to me? Never!

POZZO Yes yes, let your friend go, he stinks so. [*Silence.*] What is he waiting for?

VLADIMIR What you waiting for?

ESTRAGON I'm waiting for Godot.

[*Silence.*]

VLADIMIR What exactly should he do?

POZZO Well to begin with he should pull on the rope, as hard as he likes so long as he doesn't strangle him. He usually responds to that. If not he should give him a taste of his boot, in the face and the privates as far as possible.

VLADIMIR [*to* ESTRAGON] You see, you've nothing to be afraid of. It's even an opportunity to revenge yourself.

ESTRAGON And if he defends himself?

POZZO No no, he never defends himself.

VLADIMIR I'll come flying to the rescue.

6. The Roman goddess Fortuna, the personification of fortune, was sometimes depicted wearing a blindfold.

7. The stage itself is often referred to as "the boards."

ESTRAGON Don't take your eyes off me. [*He goes towards* LUCKY.]

VLADIMIR Make sure he's alive before you start. No point in exerting yourself if he's dead.

ESTRAGON [*bending over* LUCKY] He's breathing.

VLADIMIR Then let him have it.

[*With sudden fury* ESTRAGON *starts kicking* LUCKY, *hurling abuse at him as he does so. But he hurts his foot and moves away, limping and groaning.* LUCKY *stirs.*]

ESTRAGON Oh the brute!

[*He sits down on the mound and tries to take off his boot. But he soon desists and disposes himself for sleep, his arms on his knees and his head on his arms.*]

POZZO What's gone wrong now?

VLADIMIR My friend has hurt himself

POZZO And Lucky?

VLADIMIR So it is he?

POZZO What?

VLADIMIR It is Lucky?

POZZO I don't understand.

VLADIMIR And you are Pozzo?

POZZO Certainly I am Pozzo.

VLADIMIR The same as yesterday?

POZZO Yesterday?

VLADIMIR We met yesterday. [*Silence*] Do you not remember?

POZZO I don't remember having met anyone yesterday. But tomorrow I won't remember having met anyone today. So don't count on me to enlighten you.

VLADIMIR But—

POZZO Enough! Up pig!

VLADIMIR You were bringing him to the fair to sell him. You spoke to us. He danced. He thought. You had your sight.

POZZO As you please. Let me go! [VLADIMIR *moves away.*] Up! [LUCKY *gets up, gathers up his burdens.*]

VLADIMIR Where do you go from here.

POZZO On. [LUCKY, *laden down, takes his place before* POZZO.] Whip! [LUCKY *puts everything down, looks for whip, finds it, puts it into* POZZO'*s hand, takes up everything again.*] Rope!

[LUCKY *puts everything down, puts end of rope into* POZZO'*s hand, takes up everything again.*]

VLADIMIR What is there in the bag?

POZZO Sand. [*He jerks the rope.*] On!

VLADIMIR Don't go yet.

POZZO I'm going.

VLADIMIR What do you do when you fall far from help?

POZZO We wait till we can get up. Then we go on. On!

VLADIMIR Before you go tell him to sing.

POZZO Who?

VLADIMIR Lucky.

POZZO To sing?

VLADIMIR Yes. Or to think. Or to recite.

POZZO But he is dumb.

VLADIMIR Dumb!

POZZO Dumb. He can't even groan.

VLADIMIR Dumb! Since when?

POZZO [*suddenly furious*] Have you not done tormenting me with your accursed time! It's abominable! When! When! One day, is that not enough for you, one day he went dumb, one day I went blind, one day we'll go deaf, one day we were born, one day we shall die, the same day, the same second, is that not enough for you? [*Calmer*] They give birth astride of a grave, the light gleams an instant, then it's night once more. [*He jerks the rope.*] On!

[*Exeunt*[8] *Pozzo and Lucky. Vladimir follows them to the edge of the stage, looks after them. The noise of falling, reinforced by mimic of Vladimir, announces that they are down again. Silence. Vladimir goes towards Estragon, contemplates him a moment, then shakes him awake.*]

ESTRAGON [*wild gestures, incoherent words. Finally*] Why will you never let me sleep?

VLADIMIR I felt lonely.

ESTRAGON I was dreaming I was happy.

VLADIMIR That passed the time.

ESTRAGON I was dreaming that—

VLADIMIR [*violently*] Don't tell me! [*Silence*] I wonder is he really blind.

ESTRAGON Blind? Who?

VLADIMIR Pozzo.

ESTRAGON Blind?

VLADIMIR He told us he was blind.

ESTRAGON Well what about it?

VLADIMIR It seemed to me he saw us.

ESTRAGON You dreamt it. [*Pause*] Let's go. We can't. Ah! [*Pause*] Are you sure it wasn't him?

VLADIMIR Who?

ESTRAGON Godot.

VLADIMIR But who?

ESTRAGON Pozzo.

VLADIMIR Not at all! [*Less sure*] Not at all! [*Still less sure*] Not at all!

ESTRAGON I suppose I might as well get up. [*He gets up painfully.*] Ow! Didi!

VLADIMIR I don't know what to think any more.

ESTRAGON My feet! [*He sits down again and tries to take off his boots.*] Help me!

VLADIMIR Was I sleeping, while the others suffered? Am I sleeping now? Tomorrow, when I wake, or think I do, what shall I say of today? That with Estragon my friend, at this place, until the fall of night, I waited for Godot? That Pozzo passed, with his carrier, and that he spoke to us? Probably. But in all that what truth will there be? [ESTRAGON, *having struggled with his boots in vain, is dozing off again.* VLADIMIR *looks at him.*] He'll know nothing. He'll tell me about the blows he received and I'll give him a carrot. [*Pause*] Astride of a grave and a difficult birth. Down in the hole, lingeringly,

8. [They] exit (Latin).

the grave-digger puts on the forceps.[9] We have time to grow old. The air is full of our cries. [*He listens.*] But habit is a great deadener. [*He looks again at* ESTRAGON.] At me too someone is looking, of me too someone is saying, He is sleeping, he knows nothing, let him sleep on. [*Pause*] I can't go on! [*Pause*] What have I said?

[*He goes feverishly to and fro, halts finally at extreme left, broods. Enter* BOY *right. He halts. Silence.*]

BOY Mister . . . [VLADIMIR *turns.*] Mister Albert . . .

VLADIMIR Off we go again. [*Pause*] Do you not recognize me?

BOY No Sir.

VLADIMIR It wasn't you came yesterday.

BOY No Sir.

VLADIMIR This is your first time.

BOY Yes Sir.

[*Silence.*]

VLADIMIR You have a message from Mr. Godot.

BOY Yes Sir.

VLADIMIR He won't come this evening.

BOY No Sir.

VLADIMIR But he'll come tomorrow.

BOY Yes Sir.

VLADIMIR Without fail.

BOY Yes Sir.

[*Silence.*]

VLADIMIR Did you meet anyone?

BOY No Sir.

VLADIMIR Two other . . . [*He hesitates.*] . . . men?

BOY I didn't see anyone, Sir.

[*Silence.*]

VLADIMIR What does he do, Mr. Godot? [*Silence*] Do you hear me?

BOY Yes Sir.

VLADIMIR Well?

BOY He does nothing, Sir.

[*Silence*]

VLADIMIR How is your brother?

BOY He's sick, Sir.

VLADIMIR Perhaps it was he came yesterday.

BOY I don't know, Sir.

[*Silence*]

VLADIMIR [*softly*] Has he a beard, Mr. Godot?

BOY Yes Sir.

VLADIMIR Fair or . . . [*He hesitates.*] . . . or black?

BOY I think it's white, Sir.

[*Silence.*]

VLADIMIR Christ have mercy on us!

[*Silence.*]

9. An instrument for grasping (obstetrical forceps help pull a baby from the birth canal).

BOY What am I to tell Mr. Godot, Sir?

VLADIMIR Tell him . . . [*He hesitates.*] . . . tell him you saw me and that . . . [*He hesitates.*] . . . that you saw me. [*Pause.* VLADIMIR *advances, the* BOY *recoils.* VLADIMIR *halts, the* BOY *halts. With sudden violence.*] You're sure you saw me, you won't come and tell me tomorrow that you never saw me!

[*Silence.* VLADIMIR *makes a sudden spring forward, the* BOY *avoids him and exit running. Silence. The sun sets, the moon rises. As in Act 1.* VLADIMIR *stands motionless and bowed.* ESTRAGON *wakes, takes off his boots, gets up with one in each hand and goes and puts them down center front, then goes towards* VLADIMIR.]

ESTRAGON What's wrong with you?

VLADIMIR Nothing.

ESTRAGON I'm going.

VLADIMIR So am I.

ESTRAGON Was I long asleep?

VLADIMIR I don't know.

[*Silence.*]

ESTRAGON Where shall we go?

VLADIMIR Not far.

ESTRAGON Oh yes, let's go far away from here.

VLADIMIR We can't.

ESTRAGON Why not?

VLADIMIR We have to come back tomorrow.

ESTRAGON What for?

VLADIMIR To wait for Godot.

ESTRAGON Ah! [*Silence.*] He didn't come?

VLADIMIR No.

ESTRAGON And now it's too late.

VLADIMIR Yes, now it's night.

ESTRAGON And if we dropped him? [*Pause*] If we dropped him?

VLADIMIR He'd punish us. [*Silence. He looks at the tree.*] Everything's dead but the tree.

ESTRAGON [*looking at the tree*] What is it?

VLADIMIR It's the tree.

ESTRAGON Yes, but what kind?

VLADIMIR I don't know. A willow.

[ESTRAGON *draws* VLADIMIR *towards the tree. They stand motionless before it. Silence.*]

ESTRAGON Why don't we hang ourselves?

VLADIMIR With what?

ESTRAGON You haven't got a bit of rope?

VLADIMIR No.

ESTRAGON Then we can't.

[*Silence.*]

VLADIMIR Let's go.

ESTRAGON Wait, there's my belt.

VLADIMIR It's too short.

ESTRAGON You could hang on to my legs.

VLADIMIR And who'd hang on to mine?

ESTRAGON True.

VLADIMIR Show all the same. [ESTRAGON *loosens the cord that holds up his trousers which, much too big for him, fall about his ankles. They look at the cord.*] It might do at a pinch. But is it strong enough?

ESTRAGON We'll soon see. Here.

[*They each take an end of the cord and pull. It breaks. They almost fall.*]

VLADIMIR Not worth a curse.

[*Silence.*]

ESTRAGON You say we have to come back tomorrow?

VLADIMIR Yes.

ESTRAGON Then we can bring a good bit of rope.

VLADIMIR Yes.

[*Silence.*]

ESTRAGON Didi.

VLADIMIR Yes.

ESTRAGON I can't go on like this.

VLADIMIR That's what you think.

ESTRAGON If we parted? That might be better for us.

VLADIMIR We'll hang ourselves tomorrow. [*Pause*] Unless Godot comes.

ESTRAGON And if he comes?

VLADIMIR We'll be saved.

[VLADIMIR *takes off his hat* (LUCKY'*s*), *peers inside it, feels about inside it, shakes it, knocks on the crown, puts it on again.*]

ESTRAGON Well? Shall we go?

VLADIMIR Pull on your trousers.

ESTRAGON What?

VLADIMIR Pull on your trousers.

ESTRAGON You want me to pull off my trousers?

VLADIMIR Pull ON your trousers.

ESTRAGON [*realizing his trousers are down*] True. [*He pulls up his trousers.*]

VLADIMIR Well? Shall we go?

ESTRAGON Yes, let's go.

[*They do not move.*]

Curtain.

WOLE SOYINKA

b. 1934

An active writer for more than five decades, Wole Soyinka is widely regarded as Africa's foremost dramatist and one of the most compelling contemporary writers in English more generally, a judgment affirmed by his being awarded the Nobel Prize in Literature in 1986. Though he is also an accomplished poet, novelist, and essayist, Soyinka's worldwide acclaim rests mainly on his dramatic oeuvre. His plays make use of the rituals and festivals of Nigeria's Yoruba culture and are marked by Nigeria's volatile history, but they also reflect the influences of other cultures, such as that of classical Greece. Soyinka has been one of the continent's most outspoken critics of abuses of power, in Nigeria and elsewhere, even as he has crafted plays that cannot be tied to a particular political creed. For many, his most significant achievement is the creation of a new form of tragedy that draws on both Western and Yoruba traditions, a form that is perhaps most fully realized in *DEATH AND THE KING'S HORSEMAN* (1975).

During Soyinka's formative years, Nigeria was in its last decades of British rule. Consequently, Soyinka received a traditional education in English, first at an elite grammar school and then at Government College, Ibadan, where he excelled in the study of various Western literatures, including French and Greek. He continued his education in England, where he studied drama at the University of Leeds. In Leeds and later in London, Soyinka also intensified his engagement with the theater and wrote his first plays, which helped win him a research grant and begin his swift rise as a dramatist. He returned to Nigeria in 1960, the year of its independence from Britain and the start of a period of intense conflict between different regions of the country. Over the next few years, Soyinka founded theater groups; wrote fiction and verse as well as plays for stage, television, and radio; and taught as a university lecturer in English. At the same time, he attempted to prevent the civil war that ultimately broke out in 1967 when the southeast of Nigeria declared its independence as Biafra; these efforts led to his imprisonment. He spent much of his two years of detention in solitary confinement, an experience he later described in one of his autobiographical prose works, *The Man Died: Prison Notes of Wole Soyinka* (1972). His subsequent career has been marked by a series of exiles and returns. Soyinka has taught at the University of Cambridge and Yale University and has directed shows in Europe and the United States, but his most sustained project has been the fostering of Nigeria's literary culture and democracy.

The clearest indications of Soyinka's changing attitude toward nationalism and cultural autonomy can be found in his essays. Writing in the sixties, Soyinka was often critical of those seeking an "authentic" culture that existed before Europeans colonized Africa, and focused instead on cultural mixture. By the 1970s, however, he had turned more fully to Yoruba culture—to which he was exposed early, despite his mother's fervent Christianity—as a resource for drama. In the 1980s, as Soyinka once more became disenchanted with Nigeria's political realities, he placed less emphasis on Yoruba culture. His critical writings thus chart a path through the cultural struggles of a former colony dealing with an imposed culture that has now fused with local ones; after the terrible experience of colonialism, Western and indigenous cultures had become permanently intertwined. Soyinka's relation to colonialism was further complicated by his decision to write in English, albeit an English shot through with metaphors, idioms, and sayings from Yoruba. At various times in his career, he advocated the use of Swahili throughout the continent as a lingua franca to replace the languages of Africa's former European colonizers, but this proposal won few followers.

Soyinka's oeuvre oscillates between tradition and modernity. His earliest plays, *The Swamp Dwellers* (1958) and *The Lion and the Jewel* (1959), present a critique of traditional Yoruba practices and social structures as they come under increasing pressure from forces of modernization both from within and from without. Each play contains a village priest or ruler who opposes modernization and who cunningly seeks to hold on to vestiges of power predicated on the old ways. Soyinka clearly does not endorse this defensive rejection of modernization, although he recognizes the pain that accompanied the transformation of the Nigerian hinterland. Ultimately, these plays satirize the attempt to preserve the old at all cost. A similar critique is developed in *The Trials of Brother Jero* (1960) and *Jero's Metamorphosis* (1973), two plays that revolve around a pseudo-prophet who attracts followers solely for his own economic gain and who is ready to employ every trick possible to outsmart his rivals. In other works, Soyinka is more fully concerned with the social reality of the outcast. In *The Road* (1965), one of his best plays, a number of lowlifes are assembled around a figure called Professor, who is akin to the sham prophet Jero. As Professor ekes out a living by forging documents, he is also engaged in an unlikely quest for spiritual enlightenment. These plays show that modernity is not something imposed onto Yoruba culture from the outside but a force at work within it.

Some of Soyinka's plays aim squarely at Nigerian politics—for example, *From Zia, with Love* (1992), which harshly indicts the dictatorship—but his best-known plays avoid direct political engagement, seeking instead to weave together different cultures and traditions. In his drama, Soyinka has continually insisted on the affinities between Greek and Yoruba tragedy. Most significantly, he has related the Yoruba god Ogun, the deity to whom he himself feels closest, to the Greek god Dionysus, who is connected with the origins of Greek tragedy. This attempt to forge new forms of tragedy out of Western and African traditions led to a long-standing controversy between Soyinka and a group of Nigerian intellectuals and critics—dubbed by Soyinka the "Leftocracy"—who accused him of seeking universal human meaning while ignoring the specifics of Nigeria's political and social situation after independence.

The tensions between political drama and tragedy as well as the tensions between the use of Western and Yoruba traditions are most visible in Soyinka's adaptations of EURIPIDES' *The Bacchae* (406 B.C.E.) and of BERTOLT BRECHT's *The Threepenny Opera* (1928). *The Bacchae of Euripides* (1973) provided Soyinka with an occasion to gauge the similarities and differences between Greek and Yoruba myths. Soyinka's Dionysus is less vindictive than Euripides', and his play displays a broader social range (its chorus is made up of slaves). Yet he shares with Euripides the attempt to connect drama to its lost origin in ritual. Brecht's *Threepenny Opera* is much more overtly political; *Opera Wonyosi* (1977) replaces the underworld of London, which Brecht himself had borrowed from the eighteenth-century British playwright John

Gay, with a politically corrupt West Africa. In both adaptations, Soyinka demonstrates the power of translation and transposition, encouraging cultural mixture and cross-fertilization in a way that respects the integrity of different traditions and practices.

Soyinka's project of inventing a new tragic form culminates in *Death and the King's Horseman*, a play based on a historical incident. In 1946, a British colonial district officer interrupted the ritual suicide of a village notable, the King's Horseman—a suicide prescribed by the Yoruba religious and social system—without realizing how his interference would affect the village and, most importantly, the King's Horseman's son, who is also his protégé. This historical incident thus ties the officer, the King's Horseman, and his son in an inextricable and fatal knot. The officer himself is presented as a relatively two-dimensional figure, distinguished mainly by his colonial arrogance: Simon Pilkings interferes with local customs without knowing anything about their role in the social order or their religious significance. As a result, some critics have read the play as a defense of Yoruba customs. In his author's note, however, Soyinka takes issue with all readings that reduce the play to a simple "clash of cultures"; indeed, the play spends considerable energy trying—and failing—to bridge the gulf between them.

The two cultures are connected by various mediating figures, who participate in or have knowledge of both worlds. The officer, for example, depends on his Yoruba employees for information about local customs and religion. While Pilkings, who arrogantly dismisses their culture, often finds it difficult to interpret what his informants say, his wife is somewhat more open-minded and thus more aware of the inescapable cultural clash. The most competent intermediary is Olunde, the son of Elesin, the King's Horseman. Sent by Pilkings to England to study medicine against his father's wishes, Olunde has now returned for his father's burial. Although he is Westernized (as evidenced by the suit he wears), he does not dismiss the requirement that his father commit suicide, knowing how deeply the ritual is woven

British colonial administrators meeting tribal representatives in Lagos, Nigeria, ca. 1900.

into the social fabric of the village. In eloquently criticizing the folly of the colonial officer's attempt to stop the ritual, he serves as an authoritative commentator on the play's main conflict. Events take a tragic turn at precisely the moment when the son feels forced to abandon his role as mediator and instead become a participant.

Even as Soyinka emphasizes the significance of the Yoruba custom and Elesin's social position, he also highlights the customs and social rituals of the British colonizers. Jane, the colonial officer's wife, approvingly recounts the story of a British captain's suicide, condoned because it was deemed heroic. At the same time, Soyinka contrasts Yoruba dances with a masque held by the British, who dress in costumes to attend a ball that evokes European court culture and its rigid hierarchies. Each culture thus has a place for suicide and for masked dance. To intertwine the two cultures even more closely, Soyinka has each imitate the other. At one point, a group of village women and girls mock the idioms and intonation of their colonial rulers. At another, we see the Pilkingses appear in sacred costumes associated with the Yoruba dead, mimicking ritual movements (as best they can) to amuse their European audience.

Soyinka's interest in different forms of ritual is part of an undertaking that informs his entire oeuvre, including *Death and the King's Horseman*: the creation of a total theater. Like many other theater artists of the nineteenth and twentieth centuries, Soyinka employs as many different modes of expression as possible, seeking to bring together song, poetry, dance, speech, ritual, and music. In this play, we encounter a variety of sounds and instruments—for example, the royal drums, which weave together the traditional rhythms of wedding and death and delineate the play's tragic trajectory; different dance interludes, including the gripping suicidal dance of the King's Horseman; and different Western musical pieces, such as the tango blaring from a gramophone at the colonial officer's house and a band playing "Rule Britannia" in honor of the Prince, who is visiting the colony. But unlike some makers of total theater, Soyinka is not interested in unifying these various traditions of music, dance, and theater into one seamless whole. Rather, the play thrives on their collisions, interchanges, and mutual imitations.

The different forms of ceremony, ritual, and dance that make up this complex play are mirrored and reinforced by its unusual language and poetry. Certain Yoruba songs that accompany the play's central event, the ritual suicide, are rendered in poetic English. Like all of the utterances of the non-British characters, they are informed by the syntax, idioms, expressions, proverbs, and metaphors of Yoruba. The result is a multilayered English that takes on deeper meaning as it draws on the Yoruba world—its flora, fauna, social structure, and cosmology. The play juxtaposes and blends different languages as thoroughly as it intermingles different forms of theater and performance.

This commingling is perhaps the most important feature of *Death and the King's Horseman*. For while the play certainly shows the violence that occurs at a moment of cultural contact between the British and

A Yoruba tribal leader, 1960.

Yoruba cultures, it refuses to blame all problems on their clash. Each culture has internal tensions. Thus Yoruba culture, for Soyinka, is never simply an authentic and monolithic given that is then, in a second step, set against the putatively modern British culture. He instead views Yoruba culture as having itself undergone a process of modernization, making it a culture compatible with the international, cosmopolitan world represented by Olunde, the most articulate figure in the play. At the same time, Soyinka points to tradition and even ritualistic aspects of British culture. In this way, both Yoruba culture and British culture are divided between tradition and modernization, though Soyinka never lets us forget which one has suppressed and belittled the other.

The attempt to show the different forms of modernization at work in Yoruba and British culture stands behind the mythic construction of this tragedy, which rests on the assumption that the Yoruba gods and the Greek gods are somehow compatible or comparable. It was a project conceived as a response to the more simplistic forms of postcolonial nationalism, which took shape as incipient nations sought to create distinct national traditions in isolation. At the same time, Soyinka is trying to dismantle the vestiges of colonialism—specifically, the assumption that Western culture has a unique claim to being modern and that in order for Yoruba culture to become modern it would have to adapt Western customs, religion, and culture.

Death and the King's Horseman has sometimes been accused of nostalgically privileging the Yoruba ritual by contrasting it favorably with the ignorance of the colonial officer, but Soyinka's complex mixing of the different ritualistic practices shows that no false nostalgia is in fact at work. Like many other works of modernism, written by former colonizers and colonized alike, his plays display not just a fascination with premodern mythology and ritual but also an awareness that such myths and rituals can never be recovered in the present. Just as Richard Wagner sought to relate his operatic artwork of the future to a mythic German past and James Joyce fashioned his groundbreaking novel after Homer, so Soyinka's play gains its strength by invoking but not embracing different ritual practices. While its characters accept and perform the ritual, Soyinka's play itself is and remains a modern work, albeit one with living roots in the past. M.P.

Death and the King's Horseman

Dedicated
In Affectionate Greeting
to
My Father, Ayodele
who lately danced, and joined the Ancestors.

Author's Note

This play is based on events which took place in Oyo,[1] ancient Yoruba city of Nigeria, in 1946. That year, the lives of Elesin (Olori Elesin), his son, and the Colonial District Officer intertwined with the disastrous results set out in the play. The changes I have made are in matters of detail, sequence, and of course characterisation. The action has also been set back two or three years to while the war was still on,[2] for minor reasons of dramaturgy.

The factual account still exists in the archives of the British Colonial Administration. It has already inspired a fine play in Yoruba (Oba Wàjà[3]) by Duro Ladipo. It has also misbegotten a film by some German television company.

The bane of themes of this genre is that they are no sooner employed creatively than they acquire the facile tag of 'clash of cultures', a prejudicial label which, quite apart from its frequent misapplication, presupposes a potential equality *in every given situation* of the alien culture and the indigenous, on the actual soil of the latter. (In the area of misapplication, the overseas prize for illiteracy and mental conditioning undoubtedly goes to the blurb-writer for the American edition of my novel *Season of Anomy*[4] who unblushingly declares that this work portrays the 'clash between old values and new ways, between western methods and African traditions'!) It is thanks to this kind of perverse mentality that I find it necessary to caution the would-be producer of this play against a sadly familiar reductionist tendency, and to direct his vision instead to the far more difficult and risky task of eliciting the play's threnodic[5] essence.

One of the more obvious alternative structures of the play would be to make the District Officer the victim of a cruel dilemma. This is not to my taste and it is not by chance that I have avoided dialogue or situation which would encourage this. No attempt should be made in production to suggest it. The Colonial Factor is an incident, a catalytic incident merely. The confrontation in the play is largely metaphysical, contained in the human vehicle which is Elesin and the universe of the Yoruba mind—the world of the living, the dead and the unborn, and the numinous passage which links all: transition. *Death and the King's Horseman* can be fully realised only through an evocation of music from the abyss of transition.

W.S.

1. A city in western Nigeria, about 100 miles north of Lagos.
2. That is, World War II.
3. *The King Is Dead* (1964).
4. Published in New York in 1974 (London, 1973).
5. Resembling a threnody, or song of lament for the dead.

CHARACTERS

PRAISE-SINGER
ELESIN, Horseman of the King
IYALOJA, 'Mother' of the market
SIMON PILKINGS, District Officer
JANE PILKINGS, his wife
SERGEANT AMUSA
JOSEPH, houseboy to the Pilkingses
BRIDE
H.R.H. THE PRINCE
THE RESIDENT[6]
AIDE-DE-CAMP
OLUNDE, eldest son of Elesin

DRUMMERS, WOMEN, YOUNG GIRLS, DANCERS AT THE BALL

The play should run without an interval. For rapid scene changes, one adjustable outline set is very appropriate.

Act 1

A passage through a market in its closing stages. The stalls are being emptied, mats folded. A few WOMEN *pass through on their way home, loaded with baskets. On a cloth-stand, bolts of cloth are taken down, display pieces folded and piled on a tray.* ELESIN OBA *enters along a passage before the market, pursued by his* DRUMMERS *and* PRAISE-SINGERS. *He is a man of enormous vitality, speaks, dances, and sings with that infectious enjoyment of life which accompanies all his actions.*

PRAISE-SINGER Elesin o! Elesin Oba! Howu![7] What tryst is this the cockerel goes to keep with such haste that he must leave his tail behind?

ELESIN [*slows down a bit, laughing*] A tryst where the cockerel needs no adornment.

PRAISE-SINGER O-oh, you hear that my companions? That's the way the world goes. Because the man approaches a brand new bride he forgets the long faithful mother of his children.[8]

ELESIN When the horse sniffs the stable does he not strain at the bridle? The market is the long-suffering home of my spirit and the women are packing up to go. That Esu[9]-harassed day slipped into the stewpot while we feasted. We ate it up with the rest of the meat. I have neglected my women.

PRAISE-SINGER We know all that. Still it's no reason for shedding your tail on this day of all days. I know the women will cover you in damask and *alari*[1] but when the wind blows cold from behind, that's when the fowl knows his true friends.

6. The ranking British officer in a province.
7. Why have you come? (Yoruba greeting). *Oba:* King (Yoruba).
8. Traditionally, Yoruba men had multiple wives.
9. The Yoruba trickster god.
1. A rich, woven cloth, brightly coloured [Soyinka]. *Damask:* a lustrous patterned fabric.

ELESIN Olohun-iyo![2]

PRAISE-SINGER Are you sure there will be one like me on the other side?

ELESIN Olohun-iyo!

PRAISE-SINGER Far be it for me to belittle the dwellers of that place but, a man is either born to his art or he isn't. And I don't know for certain that you'll meet my father, so who is going to sing these deeds in accents that will pierce the deafness of the ancient ones. I have prepared my going—just tell me: Olohun-iyo, I need you on this journey and I shall be behind you.

ELESIN You're like a jealous wife. Stay close to me, but only on this side. My fame, my honour are legacies to the living; stay behind and let the world sip its honey from your lips.

PRAISE-SINGER Your name will be like the sweet berry a child places under his tongue to sweeten the passage of food. The world will never spit it out.

ELESIN Come then. This market is my roost. When I come among the women I am a chicken with a hundred mothers. I become a monarch whose palace is built with tenderness and beauty.

PRAISE-SINGER They love to spoil you but beware. The hands of women also weaken the unwary.

ELESIN This night I'll lay my head upon their lap and go to sleep. This night I'll touch feet with their feet in a dance that is no longer of this earth. But the smell of their flesh, their sweat, the smell of indigo[3] on their cloth, this is the last air I wish to breathe as I go to meet my great forebears.

PRAISE-SINGER In their time the world was never tilted from its groove, it shall not be in yours.

ELESIN The gods have said No.

PRAISE-SINGER In their time the great wars came and went, the little wars came and went; the white slavers came and went, they took away the heart of our race, they bore away the mind and muscle of our race. The city fell and was rebuilt; the city fell and our people trudged through mountain and forest to found a new home but—Elesin Oba do you hear me?

ELESIN I hear your voice Olohun-iyo.

PRAISE-SINGER Our world was never wrenched from its true course.

ELESIN The gods have said No.

PRAISE-SINGER There is only one home to the life of a river-mussel; there is only one home to the life of a tortoise; there is only one shell to the soul of man; there is only one world to the spirit of our race. If that world leaves its course and smashes on boulders of the great void, whose world will give us shelter?

ELESIN It did not in the time of my forebears, it shall not in mine.

PRAISE-SINGER The cockerel must not be seen without his feathers.

ELESIN Nor will the Not-I bird[4] be much longer without his nest.

PRAISE-SINGER [*stopped in his lyric stride*] The Not-I bird, Elesin?

ELESIN I said, the Not-I bird.

PRAISE-SINGER All respect to our elders but, is there really such a bird?

ELESIN What! Could it be that he failed to knock on your door?

2. Praise-singer (Yoruba).

3. A costly blue dye made from plants and used by royalty in Africa.

4. A bird whose call resembles the Yoruba phrase that means "not I."

PRAISE-SINGER [*smiling*] Elesin's riddles are not merely the nut in the kernel that breaks human teeth; he also buries the kernel in hot embers and dares a man's fingers to draw it out.

ELESIN I am sure he called on you, Olohun-iyo. Did you hide in the loft and push out the servant to tell him you were out?

[ELESIN *executes a brief, half-taunting dance. The* DRUMMER *moves in and draws a rhythm out of his steps.* ELESIN *dances towards the market-place as he chants the story of the Not-I bird, his voice changing dexterously to mimic his characters. He performs like a born raconteur, infecting his retinue with his humour and energy. More* WOMEN *arrive during his recital, including* IYALOJA.]

Death came calling.
Who does not know his rasp of reeds?
A twilight whisper in the leaves before
The great araba[5] falls? Did you hear it?
Not I! swears the farmer. He snaps
His fingers round his head, abandons
A hard-worn harvest and begins
A rapid dialogue with his legs.

'Not I,' shouts the fearless hunter, 'but—
It's getting dark, and this night-lamp
Has leaked out all its oil. I think
It's best to go home and resume my hunt
Another day.' But now he pauses, suddenly
Lets out a wail: 'Oh foolish mouth, calling
Down a curse on your own head! Your lamp
Has leaked out all its oil, has it?'
Forwards or backwards now he dare not move.
To search for leaves and make *etutu*[6]
On that spot? Or race home to the safety
Of his hearth? Ten market-days have passed
My friends, and still he's rooted there
Rigid as the plinth of Orayan.[7]

The mouth of the courtesan barely
Opened wide enough to take a ha'penny *robo*[8]
When she wailed: 'Not I.' All dressed she was
To call upon my friend the Chief Tax Officer.
But now she sends her go-between instead:
'Tell him I'm ill: my period has come suddenly
But not—I hope—my time.'

Why is the pupil crying?
His hapless head was made to taste

5. A silk-cotton tree (Yoruba), which yields the fiber kapok.
6. Placatory rites or medicine [Soyinka's].
7. A tall landmark in Ile-Ife, ancestral home of the Yoruba. Orayan was a son of Oduduwa, first Yoruba king, and progenitor of all subsequent kings.
8. A delicacy made from crushed melon seeds, fried in tiny balls [Soyinka's].

The knuckles of my friend the Mallam.[9]
'If you were then reciting the Koran
Would you have ears for idle noises
Darkening the trees, you child of ill omen?'
He shuts down school before its time
Runs home and rings himself with amulets.

And take my good kinsman Ifawomi.
His hands were like a carver's, strong
And true. I saw them
Tremble like wet wings of a fowl
One day he cast his time-smoothed *opele*[1]
Across the divination board. And all because
The suppliant looked him in the eye and asked,
'Did you hear that whisper in the leaves?
'Not I,' was his reply; 'perhaps I'm growing deaf—
Good-day.' And Ifa spoke no more that day
The priest locked fast his doors,
Sealed up his leaking roof—but wait!
This sudden care was not for Fawomi
But for Osanyin,[2] courier-bird of Ifa's
Heart of wisdom. I did not know a kite
Was hovering in the sky
And Ifa now a twittering chicken in
The brood of Fawomi the Mother Hen.

Ah, but I must not forget my evening
Courier from the abundant palm, whose groan
Became Not I, as he constipated down
A wayside bush. He wonders if Elegbara[3]
Has tricked his buttocks to discharge
Against a sacred grove. Hear him
Mutter spells to ward off penalties
For an abomination he did not intend.
If any here
Stumbles on a gourd of wine, fermenting
Near the road, and nearby hears a stream
Of spells issuing from a crouching form,
Brother to a *sigidi*,[4] bring home my wine,
Tell my tapper[5] I have ejected
Fear from home and farm. Assure him,
All is well.

PRAISE-SINGER In your time we do not doubt the peace of farmstead and home, the peace of road and hearth, we do not doubt the peace of the forest.

9. A teacher of Islamic doctrine (Hausa).
1. String of beads used in Ifa divination [Soyinka].
2. Patron deity of diviners. *Fawomi:* a reference to Ifa, the Yoruba god of divination.
3. Another name for Esu, the trickster god.
4. A squat, carved figure, endowed with the powers of an incubus [Soyinka], which is a demon that lies on people in their sleep.
5. The person who collects the sap of palm trees, which is fermented into wine.

ELESIN There was fear in the forest too.
Not-I was lately heard even in the lair
Of beasts. The hyena cackled loud Not I,
The civet[6] twitched his fiery tail and glared:
Not I. Not-I became the answering-name
Of the restless bird, that little one
Whom Death found nesting in the leaves
When whisper of his coming ran
Before him on the wind. Not-I
Has long abandoned home. This same dawn
I heard him twitter in the gods' abode.
Ah, companions of this living world
What a thing this is, that even those
We call immortal
Should fear to die.

IYALOJA But you, husband of multitudes?

ELESIN I, when that Not-I bird perched
Upon my roof, bade him seek his nest again,
Safe, without care or fear. I unrolled
My welcome mat for him to see. Not-I
Flew happily away, you'll hear his voice
No more in this lifetime—You all know
What I am.

PRAISE-SINGER That rock which turns its open lodes
Into the path of lightning. A gay
Thoroughbred whose stride disdains
To falter though an adder reared
Suddenly in his path.

ELESIN My rein is loosened.
I am master of my Fate. When the hour comes
Watch me dance along the narrowing path
Glazed by the soles of my great precursors.
My soul is eager. I shall not turn aside.

WOMEN You will not delay?

ELESIN Where the storm pleases, and when, it directs
The giants of the forest. When friendship summons
Is when the true comrade goes.

WOMEN Nothing will hold you back?

ELESIN Nothing. What! Has no one told you yet?
I go to keep my friend and master company.
Who says the mouth does not believe in
'No, I have chewed all that before?' I say I have.
The world is not a constant honey-pot.
Where I found little I made do with little.
Where there was plenty I gorged myself.
My master's hands and mine have always
Dipped together and, home or sacred feast,
The bowl was beaten bronze, the meats

6. A weasel-like carnivorous mammal (especially the species native to Africa).

So succulent our teeth accused us of neglect.
We shared the choicest of the season's
Harvest of yams. How my friend would read
Desire in my eyes before I knew the cause—
However rare, however precious, it was mine.

WOMEN The town, the very land was yours.

ELESIN The world was mine. Our joint hands
Raised houseposts of trust that withstood
The siege of envy and the termites of time.
But the twilight hour brings bats and rodents—
Shall I yield them cause to foul the rafters?

PRAISE-SINGER Elesin Oba! Are you not that man who
Looked out of doors that stormy day
The god of luck limped by, drenched
To the very lice that held
His rags together? You took pity upon
His sores and wished him fortune.
Fortune was footloose this dawn, he replied,
Till you trapped him in a heartfelt wish
That now returns to you. Elesin Oba!
I say you are that man who
Chanced upon the calabash[7] of honour
You thought it was palm wine and
Drained its contents to the final drop.

ELESIN Life has an end. A life that will outlive
Fame and friendship begs another name.
What elder takes his tongue to his plate,
Licks it clean of every crumb? He will encounter
Silence when he calls on children to fulfill
The smallest errand! Life is honour.
It ends when honour ends.

WOMEN We know you for a man of honour.

ELESIN Stop! Enough of that!

WOMEN [*puzzled, they whisper among themselves, turning mostly to* IYALOJA] What is it? Did we say something to give offence? Have we slighted him in some way?

ELESIN Enough of that sound I say. Let me hear no more in that vein. I've heard enough.

IYALOJA We must have said something wrong. [*Comes forward a little.*] Elesin Oba, we ask forgiveness before you speak.

ELESIN I am bitterly offended.

IYALOJA Our unworthiness has betrayed us. All we can do is ask your forgiveness. Correct us like a kind father.

ELESIN This day of all days . . .

IYALOJA It does not bear thinking. If we offend you now we have mortified the gods. We offend heaven itself. Father of us all, tell us where we went astray. [*She kneels, the other women follow.*]

7. A drinking vessel made from a gourd.

ELESIN Are you not ashamed? Even a tear-veiled
Eye preserves its function of sight.
Because my mind was raised to horizons
Even the boldest man lowers his gaze
In thinking of, must my body here
Be taken for a vagrant's?

IYALOJA Horseman of the King, I am more baffled than ever.

PRAISE-SINGER The strictest father unbends his brow when the child is penitent, Elesin. When time is short, we do not spend it prolonging the riddle. Their shoulders are bowed with the weight of fear lest they have marred your day beyond repair. Speak now in plain words and let us pursue the ailment to the home of remedies.

ELESIN Words are cheap. 'We know you for
A man of honour.' Well tell me, is this how
A man of honour should be seen?
Are these not the same clothes in which
I came among you a full half-hour ago?

[*He roars with laughter and the* WOMEN, *relieved, rise and rush into stalls to fetch rich cloths.*]

WOMEN The gods are kind. A fault soon remedied is soon forgiven. Elesin Oba, even as we match our words with deed, let your heart forgive us completely.

ELESIN You who are breath and giver of my being
How shall I dare refuse you forgiveness
Even if the offence were real.

IYALOJA [*dancing round him. Sings*]
He forgives us. He forgives us.
What a fearful thing it is when
The voyager sets forth
But a curse remains behind.

WOMEN For a while we truly feared
Our hands had wrenched the world adrift
In emptiness.

IYALOJA Richly, richly, robe him richly
The cloth of honour is *alari*
Sanyan is the band of friendship
Boa-skin[8] makes slippers of esteem

WOMEN For a while we truly feared
Our hands had wrenched the world adrift
In emptiness.

PRAISE-SINGER He who must, must voyage forth
The world will not roll backwards
It is he who must, with one
Great gesture overtake the world.

WOMEN For a while we truly feared
Our hands had wrenched the world
In emptiness.

PRAISE-SINGER The gourd you bear is not for shirking.
The gourd is not for setting down

8. That is, snake skin. *Sanyan:* a richly valued woven cloth [Soyinka].

At the first crossroad or wayside grove.
Only one river may know its contents.

WOMEN We shall all meet at the great market[9]
We shall all meet at the great market
He who goes early takes the best bargains
But we shall meet, and resume our banter.

[ELESIN *stands resplendent in rich clothes, cap, shawl, etc. His sash is of a bright red* alari *cloth. The* WOMEN *dance round him. Suddenly, his attention is caught by an object offstage.*]

ELESIN The world I know is good.

WOMEN We know you'll leave it so.

ELESIN The world I know is the bounty
Of hives after bees have swarmed.
No goodness teems with such open hands
Even in the dreams of deities.

WOMEN And we know you'll leave it so.

ELESIN I was born to keep it so. A hive
Is never known to wander. An anthill
Does not desert its roots. We cannot see
The still great womb of the world—
No man beholds his mother's womb—
Yet who denies it's there? Coiled
To the navel of the world is that
Endless cord that links us all
To the great origin. If I lose my way
The trailing cord will bring me to the roots.

WOMEN The world is in your hands.

[*The earlier distraction, a beautiful* YOUNG GIRL, *comes along the passage through which* ELESIN *first made his entry.*]

ELESIN I embrace it. And let me tell you, women—
I like this farewell that the world designed,
Unless my eyes deceive me, unless
We are already parted, the world and I,
And all that breeds desire is lodged
Among our tireless ancestors. Tell me friends,
Am I still earthed in that beloved market
Of my youth? Or could it be my will
Has outleapt the conscious act and I have come
Among the great departed?

PRAISE-SINGER Elesin-Oba why do your eyes roll like a bush-rat who sees his fate like his father's spirit, mirrored in the eye of a snake? And all these questions! You're standing on the same earth you've always stood upon. This voice you hear is mine, Oluhun-iyo, not that of an acolyte in heaven.

ELESIN How can that be? In all my life
As Horseman of the King, the juiciest
Fruit on every tree was mine. I saw,
I touched, I wooed, rarely was the answer No.

9. That is, in the afterlife.

The honour of my place, the veneration I
Received in the eye of man or woman
Prospered my suit and
Played havoc with my sleeping hours.
And they tell me my eyes were a hawk
In perpetual hunger. Split an iroko[1] tree
In two, hide a woman's beauty in its heartwood
And seal it up again—Elesin, journeying by,
Would make his camp beside that tree
Of all the shades in the forest.

PRAISE-SINGER Who would deny your reputation, snake-on-the-loose in dark passages of the market! Bed-bug who wages war on the mat and receives the thanks of the vanquished! When caught with his bride's own sister he protested—but I was only prostrating myself to her as becomes a grateful in-law. Hunter who carries his powder-horn on the hips and fires crouching or standing! Warrior who never makes that excuse of the whining coward—but how can I go to battle without my trousers?—trouserless or shirtless it's all one to him. Oka[2]-rearing-from-a-camouflage-of-leaves, before he strikes the victim is already prone! Once they told him, Howu, a stallion does not feed on the grass beneath him: he replied, true, but surely he can roll on it!

WOMEN Ba-a-a-ba O!

PRAISE-SINGER Ah, but listen yet. You know there is the leaf-nibbling grub and there is the cola-chewing beetle; the leaf-nibbling grub lives on the leaf, the cola-chewing beetle lives in the colanut. Don't we know what our man feeds on when we find him cocooned in a woman's wrapper?

ELESIN Enough, enough, you all have cause
To know me well. But, if you say this earth
Is still the same as gave birth to those songs,
Tell me who was that goddess through whose lips
I saw the ivory pebbles of Oya's[3] river-bed.
Iyaloja, who is she? I saw her enter
Your stall; all your daughters I know well.
No, not even Ogun[4]-of-the-farm toiling
Dawn till dusk on his tuber patch
Not even Ogun with the finest hoe he ever
Forged at the anvil could have shaped
That rise of buttocks, not though he had
The richest earth between his fingers.
Her wrapper was no disguise
For thighs whose ripples shamed the river's
Coils around the hills of Ilesi.[5] Her eyes
Were new-laid eggs glowing in the dark.
Her skin . . .

1. A large tree of the mulberry family, sometimes called African teak; according to Yoruba folklore, its denser, multicolored heartwood is inhabited by an impish spirit.
2. A snake.
3. The goddess of the Niger River and of winds.
4. The god of iron and war, and patron of blacksmiths. Soyinka compares him to various gods and figures from Greek myth—Apollo, Prometheus, and especially Dionysus, the god of fertility and wine, and patron of theater.
5. A town in western Nigeria.

IYALOJA Elesin Oba . . .
ELESIN What! Where do you all say I am?
IYALOJA Still among the living.
ELESIN And that radiance which so suddenly
Lit up this market I could boast
I knew so well?
IYALOJA Has one step already in her husband's home. She is betrothed.
ELESIN [*irritated*] Why do you tell me that?

[IYALOJA *falls silent. The* WOMEN *shuffle uneasily.*]

IYALOJA Not because we dare give you offence Elesin. Today is your day and the whole world is yours. Still, even those who leave town to make a new dwelling elsewhere like to be remembered by what they leave behind.

ELESIN Who does not seek to be remembered?
Memory is Master of Death, the chink
In his armour of conceit. I shall leave
That which makes my going the sheerest
Dream of an afternoon. Should voyagers
Not travel light? Let the considerate traveller
Shed, of his excessive load, all
That may benefit the living.

WOMEN [*relieved*] Ah Elesin Oba, we knew you for a man of honour.
ELESIN Then honour me. I deserve a bed of honour to lie upon.
IYALOJA The best is yours. We know you for a man of honour. You are not one who eats and leaves nothing on his plate for children. Did you not say it yourself? Not one who blights the happiness of others for a moment's pleasure.

ELESIN Who speaks of pleasure? O women, listen!
Pleasure palls. Our acts should have meaning.
The sap of the plantain never dries.
You have seen the young shoot swelling
Even as the parent stalk begins to wither.
Women, let my going be likened to
The twilight hour of the plantain.

WOMEN What does he mean Iyaloja? This language is the language of our elders, we do not fully grasp it.
IYALOJA I dare not understand you yet Elesin.

ELESIN All you who stand before the spirit that dares
The opening of the last door of passage,
Dare to rid my going of regrets! My wish
Transcends the blotting out of thought
In one mere moment's tremor of the senses.
Do me credit. And do me honour.
I am girded for the route beyond
Burdens of waste and longing.
Then let me travel light. Let
Seed that will not serve the stomach
On the way remain behind. Let it take root
In the earth of my choice, in this earth
I leave behind.

IYALOJA [*turns to* WOMEN] The voice I hear is already touched by the waiting fingers of our departed. I dare not refuse.

WOMEN But Iyaloja . . .

IYALOJA The matter is no longer in our hands.

WOMAN But she is betrothed to your own son. Tell him.

IYALOJA My son's wish is mine. I did the asking for him, the loss can be remedied. But who will remedy the blight of closed hands on the day when all should be openness and light? Tell him, you say! You wish that I burden him with knowledge that will sour his wish and lay regrets on the last moments of his mind. You pray to him who is your intercessor to the world—don't set this world adrift in your own time; would you rather it was my hand whose sacrilege wrenched it loose?

WOMAN Not many men will brave the curse of a dispossessed husband.

IYALOJA Only the curses of the departed are to be feared. The claims of one whose foot is on the threshold of their abode surpasses even the claims of blood. It is impiety even to place hindrances in their ways.

ELESIN What do my mothers say? Shall I step
Burdened into the unknown?

IYALOJA Not we, but the very earth says No. The sap in the plantain does not dry. Let grain that will not feed the voyager at his passage drop here and take root as he steps beyond this earth and us. Oh you who fill the home from hearth to threshold with the voices of children, you who now bestride the hidden gulf and pause to draw the right foot across and into the resting-home of the great forebears, it is good that your loins be drained into the earth we know, that your last strength be ploughed back into the womb that gave you being.

PRAISE-SINGER Iyaloja, mother of multitudes in the teeming market of the world, how your wisdom transfigures you!

IYALOJA [*smiling broadly, completely reconciled*] Elesin, even at the narrow end of the passage I know you will look back and sigh a last regret for the flesh that flashed past your spirit in flight. You always had a restless eye. Your choice has my blessing. [*To the* WOMEN] Take the good news to our daughter and make her ready. [*Some* WOMEN *go off.*]

ELESIN Your eyes were clouded at first.

IYALOJA Not for long. It is those who stand at the gateway of the great change to whose cry we must pay heed. And then, think of this—it makes the mind tremble. The fruit of such a union is rare. It will be neither of this world nor of the next. Nor of the one behind us. As if the timelessness of the ancestor world and the unborn have joined spirits to wring an issue of the elusive being of passage . . . Elesin!

ELESIN I am here. What is it?

IYALOJA Did you hear all I said just now?

ELESIN Yes.

IYALOJA The living must eat and drink. When the moment comes, don't turn the food to rodents' droppings in their mouth. Don't let them taste the ashes of the world when they step out at dawn to breathe the morning dew.

ELESIN This doubt is unworthy of you Iyaloja.

IYALOJA Eating the awusa nut[6] is not so difficult as drinking water afterwards.

6. A walnutlike seed that is eaten or used to produce oil. Raw, it has a bitter flavor.

ELESIN The waters of the bitter stream are honey to a man
Whose tongue has savoured all.

IYALOJA No one knows when the ants desert their home; they leave the mound intact. The swallow is never seen to peck holes in its nest when it is time to move with the season. There are always throngs of humanity behind the leave-taker. The rain should not come through the roof for them, the wind must not blow through the walls at night.

ELESIN I refuse to take offence.

IYALOJA You wish to travel light. Well, the earth is yours. But be sure the seed you leave in it attracts no curse.

ELESIN You really mistake my person Iyaloja.

IYALOJA I said nothing. Now we must go prepare your bridal chamber. Then these same hands will lay your shrouds.

ELESIN [*exasperated*] Must you be so blunt? [*Recovers.*] Well, weave your shrouds, but let the fingers of my bride seal my eyelids with earth and wash my body.

IYALOJA Prepare yourself Elesin.

[*She gets up to leave. At that moment the* WOMEN *return, leading the* BRIDE. ELESIN'*s face glows with pleasure. He flicks the sleeves of his agbada*[7] *with renewed confidence and steps forward to meet the group. As the girl kneels before* IYALOJA, *lights fade out on the scene.*]

Act 2

The verandah of the District Officer's bungalow. A tango is playing from an old hand-cranked gramophone and, glimpsed through the wide windows and doors which open onto the forestage verandah are the shapes of SIMON PILKINGS *and his wife,* JANE, *tangoing in and out of shadows in the living room. They are wearing what is immediately apparent as some form of fancy dress.*[8] *The dance goes on for some moments and then the figure of a* 'NATIVE ADMINISTRATION' POLICEMAN *emerges and climbs up the steps onto the verandah. He peeps through and observes the dancing couple, reacting with what is obviously a long-standing bewilderment. He stiffens suddenly, his expression changes to one of disbelief and horror. In his excitement he upsets a flowerpot and attracts the attention of the couple. They stop dancing.*

PILKINGS Is there anyone out there?

JANE I'll turn off the gramophone.

PILKINGS [*approaching the verandah*] I'm sure I heard something fall over. [*The* CONSTABLE *retreats slowly, open-mouthed as* PILKINGS *approaches the verandah.*] Oh it's you Amusa. Why didn't you just knock instead of knocking things over?

AMUSA [*stammers badly and points a shaky finger at his dress*] Mista Pirinkin . . . Mista Pirinkin . . .

PILKINGS What is the matter with you?

JANE [*emerging*] Who is it dear? Oh, Amusa . . .

PILKINGS Yes it's Amusa, and acting most strangely.

AMUSA [*his attention now transferred to* MRS PILKINGS] Mammadam . . . you too!

7. A flowing, wide-sleeved robe worn by important men.

8. That is, costumes.

PILKINGS What the hell is the matter with you man!

JANE Your costume darling. Our fancy dress.

PILKINGS Oh hell, I'd forgotten all about that. [*Lifts the face mask over his head showing his face. His wife follows suit.*]

JANE I think you've shocked his big pagan heart bless him.

PILKINGS Nonsense, he's a Moslem. Come on Amusa, you don't believe in all this nonsense do you? I thought you were a good Moslem.

AMUSA Mista Pirinkin, I beg you sir, what you think you do with that dress? It belong to dead cult, not for human being.

PILKINGS Oh Amusa, what a let down you are. I swear by you at the club you know—thank God for Amusa, he doesn't believe in any mumbo-jumbo. And now look at you!

AMUSA Mista Pirinkin, I beg you, take it off. Is not good for man like you to touch that cloth.

PILKINGS Well, I've got it on. And what's more Jane and I have bet on it we're taking first prize at the ball. Now, if you can just pull yourself together and tell me what you wanted to see me about . . .

AMUSA Sir, I cannot talk this matter to you in that dress. I no fit.

PILKINGS What's that rubbish again?

JANE He is dead earnest too Simon. I think you'll have to handle this delicately.

PILKINGS Delicately my . . . ! Look here Amusa, I think this little joke has gone far enough hm? Let's have some sense. You seem to forget that you are a police officer in the service of His Majesty's Government. I order you to report your business at once or face disciplinary action.

AMUSA Sir, it is a matter of death. How can man talk against death to person in uniform of death? Is like talking against government to person in uniform of police. Please sir, I go and come back.

PILKINGS [*roars*] Now! [AMUSA *switches his gaze to the ceiling suddenly, remains mute.*]

JANE Oh Amusa, what is there to be scared of in the costume? You saw it confiscated last month from those *egungun*[9] men who were creating trouble in town. You helped arrest the cult leaders yourself—if the juju[1] didn't harm you at the time how could it possibly harm you now? And merely by looking at it?

AMUSA [*without looking down*] Madam, I arrest the ringleaders who make trouble but me I no touch *egungun*. That *egungun* itself, I no touch. And I no abuse 'am. I arrest ringleader but I treat *egungun* with respect.

PILKINGS It's hopeless. We'll merely end up missing the best part of the ball. When they get this way there is nothing you can do. It's simply hammering against a brick wall. Write your report or whatever it is on that pad Amusa and take yourself out of here. Come on Jane. We only upset his delicate sensibilities by remaining here.

[AMUSA *waits for them to leave, then writes in the notebook, somewhat laboriously. Drumming from the direction of the town wells up.* AMUSA *listens, makes a movement as if he wants to recall* PILKINGS *but changes his mind. Completes his note and goes. A few moments later* PILKINGS *emerges, picks up the pad and reads.*]

9. Ancestral masquerade [Soyinka]. The spirits of the dead are believed to temporarily possess those wearing these costumes.

1. Magic associated with fetish objects.

PILKINGS Jane!

JANE [*from the bedroom*] Coming darling. Nearly ready.

PILKINGS Never mind being ready, just listen to this.

JANE What is it?

PILKINGS Amusa's report. Listen. 'I have to report that it come to my information that one prominent chief, namely, the Elesin Oba, is to commit death tonight as a result of native custom. Because this is criminal offence I await further instruction at charge office. Sergeant Amusa.'

[JANE *comes out onto the verandah while he is reading.*]

JANE Did I hear you say commit death?

PILKINGS Obviously he means murder.

JANE You mean a ritual murder?

PILKINGS Must be. You think you've stamped it all out but it's always lurking under the surface somewhere.

JANE Oh. Does it mean we are not getting to the ball at all?

PILKINGS No-o. I'll have the man arrested. Everyone remotely involved. In any case there may be nothing to it. Just rumours.

JANE Really? I thought you found Amusa's rumours generally reliable.

PILKINGS That's true enough. But who knows what may have been giving him the scare lately. Look at his conduct tonight.

JANE [*laughing*] You have to admit he had his own peculiar logic. [*Deepens her voice.*] How can man talk against death to person in uniform of death? [*Laughs.*] Anyway, you can't go into the police station dressed like that.

PILKINGS I'll send Joseph with instructions. Damn it, what a confounded nuisance!

JANE But don't you think you should talk first to the man, Simon?

PILKINGS Do you want to go to the ball or not?

JANE Darling, why are you getting rattled? I was only trying to be intelligent. It seems hardly fair just to lock up a man—and a chief at that—simply on the er . . . what is the legal word again?—uncorroborated word of a sergeant.

PILKINGS Well, that's easily decided. Joseph!

JOSEPH [*from within*] Yes master.

PILKINGS You're quite right of course, I am getting rattled. Probably the effect of those bloody drums. Do you hear how they go on and on?

JANE I wondered when you'd notice. Do you suppose it has something to do with this affair?

PILKINGS Who knows? They always find an excuse for making a noise . . . [*Thoughtfully*] Even so . . .

JANE Yes Simon?

PILKINGS It's different Jane. I don't think I've heard this particular—sound—before. Something unsettling about it.

JANE I thought all bush drumming sounded the same.

PILKINGS Don't tease me now Jane. This may be serious.

JANE I'm sorry. [*Gets up and throws her arms around his neck. Kisses him. The* HOUSEBOY *enters, retreats and knocks.*]

PILKINGS [*wearily*] Oh, come in Joseph! I don't know where you pick up all these elephantine notions of tact. Come over here.

JOSEPH Sir?

PILKINGS Joseph, are you a Christian or not?

JOSEPH Yessir.

PILKINGS Does seeing me in this outfit bother you?

JOSEPH No sir, it has no power.

PILKINGS Thank God for some sanity at last. Now Joseph, answer me on the honour of a Christian—what is supposed to be going on in town tonight?

JOSEPH Tonight sir? You mean the chief who is going to kill himself?

PILKINGS What?

JANE What do you mean, kill himself?

PILKINGS You do mean he is going to kill somebody don't you?

JOSEPH No master. He will not kill anybody and no one will kill him. He will simply die.

JANE But why Joseph?

JOSEPH It is native law and custom. The King die last month. Tonight is his burial. But before they can bury him, the Elesin must die so as to accompany him to heaven.

PILKINGS I seem to be fated to clash more often with that man than with any of the other chiefs.

JOSEPH He is the King's Chief Horseman.

PILKINGS [*in a resigned way*] I know.

JANE Simon, what's the matter?

PILKINGS It would have to be him!

JANE Who is he?

PILKINGS Don't you remember? He's that chief with whom I had a scrap some three or four years ago. I helped his son get to a medical school in England, remember? He fought tooth and nail to prevent it.

JANE Oh now I remember. He was that very sensitive young man. What was his name again?

PILKINGS Olunde. Haven't replied to his last letter come to think of it. The old pagan wanted him to stay and carry on some family tradition or the other. Honestly I couldn't understand the fuss he made. I literally had to help the boy escape from close confinement and load him onto the next boat. A most intelligent boy, really bright.

JANE I rather thought he was much too sensitive you know. The kind of person you feel should be a poet munching rose petals in Bloomsbury.[2]

PILKINGS Well, he's going to make a first-class doctor. His mind is set on that. And as long as he wants my help he is welcome to it.

JANE [*after a pause*] Simon.

PILKINGS Yes?

JANE This boy, he was the eldest son wasn't he?

PILKINGS I'm not sure. Who could tell with that old ram?

JANE Do you know, Joseph?

JOSEPH Oh yes madam. He was the eldest son. That's why Elesin cursed master good and proper. The eldest son is not supposed to travel away from the land.

JANE [*giggling*] Is that true Simon? Did he really curse you good and proper?

PILKINGS By all accounts I should be dead by now.

2. The district of central London in which the British Museum and the University of London are located; it has long been associated with art and literary culture, notably the Pre-Raphaelites in the 19th century and Virginia Woolf and the "Bloomsbury Group" in the 20th.

JOSEPH Oh no, master is white man. And good Christian. Black man juju can't touch master.

JANE If he was his eldest, it means that he would be the Elesin to the next king. It's a family thing isn't it Joseph?

JOSEPH Yes madam. And if this Elesin had died before the King, his eldest son must take his place.

JANE That would explain why the old chief was so mad you took the boy away.

PILKINGS Well it makes me all the more happy I did.

JANE I wonder if he knew.

PILKINGS Who? Oh, you mean Olunde?

JANE Yes. Was that why he was so determined to get away? I wouldn't stay if I knew I was trapped in such a horrible custom.

PILKINGS [*thoughtfully*] No, I don't think he knew. At least he gave no indication. But you couldn't really tell with him. He was rather close[3] you know, quite unlike most of them. Didn't give much away, not even to me.

JANE Aren't they all rather close, Simon?

PILKINGS These natives here? Good gracious. They'll open their mouths and yap with you about their family secrets before you can stop them. Only the other day . . .

JANE But Simon, do they really give anything away? I mean, anything that really counts. This affair for instance, we didn't know they still practised that custom did we?

PILKINGS Ye-e-es, I suppose you're right there. Sly, devious bastards.

JOSEPH [*stiffly*] Can I go now master? I have to clean the kitchen.

PILKINGS What? Oh, you can go. Forgot you were still there.

[JOSEPH *goes.*]

JANE Simon, you really must watch your language. Bastard isn't just a simple swear-word in these parts, you know.

PILKINGS Look, just when did you become a social anthropologist, that's what I'd like to know.

JANE I'm not claiming to know anything. I just happen to have overheard quarrels among the servants. That's how I know they consider it a smear.

PILKINGS I thought the extended family system took care of all that. Elastic family, no bastards.

JANE [*shrugs*] Have it your own way.

[*Awkward silence. The drumming increases in volume.* JANE *gets up suddenly, restless.*]

That drumming Simon, do you think it might really be connected with this ritual? It's been going on all evening.

PILKINGS Let's ask our native guide. Joseph! Just a minute Joseph. [JOSEPH *reenters.*] What's the drumming about?

JOSEPH I don't know master.

PILKINGS What do you mean you don't know? It's only two years since your conversion. Don't tell me all that holy water nonsense also wiped out your tribal memory.

JOSEPH [*visibly shocked*] Master!

3. Secretive, taciturn.

JANE Now you've done it.

PILKINGS What have I done now?

JANE Never mind. Listen Joseph, just tell me this. Is that drumming connected with dying or anything of that nature?

JOSEPH Madam, this is what I am trying to say: I am not sure. It sounds like the death of a great chief and then, it sounds like the wedding of a great chief. It really mix me up.

PILKINGS Oh get back to the kitchen. A fat lot of help you are.

JOSEPH Yes master. [*Goes.*]

JANE Simon . . .

PILKINGS Alright, alright. I'm in no mood for preaching.

JANE It isn't my preaching you have to worry about, it's the preaching of the missionaries who preceded you here. When they make converts they really convert them. Calling holy water nonsense to our Joseph is really like insulting the Virgin Mary before a Roman Catholic. He's going to hand in his notice tomorrow you mark my word.

PILKINGS Now you're being ridiculous.

JANE Am I? What are you willing to bet that tomorrow we are going to be without a steward-boy? Did you see his face?

PILKINGS I am more concerned about whether or not we will be one native chief short by tomorrow. Christ! Just listen to those drums. [*He strides up and down, undecided.*]

JANE [*getting up*] I'll change and make us some supper.

PILKINGS What's that?

JANE Simon, it's obvious we have to miss this ball.

PILKINGS Nonsense. It's the first bit of real fun the European club has managed to organise for over a year, I'm damned if I'm going to miss it. And it is a rather special occasion. Doesn't happen every day.

JANE You know this business has to be stopped Simon. And you are the only man who can do it.

PILKINGS I don't have to stop anything. If they want to throw themselves off the top of a cliff or poison themselves for the sake of some barbaric custom what is that to me? If it were ritual murder or something like that I'd be duty-bound to do something. I can't keep an eye on all the potential suicides in this province. And as for that man—believe me it's good riddance.

JANE [*laughs*] I know you better than that Simon. You are going to have to do something to stop it—after you've finished blustering.

PILKINGS [*shouts after her*] And suppose after all it's only a wedding. I'd look a proper fool if I interrupted a chief on his honeymoon, wouldn't I? [*Resumes his angry stride, slows down.*] Ah well, who can tell what those chiefs actually do on their honeymoon anyway? [*He takes up the pad and scribbles rapidly on it.*] Joseph! Joseph! Joseph! [*Some moments later* JOSEPH *puts in a sulky appearance.*] Did you hear me call you? Why the hell didn't you answer?

JOSEPH I didn't hear master.

PILKINGS You didn't hear me! How come you are here then?

JOSEPH [*stubbornly*] I didn't hear master.

PILKINGS [*controls himself with an effort*] We'll talk about it in the morning.

I want you to take this note directly to Sergeant Amusa. You'll find him at the charge office.[4] Get on your bicycle and race there with it. I expect you back in twenty minutes exactly. Twenty minutes, is that clear?

JOSEPH Yes master. [*Going*]

PILKINGS Oh er . . . Joseph.

JOSEPH Yes master?

PILKINGS [*between gritted teeth*] Er . . . forget what I said just now. The holy water is not nonsense. *I* was talking nonsense.

JOSEPH Yes master. [*Goes.*]

JANE [*pokes her head round the door*] Have you found him?

PILKINGS Found who?

JANE Joseph. Weren't you shouting for him?

PILKINGS Oh yes, he turned up finally.

JANE You sounded desperate. What was it all about?

PILKINGS Oh nothing. I just wanted to apologise to him. Assure him that the holy water isn't really nonsense.

JANE Oh? And how did he take it?

PILKINGS Who the hell gives a damn! I had a sudden vision of our Very Reverend MacFarlane drafting another letter of complaint to the Resident about my unchristian language towards his parishioners.

JANE Oh I think he's given up on you by now.

PILKINGS Don't be too sure. And anyway, I wanted to make sure Joseph didn't 'lose' my note on the way. He looked sufficiently full of the holy crusade to do some such thing.

JANE If you've finished exaggerating, come and have something to eat.

PILKINGS No, put it all away. We can still get to the ball.

JANE Simon . . .

PILKINGS Get your costume back on. Nothing to worry about. I've instructed Amusa to arrest the man and lock him up.

JANE But that station is hardly secure Simon. He'll soon get his friends to help him escape.

PILKINGS A-ah, that's where I have out-thought you. I'm not having him put in the station cell. Amusa will bring him right here and lock him up in my study. And he'll stay with him till we get back. No one will dare come here to incite him to anything.

JANE How clever of you darling. I'll get ready.

PILKINGS Hey.

JANE Yes darling.

PILKINGS I have a surprise for you. I was going to keep it until we actually got to the ball.

JANE What is it?

PILKINGS You know the Prince[5] is on a tour of the colonies don't you? Well, he docked in the capital only this morning but he is already at the Residency. He is going to grace the ball with his presence later tonight.

JANE Simon! Not really.

4. Police station.

5. Prince Henry, duke of Gloucester (1900–1974), the uncle of the future Queen Elizabeth II, toured Ceylon (Sri Lanka), India, and North Africa in 1942.

PILKINGS Yes he is. He's been invited to give away the prizes and he has agreed. You must admit old Engleton is the best Club Secretary we ever had. Quick off the mark that lad.

JANE But how thrilling.

PILKINGS The other provincials are going to be damned envious.

JANE I wonder what he'll come as.

PILKINGS Oh I don't know. As a coat-of-arms perhaps. Anyway it won't be anything to touch this.

JANE Well that's lucky. If we are to be presented I won't have to start looking for a pair of gloves. It's all sewn on.

PILKINGS [*laughing*] Quite right. Trust a woman to think of that. Come on, let's get going.

JANE [*rushing off*] Won't be a second. [*Stops.*] Now I see why you've been so edgy all evening. I thought you weren't handling this affair with your usual brilliance—to begin with that is.

PILKINGS [*his mood is much improved*] Shut up woman and get your things on.

JANE Alright boss, coming.

[PILKINGS *suddenly begins to hum the tango to which they were dancing before. Starts to execute a few practice steps. Lights fade.*]

Act 3

A swelling, agitated hum of women's voices rises immediately in the background. The lights come on and we see the frontage of a converted cloth stall in the market. The floor leading up to the entrance is covered in rich velvets and woven cloth. The WOMEN *come on stage, borne backwards by the determined progress of Sergeant* AMUSA *and his two* CONSTABLES *who already have their batons out and use them as a pressure against the* WOMEN. *At the edge of the cloth-covered floor however the* WOMEN *take a determined stand and block all further progress of the men. They begin to tease them mercilessly.*

AMUSA I am tell you women for last time to commot my road.[6] I am here on official business.

WOMAN Official business you white man's eunuch? Official business is taking place where you want to go and it's a business you wouldn't understand.

WOMAN [*makes a quick tug at the* CONSTABLE*'s baton*] That doesn't fool anyone you know. It's the one you carry under your government knickers[7] that counts. [*She bends low as if to peep under the baggy shorts. The embarrassed* CONSTABLE *quickly puts his knees together. The* WOMEN *roar.*]

WOMAN You mean there is nothing there at all?

WOMAN Oh there was something. You know that handbell which the whiteman uses to summon his servants . . . ?

AMUSA [*he manages to preserve some dignity throughout*] I hope you women know that interfering with officer in execution of his duty is criminal offence.

WOMAN Interfere? He says we're interfering with him. You foolish man we're telling you there's nothing to interfere with.

6. Come out of my road (pidgin English); that is get out of my way.

7. Woman's underpants; here, a contemptuous reference to the khaki shorts worn by colonial policemen.

AMUSA I am order you now to clear the road.

WOMAN What road? The one your father built?

WOMAN You are a Policeman not so? Then you know what they call trespassing in court. Or—[*Pointing to the cloth-lined steps*]—do you think that kind of road is built for every kind of feet.

WOMAN Go back and tell the white man who sent you to come himself.

AMUSA If I go I will come back with reinforcement. And we will all return carrying weapons.

WOMAN Oh, now I understand. Before they can put on those knickers the white man first cuts off their weapons.

WOMAN What a cheek! You mean you come here to show power to women and you don't even have a weapon.

AMUSA [*shouting above the laughter*] For the last time I warn you women to clear the road.

WOMAN To where?

AMUSA To that hut. I know he dey dere.

WOMAN Who?

AMUSA The chief who call himself Elesin Oba.

WOMAN You ignorant man. It is not he who calls himself Elesin Oba, it is his blood that says it. As it called out to his father before him and will to his son after him. And that is in spite of everything your white man can do.

WOMAN Is it not the same ocean that washes this land and the white man's land? Tell your white man he can hide our son away as long as he likes. When the time comes for him, the same ocean will bring him back.

AMUSA The government say dat kin' ting[8] must stop.

WOMAN Who will stop it? You? Tonight our husband and father will prove himself greater than the laws of strangers.

AMUSA I tell you nobody go prove anyting tonight or anytime. Is ignorant and criminal to prove dat kin' prove.

IYALOJA [*entering, from the hut. She is accompanied by a group of* YOUNG GIRLS *who have been attending the* BRIDE] What is it Amusa? Why do you come here to disturb the happiness of others.

AMUSA Madame Iyaloja, I glad you come. You know me, I no like trouble but duty is duty. I am here to arrest Elesin for criminal intent. Tell these women to stop obstructing me in the performance of my duty.

IYALOJA And you? What gives you the right to obstruct our leader of men in the performance of his duty?

AMUSA What kin' duty be dat one Iyaloja.

IYALOJA What kin' duty? What kin' duty does a man have to his new bride?

AMUSA [*bewildered, looks at the* WOMEN *and at the entrance to the hut*] Iyaloja, is it wedding you call dis kin' ting?

IYALOJA You have wives haven't you? Whatever the white man has done to you he hasn't stopped you having wives. And if he has, at least he is married. If you don't know what a marriage is, go and ask him to tell you.

AMUSA This no to wedding.

IYALOJA And ask him at the same time what he would have done if anyone had come to disturb him on his wedding night.

AMUSA Iyaloja, I say dis no to wedding.

8. That kind of thing (pidgin English).

IYALOJA You want to look inside the bridal chamber? You want to see for yourself how a man cuts the virgin knot?

AMUSA Madam . . .

WOMAN Perhaps his wives are still waiting for him to learn.

AMUSA Iyaloja, make you tell dese women make den no insult me again. If I hear dat kin' insult once more . . .

GIRL [*pushing her way through*] You will do what?

GIRL He's out of his mind. It's our mothers you're talking to, do you know that? Not to any illiterate villager you can bully and terrorise. How dare you intrude here anyway?

GIRL What a cheek, what impertinence!

GIRL You've treated them too gently. Now let them see what it is to tamper with the mothers of this market.

GIRL Your betters dare not enter the market when the women say no!

GIRL Haven't you learnt that yet, you jester in khaki and starch?

IYALOJA Daughters . . .

GIRL No no Iyaloja, leave us to deal with him. He no longer knows his mother, we'll teach him.

[*With a sudden movement they snatch the batons of the two* CONSTABLES. *They begin to hem them in.*]

GIRL What next? We have your batons? What next? What are you going to do?

[*With equally swift movements they knock off their hats.*]

GIRL Move if you dare. We have your hats, what will you do about it? Didn't the white man teach you to take off your hats before women?

IYALOJA It's a wedding night. It's a night of joy for us. Peace . . .

GIRL Not for him. Who asked him here?

GIRL Does he dare go to the Residency without an invitation?

GIRL Not even where the servants eat the left overs.

GIRL [*in turn. In an 'English' accent*] Well well it's Mister Amusa. Were you invited? [*Play-acting to one another. The older* WOMEN *encourage them with their titters.*]

—Your invitation card please?
—Who are you? Have we been introduced?
—And who did you say you were?
—Sorry, I didn't quite catch your name.
—May I take your hat?
—If you insist. May I take yours? [*Exchanging the* POLICEMEN*'s hats*]
—How very kind of you.
—Not at all. Won't you sit down?
—After you.
—Oh no.
—I insist.
—You're most gracious.
—And how do you find the place?
—The natives are alright.
—Friendly?
—Tractable.
—Not a teeny-weeny bit restless?
—Well, a teeny-weeny bit restless.
—One might even say, difficult?

—Indeed one might be tempted to say, difficult.
—But you do manage to cope?
—Yes indeed I do. I have a rather faithful ox called Amusa.
—He's loyal?
—Absolutely.
—Lay down his life for you what?
—Without a moment's thought.
—Had one like that once. Trust him with my life.
—Mostly of course they are liars.
—Never known a native to tell the truth.
—Does it get rather close[9] around here?
—It's mild for this time of the year.
—But the rains may still come.
—They are late this year aren't they?
—They are keeping African time.
—Ha ha ha ha
—Ha ha ha ha
—The humidity is what gets me.
—It used to be whisky.
—Ha ha ha ha
Ha ha ha ha
—What's your handicap old chap?
—Is there racing by golly?
—Splendid golf course, you'll like it.
—I'm beginning to like it already.
—And a European club, exclusive.
—You've kept the flag flying.
—We do our best for the old country.
—It's a pleasure to serve.
—Another whisky old chap?
—You are indeed too too kind.
—Not at all sir. Where is that boy? [*With a sudden bellow*] Sergeant!

AMUSA [*snaps to attention*] Yessir!

[*The* WOMEN *collapse with laughter.*]

GIRL Take your men out of here.

AMUSA [*realising the trick, he rages from loss of face*] I'm give you warning . . .

GIRL Alright then. Off with his knickers! [*They surge slowly forward.*]

IYALOJA Daughters, please.

AMUSA [*squaring himself for defence*] The first woman wey touch me . . .

IYALOJA My children, I beg of you . . .

GIRL Then tell him to leave this market. This is the home of our mothers. We don't want the eater of white left-overs at the feast their hands have prepared.

IYALOJA You heard them Amusa. You had better go.

GIRL Now!

AMUSA [*commencing his retreat*] We dey go now, but make you no say we no warn you.

GIRL Now!

9. Stifling, hot.

GIRL Before we read the riot act[1]—you should know all about that.

AMUSA Make we go. [*They depart, more precipitately.*]

[*The* WOMEN *strike their palms across in the gesture of wonder.*]

WOMEN Do they teach you all that at school?

WOMAN And to think I nearly kept Apinke away from the place.

WOMAN Did you hear them? Did you see how they mimicked the white man?

WOMAN The voices exactly. Hey, there are wonders in this world!

IYALOJA Well, our elders have said it: Dada may be weak, but he has a younger sibling who is truly fearless.[2]

WOMAN The next time the white man shows his face in this market I will set Wuraola[3] on his tail.

[*A* WOMAN *bursts into song and dance of euphoria—'Tani l'awa o l'ogbeja? Kayi! A l'ogbeja. Omo Kekere l'ogbeja.*[4] *The rest of the* WOMEN *join in, some placing the* GIRLS *on their back like infants, others dancing round them. The dance becomes general, mounting in excitement.* ELESIN *appears, in wrapper only. In his hands a white velvet cloth folded loosely as if it held some delicate object. He cries out.*]

ELESIN Oh you mothers of beautiful brides! [*The dancing stops. They turn and see him, and the object in his hands.* IYALOJA *approaches and gently takes the cloth from him.*] Take it. It is no mere virgin stain, but the union of life and the seeds of passage. My vital flow, the last from this flesh is intermingled with the promise of future life. All is prepared. Listen! [*A steady drumbeat from the distance.*] Yes. It is nearly time. The King's dog has been killed. The King's favourite horse is about to follow his master. My brother chiefs know their task and perform it well. [*He listens again.*]

[*The* BRIDE *emerges, stands shyly by the door. He turns to her.*]

Our marriage is not yet wholly fulfilled. When earth and passage wed, the consummation is complete only when there are grains of earth on the eyelids of passage. Stay by me till then. My faithful drummers, do me your last service. This is where I have chosen to do my leave taking, in this heart of life, this hive which contains the swarm of the world in its small compass. This is where I have known love and laughter away from the palace. Even the richest food cloys when eaten days on end; in the market, nothing ever cloys. Listen. [*They listen to the drums.*] They have begun to seek out the heart of the King's favourite horse. Soon it will ride in its bolt of raffia[5] with the dog at its feet. Together they will ride on the shoulders of the King's grooms through the pulse centres of the town. They know it is here I shall await them. I have told them. [*His eyes appear to cloud. He passes his hand over them as if to clear his sight. He gives a faint smile.*] It promises well; just then I felt my spirit's eagerness. The kite[6] makes for wide spaces and the

1. The act of Parliament (1716) that enabled local authorities to declare a group unlawfully assembled; before the law could be enforced, a proclamation ordering them to disperse had to be read.

2. Dada, the mythical king of Oyo and god of vegetables, abdicated in favor of his fierce younger brother Shango, who was god of lightning.

3. A common Yoruba girl's name; it means "rich gold."

4. Who says we haven't a defender? Silence! We have our defenders. Little children are our champions [Soyinka's translation].

5. The fiber of raffia palms, used to fringe the masks of *egungun* and make their skirts.

6. One of a number of birds in the family that includes hawks.

wind creeps up behind its tail; can the kite say less than—thank you, the quicker the better? But wait a while my spirit. Wait. Wait for the coming of the courier of the King. Do you know, friends, the horse is born to this one destiny, to bear the burden that is man upon its back. Except for this night, this night alone when the spotless stallion will ride in triumph on the back of man. In the time of my father I witnessed the strange sight. Perhaps tonight also I shall see it for the last time. If they arrive before the drums beat for me, I shall tell them to let the Alafin[7] know I follow swiftly. If they come after the drums have sounded, why then, all is well for I have gone ahead. Our spirits shall fall in step along the great passage. [*He listens to the drums. He seems again to be falling into a state of semi-hypnosis; his eyes scan the sky but it is in a kind of daze. His voice is a little breathless.*] The moon has fed, a glow from its full stomach fills the sky and air, but I cannot tell where is that gateway through which I must pass. My faithful friends, let our feet touch together this last time, lead me into the other market with sounds that cover my skin with down yet make my limbs strike earth like a thoroughbred. Dear mothers, let me dance into the passage even as I have lived beneath your roofs. [*He comes down progressively among them. They make way for him, the* DRUMMERS *playing. His dance is one of solemn, regal motions, each gesture of the body is made with a solemn finality. The* WOMEN *join him, their steps a somewhat more fluid version of his. Beneath the* PRAISE-SINGER*'s exhortations the women dirge 'Alẹ lẹ le, awo mi lọ.'*[8]]

PRAISE-SINGER Elesin Alafin, can you hear my voice?
ELESIN Faintly, my friend, faintly.
PRAISE-SINGER Elesin Alafin, can you hear my call?
ELESIN Faintly my king, faintly.
PRAISE-SINGER Is your memory sound Elesin?
Shall my voice be a blade of grass and
Tickle the armpit of the past?
ELESIN My memory needs no prodding but
What do you wish to say to me?
PRAISE-SINGER Only what has been spoken. Only what concerns
The dying wish of the father of all.
ELESIN It is buried like seed-yam in my mind.
This is the season of quick rains, the harvest
Is this moment due for gathering.
PRAISE-SINGER If you cannot come, I said, swear
You'll tell my favourite horse. I shall
Ride on through the gates alone.
ELESIN Elesin's message will be read
Only when his loyal heart no longer beats.
PRAISE-SINGER If you cannot come Elesin, tell my dog.
I cannot stay the keeper too long
At the gate.
ELESIN A dog does not outrun the hand
That feeds it meat. A horse that throws its rider

7. The title of the paramount king of the Yoruba (that is, the deceased king); thus "Elesin Alafin," below, means "King's Horseman."

8. Night has fallen, the seasoned initiate is leaving (Yoruba).

Slows down to a stop. Elesin Alafin
Trusts no beasts with messages between
A king and his companion.

PRAISE-SINGER If you get lost my dog will track
The hidden path to me.

ELESIN The seven-way crossroads[9] confuses
Only the stranger. The Horseman of the King
Was born in the recesses of the house.

PRAISE-SINGER I know the wickedness of men. If there is
Weight on the loose end of your sash, such weight
As no mere man can shift; if your sash is earthed
By evil minds who mean to part us at the last . . .

ELESIN My sash is of the deep purple *alari*;
It is no tethering-rope. The elephant
Trails no tethering-rope; that king
Is not yet crowned who will peg an elephant—
Not even you my friend and King.

PRAISE-SINGER And yet this fear will not depart from me
The darkness of this new abode is deep—
Will your human eyes suffice?

ELESIN In a night which falls before our eyes
However deep, we do not miss our way.

PRAISE-SINGER Shall I now not acknowledge I have stood
Where wonders met their end? The elephant deserves
Better than that we say 'I have caught
A glimpse of something'. If we see the tamer
Of the forest let us say plainly, we have seen
An elephant.

ELESIN [*his voice is drowsy*]
I have freed myself of earth and now
It's getting dark. Strange voices guide my feet.

PRAISE-SINGER The river is never so high that the eyes
Of a fish are covered. The night is not so dark
That the albino[1] fails to find his way. A child
Returning homewards craves no leading by the hand.
Gracefully does the mask regain his grove at the end of the day . . .
Gracefully. Gracefully does the mask dance
Homeward at the end of the day, gracefully . . .

[ELESIN's *trance appears to be deepening, his steps heavier.*]

IYALOJA It is the death of war that kills the valiant,
Death of water is how the swimmer goes
It is the death of markets that kills the trader
And death of indecision takes the idle away
The trade of the cutlass blunts its edge
And the beautiful die the death of beauty.
It takes an Elesin to die the death of death . . .

9. A symbol of confusion; in Yoruba folklore, the trickster god, Esu Elegba, is often found at such a crossroads.

1. Yoruba view albinism as a handicap (while believing that handicapped people are sacred to the creator of humans).

Only Elesin . . . dies the unknowable death of death . . .
Gracefully, gracefully does the horseman regain
The stables at the end of day, gracefully . . .

PRAISE-SINGER How shall I tell what my eyes have seen? The Horseman gallops on before the courier, how shall I tell what my eyes have seen? He says a dog may be confused by new scents of beings he never dreamt of, so he must precede the dog to heaven. He says a horse may stumble on strange boulders and be lamed, so he races on before the horse to heaven. It is best, he says, to trust no messenger who may falter at the outer gate; oh how shall I tell what my ears have heard? But do you hear me still Elesin, do you hear your faithful one?

[ELESIN *in his motions appears to feel for a direction of sound, subtly, but he only sinks deeper into his trance-dance.*]

Elesin Alafin, I no longer sense your flesh. The drums are changing now but you have gone far ahead of the world. It is not yet noon in heaven; let those who claim it is begin their own journey home. So why must you rush like an impatient bride: why do you race to desert your Olohun-iyo?

[ELESIN *is now sunk fully deep in his trance, there is no longer sign of any awareness of his surroundings.*]

Does the deep voice of *gbedu*[2] cover you then, like the passage of royal elephants? Those drums that brook no rivals, have they blocked the passage to your ears that my voice passes into wind, a mere leaf floating in the night? Is your flesh lightened Elesin, is that lump of earth I slid between your slippers to keep you longer slowly sifting from your feet? Are the drums on the other side now tuning skin to skin with ours in *osugbo?*[3] Are there sounds there I cannot hear, do footsteps surround you which pound the earth like *gbedu,* roll like thunder round the dome of the world? Is the darkness gathering in your head Elesin? Is there now a streak of light at the end of the passage, a light I dare not look upon? Does it reveal whose voices we often heard, whose touches we often felt, whose wisdoms come suddenly into the mind when the wisest have shaken their heads and murmured: It cannot be done? Elesin Alafin, don't think I do not know why your lips are heavy, why your limbs are drowsy as palm oil in the cold of harmattan.[4] I would call you back but when the elephant heads for the jungle, the tail is too small a handhold for the hunter that would pull him back. The sun that heads for the sea no longer heeds the prayers of the farmer. When the river begins to taste the salt of the ocean, we no longer know what deity to call on, the river-god or Olokun.[5] No arrow flies back to the string, the child does not return through the same passage that gave it birth. Elesin Oba, can you hear me at all? Your eyelids are glazed like a courtesan's, is it that you see the dark groom and master of life? And will you see my father? Will you tell him that I stayed with you to the last? Will my voice ring in your ears awhile, will you remember Olohun-iyo even if the music on the other side surpasses his mortal craft? But will they know you over there? Have they eyes to gauge your worth, have they the heart to love you, will they

2. A deep-timbred royal drum [Soyinka].
3. Secret "executive" cult of the Yoruba; its meeting place [Soyinka].
4. A dry, dust-bearing seasonal wind that blows into West Africa from the Sahara Desert.
5. The god of the ocean.

know what thoroughbred prances towards them in caparisons[6] of honour? If they do not Elesin, if any there cuts your yam with a small knife, or pours you wine in a small calabash, turn back and return to welcoming hands. If the world were not greater than the wishes of Olohun-iyo, I would not let you go . . .

[*He appears to break down.* ELESIN *dances on, completely in a trance. The dirge wells up louder and stronger.* ELESIN'*s dance does not lose its elasticity but his gestures become, if possible, even more weighty. Lights fade slowly on the scene.*]

Act 4

A Masque.[7] *The front side of the stage is part of a wide corridor around the great hall of the Residency extending beyond vision into the rear and wings. It is redolent of the tawdry decadence of a far-flung but key imperial frontier. The couples in a variety of fancy-dress are ranged around the walls, gazing in the same direction. The guest-of honour is about to make an appearance. A portion of the local police brass band with its white conductor is just visible. At last, the entrance of Royalty. The band plays 'Rule Britannia',*[8] *badly, beginning long before he is visible. The couples bow and curtsey as he passes by them. Both he and his companions are dressed in seventeenth-century European costume. Following behind are the* RESIDENT *and his partner similarly attired. As they gain the end of the hall where the orchestra dais begins the music comes to an end. The* PRINCE *bows to the guests. The band strikes up a Viennese waltz and the* PRINCE *formally opens the floor. Several bars later the* RESIDENT *and his companion follow suit. Others follow in appropriate pecking order. The orchestra's waltz rendition is not of the highest musical standard.*

Some time later the PRINCE *dances again into view and is settled into a corner by the* RESIDENT *who then proceeds to select couples as they dance past for introduction, sometimes threading his way through the dancers to tap the lucky couple on the shoulder. Desperate efforts from many to ensure that they are recognised in spite of, perhaps, their costume. The ritual of introductions soon takes in* PILKINGS *and his wife. The* PRINCE *is quite fascinated by their costume and they demonstrate the adaptations they have made to it, pulling down the mask to demonstrate how the* egungun *normally appears, then showing the various press-button controls they have innovated for the face flaps, the sleeves, etc. They demonstrate the dance steps and the guttural sounds made by the* egungun, *harass other dancers in the hall,* MRS PILKINGS *playing the 'restrainer'*[9] *to* PILKINGS' *manic darts. Everyone is highly entertained, the Royal Party especially who lead the applause.*

At this point a liveried footman comes in with a note on a salver and is intercepted almost absent-mindedly by the RESIDENT *who takes the note and reads it. After polite coughs he succeeds in excusing the* PILKINGS *from the* PRINCE *and takes them aside. The* PRINCE *considerately offers the* RESIDENT'*s wife his hand and dancing is resumed.*

On their way out the RESIDENT *gives an order to his* AIDE-DE-CAMP. *They come into the side corridor where the* RESIDENT *hands the note to* PILKINGS.

RESIDENT As you see it says 'emergency' on the outside. I took the liberty of opening it because His Highness was obviously enjoying the entertainment. I didn't want to interrupt unless really necessary.

6. Ornamental cloths spread over the saddle or harness of horses.
7. That is, a masquerade, or elaborate masked ball (a European entertainment).
8. A patriotic song (1740); its words, taken from James Thomson's poem of the same title, are set to music by Thomas Arne.
9. The person who exercises a restraining influence on the wild movements of the main dancer.

PILKINGS Yes, yes of course, sir.

RESIDENT Is it really as bad as it says? What's it all about?

PILKINGS Some strange custom they have sir. It seems because the King is dead some important chief has to commit suicide.

RESIDENT The King? Isn't it the same one who died nearly a month ago?

PILKINGS Yes sir.

RESIDENT Haven't they buried him yet?

PILKINGS They take their time about these things, sir. The preburial ceremonies last nearly thirty days. It seems tonight is the final night.

RESIDENT But what has it got to do with the market women? Why are they rioting? We've waived that troublesome tax haven't we?

PILKINGS We don't quite know that they are exactly rioting yet sir. Sergeant Amusa is sometimes prone to exaggerations.

RESIDENT He sounds desperate enough. That comes out even in his rather quaint grammar. Where is the man anyway? I asked my aide-de-camp to bring him here.

PILKINGS They are probably looking in the wrong verandah. I'll fetch him myself.

RESIDENT No no you stay here. Let your wife go and look for them. Do you mind my dear . . . ?

JANE Certainly not, your Excellency. [*Goes.*]

RESIDENT You should have kept me informed, Pilkings. You realise how disastrous it would have been if things had erupted while His Highness was here.

PILKINGS I wasn't aware of the whole business until tonight sir.

RESIDENT Nose to the ground Pilkings, nose to the ground. If we all let these little things slip past us where would the empire be eh? Tell me that. Where would we all be?

PILKINGS [*low voice*] Sleeping peacefully at home I bet.

RESIDENT What did you say Pilkings?

PILKINGS It won't happen again sir.

RESIDENT It mustn't Pilkings. It mustn't. Where is that damned sergeant? I ought to get back to His Highness as quickly as possible and offer him some plausible explanation for my rather abrupt conduct. Can you think of one, Pilkings?

PILKINGS You could tell him the truth, sir.

RESIDENT I could? No no no Pilkings, that would never do. What! Go and tell him there is a riot just two miles away from him? This is supposed to be a secure colony of His Majesty, Pilkings.

PILKINGS Yes, sir.

RESIDENT Ah, there they are. No, these are not our native police. Are these the ring-leaders of the riot?

PILKINGS Sir, these are my police officers.

RESIDENT Oh, I beg your pardon officers. You do look a little . . . I say, isn't there something missing in their uniform? I think they used to have some rather colourful sashes. If I remember rightly I recommended them myself in my young days in the service. A bit of colour always appeals to the natives, yes, I remember putting that in my report. Well well well, where are we? Make your report man.

PILKINGS [*moves close to* AMUSA, *between his teeth*] And let's have no more superstitious nonsense from you Amusa or I'll throw you in the guardroom for a month and feed you pork![1]

RESIDENT What's that? What has pork to do with it?

PILKINGS Sir, I was just warning him to be brief. I'm sure you are most anxious to hear his report.

RESIDENT Yes yes yes of course. Come on man, speak up. Hey, didn't we give them some colourful fez hats with all those wavy things, yes, pink tassels . . .

PILKINGS Sir, I think if he was permitted to make his report we might find that he lost his hat in the riot.

RESIDENT Ah yes indeed. I'd better tell His Highness that. Lost his hat in the riot, ha ha. He'll probably say well, as long as he didn't lose his head. [*Chuckles to himself.*] Don't forget to send me a report first thing in the morning young Pilkings.

PILKINGS No sir.

RESIDENT And whatever you do, don't let things get out of hand. Keep a cool head and—nose to the ground Pilkings. [*Wanders off in the general direction of the hall.*]

PILKINGS Yes, sir.

AIDE-DE-CAMP Would you be needing me sir?

PILKINGS No thanks Bob. I think His Excellency's need of you is greater than ours.

AIDE-DE-CAMP We have a detachment of soldiers from the capital sir. They accompanied His Highness up here.

PILINGS I doubt if it will come to that but, thanks, I'll bear it in mind. Oh, could you send an orderly with my cloak.

AIDE-DE-CAMP Very good sir. [*Goes.*]

PILKINGS Now sergeant.

AMUSA Sir . . . [*Makes an effort, stops dead. Eyes to the ceiling.*]

PILKINGS Oh, not again.

AMUSA I cannot against death to dead cult. This dress get power of dead.

PILKINGS Alright, let's go. You are relieved of all further duty Amusa. Report to me first thing in the morning.

JANE Shall I come Simon?

PILKINGS No, there's no need for that. If I can get back later I will. Otherwise get Bob to bring you home.

JANE Be careful Simon . . . I mean, be clever.

PILKINGS Sure I will. You two, come with me. [*As he turns to go, the clock in the Residency begins to chime.* PILKINGS *looks at his watch then turns, horror-stricken, to stare at his wife. The same thought clearly occurs to her. He swallows hard. An orderly brings his cloak.*] It's midnight. I had no idea it was that late.

JANE But surely . . . they don't count the hours the way we do. The moon, or something . . .

PILKINGS I am . . . not so sure.

1. The eating of pork is forbidden to Muslims by the Qur'an.

[*He turns and breaks into a sudden run. The two* CONSTABLES *follow, also at a run.* AMUSA, *who has kept his eyes on the ceiling throughout waits until the last of the footsteps has faded out of hearing. He salutes suddenly, but without once looking in the direction of the woman.*]

AMUSA Goodnight madam.

JANE Oh. [*She hesitates.*] Amusa . . . [*He goes off without seeming to have heard.*] Poor Simon . . . [*A figure emerges from the shadows, a young black man dressed in a sober western suit. He peeps into the hall, trying to make out the figures of the dancers.*] Who is that?

OLUNDE [*emerging into the light*] I didn't mean to startle you madam. I am looking for the District Officer.

JANE Wait a minute . . . don't I know you? Yes, you are Olunde, the young man who . . .

OLUNDE Mrs Pilkings! How fortunate. I came here to look for your husband.

JANE Olunde! Let's look at you. What a fine young man you've become. Grand but solemn. Good God, when did you return? Simon never said a word. But you do look well Olunde. Really!

OLUNDE You are . . . well, you look quite well yourself Mrs Pilkings. From what little I can see of you.

JANE Oh, this. It's caused quite a stir I assure you, and not all of it very pleasant. You are not shocked I hope?

OLUNDE Why should I be? But don't you find it rather hot in there? Your skin must find it difficult to breathe.

JANE Well, it is a little hot I must confess, but it's all in a good cause.

OLUNDE What cause Mrs Pilkings?

JANE All this. The ball. And His Highness being here in person and all that.

OLUNDE [*mildly*] And that is the good cause for which you desecrate an ancestral mask?

JANE Oh, so you are shocked after all. How disappointing.

OLUNDE No I am not shocked Mrs Pilkings. You forget that I have now spent four years among your people. I discovered that you have no respect for what you do not understand.

JANE Oh. So you've returned with a chip on your shoulder. That's a pity Olunde. I am sorry.

[*An uncomfortable silence follows.*]

I take it then that you did not find your stay in England altogether edifying.

OLUNDE I don't say that. I found your people quite admirable in many ways, their conduct and courage in this war[2] for instance.

JANE Ah yes, the war. Here of course it is all rather remote. From time to time we have a black-out drill just to remind us that there is a war on. And the rare convoy passes through on its way somewhere or on manoeuvres. Mind you there is the occasional bit of excitement like that ship that was blown up in the harbour.[3]

OLUNDE Here? Do you mean through enemy action?

2. That is, World War II.

3. Perhaps a reference to a tragic incident that involved no heroism: on December 5, 1942, when three British naval trawlers were moored in the harbor at Lagos, an oil spill caught fire. The ships exploded, killing about 200 men.

JANE Oh no, the war hasn't come that close. The captain did it himself. I don't quite understand it really. Simon tried to explain. The ship had to be blown up because it had become dangerous to the other ships, even to the city itself. Hundreds of the coastal population would have died.

OLUNDE Maybe it was loaded with ammunition and had caught fire. Or some of those lethal gases they've been experimenting on.

JANE Something like that. The captain blew himself up with it. Deliberately. Simon said someone had to remain on board to light the fuse.

OLUNDE It must have been a very short fuse.

JANE [*shrugs*] I don't know much about it. Only that there was no other way to save lives. No time to devise anything else. The captain took the decision and carried it out.

OLUNDE Yes . . . I quite believe it. I met men like that in England.

JANE Oh just look at me! Fancy welcoming you back with such morbid news. Stale too. It was at least six months ago.

OLUNDE I don't find it morbid at all. I find it rather inspiring. It is an affirmative commentary on life.

JANE What is?

OLUNDE That captain's self-sacrifice.

JANE Nonsense. Life should never be thrown deliberately away.

OLUNDE And the innocent people round the harbour?

JANE Oh, how does one know? The whole thing was probably exaggerated anyway.

OLUNDE That was a risk the captain couldn't take. But please Mrs Pilkings, do you think you could find your husband for me? I have to talk to him.

JANE Simon? Oh. [*As she recollects for the first time the full significance of* OLUNDE*'s presence.*] Simon is . . . there is a little problem in town. He was sent for. But . . . when did you arrive? Does Simon know you're here?

OLUNDE [*suddenly earnest*] I need your help Mrs Pilkings. I've always found you somewhat more understanding than your husband. Please find him for me and when you do, you must help me talk to him.

JANE I'm afraid I don't quite . . . follow you. Have you seen my husband already?

OLUNDE I went to your house. Your houseboy told me you were here. [*He smiles.*] He even told me how I would recognise you and Mr Pilkings.

JANE Then you must know what my husband is trying to do for you.

OLUNDE For me?

JANE For you. For your people. And to think he didn't even know you were coming back! But how do you happen to be here? Only this evening we were talking about you. We thought you were still four thousand miles away.

OLUNDE I was sent a cable.

JANE A cable? Who did? Simon? The business of your father didn't begin till tonight.

OLUNDE A relation sent it weeks ago, and it said nothing about my father. All it said was, Our King is dead. But I knew I had to return home at once so as to bury my father. I understood that.

JANE Well, thank God you don't have to go through that agony. Simon is going to stop it.

OLUNDE That's why I want to see him. He's wasting his time. And since he has been so helpful to me I don't want him to incur the enmity of our people. Especially over nothing.

JANE [*sits down open-mouthed*] You . . . you Olunde!

OLUNDE Mrs Pilkings, I came home to bury my father. As soon as I heard the news I booked my passage home. In fact we were fortunate. We travelled in the same convoy as your Prince, so we had excellent protection.

JANE But you don't think your father is also entitled to whatever protection is available to him?

OLUNDE How can I make you understand? He *has* protection. No one can undertake what he does tonight without the deepest protection the mind can conceive. What can you offer him in place of his peace of mind, in place of the honour and veneration of his own people? What would you think of your Prince if he refused to accept the risk of losing his life on this voyage? This . . . showing-the-flag tour of colonial possessions.

JANE I see. So it isn't just medicine you studied in England.

OLUNDE Yet another error into which your people fall. You believe that everything which appears to make sense was learnt from you.

JANE Not so fast Olunde. You have learnt to argue I can tell that, but I never said you made sense. However clearly you try to put it, it is still a barbaric custom. It is even worse—it's feudal! The king dies and a chieftain must be buried with him. How feudalistic can you get!

OLUNDE [*waves his hand towards the background. The* PRINCE *is dancing past again—to a different step—and all the guests are bowing and curtseying as he passes*] And this? Even in the midst of a devastating war, look at that. What name would you give to that?

JANE Therapy, British style. The preservation of sanity in the midst of chaos.

OLUNDE Others would call it decadence. However, it doesn't really interest me. You white races know how to survive; I've seen proof of that. By all logical and natural laws this war should end with all the white races wiping out one another, wiping out their so-called civilisation for all time and reverting to a state of primitivism the like of which has so far only existed in your imagination when you thought of us. I thought all that at the beginning. Then I slowly realised that your greatest art is the art of survival. But at least have the humility to let others survive in their own way.

JANE Through ritual suicide?

OLUNDE Is that worse than mass suicide? Mrs Pilkings, what do you call what those young men are sent to do by their generals in this war? Of course you have also mastered the art of calling things by names which don't remotely describe them.

JANE You talk! You people with your long-winded, roundabout way of making conversation.

OLUNDE Mrs Pilkings, whatever we do, we never suggest that a thing is the opposite of what it really is. In your newsreels I heard defeats, thorough, murderous defeats described as strategic victories. No wait, it wasn't just on your newsreels. Don't forget I was attached to hospitals all the time. Hordes of your wounded passed through those wards. I spoke to them. I spent long evenings by their bedsides while they spoke terrible truths of the realities of that war. I know now how history is made.

JANE But surely, in a war of this nature, for the morale of the nation you must expect . . .

OLUNDE That a disaster beyond human reckoning be spoken of as a triumph? No. I mean, is there no mourning in the home of the bereaved that such blasphemy is permitted?

JANE [*after a moment's pause*] Perhaps I can understand you now. The time we picked for you was not really one for seeing us at our best.

OLUNDE Don't think it was just the war. Before that even started I had plenty of time to study your people. I saw nothing, finally, that gave you the right to pass judgement on other peoples and their ways. Nothing at all.

JANE [*hesitantly*] Was it the . . . colour thing? I know there is some discrimination.

OLUNDE Don't make it so simple, Mrs Pilkings. You make it sound as if when I left, I took nothing at all with me.

JANE Yes . . . and to tell the truth, only this evening, Simon and I agreed that we never really knew what you left with.

OLUNDE Neither did I. But I found out over there. I am grateful to your country for that. And I will never give it up.

JANE Olunde please . . . promise me something. Whatever you do, don't throw away what you have started to do. You want to be a doctor. My husband and I believe you will make an excellent one, sympathetic and competent. Don't let anything make you throw away your training.

OLUNDE [*genuinely surprised*] Of course not. What a strange idea. I intend to return and complete my training. Once the burial of my father is over.

JANE Oh, please . . . !

OLUNDE Listen! Come outside. You can't hear anything against that music.

JANE What is it?

OLUNDE The drums. Can you hear the changes? Listen.

[*The drums come over, still distant but more distinct. There is a change of rhythm, it rises to a crescendo and then, suddenly, it is cut off. After a silence, a new beat begins, slow and resonant.*]

There, it's all over.

JANE You mean he's . . .

OLUNDE Yes, Mrs Pilkings, my father is dead. His will-power has always been enormous; I know he is dead.

JANE [*screams*] How can you be so callous! So unfeeling! You announce your father's own death like a surgeon looking down on some strange . . . stranger's body! You're just a savage like all the rest.

AIDE-DE-CAMP [*rushing out*] Mrs Pilkings. Mrs Pilkings. [*She breaks down, sobbing.*] Are you all right, Mrs Pilkings?

OLUNDE She'll be all right. [*Turns to go.*]

AIDE-DE-CAMP Who are you? And who the hell asked your opinion?

OLUNDE You're quite right, nobody. [*Going*]

AIDE-DE-CAMP What the hell! Did you hear me ask you who you were?

OLUNDE I have business to attend to.

AIDE-DE-CAMP I'll give you business in a moment you impudent nigger. Answer my question!

OLUNDE I have a funeral to arrange. Excuse me. [*Going*]

AIDE-DE-CAMP I said stop! Orderly!

JANE No, no, don't do that. I'm alright. And for heaven's sake don't act so foolishly. He's a family friend.

AIDE-DE-CAMP Well he'd better learn to answer civil questions when he's asked them. These natives put a suit on and they get high opinions of themselves.

OLUNDE Can I go now?

JANE No no don't go. I must talk to you. I'm sorry about what I said.

OLUNDE It's nothing, Mrs Pilkings. And I'm really anxious to go. I couldn't see my father before, it's forbidden for me, his heir and successor, to set eyes on him from the moment of the King's death. But now . . . I would like to touch his body while it is still warm.

JANE You will. I promise I shan't keep you long. Only, I couldn't possibly let you go like that. Bob, please excuse us.

AIDE-DE-CAMP If you're sure . . .

JANE Of course I'm sure. Something happened to upset me just then, but I'm alright now. Really.

[*The* AIDE-DE-CAMP *goes, somewhat reluctantly.*]

OLUNDE I mustn't stay long.

JANE Please, I promise not to keep you. It's just that . . . oh you saw yourself what happens to one in this place. The Resident's man thought he was being helpful, that's the way we all react. But I can't go in among that crowd just now and if I stay by myself somebody will come looking for me. Please, just say something for a few moments and then you can go. Just so I can recover myself.

OLUNDE What do you want me to say?

JANE Your calm acceptance for instance, can you explain that? It was so unnatural. I don't understand that at all. I feel a need to understand all I can.

OLUNDE But you explained it yourself. My medical training perhaps. I have seen death too often. And the soldiers who returned from the front, they died on our hands all the time.

JANE No. It has to be more than that. I feel it has to do with the many things we don't really grasp about your people. At least you can explain.

OLUNDE All these things are part of it. And anyway, my father has been dead in my mind for nearly a month. Ever since I learnt of the King's death. I've lived with my bereavement so long now that I cannot think of him alive. On that journey on the boat, I kept my mind on my duties as the one who must perform the rites over his body. I went through it all again and again in my mind as he himself had taught me. I didn't want to do anything wrong, something which might jeopardise the welfare of my people.

JANE But he had disowned you. When you left he swore publicly you were no longer his son.

OLUNDE I told you, he was a man of tremendous will. Sometimes that's another way of saying stubborn. But among our people, you don't disown a child just like that. Even if I had died before him I would still be buried like his eldest son. But it's time for me to go.

JANE Thank you. I feel calmer. Don't let me keep you from your duties.

OLUNDE Goodnight, Mrs Pilkings.

JANE Welcome home. [*She holds out her hand. As he takes it footsteps are heard approaching the drive. A short while later a woman's sobbing is also heard.*]

PILKINGS [*off*] Keep them here till I get back. [*He strides into view, reacts at the sight of* OLUNDE *but turns to his wife.*] Thank goodness you're still here.

JANE Simon, what happened?

PILKINGS Later Jane, please. Is Bob still here?

JANE Yes, I think so. I'm sure he must be.

PILKINGS Try and get him out here as quickly as you can. Tell him it's urgent.

JANE Of course. Oh Simon, you remember . . .

PILKINGS Yes yes. I can see who it is. Get Bob out here. [*She runs off.*] At first I thought I was seeing a ghost.

OLUNDE Mr Pilkings, I appreciate what you tried to do. I want you to believe that. I can tell you it would have been a terrible calamity if you'd succeeded.

PILKINGS [*opens his mouth several times, shuts it*] You . . . said what?

OLUNDE A calamity for us, the entire people.

PILKINGS [*sighs*] I see. Hm.

OLUNDE And now I must go. I must see him before he turns cold.

PILKINGS Oh ah . . . em . . . but this is a shock to see you. I mean er thinking all this while you were in England and thanking God for that.

OLUNDE I came on the mail boat. We travelled in the Prince's convoy.

PILKINGS Ah yes, a ah, hm . . . er well . . .

OLUNDE Goodnight. I can see you are shocked by the whole business. But you must know by now there are things you cannot understand—or help.

PILKINGS Yes. Just a minute. There are armed policemen that way and they have instructions to let no one pass. I suggest you wait a little. I'll er . . . give you an escort.

OLUNDE That's very kind of you. But do you think it could be quickly arranged?

PILKINGS Of course. In fact, yes, what I'll do is send Bob over with some men to the er . . . place. You can go with them. Here he comes now. Excuse me a minute.

AIDE-DE-CAMP Anything wrong sir?

PILKINGS [*takes him to one side*] Listen Bob, that cellar in the disused annexe of the Residency, you know, where the slaves were stored before being taken down to the coast . . .

AIDE-DE-CAMP Oh yes, we use it as a storeroom for broken furniture.

PILKINGS But it's still got the bars on it?

AIDE-DE-CAMP Oh yes, they are quite intact.

PILKINGS Get the keys please. I'll explain later. And I want a strong guard over the Residency tonight.

AIDE-DE-CAMP We have that already. The detachment from the coast . . .

PILKINGS No, I don't want them at the gates of the Residency. I want you to deploy them at the bottom of the hill, a long way from the main hall so they can deal with any situation long before the sound carries to the house.

AIDE-DE-CAMP Yes of course.

PILKINGS I don't want His Highness alarmed.

AIDE-DE-CAMP You think the riot will spread here?

PILKINGS It's unlikely but I don't want to take a chance. I made them believe I was going to lock the man up in my house, which was what I had planned to do in the first place. They are probably assailing it by now. I took a roundabout route here so I don't think there is any danger at all. At least not before dawn. Nobody is to leave the premises of course—the native employees I mean. They'll soon smell something is up and they can't keep their mouths shut.

AIDE-DE-CAMP I'll give instructions at once.

PILKINGS I'll take the prisoner down myself. Two policemen will stay with him throughout the night. Inside the cell.

AIDE-DE-CAMP Right sir. [*Salutes and goes off at the double.*]

PILKINGS Jane. Bob is coming back in a moment with a detachment. Until he gets back please stay with Olunde. [*He makes an extra warning gesture with his eyes.*]

OLUNDE Please, Mr Pilkings . . .

PILKINGS I hate to be stuffy old son, but we have a crisis on our hands. It has to do with your father's affair if you must know. And it happens also at a time when we have His Highness here. I am responsible for security so you'll simply have to do as I say. I hope that's understood. [*Marches off quickly, in the direction from which he made his first appearance.*]

OLUNDE What's going on? All this can't be just because he failed to stop my father killing himself.

JANE I honestly don't know. Could it have sparked off a riot?

OLUNDE No. If he'd succeeded that would be more likely to start the riot. Perhaps there were other factors involved. Was there a chieftancy dispute?

JANE None that I know of.

ELESIN [*an animal bellow from off*] Leave me alone! Is it not enough that you have covered me in shame! White man, take your hand from my body!

[OLUNDE *stands frozen to the spot.* JANE, *understanding at last, tries to move him.*]

JANE Let's go in. It's getting chilly out here.

PILKINGS [*off*] Carry him.

ELESIN Give me back the name you have taken away from me you ghost from the land of the nameless!

PILKINGS Carry him! I can't have a disturbance here. Quickly! stuff up his mouth.

JANE Oh God! Let's go in. Please Olunde. [OLUNDE *does not move.*]

ELESIN Take your albino's[4] hand from me you . . .

[*Sounds of a struggle. His voice chokes as he is gagged.*]

OLUNDE [*quietly*] That was my father's voice.

JANE Oh you poor orphan, what have you come home to?

[*There is a sudden explosion of rage from offstage and powerful steps come running up the drive.*]

PILKINGS You bloody fools, after him!

[*Immediately* ELESIN, *in handcuffs, comes pounding in the direction of* JANE *and* OLUNDE, *followed some moments afterwards by* PILKINGS *and the* CONSTABLES. ELESIN, *confronted by the seeming statue of his son, stops dead.* OLUNDE *stares above his head into the distance. The* CONSTABLES *try to grab him.* JANE *screams at them.*]

JANE Leave him alone! Simon, tell them to leave him alone.

PILKINGS All right, stand aside you. [*Shrugs.*] Maybe just as well. It might help to calm him down.

[*For several moments they hold the same position.* ELESIN *moves a step forward, almost as if he's still in doubt.*]

4. A term of abuse when applied to a white person.

ELESIN Olunde? [*He moves his head, inspecting him from side to side.*] Olunde! [*He collapses slowly at* OLUNDE*'s feet.*] Oh son, don't let the sight of your father turn you blind!

OLUNDE [*he moves for the first time since he heard his voice, brings his head slowly down to look on him*] I have no father, eater of left-overs.

[*He walks slowly down the way his father had run. Light fades out on* ELESIN, *sobbing into the ground.*]

Act 5

A wide iron-barred gate stretches almost the whole width of the cell in which ELESIN *is imprisoned. His wrists are encased in thick iron bracelets, chained together; he stands against the bars, looking out. Seated on the ground to one side on the outside is his recent bride, her eyes bent perpetually to the ground. Figures of the two* GUARDS *can be seen deeper inside the cell, alert to every movement* ELESIN *makes.* PILKINGS *now in a police officer's uniform, enters noiselessly, observes him a while. Then he coughs ostentatiously and approaches. Leans against the bars near a corner, his back to* ELESIN. *He is obviously trying to fall in mood with him. Some moments' silence.*

PILKINGS You seem fascinated by the moon.

ELESIN [*after a pause*] Yes, ghostly one. Your twin-brother up there engages my thoughts.

PILKINGS It is a beautiful night.

ELESIN Is that so?

PILKINGS The light on the leaves, the peace of the night . . .

ELESIN The night is not at peace, District Officer.

PILKINGS No? I would have said it was. You know, quiet . . .

ELESIN And does quiet mean peace for you?

PILKINGS Well, nearly the same thing. Naturally there is a subtle difference . . .

ELESIN The night is not at peace, ghostly one. The world is not at peace. You have shattered the peace of the world for ever. There is no sleep in the world tonight.

PILKINGS It is still a good bargain if the world should lose one night's sleep as the price of saving a man's life.

ELESIN You did not save my life, District Officer. You destroyed it.

PILKINGS Now come on . . .

ELESIN And not merely my life but the lives of many. The end of the night's work is not over. Neither this year nor the next will see it. If I wished you well, I would pray that you do not stay long enough on our land to see the disaster you have brought upon us.

PILKINGS Well, I did my duty as I saw it. I have no regrets.

ELESIN No. The regrets of life always come later.

[*Some moments' pause.*]

You are waiting for dawn white man. I hear you saying to yourself: only so many hours until dawn and then the danger is over. All I must do is to keep him alive tonight. You don't quite understand it all but you know that tonight is when what ought to be must be brought about. I shall ease your mind even more, ghostly one. It is not an entire night but a moment of the night, and that moment is past. The moon was my messenger and guide. When it reached a certain gateway in the sky, it touched that moment for which my whole life has been spent in blessings. Even I do not know the gateway. I have stood here and scanned the sky for a glimpse of that door but, I cannot see it. Human eyes are useless for a search of this nature. But in the house of *osugbo,* those who keep watch through the spirit recognised the moment, they sent word to me through the voice of our sacred drums to prepare myself. I heard them and I shed all thoughts of earth. I began to follow the moon to the abode of the gods . . . servant of the white king, that was when you entered my chosen place of departure on feet of desecration.

PILKINGS I'm sorry, but we all see our duty differently.

ELESIN I no longer blame you. You stole from me my first-born, sent him to your country so you could turn him into something in your own image. Did you plan it all beforehand? There are moments when it seems part of a larger plan. He who must follow my footsteps is taken from me, sent across the ocean. Then, in my turn, I am stopped from fulfilling my destiny. Did you think it all out before, this plan to push our world from its course and sever the cord that links us to the great origin?

PILKINGS You don't really believe that. Anyway, if that was my intention with your son, I appear to have failed.

ELESIN You did not fail in the main thing ghostly one. We know the roof covers the rafters, the cloth covers blemishes; who would have known that the white skin covered our future, preventing us from seeing the death our enemies had prepared for us. The world is set adrift and its inhabitants are lost. Around them, there is nothing but emptiness.

PILKINGS Your son does not take so gloomy a view.

ELESIN Are you dreaming now, white man? Were you not present at the reunion of shame? Did you not see when the world reversed itself and the father fell before his son, asking forgiveness?

PILKINGS That was in the heat of the moment. I spoke to him and . . . if you want to know, he wishes he could cut out his tongue for uttering the words he did.

ELESIN No. What he said must never be unsaid. The contempt of my own son rescued something of my shame at your hands. You have stopped me in my duty but I know now that I did give birth to a son. Once I mistrusted him for seeking the companionship of those my spirit knew as enemies of our race. Now I understand. One should seek to obtain the secrets of his enemies. He will avenge my shame, white one. His spirit will destroy you and yours.

PILKINGS That kind of talk is hardly called for. If you don't want my consolation . . .

ELESIN No white man, I do not want your consolation.

PILKINGS As you wish. Your son, anyway, sends his consolation. He asks your forgiveness. When I asked him not to despise you his reply was: I cannot judge him, and if I cannot judge him, I cannot despise him. He wants to come to you and say goodbye and to receive your blessing.

ELESIN Goodbye? Is he returning to your land?

PILKINGS Don't you think that's the most sensible thing for him to do? I advised him to leave at once, before dawn, and he agrees that is the right course of action.

ELESIN Yes, it is best. And even if I did not think so, I have lost the father's place of honour. My voice is broken.

PILKINGS Your son honours you. If he didn't he would not ask your blessing.

ELESIN No. Even a thoroughbred is not without pity for the turf he strikes with his hoof. When is he coming?

PILKINGS As soon as the town is a little quieter. I advised it.

ELESIN Yes white man, I am sure you advised it. You advise all our lives although on the authority of what gods, I do not know.

PILKINGS [*opens his mouth to reply, then appears to change his mind. Turns to go. Hesitates and stops again*] Before I leave you, may I ask just one thing of you?

ELESIN I am listening.

PILKINGS I wish to ask you to search the quiet of your heart and tell me—do you not find great contradictions in the wisdom of your own race?

ELESIN Make yourself clear, white one.

PILKINGS I have lived among you long enough to learn a saying or two. One came to my mind tonight when I stepped into the market and saw what was going on. You were surrounded by those who egged you on with song and praises. I thought, are these not the same people who say: the elder grimly approaches heaven and you ask him to bear your greetings yonder; do you really think he makes the journey willingly? After that, I did not hesitate.

[*A pause.* ELESIN *sighs. Before he can speak a sound of running feet is heard.*]

JANE [*off*] Simon! Simon!

PILKINGS What on earth . . . ! [*Runs off.*]

[ELESIN *turns to his new wife, gazes on her for some moments.*]

ELESIN My young bride, did you hear the ghostly one? You sit and sob in your silent heart but say nothing to all this. First I blamed the white man, then I blamed my gods for deserting me. Now I feel I want to blame you for the mystery of the sapping of my will. But blame is a strange peace offering for a man to bring a world he has deeply wronged, and to its innocent dwellers. Oh little mother, I have taken countless women in my life but you were more than a desire of the flesh. I needed you as the abyss across which my body must be drawn, I filled it with earth and dropped my seed in it at the moment of preparedness for my crossing. You were the final gift of the living to their emissary to the land of the ancestors, and perhaps your warmth and youth brought new insights of this world to me and turned my feet leaden on this side of the abyss. For I confess to you, daughter, my weakness came not merely from the abomination of the white man who came violently into my fading presence, there was also a weight of longing on my earth-held limbs. I would have shaken it off, already my foot had begun to lift but then, the white ghost entered and all was defiled.

[*Approaching voices of* PILKINGS *and his wife.*]

JANE Oh Simon, you will let her in won't you?

PILKINGS I really wish you'd stop interfering.

[*They come into view.* JANE *is in a dressing-gown.* PILKINGS *is holding a note to which he refers from time to time.*]

JANE Good gracious, I didn't initiate this. I was sleeping quietly, or trying to anyway, when the servant brought it. It's not my fault if one can't sleep undisturbed even in the Residency.

PILKINGS He'd have done the same thing if we were sleeping at home so don't sidetrack the issue. He knows he can get round[5] you or he wouldn't send you the petition in the first place.

JANE Be fair Simon. After all he was thinking of your own interests. He is grateful you know, you seem to forget that. He feels he owes you something.

PILKINGS I just wish they'd leave this man alone tonight, that's all.

JANE Trust him Simon. He's pledged his word it will all go peacefully.

PILKINGS Yes, and that's the other thing. I don't like being threatened.

JANE Threatened? [*Takes the note.*] I didn't spot any threat.

PILKINGS It's there. Veiled, but it's there. The only way to prevent serious rioting tomorrow—what a cheek!

JANE I don't think he's threatening you Simon.

PILKINGS He's picked up the idiom alright. Wouldn't surprise me if he's been mixing with commies or anarchists over there. The phrasing sounds too good to be true. Damn! If only the Prince hadn't picked this time for his visit.

JANE Well, even so Simon, what have you got to lose? You don't want a riot on your hands, not with the Prince here.

PILKINGS [*going up to* ELESIN] Let's see what he has to say. Chief Elesin, there is yet another person who wants to see you. As she is not a next-of-kin I don't really feel obliged to let her in. But your son sent a note with her, so it's up to you.

ELESIN I know who that must be. So she found out your hiding-place. Well, it was not difficult. My stench of shame is so strong, it requires no hunter's dog to follow it.

PILKINGS If you don't want to see her, just say so and I'll send her packing.

ELESIN Why should I not want to see her? Let her come. I have no more holes in my rag of shame. All is laid bare.

PILKINGS I'll bring her in. [*Goes off.*]

JANE [*hesitates, then goes to* ELESIN] Please, try and understand. Everything my husband did was for the best.

ELESIN [*he gives her a long strange stare, as if he is trying to understand who she is*] You are the wife of the District Officer?

JANE Yes. My name, is Jane.

ELESIN That is my wife sitting down there. You notice how still and silent she sits? My business is with your husband.

[PILKINGS *returns with* IYALOJA.]

PILKINGS Here she is. Now first I want your word of honour that you will try nothing foolish.

ELESIN Honour? White one, did you say you wanted my word of honour?

PILKINGS I know you to be an honourable man. Give me your word of honour you will receive nothing from her.

ELESIN But I am sure you have searched her clothing as you would never dare touch your own mother. And there are these two lizards of yours who roll their eyes even when I scratch.

PILKINGS And I shall be sitting on that tree trunk watching even how you blink. Just the same I want your word that you will not let her pass anything to you.

5. That is, circumvent, cajole.

ELESIN You have my honour already. It is locked up in that desk in which you will put away your report of this night's events. Even the honour of my people you have taken already; it is tied together with those papers of treachery which make you masters in this land.

PILKINGS Alright. I am trying to make things easy but if you must bring in politics we'll have to do it the hard way. Madam, I want you to remain along this line and move no nearer to the cell door. Guards! [*They spring to attention.*] If she moves beyond this point, blow your whistle. Come on Jane. [*They go off.*]

IYALOJA How boldly the lizard struts before the pigeon when it was the eagle itself he promised us he would confront.

ELESIN I don't ask you to take pity on me Iyaloja. You have a message for me or you would not have come. Even if it is the curses of the world, I shall listen.

IYALOJA You made so bold with the servant of the white king who took your side against death. I must tell your brother chiefs when I return how bravely you waged war against him. Especially with words.

ELESIN I more than deserve your scorn.

IYALOJA [*with sudden anger*] I warned you, if you must leave a seed behind, be sure it is not tainted with the curses of the world. Who are you to open a new life when you dared not open the door to a new existence? I say who are you to make so bold? [*The* BRIDE *sobs and* IYALOJA *notices her. Her contempt noticeably increases as she turns back to* ELESIN.] Oh you self-vaunted stem of the plantain, how hollow it all proves. The pith is gone in the parent stem, so how will it prove with the new shoot? How will it go with that earth that bears it? Who are you to bring this abomination on us!

ELESIN My powers deserted me. My charms, my spells, even my voice lacked strength when I made to summon the powers that would lead me over the last measure of earth into the land of the fleshless. You saw it, Iyaloja. You saw me struggle to retrieve my will from the power of the stranger whose shadow fell across the doorway and left me floundering and blundering in a maze I had never before encountered. My senses were numbed when the touch of cold iron came upon my wrists. I could do nothing to save myself.

IYALOJA You have betrayed us. We fed you sweetmeats such as we hoped awaited you on the other side. But you said No, I must eat the world's leftovers. We said you were the hunter who brought the quarry down; to you belonged the vital portions of the game. No, you said, I am the hunter's dog and I shall eat the entrails of the game and the faeces of the hunter. We said you were the hunter returning home in triumph, a slain buffalo pressing down on his neck; you said wait, I first must turn up this cricket hole with my toes. We said yours was the doorway at which we first spy the tapper when he comes down from the tree, yours was the blessing of the twilight wine, the purl[6] that brings night spirits out of doors to steal their portion before the light of day. We said yours was the body of wine whose burden shakes the tapper like a sudden gust on his perch. You said, No, I am content to lick the dregs from each calabash when the drinkers are

6. A liquor made by infusing bitter herbs in beer or ale. *Twilight wine:* that is, the finest wine; palm wine tapped before dawn is believed to be especially fresh and potent.

done. We said, the dew on earth's surface was for you to wash your feet along the slopes of honour. You said No, I shall step in the vomit of cats and the droppings of mice; I shall fight them for the left-overs of the world.

ELESIN Enough Iyaloja, enough.

IYALOJA We called you leader and oh, how you led us on. What we have no intention of eating should not be held to the nose.

ELESIN Enough, enough. My shame is heavy enough.

IYALOJA Wait. I came with a burden.

ELESIN You have more than discharged it.

IYALOJA I wish I could pity you.

ELESIN I need neither your pity nor the pity of the world. I need understanding. Even I need to understand. You were present at my defeat. You were part of the beginnings. You brought about the renewal of my tie to earth, you helped in the binding of the cord.

IYALOJA I gave you warning. The river which fills up before our eyes does not sweep us away in its flood.

ELESIN What were warnings beside the moist contact of living earth between my fingers? What were warnings beside the renewal of famished embers lodged eternally in the heart of man. But even that, even if it overwhelmed one with a thousandfold temptations to linger a little while, a man could overcome it. It is when the alien hand pollutes the source of will, when a stranger force of violence shatters the mind's calm resolution, this is when a man is made to commit the awful treachery of relief, commit in his thought the unspeakable blasphemy of seeing the hand of the gods in this alien rupture of his world. I know it was this thought that killed me, sapped my powers and turned me into an infant in the hands of unnamable strangers. I made to utter my spells anew but my tongue merely rattled in my mouth. I fingered hidden charms and the contact was damp; there was no spark left to sever the life-strings that should stretch from every fingertip. My will was squelched in the spittle of an alien race, and all because I had committed this blasphemy of thought—that there might be the hand of the gods in a stranger's intervention.

IYALOJA Explain it how you will, I hope it brings you peace of mind. The bush-rat fled his rightful cause, reached the market and set up a lamentation. 'Please save me!'—are these fitting words to hear from an ancestral mask? 'There's a wild beast at my heels' is not becoming language from a hunter.

ELESIN May the world forgive me.

IYALOJA I came with a burden I said. It approaches the gates which are so well guarded by those jackals whose spittle will from this day be on your food and drink. But first, tell me, you who were once Elesin Oba, tell me, you who know so well the cycle of the plantain: is it the parent shoot which withers to give sap to the younger or, does your wisdom see it running the other way?

ELESIN I don't see your meaning Iyaloja?

IYALOJA Did I ask you for a meaning? I asked a question. Whose trunk withers to give sap to the other? The parent shoot or the younger?

ELESIN The parent.

IYALOJA Ah. So you do know that. There are sights in this world which say different Elesin. There are some who choose to reverse the cycle of our being. Oh, you emptied bark that the world once saluted for a pith-laden being, shall I tell you what the gods have claimed of you?

[*In her agitation she steps beyond the line indicated by* PILKINGS *and the air is rent by piercing whistles. The two* GUARDS *also leap forward and place safe-guarding hands on* ELESIN. IYALOJA *stops, astonished.* PILKINGS *comes racing in, followed by* JANE.]

PILKINGS What is it? Did they try something?

GUARD She stepped beyond the line.

ELESIN [*in a broken voice*] Let her alone. She meant no harm.

IYALOJA Oh Elesin, see what you've become. Once you had no need to open your mouth in explanation because evil-smelling goats, itchy of hand and foot, had lost their senses. And it was a brave man indeed who dared lay hands on you because Iyaloja stepped from one side of the earth onto another. Now look at the spectacle of your life. I grieve for you.

PILKINGS I think you'd better leave. I doubt you have done him much good by coming here. I shall make sure you are not allowed to see him again. In any case we are moving him to a different place before dawn, so don't bother to come back.

IYALOJA We foresaw that. Hence the burden I trudged here to lay beside your gates.

PILKINGS What was that you said?

IYALOJA Didn't our son explain? Ask that one. He knows what it is. At least we hope the man we once knew as Elesin remembers the lesser oaths he need not break.

PILKINGS Do you know what she is talking about?

ELESIN Go to the gates, ghostly one. Whatever you find there, bring it to me.

IYALOJA Not yet. It drags behind me on the slow, weary feet of women. Slow as it is Elesin, it has long overtaken you. It rides ahead of your laggard will.

PILKINGS What is she saying now? Christ! Must your people forever speak in riddles?

ELESIN It will come white man, it will come. Tell your men at the gates to let it through.

PILKINGS [*dubiously*] I'll have to see what it is.

IYALOJA You will. [*Passionately*] But this is one oath he cannot shirk. White one, you have a king here, a visitor from your land. We know of his presence here. Tell me, were he to die would you leave his spirit roaming restlessly on the surface of earth? Would you bury him here among those you consider less than human? In your land have you no ceremonies of the dead?

PILKINGS Yes. But we don't make our chiefs commit suicide to keep him company.

IYALOJA Child, I have not come to help your understanding. [*Points to* ELESIN.] This is the man whose weakened understanding holds us in bondage to you. But ask him if you wish. He knows the meaning of a king's passage; he was not born yesterday. He knows the peril to the race when our dead father, who goes as intermediary, waits and waits and knows he is betrayed. He knows when the narrow gate was opened and he knows it will not stay for laggards who drag their feet in dung and vomit, whose lips are reeking of the left-overs of lesser men. He knows he has condemned our King to wander in the void of evil with beings who are enemies of life.

PILKINGS Yes er . . . but look here . . .

IYALOJA What we ask is little enough. Let him release our King so he can ride on homewards alone. The messenger is on his way on the backs of women. Let him send word through the heart that is folded up within the bolt. It is the least of all his oaths, it is the easiest fulfilled.

[*The* AIDE-DE-CAMP *runs in.*]

PILKINGS Bob?

AIDE-DE-CAMP Sir, there's a group of women chanting up the hill.

PILKINGS [*rounding on* IYALOJA] If you people want trouble . . .

JANE Simon, I think that's what Olunde referred to in his letter.

PILKINGS He knows damned well I can't have a crowd here! Damn it, I explained the delicacy of my position to him. I think it's about time I got him out of town. Bob, send a car and two or three soldiers to bring him in. I think the sooner he takes his leave of his father and gets out the better.

IYALOJA Save your labour white one. If it is the father of your prisoner you want, Olunde, he who until this night we knew as Elesin's son, he comes soon himself to take his leave. He has sent the women ahead, so let them in.

[PILKINGS *remains undecided.*]

AIDE-DE-CAMP What do we do about the invasion? We can still stop them far from here.

PILKINGS What do they look like?

AIDE-DE-CAMP They're not many. And they seem quite peaceful.

PILKINGS No men?

AIDE-DE-CAMP Mm, two or three at the most.

JANE Honestly, Simon, I'd trust Olunde. I don't think he'll deceive you about their intentions.

PILKINGS He'd better not. Alright then, let them in Bob. Warn them to control themselves. Then hurry Olunde here. Make sure he brings his baggage because I'm not returning him into town.

AIDE-DE-CAMP Very good, sir. [*Goes.*]

PILKINGS [*to* IYALOJA] I hope you understand that if anything goes wrong it will be on your head. My men have orders to shoot at the first sign of trouble.

IYALOJA To prevent one death you will actually make other deaths? Ah, great is the wisdom of the white race. But have no fear. Your Prince will sleep peacefully. So at long last will ours. We will disturb you no further, servant of the white King. Just let Elesin fulfil his oath and we will retire home and pay homage to our King.

JANE I believe her Simon, don't you?

PILKINGS Maybe.

ELESIN Have no fear ghostly one. I have a message to send my King and then you have nothing more to fear.

IYALOJA Olunde would have done it. The chiefs asked him to speak the words but he said no, not while you lived.

ELESIN Even from the depths to which my spirit has sunk, I find some joy that this little has been left to me.

[*The* WOMEN *enter, intoning the dirge 'Alẹ lẹ lẹ' and swaying from side to side. On their shoulders is borne a longish object roughly like a cylindrical bolt, covered in cloth. They set it down on the spot where*

IYALOJA *had stood earlier, and form a semi-circle round it. The* PRAISE-SINGER *and* DRUMMER *stand on the inside of the semi-circle but the drum is not used at all. The* DRUMMER *intones under the* PRAISE-SINGER*'s invocations.*]

PILKINGS [*as they enter*] What is *that*?

IYALOJA The burden you have made white one, but we bring it in peace.

PILKINGS I said *what* is it?

ELESIN White man, you must let me out. I have a duty to perform.

PILKINGS I most certainly will not.

ELESIN There lies the courier of my King. Let me out so I can perform what is demanded of me.

PILKINGS You'll do what you need to do from inside there or not at all. I've gone as far as I intend to with this business.

ELESIN The worshipper who lights a candle in your church to bear a message to his god bows his head and speaks in a whisper to the flame. Have I not seen it ghostly one? His voice does not ring out to the world. Mine are no words for anyone's ears. They are not words even for the bearers of this load. They are words I must speak secretly, even as my father whispered them in my ears and I in the ears of my first-born. I cannot shout them to the wind and the open night-sky.

JANE Simon . . .

PILKINGS Don't interfere. Please!

IYALOJA They have slain the favourite horse of the King and slain his dog. They have borne them from pulse to pulse centre of the land receiving prayers for their King. But the rider has chosen to stay behind. Is it too much to ask that he speak his heart to heart of the waiting courier? [PILKINGS *turns his back on her.*] So be it, Elesin Oba, you see how even the mere leavings are denied you. [*She gestures to the* PRAISE-SINGER.]

PRAISE-SINGER Elesin Oba! I call you by that name only this last time. Remember when I said, if you cannot come, tell my horse. [*Pause.*] What? I cannot hear you? I said, if you cannot come, whisper in the ears of my horse. Is your tongue severed from the roots Elesin? I can hear no response. I said, if there are boulders you cannot climb, mount my horse's back, this spotless black stallion, he'll bring you over them. [*Pauses.*] Elesin Oba, once you had a tongue that darted like a drummer's stick. I said, if you get lost my dog will track a path to me. My memory fails me but I think you replied: My feet have found the path, Alafin.

[*The dirge rises and falls.*]

I said at the last, if evil hands hold you back, just tell my horse there is weight on the hem of your smock. I dare not wait too long.

[*The dirge rises and falls.*]

There lies the swiftest-ever messenger of a king, so set me free with the errand of your heart. There lie the head and heart of the favourite of the gods, whisper in his ears. Oh my companion, if you had followed when you should, we would not say that the horse preceded its rider. If you had followed when it was time, we would not say the dog has raced beyond and left his master behind. If you had raised your will to cut the thread of life at the summons of the drums, we would not say your mere shadow fell across the gateway and took its owner's place at the banquet. But the hunter, laden with slain buffalo, stayed to root in the cricket's hole with his toes.

What now is left? If there is a dearth of bats, the pigeon must serve us for the offering. Speak the words over your shadow which must now serve in your place.

ELESIN I cannot approach. Take off the cloth. I shall speak my message from heart to heart of silence.

IYALOJA [*moves forward and removes the covering*] Your courier Elesin, cast your eyes on the favoured companion of the King.

[*Rolled up in the mat, his head and feet showing at either end, is the body of* OLUNDE.]

There lies the honour of your household and of our race. Because he could not bear to let honour fly out of doors, he stopped it with his life. The son has proved the father, Elesin, and there is nothing left in your mouth to gnash but infant gums.

PRAISE-SINGER Elesin, we placed the reins of the world in your hands yet you watched it plunge over the edge of the bitter precipice. You sat with folded arms while evil strangers tilted the world from its course and crashed it beyond the edge of emptiness—you muttered, there is little that one man can do, you left us floundering in a blind future. Your heir has taken the burden on himself. What the end will be, we are not gods to tell. But this young shoot has poured its sap into the parent stalk, and we know this is not the way of life. Our world is tumbling in the void of strangers, Elesin.

[ELESIN *has stood rock-still, his knuckles taut on the bars, his eyes glued to the body of his son. The stillness seizes and paralyses everyone, including* PILKINGS *who has turned to look. Suddenly* ELESIN *flings one arm round his neck, once, and with the loop of the chain, strangles himself in a swift, decisive pull. The* GUARDS *rush forward to stop him but they are only in time to let his body down.* PILKINGS *has leapt to the door at the same time and struggles with the lock. He rushes within, fumbles with the handcuffs and unlocks them, raises the body to a sitting position while he tries to give resuscitation. The* WOMEN *continue their dirge, unmoved by the sudden event.*]

IYALOJA Why do you strain yourself? Why do you labour at tasks for which no one, not even the man lying there, would give you thanks? He is gone at last into the passage but oh, how late it all is. His son will feast on the meat and throw him bones. The passage is clogged with droppings from the King's stallion; he will arrive all stained in dung.

PILKINGS [*in a tired voice*] Was this what you wanted?

IYALOJA No child, it is what you brought to be, you who play with strangers' lives, who even usurp the vestments of our dead, yet believe that the stain of death will not cling to you. The gods demanded only the old expired plantain but you cut down the sap-laden shoot to feed your pride. There is your board, filled to overflowing. Feast on it. [*She screams at him suddenly, seeing that* PILKINGS *is about to close* ELESIN*'s staring eyes.*] Let him alone! However sunk he was in debt he is no pauper's carrion abandoned on the road. Since when have strangers donned clothes of indigo before the bereaved cries out his loss?

[*She turns to the* BRIDE *who has remained motionless throughout.*]

Child.

[*The girl takes up a little earth, walks calmly into the cell and closes* ELESIN*'s eyes. She then pours some earth over each eyelid and comes out again.*]

IYALOJA Now forget the dead, forget even the living. Turn your mind only to the unborn.

[She goes off, accompanied by the BRIDE. *The dirge rises in volume and the* WOMEN *continue their sway. Lights fade to a black-out.]*

The End

JUDITH THOMPSON

b. 1954

With the premiere of her first play, *THE CRACKWALKER*, at Toronto's Theatre Passe Muraille in 1980, Judith Thompson emerged as a major new voice in Canadian theater. A professionally trained actor, Thompson discovered while at Canada's National Theatre School that her greatest interest lay in examining the "huge chasm between the social persona and the inner life" of the individual, and that she could "find out who people really are" better as a playwright than as a performer. Thompson's deep understanding of the actor's craft and the process of character development undergirds her dramaturgy and has contributed immeasurably to her success as a dramatist known for vivid portraiture. The experience of acting in David Mamet's *Sexual Perversity in Chicago* (1974) also inspired in her a taste for freedom in both dramatic language and structure that has enabled her to build plays not by constructing a plot but rather by exploring characters' voices. Monologues remain central to each of her subsequent dramas, revealing her characters' complex psychology and motivations as she examines the dynamic interplay between social forces and individual behavior. *The Crackwalker* reflects a number of Thompson's other concerns, including her Catholic upbringing, her engagement with the family as a structural unit in society, her understanding of Canadian nationalism, and her acute sensitivity to the interplay of gender, race, and class in contemporary Canadian culture. Alternately naturalistic and dreamlike, Thompson's writing conforms to no preestablished structures. Her goal as a playwright mirrors the goal of the actor: to harness varying theatrical techniques in order to convey truth in performance.

Thompson was born in Montreal but grew up mostly in Kingston, Ontario, where her father, William Robert Thompson, a researcher in the field of behavioral genetics, chaired the Department of Psychology at Queen's University. Her mother Mary, who worked both as a theater artist and part-time as an English teacher, often took her daughter to see plays. After graduating from Queen's University in 1976, Thompson enrolled in the three-year acting program at the National Theatre School in Montreal—training that provided a creative foundation for her subsequent writing. She married Gregor Campbell in 1983, and they have five children. Thompson has twice received the prestigious Governor General's Award for Drama, for *White Biting Dog* in 1984 and for the collection *The Other Side of the Dark* in 1989; in addition, she has won the Floyd S. Chalmers Canadian Play Award, for *I Am Yours* in 1987 and for *Lion in the Streets* in 1991. Most recently, she received the Susan Smith

Blackburn Prize in 2008 for her play *Palace of the End.* Although she has worked in film, television, and radio as well as in fiction, Thompson feels most drawn to live theater. She has developed an ongoing working relationship with the Tarragon Theatre in Toronto, and she also teaches playwriting at the University of Guelph. Like a number of prominent contemporary dramatists, Thompson has chosen to direct the premieres of her more recent works, seeking both to protect her artistic vision and to continue to develop her scripts through the production process.

Unlike such other notable contemporary Canadian dramatists as Michel Tremblay, whose plays are strongly associated with his position as a Québécois writer, or Sharon Pollock, whose writing has been championed for its political force, or George F. Walker, known for his comedic, postmodern sensibility, Thompson continues to produce work that is elusive and cryptic. Hers is a theater of stark images and dreamscapes, of haunting symbols juxtaposed to raw brutality, of emotional intensity and corporeal intimacy interspersed with banality and the quotidian. And whereas such early plays as *The Crackwalker, I Am Yours,* or *Lion in the Streets* provided her middle-class audiences with some distance from her visceral representations of the under class, she has more recently challenged that separation and threatened their complacency in such pieces as *Sled* (1997) and *Perfect Pie* (2000). Refusing to lessen the reality of her characters' lives through artificial catharsis or well-made narrative closure, Thompson relies on her dramas' challenging style and content to change her audience.

In *The Crackwalker,* Thompson demands our immediate and fixed attention. From the play's very first moments, we must work to understand simply what the characters are saying, as well as what and who they are talking about. Thompson takes the notion of starting in medias res to extremes. She never provides easy exposition, instead plunging directly into the maelstrom of her characters' lives. We can discern that Theresa is struggling to achieve what she imagines as a normal life from within the confines of an imperfect social services system. Her friend Sandy faces challenges of her own, especially in her relationship with the volatile Joe. And Alan, Theresa's boyfriend, grapples, as does Joe, with the meaning of manhood and with social expectations that at times become overwhelming. As Alan's life unravels, he is haunted by the presence of a Native American man, the titular Crackwalker, who has reached the true nadir of contemporary existence.

Working for the Canadian government's Adult Protective Services agency in Kingston one summer, Thompson had met a girl who became the basis for Theresa: she "was borderline mentally handicapped and . . . had this wonderful way of speaking and a wonderful purity about her." Theresa's opening monologue is much more than a "stream of consciousness" outpouring; Thompson uses this character's frankness and ebullience to reveal her complex relationship to sexuality, to religion, and to the state. Theresa's speech careers from disputing the charge that she "was suckin off queers down the Lido for five bucks" to her lack of respect for "sosha workers" to her rejection of enforced religion: "I don't like readin no stupid Bible!" Through this address, Theresa emerges as both a fully realized character and an individual buffeted by social forces and interpersonal dynamics completely beyond her control.

In the scenes that follow, Thompson intersperses brief dialogic exchanges with other monologues to explore the relationships between her characters and to reveal the demons that haunt each of them. Sandy, a modern-day Everywoman, struggles with received ideas of femininity and social status, questions her commitment to her abusive boyfriend Joe, and grapples with her precarious economic position. But she never goes so far as to interrogate the social values she has embraced. She simply adjusts her perceptions—even though she may recognize their inadequacy—in order to carry on, as in her closing description of the funeral of Theresa and Alan's baby, Danny: "And they had a big wreath of flowers around his neck so's to hide the strangle—you know the kind you put on your door at Christmas? Like that. It was kinda nice." A moment later she adds,

"The flowers never hid it they just made ya look harder."

Thompson creates subtle parallels between the conventions of femininity to which Sandy adheres and the world of male bonding, petty crime, and bravado that Joe inhabits. Narrating the events surrounding the death of a friend in a car crash, Joe observes that they "never *talked* about shit, it was the shit we done together made us good buddies. Just doin stuff with a guy you know you're thinkin the same." Joe's notions of masculinity and of how to survive in a culture of disenfranchisement are shared by Alan, but Alan also feels compelled to realize the ideals of the nuclear family to prove his worth as a man. He selects the mentally retarded Theresa, whom he sees as his "angel" and like "that madonna lady," to be his wife and the mother of his child. But his choice epitomizes the radical disjunction between these characters' visions of participating in the dominant culture and the impossibility of achieving those visions. The unraveling of Alan's dream starkly reveals the psychic and social costs of such unrealistic expectations.

As the description above makes clear, *The Crackwalker,* like a number of Thompson's plays, is brutal, unflinching, and potentially offensive in its themes and dialogue. She readily acknowledges that her plays can disturb audiences, precisely because they reveal what people mask in their everyday social interactions: "Our whole society is founded on denial. Denial of murdering the Native people, denial of oppressing women. . . . Once secrets are exposed . . . and people hate to turn red and be exposed—then they will hate you for it." Moreover, Thompson insists that to be effective, her works must be as frank and elemental as possible:

> Theatre has to be embarrassing, and theatre has to be slovenly. . . . When I have young babies I like to let my breast milk leak through my blouse in public at nice restaurants. . . . And the looks of disgust on people's faces are the same looks [as the ones] on the people that walk out of my plays. I've let something leak that's not supposed to be leaking.

Thompson frequently uses such metaphors, as corporeal states and bodily functions figure largely both in her characters' speech and in her own commentary on her creative process. Several of her plays, most notably *Tornado* (1987; rev. 1992), feature a character who, like Thompson, is epileptic. Thompson's experiences with epilepsy have profoundly affected her perspectives on life, consciousness, and the relationship between mind and body. Most strikingly, she perceives her illness in social as well as physical terms, linking her seizures to her identity as a woman and as a writer. She writes eloquently of her need, as a Catholic girl, to don a series of masks so that she might hide and preserve another self more resistant to social strictures. This stranger within, Thompson explains, manifested itself first in awkward, unfeminine physicality and then, starting at age nine, in epilepsy. Thompson's acute sensitivity, through her illness, to what she calls "contact with the dark" enables her to capture the fluidity of psychic states. Remarkable moments result, such as Alan's description of his loss of control over the frightening scenes in his mind that opens act 2 of *The Crackwalker*: "Fuck I'll be doin the dishes where I'm workin down the Tropicana there and it's like pictures burning holes in my brain I try all the time to like put other pictures over top of that, nice things that I really get off on, eh, that I really like[.]" As horrific images overpower him, Alan comes ever closer to what Thompson elsewhere calls "the abyss": "The abyss is death. It's what you don't know. . . . You see an abyss when you're falling, in that dream where you're falling and falling and there's no bottom." The threat of the abyss pervades Thompson's dramaturgy; each of her characters struggles—some successfully, others not—to retain a sense of normalcy and autonomy against its magnetic power.

The figure of the Crackwalker, the play's eponymous metaphor and the character who haunts its periphery, is inextricably linked to the abyss. Thompson based the Crackwalker, as she had Theresa, on a real person—a Kingstonian known for his obsessive avoidance of sidewalk cracks. "That guy walkin down street lookin at the

Randy Hughson as Alan and Debra Kirshenbaum as Theresa, in the 1990 performance of *The Crackwalker* at the Tarragon Theatre in Toronto, Ontario.

sidewalk" gives Sandy "the creeps," but, significantly, he is the individual with whom Alan may most closely identify, despite his feelings of revulsion. His name reminds us of children's games of daring, threat, and taboo—"step on a crack and you break your mother's back"—perhaps best captured by A. A. Milne in his poem "Lines and Squares" (1924), which warns against bears "Who wait at the corners all ready to eat / The sillies who tread on the lines of the street." The bears

try to pretend that nobody cares
Whether you walk on the lines or
squares.
But only the sillies believe their talk;
It's ever so portant how you walk.

Milne's portrait of intelligent beasts lurking in the urban landscape resonates with Thompson's images of ever-present danger. Threats of psychic chaos, sexual violation, economic deprivation, and social ostracism permeate her dramatic world. Moreover,

Milne's verse suggests a connection between social conformity—staying "in the squares"—and personal safety that Thompson both understands and deconstructs. In Thompson's theater, of course, the human beast is the most unpredictable and potentially violent presence in either the urban jungle or the Canadian wilderness.

Thompson's interest in the unpredictable and unknown has also led her to actively resist the seamless linear plots and characterological arcs that we identify with conventional dramaturgy. She creates for each character a unique voice, distinguishable by vocabulary, intonational patterns, and grammar. The Canadian critic Alan Filewod notes that Thompson's characters "move in and out of private worlds that are constructed through language; at the same time, language marks the social environments through which the characters have passed." Her plays take shape through the dramatization of strategic moments—some comic, some horrific, some banal—designed to reveal the complexity of the individuals she portrays. She leaves it to her audience to connect these moments and to find meaning created by scenic juxtapositions, idiosyncratic dialogue, and evocative imagery.

For some critics, Thompson's decision to position a number of her characters—especially women—as victims, or as individuals who unquestioningly accept dominant social structures, renders her dramaturgy politically problematic. Thompson argues, however, that one must examine "an issue that's *true,* and until you examine what *is,* what exists, you can't do anything about it." When asked what impact she would like to have on her audience, Thompson explains that she wants "to hold a mirror up to all of us" to ensure a "forced confrontation with the self." Only in a moment of awakening can theater, for Thompson, truly become powerful. "The coma lifting, then, becomes political. Art is political, should be political, but only in this really essential way." Psychically charged, visceral as well as lyrical, sexually frank, emotionally turbulent, and uncompromising in its social convictions, Thompson's playwriting exemplifies the contemporary theater at its most elemental, powerful level.

J.E.G.

The Crackwalker

CHARACTERS

THERESA
SANDY
ALAN
JOE
The MAN

1.1

THERESA Shut up, mouth, I not goin back there no more noway, I'm goin back to Sandy's! [*To audience*] You know what she done to me? She make me go livin with her up on Division[1] near Chung Wah's, cause she say I come from God, eh, then she go lookin in my room every night see if I got

1. Division Street, the main commercial thoroughfare in Kingston, Ontario.

guys in there cause Bonnie Cain told her I was suckin off queers down the Lido for five bucks; I wasn't doin it anyways Bonnie Cain was doin it I was just watchin. So last night, eh, I'm up there with a friend of mine, Danny, he a taxi driver—we're just talkin, eh, we weren't doin nothin, and so she come up and knock on the door and she say, "Trese I know you got someone in there" and I go "No Mrs. Beddison ain't nobody in here," and she start goin on about God and that, and how she knowed cause she got a six feelin[2] in her, so I get scared, eh, so I tell Danny to get in the closet. We don't got no clothes on, eh, so I put his jeans and that under the bed and I get under the covers like I'm sleepin and I go "S'kay Mrs. Beddison you could come in now." So she come in lookin at me like a stupid bitch and she say she knowed there was somebody in there cause she heard talkin and I says "You feelin okay Mrs. Beddison, ain't nobody here cept me and I sleepin," then she start goin near the closet, eh, and Danny start laughin. Well she runup the closet and she pullin on the door and I'm pullin on her arm and I'm saying "Trust me Mrs. Beddison, ya gotta trus me," cause the sosha workers are always goin on about trus and that, eh, but she don't listen, she open the door and there's Danny standin stripped naked. Well that whoredog Beddison start screamin God words at him, eh, so he takes off outa the house and she takes off after him and I got his pants, eh, so I throw em out the window case he catch em and then I bawlin. I bawlin on the bed and ya know what she make me do? She make me take a bath! A bubble bath like for the baby! All bubbles and that! Then she make me put on her stupid dressin robe itch my skin and smell like chocolate bars and that and she take me to where she livin and you know what she make me do? She make me read the Bible! I don't like readin no stupid Bible! Ya get a stomachache doin that, ya do! Stupid hose bag. I'm not goin back there no more no way, I'm goin back to Sandy's.

1.2

[SANDY *and* JOE'*s apartment.* SANDY *is scrubbing the floor furiously.* THERESA *appears, joyous, carrying a plastic bag containing all of her belongings. As she has not seen* SANDY *in several weeks, she is very excited.*]

THERESA Hi Sandy, how ya doin!!

[SANDY *does not look at* THERESA.]

SANDY What are you doin here?

THERESA I come callin on ya!

[*In the following sequence,* SANDY'*s anger builds. At first, however, it contains an element of teasing.*]

SANDY I don't want no houndogs callin on me. [*Continues scrubbing*]

THERESA I not a houndog!

SANDY Yes, y'are.

THERESA No I not.

SANDY Whoredog houndog that's what you are.

THERESA [*laughs, delighted*] Sanny!

SANDY [*pointing backwards*] And get your whorepaws offa my sofa.

2. That is, had an intuition via a "sixth sense."

THERESA [*jumps, removes hand, gasps*] Sanny, like I don't mean to bug ya or nothin [*Eating donut from bag*] but like I don't get off on livin where I'm livin no more so I come back here sleepin on the couch, okay?

SANDY I not keepin no cowpies[3] here.

THERESA I not a cowpie!

SANDY [*faces her*] Would you get out of my house?

THERESA Why, what I done?

SANDY . . . Ya smell like cookin fat—turns my gut.

THERESA That only cause I eatin chip from the chipwagon![4]

SANDY I don't care what it's cause of, get your whoreface out of here.

THERESA Why, why you bein ugly for?

SANDY You tell me and then we'll both know.

THERESA What.

SANDY Don't think nobody seen ya neither cause Bonnie Cain seen ya right through the picture window!

[THERESA *claps a hand to her mouth in "uh-oh."*]

On my couch that I paid for with my money.

THERESA Wha—

SANDY With *my husband!*

THERESA No way, Sanny.

SANDY [*unable to contain her anger any longer*] You touch my fuckin husband again and I break every bone in your body!

THERESA Bonnie Cain lyin she lyin to ya she think I took twenty buck off her she tryin to get me back.

SANDY [*starts speaking after "she lying to ya"*] That's bullshit Therese cause Bonnie Cain don't lie and you know she don't.

THERESA You don't trus me.

SANDY Fuckin right.

THERESA I never done it.

SANDY Pretty bad combination, Trese, a retarded whore.

THERESA That's a load of bullshit Sanny, I *not retarded*.

SANDY Just get out of my house and don't come back. [*Pushes her.*]

THERESA No I never I never done it! [*In angry indignation she pushes back.*]

SANDY Trese Joe told me, he told me what the two of youse done!

THERESA Oh.

SANDY Lyin whore, look at ya make me sick. Wearin that ugly dress thinkin it's sexy cause it shows off your fat tits and those shoes are fuckin stupid ya can't even walk in them.

THERESA I know.

[SANDY *stares at* THERESA. THERESA *does not move.*]

SANDY [*with an air of resignation, tiredness*] Just get out, okay?

THERESA I never wanted it, Sanny, I never wanted it he come in he made me.

SANDY Bull Trese.

THERESA He did I sleepin I sleepin there havin dreams I seen this puppy and he come in and tie me up and push it in me down my hole.

SANDY What?

3. Piles of cow manure.
4. Vendor's cart selling chips (french fries).

THERESA He tie me all up with strings and that and he singin Ol Macdonel Farm and he say he gonna kill me if I don't shut up so I be quiet and he done it he screw me.

SANDY Are you shittin me?

THERESA And—and—and he singin and he take his jean down and it all hard and smellin like pee pee and he go and he put it in my mouth.

SANDY He could do twenty for that.

THERESA Don't send him up the river[5] Sanny he didn't mean nothin.

SANDY Horny bastard he's not gettin into me again.

THERESA Me neither Sanny he tries anything I just run up to Tim Hortons[6] get a fancy donut.

SANDY Oh he won't be cheatin on me again.

THERESA How come Sanny, you tell him off?

SANDY Fuckin right I did. After Bonnie tole me, I start givin him shit, eh, and he takes the hand to me callin me a hag and sayin how he liked pokin you bettern that and look. [*Reveals bruise.*]

THERESA Bassard.

SANDY He's done it before, but he won't do it again.

THERESA Why, Sanny, you call the cops on him?

SANDY *Right.*

THERESA Did ya—

SANDY Ya know my high heels? The shiny black ones I got up in Toronto?

THERESA Yeah, they're sharp.

SANDY [*obviously enjoying telling the story*] And he knows it, too. After he beat up on me he takes off drinkin, comes back about three just shitfaced, eh, and passes out cold? Well I'm there lookin at him snorin like a pig and I says to myself "I'm gonna get this bastard," I'm thinkin of how when I seen my heels sittin over in the corner and then I know what I'm gonna do. So I take one of the heels and go over real quiet to where he's lyin, and ya know what I do? I take the heel and I rip the holy shit out of his back with it.

THERESA JEEZ DID HE WAKE UP?

SANDY Fuckin right he did. You shoulda seen him, first I guess he thought he was dreamin, eh, so he just lies there makin these ugly noises burpin and that? And then he opens his eyes, and puts his hands up like a baby eh, and *then* I *seen* him *see* the heel. Well I take off right out the back door and he's comin after me fit to kill his eyes is all red he's hissin I am scared shitless; well he gets ahold of me and I says to myself "Sandy this is it. This is how you're gonna die. You got the bastard back and now you're gonna die for it." Well he is just about to send me to the fuckin angels when he stops; just like that and turns around and goes on to bed.

THERESA How come he done that, Sanny?

SANDY I didn't know at first either, then I figured it out. Cuttin him with the heel was the smartest thing I done. Ya see, he wasn't gonna kill me cause he don't want to do time, eh, and he knew if he just beat up on me he'd

5. That is, to prison (an expression that originated in New York City, which sent convicts up the Hudson River to Sing Sing Prison in Ossining, New York).

6. A chain of doughnut shops founded and mainly located in Canada.

never get no more sleep cause I'd do it again. He knows it. He don't dare take a hand to me again, no way. Either he takes off, or he stays and he treats me nice.

THERESA Did you talk to him later?

SANDY I ain't seen him for three days. But we ate together before he took off, I fixed him up some tuna casserole and we ate it; we didn't say nothin, though. It don't matter, we sometimes go a whole week without talkin, don't mean we're pissed off at each other.

THERESA Al and I talkin all the time when we go out.

SANDY We did too when we first started goin together. After a while ya don't have to talk cause you always know what they're gonna say anyways. Makes ya sick sometimes. What are you bawlin for?

THERESA I'm sorry Joe done that to me, Sanny.

SANDY He's like that, he's a prick.

THERESA S'okay if I come livin here then?

SANDY . . . Sure, I don't care.

THERESA Thank you Sanny.

SANDY I like the company.

THERESA Don't say nothin to Al, eh?

SANDY What if I tell him what Bonnie Cain tole me about you blowin off queers down the Lido?

THERESA Oh no, Sanny, don't say bout that.

SANDY I guess old fags in Kingston are pretty hard up.

THERESA You want a donut, Sanny?

SANDY No. What kind ya got.

THERESA Apple fritters.

SANDY Jeez, Therese, ya ever see how they make them things?

THERESA No, I never worked up there.

SANDY It'd make ya sick.

THERESA I love em.

SANDY I know ya do, you're a pig.

THERESA Fuck off. . . . Only kiddin.

SANDY You watch your mouth.

THERESA You love Joe still?

SANDY I don't know. I used to feel like we was in the fuckin movies. Member that show *Funny Girl* where Barbra Streisand and Omar Sharif are goin together?[7]

THERESA She hardly[8] sing pretty.

SANDY Well remember that part where they start singin right on the boat, singin to each other?

THERESA Yeah.

SANDY We done that once. We'd been up at the Manor, eh, Chesty Morgan[9] was up there so we'd just been havin a hoot, eh, and Joe wants to go over to the General Wolfe to see the Mayor, so we get on the Wolfe Island[1] ferry

7. *Funny Girl* is a 1968 movie musical, starring Streisand (b. 1942) and Sharif (b. 1932).
8. Really.
9. Polish-born stripper (b. 1928?) who made two campy sexploitation films in 1974 and toured clubs throughout North America.
1. The largest of the Thousand Islands, located at the northeast end of Lake Ontario, where the St. Lawrence River begins; ferry service runs to the island from Kingston.

and we're laughin and carryin on and that and then we start singin, right on the bow of the Wolfe Island ferry.

THERESA Jeez.

SANDY We didn't care when we were doin it though, we didn't give a shit what anyone was thinkin, fuck em we were havin fun.

THERESA I love singin.

SANDY Joe really done that to you?

THERESA What?

SANDY *Raped* ya.

THERESA Don't like talkin about it Sanny.

SANDY *Trese.*

THERESA He done it when I never wanted it it's true.

SANDY It is, eh?

THERESA S'true, Sanny. Don't tell Joe, eh?

SANDY I mighta known it.

THERESA Still okay if I sleepin here though?

SANDY You're gonna have to do the housework while I'm workin for Nikos.

THERESA How come you workin down there I thought you didn't like Nikos?

SANDY I get off on corned beef on rye, arsewipe, what d'ya think I need the fuckin money.

THERESA Ain't Joe drivin for Amey's[2] no more?

SANDY No.

THERESA What's he doin?

SANDY Fuckin the dog,[3] I don't know.

THERESA Bassard.

SANDY I know. Gimme a bite of that.

THERESA I not really retarded am I Sanny?

SANDY Just a little slow.

THERESA Not like that guy walkin down street lookin at the sidewalk?

SANDY Jeez he give me the creeps.

THERESA He hardly got the long beard, eh?

SANDY I know.

THERESA Not like him, eh Sanny?

SANDY No. No, I tole ya Therese, you're just a little slow.

THERESA Oh.

[JOE *and* ALAN *barge in with a hot*[4] *motorbike. They start quickly, efficiently taking it apart and packing the parts.* SANDY *and* THERESA *stand there stupefied.*]

JOE Ya hoo! We got ourselves a shit-hot mother!

ALAN Did we *ever!*

JOE Okay nice and easy we don't want to mark this babe.

ALAN Like this?

JOE That's right buddy—fuckin back door wide open shit that dog just sittin there waggin its tail at us.

ALAN He wanted to be buddies with us.

JOE I just about shit it was fuckin *helpin* us.

2. A taxi company in Kingston.
3. Doing nothing (slang).
4. Stolen.

THERESA What kinda dog was it Al, one of them golden?

JOE A shepherd.

ALAN A German shepherd a police dog.

JOE A fuckin *screw*[5] dog.

SANDY You're not bringin Martin over here.

JOE How's my pussycake doin? Eh? [*Kisses* SANDY.] Eh pussycake?

SANDY I says you're not bringin Martin over here.

JOE Don't worry babe we're meetin him over to the Shamrock he ain't comin here.

ALAN Down the Beachcomber Room.

THERESA That's hardly nice down there all them trees and that?

ALAN You like it there?

THERESA I love it.

ALAN I'll take ya there sometime.

SANDY Where you been the last three nights?

JOE Paintin the town brown honeysuck whata you been doin?

SANDY I said where were ya for three nights in a row?

JOE Out with the Mayor, poochie, spookin out the Royal.

THERESA You not out with him he dead.

ALAN Theresa.

THERESA He is dead.

ALAN Joe's only kiddin, Trese.

SANDY You tell me where ya been or you're out on your car. I said where were ya the last three nights?

JOE Just hold on to your pants sugar crack first things first. [*Madly working on the bike*]

ALAN This is big bucks ya know.

SANDY You don't have to tell me cause I know. I know where ya were you were down the Embassy pissin our money away.

THERESA Them ugly old Greeks down there anyways.

ALAN You were takin Papa's *shirt*, eh Joe?

SANDY I'll tell ya somethin about gamblers youse do it just so's you could lose it's true that's why.

JOE Well fuck me blind I never knew that. Did you know that Al?

ALAN Nope, I never heard of that.

JOE Thars pretty good commander, where'd ya get that offa?

SANDY It happened to be in the *Reader's Digest*, arsewipe, and it was written by a doctor, Doctor John Grant, and I guess he knows what he's talkin about.

JOE Oooooh *Reader's Digest*, shit-for-brains is going smart on us.

THERESA She not a shit-for-brains you stupid.

JOE You simmer down there burger.

SANDY Is that where ya were, pissin away my money?

JOE [*completes a physical action*] Gotcha.

SANDY Eh?

JOE Hand me the pliers, would ya?

SANDY [*screeching*] I said where were ya Joe!

5. Prison guard (slang).

[JOE *spits his mouthful of beer in her face.* ALAN *laughs and laughs.*]

That's cute.

THERESA Stupid dummy-face.

[JOE *spits on* ALAN. ALAN *laughs, spits back.*]

SANDY You are cut off and I mean it.

JOE From what, bitch, your ugly box?

[SANDY *exits to clean up.*]

Don't know what she's so pissed off at nice brew in the face cool ya right down.

THERESA I'm movin back here Joe Sanny said I could.

ALAN She did?

JOE Is that right.

THERESA Sleepin on the couch that okay Joe?

JOE Sure, fuck, I don't care, long as the two of youse don't gang up on me.

ALAN Two women together always do.

THERESA What do two women do?

ALAN You know, gang up on the guy.

SANDY [*entering*] Only if he got it comin to him.

JOE Do I get it comin to me commander?

SANDY You're fuckin right you do.

JOE Little diesel dyke this one see what she done to me?

ALAN Holy Jeez!

JOE She's a live one all right Pearl Lasalle[6] the second.

THERESA She not like Pearl Lasalle Pearl Lasalle ugly lookin.

JOE She fights like her though don't ya honey suck? What's for supper I'm starvin.

SANDY Nothin.

JOE What?

SANDY You don't bring in money we don't get no supper.

JOE Well fuck—don't we got stuff for samiches?

SANDY Nope.

JOE Well fuck I'm goin over to Shirley's.

SANDY When.

JOE Right now fuck.

SANDY Take your stuff with ya.

JOE Would ya sit on this first I want fish for supper.

SANDY Pig. I says take your stuff with ya and get out.

JOE You for real?

SANDY Fuckin right.

JOE All right I been wantin out of this hole. Thanks babe.

SANDY Is that right?

JOE Take care. [*Starts to go.*]

SANDY You could get in a lot of trouble rapin a retard Joe.

JOE Pardon.

SANDY I said you could get in a lot of trouble rapin a retard.

6. The name of a woman living in Kingston when the play was written—a "diesel dyke" (lesbian with a masculine appearance) well-known locally both as a heavily tattooed ex-convict and as the kindly, loving mother of five children.

[THERESA *is motioning No! No! No! to* SANDY.]

JOE Yeah that's right you would. So?

SANDY You'll be up the river for twenty years when I tell the cops what you done, Joe.

ALAN Over fifty[7] don't get you twenty years no way no way!

SANDY I'm not talkin bout the bike.

JOE What? What are ya talkin about eh?

SANDY About rapin a retard.

JOE What?

SANDY About rapin Theresa.

JOE What?

SANDY About rapin Theresa with me in the next room.

JOE Rape? Rape? Who told you that did Theresa tell you that?

SANDY Yeahhh.

THERESA No no Sanny not rape I only said he done it when I never wanted it.

JOE Did you tell my wife that I raped you Theresa? [THERESA *doesn't answer.*] Did you say that? Eh? [*Grabs her.*] Eh?

THERESA I never—leave me alone you big ugly cock—

JOE I'll tell you somethin about your little girlfriend buddy. I'll tell you something about this little—

ALAN It don't matter, Joe, it—it—it just don't matter nobody don't believe her anyways.

JOE This little girl who's callin rape was sittin on that couch beggin for it.

ALAN She never.

SANDY Theresa?

JOE It's true. I come in piss drunk I'm passed out on the floor and there she is down on all fours shovin her big white ass in my face.

THERESA No I never.

JOE Big white bootie right in the face.

THERESA Go away.

JOE Tell em like it was Trese, and no crossin fingers.

THERESA I never say that Sanny, I never mean he rape me!

SANDY Theresa is he tellin the truth?

ALAN Theresa you never done that, did ya? Shown him your bum?

JOE This is your last chance, burger, now tell the fuckin truth or I get serious.

SANDY Don't lie to me Theresa. I can forgive a lot of things but not a lie.

ALAN You can tell the truth, Theresa, I'll take care of ya.

SANDY Eh, Trese?

[*Pause.*]

THERESA [*laughing*] Who farted?

ALAN I never did.

JOE Eh Theresa?

ALAN It's—it's okay, Joe it's—she—she can't handle her booze yet she was probably drunk or sniffin[8] and you was drunk and it don't matter, it just don't matter I'll be stayin with her all the nights from now I'm gonna take

7. That is, theft of property worth more than $50—the threshold for distinguishing categories of theft in Canada's criminal code until 1971.

8. That is, sniffing glue.

care of her it won't happen again she won't never say nothin bout ya again I promise.

THERESA You stayin with me all nights from now Al?

ALAN I'm takin care of ya. I'm—

SANDY Could youse leave us alone, please.

ALAN Who, me and Theresa?

SANDY If you don't mind.

ALAN Sure, sure. We—

THERESA Wait for me Al I wanna get some chocolate bars and that I starvin . . . well I am I didn't have no dinner.

JOE You. You watch your mouth, eh?

SANDY Would youse just take off?

[ALAN *pulls* THERESA *out.*]

THERESA See youse later don't do nothin I wouldn't do.

1.3

[ALAN *and* THERESA *exit.* JOE *is furious and trying to cool down. His back is to* SANDY. *She is aware of his anger. She picks something up off the kitchen floor and starts to take it in to the kitchen.* JOE *grabs her as she tries to pass him and throws her to the floor.*]

JOE You CUNT.

SANDY Keep away from me—

JOE I'm a fuckin rapist cause a fuckin retard SAYS so?

SANDY Touch me again and you go to your goddamn grave!

JOE FUCK maybe I'm the maniac been carvin all the TELLERS out in SASKATOON![9] [*Makes monster face and noise.*]

SANDY Go jump in a hole.

JOE [*grabs her, hard*] What is fuckin with your BRAIN, woman?

SANDY I didn't mean it.

JOE It was a *joke?*

SANDY I was just—you said you liked her better.

JOE What?

SANDY You said you liked—pokin her better.

JOE [*laughs, almost hysterically*] So I go to the joint.

SANDY I wasn't gonna tell nobody—

JOE You're a fuckin CROW, you know that?

SANDY I was just—seein—

JOE [*thrusting her away*] Get away from me.

[SANDY *starts to run toward him, trying to scream but the sound is muffled and distorted by a stomach seizure which stops her about three feet away from* JOE.]

You got your upset stomach again?

SANDY Bastard.

JOE [*looks her up and down*] You just give me a hard-on.

[SANDY *spits on him.*]

9. The largest city of the province of Saskatchewan, in western Canada.

Hewww you like it when I'm rough with ya, don't ya? Eh? [*Moves her roughly, whispers.*] Makes your nips stand up when I'm rough with ya.

[SANDY*'s hands are still raised.* SANDY *and* JOE *are a foot apart throughout the interchange.* SANDY *looks at him with hatred.*]

What, you don't want it? Okay, see ya later!

[*He starts to leave.*]

SANDY [*head down*] Joe.

JOE What can I do for ya?

[SANDY *smiles.*]

Oh, ya do want it. Okay, why—why—don't ya take that blouse there off?

[*She removes her blouse.*]

Hm. And the skirt.

[*She removes her skirt. She is left in a bra and pantyhose with a low crotch. He nods, looking her up and down.*]

How come ya like it like this? Eh? [*Shakes his head.*] I gotta be somewhere.

[JOE *exits.* SANDY *remains onstage, not moving. Lights out quickly.*]

1.4

[THERESA *and* ALAN *are in a restaurant.*]

THERESA Where d'ya think Joe took off to?

ALAN I don't know probably drinkin, maybe the Shamrock.

THERESA You think they're splitting up?

ALAN I hope not.

THERESA Me too. I love Sandy, she my best girlfriend.

ALAN I—Joe—he and me are good buddies, too. They go good together anyways.

THERESA Could I have a donut?

ALAN What kind, chocolate? I know you like chocolate.

THERESA I love it.

ALAN Sandy's nuts, you're not fat.

THERESA Don't say nothin about it.

ALAN You're not.

THERESA I don't like talkin about it.

ALAN Here. Two chocolate donuts.

THERESA Thank you Alan.

ALAN Jesus you're a good lookin girl. You're the prettiest lookin girl I seen.

THERESA Don't talk like that.

ALAN I love screwin with ya. Do you like it with me?

THERESA I don't know—don't ask me that stuff dummy-face.

ALAN I like eatin ya out ya know.

THERESA Shut your mouth people are lookin don't talk like that stupid-face.

ALAN Nobody's lookin. Jeez you're pretty. Just like a little angel. Huh. Like a—I know. I know. I'm gonna call you my little angel from now on. People gonna see ya and they're gonna go "There's Trese, she's Al's angel!"

THERESA Who gonna say them things?

ALAN Anybody.

THERESA They are?

ALAN Yup.

THERESA You're a dummy-face.

ALAN So beautiful.

THERESA Stop it Al you make me embarrass.

ALAN You're—I was always hopin for someone like you—always happy always laughin and that.

THERESA I cryin sometimes ya know.

ALAN Yeah but ya cry the same way ya laugh. There's somethin—I don't know—as soon as I seen ya I knew I wanted ya. I wanted to marry ya when I seen ya.

THERESA When, when did you say that?

ALAN I never said nothin, I just thought it, all the time.

THERESA We only been goin together for a little while, you know.

ALAN Let's get married.

THERESA Al stop lookin at me like that you embarrassin me.

ALAN Sorry. Did you hear me?

THERESA Yeah. Okay.

ALAN When.

THERESA Tuesday. I ask my sosha worker to come.

ALAN No. Just Joe and me and you and Sandy. Just the four of us. I want Joe to be my best man.

THERESA Sandy could be the flower girl. Uh. Oh.

ALAN What?

THERESA Hope you don't want no babies.

ALAN Why. I do! I do want babies! I get on with babies good!

THERESA Not sposda have none.

ALAN How come? Who told you that?

THERESA The sosha worker, she say I gotta get my tubes tied.[1]

ALAN What's that?

THERESA Operation up the hospital. They tie it up down there so ya won't go havin babies.

ALAN They can't do that to you no way!

THERESA I know they can't but they're doin it.

ALAN They don't have no *right.*

THERESA Yah they do Al I slow.

ALAN Slow? I don't think you're slow who told YOU that?

THERESA I ain't a good mum Al I cant help it.

ALAN Who said you ain't a good mum?

THERESA All of them just cause when I took off on Dawn.

ALAN Who's Dawn?

THERESA The baby, the other baby.

ALAN You never had a baby before did ya? Did ya?

THERESA Las—

ALAN You didn't have no other man's baby did ya? With another guy?

[*Pause.*]

THERESA No, it's Bernice's.

1. That is, be sterilized by tubal ligation; in some provinces of Canada, from the 1930s up through the 1970s, people with mental disabilities were routinely sterilized.

ALAN Who's Bernice?

THERESA My cousin my mum's sister.

ALAN Well how come you were lookin after her baby?

THERESA Cause she was sick up in hospital. Jeez Al.

ALAN Well—what happened whatdja do wrong?

THERESA Nothin it wasn't my fault just one Friday night I was sniffin, eh, so I took off down to the plaza and I leave the baby up the room, eh, I thought I was comin right back, and I met this guy and he buyin me drinks and that then I never knew what happened and I woke up and I asked somebody where I was and I was in Ottawa!

ALAN He took you all the way up to Ottawa? That bastard.

THERESA I never seen him again I thumbed back to Kingston. [*Crying*] I come back to the house and the baby's gone she ain't there so I bawlin I goin everywhere yellin after her and never found nothin then I see Bonnie Cain and she told me they took her up the Children's Aid she dead. So I go on up the Aid and they say she ain't dead she live but they not givin her back cause I unfit.

ALAN Jeez.

THERESA I ain't no more Al I don't sniff or nothin.

ALAN Them bastards.

THERESA Honest.

ALAN I know. I know ya don't and we're gonna have a baby and nobody ain't gonna stop us. We're gonna have our own little baby between you and me and nobody can't say nothin bout it. You're not goin to no hospital, understand?

THERESA But Al she say she gonna cut off my pension check if I don't get my tubes tied.

ALAN Fuck the pension check you're not goin to no hospital.

THERESA Okay Al.

ALAN Come here. You're not goin to no hospital.

THERESA You won't let em do nothin to me, will ya Al?

ALAN Nope. You're my angel and they ain't gonna touch you. . . . Hey! I know what ya look like now!

THERESA What, an angel?

ALAN That—that madonna lady; you know them pictures they got up in classrooms when you're a kid? Them pictures of the madonna?

THERESA The Virgin Mary?

ALAN Yeah. Her.

THERESA I love her I askin her for stuff.

ALAN Yuh look just like her. Just like the madonna. Cept the madonna picture got a baby in it.

THERESA It do?

ALAN She's holdin it right in her arms. You too, maybe, eh? Eh? Hey! Let's go up to the Good Thief.[2]

THERESA Al I don't know you goin to church! You goin every Sunday?

2. That is, the Church of the Good Thief, a Roman Catholic church in Kingston. The "Good Thief," traditionally given the name Dismas, was the robber crucified with Jesus who repented and asked Jesus to "remember me when thou comest into thy kingdom" (Luke 23.42).

ALAN No I never went since I was five I just want to go now. We'll go and we'll—we'll like have a party lightin candles[3] and that a party for gettin married!

THERESA I love lightin candles.

ALAN Maybe the Father's gonna be there. They're always happy when someone's gettin married we could tell him!

THERESA Al I gettin sleepy.

ALAN Well after we party I'm gonna put ya right down to sleep over at Joe's. I won't try nothin or nothin.

THERESA What if Sandy be piss off.

ALAN No Trese, they said we could stay there together. The two of us. And we're gonna.

THERESA Okay . . . really I lookin like that madonna?

ALAN Just like her. Just like her.

[*He is rocking her in his arms. Lights fade.*]

1.5

JOE Me and the Mayor we'd pick up a couple steak hoagies, and a case of twenty-four, head up to Merton on the hogs[4]—catch some shit group—you know, Mad Dog Fagin, Grapes of Wrath, somethin, get shitfaced then go back to Kingston, pick us up some juicy pie down at Lino's or Horny Tim's,[5] drive it out to middle road, fuck it blind, and have em home by one o'clock. Then we'd go down and catch the last ferry to the island and fuckin ride from one end to the other all fuckin night. Seven o'clock we'd go into Lou's have us some home fries and a couple eggs easy over then head on back to work in Kingston. That was when I was drivin a Cat[6] makin a shitload of money just a shitload. Huh—the Mayor was fuckin crazy wasn't nothin he wouldn't do nothin he was smart too he went to university in the States even, he just didn't give a shit about it, you know? He had about a hundred books I seen em all filled with words that long [*Measures two feet*] he knew what they meant, too, every one of them but he never let on, ya know? He never let on he knew so much . . . we never *talked* about shit, it was the shit we done together made us good buddies. Just doin stuff with a guy you know you're thinkin the same. Anybody touched him I woulda killed them and same goes for him . . . he was a damn good driver too but he wasn't *drivin,* Martin was. Fuckin Martin fuckin stoned on STP.[7] Martin—Martin wasn't an asshole, but he stupid you know? Jeez he was stupid. So this Friday night we'd all gotten pissed up the Manor, eh, then we all went over to the island just to fuck around and to see the Mayor's sister, Linda, who was workin at the General Wolfe waitin on tables. So Bart, that was his real name, Bart and me and Martin had all got these new boots over at the A1 men's store really nice you know,

3. In Catholic churches, worshippers light votive candles to symbolize and extend their prayers and to honor the saint before whose image the candle is lit.
4. That is, Harley-Davidson motorcycles.
5. Nickname for the Tim Hortons chain of doughnut shops.
6. That is, a piece of construction equipment (a Caterpillar).
7. A synthetic hallucinogen—a forerunner of ecstasy—introduced in the late 1960s (the initials stand for "serenity, tranquility, peace").

all leather, real solid a hundred bucks a pair so we wanted to show em off to Linda, you know, bug her. So Bart gets in there and he's jumpin on tables, eatin all the limes and cherries and that for the drinks singin some gross song about his love boots, he called them. Fuck it was funny—we were killin ourselves but Linda she wasn't laughin her boss was gettin pissed off so she told Bart, she goes "Bart, get the fuck out of here I think your goddamn boots are shit." That's what she said. So he give her a big kiss right in front of her boss and we take off in Martin's car. Me and the Mayor in the backseat, Martin and his girlfriend in the front. Well we're headin down the road goin south it's dark but it ain't wet and the last thing I remember Bart looks at me and he says "I wonder what it's like to fuck an angel" and *bang* everything goes fuckin black. When I come to I'm in the fucking ambulance goin across to Kingston and Bart's lyin there beside me dead only I didn't know it and there's his sister Linda right there in the ambulance. I don't know how she got there—she's all red all black under her eyes and that and she's bawlin just bawlin up a storm and she's huggin his legs and she's sayin something only I can't make out what she's sayin I can't make it out I was so out of it I'm thinkin I'm gonna die I'm thinkin I'm gonna die if I don't make out what she's sayin so I kept tryin to make it out and she kept sayin it and then I knew what she was sayin and you know what it was? . . . She was sayin she did like his boots. "I do like your boots Bart I do like your boots Bart I do like your boots I do like your fuckin boots I do like your boots I do like your boots I do like your boots. . . ." She wouldn't fuckin stop it.

1.6

[ALAN *and* THERESA *are sound asleep. The room is sometimes lit by passing cars. Noise of people on the street.* THERESA'S *steady breathing. Suddenly we hear* JOE, *very drunk, half singing. As soon as* ALAN *hears him he springs into his jeans, legs shaking, and awkwardly tries to light a cigarette. His heart is racing.* JOE *enters.*]

ALAN Hey Joe.

JOE Jeeeeeeezus you gimme a scare what are you doin here?

ALAN Stayin with Trese member? Member ya said I could? The—the mum's got company—in from Windsor.[8]

JOE *Windsor.* What a fuckin hole.

ALAN Yeah it's hot down there—in the summer—

JOE Look what I found in the fuckin hallway. Cheese samich with a bloody Kleenex stuck to it.

[*This makes* ALAN *very sick.*]

ALAN Jeezus who put it there.

JOE I was thinkin maybe the wife left out a little snack for me. Ya want some? Blood'n Cheez Whiz[9] samich? Hey hey hey it's hardly good.

ALAN Hey no—no—no thank you. No way.

8. An industrial city in the southwest corner of Ontario (across the Detroit River from Detroit, Michigan).

9. A processed cheese food, sold by Kraft since the 1950s.

JOE What, you don't like eatin blood or somethin?

ALAN I never tried it.

JOE Were you screwin that?

ALAN No! No I mean no I was just I—

JOE Why the hell not?

ALAN Oh no I mean I was eh, like I was a couple hours ago, but not right before ya came in I wasn't.

JOE Jeez you're strange. How come ya got dressed you goin out?

ALAN No—no I'm not goin out—I—I couldn't fuckin sleep, you know? Ya know what that's like? Ya just keep turnin and can't lie right? So I thought I'd wait up and just shoot the shit with you when ya came in.

JOE Strange-o.

ALAN I guess so. Did-dju play tonight?

JOE Papadapa dies!

ALAN He—he was cheatin again?

JOE Fuckin right he was.

ALAN He dies.

JOE Greasy fuck. Fuck once I seen Edwards get him in a half Nelson an he was so greasy he slipped out!

ALAN Ewwww.

JOE Slipped right out. Slimy bastard right in the middle of the game I turn to him and I says "Papa" I says, "Don't fuck with me, just don't fuck with me."

ALAN That's hardly good. Huh. What did he say?

JOE Nothin. He just made one of them noises.

ALAN What, what the ones with their mouth like this? Like a chicken does?

JOE Hah. Yeah it is kinda like a chicken. Gives me the creeps.

ALAN Yeah. Yeah, they do that all the time and the one I worked for, Andy? He *stunk* too, he smelled like matches, you know? After ya light a match?

JOE He's gettin it.

ALAN Yeah?? Yeah? Who's gonna give it to him, are you? Are you gonna give it to him Joe? I'll help ya I hate the bastard. I hate him.

JOE Buddy I am pleadin the Fifth. Fuuuck. [*Singing*] "I gotta get outtaaa this place if it's the lassst . . ."[1]

ALAN I know what ya mean, Joe. Too—too—too bad there weren't no late movie on or something—hah—Mr. Ed or somethin.

JOE Who's he when he's at home?

ALAN Mr. Ed? The talkin horse, don't ya remember? "A horse is a horse of course of course and no one . . ."[2]

JOE Hey [*Indicating bedroom*] w'she bawlin or did she go out?

ALAN Sleepin when we come in I think.

JOE She's a good woman buddy.

ALAN I know she is Joe. So's Trese.

1. A paraphrase of "We Gotta Get Out of This Place" (1965), a hit song recorded by the Animals (written by Barry Mann and Cynthia Weil); the line ends "thing we ever do." *Pleadin the Fifth*: invoking the right against self-incrimination guaranteed by the Fifth Amendment of the U.S. Constitution.

2. The opening lyrics of the theme song to *Mister Ed* (written by Jay Livingston and Ray Evans), an American television sitcom (1961–66).

JOE Are you sure, buddy?

ALAN Oh—that was—she—she didn't mean nothin honest Joe she she just don't think sometimes, ya know?

JOE That mouth of hers is gonna send her up shit creek one day ain't it burger?

ALAN You—you want a smoke?

JOE Whaddya got—menthol, fuck, I can't smoke that shit.

ALAN I know—I didn't buy em a guy a guy give em to me.

JOE Hey hamburger sorry for wakin ya.

THERESA I not a hamburger.

JOE Ooooh I thought ya was!

THERESA You shut up I sleepin.

JOE Okay burger queen. Yeah. Yeah buddy she's okay too.

ALAN Thank you, Joe. So's Sandy.

JOE She never fucked around on me, you know.

ALAN No?

JOE Not once. [*Goes to window and leans out*] What a fuckin hole this is eh? . . . K fuckin O.[3] [*Yells out window*] Fuuuuuuck.

[SANDY *enters.*]

SANDY Would you shut it?

JOE [*singing*] "I gotta get out of this place."

SANDY Why don't ya then ya big pig.

JOE I told ya woman don't go callin me pig in public. Jeez she got an ugly mouth, eh?

SANDY You're shitfaced, Joe, go on and pass out.

JOE You make me wanta piss my pants.

SANDY Just go on makin a fool of yourself.

JOE Down woman, me and my pal Al is gonna head up to Horny Tim's and we're gonna pick us up some taileroooonie! Then we're gonna go on over to the quarry and we're gonna get ourselves sucked and fucked

SANDY You're not proud, are ya.

[JOE *bumps into something, falls.* SANDY *starts to pick him up.*]

JOE You never fooled around on me, did ya?

SANDY Nope. I never . . . did.

JOE [*sings*] "She's a hooo-o-o-o-nky tonk womannnn gimme [*Goes to bedroom.*] gimme gimme the [*Fading*] honky tonk wom . . ."[4]

[ALAN *goes to the window and silently mouths "Fuuuuck," in imitation of* JOE. *He turns on TV, crouches on sofa, and sings softly, but can't remember the whole song.*]

ALAN Nobody—nobody here—but us chickens, nobody here but us guys don't—don't bother me we got work—to do we got stuff to do and eggs to lay—we're busy—chickens[5]—[*He pretends to be a car, makes sounds, mimes a steering wheel.*] Neeowwwwwwwwwwww. Whaaaaaa. Fhrhuuummmm. Atta girl.

3. That is, Kingston, Ontario.
4. A paraphrase of the Rolling Stones song "Honky Tonk Woman" (1969).
5. A paraphrase of the rhythm-and-blues song "Ain't Nobody Here But Us Chickens" (1946; written by Alex Kramer and Joan Whitney).

1.7

[Later, SANDY *brings in bedding to sleep on sofa, turns on lamp, turns off TV, lights cigarette, sits on sofa.]*

SANDY He pukes all over the fuckin bed.

ALAN Oooh shit.

SANDY Funny.

ALAN I'm—I'm sorry Sandy I didn't mean to laugh at ya.

SANDY Can I ask you a personal question?

ALAN Yeah, yeah sure—what?

SANDY Am I gettin ugly lookin?

ALAN What?

SANDY You know, mean lookin, uglier lookin.

ALAN Shit no, jeez—you—you look nice I think ya do! Who, who said that?

SANDY No one. Are ya sure?

ALAN Sure, sure I am you're a good looker I even heard people say ya was.

SANDY Who, who said that?

ALAN Alf. Alf said ya was.

SANDY His folks are loaded.

ALAN I know!

SANDY Did—did Joe ever say anything?

ALAN Joe? What about?

SANDY About me gettin ugly, *arsewipe*.

ALAN No, no Joe never said nothin.

SANDY Are ya sure?

ALAN Yeah. Yeah he never—he never said nothin! No! Why?

SANDY None of your business.

ALAN What's buggin you, you got your pains?

SANDY No, I don't got my *pains* but I'm gonna get em if youse—if youse—well—no offence or nothin but when are youse gettin outa here anyways?

ALAN Soon as I get up the money I—wh—why is—is it buggin you me and Trese sleepin over?

SANDY Yeah. Yeah, it is it's—it's me and Joe gotta have—have some privacy, ya know? Ya know?

ALAN Yeah. Yeah I do I—I'll be out soon what can I say, we'll be out as soon as I got the cash.

SANDY I never heard of screwin your girlfriend on your buddy's floor.

ALAN I'll be out as soon as I got the cash, okay?

SANDY It's just strange you goin with Trese on our floor.

ALAN I know it's strange I know I'm strange I'm strange okay?

SANDY I know you're fuckin strange all right.

ALAN You're smokin too much. You're smokin too much.

SANDY Look who's talkin.

ALAN Well at least I know I'm doin it you don't even know. [*Takes drag off cigarette.*]

SANDY You're fuckin nuts, you know that, nuts.

ALAN I may be nuts but I fuckin know what I'm doin. I know I'm killin myself smokin these I know it so I'm throwin them away okay? I'm throwin them away!

[ALAN *rips up his cigarettes and takes* SANDY'*s cigarette out of her mouth.*]

Fuckin killsticks!

SANDY [*tries to stop him*] Stop it you—fuckin don't you touch me—you fucker you give me back the cash for those right now right now hear?

ALAN No! No Sandy I can't I don't have the money I gotta save it so I can fuck off outa this *hole* I don't have money okay??

SANDY [*starts to back out the door shaking head*] You're nuts Al—

ALAN [*grabs her back into the room*] I am not nuts. I am not nuts you understand? I just decided now I'm gonna quit smoking that's all. I got a flash in my head of my old man tryin to take his breath tryin to find the fuckin air and not gettin it fuckin all hunched over so's he wouldn't drown to death his his his feet all puffed all that shit all that shit comin out of his mouth and they wouldn't even clean it cause they said he couldn't get nothin cause he was gonna die so he had all this shit comin out of his mouth and and I know he didn't like it cause he was clean—all the *time* he was washin—and then when he's dyin they don't give a shit about his goddamn mouth with all the fuck comin out of it and they got a goddamn vacuum cleaner goin—we can't hear nothin and he keeps sort of movin forward movin ahead in his chair like when you're tryin not to crash out at the show so ya keep movin forward? He didn't want to go he didn't want to go at all and he went cause of these. Cause of these goddamn ugly white killsticks these! [*Shows her cigarette, lets her go.*] See? See why ya can't smoke? See?

SANDY [*very moved by* ALAN*'s speech; speaks quietly*] I don't know who the fuck you think you are tearin up the place just cause you seen your old man fuckin croak.

ALAN You don't know what it's like, man, you don't know what it's like till you been there don't you talk.

SANDY Don't tell me what I know, arsewipe, don't you tell me nothin. I seen my mum go, I sat by her bed for three fuckin months and I don't go carryin on like a three-year-old.

ALAN It wasn't the same I'm tellin ya it couldna been the same.

SANDY And I'm a woman and I don't go cryin about it I never cried about it once.

ALAN I'm not cryin about it I never cried about it I'm just tellin ya why not to smoke.

SANDY You're just tellin me shit. Jeez if Joe seen you just now he'd think you were some kind of fag.

ALAN I'm not a fag that's one thing I'm not I'm not a fag.

SANDY Then start acting like a fuckin man.

ALAN I'm not a fag you take that back.

SANDY I'm not takin nothin back for no baby.

ALAN I said take that back you ugly bitch.

[ALAN *grabs her.* SANDY *throws him to the floor.*]

SANDY You're sad, you know that? You don't scare nobody.

ALAN I'm no fag.

SANDY [*goes back to lie on couch*] I seen ten-year-olds fight better than you.

ALAN Why?

SANDY Why what?

ALAN Why don't I scare nobody?

SANDY Cause you're a wimp that's why. Like one of them dogs that starts shakin when ya go to pat it.

ALAN How come?
SANDY How am I supposed to know?
ALAN Don't say nothin to Joe, eh?
SANDY What, about takin a fit?
ALAN About you thinkin I'm like one of them dogs.
SANDY I won't.
ALAN Or Trese.
SANDY Don't worry about it.
ALAN You watched your mum go?
SANDY Big deal.
ALAN Couldna been the same.
SANDY It's all the same.
ALAN Don't you feel nothin?
SANDY Well I'm not a baby like you.
ALAN No.
SANDY Anyways, bein dead ain't no different from livin anyway.
ALAN How do you know?
SANDY I just know. It's just like movin to Brockville or Oshawa[6] or somethin. It ain't that different.
ALAN Oh no. Oh no you're wrong I think you're wrong there.
SANDY No I'm not.
ALAN Yes you are.
SANDY You don't know shit Al.
ALAN I do I do know some things and I know that. I know it's different.
SANDY Get out of my house.
ALAN I'm goin I didn't want to stay anyways it *smells* funny in here.
SANDY Garbage stinks up a place.
ALAN And Sandy.
SANDY *What.*
ALAN No offence or nothin, but you—you—are—you are gettin ugly lookin.

[SANDY *looks at him.*]

See ya.

1.8

[JOE, SANDY, ALAN, THERESA *sitting in bar. Otis Redding's "I've Been Loving You Too Long"*[7] *is playing.*]

JOE That's a shit-hot tune. Too bad he died.
ALAN Did he die?
JOE That's right. In a fuckin motel.
ALAN That's too bad.
JOE Too bad Jimi Hendrix died too.
ALAN Yeah. Oh *yeah.* [*Sings, drums*] "Scuse me while I kiss the sky!"[8]

6. A town and a city, respectively, in southeast Ontario.
7. A hit song (1965) written by Jerry Butler and Otis Redding (1941–1967), an American soul singer; he died in a plane crash.
8. A line from the song "Purple Haze" (1966), by Jimi Hendrix (1942–1970), an American rock song writer and guitarist; he died of a drug overdose.

JOE Did youse know if Hendrix hadda lived he was gonna join up with ELP?

SANDY I seen them, Emerson, Lake and Palmer,[9] down in Montreal.

JOE Ya know what they woulda, been called if Hendrix hadda joined up with them?

ALAN Hendrix, and . . .

JOE [*spells it out*] H.E.L.P. *Help*. And you fuckin would need help hearin those two play together.

ALAN Fuck would ya ever.

JOE Fuckin straight.

ALAN Would ya ever. Fuck, your brain'd die.

JOE H.E.L.P. *Help*.

THERESA I wouldn't need no help.

SANDY You don't got no ear for music.

THERESA I do so.

ALAN She sings and that all the time.

THERESA I seen Jerry uptown he got a job workin for Wilmot's.

SANDY That right eh.

JOE Splinter what a cocksuck.

[*Restless,* JOE *goes to the jukebox, presses button.* JOE *walks to the urinal. After a moment,* ALAN *follows.*]

THERESA He be workin with all that ice cream all the time.

[*Pause.*]

SANDY He could hardly munch out.

THERESA I love ice cream.

SANDY Just munch right out.

1.9

[JOE *and* ALAN. *In urinal of bar.*]

ALAN Those two guys together. Geez! [*Shaking head in disbelief*]

JOE I'm goin buddy I'm takin off.

ALAN Where ya goin?

JOE That's for me to know.

ALAN Oh. Sorry. How—how come gettin sick of Kingston?

JOE Got me a job drivin a Cat.

ALAN Jeez. You make a lot of cash doin that.

JOE Nice work if you can get it.

ALAN Nice work if you can get it.

JOE Make a shitload of money.

ALAN That's hard to do, drivin one of them things, ain't it?

JOE They're mother fuckers.

ALAN Jeez fuck where'd ya learn how to do that anyways?

JOE Hymie Beach.[1]

ALAN WOW, I never knew that. You live down there?

9. An English rock group, popular in the 1970s, consisting of Keith Emerson (b. 1944), Greg Lake (b. 1948), and Carl Palmer (b. 1950).

1. A derogatory reference to Miami Beach, Florida; *hymie* is an offensive term for a Jew.

JOE Sure, shared a motel room with this creep who later turned out to be a queer boy. Started sayin stuff about my dink and that when I got out of the shower. "Is it always that long?"

ALAN Fuckin queers.

JOE I know.

ALAN They just make me—feel like pukin—

JOE I sent that one through the fuckin wall.

ALAN Did ya?

JOE Fuckin right.

ALAN I hate em.

[*Pause.*]

JOE Don't say nothin to Sandy.

ALAN Don't she know?

[JOE *shakes his head.*]

What if something happens—she gets cancer or somethin?

JOE What?

ALAN Them things happen, I've heard of them.

JOE . . . I'll let ya know where I am.

ALAN Hey—I'd like to do that kind of shit.

JOE You should come out. You could get on a site dry-wallin or somethin.

ALAN They just take anybody?

JOE Sure.

ALAN No, no way.

JOE Suit yourself.

ALAN Hey—I forgot to tell ya, Cathy Yachuk jumped offa the Brock Towers![2]

JOE What?

ALAN Jumped right onto her feet Martin was sayin, fucked em up so bad they hadda take a piece of her bum and glue it on to her f-f-feet—so's she could walk on them.

JOE How come she done that?

ALAN She seen a white light in front of her, tellin her!

JOE Fuckin whore . . . yuh, I'm gettin right out of this hole.

ALAN You comin back ever?

JOE How'm I sposda know?

1.10

[ALAN *on way to work, stumbles out door. There is an Indian* MAN *on the street, his wrists bleeding heavily. He is ambling past* ALAN. *He is very drunk.*]

ALAN Hey buddy—hey can I do something for ya?

MAN [*drunk, mumbling*] Please . . .

ALAN Hey, want a smoke?

MAN Yeah. Give me a smoke.

ALAN What are ya lookin for man?

MAN Fuckers took it fuckers.

ALAN Who? Did somebody jump ya? Eh? Did somebody jump ya?

2. A high-rise apartment complex in Scarborough (now a district of Toronto), Ontario.

MAN Yaah. Some guys. Buncha Indians—fuckin Indians.

ALAN Hey man you're an Indian aren't ya?

MAN [*giggling*] Don't burn the fish bones! Don't burn the fish bones!

ALAN That's okay man my fiancee she's Indian. Therese. I like Indians it's okay.

MAN [*weeping like a girl*] Stupid fuckin Indians.

ALAN Hey. Hey don't cry. Is it hurtin bad? Please—just stay here—I'll call an ambulance. Stay. [*Starts to walk to phone, holds up hand.*] Stay.

MAN [*sits up, screams a death scream*] Aaaahh!

[ALAN *comes back, takes off his own shirt, ties it around the* MAN's *wrist to stop the bleeding. The* MAN *sees a vision.*]

Devil-baby-eyes-devil-baby-eyes. Please. Please. Mercy. Mercy. Hand. Gimme your hand. Hand. Please.

ALAN What? You want me to hold your hand? Okay.

[MAN *takes* ALAN's *hand, starts rubbing it in a sexual way.* ALAN *doesn't know what to do.*]

MAN [*urgently*] Hey. Hey. Hey.

ALAN What, what is it, buddy?

MAN Hey. [*Makes intercourse motion with fingers.*] Let's tear off a piece. Come on let's tear off a piece. Rip off a piece. Come on.

ALAN Stupid cocksuker!

[ALAN *flings* MAN *away, but* MAN *clings to his leg.*]

Get off me you fucker! Get offfffffff me! [*He runs.*]

MAN [*lies on street, giggling*] Pleeeease. [Giggles.]

[ALAN *jumps back to* SANDY's *living room where* THERESA *is asleep at his feet.*]

ALAN [*yells*] Dieeeeeeeeeee!

1.11

[*It is the middle of the night.*]

ALAN Therese?

THERESA Yeah?

ALAN Do you ever start thinkin ugly thoughts before ya go to sleep?

THERESA No, do you?

ALAN Yeah.

THERESA Like what?

ALAN Like fallin down and your teeth hittin the sidewalk.

THERESA Ewwwww.

ALAN Sometimes I even think of someone takin out my spine, like they do with a shrimp.

THERESA You crazy stupid-face, go sleepin and think of nice stuff.

ALAN Like what.

THERESA Donuts and the Wolfe Island ferry and that. Stuff like that.

ALAN Huh. I love ya Trese.

THERESA Madonna.

2.1

ALAN Did you ever start thinkin somethin, and it's like ugly . . . ? And ya can't beat it out of your head? I wouldn't be scared of it if it was sittin in front of me, I'd beat it to shit—nothin wouldn't stop me—but I can't beat it cause it's in my head fuck. It's not like bein crazy, it's just like thinkin one thing over and over and it kinda makes ya sick. Like when I was a kid and I used to have these earaches all the time, you know? And I would keep thinkin it was like a couple of garter snakes with big ugly teeth all yellow, like an *old* guy's teeth and there they were the two of them suckin and bitin on my eardrum with these yellow teeth. Makin noises like a cat eatin cat food. I could even hear the fuckin noises. [*Makes the noise.*] Like that. Just made me wanta puke thinkin that—made the pain worse I'd think of their eyes, too, that made me sick, black eyes lookin sideways all the time while they keep suckin and chewin on my eardrum. Fuck. Do youse know what I mean? No offense or nothin I don't mean no offense I wish youse all good luck in your lives. I was just—like I just wanted to know if any of youse like knew of a medicine or somethin ya might take for this—they gotta have somethin cause the one I'm thinkin of now is even worse it's fuckin bad it's it's somethin Bonnie Cain told me about this nurse she knows goin out to Enterprise out to one of the farms out there these folks were on the dole[3] so she goes up to see if the kids got colds and that, and the wife, all small with her teeth all black takes her into the warsh room and tells her she got somethin wrong down in her woman's part. And Bonnie said this nurse lifted up this woman's skirt and you know what she seen? Like a cauliflower growin out of her thing! A cauliflower! Fuck! And ya know the worst part of it? When ya cut it it bleeds! It grows blood and that! It just happened last summer too, last fuckin summer in July! . . . How'd she go—like how'd she pee? Fuck I'll be doin the dishes where I'm workin down the Tropicana there and it's like pictures burning holes in my brain I try all the time to like put other pictures over top of that, nice things that I really get off on, eh, that I really like like—like lambs in a field, you know, with the black on their faces? Like baby sheep? I always liked them whenever I seen one in a field or someplace I always laughed at them so stupid lookin and cute fuck—I never told the other guys they were there case they burn them or something. Anyways I try puttin pictures of these baby sheep over top of the cauliflower and I'll do it and it's okay for a second then the lamb its eyes'll go all funny like slits lookin sideways just like them snakes and then it'll open its mouth and there'll be them long sharp teeth and a bunch of worms inside and the nice little sheep goes all ugly on me and the cauliflower comes back worse than ever like it ate the sheep or somethin. . . . Maybe if I could just have a car or get back to workin on cars, you know? Or get into Dragmasters,[4] then maybe I'd stop thinkin of these things. I don't know. I'm lookin for somebody who knows, that's why I'm askin youse I don't know. I wish I did. [*Pause*] If it was in front of me I'd beat it to shit, you know?

3. On public assistance or welfare. *Enterprise*: a small town northwest of Kingston.

4. A club devoted to racing motorcycles (especially Harley-Davidsons).

2.2

[ALAN *and* THERESA *at home.* ALAN *comes in after work.* THERESA *is watching television, laughing.*]

ALAN Did ya do it did ya get it done?

THERESA You got somethin on your mouth Al.

ALAN [*wipes*] What was it?

THERESA Look like cream from one of them Joe Louis.[5]

ALAN What I got on my face don't matter, Trese, I asked ya a question.

THERESA What?

ALAN Did ya get what I told ya done?

THERESA Readin writin?

ALAN Yes.

THERESA Shhhh baby sleepin Al.

ALAN Did—let's see. Awwwww hey Danny! He's not sleepin! Hey ya little bugger how ya doin—this is your dad—this is your dad speakin, ya know me? Hey? He does, he knows me. Don't ya Danny. Hey Danny did your angel mummy do what daddy asked her to? Eh? Yes? She did? Oh thank you Danny you are the most neatest cutest little baby boy—what's that on his chin?

THERESA From eatin milk.

ALAN Theresa you don't *eat* milk you drink it.

THERESA I know.

ALAN There. Wipe that ugly milk offa ya. Eh Danny? You are my little bugger and I'm your daddy! Hey! Your mummy gonna show me what she done! Okay mummy, now show me what ya done.

THERESA I lost it.

ALAN How could you lose it?

THERESA I done it, Al, but I lost it.

ALAN *Theresa.* Theresa I'm gonna try not to get mad at ya but ya can't keep doin this to me! Every day you're tellin me ya lost your homework!

THERESA Maybe someone take it.

ALAN Theresa don't you understand I am tryin to improve my family.

THERESA [*coyly*] Al.

ALAN What.

THERESA [*delighted*] You shoulda seen the pooh I done today it was hardly long!

ALAN Theresa, married ladies with babies ain't supposed to say things like that!

THERESA Sorry.

ALAN Danny could hear ya ya know.

THERESA I don't think he hear Al I think he deaf.

ALAN What?

THERESA I shoutin in his ear he don't do nothin.

ALAN Trese ya don't go shoutin in babies' ears!

[THERESA *kisses* ALAN. *He melts.*]

THERESA I love ya Al.

5. A Canadian packaged snack cake.

ALAN You know I love you don't ya you know it—more than anything in this whole world you and Danny boy.

THERESA I know Al. How many dishes you done today?

ALAN Two hundred and twenty-three.

THERESA Jeez.

ALAN Yup. That's ten more than yesterday.

THERESA Jeez.

2.3

[**THERESA** *has been sleeping over at* **SANDY**'s *because* **SANDY** *is scared. Cat scream.*]

SANDY What's that noise. Trese wake up. Hear that?

THERESA What?

SANDY Listen—oh Jesus what is it?

THERESA Maybe it Charlie Manson.[6]

SANDY Oh shut up you watch too much TV.

THERESA Maybe it a pussy cat.

SANDY Hello? Hello? Anybody there? Trese hand me somethin. The lamp.

THERESA Why?

SANDY Shut your mouth and don't ask questions.

THERESA Okay okay here.

SANDY Okay. You get the knife from the top drawer just in case he comes in here.

THERESA Who Charlie Manson.

SANDY Don't say that name Trese. Scream if anybody comes . . .

THERESA I will Sanny.

[**SANDY** *goes to other room. She screams a primal scream.*]

SANDY [*returns*] It was nothin.

THERESA How come?

SANDY Cause.

THERESA How come my baby never smilin?

SANDY Are ya doin what the workers tell ya?

THERESA Al do it he don't let me do nothin.

SANDY Why?

THERESA He smarter.

SANDY I guess so.

THERESA He love Danny. He wash him with soap and he feed him and he huggin him.

SANDY What's he feedin him.

THERESA Bologna.

SANDY At four months?

THERESA He love it.

SANDY Oh Christ. Don't ya have baby food.

THERESA I don't know.

SANDY What am I gonna do with you?

THERESA I'm glad I stayin here. Al cryin nights.

6. An American cult leader (b. 1934); he led his "family" in committing multiple murders in 1969 and was sentenced to death (later commuted to life in prison) in 1971.

SANDY How come?

THERESA I don't know. I tell him nothin's wrong everything fine but he keep cryin.

SANDY Trese do ya think Joe'll come back?

THERESA He proly comin back next Friday.

SANDY If he do, he can go to hell.

THERESA Bonnie Cain say he never comin back.

SANDY She did?

THERESA She don't know nothin. He comin back.

SANDY I got a letter.

THERESA Ya did?

SANDY I burnt it though, didn't read it.

THERESA Sandy you depress?

SANDY No. I just don't like stayin alone nights it ain't good for ya.

THERESA You could come stayin with us.

SANDY Uh uh. No way. I don't want to see no baby eatin bologna.

THERESA Oh.

SANDY You get in some baby food, Trese, or I'm reporting ya to the social worker.

THERESA Okay.

SANDY Okay?

THERESA I'm gonna.

SANDY You go on to sleep. Now.

THERESA Night Sandy. Don't go havin no bad dreams.

SANDY Night.

[THERESA *falls asleep instantly.* SANDY *stays awake, staring out.*]

2.4

[ALAN *has just been fired from his dishwashing job. He is thrown out of a door, real or imaginary, onto a busy street. He has stolen an egg, which he carries in his hand.*]

ALAN [*holding up egg as pointer*] I was quittin anyways, ya bastards, there's white worms in the hamburg, I *seen* em, there's white worms in the hamburg! [*More quietly, to himself*] I seen em wiggle—[*Turning to audience, in threatening tones*] There wasn't no egg on that pan, sir, there wasn't no egg on that frypan.

[ALAN *stares at the audience for a moment, gets the idea to throw the egg at the door and turns very slowly towards door. Then in a flash, starts to throw the egg but instead, cracks it over his head. He puts the shell in his pocket, sees somebody in the distance, sticks down his hair, leans onto the sewer and discovers the Indian* MAN *with a bottle.* ALAN *grabs it and takes a sip.*]

MAN Man, who is standing between two girly-girls in the whirly-burl.

ALAN Oh why don't ya just shut up . . .

MAN [*pointing at constellation in the sky*] Double devil—stuck together—cha cha cha!

[JOE *appears, wearing a new coat and a hat that says "SUCCESS."* ALAN *rushes to greet him. By the end of the scene, they reach the entrance to* SANDY'*s apartment.*]

ALAN Jesus Joe! Joe! Hey Joe, how're ya doin?

JOE Hey buddy how are you?

ALAN Okay, you know, hangin on. You—when did ya get back?

JOE Just now, buddy, but not for long. I'm moving Sandy out there with me.

ALAN No kidding? It's pretty good out there?

JOE It's a great place, man, lots of work, nice people. Hell of a lot better than this hole, I'm tellin you.

ALAN Yeah? Does Sandy know you're back?

JOE Nope. I'm gonna surprise her. She'll be happy as hell to see me. Then the two of us are gonna take right off.

ALAN That right? . . . Hey me and Theresa got a kid—a little boy, Danny.

JOE Is that right? Danny, huh? So how do you like bein a father?

ALAN It's all right, man. I like it. I make a good father I guess.

JOE Yeah? . . . Well, I better head off.

ALAN Hey—Joe—I got somethin to tell ya.

JOE Is this a long story or a short one?

ALAN Not too long—d'ju hear about Boyd's GTO?[7]

JOE What the one that used to be parked on Johnson below Division?

ALAN Yeah, you know, green with chrome mags and chrome cut-outs.[8]

JOE Yeah. What a fuckin beast. What about it?

ALAN He totalled it.

JOE Hah. Well it was a shitty-lookin car anyways.

ALAN Yeah but fuck it had—it had them high lift cam solid lifters, and, and high compression kit and—

JOE You name it.

ALAN He had it. Yup. Hey—did you know it had four fuckin carbs?[9]

JOE Eat shit.

ALAN No kiddin, four! But you know how come he kept it lookin so shitty?

JOE Beats me.

ALAN So the cops wouldn't notice. They all knew, though eh, they knew what he had. Fuck that thing was fast he used to shoot the main drag doin one-fifty.

JOE Yeah? That's fast.

ALAN Fuckin fast. You know how he totalled it?

JOE No.

ALAN Fuck it was funny. We were gettin polluted up at the Manor, eh, and Alfie decides he's gonna go up to Gan. He was about half pissed I guess. So parently he tries to pass three or four cars same time except one of em happens to be a truck goin left. So I guess he almost makes it but the truck catches him by his back right fender and spins him. Huh. Flipped the car six fuckin times.

JOE Jeez. How is he?

ALAN Alfie? He's okay now but he got stabbed in the heart with the rearview mirror. Had an operation.

7. A Pontiac high-performance V-8 coupe (often considered the first "muscle car"), originally built from 1964 to 1974.

8. Magnesium alloy wheels and chrome ornaments.

9. Although most cars have only one carburetor, it was not unusual for high-performance V-8 engines to have four.

JOE That right?

ALAN Chuck was with him and—

JOE The Scotty?

ALAN Yeah and he just jumped out and never even had a scratch on him. What's that a present for the wife?

JOE Yeah. That Charlie perfume[1] shit.

ALAN Hardly nice. Yeah, that's nice stuff. Women—they like that kinda stuff.

JOE I know. Smells shitty to me.

ALAN Yeah.

JOE Well I gotta move buddy catch you later.

ALAN Hey! Hey!

[*From his pocket,* ALAN *takes an ornamental iron monk with a hard-on It is wrapped in newspaper.*]

Here.

JOE What's this?

ALAN Just somethin.

JOE Oh yeah. I seen one of these. Well I'm gone.

ALAN See ya. . . . Bye Joe!

2.5

[SANDY *and* JOE *seated at a table.*]

SANDY I got a fucking hole in my gut cause of you.

JOE Who told ya that.

SANDY Doctor Scott.

JOE He don't know what he's talking about.

SANDY Hurtin me all the time I had pain.

JOE Not no more. Not no more ya won't.

SANDY I was takin pills even—prescription!

JOE I told ya babe I feel bad.

SANDY I never done nothin to you *why??*

JOE Ewwww Christ I missed your body there was times I wanted ya so bad I could taste ya. I'd lie in bed there and think about you and what ya looked like stripped naked, think about your nice titties.

SANDY Two old bags.

JOE *Nothin* them are peaches.

SANDY Bullshit. I'm not goin back with ya.

JOE Yes you are.

SANDY Can't push me around no more.

JOE Come on just try it a couple weeks if ya don't like it you can fuck off.

SANDY Won't be nothin different.

JOE It's gotta be different.

SANDY It'll be the same as before, beatin up on me.

JOE No way.

SANDY How the fuck do I know?

JOE Cause it's fuckin true that's how.

1. A perfume made by Revlon, introduced in 1973 and marketed to working women.

SANDY I hate you. I hated you all the time you was gone.

JOE I know.

SANDY I woulda laughed if you hadda died.

JOE I never did.

SANDY I know.

JOE So.

[*Pause.*]

SANDY How come ya want me back.

JOE Don't know. It's dog shit when you're gone.

SANDY Then why'd ya stay so long.

JOE Shit Sandy.

SANDY I was up nights shakin.

JOE Scared of the crackwalker[2] were ya?

SANDY He never hurt nobody.

JOE I missed makin it with ya. Did ya miss it with me?

SANDY I didn't have no one.

JOE That's cause you're mine.

SANDY Is that right.

JOE [*opens her gift*] Here. Smell that.

SANDY Hmmn.

JOE You told me you like that shit.

SANDY It's okay.

JOE Soooo. You been workin for Nikos?

SANDY Some.

JOE What else you been doin?

SANDY Learned how to make a new drink.

JOE What, rum and Coke?

SANDY That's not new.

JOE What, dough brain.

SANDY A Dirty Mother, asshole.

JOE A dirty mother asshole, what's that?

SANDY A Dirty Mother! It's tequila, crème de cacao, and milk. It's hardly good.

JOE Sounds like a chocky milkshake from Mexico.

SANDY Arsewipe. I got a batch made up in the fridge, you want one?

JOE Yeah, okay. I'll try one. Gimme a beer with it though.

SANDY [*goes to the kitchen; from kitchen*] You should give Al a call he's in a bad way.

JOE Yeah I seen him he looked like shit.

SANDY They got a kid, Danny.

JOE He was tellin me.

SANDY It's a medical retard.

JOE Fuuuuck.

SANDY It don't ever move its face—like a doll.

JOE See this thing he give me?

SANDY What is it?

JOE I don't know. An iron monk with a hard-on?

2. An allusion to a resident of Kingston known for his obsessive avoidance of sidewalk cracks (see the introduction to this play).

SANDY Jeez where'd he get that, up at Van's?

JOE I guess so. [SANDY *brings in tray.*] Well fuckin jumpqueen, eh, where'd ya get them glasses?

SANDY My girlfriend Gail she scoffed[3] em offa the 401 Inn.

JOE Fuckin eh.

SANDY They'd cost ya, ya know.

JOE Hmmm. That's, ahhh that's a shit-hot drink.

SANDY Me and Gail drink it all the time when we go out.

JOE It's not bad.

SANDY We always order it only none of em knows how to make it so we have to tell them.

JOE Yeah?

SANDY I can make any kind of drink now she taught me.

JOE What're you doin two women goin drinkin alone together.

SANDY Who said we were alone?

JOE Come here.

SANDY Joe it ain't like that no more.

JOE Who said it ain't.

SANDY I did. Keep your paws offa me.

JOE Jeez you're lookin good.

SANDY I'm doin my eyeliner different.

JOE Yeah?

SANDY Makes my eyes look bigger.

JOE Nice.

SANDY I know.

2.6

[ALAN *and* THERESA'S *place.* THERESA *is playing with the baby. There are tea things set out. The baby does not respond to anything.*]

THERESA Beebeebeebee. . . . How come you not drinkin your tea, beebee? You got a bad cold? Poor beebee. [*Singing*] My little baby is my baby my little Danny is my angel baby I take care of him, and he don't cry or nothin and he ain't never gonna have the crib death neither—[*Speaking*] No way Danny, cause I love ya. Al loves ya too but he a bastard sometime I know he don't talk nice in front of you sometime—don't you go goin into one of them deep sleeps beebee—no—hey! Hey baby Danny! Wake up cause that's how them other babies got the crib death! From sleepin too deep! S'true! You darlin little baby! You mine! That sosha worker's hardly nice, eh? Look! [*Dangles Joe Louis wrapper in front of Danny.*] Look at that baby, you like that? Eh? It's hardly pretty! You come on, come on, gimme a smile beebee; you thinkin too much just like Al that why you so serious all the time. Ohhhhh baby [*She rocks him.*] so soff. Skin hardly soff. Hey! I, look like that madonna lady and she holdin baby Jesus just like I holdin you so you mus look like Jesus! Baby Jesus! Oooohhh Danny you my beebee Jesus and I the Madonna lady and Al maybe he Joseph, he make stuff outa wood. You like a little horsey made outa wood carry you down Princess Street

3. Stole.

when we go to the S & R?[4] I love ya beebee. That a little smile? Oh! Oh baby baby Jesus I love Ya!

ALAN [*comes blasting through the door, starts tearing up the place—medicines, creams, clothes, everything*] No fuckin social worker's gonna fuckin tell me how to run my fuckin life! I don't take this fuckin shit from nobody! Nobody don't tell me what to do and nobody don't tell me how to take care of my baby never! That means you too you fuckin woman—I'm not takin any shit from you neither! There. We're not using any of their cocksucking medicine—they'll try to kill you with it!

THERESA Al! Al stop it!

ALAN They did they killed my dad with all their fuckin medicine! He didn't have no hair and he didn't have no flesh just bones all over and ugly and yellow. No way Therese no way you could stop me I'm throwin it all fuckin out! Out the window, watch! There! It's out the window! Danny! Hey Danny my boy my own son see? You don't have to be takin any of that ugly tastin shit no more!

THERESA But he gonna get numona[5] if he don't take his medicine doctor say so! Nurse say he hafta take it three time a day or he gettin worse! Doctor sees you done that he won't give us no more medicine for Danny! You bassard! You bassard! [*She hits him.*]

ALAN Arsewipe! Don't you know nothin? Don't you know them doctors make money offa sick babies? That's why they like to keep em sick with all them medicines! So they make more fuckin money!

THERESA I don't believe ya. Doctors are nice they wouldn't go makin babies sick!

ALAN Jeez you're a dumbrain sometimes, Therese, they don't give a fuck about our fuckin baby so long as they get their TVs and golf clubs and that. They care dick! That's why they give em this poison so the baby stay sick!

THERESA It not poison, it good for ya, the nurse say so! She don't even have no TV, she tole me. So you're crazy I know that stuff good for Danny he gettin better already!

ALAN That baby ain't gettin no better you stupid woman you know it ain't. It looks strange. It don't look right and that's cause they're givin it all them fuckin medicines! Fuck them! So no more!

THERESA Really would them doctors do that? Really?

ALAN Fuckin right they would. Bastards.

THERESA Bastards. How come? How come they hurtin my little baby?

ALAN Money. Money and bucks. Cocksuckers.

THERESA Well what we gonna do about all his snifflin and that?

ALAN Well I know what to do the social worker even said I did. He said I was a great father and you even heard him. I was a great father.

THERESA S'true Alan.

ALAN Well, it got a cold, right? So if ya got a cold, ya gotta get warm, what else? It's fuckin simple and them doctors always do everything to make it harder! Fuck! So all we do, is ahh—turn on the oven! It's easy! Here. Put it to about five hundred—there—and open the door like that—and—now bring him over—

4. A hardware store on Princess Street in Kingston.

5. Pneumonia.

THERESA Why? What you gonna do?

ALAN Just bring the baby over, Trese. Do what I tell ya!

THERESA Al you not cooking the baby, are ya? [*Weeping with confusion*]

ALAN [*laughs*] Huh. Wait'll I tell Joe that he'll laugh. Cookin the baby. Right. Jesus arsehole it's just like at the farm back in Picton[6] when mum used to sit by the stove with Ronny to warm him up that's all! It's easy! If a guy's got a cold, warm him up!

THERESA Oh. Don't make it too hot though.

ALAN Keep out of it, woman. [*Places crib as close to stove as he can get it.*] There. There ya go Danny! How you doin anyway you little bugger—that's right it's your daddy he come to make you better! Getcha away from all them fuckin doctors! That's right.

THERESA Al he's coughin! Cant we get back some of that cough syrup?

ALAN Listen stupid we're not usin any of that stuff I told ya! Didn't ya hear me or what? Listen. If he's coughin we'll just get that Vicks vapour rub[7] that my old man used to use.

THERESA That stuff smell too much!

ALAN If it's good enough for my old man it's good enough for my baby Therese. He used to put it all over his chest and his cough be gone the next day. Here.

[*He puts a whole jar of Vicks over the baby's body.*]

THERESA Al you puttin too much!

ALAN Don't tell me what to do! Shut up! I know what I'm doin I told ya the social worker said I was a great father! So shut up!

[*He holds the baby up. It is glistening with the stuff.*]

There. You're gonna be just fine now baby.

THERESA Al you sure it ain't too much?

ALAN Shhhhh. He's goin to sleep. Come here. I got somethin for ya.

THERESA You did? What'dja get donuts?

ALAN [*opens perfume—orange, cheap, and it has broken in the package*] Shit. It broke on me. It's okay though here I'll put it in a glass. [*He does so.*] There. [*Hands it to her.*]

THERESA Smell that. That's hardly beautiful Al. Thank you I love perfume.

ALAN I know ya do. Ya like it?

THERESA I love it. It hardly smells nice.

ALAN [*caresses her*] Guess why I brung it?

THERESA Why?

ALAN I love you and you're my angel madonna.

THERESA A-l-l-l-l-l.

ALAN It's true. Come here angel. Hey. Eh hey. You know I love makin love to ya. I love fuckin you and chewin ya out. [*Whispers*] I do.

THERESA I know.

[ALAN *starts to undress her. They start necking on the floor next to the baby.* THERESA *stops suddenly.*]

Oh oh.

6. A small town in southeast Ontario, about 40 miles from Kingston.

7. Vicks VapoRub, a topical analgesic and cough suppressant.

ALAN What?

THERESA We can't do it Al.

ALAN Don't matter if you're bleedin.

THERESA No I can't do it till I get my new IUD in. Or I get pregnant again doctor say so!

ALAN Fuck the goddamn doctors! Goddamn doctors trying to run my life saying I can't make love to my own woman to my own wife fuck em fuck em. I don't care if you get pregnant we're gonna do it when we want and no doctor's gonna tell us nothin.

THERESA No! No Alan, please! Get off me you bastard we're not doin it today no way! No! Get offa me or I callin the cops.

ALAN [*he hits her, sends her across the room*] You stupid dumb cunt Indian bitch face fat fat retarded whore. I don't want ya anyways! [*He collapses on floor, now meeker, almost whiny.*] Alls I wanted was a little lovin anyways there's nothin wrong with that? A man is sposda get lovin from his woman ain't he? That is how come ya get married, ain't it? All I wanted was a little lovin that's all . . . that's alllll.

[*The baby is crying.*]

Look what you done woman you makin the baby cry! You stupid bitch!

[THERESA *gets up to go to the baby.*]

No! No you stay down I'm the only one who can make him stop cryin. Watch. Hey baby. Hey baby here's your daddy. He's a great daddy, huh? Eh?

[*The baby is screaming.*]

THERESA Take it away from the stove Alan! Take it away from the stove!

ALAN [*to* THERESA] Shhhhh. [*To baby*] Come on baby stop that cryin daddy don't like it when you cryin! Shhhh. Now shhhhhh. Gonna buy you a car when you get older—what kind you want, a Monte Carlo?[8] Okay. I'm gonna get you a Monte Carlo. You wait, I'm gonna get work in a station and I'm gonna buy my own and I'm gonna get you anything you want. Okay? Now shhhhhhhh. Stop cryin I'm gonna get you a Monte Carlo didn't ya hear me? Didn't ya? Shhhhhh. Be quiet your mum is tryin to sleep, okay? Shhhhhh! Come on, come on. My little Danny boy baby. Come onnnn. Shhhhhhhh!

[*On the last "shhh" he squeezes the baby's neck till it dies.*]

Shhhhhh.

[*From now on he is very wooden, like a sleepwalker. Looks at* THERESA, *who is watching in wonder.*]

It's okay. It's okay it's not cryin anymore. See. It's quiet now. It's not cryin. I—I—I done it, see? See? I'm a good father he—you know how come he stopped? Cause I told him he was gonna get a Monte Carlo.

THERESA What's that?

ALAN It's a kind of car. It's a place too. One of them south sea islands. Maybe we'll go there, eh? Anyways I gotta go I gotta meet somebody . . . see ya.

[ALAN *goes.* THERESA *looks after him.*]

8. A Chevrolet coupe, designed as a midsize luxury car (introduced in 1970). Monte Carlo is a district of Monaco—a glamorous resort on the French Riviera.

2.7

[JOE *and* SANDY'S. ALAN, JOE, *and* SANDY *are watching a Leafs*[9] *hockey game on television.* ALAN *is sitting away from* JOE *and* SANDY, *and he is smoking and loudly eating barbecue chips.* JOE *and* SANDY *are very much involved with each other and the game, and they virtually ignore* ALAN.]

JOE Go go go you fucker—Bunnyfuck what are you fuckin doin—*get him off Nykoluk get him off the ice fuck.*

ALAN Imlach dies.

[JOE *does not respond.*]

IMLACH DIES!!

JOE Oh LAROCQUE—come on Sittler put that mother in come on come on FUCK OFF PERREAULT, do it Daryl hey Martin Martin put it in put it ALL RIGHT! [*Jumps up.*] ALL FUCKING RIGHT!

[ALAN *jumps up with* JOE, *leans into the TV, his face only one inch away from the screen, screams, wagging his head.*]

ALAN ALLLLL FUCKIN RIGHT!

[*Looks back at* JOE *with a little laugh.*]

SANDY [*jocularly*] Take a bird why don't ya?

[ALAN *continues yelling into TV.*]

JOE Hey Al don't scare the TV away he—

[THERESA *appears in the doorway with a bag in her hand. She is reminiscent of Cassandra in* The Trojan Women.[1]]

THERESA YOU TOLE HIM YOU GIVE HIM A MONTE CARLO AND YA DON'T EVEN DRIVE ONE. *YA DON'T EVEN DRIVE ONE.*

[*Her presence is so strong that she immediately captures their attention.*]

I not goin screwin with ya no more Al, no way. No way! You stoppem breathin. I tell him "Breathin baby, breathin" and he not cause *you stoppenim.*

ALAN [*looking away from* THERESA] She's lyin you guys, stop your lyin.

THERESA You goin up the river to Penetang[2] Al, you goin there tomorrow and you never comin out for what you done you not goin back with me I goin with Ron Harton he better than you he not stoppem breathin, he still livin up on Division up at Shuter's? I callin him up and I goin steady with him he better lookin you funny lookin I screwin him.

ALAN YOU lyin fat COW you don't know what you're fuckin talkin about crazy fucking whore-bag—LIAR!

9. The Toronto Maple Leafs. In the following exchange, Joe and Alan refer to several members of the Maple Leafs: Michel "Bunny" Laroque, goalie (1980–81, 1981–83); Mike Nykoluk, head coach (1980–84); George "Punch" Imlach, general manager (1979–81); Darryl Sittler, center (1970–82); and Terry Martin, forward (1979–80, 1980–84). Gilbert Perreault was a standout center for the Buffalo Sabres (1970–87).

1. In Euripides' play *The Trojan Women* (415 B.C.E.), Cassandra enters joyfully, despite her enslavement to Agamemnon, because she prophesies his death (it is her curse that her prophecies are never believed).

2. Penetanguishene, Ontario, location of a maximum-security hospital for the criminally insane.

[ALAN *knocks* THERESA *to the floor, hesitates, grabs two glasses half-full of Dirty Mother, and runs off.* JOE *follows.*]

THERESA You got a donut, Sanny, gimme a donut.

SANDY What have ya got in the bag Trese.

THERESA Ivy, Ivy gimme the bag, I not givin it.

SANDY What's in it, though.

THERESA I takin him up the graveyard.

SANDY What for.

THERESA I puttin him with Grandma down St. Mary's Sanny, see ya later.

SANDY [*stepping in front of* THERESA*'s exit*] Wait a minute what—

THERESA Fuck off Sanny.

SANDY What's inside it.

[THERESA *giggles.* SANDY *touches the bag, flinches.*]

I'm callin the cops.

THERESA Agghhhhh. You fuckin call anyone I takin one of my fits.

SANDY I'm shakin in my shoes, Trese. [*Begins to dial.*]

THERESA [*grabs* SANDY, *rips phone from wall*] You not callin—

SANDY [*gets up, begins to exit, turns around, points at* THERESA] You're not here when I get back and I'm tellin Ron Harton what ya done down the Lido, ya hear me?

[THERESA *stares at* SANDY *in horror.*]

I will, too.

THERESA Okay.

SANDY I mean it. [*Exits.*]

THERESA [*to baby in bag*] It okay, Danny, don't you be cryin now, you with baby Jesus sittin on the cloud and the Virgin lookin like me she with ya she sittin there wearin that long blue dress goin down to her feet hardly pretty, eh? . . . Danny? You still live? You breathin if I breathin into ya? S'okay I'm your mum! [*Tries to breathe into baby.*] Danny? You dead, eh? You not live. You never comin back, eh. [*Puts bag to side, picks up severed phone, does not dial.*] Hi Janus won't be doin readin writin today. Somethin happen. Just somethin. The baby die. The baby die. Up at Sanny's. Okay okay I waitin . . . Ron Harton still livin up at Shuter's? [*Hangs up the phone, and picks it up immediately.*] C'I speak to Ron please? Hi Ron, its Trese. S'okay if we start goin together I love ya. Okay, see ya Tuesday.

[SANDY *enters, breathless, leans against the door. She cannot look at* THERESA.]

SANDY Don't want you tellin no stories to the cops, you hear me? Want you to tell em the truth exactly like it happened, okay?

THERESA Don't like ya no more, Sanny.

SANDY S'too bad.

THERESA You a dirty faggot.

SANDY Right.

THERESA Not my friend no more!

SANDY Okay . . .

THERESA I not talkin to YOU.

[*She turns her back to* SANDY. *She is crying.* SANDY *notices.*]

SANDY You should come out to Calgary[3] sometime—visit.

THERESA No Sanny, I workin!

SANDY What?

THERESA [*tells story joyously with no trace of grief*] Down at Kresge's[4] up with Ivy. Hah! She hardly funny she hardly get pissed off when I eatin icin she yellin "Trese, if you eat one more chocolate icin I tellin Charlie" so I go "You tellin Charlie I tellin on you, Ivy, snitchin butter tarts!" They're hardly good, though, them tarts. Ivy English. . . . Sorry I can't comin with ya out west, Sanny . . . Ivy be piss off.

2.8

[ALAN *and Indian* MAN *on warm air vent.* ALAN *is leaning against wall. He is clanging two glasses together. This produces a spooky sound.*]

ALAN [*pointing to* MAN] You fuckin touch me and I'll break your head.

MAN Hee hee hee Church'n Mondee all dee Mondee hee hee hee!

ALAN I will break your fuckin head in!

MAN [*starts happily, becomes angry as he remembers incident with a paramedic who denied him phenobarbital*] Breakin my fa fa pheno phenobarbidoll[5]—barbidoll—NIGGER, YOU NIGGER!

ALAN Shut it you fuck, just shut it.

[MAN *in panic, rushes toward the audience.*]

MAN SHUT THE WINDOW, SHUT THE WINDOW, SHUT THE WINDOW . . .

[*Laughs.*]

ALAN Nothing's funny, okay, so—just—STOP LAUCHIN. Just pass out will ya, can't ya just pass out? [MAN *vomits on* ALAN's *sock.*] Ahhhh fuck you goddamn *shit*. SHIT! Eecchh you keep your puke to yourself you old fuck! [*Crouches, rocking.*] I could drive a Monte Carlo I know I could. [*Rubbing glasses together*]

[JOE *enters, looking for* ALAN, *spots him, then crosses to him.*]

JOE Al?

ALAN Joe!

JOE Look—ah—

ALAN She's lyin Joe, I could drive a Monte Carlo.

JOE Al?

ALAN I could *drive one easy.*

JOE You could drive any car on the road. Now why don't you come on—

ALAN I—I—I can't.

JOE Why not?

ALAN I—I—I'm too cold, you know? I'm freezin.

JOE You're okay, ya probably got a flu, ya got a bug, okay?

ALAN No, no, I don't got a bug I'm just cold, he puked on me.

3. A large city (about 1,800 miles from Kingston) in southern Alberta, a western province of Canada.

4. A department store; the chain operated in Canada between 1929 and 1994.

5. That is, phenobarbital, a sedative commonly prescribed to treat sleeping disorders and seizures.

JOE So he puked on ya Martin used to puke on ya all the time. Come on—come on out of that shit pit and I'll get ya a coffee.

ALAN NO. No, I don't want to, I just don't want to, okay?

JOE Suit yourself. [*Turns his back on* ALAN, *starts to leave.*]

ALAN I done what I done and I done it and I fucked it up so I'm payin for it, get it? I'm payin for it.

JOE I don't know what ya done.

ALAN Sorry, Joe.

[JOE *looks at him, can't think of what to say.*]

Joe.

JOE Yeah.

ALAN Could ya do one thing?

JOE What.

ALAN Tell her I could drive a Monte Carlo. Easy.

JOE I will.

ALAN Bye Joe. [*Crouches in previous position, zipping and unzipping his jacket.*] "Nobody here—but us chickens—nobody here but us guys—don't bother me we got work to do and eggs to lay—and guys to see—"

MAN SHHHHHHHHHHHHhhhhhhhhh. [*With no motion, just the sound*]

2.9

SANDY I think it's better off dead. I'm not kiddin ya I'm serious. It don't hurt babies to be dead they go straight on up to heaven no hell no purgatory no nothin *no problems.* Cause their souls are still white as snow—they ain't had the time to get them black and ugly. Not like the rest of us—oh no if a baby dies he's just fine he don't even know he's dead. Youse shoulda seen him lyin there in that casket he looked fine. They had them little pajamas on him Trese got up at the S & R, the ones with all them dogs chasin cats all over, all yellow? They hardly looked sweet. And they had a big wreath of flowers around his neck so's to hide the strangle—you know the kind you put on your door at Christmas? Like that. It was kinda nice. We all lined up to take a look at him too—first time he got so much attention in his life—nobody broke up or nothin not even Trese. In fact I was scared she was gonna break up laughin. I'm not kiddin ya it don't bug her at all the kid's gone. Jeez y'know I don't know what goes on inside that girl but it ain't what's goin on inside the rest of us. She only got one thing on her mind now that's goin after Ron Harton. Don't ask me *why,* he looks like the fucking wrath of God. He's a pig too. I don't blame Trese though, I still feel for her even—fuck—this old bag sittin behind me was goin on about how come Trese never went to the hairdressers, you know what her hair is like, eh, right in the middle of the service, so I turn around and I says, "You're gonna hardly think of goin to the hairdressers when your own baby's just been killed by your own husband, ya fuckin old hag." I called her that too, right to her face. Oh yeah I'll stand up for a friend, anytime. I'll tell ya who else I stood up for at that service . . . Al, and he done it. Oh yeah, I still consider him a friend. No matter what he done, nobody can say what happened in that room; so I walk into the funeral parlour, and I take one of them cookies they got lyin out, you know, just tea biscuits, and I turn around and who's standin behind me lookin me right in the eye but that goddamn Bonnie Cain. She comes up close her breath just reekin and she says to me how she seen the whole thing from the window and how he done it with a plastic bag one of them Glad bags and how Trese was lookin on and laughin. That goddamn holy bitch. "You lie" I says to her and I grab her by the tit and I says "You fuckin hound dog one more word outa you and I send you to your goddamn grave. . . ." He never done it with a plastic bag he done it with his hands. I woulda I woulda broke every bone in her fuckin body and she knowed it too. *She* didn't say nothin more. Jeez I'll be glad to get outa this hole I'm tellin ya. I won't miss it neither I won't even dream about it. I won't. I worry about Trese but she'll be okay, you know? She'll—she'll go back down the Lido, start blowin off old queers again for five bucks. It's still open it won't never close. . . . They had them flowers round Danny's neck so's to hide the strangle but I seen it. The flowers never hid it they just made ya look harder, ya know? They just made ya look harder.

2.10

[*Small struggle off stage.* THERESA *runs on stage.*]

THERESA Stupid old bassard don't go foolin with me you don't even know who I look like even. You don't even know who I lookin like.

AUGUST WILSON

1945–2005

OF the many African American dramatists who have written for the theater since Lorraine Hansberry's acclaimed *A Raisin in the Sun* (1959), none has enjoyed more popular and critical success than August Wilson. *Ma Rainey's Black Bottom* (1984), the first of Wilson's plays to reach Broadway, won the New York Drama Critics' Circle Award for best new play; ***FENCES*** (1985) received numerous honors, including the Tony Award for Best Play and the Pulitzer Prize; and *The Piano Lesson* (1987) won Wilson another Drama Critics' Circle Award and a second Pulitzer. Subsequent plays, which continued Wilson's stated project of dramatizing African American history throughout the twentieth century one decade at a time, have also received widespread acclaim. Few dramatists, white or black, have matched Wilson's historical and sociological ambition or so minutely examined the dynamics, memories, and traumas that constitute the twentieth-century African American community.

Wilson was born Frederick August Kittel on April 27, 1945, in the Hill District, a largely African American neighborhood of Pittsburgh, where all but one of his major plays are set. The fourth of six children, he was the son of a black mother and a white German baker who was absent throughout his childhood. The family had little money, relying mainly on welfare and on Daisy Wilson Kittel's earnings as a janitor. When his father, whose name he bore, died in 1965, the future writer began calling himself August Wilson, thereby choosing to identify with the African American side of his family. By that point in his life, Wilson had had ample opportunity to learn what such an identity meant in the civil rights–era United States. In 1959 his mother and her second husband, a black man named David Bedford who worked in the city Sewer Department and would provide a model for Troy in *Fences,* had moved the family to a predominantly white neighborhood. Wilson's teenage years took him from one high school to another until, the target of racist remarks and ostracism, he dropped out of school for good in tenth grade when a teacher accused him of plagiarism, insisting that his paper on Napoleon was so good that one of his sisters must have written it.

Unwilling to tell his parents what he had done, Wilson spent much of his free time in a public library; there, in the "Negro Section," he discovered the works of such African American writers as Langston Hughes, Ralph Ellison, and James Baldwin. Wilson later recalled in an interview that he derived comfort from the fact that black people wrote books, adding that he "used to dream about being part of the Harlem Renaissance." After serving one year in the U.S. Army and spending two years working odd jobs, he took major steps toward realizing his ambition in 1965 when he moved from his mother's house into a rooming house back in the Hill District, bought himself a typewriter, and changed his name. The move immersed Wilson in a culturally and socially vibrant African American community, and from the musicians, artists, ex-convicts, and workers he encountered he absorbed the personalities, behaviors, and stories that would later appear in his plays. Wilson also learned the rich and varied vernacular of this black community, marked by cadences and idioms that mixed northern and southern, urban and rural.

Wilson's early years as a writer coincided with a shift in politics and culture as the forms of social and artistic protest that characterized the late 1950s and early 1960s were replaced by the more radicalized politics of black separatism, cultural nationalism, and the black power movement. By 1965 the playwright Amiri Baraka, who had begun his career as the Beat poet LeRoi Jones, had written such incendiary plays as *Dutchman* (1964) and *The Slave* (1964) and was calling for a "Black Revolutionary Theater." Wilson was deeply influenced by black cultural nationalism and its project of celebrating African American culture and developing institutions where this culture could be nurtured and shared within the black community. In 1968 he co-founded the Black Horizons Theatre in Pittsburgh to raise black consciousness and help politicize the community. The new theater put on the plays of Baraka and other playwrights of the Black Arts movement, and Wilson tried his hand at playwriting for the first time.

These attempts at one-act dramas were not successful; indeed, not until the mid-1970s would Wilson devote himself seriously to the theater. A 1976 work based on the life and death of 1920s blues musician Blind Lemon Jefferson, *The Homecoming,* became Wilson's first produced play, and other playscripts followed; they included a 1977 musical satire about the white nineteenth-century rustler Black Bart and *Jitney!* (1979), a play set in a gypsy cab station in his native Pittsburgh. In 1978 Wilson moved to St. Paul, Minnesota, where he became associated with the Playwright's Center in Minneapolis; among other jobs, he wrote short educational plays for a theater troupe affiliated with the Science Museum of Minnesota. The breakthrough for this relatively unknown playwright came when he developed early material he had written on Ma Rainey into *Ma Rainey's Black Bottom* and submitted the completed play to the Eugene O'Neill Theater Center's Playwright's Conference in Connecticut. The play was accepted for staged reading and Wilson was introduced to Lloyd Richards, who would serve as his mentor and director in subsequent projects. After a process of workshop revisions, *Ma Rainey* premiered at the Yale Repertory Theatre in April 1984, and moved to Broadway in October of the same year.

As *Ma Rainey* was winning praise among the theatergoing public, Wilson's *Fences* and an early version of *Joe Turner's Come and Gone* had already been presented in staged readings and workshops. By that time, Wilson was fully embarked on the project that he would complete twenty years later: tracing the history of twentieth-century black America through a cycle of ten plays set in each decade of the century. The result is a remarkable panorama of modern African American history. *Ma Rainey's Black Bottom,* the only play in the cycle not set in Pittsburgh, takes place in a Chicago recording studio in 1927. Most of the action of *Fences* takes place in Troy Maxson's backyard in 1957, while *Joe Turner's Come and Gone* (1986) is set in a boardinghouse in 1911. *The Piano Lesson* (1987), which deals with the conflict between brother and sister over a 135-year-old piano that has been central to their family's history, takes place in 1936. *Two Trains Running* (1990) is set in a Pittsburgh restaurant in 1969; *Seven Guitars* (1996) deals with the causes and repercussions of a young guitar player's death in 1948. A revised version of *Jitney* (which premiered in 1996), takes place in 1977, and *King Hedley II* (1999) explores the breakdown of the black family and community in the 1980s. *Gem of the Ocean* (2003), which is set in 1904, is dominated by the figure of Aunt Ester, a 287-year-old community elder and seer who arrived on the first shipload of American slaves in 1619. *Radio Golf,* which premiered six months before Wilson's death from cancer in 2005, centers on a plan to redevelop Pittsburgh's Hill District proposed in the 1990s.

With its broad historical ambitions, Wilson's history of a people invites comparison to the cycle plays of the medieval mystery guilds presented at York, Wakefield, and elsewhere. Wilson's plays similarly stand firmly on their own yet acquire wider meanings when viewed or read in relation to each other. The historical backdrop, or metanarrative, of these plays is certainly epic in scope. Like Hansberry, Wilson takes on the legacy of the Great Migration—the movement of black Americans who left the poverty and economic limitations of the Mississippi Delta and other parts of the South for Chicago, Cleveland, New York, and other northern cities in the largest demographic shift in U.S. history. Though this migration spanned the years between 1900 and 1970 (the year that black Americans started returning to the South), its peak came during World War I and the 1920s. In his brief introduction to *Fences*, Wilson describes how the "descendants of African slaves," pursuing the same hopes and dreams as European immigrants, found a very different reception in the cities of the North, and how hard they worked to make their lives, now spent "in shallow, ramshackle houses made of sticks and tar paper," into something free and dignified. Plays such as *Joe Turner's Come and Gone, Fences*, and *The Piano Lesson* examine the impact of the Great Migration on the generations that undertook it and those that followed. In doing so, they also look back to a past whose traumas and histories constitute the horizons of urban African American racial memory: the life of southern sharecroppers during Reconstruction, when the hopes of emancipation confronted the realities of socialized racism; the uncountable brutalities of slavery; the hardships of the Middle Passage; and, at the farthest reach, Africa and its forms of community, culture, and identity. As Wilson himself has commented, "When your back is pressed to the wall you go to the deepest part of yourself, and there's a response—it's your great ancestors talking. It's blood memory."

Their identities fragmented to varying degrees, Wilson's characters carry this history with them in the form of conflicting needs, drives, and behaviors. Such conflicts particularly affect Wilson's male characters. Negotiating their way through a society uncomfortable with their presence, they move, often compulsively, from place to place, relationship to relationship, seeking a haven in the world and some balm for their restless psyches. They fall in and out of jobs and end up so regularly in jail (or the "workhouse") that being arrested becomes a kind of initiation ritual. All of Wilson's characters, male and female, are haunted by the experiences of their parents and ancestors, and they seek, in sometimes self-defeating and contradictory ways, to escape or redeem this inheritance. In *The Piano Lesson*, Berniece and Boy Willie struggle for control of the family piano, each with a different understanding of what its painful history means to the present: Boy Willie wants to sell the piano and put the money toward purchasing the plantation where their great-grandparents had worked as slaves, while Berniece is equally determined to preserve the representations of family members that their great-grandfather had carved into the piano's legs after the relatives had been sold away. The siblings' struggle with the past comes to a head when Boy Willie fights the ghost of Sutter, the slave owner who controlled their ancestors' fate, in the play's final scene.

Wilson's dual interests in the present and the historical memories that inform it have driven certain stylistic and formal choices in the composition of his plays. Though he was influenced by Baraka's writing, Wilson chose not to employ the confrontational aesthetic of the Black Revolutionary Theater movement in his own drama. Nor has he pursued the antitheatrical styles and techniques through which some other contemporary black playwrights (such as Adrienne Kennedy, Ntozake Shange, and SUZAN-LORI PARKS) subvert the representational conventions that have traditionally governed the staging of African Americans. Wilson's drama draws on realism as an aesthetic; stylistically, his plays resemble those of Eugene O'Neill, ARTHUR MILLER, and others in the American mainstream. Yet at the same time that Wilson's plays display an almost ethnographic attention to the lives of his characters, detailing their material world and social codes with a range and specificity that recall the nineteenth-century realist novel, their realism is neither simple nor seamless. Wilson's settings—a backyard, a drawing room, a cab station—are based in the everyday, but they are invested with memory, history, and myth. For one thing, the dramatic present of Wilson's plays is expanded through the act of storytelling as characters narrate individual and family history, legends, and dreams. Several scholars have noted the similarities between Wilson's raconteurs and the West African griot, or storyteller, who preserved and transmitted the oral tradition of families and communities. In their access to traumatic memory and visionary revelation, these characters—such as Herald Loomis in *Joe Turner's Come and Gone,* with his trancelike vision of bones rising from the ocean waves and re-forming as bodies on the shore—introduce myth and the supernatural to Wilson's plays. In this respect, they are related to other figures created by Wilson whose presence unsettles the boundaries of realism—characters such as Aunt Ester, the centuries-old seer who has a presence, onstage and off, in several of his plays; Hedley in *Seven Guitars,* who is obsessed by visions about his dead father and the belief that he will father the Messiah; and Troy Maxson's brother Gabe in *Fences,* who, having suffered a brain injury in World War II, carries a trumpet and believes that he is the archangel Gabriel. Traversed by characters such as these, history in August Wilson's twentieth-century chronicle becomes actual and mythic at the same time.

There is certainly something mythic and outsized about the protagonist of *Fences,* Wilson's most widely known play. The name "Troy" calls to mind the embattled city of Homer's *Iliad,* while "Maxson" (Max-son) evokes the idea of patrilineal succession so central to heroic sagas. Like Babe Ruth, Josh Gibson, and the other baseball legends in whose company he places himself, Troy is larger than life; as Wilson notes, "[t]ogether with his blackness, his largeness informs his sensibilities and the choices he has made in his life." In a play profoundly concerned with space, ownership, and boundaries, Troy's presence dominates the stage even when he is absent from a particular scene; as a glance at the character list indicates, the other characters are defined primarily in terms of their relationship to him. Boasting that he "wrestled with Death" when he was seriously ill in the hospital, Troy displays the same indomitability in his job as a garbage collector, confronting his boss to ask why only whites drive the trucks while blacks lift the garbage. His passions in life are women and baseball, and it is not always clear which comes first. Troy learned baseball while in prison for killing a man, and upon his release he played in the Negro League, the circuit of teams for black ballplayers; none played in the major leagues until Jackie Robinson joined the Brooklyn Dodgers in 1947. Negro League teams, which often drew crowds as large as those that watched their white counterparts, featured some of the best players in the history of the sport—including Josh Gibson, the so-called black Babe Ruth, who played for the powerful Homestead Grays, based in a steel mill town adjacent to Pittsburgh. As the archetypal American pastime, baseball serves as a powerful

James Earl Jones as Troy in the world premiere of *Fences* at the Yale Repertory Theatre, 1985.

symbol in *Fences* of the exclusion of black Americans from the country's social and cultural institutions. Unfortunately for Troy, by the time baseball's color line had been breached and black players gradually began playing for major league teams, he was too old to be one of them. At age fifty-three, he carries his baseball past with him as a bitter reminder of racial oppression and as a metaphor of his battles against an antagonistic life: for him, "Death ain't nothing but a fastball on the outside corner."

Troy's personality was forged in his relationship with his father, an embittered and abusive sharecropper who towered over his children and drove Troy away with a particularly ugly explosion of violence. From his father Troy learns responsibility, but it is a responsibility born of hardness, not love. When applied to his two sons, it is accompanied by a rigid sense of authority and a demand that they live their lives with the pressure-forged self-denial he has been forced to accept in his. In different ways, both Lyons (who aspires to be a musician) and Cory (a high school football star) resist this narrow definition of life's possibilities. Cory's desire to win a scholarship to play football in college reflects the changing place of black athletes in American sports: in 1957, the year the play opens, the running back Jim Brown was declared the National Football League's Most Valuable Player and the Milwaukee Braves won the World Series, defeating the New York Yankees behind the hitting of Hank Aaron (who would eventually break Babe Ruth's revered lifetime home run record). As Troy's wife Rose explains to him, "The world's changing around you and you can't even see it." But Troy is the product of a different world. Unable to perceive an alternative to the father-son struggle that he himself was forced to endure and scarred by the deprivations he faced, Troy becomes the father he ran away from, standing in the way of a younger generation's new opportunities and driving away those he loves. Resenting the self-sacrifice, suffering, and disappointment that he has nonetheless worked into a code of living, he betrays his younger son, wife, and brother.

With its psychologically embattled patriarch, urban backyard setting, and other details of plot and action, *Fences* bears more than casual resemblance to ARTHUR MILLER's *Death of a Salesman* (1949). Like the earlier play, *Fences* revolves around questions of masculinity: what the social performance of maleness consists of, how it is transmitted (or not transmitted) from fathers to sons, how it relates to social models of femaleness. Their economic and social disempowerment has made the task of fulfilling traditional male roles particularly fraught for African American men. Like Biff Loman, Cory must negotiate the boundaries of his own identity, and thereby become a man, in the shadow of his father's frustrated and defensive masculinity: "It would wrap around you and lay there until you couldn't tell which one was you anymore." He is not alone in struggling against Troy. Rose, one of only two female characters in the play, must confront her failure to meet all of her husband's needs and affirm, in the process, her own need for selfhood. Critics have been divided over the status of the women Wilson created, who inhabit a dramatic world whose orientation is largely determined by male preoccupations. To what extent is Rose's character defined in terms of and limited by the support—psychological, domestic, sexual—that she provides her husband? To what extent, conversely, does she succeed in articulating an autonomous set of experiences, desires, and identity boundaries?

Against these psychological and sociological backdrops, the play's title resonates in complex ways. Designed both to keep people in and to keep them out, the backyard fence represents the many ways in which society and the human mind establish boundaries around psyches, social units, races, genders. The play's principal characters think about fences differently. Rose, who builds fences in order to "keep people in," desires a space where her family can remain protected and whole. Troy, on the other hand, constructs fences against those aspects of life that threaten his view of the world and himself. In so doing, he establishes barriers between himself and those who love him, denying himself the possibilities of growth, intimacy, and pride in the son who has tried so hard to live up to his expectations. Alone in the play's penultimate scene, all Troy can do is swing his bat, hoping to clear the fences—hit a home run—in one last act of solitary heroism.

S.G

Fences

When the sins of our fathers visit us
We do not have to play host.
We can banish them with forgiveness
As God, in His Largeness and Laws.

—AUGUST WILSON

CHARACTERS

TROY MAXSON
JIM BONO, Troy's friend
ROSE, Troy's wife
LYONS, Troy's oldest son by previous marriage
GABRIEL, Troy's brother
CORY, Troy and Rose's son
RAYNELL, Troy's daughter

Setting

The setting is the yard which fronts the only entrance to the MAXSON household, an ancient two-story brick house set back off a small alley in a big-city neighborhood. The entrance to the house is gained by two or three steps leading to a wooden porch badly in need of paint.

A relatively recent addition to the house and running its full width, the porch lacks congruence. It is a sturdy porch with a flat roof. One or two chairs of dubious value sit at one end where the kitchen window opens onto the porch. An old-fashioned icebox stands silent guard at the opposite end.

The yard is a small dirt yard, partially fenced, except for the last scene, with a wooden sawhorse, a pile of lumber, and other fence-building equipment set off to the side. Opposite is a tree from which hangs a ball made of rags. A baseball bat leans against the tree. Two oil drums serve as garbage receptacles and sit near the house at right to complete the setting.

The Play

Near the turn of the century, the destitute of Europe sprang on the city with tenacious claws and an honest and solid dream. The city devoured them. They swelled its belly until it burst into a thousand furnaces and sewing machines, a thousand butcher shops and bakers' ovens, a thousand churches and hospitals and funeral parlors and moneylenders. The city grew. It nourished itself and offered each man a partnership limited only by his talent, his guile, and his willingness and capacity for hard work. For the immigrants of Europe, a dream dared and won true.

The descendants of African slaves were offered no such welcome or participation. They came from places called the Carolinas and the Virginias, Georgia, Alabama, Mississippi, and Tennessee. They came strong, eager, searching. The city rejected them and they fled and settled along the riverbanks and under bridges in shallow, ramshackle houses made of sticks and tar paper. They collected rags and wood. They sold the use of their muscles and their bodies. They cleaned houses and washed clothes, they shined shoes, and in quiet desperation and vengeful pride, they stole, and lived in pursuit of their own dream. That they could breathe free, finally, and stand to meet life with the force of dignity and whatever eloquence the heart could call upon.

By 1957, the hard-won victories of the European immigrants had solidified the industrial might of America. War had been confronted and won with new energies that used loyalty and patriotism as its fuel. Life was rich, full, and flourishing. The Milwaukee Braves won the World Series, and the hot winds of change that would make the sixties a turbulent, racing, dangerous, and provocative decade had not yet begun to blow full.

1.1

It is 1957. TROY *and* BONO *enter the yard, engaged in conversation.* TROY *is fifty-three years old, a large man with thick, heavy hands; it is this largeness that he strives to fill out and make an accommodation with. Together with his blackness, his largeness informs his sensibilities and the choices he has made in his life.*

Of the two men, BONO *is obviously the follower. His commitment to their friendship of thirty-odd years is rooted in his admiration of* TROY*'s honesty, capacity for hard work, and his strength, which* BONO *seeks to emulate.*

It is Friday night, payday, and the one night of the week the two men engage in a ritual of talk and drink. TROY *is usually the most talkative and at times he can be crude and almost vulgar, though he is capable of rising to profound heights of expression. The men carry lunch buckets and wear or carry burlap aprons and are dressed in clothes suitable to their jobs as garbage collectors.*

BONO Troy, you ought to stop that lying!

TROY I ain't lying! The nigger had a watermelon this big. [*He indicates with his hands.*] Talking about . . . "What watermelon, Mr. Rand?" I liked to fell out![1] "What watermelon, Mr. Rand?" . . . And it sitting there big as life.

BONO What did Mr. Rand say?

TROY Ain't said nothing. Figure if the nigger too dumb to know he carrying a watermelon, he wasn't gonna get much sense out of him. Trying to hide that great big old watermelon under his coat. Afraid to let the white man see him carry it home.

BONO I'm like you . . . I ain't got no time for them kind of people.

TROY Now what he look like getting mad cause he see the man from the union talking to Mr. Rand?

BONO He come to me talking about . . . "Maxson gonna get us fired." I told him to get away from me with that. He walked away from me calling you a troublemaker. What Mr. Rand say?

TROY Ain't said nothing. He told me to go down the Commissioner's office next Friday. They called me down there to see them.

BONO Well, as long as you got your complaint filed, they can't fire you. That's what one of them white fellows tell me.

TROY I ain't worried about them firing me. They gonna fire me cause I asked a question? That's all I did. I went to Mr. Rand and asked him, "Why? Why you got the white mens driving and the colored lifting?" Told him, "What's the matter, don't I count? You think only white fellows got sense enough to

1. I nearly fell out of my tree; that is, I was amazed.

drive a truck. That ain't no paper job! Hell, anybody can drive a truck. How come you got all whites driving and the colored lifting? He told me, "Take it to the union." Well, hell, that's what I done! Now they wanna come up with this pack of lies.

BONO I told Brownie if the man come and ask him any questions . . . just tell the truth! It ain't nothing but something they done trumped up on you cause you filed a complaint on them.

TROY Brownie don't understand nothing. All I want them to do is change the job description. Give everybody a chance to drive the truck. Brownie can't see that. He ain't got that much sense.

BONO How you figure he be making out with that gal be up at Taylors' all the time . . . that Alberta gal?

TROY Same as you and me. Getting just as much as we is. Which is to say nothing.

BONO It is, huh? I figure you doing a little better than me . . . and I ain't saying what I'm doing.

TROY Aw, nigger, look here . . . I know you. If you had got anywhere near that gal, twenty minutes later you be looking to tell somebody. And the first one you gonna tell . . . that you gonna want to brag to . . . is gonna be me.

BONO I ain't saying that. I see where you be eyeing her.

TROY I eye all the women. I don't miss nothing. Don't never let nobody tell you Troy Maxson don't eye the women.

BONO You been doing more than eyeing her. You done bought her a drink or two.

TROY Hell yeah, I bought her a drink! What that mean? I bought you one, too. What that mean cause I buy her a drink? I'm just being polite.

BONO It's alright to buy her one drink. That's what you call being polite. But when you wanna be buying two or three . . . that's what you call eyeing her.

TROY Look here, as long as you known me . . . you ever known me to chase after women?

BONO Hell yeah! Long as I done known you. You forgetting I knew you when.

TROY Naw, I'm talking about since I been married to Rose?

BONO Oh, not since you been married to Rose. Now, that's the truth, there. I can say that.

TROY Alright then! Case closed.

BONO I see you be walking up around Alberta's house. You supposed to be at Taylors' and you be walking up around there.

TROY What you watching where I'm walking for? I ain't watching after you.

BONO I seen you walking around there more than once.

TROY Hell, you liable to see me walking anywhere! That don't mean nothing cause you see me walking around there.

BONO Where she come from anyway? She just kinda showed up one day.

TROY Tallahassee. You can look at her and tell she one of them Florida gals. They got some big healthy women down there. Grow them right up out the ground. Got a little bit of Indian in her. Most of them niggers down in Florida got some Indian in them.

BONO I don't know about that Indian part. But she damn sure big and healthy. Woman wear some big stockings. Got them great big old legs and hips as wide as the Mississippi River.

TROY Legs don't mean nothing. You don't do nothing but push them out of the way. But them hips cushion the ride!

BONO Troy, you ain't got no sense.

TROY It's the truth! Like you riding on Goodyears![2]

[ROSE *enters from the house. She is ten years younger than* TROY, *her devotion to him stems from her recognition of the possibilities of her life without him: a succession of abusive men and their babies, a life of partying and running the streets, the Church, or aloneness with its attendant pain and frustration. She recognizes* TROY'S *spirit as a fine and illuminating one and she either ignores or forgives his faults, only some of which she recognizes. Though she doesn't drink, her presence is an integral part of the Friday night rituals. She alternates between the porch and the kitchen, where supper preparations are under way.*]

ROSE What you all out here getting into?

TROY What you worried about what we getting into for? This is men talk, woman.

ROSE What I care what you all talking about? Bono, you gonna stay for supper?

BONO No, I thank you, Rose. But Lucille say she cooking up a pot of pigfeet.

TROY Pigfeet! Hell, I'm going home with you! Might even stay the night if you got some pigfeet. You got something in there to top them pigfeet, Rose?

ROSE I'm cooking up some chicken. I got some chicken and collard greens.

TROY Well, go on back in the house and let me and Bono finish what we was talking about. This is men talk. I got some talk for you later. You know what kind of talk I mean. You go on and powder it up.

ROSE Troy Maxson, don't you start that now!

TROY [*puts his arm around her*] Aw, woman . . . come here. Look here, Bono . . . when I met this woman . . . I got out that place, say, "Hitch up my pony, saddle up my mare . . . there's a woman out there for me somewhere. I looked here. Looked there. Saw Rose and latched on to her." I latched on to her and told her—I'm gonna tell you the truth—I told her, "Baby, I don't wanna marry, I just wanna be your man." Rose told me . . . tell him what you told me, Rose.

ROSE I told him if he wasn't the marrying kind, then move out the way so the marrying kind could find me.

TROY That's what she told me. "Nigger, you in my way. You blocking the view! Move out the way so I can find me a husband." I thought it over two or three days. Come back—

ROSE Ain't no two or three days nothing. You was back the same night.

TROY Come back, told her . . . "Okay, baby . . . but I'm gonna buy me a banty[3] rooster and put him out there in the backyard . . . and when he see a stranger come, he'll flap his wings and crow . . ." Look here, Bono, I could watch the front door by myself . . . it was that back door I was worried about.

ROSE Troy, you ought not talk like that. Troy ain't doing nothing but telling a lie.

TROY Only thing is . . . when we first got married . . . forget the rooster . . . we ain't had no yard!

2. That is, on automobile tires.
3. That is, bantam, or small (a term applied to several breeds of domestic fowl).

BONO I hear you tell it. Me and Lucille was staying down there on Logan Street. Had two rooms with the outhouse in the back. I ain't mind the outhouse none. But when that goddamn wind blow through there in the winter . . . that's what I'm talking about! To this day I wonder why in the hell I ever stayed down there for six long years. But see, I didn't know I could do no better. I thought only white folks had inside toilets and things.

ROSE There's a lot of people don't know they can do no better than they doing now. That's just something you got to learn. A lot of folks still shop at Bella's.

TROY Ain't nothing wrong with shopping at Bella's. She got fresh food.

ROSE I ain't said nothing about if she got fresh food. I'm talking about what she charge. She charge ten cents more than the A&P.[4]

TROY The A&P ain't never done nothing for me. I spends my money where I'm treated right. I go down to Bella, say, "I need a loaf of bread, I'll pay you Friday." She give it to me. What sense that make when I got money to go and spend it somewhere else and ignore the person who done right by me? That ain't in the Bible.

ROSE We ain't talking about what's in the Bible. What sense it make to shop there when she overcharge?

TROY You shop where you want to. I'll do my shopping where the people been good to me.

ROSE Well, I don't think it's right for her to overcharge. That's all I was saying.

BONO Look here . . . I got to get on. Lucille going be raising all kind of hell.

TROY Where you going, nigger? We ain't finished this pint. Come here, finish this pint.

BONO Well, hell, I am . . . if you ever turn the bottle loose.

TROY [*hands him the bottle*] The only thing I say about the A&P is I'm glad Cory got that job down there. Help him take care of his school clothes and things. Gabe done moved out and things getting tight around here. He got that job. . . . He can start to look out for himself.

ROSE Cory done went and got recruited by a college football team.

TROY I told that boy about that football stuff. The white man ain't gonna let him get nowhere with that football. I told him when he first come to me with it. Now you come telling me he done went and got more tied up in it. He ought to go and get recruited in how to fix cars or something where he can make a living.

ROSE He ain't talking about making no living playing football. It's just something the boys in school do. They gonna send a recruiter by to talk to you. He'll tell you he ain't talking about making no living playing football. It's a honor to be recruited.

TROY It ain't gonna get him nowhere. Bono'll tell you that.

BONO If he be like you in the sports . . . he's gonna be alright. Ain't but two men ever played baseball as good as you. That's Babe Ruth and Josh Gibson.[5] Them's the only two men ever hit more home runs than you.

4. The dominant U.S. supermarket chain in the 1950s.

5. Respectively, the most famous white and black hitters of the 20th century. Ruth (1895–1948), who played with the N.Y. Yankees for most of his career (1914–35), held the major-league record for home runs in a season (60) for 34 years, and the lifetime home run record (714) for 39; Gibson (1911–1947; catcher, 1930–46), who played mainly for the Homestead Grays (near Pittsburgh) in the Negro League, was known as "the black Babe Ruth"; it is estimated that in his career he hit more than 800 home runs, 75 of them in a single season.

TROY What it ever get me? Ain't got a pot to piss in or a window to throw it out of.

ROSE Times have changed since you was playing baseball, Troy. That was before the war. Times have changed a lot since then.

TROY How in hell they done changed?

ROSE They got lots of colored boys playing ball now.[6] Baseball and football.

BONO You right about that, Rose. Times have changed, Troy. You just come along too early.

TROY There ought not never have been no time called too early! Now you take that fellow . . . what's that fellow they had playing right field for the Yankees back then? You know who I'm talking about, Bono. Used to play right field for the Yankees.

ROSE Selkirk?[7]

TROY Selkirk! That's it! Man batting .269, understand? .269. What kind of sense that make? I was hitting .432 with thirty-seven home runs! Man batting .269 and playing right field for the Yankees! I saw Josh Gibson's daughter yesterday. She walking around with raggedy shoes on her feet. Now I bet you Selkirk's daughter ain't walking around with raggedy shoes on her feet! I bet you that!

ROSE They got a lot of colored baseball players now. Jackie Robinson was the first. Folks had to wait for Jackie Robinson.

TROY I done seen a hundred niggers play baseball better than Jackie Robinson. Hell, I know some teams Jackie Robinson couldn't even make! What you talking about Jackie Robinson. Jackie Robinson wasn't nobody.[8] I'm talking about if you could play ball then they ought to have let you play. Don't care what color you were. Come telling me I come along too early. If you could play . . . then they ought to have let you play.

[TROY *takes a long drink from the bottle.*]

ROSE You gonna drink yourself to death. You don't need to be drinking like that.

TROY Death ain't nothing. I done seen him. Done wrassled with him. You can't tell me nothing about death. Death ain't nothing but a fastball on the outside corner. And you know what I'll do to that! Lookee here, Bono . . . am I lying? You get one of them fastballs, about waist high, over the outside corner of the plate where you can get the meat of the bat on it . . . and good god! You can kiss it goodbye. Now, am I lying?

BONO Naw, you telling the truth there. I seen you do it.

TROY If I'm lying . . . that 450 feet worth of lying![9] [*Pause*] That's all death is to me. A fastball on the outside corner.

6. Until 1947, when Jackie Robinson (1919–1972) began playing for the Brooklyn Dodgers, no "colored" athletes had been allowed to play in baseball's minor or major leagues since the late 19th century. Initially, professional football had a few black players (1920–34), but none subsequently played for the National Football League until 1946, when four were signed.

7. George Selkirk (1908–1987), who became the Yankee's right fielder in 1935 after Ruth retired; he batted .269 in 1940 (his average was above .300 five times in the 1930s).

8. Robinson was in fact Rookie of the Year, a six-time All-Star, and the 1949 National League MVP, outstanding as both a fielder and a hitter with a career batting average of .311.

9. A ball hit this distance would be an impressive home run in any ballpark (at its deepest, no fence is more than 435 feet from home plate).

ROSE I don't know why you want to get on talking about death.

TROY Ain't nothing wrong with talking about death. That's part of life. Everybody gonna die. You gonna die, I'm gonna die. Bono's gonna die. Hell, we all gonna die.

ROSE But you ain't got to talk about it. I don't like to talk about it.

TROY You the one brought it up. Me and Bono was talking about baseball . . . you tell me I'm gonna drink myself to death. Ain't that right, Bono? You know I don't drink this but one night out of the week. That's Friday night. I'm gonna drink just enough to where I can handle it. Then I cuts it loose. I leave it alone. So don't you worry about me drinking myself to death. 'Cause I ain't worried about Death. I done seen him. I done wrestled with him.

Look here, Bono . . . I looked up one day and Death was marching straight at me. Like Soldiers on Parade! The Army of Death was marching straight at me. The middle of July, 1941. It got real cold just like it be winter. It seem like Death himself reached out and touched me on the shoulder. He touch me just like I touch you. I got cold as ice and Death standing there grinning at me.

ROSE Troy, why don't you hush that talk.

TROY I say . . . What you want, Mr. Death? You be wanting me? You done brought your army to be getting me? I looked him dead in the eye. I wasn't fearing nothing. I was ready to tangle. Just like I'm ready to tangle now. The Bible say be ever vigilant.[1] That's why I don't get but so drunk. I got to keep watch.

ROSE Troy was right down there in Mercy Hospital. You remember he had pneumonia? Laying there with a fever talking plumb out of his head.

TROY Death standing there staring at me . . . carrying that sickle in his hand. Finally he say, "You want bound over for another year?" See, just like that . . . "You want bound over[2] for another year?" I told him, "Bound over hell! Let's settle this now!"

It seem like he kinda fell back when I said that, and all the cold went out of me. I reached down and grabbed that sickle and threw it just as far as I could throw it . . . and me and him commenced to wrestling.

We wrestled for three days and three nights. I can't say where I found the strength from. Every time it seemed like he was gonna get the best of me, I'd reach way down deep inside myself and find the strength to do him one better.

ROSE Every time Troy tell that story he find different ways to tell it. Different things to make up about it.

TROY I ain't making up nothing. I'm telling you the facts of what happened. I wrestled with Death for three days and three nights and I'm standing here to tell you about it.

[*Pause.*]

Alright. At the end of the third night we done weakened each other to where we can't hardly move. Death stood up, throwed on his robe . . . had him a white robe with a hood on it. He throwed on that robe and went off

1. "Be sober, be vigilant; because your adversary the devil, as a roaring lion, walketh about, seeking whom he may devour" (1 Peter 5.8).

2. That is, agreeing to one more year of servitude, as if he were a sharecropper.

to look for his sickle. Say, "I'll be back." Just like that. "I'll be back." I told him, say, "Yeah, but . . . you gonna have to find me!" I wasn't no fool. I wasn't going looking for him. Death ain't nothing to play with. And I know he's gonna get me. I know I got to join his army . . . his camp followers. But as long as I keep my strength and see him coming . . . as long as I keep up my vigilance . . . he's gonna have to fight to get me. I ain't going easy.

BONO Well, look here, since you got to keep up your vigilance . . . let me have the bottle.

TROY Aw hell, I shouldn't have told you that part. I should have left out that part.

ROSE Troy be talking that stuff and half the time don't even know what he be talking about.

TROY Bono know me better than that.

BONO That's right. I know you. I know you got some Uncle Remus[3] in your blood. You got more stories than the devil got sinners.

TROY Aw hell, I done seen him too! Done talked with the devil.

ROSE Troy, don't nobody wanna be hearing all that stuff.

[LYONS *enters the yard from the street. Thirty-four years old,* TROY'S *son by a previous marriage, he sports a neatly trimmed goatee, sport coat, white shirt, tieless and buttoned at the collar. Though he fancies himself a musician, he is more caught up in the rituals and "idea" of being a musician than in the actual practice of the music. He has come to borrow money from* TROY, *and while he knows he will be successful, he is uncertain as to what extent his lifestyle will be held up to scrutiny and ridicule.*]

LYONS Hey, Pop.

TROY What you come "Hey, Popping" me for?

LYONS How you doing, Rose?

[*He kisses her.*]

Mr. Bono. How you doing?

BONO Hey, Lyons . . . how you been?

TROY He must have been doing alright. I ain't seen him around here last week.

ROSE Troy, leave your boy alone. He come by to see you and you wanna start all that nonsense.

TROY I ain't bothering Lyons. [*Offers him the bottle.*] Here . . . get you a drink. We got an understanding. I know why he come by to see me and he know I know.

LYONS Come on, Pop . . . I just stopped by to say hi . . . see how you was doing.

TROY You ain't stopped by yesterday.

ROSE You gonna stay for supper, Lyons? I got some chicken cooking in the oven.

LYONS No, Rose . . . thanks. I was just in the neighborhood and thought I'd stop by for a minute.

TROY You was in the neighborhood alright, nigger. You telling the truth there. You was in the neighborhood cause it's my payday.

LYONS Well, hell, since you mentioned it . . . let me have ten dollars.

3. The fictional narrator of popular black folktales compiled by the white humorist Joel Chandler Harris, beginning with *Uncle Remus: His Songs and Sayings* (1881).

TROY I'll be damned! I'll die and go to hell and play blackjack with the devil before I give you ten dollars.

BONO That's what I wanna know about . . . that devil you done seen.

LYONS What . . . Pop done seen the devil? You too much, Pops.

TROY Yeah, I done seen him. Talked to him too!

ROSE You ain't seen no devil. I done told you that man ain't had nothing to do with the devil. Anything you can't understand, you want to call it the devil.

TROY Look here, Bono . . . I went down to see Hertzberger about some furniture. Got three rooms for two-ninety-eight. That what it say on the radio. "Three rooms . . . two-ninety-eight." Even made up a little song about it. Go down there . . . man tell me I can't get no credit. I'm working every day and can't get no credit. What to do? I got an empty house with some raggedy furniture in it. Cory ain't got no bed. He's sleeping on a pile of rags on the floor. Working every day and can't get no credit. Come back here—Rose'll tell you—madder than hell. Sit down . . . try to figure what I'm gonna do. Come a knock on the door. Ain't been living here but three days. Who know I'm here? Open the door . . . devil standing there bigger than life. White fellow . . . got on good clothes and everything. Standing there with a clipboard in his hand. I ain't had to say nothing. First words come out of his mouth was . . . "I understand you need some furniture and can't get no credit." I liked to fell over. He say "I'll give you all the credit you want, but you got to pay the interest on it." I told him, "Give me three rooms worth and charge whatever you want." Next day a truck pulled up here and two men unloaded them three rooms. Man what drove the truck give me a book. Say send ten dollars, first of every month to the address in the book and everything will be alright. Say if I miss a payment the devil was coming back and it'll be hell to pay. That was fifteen years ago. To this day . . . the first of the month I send my ten dollars, Rose'll tell you.

ROSE Troy lying.

TROY I ain't never seen that man since. Now you tell me who else that could have been but the devil? I ain't sold my soul or nothing like that, you understand. Naw, I wouldn't have truck with the devil about nothing like that. I got my furniture and pays my ten dollars the first of the month just like clockwork.

BONO How long you say you been paying this ten dollars a month?

TROY Fifteen years!

BONO Hell, ain't you finished paying for it yet? How much the man done charged you?

TROY Aw hell, I done paid for it. I done paid for it ten times over! The fact is I'm scared to stop paying it.

ROSE Troy lying. We got that furniture from Mr. Glickman. He ain't paying no ten dollars a month to nobody.

TROY Aw hell, woman. Bono know I ain't that big a fool.

LYONS I was just getting ready to say . . . I know where there's a bridge for sale.[4]

4. To sell the Brooklyn Bridge proverbially demonstrates both the seller's powers of persuasion and the buyer's gullibility (a couple of turn-of-the-century confidence men did manage to pull off this swindle).

TROY Look here, I'll tell you this . . . it don't matter to me if he was the devil. It don't matter if the devil give credit. Somebody has got to give it.

ROSE It ought to matter. You going around talking about having truck with the devil . . . God's the one you gonna have to answer to. He's the one gonna be at the Judgment.

LYONS Yeah, well, look here, Pop . . . let me have that ten dollars. I'll give it back to you. Bonnie got a job working at the hospital.

TROY What I tell you, Bono? The only time I see this nigger is when he wants something. That's the only time I see him.

LYONS Come on, Pop, Mr. Bono don't want to hear all that. Let me have the ten dollars. I told you Bonnie working.

TROY What that mean to me? "Bonnie working." I don't care if she working. Go ask her for the ten dollars if she working. Talking about "Bonnie working." Why ain't you working?

LYONS Aw, Pop, you know I can't find no decent job. Where am I gonna get a job at? You know I can't get no job.

TROY I told you I know some people down there. I can get you on the rubbish if you want to work. I told you that the last time you came by here asking me for something.

LYONS Naw, Pop . . . thanks. That ain't for me. I don't wanna be carrying nobody's rubbish. I don't wanna be punching nobody's time clock.

TROY What's the matter, you too good to carry people's rubbish? Where you think that ten dollars you talking about come from? I'm just supposed to haul people's rubbish and give my money to you cause you too lazy to work. You too lazy to work and wanna know why you ain't got what I got.

ROSE What hospital Bonnie working at? Mercy?

LYONS She's down at Passavant working in the laundry.

TROY I ain't got nothing as it is. I give you that ten dollars and I got to eat beans the rest of the week. Naw . . . you ain't getting no ten dollars here.

LYONS You ain't got to be eating no beans. I don't know why you wanna say that.

TROY I ain't got no extra money. Gabe done moved over to Miss Pearl's paying her the rent and things done got tight around here. I can't afford to be giving you every payday.

LYONS I ain't asked you to give me nothing. I asked you to loan me ten dollars. I know you got ten dollars.

TROY Yeah, I got it. You know why I got it? Cause I don't throw my money away out there in the streets. You living the fast life . . . wanna be a musician . . . running around in them clubs and things . . . then, you learn to take care of yourself. You ain't gonna find me going and asking nobody for nothing. I done spent too many years without.

LYONS You and me is two different people, Pop.

TROY I done learned my mistake and learned to do what's right by it. You still trying to get something for nothing. Life don't owe you nothing. You owe it to yourself. Ask Bono. He'll tell you I'm right.

LYONS You got your way of dealing with the world . . . I got mine. The only thing that matters to me is the music.

TROY Yeah, I can see that! It don't matter how you gonna eat . . . where your next dollar is coming from. You telling the truth there.

LYONS I know I got to eat. But I got to live too. I need something that gonna help me to get out of the bed in the morning. Make me feel like I belong in the world. I don't bother nobody. I just stay with my music cause that's the only way I can find to live in the world. Otherwise there ain't no telling what I might do. Now I don't come criticizing you and how you live. I just come by to ask you for ten dollars. I don't wanna hear all that about how I live.

TROY Boy, your mama did a hell of a job raising you.

LYONS You can't change me, Pop. I'm thirty-four years old. If you wanted to change me, you should have been there when I was growing up. I come by to see you . . . ask for ten dollars and you want to talk about how I was raised. You don't know nothing about how I was raised.

ROSE Let the boy have ten dollars, Troy.

TROY [*to* LYONS] What the hell you looking at me for? I ain't got no ten dollars. You know what I do with my money. [*To* ROSE] Give him ten dollars if you want him to have it.

ROSE I will. Just as soon as you turn it loose.

TROY [*handing* ROSE *the money*] There it is. Seventy-six dollars and forty-two cents. You see this, Bono? Now, I ain't gonna get but six of that back.

ROSE You ought to stop telling that lie. Here, Lyons.

[*She hands him the money.*]

LYONS Thanks, Rose. Look . . . I got to run . . . I'll see you later.

TROY Wait a minute. You gonna say, "Thanks, Rose," and ain't gonna look to see where she got that ten dollars from? See how they do me, Bono?

LYONS I know she got it from you, Pop. Thanks. I'll give it back to you.

TROY There he go telling another lie. Time I see that ten dollars . . . he'll be owing me thirty more.

LYONS See you, Mr. Bono.

BONO Take care, Lyons!

LYONS Thanks, Pop. I'll see you again.

[LYONS *exits the yard.*]

TROY I don't know why he don't go and get him a decent job and take care of that woman he got.

BONO He'll be alright, Troy. The boy is still young.

TROY The *boy* is thirty-four years old.

ROSE Let's not get off into all that.

BONO Look here . . . I got to be going. I got to be getting on. Lucille gonna be waiting.

TROY [*puts his arm around* ROSE] See this woman, Bono? I love this woman. I love this woman so much it hurts. I love her so much . . . I done run out of ways of loving her. So I got to go back to basics. Don't you come by my house Monday morning talking about time to go to work . . . 'cause I'm still gonna be stroking!

ROSE Troy! Stop it now!

BONO I ain't paying him no mind, Rose. That ain't nothing but gin-talk. Go on, Troy. I'll see you Monday.

TROY Don't you come by my house, nigger! I done told you what I'm gonna be doing.

[*The lights go down to black.*]

1.2

The lights come up on ROSE *hanging up clothes. She hums and sings softly to herself. It is the following morning.*

ROSE [*sings*]

Jesus, be a fence all around me every day
Jesus, I want you to protect me as I travel on my way.
Jesus, be a fence all around me every day.[5]

[TROY *enters from the house.*]

ROSE [*continued*]

Jesus, I want you to protect me
As I travel on my way.

[*To* TROY] 'Morning. You ready for breakfast? I can fix it soon as I finish hanging up these clothes?

TROY I got the coffee on. That'll be alright. I'll just drink some of that this morning.

ROSE That 651 hit yesterday.[6] That's the second time this month. Miss Pearl hit for a dollar . . . seem like those that need the least always get lucky. Poor folks can't get nothing.

TROY Them numbers don't know nobody. I don't know why you fool with them. You and Lyons both.

ROSE It's something to do.

TROY You ain't doing nothing but throwing your money away.

ROSE Troy, you know I don't play foolishly. I just play a nickel here and a nickel there.

TROY That's two nickels you done thrown away.

ROSE Now I hit sometimes . . . that makes up for it. It always comes in handy when I do hit. I don't hear you complaining then.

TROY I ain't complaining now. I just say it's foolish. Trying to guess out of six hundred ways which way the number gonna come. If I had all the money niggers, these Negroes, throw away on numbers for one week—just one week—I'd be a rich man.

ROSE Well, you wishing and calling it foolish ain't gonna stop folks from playing numbers. That's one thing for sure. Besides . . . some good things come from playing numbers. Look where Pope done bought him that restaurant off of numbers.

TROY I can't stand niggers like that. Man ain't had two dimes to rub together. He walking around with his shoes all run over bumming money for cigarettes. Alright. Got lucky there and hit the numbers . . .

ROSE Troy, I know all about it.

TROY Had good sense, I'll say that for him. He ain't throwed his money away. I seen niggers hit the numbers and go through two thousand dollars in four days. Man brought him that restaurant down there . . . fixed it up real nice . . . and then didn't want nobody to come in it! A Negro go in there

5. Traditional gospel song.
6. A reference to playing the numbers, a form of illegal gambling that was popular before the advent of legal state-run lotteries.

and can't get no kind of service. I seen a white fellow come in there and order a bowl of stew. Pope picked all the meat out the pot for him. Man ain't had nothing but a bowl of meat! Negro come behind him and ain't got nothing but the potatoes and carrots. Talking about what numbers do for people, you picked a wrong example. Ain't done nothing but make a worser fool out of him than he was before.

ROSE Troy, you ought to stop worrying about what happened at work yesterday.

TROY I ain't worried. Just told me to be down there at the Commissioner's office on Friday. Everybody think they gonna fire me. I ain't worried about them firing me. You ain't got to worry about that.

[*Pause.*]

Where's Cory? Cory in the house? [*Calls.*] Cory?

ROSE He gone out.

TROY Out, huh? He gone out cause he know I want him to help me with this fence. I know how he is. That boy scared of work.

[GABRIEL *enters. He comes halfway down the alley and, hearing Troy's voice, stops.*]

TROY [*continues*] He ain't done a lick of work in his life.

ROSE He had to go to football practice. Coach wanted them to get in a little extra practice before the season start.

TROY I got his practice . . . running out of here before he get his chores done.

ROSE Troy, what is wrong with you this morning? Don't nothing set right with you. Go on back in there and go to bed . . . get up on the other side.

TROY Why something got to be wrong with me? I ain't said nothing wrong with me.

ROSE You got something to say about everything. First it's the numbers . . . then it's the way the man runs his restaurant . . . then you done got on Cory. What's it gonna be next? Take a look up there and see if the weather suits you . . . or is it gonna be how you gonna put up the fence with the clothes hanging in the yard.

TROY You hit the nail on the head then.

ROSE I know you like I know the back of my hand. Go on in there and get you some coffee . . . see if that straighten you up. Cause you ain't right this morning.

[TROY *starts into the house and sees* GABRIEL. GABRIEL *starts singing.* TROY'S *brother, he is seven years younger than* TROY. *Injured in World War II, he has a metal plate in his head. He carries an old trumpet tied around his waist and believes with every fiber of his being that he is the Archangel Gabriel. He carries a chipped basket*[7] *with an assortment of discarded fruits and vegetables he has picked up in the strip district and which he attempts to sell.*]

GABRIEL [*singing*]

Yes, ma'am, I got plums
You ask me how I sell them
Oh ten cents apiece

7. That is, a chip basket, made from roughly joined strips of split wood.

Three for a quarter
Come and buy now
'Cause I'm here today
And tomorrow I'll be gone

[GABRIEL *enters.*]

Hey, Rose!

ROSE How you doing, Gabe?

GABRIEL There's Troy . . . Hey, Troy!

TROY Hey, Gabe.

[*Exit into kitchen.*]

ROSE [*to* GABRIEL] What you got there?

GABRIEL You know what I got, Rose. I got fruits and vegetables.

ROSE [*looking in basket*] Where's all these plums you talking about?

GABRIEL I ain't got no plums today, Rose. I was just singing that. Have some tomorrow. Put me in a big order for plums. Have enough plums tomorrow for St. Peter and everybody.

[TROY *reenters from kitchen, crosses to steps.*]

[*To* ROSE] Troy's mad at me.

TROY I ain't mad at you. What I got to be mad at you about? You ain't done nothing to me.

GABRIEL I just moved over to Miss Pearl's to keep out from in your way. I ain't mean no harm by it.

TROY Who said anything about that? I ain't said anything about that.

GABRIEL You ain't mad at me, is you?

TROY Naw . . . I ain't mad at you, Gabe. If I was mad at you I'd tell you about it.

GABRIEL Got me two rooms. In the basement. Got my own door too. Wanna see my key? [*He holds up a key.*] That's my own key! Ain't nobody else got a key like that. That's my key! My two rooms!

TROY Well, that's good, Gabe. You got your own key . . . that's good.

ROSE You hungry, Gabe? I was just fixing to cook Troy his breakfast

GABRIEL I'll take some biscuits. You got some biscuits? Did you know when I was in heaven . . . every morning me and St. Peter would sit down by the gate and eat some big fat biscuits? Oh, yeah! We had us a good time. We'd sit there and eat us them biscuits and then St. Peter would go off to sleep and tell me to wake him up when it's time to open the gates for the judgment.

ROSE Well, come on . . . I'll make up a batch of biscuits.

[ROSE *exits into the house.*]

GABRIEL Troy . . . St. Peter got your name in the book. I seen it. It say . . . Troy Maxson. I say . . . I know him! He got the same name like what I got. That's my brother!

TROY How many times you gonna tell me that, Gabe?

GABRIEL Ain't got my name in the book. Don't have to have my name. I done died and went to heaven. He got your name though. One morning St. Peter was looking at his book . . . marking it up for the judgment . . . and he let me see your name. Got it in there under M. Got Rose's name . . . I ain't seen it like I seen yours . . . but I know it's in there. He got a great big book. Got everybody's name what was ever been born. That's what he told me. But I seen your name. Seen it with my own eyes.

TROY Go on in the house there. Rose going to fix you something to eat.

GABRIEL Oh, I ain't hungry. I done had breakfast with Aunt Jemimah.[8] She come by and cooked me up a whole mess of flapjacks. Remember how we used to eat them flapjacks?

TROY Go on in the house and get you something to eat now.

GABRIEL I got to go sell my plums. I done sold some tomatoes. Got me two quarters. Wanna see? [*He shows* TROY *his quarters.*] I'm gonna save them and buy me a new horn so St. Peter can hear me when it's time to open the gates.

[GABRIEL *stops suddenly. Listens.*]

Hear that? That's the hellhounds. I got to chase them out of here. Go on get out of here! Get out!

[GABRIEL *exits singing.*]

Better get ready for the judgment
Better get ready for the judgment
My Lord is coming down

[ROSE *enters from the house.*]

TROY He gone off somewhere.

GABRIEL [*offstage*]

Better get ready for the judgment
Better get ready for the judgment morning
Better get ready for the judgment
My God is coming down

ROSE He ain't eating right. Miss Pearl say she can't get him to eat nothing.

TROY What you want me to do about it, Rose? I done did everything I can for the man. I can't make him get well. Man got half his head blown away . . . what you expect?

ROSE Seem like something ought to be done to help him.

TROY Man don't bother nobody. He just mixed up from that metal plate he got in his head. Ain't no sense for him to go back into the hospital.

ROSE Least he be eating right. They can help him take care of himself.

TROY Don't nobody wanna be locked up, Rose. What you wanna lock him up for? Man go over there and fight the war . . . messin' around with them Japs, get half his head blown off . . . and they give him a lousy three thousand dollars. And I had to swoop down on that.

ROSE Is you fixing to go into that again?

TROY That's the only way I got a roof over my head . . . cause of that metal plate.

ROSE Ain't no sense you blaming yourself for nothing. Gabe wasn't in no condition to manage that money. You done what was right by him. Can't nobody say you ain't done what was right by him. Look how long you took

8. Stereotypical "mammy" from a minstrel song; in 1893 the name and image were trademarked by a pancake mix company, which for decades hired women to portray the character.

care of him . . . till he wanted to have his own place and moved over there with Miss Pearl.

TROY That ain't what I'm saying, woman! I'm just stating the facts. If my brother didn't have that metal plate in his head . . . I wouldn't have a pot to piss in or a window to throw it out of. And I'm fifty-three years old. Now see if you can understand that!

[TROY *gets up from the porch and starts to exit the yard.*]

ROSE Where you going off to? You been running out of here every Saturday for weeks. I thought you was gonna work on this fence?

TROY I'm gonna walk down to Taylors'. Listen to the ball game. I'll be back in a bit. I'll work on it when I get back.

[*He exits the yard. The lights go to black.*]

1.3

The lights come up on the yard. It is four hours later. ROSE *is taking down the clothes from the line.* CORY *enters carrying his football equipment.*

ROSE Your daddy like to had a fit with you running out of here this morning without doing your chores.

CORY I told you I had to go to practice.

ROSE He say you were supposed to help him with this fence.

CORY He been saying that the last four or five Saturdays, and then he don't never do nothing, but go down to Taylors'. Did you tell him about the recruiter?

ROSE Yeah, I told him.

CORY What he say?

ROSE He ain't said nothing too much. You get in there and get started on your chores before he gets back. Go on and scrub down them steps before he gets back here hollering and carrying on.

CORY I'm hungry. What you got to eat, Mama?

ROSE Go on and get started on your chores. I got some meat loaf in there. Go on and make you a sandwich . . . and don't leave no mess in there.

[CORY *exits into the house,* ROSE *continues to take down the clothes.* TROY *enters the yard and sneaks up and grabs her from behind.*]

Troy! Go on, now. You liked to scared me to death. What was the score of the game? Lucille had me on the phone and I couldn't keep up with it.

TROY What I care about the game? Come here, woman. [*He tries to kiss her.*]

ROSE I thought you went down Taylors' to listen to the game. Go on, Troy! You supposed to be putting up this fence.

TROY [*attempting to kiss her again.*] I'll put it up when I finish with what is at hand.

ROSE Go on, Troy. I ain't studying you.[9]

TROY [*chasing after her*] I'm studying you . . . fixing to do my homework!

ROSE Troy, you better leave me alone.

TROY Where's Cory? That boy brought his butt home yet?

ROSE He's in the house doing his chores.

TROY [*calling*] Cory! Get your butt out here, boy!

9. That is, paying any attention to you.

[ROSE *exits into the house with the laundry.* TROY *goes over to the pile of wood, picks up a board, and starts sawing.* CORY *enters from the house.*]

TROY You just now coming in here from leaving this morning?

CORY Yeah, I had to go to football practice.

TROY Yeah, what?

CORY Yessir.

TROY I ain't but two seconds off you noway. The garbage sitting in there overflowing . . . you ain't done none of your chores . . . and you come in here talking about "Yeah."

CORY I was just getting ready to do my chores now, Pop . . .

TROY Your first chore is to help me with this fence on Saturday. Everything else come after that. Now get that saw and cut them boards.

[CORY *takes the saw and begins cutting the boards.* TROY *continues working. There is a long pause.*]

CORY Hey, Pop . . . why don't you buy a TV?

TROY What I want with a TV? What I want one of them for?

CORY Everybody got one. Earl, Ba Bra . . . Jesse!

TROY I ain't asked you who had one. I say what I want with one?

CORY So you can watch it. They got lots of things on TV. Baseball games and everything. We could watch the World Series.

TROY Yeah . . . and how much this TV cost?

CORY I don't know. They got them on sale for around two hundred dollars.[1]

TROY Two hundred dollars, huh?

CORY That ain't that much, Pop.

TROY Naw, it's just two hundred dollars. See that roof you got over your head at night? Let me tell you something about that roof. It's been over ten years since that roof was last tarred. See now . . . the snow come this winter and sit up there on that roof like it is . . . and it's gonna seep inside. It's just gonna be a little bit . . . ain't gonna hardly notice it. Then the next thing you know, it's gonna be leaking all over the house. Then the wood rot from all that water and you gonna need a whole new roof. Now, how much you think it cost to get that roof tarred?

CORY I don't know.

TROY Two hundred and sixty-four dollars . . . cash money. While you thinking about a TV, I got to be thinking about the roof . . . and whatever else go wrong around here. Now if you had two hundred dollars, what would you do . . . fix the roof or buy a TV?

CORY I'd buy a TV. Then when the roof started to leak . . . when it needed fixing . . . I'd fix it.

TROY Where you gonna get the money from? You done spent it for a TV. You gonna sit up and watch the water run all over your brand new TV.

CORY Aw, Pop. You got money. I know you do.

TROY Where I got it at, huh?

CORY You got it in the bank.

TROY You wanna see my bankbook? You wanna see that seventy-three dollars and twenty-two cents I got sitting up in there?

CORY You ain't got to pay for it all at one time. You can put a down payment on it and carry it on home with you.

1. Equivalent to about $1,500 in 2008.

TROY Not me. I ain't gonna owe nobody nothing if I can help it. Miss a payment and they come and snatch it right out your house. Then what you got? Now, soon as I get two hundred dollars clear, then I'll buy a TV. Right now, as soon as I get two hundred and sixty-four dollars, I'm gonna have this roof tarred.

CORY Aw . . . Pop!

TROY You go on and get you two hundred dollars and buy one if ya want it. I got better things to do with my money.

CORY I can't get no two hundred dollars. I ain't never seen two hundred dollars.

TROY I'll tell you what . . . you get you a hundred dollars and I'll put the other hundred with it.

CORY Alright, I'm gonna show you.

TROY You gonna show me how you can cut them boards right now.

[CORY *begins to cut the boards. There is a long pause.*]

CORY The Pirates won today. That makes five in a row.

TROY I ain't thinking about the Pirates. Got an all-white team. Got that boy . . . that Puerto Rican boy . . . Clemente.[2] Don't even half-play him. That boy could be something if they give him a chance. Play him one day and sit him on the bench the next.

CORY He gets a lot of chances to play.

TROY I'm talking about playing regular. Playing every day so you can get your timing. That's what I'm talking about.

CORY They got some white guys on the team that don't play every day. You can't play everybody at the same time.

TROY If they got a white fellow sitting on the bench . . . you can bet your last dollar he can't play! The colored guy got to be twice as good before he get on the team. That's why I don't want you to get all tied up in them sports. Man on the team and what it get him? They got colored on the team and don't use them. Same as not having them. All them teams the same.

CORY The Braves got Hank Aaron and Wes Covington.[3] Hank Aaron hit two home runs today. That makes forty-three.

TROY Hank Aaron ain't nobody. That's what you supposed to do. That's how you supposed to play the game. Ain't nothing to it. It's just a matter of timing . . . getting the right follow-through. Hell, I can hit forty-three home runs right now!

CORY Not off no major-league pitching, you couldn't.

TROY We had better pitching in the Negro leagues. I hit seven home runs off of Satchel Paige.[4] You can't get no better than that!

2. Roberto Clemente (1934–1972), a Hall of Fame outfielder who played for the Pittsburgh Pirates between 1955 and his death in a plane crash; he was a twelve-time All-Star and four-time National League batting champion. He played in 111 (of 162) games in 1957.

3. Aaron (b. 1934), who spent all but the last two years of his major-league career (1954–76) with the Milwaukee (later Atlanta) Braves, was one of the greatest baseball players of all time; his best-known achievement was breaking Ruth's lifetime home run record, eventually hitting 755; in 1957 he hit 44 home runs. Covington (b. 1932), who played for the Braves (1956–61) and five other teams (1961–66), was integral to the Braves' 1957 run to the World Series.

4. The legendary Negro League pitcher (1906–1982); he began playing in the mid-1920s, and between 1948 and 1965 played for several major-league teams.

CORY Sandy Koufax.[5] He's leading the league in strikeouts.

TROY I ain't thinking of no Sandy Koufax.

CORY You got Warren Spahn and Lew Burdette.[6] I bet you couldn't hit no home runs off of Warren Spahn.

TROY I'm through with it now. You go on and cut them boards. [*Pause*] Your mama tell me you done got recruited by a college football team? Is that right?

CORY Yeah. Coach Zellman say the recruiter gonna be coming by to talk to you. Get you to sign the permission papers.

TROY I thought you supposed to be working down there at the A&P. Ain't you suppose to be working down there after school?

CORY Mr. Stawicki say he gonna hold my job for me until after the football season. Say starting next week I can work weekends.

TROY I thought we had an understanding about this football stuff? You suppose to keep up with your chores and hold that job down at the A&P. Ain't been around here all day on a Saturday. Ain't none of your chores done . . . and now you telling me you done quit your job.

CORY I'm gonna be working weekends.

TROY You damn right you are! And ain't no need for nobody coming around here to talk to me about signing nothing.

CORY Hey, Pop . . . you can't do that. He's coming all the way from North Carolina.

TROY I don't care where he coming from. The white man ain't gonna let you get nowhere with that football noway. You go on and get your book-learning so you can work yourself up in that A&P or learn how to fix cars or build houses or something, get you a trade. That way you have something can't nobody take away from you. You go on and learn how to put your hands to some good use. Besides hauling people's garbage.

CORY I get good grades, Pop. That's why the recruiter wants to talk with you. You got to keep up your grades to get recruited. This way I'll be going to college. I'll get a chance . . .

TROY First you gonna get your butt down there to the A&P and get your job back.

CORY Mr. Stawicki done already hired somebody else cause I told him I was playing football.

TROY You a bigger fool than I thought . . . to let somebody take away your job so you can play some football. Where you gonna get your money to take out your girlfriend and whatnot? What kind of foolishness is that to let somebody take away your job?

CORY I'm still gonna be working weekends.

TROY Naw . . . naw. You getting your butt out of here and finding you another job.

5. A Hall of Fame pitcher (b. 1935), for the Brooklyn (later Los Angeles) Dodgers (1955–66).

6. The Braves' left-handed and right-handed pitching aces in 1957. Spahn (1921–2003), a Hall of Famer, played all but the final year of his career (1942–65) with the Boston (later Milwaukee) Braves; Burdette (1926–2007), the MVP of the 1957 World Series, played mainly for the Braves (1951–63) but for four other teams as well (1950, 1963–67).

CORY Come on, Pop! I got to practice. I can't work after school and play football too. The team needs me. That's what Coach Zellman say . . .

TROY I don't care what nobody else say. I'm the boss . . . you understand? I'm the boss around here. I do the only saying what counts.

CORY Come on, Pop!

TROY I asked you . . . did you understand?

CORY Yeah . . .

TROY What?!

CORY Yessir.

TROY You go on down there to that A&P and see if you can get your job back. If you can't do both . . . then you quit the football team. You've got to take the crookeds with the straights.

CORY Yessir. [*Pause*] Can I ask you a question?

TROY What the hell you wanna ask me? Mr. Stawicki the one you got the questions for.

CORY How come you ain't never liked me?

TROY Liked you? Who the hell say I got to like you? What law is there say I got to like you? Wanna stand up in my face and ask a damn fool-ass question like that. Talking about liking somebody. Come here, boy, when I talk to you.

[CORY *comes over to where* TROY *is working. He stands slouched over and* TROY *shoves him on his shoulder.*]

Straighten up, goddammit! I asked you a question . . . what law is there say I got to like you?

CORY None.

TROY Well, alright then! Don't you eat every day? [*Pause*] Answer me when I talk to you! Don't you eat every day?

CORY Yeah.

TROY Nigger, as long as you in my house, you put that sir on the end of it when you talk to me!

CORY Yes . . . sir.

TROY You eat every day.

CORY Yessir!

TROY Got a roof over your head.

CORY Yessir!

TROY Got clothes on your back.

CORY Yessir.

TROY Why you think that is?

CORY Cause of you.

TROY Aw, hell I know it's 'cause of me . . . but why do you think that is?

CORY [*hesitant*] Cause you like me.

TROY Like you? I go out of here every morning . . . bust my butt . . . putting up with them crackers[7] every day . . . cause I like you? You about the biggest fool I ever saw. [*Pause*] It's my job. It's my responsibility! You understand that? A man got to take care of his family. You live in my house . . . sleep you behind on my bedclothes . . . fill you belly up with my food . . . cause you my son. You my flesh and blood. Not 'cause I like you! Cause it's

7. Poor whites (derogatory term).

my duty to take care of you. I owe a responsibility to you! Let's get this straight right here . . . before it go along any further . . . I ain't got to like you. Mr. Rand don't give me my money come payday cause he likes me. He gives me cause he owe me. I done give you everything I had to give you. I gave you your life! Me and your mama worked that out between us. And liking your black ass wasn't part of the bargain. Don't you try and go through life worrying about if somebody like you or not. You best be making sure they doing right by you. You understand what I'm saying, boy?

CORY Yessir.

TROY Then get the hell out of my face, and get on down to that A&P.

[ROSE *has been standing behind the screen door for much of the scene. She enters as* CORY *exits.*]

ROSE Why don't you let the boy go ahead and play football, Troy? Ain't no harm in that. He's just trying to be like you with the sports.

TROY I don't want him to be like me! I want him to move as far away from my life as he can get. You the only decent thing that ever happened to me. I wish him that. But I don't wish him a thing else from my life. I decided seventeen years ago that boy wasn't getting involved in no sports. Not after what they did to me in the sports.

ROSE Troy, why don't you admit you was too old to play in the major leagues? For once . . . why don't you admit that?

TROY What do you mean too old? Don't come telling me I was too old. I just wasn't the right color. Hell, I'm fifty-three years old and can do better than Selkirk's .269 right now!

ROSE How's was you gonna play ball when you were over forty? Sometimes I can't get no sense out of you.

TROY I got good sense, woman. I got sense enough not to let my boy get hurt over playing no sports. You been mothering that boy too much. Worried about if people like him.

ROSE Everything that boy do . . . he do for you. He wants you to say "Good job, son." That's all.

TROY Rose, I ain't got time for that. He's alive. He's healthy. He's got to make his own way. I made mine. Ain't nobody gonna hold his hand when he get out there in that world.

ROSE Times have changed from when you was young, Troy. People change. The world's changing around you and you can't even see it.

TROY [*slow, methodical*] Woman . . . I do the best I can do. I come in here every Friday. I carry a sack of potatoes and a bucket of lard. You all line up at the door with your hands out. I give you the lint from my pockets. I give you my sweat and my blood. I ain't got no tears.[8] I done spent them. We go upstairs in that room at night . . . and I fall down on you and try to blast a hole into forever. I get up Monday morning . . . find my lunch on the table. I go out. Make my way. Find my strength to carry me through to the next Friday. [*Pause*] That's all I got, Rose. That's all I got to give. I can't give nothing else.

[TROY *exits into the house. The lights go down to black.*]

8. An allusion to a famous wartime declaration to the British Parliament by Prime Minister Winston Churchill in May 1940: "I have nothing to offer but blood, toil, tears, and sweat."

1.4

It is Friday. Two weeks later. CORY *starts out of the house with his football equipment. The phone rings.*

CORY [*calling*] I got it! [*He answers the phone and stands in the screen door talking.*] Hello? Hey, Jesse. Naw . . . I was just getting ready to leave now.

ROSE [*calling*] Cory!

CORY I told you, man, them spikes is all tore up. You can use them if you want, but they ain't no good. Earl got some spikes.

ROSE [*calling*] Cory!

CORY [*calling to* ROSE] Mam? I'm talking to Jesse. [*Into phone*] When she say that? [*Pause*] Aw, you lying, man. I'm gonna tell her you said that.

ROSE [*calling*] Cory, don't you go nowhere!

CORY I got to go to the game, Ma! [*Into the phone*] Yeah, hey, look, I'll talk to you later. Yeah, I'll meet you over Earl's house. Later. Bye, Ma.

[CORY *exists the house and starts out the yard.*]

ROSE Cory, where you going off to? You got that stuff all pulled out and thrown all over your room.

CORY [*in the yard*] I was looking for my spikes. Jesse wanted to borrow my spikes.

ROSE Get up there and get that cleaned up before your daddy get back in here.

CORY I got to go to the game! I'll clean it up *when I get back.*

[CORY *exits.*]

ROSE That's all he need to do is see that room all messed up.

[ROSE *exits into the house.* TROY *and* BONO *enter the yard.* TROY *is dressed in clothes other than his work clothes.*]

BONO He told him the same thing he told you. Take it to the union.

TROY Brownie ain't got that much sense. Man wasn't thinking about nothing. He wait until I confront them on it . . . then he wanna come crying seniority. [*Calls*] Hey, Rose!

BONO I wish I could have seen Mr. Rand's face when he told you.

TROY He couldn't get it out of his mouth! Liked to bit his tongue! When they called me down there to the Commissioner's office . . . he thought they was gonna fire me. Like everybody else.

BONO I didn't think they was gonna fire you. I thought they was gonna put you on the warning paper.

TROY Hey, Rose! [*To* BONO] Yeah, Mr. Rand like to bit his tongue.

[TROY *breaks the seal on the bottle, takes a drink, and hands it to* BONO.]

BONO I see you run right down to Taylors' and told that Alberta gal.

TROY [*calling*] Hey Rose! [*To* BONO] I told everybody. Hey, Rose! I went down there to cash my check.

ROSE [*entering from the house*] Hush all that hollering, man! I know you out here. What they say down there at the Commissioner's office?

TROY You supposed to come when I call you, woman. Bono'll tell you that. [*To* BONO] Don't Lucille come when you call her?

ROSE Man, hush your mouth. I ain't no dog . . . talk about "come when you call me."

TROY [*puts his arm around* ROSE] You hear this, Bono? I had me an old dog used to get uppity like that. You say, "C'mere, Blue!" . . . and he just lay there and look at you. End up getting a stick and chasing him away trying to make him come.

ROSE I ain't studying you and your dog. I remember you used to sing that old song.

TROY [*he sings*]

Hear it ring! Hear it ring!
I had a dog his name was Blue.[9]

ROSE Don't nobody wanna hear you sing that old song.

TROY [*sings*] You know Blue was mighty true.

ROSE Used to have Cory running around here singing that song.

BONO Hell, I remember that song myself.

TROY [*sings*]

You know Blue was a good old dog.
Blue treed a possum in a hollow log.

That was my daddy's song. My daddy made up that song.

ROSE I don't care who made it up. Don't nobody wanna hear you sing it.

TROY [*makes a song like calling a dog*] Come here, woman.

ROSE You come in here carrying on, I reckon they ain't fired you. What they say down there at the Commissioner's office?

TROY Look here, Rose . . . Mr. Rand called me into his office today when I got back from talking to them people down there . . . it come from up top . . . he called me in and told me they was making me a driver.

ROSE Troy, you kidding!

TROY No I ain't. Ask Bono.

ROSE Well, that's great, Troy. Now you don't have to hassle them people no more.

[LYONS *enters from the street.*]

TROY Aw hell, I wasn't looking to see you today. I thought you was in jail. Got it all over the front page of the *Courier*[1] about them raiding Sefus' place . . . where you be hanging out with all them thugs.

LYONS Hey, Pop . . . that ain't got nothing to do with me. I don't go down there gambling. I go down there to sit in with the band. I ain't got nothing to do with the gambling part. They got some good music down there.

TROY They got some rogues . . . is what they got.

LYONS How you been, Mr. Bono? Hi, Rose.

BONO I see where you playing down at the Crawford Grill tonight.

ROSE How come you ain't brought Bonnie like I told you. You should have brought Bonnie with you, she ain't been over in a month of Sundays.

LYONS I was just in the neighborhood . . . thought I'd stop by.

TROY Here he come . . .

BONO Your daddy got a promotion on the rubbish. He's gonna be the first

9. A variation on "Old Blue," a traditional African American folk song.

1. The *Pittsburgh Courier,* one of the top-selling African American newspapers in the mid-20th century.

colored driver. Ain't got to do nothing but sit up there and read the paper like them white fellows.

LYONS Hey, Pop . . . if you knew how to read you'd be alright.

BONO Naw . . . naw . . . you mean if the nigger knew how to drive he'd be all right. Been fighting with them people about driving and ain't even got a license. Mr. Rand know you ain't got no driver's license?

TROY Driving ain't nothing. All you do is point the truck where you want it to go. Driving ain't nothing.

BONO Do Mr. Rand know you ain't got no driver's license? That's what I'm talking about. I ain't asked if driving was easy. I asked if Mr. Rand know you ain't got no driver's license.

TROY He ain't got to know. The man ain't got to know my business. Time he find out, I have two or three driver's licenses.

LYONS [*going into his pocket*] Say, look here, Pop . . .

TROY I knew it was coming. Didn't I tell you, Bono? I know what kind of "Look here, Pop" that was. The nigger fixing to ask me for some money. It's Friday night. It's my payday. All them rogues down there on the avenue . . . the ones that ain't in jail . . . and Lyons is hopping in his shoes to get down there with them.

LYONS See, Pop . . . if you give somebody else a chance to talk sometime, you'd see that I was fixing to pay you back your ten dollars like I told you. Here . . . I told you I'd pay you when Bonnie got paid.

TROY Naw . . . you go ahead and keep that ten dollars. Put it in the bank. The next time you feel like you wanna come by here and ask me for something . . . you go on down there and get that.

LYONS Here's your ten dollars, Pop. I told you I don't want you to give me nothing. I just wanted to borrow ten dollars.

TROY Naw . . . you go on and keep that for the next time you want to ask me.

LYONS Come on, Pop . . . here go your ten dollars.

ROSE Why don't you go on and let the boy pay you back, Troy?

LYONS Here you go, Rose. If you don't take it I'm gonna have to hear about it for the next six months.

[*He hands her the money.*]

ROSE You can hand yours over here too, Troy.

TROY You see this, Bono. You see how they do me.

BONO Yeah, Lucille do me the same way.

[GABRIEL *is heard singing offstage. He enters.*]

GABRIEL Better get ready for the Judgment! Better get ready for . . . Hey! . . . Hey! . . . There's Troy's boy!

LYONS How you doing, Uncle Gabe?

GABRIEL Lyons . . . The King of the Jungle! Rose . . . hey, Rose. Got a flower for you. [*He takes a rose from his pocket.*] Picked it myself. That's the same rose like you is!

ROSE That's right nice of you, Gabe.

LYONS What you been doing, Uncle Gabe?

GABRIEL Oh, I been chasing hellhounds and waiting on the time to tell St. Peter to open the gates.

LYONS You been chasing hellhounds, huh? Well . . . you doing the right thing, Uncle Gabe. Somebody got to chase them.

GABRIEL Oh, yeah . . . I know it. The devil's strong. The devil ain't no pushover. Hellhounds snipping at everybody's heels. But I got my trumpet waiting on the judgment time.

LYONS Waiting on the Battle of Armageddon,[2] huh?

GABRIEL Ain't gonna be too much of a battle when God get to waving that Judgment sword. But the people's gonna have a hell of a time trying to get into heaven if them gates ain't open.

LYONS [*putting his arm around* GABRIEL] You hear this, Pop. Uncle Gabe, you alright!

GABRIEL [*laughing with* LYONS] Lyons! King of the Jungle.

ROSE You gonna stay for supper, Gabe. Want me to fix you a plate?

GABRIEL I'll take a sandwich, Rose. Don't want no plate. Just wanna eat with my hands. I'll take a sandwich.

ROSE How about you, Lyons? You staying? Got some short ribs cooking.

LYONS Naw, I won't eat nothing till after we finished playing. [*Pause*] You ought to come down and listen to me play, Pop.

TROY I don't like that Chinese music. All that noise.

ROSE Go on in the house and wash up, Gabe . . . I'll fix you a sandwich.

GABRIEL [*to* LYONS, *as he exits*] Troy's mad at me.

LYONS What you mad at Uncle Gabe for, Pop?

ROSE He thinks Troy's mad at him cause he moved over to Miss Pearl's.

TROY I ain't mad at the man. He can live where he want to live at.

LYONS What he move over there for? Miss Pearl don't like nobody.

ROSE She don't mind him none. She treats him real nice. She just don't allow all that singing.

TROY She don't mind that rent he be paying . . . that's what she don't mind.

ROSE Troy, I ain't going through that with you no more. He's over there cause he want to have his own place. He can come and go as he please.

TROY Hell, he could come and go as he please here. I wasn't stopping him. I ain't put no rules on him.

ROSE It ain't the same thing, Troy. And you know it.

[GABRIEL *comes to the door.*]

Now, that's the last I wanna hear about that. I don't wanna hear nothing else about Gabe and Miss Pearl. And next week . . .

GABRIEL I'm ready for my sandwich, Rose.

ROSE And next week . . . when that recruiter come from that school . . . I want you to sign that paper and go on and let Cory play football. Then that'll be the last I have to hear about that.

TROY [*to* ROSE *as she exits into the house*] I ain't thinking about Cory nothing.

LYONS What . . . Cory got recruited? What school he going to?

TROY That boy walking around here smelling his piss . . . thinking he's grown. Thinking he's gonna do what he want, irrespective of what I say. Look here, Bono . . . I left the Commissioner's office and went down to the A&P . . . that boy ain't working down there. He lying to me. Telling me he got his job back . . . telling me he working weekends . . . telling me he working after school . . . Mr. Stawicki tell me he ain't working down there at all!

2. The final battle between the forces of God and of evil, as described in the New Testament's book of Revelation (see 16.16).

LYONS Cory just growing up. He's just busting at the seams trying to fill out your shoes.

TROY I don't care what he's doing. When he get to the point where he wanna disobey me . . . then it's time for him to move on. Bono'll tell you that. I bet he ain't never disobeyed his daddy without paying the consequences.

BONO I ain't never had a chance. My daddy came on through . . . but I ain't never knew him to see him . . . or what he had on his mind or where he went. Just moving on through. Searching out the New Land. That's what the old folks used to call it. See a fellow moving around from place to place . . . woman to woman . . . called it searching out the New Land. I can't say if he ever found it. I come along, didn't want no kids. Didn't know if I was gonna be in one place long enough to fix on them right as their daddy. I figured I was going searching too. As it turned out I been hooked up with Lucille near about as long as your daddy been with Rose. Going on sixteen years.

TROY Sometimes I wish I hadn't known my daddy. He ain't cared nothing about no kids. A kid to him wasn't nothing. All he wanted was for you to learn how to walk so he could start you to working. When it come time for eating . . . he ate first. If there was anything left over, that's what you got. Man would sit down and eat two chickens and give you the wing.

LYONS You ought to stop that, Pop. Everybody feed their kids. No matter how hard times is . . . everybody care about their kids. Make sure they have something to eat.

TROY The only thing my daddy cared about was getting them bales of cotton in to Mr. Lubin. That's the only thing that mattered to him. Sometimes I used to wonder why he was living. Wonder why the devil hadn't come and got him. "Get them bales of cotton in to Mr. Lubin" and find out he owe him money[3] . . .

LYONS He should have just went on and left when he saw he couldn't get nowhere. That's what I would have done.

TROY How he gonna leave with eleven kids? And where he gonna go? He ain't knew how to do nothing but farm. No, he was trapped and I think he knew it. But I'll say this for him . . . he felt a responsibility toward us. Maybe he ain't treated us the way I felt he should have . . . but without that responsibility he could have walked off and left us . . . made his own way.

BONO A lot of them did. Back in those days what you talking about . . . they walk out their front door and just take on down one road or another and keep on walking.

LYONS There you go! That's what I'm talking about.

BONO Just keep on walking till you come to something else. Ain't you never heard of nobody having the walking blues? Well, that's what you call it when you just take off like that.

TROY My daddy ain't had them walking blues! What you talking about? He stayed right there with his family. But he was just as evil as he could be. My

3. Under the sharecropping system that arose in the South after the Civil War, tenant farmers received their seed, tools, food and clothing, and housing on credit from landowners; after harvesting the cotton, they had to repay these charges from their share of the value of the crop.

mama couldn't stand him. Couldn't stand that evilness. She run off when I was about eight. She sneaked off one night after he had gone to sleep. Told me she was coming back for me. I ain't never seen her no more. All his women run off and left him. He wasn't good for nobody.

When my turn come to head out, I was fourteen and got to sniffing around Joe Canewell's daughter. Had us an old mule we called Greyboy. My daddy sent me out to do some plowing and I tied up Greyboy and went to fooling around with Joe Canewell's daughter. We done found us a nice little spot, got real cozy with each other. She about thirteen and we done figured we was grown anyway . . . so we down there enjoying ourselves . . . ain't thinking about nothing. We didn't know Greyboy had got loose and wandered back to the house and my daddy was looking for me. We down there by the creek enjoying ourselves when my daddy come up on us. Surprised us. He had them leather straps off the mule and commenced to whupping me like there was no tomorrow. I jumped up, mad and embarrassed. I was scared of my daddy. When he commenced to whupping on me . . . quite naturally I run to get out of the way.

[*Pause.*]

Now I thought he was mad cause I ain't done my work. But I see where he was chasing me off so he could have the gal for himself. When I see what the matter of it was, I lost all fear of my daddy. Right there is where I become a man . . . at fourteen years of age.

[*Pause.*]

Now it was my turn to run him off. I picked up them same reins that he had used on me. I picked up them reins and commenced to whupping on him. The gal jumped up and run off . . . and when my daddy turned to face me, I could see why the devil had never come to get him . . . cause he was the devil himself. I don't know what happened. When I woke up, I was laying right there by the creek, and Blue . . . this old dog we had . . . was licking my face. I thought I was blind. I couldn't see nothing. Both my eyes were swollen shut. I layed there and cried. I didn't know what I was gonna do. The only thing I knew was the time had come for me to leave my daddy's house. And right there the world suddenly got big. And it was a long time before I could cut it down to where I could handle it.

Part of that cutting down was when I got to the place where I could feel him kicking in my blood and knew that the only thing that separated us was the matter of a few years.

[GABRIEL *enters from the house with a sandwich.*]

LYONS What you got there, Uncle Gabe?

GABRIEL Got me a ham sandwich. Rose gave me a ham sandwich.

TROY I don't know what happened to him. I done lost touch with everybody except Gabriel. But I hope he's dead. I hope he found some peace.

LYONS That's a heavy story, Pop. I didn't know you left home when you was fourteen.

TROY And didn't know nothing. The only part of the world I knew was the forty-two acres of Mr. Lubin's land. That's all I knew about life.

LYONS Fourteen's kinda young to be out on your own. [*Phone rings.*] I don't even think I was ready to be out on my own at fourteen. I don't know what I would have done.

TROY I got up from the creek and walked on down to Mobile. I was through with farming. Figured I could do better in the city. So I walked the two hundred miles to Mobile.

LYONS Wait a minute . . . you ain't walked no two hundred miles, Pop. Ain't nobody gonna walk no two hundred miles. You talking about some walking there.

BONO That's the only way you got anywhere back in them days.

LYONS Shhh. Damn if I wouldn't have hitched a ride with somebody!

TROY Who you gonna hitch it with? They ain't had no cars and things like they got now. We talking about 1918.

ROSE [*entering*] What you all out here getting into?

TROY [*to* ROSE] I'm telling Lyons how good he got it. He don't know nothing about this I'm talking.

ROSE Lyons, that was Bonnie on the phone. She say you supposed to pick her up.

LYONS Yeah, okay, Rose.

TROY I walked on down to Mobile and hitched up with some of them fellows that was heading this way. Got up here and found out . . . not only couldn't you get a job . . . you couldn't find no place to live. I thought I was in freedom. Shhh. Colored folks living down there on the riverbanks in whatever kind of shelter they could find for themselves. Right down there under the Brady Street Bridge. Living in shacks made of sticks and tar paper. Messed around there and went from bad to worse. Started stealing. First it was food. Then I figured, hell, if I steal money I can buy me some food. Buy me some shoes too! One thing led to another. Met your mama. I was young and anxious to be a man. Met your mama and had you. What I do that for? Now I got to worry about feeding you and her. Got to steal three times as much. Went out one day looking for somebody to rob . . . that's what I was, a robber. I'll tell you the truth. I'm ashamed of it today. But it's the truth. Went to rob this fellow . . . pulled out my knife . . . and he pulled out a gun. Shot me in the chest. It felt just like somebody had taken a hot branding iron and laid it on me. When he shot me I jumped at him with my knife. They told me I killed him and they put me in the penitentiary and locked me up for fifteen years. That's where I met Bono. That's where I learned how to play baseball. Got out that place and your mama had taken you and went on to make life without me. Fifteen years was a long time for her to wait. But that fifteen years cured me of that robbing stuff. Rose'll tell you. She asked me when I met her if I had gotten all that foolishness out of my system. And I told her, "Baby, it's you and baseball all what count with me." You hear me, Bono? I meant it too. She say, "Which one comes first?" I told her, "Baby, ain't no doubt it's baseball . . . but you stick and get old with me and we'll both outlive this baseball." Am I right, Rose? And it's true.

ROSE Man, hush your mouth. You ain't said no such thing. Talking about, "Baby, you know you'll always be number one with me." That's what you was talking.

TROY You hear that, Bono. That's why I love her.

BONO Rose'll keep you straight. You get off the track, she'll straighten you up.

ROSE Lyons, you better get on up and get Bonnie. She waiting on you.

LYONS [*gets up to go*] Hey, Pop, why don't you come on down to the Grill and hear me play?

TROY I ain't going down there. I'm too old to be sitting around in them clubs.

BONO You got to be good to play down at the Grill.

LYONS Come on, Pop . . .

TROY I got to get up in the morning.

LYONS You ain't got to stay long.

TROY Naw, I'm gonna get my supper and go on to bed.

LYONS Well, I got to go. I'll see you again.

TROY Don't you come around my house on my payday.

ROSE Pick up the phone and let somebody know you coming. And bring Bonnie with you. You know I'm always glad to see her.

LYONS Yeah, I'll do that, Rose. You take care now. See you, Pop. See you, Mr. Bono. See you, Uncle Gabe.

GABRIEL Lyons! King of the Jungle!

[LYONS *exits.*]

TROY Is supper ready, woman? Me and you got some business to take care of. I'm gonna tear it up too.

ROSE Troy, I done told you now!

TROY [*puts his arm around* BONO] Aw hell, woman . . . this is Bono. Bono like family. I done known this nigger since . . . how long I done know you?

BONO It's been a long time.

TROY I done known this nigger since Skippy was a pup.[4] Me and him done been through some times.

BONO You sure right about that.

TROY Hell, I done know him longer than I known you. And we still standing shoulder to shoulder. Hey, look here, Bono . . . a man can't ask for no more than that. [*Drinks to him.*] I love you, nigger.

BONO Hell, I love you too . . . but I got to get home see my woman. You got yours in hand. I got to go get mine.

[BONO *starts to exit as* CORY *enters the yard, dressed in his football uniform. He gives* TROY *a hard, uncompromising look.*]

CORY What you do that for, Pop?

[*He throws his helmet down in the direction of* TROY.]

ROSE What's the matter? Cory . . . what's the matter?

CORY Papa done went up to the school and told Coach Zellman I can't play football no more. Wouldn't even let me play the game. Told him to tell the recruiter not to come.

ROSE Troy . . .

TROY What you Troying me for. Yeah, I did it. And the boy know why I did it.

CORY Why you wanna do that to me? That was the one chance I had.

ROSE Ain't nothing wrong with Cory playing football, Troy.

TROY The boy lied to me. I told the nigger if he wanna play football . . . to keep up his chores and hold down that job at the A&P. That was the conditions. Stopped down there to see Mr. Stawicki . . .

CORY I can't work after school during the football season, Pop! I tried to tell you that Mr. Stawicki's holding my job for me. You don't never want to listen to nobody. And then you wanna go and do this to me!

4. That is, for a very long time (folk expression).

TROY I ain't done nothing to you. You done it to yourself.

CORY Just cause you didn't have a chance! You just scared I'm gonna be better than you, that's all.

TROY Come here.

ROSE Troy . . .

[CORY *reluctantly crosses over to* TROY.]

TROY Alright! See. You done made a mistake.

CORY I didn't even do nothing!

TROY I'm gonna tell you what your mistake was. See . . . you swung at the ball and didn't hit it. That's strike one. See, you in the batter's box now. You swung and you missed. That's strike one. Don't you strike out!

[*Lights fade to black.*]

2.1

The following morning. CORY *is at the tree hitting the ball with the bat. He tries to mimic* TROY, *but his swing is awkward, less sure.* ROSE *enters from the house.*

ROSE Cory, I want you to help me with this cupboard.

CORY I ain't quitting the team. I don't care what Poppa say.

ROSE I'll talk to him when he gets back. He had to go see about your Uncle Gabe. The police done arrested him. Say he was disturbing the peace. He'll be back directly. Come on in here and help me clean out the top of this cupboard.

[CORY *exits into the house.* ROSE *sees* TROY *and* BONO *coming down the alley.*]

Troy . . . what they say down there?

TROY Ain't said nothing. I give them fifty dollars and they let him go. I'll talk to you about it. Where's Cory?

ROSE He's in there helping me clean out these cupboards.

TROY Tell him to get his butt out here.

[TROY *and* BONO *go over to the pile of wood.* BONO *picks up the saw and begins sawing.*]

TROY [*to* BONO] All they want is the money. That makes six or seven times I done went down there and got him. See me coming they stick out their hands.

BONO Yeah. I know what you mean. That's all they care about . . . that money. They don't care about what's right. [*Pause*] Nigger, why you got to go and get some hard wood? You ain't doing nothing but building a little old fence. Get you some soft pine wood. That's all you need.

TROY I know what I'm doing. This is outside wood. You put pine wood inside the house. Pine wood is inside wood. This here is outside wood. Now you tell me where the fence is gonna be?

BONO You don't need this wood. You can put it up with pine wood and it'll stand as long as you gonna be here looking at it.

TROY How you know how long I'm gonna be here, nigger? Hell, I might just live forever. Live longer than old man Horsely.

BONO That's what Magee used to say.

TROY Magee's a damn fool. Now you tell me who you ever heard of gonna pull their own teeth with a pair of rusty pliers.

BONO The old folks . . . my granddaddy used to pull his teeth with pliers. They ain't had no dentists for the colored folks back then.

TROY Get clean pliers! You understand? Clean pliers! Sterilize them! Besides we ain't living back then. All Magee had to do was walk over to Doc Goldblum's.

BONO I see where you and that Tallahassee gal . . . that Alberta . . . I see where you all done got tight.

TROY What you mean "got tight"?

BONO I see where you be laughing and joking with her all the time.

TROY I laughs and jokes with all of them, Bono. You know me.

BONO That ain't the kind of laughing and joking I'm talking about.

[CORY *enters from the house.*]

CORY How you doing, Mr. Bono?

TROY Cory? Get that saw from Bono and cut some wood. He talking about the wood's too hard to cut. Stand back there, Jim, and let that young boy show you how it's done.

BONO He's sure welcome to it.

[CORY *takes the saw and begins to cut the wood.*]

Whew-e-e! Look at that. Big old strong boy. Look like Joe Louis.[5] Hell, must be getting old the way I'm watching that boy whip through that wood.

CORY I don't see why Mama want a fence around the yard noways.

TROY Damn if I know either. What the hell she keeping out with it? She ain't got nothing nobody want.

BONO Some people build fences to keep people out . . . and other people build fences to keep people in. Rose wants to hold on to you all. She loves you.

TROY Hell, nigger, I don't need nobody to tell me my wife loves me, Cory . . . go on in the house and see if you can find that other saw.

CORY Where's it at?

TROY I said find it! Look for it till you find it!

[CORY *exists into the house.*]

What's that supposed to mean? Wanna keep us in?

BONO Troy . . . I done known you seem like damn near my whole life. You and Rose both. I done know both of you all for a long time. I remember when you met Rose. When you was hitting them baseball out the park. A lot of them old gals was after you then. You had the pick of the litter. When you picked Rose, I was happy for you. That was the first time I knew you had any sense. I said . . . My man Troy knows what he's doing . . . I'm gonna follow this nigger . . . he might take me somewhere. I been following you too. I done learned a whole heap of things about life watching you. I done learned how to tell where the shit lies. How to tell it from the alfalfa. You done learned me a lot of things. You showed me how to not make the same mistakes . . . to take life as it comes along and keep putting one foot in front of the other. [*Pause*] Rose a good woman, Troy.

TROY Hell, nigger, I know she a good woman. I been married to her for eighteen years. What you got on your mind, Bono?

5. American boxer (1914–1981); as world heavyweight champion (1937–49), he was the most famous black man in the United States.

BONO I just say she a good woman. Just like I say anything. I ain't got to have nothing on my mind.

TROY You just gonna say she a good woman and leave it hanging out there like that? Why you telling me she a good woman?

BONO She loves you, Troy. Rose loves you.

TROY You saying I don't measure up. That's what you trying to say. I don't measure up cause I'm seeing this other gal. I know what you trying to say.

BONO I know what Rose means to you, Troy. I'm just trying to say I don't want to see you mess up.

TROY Yeah, I appreciate that, Bono. If you was messing around on Lucille I'd be telling you the same thing.

BONO Well, that's all I got to say. I just say that because I love you both.

TROY Hell, you know me . . . I wasn't out there looking for nothing. You can't find a better woman than Rose. I know that. But seems like this woman just stuck onto me where I can't shake her loose. I done wrestled with it, tried to throw her off me . . . but she just stuck on tighter. Now she's stuck on for good.

BONO You's in control . . . that's what you tell me all the time. You responsible for what you do.

TROY I ain't ducking the responsibility of it. As long as it sets right in my heart . . . then I'm okay. Cause that's all I listen to. It'll tell me right from wrong every time. And I ain't talking about doing Rose no bad turn. I love Rose. She done carried me a long ways and I love and respect her for that.

BONO I know you do. That's why I don't want to see you hurt her. But what you gonna do when she find out? What you got then? If you try and juggle both of them . . . sooner or later you gonna drop one of them. That's common sense.

TROY Yeah, I hear what you saying, Bono. I been trying to figure a way to work it out.

BONO Work it out right, Troy. I don't want to be getting all up between you and Rose's business . . . but work it so it come out right.

TROY Aw hell, I get all up between you and Lucille's business. When you gonna get that woman that refrigerator she been wanting? Don't tell me you ain't got no money now. I know who your banker is. Mellon[6] don't need that money bad as Lucille want that refrigerator. I'll tell you that.

BONO Tell you what I'll do . . . when you finish building this fence for Rose . . . I'll buy Lucille that refrigerator.

TROY You done stuck your foot in your mouth now!

[TROY *grabs up a board and begins to saw.* BONO *starts to walk out the yard.*]

Hey, nigger . . . where you going?

BONO I'm going home. I know you don't expect me to help you now. I'm protecting my money. I wanna see you put that fence up by yourself. That's what I want to see. You'll be here another six months without me.

TROY Nigger, you ain't right.

BONO When it comes to my money . . . I'm right as fireworks on the Fourth of July.

6. Mellon National Bank, founded in Pittsburgh in 1870 by Thomas Mellon.

TROY Alright, we gonna see now. You better get out your bankbook.

[BONO *exits, and* TROY *continues to work.* ROSE *enters from the house.*]

ROSE What they say down there? What's happening with Gabe?

TROY I went down there and got him out. Cost me fifty dollars. Say he was disturbing the peace. Judge set up a hearing for him in three weeks. Say to show cause why he shouldn't be recommitted.

ROSE What was he doing that cause them to arrest him?

TROY Some kids was teasing him and he run them off home. Say he was howling and carrying on. Some folks seen him and called the police. That's all it was.

ROSE Well, what's you say? What'd you tell the judge?

TROY Told him I'd look after him. It didn't make no sense to recommit the man. He stuck out his big greasy palm and told me to give him fifty dollars and take him on home.

ROSE Where's he at now? Where'd he go off to?

TROY He's gone on about his business. He don't need nobody to hold his hand.

ROSE Well, I don't know. Seem like that would be the best place for him if they did put him into the hospital. I know what you're gonna say. But that's what I think would be best.

TROY The man done had his life ruined fighting for what? And they wanna take and lock him up. Let him be free. He don't bother nobody.

ROSE Well, everybody got their own way of looking at it I guess. Come on and get your lunch. I got a bowl of lima beans and some cornbread in the oven. Come on get something to eat. Ain't no sense you fretting over Gabe.

[ROSE *turns to go into the house.*]

TROY Rose . . . got something to tell you.

ROSE Well, come on . . . wait till I get this food on the table.

TROY Rose!

[*She stops and turns around.*]

I don't know how to say this. [*Pause*] I can't explain it none. It just sort of grows on you till it gets out of hand. It starts out like a little bush . . . and the next think you know it's a whole forest.

ROSE Troy . . . what is you talking about?

TROY I'm talking, woman, let me talk. I'm trying to find a way to tell you . . . I'm gonna be a daddy. I'm gonna be somebody's daddy.

ROSE Troy . . . you're not telling me this? You're gonna be . . . what?

TROY Rose . . . now . . . see . . .

ROSE You telling me you gonna be somebody's daddy? You telling your *wife* this?

[GABRIEL *enters from the street. He carries a rose in his hand.*]

GABRIEL Hey, Troy! Hey, Rose!

ROSE I have to wait eighteen years to hear something like this.

GABRIEL Hey, Rose . . . I got a flower for you. [*He hands it to her.*] That's a rose. Same rose like you is.

ROSE Thanks, Gabe.

GABRIEL Troy, you ain't mad at me is you? Them bad mens come and put me away. You ain't mad at me is you?

TROY Naw, Gabe, I ain't mad at you.

ROSE Eighteen years and you wanna come with this.

GABRIEL [*takes a quarter out of his pocket*] See what I got? Got a brand new quarter.

TROY Rose . . . it's just . . .

ROSE Ain't nothing you can say, Troy. Ain't no way of explaining that.

GABRIEL Fellow that give me this quarter had a whole mess of them. I'm gonna keep this quarter till it stop shining.

ROSE Gabe, go on in the house there. I got some watermelon in the frigidaire. Go on and get you a piece.

GABRIEL Say, Rose . . . you know I was chasing hellhounds and them bad mens come and get me and take me away. Troy helped me. He come down there and told them they better let me go before he beat them up. Yeah, he did!

ROSE You go on and get you a piece of watermelon, Gabe. Them bad mens is gone now.

GABRIEL Okay, Rose . . . gonna get me some watermelon. The kind with the stripes on it.

[GABRIEL *exits into the house.*]

ROSE Why, Troy? Why? After all these years to come dragging this in to me now. It don't make no sense at your age. I could have expected this ten or fifteen years ago, but not now.

TROY Age ain't got nothing to do with it, Rose.

ROSE I done tried to be everything a wife should be. Everything a wife could be. Been married eighteen years and I got to live to see the day you tell me you been seeing another woman and done fathered a child by her. And you know I ain't never wanted no half nothing in my family. My whole family is half. Everybody got different fathers and mothers . . . my two sisters and my brother. Can't hardly tell who's who. Can't never sit down and talk about Papa and Mama. It's your papa and your mama and my papa and my mama . . .

TROY Rose . . . stop it now.

ROSE I ain't never wanted that for none of my children. And now you wanna drag your behind in here and tell me something like this.

TROY You ought to know. It's time for you to know.

ROSE Well, I don't want to know, goddamn it!

TROY I can't just make it go away. It's done now. I can't wish the circumstance of the thing away.

ROSE And you don't want to either. Maybe you want to wish me and my boy away. Maybe that's what you want? Well, you can't wish us away. I've got eighteen years of my life invested in you. You ought to have stayed upstairs in my bed where you belong.

TROY Rose . . . now listen to me . . . we can get a handle on this thing. We can talk this out . . . come to an understanding.

ROSE All of a sudden it's "we." Where was "we" at when you was down there rolling around with some godforsaken woman? "We" should have come to an understanding before you started making a damn fool of yourself. You're a day late and a dollar short when it comes to an understanding with me.

TROY It's just . . . She gives me a different idea . . . a different understanding about myself. I can step out of this house and get away from the pressures and problems . . . be a different man. I ain't got to wonder how I'm gonna pay the bills or get the roof fixed. I can just be a part of myself that I ain't never been.

ROSE What I want to know . . . is do you plan to continue seeing her. That's all you can say to me.

TROY I can sit up in her house and laugh. Do you understand what I'm saying. I can laugh out loud . . . and it feels good. It reaches all the way down to the bottom of my shoes. [*Pause*] Rose, I can't give that up.

ROSE Maybe you ought to go on and stay down there with her . . . if she a better woman than me.

TROY It ain't about nobody being a better woman or nothing. Rose, you ain't the blame. A man couldn't ask for no woman to be a better wife than you've been. I'm responsible for it. I done locked myself into a pattern trying to take care of you all that I forgot about myself.

ROSE What the hell was I there for? That was my job, not somebody else's.

TROY Rose, I done tried all my life to live decent . . . to live a clean . . . hard . . . useful life. I tried to be a good husband to you. In every way I knew how. Maybe I come into the world backwards, I don't know. But . . . you born with two strikes on you before you come to the plate. You got to guard it closely . . . always looking for the curve ball on the inside corner. You can't afford to let none get past you. You can't afford a call strike.[7] If you going down . . . you going down swinging. Everything lined up against you. What you gonna do. I fooled them, Rose. I bunted. When I found you and Cory and a halfway decent job . . . I was safe. Couldn't nothing touch me. I wasn't gonna strike out no more. I wasn't going back to the penitentiary. I wasn't gonna lay in the streets with a bottle of wine. I was safe. I had me a family. A job. I wasn't gonna get that last strike. I was on first looking for one of them boys to knock me in. To get me home.

ROSE You should have stayed in my bed, Troy.

TROY Then when I saw that gal . . . she firmed up my backbone. And I got to thinking that if I tried . . . I just might be able to steal second. Do you understand after eighteen years I wanted to steal second.

ROSE You should have held me tight. You should have grabbed me and held on.

TROY I stood on first base for eighteen years and I thought . . . well, goddamn it . . . go on for it!

ROSE We're not talking about baseball! We're talking about you going off to lay in bed with another woman . . . and then bring it home to me. That's what we're talking about. We ain't talking about no baseball.

TROY Rose, you're not listening to me. I'm trying the best I can to explain it to you. It's not easy for me to admit that I been standing in the same place for eighteen years.

ROSE I been standing with you! I been right here with you, Troy. I got a life too. I gave eighteen years of my life to stand in the same spot with you.

7. That is, a called strike: a pitch at which the batter fails to swing that the umpire judges to have been within the strike zone.

Don't you think I ever wanted other things? Don't you think I had dreams and hopes? What about my life? What about me? Don't you think it ever crossed my mind to want to know other men? That I wanted to lay up somewhere and forget about my responsibilities? That I wanted someone to make me laugh so I could feel good? You not the only one who's got wants and needs. But I held on to you, Troy. I took all my feelings, my wants and needs, my dreams . . . and I buried them inside you. I planted a seed and watched and prayed over it. I planted myself inside you and waited to bloom. And it didn't take me no eighteen years to find out the soil was hard and rocky and it wasn't never gonna bloom.

But I held on to you, Troy. I held you tighter. You was my husband. I owed you everything I had. Every part of me I could find to give you. And upstairs in that room . . . with the darkness falling in on me . . . I gave everything I had to try and erase the doubt that you wasn't the finest man in the world. And wherever you was going . . . I wanted to be there with you. Cause you was my husband. Cause that's the only way I was gonna survive as your wife. You always talking about what you give . . . and what you don't have to give. But you take too. You take . . . and don't even know nobody's giving!

[ROSE *turns to exit into the house;* TROY *grabs her arm.*]

TROY You say I take and don't give!

ROSE Troy! You're hurting me!

TROY You say I take and don't give.

ROSE Troy . . . you're hurting my arm! Let go!

TROY I done give you everything I got. Don't you tell that lie on me.

ROSE Troy!

TROY Don't you tell that lie on me!

[CORY *enters from the house.*]

CORY Mama!

ROSE Troy. You're hurting me.

TROY Don't you tell me about no taking and giving.

[CORY *comes up behind* TROY *and grabs him.* TROY, *surprised, is thrown off balance just as* CORY *throws a glancing blow that catches him on the chest and knocks him down.* TROY *is stunned, as is* CORY.]

ROSE Troy. Troy. No!

[TROY *gets to his feet and starts at* CORY.]

Troy . . . no. Please! Troy!

[ROSE *pulls on* TROY *to hold him back.* TROY *stops himself.*]

TROY [*to* CORY] Alright. That's strike two. You stay away from around me, boy. Don't you strike out. You living with a full count. Don't you strike out.

[TROY *exits out the yard as the lights go down.*]

2.2

It is six months later, early afternoon. TROY *enters from the house and starts to exit the yard.* ROSE *enters from the house.*

ROSE Troy, I want to talk to you.

TROY All of a sudden, after all this time, you want to talk to me, huh? You ain't wanted to talk to me for months. You ain't wanted to talk to me last night. You ain't wanted no part of me then. What you wanna talk to me about now?

ROSE Tomorrow's Friday.

TROY I know what day tomorrow is. You think I don't know tomorrow's Friday? My whole life I ain't done nothing but look to see Friday coming and you got to tell me it's Friday.

ROSE I want to know if you're coming home.

TROY I always come home, Rose. You know that. There ain't never been a night I ain't come home.

ROSE That ain't what I mean . . . and you know it. I want to know if you're coming straight home after work.

TROY I figure I'd cash my check . . . hang out at Taylors' with the boys . . . maybe play a game of checkers . . .

ROSE Troy, I can't live like this. I won't live like this. You livin' on borrowed time with me. It's been going on six months now you ain't been coming home.

TROY I be here every night. Every night of the year. That's 365 days.

ROSE I want you to come home tomorrow after work.

TROY Rose . . . I don't mess up my pay. You know that now. I take my pay and I give it to you. I don't have no money but what you give me back. I just want to have a little time to myself . . . a little time to enjoy life.

ROSE What about me? When's my time to enjoy life?

TROY I don't know what to tell you, Rose. I'm doing the best I can.

ROSE You ain't been home from work but time enough to change your clothes and run out . . . and you wanna call that the best you can do?

TROY I'm going over to the hospital to see Alberta. She went into the hospital this afternoon. Look like she might have the baby early. I won't be gone long.

ROSE Well, you ought to know. They went over to Miss Pearl's and got Gabe today. She said you told them to go ahead and lock him up.

TROY I ain't said no such thing. Whoever told you that is telling a lie. Pearl ain't doing nothing but telling a big fat lie.

ROSE She ain't had to tell me. I read it on the papers.

TROY I ain't told them nothing of the kind.

ROSE I saw it right there on the papers.

TROY What it say, huh?

ROSE It said you told them to take him.

TROY Then they screwed that up, just the way they screw up everything. I ain't worried about what they got on the paper.

ROSE Say the government send part of his check to the hospital and the other part to you.

TROY I ain't got nothing to do with that if that's the way it works. I ain't made up the rules about how it work.

ROSE You did Gabe just like you did Cory. You wouldn't sign the paper for Cory . . . but you signed for Gabe. You signed that paper.

[*The telephone is heard ringing inside the house.*]

TROY I told you I ain't signed nothing, woman! The only thing I signed was the release form. Hell, I can't read, I don't know what they had on that paper! I ain't signed nothing about sending Gabe away.

ROSE I said send him to the hospital . . . you said let him be free . . . now you done went down there and signed him to the hospital for half his money. You went back on yourself, Troy. You gonna have to answer for that.

TROY See now . . . you been over there talking to Miss Pearl. She done got mad cause she ain't getting Gabe's rent money. That's all it is. She's liable to say anything.

ROSE Troy, I seen where you signed the paper.

TROY You ain't seen nothing I signed. What she doing got papers on my brother anyway? Miss Pearl telling a big fat lie. And I'm gonna tell her about it too! You ain't seen nothing I signed. Say . . . you ain't seen nothing I signed.

[ROSE *exits into the house to answer the telephone. Presently she returns.*]

ROSE Troy . . . that was the hospital. Alberta had the baby.

TROY What she have? What is it?

ROSE It's a girl.

TROY I better get on down to the hospital to see her.

ROSE Troy . . .

TROY Rose . . . I got to go see her now. That's only right . . . what's the matter . . . the baby's alright, ain't it?

ROSE Alberta died having the baby.

TROY Died . . . you say she's dead? Alberta's dead?

ROSE They said they done all they could. They couldn't do nothing for her.

TROY The baby? How's the baby?

ROSE They say it's healthy. I wonder who's gonna bury her.

TROY She had family, Rose. She wasn't living in the world by herself.

ROSE I know she wasn't living in the world by herself.

TROY Next thing you gonna want to know if she had any insurance.

ROSE Troy, you ain't got to talk like that.

TROY That's the first thing that jumped out your mouth. "Who's gonna bury her?" Like I'm fixing to take on that task for myself.

ROSE I am your wife. Don't push me away.

TROY I ain't pushing nobody away. Just give me some space. That's all. Just give me some room to breathe.

[ROSE *exits into the house.* TROY *walks about the yard.*]

TROY [*with a quiet rage that threatens to consume him*] Alright . . . Mr. Death. See now . . . I'm gonna tell you what I'm gonna do. I'm gonna take and build me a fence around this yard. See? I'm gonna build me a fence around what belongs to me. And then I want you to stay on the other side. See? You stay over there until you're ready for me. Then you come on. Bring your army. Bring your sickle. Bring your wrestling clothes. I ain't gonna fall down on my vigilance this time. You ain't gonna sneak up on me no more. When you ready for me . . . when the top of your list say Troy

Maxson . . . that's when you come around here. You come up and knock on the front door. Ain't nobody else got nothing to do with this. This is between you and me. Man to man. You stay on the other side of that fence until you ready for me. Then you come up and knock on the front door. Anytime you want. I'll be ready for you.

[*The lights go down to black.*]

2.3

The lights come up on the porch. It is late evening three days later. ROSE *sits listening to the ball game waiting for* TROY. *The final out of the game is made and* ROSE *switches off the radio.* TROY *enters the yard carrying an infant wrapped in blankets. He stands back from the house and calls.*

[ROSE *enters and stands on the porch. There is a long, awkward silence, the weight of which grows heavier with each passing second.*]

TROY Rose . . . I'm standing here with my daughter in my arms. She ain't but a wee bittie little old thing. She don't know nothing about grownups' business. She innocent . . . and she ain't got no mama.

ROSE What you telling me for, Troy?

[*She turns and exits into the house.*]

TROY Well . . . I guess we'll just sit out here on the porch.

[*He sits down on the porch. There is an awkward indelicateness about the way he handles the baby. His largeness engulfs and seems to swallow it. He speaks loud enough for* ROSE *to hear.*]

A man's got to do what's right for him. I ain't sorry for nothing I done. It felt right in my heart.

[*To the baby*]

What you smiling at? Your daddy's a big man. Got these great big old hands. But sometimes he's scared. And right now your daddy's scared cause we sitting out here and ain't got no home. Oh, I been homeless before. I ain't had no little baby with me. But I been homeless. You just be out on the road by your lonesome and you see one of them trains coming and you just kinda go like this . . .

[*He sings as a lullaby.*]

Please, Mr. Engineer let a man ride the line
Please, Mr. Engineer let a man ride the line
I ain't got no ticket please let me ride the blinds[8]

[ROSE *enters from the house.* TROY *hearing her steps behind him, stands and faces her.*]

She's my daughter, Rose. My own flesh and blood. I can't deny her no more than I can deny them boys. [*Pause*] You and them boys is my family. You and them and this child is all I got in the world. So I guess what I'm saying is . . . I'd appreciate it if you'd help me take care of her.

ROSE Okay, Troy . . . you're right. I'll take care of your baby for you . . . cause . . . like you say . . . she's innocent . . . and you can't visit the sins of the father upon the child. A motherless child has got a hard time.

8. Baggage cars with no end doors. This is a traditional blues song, with lyrics adapted by Wilson.

[*She takes the baby from him.*]

From right now . . . this child got a mother. But you a womanless man.

[ROSE *turns and exits into the house with the baby. Lights go down to black.*]

2.4

It is two months later. LYONS *enters from the street. He knocks on the door and calls.*

LYONS Hey, Rose! [*Pause*] Rose!

ROSE [*from inside the house*] Stop that yelling. You gonna wake up Raynell. I just got her to sleep.

LYONS I just stopped by to pay Papa this twenty dollars I owe him. Where's Papa at?

ROSE He should be here in a minute. I'm getting ready to go down to the church. Sit down and wait on him.

LYONS I got to go pick up Bonnie over her mother's house.

ROSE Well, sit it down there on the table. He'll get it.

LYONS [*enters the house and sets the money on the table*] Tell Papa I said thanks. I'll see you again.

ROSE Alright, Lyons. We'll see you.

[LYONS *starts to exit as* CORY *enters.*]

CORY Hey, Lyons.

LYONS What's happening, Cory. Say man, I'm sorry I missed your graduation. You know I had a gig and couldn't get away. Otherwise, I would have been there, man. So what you doing?

CORY I'm trying to find a job.

LYONS Yeah I know how that go, man. It's rough out here. Jobs are scarce.

CORY Yeah, I know.

LYONS Look here, I got to run. Talk to Papa . . . he know some people. He'll be able to help get you a job. Talk to him . . . see what he say.

CORY Yeah . . . alright, Lyons.

LYONS You take care. I'll talk to you soon. We'll find some time to talk.

[LYONS *exits the yard.* CORY *wanders over to the tree, picks up the bat and assumes a batting stance. He studies an imaginary pitcher and swings. Dissatisfied with the result, he tries again.* TROY *enters. They eye each other for a beat.* CORY *puts the bat down and exits the yard.* TROY *starts into the house as* ROSE *exits with* RAYNELL. *She is carrying a cake.*]

TROY I'm coming in and everybody's going out.

ROSE I'm taking this cake down to the church for the bakesale. Lyons was by to see you. He stopped by to pay you your twenty dollars. It's laying in there on the table.

TROY [*going into his pocket*] Well . . . here go this money.

ROSE Put it in there on the table, Troy. I'll get it.

TROY What time you coming back?

ROSE Ain't no use in you studying me. It don't matter what time I come back.

TROY I just asked you a question, woman. What's the matter . . . can't I ask you a question?

ROSE Troy, I don't want to go into it. Your dinner's in there on the stove. All you got to do is heat it up. And don't you be eating the rest of them cakes in there. I'm coming back for them. We having a bakesale at the church tomorrow.

[ROSE *exits the yard.* TROY *sits down on the steps, takes a pint bottle from his pocket, opens it and drinks. He begins to sing.*]

TROY

Hear it ring! Hear it ring!
Had an old dog his name was Blue
You know Blue was mighty true
You know Blue as a good old dog
Blue trees a possum in a hollow log
You know from that he was a good old dog

[BONO *enters the yard.*]

BONO Hey, Troy.

TROY Hey, what's happening, Bono?

BONO I just thought I'd stop by to see you.

TROY What you stop by and see me for? You ain't stopped by in a month of Sundays. Hell, I must owe you money or something.

BONO Since you got your promotion I can't keep up with you. Used to see you everyday. Now I don't even know what route you working.

TROY They keep switching me around. Got me out in Greentree[9] now . . . hauling white folks' garbage.

BONO Greentree, huh? You lucky, at least you ain't got to be lifting them barrels. Damn if they ain't getting heavier. I'm gonna put in my two years and call it quits.

TROY I'm thinking about retiring myself.

BONO You got it easy. You can *drive* for another five years.

TROY It ain't the same, Bono. It ain't like working the back of the truck. Ain't got nobody to talk to . . . feel like you working by yourself. Naw, I'm thinking about retiring. How's Lucille?

BONO She alright. Her arthritis get to acting up on her sometime. Saw Rose on my way in. She going down to the church, huh?

TROY Yeah, she took up going down there. All them preachers looking for somebody to fatten their pockets. [*Pause*] Got some gin here.

BONO Naw, thanks. I just stopped by to say hello.

TROY Hell, nigger . . . you can take a drink. I ain't never known you to say no to a drink. You ain't got to work tomorrow.

BONO I just stopped by. I'm fixing to go over to Skinner's. We got us a domino game going over his house every Friday.

TROY Nigger, you can't play no dominoes. I used to whup you four games out of five.

BONO Well, that learned me. I'm getting better.

TROY Yeah? Well, that's alright.

BONO Look here . . . I got to be getting on. Stop by sometime, huh?

TROY Yeah, I'll do that, Bono. Lucille told Rose you bought her a new refrigerator.

BONO Yeah, Rose told Lucille you had finally built your fence . . . so I figured we'd call it even.

TROY I knew you would.

9. That is, Green Tree, an affluent suburb of Pittsburgh.

BONO Yeah . . . okay. I'll be talking to you.

TROY Yeah, take care, Bono. Good to see you. I'm gonna stop over.

BONO Yeah. Okay, Troy.

[BONO *exits.* TROY *drinks from the bottle.*]

TROY
Old Blue died and I dig his grave
Let him down with a golden chain
Every night when I hear old Blue bark
I know Blue treed a possum in Noah's Ark.
Hear it ring! Hear it ring!

[CORY *enters the yard. They eye each other for a beat.* TROY *is sitting in the middle of the steps.* CORY *walks over.*]

CORY I got to get by.

TROY Say what? What's you say?

CORY You in my way. I got to get by.

TROY You got to get by where? This is my house. Bought and paid for. In full. Took me fifteen years. And if you wanna go in my house and I'm sitting on the steps . . . you say excuse me. Like your mama taught you.

CORY Come on, Pop . . . I got to get by.

[CORY *starts to maneuver his way past* TROY. TROY *grabs his leg and shoves him back.*]

TROY You just gonna walk over top of me?

CORY I live here too!

TROY [*advancing toward him*] You just gonna walk over top of me in my own house?

CORY I ain't scared of you.

TROY I ain't asked if you was scared of me. I asked you if you was fixing to walk over top of me in my own house? That's the question. You ain't gonna say excuse me? You just gonna walk over top of me?

CORY If you wanna put it like that.

TROY How else am I gonna put it?

CORY I was walking by you to go into the house cause you sitting on the steps drunk, singing to yourself. You can put it like that.

TROY Without saying excuse me???

[CORY *doesn't respond.*]

I asked you a question. Without saying excuse me???

CORY I ain't got to say excuse me to you. You don't count around here no more.

TROY Oh, I see . . . I don't count around here no more. You ain't got to say excuse me to your daddy. All of a sudden you done got so grown that your daddy don't count around here no more . . . Around here in his own house and yard that he done paid for with the sweat of his brow. You done got so grown to where you gonna take over. You gonna take over my house. Is that right? You gonna wear my pants. You gonna go in there and stretch out on my bed. You ain't got to say excuse me cause I don't count around here no more. Is that right?

CORY That's right. You always talking this dumb stuff. Now, why don't you just get out my way.

TROY I guess you got someplace to sleep and something to put in your belly. You got that, huh? You got that? That's what you need. You got that, huh?

CORY You don't know what I got. You ain't got to worry about what I got.

TROY You right! You one hundred percent right! I done spent the last seventeen years worrying about what you got. Now it's your turn, see? I'll tell you what to do. You grown . . . we done established that. You a man. Now, let's see you act like one. Turn your behind around and walk out this yard. And when you get out there in the alley . . . you can forget about this house. See? Cause this is my house. You go on and be a man and get your own house. You can forget about this. Cause this is mine. You go on and get yours cause I'm through with doing for you.

CORY You talking about what you did for me . . . what'd you ever give me?

TROY Them feet and bones! That pumping heart, nigger! I give you more than anybody else is ever gonna give you.

CORY You ain't never gave me nothing! You ain't never done nothing but hold me back. Afraid I was gonna be better than you. All you ever did was try and make me scared of you. I used to tremble every time you called my name. Every time I heard your footsteps in the house. Wondering all the time . . . what's Papa gonna say if I do this? . . . What's he gonna say if I do that? . . . What's Papa gonna say if I turn on the radio? And Mama, too . . . she tries . . . but she's scared of you.

TROY You leave your mama out of this. She ain't got nothing to do with this.

CORY I don't know how she stand you . . . after what you did to her.

TROY I told you to leave your mama out of this!

[*He advances toward* CORY.]

CORY What you gonna do . . . give me a whupping? You can't whup me no more. You're too old. You just an old man.

TROY [*shoves him on his shoulder*] Nigger! That's what you are. You just another nigger on the street to me!

CORY You crazy! You know that?

TROY Go on now! You got the devil in you. Get on away from me!

CORY You just a crazy old man . . . talking about I got the devil in me.

TROY Yeah, I'm crazy! If you don't get on the other side of that yard . . . I'm gonna show you how crazy I am! Go on . . . get the hell out of my yard.

CORY It ain't your yard. You took Uncle Gabe's money he got from the army to buy this house and then you put him out.

TROY [*advances on* CORY] Get your black ass out of my yard!

[TROY'S *advance backs* CORY *up against the tree.* CORY *grabs up the bat.*]

CORY I ain't going nowhere! Come on . . . put me out! I ain't scared of you.

TROY That's my bat!

CORY Come on!

TROY Put my bat down!

CORY Come on, put me out.

[CORY *swings at* TROY, *who backs across the yard.*]

What's the matter? You so bad . . . put me out!

[TROY *advances toward* CORY.]

CORY [*backing up*] Come on! Come on!

TROY You're gonna have to use it! You wanna draw that bat back on me . . . you're gonna have to use it.

CORY Come on! . . . Come on!

[CORY *swings the bat at* TROY *a second time. He misses.* TROY *continues to advance toward him.*]

TROY You're gonna have to kill me! You wanna draw that bat back on me. You're gonna have to kill me.

[CORY, *backed up against the tree, can go no farther.* TROY *taunts him. He sticks out his head and offers him a target.*]

Come on! Come on!

[CORY *is unable to swing the bat.* TROY *grabs it.*]

TROY Then I'll show you.

[CORY *and* TROY *struggle over the bat. The struggle is fierce and fully engaged.* TROY *ultimately is the stronger, and takes the bat from* CORY *and stands over him ready to swing. He stops himself.*]

Go on and get away from around my house.

[CORY *stung by his defeat, picks himself up, walks slowly out of the yard and up the alley.*]

CORY Tell Mama I'll be back for my things.

TROY They'll be on the other side of that fence.

[CORY *exits.*]

TROY I can't taste nothing. Helluljah! I can't taste nothing no more. [TROY *assumes a batting posture and begins to taunt Death, the fastball on the outside corner.*] Come on! It's between you and me now! Come on! Anytime you want! Come on! I be ready for you . . . but I ain't gonna be easy.

[*The lights go down on the scene.*]

2.5

The time is 1965. The lights come up in the yard. It is the morning of TROY'S *funeral. A funeral plaque with a light hangs beside the door. There is a small garden plot off to the side. There is noise and activity in the house as* ROSE, GABRIEL, *and* BONO *have gathered. The door opens and* RAYNELL, *seven years old, enters dressed in a flannel nightgown. She crosses to the garden and pokes around with a stick.* ROSE *calls from the house.*

ROSE Raynell!

RAYNELL Mam?

ROSE What you doing out there?

RAYNELL Nothing.

[ROSE *comes to the door.*]

ROSE Girl, get in here and get dressed. What you doing?

RAYNELL Seeing if my garden growed.

ROSE I told you it ain't gonna grow overnight. You got to wait.

RAYNELL It don't look like it never gonna grow. Dag!

ROSE I told you a watched pot never boils. Get in here and get dressed.

RAYNELL This ain't even no pot, Mama.

ROSE You just have to give it a chance. It'll grow. Now you come on and do what I told you. We got to be getting ready. This ain't no morning to be playing around. You hear me?

RAYNELL Yes, mam.

[ROSE *exits into the house.* RAYNELL *continues to poke at her garden with a stick.* CORY *enters. He is dressed in a Marine corporal's uniform, and carries a duffel bag. His posture is that of a military man, and his speech has a clipped sternness.*]

CORY [*to* RAYNELL] Hi. [*Pause*] I bet your name is Raynell.

RAYNELL Uh huh.

CORY Is your mama home?

[RAYNELL *runs up on the porch and calls through the screen door.*]

RAYNELL Mama . . . there's some man out here. Mama?

[ROSE *comes to the door.*]

ROSE Cory? Lord have mercy! Look here, you all!

[ROSE *and* CORY *embrace in a tearful reunion as* BONO *and* LYONS *enter from the house dressed in funeral clothes.*]

BONO Aw, looka here . . .

ROSE Done got all grown up!

CORY Don't cry, Mama. What you crying about?

ROSE I'm just so glad you made it.

CORY Hey Lyons. How you doing, Mr. Bono.

[LYONS *goes to embrace* CORY.]

LYONS Look at you, man. Look at you. Don't he look good, Rose. Got them Corporal stripes.

ROSE What took you so long.

CORY You know how the Marines are, Mama. They got to get all their paperwork straight before they let you do anything.

ROSE Well, I'm sure glad you made it. They let Lyons come. Your Uncle Gabe's still in the hospital. They don't know if they gonna let him out or not. I just talked to them a little while ago.

LYONS A Corporal in the United States Marines.

BONO Your daddy knew you had it in you. He used to tell me all the time.

LYONS Don't he look good, Mr. Bono?

BONO Yeah, he remind me of Troy when I first met him. [*Pause*] Say, Rose, Lucille's down at the church with the choir. I'm gonna go down and get the pallbearers lined up. I'll be back to get you all.

ROSE Thanks, Jim.

CORY See you, Mr. Bono.

LYONS [*with his arm around* RAYNELL] Cory . . . look at Raynell. Ain't she precious? She gonna break a whole lot of hearts.

ROSE Raynell, come and say hello to your brother. This is your brother, Cory. You remember Cory.

RAYNELL No, Mam.

CORY She don't remember me, Mama.

ROSE Well, we talk about you. She heard us talk about you. [*To* RAYNELL] This is your brother, Cory. Come on and say hello.

RAYNELL Hi.

CORY Hi. So you're Raynell. Mama told me a lot about you.

ROSE You all come on into the house and let me fix you some breakfast. Keep up your strength.

CORY I ain't hungry, Mama.

LYONS You can fix me something, Rose. I'll be in there in a minute.

ROSE Cory, you sure you don't want nothing. I know they ain't feeding you right.

CORY No, Mama . . . thanks. I don't feel like eating. I'll get something later.

ROSE Raynell . . . get on upstairs and get that dress on like I told you.

[ROSE *and* RAYNELL *exit into the house.*]

LYONS So . . . I hear you thinking about getting married.

CORY Yeah, I done found the right one, Lyons. It's about time.

LYONS Me and Bonnie been split up about four years now. About the time Papa retired. I guess she just got tired of all them changes I was putting her through. [*Pause*] I always knew you was gonna make something out yourself. Your head was always in the right direction. So . . . you gonna stay in . . . make it a career . . . put in your twenty years?[1]

CORY I don't know. I got six already, I think that's enough.

LYONS Stick with Uncle Sam and retire early. Ain't nothing out here. I guess Rose told you what happened with me. They got me down the workhouse. I thought I was being slick cashing other people's checks.

CORY How much time you doing?

LYONS They give me three years. I got that beat now. I ain't got but nine more months. It ain't so bad. You learn to deal with it like anything else. You got to take the crookeds with the straights. That's what Papa used to say. He used to say that when he struck out. I seen him strike out three times in a row . . . and the next time up he hit the ball over the grandstand. Right out there in Homestead Field. He wasn't satisfied hitting in the seats . . . he want to hit it over everything! After the game he had two hundred people standing around waiting to shake his hand. You got to take the crookeds with the straights. Yeah, Papa was something else.

CORY You still playing?

LYONS Cory . . . you know I'm gonna do that. There's some fellows down there we got us a band . . . we gonna try and stay together when we get out . . . but yeah, I'm still playing. It still helps me to get out of bed in the morning. As long as it do that I'm gonna be right there playing and trying to make some sense out of it.

ROSE [*calling*] Lyons, I got these eggs in the pan.

LYONS Let me go on and get these eggs, man. Get ready to go bury Papa. [*Pause*] How you doing? You doing alright?

[CORY *nods.* LYONS *touches him on the shoulder and they share a moment of silent grief.* LYONS *exits into the house.* CORY *wanders about the yard.* RAYNELL *enters.*]

RAYNELL Hi.

CORY Hi.

RAYNELL Did you used to sleep in my room?

CORY Yeah . . . that used to be my room.

RAYNELL That's what Papa call it. "Cory's room." It got your football in the closet.

[ROSE *comes to the door.*]

ROSE Raynell, get in there and get them good shoes on.

RAYNELL Mama, can't I wear these? Them other one hurt my feet.

ROSE Well, they just gonna have to hurt your feet for a while. You ain't said they hurt your feet when you went down to the store and got them.

RAYNELL They didn't hurt then. My feet done got bigger.

ROSE Don't you give me no backtalk now. You get in there and get them shoes on.

[RAYNELL *exits into the house.*]

1. The minimum years of service required for retirement benefits.

Ain't too much changed. He still got that piece of rag tied to that tree. He was out here swinging that bat. I was just ready to go back in the house. He swung that bat and then he just fell over. Seem like he swung it and stood there with this grin on his face . . . and then he just fell over. They carried him on down to the hospital, but I knew there wasn't no need . . . why don't you come on in the house?

CORY Mama . . . I got something to tell you. I don't know how to tell you this . . . but I've got to tell you . . . I'm not going to Papa's funeral.

ROSE Boy, hush your mouth. That's your daddy you talking about. I don't want hear that kind of talk this morning. I done raised you to come to this? You standing there all healthy and grown talking about you ain't going to your daddy's funeral?

CORY Mama . . . listen . . .

ROSE I don't want to hear it, Cory. You just get that thought out of your head.

CORY I can't drag Papa with me everywhere I go. I've got to say no to him. One time in my life I've got to say no.

ROSE Don't nobody have to listen to nothing like that. I know you and your daddy ain't seen eye to eye, but I ain't got to listen to that kind of talk this morning. Whatever was between you and your daddy . . . the time has come to put it aside. Just take it and set it over there on the shelf and forget about it. Disrespecting your daddy ain't gonna make you a man, Cory. You got to find a way to come to that on your own. Not going to your daddy's funeral ain't gonna make you a man.

CORY The whole time I was growing up . . . living in his house . . . Papa was like a shadow that followed you everywhere. It weighed on you and sunk into your flesh. It would wrap around you and lay there until you couldn't tell which one was you anymore. That shadow digging in your flesh. Trying to crawl in. Trying to live through you. Everywhere I looked, Troy Maxson was staring back at me . . . hiding under the bed . . . in the closet. I'm just saying I've got to find a way to get rid of that shadow, Mama.

ROSE You just like him. You got him in you good.

CORY Don't tell me that, Mama.

ROSE You Troy Maxson all over again.

CORY I don't want to be Troy Maxson. I want to be me.

ROSE You can't be nobody but who you are, Cory. That shadow wasn't nothing but you growing into yourself. You either got to grow into it or cut it down to fit you. But that's all you got to make life with. That's all you got to measure yourself against that world out there. Your daddy wanted you to be everything he wasn't . . . and at the same time he tried to make you into everything he was. I don't know if he was right or wrong . . . but I do know he meant to do more good than he meant to do harm. He wasn't always right. Sometimes when he touched he bruised. And sometimes when he took me in his arms he cut.

When I first met your daddy I thought . . . Here is a man I can lay down with and make a baby. That's the first thing I thought when I seen him. I was thirty years old and had done seen my share of men. But when he walked up to me and said, "I can dance a waltz that'll make you dizzy," I thought, Rose Lee, here is a man that you can open yourself up to and be filled to bursting. Here is a man that can fill all them empty spaces you been tipping around the edges of. One of them empty spaces was being somebody's mother.

I married your daddy and settled down to cooking his supper and keeping clean sheets on the bed. When your daddy walked through the house he was so big he filled it up. That was my first mistake. Not to make him leave some room for me. For my part in the matter. But at that time I wanted that. I wanted a house that I could sing in. And that's what your daddy gave me. I didn't know to keep up his strength I had to give up little pieces of mine. I did that. I took on his life as mine and mixed up the pieces so that you couldn't hardly tell which was which anymore. It was my choice. It was my life and I didn't have to live it like that. But that's what life offered me in the way of being a woman and I took it. I grabbed hold of it with both hands.

By the time Raynell came into the house, me and your daddy had done lost touch with one another. I didn't want to make my blessing off of nobody's misfortune . . . but I took on to Raynell like she was all them babies I had wanted and never had.

[*The phone rings.*]

Like I'd been blessed to relive a part of my life. And if the Lord see fit to keep up my strength . . . I'm gonna do her just like your daddy did you . . . I'm gonna give her the best of what's in me.

RAYNELL [*entering, still with her old shoes*] Mama . . . Reverend Tollivier on the phone.

[ROSE *exits into the house.*]

RAYNELL Hi.

CORY Hi.

RAYNELL You in the Army or the Marines?

CORY Marines.

RAYNELL Papa said it was the Army. Did you know Blue?

CORY Blue? Who's Blue?

RAYNELL Papa's dog what he sing about all the time.

CORY [*singing*]

Hear it ring! Hear it ring!
I had a dog his name was Blue
You know Blue was mighty true
You know Blue was a good old dog
Blue treed a possum in a hollow log
You know from that he was a good old dog.
Hear it ring! Hear it ring!

[RAYNELL *joins in singing.*]

CORY and RAYNELL

Blue treed a possum out on a limb
Blue looked at me and I looked at him
Grabbed that possum and put him in a sack
Blue stayed there till I came back
Old Blue's feets was big and round
Never allowed a possum to touch the ground.

Old Blue died and I dug his grave
I dug his grave with a silver spade
Let him down with a golden chain
And every night I call his name

Go on Blue, you good dog you
Go on Blue, you good dog you

RAYNELL
Blue laid down and died like a man
Blue laid down and died . . .

BOTH
Blue laid down and died like a man
Now he's treeing possums in the Promised Land
I'm gonna tell you this to let you know
Blue's gone where the good dogs go
When I hear old Blue bark
When I hear old Blue bark
Blue treed a possum in Noah's Ark.
Blue treed a possum in Noah's Ark.

[ROSE *comes to the screen door.*]

ROSE Cory, we gonna be ready to go in a minute.

CORY [*to* RAYNELL] You go on in the house and change them shoes like Mama told you so we can go to Papa's funeral.

RAYNELL Okay, I'll be back.

[RAYNELL *exits into the house.* CORY *gets up and crosses over to the tree.* ROSE *stands in the screen door watching him.* GABRIEL *enters from the alley.*]

GABRIEL [*calling*] Hey, Rose!

ROSE Gabe?

GABRIEL I'm here, Rose. Hey Rose, I'm here!

[ROSE *enters from the house.*]

ROSE Lord . . . Look here, Lyons!

LYONS See, I told you, Rose . . . I told you they'd let him come.

CORY How you doing, Uncle Gabe?

LYONS How you doing, Uncle Gabe?

GABRIEL Hey, Rose. It's time. It's time to tell St. Peter to open the gates. Troy, you ready? You ready, Troy. I'm gonna tell St. Peter to open the gates. You get ready now.

[*Gabriel, with great fanfare, braces himself to blow. The trumpet is without a mouthpiece. He puts the end of it into his mouth and blows with great force, like a man who has been waiting some twenty-odd years for this single moment. No sound comes out of the trumpet. He braces himself and blows again with the same result. A third time he blows. There is a weight of impossible description that falls away and leaves him bare and exposed to a frightful realization. It is a trauma that a sane and normal mind would be unable to withstand. He begins to dance. A slow, strange dance, eerie and life-giving. A dance of atavistic signature and ritual.* LYONS *attempts to embrace him.* GABRIEL *pushes* LYONS *away. He begins to howl in what is an attempt at song, or perhaps a song turning back into itself in an attempt at speech. He finishes his dance and the gates of heaven stand open as wide as God's closet.*]

That's the way that go!

Blackout.

DAVID HENRY HWANG

b. 1957

FROM the Filipinos who escaped from a Spanish galleon in 1763 and established villages in the Louisiana bayous to the Chinese laborers who built the transcontinental railroad in the nineteenth century to the Cambodians who fled the killing fields of the Khmer Rouge in the 1970s, Asians have come to America and have been an integral part of American history. As the United States expanded westward, a country that had defined itself in relation to Europe (and, through the institution of slavery, to Africa) found itself increasingly engaged with the Pacific region. In the Spanish-American War (1898), the United States annexed Hawaii, was granted protectorship over Guam and the Philippines, and thereby extended a colonial arm across the Pacific Ocean. As American contacts with Asia and its people deepened, popular perceptions of the East vacillated between fascination with the exotic and mysterious "Orient" and fear of the "Yellow Peril" posed by races seemingly alien to American national identity. Even as the vogue for Chinese and Japanese design flourished in the late nineteenth and early twentieth centuries, the U.S. Congress passed laws limiting Asian immigration.

Against this historical backdrop, contemporary Asian Americans—a term that generally includes those who claim origin or ancestry from East Asia, Southeast Asia, or the Indian subcontinent—have often found themselves caught between identities. Racially linked to countries with which those in later generations have had little or no contact, they inhabit a culture that has traditionally represented Asians and those of Asian descent through stereotypes: submissive lotus blossom, dragon lady, evil genius, exotic dancer, obedient servant, warmonger. In recent years, Asian American writers have challenged these stereotypes by depicting the experience of themselves and their communities in its human complexity, and the drama of David Henry Hwang and other Asian American playwrights has given this experience a powerful voice in the American theater. Since Hwang first came to the attention of the theatrical world in the late 1970s, he has written plays exploring the complicated relationship of Chinese Americans to their familial, cultural, and spiritual roots. With his 1988 play *M. BUTTERFLY*—the most critically and commercially successful play ever written by an Asian American—Hwang broadened his gaze to include the intricate (mis)perceptions that characterize the East in the Western imagination.

David Henry Hwang (pronounced "Wong") was born on August 11, 1957, in San Gabriel, California, a wealthy suburb of Los Angeles. His father, who emigrated from Shanghai and—later—Taiwan, was a successful accountant and businessman, and his mother, who was born in southern China to a family that had been converted to fundamentalist Christianity and was raised in the Philippines, was a talented pianist. Hwang would explore this family heritage in his 1996 play *Golden Child*, which is based on the story of his great-grandfather who brought Christianity to his family in China. Because of his mother's religious background and his father's desire to assimilate in his adopted country, the family did not celebrate Chinese holidays or raise their children with an awareness of their Chinese heritage. It wasn't until he was a college student that Hwang became interested in knowing more about his roots. As a child, Hwang studied violin and excelled in debating, and his talents earned him admission to an exclusive preparatory school in Hollywood Hills. Hwang would later credit music and debate as important influences on his playwriting: "Music really helps in terms of developing structure and dramatic growth, and jazz in particular helps with theatrical improvisation. . . . And my early interest in debate no doubt contributed to my theatrical interest in the opposition of ideas and the interplay of ideas in many plays."

Hwang enrolled at Stanford University in 1975 in order to study law, but by his sophomore year he decided that he wanted to write plays. When his creative writing professor explained to him that he lacked an adequate understanding of theater, he immersed himself in drama by attending the theater and reading as many plays as he could. He was particularly drawn to the drama of Sam Shepard, several of whose plays premiered during this time at the Magic Theater in nearby San Francisco. In 1978, Hwang had the opportunity to study playwriting with Shepard and the Cuban American playwright Maria Irene Fornes at the Padua Hills Playwrights Festival workshop in Claremont, California; it was during this workshop that he conceived the idea of his first play, *FOB*. The play, whose title is the acronym popularly applied to new immigrants—standing for the condescending label "fresh off the boat"—centers on the interaction of three characters: Grace, a first-generation Chinese American; her cousin Dale, a second-generation Chinese American; and Steve, a wealthy immigrant who has just arrived from Hong Kong. Set in the back room of a California restaurant, *FOB* explores the conflicts that immigrants experience as they struggle to assimilate into their new country while also retaining their cultural identity. Though its dialogue and action are clearly influenced by Shepard's plays of the 1970s, the play reveals a highly original dramatic sensibility. In addition to offering carefully drawn psychological portraits, the play dramatizes the confrontation between realism and myth. Steve imagines himself to be the Chinese god Gwan Gung, while Grace identifies with Fa Mu Lan, the mythic "woman warrior" who is the spiritual center of Maxine Hong Kingston's 1976 novel by the same name. When the two engage in a ritualized battle in the play's second act, the realistic present gives way to the timeless space of myth.

FOB was first performed in the lounge of Hwang's Stanford dorm in March 1979 as part of a festival of student plays and musicals. Hwang also submitted the play to the Eugene O'Neill National Playwrights Conference in Connecticut, where it was selected and produced that summer. After attracting the interest of Joseph Papp, producer of the off-Broadway New York Public Theater, *FOB* was produced in New York the following year and received enthusiastic reviews. As the play moved from its college production to the Public Theater, it underwent a significant change in its theatrical style. Papp and others who read the play felt that the ritualized sequence in the play's second act should be staged using the movements and visual approach of the Peking (or Beijing) Opera, a highly stylized form of Chinese theater involving drama, music, mime, dance, and acrobatics. The addition of stage conventions from Chinese opera established a theatrical equivalent to the confrontation of East and West within the play's action, and it launched Hwang's interest in the fusion of Eastern and Western theatrical traditions that would culminate seven years later in *M. Butterfly*.

After the success of *FOB*, which won an Obie Award for Best New American Play, Hwang spent a year in the Yale School of Drama graduate playwriting program.

During that time, he wrote *The Dance and the Railroad,* which was produced in New York in 1981. Set during an 1867 strike by Chinese laborers working on the first transcontinental railroad, this two-character play dramatizes the plight of early immigrants who pursued the promise of America while living as "coolies" in an alien land. Through the character of Lone, who trained in Chinese opera and practices his craft on a mountainside at the end of each day's work, the play also expands Hwang's use of Asian theatrical traditions to explore the clash of East and West. *The Dance and the Railroad,* which enjoyed widespread critical acclaim, was followed by a series of plays whose reviews were more mixed: *Family Devotions* (1981); *The House of Sleeping Beauties* and *The Sound of a Voice,* two one-act plays produced in 1983 under the title *Sound and Beauty;* and *Rich Relations* (1986). Hwang's next play, however, would overshadow all his earlier triumphs and disappointments. After a brief preview at the National Theater in Washington, D.C., *M. Butterfly* opened at Broadway's Eugene O'Neill Theatre on March 20, 1988. Lavishly staged, the play was an enormous popular and critical success; indeed, it became one of the most commercially successful nonmusical plays in Broadway history and won a number of awards, including the Tony, Drama Desk, and Outer Critics Circle awards for Best Play. In the years since *M. Butterfly,* Hwang has done collaborative work—including a musical drama titled *1000 Airplanes on the Roof* (1988) with the composer Philip Glass—produced television scripts, and written a number of screenplays. He has also continued to write for theater. In 1996, Hwang received an Obie Award for *Golden Child* (discussed above). In 2001, Hwang's updated text for the 1958 Richard Rodgers and Oscar Hammerstein II's musical *Flower Drum Song* was staged in Los Angeles before moving to Broadway.

M. Butterfly, like many of Hwang's other plays, is characterized by a blending of history and imagination. In May 1986, Hwang heard about an incident reported earlier that month in the *New York Times.* A former French diplomat named Bernard Boursicot and a Chinese opera star named Shi Pei Pu had been arrested and tried for espionage in Paris after a twenty-year sexual relationship during which Boursicot passed government information to Shi, who then passed it on to the Communist Chinese government. During the trial, it was revealed that Boursicot had believed his lover—a man who played women's roles in Chinese and Western opera—was a woman and had conducted what he thought was a heterosexual affair. Boursicot explained that he had never seen "her" naked: "He was very shy. I thought it was a Chinese custom." Intrigued by the theatrical possibilities of so incredible a story, Hwang began working on a play. The crucial moment in conceiving this new work came when he realized that the French diplomat had fallen in love not with a person but with a stereotype of Asian women. "I was driving down Santa Monica Boulevard one afternoon, and asked myself, 'What did Boursicot think he was getting in this Chinese actress?' The answer came to me clearly: 'He probably thought he had found Madame Butterfly.' "

Although Hwang had not yet seen or listened to Giacomo Puccini's opera by that name, he was familiar with the stereotype represented by its delicate, self-sacrificing heroine. *Madame Butterfly* (*Madama* in the original Italian), which premiered in Milan in 1904, was based on a 1900 one-act play by the American playwright and producer David Belasco that Puccini had seen in London (Belasco's play was itself based on a 1898 short story by John Luther Long). Both play and opera tell the story of Cio-Cio-San, a Japanese geisha known as Madame Butterfly, and the American naval lieutenant named Pinkerton who marries her during one of his tours of duty to Japan. He then leaves with his ship; and although he fails to return the following year as promised, Cio-Cio-San waits faithfully, refusing the marriage proposal of a wealthy Japanese man. When Pinkerton finally does come back to Japan, several years later, he is accompanied by a new American wife; Butterfly takes her own life, leaving behind a child that Pinkerton and his wife will bring back to the United States. In its portrait of a submissive and feminized Asia, *Madame Butterfly* exemplifies the Western fantasy of the East as an exotic realm that displays its mysteries for the West to

John Lithgow, center, as Rene Gallimard, and B. D. Wong, right, as Song Liling, in the 1988 Broadway production of *M. Butterfly.*

admire, collect, and dominate. Such a conception of the "Orient," as Edward Said argued in his influential book *Orientalism* (1978), is a Western invention, reflecting an "imaginative geography" rather than the actual sociocultural geography of Asia and its peoples. The operations of such myths, Said claimed, can be felt not only in the representations of Asians by Europeans and North Americans but in the military and political relationships between West and East that form part of the history of imperialism.

In writing what he has called a "deconstructivist *Madame Butterfly,*" Hwang established a series of parallels and counterpoints between Puccini's opera, contemporary history, and a fictionalized version of the Boursicot story. Rene Gallimard, the diplomat of Hwang's play, relives the events of his past from the cell of a Paris prison, a nightly ritual in which he seeks the understanding, and perhaps envy, of his audience for having loved and been loved by "the Perfect Woman." In order to justify his belief and the actions, he recounts the story of *Madame Butterfly*—the opera in which he first saw the singer Song Liling perform—and identifies himself with Puccini's Pinkerton in his quest for the feminine ideal of beauty and submissiveness. The power of this myth is only deepened when Song challenges its premises: "It's one of your favorite fantasies, isn't it? The submissive Oriental woman and the cruel white man." In the following scenes, Gallimard pursues the fantasy of Pinkerton and Butterfly, exulting in his apparent power over his mistress and in his initiation, after an unpromising sexual past, into the privileges of maleness.

One of the central themes of *M. Butterfly,* Hwang suggested in a 1989 interview, is "the nature of seduction, in the sense that to some degree we seduce ourselves." On the collective as well as the individual level, the West's self-seducing perceptions of the East are intimately connected to male perceptions of the female. As Song explains when he is asked about Gallimard's delusion by a Paris judge, "One, . . . when he finally met his fantasy woman, he wanted more than anything to believe that she was, in fact, a woman. And second, I am an Oriental. And being an Oriental, I could never be completely a man." Such thinking, the play suggests, accounts for the West's historic diplomatic and military failings in its encounters with the East. Advising the French ambassador about the Americans' prospects in neighboring Vietnam, Gallimard offers the disastrously misguided prediction that "Orientals will always submit to a greater force."

Hwang's exploration of seduction and misperception also extends to the play's interaction with its audience. On the level of theatrical form, *M. Butterfly* achieves an intricate counterpointing of Eastern and Western characters, impersonations, and styles. A French diplomat taking on the role of an American lieutenant interacts with a Chinese performer playing a Japanese heroine from an opera written by an Italian. Visually and aurally, the play juxtaposes the operatic traditions of Europe with the stage conventions and music of Chinese opera, complicating the audience's point of view with a sometimes jarring cultural fusion of East and West. Moreover, as a commentary on the fluidity of roles and identities, *M. Butterfly* challenges the seemingly clear-cut categories of male and female. Hwang replaced the *Madame* of Puccini's title with the letter *M.*, which stands for *Monsieur* in French but in English is more ambiguous in its gender reference. Even spectators who know the story on which the play is based can find themselves seduced by Song's performance as a woman. Accordingly, when Song removes "her" costume and makeup near the play's end, the audience witnesses the uncanny crossing of gender boundaries. When, in the play's unexpected final scene, Gallimard turns the tables on Song and rescues his fantasy from the harsh light of reality, these boundaries are rendered even more fluid and indeterminate.

M. Butterfly has not been without its critics in the Asian American community, a number of whom have charged Hwang with falling into stereotypes of his own concerning the East and indulging the theatrical exoticism that his play otherwise faults. Yet despite such critiques, the play established Hwang as one of the leading American playwrights of his generation and the most successful figure in Asian American theater. By bringing the lives and experiences of Asian Americans into the theatrical mainstream, he has helped expose the prejudices, misconceptions, and idealized images that have limited the representations of Asianness within and beyond the borders of the United States. Just as importantly, he has served as the voice of a new generation of Asian Americans who find themselves pulled between cultures and who must come to terms with their histories, myths, and traditions while making their lives in a country half a world away from their ancestors' home.

S.G.

M. Butterfly

CHARACTERS

KUROGO[1]
RENE GALLIMARD / PINKERTON
SONG LILING / BUTTERFLY
WOMAN at party
MAN 1
MAN 2
MARC / CONSUL SHARPLESS
GIRL in magazine
COMRADE CHIN / SUZUKI
HELGA
SHU-FANG
M. TOULON
RENEE
JUDGE

Playwright's Notes

A former French diplomat and a Chinese opera singer have been sentenced to six years in jail for spying for China after a two-day trial that traced a story of clandestine love and mistaken sexual identity. . . . Mr. Boursicot was accused of passing information to China after he fell in love with Mr. Shi, whom he believed for twenty years to be a woman.

—The New York Times, *May 11, 1986*

This play was suggested by international newspaper accounts of a recent espionage trial. For purposes of dramatization, names have been changed, characters created, and incidents devised or altered, and this play does not purport to be a factual record of real events or real people.

I could escape this feeling
With my China girl . . .[2]
—DAVID BOWIE & IGGY POP

SETTING: *The action of the play takes place in a Paris prison in the present, and in recall, during the decade 1960 to 1970 in Beijing, and from 1966 to the present in Paris.*

1.1

M. GALLIMARD's *prison cell. Paris. Present.*

Lights fade up to reveal RENE GALLIMARD, *65, in a prison cell. He wears a comfortable bathrobe, and looks old and tired. The sparsely furnished cell contains a wooden crate upon which sits a hot plate with a kettle, and a portable tape recorder.* GALLIMARD *sits on the crate staring at the recorder, a sad smile on his face.*

Upstage SONG, *who appears as a beautiful woman in traditional Chinese*

1. In traditional Japanese theater, black-clad stage attendants (treated as invisible).
2. From "China Girl," co-written by the English rock musician David Bowie (b. 1947) and the American rock singer Iggy Pop (b. 1947); first released on Pop's album *The Idiot* (1977), it became a hit on Bowie's album *Let's Dance* (1983).

garb, dances a traditional piece from the Peking Opera,[3] *surrounded by the percussive clatter of Chinese music.*

Then, slowly, lights and sound cross-fade; the Chinese opera music dissolves into a Western opera, the "Love Duet" from Puccini's Madame Butterfly.[4] SONG *continues dancing, now to the Western accompaniment. Though her movements are the same, the difference in music now gives them a balletic quality.*

GALLIMARD *rises, and turns upstage towards the figure of* SONG, *who dances without acknowledging him.*

GALLIMARD Butterfly, Butterfly . . .

[*He forces himself to turn away, as the image of* SONG *fades out, and talks to us.*]

GALLIMARD The limits of my cell are as such: four-and-a-half meters by five. There's one window against the far wall; a door, very strong, to protect me from autograph hounds. I'm responsible for the tape recorder, the hot plate, and this charming coffee table.

When I want to eat, I'm marched off to the dining room—hot, steaming slop appears on my plate. When I want to sleep, the lightbulb turns itself off—the work of fairies. It's an enchanted space I occupy. The French—we know how to run a prison.

But, to be honest, I'm not treated like an ordinary prisoner. Why? Because I'm a celebrity. You see, I make people laugh.

I never dreamed this day would arrive. I've never been considered witty or clever. In fact, as a young boy, in an informal poll among my grammar school classmates, I was voted "least likely to be invited to a party." It's a title I managed to hold onto for many years. Despite some stiff competition.

But now, how the tables turn! Look at me: the life of every social function in Paris. Paris? Why be modest? My fame has spread to Amsterdam, London, New York. Listen to them! In the world's smartest parlors. I'm the one who lifts their spirits!

[*With a flourish,* GALLIMARD *directs our attention to another part of the stage.*]

1.2

A party. Present.

Lights go up on a chic-looking parlor, where a well-dressed trio, two men and one woman, make conversation. GALLIMARD *also remains lit; he observes them from his cell.*

WOMAN And what of Gallimard?

MAN 1 Gallimard?

MAN 2 Gallimard!

GALLIMARD [*to us*] You see? They're all determined to say my name, as if it were some new dance.

WOMAN He still claims not to believe the truth.

MAN 1 What? Still? Even since the trial?

3. Chinese opera is a highly stylized art form involving drama, song, mime, dance, and acrobatics. *Peking*: former Westernization of Beijing.

4. That is, *Madama Butterfly* (1904), an Italian opera composed by Giacomo Puccini (1858–1924) with a libretto by Luigi Illica (1857–1919) and Giuseppe Giacosa (1847–1906); it is one of the most frequently performed of all operas.

WOMAN Yes. Isn't it mad?

MAN 2 [*laughing*] He says . . . it was dark . . . and she was very modest!

[*The trio break into laughter.*]

MAN 1 So—what? He never touched her with his hands?

MAN 2 Perhaps he did, and simply misidentified the equipment. A compelling case for sex education in the schools.

WOMAN To protect the National Security—the Church can't argue with that.

MAN 1 That's impossible! How could he not know?

MAN 2 Simple ignorance.

MAN 1 For twenty years?

MAN 2 Time flies when you're being stupid.

WOMAN Well, I thought the French were ladies' men.

MAN 2 It seems Monsieur Gallimard was overly anxious to live up to his national reputation.

WOMAN Well, he's not very good-looking.

MAN 1 No, he's not.

MAN 2 Certainly not.

WOMAN Actually, I feel sorry for him.

MAN 2 A toast! To Monsieur Gallimard!

WOMAN Yes! To Gallimard!

MAN 1 To Gallimard!

MAN 2 Vive la différence![5]

[*They toast, laughing. Lights down on them.*]

1.3

M. GALLIMARD*'s cell.*

GALLIMARD [*smiling*] You see? They toast me. I've become patron saint of the socially inept. Can they really be so foolish? Men like that—they should be scratching at my door, begging to learn my secrets! For I, Rene Gallimard, you see, I have known, and been loved by . . . the Perfect Woman.

Alone in this cell, I sit night after night, watching our story play through my head, always searching for a new ending, one which redeems my honor, where she returns at last to my arms. And I imagine you—my ideal audience—who come to understand and even, perhaps just a little, to envy me.

[*He turns on his tape recorder. Over the house speakers, we hear the opening phrases of* Madame Butterfly.]

GALLIMARD In order for you to understand what I did and why, I must introduce you to my favorite opera: *Madame Butterfly.* By Giacomo Puccini. First produced at La Scala, Milan, in 1904, it is now beloved throughout the Western world.

[*As* GALLIMARD *describes the opera, the tape segues in and out to sections he may be describing.*]

GALLIMARD And why not? Its heroine, Cio-Cio-San, also known as Butterfly, is a feminine ideal, beautiful and brave. And its hero, the man for whom she gives up everything, is—[*He pulls out a naval officer's cap from under his crate, pops it on his head, and struts about.*]—not very good-looking, not too bright, and pretty much a wimp: Benjamin Franklin Pinkerton of the

5. Long live the difference (French), an expression that specifically celebrates the difference between the sexes.

U.S. Navy. As the curtain rises, he's just closed on two great bargains: one on a house, the other on a woman—call it a package deal.

Pinkerton purchased the rights to Butterfly for one hundred yen—in modern currency, equivalent to about . . . sixty-six cents. So, he's feeling pretty pleased with himself as Sharpless, the American consul, arrives to witness the marriage.

[MARC, *wearing an official cap to designate* SHARPLESS, *enters and plays the character.*]

SHARPLESS/MARC Pinkerton!

PINKERTON/GALLIMARD Sharpless! How's it hangin'? It's a great day, just great. Between my house, my wife, and the rickshaw[6] ride in from town, I've saved nineteen cents just this morning.

SHARPLESS Wonderful. I can see the inscription on your tombstone already: "I saved a dollar, here I lie." [*He looks around.*] Nice house.

PINKERTON It's artistic. Artistic, don't you think? Like the way the shoji[7] screens slide open to reveal the wet bar and disco mirror ball? Classy, huh? Great for impressing the chicks.

SHARPLESS "Chicks"? Pinkerton, you're going to be a married man!

PINKERTON Well, sort of.

SHARPLESS What do you mean?

PINKERTON This country—Sharpless, it is okay. You got all these geisha[8] girls running around—

SHARPLESS I know! I live here!

PINKERTON Then, you know the marriage laws, right? I split for one month, it's annulled!

SHARPLESS Leave it to you to read the fine print. Who's the lucky girl?

PINKERTON Cio-Cio-San. Her friends call her Butterfly. Sharpless, she eats out of my hand!

SHARPLESS She's probably very hungry.

PINKERTON Not like American girls. It's true what they say about Oriental girls. They want to be treated bad!

SHARPLESS Oh, please!

PINKERTON It's true!

SHARPLESS Are you serious about this girl?

PINKERTON I'm marrying her, aren't I?

SHARPLESS Yes—with generous trade-in terms.

PINKERTON When I leave, she'll know what it's like to have loved a real man. And I'll even buy her a few nylons.

SHARPLESS You aren't planning to take her with you?

PINKERTON Huh? Where?

SHARPLESS Home!

PINKERTON You mean, America? Are you crazy? Can you see her trying to buy rice in St. Louis?

SHARPLESS So, you're not serious.

[*Pause.*]

PINKERTON/GALLIMARD [*as* PINKERTON] Consul, I am a sailor in port. [*As* GAL-

6. That is, *jinrikisha* (Japanese), a light, two-wheeled passenger vehicle drawn by one or two men.

7. Paper screens used as walls, partitions, or sliding doors (Japanese).

8. In traditional Japanese society, professional women trained from childhood to entertain men with singing, dancing, and conversation.

LIMARD] They then proceed to sing the famous duet, "The Whole World Over."[9]

[*The duet plays on the speakers.* GALLIMARD, *as* PINKERTON, *lip-syncs his lines from the opera.*]

GALLIMARD To give a rough translation: "The whole world over, the Yankee travels, casting his anchor wherever he wants. Life's not worth living unless he can win the hearts of the fairest maidens, then hotfoot it off the premises ASAP." [*He turns towards* MARC.] In the preceding scene, I played Pinkerton, the womanizing cad, and my friend Marc from school . . . [MARC *bows grandly for our benefit.*] played Sharpless, the sensitive soul of reason. In life, however, our positions were usually—no, always—reversed.

1.4

Ecole Nationale. Aix-en-Provence.[1] *1947.*

GALLIMARD No, Marc, I think I'd rather stay home.

MARC Are you crazy?! We are going to Dad's condo in Marseille![2] You know what happened last time?

GALLIMARD Of course I do.

MARC Of course you don't! You never know. . . . They stripped, Rene!

GALLIMARD Who stripped?

MARC The girls!

GALLIMARD Girls? Who said anything about girls?

MARC Rene, we're a buncha university guys goin' up to the woods. What are we gonna do—talk philosophy?

GALLIMARD What girls? Where do you get them?

MARC Who cares? The point is, they come. On trucks. Packed in like sardines. The back flips open, babes hop out, we're ready to roll.

GALLIMARD You mean, they just—?

MARC Before you know it, every last one of them—they're stripped and splashing around my pool. There's no moon out, they can't see what's going on, their boobs are flapping, right? You close your eyes, reach out—it's grab bag, get it? Doesn't matter whose ass is between whose legs, whose teeth are sinking into who. You're just in there, going at it, eyes closed, on and on for as long as you can stand. [*Pause*] Some fun, huh?

GALLIMARD What happens in the morning?

MARC In the morning, you're ready to talk some philosophy. [*Beat*[3]] So how 'bout it?

GALLIMARD Marc, I can't . . . I'm afraid they'll say no—the girls. So I never ask.

MARC You don't have to ask! That's the beauty—don't you see? They don't have to say yes. It's perfect for a guy like you, really.

GALLIMARD You go ahead . . . I may come later.

MARC Hey, Rene—it doesn't matter that you're clumsy and got zits—they're not looking!

9. "Dovunque al mondo" is in fact an aria sung by Pinkerton.

1. A city in southern France, about 20 miles north of Marseille. Among its universities is the École Nationale Supérieure d'Arts et Métiers (National School of Arts and Trades), an elite school of engineering.

2. France's second-largest city, an important commercial and industrial center on the Mediterranean coast.

3. Pause (theater term).

GALLIMARD Thank you very much.

MARC Wimp.

[MARC *walks over to the other side of the stage, and starts waving and smiling at women in the audience.*]

GALLIMARD [*to us*] We now return to my version of *Madame Butterfly* and the events leading to my recent conviction for treason.

[GALLIMARD *notices* MARC *making lewd gestures.*]

GALLIMARD Marc, what are you doing?

MARC Huh? [*Sotto voce*[4]] Rene, there're a lotta great babes out there. They're probably lookin' at me and thinking, "What a dangerous guy."

GALLIMARD Yes—how could they help but be impressed by your cool sophistication?

[GALLIMARD *pops the* SHARPLESS *cap on* MARC*'s head, and points him offstage.* MARC *exits, leering.*]

1.5

M. GALLIMARD*'s cell.*

GALLIMARD Next, Butterfly makes her entrance. We learn her age—fifteen . . . but very mature for her years.

[*Lights come up on the area where we saw* SONG *dancing at the top of the play. She appears there again, now dressed as Madame* BUTTERFLY, *moving to the "Love Duet."*[5] GALLIMARD *turns upstage slightly to watch, transfixed.*]

GALLIMARD But as she glides past him, beautiful, laughing softly behind her fan, don't we who are men sigh with hope? We, who are not handsome, nor brave, nor powerful, yet somehow believe, like Pinkerton, that we deserve a Butterfly. She arrives with all her possessions in the folds of her sleeves, lays them all out, for her man to do with as he pleases. Even her life itself—she bows her head as she whispers that she's not even worth the hundred yen he paid for her. He's already given too much, when we know he's really had to give nothing at all.

[*Music and lights on* SONG *out.* GALLIMARD *sits at his crate.*]

GALLIMARD In real life, women who put their total worth at less than sixty-six cents are quite hard to find. The closest we come is in the pages of these magazines. [*He reaches into his crate, pulls out a stack of girlie magazines, and begins flipping through them.*] Quite a necessity in prison. For three or four dollars, you get seven or eight women.
I first discovered these magazines at my uncle's house. One day, as a boy of twelve. The first time I saw them in his closet . . . all lined up—my body shook. Not with lust—no, with power. Here were women—a shelfful—who would do exactly as I wanted.

[*The "Love Duet" creeps in over the speakers. Special*[6] *comes up, revealing, not* SONG *this time, but a pinup girl in a sexy negligee, her back to us.* GALLIMARD *turns upstage and looks at her.*]

GIRL I know you're watching me.

4. Under the voice (Italian); that is, spoken very softly, under the breath.
5. "Viene la sera" ("Evening Is Falling"), a duet sung by Pinkerton and Butterfly at the end of act 1 of *Madama Butterfly*.
6. A stage light used at designated moments during a play for specific, highly theatrical effects.

GALLIMARD My throat . . . it's dry.

GIRL I leave my blinds open every night before I go to bed.

GALLIMARD I can't move.

GIRL I leave my blinds open and the lights on.

GALLIMARD I'm shaking. My skin is hot, but my penis is soft. Why?

GIRL I stand in front of the window.

GALLIMARD What is she going to do?

GIRL I toss my hair, and I let my lips part . . . barely.

GALLIMARD I shouldn't be seeing this. It's so dirty. I'm so bad.

GIRL Then, slowly, I lift off my nightdress.

GALLIMARD Oh, god. I can't believe it. I can't—

GIRL I toss it to the ground.

GALLIMARD Now, she's going to walk away. She's going to—

GIRL I stand there, in the light, displaying myself.

GALLIMARD No. She's—why is she naked?

GIRL To you.

GALLIMARD In front of a window? This is wrong. No—

GIRL Without shame.

GALLIMARD No, she must . . . like it.

GIRL I like it.

GALLIMARD She . . . she wants me to see.

GIRL I want you to see.

GALLIMARD I can't believe it! She's getting excited!

GIRL I can't see you. You can do whatever you want.

GALLIMARD I can't do a thing. Why?

GIRL What would you like me to do . . . next?

[*Lights go down on her. Music off. Silence, as* GALLIMARD *puts away his magazines. Then he resumes talking to us.*]

GALLIMARD Act Two begins with Butterfly staring at the ocean. Pinkerton's been called back to the U.S., and he's given his wife a detailed schedule of his plans. In the column marked "return date," he's written "when the robins nest." This failed to ignite her suspicions. Now, three years have passed without a peep from him. Which brings a response from her faithful servant, Suzuki.

[COMRADE CHIN *enters, playing* SUZUKI.]

SUZUKI Girl, he's a loser. What'd he ever give you? Nineteen cents and those ugly Day-Glo stockings? Look, it's finished! Kaput! Done! And you should be glad! I mean, the guy was a woofer![7] He tried before, you know—before he met you, he went down to geisha central and plunked down his spare change in front of the usual candidates—everyone else gagged! These are hungry prostitutes, and they were not interested, get the picture? Now, stop slathering when an American ship sails in, and let's make some bucks—I mean, yen! We are broke!

Now, what about Yamadori? Hey, hey—don't look away—the man is a prince—figuratively, and, what's even better, literally. He's rich, he's handsome, he says he'll die if you don't marry him—and he's even willing to overlook the little fact that you've been deflowered all over the place by a foreign devil. What do you mean, "But he's Japanese?" You're Japanese! You think you've been touched by the whitey god? He was a sailor with dirty hands!

7. That is, a dog, an ugly person (slang).

[SUZUKI *stalks offstage.*]

GALLIMARD She's also visited by Consul Sharpless, sent by Pinkerton on a minor errand.

[MARC *enters, as* SHARPLESS.]

SHARPLESS I hate this job.

GALLIMARD This Pinkerton—he doesn't show up personally to tell his wife he's abandoning her. No, he sends a government diplomat . . . at taxpayer's expense.

SHARPLESS Butterfly? Butterfly? I have some bad—I'm going to be ill. Butterfly, I came to tell you—

GALLIMARD Butterfly says she knows he'll return and if he doesn't she'll kill herself rather than go back to her own people. [*Beat*] This causes a lull in the conversation.

SHARPLESS Let's put it this way . . .

GALLIMARD Butterfly runs into the next room, and returns holding—

[*Sound cue: a baby crying.* SHARPLESS, *"seeing" this, backs away.*]

SHARPLESS Well, good. Happy to see things going so well. I suppose I'll be going now. Ta ta. Ciao. [*He turns away. Sound cue out.*] I hate this job. [*He exits.*]

GALLIMARD At that moment, Butterfly spots in the harbor an American ship—the *Abramo Lincoln!*[8]

[*Music cue: "The Flower Duet."*[9] SONG, *still dressed as* BUTTERFLY, *changes into a wedding kimono, moving to the music.*]

GALLIMARD This is the moment that redeems her years of waiting. With Suzuki's help, they cover the room with flowers—

[CHIN, *as* SUZUKI, *trudges onstage and drops a lone flower without much enthusiasm.*]

GALLIMARD —and she changes into her wedding dress to prepare for Pinkerton's arrival.

[SUZUKI *helps* BUTTERFLY *change.* HELGA *enters, and helps* GALLIMARD *change into a tuxedo.*]

GALLIMARD I married a woman older than myself—Helga.

HELGA My father was ambassador to Australia. I grew up among criminals and kangaroos.[1]

GALLIMARD Hearing that brought me to the altar—

[HELGA *exits.*]

GALLIMARD —where I took a vow renouncing love. No fantasy woman would ever want me, so, yes, I would settle for a quick leap up the career ladder. Passion, I banish, and in its place—practicality!

But my vows had long since lost their charm by the time we arrived in China. The sad truth is that all men want a beautiful woman, and the uglier the man, the greater the want.

[SUZUKI *makes final adjustments of* BUTTERFLY'S *costume, as does* GALLIMARD *of his tuxedo.*]

8. Abraham Lincoln (Italian).

9. "Tutti i fior?" ("All the Flowers"), a duet sung by Butterfly and her servant Suzuki in act 2 of *Madama Butterfly* at the point in the story narrated here by Gallimard.

1. Australia was originally used by Great Britain as a penal colony, and a sizable portion of the early settlers were convicts transported between 1788 and 1868.

GALLIMARD I married late, at age thirty-one. I was faithful to my marriage for eight years. Until the day when, as a junior-level diplomat in puritanical Peking, in a parlor at the German ambassador's house, during the "Reign of a Hundred Flowers,"[2] I first saw her . . . singing the death scene from *Madame Butterfly.*

[SUZUKI *runs offstage.*]

1.6

German ambassador's house. Beijing. 1960.

The upstage special area now becomes a stage. Several chairs face upstage, representing seating for some twenty guests in the parlor. A few "diplomats"— RENEE, MARC, TOULON*—in formal dress enter and take seats.*

GALLIMARD *also sits down, but turns towards us and continues to talk. Orchestral accompaniment on the tape is now replaced by a simple piano.* SONG *picks up the death scene from the point where* BUTTERFLY *uncovers the hara-kiri*[3] *knife.*

GALLIMARD The ending is pitiful. Pinkerton, in an act of great courage, stays home and sends his American wife to pick up Butterfly's child. The truth, long deferred, has come up to her door.

[SONG, *playing* BUTTERFLY, *sings the lines from the opera in her own voice—which, though not classical, should be decent.*]

SONG "Con onor muore / chi non puo serbar / vita con onore."

GALLIMARD [*simultaneously*] "Death with honor / Is better than life / Life with dishonor."

[*The stage is illuminated; we are now completely within an elegant diplomat's residence.* SONG *proceeds to play out an abbreviated death scene. Everyone in the room applauds.* SONG, *shyly, takes her bows. Others in the room rush to congratulate her.* GALLIMARD *remains with us.*]

GALLIMARD They say in opera the voice is everything. That's probably why I'd never before enjoyed opera. Here . . . here was a Butterfly with little or no voice—but she had the grace, the delicacy . . . I believed this girl. I believed her suffering. I wanted to take her in my arms—so delicate, even I could protect her, take her home, pamper her until she smiled.

[*Over the course of the preceding speech,* SONG *has broken from the upstage crowd and moved directly upstage of* GALLIMARD.]

SONG Excuse me. Monsieur . . . ?

[GALLIMARD *turns upstage, shocked.*]

GALLIMARD Oh! Gallimard. Mademoiselle . . . ? A beautiful . . .

SONG Song Liling.

GALLIMARD A beautiful performance.

SONG Oh, please.

GALLIMARD I usually—

SONG You make me blush. I'm no opera singer at all.

GALLIMARD I usually don't like *Butterfly.*

2. The so-called Hundred Flowers Campaign, a brief period (1956–57) during which the Communist authorities allowed intellectuals greater freedom of thought and speech.

3. Ritual suicide by disembowelment (Japanese).

SONG I can't blame you in the least.

GALLIMARD I mean, the story—

SONG Ridiculous.

GALLIMARD I like the story, but . . . what?

SONG Oh, you like it?

GALLIMARD I . . . what I mean is, I've always seen it played by huge women in so much bad makeup.

SONG Bad makeup is not unique to the West.

GALLIMARD But, who can believe them?

SONG And you believe me?

GALLIMARD Absolutely. You were utterly convincing. It's the first time—

SONG Convincing? As a Japanese woman? The Japanese used hundreds of our people for medical experiments during the war,[4] you know. But I gather such an irony is lost on you.

GALLIMARD No! I was about to say, it's the first time I've seen the beauty of the story.

SONG Really?

GALLIMARD Of her death. It's a . . . a pure sacrifice. He's unworthy, but what can she do? She loves him . . . so much. It's a very beautiful story.

SONG Well, yes, to a Westerner.

GALLIMARD Excuse me?

SONG It's one of your favorite fantasies, isn't it? The submissive Oriental woman and the cruel white man.

GALLIMARD Well, I didn't quite mean . . .

SONG Consider it this way: what would you say if a blonde homecoming queen fell in love with a short Japanese businessman? He treats her cruelly, then goes home for three years, during which time she prays to his picture and turns down marriage from a young Kennedy.[5] Then, when she learns he has remarried, she kills herself. Now, I believe you would consider this girl to be a deranged idiot, correct? But because it's an Oriental who kills herself for a Westerner—ah!—you find it beautiful.

[*Silence.*]

GALLIMARD Yes . . . well . . . I see your point . . .

SONG I will never do Butterfly again, Monsieur Gallimard. If you wish to see some real theatre, come to the Peking Opera sometime. Expand your mind.

[SONG *walks offstage.*]

GALLIMARD [*to us*] So much for protecting her in my big Western arms.

1.7

M. GALLIMARD*'s apartment. Beijing. 1960.*

GALLIMARD *changes from his tux into a casual suit.* HELGA *enters.*

GALLIMARD The Chinese are an incredibly arrogant people.

HELGA They warned us about that in Paris, remember?

4. The Japanese conducted gruesome medical experiments on Chinese prisoners and civilians during their World War II–era occupation of China (1937–45).

5. A member of the Massachusetts political family whose best-known members are President John F. Kennedy (1917–1963), Senator Robert F. Kennedy (1925–1968), and Senator Edward Kennedy (b. 1932).

GALLIMARD Even Parisians consider them arrogant. That's a switch.

HELGA What is it that Madame Su says? "We are a very old civilization." I never know if she's talking about her country or herself.

GALLIMARD I walk around here, all I hear every day, everywhere is how *old* this culture is. The fact that "old" may be synonymous with "senile" doesn't occur to them.

HELGA You're not going to change them. "East is east, west is west, and . . ."[6] whatever that guy said.

GALLIMARD It's just that—silly. I met . . . at Ambassador Koening's tonight—you should've been there.

HELGA Koening? Oh god, no. Did he enchant you all again with the history of Bavaria?[7]

GALLIMARD No. I met, I suppose, the Chinese equivalent of a diva.[8] She's a singer in the Chinese opera.

HELGA They have an opera, too? Do they sing in Chinese? Or maybe—in Italian?

GALLIMARD Tonight, she did sing in Italian.

HELGA How'd she manage that?

GALLIMARD She must've been educated in the West before the Revolution.[9] Her French is very good also. Anyway, she sang the death scene from *Madame Butterfly.*

HELGA *Madame Butterfly!* Then I should have come. [*She begins humming, floating around the room as if dragging long kimono sleeves.*] Did she have a nice costume? I think it's a classic piece of music.

GALLIMARD That's what *I* thought, too. Don't let her hear you say that.

HELGA What's wrong?

GALLIMARD Evidently the Chinese hate it.

HELGA She hated it, but she performed it anyway? Is she perverse?

GALLIMARD They hate it because the white man gets the girl. Sour grapes if you ask me.

HELGA Politics again? Why can't they just hear it as a piece of beautiful music? So, what's in their opera?

GALLIMARD I don't know. But, whatever it is, I'm sure it must be *old.*

[HELGA *exits.*]

1.8

Chinese opera house and the streets of Beijing. 1960.

The sound of gongs clanging fills the stage.

GALLIMARD My wife's innocent question kept ringing in my ears. I asked around, but no one knew anything about the Chinese opera. It took four weeks, but my curiosity overcame my cowardice. This Chinese diva—this unwilling Butterfly—what did she do to make her so proud?

6. "Oh, East is East, and West is West, and never the twain shall meet," from the poem "The Ballad of East and West" (1889) by the British writer Rudyard Kipling (1865–1936).

7. Germany's southernmost state, which was an independent kingdom until 1871.

8. A female opera star of the most glamorous and imperious sort (literally, "goddess"; Italian).

9. The civil war between the Nationalist government, led by Chiang Kai-shek, and the Communist rebels, led by Mao Zedong, which ended with the establishment of the People's Republic of China under Mao in 1949.

The room was hot, and full of smoke. Wrinkled faces, old women, teeth missing—a man with a growth on his neck, like a human toad. All smiling, pipes falling from their mouths, cracking nuts between their teeth, a live chicken pecking at my foot—all looking, screaming, gawking . . . at her.

[*The upstage area is suddenly hit with a harsh white light. It has become the stage for the Chinese opera performance. Two dancers enter, along with* SONG. GALLIMARD *stands apart, watching.* SONG *glides gracefully amidst the two dancers. Drums suddenly slam to a halt.* SONG *strikes a pose, looking straight at* GALLIMARD. *Dancers exit. Light change. Pause, then* SONG *walks right off the stage and straight up to* GALLIMARD.]

SONG Yes. You. White man. I'm looking straight at you.

GALLIMARD Me?

SONG You see any other white men? It was too easy to spot you. How often does a man in my audience come in a tie?

[SONG *starts to remove her costume. Underneath, she wears simple baggy clothes. They are now backstage. The show is over.*]

SONG So, you are an adventurous imperialist?

GALLIMARD I . . . thought it would further my education.

SONG It took you four weeks. Why?

GALLIMARD I've been busy.

SONG Well, education has always been undervalued in the West, hasn't it?

GALLIMARD [*laughing*] I don't think it's true.

SONG No, you wouldn't. You're a Westerner. How can you objectively judge your own values?

GALLIMARD I think it's possible to achieve some distance.

SONG Do you? [*Pause*] It stinks in here. Let's go.

GALLIMARD These are the smells of your loyal fans.

SONG I love them for being my fans, I hate the smell they leave behind. I too can distance myself from my people. [*She looks around, then whispers in his ear.*] "Art for the masses"[1] is a shitty excuse to keep artists poor. [*She pops a cigarette in her mouth.*] Be a gentleman, will you? And light my cigarette.

[GALLIMARD *fumbles for a match.*]

GALLIMARD I don't . . . smoke.

SONG [*lighting her own*] Your loss. Had you lit my cigarette, I might have blown a puff of smoke right between your eyes. Come.

[*They start to walk about the stage. It is a summer night on the Beijing streets. Sounds of the city play on the house speakers.*]

SONG How I wish there were even a tiny cafe to sit in. With cappuccinos, and men in tuxedos and bad expatriate jazz.

GALLIMARD If my history serves me correctly, you weren't even allowed into the clubs in Shanghai[2] before the Revolution.

SONG Your history serves you poorly, Monsieur Gallimard. True, there were signs reading "No dogs and Chinamen." But a woman, especially a delicate Oriental woman—we always go where we please. Could you imagine it otherwise? Clubs in China filled with pasty, big-thighed white women, while

1. A Communist slogan advocating a proletarian (working-class) art in place of the so-called elite art of Western capitalism.

2. The largest city in China; as one of the five ports opened to foreign trade and to foreign residents in the 19th century, it became the country's economic and cultural center until investment from overseas was halted by the Communist victory.

thousands of slender lotus blossoms[3] wait just outside the door? Never. The clubs would be empty. [*Beat*] We have always held a certain fascination for you Caucasian men, have we not?

GALLIMARD But . . . that fascination is imperialist, or so you tell me.

SONG Do you believe everything I tell you? Yes. It is always imperialist. But sometimes . . . sometimes, it is also mutual. Oh—this is my flat.

GALLIMARD I didn't even—

SONG Thank you. Come another time and we will further expand your mind.

[SONG *exits.* GALLIMARD *continues roaming the streets as he speaks to us.*]

GALLIMARD What was that? What did she mean, "Sometimes . . . it is mutual?" Women do not flirt with me. And I normally can't talk to them. But tonight, I held up my end of the conversation.

1.9

GALLIMARD*'s bedroom. Beijing. 1960.*

HELGA *enters.*

HELGA You didn't tell me you'd be home late.

GALLIMARD I didn't intend to. Something came up.

HELGA Oh? Like what?

GALLIMARD I went to the . . . to the Dutch ambassador's home.

HELGA Again?

GALLIMARD There was a reception for a visiting scholar. He's writing a six-volume treatise on the Chinese revolution. We all gathered that meant he'd have to live here long enough to actually write six volumes, and we all expressed our deepest sympathies.

HELGA Well, I had a good night too. I went with the ladies to a martial arts demonstration. Some of those men—when they break those thick boards—[*She mimes fanning herself.*] whoo-whoo!

[HELGA *exits. Lights dim.*]

GALLIMARD I lied to my wife. Why? I've never had any reason to lie before. But what reason did I have tonight? I didn't do anything wrong. That night, I had a dream. Other people, I've been told, have dreams where angels appear. Or dragons, or Sophia Loren[4] in a towel. In my dream, Marc from school appeared.

[MARC *enters, in a nightshirt and cap.*]

MARC Rene! You met a girl!

[GALLIMARD *and* MARC *stumble down the Beijing streets. Night sounds over the speakers.*]

GALLIMARD It's not that amazing, thank you.

MARC No! It's so monumental, I heard about it halfway around the world in my sleep!

GALLIMARD I've met girls before, you know.

MARC Name one. I've come across time and space to congratulate you. [*He hands* GALLIMARD *a bottle of wine.*]

3. That is, Asian women. The lotus blossom symbolized the practice of footbinding, which was highly eroticized in traditional Chinese culture.

4. An Italian actress (b. 1934), famous for her beauty and viewed as an international sex symbol.

GALLIMARD Marc, this is expensive.

MARC On those rare occasions when you become a formless spirit, why not steal the best?

[MARC *pops open the bottle, begins to share it with* GALLIMARD.]

GALLIMARD You embarrass me. She . . . there's no reason to think she likes me.

MARC "Sometimes, it is mutual"?

GALLIMARD Oh.

MARC "Mutual"? "Mutual"? What does that mean?

GALLIMARD You heard!

MARC It means the money is in the bank, you only have to write the check!

GALLIMARD I am a married man!

MARC And an excellent one too. I cheated after . . . six months. Then again and again, until now—three hundred girls in twelve years.

GALLIMARD I don't think we should hold that up as a model.

MARC Of course not! My life—it is disgusting! Phooey! Phooey! But, you—you are the model husband.

GALLIMARD Anyway, it's impossible. I'm a foreigner.

MARC Ah, yes. She cannot love you, it is taboo, but something deep inside her heart . . . she cannot help herself . . . she must surrender to you. It is her destiny.

GALLIMARD How do you imagine all this?

MARC The same way you do. It's an old story. It's in our blood. They fear us, Rene. Their women fear us. And their men—their men hate us. And, you know something? They are all correct.

[*They spot a light in a window.*]

MARC There! There, Rene!

GALLIMARD It's her window.

MARC Late at night—it burns. The light—it burns for you.

GALLIMARD I won't look. It's not respectful.

MARC We don't have to be respectful. We're foreign devils.

[*Enter* SONG, *in a sheer robe. The "One Fine Day"*[5] *aria creeps in over the speakers. With her back to us,* SONG *mimes attending to her toilette. Her robe comes loose, revealing her white shoulders.*]

MARC All your life you've waited for a beautiful girl who would lay down for you. All your life you've smiled like a saint when it's happened to every other man you know. And you see them in magazines and you see them in movies. And you wonder, what's wrong with me? Will anyone beautiful ever want me? As the years pass, your hair thins and you struggle to hold onto even your hopes. Stop struggling, Rene. The wait is over. [*He exits.*]

GALLIMARD Marc? Marc?

[*At that moment,* SONG, *her back still towards us, drops her robe. A second of her naked back, then a sound cue: a phone ringing, very loud. Blackout, followed in the next beat by a special up on the bedroom area, where a phone now sits.* GALLIMARD *stumbles across the stage and picks up the phone. Sound cue out. Over the course of his conversation, area lights fill in the vicinity of his bed. It is the following morning.*]

5. "Un bel dì vedremo" ("One Fine Day We Shall See"), an aria sung by Butterfly in act 2 of *Madama Butterfly*.

GALLIMARD Yes? Hello?

SONG [*offstage*] Is it very early?

GALLIMARD Why, yes.

SONG [*offstage*] How early?

GALLIMARD It's . . . it's 5:30. Why are you—?

SONG [*offstage*] But it's light outside. Already.

GALLIMARD It is. The sun must be in confusion today.

[*Over the course of* SONG*'s next speech, her upstage special comes up again. She sits in a chair, legs crossed, in a robe, telephone to her ear.*]

SONG I waited until I saw the sun. That was as much discipline as I could manage for one night. Do you forgive me?

GALLIMARD Of course . . . for what?

SONG Then I'll ask you quickly. Are you really interested in the opera?

GALLIMARD Why, yes. Yes I am.

SONG Then come again next Thursday. I am playing *The Drunken Beauty.*[6] May I count on you?

GALLIMARD Yes. You may.

SONG Perfect. Well, I must be getting to bed. I'm exhausted. It's been a very long night for me.

[SONG *hangs up; special on her goes off.* GALLIMARD *begins to dress for work.*]

1.10

SONG LILING*'s apartment. Beijing. 1960.*

GALLIMARD I returned to the opera that next week, and the week after that . . . she keeps our meetings so short—perhaps fifteen, twenty minutes at most. So I am left each week with a thirst which is intensified. In this way, fifteen weeks have gone by. I am starting to doubt the words of my friend Marc. But no, not really. In my heart, I know she has . . . an interest in me. I suspect this is her way. She is outwardly bold and outspoken, yet her heart is shy and afraid. It is the Oriental in her at war with her Western education.

SONG [*offstage*] I will be out in an instant. Ask the servant for anything you want.

GALLIMARD Tonight, I have finally been invited to enter her apartment. Though the idea is almost beyond belief, I believe she is afraid of me.

[GALLIMARD *looks around the room. He picks up a picture in a frame, studies it. Without his noticing,* SONG *enters, dressed elegantly in a black gown from the twenties. She stands in the doorway looking like Anna May Wong.*[7]]

SONG That is my father.

GALLIMARD [*surprised*] Mademoiselle Song . . .

[*She glides up to him, snatches away the picture.*]

6. A traditional Chinese opera about an imperial concubine during the Tang dynasty (set ca. 750 C.E.). Enraged that the emperor has chosen to visit a new concubine, his previous favorite drinks herself into a state of gaiety and then despondency. *The Drunken Beauty* (or *The Drunken Concubine*) was made famous by the Beijing Opera star Mei Lanfang (1894–1961), a man who specialized in female roles.

7. A Chinese American actor (1905–1961), the first Asian woman to become a film star; she often played temptresses or exotic villainesses in the 1920s and '30s.

SONG It is very good that he did not live to see the Revolution. They would, no doubt, have made him kneel on broken glass.[8] Not that he didn't deserve such a punishment. But he is my father. I would've hated to see it happen.

GALLIMARD I'm very honored that you've allowed me to visit your home.

[SONG *curtsies.*]

SONG Thank you. Oh! Haven't you been poured any tea?

GALLIMARD I'm really not—

SONG [*to her offstage servant*] Shu-Fang! Cha! Kwai-lah![9] [*To* GALLIMARD] I'm sorry. You want everything to be perfect—

GALLIMARD Please.

SONG —and before the evening even begins—

GALLIMARD I'm really not thirsty.

SONG —It's ruined.

GALLIMARD [*sharply*] Mademoiselle Song!

[SONG *sits down.*]

SONG I'm sorry.

GALLIMARD What are you apologizing for now?

[*Pause;* SONG *starts to giggle.*]

SONG I don't know!

[GALLIMARD *laughs.*]

GALLIMARD Exactly my point.

SONG Oh, I am silly. Lightheaded. I promise not to apologize for anything else tonight, do you hear me?

GALLIMARD That's a good girl.

[SHU-FANG, *a servant girl, comes out with a tea tray and starts to pour.*]

SONG [*to* SHU-FANG] No! I'll pour myself for the gentleman!

[SHU-FANG, *staring at* GALLIMARD, *exits.*]

SONG No, I . . . I don't even know why I invited you up.

GALLIMARD Well, I'm glad you did.

[SONG *looks around the room.*]

SONG There is an element of danger to your presence.

GALLIMARD Oh?

SONG You must know.

GALLIMARD It doesn't concern me. We both know why I'm here.

SONG It doesn't concern me either. No . . . well perhaps . . .

GALLIMARD What?

SONG Perhaps I am slightly afraid of scandal.

GALLIMARD What are we doing?

SONG I'm entertaining you. In my parlor.

GALLIMARD In France, that would hardly—

SONG France. France is a country living in the modern era. Perhaps even ahead of it. China is a nation whose soul is firmly rooted two thousand years in the past. What I do, even pouring the tea for you now . . . it has . . . implications. The walls and windows say so. Even my own heart, strapped inside this Western dress . . . even it says things—things I don't care to hear.

8. One of the punishments inflicted by the Communists on those viewed as "class enemies."

9. Tea, quickly please! (Chinese).

[SONG *hands* GALLIMARD *a cup of tea.* GALLIMARD *puts his hand over both the teacup and* SONG*'s hand.*]

GALLIMARD This is a beautiful dress.

SONG Don't.

GALLIMARD What?

SONG I don't even know if it looks right on me.

GALLIMARD Believe me—

SONG You are from France. You see so many beautiful women.

GALLIMARD France? Since when are the European women—?

SONG Oh! What am I trying to do, anyway?!

[SONG *runs to the door, composes herself, then turns towards* GALLIMARD.]

SONG Monsieur Gallimard, perhaps you should go.

GALLIMARD But . . . why?

SONG There's something wrong about this.

GALLIMARD I don't see what.

SONG I feel . . . I am not myself.

GALLIMARD No. You're nervous.

SONG Please. Hard as I try to be modern, to speak like a man, to hold a Western woman's strong face up to my own . . . in the end, I fail. A small, frightened heart beats too quickly and gives me away. Monsieur Gallimard, I'm a Chinese girl. I've never . . . never invited a man up to my flat before. The forwardness of my actions makes my skin burn.

GALLIMARD What are you afraid of? Certainly not me, I hope.

SONG I'm a modest girl.

GALLIMARD I know. And very beautiful. [*He touches her hair.*]

SONG Please—go now. The next time you see me, I shall again be myself.

GALLIMARD I like you the way you are right now.

SONG You are a cad.

GALLIMARD What do you expect? I'm a foreign devil.

[GALLIMARD *walks downstage.* SONG *exits.*]

GALLIMARD [*to us*] Did you hear the way she talked about Western women? Much differently than the first night. She does—she feels inferior to them—and to me.

1.11

The French embassy. Beijing. 1960.

GALLIMARD *moves towards a desk.*

GALLIMARD I determined to try an experiment. In *Madame Butterfly,* Cio-Cio-San fears that the Western man who catches a butterfly will pierce its heart with a needle, then leave it to perish. I began to wonder: had I, too, caught a butterfly who would writhe on a needle?

[MARC *enters, dressed as a bureaucrat, holding a stack of papers. As* GALLIMARD *speaks,* MARC *hands papers to him. He peruses, then signs, stamps, or rejects them.*]

GALLIMARD Over the next five weeks, I worked like a dynamo. I stopped going to the opera, I didn't phone or write her. I knew this little flower was waiting for me to call, and, as I wickedly refused to do so, I felt for the first time that rush of power—the absolute power of a man.

[MARC *continues acting as the bureaucrat, but he now speaks as himself.*]

MARC Rene! It's me!

GALLIMARD Marc—I hear your voice everywhere now. Even in the midst of work.

MARC That's because I'm watching you—all the time.

GALLIMARD You were always the most popular guy in school.

MARC Well, there's no guarantee of failure in life like happiness in high school. Somehow I knew I'd end up in the suburbs working for Renault[1] and you'd be in the Orient picking exotic women off the trees. And they say there's no justice.

GALLIMARD That's why you were my friend?

MARC I gave you a little of my life, so that now you can give me some of yours. [*Pause*] Remember Isabelle?

GALLIMARD Of course I remember! She was my first experience.

MARC We all wanted to ball her. But she only wanted me.

GALLIMARD I had her.

MARC Right. You balled her.

GALLIMARD You were the only one who ever believed me.

MARC Well, there's a good reason for that. [*Beat*] C'mon. You must've guessed.

GALLIMARD You told me to wait in the bushes by the cafeteria that night. The next thing I knew, she was on me. Dress up in the air.

MARC She never wore underwear.

GALLIMARD My arms were pinned to the dirt.

MARC She loved the superior position. A girl ahead of her time.

GALLIMARD I looked up, and there was this woman . . . bouncing up and down on my loins.

MARC Screaming, right?

GALLIMARD Screaming, and breaking off the branches all around me, and pounding my butt up and down into the dirt.

MARC Huffing and puffing like a locomotive.

GALLIMARD And in the middle of all this, the leaves were getting into my mouth, my legs were losing circulation, I thought, "God. So this is *it*?"

MARC You thought that?

GALLIMARD Well, I was worried about my legs falling off.

MARC You didn't have a good time?

GALLIMARD No, that's not what I—I had a great time!

MARC You're sure?

GALLIMARD Yeah. Really.

MARC 'Cuz I wanted you to have a good time.

GALLIMARD I did.

[*Pause.*]

MARC Shit. [*Pause*] When all is said and done, she was kind of a lousy lay, wasn't she? I mean, there was a lot of energy there, but you never knew what she was doing with it. Like when she yelled "I'm coming!"—hell, it was so loud, you wanted to go "Look, it's not that big a deal."

GALLIMARD I got scared. I thought she meant someone was actually coming. [*Pause*] But, Marc?

MARC What?

1. A French automobile manufacturing company.

GALLIMARD Thanks.

MARC Oh, don't mention it.

GALLIMARD It was my first experience.

MARC Yeah. You got her.

GALLIMARD I got her.

MARC Wait! Look at that letter again!

[GALLIMARD *picks up one of the papers he's been stamping, and rereads it.*]

GALLIMARD [*to us*] After six weeks, they began to arrive. The letters.

[*Upstage special on* SONG, *as Madame* BUTTERFLY. *The scene is underscored by the "Love Duet."*]

SONG Did we fight? I do not know. Is the opera no longer of interest to you? Please come—my audiences miss the white devil in their midst.

[GALLIMARD *looks up from the letter, towards us.*]

GALLIMARD [*to us*] A concession, but much too dignified. [*Beat; he discards the letter.*] I skipped the opera again that week to complete a position paper on trade.

[*The bureaucrat hands him another letter.*]

SONG Six weeks have passed since last we met. Is this your practice—to leave friends in the lurch? Sometimes I hate you, sometimes I hate myself, but always I miss you.

GALLIMARD [*to us*] Better, but I don't like the way she calls me "friend." When a woman calls a man her "friend," she's calling him a eunuch or a homosexual. [*Beat; he discards the letter.*] I was absent from the opera for the seventh week, feeling a sudden urge to clean out my files.

[*Bureaucrat hands him another letter.*]

SONG Your rudeness is beyond belief. I don't deserve this cruelty. Don't bother to call. I'll have you turned away at the door.

GALLIMARD [*to us*] I didn't. [*He discards the letter; bureaucrat hands him another.*] And then finally, the letter that concluded my experiment.

SONG I am out of words. I can hide behind dignity no longer. What do you want? I have already given you my shame.

[GALLIMARD *gives the letter back to* MARC, *slowly. Special on* SONG *fades out.*]

GALLIMARD [*to us*] Reading it, I became suddenly ashamed. Yes, my experiment had been a success. She was turning on my needle. But the victory seemed hollow.

MARC Hollow?! Are you crazy?

GALLIMARD Nothing, Marc. Please go away.

MARC [*exiting, with papers*] Haven't I taught you anything?

GALLIMARD "I have already given you my shame." I had to attend a reception that evening. On the way, I felt sick. If there is a God, surely he would punish me now. I had finally gained power over a beautiful woman, only to abuse it cruelly. There must be justice in the world. I had the strange feeling that the ax would fall this very evening.

1.12

Ambassador TOULON*'s residence. Beijing. 1960.*

Sound cue: party noises. Light change. We are now in a spacious residence. TOULON, *the French ambassador, enters and taps* GALLIMARD *on the shoulder.*

TOULON Gallimard? Can I have a word? Over here.

GALLIMARD [*to us*] Manuel Toulon. French ambassador to China. He likes to think of us all as his children. Rather like God.

TOULON Look, Gallimard, there's not much to say. I've liked you. From the day you walked in. You were no leader, but you were tidy and efficient.

GALLIMARD Thank you, sir.

TOULON Don't jump the gun. Okay, our needs in China are changing. It's embarrassing that we lost Indochina.[2] Someone just wasn't on the ball there. I don't mean you personally, of course.

GALLIMARD Thank you, sir.

TOULON We're going to be doing a lot more information-gathering in the future. The nature of our work here is changing. Some people are just going to have to go. It's nothing personal.

GALLIMARD Oh.

TOULON Want to know a secret? Vice-Consul LeBon is being transferred.

GALLIMARD [*to us*] My immediate superior!

TOULON And most of his department.

GALLIMARD [*to us*] Just as I feared! God has seen my evil heart

TOULON But not you.

GALLIMARD [*to us*] —and he's taking her away just as . . . [*To* TOULON] Excuse me, sir?

TOULON Scare you? I think I did. Cheer up, Gallimard. I want you to replace LeBon as vice-consul.

GALLIMARD You—? Yes, well, thank you, sir.

TOULON Anytime.

GALLIMARD I . . . accept with great humility.

TOULON Humility won't be part of the job. You're going to coordinate the revamped intelligence division. Want to know a secret? A year ago, you would've been out. But the past few months, I don't know how it happened, you've become this new aggressive confident . . . thing. And they also tell me you get along with the Chinese. So I think you're a lucky man, Gallimard. Congratulations.

[*They shake hands.* TOULON *exits. Party noises out.* GALLIMARD *stumbles across a darkened stage.*]

GALLIMARD Vice-consul? Impossible! As I stumbled out of the party, I saw it written across the sky: There is no God. Or, no—say that there is a God. But that God . . . understands. Of course! God who creates Eve to serve Adam, who blesses Solomon with his harem but ties Jezebel to a burning bed[3]—that God is a man. And he understands! At age thirty-nine, I was suddenly initiated into the way of the world.

2. That is, French Indochina, a colony established in the late 19th century that comprised present-day Laos, Cambodia, and Vietnam. It was "lost" with the French defeat at the Battle of Dien Bien Phu in 1954, ending an insurgency that had begun with Vietnam's declaration of independence in 1945.

3. A series of biblical references: see Genesis 2.21–23 and 1 Corinthians 11.8–9 (the creation of Eve), 1 Kings 11.1–3 (Solomon's wives and concubines), and Revelation 2.20–23 (the punishment of Jezebel for harlotry, as described here).

1.13

SONG LILING*'s apartment. Beijing. 1960.*

SONG *enters, in a sheer dressing gown.*

SONG Are you crazy?

GALLIMARD Mademoiselle Song—

SONG To come here—at this hour? After . . . after eight weeks?

GALLIMARD It's the most amazing—

SONG You bang on my door? Scare my servants, scandalize the neighbors?

GALLIMARD I've been promoted. To vice-consul.

[*Pause.*]

SONG And what is that supposed to mean to me?

GALLIMARD Are you my Butterfly?

SONG What are you saying?

GALLIMARD I've come tonight for an answer: are you my Butterfly?

SONG Don't you know already?

GALLIMARD I want you to say it.

SONG I don't want to say it.

GALLIMARD So, that is your answer?

SONG You know how I feel about—

GALLIMARD I do remember one thing.

SONG What?

GALLIMARD In the letter I received today.

SONG Don't.

GALLIMARD "I have already given you my shame."

SONG It's enough that I even wrote it.

GALLIMARD Well, then—

SONG I shouldn't have it splashed across my face.

GALLIMARD —if that's all true—

SONG Stop!

GALLIMARD Then what is one more short answer?

SONG I don't want to!

GALLIMARD Are you my Butterfly? [*Silence; he crosses the room and begins to touch her hair.*] I want from you honesty. There should be nothing false between us. No false pride.

[*Pause.*]

SONG Yes, I am. I am your Butterfly.

GALLIMARD Then let me be honest with you. It is because of you that I was promoted tonight. You have changed my life forever. My little Butterfly, there should be no more secrets: I love you.

[*He starts to kiss her roughly. She resists slightly.*]

SONG No . . . no . . . gently . . . please, I've never . . .

GALLIMARD No?

SONG I've tried to appear experienced, but . . . the truth is . . . no.

GALLIMARD Are you cold?

SONG Yes. Cold.

GALLIMARD Then we will go very, very slowly.

[*He starts to caress her; her gown begins to open.*]

SONG No . . . let me . . . keep my clothes . . .

GALLIMARD But. . . .

SONG Please . . . it all frightens me. I'm a modest Chinese girl.

GALLIMARD My poor little treasure.

SONG I am your treasure. Though inexperienced, I am not . . . ignorant. They teach us things, our mothers, about pleasing a man.

GALLIMARD Yes?

SONG I'll do my best to make you happy. Turn off the lights.

[GALLIMARD *gets up and heads for a lamp.* SONG, *propped up on one elbow, tosses her hair back and smiles.*]

SONG Monsieur Gallimard?

GALLIMARD Yes, Butterfly?

SONG "Vieni, vieni!"[4]

GALLIMARD "Come, darling."

SONG "Ah! Dolce notte!"

GALLIMARD "Beautiful night."

SONG "Tutto estatico d'amor ride il ciel!"

GALLIMARD "All ecstatic with love, the heavens are filled with laughter."

[*He turns off the lamp. Blackout.*]

2.1

M. GALLIMARD*'s cell. Paris. Present.*

Lights up on GALLIMARD. *He sits in his cell, reading from a leaflet.*

GALLIMARD This, from a contemporary critic's commentary on *Madame Butterfly*: "Pinkerton suffers from . . . being an obnoxious bounder whom every man in the audience itches to kick." Bully for us men in the audience! Then, in the same note: "Butterfly is the most irresistibly appealing of Puccini's 'Little Women.' Watching the succession of her humiliations is like watching a child under torture." [*He tosses the pamphlet over his shoulder.*] I suggest that, while we men may all want to kick Pinkerton, very few of us would pass up the opportunity to *be* Pinkerton.

[GALLIMARD *moves out of his cell.*]

2.2

GALLIMARD *and* BUTTERFLY*'s flat. Beijing. 1960.*

We are in a simple but well-decorated parlor. GALLIMARD *moves to sit on a sofa, while* SONG, *dressed in a chong sam,*[5] *enters and curls up at his feet.*

GALLIMARD [*to us*] We secured a flat on the outskirts of Peking. Butterfly, as I was calling her now, decorated our "home" with Western furniture and Chinese antiques. And there, on a few stolen afternoons or evenings each week, Butterfly commenced her education.

SONG The Chinese men—they keep us down.

GALLIMARD Even in the "New Society"?[6]

4. Song's Italian lines ending this scene, translated by Gallimard, are drawn from the "Love Duet" finale of act 1 of *Madama Butterfly*.

5. That is, a cheongsam (literally, "long gown"), a traditional Chinese dress with a high collar and a slit skirt.

6. In his essay "On New Democracy" (1940), Mao Zedong called for "a new society and a new state for the Chinese nation."

SONG In the "New Society," we are all kept ignorant equally. That's one of the exciting things about loving a Western man. I know you are not threatened by a woman's education.

GALLIMARD I'm no saint, Butterfly.

SONG But you come from a progressive society.

GALLIMARD We're not always reminding each other how "old" we are, if that's what you mean.

SONG Exactly. We Chinese—once, I suppose, it is true, we ruled the world. But so what? How much more exciting to be part of the society ruling the world today. Tell me—what's happening in Vietnam?[7]

GALLIMARD Oh, Butterfly—you want me to bring my work home?

SONG I want to know what you know. To be impressed by my man. It's not the particulars so much as the fact that you're making decisions which change the shape of the world.

GALLIMARD Not the world. At best, a small corner.

[TOULON *enters, and sits at a desk upstage.*]

2.3

French embassy. Beijing. 1961.

GALLIMARD *moves downstage, to* TOULON*'s desk.* SONG *remains upstage, watching.*

TOULON And a more troublesome corner is hard to imagine.

GALLIMARD So, the Americans plan to begin bombing?

TOULON This is very secret, Gallimard: yes. The Americans don't have an embassy here.[8] They're asking us to be their eyes and ears. Say Jack Kennedy signed an order to bomb North Vietnam, Laos.[9] How would the Chinese react?

GALLIMARD I think the Chinese will squawk—

TOULON Uh-huh.

GALLIMARD —but, in their hearts, they don't even like Ho Chi Minh.[1]

[*Pause.*]

TOULON What a bunch of jerks. Vietnam was *our* colony. Not only didn't the Americans help us fight to keep them, but now, seven years later, they've come back to grab the territory for themselves. It's very irritating.

GALLIMARD With all due respect, sir, why should the Americans have won our war for us back in '54 if we didn't have the will to win it ourselves?

7. On gaining its independence in 1954, Vietnam was divided into two countries: the Communist-controlled Democratic Republic of Vietnam (North Vietnam) and the U.S.-backed Republic of Vietnam (South Vietnam). In the late 1950s, Communist insurgents in the South (the Viet Cong), aided by the North, launched a guerrilla war seeking the reunification of Vietnam.

8. The United States did not establish official diplomatic relations with the People's Republic of China until 1979.

9. While campaigning for the presidency in 1960, Kennedy pledged to increase U.S. military assistance to South Vietnam in its struggle against the armed insurgency supported by the North. In 1961, his administration signed a military and economic aid treaty with South Vietnam, leading to large increases in the number of U.S. military advisers in the country (U.S. air strikes against North Vietnam and Laos would not begin until 1964).

1. Vietnamese nationalist (1890–1969), a Communist who led the struggle for independence; after the country's partition in 1954, he became president of North Vietnam. In the early 1950s, China had sent military advisers and weapons to the Vietnamese insurgents, and it supported the North in its war with the South.

TOULON You're kidding, aren't you?

[*Pause.*]

GALLIMARD The Orientals simply want to be associated with whoever shows the most strength and power. You live with the Chinese, sir. Do you think they like Communism?

TOULON I live in China. Not with the Chinese.

GALLIMARD Well, I—

TOULON *You* live with the Chinese.

GALLIMARD Excuse me?

TOULON I can't keep a secret.

GALLIMARD What are you saying?

TOULON Only that I'm not immune to gossip. So, you're keeping a native mistress. Don't answer. It's none of my business. [*Pause*] I'm sure she must be gorgeous.

GALLIMARD Well . . .

TOULON I'm impressed. You have the stamina to go out into the streets and hunt one down. Some of us have to be content with the wives of the expatriate community.

GALLIMARD I do feel . . . fortunate.

TOULON So, Gallimard, you've got the inside knowledge—what *do* the Chinese think?

GALLIMARD Deep down, they miss the old days. You know, cappuccinos, men in tuxedos—

TOULON So what do we tell the Americans about Vietnam?

GALLIMARD Tell them there's a natural affinity between the West and the Orient.

TOULON And that you speak from experience?

GALLIMARD The Orientals are people too. They want the good things we can give them. If the Americans demonstrate the will to win, the Vietnamese will welcome them into a mutually beneficial union.

TOULON I don't see how the Vietnamese can stand up to American firepower.

GALLIMARD Orientals will always submit to a greater force.

TOULON I'll note your opinions in my report. The Americans always love to hear how "welcome" they'll be. [*He starts to exit.*]

GALLIMARD Sir?

TOULON Mmmm?

GALLIMARD This . . . rumor you've heard.

TOULON Uh-huh?

GALLIMARD How . . . widespread do you think it is?

TOULON It's only widespread within this embassy. Where nobody talks because everybody is guilty. We were worried about you, Gallimard. We thought you were the only one here without a secret. Now you go and find a lotus blossom . . . and top us all. [*He exits.*]

GALLIMARD [*to us*] Toulon knows! And he approves! I was learning the benefits of being a man. We form our own clubs, sit behind thick doors, smoke—and celebrate the fact that we're still boys. [*He starts to move downstage, towards* SONG.] So, over the—

[*Suddenly* COMRADE CHIN *enters.* GALLIMARD *backs away.*]

GALLIMARD [*to* SONG] No! Why does she have to come in?

SONG Rene, be sensible. How can they understand the story without her? Now, don't embarrass yourself.

[GALLIMARD *moves down center.*]

GALLIMARD [*to us*] Now, you will see why my story is so amusing to so many people. Why they snicker at parties in disbelief. Please—try to understand it from my point of view. We are all prisoners of our time and place. [*He exits.*]

2.4

GALLIMARD *and* BUTTERFLY*'s flat. Beijing. 1961.*

SONG [*to us*] 1961. The flat Monsieur Gallimard rented for us. An evening after he has gone.

CHIN Okay, see if you can find out when the Americans plan to start bombing Vietnam. If you can find out what cities, even better.

SONG I'll do my best, but I don't want to arouse his suspicions.

CHIN Yeah, sure, of course. So, what else?

SONG The Americans will increase troops in Vietnam to 170,000 soldiers with 120,000 militia and 11,000 American advisors.

CHIN [*writing*] Wait, wait. 120,000 militia and—

SONG —11,000 American—

CHIN —American advisors. [*Beat*] How do you remember so much?

SONG I'm an actor.

CHIN Yeah. [*Beat*] Is that how come you dress like that?

SONG Like what, Miss Chin?

CHIN Like that dress! You're wearing a dress. And every time I come here, you're wearing a dress. Is that because you're an actor? Or what?

SONG It's a . . . disguise, Miss Chin.

CHIN Actors, I think they're all weirdos. My mother tells me actors are like gamblers or prostitutes or—

SONG It helps me in my assignment.

[*Pause.*]

CHIN You're not gathering information in any way that violates Communist Party principles, are you?

SONG Why would I do that?

CHIN Just checking. Remember: when working for the Great Proletarian State, you represent our Chairman Mao[2] in every position you take.

SONG I'll try to imagine the Chairman taking my positions.

CHIN We all think of him this way. Good-bye, comrade.[3] [*She starts to exit.*] Comrade?

SONG Yes?

CHIN Don't forget: there is no homosexuality in China!

SONG Yes, I've heard.

CHIN Just checking. [*She exits.*]

SONG [*to us*] What passes for a woman in modern China.

2. Mao Zedong (1893–1976) was chairman of the Central Committee of the Chinese Communist Party from 1945 until his death. *Proletarian state:* a transitional stage in the proletarian (i.e., working-class) revolution that Karl Marx and Friedrich Engels, in *Manifesto of the Communist Party* (1848), envisioned as necessary to overthrow capitalism and bring about a classless society.

3. Customary form of address among Communists.

[GALLIMARD *sticks his head out from the wings.*]

GALLIMARD Is she gone?

SONG Yes, Rene. Please continue in your own fashion.

2.5

Beijing. 1961–63.

GALLIMARD *moves to the couch where* SONG *still sits. He lies down in her lap, and she strokes his forehead.*

GALLIMARD [*to us*] And so, over the years 1961, '62, '63, we settled into our routine, Butterfly and I. She would always have prepared a light snack and then, ever so delicately, and only if I agreed, she would start to pleasure me. With her hands, her mouth . . . too many ways to explain, and too sad, given my present situation. But mostly we would talk. About my life. Perhaps there is nothing more rare than to find a woman who passionately listens.

[SONG *remains upstage, listening, as* HELGA *enters and plays a scene downstage with* GALLIMARD.]

HELGA Rene, I visited Dr. Bolleart this morning.

GALLIMARD Why? Are you ill?

HELGA No, no. You see, I wanted to ask him . . . that question we've been discussing.

GALLIMARD And I told you, it's only a matter of time. Why did you bring a doctor into this? We just have to keep trying—like a crapshoot, actually.

HELGA I went, I'm sorry. But listen: he says there's nothing wrong with me.

GALLIMARD You see? Now, will you stop—?

HELGA Rene, he says he'd like you to go in and take some tests.

GALLIMARD Why? So he can find there's nothing wrong with both of us?

HELGA Rene, I don't ask for much. One trip! One visit! And then, whatever you want to do about it—you decide.

GALLIMARD You're assuming he'll find something defective!

HELGA No! Of course not! Whatever he finds—if he finds nothing, we decide what to do about nothing! But go!

GALLIMARD If he finds nothing, we keep trying. Just like we do now.

HELGA But at least we'll know! [*Pause*] I'm sorry. [*She starts to exit.*]

GALLIMARD Do you really want me to see Dr. Bolleart?

HELGA Only if you want a child, Rene. We have to face the fact that time is running out. Only if you want a child. [*She exits.*]

GALLIMARD [*to* SONG] I'm a modern man, Butterfly. And yet, I don't want to go. It's the same old voodoo. I feel like God himself is laughing at me if I can't produce a child.

SONG You men of the West—you're obsessed by your odd desire for equality. Your wife can't give you a child, and *you're* going to the doctor?

GALLIMARD Well, you see, she's already gone.

SONG And because this incompetent can't find the defect, you now have to subject yourself to him? It's unnatural.

GALLIMARD Well, what is the "natural" solution?

SONG In Imperial China, when a man found that one wife was inadequate, he turned to another—to give him his son.

GALLIMARD What do you—? I can't . . . marry you, yet.

SONG Please. I'm not asking you to be my husband. But I am already your wife.

GALLIMARD Do you want to . . . have my child?

SONG I thought you'd never ask.

GALLIMARD But, your career . . . your—

SONG Phooey on my career! That's your Western mind, twisting itself into strange shapes again. Of course I love my career. But what would I love most of all? To feel something inside me—day and night—something I know is yours. [*Pause*] Promise me . . . you won't go to this doctor. Who is this Western quack to set himself as judge over the man I love? I know who is a man, and who is not. [*She exits.*]

GALLIMARD [*to us*] Dr. Bolleart? Of course I didn't go. What man would?

2.6

Beijing. 1963.

Party noises over the house speakers. RENEE *enters, wearing a revealing gown.*

GALLIMARD 1963. A party at the Austrian embassy. None of us could remember the Austrian ambassador's name, which seemed somehow appropriate. [*To* RENEE] So, I tell the Americans, Diem[4] must go. The U.S. wants to be respected by the Vietnamese, and yet they're propping up this nobody seminarian as her president. A man whose claim to fame is his sister-in-law[5] imposing fanatic "moral order" campaigns? Oriental women—when they're good, they're very good, but when they're bad, they're Christians.

RENEE Yeah.

GALLIMARD And what do you do?

RENEE I'm a student. My father exports a lot of useless stuff to the Third World.

GALLIMARD How useless?

RENEE You know. Squirt guns, confectioner's sugar, hula hoops[6] . . .

GALLIMARD I'm sure they appreciate the sugar.

RENEE I'm here for two years to study Chinese.

GALLIMARD Two years?

RENEE That's what everybody says.

GALLIMARD When did you arrive?

RENEE Three weeks ago.

GALLIMARD And?

RENEE I like it. It's primitive, but . . . well, this is the place to learn Chinese, so here I am.

GALLIMARD Why Chinese?

RENEE I think it'll be important someday.

4. Ngo Dinh Diem (1901–1963); as a boy, he studied in a French Catholic school and briefly entered a monastery. With U.S. support, he became prime minister of Vietnam in 1954 and president of South Vietnam in 1955. His authoritarian and corrupt rule made him widely unpopular, and he was ousted and murdered by a group of generals who had been assured that the United States would not interfere with a coup.

5. Tran Le Xian (b. 1924), the wife of Diem's brother and chief adviser, Ngo Dinh Nhu; she was known as Madame Nhu. Because Diem was unmarried, she was in effect the country's first lady. A passionate convert to Roman Catholicism, she worked for laws banning divorce, contraception, brothels, and the like and encouraged the persecution of Buddhists.

6. Hula Hoops were a brief U.S. craze in 1958, when 25 million were sold in four months.

GALLIMARD You do?

RENEE Don't ask me when, but . . . that's what I think.

GALLIMARD Well, I agree with you. One hundred percent. That's very far-sighted.

RENEE Yeah. Well of course, my father thinks I'm a complete weirdo.

GALLIMARD He'll thank you someday.

RENEE Like when the Chinese start buying hula hoops?

GALLIMARD There're a billion bellies out there.

RENEE And if they end up taking over the world—well, then I'll be lucky to know Chinese too, right?

[*Pause.*]

GALLIMARD At this point, I don't see how the Chinese can possibly take—

RENEE You know what I *don't* like about China?

GALLIMARD Excuse me? No—what?

RENEE Nothing to do at night.

GALLIMARD You come to parties at embassies like everyone else.

RENEE Yeah, but they get out at ten. And then what?

GALLIMARD I'm afraid the Chinese idea of a dance hall is a dirt floor and a man with a flute.

RENEE Are you married?

GALLIMARD Yes. Why?

RENEE You wanna . . . fool around?

[*Pause.*]

GALLIMARD Sure.

RENEE I'll wait for you outside. What's your name?

GALLIMARD Gallimard, Rene.

RENEE Weird. I'm Renee too. [*She exits.*]

GALLIMARD [*to us*] And so, I embarked on my first extra-extramarital affair. Renee was picture perfect. With a body like those girls in the magazines. If I put a tissue paper over my eyes, I wouldn't have been able to tell the difference. And it was exciting to be with someone who wasn't afraid to be seen completely naked. But is it possible for a woman to be *too* uninhibited, *too* willing, so as to seem almost too . . . masculine?

[*Chuck Berry*[7] *blares from the house speakers, then comes down in volume as* RENEE *enters, toweling her hair.*]

RENEE You have a nice weenie.

GALLIMARD What?

RENEE Penis. You have a nice penis.

GALLIMARD Oh. Well, thank you. That's very . . .

RENEE What—can't take a compliment?

GALLIMARD No, it's very . . . reassuring.

RENEE But most girls don't come out and say it, huh?

GALLIMARD And also . . . what did you call it?

RENEE Oh. Most girls don't call it a "weenie," huh?

GALLIMARD It sounds very—

RENEE Small, I know.

7. An African American songwriter, guitarist, and singer (b. 1926), a pioneer of rock-and-roll music whose hits include "Roll Over Beethoven" (1956) and "Johnny B. Goode" (1958).

GALLIMARD I was going to say, "young."

RENEE Yeah. Young, small, same thing. Most guys are pretty, uh, sensitive about that. Like, you know, I had a boyfriend back home in Denmark. I got mad at him once and called him a little weeniehead. He got so mad! He said at least I should call him a great big weeniehead.

GALLIMARD I suppose I just say "penis."

RENEE Yeah. That's pretty clinical. There's "cock," but that sounds like a chicken. And "prick" is painful, and "dick" is like you're talking about someone who's not in the room.

GALLIMARD Yes. It's a . . . bigger problem than I imagined.

RENEE I—I think maybe it's because I really don't know what to do with them—that's why I call them "weenies."

GALLIMARD Well, you did quite well with . . . mine.

RENEE Thanks, but I mean, really *do* with them. Like, okay, have you ever looked at one? I mean, really?

GALLIMARD No, I suppose when it's part of you, you sort of take it for granted.

RENEE I guess. But, like, it just hangs there. This little . . . flap of flesh. And there's so much fuss that we make about it. Like, I think the reason we fight wars is because we wear clothes. Because no one knows—between the men, I mean—who has the bigger . . . weenie. So, if I'm a guy with a small one, I'm going to build a really big building or take over a really big piece of land or write a really long book so the other men don't know, right? But, see, it never really works, that's the problem. I mean, you conquer the country, or whatever, but you're still wearing clothes, so there's no way to prove absolutely whose is bigger or smaller. And that's what we call a civilized society. The whole world run by a bunch of men with pricks the size of pins. [*She exits.*]

GALLIMARD [*to us*] This was simply not acceptable.

[*A high-pitched chime rings through the air.* SONG, *dressed as* BUTTERFLY, *appears in the upstage special. She is obviously distressed. Her body swoons as she attempts to clip the stems of flowers she's arranging in a vase.*]

GALLIMARD But I kept up our affair, wildly, for several months. Why? I believe because of Butterfly. She knew the secret I was trying to hide. But, unlike a Western woman, she didn't confront me, threaten, even pout. I remembered the words of Puccini's *Butterfly:*

SONG "Noi siamo gente avvezza / alle piccole cose / umili e silenziose."[8]

GALLIMARD "I come from a people / Who are accustomed to little / Humble and silent." I saw Pinkerton and Butterfly, and what she would say if he were unfaithful . . . nothing. She would cry, alone, into those wildly soft sleeves, once full of possessions, now empty to collect her tears. It was her tears and her silence that excited me, every time I visited Renee.

TOULON [*offstage*] Gallimard!

[TOULON *enters.* GALLIMARD *turns towards him. During the next section,* SONG, *up center, begins to dance with the flowers. It is a drunken dance, where she breaks small pieces off the stems.*]

8. Lines from the aria "vogliatemi bene" ("Ah, Love Me a Little"), sung by Butterfly in the opera's first act.

TOULON They're killing him.

GALLIMARD Who? I'm sorry? What?

TOULON Bother you to come over at this late hour?

GALLIMARD No . . . of course not.

TOULON Not after you hear my secret. Champagne?

GALLIMARD Um . . . thank you.

TOULON You're surprised. There's something that you've wanted, Gallimard. No, not a promotion. Next time. Something in the world. You're not aware of this, but there's an informal gossip circle among intelligence agents. And some of ours heard from some of the Americans—

GALLIMARD Yes?

TOULON That the U.S. will allow the Vietnamese generals to stage a coup . . . and assassinate President Diem.[9]

[*The chime rings again.* TOULON *freezes.* GALLIMARD *turns upstage and looks at* BUTTERFLY, *who slowly and deliberately clips a flower off its stem.* GALLIMARD *turns back towards* TOULON.]

GALLIMARD I think . . . that's a very wise move!

[TOULON *unfreezes.*]

TOULON It's what you've been advocating. A toast?

GALLIMARD Sure. I consider this a vindication.

TOULON Not exactly. "To the test. Let's hope you pass."

[*They drink. The chime rings again.* TOULON *freezes.* GALLIMARD *turns upstage, and* SONG *clips another flower.*]

GALLIMARD [*to* TOULON] The test?

TOULON [*unfreezing*] It's a test of everything you've been saying. I personally think the generals probably will stop the Communists. And you'll be a hero. But if anything goes wrong, then your opinions won't be worth a pig's ear. I'm sure that won't happen. But sometimes it's easier when they don't listen to you.

GALLIMARD They're your opinions too, aren't they?

TOULON Personally, yes.

GALLIMARD So we agree.

TOULON But my opinions aren't on that report. Yours are. Cheers.

[TOULON *turns away from* GALLIMARD *and raises his glass. At that instant* SONG *picks up the vase and hurls it to the ground. It shatters.* SONG *sinks down amidst the shards of the vase, in a calm, childlike trance. She sings softly, as if reciting a child's nursery rhyme.*]

SONG [*repeat as necessary*] "The whole world over, the white man travels, setting anchor, wherever he likes. Life's not worth living, unless he finds, the finest maidens, of every land . . ."[1]

[GALLIMARD *turns downstage towards us.* SONG *continues singing.*]

GALLIMARD I shook as I left his house. That coward! That worm! To put the burden for his decisions on my shoulders!

I started for Renee's. But no, that was all I needed. A schoolgirl who would question the role of the penis in modern society. What I wanted was revenge. A vessel to contain my humiliation. Though I hadn't seen her in several weeks, I headed for Butterfly's.

9. See the first note of this scene.
1. A translation of lines sung by Pinkerton in the first act of *Madama Butterfly*.

[GALLIMARD *enters* SONG*'s apartment.*]

SONG Oh! Rene . . . I was dreaming!

GALLIMARD You've been drinking?

SONG If I can't sleep, then yes, I drink. But then, it gives me these dreams which—Rene, it's been almost three weeks since you visited me last.

GALLIMARD I know. There's been a lot going on in the world.

SONG Fortunately I am drunk. So I can speak freely. It's not the world, it's you and me. And an old problem. Even the softest skin becomes like leather to a man who's touched it too often. I confess I don't know how to stop it. I don't know how to become another woman.

GALLIMARD I have a request.

SONG Is this a solution? Or are you ready to give up the flat?

GALLIMARD It may be a solution. But I'm sure you won't like it.

SONG Oh well, that's very important. "Like it?" Do you think I "like" lying here alone, waiting, always waiting for your return? Please—don't worry about what I may not "like."

GALLIMARD I want to see you . . . naked.

[*Silence.*]

SONG I thought you understood my modesty. So you want me to—what—strip? Like a big cowboy girl? Shiny pasties on my breasts? Shall I fling my kimono over my head and yell "ya-hoo" in the process? I thought you respected my shame!

GALLIMARD I believe you gave me your shame many years ago.

SONG Yes—and it is just like a white devil to use it against me. I can't believe it. I thought myself so repulsed by the passive Oriental and the cruel white man. Now I see—we are always most revolted by the things hidden within us.

GALLIMARD I just mean—

SONG Yes?

GALLIMARD —that it will remove the only barrier left between us.

SONG No, Rene. Don't couch your request in sweet words. Be yourself—a cad—and know that my love is enough, that I submit—submit to the worst you can give me. [*Pause*] Well, come. Strip me. Whatever happens, know that you have willed it. Our love, in your hands. I'm helpless before my man.

[GALLIMARD *starts to cross the room.*]

GALLIMARD Did I not undress her because I knew, somewhere deep down, what I would find? Perhaps. Happiness is so rare that our mind can turn somersaults to protect it.

At the time, I only knew that I was seeing Pinkerton stalking towards his Butterfly, ready to reward her love with his lecherous hands. The image sickened me, pulled me to my knees, so I was crawling towards her like a worm. By the time I reached her, Pinkerton . . . had vanished from my heart. To be replaced by something new, something unnatural, that flew in the face of all I'd learned in the world—something very close to love.

[*He grabs her around the waist; she strokes his hair.*]

GALLIMARD Butterfly, forgive me.

SONG Rene . . .

GALLIMARD For everything. From the start.

SONG I'm . . .

GALLIMARD I want to—

SONG I'm pregnant. [*Beat*] I'm pregnant. [*Beat*] I'm pregnant.

[*Beat*.]

GALLIMARD I want to marry you!

2.7

GALLIMARD *and* BUTTERFLY's *flat. Beijing. 1963.*

Downstage, SONG *paces as* COMRADE CHIN *reads from her notepad. Upstage,* GALLIMARD *is still kneeling. He remains on his knees throughout the scene, watching it.*

SONG I need a baby.

CHIN [*from pad*] He's been spotted going to a dorm.

SONG I need a baby.

CHIN At the Foreign Language Institute.

SONG I need a baby.

CHIN The room of a Danish girl . . . What do you mean, you need a baby?!

SONG Tell Comrade Kang—last night, the entire mission, it could've ended.

CHIN What do you mean?

SONG Tell Kang—he told me to strip.

CHIN *Strip?!*

SONG Write!

CHIN I tell you, I don't understand nothing about this case anymore. Nothing.

SONG He told me to strip, and I took a chance. Oh, we Chinese, we know how to gamble.

CHIN [*writing*] ". . . told him to strip."

SONG My palms were wet, I had to make a split-second decision.

CHIN Hey! Can you slow down?!

[*Pause*.]

SONG You write faster, I'm the artist here. Suddenly, it hit me—"All he wants is for her to submit. Once a woman submits, a man is always ready to become 'generous.'"

CHIN You're just gonna end up with rough notes.

SONG And it worked! He gave in! Now, if I can just present him with a baby. A Chinese baby with blond hair—he'll be mine for life!

CHIN Kang will never agree! The trading of babies has to be a counterrevolutionary[2] act!

SONG Sometimes, a counterrevolutionary act is necessary to counter a counterrevolutionary act.

[*Pause*.]

CHIN Wait.

SONG I need one . . . in seven months. Make sure it's a boy.

CHIN This doesn't sound like something the Chairman would do. Maybe you'd better talk to Comrade Kang yourself.

SONG Good. I will.

[CHIN *gets up to leave*.]

2. That is, undermining the goals of the Revolution of 1949.

SONG Miss Chin? Why, in the Peking Opera, are women's roles played by men?

CHIN I don't know. Maybe, a reactionary remnant of male—

SONG No. [*Beat*] Because only a man knows how a woman is supposed to act.

[CHIN *exits.* SONG *turns upstage, towards* GALLIMARD.]

GALLIMARD [*calling after* CHIN] Good riddance! [*To* SONG] I could forget all that betrayal in an instant, you know. If you'd just come back and become Butterfly again.

SONG Fat chance. You're here in prison, rotting in a cell. And I'm on a plane, winging my way back to China. Your President pardoned me of our treason, you know.

GALLIMARD Yes, I read about that.

SONG Must make you feel . . . lower than shit.

GALLIMARD But don't you, even a little bit, wish you were here with me?

SONG I'm an artist, Rene. You were my greatest . . . acting challenge. [*She laughs.*] It doesn't matter how rotten I answer, does it? You still adore me. That's why I love you, Rene. [*She points to us.*] So—you were telling your audience about the night I announced I was pregnant.

[GALLIMARD *puts his arms around* SONG*'s waist. He and* SONG *are in the positions they were in at the end of Scene 6.*]

2.8

Same.

GALLIMARD I'll divorce my wife. We'll live together here, and then later in France.

SONG I feel so . . . ashamed.

GALLIMARD Why?

SONG I had begun to lose faith. And now, you shame me with your generosity.

GALLIMARD Generosity? No, I'm proposing for very selfish reasons.

SONG Your apologies only make me feel more ashamed. My outburst a moment ago!

GALLIMARD Your outburst? What about my request?!

SONG You've been very patient dealing with my . . . eccentricities. A Western man, used to women freer with their bodies—

GALLIMARD It was sick! Don't make excuses for me.

SONG I have to. You don't seem willing to make them for yourself.

[*Pause.*]

GALLIMARD You're crazy.

SONG I'm happy. Which often looks like crazy.

GALLIMARD Then make me crazy. Marry me.

[*Pause.*]

SONG No.

GALLIMARD What?

SONG Do I sound silly, a slave, if I say I'm not worthy?

GALLIMARD Yes. In fact you do. No one has loved me like you.

SONG Thank you. And no one ever will. I'll see to that.

GALLIMARD So what is the problem?

SONG Rene, we Chinese are realists. We understand rice, gold, and guns. You are a diplomat. Your career is skyrocketing. Now, what would happen if you divorced your wife to marry a Communist Chinese actress?

GALLIMARD That's not being realistic. That's defeating yourself before you begin.

SONG We must conserve our strength for the battles we can win.

GALLIMARD That sounds like a fortune cookie!

SONG Where do you think fortune cookies come from?

GALLIMARD I don't care.

SONG You do. So do I. And we should. That is why I say I'm not worthy. I'm worthy to love and even to be loved by you. But I am not worthy to end the career of one of the West's most promising diplomats.

GALLIMARD It's not that great a career! I made it sound like more than it is!

SONG Modesty will get you nowhere. Flatter yourself, and you flatter me. I'm flattered to decline your offer. [*She exits.*]

GALLIMARD [*to us*] Butterfly and I argued all night. And, in the end, I left, knowing I would never be her husband. She went away for several months—to the countryside, like a small animal. Until the night I received her call.

[*A baby's cry from offstage.* SONG *enters, carrying a child.*]

SONG He looks like you.

GALLIMARD Oh! [*Beat; he approaches the baby.*] Well, babies are never very attractive at birth.

SONG Stop!

GALLIMARD I'm sure he'll grow more beautiful with age. More like his mother.

SONG "Chi vide mai / a bimbo del Giappon . . ."[3]

GALLIMARD "What baby, I wonder, was ever born in Japan"—or China, for that matter—

SONG ". . . occhi azzurrini?"

GALLIMARD "With azure eyes"—they're actually sort of brown, wouldn't you say?

SONG "E il labbro."

GALLIMARD: "And such lips!" [*He kisses* SONG.] And such lips.

SONG "E i ricciolini d'oro schietto?"

GALLIMARD "And such a head of golden"—if slightly patchy—"curls?"

SONG I'm going to call him "Peepee."

GALLIMARD Darling, could you repeat that because I'm sure a rickshaw just flew by overhead.

SONG You heard me.

GALLIMARD "Song Peepee"? May I suggest Michael, or Stephan, or Adolph?

SONG You may, but I won't listen.

GALLIMARD You can't be serious. Can you imagine the time this child will have in school?

SONG In the West, yes.

3. These lines and those that follow are sung by Butterfly in act 2 of *Madama Butterfly.*

GALLIMARD It's worse than naming him Ping Pong or Long Dong[4] or—

SONG But he's never going to live in the West, is he?

[*Pause.*]

GALLIMARD That wasn't my choice.

SONG It is mine. And this is my promise to you: I will raise him, he will be our child, but he will never burden you outside of China.

GALLIMARD Why do you make these promises? I want to be burdened! I want a scandal to cover the papers!

SONG [*to us*] Prophetic.

GALLIMARD I'm serious.

SONG So am I. His name is as I registered it. And he will never live in the West.

[SONG *exits with the child.*]

GALLIMARD [*to us*] It is possible that her stubbornness only made me want her more. That drawing back at the moment of my capitulation was the most brilliant strategy she could have chosen. It is possible. But it is also possible that by this point she could have said, could have done . . . anything, and I would have adored her still.

2.9

Beijing. 1966.

A driving rhythm of Chinese percussion fills the stage.

GALLIMARD And then, China began to change. Mao became very old, and his cult became very strong. And, like many old men, he entered his second childhood. So he handed over the reins of state to those with minds like his own. And children ruled the Middle Kingdom[5] with complete caprice. The doctrine of the Cultural Revolution[6] implied continuous anarchy. Contact between Chinese and foreigners became impossible. Our flat was confiscated. Her fame and my money now counted against us.

[*Two dancers in Mao suits and red-starred caps enter, and begin crudely mimicking revolutionary violence, in an agitprop[7] fashion.*]

GALLIMARD And somehow the American war went wrong too. Four hundred thousand dollars were being spent for every Viet Cong killed; so General Westmoreland's[8] remark that the Oriental does not value life the way

4. Penis (slang).
5. The Chinese name for China (in Mandarin *Zongguo*, "central state"), first used in the 11th century.
6. The Great Proletarian Cultural Revolution (1966–76), a campaign launched by Mao to rekindle revolutionary fervor by removing so-called counterrevolutionary elements from the Communist Party and society in general. Repeated purges led by the Red Guards—a mass movement composed mainly of students and of young people from the countryside, who subscribed wholeheartedly to Mao's new cult of personality—were aimed at bureaucrats, teachers and intellectuals, and writers and artists. The result was factionalism, violence, and chaos.
7. Agitation and propaganda, usually on behalf of communism and conveyed through the arts or literature (from the name of the department of the Russian Communist Party responsible for such activities).
8. William Westmoreland (1914–2005), commander of American military operations in Vietnam (1964–68) and U.S. Army chief of staff (1968–72); in the documentary *Hearts and Minds* (1974) he said, "The Oriental doesn't put the same high price on life as does the Westerner. Life is plentiful, life is cheap in the Orient."

Americans do was oddly accurate. Why weren't the Vietnamese people giving in? Why were they content instead to die and die and die again?

[TOULON *enters.*]

TOULON Congratulations, Gallimard.

GALLIMARD Excuse me, sir?

TOULON Not a promotion. That was last time. You're going home.

GALLIMARD What?

TOULON Don't say I didn't warn you.

GALLIMARD I'm being transferred . . . because I was wrong about the American war?[9]

TOULON Of course not. We don't care about the Americans. We care about your mind. The quality of your analysis. In general, everything you've predicted here in the Orient . . . just hasn't happened.

GALLIMARD I think that's premature.

TOULON Don't force me to be blunt. Okay, you said China was ready to open to Western trade. The only thing they're trading out there are Western heads. And, yes, you said the Americans would succeed in Indochina. You were kidding, right?

GALLIMARD I think the end is in sight.

TOULON Don't be pathetic. And don't take this personally. You were wrong. It's not your fault.

GALLIMARD But I'm going home.

TOULON Right. Could I have the number of your mistress? [*Beat*] Joke! Joke! Eat a croissant for me.

[TOULON *exits.* SONG, *wearing a Mao suit,*[1] *is dragged in from the wings as part of the upstage dance. They "beat" her, then lampoon the acrobatics of the Chinese opera, as she is made to kneel onstage.*]

GALLIMARD [*simultaneously*] I don't care to recall how Butterfly and I said our hurried farewell. Perhaps it was better to end our affair before it killed her.

[GALLIMARD *exits.* COMRADE CHIN *walks across the stage with a banner reading: "The Actor Renounces His Decadent Profession!" She reaches the kneeling* SONG. *Percussion stops with a thud. Dancers strike poses.*]

CHIN Actor-oppressor, for years you have lived above the common people and looked down on their labor. While the farmer ate millet—

SONG I ate pastries from France and sweetmeats from silver trays.

CHIN And how did you come to live in such an exalted position?

SONG I was a plaything for the imperialists!

CHIN What did you do?

SONG I shamed China by allowing myself to be corrupted by a foreigner . . .

CHIN What does this mean? The People demand a full confession!

SONG I engaged in the lowest perversions with China's enemies!

9. After the Tonkin Gulf Resolution (1964) gave the president authority to "take all necessary measures" to defend U.S. forces "and to prevent further aggression," the first U.S. combat troops arrived in South Vietnam, joining 16,000 military advisers. By the end of 1966, close to 400,000 troops were in Vietnam; troop strength peaked in 1968 at 540,000. The last American forces left in 1973, and South Vietnam fell to the North in 1975.

1. A suit like that worn by Mao at the ceremony founding the People's Republic of China—with a high, buttoned collar and four external pockets. It was especially common during the Cultural Revolution.

CHIN What perversions? Be more clear!

SONG I let him put it up my ass!

[*Dancers look over, disgusted.*]

CHIN Aaaa-ya! How can you use such sickening language?!

SONG My language . . . is only as foul as the crimes I committed . . .

CHIN Yeah. That's better. So—what do you want to do now?

SONG I want to serve the people.

[*Percussion starts up, with Chinese strings.*]

CHIN What?

SONG I want to serve the people!

[*Dancers regain their revolutionary smiles, and begin a dance of victory.*]

CHIN What?!

SONG I want to serve the people!!

[*Dancers unveil a banner: "The Actor Is Rehabilitated!"* SONG *remains kneeling before* CHIN, *as the dancers bounce around them, then exit. Music out.*]

2.10

A commune. Hunan Province.[2] *1970.*

CHIN How you planning to do that?

SONG I've already worked four years in the fields of Hunan, Comrade Chin.[3]

CHIN So? Farmers work all their lives. Let me see your hands.

[SONG *holds them out for her inspection.*]

CHIN Goddamn! Still so smooth! How long does it take to turn you actors into good anythings? Hunh. You've just spent too many years in luxury to be any good to the Revolution.

SONG I served the Revolution.

CHIN Serve the Revolution? Bullshit! You wore dresses! Don't tell me—I was there. I saw you! You and your white vice-consul! Stuck up there in your flat, living off the People's Treasury! Yeah, I knew what was going on! You two . . . homos! Homos! Homos! [*Pause; she composes herself.*] Ah! Well . . . you will serve the people, all right. But not with the Revolution's money. This time, you use your own money.

SONG I have no money.

CHIN Shut up! And you won't stink up China anymore with your pervert stuff. You'll pollute the place where pollution begins—the West.

SONG What do you mean?

CHIN Shut up! You're going to France. Without a cent in your pocket. You find your consul's house, you make him pay your expenses—

SONG No.

CHIN And you give us weekly reports! Useful information!

SONG That's crazy. It's been four years.

CHIN Either that, or back to rehabilitation center!

2. In southern China. *Commune*: the basic unit of China's collectivized system of agriculture (introduced in 1958 and abandoned in 1981).

3. During the Cultural Revolution, many deemed counterrevolutionary were sent to the countryside in order to be "rehabilitated" through hard labor and political reindoctrination.

SONG Comrade Chin, he's not going to support me! Not in France! He's a white man! I was just his plaything—

CHIN Oh yuck! Again with the sickening language? Where's my stick?

SONG You don't understand the mind of a man.

[*Pause.*]

CHIN Oh no? No I don't? Then how come I'm married, huh? How come I got a man? Five, six years ago, you always tell me those kind of things, I felt very bad. But not now! Because what does the Chairman say? He tells us *I'm* now the smart one, you're now the nincompoop! *You're* the blackhead, the harebrain, the nitwit! You think you're so smart? You understand "The Mind of a Man"? Good! Then *you* go to France and be a pervert for Chairman Mao!

[CHIN *and* SONG *exit in opposite directions.*]

2.11

Paris. 1968–70.

GALLIMARD *enters.*

GALLIMARD And what was waiting for me back in Paris? Well, better Chinese food than I'd eaten in China. Friends and relatives. A little accounting, regular schedule, keeping track of traffic violations in the suburbs. . . . And the indignity of students shouting the slogans of Chairman Mao at me—in French.[4]

HELGA Rene? Rene? [*She enters, soaking wet.*] I've had a . . . a problem. [*She sneezes.*]

GALLIMARD You're wet.

HELGA Yes, I . . . coming back from the grocer's. A group of students, waving red flags, they—

[GALLIMARD *fetches a towel.*]

HELGA —they ran by, I was caught up along with them. Before I knew what was happening—

[GALLIMARD *gives her the towel.*]

HELGA Thank you. The police started firing water cannons at us. I tried to shout, to tell them I was the wife of a diplomat, but—you know how it is . . . [*Pause*] Needless to say, I lost the groceries. Rene, what's happening to France?

GALLIMARD What's—? Well, nothing, really.

HELGA Nothing?! The storefronts are in flames, there's glass in the streets, buildings are toppling—and I'm wet!

GALLIMARD Nothing! . . . that I care to think about.

HELGA And is that why you stay in this room?

GALLIMARD Yes, in fact.

HELGA With the incense burning? You know something? I hate incense. It smells so sickly sweet.

4. In May 1968, student demonstrations against the French government's heavy-handed response to earlier protests grew into a massive uprising, joined by a general strike of millions of workers, seeking to end the administration of President Charles de Gaulle. The students were a mixture of radicals and leftists, including anarchists, Marxists, Trotskyites, and Maoists.

GALLIMARD Well, I hate the French. Who just smell—period!

HELGA And the Chinese were better?

GALLIMARD Please—don't start.

HELGA When we left, this exact same thing, the riots—

GALLIMARD No, no . . .

HELGA Students screaming slogans, smashing down doors—

GALLIMARD Helga—

HELGA It was all going on in China, too. Don't you remember?!

GALLIMARD Helga! Please! [*Pause*] You have never understood China, have you? You walk in here with these ridiculous ideas, that the West is falling apart, that China was spitting in our faces. You come in, dripping of the streets, and you leave water all over my floor. [*He grabs* HELGA*'s towel, begins mopping up the floor.*]

HELGA But it's the truth!

GALLIMARD Helga, I want a divorce.

[*Pause;* GALLIMARD *continues, mopping the floor.*]

HELGA I take it back. China is . . . beautiful. Incense, I like incense.

GALLIMARD I've had a mistress.

HELGA So?

GALLIMARD For eight years.

HELGA I knew you would. I knew you would the day I married you. And now what? You want to marry her?

GALLIMARD I can't. She's in China.

HELGA I see. You want to leave. For someone who's not here, is that right?

GALLIMARD That's right.

HELGA You can't live with her, but still you don't want to live with me.

GALLIMARD That's right.

[*Pause.*]

HELGA Shit. How terrible that I can figure that out. [*Pause.*] I never thought I'd say it. But, in China, I was happy. I knew, in my own way, I knew that you were not everything you pretended to be. But the pretense—going on your arm to the embassy ball, visiting your office and the guards saying, "Good morning, good morning, Madame Gallimard"—the pretense . . . was very good indeed. [*Pause*] I hope everyone is mean to you for the rest of your life. [*She exits.*]

GALLIMARD [*to us*] Prophetic.

[MARC *enters with two drinks.*]

GALLIMARD [*to* MARC] In China, I was different from all other men.

MARC Sure. You were white. Here's your drink.

GALLIMARD I felt . . . touched.

MARC In the head? Rene, I don't want to hear about the Oriental love goddess. Okay? One night—can we just drink and throw up without a lot of conversation?

GALLIMARD You still don't believe me, do you?

MARC Sure I do. She was the most beautiful, et cetera, et cetera, blasé blasé.

[*Pause.*]

GALLIMARD My life in the West has been such a disappointment.

MARC Life in the West is like that. You'll get used to it. Look, you're driving me away. I'm leaving. Happy, now? [*He exits, then returns.*] Look, I have a date tomorrow night. You wanna come? I can fix you up with—

GALLIMARD Of course. I would love to come.

[*Pause.*]

MARC Uh—on second thought, no. You'd better get ahold of yourself first.

[*He exits;* GALLIMARD *nurses his drink.*]

GALLIMARD [*to us*] This is the ultimate cruelty, isn't it? That I can talk and talk and to anyone listening, it's only air—too rich a diet to be swallowed by a mundane world. Why can't anyone understand? That in China, I once loved, and was loved by, very simply, the Perfect Woman.

[SONG *enters, dressed as* BUTTERFLY *in wedding dress.*]

GALLIMARD [*to* SONG] Not again. My imagination is hell. Am I asleep this time? Or did I drink too much?

SONG Rene?

GALLIMARD God, it's too painful! That you speak?

SONG What are you talking about? Rene—touch me.

GALLIMARD Why?

SONG I'm real. Take my hand.

GALLIMARD Why? So you can disappear again and leave me clutching at the air? For the entertainment of my neighbors who—?

[SONG *touches* GALLIMARD.]

SONG Rene?

[GALLIMARD *takes* SONG*'s hand. Silence.*]

GALLIMARD Butterfly? I never doubted you'd return.

SONG You hadn't . . . forgotten—?

GALLIMARD Yes, actually, I've forgotten everything. My mind, you see—there wasn't enough room in this hard head—not for the world *and* for you. No, there was only room for one. [*Beat*] Come, look. See? Your bed has been waiting, with the Klimt[5] poster you like, and—see? The xiang lu [incense burner] you gave me?

SONG I . . . I don't know what to say.

GALLIMARD There's nothing to say. Not at the end of a long trip. Can I make you some tea?

SONG But where's your wife?

GALLIMARD She's by my side. She's by my side at last.

[GALLIMARD *reaches to embrace* SONG. SONG *sidesteps, dodging him.*]

GALLIMARD Why?!

SONG [*to us*] So I did return to Rene in Paris. Where I found—

GALLIMARD Why do you run away? Can't we show them how we embraced that evening?

SONG Please. I'm talking.

GALLIMARD You have to do what I say! I'm conjuring you up in *my* mind!

SONG Rene, I've never done what you've said. Why should it be any different in your mind? Now split—the story moves on, and I must change.

GALLIMARD I welcomed you into my home! I didn't have to, you know! I could've left you penniless on the streets of Paris! But I took you in!

5. Gustav Klimt (1862–1918), an Austrian painter associated with exoticism and eroticism.

SONG Thank you.

GALLIMARD So . . . please . . . don't change.

SONG You know I have to. You know I will. And anyway, what difference does it make? No matter what your eyes tell you, you can't ignore the truth. You already know too much.

[GALLIMARD *exits.* SONG *turns to us.*]

SONG The change I'm going to make requires about five minutes. So I thought you might want to take this opportunity to stretch your legs, enjoy a drink, or listen to the musicians. I'll be here, when you return, right where you left me.

[SONG *goes to a mirror in front of which is a wash basin of water. She starts to remove her makeup as stagelights go to half and houselights come up.*]

3.1

A courthouse in Paris. 1986.

As he promised, SONG *has completed the bulk of his transformation, onstage by the time the houselights go down and the stagelights come up full. He removes his wig and kimono, leaving them on the floor. Underneath, he wears a well-cut suit.*

SONG So I'd done my job better than I had a right to expect. Well, give him some credit, too. He's right—I was in a fix when I arrived in Paris. I walked from the airport into town, then I located, by blind groping, the Chinatown district. Let me make one thing clear: whatever else may be said about the Chinese, they are stingy! I slept in doorways three days until I could find a tailor who would make me this kimono on credit. As it turns out, maybe I didn't even need it. Maybe he would've been happy to see me in a simple shift and mascara. But . . . better safe than sorry.

That was 1970, when I arrived in Paris. For the next fifteen years, yes, I lived a very comfy life. Some relief, believe me, after four years on a fucking commune in Nowheresville, China. Rene supported the boy and me, and I did some demonstrations around the country as part of my "cultural exchange" cover. And then there was the spying.

[SONG *moves upstage, to a chair.* TOULON *enters as a judge, wearing the appropriate wig and robes. He sits near* SONG. *It's 1986, and* SONG *is testifying in a courtroom.*]

SONG Not much at first. Rene had lost all his high-level contacts. Comrade Chin wasn't very interested in parking-ticket statistics. But finally, at my urging, Rene got a job as a courier, handling sensitive documents. He'd photograph them for me, and I'd pass them on to the Chinese embassy.

JUDGE Did he understand the extent of his activity?

SONG He didn't ask. He knew that I needed those documents, and that was enough.

JUDGE But he must've known he was passing classified information.

SONG I can't say.

JUDGE He never asked what you were going to do with them?

SONG Nope.

[*Pause.*]

JUDGE There is one thing that the court—indeed, that all of France—would like to know.

SONG Fire away.

JUDGE Did Monsieur Gallimard know you were a man?

SONG Well, he never saw me completely naked. Ever.

JUDGE But surely, he must've . . . how can I put this?

SONG Put it however you like. I'm not shy. He must've felt around?

JUDGE Mmmmm.

SONG Not really. I did all the work. He just laid back. Of course we did enjoy more . . . complete union, and I suppose he *might* have wondered why I was always on my stomach, but. . . . But what you're thinking is: "Of course a wrist must've brushed . . . a hand hit . . . over twenty years!" Yeah. Well, Your Honor, it was my job to make him think I was a woman. And chew on this: it wasn't all that hard. See, my mother was a prostitute along the Bundt[6] before the Revolution. And, uh, I think it's fair to say she learned a few things about Western men. So I borrowed her knowledge. In service to my country.

JUDGE Would you care to enlighten the court with this secret knowledge? I'm sure we're all very curious.

SONG I'm sure you are. [*Pause*] Okay, Rule One is: Men always believe what they want to hear. So a girl can tell the most obnoxious lies and the guys will believe them every time—"This is my first time"—"That's the biggest I've ever seen"—or *both,* which, if you really think about it, is not possible in a single lifetime. You've maybe heard those phrases a few times in your own life, yes, Your Honor?

JUDGE It's not my life, Monsieur Song, which is on trial today.

SONG Okay, okay, just trying to lighten up the proceedings. Tough room.

JUDGE Go on.

SONG Rule Two: As soon as a Western man comes into contact with the East—he's already confused. The West has sort of an international rape mentality towards the East. Do you know rape mentality?

JUDGE Give us your definition, please.

SONG Basically, "Her mouth says no, but her eyes say yes."

The West thinks of itself as masculine—big guns, big industry, big money—so the East is feminine—weak, delicate, poor . . . but good at art, and full of inscrutable wisdom—the feminine mystique.

Her mouth says no, but her eyes say yes. The West believes the East, deep down, *wants* to be dominated—because a woman can't think for herself.

JUDGE What does this have to do with my question?

SONG You expect Oriental countries to submit to your guns, and you expect Oriental women to be submissive to your men. That's why you say they make the best wives.

JUDGE But why would that make it possible for you to fool Monsieur Gallimard? Please—get to the point.

SONG One, because when he finally met his fantasy woman, he wanted

6. That is, the Bund, a thoroughfare along the Huangpu River in the former Shanghai International Settlement; before the Revolution, it was lined with financial institutions, hotels, and clubs as well as wharves (*Bund* is the name often given in the Far East to an embanked street along a river or sea).

more than anything to believe that she was, in fact, a woman. And second, I am an Oriental. And being an Oriental, I could never be completely a man.

[*Pause.*]

JUDGE Your armchair political theory is tenuous, Monsieur Song.

SONG You think so? That's why you'll lose in all your dealings with the East.

JUDGE Just answer my question: did he know you were a man?

[*Pause.*]

SONG You know, Your Honor, I never asked.

3.2

Same.

Music from the "Death Scene" from Butterfly *blares over the house speakers. It is the loudest thing we've heard in this play.*

GALLIMARD *enters, crawling towards* SONG*'s wig and kimono.*

GALLIMARD Butterfly? Butterfly?

[SONG *remains a man, in the witness box, delivering a testimony we do not hear.*]

GALLIMARD [*to us*] In my moment of greatest shame, here, in this courtroom—with that . . . person up there, telling the world. . . . What strikes me especially is how shallow he is, how glib and obsequious . . . completely . . . without substance! The type that prowls around discos with a gold medallion, stinking of garlic. So little like my Butterfly.

Yet even in this moment my mind remains agile, flip-flopping like a man on a trampoline. Even now, my picture dissolves, and I see that . . . witness . . . talking to me.

[SONG *suddenly stands straight up in his witness box, and looks at* GALLIMARD.]

SONG Yes. You. White man.

[SONG *steps out of the witness box, and moves downstage towards* GALLIMARD. *Light change.*]

GALLIMARD [*to* SONG] Who? Me?

SONG Do you see any other white men?

GALLIMARD Yes. There're white men all around. This is a French courtroom.

SONG So you are an adventurous imperialist. Tell me, why did it take you so long? To come back to this place?

GALLIMARD What place?

SONG This theatre in China. Where we met many years ago.

GALLIMARD [*to us*] And once again, against my will, I am transported.

[*Chinese opera music comes up on the speakers.* SONG *begins to do opera moves, as he did the night they met.*]

SONG Do you remember? The night you gave your heart?

GALLIMARD It was a long time ago.

SONG Not long enough. A night that turned your world upside down.

GALLIMARD Perhaps.

SONG Oh, be honest with me. What's another bit of flattery when you've already given me twenty years' worth? It's a wonder my head hasn't swollen to the size of China.

GALLIMARD Who's to say it hasn't?

SONG Who's to say? And what's the shame? In pride? You think I could've pulled this off if I wasn't already full of pride when we met? No, not just pride. Arrogance. It takes arrogance, really—to believe you can will, with your eyes and your lips, the destiny of another. [*He dances.*] C'mon. Admit it. You still want me. Even in slacks and a button-down collar.

GALLIMARD I don't see what the point of—

SONG You don't? Well maybe, Rene, just maybe—I want you.

GALLIMARD You do?

SONG Then again, maybe I'm just playing with you. How can you tell? [*Reprising his feminine character, he sidles up to* GALLIMARD.] "How I wish there were even a small cafe to sit in. With men in tuxedos, and cappuccinos, and bad expatriate jazz." Now you want to kiss me, don't you?

GALLIMARD [*pulling away*] What makes you—?

SONG —so sure? See? I take the words from your mouth. Then I wait for you to come and retrieve them. [*He reclines on the floor.*]

GALLIMARD Why?! Why do you treat me so cruelly?

SONG Perhaps I *was* treating you cruelly. But now—I'm being nice. Come here, my little one.

GALLIMARD I'm not your little one!

SONG My mistake. It's I who am *your* little one, right?

GALLIMARD Yes, I—

SONG So come get your little one. If you like. I may even let you strip me.

GALLIMARD I mean, you were! Before . . . but not like this!

SONG I was? Then perhaps I still am. If you look hard enough. [*He starts to remove his clothes.*]

GALLIMARD What—what are you doing?

SONG Helping you to see through my act.

GALLIMARD Stop that! I don't want to! I don't—

SONG Oh, but you asked me to strip, remember?

GALLIMARD What? That was years ago! And I took it back!

SONG No. You postponed it. Postponed the inevitable. Today, the inevitable has come calling.

[*From the speakers, cacophony:* BUTTERFLY *mixed in with Chinese gongs.*]

GALLIMARD No! Stop! I don't want to see!

SONG Then look away.

GALLIMARD You're only in my mind! All this is in my mind! I order you! To stop!

SONG To what? To strip? That's just what I'm—

GALLIMARD No! Stop! I want you—!

SONG You want me?

GALLIMARD To stop!

SONG You know something, Rene? Your mouth says no, but your eyes say yes. Turn them away. I dare you.

GALLIMARD I don't have to! Every night, you say you're going to strip, but then I beg you and you stop!

SONG I guess tonight is different.

GALLIMARD Why? Why should that be?

SONG Maybe I've become frustrated. Maybe I'm saying "Look at me, you fool!" Or maybe I'm just feeling . . . sexy. [*He is down to his briefs.*]

GALLIMARD Please. This is unnecessary. I know what you are.

SONG Do you? What am I?

GALLIMARD A—a man.

SONG You don't really believe that.

GALLIMARD Yes I do! I knew all the time somewhere that my happiness was temporary, my love a deception. But my mind kept the knowledge at bay. To make the wait bearable.

SONG Monsieur Gallimard—the wait is over.

[SONG *drops his briefs. He is naked. Sound cue out. Slowly, we and* SONG *come to the realization that what we had thought to be* GALLIMARD*'s sobbing is actually his laughter.*]

GALLIMARD Oh god! What an idiot! Of course!

SONG Rene—what?

GALLIMARD Look at you! You're a man! [*He bursts into laughter again.*]

SONG I fail to see what's so funny!

GALLIMARD "You fail to see—!" I mean, you never did have much of a sense of humor, did you? I just think it's ridiculously funny that I've wasted so much time on just a man!

SONG Wait. I'm not "just a man."

GALLIMARD No? Isn't that what you've been trying to convince me of?

SONG Yes, but what I mean—

GALLIMARD And now, I finally believe you, and you tell me it's not true? I think you must have some kind of identity problem.

SONG Will you listen to me?

GALLIMARD Why?! I've been listening to you for twenty years. Don't I deserve a vacation?

SONG I'm not just any man!

GALLIMARD Then, what exactly are you?

SONG Rene, how can you ask—? Okay, what about this?

[*He picks up* BUTTERFLY*'s robes, starts to dance around. No music.*]

GALLIMARD Yes, that's very nice. I have to admit.

[SONG *holds out his arm to* GALLIMARD.]

SONG It's the same skin you've worshiped for years. Touch it.

GALLIMARD Yes, it does feel the same.

SONG Now—close your eyes.

[SONG *covers* GALLIMARD*'s eyes with one hand. With the other,* SONG *draws* GALLIMARD*'s hand up to his face.* GALLIMARD*, like a blind man, lets his hands run over* SONG*'s face.*]

GALLIMARD This skin, I remember. The curve of her face, the softness of her cheek, her hair against the back of my hand . . .

SONG I'm your Butterfly. Under the robes, beneath everything, it was always me. Now, open your eyes and admit it—you adore me. [*He removes his hand from* GALLIMARD*'s eyes.*]

GALLIMARD You, who knew every inch of my desires—how could you, of all people, have made such a mistake?

SONG What?

GALLIMARD You showed me your true self. When all I loved was the lie. A perfect lie, which you let fall to the ground—and now, it's old and soiled.

SONG So—you never really loved me? Only when I was playing a part?

GALLIMARD I'm a man who loved a woman created by a man. Everything else—simply falls short.

[*Pause.*]

SONG What am I supposed to do now?

GALLIMARD You were a fine spy, Monsieur Song, with an even finer accomplice. But now I believe you should go. Get out of my life!

SONG Go where? Rene, you can't live without me. Not after twenty years.

GALLIMARD I certainly can't live with you—not after twenty years of betrayal.

SONG Don't be so stubborn! Where will you go?

GALLIMARD I have a date . . . with my Butterfly.

SONG So, throw away your pride. And come . . .

GALLIMARD Get away from me! Tonight, I've finally learned to tell fantasy from reality. And, knowing the difference, I choose fantasy.

SONG *I'm* your fantasy!

GALLIMARD You? You're as real as hamburger. Now get out! I have a date with my Butterfly and I don't want your body polluting the room! [*He tosses* SONG*'s suit at him.*] Look at these—you dress like a pimp.

SONG Hey! These are Armani slacks[7] and—! [*He puts on his briefs and slacks.*] Let's just say . . . I'm disappointed in you, Rene. In the crush of your adoration, I thought you'd become something more. More like . . . a woman.

But no. Men. You're like the rest of them. It's all in the way we dress, and make up our faces, and bat our eyelashes. You really have so little imagination!

GALLIMARD You, Monsieur Song? Accuse me of too little imagination? You, if anyone, should know—I am pure imagination. And in imagination I will remain. Now get out!

[GALLIMARD *bodily removes* SONG *from the stage, taking his kimono.*]

SONG Rene! I'll never put on those robes again! You'll be sorry!

GALLIMARD [*to* SONG] I'm already sorry! [*Looking at the kimono in his hands*] Exactly as sorry . . . as a Butterfly.

3.3

M. GALLIMARD*'s prison cell. Paris. Present.*

GALLIMARD I've played out the events of my life night after night, always searching for a new ending to my story, one where I leave this cell and return forever to my Butterfly's arms.

Tonight I realize my search is over. That I've looked all along in the wrong place. And now, to you, I will prove that my love was not in vain—by returning to the world of fantasy where I first met her.

[*He picks up the kimono; dancers enter.*]

GALLIMARD There is a vision of the Orient that I have. Of slender women in chong sams and kimonos who die for the love of unworthy foreign devils. Who are born and raised to be the perfect women. Who take whatever punishment we give them, and bounce back, strengthened by love, unconditionally. It is a vision that has become my life.

7. That is, expensive, designer clothing. Giorgio Armani (b. 1934) is an Italian designer of relaxed but luxurious clothes for men and women.

[*Dancers bring the wash basin to him and help him make up his face.*]

GALLIMARD In public, I have continued to deny that Song Liling is a man. This brings me headlines, and is a source of great embarrassment to my French colleagues, who can now be sent into a coughing fit by the mere mention of Chinese food. But alone, in my cell, I have long since faced the truth.

And the truth demands a sacrifice. For mistakes made over the course of a lifetime. My mistakes were simple and absolute—the man I loved was a cad, a bounder. He deserved nothing but a kick in the behind, and instead I gave him . . . all my love.

Yes—love. Why not admit it all? That was my undoing, wasn't it? Love warped my judgment, blinded my eyes, rearranged the very lines on my face . . . until I could look in the mirror and see nothing but . . . a woman.

[*Dancers help him put on the* BUTTERFLY *wig.*]

GALLIMARD I have a vision. Of the Orient. That, deep within its almond eyes, there are still women. Women willing to sacrifice themselves for the love of a man. Even a man whose love is completely without worth.

[*Dancers assist* GALLIMARD *in donning the kimono. They hand him a knife.*]

GALLIMARD Death with honor is better than life . . . life with dishonor. [*He sets himself center stage, in a seppuku[8] position.*] The love of a Butterfly can withstand many things—unfaithfulness, loss, even abandonment. But how can it face the one sin that implies all others? The devastating knowledge that, underneath it all, the object of her love was nothing more, nothing less than . . . a man. [*He sets the tip of the knife against his body.*] It is 19__. And I have found her at last. In a prison on the outskirts of Paris. My name is Rene Gallimard—also known as Madame Butterfly.

[GALLIMARD *turns upstage and plunges the knife into his body, as music from the "Love Duet" blares over the speakers. He collapses into the arms of the dancers, who lay him reverently on the floor. The image holds for several beats. Then a tight special up on* SONG, *who stands as a man, staring at the dead* GALLIMARD. *He smokes a cigarette; the smoke filters up through the lights. Two words leave his lips.*]

SONG Butterfly? Butterfly?

[*Smoke rises as lights fade slowly to black.*]

8. Ritual suicide by disembowelment (Japanese); synonymous with hara-kiri.

TONY KUSHNER

b. 1956

When *Millennium Approaches*, Part One of *Angels in America*, opened on Broadway in 1993, Tony Kushner was hailed as the savior of serious American theater. Since the 1970s, skyrocketing production costs had made it all but impossible for an ambitious nonmusical drama to survive on Broadway. Not only did Kushner defy those odds, he did so with a work of enormous scope and ambition. *Angels in America* is a two-part epic drama exploring personal identity, sexual orientation, political responsibility, AIDS, Mormonism, Judaism, and Reagan-era conservatism within an eclectic dramaturgy that mixes realism, surrealism, and the spectacular. *Millennium Approaches* received numerous awards, including the Tony Award for Best Play and the Pulitzer Prize for Drama; not surprisingly, its sequel, *Perestroika*, was similarly acclaimed. Critics compared the play to such landmark works as TENNESSEE WILLIAMS's *A Streetcar Named Desire* (1947) and ARTHUR MILLER's *Death of a Salesman* (1949). In the ensuing years, additional North American and European productions of *Angels in America* have established Kushner's reputation as the preeminent American dramatist of his generation.

The success of *Angels* also made Kushner one of the most widely known gay artists and activists of the 1990s and early 2000s. Born in 1956, in New York City, to parents who were classical musicians, and raised in Lake Charles, Louisiana, Kushner became aware of his homosexuality by the age of ten. Because of the social stigma attached to being gay, he felt unable to acknowledge his sexual orientation openly, even to his politically liberal parents. Like Joe in *Angels*, Kushner came out to his mother in a telephone call—made from a pay phone on the morning of his first graduate class at New York University (where he completed a master of fine arts in directing in 1984). Kushner's mentor at NYU was Carl Weber, a highly reputed scholar, director, and former assistant of BERTOLT BRECHT's at the Berliner Ensemble. After graduation, Kushner worked as a director at the Repertory Theatre of St. Louis and the New York Theatre Workshop. His first major play, *A Bright Room Called Day*, premiered in San Francisco in 1987 and was produced by the New York Shakespeare Festival in 1991. In 1990, Kushner received a commission to develop *Angels in America* for the Eureka Theatre in San Francisco, where *Millennium Approaches* premiered in 1991. The play subsequently moved to the Mark Taper Forum in Los Angeles, where it was performed with *Perestroika* in 1992. Both plays were produced in London at the National Theater in 1992; in New York, *Millennium Approaches* opened in 1993 and *Perestroika* in 1994.

In the years following the success of *Angels in America,* Kushner wrote a number of adaptations and plays, including *Slavs! Thinking About the Longstanding Problems of Virtue and Happiness* (1994), which features scenes that the playwright had originally intended for *Angels; Henry Box Brown, or The Mirror of Slavery* (1998), the story of an American slave who mailed himself to freedom in 1848; and the musical *Caroline, or Change* (2002). Kushner's 2001 play *Homebody/Kabul* is set in Afghanistan in 1998, during the rule of the oppressive Taliban government. *Angels in America* was made into a highly acclaimed film for television in 2003.

Labeled by Kushner "a gay fantasia on national themes," *Angels* joined a number of other plays that deal with the experience of gay men in contemporary America. Although issues of homosexuality pervade the drama of Williams and Edward Albee, the emergence of openly gay drama can be dated to 1968 and the off-Broadway production of Mart Crowley's *The Boys in the Band.* Crowley's play gave the mainstream theater its first view inside "the closet" of gay life: in this case, a Manhattan birthday party at which a group of gay men descend into alcohol-fueled self-loathing. The writing and production of gay plays accelerated in the wake of two events: the Stonewall Riots of June 1969 and the onset of the AIDS crisis in the early 1980s. In the 1960s, the police in New York often raided bars frequented by homosexuals—who were arrested for being "disorderly"—but late on June 26, 1969, gay and lesbian patrons of Greenwich Village's Stonewall Inn resisted arrest, spawning a riot; violent protests followed for several more nights. This uprising was instrumental in sparking a new phase of the gay rights movement; its emergence was accompanied by plays that depicted the personal and sexual struggles of gay male characters. Key works of the time include Martin Sherman's *Passing By* (1974) and *Bent* (1979), Lanford Wilson's *Fifth of July* (1978), Robert Patrick's *T-Shirts* (1978), and Harvey Fierstein's *Torch Song Trilogy* (1981).

In the 1980s, "AIDS plays" expanded on the conventions of earlier gay drama to explore the impact on individuals, relationships, and families of a new and devastating epidemic. Works such as Larry Kramer's *The Normal Heart* (1985) and William Hoffman's *As Is* (1985) were aggressive in expressing their anger at the relative lack of concern displayed by the Reagan administration and by Americans generally. Even more forcefully than the plays of the 1970s, AIDS plays challenged heterosexual audiences to empathize with gay characters as individuals entitled to equal rights and opportunities within society.

Despite their dramatic power, none of these plays received the attention won by *Angels in America*. The particular acclaim that greeted Kushner's play resulted, in part, from the way in which its characters, themes, and issues address the question of American national identity. This focus on Americanness invites comparison between *Angels* and Miller's *Death of a Salesman*. Produced just four years after the end of World War II, *Salesman* exposed the false myths of the "American Dream" and the vulnerability of the self-made man whose success in business and access to the good life rest on his personal charm. Produced near the end of the twentieth century, *Angels in America* likewise reveals a fundamental social betrayal—in this case, of America's founding ideals of freedom and equality. Miller's play is grounded in the history of European immigration to the United States and in the Great Depression; Kushner's is tied to the legacy of the civil rights movement in the 1960s, the rise of the gay rights movement, and the conservative backlash against both in the 1980s and early 1990s.

Yet whereas *Salesman* critiques American society through the lens of liberal humanism, *Angels* explores how those in power legislate and enforce normative assumptions about sex and sexuality, gender, race, and class. In its affirmation of social pluralism, the play embraces a decidedly postmodern understanding of identity and history. Narratives, myths, and themes that have traditionally constituted "America"—the Founding Fathers, manifest destiny, "the melting pot," the American family—no longer fit the changing demographics and experiences of contemporary life as Kushner dramatizes them. In one of the opening scenes of *Millennium Approaches,* Harper Pitt—one of the play's visionaries—

speaks of "beautiful systems dying, old fixed orders spiraling apart." Characters in *Angels in America* must rethink their identities and that of their nation within new relationships and psychological frameworks, reinterpreting the myths of America in light of more pluralistic social realities. On the eve of the third millennium, Kushner suggests, the question of what it means to be an American must be answered in ways that are at once collective and deeply individual.

The political and social breadth of *Angels in America* is matched by its stylistic expansiveness. Whereas *Death of a Salesman* helped define the tradition of American poetic realism, innovatively combining naturalistic and expressionistic elements, *Angels* employs an extraordinary collage of theatrical styles—from realism to surrealism, tragedy to farce, Brechtian political theater to the gay performance traditions of camp and drag. Ranging from the broadly political to the intensely personal and spiritual, the play balances intimately crafted scenes with an overarching epic structure, blending psychological realism together with nonrealistic dream scenes and heightened theatrical spectacle. While interweaving these styles and structures, the play also intercuts story lines cinematically, thereby encouraging the audience to see the life of each character in relation to society and to understand that such supposedly "personal" matters as sex and love are inherently political. Coining the label "Theatre of the Fabulous" for this stylistic collage, Kushner has stressed the theatrical nature of the play's scenes and effects. In his "playwright's notes," he comments: "The moments of magic . . . are to be fully realized, as bits of wonderful *theatrical* illusion—which means it's OK if the wires show, and maybe it's good that they do, but the magic should at the same time be thoroughly amazing."

Julius (third from left) and Ethel (far left) Rosenberg, who, on June 19, 1953, became the first American citizens executed for espionage.

Even as *Angels in America* has one foot in the miraculous, its other is firmly planted in the actual. Kushner's play is set in the mid-1980s during the Reagan presidency, and its cast includes characters drawn from modern American history. Most important among these is Roy Cohn, who served as chief counsel to Senator Joseph McCarthy during the Senate's anticommunist investigations of the 1950s and who, earlier, as an assistant U.S. attorney in New York, played a key role in the most sensational and controversial case of the decade's Red Scare: the prosecution of Julius and Ethel Rosenberg, a Jewish couple accused of helping to pass secrets of American nuclear research to the Soviet Union. They were convicted in 1951 and executed in 1953. Though Cohn's investigative methods were ultimately exposed as unethical, and perhaps illegal, he went on to become a powerful attorney in Washington D.C., and New York, giving behind-the-scenes advice to FBI Chief J. Edgar Hoover as well as to judges, mayors, and presidents. Throughout his career, he repudiated his familial and cultural roots, striving to become the reverse of what he was: the son of a Jewish, liberal, Democratic New York state supreme court judge. Cohn died from AIDS in 1986 but sought, to the very end, to hide his homosexuality, insisting that his ailment was "liver cancer."

Kushner juxtaposes Cohn's life with the lives of two fictional couples, one homosexual and the other heterosexual, who represent ordinary, young middle-class Americans living in New York in the mid-1980s. The homosexual couple are Louis, who works as a word processor in an office located in Roy's building, and Prior, a drag queen who has recently learned he is HIV-positive. When Prior develops full-blown AIDS, Louis's commitment to him and to their relationship shrinks as he confronts his fears of death and emotional pain. The heterosexual couple are Joe and Harper, Mormons who have moved from Utah to New York City to further Joe's legal career; Joe has become Roy's protégé, the object of his professional mentoring and almost paternal love. Joe and Harper's marriage is brought to a crisis by Roy's offer to place Joe in a job in Washington, D.C.—a position that will enable him to block Roy's threatened disbarment—and by Joe's homosexuality, with which he has struggled

Sean Chapman as Prior and Nancy Crane as the Angel in the 1992 London premiere of *Angels in America* at the Royal National Theatre.

all his life and which he must eventually acknowledge to himself and his wife. As the play unfolds, shifting focus from one story to another, the choices and actions of these characters shed light on each other. The audience sees Prior's experience of AIDS against Roy's denial of the disease, Joe's personal and professional integrity against Roy's dishonesty, Louis's abandonment of his partner against Joe's rejection of Harper, and Joe's emerging awareness of his homosexuality against Roy's repression of his own. By thus placing characters side by side, Kushner reveals their social interconnectedness and makes them symbolic of contradictions at the heart of the United States as a nation.

Joe's and Harper's Mormonism serves as one of a number of intellectual and spiritual backdrops to *Angels in America*. The one Christian religion indigenous to the United States, the Church of Jesus Christ of Latter-day Saints was founded in response to what its adherents view as a revelation that revised established Christian belief; it developed fully only after its first members journeyed to the edges of the frontier in search of the Promised Land. The metaphor of building on a past, of migrating, of crossing personal and ideological boundaries on the way to some anticipated rebirth or revelation recurs throughout *Angels:* in the opening monologue on Jewish emigration to the United States, in Joe's awakening to his sexuality, in Louis's movement away from Prior and toward Joe, and in Harper's and Prior's visions. Indeed, Kushner makes the stage itself a frontier, filling it with diverse styles that he synthesizes into a vision of social theater. As it moves between realism and nonrealism, between epic theater and spectacle, the play explores the limits of theatrical representation; at the outer reaches of those limits are the play's split scenes and dream scenes, which address social and spiritual dissolution and redemption.

Written as the cold war ended and in the waning years of the twentieth century, *Millennium Approaches* is charged with millenarian apprehension toward an unknown future. Apocalyptic foreboding occurs throughout the play, from Harper's fears about the vanishing ozone layer to terror at the pestilential specter of AIDS. *Perestroika,* the concluding part of *Angels in America,* lightens this tone somewhat, as it affirms life, community, and the possibility of personal, social, and spiritual progress. Like Kushner himself, who found himself anointed as a theatrical prophet while he moved steadily on with his writing and his activism, the play's characters seek ways to confront the world's problems while cultivating a vision of humanity's underlying grace. But though the two-part drama moves in the direction of healing, the most memorable moment in Kushner's theatrical epic is the spectacular conclusion of *Millennium Approaches*. Terrifying, beautiful, yet ambiguous, this final scene reflects the longings and fears, the restless spirituality, and the sense of the unknown that mark the turn of the millennium.

ART BORRECA

Angels in America

A Gay Fantasia on National Themes

PART ONE: MILLENNIUM APPROACHES

CHARACTERS

ROY M. COHN,[1] a successful New York lawyer and unofficial power broker.

JOSEPH PORTER PITT, chief clerk for Justice Theodore Wilson of the Federal Court of Appeals, Second Circuit.

HARPER AMATY PITT, Joe's wife, an agoraphobic with a mild Valium[2] addiction.

LOUIS IRONSON, a word processor working for the Second Circuit Court of Appeals.

PRIOR WALTER, Louis's boyfriend. Occasionally works as a club designer or caterer, otherwise lives very modestly but with great style off a small trust fund.

HANNAH PORTER PITT, Joe's mother, currently residing in Salt Lake City, living off her deceased husband's army pension.

BELIZE, a former drag queen and former lover of Prior's. A registered nurse. Belize's name was originally Norman Arriaga; Belize is a drag name that stuck.

THE ANGEL, four divine emanations, Fluor, Phosphor, Lumen, and Candle;[3] manifest in One: the Continental Principality of America. She has magnificent steel-gray wings.

Other Characters in Part One

RABBI ISIDOR CHEMELWITZ, an orthodox Jewish rabbi, played by the actor playing HANNAH.

MR. LIES, Harper's imaginary friend, a travel agent, who in style of dress and speech suggests a jazz musician; he always wears a large lapel badge emblazoned "IOTA" (The International Order of Travel Agents). He is played by the actor playing BELIZE.

THE MAN IN THE PARK, played by the actor playing PRIOR.

THE VOICE, the voice of THE ANGEL.

HENRY, ROY's doctor, played by the actor playing HANNAH.

EMILY, a nurse, played by the actor playing THE ANGEL.

1. A Jewish, New York–born lawyer (1927–1986) who attracted public attention and controversy throughout his career, most notoriously as chief counsel (1953–54) to the Permanent Subcommittee on Investigations, which, under the chairmanship of Senator Joseph McCarthy, hunted for Communists in the government and U.S. Army.

2. Diazepam (trademark), a tranquilizer that in the 1980s was the most frequently prescribed drug in the United States.

3. All terms having to do with light: *fluor,* or fluorite, is a mineral whose crystals can exhibit lumenescence; *phosphor,* or phosphorus, also emits light; and *lumen* (literally, "light" in Latin) and *candle* are both measures of light (of its intensity and flux, respectively).

MARTIN HELLER, a Reagan Administration Justice Department flackman, played by the actor playing HARPER.

SISTER ELLA CHAPTER, a Salt Lake City real estate saleswoman, played by the actor playing THE ANGEL.

PRIOR 1, the ghost of a dead Prior Walter from the 13th century, played by the actor playing JOE. He is a blunt, gloomy medieval farmer with a guttural Yorkshire accent.

PRIOR 2, the ghost of a dead Prior Walter from the 17th century, played by the actor playing ROY. He is a Londoner, sophisticated, with a High British accent.

THE ESKIMO, played by the actor playing JOE.

THE WOMAN IN THE SOUTH BRONX, played by the actor playing THE ANGEL.

ETHEL ROSENBERG,[4] played by the actor playing HANNAH.

Playwright's Notes

A DISCLAIMER: Roy M. Cohn, the character, is based on the late Roy M. Cohn (1927–1986), who was all too real; for the most part the acts attributed to the character Roy, such as his illegal conferences with Judge Kaufman during the trial of Ethel Rosenberg, are to be found in the historical record. But this Roy is a work of dramatic fiction; his words are my invention, and liberties have been taken.

A NOTE ABOUT THE STAGING: The play benefits from a pared-down style of presentation, with minimal scenery and scene shifts done rapidly (no blackouts!), employing the cast as well as stagehands—which makes for an actor-driven event, as this must be. The moments of magic—the appearance and disappearance of Mr. Lies and the ghosts, the Book hallucination, and the ending—are to be fully realized, as bits of wonderful *theatrical* illusion—which means it's OK if the wires show, and maybe it's good that they do, but the magic should at the same time be thoroughly amazing.

In a murderous time
the heart breaks and breaks
and lives by breaking.
—Stanley Kunitz[5]
"The Testing-Tree"

4. A Jewish, New York–born Communist (1915–1953); along with her husband, Julius, she was tried and executed for conspiring to give the Soviet Union information about the atomic bomb. As an assistant in the U.S. Attorney's office in New York, Roy Cohn played a prominent role in her 1951 trial.

5. An American poet (1905–2006); "The Testing-Tree" is the title poem of a collection published in 1971.

Act 1: Bad News

(*October–November 1985*)

Scene 1

[*The last days of October.* RABBI ISIDOR CHEMELWITZ *alone onstage with a small coffin. It is a rough pine box with two wooden pegs, one at the foot and one at the head, holding the lid in place. A prayer shawl embroidered with a Star of David is draped over the lid, and by the head a yarzheit*[6] *candle is burning.*]

RABBI ISIDOR CHEMELWITZ [*he speaks sonorously, with a heavy Eastern European accent, unapologetically consulting a sheet of notes for the family names*] Hello and good morning. I am Rabbi Isidor Chemelwitz of the Bronx Home for Aged Hebrews. We are here this morning to pay respects at the passing of Sarah Ironson, devoted wife of Benjamin Ironson, also deceased, loving and caring mother of her sons Morris, Abraham, and Samuel, and her daughters Esther and Rachel; beloved grandmother of Max, Mark, Louis, Lisa, Maria . . . uh . . . Lesley, Angela, Doris, Luke, and Eric. [*Looks more closely at paper.*] Eric? This is a Jewish name? [*Shrugs.*] Eric. A large and loving family. We assemble that we may mourn collectively this good and righteous woman. [*He looks at the coffin.*]

This woman. I did not know this woman. I cannot accurately describe her attributes, nor do justice to her dimensions. She was . . . Well, in the Bronx Home of Aged Hebrews are many like this, the old, and to many I speak but not to be frank with this one. She preferred silence. So I do not know her and yet I know her. She was . . . [*He touches the coffin.*] . . . not a person but a whole kind of person, the ones who crossed the ocean, who brought with us to America the villages of Russia and Lithuania—and how we struggled, and how we fought, for the family, for the Jewish home, so that you would not grow up *here*, in this strange place, in the melting pot where nothing melted. Descendants of this immigrant woman, you do not grow up in America, you and your children and their children with the goyische[7] names. You do not live in America. No such place exists. Your clay is the clay of some Litvak shtetl,[8] your air the air of the steppes—because she carried the old world on her back across the ocean, in a boat, and she put it down on Grand Concourse Avenue, or in Flatbush,[9] and she worked that earth into your bones, and you pass it to your children, this ancient, ancient culture and home. [*Little pause*]

You can never make that crossing that she made, for such Great Voyages in this world do not anymore exist. But every day of your lives the miles that voyage between that place and this one you cross. Every day. You understand me? In you that journey is.

So . . .

6. Anniversary (Yiddish); on the anniversary of a relative's death, observant Jews light a memorial candle at home and in their synagogue.

7. Non-Jewish, Gentile (Yiddish; sometimes pejorative).

8. Lithuanian village (Yiddish).

9. Two middle-class areas of New York City to which Jews moved in large numbers in the 1920s and '30s (in the Bronx and in Brooklyn, respectively).

She was the last of the Mohicans,[1] this one was. Pretty soon . . . all the old will be dead.

Scene 2

[Same day. ROY *and* JOE *in* ROY'*s office.* ROY *at an impressive desk, bare except for a very elaborate phone system, rows and rows of flashing buttons which bleep and beep and whistle incessantly, making chaotic music underneath* ROY'*s conversations.* JOE *is sitting, waiting.* ROY *conducts business with great energy, impatience, and sensual abandon: gesticulating, shouting, cajoling, crooning, playing the phone, receiver and hold button, with virtuosity and love.]*

ROY *[hitting a button]* Hold. *[To* JOE*]* I wish I was an octopus, a fucking octopus. Eight loving arms and all those suckers. Know what I mean?

JOE No, I . . .

ROY *[gesturing to a deli platter of little sandwiches on his desk]* You want lunch?

JOE No, that's OK really I just . . .

ROY *[hitting a button]* Ailene? Roy Cohn. Now what kind of a greeting is. . . . I thought we were friends, Ai . . . Look Mrs. Soffer you don't have to get . . . You're upset. You're yelling. You'll aggravate your condition, you shouldn't yell, you'll pop little blood vessels in your face if you yell. . . . No that was a joke, Mrs. Soffer, I was joking. . . . I already apologized sixteen times for that, Mrs. Soffer, you . . . *[While she's fulminating,* ROY *covers the mouthpiece with his hand and talks to* JOE.*]* This'll take a minute, *eat* already, what is this tasty sandwich here it's— *[He takes a bite of a sandwich.]* Mmmmm, liver or some . . . Here.

[He pitches the sandwich to JOE, *who catches it and returns it to the platter.]*

ROY *[back to Mrs. Soffer]* Uh huh, uh huh. . . . No, I already told you, it wasn't a vacation, it was business, Mrs. Soffer, I have clients in Haiti, Mrs. Soffer, I . . . Listen, Ailene, YOU THINK I'M THE ONLY GODDAM LAWYER IN HISTORY EVER MISSED A COURT DATE? Don't make such a big fucking . . . Hold. *[He hits the hold button.]* You HAG!

JOE If this is a bad time . . .

ROY *Bad* time? This is a *good* time! *[Button]* Baby doll, get me . . . Oh fuck, wait . . . *[Button, button]* Hello? Yah. Sorry to keep you holding, Judge Hollins, I . . . Oh *Mrs.* Hollins, sorry dear deep voice you got. Enjoying your visit? *[Hand over mouthpiece again, to* JOE*]* She sounds like a truck-driver and he sounds like Kate Smith,[2] very confusing. Nixon[3] appointed him, all the geeks are Nixon appointees . . . *[To Mrs. Hollins]* Yeah yeah right good so how many tickets dear? Seven. For what, *Cats, 42nd Street,*

1. That is, the last of her kind—an allusion to James Fenimore Cooper's novel *The Last of the Mohicans* (1826).

2. A popular American singer (1907–1986), best known for her rendition of Irving Berlin's "God Bless America" (1918); her career peaked in the 1940s, but her robust voice made her a star of radio and television from the 1930s to the 1960s.

3. Richard M. Nixon (1913–1994), thirty seventh president of the United States (1969–74); Nixon rose to national prominence in the 1940s as an ardently anticommunist Republican congressman on the House Committee on Un-American Activities.

what? No you wouldn't like *La Cage,*[4] trust me, I know. Oh for godsake . . . Hold. [*Button, button*] Baby doll, seven for *Cats* or something, anything hard to get, I don't give a fuck what and neither will they. [*Button; to* JOE] You see *La Cage?*

JOE No, I . . .

ROY Fabulous. Best thing on Broadway. Maybe ever. [*Button*] Who? Aw, Jesus H. Christ, Harry, *no*, Harry, Judge John Francis Grimes, Manhattan Family Court. Do I have to do every goddam thing myself? *Touch* the bastard, Harry, and don't call me on this line again, I told you not to . . .

JOE [*starting to get up*] Roy, uh, should I wait outside or . . .

ROY [*to* JOE] Oh sit. [*To Harry*] You hold. I pay you to hold fuck you Harry you jerk. [*Button*] Half-wit dick-brain. [*Instantly philosophical*] I see the universe, Joe, as a kind of sandstorm in outer space with winds of mega-hurricane velocity, but instead of grains of sand it's shards and splinters of glass. You ever feel that way? Ever have one of those days?

JOE I'm not sure I . . .

ROY So how's life in Appeals?[5] How's the Judge?

JOE He sends his best.

ROY He's a good man. Loyal. Not the brightest man on the bench, but he has manners. And a nice head of silver hair.

JOE He gives me a lot of responsibility.

ROY Yeah, like writing his decisions and signing his name.

JOE Well . . .

ROY He's a nice guy. And you cover admirably.

JOE Well, thanks, Roy, I . . .

ROY [*button*] Yah? Who is *this*? Well who the fuck are *you*? Hold— [*Button*] Harry? Eighty-seven grand, something like that. Fuck him. Eat me. New Jersey, chain of porno film stores in, uh, Weehawken.[6] That's—Harry, that's the beauty of the law. [*Button*] So, baby doll, what? *Cats*? Bleah. [*Button*] *Cats!* It's about cats. Singing cats, you'll love it. Eight o'clock, the theatre's always at eight. [*Button*] Fucking tourists. [*Button, then to* JOE] Oh live a little, Joe, *eat* something for Christ sake—

JOE Um, Roy, could you . . .

ROY What? [*To Harry*] Hold a minute. [*Button*] Mrs. Soffer? Mrs. . . . [*Button*] God-fucking-dammit to hell, where is . . .

JOE [*overlapping*] Roy, I'd really appreciate it if . . .

ROY [*overlapping*] Well she was here a minute ago, baby doll, see if . . .

[*The phone starts making three different beeping sounds, all at once.*]

ROY [*smashing buttons*] Jesus fuck this goddam thing . . .

JOE [*overlapping*] I really wish you wouldn't . . .

ROY [*overlapping*] Baby doll? Ring the *Post*[7] get me Suzy see if . . .

[*The phone starts whistling loudly.*]

4. Long-running musicals on Broadway in the 1980s: *Cats* (1982–2000; lyrics by T. S. Eliot and Trevor Nunn, music by Andrew Lloyd Webber); *42nd Street* (1980–89; book by Mark Bramble and Michael Stewart, lyrics by Al Dubin, music by Harry Warren); and *La Cage aux Folles* (1983–87; book by Harvey Fierstein, lyrics and music by Jerry Herman), which presents the interactions between a gay couple (the manager and the star of a drag nightclub), the manager's son, and the conservative parents of the son's fiancée.

5. The U.S. Court of Appeals, where Joe is a lawyer holding a senior administrative position.

6. A town directly across the Hudson River from New York City.

7. The *New York Post,* which by the 1980s had become a conservative tabloid.

ROY CHRIST!

JOE *Roy.*

ROY [*into receiver*] Hold. [*Button; to* JOE] *What?*

JOE Could you please not take the Lord's name in vain? [*Pause*]
I'm sorry. But please. At least while I'm . . .

ROY [*laughs, then*] Right. Sorry. Fuck.
Only in America. [*Punches a button.*] Baby doll, tell 'em all to fuck off. Tell 'em I died. You handle Mrs. Soffer. Tell her it's on the way. Tell her I'm schtupping[8] the judge. I'll call her back. I *will* call her. I *know* how much I borrowed. She's got four hundred times that stuffed up her . . . Yeah, tell her I said that. [*Button. The phone is silent.*]
So, Joe.

JOE I'm sorry Roy, I just . . .

ROY No no no no, principles count, I respect principles, I'm not religious but I like God and God likes me. Baptist, Catholic?

JOE Mormon.

ROY Mormon. Delectable. Absolutely. Only in America. So, Joe. Whattya think?

JOE It's . . . well . . .

ROY Crazy life.

JOE Chaotic.

ROY Well but God bless chaos. Right?

JOE Ummm . . .

ROY Huh. Mormons. I knew Mormons, in, um, Nevada.

JOE Utah, mostly.

ROY No, these Mormons were in Vegas.
So. So, how'd you like to go to Washington and work for the Justice Department?

JOE Sorry?

ROY How'd you like to go to Washington and work for the Justice Department? All I gotta do is pick up the phone, talk to Ed, and you're in.

JOE In . . . what, exactly?

ROY Associate Assistant Something Big. Internal Affairs, heart of the woods, something nice with clout.

JOE Ed . . . ?

ROY Meese.[9] The Attorney General.

JOE Oh.

ROY I just have to pick up the phone . . .

JOE I have to think.

ROY Of course. [*Pause*]
It's a great time to be in Washington, Joe.

JOE Roy, it's incredibly exciting . . .

ROY And it would mean something to me. You understand?

[*Little pause.*]

JOE I . . . can't say how much I appreciate this Roy, I'm sort of . . . well, stunned, I mean . . . Thanks, Roy. But I have to give it some thought. I have to ask my wife.

8. Aggressively pushing, ingratiating himself with; fucking (from Yiddish).

9. Edwin Meese III (b. 1931), who served as attorney general (1985–88) under President Ronald Reagan (1911–2004; 40th president, 1981–89).

ROY Your wife. Of course.

JOE But I really appreciate . . .

ROY Of course. Talk to your wife.

Scene 3

[*Later that day.* HARPER *at home, alone. She is listening to the radio and talking to herself, as she often does. She speaks to the audience.*]

HARPER People who are lonely, people left alone, sit talking nonsense to the air, imagining . . . beautiful systems dying, old fixed orders spiraling apart . . .

When you look at the ozone layer, from outside, from a spaceship, it looks like a pale blue halo, a gentle, shimmering aureole encircling the atmosphere encircling the earth. Thirty miles above our heads, a thin layer of three-atom oxygen molecules, product of photosynthesis, which explains the fussy vegetable preference for visible light, its rejection of darker rays and emanations. Danger from without. It's a kind of gift, from God, the crowning touch to the creation of the world: guardian angels, hands linked, make a spherical net, a blue-green nesting orb, a shell of safety for life itself. But everywhere, things are collapsing, lies surfacing, systems of defense giving way.[1] . . . This is why, Joe, this is why I shouldn't be left alone. [*Little pause*]

I'd like to go traveling. Leave you behind to worry. I'll send postcards with strange stamps and tantalizing messages on the back. "Later maybe." "Nevermore . . ."

[MR. LIES, *a travel agent, appears.*]

HARPER Oh! You startled me!

MR. LIES Cash, check, or credit card?

HARPER I remember you. You're from Salt Lake. You sold us the plane tickets when we flew here. What are you doing in Brooklyn?

MR. LIES You said you wanted to travel . . .

HARPER And here you are. How thoughtful.

MR. LIES Mr. Lies. Of the International Order of Travel Agents. We mobilize the globe, we set people adrift, we stir the populace and send nomads eddying across the planet. We are adepts of motion, acolytes of the flux. Cash, check, or credit card. Name your destination.

HARPER Antarctica, maybe. I want to see the hole in the ozone. I heard on the radio . . .

MR. LIES [*he has a computer terminal in his briefcase*] I can arrange a guided tour. Now?

HARPER Soon. Maybe soon. I'm not safe here you see. Things aren't right with me. Weird stuff happens . . .

MR. LIES Like?

HARPER Well, like you, for instance. Just appearing. Or last week . . . well never mind.

People are like planets, you need a thick skin. Things get to me, Joe stays away and now. . . . Well look. My dreams are talking back to me.

1. Beginning in the 1970s, scientists began to warn that industrial pollutants such as chlorofluorocarbons (CFCs) might concentrate in the stratosphere and deplete the ozone there, which affords protection against harmful high-energy radiation. The first "ozone hole"—a seasonal depletion—was discovered above Antarctica in 1985, and subsequent research confirmed the widespread loss of ozone.

MR. LIES It's the price of rootlessness. Motion sickness. The only cure: to keep moving.

HARPER I'm undecided. I feel . . . that something's going to give. It's 1985. Fifteen years till the third millennium. Maybe Christ will come again. Maybe seeds will be planted, maybe there'll be harvests then, maybe early figs to eat, maybe new life, maybe fresh blood, maybe companionship and love and protection, safety from what's outside, maybe the door will hold, or maybe . . . maybe the troubles[2] will come, and the end will come, and the sky will collapse and there will be terrible rains and showers of poison light, or maybe my life is really fine, maybe Joe loves me and I'm only crazy thinking otherwise, or maybe not, maybe it's even worse than I know, maybe . . . I want to know, maybe I don't. The suspense, Mr. Lies, it's killing me.

MR. LIES I suggest a vacation.

HARPER [*hearing something*] That was the elevator. Oh God, I should fix myself up, I . . . You have to go, you shouldn't be here . . . you aren't even real.

MR. LIES Call me when you decide . . .

HARPER Go!

[*The travel agent vanishes as* JOE *enters.*]

JOE Buddy?

Buddy? Sorry I'm late. I was just . . . out. Walking. Are you mad?

HARPER I got a little anxious.

JOE Buddy kiss.

[*They kiss.*]

JOE Nothing to get anxious about.

So. So how'd you like to move to Washington?

Scene 4

[*Same day.* LOUIS *and* PRIOR *outside the funeral home, sitting on a bench, both dressed in funereal finery, talking. The funeral service for Sarah Ironson has just concluded and* LOUIS *is about to leave for the cemetery.*]

LOUIS My grandmother actually saw Emma Goldman[3] speak. In Yiddish. But all Grandma could remember was that she spoke well and wore a hat.

What a weird service. That rabbi . . .

PRIOR A definite find. Get his number when you go to the graveyard. I want him to bury me.

LOUIS Better head out there. Everyone gets to put dirt on the coffin once it's lowered in.

PRIOR Oooh. Cemetery fun. Don't want to miss that.

LOUIS It's an old Jewish custom to express love. Here, Grandma, have a shovelful. Latecomers run the risk of finding the grave completely filled.

She was pretty crazy. She was up there in that home for ten years, talking to herself. I never visited. She looked too much like my mother.

PRIOR [*hugs him*] Poor Louis. I'm sorry your grandma is dead.

2. That is, the apocalyptic "end times" foretold in the New Testament's book of Revelation.

3. A Lithuanian-born American anarchist and writer (1869–1940); she championed socialism and women's rights in the United States, Russia, and Britain. Though Goldman's primary languages were Russian and German, she gave speeches in Yiddish—the lingua franca of Jews from central and eastern Europe to reach the largest audience possible.

LOUIS Tiny little coffin, huh?

Sorry I didn't introduce you to. . . . I always get so closety[4] at these family things.

PRIOR Butch.[5] You get butch. [*Imitating*] "Hi Cousin Doris, you don't remember me I'm Lou, Rachel's boy." Lou, not Louis, because if you say Louis they'll hear the sibilant S.

LOUIS I don't have a . . .

PRIOR I don't blame you, hiding. Bloodlines. Jewish curses are the worst. I personally would dissolve if anyone ever looked me in the eye and said "Feh."[6] Fortunately WASPs don't say "Feh." Oh and by the way, darling, cousin Doris is a dyke.

LOUIS No.

Really?

PRIOR You don't notice anything. If I hadn't spent the last four years fellating you I'd swear you were straight.

LOUIS You're in a pissy mood. Cat still missing?

[*Little pause.*]

PRIOR Not a furball in sight. It's your fault.

LOUIS It is?

PRIOR I warned you, Louis. Names are important. Call an animal "Little Sheba"[7] and you can't expect it to stick around. Besides, it's a dog's name.

LOUIS I wanted a dog in the first place, not a cat. He sprayed my books.

PRIOR He was a female cat.

LOUIS Cats are stupid, high-strung predators. Babylonians sealed them up in bricks. Dogs have brains.

PRIOR Cats have intuition.

LOUIS A sharp dog is as smart as a really dull two-year-old child.

PRIOR Cats know when something's wrong.

LOUIS Only if you stop feeding them.

PRIOR They know. That's why Sheba left, because she knew.

LOUIS Knew what?

[*Pause.*]

PRIOR I did my best Shirley Booth[8] this morning, floppy slippers, housecoat, curlers, can of Little Friskies; "Come back, Little Sheba, come back. . . ." To no avail. Le chat, elle ne reviendra jamais, jamais[9] . . .

[*He removes his jacket, rolls up his sleeve, shows* LOUIS *a dark-purple spot on the underside of his arm near the shoulder.*] See.

LOUIS That's just a burst blood vessel.

PRIOR Not according to the best medical authorities.

LOUIS What? [*Pause*]

Tell me.

PRIOR K.S.,[1] baby. Lesion number one. Lookit. The wine-dark kiss of the angel of death.

4. That is, secretive about his homosexuality.
5. Assertively masculine.
6. A Yiddish interjection that expresses disgust or displeasure.
7. A reference to *Come Back, Little Sheba,* a 1952 film (dir. Daniel Mann) based on William Inge's 1950 play, which takes its title from the call for a lost dog.
8. An American actor (1898–1992); she starred in the stage and film versions of *Come Back, Little Sheba*.
9. The cat, she will never, ever come back (French).
1. That is, Kaposi's sarcoma, a type of lesion associated with AIDS; it was one of the first recognized signs of HIV infection.

LOUIS [*very softly, holding* PRIOR*'s arm*] Oh please . . .

PRIOR I'm a lesionnaire. The Foreign Lesion. The American Lesion. Lesionnaire's disease.

LOUIS Stop.

PRIOR My troubles are lesion.

LOUIS Will you *stop*.

PRIOR Don't you think I'm handling this well? I'm going to die.

LOUIS Bullshit.

PRIOR Let go of my arm.

LOUIS No.

PRIOR Let go.

LOUIS [*grabbing* PRIOR, *embracing him ferociously*] No.

PRIOR I can't find a way to spare you baby. No wall like the wall of hard scientific fact. K.S. Wham. Bang your head on that.

LOUIS Fuck you. [*Letting go*] Fuck you fuck you fuck you.

PRIOR Now that's what I like to hear. A mature reaction.
Let's go see if the cat's come home.
Louis?

LOUIS When did you find this?

PRIOR I couldn't tell you.

LOUIS Why?

PRIOR I was scared, Lou.

LOUIS Of what?

PRIOR That you'll leave me.

LOUIS Oh.

[*Little pause.*]

PRIOR Bad timing, funeral and all, but I figured as long as we're on the subject of death . . .

LOUIS I have to go bury my grandma.

PRIOR Lou?

[*Pause.*]

Then you'll come home?

LOUIS Then I'll come home.

Scene 5

[*Same day, later on. Split scene:* JOE *and* HARPER *at home;* LOUIS *at the cemetery with* RABBI ISIDOR CHEMELWITZ *and the little coffin.*]

HARPER Washington?

JOE It's an incredible honor, buddy, and . . .

HARPER I have to think.

JOE Of course.

HARPER Say no.

JOE You said you were going to think about it.

HARPER I don't want to move to Washington.

JOE Well I do.

HARPER It's a giant cemetery, huge white graves and mausoleums everywhere.

JOE We could live in Maryland. Or Georgetown.

HARPER We're happy here.

JOE That's not really true, buddy, we . . .

HARPER Well happy enough! Pretend-happy. That's better than nothing.

JOE It's time to make some changes, Harper.

HARPER No changes. Why?

JOE I've been chief clerk for four years. I make twenty-nine thousand dollars a year. That's ridiculous. I graduated fourth in my class and I make less than anyone I know. And I'm . . . I'm tired of being a clerk, I want to go where something good is happening.

HARPER Nothing good happens in Washington. We'll forget church teachings and buy furniture at . . . at *Conran's* and become yuppies.[2] I have too much to do here.

JOE Like what?

HARPER I *do* have things . . .

JOE What things?

HARPER I have to finish painting the bedroom.

JOE You've been painting in there for over a year.

HARPER I know, I . . . It just isn't done because I never get time to finish it.

JOE Oh that's . . . that doesn't make sense. You have all the time in the world. You could finish it when I'm at work.

HARPER I'm afraid to go in there alone.

JOE Afraid of what?

HARPER I heard someone in there. Metal scraping on the wall. A man with a knife, maybe.

JOE There's no one in the bedroom, Harper.

HARPER Not now.

JOE Not this morning either.

HARPER How do you know? You were at work this morning. There's something creepy about this place. Remember *Rosemary's Baby?*[3]

JOE *Rosemary's Baby?*

HARPER Our apartment looks like that one. Wasn't that apartment in Brooklyn?

JOE No, it was . . .

HARPER Well, it looked like this. It did.

JOE Then let's move.

HARPER Georgetown's worse. *The Exorcist* was in Georgetown.[4]

JOE The devil, everywhere you turn, huh, buddy.

HARPER Yeah. Everywhere.

JOE How many pills today, buddy?

HARPER None. One. Three. Only three.

LOUIS [*pointing at the coffin*] Why are there just two little wooden pegs holding the lid down?

RABBI ISIDOR CHEMELWITZ So she can get out easier if she wants to.

LOUIS I hope she stays put.

2. A term that came into widespread use in the 1980s. *Conran's:* New York retailer of contemporary home furnishings marketed to young urban professionals.

3. A horror film directed by Roman Polanski (1968), based on a best-selling novel by Ira Levin (1967), in which a young couple move into a Manhattan apartment building inhabited by Satan worshippers.

4. An affluent neighborhood in Washington, D.C., that was the setting of *The Exorcist* (1973; dir. William Friedkin), a horror film adapted from William Peter Blatty's best-selling novel (1971) about a twelve-year-old girl possessed by the devil.

I pretended for years that she was already dead. When they called to say she had died it was a surprise. I abandoned her.

RABBI ISIDOR CHEMELWITZ "Sharfer vi di tson fun a shlang iz an umdankbar kind!"

LOUIS I don't speak Yiddish.

RABBI ISIDOR CHEMELWITZ Sharper than the serpent's tooth is the ingratitude of children. Shakespeare. *Kenig Lear*.[5]

LOUIS Rabbi, what does the Holy Writ say about someone who abandons someone he loves at a time of great need?

RABBI ISIDOR CHEMELWITZ Why would a person do such a thing?

LOUIS Because he has to.

Maybe because this person's sense of the world, that it will change for the better with struggle, maybe a person who has this neo-Hegelian positivist sense of constant historical progress towards happiness or perfection or something,[6] who feels very powerful because he feels connected to these forces, moving uphill all the time . . . maybe that person can't, um, incorporate sickness into his sense of how things are supposed to go. Maybe vomit . . . and sores and disease . . . really frighten him, maybe . . . he isn't so good with death.

RABBI ISIDOR CHEMELWITZ The Holy Scriptures have nothing to say about such a person.

LOUIS Rabbi, I'm afraid of the crimes I may commit.

RABBI ISIDOR CHEMELWITZ Please, mister. I'm a sick old rabbi facing a long drive home to the Bronx. You want to confess, better you should find a priest.

LOUIS But I'm not a Catholic, I'm a Jew.

RABBI ISIDOR CHEMELWITZ Worse luck for you, bubbulah.[7] Catholics believe in forgiveness. Jews believe in Guilt. [*He pats the coffin tenderly.*]

LOUIS You just make sure those pegs are in good and tight.

RABBI ISIDOR CHEMELWITZ Don't worry, mister. The life she had, she'll stay put. She's better off.

JOE Look, I know this is scary for you. But try to understand what it means to me. Will you try?

HARPER Yes.

JOE Good. Really try.

I think things are starting to change in the world.

HARPER But I don't want . . .

JOE Wait. For the good. Change for the good. America has rediscovered itself. Its sacred position among nations. And people aren't ashamed of that like they used to be. This is a great thing. The truth restored. Law restored. That's what President Reagan's done, Harper. He says "Truth exists and can be spoken proudly." And the country responds to him. We become better.

5. That is, *King Lear* (Yiddish); the line paraphrases Shakespeare's play (1605), 1.4.265–66.

6. The German philosopher Georg Wilhelm Friedrich Hegel (1770–1831), who saw in culture and civilization the logical development of consciousness, has traditionally been viewed as an idealist (i.e., his theory is not connected to external reality or the senses); but his belief in the dialectical process—that a thesis inevitably generates its antithesis, and their interaction results in a new synthesis—can lead to such positivist philosophies (i.e., systems of thought focused on observable phenomena) as the dialectical materialism connected with Marxism.

7. Literally, "little grandmother" (Yiddish); a term of endearment, often applied to children.

More good. I need to be a part of that, I need something big to lift me up. I mean, six years ago the world seemed in decline, horrible, hopeless, full of unsolvable problems and crime and confusion and hunger and . . .

HARPER But it still seems that way. More now than before. They say the ozone layer is . . .

JOE Harper . . .

HARPER And today out the window on Atlantic Avenue there was a schizophrenic traffic cop who was making these . . .

JOE Stop it! I'm trying to make a point.

HARPER So am I.

JOE You aren't even making sense, you . . .

HARPER My point is the world seems just as . . .

JOE It only seems that way to you because you never go out in the world, Harper, and you have emotional problems.

HARPER I do so get out in the world.

JOE You don't. You stay in all day, fretting about imaginary . . .

HARPER I get out. I do. You don't know what I do.

JOE You don't stay in all day.

HARPER No.

JOE Well. . . Yes you do.

HARPER That's what you think.

JOE Where do you go?

HARPER Where do *you* go? When you walk.

[*Pause, then angrily*] And I DO NOT have emotional problems.

JOE I'm sorry.

HARPER And if I do have emotional problems it's from living with you. Or . . .

JOE I'm sorry buddy, I didn't mean to . . .

HARPER Or if you do think I do then you should never have married me. You have all these secrets and lies.

JOE I want to be married to you, Harper.

HARPER You shouldn't. You never should. [*Pause*]

Hey buddy. Hey buddy.

JOE Buddy kiss . . .

[*They kiss.*]

HARPER I heard on the radio how to give a blowjob.

JOE What?

HARPER You want to try?

JOE You really shouldn't listen to stuff like that.

HARPER Mormons can give blowjobs.

JOE *Harper.*

HARPER [*imitating his tone*] *Joe.*

It was a little Jewish lady with a German accent.[8]

This is a good time. For me to make a baby.

[*Little pause.* JOE *turns away.*]

8. Ruth Westheimer (b. 1928), the German-born psychologist and sex therapist who, as "Dr. Ruth," began hosting the radio call-in program *Sexually Speaking* in New York in 1980; it became hugely successful and was soon followed by a cable television program, *The Dr. Ruth Show.*

HARPER Then they went on to a program about holes in the ozone layer. Over Antarctica. Skin burns, birds go blind, icebergs melt. The world's coming to an end.

Scene 6

[*First week of November. In the men's room of the offices of the Brooklyn Federal Court of Appeals;* LOUIS *is crying over the sink;* JOE *enters.*]

JOE Oh, um . . . Morning.
LOUIS Good morning, counselor.
JOE [*he watches* LOUIS *cry*] Sorry, I . . . I don't know your name.
LOUIS Don't bother. Word processor. The lowest of the low.
JOE [*holding out hand*] Joe Pitt. I'm with Justice Wilson . . .
LOUIS Oh, I know that. Counselor Pitt. Chief Clerk.
JOE Were you . . . are you OK?
LOUIS Oh, yeah. Thanks. What a nice man.
JOE Not so nice.
LOUIS What?
JOE Not so nice. Nothing. You sure you're . . .
LOUIS Life sucks shit. Life . . . just sucks shit.
JOE What's wrong?
LOUIS Run in my nylons.
JOE Sorry . . . ?
LOUIS Forget it. Look, thanks for asking.
JOE Well . . .
LOUIS I mean it really is nice of you. [*He starts crying again.*]
Sorry, sorry, sick friend . . .
JOE Oh, I'm sorry.
LOUIS Yeah, yeah, well, that's sweet.
Three of your colleagues have preceded you to this baleful sight and you're the first one to ask. The others just opened the door, saw me, and fled. I hope they had to pee real bad.
JOE [*handing him a wad of toilet paper*] They just didn't want to intrude.
LOUIS Hah. Reaganite heartless macho asshole lawyers.[9]
JOE Oh, that's unfair.
LOUIS What is? Heartless? Macho? Reaganite? Lawyer?
JOE I voted for Reagan.
LOUIS You did?
JOE Twice.
LOUIS Twice? Well, oh boy. A Gay Republican.
JOE Excuse me?
LOUIS Nothing.
JOE I'm not . . .
Forget it.
LOUIS Republican? Not Republican? Or . . .
JOE What?

9. Court of appeals judges and district court judges are presidential appointees who, after confirmation, hold their positions for life, and they generally hire subordinates who share their legal philosophies. During his two terms as president, Reagan appointed almost 400 federal judges.

LOUIS What?

JOE Not gay. I'm not gay.

LOUIS Oh. Sorry.

[*Blows his nose loudly.*] It's just . . .

JOE Yes?

LOUIS Well, sometimes you can tell from the way a person sounds that . . . I mean you *sound* like a . . .

JOE No I don't. Like what?

LOUIS Like a Republican.

[*Little pause.* JOE *knows he's being teased;* LOUIS *knows he knows.* JOE *decides to be a little brave.*]

JOE [*making sure no one else is around*] Do I? Sound like a . . . ?

LOUIS What? Like a . . . ? Republican, or . . . ? Do *I*?

JOE Do you what?

LOUIS Sound like a . . . ?

JOE Like a . . . ?

I'm . . . confused.

LOUIS Yes.

My name is Louis. But all my friends call me Louise. I work in Word Processing. Thanks for the toilet paper.

[LOUIS *offers* JOE *his hand,* JOE *reaches,* LOUIS *feints and pecks* JOE *on the cheek, then exits.*]

Scene 7

[*A week later. Mutual dream scene.* PRIOR *is at a fantastic makeup table, having a dream, applying the face.* HARPER *is having a pill-induced hallucination. She has these from time to time. For some reason,* PRIOR *has appeared in this one. Or* HARPER *has appeared in* PRIOR*'s dream. It is bewildering.*]

PRIOR [*alone, putting on makeup, then examining the results in the mirror; to the audience*] "I'm ready for my closeup, Mr. DeMille."[1]

One wants to move through life with elegance and grace, blossoming infrequently but with exquisite taste, and perfect timing, like a rare bloom, a zebra orchid. . . . One wants. . . . But one so seldom gets what one wants, does one? No. One does not. One gets fucked. Over. One . . . dies at thirty, robbed of . . . decades of majesty.

Fuck this shit. Fuck this shit.

[*He almost crumbles; he pulls himself together; he studies his handiwork in the mirror.*] I look like a corpse. A corpsette. Oh my queen; you know you've hit rock-bottom when even drag is a drag.

[HARPER *appears.*]

HARPER Are you. . . . Who are you?

PRIOR Who are you?

HARPER What are you doing in my hallucination?

PRIOR I'm not in your hallucination. You're in my dream.

1. The final line of *Sunset Boulevard* (1950; dir. Billy Wilder), spoken by Gloria Swanson as the delusional former silent-movie star Norma Desmond, is "All right, Mr. DeMille, I'm ready for my closeup." The pioneering film director Cecil B. DeMille (1881–1959) plays himself in the film.

HARPER You're wearing makeup.

PRIOR So are you.

HARPER But you're a man.

PRIOR [*feigning dismay, shock, he mimes slashing his throat with his lipstick and dies, fabulously tragic. Then*] The hands and feet give it away.

HARPER There must be some mistake here. I don't recognize you. You're not. . . . Are you my . . . some sort of imaginary friend?

PRIOR No. Aren't you too old to have imaginary friends?

HARPER I have emotional problems. I took too many pills. Why are you wearing makeup?

PRIOR I was in the process of applying the face, trying to make myself feel better—I swiped the new fall colors at the Clinique counter at Macy's.[2] [*Showing her*]

HARPER You stole these?

PRIOR I was out of cash; it was an emotional emergency!

HARPER Joe will be so angry. I promised him. No more pills.

PRIOR These pills you keep alluding to?

HARPER Valium. I take Valium. Lots of Valium.

PRIOR And you're dancing as fast as you can.[3]

HARPER I'm not *addicted.* I don't believe in addiction, and I never . . . well, I *never* drink. And I *never* take drugs.

PRIOR Well, smell *you,* Nancy Drew.[4]

HARPER Except Valium.

PRIOR Except Valium; in wee fistfuls.

HARPER It's terrible. Mormons are not supposed to be addicted to anything. I'm a Mormon.

PRIOR I'm a homosexual.

HARPER Oh! In my church we don't believe in homosexuals.

PRIOR In my church we don't believe in Mormons.

HARPER What church do . . . oh! [*She laughs.*] I get it.

I don't understand this. If I didn't ever see you before and I don't think I did then I don't think you should be here, in this hallucination, because in my experience the mind, which is where hallucinations come from, shouldn't be able to make up anything that wasn't there to start with, that didn't enter it from experience, from the real world. Imagination can't create anything new, can it? It only recycles bits and pieces from the world and reassembles them into visions. . . . Am I making sense right now?

PRIOR Given the circumstances, yes.

HARPER So when we think we've escaped the unbearable ordinariness and, well, untruthfulness of our lives, it's really only the same old ordinariness and falseness rearranged into the appearance of novelty and truth. Nothing unknown is knowable. Don't you think it's depressing?

PRIOR The limitations of the imagination?

HARPER Yes.

2. A chain of department stores; its flagship store is in New York City at Herald Square. *Clinique:* an upscale brand of cosmetics.

3. A play on *I'm Dancing as Fast as I Can* (1982; dir. Jack Hofsiss), a film adapted from Barbara Gordon's best-selling 1972 memoir about Valium addiction.

4. A schoolyard taunt; Nancy Drew, a wholesome teenage detective, is the heroine of a popular series that the Stratemeyer syndicate began publishing in 1930.

PRIOR It's something you learn after your second theme party: It's All Been Done Before.

HARPER The world. Finite. Terribly, terribly. . . . Well . . .

This is the most depressing hallucination I've ever had.

PRIOR Apologies. I do try to be amusing.

HARPER Oh, well, don't apologize, you . . . I can't expect someone who's really sick to entertain me.

PRIOR How on earth did you know . . .

HARPER Oh that happens. This is the very threshhold of revelation sometimes. You can see things . . . how sick you are. Do you see anything about me?

PRIOR Yes.

HARPER What?

PRIOR You are amazingly unhappy.

HARPER Oh big deal. You meet a Valium addict and you figure out she's unhappy. That doesn't count. Of course I . . . Something else. Something surprising.

PRIOR Something surprising.

HARPER Yes.

PRIOR Your husband's a homo.

[*Pause.*]

HARPER Oh, ridiculous.

[*Pause, then very quietly*] Really?

PRIOR [*shrugs*] Threshhold of revelation.

HARPER Well I don't like your revelations. I don't think you intuit well at all. Joe's a very normal man, he . . .

Oh God. Oh God. He . . . Do homos take, like, lots of long walks?

PRIOR Yes. We do. In stretch pants with lavender coifs. I just looked at you, and there was . . .

HARPER A sort of blue streak of recognition.

PRIOR Yes.

HARPER Like you knew me incredibly well.

PRIOR Yes.

HARPER Yes.

I have to go now, get back, something just . . . fell apart.

Oh God, I feel so sad . . .

PRIOR I . . . I'm sorry. I usually say, "Fuck the truth," but mostly, the truth fucks you.

HARPER I see something else about you . . .

PRIOR Oh?

HARPER Deep inside you, there's a part of you, the most inner part, entirely free of disease. I can see that.

PRIOR Is that . . . That isn't true.

HARPER Threshhold of revelation.

Home . . .

[*She vanishes.*]

PRIOR People come and go so quickly here . . .

[*To himself in the mirror*] I don't think there's any uninfected part of me. My heart is pumping polluted blood. I feel dirty.

[*He begins to wipe makeup off with his hands, smearing it around. A large gray feather falls from up above.* PRIOR *stops smearing the makeup and looks at the feather. He goes to it and picks it up.*]

A VOICE [*it is an incredibly beautiful voice*] Look up!

PRIOR [*looking up, not seeing anyone*] Hello?

A VOICE Look up!

PRIOR Who is that?

A VOICE Prepare the way!

PRIOR I don't see any . . .

[*There is a dramatic change in lighting, from above.*]

A VOICE

Look up, look up,
prepare the way
the infinite descent
A breath in air
floating down
Glory to . . .

[*Silence.*]

PRIOR Hello? Is that it? Helloooo!

What the fuck . . . ? [*He holds himself.*]

Poor me. Poor poor me. Why me? Why poor poor me? Oh I don't feel good right now. I really don't.

Scene 8

[*That night. Split scene:* HARPER *and* JOE *at home;* PRIOR *and* LOUIS *in bed.*]

HARPER Where were you?

JOE Out.

HARPER Where?

JOE Just out. Thinking.

HARPER It's late.

JOE I had a lot to think about.

HARPER I burned dinner.

JOE Sorry.

HARPER Not my dinner. My dinner was fine. Your dinner. I put it back in the oven and turned everything up as high as it could go and I watched till it burned black. It's still hot. Very hot. Want it?

JOE You didn't have to do that.

HARPER I know. It just seemed like the kind of thing a mentally deranged sex-starved pill-popping housewife would do.

JOE Uh huh.

HARPER So I did it. Who knows anymore what I have to do?

JOE How many pills?

HARPER A bunch. Don't change the subject.

JOE I won't talk to you when you . . .

HARPER No. No. Don't do that! I'm . . . I'm fine, pills are not the problem, not our problem, I WANT TO KNOW WHERE YOU'VE BEEN! I WANT TO KNOW WHAT'S GOING ON!

JOE Going on with what? The job?

HARPER Not the job.

JOE I said I need more time.

HARPER Not the job!

JOE Mr. Cohn, I talked to him on the phone, he said I had to hurry . . .

HARPER Not the . . .

JOE But I can't get you to talk sensibly about anything so . . .

HARPER SHUT UP!

JOE Then what?

HARPER Stick to the subject.

JOE I don't know what that is. You have something you want to ask me? Ask me. Go.

HARPER I . . . can't. I'm scared of you.

JOE I'm tired, I'm going to bed.

HARPER Tell me without making me ask. Please.

JOE This is crazy, I'm not . . .

HARPER When you come through the door at night your face is never exactly the way I remembered it. I get surprised by something . . . mean and hard about the way you look. Even the weight of you in the bed at night, the way you breathe in your sleep seems unfamiliar.

You terrify me.

JOE [*cold*] I know who you are.

HARPER Yes. I'm the enemy. That's easy. That doesn't change.

You think you're the only one who hates sex; I do; I hate it with you; I do. I dream that you batter away at me till all my joints come apart, like wax, and I fall into pieces. It's like a punishment. It was wrong of me to marry you. I knew you . . . [*She stops herself.*] It's a sin, and it's killing us both.

JOE I can always tell when you've taken pills because it makes you red-faced and sweaty and frankly that's very often why I don't want to . . .

HARPER Because . . .

JOE Well, you aren't pretty. Not like this.

HARPER I have something to ask you.

JOE Then ASK! ASK! What in hell are you . . .

HARPER Are you a homo? [*Pause*]

Are you? If you try to walk out right now I'll put your dinner back in the oven and turn it up so high the whole building will fill with smoke and everyone in it will asphyxiate. So help me God I will.

Now answer the question.

JOE What if I . . .

[*Small pause.*]

HARPER Then tell me, please. And we'll see.

JOE No. I'm not.

I don't see what difference it makes.

LOUIS Jews don't have any clear textual guide to the afterlife; even that it exists. I don't think much about it. I see it as a perpetual rainy Thursday afternoon in March. Dead leaves.

PRIOR Eeeugh. Very Greco-Roman.[5]

LOUIS Well, for us it's not the verdict that counts, it's the act of judgment. That's why I could never be a lawyer. In court all that matters is the verdict.

5. An adjective apparently intended to evoke stoicism and austerity.

PRIOR You could never be a lawyer because you are oversexed. You're too distracted.

LOUIS Not distracted; *ab*stracted. I'm trying to make a point:

PRIOR Namely:

LOUIS It's the judge in his or her chambers, weighing, books open, pondering the evidence, ranging freely over categories: good, evil, innocent, guilty; the judge in the chamber of circumspection, not the judge on the bench with the gavel. The shaping of the law, not its execution.

PRIOR The point, dear, the point . . .

LOUIS That it should be the questions and shape of a life, its total complexity gathered, arranged, and considered, which matters in the end, not some stamp of salvation or damnation which disperses all the complexity in some unsatisfying little decision—the balancing of the scales . . .

PRIOR I like this; very zen; it's . . . reassuringly incomprehensible and useless. We who are about to die thank you.[6]

LOUIS You are not about to die.

PRIOR It's not going well, really . . . two new lesions. My leg hurts. There's protein in my urine, the doctor says, but who knows what the fuck that portends. Anyway it shouldn't be there, the protein. My butt is chapped from diarrhea and yesterday I shat blood.

LOUIS I really hate this. You don't tell me . . .

PRIOR You get too upset, I wind up comforting you. It's easier . . .

LOUIS Oh thanks.

PRIOR If it's bad I'll tell you.

LOUIS Shitting blood sounds bad to me.

PRIOR And I'm telling you.

LOUIS And I'm handling it.

PRIOR Tell me some more about justice.

LOUIS I *am* handling it.

PRIOR Well Louis you win Trooper of the Month.

[LOUIS *starts to cry.*]

PRIOR I take it back. You aren't Trooper of the Month.
This isn't working . . .
Tell me some more about justice.

LOUIS You are not about to die.

PRIOR Justice . . .

LOUIS . . . is an immensity, a confusing vastness. Justice is God.
Prior?

PRIOR Hmmm?

LOUIS You love me.

PRIOR Yes.

LOUIS What if I walked out on this?
Would you hate me forever?

[PRIOR *kisses* LOUIS *on the forehead.*]

PRIOR Yes.

6. An echo of "We who are about to die greet you," popularly believed to be the salute of Roman gladiators to the emperor. *Zen:* exhibiting the calm associated with this meditative Japanese school of Buddhism.

JOE I think we ought to pray. Ask God for help. Ask him together . . .

HARPER God won't talk to me. I have to make up people to talk to me.

JOE You have to keep asking.

HARPER I forgot the question.

Oh yeah. God, is my husband a . . .

JOE [*scary*] Stop it. Stop it. I'm warning you.

Does it make any difference? That I might be one thing deep within, no matter how wrong or ugly that thing is, so long as I have fought, with everything I have, to kill it. What do you want from me? What do you want from me, Harper? More than that? For God's sake, there's nothing left, I'm a shell. There's nothing left to kill.

As long as my behavior is what I know it has to be. Decent. Correct. That alone in the eyes of God.

HARPER No, no, not that, that's Utah talk, Mormon talk, I hate it, Joe, tell me, say it . . .

JOE All I will say is that I am a very good man who has worked very hard to become good and you want to destroy that. You want to destroy me, but I am not going to let you do that.

[*Pause.*]

HARPER I'm going to have a baby.

JOE Liar.

HARPER You liar.

A baby born addicted to pills. A baby who does not dream but who hallucinates, who stares up at us with big mirror eyes and who does not know who we are.

[*Pause.*]

JOE Are you really . . .

HARPER No. Yes. No. Yes. Get away from me.

Now we both have a secret.

PRIOR One of my ancestors was a ship's captain who made money bringing whale oil to Europe and returning with immigrants—Irish mostly, packed in tight, so many dollars per head. The last ship he captained foundered off the coast of Nova Scotia in a winter tempest and sank to the bottom. He went down with the ship—*la Grande Geste*[7]—but his crew took seventy women and kids in the ship's only longboat, this big, open rowboat, and when the weather got too rough, and they thought the boat was overcrowded, the crew started lifting people up and hurling them into the sea. Until they got the ballast right. They walked up and down the longboat, eyes to the waterline, and when the boat rode low in the water they'd grab the nearest passenger and throw them into the sea. The boat was leaky, see; seventy people; they arrived in Halifax with nine people on board.

LOUIS Jesus.

PRIOR I think about that story a lot now. People in a boat, waiting, terrified, while implacable, unsmiling men, irresistibly strong, seize . . . maybe the person next to you, maybe you, and with no warning at all, with time only for a quick intake of air you are pitched into freezing, turbulent water and salt and darkness to drown.

7. The grand gesture (French); by tradition, the captain is the last to leave a sinking ship.

I like your cosmology, baby. While time is running out I find myself drawn to anything that's suspended, that lacks an ending—but it seems to me that it lets you off scot-free.

LOUIS What do you mean?

PRIOR No judgment, no guilt or responsibility.

LOUIS For me.

PRIOR For anyone. It was an editorial "you."

LOUIS Please get better. Please.

Please don't get any sicker.

Scene 9

[*Third week in November.* ROY *and* HENRY, *his doctor, in* HENRY's *office.*]

HENRY Nobody knows what causes it. And nobody knows how to cure it. The best theory is that we blame a retrovirus, the Human Immunodeficiency Virus. Its presence is made known to us by the useless antibodies which appear in reaction to its entrance into the bloodstream through a cut, or an orifice. The antibodies are powerless to protect the body against it. Why, we don't know. The body's immune system ceases to function. Sometimes the body even attacks itself. At any rate it's left open to a whole horror house of infections from microbes which it usually defends against.

Like Kaposi's sarcomas. These lesions. Or your throat problem. Or the glands.

We think it may also be able to slip past the blood-brain barrier[8] into the brain. Which is of course very bad news.

And it's fatal in we don't know what percent of people with suppressed immune responses.

[*Pause.*]

ROY This is very interesting, Mr. Wizard,[9] but why the fuck are you telling me this?

[*Pause.*]

HENRY Well, I have just removed one of three lesions which biopsy results will probably tell us is a Kaposi's sarcoma lesion. And you have a pronounced swelling of glands in your neck, groin, and armpits—lymphadenopathy[1] is another sign. And you have oral candidiasis[2] and maybe a little more fungus under the fingernails of two digits on your right hand. So that's why . . .

ROY This disease . . .

HENRY Syndrome.

ROY Whatever. It afflicts mostly homosexuals and drug addicts.

HENRY Mostly. Hemophiliacs are also at risk.

ROY Homosexuals and drug addicts. So why are you implying that I . . . [*Pause*] What are you implying, Henry?

HENRY I don't . . .

ROY I'm not a drug addict.

8. The physical structure and system of cellular transport mechanisms that prevent harmful chemicals in the bloodstream from reaching the brain.

9. The host of *Watch Mr. Wizard* (1951–65), a television show that explained science to children (revived on cable as *Mr. Wizard's World*, 1983–90).

1. An abnormal enlargement of the lymph nodes.

2. An infection of the mouth by the yeastlike fungus *Candida albicans*.

HENRY Oh come on Roy.

ROY What, what, come on Roy what? Do you think I'm a junkie, Henry, do you see tracks?

HENRY This is absurd.

ROY Say it.

HENRY Say what?

ROY Say, "Roy Cohn, you are a . . ."

HENRY Roy.

ROY "You are a . . ." Go on. Not "Roy Cohn you are a drug fiend." "Roy Marcus Cohn, you are a . . ."

Go on, Henry, it starts with an "H."

HENRY Oh I'm not going to . . .

ROY *With an "H,"* Henry, and it isn't "Hemophiliac." Come on . . .

HENRY What are you doing, Roy?

ROY No, say it. I mean it. Say: "Roy Cohn, you are a homosexual." [*Pause*]

And I will proceed, systematically, to destroy your reputation and your practice and your career in New York State, Henry. Which you know I can do.

[*Pause.*]

HENRY Roy, you have been seeing me since 1958. Apart from the facelifts I have treated you for everything from syphilis . . .

ROY From a whore in Dallas.

HENRY From syphilis to venereal warts. In your rectum. Which you may have gotten from a whore in Dallas, but it wasn't a female whore.

[*Pause.*]

ROY So say it.

HENRY Roy Cohn, you are . . .

You have had sex with men, many many times, Roy, and one of them, or any number of them, has made you very sick. You have AIDS.[3]

ROY AIDS.

Your problem, Henry, is that you are hung up on words, on labels, that you believe they mean what they seem to mean. AIDS. Homosexual. Gay. Lesbian. You think these are names that tell you who someone sleeps with, but they don't tell you that.

HENRY No?

ROY No. Like all labels they tell you one thing and one thing only: where does an individual so identified fit in the food chain, in the pecking order? Not ideology, or sexual taste, but something much simpler: clout. Not who I fuck or who fucks me, but who will pick up the phone when I call, who owes me favors. This is what a label refers to. Now to someone who does not understand this, homosexual is what I am because I have sex with men. But really this is wrong. Homosexuals are not men who sleep with other men. Homosexuals are men who in fifteen years of trying cannot get a pissant antidiscrimination bill through City Council. Homosexuals are men who know nobody and who nobody knows. Who have zero clout. Does this sound like me, Henry?

HENRY No.

ROY No. I have clout. A lot. I can pick up this phone, punch fifteen numbers, and you know who will be on the other end in under five minutes, Henry?

3. Acquired immune deficiency syndrome was first recognized in 1981.

HENRY The President.

ROY Even better, Henry. His wife

HENRY I'm impressed.

ROY I don't want you to be impressed. I want you to understand. This is not sophistry. And this is not hypocrisy. This is reality. I have sex with men. But unlike nearly every other man of whom this is true, I bring the guy I'm screwing to the White House and President Reagan smiles at us and shakes his hand. Because *what* I am is defined entirely by *who* I am. Roy Cohn is not a homosexual. Roy Cohn is a heterosexual man, Henry, who fucks around with guys.

HENRY OK, Roy.

ROY And what is my diagnosis, Henry?

HENRY You have AIDS, Roy.

ROY No, Henry, no. AIDS is what homosexuals have. I have liver cancer.

[*Pause.*]

HENRY Well, whatever the fuck you have, Roy, it's very serious, and I haven't got a damn thing for you. The NIH in Bethesda has a new drug called AZT[4] with a two-year waiting list that not even I can get you onto. So get on the phone, Roy, and dial the fifteen numbers, and tell the First Lady you need in on an experimental treatment for liver cancer, because you can call it any damn thing you want, Roy, but what it boils down to is very bad news.

Act 2: In Vitro

(*December 1985–January 1986*)

Scene 1

[*Night, the third week in December.* PRIOR *alone on the floor of his bedroom; he is much worse.*]

PRIOR Louis, Louis, please wake up, oh God.

[*Louis runs in.*]

PRIOR I think something horrible is wrong with me I can't breathe . . .

LOUIS [*starting to exit*] I'm calling the ambulance.

PRIOR No, wait, I . . .

LOUIS *Wait?* Are you fucking crazy? Oh God you're on fire, your head is on fire.

PRIOR It hurts, it hurts . . .

LOUIS I'm calling the ambulance.

PRIOR I don't want to go to the hospital, I don't want to go to the hospital please let me lie here, just . . .

LOUIS No, no, God, Prior, stand up . . .

PRIOR DON'T TOUCH MY LEG!

LOUIS We have to . . . oh God this is so crazy.

PRIOR I'll be OK if I just lie here Lou, really, if I can only sleep a little . . .

4. Azidothymidine or zidovudine, an antiviral drug that was the first approved (in 1987) to treat AIDS; that the government accelerate the testing process required for its approval was a major demand of early AIDS activists. *NIH*: the National Institutes of Health, the federal agency primarily responsible for supporting and conducting medical research; its headquarters are in Bethesda, Maryland.

[LOUIS *exits.*]

PRIOR Louis?

NO! NO! Don't call, you'll send me there and I won't come back, please, please Louis I'm begging, baby, please . . .

[*Screams.*] *LOUIS!!*

LOUIS [*from off; hysterical*] WILL YOU SHUT THE FUCK UP!

PRIOR [*trying to stand*] Aaah. I have . . . to go to the bathroom. Wait. Wait, just . . . oh. Oh God. [*He shits himself.*]

LOUIS [*Entering*] Prior? They'll be here in . . .

Oh my God.

PRIOR I'm sorry, I'm sorry.

LOUIS What did . . . ? What?

PRIOR I had an accident.

[*Louis goes to him.*]

LOUIS This is blood.

PRIOR Maybe you shouldn't touch it . . . me. . . . I . . . [*He faints.*]

LOUIS [*quietly*] Oh help. Oh help. Oh God oh God oh God help me I can't I can't I can't.

Scene 2

[*Same night.* HARPER *is sitting at home, all alone, with no lights on. We can bare ly see her.* JOE *enters, but he doesn't turn on the lights.*]

JOE Why are you sitting in the dark? Turn on the light.

HARPER *No.* I heard the sounds in the bedroom again. I know someone was in there.

JOE No one was.

HARPER Maybe actually in the bed, under the covers with a knife.

Oh, boy. Joe. I, um, I'm thinking of going away. By which I mean: I think I'm going off again. You . . . you know what I mean?

JOE Please don't. Stay. We can fix it. I pray for that. This is my fault, but I can correct it. You have to try too . . .

[*He turns on the light. She turns it off again.*]

HARPER When you pray, what do you pray for?

JOE I pray for God to crush me, break me up into little pieces and start all over again.

HARPER Oh. Please. Don't pray for that.

JOE I had a book of Bible stories when I was a kid. There was a picture I'd look at twenty times every day: Jacob wrestles with the angel.[5] I don't really remember the story, or why the wrestling—just the picture. Jacob is young and very strong. The angel is . . . a beautiful man, with golden hair and wings, of course. I still dream about it. Many nights. I'm . . . It's me. In that struggle. Fierce, and unfair. The angel is not human, and it holds nothing back, so how could anyone human win, what kind of a fight is that? It's not just. Losing means your soul thrown down in the dust, your heart torn out from God's. But you can't not lose.

HARPER In the whole entire world, you are the only person, the only person I love or have ever loved. And I love you terribly. Terribly. That's what's so

5. See Genesis 32.24–30.

awfully, irreducibly real. I can make up anything but I can't dream that away.

JOE Are you . . . are you really going to have a baby?

HARPER It's my time, and there's no blood. I don't really know. I suppose it wouldn't be a great thing. Maybe I'm just not bleeding because I take too many pills. Maybe I'll give birth to a pill. That would give a new meaning to pill-popping, huh?

I think you should go to Washington. Alone. Change, like you said.

JOE I'm not going to leave you, Harper.

HARPER Well maybe not. But I'm going to leave you.

Scene 3

[*One* AM, *the next morning.* LOUIS *and a nurse,* EMILY, *are sitting in* PRIOR*'s room in the hospital.*]

EMILY He'll be all right now.

LOUIS No he won't.

EMILY No. I guess not. I gave him something that makes him sleep.

LOUIS Deep asleep?

EMILY Orbiting the moons of Jupiter.

LOUIS A good place to be.

EMILY Anyplace better than here. You his . . . uh?

LOUIS Yes. I'm his uh.

EMILY This must be hell for you.

LOUIS It is. Hell. The After Life. Which is not at all like a rainy afternoon in March, by the way, Prior. A lot more vivid than I'd expected. Dead leaves, but the crunchy kind. Sharp, dry air. The kind of long, luxurious dying feeling that breaks your heart.

EMILY Yeah, well we all get to break our hearts on this one.

He seems like a nice guy. Cute.

LOUIS Not like this.

Yes, he is. Was. Whatever.

EMILY Weird name. Prior Walter. Like, "The Walter before this one."

LOUIS Lots of Walters before this one. Prior is an old old family name in an old old family. The Walters go back to the Mayflower and beyond. Back to the Norman Conquest. He says there's a Prior Walter stitched into the Bayeux tapestry.[6]

EMILY Is that impressive?

LOUIS Well, it's old. Very old. Which in some circles equals impressive.

EMILY Not in my circle. What's the name of the tapestry?

LOUIS The Bayeux tapestry. Embroidered by La Reine Mathilde.[7]

EMILY I'll tell my mother. She embroiders. Drives me nuts.

LOUIS Manual therapy for anxious hands.

EMILY Maybe you should try it.

6. An embroidery, 230 feet long, that chronicles the invasion and conquest of England by the Normans in 1066 (preserved in the Bayeux Museum in northern France). *Mayflower:* the ship that in 1620 brought the English founders of the Plymouth Colony to Massachusetts.

7. Queen Matilda (French; ca. 1031–1083), the wife of William the Conqueror (ca. 1028–1087); the tradition that attributes the creation of the Bayeux tapestry to her has little foundation.

LOUIS Mathilde stitched while William the Conqueror was off to war. She was capable of . . . more than loyalty. Devotion.

She waited for him, she stitched for years. And if he had come back broken and defeated from war, she would have loved him even more. And if he had returned mutilated, ugly, full of infection and horror, she would still have loved him; fed by pity, by a sharing of pain, she would love him even more, and even more, and she would never, never have prayed to God, please let him die if he can't return to me whole and healthy and able to live a normal life. . . . If he had died, she would have buried her heart with him.

So what the fuck is the matter with me? [*Little pause*]

Will he sleep through the night?

EMILY At least.

LOUIS I'm going.

EMILY It's one AM. Where do you have to go at . . .

LOUIS I know what time it is. A walk. Night air, good for the . . . The park.

EMILY Be careful.

LOUIS Yeah. Danger.

Tell him, if he wakes up and you're still on, tell him goodbye, tell him I had to go.

Scene 4

[*An hour later. Split scene:* JOE *and* ROY *in a fancy (straight) bar;* LOUIS *and a* MAN *in the Rambles*[8] *in Central Park.* JOE *and* ROY *are sitting at the bar; the place is brightly lit.* JOE *has a plate of food in front of him but he isn't eating.* ROY *occasionally reaches over the table and forks small bites off* JOE*'s plate.* ROY *is drinking heavily,* JOE *not at all.* LOUIS *and the* MAN *are eyeing each other, each alternating interest and indifference.*]

JOE The pills were something she started when she miscarried or . . . no, she took some before that. She had a really bad time at home, when she was a kid, her home was really bad. I think a lot of drinking and physical stuff. She doesn't talk about that, instead she talks about . . . the sky falling down, people with knives hiding under sofas. Monsters. Mormons. Everyone thinks Mormons don't come from homes like that, we aren't supposed to behave that way, but we do. It's not lying, or being two-faced. Everyone tries very hard to live up to God's strictures, which are very . . . um . . .

ROY Strict.

JOE I shouldn't be bothering you with this.

ROY No, please. Heart to heart. Want another. . . . What is that, seltzer?[9]

JOE The failure to measure up hits people very hard. From such a strong desire to be good they feel very far from goodness when they fail.

What scares me is that maybe what I really love in her is the part of her that's farthest from the light, from God's love; maybe I was drawn to that in the first place. And I'm keeping it alive because I need it.

ROY Why would you need it?

JOE There are things. . . . I don't know how well we know ourselves. I mean, what if? I know I married her because she . . . because I loved it that she

8. A wooded section in New York's Central Park, designed as a wild garden; for much of the 20th century, the Ramble was notorious as an area for homosexual cruising.

9. Observant Mormons do not drink alcohol or caffeine (or smoke).

was always wrong, always doing something wrong, like one step out of step. In Salt Lake City that stands out. I never stood out, on the outside, but inside, it was hard for me. To pass.

ROY Pass?

JOE Yeah.

ROY Pass as what?

JOE Oh. Well. . . . As someone cheerful and strong. Those who love God with an open heart unclouded by secrets and struggles are cheerful; God's easy simple love for them shows in how strong and happy they are. The saints.[1]

ROY But you had secrets? Secret struggles . . .

JOE I wanted to be one of the elect, one of the Blessed. You feel you ought to be, that the blemishes are yours by choice, which of course they aren't. Harper's sorrow, that really deep sorrow, she didn't choose that. But it's there.

ROY You didn't put it there.

JOE No.

ROY You sound like you think you did.

JOE I am responsible for her.

ROY Because she's your wife.

JOE That. And I do love her.

ROY Whatever. She's your wife. And so there are obligations. To her. But also to yourself.

JOE She'd fall apart in Washington.

ROY Then let her stay here.

JOE She'll fall apart if I leave her.

ROY Then bring her to Washington.

JOE I just can't, Roy. She needs me.

ROY Listen, Joe. I'm the best divorce lawyer in the business.

[*Little pause.*]

JOE Can't Washington wait?

ROY You do what you need to do, Joe. What *you* need. *You*. Let her life go where it wants to go. You'll both be better for that. *Somebody* should get what they want.

MAN What do you want?

LOUIS I want you to fuck me, hurt me, make me bleed.

MAN I want to.

LOUIS Yeah?

MAN I want to hurt you.

LOUIS Fuck me.

MAN Yeah?

LOUIS Hard.

MAN Yeah? You been a bad boy?

[*Pause.* LOUIS *laughs, softly.*]

LOUIS Very bad. Very bad.

MAN You need to be punished, boy?

LOUIS Yes. I do

1. That is, Mormons, members of what is officially called the Church of Jesus Christ of Latter-day Saints (the LDS Church).

MAN Yes what?

[*Little pause.*]

LOUIS Um, I . . .

MAN Yes *what*, boy?

LOUIS Oh. Yes sir.

MAN I want you to take me to your place, boy.

LOUIS No, I can't do that.

MAN No *what?*

LOUIS No sir, I can't, I . . .
I don't live alone, sir.

MAN Your lover know you're out with a man tonight, boy?

LOUIS No sir, he . . .
My lover doesn't know.

MAN Your lover know you . . .

LOUIS Let's change the subject, OK? Can we go to your place?

MAN I live with my parents.

LOUIS Oh.

ROY Everyone who makes it in this world makes it because somebody older and more powerful takes an interest. The most precious asset in life, I think, is the ability to be a good son. You have that, Joe. Somebody who can be a good son to a father who pushes them farther than they would otherwise go. I've had many fathers, I owe my life to them, powerful, powerful men. Walter Winchell, Edgar Hoover. Joe McCarthy most of all.[2] He valued me because I am a good lawyer, but he loved me because I was and am a good son. He was a very difficult man, very guarded and cagey; I brought out something tender in him. He would have died for me. And me for him. Does this embarrass you?

JOE I had a hard time with my father.

ROY Well sometimes that's the way. Then you have to find other fathers, substitutes, I don't know. The father-son relationship is central to life. Women are for birth, beginning, but the father is continuance. The son offers the father his life as a vessel for carrying forth his father's dream. Your father's living?

JOE Um, dead.

ROY He was . . . what? A difficult man?

JOE He was in the military. He could be very unfair. And cold.

ROY But he loved you.

JOE I don't know.

2. The historical Cohn, through his work on the Permanent Subcommittee on Investigations, is most closely identified with McCarthy (1908–1957), who as senator from Wisconsin (1947–57) gained national attention with his sensational and unsubstantiated claims that the State Department and other parts of the government had been infiltrated by Communists. Winchell (1897–1972) wrote a hugely popular gossip column (begun in 1924); he lost influence after he allied himself with McCarthy's anticommunist witch hunt. Hoover (1895–1972), early in his career (during the first Red Scare, 1919–20), was placed in charge of investigating suspected alien radicals; in 1924, he became director of the Bureau of Investigation (renamed the Federal Bureau of Investigation in 1935), amassing enormous and virtually unchecked power during his forty-eight years in that position. A believer in a worldwide communist conspiracy, he too was an ally of McCarthy; rumors that he was a homosexual circulated for decades.

ROY No, no, Joe, he did, I know this. Sometimes a father's love has to be very, very hard, unfair even, cold to make his son grow strong in a world like this. This isn't a good world.

MAN Here, then.
LOUIS I. . . . Do you have a rubber?
MAN I don't use rubbers.
LOUIS You should. [*He takes one from his coat pocket.*] Here.
MAN I don't use them.
LOUIS Forget it, then. [*He starts to leave.*]
MAN No, wait.
Put it on me. Boy.
LOUIS Forget it, I have to get back. Home. I must be going crazy.
MAN Oh come on please he won't find out.
LOUIS It's cold. Too cold.
MAN It's never too cold, let me warm you up. Please?
[*They begin to fuck.*]
MAN Relax.
LOUIS [*a small laugh*] Not a chance.
MAN It . . .
LOUIS What?
MAN I think it broke. The rubber. You want me to keep going? [*Little pause*] Pull out? Should I . . .
LOUIS Keep going.
Infect me.
I don't care. I don't care.
[*Pause. The* MAN *pulls out.*]
MAN I . . . um, look, I'm sorry, but I think I want to go.
LOUIS Yeah.
Give my best to mom and dad.
[*The* MAN *slaps him.*]
LOUIS Ow!
[*They stare at each other.*]
LOUIS It was a joke.
[*The* MAN *leaves.*]

ROY How long have we known each other?
JOE Since 1980.
ROY Right. A long time. I feel close to you, Joe. Do I advise you well?
JOE You've been an incredible friend, Roy, I . . .
ROY I want to be family. Familia, as my Italian friends call it. La Familia. A lovely word. It's important for me to help you, like I was helped.
JOE I owe practically everything to you, Roy.
ROY I'm dying, Joe. Cancer.
JOE Oh my God.
ROY Please. Let me finish.
Few people know this and I'm telling you this only because . . . I'm not afraid of death. What can death bring that I haven't faced? I've lived; life is the worst. [*Gently mocking himself*] Listen to me, I'm a philosopher.

Joe. You must do this. You must must must. Love; that's a trap. Responsibility; that's a trap too. Like a father to a son I tell you this: Life is full of horror; nobody escapes, nobody; save yourself. Whatever pulls on you, whatever needs from you, threatens you. Don't be afraid; people are so afraid; don't be afraid to live in the raw wind, naked, alone. . . . Learn at least this: What you are capable of. Let nothing stand in your way.

Scene 5

[*Three days later.* PRIOR *and* BELIZE *in* PRIOR*'s hospital room.* PRIOR *is very sick but improving.* BELIZE *has just arrived.*]

PRIOR Miss Thing.

BELIZE Ma cherie bichette.[3]

PRIOR Stella.

BELIZE Stella for star.[4] Let me see. [*Scrutinizing* PRIOR] You look like shit, why yes indeed you do, comme la merde![5]

PRIOR Merci.[6]

BELIZE [*taking little plastic bottles from his bag, handing them to* PRIOR] Not to despair, Belle Reeve.[7] Lookie! Magic goop!

PRIOR [*opening a bottle, sniffing*] Pooh! What kinda crap is that?

BELIZE Beats me. Let's rub it on your poor blistered body and see what it does.

PRIOR This is not Western medicine, these bottles . . .

BELIZE Voodoo cream. From the botanica 'round the block.

PRIOR And you a registered nurse.

BELIZE [*sniffing it*] Beeswax and cheap perfume. Cut with Jergen's Lotion. Full of good vibes and love from some little black Cubana witch in Miami.

PRIOR Get that trash away from me, I am immune-suppressed.

BELIZE I *am* a health professional. I *know* what I'm doing.

PRIOR It stinks. Any word from Louis?

[*Pause.* BELIZE *starts giving* PRIOR *a gentle massage.*]

PRIOR Gone.

BELIZE He'll be back. I know the type. Likes to keep a girl on edge.

PRIOR It's been . . .

[*Pause.*]

BELIZE [*trying to jog his memory*] How long?

PRIOR I don't remember.

BELIZE How long have you been here?

PRIOR [*getting suddenly upset*] I don't remember, I don't give a fuck. I want Louis. I want my fucking boyfriend, where the fuck is he? I'm dying, I'm dying, where's Louis?

BELIZE Shhhh, shhh . . .

PRIOR This is a very strange drug, this drug. Emotional lability, for starters.

BELIZE Save a tab or two for me.

3. My dear little darling (French).
4. A line spoken by Blanche DuBois to her sister Stella in Tennessee Williams's *A Streetcar Named Desire* (1947). (*Stella* means "star" in Latin.)
5. Like shit! (French).
6. Thanks (French).
7. In *A Streetcar Named Desire*, Belle Reve (Beautiful Dream; French) is the name of Blanche and Stella's ancestral home.

PRIOR Oh no, not this drug, ce n'est pas pour la joyeux noël et la bonne année, this drug she is serious poisonous chemistry, ma pauvre bichette.[8]

And not just disorienting. I hear things. Voices.

BELIZE Voices.

PRIOR A voice.

BELIZE Saying what?

[*Pause.*]

PRIOR I'm not supposed to tell.

BELIZE You better tell the doctor. Or I will.

PRIOR No no don't. Please. I want the voice; it's wonderful. It's all that's keeping me alive. I don't want to talk to some intern about it.

You know what happens? When I hear it, I get hard.

BELIZE Oh my.

PRIOR Comme ça.[9] [*He uses his arm to demonstrate.*] And you know I am slow to rise.

BELIZE My jaw aches at the memory.

PRIOR And would you deny me this little solace—betray my concupiscence to Florence Nightingale's storm troopers?[1]

BELIZE Perish the thought, ma bébé.[2]

PRIOR They'd change the drug just to spoil the fun.

BELIZE You and your boner can depend on me.

PRIOR Je t'adore, ma belle nègre.[3]

BELIZE All this girl-talk shit is politically incorrect, you know. We should have dropped it back when we gave up drag.

PRIOR I'm sick, I get to be politically incorrect if it makes me feel better. You sound like Lou. [*Little pause*]

Well, at least I have the satisfaction of knowing he's in anguish somewhere. I loved his anguish. Watching him stick his head up his asshole and eat his guts out over some relatively minor moral conundrum—it was the best show in town. But Mother warned me: if they get overwhelmed by the little things . . .

BELIZE They'll be belly-up bustville when something big comes along.

PRIOR Mother warned me.

BELIZE And they do come along.

PRIOR But I didn't listen.

BELIZE No. [*Doing Hepburn*][4] Men are beasts.

PRIOR [*also Hepburn*] The absolute lowest.

BELIZE I have to go. If I want to spend my whole lonely life looking after white people I can get underpaid to do it.

PRIOR You're just a Christian martyr.

BELIZE Whatever happens, baby, I will be here for you.

PRIOR Je t'aime.[5]

8. It doesn't give you a merry Christmas and a happy New Year . . . my poor little darling (French).

9. Like that (French).

1. That is, nurses; Nightingale (1820–1910), an English reformer whose work organizing a unit of nurses during the Crimean War won her international fame, is credited with founding modern nursing.

2. My baby, my child (French).

3. I adore you, my beautiful Negro (French).

4. That is, the American stage and film star Katharine Hepburn (1907–2003), who often portrayed independent women.

5. I love you (French).

BELIZE Je t'aime. Don't go crazy on me, girlfriend, I already got enough crazy queens for one lifetime. For two. I can't be bothering with dementia.

PRIOR I promise.

BELIZE [*touching him; softly*] Ouch.

PRIOR Ouch. Indeed.

BELIZE Why'd they have to pick on you?
And eat more, girlfriend, you really do look like shit.

[BELIZE *leaves.*]

PRIOR [*after waiting a beat*] He's gone.
Are you still . . .

VOICE I can't stay. I will return.

PRIOR Are you one of those "Follow me to the other side" voices?

VOICE No. I am no nightbird. I am a messenger . . .

PRIOR You have a beautiful voice, it sounds . . . like a viola, like a perfectly tuned, tight string, balanced, the truth. . . . Stay with me.

VOICE Not now. Soon I will return, I will reveal myself to you; I am glorious, glorious; my heart, my countenance, and my message. You must prepare.

PRIOR For what? I don't want to . . .

VOICE No death, no:
A marvelous work and a wonder[6] we undertake, an edifice awry we sink plumb and straighten, a great Lie we abolish, a great error correct, with the rule, sword, and broom of Truth!

PRIOR What are you talking about, I . . .

VOICE

I am on my way; when I am manifest, our Work begins:
Prepare for the parting of the air,
The breath, the ascent,
Glory to . . .

Scene 6

[*The second week of January.* MARTIN, ROY, *and* JOE *in a fancy Manhattan restaurant.*]

MARTIN It's a revolution in Washington, Joe. We have a new agenda and finally a real leader. They got back the Senate[7] but we have the courts. By the nineties the Supreme Court will be block-solid Republican appointees, and the Federal bench—Republican judges like land mines, everywhere, everywhere they turn. Affirmative action? Take it to court. Boom! Land mine. And we'll get our way on just about everything: abortion, defense, Central America, family values, a live investment climate. We have the White House locked till the year 2000. And beyond. A permanent fix on the Oval Office? It's possible. By '92 we'll get the Senate back, and in ten years the South is going to give us the House. It's really the end of Liberalism. The end of New Deal Socialism.[8] The end of ipso

6. See Isaiah 29.14.
7. Majority control of the U.S. Senate shifted to the Democrats in the 1986 election (Republicans gained majorities in both the House and the Senate in 1994).
8. That is, the government programs promoting economic and social welfare (and thus labeled "socialist" by opponents) of the type first instituted during the New Deal, the name given by Franklin Delano Roosevelt (1882–1945; 32nd president, 1933–45) to his domestic reform initiatives. These programs include Social Security, banking reform, and the minimum wage.

facto secular humanism.[9] The dawning of a genuinely American political personality. Modeled on Ronald Wilson Reagan.

JOE It sounds great, Mr. Heller.

MARTIN Martin. And Justice is the hub. Especially since Ed Meese took over. He doesn't specialize in Fine Points of the Law. He's a flatfoot, a cop. He reminds me of Teddy Roosevelt.[1]

JOE I can't wait to meet him.

MARTIN Too bad, Joe, he's been dead for sixty years!

[*There is a little awkwardness.* JOE *doesn't respond.*]

MARTIN Teddy Roosevelt. You said you wanted to. . . . Little joke. It reminds me of the story about the . . .

ROY [*smiling, but nasty*] Aw shut the fuck up Martin.

[*To* JOE] You see that? Mr. Heller here is one of the mighty, Joseph, in D.C. he sitteth on the right hand of the man who sitteth on the right hand of The Man.[2] And yet I can say "shut the fuck up" and he will take no offense. Loyalty. He . . .

Martin?

MARTIN Yes, Roy?

ROY Rub my back.

MARTIN Roy . . .

ROY No no really, a sore spot, I get them all the time now, these . . . Rub it for me darling, would you do that for me?

[MARTIN *rubs* ROY*'s back. They both look at* JOE.]

ROY [*to* JOE] How do you think a handful of Bolsheviks turned St. Petersburg into Leningrad in one afternoon? *Comrades.* Who do for each other. Marx and Engels. Lenin and Trotsky. Josef Stalin and Franklin Delano Roosevelt.[3]

[MARTIN *laughs.*]

ROY *Comrades*, right Martin?

MARTIN This man, Joe, is a Saint of the Right.

JOE I know, Mr. Heller, I . . .

ROY And you see what I mean, Martin? He's special, right?

MARTIN Don't embarrass him, Roy.

ROY Gravity, decency, smarts! His strength is as the strength of ten because his heart is pure![4] *And* he's a Royboy, one hundred percent.

9. A philosophy that locates value in human reason and interests, rejecting religion and the supernatural.

1. Theodore Roosevelt (1858–1919), twenty-sixth president of the United States (1901–09); between 1895 and 1897, he served as president of the New York City Board of Police Commissioners.

2. Compare Colossians 3.1 ("Christ sitteth on the right hand of God").

3. That is, symbiosis—even between supposed adversaries—is the key to success. The German political philosopher Karl Marx (1818–1883) and the German socialist Friedrich Engels (1820–1895) co-wrote the *Manifesto of the Communist Party* (1848); the Russian revolutionaries Vladimir Lenin (1870–1924) and Leon Trotsky (1879–1940) led the Bolshevik faction of socialists that triumphed in the October Revolution of 1917 (Saint Petersburg, which was a focal point of revolutionary activity, had been given the less Germanic name Petrograd in 1914; it was renamed Leningrad after Lenin died, but its original name was restored in 1991); the dictator Joseph Stalin (1879–1953), who controlled the Soviet Union from Lenin's death until his own death, and President Roosevelt became allies in World War II. *Comrades:* form of address used among Communists.

4. Paraphrase of a couplet from "Sir Galahad" (1842), by Alfred, Lord Tennyson.

MARTIN We're on the move, Joe. On the move.

JOE Mr Heller, I . . .

MARTIN [*ending backrub*] We can't wait any longer for an answer.

[*Little pause.*]

JOE Oh. Um, I . . .

ROY Joe's a married man, Martin.

MARTIN Aha.

ROY With a wife. She doesn't care to go to D.C., and so Joe cannot go. And keeps us dangling. We've seen that kind of thing before, haven't we? These men and their wives.

MARTIN Oh yes. Beware.

JOE I really can't discuss this under . . .

MARTIN Then *don't* discuss. Say yes, Joe.

ROY Now.

MARTIN Say yes I will.

ROY Now.

Now. I'll hold my breath till you do, I'm turning blue waiting. . . . *Now*, goddammit!

MARTIN Roy, calm down, it's not . . .

ROY Aw, fuck it. [*He takes a letter from his jacket pocket, hands it to* JOE.] Read. Came today.

[JOE *reads the first paragraph, then looks up.*]

JOE Roy. This is . . . Roy, this is terrible.

ROY You're telling me.

A letter from the New York State Bar Association, Martin.

They're gonna try and disbar me.

MARTIN Oh my.

JOE Why?

ROY Why, Martin?

MARTIN Revenge.

ROY The whole Establishment. Their little rules. Because I know no rules. Because I don't see the Law as a dead and arbitrary collection of antiquated dictums, thou shall, thou shalt not, because, because I know the Law's a pliable, breathing, sweating . . . *organ*, because, because . . .

MARTIN Because he borrowed half a million from one of his clients.[5]

ROY Yeah, well, there's that.

MARTIN *And* he forgot to *return* it.

JOE Roy, that's . . . You borrowed money from a client?

ROY I'm deeply ashamed.

[*Little pause.*]

JOE [*very sympathetic*] Roy, you know how much I admire you. Well I mean I know you have unorthodox ways, but I'm sure you only did what you thought at the time you needed to do. And I have faith that . . .

ROY Not so damp, please. I'll deny it was a loan. She's got no paperwork. Can't prove a fucking thing.

[*Little pause.* MARTIN *studies the menu.*]

5. Cohn was in fact disbarred in 1986 for unethical conduct, which included borrowing $109,000 from a client and not repaying her.

JOE [*handing back the letter, more official in tone*] Roy I really appreciate your telling me this, and I'll do whatever I can to help.

ROY [*holding up a hand, then, carefully*] I'll tell you what you can do.

I'm about to be tried, Joe, by a jury that is not a jury of my peers. The disbarment committee: genteel gentleman Brahmin[6] lawyers, country-club men. I offend them, to these men . . . I'm what, Martin, some sort of filthy little Jewish troll?

MARTIN Oh well, I wouldn't go so far as . . .

ROY Oh well I would.

Very fancy lawyers, these disbarment committee lawyers, fancy lawyers with fancy corporate clients and complicated cases. Antitrust suits. Deregulation. Environmental control. Complex cases like these need Justice Department cooperation like flowers need the sun. Wouldn't you say that's an accurate assessment, Martin?

MARTIN I'm not here, Roy. I'm not hearing any of this.

ROY No. Of course not.

Without the light of the sun, Joe, these cases, and the fancy lawyers who represent them, will wither and die.

A well-placed friend, someone in the Justice Department, say, can turn off the sun. Cast a deep shadow on my behalf. Make them shiver in the cold. If they overstep. They would fear that.

[*Pause.*]

JOE Roy. I don't understand.

ROY You do.

[*Pause.*]

JOE You're not asking me to . . .

ROY Sssshhhh. Careful.

JOE [*a beat,*[7] *then*] Even if I said yes to the job, it would be illegal to interfere. With the hearings. It's unethical. No. I can't.

ROY Un-ethical.

Would you excuse us, Martin?

MARTIN Excuse you?

ROY Take a walk, Martin. For real.

[MARTIN *leaves.*]

ROY Un-ethical. Are you trying to embarrass me in front of my friend?

JOE Well it is unethical, I can't . . .

ROY Boy, you are really something. What the fuck do you think this is, Sunday School?

JOE No, but Roy this is . . .

ROY This is . . . this is gastric juices churning, this is enzymes and acids, this is intestinal is what this is, bowel movement and blood-red meat—this stinks, this is *politics*, Joe, the game of being alive. And you think you're. . . . What? Above that? Above alive is what? Dead! In the clouds! You're on earth, goddammit! Plant a foot, stay awhile.

I'm sick. They smell I'm weak. They want blood this time. I must have eyes in Justice. In Justice you will protect me.

6. That is, of high social standing (Brahmans are Hindus of the highest caste).

7. Pause (theater term).

JOE Why can't Mr. Heller . . .

ROY Grow up, Joe. The administration can't get involved.

JOE But I'd be part of the administration. The same as him.

ROY Not the same. Martin's Ed's man. And Ed's Reagan's man. So Martin's Reagan's man.

And you're mine. [*Little pause. He holds up the letter.*] This will never be. Understand me? [*He tears the letter up.*]

I'm gonna be a lawyer, Joe, I'm gonna be a lawyer, Joe, I'm gonna be a goddam motherfucking legally licensed member of the bar lawyer, just like my daddy was,[8] till my last bitter day on earth, Joseph, until the day I die.

[*Martin returns.*]

ROY Ah, Martin's back.

MARTIN So are we agreed?

ROY Joe?

[*Little pause.*]

JOE I will think about it.

[*To* ROY.] I will.

ROY Huh.

MARTIN It's the fear of what comes after the doing that makes the doing hard to do.

ROY Amen.

MARTIN But you can almost always live with the consequences.

Scene 7

[*That afternoon. On the granite steps outside the Hall of Justice, Brooklyn. It is cold and sunny. A Sabrett[9] wagon is selling hot dogs. Louis, in a shabby overcoat, is sitting on the steps contemplatively eating one. Joe enters with three hot dogs and a can of Coke.*]

JOE Can I . . . ?

LOUIS Oh sure. Sure. Crazy cold sun.

JOE [*sitting*] Have to make the best of it.

How's your friend?

LOUIS My . . . ? Oh. He's worse. My friend is worse.

JOE I'm sorry.

LOUIS Yeah, well. Thanks for asking. It's nice. You're nice. I can't believe you voted for Reagan.

JOE I hope he gets better.

LOUIS Reagan?

JOE Your friend.

LOUIS He won't. Neither will Reagan.

JOE Let's not talk politics, OK?

LOUIS [*pointing to* JOE's *lunch*] You're eating *three* of those?

JOE Well . . . I'm . . . hungry.

LOUIS They're really terrible for you. Full of rat-poo and beetle legs and wood shavings 'n' shit.

JOE Huh.

lbert Cohn (1885–1959) was a New York supreme court justice, appointed by Governor Franklin Delano Roosevelt.

9. A New York–based hot dog company.

LOUIS And . . . um . . . irridium, I think. Something toxic.[1]

JOE You're eating one.

LOUIS Yeah, well, the shape, I can't help myself, plus I'm *trying* to commit suicide, what's your excuse?

JOE I don't have an excuse. I just have Pepto-Bismol.[2]

[JOE *takes a bottle of Pepto-Bismol and chugs it.* LOUIS *shudders audibly.*]

JOE Yeah I know but then I wash it down with Coke.

[*He does this.* LOUIS *mimes barfing in* JOE*'s lap.* JOE *pushes* LOUIS*'s head away.*]

JOE Are you *always* like this?

LOUIS I've been worrying a lot about his kids.

JOE Whose?

LOUIS Reagan's. Maureen and Mike and little orphan Patti and Miss Ron Reagan Jr.,[3] the you-should-pardon-the-expression heterosexual.

JOE Ron Reagan Jr. is *not* . . . You shouldn't just make these assumptions about people. How do you know? About him? What he is? You don't know.

LOUIS [*doing Tallulah*[4]] Well darling he never sucked *my* cock but . . .

JOE Look, if you're going to get vulgar . . .

LOUIS No no really I mean . . . What's it like to be the child of the Zeitgeist? To have the American Animus as your dad? It's not really a *family*, the Reagans, I read *People*,[5] there aren't any connections there, no love, they don't ever even speak to each other except through their agents. So what's it like to be Reagan's kid? Enquiring minds want to know.

JOE You can't believe everything you . . .

LOUIS [*looking away*] But . . . I think we all know what that's like. Nowadays. No connections. No responsibilities. All of us . . . falling through the cracks that separate what we owe to our selves and . . . and what we owe to love.

JOE You just. . . . Whatever you feel like saying or doing, you don't care, you just . . . do it.

LOUIS Do what?

JOE It. Whatever. Whatever it is you want to do.

LOUIS Are you trying to tell me something?

[*Little pause, sexual. They stare at each other.* JOE *looks away.*]

JOE No, I'm just observing that you . . .

LOUIS Impulsive.

JOE Yes, I mean it must be scary, you . . .

LOUIS [*Shrugs*] Land of the free. Home of the brave. Call me irresponsible.[6]

JOE It's kind of terrifying.

1. Many hot dogs contain preservatives that can be toxic in large quantities (*iridium* is a rare metallic element).
2. A product used to treat various kinds of minor digestive distress.
3. Ronald Reagan's children from his first marriage, to Jane Wyman (Maureen [1941–2001] and Michael [b. 1951]), and his second marriage, to Nancy Davis (Patti [b. 1952] and Ron [b. 1958]). Patti's estrangement from her parents made her an "orphan."
4. Imitating the husky, drawled "darling" with which the American stage and film star Tallulah Bankhead (1902–1968) customarily addressed people.
5. An American magazine that focuses on celebrities and human interest stories; it began publication in 1974.
6. The opening phrase and the title of a 1963 song (music by Jimmy Van Heusen, lyrics by Sammy Cahn). "O'er the land of the free, and the home of the brave" is the closing phrase of the refrain of "The Star-Spangled Banner," the U.S. national anthem (words by Francis Scott Key, 1814).

LOUIS Yeah, well, freedom is. Heartless, too.

JOE Oh you're not heartless.

LOUIS You don't know.
Finish your weenie.

[*He pats* JOE *on the knee, starts to leave.*]

JOE Um . . .

[LOUIS *turns, looks at him.* JOE *searches for something to say.*]

JOE Yesterday was Sunday but I've been a little unfocused recently and I thought it was Monday. So I came here like I was going to work. And the whole place was empty. And at first I couldn't figure out why, and I had this moment of incredible . . . fear and also . . . It just flashed through my mind: The whole Hall of Justice, it's empty, it's deserted, it's gone out of business. Forever. The people that make it run have up and abandoned it.

LOUIS [*looking at the building*] Creepy.

JOE Well yes but. I felt that I was going to scream. Not because it was creepy, but because the emptiness felt so *fast*.
And . . . well, good. A . . . happy scream.
I just wondered what a thing it would be . . . if overnight everything you owe anything to, justice, or love, had really gone away. Free.
It would be . . . heartless terror. Yes. Terrible, and . . .
Very great. To shed your skin, every old skin, one by one and then walk away, unencumbered, into the morning. [*Little pause. He looks at the building.*]
I can't go in there today.

LOUIS Then don't.

JOE [*not really hearing* LOUIS] I can't go in, I need . . .
[*He looks for what he needs. He takes a swig of Pepto-Bismol.*] I can't *be* this anymore. I need . . . a change, I should just . . .

LOUIS [*not a come-on, necessarily; he doesn't want to be alone*] Want some company? For whatever?

[*Pause.* JOE *looks at* LOUIS *and looks away, afraid.* LOUIS *shrugs.*]

LOUIS Sometimes, even if it scares you to death, you have to be willing to break the law. Know what I mean?

[*Another little pause.*]

JOE Yes.

[*Another little pause.*]

LOUIS I moved out. I moved out on my . . .
I haven't been sleeping well.

JOE Me neither.

[LOUIS *goes up to* JOE, *licks his napkin and dabs at* JOE*'s mouth.*]

LOUIS Antacid moustache.
[*Points to the building.*] Maybe the court won't convene. Ever again. Maybe we are free. To do whatever.
Children of the new morning, criminal minds. Selfish and greedy and loveless and blind. Reagan's children.
You're scared. So am I. Everybody is in the land of the free. God help us all.

Scene 8

[Late that night. JOE *at a payphone phoning* HANNAH *at home in Salt Lake City.]*

JOE Mom?

HANNAH Joe?

JOE Hi.

HANNAH You're calling from the street. It's . . . it must be four in the morning. What's happened?

JOE Nothing, nothing, I . . .

HANNAH It's Harper. Is Harper . . . Joe? Joe?

JOE Yeah, hi. No, Harper's fine. Well, no, she's . . . not *fine*. How are you, Mom?

HANNAH What's happened?

JOE I just wanted to talk to you. I, uh, wanted to try something out on you.

HANNAH Joe, you haven't . . . have you been drinking, Joe?

JOE Yes ma'am. I'm drunk.

HANNAH That isn't like you.

JOE No. I mean, who's to say?

HANNAH Why are you out on the street at four AM? In that crazy city. It's dangerous.

JOE Actually, Mom, I'm not on the street. I'm near the boathouse in the park.

HANNAH What park?

JOE Central Park.

HANNAH CENTRAL PARK! Oh my Lord. What on earth are you doing in Central Park at this time of night? Are you . . .

Joe, I think you ought to go home right now. Call me from home. *[Little pause]* Joe?

JOE I come here to watch, Mom. Sometimes. Just to watch.

HANNAH Watch what? What's there to watch at four in the . . .

JOE Mom, did Dad love me?

HANNAH What?

JOE Did he?

HANNAH You ought to go home and call from there.

JOE Answer.

HANNAH Oh now really. This is maudlin. I don't like this conversation.

JOE Yeah, well, it gets worse from here on.

[Pause.]

HANNAH Joe?

JOE Mom. Momma. I'm a homosexual, Momma.

Boy, did that come out awkward. *[Pause]* Hello? Hello?

I'm a homosexual. *[Pause]* Please, Momma. Say something.

HANNAH You're old enough to understand that your father didn't love you without being ridiculous about it.

JOE What?

HANNAH You're ridiculous. You're being ridiculous.

JOE I'm . . .

What?

HANNAH You really ought to go home now to your wife. I need to g This phone call. . . . We will just forget this phone call.

JOE Mom.

HANNAH No more talk. Tonight. This . . .

[*Suddenly very angry*] Drinking is a sin! A sin! I raised you better than that. [*She hangs up.*]

Scene 9

[*The following morning, early. Split scene:* HARPER *and* JOE *at home;* LOUIS *and* PRIOR *in* PRIOR'*s hospital room.* JOE *and* LOUIS *have just entered. This should be fast and obviously furious; overlapping is fine; the proceedings may be a little confusing but not the final results.*]

HARPER Oh God. Home. The moment of truth has arrived.

JOE Harper.

LOUIS I'm going to move out.

PRIOR The fuck you are.

JOE Harper. Please listen. I still love you very much. You're still my best buddy; I'm not going to leave you.

HARPER No, I don't like the sound of this. I'm leaving.

LOUIS I'm leaving.

I already have.

JOE Please listen. Stay. This is really hard. We have to talk.

HARPER We are talking. Aren't we. Now please shut up. OK?

PRIOR Bastard. Sneaking off while I'm flat out here, that's low. If I could get up now I'd beat the holy shit out of you.

JOE Did you take pills? How many?

HARPER No pills. Bad for the . . . [*Pats stomach.*]

JOE You aren't pregnant. I called your gynecologist.

HARPER I'm seeing a new gynecologist.

PRIOR You have no right to do this.

LOUIS Oh, that's ridiculous.

PRIOR No right. It's criminal.

JOE Forget about that. Just listen. You want the truth. This is the truth.

I knew this when I married you. I've known this I guess for as long as I've known anything, but . . . I don't know, I thought maybe that with enough effort and will I could change myself . . . but I can't . . .

PRIOR Criminal.

LOUIS There oughta be a law.

PRIOR There is a law. You'll see.

JOE I'm losing ground here, I go walking, you want to know where I walk, I . . . go to the park, or up and down 53rd Street, or places where . . . And I keep swearing I won't go walking again, but I just can't.

LOUIS I need some privacy.

PRIOR That's new.

LOUIS Everything's new, Prior.

JOE I try to tighten my heart into a knot, a snarl, I try to learn to live dead, just numb, but then I see someone I want, and it's like a nail, like a hot spike right through my chest, and I know I'm losing.

R Apartment too small for three? Louis and Prior comfy but not Louis Prior and Prior's disease?

Something like that.

I won't be judged by you. This isn't a crime, just—the inevitable consequence of people who run out of—whose limitations . . .

PRIOR Bang bang bang. The court will come to order.

LOUIS I mean let's talk practicalities, schedules; I'll come over if you want, spend nights with you when I can, I can . . .

PRIOR Has the jury reached a verdict?

LOUIS I'm doing the best I can.

PRIOR Pathetic. Who cares?

JOE My whole life has conspired to bring me to this place, and I can't despise my whole life. I think I believed when I met you I could save you, you at least if not myself, but . . .

I don't have any sexual feelings for you, Harper. And I don't think I ever did.

[*Little pause.*]

HARPER I think you should go.

JOE Where?

HARPER Washington. Doesn't matter.

JOE What are you talking about?

HARPER Without me.

Without me, Joe. Isn't that what you want to hear?

[*Little pause.*]

JOE Yes.

LOUIS You can love someone and fail them. You can love someone and not be able to . . .

PRIOR You *can,* theoretically, yes. A person can, maybe an editorial "you" can love, Louis, but not *you,* specifically you, I don't know, I think you are excluded from that general category.

HARPER You were going to save me, but the whole time you were spinning a lie. I just don't understand that.

PRIOR A person could theoretically love and maybe many do but we both know now you can't.

LOUIS I do.

PRIOR You can't even say it.

LOUIS I love you, Prior.

PRIOR I repeat. Who cares?

HARPER This is so scary, I want this to stop, to go back . . .

PRIOR We have reached a verdict, your honor. This man's heart is deficient. He loves, but his love is worth nothing.

JOE Harper . . .

HARPER Mr. Lies, I want to get away from here. Far away. Right now. Before he starts talking again. Please, please . . .

JOE As long as I've known you Harper you've been afraid of . . . of men hiding under the bed, men hiding under the sofa, men with knives.

PRIOR [*shattered; almost pleading; trying to reach him*] I'm dying! You stupid fuck! Do you know what that is! Love! Do you know what love means? We lived together four-and-a-half years, you animal, you idiot.

LOUIS I have to find some way to save myself.

JOE Who are these men? I never understood it. Now I know.

HARPER What?

JOE It's me.

HARPER It is?
PRIOR GET OUT OF MY ROOM!
JOE I'm the man with the knives.
HARPER You are?
PRIOR If I could get up now I'd kill you. I would. Go away. Go away or I'll scream.
HARPER Oh God . . .
JOE I'm sorry . . .
HARPER It is you.
LOUIS Please don't scream.
PRIOR Go.
HARPER I recognize you now.
LOUIS Please . . .
JOE Oh. Wait, I . . . Oh!
[*He covers his mouth with his hand, gags, and removes his hand, red with blood.*] I'm bleeding.

[PRIOR *screams.*]

HARPER Mr. Lies.
MR. LIES [*appearing, dressed in Antarctic explorer's apparel*] Right here.
HARPER I want to go away. I can't see him anymore.
MR. LIES Where?
HARPER Anywhere. Far away.
MR. LIES Absolutamento.

[HARPER *and* MR. LIES *vanish.* JOE *looks up, sees that she's gone.*]

PRIOR [*closing his eyes*] When I open my eyes you'll be gone.

[LOUIS *leaves.*]

JOE Harper?
PRIOR [*opening his eyes*] Huh. It worked.
JOE [*calling*] Harper?
PRIOR I hurt all over. I wish I was dead.

Scene 10

[*The same day, sunset.* HANNAH *and* SISTER ELLA CHAPTER, *a real estate saleswoman,* HANNAH PITT*'s closest friend, in front of* HANNAH*'s house in Salt Lake City.*]

SISTER ELLA CHAPTER Look at that view! A view of heaven. Like the living city of heaven,[7] isn't it, it just fairly glimmers in the sun.
HANNAH Glimmers.
SISTER ELLA CHAPTER Even the stone and brick it just glimmers and glitters like heaven in the sunshine. Such a nice view you get, perched up on a canyon rim. Some kind of beautiful place.
HANNAH It's just Salt Lake, and you're selling the house *for* me, not *to* me.
SISTER ELLA CHAPTER I like to work up an enthusiasm for my properties.
HANNAH Just get me a good price.
SISTER ELLA CHAPTER Well, the market's off.

7. As the headquarters of the LDS Church, Salt Lake City contains an enormous temple and many church-related buildings.

HANNAH At least fifty.

SISTER ELLA CHAPTER Forty'd be more like it.

HANNAH Fifty.

SISTER ELLA CHAPTER Wish you'd wait a bit.

HANNAH Well I can't.

SISTER ELLA CHAPTER Wish you would. You're about the only l I got.

HANNAH Oh well now.

SISTER ELLA CHAPTER Know why I decided to like you? I decid like you 'cause you're the only unfriendly Mormon I ever met.

HANNAH Your wig is crooked.

SISTER ELLA CHAPTER Fix it.

[HANNAH *straightens* SISTER ELLA'*s wig.*]

SISTER ELLA CHAPTER New York City. All they got there is tiny roo

I always thought: People ought to stay put. That's why I got my nse to sell real estate. It's a way of saying: Have a house! Stay put! It's ay of saying traveling's no good. Plus I needed the cash. [*She takes a pac f cigarettes out of her purse, lights one, offers pack to* HANNAH.]

HANNAH Not out here, anyone could come by.

There's been days I've stood at this ledge and thought about steppin ver. It's a hard place, Salt Lake: baked dry. Abundant energy; not much tel-ligence. That's a combination that can wear a body out. No harm looing someplace else. I don't need much room.

My sister-in-law Libby thinks there's radon gas[8] in the basement.

SISTER ELLA CHAPTER Is there gas in the . . .

HANNAH Of course not. Libby's a fool.

SISTER ELLA CHAPTER 'Cause I'd have to include that in the description.

HANNAH There's no gas, Ella. [*Little pause.*] Give a puff. [*She takes a furtive drag of* ELLA'*s cigarette.*] Put it away now.

SISTER ELLA CHAPTER So I guess it's goodbye.

HANNAH You'll be all right, Ella, I wasn't ever much of a friend.

SISTER ELLA CHAPTER I'll say something but don't laugh, OK?

This is the home of saints, the godliest place on earth, they say, and I think they're right. That mean there's no evil here? No. Evil's everywhere. Sin's everywhere. But this . . . is the spring of sweet water in the desert, the desert flower. Every step a Believer takes away from here is a step fraught with peril. I fear for you, Hannah Pitt, because you are my friend. Stay put. This is the right home of saints.

HANNAH Latter-day saints.

SISTER ELLA CHAPTER Only kind left.

HANNAH But still. Late in the day . . . for saints and everyone. That's all. That's all.

Fifty thousand dollars for the house, Sister Ella Chapter; don't undersell. It's an impressive view.

8. A naturally occurring radioactive gas that can cause lung cancer.

Not-Yet-Conscious, Forward Dawning

(*January 1986*)

Scene 1

[*L...ht, three days after the end of Act 2. The stage is completely da... IOR is in bed in his apartment, having a nightmare. He wakes up, si... and switches on a nightlight. He looks at his clock. Seated by the t... ear the bed is a man dressed in the clothing of a 13th-century ... squire.*]

PRIOR [*ter...l*] Who are you?

PRIOR 1 ... name is Prior Walter.

[*...use.*]

PRIOR ... name is Prior Walter.

PRIOR 1 ... know that.

PRIOR ...xplain.

PRIOR 1 You're alive. I'm not. We have the same name. What do you want me ... explain?

PRIOR A ghost?

PRIOR 1 An ancestor.

PRIOR Not *the* Prior Walter? The Bayeux tapestry Prior Walter?

PRIOR 1 His great-great grandson. The fifth of the name.

PRIOR I'm the thirty-fourth, I think.

PRIOR 1 Actually the thirty-second.

PRIOR Not according to Mother.

PRIOR 1 She's including the two bastards, then; I say leave them out. I say no room for bastards. The little things you swallow . . .

PRIOR Pills.

PRIOR 1 Pills. For the pestilence. I too . . .

PRIOR Pestilence. . . . You too what?

PRIOR 1 The pestilence[9] in my time was much worse than now. Whole villages of empty houses. You could look outdoors and see Death walking in the morning, dew dampening the ragged hem of his black robe. Plain as I see you now.

PRIOR You died of the plague.

PRIOR 1 The spotty monster. Like you, alone.

PRIOR I'm not alone.

PRIOR 1 You have no wife, no children.

PRIOR I'm gay.

PRIOR 1 So? Be gay, dance in your altogether for all I care, what's that to do with not having children?

PRIOR Gay homosexual, not bonny, blithe and[1] . . . never mind.

PRIOR 1 I had twelve. When I died.

...Bubonic plague, or the Black Death; it ... more than one-third of the population ... and Europe in the 1300s.

...lusion to the nursery rhyme that begins "Monday's child is fair of face"; one version ends "But the child born on the Sabbath Day / Is bonny and blithe and good and gay."

[*The second ghost appears, this one dressed in the clothing of an elegant 17th-century Londoner.*]

PRIOR 1 [*pointing to* PRIOR 2] And I was three years younger than him.

[PRIOR *sees the new ghost, screams.*]

PRIOR Oh God another one.

PRIOR 2 Prior Walter. Prior to you by some seventeen others.

PRIOR 1 He's counting the bastards.

PRIOR Are we having a convention?

PRIOR 2 We've been sent to declare her fabulous incipience. They love a well-paved entrance with lots of heralds, and . . .

PRIOR 1 The messenger come. Prepare the way. The infinite descent, a breath in air . . .

PRIOR 2 They chose us, I suspect, because of the mortal affinities. In a family as long-descended as the Walters there are bound to be a few carried off by plague.

PRIOR 1 The spotty monster.

PRIOR 2 Black Jack.[2] Came from a water pump, half the city of London, can you imagine? His came from fleas. Yours, I understand, is the lamentable consequence of venery . . .

PRIOR 1 Fleas on rats, but who knew that?

PRIOR Am I going to die?

PRIOR 2 We aren't allowed to discuss . . .

PRIOR 1 When you do, you don't get ancestors to help you through it. You may be surrounded by children but you die alone.

PRIOR I'm afraid.

PRIOR 1 You should be. There aren't even torches, and the path's rocky, dark, and steep.

PRIOR 2 Don't alarm him. There's good news before there's bad.
We two come to strew rose petal and palm leaf before the triumphal procession. Prophet. Seer. Revelator. It's a great honor for the family.

PRIOR 1 He hasn't got a family.

PRIOR 2 I meant for the Walters, for the family in the larger sense.

PRIOR [*singing*]
All I want is a room somewhere,
Far away from the cold night air . . . [3]

PRIOR 2 [*putting a hand on* PRIOR's *forehead*] Calm, calm, this is no brain fever . . .

[PRIOR *calms down, but keeps his eyes closed. The lights begin to change. Distant Glorious Music.*]

PRIOR 1 [*low chant*]
Adonai, Adonai,
Olam ha-yichud,
Zefirot, Zazahot,

2. Another name for bubonic plague. The worst epidemic to devastate London killed up to 100,000, or one-fifth of the city's population, in 1665–66.

3. The opening lines of "Wouldn't It Be Lo erly?"—a song from Alan Jay Lerner and Fr erick Loewe's musical *My Fair Lady* (195

Ha-adam, ha-gadol[4]
Daughter of Light,
Daughter of Splendors,
Fluor! Phosphor!
Lumen! Candle!

PRIOR 2 [*simultaneously*]
Even now,
From the mirror-bright halls of heaven,
Across the cold and lifeless infinity of space,
The Messenger comes
Trailing orbs of light,
Fabulous, incipient,
Oh Prophet,
To you . . .

PRIOR 1 and PRIOR 2
Prepare, prepare,
The Infinite Descent,
A breath, a feather,
Glory to . . .
[*They vanish.*]

Scene 2

[*The next day. Split scene:* LOUIS *and* BELIZE *in a coffee shop.* PRIOR *is at the outpatient clinic at the hospital with* EMILY, *the nurse; she has him on a pentamidine*[5] *IV drip.*]

LOUIS Why has democracy succeeded in America? Of course by succeeded I mean comparatively, not literally, not in the present, but what makes for the prospect of some sort of radical democracy spreading outward and growing up? Why does the power that was once so carefully preserved at the top of the pyramid by the original framers of the Constitution seem drawn inexorably downward and outward in spite of the best effort of the Right to stop this? I mean it's the really hard thing about being Left in this country, the American Left can't help but trip over all these petrified little fetishes: freedom, that's the worst; you know, *Jeane Kirkpatrick*[6] for God's sake will go on and on about freedom and so what does that mean, the word freedom, when she talks about it, or human rights; you have Bush[7] talking about human rights, and so what are these people talking about,

4. Hebrew terms associated with the Kabbalah, a tradition of mystical interpretation of the Hebrew Bible, though *Adonai* is a common way of referring to the Lord. *Olam hayichud:* the world of unification (i.e., unified by God); *Zefirot:* the divine emanations that represent the aspects of God visible in the world (usually *sefirot*); *Zazahot:* the three "brightnesses" (*Tzachtzachot,* often called the "splendors") that precede and govern the emanations of the sefirot; *Ha-adam, ha-gadol:* heavenly man (literally, "the great man"; Joshua 14.15).

5. Pentamidine isethionate, a drug that fights AIDS-related pneumonia.

6. An American professor of political science (1926–2006), selected by Reagan to be U.S. ambassador to the United Nations (1981–85); she criticized the Carter administration's emphasis on human rights, arguing for U.S. support of authoritarian regimes that oppose revolutionary totalitarian (Communist) regimes.

7. George H. W. Bush (b. 1924), vice president under Ronald Reagan (1981–89) and president (1989–93).

they might as well be talking about the mating habits of Venusians, these people don't begin to know what, ontologically, freedom is or human rights, like they see these bourgeois property-based Rights-of-Man-type rights[8] but that's not enfranchisement, not democracy, not what's implicit, what's potential within the idea, not the idea with blood in it. That's just liberalism, the worst kind of liberalism, really, bourgeois tolerance, and what I think is that what AIDS shows us is the limits of tolerance, that it's not enough to be tolerated, because when the shit hits the fan you find out how much tolerance is worth. Nothing. And underneath all the tolerance is intense, passionate hatred.

BELIZE Uh huh.

LOUIS Well don't you think that's true?

BELIZE Uh huh. It is.

LOUIS *Power* is the object, not being tolerated. Fuck assimilation. But I mean in spite of all this the thing about America, I think, is that ultimately we're different from every other nation on earth, in that, with people here of every race, we can't. . . . Ultimately what defines us isn't race, but politics. Not like any European country where there's an insurmountable fact of a kind of racial, or ethnic, monopoly, or monolith, like all Dutchmen, I mean Dutch people, are well, Dutch, and the Jews of Europe were never Europeans, just a small problem. Facing the monolith. But here there are so many small problems, it's really just a collection of small problems, the monolith is missing. Oh, I mean, of course I suppose there's the monolith of White America. White Straight Male America.

BELIZE Which is not unimpressive, even among monoliths.

LOUIS Well, no, but when the race thing gets taken care of, and I don't mean to minimalize how major it is, I mean I know it is, this is a really, really incredibly racist country but it's like, well, the British. I mean, all these blue-eyed pink people. And it's just weird, you know, I mean I'm not all that Jewish-looking, or . . . well, maybe I am but, you know, in New York, everyone is . . . well, not everyone, but so many are but so but in England, in London I walk into bars and I feel like Sid the Yid, you know I mean like Woody Allen in *Annie Hall*, with the payess and the gabardine coat,[9] like never, never anywhere so much—I mean, not actively despised, not like they're Germans, who I think are still terribly anti-Semitic, and racist too, I mean black-racist, they pretend otherwise but, anyway, in London, there's just . . . and at one point I met this black gay guy from Jamaica who talked with a lilt but he said his family'd been living in London since before the Civil War—the American one[1]—and how the English never let him forget for a minute that he wasn't blue-eyed and pink and I said yeah, me too, these people are anti-Semites and he said yeah but the British Jews have the clothing business all sewed up and blacks there can't get a foothold.

8. An allusion to the property-based political theory of the British philosopher John Locke (1632–1704), which influenced the framers of the U.S. Constitution.

9. In *Annie Hall* (1977), directed by and starring Allen (b. 1935), a Jew born in New York City, Allen's character imagines that his girlfriend's midwestern family sees him as a Hasid, wearing the tight-woven wool coat and *payess* (side curls; Yiddish) characteristic of that ultraorthodox Jewish sect. *Yid:* Jew (pejorative).

1. That is, not the English Civil War (1642–48).

And it was an incredibly awkward moment of just . . . I mean here we were, in this bar that was gay but it was a *pub*, you know, the beams and the plaster and those horrible little, like, two-day-old fish and egg sandwiches—and just so British, so *old*, and I felt, well, there's no way out of this because both of us are, right now, too much immersed in this history, hope is dissolved in the sheer age of this place, where race is what counts and there's no real hope of change—it's the racial destiny of the Brits that matters to them, not their political destiny, whereas in America . . .

BELIZE Here in America race doesn't count.

LOUIS No, no, that's not . . . I mean you *can't* be hearing that . . .

BELIZE I . . .

LOUIS It's—look, race, yes, but ultimately race here is a political question, right? Racists just try to use race here as a tool in a political struggle. It's not really about race. Like the spiritualists try to use that stuff, are you enlightened, are you centered, channeled, whatever, this reaching out for a spiritual past in a country where no indigenous spirits exist—only the Indians, I mean Native American spirits and we killed them off so now, there are no gods here, no ghosts and spirits in America, there are no angels in America, no spiritual past, no racial past, there's only the political, and the decoys and the ploys to maneuver around the inescapable battle of politics, the shifting downwards and outwards of political power to the people . . .

BELIZE POWER to the People![2] AMEN! [*Looking at his watch*] *OH MY GOODNESS!* Will you look at the time, I gotta . . .

LOUIS Do you. . . . You think this is, what, racist or naive or something?

BELIZE Well it's certainly *something*. Look, I just remembered I have an appointment . . .

LOUIS What? I mean I really don't want to, like, speak from some position of privilege and . . .

BELIZE I'm sitting here, thinking, eventually he's *got* to run out of steam, so I let you rattle on and on saying about maybe seven or eight things I find really offensive.

LOUIS What?

BELIZE But I know you, Louis, and I know the guilt fueling this peculiar tirade is obviously already swollen bigger than your hemorrhoids.

LOUIS I don't have hemorrhoids.

BELIZE I hear different. May I finish?

LOUIS Yes, but I don't have hemorrhoids.

BELIZE So finally, when I . . .

LOUIS Prior told you, he's an asshole, he shouldn't have . . .

BELIZE You promised, Louis. Prior is not a subject.

LOUIS You brought him up.

BELIZE I brought up hemorrhoids.

LOUIS So it's indirect. Passive-aggressive.

BELIZE Unlike, I suppose, banging me over the head with your theory that America doesn't have a race problem.

LOUIS Oh be fair I never said that.

2. A slogan of the 1960s, associated both with student protesters and with the militant Black Panthers.

BELIZE Not exactly, but . . .

LOUIS I said . . .

BELIZE . . . but it was close enough, because en that blu've just walked out and . . .

LOUIS You deliberately misinterpreted! I . . .

BELIZE Stop interrupting! I haven't been able to . . .

LOUIS Just let me . . .

BELIZE NO! What, *talk*? You've been running your nonstop since I got here, yaddadda yaddadda blah blah blah, up down hill, playing with your MONOLITH . . .

LOUIS [*overlapping*] Well, you could have joined in a time instead of . . .

BELIZE [*continuing over* LOUIS] . . . and girlfriend it is an *esome* spectacle but I got better things to do with my time than sit here listening to this racist bullshit just because I feel sorry for you that . . .

LOUIS I am not a racist!

BELIZE Oh come on . . .

LOUIS So maybe I am a racist but . . .

BELIZE Oh I really hate that! It's no fun picking on you Louis; you're so guilty, it's like throwing darts at a slab of jello, there's no satisfying thwack, just quivering, the darts just bloop in and vanish.

LOUIS I just think when you are discussing lines of oppression it gets very complicated and . . .

BELIZE Oh is that a fact? You know, we black drag queens have a rather intimate knowledge of the complexity of the lines . . .

LOUIS *Ex*–black drag queen.

BELIZE Actually ex-ex.

LOUIS You're doing drag again?

BELIZE I don't . . . Maybe. I don't have to tell you. Maybe.

LOUIS I think it's sexist.

BELIZE I didn't ask you.

LOUIS Well it is. The gay community, I think, has to adopt the same attitude towards drag as black women have to take towards black women blues singers.

BELIZE Oh my we *are* walking dangerous tonight.

LOUIS Well, it's all internalized oppression, right, I mean the masochism, the stereotypes, the . . .

BELIZE Louis, are you deliberately trying to make me hate you?

LOUIS No, I . . .

BELIZE I mean, are you deliberately transforming yourself into an arrogant, sexual-political Stalinist-slash-racist flag-waving thug for my benefit?

[*Pause.*]

LOUIS You know what I think?

BELIZE What?

LOUIS You hate me because I'm a Jew.

BELIZE I'm leaving.

LOUIS It's true.

BELIZE You have no basis except your . . .

Louis, it's good to know you haven't changed; you are still an honorary citizen of the Twilight Zone,[3] and after your pale, pale white polemics on behalf of racial sensitivity you have a flaming *fuck* of a lot of nerve calling me an anti-Semite. Now I really gotta go.

LOUIS You called me Lou the Jew.

BELIZE That was a joke.

LOUIS I didn't think it was funny. It was hostile.

BELIZE It was three years ago.

LOUIS So?

BELIZE You called yourself Sid the Yid.

LOUIS That's not the same thing.

BELIZE Sid the Yid is different from Lou the Jew.

LOUIS Yes.

BELIZE Someday you'll have to explain that to me, but right now . . . You hate me because you hate black people.

LOUIS I do not. But I do think most black people are anti-Semitic.

BELIZE "Most black people." *That's* racist, Louis, and I think most Jews . . .

LOUIS Louis Farrakhan.[4]

BELIZE Ed Koch.[5]

LOUIS Jesse Jackson.[6]

BELIZE Jackson. Oh really, Louis, this is . . .

LOUIS Hymietown! Hymietown!

BELIZE Louis, you voted for Jesse Jackson. You send checks to the Rainbow Coalition.

LOUIS I'm ambivalent. The checks bounced.

BELIZE All your checks bounce, Louis; you're ambivalent about everything.

LOUIS What's that supposed to mean?

BELIZE You may be dumber than shit but I refuse to believe you can't figure it out. Try.

LOUIS I was never ambivalent about Prior. I love him. I do. I really do.

BELIZE Nobody said different.

LOUIS Love and ambivalence are . . . Real love isn't ambivalent.

BELIZE "Real love isn't ambivalent." I'd swear that's a line from my favorite bestselling paperback novel, *In Love with the Night Mysterious*,[7] except I don't think you ever read it.

[*Pause.*]

LOUIS I never read it, no.

3. That is, in the fantasy world of *The Twilight Zone* (1959–64), Rod Serling's television series.

4. A black religious leader (b. 1933), who in 1977 became leader of the Nation of Islam (Black Muslims); beginning in the 1980s, he received public censure for statements viewed as anti-Semitic and antiwhite.

5. A Jewish New York politician (b. 1924); though popular as mayor (1978–89), early in his administration, he angered black political leaders by reorganizing the city's poverty programs, and in the 1980s, he became a vocal critic of Farrakhan and Jesse Jackson.

6. A black civil rights leader (b. 1941), who ran for president in 1984 and 1988; the 1984 revelation that he had called New York "Hymietown," together with his association—soon disavowed—with Farrakhan, damaged his reputation with Jews. After the 1984 campaign, he turned his informal "rainbow coalition" of minorities into a national social justice organization.

7. A line from Cole Porter's 1948 song "So in Love" (whose refrain begins "So taunt me and hurt me, / Deceive me, desert me, / I'm yours 'til I die"); no such novel exists.

BELIZE You ought to. Instead of spending the rest of your life trying to get through *Democracy in America.*[8] It's about this white woman whose Daddy owns a plantation in the Deep South in the years before the Civil War—the American one—and her name is Margaret, and she's in love with her Daddy's number-one slave, and his name is Thaddeus, and she's married but her white slave-owner husband has AIDS: Antebellum Insufficiently Developed Sexorgans. And there's a lot of hot stuff going down when Margaret and Thaddeus can catch a spare torrid ten under the cotton-picking moon, and then of course the Yankees come, and they set the slaves free, and the slaves string up old Daddy, and so on. Historical fiction. Somewhere in there I recall Margaret and Thaddeus find the time to discuss the nature of love; her face is reflecting the flames of the burning plantation—you know, the way white people do—and his black face is dark in the night and she says to him, "Thaddeus, real love isn't ever ambivalent."

[*Little pause.* EMILY *enters and turns off IV drip.*]

BELIZE Thaddeus looks at her; he's contemplating her thesis; and he isn't sure he agrees.

EMILY [*removing IV drip from* PRIOR*'s arm*] Treatment number . . . [*Consulting chart*] four.

PRIOR Pharmaceutical miracle. Lazarus[9] breathes again.

LOUIS Is he. . . . How bad is he?

BELIZE You want the laundry list?

EMILY Shirt off, let's check the . . .

[PRIOR *takes his shirt off. She examines his lesions.*]

BELIZE There's the weight problem and the shit problem and the morale problem.

EMILY Only six. That's good. Pants.

[*He drops his pants. He's naked. She examines.*]

BELIZE And. He thinks he's going crazy.

EMILY Looking good. What else?

PRIOR Ankles sore and swollen, but the leg's better. The nausea's mostly gone with the little orange pills. BM's pure liquid but not bloody anymore, for now, my eye doctor says everything's OK, for now, my dentist says "Yuck!" when he sees my fuzzy tongue, and now he wears little condoms on his thumb and forefinger. And a mask. So what? My dermatologist is in Hawaii and my mother . . . well leave my mother out of it. Which is usually where my mother is, out of it. My glands are like walnuts, my weight's holding steady for week two, and a friend died two days ago of bird tuberculosis;[1] bird tuberculosis; that scared me and I didn't go to the funeral today because he was an Irish Catholic and it's probably open casket and I'm afraid of . . . something, the bird TB or seeing him or . . . So I guess I'm doing OK. Except for of course I'm going nuts.

EMILY We ran the toxoplasmosis series[2] and there's no indication . . .

8. Alexis de Tocqueville's classic study of Americans and their system of government (2 vols., 1835–40).

9. Jesus' resurrection of Lazarus from the dead is described in John 11.1–44.

1. A hard-to-treat form of tuberculosis that is common in AIDS patients.

2. A series of tests for toxoplasmosis, one of the infections commonly associated with AIDS; it often affects the brain.

PRIOR I know, I know, but I feel like something terrifying is on its way, you know, like a missile from outer space, and it's plummeting down towards the earth, and I'm ground zero, and . . . I am generally known where I am known as one cool, collected queen. And I am ruffled.

EMILY There's really nothing to worry about. I think that shochen bamromim hamtzeh menucho nechono al kanfey haschino.[3]

PRIOR What?

EMILY Everything's fine. Bemaalos k'doshim ut'horim kezohar horokeea mazhirim . . .

PRIOR Oh I don't understand what you're . . .

EMILY Es nishmas Prior sheholoch leolomoh, baavur shenodvoo z'dokoh b'ad hazkoras nishmosoh.

PRIOR Why are you doing that?! Stop it! Stop it!

EMILY Stop what?

PRIOR You were just . . . weren't you just speaking in Hebrew or something.

EMILY *Hebrew?* [*Laughs.*] I'm basically Italian-American. No. I didn't speak in Hebrew.

PRIOR Oh no, oh God please I really think I . . .

EMILY Look, I'm sorry, I have a waiting room full of . . . I think you're one of the lucky ones, you'll live for years, probably—you're pretty healthy for someone with no immune system. Are you seeing someone? Loneliness is a danger. A therapist?

PRIOR No, I don't need to see anyone, I just . . .

EMILY Well think about it. You aren't going crazy. You're just under a lot of stress. No wonder . . . [*She starts to write in his chart.*]

[*Suddenly there is an astonishing blaze of light, a huge chord sounded by a gigantic choir, and a great book with steel pages mounted atop a molten-red pillar pops up from the stage floor. The book opens; there is a large Aleph*[4] *inscribed on its pages, which bursts into flames. Immediately the book slams shut and disappears instantly under the floor as the lights become normal again.* EMILY *notices none of this, writing.* PRIOR *is agog.*]

EMILY [*laughing, exiting*] Hebrew . . .

[*Prior flees.*]

LOUIS Help me.

BELIZE I beg your pardon?

LOUIS You're a nurse, give me something, I . . . don't know what to do anymore, I . . . Last week at work I screwed up the Xerox machine like permanently and so I . . . then I tripped on the subway steps and my glasses broke and I cut my forehead, here, see, and now I can't see much and my forehead . . . it's like the Mark of Cain,[5] stupid, right, but it won't heal and every morning I see it and I think, Biblical things, Mark of Cain, Judas

3. This line begins transliterated Hebrew taken from the prayer traditionally recited at funerals for the soul of the departed; the translation is "[God, full of compassion,] who dwells on high, grant true rest upon the wings of your Divine Presence, in the exalted spheres of the holy and pure, who shine as the brightness of the heavens, to the soul of Prior, who has gone to his eternal rest, for charity has been donated in remembrance of his soul."

4. The first letter of the Hebrew alphabet.

5. According to Genesis (4.1–16), the first son of Adam and Eve, whose forehead was marked by God after he killed Abel, his brother.

Iscariot and his silver and his noose,[6] people who . . . in betraying what they love betray what's truest in themselves, I feel . . . nothing but cold for myself, just cold, and every night I miss him, I miss him so much but then . . . those sores, and the smell and . . . where I thought it was going. . . . I could be . . . I could be sick too, maybe I'm sick too. I don't know.

Belize. Tell him I love him. Can you do that?

BELIZE I've thought about it for a very long time, and I still don't understand what love is. Justice is simple. Democracy is simple. Those things are unambivalent. But love is very hard. And it goes bad for you if you violate the hard law of love.

LOUIS I'm dying.

BELIZE He's dying. You just wish you were.

Oh cheer up, Louis. Look at that heavy sky out there.

LOUIS Purple.

BELIZE *Purple?* Boy, what kind of a homosexual are you, anyway? That's not purple, Mary, that color up there is [*Very grand*] *mauve*.

All day today it's felt like Thanksgiving. Soon, this . . . ruination will be blanketed white. You can smell it—can you smell it?

LOUIS Smell what?

BELIZE Softness, compliance, forgiveness, grace.

LOUIS No . . .

BELIZE I can't help you learn that. I can't help you, Louis. You're not my business. [*He exits.*]

[*Louis puts his head in his hands, inadvertently touching his cut forehead.*]

LOUIS Ow FUCK! [*He stands slowly, looks towards where* BELIZE *exited.*] Smell what?

[*He looks both ways to be sure no one is watching, then inhales deeply, and is surprised.*] Huh. Snow.

Scene 3

[*Same day.* HARPER *in a very white, cold place, with a brilliant blue sky above; a delicate snowfall. She is dressed in a beautiful snowsuit. The sound of the sea, faint.*]

HARPER Snow! Ice! Mountains of ice! Where am I? I . . .

I feel better, I do,

I . . . feel better. There are ice crystals in my lungs, wonderful and sharp. And the snow smells like cold, crushed peaches. And there's something . . . some current of blood in the wind, how strange, it has that iron taste.

MR. LIES Ozone.

HARPER Ozone! Wow! Where am I?

MR. LIES The Kingdom of Ice, the bottommost part of the world.

HARPER [*looking around, then realizing*] Antarctica. This is Antarctica!

MR. LIES Cold shelter for the shattered. No sorrow here, tears freeze.

HARPER Antarctica, Antarctica, oh boy oh boy, LOOK at this, I . . . Wow, I must've really snapped the tether, huh?

MR. LIES Apparently . . .

6. For the story of the betrayal of Jesus by Judas Iscariot, his disciple, for thirty pieces of silver, and Judas's subsequent suicide by hanging, see Matthew 26.14–15, 27.3–5.

HARPER That's great. I want to stay here forever. Set up camp. Build things. Build a city, an enormous city made up of frontier forts, dark wood and green roofs and high gates made of pointed logs and bonfires burning on every street corner. I should build by a river. Where are the forests?

MR. LIES No timber here. Too cold. Ice, no trees.

HARPER Oh details! I'm sick of details! I'll plant them and grow them. I'll live off caribou fat, I'll melt it over the bonfires and drink it from long, curved goat-horn cups. It'll be great. I want to make a new world here. So that I never have to go home again.

MR. LIES As long as it lasts. Ice has a way of melting . . .

HARPER No. Forever. I can have anything I want here—maybe even companionship, someone who has . . . desire for me. You, maybe.

MR. LIES It's against the by-laws of the International Order of Travel Agents to get involved with clients. Rules are rules. Anyway, I'm not the one you really want.

HARPER There isn't anyone . . . maybe an Eskimo. Who could ice-fish for food. And help me build a nest for when the baby comes.

MR. LIES There are no Eskimo in Antarctica. And you're not really pregnant. You made that up.

HARPER Well all of this is made up. So if the snow feels cold I'm pregnant. Right? Here, I can be pregnant. And I can have any kind of a baby I want.

MR. LIES This is a retreat, a vacuum, its virtue is that it lacks everything; deep-freeze for feelings. You can be numb and safe here, that's what you came for. Respect the delicate ecology of your delusions.

HARPER You mean like no Eskimo in Antarctica.

MR. LIES Correcto. Ice and snow, no Eskimo. Even hallucinations have laws.

HARPER Well then who's that?

[*The Eskimo appears.*]

MR. LIES An Eskimo.

HARPER An antarctic Eskimo. A fisher of the polar deep.

MR. LIES There's something wrong with this picture.

[*The Eskimo beckons.*]

HARPER I'm going to like this place. It's my own National Geographic Special![7] Oh! Oh! [*She holds her stomach.*] I think . . . I think I felt her kicking. Maybe I'll give birth to a baby covered with thick white fur, and that way she won't be cold. My breasts will be full of hot cocoa so she doesn't get chilly. And if it gets really cold, she'll have a pouch I can crawl into. Like a marsupial. We'll mend together. That's what we'll do; we'll mend.

Scene 4

[*Same day. An abandoned lot in the South Bronx. A homeless* WOMAN *is standing near an oil drum in which a fire is burning. Snowfall. Trash around.* HANNAH *enters dragging two heavy suitcases.*]

HANNAH Excuse me? I said excuse me? Can you tell me where I am? Is this Brooklyn? Do you know a Pineapple Street?[8] Is there some sort of bus or train or . . . ?

7. That is, like the television programs—mainly documentaries featuring the exploration of the natural world—produced by the National Geographic Society since 1964.

8. A street in Brooklyn Heights, a historic district of Brooklyn.

I'm lost, I just arrived from Salt Lake. City. Utah? I took the bus that I was told to take and I got off—well it was the very last stop, so I had to get off, and I *asked* the driver was this Brooklyn, and he nodded yes but he was from one of those foreign countries where they think it's good manners to nod at everything even if you have no idea what it is you're nodding at, and in truth I think he spoke no English at all, which I think would make him ineligible for employment on public transportation. The public being English-speaking, mostly. Do you speak English?

[*The* WOMAN *nods.*]

HANNAH I was supposed to be met at the airport by my son. He didn't show and I don't wait more than three and three quarters hours for *anyone*. I should have been patient, I guess, I . . . Is this . . .

WOMAN Bronx.

HANNAH Is that . . . The *Bronx*? Well how in the name of Heaven did I get to the Bronx when the bus driver said . . .

WOMAN [*talking to herself*] Slurp slurp slurp will you STOP that disgusting slurping! YOU DISGUSTING SLURPING FEEDING ANIMAL! Feeding yourself, just feeding yourself, what would it matter, to you or to ANYONE, if you just stopped. Feeding. And DIED?

[*Pause.*]

HANNAH Can you just tell me where I . . .

WOMAN Why was the Kosciuszko Bridge[9] named after a Polack?

HANNAH I don't know what you're . . .

WOMAN That was a joke.

HANNAH Well what's the punchline?

WOMAN I don't know.

HANNAH [*looking around desperately*] Oh for pete's sake, is there anyone else who . . .

WOMAN [*again, to herself*] Stand further off you fat loathsome whore, you can't have any more of this soup, slurp slurp slurp you animal, and the—I know you'll just go pee it all away and where will you do that? Behind what bush? It's FUCKING COLD out here and I . . .

Oh that's right, because it was supposed to have been a tunnel!

That's not very funny.

Have you read the prophecies of Nostradamus?[1]

HANNAH Who?

WOMAN Some guy I went out with once somewhere, Nostradamus. Prophet, outcast, eyes like . . . Scary shit, he . . .

HANNAH Shut up. Please. Now I want you to stop jabbering for a minute and pull your wits together and tell me how to get to Brooklyn. Because you know! And you are going to tell me! Because there is no one else around to tell me and I am wet and cold and I am very angry! So I am sorry you're psychotic but just make the effort—take a deep breath—DO IT!

9. A bridge that connects the Bronx and Queens (a borough that, like Brooklyn, is on Long Island); it is named for Tadeusz Kościuszko (1746–1817), a Polish military engineer who fought with distinction in America's Continental Army in the Revolutionary War.

1. Michel de Nostredame (1503–1566), a French astrologer and physician whose *Prophesies* (1555), a collection of predictions about the future, has long found a receptive audience.

[HANNAH *and the* WOMAN *breathe together.*]

HANNAH That's good. Now exhale.

[*They do.*]

HANNAH Good. Now how do I get to Brooklyn?

WOMAN Don't know. Never been. Sorry. Want some soup?

HANNAH Manhattan? Maybe you know . . . I don't suppose you know the location of the Mormon Visitor's[2] . . .

WOMAN 65th and Broadway.

HANNAH How do you . . .

WOMAN Go there all the time. Free movies. Boring, but you can stay all day.

HANNAH Well. . . . So how do I . . .

WOMAN Take the D Train.[3] Next block make a right.

HANNAH Thank you.

WOMAN Oh yeah. In the new century I think we will all be insane.

Scene 5

[*Same day.* JOE *and* ROY *in the study of* ROY*'s brownstone.* ROY *is wearing an elegant bathrobe. He has made a considerable effort to look well. He isn't well, and he hasn't succeeded much in looking it.*]

JOE I can't. The answer's no. I'm sorry.

ROY Oh, well, apologies . . .

I can't see that there's anyone asking for apologies.

[*Pause.*]

JOE I'm sorry, Roy.

ROY Oh, well, apologies.

JOE My wife is missing, Roy. My mother's coming from Salt Lake to . . . to help look, I guess. I'm supposed to be at the airport now, picking her up but . . . I just spent two days in a hospital, Roy, with a bleeding ulcer, I was spitting up blood.

ROY Blood, huh? Look, I'm very busy here and . . .

JOE It's just a job.

ROY A job? A *job? Washington!* Dumb Utah Mormon hick shit!

JOE Roy . . .

ROY *WASHINGTON!* When Washington called me I was younger than you, you think I said "Aw fuck no I can't go I got two fingers up my asshole and a little moral nosebleed to boot!" When Washington calls you my pretty young punk friend you go or you can go fuck yourself sideways 'cause the train has pulled out of the station, and you are *out,* nowhere, out in the cold. Fuck you, Mary Jane, get outta here.

JOE Just let me . . .

ROY Explain? Ephemera. You broke my heart. Explain that. Explain that.

JOE I love you. Roy.

There's so much that I want, to be . . . what you see in me, I want to be a participant in the world, in your world, Roy, I want to be capable of that, I've tried, really I have but . . . I can't do this. Not because I don't believe in

2. The Mormon Visitors' Center.

3. A subway line that, in the Bronx, runs along the Grand Concourse; it extends to Brooklyn.

you, but because I believe in you so much, in what you stand for, at heart, the order, the decency. I would give anything to protect you, but . . . There are laws I can't break. It's too ingrained. It's not me. There's enough damage I've already done.

Maybe you were right, maybe I'm dead.

ROY You're not dead, boy, you're a sissy.

You love me; that's moving, I'm moved. It's nice to be loved. I warned you about her, didn't I, Joe? But you don't listen to me, why, because you say Roy is smart and Roy's a friend but Roy . . . well, he isn't nice, and you wanna be nice. Right? A nice, nice man! [*Little pause*]

You know what my greatest accomplishment was, Joe, in my life, what I am able to look back on and be proudest of? And I have helped make Presidents and unmake them and mayors and more goddam judges than anyone in NYC ever—AND several million dollars, tax-free—and what do you think means the most to me?

You ever hear of Ethel Rosenberg? Huh, Joe, huh?

JOE Well, yeah, I guess I . . . Yes.

ROY Yes. Yes. You have heard of Ethel Rosenberg. Yes. Maybe you even read about her in the history books.

If it wasn't for me, Joe, Ethel Rosenberg would be alive today, writing some personal-advice column for *Ms.* magazine.[4] She isn't. Because during the trial, Joe, I was on the phone every day, talking with the judge . . .

JOE Roy . . .

ROY Every day, doing what I do best, talking on the telephone, making sure that timid Yid nebbish[5] on the bench did his duty to America, to history. That sweet unprepossessing woman, two kids, boo-hoo-hoo, reminded us all of our little Jewish mamas—she came this close to getting life; I pleaded till I wept to put her in the chair.[6] Me. I did that. I would have fucking pulled the switch if they'd have let me. Why? Because I fucking hate traitors. Because I fucking hate communists. Was it legal? Fuck legal. Am I a nice man? Fuck nice. They say terrible things about me in the *Nation*.[7] Fuck the *Nation*. You want to be Nice, or you want to be Effective? Make the law, or subject to it. Choose. Your wife chose. A week from today, she'll be back. SHE knows how to get what SHE wants. Maybe I ought to send *her* to Washington.

JOE I don't believe you.

ROY Gospel.

JOE You can't possibly mean what you're saying.

Roy, you were the Assistant United States Attorney on the Rosenberg case, ex-parte[8] communication with the judge during the trial would be . . . censurable, at least, probably conspiracy and . . . in a case that resulted in execution, it's . . .

4. An American feminist magazine that appeared monthly from 1972 to 1987; it resumed publication in 2001.

5. A nonentity, a loser (Yiddish); the presiding judge in the Rosenbergs' trial was Irving R. Kaufman (1910–1992).

6. The electric chair, used to execute the Rosenbergs.

7. A left-liberal American journal of culture and politics, published weekly since 1865.

8. In law, proceedings conducted in the absence of and without notice to one party, a practice that is normally prohibited (literally, "from [one] side"; Latin); see Playwright's Notes.

ROY What? Murder?

JOE You're not well is all.

ROY What do you mean, not well? Who's not well?

[*Pause.*]

JOE You said . . .

ROY No I didn't. I said what?

JOE Roy, you have cancer.

ROY No I don't.

[*Pause.*]

JOE You told me you were dying.

ROY What the fuck are you talking about, Joe? I never said that. I'm in perfect health. There's not a goddam thing wrong with me. [*He smiles.*] Shake?

[JOE *hesitates. He holds out his hand to* ROY. ROY *pulls* JOE *into a close, strong clinch.*]

ROY [*more to himself than to* JOE] It's OK that you hurt me because I love you, baby Joe. That's why I'm so rough on you.

[ROY *releases* JOE. JOE *backs away a step or two.*]

ROY Prodigal son.[9] The world will wipe its dirty hands all over you.

JOE It already has, Roy.

ROY Now go.

[ROY *shoves* JOE, *hard.* JOE *turns to leave.* ROY *stops him, turns him around.*]

ROY [*smoothing* JOE's *lapels, tenderly*] I'll always be here, waiting for you . . . [*Then again, with sudden violence, he pulls* JOE *close, violently.*] What did you want from me, what was all this, what do you want, treacherous ungrateful little . . .

[JOE, *very close to belting* ROY, *grabs him by the front of his robe, and propels him across the length of the room. He holds* ROY *at arm's length, the other arm ready to hit.*]

ROY [*laughing softly, almost pleading to be hit*] Transgress a little, Joseph.

[JOE *releases* ROY.]

ROY There are so many laws; find one you can break.

[JOE *hesitates, then leaves, backing out. When* JOE *has gone,* ROY *doubles over in great pain, which he's been hiding throughout the scene with* JOE.]

ROY Ah, Christ . . .
Andy! Andy! Get in here! Andy!

[*The door opens, but it isn't* ANDY. *A small Jewish* WOMAN *dressed modestly in a fifties hat and coat stands in the doorway. The room darkens.*]

ROY Who the fuck are you? The new nurse?

[*The figure in the doorway says nothing. She stares at* ROY. *A pause.* ROY *looks at her carefully, gets up, crosses to her. He crosses back to the chair, sits heavily.*]

ROY Aw, fuck. Ethel.

9. That is, the son who squanders his inheritance but is joyfully welcomed back home (see Luke 15.11–32).

ETHEL ROSENBERG [*her manner is friendly, her voice is ice-cold*] You don't look good, Roy.

ROY Well, Ethel. I don't feel good.

ETHEL ROSENBERG But you lost a lot of weight. That suits you. You were heavy back then. Zaftig, mit[1] hips.

ROY I haven't been that heavy since 1960. We were all heavier back then, before the body thing started. Now I look like a skeleton. They stare.

ETHEL ROSENBERG The shit's really hit the fan, huh, Roy?

[*Little pause.* ROY *nods.*]

ETHEL ROSENBERG Well the fun's just started.

ROY What is this, Ethel, Halloween? You trying to scare me?

[ETHEL *says nothing.*]

ROY Well you're wasting your time! I'm scarier than you any day of the week! So beat it, Ethel! BOOO! BETTER DEAD THAN RED![2] Somebody trying to shake me up? HAH HAH! From the throne of God in heaven to the belly of hell, you can all fuck yourselves and then go jump in the lake because I'M NOT AFRAID OF YOU OR DEATH OR HELL OR ANYTHING!

ETHEL ROSENBERG Be seeing you soon, Roy. Julius[3] sends his regards.

ROY Yeah, well send this to Julius!

[*He flips the bird in her direction,*[4] *stands and moves towards her. Halfway across the room he slumps to the floor, breathing laboriously, in pain.*]

ETHEL ROSENBERG You're a very sick man, Roy.

ROY Oh God . . . ANDY!

ETHEL ROSENBERG Hmmm. He doesn't hear you, I guess. We should call the ambulance.

[*She goes to the phone.*] Hah! Buttons! Such things they got now.

What do I dial, Roy?

[*Pause.* ROY *looks at her, then.*]

ROY 911.

ETHEL ROSENBERG [*dials the phone*] It sings!

[*Imitating dial tones*] La la la . . .

Huh.

Yes, you should please send an ambulance to the home of Mister Roy Cohn, the famous lawyer.

What's the address, Roy?

ROY [*a beat, then*] 244 East 87th.

ETHEL ROSENBERG 244 East 87th Street. No apartment number, he's got the whole building.

My name? [*A beat*] Ethel Greenglass Rosenberg.

[*Small smile*] Me? No I'm not related to Mr. Cohn. An old friend. [*She hangs up.*]

They said a minute.

ROY I have all the time in the world.

1. Plump, with (Yiddish); *Zaftig* usually means "buxom."

2. A slogan used in the 1950s to denounce Communists ("Reds") and leftists.

3. Julius Rosenberg (1918–1953), Ethel's husband.

4. Gives her the finger.

ETHEL ROSENBERG You're immortal.

ROY I'm immortal. Ethel. [*He forces himself to stand.*]
I have *forced* my way into history. I ain't never gonna die.

ETHEL ROSENBERG [*a little laugh, then*] History is about to crack wide open. Millennium approaches.

Scene 6

[*Late that night.* PRIOR*'s bedroom.* PRIOR I *watching* PRIOR *in bed, who is staring back at him, terrified. Tonight* PRIOR I *is dressed in weird alchemical robes and hat over his historical clothing and he carries a long palm-leaf bundle.*]

PRIOR I Tonight's the night! Aren't you excited? Tonight she arrives! Right through the roof! Ha-adam, Ha-gadol . . .

PRIOR 2 [*appearing, similarly attired*] Lumen! Phosphor! Fluor! Candle! An unending billowing of scarlet and . . .

PRIOR Look. Garlic. A mirror. Holy water. A crucifix.[5] FUCK OFF! Get the fuck out of my room! GO!

PRIOR I [*to* PRIOR 2] Hard as a hickory knob, I'll bet.

PRIOR 2 We all tumesce when they approach. We wax full, like moons.

PRIOR I Dance.

PRIOR Dance?

PRIOR I Stand up, dammit, give us your hands, dance!

PRIOR 2 Listen . . .

[*A lone oboe begins to play a little dance tune.*]

PRIOR 2 Delightful sound. Care to dance?

PRIOR Please leave me alone, please just let me sleep . . .

PRIOR 2 Ah, he wants someone familiar. A partner who knows his steps. [*To* PRIOR] Close your eyes. Imagine . . .

PRIOR I don't . . .

PRIOR 2 Hush. Close your eyes.

[PRIOR *does.*]

PRIOR 2 Now open them.

[PRIOR *does.* LOUIS *appears. He looks gorgeous. The music builds gradually into a full-blooded, romantic dance tune.*]

PRIOR Lou.

LOUIS Dance with me.

PRIOR I can't, my leg, it hurts at night . . .
Are you . . . a ghost, Lou?

LOUIS No. Just spectral. Lost to myself. Sitting all day on cold park benches. Wishing I could be with you. Dance with me, babe . . .

[PRIOR *stands up. The leg stops hurting. They begin to dance. The music is beautiful.*]

PRIOR I [*to* PRIOR 2] Hah. Now I see why he's got no children. He's a sodomite.

PRIOR 2 Oh be quiet, you medieval gnome, and let them dance.

5. All items believed to deter vampires.

PRIOR 1 I'm not interfering, I've done my bit. Hooray, hooray, the messenger's come, now I'm blowing off. I don't like it here.

[PRIOR 1 *vanishes.*]

PRIOR 2 The twentieth century. Oh dear, the world has gotten so terribly, terribly old.

[PRIOR 2 *vanishes.* LOUIS *and* PRIOR *waltz happily. Lights fade back to normal.* LOUIS *vanishes.*

PRIOR *dances alone.*

Then suddenly, the sound of wings fills the room.]

Scene 7

[*Split scene:* PRIOR *alone in his apartment;* LOUIS *alone in the park. Again, a sound of beating wings.*]

PRIOR Oh don't come in here don't come in . . . LOUIS!!

No. My name is Prior Walter, I am . . . the scion of an ancient line, I am . . . abandoned I . . . no, my name is . . . is . . . Prior and I live . . . *here and now,* and . . . in the dark, in the dark, the Recording Angel opens its hundred eyes and snaps the spine of the Book of Life[6] and . . . hush! Hush!

I'm talking nonsense, I . . .

No more mad scene, hush, hush . . .

[LOUIS *in the park on a bench.* JOE *approaches, stands at a distance. They stare at each other, then* LOUIS *turns away.*]

LOUIS Do you know the story of Lazarus?

JOE Lazarus?

LOUIS Lazarus. I can't remember what happens, exactly.

JOE I don't . . . Well, he was dead, Lazarus, and Jesus breathed life into him. He brought him back from death.

LOUIS Come here often?

JOE No. Yes. Yes.

LOUIS Back from the dead. You believe that really happened?

JOE I don't know anymore what I believe.

LOUIS This is quite a coincidence. Us meeting.

JOE I followed you.

From work. I . . . followed you here.

[*Pause.*]

LOUIS You followed me.

You probably saw me that day in the washroom and thought: there's a sweet guy, sensitive, cries for friends in trouble.

JOE Yes.

LOUIS You thought maybe I'll cry for you.

JOE Yes.

LOUIS Well I fooled you. Crocodile tears. Nothing . . . [*He touches his heart, shrugs.*]

[JOE *reaches tentatively to touch* LOUIS*'s face.*]

6. In Jewish tradition, the symbolic book in which all who lived are sealed each year on the Day of Atonement, Yom Kippur; in the New Testament, it contains the names of those who will not be damned on Judgment Day (Revelation 13.8, 20.12–15).

LOUIS [*pulling back*] What are you doing? Don't do that.

JOE [*withdrawing his hand*] Sorry. I'm sorry.

LOUIS I'm . . . just not . . . I think, if you touch me, your hand might fall off or something. Worse things have happened to people who have touched me.

JOE Please.

Oh, boy . . .

Can I . . .

I . . . want . . . to touch you. Can I please just touch you . . . um, here?

[*He puts his hand on one side of* LOUIS*'s face. He holds it there.*]

I'm going to hell for doing this.

LOUIS Big deal. You think it could be any worse than New York City?

[*He puts his hand on* JOE*'s hand. He takes* JOE*'s hand away from his face, holds it for a moment, then.*] Come on.

JOE Where?

LOUIS Home. With me.

JOE This makes no sense. I mean I don't know you.

LOUIS Likewise.

JOE And what you do know about me you don't like.

LOUIS The Republican stuff?

JOE Yeah, well for starters.

LOUIS I don't not like that. I *hate* that.

JOE So why on earth should we . . .

[LOUIS *goes to* JOE *and kisses him.*]

LOUIS Strange bedfellows. I don't know. I never made it with one of the damned before.

I would really rather not have to spend tonight alone.

JOE I'm a pretty terrible person, Louis.

LOUIS Lou.

JOE No, I really really am. I don't think I deserve being loved.

LOUIS There? See? We already have a lot in common.

[LOUIS *stands, begins to walk away. He turns, looks back at* JOE. JOE *follows. They exit.*]

[PRIOR *listens. At first no sound, then once again, the sound of beating wings, frighteningly near.*]

PRIOR That sound, that sound, it. . . . What is that, like birds or something, like a *really* big bird, I'm frightened, I . . . no, no fear, find the anger, find the . . . anger, my blood is clean, my brain is fine, I can handle pressure, I am a gay man and I am used to pressure, to trouble, I am tough and strong and. . . . Oh. Oh my goodness. I . . . [*He is washed over by an intense sexual feeling.*] Ooohhhh. . . . I'm hot, I'm . . . so . . . aw Jeez what is going on here I . . . must have a fever I . . .

[*The bedside lamp flickers wildly as the bed begins to roll forward and back. There is a deep bass creaking and groaning from the bedroom ceiling, like the timbers of a ship under immense stress, and from above a fine rain of plaster dust.*]

PRIOR OH!

PLEASE, OH PLEASE! Something's coming in here, I'm scared, I don't like this at all, something's approaching and I . . . OH!

[There is a great blaze of triumphal music, heralding. The light turns an extraordinary harsh, cold, pale blue, then a rich, brilliant warm golden color, then a hot, bilious green, and then finally a spectacular royal purple. Then silence.]

PRIOR *[an awestruck whisper]* God almighty . . .
Very Steven Spielberg.[7]

[A sound, like a plummeting meteor, tears down from very, very far above the earth, hurtling at an incredible velocity towards the bedroom; the light seems to be sucked out of the room as the projectile approaches; as the room reaches darkness, we hear a terrifying CRASH *as something immense strikes earth; the whole building shudders and a part of the bedroom ceiling, lots of plaster and lathe and wiring, crashes to the floor. And then in a shower of unearthly white light, spreading great opalescent gray-silver wings, the Angel descends into the room and floats above the bed.]*

ANGEL

Greetings, Prophet;
The Great Work begins:
The Messenger has arrived.

[Blackout.]

End of Part One.

7. An American film director (b. 1947), known for his use of special effects in such hits as *Close Encounters of the Third Kind* (1977), *Raiders of the Lost Ark* (1981), and *E.T.: The Extraterrestrial* (1982).

SUZAN-LORI PARKS

b. 1964

WHEN Suzan-Lori Parks was a senior at Mount Holyoke College, she wrote her first play, *The Sinner's Place*. Because, as Parks later recalled, the play's setting consisted of "a lot of dirt on stage which was being dug at," the Theater Department rejected it for production. By the time she was awarded a Pulitzer Prize in 2002 for her play *Topdog/Underdog*, however, Parks's fascination with digging—turning over the topsoil of cultural myths, sifting through the artifacts of history, unearthing the buried voices of African Americans within history—had established her as one of the American theater's foremost archaeologists. "The responsibility of a writer," the novelist James Baldwin once remarked, "is to excavate the experience of the people who produced him." Deeply concerned with forebears and inheritances, Parks's drama uncovers this experience by examining its traces and absences in the American historical imagination. "Because so much of African American history has been unrecorded, dismembered, washed out," Parks writes, "one of my tasks as playwright is to—through literature and the special strange relationship between theater and real-life—locate the ancestral burial ground, dig for bones, find bones, hear the bones sing, write it down." By "remembering" history in the double sense of retrieving and remaking it, Parks offers new theatrical possibilities for staging the dialogue between past, present, and future. Innovative (often challenging) in language, dramatic structure, and performance, her drama remains among the most startlingly original in the contemporary American theater.

Suzan-Lori Parks was born in Fort Knox, Kentucky. The daughter of an Army colonel, she moved frequently as a child and considered a number of places home: Texas, California, North Carolina, Maryland, Vermont, and Germany, where she attended German schools rather than those for the children of American military personnel. This experience of changing location—of moving between places with divergent regional and national histories and of negotiating language differences—clearly contributed to her interest in language and in the relationships between geography, history, and identity. As an undergraduate at Mount Holyoke she took a short story writing class with James Baldwin; after she gave an animated in-class reading of one of her stories, he suggested that she consider playwriting. The turn to drama was a natural one: as she explained in a 2000 interview, she felt while writing short stories that her characters were in the room with her, "standing right behind me, talking. Not telling the story, but acting it out—doing it." Despite the Theater Department's rejection of *The Sinner's Place*, Parks decided to pursue her interest in dramatic writing. Encouraged by one of her English professors, she read the plays of two pioneering African American women playwrights: Adrienne Kennedy, whose *Funnyhouse of a Negro* (1962) dramatized its protagonist's haunted consciousness on a dreamlike stage reminiscent of the stages of AUGUST STRINDBERG and Jean Genet, and Ntozake Shange, who has explored the relationship of drama, poetry, dance, and female African American identity in *for colored girls who have considered suicide / when the rainbow is enuf* (1975) and other plays. After graduating from college in 1985 with majors in English and German, Parks studied acting for a year in London.

Upon her return to the United States, Parks quickly established herself as a playwright of note. *Betting on the Dust Commander* (1987) was produced in New York, as was *Imperceptible Mutabilities in the Third Kingdom* (1989). The latter play received an Obie (Off-Broadway) Award for Best New American Play and was widely praised by critics; indeed, after seeing the play, Mel Gussow of the *New York Times* called Parks "the year's most promising playwright." *The Death of the Last Black Man in the Whole Entire World* opened the following year at the same theater, and *Devotees in the Garden of Love* was produced at the Humana Festival in Louisville in 1992. Parks's next drama, *THE AMERICA PLAY*, was given workshop productions in Washington and Dallas in 1993 before opening at the Yale Repertory Theatre and the New York Public Theater in 1994. In 1996, her play *Venus*—based on the life of Saartjie Baartman, a Khoisan African woman who, because of her large buttocks, was exhibited in the early 1800s in London and Paris as the "Hottentot Venus"—was produced at the Public Theatre in New York and received an Obie Award for Playwriting. *In the Blood* was produced in New York in 1999, and *Fucking A* premiered in Houston in 2000; both plays were inspired by Nathaniel Hawthorne's novel *The Scarlet Letter* (1850). The Pulitzer Prize–winning *Topdog/Underdog*, which features two brothers named Lincoln and Booth, opened at the Public Theater in New York in 2001 and was subsequently taken to Broadway. Parks's most ambitious theatrical project began in 2002, when the playwright decided to write one play every day for a year. The completed plays—some less than a page in length, others considerably longer—were performed by theater groups across the United States in 2006–07 as part of a cycle titled *365 Days/365 Plays*. Parks has also written the screenplay for the film *Girl 6* (1996, directed by Spike Lee) and an adaptation of Zora Neale Hurston's 1937 novel *Their Eyes Were Watching God*, which was televised in 2005. Parks's novel *Getting Mother's Body* was published in 2003.

Intricate (sometimes dense) in texture and meaning, Parks's plays have received widespread attention for their distinctive, highly theatricalized conception of language, character, and dramatic form. As befits a dramatist whose favorite writers include the modernists William Faulkner, Virginia Woolf, and James Joyce, Parks makes intricate, highly self-conscious use of the acoustic and semantic qualities of dramatic speech. Words, Parks insists, are "spells in our mouths." Driven by the cadences, syntax, and word forms of African American dialect, distinguished by frequent wordplay and by multiple meanings, the language of Parks's drama reflects her characters' complex lives and inheritance. When one of the characters in *Imperceptible Mutabilities* says "Last night I dreamed of where I comed from. But where I comed from diduhnt look like nowhere like I been," his words evoke a collective experience of migration, relocation, and lost origins. How do contemporary African Americans, descendants of those who endured the Middle Passage in the holds of slave ships, bridge the gap between Africa and North America, between the present and the history that informs it? Like the words that Parks uses, with their "thrilling histories" and "fabulous etymologies," the characters who people her plays are indelibly marked by history. They bear names such as those in *Death of the Last Black Man in the Whole Entire World:* Black Man with Watermelon, Yes and Greens Black-Eyed Peas Cornbread, And Bigger and Bigger and Bigger, Before Columbus, and Queen-then-Pharaoh-Hatshepsut. Drawing together racial stereotypes, African history, soul food, and literary references (the character And Bigger and Bigger and Bigger, for example, is named after Bigger Thomas, the protagonist of Richard Wright's 1940 novel *Native*

Son), these figures embody many of the ways in which black Americans have been represented in American history and culture.

While Parks's dramatic characters are rooted in real lives and relationships, they also function as improvised meditations, or riffs, on cultural themes and images. Not surprisingly, music—in the form of jazz, classical music, opera, and hip-hop—has played an important role in the language and structure of Parks's drama. Rejecting the linear form of traditional drama, in which action proceeds with a clear beginning, middle, and end, Parks experiments with alternative ways of structuring dramatic incidents. One of her signature devices is "repetition and revision"—the technique, popular with jazz composers and musicians (and echoing the cadence of African American oral traditions, including preaching), of repeating a phrase over and over again while varying it slightly each time. In Parks's drama, words, exchanges, and situations return with hypnotic regularity, establishing connections and counterpoints that build with a logic as much circular as linear. "Characters refigure their words," Parks declares, "and through a refiguring of language show us that they are experiencing their situation anew." The phrase that supplies the title of *The Death of the Last Black Man in the Whole Entire World*, for instance, is spoken at a number of points in the play, and this repetition mirrors that of the action, in which the central protagonist—representing one black man and every black man—is murdered over and over again. Only in the burial scene that ends the play does this repetitive cycle in African American history attain closure.

Repetition, doubling, and, again, the remembering of history are central to *The America Play*, Parks's most frequently performed work. The play is set in a "great hole" somewhere in the American West, "an exact replica" (the stage direction indicates) "of the Great Hole of History," a fictional theme park located back East where a parade of historical figures emerge and march by for the audience's entertainment. The play's protagonist, an African American man identified by his stage name, The Foundling Father, was so entranced with the marvels of history when he visited the Great Park on his honeymoon that he became determined to re-create it. After being told that he resembled Abraham Lincoln—the two "were dead ringers, more or less"—he took to reciting speeches by the famous president in costume. When someone observed that "he played Lincoln so well that he ought to be shot," The Foundling Father devised just such an act: customers pay a penny to shoot him as he sits in Ford's Theater. One after another, they select a pistol, stand in position, and, after shooting him in the head, jump to the stage yelling "Thus to the Tyrants!" or other exclamations attributed to Lincoln's assassin John Wilkes Booth

A nineteenth-century lithograph by Currier and Ives showing the assassination of Lincoln in Ford's Theatre.

(and others). The assassination is replayed over and over again while The Foundling Father recounts to the play's audience his past and his peculiar vocation.

All history repeats itself, Karl Marx famously observed: "the first time as tragedy, the second time as farce." But in an age of historical theme parks, Revolutionary and Civil War reenactments, and interactive museums (such as the Abraham Lincoln Presidential Museum in Springfield, Illinois, which opened in 2005), history is just as likely to repeat itself as theater. In *The America Play,* Parks explores the many ways in which American history—the images, texts, performances, commemorations with which we tell the story of our collective past—writes itself into the present. The Foundling Father is flanked by a pasteboard cutout and bust of Lincoln, to which he frequently gestures; he collects the pennies that bear Lincoln's profile; and he carries with him the props by which the legendary president is identified in the popular imagination: black coat, stovepipe hat, and an assortment of beards (including a blond one, which he rarely wears because it undermines the illusion). The Foundling Father quotes from the Gettysburg Address and retells the events of the fateful night in Ford's Theater, though the account he provides is based as much on tradition and hearsay as historical fact. Parks plays with the idea of historical accuracy in her footnotes to the play, which include humorous or speculative information (including a line that Mary Todd Lincoln "might have said . . . that night") as well as documented facts. In a play that features an actor impersonating a historical figure, a replay of this performance on television (in the play's second act), and scenes from the play that Lincoln was watching (*Our American Cousin* [1858] by Tom Taylor), history becomes the site of multiple performances and competing imitations. At times, original and copy seem indistinguishable from one another. Even the Great Hole of History reappears as a theme park somewhere else.

With its parade of well-known historical figures and deeds, the Great Hole provides a spectacle of American history as it has traditionally circulated and been known. But this hole in the ground also signals its absences and elisions. Reversing the nineteenth-century tradition of blackface—white actors blackening their faces in order to play African American characters—The Foundling Father's impersonation of Abraham Lincoln foregrounds the absence or marginalization of African Americans from this history. As he refers to himself as the "Lesser Known," in contrast to the "Great Man," The Foundling Father reflects on the discrepancy between the latter's fame and his own anonymity. A "digger" by trade, he discovers a more elevated calling by following in the Great Man's footsteps. Yet the reflected glory that he acquires by impersonating Lincoln only underscores the historical invisibility to which his racial identity has otherwise consigned him. Lincoln may have freed the slaves—but the idea of America that he represents has largely excluded

Reggie Montgomery, seated, as the Foundling Father, and Adriane Lenox, as a woman customer, in the 1993 premiere production of *The America Play* at the Yale Repertory Theatre.

African Americans from its originating myths, as well as from the prevailing national identity. The Foundling Father may assume the mantle of one of his country's forefathers —but as Parks's play on his name signifies, his is an illegitimate inheritance (a *foundling* is a child of unknown parentage). When one of his customers, a woman, yells "LIES!" after jumping to the stage, her accusation strikes at the heart of the national myth—the idea of America as "a new nation, conceived in Liberty, and dedicated to the proposition that all men are created equal"—that Lincoln represents.

The search for (fore)fathers in *The America Play* extends into the play's second act, set years later, when The Foundling Father's wife Lucy and son Brazil look for traces of him after his death. Marked by the rituals of grief, this act is pervaded with a sense of mourning, yet it also conveys a tone of affirmation. The Foundling Father may have "fall[en] in love with the wrong person, fall[en] in love with the wrong dream" (as Parks suggests), but his deconstructive performance of American history has been celebratory as well. By showing this history to itself through the mirror of blackness, he has claimed a space, however small, in the performance of national identity. S.G.

The America Play

THE ROLES

Act 1: THE FOUNDLING FATHER, AS ABRAHAM LINCOLN
A VARIETY OF VISITORS

Act 2: LUCY
BRAZIL
THE FOUNDLING FATHER, AS ABRAHAM LINCOLN
2 ACTORS
The Visitors in Act 1 are played by the 2 Actors who assume the roles in the passages from *Our American Cousin* in Act 2.

Place A great hole. In the middle of nowhere. The hole is an exact replica of The Great Hole of History.

SYNOPSIS OF ACTS AND SCENES

Act 1: Lincoln Act
Act 2: The Hall of Wonders

A. Big Bang
B. Echo
C. Archeology
D. Echo
E. Spadework
F. Echo
G. The Great Beyond

Brackets in the text indicate optional cuts for production.

In the beginning, all the world was America.

—JOHN LOCKE[1]

1. English philosopher and political theorist (1632–1704); the quotation is from *Two Treatises of Government* (1689).

Act 1: Lincoln Act

A great hole. In the middle of nowhere. The hole is an exact replica of the Great Hole of History.

THE FOUNDLING FATHER AS ABRAHAM LINCOLN "To stop too fearful and too faint to go."[2]

[*Rest.*[3]]

"He digged the hole and the whole held him."

[*Rest.*]

"I cannot dig, to beg I am ashamed."[4]

[*Rest.*]

"He went to the theatre but home went she."[5]

[*Rest.*]

Goatee. Goatee. What he sported when he died. Its not my favorite.

[*Rest.*]

"He digged the hole and the whole held him." Huh.

[*Rest.*]

There was once a man who was told that he bore a strong resemblance to Abraham Lincoln.[6] He was tall and thinly built just like the Great Man. His legs were the longer part just like the Great Mans legs. His hands and feet were large as the Great Mans were large. The Lesser Known had several beards which he carried around in a box. The beards were his although he himself had not grown them on his face but since he'd secretly bought the hairs from his barber and arranged their beard shapes and since the procurement and upkeep of his beards took so much work he figured that the beards were completely his. Were as authentic as he was, so to speak. His beard box was of cherry wood and lined with purple velvet. He had the initials "A.L." tooled in gold on the lid.

[*Rest.*]

While the Great Mans livelihood kept him in Big Town the Lesser Knowns work kept him in Small Town. The Great Man by trade was a President. The Lesser Known was a Digger by trade. From a family of Diggers. Digged graves. He was known in Small Town to dig his graves quickly and neatly. This brought him a steady business.

[*Rest.*]

2. An example of chiasmus, by Oliver Goldsmith, cited under "chiasmus" in *Webster's Ninth New Collegiate Dictionary* (Springfield, MA: Merriam-Webster, Inc., 1983) p. 232. Notes 4 and 5 also refer to examples of chiasmus [Parks's note]. *Chiasmus:* the syntactic inversion of the second of two parallel clauses (a rhetorical figure). The example is from "The Traveller; or, A Prospect of Society" (1794), by Goldsmith (ca. 1730–1774), an Irish-born novelist, poet, and playwright.

3. Pause.

4. *A Dictionary of Modern English Usage,* H. W. Fowler (New York: Oxford University Press, 1983) p. 86 [Parks's note]. The quotation is from Luke 16.3.

5. *The New American Heritage Dictionary of the English Language,* William Morris, ed. (Boston: Houghton Mifflin Co., 1981) p. 232 [Parks's note].

6. The sixteenth president of the United States (1809–1865; president, 1861–65), a lawyer and legislator from Illinois who was born in backwoods Kentucky; he has been acclaimed for his leadership during the Civil War (1861–65) and for his role in ending slavery.

A wink to Mr. Lincolns pasteboard cutout. [*Winks at Lincoln's pasteboard cutout.*]

[*Rest.*]

It would be helpful to our story if when the Great Man died in death he were to meet the Lesser Known. It would be helpful to our story if, say, the Lesser Known were summoned to Big Town by the Great Mans wife: "*Emergency* oh, *Emergency,* please put the Great Man in the ground"[7] (they say the Great Mans wife was given to hysterics: one young son dead others sickly:[8] even the Great Man couldnt save them: a war on then off and surrendered to. "Play Dixie I always liked that song":[9] the brother against the brother: a new nation all conceived and ready to be hatched: the Great Man takes to guffawing guffawing at thin jokes in bad plays: "You sockdologizing old man-trap!"[1] haw haw haw because he wants so very badly to laugh at something and one moment guffawing and the next moment the Great Man is gunned down. In his rocker. "Useless Useless."[2] And there were bills to pay.) "*Emergency,* oh *Emergency* please put the Great Man in the ground."

[*Rest.*]

It is said that the Great Mans wife did call out and it is said that the Lesser Known would [sneak away from his digging and stand behind a tree where he couldnt be seen or get up and] leave his wife and child after the blessing had been said and [the meat carved during the distribution of the vegetables it is said that he would leave his wife and his child and] standing in the kitchen or sometimes out in the yard [between the right angles of the house] stand out there where he couldnt be seen standing with his ear cocked. "*Emergency,* oh *Emergency,* please put the Great Man in the ground."

[*Rest.*]

It would help if she had called out and if he had been summoned been given a ticket all bought and paid for and boarded a train in his look-alike black frock coat bought on time and already exhausted. Ridiculous. If he had been summoned. [Been summoned between the meat and the vegetables and boarded a train to Big Town where he would line up and gawk at

7. Possibly the words of Mary Todd Lincoln [1818–1882] after the death of her husband [Parks's note].

8. Of the Lincolns' four sons—Robert (1843–1926), Edward (1846–1850), William (1850–1862), and Thomas, nicknamed Tad (1853–1871)—only Robert survived into adulthood. Mary Todd Lincoln has often been described as mentally unstable.

9. At the end of the Civil War, President Lincoln told his troops to play "Dixie," the song of the South, in tribute to the Confederacy [Parks's note]. The song was published in 1860 by the Ohio-born Daniel Decatur Emmett, who wrote songs for his blackface minstrel troupe, but his claim of authorship is disputed.

1. A very funny line from the play *Our American Cousin.* As the audience roared with laughter, Booth entered Lincoln's box and shot him dead [Parks's note]. *Our American Cousin* (1858), a comedy by the English dramatist and writer Tom Taylor. John Wilkes Booth (1838–1865), a renowned Shakespearean actor and a Southern sympathizer who led the conspiracy to assassinate Lincoln as he attended a performance, less than a week after the Civil War ended.

2. The last words of President Lincoln's assassin, John Wilkes Booth [Parks's note]. After shooting Lincoln, Booth leaped to the stage and broke his leg, but escaped on horseback. After soldiers and detectives found him hiding in a barn in Virginia, about 75 miles southwest of Washington, he either was shot or shot himself and died shortly thereafter.

the Great Mans corpse along with the rest of them.[3]] But none of this was meant to be.

[*Rest.*]

A nod to the bust of Mr. Lincoln. [*Nods to the bust of Lincoln.*] But none of this was meant to be. For the Great Man had been murdered long before the Lesser Known had been born. How uhboutthat. [So that any calling that had been done he couldnt hear, any summoning he had hoped for he couldnt answer but somehow not even unheard and unanswered because he hadnt even been there] although you should note that he talked about the murder and the mourning that followed as if he'd been called away on business at the time and because of the business had missed it. Living regretting he hadnt arrived sooner. Being told from birth practically that he and the Great Man were dead ringers, more or less, and knowing that he, if he had been in the slightest vicinity back then, would have had at least a chance at the great honor of digging the Great Mans grave.

[*Rest.*]

This beard I wear for the holidays. I got shoes to match. Rarely wear em together. It's a little *much*.

[*Rest.*]

[His son named in a fit of meanspirit after the bad joke about fancy nuts[4] and old mens toes his son looked like a nobody. Not Mr. Lincoln or the father or the mother either for that matter although the father had assumed the superiority of his own blood and hadnt really expected the mother to exert any influence.]

[*Rest.*]

Sunday. Always slow on Sunday. I'll get thuh shoes. Youll see. A wink to Mr. Lincolns pasteboard cutout. [*Winks at Lincoln's cutout.*]

[*Rest.*]

Everyone who has ever walked the earth has a shape around which their entire lives and their posterity shapes itself. The Great Man had his log cabin into which he was born, the distance between the cabin and Big Town multiplied by the half-life, the staying power of his words and image, being the true measurement of the Great Mans stature. The Lesser Known had a favorite hole. A chasm, really. Not a hole he had digged but one he'd visited. Long before the son was born. When he and his Lucy were newly wedded. Lucy kept secrets for the dead. And they figured what with his digging and her Confidence work[5] they could build a mourning business. The son would be a weeper.[6] Such a long time uhgo. So long uhgo. When he and his Lucy were newly wedded and looking for some postnuptial excitement: A Big Hole. A theme park. With historical parades. The size of the hole itself was enough to impress any Digger but it was the Historicity of the place the order and beauty of the pageants which marched by them the Greats on parade in front of them. From the sidelines he'd be calling "Ohwayohwhyohwayoh" and "Hello" and waving and saluting. The Hole

3. Thousands viewed Lincoln's body lying in state in the U.S. Capitol, and thousands more watched the train bearing him home to Springfield, Illinois, where he was buried.

4. That is, Brazil nuts, which were long known in some regions of the United States as "nigger toes."

5. That is, her work as someone entrusted with confidential communications.

6. A hired mourner.

and its Historicity and the part he played in it all gave a shape to the life and posterity of the Lesser Known that he could never shake.

[*Rest.*]

Here they are. I wont put them on. I'll just hold them up. See. Too much. Told ya. [Much much later when the Lesser Known had made a name for himself he began to record his own movements. He hoped he'd be of interest to posterity. As in the Great Mans footsteps.]

[*Rest.*]

Traveling home again from the honeymoon at the Big Hole riding the train with his Lucy: wife beside him the Reconstructed Historicities he has witnessed continue to march before him in his minds eye as they had at the Hole. Cannons wicks were lit and the rockets did blare and the enemy was slain and lay stretched out and smoldering for dead and rose up again to take their bows. On the way home again the histories paraded again on past him although it wasnt on past him at all it wasnt something he could expect but again like Lincolns life not "on past" but *past. Behind him.* Like an echo in his head.

[*Rest.*]

When he got home again he began to hear the summoning. At first they thought it only an echo. Memories sometimes stuck like that and he and his Lucy had both seen visions. But after a while it only called to him. And it became louder not softer but louder louder as if he were moving toward it.

[*Rest.*]

This is my fancy beard. Yellow. Mr. Lincolns hair was dark so I dont wear it much. If you deviate too much they wont get their pleasure. Thats my experience. Some inconsistencies are perpetuatable because theyre good for business. But not the yellow beard. Its just my fancy. Every once and a while. Of course, his hair was dark.

[*Rest.*]

The Lesser Known left his wife and child and went out West finally. [Between the meat and the vegetables. A monumentous journey. Enduring all the elements. Without a friend in the world. And the beasts of the forest took him in. He got there and he got his plot he staked his claim he tried his hand at his own Big Hole.] As it had been back East everywhere out West he went people remarked on his likeness to Lincoln. How, in a limited sort of way, taking into account of course his natural God-given limitations, how he was identical to the Great Man in gait and manner how his legs were long and torso short. The Lesser Known had by this time taken to wearing a false wart on his cheek in remembrance of the Great Mans wart. When the Westerners noted his wart they pronounced the 2 men in virtual twinship.

[*Rest.*]

Goatee. Huh. Goatee.

[*Rest.*]

"He digged the Hole and the Whole held him."

[*Rest.*]

"I cannot dig, to beg I am ashamed."

[*Rest.*]

The Lesser Known had under his belt a few of the Great Mans words and after a day of digging, in the evenings, would stand in his hole reciting. But the Lesser Known was a curiosity at best. None of those who spoke of his virtual twinship with greatness would actually pay money to watch him be that greatness. One day he tacked up posters inviting them to come and throw old food at him while he spoke. This was a moderate success. People began to save their old food "for Mr. Lincoln" they said. He took to traveling playing small towns. Made money. And when someone remarked that he played Lincoln so well that he ought to be shot, it was as if the Great Mans footsteps had been suddenly revealed:

[*Rest.*]

The Lesser Known returned to his hole and, instead of speeching, his act would now consist of a single chair, a rocker, in a dark box. The public was invited to pay a penny, choose from the selection of provided pistols, enter the darkened box and "Shoot Mr. Lincoln." The Lesser Known became famous overnight.

[A MAN, *as John Wilkes* Booth, *enters. He takes a gun and "stands in position": at the left side of* THE FOUNDLING FATHER, *as Abraham* LINCOLN, *pointing the gun at* THE FOUNDLING FATHER*'s head*]

A MAN Ready.

THE FOUNDLING FATHER Haw Haw Haw Haw

[*Rest.*]

HAW HAW HAW HAW

[BOOTH *shoots.* LINCOLN *"slumps in his chair."* BOOTH *jumps.*]

A MAN [*theatrically*] "Thus to the tyrants!"[7]

[*Rest.*]

Hhhh. [*Exits.*]

THE FOUNDLING FATHER Most of them do that, thuh "Thus to the tyrants!"—what they say the killer said. "Thus to the tyrants!" The killer was also heard to say "The South is avenged!"[8] Sometimes they yell that.

[A *man, the same man as before, enters again, again as John Wilkes* Booth. *He takes a gun and "stands in position": at the left side of* THE FOUNDLING FATHER, *as Abraham* LINCOLN, *pointing the gun at* THE FOUNDLING FATHER*'s head.*]

A MAN Ready.

THE FOUNDLING FATHER Haw Haw Haw Haw

[*Rest.*]

HAW HAW HAW HAW

[BOOTH *shoots.* LINCOLN *"slumps in his chair."* BOOTH *jumps.*]

A MAN [*theatrically*] "The South is avenged!"

[*Rest.*]

7. Or "Sic semper tyrannis." Purportedly, Booth's words after he slew Lincoln and leapt from the presidential box to the stage of Ford's Theatre in Washington, D.C. on 14 April 1865, not only killing the President but also interrupting a performance of *Our American Cousin,* starring Miss Laura Keene [Parks's note]. *Sic semper tyrannis:* Thus always to tyrants (Latin), adopted in 1776 as the state motto of Virginia (whose capital, Richmond, became the capital of the Confederacy). Keene (ca. 1826–1873), a London-born actress who became well-known in the United States on the stage and as a theater manager.

8. Allegedly, Booth's words [Parks's note].

Hhhh.

[*Rest.*]

Thank you.

THE FOUNDLING FATHER Pleasures mine.

A MAN Till next week.

THE FOUNDLING FATHER Till next week.

[A MAN *exits.*]

THE FOUNDLING FATHER Comes once a week that one. Always chooses the Derringer[9] although we've got several styles he always chooses the Derringer. Always "The tyrants" and then "The South avenged." The ones who choose the Derringer are the ones for History. He's one for History. As it Used to Be. Never wavers. No frills. By the book. Nothing excessive.

[*Rest.*]

A nod to Mr. Lincolns bust. [*Nods to Lincoln's bust.*]

[*Rest.*]

I'll wear this one. He sported this style in the early war years. Years of uncertainty. When he didnt know if the war was right when it could be said he didnt always know which side he was on not because he was a stupid man but because it was sometimes not 2 different sides at all but one great side surging toward something beyond either Northern or Southern. A beard of uncertainty. The Lesser Known meanwhile living his life long after all this had happened and not knowing much about it until he was much older [(as a boy "The Civil War" was an afterschool game and his folks didnt mention the Great Mans murder for fear of frightening him)] knew only that he was a dead ringer in a family of Diggers and that he wanted to grow and have others think of him and remove their hats and touch their hearts and look up into the heavens and say something about the freeing of the slaves. That is, he wanted to make a great impression as he understood Mr. Lincoln to have made.

[*Rest.*]

And so in his youth the Lesser Known familiarized himself with all aspects of the Great Mans existence. What interested the Lesser Known most was the murder and what was most captivating about the murder was the 20 feet—

[A WOMAN, *as* BOOTH, *enters.*]

A WOMAN Excuse me.

THE FOUNDLING FATHER Not at all.

[A WOMAN, *as* BOOTH, *"stands in position."*]

THE FOUNDLING FATHER Haw Haw Haw Haw

[*Rest.*]

HAW HAW HAW HAW

[BOOTH *shoots.* LINCOLN *"slumps in his chair."* BOOTH *jumps.*]

A WOMAN "Strike the tent."[1] [*Exits.*]

9. A small, easily concealed pistol with a large bore, invented ca. 1852 by the American gunsmith Henry Deringer; Booth used a derringer to shoot Lincoln in the back of the head.

1. The last words of General Robert E. Lee [1807–1870], Commander of the Confederate Army [Parks's note].

THE FOUNDLING FATHER What interested the Lesser Known most about the Great Mans murder was the 20 feet which separated the presidents box from the stage. In the presidents box sat the president his wife and their 2 friends.[2] On the stage that night was *Our American Cousin* starring Miss Laura Keene. The plot of this play is of little consequence to our story. Suffice it to say that it was thinly comedic and somewhere in the 3rd Act a man holds a gun to his head—something about despair—

[*Rest.*]

Ladies and Gentlemen: *Our American Cousin*—

[B WOMAN, *as* BOOTH, *enters. She "stands in position."*]

B WOMAN Go ahead.

THE FOUNDLING FATHER Haw Haw Haw Haw

[*Rest.*]

HAW HAW HAW HAW

[BOOTH *shoots.* LINCOLN *"slumps in his chair."* BOOTH *jumps.*]

B WOMAN [*rest*] LIES!

[*Rest.*]

L I I I I I I I I I I I I I I I I I I I I I I I I I I I I E S !

[*Rest.*]

L I I I I I I I I I I I I I I I I I I I A R R R R R R R R R R R R R R R R S !

[*Rest.*]

Lies.

[*Rest. Exits. Reenters. Steps downstage. Rest.*]

LIES!

[*Rest.*]

L I I I I I I I I I I I I I I I I I I I I I I I I I I I I E S !

[*Rest.*]

L I I I I I I I I I I I I I I I I I I I A R R R R R R R R R R R R R R R R S !

[*Rest.*]

Lies.

[*Rest. Exits.*]

THE FOUNDLING FATHER [*rest*] I think I'll wear the yellow beard. Variety. Works like uh tonic.

[*Rest.*]

Some inaccuracies are good for business. Take the stovepipe hat! Never really worn indoors but people dont like their Lincoln hatless.

[*Rest.*]

Mr. Lincoln my apologies. [*Nods to the bust and winks to the cutout.*]

[*Rest.*]

[Blonde. Not bad if you like a stretch. Hmmm. Let us pretend for a moment that our beloved Mr. Lincoln was a blonde. "The sun on his fair hair looked like the sun itself."[3]—. Now. What interested our Mr. Lesser Known most was those feet between where the Great *Blonde* Man sat, in

2. Clara Harris (1845–1883), the daughter of a U.S. senator, and her fiancée, Major Henry Rathbone (1837–1911).

3. From "The Sun," a composition by The Foundling Father, unpublished [Parks's note].

his rocker, the stage, the time it took the murderer to cross that expanse, and how the murderer crossed it. He jumped. Broke his leg in the jumping. It was said that the Great Mans wife then began to scream. (She was given to hysterics several years afterward in fact declared insane did you know she ran around Big Town poor desperate for money trying to sell her clothing? On that sad night she begged her servant: "Bring in Taddy, Father will speak to Taddy."[4] But Father died instead unconscious. And she went mad from grief. Off her rocker. Mad Mary claims she hears her dead men. Summoning. The older son, Robert, he locked her up.[5] "*Emergency*, oh, *Emergency* please put the Great Man in the ground.")

[*Enter* B MAN, *as* BOOTH. *He "stands in position."*]

THE FOUNDLING FATHER Haw Haw Haw Haw

[*Rest.*]

HAW HAW HAW HAW

[BOOTH *shoots.* LINCOLN *"slumps in his chair."* BOOTH *jumps.*]

B MAN "Now he belongs to the ages."[6]

[*Rest.*]

Blonde?

THE FOUNDLING FATHER (I only talk with the regulars.)

B MAN He wasnt blonde. [*Exits.*]

THE FOUNDLING FATHER A slight deafness in this ear other than that there are no side effects.

[*Rest.*]

Hhh. Clean-shaven for a while. The face needs air. Clean-shaven as in his youth. When he met his Mary —. Hhh. Blonde.

[*Rest.*]

6 feet under is a long way to go. Imagine. When the Lesser Known left to find his way out West he figured he had dug over 7 hundred and 23 graves. 7 hundred and 23. Excluding his Big Hole. Excluding the hundreds of shallow holes he later digs the hundreds of shallow holes he'll use to bury his faux-historical knickknacks when he finally quits this business. Not including those. 7 hundred and 23 graves.

[C MAN *and* C WOMAN *enter.*]

C MAN You allow 2 at once?

THE FOUNDLING FATHER

[*Rest.*]

C WOMAN We're just married. You know: newlyweds. We hope you dont mind. Us both at once.

THE FOUNDLING FATHER

[*Rest.*]

4. Mary Todd Lincoln, wanting her dying husband to speak to their son Tad, might have said this that night [Parks's note]. After he was shot, Lincoln was carried to a home across the street from the theater; he died the next morning.

5. In 1875, Robert had his mother committed to an insane asylum, but she was later declared legally competent. *Hears her dead men:* from the 1850s onward, Mary Todd Lincoln became increasingly interested in spiritualism, or communication with the dead (usually attempted with the help of a medium).

6. The words of Secretary of War Edwin Stanton [1814–1869], as Lincoln died [Parks's note].

C MAN We're just married.

C WOMAN Newlyweds.

THE FOUNDLING FATHER

[*Rest.*]

[*Rest.*]

[*They "stand in position." Both hold one gun.*]

C MAN AND C WOMAN Shoot.

THE FOUNDLING FATHER Haw Haw Haw Haw

[*Rest.*]

HAW HAW HAW HAW

[*Rest.*]

[*Rest.*]

HAW HAW HAW HAW

[*They shoot.* LINCOLN *"slumps in his chair." They jump.*]

C MAN Go on.

C WOMAN [*theatrically*] "Theyve killed the president!"[7]

[*Rest. They exit.*]

THE FOUNDLING FATHER Theyll have children and theyll bring their children here. A slight deafness in this ear other than that there are no side effects. Little ringing in the ears. Slight deafness. I cant complain.

[*Rest.*]

The passage of time. The crossing of space. [The Lesser Known recorded his every movement.] He'd hoped he'd be of interest in his posterity. [Once again riding in the Great Mans footsteps.] A nod to the presidents bust. [*Nods.*]

[*Rest.*]

[*Rest.*]

The Great Man lived in the past that is was an inhabitant of time immemorial and the Lesser Known out West alive a resident of the present. And the Great Mans deeds had transpired during the life of the Great Man somewhere in past-land that is somewhere "back there" and all this while the Lesser Known digging his holes bearing the burden of his resemblance all the while trying somehow to equal the Great Man in stature, word and deed going forward with his lesser life trying somehow to follow in the Great Mans footsteps footsteps that were of course behind him. The Lesser Known trying somehow to catch up to the Great Man all this while and maybe running too fast in the wrong direction. Which is to say that maybe the Great Man had to catch him. Hhhh. Ridiculous.

[*Rest.*]

Full fringe. The way he appears on the money.

[*Rest.*]

A wink to Mr. Lincolns pasteboard cutout. A nod to Mr. Lincolns bust.

[*Rest. Time passes. Rest.*]

7. The words of Mary Todd, just after Lincoln was shot [Parks's note].

When someone remarked that he played Lincoln so well that he ought to be shot it was as if the Great Mans footsteps had been suddenly revealed: instead of making speeches his act would now consist of a single chair, a rocker, in a dark box. The public was cordially invited to pay a penny, choose from a selection of provided pistols enter the darkened box and "Shoot Mr. Lincoln." The Lesser Known became famous overnight.

[A MAN, *as John Wilkes* BOOTH, *enters. He takes a gun and "stands in position": at the left side of* THE FOUNDLING FATHER, *as Abraham* LINCOLN, *pointing the gun at* THE FOUNDLING FATHER*'s head.*]

THE FOUNDLING FATHER Mmm. Like clockwork.

A MAN Ready.

THE FOUNDLING FATHER Haw Haw Haw Haw

[*Rest.*]

HAW HAW HAW HAW

[BOOTH *shoots.* LINCOLN *"slumps in his chair."* BOOTH *jumps.*]

A MAN [*theatrically*] "Thus to the tyrants!"

[*Rest.*]

Hhhh.

LINCOLN

BOOTH

LINCOLN

BOOTH

LINCOLN

BOOTH

LINCOLN

BOOTH

LINCOLN[8]

[BOOTH *jumps.*]

A MAN [*theatrically*] "The South is avenged!"

[*Rest.*]

Hhhh.

[*Rest.*]

Thank you.

THE FOUNDLING FATHER Pleasures mine.

A MAN Next week then. [*Exits.*]

THE FOUNDLING FATHER Little ringing in the ears. Slight deafness.

[*Rest.*]

Little ringing in the ears.

[*Rest.*]

A wink to the Great Mans cutout. A nod to the Great Mans bust. Once again striding in the Great Mans footsteps. Riding on in. Riding to the rescue the way they do. They both had such long legs. Such big feet. And the Greater Man had such a lead although of course somehow still "back there." If the Lesser Known had slowed down stopped moving completely gone in

8. The repetition of characters' names without dialogue indicates an extended pause, or what Parks has elsewhere described as "an elongated and heightened (rest)."

reverse died maybe the Greater Man could have caught up. Woulda had a chance. Woulda sneaked up behind him the Greater Man would have sneaked up behind the Lesser Known unbeknownst and wrestled him to the ground. Stabbed him in the back. In revenge. "Thus to the tyrants!" Shot him maybe. The Lesser Known forgets who he is and just crumples. His bones cannot be found. The Greater Man continues on.

[*Rest.*]

"*Emergency,* oh *Emergency,* please put the Great Man in the ground."

[*Rest.*]

Only a little ringing in the ears. Thats all. Slight deafness.

[*Rest.*]

[*He puts on the blonde beard.*]

Huh. Whatdoyou say I wear the blonde.

[*Rest.*]

[*A gunshot echoes. Softly. And echoes.*]

Act 2: The Hall of Wonders

A gunshot echoes. Loudly. And echoes.
They are in a great hole. In the middle of nowhere. The hole is an exact replica of The Great Hole of History.
A gunshot echoes. Loudly. And echoes. LUCY *with ear trumpet circulates.* BRAZIL *digs.*

A. BIG BANG

LUCY Hear that?
BRAZIL Zit him?
LUCY No.
BRAZIL Oh.
[*A gunshot echoes. Loudly. And echoes.*]
LUCY Hear?
BRAZIL Zit him?!
LUCY Nope. Ssuhecho.
BRAZIL Ssuhecho.
LUCY Uh echo uh huhn. Of gunplay. Once upon uh time somebody had uh little gunplay and now thuh gun goes on playing: *KER-BANG!* KERBANG-Kerbang-kerbang-(kerbang)-((kerbang)).
BRAZIL Thuh echoes.
[*Rest.*]
[*Rest.*]
LUCY Youre stopped.
BRAZIL Mmlistenin.
LUCY Dig on, Brazil. Cant stop diggin till you dig up somethin. Your Daddy was uh Digger.
BRAZIL Uh huhnnn.

LUCY

BRAZIL

[*A gunshot echoes. Loudly. And echoes. Rest. A gunshot echoes. Loudly. And echoes. Rest.*]

[LUCY Itssalways been important in my line to distinguish. Tuh know thuh difference. Not like your Fathuh. Your Fathuh became confused. His lonely death and lack of proper burial is our embarrassment. Go on: dig. Now me I need tuh know thuh real thing from thuh echo. Thuh truth from thuh hearsay.

[*Rest.*]

Bram Price for example. His dear ones and relations told me his dying words but Bram Price hisself of course told me something quite different.

BRAZIL I wept forim.

LUCY Whispered his true secrets to me and to me uhlone.

BRAZIL Then he died.

LUCY Then he died.

[*Rest.*]

Thuh things he told me I will never tell. Mr. Bram Price. Huh.

[*Rest.*]

Dig on.

BRAZIL

LUCY

BRAZIL

LUCY Little Bram Price Junior.

BRAZIL Thuh fat one?

LUCY Burned my eardrums. Just like his Dad did.

BRAZIL I wailed forim.

LUCY Ten days dead wept over and buried and that boy comes back. Not him though. His echo. Sits down tuh dinner and eats up everybodys food just like he did when he was livin.

[*Rest.*]

[*Rest.*]

Little Bram Junior. Burned my eardrums. Miz Penny Price his mother. Thuh things she told me I will never tell.

[*Rest.*]

You remember her.

BRAZIL Wore red velvet in August.

LUCY When her 2 Brams passed she sold herself, son.

BRAZIL O.

LUCY Also lost her mind. —. She finally went. Like your Fathuh went, perhaps. Foul play.

BRAZIL I gnashed for her.

LUCY You did.

BRAZIL Couldnt choose between wailin or gnashin. Weepin sobbin or moanin. Went for gnashing. More to it. Gnashed for her and hers like I have never gnashed. I woulda tore at my coat but thats extra. Chipped uh tooth. One in thuh front.

LUCY You did your job son.

BRAZIL I did my job.

LUCY Confidence. Huh. Thuh things she told me I will never tell. Miz Penny Price. Miz Penny Price.

[*Rest.*]

Youre stopped.

BRAZIL Mmlistenin.

LUCY Dig on, Brazil.

BRAZIL

LUCY

BRAZIL We arent from these parts.

LUCY No. We're not.

BRAZIL Daddy iduhnt[9] either.

LUCY Your Daddy iduhnt either.

[*Rest.*]

Dig on, son. —. Cant stop diggin till you dig up somethin. You dig that something up you brush that something off you give that something uh designated place. Its own place. Along with thuh other discoveries. In thuh Hall of Wonders. Uh place in the Hall of Wonders right uhlong with thuh rest of thuh Wonders hear?

BRAZIL Uh huhn.

[*Rest.*]

LUCY Bram Price Senior, son. Bram Price Senior was not thuh man he claimed tuh be. Huh. Nope. Was not thuh man he claimed tuh be atall. You ever see him in his stocking feet? Or barefoot? Course not. I guessed before he told me. He told me then he died. He told me and I havent told no one. I'm uh good Confidence. As Confidences go. Huh. One of thuh best. As Confidence, mmonly contracted tuh keep quiet 12 years. After 12 years nobody cares. For 19 years I have kept his secret. In my bosom.

[*Rest.*]

He wore lifts in his shoes, son.

BRAZIL Lifts?

LUCY Lifts. Made him seem taller than he was.

BRAZIL Bram Price Senior?

LUCY Bram Price Senior wore lifts in his shoes yes he did, Brazil. I tell you just as he told me with his last breaths on his dying bed: "Lifts." Thats all he said. Then he died. I put thuh puzzle pieces in place. I put thuh puzzle pieces in place. Couldnt tell no one though. Not even your Pa. "Lifts." I never told no one son. For 19 years I have kept Brams secret in my bosom. Youre thuh first tuh know. Hhh! Dig on. Dig on.

BRAZIL Dig on.

LUCY

BRAZIL

LUCY

[*A gunshot echoes. Loudly. And echoes.*]

BRAZIL [*rest*] Ff Pa was here weud find his bones.

9. That is, "isn't."

LUCY Not always.

BRAZIL Thereud be his bones and thereud be thuh Wonders surrounding his bones.

LUCY Ive heard of different.

BRAZIL Thereud be thuh Wonders surrounding his bones and thereud be his Whispers.

LUCY Maybe.

BRAZIL Ffhe sspast like they say he'd of parlayed to uh Confidence his last words and dying wishes. His secrets and his dreams.

LUCY Thats how we pass[1] back East. They could pass different out here.

BRAZIL We got Daddys ways Daddyssgot ours. When theres no Confidence available we just dribble thuh words out. In uh whisper.

LUCY Sometimes.

BRAZIL Thuh Confidencell gather up thuh whispers when she arrives.

LUCY Youre uh prize, Brazil. Uh prize.]

BRAZIL

LUCY

BRAZIL

LUCY

BRAZIL You hear him then? His whispers?

LUCY Not exactly.

BRAZIL He wuduhnt here then.

LUCY He was here.

BRAZIL Ffyou dont hear his whispers he wuduhnt here.

LUCY Whispers dont always come up right away. Takes time sometimes. Whispers could travel different out West than they do back East. Maybe slower. Maybe. Whispers are secrets and often shy. We aint seen your Pa in 30 years. That could be part of it. We also could be experiencing some sort of interference. Or some sort of technical difficulty. Ssard tuh tell.

[*Rest.*]

So much to live for.

BRAZIL So much to live for.

LUCY Look on thuh bright side.

BRAZIL Look on thuh bright side. Look on thuh bright side. Loook onnnnn thuhhhh briiiiiiight siiiiiiiide!!!!

LUCY DIIIIIIIIIIIG!

BRAZIL Dig.

LUCY

BRAZIL

LUCY Helloooo! —. Hellooooo!

BRAZIL

LUCY

BRAZIL [We're from out East. We're not from these parts.

[*Rest.*]

My foe-father, her husband, my Daddy, her mate, her man, my Pa come out here. Out West.

[*Rest.*]

1. Die.

Come out here all uhlone. Cleared thuh path tamed thuh wilderness dug this whole Hole with his own 2 hands and et cetera.

[*Rest.*]

Left his family behind. Back East. His Lucy and his child. He waved "Goodbye." Left us tuh carry on. I was only 5.

[*Rest.*]

My Daddy was uh Digger. Shes whatcha call uh Confidence. I did thuh weepin and thuh moanin.

[*Rest.*]

His lonely death and lack of proper burial is our embarrassment.

[*Rest.*]

Diggin was his livelihood but fakin was his callin. Ssonly natural heud come out here and combine thuh 2. Back East he was always diggin. He was uh natural. Could dig uh hole for uh body that passed like no one else. Digged em quick and they looked good too. This Hole here—this large one—sshis biggest venture to date. So says hearsay.

[*Rest.*]

Uh exact replica of thuh Great Hole of History!

LUCY Sshhhhhht.

BRAZIL [*rest*] Thuh original ssback East. He and Lucy they honeymooned there. At thuh original Great Hole. Its uh popular spot. He and Her would sit on thuh lip and watch everybody who was ever anybody parade on by. Daily parades! Just like thuh Tee Vee. Mr. George Washington, for example, thuh Fathuh of our Country hisself, would rise up from thuh dead and walk uhround and cross thuh Delaware and say stuff!![2] Right before their very eyes!!!!

LUCY Son?

BRAZIL Huh?

LUCY That iduhnt how it went.

BRAZIL Oh.

LUCY Thuh Mr. Washington me and your Daddy seen was uh lookuhlike of thuh Mr. Washington of history-fame, son.

BRAZIL Oh.

LUCY Thuh original Mr. Washingtonssbeen long dead.

BRAZIL O.

LUCY That Hole back East was uh theme park son. Keep your story to scale.

BRAZIL K.[3]

[*Rest.*]

Him and Her would sit by thuh lip uhlong with thuh others all in uh row cameras clickin and theyud look down into that Hole and see—ooooo—you name it. Ever-y-day you could look down that Hole and see—ooooo you name it. Amerigo Vespucci hisself made regular appearances. Marcus Garvey. Ferdinand and Isabella. Mary Queen of thuh Scots! Tarzan King of

2. Washington (1732–1799), the "Father of our Country," the first U.S. president (1789–97), crossed the Delaware from Pennsylvania on December 25, 1776, to make a surprise attack on the Hessian forces garrisoned in Trenton, New Jersey; the attack's success was an enormous boost to American morale early in the Revolutionary War.

3. That is, "OK."

thuh Apes! Washington Jefferson Harding and Millard Fillmore. Mistufer Columbus even.[4] Oh they saw all thuh greats. Parading daily in thuh Great Hole of History.

[*Rest.*]

My Fathuh did thuh living and thuh dead. Small-town and big-time. Mr. Lincoln was of course his favorite.

[*Rest.*]

Not only Mr. Lincoln but Mr. Lincolns last show. His last deeds. His last laughs.

[*Rest.*]

Being uh Digger of some renown Daddy comes out here tuh build uh like attraction. So says hearsay. Figures theres people out here who'll enjoy amusements such as them amusements He and Her enjoyed. We're all citizens of one country afterall.

[*Rest.*]

Mmrestin.

[*A gunshot echoes. Loudly. And echoes.*]

BRAZIL Woooo! [*Drops dead.*]

LUCY Youre fakin Mr. Brazil.

BRAZIL Uh uhnnn.

LUCY Tryin tuh get you some benefits.

BRAZIL Uh uhnnnnnnnn.

LUCY I know me uh faker when I see one. Your Father was uh faker. Huh. One of thuh best. There wudnt nobody your Fathuh couldnt do. Did thuh living and thuh dead. Small-town and big-time. Made-up and historical. Fakin was your Daddys callin but diggin was his livelihood. Oh, back East he was always diggin. Was uh natural. Could dig uh hole for uh body that passed like no one else. Digged em quick and they looked good too. You dont remember of course you dont.

BRAZIL I was only 5.

LUCY You were only 5. When your Fathuh spoke he'd quote thuh Greats. Mister George Washington. Thuh Misters Roosevelt.[5] Mister Millard Fillmore. Huh. All thuh greats. You dont remember of course you dont.

BRAZIL I was only 5—

LUCY —only 5. Mr. Lincoln was of course your Fathuhs favorite. Wuz. Huh. Wuz. Huh. Hearsay says he's past. Your Daddy. Digged this hole then he died. So says hearsay.

4. Brazil names figures who were instrumental in "discovering" America: King Ferdinand (1452–1516) and Queen Isabella (1451–1504), rulers of Aragón and Castile, who underwrote the expeditions of the Italian-born explorer Christopher Columbus (1451–1506), two of which the Italian navigator Amerigo Vespucci (1454–1512)—whose accounts of his voyages to the New World led to the lands being named "America"—helped outfit; he also mentions presidents both lauded—Washington and Thomas Jefferson (1743–1826; 3rd president, 1801–09)—and disparaged: Warren Harding (1865–1923; 29th president, 1921–23) and Millard Fillmore (1800–1874; 13th president, 1850–53). The story of Mary, Queen of Scots (1542–1587; r. 1542–67)—executed, after years of imprisonment, for plotting against England's Elizabeth I—was retold in drama and opera, and Tarzan, a fictional character created by Edgar Rice Burroughs in *Tarzan of the Apes* (1912), has had a long afterlife in print sequels, film, and comics.

5. Two U.S. presidents named Roosevelt, Theodore (1858–1919; 26th president, 1901–09) and his distant cousin Franklin Delano (1882–1945; 32nd president, 1933–45).

[*Rest.*]

Dig, Brazil.

BRAZIL My paw—

LUCY Ssonly natural that heud come out here tuh dig out one of his own. He loved that Great Hole so. He'd stand at thuh lip of that Great Hole: "OHWAYOHWHYOHWAYOH!"

BRAZIL "OHWAYOHWHYOHWAYOH!"

LUCY "OHWAYOHWHYOHWAYOH!" You know: hole talk. Ohwayohwhyohwayoh, just tuh get their attention, then: "Hellooo!" He'd shout down to em. Theyd call back "Hellllooooo!" and wave. He loved that Great Hole so. Came out here. Digged this lookuhlike.

BRAZIL Then he died?

LUCY Then he died. Your Daddy died right here. Huh. Oh, he was uh faker. Uh greaaaaat biiiiig faker too. He was your Fathuh. Thats thuh connection. You take after him.

BRAZIL I do?

LUCY Sure. Put your paw back where it belongs. Go on—back on its stump. —. Poke it on out of your sleeve son. There you go. I'll draw uh X for you. See? Heresuh X. Huh. Dig here.

[*Rest.*]

DIG!

BRAZIL

LUCY

BRAZIL

LUCY Woah! Woah!

BRAZIL Whatchaheard?!

LUCY No tellin, son. Cant say.

[BRAZIL *digs.* LUCY *circulates.*]

BRAZIL [*rest. Rest*] On thuh day he claimed to be the 100th anniversary of the founding of our country the Father took the Son out into the yard. The Father threw himself down in front of the Son and bit into the dirt with his teeth. His eyes leaked. "This is how youll make your mark, Son" the Father said. The Son was only 2 then. "This is the Wail," the Father said. "There's money init," the Father said. The Son was only 2 then. Quiet. On what he claimed was the 101st anniversary the Father showed the Son "the Weep" "the Sob" and "the Moan." How to stand just so what to do with the hands and feet (to capitalize on what we in the business call "the Mourning Moment"). Formal stances the Fatherd picked up at the History Hole. The Son studied night and day. By candlelight. No one could best him. The money came pouring in. On the 102nd anniversary[6] the Son was 5 and the Father taught him "the Gnash." The day after that the Father left for out West. To seek his fortune. In the middle of dinnertime. The Son was eating his peas.

LUCY

BRAZIL

LUCY

BRAZIL

LUCY Hellooooo! Hellooooo!

[*Rest.*]

6. Hearsay [Parks's note].

BRAZIL

LUCY

BRAZIL HO! [*Unearths something.*]

LUCY Whatcha got?

BRAZIL Uh Wonder!

LUCY Uh Wonder!

BRAZIL Uh Wonder: Ho!

LUCY Dust it off and put it over with thuh rest of thuh Wonders.

BRAZIL Uh bust.

LUCY Whose?

BRAZIL Says "A. Lincoln." A. Lincolns bust. —. Abraham Lincolns bust!!!

LUCY Howuhboutthat!

[*Rest.*]

[*Rest.*]

Woah! Woah!

BRAZIL Whatchaheard?

LUCY Uh—. Cant say.

BRAZIL Whatchaheard?!!

LUCY SSShhhhhhhhhhhhhhhhhhht!

[*Rest.*]

dig!

B. ECHO

THE FOUNDLING FATHER Ladies and Gentlemen: *Our American Cousin*, Act III, scene 5:

MR. TRENCHARD[7] Have you found it?

MISS KEENE I find no trace of it. [*Discovering*] What is this?!

MR. TRENCHARD This is the place where father kept all the old deeds.

MISS KEENE Oh my poor muddled brain! What can this mean?!

MR. TRENCHARD [*with difficulty*] I cannot survive the downfall of my house but choose instead to end my life with a pistol to my head!

[*Applause.*]

THE FOUNDLING FATHER OHWAYOHWHYOHWAYOH!

[*Rest.*]

[*Rest.*]

Hellloooooo!

[*Rest.*]

Hellloooooo!

[*Rest. Waves.*]

7. Asa Trenchard is the title character of *Our American Cousin*; Laura Keene played his cousin, Florence Trenchard. (The exchange paraphrases one found in scene 6, but Florence is not present and the suicide is threatened in the following scene by another character, Sir Edward Trenchard.)

C. ARCHEOLOGY

BRAZIL You hear im?

LUCY Echo of thuh first sort: thuh sound. (E.g. thuh gunplay.)

[*Rest.*]

Echo of thuh 2nd sort: thuh words. Type A: thuh words from thuh dead. Category: Unrelated.

[*Rest.*]

Echo of thuh 2nd sort, Type B: words less fortunate: thuh Disembodied Voice. Also known as "Thuh Whispers." Category: Related. Like your Fathuhs.

[*Rest.*]

Echo of thuh 3rd sort: thuh body itself.

[*Rest.*]

BRAZIL You hear im.

LUCY Cant say. Cant say, son.

BRAZIL My faux-father. Thuh one who comed out here before us. Thuh one who left us behind. Tuh come out here all uhlone. Tuh do his bit. All them who comed before us—my Daddy. He's one of them.

LUCY

[*Rest.*]

[*Rest.*]

[BRAZIL: He's one of them. All of them who comed before us—my Daddy.

[*Rest.*]

I'd say thuh creation of thuh world must uh been just like thuh clearing off of this plot. Just like him diggin his Hole. I'd say. Must uh been just as dug up. And unfair.

[*Rest.*]

Peoples (or thuh what-was), just had tuh hit thuh road. In thuh beginning there was one of those voids here and then "bang" and then *voilà!*[8] And here we is.

[*Rest.*]

But where did those voids that was here before *we* was here go off to? Hmmm. In thuh beginning there were some of them voids here and then: KERBANG-KERBLAMMO! And now it all belongs tuh us.

LUCY

[*Rest.*]

[*Rest.*]

BRAZIL This Hole is our inheritance of sorts. My Daddy died and left it to me and Her. And when She goes, Shes gonna give it all to me!!

LUCY Dig, son.

BRAZIL I'd rather dust and polish. [*Puts something on.*]

LUCY Dust and polish then. —. You dont got tuh put on that tuh do it.

BRAZIL It helps. Uh Hehm. *Uh Hehm.* WELCOME WELCOME WELCOME TUH THUH HALL OF—

LUCY Sssht.

BRAZIL

8. Literally, "see there" (French).

LUCY

BRAZIL (welcome welcome welcome to thuh hall. of. wonnndersss: To our right A Jewel Box made of cherry wood, lined in velvet, letters "A.L." carved in gold on thuh lid: the jewels have long escaped. Over here one of Mr. Washingtons bones, right pointer so they say; here is his likeness and here: his wooden teeth.[9] Yes, uh top and bottom pair of nibblers: nibblers, lookin for uh meal. Nibblin. I iduhnt your lunch. Quit nibblin. Quit that nibblin you. Quit that nibblin you nibblers you nibblin nibblers you.)

LUCY Keep it tuh scale.

BRAZIL (Over here our newest Wonder: uh bust of Mr. Lincoln carved of marble lookin like he looked in life. Right heress thuh bit from thuh mouth of thuh mount on which some great Someone rode tuh thuh rescue. This is all thats left. Uh glass tradin bead—one of thuh first. Here are thuh licked boots. Here, uh dried scrap of whales blubber. Uh petrified scrap of uh great blubberer, servin to remind us that once this land was covered with sea. And blubberers were Kings. In this area here are several documents: peace pacts, writs, bills of sale, treaties, notices, handbills and circulars, freein papers, summonses, declarations of war, addresses, title deeds, obits, long lists of dids. And thuh medals: for bravery and honesty; for trustworthiness and for standing straight; for standing tall; for standing still. For advancing and retreating. For makin do. For skills in whittlin, for skills in painting and drawing, for uh knowledge of sewin, of handicrafts and building things, for leather tannin, blacksmithery, lacemakin, horseback riding, swimmin, croquet, and badminton. Community Service. For cookin and for cleanin. For bowin and scrapin. Uh medal for fakin? Huh. This could uh been his. Zsis his? This is his! This is his!!!

LUCY Keep it tuh scale, Brazil.

BRAZIL This could be his!

LUCY May well be.

BRAZIL [*rest*] Whaddyahear?

LUCY Bits and pieces.

BRAZIL This could be his.

LUCY Could well be.

BRAZIL [*rest. Rest*] waaaaaahhhhhhhHHHHHHHHHHHHHH! HUH HEE HUH HEE HUH HEE HUH.

LUCY There there, Brazil. Dont weep.

BRAZIL WAHHHHHHHHHH!—imissim—WAHHHHHHHHHHHH!

LUCY It is an honor to be of his line. He cleared this plot for us. He was uh Digger.

BRAZIL Huh huh huh. Uh Digger.

LUCY Mr. Lincoln was his favorite.

BRAZIL I was only 5.

LUCY He dug this whole Hole.

BRAZIL Sssnuch.[1] This whole Hole.

LUCY This whole Hole.

[*Rest.*]

BRAZIL

LUCY

9. Washington's famous "wooden teeth" were in fact dentures made of ivory and of animal and human teeth.

1. Parks defines "Sssnuch" as "a fast reverse snort, a big sniff (usually accompanies crying or sneezing)."

BRAZIL

LUCY

BRAZIL

LUCY

I couldnt never deny him nothin.
I gived intuh him on everything.
Thuh moon. Thuh stars.
Thuh bees knees. Thuh cats pyjamas.

[*Rest.*]

BRAZIL

LUCY

BRAZIL Anything?

LUCY Stories too horrible tuh mention.

BRAZIL His stories?

LUCY Nope.

[*Rest.*]

BRAZIL Mama Lucy?

LUCY Whut.

BRAZIL —Imissim—.

LUCY Hhh. ((dig.))

D. ECHO

THE FOUNDLING FATHER Ladies and Gentlemen: *Our American Cousin*, Act III, scene 2:

MR. TRENCHARD You crave affection, *you* do. Now I've no fortune, but I'm biling over with affections, which I'm ready to pour out to all of you, like apple sass over roast pork.

AUGUSTA Sir, your American talk do woo me.[2]

THE FOUNDLING FATHER [*as Mrs. Mount*] Mr. Trenchard, you will please recollect you are addressing my daughter and in my presence.

MR. TRENCHARD Yes, I'm offering her my heart and hand just as she wants them, with nothing in 'em.

THE FOUNDLING FATHER [*as Mrs. Mount*] Augusta dear, to your room.

AUGUSTA Yes, Ma, the nasty beast.

THE FOUNDLING FATHER [*as Mrs. Mount*] I am aware, Mr. Trenchard, that you are not used to the manners of good society, and that, alone, will excuse the impertinence of which you have been guilty.

MR. TRENCHARD Don't know the manners of good society, eh? Wal, I guess I know enough to turn you inside out, old gal—you sockdologizing old mantrap.

[*Laughter. Applause.*]

THE FOUNDLING FATHER Thanks. Thanks so much. Snyder has always been a very special very favorite town uh mine. Thank you thank you so very much. Loverly loverly evening loverly tuh be here loverly tuh be here with you with all of you thank you very much.

[*Rest.*]

Uh Hehm. I *only* do thuh greats.

2. Parks adds this line to a passage that is otherwise quoted directly from the play.

[*Rest.*]

A crowd pleaser: 4score and 7 years ago our fathers brought forth upon this continent a new nation conceived in Liberty and dedicated to the proposition that all men are created equal![3]

[*Applause.*]

Observe!: Indiana? Indianapolis. Louisiana? Baton Rouge. Concord? New Hampshire. Pierre? South Dakota. Honolulu? Hawaii. Springfield? Illinois. Frankfort? Kentucky. Lincoln? Nebraska.[4] Ha! Lickety split!

[*Applause.*]

And now, the centerpiece of the evening!!

[*Rest.*]

Uh Hehm. The Death of Lincoln!: —. The watching of the play, the laughter, the smiles of Lincoln and Mary Todd, the slipping of Booth into the presidential box unseen, the freeing of the slaves, the pulling of the trigger, the bullets piercing above the left ear, the bullets entrance into the great head, the bullets lodging behind the great right eye, the slumping of Lincoln, the leaping onto the stage of Booth, the screaming of Todd, the screaming of Todd, the screaming of Keene, the leaping onto the stage of Booth; the screaming of Todd, the screaming of Keene, the shouting of Booth "Thus to the tyrants!," the death of Lincoln! —And the silence of the nation.

[*Rest.*]

Yes. —.The year was way back when. The place: our nations capitol. 4score, back in the olden days, and Mr. Lincolns great head. The the-a-ter was "Fords." The wife "Mary Todd." Thuh freeing of the slaves and thuh great black hole that thuh fatal bullet bored. And how that great head was bleedin. Thuh body stretched crossways acrosst thuh bed. Thuh last words. Thuh last breaths. And how thuh nation mourned.

[*Applause.*]

E. SPADEWORK

LUCY Thats uh hard nut tuh crack uh hard nut tuh crack indeed.

BRAZIL Alaska—?

LUCY Thats uh hard nut tuh crack. Thats uh hard nut tuh crack indeed. —. Huh. Juneau.

BRAZIL Good!

LUCY Go uhgain.

BRAZIL —. Texas?

LUCY —. Austin. Wyoming?

BRAZIL —. —. Cheyenne. Florida?

LUCY Tallahassee.

[*Rest.*]

Ohio.

BRAZIL Oh. Uh. Well: Columbus. Louisiana?

3. The opening sentence of Lincoln's Gettysburg Address, delivered November 19, 1863, in Gettysburg, Pennsylvania, at the dedication ceremony for a national cemetery on the site of the Civil War's bloodiest battle, fought four months earlier.

4. This list pairs states with their capitals (a pattern that continues in the next scene).

LUCY Baton Rouge. Arkansas.

BRAZIL Little Rock. Jackson.

LUCY Mississippi. Spell it.

BRAZIL M-i-s-s-i-s-s-i-p-p-i!

LUCY Huh. Youre good. Montgomery.

BRAZIL Alabama.

LUCY Topeka.

BRAZIL Kansas?

LUCY Kansas.

BRAZIL Boise, Idaho?

LUCY Boise, Idaho.

BRAZIL Huh. Nebraska.

LUCY Nebraska. Lincoln.

[*Rest.*]

Thuh year was way back when. Thuh place: our nations capitol.

[*Rest.*]

Your Fathuh couldnt get that story out of his head: Mr. Lincolns great head. And thuh hole thuh fatal bullet bored. How that great head was bleedin. Thuh body stretched crossways acrosst thuh bed. Thuh last words. Thuh last breaths. And how thuh nation mourned. Huh. Changed your Fathuhs life.

[*Rest.*]

Couldnt get that story out of his head. Whuduhnt my favorite page from thuh book of Mr. Lincolns life, me myself now I prefer thuh part where he gets married to Mary Todd and she begins to lose her mind (and then of course where he frees all thuh slaves) but shoot, he couldnt get that story out of his head. Hhh. Changed his life.

[*Rest.*]

BRAZIL (wahhhhhhhh—)

LUCY There there, Brazil.

BRAZIL (wahhhhhh—)

LUCY Dont weep. Got somethin for ya.

BRAZIL (o)?

LUCY Spade. —. Dont scrunch up your face like that, son. Go on. Take it.

BRAZIL Spade?

LUCY Spade. He woulda wanted you tuh have it.

BRAZIL Daddys diggin spade? Ssnnuch.

LUCY I swannee[5] you look more and more and more and more like him every day.

BRAZIL His chin?

LUCY You got his chin.

BRAZIL His lips?

LUCY You got his lips.

BRAZIL His teeths?

LUCY Top and bottom. In his youth. He had some. Just like yours. His frock coat. Was just like that. He had hisself uh stovepipe hat which you lack. His medals—yours are for weepin his of course were for diggin.

5. A punning combination of *I swan* (i.e., "I declare"; dialect) and *Swannee (River)*, an allusion to Stephen Foster's 1851 song "Old Folks at Home" (which presents a sentimental view of African American life in the antebellum South).

BRAZIL And I got his spade.

LUCY And now you got his spade.

BRAZIL We could say I'm his spittin image.

LUCY We could say that.

BRAZIL We could say I just may follow in thuh footsteps of my foe-father.

LUCY We could say that.

BRAZIL Look on thuh bright side!

LUCY Look on thuh bright side!

BRAZIL So much tuh live for!

LUCY So much tuh live for! Sweet land of—! Sweet land of—?

BRAZIL Of liberty!

LUCY Of liberty! Thats it thats it and *"Woah!"* Lets say I hear his words!

BRAZIL And you could say?

LUCY And I could say.

BRAZIL Lets say you hear his words!

LUCY *Woah!*

BRAZIL Whatwouldhesay?!

LUCY He'd say: "Hello." He'd say, —. "Hope you like your spade."

BRAZIL Tell him I do.

LUCY He'd say: "My how youve grown!" He'd say: "Hows your weepin?" He'd say: —Ha! He's running through his states and capitals! Licketysplit!

BRAZIL Howuhboutthat!

LUCY He'd say: "Uh house divided cannot stand!" He'd say: "4score and 7 years uhgoh." Say: "Of thuh people by thuh people and for thuh people." Say: "Malice toward none and charity toward all." Say: "Cheat some of thuh people some of thuh time."[6] He'd say: (and this is only to be spoken between you and me and him—)

BRAZIL K.

LUCY Lean in. Ssfor our ears and our ears uhlone.

LUCY

BRAZIL

LUCY

BRAZIL

BRAZIL O.

LUCY Howuhboutthat. And here he comes. Striding on in striding on in and he surveys thuh situation. And he nods tuh what we found cause he knows his Wonders. And he smiles. And he tells us of his doins all these years. And he does his Mr. Lincoln for us. Uh great page from thuh great mans great life! And you n me llsmile, cause then we'll know, more or less, exactly where he is.

[*Rest.*]

6. Some of the most famous words spoken by or attributed to Lincoln, from, respectively, his speech on June 16, 1858, to the Illinois Republican State Convention in Springfield—"A house divided against itself cannot stand" (an allusion to Mark 3.25); the beginning and the end of the Gettysburg Address—"government of the people, by the people, for the people"; his second Inaugural Address, delivered March 4, 1865—"With malice toward none; with charity for all"; and (with slight variations in wording) a speech of September 8, 1858, in Clinton, Illinois, or a remark made to a caller at the White House—"You may fool all the people some of the time; you can even fool some of the people all the time; but you can't fool all of the people all the time" (this observation, which does not appear in any surviving Lincoln documents, has also been attributed to the 19th-century American showman P. T. Barnum).

BRAZIL Lucy? Where is he?
LUCY Lincoln?
BRAZIL Papa.
LUCY Close by, I guess. Huh. Dig.
[BRAZIL *digs. Times passes.*]
Youre uh Digger. Youre uh Digger. Your Daddy was uh Digger and so are you.
BRAZIL Ho!
LUCY I couldnt never deny him nothin.
BRAZIL Wonder: Ho! Wonder: Ho!
LUCY I gived intuh him on everything.
BRAZIL Ssuhtrumpet.
LUCY Gived intuh him on everything.
BRAZIL Ssuhtrumpet, Lucy.
LUCY Howboutthat.
BRAZIL Try it out.
LUCY How uh-bout that.
BRAZIL Anythin?
LUCY Cant say, son. Cant say.
[*Rest.*]
I couldnt never deny him nothin.
I gived intuh him on everything.
Thuh moon. Thuh stars.
BRAZIL Ho!
LUCY Thuh bees knees. Thuh cats pyjamas.
BRAZIL Wonder: Ho! Wonder: Ho!
[*Rest.*]
Howuhboutthat: Uh bag of pennies. Money, Lucy.
LUCY Howuhboutthat.
[*Rest.*]
Thuh bees knees.
Thuh cats pyjamas.
Thuh best cuts of meat.
My baby teeth.
BRAZIL Wonder: Ho! Wonder: HO!
LUCY
Thuh apron from uhround my waist.
Thuh hair from off my head.
BRAZIL Huh. Yellow fur.
LUCY My mores and my folkways.
BRAZIL Oh. Uh beard. Howuhboutthat.
[*Rest.*]
LUCY WOAH. WOAH!
BRAZIL Whatchaheard?
LUCY
[*Rest.*]
[*Rest.*]
BRAZIL Whatchaheard?!
LUCY You dont wanna know.

BRAZIL

LUCY

BRAZIL

LUCY

BRAZIL Wonder: Ho! Wonder: HO! WONDER: HO!

LUCY

Thuh apron from uhround my waist.
Thuh hair from off my head.

BRAZIL Huh: uh Tee-Vee.

LUCY Huh.

BRAZIL I'll hold ontooit for uh minit.

[*Rest.*]

LUCY

Thuh apron from uhround my waist.
Thuh hair from off my head.
My mores and my folkways.
My rock and my foundation.

BRAZIL

LUCY

BRAZIL

LUCY My re-memberies—you know—thuh stuff out of my head.

[*The TV comes on.* THE FOUNDLING FATHER*'s face appears.*]

BRAZIL (ho! ho! wonder: ho!)

LUCY

My spare buttons in their envelopes.
Thuh leftovers from all my unmade meals.
Thuh letter R.
Thuh key of G.

BRAZIL (ho! ho! wonder: ho!)

LUCY

All my good jokes. All my jokes that fell flat.
Thuh way I walked, cause you liked it so much.
All my winnin dance steps.
My teeth when yours runned out.
My smile.

BRAZIL (ho! ho! wonder: ho!)

LUCY Ssssht.

[*Rest.*]

Well. Its him.

F. ECHO

A gunshot echoes. Loudly. And echoes.

G. THE GREAT BEYOND

LUCY *and* BRAZIL *watch the TV: a replay of "The Lincoln Act."* THE FOUNDLING FATHER *has returned. His coffin awaits him.*

LUCY Howuhboutthat!

BRAZIL They just gunned him down uhgain.

LUCY Howuhboutthat.

BRAZIL He's dead but not really.

LUCY Howuhboutthat.

BRAZIL Only fakin. Only fakin. See? Hesupuhgain.

LUCY What-izzysayin?

BRAZIL Sound duhnt work.

LUCY Zat right.

[*Rest.*]

THE FOUNDLING FATHER I believe this is the place where I do the Gettysburg Address, I believe.

BRAZIL

THE FOUNDLING FATHER

LUCY

BRAZIL Woah!

LUCY Howuhboutthat.

BRAZIL Huh. Well.

[*Rest.*]

Huh. Zit him?

LUCY Its him.

BRAZIL He's dead?

LUCY He's dead.

BRAZIL Howuhboutthat.

[*Rest.*]

Shit.

LUCY

BRAZIL

LUCY

BRAZIL Mail the in-vites?

LUCY I did.

BRAZIL Think theyll come?

LUCY I do. There are hundreds upon thousands who knew of your Daddy, glorified his reputation, and would like to pay their respects.

THE FOUNDLING FATHER Howuhboutthat.

BRAZIL Howuhboutthat!

LUCY Turn that off, son.

[*Rest.*]

You gonna get in yr coffin now or later?

THE FOUNDLING FATHER I'd like tuh wait uhwhile.

LUCY Youd like tuh wait uhwhile.

BRAZIL Mmgonna gnash for you. You know: teeth in thuh dirt, hands like this, then jump up rip my clothes up, you know, you know go all out.

THE FOUNDLING FATHER Howuhboutthat. Open casket or closed?

LUCY —. Closed.

[*Rest.*]

Turn that off, son.

BRAZIL K.

THE FOUNDLING FATHER Hug me.

BRAZIL Not yet.

THE FOUNDLING FATHER You?

LUCY Gimmieuhminute.

[*A gunshot echoes. Loudly. And echoes.*]

LUCY That gunplay. Wierdiduhntit. Comes. And goze.

[*They ready his coffin. He inspects it.*]

At thuh Great Hole where we honeymooned—son, at thuh Original Great Hole, you could see thuh whole world without goin too far. You could look intuh that Hole and see your entire life pass before you. Not your own life but someones life from history, you know, [someone who'd done somethin of note, got theirselves known somehow, uh President or] somebody who killed somebody important, uh face on uh postal stamp, you know, someone from History. *Like* you, but *not* you. You know: *Known.*

THE FOUNDLING FATHER "*Emergency*, oh, *Emergency*, please put the Great Man in the ground."

LUCY Go on. Get in. Try it out. Ssnot so bad. See? Sstight, but private. Bought on time but we'll manage. And you got enough height for your hat.

[*Rest.*]

THE FOUNDLING FATHER Hug me.

LUCY Not yet.

THE FOUNDLING FATHER You?

BRAZIL Gimmieuhminute.

[*Rest.*]

LUCY He loved that Great Hole so. Came out here. Digged this lookuhlike.

BRAZIL Then he died?

LUCY Then he died.

THE FOUNDLING FATHER

BRAZIL

LUCY

THE FOUNDLING FATHER

BRAZIL

LUCY

THE FOUNDLING FATHER A monumentous occasion. I'd like to say a few words from the grave. Maybe a little conversation: Such a long story. Uhhem. I quit the business. And buried all my things. I dropped anchor: Bottomless. Your turn.

LUCY

BRAZIL

THE FOUNDLING FATHER

LUCY [*rest*] Do your Lincoln for im.

THE FOUNDLING FATHER Yeah?

LUCY He was only 5.

THE FOUNDLING FATHER Only 5. *Uh Hehm.* So very loverly to be here so very very loverly to be here the town of —Wonderville has always been a special favorite of mine always has been a very very special favorite of mine. Now, I *only* do thuh greats. Uh hehm: I was born in a log cabin of humble parentage. But I picked up uh few things. Uh Hehm: 4score and 7 years ago our fathers—ah you know thuh rest. Lets see now. Yes. Uh house divided cannot stand! You can fool some of thuh people some of thuh time! Of thuh people by thuh people and for thuh people! Malice toward none and charity toward all! Ha! The Death of Lincoln! (Highlights): Haw Haw Haw Haw

[*Rest.*]

HAW HAW HAW HAW

[*A gunshot echoes. Loudly. And echoes.* THE FOUNDLING FATHER *"slumps in his chair."*]

THE FOUNDLING FATHER

LUCY

BRAZIL

LUCY

THE FOUNDLING FATHER

BRAZIL [Izzy dead?

LUCY Mmlistenin.

BRAZIL Anything?

LUCY Nothin.

BRAZIL [*rest*] As a child it was her luck tuh be in thuh same room with her Uncle when he died. Her family wanted to know what he had said. What his last words had been. Theyre hadnt been any. Only screaming. Or, you know, breath. Didnt have uh shape to it. Her family thought she was holding on to thuh words. For safekeeping. And they proclaimed thuh girl uh Confidence. At the age of 8. Sworn tuh secrecy. She picked up thuh tricks of thuh trade as she went uhlong.]

[*Rest.*]

Should I gnash now?

LUCY Better save it for thuh guests. I guess.

[*Rest.*]

Well. Dust and polish, son. I'll circulate.

BRAZIL Welcome Welcome Welcome to thuh hall. Of. Wonders.

[*Rest.*]

To our right A Jewel Box of cherry wood, lined in velvet, letters "A.L." carved in gold on thuh lid. Over here one of Mr. Washingtons bones and here: his wooden teeth. Over here: uh bust of Mr. Lincoln carved of marble lookin like he looked in life. —More or less. And thuh medals: for bravery and honesty; for trustworthiness and for standing straight; for standing tall; for standing still. For advancing and retreating. For makin do. For skills in whittlin, for skills in painting and drawing, for uh knowledge of sewin, of handicrafts and building things, for leather tannin, blacksmithery, lacemakin, horseback riding, swimmin, croquet, and badminton. Community Service. For cookin and for cleanin. For bowin and scrapin. Uh medal for fakin.

[*Rest.*]

To my right: our newest Wonder: One of thuh greats Hisself! Note: thuh body sitting propped upright in our great Hole. Note the large mouth opened wide. Note the top hat and frock coat, just like the greats. Note the death wound: thuh great black hole—thuh great black hole in thuh great head. —And how this great head is bleedin. —Note: thuh last words. —And thuh last breaths. —And how thuh nation mourns—

[*Takes his leave.*]

CARYL CHURCHILL

b. 1938

IN February 1997, Scottish scientists sparked worldwide controversy by announcing the birth of a lamb, Dolly—the first mammalian clone successfully created from an adult cell. If it was now possible to clone a sheep, could the cloning of humans be far behind? And what were the scientific, legal, and moral implications of such research? The World Health Organization soon issued a statement condemning human cloning, as did the Parliamentary Assembly of the Council of Europe. England's Human Genetics Advisory Commission produced a strongly cautionary statement in 1998; in the United States, President Bill Clinton immediately imposed a moratorium on federal funding for human cloning research and charged his National Bioethics Advisory Commission to consider cloning's broader ramifications. Its report, *Cloning Human Beings*, appeared in June 1997. The first publication of the President's Council on Bioethics, which was created by President George W. Bush in 2001, was *Human Cloning and Human Dignity: An Ethical Enquiry* (2002). The stream of commentary on the topic, in both scientific and popular publications, has only grown, fueled by the overlapping debate about the benefits and morality of embryonic stem cell research. Here, matters of scientific fact and preoccupations of science fiction seem to merge. Though researchers point to the practical obstacles that must be overcome before human cloning could become a reality, many in the general public view the perfection of this reproductive technology as imminent—a possibility that stirs both fear and fascination. The issue raises basic questions about human identity—are we the products of our genes, our environment, or both?—and has kindled the imaginations of writers. In A NUMBER (2002), the British playwright Caryl Churchill envisions that future moment when cloning has become a reality: she explores these foundational concerns on the most personal level, asking us to consider what this "brave new world" might signify for parents and children.

Churchill is among the most influential and innovative of contemporary dramatists, consistently challenging theater artists and audiences alike since the 1970s with her politically charged and technically adventurous dramaturgy. Working in a country where theater has long reflected and affected national culture and discourse, she has embraced the stage as an avenue for expressing her deeply held social convictions. For decades, her plays have conveyed with growing urgency and intensity the potential devastation—sociological, economic, environmental, and political—that those with power can wreak on the individual and on society.

Caryl Churchill came of age at a potent, transitional period in English theater: the era of the "angry young men" like John Osborne, whose *Look Back in Anger* (1956) voiced hostility toward the British class system. Born in London in 1938, Churchill spent part of her childhood in Canada but returned to England in 1955; in 1957, she went to Oxford, studying English language and literature. At the university, she began writing plays that were produced by student theater groups. Shortly after graduation, she married David Harter, a lawyer. The couple had three children in the 1960s, and Churchill speaks frankly of her struggles in attempting simultaneously to continue writing and to fulfill her family obligations. She was initially politicized not by the broader social movements of that tumultuous era but by "being discontent with [her] own way of life—of being a barrister's wife and just being at home with small children." She started composing radio plays, because working in that form afforded her both the flexibility required by her family life and a respectable outlet for her work that was relatively accessible. As Churchill later noted in an interview, it was a time when the world-renowned dramatist "[SAMUEL] BECKETT was on the radio" and when the medium was perceived as "the way to break in" to professional playwriting.

In 1972, the first of Churchill's several television plays was produced and *Owners* was staged at London's Royal Court Theatre, a venue known for its commitment to new playwrights. Two years later, Churchill became the first woman to be offered a playwriting residency with the Royal Court; more than a dozen of her plays have premiered there, including her best-known work, *Top Girls* (1982)—a clear-eyed examination of feminism and women's lives in the "me decade"—and *A Number.* Another professional relationship that was to profoundly influence Churchill's work began in 1976, when she became involved with the Joint Stock Company. It was a theater collective committed to a collaborative, improvisational production process and to creative political engagement, and the approach taken to her plays by the company's actors and director, Max Stafford-Clark, changed how she developed her scripts. Elements of Churchill's dramaturgy that critics have called nonnaturalisitic and nonlinear are rooted in this experience. Other signature devices, such as double-casting and casting across race and gender, were initially practical techniques to make fullest use of the fairly small number of actors available to her in the company. But they soon affected and became crucial to expressing her conceptualization of characters, and were frequently employed to throw into relief the social construction of identity—most notably in *Cloud 9* (1979), Churchill's breakthrough international success that hilariously exposes Victorian notions of gender, race, and class and also poignantly captures the stubborn persistence of those values to the present day. In *A Number,* the technique of casting one actor in multiple roles lends itself brilliantly to an exploration of cloning.

Shortly before her work with Joint Stock began, Churchill had also affiliated with the socialist-feminist theater group Monstrous Regiment, which took its name from the title of a sixteenth-century misogynist pamphlet by John Knox that inveighs against the "monstrous regiment of women." The group collaborated with her in staging several pieces; one was *Vinegar Tom* (1976), a gripping historical drama about the persecution of women accused of witchcraft. Over the next decade, Churchill catapulted to international renown; *Top Girls*, *Cloud 9*, *Fen* (1983), and *Serious Money* (1987) were among her plays produced throughout the English-speaking world as well as in Europe, Asia, and Latin America. Her awards include an Obie for both *Cloud 9* and *Top Girls,* the Susan Smith Blackburn Prize for both *Fen* and *Serious Money,* and the Laurence Olivier Award (the British equivalent of the Tony Award) for *Serious Money.*

Churchill has repeatedly harnessed the power of live performance to engage audiences in meaningful political debate. Together with Mark Wing-Davey, the artistic director of London's Central School of Speech and Drama, she brought students from that professional conservatory to Romania to work with students from the Caragiale Institute of Theatre and Cinema in Bucharest in developing a piece dealing with the fall of Nicolae Ceausescu and the impact of his policies on the lives of Romanian citizens. The resulting drama, *Mad Forest* (1990), captures the complexities of life under and after an oppressive political regime. *The Skriker* (1994) weaves the dark world of folktale magic together with a hard-edged consideration of contemporary female adolescence and the natural environment, as it blurs the boundaries of drama and dance. In *Far Away* (2000), Churchill creates an apocalyptic vision of a land torn apart by conflict so profound that it beggars description. And *A Number* brings us into a frightening and all-too-conceivable world where scientific advances challenge long-held assumptions about individuals' autonomy and humanity. Although Churchill wins praise for consistently innovative and provocative dramaturgy, the arc of her career also reveals her ongoing engagement with issues that particularly concern her. Some of her earliest pieces consider themes that will recur, refined, in *A Number*. The radio play *Identical Twins* (1968), for example, examines personal identity; *Not . . . Not . . . Not . . . Not . . . Not Enough Oxygen* (1971), also a radio play, envisions a dystopic future.

A Number opens in the middle of a conversation between a father and his adult son. Though the situation appears to be normal, the topic is not: the son, Bernard, has just learned that he is not an only child (as he had always believed) but one of "a number" of cloned individuals. His father, Salter, insists that the cells taken from an earlier child—also named Bernard—were supposed to be used to produce only a single clone, but "some mad scientist has illegally" created more (perhaps twenty). Both men must grapple with this revelation, which raises issues of parental responsibility and culpability, individual identity, and the meaning of family.

The first scene sets the tone for the entire play. Structured as a kind of thriller, but one that deliberately eschews narrative closure, *A Number* relies on an exceedingly spare theatrical frame to draw us into the ever-deepening mystery of what has really happened in this family. In this two-hander (a script for two actors), Salter appears in each of five short scenes, while another actor plays the original Bernard (designated B1 in the script) and two of the clones, the

Dallas Roberts, left, plays Bernard, the cloned son of Salter (Sam Shepard) in *A Number*, which imparts a terrible mathematics lesson.

Bernard we meet initially (designated B2) and the one named Michael Black. Whom are we to believe? Which version of events is true? And what kind of people are Salter, the Bernards, and Michael?

Though the play's fragmented dialogue focuses on cloning, its subject is much broader. As noted by Stephen Daldry, its director at the Royal Court, *A Number* explores what free will is, and whether genetics or environment influences it more. Scientists and philosophers have long addressed the question of how heredity and culture interact to shape the lives of humans. By envisioning three individuals developed from the same genetic material, Churchill provides an opportunity for us to explore these issues through characters who remain distinct despite resembling each other physically—even on the cellular level.

Significantly, productions of *A Number* have chosen various theatrical means to communicate these foundational concepts of sameness and individuality. In the original London production, the actor playing the sons conveyed the differences between each character simply by changing his voice and physical mannerisms. Elsewhere, actors relied on elements of costume, such as baseball hats and jackets, to signal the different personas. Some directors had these changes occur offstage, while others had the actor transform in full view of the audience, as both performers remained on stage throughout the play.

At the same time, Churchill presents the character who is "the same" in each scene as profoundly unstable. Salter is unpredictable and chameleon-like, changing not only how he describes the past but also how he behaves to suit his different sons. Critics have observed in *A Number* echoes of other contemporary dramatists—including Samuel Beckett, Harold Pinter, and Edward Albee—who have dramatized powerful yet fractured relationships within families. These connections are depicted in the play's intense, elliptical encounters between characters, whose dialogue is filled with half-sentences, interruptions, and seemingly incomplete thoughts. Early in her career, Churchill developed a structure of fast-paced, overlapping dialogue that heightened an effect evident in ANTON CHEKHOV: through simultaneous speech, characters both make their own statements and appear to comment on each other's lines, thereby providing two layers of meaning. More recently, however, Churchill has pared down her dialogue, bringing it closer to the early style of David Mamet, who has described his process of eliminating all unnecessary words from his writing. Although such dialogue may initially seem artificial, it in fact renders human speech patterns far more accurately than do the exchanges found in traditional realist drama; at the same time, it demands of actors and directors an intense engagement with subtext, and with the connection between subtext and action.

Even as *A Number* portrays a terrifying futuristic scenario, it captures family dynamics as old as humanity itself. The characterizations of B1 and B2 have led critics to reach for biblical analogies, citing Cain and Abel, or Jacob and Esau, while the relationship between Salter and his children has elicited comparisons to ARTHUR MILLER's *All My Sons* (1947) and especially to SHAKESPEARE's *King Lear* (1605) The depictions also resonate with the contemporary observation that men often struggle to communicate and express their feelings. Significantly, Churchill makes *A Number* a play that features only men. Salter's wife does not physically appear, though maternity is certainly an issue in the drama and her story is as complex as his. As in SUSAN GLASPELL's *Trifles* (1916), the key woman becomes an absent presence—a character we come to know through others' representation of her. And *A Number,* like *Trifles,* requires us to explore this absence in terms not only of the narrative but also of culture and symbolism.

Churchill further asks us to consider whether the label *parent* is applied primarily because of what one is (genetics) or because of what one does (behavior). *A Number* builds on a common fantasy: that one might return to the earliest days of a child's life and, with the benefit of hindsight, be a better parent. Though cloning appears to offer that opportunity to turn back the clock, Churchill makes clear that this is no panacea. Our mistakes—and their impact on others—can never simply be erased. We must come to grips with past errors even as we hold on to hopes for the future.

The play's final scene, in which Salter meets the clone Michael Black, provides a conclusion to Churchill's exploration of sadly damaged fathers and sons that is both poignant and ironic. Despite their previous lack of contact, their blood forms a bond, and Salter's longing for a relationship with this heretofore unknown child is palpable. As they struggle to communicate and find commonality, Michael shares with Salter some scientific truths he finds comforting: "We've got ninety-nine percent the same genes as any other person. We've got ninety percent the same as a chimpanzee. We've got thirty percent the same as a lettuce. Does that cheer you up at all? I love about the lettuce. It makes me feel I belong." Lacking traditional family ties, Michael has sought a sense of belonging elsewhere, and in *A Number*, Churchill pushes us to question not only how and where we belong, but how much we value all our connections to living beings.

J.E.G.

A Number

CHARACTERS

SALTER, a man in his early sixties
BERNARD, his son, forty
BERNARD, his son, thirty-five
MICHAEL BLACK, his son, thirty-five

The play is for two actors. One plays SALTER, the other his sons.
The scene is the same throughout, it's where SALTER lives.

Scene 1

[SALTER, *a man in his early sixties and his son* BERNARD (B2), *thirty-five.*]

B2 A number
SALTER you mean
B2 a number of them, of us, a considerable
SALTER say
B2 ten, twenty
SALTER didn't you ask?
B2 I got the impression
SALTER why didn't you ask?
B2 I didn't think of asking.
SALTER I can't think why not, it seems to me it would be the first thing you'd want to know, how far has this thing gone, how many of these things are there?
B2 Good, so if it ever happens to you
SALTER no you're right
B2 no it was stupid, it was shock, I'd known for a week before I went to the hospital but it was still

SALTER it is, I am, the shocking thing is that there *are* these, not how many but at all

B2 even one

SALTER exactly, even one, a twin would be a shock

B2 a twin would be a surprise but a number

SALTER a number any number is a shock.

B2 You said things, these things

SALTER I said?

B2 you called them things. I think we'll find they're people.

SALTER Yes of course they are, they are of course.

B2 Because I'm one.

SALTER No.

B2 Yes. Why not? Yes.

SALTER Because they're copies

B2 copies? they're not

SALTER copies of you which some mad scientist has illegally

B2 how do you know that?

SALTER I don't but

B2 what if someone else is the one, the first one, the real one and I'm

SALTER no because

B2 not that I'm *not* real which is why I'm saying they're not things, don't call them

SALTER just wait, because I'm your father.

B2 You know that?

SALTER Of course.

B2 It was all a normal, everything, birth

SALTER you think I wouldn't know if I wasn't your father?

B2 Yes of course I was just for a moment there, but they are all still people like twins are all, quins[1] are all

SALTER yes I'm sorry

B2 we just happen to have identical be identical identical genetic

SALTER sorry I said things, I didn't mean anything by that, it just

B2 no forget it, it's nothing, it's

SALTER because of course for me you're the

B2 yes I know what you meant, I just, because of course I want them to be things, I do think they're things, I don't think they're, of course I *do* think they're them just as much as I'm me but I. I don't know what I think, I feel terrible.

SALTER I wonder if we can sue.

B2 Sue? who?

SALTER Them, whoever did it. Who did you see?

B2 Just some young, I don't know, younger than me.

SALTER So who did it?

B2 He's dead, he was some old and they've just found the records and they've traced

SALTER so we sue the hospital.

B2 Maybe. Maybe we can.

SALTER Because they've taken your cells

1. Quintuplets.

B2 but when how did they?

SALTER when you were born maybe or later you broke your leg when you were two you were in the hospital, some hairs or scrapings of your skin

B2 but they didn't damage

SALTER but it's you, part of you, the value

B2 the value of those people

SALTER yes

B2 and what is the value of

SALTER there you are, who knows, priceless, and they belong

B2 no

SALTER they belong to you, they should belong to you, they're made from your

B2 they should

SALTER they've been stolen from you and you should get your rights

B2 but is it

SALTER what? is it money? is it something you can put a figure on? put a figure on it.

B2 This is purely

SALTER yes

B2 suppose each person was worth ten thousand pounds

SALTER a hundred

B2 a hundred thousand?

SALTER they've taken a person away from you

B2 times the number of people

SALTER which we don't know

B2 but a number a fairly large say anyway ten

SALTER a million is the least you should take, I think it's more like half a million each person because what they've done they've damaged your uniqueness, weakened your identity, so we're looking at five million for a start.

B2 Maybe.

SALTER Yes, because how dare they?

B2 We'd need to be able to prove

SALTER we prove you're genetically my son genetically and then

B2 because there's no doubt

SALTER no doubt at all. I suppose you didn't see one?

B2 One what? of them?

SALTER of these people

B2 no I think they'd keep us apart wouldn't they so we don't spoil like contaminate the crime scene so you don't tell each other I have nightmares oh come to think of it I have nightmares and he might have said no if he was asked in the first place

SALTER because they need to find out

B2 yes how much we're the same, not just how tall we are or do we get asthma but what do you call your dog, why did you leave your wife you don't even know the answer to these questions.

SALTER So you didn't suddenly suddenly see

B2 what suddenly see myself coming round the corner

SALTER because that could be

B2 like seeing yourself on the camera in a shop or you hear yourself on the answering machine and you think god is that what I

SALTER but more than that, it'd be it'd be

B2 don't they say you die if you meet yourself?[2]

SALTER walk round the corner and see yourself you could get a heart attack. Because if that's me over there who am I?

B2 Yes but it's not me over there

SALTER no I know

B2 it's like having a twin that's all it's just

SALTER I know what it is.

B2 I think I'd like to meet one. It's an adventure isn't it and you're part of science. I wouldn't be frightened to meet any number.

SALTER I don't know.

B2 They're all your sons.

SALTER I don't want a number of sons, thank you, you're plenty, I'm fine.

B2 Maybe after they've found everything out they'll let us meet. They'll have a party for us, we can

SALTER I'm not going to drink with those doctors. But maybe you're right you're right, take it in a positive spirit.

B2 There is a thing

SALTER what's that?

B2 a thing that puzzles me a little

SALTER what's that?

B2 I did get the impression and I know I may be wrong because maybe I was in shock but I got the impression there was this batch and we were all in it. I was in it.

SALTER No because you're my son.

B2 No but we were all

SALTER I explained already

B2 but I wasn't being quite open with you because I'm confused because it's a shock but I want to know what happened

SALTER they stole

B2 no but what happened

SALTER I don't

B2 because they said that none of us was the original.

SALTER They said that?

B2 I think

SALTER I think you're mistaken because you're confused

B2 you think

SALTER you need to get back to them

B2 well I'll do that. But I think that's what they meant

SALTER it's not what they meant

B2 ok. But that's my impression, that none of us is the original.

SALTER Then who? do they know?

B2 they're not saying, they just say we were all

SALTER they're not saying?

B2 so if I was your son the original would be your son too which is nonsense so

SALTER does that follow?

2. According to folk belief, meeting one's ghostly double (or doppelganger) is a portent of death.

B2 so please if you're not my father that's fine. If you couldn't have children or my mother, and you did in vitro[3] or I don't know what you did I really think you should tell me.

SALTER Yes, that's what it was

B2 That's all right.

SALTER Yes I know.

B2 Thank you for telling me.

SALTER Yes.

B2 It's better to know.

SALTER Yes.

B2 So don't be upset.

SALTER No.

B2 You are though

SALTER Well.

B2 I'm fine about it. I'm not quite sure what I'm fine about. There was some other person this original some baby or cluster or and there were a number a number of us made somehow and you were one of the people who acquired, something like that.

SALTER It wasn't

B2 don't worry

SALTER because the thing is you see that isn't what happened. I am your father, it was by an artificial the forefront of science but I am genetically.

B2 That's great.

SALTER Yes.

B2 So I know the truth and you're still my father and that's fine.

SALTER Yes.

B2 So what about this original? I don't quite I don't

SALTER There was someone.

B2 There was what kind of someone?

SALTER There was a son.

B2 A son of yours?

SALTER Yes.

B2 So when was that?

SALTER That was some time earlier.

B2 Some time before I was born there was

SALTER another son, yes, a first

B2 who what, who died

SALTER who died, yes

B2 and you wanted to replace him

SALTER I wanted

B2 instead of just having another child you wanted

SALTER because your mother was dead too

B2 but she died when I was born, I thought she

SALTER well I'm telling you what happened.

B2 So what happened?

SALTER So they'd been killed in a carcrash and

B2 my mother and this

3. That is, in vitro (literally, "in glass"; Latin) fertilization; in this form of assisted reproduction, eggs are fertilized in a laboratory dish and one or more are implanted in the birth mother's uterus.

SALTER carcrash

B2 when was this? how old was the child, was he

SALTER four, he was four

B2 and you wanted him back

SALTER yes

B2 so I'm just him over again.

SALTER No but you are you because that's who you are but I wanted one just the same because that seemed to me the most perfect

B2 but another child might have been better

SALTER no I wanted the same

B2 but I'm not him

SALTER no but you're just the way I wanted

B2 but I could have been a different person not like him I

SALTER how could you? if I'd had a different child that wouldn't be you, would it. You're this one.

B2 I'm just a copy. I'm not the real one.

SALTER You're the only one.

B2 What do you mean only, there's all the others, there's

SALTER but I didn't know that, that wasn't part of the deal. They were meant to make one of you not a whole number, they stole that, we'll deal with, it's something for lawyers. But you're what I wanted, you're the one.

B2 Did you give me the same name as him?

SALTER Does it make it worse?

B2 Probably.

Scene 2

[SALTER *and his other son* BERNARD (B1), *forty.*]

SALTER So they stole—don't look at me—they stole your genetic material and

B1 no

SALTER they're the ones you want to

B1 no

SALTER because what ten twenty twenty copies of you walking round the streets

B1 no

SALTER which was nothing to do with me whatsoever and I think you and I should be united on this.

B1 Let me look at you.

SALTER You've been looking at me all the

B1 let me look at you.

SALTER Bit older.

B1 No because your father's not young when you're small is he, he's not any age, he's more a power. He's a dark dark power which is why my heart, people pay trainers to get it up to this speed, but is it because my body recognises or because I'm told? because if I'd seen you in the street I don't think I'd've stopped and shouted Daddy. But you'd've known me wouldn't you. Unless you thought I was one of the others.

SALTER It's a long time.

B1 Can we talk about what you did?

SALTER Yes of course. I'm not sure where what

BI about you sent me away and had this other one made from some bit of my body some

SALTER it didn't hurt you

BI what bit

SALTER I don't know what

BI not a limb, they clearly didn't take a limb like a starfish and grow[4]

SALTER a speck

BI or half of me chopped through like a worm and grow the other

SALTER a scraping cells a speck a speck

BI a speck yes because we're talking that microscope world of giant blobs and globs

SALTER that's all

BI and they take this painless scrape this specky little cells of me and kept that and you threw the rest of me away

SALTER no

BI and had a new one made

SALTER no

BI yes

SALTER yes

BI yes

SALTER yes of course, you know I did, I'm not attempting to deny, I thought it was the best thing to do, it seemed a brilliant it was the only

BI brilliant?

SALTER it seemed

BI to get rid

SALTER it wasn't perfect. It was the best I could do, I wasn't very I was I was always and it's a blur to be honest but it was I promise you the best

BI and this copy they grew of me, that worked out all right?

SALTER There were failures of course, inevitable

BI dead ones

SALTER in the test tubes the dishes, I was told they didn't all

BI but they finally got a satisfactory a bouncing

SALTER yes but they lied to me because they didn't tell me

BI in a cradle

SALTER all those others, they stole

BI and he looked just like me did he indistinguishable from

SALTER yes

BI so it worked out very well. And this son lives and breathes?

SALTER yes

BI talks and fucks? eats and walks? swims and dreams and exists somewhere right now yes does he? exist now?

SALTER yes

BI still exists

SALTER yes of course

BI happily?

4. Starfish, or sea stars, not only are able to regrow lost arms but also can regenerate themselves from a single arm if it includes part of the central disc to which the arms are attached.

SALTER well mostly you could say

BI as happily as most people?

SALTER yes I think

BI because most people are happy I read in the paper. Did it cost a lot of money?

SALTER the procedure? to get?

BI the baby

SALTER yes.

BI Were we rich?

SALTER Not rich.

BI No, I don't remember anything rich. A lot of dust under the bed those heaps of fluff you get don't you if you look if you go under there and lie in it.

SALTER No, we weren't. But I managed. I was spending less.

BI You made an effort.

SALTER I did and for that money you'd think I'd get exclusive

BI they ripped you off

SALTER because one one was the deal and they

BI what do you expect?

SALTER from you too they it's you they, just so they can do some scientific some research some do you get asthma do you have a dog what do you call it do you

BI Who did you think it was at the door? did you think it was one of the others or your son or

SALTER I don't know the others

BI you know your son

SALTER I know

BI your son the new

SALTER yes of course

BI you know him

SALTER yes I wouldn't think he was you, no.

BI You wouldn't think it was him having a bad day.

SALTER You look very well.

BI But it could have been one of the others?

SALTER Yes because that's what I was thinking about, how could the doctors, I think there's money to be made out of this.

BI I've not been lucky with dogs. I had this black and tan bitch wouldn't do what it's told, useless. Before that I had a lurcher[5] they need too much running about. Then a friend of mine went inside could I look after, battle from day one with that dog, rottweiler pit bull I had to throw a chair, you could hit it with a belt it kept coming back. I'd keep it shut up in the other room and it barks so you have to hit it, I was glad when it bit a girl went to pat it and straight off to the vet, get rid of this one it's a bastard. My friend wasn't pleased but he shouldn't have gone in the postoffice.

SALTER No that's right. I've never wanted a dog.

BI Don't patronise me

SALTER I'm not I'm not

BI you don't know what you're doing

5. A mixed-breed dog, traditionally used by poachers to catch rabbits (British term). *Bitch:* a female dog.

SALTER I just

B1 because you go in a pub someone throws his beer in your face you're supposed to say sorry, he only had three stitches I'm a very restrained person. Because this minute we sit here there's somebody a lot of them but think of one on the electric bedsprings or water poured down his throat and jump on his stomach. There's a lot of wicked people. So that's why. And you see them all around you. You go down the street and you see their faces and you think you don't fool me I know what you're capable of. So don't start anything.

SALTER I think what we need is a good solicitor.[6]

B1 What I like about a dog it stops people getting after you, they're not going to come round in the night. But they make the place stink because I might want to stay out a few days and when I get back I might want to stay in a few days and a dog can become a tyrant to you.

[*Silence.*]

Hello daddy daddy daddy, daddy hello.

SALTER Nobody regrets more than me the completely unforeseen unforeseeable which isn't my fault and does make it more upsetting but what I did did seem at the time the only and also it's a tribute, I could have had a different one, a new child altogether that's what most people but I wanted you again because I thought you were the best.

B1 It wasn't me again.

SALTER No but the same basic the same raw materials because they were perfect. You were the most beautiful baby everyone said. As a child too you were very pretty, very pretty child.

B1 You know when I used to be shouting.

SALTER No.

B1 When I was there in the dark. I'd be shouting.

SALTER No.

B1 Yes, I'd be shouting dad dad

SALTER Was this some time you had a bad dream or?

B1 shouting on and on

SALTER I don't think I

B1 shouting and shouting

SALTER no

B1 and you never came, nobody ever came

SALTER so was this after your mum

B1 after my mum was dead this was after

SALTER because you were very little when she

B1 yes because I can only remember

SALTER you were maybe two when she

B1 and I remember her sitting there, she was there

SALTER you remember so early?

B1 she'd be there but she wouldn't help stop anything

SALTER I'm surprised

B1 so when I was shouting what I want to know

SALTER but when was this

6. In the British legal system, a lawyer who advises clients (and does not represent them, except in the lower courts).

BI I want to know if you could hear me or not because I never knew were you hearing me and not coming or could you not hear me and if I shouted loud enough you'd come

SALTER I can't have heard you, no

BI or maybe there was no one there at all and you'd gone out so no matter how hard I shouted there was no one there

SALTER no that wouldn't have

BI so then I'd stop shouting but it was worse

SALTER because I hardly ever

BI and I didn't dare get out of bed to go and see

SALTER I don't think this can have

BI because if there was nobody there that would be terrifying and if you were there that might be worse but it's something I wonder

SALTER no

BI could you hear me shouting?

SALTER no I don't

BI no

SALTER no I don't think this happened in quite the

BI what?

SALTER because I'd

BI again and again and again, every night I'd be

SALTER no

BI so you didn't hear?

SALTER no but you can't have

BI yes I was shouting, are you telling me you didn't

SALTER no of course I didn't

BI you didn't

SALTER no

BI you weren't sitting there listening to me shouting

SALTER no

BI you weren't out

SALTER no

BI so I needed to shout louder.

SALTER Of course sometimes everyone who's had children will tell you sometimes you put them to bed and they want another story and you say goodnight now and go away and they call out once or twice and you say no go to sleep now and they might call out again and they go to sleep.

BI The other one. Your son. My brother is he? my little twin.

SALTER Yes.

BI Has he got a child?

SALTER No.

BI Because if he had I'd kill it.

SALTER No, he hasn't got one.

BI So when you opened the door you didn't recognise me.

SALTER No because

BI Do you recognise me now?

SALTER I know it's you.

BI No but look at me.

SALTER I have. I am.

BI No, look in my eyes. No, keep looking. Look.

Scene 3

[SALTER *and* BERNARD (B2).]

B2 Not like me at all
SALTER not like
B2 well like like but not identical not
SALTER not identical no not
B2 because what struck me was how different
SALTER yes I was struck
B2 you couldn't mistake
SALTER no no not at all I knew at once it wasn't
B2 though of course he is older if I was older
SALTER but even then you wouldn't
B2 I wouldn't be identical
SALTER no no not at all no, you're a different
B2 just a bit like
SALTER well bound to be a bit
B2 because for a start I'm not frightening.
SALTER So what did he want did he
B2 no nothing really, not frightening not
SALTER he didn't hit you?
B2 hit? god no, hit me? do you think?
SALTER well he
B2 he could have done yes, no he shouted
SALTER shouted
B2 shouted and rambled really, rambled he's not entirely
SALTER no, well
B2 so that's what, his childhood, his life, his childhood
SALTER all kinds of
B2 has made him a nutter really is what I think I mean not a nutter but he's
SALTER yes yes I'm not, yes he probably is.
B2 He says all kinds of wild
SALTER yes
B2 so you don't know what to believe.
SALTER And how did it end up, are you on friendly
B2 friendly no
SALTER not
B2 no no we ended up
SALTER yes
B2 we ended as I mean to go on with me running away, I was glad we were meeting in a public place, if I'd been at home you can't run away in your own home and if we'd been at his I wonder if he'd have let me go he might put me in a cupboard[7] not really, anyway yes I got up and left and I kept thinking had he followed me.
SALTER As you mean to go on as in not seeing him any more
B2 as in leaving the country.
SALTER For what for a week or two a holiday, I don't
B2 leaving, going on yes I don't know, going away, I don't want to be here.

7. Closet (British term).

SALTER But when you come back he'll still

B2 so maybe I won't

SALTER but that's, not come back, no that's

B2 I don't know I don't know don't ask me I don't know. I'm going, I don't know. I don't want to be anywhere near him.

SALTER You think he might try to hurt you?

B2 Why? why do you keep

SALTER I don't know. Is it that?

B2 It's partly that, it's also it's horrible, I don't feel myself and there's the others too, I don't want to see them I don't want them

SALTER I thought you did.

B2 I thought I did, I might, if I go away by myself I might feel all right, I might feel—you can understand that.

SALTER Yes, yes I can.

B2 Because there's this person who's identical to me

SALTER he's not

B2 who's not identical, who's like

SALTER not even very

B2 not very like but very something terrible which is exactly the same genetic person

SALTER not the same person

B2 and I don't like it.

SALTER I know. I'm sorry.

B2 I know you're sorry I'm not

SALTER I know

B2 I'm not trying to make you say sorry

SALTER I know, I just am

B2 I know

SALTER I just am sorry.

B2 He said some things.

SALTER Yes.

B2 There's a lot of things I don't, could you tell me what happened to my mother?

SALTER She's dead.

B2 Yes.

SALTER I told you she was dead.

B2 Yes but she didn't die when I was born and she didn't die with the first child in a carcrash because the first child's not dead he's walking round the streets at night giving me nightmares. Unless she did die in a carcrash?

SALTER No.

B2 No.

SALTER Your mother, the thing a thing about your mother was that she wasn't very happy, she wasn't a very happy person at all, I don't mean there were sometimes days she wasn't happy or I did things that made her not happy I did of course, she was always not happy, often cheerful and

B2 she killed herself. How did she do that?

SALTER She did it under a train under a tube[8] train, she was one of those

8. Subway (British term).

people when they say there has been a person under a train and the trains are delayed she was a person under a train.

B2 Were you with her?

SALTER With her on the platform no, I was still *with* her more or less but not with her then no I was having a drink I think.

B2 And the boy?

SALTER Do you know I don't remember where the boy was. I think he was at a friend's house, we had friends.

B2 And he was how old four?

SALTER no no he was four later when I he was walking, about two just starting to talk

B2 he was four when you sent him

SALTER that's right when his mother died he was two.

B2 So this was let me be clear this was before this was some years before I was born she died before

SALTER yes

B2 so she was already always

SALTER yes she was

B2 just so I'm clear. And then you and the boy you and your son

SALTER we went on we just

B2 lived alone together

SALTER yes

B2 you were bringing him up

SALTER yes

B2 the best you could

SALTER I

B2 until

SALTER and my best wasn't very but I had my moments, don't think, I did cook meals now and then and read a story I'm sure I can remember a particularly boring and badly written little book about an elephant at sea. But I could have managed better.

B2 Yes he said something about it

SALTER he said

B2 yes

SALTER yes of course he did yes. I know I could have managed better because I did with you because I stopped, shut myself away, gave it all up came off it all while I waited for you and I think we may even have had that same book, maybe it's you I remember reading it to, do you remember it at all? it had an elephant in red trousers.

B2 No I don't think

SALTER no it was terrible, we had far better books we had

B2 Maybe he shouldn't blame you, maybe it was a genetic, could you help drinking we don't know or drugs at the time philosophically as I understand it it wasn't viewed as not like now when our understanding's different and would a different person genetically different person not have been so been so vulnerable because there could always be some genetic addictive and then again someone with the same genetic exactly the same but at a different time a different cultural and of course all the personal all kinds of what happened in your own life your childhood or things all kind of because suppose you'd had a brother with identical an identical twin say but separated at birth so you had entirely different early you see what I'm saying would he have done the same things who can say he might have been a very loving father and in fact of course you have that in you to be that because you were to me so it's a combination of very complicated and that's who you were so probably I shouldn't blame you.

SALTER I'd rather you blamed me. I blame myself.

B2 I'm not saying you weren't horrible.

SALTER Couldn't I not have been?

B2 Apparently not.

SALTER If I'd tried harder.

B2 But someone like you couldn't have tried harder. What does it mean? If you'd tried harder you'd have been different from what you were like and you weren't you were

SALTER but then later I

B2 later yes

SALTER I did try that's what I did I started again I

B2 that's what

SALTER I was good I tried to be good I was good to you

B2 that's what you were like

SALTER I was good

B2 but I can't you can't I can't give you credit for that if I don't give you blame for the other it's what you did it's what happened

SALTER but it felt

B2 it felt

SALTER it felt as if I tried I deliberately

B2 of course it felt

SALTER well then

B2 it feels it always it feels doesn't it inside that's just how we feel what we are and we don't know all these complicated we can't know what we're it's too complicated to disentangle all the causes and we feel this is me I freely and of course it's true who you are does freely not forced by someone else but who you are who you are itself forces or you'd be someone else wouldn't you?

SALTER I did some bad things. I deserve to suffer. I did some better things. I'd like recognition.

B2 That's how everyone feels, certainly.

SALTER He still blames me.

B2 There's a difference then.

SALTER You remind me of him.

B2 I remind myself of him. We both hate you.

SALTER I thought you

B2 I don't blame you it's not your fault but what you've been like what you're like I can't help it.

SALTER Yes of course.

B2 Except what he feels as hate and what I feel as hate are completely different because what you did to him and what you did to me are different things.

SALTER I was nice to you.

B2 Yes you were.

SALTER You don't have to go away. Not for long.

B2 It might make me feel better.

SALTER I love you.
B2 That's something else you can't help.
SALTER That's all right. That's all right.
B2 Also I'm afraid he'll kill me.

Scene 4

[SALTER *and* BERNARD (B1).]

SALTER So what kind of a place was it? was it
B1 the place
SALTER he was in a hotel was he or
B1 no
SALTER I thought he was in a hotel. So where was he?
B1 what?
SALTER I'm trying to get a picture.
B1 Does it matter?
SALTER It won't bring him back no obviously but I'd like I'd like you can't help feeling curious you want to get at it and you're blocked in all directions, your son dies you want his body, you want to know where his body last was when he was alive, you can't help
B1 He had a room.
SALTER In somebody's house, renting
B1 some small you know how the locals when you arrive, just a room not breakfast you'd go out for a coffee.
SALTER So was it some pretty on a harbour front or
B1 no
SALTER thinking of him on holiday
B1 in a street just a side
SALTER but of course it wasn't a holiday he was hiding he thought he was hiding. Did you go inside the room?
B1 Just a small room, rather dark, one window and the shutters
SALTER not very tidy I expect
B1 that's right, not tidy the bed not made, couple of books, bag on the floor with clothes half out of it
SALTER did he scream?
B1 and you know what he's like, not tidy, am I tidy you don't know do you but you'd guess not wouldn't you but you'd be wrong there because I'm meticulous.
SALTER What I want to know is how you actually, what you, how you got him to go off to some remote because that's what I'm imagining, you don't shoot the lodger without the landlady hearing, I don't know if you did shoot I don't know why I say shoot you could have had a knife you could have strangled, I can't think he would have gone off with you because he was frightened which is why but perhaps you talked you made him feel or did you follow him or lie in wait in some dark? and I don't know how you found him there did you follow him from his house when he left or follow him from here last time he?
B1 I didn't need to tell you it had happened
SALTER but you did so naturally I want to
B1 and I'm wishing I hadn't

SALTER no I'm glad

BI and I'm not telling you

SALTER because I won't tell anyone

BI and there's nothing more to be said.

SALTER What about the others? or is he the only one you hated because I loved him, I don't love the others, you and I have got common cause against the others don't forget, I'm still hoping we'll make our fortunes there. I'm going to talk to a solicitor, I've been too busy not busy but it's been like a storm going on I don't know what's gone on, it's not been very long ago it all started. You're not going to be a serial, wipe them all out so you're the only, back like it was at the start I'd understand that. If they do catch up with you, I'm sure they won't I'm sure you know what you're, if they do we'll tell them it was me it was my fault anyway you look at it. Don't you agree, don't you feel that? Don't stop talking to me. It wasn't his fault, you should have killed me, it's my fault you. Perhaps you're going to kill me, is that why you've stopped talking? Shall I kill myself? I'd do that for you if you like, would you like that?

I'll tell you a thought, I could have killed you and I didn't. I may have done terrible things but I didn't kill you. I could have killed you and had another son, made one the same like I did or start again have a different one get married again and I didn't, I spared you though you were this disgusting thing by then anyone in their right mind would have squashed you but I remembered what you'd been like at the beginning and I spared you, I didn't want a different one, I wanted that again because you were perfect just like that and I loved you.

You know you asked me when you used to shout in the night. Sometimes I was there, I'd sit and listen to you or I'd not be in any condition to hear you I'd just be sitting. Sometimes I'd go out and leave you. I don't think you got out of bed, did you get out of bed, because you'd be frightened what I'd do to you so it was all right to go out. That was just a short period you used to shout, you grew out of that, you got so you'd rather not see me, you wanted to be left alone in the night, you wouldn't want me to come any more. You'd nearly stopped speaking do you remember that? not speaking not eating I tried to make you. I'd put you in the cupboard do you remember? or I'd look for you everywhere and I'd think you'd got away and I'd find you under the bed. You liked it there I'd put your dinner under for you. But it got worse do you remember? There was nobody but us. One day I cleaned you up and said take him into care.[9] You didn't look too bad and they took you away. My darling. Do you remember that? Do you remember that day because I don't remember it you know. The whole thing is very vague to me. It's two years I remember almost nothing about but you must remember things and when you're that age two years is much longer, it wasn't very long to me, it was one long night out. Can you tell me anything you remember? the day you left? can you tell me things I did I might have forgotten?

BI When I was following him there was a time I was getting on the same train and he looked round, I thought he was looking right at me but he didn't see me. I got on the train and went with him all the way.

SALTER Yes? yes?

9. Under the guardianship of the state.

Scene 5

[SALTER *and* MICHAEL BLACK, *his son, thirty-five.*]

MICHAEL Have you met the others?

SALTER You're the first.

MICHAEL Are you going to meet us all?

SALTER I thought I'd start.

MICHAEL I'm sure everyone will be pleased to meet you. I know I am.

SALTER I'm sorry to stare.

MICHAEL No, please, I can see it must be. Do I look like?

SALTER Yes of course

MICHAEL of course, I meant

SALTER no no I didn't mean

MICHAEL I suppose I meant how

SALTER because of course you don't, you don't, not exactly

MICHAEL no of course

SALTER I wouldn't mistake

MICHAEL no

SALTER or I might at a casual

MICHAEL of course

SALTER but not if I really look

MICHAEL no

SALTER no

MICHAEL because?

SALTER because of the eyes. You don't look at me in the same way.

MICHAEL I'm looking at someone I don't know of course.

SALTER Maybe you could tell me a little

MICHAEL about myself

SALTER if you don't mind

MICHAEL no of course, it's where to, you already know I'm a teacher, mathematics, you know I'm married, three children did I tell you that

SALTER yes but you didn't

MICHAEL boy and girl twelve and eight and now a baby well eighteen months so she's walking and beginning to talk, I don't have any photographs on me I didn't think, there's no need for photographs is there if you see someone all the time so

SALTER are you happy?

MICHAEL what now? or in general? Yes I think I am, I don't think about it, I am. The job gets me down sometimes. The world's a mess of course. But you can't help, a sunny morning, leaves turning, off to the park with the baby, you can't help feeling wonderful can you?

SALTER Can't you?

MICHAEL Well that's how I seem to be.

SALTER Tell me. Forgive me

MICHAEL no go on

SALTER tell me something about yourself that's really specific to you, something really important

MICHAEL what sort of?

SALTER anything

MICHAEL it's hard to

SALTER yes.

MICHAEL Well here's something I find fascinating, there are these people who used to live in holes in the ground, with all tunnels and underground chambers and sometimes you'd have a chamber you'd get to it through a labyrinth of passages and the ceiling got lower and lower so you had to go on your hands and knees and then wriggle on your stomach and you'd get through to this chamber deep deep down that had a hole like a chimney like a well a hole all the way up to the sky so you could sit in this chamber this room this cave whatever and look up at a little circle of sky going past overhead. And when somebody died they'd hollow out more little rooms so they weren't buried underneath you they were buried in the walls beside you. And maybe sometimes they walled people up alive in there, it's possible because of how the remains were contorted but either way of course they're dead by now and very soon after they went in of course. And

SALTER I don't think this is what I'm looking for

MICHAEL oh, how, sorry

SALTER because what you're telling me is about something else and I was hoping for something about you

MICHAEL I don't quite

SALTER I'm sorry I don't know I was hoping

MICHAEL you want what my beliefs, politics how I feel about war for instance is that? I dislike war, I'm not at all happy when people say we're doing a lot of good with our bombing, I'm never very comfortable with that. War's one of those things, don't you think, where everyone always thinks they're in the right have you noticed that? Nobody ever says we're the bad guys, we're going to beat shit out of the good guys. What do you think?

SALTER I was hoping I don't know something more personal something from deep inside your life. If that's not intrusive.

MICHAEL Maybe what maybe my wife's ears?

SALTER Yes?

MICHAEL Because last night we were watching the news and I thought what beautiful and slightly odd ears she's got, they're small but with big lobes, big relative to the small ear, and they're slightly pointy on top, like a disney elf[1] or little animal ears and they're always there but you know how you suddenly notice and noticing that, I mean the way I love her, felt very felt what you said something deep inside. Or the children obviously, I could talk about, is this the sort of thing?

SALTER it's not quite

MICHAEL no

SALTER because you're just describing other people or

MICHAEL yes

SALTER not yourself

MICHAEL but it's people I love so

SALTER it's not what I'm looking for. Because anyone could feel

MICHAEL oh of course I'm not claiming

SALTER I was somehow hoping

MICHAEL yes

1. That is, like the ears of an elf in an animated film created by the American movie producer Walt Disney (1901–1966).

SALTER further in

MICHAEL yes

SALTER just about yourself

MICHAEL myself

SALTER yes

MICHAEL like maybe I'm lying in bed and it's comfortable and then it gets slightly not so comfortable and I move my legs or even turn over and then it's

SALTER no

MICHAEL no

SALTER no that's

MICHAEL yes that's something everyone

SALTER yes

MICHAEL well I don't know. I like blue socks. Banana icecream. Does that help you?

SALTER Dogs?

MICHAEL do I like

SALTER dogs

MICHAEL I'm ok with dogs. My daughter wants a puppy but I don't know. Is dogs the kind of thing?

SALTER So tell me what did you feel when you found out?

MICHAEL Fascinated.

SALTER Not angry?

MICHAEL No.

SALTER Not frightened.

MICHAEL No, what of?

SALTER Your life, losing your life.

MICHAEL I've still got my life.

SALTER But there are things there are things that are what you are, I think you're avoiding

MICHAEL yes perhaps

SALTER because then you might be frightened

MICHAEL I don't think

SALTER or angry

MICHAEL not really

SALTER because what does it do what does it to you to everything if there are all these walking around, what it does to me what am I and it's not even me it happened to, so how you can just, you must think something about it.

MICHAEL I think it's funny, I think it's delightful

SALTER delightful?

MICHAEL all these very similar people doing things like each other or a bit different or whatever we're doing, what a thrill for the mad old professor if he'd lived to see it, I do see the joy of it. I know you're not at all happy.

SALTER I didn't feel I'd lost him when I sent him away because I had the second chance. And when the second one my son the second son was murdered it wasn't so bad as you'd think because it seemed fair. I was back with the first one.

MICHAEL But now

SALTER now he's killed himself

MICHAEL now you feel

SALTER now I've lost him, I've lost

MICHAEL yes

SALTER now I can't put it right any more. Because the second time round you see I slept very lightly with the door open.

MICHAEL Is that the worst you did, not go in the night?

SALTER No of course not.

MICHAEL Like what?

SALTER Things that are what I did that are not trivial like banana icecream nor unifuckingversal like turning over in bed.

MICHAEL We've got ninety-nine percent the same genes as any other person. We've got ninety percent the same as a chimpanzee. We've got thirty percent the same as a lettuce. Does that cheer you up at all? I love about the lettuce. It makes me feel I belong.

SALTER I miss him so much. I miss them both.

MICHAEL There's nineteen more of us.

SALTER That's not the same.

MICHAEL No of course not. I was making a joke.

SALTER And you're happy you say are you? you like your life?

MICHAEL I do yes, sorry.

SELECTED BIBLIOGRAPHIES

TAWFIQ AL-HAKIM

In addition to the 1977 translation by M. M. Badawi included here, *Song of Death* has been translated into English by C. W. R. Long (1972) and Denys Johnson-Davies (1973). One of the most comprehensive treatments in English of Tawfiq al-Hakim and his contribution to Egyptian theater is found in Badawi's seminal work *Modern Arabic Drama in Egypt* (1987). In this study, Badawi provides a thorough overview of al-Hakim's different developmental stages as a playwright and traces his dramatic production from its earliest experiments to the last stages. *Tawfiq al-Hakim: A Reader's Guide*, ed. William Maynard Hutchins (2003), discusses al-Hakim's plays, novels, and short stories and includes an excellent annotated biography and chronology of the writer's life and work. Other studies of al-Hakim's drama include Richard Long, *Tawfiq al Hakim, Playwright of Egypt* (1979); Roger Allen, "Egyptian Drama after the Revolution" (1979); Paul Starkey, "Tawfiq Al-Hakim: Leading Playwright of the Arab World" (1989); and Ali al-Ra'i, "Arab Drama Since the Thirties," in *The Cambridge History of Arabic Literature: Modern Arabic Literature*, ed. M. M. Badawi (1992).

ARISTOPHANES

For a detailed description of the competitions and how they were staged, see Sir Arthur Pickard-Cambridge, *The Dramatic Festivals of Athens* (2nd ed., 1968). Useful overviews of the work of Aristophanes include K. J. Dover, *Aristophanic Comedy* (1972); A. M. Bowie, *Aristophanes: Myth, Ritual and Comedy* (1993); and David Konstan, *Greek Comedy and Ideology* (1995). Two thematic studies with particular relevance to *Lysistrata* are Jeffrey Henderson, *The Maculate Muse: Obscene Language in Attic Comedy* (1975; 2nd ed., 1991), and Lauren K. Taaffe, *Aristophanes and Women* (1993). John Vaio's "The Manipulation of Theme and Action in Aristophanes' *Lysistrata*" (1973) and Jeffrey Henderson's "*Lysistrata*: The Play and Its Themes" (1980) provide excellent, detailed readings of the play. The scholarly translations by Alan H. Sommerstein (2002), Jeffrey Henderson (1996), and Stephen Halliwell (1997) all offer detailed introductions and textual analysis of this complex and challenging text.

SAMUEL BECKETT

Samuel Beckett's plays are published in the United States by Grove/Atlantic and in Britain by Faber and Faber. The most complete biography of Beckett, written with the author's approval, is James Knowlson, *Damned to Fame: The Life of Samuel Beckett* (1996), which has supplemented and, in the view of most Beckett scholars, superseded Deirdre Bair's earlier *Samuel Beckett: A*

Biography (1978). Other important biographies written since Beckett's death include Anthony Cronin, *Samuel Beckett: The Last Modernist* (1996), and Lois Gordon, *The World of Samuel Beckett, 1906–1946* (1996). Among the many critical discussions of Beckett's work, the following are particularly useful to students of his plays: Hugh Kenner, *Samuel Beckett: A Critical Study* (1961; new ed., 1968); Eugene Webb, *The Plays of Samuel Beckett* (1972); John Fletcher and John Spurling, *Beckett: A Study of His Plays* (1972; 2d ed., 1978); Ruby Cohn, *Back to Beckett* (1973) and *Just Play: Beckett's Theater* (1980); John Pilling, *Samuel Beckett* (1976); S. E. Gontarski, *The Intent of Undoing in Samuel Beckett's Dramatic Texts* (1985); Steven Connor, *Samuel Beckett: Repetition, Theory and Text* (1988); Andrew K. Kennedy, *Samuel Beckett* (1989); Enoch Brater, *Why Beckett* (1989); David Pattie, *The Complete Critical Guide to Samuel Beckett* (2000); and Rónán McDonald, *The Cambridge Introduction to Samuel Beckett* (2006). Important collections of essays include Martin Esslin, ed., *Samuel Beckett: A Collection of Critical Essays* (1965); S. E. Gontarski, ed., *On Beckett: Essays and Criticism* (1986); and Lance St. John Butler and Robin J. Davis, eds., *Rethinking Beckett: A Collection of Critical Essays* (1990). Studies of Beckett's plays in performance include Dougald McMillan and Martha Fehsenfeld, *Beckett in the Theatre: The Author as Practical Playwright and Director* (1988), and Jonathan Kalb, *Beckett in Performance* (1989). Linda Ben-Zvi, ed., *Women in Beckett: Performance and Critical Perspectives* (1990), explores issues of gender in Beckett's drama with an emphasis on performance.

Resources for the study of *Waiting for Godot* include the following: Ruby Cohn, ed., *Casebook on "Waiting for Godot"* (1967); Bert O. States, *The Shape of Paradox: An Essay on "Waiting for Godot"* (1978); Lawrence Graver, *Samuel Beckett, "Waiting for Godot,"* (1989; 2nd ed., 2004); Thomas Cousineau, *"Waiting for Godot": Form in Movement* (1990); Steven Connor, ed., *"Waiting for Godot" and "Endgame,"* by Samuel Beckett (1992); and Lois Gordon, *Reading "Godot"* (2002). David Bradby, *Beckett: "Waiting for Godot"* (2001), and Jonathan Croall, *The Coming of Godot: A Short History of a Masterpiece* (2005), discuss the play's production history. Dougald McMillan and James Knowlson, eds., *The Theatrical Notebooks of Samuel Beckett,* vol. 1, *Waiting for Godot* (1993), contains the working notes that Beckett kept while directing *Godot* at Berlin's Schiller-Theater in 1975 and will be of particular interest to actors and directors of Beckett's play.

APHRA BEHN

Maureen Duffy, *The Passionate Shepherdess: Aphra Behn, 1640–89* (1977); Angeline Goreau, *Reconstructing Aphra: A Social Biography of Aphra Behn* (1980); George Woodcock, *Aphra Behn: The English Sappho* (1989); and Janet Todd, *The Secret Life of Aphra Behn* (1996) are the most recent and authoritative of a series of biographical studies. Todd's *The Sign of Angellica: Women, Writing, and Fiction, 1660–1800* (1989) documents the increasing presence and impact of women writers in England. Todd's edited volume, *Aphra Behn Studies* (1996), provides additional recent perspectives on Behn's work as a dramatist, poet, and fiction writer and further augments the Behn biographies. Heidi Hutner's edited volume, *Rereading Aphra Behn: History, Theory, and Criticism* (1993), contributes other important essays on Behn's writing in all major genres. Individual essays on her work from a range of critical perspectives abound. For comparisons of *The Rover* and *Thomaso,* see especially Jones DeRitter, "The Gypsy, *The Rover*, and the Wanderer: Aphra Behn's Revision of Thomas Killigrew" (1986), and Elaine Hobby, "No Stolen Object, but Her Own: Aphra Behn's *Rover* and Thomas Killigrew's *Thomaso*" (1999). For studies of the setting of the play, see Linda R. Payne, "The Carnivalesque Regeneration of Corrupt Economies in *The Rover*" (1998), and Dagny Boebel, "In the Carnival World of Adam's Garden: Roving and Rape in Behn's *Rover*," in *Broken Boundaries: Women and Feminism in Restoration Drama,* ed. Katherine M. Quinsey (1996). Readings that incorporate important considerations of staging and performance include Elin Diamond, "*Gestus* and Signature in Aphra Behn's *The Rover*" (1989), and John Franceschina, "Shadow and Substance in Aphra Behn's *The Rover:* The Semiotics of Restoration Performance" (1995). Mary Anne O'Donnell has compiled the useful reference volume *Aphra Behn: An Annotated Bibliography of Primary and Secondary Sources* (1986; 2nd ed., 2004). Among the growing body of historical and critical writings on Restoration drama and theater practice, see Robert D. Hume, *The Development of English Drama in the Late Seventeenth Century* (1976) and his *Rakish Stage: Studies in English Drama, 1660–1800* (1983); J. Douglas Canfield and Deborah C. Payne, eds., *Cultural Readings of Restoration and Eighteenth-Century English Theater* (1995); Laura Brown, *English Dramatic Form, 1660–1760: An Essay in Generic History* (1981); J. L. Styan, *Restoration Comedy in Performance* (1986); Mary Anne Schofield and Cecilia Macheski, eds., *Curtain Calls: British and American Women and Theater, 1660–1820* (1991); Jocelyn Powell, *Restoration Theatre Production* (1984); and Deborah Payne Fisk, ed., *The Cambridge Companion to English Restoration Theatre* (2000), which also contains a very useful bibliography. The definitive reference work for documenting performances of the period remains William Van Lennep et al., eds., *The London Stage, 1660–1800: A Calendar of Plays, Entertainments, and Afterpieces, together with Casts, Box-Receipts, and Contemporary Comment*, 5 vols. (1960–68).

BERTOLT BRECHT

Not surprisingly, the critical literature on Brecht's life and work is extensive. The person who introduced Brecht to America was Eric Bentley, who translated many of Brecht's plays, adapted them, and wrote extensively on the author. Although his not always faithful translations have been criticized, his writings on Brecht are important milestones in Brecht criticism; they include *Bentley on Brecht* (1998; 3d ed., 2008) and *The Playwright as Thinker: A Study of Drama in Modern Times* (1967). A good biography of Brecht is still Frederic Ewen's *Bertolt Brecht: His Life, His Art, and His Times* (1967). A more recent biography, John Fuegi's controversial *Brecht and Company: Sex, Politics, and the Making of the Modern Drama* (1994), argues that much of what has been viewed as original in Brecht was noncredited work by a number of others, including several of his lovers. Though exaggerated and shrill in its claims, the book nevertheless draws needed attention to the collaborative process that was undoubtedly part of Brecht's work. A good and simple introduction to Brecht's work is John Willett's *The Theatre of Bertolt Brecht: A Study from Eight Aspects* (1959; 3d ed., 1967); Martin Esslin's *Brecht: A Choice of Evils: A Critical Study of the Man, His Work, and His Opinions* (1959; 4th ed., 1984) is more ambitious and insightful. On Brecht's exile in and influence on the theater of the United States, see James Lyon's informative *Bertolt Brecht in America* (1980). Brecht's theoretical works are collected and translated by John Willett in *Brecht on Theatre: The Development of an Aesthetic* (1964; 2d ed., 1974); a good recent study of Brecht's theater is John J. White's *Bertolt Brecht's Dramatic Theory* (2004). A theoretically challenging but intriguing discussion of Brecht is Fredric Jameson's *Brecht and Method* (1998). On the use, in *The Good Woman of Setzuan*, of a Chinese setting as well as on Brecht's interest in Chinese theater, see Eric Hayot's *Chinese Dreams: Pound, Brecht, Tel Quel* (2004).

Given Brecht's immense influence on modern drama, most classic studies of that period include substantial chapters on Brecht. See, for example, Raymond Williams, *Drama from Ibsen to Brecht* (1969); Richard Gilman, *The Making of Modern Drama* (1972); and Robert Brustein, *The Theatre of Revolt: An Approach to the Modern Drama* (1964). Brecht's paradigm has also shaped studies such as Janelle Reinelt's *After Brecht: British Epic Theater* (1994) and Elin Diamond's *Unmaking Mimesis* (1997).

ANTON CHEKHOV

Numerous translations of Chekhov's plays have appeared in the past forty years, including versions by such playwrights as Michael Frayn, Trevor Griffiths, and David Mamet. While its translations are not as stageworthy as the best of these, Ronald Hingley's nine-volume edition, *The Oxford Chekhov* (1964–80), includes all of Chekhov's plays and most of his stories. Laurence Senelick's Norton Critical Edition, *Anton Chekhov's Selected Plays* (2005), contains useful annotations on *The Cherry Orchard* and other plays. Donald Rayfield's authoritative biography, *Anton Chekhov: A Life* (1997), was the first account of the playwright's life to benefit from the opening of Russian archives after the dissolution of the Soviet Union in 1991.

The following are useful studies of Chekhov's drama: Maurice Valency, *The Breaking String: The Plays of Anton Chekhov* (1966); J. L. Styan, *Chekhov in Performance: A Commentary on the Major Plays* (1971); Richard Peace, *Chekhov: A Study of the Four Major Plays* (1983); Laurence Senelick, *Anton Chekhov* (1985); Richard Gilman, *Chekhov's Plays: An Opening into Eternity* (1995); and Donald Rayfield, *Understanding Chekhov: A Critical Study of Chekhov's Prose and Drama* (1999). Toby W. Clyman, ed., *A Chekhov Companion* (1985), and Vera Gottlieb and Paul Allain, eds., *The Cambridge Companion to Chekhov* (2000), contain valuable essays on Chekhov, while Harold Bloom, ed., *Anton Chekhov* (1999), reprints a number of previously published essays on Chekhov's fiction and drama. The chapters on Chekhov in Robert Brustein, *The Theatre of Revolt: An Approach to the Modern Drama* (1964), and Richard Gilman, *The Making of Modern Drama* (1974), remain among the best discussions of the playwright's dramatic work. Donald Rayfield, *The Cherry Orchard: Catastrophe and Comedy* (1994), is a book-length study of Chekhov's final play. Laurence Senelick, *The Chekhov Theatre: A Century of the Plays in Performance* (1997), and David Allen, *Performing Chekhov* (2000), examine Chekhov's plays in performance.

CARYL CHURCHILL

Most of Caryl Churchill's produced dramas and radio scripts to date have been published singly or in collected volumes by Methuen and Nick Hern Books. Some of her very early, unproduced pieces have not yet been made publicly available. *File on Churchill,* comp. Linda Fitzsimmons (1989), contains much useful information on Churchill's biography and early career, as well as excerpts from reviews, interviews, and other commentary. No biography of Churchill has yet been published, although she has shared information on her life with interviewers. Among the most useful of these dialogues are with Kathleen Betsko and Rachel Koenig, in *Interviews with Contemporary Women Playwrights* (1987); with Laurie Stone, "Caryl Churchill: Making Room at the Top" (1983); and with Lynne Truss, "A Fair Cop" (1984).

Early full-length studies of Churchill's work include Geraldine Cousin, *Churchill: The Playwright* (1989), and Amelia Howe Kritzer, *The Plays of Caryl Churchill: Theatre of Empowerment* (1991). Elaine Aston's *Caryl Churchill* (1997; 2d ed., 2001) builds productively on this early criticism. Janelle Reinelt has also published important analyses of Churchill in *After Brecht: British Epic Theater* (1994) and in "Caryl Churchill and the Politics of Style," in *The Cambridge Companion to Modern British Women Playwrights,* ed. Elaine Aston and Reinelt (2000). *Caryl Churchill: A Casebook,* ed. Phyllis R. Randall (1988); Helene Keyssar, *Feminist Theatre: An Introduction to the Plays of Contemporary British and American Women* (1984); Elin Diamond, "(In) Visible Bodies in Churchill's Theater," in *Making a Spectacle: Feminist Essays on Contemporary Women's Theatre,* ed. Lynda Hart (1989); Austin Quigley, "Stereotype and Prototype: Character in the Plays of Caryl Churchill," in *Feminine Focus: The New Women Playwrights,* ed. Enoch Brater (1989); Frances Gray, "Mirrors of Utopia: Caryl Churchill and Joint Stock," in *British and Irish Drama Since 1960,* ed. James Acheson (1993); and Lisa Merrill, "Monsters and Heroines: Caryl Churchill's Women," in *Modern Dramatists: A Casebook of Major British, Irish, and American Playwrights,* ed. Kimball King (2001), are all worthwhile.

To date, only two published scholarly articles discuss *A Number:* Martha Montello, "Novel Perspectives on Bioethics" (2005), and Amy Strahler Holzapfel, "The Body in Pieces: Contemporary Anatomy Theatres" (2008). Most of the commentary on the play can be found in theatrical reviews and feature articles; the more insightful of these include Michael Billington, "A Number: Royal Court, London," *The Guardian* (2002); Charles Spencer, "In Short, This is a Spellbinding Triumph: First Night," *Daily Telegraph* (2002); Matt Wolf, "Magic 'Number' Reps Churchill at her Best," *Variety* (2002); Sarah Lyall, "The Mysteries of Caryl Churchill," *New York Times* (2004); Ben Brantley, "My 3 Sons: Cloning's Unexpected Results" *New York Times* (2004); and Mel Gussow, "A Play without Instructions Morphs into Another," *New York Times* (2004). An interview with the play's original director, Stephen Daldry, can be found at www.royalcourttheatre.com/files/downloads/a_number_edupack.pdf.

For discussions of human cloning and the bioethical controversy surrounding it, see John Harris, "'Goodbye Dolly?' The Ethics of Human Cloning" (1997); Meredith Wadman, "Dolly: A Decade On" (2007); Matteo Galletti, "Begetting, Cloning and Being Human: Two National Commission Reports against Human Cloning from Italy and the U.S.A." (2006); and Dan W. Brock, "Cloning Human Beings: An Assessment of the Ethical Issues Pro and Con" (1997), reprinted in *Cloning and the Future of Human Embryo Research*, ed. Paul Lauritzen (2001).

SOR JUANA INÉS DE LA CRUZ

There is no English translation of Sor Juana's complete works. Volumes of selected writings appeared in Spanish as early as 1676, but the definitive four-volume collection, edited by Alfonso Méndez Plancarte, was not published until 1951–57. The *loa* to *The Divine Narcissus* exists in three English translations, by Willis K. Jones (1966), Margaret Sayers Peden (1985), and Patricia A. Peters (1998); the Peden and Peters volumes also contain very useful critical introductions. The major critical biography of Sor Juana in English remains that of Octavio Paz, *Sor Juana, or, The Traps of Faith*, translated by Peden (1982; trans. 1988). The critical introductions to Peden's translation of Sor Juana's prose, *A Woman of Genius: The Intellectual Autobiography of Sor Juana Inés de la Cruz* (1982), and to Electa Arenal and Amanda Powell's translation of *La Respuesta* (1994), provide further insights. Gerald Flynn's volume for the Twayne series, *Sor Juana Inés de la Cruz* (1971), contains a helpful, if limited, overview of her life and works. George H. Tavard's *Juana Inés de la Cruz and the Theology of Beauty: The First Mexican Theology* (1991) considers her primarily as a religious writer, while Pamela Kirk's *Sor Juana Inés de la Cruz: Religion, Art, and Feminism* (1998) examines in her work the interrelated elements named in the subtitle. Stephanie Merrim's *Early Modern Women's Writing and Sor Juana Inés de la Cruz* (1999) and her edited collection, *Feminist Perspectives on Sor Juana Inés de la Cruz* (1991), are the primary studies for feminist considerations of Sor Juana. The essay collections *A Reader in Latina Feminist Theology: Religion and Justice* ed. María Pilar Aquino, Daisy L. Machado, and Jeanette Rodríguez (2002), and *Women, Culture, and Politics in Latin America*, by Emilie Bergmann et al. (1990), both contain useful pieces on Sor Juana in the context of Latin American studies. Comparatively little critical attention has focused on Sor Juana's *loas*, with the exception of Lee A. Daniel's *The Loa of Sor Juana Inés de la Cruz* (1994). To gain an understanding of the *loa* and the *auto sacramental* in theater history, see Melveena McKendrick, *Theatre in Spain, 1490–1700* (1989).

EURIPIDES

Preserved through a series of historical accidents, the text of *The Bacchae* contains some omissions toward the end of the play and poses other intricate problems for those trying to establish an authoritative text. Classic studies of the playwright and the play are R. P. Winnington-Ingram's *Euripides and Dionysus: An Interpretation of the "Bacchae"* (1948) and H. D. F. Kitto's *Greek Tragedy: A Literary Study* (1939). Especially attuned to intricate construction of the play is Charles Segal's *Dionysiac Poetics and Euripides' "Bacchae"* (1982), which is informed by recent trends in philosophy and literary theory. Given the play's central concern with ritual and sacrifice, many commentators have mined the play for clues about the origin of Greek tragedy. Anthropology has been an especially important influence on such studies: for example, see *Myth and Tragedy in Ancient Greece* (1972, trans. 1988) by Jean-Pierre Vernant and Pierre Vidal-Naquet. René Girard's *Violence and the Sacred* (1972, trans. 1977) uses the structural analysis of myth by the French theorist Claude Lévi-Strauss to illuminate the play. Also influenced by these theorists is Helene P. Foley's excellent *Ritual Irony: Poetry and Sacrifice in Euripides* (1985), which pays particular attention to gender. Richard Seaford's *Reciprocity and Ritual: Homer and Tragedy in the Developing City-State* (1994) relates tragedy to the political history of Athens. For information about the Dionysus festival of Athens, consult David Wiles's *Tragedy in Athens: Performing Space and Theatrical Meaning* (1997) and Sir Arthur

Pickard-Cambridge's *The Dramatic Festivals of Athens* (1953; 2nd ed., 1968). Good general introductions to all aspects of Greek tragedy are provided by *The Cambridge Companion to Greek Tragedy* (1997), edited by P. E. Easterling, and Simon Goldhill's *Reading Greek Tragedy* (1986).

EVERYMAN

A. C. Cawley's 1961 *Everyman* is the most widely cited text of the play; Cawley's introduction to this edition gives valuable background information. *The Mirror of Everyman's Salvation: A Prose Translation of the Original Everyman* ed. John Conley, Guido de Baere, H. J. C. Schaap, and W. H. Toppen (1985), includes both the text of *Everyman* and a translation of the Dutch *Elckerlijc*. Important critical studies of *Everyman* include Lawrence V. Ryan, "Doctrine and Dramatic Structure in *Everyman*" (1957); Thomas F. Van Laan, "*Everyman*: A Structural Analysis" (1963); V. A. Kolve, "*Everyman* and the Parable of the Talents" (1972); C. J. Wortham, "*Everyman* and the Reformation" (1981); Carolynn Van Dyke, "The Intangible and Its Image: Allegorical Discourse and the Cast of *Everyman*" (1982); Donald F. Duclow, "*Everyman* and the *Ars moriendi*: Fifteenth-Century Ceremonies of Dying" (1983); Phoebe S. Spinrad, "The Last Temptation of Everyman" (1985); Stanton B. Garner, Jr., "Theatricality in *Mankind* and *Everyman*" (1987); Jacqueline Vanhoutte, "When Elckerlijc Becomes Everyman: Translating Dutch to English, Performance to Print" (1995); and David Mills, "The Theaters of *Everyman*" (1995). Robert Potter's *The English Morality Play: Origins, History and Influence of a Dramatic Tradition* (1975) discusses the influential 1901 revival of *Everyman* and the play's twentieth-century reputation.

SUSAN GLASPELL

Although there is to date no complete collected edition of Susan Glaspell's dramas, C. W. E. Bigsby's selection, *Plays* (1987), reprints several of her major works (including *Trifles*) and contains a worthwhile introduction; his entry on Glaspell for the first volume of his *Critical Introduction to Twentieth-Century American Drama* (1983) is also helpful. Marcia Noe's *Susan Glaspell: Voice from the Heartland* (1983) was the first critical biography of Glaspell. More recent definitive biographies are Linda Ben-Zvi, *Susan Glaspell: Her Life and Times* (2005), and Barbara Ozieblo, *Susan Glaspell: A Critical Biography* (2000). J. Ellen Gainor, *Susan Glaspell in Context: American Theater, Culture, and Politics, 1915–48* (2001), provides readings of Glaspell's dramas within their creative, historical, and critical milieus. Linda Ben-Zvi, ed., *Susan Glaspell: Essay on Her Theater and Fiction* (1995), contains a useful section on *Trifles* and "Jury." Veronica Makowsky, *Susan Glaspell's Century of American Women: A Critical Interpretation of Her Work* (1993), focuses on female characters and themes in Glaspell's fiction and drama, while Kristina Hinz-Bode, *Susan Glaspell and the Anxiety of Expression: Language and Isolation in the Plays* (2006), examines issues of language and isolation in the playwright's dramas. Robert Károly Sarlós, *Jig Cook and the Provincetown Players: Theatre in Ferment* (1982), provides the broader historical background to Glaspell's early theatrical career, and Cheryl Black's *The Women of Provincetown, 1915–22* (2002) focuses on the artistry of Glaspell and her female colleagues. In *Midnight Assassin: A Murder in America's Heartland* (2005), Patricia L. Bryan and Thomas Wolf provide a historical analysis of the murder that was the source for Glaspell's play. Mary E. Papke, *Susan Glaspell: A Research and Production Sourcebook* (1993), is the most comprehensive bibliographic resource.

GUAN HANQING

The Yuan text of *Dou E Yuan* has been preserved in a collection of *zaju* plays published three centuries after Guan's lifetime, but there is no single authoritative written version that defines how the play has been experienced by audiences throughout China over the centuries. Like most Chinese drama, *zaju* plays present a traditional core that survives and proliferates in performance. Each *zaju* play has been excerpted, expanded, modified, and appropriated many times throughout the past seven hundred years. No *zaju* play, *Dou E Yuan* included, has a "definitive" text. For example, Ye Xianzu (1566–1641) adapted the third act of the Yuan text of *Dou E Yuan* as part of his play *Story of the Golden Lock*, which was written in the Ming dynasty form known as *chuanqi*. This play, in turn, has been adapted into numerous forms—song, storytelling, puppetry, and live theater—all of which, at some level, recognizably derive from Guan's creation. Chinese artists and audiences favor appropriating and transforming famous plays, for doing so presents old stories to contemporary audiences. These strategies are seen not as a violation of the playwright's intentions but rather as a means of keeping the text alive. Although Yang Xianyi and Gladys Yang's 1979 translation of *Dou E Yuan* included in this anthology is a nearly complete version based on the Yuan original, its title, *Snow in Midsummer* (*Liuyue xue*), is taken from that given to a number of adaptations of a single act of *Dou E Yuan*. Other versions of Guan's play can be found in *Six Yuan Plays*, trans. Jung-en Liu (1972), and *Injustice to Tou O (Tou O Yuan): A Study and Translation*, trans. Chung wen Shih (1972).

Criticism in English on Yuan drama, and more specifically on Guan Hanqing and *Dou E Yuan*, is fairly meager. Stephen H. West's article "A Study in Appropriation: Zang Maoxun's Injustice to Dou E" (1991) contains valuable information regarding the differences between the three published versions of the play. Ching-Hsi Perng's *Double Jeopardy: A Critique of Seven Yüan Courtroom Dramas* (1978) compares the play to others in its genre. Wu-chi Liu's article "Kuan Han-Ch'ing: The Man and His Life" (1990–92) sorts through the scarce evidence on the life of the playwright. J. I. Crump's *Chinese Theater in the Days of Kublai Khan* (1980) describes the performance conventions and historical context of Yuan drama. Faye Chunfang Fei's *Chinese Theories of Theater and Performance from Confucius to the Present* (1999) contains important excerpts of Chinese dramatic theory relating to Guan Hanqing and Yuan drama in general.

HROTSVIT OF GANDERSHEIM

Major studies of the medieval theater include E. K. Chambers, *The Mediaeval Stage*, 2 vols. (1903); Karl Young, *The Drama of the Medieval Church* (1933); and O. B. Hardison, Jr., *Christian Rite and Christian Drama in the Middle Ages: Essays in the Origin and Early History of Modern Drama* (1965). Anne Lyon Haight edited a useful bibliographical volume, *Hroswitha of Gandersheim: Her Life, Time, Works, and a Comprehensive Bibliography* (1965), that includes information on translations, productions, and scholarship. Among the most influential English translations of Hrotsvit are Christopher St. John, *The Plays of Roswitha* (1923); Larissa Bonfante, *The Plays of Hrotswitha of Gandersheim* (1979); and Katharina M. Wilson, *The Plays of Hrotsvit of Gandersheim* (1989), the last of which provides the text used in this anthology. Sister Mary Marguerite Butler's *Hrotsvitha: The Theatricality of Her Plays* (1960) cogently argues for the performative potential of the dramas. Bert Nagel, "The Dramas of Hrotsvit von Gandersheim" (1970), and Kenneth DeLuca, "Hrotsvit's 'Imitation' of Terence" (1974), are both significant additions to the scholarship. The chapter on Hrotsvit in Peter Dronke's *Women Writers of the Middle Ages: A Critical Study of Texts from Perpetua (d. 203) to Marguerite Porete (d. 1310)* (1984) has proven extremely influential. Feminist approaches to the dramatist include Sue-Ellen Case, "Re-Viewing Hrotsvit" (1983); M. R. Sperberg-McQueen, "Whose Body Is It? Chaste Strategies and the Reinforcement of Patriarchy in Three Plays by Hrotswitha von Gandersheim" (1993); and Patricia Demers, "*In virginea forma:* The Salvific Feminine in the Plays of Hrotsvitha of Gandersheim and Hildegard of Bingen" (1993). Among his many publications on the dramatist, Sandro Sticca's "Sacred Drama and Comic Realism in the Plays of Hrotswitha of Gandersheim" (1979) and "Hrotswitha's 'Dulcitius' and Christian Symbolism" (1970) are particularly valuable. In addition to her fine translation, Katharina M. Wilson has published two other notable volumes, *Hrotsvit of Gandersheim: The Ethics of Authorial Stance* (1988), and another collection of the nun's dramatic and nondramatic writings, *Hrotsvit of Gandersheim: A Florilegium of Her Works* (1998); she also co-edited the volume *Hrotsvit of Gandersheim: Contexts, Identities, Affinities, and Performances* (2004) with Phyllis R. Brown and Linda A. McMillin.

LANGSTON HUGHES

The most complete collection of Langston Hughes's plays can be found in volumes 5 and 6 of *The Collected Works of Langston Hughes*, ed. Arnold Rampersad (2001–04).

Five Plays, ed. Webster Smalley (1963), offers a narrower but more widely available selection of plays, including *Soul Gone Home*. The authoritative biography of Langston Hughes is Arnold Rampersad's two-volume *The Life of Langston Hughes* (1986–88; 2d ed., 2002). John Edgar Tidwell and Cheryl R. Ragar, eds., *Montage of a Dream: The Art and Life of Langston Hughes* (2007), includes a variety of essays on Hughes's life and career. The following works are useful for an understanding of Hughes the dramatist: Darwin T. Turner, "Langston Hughes as Playwright" (1968); Faith Berry, *Langston Hughes: Before and Beyond Harlem* (1983); Leslie Catherine Sanders, "'Also Own the Theatre': Representation in the Comedies of Langston Hughes" (1992); and Joseph McLaren, *Langston Hughes: Folk Dramatist in the Protest Tradition, 1921–1943* (1997). The spring 1997 issue of *The Langston Hughes Review* is devoted to Hughes's work for theater. William Miles, "Isolation in Langston Hughes' *Soul Gone Home*," in *Five Black Writers: Essays on Wright, Ellison, Baldwin, Hughes, and Le Roi Jones*, comp. Donald B. Gibson (1970), and Philip C. Kolin and Maureen Curley, "Hughes's *Soul Gone Home*" (2003), are among the few critical studies of *Soul Gone Home*.

DAVID HENRY HWANG

The standard text of *M. Butterfly* is the New American Library edition (1989), which includes Hwang's afterword on the play and its composition. The acting edition (1988) published by Dramatists Play Service contains the same afterword, as well as a discussion of the play's Broadway production and suggestions for prospective actors, directors, and designers. Douglas Street's brief but useful monograph *David Henry Hwang* (1989) contains biographical information on the playwright and an overview of his dramatic writing through *M. Butterfly*. Additional biographical information and a more current survey of Hwang's drama can be found in William C. Boles, "David Henry Hwang," in *Asian American Writers*, ed. Deborah L. Madsen (2005), vol. 312 of the *Dictionary of Literary Biography*. Miles Xian Liu, ed., *Asian American Playwrights: A Bio-bibliographical Critical Sourcebook* (2002), provides biographical backgrounds, production history, and bibliographical information on the works of Hwang and other Asian American dramatists.

Important articles on *M. Butterfly* include Robert Skloot, "Breaking the Butterfly: The Politics of David Henry Hwang" (1990); Douglas Kerr, "David Henry Hwang and the Revenge of *Madame Butterfly*," in *Asian Voices in English*, ed. Mimi Chan and Roy Harris (1991); Marjorie Garber, "The Occidental Tourist: *M. Butterfly* and the Scandal of Transvestism," in *Nationalities and Sexualities*, ed. Andrew Parker, Mary Russo, Doris Sommer, and Patricia Yaeger (1992); Karen Shimakawa, "'Who's to Say?' or, Making Space for Gender and Ethnicity in *M. Butterfly*" (1993); Foong Ling Kong's "Pulling the Wings Off Butterfly" (1994); and Hsiu-Chen Lin, "Staging Orientalia: Dangerous 'Authenticity' in David Henry Hwang's *M. Butterfly*" (1997). James S. Moy, *Marginal Sights: Staging the Chinese in America* (1993), and Josephine Lee, *Performing Asian America: Race and Ethnicity on the Contemporary Stage* (1997), explore *M. Butterfly* in the context of earlier and contemporary representations of Asian Americans in theater and in American culture.

HENRIK IBSEN

Among the early reactions to Ibsen was George Bernard Shaw's *The Quintessence of Ibsenism* (1891), which emphasizes Ibsen's concern with pressing social and political issues; William Archer's essays, collected by Thomas Postlewait in *William Archer on Ibsen: The Major Essays, 1889–1919* (1984), foreground Ibsen's poetic choices and techniques. The decisive impact of Shaw and Archer is described in detail in Thomas Postlewait's *Prophet of the New Drama: William Archer and the Ibsen Campaign* (1986). Ibsen's third major early supporter was the critic Georg Brandes, who accompanied Ibsen's career with three essays, written in the 1870s, '80s, and '90s, collected in his *Henrik Ibsen: A Critical Study* (1899). Charles Lyons's compilation, *Critical Essays on Henrik Ibsen* (1987), includes landmark essay by Ibsen's modernist admirers, among them James Joyce, E. M. Forster, and Georg Lukàcs. The wider cultural context of Ibsen's European success, as well as a wealth of personal detail, is captured in Michael Meyer's *Ibsen: A Biography* (1971). While there have been a number of excellent studies devoted to Ibsen—for example, Michael Goldman's imaginative reading of Ibsen's subtexts and psychologies in *Ibsen: The Dramaturgy of Fear* (1999)—the most influential accounts of Ibsen's impact on modern drama are to be found in studies devoted to modern drama more generally, many of which take their point of departure from Ibsen's work. Of these, Raymond Williams's *Drama: From Ibsen to Eliot* (1952; 2nd rev. ed., 1973) is the most important, discussing Ibsen's social drama and modern tragedy. Robert Brustein's *The Theatre of Revolt: An Approach to the Modern Drama* (1964) and Richard Gilman's *The Making of Modern Drama* (1974) are classics in dating the origin of a modern revolt to Ibsen's drama, as is Peter Szondi's *The Theory of the Modern Drama* (1956; trans. 1987), which measures Ibsen against Sophocles' *Oedipus the King*. In *Ibsen and Early Modernist Theatre, 1890–1900* (1997), Kirsten Shepherd-Barr situates Ibsen in the context of theater history, and Joan Templeton's *Ibsen's Women* (1997) is the first in-depth analysis of Ibsen's construction of female characters, including Hedda Gabler. *The Cambridge Companion to Ibsen*, ed. James McFarlane (1994), provides a good introduction to recent scholarship and contemporary approaches. The best book on Ibsen is Toril Moi's *Henrik Ibsen and the Birth of Modernism: Art, Theater, Philosophy* (2006).

TONY KUSHNER

Angels in America: A Gay Fantasia on National Themes (Theatre Communications Group, 1995), is the standard edition of this two-part play. James Fisher, *The Theater of Tony Kushner: Living Past Hope* (2001), is a full-length study of the development of Kushner's drama in its social, theatrical, and biographical contexts. Robert Vorlicky, ed., *Tony Kushner in Conversation* (1998), is a rich collection of biographical, critical, and backstage interviews with the playwright. Deborah R. Geis and Steven F. Kruger, eds., *Approaching the Millennium: Essays on "Angels in America"* (1997), and Per Brask, ed., *Essays on Kushner's "Angels"* (1995), provide a range of historical, critical, and theatrical perspectives on the play. In addition to the essays included in the above collections, the following articles are useful: Charles McNulty, "*Angels in America:* Tony Kushner's Theses on the Philosophy of History" (1996); Jonathan Freedman, "Angels, Monsters, and Jews: Intersections of Queer and Jewish Identity in Kushner's *Angels in America*" (1998); Daryl Ogden, "Cold War Science and the Body Politic: An Immuno/Virological Approach to *Angels in America*" (2000); and Ranen Omer-Sherman, "The Fate of the Other in Tony Kushner's *Angels in America*" (2007).

CHRISTOPHER MARLOWE

Readers who are curious about the competing texts of *Doctor Faustus* would do well to consult *Doctor Faustus, 1604–1616: Parallel Texts*, ed. W. W. Greg (1950), and Michael Warren's authoritative essay, "*Doctor Faustus:* The Old Man and the Text" (1981). The closest approximation to a standard scholarly text of the play is by Roma Gill (2nd ed., 1989). A modern edition of *The English Faust Book* has been produced by John Henry Jones (1994). Among the classic book-length studies of Marlowe that include excellent discussions of *Doctor Faustus* are Harry Levin, *The Overreacher: A Study of Christopher Marlowe* (1952); Wilbur Sanders, *The Dramatist and the Received Idea: Studies in the Plays of Marlowe and Shakespeare* (1968); and J. B. Steane, *Marlowe: A Critical Study* (1964). More provocative approaches to Marlowe and *Doctor Faustus* can be found in Michael Goldman's "Marlowe and the Histrionics of Ravishment," Stephen J. Greenblatt's "Marlowe and Renaissance Self-Fashioning," and, especially, Edward A. Snow's "Marlowe's *Doctor Faustus* and the Ends of Desire," all of which appear in *Two Renaissance Mythmakers: Christopher Marlowe and Ben Jonson*, a remarkable collection of essays edited by Alvin Kernan (1977). Lawrence Danson's, "Marlowe: The Questioner" (1982) also has special pertinence to *Doctor Faustus*. One of the more controversial and inventive scholarly engagements with *Doctor Faustus* is William Empson's posthumously published *Faustus and the Censor: The English Faust-book and Marlowe's "Doctor Faustus"* (1987). Readers looking for a similar blend of historical scholarship and high-wire speculation in a life of Marlowe should consult Charles Nicholl's *The Reckoning: The Murder of Christopher Marlowe* (1992; rev. ed., 2002).

Those in search of a more traditional biography need look no further than David Riggs's *The World of Christopher Marlowe* (2004).

ARTHUR MILLER

Arthur Miller's *Collected Plays* (1957) contains the playwright's five major plays through 1957; *The Portable Arthur Miller* (1971; rev. ed., 2003) includes a useful selection of plays from throughout his career. Published two years before the playwright's death, Martin Gottfried's *Arthur Miller: His Life and Work* (2003) is a full-length biography of Miller. An engaging overview can also be found in Enoch Brater, *Arthur Miller: A Playwright's Life and Works* (2005). Those who want an in-depth account of the playwright's life and times through the early 1980s can consult his wide-ranging and critically acclaimed autobiography, *Timebends: A Life* (1987). Important studies of Miller's plays include Sheila Huftel, *Arthur Miller: The Burning Glass* (1965); Edward Murray, *Arthur Miller, Dramatist* (1967); Leonard Moss, *Arthur Miller* (1967; rev. ed., 1980); Benjamin Nelson, *Arthur Miller: Portrait of a Playwright* (1970); Dennis Welland, *Miller the Playwright* (1979; 3d ed., 1985); Neil Carson, *Arthur Miller* (1982; 2d ed., 2008); C. W. E. Bigsby, *A Critical Introduction to Twentieth-Century American Drama*, vol. 2, *Tennessee Williams, Arthur Miller, Edward Albee* (1984); June Schlueter and James K. Flanagan, *Arthur Miller* (1987); David Savran, *Communist, Cowboys, and Queers: The Politics of Masculinity in the Work of Arthur Miller and Tennessee Williams* (1992); Alice Griffin, *Understanding Arthur Miller* (1996); and Christopher Bigsby, *Arthur Miller: A Critical Study* (2005).

Miller wrote and spoke widely on his plays and his career as a writer. Collections of his essays and interviews include *The Theater Essays of Arthur Miller*, ed. Robert A. Martin (1978; rev. ed., 1996); Matthew C. Roudané, ed., *Conversations with Arthur Miller* (1987); *Echoes down the Corridor: Collected Essays, 1944–2000*, ed. Steven R. Centola (2000); and Mel Gussow, *Conversations with Miller* (2002). Stefani Koorey, *Arthur Miller's Life and Literature: An Annotated and Comprehensive Guide* (2000), offers an extensive bibliography of books and articles on Miller's drama, as well as information on Miller's life and politics, references to theater reviews, and production information on his plays. Susan C. W. Abbotson's, *Critical Companion to Arthur Miller: A Literary Reference to His Life and Work* (2007) is also an important resource.

Among the collections of critical essays on *Death of a Salesman* are *Death of a Salesman: Text and Criticism*, ed. Gerald Weales (1967); Helene Wickham Koon, ed., *Twentieth-Century Interpretations of "Death of a Salesman": A Collection of Critical Essays* (1983); Harold Bloom, ed., *Arthur Miller's "Death of a Salesman"* (1988; updated, 2007) and *Willy Loman* (1991; updated, 2005); Matthew C. Roudané, ed., *Approaches to Teaching Miller's "Death of a Salesman"* (1995); and Stephen A. Marino, ed., *"The "Salesman" Has a Birthday": Essays Celebrating the Fiftieth Anniversary of Arthur Miller's "Death of a Salesman"* (2000). Kay Stanton, "Women and the American Dream of *Death of a Salesman*," in *Feminist Rereadings of Modern American Drama*, ed. June Schlueter (1989), is an important feminist reading of Miller's play. Brenda Murphy, *Miller: "Death of a Salesman"* (1995), is a history of *Death of a Salesman* productions during the years 1949–89, while Miller's own *Salesman in Beijing* (1984) discusses his experiences directing the play in the People's Republic of China in 1983.

MOLIÈRE (JEAN-BAPTISTE POQUELIN)

There is, to date, no definitive, complete edition of Molière's works in English, though his plays have regularly been translated into this and many other languages. Among English translations, those of the poet Richard Wilbur have long been admired; others, such as those of Maya Slater, attempt to capture more exactly the form of the French originals. The translation by Haskell M. Block (1985) includes the preface and letters to Louis XIV quoted above. The version of *Tartuffe* created for *The Norton Anthology of Drama* is by the playwright Constance Congdon, who based it on the scholarly translation of Virginia Scott. Scott's biography *Molière: A Theatrical Life* (2000) offers an accessible and balanced portrait of the artist and provides reasoned conjectures about many of the contested and unprovable details of his career. Useful introductions to seventeenth-century drama and theater include Henry Carrington Lancaster, *The Period of Molière, 1652–1672*, part 3 of *A History of French Dramatic Literature in the Seventeenth Century* (1936); Peter D. Arnott, *An Introduction to the French Theatre* (1977); John Lough, *Seventeenth-Century French Drama: The Background* (1979); Nicholas Hammond, *Creative Tensions: An Introduction to Seventeenth-Century French Literature* (1997); and Gerry McCarthy, *The Theatres of Molière* (2002). *The Molière Encyclopedia* (2002), edited by James F. Gaines, contains a wealth of useful and succinct information on the dramatist and his works. Richard Parish's edition of the play in French (1994) also includes an informative introduction and notes in English.

Full-length critical studies of Molière abound. Those with particularly helpful discussions for a consideration of *Tartuffe* include James F. Gaines, *Social Structures in Molière's Theater* (1984); Nathan Gross, *From Gesture to Idea—Esthetics and Ethics in Molière's Comedy* (1982); W. D. Howarth, *Molière: A Playwright and His Audience* (1982); J. D. Hubert, *Molière & the Comedy of Intellect* (1962); Michael S. Koppisch, *Rivalry and the Disruption of Order in Molière's Theater* (2004); Gertrud Mander, *Molière* (1967, trans. 1973); and Martin Turnell, *The Classical Moment: Studies of Corneille, Molière and Racine* (1947). Jerry Lewis Kasparek's *Molière's "Tartuffe" and the Traditions of Roman Satire* (1977) explores sources and influences, and John Cairncross's *New Light on Molière: "Tartuffe"; "Elomire hypocondre"* (1956) establishes the arguments for the 1664 performance text accepted by many scholars as definitive. Albert Bermel's *Molière's Theatrical Bounty: A New View of the Plays* (1990) considers some of the more recent, influential productions of *Tartuffe*. Christopher Braider's chapter on *Tartuffe* in his study of French drama, *Indiscernible Counterparts: The Invention of the Text in French Classical Drama* (2002), provides a most elegant and insightful contemporary reading of the play.

SUZAN-LORI PARKS

The America Play is published in *The America Play, and Other Works* (Theatre Communications Group, 1995). Those interested in further biographical information on Suzan-Lori Parks should consult the entry on her in *Contemporary Authors Online* (Thompson Gale, 2005). Though no full-length study of Parks's plays has yet appeared, useful critical discussions of *The America Play* and Parks's career as a whole include the following: Alisa Solomon, "Signifying on the Signifyin'": The Plays of Suzan-Lori Parks" (1990); Katy Ryan, "'No Less Human': Making History in Suzan-Lori Parks's *The America Play*" (1999); Harry Elam and Alice Rayner, "Echoes from the Black (W)hole: An Examination of *The America Play* by Suzan-Lori Parks," in *Performing America: Cultural Nationalism in American Theater*, ed. Jeffrey D. Mason and J. Ellen Gainor (1999); S. E. Wilmer, "Restaging the Nation: The Work of Suzan Lori Parks" (2000); Shawn-Marie Garrett, "The Possession of Suzan-Lori Parks" (2000); and Frank Haike, "The Instability of Meaning in Suzan-Lori Parks's *The America Play*" (2002).

LUIGI PIRANDELLO

As a general overview of Pirandello's life, Gaspare Guidice's *Pirandello: A Biography* (1963; abridged trans. 1975) is more measured than Domenico Vittorini's *The Drama of Luigi Pirandello* (1935), written only one year after Pirandello had received the Nobel Prize. Because of Pirandello's place in the canon of modern drama, many of the most important commentators on modern drama have devoted essays or book chapters to his work. Among the classics in the field are Eric Bentley's *The Pirandello Commentaries* (1985) and Francis Fergusson's *The Idea of the Theater, a Study of Ten Plays: The Art of Drama in Changing Perspective* (1949), which places Pirandello in relation to other modern dramatists such as George Bernard Shaw and Bertolt Brecht. The best essay on Pirandello and metatheater is by Maurizio Grande, "Pirandello and the Theatre-within-the-Theatre: Thresholds and Frames in *Cascuno a suo modo*," in *Luigi Pirandello: Contemporary Perspectives*, ed. Gian-Paolo Biasin (1999). Roger W. Oliver's *Dreams of Passion: The Theater of Luigi Pirandello* (1979) focuses on Pirandello's theory of humor and applies it to his best-known plays, including *Six Characters*. The best book-length study of Pirandello in English is Ann Hallamore Caesar's *Characters and Authors in Luigi Pirandello* (1998), which includes detailed discussions of Pirandello's aesthetic theories and also an incisive critique of his patriarchal family structures. Daniela Bini's *Pirandello and His Muse: The Plays for Marta Abba* (1998) takes a similar approach to Pirandello's late plays. Pirandello's work in the theater is captured in *Luigi Pirandello in the Theatre: A Documentary Record*, ed. Susan Bassnett and Jennifer Lorch (1993), and in A. Richard Sogliuzzo's *Luigi Pirandello, Director: The Playwright in the Theatre* (1982). The political aspects of Pirandello's work are articulated especially well by Mary Ann Frese Witt in *The Search for Modern Tragedy: Aesthetic Fascism in Italy and France* (2001).

WILLIAM SHAKESPEARE

S. Schoenbaum's *William Shakespeare: A Compact Documentary Life* (1977; rev. ed., 1987) and Stephen Greenblatt's *Will in the World: How Shakespeare Became Shakespeare* (2004) are excellent places to learn more about Shakespeare's life and career. A very useful introduction to early modern culture and theatrical practices is Russ McDonald's *Bedford Companion to Shakespeare: An Introduction with Documents* (1996; 2nd ed., 2001).

Hamlet

A. C. Bradley's classic *Shakespearean Tragedy* (1904; 3rd ed., 1992) and Bert O. States's *Hamlet and the Concept of Character* (1992) are very different but equally outstanding investigations of Hamlet as a character. Harold Bloom's *Shakespeare: The Invention of the Human* (1998) offers an accessible and in-depth discussion of the complex and self-reflective nature of the mind of Hamlet. Ernest Jones's *Hamlet and Oedipus* (1949) is a landmark psychoanalytic work that offers a comprehensive explanation for Hamlet's delay. Arthur Kinney's recent edited volume *Hamlet: New Critical Essays* (2002) includes a number of useful articles. Janet Adelman's *Suffocating Mothers: Fantasies of Maternal Origin in Shakespeare's Plays, "Hamlet" to "The Tempest"* (1992) combines feminist concerns with a psychological approach. Jacqueline Rose's "Hamlet—The Mona Lisa of Literature," originally published in 1986 and anthologized in *Shakespeare and Gender: A History*, ed. Deborah Barker and Ivo Kamps (1995), analyzes the influence of gender in interpretations of *Hamlet*.

Michael Cohen's *Hamlet in My Mind's Eye* (1989) offers a sustained, book-length reading of the play with a keen eye to performance possibilities. Stephen Greenblatt's *Hamlet in Purgatory* (2001) is a masterful treatment of the role of religious energies in the play.

Those interested in Shakespeare's representation of madness and its connection to political subversion can turn to Karin S. Coddon's "'Such Strange Designs': Madness, Subjectivity, and Treason in Hamlet and Elizabethan Culture," in *Shakespeare's Tragedies*, ed. Susan Zimmerman (1998). Carol Thomas Neely writes on madness in *Twelfth Night* and *Hamlet* in her historically informed essay "'Documents in Madness': Reading Madness and Gender in Shakespeare's Tragedies and Early Modern Culture" (1991). *Marxist Shakespeares* (2001), edited by Jean E. Howard and Scott Cutler Shershow, includes intriguing Marxist readings of *Hamlet*. Gary Taylor's "*Hamlet* in Africa 1607" in *Travel Knowledge: European "Discoveries" in the Early Modern Period*, ed. Ivo Kamps and Jyotsna G. Singh (2001), provides a fascinating account of the first non-European performance of *Hamlet* aboard a ship in Sierra Leone.

Twelfth Night

For a discussion of Shakespeare's comedies as a form influenced by popular Elizabethan festivals, see C. L. Barber's *Shakespeare's Festive Comedy: A Study of Dramatic Form and Its Relation to Social Custom* (1959). For details of Coleridge's famous interpretations, see Terence Hawkes's collection of them, *Coleridge's Writings on Shakespeare* (1959). Harold Bloom's *Shakespeare: The Invention of the Human* (1998) provides detailed characterological analyses.

Bruce Smith's *Twelfth Night, or, What You Will: Text and Contexts* (2001) offers a number of relevant texts and documents contemporaneous with the play. Jean Howard analyzes the practice of boy actors in female roles in "Cross-Dressing, the Theatre and Gender Struggle in Early Modern England" (1988), reprinted in *The Routledge Reader in Gender and Performance*, ed. Lizbeth Goodman with Jane de Gau (1998). A number of outstanding essays take up questions of gender and sexuality in *Twelfth Night*, including Dympna Callaghan's "'And All Is Semblative a Woman's Part': Body Politics and *Twelfth Night*" (1993); Stephen Greenblatt's "Fiction and Friction," in *Shakespearean Negotiations: The Circulation of Social Energy in Renaissance England* (1988); and Joseph Pequigney's "The Two Antonios and Same-Sex Love in *Twelfth Night* and *The Merchant of Venice*," in *Shakespeare and Gender: A History*, ed. Deborah Barker and Ivo Kamps (1995). *Twentieth Century Interpretations of "Twelfth Night": A Collection of Critical Essays*, ed. Walter N. King (1968), contains a number of classic assessments of the play.

GEORGE BERNARD SHAW

Throughout his lifetime, Shaw not only tried to control the presentation of his plays, he also carefully orchestrated his public persona, essentially collaborating with, if not ghostwriting, every attempt at authorized biography. Thus Michael Holroyd's four-volume *Bernard Shaw* (1988–92) may stand for some time as the only definitive and reasonably objective study of his life and work. Shaw repeatedly revised his plays even after publication; Dan Laurence's two volume *Bernard Shaw: A Bibliography* (1983) meticulously traces Shaw's complete oeuvre. *The Bodley Head Bernard Shaw: Collected Plays with Their Prefaces*, 7 vols. (1970–74), is considered the definitive edition. Laurence also edited Shaw's four-volume *Collected Letters* (1965–88), which shed important light on his plays and other writings; many additional edited volumes of letters between Shaw and individual correspondents have also been published. Shaw published selections from his critical and political writings during his lifetime; scholarly editions of his dramatic, art, and music criticism have appeared more recently. Major Shaw research archives, which include both published and unpublished materials, are located in the British Library, the Berg Collection of the New York Public Library, the Bernard F. Burgunder Collection at Cornell University, and the Harry Ransom Humanities Research Center at the University of Texas at Austin.

Shaw's astounding volume of writing is matched only by the vast body of critical writing about him and his work. The three-volume (to date) *G. B. Shaw: An Annotated Bibliography of Writings about Him*, comp. J. P. Wearing (1986–), provides a helpful starting point for research. *Shaw: The Critical Heritage*, ed. T. F. Evans (1976), includes excerpts from reviews of his plays. *The Cambridge Companion to George Bernard Shaw*, ed. Christopher Innes (1998), includes current essays that provide valuable overviews of major topics in Shaw scholarship and contains extensive bibliographical suggestions. Raymond Mander and Joe Mitchenson's *Theatrical Companion to Shaw: A Pictorial Record of the First Performances of the Plays of George Bernard Shaw* (1954) remains the best record of his works in performance.

Among many full-length studies worth consulting are Eric Bentley, *Bernard Shaw* (1947); Tracy C. Davis, *George Bernard Shaw and the Socialist Theatre* (1994); Bernard F. Dukore, *Bernard Shaw, Playwright: Aspects of Shavian Drama* (1973); J. Ellen Gainor, *Shaw's Daughters: Dramatic and Narrative Constructions of Gender* (1991); Arthur Ganz, *George Bernard Shaw* (1983); Martin Meisel, *Shaw and the Nineteenth-Century Theater* (1963); Margery M. Morgan, *The Shavian Playground: An Exploration of the Art of George Bernard Shaw* (1972); and Alfred Turco Jr., *Shaw's Moral Vision: The Self and Salvation* (1976). Shaw scholarship has also flourished in essay form. There are three journals entirely devoted to Shaw—the *Shavian*, the *Shaw Bulletin*, and *Shaw: The Annual of Bernard Shaw Studies*—but essays abound throughout the periodic literature as well as in anthologies. For discussions of *Pygmalion* in particular, readers may wish to consult Awam Amkpa, "Drama and the Languages of Postcolonial Desire: Bernard Shaw's *Pygmalion*" (1999); Milton Crane, "Pygmalion: Bernard Shaw's Dramatic Theory and Practice" (1951); J. Ellen Gainor, "Bernard Shaw and the Drama of Imperialism," in *The Performance of Power: Theatrical Discourse and Politics*, ed. Sue-Ellen Case and Janelle Reinelt (1991); Celia Marshik, "Parodying the £5 Virgin: Bernard Shaw and the Playing of *Pygmalion*" (2000); and Jean Reynolds, "Deconstructing Henry Higgins, or Eliza as Derridean 'Text'" (1994).

SOPHOCLES

Like all classical Greek tragedies, Sophocles' plays survived through a series of accidents. Generations of scholars have tried to approximate the original text, distorted by scribes, commentators, and adaptors. The recent scholarship on the playwright is extensive; it draws on newly discovered fragments of other plays, new archaeological evidence, and new insights into Greek society and culture. The French scholars Jean-Pierre Vernan and Pierre Vidal-Naquet have been especially successful, for example, in using new anthropological theories in their commentaries on the play. Their essays are collected in *Myth and Tragedy in Ancient Greece* (1972, trans. 1988). The best general introduction to Sophocles is R. P. Winnington-Ingram's *Sophocles: An Interpretation* (1980). An older classic, H. D. Kitto's *Greek Tragedy: A Literary Study* (1939), contains a good discussion of *Oedipus the King* as well as comments on the philosophical outlook of the playwright. However, Mary Whitlock Blundell's *Helping Friends and Harming Enemies: A Study in Sophocles and Greek Ethics* (1989) is a much more searching and sophisticated analysis of Sophocles in the context of Greek ethics and philosophy. Charles Segal's *Oedipus Tyrannus: Tragic Heroism and the Limits of Knowledge* (1993) also places *Oedipus the King* in the context of theories of knowledge, while David Seale, in his *Vision and Stagecraft in Sophocles* (1982), emphasizes the metaphor and role of vision and blindness in the play. Particularly influential has been Charles Segal's *Tragedy and Civilization: An Interpretation of Sophocles* (1981), which uses Sophocles to explore the relation of kinship and ritual in Greek society and culture. *Oedipus the King* has also been important for philosophers, from Aristotle, in his *Poetics* (ca. 330 B.C.E.), through G. W. F. Hegel, in his *Lectures on Aesthetics* (1835–38). It also was central in the formulation of psychoanalysis, in Sigmund Freud's *Interpretation of Dreams* (1900). For information on Greek theater, Sir Arthur Pickard-Cambridge's *The Dramatic Festivals of Athens* (1968) is still a classic, and Eric Scapo and William J. Slater have made many fragments about Greek theater available in translation in their *The Context of Ancient Drama* (1995).

WOLE SOYINKA

For an authoritative text and extensive background readings on *Death and the King's Horseman,* consult the Norton Critical Edition, edited by Simon Gikandi (2003). The general bibliography on Soyinka's work is extensive. Book-length accounts started to appear in the early 1970s—notably, Eldred Duromsimi Jones's *The Writing of Wole Soyinka* (1973; 3d ed., 1988). A more recent study, Derek Wright's *Wole Soyinka Revisited* (1993), provides a more nuanced analysis of the dramatic works; it focuses on the different theatrical categories, particularly ritual, tragedy, and satire, that are central for understanding Soyinka's work. Ketu H. Katrak's *Wole Soyinka and Modern Tragedy* (1986) examines Soyinka's attempt to create a "Yoruba tragedy." By far the best of the critical literature on the playwright is Biodun Jeyifo's *Wole Soyinka: Politics, Poetics and Postcoloniality* (2004), which analyzes the complex relations between colonial culture, independence, and literature that mark his oeuvre. Jeyifo is among those intellectuals with whom Soyinka has heatedly debated the relation between art and politics; see, for example, Soyinka's collection of essays, *Art, Dialogue, and Outrage: Essays on Literature and Culture* (1988; rev. and expanded ed., 1993). Also useful is a collection of interviews, *Conversations with Wole Soyinka*, ed. Biodun Jeyifo (2001). Other major critics to have devoted attention to Soyinka are the philosopher Anthony Appiah, in *In My Father's House: Africa in the Philosophy of Culture* (1992), and Henry Louis Gates Jr., in "Being, the Will, and the Semantics of Death" (1981). Valuable collections of essays on Soyinka include James Gibb, ed., *Critical Perspectives on Wole Soyinka* (1980), and Biodun Jeyifo, ed., *Perspectives on Wole Soyinka: Freedom and Complexity* (2001). Jonathan Peters's *A Dance of Masks: Senghor, Achebe, Soyinka* (1978) and Kole Omotoso's *Achebe or Soyinka? A Study in Contrasts* (1996) are noteworthy comparative studies of Soyinka.

AUGUST STRINDBERG

The best biography available is Michael Meyer's *Strindberg* (1985), which seeks to distinguish between Strindberg's autobiographical novels and plays and the facts of his own life, especially his three marriages. The topic of autobiography receives special focus in Michael Robinson's *Strindberg and Autobiography: Writing and Reading a Life*

(1986) and Harry G. Carlson's *Out of Inferno: Strindberg's Reawakening as an Artist* (1996). Particular attention to Strindberg the playwright is paid by Evert Sprinchorn (whose translation of *Miss Julie* in included in this volume) in *Strindberg as Dramatist* (1992), and by Egil Törnqvist, Strindberg's main Swedish interpreter, in *Strindbergian Drama: Themes and Structure* (1982). More interested in the literary and poetic dimensions of Strindberg's drama is another translator of his plays, Harry G. Carlson, in *Strindberg and the Poetry of Myth* (1982). Also commendable is Freddie Rokem's *Strindberg's Secret Codes* (2004). Given Strindberg's influence, most of the classic studies of modern drama dedicate important essays to the playwright, including Robert Brustein's *The Theatre of Revolt: An Approach to the Modern Drama* (1964), which emphasizes Strindberg's revolt against modern life, and Raymond Williams's *Drama from Ibsen to Brecht* (1968), which combines social analysis with an attention to form. An international collection of essays on Strindberg was assembled by Göran Stockenström in *Strindberg's Dramaturgy* (1988), as well as by Michael Robinson in *Studies in Strindberg* (1998). More interested in particular genres is Børge Gedsø Madsen's *Strindberg's Naturalistic Theatre: Its Relation to French Naturalism* (1962), Walter Johnson's *Strindberg and the Historical Drama* (1963), and John Ward's *The Social and Religious Plays of Strindberg* (1980). And Strindberg's influence on expressionist theater is detailed in Michael Robinson and Sven Rossel's collection *Expressionism and Modernism: New Approaches to August Strindberg* (1999). Most thoroughly dedicated to Strindberg on stage is Frederick J. Marker and Lise-Lone Marker's *Strindberg and Modernist Theatre: Post-Inferno Drama on the Stage* (2002). For analysis specifically of *Miss Julie*, see the collection edited by Egil Törnqvist and Barry Jacobs, *Strindberg's "Miss Julie": A Play and Its Transpositions* (1988).

JUDITH THOMPSON

Judith Thompson's plays are available through the Playwrights Canada Press. Though no book-length studies devoted solely to her work have appeared to date, Ric Knowles has edited two collections of essays devoted to the playwright: *Judith Thompson* (2005) and *The Masks of Judith Thompson* (2006). In addition, the journal *Canadian Theatre Review* published a special issue on Thompson, *Judith Thompson Casebook* (Winter 1996), which contains interviews, the revised script of *Tornado,* critical analyses, production commentary, and a bibliography of primary and secondary works. Chapters on Thompson can be found in Craig Stewart Walker, *The Buried Astrolabe: Canadian Dramatic Imagination and Western Tradition* (2001), and Cynthia Zimmerman, *Playwriting Women: Female Voices in English Canada* (1994). Essays on Thompson have appeared in scholarly journals, critical volumes, and the Canadian press: see especially Julie Adams, "The Implicated Audience: Judith Thompson's Anti-Naturalism in *The Crackwalker, White Biting Dog, I Am Yours* and *Lion in the Streets,*" in *Women on the Canadian Stage: The Legacy of Hrotsvit,* ed. Rita Much (1992); Diane Bessai, "Women Dramatists: Sharon Pollock and Judith Thompson," in *Postcolonial English Drama: Commonwealth Drama since 1960,* ed. Bruce King (1992); Alan Filewod, "Critical Mass: Assigning Value and Place in Canadian Drama," in *On-stage and Off-stage: English Canadian Drama in Discourse,* ed. Albert-Reiner Glaap and Rolf Althof (1996); Jennifer Harvie, "(Im) Possibility: Fantasy and Judith Thompson's Drama," in *On-stage and Off-stage*, ed. Glaap and Althof (1996); Nigel Hunt, "In Contact with the Dark" (1988); Richard Paul Knowles, "The Dramaturgy of the Perverse" (1992); Robert Nunn, "Spatial Metaphor in the Plays of Judith Thompson" (1989); Judy Steed, "Thompson Walks a Different Path Than Her Characters" (1982); and George Toles, "'Cause You're the Only One I Want': The Anatomy of Love in the Plays of Judith Thompson" (1988).

Thompson has given a number of interviews to journalists and scholars, including Judith Rudakoff in *Fair Play: 12 Women Speak: Conversations with Canadian Playwrights* (1990), Cynthia Zimmerman in "A Conversation with Judith Thompson" (1990), and Sandra Tome in "Revisions of Probability: An Interview with Judith Thompson" (1989); see also her contributions to the dialogues "Revisions: Offending Your Audience" (1992) and "Look to the

Lady: Re-examining Women's Theatre" (1995). In addition, Thompson has written several revealing essays on her life and work; see "Why Should a Playwright Direct Her Own Play?" in *Women on the Canadian Stage*, ed. Much (1992); "Second Thoughts (What I'd Be If I Were Not a Writer)" (1995); "One Twelfth" in *Language in Her Eye: Views on Writing and Gender by Canadian Women Writing in English*, ed. Libby Scheier, Sarah Sheard, and Eleanor Wachtel (1990); and "The Happy Vessel" in *Still Running—: Personal Stories by Queen's Women Celebrating the Fiftieth Anniversary of the Marty Scholarship*, ed. Joy Parr (1987).

OSCAR WILDE

While there is no standard edition of Oscar Wilde's plays, *"The Importance of Being Earnest" and Other Plays,* ed. David Raby (1995), is a useful collection. Richard Ellmann, *Oscar Wilde* (1987), is considered the authoritative biography. Studies of Wilde's career include Rodney Shewan, *Oscar Wilde: Art and Egotism* (1977); Regenia Gagnier, *Idylls of the Marketplace: Oscar Wilde and the Victorian Public* (1986); Alan Sinfield, *The Wilde Century: Effeminacy, Oscar Wilde, and the Queer Moment* (1994); Josephine M. Guy and Ian Small, *Oscar Wilde's Profession: Writing and the Culture Industry in the Late Nineteenth Century* (2000); Neil Sammells, *Wilde Style: The Plays and Prose of Oscar Wilde* (2000); John Sloan, *Oscar Wilde* (2003); and Paul L. Fortunato, *Modernist Aesthetics and Consumer Culture in the Writings of Oscar Wilde* (2007). Early critical responses to Wilde's life and work are included in Richard Ellmann, ed., *Oscar Wilde: A Collection of Critical Essays* (1969). C. George Sandulescu, ed., *Rediscovering Oscar Wilde* (1994), and Peter Raby, ed., *The Cambridge Companion to Oscar Wilde* (1997), are valuable collections of essays.

Wilde's drama is the subject of Alan Bird, *The Plays of Oscar Wilde* (1977); Katharine Worth, *Oscar Wilde* (1983); Sos Eltis, *Revising Wilde: Society and Subversion in the Plays of Oscar Wilde* (1996); and Kerry Powell, *Oscar Wilde and the Theatre of the 1890s* (1990). Joseph Donohue and Ruth Berggren, eds., *Oscar Wilde's "The Importance of Being Earnest": A Reconstructive Critical Edition of the Text of the First Production at St. James's Theatre, London, 1895* (1995), provides an extensively annotated edition of Wilde's masterpiece with an exhaustive discussion of the play's composition and manuscript history.

TENNESSEE WILLIAMS

The standard collection of Tennessee Williams's plays is *The Theatre of Tennessee Williams,* published in eight volumes by New Directions (1971–81). Additional plays from Williams's early career have been published separately. Among the several biographies of Williams, the finest is Lyle Leverich's *Tom: The Unknown Tennessee Williams* (1995), which covers the playwright's life to 1945. Students interested in Williams's life as a whole might consult Ronald Hayman, *Tennessee Williams: Everyone Else Is an Audience* (1993). Richard F. Leavitt, ed., *The World of Tennessee Williams* (1978), includes photographs, theater programs, and other documents illustrating Williams's life and career, while Philip Kolin, ed., *The Tennessee Williams Encyclopedia* (2004), contains valuable information on the playwright's works. Kenneth Holditch and Richard Freeman Leavitt's *Tennessee Williams and the South* (2002) discusses the profound influence of this region on Williams's work.

The following include valuable critical discussions of Williams's drama: Jac Tharpe, ed., *Tennessee Williams: A Tribute* (1977); Roger Boxill, *Tennessee Williams* (1987); Alice Griffin, *Understanding Tennessee Williams* (1995); Matthew C. Roudané, ed., *The Cambridge Companion to Tennessee Williams* (1997); Robert A. Martin, ed., *Critical Essays on Tennessee Williams* (1997); Philip C. Kolin, ed., *Tennessee Williams: A Guide to Research and Performance* (1998); Nancy M. Tischler, *Student Companion to Tennessee Williams* (2000); and Judith J. Thompson, *Tennessee Williams' Plays: Memory, Myth, and Symbol* (1987; rev. ed., 2002). One of the best discussions of Williams's dramatic career can be found in volume 2 of C. W. E. Bigsby, *A Critical Introduction to Twentieth-Century American Drama* (1984). The influence of Williams's homosexuality on his drama is explored in David Savran, *Communists, Cowboys, and Queers: The Politics of Masculinity in the Work of Arthur Miller and Tennessee Williams* (1992), and

John M. Clum, *Acting Gay: Male Homosexuality in Modern Drama* (1992; expanded ed., 1994).

The essays in Jordan Y. Miller, ed., *Twentieth Century Interpretations of "A Streetcar Named Desire"* (1971), are devoted exclusively to Williams's play, as are Thomas P. Adler, *"A Streetcar Named Desire": The Moth and the Lantern* (1990), and Philip C. Kolin, ed., *Confronting Tennessee Williams's "A Streetcar Named Desire": Essays in Critical Pluralism* (1993). Philip C. Kolin, *Williams: "A Streetcar Named Desire"* (2000), provides a history of *Streetcar* in performance, while Brenda Murphy's *Tennessee Williams and Elia Kazan: A Collaboration in the Theatre* (1992) examines the productions of *Streetcar* and other Williams plays directed by Kazan. Kazan's valuable directorial notes on *Streetcar* are excerpted in the *Twentieth Century Interpretations* collection mentioned above. Maurice Yacowar's *Tennessee Williams and Film* (1977) offers a useful discussion of the 1951 film version of Williams's play.

AUGUST WILSON

The plays of August Wilson's twentieth-century cycle were published in 2007 by Theatre Communications Group in a ten-volume collection. The best book-length studies of August Wilson's life and plays are Sandra G. Shannon, *The Dramatic Vision of August Wilson* (1995); Kim Pereira, *August Wilson and the African-American Odyssey* (1995); Peter Wolfe, *August Wilson* (1999); and Harry J. Elam Jr., *The Past as Present in the Drama of August Wilson* (2004). Mary L. Bogumil, *Understanding August Wilson* (1999), and Harry J. Elam Jr., "August Wilson," in *A Companion to Twentieth-Century American Drama*, ed. David Krasner (2005), are general introductions to Wilson's work, while Yvonne Shafer, *August Wilson: A Research and Production Sourcebook* (1998), and Mary Ellen Snodgrass, *August Wilson: A Literary Companion* (2004), are valuable resources for the student of Wilson's plays. Jackson R. Bryer and Mary C. Hartig, eds., *Conversations with August Wilson* (2006), contains Wilson's major interviews. Dana A. Williams and Sandra G. Shannon, eds., *August Wilson and Black Aesthetics* (2004), examines the cultural politics of Wilson as an African American writer.

Two collections of essays—Marilyn Elkins, ed., *August Wilson: A Casebook* (1994), and Alan Nadel, ed., *May All Your Fences Have Gates: Essays on the Drama of August Wilson* (1994)—present the range of critical approaches adopted by scholars analyzing Wilson's plays. Not surprising, *Fences* comes in for a large share of their discussion. Joan Fishman, "Developing His Song: August Wilson's *Fences*" (in Elkins), traces the development of Wilson's dramatic text through revisions, staged readings, and productions; Michael Awkward, "'The Crookeds with the Straights': *Fences*, Race, and the Politics of Adaptation" (in Nadel), considers *Fences* in the context of Wilson's well-publicized insistence that any film production of the play be directed by an African American. Susan Koprince, "Baseball as History and Myth in August Wilson's *Fences*" (2006), discusses the role of baseball in the play.

The black feminist scholar bell hooks has challenged the portrayal of women in Wilson's *Fences* in *Yearning: Race, Gender, and Cultural Politics* (1990). Harry J. Elam Jr., "August Wilson's Women," and Missy Dehn Kubitschek, "August Wilson's Gender Lesson" (both in Nadel), address the question of Wilson's women from feminist and other theoretical perspectives. Carla J. McDonough, *Staging Masculinity: Male Identity in Contemporary American Drama* (1997), considers the question of masculinity in Wilson's drama in the context of social issues facing urban black males.

ZEAMI MOTOKIYO

Although Zeami mentions *Atsumori* in his treatises, the earliest extant text is from the early sixteenth century. As a result, it is not possible to pinpoint the date of this play or to know if the text we have has been revised from Zeami's version. *Atsumori* was translated into French by Arthur Arrivet in 1895, but became well known in the West only in 1921 with the translation of Arthur Waley, which has been reprinted in *Masterpieces of the Orient*, ed. G. L. Anderson (1961; enlarged ed., 1977). The translation in Karen Brazell, ed., *Traditional Japanese Theater: An Anthology of Plays* (1997), has fuller stage directions than the version included here and is illustrated. That anthology also includes selections from other plays based on the Atsumori story and general information about Japanese theater. Royall Tyler's translation in *Japanese Nō Dramas* (1992) is also recommended. Zeami's treatises may be found in J. Thomas Rimer and Yamazaki Masakazu, trans., *On the Art of the Noh Drama: The Major Treatises of Zeami* (1984), and Tom Hare, trans., *Zeami: Performance Notes* (2008). Benito Ortolani, *The Japanese Theatre: From Shamanistic Ritual to Contemporary Pluralism* (1990; rev. ed., 1995), is an authoritative history of noh and other Japanese theater traditions, while Kunio Konparu, *The Noh Theatre: Principles and Perspectives* (trans. 1983), contains a useful introductory discussion of noh theater. Thomas Blenham Hare's *Zeami's Style: The Noh Plays of Zeami Motokiyo* (1986) discusses Zeami's dramatic work as a whole; Shelley Fenno Quinn's *Developing Zeami: the Noh Actor's Atunement in Practice* (2005) explores Zeami's dramatic and theatrical writings with a particular emphasis on his theory of acting. *In the Artistry of Aeschylus and Zeami: A Comparative Study of Greek Tragedy and Nō* (1989), Mae J. Smethurst presents interesting similarities in and differences between the genres.

PERMISSIONS ACKNOWLEDGMENTS

TEXT

al-Hakim, Tawfiq: *Song of Death*, translated by Mustafa Badawi, from ARABIC WRITING TODAY: DRAMA, edited by Mahmoud Manzalaoui. Reprinted by permission of The American Research Center in Egypt, Inc.

Aristophanes: *Lysistrata*, in a new translation by Nicholas Rudall. Copyright © 1991 by Ivan R. Dee, Inc.; translation copyright © 1991 by Nicholas Rudall. All rights strictly reserved, including performance and all forms of mechanical or electronic reproduction. By permission of Ivan R. Dee, Publisher.

Beckett, Samuel: *Waiting for Godot*. Copyright © 1952 by Les Éditions de Minuit. English text copyright © 1954 by Grove Press, Inc.; copyright © renewed 1982 by Samuel Beckett, now The Estate of Samuel Beckett. Used by permission of Grove/Atlantic, Inc.

Brecht, Bertolt: *The Good Woman of Setzuan*, from Eric Bentley, translator, PARABLES FOR THE THEATRE: TWO PLAYS BY BERTOLT BRECHT. Copyright © 1948, 1965, 1999 by University of Minnesota Press. Used by permission of the University of Minnesota Press.

Chekhov, Anton: *The Cherry Orchard* from THE PLAYS OF ANTON CHEKHOV, A NEW TRANSLATION by Paul Schmidt. Copyright © 1997 by Paul Schmidt. Reprinted by permission of HarperCollins Publishers.

Churchill, Caryl: *A Number*, copyright © 2002 by Caryl Churchill Ltd. Reproduced by permission of the publisher: Nick Hern Books Ltd. (UK), www.nickhernbooks.co.uk, and Theatre Communications Group (USA), www.tcg.org.

Cruz, Sor Juana Inés de la: *The Divine Narcissus*, translated by Renee Domeier and Patricia A. Peters. Copyright © 1998 by Renee Domeier and Patricia A. Peters. Used by permission of the University of New Mexico Press.

Euripides: *The Bacchae* from EURIPIDES, COMPLETE GREEK TRAGEDIES, Volume 4, edited by David Grene and Richard Lattimore. Copyright © 1992 University of Chicago Press. Used by permission of the University of Chicago Press.

Guan Hanqing: *Snow in Midsummer* from SELECTED PLAYS OF KUAN HAN CH'ING, translated by Gladys Yan. Published by Foreign Languages Press, China.

Hrotsvit of Gandersheim: *Dulcitius* from HROTSVIT OF GANDERSHEIM: A FLORILEGIUM OF HER WORKS, edited and translated by Katharina M. Wilson. Copyright © 2000 by Katharina M. Wilson. Used by permission of Boydell & Brewer Ltd.

Hughes, Langston: *Soul Gone Home* from FIVE PLAYS. Copyright © 1937 by Langston Hughes. Reprinted by permission of Harold Ober Associates, Inc.

Hwang, David Henry: *M. Butterfly*. Copyright © 1986, 1987, 1988 by David Henry Hwang. Used by permission of Dutton Signet, a division of Penguin Group (USA), Inc.

Ibsen, Henrik: *Hedda Gabler* from FOUR MAJOR PLAYS, Volume 1, translated by Rolf Fjelde. Copyright © 1965, 1992 by Rolf Fjelde. Used by permission of Dutton Signet, a division of Penguin Group (USA), Inc.

Kushner, Tony: *Angels in America: Part One: Millennium Approaches*. Copyright © 1992, 1993 by Tony Kushner. Published by Theatre Communications Group. Used by permission of Theatre Communications Group.

Marlowe, Christopher: *Doctor Faustus*. From ENGLISH RENAISSANCE DRAMA, edited by David Bevington et al. Copyright © 2002 by W. W. Norton & Company, Inc. Used by permission of W. W. Norton & Company, Inc.

Miller, Arthur: *Death of a Salesman*. Copyright © 1949, renewed © 1977 by Arthur Miller. Used by permission of Viking Penguin, a division of Penguin Group (USA), Inc.

Moliére: *Tartuffe,* translated by Constance Congdon. Copyright © 2006 by Constance Congdon. Used by permission of Constance Congdon.

Parks, Suzan-Lori: *The America Play* from THE AMERICA PLAY AND OTHER WORKS. Copyright © 1995 by Suzan-Lori Parks. Published by Theatre Communications Group. Used by permission of Theatre Communications Group.

Pirandello, Luigi: *Six Characters in Search of an Author,* from PIRANDELLO'S MAJOR PLAYS, translated by Eric Bentley. Evanston: Northwestern University Press. Used by permission.

Shakespeare, William: *Hamlet* and *Twelfth Night* from THE COMPLETE WORKS OF WILLIAM SHAKESPEARE, edited by Stanley Wells and Gary Taylor. Copyright © 2005 Oxford University Press. Used by permission of Oxford University Press.

Sophocles: *Oedipus the King* from THREE THEBAN PLAYS by Sophocles, translated by Robert Fagles. Copyright © 1982 by Robert Fagles. Used by permission of Viking Penguin, a division of Penguin Group (USA), Inc.

Soyinka, Wole: *Death and King's Horseman.* Copyright © 1975, 2003 by Wole Soyinka. Used by permission of W. W. Norton & Company and Melanie Jackson Agency, LLC.

Strindberg, August: *Miss Julie* from SELECTED PLAYS, translated by Evert Sprinchorn. Copyright © 1986 by University of Minnesota Press. Used by permission of University of Minnesota Press.

Thompson, Judith: *The Crackwalker* from THE OTHER SIDE OF THE DARK. Copyright © 1989 by Judith Thompson. Used by permission of the playwright and Playwrights Canada Press.

Williams, Tennessee: *A Streetcar Named Desire.* Copyright © 1947 by Tennessee Williams. CAUTION: Professionals and amateurs are hereby warned that *A Streetcar Named Desire*, being fully protected under the copyright laws of the United States of America, the British Empire including the Dominion of Canada, and all other countries of the Copyright Union, is subject to royalty. All rights, including professional, amateur, motion picture, recitation, lecturing, public reading, radio and television broadcasting, and the rights of translation into foreign languages are strictly reserved. Particular emphasis is laid on the question of readings, permission for which must be secured from the author's agent, Luis Sanjurjo, c/o International Creative Management, 40 West 57th Street, New York, NY 10019. Inquiries concerning the amateur acting rights of *A Streetcar Named Desire* should be directed to the Dramatists' Play Service, Inc., 440 Park Avenue South, New York, NY 10016, without whose permission in writing no amateur performance may be given.

Wilson, August: *Fences.* Copyright © 1986 by August Wilson. Used by permission of Dutton Signet, a division of Penguin Group (USA), Inc.

Zeami Motokiyo: *Atsumori* from TRADITIONAL JAPANESE THEATRE: AN ANTHOLOGY OF PLAYS, edited and translated by Karen Brazell. Copyright © 1998 Columbia University Press. Reprinted with permission of the publisher.

ILLUSTRATIONS

Introduction: p. 3: Marty Nordstrom c/o the Guthrie Theater; **p. 5:** Erich Lessing/Art Resource, NY; **p. 7:** The Granger Collection, New York; **p. 9:** Theater and Playhouse by Richard and Helen Leacroft, Methuen Publishing, Ltd; **p. 11:** Vanni/Art Resource, NY; **p. 12:** Museo Capitolino, Rome, Italy/Ancient Art and Architecture Collection Ltd./The Bridgeman Art Library; **p. 13:** Scala/Art Resource, NY; **p. 15:** Kings Visualization Lab; **p. 19**; The Philadelphia Museum of Art/Art Resource, NY; **p. 21:** Princeton University Press, 1976; **p. 23:** AFP/Getty Images; **p. 26:** Theater and Playhouse by Richard and Helen Leacroft, Methuen Publishing, Ltd.; **p. 28:** Merridew: Coventry, 1825; **p. 30:** Wikipedia Commons; **p. 33:** Wikipedia Commons; **p. 35:** Musee de la Ville de Paris, Musee Carnavalet, Paris, France/ Giraudon/The Bridgeman Art Library; **p 37:** akg-images; **p. 39:** The Art Archive; **p. 42:** akg-Images; **p. 43:** Kevin George/Alamy; **p. 46:** akg-images; **p. 47:** Lebrecht Authors; **p. 49:** Private

Collection/The Bridgeman Art Library; **p. 51:** Tate, London/Art Resource, NY; **p. 54:** akg-images; **p. 55:** akg-images; **p. 55:** Victoria & Albert Museum, London/Art Resource, NY; **p. 57:** Lebrecht Authors; **p. 59:** Picture Collection, The Branch Libraries, The New York Public Library, Astor, Lenox and Tilden Foundations; **p. 61:** Lebrecht Authors; **p. 63:** Snark/Art Resource, NY; **p. 64:** Lipnitzki/Roger Viollet/Getty Images; **p. 65:** Kurt Weill Foundation /Lebrecht Music & Arts; **p. 66:** The New York Public Library, Astor, Lenox and Tilden Foundations; **p. 67:** Franklin D. Roosevelt Library; **p. 70:** Lipnitzki/Roger Viollet/Getty Images; **p. 72:** Hulton-Deutsch Collection/Corbis; **p. 74:** W. Eugene Smith/Time & Life/Getty Images; **p. 73:** Bettmann/Corbis; **p. 76:** Julio Donoso/Corbis; **p. 79:** Nobby Clark/Hulton Archive/Getty Images

Sophocles: Bettmann/Corbis; Museo Gregoriano Etrusco, Vatican Museums/Scala/Art Resource, NY; **Aristophanes:** Bettmann/Corbis; British Museum/Art Resource, NY; **Euripides:** Museo Pio Clementino, Vatican Museums/Scala/Art Resource, NY; Kimball Art Museum/Art Resource, NY; Shmuel Magal / Sites & Photos; **Hrotsvit of Gandersheim:** Octavo Corp. and the Bridwell Library, Southern Methodist University; **Guan Han-qing:** public domain; **Zeami Motokiyo:** Werner Forman/Art Resource, NY; Wikipedia Commons; Bachmann Eckenstein, Basel; **Everyman:** Octavo Corp. and the Bridwell Library, Southern Methodist University: Lebrecht Music & Arts/The Image Works; **Christopher Marlowe:** The Granger Collection, New York; HIP / Art Resource, NY; **William Shakespeare:** Bettmann/Corbis; Snark/Art Resource, NY; Wikipedia Commons; Wikipedia Commons; Erich Lessing/Art Resource, NY; Fitzwilliam Museum, University of Cambridge; **Molière (Jean-Baptiste Poquelin):** Réunion des Musées Nationaux/Art Resource, NY; Réunion des Musées Nationaux/Art Resource, NY; Rue des Archives/The Granger Collection, NY; **Aphra Behn:** Mary Evans Picture Library/The Image Works; HIP/Art Resource, NY; Private Collection, © Philip Mould Ltd., London/The Bridgeman Art Library; **Sor Juana Ines de la Cruz:** The Granger Collection, New York; Bettmann/Corbis; Snark/Art Resource, NY; Museum Bayreuth / Alfredo Dagli Orti; **August Strindberg:** Strindberg Museum Stockholm/Alfredo Dagli Orti/The Art Archive; Strindbergsmuseet, Stockholm; **Henrik Ibsen:** Private Collection MD/The Art Archive; Nasjonal Glleriet Oslo/The Art Archive; Fales Library/New York University; **Oscar Wilde:** Culver Pictures/The Art Archive; Hulton Archive/Getty Images; courttheartre.org; **Anton Chekhov:** Hulton Archive/Getty Images; Billy Rose Theatre Division, NYPL for the Performing Arts, Astor, Lenox and Tilden Foundations; Austrian Archives/Corbis; **George Bernard Shaw:** Culver Pictures/The Art Archive; Hulton Archive/Getty Images; London Stereoscopic Company/Getty Images; **Susan Glaspell:** Photo courtesy of the Berg Collection; Photo courtesy of Daniel J. Lawrence; Billy Rose Theatre Collection, New York Public Library for the Performing Arts; **Luigi Pirandello:** Mary Evans Picture Library/Asia Media; The Art Archive; **Langston Hughes:** ©1981 Center for Creative Photography, Arizona Board of Regents. Langston Hughes, 1932. Photograph by Edward Weston; Library of Congress; **Bertolt Brecht:** Kurt Weill Foundation/Lebrecht Music & Arts; akg-images; Courtesy of Inge Steinert; **Tennessee Williams:** Baldwin H. Ward & Kathryn C. Ward/Corbis; AP/Wide World Photos; Bettmann/Corbis; **Arthur Miller:** AP/Wide World Photos; W. Eugene Smith/Getty Images; Billy Rose Collection; **Tawfiq al-Hakim:** AFP/Getty Images; akg-images; Keystone/Getty Images; **Samuel Beckett:** John Haynes/Lebrecht Music and Art Pictures; Lipnitzki/Roger Viollet/Getty Images; **Wole Soyinka:** Hulton Archive/Getty Images; Hulton-Deutsch Collection/Corbis; Eliot Ellsofon/Time Life Pictures/Getty Images; **Judith Thompson:** David Laurence; Courtesy of Judith Thompson; **August Wilson:** AP; Yale Repertory Theatre, Yale School of Drama; **David Henry Hwang:** © Joan Marcus; **Tony Kushner:** AP/Wide World Photos; Bettmann/Corbis; John Haynes/Lebrecht Music & Arts; **Suzan-Lori Parks:** © Stephanie Diani; Currier and Ives/ Bridgeman Art Library; T. Charles Erickson; **Caryl Churchill:** Gemma Levine/Hulton Archive/Getty Images; Joan Marcus/AP.

Index